THE RAPID FACT FINDER

THE RAPID
FACT FINDER

A Desk Book of Universal Knowledge

COMPILED BY

HUGH WEIDEMAN

THOMAS Y. CROWELL COMPANY, NEW YORK

Established 1834

Preface

The Rapid Fact Finder is meant to do two things. It brings together in one volume a great deal of information that is of perennial interest and value to a large number of people. And it arranges this information for quick reference so that you can find what you want efficiently and easily. Thus it is both useful and practical.

A glance at the table of contents shows how wide the scope of *The Rapid Fact Finder* is. You cannot locate this kind of information in other desk reference books, and even in multivolume encyclopedias most of the fascinating facts are buried away. You would have to search through shelves of obscure books to locate, for example, the information contained under "Gods and Goddesses" and "Gods of the World." Yet the categories of knowledge chosen for coverage are not esoteric—every area has been tested against popular demand. Reference librarians, who through the years have become familiar with the questions asked over and over by the public, were consulted to determine just what categories of facts would prove most useful. These librarians reported that the usual desk reference books, the almanacs and the dictionaries, help little in locating much of the information wanted by their patrons. *The Rapid Fact Finder*, with its scope, fills this need.

There are more than a hundred divisions of knowledge arranged in alphabetical order. Within these divisions the facts have been specially organized to speed you to the fact you want. Sometimes, for example, the information is arranged in chronological order, such as the list of Popes, for this is the way most people can best locate the particular name they need. The "Gods of the World" is arranged according to their attributes, for more often than not your question is, "Who was the goddess of love?" or, "What divinity presides over sleep and dreams?" To take another example, the "Famous Waterfalls of the World" is arranged according to height, the statistic most wanted.

The contents have been extensively cross indexed to facilitate your search. For instance, the countries of the world are listed under a category

called "Populations of the Countries of the World." But you will find
under the C's a cross reference. Look at the table of contents again before
you place the book on your desk. A familiarity with this table will reward
you time and again, since *The Rapid Fact Finder* has information in it
that you would never expect to find in so handy a volume.

There are more than a hundred thousand facts in this *Rapid Fact
Finder*. Naturally, accuracy is paramount, and every attempt has been
made to supply the most authoritative information. Many sources went
into the preparation of each category; and, though with so full a book
there are bound to be a few errors, *The Rapid Fact Finder* has been
brought to a high degree of reliability.

Whatever, then, your occupation is, you will find *The Rapid Fact
Finder* useful. It is a book of facts—nothing but facts. The compiler is
confident that this book will become one of the most used of your desk
reference books.

Table of Contents

WITH CROSS REFERENCES

THE RAPID FACT FINDER

Abbreviations

See **Degree Abbreviations; Religious Orders**

Abdications and Depositions in European Royalty Since 1910

ALFONSO XIII: King of Spain; April 14, 1931.
CAROL II: King of Rumania; September 6, 1940.
CHARLES I: Emperor of Austria; November 12, 1918.
EDWARD VIII: King of England; December 11, 1936.
FAROUK I: King of Egypt; July 26, 1952.
HUMBERT II: King of Italy; June, 1946.
LEOPOLD III: King of Belgium; January 16, 1951.
MANUEL II: King of Portugal; October, 1910.
MICHAEL I: King of Rumania; December 30, 1947.
MOHAMMED VI: Sultan of Turkey, November 23, 1922.
NICHOLAS II: Czar of Russia; March 15, 1917.
PETER II: King of Yugoslavia; November 29, 1945.
SIMEON II: King of Bulgaria; September 8, 1946.
VICTOR EMMANUEL III: King of Italy; May 9, 1946.
WILHELMINA: Queen of the Netherlands; September 4, 1948.

Academic Colors

Official Colors for Hood Linings of Major U.S. Colleges and Universities

AMHERST: Purple, white chevron.
BOSTON UNIVERSITY: Scarlet, white chevron.
BROWN: Brown, cardinal chevron.
BRYN MAWR: Maize, white chevron.
CATHOLIC UNIVERSITY: Papal yellow, white zone.
COLGATE: Maroon.
COLLEGE OF THE CITY OF NEW YORK: Lavender.
COLUMBIA: Light blue, white chevron.
CORNELL: Carnelian red, two white chevrons.
DARTMOUTH: Green.
FORDHAM: Maroon.
GEORGETOWN: Gray, blue chevron.
HARVARD: Crimson.
HOLY CROSS: Purple.
JOHNS HOPKINS: Black, gold chevron.
MASSACHUSETTS INSTITUTE OF TECHNOLOGY: Bright red, silver-gray chevron.
MIAMI UNIVERSITY, OHIO: Bright red, white chevron.
NEW YORK UNIVERSITY: Violet.
NORTHWESTERN: Purple, gold-yellow chevron.
OHIO STATE: Scarlet, silver-gray chevron.
PRINCETON: Orange, black chevron.
RADCLIFFE: Crimson, white chevron.
SMITH: White, gold chevron.
STANFORD: Cardinal.
SYRACUSE: Orange.
TEMPLE: White, cardinal-red chevron.
UNIVERSITY OF ALABAMA: Oxford crimson, white chevron.
UNIVERSITY OF CALIFORNIA: Gold, blue chevron.
UNIVERSITY OF CHICAGO: Maroon.
UNIVERSITY OF ILLINOIS: Navy blue, two orange chevrons.
UNIVERSITY OF KANSAS: Dark blue, red chevron.
UNIVERSITY OF KENTUCKY: Blue, white chevron.

UNIVERSITY OF MAINE: Light blue.
UNIVERSITY OF MICHIGAN: Maize, azure-blue chevron.
UNIVERSITY OF MINNESOTA: Old gold, maroon chevron.
UNIVERSITY OF NORTH CAROLINA: Light blue, two white chevrons.
UNIVERSITY OF OREGON: Lemon yellow, dark green chevron.
UNIVERSITY OF PENNSYLVANIA: Red, blue chevron.
UNIVERSITY OF PITTSBURGH: Navy blue, gold-yellow chevron.
UNIVERSITY OF ROCHESTER: Dandelion yellow.
UNIVERSITY OF SOUTHERN CALIFORNIA: Gold, cardinal chevron.
UNIVERSITY OF TEXAS: White above orange, parti-per chevron.
UNIVERSITY OF WASHINGTON: Purple above gold, parti-per chevron.
UNIVERSITY OF WISCONSIN: Bright red.
VASSAR: Rose, gray chevron.
WELLESLEY: Dark blue.
WILLIAMS: Royal purple.
YALE: Blue.

Faculty Department Colors
(As Registered with the Inter-Collegiate Bureau of Academic Costume)

AGRICULTURE: Maize.
ARTS AND LETTERS: White.
BUSINESS ADMINISTRATION (COMMERCE AND ACCOUNTING): Drab.
DENTISTRY: Lilac.
ECONOMICS: Copper.
EDUCATION: Light blue.
ENGINEERING: Orange.
FINE ARTS AND ARCHITECTURE: Brown.
FORESTRY: Russet.
HUMANITIES: Crimson.
LAW: Purple.
LIBRARY SCIENCE: Lemon.
MEDICINE: Green.
MUSIC: Pink.
NURSING: Apricot.
ORATORY: Silver gray.
PHARMACY: Olive green.
PHILOSOPHY: Dark blue.
PHYSICAL EDUCATION: Sage green.
PUBLIC HEALTH: Salmon pink.
SCIENCE: Golden yellow.
SOCIAL SERVICE: Citron.
SURGICAL CHIROPODY: Nile green.
THEOLOGY: Scarlet.
VETERINARY SCIENCE: Gray.

School Colors

ADELPHI COLLEGE (NEW YORK): Brown and gold.
AKRON, UNIVERSITY OF: Blue and gold.
ALABAMA, UNIVERSITY OF: Crimson and white.
ALBERTUS MAGNUS COLLEGE (CONNECTICUT): White and Yale blue.
ALBION COLLEGE (MICHIGAN): Purple and gold.
ALBRIGHT (PENNSYLVANIA): Cardinal and white.
ALFRED UNIVERSITY (NEW YORK): Purple and gold.
ALLEGHENY COLLEGE (PENNSYLVANIA): Navy blue and gold.
ALMA COLLEGE (MICHIGAN): Maroon and cream.
AMHERST COLLEGE (MASSACHUSETTS): Purple and white.

ANNAPOLIS: See U. S. Naval Academy.

ANTIOCH COLLEGE (OHIO): Blue and gold.

ARIZONA, UNIVERSITY OF: Red and blue.

ARKANSAS, UNIVERSITY OF: White and cardinal.

AUBURN COMMUNITY COLLEGE (NEW YORK): Orange and blue.

BARD COLLEGE (NEW YORK): Scarlet and white.

BARNARD COLLEGE (NEW YORK): Blue and white.

BATES COLLEGE (MAINE): Garnet.

BAYLOR UNIVERSITY (TEXAS): Green and gold.

BELOIT COLLEGE (WISCONSIN): Gold.

BOSTON COLLEGE (MASSACHUSETTS): Maroon and gold.

BOSTON UNIVERSITY (MASSACHUSETTS): Scarlet and white.

BOWDOIN COLLEGE (MAINE): White.

BOWLING GREEN STATE UNIVERSITY (OHIO): Orange and brown.

BRADLEY UNIVERSITY (ILLINOIS): Red and white.

BRANDEIS UNIVERSITY (MASSACHU-SETTS): Blue and white.

BRIAR CLIFF COLLEGE (IOWA): Gold and royal blue.

BRIDGEPORT, UNIVERSITY OF (CONNECT-ICUT): Purple and white.

BRIGHAM YOUNG UNIVERSITY (UTAH): Blue and white.

BROOKLYN COLLEGE: Maroon and gold.

BROWN UNIVERSITY (RHODE ISLAND): Brown and white.

BRYN MAWR COLLEGE (PENNSYLVANIA): Yellow and white.

BUCKNELL UNIVERSITY (PENNSYLVANIA): Orange and blue.

BUFFALO, UNIVERSITY OF: Blue and white.

BUTLER UNIVERSITY (INDIANA): Royal blue and white.

CALIFORNIA, UNIVERSITY OF: Blue and gold.

CANISIUS COLLEGE (NEW YORK): Blue and gold.

CARNEGIE INSTITUTE OF TECHNOLOGY (PENNSYLVANIA): Carnegie plaid.

CASE INSTITUTE OF TECHNOLOGY (OHIO): Brown and white.

CATHOLIC UNIVERSITY (WASHINGTON, D.C.): Yellow and white.

CHESTNUT HILL COLLEGE (PENNSYLVA-NIA): Brown and gold.

CHICAGO, UNIVERSITY OF: Maroon.

CINCINNATI, UNIVERSITY OF (OHIO): Red and black.

CITADEL, THE (SOUTH CAROLINA): Light blue and white.

CITY COLLEGE (NEW YORK): Lavender and black.

CLARK UNIVERSITY (MASSCHUSETTS): Green and white.

CLEMSON AGRICULTURAL COLLEGE (SOUTH CAROLINA): Orange and purple.

COLBY COLLEGE (MAINE): Blue and gray.

COLGATE UNIVERSITY (NEW YORK): Maroon and white.

COLORADO, UNIVERSITY OF: Silver and gold.

COLORADO A. AND M.: Green and gold.

COLUMBIA UNIVERSITY (NEW YORK): Light blue and white.

CONNECTICUT, UNIVERSITY OF: Royal blue and white.

CORNELL UNIVERSITY (NEW YORK): Carnelian and white.

CREIGHTON UNIVERSITY (NEBRASKA): White and blue.

DARTMOUTH COLLEGE (NEW HAMP-SHIRE): Green.

DAYTON, UNIVERSITY OF (OHIO): Red and blue.

DELAWARE, UNIVERSITY OF: Blue and gold.

DENVER, UNIVERSITY OF (COLORADO): Crimson and gold.

DE PAUL UNIVERSITY (ILLINOIS): Red and light blue.

DE PAUW UNIVERSITY (INDIANA): Old gold.

DETROIT, UNIVERSITY OF (MICHIGAN): Red and white.

DICKINSON COLLEGE (PENNSYLVANIA): Red and white.

DRAKE UNIVERSITY (IOWA): Blue and white.

DREXEL INSTITUTE OF TECHNOLOGY (PENNSYLVANIA): Gold and Blue.

DUKE UNIVERSITY (NORTH CAROLINA): Blue and white.

DUQUESNE UNIVERSITY (PENNSYLVA-NIA): Red and blue.

FISK UNIVERSITY (TENNESSEE): Blue and gold.

FLORIDA, UNIVERSITY OF: Orange and blue.

FORDHAM UNIVERSITY (NEW YORK): Maroon.

FRANKLIN AND MARSHALL COLLEGE (PENNSYLVANIA): Blue and white.

FURNAM UNIVERSITY (SOUTH CARO-LINA): Purple and white.

GENEVA COLLEGE (PENNSYLVANIA): White and gold.

GEORGETOWN UNIVERSITY (WASHING-TON, D.C.): Blue and gray.

GEORGE WASHINGTON UNIVERSITY (WASHINGTON, D.C.): Buff and blue.

GEORGIA, UNIVERSITY OF: Red and black.

GEORGIA INSTITUTE OF TECHNOLOGY: Gold and white.

GEORGIAN COURT COLLEGE (NEW JER-SEY): Gold and blue.

GETTYSBURG COLLEGE (PENNSYLVANIA): Orange and blue.

GRINNELL COLLEGE (IOWA): Scarlet and black.

HAMILTON COLLEGE (NEW YORK): Buff and blue.

HANOVER COLLEGE (INDIANA): Crimson and blue.

HARDIN-SIMMONS UNIVERSITY (TEXAS): Purple and gold.

HARVARD UNIVERSITY (MASSACHU-SETTS): Crimson.

HAVERFORD COLLEGE (PENNSYLVANIA): Scarlet and black.

HEIDELBERG COLLEGE (OHIO): Red, orange, and black.

HOBART AND WILLIAM SMITH COLLEGES (NEW YORK): Orange and purple.

HOFSTRA COLLEGE (NEW YORK): Blue and gold.

HOLY CROSS, COLLEGE OF THE (MASSA-CHUSETTS): Purple.

HOWARD UNIVERSITY (WASHINGTON, D.C.): Indigo and white.

HUNTER COLLEGE (NEW YORK): Lavender and white.

IDAHO, UNIVERSITY OF: Silver and gold.

ILLINOIS, UNIVERSITY OF: Orange and navy blue.

IMMACULATA COLLEGE (PENNSYLVANIA): Blue and white.

INDIANA UNIVERSITY: Cream and crimson.

IOWA, STATE UNIVERSITY OF: Old gold and black.

IOWA STATE: Cardinal and Gold.

JOHN CARROLL UNIVERSITY (OHIO): Blue and gold

JOHNS HOPKINS UNIVERSITY (MARY-LAND): Black and old gold.
JUNIATA COLLEGE (PENNSYLVANIA): Blue and old gold.
KANSAS, UNIVERSITY OF: Crimson and blue.
KANSAS STATE: Purple and white.
KENTUCKY, UNIVERSITY OF: Blue and white.
KENYON COLLEGE (OHIO): Purple and white
LAFAYETTE COLLEGE (PENNSYLVANIA): Maroon and white.
LAKE FOREST COLLEGE (ILLINOIS): Red and black.
LEBANON VALLEY COLLEGE (PENNSYLVANIA): Blue and white.
LEHIGH UNIVERSITY (PENNSYLVANIA): Brown and white.
LONG ISLAND UNIVERSITY (NEW YORK): Blue.
LOUISIANA STATE UNIVERSITY: Purple and gold.
LOUISVILLE, UNIVERSITY OF (KENTUCKY): Cardinal and black.
LOYOLA UNIVERSITY (CHICAGO): Maroon and gold.
LOYOLA UNIVERSITY OF LOS ANGELES (CALIFORNIA): Maroon and gold.
MAINE, UNIVERSITY OF: Light blue.
MANHATTAN COLLEGE (NEW YORK): Green and white.
MANHATTANVILLE COLLEGE OF THE SACRED HEART (NEW YORK): Red.
MARIETTA COLLEGE (OHIO): Navy blue and white.
MARQUETTE UNIVERSITY (MILWAUKEE): Blue and gold.
MARYCREST COLLEGE (IOWA): Blue and white.
MARYLAND, UNIVERSITY OF: Black, gold, cerise, and silver.
MARYMOUNT COLLEGE (NEW YORK): Blue, and white.
MASSACHUSETTS INSTITUTE OF TECHNOLOGY: Red and gray.
MASSACHUSETTS, UNIVERSITY OF (AMHERST): Maroon and white.
MIAMI, UNIVERSITY OF (FLORIDA): Burnt orange, Biscayne green, and white.
MIAMI UNIVERSITY (OHIO): Scarlet and white.
MICHIGAN, UNIVERSITY OF: Maize and blue.
MICHIGAN STATE: Green and white.
MIDDLEBURY COLLEGE (VERMONT): Blue and white.
MILLS COLLEGE (CALIFORNIA): Gold and white.
MINNESOTA, UNIVERSITY OF: Maroon and gold.
MISSISSIPPI, UNIVERSITY OF: Crimson and blue.
MISSISSIPPI STATE: Red and white.
MISSOURI, UNIVERSITY OF: Black and gold.
MONMOUTH COLLEGE (ILLINOIS): Red and white.
MONTANA STATE UNIVERSITY: Copper, silver, and gold.
MORAVIAN COLLEGE (PENNSYLVANIA): Blue and gray.
MOUNT HOLYOKE COLLEGE (MASSACHUSETTS): Bright blue.
MOUNT MARY COLLEGE (WISCONSIN): Blue and white.
MOUNT MERCY COLLEGE (PENNSYLVANIA): Purple and gold.
MOUNT ST. JOSEPH-ON-THE-OHIO (OHIO): Old gold and royal blue.
MOUNT ST. MARY'S COLLEGE (CALIFORNIA:) Purple and gold.
MOUNT ST. MARY'S COLLEGE (MARYLAND): Blue and white.

MOUNT ST. VINCENT-ON-HUDSON (NEW YORK): White and gold.
MUHLENBERG COLLEGE (PENNSYLVANIA): Cardinal and gray.
NAZARETH COLLEGE (MICHIGAN): Blue and white.
NAZARETH COLLEGE (NEW YORK): Purple and gold.
NEBRASKA, UNIVERSITY OF: Scarlet and cream.
NEVADA, UNIVERSITY OF: Silver and blue.
NEW HAMPSHIRE, UNIVERSITY OF: Royal blue and white.
NEW MEXICO, UNIVERSITY OF: Cherry and silver.
NEW ROCHELLE, COLLEGE OF (NEW YORK): Light blue and white.
NEW YORK CITY COLLEGE: Lavender and black.
NEW YORK UNIVERSITY: Purple and white.
NORTH CAROLINA, UNIVERSITY OF: Light blue and white.
NORTH CAROLINA STATE: Red and white.
NORTH DAKOTA, UNIVERSITY OF: Green and rose.
NORTHEASTERN UNIVERSITY (MASSACHUSETTS): Red and black.
NORTHWESTERN UNIVERSITY (ILLINOIS): Purple.
NOTRE DAME (INDIANA): Blue and gold.
NOTRE DAME COLLEGE (STATEN ISLAND, NEW YORK): Blue and white.
OBERLIN COLLEGE (OHIO): Cardinal red and Mikado yellow.
OCCIDENTAL COLLEGE (CALIFORNIA): Burnt orange and black.
OHIO STATE: Scarlet and gray.
OHIO UNIVERSITY: Green and white.
OHIO WESLEYAN UNIVERSITY: Red and black.
OKLAHOMA, UNIVERSITY OF: Crimson and cream.
OKLAHOMA A. AND M.: Orange and black.
OMAHA, UNIVERSITY OF: Red and black.
OREGON, UNIVERSITY OF: Yellow and green.
OREGON STATE: Orange and black.
PACIFIC, COLLEGE OF THE (CALIFORNIA): Orange and black.
PENN STATE: Blue and white.
PENNSYLVANIA, UNIVERSITY OF: Red and blue.
PITTSBURGH, UNIVERSITY OF (PENNSYLVANIA): Blue and gold.
POMONA COLLEGE (CALIFORNIA): Blue and white.
PORTLAND, UNIVERSITY OF (OREGON): Purple and white.
PRINCETON (NEW JERSEY): Orange and black.
PROVIDENCE COLLEGE (RHODE ISLAND): Black and white.
PURDUE (INDIANA): Old gold and black.
QUEENS COLLEGE (NEW YORK): Pale blue and silver.
RADCLIFFE COLLEGE (MASSACHUSETTS): Cherry red.
REED COLLEGE (OREGON): Richmond rose red.
REGIS COLLEGE (MASSACHUSETTS): Red and gold.
RENSSELAER POLYTECHNIC INSTITUTE (NEW YORK): Cherry and white.
RHODE ISLAND, UNIVERSITY OF: Blue and white.
RICE INSTITUTE (TEXAS): Blue and gray.
RICHMOND, UNIVERSITY OF (VIRGINIA): Blue and crimson.
ROCHESTER, UNIVERSITY OF (NEW YORK): Yellow and blue.
RUTGERS (NEW JERSEY): Scarlet.

ST. BONAVENTURE COLLEGE (NEW YORK): Brown and white.
ST. CATHERINE'S COLLEGE (MINNESOTA): Purple and gold.
ST. ELIZABETH'S COLLEGE (NEW JERSEY): Blue and gold.
ST. FRANCIS COLLEGE (PENNSYLVANIA): Brown and gold.
ST. JOHN'S UNIVERSITY (BROOKLYN): Red and white.
ST. JOSEPH'S COLLEGE FOR WOMEN (NEW YORK): White and gold.
ST. LAWRENCE UNIVERSITY (NEW YORK): Scarlet and brown.
ST. LOUIS UNIVERSITY (MISSOURI): Blue and white.
ST. MARY COLLEGE (KANSAS): Gold and white.
ST. MARY OF THE SPRINGS (OHIO): Black, white, and gold.
ST. MARY-OF-THE-WOODS (INDIANA): White and cerulean blue.
ST. MARY'S COLLEGE (KANSAS): Blue and white.
ST. MARY'S COLLEGE (MINNESOTA): Red and white.
ST. MARY'S COLLEGE, NOTRE DAME (INDIANA): Blue and white.
ST. PETER'S COLLEGE (JERSEY CITY): Peacock blue and white.
ST. ROSE'S COLLEGE (NEW YORK): Gold and white.
ST. TERESA'S COLLEGE (MINNESOTA): White and gold.
ST. THOMAS COLLEGE (MINNESOTA): Purple and gray.
ST. VINCENT COLLEGE (PENNSYLVANIA): Green and old gold.
SALEM COLLEGE (NORTH CAROLINA): White and gold.
SAN FRANCISCO, UNIVERSITY OF (CALIFORNIA): Green and gold.
SANTA BARBARA COLLEGE (CALIFORNIA): Blue and gold.
SANTA CLARA (CALIFORNIA): Crimson and white.
SARAH LAWRENCE (NEW YORK): Green and white.
SCRANTON, UNIVERSITY OF PENNSYLVANIA): Purple and white.
SETON HALL COLLEGE (PENNSYLVANIA): Blue and white.
SIENNA HEIGHTS COLLEGE (MICHIGAN): Black and silver.
SKIDMORE COLLEGE (NEW YORK): Yellow and white.
SMITH COLLEGE (MASSACHUSETTS): White and gold.
SOUTH CAROLINA, UNIVERSITY OF: Garnet and black.
SOUTH DAKOTA, UNIVERSITY OF: Vermilion and white.
SOUTHERN CALIFORNIA, UNIVERSITY OF: Cardinal and gold.
SOUTHERN METHODIST UNIVERSITY (TEXAS): Red and blue.
SOUTHWESTERN UNIVERSITY (TEXAS): Gold and black.
SPRING HILL COLLEGE (ALABAMA): Purple and white.
SPRINGFIELD COLLEGE (MASSACHUSETTS): Maroon and white.
STANFORD UNIVERSITY (CALIFORNIA): Cardinal.
SUSQUEHANNA UNIVERSITY (PENNSYLVANIA): Orange and maroon.
SWARTHMORE (PENNSYLVANIA): Garnet and white.
SWEET BRIAR COLLEGE (VIRGINIA): Pink and green.

SYRACUSE UNIVERSITY (NEW YORK): Orange.
TEMPLE UNIVERSITY (PENNSYLVANIA): Cherry and white.
TENNESSEE, UNIVERSITY OF: Orange and white.
TEXAS A. AND M.: Maroon and white.
TEXAS CHRISTIAN: Purple and white.
TEXAS, UNIVERSITY OF: Orange and white.
TOLEDO, UNIVERSITY OF (OHIO): Blue and gold.
TRINITY COLLEGE (CONNECTICUT): Blue and gold.
TUFTS UNIVERSITY (MASSACHUSETTS): Brown and blue.
TULANE UNIVERSITY OF LOUISIANA: Olive and blue.
TULSA, UNIVERSITY OF (OKLAHOMA): Red, blue, and gold.
TUSKEGEE INSTITUTE (ALABAMA): Crimson and gold.
UNION COLLEGE (NEW YORK): Garnet.
U.S., COAST GUARD ACADEMY (CONNECTICUT): Blue and white.
U.S. MERCHANT MARINE ACADEMY (NEW YORK): Blue and gray.
U.S. MILITARY ACADEMY (NEW YORK): Black, gold, and gray.
U.S. NAVAL ACADEMY (MARYLAND): Blue and gold.
U.C.L.A. (CALIFORNIA): Blue and gold.
UPSALA COLLEGE (NEW JERSEY): Blue and gray.
URSINUS COLLEGE (PENNSYLVANIA): Red, gold, and black.
UTAH, UNIVERSITY OF: Red and white.
VALPARAISO UNIVERSITY (INDIANA): Brown and gold.
VANDERBILT UNIVERSITY (TENNESSEE): Gold and black.
VASSAR COLLEGE (NEW YORK): Pink and gray.
VERMONT, UNIVERSITY OF: Green and gold.
VILLANOVA UNIVERSITY (PENNSYLVANIA): Navy blue and white.
VIRGINIA, UNIVERSITY OF: Orange and blue.
VIRGINIA MILITARY INSTITUTE: Red, white, and yellow.
VIRGINIA POLYTECHNIC INSTITUTE: Red and orange.
VIRGINIA STATE: Orange and blue.
WABASH COLLEGE (INDIANA): Scarlet.
WAKE FOREST COLLEGE (NORTH CAROLINA): Gold and black.
WASHINGTON, UNIVERSITY OF: Purple and gold.
WASHINGTON STATE: Crimson and gray.
WASHINGTON AND LEE UNIVERSITY (VIRGINIA): Blue and white.
WASHINGTON UNIVERSITY (MISSOURI): Myrtle and maroon.
WAYNE UNIVERSITY (MICHIGAN): Green and gold.
WELLESLEY COLLEGE (MASSACHUSETTS): Blue.
WESLEYAN UNIVERSITY (CONNECTICUT): Cardinal and black.
WEST POINT: See U. S. Military Academy.
WESTERN RESERVE UNIVERSITY (OHIO): Scarlet and white.
WEST VIRGINIA: Gold and blue.
WHEATON COLLEGE (MASSACHUSETTS): Blue and white.
WILLAMETTE UNIVERSITY (OREGON): Cardinal and gold.
WILLIAM AND MARY (VIRGINIA): Green, gold, and silver.
WILLIAMS COLLEGE (MASSACHUSETTS):

WISCONSIN, UNIVERSITY OF: Cardinal. Royal purple.
WOOSTER, COLLEGE OF (OHIO): Black and old gold.
WYOMING, UNIVERSITY OF: Brown and gold.
XAVIER UNIVERSITY (LOUISIANA): Gold and white.
XAVIER UNIVERSITY (OHIO): Blue and white.
YALE UNIVERSITY (CONNECTICUT): Yale blue.
YOUNGSTOWN UNIVERSITY, THE (OHIO): Red and white.

Academy Awards
See also **Awards**

Best Actor

1927-28: Emil Jannings, *The Way of All Flesh.*
1928-29: Warner Baxter, *In Old Arizona.*
1929-30: George Arliss, *Disraeli.*
1930-31: Lionel Barrymore, *A Free Soul.*
1931-32: Fredric March, *Dr. Jekyll and Mr. Hyde.*
1932-33: Charles Laughton, *The Private Life of Henry VIII.*
1934: Clark Gable, *It Happened One Night.*
1935: Victor McLaglen, *The Informer.*
1936: Paul Muni, *The Story of Louis Pasteur.*
1937: Spencer Tracy, *Captains Courageous.*
1938: Spencer Tracy, *Boys Town.*
1939: Robert Donat, *Goodbye, Mr. Chips.*
1940: James Stewart, *The Philadelphia Story.*
1941: Gary Cooper, *Sergeant York.*
1942: James Cagney, *Yankee Doodle Dandy.*
1943: Paul Lukas, *Watch on the Rhine.*
1944: Bing Crosby, *Going My Way.*
1945: Ray Milland, *The Lost Weekend.*
1946: Fredric March, *The Best Years of Our Lives.*
1947: Ronald Colman, *A Double Life.*
1948: Laurence Olivier, *Hamlet.*
1949: Broderick Crawford, *All the King's Men.*
1950: Jose Ferrer, *Cyrano de Bergerac.*
1951: Humphrey Bogart, *The African Queen.*
1952: Gary Cooper, *High Noon.*
1953: William Holden, *Stalag 17.*
1954: Marlon Brando, *On the Waterfront.*
1955: Ernest Borgnine, *Marty.*
1956: Yul Brynner, *Anastasia.*

Best Actress

1927-28: Janet Gaynor, *Seventh Heaven.*
1928-29: Mary Pickford, *Coquette.*
1929-30: Norma Shearer, *Divorcee.*
1930-31: Marie Dressler, *Min and Bill.*
1931-32: Helen Hayes, *The Sin of Madelon Claudet.*
1932-33: Katharine Hepburn, *Morning Glory.*
1934: Claudette Colbert, *It Happened One Night.*
1935: Bette Davis, *Dangerous.*
1936: Luise Rainer, *The Great Ziegfield.*
1937: Luise Rainer, *The Good Earth.*
1938: Bette Davis, *Jezebel.*
1939: Vivien Leigh, *Gone With the Wind.*
1940: Ginger Rogers, *Kitty Foyle.*
1941: Joan Fontaine, *Suspicion.*
1942: Greer Garson, *Mrs. Miniver.*
1943: Jennifer Jones, *The Song of Bernadette.*
1944: Ingrid Bergman, *Gaslight.*
1945: Joan Crawford, *Mildred Pierce.*
1946: Olivia de Havilland, *To Each His Own.*
1947: Loretta Young, *The Farmer's Daughter.*
1948: Jane Wyman, *Johnny Belinda.*

1949: Olivia de Havilland, *The Heiress.*
1950: Judy Holliday, *Born Yesterday.*
1951: Vivien Leigh, *A Streetcar Named Desire.*
1952: Shirley Booth, *Come Back, Little Sheba.*
1953: Audrey Hepburn, *Roman Holiday.*
1954: Grace Kelly, *The Country Girl.*
1955: Anna Magnani, *The Rose Tattoo.*
1956: Ingrid Bergman, *Anastasia.*

Best Supporting Actor

1936: Walter Brennan, *Come and Get It.*
1937: Joseph Schildkraut, *The Life of Emile Zola.*
1938: Walter Brennan, *Kentucky.*
1939: Thomas Mitchell, *Stagecoach.*
1940: Walter Brennan, *The Westerner.*
1941: Donald Crisp, *How Green Was My Valley.*
1942: Van Heflin, *Johnny Eager.*
1943: Charles Coburn, *The More the Merrier.*
1944: Barry Fitzgerald, *Going My Way.*
1945: James Dunn, *A Tree Grows in Brooklyn.*
1946: Harold Russell, *The Best Years of Our Lives.*
1947: Edmund Gwenn, *Miracle on 34th St.*
1948: Walter Huston, *The Treasure of Sierra Madre.*
1949: Dean Jagger, *Twelve O'Clock High.*
1950: George Sanders, *All About Eve.*
1951: Karl Malden, *A Streetcar Named Desire.*
1952: Anthony Quinn, *Viva Zapata!*
1953: Frank Sinatra, *From Here to Eternity.*
1954: Edmond O'Brien, *The Barefoot Contessa.*
1955: Jack Lemmon, *Mister Roberts.*
1956: Anthony Quinn, *Lust for Life.*

Best Supporting Actress

1936: Gale Sondergaard, *Anthony Adverse.*
1937: Alice Brady, *In Old Chicago.*
1938: Fay Bainter, *Jezebel.*
1939: Hattie McDaniel, *Gone With the Wind.*
1940: Jane Darwell, *The Grapes of Wrath.*
1941: Mary Astor, *The Great Lie.*
1942: Teresa Wright, *Mrs. Miniver.*
1943: Katina Paxinou, *For Whom the Bell Tolls.*
1944: Ethel Barrymore, *None But the Lonely Heart.*
1945: Anne Revere, *National Velvet.*
1946: Anne Baxter, *The Razor's Edge.*
1947: Celeste Holm, *Gentleman's Agreement.*
1948: Claire Trevor, *Key Largo.*
1949: Mercedes McCambridge, *All The King's Men.*
1950: Josephine Hull, *Harvey.*
1951: Kim Hunter, *A Streetcar Named Desire.*
1952: Gloria Grahame, *The Bad and the Beautiful.*
1953: Donna Reed, *From Here to Eternity.*
1954: Eva Marie Saint, *On the Waterfront.*
1955: Jo Van Fleet, *East of Eden.*
1956: Dorothy Malone, *Written on the Wind.*

Best Picture

1927-28: *Wings*, Paramount.
1928-29: *Broadway*, MGM.
1929-30: *All Quiet on the Western Front*, Universal.
1930-31: *Cimarron*, RKO.
1931-32: *Grand Hotel*, MGM.
1932-33: *Cavalcade*, Fox.
1934: *It Happened One Night*, Columbia.
1935: *Mutiny on the Bounty*, MGM.
1936: *The Great Ziegfield*, MGM.
1937: *The Life of Émile Zola*, Warner.

1938: *You Can't Take It With You*, Columbia.
1939: *Gone With the Wind*, Selznick International.
1940: *Rebecca*, Selznick International.
1941: *How Green Was My Valley*, 20th Century-Fox.
1942: *Mrs. Miniver*, MGM.
1943: *Casablanca*, Warner.
1944: *Going My Way*, Paramount.
1945: *The Lost Weekend*, Paramount.
1946: *The Best Years of Our Lives*, Samuel Goldwyn, RKO.
1947: *Gentleman's Agreement*, 20th Century Fox.
1948: *Hamlet*, Two Cities Film, Universal International.
1949: *All the King's Men*, Columbia.
1950: *All About Eve*, 20th Century-Fox.
1951: *An American in Paris*, MGM.
1952: *The Greatest Show on Earth*, Cecil B. De Mille, Paramount.
1953: *From Here to Eternity*, Columbia.
1954: *On the Waterfront*, Horizon-American Corp., Columbia.
1955: *Marty*, Hecht and Lancaster's Steven Productions, U.A.
1956: *Around the World in 80 Days*, Michael Todd.

Best Direction

1928: Frank Borzage, *Seventh Heaven*.
1928: Lewis Milestone, *Two Arabian Nights*.
1929: Frank Lloyd, *The Divine Lady*.
1930: Lewis Milestone, *All Quiet on the Western Front*.
1931: Norman Taurog, *Skippy*.
1932: Frank Borzage, *Bad Girl*.
1933: Frank Lloyd, *Cavalcade*.
1934: Frank Capra, *It Happened One Night*.
1935: John Ford, *The Informer*.
1936: Frank Capra, *Mr. Deeds Goes to Town*.
1937: Leo McCarey, *The Awful Truth*.
1938: Frank Capra, *You Can't Take It With You*.
1939: Victor Fleming, *Gone With the Wind*.
1940: John Ford, *The Grapes of Wrath*.
1941: John Ford, *How Green Was My Valley*.
1942: William Wyler, *Mrs. Miniver*.
1943: Michael Curtiz, *Casablanca*.
1944: Leo McCarey, *Going My Way*.
1945: Billy Wilder, *The Lost Weekend*.
1946: William Wyler, *The Best Years of Our Lives*.
1947: Elia Kazan, *Gentleman's Agreement*.
1948: John Huston, *The Treasure of Sierra Madre*.
1949: Joseph Mankiewicz, *A Letter to Three Wives*.
1950: Joseph Mankiewicz, *All About Eve*.
1951: George Stevens, *A Place in the Sun*.
1952: John Ford, *The Quiet Man*.
1953: Fred Zinnemann, *From Here to Eternity*.
1954: Elia Kazan, *On the Waterfront*.
1955: Delbert Mann, *Marty*.
1956: George Stevens, *Giant*.

Academy Award Winning Songs with their Composers and the Movies in Which They Were Featured

1934: "The Continental": Herb Magidson, Con Conrad; *The Gay Divorcee*; RKO.
1935: "Lullaby of Broadway"; Al Dubin, Harry Warren; *Gold Diggers of 1935*; Warners.

1936: "The Way You Look Tonight"; Jerome Kern, Dorothy Fields; *Swing Time*; RKO.
1937: "Sweet Leilani"; Harry Owens; *Waikiki Wedding*; Paramount.
1938: "Thanks for the Memory"; Leo Robin, Ralph Rainger; *Big Broadcast of 1938*; Paramount.
1939: "Over the Rainbow"; Harold Arlen, E. Y. Harburg; *The Wizard of Oz*; MGM.
1940: "When You Wish Upon a Star"; Leigit Harline, Ned Washington; *Pinocchio*; Disney-RKO.
1941: "The Last Time I Saw Paris"; Jerome Kern, Oscar Hammerstein; *Lady Be Good*; MGM.
1942: "White Christmas"; Irving Berlin; *Holiday Inn*; Paramount.
1943: "You'll Never Know"; Harry Warren, Mack Gordon; *Hello, Frisco, Hello*; 20th Century-Fox.
1944: "Swinging on a Star"; Jimmy Van Heusen, Johnny Burke; *Going My Way*; Paramount.
1945: "It Might As Well Be Spring"; Richard Rodgers, Oscar Hammerstein; *State Fair*; 20th Century-Fox.
1946: "On the Atchison, Topeka and The Santa Fe"; Johnny Mercer, Harry Warren; *The Harvey Girls*; MGM.
1947: "Zip-A-Dee-Doo-Dah"; Ray Gilbert, Allie Wrubel; *Song of the South*; Disney-RKO.
1948: "Buttons and Bows"; Jay Livingston, Ray Evans; *The Paleface*; Paramount.
1949: "Baby, It's Cold Outside"; Frank Loesser; *Neptune's Daughter*; MGM.
1950: "Mona Lisa"; Jay Livingston, Ray Evans; *Captain Cary, USA*; Paramount.
1951: "In the Cool, Cool, Cool of the Evening"; Hoagy Carmichael, Johnny Mercer; *Here Comes the Groom*; Paramount.
1952: "High Noon"; Dimitri Tiomkin, Ned Washington; *High Noon*; Kramer-United Artists.
1953: "Secret Love"; Sammy Fain, Paul Francis Webster; *Calamity Jane*; Warners.
1954: "Three Coins in the Fountain"; Sammy Cahn, Jule Styne; *Three Coins in the Fountain*; 20th Century-Fox.
1955: "Love is a Many-Splendored Thing"; Sammy Fain, Paul Francis Webster; *Love is a Many-Splendored Thing*; 20th Century-Fox.
1956: "Whatever Will Be, Will Be"; Jay Livingston, Ray Evans; *The Man Who Knew Too Much*; Paramount.

Admission, Secession, and Readmission of States to the Union of the United States of America

Thirteen Original States

1. DELAWARE: December 7, 1787.
2. PENNSYLVANIA: December 12, 1787.
3. NEW JERSEY: December 18, 1787.
4. GEORGIA: January 2, 1788.
5. CONNECTICUT: January 9, 1788.
6. MASSACHUSETTS: February 6, 1788.
7. MARYLAND: April 28, 1788.
8. SOUTH CAROLINA: May 23, 1788.
9. NEW HAMPSHIRE: June 21, 1788.
10. VIRGINIA June 25, 1788.
11. NEW YORK: July 26, 1788.
12. NORTH CAROLINA: November 21, 1789.
13. RHODE ISLAND: May 29, 1790.

Admission of States

14. VERMONT: March 4, 1791.
15. KENTUCKY: June 1, 1792.
16. TENNESSEE: June 1, 1796.
17. OHIO: February 19, 1803.
18. LOUISIANA: April 30, 1812.
19. INDIANA: December 11, 1816.
20. MISSISSIPPI: December 10, 1817.
21. ILLINOIS: December 3, 1818.
22. ALABAMA: December 14, 1819.
23. MAINE: March 15, 1820.
24. MISSOURI: August 10, 1821.
25. ARKANSAS: June 15, 1836.
26. MICHIGAN: January 26, 1837.
27. FLORIDA: March 3, 1845.
28. TEXAS: December 29, 1845.
29. IOWA: December 28, 1846.
30. WISCONSIN: May 29, 1848.
31. CALIFORNIA: September 9, 1850.
32. MINNESOTA: May 11, 1858.
33. OREGON: February 14, 1859.
34. KANSAS: January 29, 1861.
35. WEST VIRGINIA: June 20, 1863.
36. NEVADA: October 31, 1864.
37. NEBRASKA: March 1, 1867.
38. COLORADO: August 1, 1876.
39 and 40. NORTH DAKOTA and SOUTH
      DAKOTA: November 2, 1889.
41. MONTANA November 8, 1889.
42. WASHINGTON: November 11, 1889.
43. IDAHO: July 3, 1890.
44. WYOMING: July 10, 1890.
45. UTAH: January 4, 1896.
46. OKLAHOMA: November 16, 1907.
47. NEW MEXICO: January 6, 1912.
48. ARIZONA: February 14, 1912.

Secession of States

SOUTH CAROLINA: December 20, 1860.
MISSISSIPPI: January 9, 1861.
FLORIDA: January 10, 1861.
ALABAMA: January 11, 1861.
GEORGIA: January 19, 1861.
LOUISIANA: January 26, 1861.
TEXAS: February 1, 1861.
VIRGINIA: April 17, 1861.
ARKANSAS: May 6, 1861.
NORTH CAROLINA: May 20, 1861.
TENNESSEE: June 8, 1861.

Readmission of States

TENNESSEE: July 24, 1866.
ARKANSAS: June 22, 1868.
ALABAMA: June 25, 1868.
FLORIDA: June 25, 1868.
GEORGIA: June 25, 1868 (readmitted a second
      time July 15, 1870).
LOUISIANA: June 25, 1868.
NORTH CAROLINA: June 25, 1868.
SOUTH CAROLINA: June 25, 1868.
VIRGINIA: January 26, 1870.
MISSISSIPPI: February 23, 1870.
TEXAS: March 30, 1870.
GEORGIA: July 15, 1870 (readmitted a second
      time).

Most Recurrent Letters of the English Alphabet

The normal frequencies with which letters of
the English alphabet occur from most to least
frequent: E T O A N I R S H D L U C M
P F Y W G B V K J X Z Q.
The telegraphic frequencies with which the letters
of the English alphabet occur have been established in the following sequence, from most
to least frequent: E O A N I R S T D L
H U C M P Y F G W B V K X J Q Z.

American Indians
See **Indians, American**

Ancient Near East Rulers
See **Rulers**

Angels
See also **Saints; Gods and God-desses**

Choirs of Angels

ANGEL: In post-canonical and apocalyptic literature angels are grouped in varying orders,
and the hierarchy thus constructed was
adapted to Church uses by the early Christian
Fathers. In his *De Hierarchia Celesti*,
Dionysius, the Areopagite, says that there are
three great divisions of angels; each division
is subdivided into three orders or choirs, thus
making nine in all; the names are taken
from the Old Testament (Eph. I, 21, and Col.
I, 16):

I. *Councilors of the Most High*, consisting of
Seraphim, Cherubim, and Thrones.
II. *Governors*, who rule the stars and regulate
the universe, consisting of Dominations, Virtues, and Powers.
III. *Messengers of God's Will*, consisting of Principalities or Princedoms, Archangels, and Angels.

Seven Holy Angels

SEVEN HOLY ANGELS: The Seven Holy Angels are Michael and Gabriel, who are mentioned in the Bible, Raphael, who is mentioned in the Apocrypha, and Uriel, Chamuel,
Jophiel, and Zadkiel. All seven are mentioned
in the aprocryphal book of Enoch (VIII, 2).

Animals in Symbolism
See also **Horses in Legend and Fiction**

ANIMALS IN HEAVEN. According to Mohammedan legend the following ten animals have
been allowed to enter paradise. (1) Jonah's
whale; (2) Solomon's ant; (3) the ram caught
by Abraham and sacrificed instead of Isaac;
(4) the lapwing of Balkis; (5) the camel of
the prophet Saleh; (6) Balaam's ass; (7) the
ox of Moses; (8) the dog Kratim or Katmir
of the Seven Sleepers; (9) Al Borak, Mahomet's ass; and (10) Noah's dove.
ANIMALS SACRED TO SPECIAL DEITIES:
To Apollo, the wolf, the griffin, and the crow;
to Bacchus, the dragon and the panther; to
Diana, the stag; to Aesculapius, the serpent;
to Hercules, the deer; to Isis, the heifer; to
Jupiter, the eagle; to Juno, the peacock and
the lamb; to the Lares, the dog; to Mars, the
horse and the vulture; to Mercury, the cock;
to Minerva, the owl; to Neptune, the bull;
to Tethys, the halcyon; to Venus, the dove, the
swan, and the sparrow; to Vulcan, the lion.
ANIMALS IN SYMBOLISM: The lamb, the pelican, and the unicorn are symbols of Christ.

The dragon, serpent, and swine symbolize Satan and his crew. The ant symbolizes frugality and prevision; ape, uncleanness, malice, lust, and cunning; ass, stupidity; bantam cock, pluckiness, priggishness; bat, blindness; bear, ill-temper, uncouthness; bee, industry; beetle, blindness; bull, strength, straightforwardness; bulldog, pertinacity; butterfly, sportiveness, living in pleasure; camel, submission; cat, deceit; calf, lumpishness, cowardice; cicada, poetry; cock, vigilance, overbearing insolence; cow, longevity; crocodile, hypocrisy; cuckoo, cuckoldom; dog, fidelity, dirty habits; dove, innocence, harmlessness; duck, deceit (French, *canard;* a hoax); eagle, majesty, inspiration; elephant, sagacity, ponderosity; fly, feebleness, insignificance; fox, cunning, artifice; frog and toad, inspiration; goat, lasciviousness; goose, conceit, folly; gull, gullibility; grasshopper, old age; hare, timidity; hawk, rapacity, penetration; hen, maternal care; hog, impurity; horse, speed, grace; jackdaw, vain assumption, empty conceit; jay, senseless chatter; kitten, playfulness; lamb, innocence, sacrifice; lark, cheerfulness; leopard, sin; lion, noble courage; lynx, suspicious vigilance; magpie, garrulity; mole, blindness, obtuseness; monkey, tricks; mule, obstinacy; nightingale, forlornnes; ostrich, stupidity; ox, patience, strength, pride; owl, wisdom; parrot, mocking verbosity; peacock, pride; pigeon, cowardice (pigeon-livered); pig, obstinacy, dirtiness; puppy, empty-headed conceit; rabbit, fecundity; raven, ill luck; robin redbreast, confiding trust; serpent, wisdom; sheep, silliness, timidity; sparrow, lasciviousness; spider, wiliness; stag, cuckoldom; swallow, a sunshine friend; swan, grace; swine, filthiness, greed; tiger, ferocity; tortoise, chastity; turkey-cock, official insolence; turtledove, conjugal fidelity; vulture rapine; wolf, cruelty, savage ferocity, rapine; worm, cringing.

Apocrypha
See also **Bible; Scriptures**

Apocrypha (Gr. *apokryphos,* hidden; hence, of unknown authorship). Those books included in the Septuagint and Vulgate versions of the Old Testament, but which, at the Reformation, were excluded from the Sacred Canon by the Protestants, mainly on the grounds that they were not originally written in Hebrew and were not looked upon as genuine by the Jews. They are not printed in Protestant Bibles in ordinary circulation, but in the Authorized Version, as printed in 1611, they are given immediately after the Old Testament. The books are as follows;

I and II ESDRAS
TOBIT
JUDITH
THE REST OF ESTHER
WISDOM OF SOLOMON
ECCLESIASTICUS
BARUCH, WITH THE EPISTLE OF JEREMIAH
THE SONG OF THE THREE CHILDREN
THE STORY OF SUSANNA
THE IDOL BEL AND THE DRAGON
I and II MACCABEES
The New Testament also has a large number of apocryphal books more or less attached to it. These consist of later gospels and epistles, etc., as well as such recently discovered fragments as the Logia (sayings of Jesus) or the Oxyrhynchus papyrus. The best

known books of the New Testament apocrypha are:

PROTEVANGELIUM, OR THE BOOK OF JAMES
GOSPEL OF NICODEMUS, OR THE ACTS OF PILATE
THE ASCENTS OF JAMES
THE ACTS OF PAUL AND THECLA
LETTERS OF ABGARUS TO CHRIST
EPISTLES OF PAUL TO THE LAODICEANS, AND TO THE ALEXANDRINES, AND THE THIRD EPISTLE TO THE CORINTHIANS
THE TEACHING OF THE APOSTLES (DIDACHÉ)
THE THREE BOOKS OF THE SHEPHERD OF HERMAS.

The Apostles and Evangelists with Their Appropriate Symbols
See also **Pseudonyms, Nicknames, and Special Associations for Historical Persons; Religious Allusions, References, and Symbols**

APOSTLES AND EVANGELISTS: The name Apostle is used with reference to the commonly accepted list of the twelve companions of Christ, which is based on the four conflicting lists given in the New Testament gospels; sometimes Matthias, who was chosen to take the place of Judas Iscariot, is also included, as is Paul. The name is also used in a general way for the early church missionaries whose deeds are related in the *Acts of the Apostles.* The Evangelists, four in number, are the authors of the four gospels of the New Testament. Two of the Evangelists, Matthew and John, were also among the original Twelve Apostles. Little is known of the lives of the other two Evangelists, Mark and Luke.

ANDREW: A *cross decussate,* formed of two pieces of wood crossing each other in the form of the letter X, representing the shape of the cross on which he was crucified; some legends state that he was crucified on a cross of usual shape, but that the ground gave under his weight so that the cross came to rest upon one of the side arms as well as upon the foot.

BARTHOLOMEW: A flaying knife, because he was flayed to death with one.

JAMES THE GREATER (SON OF ZEBEDEE): A pilgrim's staff, with a gourd attached to it, because he is the patron of pilgrims; also a scallop shell.

JAMES THE LESS (SON OF ALPHAEUS): A club of peculiar shape, called a fuller's pole or bat, because Simeon the Fuller killed him with a blow from such a pole.

JOHN THE DIVINE (SON OF ZEBEDEE): A cup with a winged serpent flying out of it, in allusion to the cup of sorrow which he drank, according to Christ's promise; or to the legend about Aristodemos, the priest of Diana, who gave John a cup of poison from which the saint exorcised the devil, or the harm, by the sign of the cross; as an Evangelist, he is represented by an eagle soaring above the earth because his gospel testifies to the Divine Nature of Christ.

JUDAS ISCARIOT: A bag, because he had the bag and "bare what was put therein" (John XII, 6).

JUDE (identified with THADDEUS): A club, because he was martyred with a club; also a ship.

LUKE: With a pen, looking, in deep thought over a scroll, and near him a cow or ox, symbolical of Zacharias' sacrifice at the beginning of Luke's Gospel. He is also frequently shown as painting a picture, from the tradition that he painted a portrait of the Virgin.

MARK: Seated writing, and by his side a couchant winged lion. Mark begins his gospel with the sojourn of Jesus in the wilderness, amidst wild beasts, and the temptation of Satan, "the roaring lion."

MATTHEW (OR LEVI): A book, or a purse, represents him as an Apostle, because he was a tax-collector; as an Evangelist, his emblem is a man, because his gospel is concerned chiefly with the Human Nature of Christ; also a hatchet or halbert, because he was martyred at Nadabar with a halbert.

MATTHIAS: An ax, or a spear and lance, because, after being stoned, he was beheaded with a battle-ax; also a book.

PAUL: A sword, because he was beheaded with a sword, and because it signifies the good fight of the faithful Christian armed "with the sword of the spirit, which is the word of God"; the Spanish Convent of La Lisla has a sword said to be the instrument of Paul's martyrdom.

PETER: A bunch of keys, or two keys, one gold and one silver, symbolizing the power to absolve and to bind which was given to him when he was made custodian of the "keys of the kingdom of heaven" and virtual porter at the gates of heaven and of hell; also a cock, because he went out and wept bitterly when he heard the cock crow (Matt. XXVI, 75).

PHILIP: A long staff surmounted by a Latin or a Tau Cross, because he was martyred by being hung from a tall pillar; also a double cross.

SIMON (THE CANANAEAN, OR ZEALOT): A saw, because it was the instrument of his martyrdom; also two or more fishes.

THOMAS (OR DIDYMUS): An arrow, or a spear and lance, because he was pierced through the body and martyred at Meliapour; also a builder's rule or square.

Architects, Their Schools and Representative Works

ADAM, ROBERT: (1727-1792); b. England; l. England; important influence in late Georgian architecture; the Adelphi, London.

ALBERTI (LEONE BATTISTA): (1404-1472); b. Venice; l. Florence, Rome; Renaissance scholar and architect; main façade, Santa Maria Novella, Florence.

ALESSI, GALEAZZO: (1515-1572); b. Perugia; l. Genoa, Flanders; associate of Michelangelo; street of Palaces, Genoa.

AMADEO (OMODEO), GIOVANNI ANTONIO: (1447-1522); b. Pavia, Italy; l. Milan; Renaissance Gothic; central tower, Cathedral of Milan.

AMMANATI, BERTOLOMMEO: (1511-1592); b. Italy; l. Italy; influenced by Michelangelo; famous Bridge of Santa Trinita, Florence.

ANDREA DA PISA: (1270-1349); b. Pisa; l. Florence; pupil of Giovanni da Pisa; architech for the Campanile in Florence after Giotto's death.

ANDROUT (DU CERCEAU), JACQUES: (1510/15-1584); b. France; l. France; famous atelier with circle over door; leader of Renaissance (Italian) in France.

ANTHEMIUS OF TRALLES: (6th cent. A.D.); Church of Aya Sophia in Constantinople, reign of Emperor Justinian.

APOLLODORUS OF DAMASCUS: (2nd cent. B.C.); Rome; architect in the reign of Trajan and Hadrian; Foro Trajan (Trajan's Forum), Rome.

ARCHER, THOMAS: (-1743); England; pupil of Sir John Vanbrugh; Church of St. Philip, Birmingham, England.

ARNOLFO DI CAMBIO: (1232-1303); b. Siena; l. Florence; associated with Santa Croce and Palazzo Vecchio, Florence.

ASAM, COSMAS DAMIAN: (1686-1742); Germany; Baroque period; Johanneskirche, Munich.

BACON, HENRY: (1866-1924); b. America; l. America; Lincoln memorial, Washington, D.C.

BAGLIONI, BACCIO D'AGNOLO: (1462-1543); b. Florence; l. Florence; Renaissance; worked on the great hall of the Palazzo Vecchio, Florence.

BALLU, THÉODORE: (1817-1855); b. France; l. France; classicist; Hôtel-de-Ville, Paris.

BALTARD, VICTOR: (1805-1874); b. France; l. France; classicist, associate of Viollet-le-Duc; built Halles Centrales, the great market of Paris.

BAROZZIO, GIACOMO (VIGNOLA): (1507-1572); b. Milan; l. Rome; influenced by Michelangelo; important architect of the Renaissance; Villa di Papa Guilio; architect of St. Peter's, after Michelangelo.

BARRY, SIR CHARLES: (1795-1860); b. England; l. England; classicist; Houses of Parliament, London.

BASEVI, GEORGE: (Early 19th cent.); l. England; classicist; Belgrave Square, London.

BERNINI, GIOVANNI LORENZO: (1598-1680); b. Italy; l. Rome; Baroque; colonnade of the piazza of St. Peter's, Rome.

BERRUGUETE, ALONSO: (1480-1561); b. Spain; l. Spain; architect to Charles V; influenced by Italian Renaissance; worked on the Alhambra Palace.

BEYAERT, HENRI: (1823-1894); b. Belgium; l. Belgium; Banque Nationale, Brussels.

BLONDEL, FRANÇOIS: (1617/18-1686); b. France; l. France; Triumphal Arch, Porte St. Denis, Paris.

BOLOGNE, JEAN: (1524-1608); b. French Flanders; l. Florence; statuary and fountains in Boboli Gardens, Florence.

BONNANO OF PISA: (12th cent.); b. Italy; l. Pisa; Leaning Tower of Pisa.

BONO, BARTOLOMEO: (15th cent.); b. Venice; l. Venice; Later Gothic; Ca'd'Oro, Venice.

BORROMINI, FRANCESCO: (1559-1667); b. Italy; l. Rome; Baroque; architect for St. Peter's, after Bernini.

BRAMANTE (DONATO D'AGNOLO): (1444-1514); b. Urbino; l. Milan, Rome; Renaissance; the Vatican, Rome.

BRANDON, JOHN RAPHAEL: (1817-1877); b. England; l. England; English Gothic.

BROSSE, SALOMON DE: (1560-1626); b. France; l. France; architect for Maria de' Medici; Luxembourg Palace, Paris.

BRUNELLESCHI, FILIPPO DI: (1377-1446); b. Florence; l. Florence; greatest name in Florentine Renaissance architecture; cupola of the Duomo Cathedral, Florence.

BULFINCH, CHARLES: (1763-1844); b. America; l. Boston; first native architect of Boston; State House, Boston.

BULLANT, JEAN: (1512-1578); b. France; l. France; Roman classicist; effected transition from Renaissance to French Classic style; chateau at Écouen.

BURGES, WILLIAM: (1827-1881); b. England; l. England; medievalist; Cathedral of Cork, Ireland.

BURLINGTON, EARL OF: (1695-1753); b. Ireland; l. England; enthusiastic admirer of Palladio; Burlington House, London.

BURNHAM, DANIEL HUDSON: (1846-1912); b. America; l. Chicago; pioneer city planner.

BUTTERFIELD, WILLIAM: (1814-1900); b. England; l. England; Gothic style; Keble College, Oxford.

CAMPBELL, COLIN: (-1727); b. England; l. England; protégé of Earl of Burlington; Wamstead House, Essex.

CARRÈRE, JOHN MERVEN: (1858-1911; American; Carrère and Hastings, architects; U. S. Senate and House of Representatives office buildings; New York Public Library.

CAUS, SALOMON DE: (1576-1626); b. France; l. England, Germany; engineer, landscape architect; gardens at Heidelberg Castle, Germany.

CHAMBERS, SIR WILLIAM: (1726-1811); b. Sweden; l. England; classical style of Palladio; buildings of Kew Gardens, London.

CHAMBIGÉS, MARTIN: (-1532); France; Cathedral of Sens, France.

CHELLES, JEAN DE: (13th cent.); France; Earliest architectural name connected with Cathedral of Notre Dame, Paris.

CHESIPHRON OF KNOSSOS: (7th cent. B.C.); Greece; earliest architect of Ionic Temple of Artemis at Ephesus, Asia Minor.

CHRODEGAND, ST.: (8th cent.); Germany; cloister at Metz, Lothringen, Germany; the cloister became a prototype.

COCKERELL, CHARLES ROBERT: (1788-1863); b. England; l. England; classicist; Bank of England.

COSSUTIUS: (2nd cent. B. C.); Athens; Corinthian style; Temple of Olympian Zeus, Athens.

COTTE, ROBERT DE: (1656-1735); b. France; l. France; pupil of Mansart; central tower, Cathedral of Orléans.

CRONACA, IL (SIMONE DE PALLAJUOLO): (1457-1508); Florentine architect and antiquarian; St. Salvatore al Monte, Florence.

CUVILLIÉS, FRANÇOIS DE: (1698-1767); b. France; l. Bavaria; French Baroque; Residenz-theater, Munich.

DANCE, GEORGE II: (1741-1825); b. England; l. England; classicist; Newgate Prison, London.

DEINOCRATUS: (4th cent. B. C.); Macedonia; favorite architect of Alexander the Great; laid out city of Alexandria.

L'ORME, PHILIBERT DE: (1515-1570); France; principal architect of Henry II, Diane de Poitiers, Catherine de' Medici; Tuileries begun by him, Chateau of Anet.

DUC, LOUIS JOSEPH: (1802-1879); l. France; pupil of Charles Percier; reconstructed Palais de Justice, Paris.

EGINHARD: (742-814); Switzerland; director of constructions for Emperor Charlemagne; Monastery of St. Gall, Switzerland.

EIFFEL, ALEXANDER GUSTAVE: (1832-1923); France; Eiffel Tower.

ENSINGER, MATHIAS VON: (-1463); Germany; Cathedral of Ulm, Germany.

ERWIN VON STEINBACH: (13th cent.); Germany; façade of Strasbourg Cathedral.

FILARTE: (1400-1465); b. Italy; l. Italy; assistant to Ghiberti; Ospedale Maggiore, Milan.

FISCHER VON ERLACH, JOHANN BERNHARD: (1656-1723); b. Austria; educ. Rome; began Schönbrun Castle, Vienna.

FLAGG, ERNEST: (1857-1947); American; small houses.

FLORIS, CORNELIUS DE: (1518-1575); b. Belgium; l. Belgium; studied in Rome; City Hall of Antwerp.

FONTANA, CARLO: (1634-1714); b. Italy; l. Rome; pupil of Bernini, Baroque; monument to Queen Christina in St. Peter's, Rome.

FONTANA, DOMENICO: (1543-1607); b. Italy; l. Rome; influenced by Michelangelo; Villa Negroni, Rome.

FONTAINE, PIERRE FRANÇOIS LEONARD: (1763-1853); b. France; l. France; famous atelier, Percier and Fontaine, architects for Napoleon; restored and enlarged Palais Royal.

FUGA, FERDINANDO: (1699-1784); b. Italy; l. Rome; Palazzo Corsini, Rome.

FULLER, THOMAS: (1822-1898); b. England; l. Canada; Gothic Revivalist; government buildings, Ottawa.

GABRIEL, JACQUES ANGE: (1698-1782); b. France; l. France; architect to Louis XV; Petit Trianon in Garden of Versailles.

GALILEI, ALESSANDRO: (1691-1737); b. Florence; l. England, Rome; influenced by Sir Christopher Wren; façade of San Giovanni, Laterano, Italy.

GALLI DA BIBIENA, FERDINANDO: (1657-1743); b. Tuscany; l. Italy; head of da Bibiena family, all associated with theater construction; Teatro Reale, Mantua, Italy.

GAMBARELLI, BERNARDO DI MATTEO: (1427-1479); Florence; Renaissance; monument of Leonardo Bruni, Santa Croce, Florence.

GARNIER, JEAN LOUIS CHARLES: (1825-1898); b. France; l. France; classicist; Casino, Monte Carlo, Monaco.

GHIBERTI, LORENZO DE': (1378-1455); b. Florence; l. Florence; Renaissance; famous bronze doors of Baptistry, Florence.

GIACOMO DELLA PORTA: (1541-1604); b. Milan; l. Rome; important pupil of Vignola (Barozzio, Giacomo); built cupola of St. Peter's after design of Michelangelo.

GIBBS, JAMES: (1682-1754); b. Scotland; l. England; Italian Renaissance style; Radcliffe Library, Oxford.

GILBERT, CASS: (1859-1934); American; eclectic period; Woolworth Building.

GIOCONDO, FRA GIOVANNI: (died between 1515-1519); b. Verona; l. Italy, Paris; most learned monk of his time; Pont Notre Dame, Paris.

GIOTTO DI BONDONE: (1267-1337); b. Italy; l. Florence; painter and architect, the beginner of the Renaissance; campanile of Duomo Cathedral, Florence.

GOODHUE, BERTRAM GROSVENOR: (1869-1924); America; early modern architect; Capitol at Lincoln, Nebraska.

GROPIUS, WALTER: (1883-); b. Germany; l. America; Bauhaus Group; new buildings at Harvard College, Mass.

GUMPP, GEORG ANTON: (1670-1730); b. Germany; l. Germany; most important architect of German Baroque; churches and palaces in Innsbruck, Tyrol, Austria.

HANSEN, THEOPHILUS: (1813-1890); b. Copenhagen; l. Athens; classicist and medievalist; the Academy, Athens, Greece.

HARDOUIN-MANSART, JULES: (1646-1708); b. France; l. France; architect associated with Louis XIV; Versailles.

HASTINGS, THOMAS: (1860-1929); America; eclectic period; cooperative apartments, Long Island, N. Y.

HAWKSMOOR, NICHOLAS: (1661-1736); b. England; l. England; associated with Sir Christopher Wren; towers, All Souls College, Oxford.

HERRERA, JUAN DE: (-1530); b. Spain; l. Spain; favorite architect of Philip II; Church of the Escurial, Spain.

HITTORFF, JACQUES IGNACE: (1793-1867); b. Germany; l. France; pupil of Percier, neo-Grec movement; column of the Place Vendôme, Paris.

HOBAN, JAMES: (19th cent.); b. Ireland; l.

America; designer of the White House, Washington, D. C.

HOLLAND, HENRY: (1746-1806); England; Drury Lane Theater, London.

HUNT, RICHARD MORRIS: (1828-1895); b. America; l. America; Victorian period; Marble House, Newport, R. I.

ICTINUS: (5th Cent. B.C.); Greece; one of the 7 greatest architects of ancient Greece; the Parthenon, Athens.

ISODORUS OF MILETUS: (6th cent. A.D.); Constantinople; Church of St. Sophia, Constantinople.

JEFFERSON, THOMAS: (1743-1826); b. America; l. Virginia; classicist; influenced by Palladio; University of Virginia.

JONES, INIGO: (1573-1652); b. England; l. England; influenced by Palladio and classics; Covent Garden, London.

KEYSER, HENDRICK CORNELISZOON DE: (1556-1621); b. Amsterdam; l. Holland; the most important Dutch architect; monument to Erasmus, Rotterdam.

KLENZE, LEO VON: (1784-1864); Germany; studied in Páris with Charles Percier; Glyptothek, Munich.

LABROUSTE, HENRI PIERRE FRANÇOIS: (1801-1875); b. France; l. France; classicist; Library of St. Geneviève, Paris.

LANGHANS, KARL GOTTHARD: (1733-1808); Germany; classicist; Brandenburg Gate, Berlin.

LASSUS, JEAN BAPTISTE ANTOINE: (1807-1857); b. France; l. France; French Gothic style; restoration of Notre Dame, Paris.

LATROBE, BENJAMIN HENRY: (1762-1870); b. England; l. America; Capitol (he replaced Thornton), Washington, D.C.

LE BRETON, GILLES: (-1552); France; Fontainebleau.

LE CORBUSIER (CHARLES JEANNERET): (1883-); b. Switzerland; l. France; foremost contemporary architect; apartment house in Marseilles.

LEMERCIER, JACQUES: (1590-1654); b. France; l. France; worked for Cardinal Richelieu; the Sorbonne, Paris.

LESCOT, PIERRE: (1510/15-1578); b. France; l. France; first to develop use of Classic Orders in France; one wing of the Louvre.

LEVAU, LOUIS: (1612-1670); b. France; l. France; classicist; remodeled Louvre and Tuileries.

LOMBARDO, PIETRO: (1433-1515); b. Lombardy; l. Venice; Renaissance; Church of Santa Maria du Miracoli, Venice.

LUTYENS, SIR EDWIN LANDSEER: (1869-1944); b. England; l. England; Middleton Park, Oxfordshire.

McCOMB, JOHN: (1763-1853); b. Scotland; l. America; Georgian; City Hall, New York City.

MC KIM, CHARLES FOLLEN: 1847-1909); b. America; l. America; Greek, Renaissance, and Gothic derivatives; Firm of McKim, Mead and White; Savoy Plaza Hotel, New York City.

MADERNA, CARLO: (1556-1629); b. Lombardy; l. Rome; for many years Rome's leading architect; Palazzo Barberini, Rome.

MANSART, NICHOLAS FRANÇOIS: (1598-1666); b. France; l. France; mansard roof named for him; chateaux in provinces and many houses in Paris.

MASSARI, GIORGIO: (18th cent.); Venice; Ca' Rezzonico, Venice.

MEAD, WILLIAM RUTHERFORD: (1846-1928); America; firm of McKim, Mead and White; many banks and hotels; New York City.

MICHELANGELO: (1475-1564); b. Florence; l. Rome, Florence; great man of the Renaissance; Tomb of the Medicis, Florence.

MICHELOZZI DI BARTOLOMMEO: (1396-1472); b. Florence; l. Florence; Cloister of San Marco, Florence.

MONTREUIL, PIERRE DE: (13th cent.); France; principal architect of Louis IX; Sainte-Chapelle in Palais de Justice, Paris.

NASH, SIR JOHN: (1752-1835); b. England; l. England; designed Regents Park section of London.

NEPVEU, PIERRE: (-1538); France; designer of Chateau of Chambord.

NEUTRA, RICHARD: (1892-); b. Vienna; l. California; contemporary expressionist; many houses in California.

NICCOLO DA PISA: (1207?-1278); b. Pisa; l. Italy; cathedral in Siena.

OLMSTEAD, FREDERICH LAW: (1822-1903); b; America; l. America; architect for Central Park and its buildings in New York City. It remains todays as he designed it.

ORSINI, GIORGIO: (15th cent.); b. Dalmatia; l. Italy, Dalmatia; transition from Gothic to Renaissance; cathedral in Sebenico, Dalmatia.

OUD, J. J. P.: (1890-); b. Holland; l. Holland; influenced by Frank Lloyd Wright; workers' housing developments, Rotterdam.

PALLADIO, ANDREA: (1518-1580); b. Italy; l. Italy; Renaissance; Villa Rotunda, Vicenza, Italy.

PENNETHORNE, SIR JAMES: (1801-1871); b. England; l. England; classicist; University of London.

PERCIER, CHARLES: (1764-1838); b. France; l. France; famous atelier, Percier and Fontaine introduced Empire style; reconstruction in Louvre and Tuileries.

PERRAULT, CLAUDE: (1613-1688); France; l. France; physician and architect; eastern façade and famous colonnade of the Louvre.

PERUZZI, BALDASSARE: (1451-1556); b. Volterra; l. Rome; Renaissance; supt. of works at St. Peter's, Rome, Palazzo Massimi, Rome.

PHIDIAS: (5th cent. B.C.); l. Athen; sculptor and architect; supt. of buildings in Athens; Statues of Zeus and Athena, etc.

PIRANESI, GIOVANNI BATTISTA: (1720-1778); b. Venice; l. Rome; architect and engraver; famous for engravings of Roman architecture.

POPPLEMAN, MATTHÄUS DANIEL: (1662-1736); b. Dresden; l. Dresden; Baroque; the Zwinger Palace, Dresden.

POPE, JOHN RUSSELL: (1874-1937); b. America; l. America; contemporary; Roosevelt Memorial in Washington, D. C.

POST, GEORGE BROWNE: (1837-1913); b. America; l. America; New York City architect.

PUGIN, AUGUSTUS WELBY: (1813-1852); b. England; l. England; medieval rationalist; built Catholic churches and worked on Houses of Parliament.

PYTHIUS: (4th cent. B.C.); b. Greece; l. Greece; Temple of Pallas Athena, Priene, Ionia.

RAINALDI, CARLO: (1611-1691); b. Rome; l. Rome; Church of Santa Agnese, Rome.

RAPHAEL (RAFFAELLO SANTI): (1483-1520); b. Urbino; l. Rome, Florence; Renaissance painter and architect; succeeded Bramanti as architect of St. Peter's, Rome.

RENWICK, JAMES (1818-1895); b. America; l. America; Victorian; Smithsonian Institution, Washington, D.C.

RICCHINI, FRANCESCO MARIA: (17th cent.); b. Italy; l. Milan; supervising architect of Milan Cathedral (1605-1638).

RICHARDSON, HENRY HOBSON: (1838-1886); b. America; l. America; Romanesque (American); Trinity Church, Boston.

RIPLEY, THOMAS: (1685-1758); b. England; l. England; the Admiralty, London.

RIZZO, ANTONIO DE GIOVANNI: (-1498); b. Venice; l. Venice; Venetian Renaissance; Doge's Palace.

SAARINEN, ELIEL: (1873-1950); b. Norway; l. America; contemporary; Cranbrook School, Bloomfield Hills, Michigan.

SAN GALLO, ANTONIO, II: (1585-1646); b. Rome; l. Rome; Renaissance; leading Roman Architect, associated with Raphael.

SANMICHELI, MICHELE: (1487-1559); b. Verona; l. Italy; Renaissance; influenced by Raphael; churches in Verona, military fortifications in Parma, Piacenzo.

SANSOVINO, JACOPO: (1488-1570); b. Florence l. Rome, Venice; Renaissance; Library of St. Mark, Venice.

SCAMOZZI, VICENZO: (1552-1616); b. Vicenzo; l. Venice; pupil and rival of Palladio; Cathedral of Salzburg.

SCHINKEL, KARL FRIEDRICH: (1781-1841); b. Germany; l. Berlin; Muesum and Royal Theater, Berlin.

SERLIO, SEBASTIANO: (1475-1555); b. Bologna, Italy; l. Fontainebleau, France; Renaissance; Fontainebleau.

SINAN, PASHA ABDULLAH: (16th cent.); b. Turkey; l. Turkey; most influential Turkish architect; credited with mosques, minarets, palaces in Constantinople.

SMIRKE, SIR ROBERT: (1781-1867); b. England; l. England; classicist; main façade, British Museum.

SOUFFLOT, JACQUES GERMAIN: (1709-1780); b. France; l. France; Gothic; Cathedral of Rennes.

STRICKLAND, WILLIAM: (1787-1854); b. America; l. America; Greek Revivalist; Capitol at Nashville, Tenn.

STUART, JAMES: (1713-1788); b. England; l. England; neoclassicist; book, *Antiquities of Athens*, introduced Ionic capital of Erechtheum.

SULLIVAN, LOUIS HENRY: (1856-1924); b. America; l. America; eclectic and functionalist, influenced contemporary architecture in America; Carson, Pirie, Scott Store, Chicago.

TALENTI, FRANCESCO: (14th cent.); b. Italy; l. Florence; Duomo Cathedral, Florence.

TALMAN, WILLIAM: (17th cent.); b. England; l. England; Chatsworth House, Derbyshire.

TESSIN, NICODEMUS II: (1654-1728); b. Sweden; l. Sweden; studied in Italy with Bernini and Carlo Fontana; Palace of Drottningholm, Sweden.

THORNTON, DR. WILLIAM: (1759-1828); b. West Indies; l. America; designer and supervisor of Capitol, Washington, D. C.

TRESGUERRAS, FRANCISCO EDUARDO: (1745-1833); b. Mexico; l. Mexico; "Michelangelo of Mexico"; church, Nuestra Señora del Carmen, Celaya, Mexico.

UPJOHN, RICHARD: (1802-1878); b. England; l. America; Trinity Church, New York City.

VANBRUGH, SIR JOHN: (1666-1726); b. England; l. England; Blenheim Castle.

VAN DER ROHE, MIÈS (1886-); b. Aachen; l. Germany, America; Bauhaus Group; kröler (country) house, Holland.

VASARI, GIORGIO: (1511-1574); b. Italy; Florence, Rome; Renaissance; biographies of Florentine painters; architect for remodeling of Palazzo Vecchio and Palazzo Uffizi, Florence.

VIGNOLA: See Barozzio, Giacomo.

VIGNON, BARTHÉLMY: (1762-1828); b. France; l. France; Church of the Madeleine, Paris.

VIOLLET-LE-DUC, EUGÈNE EMANUEL: (1814-1879); b. France; l. Switzerland, Paris; classicist, important influence in French 19th cent. architecture; restoration and new design for Cathedral of Notre Dame, Paris.

VISCONTI, LOUIS TULLIUS JOACHIM:

(1791-1853); b. Rome; l. France; pupil of Percier; monuments and fountains of Paris; St. Supplice, Les Invalides.

WALTER, THOMAS USTICK: (1804-1887); b. America; l. America; student of William Strickland; one of the architects associated with the Capitol, Washington, added wings for the Senate and House of Representatives.

WHITE, STANFORD: (1853-1906); b. America; l. America; firm of McKim, Mead and White; New York, Newport, and Long Island mansions.

WILLIAM OF SENS: (12th cent.); b. France; l. England; medieval; cathedrals of Sens, France, and Canterbury, England.

WILLIAM OF WYKEHAM: (1324-1404); b. England; l. England; King's Chaplain and Royal Surveyor of Castles; Winchester Cathedral, England.

WREN, SIR CHRISTOPHER: (1632-1723); b. England; l. England; astronomer and classical architect; Seamen's Hospital and Observatory, Greenwich.

WRIGHT, FRANK LLOYD: (1869-); b. America; l. America; Major world influence in contemporary architecture; Imperial Hotel, Tokyo, Japan.

WYATT, JAMES: (1748-1813); b. England; l. England; Gothic style; Fonthill Abbey, Wiltshire.

YBL, NIKOLAUS VON: (-1891); most distinguished architect of Hungary.

Art and Artists
See **Paintings**

Arthur, King
See **Knights of the Round Table**

Austrian Rulers
See **Rulers**

Awards
See **Academy Awards; Hall of Fame for Great Americans; Pulitzer Prizes; New York Drama Critics' Circle Awards; Nobel Prizes; National Book Awards**

Babylonian Gods
See **Gods and Goddesses**

Ballets
See also **Characters from Ballets**

Algeranoff, Harcourt

FOR LOVE OR MONEY: 1951; music: Gilbert Vinter; costumes: John Bainbridge.

Algo, Julian

VISIONS: 1949; music: Modest Mussorgsky; décor: Julian Algo.

Allantin, Eric

DON JUAN: 1936; choreography with Fokine; music: Christoph Willibald Gluck; décor: Mariano Andrèu; première: Alhambra Theater, London.

Alonso, Alicia

ENSAYO SINFONICA: 1951; music: Johannes Brahms *(Variations on a Theme by Haydn)*; première: Metropolitan Opera House, New York.

Andes, Angelo

EL DESTINO; 1948; music: Lazareno; costumes: Hugh Stevenson.
FARRUCA DEL SACRO MONTE; 1948; music: Azagra; costumes: traditional.
JOTA TOLEDANA: 1948; music: traditional; décor: traditional; première: Sadler's Wells Theater, London.

Anisimova, N. A.

GAYNE: 1942; music: Aram Khachaturian; décor: N. Altman; première: Molotov, U.S.S.R.

Argentinita

BOLERO: 1944; music: Maurice Ravel; costumes: Frederico Rey; première: Metropolitan Opera House, New York.
GOYESCAS: 1941; music: Enrique Granados; décor: Nicolas De Molas; première: Palacio de Bellas Artes, Mexico City.

Ashton, Frederick

APPARITIONS: 1936; music: Franz Liszt; décor: Cecil Beaton; première: Sadler's Wells Theater, London.
LE BAISER DE LA FÉE: 1935; music: Igor Stravinsky; décor: Sophie Fedorovich; première: Sadler's Wells Theater, London.
CAPRIOL SUITE: 1930; music: Peter Warlock; décor: William Chappell; première: Lyric Theater, Hammersmith, London.
CINDERELLA: 1948; music: Serge Prokofiev; décor: Jean-Denis Malcles; première: Royal Opera House, Covent Garden, London.
CUPID AND PSYCHE: 1939; music: Lord Berners; décor: Sir Francis Rose; première: Sadler's Wells Theater, London.
DANTE SONATA: 1940; music: Franz Liszt; décor: Sophie Fedorovich; première: Sadler's Wells Theater, London.
DAPHNIS AND CHLOE: 1951; music: Maurice Ravel; décor: John Craxton; première: Royal Opera House, Covent Garden, London.
DEVIL'S HOLIDAY (LE DIABLE S'AMUSE): 1939; music: Vincenzo Tommasini (after Paganini); décor: Eugene Berman; première: Metropolitan Opera House, New York.
DON JUAN: 1948; music: Richard Strauss; décor: Edward Burra; première: Royal Opera House, Covent Garden, London.
DREAMS: 1935 (revival); music: George Antheil; décor: André Derain; première: Metropolitan Opera House, New York.
FAÇADE: 1931; music: William Walton; décor: John Armstrong; première: Cambridge Theater, London.
FANTASIA BRASILEIRA: 1941; music: Francisco Mignone; décor: Enrico Bianco; première: Lima, Peru.
HARLEQUIN IN THE STREET: 1937; music: François Couperin; décor: André Derain; première: Arts Theater, Cambridge (revised première: Sadler's Wells première, London, 1938).
HOMAGE TO THE QUEEN: 1953; music: Malcolm Arnold; décor: Oliver Messel; première: Royal Opera House, Covent Garden, London.

HOROSCOPE: 1938; music: Constant Lambert; décor: Sophie Fedorovich; première: Sadler's Wells Theater, London.
ILLUMINATIONS: 1950; music: Benjamin Britten *(Les Illuminations*, for Tenor and Strings); décor: Cecil Beaton; première: City Center, New York.
THE JUDGMENT OF PARIS: 1938; music: Lennox Berkeley; décor: William Chappell; première: Sadler's Wells Theater, London.
THE LORD OF BURLEIGH: 1931; music: Felix Mendelssohn (orchestration by Edwin Evans); décor: George Sheringham; première: Camargo Society, London.
MADAME CHRYSANTHÈME: 1955; music: Alan Rawsthorne; décor: Isabel Lambert; première: Royal Opera House, Covent Garden, London.
NOCTURNE: 1936; music: Frederick Delius; décor: Sophie Fedorovich; première: Sadler's Wells Theater, London.
LES PATINEURS: 1937; music: Giacomo Meyerbeer; décor: William Chappell; première: Sadler's Wells Theater, London.
PICNIC AT TINTAGEL: 1952; music: Sir Arnold Bax; décor: Cecil Beaton; première: City Center, New York.
POMONA: 1930; music: Constant Lambert; décor: Vanessa Bell; première: Camargo Society, London.
THE QUEST: 1943; music: William Walton; décor: John Piper; première: New Theater, London.
REGATTA: 1931; music: Gavin Gordon; décor: William Chappell; première: Old Vic, London.
LES RENDEZ-VOUS: 1933; music: Francois Auber; décor: William Chappell; première: Sadler's Wells Theater, London.
LA RÊVE DE LÉONOR: 1949; music: Benjamin Britten; décor: Léonor Fini.
RINALDO AND ARMIDA: 1955; music: Malcolm Arnold; décor: Peter Rice; première: Royal Opera House, Covent Garden, London.
RIO GRANDE: 1935; revision of Camargo Society's *A Day in a Southern Port* (1931); music: Constant Lambert; décor: Edvard Burra; première: Sadler's Wells Theater, London.
SCÈNES DE BALLET: 1948; music: Igor Stravinsky; décor: André Beaurepaire; première: Royal Opera House, Covent Garden, London.
SIESTA: 1936; music: William Walton; première: Sadler's Wells Theater, London.
LES SIRENES: 1946; music: Lord Berners; décor: Cecil Beaton; première: Royal Opera House, Covent Garden, London.
SYLVIA: 1952; music: Léo Delibes; décor: Robin and Christopher Ironside; première: Royal Opera House, Covent Garden, London.
SYMPHONIC VARIATIONS: 1946; music: César Franck; décor: Sophie Fedorovich; première: Royal Opera House, Covent Garden, London.
TIRESIAS: 1951; music: Constant Lambert; décor: Isabel Lambert; première: Royal Opera House, Covent Garden, London.
VARIATIONS ON A THEME OF PURCELL: 1955; music: Benjamin Britten; décor: Peter Snow; première: Royal Opera House, Covent Garden, London.
THE WANDERER: 1941; music: Franz Schubert, Franz Liszt; décor: Graham Sutherland; première: Sadler's Wells Theater, London.
THE WEDDING BOUQUET: 1937; music: Lord Berners; décor: Lord Berners; première: Sadler's Wells Theater, London.
THE WISE VIRGINS: 1940; music: Johann Sebastian Bach (orchestration by William Walton); décor: Rex Whistler; première: Sadler's Wells Theater, London.

Babilée, Jean

L'AMOUR ET SON AMOUR: 1948; music: César Franck; décor: Jean Cocteau; première: Théâtre des Champs-Elysées, Paris.
TILL EULENSPIEGEL: 1949; music; Richard Strauss; décor: Tom Keogh; première: Théâtre des Champs-Elysées, Paris.

Balanchine, George

À LA FRANÇAIX: 1951; music: Jean Françaix. (Serenade for Small Orchestra); première: City Center, New York.
ALMA MATER: 1934; music: Kay Swift (arranged by Morton Gould); décor: Eugene Dunkel; première: Avery Memorial Theater, Hartford Connecticut.
APOLLON MUSAGÈTE: 1928; music: Igor Stravinsky; décor: André Bauchant; première: Théâtre Sarah Bernhardt, Paris.
APOLLON MUSAGÈTE: 1937 (revival); music: Igor Stravinsky; décor: Stewart Chaney; première: Metropolitan Opera House, New York.
LE BAISER DE LA FÉE: 1937; music: Igor Stravinsky; décor: Alicia Halicka; première: Metropolitan Opera House, New York.
LE BAL: 1929; music: Vittorio Rieti; décor: Giorgio di Chirico; première: Royal Opera House, Covent Garden, London.
BALLET IMPERIAL: 1941; music: Peter Tchaikovsky (Piano Concerto in G Major); décor: Mstislav Doboujinsky; première: Hunter College Playhouse, New York.
BALUSTRADE: 1941; music: Igor Stravinsky (Concerto for Violin and Orchestra); décor: Pavel Tchelitchev; première: Fifty-first Street Theater, New York.
BARABAU: 1925; music: Vittorio Rieti; décor: Maurice Utrillo; première: Coliseum, London.
BAYOU: 1952; music: Virgil Thomson (Arcadian Songs and Dances); décor: Dorothy Tanning; première: City Center, New York.
LE BOURGEOIS GENTILHOMME: 1932; music: Richard Strauss (Ariadne auf Naxos); décor: Alexandre Benois; première: Théâtre de Monte Carlo.
LE BOURGEOIS GENTILHOMME: 1944 (revival); music: Richard Strauss; décor: Eugene Berman; première: City Center, New York.
BOURRÉE FANTASQUE: 1949; music: Emmanuel Chabrier; costumes: Karinska; première: City Center, New York.
CAPRICCIO BRILLANT: 1951; music: Felix Mendelssohn; costumes: Karinska; première: City Center, New York.
CARACOLE: 1952; music: Wolfgang Amadeus Mozart (Divertimento No. 15 in B Flat Major, K. 287); costumes: Christian Bérard; première: City Center, New York.
THE CARD PARTY (CARD GAME): 1937; music: Igor Stravinsky; décor: Irene Sharaff; première: Metropolitan Opera House, New York.
LA CHATTE: 1927; music: Henri Sauguet; décor: Pevsner Gabo; première: Théâtre de Monte Carlo.
CONCERTINO: 1952; music: Jean Francaix; costumes: Karinska; première: City Center, New York.
CONCERTO BAROCCO: 1941; music: Johann Sebastian Bach (Concerto in D Minor for Two Violins); décor: Eugene Berman; première: Hunter College Auditorium, New York.
LA CONCURRENCE: 1932; music: Georges Auric; décor: André Dérain; première: Théâtre de Monte Carlo.
COTILLON: 1932; music: Emmanuel Chabrier;

décor: Christian Bérard; première: Théâtre de Monte Carlo.
DANSES CONCERTANTES: 1944; music: Igor Stravinsky; décor: Eugene Berman; première: City Center, New York.
LES DIEUX MENDIANTS: 1928; music: George Frederick Handel (arranged by Sir Thomas Beecham); décor: after Léon Bakst, with costumes by Juan Gris from Les Tentations de la Bergère; première: His Majesty's Theater, London.
DIVERTIMENTO: 1947; music: Alexi Haieff; première: Hunter College Auditorium, New York.
ÉLEGIE: 1948; music: Igor Stravinsky; première: City Center, New York.
L'ERRANT: 1933; music: Franz Schubert (Wanderer Fantasy); décor: Pavel Tchelitchev; première: Metropolitan Opera House, New York.
THE FIREBIRD: 1949 (revival); music: Igor Stravinsky; décor: Marc Chagall; première: City Center, New York.
THE FOUR TEMPERAMENTS: 1946; music: Paul Hindemith; décor: Kurt Seligmann; première: Central High School of Needle Trades, New York.
HARLEQUINADE PAS DE DEUX: 1952; music: Richard Drigo; costumes: Karinska; première: City Center, New York.
IVESIANA: 1954; music: Charles Ives; première City Center, New York.
JACK-IN-THE-BOX: 1926; music: Erik Satie (orchestration by Darius Milhaud); décor: André Derain; première: Diaghilev's Ballets Russes, Théâtre Sarah Bernhardt, Paris.
JONES BEACH: 1950; choreography with Jerome Robbins; music: Juriaan Andriessen (Berkshire Symphonies); première: City Center, New York.
MAZURKA FROM A LIFE FOR THE TSAR: 1950; music: Michael Glinka; première: City Center, New York.
METAMORPHOSES: 1952; music: Paul Hindemith; costumes: Karinska; première: City Center, New York.
MOZARTIANA: 1935; music: Peter Tchaikovsky (Suite No. 4, Mozartiana); décor: Christian Bérard; première: Théâtre des Champs-Elysées, Paris.
NIGHT SHADOW (LA SONNAMBULE): 1946; music: Vittorio Rieti, after Vincenzo Bellini; décor: Dorothy Tanning; première: City Center, New York.
OPUS 34: 1954; music: Arnold Schoenberg (Music to a Scene in a Motion Picture; Suite for String Orchestra); décor: Jean Rosenthal; première: City Center, New York.
ORPHEUS: 1948; music: Igor Stravinsky; décor: Isamu Noguchi; première: City Center, New York.
ORPHEUS AND EURIDICE: 1936; music: Christoph Willibald Gluck; décor: Pavel Tchelitchev; première: Metropolitan Opera House, New York.
LA PALAIS DE CRISTAL (afterward: Symphony in C): 1947; music: Georges Bizet; décor: Léonor Fini; première: Opéra, Paris.
PAS DE DEUX ROMANTIQUE: 1949; music: Carl Maria von Weber (Concerto for Clarinet); costumes: Robert Stevenson; première: City Center, New York.
LA PASTORALE: 1925; music: Georges Auric; décor: Pedro Pruna; première: Diaghilev's Ballets Russes, Gaîté-Lyrique, Paris.
THE PRODIGAL SON: 1929; music: Serge Prokofiev; décor: Georges Rouault; première: Théâtre Sarah Bernhardt, Paris.
REMINISCENCE: 1935; music: Benjamin Godard, Henry Brant; décor: Sergei Soudeikine;

première: Metropolitan Opera House, New York.
ROMA: 1955; music: Georges Bizet; décor: Eugene Berman; première: City Center, New York.
SCOTCH SYMPHONY: 1952; music: Felix Mendelssohn; décor: Horace Armistead; première: City Center, New York.
SERENADE: 1934; music: Peter Tchaikovsky (Serenade in C Major for String Orchestra); costumes: Jean Lurçat; première: Felix M. Warburg Estate, White Plains, New York.
THE SPELLBOUND CHILD: 1946; music: Maurice Ravel (L'Enfant et les Sortilèges); décor: Aline Bernstein; première: Central High School of Needle Trades, New York.
SWAN LAKE: 1951; choreography after Lev Ivanov; music: Peter Tchaikovsky; décor: Cecil Beaton; première: City Center, New York.
SYLVIA: PAS DE DEUX: 1950; music: Léo Delibes; costumes: Karinska; première: City Center, New York.
SYMPHONIE CONCERTANTE: 1947; music: Wolfgang Amadeus Mozart (Sinfonia Concertante in E Flat, K. 364); décor: James Stewart Morcom; première: City Center, New York.
SYMPHONIE IN C (formerly Le Palais de Cristal): 1948; music: Georges Bizet; décor: Léonor Fini; première: City Center, New York.
THEME AND VARIATIONS: 1947; music: Peter Tchaikovsky (Suite No. 3); décor: Woodman Thompson; première: City Center, New York.
TRANSCENDENCE: 1934; music: Franz Liszt (orchestration: George Antheil); décor: Franklin Watkins; première: Avery Memorial Theater, Hartford, Connecticut.
THE TRIUMPH OF BACCHUS AND ARIADNE: 1948); music: Vittorio Rieti; décor: Corrado Cagli; première: City Center, New York.
THE TRIUMPH OF NEPTUNE: 1926; music: Lord Berners; subject: Sacheverell Sitwell; costumes: arranged by Prince Shervachidze from the collection of B. Pollock; première: Diaghilev's Ballets Russes, Théâtre Sarah Bernhardt, Paris.
TRUMPET CONCERTO: 1950; music: Joseph Haydn; décor: Vivienne Kerndt; première: City Center, New York.
TYL ULENSPIEGEL: 1951; music: Richard Strauss; décor: Esteban Francés; première: City Center, New York.
LA VALSE: 1951; music: Maurice Ravel (Valses Nobles et Sentimentales; La Valse); costumes: Karinska; première: City Center, New York.
VALSE FANTASIE: 1953; music: Michael Glinka; costumes: Karinska; première: City Center, New York.
WALTZ ACADEMY: 1944; music: Vittorio Rieti; décor: Oliver Smith; première: Boston Opera House.
WESTERN SYMPHONY: 1954; music: Hershy Kay; décor: John Boyt; première: City Center, New York.

Bettis, Valerie

A STREETCAR NAMED DESIRE: 1952; music: Alex North (orchestration by Rayburn Wright); décor: Peter Larkin; première: Her Majesty's Theater, Montreal.
VIRGINIA SAMPLER: 1947; music: Leo Smit; décor: Charles Elson; première: City Center, New York.

Bolender, Todd

CAPRICORN CONCERTO: 1948; music: Samuel Barber; décor: Esteban Francés; première: City Center, New York.
COMEDIA BALLETICA: 1945; music: G. B. Pergolesi; Igor Stravinsky; décor: Robert Davison; première: City Center, New York.
THE FILLY (A STABLEBOY'S DREAM): 1953; music: John Colman; décor: Peter Larkin; première: City Center, New York.
THE MIRACULOUS MANDARIN: 1951; music: Béla Bartók; décor: Alvin Colt; première: City Center, New York.
MOTHER GOOSE SUITE: 1943; music: Maurice Ravel; première: Central High Scool of Needle Trades, New York.
SOUVENIRS: 1955; music: Samuel Barber; décor: Rouben Ter-Arutunian; première: City Center, New York.
ZODIAK: 1947; music: Rudi Revil; décor: Estaban Francés; première: City Center, New York.

Bolm, Adolph

EL AMOR BRUJO: 1925; music: Manuel de Falla; décor: Rollo Peters; première: Chicago Opera Ballet.
APOLLON MUSAGÈTES: 1928; music: Igor Stravinsky; première: Auditorium, Library of Congress, Washington, D.C.
BAL DE MARIONETTES: 1925; music: Erik Satie; décor: Nicolai Remisoff; première: Chicago Opera Ballet.
CHRISTMAS CAROL: 1925; music: Ralph Vaughn Williams; décor: Nicolai Remisoff; première: Chicago Opera Ballet.
ELOPEMENT: 1924; music: Wolfgang Amadeus Mozart; décor: Nicolai Remisoff; première: Chicago Opera Ballet.
LE FARCE DU PONT NEUF: 1926; music: Jeanne Clement Herscher; décor: Jean Valmier; première: Chicago Opera Ballet.
LE FOYER DE LA DANSE: 1924; music: Emmanuel Chabrier; décor: Nicolai Remisoff; première: Chicago Opera Ballet.
LITTLE CIRCUS: 1925; music: Jacques Offenbach; décor: Nicolai Remisoff; première: Chicago Opera Ballet.
MANDRAGORA: 1925; music: Karol Szymanowsky; décor: Nicolai Remisoff; première: Chicago Opera Ballet.
MECHANICAL BALLET: 1932; music: Alexander Mossolov (The Iron Foundry); décor: John Hambleton; première: Hollywood Bowl.
PARNASSUS AU MONTMARTRE: 1926; music: Erik Satie; décor: Nicolai Remisoff; première: Chicago Opera Ballet.
PETER AND THE WOLF: 1940; music: Serge Prokofiev; décor: Lucinda Ballard; première: Center Theater, New York.
PIERROT LUNAIRE: 1926; music: Arnold Schoenberg; décor: Nicolai Remisoff; première: Chicago Opera Ballet.
THE RIVALS: 1925; music: Henry Eichheim; décor: Nicolai Remisoff; première: Chicago Opera Ballet.
SADKO: 1915; music: Nikolai Rimski-Korsakov (Under-sea Act from opera Sadko); décor: Natalia Gontcharova; première: Maryinsky Theater, St. Petersburg.
TRAGEDY OF THE "CELLO": 1927; music: Alexandre Tansman; decor: Nicolai Remisoff; première: Chicago Opera Ballet.

Boris, Ruthanna

CAKEWALK: 1951; music: Louis Moreau Gottschalk (arrangement, Hershy Kay); décor: Robert Drew; première: City Center, New York.

CIRQUE DE DEUX: 1947; music: Charles Gounod (Walpurgisnacht from Faust); décor: Robert Davison; première: City Center, New York.

KALEIDOSCOPE: 1952; music: Dmitri Kabalevsky; costumes: Alvin Colt; première: City Center, New York.

QUELQUES FLEURS: 1948; music: François Auber; décor: Robert Davison; première: Metropolitan Opera House, New York.

WILL O' THE WISP: 1953; music: Virgil Thomson (*Louisiana Story*); décor: Dorothy Tanning; première: City Center, New York.

Borlin, Jean

LA CRÉATION DU MONDE: 1923; music: Darius Milhaud; décor: Fernand Léger; première: Théâtre des Champs Élysées, Paris.

LE TOMBEAU DE COUPERIN: 1920; music: Maurice Ravel; décor: Pierre Laprade; première: Théâtre des Champs Élysées, Paris.

Bournonville, Auguste

NAPOLI: 1842; music: Niels Gade, E. Helsted, Holger Paulli; décor: Christensen; première: Theatre Royal, Copenhagen.

Caton, Edward

FÊTE CHAMPÊTRE: 1936; choreography with C. Littlefield; music: Jean-Baptiste Lully, André Grétry, Jean-Philippe Rameau; décor: A. Jarin; première: Philadelphia Ballet Company.

LOLA MONTEZ: 1947; music: Fred Witt; décor: Raoul Pène du Bois; première: City Center, New York.

SEBASTIAN: 1945; music: Gian-Carlo Menotti; décor: Oliver Smith; première: International Theater, New York.

TRIPTYCH: 1952; music: Johannes Brahms; première: Metropolitan Opera House, New York.

Chamie, Tatiana

BIRTHDAY: 1949; music: Gioachino Rossini; décor: Mstislav Doboujinsky; première: Metropolitan Opera House, New York.

Christensen, Lew

BLACKFACE: 1947; music: Carter Harman; décor: Robert Drew; première: Ballet Society, New York.

CHARADE, OR THE DEBUTANTE: 1939; music: American melodies orchestrated by Trudi Rittmann; première: Metropolitan Opera House, New York.

CON AMORE: 1953; music: Gioachino Rossini; décor: James Bodrero; première: War Memorial Opera House, San Francisco.

ENCOUNTER: 1936; music: Wolfgang Amadeus Mozart (*Haffner Serenade*); première: Bennington, Vermont.

FILLING STATION: 1938; music: Virgil Thomson; décor: Paul Cadmus; première: Avery Memorial Theater, Hartford, Connecticut.

JINX: 1942; music: Benjamin Britten (*Variations on a Theme by Frank Bridge*); décor: James Morcom; première: National Theater, New York.

PASTORELLA: 1941; music: Paul Bowles; décor: Alvin Colt; première: American Ballet, New York.

POCAHONTAS: 1936; music: Elliott Carter; costumes: Karl Free; première: Middlebury, Vermont.

Christensen, William

BACH SUITE: 1938; music: Johann Sebastian Bach; décor: Armando Agnini; première: San Francisco Ballet.

THE BARTERED BRIDE: 1936; music: Bedrich Smetana; décor: J. C. Taylor; première: Portland, Oregon.

BLUE PLAZA: 1945; choreography with Jose Manero; music: Aaron Copland; décor: Antonio Sotomayor; première: San Francisco Ballet.

BOLERO: 1936; music: Maurice Ravel; décor: J. C. Taylor; première: Portland, Oregon.

LE BOURGEOIS GENTILHOMME: 1944; music: Jean Baptiste Lully, André Grétry; première: San Francisco Ballet.

CAPRICCIO ESPAGNOL: 1935; music: Nikolai Rimski-Korsakov; décor: J. C. Taylor; première: Portland, Oregon.

CHOPINADE: 1935; music: Frédéric Chopin; première: Seattle, Washington.

COEUR DE GLACE: 1936; music: Wolfgang Amadeus Mozart; décor: J. C. Taylor; première: Portland, Oregon.

COPPELIA: 1939; choreography after Saint-Léon; music: Léo Delibes; décor: Charlotte Rider; première: San Francisco Ballet.

DR. PANTALONE: 1947; music: Domenico Scarlatti; première: San Francisco Ballet.

HANSEL AND GRETEL: 1943; music: Engelbert Humperdinck; décor: Jean de Botton; première: San Francisco Ballet.

NOW THE BRIDES: 1939; music: Fritz Berens; décor: Charlotte Rider; première: San Francisco Ballet.

OLD VIENNA: 1938; music: Johann Strauss; décor: Charlotte Rider; première: San Francisco Ballet.

PYRAMUS AND THISBE: 1945; music: Georges Enesco; décor: Russel Hartley; première: San Francisco Ballet.

ROMEO AND JULIET: 1938; music: Peter Tchaikovsky; décor: Charlotte Rider; première: San Francisco Ballet.

RUMANIAN WEDDING: 1936; music: Georges Enesco; décor: J. C. Taylor; première: Portland, Oregon.

SONATA PATHÉTIQUE: 1943; music: Ludwig van Beethoven; première: San Francisco Ballet.

SWAN LAKE: 1940; choreography after Petipa; music; Peter Tchaikovsky; décor: Eugene Orlovsky, Nicholas Pershin; première: San Francisco Ballet.

THE TRIUMPH OF HOPE: 1944; music: César Franck; décor: Jean de Botton; première: San Francisco Ballet.

WINTER CARNIVAL: music: Johann and Josef Strauss; décor: Betty Bates, De Mars; première: San Francisco Ballet.

Cobos, Antonia

MADRONOS: 1947; music: Moritz Moszkowski, Sebastian Yradier, and others; costumes: Castillo of Elizabeth Arden; première: City Center, New York.

THE MIKADO: 1954; music: Sir Arthur Sullivan; décor: Bernard La Motte; première: Lyric Theater, Baltimore.

THE MUTE WIFE: 1944; music: Niccolo Paganini (Perpetual Motion, orchestrated by Vittorio Rieti); décor: Rico Lebrun; première: International Theater, New York.

Coralli, Jean

GISELLE: 1841; choreography with Jules Perrot; music: Adolphe Adam; décor: Pierre Ciceri; première: Théâtre de l'Académie Royale de Musique, Paris.

Coudy, Douglas

FOLK DANCE: 1936; music: Emmanuel Chabrier; costumes: Charles Rain; première: Burlington, Vermont.

Cranko, John

BEAUTY AND THE BEAST: 1949; music: Maurice Ravel; décor: Margaret Kaye; première: Sadler's Wells Theater, London.
LA BELLE HÉLÈNE: 1955; music: Jacques Offenbach (orchestration by Louis Aubert and Manuel Rosenthal); décor: Vertés; première: Sadler's Wells Theater, London.
BONNE-BOUCHE: 1952; music: Arthur Oldham; décor: Osbert Lancaster; première: Royal Opera House, Covent Garden, London.
HARLEQUIN IN APRIL: 1957; music: Richard Arnell; décor: John Piper; première: Sadler's Wells Theater, London.
THE LADY AND THE FOOL: 1955 (revised version); music: Guiseppe Verdi (orchestration by Charles Mackerras); décor: Richard Beer; première: Sadler's Wells Theater, London.
PINEAPPLE POLL: 1951; music: Sir Arthur Sullivan; décor: Osbert Lancaster; première: Sadler's Wells Theater, London.
SEA CHANGE: 1940; music: Jean Sibelius; décor: John Piper.
THE SHADOW: 1953; music: Ernö Dohnányi; décor: John Piper; première: Royal Opera House, Covent Garden, London.
THE WITCH: 1950; music: Maurice Ravel (2nd Piano Concerto); décor: Dorothy Tanning.

Cunningham, Merce

THE SEASONS: 1947; music: John Cage; décor: Isamu Noguchi, première: Ballet Society, New York.

Danieli, Fred

PUNCH AND THE CHILD: 1947; music: Richard Arnell; décor: Horace Armistead; première: City Center, New York.

Dauberval, Jean

LA FILLE MAL GARDÉE: 1786; music: Johann Wilhelm Hertel; première: Bordeaux, France.

DeMille, Agnes

BLACK RITUAL: 1940; music: Darius Milhaud (La Création du Monde); décor: Nicolas de Molas; première: Century Theater, New York.
FALL RIVER LEGEND: 1948; music: Morton Gould; décor: Oliver Smith; première: Metropolitan Opera House, New York.
THE HARVEST ACCORDING: 1952; music:

Virgil Thomson; décor: Lemuel Ayres; première: Metropolitan Opera House, New York.
RODEO (THE COURTING AT BURNT RANCH); 1942; music: Aaron Copland; décor: Oliver Smith; première: Metropolitan Opera House, New York.
TALLY-HO: 1944; music: Christoph Willibald Gluck; décor: Motley; première: Philharmonic Auditorium, Los Angeles.
THREE VIRGINS AND A DEVIL: 1941; music: Ottorino Respighi (Antiche Danze ed Arie); décor: Arne Lundborg; première: Majestic Theater, New York.

Carter, Alan

THE CATCH: 1946; music: Béla Bartok; costumes: Alan Carter.

Charrat, Janine

ADAME MIROIR: 1948; music: Darius Milhaud; décor: Delvaux.
LES ALGUES: 1954; music: Guy Bernard; décor: Louis-Bertrand Castelli.
THEMES AND VARIATIONS: 1948; music: Peter Tchaikovsky.

Dale, Margaret

THE GREAT DETECTIVE: 1953; music: Richard Arnell; décor: Robb.

Dolin, Anton

AURORA'S WEDDING: 1941 (New York première); Petipa; music: Peter Tchaikovsky; décor: Michel Boronoff, after Léon Bakst.
CAPRICIOSO: 1940; music: Domenico Cimarosa; décor: Nicolas De Molas; première; Chicago Opera House.
ITALIAN SUITE: 1940; music: Domenico Cimarosa; costumes: Nicolas de Molas; première: Robin Hood Dell, Philadelphia.
QUINTET: 1940; music: Raymond Scott; décor: Lucinda Ballard; première: Center Theater, New York.
ROMANTIC AGE: 1942; music: Vincenzo Bellini; décor: Carlos Mérida; première: Metropolitan Opera House, New York.
SCÈNES DE BALLET: 1944; music: Igor Stravinsky; première: Ziegfeld Theater, New York (in Billy Rose's The Seven Lively Arts).

Dolinoff, Alexis

AUBADE: 1936; music: Francis Poulenc; décor: R. Deshays; première: Philadelphia.

Dollar, William

AIR AND VARIATIONS: 1938; music: Johann Sebastian Bach (Goldberg Variations); première: Athens, Georgia.
CONSTANTIA: 1944; music: Frédéric Chopin (F Minor Piano Concerto No. 2); décor: Horace Armistead; première: International Theater, New York.
LE COMBAT: 1949; music: Raffaello de Banfield; décor: Lauré; première: Théâtre Marigny, Paris.
THE COMBAT: 1953; music: Raffaello de Banfield; décor: Georges Wakhevitch; première: Royal Opera House, London.
THE DUEL: 1950 (revision of Le Combat); mu-

sic: Raffaello de Banfield; costumes: Robert Stevenson; première: City Center, New York.
THE FIVE GIFTS OR FIVE BOONS OF LIFE: 1943; based on the story by Mark Twain; music: Ernö Dohnányi (*Variations on a Nursery Theme*); costumes: Esteban Francés; première: Young Men's Hebrew Association, New York.
HIGHLAND FLING: 1947; music: Stanley Bate; décor: David Ffolkes; première: Ballet Society, New York.
JUKE BOX: 1941; music: Alec Wilder; décor: Tom Lee; première: American Ballet, New York:
THE LEAF AND THE WIND: 1954; music: Paul Ramseier; première: State Fair Auditorium, Dallas.
ONDINE: 1949; music: Antonio Vivaldi (violin concertos); décor: Horace Armistead; première: City Center, New York.
PROMENADE: 1936; music: Maurice Ravel (*Valses Nobles et Sentimentales*); première: Bennington, Vermont.
A THOUSAND TIMES NEIGH: 1940; music: Tom Bennett; décor: Walter Dorwin Teague; première: American Ballet Caravan, New York.

Doone, Rupert

THE ENCHANTED GROVE: 1932; music: Maurice Ravel, Claude Debussy; décor: Duncan Grant; première: Sadler's Wells Theater, London.

Eglevsky, André

SENTIMENTAL COLLOQUY: 1944; music: Paul Bowles; décor: Salvador Dali; première: International Theater, New York.

Fernandez, José

GOYESCAS: 1940; music: Enrique Granados; décor: Nicolas de Molas; première: Center Theater, New York.

Fedorova, Alexandra

MAGIC SWAN: 1941; choreography after Marius Petipa; music: Peter Tchaikovsky; décor: Eugene Dunkel; première: Metropolitan Opera House, New York.

Fokine, Michael

ACIS AND GALATEA: 1905; Fokine's first ballet, a student exercise.
THE ANIMATES GOBLINS: 1907 (earlier form of *Le Pavillon d'Armide*); music: Nicolas Tcherepnine; décor: Alexandre Benois; première: Russian Imperial Theater, St. Petersburg.
BLUEBEARD: 1941; music: Jacques Offenbach; décor: Marcel Vertés; première: Palacio de Bellas Artes, Mexico City.
CARNAVAL: 1910; music: Robert Schumann (orchestration by Rimsky-Korsakov, Glazounov, Liadov, Tcherepnine); décor: Léon Bakst; première: Pavlova Hall, St. Petersburg.
CHOPINIANA: 1908; original version of *Les Sylphides*, given at a special performance in St. Petersburg; music: Frédéric Chopin.
CLÉOPÂTRE: 1909; music: Anton Arenski (*Prelude*, Taneev; *Arrival of Cleopatra*, Rimski-Korsakov; *Veil Dance*, Glinka; *Bacchanal*,

Glazounov, from *The Seasons*; *Persian Dance*, Mussorgsky) décor: Léon Bakst; première: Théâtre du Châtelet, Paris.
LE COQ D'OR: 1914; three-act opera by Nikolai Rimsky-Korsakov, sung by singers and simultaneously mimed by dancers; décor: Natalia Gontcharova; première: Opéra, Paris.
DAPHNIS AND CHLOE: 1912; music: Maurice Ravel; décor: Léon Bakst; première: Théâtre du Châtelet, Paris.
LE DIEU BLEU: 1911; music: Reynaldo Hahn; décor: Léon Bakst; première: Théâtre de Monte Carlo.
DON JUAN: 1936; choreography with Eric Allatini; music: Christoph Willibald Gluck; décor: Mariano Andrèu; première: Alhambra Theater, London.
LES ELÉMENTS: 1937; music: Johann Sebastian Bach; décor: Dimitri Bouchène; première: London.
LES ELFES: 1924; music: Felix Mendelssohn (Overture to *A Midsummer Night's Dream*, and the Andante and Allegro from *Concerto in E Minor for Violin*); décor: Christian Bérard; première: Metropolitan Opera House, New York.
L'EPREUVE D'AMOUR (CHUNG-YANG AND THE MANDARIN): 1936; music: Wolfgang Amadeus Mozart; décor: André Derain; première: Théâtre de Monte Carlo.
LE FESTIN: 1909; music: Peter Tchaikovsky (Blue Bird from *The Sleeping Beauty*, and Finale of the Second Symphony), and Modest Mussorgsky (*Hopak*), Glinka, and Glazounov; décor: Alexandre Benois, C. Korovin, and others, première: Théâtre du Châtelet, Paris.
THE FIREBIRD: 1910; music: Igor Stravinsky; décor: Alexander Golovin, Léon Bakst; première: Opéra, Paris.
IGROUCHKA (THE RUSSIAN TOY): 1939; music: Nikolai Rimski-Korsakov (*Fantasy on Russian Themes*, Opus 33); décor: Natalia Gontcharova; première: Metropolitan Opera House, New York.
LA LEGENDE DE JOSEPH: 1914; music: Richard Strauss; décor: Madame Sert; première: Opéra, Paris.
MIDAS (LES METAMORPHOSES): 1914; music: Maximilian Steinberg; décor: Mstislav Dobouiinsky; première: Opéra, Paris.
NARCISSE: 1911; music: Nicolas Tcherepnine; décor: Leon Bakst; première: Théâtre de Monte Carlo.
PAGANINI: 1939; music: Sergei Rachmaninoff (*Rhapsody for Piano and Orchestra on a Theme by Paganini*); décor: Sergei Soudeikine; première: Royal Opera House, Covent Garden, London.
PAPILLONS: 1914; music: Robert Schumann, Nicolas Tcherepnine; décor: Mstislav Dobouijinsky; première: Opéra, Paris.
LE PAVILLON D'ARMIDE: 1909; music: Nicolas Tcherepnine; décor: Alexandre Benois; première: Théâtre du Châtelet, Paris
PETROUCHKA: 1911; music: Igor Stravinsky; décor: Alexandre Benois; première: Théâtre du Châtelet, Paris.
PRINCE IGOR: 1909; music: Alexander Borodin (Polovtsian Dances from his opera *Prince Igor*); décor: Nicolas Roerich; première: Théâtre du Châtelet, Paris.
RUSSIAN SOLDIER: 1942; music: Serge Prokofiev (*Lieutenant Kije*); décor: Mstislav Dobouijinsky; première: Boston Opera House.
SCHEHERAZADE: 1910; music: Nikolai Rimski-Korsakov (Parts I, II, and IV of his Symphonic Suite *Scheherazade*); décor: Léon Bakst; première: Opéra, Paris.
THE SPECTER OF THE ROSE: 1911; music:

Carl Maria von Weber (*Invitation to the Dance*, orchestrated by Hector Berlioz); décor: Léon Bakst; première: Théâtre de Monte Carlo.

LES SYLPHIDES: 1909; Paris première of *Chopiniana* (renamed); music: Frédéric Chopin (*Valse No. 1*, Op. 70; *Mazurka No. 2*, Op. 32; *Mazurka No. 3*, Op. 67; *Prelude No. 7*, Op. 28; *Valse No. 2*, Op. 64; *Valse No. 1*, Op. 18; orchestrations by Igor Stravinsky and others); décor: Alexandre Benois; première: Théâtre du Châtelet, Paris.

THAMAR: 1912; music: Mily Balakirev; décor: Léon Bakst; première: Théâtre des Champs Élysées, Paris.

Franca, Celia

KHADRA: 1946; music: Jean Sibelius (*Belshazzar's Feast*); décor: Honor Frost; première: Sadler's Wells Theater, London.

Walter Gore

Note: Walter Gore produced his first ballets with the Ballet Rambert, at the theater and studio conducted by Marie Rambert in Ladbroke Road, London, which has been called, since 1933, the Mercury Theater; in 1950, he did work with the new Ballet Workshop; in 1952, he worked with the New Ballet Company, and, in 1953, began, with his wife, Paula Hinton, his own ballet group.

ANTONIA: 1949; music: Jean Sibelius; décor: Harry Cordewell.

BARTLÉMAS DANCES: 1941; music: Gustav Holst; décor: William Chappell.

CAP OVER MILL: 1940; music: Stanley Bate; décor: Nadia Benois.

CARTE BLANCHE: 1953; music: John Addison; décor: Rowell.

CONCERTO BURLESCO: 1946; music: Béla Bartók (orchestration by Arthur Oldham); décor: Eve Swinstead-Smith.

CONFESSIONAL: 1941; music: Jean Sibelius; décor: Andrée Howard.

KALEIDOSCOPE: 1949; music: Johannes Brahms, Paganini; décor: Ronald Wilson.

LARGO: 1950; music: Jean Sibelius; décor: Harry Cordwell.

MR. PUNCH: 1946; music: Harold Oldham; décor: Ronald Wilson.

PARIS-SOIR: 1939; music: Francis Poulenc; décor: Eve Swinstead-Smith.

PLAISANCE: 1947; music: Leonard Rosomon; décor: Harry Cordwell.

SIMPLE SYMPHONY: 1944; music: Benjamin Britten; décor: Ronald Wilson.

VALSE FINALE: 1938; music: Gioachino Rossini (orchestrated by Benjamin Britten); décor: Sophie Fedorovich.

WINTER NIGHT: 1949 (English première); music: Sergei Rachmaninoff (*Second Piano Concerto*); décor: Kenneth Rowell.

Graham, Martha

APPALACHIAN SPRING: 1944; music: Aaron Copland; décor: Isamu Noguchi; première: Library of Congress, Washington, D.C.

Helpmann, Robert

ADAM ZERO: 1946; music: Arthur Bliss; décor: Roger Furse; première: Royal Opera House, Covent Garden, London.

THE BIRDS: 1942; music: Overture — *The Bird Actors*, by Constant Lambert; *The Birds*, by Ottorino Respighi; décor: Chiang Yee; première: New Theater, London.

COMUS: 1942; music: Henry Purcell (orchestration by Constant Lambert); décor: Oliver Messel; première: New Theater, London.

HAMLET: 1942; music: Peter Tchaikovsky; décor: Leslie Hurry; première: New Theater, London.

MIRACLE IN THE GORBALS: 1944; music: Arthur Bliss; décor: Edward Burra; première: Princes Theater, London.

Hightower, Rosella

SALOME: 1950; music: Richard Strauss; décor: Celia Hubbard; première: Théâtre des Champs Élysées, Paris.

Howard, Andrée

ASSEMBLY BALL: 1946; music: Georges Bizet; décor: Andrée Howard; première: Sadler's Wells Theater, London.

DEATH AND THE MAIDEN: 1937; music: Franz Schubert; décor: Andrée Howard; première: Duchess Theater, London.

LADY INTO FOX: 1939; music: Arthur Honegger; décor: Raymond Sovey, after designs by Nadia Benois; première: Mercury Theater, London.

MARDI-GRAS: 1946; music: Carlos Salzédo; décor: Hugh Stevenson; première: Sadler's Wells Theater, London.

A MIRROR FOR WITCHES: 1952 (based on the novel by Esther Forbes); music: Denis ApIvor; décor: Norman Adams; première: Royal Opera House, Covent Garden, London.

LE FESTIN DE L'ARAIGNÉE: 1944; music: Albert Roussel; décor: Michael Ayrton; première: New Theater, London.

VENEZIANA: 1953; music: Gaetano Donizetti (orchestration by Denis ApIvor); décor: Sophie Fedorovitch; première: Royal Opera House, Covent Garden, London.

Humphrey, Doris

EN SALON MEXICO: 1943; music: Aaron Copland; décor: Elisabeth Parsons; première: Studio Theater, New York.

Ivantzova, Elizaveta Anderson

LES NOCES: 1929 (New York première); music: Igor Stravinsky; décor: Sergei Soudeikine.

Ivanov, Lev

THE NUTCRACKER (CASSE-NOISETTE): 1892; music: Peter Ilyich Tchaikovsky; décor: M. I. Botcharov; première: Maryinsky Theater, St. Petersburg.

SWAN LAKE, ACT II: 1894; music: Peter Ilyich Tchaikovsky; décor: M. I. Botcharov, Levogt; première: St. Petersburg production.

SWAN LAKE: 1895; choreography with Marius Petipa; music: Peter Ilyich Tchaikovsky; décor: M. I. Botcharov, Levogt; première: Maryinsky Theater, St. Petersburg.

Joffrey, Robert

PAS DE DÉESSES: 1955; music: John Field; décor: after the Bouvier lithograph.

Jooss, Kurt

Note: The ballets of Kurt Jooss are produced by the Jooss Ballet at Essen, Germany.

BALLADE: 1935; music: John Colman; décor: Hein Heckroth.
THE BIG CITY: 1932; music: A. Tansuran; décor: Hein Heckroth.
CHRONICA: 1939; music: Berthold Goldschmidt; décor: Dimitri Bouchène.
COMPANY AT THE MANOR: music: Ludwig van Beethoven (orchestration by J. Cook); décor: Doris Zinklèsen.
THE GREEN TABLE: 1932; F. A. Cohen; décor: Hein Heckroth.
JOHANN STRAUSS TO-NIGHT: 1935; music: Johann Strauss (orchestration by F. A. Cohen); décor: George Kirsta.
THE MIRROR: 1938; music: F. A. Cohen; décor: Hein Heckroth.
PANDORA: 1944; music: Roberto Gerhardt; décor: Hein Heckroth.
PERSIAN BALLET: 1924; music: Egon Wellesz; décor: Hein Heckroth.
THE PRODIGAL SON: 1933; music: F. A. Cohen; décor: Hein Heckroth.
THE SEVEN HEROES: 1933; music: F. A. Cohen; décor: Hein Heckroth.
A SPRING TALE: 1939; music: F. A. Cohen; décor: Hein Heckroth.
YOUTH (JUVENTUD): 1948; music: George Frederick Handel (orchestration by Juan Orrigo Salas); décor: Juan Venturelli.

Kaplan, E. I.

THE GOLDEN AGE: 1931; music: Dmitri Schostakovitch; décor: V. M. Khodasevich; première: Bolshoi Theater, Moscow.

Kidd, Michael

ON STAGE: 1945; music: Norman Dello Joio; décor: Oliver Smith; première: Boston Opera House.

Larchiune, L. A.

THE RED POPPY: 1926; music: Reinhold Glière; décor: Michael Kurilko; première: Leningrad.

Lee, Sammy

SKYSCRAPERS: 1926; music: John Alden Carpenter; décor: Robert Edmond Jones; première: Metropolitan Opera House, New York.

Lichine, David

CAIN AND ABEL: 1946; music: Richard Wagner (from Siegfried, and Die Götterdammerung); décor: Miguel Prieto; première: Palacio de Bellas Artes, Mexico City.
THE ENCHANTED MILL: 1949; music: Franz Schubert; (orchestration by Cloez); décor: Alexandre Benois; première: Royal Opera House, Covent Garden, London.
FAIR AT SOROCHINSK: 1943; music: Modest Mussorgsky (A Night on Bald Mountain); décor: Nicolai Remisoff; première: Broadway Theater, New York.
FRANCESCA DA RIMINI: 1937; choreography with Henry Clifford; music: Peter Tschaikovsky; décor: Oliver Messel; première: Royal Opera House, Covent Garden, London.

GRADUATION BALL: 1940; music: Johann Strauss, compiled, arranged, and orchestrated by Antal Dorati; décor: Alexandre Benois; première: Theatre Royal, Sydney, Australia.
HELEN OF TROY: 1942; music: Jacques Offenbach; décor: Marcel Vertés; première: Palacio de Bellas Artes, Mexico City.
LE PAVILLON: 1936; music: Alexander Borodin; décor: Cecil Beaton; première: Metropolitan Opera House, New York.
THE PRODIGAL SON: 1939; music: Serge Prokofiev; décor: Georges Rouault; première: Sydney, Australia.
PROTÉE: 1938; music: Claude Debussy; décor: Giorgio di Chirico; première: Royal Opera House, Covent Garden, London.
THE SPHINX: 1955; music: Henri Sauguet; décor: Christian Bérard; première: Metropolitan Opera House, New York.

Lifar, Serge

Note: Except for a brief period which he spent with the New Monte Carlo Ballet, Serge Lifar has done the major part of his work with the Opéra, Paris.

ADELAIDE, OU LA LANGAGE DES FLEURS: 1938; music: Maurice Ravel (Valses Nobles et Sentimentales); décor: Maurice Brianchon; première: Théâtre du Châtelet, Paris.
AENEUS: 1938; music: Albert Roussel; décor: Moulaert.
ALEXANDER THE GREAT: 1937; music: Philippe Gaubert; décor: P. R. Larthe.
ANIMAUX MODELES: 1948; music: Francis Poulenc; décor: Roland Oudot.
ASTROLOGUE DANS LE PUITS: 1951; music: Henri Barrault; décor: Suzanne Roland-Manuel.
AUBADE: 1948; music: Francis Poulenc.
BACCHUS AND ARIADNE: 1931; music: Albert Roussel; décor: Giorgio di Chirico.
CANTIQUE DES CANTIQUES: 1938; music: Arthur Honegger, to rhythms by Lifar; décor: Paul Colin.
LE CHEVALIER ERRANT: 1950; music: Jacques Ibert; décor: Pedro Flores.
LE CHEVALIER ET LA DEMOISELLE: 1941; music: Philippe Goubert; décor: Cassandre.
CHOTA ROUSTAVELLI: 1946; music: Hansanyi, Honegger, and Tcherepnine (selected and adapted to rhythms of the choreographer;) première: New Monte Carlo Ballet.
DAPHNIS AND CLOE: 1948; music: Maurice Ravel.
DAVID TRIOMPHANT: 1936; music: Claude Debussy, Modest Mussorgsky (orchestration by Rieti); décor: Fernand Léger.
DIVERTISSEMENT: 1948; music: Peter Tchaikovsky; décor: Dmitri Bouchène.
DRAMMA PER MUSICA: 1946; music: Johann Sebastian Bach; décor: Cassandre.
ENDYMION: 1949; music: Leguerney; décor: Dmitri Bouchène.
ENTRE DEUX RONDES: 1940; music: Samuel Roussau; décor: after Edgar Dégas.
ESCALES (PORTS OF CALL): 1948; music: Jacques Ibert; décor: Denyse de Bravura.
GISELLE: 1938; choreography after Jean Coralli; music: Adolphe Adam; décor: Alexandre Benois; première: Metropolitan Opera House, New York.
GUIGNOL ET PANDORE: 1948; music: André Jolivet; décor: Dignimont.
HARNASIE: 1936; music: Karol Szymanovsky; décor: Irène Lorentowicz.
HOP-FROG: 1951; music: Raymond Loucheur; décor: Nicholas Untersettler.

ICARE: 1935; music: Rhythms by Lifar; orchestrated by J. E. Szyfer; décor: Paul-Réné Larthe; première: Opéra, Paris.
L'INCONNU: 1950; music: André Jolivet; décor: Charles Blanc.
ISTAR: 1948; music: Vincent d'Indy.
JOAN DE ZARISSA: 1942; music: Werner Egk; décor: Yves Brayer.
JURYPARY: 1934; music: Heitor Villa-Lobos; décor: R. P. du Bois.
LUCIFER: 1949; music: Delvincourt; décor: Yves Brayer.
LES MIRAGES: 1948; music: Henri Sauguet; décor: Cassandre.
LA MORT DU CYGNE: 1948; music: Frédéric Chopin.
LE NAISSANCE DES COULEURS: 1949; music: Arthur Honegger.
LES NOCES FANTASTIQUES: 1955; music: Marcel Delannoy; décor: Roger Chastel.
NOIR ET BLANC (later Suite en Blanc): 1943; music: Édouard Lalo; décor: Stephen Bundy; after Nepo.
L'ORCHESTRE EN LIBERTÉ: 1931; music: Albert Roussel.
ORIANE ET LE PRINCE D'AMOUR: 1938; music: Florent Schmitt; décor: Pedro Pruna.
PAVANE (LAS MENILLAS): 1940; music: Gabriel Fauré; décor: José Maria Sert; première: Fifty-first Street Theater, New York.
PAVANE POUR UNE INFANTE DEFUNTE: 1948; music: Maurice Ravel.
PHÈDRE: 1950; music: Georges Auric; décor: Jean Cocteau.
PRÉLUDE DOMINICAL: 1931; music: Guy Ropartz; décor: Paul Colin.
LA PRINCESSE AU JARDIN: 1942; music: Gabriel Grovlez.
PROMENADE DE ROME: 1936; music: Samuel Rousseau; décor: Décaris.
PROMETHEUS: 1929; music: Ludwig van Beethoven.
RENARD: 1929; music: Igor Stravinsky; décor: Michael Larionov.
LE ROI NU: 1936; music: Jean Français; décor: Pedro Pruna.
SALADE: 1935; music: Darius Milhaud; décor: André Derain.
SEPTUOR: 1949; music: Jean Lutèce; décor: Yves Bonnat.
SUITE EN BLANC: The revision of Noir et Blanc.
SUR LE BORYSTHÈNE: 1932; music: Serge Prokofiev; décor: Michael Larionov.
VIE DE POLICHINELLE: 1934; music: Nicholas Nabokov; décor: Pedro Pruna.
ZADIG: 1948; music: Pierre Petit; décor: Labisse.

Littlefield, Catherine

BARN DANCE: 1937; music: Louis Gottschalk, David Guion, John Powell; décor: Ralph Pinto; première: Fox Theater, Philadelphia.
BOLERO: 1936; music: Maurice Ravel; décor: Lee Gainsborough; première: Philadelphia Ballet Company.
CAFE SOCIETY: 1938; music: Ferde Grofé; décor: Carl Shaffer; première: Philadelphia Ballet Company.
CLASSICAL SUITE: 1937; music: Johann Sebastian Bach; décor: R. Deshays; première: Princeton, New Jersey.
DAPHNIS AND CHLOE: 1936; choreography after Fokine; music: Maurice Ravel; décor: A. Jarin; première: Philadelphia Ballet Company.
THE FAIRY DOLL: 1935; music: Josef Bayer; décor: A. Jarin; première: Philadelphia Ballet Company.

FÊTE CHAMPÊTRE: 1936; choreography with Edward Caton; music: Jean-Baptiste Lully, André Grétry, Jean-Philippe Rameau; décor: A. Jarin; première: Philadelphia Ballet Company.
HOME LIFE OF THE GODS: 1936; music: Erik Satie; décor: Lazar Galpern; première: Philadelphia Ballet Company.
H. P.: 1932; music: Carlos Chavez; décor: Diego Rivera; première: Philadelphia Ballet Company.
LADIES' BETTER DRESSES: 1938; music: Herbert Kingsley; décor: R. Starke; première: Chicago.
LET THE RIGHTEOUS BE GLAD: 1937; music: J. Donath; décor: Angelo Pinto; première: Philadelphia Ballet Company.
THE MINSTREL: 1935; music: Claude Debussy; décor: Angelo Pinto; première: Haverford, Pennsylvania.
MOMENT ROMANTIQUE: 1936; music: Frédéric Chopin; première: Philadelphia Ballet Company.
PARABLE IN BLUE: 1937; music: Martin Gabowitz; décor: George C. Jenkins; première: Philadelphia Ballet Company.
THE PRODIGAL SON: 1936; music: César Franck; première: Philadelphia Ballet Company.
ROMANTIC VARIATIONS: 1936; music: Camille Saint-Saëns; première: Philadelphia Ballet Company.
THE SLEEPING BEAUTY: 1937; choreography after Petipa; music: Peter Tchaikovsky; décor: R. Deshays; première: Philadelphia Ballet Company.
THE SNOW QUEEN: 1935; music: Murray Cutter; décor: A. Jarin; première: Philadelphia Ballet Company.
TERMINAL: 1937; music: Herbert Kingsley; décor: Angelo Pinto; première: Paris.
VIENNESE WALTZ: 1936; music: Johann Strauss; décor: A. Jarin; première: Philadelphia Ballet Company.

Lopez, Pilar

THE CUCKOLD'S FAIR: 1943; music: Gustavo Pittaluga; décor: Joan Junyer; première: Cleveland, Ohio.

Loring, Eugene

BILLY THE KID: 1938; music: Aaron Copland; décor: Jared French; première: Chicago Opera House.
CAPITAL OF THE WORLD: 1953; based on story by Ernest Hemingway; music: George Antheil; décor: Esteban Francés; première: Metropolitan Opera House, New York.
CITY PORTRAIT: 1939; music: Henry Brant; décor: James Morcom.
THE DUKE OF SACRAMENTO OR HOBO OF THE HILLS: 1942; music: Norman Dello Joio; décor: George Bockman; première: New Hope, Pennsylvania.
THE GREAT AMERICAN GOOF: 1940; music: Henry Brant; décor: Boris Aronson; première: Center Theater, New York.
HARLEQUIN FOR PRESIDENT: 1942; (revival of Harlequin, 1936); music: Domenico Scarlatti; première: Washington, D. C.
THE MAN FROM MIDIAN: 1942; music: Stefan Wolpe; décor: Doris Rosenthal; première: Washington, D. C.
PRAIRIE: 1942; music: Norman Dello Joio; décor: James Morcom; première: Washington, D. C.
YANKEE CLIPPER: 1937; music: Paul Bowles;

costumes: Charles Rain; première: Saybrook, Connecticut.

MacMillan, Kenneth

HOUSE OF BIRDS: 1955; music: Federico Mompou (orchestration by John Lanchberry); décor: Nicholas Georgiadis.

Manero, José

BLUE PLAZA: 1945; choreography with William Christensen; music: Aaron Copland; décor: Antonio Sotomayor; première: San Francisco Ballet.

Massine, Leonide

ALEKO: 1942; music: Peter Tchaikovsky (orchestration by Erno Rapee); décor: Marc Chagall; première: Palacio de Bellas Artes, Mexico City.
LE ASTUZIE FEMINILI: 1920; (opera ballet in three scenes later entitled *Cimarosiana);* music: Domenico Cimarosa (orchestration by Ottorino Respighi); décor: Madame Sert; première: Royal Opera House, Covent Garden. London.
BACCHANALE: 1939; music: Richard Wagner *(Tannhäuser);* décor: Salvador Dali; première: Metropolitan Opera House, New York.
THE BALL (LE BAL): 1929; music: Vittorio Rieti; décor: Giorgio di Chirico; première: Théâtre de Monte Carlo.
BEACH: 1933; music: Jean Françaix; décor: Raoul Dufy; première: Théâtre de Monte Carlo.
LE BEAU DANUBE (THE BEAUTIFUL DANUBE): 1924; music: Johann Strauss (orchestrated by Roger Desormière); décor: Vladimir Polunin, after Constantin Guys; première: Théâtre de Monte Carlo.
BOGATYRI: 1938; music: Alexander Borodin *(Symphony No. 2 in B Minor);* décor: Nathalie Gontcharova; première: Metropolitan Opera House, New York.
LA BOUTIQUE FANTASQUE (THE FANTASTIC TOY-SHOP): 1919; music: Gioachino Rossini (orchestration by Ottorino Respighi); décor: André Derain; première: Alhambra Theater, London.
CAPRICCIO ESPAGNOL: 1939; choreography with Argentinita; music: Nikolai Rimski-Korsakov; décor: Mariano Andrèu; première: Théâtre de Monte Carlo.
CHILDREN'S GAMES (JEUX D'ENFANTS): 1933; music: Georges Bizet; décor: Joan Miró; première: Théâtre de Monte Carlo.
CHOREARTEUM: 1933; music: Johannes Brahms *(Fourth Symphony);* décor: Constantin Tcherechkovitch, Eugene Lourie; première: Alhambra Theater, London.
CIMAROSIANA: See *Le Astuzie Feminili.*
CLOCK SYMPHONY: 1948; music: Joseph Haydn; décor: Christian Bérard; première: Royal Opera House, Covent Garden, London.
CONTES RUSSES (CHILDREN'S TALES): 1917; music: A. C. Liadov; décor: Michael Larionov; première: Rome (the tales were produced singly by Diaghilev's Ballets Russes and not performed in entirety until after the war).
DESTINY (LES PRESAGES): 1940; music: Peter Tchaikovsky *(Fifth Symphony);* décor: André Masson; première: Fifty-first Street Theater, New York.
DONALD OF THE BURTHENS: 1951; music: Ian Whyte; décor: Robert MacBryde, Robert Colquhoun; première: Royal Opera House, Covent Garden, London.
DON DOMINGO (DE DON BLAS): 1942; music: Sylvestre Revueltas; décor: Julio Castellanos; première: Palacio de Bellas Artes, Mexico City.
THE ENCHANTED MILL: 1949; music: Franz Schubert; décor: Alexandre Benois; première: Royal Opera House, Covent Garden, London.
LES FEMMES DE BONNE HUMEUR (THE GOOD-HUMORED LADIES): 1917; music: Domenico Scarlatti (arranged by Vincenzo Tommasini); décor: Léon Bakst; première: Teatro Constanza, Rome.
GAITÉ PARISIENNE: 1938; music: Jacques Offenbach (orchestrated by Manuel Rosenthal and Jacques Brindejonc-Offenbach); décor: Etienne de Beaumont; première: Théâtre de Monte Carlo.
HAROLD IN ITALY: 1954; music: Hector Berlioz; décor: Bernard La Motte; première: Boston Opera House.
LES JARDINS D'ARANJUEZ (originally entitled *Las Meninas): 1918; music: Gabriel Fauré* (for Madrid performance only, Ravel-Chabrier); décor: Madame Sert; première: Rome, Diaghilev's Ballets Russes.
JARDIN PUBLIC: 1935; based on a section of *The Counterfeiters,* by André Gide; music: Vladimir Dukelsky; costumes: Jean Lurçat; première: Chicago.
JEUX D'ENFANTS: See *Children's Games.*
LABYRINTH: 1941; music: Franz Schubert (C. Major Symphony); décor: Salvador Dali; première: Metropolitan Opera House, New York.
MAD TRISTAN: 1944; music: Richard Wagner (arranged by Ivan Bounitkoff); décor: Salvador Dali; première: International Theater, New York.
MAM'ZELLE ANGOT: 1943; music: Alexandre Charles Lecocq; décor: Mstislav Doboujinsky; première: Metropolitan Opera House, New York.
LES MATELOTS: 1925; music: Georges Auric; décor: Pedro Pruna; première: Théâtre Gaîté-Lyrique, Paris.
LAS MENINAS: See *Les Jardins d'Aranjuez.*
MERCURE: 1924; music: Erik Satie; décor: Pablo Picasso; première: Théâtre des Champs-Élysées, Paris.
MIDNIGHT SUN: See *SOLEIL DE NUIT.*
MOONLIGHT SONATA: 1944; music: Ludwig van Beethoven; décor: Sergei Soudeikine; première: Chicago Opera House.
THE NEW YORKER: 1940; music: George Gershwin; décor: Carl Kent, after Rea Irvin; première: Fifty-first Street Theater, New York.
NOBILISSIMA VISIONE (ST. FRANCIS): 1938; music: Paul Hindemith; décor: Pavel Tchelitchev; première: Drury Lane Theater, London.
ODE: 1928; music: Nicholas Nabokov; décor: Pavel Tchelitchev, Charbonner; première: Théâtre de Monte Carlo, Diaghilev's Ballets Russes.
PARADE: 1917; music: Erik Satie; décor: Pablo Picasso; première: Rome, Diaghilev's Ballets Russes.
LE PAS D'ACIER: 1927; music: Serge Prokofiev; décor: Iakouloff; première: Théâtre de Monte Carlo, Diaghilev's Ballets Russes.
LE PRÉSAGES: 1933; music: Peter Tchaikovsky (Fifth Symphony); décor: André Masson; première: Théâtre de Monte Carlo.
PULCINELLA: 1920; music: Igor Stravinsky, after Pergolesi; décor: Pablo Picasso; première: Opéra, Paris.
ROUGE ET NOIR: 1939; music: Dmitri Shosta-

kovitch (First Symphony); décor: Henri Matisse; première: Théâtre de Monte Carlo.
ST. FRANCIS: See *Nobilissima Visione*.
SARATOGA: 1941; music: Jaromir Weinberger; décor: Oliver Smith, Alvin Colt; première: Metropolitan Opera House, New York.
SCOULA DI BALLO: 1933; music: Luigi Boccherini, arranged by Jean Françaix; décor: Étienne de Beaumont; première: Théâtre de Monte Carlo.
SEVENTH SYMPHONY: 1938; music: Ludwig van Beethoven; décor: Christian Bérard; première: Théâtre de Monte Carlo.
SOLEIL DE NUIT: 1915; music: Nikolai Rimsky-Korsakov; décor: Michael Larionov; première: Grand Théâtre, Geneva.
THE SONG OF THE NIGHTINGALE (LE CHANT DU ROSSIGNOL): 1920; music: Igor Stravinsky; décor: Henri Matisse; première: Opéra, Paris.
SYMPHONIE FANTASTIQUE (AN EPISODE IN THE LIFE OF AN ARTIST): 1936; music: Hector Berlioz; décor: Christian Bérard; première: Royal Opéra House, Covent Garden, London.
THE THREE-CORNERED HAT (LE TRICORNE:) 1919; music: Manuel de Falla; décor: Pablo Picasso; première: Alhambra Theater, London.
UNION PACIFIC: 1934; music: Nicholas Nabokov; décor: Albert Johnson; première: Forrest Theater, Philadelphia.
VIENNA — 1814: 1940; music: Carl Maria von Weber; décor: Stewart Chaney; première: Fiftyfirst Street Theater, New York.
ZEPHYR AND FLORA: 1925; music: Vladimir Dukelsky; décor: Georges Braque; première: Théâtre de Monte Carlo, Diaghilev's Ballets Russes.

Merante, Louis

SYLVIA: 1876; music: Léo Delibes; décor: Chaperon; Chéret; Rubé; première: Théâtre de l'Opéra, Paris.

Mordkin, Mikhail

DIONYSUS: 1938; music: Alexander Glazounov; décor: Sergei Soudeikine; première: Mordkin Ballet, New York.
GISELLE: 1937; music: Adolphe Adam; décor: Sergei Soudeikine; première: Mordkin Ballet, New York.
THE GOLDFISH: 1937; music: Nicholas Tcherepnine; décor: Sergei Soudeikine; première: Mordkin Ballet, New York.
THE SLEEPING BEAUTY: 1937, after Marius Petipa; music: Peter Tchaikovsky; décor: Lee Simonson; première: Waterbury, Connecticut.
SWAN LAKE: 1911 (New York premier); choreography after Petipa; music: Peter Tchaikovsky; décor: James Fox; première: Metropolitan Opera House.
SWAN LAKE: 1937; music: Peter Tchaikovsky; décor: Lee Simonson; première: Alvin Theater, New York.
TREPAK: 1937; music: Alexandre Tcherepnine; décor: Sergei Soudeikine; première: Alvin Theater, New York.
VOICES OF SPRING: 1938; music: Johann Strauss (orchestration by Mois Zlatin); décor: Lee Simonson; première: Alvin Theater, New York.

Nijinska, Bronislava

ANCIENT RUSSIA: 1943; music: Peter Tchai-

kovsky *(Piano Concerto No. 1)*; décor: Natalia Gontcharova; première: Cleveland, Ohio.
LE BAISER DE LA FÉE: 1928; music: Igor Schubert; décor: Alexandre Benois; première: Opéra Paris.
BELOVED: 1928; music: Franz Liszt, Franz Schubert; décor: Alexandre Benois; première: Opéra, Paris.
LES BICHES: 1924; music: Francis Poulenc; décor: Marie Laurencin; première: Théâtre de Monte Carlo.
BRAHMS VARIATIONS: 1944; music: Johannes Brahms *(Handel* and *Paganini Variations);* décor: Marcel Vertès; première: International Theater, New York.
CHOPIN CONCERTO: 1939; music: Frédéric Chopin *(Concerto for Piano and Orchestra No. 1);* décor: Ignatiev; première: Hall of Music, World's Fair Grounds, New York.
CONCERTO IN E MINOR: See *Chopin Concerto.*
DANSES SLAVES ET TZIGANES: 1936; music: Alexander Dargomijsky; décor: Sergei Soudeikine; première: Metropolitan Opera House, New York.
ÉTUDE: 1943; music: Johann Sebastian Bach; décor: Boris Belinsky; première: Music Hall, Cleveland.
LES FACHEUX: 1924; music: Georges Auric; décor: Georges Braque; première: Théâtre de Monte Carlo, Diaghilev's Ballets Russes.
HARVEST-TIME: 1945; music: Henri Wieniawski; costumes: Enid Gilbert; première: Metropolitan Opera House, New York.
THE HUNDRED KISSES: 1935; music: Frédéric d'Erlanger; décor: Jean Hugo; première: Royal Opéra House, Covent Garden, London.
NIGHT ON BARE MOUNTAIN: 1926; music: Modest Mussorgsky; décor: Natalia Gontcharova; première: Théâtre de Monte Carlo, Diaghilev's Ballets Russes.
LES NOCES: 1923; music: Igor Stravinsky; décor: Natalia Gontcharova; première: Théâtre Gaîté-Lyrique, Paris.
PICTURES AT AN EXHIBITION: 1943; music: Modest Mussorgsky; décor: Boris Aronson; première: International Theater, New York.
RENARD: 1922; music: Igor Stravinsky; décor: Michael Larionov; première: Opéra, Paris, Diaghilev's Ballets Russes.
ROMEO AND JULIET: 1926; music: Constant Lambert; décor: Paintings by Joan Miró and Max Ernst (the ballet was listed as a rehearsal without scenery); première: Théâtre de Monte Carlo, Diaghilev's Ballets Russes.
SCHUMANN CONCERTO: 1951; music: Robert Schumann *(Concerto for Piano and Orchestra);* décor: Stewart Chaney; première: Metropolitan Opera House, New York.
THE SLEEPING BEAUTY (THE SLEEPING Princess): 1921; choreography after Petipa; music: Peter Tchaikovsky; décor: Léon Bakst; première: Alhambra Theater, London.
THE SNOW MAIDEN: 1942; music: Alexander Glazounov; décor: Boris Aronson; première: Metropolitan Opera House, New York.
LES TENTATIONS DE LA BERGÈRE: 1924; music: Michel de Montéclair (orchestration by Henri Casadesus); décor: Juan Gris; première: Théâtre des Champs-Élysées, Paris, Diaghilev's Ballets Russes.
LE TRAIN BLEU: 1924; music: Darius Milhaud; décor: Laurens (curtain: Picasso); première: Théâtre des Champs-Élysées, Paris, Diaghilev's Ballets Russes.

Nijinsky, Vaslav

THE AFTERNOON OF A FAUN (L'APRÈS-

MIDI D'UN FAUNE): 1912; music: Claude Debussy; décor: Léon Bakst; première: Théâtre du Châtelet, Paris.

JEUX: 1913; music: Claude Debussy; décor: Léon Bakst; première: Théâtre des Champs-Élysées, Paris.

LE SACRE DU PRINTEMPS (THE RITE OF SPRING): 1913; music: Igor Stravinsky; décor: Nicolas Roerich; première: Théâtre des Champs-Élysées, Paris.

TYL EULENSPIEGEL: 1916; music: Richard Strauss; décor: Robert Edmond Jones; première: American tour, Daghilev's Ballets Russes.

Noverre, Jean George

LES PETITS RIENS: 1778; music: Wolfgang Amadeus Mozart; première: Opéra, Paris.

Paltenghi, David

CANTERBURY PROLOGUE: 1951; music: Peter Racine Fricker; décor: Edward Burra.

THE EVE OF ST. AGNES: 1950; music: César Franck (orchestration by Geoffrey Corbett); décor: Roger Furse.

FATE'S REVENGE, OR REBELLION IN THE UPPER ROOMS: 1951; music: Peter Tranchell; décor: Ronald Ferns.

PRISMATIC VARIATIONS: 1950; music: Ludwig van Beethoven (Variations on a Theme by Diabelli); décor: Vivienne Kernot.

SCHERZI DELLA SORTE: 1951; music: Claudio Monteverdi; décor: Leslie Hurry.

Page, Ruth

ADONIS: 1944; music: Lehman Engel; première: Page-Stone Ballet, Chicago.

AN AMERICAN PATTERN: 1937; choreography with Bentley Stone; music: Jerome Moross; décor: Nicolai Remisoff; première: Page-Stone Ballet, Chicago.

AMERICANS IN PARIS: 1936; music: George Gershwin; décor: Nicolai Remisoff; première: Cincinnati, Ohio.

THE BELLS: 1946; music: Darius Milhaud; décor: Isamu Noguchi; première: Ruth Page-Bentley Stone Ballet, Chicago.

BILLY SUNDAY OR GIVING THE DEVIL HIS DUE: 1946; music: Remi Gassman; décor: Herbert Andrews; première: Mandel Hall, Chicago.

CHOPIN IN OUR TIME: 1941; music: Frédéric Chopin, Owen Haynes; première: Page-Stone Ballet, Chicago.

CINDERELLA: 1931; music: Marcel Delannoy; décor: Nicolai Remisoff; première: Page-Stone Ballet, Chicago.

FRANKIE AND JOHNNY: 1938; choreography with Bentley Stone; music: Jerome Moross; décor: Paul Du Pont; première: Great Northern Theater, Chicago.

GOLD STANDARD: 1934; music: Jacques Ibert; décor: Nicolai Remisoff; première: Page-Stone Ballet, Chicago..   .   .   .

LA GUIABLESSE: 1933; music: William Grant Still; décor: Nicolai Remisoff; première: Page-Stone Ballet, Chicago.

GUNS AND CASTANETS: 1939; choreography with Bentley Stone; music: George Bizet, Jerome Moross; décor: Clive Rickabaugh; première: Page-Stone Ballet, Chicago.

HEAR YE! HEAR YE!: 1934; music: Aaron Copland; décor: Nicolai Remisoff; première: Page-Stone Ballet, Chicago.

IBERIAN MONOTONE: 1930; music: Maurice Ravel; première: Page-Stone Ballet, Ravinia, Illinois.

LOVE SONG: 1935; music: Franz Schubert; décor: Nicolai Remisoff; première: Ruth Page-Bentley Stone Ballet, Chicago.

OAK STREET BEACH: 1929; music: Clarence Loomis; décor: Nicolai Remisoff; première: Ravinia, Illinois.

PAVANE: 1932; music: Maurice Ravel; décor: Nicolai Remisoff; première: Page-Stone Ballet, Chicago.

LES PETITS RIENS: 1946; music: Wolfgang Amadeus Mozart; décor: Robert Davison; première: Page-Stone Ballet, Chicago.

REVENGE: 1951; music: Guiseppe Verdi (based on Il Trovatore); décor: Antoine Clavé; première: Théâtre de l'Empire, Paris.

SCRAPBOOK: 1939; choreography with Bentley Stone; music: miscellaneous; décor: Clive Rickabaugh; première: Page-Stone Ballet, Chicago.

THE STORY OF THE SOLDIER: 1931; choreography with Blake Scott; music: Igor Stravinsky; décor: Nicolai Remisoff; première: Page-Stone Ballet, Chicago.

WALTZ: 1932; music: Maurice Ravel; décor: Nicolai Remisoff; première: Page-Stone Ballet, Chicago.

Patrick, Sara

UNCLE REMUS: 1934; music: Gordon Jacob; décor: Hugh Stevenson; première: Old Vic, London.

Perrot, Jules

LA ESMERALDA: 1848; music: Cesare Pugni.

GISELLE: 1841; choreography with Jean Corelli; music: Adolphe Adam; première: Théâtre de l'Académie Royale de Musique, Paris.

PAS DE QUATRE: 1845; music: Cesare Pugni; première: His Majesty's Theater, London.

Petipa, Lucien

MAMUONA: 1882; music: Édouard Lalo; première: Opéra, Paris.

Petipa, Marius

RAYMONDA: 1898; music: Alexander Glazounov; décor: Allegri, Ivanov, Lambini; première: Marvinsky Theater, St. Petersburg.

THE SEASONS: 1900; music: Alexander Glazounov; décor: Lambini; première: Maryinsky Theater, St. Petersburg.

THE SLEEPING BEAUTY: 1890; music: Peter Tchaikovsky; décor: Ivan Vsevolojsky; première: Maryinsky Theater, St. Petersburg.

SWAN LAKE: 1895; choreography with Lev Ivanov; music: Peter Tchaikovsky; décor: M. I. Botcharov; Levogt; première: Maryinsky Theater, St. Petersburg.

Petit, Roland

BALLABILE: 1950; music: Emmanuel Chabrier (orchestration by Constant Lambert); décor: Antoine Clavé; première: Royal Opera House, Covent Garden, London.

CARMEN: 1949; music: Georges Bizet; décor: Antoine Clavé; première: Prince's Theater, London.

LA CROQUEUSE DE DIAMANTES (THE WO-

MAN WHO BITES DIAMONDS); 1950; music: Jean-Michel Damase; décor: Georges Wakhevitch; première: Théâtre Marigny, Paris.
LES DEMOISELLES DE LA NUIT: 1948; music: Jean Françaix; décor: Léonor Fini; première: Théâtre Marigny, Paris.
DEVIL TAKE HER: 1948; music: Manuel Rosenthal; décor: André Derain; première: Théâtre des Champs-Élysées, Paris.
LE JEUNE HOMME ET LA MORT: 1946; music: Johann Sebastian Bach (Passacaglia and Fugue in C Minor); décor: Georges Wakhevitch; première: Théâtre des Champs-Élysées, Paris.
LE LOUP (THE WOLF): 1953; music: Henri Dutilleux; décor: Carzou; première: Théâtre des Champs-lysées, Paris.
MUSICAL CHAIRS: 1950; music: Georges Auric; décor: Georges Geffroy; première: Théâtre des Champs-Élysées, Paris.
L'OEUF A LA COQUE: 1948; music: Maurice Thiriet; décor: Stanislas Lepri; première: Théâtre des Champs-Élysées, Paris.
LE ROSSIGNOL ET LA ROSE: 1945; music: Robert Schumann; première: Théâtre des Champs-Élysées, Paris.
THE TRAVELLING PLAYERS (LES FORAINS): 1945; music: Henri Sauguet; décor: Christian Bérard; première: Théâtre des Champs-Élysées, Paris.

Pitoev, Ludmilla

A SOLDIER'S STORY: 1918; music: Igor Stravinsky; décor: René Auberjonois; première: Lausanne Theater, Switzerland.

Platoff, Marc

GHOST TOWN: 1939; music: Richard Rogers (orchestrated by Hans Spialek); décor: Raoul Pène Du Bois; première: Metropolitan Opera House, New York.

Psota, Vania

THE CEIBOS GROVE: 1944; music: Eduardo Fabini; décor: Jacob Anchutin.
SLAVONIKA: 1942; music: Anton Dvorák; costumes: Alvin Colt; première: Palacio de Bellas Artes, Mexico City.
YARA: 1946; music: Francisco Mignone; décor: Candido Portinari; première: Metropolitan Opera House, New York.

Reisinger, Julius

SWAN LAKE: 1877; music: Peter Tchaikovsky; première: Bolshoi Theater, Moscow.

Ricarda, Ana

DEL AMOR Y DE LA MUERTE (OF LOVE AND DEATH): 1949; music: Enrique Granados y Campina (from Goyescas, orchestrated by Ernest Schelling); décor: Cecilia Hubbard; première: Théâtre de Monte Carlo.

Robbins, Jerome

THE AGE OF ANXIETY: 1950; music: Leonard Bernstein (Symphony No. 2); décor: Oliver Smith; première: City Center, New York.
BALLADE: 1952; music: Claude Debussy (Six Epigraphes Antiques); décor: Boris Aronson; première: City Center, New York.
THE CAGE: 1951; music: Igor Stravinsky

(String Concerto in D); costumes: Ruth Sobatka; première: City Center, New York.
FACSIMILE: 1946; music: Leonard Bernstein; décor: Oliver Smith; première: Broadway Theater, New York.
FANCY FREE: 1944; music: Leonard Bernstein; décor: Oliver Smith; première: Metropolitan Opera House, New York.
FANFARE: 1953; music: Benjamin Britten (The Young Person's Guide to the Orchestra); première: City Center, New York.
THE GUESTS: 1949; music: Marc Blitzstein; première: City Center, New York.
INTERPLAY: 1945; music: Morton Gould (American Concertette); décor: Oliver Smith; première: Ziegfeld Theater, New York (in Billy Rose's Concert Varieties).
JONES BEACH: 1950; choreography with George Balanchine; music: Juriaan Andriessen (Berkshire Symphonies); première: City Center, New York.
PAS DE TROIS: 1947; music: Hector Berlioz (The Damnation of Faust); costumes: John Pratt; première: Metropolitan Opera House, New York.
THE PIED PIPER: 1951; music: Aaron Copland (Concerto for Clarinet and Strings); première: City Center, New York.
QUARTET: 1954; music: Serge Prokofiev (String Quartet No. 2, Opus 92); costumes: Karinska; première: City Center, New York.
SUMMER DAY: 1947; music: Serge Prokofiev (Music for Children); décor: John Boyt; première: City Center, New York.

Rodriques, Alfred

BLOOD WEDDING: 1953; music: Denis Aplvor; décor: Isabel Lambert.
ILE DE SIRÈNES: 1952; music: Claude Debussy; décor: Sainthill.

Romanoff, Boris

CHOUT: 1929 (revision); music: Serge Prokofiev; décor: Michel Larianov; première: de Basil Ballet Russe de Monte Carlo.
PRINCE GOUDAL'S FESTIVAL: 1944; music: Anton Rubinstein (The Demon); décor: Mstislav Dobujinsky; première: Théâtre du Châtelet, Paris.
LA TRAGEDIE DE SALOME: 1913; music: Florent Schmitt; décor: Sergei Soudeikine; première: Opéra, Paris .

Rosen, Heinz

LA DAME ET LA LICORNE: 1953; music: Jacques Chailly (orchestration of fifteenth, sixteenth century songs); décor: Jean Cocteau; première: Munich.

Ross, Herbert

CAPRICHOS: 1950; music: Béla Bartók; costumes: Helene Pons; première: Hunter College Auditorium, New York.
THE THIEF WHO LOVED A GHOST: 1950; choreography with John Ward; music: Carl Maria von Weber; décor: John Ward; première: Young Men's Hebrew Association, New York.

Saint-Léon, Arthur

COPPÉLIA: 1870; music: Léo Delibes; décor:

Cambon, Desplechin, Lavastre; première: Opéra, Paris.

Schwezoff, Igor

THE ETERNAL STRUGGLE: 1940; music: Robert Schumann (Etudes Symphoniques, orchestrated by Antal Dorati); décor: Kathleen and Florence Martin; première: Theater Royal, Sidney, Australia.
THE RED POPPY: 1943; music: Reinhold Glière; décor: Boris Aronson; première: Music Hall, Cleveland.

Scott, Blake

THE STORY OF THE SOLDIER: 1931; choreography with Ruth Page; music: Igor Stravinsky; décor: Nicolai Remisoff; première: Page-Stone Ballet, Chicago.

Semonoff, Simon

GIFT OF THE MAGI: 1945; music: Lukas Foss; décor: Raoul Pène Du Bois; première: Boston Opera House.
MEMORIES: 1944; music: Johannes Brahms; décor: Raoul Pène Du Bois; première: International Theater, New York.

Sergeyev, Nicholas

AURORA'S WEDDING (excerpts from The Sleeping Beauty): 1922; choreography after Marius Petipa; music: Peter Ilyich Tchaikovsky; décor: Léon Bakst; première: Opéra, Paris.

Shabelevsky, Yuerek

ODE TO GLORY: 1940; music: Frédéric Chopin (Polonaise in A Flat Major); décor: Michel Baronov; première: Center Theater, New York.

Skibine, George

THE GREY ANGEL: 1954; music: Claude Debussy; décor: Sebire.
IDYLLE: 1954; music: François Serrette; décor: Dwyne Camble.
A TRAGEDY IN VERONA: 1950; music: Peter Tchaikovsky (Romeo and Juliet Overture); décor: André Delfau; première: Théâtre de Monte Carlo.

Slavinsky, Tadeo

CHOUT: 1921; choreography with Michael Larionov; music: Serge Prokofiev; décor: Michael Larionov; première: Théâtre Gaité-Lyrique, Paris.

Solov, Zachary

MADEMOISELLE FIFI: 1952; music: Theodore Lajart; décort: Peter Larkin; première: John Hancock Hall, Boston.

Somes, Michael

SUMMER INTERLUDE: 1950; music: 16th century music, orchestrated by Ottorino Respighi; décor: Sophie Fedorovich.

Staff, Frank

CZERNYANA: 1939; music: Karl Czerny (Piano Exercises); décor: Eve Swinstead-Smith; première: Duchess Theater, London.
ENIGMA VARIATIONS: 1940; music: Edward Elgar; décor: Guy Sheppard.
FANCIULLA DELLE ROSE: 1948; music: Anton Arenski; décor: Guy Sheppard; première: Metropolitan Ballet, London.
LOVERS' GALLERY: 1947; music: Lennox Berkeley (Divertissement in B Flat); décor: George Kirsta; première: Metropolitan Ballet, London.
LA PERI: 1938; music: Paul Dukas; décor: Alexandre Benois.
PETER AND THE WOLF: 1940; music: Serge Prokofiev; décor: Guy Sheppard.
THE TARTANS: 1938; music: William Boyce; décor: William Chappell.

Staats, Leo

CYDALISE AND THE FAUN: 1923; music: Gabriel Pierné; première: Opéra, Paris.
LE FESTIN DE L'ARAIGNÉE: 1913; music: Albert Roussel; décor: Maxime Dethomas; première: Théâtre des Arts, Paris.
LA PÉRI: 1921; choreography after Coralli; music: Paul Dukas; décor: Alexandre Benois; première: Opéra, Paris.

Stone, Bentley

AN AMERICAN PATTERN: 1937; choreography with Ruth Page; music: Jerome Moross; décor: Nicolai Remisoff; première: Page-Stone Ballet, Chicago.
FRANKIE AND JOHNNY: 1938; choreography with Ruth Page; music: Jerome Moross; décor: Clive Rickabaugh; première: Page-Stone Ballet, Chicago.
GUNS AND CASTENETS: 1939; choreography with Ruth Page; music: George Bizet, Jerome Moross; décor: Clive Rickabaugh; première: Page-Stone Ballet; Chicago.
SCRAPBOOK: 1939; choreography with Ruth Page; music: miscellaneous; décor: Clive Rickabaugh; première: Page-Stone Ballet, Chicago.

Taglioni, Filoppo

LA BAYADÈRE (LE DIEU ET LA BAYADÈRE): 1830; music: François Auber; première: Opéra, Paris.
LA SYLPHIDE: 1832; music: Jean Schneitzhoeffer; première: Théâtre de l'Académie Royale de Musique, Paris.

Taras, John

CAMILLE: 1946; music: Franz Schubert, Vittorio Rieti; décor: Cecil Beaton; première: Palacio de Bellas Artes, Mexico City
DESIGN WITH STRINGS: 1948; music: Peter Tchaikovsky (Trio in A Minor); première: Wimbledon, England.
DIVERTISSEMENT: 1950; choreography after Marius Petipa; music: Peter Tchaikovsky (excerpts from The Sleeping Beauty); décor: André Delfau; première: Théâtre de Monte Carlo.
GRAZIANA: 1945; music: Wolfgang Amadeus Mozart (Concerto in G Major for Violin and Orchestra); costumes: Alvin Colt; première: Metropolitan Opera House, New York.

THE MINOTAUR: 1947; music: Elliot Carter; décor: Jean Junyer.
PERSEPHONE: 1950; music: Robert Schumann; décor: Lila de Nobili; première: Théâtre de Monte Carlo.

Theilade, Nini

THE CLOUDS (LES NUAGES): 1940; music: Claude Debussy; décor: William De Kooning; première: Metropolitan Opera House, New York.

Tudor, Antony

ADAM AND EVE: 1932; music: Constant Lambert; première: Marie Rambert Studio, Ladbroke Road, London.
CROSS-GARTERED: 1931; music: Girolamo Frescobaldi; décor: Bocquet; Burnascini; première: Marie Rambert Studio, Ladbroke Road, London.
DARK ÉLEGIES: 1937; music: Gustav Mahler (Songs on the Death of Children); décor: Raymond Sovey, after sketches by Nadia Benois; première: Duchess Theater, London.
THE DESCENT OF HEBE: 1935; music: Ernest Bloch; décor: Nadia Benois; première: Ballet Club, Mercury Theater, London.
DIM LUSTRE: 1943; music: Richard Strauss (Burlesque in D Minor for Piano and Orchestra); décor: Motley; première: Metropolitan Opera House, New York.
GALA PERFORMANCE: 1938; music: Serge Prokofiev (first movement of Concerto for Piano and Orchestra No. 3, and Classical Symphony); décor: Hugh Stevenson; première: Toynbee Hall, London.
GALLANT ASSEMBLY: 1937; music: Guiseppe Tartini; première: Mercury Theater, London.
LA GLOIRE: 1952; music: Ludwig van Beethoven (Overtures to Egmont, Coriolanus, Leonore III); décor: Gaston Longchamp; première: City Center, New York.
GOYESCAS: 1941; music: Enrique Granados (orchestration by Harold Byrns); décor: Nicolas de Molas; première: Majestic Theater, New York.
THE JUDGMENT OF PARIS: 1938; music: Kurt Weill (from The Threepenny Opera); décor: Lucinda Ballard; première: Westminster Theater, London.
THE LADY OF THE CAMELLIAS: 1951; music: Giuseppe Verdi; décor: Cecil Beaton; première: City Center, New York.
LILAC GARDEN: 1936; music: Ernest Chausson (Poème); décor: Hugh Stevenson; première Mercury Theater, London.
LYSISTRATA: 1932; music: Serge Prokofiev; décor: William Chappell; première: Marie Rambert Studio, Ladbroke Road, London.
LES MASQUES: 1933; music: Francis Poulenc; décor: Sophie Fedorovich; première: Marie Rambert Studio, Ladbroke Road, London.
NIMBUS: 1950; music: Louis Gruenberg (Concerto for Violin and Orchestra); décor: Oliver Smith; première: City Center, New York.
PARAMOUR: 1934; music: William Boyce; décor: William Chappell; première: Marie Rambert Studio, Ladbroke Road, London.
PAVANE POUR UNE INFANTE DEFUNTE: 1933; music: Maurice Ravel; décor: Hugh Stevenson, première: Marie Rambert Studio, Ladbroke Road, London.
PILLAR OF FIRE: 1942; music: Arnold Schonberg (Verklärte Nacht); décor: Jo Mielziner; première: Metropolitan Opera House, New York.
THE PLANETS: 1934; music: Gustav Holst; décor: Hugh Stevenson; première: Marie Rambert Studio, Ladbroke Road, London.
MR. ROLLS' QUADRILLES: 1932; music: traditional; décor: Susan Salaman; première: Marie Rambert Studio, Ladbroke Road, London.
ROMEO AND JULIET: 1943; music: Frederick Delius (Over the Hills and Far Away; The Walk to the Paradise Garden; Eventyr; Brigg Fair — orchestrated by Antal Dorati); décor: Eugene Berman; première: Metropolitan Opera House, New York.
SHADOW OF THE WIND: 1948; music: Gustav Mahler (Song of the Earth); décor: Jo Mielziner; première: Metropolitan Opera House, New York.
SUITE D'AIRS: 1937; music: Henry Purcell; décor: Nadia Benois; première: Mercury Theater, London.
TIME TABLE: 1941; music: Aaron Copland (Music for the Theater); décor: James Morcom; première: Hunter College Auditorium, New York.
UNDERTOW: 1945; music: William Schuman; décor: Raymond Breinin; première: Metropolitan Opera House, New York.

Valois, Ninette de

BAR AUX FOLIES BERGÈRES: 1934; music: Emmanuel Chabrier; décor: William Chappell; première: Sadler's Wells Theater, London.
THE BIRTHDAY OF OBERON: 1933; music: Henry Purcell (orchestration by Constant Lambert); décor: John Armstrong; première: Sadler's Wells Theater, London.
CEPHALUS AND PROCRIS: 1931; music: André Grétry; décor: William Chappell; première: Sadler's Wells Theater, London.
CHECKMATE: 1937; music: Arthur Bliss; décor: E. McKnight Kauffer; première: Théâtre des Champs Élysées, Paris.
LA CRÉATION DU MONDE: 1931; music: Darius Milhaud; décor: Edward Wolfe; première: Camargo Society, London.
DANSE SACRÉE ET DANSE PROFANE: 1930; music: Claude Debussy; décor: Hedley Briggs; première: Camargo Society, London (performed at the Old Vic in 1931).
DON QUIXOTE: 1950; music: Robert Gerhardt; décor: Edward Burra; première: Royal Opera House, Covent Garden, London.
DOUANES: 1932; music: Geoffrey Toye; décor: Hedley Briggs; première: Sadler's Wells Theater, London.
FÊTE POLONAISE: 1931; music: Michael Glinka; décor: O. P. Smyth; première: Sadler's Wells Theater, London.
THE GODS GO A-BEGGING: 1936; music: George Frederick Handel; décor: Hugh Stevenson; première: Sadler's Wells Theater, London.
THE HAUNTED BALLROOM: 1934; music: Geoffrey Toye; décor: Motley; première: Sadler's Wells Theater, London.
HOMMAGE AUX BELLES VIENNOISES: 1929; music: Franz Schubert; décor: O. P. Smyth; première: Old Vic, London.
THE JACKDAW AND THE PIGEONS: 1931; music: Hugh Bradford; décor: William Chappell; première: Old Vic, London.
THE JAR: 1934; music: Alfredo Casella; décor: William Chappell; première: Sadler's Wells Theater, London.
THE JEW IN THE BUSH: 1931; music: Gordon Jacob; décor: Bertrand Guest; première: Old Vic, London.
JOB: 1931; music: Ralph Vaughan Williams; décor: Gwendolen Raverat; première: Cambridge Theater, London.

NARCISSUS AND ECHO: 1932; music: Arthur Bliss; décor: William Chappell; première: Sadler's Wells Theater, London.

NURSERY SUITE: 1932; music: Edward Elgar; décor: Nancy Allen; première: Sadler's Wells Theater, London.

ORPHEUS AND EURYDICE: 1941; music: Christoph Willibald Gluck; décor: Sophie Fedorovich; première: New Theater, London.

THE PICNIC (THE FAUN): 1928; music: Ralph Vaughan Williams; décor: Hedley Briggs; première: Old Vic, London.

PROMEMADE: 1943; music: Joseph Haydn; décor: Hugh Stevenson; première: King's Theater, Edinburgh.

PROMETHEUS: 1936; music: Ludwig van Beethoven (orchestration by Constant Lambert); décor: John Banting; première: Sadler's Wells Wells Theater, London.

THE PROSPECT BEFORE US: 1940; music: William Boyce; décor: Roger Furse; première: Sadler's Wells Theater, London.

THE RAKE'S PROGRESS: 1935; music: Gavin Gordon; décor: Rex Whistler; première: Sadler's Wells Theater, London.

LE ROI NU: 1938; music: Jean Françaix; décor: Hedley Briggs; première: Sadler's Wells Theater, London.

ROUT: 1928; music: Arthur Bliss; première: Camargo Society, London.

THE SCORPIONS OF YSIT: 1932; music: Gavin Gordon; décor: Sophie Fedorovich; première: Sadler's Wells Theater, London.

SUITE DE DANSES: 1930; music: Johann Sebastian Bach (orchestration by Eugene Goossens); décor: O. P. Smyth; première: Sadlers' Wells Theater, London.

THE WISE AND FOOLISH VIRGINS: 1933; music: Kurt Atterberg; décor: William Chappell; première: Sadler's Wells Theater, London.

Viganò, Salvatore

THE CREATURES OF PROMETHEUS: 1801; music: Ludwig van Beethoven; première: Imperial Court Theater, Vienna.

Wiener, Hans

THE INCREDIBLE FLUTIST: 1938; music: Walter Piston; première: Symphony Hall, Boston.

Yerrell, Ronald

THE WATERFALL: 1954; music: Serge Prokofiev; (Violin Sonata); décor: Desmond Heeley.

Barbaric Invaders of the Roman Empire

ALANI: A Tartar people who invaded Parthia (75 a.d.); joined, or were subjugated, by the Huns, and partipicated in the Hun invasion of the Roman Empire, which was defeated by the emperor Theodosius (379-382); some retreated to the West, and advanced with the Vandals and Swevi across the Rhine into Gallia and Spain; their unity was destroyed by the advancing Visigoths, who drove part of them with the Vandals from Spain to Africa (c. 412), and absorbed the rest (c. 452).

ALEMANNI: Also All Men (i. e., men of all nations, from which Allemand, German, derives); a body of Suevi who were attacked by Caracalla (214); after several unsuccessful attempts, invaded the Roman Empire and were defeated by Emperor Aurelian in three battles (271); beaten by Julian (356-57), and by Jovinus (368); subjugated by Clovis at Tolbiac (Zulpich) in 496; ancestors of the Swabians.

BURGUNDIANS: A Gothic tribe that overran Gaul (275); driven back by Emperor Probos; returned (287) and were defeated by Maximian; returned from the Vistula and crossed the Rhine (407); advanced from Germany into France and commanded lands along the Rhone (411); established a kingdom (413) that included Burgundy, a large part of Switzerland, Alsace, Savoy, and Provence; Gondicar first king; conquered by the Franks (534); a second kingdom, including a part of the first, was founded by Gontran, son of Clotaire I of France (561).

CIMBRI: A Teutonic race from Jutland who invaded the Roman Empire (c. 120 b.c.), defeated the Roman army under Cneius Papirius Carbo (113 b.c.), under the consul Junius Silanus (109 b.c.), under the consul Cassius Longinus (who was killed) near Lake Genova (107 b.c.); and the combined armies of the consul Cneius Mallius and the proconsul Servilius near the Rhone (105 b.c.); after their allies, the Teutones, were twice beaten by Marius at Aquae Sextiae (Aix) in Gaul (102 b.c.), the Cimbri were turned back by Marius and Catulus, at Campus Raudius, when they were about to invade Italy (101 b.c.); later they were absorbed by the Teutones or Saxons.

FRANKS: The name given to the northwest German tribes who merged in 240 a.d.; identified as the Celts who occupied the left bank of the Rhine (287); as the Salians who occupied Belgium (407); invaded Gaul and other parts of the empire with various successes in the 5th century; confined to the mouth of the Rhine (482), where they established a kingdom that extended to the Seine and Loire and restricted the Visigoths to Languedoc; their vigorous leader Clovis (481) defeated Syaerius and the Gauls at Soissons (486) and the Alemanni at Tolbiac; he embraced Christianity (496); killed Alaric the Goth at Vougle, near Poitiers, consolidated his conquests from the Loire to the Pyrenees, and made his capital at Paris (507); proclamed the "Salic Law," died (511) leaving four sons.

GOTHS: The Goths emerged (180 a.d.) as a warlike people who lived along the Vistula and Oder rivers; at about this time they began to move and took possession of the coastal lands along the Black Sea, so that they effectively controlled the country between the Caspian, Pontus, Euxine, and Baltic seas; (249-251) they crossed the Danube, entered Moesia, took Phillippopolis and massacred the inhabitants, engaged the Roman troops and defeated and killed the emperor Decius (251); 18 years later they were beaten by Claudius at Naissus (afterward called Gothicus) and 320,000 of them are said to have been butchered (269); in 272 the Emperor Aurelian ceded Dacia to them; from 360, the Goths pushed east and west, consolidating their conquests and dividing into the East or Ostrogoths, of the Black Sea region, and the West, or Visigoths, of Dacia and Podolia; after the destruction of the Roman Empire of the West by Heruli, the Ostrogoths, under Theodoric, became masters of the major part of Italy and remained in power until 553, when they were finally conquered by Justinian's general, Narses; the Visigoths, forced from Dacia and Podolia by the Ostrogoths, crossed the Danube (375) and were granted Roman protection in Thrace; revolted, defeated the Roman army, and killed Emperor Valens (378); under Alaric roamed and plundered the Peloponnesus (395); invaded Italy (401); sacked Rome (409); moved into Gaul and Spain where they settled, and founded the kingdom of the Visigoths with a center at Toulouse (414-18), which was in existence until the Saracen conquest (711) of the country.

HUNS: A fierce nomadic Asian people who are said to have conquered (c. 210 b.c.) and lost (c. 90 a.d.) China; gradually spread westward, crossing the Volga, partially subjugating and uniting with the Alani on the Don; invaded Hungary (c. 376) and drove out the Goths, who had themselves advanced from the Baltic coast to the north, and the Black Sea to the south; crossed the Danube and entered Pannonia and Moesia (395); under Attila, the "Scourge of God," ravaged the Eastern Empire (445-450), exacted tribute from Constantinople, and raided Germany and France, until compacting peace with Theodosius; then invaded the Western Empire, where Attila was beaten by Aetius at Chalons (451); after defeat, Attila retired into Pannonia where he is said to have burst a blood vessel at his wedding to the beautiful Ildico (453); with the death of Attila, the unity of the Huns was broken and they disappeared with their dwindling power: the collapse of the Huns released the subject German tribes who then renewed their own attacks on Rome.

LOMBARDS: The Longobardi, a German tribe from Brandenburg, said to have been invited into Italy by Justinian as a buffer against the Goths; their chief, Alboin, established a kingdom that lasted from 568-774; Charlemagne dethroned Desiderius, their last king.

NERVII: A hostile tribe in Belgian Gaul, conquered by Julius Caesar in a bloody battle (57 b.c.) and subdued (53 b.c.).

SCLAVONIANS (SLAVONIANS): The Sclavonians originated in the ancient country of Sarmatia between the Caspian Sea and the Vistula (including Russia and Poland); the Sarmatae (Sauromatae) were among the disturbers of the peace of the early Roman Empire; they subdued the Scythians and were in turn subjugated by the Goths (3rd-4th centuries); occupied northeastern Germany after the great migration from that region, and all of the eastern territory from the mouth of the Oder R. to the Adriatic; joined the Huns and other barbarian invasions of Rome (5th century); seized Poland and Bohemia (496).

SUEVI: A warlike Gothic tribe that entered Spain with the Alani and Visigoths (c. 408); defeated by the Visigoths and absorbed (584).

TEUTONES (GERMANS): A German people who invaded Gaul with the Cimbri and destroyed two Roman armies (113 and 105 b.c.); defeated by the consul Marius at Aix (102 b.c.), where 200,000 are said to have been killed and 70,000 taken prisoner; by the end of the 2nd century a.d. the old names of the German tribes had been lost; by the 3d century, the people on the left bank of the Rhine (Swabia) were identified as the Franks, while the Saxons and Frisii lived farther north; under Theodosius (379-395), German tribes crossed the Rhine and drove the Romans from Portugal, Spain, and France.

VANDALS: A Germanic tribe that occupied Silesia and Bohemia near the borderlands of the Suevi; attacked the Roman Empire (3rd century); pressed by the Alani, moved farther west (376); joined the Suevi and Alani, ravaged Germany and Gaul, conquered the Franks, crossed the Rhine and descended through Gallia to Spain, where they subjugated the Alani and were pressed by the Visigoths (406-414); under Genseric, invaded and conquered the Roman territories in North Africa (429) and took Carthage (October, 439); established an African kingdom ruled by Genseric (429), Hilderic (523), Gelimer (531); subdued by Belisarius (534) and dispossessed by the Saracen Moors.

Battles

Note: For important battles of the American Revolution, the War of 1812, the American Civil War, the Mexican War, and the Spanish-American War see separate entries.

Decisive Battles of History (According to Professor Creasy)

In his celebrated study of the major battles of history, Sir Edward Shepherd Creasy (1812-1878) made the following selection (1851) of the "Fifteen Decisive Battles of the World," and gave his reasons for their importance:

MARATHON, 490 b.c.: The Greek victory over the Persians ended the attempt of Darius to dominate and determinate the early development of European history.

SYRACUSE, 413 b.c.: The defeat of the Athenians on the island of Sicily brought the cycle of Athenian imperialism to a close and permitted the free development of the rising power of Rome.

ARBELA, OCTOBER 1, 331 b.c.: The defeat of the Persians by Alexander of Macedon led to the downfall of the Persian Empire.

METAURUS, 207 b.c.: The defeat of the Carthaginians by Rome ended the history of Carthage as a world power and marked the emergence of Rome as the new center of military and cultural supremacy.

TEUTOBURG (TEUTOBURGERWALD), 9 a.d.: The victory af the Germans over the Romans checked Roman expansion northward and marked the emergence of the German tribes as a decisive factor in European development.

CHÂLONS, 451 a.d.: The overwhelming Roman victory over Attila and the Huns saved western Europe from the threat of further Mongolian depredations.

TOURS, OCTOBER 10, 732: Charles Martel, the "Hammer," vanquished the Saracens and prevented the Mohammedan conquest of Europe.

HASTINGS, OCTOBER 14, 1066: The successful invasion of England by the Normans under William the Conqueror determined the kind of culture which would predominate in England and, later, in the English-speaking colonies of the world.

ORLÉANS, APRIL 29, 1429: The raising of the English siege of Orléans by the French forces under Joan of Arc crippled the continental power of England and brought an end to the rule of the English Plantagenets in France.

DEFEAT OF THE SPANISH ARMADA, JULY, 1588: The defeat of the Spanish Armada ended the ambition of Philip II of Spain to establish the House of Hapsburg as the dominating influence in European affairs.

BLENHEIM, AUGUST 13, 1704: The defeat of France at Blenheim forced Louis XIV to capitulate to the English terms of the Treaty of Utrecht, which established England as the unrivaled colonial power of the world.

PULTOWA, JULY 8, 1709: The Russian victory

over the armies of Charles XII frusrated the ambitions of the "Madman of the North" and marked the emergence of Russia as a major European power.

SARATOGA, OCTOBER 17, 1777: The decisive defeat of the British forces at Saratoga marked the turning point of the American Revolution, with fateful consequences for the continued European conquest of the world.

VALMY, SEPTEMBER 20, 1792: The victory of the army of the French Republic over the reactionary powers under the leadership of the Duke of Brunswick insured the success of the French Revolution and the maintenance of political liberalism in Europe.

WATERLOO, JUNE 18, 1815: The victory of the British, German, Dutch, and Prussian forces at Waterloo undermined the imperialist ambitions of Napoleon and ushered in the era of reaction that dominated European politics through the following decades.

Selective Listing of Decisive Battles

ACTIUM: *Date:* 31 b.c.; *place:* off west coast of Greece; *victor:* Romans (Octavius Augustus); *defeated:* Egyptian fleet (Antony, Cleopatra); *result:* Octavius became undisputed ruler of the Roman Empire.

ADRIANOPLE: *Date:* July 3, 323; *place:* Turkey; *victor:* Constantine; *defeated:* Licinius; *result:* Constantine became sole emperor of both East and West.

ADRIANOPLE: *Date:* August 9, 378; place: Turkey; *victor:* Goths; *defeated:* Romans (Valens); *result:* Valens slain in worst defeat of the Romans since Cannae.

AEGATES ISLES: *Date:* March 10, 241 b.c.; *place:* islands west of Sicily; *victor:* Romans (Caius Lutatius Catulus); defeated: Carthaginian fleet (Hanno); *result:* end of First Punic War, Sicily ceded to Rome.

AGINCOURT: *Date:* October 25, 1415; *place:* northern France; *victor:* English (Henry V); *defeated:* French; *result:* Henry V of England became ruler of France.

ANZIO (WORLD WAR II): *Date:* January 22-May 19, 1944; *place:* beach in Italy near Rome; victor: Americans, British; *defeated:* Germans; *result:* the Allies successfully established a beachhead in the Cassino-Anzio area and took the offensive along the Gustav Line, while the Germans desperately tried to prevent the occupation of Rome; the collapse of the Gustav Line on May 19 was followed by the withdrawal of the Germans from Rome (June 4), which Hitler claimed was a move to prevent the destruction of the Eternal City.

ARBELA: *Date:* October 1, 331 b.c.; *place:* Assyria; *victor:* Macedonians (Alexander the Great); *defeated:* Persians (Darius III); *result:* see Creasy's "Decisive Battles of History."

ARCOLA: *Date:* November 14-17, 1796; *place:* Lombardy, Italy; *victor:* French (Napoleon); *defeated:* Austrians (Alvinza); result: French won control of Italy.

ASPERN-ESSLING: *Dtae:* May 21-22, 1809, *place:* near Vienna, Austria; *victor:* Austrians (Archduke Charles); *defeated:* French (Napoleon); *result:* Napoleon retreated after loss of 30,000 men, but the Austrian victory was short-lived.

AUSTERLITZ: *Date:* December 2, 1805; *place:* Moravia; *victor:* French (Napoleon); defeated: Austrians (Francis of Austria), Russians (Czar Alexander, General Kutusoff); *result:* led to the treaty of Presburg, by which the city-state of Venice was ceded to Italy; the principality of Eichstadt, part of Passau, the

city of Augsburg, the Tyrol, all the possessions of Austria in Swabia, in Brusgau, and Ortenau, were transferred to the Elector of Bavaria and the Duke of Würtemberg; the Dukes of Würtemberg and Baden were created kings; the freedom of the Helvetian (Swiss) Republic was guaranteed.

BALAKLAVA: *Date:* September 25, 1854; *place:* Crimea; *victor:* English (Lord Lucan, Scarlett); *defeated:* Russians (Liprandi); *result:* Lord Lucan, misunderstanding the orders of Lord Raglan, commanded Lord Cardigan and his light cavalry to charge the Russians who had re-formed behind their artillery; in this "Charge of the Light Brigade," 198 British horsemen out of 670 survived the raking fire of the Russian artillery. Some authorities declare that the victory was with the Russians, others point out that no advantage was gained by either side.

BANNOCKBURN: *Date:* June 24, 1314; *place:* Stirlingshire, Scotland; victor: Scots (Robert Bruce); *defeated:* English (Edward II); *result:* the English force of 100,000 men was routed, the English king narrowly escaped death, and half the English army was taken prisoner.

BANNOCKBURN: *Date:* June 11, 1488; *place:* Sauchieburn, near Bannockburn, Scotland; *victor:* Scots nobles; *defeated:* James III of Scotland; *result:* death in battle of James III and victory for the revolutionary party.

BATAAN (WORLD WAR II): Date: January 2-April 9, 1942; *place:* Philippine Islands; *victor:* Japanese (Yamashita); *defeated:* Americans (MacArthur, Wainwright); *result:* the American retreat to Bataan left the Japanese free to occupy Manila; on Mar. 17. Gen. MacArthur left Bataan by Presidential order because defence was hopeless; the peninsula fell to the Japanese on Apr. 9; Gen. Wainwright and 3500 soldiers and nurses withdrew to Corregidor, where, the following day, they were forced to begin the infamous 6-day 85-mile "Death March" to a Japanese prison camp.

BISMARCK SEA (WORLD WAR II): *Date:* March 2-4, 1943: *place:* the Bismarck Archipelago off New Guinea; *victor:* American fleet; *defeated:* Japanese fleet; *result:* the major naval victory, in which the Japanese lost an entire convoy of 22 ships, was part of the massive Allied effort to prevent the Japanese from landing at Port Moresby and carrying through their threatened invasion of Australia from bases at Gona and Buna on New Guinea.

BLENHEIM: *Date:* August 13, 1704; *place:* Bavaria; *victors:* English, Austrians (Duke of Marlborough, Prince Eugene); *defeated:* French, Bavarians (Tallard, Marsin); *result:* see Creasy's "Decisive Battles of History."

BORODINO: *Date:* September 7, 1812; *place:* Russia, *victor:* French (Napoleon); *defeated:* Russians (Kutusoff); *result:* each side claimed victory, but the Russians retreated and the French occupied Moscow.

BOSWORTH FIELD (WAR OF THE ROSES): *Date:* Aug. 22, 1485; *place:* Leicestershire, England; *victors:* Lancastrians, Red Rose (Earl of Richmond, later Henry VII); *defeated:* Yorkists, White Rose (Richard III); *result:* thirteenth and last battle between the Houses of York and Lancaster; Richard III was slain; it is said that the Earl of Richmond was crowned on the spot as Henry VII with the crown that Richard had lost in a hawthorne bush.

BOUVINES: *Date:* July 27, 1214; *place:* northern France; *victor:* French (Philip Augustus); *defeated:* Germans, Flemish, English (Otto IV); *result:* beginning of France as a nation.

BOYNE: *Date:* July 1, 1690; *place:* Ireland; *victor:* William III of England; *defeated:* James II of England; *result:* James II fled to France and the Protestant succession was secure in England.

BREITENFIELD: *Date:* September 7, 1631; *place:* near Leipsig, Saxony; *victor:* Swedes (Gustavus Adolphus); *defeated:* Imperialists (Tilly; *result:* see battle of Luetzen (1632).

BREITENFIELD: *Date:* October 23, 1642; *place:* near Leipsig, Saxony; *victors:* Swedes (Torstenson); *defeated:* Imperialists; *result:* confirmed the results of the Battle of Luetzen (1632).

BULGE, BATTLE OF THE (WORLD WAR II): *Date:* December 16-28, 1944; *place:* Ardennes Forest in Belgium, France, Luxembourg; *victor:* Allies (Eisenhower); *defeated:* Germans; *result:* last major German offensive; by December 28, the offensive was contained; on January 12 the German line crumbled and the campaign was carried in its final stages to German soil.

CANNAE: *Date:* August 2, 216 b.c.; *place:* Apulia, southeast Italy; *victor:* Carthaginians (Hannibal); *defeated:* Romans (Aemilius Paulus, Terentius Varro); *result:* Roman army annihilated; Aemilius Paulus slain.

CAPORETTO (WORLD WAR I): *Date:* October 24-December 26, 1917; *place:* northern Italy; *victor:* Central Powers; defeated: Italian Army; *result:* after the Italian army deserted to the Allies, the Central Powers planned a massive retaliation to knock Italy out of war; at Caporetto, they delivered the Italian forces a staggering blow; 200,000 prisoners were taken, and 2000 pieces of artillery; it was a major setback for the Allies, but English reinforcements were sent to bolster the sagging and demoralized Italian front.

CHAERONEA (CORONEA): *Date:* August 6 or 7, 338 b.c.; *place:* Boeotia; victor: Philip of Macedon; *defeated:* Athenians and allies (Tolmides); *result:* the ruin of Greece.

CHÂLONS-SUR-MARNE: *Date:* 451 a.d.; *place:* northeast France; *victors:* Romans (Aetius) and Visigoths (Theodoric); *defeated:* Huns and Ostrogoths; *result:* see Professor Creasy's "Decisive Battles of History."

CONSTANTINOPLE: *Date:* May 29, 1453; *place:* Turkey (anciently Thrace); *victor:* Turks (Mahomet II); *defeated:* city of Constantinople; *result:* the fifty-three day's siege of the city ended with the fall of the Roman Empire in the East.

CORAL SEA (WORLD WAR II): *Date:* May 4-8, 1942; *place:* off Australia; *victor:* U.S. task force; *defeated:* Japanese naval force; *result:* on May 4, planes from the American task force sank a Japanese light cruiser, two destroyers, four gunboats, and a supply vessel; on May 6 the Japanese carrier *Ryukaku* was sunk; on May 7 Japanese planes knocked out the U.S. carrier *Lexington*, and their own carrier *Shokaku* was crippled; by this first naval encounter in history fought solely with carrier-based aircraft, the Japanese were prevented from carrying further their plans for a thrust southward at Australia.

COUTRAS: *Date:* October 20, 1587; *place:* southwest France; *victor:* Henry of Navarre (later Henry IV); *defeated:* Royalists (Duc de Joyeuse); *result:* conclusion of the War of the Three Henrys (1585-87).

CRECY (CRESSY): *Date:* August 26, 1346; *place:* northern France; *victor:* English (Edward III, Edward the Black Prince); *defeat-*

ed: French (Philip of France); *result:* the great English victory, followed by the successful siege of Calais through the following year, insured the maintenance of an English foothold on continental Europe.

CULLODEN: *Date:* April 16, 1746; *place:* near Inverness, Scotland; *victor:* English (William, Duke of Cumberland); *defeated:* Scots (Young Pretender, Charles); *result:* Charles, the last of the Stuarts, was so soundly beaten that he was forced to flee into exile.

CUNAXA: *Date:* 401 b.c.; *place:* Mesopotamia; *victor:* army of Cyrus the Younger and 10,000 Greek mercenaries; *defeated:* army of King Artaxerxes Memnon; *result:* as narrated in the *Anabasis* of Xenophon, Cyrus, who had led a rebellion against his brother Artaxerxes, was slain; the Greek mercenaries had no reason to continue the fight though they were, in their engagements, successful; their leaders accepted an invitation from Artaxerxes to discuss a settlement and were treacherously slain; Xenophon took command of the troops and led them, for 215 days, through 3465 miles of rugged enemy territory until, after an absence of 15 months, he landed them home again in Greece.

CUSTOZZA (SEVEN WEEKS' WAR): *Date:* June 24, 1866; *place:* near Verona, northern Italy; *victor:* Austrians (Archduke Albrecht); *defeated:* Italians (Victor Emmanuel); *result:* the Italians recrossed the Mincio.

CUZCO: *Date:* August, 1536; *place:* Peru; *victor:* Spaniards under Pizarro; *defeated:* natives of the city; *result:* after five months' siege, the city of the Incas fell to the invading conquistadores.

DRESDEN: *Date:* August 26-27, 1813; *place:* Germany; *victor:* Russia, Prussia, Allies (Schwarzenberg); *defeated:* French (Napoleon); *result:* the Allies were badly beaten at first and withdrew, but they were pursued so far into Bohemia by the French under Vandamme that they were able to outmaneuver and cut his forces to pieces; on November 11, 1813, Marshal St. Cyr surrendered Dresden and 25,000 French troops to the Allies.

DROGHEDA: *Date:* September 12, 1649; *place:* Ireland; *victor:* Cromwell and the Parliamentarians; *defeated:* Royalists; *result:* after his successful siege of the town, Cromwell slaughtered the entire garrison of 3000, most of them English, including the governor, Sir Aston; Wexford similarly fell and the defenders were similarly butchered; Cromwell was able to leave the reduction of Ireland to other hands and returned to secure the Revolution in England.

DUNES (DUNKIRK): *Date:* June 14, 1658; *place:* dunes (or sands) near Dunkirk, northern France; *victor:* English and French (Turenne); *defeated:* Spanish (Conde); *result:* the city was put in the hands of the English, who sold it to Louis XIV on October 17 for a half-million pounds.

DUNKIRK (WORLD WAR II): *Date:* May 26-June 3, 1940; *place:* Belgium; *victor:* Germans; *defeated:* the lightning advances of the Germans through the lowlands trapped the British at Dunkirk and threatened the capture of the most effective part of the Allied army; civilian and naval craft were drafted to help in the evacuation of the troops from the trap; in the course of a week 335,000 out of 400,000 Allied troops were transported safely to England to prepare for the Battle of Britain; it is one of the rare instances in history when a defeat can truly be labeled a moral victory.

EL ALAMEIN (WORLD WAR II): *Date:* July 1-November 2, 1942; *place:* 70 miles west of Alexandria, Egypt; *victor:* British (Auchinleck, Montgomery); *defeated:* Germans, Italians (Rommel); *result:* the initial stubborn stand of the British, July 1-July 20, checked Rommel's advance toward the Nile Delta; through the summer and fall the British Eighth Army held the line and prevented the fall of Egypt; this was the high point of the German advance in North Africa; when the British broke through the German lines on November 2, they also took the initiative in the African War, and began to reverse the German successes; by May 12, 1943, the last of the German Afrika Korps was trapped on Cape Bon in Tunisia and the battle for North Africa ended.

ETHANDUN (EDINGTON): *Date:* 878 A. D.; *place:* Wiltshire, England; *victor:* West Saxons (Alfred the Great); *defeated:* Danes (Guthrum); result: the second invasion of the Danes was blunted, leading to successive victories over them by Alfred, their eventual withdrawal (897), and the consolidation of the kingdom of England around the strongholds of the victorious West Saxons.

FLODDEN FIELD: *Date:* September 9, 1513; *place:* Northumberland, England; *victor:* English (Earl of Surrey); *defeated:* Scots (James IV); *result:* the coalition of the Scots and the French (Louis XII) against the English (Henry VIII) was crippled, James IV and many of the Scots nobles were slain, and the Scots army lost nearly 10,000 men.

FONTENAY (FONTENAILLE): *Date:* June 25, 841; *place:* Burgundy; *victor:* Charles the Bold, Louis the German; *defeated:* Emperor Lothaire I (their brother); *result:* the victory, called "the judgment of God," led to the consolidation of the French monarchy.

FONTENOY: *Date:* April 30, 1745; *place:* near Tournay, Belgium; *victor:* French (Marshal Saxe); *defeated:* English, Austrians, Dutch, Hanoverians (Duke of Cumberland); *result:* losses were heavy on both sides and the outcome of the battle was not decisive, but the Allies were forced to withdraw; the initially successful advance of the English column became a classic illustration of the effective deployment of massed infantry and was imitated by the Austrians against Napoleon at Marengo (June 14, 1800).

FRIEDLAND: *Date:* June 14, 1807; *place:* Prussia; *victor:* French (Napoleon); *defeated:* Russians, Prussians; *result:* the treaty of Tilset followed this French victory, and Prussia was forced to surrender nearly half of her possessions.

GALLIPOLI (WORLD WAR I): *Date:* 1915; *place:* the Dardanelles; *victor:* Central Powers; *defeated:* Allied fleet and army; *result:* the objective of the Dardanelles campaign was to drive a wedge between Turkey and the other Central Powers, open communications with Russia, win the help of the neutral Balkan states, and so prepare for a thrust at Austria from the south; early in 1915 the Franco-British fleet was driven out of the straits by the strategically placed Turkish artillery; a land attack by the combined British, Australian, and New Zealand troops also failed to take Gallipoli; and the entire campaign was abandoned late in 1915.

GILBERT ISLANDS (WORLD WAR II): *Date:* November 20-23, 1943; *place:* Micronesia, Pacific; *victor:* U.S.; *defeated:* Japan; *result:* successful landings at Tarawa, Makin,

and Abemama completed the reoccupation of the Gilbert Islands.

GRANICUS: *Date:* May 22, 334 b.c.; *place:* river in northwest Asia Minor; *victor:* Macedonians (Alexander the Great); *defeated:* Persians; *result:* the Persian army was decimated; Sardis capitulated to Alexander; Miletus and Halicarnassus were taken by storm.

GUADALCANAL (WORLD WAR II): *Date:* August 7-September 13, 1942; *place:* Coral Sea, off Australia; *victor:* U.S. Marine Corps, Australian task force; *defeated:* Japanese; *result:* the U.S. Marines, aided by an Australian naval force, landed on Guadalcanal on Aug. 7 and succeeded in taking Tulagi and the airfield at Luriga Bay; the following day a Japanese task force tried to destroy the landing operations of the invaders and was driven off after the Australian cruiser *Canberra* and three American heavy cruisers, the *Quincy, Astoria,* and *Vincennes,* were lost; through August and the first half of September the Japanese harassed the installations at Guadalcanal by sea and air; the lull in their activity after Sept. 13 did not make the victory of the Allies conclusive, but the pressure of the Japanese drive against Australia was temporarily lowered.

HASTINGS: *Date:* October 14, 1066; *place:* a Cinque-Port in Sussex, England; *victor:* Normans (William the Conqueror); *defeated:* Saxons (Harold); *result:* see Prof. Creasy's "Decisive Battles of History."

HOHENLINDEN: *Date:* December 3, 1800; *place:* Bavaria; *victor:* French, Bavarians (Moreau); *defeated:* Austrians (Archduke John); *result:* the peace of Lunéville, which placed the northern boundary of France at the Rhine as far as the Dutch territories; recognized the independence of the Batavian, Helvetic, Ligurian, and Cisalpine republics; and confirmed the cession by Austria of the Low Countries and Ionian Islands to France, and of Milan, Mantua, and Modena to the Cisalpine Republic (October 17, 1797), in the treaty of Campo Formio.

INCHON (KOREAN WAR): *Date:* September 15, 1950; *place:* Korea; *victor:* U.S. (10th Corps); *defeated:* North Koreans; *result:* the successful amphibious landing at Inchon, the port for the Korean capital, Seoul, permitted the U.S. troops to cut behind the North Koreans and prepare for the capture of Seoul the following week.

ISSUS: *Date:* October, 333 b.c.; *place:* Asia Minor; *victor:* Macedonians (Alexander the Great); *defeated:* Persians (Darius); *result:* the Persian army suffered a second overwhelming defeat and the Queen and royal family were taken prisoners.

IVRY: *Date:* March 14, 1590; *place:* near Evreux, northwest France; *victor:* Henry IV; *defeated:* Holy League Army (Duc de Mayenne); *result:* bolstered the hold of Henry IV on the throne of France.

IWO JIMA (WORLD WAR II): *Date:* February 9 - March 16, 1945; *place:* island south of Japan; *victor:* U.S. Marines (Admiral Spruance); *defeated:* Japanese; *result:* over 4000 Marines were killed, and 15,000 wounded; the Japanese lost more than 20,000 troops; on the island was established an American base 750 miles from Tokyo.

JEMAPPES: *Date:* November 6, 1792; *place:* northwest Belgium; *victor:* French Republicans (Dumouriez); *defeated:* Austrians; *result:* first pitched battle of the French Republican army proved the ability of the National Assembly to defend itself and remain in power.

JENA AND AUERSTADT: Date: October 14,

1806; *place:* central Germany; *victor:* French (Napoleon, Davoust); *defeated:* Prussians (Prince Hohenlohe, King of Prussia); *result:* Napoleon advanced to Berlin, where he issued the Berlin Decree (Nov. 20) banning English trade.

JUTLAND (WAR WAR I): *Date:* May 31-June 1, 1916; *place:* off Denmark; *victor:* British fleet (Admirals Beatty, Jellicoe); *defeated:* German High Seas Fleet (Admiral Richard Sheer); *result:* in the only major naval battle of the war, both sides claimed victory, but the German fleet retreated to Kiel and was bottled up there by the British for the rest of the war.

KÖNIGGRATZ (SADOWA): *Date:* July 3, 1866; *place:* Bohemia; *victor:* Prussians (King William I); *defeated:* Austrians (Marshal Benedek); *result:* the victory made Prussia supreme in Germany, unified northern Germany, gave Venetia to Italy, and led to the legislative independence of Hungary.

LA HOGUE (HAGUE): *Date:* May 19, 1692; *place:* northwest France; *victor:* English, Dutch fleets (Admirals Russell, Rooke); *defeated:* French fleet (Admiral Tourville); *result:* 26 French ships were destroyed or severely damaged and French plans for an invasion of England were defeated.

LAKE TRASIMENUS (THRASYMENE): *Date:* 217 b.c.; *place:* northern Italy; *victor:* Carthaginians (Hannibal); *defeated:* Romans (Flaminius); *result:* 15,000 Romans were slain and 10,000 taken prisoner (6000 according to Livy; 15,000, according to Polybius); Hannibal's threat to Rome grew.

LANGSIDE: *Date:* May 13, 1568; *place:* southern Scotland; *victor:* Regent of Scotland, Murray; *defeated:* Mary Queen of Scots; *result:* Mary fled to England where she was shortly afterward imprisoned by Queen Elizabeth.

LEGNANO: *Date:* May 29, 1176; *place:* Lombardy; *victor:* Lombard League or Milanese and their allies; *defeated:* Emperor Frederick Barbarossa; *result:* led to the Treaty of Constance (1183), which checked the influence of Germany in Italy and gave the Free Cities a new lease on life.

LEIPZIG (LEIPSIC): *Date:* October 16-19, 1813; *place:* Saxony; *victor:* Prussians, Russians, Austrians, Swedes (Schwarzenberg); *defeated:* French (Napoleon); *result:* in this "Battle of the Nations," the French were deserted by 17 battalions of Saxons, who switched sides during the battle and threw the victory to the Allies; of the 80,000 dead on the field more than half were French; Leipzig soon fell, the rear of the French army was taken, and the King of Saxony was captured with his family.

LEPANTO: *Date:* October 7, 1571; *place:* near Corinth, Greece; *victors:* Italian, Spanish fleets (Don John of Austria); *defeated:* Turkish fleet (Áli); *result:* the progress of the Turkish invasion was checked.

LEUCTRA: *Date:* July 8, 371 b.c.; *place:* Boeotia, northern Greece; *victor:* Thebans (Epaminondas); *defeated:* Spartans (King Cleombrotus); *result:* Spartans gradually lost their controlling influence in Greece.

LEUTHEN (LISSA): *Date:* December 5, 1757; *place:* Silesia; *victor:* Prussians (Frederick); *defeated:* Austrians (Charles of Lorraine); *result:* Charles of Lorraine was vanquished and 6000 Austrians slain.

LEYTE GULF (WORLD WAR II): *Date:* October 23-26, 1944; *place:* Philippine Islands; *victor:* U.S. task force; *defeated:* Japanese fleet; *result:* largest naval battle of the war; the

Japanese used 25 ships in an attempt to break up the American invasion; 24 of these ships were lost; the Americans lost the light carrier *Princeton*, 2 escort carriers, 2 destroyers, and 1 destroyer escort; the Japanese fleet was destroyed at Leyte.

LISSA: *Date:* July 20, 1866; *place:* islands in the Adriatic; *victor:* Austrian fleet (Tegethoff); *defeated:* Italian fleet (Persano); *result:* both parties retired after the four-hour engagement; Admiral Persano was later (December 1, 1866) tried for cowardice and acquitted (Jan. 30, 1867); meanwhile, a peace treaty was signed with the Austrians at Vienna (Oct. 3) and ratified (Oct. 12).

LUETZEN (LUTZEN, ALSO LUTZENGEN): *Date:* November 16, 1632; *place* northern Germany; *victor:* Swedes (Gustavus Adolphus); *defeated:* Imperialists (Wallenstein); *result:* Gustavus was killed, but the victory of his troops assured the independence of the Protestant states of Central Europe.

LUETZEN: *Date:* May 2, 1813; *place:* northern Germany; *victor:* French (Napoleon); *defeated:* Russia, Prussia (Wittgenstein); *result:* the battles of Bautzen and Wurschen followed immediately (May 19-21), and Napoleon won both, forcing the Allies to cross the Oder River and sue for an armistice.

MAGENTA: *Date:* June 4, 1859; *place:* Lombardy; *victor:* French, Sardinians (Louis Napoleon); *defeated:* Austrians; *result:* Louis Napoleon and the King of Sardinia entered Milan (June 8); MacMahon and Regnault d'Angely were created marshals of France.

MALPLAQUET: *Date:* September 11, 1709; *place:* northern France; *victor:* Allies (Duke of Marlborough, Prince Eugene); *defeated:* French (Marshal Villars); *result:* Mons fell to the Allies.

MANTINEA: *Date:* 362 b.c.; *place:* Arcadia, Greece; *victor:* Thebans (Epaminondas); *defeated:* League of Lacedaemon, Achaia, Ellis, Athens, and Arcadia; *result:* Epaminondas was killed in the battle and, in spite of victory, Thebes lost its power in Greece.

MARATHON: *Date:* September 28 or 29, 490 b.c.; *place:* Attica; *victor:* Greeks (Miltiades, Aristides, Themistocles); *defeated:* Persians (Datis, Artaphernes); *result:* see Prof. Creasy's "Decisive Battles of History."

MARENGO: *Date:* June 14, 1800; *place:* northern Italy; *victor:* French (Napoleon); *defeated:* Austrians (Melas); *result:* Napoleon obtained twelve strong fortresses, and became master of Italy.

MARIGNANO (MALEGNANO): *Date:* September 14, 1515; *place:* near Milan, northern Italy; *victor:* French (Francis I); *defeated:* Milanese and Swiss (Duke of Milan); *result:* more than 20.000 men fell in the "Battle of the Giants;" French gained Lombardy and made concordat with Pope Leo X (1516).

MARNE, FIRST BATTLE OF THE (WORLD WAR I): *Date:* September 6-10, 1914; *place:* northern France; *victor:* French (Generals Joffre, Foch); *defeated:* Germans (General Helmuth von Moltke); *result:* the Schlieffen Plan, by which the Germans had hoped to wage a successful war on two fronts, was proved ineffective by the resistance of the Belgians, the rapid mobilization of the Russians, and English aid; the Germans were forced to retreat to the Aisne River.

MARNE, SECOND BATTLE OF THE (WORLD WAR I): *Date:* July 15 - August 7, 1918; *place:* northern France; *victor:* Allies; *defeated:* Germans; *result:* the British at the Somme, the French from Amiens to Reims, and the Americans in the Saint-Mihiel salient and the

Meuse-Argonne campaign hammered away at the German lines and forced the general retreat of the German armies all along the front in France and Belgium.

MARSTON-MOOR: *Date:* July 2, 1644; *place:* near York, England; *victor:* Parliamentary Army, Scots (Cromwell); *defeated:* Royalists (Prince Rupert, Marquis of Newcastle); *result:* Cromwell pressed for two engagements and two victories and took the artillery of Prince Rupert; the Royalists never recovered from these losses.

MASURIAN LAKES (WORLD WAR I): *Date:* September 5-15, 1914; *place:* northern Poland (then East Prussia); *victor:* Germans (Hindenburg, Ludendorff); *defeated:* Russians (Rennenkampf, Samsonov); *result:* the Germans, after driving a wedge into the Russian army as it was advancing through East Prussia and Galicia, annihilated the second wing of the Russian command. See Tannenberg.

METAURUS: *Date:* 207 b.c.; *place:* river in central Italy; *victor:* Romans (Livius, Claudius Nero); *defeated:* Carthaginians (Hasdrubal); *result:* see Prof. Creasy's "Decisive Battles of History."

MIDWAY ISLAND (WORLD WAR II): *Date:* June 4-6, 1942; *place:* Pacific, northwest of Hawaii; *victor:* U.S. fleet, air force; *defeated:* Japanese fleet, air force; *result:* in this second naval encounter in which the action was carried on entirely by aircraft and the opposing ships never sighted one another, the victory over the Japanese was decisive, and their plan to use Midway as a stepping-stone to Hawaii was frustrated; the carrier *Yorktown* was lost, as well as the Japanese carriers *Mogami* and Mikuma.

MILVIAN BRIDGE: *Date:* October 27, 312; *place:* near Rome; *victor:* Constantine; *defeated:* Maxentius; *result:* before battle Constantine claimed to have seen a fiery cross in the sky with the motto *In hoc signo vinces* ("By this sign you shall conquer"); his victory was followed by his adoption of Christianity, his becoming sole emperor of the West, and the proclamation of the Edict of Milan (313).

MOLWITZ: *Date:* April 10, 1741; *place:* Prussian Silesia; *victor:* Prussians (Frederick II); *defeated:* Imperialists; *result:* the conclusive victory at Molwitz, combined with successes at Rossbach (1757) and Leuthen (1757), made up a series of contests from which Prussia emerged as a leader of the German States.

MORGARTEN: *Date:* November 15, 1315; *place:* Switzerland; *victor:* Swiss; defeated: Austrians (Duke Leopold); *result:* the heroic stand of 1300 Swiss against 20,000 Austrians stopped the invading army that had entered the mountain pass from Zug.

MUKDEN (RUSSO-JAPANESE WAR): *Date:* 1904-05; *place:* Manchuria; *victor:* Japanese; *defeated:* Russians; *result:* the destruction of the Russian army at Mukden and the Russian navy at Isushima brought a speedy end to the war and a humiliation for the Russian regime that forced liberal concessions to the discontented People's Representatives in the Duma.

NANCY: *Date:* January 5, 1477; *place:* northeast France; *victor:* Swiss, Duke of Lorraine; *defeated:* Charles the Bold of Burgundy; *result:* Charles the Bold was slain by the Duke of Lorraine and the Swiss.

NARVA: *Date:* November 30, 1700; *place:* Esthonia; *victor:* Swedes (Charles XII); *defeated:* Russians (Peter the Great); *result:* the Swedish army defeated a force between 3-5 times larger than its own 20,000 men; Charles XII, then nineteen, was launched on his metoric

career as the "Alexander of the North;" several horses having been shot from under him at Narva, he is reported to have said: "These people seem intent on giving me exercise."

NASEBY: *Date:* June 14, 1645; *place:* Northamptonshire, England; *victor:* Parliamentarians (Cromwell, Fairfax); *defeated:* Royalists (Charles I, Prince Rupert, Lord Astley, Sir Marmaduke Langdale); *result:* Charles I, soundly beaten, fled, abandoning his baggage and cannon; nearly 5000 prisoners were taken.

NAVARINO (NAVARINE): *Date:* October 20, 1827; *place:* southwest Greece; *victor:* English, French, Russian fleets (Admiral Codrington); *defeated:* Turkish, Egyptian fleets; *result:* the Turkish and Egyptian fleets were almost totally destroyed in an encounter which Wellington called "an untoward event."

NETHERLANDS EAST INDIES (WORLD WAR II): *Date:* January 10-March 9, 1942; *place:* Bali, Borneo, Celebes, Java, Sumatra; *victor:* Japanese; *defeated:* Allies; *result:* the vast resources of the East Indies, with strategically crucial tin, rubber, and oil, as well as commercial products, passed to the Japanese; in Burma the Japanese position was stronger, and her forces were freed for the assaults against India and Australia.

NILE: *Date:* August 1, 1798; *place:* Aboukir, near Rosetta, Egypt; *victor:* British fleet (Lord Horatio Nelson); *defeated:* French fleet (Brueys); *result:* 9 French line-of-battle ships were taken, 2 burned, 2 escaped; *L'Orient* was blown up with a loss of over 900 men, including Brueys.

NORMANDY (D-DAY, WORLD WAR II): *Date:* June 6, 1944; *place:* northwest France; *victor:* Allies (Eisenhower); *defeated:* Germans; *result:* the invasion of Hitler's "European fortress" established a beachhead for the Allies through which it was possible to re-enter France and carry the war back to the Germans on the mainland; the invasion involved more than 4000 ships, 3000 planes, and 4,000,000 Allied troops.

NOVARA: *Date:* March 23, 1849; *place:* northwest Italy; *victor:* Austrians (Marshal Radetzky); *defeated:* Sardinians (King Charles Albert); *result:* total defeat for the Sardinians; Charles Albert soon abdicated in favor of his son Victor Emmanuel.

OKINAWA (WORLD WAR II): *Date:* April 1, 1945; *place:* island south of Japan; *victor:* U.S. Marines, Air Force, Navy; *defeated:* Japanese; *result:* establishment of an airbase for strikes on the mainland of Japan.

ORLÉANS: *Date:* May 8, 1429; *place* central France; *victor:* French (Joan of Arc); *defeated:* English (Duke of Bedford); result: see Prof. Creasy's "Decisive Battles of History."

PAARDEBERG (BOER WAR): *Date:* February 27, 1900; *place:* South Africa; *victor:* English (Lord Roberts); *defeated:* Boers (Cronje); *result:* English annexed Orange Free State and the Transvaal.

PEARL HARBOR (WORLD WAR II): *Date:* December 7, 1941; *place: Hawaiian Islands; victor:* Japanese Air Force; *defeated:* U.S.; *result:* on the "day of infamy," the Japanese air force struck without warning against Pearl Harbor, the Philippines, Malaya, and Hong Kong; at Pearl Harbor some 19 U.S. ships were sunk or damaged, including the battleships *Arizona, California, Oklahoma, Utah* (all sunk), *West Virginia, Nevada, Pennsylvania, Maryland, Tennessee* (all damaged), and 3000 Americans were killed; the Japanese captured Guam, Wake, and smaller U.S. island possessions; captured Hong Kong; began the invasion of the Philippines and of the Malay Peninsula; on December 8, the U.S. declared war on Japan.

PHARSALUS (PHARSALIA): *Date:* August 9, 48 b.c.; *place:* Thessaly, northern Greece; *victor:* Julius Caesar; *defeated:* Pompey; *result:* Caesar became virtual ruler of the known world.

PHILIPPI: *Date:* October, 42 b.c.; *place:* Macedonia; *victor:* Octavius Caesar, Mark Antony; *defeated:* Cassius, Brutus; *result:* Cassius and Brutus committed suicide, their armies were disbanded, and Octavius and Antony became masters of Rome.

PLASSEY: *Date:* June 23, 1757; *place:* Bengal; *victor:* British (Clive); *defeated:* Hindus (Surajah Dowlah); *result:* the victory laid the foundation for the British Empire in India.

PLEVNA: *Date:* July 29-December 10, 1877; *place:* Bulgaria; *victor:* Russians (Todleben); *defeated:* Turks (Osman Pasha); result: unconditional surrender of Osman Pasha.

PORT ARTHUR (RUSSO-JAPANESE WAR): *Date:* January 1, 1905; *place:* now Luchun, China; *victor:* Japanese army (Nogi) and fleet (Togo); *defeated:* Russians (Stoessel); *result:* rise of Japan to a world power; establishment of parliamentary forms in the Russian Duma, where the monarchy was shaken by the humiliating defeat and was forced to make liberal concessions.

PULTOWA: *Date:* July 8, 1709; *place:* Russia; *victor:* Russians (Peter the Great); *defeated:* Swedes (Charles XII); *result:* see Prof. Creasy's "Decisive Battle of History."

PYDNA: *Date:* June 22, 168 b.c.; *place:* Macedonia; *victor:* Romans (Aemilius Paulus); *defeated:* Macedonians (Perseus); *result:* Perseus, taken prisoner by the Romans, was the last king of Macedon, which now became a Roman territory..

PYRAMIDS: *Date:* July 13-21, 1798; *place:* Egypt; *victor:* French (Napoleon); *defeated:* Mamelukes; *result:* Napoleon conquered lower Egypt.

QUEBEC: *Date:* September 13, 1759; *place:* Canada; *victor:* English (Wolfe); defeated: French (Montcalm); *result:* Quebec fell to the English; both Wolfe and Montcalm fell in the battle; English gained control of French Canada.

QUIBERON BAY: *Date:* November 20, 1759; *place:* western France; *victor:* English fleet (Admiral Hawke); *defeated:* French fleet (Admiral Conflans); result: the projected French invasion of England was defeated.

RAMILLIES: *Date:* May 23, 1706; *place:* Belgium; *victor:* English (Duke of Marlborough); *defeated:* French (Elector of Bavaria, Maréchal de Villeroi; *result:* the French army was routed; Louvain and Brussels soon fell to the victors.

RAVENNA: *Date:* April 11, 1512; *place:* on the Adriatic; *victor:* French (Gaston de Foix); *defeated:* Spanish, Papal armies; *result:* De Foix, the "Thunderbolt of Italy," fell at the moment of his victory and his death signalized the decline of French power in Italy.

RIVOLI: *Date:* November 17, 1796; *place:* near Verona, northern Italy; *victor:* Austrians; *defeated:* French (Napoleon); *result:* led to second battle of Rivoli.

ROCROI (ROCROY): *Date* May 19, 1643; *place* northern France; *victor:* French (Condé); *defeated:* Spanish; *result:* the Spanish army was totally defeated, and Spain moved closer to total eclipse as a major European power.

ROSSBACH (ROSBACH; ROSEBECQUE): *Date:* November 5, 1757; *place:* Flanders; *victor:* Prussians (Frederick the Great); *defeat-*

ed: French, Imperialists (Soubise, Prince of Saxe-Hildburghausen); *result:* this major victory established Prussia as the center of power among the German States.

SADOWA: *See Königgratz.*

SAIPAN (WORLD WAR II): *Date:* June 14-July 10, 1944; *place:* Marianas; *victor:* U.S. Marines, Army (2nd, 4th Marines, 27th Inf. Div.); *defeated:* Japanese (Admiral Nagumo); *result:* Japan lost over 25,000 troops; the American losses were 2359 killed, over 11,000 wounded; the island provided a base for the assault against Japan.

SALAMANCA: *Date:* July 22, 1812; *place:* western Spain; *victor:* British (Lord Wellington); *defeated:* French (Marshal Marmont); *result:* the victory was followed by the capture of Madrid.

SALAMIS: *Date:* October 20, 480 b.c. *place:* near Athens, Greece; *victor:* Greeks (Themistocles, Eurybiades); *defeated:* Persians (Xerxes); *result:* in the great sea battle at Salamis, 310 Greek ships defeated the 2000 ships in the flotilla of the King of Persia, crippled the Persian fleet, and saved Greece from invasion.

SEDAN (FRANCO-PRUSSIAN WAR): *Date:* September 1, 1870; *place:* Meuse Valley, northeast France; *victor:* Germans (William I); *defeated:* French (Napoleon III, Marshal MacMahon); *result:* the following day the capitulation of Sedan was signed, and the French army of the North ceased to exist; the French Empire was overthrown, and the Third Republic established.

SEMPACH: *Date:* July 9, 1836; *place:* Switzerland; *victor:* Swiss (Arnold von Winkleried); *defeated:* Austrians (Duke Leopold III); *result:* both Arnold and Leopold were slain, and the freedom of Switzerland was established.

SENLAC: *Same as Hastings.*

SEVASTOPOL (SEBASTOPOL): *Date:* September 8, 1855; *place:* southwest Crimea; *victors:* French, English (Pelisser); *defeated:* Russians (Gortchakoff); *result:* ended the crimean War and Russian power in the Mediterranean.

SEVASTOPOL (WORLD WAR II): *Date:* June 5-July 1, 1941; *place:* southwest Crimea; *victor:* Germans (Von Mannstein); *defeated:* Russians; *result:* the fortress of Sevastopol, which fell after a long and bloody siege, was the key to German mastery of the Crimea.

SINGAPORE (WORLD WAR II): *Date:* February 15, 1942; *place:* Malay Peninsula; *victor:* Japanese; *defeated:* British; *result:* 70,000 British troops surrendered unconditionally and the Japanese entered and took the city; with Singapore occupied, the Japanese attack on the Netherlands East Indies was made easier, while more troops were released for the assaults on the Philippines and Java; the approach ot India was now opened, and all of Britain's eastern empire was in danger.

SMOLENSK (SMOLENSKO): *Date:* August 16-17, 1812; *place:* Russia; *victor:* French (Napoleon); *defeated:* Russians (Barclay de Tolly); *result:* Smolensk fell to the French; Czar Alexander relieved De Tolly of his command, and appointed Kutusoff as commander in chief.

SOISSONS: *Date:* 486 a.d.; *place:* France; *victor:* Merovingian Franks (Clovis); *defeated:* Romans (Syagrius); *result:* Rome lost Gaul, and the Frankish power was established.

SOLFERINO: *Date:* June 24, 1859; *place:* Lombardy; *victor:* French (Louis Napoleon, MacMahon, Niel), Sardinians (Garibaldi); *defeated:* Austrians (General Hess); *result:* the victory led to the peace signed at Villa Franca (July 12), the unification of Italy, and the annexation (1860) of Nice and Savoy.

SOMME (WORLD WAR I): *Date:* July-November, 1916; *place:* northern France; *victor:* Allies; *defeated:* Germans; *result:* the strategy of the Allied counteroffensive on the Somme was to take some of the German pressure off Verdun; the move was in desperation; but in the following March the Germans retreated to the Hindenburg Line, releasing a thousand square miles of French territory.

SPANISH ARMADA: *Date:* July 20-29, 1588; *place:* off Calais and Gravelines; *victor:* English (Lord Howard of Effingham); *defeated:* Spanish (Duke of Medina Sidonia); *result:* see Prof. Creasy's "Decisive Battles of History."

STALINGRAD (WORLD WAR II): *Date:* August 20, 1942-February 2, 1943; *place:* Russia; *victor:* Russians; *defeated:* Germans (Von Bock); *result:* the bitter battles at the outer defenses of the city, and into the suburbs, one of the bloodiest campaigns of the war, prevented German mastery of the lower Volga, the oil fields of Baku, Leningrad, and further occupation of Russia; meanwhile, the engagement of German troops in the East slowed up their offensive in the West.

SYRACUSE: *Date:* 413 b.c.; *place:* southeast Sicily; *victor:* Syracuse; *defeated:* Athenians (Nicias, Demosthenes); *result:* see Prof. Creasy's "Decisive Battles of History."

TANNENBERG (WORLD WAR I): *Date:* August 26-30, 1914; *place:* northeast Poland (then East Prussia); *victor:* Germans (Generals Hindenburg, Ludendorff); *defeated:* Russians (Generals Rennenkampf, Samsonov); *result:* as the Russian army was invading Germany from the East, the German army drove a wedge through the advancing army, isolating and annihilating one wing at Tannenberg. See Marsurian Lakes.

TESTRI: *Date:* 687 a.d.; *place:* northern France; *victor:* Austrasian Franks (Pepin of Heristal); *defeated:* Thierry III, King of Austrasia; *result:* unification of the kingdoms of the Franks and the beginnings of the Carolingian dynasty.

TEUTOBURG (TEUTOBURGERWALD; TEUTOBERG FOREST): *Date:* 9 a.d.; *place:* probably between Detmold and Paderborn; *victor:* Germans (Hermann, i. e., Arminius); *defeated:* Romans (Varus); *result:* see Prof. Creasy's "Decisive Battles of History."

THERMOPYLAE: *Date:* August 7-9, 480 b.c.; *place:* Doris, northern Greece; *victor:* Persians (Xerxes); *defeated:* Spartans, Thespians (Leonidas); *result:* after a successful three-day stand, Leonidas was betrayed by Ephialtes, a Trachinian, who showed the Persians how the Spartans could be surprised from the rear; all but a single defender were surrounded and slaughtered; even in defeat the temper of the Greeks was revealed; it was soon tried more decisively at Salamis.

TOURS: *Date:* October 10, 732; *place:* central France; *victor:* Franks (Charles Martel); *defeated:* Saracens (Abd-el-Rahman); *result:* see Prof. Creasy's "Decisive Battles of History."

TRAFALGAR: *Date:* October 31, 1805; *place:* off Cape Trafalgar, southern Spain; *victor:* British fleet (Nelson); *defeated:* French and Spanish fleets (Villeneuve, Gravina, Alva); *result:* in this great naval encounter, Horatio Nelson, commander of the *Victory*, was killed just after signaling "England expects every man will do his duty" to the rest of his fleet; Villeneuve and the other admirals were cap-

tured, and 19 of their 33 ships were taken, sunk, or disabled.

ULM: *Date:* October 17-20, 1805; *place:* Württemberg, southern Germany; *victor:* French (Marshal Ney); *defeated:* Austrians (General Mack); *result:* Ulm, with 28,000 Austrian troops, surrendered to the French.

VALMY: *Date:* September 20, 1792; *place:* northeast France; *victor:* French (Kellermann); *defeated:* Prussians (Duke af Brunswick); *result:* see Prof. Creasy's "Decisive Battles of History."

VERDUN (WORLD WAR I): *Date:* February-September 3, 1916; *place:* northeast France on Meuse R.; *victors:* Allies; *defeated:* Germans; *result:* through the first half of 1916, the Germans threw all of their forces into the attempt to break the ring of fortresses which surrounded Verdun; over 500,000 troops perished in the brutal campaign; in July the Allies began the counteroffensive at the Somme, and the Germans abandoned the assault against Verdun on Sept. 3; the following March they retreated behind the Hindenburg Line.

VIENNA: *Date:* September 12, 1683; *place:* Austria; *victor:* Poles (John Sobieski, King of Poland), Austrians; *defeated:* Turks; *result:* the Turkish siege of the city was raised, and the Turks driven back to Raab.

WAGRAM: *Date:* July 5-6 1809; *place:* near Vienna, Austria; *victor:* French (Napoleon); *defeated:* Austrians (Archduke Charles); *result:* Austria signed armistice on July 12 and a treaty (Oct. 24) that ceded all of her seacoast to France; Saxony and Bavaria were enlarged at the expense of Austria; part of Poland in Galicia was ceded to Russia; Joseph Bonaparte was recognized as King of Spain.

WATERLOO: *Date:* June 18, 1815; *place:* Belgium; *victor:* British, Dutch, Germans (Wellington) and Prussians (Blücher); *defeated:* French (Napoleon); *result:* see Prof. Creasy's "Decisive Battles of History."

WORCESTER: *Date:* September 3, 1651; *place:* England; *victor:* Parlamentarian army (Cromwell); *defeated:* Scots, Royalists (Charles II); *result:* Charles barely escaped to France; over 2000 Royalists were killed, of 8000 prisoners, most were sold as slaves to the American colonists.

YALU RIVER: *Date:* September 17, 1894; *place:* Korea-Manchuria; *victor:* Japanese fleet (Ito); *defeated:* Chinese fleet (Ting); *result:* for the first time a naval battle was fought with modern armored ships; victory led to the reorganization of Japan.

YPRES, FIRST BATTLE OF (WORLD WAR I): *Date:* October 30-November 24, 1914; *place:* northwest Belgium; *victor:* Allies; *defeated:* Germans; *result:* the Germans, striking from the Aisne R., tried to extend their lines westward, and the Allies met them at Ypres to block their maneuvers; the Allies won the race to the sea, and held Calais, Boulogne, and Dunkirk, the important communications route between England and France; but the campaign cost more than 250,000 lives on both sides.

YPRES, SECOND BATTLE OF (WORLD WAR I): *Date:* April 22-May 25, 1915; *place:* northwest Belgium; *victor:* Germans, *defeated:* British; *result:* this battle was, in a bloody War, among the bloodiest; the defeat of the British was a serious reversal; and for the first time, poison gas was used in modern warfare.

ZAMA: *Date:* 202 b.c.; *place:* near Carthage, North Africa; *victor:* Romans (Scipio Africanus); *defeated:* Carthaginians (Hannibal); *re-*

sult: brought the Second Punic War to a close with an ignominious peace for Carthage.

Battlefields
See National Battlefield Sites; National Military Parks

Bible, Versions of the
See also Apocrypha; Parables of Christ; Scriptures

Bible, Principal English Versions

AMERICAN REVISED VERSION: A separate version published in 1901, the work of the American Committee on the Revised Version. It differs in a few particulars from the Revised Version (see below).

THE AUTHORIZED VERSION: This, the version in general use in England, was made by a body of scholars working 1604-1611 at the command of King James I (hence sometimes called "King James Bible") and published in 1611. The modern Authorized Version is however, by no means an exact reprint of the version authorized by King James; a large number of typographical errors have been corrected, the orthography, punctuation, etc., have been modernized, and the use of italics, capital letters, etc., varied. The Bishops' Bible (q.v.) was used as the basis of the text, but Tyndale's, Matthew's, Coverdale's, and the Geneva translations were also followed when they agreed better with original.

THE BISHOPS' BIBLE: A version made at the instigation of Archbishop Parker (hence also called "Matthew Parker's Bible"), to which most of the Anglican bishops were contributors. It was a revision of the Great Bible (q.v.), first appeared in 1568, and by 1602 had reached its eighteenth edition. It is this edition that forms the basis of our Authorized Version. See Treacle Bible, below.

COVERDALE'S BIBLE: The first complete English Bible to be printed, published in 1535 as a translation out of Douche (German) and Latin by Myles Coverdale. It consists of Tyndale's translation of the Pentateuch and New Testament, with translations from the Vulgate, a Latin version (1527-1528) by the Italian Catholic theologian, Sanctes Pegninus, Luther's German version (1534), and the Swiss-German version of Zwingli and Leo Juda (Zurich, 1527-1529). The first edition was printed at Antwerp, but the second (Southwark, 1537) was the first Bible printed in England. Matthew's Bible (q.v.) is largely based on Coverdale's. See Bug Bible in BIBLE, SPECIALLY NAMED EDITIONS.

CRANMER'S BIBLE: The name given to the Great Bible (q.v.) of 1540. It, and later issues, contained a prologue by Cranmer, and on the wood-cut title page (by Holbein) Henry VIII is shown seated while Cranmer and Cromwell distribuet copies to the people.

CROMWELL'S BIBLE: The Great Bible (q.v.) of 1539. The title page (see Cranmer's Bible, above) includes a portrait of Thomas Cromwell.

THE DOUAI BIBLE: A translation of the Vulgate, made by English Catholic scholars in France for the use of English boys destined for the Catholic priesthood. The New Testament was published at Rheims in 1582, and the Old Testament at Douai in 1609; hence sometimes called the Rheims-Douai version. See Rosin Bible, below.

THE GENEVA BIBLE: A revision of great importance in the history of the English Bible, undertaken by English exiles in Geneva during the Marian persecutions and first published in 1560. It was the work of William Whittingham, assisted by Anthony Gilby and Thomas Sampson. Wittingham had previously (1557) published a translation of the New Testament. The Geneva version was the first English Bible to be printed in roman type instead of black letter, the first in which the chapters are divided into verses (taken by Whittingham from Robert Stephen's Greek-Latin Testament of 1537), and the first in which italics are used for explanatory and connective words and phrases (taken from Beza's New Testament of 1556). It was immensely popular; from 1560 to 1616 no year passed without a new edition, and at least two hundred are known. In every edition the word "breeches" occurs in Gen. III, 7; hence the *Geneva Bible* is popularly known as the "Breeches Bible." See Goose Bible, Placemakers Bible in BIBLE, SPECIALLY NAMED EDITIONS.

THE GREAT BIBLE: Coverdale's revision of his own Bible of 1535 (see Coverdale's Bible), collated with Tyndale's and Matthew's, printed in Paris by Regnault, and published by Grafton and Whitchurch in 1539. It is a large folio, and a splendid specimen of typography. It is sometimes called Cromwell's Bible, as it was undertaken at his direction, and it was made compulsory for all parish churches to purchase a copy. The Prayer Book version of the Psalms comes from the November, 1540, edition of the Great Bible. See also Cranmer's Bible.

KING JAMES BIBLE: The Authorized Version (q.v.).

KNOX TRANSLATION: Most important modern Roman Catholic translation, made by Ronald Knox and published 1944-50. It is based on the original Greek and Hebrew.

MATTHEW PARKER'S BIBLE: The Bishop's Bible (q.v.).

MATTHEW'S BIBLE: A pronouncedly Protestant version published in 537 as having been "truly and purely translated into English by Thomas Matthew," which was a pseudonym, adopted for purpose of safety, of John Rogers, an assistant of Tyndale. It was probably printed at Antwerp. The next is made up of the Pentateuch from Tyndale's version together with his hitherto unprinted translation of Joshua to II Chronicles inclusive and his revised edition of the New Testament, with Coverdale's version of the rest of the Old Testament and the Apocrypha. It was quickly superseded by the Great Bible (q.v.), but it is of importance as it formed the starting point for the revisions that culminated in the Authorized Version.

THE REVISED STANDARD VERSION: This is a revision of the American Revised Version of 1901 and The Authorized Version of 1611. The New Testament was published Feb. 11, 1946, and the Old Testament on Sept. 30, 1952, The Revised Standard Version was the work of the Standard Bible Committee organized by the International Council of Religious Education, an affiliation of forty Protestant denominations.

THE REVISED VERSION: A revision of the Authorized Version commenced under a resolution passed by both Houses of Convocation in 1870 by a body of twenty-five English scholars (assisted and advised by an American Committee), the New Testament published in 1881, the complete Bible in 1885, and the Apocrypha in 1895.

RHEIMS-DOUAI VERSION: See Douai Bible.

TAVERNER'S BIBLE: An independent translation by a Greek scholar, Richard Taverner, printed in 1539 (the same year as the first Great Bible) by T. Petit for T. Berthelet. It had no influence on the Authorized Version, but is remarkable for its vigorous idiomatic English and for being the first English Bible to include a third Book of Maccabees in the Apocrypha.

TYNDALE'S BIBLE: This consists of the New Testament (printed at Cologne, 1525), the Pentateuch (Marburg, Hesse, 1530 or 1531), Jonah, Old Testament lessons appointed to be read in place of the Epistles, and a MS. translation of the Old Testament to the end of Chronicles that was afterward used in Matthew's Bible (q.v.). Tyndale's revisions of the New Testament were issued in 1534 and 1535. His principal authority was Erasmus' edition of the Greek Testament, but he also used Erasmus' Latin translation of the same, the Vulgate, and Luther's German version. Tyndale's version fixed the style and tone of the English Bible, and subsequent Protestant versions of the books on which he worked should—with one or two minor exceptions—be looked upon as revisions of his, and not as independent translations.

WYCLIF'S BIBLE: The name given to two translations of the Vulgate, one completed in 1380 and the other a few years later, in neither of which was Wyclif concerned as a translator. Nicholas of Hereford made the first version as far as Baruch III, 20; who was responsible for the remainder is unknown. The second version has been ascribed to John Purvey, a follower of Wyclif. The Bible of 1380 was the first complete version in English; as a whole it remained unprinted until 1850, when the monumental edition of the two versions by Forshall and Madden appeared, but in 1810 an edition of the New Testament was published by H. H. Baber, an assistant librarian at the British Museum.

Bible, Specially Named Editions

ADULTEROUS BIBLE: The "Wicked Bible" (q.v.).

BAMBERG BIBLE: The Thirty-six Line Bible (q.v.).

THE BEAR BIBLE: The Spanish Protestant version printed at Basle in 1569; so called because the woodcut device on the title-page is a bear.

BEDELL'S BIBLE: A translation of the Authorized Version into Irish carried out under the direction of Bedell (d. 1642), Bishop of Kilmore and Ardagh.

THE BREECHES BIBLE: The Geneva Bible (see BIBLE, PRINCIPAL ENGLISH VERSIONS) was popularly so called because in it Gen. III, 7, was rendered, "The eyes of them bothe were opened . . . and they sowed figge-tree leaves together, and made themselves breeches." This reading occurs in every edition of the Geneva Bible, but not in any other version, though it is given in the then unprinted Wyclif MS. ("Ya sewiden ye levis of a fige tre and madin brechis"), and also in the translation of the Pentateuch given in Caxton's edition of Voragine's Golden Legend (1483).

THE BUG BIBLE: Coverdale's Bible (see BIBLE, PRINCIPAL ENGLISH VERSIONS) of 1535 is so called because Ps. XCI, 5, is translated, "Thou shalt not nede to be afrayed for eny bugges by night." The same reading occurs in Matthew's Bible (see BIBLES, PRINCIPAL ENGLISH VERSIONS) and its reprints; the Authorized and Revised Versions both read "terror."

COMPLUTENSIAN POLYGLOT: The great edition, in six folio volumes, containing the Hebrew and Greek texts, the Septuagint, the Vulgate, and the Chaldee paraphrase of the Pentateuch with a Latin translation, together with Greek and Hebrew grammars and a Hebrew dictionary, prepared and printed at the expense of Cardinal Ximenes, and published at Alcalá (the ancient Complutum) near Madrid, 1513-1517.

DARTMOUTH BIBLE: A recently revised and abridged edition of the King James Bible.

THE DISCHARGE BIBLE: An edition printed in 1806, containing *discharge* for *charge* in I Tim. V. 21, "I discharge thee before God . . . that thou observe these things . . ."

THE EARS TO EAR BIBLE: An edition of 1810, in which Matt. XIII, 43, reads: "Who hath ears to ear, let him hear."

THE FERRARA BIBLE: The first Spanish edition of the Old Testament, translated from the Hebrew in 1553 for the use of the Spanish Jews. A second edition was published in the same year for Christians.

THE FORTY-TWO LINE BIBLE: The "Mazarin Bible" (q.v.).

THE GOOSE BIBLE: The editions of the Geneva Bible (see BIBLE, PRINCIPAL ENGLISH VERSIONS) printed at Dort; the Dort press had a goose as its device (q.v.).

GUTENBERG'S BIBLE: The "Mazarin Bible."

THE HE BIBLE: In the two earliest editions of the Authorized Version (both 1611) there is a variation in Ruth III, 15. In the first edition (now known as the 'He Bible") the passage reads: "and he went into the city "; the second edition (known as the "She Bible" has the variant "she." "He" is the correct translation of the Hebrew, but nearly all modern editions—with the exception of the Revised Version—perpetuate the confusion and print "she."

THE IDLE BIBLE: An edition of 1809 in which "the idole shepherd" (Zesh. XI, 17) is printed "the idle shepherd." In the Revised Version the translation is "the worthless shepherd."

THE KRALITZ BIBLE: The Bible published by the United Brethren of Moravia (hence known also as the Brother's Bible) at Kralitz, 1579-1593.

THE LEDA BIBLE: The third edition (second folio) of the Bishop's Bible (see BIBLE, PRINCIPAL ENGLISH VERSIONS), published in 1572, and so called because the decoration to the initial at the Epistle to the Hebrews is a startling and incongruous woodcut of Jupiter visiting Leda in the guise of a swan. This and several other decorations in the New Testament of this edition, were from an edition of Ovid's *Metamorphoses;* they created such a storm of protest that they were never afterward used.

THE LEOPOLITA BIBLE: A Polish translation of the Vulgate by John of Lemberg (anc. Leopolis), published in 1561 at Cracow.

THE MAZARIN BIBLE: The first printed Bible (an edition of the Vulgate), and the first large book to be printed from movable metal type. It contains no date, but was printed probably in 1455, and was certainly on sale by the middle of 1456. It was printed at Mainz, probably by Fust and Schoeffer, but as it was long credited to Gutenberg — and it is not yet agreed that he was not responsible for it — it is frequently called the Gutenberg Bible. By bibliographers it is usually known as the Forty-two Line Bible (it having 42 lines to the page), to differentiate it from the Bamberg Bible of 36 lines. Its popular name is due to the fact that the copy discovered in the Mazarin Library, Paris, in 1760, was the first to be known and described.

THE MURDERERS' BIBLE: An edition of 1801 in which the misprint *murderers* for *murmurers* makes Jude 16, read: "These are murderers, complainers, walking after their own lusts . . ."

THE OLD CRACOW BIBLE: The "Leopolita Bible" (q.v.).

THE OSTROG BIBLE: The first complete Slavonic edition; printed at Ostrog, Volhynia, Russia, in 1581.

PFISTER'S BIBLE: The "Thirty-six Line Bible" (q.v.).

THE PLACE-MAKERS' BIBLE: The second edition of the Geneva Bible (see BIBLE, PRINCIPAL ENGLISH VERSIONS), 1562; so called from a printer's error in Matt. V, 9, "Blessed are the place-makers [peace-makers], for they shall be called the children of God." It has also been called the "Whig Bible."

THE PRINTERS' BIBLE: An edition of about 1702 that makes David pathetically complain that "printers [princes] have persecuted me without a cause" (Ps. CXIX, 161).

THE PROOF BIBLE (PROBE BIBEL): The revised version of the first impression of Luther's German Bible. A final revised edition appeared in 1892.

REBECCA'S CAMELS BIBLE: An edition printed in 1823 in which Gen. XXIV, 61, tells us that "Rebecca arose, and her camels," instead of "her damsels."

THE ROSIN BIBLE: The Douai Bible (see BIBLE, PRINCIPAL ENGLISH VERSIONS), 1609, is sometimes so called, because it has in Jer. VIII, 22: "Is there noe rosin in Galaad." The Authorized Version translates the word "balm," but gives "rosin" in the margin as an alternative. Compare Treacle Bible, below.

SACY'S BIBLE: A French translation, named after the translator, Louis Isaac le Maistre de Sacy, Jansenist director of Port Royal, 1650-1679.

SCHELHORN'S BIBLE: A name sometimes given to the "Thirty-six Line Bible" (q.v.).

THE SEPTEMBER BIBLE: Luther's German translation of the New Testament, published anonymously at Wittenberg in September, 1522.

THE SHE BIBLE: See The He Bible.

THE STANDING FISHES BIBLE: An edition of 1806 in which Ezek. XLVII, 10, reads: "And it shall come to pass that the fishes [instead of fishers] shall stand upon it . . ."

THE THIRTY-SIX LINE BIBLE: A Latin Bible of 36 lines to the column, probably printed by A. Pfister at Bamberg in 1460. It is also known as the Bamberg and Pfister's Bible, and sometimes as Schelhorn's, as it was first described by the German bibliographer J. G. Schelhorn, in 1760.

THE TO-REMAIN BIBLE: In a Bible printed at Cambridge in 1805 Gal. IV, 29, reads: "Persecuted him that was born after the spirit to remain, even so it is now." The words "to remain" were added in error by the compositor, the editor having answered a proofreader's query as to the comma after "spirit" with the penciled reply "to remain" in the margin. The mistake was repeated in the first

8vo edition published by the Bible Society (1805), and again in their 12mo edition dated 1819.

THE TREACLE BIBLE: A popular name for the Bishops' Bible (see BIBLE, PRINCIPAL ENGLISH VERSIONS), 1568, because in it Jer. VIII, 22, reads: "Is there no tryacle in Gilead, is there no phistion there?" Compare Rosin Bible above. In the same Bible "tryacle" is also given for "balm" in Jer. XLVI, 11, and Ezek. XXVII, 17. Coverdale's Bible (1535) also uses the word "triacle".

THE UNRIGHTEOUS BIBLE: An edition printed at Cambridge in 1653, containing the printer's error, "Know ye not that the unrighteous shall inherit [for "shall not inherit"] the King dom of God?" (1. Cor. VI, 9). The same edition gives Rom. VI, 13, as: "Neither, yield ye your members as instruments of righteousness unto sin," in place of "unrighteousness." This is also sometimes known as the "Wicked Bible."

THE WICKED BIBLE: So called because the word *not* is omitted in the Seventh Commandment, making it, "Thou shalt commit adultery." Printed at London by Barker and Lucas, 1632. The "Unrighteous Bible" (q.v.) is also sometimes called by this name.

THE WIFE-HATER BIBLE: An edition of 1810 in which the word "life" in Luke XIV, 26, is printed "wife."

WUYCK'S BIBLE: The Polish Bible authorized by the Roman Catholics and printed at Cracow in 1599. The translation was made by the Jesuit, Jacob Wuyck.

THE ZURICH BIBLE: A German version of 1530 composed of Luther's translation of the New Testament and portions of the Old, with the remainder and the Apocrypha by other translators.

Birthstones
See also Gems and the Days of the Week; Gem Stones; Planets and Their Symbolic Gems

JANUARY: Garnet; constancy.
FEBRUARY: Amethyst; sincerity.
MARCH: Aquamarine; wisdom.
APRIL: Diamond; innocence.
MAY: Emerald; love.
JUNE: Pearl; wealth.
JULY: Ruby; freedom.
AUGUST: Peridot; friendship.
SEPTEMBER: Sapphire; truth.
OCTOBER: Opal; hope.
NOVEMBER: Topaz; loyalty.
DECEMBER: Turqoise; success.

Books
See Apocrypha; Awards; Bible, Versions of the; Scriptures

Boys' Names
See Names, Most Popular for Boys

Broadway Songs
See Songs from Broadway Plays

Cabinet, President's
See Presidency

Capital Parks
See National Capital Parks

Cathedrals, Churches, Shrines, and Temples of Historic and Architectural Interest

See also **Architects, Their Schools and Representative Works**

ABBEY CHURCH OF MONT ST. MICHEL: France, c. 15th century (Gothic).
ABBEY CHURCH OF ST. DENIS: Paris, France: built 1140-1144 (transitional French Gothic).
AHMEDIYEH: See Mosque of Amed I.
ALL SAINTS' CHURCH: See Schloss-Kirche.
AMIENS CATHEDRAL: France, 1220-1288 (Gothic).
ARCHANGEL CATHEDRAL: Moscow, Russia; erected 1505-1509.
AUGUSTUS LUTHERAN CHURCH: Troppe, Pa. 1743.
AYA SOPHIA: See Santa Sophia.
AZTECS, TEMPLE OF THE: See Teocalli.
BALTIMORE CATHEDRAL: Baltimore, Maryland; built 1806-1821 (modified Classic).
BAPTIST TEMPLE: Philadelphia, established 1871.
BASILICA OF THE SACRÉ-COEUR: Paris, France; begun 1876.
BEAUVAIS CATHEDRAL: France; begun 1247 (French Gothic).
BLUE MOSQUE OF TABRIZ: Tabriz, Iran; 15th century (Byzantine plan).
CADET CHAPEL: West Point, 1908-10 (Gothic).
CANTERBURY CATHEDRAL: Kent, England, 11-15th centuries (transitional Norman-Gothic).
CATHEDRAL, HOLY TRINITY: Quebec, 1800.
CATHEDRAL DE LA VIRGIN MARIA DE LA CONCEPCION: See Columbus Cathedral.
CATHEDRAL OF AIX-LA-CHAPELLE: France, rebuilt after 10th century (Romanesque, Gothic, Classic).
CATHEDRAL OF ANTWERP: Belgium; erected 1352-1474, spire added 1518 (Gothic).
CATHEDRAL OF BONN: Germany; 11th and 13th centuries (Gothic).
CATHEDRAL OF BOURGES: See Cathedral of St. Étienne.
CATHEDRAL OF BURGOS: Spain; begun 1221 (Gothic).
CATHEDRAL OF COLOGNE: See Cologne Cathedral.
CATHEDRAL OF COMO: Italy (Gothic-Renaissance).
CATHEDRAL OF CUZCO: Peru; erected 1560-1653 (Gothic-Baroque).
CATHEDRAL OF FLORENCE: Italy; 14th century (Gothic).
CATHEDRAL OF GRANADA: Spain; begun 1520 (Gothic).
CATHEDRAL OF LAON: France; erected 1160-1205 (transitional French Gothic).
CATHEDRAL OF LE MANS: See Cathedral of St. Julien.
CATHEDRAL OF LEÓN: Spain; erected 1204-1303 (Gothic).
CATHEDRAL OF MAINZ: Hesse, Germany; begun in 11th century (Romanesque).
CATHEDRAL OF MILAN: Italy; begun 1386 (Gothic).
CATHEDRAL OF MONREALE: near Palermo, Sicily, 12th century (Norman-Sicilian).
CATHEDRAL OF MURANO (SS. MARIA E DONATA): Italy; 9th century.
CATHEDRAL OF NAPLES: Italy; erected 1272-1323 (Gothic).
CATHEDRAL OF NOTRE DAME: Paris; 1163-1240 (Gothic).
CATHEDRAL OF NOTRE DAME: Reims, France; 13th century (French Gothic).

CATHEDRAL OF NOTRE DAME: Rouen, France; 12th-15th centuries (Gothic).
CATHEDRAL OF NOYON: France; begun c. 1150 (transitional French Gothic).
CATHEDRAL OF ORVIETO: Italy; erected 1290-1330 (Gothic).
CATHEDRAL OF PARIS: See Cathedral of Notre Dame.
CATHEDRAL OF PISA: Italy; begun 11th century (Gothic).
CATHEDRAL OF REGENSBERG: Germany; erected 1275-1309; facade dating from 1500 (German Gothic).
CATHEDRAL OF REIMS: See Cathedral of Notre Dame.
CATHEDRAL OF ROUEN: See Cathedral of Notre Dame.
CATHEDRAL OF ST. ETIENNE: Bourges, France; 13th-16th centuries (Gothic).
CATHEDRAL OF ST. ISAAC: Leningrad (St. Petersburg), Russia; built 1819-1858 (Classic).
CATHEDRAL OF ST. JOHN THE DIVINE: New York, chartered 1893 (French-Gothic).
CATHEDRAL OF ST. JULIEN: Le Mans, France; 11th century (Gothic).
CATHEDRAL OF ST. MARK: See St. Mark's Church.
CATHEDRAL OF ST. PETER: See St. Peter's Church.
CATHEDRAL OF ST. STEPHEN: Vienna, Austria; 12th-15th centuries (Gothic).
CATHEDRAL (NEW) OF SALAMANCA: Spain; erected 1513-1733 (Gothic).
CATHEDRAL (OLD) OF SALAMANCA: Spain; 12th century (Romanesque).
CATHEDRAL OF SANTIAGO DE COMPOSTELA Santiago (de Compostela); Spain; erected 1078-1211 in honor of St. James, patron saint of Spain (Romanesque).
CATHEDRAL OF SENLIS: France; begun c. 1150 (transitional French Gothic).
CATHEDRAL OF SENS: France; begun c. 1150 (transitional French Gothic).
CATHEDRAL OF SEVILLE: Spain; erected 1412-1517 (Gothic).
CATHEDRAL OF SIENA: Italy; 1229-1380. (Gothic).
CATHEDRAL OF STRASBOURG: Alsace-Lorraine; begun c. 600 (Romanesque-Gothic).
CATHEDRAL OF THE ANNUNCIATION: Moscow, Russia; erected 1484-1489.
CATHEDRAL OF NOTRE DAME: Amiens, France; 13th century (French Gothic).
CATHEDRAL OF THE ASCENSION DE MARIA SANCTISSIMA: Mexico City, begun 1573.
CATHEDRAL OF THE ASSUMPTION: Moscow, 15th Century (Lombard-Byzantine).
CATHEDRAL OF THE ASSUMPTION: Vladimir, Russia; 12th century (Byzantine).
CATHEDRAL OF TOLEDO: Spain; begun 1227 (Middle Spanish Gothic).
CATHEDRAL OF TOURS: France; 15th century (late Gothic façade; Renaissance).
CATHEDRAL OF ULM: See Protestant Münster.
CATHEDRAL OF UTRECHT: Netherlands; 13th century (Gothic).
CATHEDRAL OF VERONA: Italy; 12th century (Romanesque).
CATHEDRAL OF WORMS: Germany; 11th century (Gothic).
CENTER CHURCH: New Haven, Connecticut; 1814.
CHAPELS OF ST. PETER (TOWER OF GREEN) AND ST. JOHN (WHITE TOWER): Tower of London.
CHARTRES CATHEDRAL: France; 1190-1260. (Gothic).
CHRIST CHURCH: Alexandria, Va.; 1773.

CHRIST CHURCH: Bennington, Vt.; dedicated 1762.
CHRIST CHURCH: Philadelphia, 1695; present building begun 1727, restored 1882.
CHRIST CHURCH: Schrewsbury, N.J., 1769.
CHRIST CHURCH CATHEDRAL: Oxford, England; 12th century (late Anglo-Norman).
CHRIST'S CATHEDRAL: Liverpool, England; begun 1904 (Gothic).
CHURCH OF ST. GENEVIÈVE: Paris, 1755-81 (Classical Revival).
CHURCH OF ST. JACQUES: Liège, Belgium; erected 1513-1538 (Gothic-Renaissance).
CHURCH OF ST. MARTIN: Ypres, Belgium; 13th-14th centuries (Gothic).
CHURCH OF ST. OUEN: Rouen, France; 14th-15th centuries (Gothic).
CHURCH OF ST. PETER: Louvain, Belgium; late 14th century (Gothic).
CHURCH OF SAINT-SÉVERIN: Paris; France; 13th century (Gothic).
CHURCH OF ST. SIMEON STYLITES: Kelat-Seman, Syria (Basilican type).
CHURCH OF ST. URBAIN: Troyes, France; begun 1262 (French Gothic).
CHURCH OF SAN MACLOU: Rouen, France; 15th century (flamboyant French Gothic).
CHURCH OF SANTA CROCE: Florence, Italy; designed for the Franciscans by Arnolfo di Cambio, and erected 1294-1442 (Gothic).
CHURCH OF THE BRETHREN: Germantown, Pa.; 1770-1897.
CHURCH OF THE ESCORIAL: Madrid; 1563-1657 (Classical).
CHURCH OF THE HOLY SEPULCHRE: Jerusalem; completed c. 336 a.d. (Basilican type).
CHURCH OF THE MADELEINE: Paris; France; begun 1807 (copied after the Maison Carée of Nîmes, the historic Roman temple).
CHURCH OF THE NATIVITY: Bethlehem, 327 a.d. (Basilican type).
CHURCH OF THE PILGRIMAGE: Plymouth; Mass.; 1840.
COLLEGIATE CHURCH OF ST. NICHOLAS: New York, dedicated 1872.
COLOGNE CATHEDRAL: Germany; founded 1248, completed 1880 (Gothic).
COLUMBUS CATHEDRAL: Havana, Cuba; 1724 (Spanish-American). Also called the Cathedral de la Virgin Maria de la Concepcion.
CONGREGATION MICHVEH ISRAEL: Philadelphia, 1782.
DURHAM CATHEDRAL: England; begun 1093 (Anglo-Norman).
EL HARAM: Mecca, the Hejaz, West Arabia; 8th century. Also called the Great Mosque of Mecca.
ELY CATHEDRAL (CATHEDRAL CHURCH OF ST. ETHELDREDA AND ST. PETER: England; begun 1082 (Norman-early English).
ERFURT CATHEDRAL: Germany; erected 1349-1370 (German Gothic).
EXETER CATHEDRAL: England; 1107-1328 (Gothic).
FIRST BAPTIST CHURCH: Providence; 1774.
FIRST CHURCH OF CHRIST, SCIENTIST: Boston, 1894 (Romanesque).
FIRST CONGREGATIONAL CHURCH: Salem, Mass.; 1826.
FIRST DUTCH REFORMED CHURCH: Flatbush, Brooklyn; 1654.
FIRST HUGUENOT CHURCH: New York, 1704.
FIRST PRESBYTERIAN CHURCH: Elizabeth, New Jersey; first building erected 1666.
FIRST PRESBYTERIAN CHURCH: New York, 1844 (Gothic).
FIRST PRESBYTERIAN CHURCH: Philadelphia; present building 1822.

FRAUENKIRCHE: Nuremberg, Germany; erected 1355-1361 (German Gothic).
FRIENDS' MEETING HOUSE: Philadelphia, 1804.
GLASGOW CATHEDRAL: Scotland, completed mid-15th century (Norman).
GLORIA DEI (OLD SWEDES') CHURCH: Philadelphia, 1675, rebuilt 1700.
GLOUCESTER CATHEDRAL: England; 1072-1104 (Anglo-Saxon; Gothic).
GOLDEN PAGODA: Rangoon, erected c. 588 b.c.
GRACE CHURCH: New York; 1846.
GREAT MOSQUE OF DAMASCUS: Syria; originally a Roman temple, used successively by Christians and Mohammedans as a center of worship.
GREAT (ROYAL) MOSQUE OF ISFAHAN: Persia; late 16th century.
GREAT TOSHUGU SHRINE: See the Temples of Nikko.
HAGIA SOPHIA: See Santa Sophia.
HOLY WISDOM: See Santa Sophia.
HOLYROOD CHAPEL (HOLYROOD ABBEY): Edinburgh, Scotland; built by David I in 1128.
IL GESU: Rome, Italy; begun 1568 (Mannerist).
IYEMITSU, TEMPLE OF: See the Temples of Nikko.
IYEYASU, TEMPLE OF: See the Temples of Nikko.
JOHN STREET METHODIST CHURCH: New York, 1848.
JUDSON MEMORIAL BAPTIST CHURCH: New York, 1892.
JUMMA MUSJID: Delhi, North Indian Union; 17th century.
KING'S CHAPEL: Boston, Mass.; erected 1686.
LICHFIELD CATHEDRAL: England; 13th-14th centuries (Gothic).
LINCOLN CATHEDRAL: England; begun 1192 (Early Gothic).
THE LITTLE CHURCH AROUND THE CORNER: (Protestant Episcopal Church of the Transfiguration), Fifth Avenue at 29th St., New York.
THE LITTLE CHURCH OF ENGLAND: Newport, R.I.; 1702.
LITTLE DOVER MEETING HOUSE: Dover, N.H.; 1639, succeeded by First Congregational Church, 1829.
LLANDAFF CATHEDRAL: Near Cardiff, Wales; present building erected c. 1120, restored in 19th century; (Early English).
MARTIN LUTHER'S CHURCH: See Schloss-Kirche.
MASJID-I-SHAH: Isfahan, Iran; late 16th century. Also called the Great, or Royal, Mosque of Isfahan.
MELROSE ABBEY: Scotland; ruins of Abbey rebuilt by David Bruce in 1322 (Gothic).
MERION MEETING HOUSE: Near Philadelphia; 1695.
MISSION CONCEPCION LA PURISIMA DE ACUNA: San Antonio, Texas; 1722-31.
MISSION DOLORES (SAN FRANCISCO DE ASIS SOLANO): San Francisco, Calif.; October 9, 1776.
MISSION SAN CARLOS BORROMEO: Monterey, Calif.; 1771.
MISSION SAN DIEGO: Calif.; 1769.
MISSION SAN GABRIEL THE ARCHANGEL: Near Los Angeles, Calif.; 1771.
MISSION SAN JUAN CAPISTRANO: Calif.; 1776.
MISSION SANTA BARBARA: Calif.; 1786.
MISSION, THE ALAMO: Texas, present site from 1744.
MONASTIC CHURCH AT ZWETL: Germany; 1343 (German Gothic).

MORAVIAN CHURCH: Bethlehem, Pa.; 1805.
MORMON TEMPLE: Salt Lake City, 1853-1893.
MOSQUE OF AHMED I: Constantinople; 1608-1614: Also known as Ahmediyeh.
MOSQUE OF CORDOBA: Spain; 786 (reconverted to a Christian church from 1238).
MOSQUE OF FATEHPUR SIKRI: North Indian Union; 1556-1605.
MOSQUE OF IBN TULUN: Cairo, Egypt; 879 (brick Mosque).
MOSQUE OF ISFAHAN, GREAT (ROYAL): See Masjid-i-Shah.
MOSQUE OF KAIRWAN: North Africa; late 7th century.
MOSQUE OF MECCA, GREAT: See El Haram.
MOSQUE OF OMAR: Jerusalem; 678 (domical Mosque). Also known as the Mosque of the Dome of the Rock.
MOSQUE OF SULEIMAN I, THE MAGNIFICENT: Constantinople; 1550-1556.
MOSQUE OF SULTAN HASAN: Cairo, Egypt; 1357.
MOSQUE OF THE CAVE OF MACHPELAH: Hebron, Palestine; traditionally the tomb of Abraham and Sarah.
MOSQUE OF THE DOME OF THE ROCK: See Mosque of Omar.
THE NATIONAL CATHEDRAL: Washington, D.C.; begun 1915 (Gothic).
NOTRE-DAME-DES-VICTOIRES: Quebec, Canada; 1688.
OLD DUTCH SLEEPY HOLLOW CHURCH: Tarrytown, N.Y.; 1685.
OLD JERUSALEM: Portland, Me., rebuilt 1825.
OLD MISSION CHURCH: Mackinac Island, Mich.; 1829.
OLD NORTH CHURCH: Boston, Mass.; 1723 (Georgian). Now Christ Church, Episcopal.
OLD ST. PETER'S: Rome, destroyed 1506 (Basilican type).
OLD SHIP CHURCH: Hingham, Mass.; from 1681.
OLD SOUTH CHURCH: Boston; 1690, rebuilt 1730, restored 1776.
OLD SOUTH MEETING HOUSE: Boston, Mass.; built 1729, rebuilt 1789; (plain brick structure with high wooden steeple).
OLD SOUTH CHURCH: Newburyport, Mass.; 1756.
OLD SWEDES' CHURCH: Wilmington, Del.; 1699.
OLD TENNENT CHURCH: Monmouth Battlefield, N.J.; 1751.
THE PANTHEON: Rome, c. 120 a.d.
THE PARTHENON: Athens; begun 447 b.c.
PEARL MOSQUE: Agra, Indian Union; 1646-1653.
PENNYPACK CHURCH: Pennypack, Pa.; 1688.
PETERBOROUGH CATHEDRAL (CATHEDRAL OF ST. PETER, ST. PAUL, AND ST. ANDREW): England; begun 1117 (Norman).
POLOZHENIA RIS CATHEDRAL: Moscow, Russia; erected 1484-1486. Also called the Cathedral of the Ordination of the Priests.
PRIESTS, CATHEDRAL OF THE ORDINATION OF THE: See Polozhenia Ris Cathedral.
PROTESTANT MÜNSTER: Ulm, Germany; 14th century (Gothic).
QUAKER MEETING HOUSE: Flushing, New York; 1719.
QUINCY CHURCH: Quincy, Mass.; 1827.
REIMS CATHEDRAL: See Cathedral of Notre Dame.
ROUEN CATHEDRAL: See Cathedral of Notre Dame.
ROYAL TEMPLE OF THE EMERALD BUDDHA: Bangkok, Siam; part of the Grand Palace.
ST. ALBANS: England; begun 1077 (Norman).

ST. ANDREW'S: Richmond, Staten Island, N.Y.; original building 1706.
ST. ANNE DE BEAUPRÉ: See Shrine of St. Anne de Beaupré.
ST. CLEMENT'S: Rome (Basilican type).
ST. CRISTO DE LA LUZ: Toledo, Spain; (converted Mosque).
ST. DAVID'S CATHEDRAL: Wales; c. 1180, remodeled 1328-1347 (middle pointed Gothic).
ST. GEORGE'S CHAPEL: Windsor Castle, erected by Edward III.
ST. GEORGE'S METHODIST EPISCOPAL CHURCH: Philadelphia; 1769.
SAINT-GERMAIN-DES-PRÉS: Paris, France; present church dates from 10th-11th centuries (predominantly Romanesque).
ST. GUDULE, CHURCH OF: Brussels, Belgium; founded 1010, reconstructed 13th-17th centuries (pointed Gothic).
ST. JOHN LATERAN: Rome; 324 (Basilican type).
ST. JOHN'S: Portsmouth, N.H.; 1807.
ST. JOSEPH'S CATHEDRAL: St. Augustine, Fla.; completed 1799.
ST. LOUIS CATHEDRAL: New Orleans, 1850.
ST. MARK'S CHURCH: Venice, Italy; present building mainly completed c. 1071, additional building from 12th-15th centuries (Romanesque-Byzantine-Gothic).
ST. MARK'S IN-THE-BOUWERIE: New York City; completed 1799.
ST. MICHAEL'S: Marblehead, Mass.; begun 1714.
ST. MICHAEL EVANGELICAL LUTHERAN: Philadelphia; founded 1743.
ST. PATRICK'S: Dublin; begun 1190, burned 1316, and rebuilt.
ST. PATRICK'S CATHEDRAL: New York; 1858-79 (Gothic).
ST. PAUL'S: New York, 1766.
ST. PAUL'S CATHEDRAL: London; 1675-1710 (English Renaissance).
ST. PAUL-WITHOUT-THE-WALLS: Rome, begun 380 (Basilican type).
ST. PETER'S: Albany, New York, 1859.
ST. PETER'S CHURCH: Rome, Italy; erected 1450-1612, with work on Bramante's design begun in 1506 (Renaissance).
ST. PETER'S PROTESTANT EPISCOPAL CHURCH: Philadelphia; 1758.
SAINT PIERRE, CATHEDRAL OR CHURCH OF: Geneva, Switzerland; 10th-12th centuries (Gothic).
ST. STEFANO ROTONDO: Rome; fifth century (Basilican type).
ST. STEPHEN'S CATHEDRAL: Vienna, Austria; completed 1506 (Gothic).
ST. THOMAS' CHURCH: New York City; designed 1906 (Gothic).
ST. VITALE: Ravenna, Italy; c. 536 (Basilican).
SAINTE-CHAPELLE: Paris, France; built by Louis IX, 1242-1247 (Gothic).
SS. MARIA E DONATA: See Cathedral of Murano.
SALISBURY CATHEDRAL: England; erected 1220-1260 (early English Gothic).
SAN MIGUEL CHURCH: Santa Fe, N.M.; 1636.
SAN XAVIER DEL BAC: Near Tucson, Ariz.; c. 1654.
SANTA CROCE: See Church of Santa Croce.
SANTA MARIA DEL FIORE: Florence, Italy; begun 1298 (Gothic).
SANTA MARIA DELLA SALUTE: Venice, Italy; 1630-80 (Renaissance).
SANTA MARIA LA BIANCA: Toledo, Spain; (converted Mosque).
SANTA MARIA MAGGIORE: Rome; 432 a.d. (Basilican type).

SANTA MARIA NOVELLO: Florence; erected 1278 (Gothic).

SANTA SOPHIA: Constantinople; present structure built by Emperor Justinian, 532-537, dedicated December 25, 537 (Byzantine, remodeled by the Turks after 1453 and used as a mosque). Also called Holy Wisdom, Hagia Sophia, Aya Sofia.

SCHLOSS-KIRCHE (ALL SAINTS' CHURCH): Wittenberg, Germany; 1493-1499. Called Martin Luther's Church.

SHRINE OF OUR LADY OF GUADALUPE: Guadalupe Hidalgo, near Mexico City, Mexico.

SHRINE OF OUR LADY OF LOURDES: Lourdes, Hautes-Pyrénées Department, France.

SHRINE OF SAINT ANNE DE BEAUPRÉ: 22 miles from Quebec, Canada; rebuilt 1876-1878, burned 1922, rebuilt 1923. Basilica from 1887.

SOLOMON'S TEMPLE: Jerusalem; c. 1000 b.c. -586 b.c., when it was destroyed by Nebuchadnezzar.

STRASBOURG CATHEDRAL: See Cathedral of Strasbourg.

SWAMP CHURCH: New Hanover, Pa.; 1703; present building 1768.

TELL'S CATHEDRAL: Lake Lucerne, Switzerland; 15th century.

TEMPLE OF DIANA: Ephesus (see Seven Wonders of Ancient World).

TEMPLE OF EDFU: 50 miles southeast of Thebes, Egypt; completed 57 b.c.

THE TEMPLE OF HEAVEN: Peiping, China; erected 1420.

THE TEMPLES OF NIKKO: Nikko, central Honshu, Japan; includes early Shinto temple, the Great Toshogu Shrine, a Buddhist temple c. 765, and the temple of Iyeyasu and Iyemitsu, shoguns of the Tokugawa dynasty.

TEOCALLI (TEMPLE OF THE AZTECS): Tenochtitlan (ancient name of Mexico City, Mexico).

TRINITY CHURCH: Fishkill, N.Y.; 1769.

TRINITY CHURCH: New York; begun 1841 (Gothic).

TRONDHIEM CATHEDRAL: Norway; 1066-1248 (Orgival).

THE VOTIVE CHURCH: Vienna, Austria; completed 1879.

WELLS CATHEDRAL (CATHEDRAL CHURCH OF ST. ANDREW AT WELLS): England; begun 1174 (Gothic).

WESTMINSTER ABBEY: London; 1049-1065 (Gothic).

WINCHESTER CATHEDRAL: Hampshire, England; begun 1079 (predominantly Norman).

YORK MINSTER CATHEDRAL: England; 1189 -1474 (decorated and perpendicular English Gothic).

Largest Cathedrals of Europe

Note: The figure cited is the area of the cathedral, rounded off to the nearest hundred. The Cathedral of St. John the Divine, New York, ranks in area third in size among the world's cathedrals.

ST. PETER'S (ROME): 18,000 sq. yds.
SEVILLE CATHEDRAL: 13,000 sq. yds.
MILAN CATHEDRAL: 10,000 sq. yds.
ST. PAUL'S (LONDON): 9,000 sq. yds.
ST. SOPHIA (CONSTANTINOPLE): 8,000 sq.yds.
COLOGNE CATHEDRAL: 7,000 sq. yds.

Caves of Historic and Scientific Interest

ADULLAM, CAVE OF: Cave in which David took refuge when he fled from Saul, and thither resorted to him "everyone that was in distress, and everyone that was in debt, and everyone that was discontended." (I Sam. XXII, 1, 2.)

ALABASTER CAVERN: El Dorado, Calif.; stalactite grotto of great beauty.

ALTAMIRA CAVERNS: Santander, Spain; discovered in 1879; beautiful drawings executed in color by Cro-Magnon cave dwellers over 20,000 years ago.

BASKET-MAKERS' CAVES: Rio Grande Valley; W. Texas; remains of ancient man.

BAUMAN'S HOLE: Blankenburg, Germany; bone cavern.

BIG BONE CAVE: Ky.; has yielded immense supply of fossil bones of fairly recent times.

BLUE GROTTO: Island of Capri, Italy; base of a limestone cliff with a small opening appearing above the edge of the water; inside, domelike roof, water of deep azure color illuminated by rays passing through the water from outside.

BLUE JOHN MINE: The Peak, England; stalactitical formations, pearly yellow in color.

BURNETT CAVE: N.M.; remains of ancient man.

CANDIA LABYRINTH: Islands of Crete, Greece; many chambers connected by low winding passages.

CARLSBAD CAVERNS: Guadalupe Mountains, New Mexico; open to public for less than 30 years; limestone; contains spectacular, spacious chambers.

CAVA DI TIRRENI: Compania, S. Italy; famous Benedictine monastery (founded 1025 by St. Aeferius over a cave he occupied) nearby.

CAVE OF ADELBERG: Near Trieste; famous cave of slate and limestone cut by River Peuka; inscriptions of yr. 1213 found, also strange saurian, Proteus; many winding rooms and grottoes, stalactite formations.

CAVE OF CACAHUAMILPA: Central Mexico; penetrates a chain of mountains, entrance 70' high, 150' wide; series of large, connected halls within, also large natural amphitheater inside.

CAVE OF LA PATANA: West coast of Cuba; filled with bats, cockroaches, spiders, and crawling things; ancient Indian carvings discovered.

CAVE OF MACHPELAH: Hebron, Israel; mosque built over famous cave where Abraham and Sarah are said to have been buried.

CAVE OF PETCHABURY: Near Bangkok, Thailand; extinct volcano, 4 or 5 grottoes, 2 large basalt and white colonnades, stalactites.

CAVE OF THE DOUBS: Neufchâtel, Switzerland; ancient channel of the River Tofiere.

CAVE OF THE MAELSTROM: Norway; seacarved.

CAVE OF THE VAMPIRES: Los Sabrinos, Mexico; habitat of vampire and fruit bats, entrance in canyon with large chambers and narrow passages.

CAVE OF THE WINDS: Niagara Falls, N.Y.; rocky chamber 100'×75', formed by erosion.

CAVE OF TORGHATTEN: Northern Norway; regular gallery carried through the rock, 1650' long.

CAVERN DEL GUARCHARO: Caracas, Venezuela; entrance, 80' wide, 70' high, with mass of vegetation outside and within as long as light persists; uniform size rooms, haunt of the guacharo bird.

CAVERN OF THE SIBYL: Lake Avernus, Greece; huge chasms cut out of the rock.

CAVERN TEMPLES OF INDIA: *Elephanta*, near Bombay (Brahmin); *Ellora*, near Bombay (Brahmin); *Amboli*, Island of Salsette (Buddhist); *Kamara*, Island of Salsette (Buddhist); *Carli*, Poona (Buddhist).

CAVES OF BAMEEAN: City of caves in Egypt; 8 miles of squared holes in the hills.

CAVES OF CHOW KOW LIEN: Near Peiping, China; cave where fossil Pekin Man was discovered.

CAVES OF ETRETAT: Etretat, France; white sea-front grottoes.

CAVES OF LASCAUX: Périgord, S. W. France; cave where prehistoric cave paintings were found in 1940.

CAVES OF THE DEAD SEA SCROLLS: Between the Dead Sea and Bethlehem; discovered in 1947; caves contained scrolls of parchment and copper believed to be of the Essene Sect.

CAVE TEMPLES OF EGYPT: Ipsambul; gigantic figures of Ramses, interiors painted and cut in bas-relief.

CAVE TEMPLES OF INDIA: Near Byanta and Ellora in Hyderabad State; about 30 were excavated from soft volcanic rocks by followers of Gautama Buddha about 200 b.c.; some 700 years later the caverns were enlarged and more than 30 new ones constructed by Hindus who followed the Buddhists into the region; the caves are in a cliff over 200′ high, and are adorned in columns and frescoes; within the caves are statues, some decorative, some religious; the statues carved by the Hindus represent the peak of their art.

CHOUKONTIEN CAVE: Near Peiping, China; human remains, older than Neanderthal, found 1929.

CONCORD FISSURE: Arkansas; animal remains.

CONKLINGS CAVERN: N.M.; remains of ancient man.

CORMORANT CAVE: Island of Staffa, Scotland; cavern cut by the sea, abode of cormorants.

CORYCIAN CAVE: Coast of Cilcia, Asia Minor; circular hollow surrounded by high rock; crocuses and other plants grow within; associated with Petrarch.

CORYCIAN CAVE: Mt. Parnassus, Greece; huge size, fantastic, white stalactite formations.

CUMBERLAND BONE CAVE: Md.; valuable paleontological specimens, record of thousands of years; sinkhole entrance trapped animals.

CWN PORTH: Glamorganshire, Wales; open both ends, river runs through.

DEVIL'S HOLE: Near Las Vegas, Nevada; limestone, tapered hole entrance forming natural stairway down, underground pool called Miner's Bathtub.

DEVIL'S SINK HOLE: Rocksprings, Texas; entrance, a hole 75′ wide, 200-300′ deep; huge stalactites, emerald lakes within.

DREAM CAVERN: The Peak, England; a bone cavern, skeletons of animals found.

ELDON HOLE: Derbyshire, England; penetrates vertically down from earth's surface.

ETNA CAVE: Near Caliente, Nevada; yielded material similar to Gypsum Cave.

FINGAL'S CAVE: Island of Staffa, Scotland; great hall of cavern 370′ long, 55′ wide, 117′ high; natural colonnades of basalt, 2′ wide.

FONT-DE-GAUME: Dordogne, France; cave-paintings and engravings.

FOUNTAIN OF VAUCLUSE: Avignon, France; bottomless chasm formed by cascading waters.

GRAND CAVE: See Weyer's Cave.

GRAND CAVERNS: Grottoes, Va.; open to public, beautiful formations, flat slabs of calcite crystals.

GREAT CRYSTAL CAVE: Cave region, Kentucky; huge room 80′ high, 40′ wide, 300′ long, beautiful colored stone tendrils, gypsum into flowers; discovered by Floyd Collins.

GREAT SALTPETER CAVE: E. Kentucky; source of much of the niter used for gunpowder during the War of 1812 and the Mexican War; saltpeter first mined here in 1794.

GROTTA DEL CANE: Near Naples, Italy; mephitic cave, containing noxious gases from decomposing rock; formerly used dogs to discover noxiousness, therefore the name.

GROTTA DI POSILIPO: Near Naples, Italy; tunnel of a half-mile.

GROTTE DE MORGATTE: Coast of Brittany, Bay of Douarnenz, France; entrance by boat through low narrow opening, cave very large, streaked with color, roof of green marble; size: 150′ deep, 60′ high, 70′ wide.

GROTTE DES DÉMOISELLES: Ganges, France; entrance, descent into well 20′ deep, magnificent stalactite formation resembling Gothic and Roman halls; said to be refuge of Huguenots.

GROTTE DES FROMAGES: Bertrich-Baden, Germany; basaltic columns worn by atmosphere to resemble piles of cheeses.

GROTTE DES OISEAUX: Coast of Brittanny; Bay of Douarnenz, France; 60′ deep, 2 natural arcades for entrance, accomodates 80 people.

GROTTO OF ANTIPAROS: Antiparos Island, near Trieste; remarkable stalactite and stalagmite formation, Great Hall, 120′ long, 113′ wide, 60′ high.

GROTTO OF BONIFACIO: South coast of Corsica; limestone opens to the sea, series of halls and chambers.

GROTTO OF HAN-SUR-LESSE: Near Dinant, Belgium; very old, River Lesse runs through; fantastic shapes formed by rocks and stalactites, strange acoustics, immense depth.

GROTTO OF LA BALME: Near Lyons, France; opening is like a triumphal arch into the hill; 2 chapels within, branches from the chapels called Hall of Diamonds and (pillared) Hall of the Bats.

GROTTO OF LA MADELEINE: Montpelier, France; noxious cave, narrow opening; stalactites, lake.

GROTTO OF MONSUMMANO: Montecatini, Italy; natural gallery, crystal, marble, thermal springs.

GROTTO OF THE APOCALYPSE: Shore of the Aegean Sea; supposed to be the cave of the Apostle John.

GROTTOES OF ARCY: Arcy-sur-Cure, France; small entrance to great halls and passages, stalactites; old river bed.

GROTTOES OF OSSELLES: Besançon, France; remarkable for extent and depth, fossil bones found.

GROTTOES OF SASSENAGE: Near Grenoble, France; symmetrical, lighted laterally, gushing springs.

GROTTOES OF TOURANE: Bay of Tourane, China; marble rocks broken into pinnacles and spires, gloomy entrance into well-lighted chambers (pillared).

GYPSUM CAVE: Near Las Vegas, Nev.; human remains dating back over 10,000 yrs.; early Pueblo and other Basket-maker remains; two fireplaces and drawing of ground sloth dated by radio-carbon to 8-10,000 years ago.

HOB HOLE: Whitby, England; in chalk cliffs.

"HOLE TEETH" CAVERN: Muggendorf, England; a bear cavern, abundance of fossil teeth found.

HOWE CAVERNS: N.Y.; public cavern.

ICE CAVE OF VERGY: Cluses, France; limestone, cold in summer, warm and dry in winter.

ICE CAVES: Limestone. cold and icy in summer, warm and dry in winter; caves of this kind found at ZZelitze, Hungary; *Iletske*, Ural Mountains; *Besançon*, France; *Vesoul*, France.

JAMES CAVE: Near Louisville, Ky.; supposed to have been the rendezvous of Jesse and Frank James; contains a pit called Impossible Pit.

JAVEL CAVE: Custer Co., S.W. S. Dak.; caves of limestone formation.

KENT'S CAVERN: Torquay, England; limestone; fossils found.

KHUREITUN CAVERN: Between Bethlehem and the Dead Sea; supposed to be the cave in which David found refuge from Saul. See ADULLAM.

KIRKDALE CAVE: Yorkshire, England; a bone cavern; skeletons of hundred of animals found, mostly hyenas.

KUHLOCH CAVE: Germany; resembles a church in size and shape; remains of 2500 cavern bears found.

LA CUEVA CHICA: Central Mexico; white blindfish found.

LA MOUTHE: Dordogne, France; prehistoric cave drawings.

LA PILETA: Andalusia, Spain; cave drawings.

LASCAUX CAVE: Dordogne, near Bordeaux, France; beautiful drawings executed in color by Cro-Magnon cave dwellers over 20,000 years ago.

LAVA BEDS: N. Calif.; lava and ice caves; battleground of Modoc Indian wars 1872-73.

LEATHER MAN CAVES: Conn.-N.Y. border; series of caves that were inhabited by the Leather Man, famous late 19th-cent. hermit.

LEHMAN CAVES: E. Nev., natural caves of limestone formation.

LA MADELEINE: Southwest France near Les Eyzies; tolls and carvings of the Magdalenian culture.

LE MOUSTIER: France; Neanderthal bones and flints found here gave the name to the Mousterian age of paleolithic culture.

LES EYZIES: Dordogne, France; prehistoric cave drawings.

LUC D'AUDOUBERT: Ariège, France; cave drawings.

LURAY CAVERNS: Valley of Va.; public cavern; discovered 1874; floored with limestone of Ordovician age; many beautiful caves.

MACALLISTER'S CAVE: Island of Skye, Scotland; interior pool surrounded by formations resembling white marble.

MADISON CAVE: Near Weyer's Cave, Va.; reported to have been opened commercially shortly before 18th cent., but for a brief period only. (See Weyer's Cave.)

MAMMOTH CAVE: Near Louisville, Ky.; 2 miles of grottoes; small, low entrance, great halls and chambers; "Gothic Church" holds 1500 people; bottomless pits, "Chamber of Stars," etc.

MARBLE CAVE: Ozark Mountains, Mo.; 14 rooms, marble deposits; blind cave salamanders found.

MARIENSTADT CAVE: Frederickstal, Norway; vertical fissures of unknown depth, calculated 39,866 to 59,049 feet deep.

MARK TWAIN CAVE: Hannibal, Mo.; made famous by description in *Tom Sawyer* .

MARSOULAS: Haute-Garonne, France; cave drawings.

MELROSE CAVERNS: Harrisonburg, Va.;

historic cave, used by both sides during Civil War, has name carvings on walls.

MONTESPAN CAVERN: Foothills of French Pyrenees; group of clay statues of animals carved by cave men as ancient as the artists of Lascaux.

MOTHER LODE CAVERNS: Yosemite National Park, Calif.; includes *Mercer Caverns; Moaning Cave.*

MT. CARMEL CAVE: New Jerusalem, Palestine; excavated 1929; human remains and artifacts dating from Neanderthal man to present.

OREGON CAVES: Josephine Co., S.W. Ore.; caves of limestone formation.

ORGAN CAVE: Ronceverte, West Va.; thought to be a bone cave, very large.

PASTUM CAVE: Iran; limestone cavern, inhabited for 7000 years or more by ancient cave dwellers.

PEAK CAVERN: Castleton; England; extends 2250' into mountain; a succession of lofty halls and chambers.

PORT KENNEDY AND FRANKSTOWN CAVES: Pennsylvania; animal remains.

ST. MICHAEL'S CAVE: Gibraltar; very large; myriad picturesque stalactites.

SAND CAVE: Ky.; cave where Floyd Collins was trapped and died.

SANDIA CAVE: N.M.; contained relatively modern Pueblo material at surface; beneath were artifacts of Folsom culture and remains of extinct ice-age animals; further below were remains of extinct animals such as primitive horses, mastodons and mammoths; also fireplaces and spear points established as over 25,000 years old were discovered at lowest level.

SCHOOLHOUSE CAVE: Pendleton County, W.Va.; little beauty; very difficult to climb; chasms and dark passages.

"SCHOOL OF ELIAS" CAVE: Mt. Carmel, Israel; supposed to be the cave in which Elias lived and taught.

SCRATCHELL'S CAVE: Isle of Wight, England; sandstone; arch 300' high; overhangs the beach.

SHOSHONE CAVERN: Park Co., N. W. Wy.; large cave.

SKYLINE CAVERNS: Front Royal, Va.; circular passage containing cave clusters of anthodites ("flowers").

SOUFFLEUR CAVE: Island of Mauritius; appears as a Gothic building.

SPEEDWELL MINE: N. Derbyshire, England; limestone, mile in interior of the rock, height and depth unknown.

SPY CAVE: Belgium; 2 skeletons found in 1886 are believed to be remains of paleolithic man.

SURTSHELLIR CAVERN: Iceland; 40' high; 50' wide, 5034' long; lava formation, black stalactites; further inside, crystallized icicles, rose pillars.

THOR'S CAVERN: Valley of Dovedale, The Peak, England; said to be the caves of the Druid's human sacrifices; limestone, lofty entrance, branching roof, natural window within.

TIMPANOGOS CAVE: Central Utah; limestone cavern.

TROIS FRÈRES: Ariège, France; cave drawings.

TROU DU DIABLE: Coast of Brittany, Bay of Douarnenz, France; like a huge kiln hewn out of rock, natural stovepipe.

VENTANA CAVE: S. Ariz.; yielded many records of human occupacy.

WEYER'S CAVE (GRAND CAVE): Near Waynesboro, Va.; probably oldest existing

commercial cave in America, opened to public in 1804.
WIND CAVE: Custer Co., S. W. S. Dak.; in Wind Cave National Park.
WOODMAN'S CAVE: Harz, Germany; stalactite and stalagmite formations.
WOOKEY HOLE: Wells, England; bone cave; hyena remains; chambers half in water.
WYANDOTTE CAVE: Crawford County, Ind.; a cave visited by an early group of prehistoric men. Huge stalactite pillar has been chiseled away for material.

Cemeteries
See **National Cemeteries**

Characters and Roles from Ballet
See also **Ballets**

Note: The name of the choreographer is given with each ballet title.

ACCUSED (LIZZIE BORDEN): *Fall River Legend* (De Mille).
ACHILLES' NURSE: *La Belle Hélène* (Cranko).
ACROBAT: *Aleko* (Massine).
ADAM: *Adam and Eve* (Tudor).
THE ADOLESCENT: *Seventh Symphony* (Second Movement) (Massine).
AGAMEMNON: *La Belle Hélène* (Cranko).
AGANIPPE: *Undertow* (Tudor).
AGATHE, THE WHITE CAT-GIRL: *Les Demoiselles de la Nuit* (Petit).
AJAX I: *Helen of Troy* (Lichine).
AJAX II: *Helen of Troy* (Lichine).
ALAIN: *La Fille Mal Gardée* (Dauberval-Nijinska).
ALBRECHT: *Giselle* (Coralli-Perrot).
ALDONZA: *Don Quixote* (Valois).
ALEKO: *Aleko* (Massine).
ALGERNON C. SWINBURNE: *Ghost Town* (Platoff).
ALGUIZILS: *The Three-cornered Hat* (Massine).
ALIAS: *Billy the Kid* (Loring).
ALICIA: *The Haunted Ballroom* (Valois).
ALLEGRO: *The Wanderer* (Ashton).
ALL-POWERFUL FATHER: *The Age of Anxieity* (Robbins).
ALVAREZ, LOVER OF THE QUEEN: *Bluebeard* (Fokine).
THE AMBASSADOR: *L'Epreuve d'Amour* (Fokine).
AMELFA: *Le Coq d'Or* (Fokine).
AN AMERICAN: *La Boutique Fantasque* (Massine).
AMERICAN CHAMPION: *Le Boxing* (Salaman).
AMERICAN CHILD: *La Boutique Fantasque:* (Massine).
AMERICAN SAILOR: *Les Matelots* (Massine).
AMOR: *Orpheus and Eurydice* (Balanchine).
ANARCHIST: *Paris-Soir* (Gore).
SIR ANDREW AGUECHEEK: *Twelfth Night* (Howard).
ANGELIC APPARITION: *Francesca da Rimini* (Lichine).
ANGELO, A PAGE AND LOVER OF THE QUEEN: *Bluebeard* (Fokine).
ANNE BOLEYN: *Henry VIII* (Hightower).
ANOTHER MAN: *Facsimile* (Robbins).
ANOTHER REFLECTION: *Dim Lustre* (Tudor).
ANTONIA: *The Tales of Hoffman,* motion picture version (Ashton).
APHRODITE: *Helen of Troy* (Lichine).
APHRON, PRINCE: *Le Coq d'Or* (Fokine).
APOLLO: *Mercury* (Balanchine).
APOLLO: *Orpheus* (Balanchine).

APOLLO, LEADER OF THE MUSES: *Apollon Musagètes* (Balanchine).
ARCHBISHOP: *Adam Zero* (Helpmann).
ARCHIMAGO: *The Quest* (Ashton).
ARIADNE: *Labyrinth* (Massine).
ARIEL: *The Rape of the Lock* (Howard).
ARISTOCRAT: *Mam'zelle Angot* (Massine).
ARMAND: *The Lady of the Camellias* (Tudor).
ARMANDO, LOVER OF THE QUEEN: *Bluebeard* (Fokine).
ARTHUR: *The Wedding Bouquet* (Ashton).
THE ARTIST: *Le Beau Danube* (Massine).
ASSAY OFFICER: *Ghost Town* (Platoff).
ASSISTANT TO THE SHOPKEEPER: *La Boutique Fantasque* (Massine).
ASTROLOGER: *Le Coq d'Or* (Fokine).
ATE: *Undertow* (Tudor).
THE ATHLETE: *Le Beau Danube* (Massine).
ATHLETE: *Les Biches* (Nijinsky).
AN ATTENDANT: *Souvenirs* (Bolender).
AUNT ELLA: *Laurie makes up her Mind; Oklahoma!* (De Mille).
AURORA, PRINCESS: *Sleeping Beauty* (Littlefield).
AVARICE: *The Quest* (Ashton).
BACCHANALE: *Seventh Symphony* (Fourth Movement) (Massine).
BACCHANTES: *Undertow* (Tudor).
BALLERINA: *Scènes de Ballet* (Ashton).
BANDIT WITH RED HAIR: *Carmen* (Petit).
BARBER: *Cinderella* (Ashton).
BARBER: *Mam'zelle Angot* (Massine).
THE BARMAN: *Union Pacific* (Massine).
THE BARMAN'S ASSISTANT: *Union Pacific* (Massine).
BARON: *The Clock Symphony* (Massine).
THE BARON: *Gaîté Parisienne* (Massine).
BARON: *The Rape of the Lock* (Howard).
BARON BLUEBEARD: *Bluebeard* (Fokine).
BARTENDER: *Fancy Free* (Robbins).
BAT: *La Fiancée du Diable* (Petit).
BATHERS (2): *Aleko* (Massine).
BATHILDE: *Giselle* (Coralli-Perrot).
BATSMAN: *Le Cricket* (Salaman).
BEARDED LADY: *Jinx* (Lew Christensen).
THE BEGGAR: *Devil's Holiday* (Ashton).
BEGGAR: *Miracle in the Gorbals* (Helpmann).
BELINDA: *The Rape of the Lock* (Howard).
BELL-RINGER: *Coppélia* (Merante).
THE BELOVED: *Symphonie Fantastique* (Massine).
"BENICIA BOY" HEENAN: *Ghost Town* (Platoff).
BENNO, SIEGFRIED'S FRIEND: *Swan Lake* (Mordkin, after Petipa).
BENVOLIO: *Romeo and Juliet* (Tudor).
BERTHE: *Giselle* (Coralli-Perrot).
BILLY THE KID: *Billy the Kid* (Loring).
BIRD: *Peter and the Wolf* (Bolm).
THE BIRD: *Seventh Symphony* (First Movement) (Massine).
THE BIRD-CATCHER: *The Hundred Kisses* (Nijinska).
THE BLACKAMOOR: *Petrouchka* (Fokine).
BLACK SWAN: *Swan Lake* (Act III; (Petipa).
BLACK QUEEN: *Checkmate* (Valois).
BLANCHE, WIFE OF BLUEBEARD: *Bluebeard* (Fokine).
BLANCHE DU BOIS: *A Streetcar Named Desire* (Bettis).
THE BLOND: *Fancy Free* (Robbins).
BLUEBIRD: *The Sleeping Beauty, Bluebird Variation* (Petipa).
BLUEBIRDS: *Fairy Tale Divertissement, Sleeping Beauty* (Littlefield).
BLUE BOY: *Les Patineurs* (Ashton).
BLUE SKATER: *Les Patineurs* (Ashton).
LA BOLERO: *Les Sirènes* (Ashton).
BONANZA KING COMSTOCK: *Ghost Town* (Platoff).

BOREAS: *Zephyr et Flore* (Massine).
BOW AND ARROW DANCE: A Speciality of Mikhail Mordkin.
BOY: *Jinx* (Lew Christensen).
BOY HIKER: *Ghost Town* (Platoff).
BOY IN GREY: *Voices of Spring* (Mordkin).
BOULOTTE, SIXTH WIFE OF BLUEBEARD: *Bluebeard* (Fokine).
BREAD BOY: *Harlequin in the Street* (Ashton).
THE BRIDE: *Le Baiser de la Fèe* (Balanchine).
THE BRIDE: *La Fête Étrange* (Howard).
BRIDE: *The Wise Virgins* (Ashton).
BRIDE AND GROOM: *Souvenirs* (Bolender).
BRIDEGROOM: *Le Baiser de la Fée* (Balanchine).
BRIDEGROOM'S MOTHER: *Le Baiser de la Fée* (Balanchine).
BROTHER: *Comus* (Helpmann).
THE BRUNETTE: *Fancy Free* (Robbins).
BRYAXIS: *Daphnis and Chloe* (Fokine).
BUFFOON: *Casse Noisette:* (Ivanov).
BURGOMASTER: *Coppélia* (Merante).
BURGOMASTER'S ASSISTANT: *Coppélia* (Merante).
BUTTERFLY: *Aleko* (Massine).
THE BUTTERFLY: *L'Épreuve d'Amour* (Fokine).
THE BUTTERFLY: *Le Festin de l'Araignée* (Howard).
THE BUTTERFLY: A solo dance by Pavlova.
CALCHAS: *Helen of Troy* (Fokine).
CALCHAS: *Helen of Troy* (Lichine).
THE CALIFORNIAN POPPY: A solo dance by Pavlova.
THE CALLER: *Rodeo* (De Mille).
CALLIOPE: *Apollon Musagètes* (Balanchine).
THE CAMERA MAN: *Union Pacific* (Massine).
CAMILLE: *The Lady of the Camellias* (Tudor).
CANCAN DANCERS: *La Boutique Fantasque* (Massine).
CANDY GIRL: *The Fair at Sorochinsk* (Lichine).
CANTALBUTTE: *Sleeping Beauty* (Littlefield).
LA CAPRIOCCIOSA: *The Lady and the Fool* (Cranko).
CAPTAIN: *Voices of Spring* (Mordkin).
CAPTAIN OF THE AMAZONS: *Con Amore* (Lew Christensen).
CAPTAIN OF THE GUARD: *La Bayadère* (Filippo Taglioni).
CAPTIVE PRINCESS: *On Stage!* (Kidd).
CAPULET: *Romeo and Juliet* (Tudor).
CARABOSSE: *Sleeping Beauty* (Littlefield).
CARICATURIST: *Mam'zelle Angot* (Massine).
CARMEN: *Carmen* (Petit).
CAROLINE, THE BRIDE-TO-BE: *Lilac Garden* (Tudor).
CASTOR: *Labyrinth* (Massine).
CAT: *La Chatte* (Balanchine).
THE CAT: *Cinderella* (Fokine).
THE CAT: *The Fair at Sorochinsk* (Lichine).
CAT: *Peter and the Wolf* (Bolm).
CAVALIER TO THE FRENCH BALLERINA: *Gala Performance* (Tudor).
CAVALIER TO THE ITALIAN BALLERINA: *Gala Performance* (Tudor).
CAYONETTA: *Soirée Musicale* (Tudor).
CENTIFOLIE: *Rose von Schiras* (Alexander Genée).
THE CHAMBERLAIN: *Cinderella* (Fokine).
THE CHAMPION ROPER: *Rodeo* (De Mille).
CHARLIE: *The Sailor's Return* (Howard).
CHASTITY: *St. Francis* (Massine).
CHAUFFEUR: *Les Sirènes* (Ashton).
CHIARA: *Francesca da Rimini* (Lichine).
CHIARINA: *Le Carnaval* (Fokine).
CHIEF EUNUCH: *Scheherezade* (Fokine).

THE CHIEF FURY: *Don Juan* (Fokine-Allatini).
THE CHIEF JESTER: *Don Juan* (Fokine-Allatini).
THE CHIEF NURSEMAID: *Petrouchka* (Fokine).
CHILD: *Jeux d'Enfants* (Massine).
CHILD: *Les Sirènes* (Ashton).
CHILDREN OF DARKNESS: *Dante Sonata* (Ashton).
CHILDREN OF LIGHT: *Dante Sonata* (Ashton).
CHIMERA OF ISOLDE: *Mad Tristan* (Massine).
CHINESE: *Aurora's Wedding* (Petipa).
CHIVATO: *Cuckold's Fair* (Lopez).
CHLOE: *Daphnis and Chloe* (Fokine).
CHOLERIC VARIATION: *The Four Temperaments* (Balanchine).
CHOPDAR: *La Bayadère* (Filippo Taglioni).
CHOSEN VIRGIN: *Le Sacre du Printemps* (Massine).
CHRISTMAS: A solo dance by Pavlova.
CHUNG-YANG: *L'Épreuve d'Amour* (Fokine).
CINDERELLA: *Cinderella* (Fokine).
CLEMENTINE, THE QUEEN: *Bluebeard* (Fokine).
CLEOPATRA: *Cléopâtre* (Fokine).
CLOCKMAKER: *The Clock Symphony* (Massine).
CLORINDA: *The Duel* (Dollar).
CLOWN: *Les Forains* (Petit).
COLIN: *La Fille Mal Gardée* (Dauberval-Nijinska).
COLONEL: *The New Yorker* (Massine).
COLUMBINE: *Casse Noisette* (Ivanov).
COLUMBINE: *Le Carnaval* (Fokine).
THE COMMANDER: *Don Juan* (Fokine-Allatini).
COMPANIONS OF THE PRODIGAL SON: *The Prodigal Son* (Lichine).
COMPANIONS OF VENUS (2): *Bacchanale* (Massine).
COMUS: *Comus* (Helpmann).
CONDUCTOR: *Gala Performance* (Tudor).
COPPÉLIA: *Coppélia* (Merante).
COPPÉLIUS: *Coppélia* (Merante).
COPPELIUS, DOCTOR: *The Tales of Hoffmann*, motion picture version (Ashton).
THE COSSACK CHIEF: *La Boutique Fantasque* (Massine).
THE COSSACK GIRL: *La Boutique Fantasque* (Massine).
COTYTTO: *The Masque of Comus* (Inglesby).
COUNT ANSELMO: *Scuola di Ballo* (Massine).
COUNTESS KITTY: *Les Sirènes* (Ashton).
COUNT OSCAR: *Bluebeard* (Fokine).
A COURTESAN: *Sebastian* (Caton).
COURT JESTER: *Cinderella* (Ashton).
COWBOY IN RED: *Billy the Kid* (Loring).
THE COWGIRL: *Rodeo* (De Mille).
CUCKOO: *The Birds* (Helpmann).
CUPID: *L'Amour et Son Amour* (Babilée).
CUPID: *Seventh Symphony* (Fourth Movement) (Massine).
CUPIDON: *Les Petits Riens* (Ashton).
CURLEY: *Laurie Makes Up Her Mind; Oklahoma!* (De Mille).
CUSTOMER: *The Judgment of Paris* (Tudor).
CYBELE: *Undertow* (Tudor).
CYGNET QUARTETTE: *Swan Lake* (Petipa).
CZARDAS: *Swan Lake* (Petipa).
DAEDALUS: *Icare* (Lifar).
DAGO: *Façade* (Ashton).
DANCE-HALL GIRLS: *Billy the Kid* (Loring).
DANCE MASTER: *Gaîté Parisienne* (Massine).
DANCER: *Passionate Pavane* (Ashton).
THE DANCER: *Petrouchka* (Fokine).
DANCE-STEP VARIATION: *Graduation Ball* (Lichine).

DANCING MASTER: *Que le Diable l'Emporte!* (Petit).
DANCING POODLES: *La Boutique Fantasque* (Massine).
DANDY: *Le Beau Danube* (Massine).
DANDY: *Illuminations* (Ashton).
THE DANDY: *The Three-cornered Hat* (Massine).
DANSE ARABE: *Casse Noisette* (Ivanov).
DANSE CHINOIS: *Casse Noisette* (Ivanov).
DANSE TENDRESSE: *Croquis de Mercure* (Howard).
DAPHNIS: *Daphnis and Chloe* (Fokine).
DAPERTUTTO: *The Tales of Hoffmann,* motion picture version (Ashton).
DARK ANGEL: *Orpheus* (Balanchine).
A DARK PEASANT GIRL: *Cinderella* (Fokine).
THE DAUGHTER: *Le Beau Danube* (Massine).
DAUGHTER: *Prairie* (Loring).
DAUGHTER OF THE OLD LORD: *Devil's Holiday* (Ashton).
DAWN FAIRY: *Casse Noisette,* act III (Ivanov).
DAY: *Nuages* (Theilades).
DEATH: *Death and the Maiden* (Howard).
DEATH: *Everyman* (Inglesby).
THE DEER: *Symphonie Fantastique* (Massine).
THE DEER: *Seventh Symphony* (first movement) (Massine).
LA DÉESSE DE LA DANSE (FROM MILAN): *Gala Performance* (Tudor).
DESIRE, PRINCE: *Sleeping Beauty* (Littlefield).
A DEVIL: *Three Virgins and a Devil* (De Mille).
THE DEVIL: *Devil's Holiday* (Ashton).
DIANA: *Aubade* (Lifar).
THE DIVINE GENIUS: *Paganini* (Fokine).
DOMENICO: *Francesca da Rimini* (Lichine).
DON JOSÉ: *Carmen* (Petit).
DON JUAN: *Don Juan* (Ashton).
DON JUAN: *Don Juan* (Fokine-Allatini).
DONNA ELVIRA: *Don Juan* (Fokine-Allatini).
DON QUICHOTTE: *Le Portrait de Don Quichotte* (Milloss).
DON QUIXOTÉ: *Le Chevalier Errant* (Lifar).
DON QUIXOTE: *Don Quixote* (Valois).
DOPE FIEND: *Paris-Soir* (Gore).
DORCON: *Daphnis and Chloe* (Fokine).
DOVE: *The Birds* (Helpmann).
DOWAGER: *The New Yorker* (Massine).
THE DRAGONFLY: A solo dance by Pavlova.
DRAGONFLY PRINCESS: *The Clock Symphony* (Massine).
A DRESSER: *Gala Performance* (Tudor).
DRUMMER BOY: *Graduation Ball* (Lichine).
DRUNKARD: *The Fair at Sorochinsk* (Lichine).
DUCK: *Peter and the Wolf* (Bolm).
THE DUENNA: *Don Juan* (Fokine-Allatini).
DUESSA: *The Quest* (Ashton).
THE DUKE: *Gaîté Parisienne* (Massine).
DULCINEA, LADY: *Don Quixote* (Valois).
DWARF: *Infanta* (Lichine).
DYING SWAN: A solo dance by Pavlova.
EASTERN POTENTATE: *Les Sirènes* (Ashton).
EILLEY ORUM: *Ghost Town* (Platoff).
ELDER BROTHER: *Comus* (Helpmann).
ELDEST SISTER: *Pillar of Fire* (Tudor).
ELEANORE, WIFE OF BLUEBEARD: *Bluebeard* (Fokine).
ELIHU: *Job* (Valois).
ENTRÉE DE CUPIDON: *Les Petits Riens* (dances from) (Ashton).
ENVY: *Paganini* (Fokine).
AN EPISODE IN HIS PAST: *Lilac Garden* (Tudor).
EQUESTRIAN: *Jinx* (Lew Christensen).
EROS: *Con Amore* (Lew Christensen).
EURYDICE: *Orpheus* (Balanchine).
EURYDICE: *Orpheus and Eurydice* (Balanchine).
EUSEBIUS: *Le Carnaval* (Fokine).

EVE: *Adam and Eve* (Tudor).
EVIL GENIUS: *The Tales of Hoffmann,* motion picture version (Ashton).
A FAIR PEASANT GIRL: *Cinderella* (Fokine).
THE FAIRY: *Le Baiser de la Fée* (Balanchine).
FAIRY OF BEAUTY: *Sleeping Beauty* (Littlefield).
FAIRY OF DANCE: *Sleeping Beauty* (Littlefield).
FAIRY OF GOODNESS: *Sleeping Beauty* (Littlefield).
FAIRY OF HAPPINESS: *Sleeping Beauty* (Littlefield).
FAIRY OF HOPE: *Sleeping Beauty* (Littlefield).
FAIRY OF SONG: *Sleeping Beauty* (Littlefield).
FAMINE: *Job* (Valois).
FATE: *Les Présages* (Massine).
THE FATHER: *Le Beau Danube* (Massine).
FATHER: *The Fair at Sorochinsk* (Lichine).
FATHER: *Prairie* (Loring).
THE FATHER: *The Prodigal Son* (Lichine).
FATHER OF ST. FRANCIS: *St. Francis* (Massine).
FATHER OF THE ACCUSED: *Fall River Legend* (De Mille).
FATIMA: *La Bayadère* (Filippo Taglioni).
THE FAUN: *The Afternoon of a Faun* (Nijinsky).
THE FAUN: *Helen of Troy* (Lichine).
THE FAUN: *Bacchanale* (Massine).
FAUST: *Mephisto Valse* (Ashton).
FAVORITE SLAVE: *Scheherezade* (Fokine).
FIANCÉ: *Le Baiser de la Fée* (Balanchine).
THE FIANCÉ: *Devil's Holiday* (Ashton).
LA FILLE DE TERPSISCHORE (FROM PARIS) *Gala Performance* (Tudor).
FIORA, SISTER TO THE PRINCE: *Sebastian* (Caton).
THE FIRE: *Seventh Symphony* (Fourth Movement) (Massine).
FIREBIRD: *L'Oiseau de Feu* (Fokine).
THE FIRST HAND: *Le Beau Danube* (Massine).
FIRST HUNTER: *Peter and the Wolf* (Bolm).
FIRST INTRUDER: *The Cage* (Robbins).
THE FISH: *Seventh Symphony* (first movement) (Massine).
FISHERMAN'S WIFE: *The Goldfish* (Tcherepnine).
FLEUR-DE-LYS: *La Esmeralda* (Perrot).
THE FLIRT: *Voices of Spring* (Mordkin).
A FLORENTINE BEAUTY: *Paganini* (Fokine).
A FLORENTINE YOUTH: *Paganini* (Fokine).
FLORESTAN: *Le Carnaval* (Fokine).
FLORETTA (PRINCESS HERMILIA): *Bluebeard* (Fokine).
FLORIMUND, PRINCE: *The Sleeping Beauty* (Petipa).
FLOWER GIRL: *Gaîté Parisienne* (Massine).
FLOWER VENDOR IN EMERALD: *Voices of Spring* (Mordkin).
FLOWER VENDOR IN GREEN: *Voices of Spring* (Mordkin).
FORTUNE TELLER: *Aleko* (Massine).
FOUR ACES: *The Card Game* (Balanchine).
FOUR QUEENS: *The Card Game* (Balanchine).
FRANCESCA: *Francesca da Rimini* (Lichine).
FRANKIE: *Frankie and Johnny* (Page).
FRANTZ: *Coppélia* (Merante).
FRIAR LAURENCE: *Romeo and Juliet* (Tudor).
FRIEND: *The Fair at Sorochinsk* (Lichine).
THE FRIEND: *Pillar of Fire* (Tudor).
FRIEND OF THE BRIDE: *Le Baiser de la Fée* (Balanchine).
FRIEND OF THE RAKE: *The Rake's Progress* (Valois).
FRIVOLITY: *Les Prèsages* (Balanchine).

THE GANGSTER: *Filling Station* (Christensen).
THE GARDENER: *Le Beau Danube* (Massine).
THE GARDENER: *The Hundred Kisses* (Nijinska).
THE GAY MERCHANT: *Petrouchka* (Fokine).
GENERAL: *Voices of Spring* (Mordkin).
GENERAL POLKAN: *Le Coq d'Or* (Fokine).
THE GENTLEMAN WITH HER: *Dim Lustre* (Tudor).
GENTLEMAN WITH THE ROPE: *The Rake's Progress* (Valois).
GHOULS: *The Bells* (Page).
GIANCIOTTO MALATESTA: *Francesca da Rimini* (Lichine).
GINGER CAT BARON: *Les Demoiselles de la Nuit* (Petit).
THE GIRL: *Le Baiser de la Fée* (Balanchine).
GIRL: *Jinx* (Lew Christensen).
GIRL HIKER: *Ghost Town* (Platoff).
GIRL IN BLUE: *Les Biches* (Nijinska).
GIRL IN PINK: *On Stage!* (Kidd).
GIRL LOVER: *Lady of Shalott* (Ashton).
GIRL LOVER: *Paganini* (Fokine).
GIROLAMO: *Francesca da Rimini* (Lichine).
GISELLE: *Giselle* (Coralli-Perrot).
GISELLE: *Graduation Ball* (Lichine).
GIULIETTA: *The Tales of Hoffmann*, motion picture version (Ashton).
GLOVE-SELLER: *Gaîté Parisienne* (Massine).
GODDESS OF THE DANCE (FROM MILAN): *Gala Performance* (Tudor).
THE GODS: *Seventh Symphony* (third movement) (Massine).
GOLD: *Midas* (Fokine).
THE GOLDEN COCKEREL: *Le Coq d'Or* (Fokine).
GOLDEN SLAVE: *Scheherezade* (Fokine).
GOOD DEEDS: *Everyman* (Inglesby).
THE GOOD FAIRY: *Cinderella* (Fokine).
GOSSIP: *Paganini* (Fokine).
GOSSIP COLUMNIST: *The New Yorker* (Massine).
GOULUE: *Bar aux Folies-Bergère* (Valois).
THE GOVERNOR: *The Three-cornered Hat* (Massine).
GRACE: *Orlando's Silver Wedding* (Howard).
GRANDDAUGHTER: *Cap Over Mill* (Gore).
GRANDFATHER: *Peter and the Wolf* (Bolm).
GRAND PAS D'ACTION: *Sleeping Beauty* (Petipa).
GRAVE-DIGGER: *Hamlet* (Helpmann).
THE GREEDY VIRGIN: *Three Virgins and a Devil* (De Mille).
GREEN LADY: *Our Lady's Juggler* (Howard, Salaman).
GRITZKO: *The Fair at Sorochinsk* (Lichine).
GUARDIAN SWALLOW: *Planetomania* (Inglesby).
GUIDON, PRINCE: *Le Coq d'Or* (Fokine).
GUILE: *Paganini* (Fokine).
GUINEVERE: *Francesca da Rimini* (Lichine).
THE GYPSIES: *Petrouchka* (Fokine).
THE GYPSY GIRL: *Devil's Holiday* (Ashton).
HABITUÉ: *Bar aux Folies-Bergère* (Valois).
HAGAR: *Pillar of Fire* (Tudor).
HAIRDRESSER: *Cinderella* (Ashton).
HANDYMAN: *On Stage!* (Kidd).
HARLEQUIN: *Le Carnaval* (Fokine).
HAROLDE, THE POET: *Cakewalk* (Ruthanna Boris).
HARRY: *The Sailors Return* (Howard).
THE HAT-SELLER: *Devil's Holiday* (Ashton).
THE HEAD COACHMAN: *Petrouchka* (Fokine).
THE HEAD MISTRESS: *Graduation Ball* (Lichine).
THE HEAD WRANGLER: *Rodeo* (De Mille).
HELEN: *Helen of Troy* (Lichine).
HÉLÈNE: *Robert le Diable* (Alexander Genée).
HELEN OF TROY: *La Belle Hélène* (Cranko).

HELOISE, WIFE OF BLUEBEARD: *Bluebeard* (Fokine).
THE HEN: *The Birds* (Helpmann).
HENRY VIII: *Henry VIII* (Hightower).
HERA: *Helen of Troy* (Lichine).
HERA: *Undertow* (Tudor).
HERCULES: *The Descent of Hebe* (Tudor).
HERMES: *Helen of Troy* (Fokine).
HERMES: *Helen of Troy* (Lichine).
HERMILIA, PRINCESS (FLORETTA): *Bluebeard* (Fokine).
HERO: *Bogatyri* (Massine).
HERO: *Lola Montez* (Caton).
HERO: *On Stage!* (Kidd).
HE WORE A WHITE TIE: *Dim Lustre* (Tudor).
HILARION: *Giselle* (Coralli-Perrot).
HIPPOLYTE: *Phèdre* (Lifar).
HOFFMANN: *The Tales of Hoffmann*, motion picture version (Ashton).
HOLY STRANGER: *Miracle in the Gorbals* (Helpmann).
HOPAK LEADER: *The Fair at Sorochinsk* (Lichine).
HORSE: *Aleko* (Massine).
HORTENSE, QUEEN OF THE SWAMP LILIES: *Cakewalk* (Ruthanna Boris).
HOTEL GUESTS: *Souvenirs* (Bolender).
HUNCHBACK: *Les Rendez-vous* (Ashton).
THE HUSBAND: *Khadra* (Franca).
HUSBAND: *Lysistrata* (Tudor).
HUSBAND AND WIFE: *Souvenirs* (Bolender).
THE HUSSAR: *Le Beau Danube* (Massine).
HYMEN: *Undertow* (Tudor).
ICARUS: *Icare* (Lifar).
IMPROMPTU DANCE: *Graduation Ball* (Lichine).
THE INNOCENT: *Seventh Symphony* (second movement) (Massine).
INSECT KING: *The Clock Symphony* (Massine).
ISAURE, WIFE OF BLUEBEARD: *Bluebeard* (Fokine).
ISOLDE: *Mad Tristan* (Massine).
IT WAS SPRING: *Dim Lustre* (Tudor).
IVAN: *Aurora's Wedding* (Petipa).
JACK KETCH: *Mr. Punch* (Gore).
THE JAILER: *Symphony Fantastique* (Massine).
JEAN DE BRIENNE: *Raymonda* (Petipa, Ivanov).
JENNY LIND: *Ghost Town* (Platoff).
JINX: *Jinx* (Lew Christensen).
JOB: *Job* (Valois).
JOB'S FRIEND: *Job* (Valois).
JOB'S WIFE: *Job* (Valois).
JOCKEY: *Saratoga* (Massine).
JOHNNY: *Frankie and Johnny* (Page).
THE JOKER: *Card Party* (Balanchine).
JOSEPH: *La Légende de Joseph* (Fokine).
JOSEPHINE: *The Wedding Bouquet* (Ashton).
JOTA: *The Three-cornered Hat* (Massine).
JUDD: *Laurie Makes Up Her Mind; Oklahoma!* (De Mille).
JUGGLER: *Our Lady's Juggler* (Howard, Salaman).
JULIA: *The Wedding Bouquet* (Ashton).
JULIET, DAUGHTER TO CAPULET: *Romeo and Juliet* (Tudor).
JUNO: *The Judgment of Paris* (Tudor).
KHIVRIA: *The Fair at Sorochinsk* (Lichine).
THE KING: *The Hundred Kisses* (Nijinska).
KING: *Illuminations* (Ashton).
THE KING: *Princess Aurora* (Dolin).
KING BOBICHE: *Bluebeard* (Fokine).
KING CLAUDIUS: *Hamlet* (Helpmann).
KING DODON: *Le Coq d'Or* (Fokine).
KNIGHT OF DEATH: *Bacchanale* (Massine).
THE KING OF DIAMONDS: *La Boutique Fantasque* (Massine).
THE KING OF SPADES: *La Boutique Fantasque* (Massine).

THE KING OF THE DANDIES: *Le Beau Danube* (Massine).
KINSMAN: *Everyman* (Inglesby).
KINSMAN'S WIFE: *Everyman* (Inglesby).
THE KNIGHT: *St. Francis* (Massine).
KOSTCHEI: *L'Oiseau de Feu* (Fokine).
THE LADY: *The Lady and the Fool* (Cranko).
LADY AND HER ESCORT: *Souvenirs* (Bolender).
LADY CAPULET: *Romeo and Juliet* (Tudor).
LADY DULCINEA: *Don Quixote* (Valois).
THE LADY-GAY: *Union Pacific* (Massine).
LADY MONTAGUE: *Romeo and Juliet* (Tudor).
A LADY NO BETTER THAN SHE SHOULD BE: *Tally-Ho* (De Mille).
THE LADY WITH HIM: *Dim Lustre* (Tudor).
LAERTES: *Hamlet* (Helpmann).
LAMB: *Helen of Troy* (Lichine).
LAMPITO: *Lysistrata* (Tudor).
LAMPLIGHTER: *Voices of Spring* (Mordkin).
LANCELOT: *Francesca da Rimini* (Lichine).
LAND: *Prairie* (Loring).
LANDLADY OF THE TAVERN: *Coppélia* (Merante).
LAURIE: *Laurie Makes Up Her Mind; Oklahoma!* (De Mille).
LAWYER OF MR. TAYLOR: *The Prospect Before Us* (Valois).
LEADER OF THE BACCHANTES: *Orpheus* (Balanchine).
LEADER OF THE CANCAN GIRLS: *Gaîté Parisienne* (Massine).
LEADER OF THE JUNIOR CADETS: *Graduation Ball* (Lichine).
LEADER OF THE JUNIOR GIRLS: *Graduation Ball* (Lichine).
LEADER OF THE FURIES: *Orpheus* (Balanchine).
"LEO" AOLO: *Horoscope* (Ashton).
LEPIDOPTERIST: *Promenade* (Valois).
LETO, MOTHER OF APOLLO: *Apollon Musagètes* (Balanchine).
LIEUTENANT: *Voices of Spring* (Mordkin).
LILAC FAIRY: *Sleeping Beauty* (Petipa).
LA LIONNE: *Gaîté Parisienne* (Massine).
LISETTE (LISE): *La Fille Mal Gardée* (Dauberval-Nijinska).
LITTLE KING: *The New Yorker* (Massine).
LIZZIE BORDEN: *Fall River Legend* (De Mille).
LOLA MONTEZ: *Bacchanale* (Massine).
LORD BURLEIGH: *Lord of Burleigh* (Ashton).
LORD OF THE MANOR: *Coppélia* (Merante).
THE LORD OF THE MOUNTAIN: *Cinderella* (Fokine).
THE LORD OF THE VALE: *Cinderella* (Fokine).
LOUIS II: *Bacchanale* (Massine).
LOUIS THE ILLUSIONIST: *Cakewalk* (Ruthanna Boris).
THE LOVER: *L'Epreuve d'Amour* (Fokine).
LOVER: *Lady of Shalott* (Ashton).
LOVER: *Les Masques* (Tudor).
LOVER: *Miracle in the Gorbals* (Helpmann).
LOVER OF CAROLINE: *Lilac Garden* (Tudor).
LOVERS: *Miracle in the Gorbals* (Helpmann).
THE LUSTFUL VIRGIN: *Three Virgins and a Devil* (De Mille).
LYCEION: *Daphnis and Chloe* (Fokine).
LYSISTRATA: *Lysistrata* (Tudor).
MAC, THE FILLING-STATION ATTENDANT *Filling Station* (Christensen).
MADAME CHRYSANTHÈME: *Madame Chrysanthème* (Ashton).
MADDALENA, SISTER TO THE PRINCE: *Sebastian* (Caton).
MLLE. THEODORE: *The Prospect Before Us* (Valois).
MAGICIAN: *Comus* (Helpmann).

A MAID: *Souvenirs* (Bolender).
MAIDEN: *Death and the Maiden* (Howard).
MAITRE DE BALLET: *Gala Performance* (Tudor).
MAITRE DE BALLET: *On Stage!* (Kidd).
MALVOLIO: *Cross-gartered* (Tudor).
THE MAN: *Facsimile* (Robbins).
MAN: *Prairie* (Loring).
THE MAN: *Seventh Symphony* (first movement) (Massine).
THE MAN: *Souvenirs* (Bolender).
MAN ABOUT TOWN: *Souvenirs* (Bolender).
THE MANAGER: *Le Beau Danube* (Massine).
MANDARIN: *L'Épreuve d'Amour* (Fokine).
MANDARIN: *The Fairy Queen* (Ashton).
MAN IN GREY: *Souvenirs* (Bolender).
THE MAN SHE MUST MARRY: *Lilac Garden* (Tudor).
MARGUERITE: *Mephisto Valse* (Ashton).
MARIA: *Cross-gartered* (Tudor).
MARIUCCIA: *The Good-humored Ladies* (Massine).
MARQUIS: *The Good-humored Ladies* (Massine).
MARS: *Mars and Venus* (Ashton).
MARS: *The Planets* (Tudor).
MASTER OF CEREMONIES: *Princess Aurora* (Dolin).
MASTER OF TREGENNIS: *The Haunted Ballroom* (Valois).
MAYOR OF SOROCHINSK: *The Fair at Sorochinsk* (Lichine).
MAZURKA: *Les Sylphides* (Fokine).
MAZURKA: *Vienna—1814* (Massine).
MEDUSA: *Undertow* (Tudor).
MELANCHOLIC VARIATION: *The Four Temperaments* (Balanchine).
THE MELON HAWKER: *La Boutique Fantasque* (Massine).
MENELAUS: *Helen of Troy* (Fokine).
MENELAUS: *Helen of Troy* (Lichine).
"THE MENKEN": *Ghost Town* (Platoff).
MEPHISTO: *Mephisto Valse* (Ashton).
MERCURY: *The Descent of Hebe* (Tudor).
MERCUTIO, FRIEND OF ROMEO: *Romeo and Juliet* (Tudor).
MERMAID: *Sea Legend* (Stevenson).
MERVEILLEUSE: *Promenade* (Ashton).
THE MEXICAN GIRL: *Union Pacific* (Massine).
MEXICAN SWEETHART: *Billy the Kid* (Loring).
MIDAS: *Midas* (Fokine).
THE MILLER: *The Three-cornered Hat* (Massine).
THE MILLER'S WIFE: *The Three-cornered Hat* (Massine).
MINERVA: *The Judgment of Paris* (Tudor).
THE MINOTAUR: *Labyrinth* (Massine).
MIRAKEL, DOCTOR: *The Tales of Hoffmann*, motion picture version (Ashton).
MISTRESS: *Con Amore* (Lew Christensen).
MITCH: *A Streetcar Named Desire* (Bettis).
MONTAGUE: *Romeo and Juliet* (Tudor).
MOON: *Horoscope* (Ashton).
MOONDOG, A CLOWN: *The Lady and the Fool* (Cranko).
THE MORMON MISSIONARY: *Union Pacific* (Massine).
MORTAL UNDER MARS: *The Planets* (Tudor).
MORTAL UNDER NEPTUNE: *The Planets* (Tudor).
MORTAL UNDER VENUS: *The Planets* (Tudor).
LA MORTE AMOUREUSE: *Don Juan* (Ashton).
THE MOTHER: *Le Baiser de la Fée* (Balanchine).
THE MOTHER: *Le Beau Danube* (Massine).
MOTHER: *Prairie* (Loring).

MOTHER OF BILLY THE KID: *Billy the Kid* (Loring).
MOTHER SIMONE: *La Fille Mal Gardée* (Dauberval-Nijinska).
THE MOTORIST: *Filling Station* (Christensen).
MUSICIAN: *The Rake's Progress* (Valois).
MRS. SYLVIA TEBRICK: *Lady into Fox* (Howard).
MR. PUNCH: *Mr. Punch* (Gore).
MR. TEBRICK: *Lady into Fox* (Howard).
MYRTHA, QUEEN OF THE WILIS: *Giselle* (Coralli).
NELLY BLY: *Frankie and Johnny* (Page).
NEMESIS: *Undertow* (Tudor).
NICLO THE WAITER: *The Good-humored Ladies* (Massine).
NIGHT: *The Descent of Hebe* (Tudor).
THE NIGHTINGALE: *The Birds* (Helpmann).
NINKA: *La Bayadère* (Filippo Taglioni).
NOVICE: *The Cage* (Robbins).
NUTCRACKER PRINCE: *Casse Noisette* (Ivanov).
THE NYMPH: *The Afternoon of a Faun* (Nijinsky).
THE NYMPH: *Bacchanale* (Massine).
NYMPH OF THE SPRING: *The Fairy Queen* (Ashton).
OBEDIENCE: *St. Francis* (Massine).
OBERON: *The Fairy Queen* (Ashton).
ODALISQUE: *Shcherezade* (Fokine).
ODETTA: *Swan Lake* (Mordkin, after Petipa).
ODETTE-ODILE: *Swan Lake* (Petipa).
ODILLIA: *Swan Lake* (Mordkin, after Petipa).
OEDIPUS: *La Rencontre* (Lichine).
THE OFFICER: *Gaîté Parisienne* (Massine).
OFFICIAL: *Miracle in the Gorbals* (Helpmann).
THE OLD CHARLATAN: *Petrouchka* (Fokine).
THE OLD GENERAL: *Graduation Ball* (Lichine).
OLD LADY: *Voices of Spring* (Mordkin).
THE OLD LORD: *Devil's Holiday* (Ashton).
OLD MAN: *Khadra* (Franca).
OLD MAN: *Voices of Spring* (Mordkin).
OLD PROSPECTOR: *Ghost Town* (Platoff).
THE OLD SHEPHERD: *Symphonie Fantastique* (Massine).
THE OLD WOMAN: *Devil's Holiday* (Ashton).
OLIFOUR: *La Bayadère* (Filippo Taglioni).
OLIVIA: *Twelfth Night* (Howard).
OLYMPIA, THE DOLL: *The Tales of Hoffmann*, motion picture version (Ashton).
OPHELIA: *Hamlet* (Helpmann).
ORESTES: *Helen of Troy* (Fokine).
ORESTES: *Helen of Troy* (Lichine).
ORIENTAL: *Les Sirènes* (Ashton).
ORLANDO, LOVER OF THE QUEEN: *Bluebeard* (Fokine).
ORLANDO, THE MARMELADE CAT: *Orlando's Silver Wedding* (Howard).
ORPHEUS: *Orpheus* (Balanchine).
ORPHEUS: *Orpheus and Eurydice* (Balanchine).
ORSINO: *Twelfth Night* (Howard).
ORSON HYDE, MORMON APOSTLE: *Ghost Town* (Platoff).
PAGANINI: *Paganini* (Fokine).
PALLAS ATHENE: *Helen of Troy* (Lichine).
PAN: *Aleko* (Massine).
PANTALON: *Le Carnaval* (Fokine).
PAOLO MALATESTA: *Francesca da Rimini* (Lichine).
PAPILLON: *Le Carnaval* (Fokine).
PARASSIA, KHIVRIA'S STEPDAUGHTER: *The Fair at Sorochinsk* (Lichine).
PARIS: *La Belle Hélène* (Cranko).
PARIS: *Helen of Troy* (Lichine).
PARIS, A YOUNG NOBLEMAN: *Romeo and Juliet* (Tudor).
PAS DE DEUX: *Casse Noisette* (Ivanov).

PAS DE DEUX: *Don Quichotte* (Petipa).
PAS DE DEUX: *Don Quixote* (Valois).
PAS DE DEUX: *Giselle* (Coralli, Perrot).
PAS DE DEUX: *Les Patineurs* (Ashton).
PAS DE DEUX: *Promenade* (Valois).
PAS DES PATINEUSES: *Les Patineurs* (Ashton).
PAS DE TROIS: *Promenade* (Valois).
PAS DE TROIS: *Swan Lake* (Petipa).
PAS DE SIX: *Les Patineurs* (Ashton).
PASSERS-BY: *Fancy Free* (Robbins).
PASTOR: *Fall River Legend* (De Mille).
PAT GARRETT, FRIEND OF BILLY THE KID: *Billy the Kid* (Loring).
PAVANE: *Capriole Suite* (Ashton).
PEASANT PAS DE DEUX: *Orpheus and Eurydice* (Valois).
PEDDLAR: *The Fair at Sorochinsk* (Lichine).
PERFORMER: *Gallant Assembly* (Tudor).
PERPETUUM MOBILE: *Graduation Ball* (Lichine).
PERSONAGE: *Les Masques* (Tudor).
THE PERUVIAN: *Gaîté Parisienne* (Massine).
PESTILENCE: *Job* (Valois).
PETER: *Peter and the Wolf* (Bolm).
PETROUCHKA: *Petrouchka* (Fokine).
PHÈDRE: *Phèdre* (Lifar).
PHLEGMATIC VARIATION: *The Four Temperaments* (Balanchine).
PHOEBUS DE CHATEAUPERS: *La Esmeralda* (Perrot).
PIERRE: *Madame Chrysanthème* (Ashton).
PIERROT: *Le Carnaval* (Fokine).
PINEAPPLE POLL: *Pineapple Poll* (Cranko).
PIRATE CHIEF: *Daphnis and Chloe* (Fokine, Ashton).
THE PLANT: *Seventh Symphony* (First movement (Massine).
PLAYER: *Le Rugby* (Salaman).
POET: *Les Demoiselles de la Nuit* (Petit).
POET: *Illuminations* (Ashton).
POET: *Night Shadow* (Balanchine).
POET: *Les Sylphides* (Fokine).
POLKA: *Façade* (Ashton).
POLLUX: *Labyrinth* (Massine).
POLLUX: *Undertow* (Tudor).
POLONIUS: *Hamlet* (Helpmann).
POLOVTSIAN CHIEF: *Prince Igor* (Fokine).
POLYMNIA: *Apollon Musagètes* (Balanchine).
POLYHYMNIA: *Undertow* (Tudor).
THE POOR MAN: *St. Francis* (Massine).
POPULAR SONG: *Façade* (Ashton).
POSTCARDS: *Laurie Makes Up Her Mind; Oklahoma!* (De Mille).
POVERTY: *St. Francis* (Massine).
PRAYER: *Coppélia* (Saint-Léon).
PRÉLUDE: *Les Sylphides* (Fokine).
PRIDE: *The Quest* (Ashton).
THE PRIGGISH VIRGIN: *Three Virgins and a Devil* (De Mille).
PRINCE: *Cinderella* (Ashton).
THE PRINCE: *Cinderella* (Fokine).
THE PRINCE: *The Hundred Kisses* (Nijinska).
PRINCE: *The Mermaid* (Howard, Salaman).
THE PRINCE: *Sebastian* (Caton).
PRINCE APHRON, SON OF KING DODON: *Le Coq d'Or* (Fokine).
PRINCE CHARMING: *Princess Aurora* (Dolin).
PRINCE CHARMING: *Cinderella* (Ashton).
PRINCE DESIRE: *Sleeping Beauty* (Littlefield).
PRINCE FLORIMUND: *The Sleeping Princess* (Petipa).
PRINCE GUIDON, SON OF KING DODON: *Le Coq d'Or* (Fokine).
PRINCE FROM THE EAST: *Sleeping Beauty* (Littlefield).
PRINCE FROM THE NORTH: *Sleeping Beauty* (Littlefield).

PRINCE FROM THE SOUTH: *Sleeping Beauty* (Littlefield).
PRINCE FROM THE WEST: *Sleeping Beauty* (Littlefield).
PRINCE SAPPHIRE: *Bluebeard* (Fokine).
PRINCESS: *The Clock Symphony* (Massine).
THE PRINCESS: *The Hundred Kisses* (Nijinska).
PRINCESS: *Infanta* (Lichine).
PRINCESS AURORA: *Princess Aurora* (Dolin).
PRINCESS AURORA: *The Sleeping Beauty* (Littlefield).
PRINCESS AURORA: *The Sleeping Beauty* (Petipa).
PRINCESS FLORINE: *The Sleeping Beauty, Bluebeard Variation* (Petipa).
PRINCESS HERMILIA (FLORETTA): *Bluebird* (Fokine).
THE PRODIGAL SON: *The Prodigal Son* (Balanchine).
THE PRODIGAL SON: *The Prodigal Son* (Jooss).
THE PRODIGAL SON: *The Prodigal Son* (Lichine).
PRODUCER: *Adam Zero* (Helpmann).
PROFANE LOVE: *Illuminations* (Ashton).
PROSTITUTE: *Miracle in the Gorbals* (Helpmann).
PSYCHE: *L'Amour et Son Amour* (Babilée).
PSYCHE: *The Masque of Comus, Prologue* (Inglesby).
PUDICITIA: *Undertow* (Tudor).
PUSS-IN-BOOTS: *Aurora's Wedding* (Petipa).
PUSS-IN-BOOTS AND THE LITTLE WHITE CAT: *Fairy Tale Divertissement, Sleeping Beauty* (Littlefield).
QUASIMODO: *La Esmeralda* (Perrot).
QUEEN: *Illuminations* (Ashton).
THE QUEEN: *Princess Aurora* (Dolin).
QUEEN: *Swan Lake* (Mordkin, after Petipa).
QUEEN: *Thamar* (Fokine).
QUEEN CLEMENTINE: *Bluebeard* (Fokine).
QUEEN GERTRUDE: *Hamlet* (Helpmann).
THE QUEEN OF CLUBS: *La Boutique Fantasque* (Massine).
THE QUEEN OF HEARTS: *La Boutique Fantasque* (Massine).
QUEEN OF SHEMAKHA: *Le Coq d'Or* (Fokine).
QUEEN OF THE DANCE (FROM MOSCOW): *Gala Performance* (Tudor).
QUEEN OF THE TRIBE: *The Cage* (Robbins).
QUEEN OF THE WILIS: *Giselle* (Coralli) .
RAKE: *Con Amore* (Lew Christensen).
RAKE: *The Rake's Progress* (Valois).
RALSTON: *Ghost Town* (Platoff).
THE RANCHER'S DAUGHTER: *Rodeo* (De-Mille).
RAY, THE TRUCK DRIVER: *Filling Station* (Christensen).
RED AND BLACK: *Rouge et Noir* (Massine)
RED CASTLE: *Checkmate* (Valois).
RED COAT: *The Fair at Sorochinsk* (Lichine).
THE REDHEAD: *Fancy Free* (Robbins)
REDHEADED BANDIT: *Carmen* (Petit)
RED KING: *Checkmate* (Valois).
RED KNIGHT: *Checkmate* (Valois).
RED QUEEN: *Checkmate* (Valois).
RED RIDINGHOOD AND THE WOLF: *Fairy Tale Divertissement, Sleeping Beauty* (Littlefield).
A REFLECTION: *Dim Lustre* (Tudor).
LA REINE DE LA DANSE (FROM MOSCOW): *Gala Performance* (Tudor).
THE RICH BOY: *Filling Station* (Christensen).
THE RICH GIRL: *Filling Station* (Christensen).
RIGADON: *Scuola di Ballo* (Massine).
RIMBAUD: *Illuminations* (Ashton).
RINGMASTER: *Jinx* (Lew Christensen).

ROMEO, SON OF MONTAGUE: *Romeo and Juliet* (Tudor).
RONDINE: A solo dance by Pavlova.
ROSALINDE, WIFE OF BLUEBEARD: *Bluebeard* (Fokine).
ROSALINE: *Romeo and Juliet* (Tudor).
ROSE SPIRIT: *The Specter of the Rose* (Fokine).
ROY, THE TRUCK DRIVER: *Filling Station* (Christensen).
A RUSSIAN MERCHANT: *La Boutique Fantasque* (Massine).
RUSSIAN SAILOR: *The Red Poppy* (Glière).
SABRINA: *Comus* (Helpmann).
SACHER MASOCH: *Bacchanale* (Massine).
SACHER MASOCH'S WIFE: *Bacchanale* (Massine)
SACRED LOVE: *Illuminations* (Ashton).
SAGE: *Le Sacre du Printemps* (Massine).
SAILOR: *Con Amore* (Lew Christensen).
SAILOR: *Sea Legend* (Richardson).
SAILORS (3): *Fancy Free* (Robbins).
ST. FRANCIS: *St. Francis* (Massine).
ST. GEORGE: *The Quest* (Ashton).
SALOME: *The Dance of Salome* (Franca).
SALOME: *Dance of the Seven Veils* (Petrov).
SALOME: *Salomé* (Hightower).
SAMUEL THE PROPHET: *David Triomphant* (Lifar).
SANCHO PANZA: *Don Quixote* (Valois).
SANGUINIC VARIATION: *The Four Temperaments* (Balanchine).
SAPPHIRE, PRINCE: *Bluebeard* (Fokine).
SARACEN KNIGHTS: *The Quest* (Ashton).
SATAN: *Job* (Valois).
SATAN: *Paganini* (Fokine).
SATYRISCI: *Undertow* (Tudor).
THE SATYRS (3): *Bacchanale* (Massine).
SCANDAL: *Paganini* (Fokine).
SCHLEMIL: *The Tales of Hoffmann*, motion picture version (Ashton).
SCOTSMAN: *Graduation Ball* (Lichine).
SEBASTIAN: *Sebastian* (Caton).
SECOND INTRUDER: *The Cage* (Robbins).
SECOND RED KNIGHT: *Checkmate* (Valois).
SERPENT: *Adam and Eve* (Tudor).
THE SERPENT: *Seventh Symphony* (first movement) (Massine).
THE SERVANT: *Don Juan* (Fokine-Allatini).
SERVING-MAID: *The Gods Go A-Begging* (Balanchine).
SERVING-MAID: *The Gods Go A-Begging* (Valois).
SEVEN DEADLY SINS: *Fanciulla delle Rose* (Stoff).
SEXTON: *The Fair at Sorochinsk* (Lichine).
SGANARELLE: *Don Juan* (Fokine-Allatini).
SHADOW OF THE FAIRY: *Le Baiser de la Fée* (Balanchine).
SHAHIAR: *Scheherazade* (Fokine).
SHAH ZEMAN: *Scheherazade* (Fokine).
SHEPHERD: *The Gods Go A-Begging* (Valois).
SHEPHERD-GOD: *The Gods Go A-Begging* (Valois).
SHE WORE A PERFUME: *Dim Lustre* (Tudor).
THE SHOPKEEPER: *La Boutique Fantasque* (Massine).
SIEGFRIED: *Swan Lake* (Petipa).
SIEGFRIED: *Swan Lake* (Mordkin, after Petipa).
SILENI: *Undertow* (Tudor).
THE SIREN: *The Prodigal Son* (Lichine).
SIREN OF THE SEA: *Sea Legend* (Stevenson).
SIR LANCELOT: *The Lady of Shalott* (Ashton).
SIR PLUME: *The Rape of the Lock* (Howard).
THE SISTERS OF THE PRODIGAL SON: *The Prodigal Son* (Lichine).
SIX HUNTERS: *Peter and the Wolf* (Bolm).

THE SKY: *Seventh Symphony* (First Movement) (Massine).
SLEEPWALKER: *Night Shadows* (Balanchine).
SLEIGHT OF FEET: *Cakewalk* (Ruthanna Boris).
THE SNOB: *La Boutique Fantasque* (Massine).
SOCIAL WORKER: *Miracle in the Gorbals* (Helpmann).
SPANISH BRIDE: *The Mermaid* (Howard, Salaman).
SPARROWS (TWO): *The Birds* (Helpmann).
SPECTER: *Specter of the Rose* (Fokine).
SPHINX: *La Rencontre* (Lichine).
THE SPIDER: *The Spider's Banquet (Le Festin de l'Araignée)* (Howard).
THE SPIRIT OF CREATION: *Seventh Symphony* (First Movement) (Massine).
SPIRIT OF WINE: *Comus* (Helpmann).
SPORTS GIRL: *Le Boxing* (Salaman).
SQUARE DANCE CALLER: *Rodeo* (De Mille).
STANLEY KOWALSKI: *A Streetcar Named Desire* (Bettis).
THE STATE TROOPER: *Filling Station* (Christensen).
STELLA KOWALSKI: *A Streetcar Named Desire* (Bettis).
STEPMOTHER OF THE ACCUSED: *Fall River Legend* (De Mille).
STRANGER PLAYER: *The Haunted Ballroom* (Valois).
THE STREAM: *Seventh Symphony* (First Movement) (Massine).
STREET BOY: *Miracle in the Gorbals* (Helpmann).
STREET DANCER: *Aleko* (Massine).
STREET DANCER: *The Prospect Before Us* (Valois).
STREET DANCER: *Le Beau Danube* (Massine).
THE STREET DANCERS: *Petrouchka* (Fokine).
SUGAR PLUM FAIRY: *Casse Noisette* (Ivanov).
SUITE OF THE KNIGHT OF DEATH (2): *Bacchanale* (Massine).
SUITOR: *Récamier* (Ashton).
THE SUN: *Seventh Symphony* (First Movement) (Massine).
SURVEYOR OF THE IRISH CREW: *Union Pacific* (Massine).
SWANILDA: *Coppélia* (Merante).
THE SWINEHERD: *The Hundred Kisses* (Nijinska).
SYLVIA: *Sylvia* (Merante).
THE TAILOR: *Le Roi Nu* (Lifar).
TAMBOURINE DANCER: *Don Juan* (Fokine-Allatini).
TANCRED: *The Duel* (Dollar).
TANGO: *Façade* (Ashton).
TARANTELLA DANCERS: *La Boutique Fantasque* (Massine).
TARANTELLA: *Cimarosiana* (Massine).
TERPSICHORE: *Apollon Musagètes* (Balanchine).
THEME: *The Four Temperaments* (Balanchine).
THESEUS: *Labyrinth* (Massine).
THIEF: *Con Amore* (Lew Christensen).
THOMAS: *La Fille Mal Gardée* (Dauberval-Nijinska).
THREE COMPANIONS: *St. Francis* (Massine).
THE THREE GRACES: *Bacchanale* (Massine).
THREE GRACES: *Cakewalk* (Ruthanna Boris).
THREE GYPSIES: *The Fair at Sorochinsk* (Lichine).
THREE SINGERS: *Frankie and Johnny* (Page).
THREE YOUNG GIRLS: *Souvenirs* (Bolender).
TIMID MAN: *The New Yorker* (Massine).
TORDION: *Capriol Suite* (Ashton).
TORERO: *Of Love and Death* (Ricarda).
TORTONI: *Gaîté Parisienne* (Massine).

TRAINER: *Le Boxing* (Salaman).
THE TRANSGRESSOR: *Undertow* (Tudor).
TRAPEZIST: *Circus Wings* (Salaman).
TREPAK: *Casse Noisette*, act III (Ivanov).
TRISTAN: *Mad Tristan* (Massine).
TULIP, THE NEGRESS: *The Sailor's Return* (Howard).
TUTOR: *Swan Lake* (Petipa).
THE BACHANTES: *Bacchanale* (Massine).
TWO CADETS: *Voices of Spring* (Mordkin).
TWO CUPIDS: *Bacchanale* (Massine).
TWO FRIENDS OF THE AMBASSADOR: *L'Épreuve d'Amour* (Fokine).
TWO NYMPHS: *Apollon Musagètes* (Balanchine).
TWO OTHERS SOMEWHAT WORSE: *Tally-Ho* (De Mille).
THE TWO UGLY SISTERS: *Cinderella* (Fokine).
TYBALT, NEPHEW OF LADY CAPULET: *Romeo and Juliet* (Tudor).
TYL EULENSPIEGEL: *Tyl Eulenspiegel* (Nijinsky).
UNKNOWN: *La Bayadère* (Filippo Taglioni).
URSULA: *The Haunted Ballroom* (Valois).
THE VAGABOND: *The Prodigal Son* (Lichine).
VAGABOND GIRL: *The Vagabonds* (Burke).
VALSE CAPRICE: A solo dance by Pavlova.
VAMP-DE-LUXE: *Le Boxing* (Salaman).
VENUS: *Bacchanale* (Massine).
VENUS: *La Belle Hélène* (Cranko).
VENUS: *Cakewalk* (Ruthanna Boris).
VENUS: *The Judgment of Paris* (Tudor).
VENUS: *Mars and Venus* (Ashton).
VIEUX MARCHEUR: *Bar aux Folies-Bergère* (Valois).
VIRGIN: *Fanciulla delle Rose* (Staff).
VIRTUOSO: *La Muse s'Amuse* (Howard).
VOLUPIA: *Undertow* (Tudor).
VON ROTHBART (SORCERER): *Swan Lake* (Mordkin, after Petipa).
WAITER: *The Judgment of Paris* (Tudor).
WALTZ: *Façade* (Ashton).
WALTZ: *Serenade* (Turner).
WALTZ: *Les Sylphides* (Fokine).
WAR: *Job* (Valois).
WARRIOR: *Prince Igor* (Fokine).
WHITE WITCH: *The Fair at Sorochinsk* (Lichine).
WHO WAS SHE?: *Dim Lustre* (Tudor).
WIFE OF THE MOTORIST: *Filling Station* (Christensen).
WILD PONY: *Cakewalk* (Ruthanna Boris).
WILFRID: *Giselle* (Coralli-Perrot).
THE WILIS: *Giselle* (Coralli).
WINTER: *The Fairy Queen* (Ashton).
WINTER FAIRY: *Cinderella* (Ashton).
WISE VIRGINS: *The Wise Virgins* (Ashton).
WITCH: *Le Sacre du Printemps* (Massine).
WITCH: *Selina* (Howard).
WIVES OF ORSON HYDE (5): *Ghost Town* (Platoff).
THE WOLF: *Le Loup* (Petit).
WOLF: *Peter and the Wolf* (Bolm).
WOLFGANG, SIEGFRIED'S TUTOR: *Swan Lake* (Mordkin, after Petipa).
WOMAN: *Adam Zero* (Helpmann).
THE WOMAN: *Facsimile* (Robbins).
THE WOMAN: *Seventh Symphony* (First Movement) (Massine).
THE WOMAN: *Seventh Symphony* (Second Movement) (Massine).
THE WOMAN: *Souvenirs* (Bolender).
THE WOMAN IN THE BALL DRESS: *Apparitions* (Ashton).
WOMAN ON HORSEBACK: *Virginia Sampler* (Bettis).
WOMAN WHO BITES DIAMONDS: *La Croqueuse de Diamantes* (Petit).

WOOD NYMPH: *The Dryad* (Genée).
YELLOW CAT BARON: *Les Demoiselles de la Nuit* (Petit).
YOUNGER SISTER: *The Fugitive* (Howard).
YOUNG GIRL: *Confessional* (Gore).
YOUNG GIRL: *Le Loup* (Petit).
YOUNG GIRL: *The Rake's Progress* (Valois).
YOUNG GIPSY: *Aleko* (Massine).
THE YOUNG LOVER: *Devil's Holiday* (Ashton).
YOUNG MAN: *Horoscope* (Ashton).
THE YOUNG MAN FROM THE HOUSE OPPOSITE: *The Pillar of Fire* (Tudor).
A YOUNG MUSICIAN: *Symphonie Fantastique* (Massine).
THE YOUNG SHEPHERD: *Symphonie, Fantastique* (Massine).
YOUNG WIFE: *Don Juan* (Ashton).
YOUNGEST SISTER: *Pillar of Fire* (Tudor).
A YOUTH: *Three Virgins and a Devil* (De Mille).
ZEMPHIRA: *Aleko* (Massine).
ZEMPHIRA'S FATHER: *Aleko* (Massine).
ZOBEIDE: *Scheherazade* (Fokine).
ZOLOË: *La Bayadère* (Filippo Taglioni).
ZULMA: *La Bayadère* (Filippo Taglioni).

Characters from the Great Operas

See also **Operas, Grand; Singing Voices, Types of**

Note: B=bass; BAR=baritone; M-S=mezzosoprano; C=contralto; S=soprano; T=tenor.

L'ABATE DI CHASEUIL (T): *Adriana Lecouvreur.*
THE ABBÉ (T): *Andrea Chénier.*
THE ABBESS (dancer): *Robert le Diable.*
THE ABBESS (M-S): *Suor Angelica.*
ABDALLAH (B): *Oberon.*
ABDALLO (T): *Nabucco.*
ABDULLAH (speaking role): *Oberon.*
ABIGAILLE (S): *Nabucco.*
ABIMELECH (B): *Samson and Delilah.*
ABUL HASSAN ALI EBN BEKAR (B): *The Barber of Bagdad.*
AHILLES (T): *Iphigenia in Aulis.*
ADALGISA (S): *Norma.*
ADELAIDE (M-S): *Arabella.*
ADELE (S): *Die Fledermaus.*
ADELMA (M-S): *Turandot* (Busoni).
ADINA (S): *The Elixir of Love.*
ADMETUS (T): *Alceste.*
ADOLAR (T): *Euryanthe.*
ADORNO GABRIELE (T): *Simon Boccanegra.*
ADRIANA LECOUVREUR (S): *Adriana Lecouvreur.*
ADRIANO (M-S): *Rienzi.*
AEGISTHUS (B): *Elektra.*
AELFRIDA (S): *The King's Henchman.*
AENEAS (T): *The Trojans,* Parts I, II.
AENNCHEN (S): *Der Freischütz.*
AETHELWOLD (T): *The King's Henchman.*
AFRA (C): *La Wally.*
AFRON, PRINCE (BAR): *Le Coq d'Or.*
AGAMEMNON (B): *Iphigenia in Aulis.*
AGATHE (S): *Der Freischütz.*
AGNES (M-S): *The Bartered Bride.*
AGNES (S): *Der Freischütz.*
AHMAD (B): *Mârouf.*
AH YOE (S): *L'Oracolo.*
AÏDA (S): *Aïda.*
AITHRA (S): *The Egyptian Helen.*
ALBERICH (BAR): *Das Rheingold.*
ALBERICH (BAR): *Siegfried.*
ALBERICH (BAR): *Die Götterdämmerung.*
ALBERT (B): *La Juive.*
ALBERT (BAR): *Werther.*
ALBERT HERRING (T): *Albert Herring.*

ALBIANI, PAOLO (B): *Simon Boccanegra.*
ALBINE (M-S): *Thaïs.*
ALBRECHT VON BRANDENBURG (T): *Mathis der Maler.*
THE ALCADE (B): *Maritana.*
ALCESTE (S): *Alceste.*
ALCESTIS (S): *Alceste.*
ALCINDORO (B): *La Bohème.*
ALCMENE (M-S): *The Love of Danae.*
ALESSIO (B): *La Sonnambula.*
ALFIO (BAR): *Cavalleria Rusticana.*
ALFONSO, DON (BAR): *Così Fan Tutte.*
ALFONSO XI (BAR): *La Favorita.*
ALFONSO D'ARCOS (T): *The Dumb Girl of Portici.*
ALFONSO D'ESTE (BAR): *Lucretia Borgia.*
ALFRED (T): *Die Fledermaus.*
ALFREDO GERMONT (T): *La Traviata.*
ALI (BAR): *Mârouf.*
ALICE (M-S): *Lucia di Lammermoor.*
ALICE (S): *Robert le Diable.*
ALIDORO (B): *La Cenerentola.*
ALMANZOR (speaking role): *Oberon.*
ALMAVIVA, COUNT (T): *The Barber of Seville.*
ALMAVIVA, COUNT (BAR): *The Marriage of Figaro.*
ALMAVIVA, COUNTESS (S): *The Marriage of Figaro.*
THE ALMS COLLECTOR (S): *Suor Angelica.*
ALTAIR (BAR): *The Egyptian Helen.*
ALTOUM (T): *Turandot.*
ALTOUM (B): *Turandot* (Busoni).
ALVAR, DON (T): *L'Africaine.*
ALVARO, DON (T): *La Forza del Destino.*
ALWA (T): *Lulu.*
AMANTIO DI NICOLAO (BAR): *Gianni Schicchi.*
AMBROGIO (B): *The Barber of Seville.*
AMELIA (C): *Le Coq d'Or.*
AMELIA (S): *Un Ballo in Maschera.*
AMELIA BOCCANEGRA (S): *Simon Boccanegra.*
AMFORTAS (B-BAR): *Parsifal.*
AMINTA (S): *The Silent Woman.*
AMINA (S): *La Sonnambula.*
AMNERIS (M-S): *Aïda.*
AMONASRO (BAR): *Aïda.*
AMOR (S): *Orpheus and Eurydice.*
ANAIDE (C): *Zaza.*
ANDRES (T): *The Tales of Hoffmann.*
ANDREAS (BAR): *Wozzeck.*
ANDRELOUX (M-S): *Mireille.*
ANDROMACHE (mime): *The Trojans,* Part 1.
ANFINOMO (T): *Il Ritorno d'Ulisse in Patria.*
ANGELICA, SISTER (S): *Suor Angelica.*
ANGELINA (C): *La Cenerentola.*
ANGELOTTI, CESARE (B): *La Tosca.*
ANIMAL-TAMER (PROLOGUE; RODRIG, Act II) (B): *Lulu.*
ANITA (S): *Johnny Plays On.*
ANNA (M-S): *Der Freischütz.*
ANNA (S): *La Dame Blanche.*
ANNA (C): *L'Africaine.*
ANNA, DONNA (S): *Don Giovanni.*
ANNA (S): *Intermezzo.*
ANNA (S): *Nabucco.*
ANNA (S): *The Trojans,* Part II.
ANNABELLA, DESIRE (S): *Merry Mount.*
ANNE (S): *The Rake's Progress.*
ANNIE (M-S): *Porgy and Bess.*
ANNINA (S): *La Traviata.*
ANNIUS (M-S): *The Clemency of Titus.*
ANNUNZIATA (silent): *Harlequin.*
ANTINOO (B): *Il Ritorno d'Ulisse in Patria.*
ANTONIA (S): *The Tales of Hoffmann.*
ANTONIA (S): *Tiefland.*
ANTONIDA (S): *A Life for the Czar.*
ANTONIO (BAR): *Linda di Chamounix.*
ANTONIO (B): *Lodoletta.*

ANTONIO (B): *The Marriage of Figaro.*
APOLLO (T): *Daphne.*
APPARITION OF A YOUTH (T): *The Woman without a Shadow.*
ARABELLA (S): *Arabella.*
ARBACE (T): *Idomeneo.*
ARHIBALDO (B): *The Love of Three Kings.*
ARIADNE (S): *Ariadne auf Naxos.*
ARIANE (M-S): *Ariane et Barbe-Bleue.*
ARKEL (B): *Pelléas et Mélisande.*
ARLINE (S): *The Bohemian Girl.*
THE ARMCHAIR (B): *L'Enfant et les Sortilèges.*
ARMIDE (S): *Armide.*
ARNHEIM, COUNT (B): *The Bohemian Girl.*
ARNOLD (T): *William Tell.*
ARONT (B): *Armide.*
ARRIGO (T): *The Sicilian Vespers.*
ARSACES (C): *Semiramide.*
ARTHUR JONES (BAR): *Billy Budd.*
ARTIMIDOR (T): *Armide.*
ASCANIO (M-S): *Benvenuto Cellini.*
ASCANIUS (S): *The Trojans,* Parts I, II.
ASE (C): *The King's Henchman.*
ASHBY (B): *The Girl of the Golden West.*
ASHTON, LORD HENRY (BAR): *Lucia di Lammermoor.*
ASHTON, LUCY (S): *Lucia di Lammermoor.*
ASSAD (T): *The Queen of Sheba.*
ASSUR (BAR): *Semiramide.*
ASTAROTH (S): *The Queen of Sheba.*
ASTERIA (S): *Nero.*
ASTOLFO (B): *Lucretia Borgia.*
ASTYANAX (mime): *The Trojans,* Part 1.
ATHANAEL (BAR): *Thaïs.*
AUGUSTE (T): *Zaza.*
AUNT JANE (C): *Hugh the Drover.*
AVIS (S): *The Wreckers.*
AVITO (T): *The Love of Three Kings.*
AZEMUR (S): *Semiramide.*
AZUCENA (M-S): *Il Trovatore.*
BAAL HANAN (BAR): *The Queen of Sheba.*
BABA MUSTAPHA (T): *The Barber of Bagdad.*
BABA THE TURK (M-S): *The Rake's Progress.*
BABEKAN (speaking role): *Oberon.*
BABINSKY (BAR): *Schwanda the Bagpiper.*
BACCHUS (T): *Ariadne auf Naxos.*
BACCHUS (speaking role): *Orpheus in the Underworld.*
BACULUS (B): *The Poacher.*
BADOERO, ALVISE (B): *La Gioconda.*
BALDASSARE (BAR): *L'Arlesiana.*
A BALLAD-SELLER: (T): *Hugh the Drover.*
BALOUCCI (B): *Benvenuto Cellini.*
BALSTRODE, CAPTAIN (B): *Peter Grimes.*
BALTASAR (B): *La Favorita.*
BANKS, JONATHAN (T): *Merry Mount.*
BANQUO (B): *Macbeth.*
BARAK (B-BAR): *The Woman without a Shadow.*
BARAK (BAR): *Turandot* (Busoni).
BARAK's WIFE (S): *The Woman without a Shadow.*
BARBARINA (S): *The Marriage of Figaro.*
BARBARINO (BAR): *Stradella.*
THE BARBER (BAR): *The Silent Woman.*
BARCE (S): *The Kiss.*
BARDOLPH (T): *Falstaff.*
BARNABA (BAR): *La Gioconda.*
BARONCELLO (T): *Rienzi.*
BARTOLO, DR. (B): *The Barber of Seville.*
BARTOLO, DR. (B): *The Marriage of Figaro.*
BASILIO (B): *The Barber of Seville.*
BASILIO (T): *The Marriage of Figaro.*
BASSI (BAR): *Stradella.*
THE BATS (S): *L'Enfant et les Sortilèges.*
BAYAN (T): *Russlan and Ludmilla.*
BAZAN, DON CAESAR DE (T): *Maritana.*
BÉATRICE (M-S): *Béatrice et Bénédict.*

BEKMESSER, SIXTUS (B): *Die Meistersinger.*
BEGGAR (speaking role): *The Beggar's Opera.*
BELCORE (BAR): *The Elexir of Love.*
BELLANGERE (S): *Ariane et Barbe-Bleue.*
BELLINGHAM, GOV. (B): *The Scarlet Letter.*
BELMONTE (T): *The Abduction from the Seraglio.*
BEN (BAR): *The Telephone.*
BÉNÉDICT (T): *Béatrice et Bénédict.*
BENES (B): *Dalibor.*
BENN, HARRY (T): *The Boatswain's Mate.*
BENOÎT (B): *La Bohème.*
BENSON, MRS. (M-S): *Lakmé.*
BENVOLIO (T): *Romeo and Juliet.*
BEPPE (M-S): *L'Amico Fritz.*
BEPPE (T): *Pagliacci.*
BEPPO (T): *Fra Diavolo.*
BERARDENGO, SERT (T): *Francesca da Rimini.*
BERGERAC, CYRANO DE (BAR): *Cyrano de Bergerac.*
BERNARDINO (B): *Benvenuto Cellini.*
BERSI (M-S): *Andrea Chénier.*
BERTA (OR MARCELLINA) (S): *The Barber of Seville.*
BERTHA (S): *Euryanthe.*
BERTHA (S): *Le Prophète.*
BERTRAM (B): *Robert le Diable.*
BERYLUNE (S): *Blue Bird.*
BESS (S): *Porgy and Bess.*
BETHUNE, DI (B): *The Sicilian Vespers.*
BETT, VAN (B): *Czar and Carpenter.*
BETTO DI SIGNA (B): *Gianni Schicchi.*
BIANCA (C): *The Rape of Lucretia.*
BIANCA (S): *La Rondine.*
BILLOWS, LADY (S): *Albert Herring.*
BILLY (BAR): *Billy Budd.*
BIRKENFELD, MARQUISE DE (S): *The Daughter of the Regiment.*
BITEROLF (B): *Tannhaüser.*
BLIND, DR. (T): *Die Fledermaus.*
BLONDE (S): *The Abduction from the Seraglio.*
BLUEBEARD (B): *Ariane et Barbe-Bleue.*
BLUEBEARD, DUKE (B): *Duke Bluebeard's Castle.*
BOB (BAR): *The Old Maid and the Thief.*
BOBYL (BAR): *The Snow Maiden.*
BOBYLICKA (C): *The Sow Maiden.*
BOCCANEGRA, MARIA (S): *Simon Boccanegra.*
BOCCANEGRA, SIMON (BAR): *Simon Boccanegra.*
BOISFLEURY, MARQUIS DE (BAR): *Linda di Chamounix.*
BOMBASTO, DOTTOR (B): *Harlequin.*
BOMELY (B): *Ivan the Terrible.*
BONZE, THE (B): *Le Rossignol.*
BONZE, THE (B): *Madam Butterfly.*
BORELLA (B): *The Dumb Girl of Portici.*
BORGIA, LUCRETIA (S): *Lucretia Borgia.*
BOROV (B): *Fedora.*
BORSA, MATTEO (T): *Rigoletto.*
BORSO (BAR): *Monna Vanna.*
BOSTANA (M-S): *The Barber of Bagdad.*
BOSUN (B): *Billy Budd.*
BOUILLON, PRINCE DE (B): *Adriana Lecouvreur.*
BOUILLON, PRINCESS DE (M-S): *Adriana Lecouvreur.*
BRADFORD, WRESTLING (BAR): *Merry Mount.*
BRANDER (B): *The Damnation of Faust.*
BRANDER (BAR): *Faust.*
BRANGÄNE (M-S): *Tristan and Isolde.*
BRÉTIGNY, DE (BAR): *Manon.*
BREWSTER, LOVE (S): *Merry Mount.*
BRODRIB, MYLES (BAR): *Merry Mount.*
BRODRIB, PEREGRINE (S): *Merry Mount.*
BROGNI, CARDINAL DE (BAR): *La Juive.*

BONISLAWA, COUNTESS (S): *The Beggar Student*.
BROWN, GEORGES (T): *La Dame Blanche*.
BRÜNHILDE (S): *Die Walküre; Siegfried; Die Götterdämmerung*.
BUCKLAW, LORD ARTHUR (T): *Lucia di Lammermoor*.
BUDA (S): *The Bohemian Girl*.
BUDIVOJ (BAR): *Dalibor*.
BUSSY (BAR): *Zaza*.
BUTTERFLY, MADAM (S): *Madam Butterfly*.
CABIN BOY (speaking role): Billy Budd.
THE CADI (B): *Mârouf*.
CAIUS, DR. (T): *Falstaff*.
CAIUS, DR. (B): *The Merry Wives of Windsor*.
CALAF (T): *Turandot*.
CALAF (T): *Turandot* (Busoni).
CALATRAVA, MARQUIS OF (B): *La Forza del Destino*.
CALCHAS (BAR): *Iphigenia in Aulis*.
CALIPH (BAR): *The Barber of Bagdad*.
CANIO (T): *Pagliacci*.
CAPITO, WOLFGANG (T): *Mathis der Maler*.
CAPTAIN OF THE GUARD (B): *The Bohemian Girl*.
CAPTAIN OF THE GUARD (BAR): *Maritana*.
CAPTAIN VERE (T): *Billy Budd*.
CAPULET (B): *Romeo and Juliet*.
CARLOS, DON (T): *Don Carlos*.
CARLOS, DON (BAR): *Ernani*.
CARLOS, DON (BAR): *La Forza del Destino*.
CARLOTTA (M-S): *The Silent Woman*.
CARMELA (M-S): *The Brief Life*.
CARMELA (M-S): *The Jewels of the Madonna*.
CARMEN (S): *Carmen*.
CAROLINA (S): *Il Matrimonio Segreto*.
CAROLINE, QUEEN (S): *Madame Sans-Gêne*.
CASCART (BAR): *Zaza*.
CASPAR (B): *Der Freischütz*.
CASSANDRA (S): *The Trojans*, Parts I, II.
CASSIUS (T): *Otello*.
CASTRO, JOSE (B): *The Girl of the Golden West*.
THE CAT (M-S): *L'Enfant et les Sortilèges*.
CATERINA (S): *L'Amico Fritz*.
CATHERINE (S): *Madame Sans-Gêne*.
CAVARADOSSI, MARIO (T): *La Tosca*.
CECCO DEL VECCHIO (B): *Rienzi*.
CELIO (B): *The Love for Three Oranges*.
CELLINI, BENVENUTO (T): *Benvenuto Cellini*.
CEPRANO, COUNT (B): *Rigoletto*.
CEPRANO, COUNTESS (M-S): *Rigoletto*.
CERINTO (C): *Nero*.
CHAPPELOU (T): *The Coachman of Longjumeau*.
CHARLEMAGNE (speaking role): *Oberon*.
CHARLES, VICOMTE (T): *Linda de Chamounix*.
CHARLOTTE (S): *Werther*.
CHARMEUSE, LA (S): *Thaïs*.
CHATEAUNEUF, MARQUIS DE (T): *Czar and Carpenter*.
A CHEAP-JACK (BAR): *Hugh the Drover*.
CHEAP JEWELLERY WOMAN (M-S): *A Village Romeo and Juliet*.
CHÉNIER, ANDREA (T): *Andrea Chénier*.
CHERUBINO (S): *The Marriage of Figaro*.
CHIEF OF THE SAILORS (T): *Mârouf*.
THE CHILD (M-S): *L'Enfant et les Sortilèges*.
THE CHILD'S MOTHER (C): *L'Enfant et les Sortilèges*.
CHILLINGWORTH, ROGER (BAR): *The Scarlet Letter*.
CHIM-FEN (BAR): *L'Oracolo*.
THE CHINESE CUP (C): *L'Enfant et les Sortilèges*.
CHOREBE (BAR): *The Trojans*, Parts I, II.
CHORUS, FEMALE (S): *The Rape of Lucretia*.
CHORUS, MALE (T): *The Rape of Lucretia*.

CHRISTIAN (T): *Cyrano de Bergerac*.
CHRISTINE (S): *Intermezzo*.
CHRISTOPHER COLUMBUS I (BAR): *Christopher Columbus*.
CHRISTOPHER COLUMBUS II (BAR): *Christopher Columbus*.
CHRYSOTHEMIS (S): *Elektra*.
CIECA, LA (C): *La Gioconda*.
CIECO (B: *Iris*.
CIESCA, LA (M-S): *Gianni Schicchi*.
CINNA (BAR): *La Vestale*.
CIO-CIO-SAN (MADAM BUTTERFLY) (S): *Madam Butterfly*.
CIRILLO (BAR): *Fedora*.
CIS (S): *Albert Herring*.
CLAGGART (B): *Billy Budd*.
CLAIRON (C): *Capriccio*.
CLARA (S): *Porgy and Bess*.
CLARETTA (S): *Zaza*.
CLARISSA, PRINCESS (C): *The Love for Three Oranges*.
CLAUDIO (BAR): *Béatrice et Bénédict*.
CLEMENCE (S): *Mireille*.
CLORINDA (S): *La Cenerentola*.
CLOTILDA (S): *Norma*.
CLYTEMNESTRA (C): *Iphigenia in Aulis*.
COCKBURN, LORD (T): *Fra Diavolo*.
COIGNY, COUNTESS DE (M-S): *Andrea Chénier*.
COLLATINUS (B): *The Rape of Lucretia*.
COLLINE (B): *La Bohème*.
COLONNA, GUIDO (B): *Monna Vanna*.
COLONNA, STEFFANO (B): *Rienzi*.
COLUMBINE (S): *Fête Galante*.
COLUMBINE (M-S): *Harlequin*.
THE COMMANDANT (B): *Christopher Columbus*.
THE COMMANDATORE (B): *Don Giovanni*.
COMMERCIAL COUNCILLOR (BAR): *Intermezzo*.
COMMERE (M-S): *Four Saints in Three Acts*.
COMPERE (B): *Four Saints in Three Acts*.
CONCEPCION (S): *The Spanish Hour*.
THE CONSTABLE (B): *Hugh the Drover*.
CONSTANZA (S): *The Abduction from the Seraglio*.
THE COOK (T): *Christopher Columbus*.
THE COOK (B): *The Love for Three Oranges*.
COPPELIUS (BAR): *The Tales of Hoffmann*.
CORCY, LE MARQUIS DE (T): *The Coachman of Longjumeau*.
CORENTIN, SAINT (B): *Le Roi d'Ys*.
CORENTINO (T): *Dinorah*.
CORPORAL (B): *The Daughter of the Regiment*.
CORREGIDOR, THE (DON EUGENIO DE ZUNIGA) (T): *Der Corregidor*.
COSPICUO, ABBATE (BAR): *Harlequin*.
COSSE (T): *The Huguenots*.
THE COUNSEL FOR THE PROSECUTION (speaking role): *Christopher Columbus*.
THE COUNT (BAR): *Capriccio*.
THE COUNTESS (S): *Capriccio*.
COURTOIS (B): *Zaza*.
CRAB MAN (T): *Porgy and Bess*.
CRACKSTON, BRIDGET (C): *Merry Mount*.
CREBILLON (B-BAR): *La Rondine*.
CREON (B-BAR): *Oedipus Rex*.
CRESPEL (B): *The Tales of Hoffmann*.
THE CRICKET (S): *The Cricket on the Hearth*.
CROBYLE (S): *Thaïs*.
CROWN (BAR): *Porgy and Bess*.
CUNO (B): *Der Freischütz*.
CUPIDON (S): *Orpheus in the Underworld*.
CURRA (M-S): *La Forza del Destino*.
CURZIO (T): *The Marriage of Figaro*.
DALAND (B): *The Flying Dutchman*.
DALIBOR (T): *Dalibor*.
DANAE (S): *The Love of Danae*.
DANCAIRE, LE (T): *Carmen*.

DANDINI (B): *La Cenerentola.*
DANGEVILLE, MLLE. (M-S): *Adriana Lecouvreur.*
DANIELI (T): *The Sicilian Vespers.*
DANIELLO (BAR): *Johnny Plays On.*
DANSKER (B): *Billy Budd.*
DAPERTUTTE (BAR): *The Tales of Hoffmann.*
DAPHNE (S): *Daphne.*
THE DARK FIDDLER (BAR): *A Village Romeo and Juliet.*
DA-UD (T): *The Egyptian Helen.*
DAVID (BAR): *L'Amico Fritz.*
DAVID (T): *Die Meistersinger.*
DEANE, MRS. (M-S): *Peter Ibbetson.*
DEATH (B): *Savitri.*
DELILAH (S): *The Warrior.*
DELILAH (M-S): *Samson and Delilah.*
DESDEMONA (S): *Otello.*
DES GRIEUX, CHEVALIER (T): *Manon.*
DES GRIEUX, CHEVALIER (T): *Manon Lescaut.*
LES GRIEUX, COMTE (B): *Manon.*
DÉSIRÉ (T): *Fedora.*
DESPINA (S): *Così Fan Tutte.*
DEVILSHOOF (B): *The Bohemian Girl.*
DEW FAIRY (S): *Hansel and Gretel.*
DIANA (S): *Iphigenia in Tauris.*
DIANA (S): *Orpheus in the Underworld.*
DICKSON (T): *La Dame Blanche.*
DIDO (M-S): *The Trojans,* Part II.
DIEGO, DON (T): *L'Africaine.*
DIMMESDALE, ARTHUR (T): *The Scarlet Letter.*
DINORAH (S): *Dinorah.*
DJAMILEH (M-S): *Djamileh.*
DMITRI (C): *Fedora.*
THE DOCTOR (speaking role): *Lulu.*
DOCTOR (B): *Macbeth.*
DODON, KING (BAR): *Le Coq d'Or.*
DOLCINA, SISTER (M-S): *Suor Angelica.*
DOMINIK, GRAF (BAR): *Arabella.*
DONALD (BAR): *Billy Budd.*
DONNER (B): *Das Rheingold.*
DORABELLA (S): *Così Fan Tutte.*
DOROTA (S): *Schwanda the Bagpiper.*
DOSITEO (BAR): *Nero.*
DOSITHEUS (B): *Khovantchina.*
DOT (S): *The Cricket on the Hearth.*
DOUPHOL, BARON (BAR): *La Traviata.*
THE DRAGONFLY (LIBELLULE) (M-S): *L'Enfant et les Sortilèges.*
DROLL (C): *Oberon.*
DUCHESS ELENA (S): *The Sicilian Vespers.*
DUCLOU (BAR): *Zaza.*
DUFRESNE, MME. (M-S): *Zara.*
DUFRESNE, MILIO (T): *Zaza.*
DULCAMARA (B): *The Elixir of Love.*
DULCINÉE, LA BELLE (S): *Don Quixote.*
DUMAS (BAR): *Andrea Chénier.*
DUNCAN (Silent): *Macbeth.*
DUNSTAN (BAR): *The King's Henchman.*
DUQUESNOIR, MAJOR (B): *Peter Ibbetson.*
DURHAM, LADY (S): *Martha.*
DUTCHMAN, THE (B): *The Flying Dutchman.*
EADGAR (BAR): *The King's Henchman.*
EBERBACH, COUNT OF (BAR): *The Poacher.*
EBERBACH, COUNTESS OF (C): *The Poacher.*
EBOLI, PRINCIPESSA (M-S): *Don Carlos.*
EDGAR (T): *Lucia di Lammermoor.*
EDMONDO (T): *Manon Lescaut.*
EGLANTINE (M-S): *Euryanthe.*
EISENSTEIN, BARON VON (T): *Die Fledermaus.*
EISSLINGER, ULRICH (T): *Die Meistersinger.*
ELEAZAR (T): *La Juive.*
ELECTRA (S): *Idomeneo.*
ELEKTRA (S): *Elektra.*
ELEMER, GRAF (T): *Arabella.*
ELENA (S): *Mefistofele.*

ELENA, DUCHESS (S): *The Sicilian Vespers.*
ELISABETH (S): *Tannhaüser.*
ELISETTA (S): *Il Matrimonio Segreto.*
ELISABETH OF VALOIS (S): *Don Carlos.*
ELLEN (S): *Lakmé.*
ELSA OF BRABANT (S): *Lohengrin.*
ELVINO (T): *La Sonnambula.*
ELVIRA (S): *The Dumb Girl of Portici.*
ELVIRA (S): *Ernani.*
ELVIRA (S): *I Puritani.*
ELVIRA (S): *L'Italiana in Algeri.*
ELVIRA, DONNA (S): *Don Giovanni.*
ELVIRA, DONNA (S): *Ernani.*
EMILIA (M-S): *Otello.*
EMMA (M-S): *Khovantchina.*
EMMIE (S): *Albert Herring.*
THE EMPEROR (T): *The Woman without a Shadow.*
EMPEROR OF CHINA (B): *Le Rossignol.*
THE EMPRESS (S): *The Woman without a Shadow.*
ENTERICH (BAR): *The Beggar Student.*
ERDA (C): *Das Rheingold; Siegfried.*
ERICLEA (M-S): *Il Ritorno d'Ulisse in Patria.*
ERIK (T): *The Flying Dutchman.*
ERNANI, OR JOHN OF ARAGON (T): *Ernani.*
ERNESTO (T): *Don Pasquale.*
EROCHKA (T): *Prince Igor.*
ESCAMILLO (B): *Carmen.*
EUDORA (C): *La Juive.*
EUGENIO DE ZUNIGA, DON (THE CORREGIDOR) (T): *Der Corregidor.*
EUMETE (T): *Il Ritorno d'Ulisse in Patria.*
EURIMACO (T): *Il Ritorno d'Ulisse in Patria.*
EUROPA (S): *The Love of Danae.*
EURYANTHE OF SAVOY (S): *Euryanthe.*
EURYDICE (S): *Orpheus in the Underworld.*
EVA (S): *Die Meistersinger.*
EVANDER (T): *Alceste.*
FAFNER (B): *Das Rheingold; Siegfried.*
FALCON, THE VOICE OF (S): *The Woman without a Shadow.*
FALKE, DR. (BAR): *Die Fledermaus.*
FALSTAFF (BAR): *Falstaff.*
FALSTAFF (B): *The Merry Wives of Windsor.*
FANINAL (BAR): *Der Rosenkavalier.*
FANUEL (BAR): *Nero.*
FARFALLO (B): *The Silent Woman.*
FARFARELLO (B): *The Love for Three Oranges.*
FARLAF: *Russlan and Ludmilla.*
FASOLT (B): *Das Rheingold.*
FATA MORGANA (S): *The Love for Three Oranges.*
FATIMA (M-S): *Oberon.*
FATIMAH (S): *Mârouf.*
FAUST (T): *Faust.*
FAUST (T): *Mefistofele.*
FAUST (T): *The Damnation of Faust.*
FEDERICO (T): *L'Arlesiana.*
FEDORA, PRINCESS (S): *Fedora.*
THE FELLAH (T): *Mârouf.*
FENELLA (dancer): *The Dumb Girl of Portici.*
FENENA (S): *Nabucco.*
FENTON (T): *Falstaff.*
FENTON (T): *The Merry Wiwes of Windsor.*
FEODOR (M-S): *Boris Godounov.*
FERNANDO (T): *Goyescas.*
FERNANDO (T): *La Favorita.*
FERNANDO, DON (B): *Fidelio.*
FERRANDO (T): *Così Fan Tutte.*
FERRANDO (B): *Il Trovatore.*
THE "FIAKERMILLI" (S): *Arabella.*
FIDALMA (M-S): *Il Matrimonio Segreto.*
FIDÈS (M-S): *Le Prophète.*
FIERAMOSCA (BAR): *Benvenuto Cellini.*
FIESCO, JACOPO (B): *Simon Boccanegra.*
FIGARO (BAR): *The Barber of Seville.*
FIGARO (BAR): *The Marriage of Figaro.*

FILCH (T): *The Beggar's Opera.*
FILIPIEVNA (M-S): *Eugene Onegin.*
FINN (T): *Russlan and Ludmilla.*
FIORA (S): *The Love of Three Kings.*
FIORDILIGI (S): *Così Fan Tutte.*
FIORELLO (B): *The Barber of Seville.*
THE FIRE (S): *L'Enfant et les Sortilèges.*
FIRST MATE (BAR): *Billy Budd.*
FLAMAND (T): *Capriccio.*
FLAMINIO (T): *The Love of Three Kings.*
FLAMMEN (T): *Lodoletta.*
FLAVIO (T): *Norma.*
FLEANCE (silent): *Macbeth.*
FLEVILLE (BAR): *Andrea Chénier.*
MR. FLINT (BAR): *Billy Budd.*
FLORA, MADAME (C): *The Medium.*
FLORA BERVOIX (M-S): *La Traviata.*
FLORENCE PIKE (C): *Albert Herring.*
FLORESTAN (T): *Fidelio.*
FLORESTEIN (T): *The Bohemian Girl.*
FLORIANA (S): *Zaza.*
FLOSSHILDE (C): *Das Rheingold; Die Götter-dämmerung.*
FLYING DUTCHMAN (BAR): *The Flying Dutchmann.*
FOLTZ, HANS (B): *Die Meistersinger.*
A FOOL (B): *Hugh the Drover.*
FORD (BAR): *Falstaff.*
FORD (B): *The Merry Wives of Windsor.*
FORD, ALICE (S): *Falstaff.*
FORD, ANNE (S): *Falstaff.*
FORD, MISTRESS (S): *The Merry Wiwes of Windsor.*
FORTH, SIR RICHARD (BAR): *I Puritani.*
A FORTUNE-TELLER (S): *Arabella.*
FOUCHÉ (BAR): *Madame Sans-Gêne.*
FOUQUIER-TINVILLE (BAR): *Andrea Chénier.*
FRA DIAVOLO (T): *Fra Diavolo.*
FRA MELITONE (BAR): *La Forza del Destino.*
FRANCESCA (S): *Francesca da Rimini.*
FRANCESCO (T): *Benvenuto Cellini.*
FRANK (BAR): *Die Fledermaus.*
FRANZ (B): *Lodoletta.*
FRANZ, LITTLE (silent): *Intermezzo.*
FRASQUITA (S): *Carmen.*
FRASQUITA (M-S): *Der Corregidor.*
FRAZIER (BAR): *Porgy and Bess.*
FRÉDÉRIC (BAR): *Lakmé.*
FREDERICA (C): *Luisa Miller.*
FREDERICK OF TELRAMUND (BAR): *Lohengrin.*
FREDERICO (T): *L'Amico Fritz.*
FREIA (S): *Das Rheingold.*
FREIMANN, BARONESS (S): *The Poacher.*
FRICKA (M-S): *Das Rheingold; Die Walküre.*
FRITZ KOBUS (T): *L'Amico Fritz.*
THE FROG (T): *L'Enfant et les Sortilèges.*
FROH (T): *Das Rheingold.*
FROSCH (speaking role): *Die Fledermaus.*
FRUGOLA (M-S): *Il Tabarro.*
FÜRST, WALTER (B): *William Tell.*
GABRIEL (B): *La Dame Blanche.*
GAEA (C): *Daphne.*
GALATEA (S): *The Beautiful Galatea.*
GALITSKY, PRINCE (B): *Prince Igor.*
GALITZIN, PRINCE (T): *Khovantchina.*
GARCIAS (S): *Don Quixote.*
GASPARO (T): *La Favorita.*
GASTONE DE LÉTORIÈRES (T): *La Traviata.*
GAVESTON (B): *La Dame Blanche.*
GAZELLO (B): *Lucretia Borgia.*
MR. GEDGE (BAR): *Albert Herring.*
GELLNER, VINCENZO (BAR): *La Wally.*
GENEVIÈVE (C): *Pelleas and Melisande.*
GENNARO (T): *Lucretia Borgia.*
GENNARO (T): *The Jewels of the Madonna.*
GENOVEVA, SISTER (S): *Suor Angelica.*
GÉRALD (T): *Lakmé.*
GÉRARD, CHARLES (BAR): *Andrea Chénier.*
GERMONT, ALFREDO (T): *La Traviata.*

GERMONT, GIORGIO (BAR): *La Traviata.*
GERONIMO (BUFFO): *Il Matrimonio Segreto.*
GÉRONTE (B): *Manon Lescaut.*
GERTRUDE (S): *Hansel and Gretel.*
GERTRUDE (M-S): *Romeo and Juliet.*
GESCHWITZ, GRAFIN (M-S): *Lulu.*
GESSLER (B): *William Tell.*
GHERARDINO (C): *Gianni Schicchi.*
GHERARDO (T): *Gianni Schicchi.*
GIACOMO (B): *Fra Diavolo.*
GIANETTA (S): *The Elixir of Love.*
GIANETTO (BAR): *Lodoletta.*
GIARNO (B): *Mignon.*
GIL, COUNT (BAR): *Susanna's Secret.*
GILDA (S): *Rigoletto.*
GINGERBREAD WOMAN (S): *A Village Romeo and Juliet.*
GIOCONDA, LA (S): *La Gioconda.*
GIORGETTA (S): *Il Tabarro.*
GIORGIO GERMONT (BAR): *La Traviata.*
GIOVANNA (S): *Ernani.*
GIOVANNA (M-S): *Rigoletto.*
GIOVANNI (BAR): *Francesca da Rimini.*
GIOVANNI DA PROCIDA (B): *The Sicilian Vespers.*
GIOVANNI, DON (BAR): *Don Giovanni.*
GIOVE (T): *Il Ritorno d'Ulisse in Patria.*
GIULIA (S): *Madame Sans-Gêne.*
GIULIETTA (S): *The Tales of Hoffmann.*
GIUSEPPE (T): *La Traviata.*
GIUSEPPE HAGENBACH (T): *La Wally.*
GLYN, MRS. (C): *Peter Ibbetson.*
GOBIN (T): *La Rondine.*
MR. GOBINEAU (BAR): *The Medium.*
MRS. GOBINEAU (S): *The Medium.*
GOBRIAS (T): *Nero.*
GODOUNOV, BORIS (B): *Boris Godounov.*
GOLAUD (BAR): *Pelléas et Mélisande.*
GOLDEN COCKEREL, THE (S): *Le Coq d'Or.*
GOMEZ, DON INIGO (B): *The Spanish Hour.*
GONSALVE (T): *The Spanish Hour.*
GOOSE GIRL, THE (S): *Die Königskinder.*
GORISLAVA (S): *Russlan and Ludmilla.*
GORO (T): *Madam Butterfly.*
THE GRANDFATHER CLOCK (BAR): *L'Enfant et les Sortilèges.*
GRAND INQUISITOR (B): *Don Carlos.*
GRECH (B): *Fedora.*
A GREEK CAPTAIN (B): *The Trojans, Part I.*
GREGORIO (BAR): *Romeo and Juliet.*
GREGORY (T): *Boris Godounov.*
GREGOUX, ACHILLE (T): *Peter Ibbetson.*
GREMIN, PRINCE (B): *Eugene Onegin.*
GRENVIL, DOCTOR (B): *La Traviata.*
GRETCHEN (S): *The Poacher.*
GRETEL (S): *Hansel and Gretel.*
GRIMALDO, ENZO (T): *La Gioconda.*
GRIMES, PETER (T): *Peter Grimes.*
GRITZKO (T): *The Fair at Sorochinsk.*
GUARDIANO, PADRE (B): *La Forza del Destino.*
GUBETTA (B): *Lucretia Borgia.*
GUCCIO (B): *Gianni Schicchi.*
GUGLIELMO (B): *Così Fan Tutte.*
GUICHE, DE (B): *Cyrano de Bergerac.*
GUIDO DI MONFORTE (BAR): *The Sicilian Vespers.*
GUIDON, PRINCE (T): *Le Coq d'Or.*
GUNTHER (BAR): *Die Götterdämmerung.*
GURNEMANZ (B): *Parsifal.*
GUTRUNE (S): *Die Götterdämmerung.*
GYMNASIAST, ACT II (WARDROBE-MISTRESS, ACT I) (C): *Lulu.*
HAGEN (B): *Die Götterdämmerung.*
HAGENBACH, GIUSEPPE (T): *La Wally.*
HALY (B): *L'Italiana in Algeri.*
HANEGO (T): *L'Amico Fritz.*
HANS (T): *The Bartered Bride.*
HANSEL (M-S): *Hansel and Gretel.*
A HAPPY SHADE (S): *Orfeo ed Euridice.*

HARLEQUIN (T): *Fête Galante.*
HARLEQUIN (speaking role): *Harlequin.*
HAROUN (T): *Djamileh.*
HAROUN AL-RASHID (speaking role): *Oberon.*
HARRY (TREBLE): *Albert Herring.*
HARVEY (B): *The Wreckers.*
HECTOR, GHOST OF (B): *The Trojans,* Parts I, II.
HECUBA (M-S): *The Trojans,* Part I.
HEDWIGE (S): *William Tell.*
HEINRICH (T): *Tannhaüser.*
HEINRICH (T): *The Sunken Bell.*
HELEN (S): *The Egyptian Helen.*
HELEN OF TROY (S): *Mefistofele.*
HELENUS (T): *The Trojans,* Part I.
HELFENSTEIN, GRAF VON (silent): *Mathis der Maler.*
HELFENSTEIN, GRAFIN VON (C): *Mathis der Maler.*
HELMSMAN (BAR): *Tristan and Isolde.*
HENRIETTA OF FRANCE (S): *I Puritani.*
HENRY I (B): *Lohengrin.*
HERALD (BAR): *Alceste.*
HERALD (B): *Lohengrin.*
THE HERALD (B): *The Love for Three Oranges.*
HERCULES (BAR): *Alceste.*
HERMANN (T): *Pique-Dame.*
HERMANN (B): *Tannhaüser.*
HERMIONE (S): *The Egyptian Helen.*
A HERMIT (B): *Der Freischütz.*
HERO (S): *Béatrice et Bénédict.*
HEROD (BAR): *Hérodiade.*
HEROD (T): *Salome.*
HERODIAS (C): *Hérodiade.*
HERODIAS (M-S): *Salome.*
MRS. HERRING (M-S): *Albert Herring.*
HIDROAT (BAR): *Armide.*
HIGH PRIEST (BAR): *Alceste.*
HIGH PRIEST (BAR): *Hérodiade.*
HIGH PRIEST (BAR): *Samson and Delilah.*
HIGH PRIEST (B): *The Queen of Sheba.*
HIGH PRIEST OF BABYLON (B): *Nabucco.*
HIGH PRIEST OF NEPTUNE (T): *Idomeneo*
HIGH PRIESTESS (M-S): *La Vestale.*
HINDU MERCHANT (T): *Sadko.*
HOËL (BAR): *Dinorah.*
HOFFMANN (T): *The Tales of Hoffmann.*
HOO-TSIN (B): *L'Oracolo.*
HORTENSIO (B): *The Daughter of the Regiment.*
HOUSEKEEPER (C): *The Silent Woman.*
HUBSCHER, CATERINA (S): *Madame Sans-Gêne.*
HUGH THE DROVER (T): *Hugh the Drover.*
THE HUNCHBACK (T): *The Woman without a Shadow.*
THE HUNCH-BACKED BASS FIDDLER (B): *A Village Romeo and Juliet.*
HUNDING (B): *Die Walküre.*
HUON DE BORDEAUX (T): *Oberon.*
HYLAS (T): *The Trojans,* Part II.
IAGO (BAR): *Otello.*
IBBETSON, COLONEL (BAR): *Peter Ibbetson.*
IBBETSON, PETER (T): *Peter Ibbetson.*
IDAMANTE (S): *Idomeneo.*
IDOMENEO (T): *Idomeneo.*
IDRENUS (T): *Semiramide.*
IGOR, PRINCE (BAR): *Prince Igor.*
ILIA (S): *Idomeneo.*
IMPERIAL COMMISSIONER (B): *Madam Butterfly.*
INCREDIBLE (T): *Andrea Chénier.*
INEZ (S): *La Favorita.*
INEZ (S): *L'Africaine.*
INEZ (S): *Il Trovatore.*
AN INNKEEPER (B): *Hugh the Drover.*
INNKEEPER (B): *Manon Lescaut.*
L'INNOCENTE (M-S): *L'Arlesiana.*

INTENDANT (T): *Linda di Chamounix.*
IOLAN (T): *The Pipe of Desire.*
IOPAS (T): *The Trojans,* Part II.
IPANOV, COUNT LORIS (T): *Fedora.*
IPHIGENIA (S): *Iphigenia in Aulis.*
IPHIGENIA (S): *Iphigenia in Tauris.*
IRENE (S): *Rienzi.*
IRIS (S): *Iris.*
IRMA (S): *Louise.*
IRO (T): *Il Ritorno d'Ulisse in Patria.*
ISABELLA (S): *Christopher Columbus.*
ISABELLA (C): *L'Italiana in Algeri.*
ISABELLA (S): *Robert le Diable.*
ISEPO (T): *La Gioconda.*
ISMAELE (T): *Nabucco.*
ISOLDE (S): *Tristan and Isolde.*
ISOTTA (S): *The Silent Woman.*
AN ITALIAN SINGER (S): *Capriccio.*
AN ITALIAN SINGER (S): *Capriccio.*
IVAN, CZAR (B): *Ivan the Terrible.*
IVANITCH (T): *The Fair at Sorochinsk.*
JACK (M-S): *The Wreckers.*
JACKRABBIT, BILLY (B): *The Girl of the Golden West.*
JACQUINO (T): *Fidelio.*
JAGO (B): *Ernani.*
JAHEL (BAR): *Le Roi d'Ys.*
JAKE (BAR): *Porgy and Bess.*
JANITZKY, JAN (T): *The Beggar Student.*
JAROSLAVNA (S): *Prince Igor.*
JAVETTE (C): *Manon.*
JEAN (T or S): *The Juggler of Notre Dame.*
JEMMY (S): *William Tell.*
JENNY (S): *La Dame Blanche.*
JIM (BAR): *Porgy and Bess.*
JITKA (S): *Dalibor.*
JOCASTA (M-S): *Oedipus Rex.*
JOHN (BAR): *The Cricket on the Hearth.*
JOHNNY, NIGGER (BAR): *Johnny Plays On.*
JOHN OF ARAGON, OR ERNANI (T): *Ernani.*
JOHN OF LEYDEN (T): *Le Prophète.*
JOHNSON, DICK (T): *The Girl of Golden West.*
JOHN THE BAPTIST (T): *Hérodiade.*
JOHN THE BUTCHER (B-BAR): *Hugh the Drover.*
JOKANAAN (JOHN THE BAPTIST) (BAR): *Salome.*
JONAS (T): *Le Prophète.*
JONES, BRUTUS (BAR): *The Emperor Jones.*
JOSÉ, DON (T): *Carmen.*
JOUVENOT, MLLE. (S): *Adriana Lecouvreur.*
JUAN (T): *Don Quixote.*
JUDITH (M-S): *Duke Bluebeard's Castle.*
JULIA (S): *La Vestale.*
JULIAN (T): *Louise.*
JULIET (S): *Romeo and Juliet.*
JUNIUS (BAR): *The Rape of Lucretia.*
JUNO (M-S): *Orpheus in the Underworld.*
JUPITER (BAR): *The Love of Danae.*
JUPITER (BAR): *Orpheus in the Underworld.*
JUSTIZRAT (BAR): *Intermezzo.*
KAMMERSANGER (T): *Intermezzo.*
KARNAC (BAR): *Le Roi d'Ys.*
KATINKA (S): *The Bartered Bride.*
THE KEEPER OF THE TEMPLE GATES (S or T FALSETTO): *The Woman without a Shadow.*
KEZAL (B): *The Bartered Bride.*
KHIVRIA (C): *The Fair at Sorochinsk.*
KHOVANTSKY, ANDREW (BAR): *Khovantchina.*
KHOVANTSKY, IVAN (B): *Khovantchina.*
KILIAN (T): *Der Freischütz.*
THE KING (B-BAR): *Fête Galante.*
THE KING (B): *Maritana.*
THE KING OF CLUBS (B): *The Love for Three Oranges.*
KING OF EGYPT (B): *Aïda.*

THE KING OF SPAIN (B): *Christopher Colum-
bus.*
KING OF THE OCEAN (B): *Sadko.*
KING'S SON (T): *Die Königskinder.*
KING WINTER (B): *The Snow Maiden.*
KLINGSOR (B): *Parsifal.*
KLYTEMNESTRA (M-S): *Elektra.*
KOBUS, FRITZ (T): *L'Amico Fritz.*
KONTCHAK (B): *Prince Igor.*
KONTCHAKOVNA (C): *Prince Igor.*
KOTHNER (B): *Die Meistersinger.*
KOUPAVA (M-S): *The Snow Maiden.*
KRAKENTHORP, DUCHESSE DE (S): *The
Daughter of the Regiment.*
KRONTHAL, BARON (T): *The Poacher.*
KRUSCHINA (B): *The Bartered Bride.*
KUNDRY (S): *Parsifal.*
KUNO (B): *Der Freischütz.*
KURWENAL (BAR): *Tristan and Isolde.*
KYOTO (BAR): *Iris.*
LADY-IN-WAITING TO LADY MACBETH
(S): *Macbeth.*
LAERTES (BAR): *Mignon.*
LAKMÉ (S): *Lakmé.*
LAMORAL, GRAF (B): *Arabella.*
LAMPLIGHTER (T): *Manon Lescaut.*
LARINA (M-S): *Eugene Onegin.*
LARTIGON (B): *Zaza.*
LAURA (M-S): *La Gioconda.*
LAURA (C): *Luisa Miller.*
LAURA, COUNTESS (S): *The Beggar Student.*
LAURENCE, FRIAR (B): *Romeo and Juliet.*
LAURETTA (S): *Gianni Schicchi.*
LAWRENCE (BAR): *The Wreckers.*
LAZARILLO (M-S): *Maritana.*
LAZINSKI, BOLESLAO (mime): *Fedora.*
LEANDRO (T): *Harlequin.*
LEANDRO (BAR): *The Love for Three
Oranges.*
LE BRET (B): *Cyrano de Bergerac.*
LECOUVREUR, ADRIANA (S): *Adriana Le-
couvreur.*
LEDA (C): *The Love of Danae.*
LEFEBVRE (T): *Madame Sans-Gêne.*
LEFORT, ADMIRAL (B): *Czar and Carpenter.*
LEILA (S): *The Pearl Fischers.*
LEL (T): *The Snow Maiden.*
LENSKI (T): *Eugene Onegin.*
LEONATO (B): *Béatrice et Bénédict.*
LEONORA (S): *Stradella.*
LEONORA, COUNTESS (S): *Il Trovatore.*
LEONORA DE GUZMAN (M-S): *La Favorita.*
LEONORA DI GUSMANN (S): *La Favorita.*
LEONORA, DONNA (S): *La Forza del Destino.*
LEONORE (S): *Fidelio.*
LEOPOLD, PRINCE (T): *La Juive.*
LEPORELLO (B): *Don Giovanni.*
LERMA, COUNT (T): *Don Carlos.*
LESCAUT (BAR): *Manon.*
LESCAUT (BAR): *Manon Lescaut.*
LESCAUT, MANON (S): *Manon.*
LESCAUT, MANON (S): *Manon Lescaut.*
LETORIÈRES, GASTONE DE (T): *La Traviata.*
LEUKIPPOS (T): *Daphne.*
LEUTHOLD (B): *William Tell.*
LICINIUS (T): *La Vestale.*
LILY (M-S): *Porgy and Bess.*
LINDA (S): *Linda di Chamounix.*
LINDORFF (B): *The Tales of Hoffmann.*
LINDORO (T): *L'Italiana in Algeri.*
LINETTA (C): *The Love for Three Oranges.*
LIONEL (T): *Martha.*
LISA (S): *Cyrano de Bergerac.*
LISA (S): *Pique Dame.*
LISA (S): *La Sonnambula.*
LISETTE (S): *La Rondine.*
THE LITTLE OLD MAN (ARITHMETIC) (T):
L'Enfant et les Sortilèges.
THE LITTLE OWL (S): *L'Enfant et les Sorti-
lèges.*

LIU (S): *Turandot.*
LIVEROTTO (T): *Lucretia Borgia.*
LOBAVA (M-S): *Sadko.*
LOBETANZ (T): *Lobetanz.*
LOCKIT (BAR): *The Beggar's Opera.*
LODOLETTA (S): *Lodoletta.*
LODOVICO (B): *Otello.*
LOGE (T): *Das Rheingold.*
LOHENGRIN (T): *Lohengrin.*
LOLA (M-S): *Cavalleria Rusticana.*
LOPEZ, JUAN (B): *Der Corregidor.*
LOREK (BAR): *Fedora.*
LORENZO (T): *The Dumb Girl of Portici.*
LORENZO (T): *Fra Diavolo.*
LORENZ VON POMMERSFELDEN (B): *Mathis
der Maler.*
LORIS, COUNT (T): *Fedora.*
LOTHARIO (B): *Mignon.*
LOUISE (S): *Louise.*
LOUIS VI (B): *Euryanthe.*
THE LOUIS XV CHAIR (S): *L'Enfant et les
Sortilèges.*
THE LOVER (T): *Fête Galante.*
LUCAS, TIO (BAR): *Der Corregidor.*
LUCIA (C): *Cavalleria Rusticana.*
LUCIA (S): *The Rape of Lucretia.*
LUCRETIA (C): *The Rape of Lucretia.*
LUCY (S): *The Telephone.*
LUCY LOCKIT (S): *The Beggar's Opera.*
LUDMILLA (S): *Russlan and Ludmilla.*
LUIGI (T): *Il Tabarro.*
LUISA (S): *Luisa Miller.*
LUKAS (T): *The Kiss.*
LULU (S): *Lulu.*
LUMMER, BARON (T): *Intermezzo.*
LUNA, COUNT DI (BAR): *Il Trovatore.*
LUTHER (B): *The Tales of Hoffmann.*
LYSIART (BAR): *Euryanthe.*
MACBETH (BAR): *Macbeth.*
MACBETH, LADY (S): *Macbeth.*
MACCUS (BAR): *The King's Henchman.*
MACDUFF (T): *Macbeth.*
CAPTAIN MACHEATH (T): *The Beggar's
Opera.*
MacIRTON (B): *La Dame Blanche.*
MADAME FLORA (BABA) (C): *The Medium.*
MADDALENA (C): *Rigoletto.*
MADELEINE (S): *Andrea Chénier.*
MADELEINE (S): *The Coachman of Longju-
meau.*
MADELEINE (S): *Linda di Chamounix.*
MADELON (M-S): *Andrea Chénier.*
MAFFIO ORSINI (C): *Lucretia Borgia.*
MAGDA (S): *La Rondine.*
MAGDA (S): *The Sunken Bell.*
MAGDALENA (M-S): *Die Meistersinger.*
MAGNIFICO, DON (B): *La Cenerentola.*
MAINTOP (T): *Billy Budd.*
MAITRE AMBROISE (B): *Mireille.*
MAITRE RAMON (B): *Mireille.*
MAJOR-DOMO (T): *Adriana Lecouvreur.*
MAJOR-DOMO (BAR): *Andrea Chénier.*
THE MAJOR-DOMO (B): *Capriccio.*
THE MAJOR-DOMO (T): *Christopher Colum-
bus.*
MALATESTA, DR. (BAR): *Don Pasquale.*
MALATESTINO (T): *Francesca da Rimini.*
MALCOM (T): *Macbeth.*
MALIELLA (S): *The Jewels of the Madonna.*
MALLIKA (M-S): *Lakmé.*
MALVOLIO (BAR): *Stradella.*
MAMAI, ROSA (M-S): *L'Arlesiana.*
MAMMA LUCIA (C): *Cavalleria Rusticana.*
A MANDARIN (BAR): *Turandot (Puccini).*
MANDRYKA (BAR): *Arabella.*
MANFREDO (BAR): *The Love of Three Kings.*
MANFREDO (T): *The Sicilian Vespers.*
MANRICO (T): *Il Trovatore.*
MANTUA, DUKE OF (T): *Rigoletto.*
MANUEL (BAR): *The Brief Life.*

MANUELA (M-S): *Der Corregidor.*
MANZ (BAR): *A Village Romeo and Juliet.*
MARCEL (B): *The Huguenots.*
MARCELLINA (OR BERTA) (S): *The Barber of Seville.*
MARCELLINA (S): *Fidelio.*
MARCELLINA (S): *The Marriage of Figaro.*
MARCELLO (BAR): *La Bohème.*
MARCHESE D'OBIGNY (B): *La Traviata.*
THE MACHIONESS OF MONTEFIORE (M-S): *Maritana.*
MARCO (B): *L'Arlesiana.*
MARCO (BAR): *Gianni Schicchi.*
MARCO (T): *Zaza.*
MARGARED (S): *Le Roi d'Ys.*
MARGARET (C): *Wozzeck.*
MARGIANA (S): *The Barber of Bagdad.*
MARGUERITE (S): *Faust.*
MARGUERITE (S): *La Dame Blanche.*
MARGUERITE (S): *The Damnation of Faust.*
MARGUERITE (S): *Mefistofele.*
MARGUERITE DE VALOIS (S): *The Huguenots.*
MARIA (C): *Porgy and Bess.*
MARIE (S): *The Bartered Bride.*
MARIE (S): *Czar and Carpenter.*
MARIE (S): *The Daughter of the Regiment.*
MARIE (S): *Wozzeck.*
MARINA (M-S): *Boris Godounov.*
MARITANA (S): *Maritana.*
MARK (T): *The Wreckers.*
MARK, KING (B): *Tristan and Isolde.*
MARLARDOT (T): *Zaza.*
MÂROUF (T-BAR): *Mârouf.*
MARQUIS OF MONTEFIORE (B): *Maritana.*
MARS (B): *Orpheus in the Underworld.*
MARSCHALLIN, THE: See *Werdenberg, Princess von.*
MARTHA (M-S): *Faust.*
MARTHA (S): *Khovantchina.*
MARTHA (C): *Mefistofele.*
MARTHA (M-S): *Tiefland.*
MARTI (BAR): *A Village Romeo and Juliet.*
MARTINKA (C): *The Kiss.*
MARULLO, CAVALIERE (BAR): *Rigoletto.*
MARY (C): *The Flying Dutchmann.*
MARY (S): *Hugh the Drover.*
MARY ANN: *The Boatswain's Mate.*
MASANIELLO (T): *The Dumb Girl of Portici.*
MASETTO (BAR): *Don Giovanni.*
THE MASTER OF CEREMONIES (T): *Christopher Colombus.*
THE MASTER OF CEREMONIES (T): *The Love for Three Oranges.*
MATHIEU (BAR): *Andrea Chénier.*
MATHILDE (S): *William Tell.*
MATHIS (B): *Mathis der Maler.*
MATHISEN (B): *Le Prophète.*
MATOUS (B): *The Kiss.*
MATTEO (T): *Arabella.*
MATTEO (B): *Fra Diavolo.*
MATTEO (BAR): *Harlequin.*
MAURIZIO (T): *Adriana Lecouvreur.*
MAX (T): *Der Freischütz.*
MAX (T): *Johnny Plays On.*
MAY (S): *The Cricket on the Hearth.*
MAYOR OF HORNACHUELOS (B): *La Forza del Destino.*
MEFISTOFELE (B): *Mefistofele.*
MEISTER, WILHELM (T): *Mignon.*
MELANTO (M-S): *Il Ritorno d'Ulisse in Patria.*
MELCHTHAL (B): *William Tell.*
MÉLISANDE (S): *Ariane et Barbe-Bleue.*
MÉLISANDE (S): *Pelléas et Mélisande.*
MELITONE, FRA (BAR): *La Forza del Destino .*
MELOT (T): *Tristan and Isolde.*
MENELAUS (T): *The Egyptian Helen.*
MEPHISTOPHELES (B): *The Damnation of Faust.*

MEPHISTOPHELES (B): *Faust.*
MEPHISTOFELE (B): *Mefistofele.*
MERCÉDÈS (S): *Carmen.*
MERCEDES, DONA (S): *Der Corregidor.*
MERCURY (T): *The Love of Danae.*
MERCURY (T): *Orpheus in the Underworld.*
MERCURY (B): *The Trojans*, Part II.
MERCUTIO (BAR): *Romeo and Juliet.*
MERU (BAR): *The Huguenots.*
THE MESSENGER (BAR): *Christopher Columbus.*
THE MESSENGER (B-BAR): *Oedipus Rex.*
MESSENGER OF PEACE (S): *Rienzi.*
METIFIO (BAR): *L'Arlesiana.*
MICHA (B): *The Bartered Bride.*
MICHAÉLA (S): *Carmen.*
MICHELE (BAR): *Il Tabarro.*
MICHELIN (BAR): *Zaza.*
MICHONNET (BAR): *Adriana Lecouvreur.*
MIDAS (T): *The Love of Danae.*
MIGNON (M-S): *Mignon.*
MILADA (S): *Dalibor.*
MILLER (BAR): *Luisa Miller.*
MIME (T): *Das Rheingold; Siegfried.*
MIMI (S): *La Bohème.*
MINERVA (S): *Orpheus in the Underworld.*
MINERVA (S): *Il Ritorno d'Ulisse in Patria.*
MINGO (T): *Porgy and Bess.*
MINNIE (S): *The Girl of the Golden West.*
MIRACLE, DR. (BAR): *The Tales of Hoffmann.*
MIREILLE (S): *Mireille.*
MISSAIL (T): *Boris Godounov.*
MISTRESS OF THE NOVICES (M-S): *Suor Angelica.*
MITRANUS (T): *Semiramide.*
MIZGUIR (BAR): *The Snow Maiden.*
MONICA (S): *The Medium.*
A MONK (B): *Don Carlos.*
MONOSTATOS (T): *The Magic Flute.*
MONTANO (B): *Otello.*
MONTERONE, COUNT (BAR): *Rigoletto.*
MONTFLEURY (T): *Cyrano de Bergerac.*
MORALES (B): *Carmen.*
MORBIO (BAR): *The Silent Woman.*
MORENO (B): *The Dumb Girl of Portici.*
MORFONTAINE, GUILLOT DE (B): *Manon.*
MOROSUS, HENRY (T): *The Silent Woman.*
MOROSUS, SIR (B): *The Silent Woman.*
MORPHEUS (T): *Orpheus in the Underworld.*
MORUCCIO (BAR): *Tiefland.*
MOSER, AUGUSTIN (T): *Die Meistersinger.*
MOTHER GOOSE (M-S): *The Rake's Progress.*
MUSETTA (S): *La Bohème.*
MUSICIAN (M-S): *Manon Lescaut.*
MUSIC MASTER (T): *Manon Lescaut.*
MUSTAFA (B): *L'Italiana in Algeri.*
MYLIO (T): *Le Roi d'Ys.*
MYRTALE (M-S): *Thaïs.*
MYTYL (S): *The Blue Bird.*
NACHTIGALL, CONRAD (B): *Die Meistersinger.*
NADIA (S): *The Pipe of Desire.*
NADINA (speaking role): *Oberon.*
NADIR (T): *The Pearl Fishers.*
NAINA (T): *Russlan and Ludmilla.*
NAMOUNA (speaking role): *Oberon.*
NANCY (M-S): *Albert Herring.*
NANCY (ALTO): *Hugh the Drover.*
NANCY (C): *Martha.*
NANDO (T): *Tiefland.*
NANETTA (S): *Falstaff.*
NANETTE (S): *The Poacher.*
NAPOLEON (BAR): *Madame Sans-Gêne.*
NARBAL (B): *The Trojans*, Part II.
NARRABOTH (T): *Salome.*
THE NARRATOR (speaker): *Christopher Columbus.*
NATALIA (M-S): *Zaza.*
NAVAL CAPTAIN (B): *Manon Lescaut.*
NEDDA (S): *Pagliacci.*

NEIPPERG, COUNT (T): *Madame Sans-Gêne.*
NEJATA (C): *Sadko.*
NELLA (S): *Gianni Schicchi.*
NELSON (T): *Porgy and Bess.*
NELUSKO (BAR): *L'Africaine.*
NEMORINO (T): *The Elixir of Love.*
NEREUS (T): *Mefistofele.*
NERO (T): *Nero.*
NETTUNO (B): *Il Ritorno d'Ulisse in Patria.*
NEVERS, COUNT DE (BAR): *The Huguenots.*
NICIAS (T): *Thaïs.*
NICK (T): *The Girl of the Golden West.*
NICKLAUSSE (T): *The Tales of Hoffmann.*
NICOLA (T): *Fedora.*
NICOLAO, AMANTIO DI (BAR): *Gianni Schicchi.*
NICOLETTA (M-S): *The Love for Three Oranges.*
THE NIGHTINGALE (S): *L'Enfant et les Sortilèges.*
NIGHTINGALE, THE (S): *Le Rossignol.*
NIKITA, BOYAR (T): *Ivan the Terrible.*
NILAKANTHA (B): *Lakmé.*
NINETTA (S): *The Love for Three Oranges.*
NINETTA (S): *The Sicilian Vespers.*
NINUS, GHOST OF (B): *Semiramide.*
MRS. NOLAN (M-S): *The Medium.*
NOLAN, PHILIP (T): *The Man Without a Country.*
NORINA (S): *Don Pasquale.*
NORMA (S): *Norma.*
NORMAN (T): *Lucia di Lammermoor.*
NORNS, THE (M-S): *Die Götterdämmerung.*
NOTARY (BAR): *Don Pasquale.*
THE NOTARY (BAR): *Intermezzo.*
THE NOTARY'S WIFE (S): *Intermezzo.*
NOVICE (T): *Billy Budd.*
THE NOVICE'S FRIEND (BAR): *Billy Budd.*
NURABAD (B): *The Pearl Fishers.*
NUREDDIN (T): *The Barber of Bagdad.*
NURI (S): *Tiefland.*
THE NURSE (DIE AMME) (M-S): *The Woman without a Shadow.*
NURSING SISTER (S): *Suor Angelica.*
OBERON (T): *Oberon.*
OBERTHAL, COUNT (BAR): *Le Prophète.*
OBIGNY, MARCHESE D' (B): *La Traviata.*
OCHS, BARON (B): *Der Rosenkavalier.*
OCTAVIAN (M-S): *Der Rosenkavalier.*
OEDIPUS (T): *Oedipus Rex.*
OFFICER (T): *The Bohemian Girl.*
OFFICIAL REGISTRAR (BAR): *Madam Butterfly.*
OKHRIM (BAR): *The Fair at Sorochinsk.*
OLGA (C): *Eugene Onegin.*
OLGA, COUNTESS (S): *Fedora.*
OLGA, PRINCESS (S): *Ivan the Terrible.*
OLIVIER (BAR): *Capriccio.*
OLLENDORF, COUNT (B): *The Beggar Student.*
OLYMPIA (S): *The Tales of Hoffmann.*
THE ONE-ARMED (B): *The Woman without a Shadow.*
THE ONE-EYED (B): *The Woman without a Shadow.*
ONEGIN, EUGENE (BAR): *Eugene Onegin.*
THE ORATOR (B): *The Magic Flute.*
ORDE (B): *Semiramide.*
ORDGAR (BAR): *The King's Henchman.*
ORESTES (BAR): *Elektra.*
ORESTES (BAR): *Iphigenia in Tauris.*
ORFORD, ELLEN (S): *Peter Grimes.*
ORLOFSKY, PRINCE (M-S): *Die Fledermaus.*
OROVESO (B): *Norma.*
ORPHEUS (B): *Orpheus and Eurydice.*
ORPHEUS (T): *Orpheus in the Underworld.*
ORSINI, PAOLO (B): *Rienzi.*
ORTEL, HERMANN (B): *Die Meistersinger.*
ORTRUD (M-S): *Lohengrin.*
OSAKA (T): *Iris.*

OSCAR (S): *Un Ballo in Maschera.*
OSMIN (B): *The Abduction from the Seraglio.*
OSMINA, SISTER (S): *Suor Angelica.*
OSTASIO (BAR): *Francesca da Rimini.*
OTELLO (T): *Otello.*
OTTAVIO, DON (T): *Don Giovanni.*
OTTOKAR (BAR): *Der Freischütz.*
OURRIAS (BAR): *Mireille.*
OVLOUR (T): *Prince Igor.*
PACO (T): *The Brief Life.*
PADRE GUARDIANO (B): *La Forza del Destino.*
PAGE (BAR): *The Merry Wives of Windsor.*
PAGE, ANNE (S): *The Merry Wives of Windsor.*
PAGE, MISTRESS (M-S): *Falstaff.*
PAGE, MISTRESS (M-S): *The merry Wives of Windsor.*
PAGE, MR. (B): *The Merry Wives of Windsor.*
THE PAINTER (T): *Lulu.*
PALEMON (B): *Thaïs.*
PALMATICA (M-S): *The Beggar Student.*
PALOUCKY (B-BAR): *The Kiss.*
PAMELA, LADY (M-S): *Fra Diavolo.*
PAMINA (S): *The Magic Flute.*
PANCRATIUS (speaking role): *The Poacher.*
PANG (T): *Turandot (Puccini).*
PANTALIS (C): *Mefistofele.*
PANTALONE (B): *Turandot (Busoni).*
PANTALOON (mute): *Fête Galante.*
PANTALOON (BAR): *The Love for Three Oranges.*
PANTHEUS (B): *The Trojans,* Parts I, II.
PAOLA (T): *Francesca da Rimini.*
PAOLINO (T): *Il Matrimonio Segreto.*
PAPAGENA (S): *The Magic Flute.*
PAPAGENO (BAR): *The Magic Flute.*
PAQUIRO (BAR): *Goyescas.*
PARASSIA (S): *The Fair at Sorochinsk.*
PARIS (BAR): *Romeo and Juliet.*
PARPIGNOL (T): *La Bohème.*
PARSIFAL (T): *Parsifal.*
PASCOE (B-BAR): *The Wreckers.*
PASQUALE, DON (B): *Don Pasquale.*
PASQUIER (BAR): *Peter Ibbetson.*
PASQUIER, MARY (S): *Peter Ibbetson.*
PAUL (T): *Die Tote Stadt.*
MR. PEACHAM (B): *The Beggar's Opera.*
MRS. PEACHAM (M-S): *The Beggar's Opera.*
PEDRILLO (T): *The Abduction from the Seraglio.*
PEDRO (T): *Der Corregidor.*
PEDRO (S): *Don Quixote.*
PEDRO (T): *Tiefland.*
PEDRO, DON (B): *Béatrice et Bénédict.*
PEDRO, DON (B): *Don Giovanni.*
PEDRO, DON (B): *L'Africaine.*
PELLÉAS (T): *Pelléas et Mélisande.*
PENEIOS (B): *Daphne.*
PENELOPE (C): *Il Ritorno d'Ulisse in Patria.*
PEPA (M-S): *Goyescas.*
PEPA (S): *Tiefland.*
PERFILIEVNA (M-S): *Ivan the Terrible.*
PERICHAUD (B-BAR): *La Rondine.*
PERSIDE (S): *Nero.*
PETER (BAR): *Hansel and Gretel.*
PETER (T): *Porgy and Bess.*
PETER I (BAR): *Czar and Carpenter.*
PETER IVANOFF (T): *Czar and Carpenter.*
PHANUEL (T): *Hérodiade.*
PHENICE (S): *Armide.*
PHILINE (S): *Mignon.*
PHILIP II (B): *Don Carlos.*
PIERROT (BAR): *Fête Galante.*
PIERROTO (C): *Linda di Chamounix.*
PIETRO (BAR): *The Dumb Girl of Portici.*
PIETRO (B): *Simon Boccanegra.*
PIMEN (B): *Boris Godounov.*
PINELLINO (B): *Gianni Schicchi.*
PING (BAR): *Turandot (Puccini.).*
PINKERTON (T): *Madama Butterfly.*

PINKERTON, KATE (M-S): Madama Butterfly.
PIQUE-DAME (M-S): Pique-Dame.
PISANDRO (T): Il Ritorno d'Ulisse in Patria.
PISTOL (B): Falstaff.
PIZARRO, DON (B): Fidelio.
PLUMMER, EDWARD (T): The Cricket on the Hearth.
PLUNKETT (B): Martha.
PLUTO (T): Orpheus in the Underworld.
POGNER, VEIT (B): Die Meistersinger.
POISSON (T): Adriana Lecouvreur.
POLLIONE (T): Norma.
POLICEMAN (B): The Boatswain's Mate.
A POLISH COMMANDER (BAR): A Life for the Czar.
POLLUX (T): The Love of Danae.
POLLY (S): The Beggar's Opera.
POLYXENA (S): The Trojans, Part I.
PONG (T): Turandot (Puccini).
PONTIFEX MAXIMUS (B): La Vestale.
THE POOR HORN-PLAYER (T): A Village Romeo and Juliet.
PORGY (B-BAR): Porgy and Bess.
POUSETTE (S): Manon.
PREFECT (B): Linda di Chamounix.
PREZIOSILLA (M-S): La Forza del Destino.
PRIAM (B): The Trojans, Parts I, II.
A PRIMROSE-SELLER (C): Hugh the Drover.
THE PRINCE (T): The Love for Three Oranges.
THE PRINCE (T): Lulu.
PRINCE OF PERSIA (BAR): Turandot.
PRINCE OF VERONA (B): Romeo and Juliet.
THE PRINCESS (S): L'Enfant et les Sortilèges.
THE PRINCESS (C): Suor Angelica.
PRINCIPESSA EBOLI (M-S): Don Carlos.
PRINZIVALLE (T): Monna Vanna.
PRUNIER (T): La Rondine.
PRYNNE, HESTER (S): The Scarlet Letter.
PUBLIC OPINION (M-S): Orpheus in the Underworld.
PUBLIUS (B): The Clemency of Titus.
PUCK (S): Oberon.
PYGMALION (T): The Beautiful Galatea.
PYLADES (T): Iphigenia in Tauris.
THE QUEEN (M-S): Fête Galante.
QUEEN, A (M-S): Schwanda the Bagpiper.
THE QUEEN MOTHER OF SAMARKAND (S): Turandot (Busoni).
QUEEN OF SHEMAKHA (S): Le Coq d'Or.
QUEEN OF THE NIGHT (S): The Magic Flute.
QUEEN OF SHEBA (M-S): The Queen of Sheba.
QUEEN OF THE GYPSIES (ALTO): The Bohemian Girl.
QUICKLY, MISTRESS (M-S): Falstaff.
QUINAULT (B): Adriana Lecouvreur.
QUIXOTE, DON (BAR OR B): Don Quixote.
RACHEL (S): La Juive.
RADAMES (T): Aïda.
RAFAELE (BAR): The Jewels of the Madonna.
RAGUENEAU (T): Cyrano de Bergerac.
RAIMBAUT (T): Robert le Diable.
RAIMONDO (B): Rienzi.
RAMIRO (BAR): The Spanish Hour.
RAMIRO, DON (T): La Cenerentola.
RAKEWELL, TOM (T): The Rake's Progress.
RAMBALDO (BAR): La Rondine.
RAMFIS (B): Aïda.
RANCE, JACK (BAR): The Girl of the Golden West.
RAOUL DE NANGIS (T): The Huguenots.
LT. RATCLIFFE (B): Billy Budd.
RATMIR (C): Russlan and Ludmilla.
RAUTENDELEIN (S): The Sunken Bell.
RAYMOND (B): Lucia di Lammermoor.
MR. REDBURN (BAR): Billy Budd.
RED WHISKERS (T): Billy Budd.
REGINA (S): Mathis der Maler.
REIMER VON ZWETER (B): Tannhaüser.
REMENDADO, LE (T): Carmen.

RENATO (BAR): Un Ballo in Maschera.
REPELA (B): Der Corregidor.
THE REPRESENTATIVE OF THE SAILORS (speaking role): Christopher Columbus.
REZIA (S): Oberon.
RHADAMES (T): Aïda.
RHINE MAIDENS: See Flosshilde, Wellgunde, Woglinde.
RICCARDO, DON (T): Ernani.
RICARDO (T): Un Ballo in Maschera.
RIEDINGER (B): Mathis der Maler.
RIENZI, COLA DI (T): Rienzi.
RIGOLETTO (BAR): Rigoletto.
RINALDO (T): Armide.
RINUCCIO (T): Gianni Schicchi.
ROBBINS (T): Porgy and Bess.
ROBERT (B): Hugh the Drover.
ROBERT (T): Robert le Diable.
ROBERTO (B): The Sicilian Vespers.
ROBERTSON, SIR BENNO (T): I Puritani.
ROBINSON, COUNT (B): Il Matrimonio Segreto).
ROCCO (B): Fidelio.
LA ROCHE (B): Capriccio.
RODERIGO (T): Otello.
RODOLFO (T): La Bohème.
RODRIG, ACT II (ANIMAL-TAMER, PROLOGUE) (B): Lulu.
RODRIGO (BAR): Don Carlos.
RODRIGUEZ (T): Don Quixote.
LE ROI D'YS (B): Le Roi d'Ys.
ROMEO (T): Romeo and Juliet.
ROSALIA (C): Tiefland.
ROSALINDE (S): Die Fledermaus.
ROSA MAMAI (M-S): L'Arlesiana.
ROSARIO (S): Goyescas.
ROSCHANA (C): Oberon.
ROSE (S): The Coachman of Longjumeau.
ROSE (M-S): Lakmé.
ROSETTE (S): Manon.
ROSHANA (speaking role): Oberon.
ROSINA (M-S): The Barber of Seville.
ROSSA, LA (S): Madame Sans-Gêne.
ROUCHER (B): Andrea Chénier.
ROUVEL, BARON (T): Fedora.
ROXANE (S): Cyrano de Bergerac.
ROZENN (S): Le Roi d'Ys.
RUBRIA (M-S): Nero.
RUDOLPH (T): Euryanthe.
RUDOLF (T): William Tell.
RUDOLFO (T): Luisa Miller.
RUDOLPHO, COUNT (B): La Sonnambula.
RUGGERO (T): La Rondine.
RUGGIERO (BAR): La Juive.
RUIZ (T): Il Trovatore.
RUODI (T): William Tell.
RUSSLAN (BAR): Russlan and Ludmilla.
RUSTIGHELLO (T): Lucretia Borgia.
RUTLEDGE, MARY (S): The Man Without a Country.
RUY GOMEZ, DON (B): Ernani.
SAAMCHEDDINE, PRINCESS (S): Mârouf.
SACHS, HANS (B): Die Meistersinger.
SACRISTAN (BAR): Tosca.
SADKO (T): Sadko.
THE SAILOR (T): The Poor Sailor.
SAILOR (T): Tristan and Isolde.
THE SAILOR'S FATHER-IN-LAW (B): The Poor Sailor.
THE SAILOR'S FRIEND (BAR): The Poor Sailor.
THE SAILOR'S WIFE (S): The Poor Sailor.
ST. BRIS, COMTE DE (B): The Huguenots.
SAINT CHAVEZ (T): Four Saints in Three Acts.
SAINT IGNATIUS LOYOLA (BAR): Four Saints in Three Acts.
SAINT TERESA I (S): Four Saints in Three Acts.

SAINT TERESA II (C): *Four Saints in Three Acts.*
SAINT SETTLEMENT (S): *Four Saints in Three Acts.*
SALI, AS A CHILD (S): *A Village Romeo and Juliet.*
SALI, AS A MAN (T): *A Village Romeo and Juliet.*
SALOMÉ (S): *Hérodiade.*
SALOME (S): *Salome.*
SALUD (S): *The Brief Life.*
SALUD'S GRANDMOTHER (M-S): *The Brief Life.*
SALVIATI, CARDINAL (B): *Benvenuto Cellini.*
SAMARITANA (S): *Francesca da Rimini.*
SAMIEL (speaking role): *Der Freischütz.*
SAMOSET (B): *Merry Mount.*
SAMSON (T): *Samson and Delilah.*
SAMSON (B): *The Warrior.*
SAMUELE (COUNT RIBBING) (B): *Un Ballo in Maschera.*
SANCHO PANZA (BAR): *Don Quixote.*
SANDMAN, THE (S): *Hansel and Gretel.*
SANTAREM, DON JOSE DE (BAR): *Maritana.*
SANTE (silent): *Susanna's Secret.*
SANTUZZA (S): *Cavalleria Rusticana.*
SARASTRO (B): *The Magic Flute.*
SARVAOR (B): *The Brief Life.*
SATYAVAN (T): *Savitri.*
SAVITRI (S): *Savitri.*
SCARPIA, BARON (BAR): *La Tosca.*
SCHAUNARD (BAR): *La Bohème.*
SCHICCHI, GIANNI (BAR): *Gianni Schicchi.*
SCHIGOLCH (B): *Lulu.*
SCHLÉMIL (B): *The Tales of Hoffmann.*
SCHMIDT (BAR): *Andrea Chénier.*
SCHÖN, DR. (BAR): *Lulu.*
SCHWALB, HANS (T): *Mathis der Maler.*
SCHWANDA (T): *Schwanda the Bagpiper.*
SCHWARZ, HANS (B): *Die Meistersinger.*
SCIARONNE (B): *Tosca.*
SEA NYMPH (S): *Oberon.*
SEBASTIANO (BAR): *Tiefland.*
SECOND MATE (BAR): *Billy Budd.*
SEDLEY, MRS. (C): *Peter Grimes.*
SELIKA (S): *L'Africaine.*
SELIM, PASHA (speaking role): *The Abduction from the Seraglio.*
SELLEM (T): *The Rake's Progress.*
SELVA (B): *The Dumb Girl of Portici.*
SELYSETTE (M-S): *Ariane et Barbe-Bleue.*
SEMELE (S): *The Love of Danae.*
SEMIRAMIDE (S): *Semiramide.*
SENTA (S): *The Flying Dutchman.*
A SENTRY (T): *Ivan the Terrible.*
SEOULA (B): *Prince Igor.*
SERASKIER, MME. (S): *Peter Ibbetson.*
SERENA (S): *Porgy and Bess.*
A SERGEANT (BAR): *Hugh the Drover.*
SERGEANT OF ARCHERS (B): *Manon Lescaut.*
SERGIO (BAR): *Fedora.*
SERPINA (S): *The Maid-Mistress.*
SERVILIA (S): *The Clemency of Titus.*
SEXTUS (C): *The Clemency of Titus.*
SHADOW, NICK (BAR): *The Rake's Progress.*
SHAKLOVITY (B): *Khovantchina.*
SHALLOW (BAR): *The Merry Wives of Windsor.*
SHARPLESS (BAR): *Madam Butterfly.*
A SHELLFISH SELLER (B): *Hugh the Drover.*
A SHEPHERD (C): *L'Enfant et les Sortilèges.*
THE SHEPHERD (T): *Oedipus Rex.*
SHEPHERD (S): *Tannhäuser.*
SHEPHERD (T): *Tristan and Isolde.*
A SHEPHERD GIRL (S): *L'Enfant et les Sortilèges.*
SHERASMIN (BAR): *Oberon.*
SHERIFF (BAR): *Martha.*
A SHOWMAN (BAR): *Hugh the Drover.*

SHOWMAN (T): *A Village Romeo and Juliet.*
SHUISKY, PRINCE (T): *Boris Godounov.*
SID (BAR): *Albert Herring.*
SIDONIE (S): *Armide.*
SIEBEL (S): *Faust.*
SIEGFRIED (T): *Siegfried: Die Götterdämmerung.*
SIEGLINDE (S): *Die Walküre.*
SIEGMUND (T): *Die Walküre.*
SIGNA, BETTO DI (B): *Gianni Schicchi.*
SILVA, DON RUY GOMEZ DI (B): *Ernani.*
SILVANO (BAR): *Un Ballo in Maschera.*
SILVIO (BAR): *Pagliacci.*
SIMON (T): *The Beggar Student.*
SIMONA (S): *Zaza.*
SIMONE (B): *Gianni Schicchi.*
SIMON MAGO (BAR): *Nero.*
A SINGER (BAR): *The Brief Life.*
SIRIEX, DE (BAR): *Fedora.*
SLENDER (T): *The Merry Wives of Windsor.*
THE SLIM GIRL (S): *A Village Romeo and Juliet.*
SMERALDINA (M-S): *The Love for Three Oranges.*
SMITHERS, HENRY (T): *The Emperor Jones.*
SNEGUROCHKA (S): *The Snow Maiden.*
SOBINJIN (T): *A Life for the Czar.*
SOLOMON, KING (BAR): *The Queen of Sheba.*
SOMARONA (B): *Béatrice et Bénédict.*
SOPHIE (S): *Der Rosenkavalier.*
SPALANZANI (T): *The Tales of Hoffmann.*
SPARAFUCILE (B): *Rigoletto.*
SPINELLOCCIO, MAESTRO (B): *Gianni Schicchi.*
A SPIRIT-MESSENGER (BAR): *The Woman without a Shadow.*
SPLENDIANO (T): *Djamileh.*
SPOLETTA (T): *Tosca.*
SPORTING LIFE (T): *Porgy and Bess.*
SQUEAK (T): *Billy Budd.*
THE SQUIRREL (M-S): *L'Enfant et les Sortilèges.*
STCHELKALOV (BAR): *Boris Godounov.*
STEERSMAN (T): *Tristan and Isolde.*
STEFANO (S): *Romeo and Juliet.*
STELLA (S): *The Tales of Hoffmann.*
STESHA (BOYARDIN STEPHANIDA MATOUTA) (S): *Ivan the Terrible.*
STORCH, HOFKAPELLMEISTER ROBERT (BAR): *Intermezzo.*
STRADELLA, ALESSANDRO (T): *Stradella.*
STROH, KAPELLMEISTER (T): *Intermezzo.*
STROMMINGER (B): *La Wally.*
STYX, JOHN (BAR): *Orpheus in the Underworld.*
SULAMITH (S): *The Queen of Sheba.*
SULPICE (B): *The Daughter of the Regiment.*
THE SULTAN MIRAMOLIN (T): *Christopher Columbus.*
SULTAN OF KHAITAN (B): *Mârouf.*
SUOR GENOVEVA (S): *Suor Angelica.*
SUPERINTENDENT BUDD (B): *Albert Herring.*
SUSAN (S): *Hugh the Drover.*
SUSANIN, IVAN (B): *A Life for the Czar.*
SUSANNA (S): *The Marriage of Figaro.*
SUSANNA, COUNTESS (S): *Susanna's Secret.*
SUZEL (S): *L'Amico Fritz.*
SUZUKI (M-S): *Madam Butterfly.*
SUZY (M-S): *La Rondine.*
SVIETOSAR (B): *Russlan and Ludmilla.*
SYLVESTER VON SCHAUMBERG (T): *Mathis der Maler.*
SYNDHAM, LORD (B): *Czar and Carpenter.*
TACKLETON (B): *The Cricket on the Hearth.*
TADDEO (B): *L'Italiana in Algeri.*
TALBOT, ARNOLD (T): *The Witch of Salem.*
TALBOT, LORD ARTHUR (T): *I Puritani.*
TALLAN (T): *The Wreckers.*
TALPA (B): *Il Tabarro.*
TAMINO (T): *The Magic Flute.*

TANNHAÜSER (T): *Tannhaüser.*
TARQUINIUS (BAR): *The Rape of Lucretia.*
TARTAGLIA (B): *Turandot* (Busoni).
TATIANA (S): *Eugene Onegin.*
TAUPE, MONSIEUR (T): *Capriccio.*
TAVEN (M-S): *Mireille.*
TCHEREVIK (B): *The Fair at Sorochinsk.*
TCHERNOMOR: *Russlan and Ludmilla.*
THE TEA POT (T): *L'Enfant et les Sortilèges.*
TEBALDO (S): *Don Carlos.*
TEBALDO (T): *The Sicilian Vespers.*
TELEMACO (M-S): *Il Ritorno d'Ulisse in Patria.*
TELL, WILLIAM (B): *William Tell.*
TEMPLE-WATCHMAN (B): *The Queen of Sheba.*
TERESA (S): *Benvenuto Cellini.*
TERESA (S): *La Sonnambula.*
TEWKE, PLENTIFUL (M-S): *Merry Mount.*
TEWKE, PRAISE-GOD (BAR): *Merry Mount.*
THADDEUS (T): *The Bohemian Girl.*
THAÏS (S): *Thaïs.*
THANATOS (BAR): *Alceste.*
THE THEATER DIRECTOR (B): *Lulu.*
THIRZA (M-S): *The Wreckers.*
THISBE (M-S): *La Cenerentola.*
THOAS (B): *Iphigenia in Tauris.*
TIGELLINO (B): *Nero.*
TIMUR (B): *Turandot.*
TINCA (T): *Il Tabarro.*
TINKER, FAINT-NOT (BAR): *Merry Mount.*
TIRESIAS (B): *Oedipus Rex.*
TITANIA (speaking role): *Oberon.*
TITUREL (B): *Parsifal.*
TITUS (T): *The Clemency of Titus.*
TOBY (MUTE): *The Medium.*
TODD, MISS (C): *The Old Maid and the Thief.*
TOMMASO (B): *Tiefland.*
TOMASO (COUNT HORN): *Un Ballo in Maschera.*
THE TOM CAT (BAR): *L'Enfant et les Sortilèges.*
TOMES (BAR): *The Kiss.*
TONIO (T): *The Daughter of the Regiment.*
TONIO (BAR): *Pagliacci.*
TONIOTTA (S): *Madame Sans-Gêne.*
TONUELO (B): *Der Corregidor.*
TORELLO (BAR): *Monna Vanna.*
TORQUEMADA (T): *The Spanish Hour.*
TOSCA, FLORIA (S): *La Tosca.*
TOTO (S): *Zaza.*
TOUCHA, MICHAEL ANDREIEVITCH (T): *Ivan the Terrible.*
TRABUCCO (T): *La Forza del Destino.*
MRS. TRAPES (M-S): *The Beggar's Opera.*
TRAVERS, NED (BAR): *The Boatswain's Mate.*
A TREE (B): *L'Enfant et les Sortilèges.*
TRISTAN (T): *Tristan and Isolde.*
TRISTAN, LORD (BAR): *Martha.*
TRIVULZIO (BAR): *Monna Vanna.*
TRUCHSESS VON WALDBURG (B): *Mathis der Maler.*
TRUFALDINO (T): *The Love for Three Oranges.*
TRUFFALDINO (T): *Turandot* (Busoni).
TRULOVE (B): *The Rake's Progress.*
THE TRUMPETER (B. Trombone): *The Love for Three Oranges.*
TURANDOT (S): *Turandot* (Busoni).
TURANDOT (S): *Turandot* (Puccini).
TURIDDU (T): *Cavalleria Rusticana.*
THE TURNKEY (T): *Hugh the Drover.*
TYBALT (T): *Romeo and Juliet.*
TYL, FATHER (BAR): *The Blue Bird.*
TYL, GRANDFATHER (B): *The Blue Bird.*
TYL, GRANDMOTHER (C): *The Blue Bird.*
TYL, MOTHER (C): *The Blue Bird.*
TYLTYL (S): *The Blue Bird.*
UBALDO (BAR): *Armide.*
UBERTO (B): *The Maid-Mistress.*
ULISSE (T): *Il Ritorno d'Ulisse in Patria.*

ULRICA (C): *Un Ballo in Maschera.*
UNDERTAKER (BAR): *Porgy and Bess.*
UNDINE (S): *Undine.*
MR. UPFOLD (T): *Albert Herring.*
URBAIN (S OR C): *The Huguenots.*
URSULA (C): *Béatrice et Bénédict.*
URSULA (S): *Mathis der Maler.*
VALENTINE (BAR): *Faust.*
VALENTINE (S): *The Huguenots.*
VANNA, MONNA (S): *Monna Vanna.*
VANNA, MARCO (B): *Monna Vanna.*
VALOIS, ELIZABETH DE (S): *Don Carlos.*
VANJA (C): *A Life for the Czar.*
VANUZZI (B): *The Silent Woman.*
VARLAAM (B): *Boris Godounov.*
VASCO DA GAMA (T): *L'Africaine.*
VAUDEMONT, COUNT (B): *The Sicilian Vespers.*
VEDIO (T): *Monna Vanna.*
VELEBIN, YOUSKO (B): *Ivan the Terrible.*
VENDULKA (S): *The Kiss.*
VENETIAN MERCHANT (BAR): *Sadko.*
VENUS (C): *Orpheus in the Underworld.*
VENUS (S): *Tannhaüser.*
VESPONE (silent): *The Maid-mistress.*
VIAZEMSKY, PRINCE AFANASY (T): *Ivan the Terrible.*
VIKING MERCHANT (B): *Sadko.*
VINCENT (T): *Mireille.*
VINCENZO GELLNER (BAR): *La Wally.*
VIOLETTA VALERY (S): *La Traviata.*
VITEK (T): *Dalibor.*
VITELLIA (S): *The Clemency of Titus.*
VITELLIUS (BAR): *Hérodiade.*
VITELLOZZO (B): *Lucretia Borgia.*
VIVETTA (S): *L'Arlesiana.*
THE VIZIER (BAR): *Mârouf.*
VLADIMIR (T): *Prince Igor.*
VLADISLAV (BAR): *Dalibor.*
VLASSIEVNA (ALTO): *Ivan the Terrible.*
VOEVODA POLKAN (B): *Le Coq d'Or.*
VOGELGESANG, KUNZ (T): *Die Meistersinger.*
VOICE FROM ABOVE (C): *The Woman without a Shadow.*
VOICE OF APOLLO (BAR): *Alceste.*
VOICE OF NEPTUNE (B): *Idomeneo.*
VOLKHOVA (S): *Sadko.*
VRELI (S): *A Village Romeo and Juliet.*
WAGNER (T): *Mefistofele.*
WALDNER, GRAF (B): *Arabella.*
WALLACE, JAKE (BAR): *The Girl of the Golden West.*
WALLY (S): *La Wally.*
WALTER (S): *La Wally.*
WALTER, COUNT (B): *Luisa Miller.*
WALTHER VON DER VOGELWEIDE (T): *Tannhäuser.*
WALTHER VON STOLZING (T): *Die Meistersinger.*
WALTON, LORD GAUTIER (B): *I Puritani.*
WALTON, SIR GEORGE (B): *I Puritani.*
WALTRAUTE (M-S): *Die Götterdämmerung.*
WARDROBE-MISTRESS, ACT I (GYMNASIAST, ACT II) (C): *Lulu.*
WATCHMAN (B): *Die Meistersinger.*
WATERS, MRS. (S): *The Boatswain's Mate.*
WELLGUNDE (S): *Das Rheingold; Die Götterdämmerung.*
WENZEL (T): *The Bartered Bride.*
WERDENBERG, PRINCESS VON (S): *Der Rosenkavalier.*
WERTHER (T): *Werther.*
WHEEL-OF-FORTUNE WOMAN (S): *A Village Romeo and Juliet.*
WIG-MAKER (MIME): *Manon Lescaut.*
THE WILD GIRL (M-S): *A Village Romeo and Juliet.*
WILLIAM (T): *Hugh the Drover.*
WILLOUGHBY, CLARIS (S): *The Witch of Salem.*

WILSON, REV. JOHN (B): *The Scarlet Letter.*
WIN-SAN-LUY (T): *L'Oracolo.*
WIN-SHEE (BAR): *L'Oracolo.*
WITCH (C): *Die Königskinder.*
WITCH (M-S): *Hansel and Gretel.*
WITWE BROWE (C): *Czar and Carpenter.*
WOGLINDE (S): *Das Rheingold; Die Götterdämmerung.*
WOLFRAM VON ESCHENBACH (BAR): *Tannhäuser.*
A WOMAN (S): *Alceste.*
WOOD BIRD (S): *Siegfried.*
WORDSWORTH, MISS (S): *Albert Herring.*
WOTAN (B-BAR): *Das Rheingold; Die Walküre; Siegfried.*
WOWKLE (M-S): *The Girl of the Golden West.*
WOZZECK (T): *Wozzeck.*
WURM (B): *Luisa Miller.*
XANTHE (S): *The Love of Danae.*
XENIA (S): *Boris Godounov.*
YGRAINE (S): *Ariane et Barbe-Bleue.*
YNIOLD (S): *Pelléas et Mélisande.*
YOURY, PRINCE (B): *Ivan the Terrible.*
YVETTE (S): *La Rondine.*
YVONNE (S): *Johnny Plays On.*
ZACCARIA (B): *Nabucco.*
ZACHARIAS (B): *Le Prophète.*
ZAMIEL (SPEAKING ROLE): *Der Freischütz.*
ZAZA (S): *Zaza.*
ZDENEK'S GHOST: *Dalibor.*
ZDENKA (S): *Arabella.*
ZERBINETTA (S): *Ariadne auf Naxos.*
ZERLINA (S): *Don Giovanni.*
ZERLINA (S): *Fra Diavolo.*
ZITA (M-S): *Gianni Schicchi.*
ZORN, BALTHASAR (T): *Die Meistersinger.*
ZUANE (B): *La Gioconda.*
ZULMA (C): *L'Italiana in Algeri.*
ZUNIGA (B): *Carmen.*
ZURGA (BAR): *The Pearl Fishers.*

The Characters of Shakespeare's Plays

See also Songs from Shakespeare's Plays

AARON: A Moor, beloved by Tamora; *Titus Andronicus.*
ABBOT OF WESTMINSTER: *Richard II.*
ABERGAVENNY, LORD: *King Henry VIII.*
ABHORSON: AN executioner; *Measure for Measure.*
ABRAM: Servant of Montague; *Romeo and Juliet.*
ACHILLES: A Grecian commander; *Troilus and Cressida.*
ADAM: Servant of Oliver; *As You Like It.*
ADRIAN: A lord of Naples; *The Tempest.*
ADRIANA: Wife of Antipholus of Ephesus; *The Comedy of Errors.*
AEGON: A merchant of Syracuse; *The Comedy of Errors.*
AEMILLIA: An abbess at Ephesus; *The Comedy of Errors.*
AEMILIUS: A noble Roman; *Titus Andronicus.*
AEMILIUS LEPIDUS: A Roman triumvir; *Julius Caesar.*
AENEAS: A Trojan commander; *Troilus and Cressida.*
AGAMEMNON: A Grecian general; *Troilus and Cressida.*
AGRIPPA: A friend of Caesar; *Antony and Cleopatra.*
AGRIPPA, MENENIUS: Friend of Coriolanus; *Coriolanus.*
AGUECHEEK, SIR ANDREW: *Twelfth Night.*
AJAX: A Grecian commander; *Troilus and Cressida.*

ALARBUS: Son of Tamora; *Titus Andronicus.*
ALBANY, DUKE OF: *King Lear.*
ALCIBIADES: An Athenian general; *Timon of Athens.*
ALENÇON, DUKE OF: *King Henry VI,* Part I.
ALEXANDER: Servant of Cressida; *Troilus and Cressida.*
ALEXAS: Attendant of Cleopatra; *Antony and Cleopatra.*
ALICE: *Attendant of Princess Katharine; King Henry V.*
ALONSO: King of Naples; *The Tempest.*
AMIENS: A lord attendant of the exiled Duke; *As You Like It.*
ANDROMACHE: Wife of Hector; *Troilus and Cressida.*
ANDRONICUS, MARCUS: Tribune, brother of Titus; *Titus Andronicus.*
ANDRONICUS, TITUS: General against the Goths; *Titus Andronicus.*
ANGELO: Deputy of Duke of Vienna; *Measure for Measure.*
ANGELO: A goldsmith; *The Comedy of Errors.*
ANGUS: A Scottish nobleman; *Macbeth.*
ANNE, LADY: Widow of Edward Prince of Wales; *King Richard III.*
ANNE BULLEN: Afterward Queen; *King Henry VIII.*
ANNE PAGE: Daughter of Mrs. Page; *The Merry Wives of Windsor.*
ANTENOR: A Trojan commander; *Troilus and Cressida.*
ANTIGONUS: A Sicilian lord; *The Winter's Tale.*
ANTIOCHUS: King of Antioch; *Pericles.*
ANTIOCHUS, DAUGHTER OF: *Pericles.*
ANTIPHOLUS OF EPHESUS; ANTIPHOLUS OF SYRACUSE: Twin brothers, sons of Aegeon, but unknown to each other; *The Comedy of Errors.*
ANTONIO: Brother of Leonato; *Much Ado About Nothing.*
ANTONIO: Usurping Duke of Milan; *The Tempest.*
ANTONIO: Father of Proteus; *Two Gentlemen of Verona.*
ANTONIO: The Merchant of Venice; *The Merchant of Venice.*
ANTONIO: A sea captain; *Twelfth Night.*
ANTONY, MARK: A triumvir; *Antony and Cleopatra.*
APEMANTUS: A churlish philosopher; *Timon of Athens.*
APOTHECARY, AN: *Romeo and Juliet.*
ARCHBISHOP OF CANTERBURY: *King Henry V.*
ARCHBISHOP OF CANTERBURY: Cardinal Bourchier; *King Richard III.*
ARCHBISHOP OF CANTERBURY: Cranmer; *King Henry VIII.*
ARCHBISHOP OF YORK: Thomas Rotherham; *King Richard III.*
ARCHBISHOP OF YORK: Scroop; *King Henry IV,* Parts I, II.
ARCHDUKE OF AUSTRIA: *King John.*
ARCHIBALD: Earl of Douglas; *King Henry IV,* Parts I, II.
ARCHIDAMUS: A Bohemian lord; *The Winter's Tale.*
ARIEL: An airy spirit; *The Tempest.*
ARMADO, DON ADRIANO DE: A fantastical Spaniard; *Love's Labour's Lost.*
ARRAGON, PRINCE OF: Suitor of Portia; *The Merchant of Venice.*
ARTHUR: Elder brother of King John; *King John.*
ARTIMIDORUS: A Sophist of Cnidos; *Julius Caesar.*
ARVIRAGUS: Son of Cymbeline; *Cymbeline.*
AUDREY: A country wench; *As You Like It.*

AUFIDIUS, TULLUS: Volscian general; *Coriolanus.*

AUMERLE, DUKE OF: Son of Duke of York; *King Richard II.*

AUTOLYCUS: A rogue; *The Winter's Tale.*

AUVERGNE, COUNTESS OF: *King Henry VI, Part I.*

BAGOT: Favorite of King Richard II; *King Richard II.*

BALTHAZAR: A merchant; *The Comedy of Errors.*

BALTHAZAR: Servant to Don Pedro; *Much Ado About Nothing.*

BALTHAZAR: Servant to Portia; *The Merchant of Venice.*

BALTHAZAR: Servant to Romeo; *Romeo and Juliet.*

BANISHED DUKE: *As You Like It.*

BANQUO: A general; *Macbeth.*

BAPTISTA: A rich gentleman of Padua; *The Taming of the Shrew.*

BARDOLPH: Follower of Sir John Falstaff; *King Henry IV,* Parts I, II.

BARDOLPH: A follower of Falstaff; *The Merry Wiwes of Windsor.*

BARDOLPH: Soldier in King's Army; *King Henry V.*

BARDOLPH, LORD: Enemy of the King; *King Henry IV,* Part II.

BARNARDINE: A dissolute prisoner; *Measure for Measure.*

BASSANIO: Friend of Antonio, the Merchant of Venice; *The Merchant of Venice.*

BASSET: Of the Red Rose faction; *King Henry VI,* Part 1.

BASSIANUS: Brother of Saturninus; *Titus Andronicus.*

BASTARD OF ORLEANS: *King Henry VI, Part I.*

BATES: Soldier in King's Army; *King Henry V.*

BEATRICE: Niece of Leonato; *Much Ado About Nothing.*

BEAUFORT, CARDINAL: Bishop of Winchester; *King Henry VI,* Part II.

BEAUFORT, HENRY: Bishop of Winchester; *King Henry VI,* Part I.

BEAUFORT, JOHN: · Earl of Somerset; *King Henry VI,* Part I.

BEAUFORT, THOMAS: Duke of Exeter; *King Henry VI,* Part I.

BEDFORD, DUKE OF: Brother of Henry V; *King Henry V.*

BEDFORD, DUKE OF: Regent of France; *King Henry VI,* Part I.

BELARIUS: A banished lord; *Cymbeline.*

BELCH, SIR TOBY: Uncle of Olivia; *Twelfth Night.*

BENEDICK: A young lord of Padua; *Much Ado About Nothing.*

BENVOLIO: Friend of Romeo; *Romeo and Juliet.*

BERKELEY, EARL: *King Richard II.*

BERNARDO: An officer; *Hamlet.*

BERTRAM: Count of Rousillon; *All's Well that Ends Well.*

BIANCA: Mistress of Cassio; *Othello.*

BIANCA: Sister of Katharine; *The Taming of the Shrew.*

BIGOT, ROBERT: Earl of Norfolk; *King John.*

BIONDELLO: Servant of Lucentio; *The Taming of the Shrew.*

BIRON: A lord attendant on the King of Navarre; *Love's Labour's Lost.*

BISHOP OF CARLISLE: *King Richard II.*

BISHOP OF ELY: John Morton; *King Richard III.*

BISHOP OF ELY: *King Henry V.*

BISHOP OF LINCOLN: *King Henry VIII.*

BISHOP OF WINCHESTER: Gardiner; *King Henry VIII.*

BLANCH: Niece of King John; *King John.*

BLOUNT, SIR JAMES: *King Richard III.*

BLUNT, SIR WALTER: Friend of Henry IV; *King Henry IV,* Parts I, II.

BOLINGBROKE: A conjuror; *King Henry VI,* Part II.

BOLINGBROKE: Afterward Henry IV; *King Richard II.*

BONA: Sister of the French Queen; *King Henry VI,* Part III.

BORACHIO: Follower of Don John; *Much Ado About Nothing.*

BOTTOM: The weaver; *A Midsummer Night's Dream.*

BOURCHIER, CARDINAL: Archbishop of Canterbury; *King Richard III.*

BOULT: A servant; *Pericles.*

BOURBON, DUKE OF: *King Henry V.*

BOYET: A lord attending the Princes of France; *Love's Labour's Lost.*

BRABANTIO: A senator; *Othello.*

BRAKENBURY, SIR ROBERT: Lieutenant of the Tower; *King Richard III.*

BRANDON: *King Henry VIII.*

BRUTUS, DECIUS: A Roman conspirator; *Julius Caesar.*

BRUTUS, JUNIUS: Tribune of the people; *Coriolanus.*

BRUTUS, MARCUS: A Roman conspirator; *Julius Caesar.*

BUCKINGHAM, DUKE OF: *King Henry VIII.*

BUCKINGHAM, DUKE OF: *King Richard III.*

BUCKINGHAM, DUKE OF: Of the King's Party; *King Henry VI,* Part II.

BULLCALF: A recruit; *King Henry IV,* Part II.

BULLEN, ANNE: Afterward Queen; *King Henry VIII.*

BURGH, HUBERT DE: Chamberlain to King John; *King John.*

BURGUNDY, DUKE OF: *King Henry V.*

BURGUNDY, DUKE OF: *King Henry VI.* Part I.

BURGUNDY, DUKE OF: *King Lear.*

BUSHY: Favorite of Richard II; *King Richard II.*

BUTTS, DR.: Physician to Henry VIII; *King Henry VIII.*

CADE, JACK: A rebel; *King Henry VI,* Part II.

CADWAL: Arviragus in disguise; *Cymbeline.*

CAESAR, JULIUS: *Julius Caesar.*

CAESAR, OCTAVIUS: A triumvir; *Antony and Cleopatra.*

CAITHNESS: A Scottish nobleman; *Macbeth.*

CAIUS, DR.: A French physician; *The Merry Wives of Windsor.*

CAIUS, LUCIUS: General of Roman forces; *Cymbeline.*

CAIUS MARCIUS CORIOLANUS: A noble Roman; *Coriolanus.*

CALCHAS: A Trojan Priest; *Troilus and Cressida.*

CALIBAN: A savage and deformed slave; *The Tempest.*

CALPURNIA: Wife of Caesar; *Julius Caesar.*

CAMBRIDGE, EARL OF: A conspirator; *King Henry V.*

CAMILLO: A Sicilian lord; *The Winter's Tale.*

CAMPEIUS, CARDINAL: *King Henry VIII.*

CANIDIUS: Lieutenant-general of Antony; *Antony and Cleopatra.*

CANTERBURY, ARCHBISHOP OF: Cardinal Bouchier; *King Richard III.*

CANTERBURY, ARCHBISHOP OF: Cranmer; *King Henry VIII.*

CANTERBURY, ARCHBISHOP OF: *King Henry V.*

CAPHIS: A servant; *Timon of Athens.*

CAPUCIUS: Ambassador from Charles V; *King Henry VIII.*

CAPULET: At variance with Montague; *Romeo and Juliet.*

CAPULET, LADY: Wife of Capulet; *Romeo and Juliet.*

CARDINAL BEAUFORT: Bishop of Winchester; *King Henry VI,* Part II.

CARDINAL BOURCHIER: Archbishop of Canterbury; *King Richard III.*

CARDINAL CAMPEIUS: *King Henry VIII.*

CARDINAL PANDULPH: The Pope's legate; *King John.*

CARDINAL WOLSEY: *King Henry VIII.*

CARLISLE, BISHOP OF: *King Richard II.*

CASCA: A Roman conspirator; *Julius Caesar.*

CASSANDRA: Daughter of Priam; *Troilus and Cressida.*

CASSIO: Lieutenant to Othello; *Othello.*

CASSIUS: A Roman conspirator; *Julius Caesar.*

CATESBY, SIR WILLIAM: *King Richard III.*

CATO, YOUNG: Friend of Brutus and Cassius; *Julius Caesar.*

CELIA: Daughter of Frederick; *As You Like It.*

CERES: A spirit; *The Tempest.*

CERIMON: A lord of Ephesus; *Pericles.*

CHARLES: The Dauphin; *King Henry VI,* Part I.

CHARLES: A wrestler; *As You Like It.*

CHARLES VI: King of France; *King Henry V.*

CHARMIAN: Attendant of Cleopatra; *Antony and Cleopatra.*

CHATILLON: Ambassador from France; *King John.*

CHIRON: Son of Tamora; *Titus Andronicus.*

CHORUS: As a Prologue; *King Henry V.*

CHRISTOPHER SLY: A drunken tinker; *The Taming of the Shrew.*

CHRISTOPHER URSWICK: A priest; *King Richard III.*

CICERO: A Roman senator; *Julius Caesar.*

CINNA: A poet; *Julius Caesar.*

CINNA: A Roman conspirator; *Julius Caesar.*

CLARENCE, DUKE OF: Brother of Edward IV; *King Richard III.*

CLARENCE, THOMAS, DUKE OF: Son of Henry IV; *King Henry IV,* Part II.

CLAUDIO: A young florentine lord; *Much Ado About Nothing.*

CLAUDIO: A young gentleman; *Measure for Measure.*

CLAUDIUS: King of Denmark; *Hamlet.*

CLAUDIUS: Servant of Brutus; *Julius Caesar.*

CLEOMENES: A Sicilian lord; *The Winter's Tale.*

CLEON: Governor of Tharsus; *Pericles.*

CLEOPATRA: Queen of Egypt; *Antony and Cleopatra.*

CLIFFORD, LORD: Of the King's Party; *King Henry VI,* Parts II, III.

CLIFFORD, YOUNG: Son of Lord Clifford; *King Henry VI,* Part II.

CLITUS: Servant of Brutus; *Julius Caesar.*

CLOTEN: Son of the Queen; *Cymbeline.*

CLOWN: Feste, servant to Olivia; *Twelfth Night.*

CLOWN: Servant to Mrs. Overdone; *Measure for Measure.*

COBWEB: A fairy; *A Midsummer Night's Dream.*

COLVILLE, SIR JOHN: Enemy of the King; *King Henry IV,* Part II.

COMINIUS: General against the Volscians; *Coriolanus.*

CONRADE: Follower of Don John; *Much Ado About Nothing.*

CONSTABLE OF FRANCE: *King Henry V.*

CONSTANCE: Mother of Arthur; *King John.*

CORDELIA: Daughter of Lear; *King Lear.*

CORIN: A shepherd; *As You Like It.*

CORIOLANUS, CAIUS MARCIUS: A noble Roman; *Coriolanus.*

CORNELIUS: A courtier; *Hamlet.*

CORNELIUS: A physician; *Cymbeline.*

CORNWALL, DUKE OF: *King Lear.*

COSTARD: A clown; *Love's Labour's Lost.*

COUNTESS OF AUVERGNE: *King Henry VI,* Part I.

COUNTESS OF ROUSILLON: Mother of Bertram; *All's Well that Ends Well.*

COUNT OF ROUSILLON: *All's Well that Ends Well.*

COURT: Soldier in King's Army; *King Henry V.*

CRANMER: Archbishop of Canterbury; *King Henry VIII.*

CRESSIDA: Daughter of Calchas; *Troilus and Cressida.*

CROMWELL: Servant of Wolsey; *King Henry VIII.*

CURAN: A courtier; *King Lear.*

CURIO: Attendant of the Duke of Illyria; *Twelfth Night.*

CURTIS: Servant of Petruchio; *The Taming of the Shrew.*

CYMBELINE: King of Britain; *Cymbeline.*

DAME QUICKLY: Hostess of a tavern; *King Henry IV,* Parts I, II.

DARDANIUS: Servant of Brutus; *Julius Caesar.*

DAUPHIN: Louis; *King John.*

DAVY: Servant of Shallow; *King Henry IV,* Part II.

DECIUS BRUTUS: A Roman conspirator; *Julius Caesar.*

DEIPHOBUS: Son of Priam; *Troilus and Cressida.*

DEMETRIUS: Friend of Antony; *Antony and Cleopatra.*

DEMETRIUS: In love with Hermione; *A Midsummer Night's Dream.*

DEMETRIUS: Son of Tamora; *Titus Andronicus.*

DENNIS: Servant of Oliver; *As You Like It.*

DENNY, SIR ANTHONY: King Henry VIII.

DERCETAS: Friend of Antony; *Antony and Cleopatra.*

DESDEMONA: Wife of Othello; *Othello.*

DIANA: Daughter of Willow; *All's Well that Ends Well.*

DIANA: *Pericles.*

DICK: A follower of Jack Cade; *King Henry VI,* Part II.

DIOMEDES: A Grecian commander; *Troilus and Cressida.*

DIOMEDES: Attendant of Cleopatra; *Antony and Cleopatra.*

DION: A Sicilian lord; *The Winter's Tale.*

DIONYZA: Wife of Cleon; *Pericles.*

DOCTOR BUTTS: Physician of Henry VIII; *King Henry VIII.*

DOCTOR CAIUS: A French physician; *The Merry Wives of Windsor.*

DOGBERRY: A foolish officer; *Much Ado About Nothing.*

DOLL TEARSHEET: A bawd; *King Henry IV,* Part II.

DOLABELLA: Friend of Caesar; *Antony and Cleopatra.*

DOMITIUS ENOBARBUS: Friend of Antony; *Antony and Cleopatra.*

DON ADRIANO DE ARMADO: A fantastical Spaniard; *Love's Labour's Lost.*

DONALBAIN: Son of King Duncan; *Macbeth.*

DON JOHN: Bastard brother of Don Pedro; *Much Ado About Nothing.*

DON PEDRO: Prince of Arragon; *Much Ado About Nothing.*

DORCAS: A Shepherdess; *The Winter's Tale.*

DORSET, MARQUIS OF: *King Richard III.*

DOUGLAS, EARL OF: Archibald; *King Henry IV,* Part I.

DROMIO OF EPHESUS; DROMIO OF SYRA-
CUSE: Twin brothers, attendants of the two
Antipholuses; *The Comedy of Errors.*
DUCHESS OF GLOSTER: King Richard II.
DUCHESS OF YORK: *King Richard II.*
DUCHESS OF YORK: Mother of King Edward
IV; *King Richard III.*
DUKE, THE: Living in exile; *As You Like It.*
DUKE OF ALBANY: King Lear.
DUKE OF ALENÇON: *King Henry VI,* Part I.
DUKE OF AUMERLE: Son of Duke of York;
King Richard II.
DUKE OF BEDFORD: Brother of King Henry
V; *King Henry V.*
DUKE OF BEDFORD: Regent of France; *King
Henry VI,* Part I.
DUKE OF BOURBON: *King Henry V.*
DUKE OF BUCKINGHAM: *King Henry VIII.*
DUKE OF BUCKINGHAM: *King Richard III.*
DUKE OF BUCKINGHAM: Of the King's
Party; *King Henry VI,* Part I.
DUKE OF BURGUNDY: *King Henry V.*
DUKE OF BURGUNDY: *King Henry VI,* Part I.
DUKE OF BURGUNDY: *King Lear.*
DUKE OF CLARENCE: Brother of King Ed-
ward IV; *King Richard III.*
DUKE OF CLARENCE, THOMAS: Son of King
Henry IV; *King Henry IV,* Part II.
DUKE OF CORNWALL: *King Lear.*
DUKE OF EXETER: Uncle of Henry V; *King
Henry V.*
DUKE OF EXETER: Of the King's Party; *King
Henry VI,* Part III.
DUKE OF FLORENCE: *All's Well that Ends
Well.*
DUKE OF GLOSTER: Afterward King Richard
III; *King Richard III.*
DUKE OF GLOSTER: Brother of King Henry V;
King Henry V.
DUKE OF GLOSTER: Uncle and protector of
King Henry VI; *King Henry VI,* Part III.
DUKE OF LANCASTER: Uncle of King
Richard II; *King Richard II.*
DUKE OF MILAN: Father of Silvia; *Two
Gentlemen of Verona.*
DUKE OF NORFOLK: *King Henry VIII.*
DUKE OF NORFOLK: *King Richard III.*
DUKE OF NORFOLK: Of the Duke's Party;
King Henry VI, Part III.
DUKE OF NORFOLK: Thomas Mowbray; *King
Richard II.*
DUKE OF ORLEANS: *King Henry V.*
DUKE OF OXFORD: Of the King's Party; *King
Henry VI,* Part III.
DUKE OF SOMERSET: Of the King's Party;
King Henry IV, Parts II, III.
DUKE OF SUFFOLK: *King Henry VIII.*
DUKE OF SUFFOLK: Of the King's Party;
King Henry VI, Part II.
DUKE OF SURREY: *King Richard II.*
DUKE OF VENICE: *The Merchant of Venice.*
DUKE OF VENICE: *Othello.*
DUKE OF YORK: Cousin of the King; *King
Henry V.*
DUKE OF YORK: Son of King Edward IV; *King
Richard III.*
DUKE OF YORK: Uncle of King Richard II;
King Richard II.
DULL: A constable; *Love's Labour's Lost.*
DUMAIN: A lord attendant on the King of
Navarre; *Love's Labour's Lost.*
DUNCAN: King of Scotland; *Macbeth.*
EARL BERKELEY: *King Richard II.*
EARL OF CAMBRIDGE: A conspirator; *King
Henry V.*
EARL OF DOUGLAS: Archibald; *King Henry
IV,* Part I.
EARL OF ESSEX: Geoffrey Fitz-Peter; *King
John.*
EARL OF GLOSTER: *King Lear.*

EARL OF KENT: *King Lear.*
EARL OF MARCH: Afterward King Edward
IV; *King Henry VI,* Part III.
EARL OF MARCH: Edward Mortimer; *King
Henry IV,* Part I.
EARL OF NORTHUMBERLAND: Enemy of
the King; *King Henry VI,* Part II.
EARL OF NORTHUMBERLAND: Henry Percy;
King Henry IV, Parts I, II.
EARL OF NORTHUMBERLAND: *King
Richard II.*
EARL OF NORTHUMBERLAND: Of the King's
Party; *King Henry VI,* Part III.
EARL OF OXFORD: *King Richard III.*
EARL OF PEMBROKE: Of the Duke's Party;
King Henry VI, Part III.
EARL OF PEMBROKE: William Mareshall; *King
John.*
EARL OF RICHMOND: *King Richard III.*
EARL OF SALISBURY: *King Henry V.*
EARL OF SALISBURY: *King Richard II.*
EARL OF SALISBURY: Of the York Faction;
King Henry VI, Parts I, II.
EARL OF SALISBURY: William Longsword;
King John.
EARL OF SUFFOLK: *King Henry VI,* Part I.
EARL OF SURREY: *King Henry VIII.*
EARL OF SURREY: Son of Duke of Norfolk;
King Richard III.
EARL OF WARWICK: *King Henry V.*
EARL OF WARWICK: Of the King's Party;
King Henry IV, Part II.
EARL OF WARWICK: *Of the York Faction;
King Henry VI,* Parts I, II, III.
EARL OF WESTMORELAND: Friend to King
Henry IV; *King Henry IV,* Parts I, II.
EARL OF WESTMORELAND: *King Henry V.*
EARL OF WESTMORELAND: Of the King's
Party; *King Henry VI,* Part III.
EARL OF WORCESTER: Thomas Percy; *King
Henry IV,* Parts I, II.
EARL RIVERS: *King Richard III.*
EDGAR: Son of Gloster; *King Lear.*
EDMUND: Bastard son of Gloster; *King Lear.*
EDMUND: Earl of Rutland; *King Henry VI,*
Part III.
EDMUND MORTIMER: Earl of March; *King
Henry IV,* Part I.
EDMUND OF LANGLEY: Duke of York; *King
Richard II.*
EDWARD: Prince of Wales; *King Richard III.*
EDWARD: Son to Plantagenet; *King Henry VI,*
Part II.
EDWARD EARL OF MARCH: Afterward King
Edward IV; *King Henry VI,* Part III.
EDWARD IV, KING: *King Richard III.*
EDWARD PRINCE OF WALES: Son of King
Henry VI, *King Henry VI,* Part III.
EGEHUS: Father of Hermia; *A Midsummer
Night's Dream.*
EGLAMOUR: Agent for Silvia; *Two Gentle-
men of Verona.*
ELBOW: A simple constable; *Measure for
Measure.*
ELEANOR: *Duchess of Gloster; King Henry VI,*
Part II.
ELINOR: Mother to King John; *King John.*
ELIZABETH: Queen to King Edward IV; *King
Richard III.*
ELY, BISHOP OF: John Morton; *King
Richard III.*
ELY, BISHOP OF: *King Henry V.*
EMILIA: A lady; *The Winter's Tale.*
EMILIA: Wife of Iago; *Othello.*
ENOBARBUS, DOMITIUS: Friend of Antony;
Antony and Cleopatra.
EROS: Friend of Antony; *Antony and Cleo-
patra.*
ERPINGHAM, SIR THOMAS: Officer in the
King's Army; *King Henry V.*

ESCALUS: A lord of Vienna; *Measure for Measure*.

ESCALUS: Prince of Verona; *Romeo and Juliet*.

ESCANES: A lord of Tyre; *Pericles*.

ESSEX, EARL OF: Geoffrey Fitz-Peter; *King John*.

EUPHRONIUS: An ambassador; *Antony and Cleopatra*.

EVANS, SIR HUGH: A Welsh parson; *The Merry Wives of Windsor*.

EXETER, DUKE OF: Of the King's Party; *King Henry VI*, Part III.

EXETER, DUKE OF: Uncle of Henry V; *King Henry V*.

EXILED DUKE: *As You Like It*.

FABIAN: Servant of Olivia; *Twelfth Night*.

FALCONBRIDGE, LADY: Mother of Robert and Philip; *King John*.

FALCONBRIDGE, PHILIP: Bastard son of King Richard I; *King John*.

FALCONBRIDGE, ROBERT: Son of Sir Robert Falconbridge; *King John*.

FALSTAFF, SIR JOHN: *King Henry IV*, Parts I, II.

FALSTAFF, SIR JOHN: *The Merry Wives of Windsor*.

FANG: A sheriff's officer; *King Henry IV*, Part II.

FASTOLFE, SIR JOHN: *King Henry VI*, Part I.

FEEBLE: A recruit; *King Henry IV*, Part II.

FENTON: A young gentleman; *The Merry Wives of Windsor*.

FERDINAND: King of Navarre; *Love's Labour's Lost*.

FERDINAND: Son of the King of Naples; *The Tempest*.

FESTE: A clown; *Twelfth Night*.

FITZ-PETER, GEOFFREY: Earl of Essex; *King John*.

FITZWATER, LORD: *King Richard II*.

FLAMINUS: Servant of Timon; *Timon of Athens*.

FLAVIUS: A Roman tribune; *Julius Caesar*.

FLAVIUS: Steward of Timon; *Timon of Athens*.

FLEANCE: Son of Banquo; *Macbeth*.

FLORENCE, DUKE OF: *All's Well that Ends Well*.

FLORENCE, WIDOW OF: *All's Well that Ends Well*.

FLORIZEL: Son of Polixenes; *The Winter's Tale*.

FLUELLEN: Officer in King's Army; *King Henry V*.

FLUTE: The bellowsmender; *A Midsummer Night's Dream*.

FORD, MR.: A gentleman dwelling at Windsor; *The Merry Wives of Windsor*.

FORD, MRS.: *The Merry Wives of Windsor*.

FORTINBRAS: Prince of Norway; *Hamlet*.

FRANCE, KING OF: *All's Well that Ends Well*.

FRANCE, KING OF: *King Lear*.

FRANCE, PRINCESS OF: *Love's Labor's Lost*.

FRANCISCA: A nun; *Measure for Measure*.

FRANCISCO: A lord of Naples; *The Tempest*.

FRANCISCO: A soldier; *Hamlet*.

FREDERICK: Brother of the exiled Duke; *As You Like It*.

FRIAR JOHN: A Franciscan; *Romeo and Juliet*.

FRIAR LAWRENCE: A Franciscan; *Romeo and Juliet*.

FROTH: A Foolish gentleman; *Measure for Measure*.

GADSHILL: Follower of Sir John Falstaff; *King Henry IV*, Part I.

GALLUS: Friend of Caesar; *Antony and Cleopatra*.

GARDINER: Bishop of Winchester; *King Henry VIII*.

GARGRAVE, SIR THOMAS: *King Henry VI*, Part I.

GEOFFREY FITZ-PETER: Earl of Essex; *King John*.

GEORGE: A Follower of Cade; *King Henry VI*, Part II.

GEORGE: Duke of Clarence; *King Richard III*.

GEORGE: Duke of Clarence; *King Henry VI*, Part III.

GERTRUDE: Queen of Denmark; *Hamlet*.

GHOST OF HAMLET'S FATHER: *Hamlet*.

GLANSDALE, SIR WILLIAM: *King Henry VI*, Part I.

GLENDOWER, OWEN: *King Henry IV*, Part I.

GLOSTER, DUCHESS OF: *King Richard II*.

GLOSTER, DUKE OF: Afterward King Richard III; *King Richard III*.

GLOSTER, DUKE OF: Brother to King Henry V; *King Henry V*.

GLOSTER, DUKE OF: Uncle and protector of King Henry VI; *King Henry VI*, Part III.

GLOSTER, EARL OF: *King Lear*.

GLOSTER, PRINCE HUMPHREY OF: Son of King Henry IV; *King Henry IV*, Part II.

GOBBO, LAUNCELOT: Servant of Shylock; *The Merchant of Venice*.

GOBBO, OLD: Father of Launcelot Gobbo; *The Merchant of Venice*.

GONERIL: Daughter of King Lear; *King Lear*.

GONZALO: Councillor of Naples; *The Tempest*.

GOWER: As Chorus; *Pericles*.

GOWER: Of the King's Party; *King Henry IV*, Part II.

GOWER: Officer in King's Army; *King Henry V*.

GRANDPREE: A French lord; *King Henry V*.

GRATIANO: Brother of Brabantio; *Othello*.

GRATIANO: Friend to Antonio and Bassanio; *The Merchant of Venice*.

GREEN: Favorite of King Richard II; *King Richard II*.

GREGORY: Servant of Capulet; *Romeo and Juliet*.

GREMIO: Suitor of Bianca; *The Taming of the Shrew*.

GREY, LADY: Queen of King Edward IV; *King Henry VI*, Part III.

GREY, LORD: *King Richard III*.

GREY, SIR THOMAS: A conspirator; *King Henry V*.

GRIFFITH: Gentleman-usher of Queen Katharine; *King Henry VIII*.

GRUMIO: Servant of Petruchio; *The Taming of the Shrew*.

GUIDERIUS: Son of Cymbeline; *Cymbeline*.

GUILDENSTERN: A courtier; *Hamlet*.

GUILDFORD, SIR HENRY: *King Henry VIII*.

GURNEY, JAMES: Servant of Lady Falconbridge; *King John*.

HAMLET: Prince of Denmark; *Hamlet*.

HARCOURT: Of the King's Party; *King Henry IV*, Part II.

HASTINGS, LORD: Enemy of the King; *King Henry IV*, Part II.

HASTINGS, LORD: *King Richard III*.

HASTINGS LORD: Of the Duke's Party; *King Henry VI*, Part III.

HECATE: A witch; *Macbeth*.

HECTOR: Son of Priam; *Troilus and Cressida*.

HELEN: Wife of Menelaus; *Troilus and Cressida*.

HELEN: Woman of Imogen; *Cymbeline*.

HELENA: A gentlewoman; *All's Well that Ends Vell*.

HELENA: In love with Demetrius; *A Midsummer Night's Dream*.

HELENUS: Son of Priam; *Troilus and Cressida*.

HELICANUS: A lord of Tyre; *Pericles*.

HENRY: Earl of Richmond; *King Richard III.*
HENRY BOLINGBROKE: Afterward King Henry IV; *King Richard II.*
HENRY, EARL OF RICHMOND: A youth; *King Henry VI*, Part III.
HENRY, PRINCE: Son of King John; *King John.*
HENRY, PRINCE OF WALES: Son of King Henry IV; *King Henry IV*, Parts I, II.
HENRY IV, KING: *King Henry IV*, Parts I, II.
HENRY V, KING: *King Henry V.*
HENRY VI, *King Henry VI*, Parts I, II, III.
HENRY VIII, KING: *King Henry VIII.*
HENRY PERCY: Earl of Northumberland; *King Henry IV*, Parts I, II.
HENRY PERCY: Son of Earl of Northumberland; *King Richard III.*
HENRY PERCY (HOTSPUR): Son of Earl of Northumberland; *King Henry IV*, Parts I, II.
HERBERT, SIR WALTER: *King Richard III.*
HERMIA: Daughter of Egeus; *A Midsummer Night's Dream.*
HERMIONE: Queen of Sicilia; *The Winter's Tale.*
HERO: Daughter of Leonato; *Much Ado About Nothing.*
HIPPOLYTA: Queen of the Amazons; *A Midsummer Night's Dream.*
HOLOFERNES: A schoolmaster; *Love's Labour's Lost.*
HORATIO: Friend of Hamlet; *Hamlet.*
HORNER, THOMAS: An armorer; *King Henry VI;* Part II.
HORTENSIO: Suitor of Bianca; *The Taming of the Shrew.*
HORTENSIUS: A servant; *Timon of Athens.*
HOSTESS: Character in the Induction; *The Taming of the Shrew.*
HOSTESS QUICKLY: Hostess of a tavern; *King Henry IV*, Parts I, II.
HOTSPUR (HENRY PERCY): Son of Earl of Northumberland; *King Henry IV*, Parts I, II.
HUBERT DE BURGH: Chamberlain of King John; *King John.*
HUME: A priest; *King Henry VI*, Part II.
HUMPHREY, DUKE OF GLOSTER: Uncle of King Henry VI; *King Henry VI*, Part II.
HUMPHREY, PRINCE OF GLOSTER: Son of Henry IV; *King Henry IV*, Part II.
HUNTSMEN: Characters in the Induction; *The Taming of the Shrew.*
IACHIMO: Friend of Philario; *Cymbeline.*
IAGO: Ancient of Othello; *Othello.*
IDEN, ALEXANDER: A Kentish gentleman; *King Henry VI*, Part II.
IMOGEN: Daughter of Cymbeline; *Cymbeline*
IRAS: Attendant of Cleopatra; *Antony and Cleopatra.*
IRIS: A spirit; *The Tempest.*
ISABEL: Queen of France; *King Henry V.*
ISABELLA: Sister of Claudio; *Measure for Measure.*
JACK CADE: A rebel; *King Henry VI*, Part II.
JAMES GURNEY: Servant of Lady Falconbridge; *King John.*
JAMY: Officer in King's Army; *King Henry V.*
JAQUENETTA: A country wench; *Love's Labour's Lost.*
JAQUES: A lord attendant of exiled Duke; *As You Like It.*
JAQUES: Son of Sir Rowland de Bois; *As You Like It.*
JESSICA: Daughter of Shylock; *The Merchant of Venice.*
JOAN LA PUCELLE: Joan of Arc; *King Henry VI*, Part I.
JOHN: A follower of Cade; *King Henry IV*, Part II.
JOHN, DON: Bastard brother of Don Pedro; *Much Ado About Nothing.*

JOHN, FRIAR: A Franciscan; *Romeo and Juliet.*
JOHN, KING: *King John.*
JOHN, PRINCE OF LANCASTER: Son of King Henry IV; *King Henry IV*, Parts I, II.
JOHN OF GAUNT: Duke of Lancaster; *King Richard II.*
JOHN TALBOT: Son of Lord Talbot; *King Henry VI*, Part I.
JOURDAIN, MARGERY: A witch; *King Henry VI*, Part II.
JULIA: A lady of Verona; *Two Gentlemen of Verona.*
JULIET: Daughter of Capulet; *Romeo and Juliet.*
JULIET: *Measure for Measure.*
JULIUS CAESAR: *Julius Caesar.*
JUNIUS BRUTUS: Tribune of the people; *Coriolanus.*
JUNO: A spirit; *The Tempest.*
JUSTICE SHALLOW: A country justice; *King Henry IV*, Part II.
KATHARINA: The shrew; *The Taming of the Shrew.*
KATHARINE: A Lady attending on the Princess of France; *Love's Labour's Lost.*
KATHARINE, PRINCESS: Daughter of Charles VI, King of France; *King Henry V.*
KATHARINE, QUEEN: Wife of King Henry VIII; *King Henry VIII.*
KENT, EARL OF: *King Lear.*
KING EDWARD IV: *King Richard III.*
KING HENRY IV: *King Henry IV*, Parts I, II.
KING HENRY V: *King Henry V.*
KING HENRY VI: *King Henry VI*, Parts I, II, III.
KING HENRY VIII: *King Henry VIII.*
KING JOHN: *King John.*
KING OF FRANCE: *All's Well that Ends Well.*
KING OF FRANCE: *King Lear.*
KING RICHARD II: *King Richard II.*
KING RICHARD III: *King Richard III.*
LADY ANNE: Widow of Edward Prince of Wales; *King Richard III.*
LADY CAPULET: Wife of Capulet; *Romeo and Juliet.*
LADY FALCONBRIDGE: Mother of Robert and Philip Falconbridge; *King John.*
LADY GREY: Afterward Queen of King Edward IV; *King Henry VI*, Part III.
LADY MACBETH: Wife of Macbeth; *Macbeth.*
LADY MACDUFF: Wife of Macduff; *Macbeth.*
LADY MONTAGUE: Wife of Montague; *Romeo and Juliet.*
LADY MORTIMER: Daughter of Glendower; *King Henry IV*, Part I.
LADY NORTHUMBERLAND: *King Henry IV*, Part II.
LADY PERCY: Wife of Hotspur; *King Henry IV;* Part I.
LAERTES: Son of Polonius; *Hamlet.*
LAFEU: An old lord; *All's Well that Ends Well.*
LANCASTER, DUKE OF: Uncle of Richard II; *King Richard II.*
LANCASTER, PRINCE JOHN OF: Son of King Henry IV; *King Henry IV*, Parts I, II.
LAUNCE: Servant of Proteus; *Two Gentlemen of Verona.*
LAUNCELOT GOBBO: Servant of Shylock; *The Merchant of Venice.*
LAVINIA: Daughter of Titus; *Titus Andronicus.*
LAWRENCE, FRIAR: A Franciscan; *Romeo and Juliet.*
LEAR: King of Britain; *King Lear.*
LE BEAU: A courtier; *As You Like It.*
LENNOX: A Scottish nobleman; *Macbeth.*
LEONARDO: Servant of Bassanio; *The Merchant of Venice.*
LEONATO: Governor of Messina; *Much Ado About Nothing.*

LEONATUS, POSTHUMUS: Husband of Imogen; *Cymbeline.*
LEONINE: Servant of Dionyza; *Pericles.*
LEONTES: King of Sicilia; *The Winter's Tale.*
LEPIDUS, M. AEMILIUS: A triumvir; *Antony and Cleopatra.*
LIGARIUS: A Roman conspirator; *Julius Caesar.*
LINCOLN, BISHOP OF: *King Henry VIII.*
LION: A character in the Interlude; *A Midsummer Night's Dream.*
LODOVICO: Kinsman of Brabantio; *Othello.*
LONGAVILLE: A lord attendant on the King of Navarre; *Love's Labour's Lost.*
LONGSWORD, WILLIAM: Earl of Salisbury; *King John.*
LORD, A: Character in the Prologue; *The Taming of the Shrew.*
LORD ABERGAVENNY: *King Henry VIII.*
LORD BARDOLPH: Enemy of the King; *King Henry IV,* Part II.
LORD CHIEF JUSTICE: Of the King's Bench; *King Henry IV,* Part II.
LORD CLIFFORD: Of the King's Party; *King Henry VI,* Parts II, III.
LORD FITZWATER: *King Richard II.*
LORD GREY: Son of Lady Grey; *King Richard III.*
LORD HASTINGS: Enemy of the King; *King Henry IV,* Part II.
LORD HASTINGS: *King Richard III.*
LORD HASTINGS: Of the Duke's Party; *King Henry VI,* Part III.
LORD LOVEL: *King Richard III.*
LORD MOWBRAY: Enemy of the King; *King Henry IV,* Part II.
LORD RIVERS: Brother to Lady Grey; *King Henry VI,* Part III.
LORD ROSS: *King Richard II.*
LORD SANDS: *King Henry VIII.*
LORD SAY: *King Henry VI,* Part II.
LORD SCALES: Governor of the Tower; *King Henry VI,* Part II.
LORD SCROOP: A conspirator; *King Henry V*
LORD STAFFORD: Of the Duke's Party; *King Henry VI,* Part III.
LORD STANLEY: *King Richard III.*
LORD TALBOT: Afterward Earl of Shrewsbury; *King Henry VI,* Part I.
LORD WILLOUGHBY: *King Richard II.*
LORENZO: The Lover of Jessica; *The Merchant of Venice.*
LOUIS, THE DAUPHIN: *King John.*
LOUIS, THE DAUPHIN: *King Henry V.*
LOUIS XI: King of France; *King Henry VI,* Part III.
LOVEL, LORD: *King Richard III.*
LOVELL, SIR THOMAS: *King Henry VIII.*
LUCE: Servant of Luciana; *The Comedy of Errors.*
LUCENTIO: Son of Vincentio; *The Taming of the Shrew.*
LUCETTA: Waiting-woman of Julia; *Two Gentlemen of Verona.*
LUCIANA: Sister of Adriana; *The Comedy of Errors.*
LUCILIUS: Friend of Brutus and Cassius; *Julius Caesar.*
LUCILIUS: Servant to Timon; *Timon of Athens.*
LUCIO: A Fantastic; *Measure for Measure.*
LUCIUS: A lord: flatterer of Timon; *Timon of Athens.*
LUCIUS: A servant; *Timon of Athens.*
LUCIUS: Servant of Brutus; *Julius Caesar.*
LUCIUS: Son of Titus; *Titus Andronicus.*
LUCULLUS: A lord; flatterer of Timon; *Timon of Athens.*
LUCY, SIR WILLIAM: *King Henry VI,* Part I.
LYCHORIDA: Nurse of Marina; *Pericles.*

LYSANDER: In love with Hermione; *A Midsummer Night's Dream.*
LYSIMACHUS: Governor of Mytilene; *Pericles.*
MACBETH: General of the King's Army; *Macbeth.*
MACBETH, LADY: Wife of Macbeth; *Macbeth.*
MACDUFF: A Scottish nobleman; *Macbeth.*
MACDUFF, LADY: Wife of Macduff; *Macbeth.*
MACMORRIS: Officer in King's Army; *King Henry V.*
MAECENAS: Friend of Caesar; *Antony and Cleopatra.*
MALCOLM: Son of King Duncan; *Macbeth.*
MALVOLIO: Steward of Olivia; *Twelfth Night.*
MAMILLIUS: Son of Leontes; *The Winter's Tale.*
MARCELLUS: An officer; *Hamlet.*
MARCH, EARL OF: Edward Mortimer; *King Henry IV,* Part I.
MARCIUS, YOUNG: Son of Coriolanus; *Coriolanus.*
MARCUS ANDRONICUS: Tribune, brother to Titus; *Titus Andronicus.*
MARCUS ANTONIUS: A Roman triumvir; *Julius Caesar.*
MARCUS BRUTUS: A Roman conspirator; *Julius Caesar.*
MARDIAN: Attendant of Cleopatra; *Antony and Cleopatra.*
MARESHALL, WILLIAM: Earl of Pembroke; *King John.*
MARGARELON: Bastard son of Priam; *Troilus and Cressida.*
MARGARET: Attendant of Hero; *Much Ado About Nothing.*
MARGARET: Daughter of Reignier; *King Henry VI,* Part I.
MARGARET: Queen of King Henry VI; *King Henry VI,* Part II.
MARGARET: Widow of King Henry VI; *King Richard III.*
MARGARET, QUEEN: *King Henry VI,* Part III.
MARGERY JOURDAIN: A Witch; *King Henry VI,* Part II.
MARIA: Attendant of Olivia; *Twelfth Night.*
MARIA: A lady attending on the Princess of France; *Love's Labour's Lost.*
MARIANA: Fiancée of Angelo; *Measure for Measure.*
MARIANA: Neighbor of Widow of Florence; *All's Well that Ends Well.*
MARINA: Daughter of Pericles; *Pericles.*
MARK ANTONY: A triumvir; *Antony and Cleopatra.*
MARQUIS OF DORSET: Son of Lady Grey; *King Richard III.*
MARQUIS OF MONTAGUE: Of the Duke's Party; *King Henry VI,* Part III.
MARTEXT, SIR OLIVER: A vicar; *As You Like It.*
MARTIUS: Son of Titus; *Titus Andronicus.*
MARULLUS: A Roman tribune; *Julius Caesar.*
MELUN: A French lord; *King John.*
MENAS: Friend of Pompey; *Antony and Cleopatra.*
MENECRATES: Friend of Pompey; *Antony and Cleopatra.*
MENELAUS: Brother of Agamemnon; *Troilus and Cressida.*
MENENIUS AGRIPPA: Friend of Coriolanus; *Coriolanus.*
MENTEITH: A Scottish nobleman; *Macbeth.*
MERCADE: A lord attending on the Princess of France; *Love's Labour's Lost.*
MERCUTIO: Friend of Romeo; *Romeo and Juliet.*
MESSALA: Friend af Brutus and Cassius; *Julius Caesar.*

METELLUS CIMBER: A Roman conspirator; *Julius Caesar.*
MICHAEL: A follower of Cade; *King Henry VI,* Part II.
MICHAEL, SIR: Friend of Archbishop of York; *King Henry IV,* Parts I, II.
MILAN, DUKE OF: Father of Silvia; *Two Gentlemen of Verona.*
MIRANDA: Daughter of Prospero; *The Tempest.*
MR. FORD: A gentleman dwelling at Windsor; *The Merry Wives of Windsor.*
MR. PAGE: A gentleman dwelling at Windsor; *The Merry Wives of Windsor.*
MRS. FORD: *The Merry Wives of Windsor.*
MRS. OVERDONE: A bawd; *Measure for Measure.*
MRS. PAGE: *The Merry Wives of Windsor.*
MRS. QUICKLY: Hostess of a tavern; *King Henry IV,* Parts I, II.
MRS. QUICKLY: A hostess, wife of Pistol; *King Henry V.*
MRS. QUICKLY: Servant of Dr. Caius; *The Merry Wives of Windsor.*
MONTAGUE: At variance with Capulet; *Romeo and Juliet.*
MONTAGUE, LADY: Wife of Montague; *Romeo and Juliet.*
MONTAGUE, MARQUIS OF: Of the Duke's Party; *King Henry VI,* Part III.
MONTANO: Othello's predecessor in office; *Othello.*
MONTGOMERY, SIR JOHN: *King Henry VI,* Part III.
MOONSHINE: A character in the Interlude; *A Midsummer Night's Dream.*
MOPSA: A shepherdess; *The Winter's Tale.*
MORGAN: Belarius in disguise; *Cymbeline.*
MOROCCO, PRINCE OF: Suitor of Portia; *The Merchant of Venice.*
MORTIMER, EDMUND: Earl of March; *King Henry IV,* Part I.
MORTIMER, EDMUND: Earl of March; *King Henry VI,* Part I.
MORTIMER, LADY: Daughter of Glendower; *King Henry IV,* Part I.
MORTIMER, SIR HUGH: Uncle of Duke of York; *King Henry VI,* Part III.
MORTIMER, SIR JOHN: Uncle of Duke of York; *King Henry VI,* Part III.
MORTON: Servant of Northumberland; *King Henry IV,* Part II.
MORTON, JOHN: Bishop of Ely; *King Richard III.*
MOTH: A fairy; *A Midsummer Night's Dream.*
MOTH: Page of Armado; *Love's Labour's Lost.*
MOULDY: A recruit; *King Henry IV,* Part II.
MOUNTJOY: A French herald; *King Henry V.*
MOWBRAY, LORD: Enemy of the King; *King Henry IV,* Part II.
MOWBRAY, THOMAS: Duke of Norfolk; *King Richard II.*
MUSTARDSEED: A fairy; *A Midsummer Night's Dream.*
MUTIUS: Son of Titus; *Titus Andronicus.*
NATHANIEL, SIR: A curate; *Love's Labour's Lost.*
NERISSA: Waiting-maid of Portia; *The Merchant of Venice.*
NESTOR: A Grecian commander; *Troilus and Cressida.*
NORFOLK, DUKE OF: *King Henry VIII.*
NORFOLK, DUKE OF: *King Richard II; King Richard III.*
NORFOLK, DUKE OF: Of the Duke's Party; *King Henry VI,* Part III.
NORTHUMBERLAND, EARL OF: Enemy of the King; *King Henry IV,* Part II.
NORTHUMBERLAND, EARL OF: Henry Percy; *King Henry IV,* Parts I, II.

NORTHUMBERLAND, EARL OF: *King Richard II.*
NORTHUMBERLAND, EARL OF: Of the King's Party; *King Henry VI,* Part III.
NORTHUMBERLAND, LADY: *King Henry IV,* Part II.
NURSE OF JULIET: *Romeo and Juliet.*
NYM: Soldier in King's Army; *King Henry V.*
NYM: A follower of Falstaff; *The Merry Wives of Windsor.*
OBERON: King of the Fairies; *A Midsummer Night's Dream.*
OCTAVIA: Wife of Antony; *Antony and Cleopatra.*
OCTAVIUS CAESAR: A Roman triumvir; *Julius Caesar.*
OCTAVIUS CAESAR: A Roman triumvir; *Antony and Cleopatra.*
OLD GOBBO: Father of Launcelot Gobbo; *The Merchant of Venice.*
OLIVER: Son of Sir Rowland de Bois; *As You Like It.*
OLIVIA: A rich countess; *Twelfth Night.*
OPHELIA: Daughter of Polonius; *Hamlet.*
ORLANDO: Son of Sir Rowland de Bois; *As You Like It.*
ORLEANS, DUKE OF: *King Henry V.*
ORSINO: Duke of Ilyria; *Twelfth Night.*
OSRIC: A courtier; *Hamlet.*
OSWALD: Steward of Goneril; *King Lear.*
OTHELLO: The Moor; *Othello.*
OVERDONE, MRS.: A bawd; *Measure for Measure.*
OWEN GLENDOWER: *King Henry IV,* Part I.
OXFORD, DUKE OF: Of the King's Party; *King Henry VI,* Part III.
OXFORD, EARL OF: *King Richard III.*
PAGE, ANNE: Daughter of Mrs. Page; *The Merry Wives of Windsor.*
PAGE, MR.: A gentleman dwelling at Windsor; *The Merry Wives of Windsor.*
PAGE, MRS.: *The Merry Wives of Windsor.*
PAGE, WILLIAM: Son of Mr. Page; *The Merry Wives of Windsor.*
PANDARUS: Uncle of Cressida; *Troilus and Cressida.*
PANDULPH, CARDINAL: The Pope's legate; *King John.*
PANTHINO: Servant of Antonio; *Two Gentlemen of Verona.*
PARIS: Son of Priam; *Troilus and Cressida.*
PARIS: A young nobleman; *Romeo and Juliet.*
PAROLLES: A follower of Bertram; *All's Well that Ends Well.*
PATIENCE: Woman attending Queen Katharine; *King Henry VIII.*
PATROCLUS: A Grecian commander; *Troilus and Cressida.*
PAULINA: Wife of Antigonus; *The Winter's Tale.*
PEASBLOSSOM: A fairy; *A Midsummer Night's Dream.*
PEDANT: Personating Vincentio; *The Taming of the Shrew.*
PEDRO, DON: Prince of Arragon; *Much Ado About Nothing.*
PEMBROKE, EARL OF: Of the Duke's Party; *King Henry VI,* Part III.
PEMBROKE, EARL OF: William Mareshall; *King John.*
PERCY, HENRY: Earl of Northumberland; *King Henry IV,* Parts I, II.
PERCY, HENRY: Son of Earl of Northumberland; *King Richard II.*
PERCY, HENRY (HOTSPUR): Son of Earl of Northumberland; *King Henry IV,* Parts I, II.
PERCY, LADY: Wife of Hotspur; *King Henry IV,* Part I.
PERCY, THOMAS: Earl of Worcester; *King Henry IV,* Parts I, II.

PERDITA: Daughter of Hermione; *The Winter's Tale.*

PERICLES: Prince of Thyre; *Pericles.*

PETER: A friar; *Measure for Measure.*

PETER: Horner's man; *King Henry VI*, Part II.

PETER OF POMFRET: A prophet; *King John.*

PETO: A follower of Sir John Falstaff; *King Henry IV*, Parts I, II.

PETRUCHIO: A gentleman of Verona, suitor of Katharina; *The Taming of the Shrew.*

PHEBE: A shepherdess; *As You Like It.*

PHILARIO: Friend of Posthumus; *Cymbeline*

PHILEMON: Servant of Cerimon; *Pericles.*

PHILIP: King of France; *King John.*

PHILIP FALCONBRIDGE: Bastard son of King Richard I; *King John.*

PHILO: Friend of Antony; *Antony and Cleopatra.*

PHILOSTRATE: Master of the revels; *A Midsummer Night's Dream.*

PHILOTUS: A servant; *Timon of Athens.*

PHRYNIA: Mistress of Alcibiades; *Timon of Athens.*

PIERCE OF EXTON, SIR: *King Richard II.*

PINCH: A schoolmaster and conjurer; *The Comedy of Errors.*

PINDARUS: Servant to Cassius; *Julius Caesar.*

PISANIO: Servant to Posthumus; *Cymbeline.*

PISTOL: A follower of Sir John Falstaff; *The Merry Wives of Windsor.*

PISTOL: A follower of Sir John Falstaff; *King Henry IV;* Part II.

PISTOL: A Soldier in the King's Army; *King Henry V.*

PLANTAGENET, RICHARD: Duke of York; *King Henry VI*, Parts I, II, III.

PLAYERS: Characters in *Hamlet.*

PLAYERS: Characters in the Prologue; *The Taming of the Shrew.*

POINS: A Follower of Sir John Falstaff; *King Henry IV*, Parts I, II.

POLIXENES: King of Bohemia; *The Winter's Tale.*

POLONIUS: Lord Chamberlain; *Hamlet.*

POLYDORE: Guiderius in Disguise; *Cymbeline.*

POMPEIUS SEXTUS: Friend of Antony; *Antony and Cleopatra.*

POPILIUS LENA: A Roman senator; *Julius Caesar.*

PORTIA: A rich heiress; *The Merchant of Venice.*

PORTIA: Wife of Brutus; *Julius Caesar.*

POSTHUMUS LEONATUS: Husband of Imogen; *Cymbeline.*

PRIAM: King of Troy; *Troilus and Cressida.*

PRINCE HENRY: Son of King John; *King John.*

PRINCE HUMPHREY OF GLOSTER: Son of King Henry IV, *King Henry IV*, Part II.

PRINCE JOHN OF LANCASTER: Son of King Henry IV; *King Henry IV*, Part II.

PRINCE OF ARRAGON: Suitor of Portia; *The Merchant of Venice.*

PRINCE OF MOROCCO: Suitor of Portia; *The Merchant of Venice.*

PRINCE OF WALES: Son of King Edward IV; *King Richard III.*

PRINCE OF WALES, HENRY: Afterward King Henry V; *King Henry IV*, Part II.

PRINCESS KATHARINE: Daughter of King Charles VI; *King Henry V.*

PRINCESS OF FRANCE: *Love's Labour's Lost.*

PROCULEIUS: Friend of Caesar; *Antony and Cleopatra.*

PROPHETESS: Cassandra; *Troilus and Cressida.*

PROSPERO: Rightful Duke of Milan; *The Tempest.*

PROTEUS: A gentleman of Verona; *Two Gentlemen of Verona.*

PUBLIUS: A Roman senator; *Julius Caesar.*

PUBLIUS: Son of Marcus; *Titus Andronicus.*

PUCELLE, LA: Joan of Arc; *King Henry VI*, Part I.

PUCK: A fairy; *A Midsummer Night's Dream.*

PYRAMUS: A character in the Interlude; *A Midsummer Night's Dream.*

QUEEN: Wife of Cymbeline; *Cymbeline.*

QUEEN ELIZABETH: Queen of King Edward IV; *King Richard III.*

QUEEN KATHARINE: Wife of King Henry VIII; *King Henry VIII.*

QUEEN MARGARET: Wife of King Henry VI; *King Henry VI*, Part III.

QUEEN OF KING RICHARD II: *King Richard II.*

QUICKLY, MRS.: A Hostess; Wife of Pistol; *King Henry V.*

QUICKLY, MRS.: Hostess of a tavern; *King Henry IV*, Parts I, II.

QUICKLY, MRS.: Servant of Dr. Caius; *The Merry Wives of Windsor.*

QUINCE: The carpenter; *A Midsummer Night's Dream.*

QUINTUS: Son of Titus; *Titus Andronicus.*

RAMBURES: A French lord; *King Henry V.*

RATCLIFF, SIR RICHARD: *King Richard III.*

REGAN: Daughter of King Lear; *King Lear.*

REIGNIER: Duke of Anjou; *King Henry VI*, Part I.

REYNALDO: Servant of Polonius; *Hamlet.*

RICHARD: Afterward Duke of Gloster; *King Henry VI*, Part III.

RICHARD: Son of Plantagenet; *King Henry VI*, Part II.

RICHARD, DUKE OF GLOSTER: Afterward King Richard III; *King Richard III.*

RICHARD, DUKE OF YORK: Son of King Edward IV; *King Richard III.*

RICHARD PLANTAGENET: Duke of York; *King Henry VI*, Parts I, II, III.

RICHARD II, KING: *King Richard II.*

RICHARD III, KING: *King Richard III.*

RICHMOND, EARL OF: Afterward King Henry VII; *King Richard III.*

RIVERS, EARL: Brother of Lady Grey; *King Richard III.*

RIVERS, LORD: Brother of Lady Grey; *King Henry VI*, Part III.

ROBERT BIGOT: Earl of Norfolk; *King John.*

ROBERT FALCONBRIDGE: Son of Sir Robert Falconbridge; *King John.*

ROBIN: A page of Sir John Falstaff; *The Merry Wives of Windsor.*

ROBIN GOODFELLOW (PUCK): A fairy; *A Midsummer Night's Dream.*

RODERIGO: A Venetian gentleman; *Othello.*

ROGERO: A Sicilian gentleman; *The Winter's Tale.*

ROMEO: Son of Montague; *Romeo and Juliet.*

ROSALIND: Daughter of the banished Duke; *As You Like It.*

ROSALINE: A lady attending on the Princess of France; *Love's Labour's Lost.*

ROSENCRANTZ: A courtier; *Hamlet.*

ROSS: A Scottish nobleman; *Macbeth.*

ROSS, LORD: *King Richard II.*

ROTHERAM, THOMAS: Archbishop of York; *King Richard III.*

ROUSILLON, COUNT OF: Bertram; *All's Well that Ends Well.*

ROUSILLON, COUNTESS OF: Mother of Bertram; *All's Well that Ends Well.*

RUGBY: Servant of Dr. Caius; *The Merry Wives of Windsor.*

RUMOUR: As a Prologue; *King Henry IV*, Part II.

SALARINO: Friend of Antonio and Bassanio; *The Merchant of Venice.*

SALISBURY, EARL OF: *King Henry V.*
SALISBURY, EARL OF: *King Richard II.*
SALISBURY, EARL OF: Of the York Faction; *King Henry VI*, Parts I, II.
SALISBURY, EARL OF: William Longsword; *King John.*
SAMPSON: Servant of Capulet; *Romeo and Juliet.*
SANDS, LORD: *King Henry VIII.*
SATURNINUS: Emperor of Rome; *Titus Andronicus.*
SAY, LORD: *King Henry VI*, Part II.
SCALES, LORD: Governor of the Tower; *King Henry VI*, Part II.
SCARUS: Friend of Antony; *Antony and Cleopatra.*
SCROOP: Archbishop of York; *King Henry IV;* Parts I, II.
SCROOP, LORD: A conspirator; *King Henry V.*
SCROOP, SIR STEPHEN: *King Richard II.*
SEBASTIAN: Brother of the King of Naples; *The Tempest.*
SEBASTIAN: Brother of Viola; *Twelfth Night.*
SELEUCUS: Attendant of Cleopatra; *Antony and Cleopatra.*
SEMPRONIUS: A lord, flatterer of Timon; *Timon of Athens.*
SERVILIUS: Servant of Timon; *Timon of Athens.*
SEXTUS POMPEIUS: Friend of Antony; *Antony and Cleopatra.*
SEYTON: Officer attending on Macbeth; *Macbeth.*
SHADOW: A recruit; *King Henry IV*, Part II.
SHALLOW: A country justice; *King Henry IV*, Part II.
SHALLOW: A country justice; *The Merry Wives of Windsor.*
SHYLOCK: A Jew; *The Merchant of Venice.*
SICINIUS VELUTUS: Tribune of the people; *Coriolanus.*
SILENCE: A country justice; *King Henry IV*, Part II.
SILIUS: An officer of Ventidius's army; *Antony and Cleopatra.*
SILVIA: Daughter of the Duke of Milan; *Two Gentlemen of Verona.*
SILVIUS: A shepherd; *As You Like It.*
SIMONIDES: King of Pentapolis; *Pericles.*
SIMPCOX: An impostor; *King Henry VI*, Part II.
SIMPLE: Servant of Slender; *The Merry Wives of Windsor.*
SIR ANDREW AUGUCHEEK: *Twelfth Night.*
SIR ANTHONY DENNY: *King Henry VIII.*
SIR HENRY GUILDFORD: *King Henry VIII.*
SIR HUGH EVANS: A Welsh parson; *The Merry Wives of Windsor.*
SIR HUGH MORTIMER: Uncle of Duke of York; *King Henry VI*, Part III.
SIR HUMPHREY STAFFORD: *King Henry VI*, Part II.
SIR JAMES BLOUNT: *King Richard III.*
SIR JAMES TYRREL: *King Richard III.*
SIR JOHN COLEVILLE: Enemy of the King; *King Henry IV*, Part II.
SIR JOHN FALSTAFF: *King Henry IV*, Parts I, II.
SIR JOHN FALSTAFF: *The Merry Wives of Windsor.*
SIR JOHN FASTOLFE: *King Henry VI*, Part I.
SIR JOHN MONTGOMERY: *King Henry VI*, Part III.
SIR JOHN MORTIMER: Uncle of Duke of York; *King Henry VI*, Part III.
SIR JOHN SOMERVILLE: *King Henry VI*, Part III.
SIR JOHN STANLEY: *King Henry VI*, Part II.
SIR MICHAEL: Friend of Archbishop of York; *King Henry IV*, Parts I, II.

SIR NATHANAIEL: A curate; *Love's Labour's Lost.*
SIR NICHOLAS VAUX: *King Henry VIII.*
SIR OLIVER MARTEXT: A vicar; *As You Like It.*
SIR PIERCE OF EXTON: *King Richard II.*
SIR RICHARD RATCLIFF: *King Richard III.*
SIR RICHARDT VERNON: *King Henry IV*, Part I.
SIR ROBERT BRAKENBURY: Lieutenant of the Tower; *King Richard III.*
SIR STEPHEN SCROOP: *King Richard II.*
SIR THOMAS ERPINGHAM: Officer in King's Army; *King Henry V.*
SIR THOMAS GARGRAVE: *King Henry VI*, Part I.
SIR THOMAS GREY: A conspirator; *King Henry V.*
SIR THOMAS LOVELL: *King Henry VIII.*
SIR THOMAS VAUGHAN: *King Richard III.*
SIR TOBY BELCH: Uncle of Olivia; *Twelfth Night.*
SIR WALTER BLUNT: Friend of King Henry IV, *King Henry IV*, Parts I, II.
SIR WALTER HERBERT: *King Richard III.*
SIR WILLIAM CATESBY: *King Richard III.*
SIR WILLIAM GLANSDALE: *King Henry VI*, Part I.
SIR WILLIAM LUCY: *King Henry VI*, Part I.
SIR WILLIAM STANLEY: *King Henry VI*, Part III.
SIWARD: Earl of Northumberland; *Macbeth.*
SIWARD, YOUNG: Son of Siward; *Macbeth.*
SLENDER: Cousin of Justice Shallow; *The Merry Wives of Windsor.*
SLY, CHRISTOPHER: A drunken tinker; *The Taming of the Shrew.*
SMITH THE WEAVER: A follower of Cade; *King Henry VI*, Part II.
SNARE: A sheriff's officer; *King Henry IV*, Part II.
SNOUT: The tinker; *A Midsummer Night's Dream.*
SNUG: The joiner; *A Midsummer Night's Dream.*
SOLANIO: Friend of Antonio and Bassanio; *The Merchant of Venice.*
SOLINUS: Duke of Ephesus; *The Comedy of Errors.*
SOMERSET, DUKE OF: Of the King's Party; *King Henry VI*, Parts II, III.
SOMERVILLE, SIR JOHN: *King Henry VI*, Part III.
SOUTHWELL: A priest; *King Henry VI*, Part II.
SPEED: A clownish servant; *Two Gentlemen of Verona.*
STAFFORD, LORD: Of the Duke's Party; *King Henry VI*, Part III.
STAFFORD, SIR HUMPHREY: *King Henry VI*, Part II.
STANLEY, LORD: *King Richard III.*
STANLEY, SIR JOHN: *King Henry VI*, Part II.
STANLEY, SIR WILLIAM: *King Henry VI*, Part III.
STARVELING: The tailor; *A Midsummer Night's Dream.*
STEPHANO: A drunken butler; *The Tempest.*
STEPHANO: Servant of Portia; *The Merchant of Venice.*
STRATO: Servant of Brutus; *Julius Caesar.*
SUFFOLK, DUKE OF: *King Henry VIII.*
SUFFOLK, DUKE OF: Of the King's Party; *King Henry VI*, Part II.
SUFFOLK, EARL OF: *King Henry VI*, Part I.
SURREY, DUKE OF: *King Richard II.*
SURREY, EARL OF: *King Henry VIII.*
SURREY, EARL OF: Son of Duke of Norfolk; *King Richard III.*

TALBOT, JOHN: Son of Lord Talbot; *King Henry VI*, Part I.

TALBOT, LORD: Afterward Earl of Shrewsbury; *King Henry VI*, Part I.

TAMORA: Queen of the Goths; *Titus Andronicus*.

TAURUS: Lieutenant general to Caesar; *Antony and Cleopatra*.

TEARSHEET, DOLL: A bawd; *King Henry IV*, Part II.

THAISA: Daughter of Simonides; *Pericles*.

THALIARD: A lord of Antioch; *Pericles*.

THERSITES: A deformed Grecian; *Troilus and Cressida*.

THESEUS: Duke of Athens; *A Midsummer Night's Dream*.

THISBE: A character in the Interlude; *A Midsummer Night's Dream*.

THOMAS: A friar; *Measure for Measure*.

THOMAS, DUKE OF CLARENCE: Son of King Henry IV; *King Henry IV*, Part II.

THOMAS HORNER: An armorer; *King Henry VI*, Part II.

THREE WITCHES: *Macbeth*.

THURIO: Rival of Valentine; *Two Gentlemen of Verona*.

THYREUS: Friend of Caesar; *Antony and Cleopatra*.

TIMANDRA: Mistress of Alcibiades; *Timon of Athens*.

TIME: As Chorus; *The Winter's Tale*.

TIMON: A noble Athenian; *Timon of Athens*.

TITANIA: Queen of the fairies; *A Midsummer Night's Dream*.

TITINIUS: Friend of Brutus and Cassius; *Julius Caesar*.

TITUS ANDRONICUS: General against the Goths; *Titus Andronicus*.

TITUS LARTIUS: General against the Volscians; *Coriolanus*.

TOUCHSTONE: A clown; *As You Like It*.

TRANIO: Servant of Lucentio; *The Taming of the Shrew*.

TRAVERS: Servant of Northumberland; *King Henry IV*, Part II.

TREBONIUS: A Roman conspirator; *Julius Caesar*.

TRINCULO: A jester; *The Tempest*.

TROILUS: Son of Priam; *Troilus and Cressida*.

TUBAL: A Jew, friend to Shylock; *The Merchant of Venice*.

TULLUS AUFIDIUS: Volscian general; *Coriolanus*.

TYBALT: Nephew of Capulet; *Romeo and Juliet*.

TYRREL, SIR JAMES: *King Richard III*.

ULYSSES: A Grecian commander; *Troilus and Cressida*.

URSULA: Attendant of Hero; *Much Ado About Nothing*.

URSWICK, CHRISTOPHER: A priest; *King Richard III*.

VALENTINE: Attendant of the Duke of Illyria; *Twelfth Night*.

VALENTINE: A gentleman of Verona; *Two Gentlemen of Verona*.

VALERIA: Friend of Virgilia; *Coriolanus*.

VARRIUS: Friend of Pompey; *Antony and Cleopatra*.

VARRIUS: Servant of Duke of Vienna; *Measure for Measure*.

VARRO: Servant of Brutus; *Julius Caesar*.

VAUGHAN, SIR THOMAS: *King Richard III*.

VAUX: *King Henry VI*, Part II.

VAUX, SIR NICHOLAS: *King Henry VIII*.

VELUTUS, SICINIUS: Tribune of the people; *Coriolanus*.

VENICE, DUKE OF: *The Merchant of Venice*.

VENICE, DUKE OF: *Othello*.

VENTIDIUS: A false friend; *Timon of Athens*.

VENTIDIUS: Friend of Antony; *Antony and Cleopatra*.

VERGES: A foolish officer; *Much Ado About Nothing*.

VERNON: Of the White-Rose faction; *King Henry VI*, Part I.

VERNON, SIR RICHARD: *King Henry IV*, Part I.

VINCENTIO: Duke of Vienna; *Measure for Measure*.

VINCENTIO: An old gentleman of Pisa; *The Taming of the Shrew*.

VIOLA: In love with the Duke of Illyria; *Twelfth Night*.

VIOLENTA: Neighbor of Widow of Florence; *All's Well that Ends Well*.

VIRGILIA: Wife of Coriolanus; *Coriolanus*.

VOLTIMAND: A courtier; *Hamlet*.

VOLUMNIA: Mother of Coriolanus; *Coriolanus*.

VOLUMNIUS: Friend of Brutus and Cassius; *Julius Caesar*.

WALES, HENRY, PRINCE OF: Son of King Henry IV; *King Henry IV*, Part I, II.

WALES, PRINCE OF: Son of King Edward IV; *King Richard III*.

WALTER WHITMORE: *King Henry VI*, Part II.

WART: A recruit; *King Henry IV*, Part II.

WARWICK, EARL OF: *King Henry V*.

WARWICK, EARL OF: Of the King's Party; *King Henry IV*, Part II.

WARWICK, EARL OF: Of the York Faction; *King Henry VI*, Parts I, II, III.

WESTMINSTER, ABBOT OF: *King Richard II*.

WESTMORELAND, EARL OF: Friend to King Henry IV, *King Henry IV*, Parts I, II.

WESTMORELAND, EARL OF: *King Henry V*.

WESTMORELAND, EARL OF: Of the King's Party; *King Henry VI*, Part III.

WHITMORE, WALTER: *King Henry VI*, Part II.

WILLIAM: A country fellow; *As You Like It*.

WILLIAM LONGSWORD: Earl of Salisbury; *King John*.

WILLIAM MARESHALL: Earl of Pembroke; *King John*.

WILLIAM PAGE: Son of Mrs. Page; *The Merry Wives of Windsor*.

WILLIAMS: Soldier in King's Army; *King Henry V*.

WILLOUGHBY, LORD: *King Richard II*.

WINCHESTER, BISHOP OF: Gardiner; *King Henry VIII*.

WOLSEY, CARDINAL: *King Henry VIII*.

WOODVILLE: Lieutenant of the Tower; *King Henry VI*, Part I.

WORCESTER, EARL OF: Thomas Percy; *King Henry IV*, Parts I, II.

YORK, ARCHBISHOP OF: Scroop; *King Henry IV*, Parts I, II.

YORK, ARCHBISHOP OF: Thomas Rotheram; *King Richard III*.

YORK, DUCHESS OF: *King Richard II*.

YORK, DUCHESS OF: Mother of King Edward IV; *King Richard III*.

YORK, DUKE OF: Cousin of the King; *King Henry V*.

YORK, DUKE OF: Son of King Edward IV; *King Richard III*.

YORK, DUKE OF: Uncle of King Richard II; *King Richard II*.

YOUNG CATO: Friend of Brutus and Cassius; *Julius Caesar*.

YOUNG CLIFFORD: Son of Lord Clifford; *King Henry VI*, Part II.

YOUNG MARCIUS: Son of Coriolanus. *Coriolanus*.

YOUNG SIWARD: Son of Siward; *Macbeth*.

Cheeses of The World

ABERTAM: A hard cheese from Carlsbad, Czechoslovakia, made from ewe's milk.

ALENTEJO: A soft cheese from province of Alentejo, Portugal, cylindrical in shape, and made in 3 sizes, weighing 2 oz., 1 lb., and 4 lbs. respectively; made chiefly from ewe's milk, but goat milk is often added, especially in the smaller cheeses.

ALLGÄUER RUNDKÄSE (ALLGÄUER EMMENTALER): A type of Swiss cheese from Allgau in southwest Bavarian Alps, from 5 to 5³/₄″ thick, and 150-175 lbs. in weight.

ALPIN (CLÉRIMEMBERT): Variant of Mont d'Or, from the French Alps.

ALTENBURGER: A German goat's-milk cheese, especially from Thüringen in Central Germany, where it is called Altenburger Ziegenkäse; 8″×2″, about 2 lbs. in weight.

AMBERT (FOURME D'AMBERT): A cylindrical, cow's milk, Roquefort-type cheese made locally in Central France; differs from Roquefort in that the salt is mixed with the curd rather than rubbed on the surface of the cheese.

AMERICAN: Generic term that includes Cheddar (i.e., American Cheddar), Colby, granular or stirred-curd, and washed- or soaked-curd cheeses, and sometimes Monterey or Jack.

ANCIEN IMPÉRIAL: A French cheese, 2″×1½″ eaten fresh *(Petit Carré)* as well as cured *(Carré Affiné);* the curd is prepared as for Neufchâtel, and the curing process is similar.

APPENZELLER: Made from cow's milk in Appenzell Canton, Switzerland, in Bavaria, and in Baden, and is like Swiss cheese; made from whole as well as from skim milk.

APPETITOST: Danish sour buttermilk cheese, of which small quantities are made in U.S.A.

ARMAVIR: A sour-milk cheese, resembling German hand cheese, made in the W. Caucasus from ewe's whole milk; sour buttermilk or whey is added to heated milk, the cheese pressed in forms, and ripened in a warm place.

ASADERO (OAXACA): A white, whole-milk Mexican cheese, called *asadero* (fit for roasting) because it melts easily, and, alternately, Oaxaca, for the Mexican state of Oaxaca (though it is now mostly made in the state of Jalisco); the curd is heated and cut and braided or kneaded into loaves of various sizes, from 8 oz. to 11 lbs.

ASIAGO: Originated in Asiago commune in province of Vicenza, Italy, but is also made in Carnia, Venetia, Trentino, Lombardy, and nearby areas; first made from ewe's milk and called *Pecorino di Asiago;* now made from cow's milk and is a sweet-curd, semicooked, grana-type cheese with a pungent aroma, round and flat weighing on an average 16-22 lbs.; may be used as a table cheese when not aged, and called, when it can be sliced, *Asiago di taglio* (slicing cheese); fresh Asiago is cured at least 60 days (some prefer at least 4 mos.); medium for 6 mos.; and old (used mostly as grated cheese) over a year.

ASIN (WATER): A sour-milk, washed-curd, whitish, soft, buttery, more or less ripened cheese from farms and small dairies in N. Italian mountains; contains a few large eyes; made in spring (while the cows are in green pasture), eaten in summer and fall, popular as a dessert cheese (frequently eaten with honey and fruits); cylindrical and flat, 8″×6″ about 14 lbs. in weight; when ripened 2-3 mos. extra in a special brine to give more flavor, it is called Salmistra.

BACKSTEINER: A modified Limburger-Romadur-type cheese, similar to Stangenkäse, made to a limited extent in N. Germany; called Backstein (brick) because of its shape, but is more like Limburger made from partly skimmed milk than U.S. brick cheese, though smaller and cured for a shorter time; when made in squares, it is called Quadratkäse.

BAGOZZO (GRANA BAGOZZO; BRESCIANO): A Parmesan-type cheese similar to but smaller than Reggiano and Parmigiano, with a hard yellow body, a rather sharp flavor, and (often) a red surface.

BAKERS': A skim-milk cheese much like cottage cheese, but softer, finer-grained, with more moisture and acid; the curd is usually not washed or cooked and it is drained in bags rather than in the vat; it is usually used in making such bakery products as cheese cake, pie, and pastries, but can also be creamed and eaten like cottage cheese.

BANBURY: A rich soft cheese, cylindrical in shape, about 1″ thick, popular in England in the early 19th century.

BARBEREY: A soft small cheese like Camembert, named for Barberey, near Troyes, France, and commonly called *Fromage de Troyes*.

BATTELMATT: A small Swiss-type cheese made from cow's milk in Tessin Canton, Switzerland, when the supply of milk is not enough for making large "wheels"; cylindrical and flat, 18-24″ in diameter, 3¹/₄-4″ thick, 40-80 lbs. in weight, with a softer body than Swiss and more moisture, a flavor more like Tilsiter than Swiss; ripens quickly, and is marketed within 3-4 mos.

BELGIAN COOKED: Is made like cooked cheese (Kochkäse), from curdled skim milk heated 135°-140° F, then drained in a cloth, kneaded by hand, and let to ripen, usually 10-14 days in winter, 6-8 in summer, when cream and salt are added and the mixture is heated to about 180°, stirred, and put into molds to ripen for several days; usually weighs 3¹/₂ lbs.

BELLELAY (TÊTE DE MOINE; MONK'S HEAD): A soft, blue-veined, whole-milk cheese like Gorgonzola, first made by 15th century monks in Bern Canton, Switzerland, and now an exclusive product of that area; it has a buttery consistency and can be spread on bread.

BEL PAESE ("BEAUTIFUL COUNTRY"): Trade name of the most famous of a group of uncooked, soft, sweet, mild, fast-ripened Italian table cheeses first made about 1920 in Melzo, upper Lombardy, though similar cheeses have been made in Italy for 60 years; others in the group are Bella Alpina, Bella Milano, Bel piano Lombardo, Bel Piemonte fior d'Alpe, Savoia, and Vittoria; similar European cheeses are Schönland and Fleur des Alpes; they are called butter cheese, especially in Germany, and a similar "butter" cheese is made in Canada; U.S. variants are sold under different names because of the Italian trade mark; in parts of Italy the cheeses weigh 4¹/₂ lbs. and are 5¹/₄-6″ in diameter.

BERGKÄSE: Name of a group of Alpine cheeses, chiefly of the Swiss type, including Battlemart and Piora (from Tessin Canton, Switzerland), Gruyère (Switzerland and France), Fontina (Aosta Valley, Italy), Montasio (Carinthia and environs), Walliser (Wallis Canton, Switzerland), and several others; a soft cheese called Vacherin (Fribourg Canton, Switerland) is also classed in the Bergkäse group.

BERQUARA: A Gouda-like cheese that has

been made in Sweden since the 18th century.

BERNARDE (FORMAGELLE BERNARDE): An Italian whole cow's-milk cheese with about 10% goat's milk added for flavor, a sprinkling of saffron for color, ready to eat after curing 2 mos.

BGUG-PANIR (DARALAG): An Armenian cheese made partly or entirely from skimmed ewe's milk.

BITTO: A firm semicooked Italian cheese of the Swiss group, first made in Friuli, but now also in Lombardy; similar to Fontina and Montasio; made from cow's milk, ewe's milk, or from a mixture of goat's milk and cow's milk, and from whole, slightly skimmed, or skim milk; weighs between 35-75 lbs.; has small eyes; when made from whole milk and not fully cured, it is used as a table cheese; when made from skim milk and fully cured, it is grated.

BLEU (FROMAGE BLEU): Name for a group of Roquefort-type (blue-veined) cheeses made in the Roquefort area (S. E. France) from milk other than ewe's milk; and also for Roquefort-type cheeses made elsewhere in France (outside the Roquefort area), regardless of the kind of milk used; because of the mottled, marbled, or veined appearance of the curd they are also called *fromage persillé; other* cheeses in this group are Bleu d'Auvergne, Laguiole, Gex, Gex Bressans (goat's-milk Gex), Mont Cenis, Sassenage, Septmoncel, and Saint-Flour.

BLUE, BLUE-MOLD, OR BLUE-VEINED CHEESE: Names for cheese of the Roquefort type made in U.S.A. and Canada, from cow's or goat's, rather than ewe's milk; about 7½" in diameter, 4½-5 lbs. in weight, round and flat like Gorgonzola, but smaller. Lactic starter is added to fresh clean milk, pasteurized or homogenized, and it is set with rennet at 84° F.; 1-1½ hrs. later the coagulated curd is cut, the whey drained off, and the curd placed in perforated metal hoops 7½" in diameter and 6" deep; blue-mold powder is mixed with the curd, and some salt; the hoops are turned often, for at least 24 hrs. The cheeses are dry-salted over a period 7-10 days in a room 46-48° F. with relative humidity 95%; after a week, each cheese is pierced with 40 or more ⅛" holes to let air (essential for mold growth) reach the interior. These cheeses are now placed on edge in the curing room for 3 mos. at 48°F., relative humidity 95%, and scraped or cleaned at 3-4 week intervals to reduce slime formation and growth of foreign molds on the surface; next they are wrapped in tinfoil and stored 2-3 mos. at 40° F. in a moist room; total curing period must be at least 60 days; the yield of cured cheese is 10-11 lbs. per 100 lbs. of whole milk.

BONDON: A small, unripened, whole-milk French cheese of the fresh Neufchâtel type.

BONDOST: A Swedish, farm-type, cow's-milk cheese that has also been made in a few U.S. factories, chiefly in Wisconsin, for more than 30 years; it is cylindrical, about 5" in diameter, 3-4" thick, and weighs 2½-3 lbs. Sometimes cumin or caraway seed is mixed with the curd just before it is put into the forms.

BORELLI: A small Italian cheese made from buffalo's milk.

BOUDANNE: A French cheese made from cow's milk, ripened 2-3 mos.

BOURGAIN: A type of fresh Neufchâtel, made in France, with low fat content, unsalted, relatively high moisture content; very soft, perishable; consumed locally.

BOX (FIRM): A German cheese, known in different localities as Hohenburg, Mondsee, and Weihenstephan, with mild but piquant flavor, similar to U.S. brick cheese, made from cow's whole milk, weighing 1-4 lbs.

BOX (SOFT): A minor German cheese made from partly skimmed cow's milk in the village of Hohenheim, Württemberg, often called Hohenheimer cheese and known locally as *Schachtelkäse.*

BRA: An Italian cheese named for the Piedmont village where it was first made by nomads; it is a hard, nearly white cheese with a compact texture and sharp, salty flavor, made from partly skimmed milk, weighing about 12 lbs.

BRAND: A German hand cheese made from sour milk curd that is heated to a temperature somewhat higher than usual; the curd is salted and allowed to ferment for a day, then mixed with butter, pressed, dried, and placed in kegs to ripen, where it is occasionally moistened with beer; each cheese weighs about 5 ozs.

BRICK: One of the few cheeses of American origin; made in considerable quantities in many factories, especially in Wisconsin; it is a sweet-curd, semisoft, cow's-milk cheese, with a mild but rather pungent and sweet flavor, midway between Cheddar and Limburger; softer than Cheddar, but firmer than Limburger, it is elastic and slices without crumbling; it has an open texture with numerous round and irregular shaped eyes. The name may refer to its bricklike shape or to the bricks used in pressing it.

BRICKBAT: Made from fresh milk, with a little added cream, introduced in Wiltshire, England, in the 18th century; the milk is set with rennet at about 90° F., coagulated for 2 hrs., then the curd is cut into coarse pieces, dipped into wooden forms, and finished under light pressure; the cheese can be eaten a year after being made.

BRIE: A soft, surface-ripened cheese usually made from cow's whole milk but also at times from skim or partly skim milk; first made several centuries ago in what is now the Department of Seine-et-Marne, France; quality varies with the kind of milk used. Melun, Coulommiers, and Meaux are noted for the production of Brie, which is also known locally as *fromage de Melun* and *fromage de Coulommiers;* Brie-type cheese is made also in other parts of France and in other countries, including the U.S.A. Made in three sizes; large (16" in diameter, 1½-1⅔" thick, weighing 6 lbs.), medium (about 12" in diameter, slightly thinner than large size, weighing about 3½ lbs.), and small (5½-8" in diameter, 1¼" thick, weighing about 1 lb.); some authorities identify the small size as Coulommiers or *petit moule.* Like Camembert, which it resembles, Brie is ripened partly by molds and bacteria, and probably yeasts, that grow on the surface of the cheese, but, because of differences in the details of manufacture, the internal ripening and characteristic flavor and aroma differ. Brie is perishable and must be kept under refrigeration. It ripens more normally if it is not cut; About 14 lbs. of cheese is obtained from 100 lbs. of whole milk.

BRIOLER AND WORIENER: Named for the East Prussian localities where they are made, similar to Limburger cheese from cow's whole milk; the curing period is 4-6 weeks; each cheese is 3-4" square, 2-3" thick, and weighs about 2¼ lbs.

BROCCIO (BROUSE): A Corsican cheese similar to ricotta and Ziger; fresh and sour whey are mixed and heated almost to the boiling point; the surface coagulum is skimmed off and drained on a fine mat or in a basket; keeps for a day in summer, longer in winter, and can be kept for still longer periods if salted.

BURGUNDY (FROMAGE DE BOURGOGNE): A soft, white, loaf-shaped cheese weighing about 4 lbs.

BURMEISTER: Trade name of a soft, ripened brick-type cheese made in Wisconsin.

BUTTERMILK: Made from the curd of buttermilk and is somewhat finer grained than cottage cheese, which it closely resembles.

CACCIOCAVALLO: An Italian plastic-curd (*pasta filata*) cheese first made in southern Italy, now made also in Sicily and, in summer, in N. Italy (where it is made chiefly for export). It is especially suitable for making in warm climates, as it keeps well. The cured cheese has a smooth, fine body, and the interior of the best product is white. It is made like Provolone, but has less fat, is usually not smoked, and has a different shape (Cacciocavallo is, typically, spindle-shaped, with pointed bottom, and a neck and head at top; they are tied in pairs and hung over poles to cure and look as if hung over a saddle, hence the name, meaning "cheeses on horseback." It is usually made from cow's milk, but sometimes from a mixture of cow's and ewe's; when cured 2-4 mos. it is suitable for table use; 6-12 mos. for grating; the cheeses usually weigh $4^{1}/_{2}$-$5^{1}/_{2}$ lbs.

CACCIOCAVALLO SICILIANO: A plastic-curd (*pasta filata*) cheese like the Italian Provolone and cacciocavallo, essentially a pressed Provolone; although small quantities are made in the U.S.A., it is made chiefly in Sicily, usually from cow's whole milk, but sometimes from goat's or a mixture of the two; it is said to be made always in the shape of an oblong block; each cheese weighs $17^{1}/_{2}$-26 lbs.

CACIO FIORE (CACIOTTA): A soft, yellowish, Italian cheese with a delicate, buttery flavor; it has a soft fine curd similar to Bel Paese and the Stracchino and Crescenza cheeses of Lombardy, and is made from ewe's or goat's milk, usually in the cold winter mos. Cacio fiore Aquilano is a similar cheese that is usually made in winter (January and February), a rectangular, fast-ripening Stracchino-type cheese made from ewe's milk, preferably with vegetable (*fiore*) rennet (although good results can be gotten with calf rennet). It should be eaten within a month after it is made.

CAERPHILLY: A semisoft cow's-milk cheese made in Wales, especially popular with Welch miners; it is circular and flat, about 9" in diameter, $2^{1}/_{2}$-$3^{1}/_{2}$" thick, and weighs about 8 lbs.; the cheese is white and smooth, lacks elasticity, and is granular rather than waxy when broken.

CALCAGNO: A hard Sicilian cheese, classed as a *pecorino* (ewe's milk) cheese, suitable for grating.

CAMBRIDGE (YORK): A soft English cheese, made from cow's whole milk set at 90° F. with enough rennet to coagulate it in an hour; the uncut curd is dipped into molds, and is ready to eat after standing 30 hrs.

CAMEMBERT: A soft, surface-ripened, cow's-milk cheese, first made in 1791 by Marie Fontaine (Madame Harel) at Camembert, a hamlet in the Department of Orne, France. Napoleon is said to have given the cheese its name; the industry soon extended from Orne to the Department of Calvados, and these two departments are still principal centers of production. Camembert-type cheese is made in other parts of France, and abroad, including the U.S.A. Each cheese is about $4^{1}/_{2}$" in diameter, 1-$1^{1}/_{2}$" thick, and weighs about 10 oz.; the interior is yellow and waxy, creamy, or

almost fluid in consistency depending on the degree of ripening; the rind is a thin, feltlike layer of gray mold and dry cheese interspersed with patches of reddish yellow. The cheese is made in much the same way as Brie, but the finished cheese is smaller and the characteristic flavor differs.

CAMOSUN: A semisoft, open-textured cheese that is said to resemble Gouda and Monterey.

CANNED: Refers to method of packaging, not to a kind of cheese, although cheese so packaged is usually American Cheddar.

CANQUILLOTE (FROMAGÈRE; TEMPÊTE): A skim-milk cheese made in eastern France; water, salt, eggs, and butter are mixed with the curd, and it is pressed in molds of various shapes.

CANTAL (FOURME): A hard, rather yellow cheese with a piquant flavor and firm, close body, which has been made for centuries in the Auvergne Mountains region in the Department of Cantal, France; the cheeses are about 14" in diameter and usually weigh about 75 lbs., but vary from 40-120 lbs.

CARAWAY: See Spiced cheese.

CARRÉ (CARRÉ FRAIS): Known also as *double crème carré* and *fromage double crème*, this is a small rich French cream cheese of the Neufchâtel type, about 2" square, and less than 4 oz. in weight; the larger size—$4^{1}/_{2}$-5" in diameter, 1-$1^{1}/_{2}$" thick, 10-12 oz. in weight—is similar to Camembert and Coulommiers; a similar cheese, with much preservative salt added is called *demisel*.

CARREÉ DE L'EST: Is a Camembert-type cheese made in France from either pasteurized or unpasteurized cow's whole milk.

CASIGIOLU (PENEDDA; PERA DI VACCA): A Sicilian plastic-curd cheese made like Cacciocavallo.

CASTELMANGO: An Italian blue-mold Gorgonzola-type cheese.

CHAMPOLÉON (QUEYRAS): A hard cheese similar to Canquillote, made from skim milk in the Hautes-Alps region of France.

CHANTELLE: Trade name of a semisoft, fresh cow's-milk, ripened cheese from Illinois, made and cured in a manner similar to Bel Paese.

CHAOURCE: A soft, whole-milk cheese resembling Camembert, 4" in diameter and 3" thick; named for the village of Chaource, in the Department of Aube, France.

CHASCOL (CHASCHOSIS): A hard cheese made in the Canton of Grisons in eastern Switzerland from cow's skim milk; it is from 17-20" in diameter, from $2^{3}/_{4}$-4" thick, and weighs 22-45 lbs.

CHEDDAR: Named for the village of Cheddar in Somersetshire, England, where it was first made at least as long ago as the last half of the 16th century; it was made by colonial American wives, and the first cheese factory in the U.S.A. was a Cheddar-cheese factory, established in 1851 by Jesse Williams near Rome, Oneida County, N.Y.; at present nearly 900 million lbs. of Cheddar and Cheddar-type cheese are made in U.S. each year (about 75% of the total annual U.S. cheese production). Cheddar is a hard cheese, ranging in color from near white to yellow, made from sweet, whole cow's-milk, either raw or pasteurized (if made from partly skimmed or skim milk, it must be so labeled). Cheddar is also the name of a step in the manufacturing process and also the name of the most common style, which is about $14^{1}/_{2}$" in diameter, 12" thick, and weighs between 70-78 lbs.; other styles are: Daisy, about $13^{1}/_{4}$" in diameter, slightly more than 4" thick, 21-23 lbs.; Flat or Twin, $14^{1}/_{2}$"

in diameter, slightly more than 5″ thick, 32-37 lbs.; Longhorn, 6″ in diameter, 13″ long, 12-13 lbs.; Young American, 7″ in diameter, 7″ thick, 11-12 lbs.; Picnic or Junior Twin, 9³/₄″ in diameter, 5″ thick, 11-12 lbs.; and rectangular blocks or prints, usually 14″ long, 11″ wide, 3¹/₄″ thick, and weigh 20 lbs.; and they are made in larger sizes that weigh up to 80 lbs.

CHESHIRE (CHESTER): Ranks with Cheddar as the oldest and most popular of English cheeses, dating back as early as the reign of Elizabeth I; it was first made in Chester on the River Dee, and is said to have been molded originally in the form of the famous "Cheshire Cat"; it is a firm cheese, but more crumbly and less compact than Cheddar; like Cheddar it is cylindrical; the cheeses are 14″ in diameter, 50-70 lbs. in weight; the curd may be nearly white, but more often it is colored deep yellow with annatto.

CHESHIRE-STILTON: An English cheese with the combined characteristics of Cheshire and Stilton.

CHHANA: A sour-milk cheese made in Asia from cow's whole milk.

CHIAVARI: A sour-milk cheese made from cow's whole milk in the region of Chiavari in the province of Genova, Italy.

CHRISTALINNA: A hard cheese made from cow's milk in the Canton of Grisons, Switzerland.

CHRISTIAN IX: A Danish cheese differing from Kuminost principally in size and shape; it is cylindrical and flat and weighs less than 35 lbs., and contains spices, such as caraway seed; the surface is coated with yellow paraffin or wax.

CLÉRIMBERT: See Alpin.

COLBY: Similar to Cheddar, and may be made from either raw or pasteurized milk; has a softer body and more open texture than Cheddar, with more moisture.

COLD-PACK (CLUB; COMMINUTED): Is said to have originated in U.S.A. and is usually made from carefully selected and well-aged Cheddar cheese; it is made from pasteurized milk, or from cheese that has been held for at least 60 days at a temperature of not less than 35° F., it may be made from smoked cheese, or smoked in the processing.

COLD PACK CHEESE FOOD: Prepared by grinding very fine and mixing without heating one or more lots of the same or different varieties of cheese with one or more socalled optional dairy ingredients, to which may be added one or more of the following: an acidifying agent, water, salt, color, spices, and a sweetening agent.

COMMISSION: Is made from slightly skimmed milk in the same way as Edam and is the same shape, but weighs 8 lbs., twice as much as the average Edam; it is a product of North Holland Province and of Friesland in the Netherlands.

COMTE: Made in eastern France; similar to Gruyère; weighs 100-120 lbs.

COOKED (GERMAN; KOCHKÆSE): Name for cheese that is made by heating or "cooking" the curd; in the U.S.A. the local names include cup cheese and Pennsylvania pot cheese; in N. Germany, Topfen; in Sardinia, Fresa; when properly made it has an agreeable flavor and a smooth buttery consistency like Camembert.

COON: A Cheddar cheese that is cured by a special patented method; the surface is quite dark in color, the body is crumbly, and the flavor is sharp and tangy.

CORNHUSKER: Similar to Cheddar and Colby, but has a softer body, more moisture, and takes less time to make; it was introduced by the Nebraska Agricultural Experiment Station about 1940.

COTHERSTONE (YORKSHIRE-STILTON): A blue-veined cheese made on a small scale in the valley of the Tees, in Yorkshire, in N. England, from cow's milk; similar to Stilton.

COTRONESE: A ewe's milk cheese similar to Moliterno, and native to Calabria and Lucania, Italy; said to be seasoned at times with pepper.

COTTAGE (POT; DUTCH; SCHMIERKÆSE): A soft, uncured cheese made from skim milk or from reconstituted concentrated skim milk or nonfat dry milk solids; usually some cream is mixed with the curd before it is marketed or consumed; if the cheese contains 4% or more of fat, it is called creamed cottage cheese; flavoring materials, such as peppers, olives, and pimentos, may be added.

COULOMMIERS: A soft, mold-ripened unwashed cheese, made from cow's fresh whole milk, or a mixture of evening and morning milk; originated in the vicinity of Coulommiers, in the Department of Seine-et-Marne, France; a modified kind is made in the U.S.A. and Canada; usually eaten fresh.

CREAM: A soft, rich, uncured cheese made of cream, or a mixture of cream and milk, and used as a spread for bread, in sandwiches, and with salads, similar to unripened Neufchâtel, but with higher fat content.

CREOLE: A soft, rich, unripened Cottagetype, Louisiana cheese, made by mixing equal quantities of cottage-type curd and rich cream.

CRESCENZA (CARSENZA, STRACCHINO CRESCENZA, CRESCENZA LOMBARDI): An uncooked, soft, creamy, mildly sweet, fast-ripening, yellowish cheese of the Bel Paese type, made September-April in Lombardy, N. Italy, from cow's whole milk; a similar cheese called Raviggiolo is made in Tuscany from ewe's milk.

CREUSE: A skim-milk cheese made on farms in the Department of Creuse, France; it may be aged a year or more, and then becomes very dry and firm; or it may be put to ripen in tightly closed containers lined with straw, in which case it becomes soft and yellow and acquires a sharp flavor.

DAMEN (GLOIRE DES MONTAGNES): A soft, uncured cheese made in Hungary from cow's milk.

DANISH EXPORT: A small, flattened, cylindrical cheese about the size and shape of Gouda, made in certain Danish creameries from skim milk and buttermilk.

DELFT: A spiced cheese, almost like Leyden, made in the Netherlands from partly skimmed cow's milk.

DERBY (DERBYSHIRE): A hard, sweet-curd cheese, similar to Cheddar, but not so firm and solid, more flaky when broken, with more moisture, and faster ripening; made in Derbyshire, England, from cow's whole milk; Gloucester, Leicester Warwickshire, and Wiltshire are other English cheeses similar to Derby.

DEVONSHIRE CREAM: An English cream cheese.

DOMIATI: A pickled cheese, made from whole or partly skimmed cow's or buffalo's milk; one the top Egyptian and Arabic cheeses; it is soft, white, with no openings, mild and salty in flavor when fresh and cleanly acid when cured; aged, it darkens and develops a strong flavor.

DORSET (DORSET BLUE, BLUE VINNY, BLUE VEINY): One of the hard, blue-veined English cheeses, circular, flat, 14-16 lbs. in weight, usually dry and crumbly, with a sharp and frequently acid flavor; white, with blue veining throughout; made from partly skimmed cow's milk.

DOTTER: Said to be made in Nuremberg, Germany, by mixing egg yoke with skimmed milk and then making cheese in the usual way.

DRY (SPERRKÄSE; TROCKENKÄSE): Is made from skim milk in small dairies in the E. Bavarian Alps and in the Tyrol.

DUEL: A soft, cured, cow's-milk cheese made in Austria, 2″ square, 1″ thick.

DUNLOP: A rich, white, pressed cheese made in Scotland, and formerly considered the national cheese, but now largely superseded by a cousin, Cheddar.

EDAM (MANBOLLEN; KATZENKOPF; TÊTE DE MAURE): A semisoft to hard sweet-curd cheese made from cow's milk, originally near Edam in the province of North Holland, Netherlands. It has a pleasingly mild, clean, sometimes salty, flavor, and a rather firm and crumbly body, free of holes and openings; usually shaped like a flattened ball, but in the U.S.A. made also in a loaf shape; weighs usually 3¹/₂-4¹/₂ lb., but may be 14 lb.; in the U.S.A. they are sometimes only ³/₄-1 lb.

EGG: Is made from fresh milk to which fresh eggs are added at the rate of 2-12 eggs per 6 quarts of milk; it originated in the province of Nyland, Finland.

EMILIANO: Is a very hard cheese of the Italian grana or Parmesan type, the same as Reggiano, according to some; cylindrical, with straight or slightly convex sides, 12-16″ in diameter, 6-8¹/₂″ thick, 44-66 lbs.; with dark oiled surface, and light yellow interior; flavor varies from mild to rather sharp, and the texture is granular; usually without eyes, or with a few small ones, unevenly distributed.

ENGADINE: Made in Grison Canton, Switzerland, from cow's whole milk.

ENGLISH DAIRY: A very hard cheese made in the same general way as Cheddar, but cooked longer; used some years ago, especially in the U.S.A., in cooking.

EPOISSÉ: A soft cheese made from whole or partly skimmed milk in the Department of Côte-d'Or, France.

ERIWANI (KARAB; TALI; KURINI; ELISAVETPOLEN; KASACH): Made from fresh ewe's milk, principally in the Caucasus, and salted in brine.

ERVY: A soft Camembert-like cheese named for the village of Ervy in the Department of Aube, France, where it is made; 7″ diameter, 2¹/₂″ thick, weighs about 4 lbs.

FARM: As originally made on French farms is essentially the same as cottage cheese; also called Fromage à la pie, Mou, Maigre, and Ferme.

FETA: A white, so-called pickled cheese, the principal soft cheese made by the shepherds in the mountains around Athens, Greece; usually made from ewe's milk, but sometimes from goat's.

FILLED: Made from milk or skimmed milk to which foreign fat has been added.

FIORE SARDO: A hard Italian cheese made from ewe's milk; used as a table cheese when immature and as a condiment when fully cured.

FLØTEOST: A boiled-whey cheese made in Norway, like Mysost except that it contains more fat (Fløte, in Norwegian, indicates cream).

FLOWER: A soft, cured cheese made in England from cow's whole milk with petals of different flowers, such as roses or marigolds, added.

FOGGIANO: Made in Apulia, Italy, from

ewe's milk and resembles Cotronese and Moliterno.

FONTINA: A cooked-curd, whole-milk, semisoft to hard, slightly yellow cheese with a delicate, nutty flavor and pleasing aroma, made from ewe's milk (also from cow's milk in summer), in the Aosta Valley in Piedmont, Italy, and from cow's milk in the U.S.A.

FOREZ (D'AMBERT): Made in central France, cylindrical, 10″ diameter, 6″ thick; when of good quality, is said to taste like Roquefort. It is placed on a cellar floor to cure, covered with dirt, and water is allowed to trickle over it; frequently the cheese is spoiled by undesirable mold and bacteria.

FORMAGELLE: A small, soft cheese made from ewe's or goat's milk in the mountains of N. Italy.

FORMAGGI DI PASTA FILATA: Refers to a group of Italian cheeses made by curdling the milk with rennet, warming and fermenting the curd, heating it until it is plastic, then drawing it into ropes and then kneading and shaping it, producing a cheese that is free of whey and holes or pockets of air; for this reason such cheeses keep well even in warm climates. Among the best known are Provolone, Cacciocavallo, Moliterno, Mozzarella, Provatura, and Scamorze; others are Katschkawalj and Kaskaval (Balkans), Oschtjepek and Parenica (Slovakia), and Panedda (Sardinia).

FORMAGGINI ("SMALL CHEESE"): Term applied to several kinds of small Italian cheeses; Formaggini de Lecco is a small, cylindrical dessert cheese made near Lecco, in Lombardy, from cow's milk to which some goat's milk may be added.

FRESA: A mild, sweet, soft, cooked cheese made in Sardinia from cow's milk.

FRIBOURG: A hard cheese, made like Swiss, which has migrated from Switzerland to the Po Valley.

FRIESIAN CLOVE: A spiced cheese made in the Netherlands from cow's milk that may be partly skimmed with cloves added.

FROMAGE À LA CRÈME: A soft, rich cheese that is eaten without ripening; French cream cheese is another name.

FROMAGE FORT: One of several French cooked cheeses, made in the Department of Ain.

FRÜHSTÜCK: A small Limburger-type cheese made in Germany from whole or partly skimmed cow's milk.

GAISKÄSLI: A soft cheese made from goat's milk in Germany and Switzerland.

GAMMELOST: A semisoft, blue-mold, ripened table cheese, with a rather sharp, aromatic flavor, made in Norway (principally in the counties of Hardanger and Sogn) of sour skim milk.

GAUTRIAS: Resembles Port du Salut and is made in the Department of Mayenne, France.

GAVOT: Is made from cow's, ewe's, or goat's milk in the Department of Hautes-Alps, France.

GÉROMÉ (GÉRARDMER): A soft cheese made in the Vosges mountain region of France, and in Switzerland, named from the village Gérardmer.

GEX: A hard cow's-milk cheese named for Gex, Department of Ain, France, where it has been made for over 100 years.

GIEHEIMRATH: A deep yellow cheese like a small Gouda; made in small quantities in the Netherlands.

GISLEV: A hard cheese made in Denmark from cow's milk.

GJETOST: A Norwegian boiled-whey cheese, called Ekte (genuine) Gjetost, or Geitmyost when made from goat's milk only instead of the commoner mixture of cow's and goat's milk ("Gje" indicates a goat's-milk product.)

GLOUCESTER: A hard cheese, like Derby, made in England in the county of Gloucestershire.

GLUMSE: Resembles cottage cheese and is made in western Prussia.

GOAT'S milk: Any cheese made with goat's milk instead of cow's milk, but in the usual ways.

GOMOST: A whole-milk Norwegian cheese made usually from cow's milk but sometimes from goat's milk.

GORGONZOLA (STACCHINO DI GORGONZOLA): The chief blue-green veined cheese of Italy, said to have been made in the Po Valley since 879 a.d., and named for the village of Gorgonzola, near Milan.

GOUDA: A semisoft to hard, sweet-curd cheese similar to Edam, but fatless; was first made near Gouda in the province of South Holland, Netherlands, from whole or partly skimmed cow's milk, but skimmed less than milk used in making Edam.

GOURNAY: A soft Neufchâtel-type cheese named for Gournay, Department of Seine-Inférieure, France.

GOYA: Resembles medium-cured Asiago and comes from the province of Corrientes in Argentina.

GRANA: Refers to a group of Italian cheeses that have granular body and texture, sharp flavor, very small eyes, good keeping quality, excellent shipping properties (needing no packaging).

GRANULAR, OR STIRRED-CURD: A cheese similar to Cheddar and Colby, made in considerable quantity in the U.S.A. from either raw or pasteurized milk.

GRATED CHEESE: Prepared by grinding hard, dry, cow-fat, well-aged natural cheese to a powder.

GRAY: Is made in the Tyrol from sour skim milk; interior of the cured cheese is grayish.

GRUYÈRE (GREYERZERKÄSE; GROYER): Is made from cow's whole milk much in the manner of Swiss, but is smaller, with smaller eyes, a sharper flavor, and is usually cured in a more humid curing room; named for Gruyère, Fribourg Canton, Switzerland.

GÜSSING: An Austrian cheese much like U.S. brick cheese, but made from skim milk.

HAND: A small, sour-milk surface-ripened cheese, so named because originally molded in final shape by hand; very popular among Germans.

HARZKÄSE: A type of hand cheese made in Germany.

HAUSKÄSE: A Limburger-type cheese made in a 10″-diameter disk.

HAY (FROMAGE DE FOIN): A skim-milk cheese from the Department of Seine-Inférieure, France.

HERKIMER: A Cheddar-type cheese once popular in Herkimer County, N.Y.

HERRGÅRDSOST (MANOR): A medium firm, pliable, mild, sweet, nutty, pleasant-smelling Swedish cheese, made from partly skimmed cow's milk.

HERVÉ: A Belgian Limburger-type cheese.

HOLSTEIN HEALTH: A German cooked cheese, made from sour skim milk.

HOLSTEIN SKIM-MILK (BUTTENKÄSE): Is made principally in the Prussian province of Schleswig-Holstein.

HOP (HOPFEN): A German cheese that is cured between layers of hops, very much like Nieheimer.

HVID GJETOST: A local Norwegian goat's-milk cheese.

ILHA: A rather firm cow's-milk cheese made in the Azores and shipped to Portugal.

INCANESTRATO: A plastic-curd (pasta-filata) cheese made from ewe's milk or a mixture of cow's and ewe's milk, and so named because the curd often is pressed in wicker molds (baskets), the imprint of the wicker remaining on the cheese (incanestrato=basketed).

ISIGNY: Is named for a French town, but is said to be of American origin and is made like Camembert but washed during curing to check the growth of molds on the surface.

ISLAND OF ORLÉANS (LE FROMAGE RAFFINÉ DE L'ILE D'ORLÉANS): A soft cheese with a strong characteristic flavor, made since 1679 by farmers on the island of Orléans a few miles from Quebec on the St. Lawrence River.

JOCHBERG: Is made in the Tyrol from a mixture of cow's and goat's milk.

JOSEPHINE: Is made in Silesia from cow's whole milk.

KAJMAK: A cream cheese (as the Turkish name indicates) made from ewe's milk in Siberia.

KAREISH: One of the so-called pickled cheeses made in Egypt.

KARUT: A very dry, hard, skim-milk cheese made in Afghanistan and N.W. India.

KASKAVAL: Is made from partly skimmed ewe's milk in Siebengebürgen, Rumania.

KASSERI: A hard cheese made in Greece, usually from ewe's milk.

KATSCHKAWALJ: A plastic-curd, Cacciocavallo-type cheese made from ewe's milk in Serbia, Rumania, Bulgaria, and Macedonia; Zomma, a Turkish cheese, is similar.

KEFALOTI: A hard, grating-type cheese made in Greece and Syria from either goat's or ewe's milk.

KJÆRSGAARD: A hard, skim-milk cheese made in Denmark from cow's milk.

KLOSTER (KLOSTERKÄSE): A soft, ripened, Romadur-type cheese made in Germany from cow's whole milk.

KOPANISTI: A Greek blue-mold cheese with a sharp, peppery flavor.

KOPPEN (BAUDEN): A sour-milk cheese made by herders in their huts in the Sudetic Mts. between Bohemia and Silesia.

KOSHER CHEESE: Is made especially for Jewish consumers according to Jewish dietary custom; typically it is made without animal rennet; sometimes the milk is curdled by natural souring; sometimes a starter is added; among the Kosher cheeses are soft cheeses, such as cream and cottage; Kosher Gouda; and a cheese that is made by the Limburger process but, unlike Limburger, is eaten fresh; Kosher cheese bears a label by which it can be identified.

KRUTT (KIRGISGHERKÄSE): Is made by the nomadic tribes of the middle Asiatic steppes from the skim milk of cows, goats, ewes, or even camels.

KÜHBACHER: A soft, ripened cheese made in upper Bavaria, Germany, from whole or partly skimmed cow's milk.

KUMINOST (KOMMENOST): A spiced cheese made in the Scandinavian countries from whole or partly skimmed cow's milk.

LABNEH: A sour-milk cheese made in Syria.

LAGUIOLE (GUIOLE): A hard cheese named for the village of Laguiole, Department of Aveyron, France, resembling Cantal.

LANCASHIRE: Is like Cheshire and Cheddar, but white, softer, moister, and stronger; named for the English county where it is made.

LANGRES: A soft cheese, similar to Livarot, made in N.E. France.

LAPLAND: Resembles a very hard Swiss; made by the Laplanders from Reindeer milk.

LEATHER (LEDER; HOLSTEIN DAIRY): Is similar to Holstein skim-milk cheese and is made in Schleswig-Holstein, Germany, from cow's milk, with 5-10 per cent buttermilk added.

LEICESTER: A hard, mild cheese made from cow's whole milk and first made in Leicester Co., England.

LESCIN: Is made in the Caucasus; ewes are milked directly into a skin sack, rennet added, the curd broken up, and the whey drained; the curd is put into forms and pressed lightly; when the cheese is removed from the press, it is wrapped in leaves and bound with grass ropes; after a week or two, it is unwrapped and salted with dry salt, and again wrapped in leaves for curing.

LEYDEN (KOMIJNE KAAS): A spiced cheese made in the Netherlands from partly skimmed cow's milk to which color is added.

LIEDERKRANZ: Trade name of a soft, surface-ripened cheese made from cow's whole milk, and similar to a very mild Limburger.

LIMBURGER: A semisoft. surface-ripened cheese with a characteristic strong flavor and aroma; usually it contains small irregular openings and varies in size from a 3" cube that weighs less than a lb. to a cheese 6" square and 3" thick that weighs about 2¹/₂ lbs. It was first made in the Province of Lüttich, Belgium, and is named for the town of Limburg, its first major market; now it is made in other parts of Europe (Germany, Austria) and in the U.S.A. (Wis., N.Y.). Other similar European cheeses are: Allgäuer Limburger and Stangen (Bavaria); Romadur and Hervé (Belgium); Schloss (Germany, Austria); Marienhofer and Tanzenberger (Carinthia, in Austria); Backsteiner (Germany); and Void (France).

LIPTAUER (LIPTOI): A soft, so-called pickled, ewe's-milk (sometimes 10% cow's) cheese named for the Hungarian province of Liptow, where it is made; similar local cheeses are Landoch, Zips, Siebenburger, Neusohl, Altsohl, Klencz, and Bryndza or Brynza (German: Brinsen); a kindred Macedonian cheese is Ftinoporino.

LIVAROT: A Camembert-like cow's-milk cheese, soft, 6"×1³/₄", named for Livarot, Department of Calvados, France.

LOAF: Refers to the rectangular, loaflike shape in which several cheeses are packaged and marketed.

LODIGIANO: A *grana* or Parmesan-type cheese made in the neighborhood of Lodi, Italy.

LOMBARDO: An Italian *grana* or Parmesan-type cheese similar to Lodigiano.

LORRAINE: A small, sour-milk, hard cheese named for Lorraine, Germany.

LÜNEBERG: Is, characteristically, midway between Swiss and Limburger and is made in the small mountain valleys of Vorarlberg Province, western Austria.

MACCONAIS: A small French goat's-milk cheese.

MACQUELINE: A soft Camembert-like cheese made in Oise Department, France, from whole or partly skimmed milk.

MAILE: A ewe's-milk cheese made in the Crimea.

MAILE PENER (FAT CHEESE): A Crimean ewe's-milk cheese with a crumbly, open texture and agreeable flavor.

MAINAUER: Is similar to Radolfzeller cream and to Münster; made usually from fresh whole milk on an island in Lake Constance on the German-Swiss-Austrian borders.

MAINZER HAND (MAINZER HANDKÄSE): A small, round, cured, sour-milk German cheese.

MALAKOFF: A small, soft Neufchâtel-type French cheese.

MANTECA (MANTECHE): Is really an Italian, usually whey, butter, which is enclosed in a bag of plastic-cheese curd.

MANUR: A Serbian cow's- or ewe's-milk cheese.

MAQUÉE (FROMAGE MOU): Is a soft, brick-shaped, cow's-milk, Belgian cheese.

MARCHES: A hard pecorino (ewe's-milk) cheese made in Tuscany, Italy.

MARIENHOFER: A Limburger-type cheese made in Marienhof-Pichlern, Carinthia (Kärnten), Austria.

MÄRKISCH HAND: Differs from the usual hand cheese only in that the curd is pressed in a linen sack after salting.

MAROLLES (MAROILLES): A soft cow's-milk cheese similar to Pont L'Evêque and Livarot; made in many villages in Aisne and Nord departments, France.

MASCARPONE: A soft, small, cylindrical cheese, with a fresh ricotta-like consistency; made in Lombardy, Italy.

MECKLENBURG SKIM: A hard, skim-milk cheese, originally made in Mecklenburg province, northern Germany.

MELUN (BRIE DE MELUN): A French Brie-like cheese with a somewhat firmer curd and sharper flavor than Brie, and about the size of a small Brie.

MESITRA: A soft ewe's-milk Crimean cheese.

MIGNOT: A soft, long-established (about 120 yrs.), cylindrical or cubical cheese resembling Pont L'Evêque and Livarot, made in Calvados Department, France in two types: white, which is the fresh, April-September cheese; and *passé*, the ripened cheese of the rest of the year.

MILANO (STRACCHINO DI MILANO; FRESCO; QUARDO): A soft, sweet, fast-ripening table cheese from Lombardy, Italy, classed in the group with Crescenza and similar to Bel Paese; when made in the fall, it is called Stracchino Quartirolo.

MINTZITRA: A soft ewe's-milk cheese of Macedonia.

MITZITHRA (POT): A simple, primitive cheese made by the shepherds near Athens, Greece, from the whey by-product of feta cheese.

MODENA (MONTE): A Parmesan-type cheese made in U.S.A. during World War II.

MOLITERNO: A plastic-curd (*pasta filata*) cheese, similar to Cotronese, made originally in the provinces of Calabria and Lucania, and now also in Basilicata, Italy; it is processed like Cacciocavallo and is called Pecorino Moliterno when made from ewe's milk only.

MONCENISIO: An Italian, blue-mold, Gorgonzola-type cheese.

MONDSEER SCHACHTELKÄSE: A popular Austrian Münster-type cheese with a sharp, acid flavor like mild Limburger, made from either whole or partly skimmed milk; one whole-milk variety is called Mondseer Schlosskäse.

MONOSTORER: A ewe's milk cheese made in Transylvania, Rumania.

MONTASIO: A hard cheese, like Fontina and Bitto; first made in Friuli, Italy; (formerly Friaul, Austria.

MONTAVONER: An Austrian sour-milk cheese to which dried herbs are added in processing the curd.

MOUNT CENIS: A hard, blue-mold cheese, like Gex and Septmoncel, that is made in the region of Mont Cenis, S. E. France, usually from mixed cow's, ewe's, and goat's milk; 18″ × 6-8″, weighing 25 lbs.

MONT D'OR: A soft cheese like Pont l'Evêque named for Mont d'Or, Rhône Department, France, where it is said to date back over 300 yrs.; it is made also in Eure and Oise departments, and in other places in France, usually from cow's milk to which a small quantity of goat's milk may be added (formerly it was made from goat's milk only).

MONTEREY (JACK): Was first made on farms in Monterey County, California, about 1892; the name Monterey is now the more popular, except for high-moisture Jack; it is made from pasteurized whole, partly skimmed, or skim milk; whole-milk is semisoft, partly skimmed or skim (called grating-type Monterey, or dry Jack) is hard and used for grating; high-moisture Jack is made from whole-milk by a variant process, is moister and softer thar whole-milk Monterey.

MONTHEREY: A soft, surface-ripened, cow's-milk cheese, much like Brie, made in Seine-et-Oise, France.

MOZARINELLI: An Italian cow's- or buffalo's-milk cheese.

MOZZARELLA: A soft, plastic-curd cheese made in parts of Latium and Campania in S. Italy; originally it was made only from buffalo's milk, but now it is made also from cow's milk; processing is similar to Cacciocavallo and Scamorze, but it more nearly resembles Scamorze, since it is also eaten fresh, with little or no ripening. It is irregularly spherical in shape, weighs 8 oz.-1 lb., and is used mainly in cooking. Ricotta is often made from the whey. Considerable Mozzarella is made in the U.S.A., especially in New York.

MÜNSTER (MUENSTER): A semisoft, whole-milk cheese first made in the vicinity of Münster in the Vosges Mts., W. Germany, similar to brick but with less surface smear and subjected to less surface-ripening in curing; it contains many small, artificial openings. Nearby France makes Géromé (Gérardmer), which is similar.

MYSOST: Is made in Norway, Sweden, and Denmark, and in a few U.S. factories (Ill., Mich., N.Y., Wis.), from whey obtained in the manufacture of other cheeses.

NÄGELES (FRESH): Is made in the Netherlands from cow's skim milk, is round like Derby, 16″ × 5″ thick; cloves and cumin seed are mixed with the curd.

NATURAL RINDLESS LOAF: A natural (not process) cheese that is packaged and marketed in a transparent, flexible wrapper by one of several variations of a method that was developed about 1940.

NESSEL: A soft, round, thin, cured cow's whole milk cheese made in England.

NEUFCHÂTEL (FROMAGE DE NEUFCHÂTEL): As made originally in Seine Inférieure Department, France, is a soft, mild cheese made from whole or skim milk or a mixture of milk and cream, which is eaten fresh and cured; Bondon, Malakoff, Petit Carré, Petit Suisse, are other French cheeses differing from Neufchâtel mainly in fat content, size and shape.

NIEHEIMER: A sour-milk cheese named after Nieheim, Westphalia Province, Prussia; resembles hop cheese and is similarly packed with hops for curing.

NOEKKELOST (NÖGELOST): A Norwegian spiced cheese similar to Kuminost and Dutch Leyden.

NOSTRALE: A local name for two N. W. Italian cow's-milk cheeses, Formaggio duro, a hard cheese made in spring, and Formaggio tenero, a soft, summer cheese; Raschera, from around Mondivi, Italy, is similar.

OKA: A type of Port du Salut cheese made in the Trappist Monastery at Oka, Canada.

OLD HEIDELBERG: A soft, surface-ripened cheese made in Ill., said to resemble Liederkranz.

OLIVET: A soft cow's-milk cheese named for Olivet, Department of Loiret, France, in three types: unripened summer; half-ripened blue, the most common; and ripened, made also from whole or partly skimmed milk.

OLMÜTZER QUARGEL: A small, sour-milk, spiced hand cheese from W. Austria and Bohemia, containing caraway seed; similar to Mainzer Hand.

OSCHTJEPEK (OSCHTJEPKA): A plastic-curd cheese made in Slovakia from ewe's milk.

OSSETIN (TUSCHINSK; KASACH): A cow's-milk or ewe's-milk cheese made in the Caucasus.

OVCJI SIR: Is made in the Slovenian Alps from ewe's milk.

PAGLIA: A circular, 8″ × 2″, Gorgonzola-type cheese made in Ticino Canton, Switzerland.

PAGO: Is made from ewe's milk on the Island of Pag (Italian: Pago) in Yugoslavia.

PANNARONE (STRACCHINO DI GORGONZOLA BIANCO, GORGONZOLA DOLCE): A fast-ripening Gorgonzola-type cheese with white curd but without blue veining.

PARENCIA (PARENITZA): A ewe's-milk, Cacciocavallo-type cheese of Hungary and Slovakia.

PARMESAN: The name in common use outside of Italy, and sometimes in Italy, for a group of very hard cheeses that have been made and known in that country for centuries as grana; the group includes Parmigiano, Reggiano, Lodigiano, Lombardy, Emiliano, Veneto or Venezza, and Bagozzo or Bresciano.

PARMIGIANO: One of the subvarieties of grana (commonly called Parmesan), the hard Italian grating cheeses, resembling Reggiano and made in Parma, Reggio Emilia, Modena, Mantua, and Bologna, usually between April and November.

PASTA FILATA: Italian cheeses characterized by the fact that, after the whey is drained off, the curd is immersed in hot water or hot whey and worked, stretched, and molded while it is in a plastic condition; the chief varieties are: Cacciocavallo, Provolone, Provolette (which are hard cheeses), and Mozzarella, Provole, Scamorze, and Provatura (soft, moist cheeses), but there are many others.

PATAGRAS: A hard Cuban cheese made from pasteurized whole, or slightly skimmed milk; Gouda and Patagras are almost identical and are similarly made.

PECORINO (FORMAGGIO PECORINO): Italian ewe's milk cheeses; the most common is Pecorino Romano.

PENETELEU: Is made in Rumania by the method used in making Italian Cacciocavallo.

PEPATO (SICILIANO PEPATO): Is a Romano-type spiced cheese made in S. Italy and Sicily.

PETIT SUISSE: A small, rich, unripened French cheese, similar to Carré, but fatless; made from fresh milk to which cream is added; is unsalted.

PFISTER: A Swiss-like cheese named for its Swiss inventor, Pfister Huber; made from cow's fresh skim milk.

PICKLED: Term used for cheeses to which much preservative salt has been added; usually they are soft cheeses with a white curd and are made in warm, principally Mediterranean, countries; included in the group are: Domiati and Kareish (Egypt); Feta (Greece); Telene (Turkey, Bulgaria, Greece, and in Rumania as Brândza de Braila).

PIE: Is any cheese, like bakers' or cottage cheese, which is used in making cheese pie, cheese cake, or other bakery goods.

PIMENTO: Is any cheese to which ground pimentos have been added.

PINEAPPLE: Named for its shape and its diagonal corrugated surface; said to have originated in Litchfield County, Conn., in 1845; made from a curd that is prepared as in making Cheddar or granular or stirred-curd cheese except that it is heated until it is firmer.

PIORA: A hard, Tilsiter-like, whole-milk cheese, made either of cow's or cow's and goat's milk mixed; small eyes; made in Tessin Canton, Swiss Alps.

PONT L'EVÊQUE: A soft Romadur-like cheese manufactured near Pont L'Evêque, Calvados, Normandy, France.

POONA: A whole-milk, surface-ripened, soft cheese, round and flat, 4″×1¾″, about 1 lbs. in weight said to have originated in N.Y. State about 1949.

PORT DU SALUT (PORT SALUT): A compact, elastic, cylindrical, cow's milk cheese made first about 1865 by Trappist Monks at the Abbey at Port du Salut, near Laval, Department of Mayenne, France; the Trappists have kept the process secret, but similar cheese is made outside the monastery in central and southern Europe; other abbeys in Austria, Czechoslovakia, southern Germany, and the U.S.A. (Gethsemane, Ky.) also make Port du Salut; in France cheese of this type made outside the monasteries is called St. Paulin.

POTATO: Is made in Thuringia, E. Germany, from cow's milk, or sometimes ewe's milk, or goat's milk, with mashed potatoes added to the sour-milk or renneted curd.

PRATO (QUEIJO PRATO): A pasteurized milk, semicooked, pressed, small-eyed, Goudatype cheese made in Brazil; much like the Cuban Patagras.

PRATTIGAU: A cow's skim-milk cheese named for the Prattigau Valley in Switzerland, but also made in France.

PRESTOST (SAALAND PFARR): A cow's-milk cheese made in Sweden ever since the 18th century.

PROCESS (PASTEURIZED PROCESS): Is made by grinding fine and mixing by heat and stirring one or more cheeses of the same, or two or more, varieties, together with an emulsifying agent, into a homogenous, plastic mass; cream, Neufchâtel, cottage, creamed cottage, cooked, hard-grating, semisoft, part-skim, part-skim spiced, and skim-milk cheeses are not used.

PROCESS BLENDED (PASTEURIZED PROCESS BLENDED): Is made like process cheese, but cream or Neufchâtel can also be used in mixtures of two or more kinds and neither emulsifier nor acid is added.

PROCESS CHEESE FOOD (PASTEURIZED PROCESS CHEESE FOOD): Is made like process cheese, but cream, milk, skim milk, cheese whey or whey albumin, or concentrates or mixtures of any of these, may be added; at least 51% of the finished cheese food must be cheese.

PROCESS CHEESE SPREAD (PASTEURIZED PROCESS CHEESE SPREAD): Is like process cheese food, but has more moisture and less fat and must spread at 70° F.; fruits, vegetables, or meats may be added.

PROVATURA: A soft cheese of the plastic-curd (pasta filata) type; originated in South Italy.

PROVIDENCE: A Port du Salut-type cheese made in the monastery of Bricquebec, Manche Department, France.

PROVOLE: A round, plastic-curd (pasta filata) cheese made in S. Italy from buffalo's milk.

PROVOLONE: Is a plastic-curd (pasta filata) light-colored, mellow, smooth, agreeably flavored, cuttable cheese made originally in S. Italy, but made now also in other parts of Italy and in the U.S.A. (Wis., Mich.).

PULTOST (KNAOST; RAMOST): A sour-milk cheese made in small quantities in the thinly settled mountains of Norway.

QUACHEQ: A ewe's milk cheese made in Macedonia.

QUARTIROLO: A soft cow's-milk cheese made originally in Lombardy in autumn.

QUESO ANEJO ("AGED CHEESE"): A white, round, rather dry, skim-milk Mexican cheese with a crumbly texture.

QUESO BLANCO ("WHITE CHEESE"): The principal Latin-American cheese, made from whole, partly skimmed, or skim milk; or from whole milk with cream or skim milk added.

QUESO DE BOLA: A spherical, cured, whole-milk Edam-like cheese made locally in Mexico.

QUESO DE CAVALLO: A pear-shaped Venezuelan cheese.

QUESO DE CINCHO (QUESO DE PALMA METIDA): A spherical, 8″-16″, palm-leaf wrapped, sour-milk, Venezuelan cheese.

QUESO DE CREMA: A soft brick-type cheese; one of the principal cheeses of Costa Rica; as made there in Cuba, El Salvador, Venezuela, and other Latin-American countries, it is a rich, unripened, perishable cheese of cow's milk heavily enriched with cream, frequently used as a butter substitute.

QUESO DE HOJA: A cow's-milk cheese made in Puerto Rico; when cut the thin layers of curd are distinct and look like leaves resting one on another; hence the name, meaning "leaf cheese."

QUESO DEL PAIS ("CHEESE OF THE COUNTRY"): Known also as Queso de la tierra, a white, pressed, semisoft, perishable cheese made in Puerto Rico for local consumption.

QUESO DE PRENSA: A hard cheese made in Puerto Rico from cow's whole milk.

QUESO DE PUNA: A molded cottage cheese-type Puerto Rican cheese.

QUESO FRESCO ("FRESH CHEESE"): A rather dry cottage-cheese-type cheese made in El Salvador and other Latin-American countries.

RABACAL: A cylindrical, flat, rather firm cheese made near Coimbra, Portugal, from ewe's or goat's milk.

RADENER (SKIM-MILK RUNDKÄSE): A hard cheese made in Mecklenburg, Germany, from cow's skim milk.

RADOLFZELLER CREAM: A Mainauer-type cheese made near Lake Constance, on the German-Swiss-Austrian borders.

RANGIPORT: Is like Port du Salut and comes from Seine-et-Oise Department, France.

RAVIGGIOLO: An uncooked, soft, sweet, creamy, fast-curing cheese like Crescenza, made in Tuscany, Italy, from ewe's milk.

RAYON: A special type of Swiss made in Fribourg County, Switzerland, chiefly for Italian export.

REBLOCHON: A soft French cheese, 1-2 lbs.

REGGIANO: Is like Parmigiano and Emiliano and is one of the subvarieties of grana; made first in Reggio Emilia, Italy, April-November, but now made abroad and in the U.S.A.

REINDEER MILK CHEESE: Is made to a limited extent in Norway and Sweden.

REQUEIJÃO: Is a N. Brazilian cheese made of skim-milk.

RICOTTA: Is made from the coagulable material (principally albumin) in the whey obtained in the manufacture of other cheeses, such as Cheddar, Swiss, and Provolone; it was first made in Italy and is classed as an Italian cheese, but is now made throughout central Europe, and in the U.S.A. (chiefly Wis. and N.Y.); it is also called Ziger (or Schottenziger), Recuit, Broccio, Brocotte, Serac, Ceracee, and Mejette.

RIESENGEBIRGE: A soft goat's-milk cheese made in the mountains of Bohemia.

RINNEN: A sour-milk spiced cheese made in Pomerania, Poland, since the 18th century.

RIOLA: A soft, strong-flavored cheese, made usually from ewe's or goat's milk; resembles Mont d'Or.

ROBBIOLE: A soft, rich, fast-ripening, Crescenza-type cheese made in the Italian Alps, especially in Lombardy.

ROBBIOLINI: A soft, Crescenza-type cheese made chiefly in Lombardy, Italy, in the winter from cow's milk or from a mixture of cow's milk and either ewe's or goat's.

ROCAMADUR: A small soft cheese made in S. France from ewe's milk.

ROLL: A hard, cylindrical, 9″×8″, 20-lb. English cheese made from cow's whole milk.

ROLLOT: A soft, ripened Camembert-type cheese made in Somme and Oise departments, France.

ROMADUR: A soft, ripened cheese made in S. Germany (especially Bavaria) from either whole or partly skimmed cow's milk; similar to Limburger, but smaller, has a milder aroma and contains less salt.

ROMANELLO (LITTLE ROMANO): A very hard Italian cheese usually made from partly skimmed or skim milk; the cured cheese has a sharp flavor, and is suitable for grating and use as a condiment.

ROMANO (INCANESTRATO): One of the most famous very hard Italian cheeses, originally made from ewe's milk in the grazing area of Latium, near Rome, but now also made from cow's and goat's milk and in other regions in S. Italy and in Sardinia; when made from ewe's milk, it is called Pecorino Romano; from cow's milk Vacchino Romano; and from goat's milk, Caprino Romano; Romano-type cheese from Sicily is called Sardo.

ROQUEFORT: A blue-veined, semisoft to hard cheese, named for Roquefort, Department of Aveyron, S.E. France, where it has been a major product for 200 yrs.; a French regulation limits the use of the term Roquefort to cheese made in the Roquefort areas from ewe's milk; other French cheese of the Roquefort type is called bleu cheese, and Roquefort-type cheese made in the U.S.A. and other countries is known as blue cheese; there are, also, distinctive blue-veined cheeses of England (Stilton) and Italy (Gorgonzola).

ROYAL BRABANT: A small, Limburger-type cheese made in Belgium from cow's whole milk.

RUNESTEN: Is similar to Swedish Herrgårdsost (Manor cheese); first made in Denmark, is now also made in the U.S.A. (Minn., Wy.); the cured cheese resembles Swiss cheese, but the eyes are smaller and the finished wheel is much smaller, weighing about 5 lbs.

SAANEN (WALLISER; WALLISKÄSE): A hard cheese similar to Spalen or Sbrinza, made from cow's milk in Bern and Wallis (Valais) cantons and environs, Switzerland.

SAGE: An American-type, spiced (sage-flavored) cheese made by either the Cheddar or granular or stirred-cured process and pressed in any of the shapes and sizes in which those cheeses are pressed; the curd has a green, mottled appearance throughout.

ST. BENOIT: A soft cheese similar to Olivet, made in Loiret Department, France.

ST. CLAUDE: A small, square, goat's-milk cheese made near St. Claude, Jura Department, France.

ST. MARCELLIN (FROMAGE DE CHÈVRE): A small cheese made in Isère Department, France, from goat's milk to which either ewe's or cow's milk is sometimes added.

ST. STEPHANO: A Bel Paese-type German cheese.

SALAMANA: A soft, ewe's milk cheese made in S. Europe.

SALAME: Usually refers to a large-style Provolone; Stracchino Salame and Formaggio Salame refer to soft cheeses of the Bel Paese type.

SALOIO: A hard cheese made from cow's skim milk on farms near Lisbon, Portugal.

SANDWICH NUT: Made by chopping nuts into fresh Neufchâtel or cream cheese.

SAPSAGO (SCHABZIGER; GLARNERKÄSE; GRÜNERKÄSE, KRAUTERKÄSE; GRÜNER-KRAUTERKÄSE): A small, very hard cheese, frequently dried, with a sharp, pungent flavor, light-green color, and pleasant aroma from the clover powder which is added to the curd; made from slightly sour, skim milk in Glarus Canton, Switzerland, where it dates back 500 years, and in Germany.

SARDO (SARDO ROMANO): A Romano type cheese made on the island of Sardinia.

SARRAZIN: A Roquefort-type cheese from Vaud Canton, Switzerland.

SASSENAGE: A hard, blue-veined cheese like Gex and Septmoncel, named for Sassenage, Isère Department, France.

SCAMORZE (SCARMORZE): A small, soft, mild, plastic-curd (pasta filata) cheese, first made in Abruzzi and Molise in central Italy from buffalo's milk, but now made generally in Italy, from cow's and occasionally goat's milk.

SCANNO: Is made in Abruzzi, Italy, from ewe's milk, with a black exterior and deep yellow interior, a buttery consistency, and burned flavor; often eaten with fruits.

SCHAMSER (RHEINWALD): A large (40-45 lbs.) cheese made in Graubünden Canton, Switzerland, from cow's skim milk.

SCHLESISCHE SAUERMILCHKÄSE: Is made in Silesia in much the same way as hand cheese.

SCHLOSS (SCHLOSSKÄSE): A small, soft, ripened cheese made in Germany and N. Austria, Romadur-like, similar to but milder than Limburger; in English: castle cheese.

SCHOTTENGSIED: A whey cheese made locally by Alps peasants.

SCHÜTZENKÄSE: A Romadur-type cheese made in Austria.

SCHWARZENBERGER: A Limburger-type cheese made in S. Bohemia, W. Hungary, and Austria, and popular in Austria as a beer cheese.

SÉNECTERRE: A soft, whole-milk cheese that originated in St. Nectaire, Puy-de-Dôme Department, France.

SEPTMONCEL (JURA BLEU): A hard, blue-mold cheese, much like Gex and Sassenage, named for Septmoncel, near St. Claude, Jura Department, France.

SERRA DA ESTRELLA: A rather soft, pleasantly acid-flavored, ewe's-milk (also goat's and ewe's milk mixed, or only goat's milk, and occasionally cow's milk) cheese named for the Serra da Estrella mountain range, where it is made as the most famous of Portuguese cheeses.

SILESIAN (SCHLESISCHE WEICHQUARG): Is made from cow's skim milk by a method similar to that used in making hand cheese.

SIRAZ: A Serbian semisoft cheese usually made from whole milk; the ripened cheese has a mellow and compact body.

SIR IZ MJESINE: Is made in Yugoslavia (formerly Austria) from ewe's skim milk.

SIR MASTNY: Is made in Montenegro from ewe's milk.

SIR POSNY (TORD; MRSAV): Is made in Montenegro, Yugoslavia, from ewe's skim milk.

SLIPCOTE (COLWICK): A soft cheese made from cow's whole milk in Rutlandshire Co., England, where it dates back to the 18th century.

SMOKED CHEESE: Is usually American-type or Cheddar cheese and is characterized by the flavor and aroma of smoke.

SPALEN: A very hard cow's-milk cheese that originated in Unterwalden Canton, Switzerland, where it is known also as Nidwaldner; it has a grainy texture, and a sharp, nutty flavor; if there are eyes, they are small.

SPICED CHEESE: Cheese to which one or more spices are added during the making so that the spices are evenly distributed throughout the finished cheese; spices used include caraway seed, cumin, or cumin seed, pepper, cloves, anise, and sage; among the spiced cheeses are: caraway, Kuminost (Kommenost), Noekkelost, Leyden, Friesian clove, Christian IX, Pepato, and sage (Bondost, Sapsago, and others are sometimes included).

SPITZKÄSE: A small, spiced German cheese made from cow's skim milk.

STANGENKÄSE: A German Limburger-type cheese similar to Backsteiner; made from partly skimmed cow's milk.

STEINBUSCHER: A small, soft, Romadurtype German cheese from Steinbusch, Brandenburg, with yellow surface and buttery interior.

STEPPE: First made in Russia by German colonists, is a rich, mellow cheese with a flavor like Tilsiter, but milder, and usually has small, regular eyes; it is made in Austria, Denmark, and Germany.

STILTON: A hard, mild, blue-veined, cow's-milk cheese, considered by many England's finest, first made about 1750 in Leicestershire, but named when made in Stilton, Huntingdonshire.

STRACCHINO: Generic name for several types of Italian whole-milk cheeses; Stracchino di Gorgonzola; Stracchino di Milano; Stracchino Quartirolo, Stracchino Crescenza, and Stracchino Salame or Formaggio Salame are all included.

SURATI (PANIR): A buffalo's-milk cheese named for Surat, Gujarat District, Bombay Province, India, and the most famous of India's few cheeses.

SVECIAOST: A cow's-milk cheese made in Sweden.

SWEET-CURD: Refers to U.S. cheese made by the usual Cheddar process, but with unripened milk, and a curd cut, heated, and

drained rather quickly, without waiting for the development of acidity, and the curd is not milled.

SWISS (EMMENTALER): A large, hard, pressed-curd cheese with an elastic body and mild, nutlike, sweetish flavor; best known because of the holes or eyes that develop in the curd as the cheese ripens, first made in Bern Canton, Emmental Valley, Switzerland, about the middle 15th century.

TAFFELOST: A sharp-flavored Scandinavian cheese, said to be a whey cheese like Mysost.

TAFI: A cheese from Tucuman, Argentina.

TA LEGGIO: A soft, surface-ripened, Stracchino (whole-milk) cheese, with a mold rind, first made in Taleggio Valley, Lombardy, Italy, after World War I.

TAMIE: Made by Trappists in Savoy, France; similar to Tome de Beaumont.

TANZENBERGER: A Limburger-type cheese from Carinthia, S. Austria.

TELEME (BRÂNDZA DE BRAILA): A pickled cheese made from goat's or ewe's milk in Rumania, Bulgaria, Greece, and Turkey.

TERZOLO: Distinguishes winter grana from Maggengo (April-Sptember) and Quartirolo (September-November).

TEXEL: A ewe's-milk cheese made on the island of Texel (off Netherlands).

THENAY: A soft, whole-milk cheese that resembles Camembert and Vendôme and comes from Thenay, Loir-et-Cher Department, France.

TIBET: A hard grating cheese made from ewe's milk in Tibet.

TIGNARD: A hard, blue-veined ewe's- or goat's-milk cheese from the Tigne Valley, Savoy, France; resembles Gex and Sessenage.

TILSITER (RAGNIT): A cow's-milk cheese first made by Netherlands' immigrants near Tilset in East Prussia; it is a medium-firm, slightly yellow, plastic cheese, similar to brick, with some artificial openings (and sometimes small, round eyes), mild to medium-sharp piquant flavor, similar to mild Limburger, with caraway seed sometimes added to skim-milk Tilsiter.

TOME DE BEAUMONT: Made in France from cow's whole milk.

TOPFKÄSE: A sour-milk, cooked-curd cheese made in Germany, in a modification of Topfen, the German cooked cheese.

TOSCANELLO: A very hard ewe's-milk cheese, suitable for grating, made in Tuscany, Italy.

TOUAREG: A skim-milk cheese made by Berber tribes in Africa, from Barbary States to Lake Chad.

TOULOUMISIO: A Greek cheese similar to feta.

TRAPPIST: Was first made in 1885 in a monastery near Banjaluka, Bosnia, Yugoslavia; it is like Port du Salut and Oka; pale yellow, with a mild flavor; semisoft though cured more like the hard cheeses.

TRAVNIK (ARNAUTEN; VLASIC): A soft cheese made from ewe's milk to which a small amount of goat's milk is added; introduced in Albania more than a century ago.

TRECCE: A small, plastic-curd (*pasta filata*) Italian cheese.

TROUVILLE: A soft, ripened cheese, like Pont l'Evêque; made in Normandy, France.

TROYES: Refers to two Camembert-type cheeses, Ervy and Barberey, made near Troyes, France.

TSCHIL (LEAF; TELPANIR; ZWIRN): Is made in Armenia, from either ewe's or cow's sour skim milk.

TWDR SIR: Is made in Serbia from ewe's skim milk.

TWOROG: Is a popular sour-milk Russian cheese.

URI: A hard cow's-milk cheese from Uri Canton, Switzerland.

URSEREN (ORSERA): A mild-flavored cheese from Switzerland.

VACHERIN: Name common to several different kinds of French and Swiss cheese; *Vacherin à la main* is ripened cheese with firm hard rind and very soft interior made in Switzerland, and Savoy, France, eaten with a spoon, or spread on bread; Vacherin from Fribourg Canton, Switzerland, is a soft cheese; Vacherin du Mont d'Or, as made in France resembles Livarot; *Vacherin fondu* is made like Swiss and is melted after it is cured and spices are added.

VÄSTGOTAÖST: An open-textured cheese similar to Herrgårdsost; from Västgotaöst province, Sweden.

VENDÔME: A soft, ripened Camembert-type cheese from Vendôme, Loir-et-Cher Department, France.

VENETO: An Italian grana cheese, similar to Asiago.

VILLIERS: A square, soft cheese from Haute-Marne Department, France.

VIZÉ: A hard, Romano-type cheese, but smaller, from Greece.

VOID: A soft cheese similar to Pont l'Evêque and Limburger; from Meuse Department, France.

VORARLBERG SOUR-MILK: A hard cow's-milk cheese made from either whole or skim milk in W. Austria.

WARWICKSHIRE: An English Derby-type cheese.

WASHED-CURD (SOAKED-CURD): A semi-soft to slightly firm cheese made like Cheddar but the milled curd is washed with water before it is salted.

WEISSLACKER: A soft, ripened, cow's-milk cheese, like Limburger and Backsteiner, with a white, smeary, lustrous surface; made in Bavaria.

WENSLEYDALE: A medium-hard, blue-veined, cow's whole milk cheese named for Wensleydale District, Yorkshire.

WERDER (ELBINGER): A semisoft, cow's milk cheese made on W. Prussian farms, where it is called Niederungskäse.

WEST FRIESIAN: Is made from cow's skim milk.

WESTPHALIA SOUR-MILK: A hand cheese named for Westphalia, Germany.

WHITE (FROMAGE BLANC): A skim-milk cheese made in France in the summer.

WILSTERMARSCH (HOLSTEINER MARSCH): Is made from cow's milk in Schleswig-Holstein, Germany, and is similar to Tilsiter.

WILTSHIRE: A hard, sweet-curd, Derby-type cheese named for Wiltshire, England.

WITHANIA: An East Indian cheese whose milk is coagulated with rennet obtained from withania berries.

WORIENER: See Brioler and Woriener.

YOGHURT: Yoghurt and acidophilus cheeses are made with the special bacterial-starter cultures that are used in preparing yoghurt and acidophilus fermented milks.

ZIEGEL: Is made in Austria from cow's whole milk or whole milk with as much as 15% cream added.

ZIEGER (SCHOTTENZIGER): German names for whey (whey-protein) cheese, made by precipitating the albumin in cheese whey with heat and acid; in Italy and the U.S.A. it is called ricotta.

ZOMMA: A plastic-curd, Cacciocavallo-type cheese made in Turkey; resembles Katschkawalj.

Chinese Rulers
See **Rulers**

Choreographers
See **Ballets**

Church Calendar:
Calendar of the Time
See also **Easter Dates, Movable Days of the Easter Cycle; Festivals and Holydays; International Calendar of Saints and Special Days; Liturgical Colors, Symbolism and use; Religious Allusions, References, and Symbols**

Christmas Cycle, or the Birth of Christ

Note: When Septuagesima Sunday, which begins the Paschal Cycle, is early, some of the Epiphany Sundays are transferred to the time after the 23rd Sunday after Pentecost.

1ST SUNDAY OF ADVENT: Sunday nearrest November 30) purple.
2ND SUNDAY OF ADVENT: Purple.
3RD SUNDAY OF ADVENT (GAUDETE SUNDAY): Purple or rose.
4TH SUNDAY OF ADVENT: Purple.
CHRISTMAS EVE: Purple.
CHRISTMAS DAY: (December 25) white.
SUNDAY WITHIN THE OCTAVE OF CHRISTMAS: White.
CIRCUMCISION, OR NEW YEAR'S DAY: (January 1) white.
HOLY NAME OF JESUS: (January 2, or on Sunday between January 1-6) white.
VIGIL OF EPIPHANY: (January 5) white.
EPIPHANY OF OUR LORD: (January 6) white.
FEAST OF THE HOLY FAMILY: (Sunday within the Octave of Epiphany) white.
OCTAVE OF EPIPHANY: (January 13) white.
2ND, 3RD, 4TH, 5TH, 6TH SUNDAYS AFTER EPIPHANY: Green.

Paschal Cycle, or the Redemption

Note: These feasts are usually variable, depending upon the days of the week and the date on which Easter falls.

SEPTUAGESIMA SUNDAY: (between January 8 and February 21) purple.
SEXAGESIMA SUNDAY: Purple.
QUINQUAGESIMA SUNDAY: Purple.
ASH WEDNESDAY: (between February 4 and March 10) purple.
1ST SUNDAY IN LENT: Purple.
SPRING EMBER DAYS: (Wednesday, Friday, Saturday after 1st Sunday of Lent) purple.
2ND SUNDAY IN LENT: Purple.
3RD SUNDAY IN LENT: Purple.
4TH SUNDAY IN LENT (LAETARE SUNDAY): Purple or rose.

PASSION SUNDAY: Purple.

SEVEN SORROWS OF THE BLESSED VIRGIN MARY: (Friday in Passion Week) white.

PALM SUNDAY: Purple.

HOLY OR MAUNDY THURSDAY: White.

GOOD FRIDAY: Black.

HOLY SATURDAY: Purple and white.

EASTER SUNDAY: (Between March 22 and April 25) white.

EASTER MONDAY AND TUESDAY: White.

LOW SUNDAY: White.

PATRONAGE OF ST. JOSEPH: (Wednesday after 2nd Sunday after Easter) white.

OCTAVE OF SOLEMNITY OF ST. JOSEPH: (Wednesday after 3rd Sunday after Easter) white.

ROGATION DAYS: (Monday, Tuesday, Wednesday of 5th week after Easter) purple.

ASCENSION OF OUR LORD: (Thursday following 5th Sunday after Easter) white.

OCTAVE OF THE ASCENSION: Thursday after 6th Sunday after Easter) white.

VIGIL OF PENTECOST: (Saturday after 6th Sunday after Easter) purple and red.

PENTECOST SUNDAY OR WHITSUNDAY: (Between May 10 and June 13) red.

PENTECOST MONDAY AND TUESDAY: Red.

SUMMER EMBER DAYS: (Wednesday, Friday, Saturday after Pentecost) red.

TRINITY SUNDAY: (1st Sunday after Pentecost) white.

CORPUS CHRISTI: (Thursday after Trinity Sunday) white.

SUNDAY AFTER OCTAVE OF CORPUS CHRISTI: (2nd Sunday after Pentecost). white.

OCTAVE OF CORPUS CHRISTI: White.

FEAST OF THE SACRED HEART OF JESUS: (Friday after Octave of Corpus Christi) white.

SUNDAY WITHIN THE OCTAVE OF THE SACRED HEART: (3rd Sunday after Pentecost) white.

OCTAVE OF THE SACRED HEART: White.

Pentecostal Cycle, or the Teaching of Christ

4TH TO 17TH SUNDAYS AFTER PENTECOST: Green.

EMBER DAYS OF AUTUMN: (Wednesday, Friday, Saturday after September 14) purple.

18TH TO 23RD SUNDAYS AFTER PENTECOST: Green.

FEAST OF CHRIST THE KING: (Last Sunday of October) white.

OTHER SUNDAYS AFTER PENTECOST: Green.

LAST SUNDAY AFTER PENTECOST: Green.

Cities, Epithets of
See also **Pseudonyms, Nicknames, and Special Associations for Historical Persons**

Note: Strictly speaking, a city is a large town with a corporation and cathedral; but any large town in ordinary speech. In the Bible it means a town having walls and gates. In literature and history, the metaphorical meanings of the word are extended indefinitely.

THE ATHENS OF AMERICA: Boston.

THE ATHENS OF IRELAND: Cork.

AULD REEKIE: Edinburgh, because of the local smog, and, as some say, because of the dirty streets.

THE BRIDE OF THE SEA: Venice.

CAMBALU: Peking, the chief city of Cathay, as it was called by Marco Polo in his *Voyages*.

CARLISLE: Carduel, as the city is called in the Arthurian romances.

THE CELESTIAL CITY: In *Pilgrim's Progress*, John Bunyan calls Heaven the Celestial City. Peking, China, is also known by this name.

THE CITIES OF THE PLAIN: Sodom and Gomorrah. "Abram dwelled in the land of Canaan, and Lot dwelled in the cities of the plain, and pitched his tent toward Sodom." Gen. XIII, 12.

THE CITY OF A HUNDRED TOWERS: Pavia, Italy; famous for its towers and steeples.

THE CITY OF BELLS: Strasbourg.

THE CITY OF BROTHERLY LOVE: A nickname of Philadelphia. (Gr. *philadelphia* means "brotherly love.")

THE CITY OF CHURCHES: Brooklyn, New York.

THE CITY OF DAVID: Jerusalem. So called in compliment to King David (II Sam. V, 7, 9).

THE CITY OF DESTRUCTION: In Bunyan's *Pilgrim's Progress*, the world of the unconverted. Bunyan makes Christian flee from it and journey to the "Celestial City," thereby showing the "walk of a Christian" from conversion to death.

THE CITY OF ELMS: New Haven, Conn.

THE CITY OF ENCHANTMENTS: A magical city described in the story of Beder, Prince of Persia, in the *Arabian Nights*.

THE CITY OF GOD: The subject and title of St. Augustine's famous work *(De Civitate Dei)*, in which the body of Christian believers is called the City of God, as opposed to the body of unbelievers, or City of the World.

THE CITY OF LANTERNS: A supposititious city in Lucian's *Vere Historie*, situated somewhere beyond the zodiac.

THE CITY OF LEGIONS: Caerleon-on-Usk, where King Arthur held his court.

THE CITY OF LIGHT: Paris, France, because of its countless street lights.

THE CITY OF LILIES: Florence.

THE CITY OF MAGNIFICENT DISTANCES: Washington; famous for its wide avenues and splendid vistas.

THE CITY OF MASTS: London, in reference to the shipping-traffic on the Thames River.

THE CITY OF NOTIONS: Boston.

THE CITY OF PALACES: Agrippa, in the reign of Augustus, converted Rome from "a city of brick huts to one of marble palaces." Calcutta is also called the City of Palaces, as is, with considerably less justice, Edinburgh.

THE CITY OF PEACE: Jerusalem.

THE CITY OF REFUGE: Moses, at the command of God, set apart three cities on the east of Jordan, and Joshua added three others on the west, whither any person might flee for refuge who had killed a human creature inadvertently. The three on the east of Jordan were Bezer, Ramoth, and Golan; the three on the west were Hebron, Shechem, and Kedesh (Deut. IV, 43; Josh. 1-8). By Mohammedans, Medina, in Arabia, where Mahomet took refuge when driven by conspirators from Mecca, is known as the City of Refuge. He entered not as a fugitive, but in triumph 622 a.d. Also called the City of the Prophet.

THE CITY OF ROCKS: Nashville, Tenn.

THE CITY OF ST. MICHAEL: Dumfries, Scotland, of which city St. Michael is the patron saint.

THE CITY OF SAINTS: Montreal, Canada, is so named because all the streets are named after saints. Salt Lake City, Utah, also is known as the City of the Saints, from the Mormons who inhabit it.

THE CITY OF SPINDLES: Lowell, Mass., because of the textile industries centered there.

THE CITY OF THE ANGELS: Los Angeles, in the English translation of its Spanish name.

THE CITY OF THE GOLDEN GATE: San Francisco.

THE CITY OF THE GREAT KING: Jerusalem (Psalm XLVIII, 2; Matt. V, 35).

THE CITY OF THE PROPHET: Medina. See also The City of Refuge.

THE CITY OF THE SEA: Venice.

THE CITY OF THE SEVEN HILLS: Rome, built on seven hills (urbs septacollis). The hills are the Aventine, Caelian, Capitoline, Esquiline, Palatine, Quirinal, and Viminal.

THE CITY OF THE STRAITS: Detroit, Mich., which is what the name Detroit means in French.

THE CITY OF THE SUN: Baalbec, Rhodes, and Heliopolis, which had the sun for tutelary deity, were all so called. It is also the name of a treatise on the Ideal Republic by the Dominican friar Campanella (1568-1639), similar to the Republic of Plato, Utopia of Sir Thomas More, and Atlantis of Bacon.

THE CITY OF THE THREE KINGS: Cologne; the reputed burial place of the Magi, or Three Wise Men of the East.

THE CITY OF THE TRIBES: Galway, Ireland, because the thirteen tribes, or chief families—Burke, Blake, Budkin, Martin, Athy, Browne, D'Arcy, Joyce, Kirwan, Lynch, Morris, Ffont, and Skerrett—settled there about 1235, with Richard de Burgh.

THE CITY OF THE VIOLATED TREATY: Limerick, Ireland, because of repeated violations of the treaty of October, 1691, by which the religious freedom of the Catholics was supposed to have reverted to the toleration it enjoyed under Charles II.

THE CITY OF THE VIOLET CROWN: Athens, because the violet was the favored flower in the garlands worn at Athenian festivals and "violet-crowned" was a frequent poetic title for the citizens; also, the Greek word for violet was ion, and the name is supposed to have been a punning reference to Athens as the chief European city of the Ionian race.

THE CITY OF THE WEST: Glasgow.

THE CITY OF VICTORY: Cairo, from the Egyptian name for the city, El Kahira, meaning Victorious.

THE COCKADE CITY: Petersburg, Va., in a popular designation.

COCKAGNE: London, as the city and the suburbs were called in burlesque, the source of the term "cockney." See also Lubberland.

COTTONOPOLIS: Manchester, England.

THE CREAM CITY: Milwaukee, Wis., is sometimes so called from its numerous cream-colored brick houses.

THE CRESCENT CITY: New Orleans, because the old quarter of the city curved around a bend of the Mississippi River.

THE DRISHEEN CITY: Cork, because of the blood puddings, or "drisheens," which were once a favorite breakfast dish there.

DUN EDIN: Edinburgh, as it was called by the Celts, meaning "the face of a rock."

EDIN (EDINA): Edinburgh, poetic name supposedly coined by the Scots poet, George Buchanan.

EMBRO: Edinburgh, in Scots dialect.

THE EMPIRE CITY: New York City, because of its commercial importance and because it is the metropolis of New York State, the Empire State.

THE ETERNAL CITY: Rome. This epithet occurs in Ovid, Tibullus, and many official records of the Empire; in the Aeneid (I, 79), Jupiter tells Venus that he will give the Romans imperium sine fine (an eternal empire).

THE FAIR CITY: Perth, because of its great natural and architectural beauty.

THE FALL CITY: Louisville.

THE FLOUR CITY: Rochester, N.Y.

THE FLOWER CITY: Springfield, Ill.

THE FOREST CITY: 1. Cleveland, O., because of the many ornamental trees bordering the streets; 2. Portland, Me., for its many elms and other shade trees; 3. Savannah, Ga., because its streets are thickly shaded with pride-of-India (Margosa Azedarak) trees.

THE GARDEN CITY: Chicago, because of its many beautiful private gardens.

THE GATE CITY: Keokuk, Ia., because it also is the natural gateway of the Mississippi River.

THE GRANITE CITY: Aberdeen, Scotland.

THE GIBRALTAR OF AMERICA: Quebec.

GOTHAM: New York, as it was first called by Washington and William Irving, and James K. Paulding in Salamagundi, because the inhabitants of the city seemed to the authors like such wiseacres (like the three wise men of Gotham who went to sea in a bowl).

THE HEAD OF THE WORLD: Rome.

THE HEAVENLY CITY: The New Jerusalem; paradise.

THE HOLY CITY: Each of the centers of the world religions has a city known as the Holy City: 1. Allahabad is the Holy City of India; 2. Benares, of the Hindus; 3. Cuzco, of the ancient Incas; 4. Fez, of the Western Arabs; 5. Jerusalem, of the Jews and Christians; 6. Kairwan, near Tunis, of the Mohammedans, because the tomb of the prophet's barber was built there in the Okbar Mosque; 7. Mecca and Medina, of the Mohammedans; 8. Moscow and Kiev, of the Russians, the latter as the cradle of Russian Christianity.

THE HUB OF THE UNIVERSE: Boston.

THE IMPERIAL CITY: Rome, the seat of the Empire.

THE IRON CITY: Pittsburgh.

THE KEY OF CHRISTENDOM: Buda (now Budapest), because it was the embattled outpost of Europe during the Ottoman invasions of the sixteenth century.

THE KEY OF RUSSIA: Smolensk; because the Russian stronghold offered such strong resistance to the French invasion in 1812.

LITTLE PARIS: Milan, because of its gay Parisian atmosphere.

LITTLE VENICE: Amiens, as the lower town was dubbed by Louis XI, because the Somme River intersects the narrow streets in so many places.

LOSANTVILLE: Cincinnati, the original name of the city, meaning, from the Latin roots, "the town opposite the mouth of the Licking River."

LUBBERLAND: London, by a popular designation meaning the same thing as "Cockagne," with which it was used interchangeably by English poets of the sixteenth century. See also Cockagne.

LUTETIA: Paris, in its ancient Latin name.

THE MAIDEN TOWN: Edinburgh, because it was supposedly the refuge of Pict princesses in time of war.

THE MARSH CITY: Petrograd (Leningrad)

from its low-lying situation and frequent floods.

THE MISTRESS OF THE ADRIATIC: Venice.

THE MISTRESS OF THE WORLD: Rome.

MOBTOWN: Baltimore, so called from a reputation for lawlesness.

THE MODERN ATHENS: Boston.

THE MODERN ATHENS: Edinburgh.

THE MODERN BABYLON: London.

THE MONUMENTAL CITY: Baltimore, because of the monuments it contains.

THE MOTHER OF CITIES: Balkh.

THE MOUND CITY: St. Louis, Mo., because of the many mounds in the neighborhood of the site on which the city is built.

THE NAMELESS CITY: Ancient Rome, so called from a superstition that any one who uttered its mystical name would perish.

NEW AMSTERDAM: New York, as it was called by the original Dutch settlers.

THE NIOBE OF NATIONS: Rome, used by Lord Byron in his poem, On Rome.

THE NORTHERN ATHENS: Edinburgh.

THE PETRIFIED CITY: Ishmonie, because of the many statues of men, women, children, and animals found in this city of Upper Egypt, which were popularly supposed to have once been animate.

PORKOPOLIS: Chicago, the center of the meat-packing industry.

THE PURITAN CITY: Boston, Mass., the metropolis of the Puritan settlements of New England.

THE QUAKER CITY: Philadelphia, so called from its Quaker founders.

THE QUEEN CITY: Cincinnati, O., from the days when it was the undisputed commercial center of the American West.

THE QUEEN OF CITIES: Rome.

THE QUEEN OF THE ADRIATIC: Venice.

THE QUEEN OF THE EAST: 1. Antioch, the ancient capital of Syria, residence of the Macedonian kings and of the Roman governors; 2. Batavia, as capital of the Dutch possessions in the East Indies, was also so called.

THE QUEEN OF THE LAKES: Buffalo.

THE QUEEN OF THE NORTH: Edinburgh.

THE QUEEN OF THE WEST: Cincinnati. See also the Queen City.

THE RAILROAD CITY: Indianapolis, because it was the terminus of various railroads.

THE SILENT CITY: Venice.

THE SMOKY CITY: Pittsburgh, Penn., so called from the dirt and smoke of its industries.

THE SOLAR CITY: Same as City of the Sun.

THE TREMONT, OR TRI-MOUNTAIN, CITY: Boston, because of the three hills on which the city was built.

TRINOVANT (TRINOVANTUM): London, as it was anciently called, in a corruption of Troja Nova (New Troy), the name supposedly given to the city by its legendary founder, the English King Brutus, a descendant of Aeneas. Also written Tribonant, Troynovant.

THE TWIN CITIES: Minneapolis and St. Paul, two cities of about equal importance across the Mississippi River from each other near its head in Minn.

THE TWO EYES OF GREECE: Athens and Sparta.

VENICE OF THE NORTH: 1. Stockholm, Sweden, because of its many bridges and waterways; 2. Amsterdam.

THE VENICE OF THE WEST: Glasgow, Scotland, for reasons not entirely apparent.

WEISSNICHTWO: London, as it was called by Thomas Carlyle in Sartor Resartus, from the German for "I know not where."

THE WINDY CITY: Chicago, so called from its stiff lake breezes.

Civil War, American (1861-1865), Major Battles of
See also **Battles; Admission, Secession, and Readmission of States to the Union of the United States of America**

FIRST MANASSAS (BULL RUN): Date: July 21, 1861; place: N. E. Va., about 35 mi. from Washington, D.C.; victor: Confederate troops under Gen. P. G. T. Beauregard (other Confederate officers: Joseph E. Johnston, Jubal A. Early, Richard S. Ewell, Thomas J. Jackson, James Longstreet, E. Kirby Smith); defeated: Union troops under Brig. Gen. Irwin Mc Dowell (other Union officers: Ambrose E. Burnside, B. F. Butler, Samuel P. Heintzelman, David Hunter, D. S. Miles, Robert Patterson, W. T. Sherman, Daniel Tyler). Results: the armies, with almost even forces (35,000 Union troops, 32,000 Confederate), suffered equally in lost and wounded, but the number of Union prisoners was disproportionately high; the beaten Union Army panicked and fled; for the victorious Confederates the road to Washington seemed clear; however, Beauregard used his advantage to rest his own exhausted troops, and the initial fury of the war was followed by a comparative calm with both armies held in check for almost a year. In this battle, Col. Bee of Georgia, who was later killed in the same action, earned his own immortality and confirmed a new Southern hero when he cried out to the bewildered soldiers around him: "See where Jackson stands like a stone-wall! Rally to the Virginians!"

FORTS HENRY AND DONELSON: Date: Feb. 6-16, 1862; place: Fort Henry on Tennessee R., Fort Donelson on Cumberland R., near N. boundary of Tenn., victor: at Fort Henry, February 6, Union troops under Gen. Ulysses S. Grant, and gunboats under Commodore A. H. Foote; at Fort Donelson, Feb. 8-16, Union troops under Grant, gunboats under Foote; defeated: At Fort Henry, Confederate garrison under Lloyd Tilghman; at Fort Donelson, Confederate garrison under John B. Floyd, Gideon J. Pillow, Simon B. Buchner. Result: the two forts, located twelve miles apart at points which controlled traffic on the Tennessee and Cumberland rivers, commanded one of the major approaches to Southern territory; with the fall of Fort Donelson, the Union was, for the first time, in a strategically superior position; the Confederate commander in the West, Albert Sidney Johnston, ordered a general withdrawal of his troops; the Union Army quickly pressed forward to seize important points on the Mississippi and Alabama borders; in his demand for an "unconditional surrender" of Fort Donelson, Grant established himself as the type of popular hero that was then desperately needed in the North.

JACKSON'S VALLEY CAMPAIGN: Date: March-June 9, 1862; places: Kernstown, Mc Dowell, Front Royal, Winchester, Port Republic, Cross Keys—all small communities in the Shenandoah Valley, Va., victor: Confederate forces under Thomas J. Jackson (other Confederate officers: Turner Ashby, R. S. Ewell, Edward Johnson, Richard "Dick" Turner, Chales S. Winder); defeated: Union forces under Gen. Nathaniel P. Banks (other Union officers: Irvin McDowell, J. C. Frémont, George H. Gordon, R. H. Milroy, Rufus Saxton, Robert C. Schenck, James Shields). Result: Jackson employed his forces in the Shenandoah Valley in a series of mercurial maneuvers that were meant to, and did, confuse the Union high command; as McClellan moved up the Peninsula from Yorktown (which he had taken April 5) to Richmond, a daring Southern strategy was needed to prevent the Union advance from McDowell and so making the capture of Richmond a certainty; the strategy was devised and executed by Jackson, who began a lightning advance up the Shenandoah Valley; he made it appear that he was on the way to Washington; in alarm, the Union command kept McDowell from his rendezvous with Mc Clellan, then sent him in persuit of Jackson; the ruse was succesful; Jackson kept his pursuers engaged until it was possible for him to escape to Lee at Richmond and join in the next move to destroy the Federal plan of battle.

SHILOH: Date: April 6-7, 1862; place: on the Tennessee R. in southern Tenn.; victor: Union forces under Ulysses S. Grant and Gen. Don Carlos Buell; defeated: Confederate forces under Albert Sidney Johnston and P. G. T. Beauregard (other Confederate officers: Braxton .Bragg, William J. Hardee, Leonidas Polk, with John C. Breckinridge in reserve). Result: the Confederate troops, moving undetected in the night, surprised the divisions of W. T. Sherman and B. M. Prentiss at Pittsburg Landing on the morning of April 6; at the sound of battle, Grant rushed up from his Tennessee headquarters at Savannah, but was able to do little more than watch as the Federal camps fell to the Confederates, and wait as patiently as possible for night, which would stop the fighting long enough for Buell to arrive with reinforcements; the Southern commander, Johnston, was killed that afternoon; the Union troops held their batteries until dusk, were joined by Buell before morning and resumed the battle next day with all the odds in their favor; Beauregard was forced to withdraw; Shiloh had cost the South 10,000 men in casualties and prisoners; the North lost 13,000 men; both North and South found reasons for criticizing the ways in which their generals had conducted the battle; blame fell most heavily on Grant, and he lost the prestige that he had after Forts Henry and Donelson; Gen. Henry W. Halleck assumed field command of the Union forces and began a methodical, sluggish advance down the Mississippi; on April 25, Adm. Farragut took New Orleans, foreshadowing Union control of the Mississippi; but the army of the Confederacy was still intact in the West and the bloody action of Shiloh had resulted in effective stalemate.

SEVEN DAYS' BATTLE: Date: June 26-July 1, 1862; places: Merchanicsville, Gaine's Mill, Chickahominy, Savage's Station, White Oak Swamp, Glendale, and Malvern Hill—all small Virginia localities ringing Richmond on the north and east; victors: Confederate forces under Robert E. Lee (other Confederate officers: Richard S. Ewell, A. P. Hill, D. H. Hill, Theophilus Holmes, Benjamin Huger, Thomas J. Jackson, James Longstreet, J. E. B. Stuart); defeated: Union forces under Gen. George B. McClellan (other Union officers: Fitz-John Porter, W. B. Franklin, Samuel P. Heintzelman, E. D. Keyes, G. A. McCall, George G. Meade, G. W. Morell, J. F. Rey-

nolds, Truman Seymour, E. V. Sumner, George Sykes). Result: in the series of encounters that made up the Seven Days' Battle, Union losses were: 1,734 killed, 8,062 wounded, 6,053 missing; Confederate losses were: 3,474 killed, 16,261 wounded, 875 missing; strategically, the South won the engagement; McClellan withdrew and brought the Peninsula Campaign to a close; Richmond, the Union objective, remained in Confederate control.

SECOND MANASSAS (BULL RUN): Date: August 29-30, 1862; place: N. E. Va., about 35 mi. from Washington, D.C.; victor: Confederate forces under command of Gen. Robert E. Lee (other Confederate officers: Thomas J. Jackson, James Longstreet); defeated: Union forces under Gen. John Pope (other Union officers: Irvin McDowell, Fitz-John Porter). Result: the second battle at Bull Run ended the second attempt to send a Union force to take Richmond; John Pope was given McClellan's command and moved into Virginia with 130,000 men; in desperation, Lee divided his own army, sending Jackson north to attack the Union rear and continuing his own slower advance; confused by the maneuver, Pope threw his whole force against Jackson, ignoring whatever danger might lie along the line of Lee's advance; he was wrong in his belief that he could destroy Jackson before help arrived; on August 29, Lee and Longstreet moved into position and the Union army, badly deployed, entered a disastrous battle; only an adamant stand at Henry House Hill saved Pope's army from annihilation; the Union Army withdrew toward Washington, fighting all the way; Pope's campaign against Richmond was over; of the 100,000 Union troops engaged in the fighting, 14,462 were lost; Lee lost 9112 of his 55,000 men.

ANTIETAM: Date: September 17, 1862; place: Maryland; Union forces under Gen. George B. McClellan (other Union officers: J. D. Cox, S. W. Crawford, Abner Doubleday, W. B. Franklin, G. H. Gordon, G. S. Greene, J. F. Hartranft, Joseph Hooker, J. K. F. Mansfield, George G. Meade, Fitz-John Porter, R. B. Potter, J. B. Ricketts, I. P. Rodman, E. V. Sumner); Confederate forces under Gen. Robert E. Lee (other Confederate officers: Jubal A. Early, A. P. Hill, D. H. Hill, Thomas J. Jackson, James Longstreet, Lafayette Mc Laws). Result: the battle is usually called a draw, but Lee, after holding his field through the following day, withdrew with his forces across the Potomac; the first invasion of the North was stopped; the Union forces lost 2108 men in action, and 9549 were wounded; the Confederate dead numbered 2700, and 9024 men were wounded.

VICKSBURG CAMPAIGN: Date: October 1862 —July 4, 1863; place: western Mississippi, on the Mississippi R. west of Jackson; victor: Union forces under Gen. Ulysses S. Grant (other Union officers: John A. McClernand, S. A. Hurlbut, James B. McPherson, William T. Sherman, fleet under command of David D. Potter); defeated: Confederate garrison under command of John C. Pemberton; (other Confederate officers: Braxton Bragg, Joseph E. Johnston, Kirby Smith, Richard "Dick" Taylor). Result: from the doubtful beginnings of Grant's Mississippi campaign, in themselves scarcely sufficient to sustain hope, through the succession of smaller victories, at Port Gibson, Raymond, Jackson, Champion's Hill, and Big Black River, that preceded the unconditional surrender of Vicksburg, the spirit of the North experienced the severest strain of the

war; Port Gibson, the first significant encounter of the campaign, coincided with the
first day of the disastrous engagement at
Chancellorsville; after his desultory maneuvers
through the fall and spring, success at Port
Gibson, and the immediate capitulation of
Grand Gulf, barely suggested the magnificent
stroke that Grant was about to achieve at
Vicksburg; however, as the chain of victories
extended, excitement mounted in the North,
and everything in the nature of reinforcements and supplies that would insure the
collapse of Vicksburg was lavished upon
Grant and his army; it was, in every detail,
more than the South could match; Vicksburg
capitulated on July 4; 29,491 prisoners were
delivered to the conquerors; 170 cannon, and
50,000 small arms; the South had lost 10,000
men in the campaign; the North lost as many
men, but it had also achieved its objective;
the Mississippi River passed completely out of
Confederate control; a second of the three
major Northern war aims of 1862 (to take
Richmond, to blockade the Southern ports,
and to cut the South in two by commanding
the Mississippi) was now accomplished as the
North rediscovered the leader it had preferred to forget after Shiloh.
FREDERICKSBURG: Date: December 13, 1862;
place: on the Rappahannock River in Virginia;
victors: Confederate troops under Gen.
Robert E. Lee (other Confederate officers:
A. P. Hill, D. H. Hill, James Longstreet, Thomas J. Jackson, Lafayette McLaws); defeated:
Union forces under Gen. Ambrose E. Burnside (other Union officers: W. B. Franklin,
John Gibbon, Joseph Hooker, George G.
Meade, Edwin V. Sumner). Results: after
Antietam, McClellan was again relieved of
his command of the Union Army, and replaced
by Ambrose E. Burnside; Burnside, thinking
that he saw an occasion to strike through
Fredericksburg and drive against Richmond,
planned to cross the Rappahannock on pontoon bridges; he did not get his supplies in
time from Gen. Halleck, and Lee, Longstreet, and Jackson moved in to intercept him
even before he was ready to move; on December 13, Burnside crossed over the river and
attacked the entrenched Confederates; the
assault was savage and in vain; on December
15, Burnside withdrew across the river; the
Union losses were 1284 killed, 9600 wounded,
1769 missing; the Confederate army lost 595
killed, 4061 wounded, and 653 missing.
MURFREESBORO (STONE'S RIVER): Date:
December 31, 1862—January 2, 1863; place: 30
mi. from Chattanooga, Tennessee; Union
forces: Army of the Cumberland under Gen.
William Starke Rosencrans (other Union officers: T. L. Crittenden, Jefferson C. Davis,
R. W. Johnson, A. M. McCook, Philip H. Sheridan, G. H. Thomas, H. P. Van Cleve); Confederate forces: troops under command of
Gen. Braxton Bragg (other Confederate officers: James C. Breckinridge, Patrick Cleburne,
W. J. Hardee, Leonidas Polk, Joseph Wheeler). Result: the battle began at dawn on
December 31 and continued until dark, was
resumed in the afternoon of New Year's Day,
and reached a peak of fury on January 2;
the Union lines were severely shaken during
the first two days, but held; on January 2,
Breckinridge led the Confederates in a fierce
charge that withered under Union artillery,
and the battle ended; like Antietam, it was
not a conclusive victory for either side; Union
losses amounted to 1677 killed, 7543 wounded;
1294 Confederates were killed and 7945
wounded; Bragg retreated with his forces to

Tullahoma; for the North, the indecisive action at Murfreesboro merely extended the
havoc of two weeks before at Fredericksburg
and deepened the mood of depression that
was soon to grow to desperation at Chancellorsville; the Union Army was in control of
Tennessee west of the mountains, but Chattanooga remained in Southern hands.
CHANCELLORSVILLE: Date: May 1-4, 1863;
place: Virginia, 12 mi. W. of Fredericksburg;
victor: Confederate forces under Gen. Robert
E. Lee (other confederate officers: R. E. Col-
ston, A. P. Hill, Thomas J. Jackson, Fitzhugh
Lee, W. H. F. Lee, R. E. Rodes, J. E. B.
Stuart); defeated: Union forces under Gen.
Joseph Hooker (other Union officers: Francis
C. Barlow, D. N. Couch, Charles Devens, O.
O. Howard, George G. Meade, Alfred Pleasonton, J. F. Reynolds, John Sedgwick, D. E.
Sickles, H. W. Slocum). Result: Joseph
Hooker replaced Burnside as Union Commander; on April 27 he put into operation his
own plan for taking Richmond; feinting at
Fredericksburg to divert the attention of Lee,
he moved up the Rappahannock and crossed
over behind Lee at Chancellorsville; Lee
immediately came into line, sending Jackson
around the Union Army and advancing himself from the front; Hooker met Jackson,
then Stuart, in two major engagements which
forced him to withdraw across the river; Lee
routed the token Union force that had caused
the diversion at Fredericksburg; Union losses
numbered 17,278 out of 133,868; the Confederacy lost 12,821 out of 60,892 men, a figure
which does little to reflect the incalculable
loss of Stonewall Jackson, whose death from
a wound sustained at Chancellorsville has
never been measured in terms of a simple
statement of Confederate battle statistics.
GETTYSBURG: Date: July 1-3, 1863; place:
Pennsylvania, N. of the Maryland border;
victor: Union forces under Gen. George G.
Meade (other Union officers: John Buford,
G. A. Custer, T. C. Devin, Abner Doubleday,
A. N. Duffie, E. J. Farnsworth, William
Gamble, John Gibbon, D. M. Gregg, Winfield
Scott Hancock, O. O. Howard, H. J. Kilpatric
Wesley Merritt, Alfred Pleasonton, John F.
Reynolds, John Sedgwick, D. E. Sickles, H.
W. Slocum, Adolph von Steinwehr, George
Sykes); defeated: Confederate forces under
Gen. Robert E. Lee (other Confederate offi-
cers: J. J. Archer, Richard S. Ewell, Henry
Heth, A. P. Hill, J. B. Hood, James Longstreet, Lafayette McLaws, G. E. Pickett, J. E.
B. Stuart). Result: the victories of his forces
at Fredericksburg and Chancellorsville were
positive factors in Lee's decision to launch a
second invasion of the North; on the negative
side were the statistics of his dwindling supplies, and the cold facts of his diminished
manpower and capital; on June 3 he started
north, with Harrisburg, Pennsylvania, as his
goal; one month later, on July 1, a Confederate division was surprised in Gettysburg by
two Union corps of the Federal army which
had been sent against Lee; immediately the
battle began; the Union Army moved in
around the city from the south and west, in
a line along Cemetery Ridge which extended
from Big and Little Round Top on the south
to Culp's Hill on the north; Lee approached
from the west and took up his defense on
Seminary Ridge, which ran parallel to the
Union battle line; no encounter in the entire
war matched in fury and casualties the fighting of the next two days; the early engagements encouraged Lee to think that he would
carry the field, but "Pickett's Charge" on

July 3, which left 15,000 Southern troops shattered in the valley below the Union entrenchment on Cemetery Ridge, was the turning point of the campaign and of the war; the retreat of the Confederate forces from Gettysburg was from a field where almost 28,000 men had been lost, with 3903 killed, 18,735 wounded, and 5424 missing; the Union casualties were equally severe: 3155 men were killed, 14,529 wounded, and 5365 missing.

CHICKAMAUGA: Date: September 19-20, 1863; place: Chickamauga Creek, a tributary of the Tennessee R., in N. W. Ga.; victor: Confederate forces under Gen. Braxton Bragg (other Confederate officers: John C. Breckinridge, S. B. Buckner, Patrick Cleburne, D. H. Hill, James Longstreet, Leonidas Polk; defeated: Union forces under Gen. William Starke Rosencrans (other Union officers: Absalon Baird, J. M. Brannan, T. L. Crittenden, J. C. Davis, A. M. McCook, J. S. Negley, J. M. Palmer, J. J. Reynolds, Philip H. Sheridan, G. H. Thomas, H. P. van Cleve, F. J. Wood). Result: Gen. Rosencrans placed too great reliance on a field report of one of his subordinates, drew up his battle line ineptly, and turned every omen of Union victory into a holocaust and rout; Confederate losses, in killed, wounded, and missing, were 18,454, exceeding Union losses by 2284; the North lost 3500 more men as prisoners than did the South; it was a terrible defeat, and a scarcely less terrible victory; yet neither army was really beaten; the conclusion of Chickamauga was that more could be expected of the Confederacy, and that conclusion had yet to be tried; the wearied armies prepared for the inevitable encounter at Chattanooga.

CHATTANOOGA (BATTLE ABOVE THE CLOUDS): Date: November 23-25, 1863; place: Tennessee; victor: Union forces, under command of Gen. Ulysses S. Grant, Joseph Hooker, William T. Sherman, George H. Thomas; defeated: Confederate forces under Gen. Braxton Bragg. Result: after the bloody battle at Chickamauga, Chattanooga was, even for the defeated Confederate troops, a happy encounter; for a major Civil War battle, the casualty report was astonishingly low; the Union troops, who stormed and carried a supposedly impregnable Confederate stronghold, suffered 753 deaths, while 4722 of their men were wounded, and 349 reported missing; Confederate losses amounted to 361 killed, 2160 wounded, and more than 4000 prisoners; the battle line, extending from Missionary Ridge, on the north, across the Tennessee River, then southwestward over Lookout Range to Rossville Gap on the south, was itself a setting so striking that it inspired even the combatants to record enduring impressions of the natural beauty around them; for the first time in the war all of the major elements of the Union Army, the Army of Tennessee, the Army of the Cumberland, and the Army of the Potomac, united in a single effort, under command of the four outstanding Northern generals; after his defeat, Bragg evacuated his army to Georgia; the power of the Confederacy was broken in the West, and the arena of the war shrank to the southern strongholds in a part of Mississippi, in Alabama, and in the Atlantic states.

VIRGINIA CAMPAIGN: Date: May 3—June 3 1864; places: the Wilderness, May 5-6; Spotsylvania, May 8-12; Cold Harbor, June 1-3—all south of the Rappahannock R. in Virginia; Union Army of the Potomac under command of Gen. Ulysses S. Grant (other Union officers: at the Wilderness, Ambrose E. Burnside, G. W. Getty, W. S. Hancock, John Sedgwick, J. S. Wadsworth, G. K. Warren; at Spotsylvania, Francis C. Barlow, Emory Upton; at Cold Harbor, Francis C. Barlow); Confederate forces under command of Gen. Robert E. Lee (other Confederate officers: at The Wilderness, R. S. Ewell, A. P. Hill, Micah Jenkins, James Longstreet; at Spotsylvania, Edward Johnson, James Longstreet); result: Grant crossed the Rapidan during the night of May 3, with plans to engage and destroy Lee north of Richmond, or, if Lee retreated to the Confederate capital, to seize Petersburg, cut off Richmond's supply lines, and force Lee into a fight in the open; the results of the first month of the campaign gave little indication that Grant would achieve his objectives; Lee resisted him stubbornly in the north; the battles of The Wilderness and Spotsylvania Court House were devastating, but inconclusive; undeterred, Grant sent his stubborn message to General Halleck at Washington: "I propose to fight it out along this line if it takes all summer"; then, at Cold Harbor, he sent his men into an action that he was always to regret; the bitter fighting of June 3 brought the Union casualties of the campaign to 54,926 killed and wounded; the Army of the Potomac was badly beaten; Grant retreated further south; there was power yet in the Confederacy that it would take more than a summer to reduce.

PETERSBURG: Date: June 15, 1864—April 2, 1865; place: below Appomattox River, 22 mi. S. of Richmond, Virginia; victor: Union forces under command of Gen. Ulysses S. Grant; defeated: Confederate forces under command of Robert E. Lee. Result: the siege of Petersburg was not a single battle, but a series that lasted over many months; strategically, the city commanded the southern approaches to Richmond, and was defended with as much ingenuity and material as went into the long, bloody siege; from June 15, 1864, the date of the first unsuccessful Union attack, to April 2, 1865, when Richmond and Petersburg were abandoned by their defenders, there were scores of battles and skirmishes in the neighborhood of Petersburg, as Grant methodically and remorselessly cut the railroad lines which connected Richmond to the rest of the South; when the last supply line was broken at Five Forks, below Petersburg, the defense of Richmond was over; the city was abandoned the following day.

ATLANTA: Date: July 22—September 1, 1864; places: Peach-Tree Creek, Ezra Church, Jonesboro, all localities on the outskirts of the capital of Georgia; victor: Union forces under Gen. William T. Sherman (other Union officers: O. O. Howard, James B. McPherson, G. H. Thomas); defeated: Confederate forces under Gen. John Bell Hood (other Confederate officers: Patrick Cleburne, W. J. Hardee): Result: Sherman set out from Chattanooga with 100,000 men on May 3; his objective was to split what was left of the Confederacy in two by capturing Atlanta, and then drive on as far as he could go toward the sea; in the first month of his campaign, pushing southeastward deep within enemy territory, he lost almost 12,000 men in incessant skirmishes and battles; the toll of the second month passed 7000; the battle for Atlanta began on July 22 at Peach-Tree Creek; through the following month, the armies fought around the city as Sherman continued his strategy of cutting supply lines to the city; on September 1, Hood evacuated Atlanta with his troops; Sherman occupied the city the following day; at a cost of 35,000 men, he held a major supply center of the Confederacy; for the next two months he consolidated his forces and resisted Confederate attempts to recapture Atlanta; then, on November 16, after setting fire to the city, he began the 300 mi. march between Atlanta and Savannah, living off the countryside which he laid waste behind him untill, as a Christmas present, he sent a telegram to Lincoln announcing the capture of the cotton port of the Confederacy.

Cloud Formations

ALTOCUMULUS: Mean lower level, 6500 feet.
ALTOSTRATUS: Mean lower level, 6500 feet.
CIRROCUMULUS: Mean lower level, 20,000 feet.
CIRROSTRATUS: Mean lower level, 20,000 feet.
CIRRUS: Mean lower level, 20,000 feet.
CUMULO-NIMBUS: Mean lower level, 1600 feet.
CUMULUS: Mean lower level, 1600 feet.
NIMBOSTRATUS: Mean lower level, close to sea-level.
STRATOCUMULUS: Mean lower level, close to sea-level.
STRATUS: Mean lower level, close to sea-level.

Colleges
See **Schools;** for School Colors see **Academic Colors;** for College Degrees see **Degree Abbreviations**

College Songs:
United States and Canadian
See also **Songs, Popular**

Note: Attributions to authors and composers are given only in cases where they are generally recognized.

AKRON, UNIVERSITY OF: "Close Beside Cuyahoga's Waters"; words: A. B. Church; tune: "Annie Lisle."
ALABAMA, UNIVERSITY OF: "Alabama"; words: Helen Vickers; tune: "Amici."
ALASKA, UNIVERSITY OF: "All Hail Alaska"; words: Mary J. Walker, Carl M. Franklin; music: Carl M. Franklin.
ALBERTA, UNIVERSITY OF: "Alberta"; words: adapted from original of R. K. Michael; music: C. Lambertson.
ALFRED UNIVERSITY: "On Saxon Warriors"; words and music: Monks and McCourt.
ALLEGHENY COLLEGE: "Allegheny Pep Song."
ARIZONA, UNIVERSITY OF: "All Hail, Arizona!"; words: E. C. Monroe; music: Dorothy Monroe.
ARKANSAS, UNIVERSITY OF: "Pure as the Dawn"; words: Brodie Payne; music: Henry Dougthy Tovey.
BAYLOR UNIVERSITY: "The Baylor Bears"; words and music: Will N. Payne.
BELOIT COLLEGE: "Fairest Beloit"; words: George Carpenter Clancy; music: Erma Hoag Miranda.
BOSTON COLLEGE: "For Boston"; words and music: T. J. Hurley.

BOSTON UNIVERSITY: "Boston University Hymn"; words: Daniel L. Marsh; music: John P. Marshall.
BOWDOIN COLLEGE: "Walls of Old Bowdoin"; music: Millett Dunbar.
BRIGHAM YOUNG UNIVERSITY: "Alma Mater"; words: Glenn S. Potter; music: Walt Daniels.
BROOKLYN COLLEGE: "Towers of Marble"; words: Robert Friend; music: Sylvia Fine.
BROWN UNIVERSITY: "The Brown Cheering Song"; words: Robert B. Jones; music: Howard S. Young.
BUFFALO, UNIVERSITY OF: "Where Once the Indian Trod"; words: Samuel B. Botsford; music: Walter S. Goodale.
CALIFORNIA INSTITUTE OF TECHNOLOGY: "Fight for California Tech."
CAPITAL UNIVERSITY: "O Capital"; words: George F. Dell; music: Sibelius-Mayer.
CASE INSTITUTE OF TECHNOLOGY: "Carmen Case"; words and music: Zimmerman.
CENTRE COLLEGE: "Old Centre"; to tune of: "La Marseillaise."
CHATTANOOGA, UNIVERSITY OF: "Lookout Mountain"; to tune of: "Amici."
CHICAGO, UNIVERSITY OF: "Our Chicago"; words and music: Norman Reid.
CINCINNATI, UNIVERSITY OF: "The Red and Black"; words: Curtis R. Beresford; music: Alan T. Waterman.
THE CITADEL: "On the Shores of South Carolina"; to tune of: "Annie Lisle."
CITY COLLEGE (NEW YORK): "St. Nicholas Terrace"; words: Lewis F. Mott; "Son of a Gambolier."
CLEMSON AGRICULTURAL COLLEGE: "Where the Blue Ridge"; words: A. C. Cochran; tune: "Annie Lisle."
COE COLLEGE: "Coe Loyalty"; words and music: Risser Patty May.
COLORADO, UNIVERSITY OF: "Glory, Glory Colorado"; tune of: "Battle Hymn of the Republic."
COLORADO COLLEGE: "Our Colorado"; words: A. T. French; music: E. W. Hille.
COLORADO SCHOOL OF MINES: "The Mining Engineer"; tune of: "The Son of a Gambolier."
COLUMBIA UNIVERSITY: "The Lion's Loose Again!"; words and music: M. N. Young. A. P. Guerriero, C. Bates.
COLUMBIA UNIVERSITY, TEACHERS COLLEGE: "A Song to Teachers College"; words: Clara H. Perry; music: R. A. Laslett Smith.
CORNELL UNIVERSITY: "Far Above Cayuga's Waters"; tune: "Annie Lisle."
CREIGHTON UNIVERSITY: "The White and the Blue"; words and music: Gordon Richmond.
DARTMOUTH COLLEGE: "Men of Dartmouth"; words: Richard Hovey; tune: Harry Wellman.
DAVIDSON COLLEGE: "The Red and Black"; words: W. P. Cumning; music: K. M. Scott.
DAYTON, UNIVERSITY OF: "Flyers' March"; words and music: J. B. Meiler.
DENISON UNIVERSITY: "Denison Marching Song"; words: Gordon Long; music: Henry Arnold.
DENVER, UNIVERSITY OF: "Hail to Denver U."; words: Ira Eugene Cutler; tune: "Annie Lisle."
DE PAUL UNIVERSITY: "De Paul Victory Songs"; words: J. Leo Sullivan; music: Arthur C. Becker.
DE PAUW UNIVERSITY: "A Toast to De Pauw"; words and music: Vivien Bard.

DETROIT, UNIVERSITY OF: "Detroit Victory March"; words and music: Grank McIlhargey, Richard P. Sheridan.

DRAKE UNIVERSITY: "Dear Old White and Blue"; words: Emma J. Scott; music: Clifford Bloom.

DREXEL INSTITUTE OF TECHNOLOGY: "Drexel Marching Song"; words: Frank L. Griffin; music: J. J. Coogan.

DUKE UNIVERSITY: "Blue and White"; words and music: G. E. Leftwich, Jr.

DUQUESNE UNIVERSITY: "Duquesne Pep Song"; words: William E. O'Donnell; music: James G. Borrelli.

FORDHAM UNIVERSITY: "Fordham Ram"; words and music: J. Ignatius Coveney.

GEORGETOWN UNIVERSITY: "Sons of Georgetown"; words: Robert T. Collier.

GEORGE WASHINGTON UNIVERSITY: "Hail, Alma Mater"; words: F. F. Fleming; tune: "Integer Vitae."

GEORGIA INSTITUTE OF TECHNOLOGY: "Ramblin' Wreck"; words and music: Frank Roman.

GEORGIA, UNIVERSITY OF: "Hail to Georgia"; words and music: Gaines Walter.

GETTYSBURG COLLEGE: "Loyalty Song"; words and music: B. H. Saltzer.

GONZAGA UNIVERSITY: "Gonzaga Glorious"; words and music: Wallace Orr.

GRINNELL COLLEGE: "Sons of Old Grinnell"; words and music: J. Norman Hall.

GUSTAVUS ADOLPHUS COLLEGE: "Gustavus Adolphus"; words: John Olson; music: A. W. Anderson.

HAMILTON COLLEGE: "Carissima!"; words and music: M. W. Stryker.

HANOVER COLLEGE: "Hanover Loyalty Song"; words: Edward F. Brent; music: G. M. Small.

HARVARD UNIVERSITY: (1) "Ten Thousand Men of Harvard"; words: A. Putnam; music: Murray Taylor. (2) "Fair Harvard."

HAWAII, UNIVERSITY OF: "Fight for Old Hawaii"; words and music: Don George.

HEIDELBERG COLLEGE: "Heidelberg"; words: Rev. J. F. Hartman; music: F. A. Power.

HOLY CROSS, COLLEGE OF THE: "Holy Cross, Old Holy Cross"; tune: "Maryland."

HUNTER COLLEGE: "Fame"; words: Pauline Severling; music: Frances Friedman.

IDAHO, UNIVERSITY OF: "Idaho, Mother of Mine"; words: A. H. Upham; music: David Nyvall, Jr.

ILLINOIS, UNIVERSITY OF: "Loyal Sons of Illinois"; words: G. V. Buchanan; music: Bill Donahue.

IOWA, STATE UNIVERSITY OF: "Old Gold"; words: John C. Parish.

JOHNS HOPKINS UNIVERSITY: "On the Line"; words: John M. Booker; tune: "The Dummy Line."

KANSAS, UNIVERSITY OF: "Our Team"; words and music: H. C. Taylor.

KANSAS STATE COLLEGE OF AGRICULTURE AND APPLIED SCIENCE: "Wildcat Victory"; words and music: Harry E. Erickson.

KENTUCKY, UNIVERSITY OF: "On, On, U. of K."; words: Troy Perkins; music: Carl A. Lampert.

KNOX COLLEGE: "Fight Siwash"; words and music: Robert Murphy.

LA VERNE COLLEGE: "Guide of La Verne"; words and music: E. Raymond Root, J. Truman Funderburgh.

LAFAYETTE COLLEGE: "We'll Gather by the Twilight's Glow"; words and music: Walter C. Stier.

LAKE FOREST COLLEGE: "Fight Song"; words and music: Lucius Lobdell.

LAWRENCE COLLEGE: "Viking Song"; words and music: La Vahn Maesch, Fred Trezise.

LINFIELD COLLEGE: "Hail to Linfield"; Words and music: Keith Fender.

LOUISIANA STATE UNIVERSITY: "Tiger Team of L.S.U."; words: W. G. Higginbotham; music: Castro Carazo.

LOUISVILLE, UNIVERSITY OF: "Hail to U. of L."; words and music: George A. Resta.

LOYOLA UNIVERSITY OF LOS ANGELES: "Hail Crimson Gray"; words and music: John T. Boudreau.

MC GILL UNIVERSITY: "Hail, Alma Mater."

MANHATTAN COLLEGE: "For Old Manhattan"; words and music: Donald J. Carty, William R. Carty.

MARIETTA COLLEGE: "The Navy Blue and White."

MARQUETTE UNIVERSITY: "Hail! Alma Mater"; words and music: "Liborius Semmann."

MARYLAND, UNIVERSITY OF: "Maryland, My Maryland"; words: James R. Randall; tune: "Tannenbaum."

MICHIGAN, UNIVERSITY OF: "Hurrah for Ann Arbor!".

MICHIGAN STATE COLLEGE: "Close Beside the Winding Cedars"; words: A. M. Brown; tune: "Annie Lisle."

MILLS COLLEGE: "The Gold M. C."; words: M. Cooper, M. McDermott; music: J. P. Scott.

MINNESOTA, UNIVERSITY OF: "Hail! Minnesota"; words: Truman Elwell Rickard, Arthur Upson; music: Truman Elwell Rickard.

MISSISSIPPI, UNIVERSITY OF: "Way Down South in Mississippi"; words: Mrs. A. W. Kahle; music: W. F. Kahle, revised by Ruth McNeil.

MONMOUTH COLLEGE: "Monmouth Loyalty"; words and music: Clara Schrenk.

MONTANA STATE COLLEGE: "Stand Up and Cheer"; words: Edward E. Duddy; music: Paul P. McNeely.

MONTANA STATE UNIVERSITY: "Fight, Montana"; words: John Marshall; music: Bill Kane.

NEVADA, UNIVERSITY OF: "Nevada Hail Song"; words: A. L. Higginbottom; music: Theodore H. Post.

NEWARK, UNIVERSITY OF: "Dear Newark University"; words: Frank Kingdom; music: W. Croft, "St. Anne."

NEW HAMPSHIRE, UNIVERSITY OF: "On to Victory"; words and music: Florence V. Cole.

NEW MEXICO, UNIVERSITY OF: "Hail to New Mexico"; words: George St. Clair; music: Lena C. Claude.

NEW MEXICO STATE COLLEGE: "Our Own N. M. S. C."; tune: "America the Beautiful."

NEW YORK UNIVERSITY: "The Palisades"; words and music: Duncan M. Genns.

NORTH DAKOTA, UNIVERSITY OF: "Stand Up and Cheer"; music: Paul P. McNeely.

NORTHWESTERN UNIVERSITY: "Wild Cat Song"; words and music: Donald G. Robertson.

NORTHWEST NAZARENE COLLEGE: "Victory is Sure"; words and music: Rev. E. E. Martin.

NORWICH UNIVERSITY: "The Spirit of Old N. U."; words and musik: Gus Nelson.

OBERLIN COLLEGE: "Old Oberlin Forever"; words and music: Jason Noble Pierce.

OCCIDENTAL COLLEGE: "Give Us a Song"; words: Remsen D. Bird; music: Howard Swan and Cora Lauridsen.

OHIO WESLEYAN UNIVERSITY: "Red and Black"; words and music: R. W. Wright.

OKLAHOMA, UNIVERSITY OF: "Oklahoma, Hail"; words: Mrs. A. B. Adams; musik: R. H. Richards.

OKLAHOMA A. AND M. COLLEGE: "Ride 'Em Cowboys"; words: Edgar Ward; music: John K. Long.

OREGON, UNIVERSITY OF: "Marching Oregon"; words and music: Hopkins and Young.

OREGON STATE COLLEGE: "Hail to Old O.S.C."; words and music: Harold A. Wilkins.

PACIFIC, COLLEGE OF THE: "Hail, Pacific, Hail"; words and music: Lois Warner.

PENNSYLVANIA, UNIVERSITY OF: "Ben Franklin, Esq."; words: C. I. Jenkin; music: F. G. McCollin.

PITTSBURGH, UNIVERSITY OF: "Pitt Victory Song"; words: G. Norman Reiss, Louis M. Fushan; music: Benjamin Levant.

PRINCETON UNIVERSITY: "Old Nassau"; words: H. P. Peck; music: Karl A. Langlotz.

PROVIDENCE COLLEGE: "Alma Mater"; tune: "Finlandia."

PUGET SOUND, COLLEGE OF: "College of Dreams."

REED COLLEGE: "Fair Reed"; words: William T. Foster; tune: "Believe Me, If All Those Endearing Young Charms."

REGIS COLLEGE: "Vive, Regis"; words: J. A. Ryan; music: A. S. Dimichino.

RENSSELAER POLYTECHNIC INSTITUTE: "Stephen Van Rensselaer"; words and music: E. M. Frost.

RIDER COLLEGE: "In Our Days of Youth"; words: Charles M. Callahan; music: George F. Root, "The Hazel Dell."

ROCHESTER, UNIVERSITY OF: "Rochester Marching Song"; words and music: J. S. Rodney.

RUTGERS UNIVERSITY: (1) "Loyal Sons of Rutgers." (2) "On the Banks of the Old Raritan"; words: H. N. Fuller.

ST. JOHN'S UNIVERSITY: "Down the Line"; words and music: Peter Foglia.

ST. LOUIS UNIVERSITY: "Varsity Song"; words: Paul L. Blakely; music: Alfred G. Robyn.

ST. MARY'S COLLEGE: "Fight Song"; words and music: A. Wellesley Foshay.

SAN FRANCISCO, UNIVERSITY OF: "Victory Song"; words and music: Bud Smith.

SANTA CLARA, UNIVERSITY OF: "Pep Song"; words and music: Clemens Van Perre.

SEATTLE PACIFIC COLLEGE: "Dear Old S.P.C."; words: F. F. Warren; tune: "Annie Lisle."

SMITH COLLEGE: "Oh! Fairest Alma Mater"; words: Henrietta Sperry; music: H. D. Sleeper.

SOUTH CAROLINA, UNIVERSITY OF: "We Hail Thee, Carolina"; words: Dr. George A. Wauchope; tune: "Flow Gently Sweet Afton."

SOUTH DAKOTA, UNIVERSITY OF: "Field Song"; words: J. Hyatt Downing; music: Francelia Feary.

SOUTH DAKOTA STATE COLLEGE OF AGRICULTURE: "The Yellow and Blue"; words: N. E. Hansen; music: F. J. Haynes.

SOUTHERN CALIFORNIA, UNIVERSITY OF: "Song of Troy"; words: Ralph J. Freed; music: Charles Kisco.

SOUTHERN METHODIST UNIVERSITY: "Peruna."

SOUTHWESTERN COLLEGE: "Far Above the Walnut Valley"; tune: "Annie Lisle."

STANFORD UNIVERSITY: "The Cardinal is Waving"; words and music: W. G. Paul.

SUFFOLK UNIVERSITY: "Suffolk Hail"; Elizabeth Glenn Archer; music: Roy Harlow.

SWARTHMORE COLLEGE: "Hip, Hip, Hip, For Old Swarthmore"; words and music: Herbert L. Brown.

SYRACUSE UNIVERSITY: "Where the Vale of Onondaga"; words: Junius Stevens; tune: "Annie Lisle."

TEMPLE UNIVERSITY: "Onward with Temple"; words: W. St. Clair; music: C. D. Coppes.

TENNESSEE, UNIVERSITY OF: "The Spirit of the Hill"; words and music: Sam Gobble.

TEXAS, UNIVERSITY OF: "The Eyes of Texas"; words: John Lang Sinclair.

TEXAS CHRISTIAN UNIVERSITY: "Horned Frogs, We Are All For You"; words: Mrs. Butler Smiser; music: Claude Sammis.

TOLEDO, UNIVERSITY OF: "Golden and the Blue"; words: A. W. Trettein; tune: "Annie Lisle."

TOLEDO, UNIVERSITY OF: "U. of Toledo"; words and music: David V. Conelly.

TORONTO, UNIVERSITY OF: "The Blue and White"; words: Claris Edwin Silcox; music: Clayton E. Bush.

TRINITY COLLEGE: "Fight, Trinity"; words and music: Harry W. Nordstrom.

TULANE UNIVERSITY: "Olive Green and Blue"; words and music: E. J. Williams and W. H. Ruebush.

TULSA, UNIVERSITY OF: "Hurricane Spirit Song"; words and music: Ben Henneke.

UNION COLLEGE (NEW YORK): "Song to Old Union"; words: F. H. Ludlow; tune: "Sparkling and Bright."

U.S. MILITARY ACADEMY: (1) "Fight Away." (2) "Hoo-Rah for the Army Team"; words and music: Philip Egner.

U.S. NAVAL ACADEMY: "Navy Blue and Gold"; words and music: J. W. Crosley.

UTAH, UNIVERSITY OF: "Utah Man"; tune: "Solomon Levi."

VALPARAISO UNIVERSITY: "Hail to the Brown and Gold"; tune: "How Can I Leave Thee?"

VASSAR COLLEGE: "Hark, Alma Mater"; words: Amy Wentworth Stone; music: George Coleman Gow.

VERMONT, UNIVERSITY OF: "Vermont Victorious"; words and music: Furman, Sharples, Kiljick.

VILLANOVA COLLEGE: (1) "Villanova Anthem"; words: Al Dubin; music: Joe Burke. (2) "March of the Wildcats"; words: Raymond J. McKeon, Martin L. Gill; music: Carmen Giordano.

VIRGINIA, UNIVERSITY OF: "Virginia, Hail, All Hail"; words and music: John Albert Morrow.

WALLA WALLA COLLEGE: "Walla Walla College"; words: Hayes Davis; music: Melvin Reese.

WASHINGTON, UNIVERSITY OF: "Vict'ry for Washington"; words: Tom Herbert; music: George Larson.

WASHINGTON AND JEFFERSON COLLEGE: "Ring Her Praises"; words: L. D. Hemingway; tune: "Annie Lisle."

WELLESLEY COLLEGE: "'Neath the Oaks"; words and music after "'Neath the Elms of Old Trinity."

WESTERN ONTARIO, UNIVERSITY OF: "Western"; words: Margaret Ovens; music: Walter J. Smither.

WESTERN RESERVE UNIVERSITY: "With Spirits Light"; words and music: Henry Woodruff.

WESTMINSTER COLLEGE: "Tell Me Why."

WHITMAN COLLEGE: "Whitman! Here's to You!" words and music: S. B. L. Penrose.

WICHITA, MUNICIPAL UNIVERSITY OF:
"Hail! Wichita"; words: Samuel A. Wofsy;
music: Thurlow Lieurance.
WILLAMETTE UNIVERSITY: "I Love Willa-
mette U."; arranged by Fay Sparks.
WILLIAM AND MARY, COLLEGE OF: "Vic-
tory"; words and music: Oscar E. Wilkinson.
WILLIAMS COLLEGE: "The Mountain"; words
and music: S. W. Gladden.
WISCONSIN, UNIVERSITY OF: "The Badger
Ballad"; words: Julius E. Olson; music ar-
ranged by Charles H. Miller.
WITTENBERG COLLEGE: "Wittenberg Hymn";
words and music: Robert H. Hiller.
WOOSTER, COLLEGE OF: "To Wooster U.";
words and music: Ralph E. Plumer.
WYOMING, UNIVERSITY OF: "Where the
Western Lights"; words and music: June E.
Downey.
YALE UNIVERSITY: "Yale Bingo."

Colors
See also Academic Colors; Liturgical Colors

Kinds of Color

COMPLEMENTARY COLORS: Colors that, in
combination, produce white light. Red and
green, orange and blue, violet and yellow are
complemetary.
FUNDAMENTAL COLORS: The seven colors
of the spectrum, violet, indigo, blue, green,
yellow, orange, and red. Or red, yellow, blue,
also called primary or simple colors.
SECONDARY COLORS: Those which result
from the mixture of two or more primary
or simple colors, such as green, which is a
blend of blue and yellow.

National Colors

ARGENTINA: Blue and white.
AUSTRIA: Red, white, and red.
BELGIUM: Black, yellow, and red.
BOLIVIA: Red, yellow, and green.
BRAZIL: Green and yellow.
BULGARIA: White, green, and red.
CHILE: White, blue, and red.
CHINA: Yellow ocher.
COLOMBIA: Yellow, blue, and red.
COSTA RICA: Blue, white, red, white, and
blue.
CUBA: Five horizontal stripes, blue and white.
DENMARK: Red, with white cross.
EQUADOR: Three horizontal stripes, yellow,
blue, and red, the yellow being twice the
width of the others.
FRANCE: Blue, white and red, vertical stripes.
GERMANY: Black, red and white (Imperial
and Third Reich); black, red, and gold (Re-
publican).
GREAT BRITAIN: Red, white and blue.
GREECE: Nine horizontal stripes, blue and
white.
GUATEMALA: Blue, white, and blue, vertical
stripes.
HAITI: Blue and red.
HONDURAS: Blue, white, and blue, horizontal
stripes.
IRAN: White, top edge green, bottom edge red.
IRISH FREE STATE: Orange, white, and green.
ITALY: Green, white, and red, vertical stripes.
JAPAN: White, with red disk in center, from
which spring sixteen red rays to edge.
LIBERIA: Eleven horizontal stripes, red and
white.

LUXEMBURG: Red, white, and blue.
MEXICO: Green, white, and red, vertical
stripes.
MONACO: Red and white, horizontal.
MOROCCO: Red.
NETHERLANDS: Red, white, and blue, hori-
zontal stripes.
NICARAGUA: Blue, white, and blue, horizon-
tal stripes.
NORWAY: Red, with blue cross bordered with
white.
PANAMA: Blue, white, red.
PARAGUAY: Red, white, blue, horizontal
stripes.
PERU: Red, white, and red, vertical stripes.
PORTUGAL: Blue and white.
RUMANIA: Blue, yellow, and red, vertical
stripes.
RUSSIA: Red, with yellow hammer, sickle,
and star.
SALVADOR: Nine horizontal stripes, blue
and white.
SWEDEN: Blue, with yellow cross.
SWITZERLAND: Red, with white cross.
THAILAND: Red, with a white elephant.
TURKEY: Green and red.
UNITED STATES OF AMERICA: Stars on
blue, white with red stripes.
URUGUAY: Nine horizontal stripes, blue and
white.
VENEZUELA: Yellow, blue, and red, hori-
zontal stripes.
YUGOSLAVIA: Blue, white, and red.

Colors in Symbolism

BLUE: Hope, love of divine works; (in dresses) divine contemplation, piety, sincerity.
In blazonry, azure, signifying chastity, loyalty, fidelity; it is engraved by horizontal lines.
In art (as an angel's robe) it signifies fidelity
and faith (as the robe of the Virgin Mary),
modesty and (in the Catholic Church) humi-
lity and expiation. In Church decoration,
blue and green are used indifferently for
ordinary Sundays, and blue for all weekdays
after Trinity Sunday. As a mortuary color it
signifies eternity (applied to Deity), immortality (applied to man). In metals it is represented by tin. In precious stones it is
represented by sapphire. In planets it stands
for Jupiter.
PALE BLUE: Peace, Christian prudence, love
of good work, a serene conscience.
GREEN: Faith, gladness, immortality, the resurrection of the just; (in dresses) the gladness of the faithful. In blazonry, vert, signifying love, joy, abundance; it is engraved
from left to right. In art, signifies hope, joy,
youth, spring (among the Greeks and Moors
it signifies victory). In Church decoration it
signifies God's bounty, mirth, gladness, the
resurrection, and is used indifferently with
blue for ordinary Sundays. In metals it is
represented by copper. In precious stones
it is represented by the emerald. In planets
it stands for Venus.
PALE GREEN: Baptism.
BLACK: In blazonry, sable, signifying prudence, wisdom, and constancy; it is engraved
by perpendicular and horizontal lines crossing at right angles. In art, signifies evil,
falsehood, and error. In Church decoration
it is used for Good Friday. As a mortuary
color, signifies grief, despair, death. (In the
Catholic Church violet may be substituted
for black.) In metals it is represented by lead,
In precious stones it is represented by the
diamond. In planets it stands for Saturn.

PURPLE: Justice, royalty. In *blazonry*, purpure, signifying temperance; it is engraved by lines slanting from right to left. In *art*, signifies royalty. In *metals* it is represented by quicksilver. In *precious stone* it is represented by amethyst. In *planets* it stands for Mercury.

RED: Martyrdom for faith, charity; (in dresses) divine love. In *blazonry*, gules; blood-red is called sanguine. The former signifies magnanimity and the latter fortitude; it is engraved by perpendicular lines. In *Church decorations* it is used for martyrs, for Ash Wednesday, for the last three days of Holy Week, and for Whit Sunday. In *art*, signifies passion. In *metals* it is represented by iron. In *precious stones* it is represented by ruby. In *planets* it stands for Mars.

Committees, Congressional
See **Congress of the United States**

Composers
See **Musical Compositions**

Congress of the United States

Congressional Representation, by State

ALABAMA: 9 representatives.
ARIZONA: 2 representatives.
ARKANSAS: 6 representatives.
CALIFORNIA: 30 representatives.
COLORADO: 4 representatives.
CONNECTICUT: 6 representatives.
DELAWARE: 1 representative.
FLORIDA: 8 representatives.
GEORGIA: 10 representatives.
IDAHO: 2 representatives.
ILLINOIS: 25 representatives.
INDIANA: 11 representatives.
IOWA: 8 representatives.
KANSAS: 6 representatives.
KENTUCKY: 8 representatives.
LOUISIANA: 8 representatives.
MAINE: 3 representatives.
MARYLAND: 7 representatives.
MASSACHUSETTS: 14 representatives.
MICHIGAN: 18 representatives.
MINNESOTA: 9 representatives.
MISSISSIPPI: 6 representatives.
MISSOURI: 11 representatives.
MONTANA: 2 representatives.
NEBRASKA: 4 representatives.
NEVADA: 1 representative.
NEW HAMPSHIRE: 2 representatives.
NEW JERSEY: 14 representatives.
NEW MEXICO: 2 representatives.
NEW YORK: 43 representatives.
NORTH CAROLINA: 12 representatives.
NORTH DAKOTA: 2 representatives.
OHIO: 23 representatives.
OKLAHOMA: 6 representatives.
OREGON: 4 representatives.
PENNSYLVANIA: 30 representatives.
RHODE ISLAND: 2 representatives.
SOUTH CAROLINA: 6 representatives.
SOUTH DAKOTA: 2 representatives.
TENNESSEE: 9 representatives.
TEXAS: 22 representatives.
UTAH: 2 representatives.
VERMONT: 1 representative.
VIRGINIA: 10 representatives.
WASHINGTON: 7 representatives.
WEST VIRGINIA: 6 representatives.
WISCONSIN: 10 representatives.
WYOMING: 1 representative.

Senate Standing Committees

AGRICULTURE & FORESTRY: 16 committee members.
APPROPRIATIONS: 23 committee members.
ARMED SERVICES: 15 committee members.
BANKING & CURRENCY: 15 committee members.
DISTRICT OF COLUMBIA: 9 committee members.
FINANCE: 15 committee members.
FOREIGN RELATIONS: 15 committee members.
GOVERNMENT OPERATIONS: 13 committee members.
INTERIOR & INSULAR AFFAIRS: 15 Committee members.
INTERSTATE & FOREIGN COMMERCE: 15 committee members.
JUDICIARY: 15 committee members.
LABOR & PUBLIC WELFARE: 13 committee members.
POST OFFICE & CIVIL SERVICE: 11 committee members.
PUBLIC WORKS: 11 committee members.
RULES & ADMINISTRATION: 9 committee members.

House Standing Committees

AGRICULTURE: 33 committee members.
APPROPRIATIONS: 50 committee members.
ARMED SERVICES: 39 committee members.
BANKING & CURRENCY: 29 committee members.
DISTRICT OF COLUMBIA: 25 committee members.
EDUCATION & LABOR: 27 committee members.
FOREIGN AFFAIRS: 29 committee members.
GOVERNMENT OPERATIONS: 30 committee members.
HOUSE ADMINISTRATION: 23 committee members.
INTERIOR & INSULAR AFFAIRS: 30 committee members.
INTERSTATE & FOREIGN COMMERCE: 31 committee members.
JUDICIARY: 30 committee members.
MERCHANT MARINE & FISHERIES: 29 committee members.
POST OFFICE & CIVIL SERVICE: 25 committee members.
PUBLIC WORKS: 29 committee members.
RULES: 12 committee members.
UN-AMERICAN ACTIVITIES: 9 committee members.
VETERANS' AFFAIRS: 26 committee members.
WAYS & MEANS: 25 committee members.

Congressional Declarations of War

1. WAR OF 1812: June 18, 1812.
2. MEXICAN WAR: May 13, 1846.
3. SPANISH-AMERICAN WAR: April 25, 1898.
4. WAR WITH GERMANY: April 6, 1917.
5. WAR WITH AUSTRIA: December 7, 1917.
6. WAR WITH JAPAN: December 8, 1941.
7. WAR WITH GERMANY: December 11, 1941.
8. WAR WITH ITALY: December 11, 1941.
9. WAR WITH BULGARIA: June 5, 1942.
10. WAR WITH HUNGARY: June 5, 1942.
11. WAR WITH RUMANIA: June 5, 1942.

Constellations
See also Stars

Twenty-nine North of the Zodiac

ANDROMEDA: The Chained Lady.
AQUILA: The Eagle.
AURIGA: The Charioteer.
BOÖTES: The Wagoner, or Plowman.
CAMELOPARDALIS: The Camelopard.
CANES VENATICI: The Hunting Dogs.
CASSIOPEIA: The Lady in the Chair.
CEPHEUS: Cepheus, the King.
COMA BERENICES: Berenices' Hair.
CORONA BOREALIS: The Northern Crown.
CYGNUS: The Swan.
DELPHINUS: The Dolphin.
DRACO: The Dragon.
EQUULEUS: The Colt.
HERCULES: Hercules (Kneeling).
LACERTA: The Lizard.
LEO MINOR: The Lesser Lion.
LYNX: The Lynx.
LYRA: The Lyre, or Harp.
OPHIUCHUS: The Serpent Holder. (Ophiuchus is sometimes called Serpentarius.)
PEGASUS: The Winged Horse.
PERSEUS: Perseus (the Hero, with Medusa's Head).
SAGITTA: The Arrow.
SCUTUM: The Shield.
SERPENS: The Serpent.
SERPENTARIUS: Alternate name for Ophiuchus.
TRIANGULUM: The Triangle.
URSA MAJOR: The Greater Bear.
URSA MINOR: The Lesser Bear.
VULPESCULA: The Fox (and the Goose).

Twelve Zodiacal Constellations

AQUARIUS: The Water-Bearer.
ARES: The Ram.
CANCER: The Crab.
CAPRICORNUS: The Goat.
GEMINI: The Twins.
LEO: The Lion.
LIBRA: The Balance, or Scales.
PISCES: The Fishes.
SAGITTARIUS: The Archer.
SCORPIUS (OR SCORPIO): The Scorpion.
TAURUS: The Bull.
VIRGO: The Virgin.

Forty-nine South of the Zodiac

ANTILA (PNEUMATICA): The Air Pump.
APUS (OR AVIS INDICA): Bird of Paradise (or of India).
ARA: The Altar.
ARGO NAVIS: (Carina, Malus, Puppis, Vela)[1] The Ship (the Keel, the Mast, the Stern, the Sails).
CAELUM (SCALPTORIUM): The (Engraver's) Tool.
CANIS MAJOR: The Greater Dog.
CANIS MINOR: The Lesser Dog.
CARINA: The Keel. See Argo Navis.
CENTAURUS: The Centaur.
CETUS: The Whale.
CHAMAELEON: The Chameleon.

1. Carina, Malus, Puppis, and Vela are sometimes listed as separate constellations, and sometimes grouped together into the single constellation Argo Navis. In older (Ptolomaic) star charts, Pyxis was also included as a subdivision of Argo Navis.

CIRCINUS: The Pair of Compasses.
COLUMBA (NOACHI): (Noah's) Dove.
CORONA AUSTRALIS: The Southern Crown.
CORVUS: The Crow.
CRATER: The Bowl.
CRUX AUSTRALIS: The Southern Cross.
DORADO (OR XIPHIAS): The Gilthead, or Swordfish.
ERIDANUS: The River Po.
FORNAX (CHEMICAE): The (Chemist's) Furnace, or Retort.
GRUS: The Crane.
HOROLOGUIM: The Clock.
HYDRA: The Water-Serpent, or Hydra (fem).
HYDRUS: The Water-Snake, or Sea-Serpent (masc.).
INDUS: The Indian.
LEPUS: The Hare.
LUPUS: The Wolf.
MALUS: The Mast. See Argo Navis.
MENSA (MONS MENSAE): Table Mountain.
MICROSCOPIUM: The Microscope.
MONOCEROS: The Unicorn.
MUSCA (OR APIS): The Fly (or the Bee).
NORMA: The Square and Rule.
OCTANS: The Octant.
ORION: Orion, the Hunter.
PAVO: The Peacock.
PHOENIX: Phoenix, the Fabulous Bird.
PICTOR (EQUULEUS PICTORIUS): The Painter's Easel, or Little Horse.
PISCIS AUSTRINUS: The Southern Fish.
PUPPIS: The Stern. See Argo Navis.
PYXIS (NAUTICA): The (Ship's) Compass. See Argo Navis.
RETICULUM: The Reticule, or Net.
SCULPTOR (APPARATUS SCULPTORIUS): The Sculptor's Tools.
SEXTANS: The Sextant.
TELESCOPIUM: The Telescope.
TRIANGULUM AUSTRALE: The Southern Triangle.
TUCANA: The Toucan.
VELA: The Sails. See Argo Navis.
VOLANS (Piscius Volans): The Flying Fish.

Countries of the World
See Population of the Countries of the World; Products of the World, Their Origins and Uses

Court Fools

From medieval times till the 17th century licensed fools or jesters were commonly kept at court, and frequently in the retinue of wealthy nobles. The guild "fools" of medieval times played an important part in the spread of literature and education. They formed a branch of the troubador organization. Some famous fools are:

ARCHIE ARMSTRONG: Jester of James I (English).
PATRICK BONNY: In the court of the Scottish regent Morton (James Douglas, fourth Earl of Morton), 1572.
BRUSQUET: Jester of Henri II (French).
CHICOT: Jester of Henri III and IV (French).
JENNY COLQUHOUN: Fool of Mary, Queen of Scots.
HAINCELIN COQ: Fool of Charles VI (French).
DAGONET: The fool of King Arthur.
THOMAS DERRIE: Jester of James I (English).
FEVRIAL or LE FEURIAL: Fool of Louis XII and François (French). Also known as Triboulet.
JAMES GEDDES: Fool of Mary, Queen of Scots.

ROBERT GRENE: Jester of Queen Elisabeth I (English).
THOMAS KILLIGREW: Jester of King Charles I (English).
L'ANGELY: Jester of Louis XIII (French).
GUILLAUME LOUEL: Fool of Charles VII (French).
MITTON: Fool of Charles V (French).
PATCH: Court fool of Elizabeth, wife of Henry VII (English).
PATCHE: Jester of Henry VIII (English), presented to him by Cardinal Wolsey.
PATISON: Sir Thomas More's jester. He is shown in a painting of Chancellor More by Holbein.
DICKIE PEARCE: The fool of the Duke of Suffolk, immortalized by an epitaph written by Dean Swift in 1728.
RAYERE: The fool of Henry I (English).
SCOGAN: The fool of Edward IV (English).
SIBILOT: Jester of Henri III and IV (French).
WILL SOMERS: Jester of Henry VIII (English).
THEVENIN DE ST. LEGER: Fool of Charles V (French).
TRIBOULET: Jester of Louis XII and of François I (French). This was the name given him by Rabelais and by Victor Hugo in his *Roi s'Amuse*. See Fevrial.

Cross
See **Religious Allusions, References, and Symbols**

Dates

See **Abdications and Depositions in European Royalty Since 1910; Admission, Secession, and Readmission of States to the Union of the United States of America; Architects, Their Schools and Representative Works; Awards; Ballets; Battles; Church Calendar, Calendar of the Time; Civil War, American, Battles of; Congress of the United States; Easter Dates, Movable Days of the Easter Cycle; Festivals and Holydays; Homes, American; International Calendar of Saints and Special Days; Mexican War, Battles of; Musical Compositions; Novelists and Prose Writers; Operas, Grand; Paintings; Popes; Revolutionary War, Battles of the American; Rulers; Satirists and Humorists; Spanish-American War, Battles of; Speeches and Sermons; War of 1812, Battles of**

Declarations of War, Congressional
See **Congress of the Unites States**

Degree Abbreviations

A.A.: Associate of Arts or Associate in Arts.
A.A. IN COM.: Associate of Arts in Commerce.
A.B.: *Artium Baccalaureus* (Bachelor of Arts).

A.B.ED.: Bachelor of Arts in Education.
A.B. IN BUS. AND BANK: Bachelor of Arts in Business and Banking.
A.B. IN ED.: Bachelor of Arts in Education.
A.B. IN J.: Bachelor of Arts in Journalism.
A.B. IN L.S.: Bachelor of Arts in Library Science.
A.B. IN S.SC.: Bachelor of Arts in Social Sciences.
A.B.L.S.: Bachelor of Arts in Library Science.
ADJ.A.: Adjunct in Arts.
A.E.: Agricultural Engineer.
AE.E.: Aeronautical Engineer.
AERO.E.: Aeronautical Engineer.
A.M.: Master of Arts.
A.M. IN ED.: Master of Arts in Education.
A.M.L.S.: Master of Arts in Library Science.
A.M.S.W.: Master of Arts in Social Work.
B.A.: Bachelor of Arts.
B.A.ARCH.: Bachelor of Arts in Architecture.
B.A.CH.: Bachelor of Arts in Chemistry.
B.ADM.ENG.: Bachelor of Administrative Engineering.
B.A.E.: Bachelor of Arts in Education, or Bachelor of Art Education.
B.AERO.E.: Bachelor of Aeronautical Engineering.
B.A.AG.: Bachelor of Agriculture.
B.A. IN B.A.: Bachelor of Arts in Business Administration.
B.A. IN ED.: Bachelor of Arts in Education.
B.A. IN EDUCA.: Bachelor of Arts in Education.
B.A. IN J.: Bachelor of Arts in Journalism.
B.A. IN NURS.: Bachelor of Arts in Nursing.
B.A. IN SP.: Bachelor of Arts in Speech.
B.A.J.: Bachelor of Arts in Journalism.
B.A. MUS. ED.: Bachelor of Arst in Music Education.
B.A.P.: Bachelor of Architecture and Planning.
B.APP.ARTS.: Bachelor of Applied Arts.
B.ARCH.: Bachelor of Architecture.
B.ARCH.E.: Bachelor of Architectural Engineering.
B.B.A.: Bachelor of Business Administration.
B.B.AD.: Bachelor of Business Administration.
B.B.S.: Bachelor of Business Science.
B.BUS.AD.: Bachelor of Business Administration.
B.C.E.: Bachelor of Civil Engineering.
B.C.ENG.: Bachelor of Civil Engineering.
B.CH.E.: Bachelor of Chemical Engineering.
B.CHEM.E.: Bachelor of Chemical Engineering.
B.CH.ENG.: Bachelor of Chemical Engineering.
B.COM.SC.: Bachelor of Commercial Science.
B.C.S.: Bachelor of Commercial Science.
B.D.: Bachelor of Divinity.
B.DES.: Bachelor of Design.
B.DR.ART.: Bachelor of Dramatic Art.
B.E.: Bachelor of Education, or Bachelor of Engineering, or Bachelor of Expression.
B.ED.: Bachelor of Education.
B.ED. IN PHYS.ED.: Bachelor of Education in Physical Education.
B. EDUC.: Bachelor of Education.
B.E.E.: Bachelor of Electrical Engineering.
B.EL.ENG.: Bachelor of Electrical Engineering.
B.ENG.PHYSICS.: Bachelor of Engineering Physics.
B.E.S.: Bachelor of Engineering Science.
B.F.A.: Bachelor of Fine Arts.
B.F.A. IN ED.: Bachelor of Fine Arts in Education.
B.F.A. IN MUS.: Bachelor of Fine Arts in Music.
B.F.A. IN P.S.: Bachelor of Fine Arts in Painting and Sculpturing.
B.F.A. IN SP.: Bachelor of Fine Arts in Speech.
B.F.A. MUS.: Bachelor of Fine Arts in Music.

B.IND.E.: Bachelor of Industrial Engineering.
B.J.: Bachelor of Journalism.
B.L.: Bachelor of Letters.
B.L.A.: Bachelor of Landscape Architecture.
B.LAND ARCH.: Bachelor of Landscape Architecture.
B.L. IN J.: Bachelor of Letters in Journalism.
B.LITT.: Bachelor of Literature.
B.L.S.: Bachelor of Library Science.
B.M.: Bachelor of Music, or Bachelor of Medicine.
B.M.E.: Bachelor of Mechanical Engineering, or Bachelor of Music Education.
B.MECH.ENG.: Bachelor of Mechanical Engineering.
B.MED.: Bachelor of Medicine.
B.M.ED.: Bachelor of Music Education.
B.MET.E.: Bachelor of Metallurgical Engineering.
B.MIN.E.: Bachelor of Mining Engineering.
B.M. IN P.S.M.: Bachelor of Music in Public School Music.
B.M. IN S.M.: Bachelor of Music in School Music.
B.MUS.: Bachelor of Music, or Bachelor in Music.
B.MUS.E.: Bachelor of Music Education.
B.MUS.ED.: Bachelor of Music Education.
B.MUS.EDUC.: Bachelor of Music Education.
B.N.: Bachelor of Nursing.
B.N.S.: Bachelor of Naval Science.
B.O.: Bachelor of Oratory.
B.OF ENGR.: Bachelor of Engineering.
B.OF F.A.: Bachelor of Fine Arts.
B.OF F.A. IN DR. ART.: Bachelor of Fine Arts in Dramatic Art.
B.OF PHARM.: Bachelor of Pharmacy.
B.OF VOC.ED.: Bachelor of Vocational Education.
B.PH.: Bachelor of Philosophy.
B.P.S.M.: Bachelor of Public School Music.
B.S.: Bachelor of Science.
B.S.A.: Bachelor of Science in Agriculture.
B.S.A.A.: Bachelor of Science in Applied Arts.
B.S.A.E.: Bachelor of Science in Agricultural Engineering.
B.S.AGR.: Bachelor of Science in Agriculture.
B.S.ARCH.: Bachelor of Science in Architecture
B.S.B.A.: Bachelor of Science in Business Administration.
B.S.BUS.: Bachelor of Science in Business.
B.SC.: Bachelor of Science.
B.S.C.: Bachelor of Science in Commerce.
B.S.C.E.: Bachelor of Science in Civil Engineering.
B.S.C.ENGR.: Bachelor of Science in Civil Engineering.
B.S.CH.E.: Bachelor of Science in Chemical Engineering.
B.SC.CHEM.: Bachelor of Science in Chemistry.
B.SC. IN AGR.: Bachelor of Science in Agriculture.
B.SC. IN AGR.ENG.: Bachelor of Science in Agricultural Engineering.
B.SC. IN ARCH.ENG.: Bachelor of Science in Architectural Engineering.
B.SC. IN BUS.ADM.: Bachelor of Science in Business Administration.
B.SC. IN C.E.: Bachelor of Science in Civil Engineering.
B.SC. IN CHEM.ENG.: Bachelor of Science in Chemical Engineering.
B.SC. IN COMM.ENG.: Bachelor of Science in Commercial Engineering.
B.SC. IN DENT.: Bachelor of Science in Dentistry.
B.SC. IN ED.: Bachelor of Science in Education.
B.SC. IN E.E.: Bachelor of Science in Electrical Engineering.

B.SC. IN GENERAL HOME ECON.: Bachelor of Science in General Home Economics.
B.SC. IN HOME ECON.: Bachelor of Science in Home Economics.
B.SC. IN M.E.: Bachelor of Science in Mechanical Engineering.
B.SC. IN MED.: Bachelor of Science in Medicine.
B.SC. IN NURS.: Bachelor of Science in Nursing.
B.SC. IN PHARM.: Bachelor of Science in Pharmacy.
B.SCH.MUSIC.: Bachelor of School Music.
B.S. COMM.: Bachelor of Science in Commerce.
B.S. COMMERCIAL EDUC: Bachelor of Science in Commercial Education.
B.S.D.: Bachelor of Science in Dentistry.
B.S.E.: Bachelor of Science in Engineering, or Bachelor of Science in Education.
B.S.ECON.: Bachelor of Science in Economics.
B.S.ED.: Bachelor of Science in Education.
B.S.EDUC.: Bachelor of Science in Education.
B.S.E.E.: Bachelor of Science in Electrical Engineering.
B.S.E.ENGR.: Bachelor of Science in Electrical Engineering.
B.S.ELEC.ENGR.: Bachelor of Science in Electrical Engineering.
B.S.E.M.: Bachelor of Science in Mining Engineering.
B.S.ENGIN.: Bachelor of Science in Engineering.
B.S.F.: Bachelor of Science in Forestry.
B.S.FOR.: Bachelor of Science in Forestry.
B.S.H.E.: Bachelor of Science in Home Economics.
B.S.H.EC.: Bachelor of Science in Home Economics.
B.S.HYG.: Bachelor of Science in Hygiene.
B.S.I.E.: Bachelor of Science in Industrial Engineering.
B.S. IN A.E.: Bachelor of Science in Aeronautical Engineering, or Bachelor of Science in Administrative Engineering, or Bachelor of Science in Agricultural Engineering.
B.S. IN AERO.ADM.: Bachelor of Science in Aeronautical Administration.
B.S. IN AGR.: Bachelor of Science in Agriculture.
B.S. IN AGR.ED.: Bachelor of Science in Agricultural Education.
B.S. IN AGRIC.: Bachelor of Science in Agriculture.
B.S.IN APP. ARTS.: Bachelor of Science in Applied Arts.
B.S. IN ARCH.: Bachelor of Science in Architecture.
B.S. IN ARCH. ENGR.: Bachelor of Science in Architectural Engineering.
B.S. IN ART ED.: Bachelor of Science in Art Education.
B.S. IN B.A.: Bachelor of Science in Business Administration.
B.S. IN BIOL.: Bachelor of Science in Biology.
B.S. IN BUS.: Bachelor of Science in Business.
B.S. IN BUS. ADM.: Bachelor of Science in Business Administration.
B.S. IN BUS. AND PUBLIC ADM.: Bachelor of Science in Business and Public Administration.
B.S. IN BUS.ED.: Bachelor of Science in Business Education.
B.S. IN C.: Bachelor of Science in Commerce.
B.S. IN C. AND E.: Bachelor of Science in Commerce and Economics.
B.S. IN C.E.: Bachelor of Science in Civil Engineering.
B.S. IN CH.E.: Bachelor of Science in Chemical Engineering.

B.S. IN CHEM.: Bachelor of Science in Chemistry.

B.S. IN CHEM.ENG.: Bachelor of Science in Chemical Engineering.

B.S. IN CH. ENGR.: Bachelor of Science in Chemical Engineering.

B.S. IN CHEM.ENGR.: Bachelor of Science in Chemical Engineering.

B.S. IN CIVIL ENGR.: Bachelor of Science in Civil Engineering.

B.S. IN COM.: Bachelor of Science in Commerce.

B.S. IN COM.ED.: Bachelor of Science in Commercial Education.

B.S. IN COM.ENG.: Bachelor of Science in Commercial Engineering.

B.S.IND.ED.: Bachelor of Science in Industrial Education.

B.S.IND.ENGR.: Bachelor of Science in Industrial Engineering.

B.S. IN DENT.: Bachelor of Science in Dentistry.

B.S. IN E.: Bachelor of Science in Engineering.

B.S. IN EC.: Bachelor of Science in Economics.

B.S. IN EC. AND BUS.ADM.: Bachelor of Science in Economics and Business Administration.

B.S. IN ECON.: Bachelor of Science in Economics.

B.S. IN ED.: Bachelor of Science in Education.

B.S. IN ED.-MUSIC SUPER.: Bachelor of Science in Education, Music Supervision.

B.S. IN ED.-PHYS.ED.: Bachelor of Science in Education-Physical Education.

B.S. IN EDU.: Bachelor of Science in Education.

B.S. IN EDUC.: Bachelor of Science in Education.

B.S. IN EDUCA.: Bachelor of Science in Education.

B.S. IN ED. WITH MUSIC SUPERVISION: Bachelor of Science in Education with Music Supervision.

B.S. IN E.E.: Bachelor of Science in Electrical Engineering.

B.S. IN ELEC. ENG.: Bachelor of Science in Electrical Engineering.

B.S. IN ELEC.ENGINEER.: Bachelor of Science in Electrical Engineering.

B.S. IN ELEM. ED.: Bachelor of Science in Elementary Education.

B.S. IN E.M.: Bachelor of Science in Mining Engineering.

B.S. IN ENGR.: Bachelor of Science in Engineering.

B.S. IN ENGR.PHYS.: Bachelor of Science in Engineering Physics.

B.S. IN F.S.: Bachelor of Science in Foreign Service.

B.S. IN GEN.ENG.: Bachelor of Science in General Engineering.

B.S. IN GENRL.BUS.: Bachelor of Science in General Business.

B.S. IN GEOL.: Bachelor of Science in Geology.

B.S. IN GROUP WORK ADMIN.: Bachelor of Science in Group Work Administration.

B.S. IN GROUP WORK ED.: Bachelor of Science in Group Work Education

B.S. IN HEALTH AND PHY.ED.: Bachelor of Science in Health and Physical Education.

B.S. IN HEALTH ED.: Bachelor of Science in Health Education.

B.S. IN HOME EC.: Bachelor of Science in Home Economics.

B.S. IN HOME EC.ED.: Bachelor of Science in Home Economics Education.

B.S. IN HOME ECON.: Bachelor of Science in Home Economics.

B.S. IN I.E.: Bachelor of Science in Industrial Engineering.

B.S. IN J.: Bachelor of Science in Journalism.

B.S. IN JRNL.: Bachelor of Science in Journalism.

B.S. IN L.: Bachelor of Science in Law.

B.S. IN LAB.TECH.: Bachelor of Science in Laboratory Technology.

B.S. IN LIB.ARTS.: Bachelor of Science in Liberal Arts.

B.S. IN LIB.SERVICE.: Bachelor of Science in Library Service.

B.S. IN L.S.: Bachelor of Science in Library Science.

B.S. IN M.E.: Bachelor of Science in Mechanical Engineering.

B.S. IN MEC.ARTS.: Bachelor of Science in Mechanical Arts.

B.S. IN MECH.E.: Bachelor of Science in Mechanical Engineering.

B.S. IN MECH.ENG.: Bachelor of Science in Mechanical Engineering.

B.S. IN MECH.IND.: Bachelor of Science in Mechanical Industries.

B.S. IN MED.: Bachelor of Science in Medicine.

B.S. IN MED.SC.: Bachelor of Science in Medical Science.

B.S. IN MED.TECH.: Bachelor of Science in Medical Technology.

B.S. IN MET.ENG.: Bachelor of Science in Metallurgical Engineering.

B.S. IN MINING ENG.: Bachelor of Science in Mining Engineering.

B.S. IN MINING ENGR.: Bachelor of Science in Mining Engineering.

B.S. IN MUS.: Bachelor of Science in Music.

B.S. IN N.: Bachelor of Science in Nursing.

B.S. IN N.E.: Bachelor of Science in Nursing Education.

B.S. IN NURS.: Bachelor of Science in Nursing.

B.S. IN NURSING ED.: Bachelor of Science in Nursing Education.

B.S. IN NURSING EDUC.: Bachelor of Science in Nursing Education.

B.S. IN P.A.: Bachelor of Science in Practical Arts.

B.S. IN P.A.L.: Bachelor of Science in Practical Arts and Letters.

B.S. IN P.E.: Bachelor of Science in Petroleum Engineering.

B.S. IN P.EDUC.: Bachelor of Science in Physical Education.

B.S. IN PH.: Bachelor of Science in Pharmacy.

B.S. IN PHARM.: Bachelor of Science in Pharmacy.

B.S. IN PHCY.: Bachelor of Science in Pharmacy.

B.S. IN P.H.N.: Bachelor of Science in Public Health Nursing.

B.S. IN PHY.ED.: Bachelar of Science in Physical Education.

B.S. IN P.S.M.: Bachelor of Science in Public School Music.

B.S. IN PUBLIC ADM.: Bachelor of Science in Public Administration.

B.S. IN RAD.TECHN.: Bachelor of Science in Radiological Technology.

B.S. IN R.E.: Bachelor of Science in Religous Education.

B.S. IN SC.: Bachelor of Science in Science.

B.S. IN SCHOOL L.S.: Bachelor of Science in School Library Science.

B.S. IN S.E.: Bachelor of Science in Sanitary Engineering.

B.S. IN SOC.: Bachelor of Science in Sociology.

B.S. IN SP.: Bachelor of Science in Speech.

B.S. IN S.S.: Bachelor of Science in Social Service.
B.S. IN S.SC.: Bachelor of Science in Social Science.
B.S. IN SCHOOL MUS.: Bachelor of Science in School Music.
B.S. IN SEC.SCI.: Bachelor of Science in Secretarial Science.
B.S. IN S.W.: Bachelor of Science in Social Work.
B.S. IN TEXTILE ENG.: Bachelor of Science in Textile Engineering.
B.S. IN VOC.ED.: Bachelor of Science in Vocational Education.
B.S.J.: Bachelor of Science in Journalism.
B.S.JOUR.: Bachelor of Science in Journalism.
B.S.JOUR.: Bachelor of Science in Journalism.
B.S.L.: Bachelor of Sacred Literature.
B.S.L.A.: Bachelor of Science in Landscape Architecture.
B.S.L.A. AND MED.: Bachelor of Science in Liberal Arts and Medicine.
B.S.L.A. AND NURS.: Bachelor of Science in Liberal Arts and Nursing.
B.S.L.S.: Bachelor of Science in Library Science.
B.S.M.: Bachelor of School Music.
B.S.M.E.: Bachelor of Science in Mechanical Engineering.
B.S.MECH.ENGR.: Bachelor of Science in Mechanical Engineering.
B.S.MED.: Bachelor of Science in Medicine.
B.S.MUS.: Bachelor of School Music.
B.S.N.: Bachelor of Science in Nursing.
B.S.P.A.: Bachelor of Science in Public Administration.
B.S.P.E.: Bachelor of Science in Physical Education.
B.S.PHAR.: Bachelor of Science in Pharmacy.
B.S.PHARM.: Bachelor of Science in Pharmacy.
B.S.PHYS.: Bachelor of Science in Physics.
B.S.PHYS.ED.: Bachelor of Science in Physical Education.
B.S.S.: Bachelor in Social Science.
B.S.SC.: Bachelor of Social Science.
B.S.SCHOOL SUPV.: Bachelor of Science in School Supervision.
B.S.SEC.ST.: Bachelor of Science in Secretarial Studies.
B.S.SEC.STUD.: Bachelor of Science in Secretarial Studies.
B.TH.: Bachelor of Theology.
B.V.A.: Bachelor of Vocational Agriculture.
C.E.: Civil Engineer.
CER.E.: Ceramic Engineer.
CH.E.: Chemical Engineer.
CHEM.ENG.: Chemical Engineer.
COM.E.: Commercial Engineer.
C.P.H.: Certificate in Public Health.
D.AGR.: Doctor of Agriculture.
D.B.: Bachelor of Divinity.
D.B.A.: Doctor of Business Administration.
D.C.E.: Doctor of Civil Engineering.
D.C.L.: Doctor of Civil Law.
D.C.S.: Doctor of Commercial Science.
D.D.: Doctor of Divinity.
D.D.M.: Doctor of Dental Medicine.
D.D.S.: Doctor of Dental Science, or Doctor of Dental Surgry.
D.D.SC.: Doctor of Dental Science.
D.ED.: Doctor of Education.
D.ENG.: Doctor of Engineering.
D.ENG.S.: Doctor of Engineering Science.
DENT.HYG.: Dental Hygientist.
D.M.D.: Doctor of Dental Medicine.
D.M.L.: Doctor of Modern Languages.
D.M.S.: Doctor of Medical Science.

D.P.H.: Doctor of Public Helath.
D.R.E.: Doctor of Religious Education.
DR.ENG.: Doctor of Engineering.
DR.P.H.: Doctor of Public Health.
DR.SCI.: Doctor of Science.
D.S.C.: Doctor of Surgical Chiropody.
D.SC.HYG.: Doctor of Science in Hygiene.
D.S.S.: Doctor of Social Science.
D.V.M.: Doctor of Veterinary Medicine.
ED.B.: Bachelor of Education.
ED.D.: Doctor of Education.
ED.M.: Master of Education.
E.E.: Electrical Engineer.
E.M.: Mining Engineer.
E.MET.: Metallurgical Engineer.
ENG.: Engineer.
ENG.D.: Doctor of Engineering.
ENGR.: Engineer.
F.ENG.: Forest Engineer.
FOR.: Forester.
G.ARCH.: Graduate in Architecture.
G.CP.: Graduate in Chiropody.
GEOD.E.: Geodetic Engineer.
GEOL.E.: Geological Engineer.
G. IN N.: Graduate in Nursing.
G.L.: Graduate in Law.
G.N.: Graduate Nurse.
G.PH.: Graduate in Pharmacy.
H.H.D.: Doctor of Humanities.
IND.E.: Industrial Engineer.
IND.ENGIN.: Industrial Engineer.
J.C.B.: Bachelor of Canon Law.
J.C.D.: Doctor of Canon Law.
J.C.L.: Licentiate in Canon Law.
J.D.: **Doctor of Jurisprudence, or Doctor of Law.**
J.S.D.: Doctor of Science of Law.
JUR.D.: Doctor of Jurisprudence.
JUR.SC.D.: Doctor of Science of Jurisprudence.
L.H.D.: Doctor of Humane Letters.
LITT.B.: Bachelor of Litterature.
LITT.D.: Doctor of Letters, or Doctor of Literature.
LITT.M.: Master of Letters.
LL.B.: Bachelor of Laws.
LL.D.: Doctor of Laws.
LL.M.: Master of Laws.
M.A.: Master of Arts.
M.A.E.: Master of Aeronautical Engineering, or Master of Art Education.
M.AERO.E.: Master Aeronautical Engineering.
M.A. IN CHRISTIAN ED.: Master of Arts in Christian Education.
M.A. IN ED.: Master of Arts in Education.
M.A. IN PUBLIC ADM.: Master of Arts in Public Administration.
M.A.L.D.: Master of Arts in Law and Diplomacy.
M.ARCH.: Master of Architecture.
M.ARCH. IN C.P.: Master of Architecture in City Planning.
MAR.E.: Marine Engineer.
M.B.: Bachelor of Medicine.
M.B.A.: Master in Business Administration.
M.C.E.: Master of Civil Engineering.
M.C.ENG.: Master of Civil Engineering.
M.CH.E.: Master of Chemical Engineering.
M.CH.ENG.: Master of Chemical Engineering.
M.CLIN.PSYCHOL.: Master of Clinical Psychology.
M.C.P.: Master of City Planning.
M.C.S.: Master of Commercial Science.
M.D.: Doctor of Medicine.
M.DES.: Master of Design.
M.E.: Mechanical Engineer.
MECH.E.: Mechanical Engineer.
MEC.ENG.: Mechanical Engineer.
M.ED.: Master of Education.
MED.SC.D.: Doctor of Medical Science.

M.E.E.: Master of Electrical Engineering.
M.EL.ENG.: Master of Electrical Engineering.
M.ENG.: Mining Engineer.
M.ENGRG.: Master of Engineering.
M.E.P.A.: Master in Engineering and Public Administration.
MET.E.: Metallurgical Engineer.
M.F.: Master of Forestry.
M.F.A.: Master of Fine Arts.
M.F.A.ART AND ARCH.: Master of Fine Arts in Art and Archaelogy.
M.F.A. IN ARCH.: Master of Fine Arts in Architecture.
M.F.A. IN MUS.: Master of Fine Arts in Music.
M.GYN.AND OBS.: Master in Gynecology and Obstetrics.
M.I.A.: Master of International Affairs.
M. IN ED.: Master in Education.
MINING ENG.: Mining Engineer.
M. INT.MED.: Master in Internal Medicine.
M.L.A.: Master of Landscape Architecture.
M.L.ARCH.: Master of Landscape Architecture.
M.L.D.: Master of Landscape Design.
M.M.: Master of Music.
M.M.E.: Master of Mechanical Engineering.
M.MECH.ENG.: Master of Mechanical Engineering.
M.MET.E.: Master of Metallurgical Engineering.
M.MUS.: Master of Music.
M.MUS.ED.: Master of Music Education.
M.N.: Master of Nursing.
M. OF ED.: Master of Education.
M.P.A.: Master of Public Administration.
M.P.H.: Master of Public Health.
M.P.L.: Master of Patent Law.
M.R.E.: Master of Religious Education.
M.R.ED.: Master of Religious Education.
M.R.P.: Master in Regional Planning.
M.S.: Master of Science.
M.S.A.: Master of Science in Agriculture.
M.S.ARCH.: Master of Science in Architecture.
M.SC.: Master of Science.
M.SC.D.: Doctor of Medical Science.
M.S.CH.E.: Master of Science in Chemical Engineering.
M.S.CHEM.: Master of Science in Chemistry.
M.SC. IN AGR.ENG.: Master of Science in Agricultural Engineering.
M.SC. IN ED.: Master of Science in Education.
M.SC. IN E.E.: Master of Science in Electrical Engineering.
M.SC. IN ME.: Master of Science in Mechanical Engineering.
M.SC. IN SOC.W.: Master of Science in Social Work.
M.SC.MED.: Master of Medical Science.
M.S.DENT.: Master of Science in Dentistry.
M.S.E.: Master of Science in Engineering.
M.S.H.EC.: Master of Science in Home Economics.
M.S.HYG.: Master of Science in Hygiene.
M.S. IN B.A.: Master of Science in Business Administration.
M.S. IN C.E.: Master of Science in Civil Engineering.
M.S. IN CHEM.: Master of Science in Chemistry.
M.S. IN COM.: Master of Science in Commerce.
M.S.IND.E.: Master of Science in Industrial Engineering.
M.S. IN ED.: Master of Science in Education
M.S. IN EDUC.: Master of Science in Education.
M.S. IN E.E.: Master of Science in Electrical Engineering.
M.S. IN E.M.: Master of Science in Engineering Mechanics.
M.S. IN ENG.: Master of Science in Engineering.

M.S. IN ENG'G.: Master of Science in Engineering.
M.S. IN GOV'T MANAGEMENT: Master of Science in Government Management.
M.S. IN GROUP WORK ED.: Master of Science in Group Work Education.
M.S. IN HOME EC.: Master of Science in Home Economics.
M.S. IN HYG. AND PHYS.EDUC.: Master of Science in Hygeine and Physical Education.
M.S. IN J.: Master of Science in Journalism.
M.S. IN L.S.: Master of Science in Library Science.
M.S. IN M.E.: Master of Science in Mechanical Engineering.
M.S. IN MUS.: Master of Science in Music.
M.S. IN N.E.: Master of Science in Nursing Education.
M.S. IN NURS.: Master of Science in Nursing.
M.S. IN PHY.ED.: Master of Science in Physical Education.
M.S. IN P.S.M.: Master of Science in Public School Music.
M.S. IN PUBLIC ADM.: Master of Science in Public Administration.
M.S. IN RET.: Master of Science in Retailing.
M.S. IN S.E.: Master of Science in Sanitary Engineering.
M.S. IN SOCIAL ADM.: Master of Science in Social Administration.
M.S. IN S.S.: Master of Science in Social Service.
M.S. IN S.W.: Master of Sceince in Social Work.
M.S. IN TRANS.: Master of Science in Transportation.
M.S. IN TRANS.E.: Master of Science in Transportation Engineering.
M.SOC.WK.: Master of Social Work.
M.S.P.E.: Master of Science in Physical Education.
M.S.P.H.: Master of Science in Public Health.
M.S.PHAR.: Master of Science in Pharmacy.
M.S.P.H.E.: Master of Science in Public Health Engineering.
M.S.S.: Master of Social Service, or Master of Social Science.
M.SURGERY: Master in Surgery.
M.S.W.: Master of Social Work.
M.TH.: Master of Theology.
MUS.B.: Bachelor of Music.
MUS. D.: Doctor of Music.
MUS.M.: Master of Music.
NAV.ARCH.: Naval Architect.
P.E.: Petroleum Engineer.
PED.D.: Doctor of Pedagogy.
PHAR.D.: Doctor of Pharmacy.
PH.B.: Bachelor of Philosophy.
.PH.B. IN B.A.: Bachelor of Philosophy in Business Administration.
PH.B. IN J.: Bachelor of Philosophy in Journalism.
PH.B. IN SP.: Bachelor of Philosophy in Speech.
PH.C.: Pharmaceutical Chemist.
PH.D.: Doctor of Philosophy.
PH.D. IN ED.: Doctor of Philosophy in Education.
PH.G.: Graduate in Pharmacy.
PH.L.: Licentiate in Philosophy.
PH.M.: Master of Philosophy.
PROF.ENG.: Professional Engineer.
S.B.: Bachelor of Science.
S.B. COMM.: Bachelor of Science in Commerce.
S.B. IN CHEM.: Bachelor of Science in Chemistry.
S.B. IN ED.: Bachelor of Science in Education.
S.B. IN ENGIN.: Bachelor of Science in Engineering.

S.B. IN GEOL.: Bachelor of Science in Geology.
S.B. IN MED.: Bachelor of Science in Medicine.
S.B. IN PHAR.: Bachelor of Science in Pharmacy.
SC.B.: Bachelor of Science.
SC.B. IN CHEM.: Bachelor of Science in Chemistry.
SC.B. IN ENG.: Bachelor of Science in Engineering.
SC.D.: Doctor of Science.
SC.D.MED.: Doctor of Medical Science.
SCH.MUS.B.: Bachelor of School Music.
SC.M.: Master of Science.
S.D.: Doctor of Science.
S.J.D.: Doctor of Juridical Science.
S.M.: Master of Science.
S.M. IN ENGIN.: Master of Science in Engineering.
S.SC.D.: Doctor of Social Science.
S.T.B.: Bachelor of Sacred Theology or Bachelor of Theology.
S.T.D.: Doctor of Sacred Theology.
S.T.L.: Licentiate in Sacred Theology.
S.T.M.: Master of Sacred Theology, or Master of Theology.
TH.B.: Bachelor of Theology.
TH.D.: Doctor of Theology.
V.M.D.: Doctor of Veterinary Medicine.
WOOD TECH: Wood Technologist.

Detectives in Fiction:
The Most Famous Sleuths of Fiction, Their Authors, and the Stories in Which They Appear

UNCLE ABNER: Melville Davisson Post; *Uncle Abner: Master of Mysteries* (a collection of stories).
ROGER ACKROYD: Agatha Christie; *The Murder of Roger Ackroyd.*
KOGORD AKECHI: Edogawa Rampo (Taro Hirai); *The Psychological Test and Other Stories.*
INSPECTOR RODERICK ALLEYN: Ngaio Marsh; *A Man Lay Dead; Death in Ecstacy; Vintage Murder; Overture to Death; I Can Find My Way Out; Wreath for Rivera.*
JOHN APPLEBY: Michael Innes (John I. Stewart); *Seven Suspects; Hamlet, Revenge!; Lament for a Maker; Appleby on Ararat.*
INSPECTOR ASHENDEN: W. Somerset Maugham; *Ashenden of Scotland Yard.*
PROFESSOR AUGUSTUS: S. F. X. Van Dusen and Jacques Futrelle; *The Thinking Machine.*
MR. BARNES & ROBERTS LEROY MITCHELL: Rodrigues Ottolengui; *Final Proof.*
PAUL BECK: M. McDonnell Bodkin; *Paul Beck, The Rule of Thumb Detective.*
M. RAOUL BECQ: William LeQueux; *Mysteries of a Great City.*
CAPTAIN SAM BIRGE: William Krasner; *Walk the Dark Streets; The Stag Party.*
INSPECTOR BLUNT: Mark Twain; *The Stolen White Elephant.*
COLONEL BRAXTON: Melville Davisson Post; *The Silent Witness.*
INSPECTOR BRIDIE: Margery Allingham; *Black Plumes.*
FATHER BROWN: G. K. Chesterton; *The Innocence of Father Brown* (a collection of stories); *The Father Brown Omnibus* (a collection).
MR. BURTON: Seely Regester (Metta Victor); *The Dead Letter.*
ALBERT CAMPION: Margery Allingham; *Mr.*

Campion and Others; Death of a Ghost; Flowers for the Judge; The Fashion in Shrouds; Traitor's Purse.
LETITIA CARBERRY: Mary Roberts Rinehart; *The Amazing Adventures of Letitia Carberry.*
CARNACKI: William Hope Hodgson; *Carnacki, The Ghost-Finder.*
MAX CARRADOS: Ernest Bramah; *Max Carrados; The Eyes of Max Carrados* (this title alludes to the fact that Carrados is blind, a major innovation in the world of detective fiction).
NICK CARTER: Nicholas Carter (pseudonym); *Move in the Dark; Victim of Circumstance; The Detective's Pretty Neighbor.*
CHARLIE CHAN: Earl Derr Biggers; *The Chinese Parrot; Behind That Curtain; The Black Camel; The House Without a Key; Keeper of the Keys; Charlie Chan Carries On.*
HAMILTON CLEEK: T. W. Hanshew; *The Man of Forty Faces.*
JOSHUA CLUNK: H. C. Bailey; *The Garston Murder Case.*
DR. DANIEL WEBSTER COFFEE: Lawrence Blochman; *Diagnosis Homicide.*
SERGEANT CUFF: Wilkie Collins; *The Moonstone.*
D.: Graham Greene; *The Confidential Agent.*
SUSAN DARE: Mignon G. Eberhart; *The Cases of Susan Dare.*
ARCHER DAWE: J. S. Fletcher; *The Adventures of Archer Dawe (Sleuth Hound).*
DORCAS DENE: George R. Sims; *Dorcas Dene, Detective.*
BULLDOG DRUMMOND: Herman Cyril Mc Neile; *Bulldog Drummond Returns.*
DETECTIVE JOHN DUFF: Harvey J. O'Higgins; *Detective Duff Unravels It.*
M. AUGUSTE DUPIN: Edgar Allan Poe; *The Murders in the Rue Morgue.*
MICHAEL DUVEEN: Eden Philpott; *My Adventure in the Flying Scalsman.*
HOMER EVANS: Elliot Paul; *The Mysterious Mickey Finn.*
DR. GIDEON FELL: John Dickson Carr; *The Incautious Burglar; The Three Coffins; The Murder of Sir Edmund Godfrey; The Arabian Nights Murder.*
SOLANGE FONTAINE: F. Tennyson Jesse; *The Solange Stories.*
REGGIE FORTUNE: H. C. Bailey; *Call Mr. Fortune.*
CHIEF INSPECTOR FRENCH: Freeman Willis Crofts; *Inspector French's Greatest Case; Murderers Make Mistakes.*
MAGISTRATE FROGET: Georges Simenon; *Les Nouvelles Enquêtes de Maigret.*
ANTHONY GETHRYN: Philip MacDonald; *The Rasp.*
ANTHONY GILLINGHAM: A. A. Milne; *The Red House Mystery.*
BEVERLY GRETTON: Herbert Cadette; *The Adventures of a Journalist.*
EBENEZER GRYCE: Anna Katharine Green; *The Leavenworth Case.*
PHILO GUBB: Ellis Parker Butler; *Philo Gubb.*
DR. EUSTACE HAILEY: Anthony Wynne; *Sinners Go Secretly.*
TOMMY HAMBLEDON: Manning Coles; *Drink to Yesterday; A Toast to Tomorrow.*
MIKE HAMMER: Mickey Spillane; *I, the Jury; Kiss Me Deadly.*
GABRIEL HANAUD: A. E. W. Mason; *At the Villa Rosa; The House of the Arrow; The Four Corners of the World.*
JIM HANVEY: Octavus Roy Cohen; *Jim Hanvey, Detective.*

THORPE HAZELL: Victor L. Whitechurch; *Thrilling Stories of the Railway.*

NORMAN HEAD: L. T. Meade and Robert Eustace; *The Brotherhood of Seven Kings.*

MARTIN HEWITT: Arthur Morrison; *Martin Hewitt, Investigator.*

SHERLOCK HOLMES: A. Conan Doyle. The most famous fictional detective of them all. The "Adventures of Sherlock Holmes" began with *Study in Scarlet* (1887), and continued through *The Sign of the Four* (1889). *The Adventures of Sherlock Holmes* (1892), *The Memoirs of Sherlock Holmes* (1894), *The Hound of the Baskervilles* (1902), *The Return of Sherlock Holmes* (1905), *The Valley of Fear* (1915), *His Last Bow* (1917), and *The Case Book of Sherlock Holmes* (1927). Holmes was technically an amateur, but his devastating analytical powers and his tireless pursuit of all the mysterious facts often put Scotland Yard to shame; Dr. Joseph Bell, a physician, and also one of Conan Doyle's professors, is said to have been the inspiration to the fictional character.

I: Daphne Du Maurier; *Rebecca.*

NOVEMBER JOE: Hesketh Prichard; *November Joe.*

SIR JOHN: Clemence Dane and Helen Simpson; *Enter Sir John; Re-enter Sir John.*

DR. SAM JOHNSON: Lillian de la Torre; *Dr. Sam Johnson, Detector.*

INSPECTOR JOLY: Arthur Sherburne Hardy; *Deanne and Her Friends.*

AVERAGE JONES: Samuel Hopkins Adams; *Average Jones.*

HEMLOCK JONES: Bret Harte; *Condensed Novels* (Second Series).

MONSIEUR JONQUELLE: Melville Davisson Post; *M. Jonquelle: Prefect of Police of Paris.*

PROF. CRAIG KENNEDY: Arthur B. Reeves; *The Silent Bullet.*

ASTROGEN (ASTRO) KERBY: Gelett Burgess; *The Master of Mysteries.*

MORRIS KLAW: Sax Rohmer; *The Dream Detective.*

DRURY LANE: Barnaby Ross (Ellery Queen; i.e. Frederick Dannay and Manfred B. Lee); *The Tragedies of X, Y, Z.*

M. LECOQ: Emile Gaboriau; *The Little Old Man of Batignolles.*

ARSÈNE LUPIN: Maurice Leblanc; *Arsène Lupin, Gentleman-Cambrioleur; The Eight Strokes of the Clock; 813; The Crystal Stopper; The Teeth of the Tiger.*

PAUL LYNDE: Thomas Bailey Aldrich; *Out of His Head.*

MAÎTRE MAGLOIRE: Emile Gaboriau; *The Little Old Man of Batignolles.*

INSPECTOR MAIGRET: Georges Simenon; *Les Nouvelles Enquêtes de Maigret; Maigret's Christmas; The Sailor's Rendezvous; The Saint-Fiacre Affair; Maigret to the Rescue; Maigret in New York's Underworld; Maigret Keeps a Rendezvous; Maigret Travels South; Maigret's Revolver; Patience of Maigret; No Vacation for Maigret.*

PHILIP MARLOWE: Raymond Chandler; *The Big Sleep; Farewell, My Lovely.*

SIR HENRY MARQUIS: Melville Davisson Post; *The Sleuth of St. James' Square; The Bradmoor Murder.*

PERRY MASON: Erle Stanley Gardner; The Perry Mason series (beginning with *The Case of the Velvet Claws*).

RANDOLPH MASON: Melville Davisson Post; *The Strange Schemes of Randolph Mason* (in which the first criminal lawyer of detective fiction shows up).

INSPECTOR MATHER: Graham Greene; *This Gun for Hire.*

ASEY MAYO: Phoebe Atwood Taylor; *The Cape Cod Mystery; Three Plots for Asey Mayo.*

GREAT MERLINI: Clayton Rawson; *Death from a Top Hat.*

SIR HENRY MERRIVALE: John Dickson Carr; *The Red Widow Murders; The Judas Window.*

INSPECTOR MIDWINTER (Eden Phillpotts); *The Thing at Their Heels; Who Killed Cock Robin?*

MR. MOTO: John P. Marquand; the Mr. Moto series (beginning with *No Hero*).

KENT MURDOCK: George Harmon Coxe; *Murder on Their Minds.*

DORA MYRL: M. McDonnell Bodkin; *Dora Myrl, the Lady Detective.*

MR. AND MRS. NORTH: Richard and Frances Lockridge; *Burnt Offering; Murder Out of Town; The Norths Meet Murder.*

LANCE O'LEARY: Mignon G. Eberhardt; *The Patient in Room 18.*

DETECTIVE O'MALLEY: William MacHarg; *The Affairs of O'Malley.*

BILL PARMELEE: Percival Wilde; *Rogues in Clover.*

DEPUTY PARR: Frederick Irving Anderson; *The Infallible Godahl; The Notorious Sophie Lang; Book of Murder.*

MRS. PASCHAL: Charles H. Clarke; *Revelations of a Lady Detective* (in which a lady sleuth appeared for the first time in detective fiction).

MR. PINKERTON: David Frome (Mrs. Zenith J. Brown); *The Hammersmith Murder Stories; Mr. Pinkerton Detective Stories; The Man from Scotland Yard.*

PROF. HENRY POGGIOLI: T. S. Stribling; *Clues of the Caribees.*

HERCULE POIROT: Agatha Christie; *The Mysterious Affair at Styles; ABC Murders; Murder in Three Acts; Cards on the Table; The Hollow; Perilous Journeys of Hercule Poirot (The Mystery of the Blue Train, Death on the Nile, Murder in Mesopotamia); There is a Tide; Murder in Retrospect.*

INSPECTOR POOLE: Henry Wade; *Policeman's Lot; The Duke of York's Steps.*

ELLERY QUEEN: Ellery Queen (Frederick Dannay and Manfred B. Lee); *The Adventures of Ellery Queen.*

DR. PRIESTLY: John Rhodes (C. J. C. Street); the Dr. Priestly series (beginning with *The Paddington Mystery*).

ROMNEY PRINGLE: Clifford Ashdown; *The Adventure of Romney Pringle.*

PARKER PYNN: Agatha Christie; *Mr. Parker Pynn, Detective.*

J. G. REEDER: Edgar Wallace; *The Murder Book of J. G. Reeder* (in England: *The Mind of J. G. Reeder*); *Red Aces; Mr. Reeder Returns*).

INSPECTOR RINGROSE: Eden Phillpotts; *The Grey Room; The Red Redmarynes.*

JOSEPH ROULETABILLE: Gaston Leroux; *The Mystery of the Yellow Room; La Parfum de la Dame en Noir; The Perfume of the Woman in Black.*

ARTHUR ROWE: Graham Greene; *The Ministry of Fear.*

THE SAINT: See Simon Templar.

MICHAEL SHAYNE: Brett Halliday (Davis Dresser); *Dead Man's Diary; Dinner at Dupres; A Taste for Cognac.*

ROGER SHERINGHAM: Anthony Berkeley; *Trial by Error; The Layton Murder Case; The Poisoned Chocolates Case; The Second Shot.*

SAM SPADE: Dashiell Hammett; *The Adventures of Sam Spade; The Maltese Falcon; The Glass Key.*

GAVIN STEVENS: William Faulkner; *Knight's Gambit*.
FLEMING STONE: Carolyn Wells; *The Clue*.
NIGEL STRANGEWAYS: Nicholas Blake (Cecil Day Lewis); *A Question of Proof; The Beast Must Die; The Smiler with the Knife; A Tangled Web; The Whisper in the Gloom*.
PÈRE TABARET: Emile Gaboriau; *L'Affaire Lerouge*.
TREVIS TARRANT: C. Daly King; *The Curious Mr. Tarrant*.
SIMON TEMPLAR (ALIAS THE SAINT): Leslie Charteris; *Meet—the Tiger! The Brighter Buccaneer; The Saint around the World; The Saint Steps In; The Saint Goes On; The Saint on the Spanish Main; The Saint vs. Scotland Yard*.
CHIEF INSPECTOR THEAKSTONE: Wilkie Collins; *The Queen of Hearts*.
DR. JOHN THORNDYKE: R. Austin Freeman; *The Red Thumb Mark; John Thorndyke's Cases*.
CECIL THOROLD: Arnold Bennett; *The Loot of Cities*.
TICTOCQ: O. Henry; *Rolling Stones*.
PHILIP TOLEFREE: R. A. J. Walling; *The Fatal Five Minutes*.
LUTHER TRANT: Macharg & Balmer; *The Achievements of Luther Trant*.
MR. TRENT: E. C. Bentley; *The Woman in Black* (in England; *Trent's Last Case); Trent Intervenes; Trent's Own Case*.
MR. EPHRIAM TUTT: Arthur Train; *Tutt and Mr. Tutt*.
INSPECTOR VAL: Alfred Henry Lewis; *Confessions of a Detective*.
LIEUTENANT VALCOUR: Rufus King; *Murder by the Clock*.
EUGENE VALMONT: Robert Barr; *The Triumphs of Eugene Valmont*.
PHILO VANCE: S. S. Van Dine (Willard Huntington Wright); *The Benson Murder Case; The Canary Murder Case; The Greene Murder Case; The Bishop Murder Case*.
INSPECTOR WALKER: Melville Davisson Post; *Walker of the Secret Police*.
LORD PETER WHIMSEY: Dorothy Sayers; *Whose Body?; Strong Poison; Have His Carcase; The Bone of Contention; The Documents in the Case; Murder Must Advertise; Gaudy Night; Nine Tailors*.
CALEB WILLIAMS: William Godwin; *Things As They Are*.
SUPERINTENDENT HENRY WILSON: G. D. H. Cole and M. I. Cole; *Superintendent Wilson's Holiday*.
HILDEGARDE WITHERS: Stuart Palmer; *The Penguin Pool Murder; The Puzzle of the Blue Banderilla; The Riddles of Hildegarde Withers*.
NERO WOLFE: Rex Stout; *Fer-de-Lance; The Black Mountain; And Be a Villain; Before Midnight; The Golden Spiders; Prisoner's Base; Second Confession; The Red Box; Too Many Cooks; The League of Frightened Men*.
PRINCE ZALESKI: M. P. Shiel; *Prince Zaleski*.

Drama
See **Awards; Plays, Long Runs on Broadway**

Easter Dates:
Movable Days of the Easter Cycle
See also **Church Calendar; Festivals and Holydays; International**

Calendar of Saints and Special Days

1958: Shrove Monday, Feb. 17; Shrove Tuesday, Feb. 18; Ash Wednesday, Feb. 19; Passion Sunday, March 23; Palm Sunday, March 30; Maundy Thursday, April 3; Good Friday, April 4; Easter, April 6; Rogation Sunday, May 11; Ascension, May 15; Whit Sunday or Pentecost, May 25; Whit Monday, May 26; Trinity, June 1.
1959: Shrove Monday, Feb. 9; Shrove Tuesday, Feb. 10; Ash Wednesday, Feb. 11; Passion Sunday, March 15; Palm Sunday, March 22; Maundy Thursday, March 26; Good Friday, March 27; Easter, March 29; Rogation Sunday, May 3; Ascension, May 7; Whit Sunday or Pentecost, May 17; Whit Monday, May 18; Trinity, May 24.
1960 (LEAP YEAR): Shrove Monday, Feb. 29; Shrove Tuesday, March 1; Ash Wednesday, March 2; Passion Sunday, April 3; Palm Sunday, April 10; Maundy Thursday, April 14; Good Friday, April 15; Easter, April 17; Rogation Sunday, May 22; Ascension, May 26; Whit Sunday or Pentecost, June 5; Whit Monday, June 6; Trinity, June 12.
1961: Shrove Monday, Feb. 13; Shrove Tuesday, Feb. 14; Ash Wednesday, Feb. 15; Passion Sunday, March 19; Palm Sunday, March 26; Maundy Thursday, March 30; Good Friday, March 31; Easter, April 2; Rogation Sunday, May 7; Ascension, May 11; Whit Sunday or Pentecost, May 21; Whit Monday, May 22; Trinity, May 28.
1962: Shrove Monday, March 5; Shrove Tuesday, March 6; Ash Wednesday, March 7; Passion Sunday, April 8; Palm Sunday, April 15, Maundy Thursday, April 19; Good Friday, April 20; Easter, April 22; Rogation Sunday, May 27; Ascension, May 31; Whit Sunday or Pentecost, June 10; Whit Monday, June 11; Trinity, June 17.
1963: Shrove Monday, Feb. 25; Shrove Tuesday, Feb. 26; Ash Wednesday, Feb. 27; Passion Sunday, March 31; Palm Sunday, April 7; Maundy Thursday, April 11; Good Friday, April 12; Easter, April 14; Rogation Sunday, May 19; Ascension, May 23; Whit Sunday or Pentecost, June 2; Whit Monday, June 3; Trinity, June 9.
1964 (LEAP YEAR): Shrove Monday, Feb. 10; Shrove Tuesday, Feb. 11; Ash Wednesday, Feb. 12; Passion Sunday, March 15; Palm Sunday, March 22; Maundy Thursday, March 26; Good Friday, March 27, Easter, March 29; Rogation Sunday, May 3; Ascension, May 7; Whit Sunday or Pentecost, May 17; Whit Monday, May 18; Trinity, May 24.
1965: Shrove Monday, March 1; Shrove Tuesday, March 2; Ash Wednesday, March 3; Passion Sunday, April 4; Palm Sunday, April 11; Maundy Thursday, April 15; Good Friday, April 16; Easter, April 18; Rogation Sunday, May 23; Ascension, May 27; Whit Sunday or Pentecost, June 6; Whit Monday, June 7; Trinity, June 13.
1966: Shrove Monday, Feb. 21; Shrove Tuesday, Feb. 22; Ash Wednesday, Feb. 23; Passion Sunday, March 27; Palm Sunday, April 3; Maundy Thursday, April 7; Good Friday, April 8; Easter, April 10; Rogation Sunday, May 15; Ascension, May 19; Whit Sunday or Pentecost, May 29; Whit Monday, May 30; Trinity, June 5.
1967: Shrove Monday, Feb. 6; Shrove Tuesday, Feb. 7; Ash Wednesday, Feb. 8; Passion Sunday, March 12; Palm Sunday, March 19; Maundy Thursday, March 23; Good Friday, March

24; Easter, March 26; Rogation Sunday, April
30; Ascension, May 4; Whit Sunday or Pente-
cost, May 14; Whit Monday, May 15; Trinity,
May 21.
1968 (LEAP YEAR): Shrove Monday, Feb. 26;
Shrove Tuesday, Feb. 27; Ash Wednesday,
Feb. 28; Passion Sunday, March 31; Palm
Sunday, April 7; Maundy Thursday, April 11;
Good Friday, April 12, Easter, April 14; Ro-
gation Sunday, May 19; Ascension, May 23;
Whit Sunday or Pentecost, June 2; Whit Mon-
day, June 3; Trinity, June 9.
1969: Shrove Monday, Feb. 17; Shrove Tuesday,
Feb. 18; Ash Wednesday, Feb. 19; Passion
Sunday, March 23; Palm Sunday, March 30;
Maundy Thursday, April 3; Good Friday,
April 4; Easter, April 6; Rogation Sunday,
May 11; Ascension, May 15; Whit Sunday or
Pentecost, May 25; Whit Monday, May 26;
Trinity, June 1.
1970: Shrove Monday, Feb. 9; Shrove Tuesday,
Feb. 10; Ash Wednesday, Feb. 11; Passion
Sunday, March 15; Palm Sunday, March 22;
Maundy Thursday, March 26; Good Friday,
March 27; Easter, March 29; Rogation Sunday,
May 3; Ascension, May 7; Whit Sunday or
Pentecost, May 17; Whit Monday, May 18;
Trinity, May 24.
1971: Shrove Monday, Feb. 22; Shrove Tuesday,
Feb. 23; Ash Wednesday, Feb. 24; .Passion
Sunday, March 28; Palm Sunday, April 4;
Maundy Thursday, April 8; Good Friday,
April 9; Easter, April 11; Rogation Sunday,
May 16; Ascension, May 20; Whit Sunday or
Pentecost, May 30; Whit Monday, May 31;
Trinity, June 6.
1972 (LEAP YEAR): Shrove Monday, Feb. 14;
Shrove Tuesday, Feb. 15; Ash Wednesday,
Feb. 16; Passion Sunday, March 19; Palm
Sunday, March 26; Maundy Thursday, March
30; Good Friday, March 31; Easter, April 2;
Rogation Sunday, May 7; Ascension, May 11;
Whit Sunday or Pentecost, May 21; Whit Mon-
day, May 22; Trinity, May 28.
1973: Shrove Monday, March 5; Shrove Tues-
day, March 6; Ash Wednesday, March 7; Pas-
sion Sunday, April 8; Palm Sunday, April 15;
Maundy Thursday, April 19; Good Friday,
April 20; Easter, April 22; Rogation Sunday,
May 27; Ascension, May 31; Whit Sunday or
Pentecost, June 10; Whit Monday, June 11;
Trinity, June 17.
1974: Shrove Monday, Feb. 25; Shrove Tuesday,
Feb. 26; Ash Wednesday, Feb. 27; Passion
Sunday, March 31; Palm Sunday, April 7;
Maundy Thursday, April 11; Good Friday,
April 12; Easter, April 14; Rogation Sunday,
May 19; Ascension, May 23; Whit Sunday or
Pentecost, June 2; Whit Monday, June 3; Tri-
nity, June 9.
1975: Shrove Monday, Feb. 10; Shrove Tuesday,
Feb. 11; Ash Wednesday, Feb. 12; Passion
Sunday, March 16; Palm Sunday, March 23;
Maundy Thursday, March 27; Good Friday,
March 28; Easter, March 30; Rogation Sunday
May 4; Ascension, May 8; Whit Sunday or
Pentecost, May 18; Whit Monday, May 19;
Trinity, May 25.
1976 (LEAP YEAR): Shrove Monday, March 1;
Shrove Tuesday, March 2; Ash Wednesday,
March 3; Passion Sunday, April 4; Palm Sun-
day, April 11; Maundy Thursday, April 15;
Good Friday, April 16; Easter, April 18; Ro-
gation Sunday, May 24; Ascension, May 28;
Whit Sunday or Pentecost, June 7; Whit Mon-
day, June 8; Trinity, June 14.
1977: Shrove Monday, Feb. 21; Shrove Tuesday,
Feb. 22; Ash Wednesday, Feb. 23; Passion
Sunday, March 27; Palm Sunday, April 3;
Maundy Thursday, April 7; Good Friday,

April 8; Easter, April 10; Rogation Sunday,
May 16; Ascension, May 20; Whit Sunday or
Pentecost, May 30; Whit Monday, May 31;
Trinity, June 6.
1978: Shrove Monday, Feb. 6; Shrove Tuesday,
Feb. 7; Ash Wednesday, Feb. 8; Passion Sun-
day, March 12; Palm Sunday, March 19;
Maundy Thursday, March 23; Good Friday,
March 24; Easter, March 26; Rogation Sunday,
May 1; Ascension, May 5; Whit Sunday or
Pentecost, May 15; Whit Monday, May 16;
Trinity, May 22.
1979: Shrove Monday, Feb. 26; Shrove Tuesday,
Feb. 27; Ash Wednesday, Feb. 28; Passion
Sunday, April 1; Palm Sunday, April 8; Maun-
day Thursday, April 12; Good Friday, April
13; Easter, April 15; Rogation Sunday, May
21; Ascension, May 25; Whit Sunday or
Pentecost, June 4; Whit Monday, June 5;
Trinity, June 11.
1980 (LEAP YEAR): Shrove Monday, Feb. 18;
Shrove Tuesday, Feb. 19; Ash Wednesday,
Feb. 20; Passion Sunday, March 23; Palm Sun-
day, March 30; Maundy Thursday, April 3;
Good Friday, April 4; Easter, April 6; Roga-
tion Sunday, May 12; Ascension, May 16;
Whit Sunday or Pentecost, May 26; Whit
Monday, May 27; Trinity, June 2.
1981: Shrove Monday, March 2; Shrove Tuesday,
March 3; Ash Wednesday, March 4; Passion
Sunday, April 5; Palm Sunday, April 12;
Maundy Thursday, April 16; Good Friday,
April 17; Easter, April 19; Rogation Sunday,
May 24; Ascension, May 28; Whit Sunday or
Pentecost, June 7; Whit Monday, June 8; Tri-
nity, June 14.
1982: Shrove Monday, Feb. 22; Shrove Tuesday,
Feb. 23; Ash Wednesday, Feb. 24; Passion
Sunday, March 28; Palm Sunday, April 4;
Maundy Thursday, April 8; Good Friday,
April 9; Easter, April 11; Rogation Sunday,
May 16; Ascension, May 20; Whit Sunday or
Pentecost, May 30; Whit Monday, May 31;
Trinity, June 6.
1983: Shrove Monday, Feb. 14; Shrove Tuesday,
Feb. 15; Ash Wednesday, Feb. 16; Passion
Sunday, March 20; Palm Sunday, March 27;
Maundy Thursday, March 31; Good Friday,
April 1; Easter, April 3; Rogation Sunday,
May 8; Ascension, May 12; Whit Sunday or
Pentecost, May 22; Whit Monday, May 23;
Trinity, May 29.
1984 (LEAP YEAR): Shrove Monday, March 5;
Shrove Tuesday, March 6; Ash Wednesday,
March 7; Passion Sunday, April 8; Palm Sun-
day, April 15; Maundy Thursday, April 19;
Good Friday, April 20; Easter, April 22; Ro-
gation Sunday, May 27; Ascension, May 31;
Whit Sunday or Pentecost, June 10; Whit
Monday, June 11; Trinity, June 17.

Egyptian Gods
See **Gods and Goddesses**

English Rulers
See **Rulers**

Evangelists
See **Apostles and Evangelists**

Faculty Colors
See **Academic Colors**

Father as Title
See **Pseudonyms, Nicknames, and**

Special Associations for Historical Persons

Federal Recreation Areas
See **National Parks**

Festivals, American
See **Indian Reservations** for other information about Indian Festivals

Note: The dates of many of these festivals are subject, like weather, to change—usually because of the weather. Some of the festivals are seasonal, and depend upon such natural events as the running of the sap in maple trees, or the decisions of rattlesnakes as to when to take the sun. In such cases, the best approximations of the time of the festivals are given.

Alabama

ALABAMA DEEP SEA FISHING RODEO: August, Mobile.
AZALEA FESTIVAL: Late winter-early spring, Mobile (Azalea Trail).
DIXIE PUPPY TRIAL: Mid-March, Union Springs.
MARDI GRAS: Shrove Tuesday, Mobile.
PEANUT FESTIVAL: Late October, Dothan.
STATE FAIR: Early October, Birmingham.

Arizona

ANNUAL ALL-INDIAN POW-WOW: Early July, Flagstaff.
ANNUAL APACHE INDIAN RODEO: March, San Carlos.
ANNUAL CACTUS SHOW: Third Week of February, Phoenix (Desert Botanical Gardens).
ANNUAL COCHISE COUNTY FAIR: September, Douglas.
ANNUAL HOPI ARTS AND CRAFTS SHOW: First two weeks of July, Flagstaff (Museum of Northern Arizona).
ANNUAL LIVESTOCK SHOW: March, Tucson.
ANNUAL REX ALLEN DAY: Late April of early May, Willcox.
ANNUAL RODEO: Late October, Buckeye.
ANNUAL RODEO: Last Sunday in June, Dewey.
ANNUAL RODEO: Mid-August, Payson.
ANNUAL RODEO, "LA FIESTA DE LOS VAQUEROS": Late February, Tuscon.
ANNUAL SALT RIVER VALLEY MELON HARVEST: July (depending on harvest), Glendale.
ANNUAL SOUTHSIDE SHERIFFS' POSSE RODEO: March, Chandler.
ANNUAL SOUTHWEST ALL-INDIAN POW WOW: Around July 4, Flagstaff.
ARIZONA HORSE LOVERS CLUB SPRING SHOW: Late April, Phoenix.
ARIZONA SNOW BOWL SKI RACE: New Year's Day (usually), Flagstaff.
CACTUS LEAGUE EXHIBITION BASEBALL GAMES: Second week of March; Phoenix, Tucson, Mesa, Scottsdale.
CAVALCADE OF COLOR, ASPEN FESTIVAL: Early October, statewide.
COTTON CARNIVAL: November, Casa Grande.
DESERT TREK: Mid-April, Wickenburg.

EASTER SUNRISE SERVICES: Grand Canyon (Shrine of Ages).
FEAST OF ST. FRANCIS XAVIER: December, Tucson.
FESTIVAL OF FINE ARTS: April, Tucson.
FIESTA DE LOS VAQUEROS: Late February, Tucson.
FRONTIER DAYS: Early July, Prescott.
GOLD RUSH DAYS: Last week of January, Wickenburg.
GOOD NEIGHBOR DAY: October, Bisbee.
HOPI SNAKE DANCE: August. In even years at Hotevilla, Shipolovi, Shongopovi; in odd years at Mishongnovi, Walpi.
INDIAN CEREMONIAL DANCES: Early July, Flagstaff.
LAS POSADAS: December 25, Tucson.
NATIONAL LIVESTOCK SHOW: Early January, Phoenix.
NAVAJO TRIBAL FAIR: September, Window Rock.
NORTHERN ARIZONA RODEO: Labor Day holidays. Williams.
OLD TUCSON DAYS: Mid-November, Tucson.
OPENING OF THE GUEST RANCH SEASON: October 1, Wickenburg.
OPENING OF WINTER GUEST SEASON: November 1, Tucson.
PALO VERDE FESTIVAL: May, Tucson.
PIONEER DAY CELEBRATION: July 24, Mesa, Safford, St. David, St. John.
PHOENIX DONS CLUB TREK TO SUPERSTITION MOUNTAINS (LOST DUTCHMAN GOLD MINE): February or March.
PHOENIX OPEN GOLF TOURNAMENT: First week of January.
PHOENIX WORLD CHAMPIONSHIP RODEO: Mid-March.
RAWHIDE ROUNDUP: Early March, Mesa.
ROSE FESTIVAL AND ART EXHIBIT: Early May, Tucson.
ST. JOHN'S DAY: Late June, St. John's.
SALAD BOWL FOOTBALL GAME: Christmas week, Phoenix.
SILVER SPUR RODEO: Mid-February, Yuma.
SKI CARNIVAL: Mid-November—Spring. Flagstaff.
SMOKE CEREMONIALS: First or second Saturday of August, Prescott.
SQUARE DANCE FESTIVAL AND FIDDLER'S JAMBOREE: Mid-February, Phoenix.
TOMBSTONE DAYS: Late October, Tombstone.
20-30 CLUB JUNIOR RODEO: Late January, Mesa.
TUCSON FESTIVAL: Mid-April.
YAQUI EASTER CEREMONIALS: Holy Week, Labor Day.

Arkansas

ALL-STATE HIGH SCHOOL CONCERT: Mid-March, Little Rock.
ARKANSAS LIVESTOCK SHOW AND RODEO: Early October, Little Rock.
CHRISTMAS EVE CAROLS AND PAGEANT: Hot Springs (National Park).
CROWLEY RIDGE PEACH FESTIVAL: Late July, Forest City.
EASTER SUNRISE SERVICES: Hot Springs (National Park).
INSPIRATION POINT OPERA FESTIVAL: June-July, Eureka Springs.
NATIONAL COTTON PICKING CONTEST: Early October, Blytheville.
NATIONAL DUCK CALLING CONTEST: Late November, Stuttgart.

California

ACADEMY AWARD PRESENTATIONS: March, Hollywood.
ALL-WESTERN BAND REVIEW: November, Long Beach.
ALMOND BLOSSOM FESTIVAL: Early March, Quartz Hill.
ANNUAL NATIONAL ORANGE SHOW: March, San Bernardino.
ANNUAL VINTAGE FESTIVAL: Last week of September, Sonoma.
APPLE SHOW: Early October, Boonville.
BACH FESTIVAL: Third week in July, Carmel.
BAND REVIEW: First Saturday in May, National City.
BENEDICTION DE LOS ANIMALES: Holy Saturday, Los Angeles (Olvera Street).
BLUE RIBBON HORSE SHOE: Mid-October, Sacramento (State Fair Grounds).
BUREAU OF MUSIC SUNDAY CONCERTS: May-June, Los Angeles.
CALIFORNIA (TRACK) RELAY: May, Modesto.
CAMELLIA SHOW: Early March, Sacramento.
CAMELLIA SHOW: Late February, San Diego.
CARROT FESTIVAL: Late April, Holtville.
CHERRY BLOSSOM FESTIVAL: Late March —early April, San Francisco (Golden Gate Park Conservatory).
CHERRY FESTIVAL: Mid-June, Beaumont.
CHICO RODEO: Mid-May, Chico.
CHILDREN'S BOOK AND ART FESTIVAL: Early October, San Diego.
CHINESE NEW YEAR: Two weeks after January 19, San Francisco (Chinatown).
CHRISTMAS PARADE: Thanksgiving, Hollywood.
CHRYSANTHEMUM SHOW: Late November, Glendale.
CINCO DE MAYO FIESTA: May 5, San Diego (Balboa Park).
CIVIC POPS CONCERTS: July, San Francisco.
CLAM FESTIVAL: January 1, Pismo Beach.
COLOSSEUM (TRACK) RELAYS: Mid-May, Los Angeles.
COLUMBUS DAY: Sunday of Columbus Day (October 12) Week, San Francisco.
COUNTRY DANCERS FESTIVAL: Late August, Healdsburg.
COUNTY FAIR: Mid-May, Angels Camp (Calaveras County).
CYMBIDIUM SHOW: March or April, Santa Barbara.
DAHLIA SHOW: Early August, San Diego.
DAHLIA SHOW: Late August, San Leandro.
DANISH DAYS: August, Solvang.
DATE FESTIVAL: Mid-February, Indio.
DE ANZA DAYS: Early May, Riverside.
DESERT CIRCUS: March or April, Palm Springs.
EASTER SUNRISE SERVICES: Hollywood Bowl.
EASTER SUNRISE SERVICES: Laguna Beach (Irvine Bowl).
EASTER SUNRISE SERVICES: Redlands (Redlands Bowl).
EASTER SUNRISE SERVICES: San Diego (Mount Helix, Mount Soledad, Balboa Hill, Presidio Hill).
FAIRFIELD-SUISUN RODEO: Mid-May, Fairfield.
FAR WEST TURKEY SHOW: November or December, Turlock.
FIESTA: May or June, San Fernando.
FIESTA: July 4, San Leandro.
FIESTA DE LA LUNA: Mid-July, San Diego County.

FIESTA DEL PACIFICO: Mid-July to mid-August, San Diego.
FISHING FIESTA: October, San Pedro.
FOLK DANCE FESTIVAL: Late June, Oakland (Woodminster Amphitheater).
FOUNDERS' FESTIVAL: Mid-October, Santa Cruz.
FRESNO FIESTA AND FAIR: Mid-August, San Mateo.
GOLD RUSH DAYS: Mid-October, Mojave.
GOLD RUSH FESTIVAL: Early June, Auburn.
GRAND NATIONAL LIVESTOCK EXPOSITION, HORSE SHOW AND RODEO: First two weeks of November, San Fransisco.
GREEK THEATER MUSIC FESTIVAL: Summer, Los Angeles.
GRUNION DERBY: July-August, Huntington Beach.
HALLOWEEN FESTIVAL: Anaheim.
HOLLYWOOD BOWL CONCERTS: July-August, Hollywood.
HORNED TOAD DERBY: Third Saturday in May, Coalinga.
IMPERIAL VALLEY FAIR: Early March, Imperial.
INTERNATIONAL DESERT CAVALCADE: Mid-March, Calexico.
KING CITY STAMPEDE AND RODEO: Late September, King City.
LAMB DERBY: May, Willows.
LA PURISIMA MISSION FIESTA: First Sunday in December, Lompoc.
LONE PINE STAMPEDE AND RODEO: Late April, Lone Pine.
LOS ANGELES COUNTY FAIR: September, Pomona.
MARINE WEEK: July, Santa Barbara.
MERCED COUNTY SPRING FAIR AND LIVESTOCK SHOW: May Day, Los Banos.
MID-WINTER (SAILPLANE) SOARING CHAMPIONSHIPS: Late February, San Diego (Torrey Pines).
MINERAL AND GEM SHOW: Mid-October, San Diego.
MISSION SAN DIEGO DE ALCANA FIESTA: Second Sunday in July, San Diego.
MISS UNIVERSE INTERNATIONAL BEAUTY PAGEANT: July, Long Beach.
MUSIC ACADEMY OF THE WEST SUMMER FESTIVAL: Santa Barbara.
MUSICAL ARTS SOCIETY FESTIVAL: June-August, La Jolla.
MUSIC FESTIVAL: June, Los Angeles.
NATIONAL DOLL SHOW: Mid-October, San Diego.
NATIONAL ORANGE SHOW: Late March, San Bernardino.
NORTHERN SACRAMENTO MUSIC FESTIVAL: Late April, Chico.
OJAI MUSIC FESTIVAL: May, Ojai.
OLD SAN RAFAEL FIESTA DAYS: Late August, San Rafael.
OLD SPANISH DAYS FIESTA: August, Santa Barbara.
ORCHID SHOW: Late March, San Diego.
PACIFIC COAST CHAMBER ORCHESTRA MUSIC FESTIVAL: June, Santa Barbara.
PAGEANT OF THE MASTERS: July or August, Laguna Beach.
PASO ROBLES FAIR: Mid-September.
PENTECOST FESTIVAL: Pentecost Sunday, San Diego.
PIONEER DAY: Mid-October, Paso Robles.
PIONEER DAY FESTIVAL: Early May, Burbank.
PIONEER FESTIVAL: Mid-June, Folsom.
PORTUGESE FIESTA: Late May, Point Loma.
RAISIN DAY: Second Saturday in October, Dinuba.

RAMONA (OUTDOORS DRAMA): Late April-May 1, Hemet.
REDLANDS BOWL CONCERTS: Summer, Redlands.
REDWOOD EMPIRE RODEO: Late June, Eureka.
RETURN OF SWALLOWS TO SAN JUAN CAPISTRANO MISSION: About St. Joseph's Day, March 19.
RIVERSIDE COUNTY DATE FESTIVAL AND CAMEL RACES: February, Indio.
RODEO: Labor Day weekend, Bishop.
RODEO: Mid-June, Salinas.
ROUGH WATER SWIM: Mid-August, La Jolla.
ST. PATRICK'S DAY: March 17, San Francisco.
SALMON DERBY, JULY OR AUGUST: Eureka (Humboldt Bay).
SAN DIEGO COUNTY FAIR: Late June-Early July, Del Mar.
SAN DIEGO SYMPHONY CONCERTS: Summer, San Diego (Balboa Park Bowl).
SAN JUAN CAPISTRANO DAY, DEPARTURE OF THE SWALLOWS: October 23 (usually), Mission San Juan Capistrano. See Return of the Swallows above.
SANTA ANITA RACETRACK SEASON: Late December—early March, Santa Anita.
SANTA MARIA RODEO: Early June.
SILVER BELT SKI RACES: Late April, Norden (Sugar Bowl).
SPRING FLOWER: Late April—early May, Oakland.
SPRING FLOWER SHOW: Mid-April, Pasadena (Brookside Park).
SPRING ROSE SHOW: Early April, San Diego.
STATE FAIR: Early September, Sacramento.
STOCKTON FAIR: Late August.
SYMPHONIES UNDER THE STARS: June-September, Hollywood Bowl.
TOURNAMENT OF ROSES: New Year's Day, Pasadena.
VINTAGE FESTIVALS: September-October, Throughout wine regions.
VISTACADO DAYS (AVACADO HARVEST): First week of June, Vista Annual Sonoma Rodeo, Sonoma.
WALNUT FESTIVAL: Late September, Walnut Creek.
WEST COAST (TRACK) RELAY: May, Fresno.
WILDFLOWER SHOW: Throughout May, Julian.
YELLOWTAIL FISHING DERBY: Mid-September, San Diego.

Colorado

ANNUAL ARKANSAS RIVER BOAT RACE: Third week of June, Salida.
ARAPAHO GLACIER CLIMB: Second Sunday in August, Boulder.
BLOSSOM FESTIVAL: Spring, Canon City.
BOYS' AND GIRLS' RODEO: Mid-August, La Junta.
CATTLEMEN'S DAYS: Third week of July, Gunnison.
CENTRAL CITY OPERA FESTIVAL: July-August.
CHUCK WAGON DINNERS: Mid-June to Labor Day, Colorado Springs (Garden of the Gods).
EASTER SUNRISE SERVICE: Colorado Springs (Garden of the Gods).
FALL COLOR WEEK: Mid-October, Grand Junction.
GOETHE FESTIVAL: June-September, Aspen (Institute for Humanistic Studies).
GOLD RUSH DAYS: Mid-July, Idaho Springs.
IMPERIAL HOTEL MELODRAMA: Late June—September, Cripple Creek.

INDIAN PAGEANT: Early August, Canon City (Camp Holy Cross).
KOSHARE INDIAN SUMMER FESTIVAL: Third week of July, La Junta.
LIPTON CUP REGATTA: Third week of August, Grand Lake.
NATIONAL WESTERN STOCK SHOW: Mid-January, Denver.
PEACH BLOSSOM SUNDAY: Late April. Grand Junction.
PERRY-MANSFIELD THEATER AND DANCE FESTIVAL: July-August, Steamboat Springs.
PIKES PEAK AUTO HILL CLIMB: First week of September, Colorado Springs.
PIKES PEAK OR BUST RODEO: Second week of August, Colorado Springs.
PIONEER DAY FESTIVAL: Second Monday in September, Florence.
PIONEER FESTIVAL: Early August, La Junta.
POW WOW AND RODEO: Last week of July, Boulder.
RED ROCKS MUSIC FESTIVAL: July-August, Denver.
ROCK CUP SKI RACES: March, Aspen.
RODEOS: July-September, state-wide.
ROYAL GORGE ROUNDUP: Second week of June, Canon City.
SANTA FE TRAIL DAYS: Early May, Las Animas.
SHAVANO DAYS: July 2-4, Salida.
SOUTHERN COLORADO MUSIC FESTIVAL: Late April or early May, Pueblo.
SPANISH TRAILS FIESTA AND RODEO: First week of August, Durango.
STATE FAIR: Late August, Pueblo.
SUMMER CONCERTS (DENVER SYMPHONY): Summer, Red Rocks.
WATERMELON DERBY: First week of September, Rocky Ford.
WESTERN COLORADO MUSIC FESTIVAL: Late April, Grand Junction.
WILD FLOWER WEEK: Late May, Grand Junction.
WINTER SPORTS CARNIVAL: Mid-February. Steamboat Springs.
YULE LOG CEREMONY: Sunday before Christmas, Palmer Lake.

Connecticut

ADLEY FAIR FARMS HORSE SHOW: July, Fairfield.
ALL-STATE MUSIC FESTIVAL: Last week in October, Hartford (Bushnell Memorial Hall).
AMERICAN DANCE FESTIVAL: Mid-August, New London (Connecticut College).
BRIDGEPORT POPS: Summer, Bridgeport.
CHRYSANTHEMUM SHOW: November, New Haven (East Rock Park).
CONNECTICUT SQUARE DANCE FESTIVAL: (Part of Farm and Home Week at Storrs.)
DANBURY FAIR: Early October.
FARM AND HOME WEEK: Second week in August, Storrs.
FLOWER SHOW: Late March, Hartford (West Hartford Armory).
HORSE SHOW: May, New Haven.
HORSE SHOW: October, Middleton.
HORSE SHOW, PROFESSIONAL HORSEMEN'S ASSOCIATION: June, Farmington.
HUNTER'S MARCH: Fall, Blue Trail Range, East Wallingford.
LONG ISLAND SOUND ANNUAL OPEN REGATTA: September, Guilford.
MIDGET AUTOMOBILE RACES: Saturday nights in June, Danbury (Fairgrounds).
MUSIC MOUNTAIN SERIES OF CONCERTS: July-August, Falls Village.

MUSIC-UNDER-THE-STARS: July-August, New Haven (Yale Bowl).
NORTHEASTERN REGIONAL SMALL BORE TOURNAMENT: July, Blue Trail Range, East Wallingford.
NUTMEG STATE CHAMPIONSHIP COON DOG FIELD TRIALS: First Sunday in November, West Cheshire.
OPEN ARCHERY TOURNAMENT: May, New Britain.
PRESIDENT'S CUP RIFLE MATCH: Late September, Blue Trail Range, East Wallingford.
SPRING SMALL BORE RIFLE CHAMPIONSHIP: Second week end in May, Blue Trail Range, East Wallingford.
STATE CHAMPIONSHIP GALLERY RIFLE TEAM MATCH: Late March, New Haven (Winchester Club House).
UKRANIAN FOLK DANCES AND GAMES: April, New Britain.
YALE-HARVARD ROWING RACE: Late spring, Derby or New London.

Delaware

ARDEN FAIR: Saturday before Labor Day.
ART EXHIBIT: May and November, Wilmington (Society of Fine Arts).
"BIG QUARTERLY" (NEGRO RELIGIOUS REVIVAL): August, Wilmington.
COUNTY (KENT AND SUSSEX) FAIR: Late July, Harrington.
DELAWARE DAY: December 7, state-wide observance.
DELAWARE FESTIVAL OF THE ARTS: May, state-wide observance.
DOG SHOW: September, Wilmington.
DOVER DAY: First Saturday in May, Dover.
FLOWER MARKET DAY: May, Wilmington.
FRIENDS OF OLD DRAWYER'S DAY: First Sunday in June, Odessa.
GREEK INDEPENDENCE DAY CELEBRATION: March, Wilmington.
HOMECOMING—LABOR DAY FESTIVAL (DELAWARE BREAKER SWIM): Lewes. Labor Day.
INTERNATIONAL EXHIBITION OF PHOTOGRAPHY: See National Salon of Photography below.
KENT AND SUSSEX COUNTIES FAIR: July, Harrington.
MIDDLE STATES AND DELAWARE STATE CLAY COURT TENNIS CHAMPIONSHIPS: Late June, Wilmington, (Du Pont Country Club).
NATIONAL SALON OF PHOTOGRAPHY: February, Wilmington (Society of Fine Arts).
OLD NEW CASTLE DAY: Third Saturday in May, New Castle.
PUBLIC AND PRIVATE SCHOOL ART EXHIBITION: Spring, Wilmington.
SUSSEX COUNTY OLD CHRISTMAS: January 6, Harrington.
SWEDISH COLONIAL DAY: March 29, Wilmington (Ft. Christiana State Park).
WATER FESTIVAL: July or August, Arden.
WILMINGTON FLOWER MARKET: May.

District of Columbia

AMERICAN FEDERATION OF ARTS CONVENTION: May.
ARMY DAY PARADE: April 6.
CHERRY BLOSSOM FESTIVAL: Spring.
EASTER EGG ROLLING: Easter Monday, White House lawn.
MEMORIAL DAY SERVICES: May 30.
PRESIDENTIAL INAUGURATION AND BALL: Usually on January 20 after November Presidential elections.
PRESIDENT'S CUP REGATTA: Usually third week end in September, Potomac River.

Florida

ALL-AMERICAN AIR MANEUVERS: Mid-January, Miami.
BACH FESTIVAL: Early March, Winter Park.
CAMELLIA AND TROPICAL FLOWER SHOW: Late March, St. Petersburg.
CAMELLIA SHOW: Mid-January, Pensacola.
CITRUS FRUIT FESTIVAL: Mid-February, Winter Haven.
CROSS DAY: January 6, Tarpon Springs.
EASTER SUNDAY SERVICES: St. Augustine (Spanish Fort).
FESTIVAL OF STATES: March or April, St. Petersburg.
GASPARILLA WEEK: February, Tampa.
GREATER MIAMI FISHING TOURNAMENT: Mid-December—mid-April.
HIALEAH RACING SEASON: January-March, Hialeah Park.
INTERNATIONAL BLACK DRUM RODEO: June-October, St. Augustine.
LATIN AMERICAN FIESTA: Mid-March, Tampa.
MIAMI BEACH POPS CONCERTS: June-Aug.
NATIONAL AMATEUR CHAMPIONSHIP MOTORCYCLE RACES: Mid-February, Daytona Beach.
NATIONAL OPEN SINGLES (SHUFFLEBOARD) TOURNAMENT: Mid-January, St. Petersburg (Headquarters).
NATIONAL SEA-TROUT DERBY: Mid-October—mid-February, St. Augustine.
ORANGE BOWL GAME: January 1, Miami.
PAGEANT OF LIGHT: Mid-February, Fort Myers.
POINCIANA FESTIVAL: May-June, Miami.
ST. PETERSBURG-HAVANA SAILING RACE: March.
SARA DE SOTO PAGEANT: Mid-February, Sarasota.
SHELL FAIR: Mid-March, Fort Myers (Sanibel Island).
SILVER SAILFISH DERBY: January 20—February 17, Palm Beach.
STATE FAIR: February, Tampa.
STOCK CAR RACING: Mid-February, Daytona Beach.
TARPON ROUNDUP: May-July, St. Petersburg.
TARPON TOURNAMENT: May-August, Sarasota.
TROPICANZA WEEK: April, Fort Lauderdale.
WATERMELON FESTIVAL: Mid-May, Leesburg.

Georgia

ATLANTA MUNICIPAL THEATER-UNDER-THE-STARS: July-August, Atlanta (Chastain Amphitheater).
HAM AND EGG SHOW: Mid-March, Fort Valley.
MASTERS (GOLF) TOURNAMENT: Early April, Augusta (National Golf Club).
OPEN HOUSE HOMES AND GARDENS TOURS: March-April, many cities.
STATE EXPOSITION: Mid-October, Macon.
ST. PATRICK'S DAY: March 17, Savannah.
TOBACCO FESTIVAL: Mid-July, Moultrie.
UNCLE REMUS FLOWER FESTIVAL: Mid-May, Atlanta (Wren's Nest).

WOMENS' TITLEHOLDERS OPEN GOLF CHAMPIONSHIP: Mid-March, Augusta (Country Club).

Idaho

AMERICAN DOG DERBY: February 22, Ashton.
AMERICAN LEGION RACES: Last week of March, Sun Valley Ski Club.
APPLE BLOSSOM FESTIVAL: First week of May, Payette.
BASQUE SHEPHERDS DANCE: Last week of December, Boise.
BORDER DAYS: July 4, Grangeville.
CHERRY FESTIVAL: Mid-June, Emmett.
EAST IDAHO STATE FAIR: Mid-September, Blackfoot.
4-H STOCK SHOW: Mid-August, Caldwell.
HARRIMAN CUP RACES: Last week of March, Sun Valley Ski Club.
LAKE PEND OREILLE FISHING DERBY: May—November, Sandpoint.
LEWISTON ROUNDUP: Week end after Labor Day.
LOG DRIVE FESTIVAL: Late May or early June, Priest River.
MUSIC WEEK: May, Boise.
PIONEERS' DAY: June 15, Franklin.
PIONEERS' DAY AND RODEO: Late July, St. Anthony.
ROUNDUP AND RODEO: Early September, Lewiston.
SHOSHONE SUN DANCE: Mid-July, Fort Hall Reservation (Pocatello).
SHOSHONE WARM DANCE: January or February, Fort Hall Reservation (Pocatello).
SNAKE RIVER STAMPEDE: Third week of July, Nampa.
SPEED DAY FESTIVAL: Early October, Shelley.
SUN VALLEY SKI TOURNAMENT (HARRIMAN CUP): Second week in March.
WAR BONNET ROUNDUP: Second week of August, Idaho Falls.
WESTERN STATE FAIR: Last week of August, Boise.

Illinois

ALL-AMERICAN GOLF TOURNAMENT: Early August, Chicago.
ALL-STAR FOOTBALL GAME: Late August, Chicago (Soldier's Field).
ALL-STAR ICE SHOW: Early February, Chicago (Stadium).
AMERICAN PASSION PLAY: Sundays in April-May, Bloomington.
AZALEA SHOW: February-March, Chicago (Garfield and Lincoln Park Conservatory).
BASKETBALL TOURNAMENT: December-March, Chicago.
BLOSSOMTIME FESTIVAL: May, Chicago, Grant Park.
BURGOO SOUP PICNIC: Early August, Winchester.
CHICAGOLAND MUSIC FESTIVAL: August, Chicago (Soldier's Field).
CHRISTMAS FLOWER SHOW: December-January, Chicago (Garfield and Lincoln Park Conservatory).
CHRYSANTHEMUM SHOW: November-December, Chicago (Garfield and Lincoln Park Conservatory).
COLLEGE ALL-STAR BASKETBALL CLASSIC: In season, Chicago.
EASTER AND SPRING FLOWER SHOW: April, Chicago (Garfield and Lincoln Park Conservatory).

FARM SPORTS FINALS FESTIVAL: Last week end in August, Champaign-Urbana (University of Illinois).
GRANT PARK OPEN-AIR SYMPHONY CONCERTS: July-August, Chicago.
GRAPE HARVEST FESTIVAL: Mid-September, Nauvoo.
HALLOWEEN MARDI GRAS: Pinckneyville.
HARVEST MOON DANCE FESTIVAL: Third Saturday in November, Chicago (Stadium).
HOG DAYS: September, Kewanee.
INTERNATIONAL KENNEL CLUB SHOW: Late March, Chicago.
INTERNATIONAL LIVESTOCK EXHIBITION: November or December, Chicago (International Amphitheater).
INTERNATIONAL PHOTOGRAPHY SHOW: February, Chicago (Historical Society).
INTERNATIONAL TRAVEL EXPOSITION: April, Chicago.
MILK DAY: Second Tuesday in June, Harvard.
NATIONAL CHAMPIONSHIP TOURIST TROPHY MOTORCYCLE RACES: Early September, Peoria.
NATIONAL FARM SHOW: Concurrent with International Livestock Exhibition, Chicago.
PANCAKE FESTIVAL: Third Wednesday in September, Villa Grove.
PASSION PLAY: Sundays in April-June, Zion.
PEACH FESTIVAL: Early August, Centralia.
PEACH FESTIVAL: August, Metropolis.
PET PARADE: First Saturday in June, La Grange.
PRIME BEEF FESTIVAL: September, Monmouth.
PUMPKIN FESTIVAL: Last week end in September, Eureka.
SAUERKRAUT DAY: Third Thursday in September, Forreston.
SOUTH CENTRAL DAIRY DAY AND FAIR: August, Ritchfield.
SPORTSMEN'S BOAT AND VACATION SHOW: April, Chicago (International Amphitheater).
SQUARE DANCE FESTIVAL: Summer, Chicago (Congress Street Plaza).
STATE FAIR: Mid-August, Springfield.
SUMMER FLOWER SHOW: July-August, Chicago (Garfield and Lincoln Park Conservatory).
SWIM FESTIVAL: Summer, Chicago.
TOURNAMENT OF (BOXING) CHAMPIONS: March, Chicago (Chicago Stadium).
WHEATFIELD PLOWING MATCHES: Second Saturday in September, Plainfield.
WOMEN'S BOWLING TOURNAMENT: January-March, Chicago.

Indiana

CHRISTMAS CAROL FESTIVAL: Week before Christmas, Indianapolis (Soldiers and Sailors Monument).
CORPUS CHRISTI PROCESSION: Oldenburg.
EASTER SUNRISE SERVICES: Indianapolis (Soldiers and Sailors Monument).
GOLDEN RAIN TREE FESTIVAL: Late July, New Harmony.
INDIANAPOLIS AUTOMOBILE SPEED CLASSIC: Memorial Day, Indianapolis Motor Speedway.
INTERNATIONAL DAIRY EXPOSITION: October, Indianapolis (State Fair Grounds).
INTERNATIONAL FRIENDSHIP GARDENS CONCERTS: July-August, Michigan City.
PERSIMMON FESTIVAL: Early October, Mitchell.
PUMPKIN SHOW: September-October, Versailles.

SEVEN SORROWS OF MARY PROCESSION:
Mid-September, Oldenburg.
STATE FAIR: Early September, Indianapolis
(State Fair Grounds).

Iowa

ALL-IOWA FAIR: Third week in August,
Cedar Rapids (Hawkeye Downs).
CENTRAL IOWA FAIR: Mid-September, Mar-
shalltown.
CLAY COUNTRY FAIR: Early September,
Spencer.
DAIRY CATTLE CONGRESS: Early October,
Waterloo.
DRAKE (TRACK AND FIELD) RELAYS:
Last week end in April, Des Moines.
EASTERN IOWA BAND FESTIVAL: Mid-
May, Cedar Rapids.
HOBO PARADE: Late August, Britt.
IOWA STATE SPRING MARKET HOG SHOW:
Early March, Cedar Rapids.
LITTLE MIDWEST HORTICULTURAL EXHI-
BITION: Mid-November, Ames.
MESQUAKIE INDIAN POW-WOW AND IN-
TERTRIBAL CEREMONIAL: Late August,
Tama.
MISSISSIPPI VALLEY FAIR: Mid-August,
Davenport.
NATIONAL STALLION AND SADDLE
HORSE SHOW: Mid-August, Creston.
NORTHEAST IOWA BAND JUBILEE: Late
June, Waterloo.
NORTH IOWA BAND FESTIVAL: Early June,
Mason City.
PEONY TRAIL DAYS: Early June, Dubuque.
RODEO: Mid-August, Sidney.
STATE FAIR: Late August, Des Moines.
TULIP FESTIVAL: Mid-May, Orange City.
TULIP FESTIVAL: Mid-May, Pella.
VEISHEA: Mid-May, Ames (Iowa State Col-
lege).

Kansas

CENTRAL KANSAS FREE FAIR: Late Au-
gust, Abilene.
FIESTA: Late July, Kansas City (Armour-
dale).
FREE FAIR: Second week in September,
Topeka.
GREAT SOUTHWEST FREE FAIR: Early Sep-
tember, Dodge City.
HOLY CITY CANTATA: Palm Sunday, Fort
Scott.
KANSAS DAY: January 29, state-wide ob-
servance.
KANSAS (TRACK AND FIELD) RELAYS:
Mid-April, Lawrence.
NATIONAL 4-H CLUB FAT STOCK FAIR
AND HORSE SHOW: Early October, Wichita.
NATIONAL (GREYHOUND) COURSING AS-
SOCIATION MEET: Mid-October, Abilene.
NEEWOLLAH: Halloween, Independence.
NORTH CENTRAL KANSAS FREE FAIR:
Late August-September, Belleville.
PEACE TREATY PAGEANT: Early October
at five-year intervals, Medicine Lodge.
STATE FAIR: Third week in September,
Hutchinson.
WHEAT BELT EASTER FESTIVAL: Holy
Week, Lindsborg (Bethany College).

Kentucky

AMERICAN FOLK SONG FESTIVAL: Second
Sunday in June, Ashland (Traipsin Woman
Cabin, Mayo Trail).

AUTUMN SONG FESTIVAL: Second Sunday
in October, Pikeville.
BLUE GRASS STAKES: Last Sunday of April
spring season, Lexington (Keeneland).
BREEDER'S FUTURITY: Close of October fall
season, Lexington (Keeneland).
FAT CATTLE SHOW: Early November, Louis-
ville.
HOMECOMING WEEK END: August full-moon,
London.
JUNIOR LEAGUE HORSE SHOW: Second
week in July, Lexington.
KENTUCKY DERBY: First Saturday in May,
Louisville (Churchill Downs).
LAUREL FESTIVAL: Late May, Pineville.
OLD SOUTHERN HARMONY FESTIVAL:
Fourth Sunday in May, Benton.
STATE FAIR: Early September, Louisville.
STATE HIGH SCHOOL MUSIC FESTIVAL:
Spring, Lexington (University of Kentucky)
and Bowling Green (Western State College).
TENNESSEE VALLEY HO! CRUISE: June,
Paducah.
TOBACCO FESTIVAL: Late October, Shelby-
ville.
WESTERN KENTUCKY FAIR: Third week in
July, Paducah.

Louisiana

ALL SAINTS' DAY: November 1, New Orleans.
BLESSING OF THE SHRIMP BOATS: Early
August, Morgan City.
CRESCENT CITY CONCERT ASSOCIATION:
June-July, New Orleans.
DOLL AND TOY FUND DISTRIBUTION:
Christmas, New Orleans.
FIESTA: Spring, New Orleans.
INTERNATIONAL RICE FESTIVAL: Late
October, Crowley.
MARDI GRAS: Shrove Tuesday, New Orleans.
PAN AMERICAN (MOTOR BOAT) REGATTA:
Mid-May, New Orleans.
PIROGUE DERBY: Mid-May, Lafitte.
ST. AMICO'S PILGRIMAGE: Sunday after
Easter, Donaldson.
STATE FAIR: Late October, Shreveport.
SUGAR BOWL FOOTBALL GAME: January 1,
New Orleans.
SUGAR CANE FESTIVAL: Early October,
New Iberia.
TARPON RODEO: Late August, Southwest
Pass (Mississippi Delta).
TRI-STATE SINGING CONVENTION: Late
April, Shreveport.
YAMBILEE: Mid-October, Opelousas.

Maine

ARUNDEL OPERA THEATER: July-Septem-
ber, Kennebunkport.
BANGOR-CARIBOU SKI RACE: February.
COMMUNITY CONCERT: November, Port-
land.
MAINE BROILER DAY FESTIVAL: Early
July, Belfast.
MAINE LOBSTER AND SEAFOOD FESTIVAL:
First week in August, Rockland.
NORTHERN MAINE FAIR: July, Presque Isle.
POTATO BLOSSOM FESTIVAL: July-August,
Fort Fairfield.
SKOWHEGAN FAIR: Third week in August,
Skowhegan.
STATE FAIR: September, Lewiston.
STATE OF MAINE TUNA TOURNAMENT:
Second week in August, Boothbay Harbor.
WINTER CARNIVAL AND SPORTSMEN's
SHOW: March, Presque Isle.

WINTER CARNIVAL: February, Camden.
WINTER CARNIVAL: February, Rumford.
WINTER SPORTS CARNIVAL: January, Fryeburg.

Maryland

ANTIETAM MEMORIAL DAY EXERCISES: May 30, Hagerstown.
ART AND INDUSTRIAL FAIR: September, Crisfield.
ART EXHIBITION: March or April, Museum of Art, Baltimore.
DOG SHOW: Hagerstown, September.
DUTCH PICNIC: First Saturday in August, Reisterstown.
EASTERN NATIONAL LIVESTOCK SHOW: Early November, Baltimore (Timonium State Fair Grounds).
FISHING FAIR: Mid-September, Chesaspeake Bay.
FLOWER MART: Second Wednesday in May, Baltimore (Washington Monument, Mt. Vernon Square).
GIBSON ISLAND SUMMER CARNIVAL: July, Baltimore.
GRAND NATIONAL: Third or fourth Saturday in April, Butler.
HAGERSTOWN FAIR: September.
HALLOWEEN PARADE: Easton.
HORSE SHOW: Hagerstown, September.
HOUSE AND GARDEN PILGRIMAGE: Late April, wide observance.
JUNE WEEK: Early June, U.S. Naval Academy, Annapolis.
LONG GREEN HORSE SHOW AND CARNIVAL: August, Hyde.
MARYLAND HUNT CLUB STEEPLECHASE: Last Saturday in April, Worthington Valley (Shawan).
MARYLAND REVOLVER AND PISTOL CHAMPIONSHIPS: First week end in June, Sparrows Point.
MUMMERS' PARADE: October 31, Hagerstown.
MY LADY'S MANOR STEEPLECHASE: Second or third Saturday in April, Monkton.
PREAKNESS STAKES: Second or third Saturday in May, Baltimore (Pimlico).
STATE FAIR: Early September, Baltimore (Timonium State Fair Grounds).

Massachusetts

APPLE BLOSSOM FESTIVAL: Early May, Nashota Valley.
BASS DERBY: September 15—October 15, Martha's Vineyard.
BERKSHIRE MUSIC FESTIVAL: July, Tanglewood.
BLESSING OF THE FLEET: Feast of Corpus Christi, Gloucester.
BLESSING OF THE FLEET: Feast of St. Peter (June 29), Gloucester.
BOSTON ATHLETIC ASSOCIATION MARATHON: Patriot's Day (April 19), Boston.
BOSTON PUBLIC GARDENS ARTS FESTIVAL: June.
BRANDEIS FESTIVAL OF CREATIVE ARTS: June, Waltham (Brandeis University).
BUNKER HILL DAY CELEBRATION AND PARADE: June 17, Charlestown.
CASTLE HILL JAZZ CONCERTS: July-August, Ipswich.
CASTLE HILL MUSIC FESTIVAL: July-August, Ipswich.
CHERRY BLOSSOM TIME: Late April, Arnold Arboretum, Boston.

COONAMESSET MUSIC SOCIETY FESTIVAL: September, Falmouth.
COUNTRY DANCE SOCIETY FESTIVAL: August, Pinewood.
CRAB APPLE SUNDAY: Early May, Arnold Arboretum, Boston.
DANCE FESTIVAL: Fridays and Saturdays in summer, Jacob's Pillow (Ted Shawn, director), East Lee.
EASTERN DOG SHOW: February, Boston.
EASTERN STATES EXPOSITION: September, Springfield.
ESPLANADE CONCERTS: July-August, Boston (Hatch Memorial Shell).
FAIR: September, Brockton.
FISHERMEN'S MEMORIAL DAY: Sunday in August, Gloucester.
FOREFATHERS' DAY (ANNIVERSARY OF THE PILGRIM FATHER'S LANDING): December 21, Plymouth.
GARDEN WEEK: Fourth week in May, statewide observance.
JACOB'S PILLOW DANCE FESTIVAL: July-August, Lee.
KNIGHTS OF COLUMBUS TRACK AND FIELD MEET: January, Boston.
LAUREL FESTIVAL: June, Westfield.
LENOX JAZZ FESTIVAL: July-August, Lenox.
LILAC SUNDAY: Third week in May (usually), Arnold Arboretum, Boston.
NEW ENGLAND ANTIQUES EXPOSITION: April, Boston.
NEW ENGLAND FOLK FESTIVAL: November, Boston (Y.W.C.A.).
OPENING OF BOSTON SYMPHONY "POPS" CONCERTS: May, Boston.
PATRIOTS' DAY IN MASSACHUSETTS: April 19, state-wide observation.
PLYMOUTH ROCK CENTER OF MUSIC AND DRAMA FESTIVAL: July-September, Duxbury.
PLYMOUTH ROCK FESTIVAL: Summer Saturdays, Plymouth.
PRO MUSIC ANTIQUA OF NEW YORK FESTIVAL: August, Lenox.
PROVINCETOWN ART ASSOCIATION BALL: Third week in August, Provincetown.
PROVINCETOWN COSTUME BALL: Third week in July.
RACE WEEK (YACHTS): August, Marblehead.
REVOLUTIONARY PAGEANT: April 19, Lexington.
ST. PATRICK'S DAY PARADE: March 17, Boston.
ST. PETER FIESTA: June, Gloucester.
SOUTH MOUNTAIN CHAMBER MUSIC FESTIVAL: August, Pittsfield.
SPORTSMEN'S AND BOAT SHOW: First two weeks of February, Boston.
SPRING FLOWER SHOW: Third week in March, Boston.
WAGNER CONCERTS: January, Springfield.
WORCHESTER MUSIC FESTIVAL: Last week in October.
WORCHESTER TELEGRAM-GAZETTE ANNUAL BOOK REVIEWER'S COCKTAIL PARTY: Spring, Worcester.

Michigan

ANN ARBOR MAY MUSIC FESTIVAL: Early May, Ann Arbor.
BIRLING CHAMPIONSHIP: Early July, Gladstone.
CHERRY BLOSSOM BLESSING: May, Bowers Harbor.
GOLD CUP MOTOR BOAT RACE: July, Detroit.

HARMSWORTH INTERNATIONAL MOTOR-
BOAT RACE (BRITISH INTERNATIONAL
TROPHY): Challenge event, date variable,
Detroit.
MAPLE SYRUP FESTIVAL: April, Vermont-
ville.
MICHIGAN CANOE CHAMPIONSHIP: Mid-
September, Au Sable River (Grayling to
Oscoda).
MICHIGAN SHUFFLEBOAT CHAMPION-
SHIP: Early July, Traverse City.
NATIONAL CHERRY FESTIVAL: June or
July, Traverse City.
NATIONAL SHUFFLEBOAT CHAMPION-
SHIP: Mid-July, Traverse City.
PERCH FESTIVAL: Early May, Tawas.
PLANTERS' SHOW: Early November, Petoskey.
RED FLANNEL FESTIVAL: November, Cedar
Springs.
SILVER CUP REGATTA: Late summer,
Detroit.
SKI TOURNAMENT: Last week end in Febru-
ary, Iron Mountain (Pine Mountain Ski
Slide).
SPORTS AND FOREST FESTIVAL: Late July,
Manister.
SPORTSMEN'S AND VACATION SHOW:
Early April, Detroit (Fair Grounds).
STATE FAIR: Labor Day week, Detroit.
TROUT FESTIVAL: April, Kalkaska.
TULIP TIME: Mid-May, Holland.
WINTER CARNIVAL: Week end before Wash-
ington's Birthday, Ishpeming.

Minnesota

AQUATENNIAL: Late July, Minneapolis.
BOX CAR DAYS: Labor Day, Tracy.
BUTTER DAYS FESTIVAL: Early June, Sauk
Center.
CANOE DERBY: Mid-July, Bemidji-Minne-
apolis.
CHIPPEWA POW-WOW AND FESTIVAL:
Mid-June, White Earth.
FESTIVAL OF NATIONS: Usually late May at
2-3 year intervals, St. Paul.
FIESTA: Late July, Montevideo.
FLOWER SHOW: Late August, Duluth.
FOLK DANCE FESTIVAL: Late January,
Duluth.
FOREST FESTIVAL: Late September, Inter-
national Falls.
MIDSUMMER FESTIVAL: Sunday closest to
June 24, Duluth.
POPS CONCERTS: July-September, St. Paul.
SAUERKRAUT DAY FESTIVAL: Early Sep-
tember, Springfield.
STATE FAIR: Early September, St. Paul.
WINTER CARNIVAL: Third week end in
January, St. James.
WINTER CARNIVAL: Early February, St.
Paul.
WINTER CARNIVAL: Early February, Winona.

Mississippi

BLESSING OF THE SHRIMP BOATS: Early
August, Biloxi.
HOLLY SPRINGS PILGRIMAGE: Late April,
Holly Springs.
HOUSE AND GARDEN TOUR: March-April,
Natchez.
MARDI GRAS: Shrove Tuesday, Biloxi.
MISSISSIPPI AGRICULTURAL AND INDUS-
TRIAL EXPOSITION: Mid-October, Jack-
son.
U.S. FIELD TRIAL: Mid-February, Hernando.

Missouri

AMERICAN ROYAL LIVESTOCK AND
HORSE SHOW: Third week in October,
Kansas City.
APPLE BLOSSOM FESTIVAL: Early May,
St. Joseph.
BICYCLE RACE: Third Sunday in Septem-
ber, St. Louis (Forest Park).
CHRYSANTHEMUM SHOW: November, St.
Louis (Missouri Botanical Gardens).
FUTURE FARMERS OF AMERICA: October
or November, Kansas City.
NATIONAL FOLK FESTIVAL: Early April,
St. Louis.
RIVER FESTIVAL: Mid-August, Louisiana.
ROSE GARDEN PILGRIMAGE: Late May,
Cape Girardeau.
STATE FAIR: Late August, Sedalia.
SUMMER OPERA FESTIVAL: June-Septem-
ber, St. Louis (Forest Park).
THANKSGIVING DAY MUSIC FESTIVAL:
St. Louis (Forest Park).
VEILED PROPHET PARADE AND FESTI-
VAL: First Tuesday after first Monday in
October, St. Louis.

Montana

ASSINIBORNE SUN DANCE: July, Fort Bel-
knap.
BLACKFELT MEDICINE LODGE: Late June
(usually), Browning.
CROW TRIBAL FAIR AND POW-WOW:
August, Crow Agency.
DAYS OF '49 CELEBRATION AND RODEO:
Around July 4, Roundup.
FESTIVAL OF NATIONS: Mid-August, Red
Lodge.
FLATHEADS' POW WOW: Around July 4,
Arlee.
HARVEST FESTIVAL AND CANADIAN
DAYS: Early October, Sidney.
HOME OF CHAMPIONS ANNUAL RODEO:
Around July 4, Red Lodge.
HOMESTEADERS' DAYS AND RODEO: Sec-
ond week of June, Hot Springs.
MIDLAND EMPIRE FAIR AND RODEO: Mid-
August, Billings.
MIDSUMMER FIESTA: Late June—Early July,
Helena.
MONTANA INSTITUTE OF THE ARTS
FESTIVAL: Second week of June, Virginia
City.
MONTANA SOLO AND SMALL ENSEMBLE
FESTIVAL: May, Missoula.
MUSIC FESTIVAL: Early May, Havre.
NATIONAL FRESH WATER TROUT DERBY:
Second Sunday in August, Livingston (Yel-
lowstone River).
NORTHERN CHEYENNE SUN DANCE: June,
Lame Deer.
NORTH MONTANA STATE FAIR AND
RODEO (QUEEN OF MONTANA CON-
TEST): Second week of August, Great Falls.
POTATO AND SEED SHOW: Early February,
Kalispell.
RODEO: Early June, Billings.
RODEOS: June-September, state-wide.
ROUNDUP AND RANGE RIDERS REUNION:
Last week of June (usually), Miles City.
STATE FAIR: Early August, Great Falls.
STATE SQUARE DANCE FESTIVAL: Mid-
June, Kalispell.
VIGILANTE PARADE: Early May, Helena.
WILD HORSE STAMPEDE: Mid-July, Wolf
Point.

Nebraska

AK-SAR-BEN BALL: Late October, Omaha.
AK-SAR-BEN-FESTIVAL: May-July, Omaha.
CAMP CLARKE DAYS: Mid-May, Bridgeport.
FOLK DANCE FESTIVAL: Saturday after Easter, Lincoln.
HARVEST OF HARMONY: Mid-October, Grand Island.
KING KORN KARNIVAL: Mid-September, Plattsmouth.
NATIONAL ALBINO HORSE SHOW: Early June, Naper.
NATIONAL PLOW TERRACE BUILDING CONTEST: August or September, locality varies.
OREGON TRAIL DAYS: Mid-July, Gering.
POPCORN DAYS: Late September, North Loop.
STATE FAIR: Early September, Lincoln.
STOCK SHOW AND RODEO: Early October, Omaha.

Nevada

ANNUAL FAIR AND RACE MEET: September, Elko.
HELLDORADO: May, Las Vegas.
LABOR DAY CELEBRATION: Reno.
LABOR DAY RODEO: Winnemucca.
NEVADA DAY CELEBRATION: October 31, Carson City.
PONY EXPRESS, HORSE SHOW AND RACE CELEBRATION: August, Ely.
RODEO: July 4, Reno.
SILVER STATE STAMPEDE: June, Elko.
STAMPEDE AND 49er SHOW: September, Fallon.
WINTER SPORTS: Ely (Murry Summit).

New Hampshire

DARTMOUTH WINTER CARNIVAL: Early February.
EASTERN SLOPE MUSIC FESTIVAL: Last week end in August, White Mountains.
FAIR: August, Pittsfield.
FAIR: September, Rochester.
FAIR: October, Sandwich.
FALL FOLIAGE FESTIVAL: Second week in October, Warner.
NEW ENGLAND GYPSY TOUR (MOTORCYCLE ROAD RACE): Third week end in June, Laconia.
THE OLD HOMESTEAD (by Denham Thompson): July, Swazey Center (Potash Bowl).
OLD HOME WEEK: Last week in August.
RODEO: September, Keene.
SEVEN ARTS FESTIVAL: July, Pike.
U.S. AMATEUR SKI ASSOCIATION JUMPING, CROSS-COUNTRY AND COMBINED CHAMPIONSHIPS: March, Winnipesaukee.
U.S. EASTERN SKI JUMPING AND CROSS-COUNTRY MEET: February, Hilford.
U.S. SLALOM AND DOWNHILL CHAMPIONSHIPS, CANNON MOUNTAIN: April, Franconia.
WHITE MOUNTAIN ART SHOW: August, Littleton.
WHITE MOUNTAIN SEVEN ARTS FESTIVAL: Second week in July, Pike.

New Jersey

AGRICULTURE SHOW: January, Trenton.
ART FESTIVAL: Second Saturday in May, Plainfield.

ATLANTIC CITY GARDEN PIER SYMPHONIES: July-September.
BABY PARADE: Late August, Asbury Park.
BABY PARADE: Mid-August, Ocean City.
CAMDEN COUNTY KENNEL CLUB DOG SHOW: November, Camden.
EASTERN STATES SKEET MEET: January, Morristown.
FEAST OF OUR LADY OF MOUNT CARMEL: Late July, Hammonton.
FESTIVAL OF ROSES: June, Newark.
FITE MEMORIAL MARATHON (SPEEDBOAT) RACE: Memorial Day, Ocean City.
HYDRANGEA FESTIVAL: Early July, Atlantic City.
ICE CARNIVAL: January, Morristown.
KUGLER-ANDERSON MEMORIAL (BICYCLE) RACE: Memorial Day, Somerville.
MARDI GRAS: Halloween, Vineland.
MISS AMERICA CONTEST: Week after Labor Day, Atlantic City.
MORRIS AND ESSEX COUNTY KENNEL CLUB SHOW: Saturday before Memorial Day, Madison.
MORRIS COUNTY FAIR: Late August, Morristown.
MRS. AMERICA CONTEST: Week after Labor Day, Asbury Park.
MUSIC FESTIVAL: August, Ventnor.
NATIONAL MARBLES TOURNAMENT: Late June, Asbury Park.
NATIONAL SWEEPSTAKES (SPEEDBOAT) REGATTA: Mid-August, Red Bank.
OCEAN CITY SAILBOT RACE: Early August.
SAILING OF OYSTER FLEET: September, Port Norris.
SALON OF PHOTOGRAPHY SHOW: March, Hackensack.
SCOTTISH GAMES: September, Holmdel (Brookdale Farm).
STATE FAIR: Last full week in September, Trenton.
THANKSGIVING DAY PARADE: Newark.

New Mexico

ANNUAL ASPENCADE: October 11, Ruidoso.
ANNUAL ELKS RODEO: Late May, Carlsbad.
ANNUAL FESTIVAL AND CEREMONIAL DANCES: June 24, San Juan Pueblo.
ANNUAL FIESTA: September 3-5, Santa Fe.
ANNUAL FIESTA AND HARVEST CORN DANCE: November 12, Jemez Pueblo.
ASPEN WEEK: Early October, Santa Fe.
BUFFALO OR DEW DANCE: January 1, Taos Indian Festival.
CANDLEMAS DAY CEREMONIAL DANCES: February 2, San Felipe, Cochiti, Santo Domingo Indian pueblos.
CEREMONIAL DANCE: Mid-March, Laguna Pueblo.
CHISHOLM TRAIL ROUNDUP: Last week of September, Artesia.
CITY OF BETHLEHEM CHRISTMAS PANORAMA: December 18-31, Climax Canyon (Raton).
CORN DANCE AND CEREMONIAL RACES: May 3, Taos Pueblo.
COWBOY REUNION RODEO: Early August, Las Vegas.
EASTERN NEW MEXICO STATE FAIR: September 13-17, Roswell.
FEASTDAY OF ST. PHILIP NERI (SAN FELIPE DE NERI): Sunday after May 26, Albuquerque.
FEAST OF CORPUS CHRISTI: First week of June, Sante Fe and Taos.

FIESTA AND CORN DANCE: July 14, Cochiti Indian Pueblo.
FIESTA AND DEVIL DANCE: July 2-4, Mescalero Apache Reservation.
HARVEST DANCE: Mid-September, San Ildefonso Pueblo.
INDIAN HORSE SHOW: Mid-August, Santa Fe.
INTER-TRIBAL INDIAN CEREMONIAL: Mid-August, Gallup.
JAILBREAK OF BILLY THE KID: July 19, Lincoln.
LAS CRUCES PILGRIMAGE BY TORTUGAS INDIANS: December 10-12, Las Cruces.
LINCOLN COUNTY PAGEANT: Early August, Lincoln.
NAVAJO "YEI-BE-CHI" AND FIRE DANCE: After first frost, Navajo Reservation.
OLD PECOS DANCE: Early August, Jemez Pueblo.
PASSION PLAY: Good Friday, Taos (Penitente Chapel).
PLAY DAY: Mid-April, Alamogordo (White Sands National Monument).
PROCESSION OF LOS CONQUISTADORES: Week after Feast of Corpus Christi, Santa Fe.
RODEO: Around July 4, Grants.
RODEO DE SANTA FE: July 14-17, Santa Fe.
ST. JAMES DAY FIESTA AND HARVEST CORN DANCE: November 12, Tesque.
SAN GERONIMO SUNDOWN DANCE: September 29-30, Taos Pueblo.
SAN ISIDRO FIESTA: Mid-May, Taos.
SANTA FE FIESTA: Early September.
"SHALAKO" CERMONIES AND HOUSE DANCES: Late November or early December, Zuni Pueblo.
SOUTHWESTERN CATTLE FESTIVAL: October 16-20, Clovis.
SPRING CORN DANCE: Easter Sunday and following, Cochiti, San Felipe, Santo Domingo pueblos (between Albuquerque and Santa Fe).
STATE FAIR: Late September, Albuquerque.
TAOS (TALPI) PASSION PLAY: Good Friday (Penitente Chapel).
TOWN FIESTA: September 28-29, Taos.
TRI-STATE FAIR AND FESTIVAL: October 7-8, Deming.
TRUTH OR CONSEQUENCES ANNUAL FIESTA (RALPH EDWARDS): April 15-17; place varies.

New York

ALBANY KENNEL CLUB DOG SHOW: December, Albany.
AMERICAN CHAMBER OPERA SOCIETY FESTIVAL: June, Katonah.
APPLE BLOSSOM FESTIVAL: May, Brockport.
BELMONT STAKES: Second week in June, Belmont, Long Island.
BIG FISH CONTEST: April-September, Albany.
BOYS' and GIRLS' BOOK FAIR: Late November, Museum of Natural History, New York City.
BUFFALO CIVIC ORCHESTRA SUMMER PARK CONCERTS.
BUFFALO PHILHARMONIC POPS CONCERTS: Tuesdays in July (Kleinhans Hall).
CHAMBER MUSIC FESTIVAL: August, Southampton, Long Island (Parrish Museum).
CHAUTAUQUA INSTITUTION MUSIC FESTIVAL: July-August, Chautauqua.
CHRISTMAS WEEK FLOWER SHOW: Rochester (Lamberton Conservatory).
CHRYSANTHEMUM SHOW: November, Rochester (Lamberton Conservatory).
COLUMBUS DAY PARADE: October 12, Fifth Avenue, New York City.

COUNTY FAIR: August, Gouverneur.
DAIRYLAND FESTIVAL: Late June, Watertown.
EASTERN INTERNATIONAL GLADIOLUS SHOW: Third Tuesday and Wednesday in August, Binghampton.
EASTERN STATES ROLLER SKATING CHAMPIONSHIPS: June, Brooklyn.
EASTERN STATES SPEED SKATING CHAMPIONSHIP: Late January, Saratoga Springs.
EASTER PARADE: Easter Sunday, Fifth Avenue, New York City.
EISTEDDFOD AND WELSH DAY: Early May, Utica.
EMPIRE STATE MUSIC FESTIVAL: July and August, Ellenville.
FAIR: September, Mineola, Long Island.
FEAST OF SAN GENNARO: Third week in September, Mulberry Street, New York City.
FESTIVAL OF AMERICAN MUSIC: May, Rochester (Eastman School of Music).
GOLDEN GLOVES AMATEUR BOXING TOURNAMENTS: Late February, Madison Square Garden, New York City.
GUGGENHEIM MEMORIAL CONCERTS: Summer, New York City (Central Park, Manhattan, and Prospect Park, Brooklyn).
GUILD HALL FRIENDS OF MUSIC FESTIVAL: August, East Hampton, Long Island.
HAMBLETONIAN STAKES: Early August, Goshen.
HARMONY HILL MUSIC CENTER FESTIVAL OF MODERN MUSIC: Summer, Woodstock.
HARNESS RACING: September, Saratoga Springs.
HARVEST MOON BALL: Mid-September, Madison Square Garden, New York City.
HARWOOD (MOTORBOAT) TROPHY RACE: Early September, around Manhattan Island.
INDIAN COUNCIL FIRE: September, Lake Placid.
INTERNATIONAL FLOWER SHOW: Late March, New York Coliseum, New York City.
IRISH FEIS: Early June, Fordham University Campus, Bronx, New York.
LILAC FESTIVAL.: Late May, Rochester (Highland Park).
MARDI GRAS: September, Coney Island.
MEN'S NATIONAL SINGLES TENNIS CHAMPIONSHIPS: Late August-September, Forest Hills.
MIDDLE ATLANTIC OUTDOOR SPEED SKATING CHAMPIONSHIPS: Mid-July, Newburgh (Rrecreation Park).
MORMON PAGEANT: Third week in August, Palmyra (Hill Cymorah).
NATIONAL HORSE SHOW: Early November, Madison Square Garden, New York City.
NATIONAL MOTOR BOAT SHOW: Early January, New York Coliseum, New York City.
NATIONAL MUZZLE LOADING RIFLE SHOOT: Late September, Fort Ticonderoga.
NATIONAL PUBLISHERS' (BOOK AWARD) WEEK: March, New York City.
NAUMBURG CONCERTS: May-June, New York City (Central Park).
NEW YORK STATE OUTBOARD MOTORBOAT CHAMPIONSHIP: July, Geneva.
NORTHEASTERN STATES SOARING (GLIDER) CONTEST: Early July, Elmira.
OLUF MIKKELSEN (MOTORBOAT) TROPHY: Mid-June, Hudson River between Albany and New York City.
OUTBOARD MOTOR MARATHON: May, Albany to New York.
PAGEANT OF THE FEAST OF THE GREEN CORN: August, Ticonderoga.
RACE (SAILBOAT) WEEK: Late July, Larchmont and Long Island.

REGIMENTAL PARADES: 4:30 p. m., Mondays and Tuesdays, September-October, U.S. Military Academy, West Point.
RODEO: October-November, Madison Square Garden, New York City.
ROSE FESTIVAL: Late June, Newark.
SAD VAIL ROWING REGATTA: Mid-May, Poughkeepsie.
ST. PATRICK'S DAY PARADE: March 17, Fifth Avenue, New York City.
SIDEWALK (ART) EXHIBITION: May-June, September-October, Greenwich Village, New York City.
SILVER SKATES CONTEST: Second week in January, Madison Square Garden, New York City.
SPORTSMEN'S SHOW: Late March, Buffalo.
SPORTSMEN'S SHOW: Late February, New York Coliseum, New York City.
STADIUM CONCERTS: Summer evenings, Lewisohn Stadium, New York City.
STATE FAIR: Early September, Syracuse.
THANKSGIVING DAY PARADE: Broadway, New York City.
U.S. AMATEUR ROLLER SKATING CHAMPIONSHIPS: June, New York.
WASHINGTON SQUARE SUMMER CONCERTS: August, New York City.
WESTCHESTER MUSIC FESTIVAL: April, White Plains (County Center).
WESTMINSTER KENNEL CLUB SHOW: Second week in February, Madison Square Garden, New York City.
WINTER CARNIVAL: February, Cooperstown.
WINTER CARNIVAL: Christmas Week, Lake Placid.
WINTER CARNIVAL: January-March, Saranac Lake.
WINTER CARNIVAL: Early February, Syracuse University.
WINTER CARNIVAL AND INVITATION SKI MEET: February, Watertown.
WITHERS: Mid-May, Belmont, Long Island.

North Carolina

APPLE FESTIVAL: Early September, Hendersonville.
BREVARD FESTIVAL: August, Brevard (Transylvania Music Camp).
CHEROKEE FAIR: Early October, Cherokee.
EASTERN CAROLINA SINGING CONVENTION: Third Sunday in May, Wilson.
EASTER SUNRISE SERVICES: Winston-Salem (Old Home Moravian Church, Salem Square).
FESTIVAL OF ARTS: Mid-October, Asheville.
FOX HUNTING BARBECUE: Mid-October, Sedgefield.
GARDEN TOURS: April-May, many cities.
GOURD VILLAGE GARDEN FESTIVAL: Late September, Cary.
INTERNATIONAL MOTH BOAT REGATTA: Mid-October, Elizabeth City.
THE LOST COLONY: Late June—Labor Day, Waterside Theater, Fort Raleigh (near Manteo, Roanoke Island).
MORAVIAN MUSIC FESTIVAL: June, Winston-Salem (Salem College).
MOUNTAIN DANCE AND FOLK FESTIVAL: Early August, Asheville.
NATIONAL ART EXHIBIT: Late July, Hendersonville (Huckleberry Mountain Workshop-Camp).
STATE SINGING CONVENTION: Fourth Sunday in June, Benson.
TOBACCO FESTIVAL: August, Witeville.
TRANSYLVANIA MUSIC CAMP: June-July, Brevard.

TRI-STATE SINGING CONTEST (SINGING ON THE MOUNTAIN): Fourth Sunday in June, Linville.

North Dakota

CARNEY SONG CONTEST: February 22, Grand Forks (University of North Dakota).
STATE FAIR: Late July, Minot.
UPPER MISSOURI BAND FESTIVAL: Late May, Williston.

Ohio

ALL-AMERICAN SOAP BOX DERBY: Second Sunday in August, Akron (Derby Downs).
BALDWIN WALLACE BACH FESTIVAL: May, Berea.
FARMERS' WEEK: Late March, Columbus (Ohio State University).
GRAND AMERICAN TRAP SHOOTING HANDICAP: Early August, Vandalia.
GRAPE HARVEST FESTIVAL: October, Dayton (St. Stephen's Church).
MARIETTA REGATTA: Late June, Marietta.
NATIONAL AIR RACES: Labor Day week end, Cleveland.
PUMPKIN FESTIVAL: Third week in October, Circleville.
STATE FAIR: Early September, Columbus.
SUMMER OPERA FESTIVAL: June-August, Cincinnati (Eden Park Zoo).
SUMMER POPS: Cleveland (Municipal Auditorium).

Oklahoma

AMERICAN INDIAN EXPOSITION: Mid-August, Anadarko.
EASTER SUNRISE SERVICES AND PASSION PLAY: Holy City.
FREE STATE FAIR: Early October, Muskogee.
INDIAN HOMECOMING: Mid-July, Pawnee.
INDIAN POW-WOW: Late August, Ponca City.
RATTLESNAKE ROUNDUP: O'Keene.
TWILIGHT TIME SUMMER MUSIC SERIES: Oklahoma City.

Oregon

CHERRY FESTIVAL: Mid-July, Salem.
CHIEF JOSEPHS DAYS: Last week end of July, Joseph.
CRAB FESTIVAL: Early May, Newport.
EASTERN OREGON LIVESTOCK SHOW: Early June, place varies.
FLEET OF FLOWERS: Memorial Day, Depoe.
HUCKLEBERRY FESTIVAL: August, Warm Springs Reservation.
MIRROR POND WATER PAGEANT: July 4, Bend.
MISS OREGON PAGEANT: Mid-July, Seaside.
PACIFIC INTERNATIONAL LIVESTOCK EXPOSITION: Mid-October, Portland.
PEA-HARVEST FESTIVAL: May, Milton-Freewater.
PENDLETON ROUNDUP: Mid-September, Pendleton.
PIONEER CAVALCADE: Late June, Seaside.
POWDER RIVER CAVALCADE: Early July, Baker.
RHODODENDRON FESTIVAL: Memorial Day Sunday, Florence.
RODEOS: July-September, state-wide events.

ROOT FESTIVAL: April, Warm Springs Reservation.
ROSE FESTIVAL: Mid-June, Portland.
ROUNDUP AND RODEO: Third week in September, Pendleton.
SALMON DERBY: Early September, Astoria (Columbia River).
SHAKESPEARE FESTIVAL: August, Ashland.
STATE FAIR: Labor Day week, Salem.
TIMBER CARNIVAL: Early July, Albany.
WHITE WATER PARADE: Last Sunday of April (usually), Vida-Leaburg Dam on McKenzie River.

Pennsylvania

ALL-STATE BAND CONCERT: Spring, city optional.
ANTIQUES EXPOSITION: October, Philadelphia.
APPLE BLOSSOM FESTIVAL: May, York.
APPLE BUTTER MAKING DAY: Labor Day week end, Allentown (Dorney Park).
BACH FESTIVAL: Early May, Bethlehem (Lehigh University).
BATTLE OF GETTYSBURG ANNIVERSARY CELEBRATION: July 1-3, Gettysburg.
BEAN SOUP HOMECOMING DAY: Early September, McClure.
BIG THURSDAY, COUNTRY FAIR WEEK: Mid-September, southeast Pennsylvania.
BOAT AND SPORTSMEN'S SHOW: October, Philadelphia.
BOOK FAIR: October, Philadelphia.
CEDARCREST COLLEGE MUSIC WORKSHOP AND FESTIVAL: Summer, Allentown.
CHERRY FESTIVAL: Mid-July, North East.
CLOTHESLINE ART SHOW: Spring, Philadelphia (Rittenhouse Square).
COUNTY FAIR: August, Bedford.
COUNTY FAIR: August, Morristown.
CULTURAL OLYMPICS: Spring, Philadelphia (University of Pennsylvania).
DEVON HORSE SHOW AND COUNTRY FAIR: May, Philadelphia.
DOG SHOW: Early November, Philadelphia (Kennel Club).
DOGWOOD FESTIVAL: Late April-May, Valley Forge.
EASTER SUNRISE SERVICE: Bethlehem.
EASTER SUNRISE SERVICE: Williamsport.
ELFRETH'S ALLEY DAY: First week end in June, Philadelphia.
FAIR: October, Hughesville.
FALL FLOWER SHOW: November, Schenley Park, Pittsburgh (Phipps Conservatory).
FARM SHOW: Second week in January, Harrisburg.
FEAST OF CANDLES: July 4, Lititz (Borough of).
FLAG DAY: June 14, Betsy Ross House, 239 Arch St., Philadelphia.
FLOWER SHOW: Early March, Philadelphia (Commercial Museum).
FOLK FESTIVAL: July 4, Pittsburgh.
FOUNDER'S DAY EXHIBIT: October-December, Pittsburgh (Carnegie Art Institute).
GROUNDHOG DAY CEREMONY: February 2, Quarryville.
HALLOWEEN PARADE: Allentown.
HORSE SHOW (BRYN MAWR AND CHESTER COUNTY): Last week end in September, Devon.
HORSE SHOW: July, York.
HORSE SHOW: July, Erie.
INTERSTATE FAIR: Early September, York.
INTERSTATE LAUREL FESTIVAL: June, Wellsboro.
LABOR DAY FAIR: Lock Haven.

LAUREL FESTIVAL: Mid-June, Wellsboro.
LITTLE LEAGUE BASEBALL WORLD SERIES: Late August, Williamsport.
LONGWOOD OPEN AIR THEATER SEASON: June-August, Kennett Suqare.
MAPLE DAY FESTIVAL: Late March, Meyersdale.
MEMORIAL DAY OBSERVANCE: May 30, National Military Park, Gettysburg.
MEMORIAL EXERCISES: June 30, Gettysburg.
MORAVIAN CHRISTMAS EVE VIGIL AND LOVE FEAST: Bethlehem.
MORAVIAN DAWN SERVICE: Easter Sunday, Bethlehem.
MUMMERS' PARADE AND WELSH EISTEDDFOD: January 1, Philadelphia.
MUSIC FESTIVAL: Third week in June, Municipal Stadium, Philadelphia.
NATIVITY CHRISTMAS PAGEANT: Christmas Week, Lansdowne.
NEW YEAR'S EISTEDDFOD: First week in January, Philadelphia (Girard Avenue-Welsh Presbyterian Church).
NORTHEASTERN SINGERS UNION FESTIVAL: June, city optional.
OLD FIDDLERS' PICNIC: Early August, West Chester (LENAPE PARK).
OLD SWEDES' CHURCH GARDEN FETE: May, Philadelphia.
OPENING OF PHILADELPHIA ORCHESTRA SEASON: October.
PENN RELAY CRANIVAL: Late April, Franklin Field, Philadelphia.
PENNSYLVNIA ACADEMY OF FINE ARTS ANNUAL OILS AND SCULPTURE SHOW: January, Philadelphia.
PENNSYLVANIA DUTCH DAY: Late August, Hershey.
PENNSYLVANIA FEDERATION OF SINGING SOCIETIES FESTIVAL: June, city optional.
PENNSYLVANIA RAILROAD GARDEN CLUB SHOW: Second week in September, Philadelphia (Thirtieth Street Station).
PENNSYLVANIA WEEK: Late October, statewide observance.
PHILADELPHIA INQUIRER CHARITIES TRACK MEET: Late January, Convention Hall, Philadelphia.
PUBLIC HEALTH NURSING ASSOCIATION OPEN HOUSE DAY: Second week end in May, New Hope.
RAIN DAY FESTIVAL: July 29, Waynesburg.
READING FAIR: September.
READING HORSE SHOW: May, Reading.
RITTENHOUSE SQUARE FLOWER MART: May, Philadelphia.
ROBIN HOOD DELL CONCERTS: Summer evenings, Philadelphia (Fairmount Park).
ROSE FESTIVAL: June, Reading.
SANTA LUCIA DAY: Week end nearest December 13, Philadelphia (American Swedish Historical Museum).
SCHOOLMEN'S WEEK: Late April, Philadelphia (University of Pennsylvania).
SCHUTCHING DAY: Second week end in September, Stahlstown.
SCHWENKFELDER THANKSGIVING: September 24, southeast Pennsylvania.
SPORTSMEN'S FIELD DAY: July, Williamsport.
STATE FAIR: August, Lewisburg.
STATE FARM PRODUCTS SHOW: January, Harrisburg.
STATE SKI CHAMPIONSHIPS: Early February, Laurel Mountain.
SUGARTOWN HORSE SHOW: First Saturday in May, Malvern (Fox Ridge Farms).
SUMMER MUMMERS' PARADE: August, Philadelphia.

TAMIMENT CHAMBER MUSIC FESTIVAL:
Summer, Tamiment.
TULIP FESTIVAL: Summer, Hershey.
UNCLE WIP CHRISTMAS PARADE: Thanks-
giving Day, Philadelphia.
VENANGO COUNTY FARMERS' AND FRUIT
GROWERS' FAIR: October, Franklin.
WATER CARNIVAL: August, Morristown.
WELSH EISTEDDFOD: March 17, Wilkes-
Barre.
YORK COUNTY FAIR: September, York.

Rhode Island

BERMUDA CRUISE (START): June, Newport.
FIELD DAY AND CLAM BAKE: Last Sunday
in August, Warren.
GAY NINETIES PARTY: Labor Day week end,
Newport.
NEWPORT JAZZ FESTIVAL: Two days in
July, Newport.
NEWPORT MUSIC FESTIVAL: July-August,
Newport.
STATE FAIR: Late August, Kingston.

South Carolina

AZALEA FESTIVAL: Between March-April,
Charleston (Cypress, Magnolia Middleton Gar-
dens).
STATE FAIR: Early October; place varies.
STATE MUSIC FESTIVAL: Mid-April, Rock
Hill.
WATERMELON FESTIVAL: Late June,
Hampton.

South Dakota

BLACK HILLS EXPOSITION: Mid-August,
Rapid City.
BLACK HILLS MOTORCYCLE CLASSIC:
Mid-May, Sturgis.
BLACK HILLS PASSION PLAY: Mid-June
to early September, Spearfish.
BLACK HILLS PLAYHOUSE (SUMMER
STOCK): Late June—late August, Custer
State Park.
BLACK HILLS RANGE DAYS: Mid-July,
Rapid City.
BLACK HILLS ROUNDUP: Early July, Belle
Fourche.
CORN PALACE FESTIVAL: Late September,
Mitchell.
DAYS OF 1910: Late August, Timber Lake.
DAYS OF '76 FESTIVAL: Early August, Dead-
wood Gulch.
FRONTIER DAYS: Early July, Wilmot.
GOLD DISCOVERY DAYS: Late July, Custer.
GYPSY DAY: Mid-October, Aberdeen (North-
ern State Teacher's College).
HOBO DAY: Early October, Brookings (South
Dakota State College).
LEGION RODEO: Mid-July, Huron.
MISS SOUTH DAKOTA BEAUTY CONTEST:
Mid-June, Hot Springs.
PASSION PLAY: July-August, Spearfish.
PHEASTIVAL: Mid-October, Huron.
ROSEBUD SIOUX FAIR: Late August, Rose-
bud.
SIOUX STAMPEDE RODEO: Early July,
Martin.
STATE FAIR: Mid-September, Huron.
TEPEE DAYS: Early October, Sioux Falls
(Sioux Falls College).
TRIAL OF JACK MC CALL: Mid-June to Sep-
tember (five times a week), Deadwood.

Tennessee

COTTON CARNIVAL: Mid-May, Memphis.
LAWRENCEBURG SINGING FESTIVALS:
Late March and late September.
MULE DAY: First Monday in April, Columbia.
NATIONAL FIELD TRIAL CHAMPIONSHIP:
Mid-February, Grand Junction.
NATIONAL FOX HUNT: Mid-November, usu-
ally at Paris.
RHODODENDRON FESTIVAL: Late June,
Roan Mountain.
STATE FAIR: Mid-September, Nashville.
TENNESSEE WALKING HORSE NATIONAL
CELEBRATION: Week of September 1,
Shelbyville.
WILD BOAR AND BEAR HUNTS: October-
November, Cleveland (Cherokee National
Forest).

Texas

ALL-STATE PICNIC: Mid-February, McAllen.
CITRUS FIESTA: Mid-January, Mission.
COTTON BOWL FOOTBALL GAME:
January 1, Dallas.
COWBOY REUNION: Early July, Stamford.
COWBOYS' CHRISTMAS BALL: Week before
Christmas, Anson.
EASTER BONFIRES: Holy Saturday night,
Fredericksburg.
FIESTA SAN JACINTO: Mid-April, San
Antonio.
FOREST FESTIVAL: Early October, Lufkin.
LA DANZA DE LOS MATACHINES: Decem-
ber 12, January 6, March 19, May 3, August
10, Our Lady of Guadalupe Church, San
Antonio.
LIVESTOCK SHOW: February, Houston.
LOS PASTORES: December 25—March 19, San
Antonio.
OIL PROGRESS WEEK: Second week of Oc-
tober, Abilene.
OLD FIDDLERS' CONTEST: Last Saturday in
May, Athens.
RODEO: Late January—early February, Fort
Worth.
RODEOS: June-September, state-wide events.
ROSE FESTIVAL: Early October, Tyler.
SOUTHWESTERN EXPOSITION AND FAT
STOCK SHOW: Late January—early Febru-
ary, Fort Worth.
SOUTHWESTERN SUN CARNIVAL: First
week of January, El Paso.
SQUARE DANCE FESTIVAL: First week of
May, El Paso.
STATE FAIR: Dallas.
SUN BOWL GAME AND CARNIVAL:
January 1, El Paso.

Utah

CHERRY FESTIVAL: July 4, North Ogden.
DAYS OF '47: July, Salt Lake City.
DAIRY DAY: May 14, Plain City.
GOLDEN SPIKE DAY: May 10, Ogden.
INTERMOUNTAIN SCHOOL BAND TOUR-
NAMENT: Early May, Price.
JUNIOR FAT STOCK SHOW: August, Ogden.
LAMB DAY: Mid-August, Fountain Green.
LIVESTOCK SHOW: Mid-November, Ogden.
MORMON TABERNACLE MESSIAH ORATO-
RIO: New Year's Day Sunday, Salt Lake
City.
PEACH DAY: Early September, Brigham.
PEACH DAY: Mid-September, Ferron.
PIONEER DAYS: Third week of July, Ogden.
SNOW CUP, GIANT SLALOM: December, Alta.

STATE FAIR: September, Salt Lake City.
STEEL DAY FESTIVAL: Labor Day, American Fork.
TIMPANOGOS MOUNTAIN CLIMB AND ASPEN GROVE CAMP: Saturday in July, Timpanogos Mount.
UNIVERSITY OF UTAH LIGHT OPERA FESTIVAL: July, Salt Lake City.
UTE BEAR DANCE: April, Whiterocks.

Vermont

BENNINGTON COMPOSERS' (MUSICAL) CONFERENCE: August.
CHAMPLAIN VALLEY EXPOSITION: August, Essex Junction.
COLONIAL DAY: First Wednesday in August, Castleton.
FAIR: September, Rutland.
FAIR: September, Tunbridge.
FOREST FESTIVAL WEEK: Last week in September, state-wide observance.
HORSE WEEK: First week in September, Woodstock.
MAPLE SYRUP FESTIVAL: St. Albans; seasonal.
MIDDLEBURY COLLEGE WINTER CARNIVAL: Late February, Middlebury.
MT. MANSFIELD SUGAR SLALOM: March, Stowe.
SING WEEK, TRAPP FAMILY MUSIC CAMP: July, Stowe.
VERMONT COMMUNITY FESTIVAL: Early May, Burlington.
VERMONT MUSIC FESTIVAL: Early May, Burlington.
WESTON COMMUNITY CLUB CONCERTS: Summer, Weston.
WINTER SPORTS CARNIVAL: Mid-February, Brattleboro.
WINTER SPORTS CARNIVAL: January, Woodstock.
WOMEN'S DOWNHILL, SLALOM AND COMBINED CHAMPIONSHIPS: March, Rutland.
WORLD FAIR: Third week in September, Tunbridge.

Virginia

CAPE HENRY PILGRIMAGE: Sunday nearest April 26.
DEEP RUN HUNT CUP STEEPLECHASE: First Saturday in April, Richmond.
DOG MART: October, Fredericksburg.
HISTORIC GARDEN WEEK: Late April, wide observance.
JOUSTING TOURNAMENT: Third Saturday in April, Mt. Solon's Natural Chimneys (Staunton).
MUSIC FESTIVAL: May, Charlottesville.
NATIONAL CHAMPIONSHIP MOTORCYCLE RACE: Last week end in May, Richmond.
SHENANDOAH APPLE BLOSSOM FESTIVAL: Late April or early May, Winchester.

Washington

APPLE BLOSSOM FESTIVAL: First week end in May, Wenatchee.
CALEDONIAN GAMES: First Saturday in August, Vancouver.
CLAMARAMA: Mid-May, Olympic beaches.
CLAM FESTIVAL: Late May, Long Beach.
DAFFODIL FESTIVAL: Late March—early April, Puyallup Valley.
DAIRY CONGRESS: August, Sunnyside.
DOLL AND PET PARADE: Last Saturday in August, Olympia.

INTERNATIONAL HIGHLAND GAMES: Second Saturday in August, Seattle.
LILAC TIME: Mid-May, Spokane.
LOGGERODEO CELEBRATION: About July 4, Sedro Valley.
LOGGERS JUBILEE: Mid-August, Morton.
MUSIC-UNDER-THE-STARS: July-August, Seattle.
PEACE ARCH FESTIVAL: Fourth Friday in September, Blaine.
PIONEER FESTIVAL: Last week end in July, Ferndale (Pioneer Park).
POW-WOW: About July 4, Toppenish.
RHODODENDRON FESTIVAL: Late May, Port Townsend.
RHODODENDRON TOURS: Late May, Puget Sound area.
RODEO: Early September, Ellensburg.
SALMON DERBY WEEK: Early September, Port Angeles.
SEAFAIR: First two weeks of August, Seattle.
STAMPEDE: Mid-August, Omak.
TIMBER BOWL FESTIVAL: Late June, Darrington.
TURKEY SHOW: Early December, Sunnyside.
VICTORIA HIGHLAND GAMES: Last Saturday in July, Victoria, B.C.
WATER FOLLIES CELEBRATION: Third week of July, Pasco.
WESTERN WASHINGTON STATE FAIR: Third week of September, Puyallup.

West Virginia

AGRICULTURAL AND INDUSTRIAL FAIR: September, Dunbar.
BAND FESTIVAL: Early May, Huntington.
BUCKWHEAT FESTIVAL: Second week in October, Kingwood.
DAIRY CATTLE SHOW: Early August, Weston (Jackson's Mill).
FOREST FESTIVAL: Early October, Elkins.
LILY FAMILY REUNION: Third week end in August, Flat Top.
MOUNTAIN CHOIR FESTIVAL: September, Arthurdale.
MUSIC FESTIVAL: Mid-May, Glenville.
OGLEBAY INSTITUTE OPERA WORKSHOP: July-August, Wheeling.
SOUTHERN APALACHIAN INDUSTRIAL EXHIBIT: August, Bluefield.
STATE FAIR: Labor Day week, Lewisburg.
STRAWBERRY FESTIVAL: Early June, Buckhannon.

Wisconsin

APPLE BLOSSOM DAY: May, Gays Mill.
CHEESE DAY: Every fifth September, Monroe.
CHERRY BLOSSOM SUNDAY: Last Sunday in May, Sturgeon Bay.
CHRISTMAS FLOWER SHOW: December, Milwaukee (Mitchell Park Conservatory).
CHRYSANTHEMUM SHOW: November, Milwaukee (Mitchell Park Conservatory).
EASTER LILY SHOW: Beginning Palm Sunday, Milwaukee (Mitchell Park Observatory).
GOLF TOURNAMENT: July, Milwaukee.
HIGH SCHOOL MUSIC FESTIVAL: April-May, River Falls and La Crosse.
HUSBAND-WIFE BOWLING TOURNAMENT: End of bowling season, Milwaukee.
ICE-SKATING CARNIVAL: January, Milwaukee.
INDIAN DANCE FESTIVAL: Thursdays in summer, Hayward.
MIDWINTER MUSIC CLINIC: Madison (University of Wisconsin).

MOTHER'S DAY FLOWER SHOW: May, Milwaukee (Mitchell Park Conservatory).
MUSIC FESTIVAL: Late May, Milwaukee (Auditorium).
MUSIC-UNDER-THE-STARS: June-August, Milwaukee.
ORCHID SHOW: Early February, Milwaukee (Mitchell Park Conservatory).
PENINSULA MUSIC FESTIVAL: August, Ephraim.
PRAIRIE DU CHIEN PILGRIMAGE AND FESTIVAL: Third week in May.
SOAP BOX DERBY: June, Milwaukee.
SPORTS AND VACATION SHOW: Late April, Milwaukee.
STATE FAIR: Late August, Milwaukee (State Fair Park).
STATE SOLO AND ENSEMBLE FESTIVAL: May, Madison (University of Wisconsin).
SUMMER FLOWER SHOW: Milwaukee (Mitchell Park).
SUMMER MUSIC CLINIC: July-August, Madison (University of Wisconsin).
SWISS PAGEANT AND FESTIVAL (WILLIAM TELL FESTIVAL): Labor Day week end, New Glarus.
TRI-STATE FAIR: Late August, Superior.
WINNEBAGO CEREMONIAL DANCES: Summer evenings, Upper Dells (Stand Rock Amphitheater).

Wyoming

ALL AMERICAN INDIAN DAYS (MISS AMERICAN INDIAN PAGEANT): Early August, Sheridan.
ANTELOPE DERBY: Hunting season, Rawlins.
BOTS SOTS STAMPEDE AND RODEO: Mid-July, Sheridan.
CODY RODEOS: Nightly July 5—August 31, Cody.
CODY STAMPEDE AND RODEO: July 3-4, Cody.
DAYS OF '49: Mid-June, Greybull.
FRONTIER DAYS: Late July, Cheyenne.
GIFT OF THE WATERS PAGEANT: First Sunday of August (usually), Thermopolis.
JUBILEE DAYS FESTIVAL: Mid-July, Laramie.
MUSIC FESTIVAL: Late April, Casper.
ONE-SHOT ANTELOPE HUNT: First day of season, Lander.
PIONEER DAYS: Early July, Lander.
PIONEER HISTORICAL PARADE AND RODEO: Around July 4, Lander.
ROCKY MOUNTAIN OIL SHOW: Third week of June, Casper.
SHERIDAN-WYO RODEO: Third week in July, Sheridan.
SHOSHONE FESTIVAL: August, Fort Washakie.
SHOSHONE SUN DANCE: Early July, Fort Washakie.
STATE FAIR: Early September, Douglas.
WESTERN SQUARE DANCE FESTIVAL: Third week of October, Laramie.

Festivals and Holydays
See also Church Calendar; Easter Dates, Movable Days of the Easter Cycle;; International Calendar of Saints and Special Days; Religious Allusions, References, and Symbols

NEW YEAR'S DAY: An ancient and universal day of festivity, by whatever calendar the beginning of the new year is calculated. In the calendar of the Church year, New Year's Day is celebrated as the Feast of the Circumcision. However, religious observances have never completely altered the secular nature of this holiday, and there is a direct line of relationship between the contemporary round of cocktail parties, the Feast of Fools of the Middle Ages, and the old Roman customs of routs and revelry.

CIRCUMCISION, FEAST OF THE: On January 1, the Christian churches commemorate the circumcision of the Infant Jesus, in accordance with traditional Jewish practice. It is the religious counterpart of the secular holiday on this day. See New Year's Day.

FEAST OF FOOLS, JANUARY 1: In the Middle Ages, New Year's Day was celebrated as the Feast of Fools, in honor of the ass on which Christ made his triumphal entry into Jerusalem. The entire ritual of the Church was held up to remarkable ridicule, with the Office of the Days chanted in travesty, a procession that mocked the procession of Christ into Jerusalem, all the "Amens" changed into the brayings of an ass, and the final crowning of the ass within the sanctuary of the Cathedral. (See New Year's Day.)

ST. GENEVIEVE'S DAY, JANUARY 3: St. Genevieve is the patron saint of Paris, credited with having saved the city from the barbarian invasions of Childeric and Attila. Her intercession has traditionally been sought in times of danger and plagues.

TWELFTH NIGHT OR EPIPHANY EVE, JANUARY 5: The night before the Epiphany commemorates the journey of the Magi, or Three Wise Men of the East, who followed the Christmas star to Bethlehem to bring the new-born Infant Jesus their gifts of gold, frankincense, and myrrh. Shakespeare's play, *Twelfth night*, with the comic adventures of Sir Toby Belch, Sir Andrew Aguecheek, Malvolio, and Feste, is in the traditional bright spirit of Epiphany Eve.

TWELFTH-DAY, OR EPIPHANY, JANUARY 6: The Epiphany, from a Greek verb meaning to »show forth« or »manifest,« marks the anniversary of the day when the Wise Men of the East first saw the Christ Child. It is a day of traditional merriment; in Stuart England the King re-enacted a pageant of the journey of the Magi; in countries of the Eastern Rite of the Christian churches, the ritual of the Blessing of the Waters is held on the Epiphany. Greek divers, in one well-known ceremony of this ritual, fetch for a golden cross thrown into the water by the patriarch of the church.

CARNIVAL, SUNDAY BEFORE LENT: The Carnival holiday (the name is derived from Latin words meaning "farewell to flesh") is in Christian countries the last outburst of hilarity before the Lenten season begins. The Carnival of Venice, with its legendary history of masquerades and merriment, is the most famous of the many traditional celebrations that mark Carnival Day.

PLOW MONDAY, MONDAY AFTER TWELFTH-DAY: Plow Monday marked the return of the English farmers to their fields after the long festivities of the Christmas season. It was not, however, a typical workday, and some of the spirit of the season lingered on in various local sports and feasts.

ST. AGNES' EVE, JANUARY 20: On the eve of St. Agnes, an English maiden could, with forethought, learn who her lover would be. She was required, in various versions of the ritual, to go to bed without her supper, but supplied with a certain flour-and-water cake that she had made; to eat a hard-boiled egg (shell and all); or to swallow a live herring: her expectation was that a vision of Prince Charming would appear in her dreams. Both Ben Jonson and John Keats have saluted the rites of St. Agnes' Eve in their verses.

ST. PAUL'S DAY, JANUARY 25: The weather of the entire year is held to depend upon what kind of day the anniversary of Paul's conversions turns out to be. The importance of the weather on this day is explained in an old verse:

> If St. Paul's day be fair and clear
> It doth betide a happy year.
> But if by chance it then should rain,
> It will make dear all kinds of grain;
> And if the clouds make dark the sky,
> If blustering winds do blow aloft,
> Then wars shall trouble the realm full oft.

CANDLEMAS, FEBRUARY 2: The feast of Candlemas commemorates the Purification of the Virgin Mary, a ceremony that is still participated in by women who have recently given birth. Beneath the Christian significance of the day, Candlemas is sometimes associated with the mythological quest of Ceres, the goddess of the grain, who lit her torch on this day and went in search of her daughter Proserpina, the spring-goddess, who had been abducted by Pluto and carried down to hell. In the Roman Catholic Church, Candlemas Day is the day on which all the church candles that are to be used in the coming year are blessed.

ST. BLAISE'S DAY, FEBRUARY 3: The feast of St. Blaise is marked in the Christian churches by the ceremony of blessing the throats of the faithful with holy candles, to gain the intercession of the saint in warding off diseases of the throat, a power with which he has traditionally been associated.

CHINESE NEW YEAR: The traditional Chinese New Year is celebrated on the day of the first moon, with the explosion of enough firecrackers to scare off all demons for the rest of the year.

MARDI GRAS: The Tuesday before the beginning of Lent, called Shrove Tuesday from the old English word for confessing, or "shroving," brings the festive period of the new year to an end. The name of the day, which is French for "Fat Tuesday," refers to last-minute feasts eaten everywhere in Europe before the lean days of the Lenten fast begin. The Mardi Gras of New Orleans is one of the world-famous celebrations that take place on Shrove Tuesday.

ASH WEDNESDAY: On Ash Wednesday, the Lenten season begins. In Christian churches around the world the foreheads of the faithful are marked with ashes, as a warning to be mindful of death and the last things.

LINCOLN'S BIRTHDAY, FEBRUARY 12: The birthday of Abraham Lincoln, the 16th president of the United States, is celebrated each year in the United States as a national holiday.

ST. VALENTINE'S DAY, FEBRUARY 14: The identy of St. Valentine, who may have been one of three early Christian martyrs, is uncertain, but the origin of valentines is clearly traced back to Rome, where on February 13, the feast of Februata Juno, young girls were paired off with the young men who were lucky enough to draw their names by lot from an urn.

WASHINGTON'S BIRTHDAY, FEBRUARY 22:
The birthday of the first president of the United States.

FEAST OF LANTERNS, FEBRUARY 24: In China, the Feast of Lanterns heralds the return of the sun in the person of a huge papiermâché and cloth dragon led in a triumphant night parade through streets decorated with thousands of brightly colored lanterns.

LUPERCALIA, FEBRUARY 15: In ancient Rome, the Lupercalia was a religious fertility rite in charge of the priests of Faunus, or Pan, who were called the Luperci; the priests ran (some say naked) through the neighborhood of the Palatine Hill and whipped the women they met with goatskin thongs as a sign that they would bear many children easily; in Shakespeare's play *Julius Caesar* (act I, scene 2) Mark Antony runs with the priests and Caesar bids him to remember to touch Calpurnia so that she will conceive and bear him an heir.

ST. DAVID'S DAY, MARCH 1: St. David, the patron saint of Wales, won a battle in 640 a.d. by commanding each of the men to wear a leek to distinguish the Welshmen from the Saxons in a close hand-to-hand encounter and keep them from aiding the enemy by slaughtering one another by mistake; on March 1, the Welsh commemorate this victory by wearing a leek or a daffodil; in Shakespeare's *King Henry the Fifth* (act V, scene I) Pistol makes sport of the Welsh captain, Fluellen, and the tradition of wearing a leek on St. David's Day.

PEACH BLOSSOM FESTIVAL, MARCH 3: Also called Doll Festival, the Peach Blossom Festival is a Japanese ritual in honor of the family and the monarchy; on this day Japanese girls display their famous collections of dolls (ideally 15 in number, and costumed like the entourage of the former royal household, complete down to footmen), along with replicas of blossoming peach and cherry trees.

MOTHERING SUNDAY, OR MID-LENT: The fourth Sunday in Lent is for the English a day much like Mother's Day in America; historically the anniversary dates back to the medieval practice of setting aside a day in Lent on which gifts were to be donated to Mother Church; scholars establish an even more ancient precedent, and trace the festival to ancient Greek and Roman celebrations in honor of the great nature goddess, the Magna Mater; the tradition survives in the visits that children make to their mothers on this day and in the gifts they bring.

BON, JULY 13-16: The Bon festival in Japan is held during the days when the spirits of the dead are expected to visit the altars of their ancestral homes.

EASTER: The oldest festival of the Christian Church, which celebrates the resurrection of Christ from the dead, and is symbolically, a guarantee of the redemption of mankind; the word is derived from the Anglo-Saxon *Eastre*, the goddess of the dawn, and the festival derives partly from pagan sources; Easter did not come into prominence until the 2nd and 3rd centuries of the Christian era, when question as to its exact date disturbed the Church with the bitter "quarto-deciman controversy."

APRIL FOOL'S DAY, APRIL 1: The persistent tradition about the pranks of April Fool's Day is that they originated at the time of the calendar change when some die-hards refused to date the New Year from January 1 rather than March 25 and were rewarded by their neighbors with practical jokes instead of the presents which were customarily exchanged at the end of the holiday season.

BIRTHDAY OF THE BUDDHA, APRIL 8: All of the major events in the life of Gautama Buddha, the founder of Buddhism, are traditionally celebrated on April 8, which was the day of his birth, his enlightenment, and of his achievement of Nirvana.

HOCKTIDE: Was a movable holiday dependent upon the date of Easter; for two days after the second Sunday after Easter the English countryside was transformed into a turn-and-turnabout Sadie Hawkin's kind of holiday; on Monday the men were free to round or "hock" up any available women and hold them under bail; the women had their chance to reciprocate the next day; all proceeds were contributed to the upkeep of the Church.

PATRIOTS' DAY, APRIL 18: On Patriots' Day New England re-enacts the midnight ride of Paul Revere with general pageantry.

ST. GEORGE'S DAY, APRIL 23: St. George is the patron saint of England and his feast, if less an occasion for festivity than formerly, is still associated with his special symbols, the rose, which is worn as a token, and the red cross flag, which is hung out in his honor; the feast of St. George is also kept in other parts of Europe, where he has been universally invoked as a protector against witches, devils, and monsters of all kinds as well as dragons.

PASSOVER (PESACH): The Feast of Passover, the jubilant holiday of the Jewish calendar, is celebrated with ceremonial festivity through the 15th-22d of Nisan, the first month of the ecclesiastical year (March-April), and commemorates the sparing of the Jewish children when the angel of the Lord passed in the night during the final plague of Egypt and cut down the oldest son in every house where the doorstep had not been sprinkled with the blood of the lamb.

EVE OF ST. MARK, APRIL 24: The feast of St. Mark, April 25, is a general religious holiday in Europe, but the myth of St. Mark's Eve has eclipsed the saint's day in legend and literature; in his play, *The Eve of St. Mark* (1942), Maxwell Anderson evoked the tradition that a vision of everyone who was doomed to die within the year would appear to anyone who stood on the church-porch between the hours before and after midnight on St. Mark's Eve.

ARBOR DAY: Most of the state legislatures of the United States have set aside a day between late April and early May for planting trees; the patron of these holidays is Johnny Appleseed (John Chapman), who is credited with establishing apple orchards from New-England through the midwest during his life-long pilgrimage of prayers and good works.

ROGATION DAYS: In the ecclesiastical year, the three days before Ascension Thursday, the 37-39th days after Easter, are appointed as Rogation Days, or days of special fasting and supplication; in Elizabethan England the days were devoted to a general procession around the boundaries of parishes in order to impress the public mind with their inviolability and to give the territories an annual legal status, a ceremony reminiscent of the ancient Roman Terminalia (February 23).

WALPURGIS NIGHT, APRIL 30: In their decline, the gods of the Norsemen degenerated in the popular mind into witches and warlocks and were generally credited with conducting a Witches' Sabbath each May Day Eve on the peak of Broken in the Harz Mountains.

MAY DAY, MAY 1: In ancient Rome, April was the month of flowers and was saluted with the Floralia, or Feast of Flowers; May Day observances are supposed to be a continuation of this Roman custom, and have been long associated with practices which commemorate the annual spring revival of vegetation. In the contemporary world May Day is, in Catholic countries, the beginning of the month of the Virgin Mary, and, in European countries, a Labor Day holiday which has lately been pre-empted by the Russians as a memorial observance of the Communist Revolution.

THE FINDING OF THE CROSS, MAY 3: St. Helena, the mother of Constantine the Great, is remembered in a universal Christian feast that commemorates her successful pilgrimage to the Holy Land in search of the True Cross.

ASCENSION THURSDAY: Forty days after Easter, the day on which Christ ended His earthly existence and ascended again into heaven, is marked in the ecclesiastical calendar as Ascension Day, one of the major holydays of the Church year.

FURRY DAY, MAY 8: Although the origin of the name Furry Day is vigorously disputed, being attributed variously to the Roman Floralia or Flora's Day, to an Old English word for *feast* and another one for *fair*, there persists an English holiday in Cornwall which is celebrated with a rousing Furry Dance, when the whole day is given over to a succession of ceremonial dances, house tours, and fairs which have been readily, if mysteriously, incorporated within the general spring festivities.

WHITSUNDAY (PENTECOST): The fiftieth day after Easter commemorates in the Church year the descent of the Holy Ghost upon the Apostles, when they were blessed with the gift of tongues and enabled to go abroad and preach the Gospel; the "white" in Whitsunday refers to the Baptismal robes of the received Christians. Throughout European history, it has been an annual day of lavish religious processions and pageantry.

CORPUS CHRISTI, FIRST THURSDAY AFTER TRINITY SUNDAY: The feast of Corpus Christi (the Body of Christ) dates back to the Middle Ages, and is an annual religious holiday in honor of the Blessed Sacrament, when, especially in Catholic countries, public demonstrations in the form of processions commemorate the solemn nature of the day, and are often followed by pageants, feasts, and games in the spirit of a general holiday.

MEMORIAL DAY, MAY 30: In almost all of the U.S.A. the day of commemorating all of the country's soldiers and sailors who have died in battle is a legal holiday and falls on May 30. In the South, however, Confederate Memorial Day is observed, and is dated variously April 26, May 10, May 30, and June 3; the significance of the day was originally established by the commander of the G.A.R., General John Logan, who commanded May 30, 1868, as a day for honoring the graves of the men who had died in the Civil War. Since that time, the ceremonies of the day have come to include all of the fallen of all the campaigns of U.S. battle history.

FEAST OF WEEKS, PENTECOST OR SHABUOTH: Seven weeks after the 16th of Nisan, usually the 6th and 7th of Sivan, the Jews commemorate the Day when God gave the Ten Commandments to Moses on Mount Sinai. The Date also corresponds with the Near East harvest season, and is marked by appropriately symbolic religious observances.

FLAG DAY: On June 14, 1777, Congress declared the official adoption of the flag of the United States, then thirteen alternating red and white stripes, and thirteen white stars on a blue field to commemorate the thirteen original states. The number and position of the stars was modified by the Congressional declaration of 1818, when it was agreed to add an additional star each July 4 for each new state, but to keep the original, and now honorary, pattern of the stripes. Flag Day commemorates the formal adoption of the Stars and Stripes in 1777.

MIDSUMMER, OR ST. JOHN'S EVE, JUNE 23: Midsummer, with its tangled threads of paganism and Christianity, nature and supernature, was the perfect setting for the delicate fantasy of William Shakespeare's *A Midsummer Night's Dream*. Throughout Europe, in every age, there has been recognition of the bewitching character of the summer solstice, and the Church conceded the invigorating spirit of the time by appointing the feast of St. John the Baptist to this season and singling him out as the only saint outside the Holy Family who is commemorated on his birthday, rather than on the anniversary of his death. The sun-worship of the Druids, contained by the symbols of fire and blood, erupted into action on Midsummer's Night when great bonfires blazed on the mountaintops of England and dancers circled the flames until the energy of each spark and each spirit was spent. The time is tamer now, but quaint notions here and there recall the mystic night of "the lunatic, the lover, and the poet."

INDEPENDENCE DAY, OR FOURTH OF JULY: On July 4, 1776, the Second Continental Congress declared the independence of the American Colonies from England, and the date has been accepted as the national anniversary of American independence, although the Declaration of Independence was not formally signed until August 2, 1776.

BASTILLE DAY, JULY 14: The fall, on July 14, 1789, of the Bastille, the ancient symbol of Bourbon tyranny, was the first augury of success for the French Revolution. It is a French holiday and the universal anniversary of liberal aspiration.

ST. SWITHIN'S DAY, JULY 15: Bishop Swithin of Winchester died in England in the ninth century, and legend has it that he asked to lie where, unlike Christina Rossetti, he believed that he would be able to feel the rain. So he was buried outside his church, where his spirit rested in soggy contentment until some pious monks decided to store his bones in a crypt. A terrific thunderstorm roared out the saint's displeasure, and for forty days and nights rain fell on unhappy Winchester. The curse of St. Swithin is said to operate wherever it rains on his day, an omen that a deluge is due.

LAMMAS, AUGUST 1: Lammas is traced either to the Anglo-Saxon loaf-mass (hlafmass), when Druid priests blessed the first loaves made with the wheat of the new harvest, or to a feudal "lamb mass" when a lamb was offered at mass from each church under the jurisdiction of the Cathedral of St. Peter-in-Chains (St. Peter in Vinculis) in York, England. Similar offerings continue to be made to this day. Lammastide, referred to by Shakespeare, is the season around Lammas.

ASSUMPTION DAY, AUGUST 15: The Virgin Mary was, in Christian theology, the only mortal ever to have been spared the corruption of the grave; at her death she was taken up body and soul to heaven; the anniversary of her Assumption (Latin: taking-up) is a universal feast of the Church.

ST. BARTHOLOMEW'S DAY, OR BARTHOLOMEW, AUGUST 24: Bartholomew's Day is kept alive in literature by *Bartholomew's Fair*, in which Ben Jonson satirized the Puritans, and in history by the Bartholomew's Day Massacre in Paris, 1572, when 30,000 French Protestants were butchered by order of Charles IX; but it was once an anniversary which drowned in universal merriment whatever significance the day may have had; from 1133, when the first fair was held at Smithfield, until 1822, when official intervention effectively killed the rowdy spirit of the day (Sept. 3 after the calendar change in 1752), Bartholomew Fair was the greatest fair in England and St. Bartholomew's Day the wildest.

LABOR DAY, FIRST MONDAY IN SEPTEMBER: As a day dedicated to the American working people, Labor Day is traced back to 1882 when the Central Labor Union of New York acted on a proposal of the President of the Carpenter's Brotherhood, Peter J. Mc Guire, and set aside a day of recognition of the strength and spirit of the working class; a success, the holiday was adopted as an annual affair by the National Federation of Labor Unions, which was shortly followed by the federal declaration of Labor Day as a national holiday.

NATIVITY OF THE BLESSED VIRGIN MARY, SEPTEMBER 8: The anniversary of the birth of the Blessed Virgin, instituted by Pope Servius, is a universal feast in the Catholic Church.

MICHAELMAS, SEPTEMBER 29: The victory of St. Michael the Archangel over Lucifer is commemorated on his feast day, which is universally observed in the Christian churches.

BIRTHDAY OF CONFUCIUS, SEPTEMBER 28: The great Chinese philosopher Confucius was born September 28, 551 b.c., and his birthday is a solemn feast in China.

ROSH HASHANA: The Jewish New Year is celebrated on the 1st and 2nd of Tishri; the symbol of the holiday is the shofar (shophar), or sacred ram's horn, which was blown anciently as a battle signal, or to announce sacred festivals, the Sabbath, the new moon, and the New Year, and is still sounded on Yom Kippur, the Day of Atonement, ending this first cycle of high holidays of the religious calendar.

YOM KIPPUR (DAY OF ATONEMENT): The Day of Atonement, the 10th of Tishri, is the holiest day of the Jewish religious calendar, a day of strict fast that is observed by synagogue services and prayers for the forgiveness of sins committed in the past year.

SUKKOTH (FEAST OF TABERNACLES): The symbol of Sukkoth, which is celebrated through the 15th-22nd of Tishri, is the hut or sukkah that the ancient Jewish farmers built in the fields as a night-shelter during the harvest season. Meals during the holidays are taken in a replica of the sukkah which is built in a convenient place. The spirit of the time, in private and in synagogue, is one of thankfulness to the God who protects His own, though they have only branches and leaves to shelter them.

HALLOWEEN, OCTOBER 31: All Hallow's Eve

is associated with many ancient customs, but the persistent theme of the holiday is that it is the night of the year when witches and warlocks are abroad to celebrate their wicked rites, though All Hallows refers to the hallowed ones, or saints, whose day comes with the dawn.

ALL SAINTS' DAY, NOVEMBER 1: The Christian Church commemorates, in a feast of great joy, all the legion of the blest who have risen to their heavenly reward.

ALL SOUL'S DAY, NOVEMBER 2: The feast of All Souls is a solemn day of commemoration, in Christian churches, of the souls of the dear departed.

GUY FAWKES' DAY, NOVEMBER 5: Guy Fawke's Day is to the English what the Fourth of July is to Americans, a holiday with fireworks; it commemorates the plot to blow up Parliament, November 5, 1605, when Guy Fawkes was taken and executed as a Catholic enemy of the Protestant king, and a member of a conspiracy to overthrow the government.

ARMISTICE DAY, NOVEMBER 11: All was quiet on the western front at the eleventh hour of the eleventh day of the eleventh month of the final year of the war to end all wars. The monument and the day when World War I ended in 1918 is annually observed, though, understandably, with less authority since World War II.

FEAST OF ST. MARTIN, NOVEMBER 11: The time around the Feast of St. Martin is called Martinmas, which was coincident with the final harvest, a period of general relief, which was undoubtedly contributed to the fame of Martin, who was the patron saint of innkeepers and drunkards and whose feast fell on the day of the ancient Roman Vinalia, or Feast of Bacchus.

THANKSGIVING: Thanksgiving, which is usually the fourth Thursday of November, is a U.S.A. national holiday that commemorates the safe landing of the Pilgrims at Plymouth, November 21, 1620.

BIRTHDAY OF THE PROPHET, DECEMBER 1: The anniversary of the birth of Mohammed begins a lengthy Mohammedan holiday with both religious and secular celebrations.

ADVENT: In the Church year Advent is the beginning of the Christmas season, and begins on St. Andrew's Day (November 30), or the Sunday closest.

FEAST OF THE IMMACULATE CONCEPTION, DECEMBER 8: In the Catholic Church the feast of the Immaculate Conception, in honor of the Blessed Virgin's birth, free from the stain of original sin, is a solemn high feast with joyful connotation.

SATURNALIA, DECEMBER 17: The Roman Saturnalia was held in honor of Saturn, the god of seed sowing and began on December 17; it was a period of such unrestrained festivity that the term saturnalia is still used to describe any occasion of general debauchery.

HANUKKAH (FEAST OF THE DEDICATION): In the Jewish calendar, Hanukkah is celebrated through 25th of Kislev to the 2nd of Tebet (or, when Kislev has 29 days, through the 3rd of Tebet). Historically, it commemorates the liberation of the Temple from Greek domination. The symbol of the holiday is the Menorah, the eight-branched candelabra that gives the period the alternate name of the Festival of Lights. One candle is lit each night until, at the end of nights, the entire candelabra is aglow, as was the Temple

when the eternal light was rekindled after the victory of Judas Maccabeus.

CHRISTMAS EVE, DECEMBER 24: Christmas Eve is the great period of waiting in the Christian Church, and is observed universally as an anticipation of the birth of Christ, which is commemorated at midnight.

CHRISTMAS, DECEMBER 25: The most popular day in the Christian Church calendar is the anniversary of the birth of Christ, a traditional day of rejoicing, of feasts, and of exchanging gifts; but, before the fifth century, no one was agreed as to when Christmas should fall; Venerable Bede noted that the "Angli began the year on December 25 when we now celebrate the birthday of the Lord; and the very night which is now so holy to us, they call in their tongue *modranecht*, that is, Mothers Night"; the feast shades back into Mesopotamian, Greek, Roman, and Hebrew history, which is inevitable since it falls at the winter solstice, one of the natural divisions of the year; but, though survivals cling to the Christmas customs, and new arrivals like the commercialism of the contemporary world, threaten to distort its nature and usurp its place, it remains triumphantly the focus of the Western year, the dead of winter, looking forward to the spring, and the still of the spirit looking forward to eternity.

FEAST OF STEPHEN, DECEMBER 26: The feast of St. Stephen, the first martyr was set closest to Christmas in honor of his sacrifice.

BOXING DAY: In England, Boxing Day, a legal holiday, falls on the first weekday after Christmas; it is customary for Englishmen to distribute "boxes" (tips) to employees, servants, mailmen, and charmen; the custom is said to date back to the Romans who crossed the English Channel in the time of the Caesars and put a small bribe aside in a box to help persuade the gods to grant them a favorable crossing; when they reached their destinations safely, they distributed the boxes among the poor.

HOLY INNOCENTS' DAY, DECEMBER 28: The feast of the Holy Innocents commemorates all the little children who were slain at the command of Herod because he had heard that there was One among them who would be greater than he. It is universally considered to be a bad-luck day of the calendar and everyone is warned not to begin anything on Holy Innocents' Day.

NEW YEAR'S EVE, DECEMBER 31: Like Janus, the two-faced Roman God of ends and beginnings, New Year's Eve stands at the end of the old year gloating over the past, and at the beginning of the new year musing on the future; the strategic location of the day in the calendar year has made it a natural holiday that is observed with celebrations that are like its own ambiguous nature.

First Ladies
See **Presidency**

Flora's Dial
See also **Flowers, Plants, Leaves and Their Symbolic Meanings**

A fanciful or imaginary dial supposed to be formed by the opening and closing time of flowers.

Dial of Flowers with Approximate Opening Time

The first twelve hours, a.m.:
1. (Scandinavian sowthistle closes.)
2. Yellow goats-beard.
3. Common oxtongue.
4. Hawkweed; late-flowing dandelion and wild succory.
5. White water lily, naked-stalked poppy, and smooth sowthistle.
6. Shrubby hawkweed and spotted cat's-ear.
7. White water lily, garden lettuce, and African marigold.
8. Scarlet pimpernel, mouse-ear hawkweed, and proliferous pink.
9. Field marigold.
10. Red sandwort.
11. Star of Bethlehem.
Noon. Ice plant.

The second twelve hours, p.m.:
1. Common purslane.
2. (Purple sandwort closes.)
3. (Dandelion closes.)
4. (White spiderwort closes.)
5. Julap.
6. Dark crane's-bill.
7. (Naked-stalked poppy closes.)
8. (Orange day lily closes.)
9. Cactus opuntia.
10. Purple bindweed.
11. Night-blooming catch-fly.
Midnight. (Late-flowering dandelion closes).

Dial of Flowers with Approximate Closing Time

The first twelve hours:
1. Scandinavian sowthistle.
2. (Yellow goat's-beard opens.)
3. (Common oxtongue opens.)
4. (Wild succory opens.)
5. (Several sowthistles open.)
6. (Spotted cat's-ear opens.)
7. Night-flowering catch-fly.
8. Evening primrose.
9. Purple bindweed.
10. Yellow Goats-beard.
11. Star of Bethlehem.
Noon. Field sowthistle

The second twelve hours, p.m.:
1. Red or proliferous pink.
2. Purple sandwort.
3. Dandelion or field marigold.
4. White spiderwort and field bindwort.
5. Common cat's-ear.
6. White water lily.
7. Naked-stalked poppy.
8. Orange day lily and wild succory.
9. Convolvolus linnaeus and chickweed.
10. Common nipplewort.
11. Smooth sowthistle.
Midnight. Creeping mallow and late dandelion.

First Names
See **Names**

Flowers, Plants, Leaves and Their Symbolic Meanings
See also **Flora's Dial;** *State Flowers* (under **States**); **Saints**

AMARANTH: Immortality.

ANEMONE: Frailty; anticipation.
APPLE BLOSSOM: Admiration.
ASPEN LEAF: Fear.
ASPHODEL: Death; sorrow.
BUTTERCUP: Wealth.
CALLA LILY: Pride.
CAMELLIA: Intrinsic value.
CARNATION: Rejoicing; coronation.
CHRYSANTHEMUM: Longevity.
COLUMBINE: Freedom.
CORNFLOWER: Delicacy.
COWSLIP: The beauty of youth.
CYCLAMEN: Shyness.
DAFFODIL: Unrequited love.
DAISY: Simplicity; innocence.
DANDELION: Coquetry.
FERN: Sincerity.
FORGET-ME-NOT: Faithfulness.
FOUR-LEAF CLOVER: Luck.
GERANIUM: Gentility.
GOLDENROD: Encouragement.
HEATHER: Loneliness.
HEATHER, WHITE: Good fortune.
HOLLYHOCK: Ambition.
HONEYSUCKLE: Friendship.
HYACINTH: Grief and sorrow.
IRIS: Wisdom; faith; courage. In ancient times, a symbol of Christianity.
IVY: Trustfulness; connubial love.
JASMINE: Love (Arabic).
LAUREL: Fame.
LILAC: Fastidiousness.
LILY: Purity, chastity.
LILY OF THE VALLEY: Unconscious sweetness.
LOTUS: Forgetfulness.
MARIGOLD: Contempt.
MYRTLE: Wedded bliss.
NARCISSUS: Vanity.
OAK LEAF: Patriotism; hospitality.
OLIVE BRANCH: Peace.
ORANGE BLOSSOM: Marriage.
ORCHID: Unbounded passion.
OXALIS: Pangs of regret.
PALM LEAF: Victory.
PANSY: Thought.
PEONY: Indignation.
POPPY: Sloth; oblivion.
PRIMROSE: Youth.
ROSE: Virtue; love; victory; martyrdom; peace; prosperity; silence; beauty.
ROSE, YELLOW: Jealousy.
ROSEMARY: Remembrance.
SHAMROCK: Loyalty. Also a Christian symbol for the Trinity.
SNOWDROP: Friend in need.
SUNFLOWER: Globe of light, sun.
TUBEROSE: Bereavement.
TULIP, YELLOW: Love in vain.
VIOLET: Modesty.
WALLFLOWER: Love in adversity.
WATER LILY: Purity of heart.
YEW: Death.

Fools
See **Court Fools**

Foreign Languages
See **Languages of the World**

French Rulers
See **Rulers**

Gems and Days of the Week
See also **Birthstones; Planets and Their Symbolic Gems; Gem Stones**

Note: Sometimes birthstones are determined by the day of the week on which one was born, rather than by a birth-month. The following list is a currently acceptable substitute for the standard list of birthstones by months.

SUNDAY: Diamond, or topaz.
MONDAY: Pearl, or crystal.
TUESDAY: Ruby, or emerald.
WEDNESDAY: Amethyst, or loadstone.
THURSDAY: Sapphire, or carnelian.
FRIDAY: Emerald, or cat's-eye.
SATURDAY: Diamond, or turquoise.

Gem Stones: In Order of Their Relative Hardness
See also Birthstones; Planets and Their Symbolic Gems; Gems and Days of the Week; Products of the world, their Origins and Uses

DIAMOND: *Crystallized carbon.* As a gem it is transparent. Colors range from blue-white (water-clear) through pale yellow to canary, rose (occasionally red), yellow-green to bottle-green, orange, to (rarely) blue. The fabulous "black diamond" is a variety of diamond called carbonado. Diamond is usually cut brilliant or rose-cut.

RUBY: *Corundum.* As a gem it is transparent. Colors range from rose to purplish-red, with a standard shade called pigeon's blood. Ruby is usually cut brilliant or brilliant-step cut. See Sapphire below.

SAPPHIRE: *Corundum.* As a gem it is transparent. The standard color is cornflower-blue, and the varieties of sapphire are named according to their color: Oriental Topaz is golden yellow; Oriental Emerald is green; Oriental Amethyst is purple; Fancy Sapphire is water-clear (blue-white). Sapphire is usually cut brilliant or brilliant-step cut. When it is cut cabochon, it shows, like ruby, a white star-like pattern and is called Star Sapphire.

ALEXANDRITE: *A variety of Chrysoberyl.* As a gem it is transparent. By ordinary light, the color is grass-green or blue-green; by artificial light, the color is a raspberry hue. Alexandrite is usually cut brilliant.

CHRYSOBERYL: *Beryllium aluminate with traces of iron.* As a gem it is either transparent or translucent. Colors usually range from yellow to light green, and the varieties of chrysoberyl are named according to their colors: (Oriental) Cat's Eye or Cymophane is cloudy and greenish-yellow or olive in color; Alexandrite is, according to the kind of light shining on it, green or red; Yellow Chrysoberyl is transparent and straw, olive, or golden brown in color. Chrysoberyl is usually cut cabochon or brilliant cut. See Alexandrite.

SPINEL: *Magnesium aluminate.* As a gem it is transparent. Colors range from yellow, rose, red (called spinel ruby), green, light blue to indigo, to violet. Spinel is usually cut brilliant, step cut, or brilliant-step cut.

TOPAZ: *Fluosilicate of aluminium.* As a gem it is transparent. It may be colorless, or range in color from pale to tawny yellow, orange, pale green, pale blue, pink or red (which results from heating yellow topaz), to violet. "Precious" topaz is the color of sherry wine. Topaz is usually brilliant-step cut. It is often used in signet rings.

AQUAMARINE: *Variety of beryl.* As a gem it is transparent. Colors are blue, sea-green, or green. Aquamarine is usually brilliant-step cut.

BERYL: *Beryllium and aluminum silicate.* As a gem it is transparent. The varieties of beryl are named according to their color: Emerald is green; Aquamarine is sea-green; Golden Beryl is yellow; Morganite is pink or rose. Beryl is usually table-cut, or brilliant-step cut.

EMERALD: *Variety of beryl.* As a gem it is transparent. In color it is a sharp green (called "emerald green"), or a light to dark lustrous green. Emerald is usually step cut, or cut cabochon.

TOURMALINE: *Complex subsilicate.* As a gem it is transparent. It may be colorless, or range in color from gray-yellow, pink to red, olive, brown, to blue. Tourmaline is usually cut brilliant, or brilliant-step cut.

ZIRCON: *Zirconium orthosilicate.* As a gem it is transparent. Varieties are named according to their color: Hyacinth is red to bluish blue-red; Jacinth is yellow, orange, or green; Jargoon is colorless or very pale in color. Zircon is usually rose-cut, table-cut, or cut brilliant.

PYROPE: *Variety of garnet.* As a gem it is transparent. In color it is a deep brilliant red. Pyrope is usually cut brilliant.

AGATE: *Variegated chalcedony.* As a gem it is transculent. It is composed of bands or patches of dark and light chalcedony, and varieties are named according to the pattern of the composition: Eye Agate has circular markings; Moss agate has green veins or branches inside. Agate is commonly used in carved forms and in cameos.

ALMANDINE (ALMANDITE): *Variety of garnet.* As a gem it is transparent. In color it is violet-red or crimson. Almandine is usually cut cabochon, brilliant-step cut, or cut-cabochon.

AMETHYST: *Variety of crystallized quartz.* As a gem it is transparent. Color ranges from violet to purple. Amethyst is usually brilliant-step cut, or cut cameo and intaglio.

AVENTURINE: *Variety of quartz.* As a gem it is translucent. In color it is brownish red, or green with metallic flecks. Aventurine is much used in carved forms.

BLOODSTONE (HELIOTROPE): *Variety of chalcedony.* As a gem it is opaque. In color it is dark green with red flecks or streaks. Bloodstone is commonly used in signet rings, or in carved forms.

CAIRNGORM (SMOKY QUARTZ): *Variety of quartz.* As a gem it is transparent. In color it is a smoky gray or a smoky brown. Cairngorm is usually brilliant-step cut. It is used in carved forms.

CARNELIAN: *Variety of chalcedony.* As a gem it is translucent. In color it is a wax yellow, red-brown, or orange-red. Carnelian is used in carved forms, as beads, or cut as cameos.

CAT'S EYE: *Variety of chalcedony.* As a gem it is translucent. Usual colors are shades of yellow, green, and brown. Cat's Eye is usually cut cabochon. See also (Oriental) Cat's Eye under Chrysoberyl.

CITRINE: *Black quartz.* As a gem it is transparent. The characteristic color of citrine is a pale or straw yellow, which results from heating black quartz. Citrine is usually brilliant-step cut.

CHALCEDONY: *Cryptocrystalline variety of quartz.* As a gem it is translucent. Colors range from white to yellow, to blue-gray. Chalcedony is used in beads, and in carved forms.

CHRYSOPRASE (GREEN CHALCEDONY): *Variety of chalcedony.* As a gem it is translucent. Coloring is in various bright shades of green. Chrysoprase is usually table-cut, or cut cabochon. It is often used in signet rings.

HYACINTH: *Variety of zircon.* As a gem it is transparent. Color is from red to bluish blue-red. Hyacinth is usually cut brilliant.

JACINTH: *Variety of zircon.* As a gem it is transparent. Colors range through yellow, orange, and green. Jacinth is usually cut brilliant.

JARGOON (JARGON): *Variety of zircon.* As a gem it is transparent. Jargoon is the name given to colorless zircons and to those of a very pale tinging of color. It is usually cut brilliant.

JASPER: *Variety of chalcedony.* As a gem it is opaque. Colors range through red, yellow, brown, and gray-green. Jasper is often used in signet rings, in beads, and in carved forms.

ONYX: *Variety of chalcedony.* As a gem it is translucent to opaque. Onyx is characteristically banded in white and black. It is usually cut cameo, or cut cabochon.

ROCK CRYSTAL: *Quartz.* As a gem it is transparent. It is characteristically colorless, or slightly tinged with color. Rock crystal is usually cut brilliant, rose-cut, or table-cut. It is commonly used as beads, as stones for rings, as seals, or in carved forms.

RUBELLITE: *Tourmaline.* As a gem it is transparent. Color varies from rose pink to crimson. Rubellite is usually brilliant-step cut.

GARNET: *Silicate.* As a gem it is transparent. Varieties of garnet are named according to color: Almandine (Almandite) is wine-red; Essonite is orange-red; Demantoid is green; Pyrope is blood-red; Rhodolite ranges from pink to purple. Garnet is usually cut cabochon, or rose-cut.

JADE: *Jadeite or Nephrite.* As a gem it is translucent. Colors range from white to dark green, mottled green, yellow, red, to blue-red. Jade is commonly used in carved forms and in beads. See Nephrite.

NEPHRITE (JADE): *Variety of tremolite or actinolite.* As a gem it is translucent. Colors range through white, leaf green, and black. Nephrite, a less valuable kind of jade, is commonly used in carved forms. See Jade.

PERIDOT: *Variety of chrysolite.* As a gem it is transparent. Color varies from pale yellow to deep olive. Peridot is usually cut brilliant, or step cut.

AMAZON STONE (AMAZONITE): *Variety of microcline.* As a gem it is opaque. The usual color is a blue-green. Amazon Stone is usually cut cabochon. It is used in carved forms.

ESSONITE (CINNAMON STONE; HESSONITE): *Variety of garnet.* As a gem it is transparent. Color ranges from orange-red to cinnamon-brown. Essonite is usually cut brillant-step cut.

MOONSTONE: *Feldspar.* As a gem it is translucent. Color is white, pale blue-gray, or opalescent. Moonstone is usually cut cabochon. It is often used in beads.

TURQUOISE: *Complex alumina-copper-phosphate.* As a gem it is opaque. Color ranges through green-blue, sky blue, apple green. Turquoise is usually cut cabochon. It is frequently used in carved forms.

OPAL: *Hydrated silica.* As a gem it is translucent. The standard colors are white and black, with a characteristic interior glow, and varieties are named for their colors: Fire Opal is the color of flame; Mexican Opal is a rich, lustrous green; Harlequin Opal is speckled with bright colors; Black Opal is dark gray or blue. Opal is cut cabochon.

LAPIS LAZULI: *Complex silicate.* As a gem it is opaque. Colors vary from azure to rich blue, with tinges of green, white, or yellow, or flecks of gold. Lapis lazuli is commonly used in carved forms.

PEARL: *Nacre.* Pearls may be translucent or opaque. Colors vary greatly, and include white, yellow, green, blue, purple, pink, red, brown, and black. Pearls are named according to their shape: Paragon is a perfect sphere; Robold is almost rounded; Egg Shape is an elongated oval; Pear Shaped is shaped like a pear; Drop Shape has a pointed end, like a tear, or drop of water; Baroque is irregularly shaped; Button is flattened on one side. A Blister Pearl is a pearl that comes attached to the shell. Seed Pearls are dwarf pearls. A Perle Coq is a hollow pearl, or a shell blister. Mother-of-Pearl is an inner layer of shell.

MALACHITE: *Basic carbonate of copper.* As a gem it is opaque. The usual color is a deep, lustrous green. Malachite is used in carved forms. It is also used for table-tops, and in decoration. See Azurite.

SERPENTINE: *Hydrous magnesium silicate.* As a gem it is translucent. The color is usually a dull, mottled yellow-green or gray-green. Serpentine is usually used in carved forms.

AZURITE: *Basic carbonate of copper.* As a gem it is opaque. The usual color is a deep blue. Azurite is commonly cut cabochon. It is sometimes called Blue Malachite.

CORAL: *Carbonate of lime.* Coral is opaque. Colors range from white through pink, red, and blood-red. Coral is commonly used in carved forms, or in beads.

JET: *Fossilized wood, or a mineral like coal.* Jet is opaque. In color it is a velvety black, The common uses of jet are as beads, brooches, earrings, and costume jewelry.

AMBER: *Fossil resin.* Amber is transparent or translucent. Color ranges from champagne to red-brown. Amber is usually cut cabochon. It is often used in beads, and in carved forms.

German Rulers
See **Rulers**

Girls' Names
See **Names, Most Popular for Girls**

Given Names
See **Names**

Gods and Goddesses
See also **Gods of the World, A Checklist of Their Works and Patronage; Religious Allusions, References, and Symbols**

Greek and Roman Gods

ABELLIO: Identified with Apollo as sun-god.

ACCA LARENTIA: Another name for Larenta.

ACHELOIADES: The Sirens, as daughters of Achelous.

ACHELOUS: River-god; son of Oceanus and Tethys; father of the Sirens by Melpomene; oldest of 3000 brothers; spirit of all fresh water; fought with Hercules for Deianira; **as** a bull he fought again with Hercules and lost a horn which the Naiads made into the horn of plenty. (Greek.)

ACHERON: Son of Helios Gaea; changed to the river of Hades, where the shades of the dead hover, into which Phlegethon (River of Fire) and Cocytus (River of Lament) flow.

ADEPHAGIA: Goddess of gluttony. (Greek.)

ADONIS: Son of Cinyras by his daughter Smyrna (Myrrha); Aphrodite, enchanted by his beauty, was so grieved by his death in a hunting accident that the gods allowed him to return from Hades for six months every year; returns to earth each spring, and his myth, which was celebrated in an annual festival throughout the ancient world, symbolized the death and rebirth of nature in the fall and spring of the year. (Greek.)

ADRASTIA: Another name for Nemesis.

ADRASTREA: Goddess of destiny, or inevitable fate; daughter of Zeus and Ananke; punisher of injustice. (Greek.)

AEACUS: Son of Zeus and Aegina, just ruler of the Myrmidons, who became one of three judges of the dead in Hades. See Minos, Rhadamanthus. (Greek.)

AEËTES: Son of Helios and Perse, father of Medea.

AEGA: Daughter of Helios; changed into a star by Zeus. (Greek.)

AEGAEAN: Another name for Nereus, as god of the Aegean sea.

AEGINA: Daughter of the river-god Asopus; mother of Aeacus, either by Zeus or by her father. See Aeacus.

AELLO: A Harpy; name means "tempest." See Harpies.

AEOLUS: God of the winds, ruler of the Aeolian Islands, with his palace at Strongyle (Stromboli); kept the winds in a cave and released them only by order of Zeus.

AESCULAPIUS: God of medicine; son of Apollo and Coronis; raised by the centaur Chiron on Mount Pelion after his mother was killed for her infidelity with Ischys; Zeus, fearing that he would conquer death and make men immortal, killed him with a thunderbolt and placed him among the gods. (Greek.)

AETHER: Personification of the sky; son of Chaos, or of Erebus and Nyx. (Greek.)

AGLAIA: The "bright one" of the Graces; Brilliance. See Charites.

AIDES: Another form of Hades.

AIDOS: Personification, among the Greeks, of an emotion somewhat like *noblesse oblige*. insofar as a fortunate man contemplates the lot of the less favored; also the sense of propriety that inhibits men from doing evil.

ALASTOR: The "Unforgetting One"; (1) epithet of Zeus and of other gods as avengers of wrong; (2) personification of vengeance, especially of murder that has gone undetected. (Greek.)

ALCYONE: (1) A Pleiad; daughter of Atlas and Pleione; (2) daughter of Aeolus and Enarete; wife of Cëyx; when she tried to reach the body of her drowned husband, the gods changed both of them into sea-birds, with power to calm the seas in their breeding season (The "halcyon days." (Greek.).

ALECTO: The "Unceasing One" of the Furies.

ALPHEUS: River-god of the Alpheus River, who pursued the nymph Arethusa. See Arethusa.

AMOR: Roman name for Eros.

AMPHITRITE: A Nereid (or sometimes, an Oceanid), daughter of Nereus and Doris, wife of Poseidon and therefore goddess of the sea, mother of Triton. (Greek.)

ANANKE: Personification of necessity (what must be, must be); daughter of Erebus and Nyx. (Greek.)

ANTEROS: The avenging Eros (*deus ultor*), punisher of those who failed to return the love of others; sometimes represented as the rival of Eros, who undid the work of love. (Greek.)

APHRODITE: Goddess of love; daughter, in the Iliad; of Zeus and Dione, but usually represented as springing full-grown from the foam of the sea; wife of Hephaestus; mother of Eros; most beautiful of the goddesses, lover of Ares, Dionysus, Hermes, Poseidon, Anchises (father of Aeneas), and Adonis. See Uranus.

APOLLO: Identified with the sun-god Helios, therefore Phoebus ("Bright" or "Pure") Apollo, the Olympian god of youth, beauty, poetry and music, Prophecy, and archery; son of Zeus and Leto, twin of Artemis, leader of the Muses, a deliverer and punisher of men; also called Pythian Apollo from the seat of his oracle and worship at Pytho (or Delphi). (Greek.)

APOLLYN: The "Angel of the bottomless pit," corresponding with Abaddon of the Hebrews.

AQUILO: Roman name for Boreas.

ARA: Goddess of vengeance or destruction.

ARCAS: Son of Zeus and Callisto, founder of Arcadia. See Arcturus, Boötes.

ARCTURUS (ARCTOS): Names for Arcas.

ARES: God of war; son of Zeus and Hera; lover of Aphrodite; father, by different spouses, of Meleager (the prince of Calydon), Cyncus (slain by Hercules), Parthenopaeus (one of the seven against Thebes), Alcippe (whose violator, Hamillhothius, son of Poseidon, Ares slew, thus precipitating the trial that won him an acquittal and the Areopagus, or "hill of Ares," a name); fiercest of the gods, hated even by his family; attended by Eris, Demios, Metis, Pallor, and Phobos. (Greek.)

ARETHUSA: A virgin huntress, devotee of Artemis, who was pursued by the river-god Alpheus, and changed by the goddess into a submarine river which rose again in the fountain of Arethusa on the island of Ortygia at Syracuse. (Greek.)

ARTEMIS: Goddess of the hunt, the moon, and wild nature; daughter of Zeus and Leto; twin sister of Apollo, and, like him, a deliverer and punisher, especially of women; a virgin goddess, patroness of chastity. (Greek.)

ASOPUS: River-god of the river Asopus; son of Oceanus and Tethys; father of Aegina, Evadne, and Euboea. (Greek.)

ASTERIA: Daughter of Coeus, the Titan, and Phoebe; sister of Leto, wife of Perses, mother of Hecate; changed to an island to escape the lust of Zeus.

ASTRAEUS: A Titan, husband of Eos, and father, in some accounts, of the winds and stars. (Greek.)

ASTREA: Goddess of innocence, purity, justice; daughter of Zeus and Themis; with sister, Pudicitia (Modesty), left the earth after the Golden Age, when men had become wicked, and lived among the stars as the constellation Virgo. (Greek.)

ATE: Among earliest of Greek goddesses, daughter of Eris (Strife) or Zeus, spirit of infatuation and mischief who led gods as well as men into rash and foolish actions.

ATHENA: Olympian goddess of Wisdom, the virgin (therefore also "Parthenos") battle-goddess who sprang fully grown and armed from the head of Zeus after, some say, he had eaten her "mother," Metis; patroness of the state and of prosperity, of agriculture, practical and fine arts, law courts (she is said to have instituted the Areopagus at Athens), she is also credited with first having taught men to tame horses. In the war of the Olympians and the Titans she slew the giant Pallas; hence any city which kept a statue of her, called a palladium, was guaranteed her aid as long as the statue stood; therefore her special title, Pallas Athene. (Greek.)

ATLAS: In Homeric legend, the god who held up the heavens on pillars which he supported on his back; in later myth, a Titan in rivalry with Zeus, condemned to support the heavens on his head and hands.

ATROPOS: See Moirae.

AURORA: Roman name for Eos.

AUSTER: Roman name for Notus.

BACCHANTES: See Maenads.

BACCHUS: Roman wine-god, identified with Dionysus.

BELA: Spartan equivalent of Abellio.

BELLONA: Roman name for Enyo.

BENDIS: Thracian goddess of the moon.

BOÖTES: Arcas, king of Arcadia; in the hunt, gave chase to a she-bear who was really his mother in disguise; changed by Zeus into the Little Bear (or Little Dipper) and, as a constellation, still pursues his mother across the skies. See Callisto.

BOREAS: The North Wind; son in some accounts of Astraeus and Eos; brother of Hesperus, Zephyrus, and Notus; father by Orithyia, of Zetes, Calais, and Cleopatra (wife of the Phineus whom her brothers rescued from the Harpies); depicted with beard, stern face (in keeping with reputation for rudeness), and blowing a conch shell, he is a familiar figure on old maps; also the North-northeast Wind.

BRIAREUS: See Hecatoncheires.

BRITOMARTIS: A Cretan nymph, daughter of Zeus by Carme; to escape the lust of Minos, she leaped into the sea and was deified by Artemis; identified with her patroness Artemis, she was invoked by hunters, sailors, and fishermen, and was considered to be the dispenser of happiness to men.

BROMIUS: Surname of Dionysus as the noisy god of the Bacchic rituals.

CABIRI: Mysterious gods worshiped in Thebes, Anthedon, Pergamus, and elsewhere, and with especially splendid ritual at Samothrace; sometimes identified as earth-gods and associated particularly with the Pelasgi, who established their worship throughout Greece.

CALLIOPE: Chief of the nine Muses, patroness of eloquence and epic poetry; mother of Orpheus by Apollo. See Muses.

CALLISTO: An Arcadian nymph, hunting companion of Artemis; Zeus loved her and disguised her as a she-bear to conceal her from Hera; her son, Arcas, a hunter, gave chase and, as he was about to slay her, Zeus raised both of them to the sky as constellations, where the chase goes on with Callisto as the Great Bear (Big Dipper) and her son, renamed Boötes, as the Little Bear (Little Dipper). (Greek.)

CALYPSO: A sea-nymph who entertained and tried to detain Ulysses on her island. (Greek.)

CARMENAE: Prophetic nymphs in the religion of ancient Italy; sometimes identified with the Greek Muses. See Carmenta.

CARMENTA (CARMENTIS): Most celebrated of the Carmenae, said originally to have been called Nicostrate, mother of Evander;

a temple at the foot of the Capitoline Hill and altars near the Carmentalis Gate were dedicated to her in Rome. See Carmenae.

CARPO: See Horae.

CASTOR: See Dioscuri, Tyndaridae.

CATAMITUS: Roman name for Ganymede.

CELAENO: The "Gloomy One," a Harpy.

CENTAURS: Originally a race of bull—killers from Mount Pelion in Thessaly; later represented as half-horses and half-men and said to be sons of Ixion and a phantom which Zeus created to resemble Hera, to whose love Ixion aspired; at wedding of their half-brother, Pirithous, to Hippodamia, the drunken Centaur Evrytion (Eurytus) carried off the bride; the groom's people, the Lapithae, gave fight to the Centaurs and drove them off into exile on Mount Pindus.

CENTIMANUS: Roman name for the Hecatoncheires.

CERBERUS: Guardian of the gate to hell, a dog with three heads and the tail of a serpent.

CERES: Roman name for Demeter.

CETO: Daughter of Oceanus and Gaea, mother of the Gorgons by the sea-god Phorcys.

CHAOS: Most ancient of the gods, personified the void and formless infinite from which all things came; begot Erebus and Nyx, the parents of Aether and Hemera. (Greek.)

CHARIS: In the Iliad, goddess of grace and beauty, represented as wife of Hephaestus; merges in later myth with the Charites.

CHARITES: The three Graces.

CHARON: Son of Erebus and Nyx, boatman of the river Styx, who ferried the shades of the dead to Hades. (Greek.)

CHARYBDIS: A sea-monster guarding the strait between Italy and Sicily where, as a gulf, she swallowed and threw up the ocean twice each day and preyed upon hapless sailors. See Scylla. (Greek.)

CHERA: Hera as patroness of widows.

CHIRON: A Centaur; son of Cronus and Philyra; trained by Apollo and Artemis in hunting, medicine, music, gymnastics, and prophecy, he lived on Mount Pelion and taught his skills to many of the Greek heroes, including Peleus (father of Achilles), Achilles, and Diomedes; gave his immortality to Prometheus when he was accidentally wounded by a poison arrow of his friend Hercules, and was placed by Zeus among the stars as the constellation Sagittarius. See Centaurs.

CHLORIS: Goddess of flowers; wife of Zephyrus. (Greek.)

CIRCE: A sorceress, daughter of Helios and Perse, sister of Aeëtes, Pasiphaë, and Perses; after luring men to her island home on Aeaea, she feasted them, then, by her magic, turned them into beasts. (Greek.)

CLIO: Muse of history. See Muses.

CLOTHO: See Moirae.

CLUSIUS (CLUSIVIUS): The "Shutter"; Janus as the porter of heaven. See Patulcus.

CLYMENE: (1) Daughter of Oceanus and Tethys, wife of Iapetus, mother of the Titans Atlas, Prometheus, and Epimetheus; (2) a nymph (in some accounts, a mortal) who bore Phaëton by the sun-god, Helios, and encouraged him to ask permission to drive the chariot which draws the sun daily across the heavens. (Greek.)

COCYTUS: Infernal river of Lament. See Acheron.

COELUS: Roman name for Uranus.

COEUS: A Titan, husband of Phoebe, father of Lato. See Titans.

COTTUS: See Hecatoncheires.

COTYS: A Thracian goddess, patron of a festival called the Cotyttia, similar to the worship of Cybele in Thrace; she had special devotees called Baptae, like the Corybantes who worshiped Cybele, and her festivals, introduced into Athens and Corinth, were of the same erotic and orgiastic nature.

COTYTTO: Another name for Cotys.

CRIMISSUS: A river-god, father of the hero Alcestis who founded the town of Segesta on Sicily. (Greek.)

CRIUS: A Titan, son of Uranus and Gaea. See Titans.

CRONIUS: Patronymic of Poseidon as son of Cronus.

CRONUS: Leader of the Titans; wounded and deposed his father, Uranus, and ruled the heavens with his brothers and sisters until he was, in turn, overthrown by his son, Zeus. See Titans.

CUPID: Roman name for Eros.

CYBELE: A Phrygian earth-goddess, or "great mother," identified with Rhea. See also Cotys.

CYCLOPS: (1) In Homer and in Virgil, fierce one-eyed giants (Polyphumus was the chief one) who kept sheep in the pastures of Sicily and fed on human flesh; (2) in Hesiod, Titans, three sons of Uranus and Gaea, named Arges, Brontes, and Steropes, also one-eyed, thrown into Tartarus by Cronus, but released by Zeus, and therefore so friendly to the Olympians as to supply Zeus with his characteristic thunderbolts, Hades with his helmet, and Poseidon with his trident; afterwards slain by Apollo for having given Zeus the thunderbolt that killed Aesculapius; (3) five in number, with Acamas and Pyracmon added, they were later thought to work the furnaces and forces of Hephaestus, which supplied the armor and ornament of the gods.

CYNTHIA: Another name for Diana.

DACTYLS (DACTYLI): Like the Corybantes, attendants of Cybele; they discovered iron and iron-working and, as their metrical name suggests, are thought to have brought rhythm to the Greeks; called Idean Dactyls from their home on Mount Ida.

DAPHNE: A nymph, daughter of the river-god Peneus; she was pursued by Apollo and, in answer to her prayers to her father, was turned into a laurel tree, which thereafter became the tree most sacred to Apollo. (Greek.)

DARDANUS: Son of Zeus and Electra; mythical ancestor of the Trojans and the Romans.

DEA TACITA: The Sabine goddess, Larunda, whose worship was brought to Rome by Titus Tatius after the rape of the Sabine women; identified with Larenta.

DEINO (DINO): See Graeae.

DEMAGORGON: A demiurge, hideous ruler of the spirits of hell whose very name evoked horror and dread. (Greek.)

DEMETER: With Dionysus, the great earth-deity of the Greeks; the "mother-goddess" or "Mother Earth," she was the daughter of Cronus and Rhea, and the sister-wife of Zeus, by whom she bore Persephone, the goddess of grain and harvests, and is often represented as carrying a torch, with which she searched for Persephone in the underworld. See Persephone.

DEMIOS: Personification of dread, an attendant of Ares.

DENDRITES: Dionysus as a tree-god.

DIANA: Roman name for Artemis.

DICTYNNA: Another name for Britomartis.

DIKE: See Horae.

DIONE: A Titan, sister-consort of Zeus, to whom, in one account, she bore Aphrodite; associated with Dodona, the most ancient oracle in Greece, dedicated to Zeus in Epirus. See Titans, Aphrodite.

DIONYSUS: God of wine; with Ceres, the goddess of grain, greatest among the earth-gods of the Greeks; son of Zeus by Semele, he was hated by his jealous step mother Hera and forced by her to wander madly through Egypt, Syria, and India, where he introduced the culture of grape orchards; encouraged the ecstasies and orgies of the Maenads (Bacchantes), and was therefore identified with religious fanaticism and mania.

DIOS: Another name for Zeus.

DIOSCURI: Epithet of the twins Castor and Polydeuces (Pollux) as "sons of Zeus," designating them as children of Zeus and Leda, hence, brothers of Helen of Troy with whom they were simultaneously hatched from the two eggs produced from the union of their mother and the Swan.

DIS: Roman name for Hades.

DORIS: (1) A sea-goddess, daughter of Oceanus and Thetis, sister-consort of Nereus to whom she bore the fifty Nereids; (2) one of the Nereids. See Nymphs.

DRYADS: See Nymphs.

ECHO: A nymph who distracted Hera with chatter while Zeus sported with her sisters and was changed by the suspicious goddess into an echo; later she fell in love with Narcissus and grieved so over his failure to return her affection that she pined away until nothing was left of her but her voice. (Greek.)

EILEITHYIA: Another form of Ilithyia.

EIRENE: Another form of Irene.

ELECTRA: (1) Daughter of Oceanus and Tethys; wife of Thaumas; mother of Iris and the Harpies; (2) daughter of Atlas and Pleione; a Pleiad; mother, by Zeus, of Iasion and Dardanus. (Greek.)

EMPUSA: A Thracian specter and vampire in the train of Hecate, the terror of travelers.

EMPUSA: A Thracian specter and vampire in the train of Hecate, the terror of travelers.

ENYO: Goddess of war, in the train of Ares, and represented as his sister or his wife; one of the Graeae, her name means "Horror," and she walked in a terrible company that included Panic, Terror, and Trembling. (Greek.)

EOS: Goddess of the dawn, daughter of the Titans Hyperion and Thia; wife of Tithonus; mother of Memnon; each morning she drove her chariot up the heavens from the ocean to announce the arrival of a new day.

EPIMETHEUS: A Titan, son of Iapetus and Clymene, who accepted Pandora, the first woman, as a gift from Zeus, and so brought trouble and sorrow into the life of man on earth.

EREBUS: God of the netherworld, son of Chaos, who personified the gloomy place through which the shades of the dead passed on the way to Hades; father of Aether and Hemera by his sister, Nyx. (Greek.)

ERIS: Personification of strife or discord; an attendant on Ares.

EROS: God of love; son of Aphrodite, either by Zeus, Ares, or Hermes; in some accounts a cosmic deity born from an egg produced by Nyx (Night) or, in Hesiod, the first of the gods, a representation of the force in nature that attracts things to one another and much like the life instinct, or Eros, recognized in contemporary Freudian psychology; with his quiver of arrows, some gold to kindle love in the hearts of his victims, some lead to kindle hate, Eros was often depicted as blind, and in late mythology, as a practical joker from whom neither gods nor men were safe; loved Psyche. See Anteros, Psyche, Thanatos. (Greek.)

EUMENIDES: The Furies; an ironic title, meaning literally "The good-tempered goddesses," which is just what the Eumenides were not, and used by the Greeks as a way of getting around these terrifying sisters.

EUNOMIA: See Horae.

EUPHROSYNE: One of the three Graces, whose name signifies "joy."

EURUS: The East Wind; also the Southeast Wind. See Winds.

EURYALE: See Gorgons.

EURYNOME: A Titan, daughter of Oceanus, wife of Ophion, queen-consort of Olympus until she was deposed by Rhea. See Titans.

EVANDER: Roman culture hero; son of Hermes and an Arcadian nymph called Carmenta or Tiburtis; established colony of Arcadians at Pallantium on the Tiber River, which was an original village of Rome; introduced worship of Demeter, Herakles, Pan, and Poseidon, and taught the social, civic, and cultural arts to his neighbors.

FATES: See Moirae.

FAUNA: Wife and female counterpart of Faunus.

FAUNS: Roman Satyrs. See Faunus.

FAUNUS: Roman god of fields and shepherds; son of Picus, grandson of Saturnus; father of Latinus; third king of the Laurentes; later, when the worship of Pan reached Italy, identified with Pan, just as the Fauni, his followers, became Satyrs.

FAVONIUS: Roman name for Zephyrus.

FLORA: Roman name for Chloris.

GALATEA: A sea-nymph, daughter of Nereus and Doris; the Cyclops, Polyphemus, in love with Galatea, crushed her lover Acis under a huge rock; Galatea changed the blood oozing from beneath the rock into the river Acis or Achinius, which flows at the foot of Mount Aetna. (Greek.)

GANYMEDE: Fairest of all mortals; taken by Zeus to Mount Olympus to be cupbearer of the gods. (Greek.)

GEMINI: (1) Roman name for the twins, Castor and Pollux; (2) the constellation to which Castor and Pollux were translated by Zeus. See Dioscuri, Tyndaridae.

GLAUCUS: A fisherman of Anthedon in Boeotia, Glaucus was changed by Ocean and Tethys into a sea-god after he had eaten a divine herb planted by Cronus (Saturn) and had to live in the sea; loved Scylla, the sea-nymph, but his love was unreturned (see Scylla); a patron of fishermen and sailors, with great powers of prophecy. (Greek.)

GORGONS (GORGONES): Sisters of the Graeae, and also three in number, named Euryale, Medusa, and Stheno, of whom Medusa alone was mortal; also called the Phorcydes, they were winged monsters, with claws, enormous teeth, and serpents instead of hair, and the sight of them turned onlookers to stone; after the hero Perseus killed Medusa, her head was placed in the center of Athena's shield. See Graeae.

THE GRACES: Usually three lovely maidens, the sisters Aglaia, Euphrosyne, and Thalia. They bestowed beauty and charm, and were often identified with the Muses.

GRADIVUS: Mars as Roman war-god.

GRAEAE (GRAIAE): Three sisters, "the old (or gray) ladies," daughters of Phorcys and Ceto, guardians of the Gorgons; they were Pephredo, Enyo, and Deïno (Dino), and are called the Phorcydes after their father;

white-haired at birth, they had but a single eye and a single tooth to share among themselves. (Greek.)

GRATIAE: Roman name for the Graces.

GYGES (GYES): See Hecatoncheires.

HADES (AIDES): God of the underworld; son of Cronus and Rhea; husband of Persephone; ruler of the dead; by men hated and feared above all the gods. See Demeter, Persephone.

HALCYONE: Another name for Alcyone.

HEBE: Goddess of youth; daughter of Zeus and Hera; cupbearer of the gods before Ganymede, she filled their cups with nectar; married Herakles after the hero was received among the gods.

HECATE: Daughter of Perses and Asteria, called Perseïs for her father, Hecate was a goddess of many guises; she has been represented as the last of the race of Titans who kept her powers into the reign of Zeus; she is the goddess of "three forms"—Selena in heaven, Artemis on earth, and Persephone in hell; or, as Hecate, she is the infernal aspect of a threefold Artemis, goddess of moonlight nights and, actually, Diana of the Crossways; none of these reports, however, denies her great powers, and she was respected by gods and men as the patroness of magic and witchcraft.

HECATONCHEIRES: Three monsters, each with a hundred hands, sons of Uranus and Gaea; their names were Briareus (or Aegaeon), Cottus, and Gyges (or Gyes); they are thought to have personified the roar of breaking waves and each is identified with some aspect of the winter season; thus Briareus (the "Presser") was associated with the burden of winter snow on the earth, Cottus (the "Smiter") was identified with hail, and Gyges (the "Furrower") brought to mind the weathering action of the rain. See Uranus.

HELEN OF TROY: Immortal daughter of Zeus and Leda, sister of Castor and Pollux; the rape of Helen by Paris was the cause of the Trojan war.

HELIADES: Sons and daughters of Helios, especially Lampetie, Phaethusa, and Phoebe, daughters of the nymph Clymene, who wept so bitterly at the death of their brother Phaëton that they were turned into poplartrees, and their tears into amber. (Greek.)

HEPHAESTUS: God of fire; son, in Homer, of Zeus and Hera; sometimes said to be son of Hera by no father and her answer to the birth of Athena from the head of Zeus; he was such a deformed and ugly child that Hera flung him from Olympus and he fell into the sea where he was raised by Thetis and Eurynome; returned to Olympus as artisan of the gods, whose palaces he modeled after his own, which was made of the substance of the stars; sometimes represented as living and working on a volcanic island with the Cyclops as his servants; in early myth, husband of Charis, or of Aglaia, youngest of the Charites; later represented as the husband of Aphrodite, to whose beauty his ugliness stood in opposition as one of the profoundest ironies in the scheme of creation.

HERAKLES: Son of Zeus by Alcmene, wife of Amphitryon of Thebes; because he wished to raise a hero to rule over the race of Perseus, Zeus seduced Alcmene in the form of her absent husband; but this dynasty was defeated by Hera, who had other plans for the race, and became the lifelong enemy of Herakles; when he was grown and married, she afflicted him with madness, causing him to kill his children; in desperation he went to the oracle at Delphi where he was told to bind himself to Eurystheus at Tiryns for 12 years and perform the tasks that his master set up for him; this Herakles did, and his 12 labors in the course of his bondage won him fame as the greatest hero of the Greeks; the traditional list of his 12 labors is: (1) *To skin the Nemean Lion.* This fierce monster, spawned by Typhon and Echidna, roamed the valley of Nemea, in north Argolis; invulnerable to the club and arrows of Herakles, it was finally strangled in his bare hands and the carcass was brought to Tiryns. (2) *To kill the Lernean Hydra.* Another monstrous offspring of Typhon and Echidna, the hydra lived in a swamp near the well of Amyone and preyed on the countryside of Lerna, near Argos; it had 9 heads, of which the middle one was immortal; whenever a head was struck off, two grew back in its place; Herakles, with the help of his servant Iolaus, burned the heads of the Hydra away, and buried the immortal one under a rock; then he dipped his arrows in the bile of the monster, so that their wound would be incurable. (3) *To capture the Arcadian stag.* Eurystheus ordered Herakles to bring back alive this stag with the golden antlers and brazen feet; the pursuit of the fleet and wily stag occupied an entire year, but Herakles finally brought it down with an arrow, and returned with the living beast on his shoulders. (4) *To capture the Erymanthian boar.* Ordered by Eurystheus to bring the boar back alive from Psophis, to which it had descended from Mount Erymanthus, Herakles chased the beast through the snow until it was tired enough to be snared with a net (the chase is sometimes said to have occurred in Thessaly). (5) *To clean the Augean stables.* King Augeus of Elis kept 3000 oxen in stables which had not been cleaned for 30 years; when Eurystheus ordered him to clean the stables in a day, Herakles diverted the rivers Alpheus and Peneus through the stalls and accomplished his task in the allotted time. (6) *To rout the Stymphalian birds.* These man-eating birds, with brazen claws, wings, and beaks, had feathers which they used like arrows; pets of Ares, they lived in Arcadia near Lake Stymphalus and raided the countryside; when Eurystheus ordered Herakles to drive them away, Athena gave the hero a brass rattle which he shook and so startled the birds that they took flight (in some accounts, Herakles killed them with his arrows while they were in the air). (7) *To capture the Cretan bull.* Poseidon had given the bull to King Minos of Crete, to be used as a sacrificial offering; but Minos thought the bull too beautiful to destroy, and sacrificed another instead; angry, Poseidon, drove the bull mad and Eurystheus ordered Herakles to capture it and so stop the havoc it was causing on Crete; Herakles brought the bull back on his shoulders. (8) *To capture the mares of Diomedes, King of the Bistones.* This Thracian king kept horses which he fed on human flesh; when Herakles and his companions, bidden by Eurystheus to bring the horses back alive, seized the beasts, they were pursued by Diomedes and the Bistones; in the fight that followed, the Bistones were defeated and Herakles threw the body of Diomedes to the horses, taming them with the flesh of their master. (9) *To bring back the girdle of Hippolyte, Queen of the Amazons.* Admete, daughter of Eurystheus, coveted the girdle that Hippolyte had been given by her father Ares, and Eurystheus commanded Herakles to get it for her; Herakles won the girdle after a contest sponsored by his enemy Hera, in which Hippolyte was killed. (10) *To capture the red oxen of Geryones (Geryon).* Herakles was next ordered to bring back the oxen belonging to Geryones, who was a monster with 3 bodies and 3 heads living on the western island of Erythia, where the setting rays of the sun stained the land red; on this long journey, Herakles reached the frontiers of Africa and Europe, where he raised the pillars that bear his name (at Gibralter); on Erythia he killed Geryones, as well as the monster, Eurytion, and the two-headed dog, Orthrus, who guarded the oxen; after many adventures, he returned with the oxen to Eurystheus, who sacrificed them to Hera. (11) *To procure the golden apples of the Hesperides.* Since the whereabouts of the apples, which Geae had given as a wedding gift to Hera, was a secret, this labor was particularly difficult; for Hera had entrusted the apples to the Hesperides and the dragon Ladon who lived on Mount Atlas in the land of the Hyperboreans; since Atlas was the father of the Hesperides, Herakles went and offered to relieve him of the burden of holding up the heavens if he would help in the quest; Atlas complied willingly and got the apples, but threatened to return them himself to Eurystheus and leave Herakles holding the sky; whereupon Herakles asked for and got a moment's grace in order to place a pad on his shoulder, picked up the apples and left before dim-witted Atlas realized that he was back where he had started. (12) *To bring back Cerberus from the underworld.* The last, and worst, labor led Herakles down into hell, where Hades agreed to the mission provided that Herakles used no weapons; the hero carried the terrible dog back to Eurystheus in his bare hands, and returned it the same way to the underworld. The twelfth adventure closes the canon of the labors of Herakles, but not of his adventures; his long, eventful life brought him at last to Deianira, daughter of Oeneus, his last wife, whom the dying centaur, Nessus, persuaded to give Herakles the fatal shirt steeped in the incurable poison of Herakles' arrows, with which he had himself been cut down; with the poison eating into him, Herakles erected his own funeral pyre on Mount Oeta, but was rescued by a cloud which descended upon him and carried him off to Mount Olympus where he was made immortal, married Hebe, and so won a mollified Hera as a mother-in-law.

HERCULES: Roman name for Herakles.

HERMAPHRODITUS: Son of Hermes and Aphrodite; greatgrandson of Atlas, and therefore also known as Atlantiades and Atlantius; in answer to the prayers of the nymph of the fountain of Salmacis, near Helicarnassus, who had spied and seized him at his bath, he was joined to her forever and they became one in body, retaining the characteristics of either sex. (Greek.)

HERMES: Messenger of the gods; god of eloquence, prudence and cunning; inventor of the lyre, syrinx, alphabet, numbers, astronomy, the arts of boxing, gymnastics, the sciences of weights and measures; cultivator of the olive-tree, protector of travelers; son of Zeus and Maia; shrewdest of the gods, he was also the patron of thieves, and was the god who conducted the shades of the dead to the underworld.

HESPERIDES: (1) Daughters of Zeus and Themis, or (2) in another account, daughters of Atlas and Hesperis (and called, after either parent the Atlantides or the Hesperides); either three in number (Aegle, Arethusa, and Hesperia) or four (Aegle, Arethusa, Crytheia, and Hestia), or sometimes as many as seven. However, despite these discrepancies, they were, with the dragon Ladon, the acknowledged guardians of the golden apples which Hercules had to procure in one of his labors. See Themis, Titans.

HESPERIS: Mother, by Atlas, of the Hesperides. See Hesperides.

HESPERUS: The evening star; son of Astraeus and Eos, of Cephalus and Eos, or of Atlas. See Lucifer.

HESTIA: Goddesses of the hearth; daughter of Cronus and Rhea; a virgin goddess, patron of domestic life. (Greek.)

HIMEROS: Personification of longing, an attendant on Eros.

HORAE: Daughters of Zeus and Themis, guardians of the doorways to Olympus, of the seasons, the weather, and the processes of nature; the Athenians worshiped two, Thallo, the Hora of spring, and Carpo, the Hora of Fall; Hesiod calls them Dike (Justice), Eunomia (Good Order, especially legal and political order), and Irene (Peace).

HYADES: Seven nymphs; daughters of Atlas and Pleione; sisters of the Pleiades; their parentage and number vary in different accounts, but, as seven sisters, they are named Ambrosia, Coronis, Dicne (or Thyene), Eudora, Pedile, Phytho, and Polyxo; either as a reward for nursing the infant Dionysus, or for their sisterly devotion to Hyas (sometimes said to be their father), they were placed as stars in the head of the constellation Taurus: their name means "Rainers," and the time of their rising and setting in May and November is the rainy season along the Mediterranean. (Greek.)

HYAS: Son of Atlas; either father or brother of the Hyades; killed by a wild beast in Libya; the grief of the Hyades because of his death won them a place among the stars. See Hyades.

HYGEIA (HYGEA): Goddess of health; daughter or wife of Aesculapius; a virgin goddess (Greek).

HYMEN (HYMENAEUS): God of marriage; usually said to be son of Apollo and Urania. (Greek.)

HYPERION: A Titan, father of Helios (the sun), Selene (the moon), and Eos (the dawn). See Titans.

HYPNUS (HYPNOS): God of sleep; son of Erebus and Nyx, brother of Thanatos, father of the dream-makers, Morpheus, Icelus, and Phantasus; dwelt in the Cave of Sleep in the misty, cloud-capped, eternally dark abode of the Cimmerians on the farther bank of Oceanus. (Greek.)

IAPETUS: A Titan, husband of Clymene, father of Atlas, Prometheus, and Epimetheus. See Titans.

IASION: Son of Zeus and Electra; by Demeter, father of Plutus. (Greek.)

ILITHYIA: Goddess of childbirth, either daughter of Hera, or personification of a special attribute of Hera. (Greek.)

INACHUS: Son of the Titans Oceanus and Tethys; father of Phoroneus and Io; first King of Argos; river Inachus said to have been named after him, hence called sometimes a river-god.

INO: Daughter of Cadmus and Harmonia; wife of Athamas; later changed into a sea-goddess when she leaped into the sea with the body of her dead son Melicertes, whom her husband had killed in madness; later

rescued Odysseus. See Leucothea. (Greek.)

IRENE: See Horae.

IRIS: Goddess of the rainbow; in the *Iliad*, messenger of the gods; daughter of Thaumas and Electra; sister of the Harpies; in early myth a virgin goddess; later wife of Zephyrus, mother of Eros. (Greek.)

JANUS (JANUS BIFRONS): Originally a Roman numina, a pair of divinities, who were worshiped as the sun and moon, as the names Janus (Dianus) and Jana (Diana), which are based on the same root *(dies—day)*, imply; invoked even before Jupiter in every undertaking, Janus was the god of beginnings, who opened the year and the seasons and left his name as the first month of the new year, January; a passage by the Forum, called the "temple" of Janus, was left open in wartime to show that the god was out with the troops, and closed in peacetime to keep this tutelary divinity safely at home; New Year's Day, his feast day, was celebrated by an exchange of copper coins, called *strenae*, with a double-headed Janus on one side, representing the ability of the god to see in both directions at once, both before and after. See Patulcus, Clusius, Janus Quadrifrons.

JANUS QUADRIFRONS: Literally, the four-headed Janus; Janus in his representation as the guardian of the four seasons.

JUDGES OF THE DEAD: In Greek mythology, the three judges of the dead in Hades were Aeacus, Minos, and Rhadamanthus.

JUNO: Roman name for Hera.

JUPITER (JOVE): Roman name for Zeus.

JUVENTAS: Roman name for Hebe.

KORA: Literally "maiden," an epithet for Persephone.

LACHESIS: See Moirae.

LARENTA: Mistress of Hercules and nurse of Romulus and Remus, honored in Roman religion by the annual festival of the Larentalia (Dec. 23). Also called Acca Larentia; identified with Larunda.

LARES: Roman numina, spirits of dead ancestors who were remembered as household and civic gods; there were Lares domestici, true guardians of private houses, and Lares publici who, either as Lares praestites, protected the entire city, or as Lares compitales, werved over definite sections of the city which were marked at the compita, or street-crossings; only the spirits of good men became Lares; at family meals some offering was set out for the Lares, and at family celebrations the Lararia, or compartments of the Lares, were thrown open. See Penates, Lemures.

LARUNDA: Sabine goddess identified with Larenta. Also called Dea Tacita.

LEDA: Wife of Tyndareus of Sparta; mother either by him or by Zeus, of Castor and Polydeuces (Pollux), Clytemnestra and Helen; in the popular legend, she was visited by Zeus in the form of a swan and brought forth 2 eggs; from one egg, Helen was born, from the other, the twins, her brothers. (Greek.)

LEMURES: Spirits of the dead; sometimes used as a common term for all dead souls, which were then subdivided into Lares, or the spirits of good men, and Larvae, or the spirits of evil men; more popularly identified only with the Larvae and used as a synonym for these dreaded specters who tormented the living; the Lemuralia (Lemuria) was a special Roman feast celebrated to appease the Lemures.

LENAEUS: From "lenus," wine-press or vintage, an epithet of Dionysus.

LETHE: Infernal river of Forgetfulness.

LETONA: Roman name for Leto.

LEUCE: A nymph beloved by Hades, changed by him into a white poplar tree.

LEUCOTHEA: Sea-goddess; name of Ino after she was deified. (Greek.)

LIBER: Roman name for Bacchus.

LITAE: Goddesses of good will, daughters of Zeus, assigned to undoing the harm done to others by Ate. (Greek.)

LUCIFER: (1) The morning star, or the planet Venus when seen before sunrise; identified with Hesperus, father of Ceÿx by Philonis; sometimes said to be father of the Hesperides; (2) epithet of several goddesses of light, as Artemis, Aurora, Hecate. (Greek.)

LUCINA: (1) Roman name for Ilithyia. (2) Epithet of Juno and of Diana.

LUNA: Roman name for Selene.

MAENADS: Nymphs who attended on Dionysus (Bacchus); also women who celebrated his rites, remarkable for their ecstatic abandonment.

MAIA: Eldest of the Pleiades; mother of Hermes by Zeus. See Pleiades.

MANES: In Rome, the souls of the dead departed, who were worshiped as gods; D.M.S., a common inscription on sepulchers, commemorated the Manes and stood for *Dis Manibus Sacrum.*

MARS: Roman god of war, roughly equivalent to Ares; in Roman myth, father of Romulus and Remus by the vestal virgin Rhea Silvia; hence founder of the Roman nation, and second only to Jupiter in the Roman pantheon, with the honorific title "Father Mars," and, with Jupiter and Quirinius, tutelary god of the Romans; also patron of agriculture and cattle; husband of Neria (Neriene). See Gradivus, Silvanus, Quirinus.

MEDEA: Daughter of Aeëtes, King of Colchis; famed for her powers as an enchantress, which she used to help Jason in his quest for the golden fleece; later, when Jason deserted her for Creüsa, the daughter of Creon, Medea, in rage, killed her two children and her rival, then fled to Athens, where she is said to have married King Aegeus.

MEDUSA: See Gorgons.

MELIAN (MELIC) NYMPHS: Nymphs who sprang from the blood of Uranus, after he was wounded by Cronus. See Titanus, Uranus, Cronus.

MERCURY: Roman name for Hermes.

MEROPE: (1) One of the Heliades. (2) A Pleiad, wife of Sisyphus, mother of Glaucus; in the constellation of the Pleiades the dimmest star because of her shame for having married a mortal.

METIS: Personification of prudence; daughter of Oceanus and Tethys, first wife of Zeus; with her aid Zeus became king of the gods after Metis induced Cronus to take a potion which caused him to vomit up his children, who then joined Zeus in the revolt against their father and the Titans; later Zeus, like his father before him, grew fearful of a rival, and ate Metis because she had become pregnant; Athena is said by some to have been the fetus that Zeus swallowed. See Titans, Cronus, Athena.

METIS: Personification of fear, an attendant on Ares.

MINERVA: Roman name for Athena.

MINOS: Son of Zeus and Europa, brother of Rhadamanthus, Cretan king and lawgiver, who became one of the three judges of the dead in Hades. See Aeacus, Rhadamanthus. (Greek.)

MINTHE (MINTHA): A nymph; daughter of Cocytus; loved by Hades; changed by Demeter or Persephone into the mint (mintha) plant.

MNEMOSYNE: A Titan, personification of memory, mother of the Muses by Zeus. See Titans, Muses.

MOIRAE: The Fates, three daughters of Zeus and Themis (Law), who spun, measured, and cut at will thread of a human destiny, or life; they were (1) Clotho, the spinner, who was mainly responsible for spinning the thread of life, (2) Lachesis, the Disposer of Lots, who measured the thread of life, and (3) Atropos, the Unturning (or Undeviating) One, who cut the thread of life with her fearful shears.

MOMUS: God of mockery and ridicule; in Hesiod, son of Nyx. (Greek.)

MORPHEUS: God of dreams; son of Hypnus; his name means literally the "fashioner," or "molder", because he gave form to the dreams that appear to sleepers; sometimes identified with Hypnus. (Greek.)

MORS: Roman name for Thanatos.

MULCIBER: Epithet of Vulcan, used ironically as Eumenides for the Furies. It means "the softener."

MUSES (MUSAE): In early Greek writing, the Muses merely inspired song; later they became deities who had the arts and sciences in their keeping; daughters of Zeus and Mnemosyne, they were born near Mount Olympus at Pieria where they guarded the sacred Pierian spring, the source of poetic inspiration; from an original band of three, their company expanded to nine, each with her own name and attribute; (1) Clio, the Muse of history, who is depicted either sitting or standing with an open roll of paper or a chest of books; (2) Euterpe, whose flute symbolizes her role as Muse of lyric poetry; (3) Thalia, the comic Muse, with her special symbols: the music mask, a shepherd's staff, and an ivy wreath; (4) Melpomene, the tragic Muse, who carries the tragic mask, the sword of Hercules, or a sword, is crowned with vine leaves, and wears the *cothurnus* (buskin); (5) Terpsichore, the Muse of choreography, as represented in the dances and songs of the Greek chorus; depicted with her lyre and plectrum; (6) Erato, the Muse of erotic poetry and mimicry, who also may be carrying a lyre; (7) Polyhymnia (or Polymnia), Muse of sacred poetry, who is usually depicted in an attitude of meditation; (8) Urania, the Muse of astronomy, who carries a pointer and a globe; (9) Calliope, the chief of the Muses, who is depicted with a tablet and stylus and sometimes with a roll of paper or a book.

NEMESIS: Goddess of vengeance; earlier, the measurer of happiness and misery, who afflicted with misfortunes those too liberally blessed by fate; more characteristically a punisher of crimes, like the Furies. (Greek.)

NEPTUNE (NEPTUNUS): Roman name for Poseidon.

NEREUS: A sea-god, the wise and infallible old man of the sea; son of Pontus and Gaea; husband of Doris; father of the 50 Nereids; ruled the Mediterranean from his subterranean palace. See Aegaean.

NIKE: Goddess of victory. (Greek.)

NOCTIFER: Another name for Hesperus.

NOTUS: The South Wind, bearer of fog and rain, son of Astraeus and Eos, brother of Hesperus and Zephyeus. See Winds.

NOX: Roman name for Nyx.

NUMINA: The abstract deities of the Romans before the myths of the Greeks were imported and popularized; literally, the powers that be, who were conceived without definite shape or form.

NYMPHS (NYMPHAE): The nymphs were nature spirits associated with water, trees, and mountains. They were divided into (1) sea-nymphs, who were either Oceanides, the nymphs of the great ocean, or Nereides, the daughters of Nereus, who represented only the Mediterranean Sea; (2) Naiades, who were the spirits of lakes, rivers, and springs; (3) mountain-nymphs, or Oreades, who frequented mountains and caves; (4) valley-nymphs, or Napaeae, the spirits of secluded glens; (5) tree nymphs, the Dryades and Hamadryades, who lived through the cycle of birth, growth, and death of the trees they inhabited; and (6) nymphs who were patronesses of particular places and took their names from the place with which they were associated, like the Hyades who had lived in the valley of Nysa and were therefore known also as the Nysaean nymphs.

NYSAEAN NYMPHS: See Hyades.

NYX: Goddess of night; daughter of Chaos, sister-wife of Erebus; mother of Aether, Hemera, Hypnus, and Thanatos; a deity of the underworld. See Chaos, Eros, Thanatos.

OCEANUS: A Titan, personification of the river that the Greeks supposed encircled the earth; ruler of the waters until he was replaced by Poseidon after the success of the second revolt of the gods. See Cronus, Titans, Uranus, Zeus.

ONIROS: God of dreams. (Greek.)

OPHION: A Titan, husband of Eurynome, with whom he ruled Olympus until he was deposed by Cronus. See Titans.

OPS: Roman name for Rhea.

ORCUS: Roman name for Hades.

PALAEMON: Sea-god; son of Ino;: name changed from Melicertes after he was deified. See Ino.

PALES: Roman numina, protector of flocks and shepherds whose festival, the Palilia, fell on the day Rome was founded, April 21.

PALLAS: See Athena.

PALLAS: A Titan, husband of Styx, nymph of the river Styx. See Titans.

PALLOR: Personification of terror, an attendant on Ares.

PAN: God of flocks and shepherds; usually called a son of Hermes; from Arcady, his first place of worship, his fame spread throughout Greece; inventor of the syrinx or shepherds flute, to which he kept time with the beat of his goat's feet as he led the dance of the nymphs in his native forests; feared by travelers whom, in keeping with his horns, puck-nose, and sensual mien, he enjoyed startling with sudden noises and sending on the run in "Panic" fear.

PARCAE: Roman name for the Fates. See Moirae.

PASIPHAË: Daughter of Helios and Perse, wife of Minos, mother of Androgeos, Ariadne, and Phaedra.

PATULCUS: The "Opener;" Janus as the porter of Heaven. See Clusius.

PENATES: Roman numina, worshiped as household gods, both privately within single families, and publicly when all citizens were thought of as one great family; because the Lares were included among the Penates, the names are sometimes used interchangeably; but the Lares were not the only Penates, since there was usually no more than one Lar to a family, while the Penates were conceived of as plural; common tradition held that Aeneas brought the Penates with him from Troy, and established them at Lavinium; then at Alba Longa, and finally at Rome; images of these gods were kept in the Penetralia, the center of the house; the private Penates were hearth gods, where perpetual fires burned in their honor; the table was sacred to them, and their proper portion was the saltcellar and first fruits. See Lares.

PENEUS: A river-god, son of Oceanus and Tethys; father of Daphne. (Greek.)

PEPHREDO: See Graeae.

PERSE (PERSA): Daughter of Oceanus, wife of Helios, mother of Aeëtes, Circe, Pasiphaë, and Perses. (Greek.)

PERSEPHONE: Daughter of Zeus and Demeter, wife of Hades, hence queen of the underworld; Zeus secretly pledged her to Hades, and she was abducted and carried off to hell without her mother's knowledge; in anger Demeter caused the grain to stop growing until her daughter was returned; but Persephone, having eaten the sacred pomegranate in the underworld, was doomed to go back and spend four months of the year there; the yearly drama of the departure and return of Persephone, with the accompanying sorrow and joy of Demeter, represents the cycle of the seasons in nature. See Demeter.

PERSES: Son of Helios and Perse, father of Hecate. (Greek.)

PHAËTON: A mortal, son of Helios and Clymene, who wrung from his father permission to drive the chariot of the sun, lost control of the fiery steeds, and was struck down by a thunderbolt of Zeus when he almost destroyed the earth on his wild ride. See Clymene. (Greek.)

PHLEGETHON: Infernal river of Fire. See Acheron.

PHOBOS: Personification of alarm, an attendant on Ares.

PHOEBE: Epithet of Artemis as goddess of the moon and hence female counterpart of Phoebus, the sun-god.

PHOEBE: A Titan, wife of Coeus, mother of Leto. See Titans.

PHOEBUS: See Apollo.

PHORCYDES: See Gorgons, Graeae.

PHORCYS (PHORCUS): A sea-god; son of Pontus and Gaea; father of the Graeae and Gorgones, who were called after him, Phorcydes or Phorcynides.

PICUS: Roman rustic god, famous for his powers of prophecy; son of Saturnus, father of Faunus by Canens; Circe, in love with Picus, changed him into a woodpecker because he could love no one but Pomona; he retained his prophetic talent, for the woodpecker, sacred to Mars, was credited with power to see into the future.

PLEIADES: Seven nymphs; daughters of Atlas and Pleione; sisters of the Hyades; virgin companions of Artemis; pursued by the hunter Orion, they prayed for aid and were changed to doves, then to the stars in the constellation that bears their name; they were Alcyone, Celaeno, Electra, Maia, Merope, Sterope, and Taygete. See Hyades.

PLEIONE: Daughter of Oceanus; wife of Atlas; mother of the Pleiades. See Pleiades.

PLUTO: Early epithet of Hades as giver of wealth; became in time the actual name of the god, as a way of naming Hades without using his dreaded name directly.

PLUTUS: God of wealth; son of Iasion and

Demeter; blinded by Zeus that he might distribute his gifts without favor.

PLUVIUS: Roman epithet of Jupiter as the sender of rain.

POLIAS: Epithet of Athena, as the goddess-guardian of cities, especially of Athens.

POLLUX: Roman name of Polydeuces, twin brother of Castor. See Dioscuri, Tyndaridae.

POMONA: Originally a numina, guardian of orchards, who became a goddess and, though still the patroness of fruit trees and gardens (Pomorum Patrona), was celebrated as the consort of Vertumnus, Picus, and Silvanus.

PONTUS: An ocean-god; husband of Gaea; father of Nereus.

PORTUNUS (PORTUMNUS): Roman name for Palaemon.

POSEIDON: God of the sea; with Zeus (god of the heavens), Hades (god of the underworld), one of the three gods among whom the rule of the universe was divided; son of Cronus and Rhea; husband of Amphitrite; father of Triton, Rhode, and Benthesicyme; dwelt in a palace in the sea-deeps near Aegae in Euboea. (Greek.)

PRIAPUS: God of fruitfulness, protector of flocks, bees, vines, and gardens; son of Dionysus and Aphrodite.

PROSERPINA: Roman name for Persephone.

PROTEUS: Old man of the sea; described as a son of Poseidon; king, in some accounts, of Egypt; father of Idothea, Polygonus, and Telegonus; tended the seals of Poseidon, rising from the sea at noon to sleep in the shade, where, if he could be caught and held and so prevented from assuming one of his endless variety of shapes, he would predict the future.

PSYCHE: Personification of the soul; a mortal princess, Psyche won the love of Cupid and the hatred of Venus because of her beauty; after many trials inflicted by Venus, which included sorting overnight a store-house of mixed grain seed, fleecing the golden wool of a flock of wild sheep, filling a flask from the river Styx, and a quest for Persephone in the underworld, she was immortalized at the request of Cupid, and Love (Cupid) and Soul (Psyche) were united forever.

PUDITICIA: Goddess of modesty; sister of Astrea.

QUIRINUS: (1) Mars as patron of the civic life of Rome, identified with Quirinus; (2) Sabine for "lance" or "spear," the name for Romulus, founder of Rome, after he was deified and worshiped, with Jupiter and Mars, as tutelary god of the city.

REMUS: Twin-brother of Romulus who was rescued in infancy from the Tiber River and suckled by a she-wolf; slain by Romulus because he demeaned the new city that his brother founded by leaping over the walls. See Romulus.

RHADAMANTHUS: Son of Zeus and Europa, because of his just life became one of three judges of the dead in Hades. See Aeacus, Minos. (Greek.)

RHEA: A Titan, sister and wife of Cronus, mother of Demeter, Hades, Hera, Hestia, Poseidon, and Zeus. After Cronus, fearful of a rival, devoured his children, Rhea concealed the newborn Zeus, giving her husband a stone to swallow instead, and placed her son to nurse in a cave of the Cretan demons, the Curetes. Rhea is identified with Cybele, The "great mother" goddess of Phrygia and Lydia, and with Ops, the Roman earth-goddess. She is also called the "mother of the Olympian Gods." See Titans, Uranus, Cronus.

RHODE (RHODES): Daughter of Poseidon and Helia, or of Helios and Amphitrite, or of Poseidon and Aphrodite, or of Oceanus; gave her name to the island of Rhodes; bore 7 sons to Helios.

ROMULUS: Twin-brother of Remus and son of Mars and Rhea Silvia; in infancy he was thrown into the Tiber with his brother, but the children were rescued and suckled by a she-wolf; founded and became the first king of Rome; deified by the Romans, he became identified with the patron war-god, Quirinus. See Remus.

SABAZIUS: A Phrygian god, son of Cybele or Rhea, or of Persephone by Zeus; identified with Dionysus; torn by the Titans into 7 pieces.

SALACIA: Roman goddess of the sea, wife of Neptune.

SATURN: Roman name for Cronus.

SATURNIUS: Roman patronymic for Neptune as son of Saturn.

SATYRS (SATYRI): Class of beings in Greek myth who represent the overflowing abundance of nature; sons of Hermes and Ipthima, or of the Naides; associated especially with the train of Bacchus; with bristly hair, pointed ears, snub nose, 2 small horns and a tail, they accentuated these animal characteristics by dressing in skins and hides; as field and forest gods, companions of the nymphs, they were feared by mortals; the older were called Sileni, the younger Satyrisci.

SCYLLA: A sea-nymph, beloved by Glaucus, changed by jealous Circe into a rock-bound monster who, with Charybdis on a neighboring rock, plagued the shipping lines between Italy and Sicily; she is said to have been killed by Hercules for stealing some of the oxen of Geryon, and restored to life by Phorcys. See Charybdis.

SELENE: Goddess of the moon; daughter of Hyperion and Thea; sister of Helios; became identified with Artemis as her brother did with Apollo; to her, rather than to the virginal Artemis, rightfully belongs the story of Endymion, the eternal sleeper on Mount Lathmos, by whom she is said to have had 50 daughters. (Greek.)

SEMELE: Daughter of Cadmus and Harmonia; sister of Agave, Autonoë, Ino, and Polydorus; because Zeus loved her, Hera tricked her into asking to see him in his divine form, and she was consumed by lightning when he did appear, reluctantly, as the god of thunder; Zeus saved their child, Dionysus, with whom she was pregnant, and she was later brought by her son to Olympus and deified. See Thyone.

SILENUS: The oldest of the Sileni, or elder Satyri, came in time to be known as the Silenus, or simply, Silenus; sometimes represented as a son of Pan or Gaea, rather than of Hermes; claimed as inventor of flute; a jovial sport who rode an ass because he was too old to walk, he was in the power of mortals when drunk or sleeping, and, if surrounded with chains of flowers, could be made to speak his inspired prophecies. See Satyrs.

SILVANUS: Mars as Roman rustic god, guardian of cattle; originally a numina, patron of farmers and woodsmen.

SIMAETHUS: A nymph; wife of Faunus; mother of Acis.

SIRENS (SIRENES): Sea-nymphs with power to cast a spell over anyone who heard them singing; called daughters of Phorcus, of Achelous and Sterope, of Terpsichore, of Melpomene, of Calliope, or of Gaea, their identity is as uncertain as their parentage; sometimes represented as two sisters, Aglaopheme and Thelxiepia, sometimes as three, Aglaope, Pisinöe, and Thelxiepia (or Leucosia, Ligia, and Parthenope); encountered by Ulysses in his wandering, and by the Argonauts. (Greek.)

SOMNUS: Roman name for Hypnus.

STHENO: See Gorgons.

STYX: Infernal River where Charon ferries the souls of the dead; chief river of Hades, which it encircled seven times. See Acheron.

SWAN: Zeus, in the form of a swan, was the father of Castor and Polydeuces (Pollux) and Helen by Leda. See Dioscuri, Leda.

SYLVANUS: Same as Silvanus.

TARTARUS: Roman name for Hades.

TELECHINES: A tribe descended from Poseidon or Thalassa, variously represented as (1) cultivators of the soil; (2) sorcerers, with looks that killed, power to control the elements, and even power over life, which they could destroy with a mixture of Stygian water and sulphur; (3) as artists and artisans, workers in brass and iron, and patrons of useful arts and cultural institutions. (Greek.)

TELLUS: Roman name for Gaea.

TERMINUS: A Roman numina, custodian of boundaries and frontiers; by order of Numa, second king of Rome, everyone is said to have been required to mark the boundaries of his property with stones dedicated to Jupiter, where annual sacrifice was to be made on the feast of the Terminalia; the worship of Terminus grew out of this custom; the original Terminus of the Roman state was between the fifth and sixth milestones at Festi, on the Laurentum road; another stood in the Temple of Jupiter in the Capitol.

TETHYS: A Titan, sister and wife of Oceanus, hence, goddess of the ocean until Zeus put Amphitrite in her place; mother of Metis, of the Oceanides (or sea-nymphs), and of all the river-gods; fostermother of Hera. See Titans, Nymphs.

THALIA: One of the three Graces, whose name signifies "bloom." (Greek.)

THALLO: See Horae.

THANATOS: God of death; son of Nyx (Night), brother of Hypnus (Sleep); a deity of the underworld; in contemporary Freudian psychology, the death instinct, a destructive energy directed inward against the self, and, when frustrated by Eros, outward against others. See Eros. (Greek.)

THAUMAS: Son of Pontus and Gaea; husband of the sea-nymph Electra; father of Iris and the Harpies. (Greek.)

THEMIS: A Titan, the personification of justice and law; counselor and consort of Zeus; by him, mother of the Moirae, the Horae, and in some accounts, of the Hesperides; represented tradition and social order; is said to have held the Delphic oracle after Gaea and before Apollo. See Titans.

THIA: A Titan, sister and wife of Hyperion, mother of Helios (the sun), Selene (the moon) and Eos (the dawn); hence, the female principle of light. See Titans.

THYONE: Selene, after Dionysus brought her from Hades to Olympus and had her made a goddess.

TITANS: The elder gods of the Greeks, huge and powerful sons and daughters of Uranus and Gaea, who came to power when Cronus wounded and overthrew his father. Besides their leader, Cronus, the Titans whose names occur in mythology include: Atlas, Coeus, Crius, Dione, Epimetheus, Eurynome,

Hyperion, Iapetus, Leto, Maia, Mnemosyne, Oceanus, Ophion, Pallas, Phoebe, Prometheus, Rhea, Tethys, Themis, and Thia.

TRITON (TRITONS): A sea-god, son of Poseidon and Amphitrite (or, sometimes, the Harpy Celaeno); lived in the submarine palace near Aegae; part man, part fish; blew on a conch shell to soothe the waves; sometimes represented as plural. (Greek.)

TYCHE: Goddess of fortune; represented as steersman of the rudder that guided the affairs of the world, and as a ball, symbolizing the fitfulness of her gifts. (Greek.)

TYNDARIDAE: Patronymic of Castor and Polydeuces (Pollux) as sons of Tyndareus, king of Lacedaemon, and Leda; Castor was a famous tamer of horses, Polydeuces a famous boxer. See Dioscuri. (Greek.)

UPIS: (1) Artemis as the patroness of women in labor; (2) a nymph, nurse of Artemis, who later joined the train of her foster child; (3) father of Artemis. (Greek.)

URANUS: The personification of the heavens, among the most ancient of the gods; son or husband of Gaea (Terra, in Latin, or Earth) father of the Titans, the Cyclops, the Hecatoncheires, and, in Cicero, of Mercury (Hermes) by Dia and Venus (Aphrodite) and by Hemera; hating his monstrous children, the Hecatoncheires, he imprisoned them in Tartarus, but Gaea conspired with the Titans and the Cyclops to release them; Cronus, a Titan, castrated his father and from the blood of his wound sprang the Giants, the Erinyes (Furies), and in some accounts, the satyr, Silenus, the Melic nymphs, and Aphrodite, who is represented as springing from the foam as he washed his wound in the sea.

VENUS: Roman name for Aphrodite.

VESPER: Another name for Hesperus.

VESTA: Roman name for Hestia.

VICTORIA: Roman name for Nike.

VULCAN (VULCANUS): Roman name for Hephaestus.

VULTURNUS: Sometimes given as alternative Roman name for Eurus.

WINDS: The Greeks personified the four winds as Boreas (North Wind), Notus (South Wind), Eurus (East Wind), Zephyrus (West Wind); Roman names for the same winds were Aquilo, Auster, Eurus (sometimes Vulturnus), and Favonius; the winds were kept in caves by Aeolus. See Aeolus, Boreas, Notus, Eurus, Zephyrus.

ZAGREUS: Another name for the mystic Dionysus, born to Persephone by Zeus in the form of a dragon; the Titans tore him apart, and Athena carried his heart to Zeus; worshiped as a bull-god in the fertility rites of the Orphics.

ZELUS: Personification of strife and zeal; son of Pallas and Styx, brother of Nike (Victory).

ZEPHYRUS: The West Wind; in Hesiod, son of Astraeus and Eos, therefore brother of Hesperus and Notus; in some accounts, son of Aeolus and Eos; described in Homer as living with Boreas in a cave of Mount Haemus in Thrace; by the Harpy, Podarge, father of Achilles' horses Xanthus and Balius; by his wife, Chloris, father of Carpus. See Winds.

ZEUS: The supreme Olympian god; son of Cronus and Rhea; brother of Poseidon, Hades, Hestia, Demeter; brother-husband of Hera; ruler of the heavens, with his throne on Mt. Olympus; father of gods and men; source of all things; the thunder and the lightning were his arms, and he created storms and tempests by shaking his aegis; led the revolt of the gods against Cronus and so became chief over his brothers and sisters; father of Ares, Hephaestus, Ilithyia, and Hebe by Hera; of Athena by Metis; of the Horae and Moerae by Themis; of the Charites (Graces) by Eurynome; of Persephone by Demeter; of the Muses by Mnemosyne; of Apollo and Artemis by Leto; often, enamored of a beautiful mortal, he would strive to elude the ever-watchful eye of Hera and pursue his passion in peace; among his famous amours were those with Aegina, mother of Aeacus, king of the Myrmidons; with Callisto, whom Hera changed into a bear; with Danaë, whom he visited as a shower of gold; with Europa, whom he carried off in the form of a bull; with Io, to whom he appeared as a cloud; with Leda, whom he visited as a swan; with Leto, mother of Artemis and Apollo; with Semele, mother of Dionysus, who was burned to ashes when he appeared to her, at her insistence, as the god of thunder. See Cronus, Metis.

Norse Gods and Elements of Norse Mythology

ABUNDANTIA: Same name as Abundia.

ABUNDIA: Fulla as a personification of the fullness of the earth.

AEGIR: God of the sea; husband of Ran; father of Wind and Waves; a cruel and capricious deity who ruled independently of the Aesir and was not considered a member of the royal family; causer and quieter of tempests.

AESIR: In Norse mythology, a collective name for the gods as rulers and sustainers of the world. Odin was the principal Asa, and in his throne room in Glads-heim, sat heigher than the other 12 major male deities who made up the supreme pantheon. These 12 gods, each of whom maintained a private throne room, were: Balder, Bragi, Forseti, Frey, Heimdall, Hodur, Thor, Tyr, Uller, Vali, Ve, and Vidar.

AFI: Grandfather; husband of Amma, and fosterfather of Karl.

AFTERNOON: Personification of the time after noon; guardian of this time of day.

AI: Great-grandfather; husband of Edda, and fosterfather of Thrall.

AKU-THOR: Thor as charioteer, when he was on his rounds as thunder-god.

ALBERICH: In German mythology, king of the dwarfs and elves and chief of the Niblungs (Nibelungs). Identified with Oberon.

ALF-HEIM: The home of the elves and fairies, suspended between heaven and earth.

ALI: Same as Vali.

ALLFATHER: All-powerful being, uncreated and unseen, who existed from the beginning in the unbroken darkness before air, earth, or sea came into existence; later identified with Odin.

ALSVIN: The rapid-goer; one of the team of horses that drew the chariot of the sun. See Arvakr.

AMMA: Grandmother; wife of Afi; by Riger, mother of Karl, and ancestress of the agricultural class.

ANDHRIMNIR: The cook of the gods. See Eldhrimnir, Saehrimnir.

ANDVARANAUT: The ring of the dwarf Andvari, which Sigurd took from Regin and gave to Brynhild in pledge of their engagement.

ANDVARI: In the Eddas, king of the dwarfs, from whom Loki took the treasure of the

dwarfs, the Helmet of Dread, and the magic ring Andvaranaut.

ANGUR-BODA: Omen of evil; a giantess whom Loki secretly married in Jotun-heim; by him, mother of the serpent Iörmungandr, the Fenris Wolf, and Hel; also mother of Gerd; on the eve of Ragnarok she fed her monstrous grandchildren on the brains and marrow of murderers and adulterers as the world grew wickeder and the last day was ready to dawn.

ANNAR: Second husband of the goddess Nott; father of Jord.

ARVAKR: The earth-waker; a steed that drew the chariot of the sun. See Alsvin, Svalin.

ASA: A single Aesir was an Asa.

ASA-BRIDGE: Another name for Bifrost.

ASABRU: The rainbow that, as Bifrost, formed the bridge of the gods; made of fire, water, and air, quivering and changing color, it supported only the gods who journeyed across it to earth and to the Urdar Well where their daily council was held; Thor, alone of the gods, was too heavy to walk on the rainbow.

ASGARD: The home of the gods.

ASK (ASH, ASKE): The ash tree, or block of ash wood, found by Odin, Vili, and Ve (or Odin, Hoenir, and Loki), and fashioned into the first man. See Embla.

ASYNJUR: A collective name for the 24 goddesses of Norse mythology.

AUD: Son of the goddess Nott by her first husband, Naglfari; stepbrother of Jord and Dag.

AUDHUMLA: The nourisher; a gigantic cow produced from the interaction of elemental ice and fire; suckled Ymir with her milk and freed Buri from an ice block which she licked for salt.

AUSTRIA: A dwarf; personification of the East. See Nordri.

BALDER (BALDR): An Asa; a sun-god, fountain of light; son of Odin and Frigga, twin of Hodur; husband of Nanna; fairest and most loved of the gods; when the rumor reached Asgard that he would be the son of Odin whom Rossthief had predicted must die, all of nature vowed to Frigga that it would never do Balder harm; all except the mistletoe, which Loki fashioned into a spear and, through the agency of the blind Hodur, struck Balder down; with his wife Balder was burned in a great funeral pyre, and his shade descended to Hel.

BALMUNG: Siegfried's sword, forged by Wieland the Smith (Volund).

BE'AL: The principal god of the Druids.

BEAV: Name for Vali.

BELTANE: The spring festival of the Druids, held annually at the beginning of May; name means the "fire of god," because the seasonal return of the sun, identified with the god Be'al, was saluted with great bonfires burned on the mountaintops.

BERGELMIR: A frost giant, son of Thrudgelmir; lone survivor of the first race of giants, founder of Jotun-heim.

BERSERKER: Warrior so inspired by Odin that he led a charmed life on the battlefield and could perform acts of superhuman bravery although he was naked (berserker= bare sark or shirt) and weaponless.

BERTHA (BRECHTA): Frigga as guardian of the Heimchen, or souls of unborn children; as patroness of agriculture, and as legendary ancestress of several royal families, especially Bertha Broadfoot, mother of Charlemagne, who developed a particularly large and flat foot by constant treadling of her spinningwheel.

BESTLA: A giantess; daughter of Bolthorn; wife of Borr; mother of Odin, Vili, and Ve.

BEYGGVIR: Personification of chaff; husband of Beyla; attendant of Frey as an agricultural and fertility god.

BEYLA: Personification of manure; wife of Beyggvir; attendant on Frey as an agricultural and fertility god.

BIFROST: The bridge of the gods that stretched from edge to edge of Nifl-heim and arched high above Midgard. See Asabru.

BIL: The waning moon; child companion of Mani from a cruel father who made her and her brother Kiuki carry water all night long; original Jill of Jack and Jill.

BILLING: King of the Ruthenes; father of Rinda.

BILSKIRNIR: Lightning; the palace of Thor in Thrud-vang; in the 540 halls of this great palace, the largest in Asgard, Thor entertained the souls of dead thralls, of whom he was special patron.

BLACK DWARFS: Same as Dwarfs.

BLODUG-HOFI: Frey's fearless horse, which passed through fire and water without balking.

BODEN: The bowl of propitiation, companion to Sol, in which the dwarfs stored part of Kvasir's blood. See Kvasir.

BOLTHORN: The thorn of evil; a frost giant, father of Bestla; the marriage of Bestla and the god Borr introduced the tragic flaw, mortality, into the history of the Northern gods and made the Götterdämmerung (twilight of the gods) inevitable.

BORR: The personification of birth; oldest son of Buri; husband of the giantess Bestla; father of Odin, Vili, and Ve.

BOUS: Vali as patron and sustainer of the peasant class.

BRAGI: An Asa, god of poetry eloquence and song; son of Odin and Gunlod; husband of Idun; possessed a magic golden harp on which he played his enchanting music.

BREIDABLIK: The immaculate, resplendent, sunlit palace of Balder in Asgard.

BRISINGA-MEN: The gold necklace the dwarfs made for Freya.

BROCKEN (BLOCKSBERG): The mountain peak of the Harz mountains where the witches and demons celebrated the Walpurgisnacht (Walpurgis Night).

BRUNHILD (BRÜNNHILDE; BRYNHILD): A heroine of Teutonic and Scandinavian legend; (1) in the *Nibelungenlied* she is the queen of Issland, who makes a wow never to marry any man except the one who can beat her in three trials of skill and strength: hurling a spear, throwing a stone, and jumping. With the aid of Siegfried, who was equipped with a magic cape that made him invisible, Gunther, king of Burgundy, fulfilled the conditions of the contest and won Brunhild; later the aid of Siegfried was needed again when the new Queen proved too much of a shrew for her husband to manage; by depriving her of a magic ring and a magic girdle which she possessed, Siegfried effected a reconciliation between the royal couple; (2) In the *Volsunga Saga*, Brunhild is a Valkyr (Valkyrie), and perhaps a daughter of Odin, who is banished by the god for changing the course of a battle and giving victory to the side that should have lost; Odin placed her in Hindarfiall where, stung with the Thorn of Sleep, she was surrounded by a wall of fire and was doomed to stay there until discovered and freed by the man who would be her lover; it is this version of the story that was adapted by Wagner in his cycle of operas, *The Ring of the Nibelung (Der Ring des Nibelungen)*. See Sigurd, Siegfried, Nibelungenlied.

BRUNNAKER: Sacred grove of Idun in Asgard.

BRYNHILD: Variant of Brunhild as heroine of the Volsunga Saga.

BURI: The producer; freed from an ice block by the dawn cow, Audhumla; first of the gods; father of Borr; waged the primeval war against the first giants, then married the giantess Bestla, who bore to him Odin, Vili, and Ve.

CHERU: A sword-god; identified with Tyr and Heimdall; chief god of the Cheruski, in whose mythology he was also a sun-god. See Cheru's Sword.

CHERU'S SWORD: A magic sword that guaranteed military supremacy to its wielder. Same as Tyr's Sword.

CHILDREN OF THE MIST: The Nibelungs, or Nibelungers.

DAG: Personification of the day; radiant son of the goddess Nott by her third husband Dellinger; stepbrother of Aud and Jord; appointed by the gods to drive the bright chariot of day. See Skin-faxi.

DAIN: One of the four sacred stags that pastured in the branches of Yggdrasil, dropping honey dew on the earth from their horns and supplying water for all the rivers of the world; the other 3 stags were Dvalin, Duneyr, and Durathor.

DELLINGER: God and personification of the dawn; third husband of Nott; father of Dag.

DISES: Same as Idises.

DONAR: Another name for Thor.

DRAUPNIR: Magic ring of Odin, symbol of fruitfulness.

DRUIDS: Priests of the Norsemen; also called Godi; a prime function of the Druids was to sarifice hostages of war on their sacred altars, or dolmens, which were consecrated to the god Tyr.

DUNEYR: See Dain.

DURATHOR: See Dain.

DVALIN: See Dain.

DWARFS: The dark, cunning, malevolent inhabitants of Svart-alfa-heim who were bred as maggots in the decaying flesh of the giant Ymir and endowed by the gods with human form and superhuman intelligence; miners of gold, silver, and jewels, which they stored in secret crevices of their subterranean home. See Elves.

EAGOR: Anglo-Saxon for Aegir.

EASTRE: Saxon goddess of spring, identified with Frigga, from whose name Easter is derived. Also Ostara.

EDDA: Great grandmother; wife of Ai; by Riger, mother of Thrall, and ancestress of the class of thralls, or serfs.

EDDAS: An Icelandic, or Old Norse, cycle of literature in which the history of the Northern gods has its most permanent and coherent record; Edda, which is derived either from the name of the great-grandmother in the Old Norse poem *Rigsthul*, or from the Old Norse word *odhr*, meaning poetry, is given to two different works or collections: The Elder, or Poetic Edda, and The Younger, or Prose, Edda; The Elder Edda was discovered in 1643 and is dated from the 9th-13th centuries, the final compilation being attributed to a Christian priest, Saemund (Sigmund) Sigfusson (d. 1133), and known also as Saemund's Edda; The Prose Edda, written in prose and verse by Snorri Sturluson (d. 1242), retells, chiefly in prose, the parts of The Poetic Edda that describe the creation of the world and of man, and the genealogy, lives, and fates of the gods; it consists of the *Gylfaginning* (an epitome of Scandinavian mythology), the *Bragaraeour* (or sayings of Bragi), the *Skaldskaparmal* (or glossary of poetical expressions), the *Hattatal* (or list of meters, with examples of all known forms of verse), and a preface that outlines the origins and history of poetry, with references to celebrated poets and their works.

EINHERIAR: Warriors who fell in battle and were chosen from the field by the Valkyries (Valkyrs) to live with Odin in Valhalla. See Valhalla, Valkyries.

EINMYRIA: Personification of ashes; daughter of Loki and Glut; sister of Eisa.

EIRA: Attendant of Frigga; was a skilled physician and taught women the uses of simples to cure wounds and diseases.

EISA: Personification of embers; daughter of Loki and Glut; sister of Einmyria.

ELB (ELF): Water-god of the River Elb.

ELBEGAST: Another name for Andvari.

ELDHRIMNIR: The great caldron in which Andhrimnir cooked the sacred boar Saehrimnir.

ELLI: Personification of old age; nurse of Utgard-loki, who beat Thor in a wrestling match, since even a god cannot resist old age.

ELVES (OR LIGHT ELVES): The fair, good, benevolent inhabitants of Alf-heim who were bred as maggots in the decaying flesh of the giant Ymir and endowed by the gods with human form and superhuman intelligence; attendants on plants and flowers; companions of birds and butterflies, they danced in the moonbeams and in magic circles on the grass. See Dwarfs.

ELVIDNER: Misery; the Hall of Hel.

EMBLA: The elm tree, or block of elm wood, fashioned by the gods into the first woman. See Ask.

ER: A sword-god; identified with Tyr and Heimdall.

ERLKONIG: King of the elves (Elfen Konig).

ERNA: Wife of Jarl; prototype of women of the ruling class.

EVENING: Personification of evening; guardian of his time of night.

FADIR: Father; husband of Modir, and foster father of Jarl.

FAFNIR: A giant which, in the form of a dragon, guarded a treasure belonging to the Nibelungs and was killed by Siegfried.

FAIRIES: Another name for the Light Elves. See Elves.

FENRIS WOLF: Offspring of Loki and Angur-Boda; a hideous monster fated to swallow Odin on the last day of the gods and effect the fall of the house of Asgard; until released by Loki on the day of battle, kept chained by the gods after Tyr lost his right hand in the effort to capture the beast; sire of Hati, Managarm, and Skoll.

FENSALIR: Frigga's palace, the hall of mists or of the sea, where she spun golden thread and wove webs of gaily colored clouds, using her jeweled spinning wheel or distaff.

FINNS: In Norse mythology, a polar people with power to control the winds and storms that came from the north.

FIORGYN: A giantess, sometimes represented as the mother of Frigga.

FLYGIE: A spirit, much like a Guardian Angel, assigned to watch over and guide a person through life; everyone had his own special Flygie, which had the definite shape either of a man or beast and yet remained invisible or undetected by its ward until he

was at the point of death, when the Flygie revealed itself; in rare instances a living man was permitted a vision of his Flygie.

FORENOON: Personification of the time before noon; guardian of his time of day.

FORNJOTNR: Another name for Ymir.

FORSETI: An Asa, god of justice and righteousness; son of Balder and Nanna; wisest, mildest and most persuasive of the gods, he was chosen to administer the eternal law and to decide the cases of both gods and men; dwelt in Asgard in the resplendent gold and silver palace Glitner.

FREKI: Sacred hunting hound (or wolf) of Odin. See Geri.

FREY (FREYR): An Asa, god of sunshine and summer showers; son of Niörd by Nerthus or Skadi; brother of Freya; born in Vanaheim, but welcomed to Asgard and given Alfheim as his province; husband of Gerda; father of Fiolnir; his powers overlap those of other gods and he is represented as a patron of sailors and, most particularly, of crops.

FREYA: Goddess of love and beauty; daughter of Niörd either by Nerthus or Skadi; sister of Frey; wife of Odur, mother of Hnoss and Gersemi; fairest and most loved of the goddesses; also represented as leader of the Valkyrs; born in Vana-land she was nonetheless royally received in Asgard and given Folkvang as her province and Sessrymir, the spacious, as her palace; from her name and her feast-day, the word Friday is derived.

FRIGGA (FRIGG, FREIJA): Queen of the gods; daughter of Nott or of the giantess Fiorgyn; sister of Jord; second wife of Odin; mother of Balder, Hermod, and perhaps Tyr; goddess of the atmosphere and clouds, of conjugal and motherly love; patroness of married couples and parents.

FRO: German name for Frey.

FULLA: Attendant or sister of Frigga; keeper of Frigga's jewel box; confidante and adviser of the goddess; her hair represented the Golden Grain.

FUNFENG: Servant of Aegir, the sea-god, whom Loki slew and so precipitated his own expulsion from Asgard.

GAMBANTEIN: The sacred staff, or wand, of Hermod.

GARN: Savage, blood-smeared dog that guarded Hel-gate, the entrance to the palace of Hel.

GELGIA: The handle end of the magic fetter Gleipner, which was drawn through the rock Gioll and fastened to the boulder Thviti, to chain up the Fenris Wolf until Ragnarok.

GERDA: Personification of the Northern Lights (aurora borealis), or, sometimes, of the winter earth; daughter of the frost-giant Gymir and Angur-Boda; wife of Frey; mother of Fiolnir.

GERI: Sacred hunting hound (or wolf) of Odin. See Freki.

GERSEMI: Daughter of Freya and Odur; sister of Hnoss; so fair were these two girls that they gave their names as titles for everything that was beautiful.

GIALLAR BRIDGE: Glass bridge over the river Gioll, the outer boundary of Hel.

GIALLAR-HORN: The horn of Heimdall, with which he announced, in soft notes, the passings of the gods; on Ragnarok Heimdall anticipated the twilight of the gods with a shattering blast on this same sacred horn.

GINNUNGA-GAP: At the dawn of time, the great, gloomy fathomless abyss in the center of space.

GIOLL: When the gods tied up the Fenris

Wolf, this was the rock through which the magic chain, Gleipnir, was drawn before being fastened to the buried boulder Thviti.

GLADS-HEIM: The 12-throned council room of the gods. See Valaskialf.

GLASIR: Sacred grove of Asgard where the leaves of the trees were of shimmering red gold and Odin had his third heavenly palace, Valhalla. See Glads-heim, Valaskialf, Valhalla.

GLAUR: Personification of glow; probably son of Surtr; husband of Sol.

GLEIPNIR: Magic halter of sheerest silk which was spun by the Black Dwarfs as a fetter for the Fenris Wolf after the powerful chains Laeding and Droma had been tried and failed. See Gelgia.

GLUT: Personification of glow; first wife of Loki; mother of Eisa and Einmyria.

GNA: Messenger of Frigga; rode on the swift horse Hofvarpnir.

GNOMES: Another name for the Black Dwarfs.

GODE (FRAU): Name for Frigga as the female counterpart of Wuotan or Woden.

GODI: The Druids.

GONDEMAR: Another name for Andvari.

GRAM: Sigurd's sword, which Odin had driven into a log with the prediction that none but a great hero would draw it out; the sword was extracted by Sigmund, the father of Sigurd, who, at his death, bequeathed Gram to his son.

GRANE: Alternate name for Sigurd's horse Greyfell.

GREYFELL: Sigurd's horse, descended from Sleipnir, the steed of Odin.

GRID: Personification of matter; a giantess, wife of Odin and mother of Vidar.

GULLFAXI: The golden-maned horse Thor gave to his son Magni.

GULLIN-BURSTI: The golden-bristled boar, symbol of the sun, which the Black Dwarfs gave to Frey.

GUNGNIR: The sacred spear of Odin, which made all oaths sworn upon it unbreakable; fashioned by Odin from a branch of Yggdrasil.

GUNLOD: Daughter of the giant Suttung; guardian of the vessels of Kvasir's blood, which her father stole from the dwarfs; Odin wooed and wed her to get possession of the magic blood; the child of their marriage was Bragi. See Kvasir, Kvasir's Blood.

GYMIR: The hider; another name for Aegir.

HAGEDISES: Same as Dises, Idises.

HALLINSKIDE: Another name for Heimdall.

HATI: Hatred; the wolf that incessantly pursued and threatened to devour the sun and moon. See Mani, Skoll, Sol.

HEIDRUN: Sacred goat of Odin; pastured in the branches of Yggdrasil and supplied the heavenly mead of the gods.

HEIMDALL: An Asa, watchman of the gods, who was posted as sentinel on Bifröst; son of Odin and the Waves, the nine daughters of Aegir and Ran, who, in a single corporate action, gave birth to Odin's child; through Heimdall, the Aesir were related to the ruling house of the kingdom of Ocean, but this did not give them power to control what happened there. See Aegir, Giallar-horn.

HEL (HELA): Goddess of death; daughter of Loki and Angur-Boda; personification of pain; her body was half black and half blue; like her blood relations the serpent Iörmungandr and the Fenris Wolf, she did not disdain a feast of human brains and marrow; banished by Odin to Nifl-heim, she established and ruled the horrific kingdom of the dead.

HERMOD: Messenger of the gods; son and

envoy of Odin, with some of the attributes of a battle-god.

HERU: A sword-god; identified with Tyr and Heimdall.

HIUKI: The waxing moon; child-companion of Mani; snatched by Mani from a cruel father who made him and his sister Bil carry water all night long; original Jack of Jack and Jill.

HLER: The shelterer; another name for Aegir.

HLORA: Personification of heat; with Vingnir, guardian of young Thor.

HLORRIDI: Name of Thor as ward of Hlora.

HNOSS: Lovely daughter of Frea and Odur; sister of Gersemi.

HODUR (HODR): An Asa; god of darkness; son of Odin and Frigga; a sullen deity, represented as blind to characterize his nature; tricked by Loki into slaying Balder, he was in turn killed by Vali, who was the agent chosen by fate to avenge Balder's death; resurrected and reconciled to Balder after Ragnarok.

HOENIR: In some accounts it was Hoenir, instead of Vili, who helped in the creation of the first man and woman and endowed them with reason and motion; sometimes represented as an Asa, Hoenir lost his option on a palace in Asgard when he went as a hostage to Vana-heim after the dawn-age war between the Aesir and the Vanas; but he is also said to have returned after Ragnarok to help in the reclamation of the earth.

HOFVARPNIR: The hoof-thrower; the horse Gna rode on her errands to find out for Frigga what was going on in the world.

HOLDA (HULDA; FRAU HOLLE): Other names for Frigga; as Holda, Frigga is said to have given flax to mankind and also lessons in how to use it. See also Venus, Frau.

HOLLER: German name for Uller as husband of the goddess Holda, the beneficent counterpart of Frigga; as a blanket of winter snow he is represented as covering, shielding, and fertilizing the fair earth, Holda, in anticipation of the following spring.

HRAESVELGR: The corpse swallower; a giant clad in eagle plumes, he sat at the northernmost edge of the heavens and created the blasts of cold wind by beating his wings or arms.

HRIM-FAXI: Frost-mane; sable steed that drew the dark chariot of night (Nott), from whose waving mane dew and hoar-frost dripped upon the earth.

HRIM-THURS (HRIMTHURSEN): The ice-giants. See Ymir.

HROTHI: Sword of Fafnir.

HUGI: Personification of thought; son of the giant Utgard-loki, who beat Thialfi in a foot-race, since even a god could not run faster than thought.

HUGIN: A raven, personification of thought; sat on Odin's shoulder and was sent out into the world every morning to bring back news of what was going on there.

HULDRA: Another name for Frigga.

HVERGILMIR: The exhaustless spring, rising in Nifl-heim, which fed the 12 great Elivagar, or rivers of ice; one of the original and most important of the geological concepts in the cosmology of the Norsemen; it was located at the deepest root of Yggdrasil, at the remotest point of the underworld; there the giant serpent Nidhung lived and interrupted his remorseless gnawing at the tree of life only long enough to feed on the flesh and bones of the damned who, in their hideous journey through Hel, were finally swept into the seething caldron of Hvergelmir.

HYNDLA: A sorceress.

IARN-GREIPER: The iron gauntlet Thor used to grip his red-hot hammer, Miölnir, symbol of his thunderbolts.

IARNSAXA: Stone of iron; a giantess, wife of Thor, mother of Magni and Modi.

IDAVOLD: A broad, sacred plain high above the earth, on the far side of the stream Ifling, where Asgard, the home of the gods, was situated; the green plain of Ida, playground of the gods.

IDISES: Prophetesses; later witches. See Vala.

IFING: The sacred river, whose waters never froze, which separated earth from the home of the gods. See Idavold.

IDUN: Goddess of spring, daughter of the dwarf, Ivald; sister of the dwarfs who made the sacred weapons of the gods in Svart-alfa-heim; discovered by Bragi in his wanderings through the forests, she returned to Asgard with him as his wife; as goddess of eternal youth, she possessed a basket of magic apples that rejuvenated all who ate of them; the giant Liassi kidnaped her and her precious fruit and escaped to Thrym-heim where she was kept prisoner until her release by Loki; this adventure is a representation of Idun as a goddess of the vegetation that dies each winter, and revives each spring. See Thiassi.

IÖRMUNGANDR: The Midgard serpent, off-spring of Loki and Angur-Boda; banished to the sea by Odin, it churned up tempests until Ragnarok, when, with all the forces of evil, it joined the assault against Asgard; slain by Thor in the battle with the gods. Iörmungandr also indirectly slew Thor when the god was drowned in the flood of venom gushing from the wound he had dealt the serpent.

IRMIN: Saxon god who rode his chariot across Irmin's Way, or the Milky Way; his statue, the Irminsul, was destroyed by Charlemagne near Paderborn in 772; identified with Odin, the chariot formed part of the Great Bear constellation, which is also called Odin's Wain (or Wagon) and Charles' Wain (after Charlemagne).

IRONWOOD: Wood of trees with iron-leaves which was passed on the way to Nifl-heim.

JARL: Prototype of the aristocrat; husband of Erna; father of Konur, legendary first king of Denmark.

JORD: The primeval earth; daughter of Night or of the giantess Fiorgyn; first wife of Odin, by whom she bore Thor; halfsister of Aud and Dag.

JOTUN-HEIM: The home of the giants; founded by Bergelmir and his wife, lone survivors of the first war between the giants and the gods, and ancestors of the entire line of evil frost giants. See Ymir.

KARL: Prototype of the farmer or agricultural class of mankind; husband of Snor. See Amma.

KOBOLDS: Another name for the black dwarfs.

KVASIR: A culture hero who was born of the sacred spit that sealed the dawn-age peace treaty between the Aesir and Vanas; inordinately wise and good, Kvasir wandered across the earth dispensing wisdom and kindness until he was slain by the dwarfs Fialir and Galar, who then drew off and stored his blood in the three vessels Od-hroerir, Son, and Boden; mixed with honey this blood, when drunk, inspired song so sweet that it had the power to enchant every listener.

KVASIR'S BLOOD: A magic potion of honey and blood, mixed by the dwarfs; conferred supernatural powers of inspiration. It was drunk by Odin. See Kvasir.

LAGA: Same as Saga.

LANDVIDI: The wide land; the home of Vidar in the virgin forest.

LAURIN: Another name for Andvari.

LERAD: The peacegiver; the topmost branch of Yggdrasil, which shaded Odin's hall.

LIGHT ELVES: See Elves.

LODUR: Another name for Loki.

LOFN: Personification of praise or love; attendant of Frigga with the special duty of removing all obstacles from the path of true love.

LOGI: Personification of wildfire; son of the giant Utgard-loki (Skrymir) who bested Loki in a drinking bout, since even a god could not drink more than fire.

LOKI: God of fire, mischief, and sin; identified as a dawn-age deity, son of Ymir and brother of Kari, Hler, and Ran; or as son of the giant Farbauti by Lavfeia (Leafy Isle) or Nal (Vessel); father of Eisa and Einmyria by Glut; of Hel, Iörmungandr, and the Fenris Wolf by Angur-Boda; of Narve and Vali (not the avenger of Balder's death) by Sigyn; perpetual disturber of the peace and projects of the gods; leader of the traitors within Asgard who, at Ragnarok, unleashed the Fenris Wolf and so accomplished the twilight of the gods.

LORELEI: Water sprite of St. Goar on the Rhine who sang so sweetly to the sailors on the ships passing by that she caused them to forget their courses and crash to death on the rocky shores nearby.

MAGNI: Personification of strength; son of Thor and Iarnsaxa; brother of Modi.

MANA-HEIM: The home of man; another name for Midgard.

MANI: Personification of the moon; son of Mundilfari; brother of Sol; appointed by the gods to guide the moon through the heavens. See Bil, Hivki.

MEGIN-GIORD: Magic belt of Thor; doubled and redoubled his prodigious strength with every notch he took it on.

MIDGARD: The middle garden, or earth; fashioned by the sons of Borr from the flesh of the frost giant Ymir.

MIDNIGHT: Personification of midnight; guardian of his time of night.

MIDGARD SERPENT: Iörmungandr.

MIMIR: Keeper of the spring whose waters gave the drinker knowledge of the future; in exchange for a drink of the sacred water, Mimir demanded and got one of Odin's eyes, which was dropped by the god into the spring; Odin was always represented afterward as one-eyed, which is symbolic of the sun.

MIMIR'S WELL: The ocean.

MIÖLNIR: The crusher; the magic hammer of Thor.

MODGUD: The skeleton who guarded the Gialler-bridge and collected a toll of blood from the shades of the dead as they passed her lair on their way to Hel.

MODI: Personification of courage; son of Thor and Iarnsaxa; brother of Magni.

MODIR: Mother; wife of Fadir; by Riger, mother of Jarl, and ancestress of aristocrats.

MORNING: Personification of morning; guardian of his time of day.

MOSS MAIDENS: Wood nymphs, representations of the autumn leaves whirled away by the winter wind; sometimes the "game" pursued in the Wild Hunt.

MUNDILFARI: A giant; father of Sol and Mani.

MUNIN: A raven, personification of memory; reported to Odin the news of the world. See Hugin.

MUSPELLS-HEIM: The world of elemental fire, located opposite Nifl-heim, guarded by Surtr, the flame giant.

NAGLFAR: The ship made by the Giants out of dead men's nails, on which they will sail, at Ragnarok, to give battle to the gods.

NAGLFARI: First husband of the goddess Nott; father of Aud.

NAIN: The subterranean kingdom of the dwarf of death; also the dwarf himself.

NANNA: Personification of blossoms and the flowering cycle of plants; wife of Balder, mother of Forseti; accompanied the shade of Balder to Hel and dwelt there with him until after the twilight of the gods, then returned to revitalize the devastated earth.

NASTROND: In Hel, the strand of corpses, washed by rivers of gelid venom, that the shades of the damned crossed on the way to the caldron Hvergelmir.

NERTHUS: In German myth, Frigga as Mother Earth; but, in Scandinavian tradition, an independent deity who was the sister and first wife of Niörd and the mother, rather than Skadi, of Frey and Freya.

NIBELUNGENLIED, THE: A Middle High German epic poem based on the Scandinavian legends of the Volsunga Saga and the Eddas and written in its final form by an unknown South German poet of the early thirteenth century. The Nibelungs or Nibelungers were a race of Scandinavian dwarfs who dwelt in Nibelheim, the land of perpetual mist, ruled by King Nibelung; they owned a fabulous hoard of gold and jewels which was in the keeping of the dwarf Alberich; Siegfried, the hero of the first part of the poem, slew the dragon that guarded the treasure and won possession of the gold and also the title of Niblung (a name used also for his followers and for the Burgundians who eventually came to own the treasure); he gave the treasure to his bride Kriemhild as a wedding present; the gold excited the greed of Hagan, who killed Siegfried, but Kriemhild escaped with the treasure to Worms, where she was overtaken by Hagan and Gunther, who robbed her and buried the gold in the Rhine; in turn, they were caught and killed when they refused to reveal where the gold was, and so it remained forever in the keeping of the Rhine Maidens; the second part of the poem tells of the marriage of Kriemhild to King Etzel (Attila), the visit of the Burgundians to the court of the Huns, and the tragic deaths of all of the major characters in fulfillment of the fatal necessity which controls all things; the first part of the Nibelungenlied is divided into nineteen lays, comprising 1188 four-line stanzas; the second part contains thirty lays; the Scandinavian version of the same legend is known as the Volsunga Saga.

NIBELUNGS (NIBLUNGS): The dwarfs or demons who lived in Niblung, the land of mist, ruled by the wizard king and queen Giuki and Grimhilde; through the magic of Grimhilde, Sigurd was drugged into forgetfulness and married to Gudrun, and the stage was set for the wrath and revenge of the Valkyr (Valkyrie) Brunhild. See Brunhild, Sigurd, Nibelungenlied.

NICORS: Sea monsters.

NIDHUG: The dragon that lived in the seething caldron Hvergelmir and gnawed at the roots of Yggdrasil, hoping to bring the tree down and effect the twilight of the gods.

NIFL-HEIM: The world of mist and darkness, north of Ginnunga-gap, where the spring, Hvergelmir, rose.

NIGHT DWARFS: Same as Black Dwarfs.

NIÖRD: A Van, god of the winds and coastal waters; husband, in some accounts, or Nerthus, in others, of Skadi; father of Frey and Freya; dwelt in the marine palace of Noatun, which became a temporary residence when he went to Asgard as a hostage after the dawn-age war between the Aesir and Vanas; also a personification of summer, and his sway over the ocean was therefore a beneficent one, since he was invoked to quiet the winter squalls stirred up by Aegir; patron of ships, fishing, commerce, and agriculture, he is represented as a handsome, kindly companion of sea-gulls, swans, and seals, and the gardener of all marine vegetation.

NIP: Personification of the buds and budding cycle of plants; mother of Nanna.

NIXIES (NEKARS): Stromkarls.

NOON: Personification of noon; guardian of his time of day.

NORDRI: A dwarf; after the sons of Borr raised the skull of Ymir as the heavenly vault above the ocean and earth, Nordri (North), Sudri (South), Austri (East), and Westri (West) were stationed as guards and supporters of the four corners.

NORNS (NORNEN): Goddesses of fate; in particular the three daughters of Wyrd, the elder spirit of destiny, who were named Skuld, Urd, and Verdandi, and entered the world with sin, when the Golden Age was over; in their keeping was the vast web of fate, which they wove with threads of many colors from white to black, depending on what was about to happen; even the gods could not question their decrees, nor could they themselves, for they spun blindly, according to the will of the eternal Orlog; there were, in fact, many Norns, who were much like the guardian angels of the Christian age, but the name has come to be applied almost exclusively to the daughters of Wyrd. See Skuld, Urd, Verdandi.

NOTT: Goddess and personification of night; thrice-wed daughter of the giant, Norvi; wife of Naglfari by whom she bore Aud; of Annar by whom she bore Jord; and of Dellinger by whom she bore Dag; appointed by the gods to drive the dark chariot of night. See Hrimfaxi.

OBERON (AUBERON): In English and French mythology, king of the dwarfs and elves (or fairies), husband of Titania, leader of the fairy revels on Midsummer Night. Identified with Andvari.

OD-HROERIR: The kettle of inspiration in which the dwarfs stored part of Kvasir's Blood. See Kvasir.

ODIN (WODEN, WUOTAN): The supreme Asa, god of gods, who ruled gods and men from his throne in Asgard; father by Jord, of Thor; by Frigga, of Balder, Hermod, and perhaps of Tyr; by Rinda, of Vali; by Grid, of Vidar; by Gunlod, of Bragi; by the Waves, of Heimdall; he is also represented as the husband of Saga and Skadi; as battle-god, he led the Valkyrs; as god of wisdom, he was inventor and patron of runes; patron of the hunt, especially the Wild Hunt; personification of the heavens.

ODUR: Representation of the summer sun; husband of Freya; father of Hnoss and Gersemi; symbol also of erotic passion and sensual pleasure, he is said to have all but broken Freya's heart when he suddenly deserted her and followed the lure of his desire so far that only a goddess as determined as she could ever have brought him back.

OLLER: Same as Uller.

ORGELMIR (SEETHING CLAY): Another name for Ymir.

ORLOG: The eternal law of the universe, without beginning or end, whose inscrutable will determined the fate of all things, even of the gods.

OSTARA: Form of Eastre.

QUICKBORN: Frigga's magic fountain of youth.

RAGNAROK: The twilight of the gods.

RAINBOW BRIDGE: Bifröst.

RAN: Goddess of the sea; wife of Aegir; mother of Wind and Waves; also goddess of death for those drowned at sea; a malicious deity who spread her nets for passing ships and drew her catches of cargoes and crews down to her submarine palace.

RATATOSK: The branch borer; a squirrel that scampered up and down the branches of Yggdrasil carrying tales from the eagle on top to the dragon, Nidhug, below and stirring up trouble between the two. See Nidhug, Vedfolnir.

RATI: The auger of Odin.

REIFRIESEN: The Hrim-thurs, or Hrimthursen.

RIGER: Heimdall as the ancestor of the social classes of mankind. See Amma, Edda, Modir.

RINDA: Personification of the ice-bound winter-earth; daughter of Billing, king of the Ruthenes; in fulfillment of the prophecy of Rossthief, wife of Odin after he had succeded in thawing her chilly nature with unusually ardent and determined advances; mother of Vali.

RINGHORN: Balder's ship; became his pyre in an elaborate "Viking's funeral" which the gods solemnized after he was murdered by Hodur.

RIVERS OF HEL: The principal rivers of Hel were: the Elivagar, twelve streams that rose in the spring Hvergelmir, and turned to roaring avalanches of ice as they rolled down Ginnunga-gap; the Leipter, by which the Northmen swore the oaths they dared not break; the Slid, a churning torrent of bristling swords; and the Gioll, the water boundary of Nifl-heim, arched by the Giallar Bridge.

ROSSTHIEF: Horse-thief; a giant Finn with prophetic powers who predicted to Hermod the death of Balder, Odin's marriage to Rinda, and the birth of Vali, who would avenge Balder's death.

RUNES: Early alphabet of the Northmen, at first invested with magical properties and used in divination; in later times they became the customary alphabet for keeping records; old Finnish and Norse poetry are also called runes.

RUTHENES: The Russians.

SAEHRIMNIR: The sacred boar that was killed, dressed, and eaten daily, supplied ample meat for all the meals of Asgard, and came to life again in time for the next meal. See Andhrimnir, Eldhrimnir.

SAGA: Goddess of history, who lived in the crystal palace of Sokvabek under a cool, ever-running river; Odin visited Saga daily and she is sometimes represented as among his wives.

SAMH'IN: The fall festival of the Druids, held annually on November 1 (Halloween) and means the "fire of peace" because all matters demanding judicial decision were brought before the central conclave of the Druidic order and settled; then all the neighborhood fires, which had been extinguished for the festival, were relit with brands from a sacred fire newly kindled for the ceremonies.

SAXNOT: Saxon sword-god, identified with Tyr.

SCALDS: Northern poets who left the Eddas and Sagas as records of their songs.

SIEGFRIED: Hero of the first part of the Old German epic, the *Nibelungenlied;* son of Siegmund and Seglinde, king and queen of the Netherlands; slew the dragon guarding the treasure of the Nibelungs and, bathed in the blood of the dying monster, was rendered invulnerable except for a spot between his shoulder-blades where a linden leaf had unfortunately lodged; won the gold and jewels of the treasure hoard and was gifted by the dwarf Alberich with a cloak which made him invisible and a sword, Balmung, forged by Wieland the Smith, which made him invincible; married Kriemhild, sister of Gunther, King of Burgundy; with the help of his magic cape, wooed Brunhild, Queen of Issland, in behalf of Gunther; treacherously slain by Hagan, who stole the Nibelung treasure and buried it in the Rhine.

SIF: An earth-goddess, second wife of Thor; famous for her long golden hair; Loki stole her hair and was forced to beg a new head from the dwarfs; the hair is said to represent the grass which annually disappears and returns to earth; mother by Thor, of Lorride and Thrud, and by an unidentified husband, of Uller.

SIGMUND (SIEGMUND): Son of Volsung, father of Sigurd in the Volsunga Saga.

SIGURD: In the Volsunga Saga, the name under which Siegfried, the hero of the *Nibelungenlied,* appears.

SKADI: Goddess of winter; daughter of the giant, Thiassi; wife of Odin, of Niörd, and of Uller; after her marriage to Niörd, the god of summer, the ill-matched couple found they could never agree, and so parted amicably; with the winter-god Uller, the winter-goddess was on an even footing, and freer to pursue her accustomed pleasures as goddess of the hunt and patroness of hunters and sleigh-riders.

SKIDBLADNIR: The magic ship of Frey, which never lacked for a favorable wind, and could be expanded or shrunk to any size, from a man-of-war to a pea; symbol of the clouds.

SKIN-FAXI: Shining-mane; the white steed that drew the bright chariot of day (Dag), from whose waving mane beams of light flashed in all directions and lit up the world.

SKIRNIR: Favorite servant of Frey; assisted the god in winning Gerda as his wife.

SKOLL: Repulsion; wolf that incessantly pursued and threatened to devour the sun and moon. See Hati, Mani, Sol.

SKRYMIR: A giant who lived in Utgard and, as Utgard-loki, beat Odin and Loki in a number of contests of endurance. See Hugi, Logi.

SKULD: A Norn; the intriguingly veiled and temperamental sister of Urd and Verdandi, who undid the web her two co-workers wove on the loom of destiny; personification of the future, who gazed in the direction away from Urd and guarded her awful secrets in a book with uncut leaves, or a scroll that had never been unrolled. See Norns.

SLEIPNIR: Eight-footed gray horse of Odin.

SNOR: Wife of Karl; prototype of women of the agricultural class.

SNOTRA: Goddess of virtue, an attendant on Frigga; she had mastered all knowledge.

SOL: Personification of the sun; daughter of Mundilfar; sister of Mani; wife of Glaur; appointed by the gods to guide the sun through the heavens.

SON: The bowl of expiation in which the dwarfs stored part of Kvasir's Blood. See Kvasir.

STROMKARLS: Gentle male water-gods, counterparts of Undines.

SUDRI: A dwarf, personification of the South. See Nordri.

SUMMER: God and personification of the summer season; descendant of Svasud, the gentle. See Winter.

SURTR: The flame giant who guarded Muspellsheim and showered Ginnunga-gap with sparks from his fiery sword; personification of the fire element that in Norse mythology acted with the elemental ice to bring the world into being.

SVADILFARE: Magnificent workhorse of the unidentified giant who offered to build an impregnable fortress for the gods in Asgard, with no assistants except Svadilfare, if the gods would agree to give him the sun, moon, and Freya, as his wages; thinking the task impossible the gods agreed and had to employ Loki to defeat the project when the giant was nearly finished; in rage the giant threatened the gods and they slew him, thus committing the original sin, or unpardonable act of injustice, which, like the crime of Atreus in the Greek cycle of myths about his fated house, demanded expiation and so threw the shadow of doom across Asgard and anticipated the inevitable downfall of the gods.

SVALIN: The cooler; a shield placed by the gods before the sun chariot to keep the steeds Arvakr and Alsvin from burning up.

SVART-ALFA-HEIM: The underground home of the Black Dwarfs.

SVASUD: The mild and lovely one; forebear of Summer.

SYN: Personification of truth who guarded the door to Frigga's palace and presided over all tribunals and trials.

TANNGNIOSTR: Tooth-cracker; one of the goats that drew the brazen chariot of Thor. See Tanngrisnr.

TANNGRISNR: Tooth-gnasher; the goat, that, in team with Tanngniostr, pulled the chariot of Thor.

TARNKAPPE: The red caps, worn by the dwarfs, that made them invisible.

THIALFI: Servant of the giant Utgard-loki (Skrymir).

THIASSI: A Hrim-thurs; personification of the winter wind; father of Skadi; kidnaped Idun, the goddess of youth, to get control of her magic apples; when Loki stole the goddess back again, Thiassi followed him to the walls of Asgard, and was there set upon and slain by the gods, who then placed his eyes in the sky as a constellation of stars to placate his infuriated and dangerous family.

THOR: An Asa, god of thunder; son of Odin by Jord or Frigga; raised by Vingnir and Hlora, the personifications of sheet lightning; reigned in Asgard in the province of Thrudvang; husband of Iarnsaxa who bore him Magni and Modi, and of Sif who bore him Lorride and Thrud; red-bearded patron of the Yule-tide, in which it was customary to burn an oak log in his honor, he has left his name in Thursday, or Thor's Day.

THRALL: Prototype of the thralls, or serfs; husband of Thyr. See Edda.

TRUDGELMIR: A frost giant; son of Ymir; father of Bergelmir.

THRUD-VANG (THRUD-HEIM): Seat of Bilskirnir, the palace of Thor.

THRYM-HEIM: Land of the storm giant Thiassi.

THVITI: The sunken boulder that anchored the leash on the Fenris Wolf to the core of the earth. See Fenris Wolf.

THYR: Wife of Thrall; prototype of female workers of the laboring class.

TITANIA: Queen of the fairies (elves) and dwarfs; wife of Oberon.

TIU: Another name for Tyr, from which Tuesday, or Tiu's Day, is derived.

TROLLS: Another name for the black dwarfs.

TROLLWEIBER: Ghosts who rode the earth by night on wolves that wore snakes as bridles.

TYR: An Asa, god of war; son of Odin by Frigga or by a giantess who personified the raging sea; represented as a companion of the Valkyrs; in the struggle to chain up the fierce Fenris Wolf, Tyr lost his right arm, and his one-handedness was symbolic of the fortunes of war which could go only one way; a sword-god, patron of athletic contests and all sports. See Fenris Wolf.

ULLER (OLLER, ULLR): An Asa, god of winter; son of Sif, stepson of Thor; also patron of the hunt, especially the Wild Hunt, and god of death; as god of winter, his power was second only to Odin's and he reigned supreme in his season, when he supplanted and drove Odin into exile; he kept his palace, or lodge, in Ydalir, the valley of the yews. See Vulder, Holler, Skadi.

UNDINES: Female water-goddesses or spirits, with the torsos of women and the tails of fishes; counterparts of the Stromkarls.

URD: A Norn; the haggard sister of Skuld and Verdandi, she personified the past, constantly looking behind her to find it. See Wurd.

URDAR: The sacred fountain of Asgard.

UTGARD-LOKI: The giant Skrymir.

VALA: The Norns as prophetesses; used to designate women who were credited with power to forsee the future, and came in later ages to be called witches.

VALASKIALF: Throne room of Odin where his throne Hlidskialf stood. See Glads-heim, Glasir.

VALFATHER: Title of Odin.

VALHALLA: The hall of the chosen slain; one of 3 palaces of Odin; above the main gate sat an eagle that could see the whole world at a glance; 540 doors, through which 800 warriors all abreast could pass, led within; light was furnished by the glitter of the spears of which the walls were made; golden shields served as a roof; at long tables, the Einheriar, the favorite guests of Odin, were wined and dined. See Einheriar, Valkyries.

VALI: An Asa; god of eternal light, whose month, between mid-January and mid-February, is Liosberi, the light-bringing, represented by the sign of the bow, the characteristic emblem of Vali; son of Odin and Rinda; fated to avenge the death of Balder and, with Vidar, to rule the earth after Ragnarok; lived in Valaskialf with Odin.

VALKYRIES (VALKYRS): Choosers of the slain; nine beautiful maidens, attendants on Odin, who chose half the dead warriors from the fields of battle, and led them across the rainbow bridge Bifröst to live with the gods in Valhalla. See Valhalla, Einheriar.

VAN: A single Vanas was a Van.

VANADIS (VANABRIDE): A name for Freya as a native of Vana-heim.

VANAHEIM: The home of the Vanes.

VANAS: The sea and wind gods who dwelt in Vana-heim and ruled their domains independently from the Aesir; in early times they waged a war with the other gods, but the parties had come to terms and agreed to live in peace, after Niörd, a Van, came to live with his children Frey and Freya in Asgard, while the Asa Hoenir, brother of Odin, went to live in Vanaheim.

VARA: Attendant of Frigga; rewarded those who kept their word and punished perjurers.

VASUD: Personification of the icy wind; father of Vindsual; grandfather of Winter.

VE: Personification of holiness or the holy spirit; son of Bolthorn and Bestla; brother of Odin and Vili; helped kill the giant Ymir at the dawn of time, and helped in the creation of the earth and of the first man and woman, to whom he gave the gifts of senses, expression, and speech. See Ymir.

VEDFOLNIR: The falcon that perched between the eyes of the eagle sitting on the top most bough of Yggdrasil and reported to Odin all that he saw in heaven, on earth, and in the underworld. See Lerad.

VENUS, FRAU: As Frau Venus, Holda (or Frigga) is represented as living in a cave in Horselberg in Thuringia to which she lured men, kept them her prisoners, and drugged their senses with all kinds of pleasures; her most famous victim was, in later myth, Tannhäuser.

VERDANDI: A Norn; the gay and resolute sister of Urd and Skuld, who gazed fearlessly ahead, along the path she was about to take.

VIDAR (VITHAR): An Asa, god of the forests and the elements; son of Odin by the giantess Grid; called the "silent one" from his association with the brooding woods; fated to survive the holocaust of Ragnarok and return to rule and regenerate the earth; hence, like Adonis to the Greeks and Osiris to the Egyptians, a Northern symbol of the power of the earth to survive the winter and revive with the coming of spring; lived and ruled Landvidi.

VIGRID: Field of the last battle between the giants and the gods.

VIKING'S FUNERAL: The burial ceremony for a dead hero, in which the corpse and worldly possessions of the dead man were placed on a raft or float (a symbol for a ship), set afire, and left to drift until consumed by fire and water. In his novel *Beau Geste* Percival Christopher Wrenn made dramatic use of the Viking's Funeral as a memorial to some contemporary "vikings."

VILI: Personification of will; son of Bolthorn and Bestla; brother of Odin and Ve; with his father and brothers accomplished the deaht of Ymir in the initial struggle between the gods and giants; with Odin and Ve shared in the creation of the earth and of the first man, Ask (Aske, Ash), and the first woman, Embla, to whom he gave the gifts of reason and motion. See Ymir.

VINDSUAL: Son of Vasud; father of Winter.

VINGNIR: The winged (one); with Hlora, guardian of young Thor.

VINGOLF: Another name for Valhalla.

VINGTHOR: Name of Thor as ward of Vingnir.

VJOFN: Attendant of Frigga, with the special duty of softening hard hearts, promoting peace among men, and patching up quarrels between husbands and wives.

VOLLA: Same as Fulla.

VOLUND (WAYLAND, OR WIELAND, THE SMITH): A mortal who, with his brothers Egil and Slagfinn, surprised, captured, and enchanted the Valkyrs, Olrun, Alvit, and Suanhit; the brothers each married a battle-maiden, only to lose his wife when the nine-year spell of the Valkyrs ended, and the wives returned to Asgard; after many adventures, which exercised his skills as a blacksmith, Volund was reunited with his wife in Alf-heim where he became armorer to the gods; among the weapons he forged were Balmung, the sword of Sigmund; Joyeyse, the

sword of Charlemagne; Miming, the sword of his son Heime.

VOLSUNG: Great-grandson of Odin and grandfather of Sigurd, whose birth, adventures, and death are related in the opening of the *Volsunga Saga*.

VOLSUNGA SAGA: Scandinavian prose version of the Germanic epic, the *Nibelungenlied*, differing somewhat in the names of the characters and the details of their adventures; the hero is Sigurd, who is raised by Regin the Smith and slavs the dragon Fafnir; he is the hero fated to release the Valkyr, Brynhild, from the spell cast upon her by Odin; marries Brynhild but, on his journeys, is drugged by Grimhild, Queen of the Nibelungs, and married to the princess, Gudrun, helps prince Gunnar to win Brynhild and return with the Valkyr to the land of the Nibelungs; there the appearance of his first wife breaks his own enchantment, but the four lovers are so enmeshed in their tangled allegiances that there is none but a tragic exit for them; in rage, Brynhild plots and encompasses the murder of Sigurd, then kills herself and is burned with his corpse on the same funeral pyre.

VOL: The river of blood that flowed from the Fenris Wolf when the gods chained him up and stuck a sword in his mouth to stifle his howling.

VOR: Faith; attendant of Frigga; knew everything that was to happen in the world.

VULDER: Anglo-Saxon name for Uller.

WALPURGISNACHT: The night of revelry and riot celebrated by the witches and demons on the Brocken, or Blocksberg, a peak of the Harz Mountains, every May Day eve, the feast of Saint Walburga.

WAVES (WAVE MAIDENS): Nine daughters of Aegir and Ran, who sported with their brother Wind across the surface of the sea; wives of Odin, and corporate mother of Heimdall; they were named Atla, Augeia, Aurgiafa, Egia, Gialp, Greip, Iarnsaxa, Sindur, and Ulfrun.

WESTRI: A dwarf; personification of the West. See Nordri.

WHITE LADY: Frigga as Bertha.

WILD HUNT: The passage, like the winds of a storm, of disembodied spirits led by Odin, the Wild Hunter; also called Woden's Hunt, the Raging Hose, Gabriel's Hounds, and Asgardreia, the chase was after a visionary boar, wild horse, maidens, or wood nymphs. In England it was called Herlathing because Herla, a mythical king was the supposed leader; in northern France it was the Mesnee d'Hellequin, from Hel, the goddess of death. In the Middle Ages it became known as Cain's Hunt and Herod's Hunt after the restless spirits of the murderers of Abel and of John the Baptist and the Holy Innocents. Charlemagne, Barbarossa, King Arthur, or notorious sinners like the squire of Rodenstein and Hans von Hackelberg, have also been represented as leaders of the Wild Hunt.

WILD HUNTER (HUNTSMAN): Odin as leader of disembodied spirits. See Wild Hunt.

WIND: Prince of the sea, son of Aegir, the sea-god, and the sea goddess, Ran; brother of the Waves.

WINTER: God and personification of the winter season. Son of Vindsual; grandson of Vasud; enemy of Summer.

WODE, FRAU: See Gode.

WOTAN (WUOTAN): Another name for Odin.

WODEN: Saxon name of Odin, from which form Wednesday is derived.

WURD: The weird one; another name for Urd;

the Three Weird Sisters in Shakespeare's
Macbeth are all called by the title that belongs to Urd, the Norn, or Fate, who represented the past.

WYRD: Goddess of fate; mother of the Norns.

YGGDRASIL: The huge evergreen ash tree
created by Allfather and fashioned into the
tree of the universe, of time, and of life;
with roots in the underworld by the spring
Hvergelmir, in the earth by Mimir's Well,
and in heaven by the Urdar fountain, this
massive tree encompassed and overshadowed
all of creation.

YMIR: Giant produced by the action of heat
and cold on the hoar (rime) and icebergs in
the great central abyss, Ginnunga-gap; a
Hrim-thurs; suckled in the dawn of time by
the cow Audhumla; father of Thrudgelmir;
when he was slain in the first war between
the gods and the frost giants, all of the
giants except his grandson, Bergelmir, were
drowned in the flood of his gushing blood;
from his corpse the sons of Borr fashioned
the world; also called Orgelmir. See Surtr,
Buri.

ZIU: Variant of Tiu, as chief of the Swabian
gods.

ZWERGE: The dwarfs.

Major Gods and Goddesses of Babylon, Egypt, India, and the Orient

ADAD: Storm-god of the Babylonians; formed
with Sin and Shamash the second major triad
of gods; he was a prime-mover of the Storm
which caused the Flood; his centers of worship were in Babylon, Borsippa, Ashur, and
Aleppo; his symbols were the lightning and
the ax, his sacred number 6, his sacred animal the bull.

AGNI: Hindu god of fire, who is represented,
like the Roman Janus, as two-faced, in symbolism of his benevolent and malevolent
attributes.

AHA: Popular domestic god of the Egyptians,
similar to the dwarf-god Bes; his name means
Fighter, and his image on knives made them
powerful weapons against demons.

AHI: In Vedic myth, the serpent corresponding to the Hindu drought-demon, Vritra, which
engages Indra in mortal combat.

AHRIMAN: The principle of evil in the dualistic system of Zoroaster; as the enemy and
opposite of Ormazd, the Good Principle,
Ahriman will eventually be overthrown.

AHURA MAZDA: Same as Mazda.

AIN SOPH: The Supreme Spirit of Judaism,
similar to the Shakti of Brahminism.

AKHET: Egyptian goddess, personification of
the flood-season.

ALLAH: In Arabic, *al-ilah*, i.e., Worthy to be
Adored, the Arabic name used by the Moslems for God.

ALLATU: Semitic form of Ereshkigal.

ALOKA: Hindu goddess, personification of
light.

AMAUNET: See Ogdoad.

AMENHOTEP: King Amenhotep I of Egypt
who, after his death, was worshiped as a
local, popular deity in Thebes, where his
tomb is located.

AMENOTHES PAAPIOS: Greek name for
Amenhotep, son of Hapu, and Grand Vizier
of King Amenhotep III, who was deified and
worshiped after his death in various popular
Egyptian and Greek cults. See Imuthes.

AMENTET: Egyptian goddess, personification
of the West.

AMMON: Greek equivalent of Amun, as popularized by Herodotus.

AMON-RE (AMONRE): Supreme god of the
Empire which was founded on the conquests
of the XVIIIth Dynasty of Thebes; the new
rulers submerged the regnant god Re in their
own deity Amun and elevated the composite
god to leadership of the pantheon.

AMUM: See Ogdoad.

AMUN (AMEN, AMON): One of the Egyptian
creator-gods, worshiped in early times at
Hermopolis, later translated to Thebes, where
he became the local patron, and finally merged
with Re to become the supreme god of the
pantheon; his early representation was with
the head of a ram, symbolizing his function
as fertility-god; as such he was the Jupiter
Ammon of classical reference and was patron
of the Ammon Oracle in the Libyan desert;
his later image was as a man wearing on his
head a disc surmounted by two ostrich
plumes (an elaboration of his more primitive
ram's horns); in the Theban period, he headed
the divine triad of which his wife, Mut, and
Khons (Khonsu), his son, were the subordinate members.

ANAHITA: Persian goddess of war and fertility.

ANANTA: In Hindu myth, the serpent of eternity, who will support Vishnu on its back
at the end of the Kali Yuga, or present age
of the world, while from the stomach of the
god grows a lotus in which Brahma will
appear to recreate the world.

ANAT (ANATH): Semitic goddess of war, conceived by the early Jews as a consort of
Yahve, and also adopted and worshiped by
the Egyptians, who called her a daughter of
Re.

ANDJETI: Primitive Egyptian god, patron of
Djedu, who was later identified with Osiris.

ANUNIT: Babylonian goddess of war.

ANTU: In Babylonian religion, the early consort of Anu, mother of the Anunnaki and
Asakki.

ANU: In Babylonian religion, father and king
of the gods, ruler of the heavens; son of
Apsu and Tiamat; husband of Antu, and,
later, of Ishtar (Innina); father, by Antu, of
the Anunnaki and the seven evil Assaki
(demons); in Sumerian, Anu means "heaven;"
the home of Anu was in the third heaven; to
him was assigned the Equatorial region of the
heavens for his special dominion; his symbol
was the sacred shrine surmounted by the divine
horned cap, his sacred animal the heavenly
bull, his sacred number 60; with Enlil and
Enki, he formed the supreme triad of Babylonian deities.

ANUBIS: Greek form of Anupew, the Egyptian
name of the early "dog-god" of Upper Egypt,
who was from early times worshiped as god
of the dead and protector of tombs; later,
as attendant to Osiris in the underworld, he
kept the scales on which the hearts of the
dead were weighed against Truth in judgment
of their earthly deeds.

ANUKET (ANUKIT): In Egyptian myth, consort of the god Khnum, and member of the
divine triad of Elephantine.

ANUNNAKI: Apparently a collective term for
the Babylonian gods of the heaven, earth,
and the underworld; Enlil is called King of
the Anunnaki. See Igigi. Also, simply the
underworld gods af Babylonian religion, offspring of Anu and Antu.

APEPI: In Egyptian myth, serpent-leader of
the demons who daily assaulted the sun and
were daily driven back, a dramatic representation of the succession of night and day.

APIS: Greek form of Hapi, the Egyptian bull

whose worship is traced as far back as the 1st Dynasty at Memphis; in the New Kingdom, he was considered an embodiment or "repetition" of Ptah, but gradually, became identified with the funerary cult of Osiris and finally merged with Osiris into the deity Usar-hape; as Usar-hape, he was discovered by the Greek colony of Memphis and renamed Osorapis. See Osorapis, Sarapis.

APSU: God of the underworld ocean in ancient Babylonian myth.

ARCHANGEL: An angel of the highest rank; in the Koran, the four great angels are Gabriel, who typifies revelation and inspiration, Michael, who represents war, Azrael, or the angel of death, and Azrafil, or the awakener.

ARJUNA: Hero of the Mahabharata.

ARURU: In early Babylonian mythology, the mother-goddess who assisted Enlil in the creation of mankind. See Ninmach.

ASAKKI: Seven evil demons of Babylonian religion, offspring of Anu and Antu.

ASH: In Egyptian myth, an anthropomorphic deity, sometimes represented with the head of a hawk, who was probably a local cult god of the Libyan border.

ASHIMA: A Semitic goddess who was, until the 6th century b.c., considered as a consort of Yahve.

ASHUR: Supreme god and god of war of Assyria, where he assumed the functions of Enlil and Marduk and had as his consort Ishtar; his symbol was the winged disc encircling a bust of the god in the act of shooting an arrow.

ASTARTE: The Phoenician goddess of fertility and sexual love, identified with Ishtar and Aphrodite, and, through literary allusions, with Semele and Artemis as a moon-goddess; an Egyptian cult of the goddess also existed in Memphis, where she absorbed some of the characteristics of native Egyptian deities, and was even identified as a daughter of Ptah.

ATAR: Iranian god of fire.

ATARGATIS: Syrian mother-goddess.

ATON (ATEN): The material character of the sun-god, Re, as the actual sun-disc, promoted by Amenhotep IV (Akhnaton, Ekhnaton, Ikhnaton) as the symbol of his monotheistic reformation during the 14th century b.c.

ATTIS (ATYS): Syrian savior-god; son of the virgin Nana; he was killed by a wild boar in a symbolical death which, like the death of Adonis in Greek mythology, represents the annual death and revival of vegetation on the earth.

ATUM: Egyptian creator-god, originally from Heliopolis, represented in early times as the oldest, at one time the only, and therefore the self-created of the gods; absorbed finally into Re, and depicted in sun-worship as the setting sun.

BAAL (BEL, BEEL): A Semitic word meaning lord or possessor; the Israelites used Baal when referring to a variety of gods (including Yahweh), and so brought upon themselves the anger of their prophets for straying from the worship of the One True God.

BAALZEBUB: The Semitic "Lord of Flies."

BABBAR: Early Sumerian name for Shamash.

BASTET (BAST): Egyptian cat-goddess whose popular cult, centered in Bubastis, dated back to early times, and was probably first associated with the lioness rather than the cat; Herodotus describes a festival of Bastet in his history.

BEELZEBUB: The Biblical oracle deity of the Ekron, a city of the Philistines.

BELPHEGOR: Moabite deity, noted for his licentiousness.

BES: A dwarfish, bandy-legged, domestic god of the Egyptians, whose image, worn on the body, had powerful talismanic properties.

BHAVANI: See Prthivi.

BRAHMA: The supreme god of the Hindus, the soul or essence of all things, uncreated, immaterial, beyond space and time, who is himself being, intelligence, and happiness. As creative energy, Brahma is quiescent, and will remain so until the end of Kali Yuga, or present age of the world; therefore he maintains neither temple nor altar. He is represented with four heads, holding in one hand a copy of the Vedas, in another a vessel of lustral water, in a third a spoon for pouring the water, and in his fourth hand is a rosary. Husband of Sarasvati. See also Sacti, Vahana.

BUCHIS: Sacred bull of the Egyptians.

CYBELE: A Phyrigian goddess, personification of the fruitful earth; consort of Attis.

DAGON: Supreme god of the Philistines, whose worship was also adopted by the Phoenicians; represented originally as half-man and half-fish, he became in time an agricultural god.

DAITYAS: The Demons in Vedic religion.

DEDUN: Nubian war-god, described as the incense bringer or bearer, who was absorbed into the worship of the Egyptian Khnum.

DEVA: In Hindu and Buddhist mythology, a beneficent spirit of the light and air, but, among the Persians, evil spirits and demons.

DUAMUTEF: Son of the Egyptian god Horus, in whose keeping was one of the four jars in which the viscera of the embalmed dead were stored.

DUMU-ZI: Sumerian name for Tammuz.

DURGA: See Prthivi.

DYAUS: In Vedic myth, the god of the bright sky, who is sometimes addressed as a supreme god. Also called Dyaush-Pitir.

EA: Later name for Enki.

EBLIS: In Mohammedan theology, leader of the fallen angels.

ENKI (EA): In Babylonian religion, god of the waters, who made up, with Anu and Enlil, the supreme triad of deities; husband of Damkina; father of Marduk; his home was in the Apsu, the underworld ocean which supported the earth; the center of his cult was in the temple of Eengurra in Eridu; to him were assigned the heavens south of the Equator; his symbols were the ram's head and the mythical goat-fish with the head of a goat and body of a fish, and the constellations Pisces and Aquarius; his sacred number was 40; patron of wisdom, Enki instructed men in the arts and crafts and was keeper of the secrets of magic.

ENLIL (ELLIL): Ruler of the earth in Babylonian religion, whose name means storm or wind; with Anu and Enki made up the supreme triad of Babylonian deities; in early times, the principal god of the triad, later surpassed by Anu and dropped to second place in the heavenly hierarchy; husband of Ninlil; the center of his cult was the temple Ekur (House of the Mountain) in Nippur; to him were assigned the heavens north of the Equator; his astrological symbol was the Pleiades, his sacred number 50; an ambiguous deity who is sometimes represented as the creator of mankind, and sometimes as the god who sent the Flood to destroy all of the earth, including every man; keeper of the tablets of destiny, with control over the fate of all things.

ERESHKIGAL: Goddess and ruler of the under-

world in Babylonian mythology; wife of
Nergal; her chief center of worship was at
Cuthah.

ERNUTET: In Egyptian myth, personification
of the harvest, represented as a cobra, or
cobraheaded woman; identified with Renenet.

ERSHOP: A Semitic Ba'al who came with
prisoners of war to Egypt and absorbed
some of the attributes of Egyptian deities,
particularly the function of Ptah as the god
to whom prayers and petitions were addressed;
represented with a high, tasseled conical cap,
holding a shield and spear in his left hand
and a mace in his right.

ESET: Egyptian form of the name Isis.

GANAPATI: Another name for Ganesa.

GANDHARVAS: The semi-divine minstrels of
the gods of India whose home is the sky and
the regions of air.

GANESA (GANESHA): The Hindu elephant-
headed god of wisdom, who is invoked, like
the Greek Muses, at the beginning of literary
works; son of Siva and Parvati.

GARUDA: The vehicle of Vishnu in Hindu
myth, represented as kings of birds, half-
man and half-bird.

GEB (SEB): God of the earth in Egyptian myth;
husband of Nut; father of Set, Osiris, and
Isis; often represented as an oarsman of the
sun-boat. See Nut.

GWYDION: Cymric god of the sky, the magician who taught men the arts and crafts of
civilization.

GWYN (GWYNN): Cymric god of the underworld, and king of the Welsh fairies; son of
Nudd (Lludd); a great hunter and woodsman, he is represented by his special symbol,
the owl.

HA: In Egyptian myth, the god who personified the desert, specifically the Libyan desert.

HADAD: Syrian name for Adad.

HAPI: See Apis.

HAPY: Son of the Egyptian god Horus, in
whose keeping was one of the four jars in
which the viscera of the embalmed dead
were stored.

HARAKHTE: In Egyptian myth, the Horus of
the Horizon, a transitional deity who represented the conquest of the Horus-worshiping
Upper Egyptian kings over the Re-worship-
ing Lower Egyptians; finally called Re-
Harakhte when the merger of the two peoples
was complete.

HAROËRIS (HAR-WER): Horus the Elder,
Greek and Egyptian title used to designate
various temples of the Horus cult.

HARPOCRATES (HAR-PE-KHRAD): Horus
the Child, Greek and Egyptian title for the
son of Osiris and Isis.

HARSAPHES (HARSHAF): Primitive ram-god
of Herakleopolis Magna in Upper Egypt,
known only by this title which means "He
who is on his lake."

HATHOR: Sky-goddess of the Egyptians, represented from early times as a tree or a
pillar in various places, bust most enduringly
as a cow-goddess whose head was often a
cow's head, with a disc mounted between the
horns; also the goddess of love and social
joy, functioning in various temple ceremonies as the consort of Amun.

HATMEHIT: Fish-goddess of Lower Egypt.

HAUNET: See Ogdoad.

HAURON: Originally a Semitic deity who
migrated to Egypt, was represented, like
Horus, as a falcon, and was associated with
the Great Sphinx of Memphis.

HEDJ-WER (HEDJWEREW): Baboon-god of
the early Egyptians whose name, which is actually a late title, means the Great White One,

or Whitest of the Great Ones.

HEKET: Egyptian fertility goddess, represented
as a frog; at Antinoupolis, she was the consort of Khnum.

HERMES AËRIOS: Greek name for the Egyptian
Show.

HIKE: The magic powers of the sun-god, Re,
personified as one of the gods acting as the
crew of the sun-boat.

HOR-SHED: An Egyptian deity in whom the
characteristics of the culture hero, Shed, and
the young Horus were merged; represented
as a naked child astride the heads of two
crocodiles, his hands filled with snakes, scorpions, a lion, and a gazelle, against which
his image had talismanic powers.

HORUS: Egyptian hawk- or falcon-headed god,
represented from early times as a sky-god;
his origins are obscure, and he has many
different forms, but he is most prominent as
the god of the rising sun, and, as the son of
Osiris and Isis, the slayer of his uncle Set in
revenge for the murder of Osiris; father of
the funerary brothers Duamutef, Hapy, Imset,
and Kebehsenuf.

HU: The word of the sun-god, Re, specifically
his commands and creative ordinances; conceived as one of the crewmen of the sun-boat.

HUH: See Ogdoad.

HUITZILOPOCHTLI: Blood-thirsty Aztec god,
to whom annual human sacrifices were made.

IAH: An Egyptian moon-god.

IBLIS: In Mohammedan theology, the fallen
angel who became chief of the Mohammedan
evil spirits.

IGIGI: Apparently a collective term for the
Babylonian gods of heaven, earth, and the
underworld; Anu, Ashur, and Marduk are
called King of the Igigi. See Anunnaki.

IMIUT: Early Egyptian god, identified with
Anubis, whose fetish was an inflated animal
skin hanging from a pole.

IMSET: Son of the Egyptian god Horus, in
whose keeping was one of the four jars in
which the viscera of the embalmed dead
were stored.

IMUTHES: Greek name for Imhotep, vizier
and court architect of King Djoser, who was
deified and worshiped after his death in
various popular Egyptian and Greek cults.
See Amenothes Paapios.

INARI: Goddess of vegetation in Shintoism
(Japanese).

INDRA: Hindu fertility-god and war-god,
slayer of the drought-demon Vritra; he lived
with the Apsaras or nymphs on Mt. Muru,
the Olympus-like mountain thought to lie
north of the Himalayas.

INNINA: Sumerian name for Ishtar.

IRRA: Plague-god in Babylonian mythology,
an implacable enemy of man, who is often
associated with Nergal.

ISHTAR (INNINA): The most popular goddess
of the Babylonian and Assyrian pantheon,
goddess of Love and procreation, and of war;
associated with the second triad of gods, Sin,
Shamash, and Adad, but later consort of Anu;
daughter of Sin; sister-wife of Tammuz, in
search of whom she descended to the underworld; her chief center of worship was at
Erech; her symbol was an eight- or sixteen-
pointed star; Venus (Dilbat) and Sirius were
her stars; her sacred number was 15; usually
represented either as riding on or accompanied by her sacred beast, the lion.

ISHVARA: In the popular Hindu cult, the
savior-god, whose counterpart is Brahma in
philosophical speculation.

ISIS (ESET): The most popular of the Egyptian
goddesses of fertility and motherhood; daugh-

ter of Geb and Nut; sister and wife of Osiris, whose search for the dismembered and scattered parts of her husband's body is celebrated in the principal Egyptian resurrection myth; mother of Horus; often identified with Hathor and represented with the head of a cow; the worship of Isis spread to Greece and Rome; in Rome she was also the patroness of sailors and travelers.

ISRAFIL: Moslem angel of music, who will sound the Ressurection Trumpet on the last day.

JACA: The evil spirit or devil of Cingalese myth.

JAMSHID (JAMSHYD): In Persian myth, the Genii King whose golden cup was filled with the elixir of life; the fifth quatrain of The Rubaiyat refers to the Seven-Ringed Cup of Jamshyd.

JIZO: A Japanese god, formerly of China, whose special province is the care of little children.

JUPITER AMMON: An Egyptian deity, worshiped at the Siwa oasis in the Libyan desert, where he was patron of one of the most famous oracles of the ancient world; usually represented with ram's horns, he combined the characteristics of the Egyptian Amun and the Roman Jupiter; it was the oracle of Jupiter Ammon which predicted to Alexander the Great, during his visit in 332 b.c., that he would conquer the world.

KAHWET: See Ogdoad.

KAMA (KAMADEVA): Hindu god of love, represented as owning ten fetters or bonds of desire, all of which must be broken by the Buddhist disciple; he is pictured as a handsome youth who rides a parrot or a dove in company with a train of nymphs; he is armed with a sugarcane bow, strung with a cord of bees, and each of his arrowheads is a different and meaningful flower.

KALI: See Prthivi.

KEBEHSENUF: Son of the Egyptian god Horus, in whose keeping was one of the four jars in which the viscera of the embalmed dead were stored.

KEBHOWET: Egyptian goddess personifying the Cold Water Libation, which, as keeper of cool water, she prepared daily for the sun-god in his temples; this function was later assumed by Horus and Thoth.

KEDESH: Semitic goddess of love and beauty, concubine of the gods, who migrated to Egypt in the period of the Empire.

KHEM: In Egyptian religion, the personification of generation and reproduction, a manifestation of universal life metamorphosed into the person of a god whom the Greeks identified with Pan when they called his center of worship at Chemmis Panopolis, or the City of Pan; also identified with the Egyptian garden-god Ranno.

KHENTEKHTAY: Egyptian falcon- or hawk-god of Athribis in Lower Egypt who was finally identified with Horus; his sons assisted the sons of Horus in the later embalming ritual sponsored by Anubis.

KHENTI-AMENTIU: Early funerary god of the Egyptians, represented as a recumbent dog; his name, Foremost of the Westerners, refers to the dominant Egyptian belief that the abode of the dead was in the West, where the sun set; later merged with Osiris.

KHEPERA: An Egyptian creator-god, identified with sun-worship as the morning sun; sometimes represented as the self-produced Father of the Gods; his symbol was the scarab beetle.

KHERTY: Egyptian ram-god of Lower Egypt, represented in the form of a recumbent mummy.

KHNUM (KHNEMU): The ram-god of Elephantine; represented in early Egypt myth as the divine potter who fashioned the first man out of clay; with his consorts, Anuket and Satet, he made up the triad of gods of Elephantine.

KHONS (KHENSU): Egyptian moon-god and god of healing; son of Amun and Mut with whom he formed the divine triad of Thebes.

KINGU: In ancient Babylonian myth, consort of Tiamat.

KRISHNA: An avatar of Vishnu, whose exploits are celebrated in the Bhagavad-gita, in which the Way of Religious Devotion, or Bhakti, is set forth; Krishna himself was possibly a hero who was later deified.

KUAN LIN: See Kwannon.

KUK: See Ogdoad.

KWANNON (KUAN LIN): In Chinese and Japanese Buddhism, a female bodhisattva worshiped as goddess of mercy and love.

KWEI: The spirits and ghosts of Chinese folklore.

LABBU MONSTER: In Babylonian creation myths, a primeval evil force which represented the rampaging water of the Tigris-Euphrates and had to be destroyed or controlled before the lives of the gods or of men were possible.

LAKSHMI (SRI): Hindu goddess of beauty and wealth, who also represents the fortunes of kingdoms and kings; wife of Vishnu. Also called Maha Lakshmi.

LLUDD: See Nudd.

MA'AT (MA'ET): Egyptian goddess who personified Right or Truth; daughter of the sun-god, Re; represented as standing on the prow of the sun-boat as it sailed across the sky; symbolized by the ostrich feather, against which the hearts of the dead were weighed in judgment before Osiris in the underworld.

MAFDET: Early Egyptian cat- or mongoose-goddess, the Lady of the Castle, who protected her suppliants against snake-bites.

MAHA LAKSHMI: See Lakshmi.

MANU: Hindu Noah.

MARA: Personified principle of evil of Hindu and Buddhist theology.

MARDUK: A Babylonian sun-god, tutelary god of Babylon; son of Enki; consort of Zarpanit; father of Nebo; came in time to absorb many of the attributes of the earlier gods; he is assigned, in creation myths, the role of defending the gods against Tiamat, the primitive Chaos-monster, whom he slays and splits in two, creating the heavens from one part of her body and the oceans from the other, and winning by his exploits kingship of the gods, with authority equal to Anu's.

MARUTS: Vedic storm-gods, companions of Vayu.

MAZDA (AHURA MAZDA): The supreme god of the Zoroastrian Zend-Avesta.

MELKARTH (MELCARTH): The patron or tutelary deity (Baal) of Tyre in Phoenicia, identified with Moloch and Milcom.

MERSEGER: In Egyptian myth, the cobra-goddess of Thebes; as guardian of the Necropolis, or City of the Dead, the silence-loving Mistress of the West was also called Ta-dehnet.

MILCOM: An Ammonite deity, identified with Moloch, and with the Phoenician Melkarth.

MIN: Egyptian god of fertility; like Ptah and Osiris, represented as mummiform; as god of procreation, his symbol was ithyphallic; his sacred plant was the lettuce, which was carried in harvest festival processions, the most important of the god's annual "comings-forth."

MITHRA MITHRAS: Persian god of light whose worship extended to Rome during the period of the early Empire.

MOLOCH: A Semitic deity identified with Melkarth of the Phoenicians; the Biblical "abomination of the Ammonites," with a reputation for demanding human sacrifices.

MONT (MONTU): Egyptian god of war, represented as a hawk- or falcon-headed man crowned with a solar disc; his sacred animal was the bull; originally centered at El-Mont, his cult spread to Thebes, Medamud, and Tod.

MUMMU: Craftsman-god of the Babylonians, attendant on Enki.

MUKTI: See Moksha.

MUT (MAUT): Vulture-headed consort of Amun, forming with him and Khons the Theban triad of gods.

NANDI: Hindu goddess of joy.

NANNAR: Early name for Sin.

NANTAR: Messenger of Ereshkigal, herald of death, in whose train were sixty diseases which he had in his power to release against mankind.

NAPRI: Egyptian goddess who personified Corn.

NARAYANA: In Hindu myth, the divine spirit of the Balm, represented as a comely youth lying on a floating or swimming snake and with his toe in his mouth.

NAUNET: See Ogdoad.

NEKHEBET (NEKHEBT): Vulture-goddess of Enkhab (El-Kab) who became tutelary goddess of the Upper Egyptian Kingdom in the predynastic period.

NEBO: Babylonian god of writing; son of Marduk; consort of Tashmetu.

NEITH: Lower Egyptian goddess of the hunt, of war, and of the upper heavens; identified also as goddess of wisdom; represented from early times as two arrows crossed over a shield, and, later, as a woman wearing the crown of Lower Egypt and bearing in her left hand a lotus scepter.

NEPHTYS: In Egyptian mythology, daughter of Geb and Nut, sister-consort of Set, assistant to Isis, her sister, in the rites of her slain brother, Osiris.

NERGAL: God of the underworld in Babylonian myth; husband of Ereshkigal; spent six months of every year on the earth where he represented the evil side of Shamash and was the sun-god's agent when Shamash visited men with plagues, wars, devastation and floods

NINGAL: Wife of Sin in Babylonian mythology; mother of Shamash.

NINGIZZIDA: In Sumerian mythology, a god of the underworld, friend and companion of Tammuz.

NINKHURSAGGA: See Ninmach.

NINMACH: Mother-goddess of the early Babylonians, patroness of childbirth. Known also as Nintu, Ninkhursagga, and Aruru.

NINTU: See Ninmach.

NUB: Egyptian goddess who personified Gold.

NUDD (LLUDD): Gaelic and Cymric names of the sky- and sun-god; father of Gwyn; identified with the mythical Lud, King of Briton.

NUN: The limitless watery deep of Egyptian cosmology, personified as the first self-produced god. See Ogdoad.

NUSKU: The Babylonian fire-god, chief minister of Enlil.

NUT: In Egyptian myth, the goddess who personified the sky; wife of Geb; mother of Set, Osiris, and Isis; represented as the figure of a woman, often spangled with stars, bending over and encompassing the body of her husband, the earth.

OGDOAD: A group or set of eight; specifically, in Egyptian mythology, the four sets of male and female principles, Amum and Amaunet, Huh and Haunet, Kuk and Kahwet, Nun and Naunet, who spun the world out of their own elemental substances.

OM: In Hindu mysticism, the key to Reality, a symbol which is contemplated by all sects; it is represented as the divine force of creation, the Logos, and the All which sums up, in the single sound, the Absolute, the Relative, and all that lies between.

ONURIS: Egyptian tutelary god of This, identified with Shed.

ORMAZD (AHURA MAZDA): The supreme god of Zoroastrianism, creator of the world, holy, wise, just, and good, whose later association was with the principle of good as opposed to the principle of evil, or Ahriman; represented as a bearded man encircled by a winged disc.

OSIRIS: Egyptian god of the Kingdom of Death; son of Geb and Nut; brother of Set; brother-husband of Isis; father of Horus; originally centered at Djedu, the cult of Osiris spread down the Delta, and the center was transferred to Abydos; represented as mummiform, the figure of Osiris was invested with regal trappings, he was closely associated with the fates of kings, his resurrection from the dead prefiguring their own, and is thought to have been an historical king who was eventually deified; the annual overflow of the Nile is dramatized in his myth as a nature-god; as a fertility-god, he is the chief figure of the great Egyptian resurrection myth, in which he is slain and dismembered by Set, the parts of his body discovered and buried by Isis, his death revenged by Horus, and his body finally reunited and revived when he ate, through magic, the eye of Horus; as king of the underworld, he was judge of the dead and supreme funerary god, in which capacity his worship was spread throughout the Mediterranean world during the period of the Roman Empire.

OSORAPIS: Greek name for Usar-Hape, as Apis was called by the Egyptians at Memphis after he had become identified with the Osiris cult; the Greek colony in the city adopted the bull god under their own name, giving Ptolemy I grounds for the decision which transformed the god finally into the cult-deity, Sarapis. See Sarapis.

PRAJAPATI: Hindu creator of the world.

PROYET: Egyptian goddess of Spring.

PRTHIVI: The Mother-earth of Hindu myth, wife of Siva; as Durga or Kali, she is the goddess of Saktism, or worship of the female principle in nature, which is celebrated with obscene rites accompanied by bloody, sometimes human, sacrifice; as Kali, she functions with Siva as an avenging deity and her symbol is a rope with which she strangles evil-doers. Known also as Bhavani. See Sacti.

Ptah: Creator-god of the Egyptians, father of the gods and of men, architect of the world; represented as an idol in the wrappings of a mummy; his cult was centered at Memphis.

PUSHAN: A sun-god of the Vedic religion.

QEB: Variant of Geb.

QUETZALCOATL: The Feather-Serpent, a pre-Aztec sun-god of Mexico; when the Spaniards began their conquest of Mexico, they were supposed by the Mexicans to represent this god, whose second-coming was promised in their religion; consequently, the natives offered little resistance and fell victim to the greed of the Conquistadors.

RAKSHASAS: Storm demons in Hindu mythology; also agents of destruction.

RAMA: The hero of the Ramayana who defeats the demon Rabana; also the name of a religious sect of Vaishnavism, the Ramaites, of the 8th century a.d.

RANNO: Garden-god of the Egyptians, patron of wine-press and of gardening and farming tools, which were often decorated with his image in the form of an asp; identified by the Greeks with Priapus and by the Egyptians with Khem.

RASHNU: In Zoroastrian religion, the Spirit of Truth who will hold the scales in the Last Judgment.

RE (RA): Supreme god of Egypt, worshiped as the principal sun-god, representing the full noon-day sun; son of Nut; depicted in early times as a hawk- or falcon-headed man crowned with the solar-disc and uraeus, or cobra, symbol, as a lion or cat and, progressively, as the celestial body or winged solar disc; the center of his cult was at Heliopolis; when the idea of kingship was identified with solar religion, the Kings of Egypt called themselves Sons of Re; his cult was finally eclipsed and absorbed by the funerary cult of Osiris.

RENENET: In Egyptian myth, personification and goddess of nursing, whose function was the safe delivery and welfare of infants; later assumed the personification of riches and fortune, and became identified with the goddess Ernutet.

RESHEP: Another name for Ershop.

RESHEPH: Syrian name for Adad.

RIMMON: Old Testament name for Adad.

RONPET: Egyptian goddess who personified the Year.

SACTI (SAKTI): In Hindu myth, a wife of a god. The sacti of the Trimurti were: of Brahma, Sarasvati; of Vishnu, Lakshmi; of Siva, Prthivi.

SAKTI: Wife of Siva; as the energizing force in the world, she is regarded by the Hindus as the divine complement of the passive and contemplative Siva, and therefore patron of the creative functions revealed in evolution.

SAKTISM (SACTISM): In Hindu religion, worship of the female principle in nature, often accompanied by obscene and bloody rites. See Prthivi.

SARAPIS: Through the desire of Ptolemy I to absorb the Greek colonists in Egypt into his kingdom, the god Osorapis was chosen as a representative deity who would win favor with both Egyptians and Greeks; a new image for the old god was imported from Asia Minor, and the name Sarapis was invented for the occasion; as Sarapis, the novel old god became more popular than ever; the Greeks identified him with Pluto and built a temple for him, the Serapeum, in Alexandria; the Egyptians renamed the cemetery of the sacred bulls at Memphis, calling it also the Serapeum; with the Roman conquest, the god migrated to Italy, and as far eastward as the Greek colonies on the Black Sea; during the reign of Caligula, a temple to Isis and Sarapis was built in Rome, and the Roman cult of these two deities survived until the end of paganism; in Egypt the worship of the god progressed so far that, by the 3rd Century, he was regarded almost as a sun-god.

SARASVATI: Hindu goddess of poetry, wisdom, eloquence, and fine arts; wife of Brahma. See Sacti.

SATAN: The evil principle of the ancient Israelites, similar to and probably derived from Babylonian beliefs, just as Christianity absorbed a belief in Satan from the gospels.

SATI (SATET): Queen of the Egyptian gods and goddess of the lower heaven; consort of Khnum, forming with him and Anuket the triad of gods of Elephantine; represented with the horns of a cow.

SAVITAR: One-handed sun-god of Vedic myth.

SEB: Variant of Geb.

SEBEK: Egyptian crocodile-god, represented as a man with the head of a crocodile.

SED: Early Egyptian dog-god, identified with Upuaut.

SET (SETEKH; SETH): Egyptian god of the atmosphere, from whose body emerged iron and flint; possibly the older of the gods; son of Geb and Nut; brother of Osiris; husband of Tefnut; originally centered in Enboyet (Ombos), the cult of Set spread until it met and rivalled the cult of Horus, son of Osiris, and was followed by the transformation of Set into the evil god who murdered his brother and was himself slain by his nephew; represented in early times as a donkey-god, his form became increasingly fabulous and at last wholly mythical.

SEVEN JAPANESE GODS OF HAPPINESS (OR LUCK): Benten; Bishamon; Daikoku; Ebisu; Fuku-roku-yu; Hotei; Jurojin.

SHAITAN: Arabic devil or spirit of evil.

SHAMASH: Sun-god of the Babylonians; son of Sin and Ningal; with Sin and Adad, formed the second major triad of Babylonian divinities; his chief centers of worship were at Sippar and Larsa; his symbol was a solar disc surrounding a four-pointed star with rays emerging from between the points, or, in Assyria, a winged solar disc; his sacred number was 20; patron of truth and justice in the communal life of man; he was also, with Adad, concerned with giving and interpreting oracles.

SHED: The Savior, a tutelary god of Egypt, whose fame as a hunter made his image a potent talisman against snakes, scorpions, and crocodiles. See Hor-Shed.

SHEN: Good spirits in Chinese folklore.

SHESMU: Egyptian god who personified Wine-pressing.

SHOMU: Egyptian god of Summer.

SHOW (SHU): Egyptian god of the air, first son of Atum, brother of Tfenet, father of the rest of the gods, and of all of life; in early cosmology, regarded as separating earth and sky and holding them apart by filling the space between his own presence; in later sun-worship, he figured as the atmosphere, or, more particularly, as the sun at twilight, or as twilight.

SHOY: Egyptian god who personified Fate or Destiny.

SHULMANN: Identified as the Assyrian counterpart of Ninurta.

SIN: Moon-god of the Babylonians; in Sumeria, represented as son of Enlil; husband of Ningal; father of Shamash; patron of the calendar, who set the periods of the days, months, and years; also a vegetation-god, with special concern for fertility in cattle; his centers of worship were at Ur and Harran; his symbol was the crescent, his sacred number 30; he is represented with a beard of lapis-lazuli and mounted on his sacred beast, the winged bull.

SIVA (SHIVA): Hindu god of reproduction and dissolution whose symbol, the linga, represents the universal creative force; with Brahma and Vishnu he forms the third of the great triad of Hinduism (from Sanskrit çiva, meaning happy); husband of Prthivi;

represented as white in color, he is sometimes carrying a trident and the rope, or *pasha*, with which he strangles sinners; around his neck Siva wears a strand of human skulls, and his earrings are snakes; he is girt in a tiger's skin and from his forehead flows the sacred river Ganges. See Trimurti, Sacti, Vahana.

SOKAR (SOKER): Funerary deity of the Egyptian neighborhood of Memphis, represented as mummiform, with the head of a hawk or falcon; identified finally with Ptah, the god of Memphis, as Ptah-Sokar, and sometimes with Osiris; in sun-worship, he was thought of as the sun at night.

SOKHET: Egyptian goddess who represented the Cultivable Plain or Arable Land.

SOMA: In Vedic myth, the personification of the liquor of the Soma plant, who was represented as the sustainer of both gods and of men, and of their worlds.

SRI: See Lakshmi.

SUN-GODS, EGYPTIAN: In Egyptian myth, all of the phases of the sun were worshiped, each as a different deity: Re was the sun at full strength; Horus, the rising-sun; Khepera, the morning sun; Atum, the setting sun; Show, the sun at twilight; Sokar, the sun at night, and Aton, the solar disc.

SURYA: Vedic sun-god, who dwelt, like the Greek Helios, in the body of the sun; son and consort of the dawn goddess, Ushas.

TA-DEHNET: Another name for the Egyptian cobra-goddess, Merseger, which refers to her temple on the mountain-peak (Kurn) guarding the Valley of the Kings.

TAMMUZ: Vegetation-god of the early Sumerians, who is represented as descending to the underworld where he is sought out by his sister-wife, Ishtar, and brought back to the earth; the descent and return of Tammuz represents the annual death and revival of vegetation on the earth, and was the basis of the later Babylonian New Year Festival.

TASHMETU: Personification of hearing; consort of Nebo in Babylonian myth.

TAYET: Egyptian goddess who personified the art of weaving.

TESHUB: Hittite name for Adad.

TFENET: Egyptian goddess of moisture, daughter of Atum, twin and wife of Show, mother of the gods and of all of life.

THOTH: Ibis-headed scribe of the Egyptian gods, patron of wisdom and magic, god of the moon, who assisted with Osiris in the underworld at the judgment of the dead; the first month of the calendar of the New Kingdom was Thoth; his sacred animal was the baboon.

TIAMAT: In ancient Babylonian myth, goddess of chaos; consort of Kingu; in the epics, Marduk destroys her in single combat and fashions the world from her body.

TOËRIS (TWERET): Greek and Egyptian names for the domestic fertility goddess of Egypt, represented as a pregnant hippopotamus standing on hind-leg.

THE TRIMÛRTI: The Brahmanic triad of gods, consisting of Brahma, the creator, Vishnu, the preserver, and Siva, the destroyer. The three are not independent, but are merely phases or personified powers of the supreme and inscrutable Brahm.

TYPHON: Identified by the Greeks with the Egyptian god Set, Typhon was the monster who married Echidna and spawned Cerberus, the Sphinx, the Chimera, and many other of the classical prodigies; son of Typhoeus, and therefore, by the genealogy of Hesiod, grandchild of Tartarus and Gaea (or of Hera

alone), he came to be identified with his father and assumed the family attribute of having a hundred heads and multiple horrible voices and eyes; the original Typhoeus was struck down by a thunderbolt of Zeus and buried beneath Mt. Etna, where he continued to make his unwelcome presence felt as the genius of the volcano.

UMA: In Hindu myth, goddess of light and beauty, and wife of Siva.

UPUAUT: Early Egyptian dog-god of Siut, whose name means the "way-opener"; identified with Sed.

USUR-HAPE: See Apis, Osorapis.

USHAS: Goddess of the dawn in Vedic myth, mother and wife of the sun-god, Surya.

UTNAPISHTIM: Babylonian hero of the Noah legend, who was forewarned by Enki and so built a ship and escaped the coming Flood.

UTU: Early Sumerian name for Shamash.

VAE: In Vedic myth, goddess of speech, and wife of Brahma.

VAHANA: In Hindu myth, the vehicle of a god. The vehicles of the Trimûrti were: of Brahma, the goose; of Vishnu, Garuda, king of birds, half-man and half-bird; of Siva, a white bull.

VARANU: In Hindu Vedic religion, the sky-god or god of righteousness; Indra and other gods of sacrifice took his place in later times.

VAYU: Vedic god of the wind and the air, companion of the Maruts, or storm-gods.

VISHNU: In Hindu myth, the preserver, the sustaining power of the divine spirit; husband of Lakshmi, represented as blue in color. See Trimûrti, Sacti, Vahana.

WEDJOYET: Tutelary goddess of the Kingdom of Lower Egypt, whose symbol was the cobra.

WER: The Great One, a sky- and light-god of early Egypt, later identified with Horus.

YAMA: Hindu god of the dead, regarded as the mythical ancestor of the Indo-Aryans and, as Yima, the ancestor of the Iranian-Aryans.

YAZATAS: The angels in Zoroastrian religion.

YIMA: Another name for Yama.

ZALTU: In Babylonian myth, personification of Strife, created by Ea as counterpart to the violence of Ishtar.

ZARATHUSTRA: See Zoroaster.

ZARPANIT: In Babylonian myth, consort of Marduk.

ZU-BIRD: The Storm-Bird in Babylonian mythology, represented as half-bird and half-man, who stole the tablets of destiny from Enlil.

Gods of the World: A Checklist of Their Works and Patronage with the Heavens and Hells of Different World Religions

Gods of Archery

APOLLO: Greek.
ULLR: Norse.
VILI: Norse.
YARRI: Hittite.

Gods of Arts, Sciences, Culture, and Civilization

APIS: Egyptian.
APOLLO: Greek.
APOLLO CITHAROEDUS: Greek.
APOLLO MUSAGETES (APOLLO AS LEADER OF THE MUSES): Greek.
BRAGI: Norse.
CREDNE: Irish.

CRONUS: Greek.
THE CYCLOPS: Greek.
DAGDA: Gaelic.
DAIKOKU: Japanese.
DANH-GBI: Ewe.
DIONYSUS: Greek.
EA: Babylonian.
EL-LAL: Patagonian.
ENKI: Sumerian.
GANESA: Hindu.
GOIBNIU: Irish.
GOVANNON: Celtic.
HEPHAESTUS: Greek.
HERMES: Greek.
HERMES TRISMEGISTUS: Egyptian.
IKTO: Sioux.
IMHOTEP: Egyptian.
ISRAFEL: Mohammedan.
ITALAPAS: Chinook.
KABTA: Sumerian.
KOSHAR: Canaanite.
LUCHTA: Irish.
MANABOZHO: Algonquin.
MERCURY: Roman.
MUSHADAMMA: Sumerian.
ODIN: Norse.
OGMA: Gaelic.
PAN: Greek.
PILUMNUS: Etruscan.
SATURN: Roman.
SIVA: Hindu.
SUA: Muysca.
TANE-MAHUTA (TANE'): Polynesian.
TENJIN: Japanese.
THOTH: Egyptian.
TIR: Zoroastrian.
TVASHTAR: Vedic.
VIRACOCHA: Inca.
VULCAN: Roman.
WEN-CHANG: Chinese.
ZEUS BASILEUS: Greek.
ZEUS HIKESIOS: Greek.
ZEUS PANHELLENIOS: Greek.
ZEUS PHATRIOS: Greek.
ZEUS XENIOS: Greek.
ZUME: Paraguay Indian.

Godesses of Arts, Sciences, Culture, and Civilization

AMA-TERASU: Japanese.
ATHENA: Greek.
BELISAMA: Gallic.
BENTEN: Japanese.
BRIGHIT: Gaelic.
CALLIOPE (A MUSE): Greek.
CERES: Roman.
CLIO (A MUSE): Greek.
CYBELE: Phrygian.
DEMETER: Greek.
ERATO (A MUSE): Greek.
EUNOMIA: Greek.
EUTERPE (A MUSE): Greek.
MELPOMENE (A MUSE): Greek.
MINERVA: Roman.
THE MUSES: Greek.
PERCHTA: Germanic.
POLYHYMNIA (A MUSE): Greek.
SA: Egyptian.
SALUS: Etruscan.
SARASVATI: Hindu.
SEFKH: Egyptian.
STRENIA: Sabine.
TERPSICHORE (A MUSE): Greek.
THALIA (A MUSE): Greek.
URANIA (A MUSE): Greek.
VACH: Vedic.
XOCHIQUETZAL: Aztec.

Gods of Athletes

POLYDEUCES: Greek.
CASTOR: Greek.
ZEUS: Greek.

Gods of Beauty

ANGUS (AENGUS; OENGUS): Gaelic.
APOLLO: Greek.
BALDUR: Norse.

Goddesses of Beauty

AGLAIA (A CHARITE): Greek.
APHRODITE: Greek.
ASHTARTH: Canaanite.
ASTARTE: Phoenician.
ATARGATIS: Semitic.
CHARIS: Greek.
THE CHARITES: Greek.
DEA SYRIA: Roman.
DERCETO: Greek.
EUPHROSYNE (A CHARITE): Greek.
FREYA: Norse.
THE GRACES: Roman.
ISHTAR: Babylonian.
LAKSHMI: Hindu.
TURAN: Etruscan.
THALIA (A CHARITE): Greek.
VENUS: Roman.

Gods of Bees

PAN: Greek.
PRIAPUS: Greek.

Gods of Boundaries

JUPITER TERMINUS: Roman.
SILVANUS: Roman.
SUNDI-PENNU: Khond.
TERMINUS: Roman.

Gods of Childbirth

JIZO: Japanese.

Goddesses of Childbirth and Motherhood

APET: Egyptian.
CARMENTA (CARMENTIS): Roman.
DIANA: Roman.
EGERIA: Roman.
JUNO LUCINA: Roman.
KOUROTROPHOS: Greek.
LUCINA: Roman.
NIN-KHURSAG: Sumerian.
PARTULA: Roman.
RUMINA: Roman.
SAMAIYA: Dom.
SARPANIT: Babylonian.
SENEB: Egyptian.
SHASTI: Hindu.
THALNA: Etruscan.
UPIS: Greek.

Goddesses of Compassion

KWAN MON: Japanese.
KWAN YIN: Buddhist.

Gods of Creation

AHSONNUTLI: Navaho.
ANSHAR: Babylonian.
APSU: Babylonian.
ATIUS TIRAWA: Pawnee.
AWONAWILONA: Zuñi.
AWONDO: Munshi.
BA'AL SHAMIN: Syrian.
BATARA-GURU: Batak.
BE'AL: Druid.
BRAHMA: Hindu.
BURI: Norse.
CRONOS: Greek.
DEMIURGUS: Greek.
THE DINGRI: Sumerian.
DYAUS-PITRI: Vedic.
EL: Babylonian.
EL: Canaanite.
EL-LAL: Patagonian.
ESAUGETUH EMISSEE: Creek.
HOBAL: Arabic.
IKANAM: Chinook.
KATONDA: Baganda.
KHNEMU: Egyptian.
KYUMBI: Wapare.
KULOSKAP: Algonquin.
KUMARBI: Hurrian.
KUMARPISH: Hittite.
KUMARVE: Khurrish.
LEZA: Bantu.
LUBU-LANGI: Malayan.
MANITO: Algonquin.
MEKE MEKE: Polynesian.
MONAN: Tupi-Guarani.
MULUNGU: Yaos.
NOURALI: Australian.
NSAMBE: Fan.
PACHACAMAC: Inca.
PAMULAK MANOBO: Bagobos.
PASE-KAMUI: Ainu.
POON-KOO-WONG: Chinese.
PRAJAPATI: Vedic.
PTAH: Egyptian.
QAT: Fijian.
RANGI-POTIKI: Polynesian.
RUHANGA: Banyoro.
SATURN: Roman.
SHINGRAWA: Kachin.
TANE-MAHUTA (TANE'): Polynesian.
TANGAROA: Maori.
TEZCATLIPOCA: Aztec.
TIGYAMA: Bagoto.
UWOLOWU: Slave Coast.
VATEA: Polynesian.
VE: Norse.
VILI: Norse.
VIRACOCHA: Inca.
WAKONDA: Sioux.
WUNI: Nankanni.
ZANAHARY: Malagasy.

Goddesses of Creation

ALLAT: Arabian.
ARURU: Babylonian.
ATAENSIC: Huron.
CERIDWEN: Druid.
EKA ABASSI: Ibibo.
KISHAR: Babylonian.
MEHURT: Egyptian.
MESUKKUMMIK O-KWI: Ottawa.
NUSTOO: Dravidian.
NIN-LIL: Babylonian.
PAPA-TU-A-NUKU: Polynesian.

Gods and Goddesses of Culture and Civilization
See Gods and Goddesses of Arts, Sciences, Culture, and Civilization

Gods of Cunning

HERMES: Greek.
MERCURY: Roman.

Cup-bearer of the Gods

GANYMEDE: Greek.
HEBE: Greek. Hebe, goddess of youth, was cup-bearer of the gods before Ganymede.

Gods of Dawn

THE ASVINS: Vedic.
ATARAPA: Polynesian.
LUG: Celtic.
SHAHAR: Canaanite.

Goddesses of Dawn

AURORA: Roman.
CHASCA: Inca.
EASTRE: Teutonic.
EOS: Greek.
MATUTA: Roman.
SARANYU: Hindu.
THESAN: Etruscan.
USHAS: Hindu.

Gods of Day

ATA-HIKURTANGI: Polynesian.
SHERI: Sumerian.

Goddesses of Day

HEMERA: Greek.

Gods of Commerce

HERMES: Greek.
MERCURY: Roman.
TACATECUTLI: Aztec.
THURMS: Etruscan.

Gods of Death and the Underworld
See also Heavens and Hells below

AHKTUNOWIHIO: Cheyenne.
AMEI AWA: Kayan.
ANUBIS: Egyptian.
APOLLO: Greek.
ARAWN: Cymric.
AZRAEL: Hebrew, Mohammedan.
BHOLANATH: Dom.
CAMAZOTZ: Central American Indian.
CHARON: Greek.
CHARUN: Etruscan.
CROMM CRUACH: Irish.
DEMAGORGON: Greek.
DENGDIT: Dinka.
DIONYSUS: Greek.
DIS: Roman.
DONN: Irish.
EMMA-O: Buddhist (Japanese).
ENMESHARA: Babylonian.
THE FOMOIRE: Irish.
GWYNN: Cymric.

HADES: Greek.
HAK: Egyptian.
HAVGAN: Cymric.
HERMES PSYCHOPOMPOS: Geek.
HERSHEF: Egyptian.
HORON: Canaanite.
INDAGARRA: Wa-twa.
JUPITER STYGIUS (PLUTO): Roman.
KALMA: Finnish.
KAMI: Japanese.
THE KATCINAS: Hopi.
KHENTAMENTIU: Egyptian.
KULMU: Etruscan.
MAHNESH: Etruscan.
MANA: Finnish.
MANAWYDDAN: Cymric.
MANTUS: Etruscan.
MAUI-TIKITIKI-A-TARANGA: Polynesian.
MERCURY: Roman.
MICTLANTECUTLI: Aztec.
MIDIR (MIDER): Gaelic.
MIRU: Polynesian.
MORS: Roman.
MOT: Canaanite.
NERGAL: Assyrian.
NURUNDERI: Australian.
ORPHEUS: Greek.
ORCUS: Roman.
SERAPIS: Egyptian.
ONI: Japanese.
OSIRIS: Egyptian.
PLUTO: Greek.
PSYCHOPOMPOS (HERMES): Greek.
PUSHAN: Vedic.
PWYLL: Cymric.
RAKSHAS: Hindu.
RASHNU: Zoroastrian.
SARAMA: Hindu.
SOKER: Egyptian.
SUPAY: Inca.
TEUTATES: Gallic.
THANATOS: Greek.
THOTH: Egyptian.
TIR: Zoroastrian.
TI-TSANG: Chinese.
TORNGARSUK: Eskimo.
TUAMATEF: Egyptian.
TUNG AK: Eskimo.
VANTH: Etruscan.
YAMA: Hindu.
YEN-LO-WANG: Chinese.
YIMA: Persian.
YUM CIMIL: Mayan.
ZEUS MEILICHIOS: Greek.

Goddesses of Death and the Underworld
See also *Heavens and Hells* below

ALLATU: Babylonian.
APHRODITE: Greek.
ATAENSIC: Huron.
BELIT-SERI: Sumerian.
BURING UNE: Borneo.
CHUMA: Slav.
CULSU: Etruscan.
DAMKINA: Babylonian.
HECATE: Greek.
HEL: Norse.
HINE-A-TE-PO: Polynesian.
HINE-NUI-TE-PO: Polynesian.
HINE-RUAKI-MOE: Polynesian.
HOLDA: Norse.
INNINI: Sumerian.
KALI: Hindu.
KHON-MA: Tibetan.
LIBITINA: Roman.
MANIA: Etruscan.

MARI: North India.
MERAU: Polynesian.
MERSEGRET: Egyptian.
NEBTA: Egyptian.
NENIA: Roman.
NEPHTYS: Egyptian.
NINAZU: Assyrian.
PERSEPHONE: Greek.
PROSERPINA: Roman.
RAN: Norse.
SEKHET: Egyptian.
TAOURT: Egyptian.
TEOYAOMIQUI: Aztec.
TETHRA: Irish.
VIELONA: Lett.
YAMI: Hindu.

Gods of Disinterestedness

EBISU: Japanese.

Gods of Dreams and Sleep

HERMES: Greek.
HYPNOS: Greek.
MAKHIR: Babylonian.
MERCURY: Roman.
MORPHEUS: Roman.
ONIROS: Greek.
SOMNUS: Roman.
UNI: Finnish.
UNKTAHE: Dakota.
UTAMO: Finnish.

Gods of Earth

THE CABIRI: Pelasgian.
CONSUS: Roman.
DAGAN: Semitic.
DAGDA: Gaelic.
DHARNI MATA: Dravidian.
ENUA: Polynesian.
GEB: Egyptian.
HOW-TOO: Chinese.
JUMO: Finnish.
KOBOLD: Teutonic.
KUMARBI: Hurrian.
KUMARPISH: Hittite.
KUMARVE: Khurrish.
NERTHUS: Teutonic.
OBASSI NSI: Ekoi.
OHONAMOCHI: Japanese.
SATURN: Roman.
TEGID VOHEL: Druid.
WHEN-UA: Maori.

Goddesses of Earth

AJYSYT: Yakut.
ANATA: Babylonian.
ANYIGBA: Togoland.
ARMAITA: Zoroastrian.
ASASE AY: Ashanti.
AWITELIN TSITA: Zuni.
COATLICUE: Aztec.
CYBELE: Phrygian.
DAMIA: Greek.
DAMKINA: Babylonian.
DANU: Gaelic.
DEMETER: Greek.
DESPOINA: Greek.
DIANA: Roman.
DIONE: Greek.
DON: Cymric.
FAUNA: Latin.
GAEA: Greek.

GUAMAONOCON: Antillean.
HECATE: Greek.
HERTHA: Norse.
ISHTAR: Babylonian.
KORE (PERSEPHONE): Greek.
MAAN-EMO: Finnish.
MAMA ALLPA: Peruvian.
MESUKKUMMIK O-KWI: Ottawa.
MUKYLCIN: Wotyak.
PAPA: Maori.
PERCHTA: Germanic.
PERSEPHONE (KORE): Greek.
PRITHIVI: Vedic.
RHEA: Greek.
SEDNA: Egyptian.
SEMELE: Greek.
TARI PENNU: Khond.
TELLUS MATER: Roman.
TERRA: Roman.
UMA: Hindu.
USI-AFU: Timor.
ZEMYNA: Lett.

Gods of Evil

AHI: Vedic.
AHRIMAN: Zoroastrian.
AL: Persian.
ALP: Teutonic.
THE ANU: Polynesian.
THE ANUNNAKI: Babylonian.
APOCATEQUIL: Peruvian.
ASMODEUS: Jewish.
ASURA: Vedic.
AWONDO: Munshi.
BA'AL SHAMIN: Syrian.
BOHSUN: Ashanti.
BUSO: Bagobos.
THE DAEVA: Zoroastrian.
THE DAITYAS: Hindu.
THE DASYUS: Vedic.
DIBBARRA: Babylonian.
EMPUSA: Thracian.
ENIGOHATGEA: Iroquois.
THE FENG-SHUI: Chinese.
THE FOMOIRE: Irish.
GUECUBU: Araucanian.
HIISI: Finnish.
IBLIS: Mohammedan.
IRA: Babylonian.
JINNI: Mohammedan.
JUTAS: Finnish.
KAKODAEMON: Greek.
KEREMET: Wotyak.
KUKULCAN: Mayan.
LEMPO: Finnish.
LOKI: Norse.
LUCIFER: Christian.
MAHAKALI: Banjara.
THE MASKIM: Chaldean.
MUURUP: Wiradjuri.
MUZUNGA MAYA: Mozambique.
NAMTARU: Babylonian.
NERGAL: Assyrian.
NIX: Teutonic.
NYANG: Madagascar.
PHOOKA: Irish.
PILWIZ: Teutonic.
PIRU: Finnish.
THE RAKSHAS: Hindu.
RESHEPH: Canaanite.
SATAN: Judeo-Christian.
SET: Egyptian.
SETEBOS: Patagonian.
SHANKPANNA: Yorubas.
SIBI: Babylonian.
TAWISKARON: Iroquois.
THE TITANS: Greek.
TU-MATAUENGA (TU'): Polynesian.

ZELUS: Greek.
ZOTZ: Mayan.

Goddesses of Evil

AËLLO (A HARPY): Greek.
ATE: Greek.
CELAENO (A HARPY): Greek.
DISCORDIA: Roman.
ERIS: Greek.
FEBRIS: Roman.
THE HARPIES: Greek.
KALI: Hindu.
KELPIE: Caledonian.
LILITH: Assyrian.
MANIA: Etruscan.
MATA: Gond.
MEFITIS: Roman.
OCYPETE (A HARPY): Greek.
PARBUTTA: Hindu.
RAN: Norse.
SITALA: Kachhi.
TAOURT: Egyptian.
TARI PENNU: Khond.
TORU-GUENKET: Tupi.

Gods of Fate and Fortune

ALASTOR: Greek.
ANU: Babylonian.
BA'AL SHAMIN: Syrian.
GAD: Semitic.
HADU: Teutonic.
SILA: Alaska-Greenland Eskimo.
TA CHUE: Korean.

Goddesses of Fate and Fortune

ADRASTEA: Greek.
AGLAIA: Greek.
ALECTO: Greek.
ANANKE: Greek.
ANNA KUARI: Oraon.
ARA: Greek.
ATAENSIC: Huron.
ATROPOS: Greek.
THE CHARITES: Greek.
CLOTHO: Greek.
DECUMA: Roman.
THE DIRAE: Roman.
THE ERINYES: Greek.
EUPHROSYNE: Greek.
THE FATES: Roman.
FATUM: Roman.
FORTUNA: Roman.
THE FURIES: Latin.
THE GRACES: Roman.
LACHESIS: Greek.
LAKSHMI: Hindu.
LASA: Etruscan.
MEAN: Etruscan.
MEGAERA: Greek.
MENRVA: Etruscan.
MOERA: Greek.
MORTA: Roman.
NECESSITAS: Roman.
NEMESIS: Greek.
NONA: Roman.
THE NORNS: Norse.
NORTIA: Etruscan.
THE PARCAE: Greek.
SEDNA: Eskimo.
SKULD: Norse.
TARI PENNU: Khond.
THALIA: Greek.
TISIPHONE: Greek.
TYCHE: Greek.

URDUR: Norse.
VENUS FELIX: Roman.
VERTHANDI: Norse.

Gods of Fertility

AGDESTIS: Phrygian.
BA'AL: Semitic.
CHITOMÉ: Congo.
DANH-GBI: Ewe.
DIONYSUS: Greek.
FREY: Norse.
HAPI: Egyptian.
HENO: Iroquois.
IOSKEHA: Huron.
ITZAMNA: Mayan.
KEREMET: Wotyak.
KHEM: Egyptian.
KHEPERA: Egyptian.
MAUI-TIKITIKI-A-TARANGA: Polynesian.
MAZZEBAH: Canaanite.
MIN: Egyptian.
MITHRA (MITHRAS): Persian.
MUTINUS: Roman.
NEFER-TUM: Egyptian.
NERTHUS: Teutonic.
PARJANYA: Vedic.
PRIAPUS: Greek.
PUSHAN: Vedic.
RATUMAINBULU: Fijian.
SABAZIOS: Phrygian-Thracian.
SANDAN: Cappadocian.
TAARA: Esthonian.
TANE-MAHUTA (TANE'): Polynesian.
THE TUATHA DE DANANN: Gaelic.
VIRACOCHA: Inca.

Goddesses of Fertility

ABUNDANTIA: Roman.
ANAHITA: Zoroastrian.
ANAITIS: Armenian.
ANGET: Egyptian.
ARTEMIS: Greek.
ASHTARTH: Canaanite.
ASHTORETH: Phoenician.
ATARGATIS: Syrian.
ATHEH: Tarsus.
AUDHUMLA: Norse.
AWITELIN TSITA: Zuni.
BASTET: Egyptian.
BAU: Babylonian.
BELTIS: Babylonian.
BONA DEA: Roman.
BRIGHIT: Gaelic.
CYBELE: Phrygian.
DANU: Gaelic.
DEA DIA: Roman.
DEA SURIA: Roman.
DEMETER: Greek.
DIANA: Roman.
GOURI: Hindu.
HERA: Greek.
HOLDA: Norse.
INNINA: Sumerian.
ISHTAR: Babylonian.
ISIS: Egyptian.
JUNO: Roman.
MA: Comanan.
MAGNA MATER: Anatonian.
MEHURT: Egyptian.
MEZTLI: Aztec.
MUKYLCIN: Wotyak.
MYLITTA: Babylonian.
NEHALENNIA: Germanic.
NENATTASH: Hittite.
NINTUD: Sumerian.
OPS: Roman.
PERCHTA: Germanic.

SARPANIT: Babylonian.
SHAUSHKA: Hurrian.
VENUS: Roman.
ZIZA: Teutonic.

Gods of Fire

AGNI: Vedic.
AGNISH: Hittite.
ATAR: Zoroastrian.
DSO: Slave Coast.
FUDO: Japanese.
GIBIL: Chaldean.
GIRRU: Babylonian.
HEPHAESTUS: Greek.
HINE-I-TEPAKA: Polynesian.
MILCOM: Ammonite.
MOLOCH: Phoenician.
NDAUTHINA: Fijian.
NUSKU: Sumerian.
SHU-LU-WIT-SI: Zuni.
TATEVALI: Huichol.
VULCAN: Roman.
THE YEI: Navaho.

Goddesses of Fire

BRIGHIT: Gaelic.
FORNAX: Roman.
HINE-KAIKOMAKA: Polynesian.
MAHU-IKA: Maori.
PELE: Hawaiian.

Gods of Fishes

APU-KO-HAI: Polynesian.
EBISU: Japanese.
IKA-TERE: Polynesian.
NÚADU AIRGETLÁM: Irish.
OPOCHTLI: Mexican.
PUNGA: Polynesian.
RONGO-MAI: Polynesian.
UKUPANIPO: Hawaiian.
YEMAN'GNYEM: Siberian.

Goddesses of Fishes

YAUMAU-HADAKU: Samoyed.

Gods of Flocks, Shepherds, and Stables

APOLLO CRIOPHORUS: Greek.
DUMUZI: Sumerian.
GOHELI PENU: Madras.
INNUS: Roman.
FAUNUS: Roman.
MARS: Roman.
MOCCUS: Gallic.
MULLO: Gaelic.
MUTINUS: Roman.
NEPTUNE: Roman.
PAN: Greek.
POSEIDON: Greek.
PUSHAN: Vedic.
PRIAPUS: Greek.
SILVANUS: Roman.
SUMUGAN: Sumerian.
TAMMUZ: Babylonian.
TAPIO: Finnish.

Goddesses of Flocks, Shepherds, and Stables

ASHTARTH: Canaanite.

EPONA: Gallic.
HIPPONA: Roman.
PALES: Roman.

THE TUATHA DE DANANN: Gaelic.
ZEUS: Greek.
ZEUS PISTIOS: Greek.

Goddesses of Flowers

CHLORIS: Greek.
FERONIA: Etruscan.
FLORA: Roman.
KWAN YIN: Chinese.

Gods and Goddesses of Fortune
See *Gods and Goddesses of Fate and Fortune*

Goddesses of Good, Right, Justice, and Truth

ASTRAEA: Greek.
DESPOINA: Modern Greek.
DIKE: Greek.
FIDES: Roman.
THE LITAE: Greek.
MA'ET: Egyptian.
TARA: Mahayana Buddhism.
THEMIS: Greek.

Gods of Gardens

VERTUMNUS: Roman.

Gods of Happiness

BISHAMON: Japanese.
DAIKOKU: Japanese.
EBISU: Japanese.
FUKUROKUJU: Japanese.
HOTEI: Japanese.
JUROJIN: Japanese.
OMACATL: Mexican.
SHOU-HSING: Chinese.

Goddesses of Gardens

HORTA: Etruscan.
VENUS: Roman.
VOLTUMNA: Etruscan.

Goddesses of Happiness

BENTEN: Japanese.
BRITOMARTIS: Cretan.
EUPHROSYNE: Greek.
HATHOR: Egyptian.
SAMKHAT: Babylonian.
UZUME: Japanese.

Gods of Gates, Thresholds, and Doors

CULSANS: Etruscan.
NI-O: Japanese.
JANUS: Roman.
THE PENATES: Roman.
SHEN-SU: Chinese.
VATTUMA: Hindu.
VASTOSHPATI: Hindu.

Gods and Goddesses of the Harvest
See *Gods and Goddesses of Vegetation and Harvest*

Gods and Goddesses of Healing
See *Gods and Goddesses of Medicine and Healing*

Gods of Good, Right, Justice, and Truth

AMSHASPAND: Zoroastrian.
ATAGO: Japanese.
AWONDO: Munshi.
BABBAR: Sumerian.
BALDUR: Norse.
BISHAMON: Japanese.
DAGDA: Irish.
DARMADEVA: India.
DOC-CU'O'C: Annamese.
ENIGORIO: Iroquois.
THE FENG-SHUI: Chinese.
FIDIUS DIUS: Latin.
FORSETI: Norse.
INAR: Hittite.
JUPITER FIDIUS: Roman.
THE KATCINAS: Hopi.
LUBU-LANGI: Malayan.
MARDUK: Babylonian.
MERODACH: Babylonian.
MISHOR: Canaanite.
MITHRA (MITHRAS): Persian.
NUSKU: Babylonian.
OGMA: Gaelic.
OKI: Huron.
ORMAZD: Zoroastrian.
PAMALAK MANOBO: Bagobos.
RASHNU: Zoroastrian.
SEDEQ: Canaanite.
SHEMESH: Canaanite.
SILA: Alaska-Greenland Eskimo.
TEHARONHIAWAGON: Iroquois.
TIWAZ: Teutonic.
TORU-SHOM-PEK: Tupi.

Gods of the Hearth

KULSHESH: Etruscan.
TSAO SHEN: Chinese.

Goddesses of the Hearth

ASPELENIE: Slav.
BRIGHIT: Gaelic.
FORNAX: Roman.
HESTIA: Greek.
VESTA: Roman.

Goddesses of Hope

SPES: Roman.

Gods of the Hunt

ABOG: Bagobos.
NIN: Assyrian.
OPOCHTLI: Mexican.
TSUL KALU: Cherokee.
ULLR: Norse.

Goddesses of the Hunt

ANATH: Canaanite.
ARTEMIS: Greek.
BELTIS: Babylonian.
BRITOMARTIS: Cretan.
DIANA: Roman.
VACUNA: Sabine.

Gods of Irrigation

ASHTAR: Canaanite.
ENKIMDU: Sumerian.
TAMMUZ: Babylonian.

Gods and Goddesses of Justice
See *Gods and Goddesses of Good, Right, Justice, and Truth*

Goddesses of Liberty

FERONIA: Roman.
LIBERTAS: Roman.

Gods of Light

AETHER: Greek.
AO-NUI: Polynesian.
AO-ROA: Polynesian.
APOLLO: Greek.
BALDUR: Norse.
GANDHARVA: Hindu.
HYPERION: Greek.
IOSKEHA: Huron.
MANABOZHO: Algonquin.
MICHABO: Algonquin.
MITHRA: Persian.
NUSKU: Babylonian.
OANNES: Chaldean.
PHOEBUS APOLLO: Greek.
SHOW: Egyptian.
TANGAROA: Maori.
TANE-MAHUTA (TANE'): Polynesian.
THE TUATHA DE DANANN: Gaelic.

Goddesses of Light

CUPRA: Etruscan.
NANNA: Norse.
ROHE: Polynesian.
TAFNE: Egyptian.
THALNA: Etruscan.

Gods of Longevity

JUROJIN: Japanese.
SHOU-HSING: Chinese.

Gods of Love

AIZEN MYO-O: Japanese.
AMOR: Roman.
ANGUS (AENGUS; OENGUS): Gaelic.
CUPID: Roman.
EROS: Greek.
FREYR: Norse.
KAMA: Hindu.
LEMPO: Finnish.

Goddesses of Love

ALITTA: Arabian.

APHRODITE: Greek.
ASHTARTH: Canaanite.
ASHTORETH: Phoenician.
ASTARTE: Phoenician.
ATARGATIS: Semitic.
BENTEN: Japanese.
COTYTTO: Phrygian.
DEA SYRIA: Roman.
DERCETO: Greek.
FREYA: Norse.
HATHOR: Egyptian.
MYLITTA: Babylonian.
NENATTASH: Hittite.
SHAUSHKA: Hurrian.
TURAN: Etruscan.
VENUS: Roman.
XOCHIQUETZAL: Aztec.

Gods of Marriage

BHAGA: Vedic.
HYMEN: Greek.

Goddesses of Marriage

DEMETER: Greek.
FRIGGA: Norse.
HERA: Greek.
JUNO PRONUBA: Roman.

Gods of Medicine and Healing

AESCULAPIUS: Greek.
APOLLO: Greek.
BELENUS: Druid.
CHIRON THE CENTAUR: Greek.
DIANCÉCHT: Irish.
EA: Babylonian.
ESHMUN: Semitic.
THE ICHEIRI: Carib.
KHONS: Egyptian.
MARDUK: Babylonian.
MUNU: Finnish.
OANNES: Chaldean.

Goddesses of Medicine and Healing

ANGITA: Latium.
ATHENA HYGEIA: Greek.
AYA: Hurrian.
CUCHAVIVA: Muysca.
EIR: Teutonic.
GULA: Chaldean.
HYGEIA: Greek.
KULITTASH: Hittite.
MINERVA: Roman.
PANACEA: Greek.
SALUS: Etruscan.
STRENIA: Sabine.
TETEO-INNAN: Mexican.

Goddesses of Memory

MNEMOSYNE: Greek.

Messengers of the Gods

GEPHEN: Canaanite.
GNA: Norse.
HERMES: Greek.
MERCURY: Roman.
MUKISHANUSH: Hittite.
NINSHUBUR: Sumerian.
SARAMA: Hindu.

THURMS: Etruscan.
UGAR: Canaanite.

Messengers (Goddesses) of the Gods

IRIS: Greek.

Goddesses of Modesty

PUDICITIA: Roman.

Gods of the Moon

AAH: Egyptian.
AH: Egyptian.
ANINGAHK: Eskimo.
ARMA: Hittite.
ENZU: Chaldean.
GLETI: Dahoman.
KASKU: Protohattic.
KHONS: Egyptian.
KUSHAH: Hurrian.
MARAMA: Polynesian.
MAUI-TIKITIKI-A-TARANGA: Polynesian.
MISOR: Phoenician.
NANNA: Chaldean.
SIN: Babylonian.
SOMA: Vedic.
TARAI: Andaman Islands.
TSUKI-YO-MI: Japanese.
YAREAH: Canaanite.
ZADEK: Phoenician.

Goddesses of the Moon

ARDUINA: Gallic.
ARTEMIS: Greek.
ASHTORETH: Syrian.
ASTARTE: Phoenician.
BENDIS: Thracian.
BASTET: Egyptian.
DEA COELESTIS: Roman.
DIANA: Roman.
FUNAN: Timoreese.
HECATE: Greek.
HERA: Greek.
HINA-KEHA: Polynesian.
HINA-URI (HINA'): Polynesian.
IO: Polynesian.
JUNO CAELESTIS: Roman.
LALA: Etruscan.
LUNA: Roman.
MEZTLI: Aztec.
NIKKAL: Hurrian.
NIN-GAL: Sumerian.
NING-BONGA: Dravidian.
PAJAU YAN: Cham.
SELENE: Greek.
TANITH: Carthaginian.
TORU-GUENKET: Tupi.

Goddesses of Motherhood
See Goddesses of Childbirth and Motherhood

Gods of Night

ARICOUTE: Tupi.
BALOR: Celtic.
EREBUS: Greek.
THE FOMOIRE: Irish.
HODUR: Norse.
HURRI: Sumerian.
IOLOKIAMO: Orinoco Indian.

PO-NUI: Polynesian.
PO-ROA: Polynesian.
SUMMANUS: Etruscan.
TEZCATLIPOCA: Aztec.

Goddesses of Night

BUTO: Egyptian.
HINE-NUI-TE-PO: Maori.
LILITH: Assyrian.
NOX: Roman.
NYX: Greek.

Gods of Peace

BALDUR: Norse.
FORSETI: Norse.

Goddesses of Peace

ATHENA: Greek.
IRENE: Greek.
NERTHUS: Teutonic.
PAX: Roman.

Gods of Ports and Harbors

PALAEMON: Greek.
PORTUNUS: Roman.

Gods of Prophecy

APOLLO: Greek.
BAI ÜLGEN: Altaic.
BEELZEBUB: Ekonite.
FAUNUS: Latin.
PROTEUS: Greek.
SHAMASH: Babylonian.

Goddesses of Prophecy

ALBUNEA: Roman.
THE BANSHEES: Irish.
BATHKOL: Hebrew.
THE CAMENAE: Roman.
CARMENTA (CARMENTIS): Roman.
CREUSA: Roman.
MÂ (MÂ-BELLONA): Cappadocian-Roman.
MAHAKALI: Banjara.
NINA: Babylonian.

Gods of the Rainbow

ANYI-EWO: Ewe.
KAHU-KURA: Polynesian.
LA'A-MAOMAO: Samoan.
UENUKU: Polynesian.

Goddesses of the Rainbow

CUCHAVIVA: Muysca Indian (South America).
IRIS: Greek.
IXCHEL: Mayan.

Goddesses of Rumor

FAMA: Roman.

Goddesses of Salt

HUIXTOCIHUATL: Aztec.

Gods of Satire

MOMUS: Greek.

Gods and Goddesses of Sciences
See *Gods and Goddesses of Arts, Sciences, Culture, and Civilization*

Gods and Goddesses of Seafarers
See *Gods and Goddesses of Wayfarers and Seafarers*

Gods of the Seasons

KOSTRUBONKO: Little Russian.
PHUPHLUNS: Etruscan.
VERTUMNUS: Roman.

Goddesses of the Seasons

THE HORAE: Greek.
VOLTUMNA: Etruscan.

Goddesses of Sex

TLAZOLTEOTL: Aztec.

Goddesses of Ships

FRIGGA: Norse.

Gods of Silence

HARPOCRATES: Egyptian.
VIDUR: Norse.

Goddesses of Silence

ANGERONA: Roman.
ARANYANI: Vedic.
MERSEKER: Egyptian.

Gods of Sky and Air

AMBA: Senegalese.
ANA: Sumerian.
ANU: Babylonian.
ANU-MATAO: Polynesian.
ANU-MATE: Polynesian.
ANU-WHAKARERE: Polynesian.
ANU-WHAKATORO: Polynesian.
ART-TOYON-AGA: Yakut.
ASISTA: Nandi.
AWONDO: Munshi.
BAAL: Canaanite.
CAMULUS: Gallic.
COEL: Cymric.
COELUS: Roman.
COTOKINUNWU: Hopi.
HEAMMAWIHIO: Cheyenne.
HEIMDAL: Norse.
HOMI: Hottentot.
INANNA: Sumerian.
JANUS: Roman.
LLUD: Cymric.
MAWU: West African.
NGOC HOANG: Chinese.
NUDD: Gaelic.
NUM: Samoyed.
OLORUN: African.
OSA: African.

ONYAME: Ashanti.
OSOWO: African.
PO-THEN: Thai.
QUETZALCOATL: Aztec.
RANGI: Maori.
RUWA: Wachagga.
SILAP INUA (SILA): Eskimo.
TARKU: Hittite.
TAWHAKI: Maori.
TENGRI: Mongolian.
TSUI-GOAM: Hottentot.
UKKO: Finnish.
URANUS: Greek.
VARANU: Hindu.
VIDUR: Norse.
WE: African.
YULGEN: Turkish.

Goddesses of Sky and Air

ALITTA: Arabian.
APHRODITE URANIA: Greek.
ASTARTE: Phoenician.
AZER-AVA: Moksha.
DEA COELESTIS: Roman.
DEBAN: Agaos.
FRIGGA: Norse.
HATHOR: Egyptian.
MYLITTA: Assyrian.
NEITH: Egyptian.
NUT: Egyptian.
TANITH: Carthaginian.

Gods of Stars

ATOUAHI: Polynesian.
FAOUROUA: Polynesian.
THE IGIGI: Babylonian.

Goddesses of Stars

ASTARTE: Phoenician.
HERA: Greek.
HESPERUS: Roman.
NANA: Sumerian.
VENUS: Roman.

Gods and Goddesses of Shepherds
See *Gods and Goddesses of Flocks, Shepherds, and Stables*

Gods and Goddesses of Stables
See *Gods and Goddesses of Flocks, Shepherds, and Stables*

Storm, Thunder, Earthquake, and Volcano Gods

ADAD: Babylonian.
AEOLUS: Greek.
AMMA: Senegalese.
AO-KAHIWAHIWA: Polynesian.
AO-KANAPANAPA: Polynesian.
AO-NUI: Polynesian.
AO-PAKAKINA: Polynesian.
AO-PAKAREA: Polynesian.
AO-POTANGO: Polynesian.
AO-POURI: Polynesian.
AO-ROA: Polynesian.
AO-TAKAWE: Polynesian.
AO-WHEKERE: Polynesian.
AO-WHETUNA: Polynesian.
APU-HAU: Polynesian.
APU-MATANGI: Polynesian.

ASGAYA GIGAGEI: Cherokee.
ATHARVAN: Iranian.
AWHIOWHIO: Polynesian.
BAAL: Canaanite.
THE BACABS: Mayan.
BAGBA: Togo.
BILIKU: Andaman Islands.
BOBOWISSI: Gold Coast.
CUN: Andean Indian.
DATTA: Luwain.
DONAR: Teuton.
EN-LIL: Sumerian.
ESSEGHE-MALAN: Buriat.
FAATI'U: Samoan.
THE FOMOIRE: Irish.
HAOKAH: Sioux.
HANUI-O-RANGI: Polynesian.
HEBESIO: Awuna.
HENO: Iroquois.
HERCLE: Etruscan.
HURAKAN: Mayan.
ILLAPA: Peruvian.
INDRA: Vedic.
ISHKUR: Sumerian.
ITZAMMA: Mayan.
JUPITER DOLICHENUS: Hittite.
JUPITER FULGUR: Roman.
JUPITER FULMINATOR: Roman.
JUPITER PLUVIUS: Roman.
JUPITER SERENATOR: Roman.
JUPITER TONANS: Roman.
KARI: Negrito.
THE KATCINAS: Hopi.
KHEBIOSO: Ewe.
KILAT: Bagobos.
KUKULU: Lower Guinea, West Africa.
LA'A-MAOMAO: Polynesian.
MABOYA: Carib.
MAFUIE: Samoan.
THE MATA KODOU: Upper Nile.
MAUI: Polynesian.
MIXCOATL: Mexican.
MÓOOI: Tonga Islanders.
MULUNGU: Bantu.
MURA-MURAS: Dieri..
NAMVULU VUMU: Congo.
NDENGEI: Fijian.
NIRIG: Babylonian.
OBUMO: Gold Coast.
PARJANYA: Vedic.
PERKUNAS: Lithuanian.
PERUN: Slav.
PIDZU PENNU: Kanah.
PILLAN: Chilean.
QOZAH: Arabian.
RAKA: Polynesian.
RESHEPH: Egyptian.
RUA-AI-MOKO: Polynesian.
RUAN-MOKO (RU'): Polynesian.
SENDU BIR: North India.
SOGBLE: Hos.
SUMMANUS: Etruscan.
SUSA-NO-WO: Japanese.
TAARA: Esthonian.
TARANIS: Gallic.
TARKU: Hittite.
TARU: Protohattic.
TAWHIRI-MATEA: Polynesian.
TESHUB: Hurrian.
THEISPAS: Urartian.
THOR: Norse.
TISHTRYA: Iranian.
TLALOC: Aztec.
TOHIL: Quiche.
TUPAN: Botocudo.
UA: Polynesian.
USONDO: Zulu.
VEJOVIS: Etruscan.
VUL: Babylonian.
WAUKHEON: Dakota.

WHATI-TIRI: Polynesian.
YU SHUH: Chinese.
ZAYAN: Buriat.
ZU-BIRD: Babylonian.

Storm, Thunder, Earthquake, and Volcano Goddesses

AZER-AVA: Moksha.
CHALCHIHUITLICUE: Aztec.
THE HYADES: Greek.
PELE: Hawaiian.
SODZA: Hos.

Gods of the Sun

AMON-RE: Egyptian.
ANHER: Egyptian.
APLU: Etruscan.
APOLLO: Greek.
ARTINIS: Urartian.
ASISTA: Nandi.
ATON: Egyptian.
ATHTAR: Minaean.
ATUN: Egyptian.
BA'AL-MELKARTH: Phoenician.
BARBAR: Sumerian.
BE'AL: Druid.
BELENUS: Druid.
BELLA PENNU: Khond.
BHAGAWAN: Oranon.
BOCHICA: Chibcha.
BORAM: Bhuiyas.
DAINIZ-NO-RAI: Japanese.
DHARME: Oraon.
DONGOR GOMOIJ: Kurku.
ESHMUN: Semitic.
GARUDA: Hindu.
GUGUS: Gallic.
HAMARCHIS: Egyptian.
HELIOGABALUS: Semitic.
HELIOS: Greek.
HORUS: Egyptian.
ISHUM: Babylonian.
ISTANU: Hittite.
KLESEAKARKL: Nutka.
LISSA: Dahoman.
LUGH: Celtic.
MARDUK: Babylonian.
MAUI-TIKITIKI-A-TARANGA: Polynesian.
MENTU: Egyptian.
MISOR: Phoenician.
MITHRA: Persian.
NERGAL: Assyrian.
NINGIRSU: Babylonian.
NINIB: Babylonian.
NUDD: Gaelic.
NYAN: West African.
PHOEBUS APOLLO: Greek.
QUETZALCOATL: Aztec.
RE: Egyptian.
SANTA: Luwian.
SAVITAR: Vedic.
SHALEM: Canaanite.
SHAMASH: Babylonian.
SHEMESH: Canaanite.
SHIMEGI: Hurrian.
SING-BONGA: Bihor.
SOL: Roman.
SUA: Muysca.
SULIS: Celtic.
SURYA: Hindu.
TAMA-NUI-TE-RA (RA'): Polynesian.
TAMMUZ: Babylonian.
TIOMONDONAR: Tupi.
TONATIUH: Aztec.
TORU-SHOM-PEK: Tupi.
THE TUATHA DE DANANN: Gaelic.

UPU-LERA: New Guinea.
USIL: Etruscan.
USI-NENO: Timor.
VIVASVAT: Vedic.
ZADEK: Phoenician.

Goddesses of the Sun

AMA-TERASU: Japanese.
AYA: Hurrian.
GULA: Babylonian.
GULA: Chaldean.
HEPAT: Hittite.
SEKHET: Egyptian.
SHAPASH: Canaanite.
WURUSEMU: Protohattic.

Supreme Gods

ADONAI: Hebrew.
AHRIMAN: Zoroastrian.
AHSONNUTLI: Navaho.
ALLAH: Mohammedan.
AMON: Egyptian.
ANA: Sumerian.
ANSHAR: Babylonian.
ANU: Babylonian.
APOCATEQUIL: Peruvian.
ART-TOYON-AGA: Yakut.
ASHUR: Assyrian.
ASISTA: Nandi.
ATAHOCAN: Algonquian.
ATON: Egyptian.
ATHTAR: Minaean.
ATIUS TIRAWA: Pawnee.
AWONAWILONA: Zuni.
AWONDO: Munshi.
BA'AL SHAMIN: Syrian.
BAI ULGEN: Altaic.
BATARA-GURU: Batak.
BE'AL: Druid.
BELLA PENNU: Khond.
BORAM: Bhuiyas.
BRAHMA: Hindu.
CHITOMÉ: Congo.
CRONUS: Greek.
CUKU: Ibos.
DHARMI: Oranon.
DUSHARA: Nabataean.
EL: Canaanite.
EL-LAL: Patagonian.
ENSOPH: Cabalistic.
GAUTAMA: Buddhistic.
GOD: Christian.
IMANA: Warundi.
INDAGARRA: Wa-twa.
IO: Polynesian.
IOCAUNA: Antillean.
JEHOVAH: Judeo-Christian.
JUMALA: Finnish.
JUOK: Shilluk.
JUPITER: Roman.
JURUPARI: Uaupe.
KAMUI: Ainu.
KATONDA: Baganda.
KHALDI: Urartian.
KHUTSAU: Ossete.
KLESEAKARKL: Nutka.
KULOSKAP: Algonquian.
LEZA: Bantu.
LUBU-LANGI: Malayan.
MATOWELIA: Mohave.
MEKE MEKE: Polynesian.
MICHABO: Algonquian.
MULA DYADI: Batak.
NGAI: Masai.
NISROCH: Assyrian.
NOURALI: Australian.

OBASHI: Cameroons.
ODIN: Norse.
ORMAZD: Zoroastrian.
PACHACAMAC: Inca.
PARAMESVARA: Banjara.
PASE-KAMUI: Ainu.
PATOL: Mayan.
PTAH: Egyptian.
QUAHOOTZE: North American Indian.
RE (RA): Egyptian.
SAATO: Samoan.
SANTA: Luwian.
SATURN: Roman.
SHANG-TI: Chinese.
SIANG-TIEI: Korean.
SING-BONGA: Bihor.
SKAMBHA: Vedic.
TARONHIAWAGON: Iroquois.
TARU: Protohattic.
TAWHIRI-MA-TEA: Maori.
TELECHINES: Greek.
TEN GERIS: Buriat.
TESHUB: Hurrian.
THAGYA MIN NAT: Burmese.
THAKUR: Santal.
TINA: Etruscan.
TORNGARSOAK: Labrador Eskimo.
UPU-LERA: Papuan.
UWOLOWU: Slave Coast.
VIRACOCHA: Inca.
WAQ: Gallas.
WENI: Builsa.
WUNI: Nankanni.
YAHWEH: Hebrew.
YRYN-AJY-TOJON: Yakut.
ZAMBI: Bantu.
ZAMOLXIS: Getae.
ZANAHARY: Malagasy.
ZEUS: Greek.
ZIPARWA: Palaic.

Supreme Goddesses

AA: Babylonian.
ALAGHOM NAOM: Mayan.
ALLAT: Arabian.
ASHERATH: Canaanite.
ASTARTE: Phoenician.
ATARGASTIS: Syrian.
ATHEH: Tarsus.
CUPRA: Etruscan.
DIONE: Greek.
HEPAT: Hurrian.
HERA: Greek.
JUNO: Roman.
KISHAR: Babylonian.
MARI: North India.
NINTUD: Sumerian.
NZAMBI: Bakongo.
RHEA: Greek.
SATI: Egyptian.

Gods of Theft and Thieves

GANDAK: Dom.
HERMES: Greek.
MERCURY: Roman.

Goddesses of Theft and Thieves

LAVERNA: Roman.

Gods and Goddesses of Thresholds
See *Gods and Goddesses of Gates, Thresholds, and Doors*

Gods and Goddesses of Thunder
See Gods and Goddesses of Storms, Thunder, Earthquakes, and Volcanoes

Gods of Touch

HU: Egyptian.

Gods and Goddesses of Truth
See Gods and Goddesses of Good, Right, Justice, and Truth

Goddesses of Twilight

MENRVA: Etruscan.

Gods of Vegetation and Harvest

ADONIS: Syrian.
AIYANAR: Southern India.
AKA-KANET: Araucanian.
AMEI AWA: Kayan.
ATTIS (ATYS): Phrygian.
APOLLO: Greek.
BHAIRON: Kunbi.
BHUMIYA North India.
BORMUS: Mariandynian.
CACHIMANA: Orinoco Indian.
CONSUS: Roman.
CRONUS: Greek.
DAGAN: Canaanite.
DENDRITES: Greek.
DIONYSUS: Greek.
ENMESHARA: Babylonian.
THE FAUNI: Roman.
FAUNUS: Latin.
FE JOKOO: African.
FREY: Norse.
GHANSYAM DEO: Gond.
HAUMIA-TIKITIKI: Polynesian.
HUNTIN: West African.
HYACINTHUS: Greek.
KHALKISH: Hittite.
LINUS: Phoenician.
LITYERSES: Phrygian.
THE LJESCHIE: Russian.
MANEROS: Egyptian.
MARS: Roman.
MAUI-TIKITIKI-A-TARANGA: Polynesian.
MAZZEBAH: Canaanite.
MUTINUS: Roman.
NEPRA: Egyptian.
NINGIRSU: Babylonian.
ONATAH: Iroquois.
PICUMNUS: Etruscan.
PRIAPUS: Greek.
PUWE-WAI: Javanese.
RATUNMAINBULU: Fijian.
SATURN: Roman.
THE SATYRI: Greek.
SHEN NUNG: Chinese.
SILVANUS: Roman.
SIVA: Hindu.
SUMUGAN: Sumerian.
TAMMUZ: Babylonian.
TANEMAHUTA: Maori.
TANI: Society Islands.
TAPIO: Finnish.
TELEPINUSH: Hittite.
VIDAR: Norse.
XIPE TOTEC: Mexican.
THE YEI: Navaho.
YINUKATSISDAI: Hupa.

Goddesses of Vegetation and Harvest

ARSIYA: Canaanite.
ARTEMIS: Greek.
ASHERAH: Canaanite.
AXO-MAMA: Peruvian.
BAU: Babylonian.
BONA DEA: Roman.
CENTEOTL: Mexican.
CERES: Roman.
CHICOMECOHUATL: Aztec.
COCA-MAMA: Peruvian.
CUCHAVIVA: Muysca.
DAMIA: Greek.
DANU: Gaelic.
DEA DIA: Roman.
DEMETER: Greek.
DIANA: Roman.
DON: Cymric.
THE DRYADS: Greek.
GAURI: Hindu.
HALKI: Hittite.
THE HAMADRYADS: Greek.
INARI: Japanese.
KAIT: Protohattic.
KORE (PERSEPHONE): Greek.
MAMA ALLPA: Peruvian.
MAWA SODZA: Hos.
NIDABA: Sumerian.
OMONGA: Timoreese.
OPS: Roman.
PADMAVATI: Hindu.
PANI: Maori.
PARVATI: Hindu.
PERSEPHONE (KORE): Greek.
POMONA: Roman.
PO-NAGAR: Cham.
QUINOA-MAMA: Peruvian.
RANNU: Egyptian.
SANING SARI: Minangkabauer.
SIEN-TSAN: Chinese.
TOYO-UKE-BIME: Japanese.
UKE-MOCHI: Japanese.
VACUNA: Sabine.
XILONEN: Aztec.
ZARA-MAMA: Peruvian.

Gods of Victory

JUPITER FERETRIUS: Roman.
MITHRA (MITHRAS): Persian.
ZEUS: Greek.

Goddesses of Victory

BUDDUD: Druid.
NIKE: Greek.
VACUNA: Sabine.
VENUS VICTRIX: Roman.
VICTORIA: Roman.

Gods of War and Battle

ALBIOREX: Gallic.
APOLLO BOEDROMIOS: Greek.
ARES: Greek.
ASHTABI: Hurrian.
BOK GLAIH: Malayan.
CAMAXTLI: Mexican.
CAMULUS: Gallic.
CHEMOSH: Moabitic.
COEL: Celtic.
EPUNAMUN: Chilean.
FE'E: Samoan.
GISH: Kafir.
HESUS: Gallic.
HUITZILOPOCHTLI: Aztec.

IRA: Babylonian.
JUPITER STATOR: Roman.
KARTTIKEYA: Hindu.
KUAN YU: Chinese.
MARS: Roman.
MARU: Polynesian.
NIN: Assyrian.
NINGIRSU: Babylonian.
ONURIS: Egyptian.
PHOBOS: Greek.
QUAHOOTZE: North American Indian.
QUIRINUS: Roman.
ROMULUS: Roman.
SHUWALIYATTA: Hurrian.
SULINKATTE: Protohattic.
TIWAZ: Teutonic.
TU-MATAUENGA (TU'): Polynesian.
TYR: Norse.
WURUNKATTE: Protohattic.
YARRI: Hittite.
ZABABA: Sumerian.

Goddesses of War and Battle

ANATH: Semitic.
APHRODITE AREIA: Greek.
ASHTARTH: Canaanite.
ATHENA: Greek.
BADB (BODB): Irish.
BELLONA: Roman.
BELTIS: Babylonian.
COATLICUE: Aztec.
ENYO: Greek.
JUNO QUIRITIS: Roman.
MĀ (MĀ-BELLONA): Cappadocian-Roman.
MINERVA: Roman.
MORRIGAN (MORRIGU): Irish.
PARBUTTA: Hindu.
SHAUSHKA: Hurrian.
THE VALKYRIE: Norse.

Gods of Water

ACHELOUS: Greek.
ACHERON: Greek.
AEGIR: Norse.
AHTO: Finnish.
ALPHEUS: Greek.
AMPHITRYON: Greek.
APAM NEPAT: Persian.
APSU: Babylonian.
ARUNASH: Hittite.
ASOPUS: Greek.
ASTERION: Greek.
BAHU: Egyptian.
CANOPUS: Egyptian.
DYLAN: Cymric.
EA: Babylonian.
ENBILULU: Sumerian.
ENKI: Sumerian.
FONS: Roman.
GLAUCUS: Greek.
HAPI: Egyptian.
HU: Celtic.
HYMIR: Norse.
INACHUS: Greek.
JEBISU: Japanese.
KHNUM: Egyptian.
LER: Gaelic.
LLYR: Cymric.
MUKASA: Baganda.
MUNT: Egyptian.
NEPTUNE: Roman.
NER: Druid.
NEREUS: Greek.
NETHUNS: Etruscan.
NILUS: Egyptian.
NIX: Teutonic.

NUN: Egyptian.
OANNES: Chaldean.
OCEANUS: Greek.
OHO-WATA-TSU-MI: Japanese.
PARA-WHENUA-MEA: Polynesian.
PENEUS: Greek.
PHORCYS: Greek.
PONTUS: Greek.
POSEIDON: Greek.
PROTEUS: Greek.
SUITENGU: Japanese.
TANGAROA: Polynesian.
TRITON: Greek.
VARANU: Hindu.
YAM: Canaanite.

Goddesses of Water

AMPHITRITE: Greek.
ALBUNEA: Roman.
ANQET: Egyptian.
APHRODITE: Greek.
ARTEMIS: Greek.
ASHERATH: Canaanite.
ATAENSIC: Huron.
BOANN: Gaelic.
CALYPSO: Greek.
THE CAMENAE: Roman.
CARMENTA (CARMENTIS): Roman
CERTO: Greek.
CYMODOCE: Greek.
DERCETO: Syrian.
DIANA: Roman.
DORIS: Greek.
DOTO: Greek.
ERUA: Babylonian.
EURYNOME: Greek.
FERONIA: Roman.
GALATEA: Greek.
HALCYONE: Greek.
IDA: Roman.
JUTURNA: Roman.
KELPIE: Caledonian.
LEUCOTHEA: Greek.
MARICA: Roman.
THE NAIADS: Roman.
THE NEREIDS: Greek.
NINA: Babylonian.
NJAI: Javanese.
THE NYMPHS: Greek.
THE OCEANIDES: Greek.
THE OREADS: Greek.
RAN: Norse.
SALACIA: Greek.
SEDNA: Eskimo.
SIRARA: Sumerian.
THE SIRENS: Greek.
TAKÁNAKAPSÂLUK: Iglulik Indian.
TALLIYA: Canaanite.
TETHYS: Greek.
THETIS: Greek.
TIAMAT: Babylonian.
UNDINE: Germanic.
WELLAMO: Finnish.

Gods of Wayfarers and Seafarers

APOLLO AGYIEUS: Greek.
CASTOR: Greek.
FAUNUS: Roman.
HERMES: Greek.
HSING SHEN: Chinese.
KOMPIRA: Japanese.
MERCURY: Roman.
NJORD: Norse.
OGMA: Irish.
POLYDEUCES (POLLUX): Greek.
PUSHAN: Vedic.

SARAMA: Hindu.
TRITON: Greek.
YACATECUTLI: Aztec.
YEMAN'GNYEM: Siberian.

Goddesses of Wayfarers and Seafarers

ISIS: Egyptian.
NEHALENNIA: Germanic.

Gods of Wealth

BHAGA: Vedic.
BISHAMON: Japanese.
DAIKOKU: Japanese.
FUKUROKUJU: Japanese.
JAMBHALA: Tibetan.
KUVERA: Hindu.
LUNG: Chinese.
MAMMON: Syrian.
PITTERI PENNU: Khond.
PLUTO: Greek.
PLUTUS: Greek.
PUKE: Lett.
PUSHAN: Vedic.
SHOU-HSING: Chinese.
TSAI SHEN: Chinese.
URCAGUAY: Peruvian.

Goddesses of Wealth

BENTEN: Japanese.
SRI: Hindu.
STRENIA: Sabine.

Gods of Wine

BACCHUS: Greek.
DIONYSUS: Greek.
JUPITER: Roman.
LENAEUS: Cretan.
LIBER: Roman.

Goddesses of Winter

GERTHR: Norse.
ZIMARZLA: Russian.

Gods of Wisdom

A'A: Hurrian.
ATLAS: Greek.
BALDUR: Norse.
CONSUS: Roman.
ELATHA: Irish.
ENKI: Sumerian.
FUDO: Japanese.
GANESA: Hindu.
HERMES TRISMEGISTUS: Egyptian.
IMHOTEP: Egyptian.
MANJUÇRI: Ningma Lamaism, Tibet.
MIMIR: Norse.
NEBO: Chaldean.
OANNES: Chaldean.
ODIN: Norse.
PAMALAK MANOBO: Bagobos.
SA: Egyptian.
SILA: Alaska-Greenland Eskimo.
SIN: Babylonian.
THOTH: Egyptian.
TIKI: Maori.
VRIHASPATI: Vedic.

Goddesses of Wisdom

ALAGHOM NAOM: Mayan.
ATHENA: Greek.
BRIGHIT: Gaelic.
THE DAKINIS: Kagyud Lamaism, Tibet.
EGERIA: Roman.
FAUNA: Latin.
KAMRUSEPA: Hittite.
KATAHZIPURI: Protohattic.
METIS: Greek.
MINERVA: Roman.
SARASVATI: Hindu.

Gods of Youth

ANGUS (AENGUS; OENGUS): Gaelic.
APOLLO: Greek.

Goddesses of Youth

HEBE: Greek.
IDUNA: Norse.
JUVENTAS: Roman.

Gods Who Die
(Dying Gods)

ADONIS: Semitic.
THE AESIR (EXCEPT VIDAR): Norse.
AMMON: Egyptian.
ANHOURI: Egyptian.
APOLLO: Greek.
ATTIS (ATYS): Phrygian.
BORMUS: Mariandynian.
CHINIGCHINICH: Acagchemem.
CHITOMÉ: Congo.
DIONYSUS: Greek.
ERICHTHONIUS: Greek.
HEITSI-EIBIB: Hottentot.
HIPPOLYTUS: Greek.
HUITZILOPOCHTLI: Aztec.
KOSTROMA: Russian.
KOSTRUBONKO: Little Russian.
KUPALO: Russian.
LADA: Russian.
LINUS: Phoenician.
LITYERSES: Phrygian.
MANEROS: Egyptian.
MITHRA (MITHRAS): Persian.
ORPHEUS: Greek.
OSIRIS: Egyptian.
TAMMUZ: Assyro-Babylonian.
TELIPINU: Hittite.
TEZCATLIPOCA: Aztec.
TOUMOU: Egyptian.
VIRIBUS: Roman.
XIPE TOTEC: Mexican.
YARILO: Russian.
ZAGREUS: Cretan.
ZEUS: Greek.

Goddesses Who Die
(Dying Goddesses)

CHICOMECOHUATL: Aztec.
KWAN YIN: Chinese.

HEAVENS

AALU: Egyptian.
ASGARD: Norse.
AVALON: Celtic.
BEHESTH: Persian.

BULOTU: Samoan.
DYAUS: Vedic.
ELYSIUM: Greek.
GLADSHEIM: Norse.
HARA-BEREZAITI: Zoroastrian.
ISLAND OF THE HESPERIDES: Greek.
JÖRD LIFANDA MANNA: Norse.
ODAINS-AKR: Norse.
PO: Polynesian.
RAJ: Slav.
SID: Celtic.
TAKAMA-NO-HARA: Japanese.
TOO'GA: Bushmen.
VALHALLA: Norse.
VARA: Iranian.

HELLS

ACHERON: Roman.
AMENTI: Egyptian.
ANNWN: Cymbric.
ARALU: Babylonian.
AVERNUS: Roman.
DUAT: Egyptian.
EREBUS: Roman.
GEHENNA: Semitic.
HADES: Greek.
HEL: Teutonic.
HIKU-TOIA: Polynesian.
KIBU: Polynesian.
KINGDOM OF ERLIK: Yukaghir.
MBULU: Fijian.
NARAKA: Hindu.
NAV: Slav.
ORCUS: Roman.
PEKLO: Slav.
PO (TE PO): Polynesian.
PULOTU: Samoan.
SA-LE-FEE: Samoan.
SHEOL: Hebrew.
TECH DUINN: Irish.
UNUGI: Sumerian.
XIBALBA: Mayan.
YOMI: Japanese.
YOMOTSU-KUNI: Japanese.

Greek Gods
See **Gods and Goddesses**

Greek Rulers
See **Rulers**

Hall of Fame for Great Americans With Years When Candidates Were Admitted

Established 1900 at New York University

ADAMS, JOHN: Statesman, 1900.
ADAMS, JOHN QUINCY: Statesman, 1905.
AGASSIZ, LOUIS: Scientist, 1915.
ANTHONY, SUSAN B.: Woman suffrage leader, 1950.
AUDUBON, JOHN JAMES: Scientist, 1900.
BANCROFT, GEORGE: Historian, 1910.
BEECHER, HENRY WARD: Preacher, 1900.
BELL, ALEXANDER GRAHAM: Inventor, 1950.
BOONE, DANIEL: Explorer, 1915.
BOOTH, EDWIN: Actor, 1925.
BROOKS, PHILLIPS: Preacher, 1910.
BRYANT, WILLIAM CULLEN: Author, 1910.
CHANNING, WILLIAM ELLERY: Preacher, 1900.
CHOATE, RUFUS: Jurist, 1915.

CLAY, HENRY: Statesman, 1900.
CLEMENS, SAMUEL L.: Author, 1920.
CLEVELAND, GROVER: Statesman, 1935.
COOPER, JAMES FENIMORE: Author, 1910.
COOPER, PETER: Philanthropist, 1900.
CUSHMAN, CHARLOTTE S.: Actress, 1915.
EADS, JAMES B.: Engineer, 1920.
EDWARDS, JONATHAN: Theologian, 1900.
EMERSON, RALPH WALDO: Author, 1900.
FARRAGUT, DAVID G.: Sailor, 1900.
FOSTER, STEPHEN COLLINS: Ballad composer, 1940.
FRANKLIN, BENJAMIN: Statesman, 1900.
FULTON, ROBERT: Inventor, 1900.
GIBBS, JOSIAH WILLARD: Physicist, 1950.
GORGAS, WILLIAM CRAWFORD: Surgeon, 1950.
GRANT, ULYSSES S.: Soldier, 1900.
GRAY, ASA: Scientist, 1900.
HAMILTON, ALEXANDER: Statesman, 1915.
HAWTHORNE, NATHANIEL: Author, 1900.
HENRY, JOSEPH: Scientist, 1915.
HENRY, PATRICK: Statesman, 1920.
HOLMES, OLIVER WENDELL: Author, 1910.
HOPKINS, MARK: Educator, 1915.
HOWE, ELIAS: Inventor, 1915.
IRVING, WASHINGTON: Author, 1900.
JACKSON, ANDREW: Statesman, 1910.
JACKSON, THOMAS JONATHAN: American Confederate general, 1955.
JEFFERSON, THOMAS: Statesman, 1900.
JONES, JOHN PAUL: Sailor, 1925.
KENT, JAMES: Jurist, 1900.
LANIER, SIDNEY: Poet, 1945.
LEE, ROBERT E.: Soldier, 1900.
LINCOLN, ABRAHAM: Statesman, 1900.
LONGFELLOW, HENRY W.: Author, 1900.
LOWELL, JAMES RUSSEL: Author, 1905.
LYON, MARY: Educator, 1905.
MADISON, JAMES: Statesman, 1905.
MANN, HORACE: Educator, 1900.
MARSHALL, JOHN: Jurist, 1900.
MAURY, MATTHEW F.: Scientist, 1930.
MITCHELL, MARIA: Scientist, 1905.
MONROE, JAMES: Statesman, 1930.
MORSE, SAMUEL F. B.: Inventor, 1900.
MORTON, WILLIAM T. G.: Physician, 1920.
MOTLEY, JOHN LOTHROP: Historian, 1910.
NEWCOMB, SIMON: Scientist, 1935.
PAINE, THOMAS: Author, 1945.
PALMER, ALICE FREEMAN: Educator, 1920.
PARKMAN, FRANCIS: Historian, 1915.
PEABODY, GEORGE. Philanthropist, 1900.
PENN, WILLIAM: Colonizer, 1935.
POE, EDGAR ALLAN: Author, 1910.
REED, WALTER: Surgeon, 1945.
ROOSEVELT, THEODORE: Statesman, 1950.
SAINT-GAUDENS, AUGUSTUS: Sculptor, 1920.
SHERMAN, WILLIAM TECUMSEH: Soldier, 1905.
STORY, JOSEPH: Jurist, 1900.
STOWE, HARRIET BEECHER: Author, 1910.
STUART, GILBERT CHARLES: Painter, 1900.
WASHINGTON, BOOKER T: Educator, 1945.
WASHINGTON, GEORGE: Statesman, 1900.
WEBSTER, DANIEL: Statesman, 1900.
WESTINGHOUSE, GEORGE: Inventor, 1955.
WHISTLER, J. A. MCNEILL: Painter, 1930.
WHITMAN, WALT: Author, 1930.
WHITNEY, ELI: Inventor, 1900.
WHITTIER, JOHN GREENLEAF: Author, 1905.
WILLIAMS, ROGER: Colonizer, 1920.
WILLARD, EMMA: Educator, 1905.
WILLARD, FRANCES ELIZABETH: Reformer, 1910.
WILSON, WOODROW: Statesman, 1950.
WRIGHT, WILBUR: Inventor, 1955.

Heavens and Hells
See **Gods and Goddesses: A Checklist of Their Works and Patronage; Religious Allusions, References, and Symbols**

Herbs and Their Uses

ACONITE: Any plant of the genus *Aconitum*, but particularly *Aconitum napellus*, or Monkshood; though poisonous, all parts of the plant are used in medicine, chiefly as a heart and respiratory sedative; some applications for the pains of neuralgia and rheumatism are derived from Monkshood.

AGRIMONY: Any plant of the genus *Agrimonia*, but particularly the European Agrimony, *Agrimonia eupatoria*; the leaves of the plant are used to make a tonic tea, and also as the base of a mouth rinse; a yellow dye is extracted from the leaves.

ALKANET: The plant and root of the Real Alkanet, or *Alkanna tinctoria*, which is native to Europe and is the source of alkannin, a red powder used in dye-making; also known as Dyer's Bugloss.

ANGELICA: Any plant of the genus *Angelica*, but particularly *Angelica archangelica*, or Garden Angelica; the leafstalks are candied and used in preserves; the fruit and roots furnish flavoring for liqueurs and wines, and a base for perfumes, are eaten as vegetables, used medicinally in a tea; in Norway, a bread is made from the roots.

ANISE: *Pimpinella anisum*, a native of Egypt, but grown universally for its seeds, leaves, and flowers; the seeds, or fruit, are powdered and used as flavoring in baking, and in sauces, stews, and soups; they also provide flavor for cough medicines, and for various liqueurs (particularly Anisette) as well as a base for soaps and perfumes; the leaves are used in fresh salads, and the oil in the preparation of antiseptics.

BALM: Any plant of the genus *Melissa*, but particularly *Melissa officinalis*, known variously as Lemon Balm, Sweet Balm; the leaves are used as a flavoring for sauces, stews, soups, salads, and dressings, in a tea, in medicine as an agent to induce sweating, as a base for perfumes, ointments, and polishes, and in making liquers (especially Benedictine and Chartreuse).

BASIL: Any of several aromatic plants, but particularly species of the genus *Ocimum*, as *Ocimum basilicum*, Sweet Basil, and *Ocimum minimum*, Bush Basil, and *Ocimum crispum*, Curly Basil; the leaves are used as flavoring for soups, stews, and salads, and yield an oil which is a base for perfumes; Basil is used medicinally as a stimulant, as well as in making Basil Vinegar.

BEDSTRAW: Any herb of the genus *Galium*, but particularly *Galium verum*, Yellow Bedstraw, and *Galium mollugo*, White Bedstraw; the flower is used in coloring cheese and butter, the root as a red dye, the stalk and leaves as an agent for curdling milk.

BAY LEAF: The dried leaf of the Sweet Bay or Bay Laurel, *Laurus nobilis*, which is used in cooking as a flavoring and industrially in making perfumes; the oil is used medicinally in preparations for the external treatment of rheumatism.

BENE; BENNE: See Sesame.

BERGAMOT, RED: A North American Mint, *Monarda didyma*, which yields an oil used in making perfumes, hair preparations, and, medicinally, as a stimulant.

BLESSED THISTLE: *Cnicus benedictus*, named for its uses as a healing agent in fevers and dyspepsia; the leaves and seeds are used in making Vermouth.

BONESET: Any of several American herbs of the genus *Eupatorium*, but particularly *Eupatorium perfoliatum*, whose leaves and flowers once had wide vogue as a laxative and emetic.

BORAGE: A native European herb, *Borago officinalis*, now widely naturalized, whose leaves are used in pickles and salads, in claret cup as a beverage, as a laxative, and in preparations for rheumatism and skin-diseases; the flowers are mixed with other petals and spices and used as a household deodorant, or potpourri, and may be candied for uses in confectionery.

BUGBANE: A perennial herb, *Cimicifuga racemosa*, with an odor noxious to insects, particularly bedbugs; also used as a sedative, and in treatments for rheumatism, dropsy, asthma, and other ailments.

BUGLEWEED: Any Mint of the genus *Lycopus*, but particularly *Lycopus virginicus*, with medicinal use as a mild narcotic and as a tonic.

BUGLOSS: Any plant of the genus *Anchusa*, but particularly *Anchusa officinalis*, or Common Alkanet, *Anchusa azurea*, or Italian Bugloss, and *Echium vulgare*, or Blueweed; the plants are used medicinally to induce sweating, as laxatives, astringents, and tonics.

BURNET: Any plant of the genus *Sanguisorba*, but particularly *Sanguisorba minor*, or Salad Burnet, which is used in salads and beverages, and medicinally as a astringent, and *Poterium Sanguisorba*, the Common Burnet, which is also used in salads and beverages.

BUTTERFLY WEED: *Asclepias tuberosa*, a milkweed with orange blossoms, whose root is used medicinally to induce sweating and as an expectorant.

CALENDULA: The Common Pot Marigold, *Calendula officinalis*, whose dried orange flowers are used medicinally in preparation of applications for wounds, cuts, and bruises, as a laxative, and to induce sweating; the flowers are also used in soups and stews, and as a coloring agent.

CARAWAY: An aromatic, *Carum carvi*, whose seeds are used in cooking, in confectionery, and in making liqueurs (especially Kümmel); the leaves are sometimes used in salads; the roots are boiled and eaten as vegetables.

CARDOON: *Cynara cardunculus*, a relative of the artichoke, whose roots may be blanched and eaten like celery, or, with the stalks and leaf-veins, stewed as vegetables; the plant yields rennet used to curdle milk in cheesemaking, and is the source of a yellow dye.

CATMINT; CATNIP: *Nepeta cataria*, whose leaf is used in a hot tea for fevers or as a sedative, and fresh or dry are a tonic for cats; the plant is also used as bee forage.

CAMOMILE; CHAMOMILE: Any plant of the genus *Anthemis*, but particularly *Anthemis nobilis*, the Roman (or English) Camomile, or of the related genera *Matricaria* and *Chamomilla*, but particularly *Matricaria chamomilla*, or German Camomile; the flowers are used medicinally as sedatives and to reduce fevers, to counteract spasms and gas; the oil is used in making perfumes, and the oil of the German Camomile is also a solvent for platinum chloride; a rinse prepared from the flowers is said to preserve the natural highlights of the hair.

CHERVIL: An aromatic herb, *Anthriscus Cerefolium*, whose leaves are used as flavoring and seasoning, in sauces, soups, and salads, and as a garnish much like parsley; it is also used medicinally as an application for bruises.

CHICORY: A common perennial, *Cichorium intybus*, native to Europe, whose roots, ground and roasted, are used to sharpen the flavor of coffee; the leaves are blanched and used in salads. Also called Succory.

CHIVES: *Allium schoenoprasum*, a relative of the onion family, whose bulb is used as a substitute for onion; the leaves are used in salads.

CLARY: An aromatic herb, *Salvia sclarea*, native to southern Europe, and very popular in England as a potherb; it is used as a fixative in making perfume, as a flavoring for beer, and as a wine.

CICELY: Any of several herbs of various genera, but particularly *Myrrhis odorata*, Sweet Cicely, whose seed yields an oil used in making Chartreuse; the roots may be boiled and eaten as vegetables.

COLTSFOOT: A perennial herb, *Tussilago farfara*, native to Europe, whose leaves and flowers are used in preparations for coughs, asthma, bronchitis, and other pulmonary disorders; the leaves are sometimes dried and used as a substitute for tobacco.

CORIANDER: *Coriandrum sativum*, indigenous to southern Europe, whose seeds are extensively used as a flavoring in cooking, baking, confectionery, in the making of liqueurs (particularly Chartreuse) and gin, in perfumery, and medicinally as a stomachic and to counteract gas.

CORNFLOWER: A native European plant, *Centaurea cyanus*, whose blue flowers yield a juice used variously as an ink, as a tonic, and as an eyewash. Called also Bluebottle and Bachelor's Button.

COSTMARY: An aromatic herb, *Chrysanthemum balsamita*, whose leaves may be used in flavoring ale and beer, in salads, or as a potherb, and, medicinally, as a preparation for counteracting catarrh.

CUMIN: A native of Egypt and Syria, *Cuminum cuminum*, whose seeds are dried and used like Caraway; it was once a widely cultivated European spice, but has now been widely replaced by Caraway; in the East it is still generally used in making curry powder.

DIGITALIS: The Purple Foxglove, *Digitalis purpurea*, whose dried leaves are used medicinally as a cardiac and diuretic.

DILL: A European herb, *Anethum graveolens*, whose seeds are widely used in pickles and vinegar, in soups and gravies, in baking, and as a source of an oil in perfumery; the leaves are sometimes used as flavoring for salads and soups; the seeds are also used medicinally as a stimulant and to counteract gas.

ELECAMPANE: A native European plant, naturalized in the U.S., *Inula helenium*, whose root is used in confectionery, in flavoring liqueurs (particularly Absinthe), and in preparations for pulmonary disorders, in veterinary medicines, and as a dye.

FENNEL: A perennial European herb, *Foeniculum vulgare*, or Common Fennel, whose leaves may be blanched and used in salads, as a garnish, or boiled as a potherb; the seeds are widely used as flavoring, and yield an oil useful in making soap, in perfumery, and in flavoring liqueurs (particularly Absinthe); the seeds also have medicinal value in preparations for diseases of the chest organs, for correcting gas, and as eyewashes.

FENNEL-FLOWER: Any herb of the genus *Nigella*, but particularly *Nigella sativa*, whose black, spicy seeds are used, especially in India, as a condiment and as a flavoring.

FENUGREEK: An annual herb, native to Asia, *Trigonella foenum-graecum*, whose aromatic seeds are used in making curry; the seeds are also used medicinally in the preparation of poultices and ointments.

FEVERFEW: A perennial European plant, *Chrysanthemum parthenium*, whose leaves and flowers have long been used medicinally in preparations for fevers and for nervous aches and pains.

FLAX: A plant of the genus *Linum*, but particularly *Linum usitatissimum*, or Common Flax, whose seeds are crushed and used medinally in poultices, for laxatives, and for treating burns; the seeds and fibers also have important commercial and industrial uses as the sources of linseed oil and of linen.

FOXGLOVE, PURPLE: See Digitalis.

FRAXINELLA: A Eurasian perennial herb, *Dictamnus albus*, commonly called Gas Plant, because its flowers yield a gas which is inflammable in hot weather; the root is used medicinally in preparations for fevers and is also drunk as a tea.

FUMITORY: Any plant of the genus *Fumaria*, but particularly *Fumaria officinalis*, used as an agent to counteract scurvy; the flowers yield a yellow dye used for coloring wool.

GARLIC: A European bulbous herb, *Allium sativum*, used extensively as flavoring in cooking and in salads; the bulb has major medicinal uses as a stimulant, expectorant, diuretic, and antispasmodic.

GERMANDER: Any plant of the genus *Teucrium*, but particularly *Teucrium chamaedrys*, or Wall Germander, used as an agent to counteract scurvy.

GOOD KING HENRY: A European plant, naturalized in the U.S., *Chenopodium bonushenricus*, used as a potherb, and, medicinally, as a laxative.

HOLLYHOCK: A perennial herb, native to China, *Althea rosea*, whose flowers yield a coloring agent used in wine-making; the medicinal uses of Hollyhock are as counteractions of inflammation.

HOREHOUND: A native European Mint, naturalized in the U.S., *Marrubium vulgare*, whose top leaves furnish a medicine used in many forms for pulmonary disorders; the dried leaves are used in making tea.

HOUSELEEK: A native European succulent plant, *Sempervivum tectorum*, whose leaves are applied directly to burns and inflammations of the skin.

HYSSOP: An aromatic and pungent European mint, *Hyssopus officinalis*, whose leaves yield an oil used in perfumery, in flavoring liqueurs (especially Chartreuse); the leaves are sometimes used in salads, and also furnish medicines for coughs, tonics, and laxatives.

INDIGO, WILD: *Baptisia tinctoria*, an American plant of the genus *Baptisia*, whose roots are used medicinally in treatments for typhoid and scarlet fever, for diphtheria, to induce vomiting, and as a general antiseptic.

INDIGO, BLUE FALSE: *Baptisia australis*, a plant of the southwestern U.S., of the genus *Baptisia*, whose roots are used medicinally to induce vomiting.

LARKSPUR: Any plant of the genus *Delphinium*, but particularly *Delphinium ajacis*; both the seeds and the flowers are poisonous; the seeds are used medicinally in preparations for asthma, and as a toxic for body lice; the flowers are used medicinally in preparations for dysentery, dropsy, and gout.

LAVENDER: Any plant of the genus *Lavan-*

dula, but particularly the European Mint *Lavandula officinalis* whose spikes yield the aromatic oil known as Oil of Lavender used in perfumery and in medicines as a stimulant and to counteract gas; other useful species of lavender are *Lavandula spica*, or Spike Lavender, *Lavandula vera*, or True Lavender (also called English Lavender), and *Lavandula stoechas*, or French Lavender.

LEMON VERBENA: A small shrub, *Lippia citriodora*, native to South America, whose leaves are used medicinally as a sedative, and as a curative for fevers and gas, and also in perfumery.

LILY-OF-THE-VALLEY: A perennial herb, *Convallaria majalis*, whose roots, flowers, and leaves are used as a cardiac; the flowers and leaves are also used medicinally as a laxative and as an agent to induce vomiting.

LOVAGE: A European herb, *Levisticum officinale*, once widely used as a domestic remedy to reduce gas, or to cause perspiration, but now restricted to the flavoring and confectionery uses of the seeds; the stalks may be blanched and eaten like celery, and the flowers and leaves yield an oil used in perfumery.

MADDER: A Eurasian herb, *Rubia tinctorum*, whose roots are used as a dyestuff.

MARJORAM: Any plant of the genera *Origanum* and *Marjorana*, but particularly *Origanum vulgare*, or Wild Marjoram, *Marjorana hortensis*, or Sweet Marjoram, and *Marjorana onites*, or Pot Marjoram; the leaves are used as flavoring ·and in cooking, the oil in perfumery and soap-making, and the flowers yield a dyestuff; Marjoram is used for making tea, and was once widely cultivated for the medicinal value of the tea in relieving headache and asthma; Wild Marjoram is used as a stimulant and as a tooth-ache drop.

MARSH MALLOW: A European perennial herb, *Althea officinalis*, used medicinally as a demulcent; the root liquid, once used as the base of the confectionery marshmallow, is now a curative for sore throat.

MINT: A plant of the genus *Mentha*, or, more generally, of the family *Lamiaceae*, but particularly *Mentha piperita*, or Peppermint, *Mentha spicata*, or Spearmint, *Mentha rotundifolia*, or Apple Mint, *Mentha arvensis*, or Corn Mint, and *Mentha citrata*, or Orange Mint; the mints are cultivated for their essential oils which have many various uses in cooking, medicine, perfumery, liqueur-making, and confectionery.

MONKSHOOD: See Aconite.

MUGWORT: A perennial herb, native to Eurasia, *Artemisia vulgaris*, or any of several similar American species, but particularly *Artemisia lactiflora*, or White Mugwort, and *Artemisia ludoviciana*, or Western Mugwort; the whole herb is used medicinally as a tonic.

MULLEIN: Any herb of the genus *Verbascum*, but particularly *Verbascum thapsus*, or Great Mullein, and *Verbascum blattaria*, or Moth Mullein; the leaves are used medicinally in pulmonary disorders, and also for poultices.

MUSTARD: Any of several species of the genus *Brassica*, but particularly *Brassica nigra*, or Black Mustard, *Brassica alba*, or White Mustard, which are widely cultivated for their seeds; Oil of Mustard is made from a preparation of mixed Black and White Mustard Seeds and is used in making soap, salad oils, and lubricants; mustard is a stimulant and diuretic and is used to induce vomiting; Black Mustard is a general antiseptic, and White is used for pulmonary disorders, for gas, as a gargle, and as a laxative; the leaves of the White Mustard are used in salads.

NASTURTIUM: Any plant of the genus *Tropaeolum*, but particularly *Tropaeolum majus*, whose seeds are used in pickles, and leaves and flowers in salads.

PARSLEY: A European garden herb, *Petroselinum hortense*, whose leaves have major culinary uses as a flavoring for soups, stews, and as a garnish for salads and are used medicinally as a vulnerary; the herb is used as a coloring agent in wines and cheeses, and an oil, extracted from the fruit, is used in drugs; an imitation Absinthe is made from Parsley.

PENNYROYAL: A European Mint *Mentha pulegium* used medicinally as an antispasmodic and to induce menstruation, or the American Pennyroyal, *Hedeoma pulegioides*, with similar medicinal properties.

PERILLA: A small genus of Asiatic plants, but particularly *Persilla frutescens crispa*, or Beefsteak Plant, cultivated for ornamentation and for the oil from its seeds which is used in the U.S. as a drying agent in paints.

PIMPERNEL: Any plant of the genus *Anagallis*, but particularly *Anagallis arvensis* which is used medicinally to induce sweat and as an expectorant, and was formerly widely used as a domestic remedy.

POPPY, OPIUM: A Eurasian perennial herb, *Papaver somniferum*, whose seeds have various uses as bird food, or as a source of an oil used in cooking, but is cultivated especially for the juice, extracted from the pod, which is the source of opium.

PRIMROSE: Any plant or flower of the genus *Primula*, especially *Primula veris*, or Cowslip, which is used medicinally to induce vomiting, and to reduce pain.

PYRETHRUM: Any of several garden plants of the genus *Chrysanthemum*, but particularly *Chrysanthemum cinerariaefolium*, whose flowers are cultivated for use as an insecticide.

RAMPION: A European plant of the genus *Campanula*, *Campanula rapunculus*, or Bellflower, whose roots are boiled and eaten as vegetables, and whose leaves are used in salads.

ROSE GERANIUM: Any of several South African herbs of the genus *Pelargonium*, but particularly *Pelargonium graveolens*, which yields an oil used in perfumery.

ROSEMARY: A shrub, *Rosmarinus officinalis*, of southern Europe and the Near East, whose leaves are used in perfumery and cosmetics, in cooking, and, medicinally, as an antispasmodic and to induce menstruation.

RUE: A perennial woody herb, *Ruta graveolens*, which was formerly widely used as a domestic remedy and as a seasoning, but contemporary uses, other than as ornamentation, are few; the Italians are reported to have used the leaves in salads, and also in an eyewash, but in Italy, too, the practical uses of the plants have diminished drastically since the time when Rue was a sovereign remedy among the ancient Romans.

SAFFLOWER: An herb, indigenous to Europe, *Carthanus tinctorius*, whose flowers yield a red dyestuff of many used in tinting fabrics, as a coloring agent for foods and beverages, in confectionery, and in cosmetics; when used medicinally as a drug, the same product is a laxative; the oil of the seeds is a drying agent in paints.

SAFFRON: A species of crocus, *Crocus sativus*, whose orange stigmas are dried and used as a coloring agent in foods and beverages, and as a dyestuff; the same product is used medicinally in treating nervous disorders.

SAGE: Any Mint of the genus *Salvia*, but particularly, *Salvia officinalis*, or Garden Sage, whose leaves are used as flavoring for foods, as a seasoning, in making sage tea and wine, in perfumery and soap-making, and medicinally as an astringent, an expectorant, a sudorific, and as a curative for fevers and nervous spells; the fresh leaves are also recommended as a dentifrice and as a gum-conditioner.

SAMPHIRE: A fleshy plant, native to Europe, *Crithmum maritimum*, whose leaves may be pickled and kept for salads.

SANTONICA: The European wormwood, *Artemisia pauciflora*, whose flowers are dried and used medicinally as a vermifuge.

SAVORY: Any plant of the genus *Satureia*, but particularly *Satureia hortensis*, or Summer Savory, and *Satureia montana*, or Winter Savory, which are in general use in cooking; the leaves are used in sauces, salads, stews, and stuffings, or as a garnish; or they can be dried and used in syrups and preserves; Summer Savory has the more delicate flavor, and is also used medicinally in herbal, or aromatic, baths.

SENNA, AMERICAN (WILD): The leaves of *Cassia marilandica*, or American Savory, are dried and used as a purgative; other species of Senna, *Cassia acutifolia* and *Cassia augustifolia*, are similarly used.

SESAME: *Sesamum indicum*, a native East Indian herb; the seeds yield an oil with major industrial uses in the making of soap, margarine, ink, cosmetics, salves, liniments, and laxatives; the oil is also used in cooking, while the seeds are used in baking.

SKIRRET: The roots of *Sium sisarum*, or Skirret, may be boiled and eaten as vegetables, sometimes with the medicinal purpose of relieving chest diseases.

SNAKEROOT: See Bugbane.

SNAKEROOT, VIRGINIA: The roots of *Aristolochia serpentina*, or Virginia Snakeroot, are used in a preparation for treating snakebites.

SORREL: Any plant of the genus *Rumex*, but particularly *Rumex scutatus*, or French Sorrel, and *Rumex Acetosa*, or Common Sorrel, whose leaves are used in soups, stews, and salads, and medicinally as a curative for scurvy.

SOUTHERNWOOD: A shrubby wormwood, native to Europe, *Artemisia abrotanum*, whose fragrant leaves are stored with clothing to prevent moths; the leaves are also used for various medicinal purposes, such as herbal baths, astringents, and as a vermifuge; they are also sometimes used as a flavoring in cooking, and are said to be used similarly in making wine.

SPEEDWELL: Any herb of the genus *Veronica*, of the figwort family, but particularly *Veronica officinalis*, or Common Speedwell, which has many medicinal uses in treatments for rheumatism, gout, pulmonary disorders, and skin diseases, and is also used in making Vermouth.

SUCCORY: Another name for Chicory.

TANSY: Any plant of the genus *Tanacetum*, but particularly the aromatic, bitter *Tanacetum vulgare*, whose leaves are used medicinally as a tonic and vulnerary, as a flavoring in cooking, in perfumery, and in making liqueurs (especially Chartreuse).

TARRAGON: A herb, native to Europe, *Artemisia dracunculus*, whose leaves, usually when fresh, are used as flavoring in salads, sauces, preserves, and confectionery, and, particularly, in making tarragon vinegar; the fresh leaves also contain an essential oil which is used in perfumery.

THRIFT: Any plant of the genus *Statice*, but

particularly *Statice armeria*, whose pink and white flowers make attractive garden ornamentation; the flowers are sometimes used medicinally to relieve urinary disorders.

THYME: Any Mint of the genus *Thymus*, but particularly *Thymus serpyllum*, or Wild Thyme, *Thymus vulgaris*, or Garden Thyme, and *Thymus citriodorus*, or Lemon Thyme, whose leaves, either fresh or dried, are widely used as a flavoring for sauces, soups, stews, stuffings, and preserves; thyme yields an essential oil, Oil of Thyme, with astringent properties of many uses in medicine, such as in anesthetics, deodorants, dentrifices, and gargles; the oil is an ingredient in perfumery and soap-making, and is also used in making liqueurs (especially Benedictine).

VALERIAN: Any perennial of the genus *Valeriana*, but particularly *Valeriana officinalis*, the Common Valerian of Garden Heliotrope, whose roots are used medicinally as a sedative, antispasmodic, and to counteract gas; it is also used in perfumery.

WOAD: An herb, *Isatis tinctoria*, of the European mustard family, whose leaves yield a blue dyestuff formerly in general use in pure form (the same blue dye that was used ceremonially as a body ornament by the ancient Celts of the British Isles), but now usually added to black dye and indigo as a fixative; the leaf and stem have medicinal properties as an astringent.

WOODRUFF: A European herb, *Asperula odorata*, whose leaves are used in perfumery and in flavoring wines and liqueurs. Also known as Sweet Woodruff.

WORMWOOD: A woody herb, native to Europe, of the genus *Artemisia*, but particularly *Artemisia absinthium*, whose leaves yield the acrid green oil used in making Absinth; the leaves also have medicinal properties and are used in treatments for fevers, rheumatism, as a vermifuge, and as an antiseptic.

YARROW: *Achillea millefolium*, or Common Yarrow, a Eurasian herb of the aster family, used medicinally as a laxative; the flowers are used in treatments for uterine disorders and catarrh.

Hindu Gods
See **Gods and Goddesses**

Historic Sites
See **National Historic Sites; National Federal Historic Sites; National Historic Parks**

Holy Roman Emperors
See **Rulers**

Homes, American
See also **Architects, Their Schools and Representative Works**

BLOCKHOUSES: 1675-1677; New England; square fort, second story overhangs with thick protective walls, square-hewn timbers, pyramidal roof, very small windows.

BRICK ROW HOUSES: 1776; Baltimore, Philadelphia; arch. Robert Mills; houses of unified design, brick-fronted with 3 marble steps. Attached.

CALIFORNIA BUNGALOW: 1900; Calif., Conn.; archs. Greene and Greene; shingle style tradition, open planning, plank and beam construction, redwood.

CAPE COD HOUSE: Middle 17th cent.—18th cent.; Cape Cod, Nantucket, Martha's Vineyard; low one-story eaves, white clapboard or shingle outsides, large central chimney.

CHURRIGUERESQUE: Early 18th cent.; Spanish Southwest; influence of Manuel Churriquera; baroque Spanish, abundant with extravagant form, color, murals, ornateness, broken cornices, squirming volutes.

CLASSIC: 1893-1917; New York City, Boston; firm of McKim, Meade and White; consistent use of Greek, Roman, Renaissance, and Gothic derivatives in building design.

CONCRETE AND MASONRY HOUSE: 1900; arch. Frank Lloyd Wright; beginnings of truly American architecture in the proper use of concrete and stucco. Reinforced concrete frame, flattened arch replaces horizontal or rounded. Roof becomes flat. Soundproof.

DOWNING'S COTTAGE STYLE: 1860-1880; wealthy suburbs; arch. Andrew Jackson Downing; wood and stucco, traceried eaves, lattice windows, Gothic and Renaissance detail with porticos and gables.

DUTCH COLONIAL: Middle 17th cent.; New Amsterdam and Hudson Valley; Holland inspired; red or yellow brick, stepped gable roof rising to chimney, small-paned windows, 2½-3½ stories high, doors on several stories.

DYMAXION HOUSE: See Fuller House.

EASTLAKE HOUSES: 1860-1880; widespread; Charles L. Eastlake, English architect and designer; house's interior and exterior under his influence, overdesigned. Gambrel roofs of different shapes and colors, bays, oriels, jigsaw work, high narrow windows with diamond panes; 2-story porches.

ENGLISH WIGWAM: 1620; Va., New England; round-roof structure of oblong plan covered with mats. Doors.

FEDERAL STYLE: Post-Revolution (1784); Salem, Mass.; arch. Asher Benjamin; walls, flush board or painted white on stucco, abstract classical smoothness geometric in effect, Federal doorway, eliptical fanlight sided by slender Adams-influenced columns.

FRAME HOUSE: 1893; widespread; houses built by means of timber or scantling inside, covered outside with boarding or shingle.

FRENCH CREOLE: 18th—early 19th cent.; La.; houses raised 6-8 feet on closed-in brick piers; outside staircase rising to open main floor gallery or porch surrounding house. Slender columns support hipped roof with narrow dormer windows. French windows on porch, outer blinds.

FRENCH STYLE (THIRD EMPIRE): 1860-1880; homes of the wealthy in large cities, Newport, etc.; arch. Richard Hunt; mansard roofs with dormers, ornate columns and pediments, pseudo-Renaissance cupolas, heavy walls, overornamented.

FULLER HOUSE: 1946; Wichita, Kan.; arch. Richard Buckminster Fuller; circular, metal, built around and suspended vertically by shrouds from a central mast-like structure housing the building services, windows of acrylic plastic; successor to prefabricated Dymaxion house, earlier design of the architect.

FUNCTIONAL HOUSE: 1893; Chicago; arch. Louis Sullivan; movement developed from Sullivan's "form follows function" in hope of creating an American style. Ornament called "modernistic."

GEORGIAN (EARLY): Before 1750; Eastern seaboard; wood, plain clapboard, unbroken façade, quoined corners, no entrance portico, front door with rectangular transom, scroll pediment over door, small-paned windows,

plain or corniced, single arched window on stair landing, steep roof pitch.

GEORGIAN (LATE): After 1750; Eastern seaboard; Robert Adams influence; rusticated wood, projecting central pavilion, corners marked by giant pilasters, small entrance portico, front door, semicircular fanlight over; windows, fewer and large-paned, pedimented windows, Palladian windows for stairlanding; lower roof pitch, balustraded roof decks, arched dormer windows.

GOTHIC REVIVAL: 1820-1860 (Romantic period); interspersed with Greek Revival throughout the States; medieval architecture, pointed arch, supporting buttresses, effect of lightness and flexibility.

GREEK REVIVAL: 1820-1860; Me. to Ga., low Miss., Northwest; arch. William Strickland; white, classic portico (Doric or Ionic), temple form, surrounding peristyle of columns.

GREIGO ROMANO: Late 18th cent.; La.; Spanish formal style of Philip II with French influence in mansard roofs, balconies.

HALF-TIMBERED HOUSE: Early 17th cent.; New England, Pa.; medieval influence, timber frame with spaces filled in with masonry.

LOG HOUSES: 18th cent. on; introduced by German & Swedish colonists, Scotch-Irish made the "log cabin" the symbol of frontier America; round logs laid horizontally on one another, notched corners, protruding ends, spaces chinked with moss or clay.

MODERN HOUSE: 1932; Chicago; arch. Louis Sullivan, Frank Lloyd Wright influenced by Bauhaus;
1. Building in terms of volume, space enclosed by planes or surfaces as opposed to mass.
2. Regularity (vertical, horizontal) and repetition as basis of composition.
3. Flexibility in building plan.
4. Technical perfection and fineness of proportion.
"Machine for living."

MOORISH-GOTHIC: Early 19th cent.; Calif.; gothic medievalism with Moorish detail of decoration.

NEOCLASSIC: 1780-1790; vogue that swept the Western World; arch. James Stuart; use of Ionic column of Erechtheum rather than standard Renaissance Ionic.

NEW ENGLAND COLONIAL: 1650; Conn., Mass., R. I.; original one room, expanding units added, oak frame, timbered and boarded interior, clapboard outside, massive brick fireplace, leaded diamond-pane windows, steep roofed.

PALLADIAN STYLE: Post-Revolution; Va. mansions; Thomas Jefferson, Benjamin Latrobe influenced by Andrea Palladio; square mass enclosing a circular domed rotunda fronted by classical porticoes on 4 sides.

PENNSYLVANIA DUTCH: 18th cent.; Pa., York and Lancaster counties, Lehigh Valley; rough stone walls, brownstone quoins at corners, 2 stories, flared projecting eaves.

PLATERESQUE: 1820-1830; Monterey, San Francisco; resembling silversmith style of metal work; refers to the ornate decoration.

POPINJAY COLONIAL: 1900-1920; widespread; naïve use of "colonial" in Eclectic period; interpreted as anything with white columns, cornice, green blinds.

PREFABRICATED HOUSE: 1941; widespread; war influenced; quickly erected, demountable housing, plywood, canvas, synthetic materials.

PUEBLO: 900-1200; N. M.; communal edifices of stone and adobe, receding terraces.

QUEEN ANNE: 1876-1896; Newport, Short Hills (N. J.), etc.; influenced by Robert Shaw, English architect; shingle and brick, high clustered chimneys, rough-cast gables, horizontal window bands with spaces filled with half-timbered design.

QUEEN ANNE COLONIAL: 1869-1876; Newport; arch. Charles McKim; remodeled colonial into modified Queen Anne, adding bay windows, living halls, stair combinations.

ROMANESQUE REVIVAL: 1876-1896; Boston, N. Y.; arch. Henry Hobson Richardson; romantic and picturesque mass with a rich texture, hewn stone or rough brick with carvings, high roofs, clustered windows, deeply arched doorways.

ROMAN REVIVAL: Early 19th cent.; Va.; Palladian interpreted with freedom; 2-story classic portico topped by pediments.

ROMANTIC STYLE: 1860-1880; Newport, etc.; Charles Eastlake, Richard Hunt, Andrew Downing; parvenu period drawing on foreign romantic design; French Chateau, Swiss Chalet, Elizabethean Half-timbered, Italian Villa, Moorish Castle, Crenelated Tower, etc.

SOUTHERN COLONIAL: 17th cent.; 500 miles along Atlantic Coast, Delaware River to Savannah River;
1. Farmhouses, weatherboards, clay wall filling, wide exterior chimney, gable roof.
2. Brick construction, bricks very plentiful, plan similar to frame houses.

SOUTHERN PLANTATION: 18th cent.; S. C.; English influence; columned entrance porticoes, recessed central bay permitting porch; roof double-hipped, entrance door and window above framed by pilasters and pediments; double flight of steps. Brick or frame.

SPANISH COLONIAL: 16th cent.; Fla.; expressed absolutism and aristocracy; 2 stories, thick lower wall of coquina limestone; second story frame construction with clapboard siding. Hipped tile roof covers second-story porches at ends.

SPANISH-MEXICAN: 1609-1846; N. M.; blend of Spanish and Indian influences.

SPANISH MISSION: 1769-1826; Calif., Tex.; arch. Fermin de Lasuen; quadrangle of buildings surrounding open patio, adobe brick (clay, sand, water) construction, red-tiled roofs (tiles half-cylinder).

TIDEWATER COLONIAL: Early 18th cent.; Williamsburg, Va.; arch. Richard Taliaferro; aristocracy, wealth, and mild climate influenced separate units, kitchen, slave quarters; smoke-house along with main house. Early Georgian simplicity, red brick, 2 stories, hipped roof, balanced chimneys.

VICTORIAN GOTHIC: 1860-1880; influence widespread over the States; archs. James Renwick, Richard Hunt; brownstone or wood structures, elaborate entrances, porches, piazzas, gothic-centered arches, gables, bay windows, towers and turrets, decorative bargeboards.

Horses in Legend and Fiction
See also **Animals in Symbolism**

AL BORAK: The "horse" that conveyed Mahomet from the earth to the seventh heaven. It was milk-white, had the wings of an eagle, and a human face, with horse's cheeks. Every pace it took was equal to the farthest range of human sight. The name is Arabic for "the lightning."

ALIGERO CLAVILENO: The "wooden-pin wing-horse" that Don Quixote and Sancho Panza

mounted to rescue Dolorida and her companions.

ARION: (Gk. martial) Hercules' horse, which was given to Adrastus. Also, the fleet, talking horse, with right feet like a man's, created by Neptune when he struck the earth with his trident.

ARUNDEL: (Fr. *hirondelle*, swallow). The horse of the famous knight of chivalric romances, Bevis of Southampton, which was, as his name implies, swift as a swallow.

BAJARDO: (The same name as Bayard, see below). In *Orlando Furioso*, Rinaldo's horse, of a bright bay color, and once the property of Amadis of Gaul. He was found by Malagigi, the wizard, in a cave guarded by a dragon, which the wizard slew. According to tradition he is still alive, but flees at the approach of man, so that no one can ever hope to catch him.

BANK'S HORSE: See Marocco, below.

BARBARY: See Roan Barbary.

BAVIECA: (Sp. Simpleton.) The Cid's horse. He survived his master two years and a half, during which time no one was allowed to mount him. He was buried before the gate of the monastery at Valencia, and two elms were planted to mark the site. So called because, when Rodrigo in his youth was given the choice of a horse, he passed by the most esteemed ones and selected a rough colt; whereupon his godfather called the lad a *bavieca*, and Rodrigo transferred the name to his horse.

BAYARD: (Bay colored), the horse of the four sons of Aymon, which grew larger or smaller as one or more of the four sons mounted it. According to tradition one of the hoofprints may still be seen in the forest of Soignes, and another on a rock near Dinant. The same name as Bajardo, above.

BEVIS: Marmion's horse, in Scott's poem. The word is Norse, and means swift.

BLACK BEAUTY: Anna Sewall tells the story of Black Beauty in *Black Beauty, His Grooms and Companions*, which is also an eloquent plea for kindness toward all animals.

BLACK BESS: The celebrated mare which carried the highwayman, Dick Turpin, on his trip from London to York.

BLACK HORSE: In the Apocalypse (*Revelation*), the horse of Famine.

BORAK: See Al Borak.

BRAZEN HORSE: Cambuscan, the King of Sarra in Tartary—in Chaucer's unfinished *Squire's Tale*—had a daughter named Canace. On her birthday the King of Arabia and India sent Cambuscan a "steed of brass, which, between sunrise and sunset, would carry its rider to any spot on earth." All that was required was to whisper the name of the place in the horse's ear, mount upon his back, and turn a pin set in his ear. When the rider had arrived at the place required, he had to turn another pin, and the horse instantly descended; and, with another screw of the pin, vanished till it was again required. Milton refers to the story in his *Il Penseroso*.

BRIGADORE (OR BRIGLIADORE): (Golden Bridle), Sir Guyon's horse, in Spenser's *Faerie Queene* (V. II, etc.). It had a distinguishing spot in its mouth, like a horseshoe. Orlando's famous charger, second only to Bajardo in swiftness and wonderful powers, had the same name—Brigliadoro.

BRONZOMARTE: The steed of Sir Launcelot Greaves in Tobias Smollett's travesty of Don Quixote, *The Adventures of Launcelot Greaves* described as "a fine mettlesome sorrel who had got good blood in him."

BUCEPHALUS: (Bull-headed, from Gk. words for bull and head). The celebrated horse of Alexander the Great, who was the first to break him in, in fulfillment of the condition stated by an oracle as necessary for gaining the crown of Macedon; no one except Alexander could ever mount Bucephalus, but the horse even knelt down to take up his master; when he died, at the age of thirty, he was buried in a special mausoleum that Alexander named the Bucephala.

THE CENTAURS: In Greek myth, the wild descendants of Ixion, who were half-horse and half-man and lived in the mountains of Thessaly. See also Chiron.

CHIRON: In Greek myth, the most famous of the centaurs, son of Cronus and Philyra, who was expert in the arts of medicine, tutor of Aesculapius and Achilles, and metamorphosed by Zeus into the constellation Sagittarius. See also Centaurs.

DAPPLE: In Cervante's Don Quixote, the dappled ass of Sancho Panza.

DARK HORSE: A racing term for a promising but untried horse, whose merits are kept secret from betters and bookies. In politics the term is reserved for candidates put up at the last minute.

FADDA: Mahomet's white mule.

FRONTINO: In the romances of chivalry, the horse of Ruggiero (Rogero), described by Cervantes in Don Quixote as "the renowned Frontino, which Bradamante purchased at so high a price, "in allusion to the adventures of the Christian Amazon, Ruggiero's mistress, 'whose story is told at length in the last book of Orlando Furioso.

GIFT HORSE: Don't look a gift horse in the mouth, goes the popular saying; that is, never ask how much a present really costs. Latin: Noli equi dentes inspicere donati. Scholastic Latin: Si quis det mannos pe quoere in dentibus annos. Italian: A cavallao daio non guardar in bocca. French: A cheval donné il ne faut pas regarder aux dents. Spanish: A caballo dato no le mirem el diente.

GRANE (GRANI): In Scandinavian an Teutonic legends, and especially in the Nibelungenlied, the marvelously swift horse of Siegfried, named for his gray-colored coat.

THE HIPPOGRIFFON OF ASTOLPHO: Astolpho (Astolfo), the English cousin of Orlando in the romances of chivalry who is made to cure Orlando's madness in Orlando Furioso by bringing back the hero's lost wits in a vial from the moon, is represented as riding on a fabulous flying horse.

HOFVARPNIR: In Norse mythology, the horse ridden by Gna, the messenger of Frigga, when she was sent out by the goddess on missions of inquiry and inspection.

HRIM-FRAXI: In Norse mythology, the sable steed that drew the black chariot of night and dropped dew and hoarfrost on the earth from his waving mane.

MAROCCO: Bank's performing horse, famous in the late Elisabethan period, and frequently mentioned by the dramatists. Its shoes were of silver, and one of its exploits was to mount the steeple of St. Paul's.

PALE HORSE: In the Apocalypse (Revelation), the horse of Death.

PASSETREUL: In the Arthurian legends, the horse of Sir Tristram.

PEGASUS: (Gk. "born near the source of the ocean.") In Greek and Roman myth, the winged horse which sprang from the blood of Medusa and belonged to Apollo and the Muses. Perseus rode him to the rescue of Andromeda.

At the rap of his hoof, the fountain Hippocrene burst forth on Mount Helicon. Bellerophon caught him and destroyed the Chimera with his aid, but when he tried to ride him to heaven, Pegasus threw his rider, mounted alone to the stars, and was there changed into a constellation.

RABICANO (OR RABICAN): Argalia's horse in Orlando Innamorato, and Astolpho's horse in Orlando Furioso. Its dam was Fire, its sire Wind; it fed on unearthly food. The word means a horse with a "dark tail but with some white hairs."

RED HORSE: In the Apocalypse (Revelation), the horse of Slaughter.

REKSH: In Persian legend, and in Matthew Arnold's Sohrab and Rustum, Rustum's horse.

ROAN BARBARY: The favorite horse of King Richard II.

"When Bollingbroke rode on Roan Barbary
That horse that thou so often has bestrid."
Shakespeare: Richard II, V, 5.

ROSINANTE: ("Formerly a hack"), Don Quixote's horse, all skin and bone.

SEIAN HORSE: A term for a possession that invariably brought ill luck with it. Hence the Latin proverb Ille homo habet equum Seianum. Cneius Seius had an Argive horse, of the breed of Diomed, of a bay color and surpassing beauty, but it was fatal to its possessor. Seius was put to death by Mark Antony. Its next owner, Cornelius Dolabella, who bought it for 100,000 sesterces, was killed in Syria during the civil wars. Caius Cassius, who next took possession of it, perished after the battle of Philippi by the same sword that stabbed Caesar. Antony had the horse next, and after the battle of Actium slew himself. Like the gold of Tolosa and Hermione's necklace, the Seian or Sejan horse was a fatal possession.

SKIN-FRAXI: In Norse mythology, the white steed that drew the bright chariot of day and flashed beams of light throughout the world from his waving mane.

SLEIPNIR: Odin's gray horse, which had eight legs and could traverse either land or sea. The horse typifies the wind that blows over land and water from eight principal points.

TROJAN HORSE: See Wooden Horse of Troy, below.

VEGLIANTINO: Orlando's horse in the legends about the hero of Orlando Furioso and Orlando Innamorrato; his more celebrated steed was Brigliadore.

WHITE HORSE: In the Apocalypse (Revelation), the horse of Conquest.

WOODEN HORSE: A legendary enchanted horse that could be directed by a peg turned by the rider and could fly through the air. Cambuscan had such a horse, but it was of brass. See Aligero Clavilena: "This very day may be seen in the king's armory the identical peg with which Peter of Provence turned his Wooden Horse, which carried him through the air. It is rather bigger than the pole of a coach, and stands near Babieca's saddle." Don Quixote, Pt. I, Bk. IV, 19.

WOODEN HORSE OF TROY: Virgil tells us that Ulysses had a monster wooden horse made after the death of Hector, and gave out that it was an offering to the gods to secure a prosperous voyage back to Greece. The Trojans dragged the horse within their city, but it was full of Grecian soldiers, who at night stole out of their place of concealment, slew the Trojan guards, opened the city gates, and set fire to Troy. Menelaus was one of the Greeks shut up in it. It was made by Epeios.

XANTHUS: (Golden-hued) Achilles' horse

which, after an undeserved scolding by his master, warned the hero that the day of death was near.

House Standing Committees
See Congress of the United States

Indians, American

CHIEF FAMILIES OF AMERICAN INDIANS

Algonquin; Caddoan; Déné; Iroquois; Muskhogean; Penutian; Siouan; Uto-Aztecan.

Major Tribes of the Chief Families of American Indians

Algonquin Family

ATLANTIC SLOPE: Abnaki; Algonquin (Algonkin); Delaware; Mahican; Massachusetts; Micmac; Montagnais; Narraganset; Naskapi; Pequot; Powhatan; Wampanoag.
CALIFORNIAN: Wiyot; Yurok.
CENTRAL REGION: Cree; Fox; Illinois; Kickapoo; Menomini; Miami; Ojibway; Ottowa; Potawatomi; Sauk; Shawnee.
PLAINS INDIANS: Arapaho; Blackfoot; Blood; Cheyenne; Gros Ventre (Atsina); Piegan; Plains Cree.
PUTATIVE MEMBERS: Flathead; Kalispel; Siletz; Spokan; Wenatchi.

Caddo Family

ARIKARA.
CADDO: Kichai; Tawakoni; Waco; Wichita.
PAWNEE: Chaui; Kitkahaxki; Pitahauirata; Skidi.

Déné Family

ATHABASCAN: Ahtena (Atnas; Copper River); Bear Lake (Satudene; Great Bear Lake); Beaver (Tsattine); Carrier (Takulli); Chilcotin (Tsilkotin); Chipewyan; Dogrib (Thlingchadinne); Han (Hankutchin); Hare (Kawchodinne); Ingalik (Kaiyuhkhotana); Kaska (Nahani); Koyukon (Unakhotana; Tenas); Kutchin (Loucheux; Dindjie); Mountain (Montagnais; Montagnard); Nabesna (Nabesnatana; Upper Tanana); Nicola (Stuichamukh); Sarsi (Sarcee); Sekani (Tsekehne); Slaves (Slaves); Tahltan; Tanaina (Knaiakhotana; Kenaitze); Tanana (Nukluktanas; Lower Tanana); Tsetsaut; Tutchone (Tutchone-Kutchin); Yellow Knife (Tatsanottine; Copperknife).
NORTH PACIFIC COAST: Haida; Tlingit (Auk; Chilkat; Sitka; Stikine; Taru; Tongas; Yakutat; etc.); Tsimshian (Chimmesyan).
UNITED STATES DÉNÉ: Northern Group (Hupa; Kato; Tolowa); Southern Group (1—San Carlos: White Mountain, Chiricahua, Mescalero, Navaho; 2—Jicarilla: Kiowa Apache).

Iroquois Family

NORTHERN TRIBES—SIX NATIONS: Cayuga; Mohawk; Oneida; Onondaga; Seneca; Tuscarora.
INDEPENDENTS: Erie; Huron or Wyandot; Neutrals; Susquehanna or Conestoga.
SOUTHERN: Cherokee.

Muskhogean Family

MUSKOHEGAN: Alibamu; Apalachee; Chickasaw; Choctaw; Koasati; Lower Creek; Natchez; Seminole; Taensa; Tunica; Upper-Creek.

Penutian Family

CALIFORNIAN: Costanoan; Maidu; Miwok; Wintun; Yokut.
CAYUSE: Molala.
CHINOOKAN: Clatsop; Chinook; Wasco; Wishran.
KLAMATH: Modoc.
MEXICAN: Huave; Jicquean; Lencan; Mixe; Payan; Zoque.
SHAHAP TIN: Klikitat; Nez Percé; Paloos; Topinish; Umatilla; Wallawalla; Warm Springs; Yakima.

Siouan Family

ASSINIBOIN OR STONEY.
DAKOTA TRIBES: Eastern Dakota; Santee-Dakota; Teton-Dakota; Yankton.
LOWER MISSOURI: Iowa; Kansas; Omaha; Osage; Oto; Ponca.
STRAGGLERS: Biloxi; Catawba; Quapaw; Tutelo; Winnebago.
UPPER MISSOURI: Crow; Hidatsa; Mandan.

Uto-Aztecan Family

KIOWA.
MAYA BRANCH: Many tribes in Yucatan and Guatemala.
NAHUATLAN OR AZTEC BRANCH: Aztec; Cora; Opata; Papago; Pima; Yaqui.
SHOSHONEAN BRANCH: Bannock, Ida., Chemehuevi, Ariz., Nev.; Comanche, Okla.; Hopi; Ariz.; Kern River Tribes, Calif.; Mission Tribes, Calif.; Mono Tribes, Calif.; Paiute, Nev.; Panamint, Nev.; Snake, Ida.; Ute, Ut. and Colo.; Wind River, Wy.
TANOAN BRANCH: Pueblo villages of: Hano; Isleta; Jemez; Nambe; Picuris; Pojoaque; Sandia; San Ildefonso; San Juan; Santa Clara; Taos; Tesuque.

Iroquois Confederacy of the Five Nations

Cayuga; Mohawk; Oneida; Onondaga; Seneca.

Iroquois Confederacy of the Six Nations

Cayuga; Mohawk; Oneida; Onondaga; Seneca; Tuscarora.

AMERICAN INDIANS: THEIR TRIBES AND STATES

Alabama

ABIHKA: See Creek Confederacy and Muskogee.
ALABAMA: Perhaps from native word "albina," meaning "to camp," or "alba amo," "weed gatherer," referring to the black drink; belonged to S. division of the Muskhogean stock and was perhaps connected with the lost tongues of the Musklasa and Tuskegee; closely

related to Koasati and more remotely to Hitchiti and Choctaw; lived mainly on upper course of Alabama R.; pop. in 1715, 770.

APALACHEE: Some lived for a time with Lower Creeks and perhaps in Ala.; after 1715, settled on Chattahoochee R. in Russell County before pushing with Creeks across the Miss.

ATASI: A division or subtribe of the Muskogee.

CHATOT: Driven from Fla. and settled near Mobile before moving to La.

CHEROKEE: In late 18th century some Cherokees reached Muscle Shoals by pushing down the Tennessee R. and constituted the Chickamauga band; all their territory was surrendered 1807-1835.

CHICKASAW: Had a few settlements in N.W. Ala. where the state crossed their hunting grounds.

CHOCTAW: Hunted and held, at least for a while, parts of S.W. Ala. beyond the Tombigbee.

CREEK CONFEDERACY: The loose organization that dominated politics in Ga. and Ala. from ancient times centered on a group of tribes called Muskogee; Carolina colonists called all of these peoples Creeks because of their contacts with the body living on the present Ocmulgee R., which the Europeans called Ochese Creek; the Creeks were early divided geographically into two parts, one called Upper Creeks, on the Coosa and Tallapoosa Rivers; the other, Lower Creeks, on the lower Chattahoochee and Ocmulgee; the former were also divided at times into the Coosa branch or Abihka and the Tallapoosa branch, and the two were called Upper and Middle Creeks respectively; the dominant Muskogee gradually gathered about them and even under them the Apalachicola, Hitchiti; Okmulgee, Sawokli, Chiaha, Osochi, Yuchi, Alabama, Tawasa, Pawokti, Muklasa, Koasati, Tuskegee, a part of the Shawnee, and for some time Yamasee, not counting broken bands and families from various quarters; the first seven of these tribes were for the most part among the Lower Creeks, the rest with the Upper Creeks.

EUFAULA: A division or subtribe of the Muskogee.

FUSHATCHEE: A division of the Muskogee.

HILIBI: A division or subtribe of the Muskogee.

HITCHITI: Lived for a long time near and within Alabama along the S.E. border.

KAN-HATKI: A division of the Muskogee.

KEALEDJI: A division of the Muskogee.

KOASATI: Meaning unknown; belonged to S. Muskhogean linguistic group, and were particularly close to the Alabama; lived just below and east of the point where the Coosa and Tallapoosa join to form the Alabama, as the survival of their name in Coosada Creek and Station indicates.

KOLOMI: A division of the Muskogee.

MOBILE: Meaning unknown, but suggested as Choctaw "moeli," "to paddle," since Mobile is pronounced *moila* by the Indians; it is the Mabila, Mavilla, Mauilla, or Mauvila of the De Soto chroniclers; closely connected with the language of the Choctaw, and a trade jargon based upon Choctaw or Chickasaw was called by this name; lived on W. side of Mobile R. a few miles below the Alabama-Tombigee river junction when the French settled the seacoast of Alabama; in 16th cent., when De Soto fought them, the pop. was perhaps 6000-7000; in 1650, 2000 Mobile and Tohome; in 1702, with the Naniaba included, 100 warriors.

MULASKA: Meant in Alabama and Choctaw "friend," or "people of one nation"; related

to the Koasati Alabama, or Choctaws, rather than to Muskogees; lived on the S. bank of the Tallapoosa River in Montgomery; population in 1760, 50 men; in 1792, 30.

MUSKOGEE: Usually referred to as Creeks; a division of the Muskhogean family of languages; lived in towns from Atlantic coast of Ga. to central Ala.; in 1715, a census by S. C. government estimated all of the Creeks, exclusive of the Alabama, Yuchi, Shawnee, Apalachicola, and Yamasee, to number 6522; U.S. census of 1930, which included the Alabama and Koasati Indians of Tex. and La. among others, totaled 9083.

NAPOCHI: Belonged to S. division of Muskhogeans proper, probably closest to the Choctaw; lived along Black Warrior R.; no estimate of numbers.

NATCHEZ: One section of the Natchez Indians settled among the Abihka Creeks near Coosa R. after 1731 and went to Okla. a century later with the rest of the Creeks.

OKCHAI: A division of the Muskogee.

OKMULGEE: A Creek tribe and town of the Hitchiti connection.

OSOCHI: Supposedly spoke Muskogee, but may have been originally part of the Timucua; centered in the great bend of the Chattahoochee R., Russell Co., Alabama, near the Chiaha; population (male) in 1750, 30; in 1792, 52.

PAKANA: A division of the Muskogee.

PAWOKTI: Moved from Florida to the neighborhood of Mobile with the Alabama Indians; established town on upper course of Alabama R.; finally were absorbed into Alabama division of Creek Confederacy.

PILTHLAKO: Division of the Creeks, probably related to the Muskogee, possibly a division of the Okchai.

SAWOKLI: Possibly "raccoon people" in the Hitchiti language; belonged to Muskhogean linguistic stock and to the subdivision called Atcik-hata; lived on the Chattahoochee R. in N.E. Barbour Co., Ala.

SHAWNEE: In 1716 a band of Shawnee from Savannah R. moved to the Chattahoochee and later to the Tallapoosa, where they remained until early in the 19th cent.; a second band settled near Sylacauga in 1747 and remained there until some time before 1761, when they returned north.

TAENSA: Moved from Louisiana in 1715 and were given a location about two leagues from the French fort at Mobile, one which had been recently abandoned by the Tawasa, along a watercourse which was named from them Tensaw R.; soon after the cession of Mobile to Great Britain, the Taensa returned to Louisiana.

TOHOME: Belonged to the southern branch of the Muskhogean linguistic group, their closest relatives being the Mobile; lived about Mc Intosh's Bluff on the W. bank of the Tombigbee R., some miles above its junction with the Alabama.

TUKABAHCHEE: One of the four head tribes of the Muskogee.

TUSKEGEE: Language unknown, but it was probably affiliated with the Alabama, and hence with the southern branch of the Muskhogeans; the tribe's later and best-known location was on the point of land between the Coosa and Tallapoosa Rivers, but in 1685 part of them were on the Chattahoochee R. near modern Columbus and the rest were on the upper Tennessee near Long Island.

WAKOKAI: A division or subtribe of the Muskogee.

WIWOHKA: A division of the Muskogee made up from several different sources.

YAMASEE: Shortly after 1715 a band of Yamasee was on Mobile Bay at the mouth of the Deer R.; possibly the same band afterward appeared among the Upper Creeks, and still later moved across to the Chattahoochee R. and then to W. Florida, where in 1823 they constituted a Seminole town.

YUCHI: Shifted from the Savannah to Uchee Creek in Russell County between 1729 and 1740 and continued there until the westward migration of the Creek Nation.

Arizona

APACHE: Bands occupied Gila R. region and periodically overran much of the state.

COCOPA: Belonged to the Yuman linguistic family, a branch of the Hokan stock; lived about the mouth of the Colorado R.; population in 1776, 3000; in 1937, 41 in the U.S.

HALCHIDHOMA: Belonged to Yuman branch of the Hokan linguistic stock; lived along the Colorado R. near mouth of the Gila; population in 1770, 1000.

HALYIKWAMAI (JALLICUMAY, QUIGYUMA, TLALLIGUAMYAS, KIKIMA): Belonged to Yuman linguistic stock, with dialect close to Cocopa and Kohuana; lived along the Colorado R. near the mouth of the Gila; were probably absorbed finally by the Cocopa or another Yuman people.

HAVASUPAI: Means "blue (or green) water people," abbreviated into Supai; belong to the Yuman branch of the Hokan linguistic stock, closely connected with the Walapai, and next with the Yavapai; occupy Cataract Canyon of the Colorado R., N.W. Ariz.; population in 1680, about 300; in 1937, 208.

HOPI: From their own name Hópitu, "peaceful ones," or Hópitu-shinumu, "peaceful all people"; constitute a peculiar dialectal division of the Shoshonean branch of the Uto-Aztecan linguistic family, the only Shoshonean people who are known to have adopted a Pueblo culture, though the Tanoans may be of remote Shoshonean relationship; live on Three Mesas in N.E. Ariz.; population in 1680, 2800; in 1930 U.S. census, 2752.

KOHUANA (CAJUENCHE, CAWINA, QUO-KIM): Belonged to Yuman branch of the Hokan linguistic stock, spoke the Cocopa dialect, and were closely connected with the Halyikwamai; lived on E. bank of the Colorado R. below the mouth of the Gila, near the Halyikwamai, extending south into southern Calif., next to the eastern Diegueno; population in 1680, 3000; in 1883, 36.

MARICOPA: Belonged to Yuman linguistic stock, a part of the Hokan family, most closely related to the Yuma tribe proper and the Halchidhoma; live on the Gila R. with and below the Pima, to the mouth of the river; population in 1680, 2000; in 1937, 339.

MOHAVE (AMOJAVE, JAMAJABS): From a native word hamakhava, referring to the Needles and signifying "Three Mountains"; belonged to Yuman linguistic family; live on both sides of the Colorado R. between the Needles and Black Canyon; population in 1680, 3000; in 1937, 856.

NAVAHO: Occupied N.E. section of Arizona.

PAIUTE: The southern or true Paiute occupied or hunted over the northern sections of Ariz.

PAPAGO: Means "bean people," from papáh, "beans," and octam "people"; belong to the Piman branch of the Uto-Aztecan linguistic stock and are very close to the Pima; live S.

and S.E. of the Gila R., especially S. of Tucson; in the main and tributary valleys of the Santa Cruz R., and extending W. and S.W. across the desert waste called the Papagueria, into Sonora, Mexico; population in 1680, 6000; in 1937, 6305.

PIMA: Means "no" in Nevome dialect, and was ineptly applied by early missionaries; give their name to the Piman linguistic stock of Powell, a subdivision of the Uto-Aztecan stock, including the Nahuatlan and Shoshonean families; live in the Gila and Salt River valleys; population in 1680, 4000; in 1937, 5170.

QUAHATIKA (KOHATK): Belonged to the Piman division of the Uto-Aztecan stock, closely related to the Pima; live in the S. Ariz. desert, 50 miles south of the Gila R.

SOBAIPURI: Closely connected with, if not a part of, the Papago, of the Piman division of the Uto-Aztecan linguistic stock; lived in the main and tributary valleys of the San Pedro and Santa Cruz Rivers, between the mouth of the San Pedro and the ruins of Casa Grande, and possibly E. into S. Arizona; population in 1680, 600; now extinct.

TONTO: A name applied indiscriminately to a number of distinct groups of Apache and Yuman peoples; is said to have been used collectively of an Indian group that actually included Yavapai, Yuma, and Maricopa, with some Pinaleño Apache, and was placed on the Verde R. Reservation, Arizona, in 1875, then transferred to San Carlos Reservation the same year; also used in reference to descendants of Yavapai men and Pinaleño women.

WALAPI: From xáwalapáiy, "pine-tree folk"; belonged to Yuman branch of Hokan linguistic stock, closest to the Havasupai; lived on middle course of the Colorado R., above the Mohaves, between Sacramento Wash and National Canyon and Island, and S. almost to Bill Williams Fork; population in 1680, 700; in 1937, 454.

YAVAPAI: Belonged to Yuman branch of the Hokan linguistic family, closest to the Havasupai and Walapai; lived in W. Arizona from Pinal and Mazatsal Mts., to the Halchidhoma and Chemehuevi country around Colo., and from Williams and Santa Maria Rivers, including valleys of smaller branches, to the Gila R. population in 1680, 600-1500; in 1937, 194.

YUMA: A chief tribe of the old Yuman linguistic stock, to which they gave their name; closest to the Maricopa and Halchidhoma; the Yuman stock is now considered a part of the larger Hokan family; lived on either side of the Colorado R. above the Cocopa, about 50-60 miles from the mouth, near the junction of the Gila R., and Ft. Yuma; population in 1776, 3000-3500; in 1937, 848.

Arkansas

CADDO: Are treated under five heads: Adai and the Natchitoches Confederacy in La., Eyeish and the Hasinai Confederacy in Ark., and the Kadohadacho Confederacy in Texas; tribes of the Kodohadacho Confederacy are the only ones known to have lived in Ark.

CAHINNIO: One of the tribes connected with the Kadohadacho Confederacy.

CHEROKEE: Some lived in Arkansas while they were on their way from their old territories in Okl., and a tract of land in N.W. Ark. was granted them by treaty in 1817; they receded it to the U.S. in 1828.

CHICKASAW: Passed through Arkansas on their way to Okl., but owned no land there.

CHOCTAW: Had a village on the lower course of the Ark. R. in 1805 and owned a large strip of territory in the western part of the state, granted to them by a treaty of Doak's Stand, 1820; they surrendered the latter in a treaty concluded at Washington, 1825.

ILLINOIS: When Europeans first descended the Mississippi, an Illinois division known as Michigamea, "Big Water" was settled in N.E. Ark. about a lake known by their name, probably the present Big Lake in Mississippi County; they had probably come from the region of Ill. only a short time before, perhaps from a village entered on some old maps as "the village of the Michigamea"; toward the end of the 17th cent. they were driven north again by the Quapaw or Chicasaw and united with the cognate Kaskaskia.

KASKINAMPO: Appear to have been encountered in 1541 by De Soto in what is now the state of Ark.

MICHIGAMEA: See Ill., above.

MOSOPELEA: See Ofo.

OFO: If these are the Mosopelea, as seems assured, they appear to have lived for a short time near the end of the 17th cent. in the neighborhood of the Quapaw on the lower course of the Ark. R. before moving farther south.

OSAGE: Hunted over much of the N. and particularly N.W. part of Ark. and claimed all lands now included in the state as far south as the Ark. R.; they ceded most of their claims to the U.S. in a treaty signed at Fort Clark, La. Territory, in 1808, and the remainder by treaties in 1818 and 1825.

QUAPAW: Meaning "downstream people," they were known by some form of this word to the Omaha, Ponca, Kansa, Osage, and Creeks; of Siouan linguistic stock, lived at or near the mouth of the Ark. R.; population 2500 in 1650, 1400 in 1750, 500 in 1829, 175 in 1885, and 222 in 1930.

TUNICA: The Tunica, or some tribe speaking their language, lived in Ark. in the time of De Soto; it is not unlikely that the Pacaha or Capaha, who have often been identified with the Quapaw, were one of these; in later historic times they camped in the N.W. part of La. and probably in nearby sections of Ark.

YAZOO: Like the Tunica, this tribe probably camped at times in N.E. La. and S.E. Ark., but there is no direct evidence of the fact.

California

ACHOMAWI: From adsuma or achoma, "river"; are classed with the Hokan family; lived in valley of the Pit R. from about Montgomery Creek (Shasta Co.) to Goose Lake on the Oregon line, except Burney, Hat, and Horse or Dixie Valley Creeks.

ALLIKLIK: Belonged to Californian group of Shoshonean division of Uto-Aztec linguistic stock, closest to the Serrano; lived on upper Santa Clara R.

ATSUGEWI: With the Achomawi, constituted the Palaihnihan or eastern group of the Shastan stock, now placed in the Hokan family; lived on Burney, Hat, and Dixie Valley or Horse Creeks.

BEAR RIVER INDIANS: No name survives for this group living along Bear R. in Humboldt Co.; they belonged to the Athapascan linguistic family, closest to the Mattole,

Sinkyone, and Nongatl tribes to the S. and E.

CAHUILLA (KAWIA): Belonged to the southern Calif. group of the Shoshonean division of the Uto-Aztecan stock; lived chiefly in inland basin between the San Bernardino Range and the range extending S. from Mt. San Jacinto; population in 1770, 2500; in 1910, 800.

CHEMEHUEVI: Part of the true Paiute and associated with them and the Ute in a single linguistic subdivision of the Shoshonean division of the Uto-Aztecan linguistic stock; lived anciently in E. Mojave desert; later settled on Cottonwood Island, in Chemehuevi Valley, and at other points on the Colorado R.; population in ancient times, 500-800; in 1910, 355.

CHETCO: Penetrated slightly across Calif. border from home in Oregon.

CHILULA: Corruption of Yurok Tsulu-la, "people of Tsulu"—the Bald Hills; with the Hupa and Whilkut, formed one group of the Athapascan linguistic stock; lived on or near lower Redwood Creek from near island edge of heavy Redwood belt to a few miles above Minor Creek; population before white contact, 500-600; two or three families survive.

CHIMARIKO: From chimar, "person"; classed now in the Hokan linguistic family; lived on canyon of the Trinity R. from mouth of New R. to Canyon Creek; population in 1849, 250; a few mixed-bloods survive.

CHUMASH: Classed now with the Hokan family; occupied three northern islands of Santa Barbara group (they are called popularly Santa Barbara Indians), the coast from Malibu Canyon to Estero Bay and inland to the range dividing the drainage of the Great Valley from the coast, except to the W. where their frontier was the watershed between the Salinas and the Santa Maria and Short Coast streams, and on the E. where some small fragments had occupied part of the most southerly drainage of the San Joaquin-Kern system; population in 1770, 10,000; in 1910, 38; in 1930, 14.

COSTANOAN: From Spanish costaños, "coast people"; formed one division of the Penutian linguistic stock; lived on the coast between San Francisco Bay and Point Sur, and inland to about Mount Diablo Range; population in 1770, 7000; now extinct.

CUPEÑO: Spoke a dialect belonging to the Luiseno-Cahuilla branch of the Shoshonean division of the Uto-Aztec linguistic stock; lived in the mountains district at the headwaters of San Luis Rey R., about 10×15 miles wide; population in 1770, about 500; in 1910, 150.

DAKUBETEDE: Penetrated Calif. slightly over the southern border of Oregon.

DIEGUEÑO: From the name of the Mission of San Diego; belonged to the central division of the Yuman linguistic group; lived, in northern group, in E. part of San Diego Co., extending S. indefinitely into Mexican state of Baja Calif.; and, in southern group, in modern districts of Campo, La Posta, Manzanita, Guyapipe, and La Laguna, and whose territory in Baja Calif.; population in 1770 (with Kamia), 3000; in 1930, 322.

ESSELEN: Classed in Hokan linguistic family; lived on upper Carmel R., Sur R., and the coast from Point Lopez practically to Point Sur; population in 1770, 500; now extinct.

FERNANDO: Named from the San Fernando Mission in Los Angeles Co.; belonged to Californian section of Shoshonean division of Uto-Aztecan linguistic stock, closest to the Gabrielino; lived in the Los Angeles R.

valley above Los Angeles; population in 1770 (with the Gabrielino and Nicoleno), 5000; now virtually extinct.

GABRIELINO: From San Gabriel, one of the two Franciscan missions in Los Angeles Co.; belonged, with closely related Fernandeño, to Californian branch of the Shoshonean division of the Uto-Aztecan stock; lived in San Gabriel R. valley, around Los Angeles, and through half of Orange Co. southward, or Santa Catalina Island, and probably San Clemente; population in 1770 (with Fernandeno and Nicoleno), 5000; now virtually extinct.

HALCHIDHOMA: Lived on middle Col. (see under Ariz.).

HUCHNOM: Belonged to Yukian linguistic stock; lived in South Eel R. valley from Hullville almost to mouth, in Tomki Creek valley, and Deep or Outlet Creek; population in 1770, 500; in 1910, 7 full-bloods, and 8 half-breeds.

HUPA: Belonged to Athapascan linguistic stock, forming a tight linguistic group with the Chilula and Whilkut; lived on middle course of Trinity R. and branches, particularly through 8-mile Hupa (Hoopa) Valley, and on New R.; population in 1770, 1000; in 1937, 575.

JUANEÑO: From the Mission San Juan Capistrano; belonged to Shoshonean branch of Uto-Aztecan linguistic stock; lived from Pacific Ocean to crest of southern continuation of the Sierra Santa Ana; southward, toward the Luiseno, the boundary ran between the San Onofre and Las Pulgas; on the north, toward the Gabrielino, it is said to have followed Alisos Creek; population in 1770, 1000; in 1910, 16.

KAMIA: Belonged to Yuman stock of Powell, now classed as a subdivision of the Hokan family; lived in Imperial Valley, and on banks of sloughs connecting it with the Colorado R.

KAROK: Now classed in the Hokan linguistic family; lived on middle course of Klamath R. between the Yurok and Shasta and all of the branches of the Klamath except the upper course of Salmon R.; population in 1770, about 1500; in 1930, 755.

KATO: Means "lake" in Pomo; belonged to Athapascan linguistic stock; lived on upper course of South Fork of Eel R.; population in 1770, 500; now 50.

KAWAIISU: Belonged to Shoshonean branch of Uto-Aztecan linguistic family; lived in Tehachapi Mts.; population, anciently, about 500; in 1925, about 150.

KITANEMUK: Belonged to Shoshonean division of Uto-Aztecan linguistic stock, and to a subgroup which included Alliklik, Vanyume, and Serrano; lived on upper Tejon and. Paso Creeks, streams on rear sides of the Tehachapi Mts. in the same vicinity, and the small creeks draining the N. slope of the Liebre and Sawmill Range, with Antelope Valley and the westernmost end of the Mohave desert; population in 1770, 3500 (Serrano, Vanyume, Kitanemuk, and Alliklik); in 1910, 150.

KONOMIHU: Most eccentric of the Shastan group of tribes of the Hokan linguistic family; lived in lands around forks of the Salmon R.

KOSO: Formed westernmost extension of Shoshone-Comanche branch of Shoshonean division of Uto-Aztecan linguistic stock; lived on barren land in S.E. between the Sierra and the Nev. state line, including Owens Lake, the Coso, Argus, Panamint, and Funeral Mts., and the intervening valleys; population, anciently, about 500; today, 100-500.

LASSIK: From name of a chief; belonged to Athapascan linguistic family, closest to southern neighbors, the Nongatl; lived on stretch of the Eel R., from above mouth of South Fork almost to Kekawaka Creek; also on Dobbins Creek, and Soldier Basin at the head of Mad R.; population in 1770 (with the Nongatl and Sinkyone), 2000; in 1910, 100.

LUISEÑO: From name of Mission San Luis Rey de Francia; belonged to Shoshonean division of Uto-Aztecan linguistic family; lived in S. part of the state from the coast toward, but to the W. of, the divide extending S. from Mount San Jacinto; bounded N. by cognate Juaneño, Gabrielino, and Serrano, and S. by the Diegueño; population in 1770, not more than 4000; today, less than 500.

MAIDU: Means "person"; classed in the Penutian linguistic family; lived in drainage areas of the Feather and American rivers; population in 1770, about 9000; in 1930, 93.

MATTOLE: One of the primary division of Indians of Athapascan stock living in Calif.; lived on Bear R. and Mattole R. drainages; also on a few miles along Eel R. and its Van Dusen Fork just above Wiyot; population in 1770, 500; in 1910, 34 (of whom 10 were fullbloods).

MIWOK: Means "people"; classed as subdivision of Penutian linguistic family; lived (1) mainly on W. slope of Sierra Madre between Fresno and Consumnes rivers where the valley is cut by the deltas of the San Joaquin and Sacramento; (2) on the coast, from Golden Gate N. to Duncan's Point and E. to Sonoma Creek; and (3) near Lake Miwok in the basin of Clear Lake, the S. bank of Cache Creek, the lake outlet, and a short distance beyond; population in 1770, 11,000; in 1930, 491.

MODOC: Penetrated N. border of Calif. from Oregon.

MOHAVE: Held some territory near Col. R.

NICOLEÑO: From San Nicolas, easternmost of Santa Barbara Islands; belonged to Shoshonean division of Uto-Aztecan linguistic stock; lived on San Nicolas Island.

NONGATL: Belonged to Athapascan linguistic family, closest to Lassik; lived in land drained by three right-hand affluents of Eel R.—Yager Creek, Van Dusen Fork, and Larrabee Creek—and on upper Mad R.; population in 1770 (with Sinkyone and Lassik), 2000; in 1910, 100.

OKWANUCHU: Belonged to Shastan division of Hokan linguistic stock; lived on upper Sacramento from about Salt and Boulder Creeks to headwaters; and on McCloud R. and Squaw Creek above their junction.

PAIUTE, NORTHERN (PAVIOTSO): Held part of the Sierra in S.E. Calif., desert country to the east, and an extreme N.E. strip of land.

PANAMINT: Shoshonean tribe of southern Calif.

PATWIN: Means "person"; the southernmost and most diverse dialectic division of the former Wintun (Copehan) linguistic family, now classed as Penutian stock; lived in W. Sacramento Valley, from San Francisco Bay to just below Willows, on both sides of the Sacramento R. to N. boundaries of their own territory.

POMO: Classed with Hokan family; lived on Pacific coast between Cleone and Duncan's Point, and inland, with a few breaks, to Clear Lake; a detached group lived on Stony Creek; population in 1770, 8000; in 1930, 1143.

SALINAN: From the Salinas R.; classed with Hokan family; lived from about headwaters of the Salinas (or perhaps only from Santa

Margarita Divide) N. to Santa Lucia Peak and an undiscovered point in the valley S. of Soledad; and from the sea probably to the main crest of the coast range; population in 1770, 2000-3000; now extinct.

SERRANO: From Spanish "mountaineers"; belonged to Shoshonean division of Uto-Aztecan linguistic stock; lived in San Bernardino Range; somewhere to the north; the San Gabriel Mts. or Sierra Madre W. to Mt. San Antonio; and probably a tract of fertile lowland S. of the Sierra Madre, from about Cucamonga E. to above Mentone and as far as San Gorgonio Pass; population, anciently, 1500; in 1910, 118.

SHASTA: Part of Shastan division of Hokan linguistic stock; lived on Klamath R. between Indian and Thompson Creeks to just above Fall Creek; also in the drainage areas of two tributaries of the Klamath-Scott R. and Shasta R.—and a tract on the N. side of the Siskiyous in Ore. on the affluents of Rogue R. known as Stewart R. and Little Butte Creek; population in 1770, 2000; in 1910, 100.

SINKYONE: A tribe of the southern Californian group of Athapascan family; lived on South Fork of Eel R. and its branches and the nearby coast from near Four Mile Creek to Usal Lagoon.

TOLOWA: One of the divisions into which the Calif. peoples of the Athapascan linguistic stock are divided. but closely connected with the Athapascan tribes of Ore. immediately to the north; lived on Crescent Bay, Lake Earl, and Smith R.; population in 1770, 450-1000; in 1910, 121.

TUBATULABAL: From Shoshone "pine-nut eaters"; as Kern River Shoshoneans, given a position as a major division of the Shoshonean branch of the Uto-Aztecan linguistic family; lived in upper Kern River Valley; population in 1770, estimated at 1000; in 1910, 105.

VANYUME: Belonged to Shoshonean division of Uto-Aztecan linguistic stock; lived on Mohave R.; now extinct.

WAILAKI: Means "north language"; belonged to Athapascan linguistic stock and to southern Calif. group; lived on Eel R. from Lassik territory to Big Bend, several W. side streams, and Kekawaka Creek on E. side; and all of North Fork except the head; population in 1770, 1000; in 1910, 227.

WAPPO: Corruption of Spanish *guapo* "brave"; a very eccentric form of speech of the Yukian linguistic family; lived on headwaters of Napa R. and Pope and Putah Creeks, and a stretch of Russian R.; population in 1770, 1000; in 1910, 73.

WASHO: Ranged over land near angle in E. border of Calif.

WHILKUT: From Hupa Hoilkut-hoi; belonged to Hupa dialectic group of Athapascan linguistic family; lived on upper part of Redwood Creek above Chilula Indians and Mad R. except in lowest course, up to Iaqua Butte; population, anciently, 500; in 1910, 50 full-bloods.

WINTU: Means "people"; classed as part of Penutian family; lived in upper Sacramento valleys and upper Trinity R. north of Cottonwood Creek, from Cow Creek on E., to South Fork of the Trinity on the W.

WINTUN: Means "people"; classed in Penutian family; lived on W. side Sacramento Valley from river to coast range, and from Cottonwood Creek on N. to about latitude of Afton and Stonyford on S.; population in 1770, 12,000; in 1910, 1000.

WIYOT: Properly the name of one of the three Wyot (Wiyot) districts but extended by most

of their neighbors over the whole people; not definitely assigned to a family and considered variously an independent Wishoskan stock, or, combined with the Yurok as the Tirwan; or, related to the great Algonquian family of the East; lived on lower Mad R., Humboldt R., and lower Eel R.; population .in 1770, 1000; in 1910, 100.

YAHI: Means "person"; constituted southernmost group of Yahan division of Hokan linguistic stock; lived on Mill and Deer Creeks.

YANA: Means "person"; classed with larger Hokan family; with the Yani, extended from Pit R. to Rock Creek, and from edge of upper Sacramento Valley to headwaters of E. tributaries of the Sacramento R.; population in 1770 (including Yahi), 1500; in 1930, 9.

YOKUTS: Means "person"; classed as a part of Penutian stock; lived on whole floor of San Joaquin Valley from mouth of San Joaquin R. to foot of Tehachapi, and the nearby lower slopes or foothills of the Sierra Nevada, up to a few thousand feet, from Fresno R. S.; population in 1770, 18,000; in 1930, 1145.

YUKI: Means "stranger" or "foe"; constituted an independent stock called Yukian; lived in all the land lying in the drainage of Eel R. above North Fork, except for a stretch on South Eel R. where their allies, the Huchnom, were located; population in 1770, 2000; in 1930 (with coast Yuki and Huchnom), 177.

YUKI, COAST (UKHOTNO'M): Ukhotno'm, or "ocean people," is the name by which the Coast Yuki are known to the Yuki of the interior, with whom they are linked more closely than with the Huchnom; they lived along the Pacific Coast from Cleone to midway between Rockport and Usal and inland to the divide between the coast streams and Eel R.; population in 1770, 500; in 1910, 5.

YUMA: Extended into extreme S.E. corner of the state from Ariz.

YUROK: Means "downstream"; without definite status, and regarded variously as an independent stock, combined with the Wiyot into the Ritwan family, or as a part of the great Algonquian family of the E.; lived on lower Klamath R. and along the coast N. and S.; population in 1770, 2500; in 1930, 471.

Colorado

APACHE: Bands raided in Col. from time to time, but only the Jicarilla were occupants (see below).

ARAPAHO: Ranged over E. Col.

BANNOCK: Roamed N.W. Col. with the Shoshone.

CHEYENNE: Ranged E. Col.

COMANCHE: Ranged E. Col.

JICARILLA: From Spanish, meaning "little basket" after the basket-weaving skill of the women; one of the so-called Apache tribes, of the Athapascan linguistic stock, but constituting, with the Lipan, a group distinct from the Apache proper; lived in S.E. Col. and N. N. M., but have ranged into nearby Kan., Okl., and Tex.; population in 1845, 800; in 1937, 714.

KIOWA: Ranged E. Col.

KIOWA APACHE: Always hunted and warred with the Kiowa.

NAVAHO: Lived just S. of Col. border, occasionally crossing over.

PUEBLOS: The ancestors of the Pueblos must have lived where the pueblo and cliff ruins of Col. are today.

SHOSHONE: Ranged N.W. Col.
UTE: Formerly occupied all of Central and W. Col.

Connecticut

MAHICAN: N.W. Litchfield Co. was occupied by the Wawyachtonoc, a tribe of the Mahican Confederacy of the upper Hudson, though their main seats were in Columbia and Dutchess counties, N. Y.

MOHEGAN: From an Indian word meaning "wolf"; they were probably a branch of the Mahican, and are said to have invaded Conn. from the W. (N.Y.), at about the same time as the Pequot; belonged to Algonquian linguistic family; originally they occupied most of the upper valley of the Thames and its branches, and later claimed some of the territory of the Nipmuc, Connecticut R. tribes, and (formerly) Pequot. Population in 1600, 2200; in 1705, 750; in 1804, 84; in 1910, 22.

NIANTIC, WESTERN: On seacoast from Niantic Bay to Conn. R.; pop. in 1600, 600; in 1761, 85.

NIPMUC: Some bands extended into N.W. Conn.

PEQUOT: "Destroyers"; occupied coast of New London Co. from Niantic R. nearly to R.I. state line; until driven out by the Narraganset, they extended into R.I. as far as Wecapaug R. pop. in 1600, 2200; in 1674, 1500; in 1762, 140; in 1910, 66.

WAPPINGER: Valley of Conn. R. was home of a number of bands that might be called Mattabesec after the name of the most important; all were a part of the Wappinger.

Delaware

DELAWARE: The Unalachtigo division of the Delaware occupied all the northern parts of this state when it was first visited by Europeans.

NANTICOKE: Bodies of Indians classed under this general head extended into the southern and western sections. Unalachtigo and Nanticoke are two forms of the same word, though, as differentiated, they have been applied to distinct tribes.

Florida

ACUERA: Belonged to Timucuan or Timuquanan linguistic division of Muskhogean linguistic family; lived about headwaters of Ocklawaha R.

AGUACALEYQUEN: See Utina.

AIS: Believed to have spoken language similar to that of the Calusa, and to have been connected with Muskhogean stock; lived along Indian R. on E. coast of peninsula; in 1650, largest part of 1000 in group of tribes listed as Tekesta, Guacata, and Jaega; in 1728, 52 were reported.

ALABAMA: Bands lived near Apalachicola R. early in 18th cent., until driven out in 1708; part returned for short time after Creek-American War.

AMACANO: Tribe or band connected with Yamasee, placed with Chine and Caparaz in mission on Apalachee coast in 1674; pop., all together, 300.

AMACAPIRAS: See Macapiras.

APALACHE: Means perhaps "people on the other side," or "helper"; belonged to Muskhogean linguistic stock; lived near Tallahassee; pop. in 1650, 7000; in 1715, 1000; in 1758. 100; in 1832, 50.

APALACHICOLA: Lived at times below boundary line of state, and gave their name to river that cuts the panhandle of Fla.

CALUSA: Probably belonged to Muskhogean stock; lived on W. coast southward of Tampa Bay, including Florida Keys; Indians about Lake Okeechobee, though distinct, seem also to have been Calusas; pop. in 1650, 3000.

CAPARAZ: Small band, with Amacano and Chine bands, in mission on Apalachee coast in 1674; possibly survivors of Capachequi mentioned by De Soto; pop., 300.

CHATOT: Belonged to southern division of Muskhogean stock; lived west of Apalachicola R., perhaps near middle course of the Chipola; pop. in 1674, 1200-1500; in 1725-26, 140.

CHIANA: A tribe of Creeks of whom a few came to Fla. before the Creek-American War; are said to have occupied "Beech Creek" on Suwannee R. in 1817, which may have been Fulemmy's Town or Pinder Town.

CHILUCAN: In 1776 in list of Indians in Fla. missions; possibly connected with Timucuans.

CHINE: Small band in San Luis doctrina on Apalachee coast in 1674; may have moved later into Apalachee country and been listed in 1680 as the mission San Pedro de los Chines. See Caparaz.

CREEKS: See Alabama, Chiana, Hitchiti, Mikasukee, Muskogee, Oconee, Sawokli, Tawasa and Yuchi.

FRESH WATER INDIANS: Also called the "Agua Dulce" Indians, these people lived in 7-9 neighboring towns; native equivalent of their name is not known; belonged, like the Acuera, to the Timucuan linguistic division of the Muskhogean linguistic family; lived in coast district of E. Fla. between St. Augustine and Cape Canaveral.

GUACATA: Classified with S. Fla. peoples; lived around St. Lucie R. in St. Lucie and Palm Beach counties.

GUALE: In late times many were driven from their Georgian country into Fla.

HITCHITI: Large numbers of Hitchiti-speaking peoples crossed into Fla. after destruction of earlier tribes of the Peninsula, so that up to Creek-American War, Hitchiti was spoken by most Seminoles; true Hitchiti seem not to have been very active in this early movement, but they later established the settlements of Attapulgas (or Atap-halgi) and perhaps other of the so-called Fowl Towns.

ICUFUI: Probably of the Timucuan group; lived on mainland and possibly in S.E. Ga.; near border between the Timucua and the strictly Muskhogean populations.

JEAGA: Classified with tribes of S. Fla., and perhaps of Muskhogean division proper; lived on Jupiter Inlet, on E. coast.

KOASATI: Band appears from 1823 map to have joined the Seminole in Fla. and established settlement in "Coosada Old Town" on middle course of Choctawhatchee R.

MACAPIRAS (AMACAPIRAS): Small tribe (24) brought with some Pohoy to St. Augustine missions in 1726, apparently from S.W. coast.

MIKASUKI: Belonged to the Hitchiti-speaking branch of the Muskhogean linguistic family; their earliest known home was about Miccocukee Lake in Jefferson Co.

MOCOCO (MUCOCO): Belonged most probably to the Timucuan division of the Muskhogean linguistic stock; lived about the head of Hillsboro Bay.

MUKLASA: A small Creek town whose inhabitants were probably related by speech to the Alabama and Koasati, said to have gone to Fla. after the Creek War.

MUSKOGEE: The first true Creeks or Muskogee to enter Fla. were probably a band of Eufaula Indians who made a settlement (1761) some distance above Tampa Bay; but the great Muskogee immigration came after the Creek-American War; they came from many towns, but especially from those on the Tallapoosa R., and gave the final tone and characteristic language to the Fla. emigrants who had previously been mainly of Hitchiti connection; therefore the so-called Seminole language is Mushkogee, with possibly a few minor changes in the vocabulary.

OCALE (ETOCALE): Lived in Marion County or Levy County N. or the bend of the Withlacoochee R.

OCITA: See Pohoy.

OCONEE: Left Chattahoochee about 1750, moved into Fla., and established themselves on the Alachua Plain, constituting the first large band of N. Indians to settle in Fla.; their chiefs came to be recognized as head chiefs of the Seminole.

ONATHEAQUA: Appear in the chronicles of Laudonnière and Le Moyne as one of the two main Timucua tribes in N.W. Fla., the other being the Hostaqua or Yustaga.

OSOCHI: A Creek division thought to have originated in Fla.

PAWOKTI: Probably affiliated either with the Tawasa or the Ala., and therefore speaking a Muskhogean dialect (using Muskhogean in the extended sense); earliest records place them W. of Choctawwhatchee R., near the Gulf of Mexico.

PENSACOLA: Means "Hair people"; belonged to the Muskhogean stock and spoke a dialect close to Choctaw; lived around Pensacola Bay; population in 1725, 40 men.

POHOY (POOY, POSOY): Evidently were closely affiliated with the Timucuan division of the Muskhogean linguistic stock; lived on S. shore of Tampa Bay; population in 1680, 300.

POTANO: Lived in Alachua County; see Utina; population in 1650, 3000.

SATURIWA: Lived about mouth of St. John's R., and perhaps on Cumberland I.; see Utina.

SAWOKLI: Were a division of Creek Indians belonging to the Hitchiti-speaking group, and all seem to have once lived in Fla., before moving up around the Lower Creeks (in Ala.).

SEMINOLE: Means "one who has camped out from the regular towns"; just before the last Seminole War, the Seminole removed from the Creek Towns where they constituted a fair representation of the population (perhaps two-thirds were Creek proper or Muskogee, and the remaining third Indians of the Hitchiti-speaking towns, Alabama, Yamasee, and a band of Yuchi); population, before Creek-American War, about 2000; after, about 5000; in 1930, 2048.

SURRUQUE: Probably of the Timucuan linguistic group; lived around Cape Canaveral.

TECATACURU: Lived on Cumberland Island; see Utina.

TAWASA: Spoke a dialect belonging to the Timucuan division of the Muskhogean linguistic family; lived, in 1706-07, about the latitude of the Chattahoochee-Flint R. junction in W. Fla.

TEKESTA (TEQUESTA): May have spoke Muskhogean; lived around Miami.

TIMUCUA: See Utina.

TOCOBAGA: Lived about Old Tampa Bay; see Utina.

UCITA: See Pohoy.

UTINA (TIMUCUA): The Timucuan subdivision of the Muskhogean linguistic stock; lived from the Suwannee to the St. Johns, and eastward of the latter (some subdivisions should be rated as independent tribes; see Georgia); population in 1650, 13,000 (including 3000 Potano, 1000 Hostaqua, 8000 Timucua proper and their allies, and 1000 Tocobaga); shortly after 1836, 0.

YAMASEE: Some tribes affiliated with the Yamasee settled in the Apalachee country in the latter part of the 17th cent.

YUCHI: A body settled W. of the Apalachicola R. in 17th cent., later moving N. to join the Creeks (before 1761); later, some E. Yuchi joined the Seminole and in 1823 had a settlement called Tallahassee or Spring Gardens 10 miles from Volusia, and probably moved to Oklahoma at the end of the last Seminole War.

YUFERI: The name of a town or group of towns from somewhere near Cumberland Island, and perhaps in Ga.

YUI: Lived on the mainland 14 leagues inland from Cumberland Island, and probably in S.E. Ga.; population in 1602, more than 1000.

YUSTAGA: Probably belonged to the Timucuan branch of the Muskhogean linguistic stock; lived between Aucilla and Suwannee Rivers, toward the coast; population in 1928, 1000.

Georgia

APALACHEE: After 1704, fleeing from the English and Creeks, established village just below Augusta; moved back to Fla. after 1715.

APALACHICOLA: Means "people of the other side"; belonged to Muskhogean linguistic family; lived along Apalachicola R., and by source at junction of Chattahoochee and Flint Rivers; pop. in 1715, 214; in 1832, 239.

CHATOT: Lived at times in S.W. part of state.

CHEROKEE: From early times in N. and N.E. parts of state, probably after Creeks occupied same area.

CHIAHA: Belonged to Muskhogean linguistic stock; in early times, one band lived on Burns Island in Tenn., one in E. Ga. near coast; later they lived on middle course of Chattahoochee R.

CHICKASAW: A band lived near Augusta from 1723-76; then moved among Lower Creeks.

CREEKS: In 16th century, probably large part of tribes later forming Creek Confederacy lived on Ga. coast; after 1650, most were on Chattahoochee and Ocmulgee rivers, and later were called Lower Creeks; after Yamasee War in 1715, lived on Ga. and Ala. sides of Chattahoochee until migration to Oklahoma in 19th cent.

GUALE: Belonged most probably to Muskhogean family; lived on Ga. coast between St. Andrew's Sound and Savannah R.

HITCHITI: Belonged to Muskhogean linguistic family; lived earlier on lower course of Ocmulgee R., later in Chattahoochee County; pop. in 1832, 381.

KASIHTA: One of most important divisions of the Muskogee, possibly the Cofitachequi of the De Soto narratives.

OCONEE: Belonged to Muskhogean linguistic stock; lived just below Rock Landing on Oconee R., Ga. (see also Fla.). Pop. in 1675, 200.

OKMULGEE: Means "where water boils up"; belonged to Muskhogean linguistic stock; lived in great bend of Chattahoochee R., Russell Co., Ala.; earlier near Macon; pop. in 1822, 220.

OSOCHI: Part of Lower Creeks living for time in S.W. Georgia.

SAWOKLI: Part of Creeks in Hitchiti-speaking group of towns along the S.E. Alabama border.

SHAWNEE: A Shawnee band from the Cumberland settled on Savannah R. around 1680 and drove off the Westo Indians who had been harrassing the new colony of S. Carolina; stayed long enough in the neighborhood of Augusta to give their name to the Savannah R., but between 1707-1731 completed migration to Pennsylvania (see S. Carolina, Tennessee).

TAMATHLI: Possibly means "flying creatures," i.e. birds; belonged to Atsik-hata group in Creek Condefederacy; lived in S.W. Ga. and nearby Fla.; pop. in 1822, 220.

TIMUCUA: Evidently occupied Cumberland Island and part of adjacent mainland, as well as N. and cent. Florida.

YAMASEE: Spoke a Muskhogean dialect; lived on Ocmulgee R., not far above juncture with Oconee, and ranged inland; pop. in 1715, 1215.

YUCHI: Constituted a linguistic stock, the Uchean, distinct from all others, though structurally similar to language of Muskhogean and Siouan families; located early in E. Tenn., east beyond Manchester, west to Muscle Shoals; a main center is thought to have been on Hiwassee R., with settlements N. to Green R., Ky.; later, part settled in N. Fla., near Eucheanna, and another part on Savannah and Ogeechee rivers; population may have been more than 5000 in 1525; in 1930 census, 216.

YUFERA: Reported on Cumberland Island and inland into Ga. (See Fla.).

Idaho

BANNOCK: From their own name Banakwut; belonged to Shoshonean branch of the Uto-Aztecan linguistic stock, a detached branch of Northern Paiute; lived in historic times in S.E. Idaho, ranging into W. Wy., between lat. 40° N. and 45° N., and from long. 113° W. east to the main chain of the Rockies; spread at times down Snake R., and some as far north as the Salmon R., and even into S. Montana; population in 1829 (probably including Shoshone) 8000; in 1937, 342.

KALISPEL: Belonged to the interior division of the Salishan family; lived on Pend Oreille R. and Lake, Priest Lake, and the lower course of Clark's Fork; population in 1780, 1200; in 1937, 97.

KUTENAI: Occupied extreme northern part of Ida.

NEZ PERCE: Means, in French, "pierced nose"; a tribe of the Shahaptian division of the Shapwailutan linguistic stock, to which they gave the name commonly applied to them by Salish tribes; occupied large part of central Ida., and parts of S.E. Washington and N.E. Ore.; population in 1780, 4000; in 1930, 4119.

PAIUTE, NORTHERN: Entered S.W. Idaho at times.

PALOUSE: Extended up the Palouse R. into Idaho.

SALISH, OR FLATHEAD: Visited Idaho to some extent.

SHOSHONE, NORTHERN: Belonged to the Shoshone-Comanche dialectic group of the Shoshonean division of the Uto-Aztecan lin-

guistic family; lived in E. Ida., except territory held by Bannock; W. Wyo.; and N.E. Ut.; population in 1845 (with Western Shoshone) 4500; in 1937, 1201.

SKITSWISH: Belonged to the inland division of the Salishan stock, closest to the Kalispel or Pend d'Oreilles; lived on the headwaters of the Spokane R., a little above Spokane Falls to sources; including Coeur d'Alene Lake and all its tributaries, and the head of the Clearwater; population in 1780, 1000-4000; in 1937, 608.

SPOKAN: Extended a few miles into Idaho. along the western border.

Illinois

CHIPPEWA: Tribal representatives were parties to the treaties made in 1795, 1816, 1829, and 1833 giving Illinois lands to the whites.

DELAWARE: Passed across Illinois while being slowly crowded W. by the whites.

FOXES: Together with the Sauk, drove the Illinois Indians from the N.W. part of the state in the latter half on the 18th cent. and took their places, but ceded the territory to the U.S. in 1804.

ILLINOIS: A native word signifying "men," "people"; belonged to the Algonquian stock and were more closely connected with the Chippewa than with any other Algonquian tribe except the Miami; in historic times lived principally along the Ill. and Miss. rivers, one division, the Michigamea, being as far south as N.E. Ark.; population 8,000 in 1650, 1500-2000 in 1750; and 150 in 1800.

KICKAPOO: After helping to destroy the Illinois settled on Vermillion R. and extended territories to the Ill. R.; ceded this land to the U.S. in 1819.

MIAMI: In early times had a town on the site of Chicago; later their territorial claims covered parts of the eastern sections of the state.

OTTAWA: Worked down to the northernmost part of the state in the 18th cent.

POTAWATOMI: Succeeded the Miami in the region of Chicago, and, after the destruction of the Illinois, occupied still more territory in the N.E. part of the state.

SAUK: Assisted their relatives the Foxes in expelling the Illinois from the Black Rock region, and both occupied this land until it was ceded to the whites; they then moved farther west.

SHAWNEE: Lived for a while in southern Ill.

WINNEBAGO: Tribal representatives were parties to an Ill. land cession in 1829.

WYANDOT: Representatives were parties to the Treaty of Greenville, 1795.

Indiana

CHIPPEWA: Tribal representatives appear as parties to the Treaty of Greenville and others made in 1817 and 1821 by which lands in Ind. were ceded to the whites.

DELAWARE: Most of whom were then living in Ohio, received permission about 1770 from the Miami and Piankashaw to occupy that land in Ind. between the Ohio and White rivers, where at one time they had six villages; in time, all moved to Miss., Kan., and Okla.

ERIE: Tribal territory may once have extended into the N.E. part of the state.

ILLINOIS: Tribal representatives were parties to the Treaty of Greenville, 1795.

IROQUOIS: Particularly the westernmost Iroquoian tribe, the Seneca, drove the earlier Indian occupants out of Ind., yet they themselves seem to have had few settlements in the state.

KICKAPOO: Undoubtedly occupied some of W. Indiana for brief periods.

MIAMI: Their name is thought to be derived from the Chippewa word *omaumeg*, signifying "people on the peninsula," but according to their own traditions, it came from the word for pigeon; the name used by themselves, as recorded and often used by early writers, is Twightwees, derived from the cry of a crane; belonged to Algonquian linguistic stock; first known near Green Bay, Wis., and moved gradually S. and E. to the Miami R. and perhaps as far as the Scioto; after the peace of 1763 they abandoned their eastern territories and retired to Indiana; took part in all subsequent wars in this section but began to dispose of their lands after the War of 1812, and had parted with most of them by 1838, the U.S. agreeing to give them new lands W. of Mississippi; of the six Miami bands, two, the Piankashaw and Wea, are considered as tribes.

MOSOPELEA: Territory probably extended into the extreme S.E. part of Indiana, before the tribe left its land N. of the Ohio.

NEUTRALS: Territory may have extended slightly into the N.E. part of the state.

OTTAWA: Tribal representatives appear as parties to the Treaty of Greenville, 1795, and to others in 1817 and 1821 by which Ind. lands were ceded to the U.S.

POTAWATOMI: Pushed into the N. part of the state during the 18th cent. and were in occupancy until they ceded their lands to the U.S. in the first half of the 19th cent.

SENECA: See Iroquois.

SHAWNEE: Had an ancient town in Posey County at the junction of the Wabash and Ohio; later had settlements along the S. and E. borders, and the soil of Ind. was the scene of the activities of the Shawnee Prophet and his brother Tecumseh until after Gen. Harrison's victory at Tippecanoe.

WYANDOT: Tribal representatives were parties to the Treaty of Greenville, 1795.

Iowa

CHIPPEWA: Ceded lands in Ia. in 1846.

DAKOTA: Moved in behind the Iowa until forced to retreat from the Sauk and Fox about the time of the Black Hawk War.

FOXES: In 1804-32 completed total migration of the tribe to Ia.; in 1842 they moved to Kansas, but returned in full force by 1859 and bought land near Tama City where they still live.

ILLINOIS: The confederacy of Algonquian tribes known as the Illinois included the Cahokia, Kaskaskia, Michigamia, Moingwena, Peoria, and Tamaroa; its center was in Ill. and nearby Ia. and Wis.; Franquelin (1688) placed the Peoria on the upper Ia. R., but, according to Marquette (1673), they were near the mouth of the Des Moines with the Moingwena (from whom the name Des Moines is derived) when he went down the Miss. R., and near Peoria, Ill. when he came back up again.

IOWA: Belonged to the Siouan linguistic stock of the Chiwere subdivision, with the Oto and Missouri; lived generally within the state of. Indiana; population in 1760, 1100; Lewis and Clark counted 800 in 1804; the census of 1930 returned a total of 154.

MISSOURI: Are connected with the Ia. in origin and history.

MOINEWENA: See Illinois, above.

OMAHA: Roamed W. Ia. before moving into Neb.

OTO: See Iowa, above.

OTTAWA: Were in the party that ceded Iowa to whites in 1846.

PEORIA: See Illinois, above.

PONCA: Were with the Omaha in W. Iowa.

POTAWATOMI: Settled in W. Ia. before moving to Kan.

SAUK: Moved into Ia. after the Black Hawk War (1832), and went on to Kan. in 1842.

WINNEBAGO: Moved to the Neutral Ground in Ia. granted to them by treaty of September 15, 1832, but left for Minn. in 1848.

Kansas

APACHE: See Jicarilla.

ARAPAHO: Ranged over much of W. Kan. at one time.

CHEROKEE: By the treaty of New Echota, the Cherokee obtained title to lands in S.E. Kansas, in the "neutral land," and along the southern border, but they were receded to the U.S. government in 1866.

CHEYENNE: Ranged western Kan. at one time.

CHIPPEWA: In 1839 the Swan Creek and Black R. bands of Michigan Chippewa arrived at lands on the Osage R., Kan., which they had by grant from 1836; in 1866 they moved to Cherokee country in Okla. and merged with the host tribe.

COMANCHE: Ranged western Kan.

DELAWARE: Were given land in N.E. Kan. in 1829 which they surrendered by treaties in 1854, 1860, and 1866, agreeing, in 1867, to live with the Cherokees in Okl.; some of the land had been given to a body of Munsee ("Christian Indians"), who sold it in 1857 and went, for the most part, to live with the Cherokee in Okl.

FOXES: Lived briefly on an eastern Kan. reservation, but returned to Ia. in about 1859.

ILLINOIS: Were assigned a reservation near Paola in 1832, but transferred to N.E. Oklahoma in 1867.

IOWA: Were assigned a reservation in N.E. Kan. in 1836, where some have remained.

IROQUOIS: Were, with some Munsee, Macican, and S. New England Indians, assigned a reservation in Kan. in 1838, but few accepted and the lands were later forfeited.

JICARILLA: From their homes in Colorado and New Mexico, ranged through Texas, Oklahoma, and Kansas; one of the "Apache" tribes.

KANSA: Derives from the name of a major subdivision of the tribe; belonged, with the Osage, Quapaw, Omaha, and Ponca, to the Dhegiha subdivision of the Siouan linguistic stock; lived in general along the Kan. R.; population in 1780, 3000; in 1937, 515.

KICKAPOO: Were assigned a reservation in Kansas in 1832.

KIOWA: Means "principal people"; were connected with the Tanoan stock and probably also with the Shoshonean; lived in an area which covered parts of Okla., Kan., Col., N. Mex., and Tex.; population in 1780, 2000; in 1937, 2263.

KIOWA APACHE: Name derived from the Kiowa and from similarity of their dialect to better-known Apache dialects, though the tribes were unrelated; belonged to the Athapascan linguistic family, closest to the Jacarilla and Lipan (Hoijer); lived with and near the Kiowa from time of earliest records; population in 1780, 300; in 1937, 340.

MIAMI: The Piankashaw and Wea subdivisions of the Miami were assigned lands in Eikan with the Illinois in 1832, and were joined in 1840 by the rest of the Miami; in 1867 they went with the Illinois to Okla.

POTAWATOMI: In 1840 the Potawatomi of the Woods moved to the Osage R. lands S.W. of the Missouri which the U.S. government granted them in 1837; the lands were receded in 1846 in exchange for a reserve between the Shawnee and Delaware (Shawnee Co.); they were joined in 1847-48 by the Prairie Potawatomi who had moved down progressively from Wisc. and from the reservation assigned to them in S.W. Ia. by the Treaty of Chicago (1833), and by the Mich. Potawatomi (c. 1850); by 1871 the Potawatomi of the Woods had removed to new lands in Okla.

QUAPAW: Ceded (1867) their reserve in Indian Territory, including the S.E. tip of Kansas, which they had held from 1833.

SAUK: With the Fox, occupied a reserve in E. Kan., but moved to Okla. in 1867.

MISSOURI: Were with the Oto when they lived in Kan.

MUNSEE: Owned land in Kan. 1854-59.

OSAGE: Ceded lands in S.E. Kan. in 1825, 1865, and 1870.

OTO: Lived on the E. Kan. border several times in their later history.

OTTAWA: Signed treaties in 1867 and 1872 about the disposition of lands on Marais des Cygnes or Osage R., which two bands of them had been granted in 1831; Ottawa bands lived (1832-65) at Blanchard's Fork and Roche de Boeuf before removing to Oklahoma.

PAWNEE: Occupied the valley of the Republican Fork of the Kan. R.

SHAWNEE: Lived (1825-54) on a reserve along the S. bank of the Kansas R., W. of the Mo. border, which was receded to the U.S. government when the Shawnee removed to Okla.

WYANDOT: Bought Miss. R. Delaware lands in E. Kan. in 1843 and held them until 1850; others owned Okla. border lands which they receded in 1867.

Kentucky

CHEROKEE: Claimed some land in S.E. Ky. and traces of their type of culture and said to be found in archeological remains along the upper course of the Cumberland, but no permanent Cherokee settlement is known to have existed in historic times within the state.

CHICKASAW: Claimed the westernmost end of Ky., and at a very early period they had a settlement on the lower course of the Tenn. R., either in Ky. or Tenn.

MOSOPELEA: May have lived within the boundaries of Kentucky for a brief time, perhaps at the mouth of the Cumberland R. when they were on their way from Ohio to the lower Mississippi.

SHAWNEE: Had more to do with Ky. in early times than any other tribe, but maintained few villages in the state for a long period; their more permanent settlement were farther S. about Nashville; the tribe crossed and recrossed the state several times in its history and used it still more frequently as a hunting ground.

YUCHI: According to some early maps, had a town in Ky. on the present Green R.

Louisiana

ACOLPISSA: "Those who listen and see," indicating possibly "borderers" or "scouts"; belonged to the Muskhogean linguistic family and evidently spoke a language closely related to Choctaw and Chickasaw; closest relatives were the Tangipakoa; earliest known location was on the Pearl R. about eleven miles above its mouth; population 300 warriors in 1699, 200 in 1722.

ADAI: Of Caddoan stock; lived near the present Robeline in Natchitoches Parish; population 400 in 1698, 27 in 1825.

ALABAMA: Some of this tribe moved to La. shortly after the territory E. of the Miss. was abandoned by the French; most of them finally passed on to Tex., but a few are still settled in the S.W. part of the state.

APALACHEE: A band of Apalachee moved from the neighborhood of Mobile to La. in 1764, remained for a short time on the Miss. R. and then moved up to the Red R., where they obtained a grant of land along with the Taensa; later they sold this land and part of them probably moved to Okla., but others remained in La. and joined other tribes.

ATAKAPA: "Man-eater," because they and some of the Indians W. of them at times ate the flesh of their enemies; belonged to one family with the Chitimacha, their eastern neighbors, and probably the Tunican group on the Mississippi, the whole being called the Tunican stock; extended along the coast of La. and Tex. from Vermilion Bayou to and including Trinity Bay; population 2000 in 1650.

AVOYEL: Signifies probably "people of the rocks," referring to flint, and very likely applied to them because they were middlemen in supplying the Gulf coast with flint; spoke a dialect of the Natchez group of the Muskhogean linguistic family; lived near the present Marksville, La.; population in 1698, 280 warriors.

BAYOGOULA: "Bayou people," either from their location or from the fact that their tribal emblem was the alligator; their language was of the southern Muskhogean division, not far removed from Houma and Choctaw; lived near present Bayou Goula, in Iberville Parish.

BILOXI: Settled in La. about 1764, and a very few are still living there.

CADDO: The Caddo Indians are given under five different heads: the Adai and the Natchitoches Confederacy in La.; the Eieish, the Hasinai Confederacy, and the Kadohadacho Confederacy in Tex.

CHATOT: Entered La. about 1764, lived for a while on Bayou Boeuf, and later moved to the Sabine R., after which nothing more is heard of them. (See Fla.)

CHAWASHA: One of the Chitimacha division of the Tunican linguistic stock; lived on Bayou La Fourche and eastward to the Gulf of Mexico and across the Mississippi.

CHITIMACHA: Perhaps derived from the name of the Grand R. in the native tongue, though it has been interpreted through the Choctaw language as meaning "those who have pots"; they have given their name to a group of languages under the Tunican linguistic stock, including also the Chawasha and Washa; lived on the Grand R., Grand Lake, and lower course of Bayou La Teche; population in 1650, 3000.

CHOCTAW: Began moving into La. not long after the settlement of New Orleans, at first temporarily, but later for permanent occupancy, especially after the territory E. of the Miss. had been ceded to Great Britain; some settled on the N. shores of Lake Pontchartrain, where a few still remain, while other bands established themselves on the Nezpique, Red R., Bayou Boeuf, and elsewhere; most of these drifted in time to the Choctaw Nation of Okla., but a few families are still scattered about La.

DOUSTIONI: A small tribe of the Natchitoches Confederacy.

HOUMA: About 1706, moved from the Miss.-La. border into La., where their descendants remain to the present day.

KOASATI: Part of this tribe entered La. near the end of the 18th cent. and lived on the Red R. and in the W part of the state; the largest single band now lives N.E. of Kinder, La.

KOROA: Camped, hunted, and had at times more permanent settlements in N.E. Louisiana.

MUGULASHA: Formerly lived in the same town as the Bayogoula on the lower course of the Mississippi; some early writers state that they were identical with the Quinipissa.

MUSKOGEE: The true Muskogee were represented by one band, a part of the Pakana tribe, which moved into the colony about 1764; they were settled on the Calcasieu R. in 1805; later they seem to have united with the Alabama now living in Polk County, Texas; there are no known survivors at the present day.

NATCHEZ: Attacked by the French after they had destroyed the Natchez post, this tribe escaped into Louisiana and fortified themselves at Sicily Island from which most of them again escaped; a part under the chief of the Flour Village attacked the French post Natchitoches from their town, and entrenched themselves in it; St. Denis, commander of that post, attacked them, however, having been reinforced by some Caddo and Atakapa, and inflicted upon them a severe defeat; after this, no considerable number of Natchez seem to have remained in Louisiana.

NATCHITOCHES CONFEDERACY: *Natchitoches* is generally supposed to be derived from *nashitosh*, the native word for pawpaw, but an early Spanish writer, Jose Antonio Pichardo, was told that it was from a native word *nacicit* signifying "a place where the soil is the color of red ocher," and that it was applied originally to a small creek in their neighborhood running through red soil; belonged to the Caddo division of the Caddoan linguistic stock, their nearest relatives being the Indians of the Kadohadacho and Hasinai Confederacy; population about 1000 before contact with the whites.

OFO: Entered Louisiana some time in the latter half of the 18th cent. and finally united with the Tunica, settling with them at Marksville.

OKELOUSA: "Black water"; most probably of Muskhogean linguistic stock; moved about considerably, their best determined location being on the western side of the Mississippi, back of and above Point Coupée.

OPELOUSA: Probably from Mobilian and Choctaw *aba lusa*, "black above," meaning black-headed or black-haired; probably belonged to the Ata Kapan group of tribes; lived near the present Opelousa; population, 130 warriors in 1715, 40 in 1805, 20 in 1814.

OUACHITA: A tribe of the Natchitoches Confederacy.

PASCAGOULA: Entered Louisiana about 1764 and lived on the Red R. and Bayou Boeuf; subsequent history is uncertain.

QUAPAW: Lived with the Kadohadacho from 1823 to 1833 on a southern affluent of the Red R.

QUINIPISSA: "Those who see," perhaps meaning "scouts," or "outpost"; belonged to the southern division of the Muskhogean stock, and probably were very closely related to the Choctaw; lived on the western bank of the Mississippi, some distance from New Orleans.

TAENSA: Probably a place name; one of the three known tribes of the Natchez division of the Muskhogean stock; lived at the western end of Lake St. Joseph, in Taensa Parish; total population about 800 in 1698.

TANGIPAHOA: Meaning probably "corncob gatherers," or "corncob people"; belonged to the southern division of the Muskhogean stock; lived probably on the present Tangipahoa R., Tangipahoa Parish.

TAWASA: Some Tawasa accompanied the Alabama to Louisiana, but not until after the separate existence of the tribe had ended.

WASHA: Appear oftenest in literature in the French form *Ouacha*, the meaning unknown; their nearest relatives were the Chawasha, and both belonged to the Chitimachan branch of the Tunican linguistic family; earliest known location was on Bayou La Fourche, perhaps near the present Labadieville, Assumption Parish; population in 1715, 50 warriors.

YATASI: A tribe of the Natchitoches Confederacy.

Maine

MALECITE: Moved into N.E. Maine from Canada.

PASSAMAQUODDY: "Those who pursue the pollock," or, "pollock-plenty-place"; belonged to the Algonquian linguistic family; lived on Passamaquoddy Bay, St. Croix River, and the Scoodic Lakes; pop. 150 in 1726; 130 in 1804; 386 in 1910.

PENNACOOK: The Accominta and Newichawanoc of extreme S.W. part of state belonged to this tribe.

PENOBSCOT: Belonged to Algonquian linguistic family; lived on both sides of Penobscot Bay and in entire drainage area of Penobscot River; pop. 650 in 1726; 1000 in 1736; 700 in 1753; 700 in 1765; 350 in 1786; 301 in 1930.

Maryland and District of Columbia

CONOY: Probably a synonym of Kanawha, but meaning is unknown; also spelled Canawese and Ganawese; belonged to Algonquian linguistic family; lived between Potomac R. and western shore of Chesapeake Bay; pop. 2000 in 1600; 150 in 1765.

DELAWARE: Occupied or at least hunted some territory in extreme N.E. part of state.

NANTICOKE: "Tidewater people"; belonged to the Algonquian linguistic family; included (broadly) all of the Indians of eastern shore of Md. and S. Delaware.

POWHATAN: The Accohanoc Indians of the panhandle of Va., who extended over into Worcester Co., were the only representatives of the Powhatan Indians in Md., though the Conoy were closely related to them.

SHAWNEE: Settled temporarily in W. Md. near the Potomac and in the N.E. part of the state on the Susquehanna.

SUSQUEHANNA: Lived along and near the Susquehanna R.

Massachusetts

MAHICAN: Ranged over most of Berkshire Co., represented mainly by Housatonic or Stockbridge Indians.

MASSACHUSETS: "At the range of hills," meaning the hills of Milton; belonged to Algonquian linguistic family; lived in region of Massachusetts Bay between Salem on N. and Marshfield and Brocton on S. Later they claimed lands beyond Brocton as far as the Great Cedar Swamp, formerly under control of the Wampanoag; pop. 3000 in 1600; in 1631 reduced to 500, and soon considerably below, by smallpox.

NAUSET: Inhabited all of Cape Cod except extreme western end; probably formed one group with Massachusets; pop. in 1600, 1200; in 1621, 500; in 1767, 292; in 1930, 200-300.

NIPMUC: From Nipmaug, "fresh-water fishing place"; belonged to Algonquian linguistic family; occupied cent. plateau of Massachusetts, particularly S. Worcester Co., and extended into N. Rhode Island and Connecticut; population in 1650; 500; in 1910, 81.

PENNACOOK: Lived in N.E. part of Mass., represented by Agawam, Nashua, Naumkeag, Pentucket, Wachuset, Wamesit, Weshacum tribes.

POCOMTUC: Belonged to Algonquian linguistic family; located in present counties of Franklin, Hampshire, and Hampden, and in neighboring Conn. and Vt. Pop. in 1600, 1200; in 1910, perhaps 23.

WAMPANOAG: "Eastern people"; belonged to Algonquian linguistic family; occupied R.I. east of Narragansett Bay, Bristol Co., Mass., S. Plymouth Co. below Marshfield and Brocton, extreme W. part of Barnstable (Indians of Martha's Vineyard should also be added to them); pop. in 1600, 2400; epidemic of smallpox in 1617; in 1700, 400; in 1861, 300, exclusive of Martha's Vineyard Indians.

Michigan

CHIPPEWA: At a very early period lived about Sault Ste. Marie and on the N. Shore of Lake Michigan.

FOXES: Probably lived in the state at an early period.

HURONS: See Wyandot.

KICKAPOO: Probably lived in the state at an early period.

MENOMINEE: Ceded its claim to a portion of the upper peninsula of Michigan in 1836.

MIAMI: At one time occupied the valley of the St. Joseph R. and other parts of the S. Michigan border.

NEUTRALS: Bands of the Neutral Nation extended, in the 17th cent., into what is now S.E. Michigan.

NOQUET: Meaning probably "bear foot," another name for the Bear gens in Chippewa; the Bear gens may have been prominent in this tribe; thought to be related to the Menominee of the Algonquian linguistic family; lived near Big Bay de Noquet and Little Bay de Noquet and extending across the N. peninsula of Michigan to Lake Superior.

OTTAWA: Native word meaning "to trade"; belonged to Algonquian linguistic stock, related to Chippewa and Potawatomi; first record of home is from Manitoulin Island and Georgian Bay area; later moved to Michigan; population in 1600, 6000; census of 1930 counted 1745.

POTAWATOMI: Means "people of the place of fire," and therefore called the Fire Nation; belonged to the Algonquian linguistic family, closely related to Chippewa and Ottawa; ancestral home was the lower peninsula of Michigan; population in 1650, 4000; U.S. census of 1930 counted 1854; in 1937, 4133.

SAUK: Lived about Saginaw Bay before contact with Europeans, and were probably driven beyond Lake Michigan by the Ottawa and Neutral Nation alliance.

WYANDOT: Lived briefly at different Michigan places, such as Michilimackinac and Detroit, after being dispossessed by the Iroqois.

Minnesota

ARAPAHO: Are said to have lived once along the Red R. in present North Dakota and Minnesota (see under Wyoming).

CHEYENNE: Are traced through their earliest records to the part of Minnesota bounded by the Mississippi, Minnesota, and Red rivers; later moved to the Sheyenne branch of the Red R., North Dakota.

CHIPPEWA (OJIBWA): Means "to roast until puckered up," after the puckered seam in their moccasins; the type tribe of one of the two largest divisions of the Algonquian linguistic stock; associated early with the Sault Ste. Marie area, later extending over the northern shore of Lake Huron and both shores of Lake Superior, well into the northern interior, and as far W. as the Turtle Mts., N.D.; population in 1650, 35,000; U.S. census of 1930 gives 21,549, including 9,495 in Minnesota, 4,437 in Wisconsin, 3,827 in North Dakota, 1,865 in Michigan, and 1,549 in Montana.

DAKOTA: Were first known to Europeans in S. Minnesota, and, even when they ceded their lands in 1863, retained rights to the Red Pipestone Quarry.

FOXES: Were party to an 1830 treaty which ceded Minnesota lands to the whites.

IOWA: Are said to have once lived near Red Stone Quarry in S.W. Minnesota, and were at the mouth of Minnesota R. when the Dakota arrived there, near the mouth of the Blue Earth R. just before Le Sueur arrived in 1701.

MISSOURI: Were party to the 1830 treaty which ceded Minnesota lands to the whites.

OMAHA: Once lived near Red Pipestone Quarry.

OTO: Are said once to have shared the ownership of Blue Earth R. with the Iowa and western Dakota.

OTTAWA: Once wintered on Lake Pepin.

PONCA: Were once probably in S.W. Minnesota.

SAUK: Were represented in an 1830 treaty which ceded Minnesota lands to the whites.

WINNEBAGO: Some lived in Minnesota, 1848-62, after surrendering their reservation in Iowa Territory.

WYANDOT: Visited borders of Minnesota briefly with the Ottawa.

Mississippi

ACOLAPISSA: When first known, lived on the Pearl R. partly in what is now Mississippi, partly in Lousiana, but in later times they most were closely associated with Louisiana.

BILOXI: Apparently a corruption of their own name Taneks Anya, "first people"; Creek name, Poluksalgi; belonged to the Siouan linguistic family; earliest historical location was on the lower course of the Pascagoula R.; population 420 in 1698, 175 in 1720, and 105 in 1805.

CAPINANS: The name of a body of Indians connected in French references with the Biloxi and Pascagoula and probably a branch of one of them.

CHAKCHIUMA: *Shaktci homma*, meaning "red crawfish (people)"; spoke a dialect closely related to Choctaw and Chicasaw; their nearest relatives were the Houma, who evidently separated from them in very recent times; in the 18th cent. on the Yalobusha R. where it empties into the Yazoo, but at an early period extending to the head of the Yalobusha and eastward between the territories of the Choctaw and Chickasaw tribes as far as West Point.

CHICKASAW: Closely connected with the Choctaw and one of the principal tribes of the Muskhogean group; in northern Mississippi, principally in Pontotoc and Union Counties; population 1900 in 1715, 3600 in 1829, 4204 in 1910, and 4745 in 1930.

CHOCTAW: Largest tribe of the southern Muskhogean branch; linguistically, but not physically, most closely allied with the Chickasaw and after them with the Alabama; nearly all Choctaw towns in the S.E. part of Mississippi though they controlled the ad joining territory in the present state of Alabama; the small tribes of Mobile were sometimes called Choctaw; population 19,554 in 1831, 15,917 in 1910, and 17,757 in 1930.

CHOULA: "Fox" in Chickasaw and Choctaw; there is some reason to believe the name was applied to a part of the Ibitoupa tribe.

GRIGRA: Name said to have been given them from the frequent occurrence of these two syllables in their speech; they are sometimes referred to as the "Gray Village" of the Natchez; an *r* in their language suggests a probable relationship with the Tunican tribes; formed one of the Natchez villages on St. Catherines Creek, Mississippi.

HOUMA: Literally "red" but evidently an abbreviation of *shaktci homma*, "red crawfish"; spoke a Muskhogean language much like Choctaw, and their red crawfish emblem indicates that they had separated from the Chakchiuma; earliest known location was on the E. side of the Mississippi R. some miles inland and close to the Mississippi-Louisiana border, perhaps near the present Pinckney, Mississippi; population 1000 in 1650, 270-300 in 1739, and 60 in 1803.

IBITOUPA: Meaning probably, people "at the source of" a stream or river; their language was probably Muskhogean, and closely related to Chakchiuma, Chickasaw, and Choctaw; lived on the Yazoo R. in the present Holmes County, perhaps between Abyatche and Chicopa Creeks.

KOASATI: A band of Koasati moved from Alabama to the Tombigbee R. in 1763, but returned to their old country a few years later, impelled by the hostilities of their new neighbors.

KOROA: Most probably belonged to the Tunican linguistic group; appear most frequently in association with the Yazoo on the lower course of the Yazoo R., but at the very earliest period were on the banks of the Mississippi or in the interior of Louisiana on the other side of the river.

MOCTOBI: The name appears in the narratives of the first settlement of Louisiana, in 1699, applied to a tribe living with or near the Biloxi and Pascagoula; it is perhaps the name of the latter in the Biloxi language, or a subdivision of the Biloxi themselves.

NATCHEZ: The largest of three tribes speaking closely related dialects, the other two being the Taensa and Avoyel, and this group was remotely connected to a great Muskhogean family; their historic seat was along St. Catherines Creek, and a little E. of the present city of Natchez; population in 1650, 4500; 1731, 300 warriors.

OFO (OFOGOULA): Another name for Mosopelea, called "Dog People" by some tribes.

OKELOUSA: A tribe living at one time in N. Mississippi.

PASCAGOULA: "Bread people," probably Muskhogeans, although closely associated with the Siouan Biloxi; earliest known location was on the river that still bears their name, about 40 mi. from its mouth; population 455 in 1698, 240 in 1822.

PENSACOLA: Moved inland from Pensacola Bay near the end of the 17th cent. and in 1725-26 had established themselves near the Biloxi on the Pearl R.

QUAPAW: When discovered by the French in 1673, one of their towns was on the E. side of the Mississippi, but before 1700 it moved to the western bank.

TAPOSA: Probably Muskhogean stock; their earliest location on the Yazoo R. a few miles above the Chakchiuma.

TIOU: Belonged to the Tunica linguistic group of the Tunican family; their earliest location was near the upper course of the Yazoo R.; later they lived a little south of the Natchez and then among them.

TUNICA: "The people," or "those who are the people"; the leading tribe of the Tunica group of the Tunican stock, the latter including also the Chitimacha and Atakapa; lived on the lower course of the Yazoo R., on the south side about 10 mi. from its mouth; population 2000 in 1650, 460 in 1719, and 50-60 in 1803.

YAZOO: Probably belonged to the Tunican group and stock; lived on the S. side of the Yazoo R. about 10 mi. from its mouth.

Missouri

CADDO: Are connected by archeological evidence to the early history of Missouri.

DAKOTA: Were included in the treaty-makers of 1830, who ceded Missouri lands to the whites.

DELAWARE: In 1818-29 held S. Missouri lands by treaty.

FOXES: Sent delegates to the treaty conferences in 1804 and 1830, which ceded Indian lands to the U.S. government.

ILLINOIS: Once lived along E. Missouri borders.

IOWA: Once lived in Missouri north of the Missouri R.

KICKAPOO: Lived briefly in Missouri before moving on to Kansas.

MISSOURI: Means "(people having) dugout canoes," or "(people having) wooden canoes"; lived on the Missouri on the S. bank near the mouth of the Grand R.; belonged, with the Iowa and Oto, to the Chiwere division of the Siouan linguistic family; population in 1780, 1000; 13 Indians of the Missouri tribe were returned by the census of 1910.

OMAHA: Were party to the 1830 treaty that ceded Missouri lands to the U.S. government.

OSAGE: Were the chief members of the Dhegiha division of the Siouan linguistic stock; lived on Osage R., Missouri, but a small number of "Little Osage" was on the Missouri R. near the Missouri Indians; population in 1780, 6200; in 1937, 3649.

OTO: Entered Missouri with the Missouri Indians, later moving on to Kansas.

SAUK: Were party to the 1804 and 1830 treaties that ceded Missouri lands to the U.S. government.

SHAWNEE: Some settled near Cape Girardeau early in the 18th cent., but ceded their lands to the U.S. government in 1825.

Montana

ARAPAHO: Occupied or camped in S.E. Montana at different times.

ARIKARA: Some hunted in E. Montana.

ASSINIBOIN: From Chippewa, meaning "one who cooks by the use of stones"; belonged to Siouan linguistic family, a branch of the Dakota, sprung from the Yanktonai, whose dialect they spoke; associated chiefly with the valleyes of the Saskatchewan and Assiniboin Rivers, Canada; in U.S. occupied territory N. of the Milk and Missouri rivers as far east as the White Earth; population in 1780, 10,000; in 1904, 2605.

ATSINA: Were a part of the Arapaho, of the Algonquian linguistic family; lived on the Milk R. and nearby parts of the Missouri in Montana, ranging N. to she Saskatchewan; population in 1780, 3000; in 1937, 809.

BANNOCK: Ranged W. Montana.

BLACKFEET: See Siksika.

CHEYENNE: Frequently entered E. Montana; Northern Cheyenne finally granted reservation in Montana.

CHIPPEWA: Began to move to Montana in recent times, the census of 1910 counting 486.

CREE: In recent times some Cree have settled in Montana, the 1910 census counting 309.

CROW: A translation, through French (gens des corbeaux), of their own name Absaroke, "crow-, sparrowhawk-, or bird-people"; belonged to Siouan linguistic stock, closest to the Hidatsa; lived on the Yellowstone R. and branches, as far north as Musselshell and S. to Laramie Fork on the Platte, but chiefly on three southern tributaries of the Yellowstone, the Powder, Wind, and Big Horn Rivers; population in 1780, 4000; in 1937, 2173.

DAKOTA: Hunted and warred in Montana at times.

HIDATSA: With the Arikara and Mandan, ceded Montana lands to the U.S. government in 1869 and 1880.

KALISPEL: Visited W. Montana at times, finally settling in Flathead Reservation.

KIOWA: Reportedly lived once in S.E. Montana.

KUTENAI: Regarded by some linguistics as remote relatives of the Algonquians and Salishans, but also placed in a distinct stock called Kitunahan; lived on Kootenay R., Kootenay Lake, Arrow Lake, and the upper course of the Columbia R., except bend between Donald and Revelstoke; in S.E. British Columbia; N.W. Montana; N.E. Washington, and northern tip of Idaho; in modern times S.E. to Flathead Lake; population in 1780, 1200; in 1937, 118 in Idaho.

MANDAN: Ceded Montana lands in treaties in 1869 and 1880.

NEZ PERCÉ: Sometimes entered S.W. Montana in small numbers.

PIEGAN: Southernmost tribe of the Siksika.

SALISH: Properly a place name, with the last syllable, -ish, "people"; belonged to interior division of the Salishan linguistic family, to which they gave their name; lived in W. Montana originally, extending from Rockies S. to the Gallatin, E. to Crazy Mt. and Little Belt Ranges, N. to hill country above Helena; later centered around Flathead Lake; population in 1780, above 600; in 1905, 557.

SEMATUSE: Identified as a former tribe of the Salishan stock, closely related to the Salish tribe, but this is disputed.

SHOSHONE: Once ranged E. Montana north to the Milk R.

SIKSIKA: Meaning "black feet," the more popular name of the tribe, attributed to the discoloration of their feet by ashes of prairie fires, but more probably from their black moccasins; belonged to Algonquian linguistic stock; lived between North Saskatchewan R., Canada, and S. headstreams of the Missouri in Montana, and from long. 105° W. to Rocky Mts. population in 1780, 15,000; in 1937, 4242.

SPOKAN: In 1910, 134 were reported as living in Montana.

TUNAHE (TUNA'XE): Either an extinct Salishan tribe of W. central Montana, or a former eastern or plains band of the Kutenai Indians which gave its name to the tribe.

Nebraska

ARAPAHO: Ranged widely over western Nebraska.

ARIKARA: Lived anciently with the Skidi Pawnee in Nebraska, and returned to the same tribe for two years after 1823.

CHEYENNE: Ranged the W. part of the state.

COMANCHE: Before moving S., lived at some early date in W. Nebraska.

DAKOTA: Conducted constant raids into the state.

FOXES: Were party to an 1830 land cession.

IOWA: Accompanied the Omaha to South Dakota from Minnesota, then to Nebraska, but continued S.E. into Iowa.

KANSAS: Were parties to an 1825 land cession.

KIOWA: Once lived on W. border of Nebraska, before following the Comanche S.

MISSOURI: Lived for a time S. of Platte R. to escape the Sauk and Fox in Missouri.

OMAHA: Means "those going against the wind"; belonged to the section of the Siouan stock that included the Ponca, Kansa, Osage, and Quapaw; lived in N.E. Nebraska on the Missouri R.; population in 1780, 2800; in 1932, 1684.

OTO: From a Watcota word meaning "lechers"; formed, with the Iowa and Missouri, the Chiwere group of the Siouan linguistic family, closely connected with the Winnebago; their usual historical location was on the lower Platte, or the nearby banks of the Missouri; population in 1780, 900; in 1937, 756 were reported in Oklahoma.

PAWNEE: Were one of the chief tribes of Caddoan linguistic stock; the Arikara were an offshoot and the Wichita were more closely related to them than were the Caddo; lived on the middle course of the Platte R. and the Republican Fork of the Kansas R.; population in 1780, 10,000; in 1937, 956 were reported.

PONCA: Spoke practically the same language as the Omaha, forming with them, the Osage, Kansa, and Quapaw, the Dhegiha group of the Siouan linguistic family; lived on the right bank of the Missouri at the mouth of the Niobrara; population in 1780, 800; in 1937, the U.S. Indian Office gave 825 in Oklahoma and 397 in Nebraska.

SAUK: Were party to the 1830 cession of Nebraska lands.

WINNEBAGO: Some settled near the Omaha after fleeing from the Dakota in Minnesota in 1862, and were later assigned a reservation.

Nevada

KOSO: Sometimes ranged into Nevada from California.

PAIUTE, NORTHERN (PAVIOTSO): Constituted, with the Bannock, one dialectic group of the Shoshonean branch of the Uto-Aztecan stock; covered W. Nevada, S.E. Oregon, and strip of California E. of the Sierra Nevada as far S. as Owens Lake (exclusive of the Washo territory); population in 1845 (with Southern Paiute), 7500; in 1937, 439.

PUEBLO: Archeological evidence exists of prehistoric occupation of S. Nevada by Pueblo.

SHOSHONE, WESTERN: Western Shoshone occupied N.E. Nevada to the Reese River Valley.

UTE: Claimed a small part of E. Nevada.

WASHO: From Washiu, meaning "person"; are thought to have been related to some Californian tribes, either the Chumash, or in the Hokan linguistic family; lived on the Truckee R. down to the Meadows; Carson R. down to first large canyon below Carson City; borders of Lake Tahoe; and Sierra and Nevada Valleys as far as first range S. of Honey Lake, California; population in 1845, 1000; in 1937, 629.

New Hampshire

ABNAKI: Parts of Grafton Co. were occupied by the Ossipee and Pequawket bands, affiliated with the Sokoki of the Abnaki tribe.

PENNACOOK: "At bottom of hill (or highland)" or "down hill"; belonged to Algonquian linguistic family; occupied S. and cen. N. H., N.E. Massachusetts, and S. Me.

New Jersey

DELAWARE: From Lord Delaware, second governor of Virginia; belonged to Algonquian linguistic family; occupied all of N.J., W. Long Island, all of Staten and Manhattan Islands, and neighboring parts of the mainland, along with other portions of N.Y. W. of the Hudson, and parts of E. Pa. and N. Del. (see also Del., Ill., Ind., Kan., Md. and D. of C., Mo., N.Y., O., Pa., Okla., and the Munsee under Kan., Okla., and Wis.); pop. in 1600, more than 8000; in 1910, 985; in 1937, 140.

New Mexico

APACHE: Probably from apachu, "enemy," the Zuni name for the Navaho, who were called "Apaches de Nabaju" by the first Spaniards in New Mexico; with the Navaho, the Apache constituted the western group of the southern division of the Athapascan linguistic stock; lived in S. New Mexico and Arizona, W. Texas, and S.E. Colorado, also ranging over much of New Mexico; population in 1680, 5000; in 1937, 6916.

COMANCHE: Raided New Mexico territory repeatedly during the Spanish period.

JEMEZ: Corruption of Hamish or Haemish, the Keresan name of the pueblo; with the defunct Pecos, the Jemez constituted a distinct group of the Tanoan linguistic family now a part of the Kiowa-Tanoan group; lived on the N. 'bank of the Jemez R., about 20 miles N.W. of Bernalillo; population in 1680, 2500; in 1937, 648.

JICARILLA: An Apache tribe which ranged over N.E. New Mexico.

KERESAN PUEBLOS: Keresan is an adaptation of Keres, which is what the Indians call themselves; constitute an independent stock; live on the Rio Grande, in N.E. New Mexico between the Rio de Los Frijoles and the Rio Jemez, and from the pueblo of Sia on the Rio Jemez to the mouth of the river; population in 1760, 3956; in 1937, 5781.

KIOWA: Raided in and across New Mexico in the Spanish and early American periods.

KIOWA APACHE: An Athapascan tribe incorporated into and accompanying the Kiowa.

LIPAN: The easternmost of the Apache tribes.

MANSO: From a Spanish word meaning "mild"; belonged to the Tanoan division of the Kiowa-Tanoan linguistic stock; lived about Mesilla Valley, near present Las Cruces, New Mexico; population in 1668, upward of 1000; few remain.

NAVAHO (NAVAJO): Derives from Tews Navahu, referring to a large area of cultivated land and applied to a former Tewa pueblo, then, by extension, to the Navaho, who intruded on the Tewa domain and were known to the Spaniards as "Apaches de Navajo" to distinguish them from other so-called Apache bands; with the Apache tribes, constituted the southern division of the Athapascan linguistic family; lived in N. New Mexico and Arizona, with some extension into Colorado and Utah; population in 1680, 8000; in 1937, 44,304.

PECOS: Derives from Péaku, the Keresan name of the pueblo; belonged to the Jemez division of the Tanoan linguistic family, itself a part of the Kiowa-Tanoan stock; lived on the upper branch of the Pecos R., about 30 miles S.E. of Santa Fe; population in 1540, 2000-2500; in 1910, 0.

PIRO PUEBLOS: A division of the Tanoan linguistic family, in turn a part of the Kiowa-Tanoan stock; in early 17th cent., comprised two divisions, one in the Rio Grande Valley from the present town of San Marcial, Socorro Co., northward to within 50 miles of Albuquerque, where the Tiwa settlements began; the other, called sometimes Tompiros and Salineros, occupying an area E. of the Rio Grande around the Salt Lagoons, or Salinas, where they adjoined the eastern group of Tiwa settlements on the south; population in the 16th cent., 9000; now, 60.

PUEBLO INDIANS: General name for S.W. Indians who lived in stone buildings rather than more fragile shelters, pueblo being the Spanish name for "town" or "village"; it is not a tribal or a stock name; the Pueblos belonged to four distinct stocks.

SHUMAN: Lived at various times within or near the S. and E. borders of New Mexico.

TEWA PUEBLOS: Tewa is from a Keres word meaning "moccasins"; constituted a major division of the Tanoan linguistic family, itself a part of the Kiowa-Tanoan stock; lived along the valley of the Rio Grande in N. New Mexico, with one pueblo, Hano, in Hopi country in Arizona; population in 1680, 3600;

in 1910, 968; in 1937, 1708, not including the
Hano.

TIWA PUEBLOS: Tiwa is from *tiwan* (pl. *ti-wesh*), their own name, which is alternately
spelled Tebas, Tigua, Tiguex, Tihuas, Chiguas;
a division of the Tanoan linguistic family, itself a part of the Kiowa-Tanoan stock; formed
three geographic divisions, one at Taos and
Picuris (the northernmost New Mexican
pueblos), on the upper Rio Grande; one at
Sandia and Isleta, respectively N. and S. of
Albuquerque; the third in the pueblos of
Isleta del Sur and Senecú del Sur near El
Paso, in Texas and Chihuahua, Mexico, respectively; population in 1680, 12,200; in 1937,
2122.

UTE: Close along the northern border of New
Mexico, frequently raiding across.

ZUÑI (JUÑI): Is a Spanish adaptation of the
Keresan Sünyyitsi, or Sünyitsa, of unknown
meaning; constituted the Zuñian linguistic
stock; lived on N. bank of upper Zuñi R.,
Valencia Co.; population in 1630, 10,000; in
1680, 2500; in 1923, 1911; in 1937, 2080.

New York

DELAWARE: Bands of two of main divisions
of the Delaware Indians, the Munsee and
Unami, extended into parts of N.Y. state, including Manhattan Island.

ERIE: Occupied parts of Chautauqua and Cat-
taraugus Counties.

IROQUOIS: "Real adders"; belonged to Iroquoian linguistic family; lived in upper and central part of Mohawk Valley and lake region
of cen. New York; after obtaining guns from
the Dutch, the Iroquois acquired a dominating influence among the Indians from Me.
to the Miss. and between the Ottawa and
Cumberland Rivers; pop. in 1600, 5500; in
1685, 16,000; in 1923, 20,051.

MAHICAN: "Wolf," variant of Mohegan, but
not same tribe; belonged to Algonquian linguistic family; lived on both banks of upper
Hudson from Catskill Creek to Lake Champlain and eastward to include the valley of
the Housatonic.

MOHEGAN: See Connecticut.

MONTAUK: Name of uncertain meaning; belonged to Algonquian linguistic family; lived
in eastern and central parts of Long Island;
pop. 6000 in 1600; 30 in 1829.

NEUTRALS: So called by the French because
they remained neutral during the later wars
between the Iroquois and Huron; belonged
to Iroquoian linguistic family; lived in S.
Ontario, W. N.Y., N.E. Ohio, S.E. Mich.; pop.
in 1600, 10,000; in 1653, 800.

SAPONI: Some years after leaving Ft. Chris-
tanna, Va., the Saponi settled among the
Iroquois and were formally adopted by the
Cayuga tribe in 1753.

TUSCARORA: After their defeat in the Tuscarora War (1712-13), bands of this tribe began moving north; in the course of time the
majority settled in N.Y. state, so that
the Iroquois came to be known as the Six
Nations instead of the Five Nations.

TUTELO: Accompanied the Saponi from Virginia and were adopted by the Cayuga at
the same time.

WAPPINGER: "Easterners"; belonged to the
Algonquian linguistic family; lived on E.
band of Hudson R. from Manhattan Is. to
Poughkeepsie and in territory E. to Connecticut Valley; pop. 3000 in 1600.

WENROHRONON: "The people of the place
of floating scum," from oil-spring of the
town of Cuba, Allegany Co., belonged to
Iroquoian linguistic family.

North Carolina

BEAR RIVER INDIANS: Associated with Algonquian tribes; may have been part of the
Machapunga.

CAPE FEAR INDIANS: Named from Cape
Fear; belonged to eastern Siouan tribes;
lived on Cape Fear River; pop. 1000 in 1600;
206 in 1715; 30 in 1808.

CATAWBA: Occupied parts of S.W. N. Carolina near Catawba R.

CHERAW (SARA): Belonged to Siouan linguistic family (uncertain); lived at head of Saluda
R. in Pickens and Oconee counties, S.C.,
whence they removed at an early date to
present Henderson, Polk, and Rutherford
counties, N.C.; pop. 1200 in 1600, probable.

CHEROKEE: In mountainous parts of state
and in the West (see Tenn.).

CHOWANOC: "(People) at the south"; belonged to Algonquian linguistic family; lived on
Caowan R. about junction of Meherrin and
Blackwater rivers; pop. 1500 in 1600; 5 in
1755.

CORE (OR CORANINE): Thought to be of
Algonquian linguistic family; lived on peninsula S. of Neuse R. in Carteret and Craven
counties; pop. 1000 in 1600.

ENO: "To dislike," "mean," "contemptible" (perhaps); probably of Siouan linguistic family;
lived on Eno River in present Orange and
Durham counties.

HATTERAS: Belonged to Algonquian linguistic family; lived along sand banks about
Cape Hatteras E. of Pamlico Sound, and frequented Roanoke Island.

KEYAUWEE: Thought to have been of Siouan
linguistic family; lived at points of meeting
of present Guilford, Davidson, and Randolph
counties; pop. 500 in 1600.

MACHAPUNGA: "Bad dust," "bad dirt"; belonged to Algonquian linguistic family; lived
in present Hyde Co. and probably also in
Washington, Tyrrell, and Dare counties, and
part of Beaufort; pop. 1200 in 1600; probably
less than 100 in 1701.

MEHERRIN: From Va. into Northampton and
Hertford counties.

MORATOK: From a place name; belonged to
Algonquian linguistic family; lived on Roanoke R.

NATCHEZ: Part sought refuge with Cherokees
after French broke up their tribe; most appear to have lived along Hiwassee R.; moved
with Cherokee to Oklahoma reservation.

NEUSIOK: Probably a place name; possibly
Algonquian, possible Iroquoian; lived on lower
Neuse R., particularly on S. side, in Craven
and Cartaret counties.

OCCANEECHI: When they lived on Roanoke
R., Va., they probably ranged over into
Warren, Halifax, and Northampton counties,
N.C. In 1701 they were in Orange Co., N.C.

PAMLICO: Belonged to Algonquian linguistic
family; lived on Pamlico R.

SAPONI: Lived on Yadkin R. and in other
parts of state for a certain period. (See Va.)

SHAKORI: Belonged to Siouan linguistic family; moved frequently, but probably centered
in the courses of Shocco and Big Shocco
Creeks in present Vance, Warren, and Franklin counties.

SARA: See Cheraw.

SISSIPAHAW: Of Siouan linguistic family;
lived about present Saxapahaw on Haw R.

in lower part of Alamance Co.; pop. 800 in 1600.

SUGEREE: Occupied parts of Mecklenburg Co.

TUSCARORA: "Hemp gatherers"; belonged to Iroquoian linguistic family; lived on Roanoke, Tar, Pamlico, and Neuse rivers (see also Pa. and N.Y.); pop. 5000 in 1600; 400 in 1796; 828 in 1885.

TUTELO: For a while on upper Yadkin and later in Bertie Co.

WACCAMAW: Into state from head of Waccamaw R.

WATEREE: Said in 1670 to be on upper Yadkin.

WAXHAW: Into Union Co. from S. Carolina.

WEAPEMEOC (YEOPIM): Of Algonquian linguistic family; lived in most of present Currituck, Camden, Pasquotank, and Perquimans counties, and part of Chowan Co. N of Albemarle Sound. In the time of the Raleigh colony, the Weapemeoc had 700-800 warriors.

WOCCON: Belonged to Siouan linguistic family; lived between Neuse R. and one of its affluents, perhaps at about the present Goldsboro, Wayne Co.; pop. in 1600, 600.

YADKIN: Probably to Siouan linguistic family; on Yadkin R.

YEOPIM: See Weapemeoc.

North Dakota

ARIKARA: Means "horns," or "elk," because two pieces of bone were let to stick up from their hair; belonged to the Caddoan linguistic stock; lived at different places on the Missouri R. between Cheyenne R., S. Dakota and Ft. Berthold, N. Dakota; population in 1780, 3000; the U.S. Indian Office census of 1937 listed 616.

ASSINIBOIN: Often descended from Canada on war missions, but did not establish permanent camps in North Dakota.

CHEYENNE: Settled on the Sheyenne Fork of the Red R. during their migration from Minnesota, but later left the state.

CHIPPEWA: Pushed W. to the Turtle Mts., which gave their name to a Chippewa band.

DAKOTA: Some settled at different times in E., S., and S.W. North Dakota, during their westward migration from Minnesota, and part of the Standing Rock Agency is within North Dakota.

HIDATSA: Belonged to Siouan linguistic stock, closely related to the Crow; lived at various points on the Missouri between the Heart and Little Missouri rivers; population in 1780, 2500; in 1937, 731.

MANDAN: Belonged to Siouan linguistic stock; lived near the Hidatsa on the Missouri, between Heart and Little Missouri rivers; population in 1780, 3600; in 1937, 345.

Ohio

CHIPPEWA: Tribal representatives appear as parties to the Treaty of Greenville, 1795, and to treaties concluded in 1807 and 1817, by which lands in Ohio were relinquished to the whites.

DELAWARE: Lived in Ohio for a considerable period in the course of their migration W. under white pressure.

ERIE: Meaning "long tail" in Iroquois, and referring to the panther, from which circumstance they are often referred to as the Cat Nation; belonged to the Iroquoian linguistic family; lived throughout N. Ohio, except possibly in the N.W. corner, and in portions of N.W. Pennsylvania and W. New York; in the S.E. part of the state they perhaps reached the Ohio R.

HONNIASONT: Occupied parts of the eastern fringe of Ohio after it had been incorporated into the Iroquois, and perhaps before.

ILLINOIS: Tribal representatives were parties to the Treaty of Greenville, by which lands in the state were relinquished to the whites.

IROQUOIS: After the destruction or dispersal of the Erie and other native tribes, many Iroquois settlements were made in Ohio, particularly by the westernmost tribe, the Seneca; some of these so-called Iroquois villages were no doubt occupied by people of formerly independent nations.

KICKAPOO: Tribal representatives were parties to the Treaty of Greenville.

MIAMI: After the original tribes of Ohio had been cleared away, some Miami worked their way into the state, particularly into the W. and N. parts, and they gave their name to three Ohio rivers, the Miami, Little Miami, and Maumee.

MOSOPELEA: Spoke a Siouan dialect most closely related to Biloxi and Tutelo and secondarily to Dakota; when the French first heard of them they were in S.W. Ohio, but their best-known historical location was on the lower Yazoo, close to the Yazoo and Koroa Indians.

NEUTRALS: The Neutral Nation may have occupied a little territory in the extreme N.W. of the state.

OFO: Another name for Mosopelea, called "Dog People" by some tribes.

OTTAWA: In the 18th cent. worked their way into the N. part of the states and established settlements along the shore of Lake Erie.

POTAWATOMI: Tribal representatives were parties to the Treaty of Greenville, 1795, and others made in 1805, 1807, and 1817, by which lands were ceded to the whites.

SENECA: See Iroquois, under New York.

SHAWNEE: It is probable that some were in Ohio at very early periods; after they had been driven from the Cumberland Valley by the Chicasaw and Cherokee shortly after 1714, they worked their way N. into Ohio, and, as they were joined by the former eastern and southern bands, Ohio became the Shawnee center until after the Treaty of Greenville.

WYANDOT: Meaning perhaps "islanders," or "dwellers on a peninsula"; at an early date usually known as Huron, a name given by the French from huré, "rough," and the deprecating suffix -on; belonged to the Iroquoian linguistic family; earliest known location of the Huron proper was the St. Lawrence Valley and the territory of the present province of Ontario, from Lake Ontario across to Georgian Bay; the Tionontati were just W. of them on Lake Huron; population in 1600, 10,000 Huron and 8,000 Tionontati.

Oklahoma

ALABAMA: Some accompanied the Creeks to Oklahoma in the early 19th cent. and settled near Weleetka.

APACHE: A name given to a group of tribes which included the Jicarilla in Colorado; the Kiowa Apache in Kansas, the Lipan in Texas, and the Apache in New Mexico.

APALACHEE: A few moved to Oklahoma from Alabama or Louisiana.

ARAPAHO: Ranged western Oklahoma in early times; the Southern Arapaho were given a reserve and later alloted land in severalty in W. central Oklahoma with the Southern Cheyenne.

BILOXI: A few moved to Oklahoma and lived with the Choctaw and Creeks.

CADDO: Moved to Oklahoma in 1859 and were given a reserve in the S.W. near Anadarko.

CHEROKEE: Moved to large reserve in N.E. Oklahoma in 1838-39; after 70 years of tribal rule there, they were allotted lands in severalty and became U.S. citizens.

CHEYENNE: See Arapaho, above.

CHICKASAW: Moved to Oklahoma (1822-40); are now U.S. citizens.

CHOCTAW: Most moved to Oklahoma at about the same time as the Chickasaw and are now U.S. citizens.

COMANCHE: Lived in W. Oklahoma in later history; were given a reserve in the S.W., and finally land in severalty when they became U.S. citizens.

CREEKS: The tribes of the Creek Confederacy moved to Oklahoma 1836-41, and were given a reserve in the N.E.; early in the present century they were allotted lands in severalty and became U.S. citizens.

DELAWARE: Part were removed from Kansas in 1867 to N.E. Oklahoma and incorporated with the Cherokee Nation; part is with the Caddo and Wichita in S.W. Oklahoma.

FOXES: A few came to Oklahoma with the Sauk in 1867.

HITCHITI: A subtribe of the Creek Confederacy.

ILLINOIS: Survivors, chiefly Peoria and Kaskaskia, moved to reserve in N.E. Oklahoma in 1868.

IOWA: Part of the Kansan Iowa were given a central Oklahoma reserve in 1883 and allotted land in severalty in 1890.

IROQUOIS: Some, with Tuscarora, Wyandot, and probably Erie Nation Indians, were given a reserve in N.E. Oklahoma as so-called Seneca people; their descendents are now U.S. citizens.

JICARILLA: An Athapascan tribe who ranged in early times over W. Oklahoma and were known as Apache.

KANSA: Were moved to Oklahoma in 1873 and given a reserve in the N.E.

KICHAI: Moved to the headwaters of the Trinity from their early home on the Red R., but fled N. from the Texans in 1859 and lived with the Wichita near Anadarko.

KICKAPOO: Some were moved back from Mexico in 1873 and settled in central Oklahoma where they were in time joined by most of the tribe.

KIOWA AND KIOWA APACHE: Formerly ranged over W. Oklahoma.

KOASATI: A tribe of the Creek Confederacy who were removed to N.E. Oklahoma and settled in the W. Creek territory there.

LIPAN: The easternmost band of Apache, some of whom are with the Tonkawa.

MIAMI: In the group of Miami who were removed from Indiana and given a reserve with the Illinois in N.E. Oklahoma were both Piankashaw and Wea.

MIKASUKI: Some came to Oklahoma with the Seminole and maintained their own Square Ground until 1914.

MISSOURI: Survivors came to Oklahoma with the Oto in 1882.

MODOC: Part were sent to the Quapaw Reservation after the Modoc War (1873).

MUKLASA: A small Creek division that is said to have kept its identity in Oklahoma.

MUNSEE: A few came with the Delaware proper to Oklahoma, where 21 were counted in 1910.

MUSKOGEE: The name of the chief tribe or group of the Creeks.

NATCHEZ: Some came with the Creeks to Oklahoma and settled near Eufaula, later merging with the rest of the Creek population; others settled in the Cherokee Nation near the Illinois R., where a few still maintain their identity.

NEZ PERCÉ: Chief Joseph's band was sent to Oklahoma in 1878, but the climate was too much for them, and they were transferred to Colville Reservation (Idaho) in 1885.

OKMULGEE: A Creek tribe and town of the Hitchiti division of the Nation.

OSAGE: Once owned most of N. Oklahoma, and still hold a large N.E. reservation, though they have been allotted lands in severalty.

OTO: Part moved to the Sauk and Fox land in Oklahoma in 1880, and were followed in 1882 by the rest.

OTTAWA: Some finally settled in N.E. Oklahoma about 1868.

PAWNEE: Moved to Oklahoma in 1876 and given a reserve in N. central part of the state, where they have been allotted lands in severalty.

PEORIA: See Illinois above.

PIANKASHAW: See Miami.

PONCA: Were forcibly moved to Oklahoma in 1877, and the greater part settled near the Osage in the N.E.

POTAWATOMI: The Potawatomi of the Woods were moved from Kansas (1867-81) and given a reserve in the central part of Oklahoma.

QUAPAW: Ceded all their S.E. Kansas lands in 1867 and have confined themselves to the N.E. Oklahoma lands they were granted in 1833, though a large number have moved to the Osage reserve.

SAUK: Exchanged their Kansas land in 1867 for the central Oklahoma lands they still occupy.

SEMINOLE: Most were removed to Oklahoma after the Seminole War in Florida.

SENECA: See Iroquois.

SHAWNEE: The Absentee Shawnee moved to central Oklahoma from Kansas in 1845; a second band to N.E. Oklahoma in 1867; the third and largest section moved to the Cherokee lands in 1869.

TAWAKONI: Belonged to the Caddoan linguistic stock, most closely connected with the Wichita; lived on the Canadian R. N. of the upper Washita; population in 1772 included about 220 warriors; the 1910 census reported a lone survivor of the tribe.

TAWEHASH: Belonged to the Caddoan linguistic stock, closely related to the Wichita, Tawakoni, Waco, and Yscani; earliest known home was on the Canadian R. N. of the Washita headwaters.

TONKAWA: Survivors were moved to Oklahoma in 1884, settled on a reserve near Ponca, and eventually allotted lands in severalty.

TUSKEGEE: A Creek division, thought to be connected linguistically to the Alabama, which moved W. with the Creek Confederacy and settled in N.W. Oklahoma.

WACO: Closely related to the Tawakoni of the Wichita group of tribes belonging to the Caddoan stock; originally they lived with the Wichita in Oklahoma, but first appear in connection with their village on the site of present Waco, Texas; population in 1859, 171; in 1910, 5.

WEA: See Miami.

WICHITA: From wits, "man"; were a principal tribe of the Caddoan linguistic family; are certainly traced to the Canadian R. N. of the headwaters of the Washita; population in 1780, 3200; in 1937, 385.

WYANDOT: Part, including old Tionontati, moved from Kansas to N.E. Oklahoma in 1867.

YSCANI (ASCANI, HYSCANI, IXCANI): A confederated Wichita tribe of the Caddoan linguistic family; are mentioned first along with the Wichita and allied tribes on the S. Canadian in the later Chickasaw territory, but part lived 60 leagues farther to the N.W.; in 1772 their village was reported to have 60 warriors; about 1782, 90 families were counted in the tribe.

YUCHI: United and came W. with the Creeks.

Oregon

AHANTCHUYUK: Belonged to Kalapooian linguistic stock; lived on and about Pudding R., which flows into the Willamette about 10 miles S. of Oregon City.

ALSEA: Belonged to Yakonan linguistic stock; lived on the Alsea R. and Bay; population in 1780, 6000; in 1930, 9.

ATFALATI (FALLATAHS): Belonged to northern dialectic branch of Kalapooian linguistic family; lived on Atfalati plains, the hills about Forest Grove and around Wapato; said to have reached as far as Portland; population in 1910, 44.

BANNOCK: Came over eastern borders between the Powder and Owyhee Rivers in recent times.

CALAPOOYA: Belonged to Calapooya dialectic division of Kalapooian linguistic stock; lived on headwaters of the Willamette R. including McKinzie, Middle, and W. Forks.

CAYUSE: Considered a branch of the Shapwailutan family; lived about heads of Walla Walla, Umatilla, and Grande Ronde rivers, from Blue Mts. to Deschutes R., Washington and Oregon; population in 1780, 500; in 1937, 370.

CHASTACOSTA: Belonged to Athapascan stock; lived on lower Illinois R., in either side of the Rogue R. for some distance above junction with the Illinois, and farther still up the N. bank; population in 1937, 30.

CHELAMELA: Belonged to Calapooya dialectic division of Kalapooian linguistic stock; lived on Long Tom Creek, a western tributary of the Willamette R.

CHEPENAFA: Belonged to Calapooya dialectic division of the Kalapooian linguistic stock; lived at forks of St. Mary's Creek, near Corvallis; population in 1910, 24.

CHETCO: Means "close to the mouth of the stream"; belonged to Athapascan linguistic stock; lived around the mouth of the Chetko R., upstream for 14 miles, and on the Winchuck R.

CLACKAMAS: Belonged to Chinookan linguistic stock and to a dialectic division that has their name; lived on the Clackamas R., claiming land from near the mouth almost to Oregon City and E. to the Cascade Mts., population in 1780, 2500; in 1930, 561.

CLATSKANIE: Belonged to Athapascan linguistic stock; are thought to have once occupied and abandoned the prairies along the Chehalis R. because of game failure, then to have crossed the Columbia and lived in the mountains near Clatskanie R., with which they are associated; they levied tolls from everyone using the Columbia R.; population in 1780, 1600; in 1910, 3.

CLATSOP: Means "dried salmon"; belonged to the lower Chinook dialectic division of Chin-

ookan linguistic stock; lived around Cape Adams, on S. side of the Columbia R., to Tongue Point upstream and southward on the Pacific coast to Tillamook Head.

CLOWWEWALLA: Belonged to Clackamas division of Chinookan linguistic stock; lived at falls of the Willamette R.; population in 1780, 900; now extinct.

DAKUBETEDE: Belonged to Athapascan linguistic stock; lived on the Applegate R.

HANIS: Formed one dialectic group of Kusan linguistic family, the other being Miluk; lived on the Coos R. and Bay.

KLAMATH: With the Modoc, constituted the Lutumian division of Shapwailutan linguistic family; lived on upper Klamath Lake, Klamath Marsh, and Williamson and Sprague Rivers; population in 1780, 800-1200; in 1937, 1912.

KUITSH: Belonged to Yakonan linguistic stock; lived on lower Umpqua R.

LATGAWA: Means "those living in the uplands"; with the Takelma proper, constituted the Takilman linguistic family which, in turn, was probably affiliated with the Shastan stock; lived on upper Rogue R. eastward about Table Rock and Bear Creek, and around Jacksonville.

LOHIM: Reputedly a band of Shoshoneans entering Oregon at a late period; lived on Willow Creek, a southern affluent of the Columbia.

LUCKIAMUTE (LAKMIUT): Belonged to Calapooya dialectic division of Kalapooian linguistic stock; lived on the Luckiamute R.; population in 1905, 28; in 1910, 8.

MILUK (LOWER COQUILLE): Spoke the southern of two dialects of Kusan linguistic family, related remotely to Yakonan stock; lived at the mouth of the Coquille R.

MISHIKHWUTMETUNNE: Means "people who live on the stream called Mishi"; belonged to Athapascan linguistic stock, closest to the Tutuni; lived on upper Coquille R.

MODOC: From Moatokni, meaning "southerners"; with the Klamath, constituted the Lutuamian division of Shapwailutan linguistic stock; lived on Little Klamath Lake, Modoc Lake, Tule Lake, Lost River Valley, and Clear Lake, at times eastward to Goose Lake; population in 1780, 400-800; in 1937, 329.

MOLALA: With the Cayuse, constituted the Waiilapuan division of Shapwailutan linguistic stock; lived earlier in Deschutes R. valley, but were driven W. by hostile tribes into the valleys of the Molala and Santiam Rivers; part settled in the S. about the headwaters of the Umpqua and Rogue Rivers; population in 1849, 100; in 1910, 31.

MULTNOMAH: Belonged to Clackamas division of Chinookan linguistic stock; lived around Sauvies Island.

NALTUNNETUNNE: Small Athapascan tribe between the Tutuni and Chetco.

NEZ PERCÉ: Extended into N.E. Oregon.

AIUTE, NORTHERN (PAVIOTSO): Occupied S.E. Oregon and once extended northward through Powder R. Valley and upper John Day R. until driven back by Shahaptians.

SANTIAM: Belonged to Calapooya dialectic division of Kalapooian linguistic stock; lived on the Santiam R.; in 1906, 23; in 1910, 9.

SHASTA: Extended from California into territory watered by Jenny Creek.

SILETZ: Belonged to Salishan linguistic stock; lived on the Siletz R.

SIUSLAW: Belonged to Siuslawan division of Yakonan linguistic stock; lived around Siuslaw R.; population in 1910, 7.

SKILLOOT: Occupied part of Oregon opposite mouth of the Cowlitz R.

SNAKE: See Paiute, Northern, under *Nevada*.

TAKELMA: Means "those dwelling along the river"; with the Latgawa, constituted the Takilman linguistic stock; lived on middle course of the Rogue R. from above the Illinois R. to near Grant's Pass and on tributaries of the Rogue R. between these limits and upper course of Cow Creek; also S., almost to California.

TALTUSHTUNTUDE: Belonged to Athapascan linguistic stock; lived on Galice Creek.

TENINO: Constituted a division of the Shahaptian branch of Shapwailutan linguistic stock; by treaty of 1855, settled on Yakima Reservation, Washington.

TILLAMOOK: Means in Chinook "people of Nekelim (or Nehalem)"; were principal tribe in Oregon which belonged to the Salishan linguistic family, coastal division; lived on the coast from Hehalem to Salmon Rivers; population in 1805, 2200; in 1930, 12.

TUTUNI: Belonged to Athapascan linguistic stock, closest to the Mishikhwutmetunne; lived on lower Rogue R. and Pacific coast N. and S. of its mouth; population in 1854, 1311; in 1910, 383.

TYIGH: Belonged to Tenino branch of Shahaptian division of Shapwailutan linguistic stock; lived about Tygh and White rivers.

UMATILLA: Belonged to Shahaptian division of Shapwailutan linguistic stock; lived on the Umatilla R. and banks of the Columbia near mouth of the Umatilla.

UMPQUA: Belonged to Athapascan linguistic stock; lived on upper Umpqua R., E. of the Kuitsh; population in 1846, about 400; in 1937, 43.

WALLAWALLA: Extended a little into N.E. Oregon.

WALPAPI: Part of Northern Paiute, commonly called Snakes.

WASCO: From *wacq!ó*, meaning "cup or small bowl of horn," referring to cup-shaped rock near main tribal village; belonged to upstream branch of Chinookan linguistic stock, closest to Wishram; lived near The Dalles, in Wasco Co.; population in 1882, 900; in 1937, 227.

WATLALA: Belonged to Chinookan linguistic stock and Clackamas dialectic group; lived at Cascades of Columbia R. down to mouth of the Willamette R.

YAHUSKIN: One of two chief peoples in Oregon of Northern Paiute division of the Shoshonean, and therefore Uto-Aztecan linguistic stock (see Nevada).

YAMEL (YAM HILL): With the Atfalati, belonged to northern dialectic division of the Kalapooian linguistic stock; lived on the Yamhill R., population in 1910, 5.

YAQUINA: One of the tribes of the Yakonan linguistic stock to which they gave their name; lived about Yaquina R. and Bay; population in 1910, 19.

YONCALA: From Ayankeld, or Tch' Ayankeld, meaning "those living at Ayankelde"; were the southernmost tribe of the Kalapooian linguistic stock, forming one of the three dialectic divisions; lived on Elk and Calapooya Creeks; tributaries of the Umpqua R.; population in 1910, 11.

Pennsylvania

DELAWARE: In early times in E. Pa., along Delaware R., later for a time on the Susquehanna and headwaters of the Ohio.

ERIE: Extreme N.W. corner of state.

HONNIASONT: "Wearing something round the neck"; belonged to Iroquoian linguistic family.

IROQUOIS: In early times only as hunters, later settled.

SALUDA: A band of "Saluda" Indians from S. Carolina moved to Conestoga in 18th cent. They may have been Shawnee.

SAPONI: Majority lived at Shamokin for a few years some time after 1740, but then continued on to join the Iroquois.

SHAWNEE: Bands of Shawnee were temporarily located at Conestoga, Sewickley, and other points in Pa.

SUSQUEHANNA: A shortened form of Susquehannock, meaning unknown; belonged to Iroquoian linguistic family; lived on Susquehanna R. in N.Y., Pa., and Md.; pop. in 1600, 5000; in 1648, 550 warriors.

TUSCARORA: Stopped for time in Susquehanna Valley on way to join Iroquois bands in N.Y.

TUTELO: Most of these Indians lived at Shamokin with the Saponi and accompanied them to the Iroquois nation.

WENROHRONON: Occupied some parts of the state along the N.E. border.

Rhode Island

ABNAKI: Probably Wabnaki, "those living at the sunrise," "those living at the east," "easterners"; belonged to the Algonquian linguistic family; pop. 3000 in 1600; sometimes name includes Malecite, Penokcot, Pennacook.

NARRAGANSET: "People of the small point"; belonged to Algonquian linguistic family; occupied greater part of R.I. W. of Narragansett Bay, between Providence and Pawcatuck Rivers; pop. in 1600, 4000, including E. Niantic; in 1812, 140; in 1910, 16.

NIANTIC, EASTERN: "At a point of land on a (tidal) river or estuary"; occupied W. coast of Conn.; E. and W. Niantic were parts of one original tribe split in two, perhaps by the Pequot; nearest relatives of both probably the Narraganset.

NIPMUC: The Coweset and some other bands of Nipmuc extended into N.W. part of state, but most of these were under domination of Narraganset.

PEQUOT: Originally occupied some lands in W. R.I. of which the Narraganset dispossessed them.

WAMPANOAG: Occupied mainland sections of R.I. E. of Narragansett Bay and Providence River; at one period held island which gives state name, but were driven by Narraganset.

South Carolina

CATAWBA: Belonged to Siouan linguistic family; lived in York and Lancaster Counties mainly, but extended as far as North Carolina and Tennessee; pop. in 1600, 5000; in 1752, 1000; in 1775, 400; in 1930, 166.

CHEROKEE: Occupied extreme N.W. part of state.

CHIAHA: Lived in state at times.

CHICKASAW: In 1753 a body of Chickasaw settled on state side of Savannah R.; moved to Augusta in 1757; sided against Colonies in Revolution and their lands were confiscated (1783). See Mississippi.

CONGAREE: Spoke a Siouan dialect, related to Catawba; lived on Congaree R., centering around present capital city, Columbia; pop. in 1600, 800; in 1715, 40.

CREEKS: In time of De Soto, the Creeks occupied several towns near the Savannah R., and were often found until much later in the provincial towns of the area.

CUSABO: Means possibly "Coosawhatchie River (people)"; belonged to Muskhogean linguistic family; lived in southernmost S. Carolina between Charleston Harbor and Savannah R., in valleys of the Ashley, Edisto, Ashepoo, Combahee, Salkehatchie, and Coosawatchie rivers.

ENO: Moved into northern part of state after 1716, and perhaps united with Catawbas.

KEYAUEE: Settled on Pee Dee after 1716; probably united with Catawbas.

NATCHEZ: A band lived near Four Hole Springs for several years' up to 1744.

PEDEE: Probably belonged to Siouan linguistic family; lived on Great Pee Dee R., particularly in middle course; pop. in 1600, 600.

SALUDA: Probably Shawnees, of Algonquian linguistic family; lived on Saluda R.

SANTEE: Means "the river," or "the river is there"; belonged most probably to Siouan linguistic family; lived on middle course of Santee R.; pop. in 1600, 1000; in 1715, 80-85.

SEWEE: Perhaps, means "island"; belonged most probably to Siouan linguistic family; lived in lower course of Santee R., westward to Monks Corner, Berkeley County; pop. 1600, 800; in 1715, 57.

SHAKORI: Probably moved down with Enos after 1716 and united with Catawbas.

SHAWNEE: About 1680, a band settled on Savannah R. and settled near Augusta; by 1731 all had moved to Pennsylvania.

SISSIPAHAW: May have been in state in 1569.

SUGEREE: Possibly means "people stingy," "spoiled," or "of river whose-water-cannot-be-drunk"; probably belonged to Siouan linguistic family; lived around Sugar Creek in York County, S. C., and Mecklenburg County, N. C.

WACCAMAW: Probably of Siouan linguistic family; lived on Waccamaw R., and lower course of Pee Dee; pop. in 1600, 900 (smaller tribes included).

WATEREE: Possibly means "to float on the water"; probably of Siouan linguistic stock; lived most probably on Wateree R., below Camden; pop. in 1600, 1000.

WAXHAW: Probably belonged to Siouan linguistic family; lived in Lancaster County, S. C., and Union and Mecklenburg counties, N. C.; included in 5000 Catawbas estimated for 1600.

WINYAH: Probably belonged to Siouan linguistic family; lived on Winyah Bay, Black River, and on lower course of Pee Dee; pop. in 1715, 106.

YAMASEE: Probably moved back and across S. border of state; from 1687-1715 settled on N. side of Savannah R.

YUCHI: Entered S.C. probably after 1661; band high up on Savannah R. until 1716; another body settled later between Silver Bluff and Ebenezer Creek; between 1729-1751 completed westward evacuation to join Creeks.

South Dakota

ARAPAHO: Are traditionally associated with the Black Hills.

ARIKARA: Stopped along the Missouri R. during their migration northward after splitting from the Skidi Pawnee.

CHEYENNE: Means, in Dakota, "people of alien speech," or "red talkers"; Cheyenne was one of the three most aberrant languages of the Algonquian linguistic family, shared by no tribe except the Sutaio, whose speech differed only in minor points; were associated with the Cheyenne R. and the Black Hills in South Dakota, but are notorious for their nomadic habits; population in 1780, 3500; in 1937, 1561 Northern Cheyenne and 2836 Southern Cheyenne and Arapaho together.

DAKOTA: Means "allies" in the Santee or eastern dialect; belonged to the Siouan linguistic family, most closely related to the Hidatsa; lived by the Mississippi in S. Minnesota, N.W. Wisconsin, and nearby Iowa, and gradually extended their holdings westward; population in 1780, 25,000; in 1937, 33,625.

KIOWA: Occupied the Black Hills before the Sutaio and Cheyenne.

MANDAN: Are said to have lived along the Missouri R. before migrating to North Dakota.

OMAHA: Were driven from Minnesota to the Missouri in South Dakota and were later forced by the Dakota downstream to Nebraska.

PONCA: Came with the Omaha from Minnesota, but left them and settled for a time in the Black Hills; then returned to the Missouri and settled in Nebraska.

SUTAIO: Belonged to the Algonquian linguistic stock, related most closely to the Cheyenne; were first known to the Whites as living between the Missouri R. and Black Hills.

WINNEBAGO: Lived for a time on Crow Creek reservation after leaving Minnesota in 1862; then took refuge with the Omaha.

Tennessee

CATAWBA: Lived among the Cherokee for a brief period in their later history and they may have occupied lands in Tennessee at that time; may have been in E. Tennessee at a more remote epoch.

CHEROKEE: Meaning possibly from Creek tciloki, "people of a different speech"; their language is the most aberrant form of speech of the Iroquoian linguistic family; from the earliest times of which we have any certain knowledge, the Cherokee have occupied the highest districts of the S. end of the Appalachian chain, mainly in the states of Tennessee and North Carolina, but including also parts of South Carolina, Georgia, Alabama, and Virginia; there seems to have been a Cherokee migration legend something like that of the Creeks, according to which the tribe entered their historic seats from some region toward the N.E.; population 22,000 in 1650, 20,000 in 1729, 22,500 in 1838, 19,000 in 1885, 31,489 in 1910, 36,432 in 1923, and 45,238 in 1930.

CIAHA: A part of this tribe was encountered by De Soto in 1540, probably on what is now Burns Island.

CHICKASAW: In historic times claimed the greater part of W. Tennessee, and twice drove Shawnee Indians from the Cumberland Valley, the first time with the help of the Cherokee, according to the claim of the latter; at an early date they had a settlement on the lower Tennessee R., but it is doubtful whether this was in Tennessee or Kentucky.

KASKINAMPO: Meaning unknown, though -nampo may be the Koasati word for many; their best known historic location was on the lower end of an island in the Tennessee R., probably the one now called Pine Island.

MOSOPELEA: Probably established themselves on the Cumberland R. and at one or two points on the Tennessee shore of the Mississippi, on their way from Ohio to Mississippi.

MUSKOGEE: Some of them probably occupied part of Tennessee in prehistoric times, and at a later date their war parties constantly visited the area.

NATCHEZ: After being driven from Mississippi and Louisiana, one band of Natchez lived among the Cherokee.

OFO: See Ofo, under *Mississippi* and *Ohio*.

SHAWNEE: Meaning "southerners," the best-known variants of the name being the French *Chaouanons*, and that which appears in the name of the Savannah R.; belonged to the Algonquian linguistic stock, their closest relatives being the Fox, Sauk, and Kickapoo; there was scarcely a tribe that divided as often, or moved so much as the Shawnee, but one of the earliest historic seats of the people as a whole was on the Cumberland R.; indications are they migrated there from the N. not long previous to the historic period; population in 1650, 3000; 1910, 1338; 1930, 1161.

TALI: A tribe met by De Soto near the great bend of the Tennessee and found in the same region by the earliest English and French explorers, living in what is now northern Alabama and perhaps also in Tennessee; it is probable they were part of the Creeks.

TUSKEGEE: One band formed a settlement or settlements in the Cherokee nation.

YUCHI: Most probably lived at one period in and near the mountains of E. Tennessee, though one band of them was on the Tennessee R. just above Muscle Shoals and there is evidence that they once occupied the Hiawassee Valley.

Texas

AKOKISA: The Atakapa living in S.E. Texas between Trinity Bay and Trinity R. and Sabine R.

ALABAMA: Some came to Texas in early 19th cent., where the largest single body of Alabama still lives in Polk Co.

ANADARKO: A tribe or band of the Hasinai Confederacy.

APACHE: In early times the Jicarilla and other Apache raided across the N.W. and W. boundaries of Texas, but only the Lipan established headquarters within the state.

ARANAMA: Were associated sometimes with the Karankawa in the Franciscan missions, but were said to be distinct from them.

ATAKAPA: See also under Louisiana, and reference to Akokisa above.

BIDAI: Are thought to have been of the Atakapan linguistic stock; lived on the middle course of the Trinity R. about Bidai Creek and to the W. and S.W.; population in 1690, 500; in 1805, 10.

BILOXI: Some were in Texas before 1828; a band camped on the Little R., a tributary of the Brazos, about 1846, and afterward occupied a village on Biloxi Bayou in Angelica Co., but later went to Louisiana or Oklahoma.

CADDO: Tribes included the Adai and the Natchitoches Confederacy (see under *Louisiana*); and the Eyeish, the Hasinai Confederacy, and the Kadohadacho Confederacy in Texas.

CHEROKEE: A chief called Bowl led a band of Cherokee into Texas early in the 19th cent., but he was driven back and killed by the Texans.

CHOCTAW: Twelve hundred Choctaw were reported on the Sabine and Neches rivers in 1822; the Yowani Choctaw were admitted among the Caddo there; all of the Choctaw finally moved to Oklahoma.

COAHUILTECAN TRIBES: Name comes from the Mexican state of Coahuila, where the tribes lived as well as in Texas; includes all the tribes known to have belonged to the Coahuiltecan linguistic family and some supposed on circumstantial evidence to be a part of it; most of the so-called Tamaulipecan family of Mexico were probably related to the Coahuiltecan tribes, as were probably also, if more distantly, the Karankawan and Tonkawan groups; spread over E. Coahuila, Mexico, and almost all Texas W. of San Antonio R. and Cibolo Creek; population in 1690, 15,000.

COMANCHE: Belonged to the Shoshonean linguistic family, a branch of Uto-Aztecan, its tongue being almost identical with that of the Shoshoni; lived in N.W. Texas and beyond as far as the Arkansas R.; population in 1690, 7000; in 1937, 2213.

CREEKS: See Muskogee, under *Alabama*.

DEADOSE: Atakapa tribe or subtribe in S. central Texas.

EYEISH (HAISH): Belonged to the Caddoan linguistic stock, closely related to the Adai and the peoples of the Kadohadacho and Hasinai confederacies; lived on Ayish Creek, N.E. Texas, between the Sabine and Neches rivers; population in 1779, 20 families; in 1828, 160 families.

HAINAI: Prominent band of the Hasinai Confederacy.

HASINAI CONFEDERACY: Means "our own folk"; also appears as Assinay or Cenis; one of the major divisions of the Caddo; lived in N.E. Texas between the headwaters of the Neches and Trinity rivers; population in 1690, estimated at 4000; in 1937, 967.

ISLETA DEL SUR: See Pueblos, under *New Mexico*.

JICARILLA: Ranged into Texas at times.

KADOHADACHO CONFEDERACY: Means "real chiefs," *kadi* being word for "chief," and the root of the word *Caddo;* belonged to the Caddo division of the Caddoan linguistic stock; lived in N.E. Texas and S.W. Arkansas at the Great Bend of the Red R., though they are usually associated with the Caddo Lake region which they later occupied; population 1700-1709, estimated at 2000-2500; in 1937, 967.

KARANKAWAN TRIBES: An independent linguistic stock, seemingly most closely connected with the Coahuiltecan group; lived on the Gulf of Mexico between Trinity and Arkansas Bays.

KICHAI (KITSEI): A tribe of the Caddoan stock whose language lay midway between Wichita and Pawnee; lived on the upper waters of Trinity R. and between Trinity and Red rivers; population in 1690, 500; in 1910 census, 10.

KIOWA: Ranged across N. Texas.

KOASATI: By 1850 most of the Koasati were in Texas on the Neches and Trinity (earlier on the Sabine) rivers; a pestilence drove the survivors back to Louisiana, where the largest body still lives; about 10 lived with the Alabama in Polk Co., in 1912.

LIPAN: From Ipa-N'de, and apparently a personal name; N'de means "people"; one of the tribes of the Athapascan linguistic stock to which the general name Apache was applied;

formed one linguistic group with the Jicarilla; formerly ranged from the Rio Grande
in New Mexico over E. New Mexico and W.
Texas, S.E. to the Gulf of Mexico; population
in 1690, 500; in 1910 census, 28.

MUSKOGEE: A few came to Texas in the 19th
cent.

NABEDACHE; NACACHAU; NACANISH; NA-
COGDOCHE; NADACO; NAMIDISH; NE-
CHAUI; NECHES; and one section of the
NASONI: Small bands or tribes belonging
to the Hasinai Confederacy.

NANATSOHO; NASONI (UPPER): Small bands
or tribes connected with the Kadohadacho
Confederacy.

PAKANA: A Muskogee division.

PASCAGOULA: Bands entered Texas from
Louisiana early in the 19th cent., one living
for a long time on Biloxi Bayou, a branch
of the Neches; all had disappeared in 1912
except two half-Pascagoula with the Alabama in Polk Co.

PATIRU: Associated with the Akokisa, Bidai
and Deadose in San Ildefonso Mission W.
of the Trinity R., believed to have spoken
an Atakapan language, and to have lived
formerly along Caney Creek.

PUEBLOS ISLETA DEL SUR AND SENECÚ
DEL SUR: Near El Paso, are both settlements composed mainly of Indians brought
back by Gov. Otermin in 1681 after an unsuccessful attempt to subdue the Pueblo
Indians of the Rio Grande; Senecú was actually in Chihuahua, Mexico; the people of
these pueblos are now almost completely
Mexicanized. (See New Mexico.)

QUAPAW: Lived with the Caddo Indians in
N.W. Louisiana and N.E. Texas (1823-33), the
Imaha band considered a constituent element
of the Caddo Confederacy.

SENECÚ DEL SUR: See Pueblos, above.

SHAWNEE: A band entered Texas briefly in
mid 19th cent., but were later moved to
Oklahoma.

SHUMAN (JUMANO, HUMANO): Eastern division was once classified as Caddoan stock,
but is now considered Uto-Aztecan; the
western section was classed, erroneously, as
Tanoan; lived in early times along the Rio
Grande between the mouth of the Concho
and El Paso, extending W. as far as the
Casas Grandes in Chihuahua; later some entered the W. Texas plains and E. New Mexico.

SOACATINO (XACATIN): Met by De Soto in
N.W. Louisiana or N.E. Texas and, though
Caddo, not definitely identified with a known
Caddo tribe.

TAWAKONI: A subdivision of the Wichita, or
a tribe closely affiliated with them.

TONKAWAN TRIBES: Constituted a distinct
linguistic family, with affinities for the Coahuiltecan and probably Karankawan and
Tunican groups; lived in central Texas from
Cibolo Creek on the S.W. to within a few
miles of the Trinity R. on the N.E.; population in 1690, 1600; in 1937, 51.

WACO: A subtribe or tribe of the Wichita
group; lived briefly near Waco before moving
to Oklahoma.

WICHITA: Lived, for a long time, on either
side of the Red R. in N. Texas.

Utah

BANNOCK: Ranged N. Utah to the Uintah
Mts., and beyond Great Salt Lake.

GOSIUTE: Small body of Indians in region
around Great Salt Lake.

NAVAHO: At times occupied small part of
S.E. Utah, to the San Juan R.

PAIUTE, SOUTHERN: Occupied S.W. Utah
(see also reference under Paiute, Northern
in Nevada.

SHOSHONE, WESTERN: Extended into N.
Utah; they included the Gosiute (see reference
under Shoshone, Northern in Idaho, and also
Gosiute above).

UTE: Belonged to Shoshonean division of the
Uto-Aztecan linguistic stock, closest to the
true Paiute, Kawaiisu, and Chemehuevi; lived
in central and W. Colorado and all of E.
Utah, including E. Salt Lake Valley and Utah
Valley and into drainage area of the San
Juan R. in New Mexico; population in 1845,
4500; in 1937, 2163.

Vermont

ABNAKI: A band known as the Missiassik was
at one time settled on Missisquoi R. in
Franklin Co.

MAHICAN: Bands of the Mahican hunted in
S.W. and W. parts of Vt., making temporary
settlements from time to time. One Mahican
village (Winooskeek) is thought to have been
located at mouth of Winooski R.

PENNACOOK: Lived on E. margins of Vt., and
hunted considerably within borders.

POCOMTUC: Northernmost bands of the Pocomtuc extended into S. parts of Vt.

Virginia

CHEROKEE: Claimed territory in extreme S.W.
part of state; it was at least part of their
hunting territory if not their home.

MANAHOAG: "They are very merry" (improb-
able); belonged to Siouan linguistic family;
lived in N. Va. between falls of the rivers
and mts. E. and W. and the Potomac and
N. Anna rivers N. and S.; pop. 1500 in 1600,
perhaps.

MEHERRIN: Belonged to Iroquoian linguistic
family; lived along Meherrin R. on Va.-N.
Carolina border; pop. 700 in 1600.

MONACAN: "Digging stick" or "spade" (possible); belonged to Siouan linguistic family;
lived on upper waters of James R. above
falls at Richmond; pop. in 1600, 1200 doubtful.

NAHYSSAN: Belonged to Siouan linguistic
family; lived on left bank of James R., about
1½ mi. upstream from Wingina, in Nelson Co.

NOTTAWAY: "Adders"; belonged to Iroquoian
linguistic family; lived on Nottaway R. in
S.E. Virginia, pop. in 1600, 1500; in 1825, 47.

OCCANEECHI: Belonged to Siouan linguistic
family; lived on middle and largest island in
Roanoke R., near site of Clarksville, Mecklenburg Co., Va.; pop. in 1600, 1200.

POWHATAN: "Falls in a current of water";
belonged to Algonquian linguistic family;
lived in tidewater section of Va. from Potomac R. to divide between James R. and
Albemarle Sound, and the territory of the
present eastern shore of Va.; pop. in 1600,
9000.

SAPONI: "Shallow water"; belonged to Siouan
linguistic family; lived probably on banks of
Riuawna, in Albemarle Co., directly N. of
the U. of Va., and about ½ mi. up the river
from the present bridge of the Southern Ry.;
pop. in 1600, 2700.

SHAKORI: Seem to have lived in Va. at one
time.

SHAWNEE: For a time in Shenandoah Valley.

TUTELO: Belonged to Siouan linguistic family; lived near Salem, Va., though Big Sandy R. at one time bore their name and may have been an earlier seat.

Washington

CATHLAMET: Belonged to Chinookan stock; lived on S. bank near the mouth of the Columbia R., between Tongue Point and Puget Sound, and on N. bank from the mouth of Grays Bank to a little E. of Oak Point; population in 1780, 450; now extinct.

CATHLAPOTLE: Means "people of Lewis River"; belonged to Chinookan linguistic stock; lived on the lower Lewis R. and on S.E. side of the Columbia R. in Clarke Co.; population in 1780, 1300; in 1806, 900.

CAYUSE: Lived near heads of Wallawalla, Umatilla, and Grande Ronde rivers, from Blue Mts. to Deschutes R., Washington and Oregon.

CHEHALIS: Means "sand"; belonged to coastal division of Salishan linguistic family, closest to the Humptulips, Wynoochee, and Quinault; lived on lower Chehalis R., and S. side of Grays Bay; later occupied Chinook lands near Willapa Bay.

CHELAN: Name derives from Chelan Lake; were an interior Salish tribe speaking the Wenatchee dialect; lived at outlet of Lake Chelan.

CHILLUCKITTEQUAW: Belonged to Chinookan linguistic stock: Lewis and Clark reported finding them in Klickitat and Skamania Counties, on N side of the Columbia R., from 10 miles below the Dalles to the Cascades; population in 1780, 3000.

CHIMAKUM: With the Quileute and Hoh, constituted the Chimakuan linguistic stock; which was probably connected with the Salishan stock; lived on peninsula between Hood's Canal and Port Townsend; population in 1780, 400; in 1910, 3.

CHINOOK: From Tsinúk, their Chehalis name; belonged to Lower Chinook division of the Chinookan family; lived on the N. side of Columbia R. from the mouth to Grays Bay (not Grays Harbor), and northward on the seacoast to Willipa or Shoalwater Bay; population in 1780 (with Killaxthokl), 800; now extinct.

CLACKAMAS: Said to have lived on either side of the Columbia R.

CLALLAM: Means "strong people"; belonged to the coastal division of the Salishan linguistic stock, closest to the Songish; lived on the S. side of the Strait of Juan de Fuca, between Port Discovery and the Hoko R.; later occupied Chimakum and lower Vancouver Island; population in 1780, 2000; in 1937, 764.

CLALSKANIE: See Clalskanie, under Oregon.

COLUMBIA (SINKIUSE-COLUMBIA): Named for their former connection with the Columbia R.; belonged to inland division of the Salishan linguistic stock, closest to the Wenatchee and Methow; lived on the E. bank of the Columbia R. from Ft. Okanogan to Pt. Eaton, then on Columbia Reservation; one band is now in Colville Reservation; population in 1780 (with Pisquow), 1000-10,000; in 1910, 52.

COLVILLE: Named after Ft. Colville, the memorial to London Governor Colville of the Hudson's Bay Company (1825); belonged to inland division of the Salishan linguistic stock, in the same branch with the Okanagon, Sanpoil, and Senijextee; lived on the Colville R. and the Columbia R. between Kettle Falls and Hunters; population in 1780, 1000-2500; in 1937, 322.

COPALIS: Belonged to the coastal division of the Salishan linguistic family; lived on the Copalis R. and Pacific Coast between the mouth of Joe Creek and Grays Harbor; population in 1805, 200; in 1888, 5.

COWLITZ: Belonged to the coastal division of the Salishan linguistic family; lived on the lower and middle courses of the Cowlitz R., later on Chehalis and Puyallup reservations.

DUWAMISH: From a place name; belonged to Nisqually dialectic group of the coast division of the Salishan linguistic stock; population in 1780 (with Suquamish and other tribes), 1200; in 1910, 20.

HOH: Spoke the Quileute language; lived on the Hoh R. on the W. coast of Washington; population in 1780 (with Quileute), 500; in 1905, 62.

HUMPTULIPS: Said to mean "chilly region"; belonged to the coastal division of the Salishan linguistic stock; closest to the Chehalis; lived on the Humptulips R., part of Grays Harbor, including Hoquiam Creek and Whiskam R.; population in 1888, 18; in 1904, 21.

KALISPEL: Extended over the E. border from Idaho.

KLICKITAT: In Chinook "beyond," referring to the Cascade Mts.; belonged to the Shahaptian division of Shapwailutan linguistic family; population in 1780 (with Taitnapam), 600; in 1910, 405.

KWAIAILK: Belonged to the coastal division of the Salishan linguistic family, closest to the Cowlitz and Chehalis; lived on the upper Chehalis R.; population in 1855, 216.

KWALHIOQUA: Means in Chinook, "a lonely place in the woods"; belonged to Athapascan linguistic stock; lived on the upper course of the Willopah R., and the S. and W. headwaters of the Chehalis; population in 1780, 200; now extinct.

LUMMI: Belonged to the coastal division of the Salishan linguistic family; lived on upper Bellingham Bay, and near the mouth of the Noonsack R., until finally placed on the Lummi Reservation; population in 1780 (with Samish and Noonsack), 1000; in 1937, 661.

MAKAH: Means "cape people"; belonged to Nootka branch of the Wakashan linguistic family; lived about Cape Flattery, claiming Tatoosh Island, and the coast E. to the Hoko R., and south to Flattery Rocks; now on Makah Reservation; population in 1780 (with the Ozette), 2000; in 1937, 407.

METHOW: Spoke a dialect of the interior division of the Salishan linguistic stock; lived on the Methow R.

MICAL: Were a branch of the Shahaptian tribe called Pshwanwapam; lived on the upper Nisqually R.

MUCKLESHOOT: Belonged to the Nisqually dialectic group of the coastal division of the Salishan linguistic family; lived on the White R., from Kent eastward to the mountains, and may have held the Green R.

NEKETEMEUK: A problematic tribe, said by those who believe that they ever really existed to have been a Salishan tribe living near The Dalles.

NESPELEM: A division of the Sanpoil.

NOONSACK: Means "mountain men"; belonged to the coastal division of the Salishan linguistic family; lived on the Noonsack R., Whatcom Co.; population in 1906, 200; in 1937, 239.

NTLAKYAPAMUK: Southern bands roamed through Washington.

OKANOGAN: From Okanaqen (Okanaqenix, Okinaqen), a place on the Okanogan R. at the mouth of the Similkameen, near Okanogan Falls, which is said to have been the tribal headquarters, and even the origin of the entire tribe; belonged to the interior division of the Salishan stock; lived above the mouth of the Similkameen R. on the Okanogan R. as far as Canadian border, and along the shores of Okanagan Lake in British Columbia; population in 1780, 2000; in 1906, 1351.

OZETTE: Were a southern branch of the Makah, belonging to the Nootka branch of the Wakashan linguistic family; lived on Ozette Lake and Ozette R. in Clallam Co.; in 1937, 1.

PALOUSE: Belonged to the Shahaptian division of the Shapwailutan linguistic stock, closest to the Nez Percé; lived in the Palouse R. Valley in Washington and Idaho and on a small section of the Snake R., eastward to the Camas grounds near Moscow, Idaho; included in the Yakima Treaty (1855), they have as yet declined the obligations and the offer of a reservation; population in 1780, 5400; in 1910, 82.

PSHWANWAPAM: Means "the stony ground"; belonged to the Shahaptian division of the Shapwailutan linguistic family; lived on the upper Yakima R.

PUYALLUP: From Pwiyalap, the native name of the Puyallup R.; belonged to the Nisqually dialect group of the coastal division of the Salishan linguistic family; lived at the mouth of the Puyallup R. and the nearby coast, including Carr Inlet and the southern part of Vashon Island; population in 1937, 322.

QUEETS (QUAITSO): Belonged to the coastal division of the Salishan linguistic family, closest to the Quinault; lived on the Queets R. and branches; population in 1805, 250; in 1909, 62.

QUILEUTE: With the Hoh and Chimakum, constituted the Chimakuan linguistic family; lived on Quilayute R. on W. coast of Washington; now on Quileute and Makah Reservations; population in 1780 (with Hoh), 500; in 1937, 284.

QUINAULT: A corruption of Kwinail, which was the largest settlement on the site of present Taholah village at the mouth of the Quinault R.; belonged to the coastal division of the Salishan linguistic family; lived in the valley of the Quinault R. and on the Pacific coast between Raft R. and Joe Creek; population in 1805, less than 800; in 1937, 1228.

SAHEHWAMISH: Belonged to the Nisqually dialectic group of the coastal division of the Salishan linguistic stock; lived on inmost inlets of Puget Sound; population in 1780, 1200; in 1907, 780.

SAMISH: Belonged to the coastal division of the Salishan linguistic family; lived on Samish Bay and Samish Island, Guemes Island, and N.W. part of Fidalgo Island; now on the Lummi Reservation.

SANPOIL: Belonged to the inland division of the Salishan linguistic stock; lived on the Sanpoil R. and Nespelem Creek, and on the Columbia R. below Big Bend; now on Sanpoil and Colville Reservations; population in 1780, 800-1700; in 1937, 202.

SATSOP: Belonged to the coastal division of the Salishan linguistic family; lived on the Satsop R., a branch of the Chehalis; population in 1888, 12.

SEMIAHMOO: Belonged to the coastal divi-sion of the Salishan linguistic stock; lived about Semiahmoo Bay in N.W. Washington and S.W. British Columbia; population in 1843, 300; in 1909, 38 (all in Canada).

SENIJEXTEE: Belonged to the inland division of the Salishan linguistic stock, closest to the Sanpoil; lived on either side of the Columbia R. from Kettle Falls to Canada, the valley of the Kettle R., Kootenay R. from mouth to the first falls, and near Arrow Lakes, B.C.; population in 1780, 500; in 1909, 342 (on Colville Reservation).

SINKAIETK: Classified with the Okanogan and called Lower Okanogan, both being dialectic groups of interior Salishan Indians; lived on the Okanogan R., from its mouth to the mouth of the Similkameen.

SINKAKAIUS: Means "between people"; belonged to the interior division of Salishan linguistic stock; lived between the Columbia R. and the Grand Coulee near Waterville.

SKAGIT: Belonged to the coastal division of Salishan linguistic stock; lived on Skagit and Stillaguamish Rivers except at mouths; population in 1853, 300; in 1937, 200.

SKILLOOT: Belonged to Clackamas dialectic division of the Chinookan linguistic family; lived on either side of the Columbia R.; population in 1806, 2500; now extinct.

SKIN: From a town name; belonged to the Shahaptian division of Shapwailutan linguistic stock; lived on the Columbia R. from The Dalles to a point 75 miles above.

SNOHOMISH: Belonged to the Nisqually dialectic group of the coastal division of the Salishan linguistic stock; lived on lower Snohomish R. and S. end of Whidbey Island.

SNOQUALMIE: Belonged to the Nisqually branch of the coastal division of the Salishan linguistic family; lived on the Snoqualmie and Skykomish Rivers.

SPOKAN: Belonged to the inland division of Salishan linguistic stock; closest to the Kalispel, Pend d'Oreilles, Sematuse, and Salish; lived on the Spokane and Little Spokane Rivers, perhaps as far S. as Cow Creek, and N. to all the feeders of the Spokane R.; population in 1780, 1400-2500; in 1937, 847.

SQUAXON (SQUAKSON): Belonged to the Nisqually branch of the coast division of the Salishan linguistic family; lived on North Bay, Puget Sound.

SUQUAMISH: Belonged to the Nisqually branch of the coastal division of Salishan linguistic stock, closest to the Duwamish; Seattle was the famous chief of both tribes; lived on the W. side of Puget Sound; population in 1857, 441; in 1937, 168.

SWALLAH: Belonged to the coastal division of Salishan linguistic family; lived on Orcas Island and San Juan Island and the group to which they belong.

SWINOMISH: Belonged to the coastal division of Salishan linguistic family; lived on N. part of Whidbey Island and about the mouth of the Skagit R.

TAIDNAPAM (UPPER COWLITZ): Belonged to Shahaptian division of the Shapwailutan linguistic family; lived on headwaters of the Cowlitz R., perhaps as far as headwaters of the Lewis R.

TWANA: Constituted one dialectic group of the coastal division of the Salishan stock; lived on both sides of Hood's Canal; now on the Skokomish Reservation.

WALLA WALLA: Means "little river"; belongs to Shahaptian division of the Shapwailutan linguistic stock; closely related to the Nez Percé; lived on the lower Walla Walla R.

(except perhaps in the Cayuse area around Whitman), and for a short span along the Columbia and Snake rivers, near their junction, in Washington and Oregon; now on the Umatilla Reservation, Oregon.

WANAPAM: Belonged to the Shahaptian division of Shapwailutan linguistic stock, closest to the Palouse; lived in bend of Columbia R. between Priest Rapids and some distant point below the Umatilla R. mouth, and E. of the Columbia N. of Pasco; population in 1780, 1800.

WATLALA: Occupied the N. side of the Columbia R. from Cascades to Skamania and perhaps to Cape Horn, and a larger area on the S. side.

WAUYUKMA: Belonged to Shahaptian division of the Shapwailutan linguistic family, closest to the Palouse; lived on the Snake R. below mouth of the Palouse R.

WENATCHEE: Belonged to inland division of the Salishan linguistic family, closest to the Sinkiuse-Columbia Indians; lived on Methow and Wenatchee Rivers and Chelan Lake; now under Colville Agency; population in 1780, over 1400; in 1910, 52.

WISHRAM: Belonged to Chinookan stock, and spoke the same dialect as the Wasco; lived on N. side of the Columbia R. in Klickitat Co.; population in 1780, 1000-1500; in 1937, 124.

WYNOOCHEE: Closely connected with Chehalis Indians and belonged to the coastal division of Salishan linguistic stock; lived on Wynoochee, which flows into the Chehalis.

YAKIMA: Means "runaway"; belonged to Shahaptian division of the Shapwailutan linguistic family; lived on lower Yakima R.

West Virginia

MONETON: "Big water" people; belonged to Siouan linguistic family; lived on lower course of Kanawha R.

CHEROKEE: (see Tennessee) CONOY, (see Maryland and District of Columbia), DELAWARE (see New Jersey), HONNIASONT and SUSQUEHANNA (see Pennsylvania), and SHAWNEE (see Tennessee): All settled in various parts of W. Va. from time to time, but none was established there at an early date for an appreciable period except perhaps the Conoy, whose name appears to be perpetuated in that of the Kanawha R.

Wisconsin

CHIPPEWA: Pushed into Wisconsin in last half of 17th cent.; later drove the Foxes from the northern part of the state and occupied these lands.

DAKOTA: Lived very early in N.W. Margin of Wisconsin.

FOXES: Belonged to Algonquian family in the same group with the Sauk and Kickapoo; lived near Lake Winnebago or along the Fox R.; Lewis and Clark counted 1200 Fox in 1805; in 1930 there were 887 Sauk and Fox.

HOUSATONIC: See Stockbridges.

ILLINOIS: Probably occupied S. and S.W. Wisconsin at some time.

IOWA: The Winnebago are reportedly the mother tribe of the Iowa, Oto, and Missouri, all of whom are thought to have stopped in Wisconsin during their migration southward.

IROQUOIS: Were ancient enemies of the Wisconsin Indians, and the Oneida were later given a reservation in the state.

KICKAPOO: Derived from Kiwegapaw, meaning "he stands about," "he moves about, standing now here, now there"; belonged to Algonquian linguistic stock, in a group with the Foxes and Sauk; may have lived near the Sauk in lower Michigan peninsula; by 1670 they occupied the portage between Fox and Wisconsin rivers, probably near Alloa; later they settled near the Milwaukee R., and gradually began the migrations which took part of them as far as Mexico; population in 1650, 2000; in 1930 census, 523.

MAHICAN: See Stockbridges.

MASCOUTEN: The Prairie Band of the Potawatomi, and also the Peoria Band of Illinois who lived in early times by the Kickapoo.

MENOMINEE: Means "wild rice men," derived from the lake wild rice which was their diet; belonged to the Algonquian linguistic family, close to the Cree and Foxes; lived near the Menominee R., Wisconsin; population in 1650, 3000; the U.S. Indian Office Report of 1937 counted 2221.

MIAMI: Lived in S. Wisconsin at time of early French explorations, but later moved from the state.

MISSOURI: See Iowa.

MUNSEE: Some moved into Wisconsin with the Stockbridges.

NOQUET: Were possibly related to the Menominee or Chippewa, and are thought to have extended at times into N.E. Wisconsin.

ONEIDA: See Iroquois.

OTO: See Iowa.

OTTAWA: Lived for a time in Wisconsin after fleeing from the Iroquois, on islands at the mouth of Green Bay, on the Black R., and at Chequamegon Bay.

POTAWATOMI: Were known by the early French explorers to have occupied the islands at the mouth of Green Bay before beginning to migrate S.

SAUK: Derives from osakiwug, meaning "people of the outlet," or "people of the yellow earth"; belonged to Algonquian linguistic stock, in same group with the Foxes and Kickapoo; lived on upper Green Bay and lower Fox R.; population in 1650, 3000; in 1937 the U.S. Indian office listed 126 Sauk and Fox in Kansas, and 861, chiefly Sauk, in Oklahoma.

STOCKBRIDGES: Name for Indians who belonged to the Housatonic and other tribes of Mahican group, who were placed on a Green Bay reservation in 1833 with the Oneida and some Munsee; in 1856 most of them moved to the reservation they now occupy W. of Shawano.

TIONONTATI: A few lived in Wisconsin as Wyandot.

WINNEBAGO: Means in Fox and Sauk "people of the filthy water"; belonged to the Siouan linguistic family, in the Chiwere subdivision with the Iowa, Oto, and Missouri; lived on S. side of Green Bay and inland to Lake Winnebago; population in 1650, 3800; in 1937 U.S. Indian Office census, 1456 in Wisconsin and 1212 in Nebraska.

WYANDOT: Part fled from the Irouqois to Michilimackinac, then to Green Bay, with some Ottawa.

Wyoming

ARAPAHO: With their near neighbors the Atsina, the most aberrant group of the Algonquian linguistic stock; occupied different regions in historic period, but are closely identified with N.E. Wyoming, where the main body long resided and was finally given a reserve; population in 1780, 3000; in 1930, 1241.

BANNOCK: Some ranged W. Wyoming.

CHEYENNE: Long allied with Arapaho, hunted and warred in E. Wyoming.

COMANCHE: Probably occupied Wyoming lands before moving S.

CROW: Occupied the valleys of Powder, Wind, and Big Horn rivers, and ranged southward to Laramie (see *Montana*).

DAKOTA: Ranged into Wyoming territory but had no permanent settlements there.

KIOWA: Reportedly lived for a time in or near the Black Hills before moving S.

KIOWA APACHE: Shared activities with the Kiowa.

PAWNEE: Hunted and warred in Wyoming at times.

SHOSHONE: Northern Shoshone once occupied W. Wyoming.

UTE: Lived just S. of Wyoming, occasionally entering to hunt or to fight.

Indians, Some Famous American

BIRD WOMAN: See Sacajawea.

BLACK HAWK: (1767-1838) chief of the Sauk (or Sac), an Algonkin tribe in what is now Illinois; sided with English in War of 1812; opposed sale of Indian lands to white settlers pushing west after the War; finally crossed back east of Mississippi River and led attack (1832) which came to be called Black Hawk War (Abraham Lincoln was among American troops fighting Black Hawk); after defeat, he was kept in Ft. Monroe, Va., then finally released; wrote autobiography (1833).

BLUE JACKET: chief of the Shawnee, an Algonkin tribe of the Ohio territory; believed to have led the confederation of Indian tribes that engaged (1794) General Anthony Wayne in the battle of Fallen Timbers (now Maumee, Ohio); deserted by their English allies, the Indians were defeated and accepted a truce that cost them the greater part of Ohio and part of Indiana.

BRANT, JOSEPH: (1742?-1807) chief of the Mohawks, a tribe of the Iroquois confederation, in New York state between Utica and Albany; educated in colonial charity school in Conn.; baptized in Anglican Episcopal Church (hence his English name); sided with British in Revolution, leading Indian troops at battle of Oriskany (1777); organized Cherry Valley Massacre (1778); conducted raids in Mohawk Valley; negotiated treaty with British for indemnification of Iroquois lands lost in Revolution (1785); portrait painted in Indian dress by George Romney (1734-1802), during visit to England; Indian name: Thayendanegea.

CANONCHET: Algonkin warrior and leader, allied to King Philip in series of wars waged against the New England colonists (1675-1676); captured and condemned, he said that he was not unhappy to die before his heart had grown soft, or he had ever said anything unworthy of himself.

CAPTAIN JACK: See Keintpoos.

COCHISE: six-foot chief of Chiricachua Apaches, of the Athabascan family of the Southwest; accused falsely of kidnaping (1861) a white boy (Mickey Free) from ranch near Ft. Buchanan; resented attempts to detain him and nurtured special hatred for white men ("I was at peace with the whites until they tried to kill me for what other Indians did; now I live and die at war with them."); went on warpath, burning 13 white

men alive, torturing 5 to death, dragging 15 to death at the end of a lariat; peace talk with Gen. Gordon Granger at Indian Agency at Canada Alamosa (1871); returned home to southern Arizona shortly after with warriors.

CORNPLANTER: (1735?-1836) chief of the Seneca, a tribe of the Iroquois confederation in New York state; said to have been a half-breed, by a Dutch father; sided with British in Revolution, but in sympathy with Americans in War of 1812; statesman among Indian leaders, he negotiated many treaties and was invited to audiences with Washington and Gen. Anthony Wayne; monument erected to him in Pennsylvania. Also known as John O'Bail.

CRAZY HORSE: (1849?-1877) chief of the Oglalas, a subtribe of the Teton-Dakota of the Sioux family, living in the Dakotas, Missouri, Nebraska, and Wyoming; with Sitting Bull and Gall, attacked Custer in the battle of Little Big Horn (June 25, 1876); surrendered, but was killed while trying to escape; Indian name: Uitco.

GALL: (1840?-1894) chief of the Teton-Dakota (Hunkpapa) tribe of the Sioux family; refused to return from Big Horn Buffalo Grounds (1876) when hunting permits by U.S. government expired; joined with Sitting Bull and Crazy Horse in attack on Gen. George A. Custer (1839-1876) at battle of Little Big Horn (June 25, 1876) where, in the famous "Last Stand," all of Custer's command was wiped out; fled with his band to Canada; reconciled to whites and became (1889) Judge of Court of Indian Offenses of the Indian Agency.

GERONIMO: (1829-1909) chief of the Apache tribe of the Déné family; born in Arizona; participated in raids from 1850; captured and sent to reservation (1883); escaped and resumed terrorism; surrendered voluntarily (1886) and sent to Florida prison, then military reservation at Ft. Sill, Oklahoma; baptized (1903) in Dutch Reformed Church; dictated autobiography (1906); for 40 years the scourge of the western plains.

HIAWATHA: (fl. 1500) a Mohawk (tribe of the Iroquois family) who lived in the Mohawk Valley of New York State; legendary founder of league of the Five Nations (Cayuga, Mohawk, Oneida, Onondaga, Seneca) from among the warring tribes of the Mohawk Valley and Finger Lakes District in New York State; title figure of poem by Henry Wadsworth Longfellow, "The Song of Hiawatha" (1855).

JOHN O'BAIL: See Cornplanter.

JOSEPH CHIEF: chief of the Nez Percé of Shahaptin tribe of the Penutian family, which lived in Washington, Oregon, and Montana; refused (1877) to comply with treaty of 1863 which consigned his people to a reservation; took command of the resistance; fought running battles at White Bird Canyon, Idaho (June 16, 1877); Clear Water River; Billings, Montana; and Bear Paw Mountains, near Chinook, Montana, where he was finally defeated; died at Colville Reservation, Washington, Sept. 21, 1904; is remembered for his touching speech of surrender, which ends: "Hear me, my chiefs. I am tired. My heart is sick and sad. From where the sun now stands I will fight no more forever."

KEINTPOOS (KINTPUASH) CAPTAIN JACK): a chief of Modoc tribe (of the Penutian family) living in southern Oregon; in 1870 fled with Modocs from reservation to California; took refuge in Lava Beds south of Tule Lake; refused orders to return and attacked troops sent after him; went on warpath, burning farms and harassing settlers; leader of Indians through the Modoc War; captured May 31, 1873; tried, and hanged October, 1873.

KEOKUK: (1770?-1848) chief of the Sauk (or Sac), an Algonkin tribe, in what is now Illinois; contemporary of Black Hawk; favored peaceful treaties with the American settlers, using his powers as orator to effect truce between the Sauk and the Sioux (1837), travelling to Washington to present Sauk case in land dispute between the tribes; in 1883 his body was disinterred and moved to Keokuk, Iowa, his namesake; bronze bust has been erected in his memory in Washington.

LILY OF THE MOHAWKS: See Tekakwitha.

LITTLE TURTLE: chief of the Miamis, an Algonkin tribe of the Ohio territory; leader in defeat of Gen. Harmer, who had been sent by Washington (1790) to subdue the tribes that were being encouraged by the English to continue their raids against the American settlements in the Old Northwest; contributed to rout of the army of Gen. St. Clair the following year, when the Iroquois joined the war against the Americans.

LOGAN (SOMETIMES JOHN OR JAMES LOGAN): (1725?-1780) chief of the Mingo, an independent band of the Iroquois family (but associated with Algonkins) living in Pennsylvania; said to have been a half-breed of French parentage; infuriated when some of his people (including relatives) were attacked and killed by white settlers in the Yellow Creek Massacre (1774), he retaliated with raids until Gov. Dunmore of Virginia begged a peace settlement; replied with a famous speech that Jefferson compared to the orations of Demosthenes and Cicero; murdered by his nephew (1780); monument erected near Circleville, Ohio, where speech was delivered; Indian name: Tahgahjute.

MASSASOIT: (D. 1661) chief of Wampanoags, a tribe of Algonkins living in Cape Cod area of Massachusetts; was friendly to the Plymouth colony, and taught the Pilgrims how to raise corn; entered into peace treaty with the colonists in 1621; father of King Philip.

OSCEOLA: (1800?-1838) chief of the Seminoles, a tribe of the Muskhogean family, which is thought to have lived in southern Georgia and Florida; organized and led the Second Seminole War (1835-37); tricked into appearing at a peace conference, he was seized by the U.S. Army and imprisoned in Ft. Moultrie, South Carolina, where he died; the furious Seminoles continued to fight until sued for a true peace.

PETALASHARO I: (1797?-1852) leader of the Pawnee, a tribe of the Caddo family, living in Nebraska; celebrated as a religious reformer because of his efforts to end the ritual of human sacrifice in the tribal ceremony dedicated to the Morning Star; when a Comanche maiden was brought to the sacrificial altar, Petalasharo suddenly seized her and carried her back to her own people; the practice of human sacrifice was soon officially ended.

PHILIP, KING: succeeded to leadership of Wampanoags in 1662, after death of his father, Massasoit; as the Plymouth colony expanded, tension mounted between his tribe and the whites, leading to the deaths of 3 Wampanoags in 1675; Philip retaliated by waging war (King Philip's War, 1675-1676), and was himself killed on August 12, 1676; Indian name: Metacomet.

POCAHONTAS: (1595?-1617) chieftain's daughter of the Powhatan league of tribes of the Algonkin family, occupying the territory where the English established their first colony in Virginia; father, Powhatan; saved life of colonial leader John Smith (1580-1631); married (1614) tobacco farmer, John Rolfe (1585-1622); died in England; Indian name: Matoaka; Christian name: Rebecca.

PONTIAC: chief of the Ottawas, an Algonkin tribe of the Ohio territory, a leader in the French and Indian War (1754-1763), on side of French; continued hostilities after the fall of Quebec (1763), and rallied the Delawares, Miamis, Ojibways, Ottawas, Potawatomis, and Shawnees to destructive raids on the English colonies throughout the area from Michigan to Pennsylvania, in action called the Pontiac Conspiracy; deserted by the French and his allies, he finally made peace with the English (1766) and retreated to St. Louis, where he was murdered (1769).

POWHATAN: (1550-1618) chief of Powhatan league of Algonkin tribes in territory that is now state of Virginia; father of Pocahontas; Indian name: Wa-hun-sen-a-cawh.

PROPHET: See Tenskwatawa.

RED CLOUD: (1822-1909) chief of the Teton-Dakota tribe of the Sioux family, which was concentrated in the Black Hills (South Dakota, Wyoming); suspected of leading outbreak in Minnesota in 1862; raided U.S. operations trying to establish Fts. Kearney and Fetterman; fell into the ambush of the Wagon Box Fight (1867) near Sheridan, Wyoming; negotiated peace (1869); later retired to Pine Ridge Reservation in South Dakota.

RED EAGLE: (1780?-1824) chief of the Creeks, a tribe of the Muskhogean family (Alabama); encouraged by British in War of 1812, led attack on Ft. Mims (Aug. 30, 1813) and slaughtered garrison of 500, including women and children; opposed by Gen. Andrew Jackson in Creek War (1813-1814), and finally defeated at Horseshoe Bend (Jan. 27, 1814); withdrew to Monroe County, Alabama, after treaty of peace; American name: William Weatherford.

RED JACKET: (1756?-1830) chief of the Senecas, tribe of the Iroquois confederation in New York state; fought with British in Revolution, with Americans in War of 1812; sought friendship between Indians and whites on basis of end to further expansion by the settlers and mutual cultural integrity.

RED WING: (1750?-1825) chief of the Eastern Dakota tribe of the Sioux family, living in the Minnesota territory; sided with the British in the War of 1812, but reconciled later with U.S.; Red Wing, Minnesota is his namesake.

SACAJAWEA (OR SACAGAWEA: BIRD WOMAN): (1787?-1812) a woman of the Snake or Shoshoni tribe of the Uto-Aztecan family, which lived in Montana and Idaho; seized by war party of Hidatsas, and carried off at age 14 to North Dakota; a French-Canadian fur-trapper, Toussaint Charbonneau, adopted and later married her (1804) as his second wife; in same year Charbonneau was taken on by Lewis and Clark as guide and interpreter, with provision that his wife, who knew the country, go along; accompanied the expedition as guide; died Dec. 20, 1812, at age 25.

SEQUOIA (SEQUOYA, OR SEQUOYAH): (1760?-1843) leader of the Eastern Cherokees, a tribe of the Iroquois family then living in Tennessee; said to be half-breed son of a white trader named George Guess (Gist; Guest), whose name he later assumed; crippled accidentally, Sequoia was an intellectual and moral, rather than military, leader of his people; invented (begun 1809) an alphabet (syllabary) to teach writing to the Cherokees, which was adoped (1821) and became basis of newspaper (1827); traveled and lectured to Cherokees west of Mississippi; negotiated treaties with American government; Sequoia tree of California named in his honor.

SITTING BULL: (1834?-1890) a chief of the Te-ton-Dakota tribe of the Sioux family; refus-ed, with Gall and Crazy Horse, to return to reservations after the buffalo-hunting season (1875-76) in the Big Horn country; fell upon the soldiers sent with Gen. George A. Custer to bring them back to the Black Hills; anni-hilated the U.S. troops in Custer's Last Stand at battle of Little Big Horn (June 25, 1876); fled with band to Canada, but returned to U.S. custody when the English and the Canadian Indians refused to help; active again in Indian trouble of 1890; finally caught and executed.

SQUANTO: (D. 1622) chief of the Massachuset tribe of the Algonquian family living in region of Massachusetts Bay between Salem and Brocton; befriended the settlers of the Plymouth Colony and taught them how to plant and grow corn; name has passed into English as *squantum,* meaning a picnic or party, specifically, a chowder party.

TAHGAHJUTE: See Logan.

TAMENEND: (C. 1685) chief of the Delawares, an Algonkin tribe that lived in the valley of the Delaware River; he was held in such esteem that he came to be called St. Tam-many; so legendary was his virtue that he was chosen as patron of a white society that was organized in 1772 as the "Sons of King Tammany"; when veterans of the Revolution organized (c. 1786), they called themselves the Tammany Society; from this group, with its headquarters at Tammany Hall, grew the dominant political organization in New York state.

TAMMANY, SAINT: See Tamenend.

TECUMSEH: (D. 1813) chief of the Shawnees, an Algonkin tribe of the Ohio territory; fought with Blue Jacket against army of Gen. Wayne (1794); attempted to organize Indian tribes from Minnesota to Louisiana into a federation that would live in peace with both the Americans and British; but his broth-er, Tenskwatawa, took adventage of Tecum-seh's peace mission to cause Gen. William Henry Harrison to engage the Indians in ac-tion at Tippecanoe River (1811); Tecumseh fled to Canada, joined the British in the War of 1812, was killed in action (1813) between army of Gen. Harrison and the British under Gen. Proctor in Battle of Thames.

TEKAWITHA: (1656-1680) a young woman of the Mohawks, a tribe of the Iroquois family, living in New York state; with Garaconthie, one of the earliest, and the most celebrated, of the Jesuit converts in New York state; received instruction (1667) in Christianity and baptized; is known as the Lily of the Mohawks because of her outstanding piety.

TENSKWATAWA: a Shawnee, brother of Te-cumseh; the medicine man of his tribe, he was known as the Prophet; ignoring the commands of Tecumseh, he provoked the Americans to war and led the alliance against Gen. Harrison at Tippecanoe (1811).

THAYENDANEGEA: See Brant, Joseph.

WANETA: (1795?-1848) chief of the Yanktonai, a Dakota tribe of the Sioux family, inhabit-ing South Dakota; fought with the British against the Americans in the War of 1812; in 1820 planned a further war against U.S., but was seized and imprisoned at Ft. Snelling,

Minnesota; finally renounced his allegiance to England and became leader of his people in negotiations with U.S.; portrait painted (1832) by George Catlin (1796-1872).

WEATHERFORD, WILLIAM: See Red Eagle.

Indian Reservations
For information about national recreation areas see listings under **National**

Indian reservations of the United States are not recreational areas in the ordinary sense of the word. But many of them are tourist attractions. Ceremonials, architecture, arts and crafts, and other aspects of Indian culture are of great interest.

Indian reservations vary in size from a few hundred acres to the huge Navajo Reservation (three times the size of the state of Massachu-setts). These areas, the last remnants of the vast Indian holdings that once included most of what has become the United States, have been re-served to them by treaties and statutes. Indians are not required to remain on reservations, and thousands of them have settled in towns and cities from coast to coast. They are not supported by the Federal government, but earn their living like other citizens of the United States. Indian ceremonials are held at all times of the year, although summer and early fall are the principal seasons. Ceremonials of particular in-terest include: the Flagstaff Indian Ceremonial (Arizona), July 3-4-5; the Gallup Inter-tribal Ceremonial (New Mexico), the Hopi Snake Dance (Arizona), the Pueblo Corn Dances (New Mex-ico), the Anadarko Indian Fair (Oklahoma), in August; the Crow Fair (Montana), in Septem-ber; the Cherokee Indian Fair (North Carolina), in October; the Navajo Yeibechai dances (Ari-zona and New Mexico), in November; and the Zuni Shalako (New Mexico), in December.

Museums maintained by the Indian Service, illus-trating Indian history and culture, are: Museum of the Plains Indians at Browning, Mont.; Sioux Museum at Rapid City, S. D.; Papago Indian Museum at Sells, Ariz.; and the Oklahoma Tribes Museum at Anadarko, Okla. Schools specializing in arts and crafts are: the Santa Fe Indian School, Santa Fe, N. Mex.; the Haskell Institute, Lawrence, Kans.; the Sequoyah Indian School, Tahlequah, Okla.; and the Pine Ridge Indian School at Pine Ridge, S. D.

Industry
See **Products of the World**

International Calendar of Saints and Special Days
See also **Church Calendar; Easter Dates, Movable Feasts of the Easter Cycle; Festivals and Holy-days; Religious Allusions, Refer-ences, and Symbols** (for Holydays of Obligation)

January

JAN. 1: Circumcision.

JAN. 2: St. Basil; Octave Day of St. Stephen; Holy Name of Jesus.

JAN. 3: St. Genevieve; Octave Day of St. John.

JAN. 4: SS. Prisca, Priscus, Rigobert; Octave Day of Holy Innocents.
JAN. 5: SS. Amelia, Simeon Stylites.
JAN. 6: Epiphany.
JAN. 7: SS. Melanie, Lucian.
JAN. 8: Holy Family.
JAN. 9: SS. Fillan, Julian, Marcellus.
JAN. 10: St. William.
JAN. 11: SS. Hortense, Hyginus.
JAN. 12: SS. Arcadius, Lucienne.
JAN. 13: SS. Kentigern, Veronica.
JAN. 14: SS. Felix of Nola, Hilary.
JAN. 15: SS. Maur (Maurus), Paul the First Hermit.
JAN. 16: SS. Honoré, Marcellus.
JAN. 17: St. Anthony Abbot.
JAN. 18: St. Beatrice; Feast of Chair of St. Peter at Rome.
JAN. 19: SS. Abachum, Audifax, Canute, Marius, Martha (Martyr), Sulpice.
JAN. 20: SS. Fabian, Sebastian.
JAN. 21: St. Agnes.
JAN. 22: SS. Anastasius, Vincent.
JAN. 23: SS. Emerentiana, Raymund of Pennafort.
JAN. 24: St. Timothy.
JAN. 25: Conversion of St. Paul.
JAN. 26: SS. Paul, Polycarp.
JAN. 27: SS. John Chrysostem, Julien.
JAN. 28: SS. Charlemagne, Peter Nolasco; Second Feast of St. Agnes.
JAN. 29: St. Francis de Sales.
JAN. 30: St. Martina.
JAN. 31: SS. John Bosco, Marcella.

February

FEB. 1: SS. Bridget of Kildare, Ignatius of Antioch.
FEB. 2: Purification of B.V.M.
FEB. 3: St. Blaise.
FEB. 4: SS. Andrew Corsini, Gilbert, Joseph Leonissa.
FEB. 5: St. Agatha.
FEB. 6: SS. Dorothy, Titus.
FEB. 7: St. Romuald Abbot.
FEB. 8: SS. Irma, John of Matha.
FEB. 9: SS. Apollonia, Cyril of Alexandria.
FEB. 10: St. Scholastica.
FEB. 11: St. Hortense; Our Lady of Lourdes.
FEB. 12: St. Eulalia; Holy Seven Founders (of Servites).
FEB. 13: St. Lézin.
FEB. 14: SS. Joan Valois, Valentine.
FEB. 15: SS. Faustinus, Jovita.
FEB. 16: Bl. Philippa.
FEB. 17: Bls. Andrew, Luke, Peter.
FEB. 18: SS. Bernadette, Simeon.
FEB. 19: St. Gabinius.
FEB. 20: SS. Olean, Sylvain.
FEB. 21: SS. Felix, Pepin.
FEB. 22: SS. Isabelle, Margaret of Cortona; Feast of Chair of St. Peter at Antioch.
FEB. 23: SS. Gerard, Peter Damian.
FEB. 24: SS. Ethelbert, Matthias.
FEB. 25: SS. Leander, Matthias (in leap year).
FEB. 26: St. Nestor.
FEB. 27: SS. Gabriel (of Our Lady of Sorrows), Honorine.
FEB. 28: St. Theophilus; Bls. Antonia, Louise.
(FEB. 29) St. Oswald.

March

MAR. 1: SS. Aubin, David of Wales.
MAR. 2: St. Simplice.
MAR. 3: St. Marimus.
MAR. 4: SS. Casimir; Lucius.

MAR. 5: St. John-Joseph.
MAR. 6: SS. Colette, Felicitas, Perpetua.
MAR. 7: St. Thomas Aquinas.
MAR. 8: St. John of God.
MAR. 9: SS. Catherine Banonia, Constantine of Cornwall, Frances of Rome.
MAR. 10: Holy Forty Martyrs (of Sebaste, frozen to death at command of emperor Licinius, a.d. 320, in Armenia).
MAR. 11: St. Constant.
MAR. 12: St. Gregory the Great.
MAR. 13: SS. Euphrasia, Patricia.
MAR. 14: St. Mathilda.
MAR. 15: SS. Longinus, Louise de Marillac, Zachary.
MAR. 16: St. Papas.
MAR. 17: St. Patrick.
MAR. 18: SS. Alexander, Cyril of Jerusalem.
MAR. 19: St. Joseph.
MAR. 20: St. Joachim.
MAR. 21: St. Benedict Abbot.
MAR. 22: SS. Bennvente, Catherine Flisca Adorna, Leah.
MAR. 23: SS. Catherine of Sweden, Victor.
MAR. 24: St. Gabriel the Archangel.
MAR. 25: Annunciation of B.V.M.
MAR. 26: St. Emmanuel.
MAR. 27: St. John Damascene.
MAR. 28: St. John Capistran.
MAR. 29: SS. Cyril, Eustache.
MAR. 30: St. Amadeus.
MAR. 31: Station at St. John Lateran.

April

APR. 1: St. Hugues.
APR. 2: St. Francis of Paula.
APR. 3: St. Irene.
APR. 4: SS. Adele, Benedict Moor, Isidore.
APR. 5: St. Vincent Ferrer.
APR. 6: St. Celestine.
APR. 7: St. George.
APR. 8: St. Albert, Bl. Julie Billiart.
APR. 9: St. Hugh.
APR. 10: SS. Fulbert, Terence.
APR. 11: St. Leo the Great.
APR. 12: SS. Jules, Zemo.
APR. 13: SS. Hermenegild, Ida.
APR. 14: SS. Justin, Maximus, Tiburtius, Valerian.
APR. 15: St. Paternus.
APR. 16: St. Benedict Joseph-Labre, Odette.
APR. 17: St. Anicetus.
APR. 18: St. Parfait; Bl. Andrew Hibernocus.
APR. 19: Bls. Conrad, Mark.
APR. 20: SS. Theodore, Sulpicius.
APR. 21: SS. Anselm, Conrad Parzham.
APR. 22: SS. Caius, Soter.
APR. 23: St. George the Great Martyr, Bl. Giles of Assisi.
APR. 24: SS. Fidelis of Sigmaringen, Gaston.
APR. 25: St. Mark the Evangelist.
APR. 26: SS. Cletus, Frederick, Marcellinus.
APR. 27: SS. Fernand, Peter Canisius, Thuribius of Mogrobejo.
APR. 28: SS. Paul of the Cross, Vitalis.
APR. 29: SS. Peter of Verona, Robert.
APR. 30: SS. Ludovic, Catherine of Siena.

May

MAY 1: SS. James, Philip.
MAY 2: St. Athanasius.
MAY 3: SS. Alexander Pope, Eventius, Juvenal, Theodolus; Finding of the Holy Cross.
MAY 4: St. Monica.
MAY 5: St. Pius V.
MAY 6: St. John, Apostle and Evangelist, Be-

fore the Latin Gate (commemorates attempt to boil John in oil before the Latin Gate).
MAY 7: St. Stanislaus Bishop.
MAY 8: Apparition of St. Michael Archangel.
MAY 9: St. Gregory Nazianzen.
MAY 10: SS. Antonius, Epimachus, Gordian, Solangia.
MAY 11: SS. Gildas, Lucia Filippini.
MAY 12: SS. Achilleus, Domitilla, Nereus, Pancras; Feast of St. Joan of Arc May 12 (or 2nd Sunday in May).
MAY 13: SS. Robert Bellarmine, Servais.
MAY 14: St. Boniface of Tarsus.
MAY 15: SS. Denise, John Baptist de la Salle.
MAY 16: SS. Brendan the Voyager, Honoré, Ubaldus.
MAY 17: St. Paschal Baylon.
MAY 18: SS. Felix of Cantalice, Juliette, Venantius.
MAY 19: SS. Peter Celestine, Pudentia, Theophilus of Corte, Yves.
MAY 20: St. Bernardine of Siena.
MAY 21: St. Gisèle.
MAY 22: SS. Emile, Rita of Cascia.
MAY 23: St. Didier.
MAY 24: Bls. John, John Cetina, Peter.
MAY 25: SS. Gregory VII, Madeleine Sophie Barat, Urban.
MAY 26: SS. Eleutherius Pope, Mary Ann of Jesus, Philip Neri.
MAY 27: St. Bede, John I Pope.
MAY 28: SS. Augustine of Canterbury, Francis.
MAY 29: SS. Mary Magdelene dei Pazzi, Maxim; Bls. Stephen, Raymond.
MAY 30: SS. Felix I Pope, Ferdinand the King.
MAY 31: St. Angela Merici, Petronilla.

June

JUNE 1: St. Fortunatus.
JUNE 2: SS. Elmo, Emilie, Erasmus, Marcellinus, Peter.
JUNE 3: St. Clothilde.
JUNE 4: SS. Emma, Francis Caracciolo.
JUNE 5: SS. Boniface of Germany, Yvonne.
JUNE 6: St. Norbert.
JUNE 7: St. Claude.
JUNE 8: SS. Columba, Médard.
JUNE 9: SS. Felician, Primus.
JUNE 10: St. Margaret, Queen of Scotland.
JUNE 11: St. Barnabus.
JUNE 12: SS. Basilides, Cyrinus, John of St. Facundus, Nabor, Nazarius.
JUNE 13: St. Anthony of Padua.
JUNE 14: SS. Basil, Anastasius.
JUNE 15: SS. Crescentia, Guy, Modestus, Vitus.
JUNE 16: SS. Benno, John Francis Regis.
JUNE 17: St. Hervé.
JUNE 18: SS. Ephrem the Syrian, Florentine, Marcellianus, Mark.
JUNE 19: SS. Gervais, Juliana Falconieri, Protase.
JUNE 20: St. Silverius Pope.
JUNE 21: SS. Aloysius Gonzaga, Raoul.
JUNE 22: SS. Alban, Paulinus.
JUNE 23: SS. Alice, Joseph Cafasso.
JUNE 24: Nativity of St. John the Baptist.
JUNE 25: SS. Prosper, William Abbot.
JUNE 26: SS. David, John and Paul (Martyrs).
JUNE 27: St. Ladislas.
JUNE 28: St. Irenaeus.
JUNE 29: SS. Peter, Paul.
JUNE 30: St. Emilienne; Commemoration of St. John the Apostle.

July

JUL. 1: Feast of the Precious Blood.

JUL. 2: Visitation of Our Lady; SS. Processus, Martinian.
JUL. 3: SS. Anatole, Leo II.
JUL. 4: SS. Bertha, Martin of Bullions.
JUL. 5: SS. Anthony, Mary Zaccaria, Zoe.
JUL. 6: St. Maria Goretti.
JUL. 7: SS. Cyril, Eliane, Fermin, Methodius.
JUL. 8: SS. Elizabeth Queen of Portugal, Virginia.
JUL. 9: St. Blanche.
JUL. 10: SS. Felicity, Holy Seven Brothers, Rufina, Secunda.
JUL. 11: SS. Pius I, Olga.
JUL. 12: SS. Felix, John Gualbert, Nabor.
JUL. 13: SS. Anacletus, Francis Solanus, Joel.
JUL. 14: St. Bonaventure.
JUL. 15: SS. Henry the Emperor, Swithin.
JUL. 16: St. Alain; Our Lady of Mt. Carmel.
JUL. 17: St. Alexius.
JUL. 18: SS. Camillus of Lellis, Symphorosa and her 7 Sons, Thenew.
JUL. 19: St. Vincent de Paul.
JUL. 20: SS. Jerome Emilian, Margaret.
JUL. 21: SS. Praxedes, Victor.
JUL. 22: St. Mary Magdalene.
JUL. 23: SS. Apollinaris, Lawrence Brindisi.
JUL. 24: SS. Christina, Francis Solano, Liborius.
JUL. 25: SS. Christopher, James the Greater Apostle.
JUL. 26: St. Anne.
JUL. 27: SS. Nathalia, Pantaleon.
JUL. 28: SS. Celsus, Innocent I, Nazarius, Victor I.
JUL. 29: SS. Beatrice, Faustinus, Felix II, Martha, Simplicius.
JUL. 30: SS. Abdon and Sennen.
JUL. 31: SS. Germain, Ignatius of Loyola.

August

AUG. 1: St. Peter's Chains; Holy Maccabees.
AUG. 2: St. Alphonsus de Liguori; Stephen Pope.
AUG. 3: St. Geoffrey; Finding of Body of St. Stephen the First Martyr.
AUG. 4: St. Dominic.
AUG. 5: Our Lady of the Snows.
AUG. 6: Transfiguration; SS. Agapitus Deacon, Felicissimus, Sixtus II.
AUG. 7: St. Cajetan (Gaétan); Donatus.
AUG. 8: SS. Cyriacus, Justin, Largus, Smaragdus.
AUG. 9: SS. Emidius, John Mary Vianney; Romanus.
AUG. 10: St. Lawrence.
AUG. 11: SS. Susanna, Tiburtius.
AUG. 12: St. Clare (Claire).
AUG. 13: SS. Cassian, Hippolytus.
AUG. 12: SS. Eusebius, Ghislain.
AUG. 15: Assumption of B.V.M.
AUG. 16: SS. Armella, Joachim, Roch (Roque).
AUG. 17: SS. Elise, Hyacinth, Rocco.
AUG. 18: SS. Agapitus, Helen.
AUG. 19: SS. Flavian, John Eudes.
AUG. 20: SS. Bernard Abbot, Stephen of Hungary.
AUG. 21: SS. Bernadette, Jane Francis 'de Chantal.
AUG. 22: SS. Hippolytus, Philibert; Symphorian, Timothy.
AUG. 23: SS. Philip Benizi, Sidonia.
AUG. 24: St. Bartholomew.
AUG. 25: St. Louis the King.
AUG. 26: SS. Privatus, Zephyrinus.
AUG. 27: SS. Armand, Joseph Calasanctius.
AUG. 28: SS. Augustine, Hermes.
AUG. 29: Beheading of St. John the Baptist; St. Sabina.
AUG. 30: SS. Adauctus, Felix, Fiacre, Rose of Lima.
AUG. 31: SS. Aristide, Raymond Nonnatus.

September

SEPT. 1:   St. Giles Abbot; Holy Twelve Brothers.
SEPT. 2:   SS. Lazarus, Stephen King of Hungary.
SEPT. 3:   SS. Gregory, Pius X.
SEPT. 4:   St. Rose of Viterbo.
SEPT. 5:   SS. Bertin, Eleutherius, Lawrence Justinian.
SEPT. 6:   St. Donatien.
SEPT. 7:   SS. Cloud, Regina.
SEPT. 8:   Nativity of B.V.M.; St. Adrian.
SEPT. 9:   SS. Gorgonius, Omer, Peter Claver.
SEPT. 10: SS. Aubert, Nicholas of Telentino.
SEPT. 11: SS. Hyacinth Martyr, Protus.
SEPT. 12: St. Perpetua; Holy Name of Mary.
SEPT. 13: SS. Aime, Eulogius.
SEPT. 14: Exaltation of the Holy Cross.
SEPT. 15: Seven Dolors of the B.V.M.; S. Nicomedes, Valerian.
SEPT. 16: SS. Cornelius, Cyprian, Euphemia, Germinianus, Lucy.
SEPT. 17: Stigmata of St. Francis; St. Lambert.
SEPT. 18: SS. Joseph of Cupertino, Sophie.
SEPT. 19: SS. Januarius, Gustave.
SEPT. 20: St. Eustace.
SEPT. 21: St. Matthew the Apostle.
SEPT. 22: SS. Maurice, Thomas of Villanova.
SEPT. 23: SS. Linus, Thecla.
SEPT. 24: Our Lady of Ransom; St. Pacificus.
SEPT. 25: St. Firmin.
SEPT. 26: SS. Cyprian, Isaac Jogues, John de Brebeuf and Companions, Justina.
SEPT. 27: SS. Cosmas and Damian; Eleazer.
SEPT. 28: St. Wenceslaus.
SEPT. 29: Dedication of St. Michael the Archangel.
SEPT. 30: St. Jerome.

October

OCT. 1:   St. Remigius (Rémi).
OCT. 2:   Guardian Angels.
OCT. 3:   St. Theresa of the Infant Jesus (Little Flower).
OCT. 4:   St. Francis of Assisi.
OCT. 5:   SS. Constant, Placidus.
OCT. 6:   SS. Bruno, Faith, Mary-Francis.
OCT. 7:   SS. Apuleius, Bacchus, Marcellus, Mark Pope, Serge (Sergius); Holy Rosary.
OCT. 8:   St. Bridget of Sweden.
OCT. 9:   SS. Dionysius ' (Denis), Eleutherius, John Leonard, Rusticus.
OCT. 10: SS. Daniel, Florent, Francis Borgia.
OCT. 11: SS. Kenny, Placidus; Maternity of B.V.M.
OCT. 12: St. Wilfred.
OCT. 13: SS. Edward the King, Seraphin.
OCT. 14: SS. Callistus, Feuillen.
OCT. 15: St. Teresa of Avila.
OCT. 16: SS. Hedwig, Leopold.
OCT. 17: SS. Audrey, Margaret Mary Alacoque.
OCT. 18: St. Luke the Evangelist.
OCT. 19: SS. Frideswide, Laura, Peter of Alcántara.
OCT. 20: SS. Aurelian, John Cantius.
OCT. 21: SS. Celine, Hilarion, Ursula.
OCT. 22: SS. Lydia, Melanius.
OCT. 23: Bls. Josephine, Mary Clotilde Angela.
OCT. 24: St. Raphael the Archangel.
OCT. 25: SS. Chrysanthus, Crispin and Crispian, Daria.
OCT. 26: St. Evaristus.
OCT. 27: Bl. Contard.
OCT. 28: Holy Apostles Simon and Jude.
OCT. 29: SS. Narcissus, Rudolphe.
OCT. 30: St. Arsene.
OCT. 31: St. Quentin.
LAST SUNDAY IN OCT.: Christ the King.

November

NOV. 1:   All Saints; St. Mathurin.
NOV. 2:   All Souls.
NOV. 3:   St. Hubert, Bl. Martin de Porres.
NOV. 4:   SS. Agricola of Bologna, Charles Borromeo, Vitalis of Bologna.
NOV. 5:   Sacred Relics; St. Sylvia.
NOV. 6:   St. Leonard.
NOV. 7:   St. Ernest.
NOV. 8:   Four Crowned Martyrs; St. Godefroy.
NOV. 9:   SS. Mathurin, Theodore.
NOV. 10: SS. Andrew Avellino, Bebiana, Juste, Nympha, Respicius, Tryphon.
NOV. 11: St. Martin the Bishop.
NOV. 12: SS. Martin Pope, Mennas, René.
NOV. 13: SS. Didacus, Stanislas Koska.
NOV. 14: SS. Josaphat, Philomena.
NOV. 15: SS. Albert the Great, Eugenia.
NOV. 16: SS. Agnes of Assisi, Edme, Gertrude.
NOV. 17: St. Gregory the Wonder Worker (Bishop).
NOV. 18: St. Maxime.
NOV. 19: SS. Elizabeth of Hungary, Philippina Duchesne, Pontianus.
NOV. 20: SS. Edmund, Felix of Valois.
NOV. 21: Presentation of the B.V.M.
NOV. 22: St. Cecilia.
NOV. 23: SS. Clement of Rome; Felicitas and her Seven Sons.
NOV. 24: SS. Chrysogonus, Flora, John of the Cross.
NOV. 25: St. Catherine of Alexandria.
NOV. 26: SS. Delphine, Peter of Alexandria, Sylvester.
NOV. 27: St. Severinus.
NOV. 28: SS. Catharine Labouré, James of the Marches, Stephanie.
NOV. 29: St. Saturninus.
NOV. 30: St. Andrew the Apostle.

December

DEC. 1:   St. Eloi (Eligius).
DEC. 2:   SS. Bibiana, Vivian.
DEC. 3:   St. Francis Xavier.
DEC. 4:   SS. Barbara, Peter Chrysologus.
DEC. 5:   St. Sabbas.
DEC. 6:   St. Nicholas of Myra.
DEC. 7:   St. Ambrose.
DEC. 8:   Immaculate Conception.
DEC. 9:   St. Leocadie.
DEC. 10: SS. Melchiades, Valerius; Our Lady of Loreto.
DEC. 11: SS. Damasus, Daniel.
DEC. 12: Our Lady of Guadalupe.
DEC. 13: SS. Lucy, Odile.
DEC. 14: St. Florian.
DEC. 15: St. Mesmin.
DEC. 16: SS. Adelaide, Eusebius.
DEC. 17: SS. Lazarus, Yolande.
DEC. 18: SS. Gatien, Rufus, Zosimus; Virgin of the Lonely (Soledad).
DEC. 19: SS. Fausta, Timoleon.
DEC. 20: SS. Eugene, Liberatus.
DEC. 21: St. Thomas the Apostle.
DEC. 22: SS. Frances Cabrini (Mother Cabrini), Honoratus.
DEC. 23: St. Victoria.
DEC. 24: St. Irmine.
DEC. 25: Christmas; St. Anastasia.
DEC. 26: St. Stephen (Étienne) the First Martyr.
DEC. 27: St. John the Evangelist.
DEC. 28: Holy Innocents.
DEC. 29: SS. Eleanor, Thomas of Canterbury (à Becket).
DEC. 30: St. Roger.
DEC. 31: St. Sylvester.

Italian Rulers
See **Rulers**

Jesus Christ
See **Parables of Christ; Saints**

Justices of the United States Supreme Court

Chief Justices

JAY, JOHN: 1789-1795.
RUTLEDGE, JOHN: 1795.
ELLSWORTH, OLIVER: 1796-1799.
MARSHALL, JOHN: 1801-1835.
TANEY, ROGER B.: 1836-1864.
CHASE, SALMON P.: 1864-1873.
WAITE, MORRISON R.: 1874-1888.
FULLER, MELVILLE W.: 1888-1910.
WHITE, EDWARD D.: 1910-1921.
TAFT, WILLIAM H.: 1921-1930.
HUGHES, CHARLES E.: 1930-1941.
STONE, HARLAN F.: 1941-1946.
VINSON, FREDERICK M.: 1946-1953.
WARREN, EARL: 1953-

Associate Justices

BLAIR, JOHN: 1789-1796.
CUSHING, WILLIAM: 1789-1810.
RUTLEDGE, JOHN: 1789-1791.
WILSON, JAMES: 1789-1798.
IREDELL, JAMES: 1790-1799.
JOHNSON, THOMAS: 1791-1793.
PATERSON, WILLIAM: 1793-1806.
CHASE, SAMUEL: 1796-1811.
WASHINGTON, BUSHROD: 1798-1829.
MOORE, ALFRED: 1799-1804.
JOHNSON, WILLIAM: 1804-1834.
LIVINGSTON, HENRY B.: 1806-1823.
TODD, THOMAS: 1807-1826.
STORY, JOSEPH: 1811-1845.
DUVAL, GABRIEL: 1811-1836.
THOMPSON, SMITH: 1823-1843.
TRIMBLE, ROBERT: 1826-1828.
MC LEAN, JOHN: 1829-1861.
BALDWIN, HENRY: 1830-1844.
WAYNE, JAMES M.: 1835-1867.
BARBOUR, PHILIP P.: 1836-1841.
CATRON, JOHN: 1837-1865.
MC KINLEY, JOHN: 1837-1852.
DANIEL, PETER V.: 1841-1860.
NELSON, SAMUEL: 1845-1872.
WOODBURY, LEVI: 1845-1851.
GRIER, ROBERT C.: 1846-1870.
CURTIS, BENJAMIN R.: 1851-1857.
CAMPBELL, JOHN A.: 1853-1861.
CLIFFORD, NATHAN: 1858-1881.
DAVIS, DAVID: 1862-1877.
MILLER, SAMUEL F.: 1862-1890.
SWAYNE, NOAH H.: 1862-1881.
FIELD, STEPHEN J.: 1863-1897.
STRONG, WILLIAM: 1870-1880.
BRADLEY, JOSEPH P.: 1870-1892.
HUNT, WARD: 1873-1882.
HARLAN, JOHN M.: 1877-1911.
WOODS, WILLIAM B.: 1880-1887.
MATTHEWS, STANLEY: 1881-1889.
BLATCHFORD, SAMUEL: 1882-1893.
GRAY, HORACE: 1882-1902.
LAMAR, LUCIUS Q. C.: 1888-1893.
BREWER, DAVID J.: 1889-1910.
BROWN, HENRY B.: 1890-1906.
SHIRAS, GEORGE, JR.: 1892-1903.
JACKSON, HOWELL E.: 1893-1895.
WHITE, EDWARD D.: 1894-1910.

PECKHAM, RUFUS W.: 1896-1909.
MC KENNA, JOSEPH: 1898-1925.
HOLMES, OLIVER W.: 1902-1932.
DAY, WILLIAM R.: 1903-1922.
MOODY, WILLIAM H.: 1906-1910.
HUGHES, CHARLES E.: 1910-1916.
LURTON, HORACE H.: 1910-1914.
VAN DEVANTER, WILLIS: 1910-1937.
LAMAR, JOSEPH R.: 1911-1916.
PITNEY, MAHLON: 1912-1922.
MC REYNOLDS, JAMES C.: 1914-1941.
BRANDEIS, LOUIS D.: 1916-1939.
CLARKE, JOHN H.: 1916-1922.
SUTHERLAND, GEORGE: 1922-1938.
BUTLER, PIERCE: 1923-1939.
SANFORD, EDWARD T.: 1923-1930.
STONE, HARLAN F.: 1925-1941.
ROBERTS, OWEN J.: 1930-1945.
CARDOZO, BENJAMIN N.: 1932-1938.
BLACK, HUGO L.: 1937-
REED, STANLEY F.: 1938-
DOUGLAS, WILLIAM O.: 1939-
FRANKFURTER, FELIX: 1939-
MURPHY, FRANK: 1940-1949.
BYRNES, JAMES F.: 1941-1942.
JACKSON, ROBERT H.: 1941-1954.
RUTLEDGE, WILEY B., JR.: 1943-1949.
BURTON, HAROLD H.: 1945-
CLARK, TOM C.: 1949-
MINTON, SHERMAN: 1949-1956.
HARLAN, JOHN MARSHALL: 1955-
BRENNAN, WILLIAM J., Jr.: 1956-
CHARLES WHITTAKER: 1956-

Knights of the Round Table

THE ROUND TABLE of the Arthurian romances was reportedly made by Merlin at Carduel for Uther Pendragon. Uther gave it to King Leodegraunce, of Cameliard, who gave it to King Arthur when the latter married Guinevere, his daughter. It was circular to prevent any jealousy on the score of precedency; it seated 150 knights, and a place was left in it for the Holy Grail. The first reference to it is in Wace's *Roman de Brut* (1155), but the fullest legendary details are from Malory's *Le Morte d'Arthur*, III, i and ii.
KNIGHTS OF THE ROUND TABLE: According to Malory (*Le Morte d'Arthur*, III, i, ii), there were 150 knights who had "sieges" at the table. King Leodegraunce brought 100 when, at the wedding of his daughter Guinevere, he gave the table to King Arthur. Merlin's followers filled up twenty-eight of the vacant seats, and the King elected Gawain and Tor; the remaining twenty were left for those who might prove worthy. Of all the knights of King Arthur's court there were, however, always twelve who held positions of the highest honor. The twelve vary in different accounts, but the following names hold the most conspicuous places:

(1) LANCELOT, (2) TRISTRAM, (3) LAMO-
  RACKE: The three bravest.
(4) TOR: The first made.
(5) GALAHAD: The chaste.
(6) GAWAIN: The courteous.
(7) GARETH: The big-handed.
(8) PALOMIDES: The Saracen or unbaptized.
(9) KAY: The rude and boastful.
(10) MARK: The dastard.
(11) MODRED: The traitor.
THE TWELFTH: He must be selected from one of the following knights, all of whom are seated with the prince in the frontispiece at-

tached to Malory's *Le Morte d'Arthur* (published 1470): SIRS ACOLON, BALLAMORE BELEOBUS, BELVOURE, BERSUNT, BORS, ECTOR DE MARIS, EWAIN, FLOLL, GAHERIS, GALOHALT, GRISLET, LIONELL, MARHAUS, PAGINET, PELLEAS, PERCIVAL, SAGRIS, SUPERABILIS, and TURQUINE.

The World's Great Lakes in the Order of Comparative Size

CASPIAN SEA*: 169,350 sq.mi.; Asia-Europe.
SUPERIOR: 31,820 sq.mi.; North America.
VICTORIA NYANZA: 26,800 sq.mi.; Africa.
ARAL SEA*: 26,200 sq.mi.; Asia.
HURON: 23,000 sq.mi.; North America.
MICHIGAN: 22,400 sq.mi.; North America.
BAIKAL: 13,200 sq.mi.; Asia.
TANGANYIKA: 12,500 sq.mi.; Africa.
GREAT BEAR LAKE: 12,200 sq.mi.; North America.
NYASA: 11,000 sq.mi.; Africa.
GREAT SLAVE LAKE: 10,800 sq.mi.; North America.
ERIE: 9,940 sq.mi.; North America.
WINNIPEG: 9,450 sq.mi.; North America.
ONTARIO: 7,540 sq.mi.; North America.
BALKHASH: 7,150 sq.mi.; Soviet Central Asia.
LADOGA: 7,000 sq.mi.; U.S.S.R., Europe.
MARACAIBO*: 6,300 sq.mi.; South America.
CHAD: 5,000-10,000 sq.mi.; Africa.
ONEGA: 3,764 sq.mi.; Soviet Russia, Europe.
EYRE*: 3,700 sq.mi.; Australia.
TITICACA: 3,500 sq.mi.; South America.
RUDOLF: 3,475 sq.mi.; Africa.
NICARAGUA: 3,000 sq.mi.; Central America.
ATHABASKA: 2,900 sq.mi.; North America.
REINDEER: 2,440 sq.mi.; North America.
GREAT SALT LAKE*: 2,360 sq.mi.; North America.
ISSYK KUL*: 2,250 sq.mi.; Soviet Central Asia.
TORRENS*: 2,200 sq.mi.; Australia.
VENER (VÄNERN): 2,150 sq.mi.; Sweden, Europe.
NETTILLING: 2,100 sq.mi.; North America.
WINNIPEGOSIS: 2,086 sq.mi.; North America.
TUNGTING HU: 2,000-4,000 sq.mi.; China, Asia.
ALBERT NYANZA: 2,000 sq.mi.; Africa.
HELMAND (HAMUN-I-HELMAND)*: 2,000 sq. mi.; Iran, Asia.
LAKE OF THE WOODS: 1,851 sq.mi.; U.S.— Canada, North America.
MANITOBA: 1,800 sq.mi.; North America.
NIPIGON: 1,730 sq.mi.; Canada, North America.
DUBAWNT: 1,654 sq.mi.; North America.
BANGWEULU: 1,600-1,900 sq.mi.; Africa.
GAIRDNER: 1,600 sq.mi.; Australia.
URMIA*: 1,500-2,300 sq.mi.; Iran, Asia.
VAN*: 1,500 sq.mi.; Turkey, Asia.
PEIPUS: 1,350 sq.mi.; Soviet Russia, Europe.
TANA: 1,100 sq.mi.; Africa.
VÄTTERN (VETTER): 733 sq.mi.; Sweden, Europe.
GOKCHA (SEVAN): 540 sq.mi.; Armenian S.S.R.; Europe.
MÄLAR (MÄLAREN): 440 sq.mi.; Sweden, Europe.
DEAD SEA*: 370 sq.mi.; Palestine-Transjordan, Asia.
BALLATON (PLATTENSEE): 266 sq.mi.; Hungary, Europe.

* Indicates salt lake.

LAKE OF GENEVA (LEMAN): 225 sq.mi.; Switzerland-France, Europe.
LAKE CONSTANCE (BODEN SEE): 207 sq. mi.; Germany-Austria-Switzerland, Europe.

Languages of the World By Countries and Number of Speakers

Africa

ALGERIA: 9,620,000; Arabic, Berber, French.
ANGLO-EGYPTIAN SUDAN: 8,820,000; Arabic; Kushitic; Sudanese-Guinean.
ANGOLA: 4,280,000; Bantu, Portuguese.
BASUTOLAND: 627,000; Bantu, English.
BECHUANALAND: 296,000; Bantu, English.
BELGIAN CONGO: 12,600,000; Bantu, Sudanese-Guinean, French, Flemish.
BRITISH CAMEROONS: 1,500,000; Bantu, Sudanese-Guinean, English.
BRITISH SOMALILAND: 640,000; Kushitic, English.
BRITISH TOGOLAND: 416,000; Arabic, Berber, Sudanese-Guinean, English.
CAPE VERDE ISLANDS: 172,000; Portuguese.
COMORO ISLANDS: 170,000; Arabic, French.
EGYPT: 22,934,000; Arabic, Kushitic, Sudanese-Guinean (Nubian), English, French, Greek, Italian.
ERITREA: See Ethiopia and Eritrea.
ETHIOPIA AND ERITREA: 20,000,000; Ethiopian, Kushitic, Sudanese-Guinean, Italian.
FRENCH CAMEROONS: 3,146,000; Bantu, Sudanese-Guinean, French.
FRENCH EQUATORIAL AFRICA: 4,680,000; Sudanese-Guinean, Arabic, Bantu, French.
FRENCH MOROCCO: 8,495,000; Arabic, Berber, French.
FRENCH SOMALILAND: 63,000; Kushitic, French.
FRENCH TOGOLAND: 1,080,000; Arabic, Berber, Sudanese-Guinean, French.
FRENCH WEST AFRICA: 18,729,000; Arabic, Berber, Sudanese-Guinean, French.
GAMBIA, COLONY AND PROTECTORATE: 285,000; Sudanese-Guinean, English.
KENYA, COLONY AND PROTECTORATE: 6,048,000; Sudanese-Guinean, English.
LIBYA: 1,105,000; Arabic, Berber, Italian.
LIBERIA: 1,250,000; Sudanese-Guinean, English.
MADAGASCAR (EXCLUDING DEPENDENCIES): 4,776,000; Indonesian (Malagasy), French.
MAURITIUS (EXCLUDING DEPENDENCIES): 549,000; Hindustani, English, French.
MOZAMBIQUE: 6,030,000; Bantu, Portuguese.
NIGERIA: 31,254,000; Sudanese-Guinean, English.
NORTHERN RHODESIA: 2,130,000; Bantu, English, Afrikaans.
NYASALAND: 2,540,000; Bantu, English, Afrikaans.
PORTUGUESE GUINEA: 541,000; Sudanese-Guinean, Portuguese.
RÉUNION: 278,000; French.
RUANDA-URUNDI: 4,280,000; Bantu, Sudanese-Guinean, French, Flemish.
SAÕ TOMÉ AND PRINCIPE: 58,000; Bantu, Portuguese.
SEYCHELLES: 39,000; English, French.
SIERRA LEONE: 2,050,000; Sudanese-Guinean, English.
SOMALIA (ITALIAN TRUST): 1,280,000; Kushitic, Italian.
SOUTHERN RHODESIA: 2,399,000; Bantu, English, Afrikaans.

SOUTH WEST AFRICA: 458,000; Bantu, Hottentot-Bushman, English, German.
SPANISH GUINEA: 208,000; Bantu, Spanish.
SPANISH MOROCCAN PROTECTORATE: 1,045,000; Arabic, Berber, Spanish.
SPANISH POSSESSIONS IN NORTH AFRICA: 143,184; Arabic, Spanish.
SPANISH WEST AFRICA: 83,000; Arabic, Spanish.
SWAZILAND: 217,000; Bantu, English.
TANGANYIKA: 8,324,000; Bantu, English.
TANGIER: 183,000; Arabic, French, Spanish, English.
TUNISIA: 3,745,000; Arabic, Berber, French, Italian.
UGANDA: 5,508,000; Bantu, Sudanese-Guinean, English.
UNION OF SOUTH AFRICA: 13,669,000; Bantu, Hottentot-Bushman, English, Afrikaans.
ZANZIBAR AND PEMBA: 278,000; Bantu, Swahili, English.

Asia

ADEN COLONY: 140,000; Arabic, some English.
ADEN PROTECTORATE: 650,000; Arabic, some English.
AFGHANISTAN: 12,000,000; Pushtu, Persian.
ASSOCIATED STATES OF CAMBODIA, LAOS, AND VIET-NAM: See Cambodia; Laos; Viet-nam.
BAHREIN: 120,000; Arabic, some English.
BHUTAN: 623,000; Indo-Aryan, Tibetan dialects.
BRITISH BORNEO: See Brunei; North Borneo; Sarawak.
BRUNEI: 56,000; Indonesian, English.
BURMA: 19,434,000; Burmese, English.
CAMBODIA: 4,358,000; Khmer, Tao.
CEYLON: 8,589,000; Singhalese (in south) Tamil (in north), English.
CHINA: 582,603,000; Chinese, Tibetan, Thai; Ural-Altaic dialects in Chinese Turkistan and Mongolia; some English, Japanese.
CYPRUS: 520,000; Cyprus; some English, Turkish.
HONG KONG: 2,340,000; Chinese; some English, Japanese.
INDIA: 381,690,000; Indo-Aryan dialects (north) Dravidian dialects (south); some Munda, English.
INDONESIA: 81,900,000; Indonesian, Papuan.
IRAN: 21,146,000; Persian, Kurdish, some French.
IRAQ: 5,200,000; Arabic, Kurdish, Turkish.
ISRAEL: 1,748,000; Hebrew, Arabic, English.
JAPAN: 89,100,000; Japanese, some Ainu.
JORDAN: 1,427,000; Arabic, some English.
KOREA, NORTH AND SOUTH: 28,000,000; Korean, Japanese.
KUWAIT: 203,000; Arabic; some English.
LAOS: 1,425,000; Khmer, Tao.
LEBANON: 1,425,000; Arabic, French.
MACAU: 200,000; Chinese, some Portuguese.
MALAYA, FEDERATION OF: 6.058,000; Malayan, Chinese, Mon-Khmer, English.
MALDIVE ISLANDS: 89,000; Arabic, Senghalese, Dravidian dialects.
MONGOLIAN PEOPLE'S REPUBLIC: 1,000,000; Mongolian; Russian.
MUSCAT AND OMAN: 550,000; Arabic.
NEPAL: 8,431,537; Indo-Aryan; Tibetan dialects.
NORTH BORNEO: 370,000; Indonesian, English.
OMAN: See Muscat and Oman.
PAKISTAN: 82,439,000; Indo-Aryan dialects.
PALESTINE: 325,000; Arabic; some English, Hebrew.

PHILIPPINES: 21,849,000; Indonesian dialects, English, Spanish.
PORTUGUESE INDIA: (Damão, Diu, Goa) 644,000 Indo-Aryan dialects.
PORTUGUESE TIMOR: 469,000; Indonesian, Portuguese.
QATAR: 35,000; Arabic.
RYUKYU ISLANDS: 798,000; Japanese, Luchuan, some English.
SARAWAK: 614,000; Indonesian, English.
SAUDI ARABIA: 7,000,000; Arabic.
SINGAPORE: 1,411,000; Chinese, English, Hindi, Malayan.
SYRIA: 4,145,000; Arabic, French.
THAILAND: 20,302,000; Thai, Mon-Khmer dialects.
TRUCIAL OMAN: 80,000; Arabic.
TURKEY: 24,122,000; Turkish; Armenian, Kurdish.
VIET-NAM: 26,300,000; Khmer, Tao.
YEMEN: 4,500,000; Arabic.

Europe

ALBANIA: 1,394,000; Albanian, some Greek, Italian, Serbo-Croatian, Turkish.
ANDORRA: 6,000; Catalan, French, Spanish.
AUSTRIA: 6,974,000; German.
BELGIUM: 8,868,000; Flemish, French.
BULGARIA: 7,548,000; Bulgarian, some Turkish.
CZECHOSLOVAKIA: 13,089,000; Czech and Slovak; some German, Hungarian, Ukrainian.
DENMARK: 4,439,000; Danish, German.
ESTHONIA: See Union of Soviet Socialist Republics.
FINLAND: 4,241,000; Finnish; some German, Russian, Swedish.
FRANCE: 43,274,000; French.
GERMANY: 70,190,000; German.
GIBRALTER: 25,000; Spanish, English.
GREECE: 7,973,000; Greek; some Albanian, Bulgarian, Turkish.
HUNGARY: 9,805,000; Hungarian; some German, Rumanian, Slovak.
ICELAND: 158,000; Icelandic; Danish.
IRELAND, REPUBLIC OF: 2,909,000; English; Irish Gaelic (Erse).
ITALY: 48,016,000; Italian.
LATVIA: See Union of Soviet Socialist Republics.
LIECHTENSTEIN: 15,000; German.
LITHUANIA: See Union of Soviet Socialist Republics.
LUXEMBOURG: 309,000; German, French.
MONACO: 22,000; French, Italian.
NETHERLANDS: 10,751,000; Dutch; some English, French, German.
NORWAY: 3,425,000; Norwegian, Lapp; some English, German.
POLAND: 27,278,000; Polish; some German, Russian, Yiddish.
PORTUGAL: 8,756,000; Portugese, Spanish.
ROMANIA: 17,000,000; Rumanian; some Bulgarian, German, Hungarian.
RUSSIA: See Union of Soviet Socialist Republics.
SAN MARINO: 14,000; Italian.
SPAIN: 28,976,000; Spanish; some Basque, Catalan, Portuguese.
SWEDEN: 7,262,000; Swedish, Lapp; some German.
SWITZERLAND: 4,977,000; Italian, French, German, Rumansh.
UNION OF SOVIET SOCIALIST REPUBLICS: 200,200,000. Of an estimated 130 languages spoken within the U.S.S.R., the chief languages are: Great Russian, White Russian, Ukrainian, Byelorussian, Uzbek, Tartar, Kazakh,

Armenian, Azerbaijan, Georgian, Latvian, Lithuanian, and Esthonian (Finno-Ugrian).
UNITED KINGDOM: 51,215,000; English, Welsh, Gaelic.
YUGOSLAVIA: 17,628,000; Serbo-Croatian, Slovene; some Albanian, Bulgarian, German, Hungarian, Italian, Rumanian.

North America

ALASKA: 209,000; English.
BAHAMAS: 94,000; English.
BERMUDAS: 41,000; English.
BRITISH HONDURAS: 79,000; English, Spanish.
CANADA: 15,601,000; Predominately English; French spoken by about 3-3$^1/_2$ millions in Ontario and Quebec.
CANAL ZONE: 53,000; English, Spanish.
COSTA RICA: 951,000; Spanish.
CUBA: 5,829,000; Spanish.
DOMINICAN REPUBLIC: 2,404,000; Spanish.
EL SALVADOR: 2,193,000; Spanish.
GREENLAND: 26,000; Danish.
GUADALOUPE AND DEPENDENCIES: 230,000; French.
GUATEMALA: 3,258,000; Spanish.
HAITI: 3,305,000; French.
HONDURAS: 1,660,000; Spanish.
JAMAICA (WITHOUT DEPENDENCIES): 1,550,000; English.
LEEWARD ISLANDS: 128,000; English.
MARTINIQUE: 240,000; French.
MEXICO: 29,679,000; Spanish.
NICARAGUA: 1,245,000; Spanish.
PANAMA: 910,000; Spanish.
PUERTO RICO: 2,263,000; Spanish, English.
U.S.A.: 165,271,000; English.
VIRGIN ISLANDS: 24,000; English, Danish.
WINDWARD ISLANDS: 308,000; English.

Oceania

AMERICAN SAMOA: 22,000; Polynesian, English, German.
AUSTRALIA: 9,248,000; English, some native Australian.
BRITISH SOLOMON ISLANDS: 103,000; Melanesian, English.
CAMPBELL ISLAND: See New Zealand.
CAROLINE ISLANDS (CAROLINES): See Pacific Islands.
COOK, NIUE, AND TOKELAU ISLANDS: 23,000; Polynesian, English.
FIJI: 339,000; Melanesian, Hindustani, English.
FRENCH OCEANIA: 69,000; Polynesian, French.
GILBERT AND ELLICE ISLANDS: 40,000; Micronesian, Polynesian, English.
GUAM: 36,000; Micronesian, English.
HAWAII: 560,000; Polynesian, Chinese, English, Japanese, Korean.
KERMADEC ISLANDS: See New Zealand.
MARIANA ISLANDS (MARIANAS): See Pacific Islands.
MARSHALL ISLANDS: See Pacific Islands.
NAURU: 4,000; Micronesian; Chinese, English.
NETHERLANDS NEW GUINEA: 700,000; Papuan, Dutch.
NEW CALEDONIA AND DEPENDENCIES: 63,000; Melanesian, English, French.
NEW GUINEA (AUSTRALIA): 1,254,000; Papuan, English.
NEW HEBRIDES: 54,000; Melanesian, English, French.
NEW ZEALAND (INCL. CAMPBELL AND

KERMADEC ISLANDS): 2,136,000; English, some Polynesian, Maori.
NIUE: See Cook, Niue, and Tokelau Islands.
NORFOLK: 1,000; English.
PACIFIC ISLANDS (U.S. TRUST: INCLUDES MARIANA, CAROLINE, AND MARSHALL ISLANDS): 64,000; Micronesian, Malayo-Polynesian; Spanish, English.
PAPUA: 446,000; Papuan, English.
TOKELAU ISLANDS (UNION ISLANDS) See Cook, Niue, and Tokelau Islands.
TONGA: 54,000; Polynesian, English.
UNION ISLANDS: See Tokalau Islands.
WESTERN SAMOA: 97,000; Polynesian, French.

South America

ARGENTINA: 19,111,000; Spanish.
BOLIVIA: 3,198,000; Spanish.
BRAZIL: 58,456,000; Portuguese.
BRITISH GUIANA: 485,000; English.
CHILE: 6,761,000; Spanish.
COLOMBIA: 12,657,00; Spanish.
ECUADOR: 3,675,000; Spanish.
FRENCH GUIANA: 28,000; French.
PARAGUAY: 1,565,000; Spanish.
PERU: 9,396,000; Spanish.
SURINAM: 225,000; Dutch.
URUGUAY: 2,615,000; Spanish.
VENEZUELA: 5,774,000; Spanish.

Light Opera and Musical Comedy
See Songs from Broadway Plays

Liturgical Colors: Symbolism and Use
See also Colors in Symbolism; Academic Colors; Church Calendar

WHITE: Life, innocence, purity, glory, and joy; used on All Saints Day (November 1), Christmas (December 25), Circumcision (January 1), Easter, Feast of the Annunciation (March 25), Feast of the Purification (February 2), feasts of saints who were not martyrs, Nativity of St. John the Baptist (June 24), Trinity Sunday.
RED: Fire and blood; symbolizes burning charity and the sacrifice of martyrs; used on Corpus Christi, Elevation of the Cross, (May 2), feasts of the apostles and martyrs, Finding of the Cross (September 14), Holy Innocents (December 28), Whitsunday or Pentecost.
GREEN: Hope of eternal life, because it is the color of plants and trees; proper on all sundays that are not specific festivals.
VIOLET: Affection and melancholy; used during Advent (the four weeks preceding Christmas), on all Penitential Days, except Good Friday, All Souls Day (November 2), Lent, Rogation Days.
BLACK: Mourning, symbolizing death; used on Good Friday and in masses for the dead.

Memorial Park
See National Memorial Park

Memorials
See National Memorials

Mexican War Battles
See also **Battles**

1846

APRIL 25: Fort Brown, Texas; Mexican troops under Gen. Arista crossed the Rio Grande and wiped out American scouting party commanded by Capt. Thornton.

MAY 8: Palo Alto: Americans commanded by Gen. Zachary Taylor defeated the Mexicans.

MAY 9: Resaca de la Palma: Americans (Gen. Zachary Taylor) drove the Mexicans across the Rio Grande.

MAY 18: Matamoras, Mexico, seized by Gen. Taylor after he crossed the Rio Grande.

JUNE 14: Bear Flag Revolt. American settlers in Sacramento Valley, Calif., under leadership of William B. Ide, seized Sonoma, declared their independence, and raised a new flag—a grizzly bear and star on a white field, with the words California Republic; two weeks later, on June 25, Lt. John Charles Frémont reached Sonoma and took command of the rebellion.

JULY 7: Monterey, California, surrendered to Com. John D. Sloat.

JULY 9: Americans, under Capt. John Montgomery took San Francisco.

AUGUST 13: Americans under Com. Stockton and Lt. Frémont, seized Los Angeles.

AUGUST 18: Col. Stephen Watts Kearny captured Santa Fe, New Mexico; New Mexico proclaimed a territory of the Union.

SEPTEMBER 21-23: Monterey, Mexico, besieged by Americans (Gen. Zachary Taylor).

SEPTEMBER 24: Monterey, Mexico, fell to Americans; American casualties in the campaign were 488 in killed and wounded; Mexican causalties reached 367.

SEPTEMBER 23-30: California counterrevolution: Mexicans directed by Capt. José Maria Flores revolted and drove Americans from Los Angeles, Santa Barbara, and San Diego.

SEPTEMBER 26: Tabasco, Mexico, bombarded by U.S. ships.

OCTOBER 25: Tabasco again bombarded by U.S. ships.

NOVEMBER 16: Saltillo, Mexico, captured by Americans (Gen. Zachary Taylor).

DECEMBER 6: San Pasqual, California; Army of the West, an American expedition from Ft. Leavenworth, commanded by Stephen W. Kearney, engaged and defeated Mexicans, then went on to San Diego.

DECEMBER 25: Battle of El Brazito; American expeditionary force (Col. Alexander Doniphan) defeated Mexicans.

DECEMBER 27: Americans (Col. Doniphan) occupied El Paso.

DECEMBER 29: Victoria, Mexico, fell to Americans (Gen. Zachary Taylor).

1847

JANUARY 8: San Gabriel, Mexico, bombarded by U.S. vessels.

JANUARY 8-9: Gen. Kearney defeated Mexicans in battles along the San Gabriel River.

JANUARY 13: Mexican army in California (Andres Pico) surrendered to Americans (Lt. Frémont) on terms of Treaty of Cahuenga, ending the war in California.

FEBRUARY 23: Buena Vista; Mexicans (Gen. Santa Ana) defeated by Americans (Gen. Zachary Taylor).

FEBRUARY 28: Battle of the Sacramento: Americans (Col. Doniphan) defeated Mexicans.

MARCH 1: Americans (Col. Doniphan) occupied Chihuahua.

MARCH 9: American invasion force (Gen. Winfield Scott) landed below Vera Cruz.

MARCH 22: Vera Cruz bombarded by U.S. vessels.

MARCH 27: Vera Cruz surrendered to Americans (Gen. Winfield Scott).

MARCH 30: Alvarado and Flacotalpan surrendered to Americans.

APRIL 18: Tuspan taken by U.S. ships; battle of Cerro Gordo won by Americans (Gen. Winfield Scott).

APRIL 20: Jalapa fell to Americans (Gen. Winfield Scott).

APRIL 22: Perote fell to Americans (Gen. Winfield Scott).

MAY 15: Mexicans defeated at Puebla; Americans (Gen. Winfield Scott) occupied city 200 mi. from Mexico City.

JUNE 15: Bombardement by U.S. ships near Tabasco.

AUGUST 7-10: U.S. forces left Puebla and advanced on Mexico City.

AUGUST 19-20: Contreras, Churubusco, and San Antonio: Mexicans defeated by Americans (Gen. Winfield Scott).

SEPTEMBER 8: Molino del Rey; Americans, with heavy casualties, defeated Mexicans.

SEPTEMBER 12-13: Chapultepec, Mexico, bombarded and taken by Americans (Gen. Winfield Scott).

SEPTEMBER 14: Mexico City surrendered.

1848

FEBRUARY 2: Treaty of Guadalupe Hidalgo: by terms of the peace treaty that ended the Mexican War, New Mexico and California were ceded by Mexico to the U.S.A. with all of Texas north of the Rio Grande (including parts of the present states of Arizona, Colorado, Nevada, and Utah); Mexico was indemnified 15 million dollars for the loss of these possessions (1,193,061 sq.mi. of territory).

Monuments
See **National Monuments**

Movies with Notable Musical Scores
See also **Musical Compositions**

ABE LINCOLN IN ILLINOIS: Music by Roy Denslow Webb; RKO; 1939.

ACTION IN THE NORTH ATLANTIC: Music by Adolph Deutsch; Warners; 1943.

ADDRESS UNKNOWN: Music by Ernst Toch; Columbia; 1944.

ADVENTURES OF DON JUAN: Music by Max Steiner; Warners; 1949.

ADVENTURES OF ROBIN HOOD: Music by Erich Wolfgang Korngold; Warners; 1938.

AIR FORCE: Music by Franz Waxman; Warners; 1944.

ALEXANDER'S RAGTIME BAND: Music by Alfred Newman; 20th Century-Fox; 1938.

ALI BABA AND THE FORTY THIEVES: Music by Edward Wald; Universal; 1944.

ALICE IN WONDERLAND: Music by Dimitri Tiomkin; Paramount; 1934.

ALL ABOUT EVE: Music by Alfred Newman, 20th Century-Fox; 1950.

ALL THIS, AND HEAVEN TOO: Music by Max Steiner; Warners; 1940.

AN AMERICAN GUERILLA IN THE PHILIPPINES: Music by Lionel Newman; 20th Century-Fox; 1950.

AN AMERICAN IN PARIS: Music by Johnny Green; MGM; 1950.

AN AMERICAN ROMANCE: Music by Louis Gruenberg; MGM; 1944.

ANASTASIA: Music by Alfred Newman; 20th Century-Fox; 1956.

ANCHORS AWEIGH: Music by Georgie Stoll (orchestrations, Axel Stordahl); MGM; 1945.

AND NOW TOMORROW: Music by Victor Young; Paramount; 1944.

AND THEN THERE WERE NONE: Music by Mario Castelnuovo-Tedesco; Popular Pictures, René Clair; 1945.

ANGELS OVER BROADWAY: Music by George Antheil; Columbia; 1940.

ANNA AND THE KING OF SIAM: Music by Bernard Herrmann; 20th Century-Fox; 1946.

ANNIE GET YOUR GUN: Music by Adolph Deutsch, based on score by Irving Berlin; MGM; 1950.

ANOTHER PART OF THE FOREST: Music by Daniele Amfitheatrof; Universal-International; 1948.

THE ARNELO AFFAIR: Music by George Bassman; MGM; 1947.

AROUND THE WORLD IN EIGHTY DAYS: Music by Victor Young; UA-Michael Todd; 1956.

ARSENIC AND OLD LACE: Music by Leo F. Forbstein and Hugo Friedhofer; Warners; 1944.

ANTHONY ADVERSE: Music by Erich Wolfgang Korngold; Warners; 1936.

THE ASPHALT JUNGLE: Music by Miklos Rozsa; MGM; 1950.

THE BAD SEED: Music by Alex North; Warners; 1956.

BAHAMA PASSENGE: Music by David Buttolph; Paramount; 1942.

BAMBI: Music by Alexander Lang Steinert; Walt Disney; 1941.

THE BARRETTS OF WIMPOLE STREET: Music by Bronislau Kaper; MGM; 1957.

BATHING BEAUTY: Music by Johnny Green; MGM; 1944.

BEAUTY AND THE BEAST (LA BELLE ET LA BÊTE): Music by George Auric; Lopert Films; 1946.

BEDTIME STORY: Music by Werner Richard Heymann; Columbia; 1941.

THE BLACK ROSE: Music by Richard Addinsell; 20th Century-Fox; 1950.

BLOOD AND SAND: Music by Alfred Newman; 20th Century-Fox; 1941.

BOYS RANCH: Music by Nathaniel Shilkret; MGM; 1946.

BOYS TOWN: Music by Edward Wald; MGM; 1936.

THE BRAVE ONE: Music by Victor Young; RKO; 1956.

BRIGHAM YOUNG: Music by Alfred Newman; 20th Century-Fox; 1940.

BROADWAY RHYTHM: Music by Johnny Green; MGM; 1943.

THE BUCCANEER: Music by George Antheil; Paramount; 1938.

BUFFALO BILL: Music by David Buttolph; 20th Century-Fox; 1943.

BUS STOP: Music by Alfred Newman; 20th Century-Fox; 1956.

CAGED: Music by Max Steiner; Warners; 1950.

CALCUTTA: Music by Victor Young; Paramount; 1945.

THE CANTERVILLE GHOST: Music by George Bassman; MGM; 1944.

CAPTAIN FROM CASTILE: Music by Alfred Newman; 20th Century-Fox; 1947.

CAPTAINS COURAGEOUS: Music by Franz Waxman; MGM; 1937.

CAROUSEL: Music by Alfred Newman (based on score by Rodgers & Hammerstein II); 20th Century-Fox; 1956.

CASABLANCA: Music by Max Steiner; Warners; 1942.

THE CAT AND THE CANARY: Music by Ernst Toch; Paramount; 1938.

CHAD HANNA: Music by David Buttolph; 20th Century-Fox; 1940.

CHARGE OF THE LIGHT BRIGADE: Music by Max Steiner; Warners; 1936.

CHARLIE CHAN AT THE OPERA: Music by Oscar Levant; 20th Century-Fox; 1936.

CHEAPER BY THE DOZEN: Music by Lionel Newman; 20th Century-Fox; 1950.

CHINA SKY: Music by Leigh Harline; RKO; 1944.

CINERAMA HOLIDAY: Music by Jack Shaindlin; Stanley-Warner Cinerama Corp.; 1955.

CITIZEN KANE: Music by Bernard Herrmann; RKO; 1940.

CITY WITHOUT MEN: Music by David Raskin; Columbia; 1942.

CLAUDIA: Music by Alfred Newman, Charles Henderson; 20th Century-Fox; 1943.

CLAUDIA AND DAVID: Music by Cyril J. Mockridge; 20th Century-Fox; 1946.

CLIMAX: Music by Edward Wald; Universal; 1944.

THE CLOCK: Music by George Bassmann; MGM; 1945.

COME TO THE STABLE: Music by Cyril J. Mockridge; 20th Century-Fox; 1949.

COMMAND DECISION: Music by Miklos Rozsa; MGM; 1949.

COMMANDOES STRIKE AT DAWN: Music by Louis Gruenberg; Columbia; 1942.

CONQUEST: Music by Herbert Stothart; MGM; 1937.

THE CONSTANT NYMPH: Music by Erich Wolfgang Korngold; Warners; 1942.

THE CORSICAN BROTHERS: Music by Dimitri Tiomkin; United Artists; 1941.

CORVETTE K-225: Music by David Buttolph; Universal; 1943.

COUNTER ATTACK: Music by Louis Gruenberg; Columbia; 1945.

CRY HAVOC: Music by Daniele Amfitheatrof; MGM; 1943.

DAMSEL IN DISTRESS: Music by George Gershwin; RKO; 1937.

DARK MOUNTAIN: Music by Willy Stahl; Pine & Thomas; 1944.

DAVID COPPERFIELD: Music by Herbert Stothart; MGM; 1934.

DAYS OF GLORY: Music by Daniele Amfitheatrof; RKO; 1944.

DEADLINE AT DAWN: Music by Hans Eisler; RKO; 1945.

THE DEEP BLUE SEA: Music by Muir Mathieson; London-20th Century-Fox; 1955.

DELIGHTFULLY DANGEROUS: Music by Morton Gould; United Artists; 1945.

DESTINATION MOON: Music by Leith Stevens; George Pal-United Artists; 1950.

THE DEVIL AND DANIEL WEBSTER (ALL THAT MONEY CAN BUY): Music by Bernard Herrmann; RKO; 1941.

DEVIL MAY CARE: Music by Herbert Stothart; MGM; 1930.

DIAL M FOR MURDER: Music by Dimitri Tiomkin; Warners; 1955.

DIARY OF A CHAMBERMAID: Music by Michel Michelet; United Artists; 1945.

DEVOTION: Music by Erich Wolfgang Korngold; Warners; 1943.

DIANE: Music by Miklos Rozsa; MGM; 1955.

DR. RENAULT'S SECRET: Music by David Raskin; 20th Century-Fox; 1941.

DOLWYN: Music by John Greenwood; London; 1949.

DOUBLE INDEMNITY: Music by Miklos Rozsa; Paramount; 1945.

A DOUBLE LIFE: Music by Miklos Rozsa; Universal; 1948.

DOWN TO EARTH: Music by Mario Castelnuovo-Tedesco; Columbia; 1947.

DRAGON SEED: Music by Herbert Stothart; MGM; 1944.

DRAGONWYCK: Music by Alfred Newman; 20th Century-Fox; 1945.

DUEL IN THE SUN: Music by Dimitri Tiomkin; Selznick; 1946.

EASTER PARADE: Music by Johnny Green; MGM; 1948.

EAST OF EDEN: Music by Leonard Rosenman; Warners; 1955.

EASY TO WED: Music by Johnny Green; MGM; 1945.

THE EDGE OF DARKNESS: Music by Franz Waxman; Warners; 1943.

THE EGYPTIAN: Music by Alfred Newman; 20th Century-Fox; 1954.

THE ENCHANTED COTTAGE: Music by Roy Denslow Webb; RKO; 1945.

ESCAPE ME NEVER: Music by Sir William Walton; British & Dominions; 1935.

ESCAPE ME NEVER: Music by Erich Wolfgang Korngold; Warners; 1946.

THE EVE OF ST. MARK: Music by Emil Newman; 20th Century-Fox; 1944.

FAITHFUL IN MY FASHION: Music by Nathaniel Shilkret; MGM; 1946.

FALLEN ANGEL: Music by David Raskin; 20th Century-Fox; 1945.

THE FALLEN SPARROW: Music by Roy Denslow Webb; RKO; 1943.

THE FAN (LADY WINDERMERE'S FAN): Music by Daniele Amfitheatrof; 20th Century-Fox; 1949.

FATHER OF THE BRIDE: Music by Adolph Deutsch; MGM; 1950.

FIGHTER SQUADRON: Music by Max Steiner; Warners; 1948.

THE FIGHT FOR LIFE: Music by Louis Gruenberg; Pare Lorentz-U.S. Film Service; 1940.

THE FIGHTING LADY: Music by David Buttolph; 20th Century-Fox; 1944.

FIREFLY: Music by Herbert Stothart; MGM; 1937.

FIRE OVER ENGLAND: Music by Richard Addinsell; United Artists; 1937.

FIRST COMES COURAGE: Music by Ernst Toch; Columbia; 1943.

FIVE GRAVES TO CAIRO: Music by Miklos Rozsa; Paramount; 1944.

THE FLAME AND THE ARROW: Music by Max Steiner; Warners; 1950.

FLAMINGO ROAD: Music by Max Steiner; Warners; 1949.

FLESH AND FANTASY: Music by Alexandre Tansman; Universal; 1942.

FORCE OF EVIL: Music by David Raskin; MGM-Enterprise; 1949.

A FOREIGN AFFAIR: Music by Frederick Hollander; Paramount; 1948.

FOREIGN CORRESPONDENT: Music by Alfred Newman; Walter Wanger-United Artists; 1940.

FOREVER AMBER: Music by Alfred Newman; 20th Century-Fox; 1947.

FORT APACHE: Music by Richard Hageman; Argosy; 1948.

FOR WHOM THE BELLS TOLLS: Music by Victor Young; Paramount; 1943.

THE FOUNTAINHEAD: Music by Max Steiner; Warners; 1949.

FOUR DAUGHTERS: Music by Max Steiner; Warners; 1938.

FOUR FEATHERS: Music by Miklos Rozsa; Alexander Korda-United Artists; 1939.

FOUR WIVES: Music by Max Steiner; Warners; 1940.

FRENCHMAN'S CREEK: Music by Victor Young; Paramount; 1944.

THE FRIENDLY PERSUASION: Music by Dimitri Tiomkin; Allied Artists; 1956.

THE FUGITIVE: Music by Richard Hageman; Argosy; 1947.

THE GARDEN OF ALLAH: Music by Max Steiner; Selznick-United Artists; 1936.

THE GENERAL DIED AT DAWN: Music by Werner Janssen; Paramount; 1936.

THE GHOST AND MRS. MUIR: Music by Bernard Herrmann; 20th Century-Fox; 1947.

THE GHOSTBREAKERS: Music by Ernst Toch; Paramount; 1939.

GIANT: Music by Dimitri Tiomkin; Warners; 1956.

THE GLASS MENAGERIE: Music by Max Steiner; Charles F. Feldman Group-Warners; 1950.

GOLDEN BOY: Music by Victor Young; Columbia; 1939.

GOLDEN EARRINGS: Music by Victor Young; Paramount; 1947.

GOLDWYN FOLLIES: Music by George Gershwin; United Artists; 1937.

GONE WITH THE WIND: Music by Max Steiner; Selznick International; 1939.

THE GOOD EARTH: Music by Herbert Stothart; MGM; 1937.

THE GRAPES OF WRATH: Music by Alfred Newman; 20th Century-Fox; 1940.

THE GREAT DICTATOR: Music by Meredith Willson; United Artists; 1940.

GREAT EXPECTATIONS: Music by Walter Goehr; Cineguild; 1947.

THE GREAT GARRICK: Music by Adolph Deutsch; Warners; 1937.

THE GREAT JOHN L.: Music by Victor Young; Bing Crosby-United Artists; 1945.

THE GREAT WALTZ: Music by Dimitri Tiomkin; MGM; 1937.

THE GREEN YEARS: Music by Herbert Stothart; MGM; 1946.

GUADALCANAL DIARY: Music by Emil Newman, David Buttolph; 20th Century-Fox; 1943.

GUEST WIFE: Music by Daniele Amfitheatrof; United Artists; 1945.

GULLIVER'S TRAVELS: Music by Victor Young; Paramount; 1939.

GUNGA DIN: Music by Alfred Newman; RKO; 1939.

GUYS AND DOLLS: Music by Cyril J. Mockridge; Samuel Goldwyn; 1955.

HAIL THE CONQUERING HERO: Music by Werner Richard Heymann; Paramount; 1945.

THE HAIRY APE: Music by Michel Michelet; United Artists; 1945.

HALF ANGEL: Music by Lionel Newman; 20th Century-Fox; 1950.

HAMLET: Music by Sir William Walton; Two Cities Films; 1948.

HANGMEN ALSO DIE: Music by Hans Eisler; United Artists; 1943.

HANGOVER SQUARE: Music by Bernard Herrmann; 20th Century-Fox; 1944.

HAPPY LAND: Music by Cyril John Mockridge; 20th Century-Fox; 1943.

THE HEIRESS: Music by Aaron Copland; Paramount; 1949.

HENRY V: Music by Sir William Walton; Two Cities Films; 1944.

THE HIGH AND THE MIGHTY: Music by Dimitri Tiomkin; Paramount; 1954.

HIGH NOON: Music by Dimitri Tiomkin; Stanley Kramer-United Artists; 1952.

HIGH SIERRA: Music by Adolph Deutsch; Warners; 1940.

HIGH SOCIETY: Music by Cole Porter; MGM; 1956.

HITLER'S CHILDREN: Music by Roy Denslow Webb; RKO; 1942.

HITLER GANG: Music by David Buttolph; Paramount; 1944.

HOLD THAT BLOND: Music by Werner Richard Heymann; Paramount; 1945.

HOLY MATRIMONY: Music by Emil Newman; 20th Century-Fox; 1943.

THE HOMESTRETCH: Music by Alfred Newman; 20th Century-Fox; 1947.

HOODLUM SAINT: Music by Nathaniel Shilkret; MGM; 1945.

THE HORN BLOWS AT MIDNIGHT: Music by Franz Waxman; Warners; 1944.

HOTEL IMPERIAL: Music by Richard Hageman; Paramount; 1939.

HOUSEKEEPER'S DAUGHTER: Music by Amedeo De Filippi; Columbia; 1938.

HOUSE ON 92ND STREET: Music by David Buttolph; 20th Century-Fox; 1945.

HOW GREEN WAS MY VALLEY: Music by Alfred Newman; 20th Century-Fox; 1941.

THE HOWARDS OF VIRGINIA: Music by Richard Hageman; Columbia; 1940.

HUMORESQUE: Music by Leo F. Forbstein; Warners; 1947.

THE HUNCHBACK OF NOTRE DAME: Music by Alfred Newman; RKO; 1939.

HURRICANE: Music by Alfred Newman; Samuel Goldwyn; 1937.

IF I WERE KING: Music by Richard Hageman; Paramount; 1938.

I'LL BE SEEING YOU: Music by Daniele Amfitheatrof; Selznick International; 1944.

IMMORTAL SERGEANT: Music by David Buttolph; 20th Century-Fox; 1942.

THE INFORMER: Music by Max Steiner; RKO; 1935.

IN OLD CALIFORNIA: Music by David Buttolph; Republic; 1942.

IN OLD CHICAGO: Music by Louis Silvers; 20th Century-Fox; 1938.

IN PERSON: Music by Oscar Levant; RKO; 1935.

INSPECTOR GENERAL: Music by Johnny Green; MGM; 1949.

IT'S A WONDERFUL LIFE: Music by Dimitri Tiomkin; Liberty Films; 1947.

IVANHOE: Music by Miklos Rozsa; MGM.

JACARE: Music by Miklos Rozsa; United Artists; 1943.

JANE EYRE: Music by Bernard Herrmann; 20th Century-Fox; 1943.

JOHNNY ANGEL: Music by Leigh Harline; RKO; 1945.

JOHNNY BELINDA: Music by Leo F. Forbstein; Warners; 1948.

JUAREZ: Music by Erich Wolfgang Korngold; Warners; 1939.

THE JUNGLE BOOK: Music by Miklos Rozsa; Korda; 1942.

KEYS OF THE KINGDOM: Music by Alfred Newman; 20th Century-Fox; 1944.

THE KING AND I: Music by Alfred Newman; 20th Century-Fox; 1956.

KING KONG: Music by Max Steiner; RKO; 1933.

KINGS ROW: Music by Erich Wolfgang Korngold; Warners; 1941.

KISMET: Music by Herbert Stothart; MGM; 1944.

KITTY FOYLE: Music by Roy Denslow Webb; RKO; 1940.

KNICKERBOCKER HOLIDAY: Music by Werner Richard Heymann; United Artists; 1944.

LADIES IN RETIREMENT: Music by Ernst Toch; Columbia; 1941.

LASSIE COME HOME: Music by Daniele Amfitheatrof; MGM; 1943.

THE LATE GEORGE APLEY: Music by Alfred Newman; 20th Century-Fox; 1947.

LEAVE HER TO HEAVEN: Music by Alfred Newman; 20th Century-Fox; 1945.

THE LETTER: Music by Max Steiner; Warners; 1940.

A LETTER FOR EVIE: Music by George Bassman; MGM; 1945.

LETTER FROM AN UNKNOWN WOMAN: Music by Daniele Amfitheatrof; Rampart-Universal; 1948.

LETTER TO THREE WIVES: Music by Alfred Newman; 20th Century-Fox; 1949.

LET US LIVE: Music by Karol Rathaus; Columbia; 1939.

LIFEBOAT: Music by Emil Newman; 20th Century-Fox; 1944.

THE LIGHT THAT FAILED: Music by Victor Young; Paramount; 1939.

LILAC TIME: Music by Nathaniel Shilkret; First National; 1928.

LILI: Music by Bronislau Kaper; MGM; 1953.

LIMELIGHT: Music by Charles Chaplin; Celebrated-United Artists; 1952.

THE LONG VOYAGE HOME: Music by Richard Hageman; United Artists; 1942.

LOST ANGEL: Music by Daniele Amfitheatrof; MGM; 1943.

LOST HORIZON: Music by Dimitri Tiomkin; Columbia; 1937.

LOST PATROL: Music by Max Steiner; RKO; 1934.

LOST WEEKEND: Music by Miklos Rozsa; Paramount; 1945.

LOVE AFFAIR: Music by Roy Denslow Webb; RKO; 1938.

LOVE IS A MANY-SPLENDORED THING: Music by Alfred Newman; 20th Century-Fox; 1955.

LOVE LETTERS: Music by Victor Young; Paramount; 1945.

THE LOVES OF CARMEN: Music by Mario Castelnuovo-Tedesco; Beckworth-Columbia; 1948.

LUCK OF THE IRISH: Music by Cyril J. Mockridge; 20th Century-Fox; 1948.

LUST FOR LIFE: Music by Miklos Rozsa; MGM; 1956.

MACBETH: Music by Jacques Ibert; Mercury Prod.; 1948.

MADAME BOVARY: Music by Miklos Rozsa; MGM; 1949.

MADAME CURIE: Music by Herbert Stothart; MGM; 1943.

THE MAGNIFICENT AMBERSONS: Music by Bernard Herrmann; RKO; 1941.

THE MAGNIFICENT YANKEE: Music by David Raskin; MGM; 1950.

MAIN STREET TODAY: Music by David Raskin; MGM; 1943.

MAJOR BARBARA: Music by Sir William Walton; Gabriel Pascal; 1941.

THE MALTESE FALCON: Music by Adolph Deutsch; Warners; 1941.

MAN FROM TEXAS: Music by George Bassman; MGM; 1947.

MAN HUNT: Music by Alfred Newman; 20th Century-Fox; 1941.

THE MAN I LOVE: Music by Leo Forbstein; Warners; 1947.

THE MAN WHO KNEW TOO MUCH: Music by Bernard Herrmann; Filwite-Paramount; 1956.

THE MAN WITH THE GOLDEN ARM: Music by Elber Bernstein; Carlyle-United Artists; 1955.

MARTY: Music by Roy Denslow Webb; Hecht-Lancaster-United Artists; 1955.

MARY, QUEEN OF SCOTS: Music by Nathaniel Shilkret; RKO; 1936.

THE MASK OF DIMITRIOS: Music by Adolph Deutsch; Warners; 1944.

MAYTIME: Music by Herbert Stothart; MGM; 1937.

A MEDAL FOR BENNY: Music by Victor Young; Paramount; 1944.

MEET JOHN DOE: Music by Dimitri Tiomkin; Warners; 1941.

THE MEN IN HER LIFE: Music by David Raskin; Columbia; 1942.

THE MERRY WIDOW: Music by Herbert Stothart; MGM; 1934.

MILDRED PIERCE: Music by William Allwyn; Warners; 1945.

THE MIRACLE OF OUR LADY OF FATIMA: Music by Max Steiner; Warners; 1952.

MIRACLE ON 34TH STREET: Music by Alfred Newman; 20th Century-Fox; 1947.

MISSION TO MOSCOW: Music by Max Steiner; Warners; 1943.

MR. IMPERIUM: Music by Johnny Green; MGM; 1950.

MR. SKEFFINGTON: Music by Franz Waxman; Warners; 1944.

MR. SMITH GOES TO WASHINGTON: Music by Dimitri Tiomkin; Columbia; 1938.

MRS. MINIVER: Music by Herbert Stothart; MGM; 1942.

MISS SUSIE SLAGEL'S: Music by Daniele Amfitheatrof; Paramount; 1945.

MOBY DICK: Music by Louis Levy; Warners; 1956.

THE MOON AND SIXPENCE: Music by Dimitri Tiomkin; United Artists; 1939.

THE MORE THE MERRIER: Music by Leigh Harline; Columbia; 1943.

MOTHER WORE TIGHTS: Music by Alfred Newman; 20th Century-Fox; 1947.

MOULIN ROUGE: Music by George Auric; Romulus-United Artists; 1953.

THE MOUNTAIN: Music by Daniele Amfitheatrof; Paramount; 1956.

MOURNING BECOMES ELECTRA: Music by Richard Hageman; RKO; 1947.

MUTINY ON THE BOUNTY: Music by Herbert Stothart; MGM; 1935.

MY DARLING CLEMENTINE: Music by Alfred Newman; 20th Century-Fox; 1946.

MY FAVORITE BLOND: Music by David Buttolph; Paramount; 1942.

MY FAVORITE WIFE: Music by Roy Denslow Webb; RKO; 1939.

MY LIFE WITH CAROLINE: Music by Werner Richard Heymann; RKO; 1940.

MY SON, MY SON: Music by Edward Wald; United Artists; 1939.

NATIONAL VELVET: Music by Herbert Stothart; MGM; 1945.

NAUGHTY MARIETTA: Music by Herbert Stothart; MGM; 1935.

NAVY BLUE AND GOLD: Music by Edward Wald; MGM; 1937.

NAVY WAY: Music by Willy Stahl; Pine & Thomas; 1944.

THE NEXT VOICE YOU HEAR: Music by David Raskin; MGM; 1950.

NIGHTMARE ALLEY: Music by Cyril J. Mockridge; 20th Century-Fox; 1947.

NIGHT MUST FALL: Music by Edward Wald; MGM; 1937.

NINOTCHKA: Music by Werner Richard Heymann; MGM; 1939.

NOBODY LIVES FOREVER: Music by Adolph Deutsch; Warners; 1944.

NONE BUT THE LONELY HEART: Music by Hans Eisler; RKO; 1944.

NONE SHALL ESCAPE: Music by Ernst Toch; Columbia; 1943.

NORTHERN PURSUIT: Music by Adolph Deutsch; Warners; 1942.

THE NORTH STAR: Music by Aaron Copland; Samuel Goldwyn; 1943.

NOTHING SACRED: Music by Oscar Levant; Selznick; 1937.

NOW, VOYAGER: Music by Max Steiner; Warners; 1942.

OBJECTIVE BURMA: Music by Franz Waxman; Warners; 1945.

ODD MAN OUT: Music by William Allwyn; J. Arthur Rank; 1947.

OF HUMAN BONDAGE: Music by Erich Wolfgang Korngold; Warners; 1945.

OF MICE AND MEN: Music by Aaron Copland; Halpach, Inc., 1939.

OLD AQUAINTANCE: Music by Franz Waxman; Warners; 1943.

ONCE IN A BLUE MOON: Music by George Antheil; Paramount; 1935.

ONE MAN'S NAVY: Music by Nathaniel Shilkret; MGM; 1945.

ONE NIGHT TO REMEMBER: Music by Werner Richard Heymann; Columbia; 1943.

ON THE WATERFRONT: Music by Leonard Bernstein; Horizon-20th Century-Fox; 1954.

O.S.S.: Music by Daniele Amfitheatrof; Paramount; 1946.

OUR HEARTS WERE YOUNG AND GAY: Music by Werner Richard Heymann; Paramount; 1944.

OUR TOWN: Music by Aaron Copland; United Artists-Sol Lesser; 1940.

THE OX-BOW INCIDENT: Music by Cyril John Mockridge; 20th Century-Fox; 1942.

PARIS CALLING: Music by Richard Hageman; Universal; 1941.

PARIS UNDERGROUND: Music by Alexandre Tansman; Constance Bennett-United Artists; 1945.

PETER IBBETSON: Music by Ernst Toch; Paramount; 1935.

THE PHANTOM HORSE: Music by Seitaro Omori, Koji Shima; Ed Harrison; 1956.

PHANTOM OF THE OPERA: Music by Edward Wald; Universal; 1943.

PICNIC: Music by George Duning; Columbia; 1956.

PINKY: Music by Alfred Newman; 20th Century-Fox; 1949.

PINOCCHIO: Songs by Leigh Harline; Walt Disney; 1940.

A PLACE IN THE SUN: Music by Franz Waxman; Paramount; 1951.

THE PLAINSMAN: Music by George Antheil; Paramount; 1937.

PLYMOUTH ADVENTURE: Music by Miklos Rozsa; MGM; 1952.

THE POSTMAN ALWAYS RINGS TWICE: Music by George Bassman; MGM; 1946.

PRIDE OF THE YANKEES: Music by Leigh Harline; Goldwyn; 1942.

THE PRIVATE AFFAIRS OF BEL AMI: Music by Darius Milhaud; Enterprise; 1947.

PRIVATE LIVES OF ELIZABETH AND ESSEX: Music by Erich Wolfgang Korngold; Warners; 1939.

QUALITY STREET: Music by Roy Denslow Webb; RKO; 1936.

QUICKSAND: Music by Louis Gruenberg; Stiefel-United Artists; 1950.

QUO VADIS: Music by Miklos Rozsa; MGM; 1951.

THE RAINMAKER: Music by Alex North; Paramount; 1956.

THE RAINS CAME: Music by Alfred Newman; 20th Century-Fox; 1939.

THE RAZOR'S EDGE: Music by Alfred Newman; 20th Century-Fox; 1946.

REAP THE WILD WIND: Music by Victor Young; Paramount; 1941.

REAR WINDOW: Music by Franz Waxman; Paramount; 1954.

REBECCA: Music by Franz Waxman; Selznick International; 1939.

THE RED HOUSE: Music by Miklos Rozsa; Thalia; 1947.

RED LIGHT: Music by Dimitri Tiomkin; Roy del Ruth-United Artists; 1949.

THE RED PONY: Music by Aaron Copland; Feldman-Milestone-Republic; 1949.

RED RIVER: Music by Dimitri Tiomkin; Monterey-United Artists; 1948.

THE RED SHOES: Music by Brian Easdale; Archers-Eagle Lion; 1948.

THE REFORMER AND THE REDHEAD: Music by Alfred Newman; 20th Century-Fox; 1949.

RICHARD III: Music by Sir William Walton; London Films; 1955.

RINGS ON HER FINGERS: Music by Cyril John Mockridge; 20th Century-Fox; 1942.

THE RIVER: Music by M. A. Partha Sarathy; Oriental International-United Artists; 1951.

THE ROAD BACK: Music by Dimitri Tiomkin; Universal; 1936.

THE ROBE: Music by Alfred Newman; 20th Century-Fox; 1953.

THE ROGUE SONG: Music by Herbert Stothart; MGM; 1930.

ROMANCE OF ROSY RIDGE: Music by George Bassman; MGM; 1947.

ROMEO AND JULIET: Music by Herbert Stothart; MGM; 1936.

THE ROOSEVELT STORY: Music by Jack Shaindlin; Tola; 1947.

ROSE MARIE: Music by Herbert Stothart; MGM; 1936.

THE ROSE TATTOO: Music by Alex North; Paramount; 1955.

A ROYAL SCANDAL: Music by Alfred Newman; 20th Century-Fox; 1945.

ROYAL WEDDING: Music by Johnny Green; MGM; 1950.

RUBY GENTRY: Music by Heinz Roemheld; Bernhard-Vidor-20th Century-Fox; 1953.

RULERS OF THE SEA: Music by Richard Hageman; Paramount; 1939.

SABRINA: Music by Frederick Hollander; Paramount; 1954.

THE SAILOR TAKES A WIFE: Music by Johnny Green; MGM; 1945.

SALOME, WHERE SHE DANCED: Music by Edward Wald; Universal; 1945.

SAMSON AND DELILAH: Music by Victor Young; Cecil B. De Mille-Paramount; 1949.

SAN FRANCISCO: Music by Herbert Stothart; MGM; 1936.

SARATOGA TRUNK: Music by Max Steiner; Warners; 1943.

SCANDAL IN PARIS: Music by Hans Eisler; United Artists; 1945.

SCOTT OF THE ANTARCTIC: Music by Ralph Vaughan Williams; Ealing Studios-Eagle Lion Films; 1949.

THE SCOUNDREL: Music by George Antheil; Paramount; 1935.

THE SEA HAWK: Music by Erich Wolfgang Korngold; Warners; 1940.

THE SEA OF GRASS: Music by Herbert Stothart; MGM; 1946.

SEARCHING WIND: Music by Victor Young; Paramount; 1946.

THE SECRET LIFE OF WALTER MITTY: Music by David Raskin; Samuel Goldwyn; 1947.

THE SEPTEMBER AFFAIR: Music by Victor Young; Hal Wallis-Paramount; 1950.

THE SEVENTH CROSS: Music by Roy Denslow Webb; MGM; 1944.

SHADOW OF A DOUBT: Music by Dimitri Tiomkin; Universal; 1940.

SHALL WE DANCE?: Music by George Gershwin; RKO; 1937.

SHANE: Music by Victor Young; Paramount; 1953.

SHANGHAI GESTURE: Music by Richard Hageman; United Artists; 1942.

SHE WORE A YELLOW RIBBON: Music by Richard Hageman; Argosy-RKO; 1949.

SHOCK: Music by David Buttolph; 20th Century-Fox; 1946.

SINCE YOU WENT AWAY: Music by Max Steiner; Selznick International; 1944.

SISTER KENNY: Music by Alexandre Tansman; RKO; 1946.

THE SKY'S THE LIMIT: Music by Leigh Harline; RKO; 1943.

SMOKY: Music by David Raskin; 20th Century-Fox; 1945.

THE SMUGGLERS (THE MAN WITHIN): Music by Clifton Parker; Sidney Box-Eagle-Lion; 1947.

SNOW WHITE: Background music by Leigh Harline; Walt Disney; 1938.

SO ENDS OUR NIGHT: Music by Louis Gruenberg; Loew-Lewin; 1943.

SOMEWHERE IN THE NIGHT: Music by David Buttolph; 20th Century-Fox; 1946.

SONG OF BERNADETTE: Music by Alfred Newman; 20th Century-Fox; 1943.

SONG OF THE SOUTH: Music by Daniele Amfitheatrof; Walt Disney; 1946.

SONG TO REMEMBER: Music by Miklos Rozsa; Columbia; 1945.

SPANISH EARTH: Music by Mark Blitzstein and Virgil Thomson; Contemporary Historians, Inc.; 1937.

SPANISH MAIN: Music by Hans Eisler; RKO; 1945.

SPECTER OF THE ROSE: Music by George Antheil; Republic Pictures; 1946.

SPELLBOUND: Music by Miklos Rozsa; Selznick; 1945.

THE SPIRAL STAIRCASE: Music by Roy Denslow Webb; RKO; 1945.

STAGE DOOR: Music by Roy Denslow Webb; RKO; 1937.

THE STAR: Music by Victor Young; Thor-20th Century-Fox; 1952.

A STAR IS BORN: Music by Max Steiner; Selznick-United Artists; 1937.

STARS AND STRIPES FOREVER: Music by Alfred Newman; 20th Century-Fox; 1952.

STARS IN MY CROWN: Music by Adolph Deutsch; MGM; 1950.

THE STORY OF DR. WASSEL: Music by Victor Young; Paramount; 1944.

THE STORY OF GI JOE: Music by Louis Applebaum; Lester Cowan; 1945.

STRANGE LOVE OF MARTHA IVERS: Music by Miklos Rozsa; Paramount; 1946.

THE STRANGER OF THE SWAMP: Music by Alexander Lang Steinert; PRC; 1945.

THE STRATTON STORY: Music by Adolph Deutsch; MGM; 1949.

A STREETCAR NAMED DESIRE: Music by Alex North; Warners; 1951.

STREET SCENE: Music by Alfred Newman; Samuel Goldwyn; 1931.

THE SULLIVANS: Music by Alfred Newman; 20th Century-Fox; 1944.

SUMMER STOCK: Music by Johnny Green; MGM; 1950.

SUMMER STORM: Music by Karl Hajos; Angelus-United Artists; 1944.

SUSAN AND GOD: Music by Herbert Stothart; MGM; 1940.

SUSPENSE: Music by Daniele Amfitheatrof; Monogram; 1946.

SUSPICION: Music by Franz Waxman; RKO; 1942.

THE SWAN: Music by Bronislau Kaper; MGM; 1956.

TALL IN THE SADDLE: Music by Roy Denslow Webb; RKO; 1944.

TAMPICO: Music by David Raskin; 20th Century-Fox; 1943.

TEA AND SYMPATHY: Music by Adolph Deutsch; MGM; 1956.

TEAHOUSE OF THE AUGUST MOON: Music by Saul Chaplin; MGM; 1956.

THE TEN COMMANDMENTS: Music by Elmer Bernstein; Paramount; 1956.

TENDER COMRADE: Music by Leigh Harline; RKO; 1943.

TENTH AVENUE ANGEL: Music by Nathaniel Shilkret; MGM; 1946.

TEST PILOT: Music by Franz Waxman; MGM; 1938.

THELMA: Music by Willy Stahl; Robins Engle; 1922.

THEY DRIVE BY NIGHT: Music by Adolph Deutsch; Warners; 1940.

THEY KNEW WHAT THEY WANTED: Music by Alfred Newman; RKO; 1940.

THEY SHALL HAVE MUSIC: Music by Alfred Newman; Samuel Goldwyn-United Artists; 1939.

THEY WON'T FORGET: Music by Adolph Deutsch; Warners; 1937.

THE THIEF OF BAGDAD: Music by Miklos Rozsa; Alexander Korda; 1940.

THE THIRD MAN: Zither music by Anton Karas; London Film; 1949.

THIS GUN FOR HIRE: Music by David Buttolph; Paramount; 1942.

THIS THING CALLED LOVE: Music by Werner Richard Heymann; Columbia; 1940.

THIS WOMAN IS MINE: Music by Richard Hageman; Universal; 1940.

THE THREE GODFATHERS: Music by Richard Hageman, Argosy; 1948.

THREE STRANGERS: Music by Adolph Deutsch; Warners; 1945.

THUNDERHEAD: Music by Emil Newman; 20th Century-Fox; 1945.

THUNDER ROCK: Music by Hans May; Charter Film; 1944.

A TICKET TO TOMAHAWK: Music by Lionel Newman; 20th Century-Fox; 1950.

'TIL WE MEET AGAIN: Music by David Buttolph; Paramount; 1944.

TIMBER QUEEN: Music by Willy Stahl; Pine & Thomas; 1944.

TIN PAN ALLEY: Music by Alfred Newman; 20th Century-Fox; 1940.

THE TITAN: Music by Alois Melichar; Flaherty-United Artists; 1950.

TO BE OR NOT TO BE: Music by Werner Richard Heymann; Lubitch-Korda; 1942.

TO EACH HIS OWN: Music by Victor Young; Paramount; 1945.

TOGETHER AGAIN: Music by Werner Richard Heymann; Columbia; 1945.

TOMORROW IS FOREVER: Music by Max Steiner; International; 1945.

TONIGHT WE RAID CALAIS: Music by Cyril John Mockridge; 20th Century-Fox; 1943.

TRAPEZE: Music by Muir Mathieson; United Artists; 1956.

TREASURE ISLAND: Music by Clifton Parker; Disney-RKO; 1950.

THE TREASURE OF SIERRA MADRE: Music by Max Steiner; Warners; 1948.

THE TWO MRS. CARROLLS: Music by Franz Waxman; Warners; 1945.

TWO SMART PEOPLE: Music by George Bassman; MGM; 1946.

UNCERTAIN GLORY: Music by Adolph Deutsch; Warners; 1943.

UNCHAINED: Music by Alex North; Hall Bartlett-Warners; 1955.

UNDER CAPRICORN: Music by Richard Addinsell; Transatlantic-Warners; 1949.

THE UNDYING MONSTER: Music by David Raskin; 20th Century-Fox; 1942.

THE UNINVITED: Music by Victor Young; Paramount; 1943.

THE UNSEEN: Music by Ernst Toch; Paramount; 1944.

TWO YEARS BEFORE THE MAST: Music by Victor Young; Paramount; 1944.

THE VIRGINIAN: Music by Daniele Amfitheatrof; Paramount; 1945.

VIVA VILLA: Music by Herbert Stothart; MGM; 1933.

VOICE IN THE WIND: Music by Michel Michelet; United Artists; 1944.

WAGON MASTER: Music by Richard Hageman; Argosy-RKO; 1950.

WAKE ISLAND: Music by David Buttolph; Paramount; 1942.

WALK IN THE SUN: Music by Earl Robinson; 20th Century-Fox; 1940.

THE WAY OF ALL FLESH: Music by Victor Young; Paramount; 1939.

WE WERE STRANGERS: Music by George Antheil; Horizon-Columbia; 1949.

WEEKEND AT THE WALDORF: Music by Johnny Green; MGM; 1945.

THE WESTERNER: Music by Dimitri Tiomkin; Samuel Goldwyn; 1937.

WESTERN UNION: Music by David Buttolph; 20th Century-Fox; 1941.

WESTWARD HO, THE WAGONS!: Music by George Bruns; Disney-Buena Vista; 1956.

WHERE DO WE GO FROM HERE? Music by Kurt Weill; 20th Century-Fox; 1945.

WHERE THE SIDEWALK ENDS: Music by Lionel Newman; 20th Century-Fox; 1950.

WHIRLPOOL: Music by Alfred Newman; 20th Century-Fox; 1949.

THE WHITE TOWER: Music by Roy Denslow Webb; RKO; 1950.

THE WINDOW: Music by Roy Denslow Webb; RKO; 1949.

WINTER MEETING: Music by Max Steiner; Warners; 1948.

WINTERSET: Music by Nathaniel Shilkret; RKO; 1936.

THE WIZARD OF OZ: Music by Herbert Stothart; MGM; 1939.

A WOMAN'S FACE: Music by Bronislau Kaper; MGM; 1941.

THE WOMEN: Music by Edward Wald; MGM; 1936.

WUTHERING HEIGHTS: Music by Alfred Newman; Samuel Goldwyn; 1939.

THE YEARLING: Music by Herbert Stothart; MGM; 1946.

YOU AND ME: Music by Kurt Weill; Paramount; 1938.

THE YOUNG STRANGER: Music by Leonard Rosenman; RKO; 1957.

YOUNG TOM EDISON: Music by Edward Wald; MGM; 1937.

YOU WERE NEVER LOVELIER: Music by Leigh Harline; Columbia; 1942.

Musical Compositions

See also **Popular Names of Musical Compositions; Movies with Notable Scores; Operas, Grand; Pulitzer Prizes; Songs from Broadway Plays**

ADAM, CHARLES ADOLPHE (1803-1856):

Giselle (Ballet Music); *Si J'Etais Roi* Overture.

ALBENIZ, ISAAC (1860-1909): Cantos de España, Opus 232; Catalonia Suite; España, Opus 165; Iberia Suite.

ALBINONI, TOMMASO (1674?-1745?): Adagio for Strings & Organ; Concerto a cinque in B Flat Major, Opus 5, No. 1; Concerto a cinque in D Minor, Opus 5, No. 7; Concerto a cinque in C Major, Opus 5, No. 12; Concerto a cinque, Opus 9, No. 12; Concerto for Oboe in B Flat Major, Opus 7, No. 3; Concerto for Oboe in D Major, Opus 7, No. 6; Concerto for Oboe in F Major, Opus 7, No. 9; Concerto for Oboe in C Major, Opus 7, No. 12; Concerto for Oboe in D Minor, Opus 9, No. 2; Concerto for Strings in D Major; Concerto for Violin in D Major, Opus 9, No. 7; Sonata in G Minor (Strings) Opus 2, No. 6; Trio Sonata in A Major for 2 Violins & Continuo, Opus 1, No. 3.

ANDERSON, LEROY (1908-   ): Irish Suite; Scottish Suite.

ANTHEIL, GEORGE (1900-   ): *Ballet Mécanique* for Percussion Instruments; *Capital of the World* (Ballet Music); Fragments (8) from Shelley (Chorus); *McKonkey's Ferry* Overture; Serenade No. 1 for Strings; Sonata No. 2 for Violin; Songs of Experience (William Blake); Symphony No. 5; Valentine Waltzes for Piano.

ARBOS, ENRIQUE FERNANDEZ (1863-1939): Tangoes for Violin and Piano, Opus 6.

ARCHANGELSKY, ALEXANDER (1846-1924): Divine Liturgy of St. John Chrysostom; Mass for the Dead.

ARENSKY, ANTON (1861-1906): Children's Suite, Opus 65; Fantasie on Epic Russian Songs for Piano and Orchestra, Opus 49; Quintet in D for Piano and Strings, Opus 51; Silhouettes, Opus 23 (Suite No. 2 for Orchestra); Variations on a Theme by Tchaikovsky for String Orchestra, Opus 35A.

ARIOSTI, ATTILIO (1666-1740): Lesson 5 in E Minor for Viola d'Amore.

ARNE, THOMAS AUGUSTINE (1710-1778): *Comus* (Masque); *Thomas and Sally* (Opera).

ARNELL, RICHARD (1917-   ): Concerto for Violin and Orchestra in One Movement; Fantasia for Orchestra; Overture: *The New Age;* Overture: "1940"; *Punch and the Child* for Orchestra; String Quartets Nos. 1-3; Symphonies Nos. 1-3.

ARRIAGA, JUAN (1806-1825): *Agar* (Cantata); *Los Esclavos Felices* Overture; Sinfonia in D Major.

ARRIETA, PASCUAL (1823-1894): *Isabel la Catolica o sea la conquista de Granada* (Zarzuela); *Marina* (Zarzuela).

AUBERT, LOUIS (1877-   ): *La Habanera* (Orchestra); Songs for Voice and Piano.

AURIC, GEORGE (1899-   ): *Fontaine de Jouvence,* Suite; *Malborough s'en va-t'en* for Orchestra.

BACH, JOHANN CHRISTIAN (1735-1782): Canzonette a Due, Opus 4; Concerto in F Major for Organ, Opus 7, No. 2; Concerto in E Flat Major for Harpsichord, Opus 7, No. 5; Concerto in C Minor for Cello; Quintet in D Major (Flute, Oboe, Violin, Cello, Harpsichord); Quintet in F Major for Oboe, Violin, Viola, Cello, & Harpsichord; Quintet in B Flat Major for Flute, Oboe, Violin, Viola, & Continuo; Sinfonia No. 4 in D Major; Sinfonia Concertante in A Major for Violin and Cello; Sinfonia Concertante for Two Violins, Oboe, and Orchestra; Sonata in G Major for 2 Pianos; Sonatas in D Major

and G Major for Flute & Harpsichord; Symphony in E Major, Opus 9, No. 2; Symphony in E Flat Major for Double Orchestra, Opus 18, No. 1; Symphony in B Flat Major, Opus 18, No. 2 *(Lucio Silla)*; Symphony in D Major, Opus 18, No. 3; Symphony in D Major, Opus 18, No. 4; Vauxhall Songs.

BACH, JOHANN SEBASTIAN (1685-1750): Adagio for Strings; Air from Suite No. 3 ("Air on the G String"); Allabreve in D Major for Organ; Anna Magdalena Book for Harpsichord; Arioso for Strings; Art of The Fugue (in arrangements for Harpsichord, 2 Pianos, or Orchestra); Ascension Oratorio; Brandenburg Concerto No. 1 in F Major; Brandenburg Concerto No. 2 in F Major; Brandenburg Concerto No. 3 in G Major; Brandenburg Concerto No. 4 in G Major; Brandenburg Concerto No. 5 in D Major; Brandenburg Concerto No. 6 in B Flat Major; Canonic Variations on "Vom Himmel hoch" for Organ; Cantata No. 1 ("Wie schön leuchet der Morgenstern"); Cantata No. 4 ("Christ lag in Todesbanden"); Cantata No. 11 ("Lobet Gott in seinen Reichen"); Cantata No. 19 ("Es erhub sich ein Streit"); Cantata No. 21 ("Ich hatte viel Bekümmernis"); Cantata No. 31 ("Easter Cantata"); Cantata No. 34 ("O ewiges Feuer"); Cantata No. 39 ("Brich dem Hungrigen dein Brot"); Cantata No. 41 ("Jesu sei gepreist"); Cantata No. 42 ("Am Abend aber desselbigen Sabbats"); Cantata No. 46 ("Schauet doch und sehet"); Cantata No. 50 ("Nun ist das Heil"); Cantata No. 51 ("Jauchzet Gott"); Cantata No. 53 ("Schlage doch"); Cantata No. 54 ("Widerstehe doch"); Cantata No. 56 ("Ich will den Kreuzstab gerne tragen"); Cantata No. 60 ("O Ewigkeit, du Donnerwort"); Cantata No. 63 ("Christmas Cantata"); Cantata No. 65 ("Sie werden aus Saba alle kommen"); Cantata No. 67 ("Halt in Gedächtnis Jesum Christ"); Cantata No. 70 ("Wachet, betet"); Cantata No. 78 ("Jesu, der du meine Seele"); Cantata No. 79 ("Gott der Herr ist Sonn' und Schild"); Cantata No. 80 ("Ein' feste Burg"); Cantata No. 82 ("Ich habe genug"); Cantata No. 104 ("Du Hirte Israel, höre"); Cantata No. 105 ("Herr, gehe nicht ins Gericht"); Cantata No. 106 ("Gottes Zeit"); Cantata No. 107 ("Actus Tragicus"); Cantata No. 112 ("Der Herr ist mein getreuer Hirt"); Cantata No. 122 ("Das neugeborne Kindelein"); Cantata No. 133 ("Ich freue mich in dir"); Cantata No. 140 ("Wachet auf, ruft uns die Stimme"); Cantata No. 146 ("Wir mussen durch viel Trubsal"); Cantata No. 158 ("Easter Cantata"); Cantata No. 161 ("Komm, du süsse Todesstunde"); Cantata No. 170 ("Vergnugte Ruh"); Cantata No. 185 ("Barmherziges Herze der ewigen Liebe"); Cantata No. 189 ("Meine Seele ruhmt und preist"); Cantata No. 200 ("Bekennen will ich seinen Namen"); Cantata No. 201 ("Phoebus und Pan"); Cantata No. 202 ("The Wedding"); Cantata No. 203 ("Amore Traditore"); Cantata No. 205 ("Der zufriedengestellte Aeolus"); Cantata No. 209 ("Non sa che sia dolore"); Cantata No. 211 ("Coffee"); Canzona in D Minor (Organ); Capriccio on the Departure of a Beloved for Violin (transcriptions for Piano, Guitar, Orchestra); Christmas Oratorio; Chromatic Fantasy & Fugue in D Minor (Harpsichord); Concerto No. 1 in D Minor for Harpsichord; Concerto No. 2 in E Major for Harpsichord; Concerto No. 3 in D Major for Harpsichord; Concerto No. 4 in A Major for Harpsichord; Concerto No. 5 in F Minor for Harpsichord; Concerto No. 6 in F Major for Harpsichord; Concerto No. 1 in C Minor for 2 Harpsichords; Concerto No. 2 in C Major for 2

Harpsichords; Concerto No. 1 in D Minor for 3 Harpsichords; Concerto No. 2 in C Major for 3 Harpsichords; Concerto in A Minor for 4 Harpsichords; Concerto in D Minor for Organ; Concerto No. 1 in A Minor for Violin; Concerto No. 2 in E Major for Violin; Concerto in D Minor for Violin; Concerto in G Minor for Violin; Concerto in D Minor for Two Violins; Concerto in C Minor (D Minor) for Violin and Oboe; Concerto in A Major for Oboe d'Amore, Strings, & Continuo; Concerto in A Minor for Flute, Violin, & Harpsichord; Concerto in D Minor (after Marcello) for Harpsichord solo; Concertos (6) (after Vivaldi) for Harpsichord solo; Easter Oratorio; English Suite No. 1 in A Major for Harpsichord; English Suite No. 2 in A Minor for Harpsichord; English Suite No. 3 in G Minor for Harpsichord; English Suite No. 4 in F Major for Harpsichord; English Suite No. 5 in E Minor for Harpsichord; English Suite No. 6 in D Minor for Harpsichord; Fantasia in C Minor, BWV 562, for Organ; Fantasia in G Major, BWV 572, for Organ; Fantasia in C Minor, BWV 906, for Organ; Fantasia in C Minor, BWV 919, for Organ; Fantasia in A Minor, BWV 920, for Organ; Fantasia in A Minor, BWV 922, for Organ; Fantasia and Fugue in C Minor, BWV 537, for Organ; Fantasia & Fugue in G Minor, BWV 542, for Organ; Fantasia & Fugue in A Minor, BWV 904, for Organ; Fantasia-Rondo in C Minor, BWV Anh. 86, for Organ; French Suite No. 1 in D Minor for Harpsichord; French Suite No. 2 in C Minor for Harpsichord; French Suite No. 3 in B Minor for Harpsichord; French Suite No. 4 in E Flat Major for Harpsichord; French Suite No. 5 in G Major for Harpsichord; French Suite No. 6 in E Major for Harpsichord; Fughetta & Chorale-Prelude on "Dies sind die hell'gen zehn Gebot'" for Organ; Fugue in A Minor for Organ; Fugue in D Minor for Organ; Fugue in G Major for Organ; Fugue in G Minor, BWV 578, for Organ; Fugue in G Minor for Organ; Goldberg Variations for Harpsichord; Italian Concerto for Harpsichord; Jesu Joy of Man's Desiring (arrangements for Organ, Piano, Orchestra); Magnificat in D Major for Soli, Chorus, and Orchestra; Mass in B Minor; Missa Brevis No. 1 in F Major; Missa Brevis No. 2 in A Major; Missa Brevis No. 3 in G Minor; Missa Brevis No. 4 in G Major; Motet No. 1 ("Singet dem Herrn"; Motet No. 2 ("Der Geist hilft"); Motet No. 3 ("Jesu, meine Freude"); Motet No. 4 ("Furchte dich nicht"); Motet No. 5 ("Komm, Jesu, komm"); Motet No. 6 ("Lobet den Herrn, alle Heiden"); Partita No. 1 in B Flat Major for Harpsichord; Partita No. 4 in D Major for Harpsichord; Partita No. 6 in E Minor for Harpsichord; Partita No. 1 in B Minor for Violin unaccompanied; Partita No. 2 in D Minor for Violin unaccompanied; Partita No. 3 in B Minor for Violin unaccompanied; Partita in E Minor for Violin and Piano; Passacaglia and Fugue in C Minor for Organ; Pastorale in F Major for Organ; Praeludium, Fugue, & Allegro in E Flat Major for Organ; Prelude in C Major for Organ; Prelude in D Major for Organ; Prelude in D Minor for Organ; Prelude & Fugue in B Minor for Organ; Prelude & Fugue in C Major, BWV 547, for Organ; Prelude & Fugue in C Minor, BWV 537, for Organ; Prelude & Fugue in C Minor, BWV 546, for Organ; Prelude & Fugue in D Major, BWV 532, for Organ; Prelude & Fugue in E Minor, BWV 548, for Organ; Prelude & Fugue in E Minor, BWV 533, for Organ; Prelude

& Fugue in E Flat Major ("St. Anne") for Organ; Prelude & Fugue in F Minor, BWV 534. for Organ; Prelude & Fugue in G Major, BWV 541 ("Great"), for Organ; Prelude & Fugue in A Major, BWV 536, for Organ; Prelude & Fugue in A Minor, BWV 894, for Organ; Prelude & Fugue in A Minor, BWV 543, for Organ; Prelude & Fugue in B Minor, BWV 544, for Organ; Sanctus No. 1 in C Major for Soli, Chorus, and Orchestra; Sanctus No. 2 in D Major for Soli, Chorus, and Orchestra; Sanctus No. 3 in D Minor for Soli, Chorus, and Orchestra; Sanctus No. 4 in G Major for Soli, Chorus, and Orchestra; Sonata in D Major for Harpsichord & Violin No. 3 in E Major for Harpsichord & Violin; Sonata No. 5 in F Minor for Harpsichord & Violin; Sonata No. 1 in G Minor for Violin unaccompanied; Sonata No. 2 in A Minor for Violin unaccompanied; Sonata No. 3 in C Major for Violin unaccompanied; Sonata in G Minor for Violin; Sonata in E Minor for Violin & Continuo; Sonata in G Major for Violin & Continuo; Sonata in C Major for 2 Violins & Continuo, BWV 1037; Sonatas Nos. 1-3 for Viola da Gamba & Harpsichord; Sonata No. 4 in C Major, for Flute & Continuo, BWV 1033; Sonata No. 5 in E Minor for Flute & Continuo, BWV 1034; Sonata No. 6 in E Major for Flute & Continuo, BWV 1035; Sonata No. 7 in G Minor for Flute & Harpsichord, BWV 1020; Sonata in G Major for Flute, Violin, & Continuo; St. John Passion for Soli, Chorus, and Orchestra; St. Matthew Passion for Soli, Chorus, and Orchestra; Suite No. 1 in G Major for Cello unaccompanied; Suite No. 2 in D Minor for Cello unaccompanied; Suite No. 3 in C Major for Cello unaccompanied; Suite No. 4 in E Flat Major for Cello unaccompanied; Suite No. 5 in C Minor for Cello unaccompanied; Suite No. 6 in D Major for Cello unaccompanied; Suite No. 1 in C Major for Orchestra; Suite No. 2 in B Minor for Flute and Strings; Suite No. 3 in D Major for Orchestra; Suite No. 4 in D Major for Orchestra; Suite No. 1 in G Minor for Lute; Suite No. 2 in E Minor for Lute; Toccata in E Major, BWV 566, for Organ; Toccata in C Minor, BWV 911, for Harpsichord; Toccata in D Major, BWV 912, for Harpsichord; Toccata in D Minor, BWV 913, for Harpsichord; Toccata in F Sharp Minor, BWV 910, for Harpsichord; Toccata in E Minor, BWV 914, for Harpsichord; Toccata in G Major, BWV 916, for Harpsichord; Toccata in G Minor, BWV 915, for Harpsichord; Toccata, Adagio, and Fugue in C Major for Organ; Toccata and Fugue in D Minor, BWV 538, for Organ; Toccata and Fugue in F Major, BWV 540, for Organ; Toccata and Fugue in D Minor, BWV 565, for Organ; Trio Sonata No. 1 in E Flat Major for Organ; Trio Sonata No. 2 in C Minor for Organ; Trio Sonata No. 3 in D Minor for Organ; Trio Sonata Nr. 4 in E Minor for Organ; Trio Sonata No. 5 in C Major for Organ; Trio Sonata No. 6 in G Major for Organ; Trio Sonata in D Minor for Flute, Oboe, and Harpsichord; Variations on "O Gott, Du Frommer Gott" for Organ; Variations on "Sei gegrüsset, Jesu gütig" for Organ; Well-Tempered Clavier, Books I and II, for Harpsichord; *The Wise Virgins* (Ballet, arranged by William Walton).

BACH, KARL PHILLIP EMMANUEL (1714-1788): Chromatic Fantasy for Harpsichord; Concerto in D Major for Orchestra; Concerto in C Minor for Piano (1753); Concerto in D Major for Piano; Concerto in D Minor

for Piano; Concerto in A Minor for Piano;
Concerto in G Major for Flute; Concerto
in A Minor for Flute; Duo in E Minor for
Two Clarinets; Magnificat in D Major for
Soli, Chorus, and Orchestra; Quartet in G
Major for Strings; Sonata in C Minor for
Piano; Sonata in D Major for Piano; Sonata
in E Minor for Piano; Symphony No. 1 in
D Major; Symphony No. 3 in C Major; Sym-
phony in D Minor; Trio Sonata in B Flat
Major for Strings; Trio Sonata in B Flat
for Clarinet, Cembalo, and Bassoon; Trio
Sonata in E Flat for Clarinet, Cembalo, and
Bassoon; Trio in B Minor for Strings; Trio
in B Flat Major for Flute, Violin, and Harp-
sichord.

BACH, WILHELM FRIEDEMANN (1710-1784):
Fugue in D Minor for Piano; Fugue in F Flat
Major for Piano; Sonata in F Major for
Flute, Violin, and Harpsichord.

BALAKIREV, MILI ALEKSEEVICH (1837-
1910): Incidental Music to *King Lear;* *Isla-
my,* Fantasy for Piano (or Orchestra); Overture on Three Russian Themes; *Russia,* Symphonic Poem; *Tamar,* Symphonic Poem.

BARBER SAMUEL (1910-): Adagio for
String Orchestra, Opus 11; Commando
March for Winds; Concerto for Violin, Opus
14; *Dover Beach,* for Voice and String Quar-
tet; Essay No. 1 for Orchestra, Opus 12;
Essay No. 2 for Orchestra, Opus 12; Hermit
Songs for Voice and Orchestra; *Medea,* Opus
23 (Ballet); Music for a Scene from Shelley;
Quartet in B Minor for Strings; Quartet in
D Major for Strings, Opus 11; *The School
for Scandal* Overture; Serenade for String
Quartet; Sonata for Cello and Piano, Opus 6;
Souvenirs (two Pianos); *A Stopwatch and
an Ordnance Map,* for Men's Chorus and
Kettledrums; Symphony in One Movement,
Opus 9; Symphony No. 2, Opus 19; *The Vir-
gin Martyrs,* for Chorus.

BARTÓK, BÉLA (1881-1945): Allegro Barbaro,
for Piano; Bagatelles, Op. 6, for Piano; *Blue-
beard's Castle* (Opera); Bulgarian Dances,
for Piano; Burlesques, Opus 8c, for Piano;
Cantata Profana; Concerto No. 2 for Piano;
Concerto No. 3 for Piano; Concerto for
Viola; Concerto for Violin; Concerto for
Orchestra; Contrasts for Violin, Clarinet,
and Piano; *Deux Images* for Orchestra;
Divertimento for Strings; Duets for Two
Violins; Easy Pieces for Piano; Elegies, Opus
8b, for Piano; Fantasy for Piano; Hungarian
Folk Songs for Voice and Piano; Hungarian
Peasant Songs for Piano; Little Pieces for
Piano; *Mikrokosmos,* for Piano; *The Miracu-
lous Mandarin,* Suite for Orchestra; Music
for Strings, Percussion, and Celesta; Out
of Doors Suite, for Piano; Portraits for Or-
chestra, Opus 5; Quartet No. 1 in A Minor,
Opus 7, for Strings; Quartet No. 2 in A Mi-
nor, Opus 17, for Strings; Quartet No. 3, for
Strings; Quartet No. 4, for Strings; Quartet
No. 5, for Strings; Quartet No. 6, for Strings;
Rhapsody No. 1 for Violin and Orchestra;
Rhapsody No. 2 for Violin and Orchestra;
Rondos on Folk Tunes, for Piano; Rumanian
Christmas Carols, for Piano; Rumanian Dan-
ces, for Piano; Rumanian Folk Dances, for
Piano; Sketches, Opus 9, for Piano; Slovak
Folk Songs, for Chorus; Sonata for Piano
(1926); Sonata for Two Pianos and Percus-
sion; Sonata for Violin unaccompanied; So-
nata No. 1 for Violin and Piano; Sonata
No. 2 for Violin and Piano; Sonatina in D
Major for Piano; Songs, Opus 16, for Voice
and Piano; Suite No. 1 for Orchestra, Opus
3; Suite No. 2 for Orchestra, Opus 4; Suite

for Piano, Opus 14; Village Scenes, for Voice
and Piano; *The Wooden Prince* (Ballet Suite).

BATESON, THOMAS (1570-1630): Madrigals.

BATH, HUBERT (1883-1945): Cornish Rhapsody, for Piano and Orchestra.

BAUER, MARION (1887-   ): Concerto for
Piano and Orchestra, Opus 36; Fantasia
Quasi una Sonata for Violin and Piano; Prel-
ude and Fugue for Flute and Strings; Sonata
for Viola and Piano, Opus 22; Sonata No. 1
for Violin, Opus 14; Sonatina for Oboe and
Piano, Opus 32a; Suite for String Orchestra,
Opus 34; Trio Sonata, Opus 40.

BAX, ARNOLD (1883-1953): Coronation
March; *The Garden of Fand,* Symphonic
Poem; *London Pageantry,* Symphony; *November Woods,* Symphonic Poem; Quintet
for Oboe & Strings; Quintet for Strings and
Harp; Romantic Overture; *Tintagel,* Symphonic Poem; Trio for Harp, Flute, and Viola.

AYER, JOSEF (1852-1913): *Die Puppenfee* (Ballet Music).

BEETHOVEN, LUDWIG VAN (1770-1827):
Ah, Perfido! Opus 65, for Voice and Orches-
tra; Andante Favori in F Major, for Piano;
"An die ferne Geliebte" (*"To the Distant
Beloved"*), Six Songs, Opus 98; Bagatelles
for Piano; Choral Fantasy in C Minor for
Piano, Chorus, and Orchestra; *Christ on the
Mount of Olives,* Opus 85, for Soli, Chorus,
and Orchestra; Concerto in E Flat Major for
Piano (1784); Concerto No. 1 in C Major for
Piano, Opus 15; Concerto No. 2 in B Flat
Major for Piano, Opus 19; Concerto No. 3
in C Minor for Piano, Opus 37; Concerto
No. 4 in G Major for Piano, Opus 58; Con-
certo No. 5 in E Flat Major for Piano, Opus
73 ("Emperor"); Concerto in D Major, Opus
61 (transcribed for piano); Concerto in D
Major for Violin, Opus 61; Concerto in C
Major, Opus 56 ("Triple"); *Consecration of
the House* Overture, Opus 124; Contradances
for Orchestra; *Coriolan* Overture; *The Creatures of Prometheus* Overture; Duet in E
Flat for Viola and Cello; Duos for Clarinet
and Bassoon; *Egmont* Overture; Elegischer
Gesang, Opus 118, for Voices and Strings;
Fidelio Overture; Gellert Lieder, Opus 48
for Voice and Piano; German Dances for
Orchestra; Grosse Fugue for Strings, Opus
133; *King Stephen* Overture; *Leonore* Overture, No. 1; *Leonore* Overture, No. 2; *Leonore* Overture No. 3; Marches, Opus 45, for
Piano; Minuets for the Redoutensaal; Missa
Solemnis in D Major, Opus 123; Musik zu
einem Ritterballet; *Namensfeier* Overture;
Octet in E Flat Major for Winds, Opus 103;
Pieces (5) for Piano, Opus Posthumous; Polo-
naise in C Major for Piano, Opus 89; Quartet in C Major for Strings, Opus 2, No. 3;
Quartet for Strings, Opus 14, No. 1; Quartet in E Flat Major for Piano and Strings,
Opus 16; Quartet No. 1 in F Major for
Strings, Opus 18, No. 1; Quartet No. 2 in G
Major for Strings, Opus 18, No. 2; Quartet
No. 3 in D Major for Strings, Opus 18, No.
3; Quartet No. 4 in C Minor for Strings,
Opus 18, No. 4; Quartet No. 5 in A Major
for Strings, Opus 18, No. 5; Quartet No. 6
in B Flat Major for Strings, Opus 18, No.
6; Quartet No. 7 in F Major for Strings,
Opus 59, No. 1; Quartet No. 8 in E Minor
for Strings, Opus 59, No. 2; Quartet No. 9
in C Major for Strings, Opus 59, No. 3;
Quartet No. 10 in E Flat Major for Strings,
Opus 74; Quartet No. 11 in F Minor for
Strings, Opus 95; Quartet No. 12 in E Flat
Major for Strings, Opus 127; Quartet No. 13
in B Flat Major for Strings, Opus 130; Quartet No. 14 in C Sharp Minor for Strings,

Opus 131; Quartet No. 1 in E Flat Major for Piano and Strings, Opus 152; Quartet No. 2 in D Major for Piano and Strings, Opus 152; Quartet No. 3 in C Major for Piano and Strings, Opus 152; Quintet in E Flat Major for Strings (two violas), Opus 4; Quintet in E Flat Major for Piano and Winds, Opus 16; Quintet in C Major for Strings (two violas), Opus 29; Quintet for Oboe, Horns, and Bassoon; Romance Cantabile for Piano and Orchestra; Romance No. 1 in G for Violin and Orchestra, Opus 40; Romance No. 2 in F for Violin and Orchestra, Opus 50; Rondino in E Flat Major (Grove 154) for Winds; Rondo a Capriccio for Piano, Opus 129; Rondo No. 1 in C Major for Piano, Opus 51; Rondo in B Flat Major for Piano, Opus Posthumous; *The Ruins of Athens* for Soli, Chorus, and Orchestra, Opus 113; Septet in E Flat Major for Strings and Winds, Opus 20; Serenade in D Major for Flute, Violin, & Viola, Opus 25; Sextet in E Flat Major for Winds, Opus 71; Sextet in E Flat Major for Strings and 2 Horns, Opus 81b; Sonata for Cello No. 1 in F Major, Opus 5, No. 1; Sonata for Cello No. 2 in G Minor, Opus 5, No. 2; Sonata for Cello No. 3 in A Major, Opus 69; Sonata for Cello No. 4 in C Major, Opus 102, No. 1; Sonata for Cello No. 5 in D Major, Opus 102, No. 2; Sonata in F Major for Horn, Opus 17; Sonata No. 1 in F Minor for Piano, Opus 2, No. 1; Sonata No. 2 in A Major for Piano, Opus 2, No. 2; Sonata No. 3 in C Major for Piano, Opus 2, No. 3; Sonata No. 4 in E Flat Major for Piano, Opus 7; Sonata No. 5 in C Minor for Piano, Opus 10, No. 1; Sonata No. 6 in F Major for Piano, Opus 10, No. 2; Sonata No. 7 in D Major for Piano, Opus 10, No. 3; Sonata No. 8 in C Minor for Piano, Opus 13 ("Pathétique"); Sonata No. 9 in E Major for Piano, Opus 14, No. 1; Sonata No. 10 in G Major for Piano, Opus 14, No. 2; Sonata No. 11 in B Flat Major for Piano, Opus 22; Sonata No. 12 in A Flat Major for Piano, Opus 26; Sonata No. 13 in E Flat Major for Piano, Opus 27, No. 1; Sonata No. 14 in C Sharp Minor for Piano, Opus 27, No. 2 ("Moonlight"); Sonata No. 15 in D Major for Piano, Opus 28 ("Pastorale"); Sonata No. 16 in G Major for Piano, Opus 31, No. 1; Sonata No. 17 in D Minor for Piano, Opus 31, No. 2 ("Tempest"); Sonata No. 18 in E Flat Major for Piano, Opus 31, No. 3; Sonata No. 19 in G Minor for Piano, Opus 49, No. 1; Sonata No. 20 in G Major for Piano, Opus 49, No. 2; Sonata No. 21 in C Major for Piano, Opus 53 ("Waldstein"); Sonata No. 22 in F Major for Piano, Opus 54; Sonata No. 23 in F Minor for Piano, Opus 57 ("Appassionata"); Sonata No. 24 in F Sharp Major for Piano, Opus 78; Sonata No. 25 in G Major for piano, Opus 79; Sonata No. 26 in E Flat Major for Piano, Opus 81a ("Les Adieux"); Sonata No. 27 in E Minor for Piano; Opus 90; Sonata No. 28 in A Major for Piano, Opus 101; Sonata No. 29 in B Flat Major for Piano, Opus 106 ("Hammerklavier"); Sonata No. 30 in E Major for Piano, Opus 109; Sonata No. 31 in A Flat Major for Piano, Opus 110; Sonata No. 32 in C Minor for Piano, Opus 111; Sonata in D Major for Piano, Four Hands, Opus 6; Sonata for Violin No. 1 in D Major, Opus 12, No. 1; Sonata for Violin No. 2 in A Major, Opus 12, No. 2; Sonata for Violin No. 3 in E Flat Major Opus 12; Sonata for Violin No. 4 in A Minor, Opus 23; Sonata for Violin No. 5 in F Major, Opus 24 ("Spring"); Sonata for Violin No. 6 in A Major, Opus 30, No. 1;

Sonata for Violin No. 7 in C Minor, Opus 30, No. 2; Sonata for Violin No. 8 in G Major Opus 30, No. 3; Sonata for Violin No. 9 in A Major, Opus 47 ("Kreutzer"); Sonata for Violin No. 10 in G Major, Opus 96; Symphony No. 1 in C Major, Opus 21; Symphony No. 2 in D Major, Opus 36; Symphony No. 3 in E Flat Major, Opus 55 ("Eroica"); Symphony No. 4 in B Flat Major, Opus 60; Symphony No. 5 in C Minor, Opus 67; Symphony No. 6 in F Major, Opus 68 ("Pastorale"); Symphony No. 7 in A Major, Opus 92; Symphony No. 8 in F Major, Opus 93; Symphony No. 9 in D Minor, Opus 125 ("Choral"); Symphony in C Major ("Jena"); Symphony, Opus 91 ("Wellington's Victory"); Trio for Strings No. 2 in G Major, Opus 9, No. 1; Trio for Strings No. 3 in D Major, Opus 9, No. 2; Trio for Strings No. 4 in C Major, Opus 9, No. 3; Trio for Piano, Violin, & Cello No. 1 in E Flat Major, Opus 1, No. 1; Trio for Piano, Violin & Cello No. 2 in G Major, Opus 1, No. 2; Trio for Piano, Violin, & Cello No. 3 in C Minor, Opus 1, No. 3; Trio for Piano, Violin, & Cello No. 4 in B Flat Major, Opus 11; Trio for Piano, Violin, & Cello No. 5 in D Major, Opus 70, No. 1 ("Ghost"); Trio for Piano, Violin, & Cello No. 6 in E Flat Major, Opus 70, No. 2; Trio for Piano, Violin, & Cello No. 7 in B Flat Major, Opus 97 ("Archduke"); Trio for Piano, Violin, & Cello No. 8 in B Flat Major, Opus Posthumous; Trio in B Flat Major for Piano, Clarinet, & Cello, Opus 11; Trio in C Major for 2 Oboes & English Horn, Opus 87; Trio in G Major for Flute, Bassoon, and Piano; Variations & Fugue in E Flat Major, Opus 35 ("Eroica"), for Piano; Variations in F Major on "Ein Mädchen," for Piano and Cello, Opus 66; Variations for Flute & Piano, Opus 105, Opus 107; Variations on a Theme by Diabelli, for Piano, Opus 120; Variations in G Major on "Judas Maccabeus," Piano and Cello; Variations in E Flat Major on "Bei Männern," for Piano and Cello; Variations on Mozart's "La ci darem la mano," two Oboes and English Horn; Variations in C Minor for Piano; Variations in D Major for Piano; Viennese Dances for Orchestra.

BENJAMIN, ARTHUR (1893-   ): Sonatina for Violin & Piano.

BEREZOWSKY, NIKOLAI (1900-1953): Christmas Overture; Concerto for Harp; Concerto for Viola; Concerto Lirico for Cello; Hebrew Suite; Sonata for Piano; Quintet for Woodwinds, No. 1; Quartet for Strings; Quartet for Strings, Opus 16; Quartet for Strings with Orchestra; Sextet for Strings; Suite for Wind Quintet, Opus 11; Symphonies Nos. 1-4.

BERG, ALBAN (1885-1935): Chamber Concerto for Violin, Piano, and Winds; Concerto for Violin; Four Pieces for Clarinet and Piano, Opus 5; Quartet, Opus 3, for Strings.

BERGER, ARTHUR (1912-   ): Duo for Cello and Piano; Partita for Piano; Quartet in C Major for Woodwinds (Flute, Oboe, Clarinet, Bassoon) (1941); Serenade for Orchestra in One Movement; Words for Music Perhaps, Three Songs from the Yeats Cycle for High Voice and Piano.

BÉRIOT, CHARLES AUGUSTE DE (1802-1870): Concertos (7) for Violin; Duos Brilliants for Piano and Violin; Scene de Ballet for Violin, Opus 100; Variations (11) for Violin.

BERKELEY, LENNOX RANDAL (1903-   ): Serenade for Strings; Sonatina for Violin and Piano; Theme and Variations for Violin and Piano.

BERLIOZ, HECTOR (1803-1869) *Beatrice and Benedict* Overture; *Benvenuto Cellini* Overture; *Le Corsaire* Overture; *The Damnation of Faust,* Opus 24, Dramatic Legend for Soli, Chorus, and Orchestra; *L'Enfance du Christ,* Opus 25, for Soli, Chorus, and Orchestra; *Les Francs-Juges* Overture; Funeral March —Last Scene of *Hamlet,* Opus 18, No. 3; Funeral and Triumphal Symphony, Opus 15; *Harold in Italy,* Opus 16, for Orchestra and Viola; *King Lear* Overture, Opus 4; *Lelio* (Symphonie Fantastique, Part 2); *Les Nuits d'Eté,* Opus 7 (Song Cycle); Requiem; *The Roman Carnival* Overture, Opus 9; *Romeo and Juliet,* Opus 17, a Dramatic Symphony; Symphonie Fantastique, Opus 14; Te Deum; Trojan March; *Waverly* Overture, Opus 1.

BERNERS, LORD (1883-1950): *Cupid and Psyche* (Ballet); **Fantaisie Espagnole for Orchestra**; Funeral Marches (3) for Piano; *Luna Park* (Ballet); Music for Piano; *The Triumph of Neptune* (Ballet); *The Wedding Bouquet* (Ballet).

BERNSTEIN, LEONARD (1918-   ): Anniversaries (7) for Piano; *Candide* Overture; *Facsimile* (Ballet); *Fancy Free* (Ballet); Serenade for Violin, Strings, and Percussion; Sonata for Clarinet and Piano; Symphony, "Jeremiah."

BERWALD, FRANZ ADOLF (1796-1868): Symphonies 1-3.

BINCHOIS, EGIDIUS (GILLES DE BINCHE) (c. 1400-1460): Masses (7); Sacred Songs; Secular Chansons (52).

BIZET, GEORGES (1838-1875): *L'Arlésienne* Suite No. 1; *L'Arlésienne* Suite No. 2; *Danse Bohémienne* for Orchestra; *Djamileh* (Ballet Music); *The Fair Maid of Perth* Suite: *Jeux d'Enfants,* Opus 22, for Orchestra; *Patrie* Overture; *Roma* Suite; Symphony in C Major.

BLISS, ARTHUR (1891-   ): *Checkmate* Ballet; A Color Symphony; Concerto for Violin & Orchestra; *Madame Roy,* for Voice and Chamber Orchestra; *Miracle in the Gorbals* (Ballet Suite); Quartet for Strings; Quartet for Clarinet and Oboe; *Rout,* for Voice and Chamber Orchestra; Sonata for Violin; Theme and Cadenza for Violin and Orchestra.

BLITZSTEIN, MARC (1905-   ): *Freedom Morning,* Symphonie Poem; *Native Land,* Film Suite.

BLOCH, ERNEST (1880-   ): *Adonai Elohim* —From Israel, for 2 Sopranos, 2 Altos, Bass, Orchestra (or Piano); *Baal Shem,* for Violin and Piano; Concerto for Violin and Orchestra; Concerto Grosso for Strings and Piano Obligato; Episodes (4) for Piano, Strings, and Wind Instruments; *Evocations,* Symphonic Suite; *From Jewish Life,* for Cello and Piano; *In the Mountains,* Piano Trio or String Quartet; Israel Symphony for 2 Sopranos, 2 Altos, Bass, and Orchestra; *Méditation Hébraïque* for Cello and Piano; Pieces for Children (Piano); *Processional* for Viola and Piano; Quartets Nos. 1-4 for Strings; Quintet for Piano and Strings; *Schelomo*—Hebrew Rhapsody for Cello and Orchestra; Sacred Service for Baritone, Mixed Chorus, Orchestra or Organ; Sonata No. 1 for Violin; Sonata No. 2 for Violin and Piano ("Poème Mystique"); Sonata for Piano; Suite for Viola and Piano; Suite Hébraïque, for Viola and Piano; Three Landscapes, String Quartet; *Voice in the Wilderness,* Symphonic Poem for Cello and Orchestra.

BLODEK, VILÉM (1834-1874): Concerto for Flute; Mass; Overture; Quartets for Men's Voices; *V Studni (In the Well),* comic opera in one act.

BLOW, JOHN (c. 1648-1708): *Awake, Awake, My Lyre,* for Soli, Chorus, and Orchestra; Ode on the Death of Henry Purcell; *Venus and Adonis,* for Soli Voices, Chorus, and Orchestra.

BOCCHERINI, LUIGI (1743-1805): Concerto in B Flat Major for Cello; Concerto in D Major for Cello; Concerto in D Major for Flute and Strings; Overture in D Major; Pastorale (from Quintet No. 4 in D Major; Opus 37); Quartet in B Flat Major for Strings, Opus 1, No. 2; Quartet in D Major for Strings, Opus 6, No. 1; Quartet No. 8 in A Major for Strings, Opus 33, No. 6; Quartet in A Major for Strings, Opus 39, No. 3; Quartet in A Major for Strings, ·Opus 39, No. 8; Quartet in E Flat Major for Strings, Opus 40, No. 2; Quartet in E Flat Major for Strings, Opus 58, No. 2; Quartet in E Flat Major for Strings, Opus 58, No. 3; Quartet in B Minor for Strings, Opus 58, No. 4; Quintet No. 1 in A Major for Piano and Strings, Opus Posthumous; Quintet No. 4 in D Minor for Piano and Strings, Opus Posthumous; Quintet in C Major for Strings; Quintet in E Flat Major for Flute & Strings; Quintet No. 1 in D Major for Guitar and Strings; Quintet in E Minor for Guitar & Strings, Opus 50, No. 3; Sextet in E Flat Major for Strings, Opus 24, No. 1; Sextet in E Flat Major for Strings, Opus 41; Sinfonia Concertante in G Major; Sonata No. 6 in A Major for Cello; Symphony in C Major, Opus 16, No. 3; Symphony in B Major ("Funeral"); *La Tiranna Spagnola,* Opus 44, No. 4, for String Quartet; Trio in G Minor, Opus 9, No. 5, for Strings; Trio in G Major, Opus 39, No. 2, for Strings; Trios for Strings, Opus 35 (No. 1, F Minor; No. 2, G Major; No. 3, E Flat Major; No. 4, D Major; No. 5, C Minor; No. 6, E Major).

BOIELDIEU, FRANÇOIS ADRIEN (1775-1834): *The Caliph of Bagdad* Overture; *La Dame Blanche* Overture.

BOISMORTIER, JOSEPH BODIN DE (1691-1755): Concerto in A Minor for 5 Flutes, Opus 15, No. 2.

BONONCINI, GIOVANNI BATTISTA (1660-?1750): Cantate e Duetto, for George I (1721); Divertimenti for Harpsichord (1722); Divertimento da Camera in C Minor for Flute and Harpsichord; Sonatas or Chamber Airs for two Violins and a Bass (1732).

BONPORTI, ANTONIO FRANCESCO (1660-1740): Concerto in D Major for Strings, Opus 11, No. 8; Recitative for Violin and Strings.

BORODIN, ALEXANDER (1833-1887): *In the Steppes of Central Asia,* Symphonic Poem; Nocturne for String Orchestra (arranged by Sargent); Polovetsian Dances (from *Prince Igor);* Quartet No. 2 in D Major, for Strings; Quintet for Piano, Opus Posthumous; Suite for Piano; Symphony No. 1 in E Flat Major; Symphony No. 2 in B Minor; Symphony No. 3 in A Minor (unfinished); Trio for Strings, Opus Posthumous.

BOTTESINI, GIOVANNI (1821-1889): Grand Duo Concertant for Violin, Double Bass, & Piano.

BOWLES, PAUL (1911-   ): Canciones Espanolas, Four Songs; *Facsimile* (Ballet); Mediodia for Flute, Clarinet, Trumpet, Piano, and Strings; *Music for a Farce,* for Clarinet, Trumpet, Piano, and Percussion); *Pastorella* (Ballet); A Picnic Cantata; Romantic Suite for 6 Wind and String Instruments, Percussion, and Piano; *Scènes d'Anabase* for Tenor, Oboe, and Piano; Sonata for Flute and Piano; Sonata for Oboe and Clarinet; Sonata for

Two Pianos; Suite for Small Orchestra; Suite for Two Pianos: *Yankee Clipper* (Ballet).

BRAHMS, JOHANNES (1833-1897): Academic Festival Overture, Opus 80; Allegro for Violin and Piano; Alto Rhapsody, Opus 53, for Voice and Orchestra; Ave Maria, for Female Chorus and Orchestra or Organ, Opus 12; Ballades, Opus 10, for Piano; Ballade in G Minor, Opus 118, for Piano; Capricci and Intermezzi, Opus 76, for Piano; Cappricci and Intermezzi, Opus 116, for Piano; Chorale Preludes, Opus 122, for Organ; Concerto No. 1 in D Minor for Piano, Opus 15; Concerto No. 2 in B Flat Major for Piano, Opus 83; Concerto in D Major for Violin, Opus 77; Concerto in A Minor, Opus 102 ("Double"), for Violin and Cello; Funeral Hymn for Chorus and Winds, Opus 13; German Requiem, Opus 45, for Soli, Chorus, and Orchestra; Gesang der Parzen, for Chorus and Orchestra; Hungarian Dances for Orchestra; Intermezzi, Opus 117, for Piano; Intermezzi, Ballade, and Romance, Opus 118, for Piano; Intermezzi and Rhapsodie, Opus 119, for Piano; Liebeslieder Waltzes, Opus 52, for Piano, four hands, and four Solo Voices; Marienlieder, Opus 22, for Chorus; Nänie, Opus 82, for Chorus and Orchestra; Neue Liebeslieder Waltzes, Opus 65, for Piano four hands, and four Solo Voices; Quartet No. 1 in G Minor (Piano) Opus 25; Quartet No. 2 in A Major (Piano) Opus 26; Quartet No. 3 in C Minor (Piano) Opus 60; Quartet No. 1 in C Minor, Opus 51, No. 1, for Strings; Quartet No. 2 in A Minor, Opus 51, No. 2, for Strings; Quartet No. 3 in B Flat Major, Opus 67, for Strings; Quintet in F Minor (Piano) Opus 34; Quintet No. 1 in F Major (String) Opus 88; Quintet No. 2 in G Major (String) Opus 111; Quintet in B Minor for Clarinet & Strings, Opus 115; Rhapsodies, Opus 79, for Piano; Rhapsody in E Flat Major, Opus 119, for Piano; *Rinaldo* (Cantata); Romance in F Major, Opus 118, for Piano; Scherzo in E Flat Minor for Piano, Opus 4; *Schicksalslied (Song of Destiny)* for Chorus and Orchestra, Opus 54; Serenade No. 1 in D Major, Opus 11, for Orchestra; Serenade No. 2 in A Major, Opus 16, for Orchestra; Sextet in B Flat Major, Opus 18, for Strings; Sonata in C for Piano, Opus 1; Sonata No. 2 in F Sharp Minor for Piano, Opus 2; Sonata No. 3 in F Minor for Piano, Opus 5; Sonata in F Minor for 2 Pianos, Opus 34; Sonata No. 1 in G Major for Violin, Opus 78 ("Rain"); Sonata No. 2 in A Major for Violin, Opus 100; Sonata No. 3 in D Minor for Violin, Opus 108; Sonata No. 1 in E Minor for Cello, Opus 38; Sonata No. 2 in F Major for Cello, Opus 99; Sonata No. 1 in F Minor for Viola, Opus 120; Sonata No. 2 in E Flat Major for Viola, Opus 120; Sonata No. 1 in F Minor for Clarinet, Opus 120; Sonata No. 2 in E Flat Major for Clarinet, Opus 120; Songs for Alto, Viola, and Piano, Opus 91; Songs for Women's Voices, Opus 17; Symphony No. 1 in C Minor, Opus 68; Symphony No. 2 in D Major, Opus 73; Symphony No. 3 in F Major, Opus 90; Symphony No. 4 in E Minor, Opus 98; Tragic Overture, Opus 81; Trio in B Major for Piano, Violin, and Cello, Opus 8; Trio in C Major, Opus 87, for Strings; Trio in C Minor, Opus 101, for Strings; Trio in A Major (Piano) Opus Posthumous; Trio in A Minor, for Clarinet, Cello, & Piano, Opus 114; Trio in E Flat Major, for Piano, Violin, & Horn, Opus 40; Variations on a Theme of Schumann, Opus 9, for Piano; Variations & Fugue on a Theme of Handel, Opus 24, for Piano; Variations on a Theme of Paganini, Opus 35, for Piano; Variations on a Theme of Haydn, Opus 56a, for Orchestra; Variations on a Theme of Haydn, Opus 56b, for two Pianos; Vier Ernste Gesänge for Voice and Piano; Waltzes, Opus 39, for Piano; Zigeunerlieder, Opus 103, for Vocal Quartet and Piano.

BRANT, HENRY (1913-) *Angels and Devils*, for Flute and Orchestra of Flutes; Choral Preludes for Orchestra; *City Portrait* (Ballet); Concerto for Flute and Orchestra; *Dedication in Memory of a Great Man*, for Orchestra; Fantasy and Caprice for Violin and Orchestra; *Galaxy 2*, for Chamber Orchestra; *Gallopjig Colloquy*, Scherzo Ballad for Orchestra; *Good Weather* Overture; *The Great American Goof* (Ballet); Intrada and Ricercata for Orchestra; Prelude and Fugue for Orchestra; *Signs and Alarms* for Chamber Orchestra; Sonata for Two Pianos; Suite for Flute and String Quartet; Symphony in B.

BRETON, TOMAS (1850-1923): *La Verbena de la Paloma* for Soli, Chorus, and Orchestra.

BRÉVAL, JEAN-BAPTISTE (1765-1825): Concertos (8) for Cello; Sonata in G Major for Cello; Symphonies (8).

BRITTEN, BENJAMIN (1913-): A Ceremony of Carols, for Choir and Harp; Diversions on a Theme for Piano (Left Hand) & Orchestra; Fantasy for Oboe and Strings, Opus 2; Folk Songs of the British Isles, for Voice and Piano; Holy Sonnets of John Donne, Opus 35, for Tenor and Piano; Hymn to St. Cecilia, for Chorus; *Les Illuminations de Rimbaud*, for Tenor and Orchestra; *Matinées Musicales*, for Orchestra; Metamorphoses after Ovid, Opus 49, for Oboe; Quartet No. 1 in D Major, Opus 25, for Strings; *Rejoice in the Lamb*, for Chorus; *Saint Nicholas* (Cantata); Serenade for Tenor, Horn, & Strings; Seven Sonnets of Michelangelo, Opus 22, for Tenor and Piano; A Simple Symphony, Opus 4; Sinfonia da Requiem; *Soirées Musicales*, for Orchestra; Song Cycle, for Voice and Piano; Te Deum in C Major, for Chorus and Organ; Variations on a Theme of Frank Bridge, Opus 10, for Orchestra; The Young Person's Guide to the Orchestra, Opus 34, for Narrator and Orchestra.

BRUCH, MAX (1838-1920): Canzone, Opus 55, for Cello and Orchestra; Concerto No. 1 in G Minor for Violin, Opus 26; Concerto No. 2 in D Minor for Violin, Opus 44; *Kol Nidre*, Opus 47, for Cello and Orchestra; Scottish Fantasy, Opus 46, for Violin and Orchestra.

BRUCKNER, ANTON (1824-1896): Intermezzo for String Quintet; Mass No. 2 in E Minor; Overture in G Minor; Psalm No. 112 (Chorus and Orchestra); Psalm No. 150 (Chorus and Orchestra); Quintet in F Major for Strings; Symphony in D Minor, Opus Posthumous ("Youth"); Symphony No. 1 in C Minor; Symphony No. 2 in C Minor; Symphony No. 3 in D Minor; Smphony No. 4 in E Flat Major ("Romantic"); Symphony No. 5 in B Flat Major; Symphony No. 6 in A Major; Symphony No. 7 in E Major; Symphony No. 8 in C Minor; Symphony No. 9 in D Minor; Te Deum, for Solo Voices, Chorus, and Orchestra.

BURKHARD, WILLY (1900-): Toccata for 4 Winds, Percussion, & Strings, Opus 86.

BUSONI, FERRUCCIO (1866-1924): Concerto for Clarinet; Concerto for Violin, Opus 35a; Fantasia Contrappuntistica, for Piano.

BUXTEHUDE, DIETRICH (1637-1707): Cantata ("Aperite mihi portas justitiae"); Cantata ("In dulci jubilo"); Cantata ("Jubilate Domino"); Cantatas ("Lauda Sion"; "Jesu,

Meine Freude"); Cantatas (Solo) ("Singet dem Herrn"; "Herr, auf Dich"; Canzonas for Organ; Canzonettas for Organ; Chaconnes for Organ; Chorale Fantasias for Organ; Chorale Variations for Organ; Passacaglia for Organ; Prelude, Fugue, & Chaconne in C Major for Organ; Prelude & Fugue in G Minor for Organ; Preludes & Fugues for Organ; Toccata and Fugue in F Major for Organ.

BYRD, WILLIAM (1543-1623): The Great Service, for Chorus; Mass for Four Voices; Mass for Five Voices; Songs for Voice & Viols.

CAGE, JOHN (1912-   ): Amores for Three Players; Book of Music for Two Pianos; Construction in Metal for Seven Players, Percussion Orchestra; Imaginary Landscapes 1-3, for Electrical Orchestra with Percussion; March for Five Players; Quartet for Strings; Second Construction, for Four Players; Three Dances for Two Pianos.

CAPLET, ANDRÉ (1878-1925) The Masque of the Red Death, for Harp and Orchestra.

CARCASSI, MATTEO (1792-1853): Melodious Studies for Guitar, Opus 60.

CARISSIMI, GIACOMO (1605-1674): Balthazar (Oratorio); Jephte (Oratorio); Jonas (Oratorio); Judicium Salomonis (Oratorio).

CARPENTER, JOHN ALDEN (1876-1951): Adventures in a Perambulator, Suite for Orchestra; Birthday of the Infanta (Ballet); Concertino for Piano and Orchestra; Concerto for Violin and Orchestra; Danse Suite for Orchestra; Krazy Kat (Ballet); Quartet for Piano and String Quartet; Quartet for Strings; The Seven Ages, Symphonic Suite for Orchestra; Skyscrapers (Ballet); Songs of Faith, for Mixed Chorus and Orchestra; Songs of Freedom, for Unison Chorus and Orchestra: Symphony I; Symphony II.

CARTER, ELLIOTT (1908-   ): First String Quartet; Holiday Overture; The Minotaur (Ballet Suite); Pastoral for English Horn and Piano; Pocahontas (Ballet); Quintet for Woodwinds; Second String Quartet; Sonata for Flute and Piano; Sonata for Piano; Symphony No. 1.

CASELLA, ALFREDO (1883-1947): L'Adieu à la Vie, 4 Hindu Lyrics from the Gitanjali of Tagore; Italia, Opus 11, Rhapsody for Orchestra; Pieces (5) for String Quartet; Scarlattiana, for Piano and Orchestra; Serenade for Small Orchestra; Sonata for Harp, Opus 68.

CASTELNUOVO-TEDESCO, MARIO (1895-   ): An American Rhapsody, for Orchestra; Concerto for Guitar and Orchestra; Concerto No. 2 for Violin ("The Prophets"); Cypresses, for Orchestra; Le Danze del Re David, for Piano; Divertimento for Two Flutes; Figaro, for Violin and Orchestra; Overture to King John; Quintet for Guitar & Strings, Opus 143; Serenade for Guitar and Orchestra; Sonata for Clarinet and Paino; Sonata for Violin and Viola.

CATALIAN, ALFREDO (1854-1893): A Sera, for Orchestra; Ero e Leandro, Symphonic Poem; Serenatella, for Orchestra; Silenzo e Contemplazione, for Orchestra.

CAVALLI, PIETRO FRANCESCO (1602-1676): Giudizio Universale for Solo Voices, Chorus, and Orchestra.

CHABRIER, EMMANUEL (1841-1894): A la Musique, for Chorus and Orchestra; Bourrée Fantasque, for Piano; Une Education Manquée (Operetta); España, Rhapsody for Orchestra; Gwendoline Overture, for Orchestra; Habanera, Orchestral Suite; Idyll, for Piano; Marche de Fête, for Orchestra; Marche Française, for Orchestra; Marche Joyeuse, for Orchestra; Pieces for Piano; Pièces Pitto-

resques, for Piano; Suite Pastorale, for Orchestra.

CHAPÍ, RUPERTO (1851-1909): Zarzuelas (155) including: El Barquillero; La Bruja; El Punao de Rosas; La Revoltosa; La Tempestad.

CHARPENTIER, MARC-ANTOINE (1634-1704): Mass and Symphony "Assumpta est Maria"; Medée, for Solo Voices and Instruments; Messe de Noël; Midnight Mass; La Reniement de St. Pierre (Oratorio).

CHAUSSON, ERNEST (1855-1899): Chanson Perpétuelle, for Voice and Orchestra; Concerto in D for Violin, Piano, & String Quartet, Opus 21; Hymne védique, for Chorus and Orchestra, Opus 19, for Voice and Orchestra (or Piano); Poème de l'Amour et de la Mer, Opus 19, for Voice and Orchestra (or Piano); Poème, for Violin & Orchestra, Opus 25; Quartet for Strings; Un Soir de Fête, Orchestra; Symphony in B Flat Major, Opus 20; Trio in G Minor, Opus 3, for Strings; Viviane, Symphonic Poem, Opus 5.

CHAVEZ, CARLOS (1899-   ): Corrido de "El Sol," for Orchestra; Obertura Republicana; Sinfonia India; Sonatina for Violin & Piano; Toccata for Percussion; Tree of Sorrow, for a capella Choir.

CHERUBINI, LUIGI (1760-1842): Fugal Suite in D Major, for Flute and Strings; La Liberta a Nice, Vocal Duets with Piano; Mass in C Major; Requiem Mass in C Minor; Sonatas for Piano; Symphony in D Major.

CHOPIN, FRÉDÉRIC (1810-1849): Allegro de Concert, for Piano, Opus 46; Andante Spianato, for Piano; Ballade No. 1 in G Minor, for Piano; Ballade No. 2 in F Major, Opus 38, for Piano; Ballade No. 3 in A Flat Major, for Piano; Ballade No. 4 in F Minor, for Piano; Barcarolle in F Sharp Major, Opus 60, for Piano; Berceuse in D Flat Major, Opus 57, for Piano; Bolero for Piano, Opus 19; Concerto No. 1 in E Minor for Piano and Orchestra, Opus 11; Concerto No. 2 in F Minor for Piano and Orchestra, Opus 21; Duo Concertante on Themes from Robert le Diable, for Piano and Cello; Ecossaises (3) Opus 72, for Piano; Etudes, Opera 10, 25, and Posthumous, for Piano; Fantasie in F Minor, Opus 49, for Piano; Fantasie-Impromptu in C Sharp Minor, Opus 66, for Piano; Grande Polonaise, Opus 22, for Piano and Orchestra; Impromptus, Opera 29, 36, 51, for Piano; Introduction and Polonaise, for Piano and Cello, Opus 3; Krakowiak Rondo, Opus 14, for Piano and Orchestra; Marche funèbre, Opus 72, for Piano; Mazurkas, Opera 6, 7, 17, 24, 30, 33, 41, 50, 56, 59, 63, 67, 68, and Posthumous for Piano; Morceau de concert sur la Marche le Puritains de Bellini; Nocturnes, Opera 9, 15, 27, 32, 37, 48, 55, 62, 72, for Piano; Polonaises, Opera 26, 40, 44, 53, 61, 71, and Posthumous, for Piano; especially: Polonaise No. 6 in A Flat Major, Opus 53 ("Heroic"), and Polonaise No. 7 in A Flat Major, Opus 61 ("Fantasie"); Preludes (24), Opus 28, for Piano; Rondo in C Major, Opus 73, for two Pianos; Scherzo No. 1 in B Minor, Opus 20, for Piano; Scherzo No. 2 in B Flat Minor, Opus 31, for Piano; Scherzo No. 3 in C Sharp Minor, Opus 39, for Piano; Scherzo No. 4 in E Major, Opus 54, for Piano; Sonata No. 1 in G Minor for Piano, Opus 4; Sonata No. 2 in B Flat Minor for Piano, Opus 35; Sonata No. 3 in B Minor for Piano, Opus 58; Songs Opus 74, for Voice and Piano; Les Sylphides (Ballet); Tarantelle, Opus 43, for Piano; Trio in G Minor, Opus 8, for Strings and Piano; Variations dans l'Hexaméron, for Piano; Variations on "La ci darem la mano," Opus

2, for Piano and Orchestra; Variations on a Theme of Hérold, Opus 12, for Piano; Waltzes, Opera 18, 34, 42, 64, 69, 70, and Posthumous for Piano.

CIMAROSA, DOMENICO (1749-1801): Cantatas; Concerto for Oboe and Strings; Concerto in G Major for 2 Flutes; Masses; Oratorios (2); Symphonies (7).

CLEMENTI, MUZIO (1752-1832): Sonata in F Minor, Opus 14, for Piano; Sonata in F Sharp Minor, Opus 26, No. 2, for Piano; Sonata in G Minor, Opus 34, for Piano; Sonata in B Minor, Opus 40, No. 2, for Piano; Sonatinas, Opus 36, for Piano; Sonatinas, Opus 37, for Piano; Symphony in D Major, No. 2.

CONUS, GEORGE (GEORGY EDUARDO-VITCH KONIUS) (1862-1933): Cantata in Memory of Alexander III, Opus 8; Concerto in E Minor for Violin; *Daita* (Ballet); *La forêt bruisse*, Symphonic Poem after Vladimir Korolenko, Opus 30; *From the World of Illusion*, Symphonic Poem, Opus 23; *Scènes enfantines*, Suite for Orchestra and Chorus, Opus 1.

COATES, ERIC (1886-   ) *4 Centuries* Suite, for Orchestra; *London Suite*, for Orchestra; *Three Bears*, Orchestral Fantasy; *The 3 Elizabeths* Suite, for Orchestra.

COPLAND, AARON (1900-   ): *Appalachian Spring* (Ballet Suite); *As It Fell Upon a Day*, for Soprano, Flute, and Clarinet; *Billy the Kid* (Ballet Suite); Concerto for Piano ("Jazz Concerto"); Concerto for Clarinet and Strings; *Cortège Macabre*, for Orchestra (from *Grogh*); *Danzon Cubano*, for two Pianos; Elegies for Violin and Viola; *Fanfare for the Common Man*, for Percussion and Brass; Four Piano Blues; *In the Beginning*, for a capella Chorus; Passacaglia (1922), for Piano; Piano Variations; Poems of Emily Dickinson, for Voice and Piano; Quartet for Piano and Strings; *Rodeo* (Ballet); *El Salon Mexico*, for Orchestra; Sextet for String Quartet, Clarinet, and Piano; Sonata for Piano (1941); Symphony No. 3; Trio, *Vitebsk*, for Violin, Cello, and Piano; Two Pieces for String Orchestra.

CORELLI, ARCANGELO (1653-1713): Concerto in F Major for Oboe; Concerto Grosso No. 1 in D Major, Opus 6, for Strings; Concerto Grosso No. 2 in F Major, Opus 6, for Strings; Concerto Grosso No. 3 in C Minor, Opus 6, for Strings; Concerto Grosso No. 4 in D. Major, Opus 6, for Strings; Concerto Grosso No. 5 in B Flat Major, Opus 6, for Strings; Concerto Grosso No. 6 in F Major, Opus 6, for Strings; Concerto Grosso No. 7 in D Major, Opus 6, for Strings; Concerto Grosso No. 8 in G Minor, Opus 6 ("Christmas"), for Strings; Concerto Grosso No. 9 in F Major, Opus 6, for Strings; Concerto Grosso No. 10 in C Major, Opus 6, for Strings; Concerto Grosso No. 11 in B Flat Major, Opus 6, for Strings; Concerto Grosso No. 12 in F Major, Opus 6, for Strings; Suonate (12) a violino e violone o cembalo, Opus 5 (1700). Suonate a tre (12), due violini e violone col basso per l'organo, Opus 1 (1683); Suonate a tre (12), due violini e violone col basso per l'organo, Opus 3 (1689); Suonate da camera a tre (12), due violini, violoncello e violone o cembalo, Opus 2 (1685); Suonate da camera a tre (12), due violini e violone o cembalo, Opus 4 (1694).

COUPERIN, FRANCOIS (1668-1733): Concerts Royaux Nos. 1-4, for Flute, Cello, and Harpsichord; Pieces for Harpsichord, four books (1713, 1716, 1722, 1730); Mass for the Parishes (Organ); Motet de Sainte Suzanne, for Solo Voices, Chorus, and Orchestra;

Pieces en Concert for Cello and Orchestra. (Arrangement of Harpsichord pieces by Bazelaire); *Le Parnasse ou l'Apothéose de Corelli*, trio Sonata, two Violins and Harpsichord; *La Steinquerque*, trio Sonata for two Violins and Harpsichord; Tenebrae Services, Voices and Organ.

COUPERIN, LOUIS (1626-1661): Pièces de Clavecin.

COWELL, HENRY (1897-   ): Communication, for Orchestra; *Atlantis* (Ballet); *The Building of Banba* (Ballet); Celtic Set for Orchestra; Concerto for Piano and Orchestra; Concerto Piccolo for Piano and Band; Fiddler's Jig, for Orchestra; Four Continuations for Full String Orchestra; Hymn and Fuguing Tune No. 1 for Band; Hymn and Fuguing Tunes Nos. 2 and 5 for String Orchestra; Hymn and Fuguing Tune No. 3 for Full Orchestra; Irish Suite in Three Movements for Orchestra; Pastoral and Fiddler's Delight, for Orchestra; Prelude for Violin & Harpsichord; Reel Irish for Full Band; Saturday Night in the Firehouse, for Orchestra; Sonata No. 1 for Violin & Piano (1945); Suite for Piano and String Orchestra; Symphonic Set, Opus 17; Symphony No. 2 (Anthropos); Symphony No. 3 (Gaelic); Symphony No. 4; Symphon No. 7; Symphony No. 10; Symphony No. 11; Toccata for Flute. Soprano, Cello, & Piano; Vestiges, for Orchestra.

CRESTON, PAUL (1906-   ): Choric Dances, Opus 17B for Orchestra; Concerto for E Flat Alto Saxophone and Orchestra, Opus 26; Dance Overture; Dance Variations, for Soprano and Orchestra, Opus 32; *Dawn Mood*, Opus 36, for Orchestra; *Frontiers*, Opus 34, for Orchestra; Invocation and Dance, Opus 68, for Orchestra; Pastorale and Tarantella, Opus 28, for Orchestra; Prelude and Dance, Opus 25, for Orchestra; Quartet for Strings, Opus 8; Sonata for Alto Saxophone and Piano, Opus 19; Sonata for Piano, Opus 9; Suite for Viola and Piano, Opus 13; Suite for Violin and Piano; Opus 18; Symphony No. 1, Opus 20; Symphony No. 2, Opus 35; Three Poems from Walt Whitman for Cello and Piano; Threnody, Opus 16, for Orchestra.

CUI, CÉSAR (1835-1918): Marche Solonelle, for Orchestra, Opus 18; Quartet for Strings in C Minor, Opus 45; Scherzo for Orchestra, Opus 1; Suite Concertante for Violin and Orchestra; Opus 25; Suite Miniature for Orchestra, Opus 20; Suite No. 2 for Orchestra, Opus 38; Suite No. 3 for Orchestra, Opus 40; Suite No. 4 for Orchestra, Opus 42 ("In modo populare"); Tarantella, Opus 12, for Orchestra.

DAHL, INGOLF (1912-   ): Allegro and Arioso for Flute, Oboe, Clarinet, Horn, and Bassoon; Concerto a Tre, for Clarinet, Violin, and Cello; *The Deep Blue Devil's Breakdown*, for 2 Pianos, 8 Hands; Duo for Cello and Piano; Music for 5 Brass Instruments, 2 Trumpets, Horn, and 2 Trombones; Rondo for Piano Four Hands; Suite for Piano; Variations on a Swedish Folktune for Flute Solo.

DANZI, FRANZ (1763-1826):   128th Psalm for Chorus and Orchestra; Quintets for Wind Instruments, Opus 56, Nos. 1 & 2; Quintet for Winds, Opus 67, No. 1; Sonatas (2) for Horn and Piano.

DEBUSSY, CLAUDE ACHILLE (1862-1918): *L'Ange Gris* (Ballet Suite) (arrangement of Suite Bergamasque); Arabesques, for Piano; *Ariettes Oubliées*, for Voice and Piano (after poems by Verlaine); Berceuse héroïque for the King of Belgium, 1915), for Piano. *La Boîte à Joujoux* (Ballet); Chansons de Bilitis, three Songs with Piano; *Children's Corner Suite,* for Piano; Cinq Poèmes (Baudelaire), Voice and Piano; *Crimen Amoris* (Ballet), *La Damoiselle Elue,* Cantata; Danses Sacrée et Profane, for Harp and Orchestra; *D'Un Cahier d'Esquisses,* for Piano; *En Blanc et Noir,* for two Pianos; *L'Enfant Prodigue,* Cantata; *Estampes (Pagodes; La Soirée dans Grenade; Jardins sous la pluie),* for Piano; Etudes (Books 1 & 2), for Piano; Fantasy for Piano and Orchestra; *Images* (two sets: 1st set: *Reflets dans l'eau; hommage a Rameau; Mouvement;* 2nd set: *Cloches à travers les feuilles; Et la lune descend sur le temple qui fut; Poissons d'or),* for Piano; *Images (Gigues; Iberia; Rondes de Printemps),* for Orchestra; *L'Isle Joyeuse,* for Piano; *Jeux: Poème Dansée* (Ballet); *Marche Ecossaise,* for Orchestra; *Le Martyre de St. Sebastien,* a Mystery (Solo Voices, Chorus, Orchestra); *Masques,* for Piano; *La Mer,* 3 Symphonic Sketches *(De l'aube à midi sur la mer; Jeux de vagues; Dialogue du vent et de la mer),* Orchestra; Nocturnes *(Nuages, Fêtes; Sirènes)* for Orchestra; Noël des *Enfants qui n'ont plus de Maison* for Voice and Piano (or Orchestra); Petite Suite, for Piano Duet (also Orchestra); *Pour le piano* (Prélude; Sarabande; Toccata); *Prelude to the Afternoon of a Faun,* Orchestra; Preludes, Book 1 *(Danseuses de Delphes; Voiles; Le Vent dans la plaine; Les sons et les parfums tournent dans l'air du soir; Les Collines d'Anacapri; Des pas sur la neige; Ce qu'a vu le vent d'Ouest; La Fille aux cheveux de lin; La Sérénade interrompue; La Cathédrale engloutie; La Danse de Puck; Minstrels)* for Piano; Preludes, Book 2 *(Brouillards; Feuilles mortes; La puerta del Vino; Les fées sont d'exquises danseuses; Bruyères; General Lavine — eccentric; La Terrasse des audiences du clair de lune; Ondine; Hommage a S. Pickwick, Esq., P.P.M.P.C.; Canope; Les Tierces alternées; Feux d'artifice),* for Piano; *Printemps* (Symphonic Suite); *Proses lyriques,* for Voice and Piano; Quartet in G Minor, Opus 10, for Strings; *Rêverie,* for Piano; Rhapsody No. 1 for Clarinet & Piano; Rhapsody for Saxophone and Orchestra; *Six Epigraphes Antiques* for Piano duet; Sonata No. 1 in D Minor for Cello; Sonata No. 2 for Flute, Viola, and Harp; Sonata No. 3 in G Minor for Violin; Suite Bergamasque (Prélude; Menuet; *Clair de lune; Passepied),* for Piano; *Syrinx,* for Flute Solo; Valse: *La plus que lente,* for Piano.

DELIBES, LÉO (1836-1891): *Alger,* Cantata; Choruses for Men's and Women's Voices; *Coppélia* (Ballet); Melodies (15), Songs with Piano; *Naila Waltz,* for Piano or Orchestra; *La Source* (Ballet); *Sylvia* (Ballet).

DELIUS, FREDERICK (1863-1934): *Appalachia,* Variations for Orchestra with final Chorus; *Brigg Fair,* for Orchestra; Caprice and Elegy for Cello and Orchestra; *Eventyr,* for Orchestra; *Hassan* (Serenade), for Cello and Piano; *In a Summer Garden,* for Orchestra; Lebenstanz, for Orchestra; Legend, for Violin and Orchestra; A Mass of Life, for Solo Voices, Chorus, and Orchestra; *North Country Sketches,* for Orchestra; *On Hearing the First Cuckoo in Spring,* for Orchestra; *Over the Hills and Far Away,* for Orchestra; *Paris,* a Nocturne for Orchestra; *Sea Drift* for Baritone, Chorus, and Orchestra (after Walt Whitman); Sonata No. 2 for Violin; Sonata No. 3 for Violin; Sonata for Cello & Piano; *A Song of Summer,* for Orchestra; *The Song of the High Hills,* for Orchestra with final Chorus; Songs of Sunset, for Solo Voices,

Chorus, and Orchestra; *Summer Night on the River,* for Orchestra; *The Walk to the Paradise Garden;* for Orchestra.

DELLO JOIO, NORMAN (1913-): American Landscape, for Orchestra; Concertino for Flute; Concertino for Harmonica; Concertino for Piano; *The Duke of Sacramento* (Ballet); Magnificat for Orchestra; Meditations on Ecclesiastes, for Orchestra; *On Stage* (Ballet); *Prairie* (Ballet); Ricercari, for Piano and Orchestra; Sinfonietta for Orchestra; Sonata No. 1 for Piano; Sonata No. 2 for Piano; Sonata No. 3 for Piano; Suite for Piano; *To a Lone Sentry,* for Orchestra; *The Triumph of St. Joan,* Symphony; Variations and Capriccio for Violin and Piano.

DIABELLI, ANTON (1781-1858): Sonatinas, Opus 168; Trio for Flute, Viola, & Guitar.

DIAMOND, DAVID (1915-): Concerto for Chamber Orchestra; Concerto for Violin and Orchestra; Hommage à Satie, for Chamber Orchestra; Music for Double String Orchestra, Brass, and Tympani; Quartet for Piano and String Trio; Rounds for String Orchestra; Sonata for Cello and Piano; Sonata for Violin and Piano; Symphonies Nos. 1-4; Trio for Strings; *Tom* (Ballet).

DISTLER, HUGO (1908-1942): *The Christmas Story,* Opus 10, Cantata.

DITTERSDORF, KARL DITTERS VON (1739-1799): Concerto Grosso for Strings and Orchestra; Concerto in A Major for Harp; Divertimento: *Il combattiment del l'umani passioni; Divertissements* (12) for 2 Violins and Cello; *Esther* (Oratorio); Operas (28); Partitas (3) for Wind Quintet; Preludes (72) for Piano; *The Rescue of Andromeda by Perseus* for Oboe and Orchestra; Sonatas (12) for Piano 4 Hands; Symphony in A Minor; Symphony in C Major; Symphony in E Flat Major; Symphonies (12) for Orchestra on Ovid's *Metamorphoses* (6 extant).

DOHNÁNYI, ERNST VON (1877-): Concerto for Piano and Orchestra in E Minor, Opus 5; Im Lebenslenz (6 Songs), Opus 16; Klavierstücke (5), Opus 3; Konzertstück for Violin and Orchestra, Opus 12; Overture Zriniji, Opus 2; Passacaglia for Piano, Opus 6; Quartet for Strings in A Minor, Opus 7;, Quartet No. 2 in D Flat Major, Opus 15, for Strings; Quartet No. 3 in A Minor, Opus 33, for Strings; Quintet for Piano in C Minor, Opus 1, Quintet No. 2 in E Flat Major for Piano, Opus 26; Four Rhapsodies, Opus 11, for Piano; *Ruralia Hungarica,* Five Pieces for Orchestra; Serenade in C Major, Opus 10, for Strings; Sonata in C Sharp Minor for Violin, Opus 21; Suite in F Sharp Minor, Opus 19, for Orchestra; Smphony No. 1 in F; Symphony No. 2 in D Minor, Opus 9; Symphonic Minutes, Opus 36; Variations in G for Piano, Opus 4; Variations on a Nursery Theme for Piano & Orchestra; *Winterreigen* (10 Bagatelles for Piano), Opus 13.

DONIZETTI, GAETANO (1797-1848): Masses (6); Quartets (12) for Strings; Requiem Mass; Sinfonia Concertante in B Flat Major.

DONOVAN, RICHARD (1891-): *New England Chronicle,* for Orchestra; Ricercare for Oboe and Strings; Serenade for Oboe, Violin, Viola, and Violoncello; Sextet for Wind Instruments and Piano; *Smoke and Steel,* Symphonic Poem; Soundings for Trumpet, Bassoon, Percussion; Suite for Oboe and Strings; Symphony for Chamber Orchestra; Trio for Violin, Cello, and Piano; Wood-Notes for Flute, Harp, and String Orchestra.

DOWLAND, JOHN (1568-1626): Books 1, 2, and 3 of Songes or Ayres, for Voices, Lute, and Bass Viol; *Lachrymae, or Seven Teares, figured in seven passionate Pavans,* for Lute and Strings.

DRAESEKE, FELIX (1835-1913): Adventlied for Solo Voices, Chorus, and Orchestra, Opus 30; *Christus,* Trilogy and Prelude (Oratorio); Concertstück for Cello with Orchestra, Opus 49; Grand Mass in F Sharp Minor, for Solo Voices, Chorus, and Orchestra, Opus 60; Missa a cappella, Opus 85; Quartet for Strings in C Minor, Opus 27; Quartet for Strings in E Minor, Opus 35; Quartet No. 3 in C Flat Minor for Strings; Requiem in B Minor, Opus 22; Serenata in D for Small Orchestra, Opus 49: Symphony No. 1 in G, Opus 12; Symphony No. 2 in F, Opus 25; Symphonia Comica (Symphony No. 4 in E Minor), Opus 40; Symphonia Tragica (Symphony No. 3 in C, Opus 40).

DRAGONETTI, DOMENICO (1763-1846): Concerto for Double Bass with Piano.

DUBOIS, FRANÇOIS CLÉMENT THÉODORE (1837-1924): *Adonis,* Symphonic Poem; *Atala,* Cantata; Concert Overture in D; Concerto-Capriccio for Piano; Fantaisie Triomphale, for Organ and Orchestra; *La Farandole* (Ballet); Hymne Nuptiale, for Orchestra; Marche héroïque de Jeanne d'Arc, for Orchestra; Méditation-Prière for Strings, Oboe, Harp, and Organ; *Notre Dame de la Mer,* Symphonic Poem; *Le Paradis perdu,* Oratorio; Petites pièces (4) for Orchestra; *The Seven Last Words,* Oratorio.

DUFAY, GUILLAUME (1400-1474): Missa Caput; Sacred Songs (5).

DUKAS, PAUL (1865-1935)M) *Götz von Berlichingen* Overture; *King Lear* Overture; *La Péri* (Ballet); *Polyeucte* Overture; Prélude élégiaque for Piano; Sonata for Piano in E Flat Minor; *The Sorcerer's Apprentice,* Scherzo for Orchestra; Symphony in C Major; Variations, Interlude and Finale on a Theme of Rameau, for Piano; Villanelle, for Horn and Piano.

DUNSTABLE, JOHN (c.1370-1453): Gloria; Hymns (3); Motets; *O Rosa Bella,* 3-part Chanson.

DUPRÉ, MARCEL (1886-): Passion Symphony, Opus 23, for Organ; Prelude & Fugue in G Minor for Organ; Stations of the Cross, Opus 29, for Organ; Variations sur un Noël, for Organ

DURANTE, FRANCESCO (1684-1755): Concerto No. 1 in F Minor for Strings; Concerto No. 5 in A Major for Strings; Concerto in G Major for Strings; Divertimento in F Minor for Strings; *Lamentations of Jeremiah;* Madrigals (12); Masses (13); Motets (16); Pastoral Mass; Psalms (16); Sonatas (6) for Harpsichord.

DUTILLEUX, HENRI (1916-): *Le Loup* (Ballet).

DVORAK, ANTON (1841-1904): *America's Flag,* Cantata; Biblische Lieder, Opus 99, for Voice and Piano; Carnival Overture, Opus 92, for Orchestra; Concerto in G Minor for Piano, Opus 33; Concerto in A Minor for Violin, Opus 53; Concerto in B Minor for Cello, Opus 104; *Dumky,* for Violin, Cello and Piano, Opus 90; *The Golden Spinning Wheel,* Opus 109, for Orchestra; Husktska Overture, Opus 67; *In der Natur* Overture, Opus 91; *The Jacobin* (Symphonic Suite); Legends, Opus 59, for Orchestra; Liebslieder, Opus 83, for Voice and Piano; *Magic* Overture; Mazurkas for Piano, Opus 56; *Mein Heim,* Overture, Opus 62; *The Midday Witch,* Opus 108, for Orchestra; Moravian Duets, Opus 32, for voices and Piano; Notturno for Strings, Opus 40, *Othello*

Overture, Opus 93, for Orchestra; Quartet in E Flat Major (Strings), Opus 51; Quartet in E Flat Major (Piano), Opus 87; Quartet in F Major (Strings), Opus 96; Quartet in A Flat Major (Strings), Opus 105; Quartet in G Major (Strings), Opus 106; Quintet in G Major (Double Bass), Opus 77; Quintet in A Major (Piano), Opus 81; Quintet in E Flat Major (Viola), Opus 97; Requiem, Opus 89; Rhapsodie in A Minor, Opus Posthumous, for Orchestra; Romantic Pieces for Violin, Opus for Orchestra, Opus 66; Serenade in E Major, Opus 22, for Strings; Slavonic Dances, Opus 46 and Opus 72, for Orchestra; Slavonic Rhapsodies for Orchestra (No. 1 in D Major; No. 2 in G Minor; No. 3 in A Major), Opus 45; Sonata in F Major for Violin, Opus 57; *The Specter's Bride,* Cantata for Soli, Chorus, and Orchestra, Opus 69; Stabat Mater, Opus 58, for Soli, Chorus, and Orchestra; Suite in D Major for Orchestra (Preludium, Polka, Minuet, Romance, Furiant), Opus 39 ("Czech Suite"); Symphonic Variations on an original Theme for Orchestra, Opus 78; Symphony No. in D Major, Opus 60; Symphony No. 2 in D Minor, Opus 70; Symphony No. 3 in F Major, Opus 76; Symphony No. 4 in G Major, Opus 88; Scherzo Capriccioso 75; *Rusalka* (Opera); Symphony No. 5 in E Minor, Opus 95 ("From the New World"); Symphony in E Flat, Opus Posthumous; Terzetto in C Major, Opus 74, for Strings; Trio in F Minor, Opus 65, for Strings; Trio in E Minor, Opus 90, for Strings; Two Piano Pieces (Berceuse, Capriccio), Opus Posthumous; *Waldesruhe,* for Cello and Orchestra; Waltzes for Piano, Opus 54; *The Watersprite,* Symphonic Poem, Opus 107; *Wood Dove,* Symphonic Poem, Opus 110; Zigeunerlieder, Opus 55, for Voice and Piano (or Orchestra).

ECCLES, HENRY (1670-1742): Sonata in G Minor for Violin; Twelve Solos for Violin.

ELGAR, SIR EDWARD (1857-1934): *The Apostles,* Opus 49 (Oratorio); *The Black Knight,* Opus 25 (Cantata); *The Carillon,* Opus 75 (Recitation with Orchestra); *Chanson de Matin,* Opus 15, No. 2 for Orchestra; *Chanson de Nuit,* Opus 15, No. 1 for Orchestra; *Cockaigne* Overture, Opus 40; Concerto in B Minor for Violin, Opus 61; *The Dream of Gerontius,* Opus 38, Oratorio; *Enigma* Variations, Opus 36, for Orchestra; *Falstaff,* Opus 68 (Symphonic Study); *Froissart,* Overture, Opus 19, for Orchestra; *In the South,* Opus 50 for Orchestra; *The Kingdom,* Opus 51 (Oratorio); *The Light of Life,* Opus 29 (Oratorio); *Polonia,* Opus 76 (Symphonic Prelude); Pomp and Circumstance Marches (1-5); Quartet in E Minor, Opus 83, for Strings; *Scenes from the Bavarian Highlands,* for Chorus and Orchestra, Opus 27; *Sea Pictures,* Opus 37, for Voice and Orchestra; Serenade for Strings in E Minor, Opus 20; Sonata in E Minor for Violin, Opus 82; *Sospiri,* Adagio for String Orchestra, Harp, and Organ, Opus 70; Spanish Serenade for Chorus and Orchestra, Opus 23; *The Spirit of England,* for Chorus and Orchestra, Opus 80; Symphony No. 1 in A Flat, Opus 55; Symphony No. 2 in E Flat, Opus 63; *Wand of Youth* (Suite No. 1), Opus 1a, for Orchestra; *Wand of Youth* (Suite No. 2), Opus 1b, for Orchestra.

ENESCO, GEORGES (1881-1955): Dixtuor for Winds and Orchestra; Octet for Strings in C Major; Rumanian Rhapsody No. 1 in A Major, Opus 11, for Orchestra; Rumanian Rhapsody No. 2 in D Major, for Orchestra; Sonata No. 3 in A Minor for Violin, Opus 25.

ESPLÁ, OSCAR (1889-): Sonata Espanola, Opus 53, for Piano.

FALLA, MANUEL DE (1876-1946): *El Amor Brujo (Love by Witchcraft)* (Ballet); Concerto for Harpsichord and small Orchestra; *Homenajes*, for Orchestra; *Master Peter's Puppet Show* (Puppet Opera) for Singers and Chamber Orchestra; *Nights in the Gardens of Spain*, for Piano and Orchestra; Pièces Espagnoles, for Piano; Ritual Fire Dance (extract from *El Amor Brujo*), for Piano or Orchestra; Suite Populaire Espagnole, for Cello and Piano; *The Three-cornered Hat* (Ballet); *Le Tombeau de Claude Debussy*, for Guitar; *La Vida Breve* (Opera).

FAURÉ, GABRIEL (1845-1924): Ballade for Piano and Orchestra, Opus 19; Barcarolle No. 2 in G Major, Opus 41, for Piano; Barcarolle No. 6 in E Flat Major, Opus 70, for Piano; *La Bonne Chanson*, Opus 61, No. 1, for Voice and Piano; *La Chanson d'Eve*, for Voice and Piano; *Choeur des Djinns; Dolly*, Opus 56, for Orchestra; Elegy for Piano; *L'Horizon Chimérique*, Opus 113, for Voice and Piano; Impromptus (5) for Piano; Impromptu for Harp Solo; Masques et Bergamasques, Opus 112, for Orchestra; Les Melodies de Venise, Opus 58, for Voice and Piano; *La Naissance de Venus*, for Solo Voices, Chorus, and Orchestra; Nocturnes for Piano; Papillons, for Piano and Cello; Pavane, Opus 50, for Orchestra and Chorus; *Pélléas et Mélisande*, Suite Opus 80, for Orchestra; Quartet in E Minor, Opus 121, for Strings; Quartet No. 1 in C Minor (Piano), Opus 15; Quartet No. 2 in G Minor (Piano); Quintet No. 2 in C Minor (Piano), Opus 115; Requiem; Sonata No. 1 in A Major for Violin, Opus 13; Sonata No. 2 in E Minor for Violin, Opus 108; Sonata No. 1 in D Minor for Cello, Opus 109; Sonata No. 2 in G Minor for Cello, Opus 117; Suite for Orchestra in F; Symphony in D Minor; Theme and Variations in C Sharp Minor, Opus 73, for Piano; Trio in D Minor, Opus 120, for Strings.

FINE, VIVIAN (1914-): Concerto for Piano and Orchestra; Danse Suite for Orchestra; Music for Piano; *Mutability* (Song Cycle); *Opus 51* (Ballet); Partita for Woodwind Quintet; Piano Suite in E Flat; Prelude for String Quartet; Quartet for Strings (1952); *Race of Life* (Ballet); Suite for Oboe and Piano; Suite for Violin; *We Too Are Exiles* (Ballet).

FOOTE, ARTHUR (1853-1937): Suite in E Major, String Orchestra.

FOSS, LUKAS (1922-): Concerto No. 2 for Piano; *Gift of the Magi* (Ballet); *The Jumping Frog of Calaveras County* (Opera); A Parable of Death, for Narrator, Tenor, Chorus, Piano, Percussion, and Strings; *The Prairie* Symphonic Piece for Orchestra); Set of Three Pieces for Two Pianos; Song of Anguish for Baritone and Orchestra; *The Song of Songs* for Soprano and Orchestra; Symphony in G.

FOSTER, STEPHEN (1826-1864): Songs: Open Thy Lattice, Love; The Louisiana Belle; Old Uncle Ned; O Susanna; My Old Kentucky Home; Old Dog Tray; Massa's in the Cold, Cold, Ground; Gentle Annie; Willie; We Have Missed You; I Would Not Die in Springtime; Come Where My Love Lies Dreaming; Old Black Joe; Ellen Boyne; The Old Folks at Home; Nellie Was a Lady; O, Boys, Carry Me 'Long; Nellie Bly; Nancy Till; Laura Lee; Maggie By My Side; Beautiful Dreamer; Jeannie With the Light Brown Hair; Camptown Races; Carry Me Back to Old Virginny; Away Down South.

FRANCAIX, JEAN (1912-): Concertino for

Piano and Orchestra; *The Emperor's New Clothes* (Ballet); Quintet for Winds; Serenade Bea, for Strings.

FRANCK, CÉSAR (1822-1890): Andantino for Organ; Ballade for Piano; Cantabile (Organ); *Le Chasseur Maudit (The Accursed Hunter)* Symphonic Poem for Orchestra; Chorales for Organ: No. 1 in E; No. 2 in B Minor; No. 3 in A Minor; Choruses (4); *Les Djinns*, Symphonic Poem for Orchestra; *Les Eoliedes*, Symphonic Poem for Orchestra; Fantasie in C Major for Organ, Opus 16; Fantasie in A Major for Organ; Finale in B Flat Major for Organ, Opus 21; Grande Pièce Symphonique for Organ, Opus 17; Messe à Trois voix, with Organ, Harp, Violincello, and Contrabassoon; Messe Solenelle; Motets (4); Offertoires (4); Oratorios: *(Ruth; La Tour de Babel; Rédemption; Les Béatitudes; Rebecca)*; L'Organiste (posthumous pieces); Pastorale for Organ, Opus 19, No. 4; Petites Pièces (44) for Organ; Pièce Héroïque for Organ; Prelude, Aria, and Finale, for Piano; Prelude, Chorale, & Fugue, for Piano; Prelude, Fugue, and Variation, for Organ, Opus 18; Prière, for Organ; Préludes et Prières (3 Vols.), for Organ; *Le Procession*, Song arranged for Orchestra; Psaume CL for Chorus, Organ, and Orchestra; *Psyché*, Symphonic Poem for Chorus and Orkestra; Quartet in D Major for Strings; Quintet in F Minor (Piano); *Rédemption* (Symphonic Interlude); Sonata in A Major for Violin & Piano; Songs (14); Symphonic Variations for Piano and Orchestra; Symphony in D Minor; Trio in F Sharp Major, Opus 1, No. 1.

FREDERICK THE GREAT (FRIEDRICH II) (1712-1786): Concerto in C Major for Flute; Overture to *Acis and Galathea*; Sonatas for Flute & Harpsichord.

FRESCOBALDI, GIROLAMO (1583-1643): Arie musicali a piu voci (1630); Capricci sopra diversi soggetti (1624); Fiori Musicali, for Organ; Five Canzoni per Sonar; Il 20 libri de toccate, canzoni, versi d'inni, magnificat, gagliardi, correnti ed altre partite d'intav. di cembalo ed organo (1616); Ricercari e canzoni francesci (1615); Toccate e partite d'intavolatura di cembalo (1615); Toccata per l'Elevazioni, arranged for Orchestra.

FUERSTENAU, JOHANN CASPAR (1722-1819): Suite for Flute & Guitar, Opus 35.

FUX, JOHANN JOSEPH (1660-1741): Dies Irae (2); Masses (50-including the Missa Canonica); Oratorios (29-including Concentus Musicoinstrumentalis a 7); Requiems (3); Sacred sonatas (38); Vespers and Psalms (57).

GABRIELSKI, JOHANN WILHELM (1791-1846): March & Trio for Orchestra & Toy Instruments.

GALUPPI, BALDASSARE (1706-1785):Concerto No. 2 in B Flat Major ("A Quattro"), for Strings; Concerto No. 6 in C Minor ("A Quattro"), for Strings; Quartet in G Minor, for Strings.

GANNE, LOUIS-GASTON (1862-1923): Les Ailes (Ballet); Au Japon (Ballet); Cocorico (Vaudeville); Les Colles de Femmes (Vaudeville); Hans, le Joueur de Flûte (Vaudeville); Phryne (Ballet); Rabelais (Vaudeville); Rhodope (Vaudeville); Les Saltimbanques (Vaudeville).

GEMINIANI, FRANCESCO (1667-1762): Concerti Grossi, Opus 2, for Strings; Concerti Grossi, Opus 3, for Strings; Concerti Grossi, Opus 4, for Strings; Concerti Grossi, Opus 6, for Strings; Concerti Grossi, Opus 7, for Strings; Soli (6) for Cello, Opus 5; Soli for Violin (12), Opus 1; Sonata in B Flat Major for Violin unaccompainied; Sonatas for Violin (12), Opus 11; Trios (12) for 2 Violins and Cello.

GERMAN, EDWARD (1862-1936): Bolero for Violin and Orchestra; Commemoration, an English Fantasia for Orchestra; Coronation March and Hymn; Funeral March in D Minor for Orchestra; Gypsy Suite, for Orchestra; Hamlet (Symphonic Poem); Henry VIII Dances for Orchestra; Merrie England (Opera); Nell Gwynn Dances, for Orchestra; Pastorale and Bourrée for Oboe and Piano; Rhapsody on March Themes, for Orchestra; Scotch Sketch for Cello and Piano; The Seasons (Symphonic Suite); Serenade for Voice, Piano, Oboe, Clarinet, Bassoon, and Horn; Sketches (3) for Cello and Piano; Suite for Flute and Piano; Suite in D Minor for Orchestra; Symphony in A Minor; Symphony in E Minor; Welsh Rhapsody for Orchestra.

GERSHWIN, GEORGE (1898-1937): An American in Paris, for Orchestra; Concerto in F for Piano and Orchestra; Cuban Overture; Preludes for Piano (or Orchestra); Rhapsody in Blue, for Piano and Orchestra; Rhapsody No. 2 for Piano and Orchestra.

GESUALDO, CARLO (c.1560-1613): Madrigals (6 vols.) a 5.

GIARDINI, FELICE DE (1716-1796): Concertos (2) for Violin; Quintets (6) for Piano; Quintets (12) for Strings; Ruth, Oratorio; Soli for Violin (5); Sonata a Tre for Strings; Sonatas (6) for Piano and Violin.

GIBBONS, ORLANDO (1583-1625): Fantasias Nos. 1 & 2 for Viols.

GILLIS, DON (1912-): The Alamo (Symphonic Poem); Cowtown (Orchestral Suite); The Man Who Invented Music, for Orchestra; The Panhandle (Orchestral Suite); Portrait of a Frontier Town, for Orchestra; Prairie Poem, for Orchestra; The Raven (Symphonic Poem); String Quartets (5); Symphony No. 1 (An American Symphony); Symphony No. 2 (A Symphony of Faith); Symphony No. 3 (A Symphony for Free Men); Symphony No. 4; Symphony Nr. 5; Symphony No. 5½.

GILSON, PAUL (1865-1942): David, for Solo Voices, Chorus, and Orchestra; La Destinée, Symphonic Poem; Fantasy on Canadian Folk-Themes, for Orchestra; Francesca da Rimini, a Dramatic Cantata; Halia, Symphonic Poem; Humoresques (2) for Woodwinds; La Mer, a Symphony; Norwegian Suite for Strings; Scotch Dances for Orchestra; Scotch Rhapsody for Orchestra; Septet for Woodwinds; Suite Pastorale for Orchestra; Les Suppliantes, for Solo Voices, Chorus, and Orchestra.

GLAZOUNOV, ALEXANDER (1865-1936): Carnaval Overture, Opus 45; Christmas Singers ("Les Chanteurs de Noel"), for Strings; Concerto No. 1 in F Minor for Piano, Opus 92; Concerto in A Minor for Violin, Opus 82; Concerto for Saxophone; Élegie for Orchestra, Opus 8 (A la memoire d'un héros); Mazurka for Orchestra, Opus 18; Oberek, for Violins; Overture No. 1 on Greek Themes, Opus 3; Overture No. 2 on Greek Themes, Opus 6; Prelude and 2 Mazurkas for Piano, Opus 25; Quartet for Strings in D Major, Opus 1; Quartet No. 2 in F for Strings, Opus 10; Raymonda (Ballet); Ruses d'Amour, Opus 61 (Ballet); Scènes de Ballet, Opus 52; The Sea, Fantasy for Orchestra, Opus 28; The Seasons, Opus 67 (Ballet); Serenade for Orchestra, Opus 7; Sonata in E Minor for Piano, Opus 75; Stenka Razin, Opus 13 (Symphonic Poem); Suite Charactéristique, for Orchestra, Opus 9; Suite on S.A.C.H.A. for Piano, Opus 2; Symphony No. 1 in E, Opus 5; Symphony No. 2 in F Sharp Minor, Opus 16; Symphony No. 3 in D, Opus 33; Symphony No. 4 in E Flat, Opus 48; Symphony No. 5 in B Flat Major, Opus 55; Symphony No. 6 in C Minor, Opus 58; Symphony No. 7 in F Major, Opus 77; Symphony No. 8 in E Flat, Opus 83; Valse de Concert No. 1, Opus 47, for Orchestra; Valse de Concert No. 2 in F, Opus 51, for Orchestra.

GLIÈRE, REINHOLD (1875-1956): The Bronze Horseman (Ballet); Concerto in E Flat Major for Harp; Concerto for Horn and Orchestra, Opus 91; Die Sirenen, Symphonic Poem, Opus 33; Octet for Strings in D, Opus 5; Quartet for Strings in A, Opus 12; Quartet for Strings in G, Opus 20; The Red Poppy (Ballet); Romance for Violin and Orchestra, Opus 3; Sextet for Strings in F Minor, Opus 1; Sextet for Strings in B Minor, Opus 7; Sextet for Strings in C, Opus 11; Suite, Opus 13, for Orchestra; Symphony No. 1 in E Flat Major, Opus 8; Symphony No. 2 in C, Opus 25; Symphony No. 3, Opus 42 ("Ilya Mourometz"); Triumphant Overture, Opus 72.

GLINKA, MICHAEL (1803-1857): Jota Aragonesa, Capriccio Brilliant, for Orchestra; La Kamarinskaja, Fantasia for Orchestra; A Life for the Czar (Ballet Music); Minuet for String Quartet; Polonaises (2) for Orchestra; Quartet for Strings; Russlan and Ludmilla Overture; Sextet for Piano and Strings; Souvenir d'une nuit d'été à Madrid, for Orchestra; Trio for Piano, Clarinet, and Bassoon; Trio Pathétique for Violin, Cello, and Piano; Variations in F Major for Piano.

GLUCK, CHRISTOPH WILLIBALD (1714-1787): Concerto in G Major for Flute & Orchestra; Don Juan (Pantomime Ballet); Fruhlingsfeier ("Spring Festival"), for Chorus and Orchestra; L'Ivrogne Corrigé ("The Reformed Drunkard") (Opera); Iphigenia in Aulis Overture.

GOEB, ROGER (1914-): Quintet for Woodwinds; Symphony No. 3; Three American Dances for Orchestra.

GOLDMARK, KARL (1830-1915): Concerto for Violin in A Minor, Opus 28; Concerto No. 2 for Violin; Der gefesselte Prometheus Overture, Opus 38; Im Frühling Overture, Opus 36; Penthesilia Overture, Opus 31; Quartet in B Flat for Strings, Opus 8; Quintet for Strings in A Minor, Opus 9; Rustic Wedding Symphony, Opus 26; Sakuntala Overture, Opus 13; Sappho Overture, Opus 44; Scherzo in E Minor for Orchestra, Opus 19; Sonata in D for Piano and Violin, Opus 19; Sturm und Drang, Piano Pieces, Opus 5; Suite in E for Piano and Violin, Opus 43; Symphony, Opus 26 (Die ländliche Hochzeit); Symphony in E Flat, Opus 35; Zriny, Symphonic Poem.

GOTTSCHALK, LOUIS MOREAU (1829-1869): The Banjo, for Piano; Cakewalk (Ballet); Creole Ballads for Piano; Cuban Dances for Piano; Escenas campestres cubanas, for Orchestra; Gran Marcha solemne, for Orchestra; Gran Tarantella, for Orchestra; Montevideo, Symphony; La Nuit des tropiques, Symphony.

GOULD, MORTON (1913-): Ballad for Band; Cantata for Chorus and Chamber Orchestra; Chorale and Fugue in Jazz for 2 Pianos and Orchestra; Concerto for Orchestra; Concerto for Viola and Orchestra; Fall River Legend (Ballet); Harvest, for Orchestra; Interplay for Piano and Orchestra; Latin American Symphonette; Manhattan Serenade for Piano; Minstrel Show, for Orchestra; Pavane for Piano; Piano Concerto for Chamber Orchestra; Rhapsodies on Familiar Themes for Piano and Orchestra; Rhapsodies for Piano and Orchestra; Sonatas Nos. 1-3 for Piano; Spirituals for Orchestra; Suite for Violin; Symphonies Nos. 1-3; Swing Symphonietta for Orchestra.

GOUNOD, CHARLES FRANÇOIS (1818-1893: *A la Frontière* (Cantata); *Biondina*, Song Cycle for Voice and Piano; *Fernand*, Cantata; *La Rédemption*, Sacred Trilogy; Little Symphony in B Minor for Winds; *Marie Stuart and Rizzio*, Cantata; Mass: Angeli custodes; Mass of St. Cecilia; Méditation (Ave Maria) on the First Prelude of Bach's *Well-Tempered Clavicord;* Messe à Jeanne d'Arc; Messe solonnelle; *Mors et Vita,* Sacred Trilogy; Quartet No. 3 in A Minor for Strings; Stabat Mater, with Orchestra; *Tobie* (Oratorio).

GRANADOS, ENRIQUE (1867-1916): *A la Cubana,* for Piano; *Cuentos Para la Juventud,* Piano pieces; *Dante,* Symphonic Poem; Escenas Romanticas, for Piano; *Goyescas,* for Piano; *El Pelele,* for Piano; Marche militaire, for Piano; *La Nit del Mort,* Symphonic Poem; Spanish Dances, Piano pieces; Valses poeticos, Piano pieces.

GRÉTRY, ANDRÉ (1741-1813): *Céphale et Trocris* (Ballet Music); Confiteor; De Profundis; Quartets (2) for Piano, Flute, Violin and Bass; Quartets (6) for Strings; Requiem; Sonatas (6) for Piano; Symphonies Nos. 1-6.

GRIEG, EDVARD (1843-1907): Ballade in G Minor for Piano, Opus 24; Children's Songs (7) for Piano, Opus 61; Concerto in A Minor for Piano, Opus 16; Elegiac Melodies (2) for Strings, Opus 34; Funeral March in Memory of His Father; Funeral March in Memory of Nordraak; Improvisations (2), Piano Pieces, Opus 29; *In Autumn,* Opus 11, Overture; *Lieder aus Fjeld und Fjord,* Opus 44; Lyric Pieces for Piano, Op. 12, 38, 43, 47, 54, 57, 62, 65, 68, 71; Melodies for String Orchestra, Opus 53; Norwegian Dances, Opus 35, for Orchestra; Norwegian Folksongs and Dances, Opus 17; Norwegian Peasant Danses, Opus 72 ("Slatter"), for Piano; Old Norwegian Romance with Variations, Opus 51, for Two Pianos; *Peer Gynt* Suites Nos. 1 & 2; Quartet in G Minor, Opus 27, for Strings; *Sigurd Jorsalfar* Suite, Opus 56, for Orchestra; Sonata in E Minor for Piano, Opus 7; Sonata in G For Piano and Violin, Opus 13; Sonata No. 1 in F Major for Violin, Opus 8; Sonata No. 3 in C Minor for Violin, Opus 45; Suite for String Orchestra *(Aus Holberg's Zeit),* Opus 40; Symphonic Dances, Opus 64, for Piano Duet; Symphonic Pieces (2), Opus 14, for Piano Duet; *Wedding Day at Troldhaugen* for Orchestra.

GRIFFES, CHARLES T. (1884-1920): Bacchanale, Opus 6, No. 3, for Orchestra; Fantasy Pieces (3), Opus 6, for Piano; Five Old Chinese and Japanese Songs for Voice and Orchestra; *The Lament of Ian the Proud,* for Voice and Orchestra; Nocturne for Orchestra; Pieces for Piano (10) (includes the selections in *Roman Sketches); The Pleasure Dome of Kubla Khan,* Tone Poem for Orchestra; Poem for Flute and Orchestra; *Roman Sketches,* Suite for Piano, Opus 7 ("Clouds", "The Fountain of the Aqua Paola", "The White Peacock", "The Vale of Dreams"); *Sho-Jo,* Music for a Japanese Mime Play; Sonata for Piano; Songs for Voice and Orchestra (24) (includes "The Lament of Ian the Proud" and "Thy Dark Eyes to Mine", settings to poems by Fiona MacLeod, and "We'll to the Woods and Gather May" and "Symphony in Yellow"); Three Poems of Fiona McLeod, Opus 11, for Orchestra; Tone Pictures (3), Opus 5, for Piano.

GROFÉ, FERDE (1892-): *Atlantic Crossing,* for Narrators and Orchestra; *Aviation* Suite, for Orchestra; *Death Valley* Suite, for Orchestra; *Grand Canyon* Suite, for Orchestra; *Henry Hudson* Suite, for Orchestra; *Hollywood* Suite, for Orchestra; *Mississippi* Suite, for Orchestra; *Table d'Hote,* for Flute, Violin, and Viola; *Tabloid* Suite, for Orchestra.

HAESSLER, JOHANN WILHELM (1747-1822): Grand Gigue in D Minor, Opus 31, for Piano.

HAHN, REYNALDO (1875-1947): *Béatrice d'Este* (Ballet); *Le Bois Sacré* (Ballet); *Le Dieu Bleu* (Ballet); *Nuit d'amour bergamasque, Symphonic Poem; La Pastorale de Noël, a* Christmas mystery; *Promethée triomphant,* Symphonic Poem; Songs in Gray *(Chansons Grises)* for Voice and Piano.

HAIEFF, ALEXANDER (1914-): Concerto for Piano & Orchestra; Divertimento for Small Orchestra; Juke Box Pieces (4) for Piano, Piano Pieces (5); Quartet No. 1 for Strings; Serenade for Oboe, Clarinet, Bassoon, and Piano; Sonata for Two Pianos (1945); Suite for Violin and Piano.

HAINDL, FRANZ SEBASTIAN (1727-1812): Symphony in G Major.

HALFFTER, ERNESTO (1905-): *El Cojo Enamorado,* for Orchestra; Sinfonietta in D Major.

HALVORSEN, JOHAN (1864-1935): Cantata for the Coronation of King Haakon; Concerto for Violin; *Fossegrimen* Suite, Opus 21, for Orchestra; Norwegian Rhapsody No. 1, for Orchestra; Passacaglia (by Handel), arranged for Violin and Viola; Suite Ancienne, Opus 31, for Orchestra.

HANDEL, GEORGE FREDERICK (1685-1759): *Acis & Galatea* (Secular Oratorio); *Alcina* (Dream Music), for Orchestra; *Alexander's Feast* (Ode for Chorus and Orchestra); Anthems (Psalms 42 and 68) for Solo Voices, Chorus, and Orchestra; *Apollo e Dafne,* for Solo Voice and Orchestra; *Belshazzar* (Oratorio); Concerto in C Major for Orchestra ("Alexanderfest"); Concertos Nos. 1-6 for Orchestra, Opus 3; Concerto in D Major for Orchestra (arr. Ormandy); Concerto in F Major for Strings and Winds; Concertos for Organ or Harpsichord, Nos. 1-6, Opus 4; Concertos for Organ or Harpsichord, Nos. 1-6, Opus 7; Concerto No. 13 in F Major for Harpsichord or Organ; Concerto No. 14 in A Major for Harpsichord or Organ; Concerto No. 19 in D Minor for Harpsichord or Organ; Concerto in G Minor for Oboe and Strings; Concerto in E Flat Major for Oboe and Strings; Concerto in B Flat Major for Oboe and Strings; Concerto in b flat Major for Viola; Concerto in B Minor for Viola; Concerto in G Minor for Viola; Concerto for Horns and Side-drums; Concerto for Trumpets and Horn; Concerto Grosso No. 1 in G Major, Opus 6; Concerto Grosso No. 2 in F Major, Opus 6; Concerto Grosso No. 3 in E Minor, Opus 6; Concerto Grosso No. 4 in A Minor, Opus 6; Concerto Grosso No. 5 in D Major, Opus 6; Concerto Grosso No. 6 in G Minor, Opus 6; Concerto Grosso No. 7 in B Flat Major, Opus 6; Concerto Grosso No. 8 in C Minor, Opus 6; Concerto Grosso No. 9 in F Major, Opus 6; Concerto Grosso No. 10 in D Minor, Opus 6; Concerto Grosso No. 11 in A Major, Opus 6; Concerto Grosso No. 12 in B Minor, Opus 6; Dettingen "Te Deum," for Chorus and Orchestra; *The Faithful Shepherd* Suite (arr. Beecham), for Orchestra; *Faramondo* Overture; Festival Suite (arr. Fekete), for Orchestra; Forest Music, for Harpsichord; Fugues (6) for Harpsichord; *Israel in Egypt* (Oratorio); Italian Cantatas; *Judas Maccabaeus* (Oratorio); *L'allegro, il penseroso, ed il moderato* (Ode); Largo (from *Xerxes),* for Orchestra; *Messiah* (Oratorio); Occasional Oratorio; Ode for St. Cecilia's Day, for Solo Voices, Chorus, and Orchestra; Passacaglia (arr. Halvorsen), for Violin and Viola; *Rodelinda* (Oratorio); Royal Fireworks Music; for Orchestra; *Saul* (Oratorio); *Semele* (Oratorio); *Solomon* (Oratorio); Sonatas Nos. 1-6 for Violin, Opus 1; Sonatas for Flute and Harpsichord, Opus 1; Sonata No. 4 in B Flat Major for 2 Violins & Continuo, Opus 2, No. 4; Sonata No. 5 in F Major for 2 Violins & Continuo, Opus 2, No. 5; Sonata No. 8 in G Minor for 2 Violins & Continuo, Opus 2, No. 8; Sonata No. 9 in E Major for 2 Violins & Continuo, Opus 2, No. 9; Sonata No. 11 in D Major for 2 Violins & Continuo, Opus 5, No. 2; Sonata No. 12 in E Minor for 2 Violins Continuo, Opus 5, No. 3; *Sosarme* (Opera); *St. John Passion; Suites of Pieces* (3 sets) for Harpsichord; *The Triumph of Time and Truth,* Oratotio; *Water Music,* for Orchestra.

HANDL, JACOB (1550-1591):Ascendit Deus, for a cappella Choir.

HANSON, HOWARD (1896-   ): The Cherubic Hymn, for Chorus and Orchestra; Chorale and Alleluia, for Winds; Concerto da Camera, Opus 7, for Piano and String Quartet; Concerto for Organ, Strings, & Harp; *Exaltation,* Symphonic Poem; Fantasy Variations on a Theme of Youth, for Orchestra; *Lux Aeterna,* Symphonic Poem; North and *West,* Symphonic Poem; *Pan and the Priest,* Symphonic Poem; Pastorale for Orchestra; Quintet in F Minor, Opus 6, for Piano and String Quartet; Serenade for Flute, Strings, and Harp; Songs from "Drum Taps," for Chorus and Orchestra (text Walt Whitman); Symphonic Legend; Symphonic Rhapsody for Orchestra; Symphony No. 1 (Nordic); Symphony No. 2 (Romantic); Symphony No. 3, Opus 33; Symphony No. 4, Opus 34; Symphony No. 5.

HARRIS, ROY (1898-   ): *Abraham Lincoln Walks at Midnight,* for Voice and Chamber Orchestra; Concerto for Piano, Clarinet and String Quartet; Fantasy for Piano and Orchestra; First Piano Concerto with Band; First String Quartet; *From This Earth* (Ballet); Second String Quartet; Sonata for Violin and Piano; String Sextet for 2 Violins, 2 Violas, and 2 Cellos; Symphony 1933; Symphony No. 1; Symphony No. 2; Symphony No. 3; Symphony No. 4 (Folk Song) for Chorus and Orchestra; Symphony No. 5; Symphony No. 6, after the Gettysburg Address; Symphony No. 7; Third String Quartet; Trio for Violin, Cello, and Piano; Viola Quintet, (Viola and String Quartet); Violin Sonata (Violin and Piano); *What So Proudly We Hail* (Ballet).

HARRISON, LOU (1917-   ): Mass; Suite No. 2 for String Quartet; Suite for Violin, Piano, & Orchestra; Suite for Cello and Harp.

HAUER, JOSEF MATTHIAS (1883-   ): Hoelderlin Lieder for Piano, Opus 32.

HAYDN, FRANZ JOSEPH (1732-1809): Credited with from 104-125, or more, symphonies, an estimate complicated by the fact that Haydn himself included over 60 of his divertimenti, cassations, sextets, and other compositions, as symphonies; his other instrumental works include: violin concertos (9), cello concertos (6), concertos for baritone, doublebass, lira, flute, or horn (16), string quartets (77), trios for strings and other instruments excluding the piano (32), compositions for baritone (175), Violin sonatas (4), duets for violin and viola (6), nocturnes for lira (7), concertos for harpsichord or piano (20), piano concertos: with violin and cello (35), with

flute and cello (3), sonatas and divertimenti for harpsichord or piano (53), and for harpsichord or piano with violin (4); his vocal compositions include oratorios (3), cantatas, masses (14), Te Deums (2), a Stabat Mater, offertories (13), motets, arias, operas (3), Italian comedies (4), Italian opera buffa (13), marionette operas (5), incidental music to plays, the unfinished *Orfeo,* The Ten Commandments in canonform, German songs (36), canzonets (12), Scotch and Welsh folksongs, the (former) Austrian National Anthem; Haydn also wrote numerous minor pieces for instruments and voices; the following list of compositions includes those of his works which are chiefly heard today: Andante con Variazioni in F Minor for Piano; *Ariana a Naxos,* Cantata for Solo voice and Piano; Concertino in C Major for Harpsichord; Concerto in D Major for Harpsichord, Opus 21; Concerto in G Major for Harpsichord; Concerto in F Major for Harpsichord; Concerto in C Major for Violin; Concerto in F Major for Violin & Harpsichord; Concerto No. 1 in D Major for Cello, Opus 101; Concerto in D Major for Flute; Concerto in E Flat Major for Trumpet; *The Creation* (Oratorio); *Deutschlands Klage auf den Tod Friedrichs des Grossen,* Cantata for Solo Voice and Baritone; Divertimento No. 1 in B Flat Major for Harpsichord or Piano; Divertimento No. 2 in A Major for Harpsichord or Piano, Opus 31; Divertimento No. 3 in G Major for Harpsichord or Piano, Opus 31; Divertimento in C Major, for Harpsichord or Piano; Divertimento in D Major, for Harpsichord or Piano; Divertimento in F Major for Harpsichord or Piano; Divertimento in G Major for Harpsichord or Piano; Divertimento a 6 Stromenti in E Flat Major; *Il ritorno de Tobia* (Oratorio); Italian Overture; *The Man in the Moon* (Opera); Mass in E Flat Major (Great Organ Mass); Minuets ("Hofball"); Missa Brevis in F Major; Missa St. Joannis de Deo; Missa Solemnis in B Flat Major; Missa Solemis in D Minor; Octet in F Major; Overture in D Major; *Philemon and Baucis* (Opera); Quartet in F Major for Strings, Opus 3, No. 5; Quartet in F Minor for Strings, Opus 20, No. 5; Quartet in E Flat Major for Strings, Opus 33, No. 2; Quartet in C Major for Strings, Opus 33, No. 3; Quartet in C Major for Strings, Opus 64, No. 1; Quartet in B Minor for Strings, Opus 64, No. 2; Quartet in B Flat Major for Strings, Opus 64, No. 3; Quartet in G Major for Strings, Opus 64, No. 4; Quartet in D Major for Strings, Opus 64, No. 5; Quartet in E Flat Major for Strings, Opus 64, No. 6; Quartet in F Major for Strings, Opus 74, No. 2 ("Imperial"); Quartet in G Major for Strings, Opus 76, No. 1; Quartet in D Minor for Strings, Opus 76, No. 2 ("Quinten"); Quartet in C Major for Strings, Opus 76, No. 3 ("Emperor"); Quartet in B Flat Major for Strings, Opus 76, No. 4 ("Sunrise"); Quartet in D Major for Strings, Opus 76, No. 5; Quartet in E Flat Major for Strings, Opus 76, No. 6; Quartet in G Major for Strings, Opus 77, No. 1; Quartet in F Major for Strings, Opus 77, No. 2; Scherzando in F Major for Strings; Scotch Songs for Solo Voice; *The Seasons* (Oratorio); Serenades (3) for Wind Band; *The Seven Last Words of Christ,* Opus 51 (String Quartet); *The Seven Last Words of Our Savior on the Cross* (Oratorio); Sonata for Piano No. 5 in C Major; Sonata for Piano No. 6 in G Major; Sonata for Piano No. 8 in A Flat Major; Sonata for Piano No. 9

in D Major; Sonata for Piano No. 10 in G Major; Sonata for Piano No. 23 in F Major; Sonata for Piano No. 25 in C Minor; Sonata for Piano No. 30 in A Major; Sonata for Piano No. 34 in E Minor; Sonata for Piano No. 37 in D Major; Sonata for Piano No. 50 in C Major; Sonata in C Major for Cello; Symphony No. 7 in C Major ("Noon"); Symphony No. 12 in E Major; Symphony No. 22 in E Flat Major ("the Philosopher"); Symphony No. 23 in G Major; Symphony No. 29 in E Major; Symphony No. 30 in C Major ("Alleluja"); Symphony No. 44 in E Minor ("Trauer"); Symphony No. 45 in F Sharp Minor ("Farewell"); Symphony No. 48 in C Major ("Maria Theresa"); Symphony No. 49 in F Minor ("La Passione"); Symphony No. 53 in D Major ("Imperial"); Symphony No. 54 in G Major; Symphony No. 64 in A Major; Symphony No. 67 in F Major; Symphony No. 70 in D Major; Symphon No. 85 in B Flat Major ("La Reine"); Symphony No. 86 in D Major; Symphony No. 88 in G Major; Symphony No. 91 in E Flat Major; Symphony No. 92 in G Major ("Oxford"); Symphony No. 93 in D Major; Symphony No. 94 in G Major ("Surprise"); Symphony No. 95 in C Minor; Symphony No. 96 in D Major ("Miracle"); Symphony No. 97 in C Major; Symphony No. 98 in B Flat Major; Symphony No. 99 in E Flat Major; Symphony No. 100 in G Major ("Military"); Symphony No. 101 in D Major ("Clock"); Symphony No. 102 in B Flat Major; Symphony No. 103 in E Flat Major ("Drum Roll"); Symphony No. 104 in D Major ("London"); Toy Symphony; Trios for Strings, Opus 53 No. 1 in G; No. 2 in B Flat; No. 3 in D; Trio No. 1 in G Major for Violin, Cello, & Piano ("Gypsy Rondo"); Trio No. 2 in F Sharp Minor for Violin, Cello, & Piano; Trio No. 3 in C Major for Violin, Cello, & Piano; Trio No. 5 E Flat Major for Violin, Cello, & Piano; Trio No. 10 in E Minor for Violin, Cello, & Piano; Trio No. 16 in G Minor for Violin, Cello, & Piano; Trio No. 17 in G Minor for Violin, Cello, & Piano; Trio No. 24 in A Flat Major for Violin, Cello, Piano; Trio No. 28 in G Major for Violin, Cello, & Piano; Trio No. 30 in D Major for Violin, Cello, & Piano.

HAYDN, MICHAEL (1737-1806): Church Music (360 compositions, including oratorios, masses, cantatas, graduals, requiems); Concerto in B Flat Major for Violin; Concerto for Viola, Piano, & Orchestra; Concerto in D Major for Flute; Divertimento in C Major for Strings; Organ Pieces (50); Quintets (3) for Strings; Sextet for Strings; Symphonies (30); Symphony in C Major; Symphony in G Major; Turkish Suite (from Zaïre), for Orchestra.

HELLER, STEPHEN (1814-1888): Album for the Young, Opus 138, for Piano; Ballades (3), for Piano, Opus 115; Balletstücke for Piano, Opus 111; Bergeries (3), Opus 106 (for Piano); Dans les bois (Piano pieces), Opera 86, 128, 136; Etudes, Opera 16, 45, 46, 47, 90, 125 (for Piano); Nuits Blanches, Opus 82 (for Piano); Préludes, Opus 117 (for Piano); Promenades d'un solitaire, Opera 78, 80, 89 (for Piano); Tablettes d'un solitaire, Opus 153 (for Piano); Tarantelles, Opera 53, 61, 137 (for Piano); Traumbilder, Opus 79 (for Piano); Voyage autour de ma chambre, Opus 140 (for Piano).

HILL, EDWARD BURLINGAME (1872-): Launcelot and Guinevere, Symphonic Poem; Prelude for Orchestra; Quintet for Clarinet and String Quartet; Sextet for Wind Instruments and Piano in B Flat Major; Sonata for Flute

and Piano in E Flat; Stevensoniana Suite No. 1, Opus 24; Stevensoniana Suite No. 2; String Quartet in C Major, Opus 40; Symphony No. 1 in B Flat Major; Symphony No. 2 in C Major; Symphony No. 3 in G Major, Opus 41.

HINDEMITH, PAUL (1895-1957): Concert Music for Strings and Brass, Opus 50; Concerto for Cello and Orchestra; Concerto for Piano and Orchestra; Concerto in D Major for Mandolin; Cupid and Psyche Overture; Das Marienleben, for Voice and Piano, Opus 27; The Demon (Pantomime Ballet); Die Harmonie der Welt, for Orchestra; Education Music for Instrumental Ensemble, Opus 44; Geistliche Motette, for Voice and Piano; The Harp That Once Through Tara's Hall, for Mixed Chorus, Piano or Harp, and Strings; Kammermusik No. 1, Opus 24, No. 1; Kammermusik No. 2, Opus 24, No. 2; Little Piano Pieces, Opus 45, No. 4; Ludus Tonalis, 12 Piano Fugues with Preludes, Interludes, and Postludes; Mathis der Maler (Symphonic Suite derived from Opera); Morgenmusik for Brass Ensemble; Nine English Songs, Cycle for Voice and Piano; Nobilissima Visione, for Orchestra; Pieces (5), for Strings; Quartet No. 1 in F Minor, Opus 10, for Strings; Quartet No. 3, Opus 22, for Strings; Quartet for Clarinet, Violin, Cello, & Piano; Sonata for English Horn and Piano; Sonata No. 1 for Piano; Sonata No. 2 for Piano; Sonata No. 3 for Piano; Sonata for Piano 4 Hands (1938); Sonata No. 1 for Organ (1937); Sonata No. 2 for Organ (1937); Sonata No. 3 for Organ (1940); Sonata for Viola & Piano, Opus 11, No. 4; Sonata for Cello and Piano, Opus 11, No. 3; Sonata for Flute and Piano, Sonata for Clarinet and Piano (1939); Sonata for Bassoon and Piano; Sonata for Trombone and Piano; Sonata for Trumpet and Piano; String Quartet, 1943; Symphonic Dance; Symphonic Metamorphoses on Themes by Carl Maria von Weber; Symphony in D Major for Orchestra & Children's Instruments; Symphony in E Flat; Theme with Four Variations (The Four Temperaments) for Piano and Strings; Trauermusik for Viola and Orchestra; Trio No. 1 for Strings, Opus 34 (1924); Trio No. 2 for Strings (1933); When Lilacs Last in the Dooryard Bloomed, for Alto, Baritone, Mixed Chorus, and Orchestra.

HOLST, GUSTAV (1874-1934): Costwolds Symphony; Fugal Overture for Orchestra; Oriental Suite; The Perfect Fool (Ballet); The Planets, Opus 32 (Orchestral Suite); Suites No. 1 in E Flat Major; No. 2 in F Major, Opus 28 (for Band).

HONNEGGER, ARTHUR (1892-1955): Chant de Joie, for Orchestra; A Christmas Cantata; Concerto da camera for Flute and English Horn; Danse de la Chèvre for Flute unaccompanied; Le Dit des jeux du monde (Masque); Horace Victorieux, a Mimed Symphony; King David (Oratorio); Mouvement Symphonique No. 3; Nicolas la Flue, a Dramatic Legend for Mixed Voices and Orchestra; Orchestral Prelude to Aglavaine et Selysette, by Maurice Maeterlinck; Pacific 231, for Orchestra; Pastorale d'Eté, for Orchestra; Petite Suite for Flute, Violin, & Piano; Rapsodie (for Winds); Rugby (for Orchestra); Semiramis (Ballet); Sonata for Clarinet & Piano; Sonata for Violin Unaccompanied; Symphony No. 2 for Strings and Trumpet; Symphony No. 3, for Large Orchestra; Symphony Nr. 5; The Tempest: Prelude for Orchestra.

HOVHANESS, ALAN (1911-): Arevakal, for Orchestra; Duet for Violin & Harpsichord; The Flowering Peach (Orchestral Suite); Kaldis, for Piano and Orchestra; *King Vahaken* ("Is There Survival"), for Orchestra; Music for Piano; Orbit No. 1, for Orchestra; Prelude and Quadruple Fugue, for Orchestra.

HOWE, MARY (1882-): American Piece for Orchestra; *Cards* (Ballet); *Castellana*, for 2 Pianos and Orchestra; Dirge for Orchestra; Paean for Orchestra; *Potomac*, for Orchestra; Quatuor, String Quartet; *Sand*, for Orchestra (arranged for Chamber Orchestra) Sonata in D for Violin and Piano; *Stars* and *Whimsey*, for Chamber Orchestra; Suite for Piano and String Quartet; Three Pieces after Emily Dickinson for String Quartet.

HUMMEL, JOHANN (1778-1837): Concerto in A Minor for Piano, Opus 85; Quartet in G Major for Strings, Opus 30, No. 2; Septet in D Minor, Opus 74.

HUMPERDINCK, ENGELBERT (1854-1921): Moorish Rhapsody, for Orchestra.

IBERT, JACQUES (1890-): *Les Amours de Jupiter*, for Orchestra; *Capriccio* for Orchestra; Concertino da camera for Saxophone; Divertissement for Orchestra; *Escales (Ports of Call)*, for Orchestra; Histoires for Piano; A Louisville Concerto, for Orchestra; Suite Elizabethane for Orchestra; Suite Symphonique ("Impressions of Paris"); Trio for Violin, Cello, and Harp; Trois Pièces Brèves for Winds.

IMBRIE, ANDREW (1921-): *Chant de folie*, for Chorus and Orchestra, after *The Ballad of Reading Gaol*, by Oscar Wilde; *Diane de Poitiers* (Bellet); *L'Eventail de Jeanne* (Ballet); *Gold Standard* (Ballet); Quartet in B Flat Major for Strings; *Les Rencontres* (Ballet).

d'INDY, VINCENT (1851-1931): Istar Variations, for Orchestra; *Jour d'Eté a la Montagne*, for Orchestra, Opus 61; Suite for Trumpet, 2 Flutes, & Strings, Opus 24; Symphony for Orchestra and Piano on a French Mountain Song, Opus 25.

IRELAND, JOHN (1879-): Concertino Pastorale for Strings.

IVES, CHARLES (1874-1954): *Aeschylus and Sophocles*, for Voice, String Quartet, and Piano; First Orchestral Set; Overture No. 3 for Orchestra; Psalm No. 67: Come Ye Thankful People, Come, for Choir and Orchestra; Quartet No. 2 for Strings; Scherzo, No. 2 for Woodwinds and Strings; Second Orchestral Set; Sonata No. 1 for Piano; Sonata No. 2 for Piano (Concord, Mass.); Sonata No. 1 for Violin and Piano; Sonata No. 2 for Violin and Piano; Sonata No. 3 for Violin and Piano; Sonata No. 4 for Violin and Piano; Song Cycle No 4 with Small Chamber Orchestra; Symphony Holidays; Symphony No. 2; Symphony No. 3; *Three Places in New England*, for Orchestra; *Tone Roads No. 3* for Chamber Orchestra; *The Unanswered Question*, for Orchestra.

JACOBI, FREDERICH (1891-1952): Concertino for Piano and Strings; Concerto for Violin and Orchestra; Concerto for Violincello and Orchestra; *The Eve of St. Agnes*, for Orchestra; Four Dances from *The Prodigal Son*, for Orchestra; *Hagiographia*, for String Quartet and Piano; Indian Dances for Orchestra; Music Hall Overture; Night Piece for Flute and Small Orchestra; Ode for Orchestra; Rhapsody for Harp and String Orchestra; String Quartet; String Quartet No. 2; Symphony; Two Assyrian Prayers, for Soprano or Tenor and Orchestra.

JAMES, PHILIP (1890-): *Bret Harte*, Overture for Orchestra; *Gwallia*, Rhapsody for Orchestra; *Judith* (Ballet); Kammersymphonie; Sea Sketches for Bass-Baritone and Orchestra; Sinfonietta for Chamber Orchestra;

Suite for Chamber Orchestra; Suites 1 and 2 for String Orchestra; Symphony No. 1.

JANÁČEK, LEOŠ (1854-1928): *Concertino* for Orchestra; *Diary of One Who Vanished*, for Voices and Piano; *Dumka* for Violin & Piano; Festival Mass; *From a House of the Dead* (Opera); Quartet for Strings No. 2 ("Intimate Letters"); Sinfonietta; Slavonic Mass; Sonata for Violin & Piano; Suite for String Orchestra; *Taras Bulba*, for Orchestra; *Youth*, for String Orchestra.

JÄRNEFELT, ARMAS (1869-): *Åbo slott*, for Chorus and Orchestra; *Heimatklang* (Symphonic Fantasy); *Korsholm* (Symphonic Poem); *Loula vuoksella*, for Chorus and Orchestra; Praeludium, for Orchestra; Serenade, for Orchestra; *Suomen synty*, for Chorus and Orchestra; Symphonic Fantasy.

JENKINS, JOHN (1592-1678): Fancies for Viols; The Fleece Tavern Rant; The Lady Katharine Audley's Bells (The Five Bell Consort), for Viols; The Mitter Rant; Pavane for 4 Viols; The Peterborough Rant; Sonatas (12) for 2 Violins and a Bass, with a Thorough Bass for the Organ or Theorbo.

JEUNE, CLAUDIN LE (c.1530-1602): Psalms of David (40); Te Deum.

JOHNSON, HUNTER (1906-): Adagio for Strings; Andante for Flute and Strings; Concerto for Piano and Small Orchestra; *Deaths and Entrances* (Ballet); Elegy for Clarinet and Strings; *Letter to the World* (Ballet); Piano Sonata; Prelude for Orchestra; Symphony No. 1.

JOLIVET, ANDRÉ (1905-): Andante for Strings; *Calirrhoë*, Cantata; *Comala*, Cantata; Concertino for Trumpet, Piano, and Strings; Concerto for Piano and Orchestra; Concerto for Orchestra, Opus 124; Epithalame for 3 Violins and Orchestra; *Lalla Rookh* (Symphonic Poem); Meditation for English Horn and Orchestra; Poème for Violoncello and Orchestra; Prelude and Dance for Orchestra Quartet in E Flat for Piano, Opus 23; Sonata for Violin in D, Opus 27; Sonata for Violin in E, Opus 34; Suite No. 3 for Orchestra; Trio for Piano in B Minor; Trio for Piano, Violin and Viola in F Sharp Minor, Opus 30.

JONGEN, LEON (1885-): *Malaise, for Orchestra*; *La Nuit de Noël*, Cantata.

JOSQUIN DES PRÉS (c.1445-1521): De Profundis, for Choir; Masses: L'omme armé, La sol fa re mi; Gaudeamus; L'omme armé, sexti toni; Hercules, dux Ferrarae; Malheur me bat; Lami Baudichon; Pange lingua; Una musque de Buscaya; D'ung aultre amor; Mater patris; Faysans regrets; Ad fugam; Di dadi; De Beata Virgine; Sine nomine.

JOSTEN, WERNER (1888-): *A Une Madone*, for Tenor Solo and Orchestra, after Baudelaire; *Batoula* (Ballet); Concerto Sacro No. 1 for String Orchestra and Piano; Concerto Sacro No. 2 for String Orchestra and Piano; *Endymion* (Ballet); *Joseph and His Brethren* (Ballet); *Jungle* (Ballet); Jungle, for Orchestra; Serenade for Orchestra; Symphony for Strings; Symphony in F; Sonata for Cello and Piano; Sonata for Piano; Sonata for Violin and Piano; Sonatina for Violin and Piano; Trio for Oboe, Clarinet, and Bassoon; Trio for Violin, Viola, and Cello.

KABALEVSKY, DMITRI (1904-): *Colas Breugnon* Suite; *The Comedians*, Opus 26, for Orchestra; Concerto No. 2 in G Minor for Piano and Orchestra, Opus 23; Concerto No. 3 for Piano; Concerto for Violin, Opus 48; Concerto for Cello, Opus 49; *The Golden Spikes* (Ballet); *Our Great Fatherland*, a Cantata for Choir, Soli, and Orchestra; *The*

People's Avengers, Suite for Chorus and Orchestra; *Poem of Struggle,* for Chorus and Orchestra; Preludes (24) for Piano; Preludes (3), Opus 38, for Piano; Quartet No. 2 in G Minor, Opus 44, for Strings; Sonata No. 2 for Piano, Opus 45; Sonatina in C Major for Piano, Opus 13, No. 1; Symphony No. 2, Opus 19; *Taras' Family,* for Soloists, Chorus, and Orchestra.

KALINNIKOFF, VASSILI (1866-1901): *Cedar and Palm* (Symphonic Poem); *The Nymphs* (Symphonic Poem); Overture and Entractes (4) to *Tsar Boris; Russalka,* Ballade for Solo Voices, Chorus, and Orchestra; Symphony No. 1 in G Minor; Symphony No. 2 in A Major; Prologue to *1812,* an Overture for Orchestra.

KARLOWICZ, MIECYSLAW (1876-1909): Concerto in A Major for Violin and Orchestra, Opus 8; Lithuanian Rhapsody for Orchestra, Opus 11; Old, Old Songs, Opus 10; Präludium und Doppelfuge for Piano, Opus 5; *Returning Waves* (Symphonic Poem); Sonata for Piano, Opus 6; *Stanislav and Anna of Oswiecim* (Symphonic Poem), Opus 12; Symphony in E Minor, Opus 7.

KAY, ULYSSES (1917-): Concerto for Oboe; *Danse Calinda* (Ballet); Evocation for Concert for Band; Quintet for Flute and String Quartet; Round Dance and Polka, for Orchestra; Sinfonietta for Orchestra; Suite for Brass Choir; Suite in B for Oboe and Piano.

KENNAN, KENT (1913-): Concertino for Piano and Orchestra; Dance Divertimento for Orchestra; Night Soliloquy, for Flute and Orchestra; Quintet for Piano and Strings; Symphony.

KERLL, JOHANN CASPAR (1627-1693): Music for Organ.

KERN, JEROME (1885-1945): *Mark Twain* (Portrait for Orchestra).

KERR, HARRISON (1889-): Contrapunctal Suite for Orchestra; Dance Suite for Orchestra; Sonatas (2) for Piano; String Quartet; Symphony No. 1; Symphony No. 2; Symphony No. 3; Trio for Violin, Cello, and Piano.

KHACHATURIAN, ARAM (1903-): *Battle for Stalingrad* (Orchestral Suite); Concerto for Cello (1946); Concerto for Piano and Orchestra; Concerto for Violin; *Gayne Ballet* Suites Nos. 1, 2, & 3; *Masquerade* Suite, for Orchestra; Symphony No. 2; Trio for Clarinet, Violin, and Piano.

KHRENNIKOV, TIKHON (1913-): *Much Ado about Nothing* Suite, for Orchestra; Symphony No. 1, Opus 4; Concerto for Piano; Five Pieces for Piano; Three Pieces for Piano.

KIRCHNER, LEON (1919-): Quartet No. 1 for Strings; Sonata Concertante for Violin & Piano; Trio for Violin, Cello, & Piano.

KLUGHARDT, AUGUST (1847-1902): Fantasy Pieces (5) for Piano, Oboe, and Cello; *Die Grablegund Christi,* Opus 50 (Oratorio); *Judith,* Opus 85 (Oratorio); *Lenore* (Symphonic Poem); Quintet for Winds, Opus 79; Symphony No. 1 in F Minor, Opus 34; Symphony No. 2 in D, Opus 37; Symphony No. 3 in C Minor, Opus 57; Symphony No. 4 in C Minor, Opus 71; *Die Zerstörung Jerusalems,* Opus 75 (Oratorio).

KODALY, ZOLTAN (1882-): Concerto for Orchestra, Duo for Violin and Cello, Opus 7; Galanta Dances, for Orchestra; *Háry János* Suite; Marosszek Dances for Piano (or Orchestra); Missa Brevis; Peacock Variations for Orchestra; Piano Pieces (7), Opus 11; Psalmus Hungaricus, Opus 13, for Tenor, Chorus, and Orchestra; Quartet No. 1 for Strings, Opus 2; Quartet No. 2 for Strings, Opus 10; Sappho's Love Song; At Night;

The Forest, for Voice and Piano; Serenade for Strings, Opus 12; Sonata for Cello and Piano, Opus 4; Sonata for Cello Unaccompanied, Opus 8; Te Deum; Theater Overture.

KOHS, ELLIS (1916-): Concerto for Piano and Orchestra; Concerto for Orchestra; Concerto for Viola and String Nonet; Sonatina for Bassoon and Piano; String Quartet; Symphony No. 1.

KORNGOLD, ERICH (1897-1957): Concerto in D Major for Violin, Opus 35; *Tomorrow,* Opus 33 (Symphonic Poem).

KREISLER, FRITZ (1875-): Quartet in A Minor, for Strings.

KRENEK, ERNST (1900-): Bagatelles (4) for Piano 4 Hands, Opus 70; *The Ballad of the Railroads,* English Song Cycle; Concerto No. 3 for Piano and Orchestra; Concerto for Violin, Piano, & Orchestra; Fiedellieder, Opus 64, for Voice and Piano; Lamentations of Jeremiah The Prophet, Opus 93, for a Cappella Choir; Pieces for Piano; *The Seasons,* Opus 36, for a Cappella Choir; Seventh String Quartet, Opus 96; Sonata for Organ, Opus 92; Sonata No. 3 for Piano, Opus 92, No. 4; Sonata No. 4 for Piano; Sonata No. 5 for Piano; Sonata for Violin and Piano; Sonata for Viola Solo, Opus 92, No. 3; Sonatina for Flute and Clarinet or Viola, Opus 92, No. 2; Suite for Cello Solo, Opus 84; Symphonic Elegy for String Orchestra; Symphonic Piece for String Orchestra, Opus 86; *Tricks and Trifles,* for Orchestra; Trio for Violin, Clarinet, and Piano; Variations on a North Carolina Folk Song "I Wonder as I Wander," Opus 94.

KREUTZER, RODOLPHE (1780-1849): Concertos (19) for Violin; Double Concertos (2); *Etudes ou Caprices* (40) for Violin Solo; String Quartets (15); String Trios (15); Symphonie concertante for Violin and Cello with Orchestra.

KUHLAU, FRIEDRICH (1786-1832): Sonatinas for Piano, Opus 20, No. 3; Opus 55, Nos. 1, 2, 3; Opus 59, No. 1; Opus 88, No. 2.

LALANDE, MICHEL-RICHARD DE (1657-1726): Christe, Redemptor Omnium, for Chorus; De Profundis, for Solo Voices, Chorus, and Orchestra; Incidental Music to Molière's *Mélicerte;* Motets (60) for Choir and Orchestra; Symphonies pour les Soupers du Roy.

LALO, EDOUARD (1823-1892): Allegro Symphonique for Orchestra; Aubade-allegretto, for Orchestra; Concerto in C Minor for Piano and Orchestra; Concerto in F Major for Violin; Concerto in D Minor for Cello; Concerto Russe for Violin and Orchestra; Divertissement for Orchestra; *Fiesque* Overture; Litanies de la Sainte-Vierge, for Mixed Chorus and Orchestra; *Namouna* (Ballet Suites Nos. 1 & 2); Norwegian Fantasy for Violin and Orchestra; O Salutaris, for 3-part Female Chorus and Organ; Quartet in E Flat for Strings, Opus 19 (revised 1880 as Opus 45); Romance Serenade, for Violin and Orchestra; Scherzo for Orchestra; Sonata for Cello and Piano; Sonata for Violin and Piano, Opus 12; Symphonie Espagnole, for Violin and Orchestra, Opus 21; Symphony No. 2 in G Minor; Trio in A Minor for Piano, Opus 26; Trio in B Minor for Piano; Trio in C Minor for Piano, Opus 7.

LAMBERT, CONSTANT (1905-1951): Concerto for Piano and 9 Instruments; Horoscope (Ballet); *Rio Grande,* for Piano, Chorus, and Orchestra; Songs by Li-Po, for Voice and Orchestra.

LANNER, JOSEPH (1801-1843): Banquet-Polonaise, Opus 135, for Orchestra; Bolero for Orchestra; Cotillons (6), for Orchestra; *Der*

Preis Einer Lebensstunde Overture, Opus 130; Galops (25), for Orchestra; Ländler (25), for Orchestra; Marches (3), for Orchestra; Mazurkas (8), for Orchestra; Polkas (3), for Orchestra; Quadrilles (10), for Orchestra; Tarantella, Opus 187, for Orchestra; Waltzes (106), for Orchestra.

LASSUS, ORLANDO (1530-1594): Lamentations of Jeremiah, for Chorus; Missa "Puisuqe j'ay perdue"; Psalmi Davidis poenitentiales; Psaumes de la Penitence a 5 Voix.

LECLAIR, JEAN-MARIE (1697-1764): Concerti grossi for 3 Violins, Viola, Cello, and Organ; Duos for Violins; Sonata in G Major for Violin, Opus 2, No. 5; Sonata in D Major for Violin, Opus 9, No. 3; Sonatas (48) for Violin with Continuo; Trios (6) for 2 Violins with Bass.

LA VIOLETTE, WESLEY (1894-): Dedications, Concerto for Violin; Double Concerto for String Quartet and Orchestra; Fourth Symphony (band); Largo Lyrico, for String Orchestra; Music fron the High Sierras, for Orchestra; Nocturne for Orchestra; *Osiris,* for Orchestra; Piano Concerto; Piano Quintet; Quintet for Flute and String Quartet; Requiem for Orchestra; Second (Children) Symphony; Serenade for Flute and String Quartet; String Quartets Nos. 1-3; Symphony; Violin Concerto No. 2.

LECOCQ, ALEXANDRE CHARLES (1832-1918): Aubade for Piano; Gavotte for Piano; *Les Fantoccini,* Ballet-Pantomime for Piano; *Les Miettes,* 24 Morceaux de genre for Piano.

LECOUONA, ERNESTO (1896-): *Andalucia* (Suite Espagnole), for Piano; *El Cafetal* for Solo Voices, Chorus, and Orchestra; Danzas Afro-Cubanas for Piano; Danzas Cubanas for Piano; Malaguena, for Orchestra; *Maria La O,* for Solo Voices, Chorus, and Orchestra; *Rosa La China,* for Solo Voices, Chorus, and Orchestra;.

LEKEU, GUILLAUME (1870-1894): Adagio for String Orchestra (without Double Bass); *Andromède* for Solo Voices, Chorus, and Orchestra; *Fantaisie symphonique sur deus airs populaires angevins;* First Symphonic Study, *Chant de triomphale délivrance;* Quartet for Piano (completed by D'Indy); Second Symphonic Study, *Sur le second Faust;* Sonata for Cello and Piano (completed by D'Indy); Sonata in G Major for Violin; Trio for Piano.

LEO, LEONARDO (1694-1744): Concertos (6) for Cello, with two Violins, and Bass; Grand Miserere, for Double Choir (8-part) a cappella; Masses (5); Oratorios (6).

LIADOFF, ANATOL (1855-1914): *Baba Yaga* Symphonic Poem for Orchestra, Opus 56; Ballade for Orchestra, Opus 21b; Ballade for Piano, Opus 21; Choruses with Orchestra to Maeterlinck's *Soeur Béatrice,* Opus 60; Choruses with Orchestra to Schiller's *Die Braut von Messina,* Opus 28; Deux Morceaux for Piano, Opus 31; Four Arabesques for Piano, Opus 7; Four Preludes for Piano, Opus 13; Glorification, for Orchestra; Intermezzo for Piano, Opus 7; Intermezzo for Piano, Opus 8; *Kikimora,* Symphonic Poem for Orchestra, Opus 63; *Le lac enchanté,* Symphonic Poem for Orchestra, Opus 62; Mazurka for Orchestra, Opus 19; Novellette for Piano, Opus 20; Polonaise for Orchestra, Opus 49; Polonaise for Orchestra, Opus 55; Prelude and Mazurka for Piano, Opus 28; Russian Folk Songs, for Orchestra; Scherzo for Orchestra; Opus 16; Six Morceaux for Piano, Opus 3; Three Preludes for Piano, Opus 28.

LISZT, FRANZ (1811-1886): *Ab irato,* étude de perfection, for Piano; *Années de Pèlerinage* —Italy, for Piano; *Années de Pèlerinage*— Switzerland, for Piano; Apparitions (3) for Piano; Ballades (2) for Piano; *Battle of the Huns* (Symphonic Poem No. 11); *Bénédiction de Dieu dans le solitude,* for Piano; Berceuse for Piano; *La Campanella* (Paganini Étude No. 3), for Piano; Caprice-Waltzes (3), for Piano; *Ce qu'on entend sur la montagne,* Symphonic Poem (after Victor Hugo); *Christus,* Oratorio; Concerto No. 1 in E Flat Major for Piano; Concerto No. 2 in A Major, for Piano; Concerto Pathétique in E Minor (Concert Solo, for Piano); Consolations (6), for Piano; Dante Sonata *(Après une lecture de Dante),* for Piano; Dante Symphony; *Die Ideale,* Symphonic Poem, (after Schiller); *Die Legende von der Leiligen Elisabeth,* Oratorio; Élégies (2), for Piano; Études (6) (after Paganini) for Piano; *Études d'exécution transcendante,* for Piano; Fantasia & Fugue on B.A.C.H., for Organ; Fantasia & Fugue on "Ad Nos, Ad Salutarem Undam," for Organ; A Faust Symphony; *Festklänge* (Symphonic Poem No. 7); Festmarsch for Orchestra; Festvorspiel for Orchestra; Feuilles d'Album (3), for Piano; Fountains at the Villa d'Este, for Piano; *Funérailles,* for Piano; Gaudeamus igitur, for Orchestra with Solo Voices and Chorus; Gloria & Credo (from an Organ Mass); *Gnomenreigen,* concert-étude for Piano; Grand Galop chromatique for Piano; Grandes Études de Concert Nos. 1-3 for Piano; *Hamlet* (Symphonic Poem No. 10); *Harmonies poétiques et religieuses* (10), for Piano; *Heroïde funèbre,* Symphonic Poem; *Huldigungsmarsch,* for Orchestra; *Hungaria* (Symphonic Poem No. 9); *Hungaria,* for Solo Voices, Chorus, and Orchestra; Hungarian Fantasia for Piano and Orchestra; Hungarian Rhapsodies (15) for Piano; *L'hymne de Pape,* for Piano; Künstler, Festzug for Orchestra; *Le lac enchanté,* Opus 62, Symphonic Poem; *Légendes* (2) for Piano (St. François d'Assise, St. François de Paul); Liebesträume (3), for Piano; *Masonyi's Grabgeleit,* for Piano; *Mazeppa* (Symphonic Poem No. 6); Mazurka brilliante for Piano; Mephisto Waltz, for Piano (or Orchestra); Missa Choralis; *Orpheus* (Symphonic Poem No. 4); Polish Songs (6) for Piano (after Chopin); Polonaise No. 2 in E Major for Piano; *Les Préludes* (Symphonic Poem No. 3); *Prometheus* (Symphonic Poem No. 5); Rákoczy March, for Orchestra; Rhapsodie Espagnole, for Piano; *Rigoletto* (Paraphrase de Concert), for Piano; Scherzo and March for Piano; Soirées de Vienne, for Piano; Sonata in B Minor for Piano; *Sonetto del Petrarca No. 104,* for Piano; *Tasso, Lament and Triumph* (Symphonic Poem No. 2); *Totentanz,* for Piano and Orchestra; Valse Impromptu for Piano; Variations on the Bach Prelude "Weinen, Klagen," for Piano; *Via crucis,* for Piano; *Von der Wiege bis zum Grabe,* Symphonic Poem (after Michael Zichy); *Vom Fels zum Meer,* Deutscher Siegesmarsch for Orchestra; *Waldesrauschen,* concert-étude for Piano; *Weihnachtsbaum* (12 Pieces), for Piano.

LITOLFF, HENRY CHARLES (1818-1891): *Chant des Belges* Overture, Opus 101; Concerto-symphonies (5) for Piano with Orchestra, Opus 15; Eroica Violin-Concert, Opus 42; Études de concert (6) for Piano, Opus 35; *Les Girondistes* Overture, Opus 80; *Les Guelfes* Overture, Opus 99; *Robespierre* Overture, Opus 55; *Ruth and Booz,* Oratorio; Szenen aus Goethe's Faust, for Solo Voices, Chorus, and Orchestra, Opus 103.

LOCATELLI, PIETRO (1693-1764): L'arte del violini, for 2 Violins, Viola, Cello, and

Continuo (12 Concertos and 24 Caprices), Opus 3; L'arte di nuova modulazione (Caprices énigmatiques), Opus 9; Concerti a quattro (6), Opus 7 for Strings; Concerto da camera; Concertos (6), for Violin, Opus 4; Concerti Grossi for Strings, Opus 1, Nos. 1-12; Contrasto armonico, 4-part concerti for Strings, Opus 10; Elegiac Symphony ("Trauersymphonie"); Sonata in F Minor for Violin ("Au Tombeau"); Sonata in F Major for Flute, Opus 2, No. 8; Sonatas (12) for Violin, Opus 6; Trios (6) for Strings, Opus 5.

LOCKE, MATTHEW (c. 1632-1677): Consort of Four Parts for Viols.

LOEFFLER, CHARLES MARTIN (1861-1935): Divertimento for Violin with Orchestra; Divertissement espagnole for Orchestra and Saxophone; Memories of My Childhood (Symphonic Poem); The Mystic Hour, Symphony for Orchestra and Male Chorus; A Pagan Poem, after Virgil (Symphonic Poem); Poem for Orchestra (»La Bonne Chanson«), after Verlaine; Rhapsodies (2) for Oboe, Viola, Cello, Double-Bass, and Harp; Les veillées de l'Ukraine, Suite in 4 movements for Violin and Full Orchestra, after Gogol.

LOEILLET, JEAN BAPTISTE (1680-1730): Sonata in B Flat Major for Violin & Harpsichord; Sonata in F Sharp Minor for Cello & Harpsichord; Sonata in C Minor for Flute, Oboe, & Harpsichord; Sonata in G Minor for Recorder & Harpsichord; Trio Sonata in G Major for Strings; Trio Sonata in B Minor for Strings.

LOPATNIKOFF, NIKOLAI (1903-): Concertino for Orchestra, Opus 30; Concerto for Violin and Orchestra, Opus 26; Opus Sinfonicum for Orchestra; Sonata No. 2 for Violin and Piano, Opus 32; Symphonietta, Opus 27; Symphony No. 2, Opus 24; Variations & Epilogue for Cello & Piano.

LORTZING, GUSTAV ALBERT (1801-1851): Die Himmelfahrt Christi, Oratorio; Undine (Ballet Music); Zar und Zimmermann (Ballet Music).

LÜBECK, VINCENTIUS (1654-1740): Cantatas (2); Preludes & Fugues Nos. 1-6 for Organ.

LUENING, OTTO (1900-): Americana for Orchestra, Opus 28; Coal Scuttle Blues for Two Pianos (with Ernst Bacon); Concertino for Flute, Harp, Celesta, and Strings, Opus 16; Dirge for Orchestra; Divertimento for Orchestra, Opus 23; Emily Dickinson Song Cycle; Fantasias (2) for Orchestra; Fantasy in Space for Tape Recorder; Invention for Tape Recorder; Kentucky Rondo for Orchestra; Low Speed for Tape Recorder; Second String Quartet, Opus 14; Serenade for Orchestra; Sonata for Violin and Piano, Opus 1; The Soundless Song, for Soprano, String Quartet, Piano, Flute, and Clarinet, Opus 11; String Quartet with Clarinet obbligato, Opus 4; Suite for Cello and Piano; Symphonic Fantasia for Orchestra; Symphonic Poem, Opus 5; Symphonic Poem, Opus 15; Third String Quartet, Opus 20; Wisconsin Suite, for Orchestra.

LUIGINI, ALEXANDRE CLÉMENT (1850-1906): Anges et Démons (Ballet); Arlequin Ecolier (Ballet); Ballet Egyptien, for Orchestra; Le Bivouac (Ballet); Dauritha (Ballet); Les Écharpes (Ballet; Le Meunier (Ballet); Les Noces d'Ivanovna (Ballet); Quartets (3) for Strings; Romance symphonique, for Orchestra; Rose et Papillon (Ballet); Rayon d'or (Ballet).

LULLY, JEAN-BAPTISTE (1632-1687): Airs for Violin; Four-part mass a Cappella; Miserere; Noce Villageoise (Ballet Suite, arranged Manuel Rosenthal); Notturno, for Orchestra; Symphonies for Violin; Te Deum; Trios for Violins.

McBRIDE, ROBERT GUYN (1911-): Depression, Sonata for Violin and Piano; Mexican Rhapsody, for Orchestra; Popover for Clarinet and Orchestra; Prelude to a Tragedy for Orchestra; Pumpkin Eaters Little Fugue; Punch and the Judy, Suite for Orchestra; Quintet for Oboe & Strings; Strawberry Jam Home-Made) for Orchestra; Workout for Chamber Orchestra (15 instruments); Workout for Oboe and Piano.

McDONALD, HARL (1899-1955): The Arkansas Traveler, for Orchestra; Bataan, Symphonic Poem; Chameleon Variations for Orchestra; Concerto for Violin and Orchestra; Fantasy for String Quartet; From Childhood Suite, for Harp and Orchestra; Mohave, Symphonic Fantasy; My Country at War, Symphonic Suite; Quartet on Negro Themes for Chamber Orchestra; Santa Fe Trail, Symphony No. 1; Symphony No. 2 (Rhumba); Symphony No. 3, Tragic Cycle; Symphony No. 4; Trio in G Minor for Piano, Violin, and Callo; Trio No. 2 for Chamber Orchestra.

MACDOWELL, EDWARD (1861-1908): Concerto No. 1 in A Minor for Piano, Opus 15; Concerto No. 2 in D Minor for Piano, Opus 23; Fireside Tales, for Piano, Opus 61; New England Idyls, for Piano, Opus 62; Sea Pieces, for Piano, Opus 55; Sonata Eroica for Piano, Opus 50; Sonata Tragica for Piano, Opus 45; Suite No. 1, for Orchestra; Suite No. 2, for Orchestra, Opus 48 ("Indian"); Witches Dance, for Piano, Opus 17, No. 2; Woodland Sketches, for Piano. Opus 51.

MACHAUT, GUILLAUME DE (c. 1300-1377): Ballades (Songs); Motets; Notre Dame Mass; Rondeaux (Songs); Virelais (Songs).

McPHEE, COLIN (1901-): Bali, for Orchestra; Balinese Ceremonial Music for Pianos; Concerto for Piano and Orchestra; Concerto for Piano and Wind Octet; Saraband for Orchestra; Sonatina for 2 Flutes, Clarinets, Trumpets, and Piano; Symphony in One Movement; Tabuh-Tabuhan, for 2 Pianos and Orchestra.

MADLSEDER, NONNONUS (1730-1797): Symphony in D Major.

MAHLER, GUSTAV (1860-1911): Kindertotenlieder, Song Cycle (5 songs) with Orchestra; Das Klagende Lied (Song of Lament) for Solo Voices, Chorus, and Orchestra; Das Lied von der Erde (3 songs for Tenor, 3 songs for Alto), Posthumous; Rübezahl, a Märchenspiel; Songs from Ruckert; Songs of a Wayfarer, Song Cycle (4 songs) with Orchestra; Songs of Youth, 3 Books of early songs with Piano; Symphony No. 1 in D Major; Symphony No. 2 in C Minor; Symphony No. 3 in D Minor; Symphony No. 4 in G Major; Symphony No. 5 in C Sharp Minor; Smphony No. 6 in A Minor; Symphony No. 7 in B Minor; Symphony No. 8 in E Flat Major; Symphony No. 9 in D Minor; Symphony No. 10 in F Sharp Major; The Youth's Magic Horn, Song Cycle (12 songs) with Orchestra.

MALAT, JAN (1843-1915): Slavonic Girls (Orchestral Suite).

MALIPIERO, G. FRANCESCO (1882-): Concerto for Violin; Poemi Asolani, for Piano; Quartet for Strings No. 4; Quartet for Strings No. 7; Rispetti e Strambotti, for Strings; Sonata a Cinque for Strings; Symphony No. 7.

MANCINI, FRANCESCO (1674-1739): Concerto a quattro in E Minor for Harpsichord and Orchestra.

MARAIS, MARIN (c. 1656-1728): Pieces for Viola da Gamba and Harpsichord, 5 Books;

Pieces for 2 Violas da Gamba & Harpsichord; Trios for Violin, Flute, and Viola da Gamba; Trios for Violin, Viola da Gamba, and Harpsichord.

MARCELLO, BENEDETTO (1686-1739): Aria in A Minor for Strings; Concerto in C Minor for Oboe and Strings; Concerto Grosso in F Major, Opus 1, No. 4; Estro poetico-armonico; Parafrasi sopra in cinquanta primi Salmi, for 1-4 Voices, with Basso continuo for Organ or Harpsichord (a few with Cello Obligato, or 2 Violins); Sonatas for Viola da Gamba & Harpsichord, Opus 1; Sonata in B Minor for Flute, Opus 1, No. 4

MARTIN, FRANK (1890-): Concerto for Harpsichord & Small Orchestra; Concerto for Violin; Jedermann (6 Monologues) for Voice and Piano; Passacaille for Strings.

MARTINI, GIOVANNI BATTISTA (1706-1784): Concerto in F Major for Piano; Duetti da camera a diversi voci; Sonate (18) d'intavolatura per l'organo e cembalo.

MARTINU, BOHUSLAV (1891-): Concerto for String Quartet and Orchestra; Concerto for 2 Pianos and Orchestra; Concerto for Violin and Orchestra; Concerto Grosso; Intermezzo for Orchestra; Madrigal Sonata for Flute, Violin, and Piano; Memorial to Lidice, for Orchestra; Partita for String Orchestra (Suite ?); Quintet for Strings and Piano; Les Ritournelles, for Piano; Serenade for Orchestra; Sonata No. 3 for Violin; Sonata for Flute and Piano; Suite Concertante for Violin and Orchestra; Symphonies Nos. 1-4; Thunderbolt P-47, for Orchestra; Trio for Flute, Cello, and Piano.

MASON, DANIEL GREGORY (1873-): Chanticleer Overture, Opus 27; Russians, for Baritone and Orchestra, Opus 18; Sonata for Clarinet and Piano, Opus 14; String Quartet on Negro Themes, Opus 19; Symphony No. 1 in C Minor, Opus 11; Symphony No. 2 in A Major, Opus 30; Symphony No. 3 (A Lincoln Symphony), Opus 35; Violin Sonata, Opus 5.

MASSENET, JULES (1842-1912): Le Carillon (Ballet); Le Cid (Ballet Suite); La Cigale (Ballet); Concerto in E Flat Major for Piano and Orchestra; Devant la Madone, for Orchestra; Espada (Ballet); Fantasy for Cello and Orchestra; Marche solonnelle, for Orchestra; Oratorios (Mary Magdalene; Eve; The Promised Land); Parade militaire, for Orchestra; Phèdre Overture; Les Rosati, for Orchestra; Scènes Alsaciennes (Orchestral Suite No. 7); Scènes Pittoresques (Orchestral Suite No. 4); Thaïs (Ballet Music); Visions, Symphonic Poem; Werther Overture.

MATTHESON, JOHANN (1681-1764): Flute Sonatas (12); Mass; Operas (8); Oratorios and Cantatas (24); Passion; Sonata in E Minor for Violin; Suites for Harpsichord; Violin sonatas.

MEDTNER, NICOLAI (1880-1951): Märchen-Sonate in D Minor and Sonata in E Minor, Opus 25, for Piano; Sonata in F Minor for Piano, Opus 5; Sonata in G Minor for Piano, Opus 22; Sonata-Ballade for Piano, Opus 27; Sonata-Triaden in A Flat, D Minor, and C, Opus 11, for Piano.

MEHUL, ETIENNE HENRI (1763-1817): Les Amazons, ou la fondation de Thèbes (Ballet); Le Chasse de Jeune Henri Overture; La journée aux aventures (Ballet); L'Oriflamme (Ballet); Persée et Andromède (Ballet); Le Prince troubadour (Ballet); Le rétour d'Ulysse (Ballet); Sonata in A Major for Piano, Opus 1, No. 3; Symphony No. 1 in C Minor; Timoleon Overture; Le Trésor Supposè Overture.

MENASCE, JACQUES DE (1905-): Concerto No. 2 for Piano and Orchestra; Divertimento

on a Children's Song, for Piano and Orchestra; Petite Suite pour le Piano; Pour une princesse, Song Cycle for Piano; Sonatina No. 2 for Piano; Third Sonatina for Piano.

MENDELSSOHN, FELIX (1809-1847): Allegro Brillant in A Major for Piano, Opus 92; Andante & Variations in B Flat Major for Piano, Opus 83a; Andante, Scherzo, Capriccio & Fugue for Strings, Opus 81; An die Künstler (To the Sons of Art), Opus 68, for Male Chorus, and Brass; Calm Sea & Prosperous Voyage, for Orchestra; Capriccio Brillant, Opus 22, for Piano with Orchestra; Children's Pieces (6) for Piano, Opus 72; Concert Pieces for Horn, Clarinet, Piano, Opus 113, Opus 114; Concerto No. 1 in G Minor for Piano, Opus 25; Concerto No. 2 in D Minor for Piano, Opus 40; Concerto in E Flat Major for 2 Pianos; Concerto in D Minor for Violin; Concerto in E Minor for Violin, Opus 64; Die Erste Walpurgisnacht, Ballade for Solo Voices, Chorus, and Orchestra, Opus 60; Elijah, Opus 70 (Oratorio); Festgesänge (2) for Male Chorus and Orchestra; Fingal's Cave Overture (Hebrides), for Orchestra; Lobgesang, Opus 52 ("Hymn of Praise") (Symphony-Cantata); A Midsummer Night's Dream, Overture and Incidental Music, for Orchestra; Octet in F Flat Major for Strings, Opus 20; Psalm 95 for Solo Voices, Chorus, and Orchestra, Opus 46; Psalm 115 for Solo Voices, Chorus, and Orchestra, Opus 31; Prelude and Fugue in C Minor for Organ; Quartet No. 1 in E Flat Major for Strings, Opus 12; Quartet No. 2 in A Minor for Strings, Opus 13; Quartet No. 3 in D Major for Strings, Opus 44, No. 1; Quartet No. 4 in E Minor for Strings, Opus 44, No. 2; Quartet No. 5 in E Flat Major for Strings, Opus 44, No. 3; Quartet in F Minor (Piano), Opus 2; Quintet No. 1 in A Major for Strings, Opus 18; Quintet No. 2 in B Flat Major for Strings, Opus 87; Rondo Brillant in E Flat Major for Piano, Opus 29; Rondo Capriccioso for Piano, Opus 14; Ruy Blas Overture, for Orchestra; Die Schöne Melusine Overture, Opus 21, for Orchestra; Sextet for Piano, Violin, 2 Violas, Cello, & Bass, Opus 110; Sonata No. 1 in F Minor for Organ, Opus 65; Sonata No. 2 in C Minor for Organ, Opus 65; Sonata No. 3 in A Major for Organ, Opus 65; Sonata No. 6 in D Minor for Organ, Opus 65; Sonata in F Minor for Violin and Piano, Opus 5; Sonata No. 1 in B Flat Major for Cello, Opus 45; Sonata No. 2 in D Major for Cello, Opus 58; Songs for Voice and Piano; Songs without Words, for Piano, Opera 19b, 30, 38, 53, 62, 67, 85, 102; St. Paul Oratorio, Opus 36; Symphony No. 1 in C Minor, Opus 11; Symphony No. 2, Opus 52 (Lobgesang); Symphony No. 3 in A Minor, Opus 56; ("Scotch"); Symphony No. 4 in A Major, Opus 90 ("Italian"); Symphony No. 5 in D Major, Opus 107 ("Reformation"); Trio No. 1 in D Major (Piano, Violin, Cello), Opus 49; Tu es Petrus; for 5-part Chorus or Orchestra; Variations after Liszt, for Piano; Variations Sérieuses in D Minor for Piano, Opus 54; The Wedding March, for Piano; The Wedding of Camacho Overture.

MENNIN, PETER (1923-): Concertino for Flute, Strings, and Percussion; Folk Overture, for Orchestra; Piano Sonata; Quartet No. 1, for Strings; Quartet No. 2, for Strings; Symphonies Nos. 1-3.

MENOTTI, GIAN-CARLO (1911-): Amelia al Ballo Overture; Concerto for Violin; Piano Concerto in F; Sebastian (Ballet); Trio for a House Warming Party, for Piano, Cello, and Flute.

MESSAGER, ANDRÉ CHARLES PROSPER (1853-1929): *Les Deux Pigeons* (Ballet); *Isoline* (Ballet Suite); Symphony; Pages Célèbres, Pages Oubliées, for Voice and Orchestra; *Véronique* Overture.

MESSIAEN, OLIVIER (1908-): Le Banquet Celeste, for Organ; Messe de la Pentecôte; Préludes (2) for Piano; Three Organ Pieces; Vision de L'Amen, for 2 Pianos.

MEYERBEER, GIACOMO (1791-1864): *L'Africaine* (Overture; Marche Indienne); Chorus to the *Eumenides* of Aeschylus; *Der Genius der Musik am Grabe Beethovens*, Cantata; Fackeltänze (4) for Wind Band; Gutenberg Cantata; *Les Huguenots* Overture; *Marisa und ihr Genius*, Cantata; Ode to Rauch, for Solo Voices, and Orchestra; *Le Pardon de Ploermel* Overture; *Les Patineurs* (Ballet Music); *Le Prophète* (Waltz; Quadrille des Patineurs; Galop; Coronation March); Sacred Odes (7) by Klopstock for 4 Voices a cappella; Serenade: *Brautgeleite aus der Heimat*, for 8 Voices unaccompanied; *Struensee*, Incidental Music.

MIASKOVSKY, NICOLAI (1881-1950): Concerto for Violin, Opus 44; Concerto for Cello, Opus 66; Divertimento for Orchestra, Opus 80; Lyric Concertino in G Major for Orchestra, Opus 32, No. 3; Overture in G Major; Symphony No. 16 in F Major, Opus 39; Symphony No. 21 in F Sharp Minor, Opus 51; Symphony No. 27.

MILHAUD, DARIUS (1892-): Air for Viola and Orchestra; *Les Amours de Ronsard*, 4 Songs for Soprano and Orchestra; *Le Bal Martiniquais*, for Orchestra or Two Pianos; *The Bells* (Ballet); *Le Boeuf sur le Toit*, for Orchestra; *Cain and Abel*, for Narrator and Orchestra; *La Cheminée du Roi René*, for Winds; Concertino d'automne, for Piano 4 Hands; Concertino d'Eté, for Viola and Chamber Orkestra; Concerto for Clarinet and Orchestra; Concerto for Two Pianos and Orchestra; Concerto No. 1 for Piano; Concerto No. 2 for Piano and Orchestra; Concerto No. 2 for Violin and Orchestra; Concerto No. 4 for Piano; Concerto for Percussion and Small Orchestra; *La Création du Monde*, for Orchestra; Fanfare de la Liberté for Orchestra; Four Sketches for Orchestra; The Household Muse, Orchestral or Piano Suite; *Jeux de Printemps* (Ballet); Kaddish, for Solo Voice, Chorus ad lib., and Organ; Kentuckiana, for Orchestra; Mills Fanfare, for String Orchestra; Opus Americanum No. 2 (Ballet Suite); Pastorale for Oboe, Clarinet, and Bassoon; Poèmes Juifs, for Voice and Piano; Quatre Chants de Misère, Song Cycle; Quartet for Strings (1912); Quartet for Strings No. 12; Quartet for Strings No. 1 (1951); Quintet for Strings No. 2 (1952); Sacred Service, for Solo Voices, Choir, and Organ; Saudades do Brazil (Suite of Dances) for Piano (or Orchestra); Scaramouche, for Two Pianos; Sonata for Flute, Oboe, Clarinet, and Piano; Sonata for Violin and Harpsichord; Sonatina for Clarinet & Piano; Sonatina for Flute and Piano; Sonatina for 2 Violins; Sonata No. 2 for Violin and Piano; String Quartet No. 10 (Birthday Quartet); String Quartet No. 11; String Quartet No. 12; Suite for Winds after Corrette; Suite Française for Orchestra; Suite Provençale for Orchestra, Symphonic Band, or Piano 4 Hands; Suite for Violin, Clarinet, and Piano; Symphony No. 1; Symphony No. 2; Symphony No. 4 for Strings; Symphony No. 4 (1948 Revision); Third Symphony with Choir; Touches Blanches and Touches Noires, for Piano; Two Sketches for Winds.

MOMPOU, FEDERICO (1893-): Impresiones Intimas, for Piano; Scènes d'enfants, for Piano.

MONTEVERDI, CLAUDIO (1567-1643): Ballet-Madrigal Ferdinand III; Beatus Vir, for Solo Voices, Chorus, and Orchestra; Concerto for Tenor and Strings; Iro's Air (*Ulysses*); Laetatus Sum (Psalm for Chorus, Organ, & Orchestra); *Lagrime d'Amante al Sepolcro dell' Amata* (Madrigals); Laudate Dominum, Solo Voices, Chorus, and Orchestra; Madrigals (eight books of 5-part vocal pieces); Madrigals on Texts from "Il Pastor Fido"; Magnificat; Messa a 4 Voci da Cappella (1651); Sonata a 8 sopra "Sancta Maria ora pro nobis"; *Tirsi e Clori* (Ballo Concertante); Ut Queant, for Solo Voices, Chorus, and Orchestra; Vespro della Beata Vergine (1610), for Solo Voices, Chorus, and Orchestra.

MOORE, DOUGLAS (1893-): Ballade of William Sycamore, for Baritone, Flute, Trombone, and Piano; Cotillion Suite, for Orchestra; Down East Suite, for Violin and Piano; Farm Journal, for Orchestra; Four Museum Pieces for Orchestra; *Moby Dick*, for Orchestra; *Pageant of P. T. Barnum*, for Orchestra; Quartet for Strings; Quintet for Clarinet and Strings; Quintet for Woodwinds and Horn; A Symphony of Autumn; Symphony No. 2 in A Major.

MORLEY, THOMAS (1557-1603): Canzonets, or Little Short Songs to Three Voices (1593); The Firsk Book of Airs, or Little Short Songs to Sing and Play to the Lute with the Bass Viol (1597), (containing "It was a lover and his lass" from Shakespeare's *As You Like It);* The First Book of Ballads to Five Voices (1595); The First Book of Canzonets to Two Voices (1595); Madrigals to Four Voices (1594).

MOSSOLOV, ALEXANDER (1900-): Iron Foundry, for Orchestra.

MOSZKOWSKI, MORITZ (1854-1925): *Aus aller Herren Länder*, for Orchestra, Opus 23; Concerto for Piano in E, Opus 59; Concerto for Violin, Opus 30; En Automne, for Piano Opus 36, No. 4; *Jeanne d'Arc*, Opus 19, Symphonic Poem; *Laurin* (Ballet); Phantastischer Zug, for Orchestra; Spanish Dances for Piano; Suite for 2 Violins and Piano, Opus 71; Suite in F for Orchestra, Opus 39; Suite in G Minor for Orchestra, Opus 47.

MOZART, LEOPOLD (1719-1787): Cassatio in G Major (Toy Symphony); Der Morgen und der Abend, Piano Pieces (12); Oratorios (12); Symphonies (18 published); Trio Sonatas (6) for 2 Violins with Basso Continuo.

MOZART, WOLFGANG AMADEUS (1756-1791); Adagio in E Major for Violin, K. 261; Adagio in B Minor for Piano, K. 540; Adagio in C Major for Organ, K. 580a; Adagio in C Major for Organ, K. 617a; Adagio and Allegro in F Minor for Organ, K. 594; Adagio & Fugue in F Minor for Strings, K. 404a; Adagio and Fugue in C Minor for Organ, K. 546; Adagio for Glass Harmonica, K. 617a; Adagio and Rondo for Glass Harmonica, Flute, Oboe, Viola, and Cello, K. 617; Allegro in B Flat Major for Piano, K. 3; Allegro in G Minor for Piano, K. 312; Andante in C Major for Flute & Orchestra, K. 315; Andante in F Major for Piano, K. 616; Andante Con Variazione in G Major for Piano Duet, K. 501; Andante for Mechanical Organ, K. 616; Andantino in E Flat Major for Piano, K. 236; Cadenzas (35) to Piano Concertos; Canons (20) (2-12 Voices); Cantatas (*Davidde penitente, Maurerfreude* (Masonic), *Kleine Freimaurercantate*); Capriccio in C Major for Piano, K. 395; Cassation No. 1 in G Major for Orchestra, K. 63; Cassation in B Flat

Major for Orchestra, K. 99; Cassation in E Flat Major for Orchestra; Cassazione: Quartet for Oboe, Clarinet, Horn, & Bassoon; Chorus, 3-part, with Organ; Comic Duet for Soprano and Bass; Comic Terzet with Piano; Concert Aria for Alto with Orchestra; Concert Arias (27) for Soprano and Orchestra; Concert Aria and Rondo (1) for Soprano and Orchestra; Concert Arias (8) for Tenor with Orchestra; Concert Arias (5) and Arietta for Bass with Orchestra; Concerto for Piano, No. 1 in F Major, K. 37; Concerto for Piano, No. 2 in B Flat Major, K. 39; Concerto for Piano, No. 3 in D Major, K. 40; Concerto for Piano, No. 4 in G Major, K. 41; Concerto for Piano, No. 5 in D Major, K. 175; Concerto for Piano, No. 6 in B Flat Major, K. 238; Concerto for Three Pianos, No. 7 in F Major, K. 242; Concerto for Piano, No. 8 in C Major, K. 246; Concerto for Piano, No. 9 in E Flat Major, K. 271; Concerto for Two Pianos, No. 10 in E Flat Major, K. 365; Concerto for Piano, No. 11 in F Major, K. 413; Concerto for Piano, No. 12 in A Major, K. 414; Concerto for Piano, No. 13 in C Major, K. 415; Concerto for Piano, No. 14 in E Flat Major, K. 449; Concerto for Piano, No. 15 in B Flat Major, K. 450; Concerto for Piano, No. 16 in D Major, K. 451; Concerto for Piano, No. 17 in G Major, K. 453; Concerto for Piano, No. 18 in B Flat Major, K. 456; Concerto for Piano, No. 19 in F Major, K. 459; Concerto for Piano, No. 20 in D Minor, K. 466; Concerto for Piano, No. 21 in C Major, K. 467; Concerto for Piano, No. 22 in E Flat Major, K. 482; Concerto for Piano, No. 23 in A Major, K. 488; Concerto for Piano, No. 24 in C Minor, K. 491; Concerto for Piano, No. 25 in C Major, K. 503; Concerto for Piano, No. 26 in D Major, K. 537 ("Coronation"); Concerto for Piano, No. 27 in B Flat Major, K. 595; Concertos for Piano in D; G; E Flat, K. 107 (after J. C. Bach); Concerto for Violin, No. 1 in B Flat Major, K. 207; Concerto for Violin, No. 2 in D Major, K. 211; Concerto for Violin, No. 3 in G Major, K. 216; Concerto for Violin, No. 4 in D Major, K. 218; Concerto for Violin, No. 5 in A Major, K. 219 ("Turkish"); Concerto for Violin, No. 6 in E Flat Major, K. 268; Concerto for Violin, No. 7 in D Major, K. 271a; Concerto for Flute in G Major, K. 313; Concerto for Flute in D Major K. 314; Concerto for Flute and Harp in C Major, K. 299; Concerto for Clarinet in A, K. 622; Concerto for Bassoon in B Flat Major, K. 191; Concerto for Horn in D Major, K. 412; Concerto for Horn in E Flat Major, K. 417; Concerto for Horn in E Flat Major, K. 447; Concerto for Horn in E Flat Major, K. 496; Contradances for Orchestra; De Profundis; Divertimento in E Flat Major for Orchestra, K. 113; Divertimento in D Major, for Orchestra, K. 131; Divertimento in D Major for Orchestra, K. 136; Divertimento in B Flat Major for Orchestra, K. 137; Divertimento in F Major, for Orchestra, K. 138; Divertimento in E Flat Major for Orchestra, K. 166; Divertimento in B Flat Major for Orchestra, K. 186; Divertimento in C Major for Orchestra, K. 187; Divertimento in C Major for Orchestra, K. 188; Divertimento in D Major for Orchestra, K. 205; Divertimento in B Flat Major for Orchestra, K. 240; Divertimento in F Major for Orchestra, K. 247; Divertimento in D Major for Orchestra, K. 251; Divertimento in E Flat Major for Orchestra, K. 252; Divertimento in F Major for Orchestra, K. 253; Divertimento in B Flat Major for Orchestra, K. 270; Divertimento in B Flat Major

for Orchestra, K. 287; Divertimento in E Flat Major for Orchestra, K. 289; Divertimento in D Major for Orchestra, K. 334; Divertimento in E Flat Major for Violin, Viola, & Cello, K. 563; Divertimento in E Flat Major for Orchestra, K. Anh. 226; Divertimento in B Flat Major for Orchestra, K. Anh. 227; Dixit et Magnificat for chorus and Orchestra, K. 193; Duo No. 1 in G Majo for Violin & Viola, K. 423; Eine kleine Nachtmusik, (String Quintet) K. 525; Exsultate Jubilate (Motet), K. 165; Fantasia in C. Minor for Piano, K. 396; Fantasia in D Minor for Piano, K. 397; Fantasia in C Minor for Piano, K. 475; Fantasia in F Minor for Organ, K. 608; Fantasy & Fugue in C Major for Piano, K. 394; Fugue in G Minor for Piano, K. 401; Funeral March in C Minor for Piano, K. 453a; German Church Songs (2); German Dances for Piano (or Orchestra); German Warsong; Gigue in G Major for Piano, K. 574; Gradual; Hymns (2); *Idomeneo* Overture; *Il Re Pastore* Overture; Kyrie in D Minor for 4 Voices, K. 341 ("Muenchener"); Litaniae de Venerabili Altaris Sacramento, K. 243; Litaniae Laurentanae in D Major, K. 195; March in F Major for Orchestra, K. 248; March in D Major for Orchestra, K. 249 ("Haffner"); Marches Nos. 1 & 2, for Orchestra, K. 335; Masonic Funeral Music, K. 477, for Orchestra; Mass in F Major, K. 192; Mass in D Major, K. 194 ("Missa Brevis"); Mass in C Major, K. 257 ("Credo Mass"); Mass in C Major, K. 317 ("Coronation"); Mass in C Minor, KV. 427 ("The Great"); Memorial Service; Minuets for Piano, K. 1, 2, 4, 5, 94; Minuet in D Major for Piano, K. 355; Minuets for Orchestra, K. 568, 599; Miserere; Motet for Soprano Solo (Church Music); A Musical Joke for Orchestra, K. 522; Minuets (2) with Contradances, for Orchestra, K. 463; Notturni (6) for Voices & Winds; Offertories (9); Offertorium pro Festo Sti. Joannis Baptistae, K. 72; Overture in B Flat Major for Orchestra, K. 311a ("Paris"); Passion Cantata; *Les Petits Riens* (Ballet Music); Quartet in G Major for Strings, K. 80; Quartet in D Major for Strings, K. 155; Quartet in G Major for Strings, K. 156; Quartet in C Major for Strings, K. 157; Quartet in F Major for Strings, K. 158; Quartet in B Flat Major for Strings, K. 159; Quartet in E Flat Major for Strings, K. 160; Quartet in F Major for Strings, K. 168; Quartet in F Major for Strings, K. 169; Quartet No. 1 in A Major for Strings, KA 212; Quartet No. 2 in B Flat Major for Strings, KA 210; Quartet No. 3 in C Major for Strings, KA 211; Quartet No. 4 in E Flat Major for Strings, KA 213; Quartet No. 10 in C Major for Strings, K. 170; Quartet No. 11 in E Flat Major for Strings, K. 171; Quartet No. 12 in B Flat Major for Strings, K. 172; Quartet No. 14 in G Major for Strings, K. 387; Quartet No. 15 in D Minor for Strings, K. 421; Quartet No. 16 in E Flat Major for Strings, K. 428; Quartet No. 17 in B Flat Major for Strings, K. 468 ("The Hunt"); Quartet No. 18 in A Major for Strings, K. 464; Quartet No. 19 in C Major for Strings, K. 465 ("Dissonant"); Quartet No. 20 in D Major for Strings; K. 499; Quartet No. 21 in D Major for Strings, K. 575; Quartet No. 22 in B Flat Major for Strings, K. 589; Quartet No. 23 in F Major for Strings, K. 590; Quartet No. 1 in G Minor (Piano), K. 478; Quartet No. 2 in E Flat Major (Piano), K. 493; Quartet in D Major for Flute and Strings, K. 285; Quartet in C Major for Flute and Strings, K. 285b; Quartet in A Major for Flute and Strings, K. 298; Quartet in F Major for Oboe and Strings, K. 370; Quintet in B Flat Major for Strings, K. 46; Quintet in B Flat Major for Strings, K. 174; Quintet in C Minor for Strings, K. 406; Quintet in E Flat Major for Horn, K. 407; Quintet in C Major for Strings, K. 515; Quintet in G Minor for Strings, K. 516; Quintet in D Major for Strings, K. 593; Quintet in E Flat Major for Strings, K. 614; Quintet in E Flat Major (Piano), K. 452; Quintet in A Major for Clarinet, K. 581; Regina Coeli (3); Requiem, K. 626; Rondo for Soprano, K. 490; Rondo in B Flat Major for Violin, K. 269; Rondo in C Major for Violin, K. 373; Rondo in D Major for Piano, K. 382; Rondo in A Major for Piano, K. 386; Rondo in D Major for Piano, K. 485; Rondo in F Major for Piano, K. 494; Rondo in A Minor for Piano, K. 511; Serenade No. 4 in D Major for Orchestra, K. 203; Serenade No. 6 in D Major for Orchestra, K. 239 ("Serenata Notturna"); Serenade No. 7 in D Major for Orchestra, K. 250 ("Haffner"); Serenade No. 9 in D Major for Orchestra, K. 320 ("Post Horn"; Serenade No. 10 in B Flat Major for Orchestra, K. 361; Serenade No. 11 in E Flat Major for Orchestra, K. 375; Serenade No. 12 in C Minor for Orchestra, K. 388; Sinfonia Concertante in E Flat Major, K. 364; Sinfonia Concertante in E Flat Major, K. 297b (K. Anh. 9); Sonatas (17) for Organ, usually with 2 Violins and Cello; Sonata for Piano No. 1 in C Major, K. 279; Sonata for Piano No. 2 in F Major, K. 280; Sonata for Piano No. 3 in B Flat Major, K. 281; Sonata for Piano No. 4 in E Flat Major, K. 282; Sonata for Piano No. 5 in G Major, K. 283; Sonata for Piano No. 6 in D Major, K. 284; Sonata for Piano No. 7 in C Major, K. 309; Sonata for Piano No. 8 in A Minor, K. 310; Sonata for Piano No. 9 in D Major, K. 311; Sonata for Piano No. 10 in C Major, K. 330; Sonata for Piano No. 11 in A Major, K. 331; Sonata for Piano No. 12 in F Major, K. 332; Sonata for Piano No. 13 in B Flat Major, K. 333; Sonata for Piano No. 14 in C Minor, K. 457; Sonata for Piano No. 15 in C Major, K. 494; Sonata for Piano No. 15 in C Major, K. 545; Sonata for Piano in F Major, K. 547a; Sonata for Piano No. 16 in B Flat Major, K. 570; Sonata for Piano No. 17 in D Major, K. 576 ("Trumpet"); Sonata for Piano No. 1 in G Major for Piano 4 Hands, K. 357; Sonata No. 2 in B Flat Major for Piano 4 Hands, K. 358; Sonata No. 3 in D Major for Piano 4 Hands, K. 381; Sonata No. 4 in F Major for Piano 4 Hands, K. 497; Sonata No. 5 in C Major for Piano 4 Hands, K. 521; Sonata in D Major for Two Pianos, K. 448; Sonata for Violin in G Major, K. 11; Sonata for Violin in C Major, K. 296; Sonata for Violin in G Major, K. 301; Sonata for Violin in E Flat Major, K. 302; Sonata for Violin in E Minor, K. 304; Sonata for Violin in D Major, K. 306; Sonata for Violin in F Major, K. 377; Sonata for Violin in B Flat Major, K. 378; Sonata for Violin in G Major, K. 379; Sonata for Violin in E Flat Major, K. 380; Sonata for Violin in B Flat Major, K. 454; Sonata for Violin in E Flat Major, K. 481; Sonata for Violin in A Major, K. 526; Sonata in B Flat Major for Bassoon & Cello, K. 292; Song with Chorus and Organ; Songs (34) for Solo Voice with Piano; Suite in C Major for Piano, K. 399; Symphony No. 1 in E Flat Major, K. 16; Symphony No.

2 in B Flat Major, K. 17; Symphony No. 3 E Flat Major, K. 18; Symphony No. 4 in D Major, K. 19; Symphony No. 5 in B Flat Major, K. 22; Symphony No. 6 in F Major, K. 43; Symphony No. 7 in D Major, K. 45; Symphony No. 8 in D Major, K. 48; Symphony No. 9 in C Major, K. 73; Symphony No. 10 in G Major, K. 74; Symphony No. 11 in D Major, K. 84; Symphony No. 12 in G Major, K. 110; Symphony No. 13 in F Major, K. 112; Symphony No. 14 in A Major, K. 114; Symphony No. 15 in G Major, K. 124; Symphony No. 16 in C Major, K. 128; Symphony No. 18 in F Major, K. 130; Symphony No. 19 in E Flat Major, K. 132; Symphony No. 20 in D Major, K. 133; Symphony No. 21 in A Major, K. 134; Symphony No. 22 in C Major, K. 162; Symphony No. 23 in D Major, K. 181; Symphony No. 24 in B Flat Major, K. 182; Symphony No. 25 in G Minor, K. 183; Symphony No. 26 in E Flat Major, K. 184; Symphony No. 27 in G Major, K. 199; Symphony No. 28 in C Major, K. 200; Symphony No. 29 in A Major, K. 201; Symphony No. 30 in D Major, K. 202; Symphony No. 31 in D Major, K. 297 ("Paris"); Symphony No. 32 in G Major, K. 318; Symphony No. 33 in B Flat Major, K. 319; Symphony No. 34 in C Major, K. 338; Symphony No. 35 in D Major, K. 385 ("Haffner"); Symphony No. 36 in C Major, K. 425 ("Linz"); Symphony No. 37 in G Major, K. 444; Symphony No. 38 in D Major, K. 504 ("Prague"); Symphony No. 39 in F Flat Major, K. 543; Symphony No. 40 in G Minor, K. 550; Symphony No. 41 in C Major, K. 551 ("Jupiter"); Tantum Ergo (2); Te Deum; Trio No. 1 in G Major, K. 496, for Piano, Violin, and Cello; Trio No. 2 in B Flat Major, K. 502, for Piano, Violin, and Cello; Trio No. 3 in E Major, K. 542, for Piano, Violin, and Cello; Trio No. 4 in C Major, K. 548, for Piano, Violin, and Cello; Trio No. 5 in G Major, K. 564, for Piano, Violin, and Cello; Trio No. 6 in B Flat Major, K. 254, for Piano, Violin, and Cello; Trio in E Flat Major for Clarinet, Viola, & Piano, K. 498; Variations on a Dutch Air, for Piano, K. 24; Variations on "William of Nassau," for Piano, K. 25; Variations in F Major, for Piano, K. 54; Variations on a Minuet of Fischer, for Piano, K. 179; Variations on an Arietta of Salieri, for Piano K. 180; Variations on "Lison dormait," for Piano, K. 264; Variations on "Ah, vous dirai-je, Maman," for Piano, K. 265; Variations on a March by Grétry, for Piano, K. 352; Variations on "La Belle Françoise," for Piano, K. 353; Variations on "Je Suis Lindor," for Piano, K. 354; Variations on "Hélas, j'ai perdu mon amant," for Piano and Violin, K. 360; Variations on "Salve tu, Domine," for Piano, K. 398; Variotons on "Unser Dummer Pobel Meint," Piano, K. 455; Variations on "Come un agnello," for Piano, K. 460; Variations on an Allegretto, for Piano, K. 500; Variations on a Minuet of Duport, for Piano, K. 573; Variations on "Ein Weib ist das herrlichste Ding," for Piano, K. 613; Veni Sancte; Vesperae de Dominica, K. 321, for Solo Voices, Choruses, and Orchestra.

MUFFAT, GEORG (C. 1645-1704): Concerti Grossi, for Strings; Organ Works; Sonatas for Various Instruments; Suites for Orchestra.

MUSSORGSKY, MODEST (1835-1881): *The Defeat of Sennacherib*, for Chorus and Orchestra; Intermezzo in Modo Classico in B Minor, for Orchestra; *Night on Bald Mountain* (Symphonic Fantasy); *The Nursery*, for Voice and

Piano; *Pictures at an Exhibition*, for Piano (or Orchestra); Scherzo in B, for Orchestra; Songs and Dances of Death, for Voice and Piano; Sunless Cycle, for Voice and Piano; Turkish March, for Orchestra.

NIELSEN, CARL (1865-1931): Commotio for Organ, Opus 58; Concerto for Clarinet and Orchestra, Opus 57; Concerto for Flute and Orchestra; Little Suite for Strings, Opus 1; *Maskerade* Overture; Motets (3) for Mixed Voices; Quartet No. 2 in F Minor for Strings, Opus 5; Quartet No. 4 in F Major for Strings, Opus 44; Quintet for Winds, Opus 43; Symphony No. 1 in G Minor, Opus 7; Symphony No. 3, Opus 27 ("Sinfonia Espansiva"); Symphony No. 5; Symphony No. 6 ("Sinfonia Semplice").

NIN, JOAQUIN (1879-): Chants d'Espagne, for Violin and Piano.

NYSTROEM, GÖSTA (1890-): *The Merchant of Venice* (Theater Suite No. 4); Songs at the Sea, for Voice and Orchestra.

OFFENBACH, JACQUES (1819-1880): *La Belle Hélène* Overture; *Bluebeard* Overture and Suite; Chanson de Fortunio (for De Musset's *Chandelier); Fantasia for Orchestra; Gaîté Parisienne* (Ballet); *La Grande Duchesse de Gerolstein* Overture; *Helen of Troy* (Ballet Suite); *A Marriage by Lantern Light* Overture; *Orpheus in the Underworld* Overture; *Le Papillon* (Ballet-Pantomime).

ONSLOW, GEORGE (1784-1852): Nonet for Wind and String Ensemble, Opus 77; Piano Trios (10); Quintet for Wind Instruments, Opus 81; Septet for Piano, Flute, Oboe, and Strings; Sextet for Piano & Wind Instruments, Opus 79; Sextet for Piano, Flute, Oboe, and Strings; Solo Scena for Bass with Orchestra; Sonatas for Piano and Cello (3); Sonatas for Piano and Cello (3); String Quartets (36); String Quintets (34); Symphonies Nos. 1-4.

ORFF, CARL (1895-): *Antigone,* Orchestral Setting of Holderlin's translation of Sophocles; *Carmina Burana* (Secular Songs), a Scenic Oratorio; *Catulli Carmina,* for Solo Voices, 4 Pianos, Percussion; *Trionfo di Afrodite, for* Solo Voices, Chorus, and Orchestra.

PADEREWSKI, IGNAZ JAN (1860-1941): Album de Mai, scènes romantiques, for Piano, Opus 10; Chants du Voyageur, for Piano, Opus 8; Concerto in A Minor for Piano, Opus 17; Danses Polonaises, Opus 5, for Piano; Danses polonaises, Opus 9, for Piano; Deux Morceaux, Prelude and Minuet, Opus 1, for Piano; Elegie for Piano, Opus 4; Fantasie Polonaise for Piano & Orchestra, Opus 19; Introduction and toccata for Piano, Opus 6; Krakowiak for Piano, Opus 3; Legende No. 2 for Piano, Opus 20; Symphony in B Minor, Opus 24.

PAGANINI, NICCOLO (1782-1840): Caprices (24) for Violin Solo, Opus 1; *Il Carnevale di Venezia,* 20 Variations, Opus 10; Concert allegro moto perpetuo, Opus 11; Concerto in E Flat for Violin in D, Opus 6; Concerto for Violin in B Minor with Rondo à la Clochette (La Campanella), Opus 7; Concerto No. 4 in D Minor for Violin; Grand quartets (3), for Violin, Viola, Guitar, and Cello, Opera 4, 5; Quartet in E Major, for Strings; Sonatas (6) for Violin and Guitar, Opera 2, 3; *Le Streghe (Witches' Dance)* Variations on a theme by Simone Mayr, Opus 8; Variations on the G String on Rossini's *Moses.*

PAINE, JOHN KNOWLES (1839-1906): Prelude to Sophocles' Tragedy *Oedipus Rex,* Opus 35.

PAISIELLO, GIOVANNI (1740-1816): Concerto in C Major for Harpsichord; Concerto a cinque for Strings; Concertos (6) for Piano;

Dixit; Five-part Masses (2); Funeral March for General Hoche; Magnificat; Masses (30) for Double Choir and 2 Orchestras; Miserere; Passion Oratorio; Quartets (12) for Piano and Strings; Quartets (6) for Strings; *La Scuffiara* Overture; Solemn Masses (3) for Double Choir and 2 Orchestras; Sonata and Concerto for Harp; Symphonies No. 1-12; Te Deum for Double Choir and 2 Orchestras.

PALESTRINA, GIOVANNI PIERLUIGI DA (1525-1594): Hymns and Offertories a 4-5 (113); Improperia for Holy Week; Lamentations (9), each in several settings a 4-8; Litanies (10); Magnificat; Masses a 4-8 (93); Missa "Assumpta est Maria"; Missa "Iste Confessor"; Missa Sine Nomine; Missa Papae Marcelli; Missa "Veni Sponsa Christi"; Motets a 4-12 (181); Psalms (4); Sacred Italian Madrigals (56); Secular Italian Madrigals (83).

PALMER, ROBERT (1915-): Concerto for Five Instruments (Flute, Violin, Clarinet, English Horn, and Cello); K. 19-Elegy for Thomas Wolfe, for Orchestra; Quartet for Piano and Strings; Sonata for Piano; Sonata for Violin and Piano; Symphonic Variations for Large Orchestra; Trios 1 and 2 for Violin, Viola, and Cello; Variations, Chorale, and Fugue for Orchestra.

PALMGREN, SELIM (1878-): Ballade for Piano, Opus 18; Concerto in C Sharp Minor for Piano; Concerto in G Minor for Piano; Fantasy for Piano, Opus 6; Finnish Lyrics (12) for Piano, Opus 22; Finnish Suite for Piano, Opus 24; *Floden,* Symphonic Poem; *May Night,* for Piano; Preludes (24) for Piano, Opus 17; Sonata in D Minor for Piano.

PARADISI, PIETRO DOMENICO (1707-1791): Sonatas (12) for Harpsichord; Toccata in A Major for Harpsichord.

PERGOLESI, GIOVANNI BATTISTA (1710-1736): Cantatas (6) with String Accompaniment; Concerto No. 1 in G Major for String Orchestra; Concerto No. 2 in G Major for String Orchestra; Concerto No. 3 in A Major for String Orchestra; Concerto No. 4 in F Minor for String Orchestra; Concerto No. 5 in E Flat Major for String Orchestra; Concerto No. 6 in B Flat Major for String Orchestra; Concerto in G Major for Flute and Orchestra; *Giasone,* Cantata; Masses (2) for 5-Part Chorus with Orchestra; *The Nativity,* Oratorio; *Orfeo,* Cantata; *Salve Regina;* Sinfonia for Cello and Bass; Sonata No. 12 for Violin; Sonata in Stile di Concerto; Stabat Mater, for Soprano and Alto with String Orchestra and Organ; Trio Sonatas (30) for two Violins with Bass; Trio Sonata with String Orchestra.

PEROTINUS (c.1180-1236): Salvatoris Hodie, for Chorus; Viderunt Omnes, for Chorus.

PERSICHETTI, VINCENT (1915-): Concert for Piano 4 Hands, Opus 56; Divertimento for Band; *The Hollow Men,* for Trumpet and String Orchestra; Pastoral for Winds; Poems for Piano, Books 1 and 2; Psalm, for Band; Quintet for Piano and Strings; Symphonies Nos. 1-4; Trio for Violin, Cello, and Piano.

PETRASSI, GOFFREDO (1904-): *Don Quixote* (Ballet Suite).

PEZEL, JOHANN (1639-1694): Sonatas for Brass.

PFITZNER, HANS (1869-1949): *Das Christelflein* Overture; *Katchen von Heilbronn* Overture; Kleine Sinfonie, Opus 44; Symphony in C Major, Opus 46; Symphony in C Sharp Minor; Three Preludes from *Palestrina,* for Orchestra.

PHILLIPS, BEVVILL (1907-): Concerto for Piano and Orchestra; Music for Strings; Nine by Nine, Sonata for Piano; *Play Ball* (Ballet);

Princess and Puppet (Ballet); Selections from McGuffey's Reader, for Orchestra; Sonata for Cello and Piano; String Quartet No. 1; Symphony Concertante.

PICK-MANGIAGALLI, RICCARDO (1882-1949): Fugues for String Quartet.

PIERNÉ, GABRIEL (1863-1937): Sonata for Violin and Piano, Opus 46.

PIJPER, WILLEM (1894-1947): Concerto for Piano; Epigrams (6) for Orchestra; Symphony No. 3.

PISTON, WALTER (1894-): Chromatic Study on the Name of Bach, for Organ; Concerto for Orchestra; Concerto for Violin and Orchestra; Concertino for Pianoforte and Chamber Orchestra; Divertimento for Nine Instruments; *The Incredible Flutist* (Ballet); Partita for Violin, Viola, and Organ; Prelude and Fugue for Orchestra; Quintet for Flute and String Quartet; Sinfonietta; Sonata for Violin and Piano; Sonatina for Violin and Harpsichord; Suite for Orchestra; Symphonies Nos. 1-4; Trio for Violin, Cello, & Piano; *Tunbridge Fair*, for Band.

PIZZETTI, ILDEBRANDO (1880-): Cello Concertos (4); Concerto (2) for Piano; *Danza Bassa Dello Sparviero*, for Orchestra; Grand Sonatas (6) for Piano Solo; *La Pisanella*, for Orchestra; Quartets (6) for Flute and Strings; Septet for Strings with 2 Horns; Sextet for 2 Violins, 2 Violas, Cello, and Double-Bass; Sonatas for Piano 4 Hands; String Quartets (45); String Quintets, Books 1-5; Symphonies (29); Symphonies Concertantes (7), for 2 Violins, for Strings, for Strings and Wind, for Wind, or for Piano and Violin.

PLEYEL, IGNAZ (1757-1831): Symphony Concertante No. 5.

PONCHIELLI, AMILCARE (1834-1886): Dance of the Hours (from *La Gioconda),* for Orchestra.

POPOV, GABRIEL (1904-): Symphony No. 2 ("Patria").

PORPORA, NICCOLA (1686-1767): Arie for Cello and Strings; Cantatas for Voice with Harpsichord; Fugues (6) for Harpsichord; Sinfonie (6) da camera for 2 Violins, Cello, and Bass; Sonatas (12) for Violin with Bass.

PORTER, QUINCY (1897-): Concerto Concertante for Two Pianos; Dance in Three Time, for Orchestra; Incidental Music to *Sweeney Agonistes* (T. S. Eliot) and 3 Greek Mimes for String Quartet, Voices, and Percussion; Quartet No. 6, for Strings; Sonata for Horn and Piano; Sonata for Horn (or Cello) and Piano; Sonata No. 2 for Violin and Piano; String Quartets Nos. 1-7; Suite in C Minor for Orchestra; Symphony No. 1; Ukrainian Suite for Strings.

POULENC, FRANCIS (1899-): Aubade, Choreographic Concerto for Piano and 18 Instruments; *Le Bal Masqué*, for Voice and Orchestra; *Les Biches* (Ballet); *Cocardes* (Ballet); Concerto for Piano and Orchestra; Concerto in G Minor for Organ, Strings, & Tympani; Concerto in D Minor for Two Pianos and Orchestra; *Diana* (Ballet); *Football* (Ballet); *Les Mamelles de Tiresias* (Opera); *Les Mariés de la Tour Eiffel* (Ballet); Mouvements Perpetuels, for Piano; Nocturne in D Major, for Piano; Rhapsodie Nègre; Sextette for Piano and Winds; *Soirée Française* for Voice and Piano; *Les Soirées de Nazelles*, for Piano; *Sonata for Piano 4 Hands*; Sonata for Two Pianos; Sonata for Trumpet, Trombone, and Horn; Suite Française, for Piano; Trio for Piano, Oboe, and Bassoon.

PROKOFIEV, SERGE (1891-1953): *Alexander Nevsky (Cantata, Opus 78); Chout* Ballet,

Opus 21 ("Buffoon"); *Cinderella* (Ballet); *Cinderella* (Waltz); Classical Symphony in D Major, Opus 25; Concerto No. 1 in D Flat Major for Piano, Opus 10; Concerto No. 3 in C Major for Piano, Opus 26; Concerto No. 5 in G Major for Piano, Opus 55; Concerto No. 1 in D Major for Violin, Opus 19; Concerto No. 2 in G Minor for Violin, Opus 63; Divertimento, Opus 43, for Orchestra; *The Gambler* (4 Portraits) for Orchestra; *Lieutenant Kije* Suite, Opus 60; March (from *Love for Three Oranges); Music for Children*, for Piano; *On Guard* (Oratorio); Overture on Hebrew Themes, Opus 34, for Clarinet, Piano, and String Quartet; *Peter and the Wolf*, Orchestral Fairy Tale for Children, Opus 67; Prelude in C Major, for Harp, Opus 12 No. 7; *The Prodigal Son* (Ballet), Opus 46; Quartet No. 1 for Strings, Opus 50; Quartet No. 2 in F Major for Strings, Opus 92; Quintet for Strings, Opus 39; *Romeo and Juliet*, Opus 64 (Ballet); Scythian Suite for Orchestra, Opus 20; *Semyon Kotko* (Orchestral Suite); Sinfonietta, Opus 5/48; Sonata No. 2 in D Minor for Piano, Opus 14; Sonata No. 3 in A Minor for Piano, Opus 28; Sonata No. 4 in C Minor for Piano, Opus 29; Sonata No. 5 in C Major for Piano, Opus 38; Sonata No. 6 for Piano, Opus 82; Sonata No. 7 for Piano, Opus 83; Sonata No. 8 for Piano, Opus 84; Sonata No. 9 in C Major for Piano, Opus 103; Sonata in F Minor for Violin, Opus 80; Sonata in D Major for Violin, Opus 94; Sonata for 2 Violins, Opus 56; Sonata for Cello, Opus 119; *The Stone Flower* Ballet ("Gypsy Fantasy"); *The Stone Flower* ("Wedding Suite"); *Summer Day*, Children's Suite for Little Symphony, Opus 65B; Symphony No. 4 in C Major, Opus 47; Symphony No. 5 in B Flat Major, Opus 100; Symphony No. 6 in E Flat Minor, Opus 111; Symphony No. 7; Toccata in D Minor, for Piano, Opus 11; *The Ugly Duckling*, for Voice and Orchestra, Opus 18· *Visions Fugitives, for Piano, Opus 22; Winter Holiday*, for Chorus and Orchestra.

PURCELL, HENRY (c. 1658-1695): Anthems; Birthday Odes for Queen Mary; Chaconne in G Minor ("Great"), for String; Chaconne in G Minor ("London"), for Strings; *Come Ye Sons of Art*, for Solo Voices, Chorus, and Orchestra; Death of Dido, from *Dido and Aeneas* (Voice and Orchestra); *The Fairy Queen* (Incidental Music); Fantasies in Three, Four, & Five Parts, for Viols; Odes (3) for St Cecilia's Day; Suites for Harpsichord; *Timon of Athens* (Masque); Trio Sonatas (22), for 2 Violins and Continuo; Trumpet Voluntary, for Organ; Welcome Songs (29), including the Yorkshire Feast Song.

QUANTZ, JOHANN JOACHIM (1697-1773): Concerto No. 17 in D Major for Flute; Concerto in G Major for Flute; Concertos (300) for One and Two Flutes and Orchestra; Flute Pieces (200); Neue Kirchenmelodien; Sei Duetti for Flutes; Sonatas for Flute & Harpsichord.

RABAUD, HENRI (1873-1949): Concertino for Cello and Piano; Divertissement sur des chansons russes, for Orchestra, Opus 2; Eclogue, Poème Virgilien, Opus 6; *Job* (Oratorio); *Mârouf* (Ballet Music); *La procession nocturne*, Symphonic poem after Lenau, Opus 6; Quartet for Strings in G Minor, Opus 3; Symphony No. 2 in E Minor, Opus 5.

RACHMANINOFF, SERGEI (1873-1943): *The Bells*, Opus 35, for Chorus and Orchestra, after Poe; Concerto No. 1 in F Sharp Minor for Piano, Opus 1; Concerto No. 2 in C Minor for Piano, Opus 18; Concerto No. 3 in D Minor for Piano, Opus 30; Concerto No. 4 in G Minor for Piano, Opus 40; Etudes Tableaux for Piano, Opus 39; *The Isle of the Dead*, Opus 29, Tone Poem; Polka de W. R., for Piano; Preludes for Piano; Quartet in G Minor for Strings; Rhapsody on a Theme of Paganini, for Piano and Orchestra, Opus 43; Romance in E Flat Major for Piano, Opus 8, No. 2; Sonata No. 1 for Piano, Opus 28; Sonata No. 2 in B Flat Minor for Piano, Opus 36; Sonata in G Minor for Cello, Opus 19; Suite No. 1 for Two Pianos, Opus 5 ("Fantasy"); Suite No. 2 for Two Pianos, Opus 17; Symphonic Dances, for Orchestra; Symphony No. 1 in D Minor, Opus 13; Symphony No. 2 in E Minor, Opus 27; Symphony No. 3 in A Minor, Opus 44; Variations on a Theme of Chopin for Piano, Opus 22; Variations on a Theme of Corelli for Piano, Opus 42; Vocalise, Opus 34, No. 14, for Orchestra.

RAMEAU, JEAN PHILIPPE (1683-1764): *Diane et Acteon*, Cantata; *L'Impatience*, Cantata; *Les Paladins*, Suites Nos. 1 & 2 for Orchestra; Pièces de clavecin en concerts (with Violin or Flute, and Viol or Second Violin) (1741); Suites of Pieces for Harpsichord.

RAVEL, MAURICE (1875-1937): *Adélaide ou le langage des fleurs* (Ballet after *Valses nobles et sentimentales*); *Alborado del Gracioso*; for Orchestra; *Une Barque sur l'Ocean* for Orchestra; *Bolero*, for Orchestra; *Chansons Madécasses*, for Voice and Piano; *Chants Populaires*, for Voice and Piano; Concerto in G Major for Piano and Orchestra; Concerto for the Left Hand (Piano and Orchestra); *Daphnis et Chloë* (Ballet); *L'Enfant et les Sortilèges* (Opera); Five Greek Songs for Voice and Piano; *Gaspard de la Nuit*, for Piano; Hebrew Songs for Voice and Piano; *L'Heure Espagnole* (Opera); *Histoires Naturelles*, for Voice and Piano; Introduction and allegro for Harp, Flute, Clarinet, and String Quartet; *Jeux d'Eau*, for Piano; Menuet Antique, for Piano (or Orchestra); Menuet sur le Nom de Haydn, for Piano; *Miroirs*, for Piano *(Noctuelles; Oiseaux tristes; Une Barque sur l'Ocean; Alborado del Gracioso; La Vallée des Cloches);* Mother Goose Suite (originally 5 Children's Pieces for Piano 4 Hands, orchestrated in 1912 as a Ballet) *Pavane pour une Infante Défunte*, for Piano (or Orchestra); Pièce en Forme de Habanera, for Piano and Violin (or Cello); Poèmes de Stéphane Mallarmé; for Voice and Orchestra; Prelude in A Minor (1913), for Piano; Quartet in F for Strings; Rhapsodie Espagnole, Symphonic Suite; Shérérazade, for Voice and Orchestra; Sonata for Violin and Piano; Sonata for Violin and Cello; Sonatine for Piano; *Le Tombeau de Couperin*, Suite for Piano (or Orchestra); Trio in A Minor for Piano and Strings; Tzigane, Rhapsody for Violin and Orchestra; La Valse, a Choreographic Poem for Two Pianos or Orchestra; Valses Nobles et Sentimentales, for Piano (or Orchestra).

RAWSTHORNE, ALAN (1905-): Concerto No. 2 for Piano.

REED, H. OWEN (1910-): *Evangeline*, Orchestral Suite; *La Fiesta Mexicana*, for Wind Ensemble; *The Masque of the Red Death* (Ballet-Pantomime); Overture; Piano Sonata; String Quartet; Symphonic Dance; Symphony No. 1.

REGER, MAX (1873-1916): Aria, Opus 103a, for Violin and Piano; Ballet Suite, Opus 130 (Orchestra); Chorale Preludes, Opus 67, for Organ; Quintet in A Major for Clarinet and Strings, Opus 146; Serenade for Orchestra, Opus 95; Six Preludes and Fugues for Piano, Opus 99; Sonata No. 2 for Cello uanccompanied Opus 131c; Sonatines in F and A for Piano, Opus 89; Suite in G Major for Cello unaccompanied; Variations & Fugue on a Merry Theme of Hiller, for Orchestra, Opus 100; Variations & Fugue on an Original Theme, for Organ, Opus 73; Variation and Fugue on a Theme by Bach, for Piano, Opus 81; Variations and Fugue on a Theme by Beethoven, for 2 Pianos, Opus 86; Variations & Fugue on a Theme by Mozart, Opus 132, for Orchestra.

REICHA, ANTON (1770-1836): Decet for 5 Stringed and 5 Wind Instruments; Octet for 4 Stringed and 4 Wind Instruments; Overture; Quartet for 4 Flutes; Quartet (6) for Flute and Strings; Quartets (20) for Strings; Quintet for Clarinet; Quintet No. 2 in E Flat Major for Winds, Opus 88, No. 2; Quintet No. 9 in D Minor for Winds, Opus 91, No. 3; Quintets (24) for Flute, Oboe, Clarinet, Horn, and Bassoon; Quintets for Strings (5); Sonatas (12) for Violin and Piano; Symphonies (2); Trios (24) for 3 Horns; Trios (6) for Strings.

REINAGLE, ALEXANDER (1756-1809): Sonata in E Major for Piano.

RESPIGHI, OTTORINO (1879-1936): Ancient Airs and Dances, for Harp; *The Birds*, for Orchestra; *Brazilian Impressions*, for Orchestra; *Church Windows*, for Orchestra; Concerto Gregoriano, for Violin and Orchestra; *The Fountains of Rome*, for Orchestra; *The Pines of Rome*, for Orchestra; Quartet for Strings ("Doric"); *Roman Festivals*, for Orchestra; Rossiniana for Orchestra; *Il Tramonto*, for Voice and String Quartet; *Trittico Botticelliano*, for Orchestra.

REVUELTAS, SYLVESTRE (1899-1940): Cuauhnahuac, for Orchestra; Ocho por Radio (8 Musicians Broadcasting), for Orchestra; Sensemaya, for Orchestra; Songs for Voice and Piano; Three Pieces for Violin and Piano.

RICHTER, FRANZ XAVER (1709-1789): Concertos for Piano with String Orchestra (6); Duets for Flute (6); Quartets for Strings (6); Sonatas for Flute with Basso Continuo (6); Symphonies (69); Trios for Flute and Violin (8); Trio Sonatas for 2 Violins with Basso Continuo (12).

RIEGGER, WALLINGFORD (1885-): New Dance, for Orchestra; Quartet No. 2 for Strings; Quintet for Winds, Opus 51; Sonatina for Violin & Piano; Symphony No. 3.

RIETI, VITTORIO (1898-): Madrigale for Orchestra; *The Night Shadow* (Ballet); *Oedipus* (Ballet); Partita for Harpsichord, Strings, and Winds; Sinfonia Tripartita (Fourth Symphony); Sonata for Winds; Suite Champêtre for 2 Pianos; *Waltz Academy* (Ballet).

RIMSKY-KORSAKOV, NICOLAI (1844-1908): Capriccio Espagnol, Opus 34, for Orchestra; *Christmas Eve* (Orchestral Suite); Concerto in C Sharp Minor for Piano, Opus 30; *Conte féerique, for Orchestra, Opus 29; Le Coq d'Or Suite; Cortège des Nobles (from Mlada)* for Orchestra; *Dragonflies (Stekosy),* for 3-part Female Chorus and Orchestra, Opus 53; Fantaisie de concert in B Minor for Violin and Orchestra, Opus 33; Fantasy on Russian Themes, Opus 33, for Violin and Orchestra; Fantasy on Serbian Themes, Opus 6, for Orchestra; *Ivan the Terrible* Suite; Khorovod, for Strings; *Legend of the Invisible City of Kitzeh* Suite; *May Night* Overture; *Musikalische Bilder*, Suite from opera *Tsar Saltan*, Opus 57; *On the Tomb (Nad mogiloi)* for Orchestra, Opus 61; Quartet for Strings in F, Opus 12; Quintet in

B Flat Major for Piano and Winds; Russian
Easter Overture, Opus 36; *Sadko*, Symphon-
ic Poem, Opus 5; Scheherazade. Symphonic
Suite after "The Thousand and One Nights,"
Opus 35; *Skazka*, Opus 29, for Orchestra;
Slava (Glory) for Mixed Chorus and Orchestra,
Opus 21; The Song About Alexis (Stich ob
Aleksieie), for Mixed Chorus and Orchestra,
Opus 20; Suite for Cello and Piano, Opus 37;
Symphonietta on Russian Themes in A Minor,
Opus 31; Symphony No. 1 in E Minor,
Opus 1; Symphony No. 2, Opus 9 ("Antar");
Symphony No. 3 in C, Opus 32; Trio in
C Minor for Violin, Cello, and Piano; *Tsar
Saltan* Suite (See Musikalische Bilder).
RIVIER, JEAN (1896-): Symphony No. 2 for
Strings.
ROBINSON, EARL (1910-): Ballad for Amer-
icans, for Solo Voice, Mixed Chorus, and
Orchestra; *The Lonesome Train*, for Mixed
Chorus and Orchestra; Rhapsody in Brass,
for Trumpets and Trombone; *Sandhog*, for
Narrator, Vocal and Piano; Symphonic Frag-
ment for Chamber Orchestra; *Tower of Babel*,
for Mixed Chorus and Orchestra.
RODGERS, RICHARD (1902-): *Out of My
Dreams* (Ballet from *Oklahoma!*); *Slaughter
on Tenth Avenue* (Ballet); *Victory at Sea*,
Orchestral Suite.
ROGERS, BERNHARD (1893-): *Adonais*,
Poem for Orchestra; *Amphitryon*, Overture;
Japanese Landscapes, Orchestral Suite; *Pinoc-
chio*, for Orchestra; *Prelude to Hamlet*; Quar-
tet for Strings in D Minor; Soliloquy for
Flute and Strings; *The Song of the Nightin-
gale*, for Orchestra; Symphonies Nos. 1-4;
Three Japanese Dances, for Mezzo Soprano
and Orchestra; Two American Frescoes, for
Orchestra.
ROREM, NED (1923-): Sonata No. 2 for
Piano.
ROSENMÜLLER, JOHANN (c. 1620-1684):
Kernsprüche mehrentheils aus heiliger Schrift,
motets a 3-7 with instruments and continuo;
Trio Sonata No. 2 in E Minor, Strings &
Continuo; Sonate (42) de camera a 5 Stro-
menti; Studentenmusik von 3 und 5 Instru-
ment (Dance Music); Suite No. 9 in C Minor
from Studentenmusik.
ROSETTI, FRANCESCO (1750-1792): Concer-
tino in E Flat Major for Bassoon; Concertos
(4) for Clarinet; Concertos (4) for Flute;
Concertos (3) for Horns; Concertos (2) for
2 Horns, Oratorios *(Der sterbende Jesus,
Jesus in Gethsemane)*; Quartets (9) for Strings;
Requiem, Sextet for Flute, 2 Horns, and
Strings; Symphonies (34).
ROSSINI, GIOACCHINO (1792-1868): *La
Boutique Fantasque* (arr. Respighi) for Or-
chestra; Chant de Titans, for 4 Basses with
orchestra; *La Gazza Ladra* Overture; *Italian
Woman in Algiers* Overture; *The Journey to
Rheims* Overture; Messe Solennelle; O Salu-
taris for Vocal Quartet; Quartets for Wind
Instruments; Quoniam for Solo Bass with
Orchestra; *La Scala di Seta* Overture; *Semi-
ramide* Overture; *The Siege of Corinth* Over-
ture; *Il Signor Bruschino* Overture; Soirées
musicales (8 ariettas and 4 duets); Sonatas
Nos. 1-4 for Strings; Stabat Mater; *Tancredi*
Overture; Tantum Ergo, for 3 Male Voices
with Orchestra; *Il Turco in Italia* Overture;
William Tell (Ballet Music); *William Tell*
Overture.
ROUSSEL, ALBERT (1869-1937): *Bacchus et
Ariane*, Suites Nos. 1 & 2, Opus 43; Con-
certo for Piano, Opus 36; Concerto for Small
Orchestra, Opus 34; Divertissement for Wind
Instruments, Opus 6; *Evocations*, Three Sym-
phonic Sketches, Opus 15; Petite Suite, Opus

39, for Orchestra; *Le Poème de la Forêt*,
Symphony, Opus 7; Résurrection, Symphonic
Prelude, Opus 4; *The Sandman*, for Orches-
tra; *The Spider's Feast*, Opus 17 (Ballet
Pantomime); Sinfonietta for Strings, Opus 52;
Symphony No. 3 in G Minor, Opus 42; Trio
for Flute, Viola, & Cello, Opus 40.
ROZSA, MIKLOS (1907-): Concerto for
String Orchestra, Opus 17; Concerto for
Violin; *The Jungle Book* Suite, for Orchestra;
Quo Vadis Suite; *The Red House* Suite;
Spellbound Concerto; Theme, Variations, and
Finale for Orchestra, Opus 13; *The Thief of
Bagdad* Suite; *To Everything There is a
Season*, Motet for Mixed Chorus a cappella.
RUBBRA, EDMUND DUNCAN (1901-):
Missa in Honorem Sancti Dominici, Opus 66;
Sonata No. 2 for Violin.
RUBINSTEIN, ANTON (1830-1894): Caprice
Russe for Piano with Orchestra, Opus 102;
Concerto No. 4 in D Minor for Piano, Opus
70; Concerto for Violin in G, Opus 46;
Fantasia Eroica, for Piano with Orchestra,
Opus 110; Kammenoi-Ostrow, the Stone Is-
land with Palace in the Neva, 24 Pictures
for Piano Solo; *La Russie*, Symphonic Poem;
Suite for Orchestra in 6 Movements, Opus
119; Symphonies Nos. 1-6 (in F, Opus 40; in
C, Opus 42; in A, Opus 56; in D Minor,
Opus 95; in G Minor, Opus 107; in A Minor,
Opus 111).
RUGGLES, CARL (1876-): *Evocations*
(4 Chants for Piano); Men and Angels, for
Orchestra; Men and Mountains ("Lilacs"),
for Orchestra; Organum for Orchestra; Por-
tals, for String Orchestra; Sun Treader, for
Orchestra; Vox Clamans in Deserto, for Solo
Voice and Chamber Orchestra.
RUST, FRIEDRICH WILHELM (1749-1796):
Sonata for Viola.
SACCHINI, ANTONIO MARIA GASPERE
(1730-1786): *Oedipo a Colono* Overture.
SAINT-SAENS, CAMILLE (1835-1921): Allegro
Appassionato for Piano, Opus 70; Bacchanale
(*Samson et Dalila*), for Orchestra; Caprice
Andalouse, for Violin and Orchestra, Opus 122;
Caprice Arabe, for 2 Pianos, Opus 96;
Caprice Héroique, for 2 Pianos, Opus 106;
Caprice on Danish and Russian Airs, Opus
79, for Piano and 3 Winds; *Carnival of the
Animals*, for 2 Pianos and Orchestra; Christ-
mas Oratorio; Concert Piece for Harp and
Orchestra, Opus 154; Concerto No. 2 in G
Minor for Piano, Opus 22; Concerto No. 4 in
C Minor for Piano, Opus 44; Concerto No.
5 in F Major for Piano, Opus 103; Concerto
No. 3 in B Minor for Violin, Opus 61;
Concerto No. 1 in A Minor for Cello, Opus
33; *Danse Macabre*, Opus 40 (Symphonic
Poem); Fantasy for Violin and Harp, Opus
124; *Henry VIII* Ballet Music; Introduction
and Rondo Capriccioso, Opus 28, for Violin
and Orchestra; *Le Jeunesse d'Hercule*, Opus
50 (Symphonic Poem); Messe solonnelle, for
Solo Voices, Chorus, and Orchestra, Opus 4;
Les Noces des Promethée, Cantata for Solo
Voices, Chorus, and Orchestra, Opus 19;
Omphale's Spinning Wheel, Opus 31 (Sym-
phonic Poem); Overture de Fête, Opus
133; *Phaéton*, Opus 39 (Symphonic Poem);
Polonaise for 2 Pianos, Opus 77; *La Prin-
cesse Jaune* Overture; Rapsodie d'Auvergne,
for Piano and Orchestra, Opus 73; Rhapsodie
Brétonne, for Orchestra, Opus 7b; *Samson
and Delilah* (Ballet Music); Septet in E
Flat Major, Opus 65, for String Quartet,
Trumpet, and Piano; Six Bagatelles for Piano,
Opus 3; Sonata No. 1 in D Minor for
Violin, Opus 75; Sonata for Clarinet & Piano;
Symphony No. 1 in E Flat, Opus 2; Sym-

phony No. 2 in A Minor, Opus 55; Symphony No. 3 in C Minor, Opus 78; Three Preludes and Fugues for Organ, Opus 99; Valse gaie, for Piano, Opus 139; Valse Mignonne, for Piano, Opus 104; Variations on a Theme of Beethoven, Opus 35, for 2 Pianos; *Wedding Cake*, Opus 76, Caprice-Valse for Piano and String Orchestra.

SALIERI, ANTONIO (1750-1825): *Axur, Re d'Ormus* Overture.

SALZEDO, CARLOS (1885-): Bolmimbrie, for 7 Harps; Dances for Harp; Four Preludes to the Afternoon of a Telephone, for 2 Harps; Panorama, Suite for Harp Solo; Pentacle, for 2 Harps.

SAMMARTINI, GIOVANNI BATISTA (1700-1775): Concerto Grosso, Opus 11, No. 4, for Strings; Sonata in G Major for Cello & Continuo.

SARASATE, PABLO (1844-1908): Airs Ecossais, for Violin and Orchestra, Opus 34; Chansons Russe, for Violin and Orchestra, Opus 49; La Chasse, for Violin and Orchestra, Opus 44; Fantasia on *Carmen*, for Violin and Orchestra; Fantasia on *Faust*, for Violin and Orchestra; Jota de San Fermin, for Violin and Orchestra, Opus 36; Navarra, for 2 Violins and Orchestra, Opus 33; Nocturne-Sérénade, for Violin and Orchestra, Opus 45; Peteneras, Caprice for Violin and Orchestra, Opus 35; Rêve, for Violin and Orchestra, Opus 53; Spanish Dances, Opera, 32, 37, 38, 41, 42, 43, for Violin and Orchestra; Spanish Dances for Violin and Piano, Opera 21, 23, 26, 27, 28, 29, 30, 39; Zigeunerweisen, for Violin and Orchestra, Opus 20, No. 1.

SATIE, ERIK (1866-1925): Aperçus désagréables, for Piano; Enfantines, for Piano; En Habit de Cheval, for 2 Pianos; Gymnopédies for Piano (or Orchestra); Mass for the Poor; *Parade* (Ballet); Pièces froids, for Piano; *Socrate* (Symphonic Drama); Three Pieces in the Shape of a Pear, for 2 Pianos; *Uspud* (Ballet).

SCARLATTI, ALESSANDRO (1659-1725) Cantatas (over 600), Concerto No. 3 in F Major for Strings; Concerto No. 6 in F Major for Strings; Quartet in D Minor, for Strings; Quartettino, for Recorder, Violin, Oboe, Harpsichord and Cello; St. John Passion; Sinfonia No. 5 in D Minor; Stabat Mater; *Su le sponde del Tebro* (Cantata); Trio Sonata in F Major, for Recorder, Oboe, & Continuo.

SCARLATTI, DOMENICO (1685-1757) *The Good Humored Ladies* (Ballet Suite); Sonatas for Harpsichord (555); Sonatas for Violin & Harpsichord.

SCHILLINGS, MAX VON (1868-1933): Festlicher Marsche for Military Band, Opus 27; Glockenlieder, for Solo Voice and Orchestra, Opus 22· Hochzeitglocken, for Baritone, Chorus and Orchestra, Opus 26; *Meergruss and Seemorgen*, Symphonic Fantasies, for Orchestra, Opus 6; Songs, Opera 1, 2, 4, 7, 13, 14, 16, 17, 19.

SCHMITT, FLORENT (1870-): *En Été*, for Orchestra, Opus 3; *Ourvaçi* (Ballet); *Le Palais hanté*, Symphonic Study after Poe, Opus 49; Psalm XLVII, for Solo Voices, Chorus, and Orchestra; *Reflets d'Allemagne*, Orchestral Suite, Opus 28; Rhapsodie Viennoise, for Orchestra, Opus 53; *La Tragédie de Salomé*, Opus 50 (Ballet).

SCHNABEL, ARTUR (1882-1951): Concerto for Piano; Piano Pieces; Piece in 7 Movements, for P ano; Youth P ece, for Piano.

SCHÖNBERG, ARNOLD (1874-1951): Begleitmusik, for Orchestra, Opus 34; Canon for

String Quartet; Concerto for Piano and Orchestra, Opus 42; Concerto for String Quartet and Orchestra; Concerto for Violin and Orchestra, Opus 36; *Das Buch der hängenden Garten*, Opus 15, for Voice and Piano; Early Songs, Opera, 2, 3, 6, 14; *Erwartung*, Monodrama) Opus 17; Five Pieces for Orchestra; *Gurrelieder*, for Solo Voices, Chorus, and Orchestra; Herzgewächse, for Voice and Orchestra, Opus 20; Kammersymphonie No. 2; Kol Nidre, for Chorus and Orchestra; The New Classicism, for Solo Voices, Chorus, and Orchestra, Opus 28, No. 3; Ode to Napoleon Buonaparte for Reciter, String Quartet, or String Quartet and Piano; Piano Pieces, Opera 11, 25; Piano Pieces, Opus 33a & 33b; Pierrot Lunaire, for Voice and Chamber Ensemble; Quartet No. 1 in D Minor for Strings, Opus 7; Quartet No. 2 in F Sharp Minor for Strings, Opus 10; Quartet No. 3 for Strings, Opus 30; Quartet No. 4 for Strings, Opus 37; Serenade for Baritone and Instrumental Septet, Opus 24; Songs, Opus 48, for Voice and Piano; Suite for String Orchestra; A Survivor from Warsaw, for Narrator, Chorus, and Orchestra; Theme and Variations for Band, Opus 43; Theme and Variations for Orchestra, Opus 43b; Variations on a Recitative for Organ, Opus 40; Verklärte Nacht, Opus 4, for String Sextet or String Orchestra.

SCHUBERT, FRANZ (1797-1828): Adagio and Rondo for Piano, Opus 145; Allegretto in C Minor, for Piano; Andantino varié in B Minor, for Piano, Opus 84, No. 1; Auf dem Wasser zu singen, Barcarolle, Song with Piano; Deutsche Messe for 4-Part Mixed Chorus with Organ; *Die Schöne Müllerin*, Opus 25, Song Cycle of 20 Numbers with Piano; Divertissement à l'Hongroise, for Piano 4 Hands, Opus 54; Eine kleine Trauermusik, for Winds; Fantasia in C Major for Piano and Orchestra, Opus 15 ("Wanderer"); Fantasia in F Minor for Pianos, Opus 103; Gastein Symphony; German Dances for 2 Pianos (or Orchestra); Gesang der Geister über den Wassern, Opus 167, for Male Voices and Orchestra; Grand Duo for Piano Four Hand, Opus 140; *Der Hausliche Krieg*, for Solo Voices, Chorus, and Orchestra; Hommage aux belles Viennoises, Waltz for Piano, Opus 67; Hymn to the Sun, for Piano and Chorus; Impromptus for Piano, Opus 90 and Opus 142; Introduction and Variations for Flute and Piano, Opus 160; Italian Overtures in C Major and D Major, for Orchestra; Italian Songs; Ländler for Piano; Lebensstürme, for Piano 4 Hands, Opus 144; March in E Major for Piano; Marche Caracteristique in C Major for Pianos, Opus 121, No. 1; Marche Militaire, for Piano; Mass in A Flat Major; Mass in E Flat Major; Mass in G Major; Minuets for Orchestra; Minuet and Finale in F Major for Winds; Miriam's Siegesgesang for Solo, Chorus, and Piano; Moments Musicaux, for Piano, Opus 94; Nocturne for Cello and Piano in E Flat, Opus 148; Notre amitié, Rondo in D, for Piano 4 Hands, Opus 138; Octet for Strings, Horn, Bassoon, and Clarinet, Opus 166; Phantasie in C for Piano, Opus 159; Polonaises for Piano 4 Hands; Quartet No. 1 in B Flat Major for Strings; Quartet No. 2 in C Major for Strings; Quartet No. 3 in B Flat Major for Strings; Quartet No. 8 in B Flat Major for Strings; Quartet No. 10 in E Flat Major for Strings, Opus 125, No. 1; Quartet No. 11 in E Major for Strings, Opus 125, No. 2; Quartet No. 13 in A Minor for Strings, Opus 29; Quartet No. 14 in D Minor for Strings, Opus Posthumous

("Death and the Maiden"); Quartet No. 15 in G Major for Strings, Opus 161; Quartet in G Major for Flute, Guitar, Viola, and Cello; Quartettsatz in C Minor for Strings, Opus Posthumous; Quintet in A Major (Piano), Opus 114 ("Trout"); Quintet in C Major (Cello), Opus 163; Rondo in A Major for Pianos, Opus 107; Rondo in D Major for 2 Pianos, Opus 138; Rondo in A Major for Violin and Strings; Rondo brillant in B Minor for Piano and Violin, Opus 70; *Rosamunde*, Opus 26 (Ballet Music No. 2); *Rosamunde* Overture ("Alfonso und Estrella"); *Rosamunde* Overture ("The Magic Harp"); Scherzos for Pianos in B Flat Major and D Flat Major; Schwanengesang, for Voice and Piano; Snow White Suite (arr. Fekete); Sonata in A Major for Piano, Opus Posthumous; Sonata in B Flat Major for Piano, Opus Posthumous; Sonata in C Minor for Piano, Opus Posthumous; Sonata in E Major for Piano; Sonata in F Minor for Piano; Sonata in B Flat Major for Piano 4 Hands, Opus 30; Sonata in A Minor for Piano, Opus 42; Sonata in D Major for Piano, Opus 53; Sonata in G Major for Piano, Opus 78 ("Fantasy"); Sonata in A Major for Piano, Opus 120; Sonata in E Flat Major for Piano, Opus 122; Sonata in A for Piano, Opus 137; Sonata in A Minor for Piano, Opus 143; Sonata in B Flat Major for Piano, Opus 147; Sonata in A Minor for Piano, Opus 164; Sonata in C Major for Piano (1815); Sonata No. 1 in D Major for Violin, Opus 137 (Sonatina); Sonata No. 2 in A Minor for Violin, Opus 137; Sonata No. 3 in G Minor for Violin, Opus 137; Sonata No. 5 in A Major for Violin, Opus 162 ("Duo"); Sonata in A Minor for Cello, Opus Posthumous ("Arpeggione"); Songs for Male Chorus; Symphony in E Major (arr. Weingartner); Symphony No. 1 in D Major; Symphony No. 2 in B Flat Major; Symphony No. 3 in D Major; Symphony No. 4 in C Minor ("Tragic"); Smphony No. 5 in B Flat Major; Symphony No. 6 in C Major; Symphony No. 7 (9) in C Major ("The Great"); Symphony No. 8 in B Minor ("Unfinished"); Tantum Ergo (2) for 4-Part Mixed Chorus with Orchestra; Trio No. 1 in B Flat Major, Opus 99, for Piano and Strings; Trio No. 2 in E Flat Major, Opus 100, for Piano and Strings; Valses Nobles, for Piano, Opus 77; Valses sentimentales (34), for Piano, Opus 50; Variations in A Flat Major for Piano 4 Hands, Opus 35; Variations in B Flat Major for Piano 4 Hands, Opus 82, No. 2; Variations on a Theme of Diabelli, for Piano; *Die Winterreise*, for Voice and Piano.

SCHUMAN, WILLIAM (1910-): Concerto for Violin and Orchestra; *George Washington Bridge*, for Band; Prayer for Orchestra in Time of War; Quartets Nos. 1-4, for Strings; Symphonies Nos. 1-6; *This Is Our Time*, Secular Cantata No. 1 for Mixed Chorus and Orchestra; *Undertow* (Choreographic Episodes); *Voyage*, for Piano.

SCHUMANN, CLARA (1819-1896): Caprices in Waltz Form for Piano, Opus 2; Concerto in A Minor for Piano, Opus 7; Flüchtige Stücke, for Piano, Opus 15; Impromptu for Piano, *Souvenir de Vienne*, Opus 9; Lieder for Piano from Rollet's *Jucunde*, Opus 23; Polonaises for Piano, Opus 1; Preludes and Fugues for Piano, Opus 16; Romances, for Piano, Opus 11; Romances, for Piano, Opus 21; Romances, for Piano and Violin, Opus 22; Scherzo No. 1 for Piano, Opus 10; Scherzo No. 2 in C Minor, for Piano, Opus 14;

Trio in G Minor for Piano and Strings, Opus 17.

SCHUMANN, ROBERT (1810-1856): Abegg Variations for Piano, Opus 1; Adagio & Allegro for Cello, Opus 70; Album for the Young, for Piano, Opus 68; Andante and Variations in B Flat Major, for 2 Pianos, Opus 46; Arabesque for Piano, Opus 18; Ballszenen, 9 pieces for Piano Duet, Opus 109; Blumenstück, for Piano, Opus 19; Bunte Blätter, for Piano, Opus 99; *Carnaval*, for Piano, Opus 9; Concert Allegro in D Minor for Piano & Orchestra, Opus 134; Concerto in A Minor for Piano, Opus 54; Concerto in A Minor for Cello, Opus 129; Davidsbündler Dances, for Piano Opus 6; *Dichterliebe*, for Voice and Piano, Opus 48; *Die Braut von Messina*, Concert Overture, Opus 100; Fantasie in C Major for Piano, Opus 17; Fantasiestücke for Piano, Opus 12; Fantasiestücke for Piano and Clarinet, Opus 73; Fantasy for Violin and Orchestra, Opus 131; Faschingsschwank aus Wien, for Piano, Opus 26; Festouvertüre, Opus 123; Four Sketches for Organ, Opus 58; Frauenliebe und Leben, for Voice and Piano, Opus 42; Fugues (6) on B.A.C.H. for Piano or Organ, Opus 60; Fünf Stücke im Volkston, for Cello and Piano, Opus 102; *Hermann und Dorothea*, Concert Overture, Opus 136; Humoreske, for Piano, Opus 20; Impromptus on a Theme by Clara Wieck, for Piano, Opus 5; Intermezzi, for Piano, Opus 4; Introduction and Allegro Appassionato, for Piano and Orchestra, Opus 92; *Julius Caesar*, Concert Overture, Opus 128; Kinderball, for Piano Duet, Opus 130; Kinderscenen for Piano, Opus 15; Konzertstück for 4 Horns and Orchestra, Opua 86; Kreisleriana, for Piano, Opus 16; Liederkreis, for Voice and Piano, Opus 24; Liederkreis, for Voice and Piano, Opus 39; *Manfred* Overture, Opus 115; Märchenerzählungen, for Piano, Clarinet, Viola, Opus 132; Motet, *Verzweifle nicht im Schmerzenstal*, for Double Male Chorus (Organ ad lib), Opus 93; Myrthen, for Voice and Piano, Opus 25; Nachtstücke for Piano, Opus 23, Noveletten for Piano, Opus 21; Novelette No. 2 in D Major for Piano, Opus 21; Novelette No. 4 in D Major for Piano, Opus 21; Novelette No. 8 in F Sharp Minor for Piano, Opus 21; Overture, Scherzo, and Finale for Orchestra, Opus 52; Papillons, for Piano, Opus 2; The Prophet Bird, for Piano, Opus 82, No. 7; Quartet in A Minor for Strings, Opus 41, No. 1; Quartet in F Major for Strings, Opus 41, No. 2; Quartet in A Major for Strings, Opus 41, No. 3; Quartet in E Flat Major for Piano & Strings, Opus 47; Quintet in E Flat Major for Piano and Strings, Opus 44; Romances, for Piano, Opus 28; Romance in F Sharp Major for Piano, Opus 28, No. 2; Scherzo, Gigue, Romanze, und Fughetta for Piano, Opus 32; Sonata No. 1 in F Sharp Minor for Piano, Opus 11; Sonata No. 2 in F Minor for Piano, Opus 14; Sonata No. 3 in G Minor for Piano, Opus 22; Sonatas (3) for Piano, for the Young, Opus 118; Sonata No. 1 in A Minor for Violin, Opus 105; Studies for Piano after Caprices by Paganini, Opus 3; Symphonic Etudes, Opus 13, for Piano; Symphony No. 1 in B Flat Major, Opus 38 ("Spring"); Symphony No. 2 in C Major, Opus 61; Symphony No. 3 in E Flat Major ("Rhenish"); Symphony No. 4 in D Minor, Opus 120; Toccata in C Major, Opus 7, for Piano; Trio No. 1 in D Minor, for Piano and Strings, Opus 63; Trio No. 2 in F Major, for Piano and Strings, Opus 80;

Waldscenen for Piano, Opus 82; Warum, for Piano.

SCHÜTZ, HEINRICH (1585-1672): Cantiones Sacraea 4 with Continuo; Die 7 Worte Christi am Kreuz; Italian Madrigals; Kleine Geistliche Konzerte; Mehrchörige Psalmer, with Instruments and Continuo; Motets; Musicalische Exequien, for Solo Voices, Chorus, and Orchestra; Psalmen Davids deutsch durch Cornelium Beckern in 4 Stimmen gestellt; Sacred Choral Music, including Musicalia ad chorum sacrum with continuo (1648); Symphoniae Sacrae, for Voices and Instruments; St. John Passion, for Solo Voices, Chorus, and Orchestra; St. Matthew Passion; Weihnachts-Historie, for Solo Voices, Chorus, and Orchestra.

SCRIABIN, ALEXANDER (1872-1915): Concerto in F Sharp Minor for Piano, Opus 20; Poem of Ecstasy, Opus 54, for Orchestra; Prometheus: The Poem of Fire, Opus 60, for Orchestra; Sonata No. 3 in F Sharp Minor for Piano, Opus 23; Sonata No. 4 in Sharp Major for Piano, Opus 30; Symphony No. 2 in C Minor, Opus 29; Symphony No. 3 in C Major, Opus 43 ("Divine Poem").

SESSIONS, ROGER (1896-): The Black Maskers, Orchestral Suite; Chorale No. 1 for Organ; Chorale Preludes (4) for Organ; Concerto for Violin; From My Diary, for Violin and Piano; Quartet No. 1 for Strings; Quartet No. 2 for Strings; Sonata for Piano; Sonata No. 2 for Piano; Symphony No. 1; Symphony No. 2; Turn O Libertad, for Mixed Chorus and Piano 4 Hands.

SHAPERO, HAROLD (1920-): Nine Minute Overture; Serenade in D for String Orchestra; Sonata for Piano 4 Hands; Sonata for Violin and Piano; Symphony for Classical Orchestra; Three Amateur Sonatas for Piano; Three Pieces for Three Pieces, Flute, Clarinet, Bassoon; Trumpet Sonata for Trumpet and Piano.

SHAW, OLIVER (1779-1848): For the Gentlemen Suite, for Winds; Psalms and Ballads: Mary's Tears, The Inspiration, Sweet Little Ann, The Death of Percy.

SHOSTAKOVITCH, DMITRI (1906-): The Age of Gold, Opus 22 (Ballet); Ballet Russe; Ballet Suites Nos. 1, 2, 3; Children's Piano Pieces; Concerto for Piano and Orchestra, Opus 35; Concerto for Violin, Opus 99; Fall of Berlin Suite, for Orchestra; Fantastic Dances (3) for Piano; Preludes (24) for Piano; Preludes & Fugues for Piano, Opus 87; Quartet No. 1 for Strings, Opus 49; Quartet No. 2 for Strings, Opus 69; Quartet No. 4 for Strings, Opus 83; Quartet No. 5 for Strings, Opus 92; Quintet for Piano and Strings, Opus 57; Sonata No. 2 in B Minor for Piano, Opus 64; Song of the Forests, for Solo Voices, Chorus, and Orchestra, Opus 81; Symphony No. 1 in F Major, Opus 10; Symphony No. 5, Opus 47; Symphony No. 6, Opus 53; Symphony No. 7, Opus 60 ("Leningrad"); Symphony No. 9, Opus 70; Symphony No. 10 in E Minor, Opus 93; Trio in E Minor for Piano and Strings, Opus 67.

SIBELIUS, JAN (1865-1957): Atenarnes Sång (Song of the Athenians), for Male Chorus, Horn, Septet, Cymbals, Triangle, and Drum, Opus 31; The Bard, Opus 64, Symphonic Poem; Belsazars Gastmal, from the music to Belsazar, Opus 51; Canzonetta for String orchestra, Opus 62a; Concerto in D Minor for Violin, Opus 47; Dance Intermezzo, Opus 45, No. 2 (Orchestra); En Saga (A Legend), Opus 9, Symphonic Poem; Festivo, for Orchestra; Finlandia, Opus 26, Symphonic Poem;

Four Historic Scenes, Orchestral Suite, Opus 66; In Memoriam, Funeral March, Opus 59; Karelia Overture, Opus 10; Karelia Suite, Opus 11 (Orchestra); King Christian II Suite, Opus 27; Lemminkainen Suite (Orchestra); Lemminkainen's Return, Opus 22, No. 4 (Orchestra); Luonnotar, Symphonic Poem with Soprano Solo, Opus 70; Nightride and Sunrise, Opus 55, Symphonic Poem; The Oceanides, Opus 73, Symphonic Poem; Pelléas and Mélisande, Opus 46, Suite for Small Orchestra; Pohjola's Daughter, Opus 49, Symphonic Fantasy; Quartet in D Minor for Strings, Opus 56 ("Voces Intimae"); Rakastava Opus 14; Suite for Strings and Tympani; Romance in C Major for String Orchestra, Opus 42; Spring Song, Opus 16 (Orchestra); The Swan of Tuonela, Opus 22, No. 3, for Orchestra; Symphony No. 1 in E Minor, Opus 39; Symphony No. 2 in D Major, Opus 43; Symphony No. 3 in C Major, Opus 52; Symphony No. 4 in A Minor, Opus 63; Symphony No. 5 in E Flat Major, Opus 82; Symphony No. 6 in D Minor, Opus 104; Symphony No. 7 in C Major, Opus 105; Papiola, Opus 112, for Orchestra; The Tempest, Opus 109 (Prelude), for Orchestra; Valse Romantique for Small Orchestra, Opus 64; Valse Triste, from Incidental Music to Kuolema, Opus 44.

SIEGMEISTER, ELIE (1909-): American Holiday, for Orchestra; American sonata for Piano; Ozark Set, for Orchestra; Prairie Legend, for Orchestra; Rhapsody for Orchestra; Sonata for Violin and Piano; Strange Funeral in Braddock, for Solo Voice and Orchestra; String Quartet; Sunday in Brooklyn, for Orchestra; A Walt Whitman Overture, for Orchestra; Western Suite, for Orchestra; Woodwind Quintet.

SINDING, CHRISTIAN (1856-1941): Episodes Chevaleresque, Orchestral Suite, Opus 35; Legende for Violin and Orchestra, Opus 46; Rondo infinito, for Orchestra, Opus 42; Rustle of Spring, for Orchestra; Serenades (2) for 2 Violins and Piano, Opus 56, Opus 92; Suite in A Minor for Violin and Orchestra, Opus 10; Symphony in D Minor, Opus 21; Symphony in D, Opus 85.

SIQUEIRA, JOSE (1907-): Xango (Brazilian Negro Cantata).

SKILTON, CHARLES SANFORD (1868-1941): American Indian Fantasie for Cello and Orchestra; The Guardian Angel, Oratorio; Indian Dances for Orchestra (Deer Dance, War Dance); Overture in E Minor for Cello and Orchestra; Sonatina for Violin and Piano; The Witches' Daughter, Cantata.

SMETANA, BEDRICH (1824-1884): Am Seegstade, Concert Etude for Piano; The Bartered Bride Overture; Blaník, Symphonic Poem from the Cycle Má Vlast; Bohemian Dances, for Piano (or Orchestra); Fantasy for Violin and Orchestra; Festmarch in honor of Shakespeare's Tercentennial; From Bohemia's Meadows and Forests (Zčeských luhův a hajův), Symphonic Poem from the Cycle Má Vlast; The High Castle (Vyšehrad), Symphonic Poem from the Cycle Má Vlast; Libussa Overture; The Moldau (Vltava), Symphonic Poem from the Cycle Má Vlast; My Fatherland (Má Vlast), Cycle of Six Symphonic Poems; Polkas (3 sets), for Piano; Quartet in C for Strings; Quartet in E Minor for Strings ("From my Life"); Quartet in F for Strings; Richard III, Symphonic Poem; Sárka, Symphonic Poem from the Cycle Má Vlast; Tábor (The Camp), Symphonic Poem from the Cycle Má Vlast; Trio in G Minor for Strings, Opus 15; Triumph

Symphony; *Wallenstein's Camp*, Opus 14, Symphonic Poem; Wedding Scenes, for Orchestra.

SOR, FERNANDO (1778-1839): Studies and Variations for Guitar.

SPELMAN, TIMOTHY MATHER (1891-): *Barbaresques*, Orchestral Suite; *Five Whimsical Serenades* for String Quartet or Piano Suite; *Florentine Sketches*, Orchestral Suite; *Le Pavillon sur l'Eau*, for Flute, Harp, and Strings; *Saints' Days*, Symphonic Suite; Symphony in G Minor; *The Vigil of Venus*, for Soprano and Baritone, Chorus, and Orchestra.

SPOHR, LOUIS (1784-1859): Concertantes (2) for Violin and Orchestra; Concerto No. 7 in E Minor for Violin, Opus 38; Concerto No. 8 in A Minor for Violin, Opus 47; Concerto No. 9 in A Minor for Violin, Opus 47; Concerto in F Minor for Clarinet; Concerto for Quartet, Opus 131; *Faust* Overture; Grande Polonaise for Violin and Orchestra; *Jessonda* Overture; Nonet in F Major, Opus 31, for Violin, Viola, Cello, Double Bass, Flute, Oboe, Clarinet, Bassoon, and Horn; Overtures (8); Songs (6) for Mezzo, Clarinet, and Piano; Symphonies Nos. 1-9 (No. 1 in E Flat, Opus 20; No. 2 in D Minor, Opus 49; No. 3 in C Minor, Opus 78; No. 4 in F, Opus 86; No. 5 in C Minor, Opus 102; No. 6 in G, Opus 116; No. 7 in C, Opus 121; No. 8 in G Minor, Opus 137; No. 9 in B Minor, Opus 143).

STAINER, SIR JOHN (1840-1901): *The Crucifixion*, Cantata: *The Daughter of Jairus*, Cantata; *Gideon*, Oratorio; *St. Mary Magdalene*, Cantata.

STAMITZ, KARL (1746-1801): Concerto in D Major for Flute; Concerto in G Major for Flute; Concerto for Clarinet & Bassoon; Concertos (7) for Violin; Quartet for Winds, Opus 8, No. 2; Quartets for Strings, Opera 4, 7, 10, 13, 14, 15; Sinfonia Concertante in F Major; Symphonies (70); Symphony for Two Orchestras, Trios (6) for 2 Violins with Bass.

STEHMAN, JACQUES (1912-): Chant Funèbre, for Orchestra; Symphonie de Poche, for Orchestra.

STEIN, LEON (1910-): Concerto in A Minor for Violin and Orchestra; *Doubt* (Ballet); *Exodus* (Ballet); Hassidic Dances (3) for Orchestra; Passacaglia for Orchestra; Prelude and Fugue for Orchestra; Quartets (2) for Strings; Sinfonietta for String Orchestra; Suite for String Quartet; Symphony No. 1 in C; Symphony No. 2 in E Minor; Tryptych for Orchestra (after 3 poems by Walt Whitman).

STICH, JOHANN WENZEL (1746-1803): Concertos (14) for Horn; Duets for 2 Horns, and for Horn and Double Bass; Hymne à la liberté, with Orchestra; Quartets (24) for Horn and Strings; Quartet in F Major for Horn & Strings; Quintet for Horn, Flute, and Strings; Sextet for Horn, Clarinet, Bassoon, and Strings; Trios (20) for 3 Horns.

STRADELLA, ALESSANDRO (c. 1645-1682): *Il Barcheggio*, Cantata; *Susanna*, Oratorio; *San Giovanni Battista*, Oratorio; Trio Sonatas, for Strings & Continuo.

STRAUSS, JOHANN (1825-1899): *Le Beau Danube* (Ballet Suite); Dances (500) (including: The Beautiful Blue Danube; Roses from the South; Künstlerleben; Wiener Blut; The 1,001 Nights; Wine, Women, and Song; and Tales From the Vienna Woods); *Die Fledermaus* Overture; *Graduation Ball* (Ballet); *The Gypsy Baron* Overture; Perpetuum Mobile, Musical Joke, Opus 257; Treasure Waltz from *Der Zigeunerbaron*.

STRAUSS, JOHANN, SR. (1804-1849): Cotillons and Contre-danses (6); Galops (24); Marches (18); Polkas (13); Potpourris (6); Quadrilles (32); Waltzes (152) (including: Lorelei; Gabrielen; Taglioni; Cäcilien; Victoria; Kettenbrücken; and Bajaderen Walzer; Electrische Funken; Mephistos Höllenrufe, and Donau-Lieder).

STRAUSS, JOSEPH (1827-1870): Dances, Op. 1-283.

STRAUSS, RICHARD (1864-1949): An Alpine Symphony, Opus 64; *Also Sprach Zarathustra*, Opus 30, Tone Poem; *Aus Italien*, Opus 16, Symphonic Fantasy; *Le Bourgeois Gentilhomme* Suite, Opus 60; Burlesque in D Minor, for Piano and Orchestra; Concerto in D Minor for Violin, Opus 8; Concerto for Oboe and Small Orchestra; Concerto No. 1 in E Flat Major for Horn, Opus 11; Dance Suite after Couperin (1923), for Orchestra; *Death and Transfiguration*, Opus 24, Symphonic Poem; Divertimento after Couperin, Opus 86, for Orchestra; *Don Juan*, Opus 20, Symphonic Poem; *Don Quixote*, Fantastic Variations on a Theme of Knightly Character, Opus 35; Duet-Concertino for Clarinet and Bassoon; *Ein Heldenleben*, Opus 40, Tone Poem; Festmarsch in E Flat Major, Opus 1, for Orchestra; Four Last Songs, for Voice and Orchestra; *Josephslegende* (Ballet), Opus 63; *Macbeth*, Opus 23, Symphonic Poem; Metamorphoses, for Orchestra; *Der Rosenkavalier* Suite; *Salome* "Dance of the Seven Veils"), for Orchestra; *Schlagobers*, Opus 70 (Ballet); Serenade in E Flat Major, for Woodwinds, Opus 7; Sonata in B Minor for Piano, Opus 5; Sonata in E Flat Major for Violin, Opus 18; Sonata for Cello and Piano, Opus 6; Songs (including: Zueignung; Die Nacht; and Allerseelen, Opus 10; Ständchen and Barcarole, Opus 17; Breit über mein Haupt, Opus 19; Cäcilie; Heimliche Aufforderung; and Morgen, Opus 27; Traum durch die Dämmerung, Opus 29; Ich trage meine Minne, Opus 32); Suite in B Flat Major, Opus 4, for Winds; Symphonia Domestica, Opus 53; Symphony in F Minor, Opus 12; Symphony in E Flat Major for Winds, Opus Posthumous; *Taillefer* (Ballet for Chorus, Soloists, and Orchestra); *Till Eulenspiegel's Merry Pranks*, Opus 28, Tone Poem; Wanderers Sturmlied, Opus 14, for 6-Part Mixed Chorus and Orchestra.

STRAVINSKY, IGOR (1882-): *Apollon Musagètes (Ballet); Les Abeilles* (Ballet); *Le Baiser de la Fée* Ballet; Cantata (1952); Capriccio for Piano & Orchestra; *Chant du Rossignol*, Symphonic Poem; Chant Funèbre, Opus 6; Circus Polka (originally for Band, later Orchestrated); Concertino for String Quartet; Concerto for Piano & Wind Orchestra; Concerto for Two Solo Pianos; Concerto in D Major for Violin; Concerto in D Major for Strings; Danses concertantes (Ballet); Dumbarton Oaks Concerto, for Chamber Orchestra; Duo Concertant for Violin and Piano; Ebony Concerto; Elegie for Unaccompanied Violin; *Le Faune et la Bergère*, for Voice with Orchestra, Opus 2; *Feu d'artifice*, Fantasy for Orchestra, Opus 4; *The Firebird* (Ballet); *L'Histoire du Soldat* (Play with Music); In Memoriam Dylan Thomas, for Solo Voice and Chamber Ensemble; *Jeu de Cartes* (Ballet); Mass; *Les Noces* for Solo Voices, Choir and Orchestra; Norwegian Moods, Four Episodes for Orchestra; Octet for Wind Instruments; Ode (Eulogy-Eclogue-Epitaph), for Orchestra; *Oedipus Rex* (for Narrator, Solo Voices, Chorus, and Orchestra; *Petrouchka* (Ballet); Piano Rag Music; Pieces for Solo Clarinet; Pieces for String Quartet *(1914); Pulcinella* Suite (Ballet); *Renard for* Solo Voices, Chorus, and Orchestra; *Les rois des étoiles,* for Chorus and Orchestra; Russian Maiden's Song, for Violin and Piano; *Le Sacre du Printemps,* Pictures of Pagan Russia (Ballet); Scènes de ballet, for Orchestra; Scherzo fantastique, for Orchestra, Opus 3; Scherzo a la Russe, for Orchestra; Septet for Chamber Ensemble; Sonata for Piano; Sonata for Two Pianos; Songs (3) on Japanese Poems; Symphony No. 1 in E Flat Major, Opus 1; Symphony in C; Symphony of Psalms, for Chorus and Orchestra; Symphonies for Wind Instruments; Tango for Piano or Two Pianos; Three Easy Pieces (1917), for Piano Duet.

SUK, JOSEF (1874-1935) Dramatic Overture; *Ein Sommermärchen,* Opus 29, Symphonic Poem; Elegie for Violin and Cello, with String Quartet, Harmonium, and Harp. (Opus 23); Fantasie for Violin and Orchestra, Opus 24; Pieces (4) for Violin and Piano, Opus 17; *Praga,* Symphonic Poem, Opus 26; Scherzo fantastique for Orchestra, Opus 25; Serenade for String Orchestra, Opus 6; Symphony in E, Opus 14; Symphony in E Minor, Opus 27.

SULLIVAN, SIR ARTHUR S. (1842-1900): *Henry VIII* (Shakespeare), Incidental Music; Light Opera, in collaboration with William S. Gilbert (1836-1911) *(The Gondoliers; Iolanthe; The Mikado; Patience; H. M. S. Pinafore; The Pirates of Penzance; Princess Ida; Ruddigore; The Sorcerer; Trial by Jury; The Yeomen of the Guard); The Tempest* (Shakespeare), Incidental Music.

SUPPÉ, FRANZ VON (1820-1895): *The Beautiful Galatea* Overture; *Boccaccio* Overture; *Fatinitza* Overture; *Jolly Robbers* Overture; *Light Cavalry* Overture; Missa Dalmatica; *Morning, Noon, and Night in Vienna* Overture *Pique Dame* Overture; *Poet and Peasant* Overture; Requiem: L'estremeo quidrizio; Symphony.

SVENDSEN, JOHAN SEVERIN (1840-1911): *Carnival in Paris,* for Orchestra; *Norwegian Artists' Carnival,* for Orchestra, Opus 12; Norwegian Rhapsodies for Orchestra, No. 2, Opus 19; No. 3, Opus 21; Romance in G Major for Violin and Orchestra, Opus 26; Symphony No. 2 in B Flat Major, Opus 15.

SWEELINCK, JAN PIETERSZOON (1562-1621): Music for Harpsichord; Toccata in A Minor for Organ; Variations on "Mein junges Leben hat ein End" for Organ; Variations on "Unter den Linden grüne" for Organ.

SYLVA, JOHANN ELIAS DE (1716-1797): Symphonie Concertante for Piano & Orchestra, Opus 60; Symphony in D Major.

SZYMANOWSKI, KAROL (1883-1937): Concert Overture; Concerto for Violin and Orchestra, Opus 35; Etude in B Flat Minor for Piano, Opus 4, No. 3; *The Fountain of Arethusa,* for Violin and Piano; Preludes for Piano, Opus 1; Quartet in C Major for Strings, Opus 37; Romanze for Violin and Piano, Opus 23; Sonata in C Minor for Piano, Opus 8; Sonata in A for Piano, Opus 21; Sonata in D Minor for Violin, Opus 9; Songs, Opera 7, 11, 17, 22; Symphony in B; Symphony in F Minor; Variations for Piano, Opus 3, Opus 10.

TALLIS, THOMAS (1505-1585): *The Lamentations of Jeremiah,* for Chorus; Nata Lux de Lumine, Cantiones Sacrae No. 8; Short Service; Spem in alium non habui, Song of 40 parts for 8 5-part Choirs.

TANEYEV, SERGIUS (1856-1915): Suite de

Concert for Violin and Orchestra, Opus 28; Symphony No. 1 in C Minor, Opus 12.

TANSMAN, ALEXANDRE (1897-): Adagio and Allegro for Orchestra; Four Impressions for Woodwind Octet; *He, She, and I* (Ballet); *Isiah, the Prophet,* for Choir and Orchestra; Polish Rhapsody, for Orchestra; Serenades (3) for Orchestra; Symphonies Nos. 1-7; Triptych, for Strings; Variations on a Theme by Frescobaldi, for String Orchestra.

TARTINI, GIUSEPPE (1692-1770): Concerto in D Minor for Violin and Strings; Concerto in E Major for Violin and Strings; Concerto in F Major for Violin; Concerto No. 58 in F Major; Concerto in A Minor for Violin; Concerto in A Major for Cello & Strings; Quartet in D Major for Strings; Sonata in A Minor for Violin and Harpsichord; Sonata in B Minor for Violin and Harpsichord; Sonata in B Flat Major for Violin and Harpsichord; Sonata in D Major for Violin and Harpsichord; Sonata in G Major for Violin and Harpsichord: Sonata in G Minor ("Devil's Trill") for Violin and Harpsichord; Variations on a Theme of Corelli for Cello and Harpsichord.

TAYLOR, DEEMS (1885-): *Circus Day,* Opus 18, Orchestral Fantasy; *Through the Looking Glass,* Opus 12, Orchestral Suite.

TCHAIKOVSKY, PETER ILYICH (1840-1893): Album for the Young for Piano, Opus 39; Andante Cantabile (from String Quartet, Opus 11) for Orchestra; *Aurora's Wedding* (Ballet); Autumn Song, for Orchestra; Capriccio Italien, Opus 45, for Orchestra; Concert Fantasy for Piano and Orchestra, Opus 56; Concerto No. 1 in B Flat Minor for Piano, Opus 23; Concerto No. 2 in G Major for Piano, Opus 44; Concerto in D Major for Violin, Opus 35; 1812 Overture; Fantasia, for Orchestra; *Francesca da Rimini,* Opus 32, Orchestral Fantasy); *Hamlet,* Opus 67a (Overture-Fantasia); Liturgical Music; *Manfred,* Opus 58, Symphonic Poem; Marche Slave, for Orchestra; Meditation (Opus 42) for Violin and Piano; *The Months,* Twelve Pieces for Piano, Opus 37a; *Nutcraker* Suites, Nos. 1 and 2; Piano Pieces, Opus 19; Piano Pieces, Opus 40; Quartet No. 1 in D Major for Strings, Opus 11; Quartet No. 2 in F Major for Strings, Opus 22; Romance in F Minor for Piano, Opus 5; *Romeo and Juliet* (Fantasy Overture); *Souvenir de Hapsal* for Piano, Opus 2; *Souvenir d'un lieu cher,* 3 pieces for Violin and Piano, Opus 42; Serenade in C Major for Orchestra, Opus 48; Sérénade Mélancolique for Violin and Orchestra, Opus 26; *Sleeping Beauty* (Ballet); *The Snow Maiden,* Incidental Music; Sonata in G Major for Piano, Opus 37; *Souvenir de Florence,* Opus 70, Suite for Strings; *The Storm* Overture, Opus 76; Suite No. 1 in D Minor for Orchestra, Opus 43; Suite No. 2 in C Major, for Orchestra, Opus 53; ("Caracteristique"); Suite No. 3 in G Major for Orchestra, Opus 55; Suite No. 4 in G Major, for Orchestra, Opus 61 ("Mozartiana"); *Swan Lake* (Ballet): Symphony No. 1 in G Minor, Opus 13 ("Winter Reveries"); Symphony No. 2 in C Minor, Opus 17 ("Little Russian"); Symphony No. 3 in D Major, Opus 29, ("Polish"); Symphony No. 4 in F Minor, Opus 36; Symphony No. 5 in E Minor, Opus 64; Symphony No. 6 in B Minor, Opus 74 ("Pathetique"); *The Tempest,* Opus 18 (Symphonic Fantasia); Theme and Variations (from Suite No. 3), for Orchestra; Trio in A Minor (Piano, Violin, Cello), Opus 50; Two Piano Pieces (Nocturne and Humoreske), Opus 10; Variations on a Rococo Theme, for Cello & Orchestra, Opus 33; Waltz Scherzo.

TCHEREPNINE, ALEXANDER (1899-): Arabesques, for Piano; Bagatelles for Piano, Opus 5; Nocturne in G Sharp Minor for Piano; Sonata Romantique for Piano, Opus 4; Trio, Opus 34, for Strings.

TELEMANN, GEORG PHILIPP (1681-1767): Cantatas (Der Schulmeister; Das Glück; Die Landlust); Church Music with Organ or Orchestra (about 3000 pieces); Concerto in G Major for Viola; Concerto in A Minor for 2 Flutes; Concerto in B Flat Major for 2 Flutes; Concerto in F Minor for Oboe & Strings; Fantasias for Harpsichord; Oratorios: Der Tag des Gerichts; Ino); Overtures (600); Partita No. 5 in E Minor for Oboe and Harpsichord; Partita in G Major for Recorder & Continuo; Passions (44); Pimpinone ("The Unequal Marriage") (Opera); Quartet in D Minor for 3 Flutes & Continuo; Sonata in A Minor for Violin; Sonata in G Minor for Violin; Sonata in C Minor for Oboe and Harpsichord; Sonata in C Minor for Recorder, Oboe, & Harpsichord; Sonata in E Minor, for Recorder, Oboe, and Harpsichord; Sonata in G Major for Viola da Gamba & Continuo; Sonata a Tre in D Major for Flute, Gamba, & Continuo; Sonata Polonaise No. 2 for Violins & Continuo; Suite in D Major, for Orchestra; Suite in A Minor for Flute and Strings; Trio Sonata in E Major for Violins & Continuo; Trio in E Minor for Flute, Oboe, & Continuo; Trio Sonatas & Duetto for Flute, Violin, & Continuo.

TEMPLETON, ALEC (1909-): Quartet No. 1 for Strings; Trio for Flute, Oboe, & Piano.

THOMAS, AMBROISE (1811-1896): Les Archers de Bouvines, 4-part Male Chorus; The Atlantic, 4-part Male Chorus; Betty (Ballet); Le chant des amis, 4-part Male Chorus; Fantaisie for Piano and Orchestra; Le Forgeron, 4-part Male Chorus; France! France! 4-part Male Chorus; Hommage à Boieldieu, Cantata; Marche religieuse; Messe solennelle; Motets (3) with Organ; Neapolitan canzonets (6); La nuit du Sabbat, 4-part Male Chorus; Paris, 4-part Male Chorus; Quartet in E for Strings; Quintet in F for Strings; Raymond Overture; Requiem; The Roman Carnaval, 4-part Male Chorus; Le Salut aux chanteurs, 4-part Male Chorus; The Temple of Peace, 4-part Male Chorus; La Tempête (Ballet); Les Traîneaux, 4-part Male Chorus; Trio in D Minor for Strings; Le Tyrol, 4-part Male Chorus; La Vapeur, 4-part Male Chorus.

THOMPSON, RANDALL (1899-): Jazz Piano, for Piano and Orchestra; The Piper at the Gates of Dawn, for Orchestra; Quartet No. 1 in D Minor for Strings; Sonata for Piano and Chamber Orchestra; Suite for Oboe, Clarinet, and Viola; Suite for Piano and Chamber Orchestra; Symphony No. 1; Symphony No. 2 in E Minor; The Testament of Freedom, for Men's Voices with Piano (or Orchestra or Band).

THOMSON, VIRGIL (1896-): Acadian Songs & Dances (from The Louisiana Story); Capital, Capitals, for Four Men and Piano; Election Day, Orchestral Suite; Filling Station (Ballet); Five Songs from William Blake for Voice and Orchestra; Forty Portraits for Violin, Violin and Piano, Piano Solo; Quartet No. 2 for Strings; Serenade in Five Movements for Flute and Violin; Sonata da Chiesa for 5 Instruments; Stabat Mater, for Soprano and String Quartet; Suite for Orchestra, No. 1; Suite for Orchestra, No. 2; Symphony on a Hymn Tune; Symphony No. 2; Synthetic Waltzes for Piano; Three Pictures for Orchestra.

TOCH, ERNST (1887-): Big Ben, Variationphantasy on the Westminster Chimes, for Orchestra; Chinese Flute, for Orchestra; Circus Overture; The Idle Stroller, Suite for Orchestra; Pinocchio, a Merry Overture; Poems to Martha, Quintet for Voice and Strings, Opus 66; Quintet for Piano and Strings, Opus 64; Studies for Beginners, for Piano, Opus 59; Symphony No. 3, Opus 75; Trio for Violin, Viola, and Cello.

TOMKINS, THOMAS (1572-1656): Balletti da camera a 3 violini e bass continuo, Opus 1; Music for Organ & Harpsichord; Sinfonie a 2-4 stromenti, Opus 3.

TORELLI, GIUSEPPE (c. 1660-1708): Concerto in D Minor for Violin, Strings & Continuo; Concerti Grossi Nos. 1-12, Opus 8, for Strings.

TURINA, JOAQUIN (1882-1949): Canto a Sevilla, for Voice and Orchestra; Ciclo Pianistico, for Piano; Danzas Fantasticas, for Piano and Orchestra; Danzas Gitanas, for Piano; Le Jeudi Saint a Minuit, for Piano; Mujeres Espanolas, for Piano, Opus 17; Music for Guitar; Ninerias (Petite Suite pour Piano); La Oracion del Torero, Opus 8, for String Quartet (or Orchestra); Poema Fantastico, for Piano, Opus 98; La Procesion del Rocio, for Orchestra; Recuerdos de la Antigua Espana, for Piano; Rhapsodia Symphonica, for Piano and Orchestra; Scene Andalouse, for Piano, Viola, and Strings; Singonia Sevillana.

VALENTINI, GIUSEPPE (1681-1740): Sonata No. 4 in E, for Cello and Continuo.

VALERIUS, ADRIANUS (1575-1625): Songs, for Choir.

VARÈSE, EDGARD (1885-): Ameriques, for Orchestra; Arcana, for Orchestra; Density 21.5, for Solo Flute; Equatorial, for Organ, Percussion, Brass, Theremin Instrument, and Baritone Voice; Espace, for Orchestra; Hyperprism, for Chamber Orchestra; Integrales, for Percussion Orchestra; Ionization, for 13 Percussion Players; Metal, for Soprano and Orchestra; Octandre, for Percussion Orchestra; Offrandes, for Soprano Voice and Chamber Orchestra; Symphony with Chorus.

VAUGHAN WILLIAMS, RALPH (1872-): Boldrewood, Orchestral Impressions; Bucolic Suite for Orchestra; Concerto Academico in D Minor for Violin; Concerto for Oboe and Strings; Fantasia for Piano and Orchestra; Fantasia on Greensleeves, for Orchestra; Fantasia on the Old 104th Psalm Tune, for Piano, Chorus, and Orchesrta; Fantasia on a Theme by Tallis for String Orchestra; Five Mystical Songs for Baritone Solo and Mixed Chorus; Five Tudor Portraits for Chorus and Orchestra; Flos Campi, for Viola, Chorus and Orchestra; For All the Saints, a Hymn; The Garden of Proserpine, for Mixed Chorus; Harnham Down, Orchestral Impressions; Heroic Elegy, for Orchestra; The House of Life (Rossetti), Song Cycle; Job: A Masque for Dancing; Mass in G Minor for Chorus and Orchestra; Old King Cole (Ballet Suite); On Wenlock Edge, Song Cycle for Tenor Voice, String Quartet, and Piano; Quartet for Strings in C Minor; Quartet for Strings in G Minor; Quintet in G Minor for Piano, with Violin, Clarinet, Cello, and Horn; Quintet in C Minor, with Violin, Viola, Cello, and Double Bass; Sancta Civitas ("The Holy City"), Cantata; Sea Chantys (3) for Chorus; A Sea Symphony (Whitman) for Solo Voices and Chorus; Serenade for Small Orchestra; Serenade to Music for 16 Solo Voices and Orchestra; Sonata in A Minor for Violin; Songs from Pilgrim's Progress for Solo Voices and Piano; Songs of

Travel (Stevenson), Song Cycle for Voice and Piano; Suite of English Folk Songs; Symphony No. 1 ("A Sea Symphony"); Symphony No. 2 ("London"); Symphony No. 3 ("Pastoral"); Symphony No. 4 in F Minor; Symphony No. 5 in D Major; Symphony No. 6 in E Minor; Symphony No. 7 ("Antarctica"); Symphony No. 8 in D Minor; Three Nocturnes for Baritone Solo; Three Norfolk Rhapsodies in E Minor, D Minor, and G Minor, for Orchestra; Three Studies in English Folk Songs for Violin and Piano; Toccata Marziale, for Winds; *Towards the Unknown Region* (Whitman), for Mixed Chorus; *The Wasps*, Incidental Music (Orchestra); *Willow Wood*, Cantata for Baritone and Female Chorus.

VERDI, GIUSEPPE (1813-1901): *Aïda* Prelude; *Aïda* (Ballet Music); Composizioni da Camera, for Soprano and Piano; Concertos (6) and Variations for Piano; *La Forza del Destino* Overture; *Guarda che bianca luna*, Nocturne for Soprano, Tenor, and Bass, with Flute Obligato; Hymn of the Nations, for Choir and Orchestra; *The Lady and the Fool* (Ballet Suite); *Luisa Miller; Manzoni Requiem; Messa; Nabucco* Overture; Pater Noster, for 5-part Chorus a capella; Quartet in E Minor for Strings; Quattro Pezzi sacri (Ave Maria and Stabat Mater for Mixed Chorus a capella; Laudi alle Vergine Maria for Female Chorus a cappella; Te Deum for Double Chorus with Orchestra); Requiem, for Solo Voices, Choir, and Orchestra; Songs for Bass: *L'Esule* and *La Seduzione*; Symphonies (2); Tantum Ergo (3); Te Deum, for Double Chorus with Orchestra; *I Vespri Siciliani* Overture.

VERRALL, JOHN WEEDON (1908-): *The Children*, Overture for Orchestra; Concert Piece for Strings and Horn; *Portrait of a Man*, for Orchestra; Prelude & Allegro for Strings; Quartet No. 4 for Strings; Serenade for Clarinet, Horn, and Bassoon; Six Variations for Orchestra; Sonata for Horn and Piano; Sonata for Viola and Piano; Symphonies Nos. 1 and 2; Trio for Strings (2 Violins, Viola).

VICTORIA, TOMAS LUIS DE (c. 1558-1611): Hymni totius anni a 4, with 4 psalms a 8; Magnificats a 4, with 4 antiphones to the Virgin; Masses a 4-8; Missa Dominicalis; Missa Pro Defunctis & Magnificat IV Toni; Motet: Jesu, dulcis memoria (Hymnus for 4 Voices on the hymn of St. Bernard of Clairvaux); Motetta festorum totius anni cum communi sanctorum a 5-8; Officium defunctorum sex vocibus: Requiem for the Empress; Officium hebdomadae sanctae; O Magnum Mysterium (Mass); O Quam Gloriosum (Mass).

VIEUXTEMPS, HENRI (1820-1881): Andante and Rondo for Violin and Piano, Opus 27; Ballade et Polonaise for Violin and Orchestra, Opus 38; Concerto No 2 in E for Violin and Orchestra, Opus 10; Concerto No. 5 in A Minor for Violin, Opus 37; Fantasia appassionata for Violin and Orchestra, Opus 35; Fantaisie Caprice, Opus 11, for Violin and Orchestra; Grosse Fantasie über slavische Volksmelodien for Violin and Piano, Opus 27; Hommage à Paganini, for Violin and Piano, Opus 9; Marche funèbre for Violin and Piano, Opus 58; Old England, Caprices on English Airs of the 16th and 17th centuries, for Violin and Orchestra, Opus 42; Sonata in D for Violin and Piano, Opus 12; Souvenirs de Russie, Fantasy for Violin and Orchestra, Opus 21; Suite in B Minor, for Violin and Piano, Opus 43.

VILLA-LOBOS, HEITOR (1887-): Ave Maria No. 20 for Chorus; The Baby's Family, for Piano; Bachianas Brasileiras No. 1, for Chamber Orchestra; Bachianas Brasileiras No. 3, for Piano and Strings; Bachianas Brasileiras No. 4, for Piano; Bachianas Brasileiras No. 5, for Voice and Orchestra; Bachianas Brasileiras No. 6 for Flute and Bassoon; Bashianas Brasileiras No. 8, for Orchestra; The Children's Doll Suite, for Piano; Chôros No. 2, for Flute and Clarinet; Chôros No. 4, for Chamber Orchestra; Chôros No. 5, for Piano; Chôros No. 6, for Orchestra; Chôros No. 7, for Chamber Orchestra; Cirandas, for Piano; Concerto for Piano and Orchestra; Duo for Violin and Viola; Momoprecoce for Piano; Nonetto, for Chorus; *The Origin of the Amazon River*, for Orchestra; Poeme Singelo, for Piano; Preludes (5), for Guitar; Quintette en forme de Chôrus, for Winds; Quatuor, for Chorus; Rude Poeme, for Piano; Saudades das Selvas Brasileiras, for Piano; Serestas (Brazilian Serenades), for Voice; Suite Floral, for Piano, Opus 97; The Three Maries, for Piano; Uirapurú, for Orchestra.

VINCI, LEONARDO DA (1690-1730): Danza Antiche for Strings.

VIOTTI, GIOVANNI BATTISTA (1753-1824): Concertantes (2) for 2 Violins; Concertos (29) for Violin, especially Concerto No. 22 in A Minor; Divertissements (3) for Violin alone; Duos (51) for 2 Violins; Nocturnes for Violin and Piano; Quartets (21) for Strings; Sonata for Piano; Sonatas for Violin and Piano.

VITALI, GIOVANNI BATTISTA (c. 1665-1697): Chaconne for Violin and Figured Bass.

VIVALDI, ANTONIO (c. 1675-1741): *Beatus Vir* (Oratorio); Concerti Grossi Nos. 1-12 for Strings, Opus 3 ("L'Estro Armonico"); Concertos Nos. 1-12 for Violin, Strings, & Continuo, Opus 4 ("La Stravaganza"); Concertos Nos. 1-12 for Violin, Opus 8 ("Il Cimento"); Concertos Nos. 1-12 for Violin, Strings, & Continuo, Opus 9 ("La Cetra"); Concertos Nos. 1-6 for Flute, Opus 10 (No. 2 in G Minor: "La Notte; No. 3 in D Major "The Bullfinch"; Concerto in C Major for Orchestra ("San Lorenzo"); Concerto in C Major for Violin, 2 Cellos, Strings, & Harpsichord; Concerto in C Major for 2 Flutes; Concerto in C Major for 2 Trumpets; Concerto in C Major for Bassoon; Concerto in C Minor for Violin ("Il Sospetto"); Concerto in C Minor for 2 Violins, Harpsichord, and Strings; Concerto in D Major for 2 Violins & 2 Cellos; Concerto in D Minor for Viola d'Amore; Concerto in D Minor for Strings & Harpsichord ("Madrigalesco"); Concerto in E Major for Violin ("Il Riposo"); Concerto in E Flat Major for Violin, Opus 33, No. 1; Concerto in E Flat Major for 2 Trumpets; Concerto in F Major for 3 Violins and Strings; Concerto in G Major for Strings and Cembalo ("Alla Rustica"); Concerto in G Major for Cello, Strings, and Cembalo; Concerto in G Minor for Violin, Opus 12, No. 1; Concerto in G Minor for 2 Violins, Cello, & Strings; Concerto in G Minor for Flute, Oboe, & Bassoon; Concerto in G Minor ("For the Dresden Orchestra"); Concerto in A Major for Viola d'Amore; Concerto in A Minor for 2 Violins; Concerto in A Minor for 4 Violins; Concerto in A Minor for Viola d'Amore, Strings, and Cembalo; Concerto in A Minor for Bassoon, Strings, & Harpsichords; Concerto in B Flat Major for Violin ("Funebre"); Concerto in B Flat Major for 2 Violins; Concerto in B Flat Major for Bassoons & Strings ("La Notte"); Concerto in B Flat Major for Oboe & Violin; Dixit (Psalm 109), for Solo Voices, Chorus, and Orchestra; Gloria, for Solo Voices, Chorus, and Orchestra; In Honore del Principe Darmstadt, for Voice and Orchestra; *Juditha Triumphans*, for Solo Voices, Chorus, and Orchestra; *Laudate Pueri*, for Solo Voices, Chorus, and Orchestra; *La Ninfa e Il Pastore* ("Serenata A Tre"), Solo Voices and Orchestra; Salve Regina, for Voice and Orchestra; *The Seasons* for Violin and Orchestra, Opus 8; Stabat Mater; Symphony for Strings in B Minor ("Al Santo Sepolcro").

WAGNER, RICHARD (1813-1883): Bacchanale from *Tannhäuser*, Brünnehilde's Immolation from *Die Götterdämmerung*; *Die Meistersinger*: Prelude; A Faust Overture; *The Flying Dutchman* Overture; Funeral Music from Die Götterdämmerung; Klingsor's Magic and Flower Maidens' Scene from *Parsifal*; *Lohengrin*: Prelude, Act I; *Lohengrin*: Prelude, Act III; *Magic Fire Music*, Act III, *Die Walküre*; *The Ride of the Valkyries*, Act III, *Die Walküre*; *A Siegfried Idyl*; *Tannhäuser* Overture; Transformation Scene from *Parsifal*; *Tristan and Isolde*: Prelude and Love Death; Waldweben (Forest Murmurs) from *Siegfried*; *Wesendonck Songs for Soprano* and Orchestra (or Piano).

WALDTEUFEL, EMIL (1837-1912): The Skaters Waltz.

WALTON, SIR WILLIAM (1902-): *Belshazzar's Feast*, for Solo Voice, Chorus, and Orchestra; Concerto for Violin and Orchestra; Concerto for Viola; Coronation Marches for Orchestra; *Façade* (Ballet); Orb and Sceptre, for Orchestra; *Portsmouth Point* Overture; Quartet in A Minor for Strings; Quartet for Piano & Strings; *Scapino* (A Comedy Overture); Siesta for Orchestra; Sonata for Violin and Piano; *The Wise Virgins* (Ballet Suite).

WARD, ROBERT (1917-): Adagio & Allegro for Orchestra; Jubilation Overture; Symphony No. 3.

WAXMAN, FRANZ (1906-): Sinfonietta for Strings and Tympani.

WEBER, CARL MARIA VON (1786-1826): *Abu Hassan*, Singspiel; *Battle and Victory* (Cantata); Concerto No. 1 in C Major for Piano, Opus 11; Concerto No. 2 in E Flat Major for Piano, Opus 32; Concerto No. 1 in F Minor for Clarinet, Opus 73; Concerto No. 2 in E Major for Clarinet, Opus 74; Concertino in C Minor for Clarinet, Opus 26; Concerto in F Major for Bassoon, Opus 75; *Euryanthe* Overture; Grand Duo Concertante, Opus 48, for Clarinet and Piano; *Invitation to the Dance*, for Orchestra, Opus 65; Konzertstück in F Minor for Piano and Orchestra; Pieces for Piano 4 Hands; *Preciosa* Overture; Sonata No. 1 in C Major for Piano, Opus 24; Sonata No. 2 in A Flat Major for Piano, Opus 39; Sonata No. 4 in E Minor for Piano, Opus 70; Sonatas Nos. 1-6 for Violin, Opus 10; Symphony No. 1 in C Major; Symphony No. 2 in C Major.

WEBER, BEN (1916-): Symphony on Poems of William Blake, Opus 33.

WEBERN, ANTON (1883-1945): Five Movements for String Quartet; Piano Variations; Second Cantata, to the Child of God; String Trio, Opus 20; String Quartet; Symphony; Variations for Piano and Orchestra.

WEIGL, KARL (1881-1949): Fifth Symphony in C Minor (Apocalyptic); Fourth Symphony in F Minor; Quartet No. 1 in A For Strings, Opus 4; Quartet No. 6 in C Major for Strings, Opus 37; Rhapsody in C Minor for Piano and Orchestra; Sinfonische Fantasie, Opus 16; Sonata for Viola, Opus 38; Symphony in E Flat, Opus 5; Trio in D Minor for Violin, Cello, and Piano; *Vienna, the City That Was*; Dances from Old Vienna

for Orchestra; Songs, Opus 36, for Voice and String Quartet.

WEILL, KURT (1900-1950): *The Ballad of Magna Charta*, Cantata; Concerto for Violin & Wind Orchestra, Opus 12.

WEINBERGER, JAROMIR (1896-): *Schwanda* (Polka and Fugue), for Orchestra.

WEISS, KAREL (1862-): Bohemian Dance No. 3 for Orchestra.

WIDOR, CHARLES (1845-1937): Symphony No. 5 in F Minor, Opus 42, No. 1; Symphony No. 6 in G Minor, Opus 42, No. 2; Symphony No. 9 ("Gothique"); Symphony No. 10 ("Romane"); Variations from Symphonie Gothique.

WIENIAWSKI, HENRI (1835-1880): Caprices for Violin in A Major, E Flat Major; Concerto No. 2 in D Minor, Opus 22 for Violin and Orchestra; Polonaises for Violin in A Major, in D Major; Scherzo-Tarantelle, Opus 16, for Violin; Souvenir de Moscou, Opus 6, for Violin.

WILBYE, JOHN (1574-1638): Madrigals.

WOLF, HUGO (1860-1903): Gedichte von Erchendorff, 20 poems, 1886-88, Songs; Gedichte von Goethe, 51 poems, 1888-89, Songs; Gedichte von Mörike, 53 poems, 1888, Songs; Italian Serenade for String Quartet; Italienisches Liederbuch, 46 poems, 1896; Lieder nach verschiedenen Dichtern, 31 poems, 1877-97, Songs; Songs: Zwölf Lider aus Jugendzeit (1877-78); Spanisches Liederbuch, 44 poems, 1889-90, Songs.

WOLF-FERRARI, ERMANNO (1876-1948): Impromptus for Piano, Opus 13; Kammersymphonie in B Flat, Opus 8; Quintet in D Flat for Piano, Opus 6; Serenade for String Orchestra; Sonata for Violin in G Minor, Opus 1; Trio for Piano in D, Opus 5; Trio in F Sharp Major for Piano, Opus 7.

WOLKENSTEIN, OSWALD VON (c. 1377-1445): Lieder, for Voices and Instruments.

YSAYE, EUGENE (1858-1931): Sonata No. 3 in E Minor for Solo Violin, Opus 27; Sonata No. 4 in D Minor for Solo Violin, Opus 27.

Musical Instruments, Classification of

See also **Oriental Orchestra; Symphony Orchestra**

Classification of Musical Instruments

AUTOPHONES OR IDIOPHONES: Are instruments made of materials that are naturally resonant and need only the action of a player, whether by striking, plucking, rubbing, blowing, or stamping, to produce sound.

MEMBRANOPHONES: Are instruments that produce sound by the vibration of membranes or skins stretched over openings and struck, rubbed, blown, or oscillated; the largest category of membranophones is composed of drums.

CHORDOPHONES: Are instruments with strings that are set vibrating by plucking, striking, rubbing, and by the simple or regulated action of air currents.

AEROPHONES: Are instruments that produce sound by the vibrations of an air column through contact with some device or appliance such as a whistle-head, or reed, or by the compressed lip action of the player.

ELECTROPHONES: Are either electromechanical and produce sound by ordinary vibrations which are changed from mechanical to electric, or radioelectric and produce sound by altering the distinct frequency of an oscillating electric circuit.

Class I
Autophones or Idiophones

BY STRIKING (CONCUSSION INSTRUMENTS: Castanets (one-handed—clashed directly); cymbals (two-handed-clashed directly); rattles (strung, sliding, contained—shaken directly); bells (empty, clapper; suspended, resting; single, in sets or chimes—struck directly); litophones or sonorous rocks (struck directly); metallophones or gongs (struck directly); triangle (struck directly with iron rod); xylophones (wood or metalstruck directly); carillons (keyboard, foot); dulcitone keyboard); clock chimes (automatic).
BY PLUCKING: Jaw's or Jew's harp (plucked directly with finger); notched rattles (tongue oscillated by ratchet wheel); claviola (keyboard); musical boxes (automatic).
BY RUBBING OR FRICTION: Musical glasses or glass harmonica (rubbed directly with moistened fingers); nail violin, nail harmonica (bow); clavicylinder (keyboard); barrel Aiuton, nagelklavier (automatic).
BY BLOWING: Cracker glass, or Schall glass (vibrated directly by player's breath); aeolsklavier (automatic).
BY STAMPING: Stamping pit (stamped with feet); stamping gourds, stamping sticks, stamping tubes (pounded against ground).

Class II
Membranophones

BY STRIKING (PERCUSSION INSTRUMENTS): Tambourine (rim-frame jingling drum—struck directly with hand); timbrel (rimframe, usually hoop-shaped drum, predecessor of Tambourine); bass or Turkish drum (cylinder frame—struck directly with heavy stick); tenor drum (cylinder frame—struck directly); side drum (cylinder frame—struck directly); kettle drum (bowl frame—struck directly); handle drum (whirled by handle with a ratchet wheel to engage hammers); pedal drum (pedal); barrel drum (automatic).
BY FRICTION: Rommelpot (stick in drum head rubbed directly with moistened fingers to set up vibrations); brummtopf (cord in drum head rubbed to cause vibrations); waldteufel, or forest devil (friction cord in drum head attached to rod and whirled to set up vibrations.
BY BLOWING (SYMPATHETIC OR CO-VIBRATION): Kazoo, mirliton (breath of player vibrated by stretched membrane); onion flute, flûte eunuque (breath of player vibrated by stretched membrane).
BY VIBRATION: Gourd xylophone or marimba (gourd resonator under each bar amplifies sound when bar is struck); gramaphone (automatic).

Class III
Chordophones

BY PLUCKING: Harp (many open strings running vertically to soundboard); lyre (box, or bowl; neckless; open strings; plucked or bowed); musical bow (separate resonator, gourd, or mouth; neckless; open string); psaltery (neckless; open, usually gut-string);

zither (neckless; fretted string); cithara, or cither (neck—plucked directly); guitar (neck—plucked directly); lute (neck—plucked directly); harpsichord (keyborard); virginal (keyboard); barrel spinet (automatic).
BY STRIKING: Dulcimer (neckless—struck directly); tambourin à cordes, tambourin du Béarn (neckless—struck directly); clavichord (keyboard—struck directly); piano (keyboard struck directly); pianola (automatic—struck directly).
BY FRICTION: Crwth (ancient Welsh bowed lyre, neckless); harpa, talharpe, or tannenharfe (archaic Scandanavian bowed lyre; neckless); rebec (neck, bowed); viol (neck, bowed); violin (neck, bowed) marine trumpet, tromba marina, or trumscheit (neck, bowed); hurdygurdy (keyboard); nyckelfiol or nyckel harpa (Swedish keyboard instrument); celestina (automatic); violina (automatic).
BY AIR: Aeolian harp (neckless-played directly by the winds); anemocorde or aeroclavicorde (keyboard).

Class IV
Aerophones

BY COMPRESSED LIPS OF PLAYER, OR LIP-VOICED; Natural horn (simple conical tube with holes); ophicleide or keyed serpent (conical tube with holes, a large key bugle, now replaced by the valve tuba of the modern orchestra); slide horn (conical tube with slide); cornet (conical tube, valved); valve horn (conical tube); natural trumpet (simple cylindrical tube); keyed trumpet (cylindrical tube with holes); slide trombone (cylindrical tube); slide trumpet (cylindrical tube); valve trombone (cylindrical tube); valve trumpet (cylindrical tube).
BY OSCILLATING A REED, OR REED-VOICED; Clarinet (cylindrical tube with single reed, tongue vibrating on frame); krumhorn (cylindrical tube with double reed); saxophone (conical tube with single reed); oboe (conical tube with double reed); bassoon (conical tube with double reed); mouth organ or Mundharmonika (free reed, tongue vibrating within frame); bagpipe (with finger holes, chanter, and usually double reed, voiced indirectly); harmonium (keyboard, free reeds, voiced indirectly); accordion, or Ziehharmonika (keyboard, free reeds, voiced indirectly); regal (small reed organ, voiced indirectly); barrelorgan (automatic).
FLUE-VOICED; Panpipe or syrinx (several simple vertical flutes bound together, open or end-stopped); kaval (simple vertical open tube, end blown; Slovakian); flageolet, flautino, or flauto piccolo (whistle-blown); recorder, blockflöte, flauto dolce, flûte douce (inverted conical bore, seven front holes, one high dorsal hole, whistle-blown); transverse flute (side-blown); ocarina (globular beaked flute with whistle head and eight fingerholes); pipe organ (keyboard, voiced indirectly); bird organ (automatic, voiced indirectly).

Class V
Electrophones

BY OSCILLATION (HETERODYNE FREQUENCY): Thereminvox or Aetherophone (1924) (frequency controlled directly by player's hand); Electronde (frequency controlled directly by player); Trautonium (1930) (frequency controlled directly by elementary keyboard; monophonic); Hellertion (1928) (frequency controlled directly by a type of elementary keyboard; polyphonic); radio organ (Paris, 1932) (frequency controlled indirectly by keyboard, seventy-six stops, three manuals, pedal; polyphonic).

ELECTROMAGNETIC: Hammond Organ (1939) (frequency controlled indirectly by keyboard; polyphonic).

ELECTROSTATIC: Compton Organ (frequency controlled indirectly by keyboard; polyphonic).

Names, Most Popular Boys'

AARON: (Heb) enlightened; otherwise, mountaineer.
ABEL:(Heb) breath; vapor; vanity.
ABIEL: (Heb) father of strength.
ABIJAH: (Heb) Jehovah is father. Dim. Biji.
ABNER: (Heb.) father of light.
ABRAHAM: (Heb.) father of a multitude. Dims. Abe, Abie.
ABRAM: (Heb.) father of elevation. Dims. Abe, Abie.
ABSALOM: (Heb.) father of peace.
ADALBERT: (Gk.) see Albert, Ethelbert.
ADAM: (Heb.) earth man; red man; red earth. Dim. Ad.
ADOLPHUS: (Ger.) noble wolf; noble hero. Dim. Adolf, Adolph.
ADRIAN: (Lat.) of Adria (Italy). See Hadrian.
AENEAS: (Lat.) commended.
ALAN: (Celt.) harmony; otherwise, (Slav.) hound. Perhaps form of Hilary. Also, Allan, Allen. Dim. Al.
ALARIC: (Ger.) ruler; noble ruler; all-rich.
ALASTAIR: Scots form of Alexander. Also, Alister.
ALBERT: (Ger.) illustrious; nobly bright; all bright. Dims. Bert, Bertie.
ALBION: (Celt.) land of white cliffs. Old and poetic name for England.
ALDOUS: (Ger.) old.
ALEXANDER: (Gk.) helper of men; defender. Dims. Alec, Aleck, Alex, Sanders, Sandy.
ALEXIS: (Gk.) help; defense.
ALFONSO: See Alphonsus.
ALFRED: (Ger.) helper; counselor; an elf (wizard) in council. Dims. Alf, Alfie.
ALGERNON: (O.F.) Whiskered. Dim. Algie.
ALLAN: See Alan.
ALMERIC: (Ger.) work; rule. Form of Emery.
ALONZO: Same as Alfonso.
ALOYSIUS: (Lat.) Grace. Also, Aloys.
ALPHEUS: (Gk.) deputy.
ALPHONSUS: (Ger.) all-ready; willing; brave. Also, Alfonso, Alphonso.
ALVAN: (Heb.) iniquity. Also, Alvah.
ALVIN: (Ger.) winning all. Also, Alwin.
AMADEUS: (Lat.) lover of god.
AMARIAH: (Heb.) whom God (Jehovah) promised.
AMASA: (Heb.) bearer of burden.
AMBROSE: (Gk.) divine; immortal.
AMOS: (Heb.) strong; courageous; burden.
ANASTASIUS: (Gk.) rising up.
ANDREW: (Gk.) manly; courageous; strong. Dims. Andy, Drew.
ANEURIN: (Welsh)) honorable. Also, Aneirin. Dim. Nye.
ANGUS: (Gaelic) choice.
ANSELM: (Ger.) protection of God.
ANTHONY: (Lat.) praiseworthy; priceless. Also Antony. Dim. Tony.
ARCHIBALD: (Ger.) outstandingly bold; holy prince. Dims. Archie, Baldie.
ARNOLD: (Ger.) strong as an eagle. Dim. Arnie.

ARTEMAS: (Gk.) gift of Artemis (Diana).
ARTHUR: (Celt.) high; noble. Dims. Art, Artie.
ASA: (Heb.) physician; healer.
ASAHEL: (Heb.) made of God.
ASAPH: (Heb.) collector.
ASHER: (Heb) happy; fortunate.
ASHUR: (Heb.) black; blackness.
ATHANASIUS: (Gk.) immortal.
ATHELSTAN: (O.E.) noble stone.
AUBREY: (Ger.) ruler of spirits.
AUGUSTINE: (Lat.) belonging to Augustus (the Roman Emperor). Also, Augustin. Dims. Austin, Gus, Gussie.
AUGUSTUS: (Lat.) exalted; majestic; imperial. Dims. Augie. Gus, Gussie.
AURELIUS: (Lat.) golden.
AUSTIN: Dim. of Augustine.
AYLMER: (Ger.) renowned; famous. Also. Elmer.
ALWYN: (Ger.) noble friend.
BALDWIN: (Ger.) bold winner; bold friend.
BAPTIST: (Gk.) purifier.
BARDOLPH: (Ger.) bright wolf. Also, Bardolf.
BARNABAS: (Heb.) son of exhortation, or consolation. Also, Barnaby. Dim. Barney.
BARNARD: Same as Bernard.
BARRY: (Irish) spear.
BARTHOLOMEW: (Heb.) son of Talmai; brotherly; otherwise, warlike son. Dim. Bart.
BASIL: (Gk.) kingly; royal.
BENEDICT: (Lat.) blessed. Also, Benedick, Bennet, Bennett.
BENJAMIN: (Heb.) son of the right hand. Dims. Ben, Bennie, Benny.
BENNET: same as Benedict.
BERNARD: (Ger.) bold as a bear; strong bear. Also, Barnard. Dim. Barney.
BERTRAM: (Ger.) bright raven; fair; illustrious. Dims. Bert, Bertie.
BILL: Dim. of William.
BLAISE: (Fr.) sprouting forth.
BOB: Dim. of Robert.
BONIFACE: (Lat.) benefactor.
BORIS: (Russ.) fighter.
BRIAN: (Celt.) strong.
BRUCE: From surname.
BRUNO: (Ger.) brown.
BURT: (Scots) from surname.
BURTON: From a place name. Dims. Bertie, Burt.
CADWALLADER: (Celt.) battle-arranger.
CAESAR: (Lat.) hairy; blue-eyed; also, born through Caesarean operation.
CALEB: (Heb.) bold; impetuous; otherwise, dog.
CALVIN: (lat.) bald. Dim. Cal.
CANDIDE: (Lat.) white; pure; innocent.
CARL: Form of Charles.
CASIMIR: (Polish) peacemaker.
CASPER: Form of Jasper. Also, Caspar.
CECIL: (Lat.) dim-sighted.
CEDRIC: Literary name derived from character in Sir Walter Scott's *Ivanhoe*.
CEPHAS: (Aramaic) stone.
CHARLES: (Ger.) noble-spirited; manly; strong. Dims. Charlie, Charley.
CHESTER) (Lat.) warlike; or, fort.
CHRISTIAN: (Lat.) belonging to Christ; follower of Christ. Dims. Chris, Christie, Christy.
CHRISTOPHER: (Gk.) Christ-bearer. Dims. Chris, Christie, Christy, Kester, Kit.
CLARENCE: (Lat.) illustrious; bright. Also, Clarence.
CLAUDE: (Lat.) lame. Also, Claud, Claudius.
CLEMENT: (Lat.) mild-tempered, even-tempered; merciful. Dim. Clem.
CLIVE: (Eng.) from surname.
COELIUS: (Lat.) heavenly.
COLIN: (O. E.) peasant; otherwise, from Nicholas.

CONRAD: (Ger.) able counselor.
CONSTANT: (Lat.) constant; firm; faithful.
CONSTANTINE: (Lat.) resolute; firm; faithful.
CORNELIUS: (Lat.) horn (uncertain). Dim. Corny.
COSMO: (Gk.) order.
CRISPIN: (Lat.) curly-headed. Also, Crispian, Crispus.
CURTIS: (O.F.) courteous. Dim. Curt.
CUTHBERT: (O. E.) notably splendid.
CYPRIAN: (Gk.) of the island of Cyprus.
CYRIL: (Gk.) lordly.
CYRUS: (Persian) sun: throne. Dim. Cy.
DAMIAN: (Gk.) tamer.
DANIEL: (Heb.) divine judge; God is my judge. Dims. Dan, Danny.
DARIUS: (Persian) preserver.
DAVID: (Heb.) beloved. Dims. Dave, Davy.
DEMETRIUS: (Gk.) belonging to Demeter (Ceres), the earth goddess; sprung from the earth.
DENNIS: Form of Dionysius. Also, Denis.
DEREK: Form of Theodoric. Also, Derrick, Derrick, Diedrik, Dietrich.
DESMOND: (Irish) from surname.
DEXTER: (Lat.) right hand; fortunate.
DICK: Dim. of Richard.
DION: Dim. of Dionysius.
DIONYSIUS: (Gk) belonging to Dionysius (Bacchus), the wine god. Also, Denis, Dennis, Dion.
DOMINIC: (Lat.) belonging to the Lord. Also, Dominick. Dim. Dom.
DONALD: (Celt.) proud chief; ruler of the world. Dims. Don, Donnie.
DOUGLAS: (Celt.) dark gray. Dims. Doug, Dougie, Dug.
DUNCAN: (Celt.) brown chief; brown warrior.
DUNSTAN: (O. E.) hill-stone.
DWIGHT: From surname.
EAMON: (Irish) form of Edmund.
EBEN: (Heb.) stone.
EBENEZER: (Heb.) stone of help, or salvation.
ED: Dim. of Edgar, Edmund, Edward.
EDGAR: (O. E.) giver of happiness; happy spear. Dims. Ed, Eddie, Eddy, Ned, Neddy.
EDMUND: (O. E.) defender of happiness, or property. Dims. Ed, Eddie, Eddy, Ned, Neddy.
EDWARD: (O. E.) guardian of happiness; rich guardian. Dims. Ed, Eddie, Eddy, Ned, Neddy.
EDWIN: (O. E.) gainer of happiness: happy friend. Dims. Ed, Eddie, Eddy, Ned, Neddy.
EGBERT: (O. E.) bright sword; famous swordsman. Dim. Bert.
ELBERT: Form of Albert.
ELDRED: (O. E.) great counsel; terrible. Also, Aldred.
ELEAZER: (Heb.) whom God helps, or helped.
ELI: (Heb.) exalted; or, foster son.
ELIAS: form of Elijah.
ELIHU: (Heb.) God the Lord.
ELIJAH: (Heb.) Jehovah is my God.
ELISHA: (Heb.) God is my salvation.
ELLIS: (Heb.) form of Elisha.
ELMER: (O. E.) form of Aylmer.
EMERY: (Ger.) work, rule. Also, Emmery, Emory.
EMLYN: (Welsh) diligent.
EMMANUEL: (Heb.) God with us. Also, Immanuel.
ENOCH: (Heb.) consecrated; dedicated; skilled.
ENOS: (Heb.) man.
EPHRAIM: (Heb.) very fruitful; double fruitfulness.
ERASMUS: (Gk.) beloved; lovable. Dim. Ras.
ERIC: (O. N.) brave; powerful; rich.
ERNEST: (Ger.) earnest. Dims. Ern, Ernie.
ERNST: (Ger.) form of Ernest.

ETHAN: (Heb.) strength; firmness.
ETHELBERT: (O. E.) nobly bright. Dim. Bert.
EUGENE: (Gk.) Wellborn; noble. Dim. Gene, Genie.
EUSEBIUS: (Gk.) pious.
EUSTACE: (Gk.) fruitful.
EVAN: (Celt.) young warrior.
EVELYN: Form of Evelina, used as both male and female.
EVERARD: (Ger.) strong as a boar.
EWEN: (Gaelic) youth. Also, Ewan.
EZEKIEL: (Heb.) strength of God. Dim. Zeke.
EZRA: (Heb.) help.
FABIAN: (Lat.) belonging to Fabius.
FARQUHAR: (Gaelic) manly.
FELIX: (Lat.) happy.
FERDINAND: (Ger.) brave; valiant, risks life. Also, Fernando. Dim. Ferdie.
FERGUS: (Gaelic) most choice.
FINLAY: (Gaelic) sunbeam.
FRANCIS: (Ger.) free. Dim. Frank.
FREDERICK: (Ger.) peaceful ruler; abounding in peace. Dims. Fred, Freddie, Freddy.
GABRIEL: (Heb.) strong man of God; strength. Dim. Gabe.
GAMALIEL: (Heb.) recompense of God.
GARRET: (Ger.) firm spear; good spearsman. Also, Gareth, Garrett, Gerald, Gerard.
GAVIN: (Welsh) hawk. Also, Gawain.
GENE: Dim. of Eugene.
GEOFFREY: (Ger.) at peace with God; joyful. Also, Jeffrey. Dim. Jeff.
GEORGE: (Gk.) landholder; husbandman. Dims. Georgie, Geordie, Dod.
GERALD: (Ger.) spearman. Also, Gerard. Dims. Gerry, Jerry.
GERARD: (Ger.) strong with the spear. Dims. Gerry, Jerry.
GERSHOM: (Heb.) exile.
GERVASE: (Ger.) spear-servant. Also, Jervis.
GIDEON: (Heb.) destroyer; woodsman.
GILBERT: (Ger.) famous; yellow-bright. Dims. Bert, Gil.
GILES: (Gk.) shield-bearer; otherwise, kid.
GODARD: (Ger.) pious; virtuous.
GODFREY: (Ger.) at peace with God.
GODWIN: (O. E.) friend of God; otherwise, good fighter.
GORDON: (Celt.) generous hospitality. From surname. Also, Gordan, Gorden.
GRAHAM: (Scots) from surname.
GREGORY: (Gk.) watchful.
GRIFFITH: (Welsh) red brown; otherwise, with great faith.
GUSTAVUS: (Ger.) warrior; hero; or, staff of meditation.
GUY: (F.) leader.
HADRIAN: (Lat.) from place name in Latin, "black earth." Same as Adrian.
HAL: Dim. of Harold.
HANNIBAL: (Punic) grace of Baal (sun god of the Chaldean trinity).
HAROLD: (Ger.) general of an army. Dims. Hal, Harry.
HARRY: Dim. of Harold, Henry.
HECTOR: (Gk.) holding fast.
HENRY: (Ger.) head of a house; chief. Dims. Hal, Hank, Harry, Hen, Henny.
HERBERT: (O. E.) glory of the army; or, glorious army. Dims. Bert, Bertie, Herb, Herbie.
HERCULES: (Lat.) pride of Hera (Juno), goddess wife of Zeus (Jupiter). Also, Heracles, Herakles.
HERMAN: (Ger.) warrior. Also, Hermann.
HEZEKIAH: (Heb.) strength of the Lord.
HILARY: (Lat.) cheerful; merry.
HILDEBRAND: (Ger.) battle sword.
HIRAM: (Heb.) high born; most noble. Dims. Hi, Hy.

HORACE: (Lat.) sunlight (uncertain). Also, Horatio.
HOSEA: (Heb.) salvation.
HOWELL: (Celt.) sound; whole.
HUBERT: (Ger.) bright-spirited; bright-souled. Dims. Bert, Bertie.
HUGH: (Ger.) mind; spirit. Also, Hew, Hugo. Dim. Hughie.
HUGO: Same as Hugh.
HUMBERT: (Ger.) bright.
HUMPHREY: (Ger.) guardian of the peace, or of the home. Also, Humphry.
HYACINTH: (Gk.) from name of the flower.
IAN: Gaelic form of John.
ICHABOD: (Heb) the glory has departed.
IGNATIUS: (Gk.) ardent; fiery.
IGOR: (Russ.) alertness.
IMMANUEL: Same as Emmanuel.
INGRAM: (Ger.) raven.
INIGO: May be Spanish form of Ignatius.
IRA: (Heb.) watchful; vigilant.
ISAAC: (Heb.) laughter. Also, Isaak. Dims. Ike, Iky.
ISAIAH: (Heb.) salvation of the Lord.
ISIDORE: (Gk.) gift of Isis (Egyptian goddess). Dim. Izzy.
ISRAEL: (Heb.) God prevails; otherwise, soldier of God. Dim. Izzy.
IVAN: Russian form of John.
IVOR: (Celt.) yew tree. Also, Ifor, Ivo, Yvor.
JABEZ: (Heb.) he will cause pain.
JACK: Dim. of John.
JACOB: (Heb.) supplanter; follower. Dims. Jake, Jakie.
JAIRUS: (Heb.) he will enlighten.
JAMES: (Heb.) supplanter; follower. Same as Jacob. Dims. Jamie, Jim, Jimmie, Jimmy.
JAN: Dim. of John.
JAPETH: (Heb.) enlargement.
JARED: (Heb.) descent.
JASON: (Gk.) healer.
JASPER: (Persian) treasurer (uncertain).
JEDEDIAH: (Heb.) beloved of Jehovah. Also, Jedidiah.
JEFFREY: Form of Geoffrey, Godfrey.
JEHTRO: (Heb.) Jehovah is his father.
JEREMIAH: (Heb.) exalted of the Lord. Also, Jeremias, Jeremy.
JEROME: (Gk.) holy name. Dim. Jerry.
JERRY: Dim. of Jeremiah, Gerald, Gerard, Jerome.
JERVIS: Same as Gervase.
JESSE: (Heb.) Jehovah is.
JETHRO: (Heb.) abundance.
JIM: Dim. of James.
JOAB: (Heb.) Jehovah is his father.
JOB: (Heb.) afflicted; hated; persecuted.
JOCELYN: (Ger.) of the stock of the gods. Also, Jocelin.
JOCK: Dim. of John.
JOE: Dim. of Joseph.
JOEL: (Heb.) the Lord is God; Jehovah is God.
JOHN: (Heb.) grace of God; God has favored; Jehovah's favor. Dims. Jack, Jackie, Jacky, Jan, Jock, Johnnie, Johnny.
JONAH: (Heb.) dove. Also, Jonas.
JONATHAN: (Heb.) Jehovah's gift; gift of God.
JOSEPH: (Heb.) He (Jehovah) shall add; God shall add. Dims. Joe, Joey.
JOSHUA: (Heb.) God of salvation. Dim. Josh.
JOSIAH: (Heb.) Jehovah heals. Also, Josias.
JOTHAM: (Heb.) the Lord is upright.
JUAN: Spanish form of John.
JUDE: (Heb.) Jehovah leads; otherwise, confession. Also, Judah.
JULIAN: (Lat.) belonging to Julius. Dim. Jule.
JULIUS: (Lat.) soft-haired. Dim. Jule.

JUSTIN: (Lat.) just. Also, Justus.
KEITH: (Scots) from a place name.
KENELM: (A. S.) defender of his family.
KENNETH: (Celt.) commander; leader; or, handsome leader. Dims. Ken, Kennie.
KENT: (Eng.) from place name of English county.
KERMIT: (Celt.) free (uncertain).
KESTER: (Celt.) dim. of Christopher.
KEVIN: (Irish) handsome.
KING: (A. S.) ruler.
KIRBY: (A. S.) church town; otherwise, from a place name.
KIRK: (Scots) church.
KIT: Dim. of Christopher.
KNUT: (Danish) race; kind.
KONRAD: Same as Conrad.
KURT: Dim. of Conrad. Konrad.
LABAN: (Heb.) white.
LAMBERT: (Ger.) illustrious landholder.
LANCELOT: (Ger.) little lance; warrior; servant. Also, Launcelot. Dim. Lance.
LAURENCE: (Lat.) crowned with laurel. Also, Lawrence. Dim. Larry.
LAZARUS: (Heb.) whom God helps; otherwise, destitute of help.
LEANDER: (Gk.) lion-man.
LEE: (Celt.) gentle being.
LEIGH: (O. E.) beauty of the wayside.
LEMUEL: (Heb.) consecrated to God; otherwise, created by God. Dim. Lem.
LEO: (Lat.) lion. Also, Leon. Dim. Lee.
LEONARD: (Ger.) strong as a lion; brave as a lion. Dim. Len, Lennie.
LEONIDAS: (Gk.) lion-like.
LEOPOLD: (Ger.) champion of the people.
LESLIE: (O. E.) lessee; otherwise, from a place name. Also, Lesley. Dim. Lee.
LESTER: (O. E.) lustrous.
LEVI: (Heb.) adhesion.
LEWIS: (Ger.) bold warrior; famous warrior. Dim. Lew.
LIAM: Irish form of William.
LINUS: (Gk.) flaxen-haired.
LIONEL: (Lat.) young lion.
LLEWELLYN: (Welsh) lightning. Also, Llewellyn.
LLOYD: (Welsh) gray.
LODOWICK: Form of Ludovic.
LORENZO: Same as Laurence.
LOT: (Heb.) veil; covering.
LOUIS: (Ger.) famous warrior. Also, Lewis.
LUCAS: Form of Luke.
LUCIAN: (Lat.) belonging to Lucius. Also, Lucien.
LUCIUS: (Lat.) light.
LUCRETIUS: (Lat.) gain.
LUDOVIC: From Ludovicus, Latin form of Lewis. Also, Aloysius.
LUKE: (Lat.) abbreviation of a Latin name, Eucanus or Lucilius; otherwise, light. Also, Lucas.
LUTHER: (Ger.) famous warrior; illustrious warrior.
LYNN: (Eng. family name); form same as feminine.
MADOC: (Welsh) fortunate; good; beneficent.
MAGNUS: (Lat.) great.
MALACHI: (Heb.) messenger of the Lord; My (Jehovah's) messenger. Also, Malachy.
MALCOLM: (Celt.) follower of Saint Columba.
MALISE: (Celt.) servant of Jesus.
MANASSEH: (Heb.) forgetfulness.
MANUEL: Form of Emmanuel.
MARCELLUS: Dim. of Marcus.
MARCIUS: Form of Marcus.
MARCUS: (Lat.) hammer; mallet; otherwise, sprung from Mars. Also, Mark.
MARK: Form of Marcus.

MARMADUKE: (Celt.) mighty noble. (uncertain). Dim. Duke.
MARTIN: (Lat.) of Mars; warlike.
MATTHEW: (Heb.) gift of Jehovah. Dim. Mat, Mattie.
MATTHIAS: Same as Matthew.
MAURICE: (Lat.) Moorish; dark-colored; swarthy. Also, Morris.
MAXIMILIAN: (Lat.) the greatest Aemilianus. Dim. Max.
MERLIN: (Welsh) legendary medieval magician.
MICAH: (Heb.) Godlike; otherwise, who is like the Lord?
MICHAEL: (Heb.) Godlike; who is like God? Dim. Mike.
MILES: (Ger.) merciful; otherwise, (Lat.) soldier.
MONTAGUE: From a surname. Also, Montagu. Dim. Monty.
MORDECAI: (Heb.) consecrated to Marduk (chief god of Babylonian pantheon).
MORGAN: (Welsh) sea-dweller.
MORRIS: Form of Maurice.
MORTIMER: (O. F.) Ever-living.
MORTON: (O. E.) unsatisfied.
MOSES: (Heb.) taken from the water. Dim. Mose.
MUNGO: (Celt.) dear one; or, name for Saint Kentigern.
MURDOCH: (Gaelic) seafarer. Also, Murdo, Murdock.
MYLES: Form of Miles.
NAHUN: (Heb.) consolation; comforting.
NANTY: Dim. of Anthony.
NAPOLEON: (Gk.) lion of the forest grove.
NAT: Dim. of Nathan, Nathaniel.
NATHAN: (Heb.) gift; given. Dim. Nat.
NATHANIEL: (Heb.) gift of God. Also, Nathanael. Dim. Nat.
NED: Dim. of Edgar, Edmund, Edwin. Also, Neddie, Neddy.
NEHEMIAH: (Heb.) whom God (Jehovah) comforts; or, comfort of the Lord.
NEIL: (Gaelic) chieftain; champion; otherwise, (Lat.) dark; swarthy. Also, Neal.
NEVILLE: From a surname.
NICHOLAS: (Gk.) victory of the people. Also, Nichol, Nicol, Nicolas. Dims. Colin, Nick, Nickie, Nicky.
NICODEMUS: (Gk.) victory of the people.
NIGEL: (Celt.) champion.
NOAH: (Heb.) Long-lived; rest; comfort.
NOEL: (F.) Christmas.
NORMAN: (ger.) northman; native of Normandy; otherwise, a Fate.
OBADIAH: (Heb.) servant of the Lord (Jehovah).
OBED: (Heb.) serving God (Jehovah).
OCTAVIUS: (Lat.) eighth born. Also, Octavus.
OLAF: (O. N.) after Saint Olaf.
OLIVER: (Lat.) olivetree. Dims, Noll, Nollie, Ollie.
OLIVEN: (Welsh) white path.
ORESTES: (Gk.) mountaineer.
ORLANDO: Form of Roland.
ORSON: (Lat.) bear.
OSBERT: (O. E.) light of God.
OSCAR: (Celt.) leaping warrior.
OSMUND: (Ger.) protection of God.
OSWALD: (Ger.) power of God.
OTTO: (Ger.) rich; otherwise, giant. Also, Otho.
OWEN: (Celt.) young warrior; otherwise, lamb.
PADDY: Dim. of Patrick.
PAT: Dim. of Patrick.
PATRICK: (Lat.) patrician; a noble. Dim. Paddy, Pat.
PAUL: (Lat.) little. Also, Paulus.
PELEG: (Heb.) division.
PERCIVAL: (Lat.) courteous. Dim. Perse.

PERCY: Dim. of Percival; otherwise, a surname.
PEREGRINE: (Lat.) traveler; pilgrim; stranger.
PETER: (Gk.) rock. Dim. Pete, Petey.
PHELIM: (Celt.) ever good.
PHILANDER: (Gk.) lover of men.
PHILEMON: (Gk.) loving; friendly.
PHILIP: (Gk.) lover of horses. Dims. Phil, Pip.
PHINEAS: (Heb.) mouth of brass; oracle; otherwise, Negro. Also, Phinehas.
PIP: Dim. of Philip.
PIUS: (Lat.) pious; dutiful.
POMPEY: (Lat.) showy.
PRESERVED: (Eng.) redeemed.
QUARTUS: (Lat.) fourth born.
QUENTIN: (Lat.) fifth born. Also, Quintin, Quintus.
QUINCY: (Lat.) name of a Roman gens.
QUINTILIAN: (Lat.) name of a Roman gens.
RALPH: (Ger.) famous wolf, or, hero. From Rudolphus.
RANALD: Form of Reginald.
RANDOLPH: Form of Rudolphus. Also, Randal, Randall. Dim. Randy.
RAOUL: French form of Ralph.
RAPHAEL: (Heb.) the healing of God; otherwise, God has healed.
RASMUS: Dim. of Erasmus.
RASTUS: Dim. of Erastus.
RAY: Dim. of Raymond.
RAYMOND: (Ger.) wise protector; mighty protector. Also, Raymund. Dim. Ray.
RAYNER: (Ger.) great counselor.
REDMOND: (O. E.) ambitious.
REGINALD: (O. E.) strong ruler. Also, Ranald, Reynold, Ronald. Dims. Reg, Reggie, Rex.
RENÉ: (F.) reborn.
REUBEN: (Heb.) behold, a son; otherwise, renewer. Dim. Rube.
REUEL: (Heb.) friend of God.
REX: (Lat.) king. Otherwise, dim. of Reginald.
REYNOLD: Form of Reginald.
RHETT: Literary name, after Rhett Butler, hero of Margaret Mitchell's novel, Gone with the Wind.
RHYS: (Welsh) adventurer.
RICHARD: (Ger.) king; strong ruler; powerful. Dims. Dick, Dickie, Dicky.
ROBERT: (Ger.) bright in fame. Dims. Bob, Bobbie, Bobby, Rob, Robbie, Robby, Robin.
ROBIN: Dim. of Robert.
RODERICK: (Ger.) rich in fame. Also, Roderic. Dims. Rod, Roddie, Rurik.
RODNEY: (O. R.) passing fair; otherwise, a surname.
RODOLPH: Same as Rudolph.
RODOLPHUS: Same as Rudolphus.
ROGER: (Ger.) famous with the spear. Dims. Hodge, Hodgkin.
ROLAND: (Ger.) fame of the land. Also, Rowland.
ROLF: Dim. of Rudolph. Also, Rolfe.
RONALD: Form of Reginald.
RORY: (Irish) red.
ROY: (Gaelic) red-haired; otherwise, (F.) king.
ROYAL: (F.) king. Dim. Roy, Roy-Roy.
RUDOLPH: (Ger.) famous wolf, or, hero; courageous. Also, Ralph, Randal, Randolph, Rodolph, Rudolphus. Dims. Rolf, Rudy.
RUFUS: (Lat.) red: red-haired. Dim. Rufe.
RUPERT: Form of Robert.
RURIK: Form of Roderick.
Sal: Dim. of Salvador, Salvatore.
SALMON: (Heb.) shady.
SALVADOR: (Sp.) Savior. Dim. Sal.
SALVATORE: (It.) Savior. Dim. Sal.
SAMSON: (Heb.) splendid sun; otherwise, child of the sun. Also, Sampson.

SAMUEL: (Heb.) heard by God; otherwise, name of God. Dims. Sam, Sammy.
SANCHO: (Sp.) holy. Also, Sanchez.
SANDERS: Dim. of Alexander.
SASCHA: (Russian) dim. of Alexander.
SAUL: (Heb.) asked for.
SEAMUS: Gaelic form of James. Also, Seumas.
SEAN: Irish form of John.
SEBA: (Heb.) eminent.
SEBASTIAN: (Gk.) venerable; reverend.
SECUNDUS: (Lat.) second born.
SEPTIMUS: (Lat.) seventh born.
SERENUS: (Lat.) calm; peaceful; serene. Also, Sereno.
SERLE: (O. E.) armor. Also, Searle.
SETH: (Heb.) appointed.
SEUMAS: Form of Seamus.
SEXTUS: (Lat.) sixth born.
SHAMUS: Form of Seamus, Seumas.
SHANE: Form of Sean.
SIDNEY: From a surname. Also, Sydney.
SIEGFRIED: (Ger.) victorious peace. Also, Sigurd.
SIGISMUND: (Ger.) conquering protection. Also, Siegmund, Sigmund, Zigmund, Zygmund. Dims. Sig, Siggie, Zig, Ziggie, Zyg, Zyggie.
SIGURD: Form of Siegfried.
SILAS: Form of Silvanus.
SILVANUS: (Lat.) rustic; woodsman; forester. Also, Silas, Silvius, Sylvester, Sylvius. Dim. Sil.
SILVESTER: Form of Silvanus. Also, Sylvester.
SIMON: (Heb.) peaceful. Dim. Sol.
STANISLAS: (Polish) martial fame. Also, Stanislaus.
STANLEY: From a surname. Dim. Stan.
STEPHEN: (Gk.) crown; garland. Dim. Steenie, Steve.
SYDNEY: Same as Sidney.
SYLVANUS: Form of Silvanus.
SYLVESTER: Form of Silvester.
TAM: Dim. of Thomas.
TED: Dim. of Edward, Theodore. Also, Teddy.
TERENCE: (Lat.) tender. Dim. Terry.
TERRY: Dim. of Terence.
TEX: From the state of Texas, USA.
THADDEUS: (Heb.) wise one; otherwise, devout. Also, Thaddaeus. Dims. Tad, Thad.
THEOBALD: (Ger.) champion of the people. Dim. Theo.
THEODORE: (Gk.) gift of the gods. Dims. Ted, Teddy.
THEODORIC: (Gk.) power among the people. Dims. Derek, Derrick.
THEODOSIUS: (Gk.) divine gift.
THEOPHILUS: (Gk.) loved by God; or, love of God.
THERON: (Gk.) hunter.
THOMAS: (Heb.) twin. Dims. Tom. Tommy.
THORSTEIN: Form of Thurston.
THURSTON: (O. N.) Thor's stone. Also, Thorstein.
TIMOTHY: (Gk.) God-fearing. Dims. Tim, Timmy.
TITUS: (Lat.) safe; otherwise, (Gk.) (uncertain).
TOBIAS: (Heb.) distinguished by the Lord; otherwise, Jehovah is good. Also, Tobiah. Dim. Toby.
TONY: Dim. of Anthony.
TRACY: From a surname.
TRISTRAM: (Celt.) tumult; otherwise, (Lat.) grave, pensive, sorrowful. Also, Tristan.
ULRIC: (Ger.) ruler of the wolf.
ULYSSES: (Latin form of Greek name Odysseus) hater. Dim. 'Lyss.
URBAN: (Lat.) of the city; courteous; polite.
URIAH: (Heb.) the Lord's light, or fire.
URIEL: (Heb.) light of God (Jehovah).

VALENTINE: (Lat.) strong; healthy.
VERE: From a surname.
VERNON: (Fr. place name).
VICTOR: (Lat.) conqueror. Dims. Vic. Vick.
VINCENT: (Lat.) conquering; victorious. Dims. Vin, Vinny.
VIVIAN: (Lat.) lively. Also, Vivien, Vyvian, Vyvyen.
WALDO: (Ger.) strong.
WALTER: (Ger.) strong warrior; otherwise, wood master. Dims. Walt, Wat.
WAT: Dim. of Walter.
ALBERT: (Ger.) wellborn.
WILFRED: (Ger.) peace-winner. Also, Wifred.
WILHELM: Ger. form af William.
WILLIAM: (Ger.) resolute helmet; protection; defender. Dims. Bill, Billy, Will, Willie, Willy.
WINFRED: (Welsh or O. E.) peace winner. Dim. Winnie.
WINSTON: From a surname. Dim. Winnie.
XAVIER: (Sp.) fascinating.
YVES: French form of Ivor. Also, Yve.
ZABDIEL: (Heb.) gift of God.
ZACCHEUS: Form of Zachariah.
ZACHARIAH: (Heb.) remembered by the Lord (Jehovah). Also, Zachary. Dim. Zack.
ZEBEDIAH: (Heb.) gift of the Lord. Also, Zebedee.
ZECHARIAH: From af Zachariah.
ZEDEKIAH: (Heb.) justice of the Lord (Jehovah); otherwise, Jehovah is righteous.
ZENAS: (Gk.) gift of Zeus (Jupiter).
ZEPHANIAH: (Heb.) hid of the Lord (Jehovah). Dim. Zeph.

Names, Most Popular Girls'

ABIGAIL: (Heb.) joy of the father; or, father rejoiced. Dims. Abbie, Abby, Gail, Gale.
ADA: Dim. of Adelaide.
ADELAIDE: (Ger.) princess; wellborn.
ADELE: (Ger.) wellborn; noble. Also, Adela, Adelia.
ADELINA: (Ger.) wellborn. Also, Adeline. Dims. Addie, Addy.
ADRIAN: (Lat. of Adria, a Latin place name. Same as Adrian, when used as male name. Also, Adriana, Adrianna, Adrien, Adrienne.
AGATHA: (Gk.) good; kind. Dim. Aggie, Aggy.
AGNES: (Gk.) chaste; innocent; pure. Dims. Aggie, Aggy, Nancy.
AILEEN: Form of Helen; otherwise, (Irish) peasant. Also, Eileen.
ALBERTA: Fem. of Albert.
ALETHEA: (Gk.) truth.
ALEXANDRA: Fem. of Alexander.
ALEXIS: (Gk.) helper. Also, Alexia.
ALICE: (Gk.) truth; nobility. Dims. Allie, Ally, Ellie, Elsie.
ALICIA: Form of Alice.
ALINE: Form of Adeline.
ALISON: Scots form of Alice.
ALMA: (Lat.) fostering; nourishing; loving.
ALMIDA: (Byzantine) power of love.
ALMIRA: (Arabic) princess; lofty (uncertain).
ALONA: (Celt.) exceedingly beautiful.
ALTHEA: (Gk.) healer.
AMABEL: (Lat.) lovable. Also, Mabel.
AMALIA: Form of Amelia.
AMANDA: (Lat.) worthy of love.
AMARYLLIS: (Lat.) rustic sweetheart.
AMELIA: (Ger.) busy; energetic.
AMY: (F.) beloved.
ANASTASIA: (Gk.) immortal; resurrection.
ANCILLA: (lat.) handmaid.
ANDRINA: Fem. of Andrew.
ANGELA: (Gk.) angel; messenger.
ANGELICA: (Gk.) angelic.

ANGELINA: (Gk.) lovely; angelic. Also, Angeline. Dims. Angie, Lina.
ANITA: (Sp.) gracious. Dim. Nita.
ANN: (Heb.) grace. Also, Anna, Anne. Dims. Annette, Annie, Nan, Nancy, Nina.
ANNABEL: (Heb.) gracefully beautiful. Also, Annabella, Annabelle.
ANNETTE: Dim. of Ann. Dims. Annie, Nan, Nancy, Net, Nettie, Netty, Nina.
ANTHEA: (Gk.) flowery.
ANTOINETTE: Dim. of Antonia. Dims. Net, Nettie, Netty, Toinette.
ANTONIA: Fem. of Anthony. Dims. Antoinette, Net, Nettie, Netty.
APRIL: (Lat.) from the name of the month, meaning to open.
ARABELLA: (Lat.) fair altar; otherwise, (Arabian) woman. Dims. Bell, Bella, Belle.
ARIADNE: (Gk.) holy one.
ARIANA: Form of Ariadne.
ARTEMISIA: (Gk.) gift of Artemis (Diana), goddess of the hunt.
ASPASIA: (Gk.) welcome.
ASTRID: (Norse) strength of the gods.
ATALANTA: (Gk.) equal.
AUDREY: (Ger.) noble.
AUGUSTA: Fem. of Augustus.
AURELIA: Fem. of Aurelius.
AURORA: (Lat.) from Aurora, Roman goddess of the dawn.
AVIS: (Ger.) refuge from strife. Also, Avice.
BARBARA: (Gk.) foreign; strange; stranger.
BEATRICE: (Lat.) happy. Also, Beatrix. Dims. Bea, Beattie, Beatty, Bee, Trix, Trixie.
BECKY: Dim. of Rebecca.
BEDELIA: Form of Bridget.
BELINDA: (Ger.) serpent; otherwise, (uncertain).
BELL: Dim. of Arabella, Isabella, etc. Also, Bella, Belle.
BERENICE: (Gk.) bringing victory. Also, Bernice.
BERTHA: (Ger.) bright; beautiful; famous. Dims. Bertie, Berty.
BERYL: (Gk.) brilliant. Same as the jewel.
BESS: Dim. of Elizabeth.
BETH: Dim. of Elizabeth.
BETHIA: (Heb.) daughter of Jehovah.
BETSY: Dim. of Elizabeth.
BETTE: Dim. of Elizabeth.
BETTY: Dim. of Elizabeth.
BEULAH: (Heb.) land of rest: otherwise, married. Also, Beula.
BIANCA: (It.) white.
BIDDY: Dim. Bridget.
BLANCHE: (Ger.) white. Also, Blanch.
BOADICEA: (O. E.) queenly; regal.
BRENDA: (O. N.) sword.
BRIGID: (Celt.) bright; otherwise, strength. Also, Bridget.
BRONWEN: (Welsh) pure of heart.
CAMILLA: (Lat.) attendant at a sacrifice; otherwise, above suspicion.
CANDIDA: (Lat.) white; pure; innocent.
CARLOTTA: Form of Charlotte.
CARMEL: (Heb.) garden.
CAROL: Form of Caroline. Also, Carole.
CAROLA: Fem. of Charles.
CAROLINE: (Ger.) noble-spirited. Dims. Carol, Carrie, Lina.
CATHERINE: (Gk.) pure. Also, Catharina, Catherina, Katharine, Katherine, Katharina, Katherina, Katrina. Dims. Cathie, Cathy, Kate, Katie, Kathie, Kathy, Katy, Kit, Kittie, Kitty.
CECILIA: Fem. of Cecil. Also, Cecily, Cicely. Dims. Cis, Cissie, Cissy.
CELESTINE: (Lat.) heavenly.
CELIA: Fem. of Coelius.
CHARITY: (Lat.) kindness. Dim. Cherry.

CHARLOTTE: Fem. of Charles. Dims. Lettie, Letty, Lottie, Lotty.
CHLOE: (Gk.) blooming; green herb.
CHRISTABEL: (Gk.) fair Christian.
CHRISTIANA: Fem. of Christian. Also, Christina, Christine. Dims. Chris, Chrissie, Teenie, Tina.
CICELY: Form of Cecilia.
CLAIRE: Form of Clara. Also, Clare.
CLARA: (Lat.) bright; illustrious. Also, Claire, Clare.
CLARIBEL: (Lat.) brightly fair.
CLARICE: Form of Clara.
CLARISSA: (Lat.) most fair. Form of Clara.
CLAUDETTE: Fem. of Claudius.
CLAUDIA: Fem. of Claudius.
CLEMENTINE: Fem. of Clement. Also, Clementina.
CLEOPATRA: (Gk.) famous; celebrated.
CLOTILDA: (Ger.) fair-minded. Also, Clothilda.
COLETTE: Fem. of Nicholas. Dim. Nicolette.
CONSTANCE: (Ger.) bright; beautiful; famous. Dim. Cornie.
CORA: Form of Corinna.
CORDELIA: (Lat.) warmhearted.
CORINNA: (Gk.) maiden. Also, Corinne.
CORNELIA: Fem. of Cornelius. Dims. Cornie, Nellie.
CYNTHIA: (Gk.) of Mount Cynthus, in association with the goddess Artemis (Diana).
DAISY: (A. S.) after the flower, meaning "the eye of the day."
DAPHNE: (Gk.) laurel.
DEBORAH: (Heb.) bee. Dims. Deb, Debbie.
DEIRDRE: (Celt.) heroine in Irish mythology, the beautiful and fated Deirdre of the Sorrows. Dim. Dee Dee.
DELIA: (Gk.) of the island of Delos, in association with the birthplace of Artemis (Diana).
DENISE: Fem. of Dennis.
DIANA: (Lat.) goddess of the moon and the chase in Roman mythology. Dims. Di, Die.
DILYS: (Welsh) true; faithful.
DINAH: (Heb.) judged. Also, Dina.
DOLORES: (Sp.) sorrows; sorrowful. Dim. Lola.
DORA: Dim. of Dorothy, Theodora.
DORCAS: (Gk.) gazelle.
DOREEN: Irish form of Dorothy.
DORINDA: Form of Dorothy.
DORIS: (Gk.) sea nymph.
DOROTHY: (Gk.) gift of the gods. Also, Dorothea, Dorinda. Dims. Doll, Dolly, Dora, Dottie, Dotty.
DRUSILLA: (Lat.) strengthening; otherwise, dewy-eyed.
DULCIE: (Lat.) sweet.
EDITH: (O. E.) happiness; otherwise, rich gift. Also, Edyth, Edythe. Dims. Edie, Edy.
EDNA: (Heb.) pleasure.
EFFIE: Dim. of Euphemia.
EILEEN: Irish form of Helen.
EIRENE: Form of Irene.
ELAINE: (O. F.) form of Helen.
ELEANOR: Form of Helen. Also, Elinor. Dims. Ella, Nell, Nellie, Nora.
ELENA: Form of Helen.
ELFREDA: (O. E.) fairy strength.
ELGIVA: (O. E.) noble gift.
ELIZA: Form of Elizabeth.
ELIZABETH: (Heb.) consecrated to God; worshiper of God; or, God is my satisfaction. Also, Elisabeth, Eliza. Dims. Bess, Bessie, Bessy, Beth, Betsy, Bette, Betty, Elsie, Libby, Lisbeth, Liza, Lizzie.
ELLA: Dim. of Eleanor; or of Arabella, Isabella, etc.
ELLEN: Form of Helen.
ELMA: Contraction of Elizabeth Mary.
ELOISE: Form of Heloise. Also, Eloisa.
ELSA: Dim. of Alice, Elizabeth.

ELSIE: Dim. of Alice, Elizabeth.
ELSPETH: Scots form of Elizabeth.
ELVIRA: (Lat.) white; otherwise, (Sp.) fairy counsel.
EMELINE: (Ger.) energetic; industrious. Also, Emmeline.
EMERALD: (F.) after the name of the jewel.
EMILY: (Lat.) industrious. Also, Emilia.
EMMA: (Ger.) universal. Dim. Em, Emmie, Emmy.
ENA: (Irish) fire.
ENID: (Welsh) patient.
ERMYNTRUDE: (Ger.) strength of the god Ermin. Also, Irmentrude. Dims. Ernie, Erny.
ERNESTINE: Fem. of Ernest. Dim. Tina.
ESME: (F.) beloved.
ESMERALDA) (Sp.) emerald.
ESTELLE: (Lat.) star. Also, Estella. Dim. Stella.
ESTHER: (Persian) star. Also, Hester. Dims. Hetty, Tess.
ETHEL: (O. E.) noble.
ETHELDREDA: (O. E.) noble power.
ETHELINDA: (Ger.) noble snake. Also, Ethelind.
ETTA: Dim. of Henrietta.
EUDORA: (Gk.) good gift.
EUGENIA: Fem. of Eugene.
EUGÉNIE: French form of Eugene.
EULALIA: (Gk.) sweet-speaking.
EUNICE: (Gk.) bright victory; commended.
EUPHEMIA: (Gk.) of good report. Dim. Effie.
EVADNE: (Gk.) sacrifice.
EVANGELINE: (Gk.) bringing good news.
EVE: (Heb.) life. Also, Eva.
EVELEEN: Irish form of Eva.
EVELINA: (Celt.) agreeable. Also, Eveline.
EVELYN: Form of Evelina.
FABIA: Fem. of Fabian.
FAITH: (Lat.) faith.
FANNY: Dim. of Frances. Also, Fannie.
FAUSTINA: (Lat.) lucky; fortunate.
FAWN: (Lat.) young deer.
FAY: (F.) fairy; otherwise, (Lat.) faith. Also, Faye.
FEDORA: Form of Theodora.
FELICIA: Fem. of Felix. Also, Felice, Felise.
FELICITY: Fem. of Felix.
FERN: From name of plant; otherwise, dim. of Fernanda. Also, Ferne.
FERNANDA: Fem. of Ferdinand.
FIDELIA: (Lat.) faithful. Also, Fidele.
FIFI: Dim. of Josephine.
FIONA: (Gaelic) fair; white.
FLAVIA: (Lat.) golden yellow.
FLEUR: (F.) Flower.
FLORA: (Lat.) flower. Also, Floris.
FLORENCE: (Lat.) blooming. Dims. Flo, Flossie, Flossy.
FRANCES: Fem. of Francis. Dims. Fanny, Frankie.
FREDA: (Ger.) peace. Also, Frieda.
FREDERICA: Fem. of Frederick. Dims. Freddie, Freddy, Frieda.
FREYA: (Norse) after Freya, Norse goddess of love: Freya's Day = Friday.
FRIEDA: See Freda.
FRITZI: Fem. of Fritz.
GABRIELLE: Fem. of Gabriel.
GAIL: Dim. of Abigail. Also, Gaile, Gale, Gayl, Gayle.
GARNET: From the name of the jewel.
GAY: (F.) merry; happy.
GEMMA: (Lat.) jewel.
GENE: Form of Jean; otherwise, dim. of Eugenia. Also, Genia.
GENEVIEVE: (Celtic) white; magic sighs.
GEORGIA: Fem. of George; otherwise, a place name, after state of Georgia (U.S.A.).

GEORGIANA: Fem. of George. Also, Georgianna, Georgina. Dims. Georgia, Georgie.
GERALDINE: Fem. of Gerald.
GERMAINE: (Lat.) german.
GERTRUDE: (Ger.) spear-maiden; spear-strength. Dims. Gert, Gertie, Trude, Trudi, Trudy.
GILDA: (Ger.) golden; otherwise, (Celtic) servant of God.
GINGER: Dim. of Virginia.
GISELLE: (Ger.) pledge. Also, Gisele, Gisella.
GLADYS: (Celtic) princess; otherwise, (Welsh) form of Claudia.
GLENDA: Fem. of Glen. Also, Glynis.
GLORIA: (Lat.) glory.
GLYNIS: Form of Glenda.
GOLDA: (Ger.) gold. Dim. Goldie, Goldy.
GRACE: (Lat.) grace; favor. Dim. Gracie.
GREER: Fem. of Gregory.
GRETA: German dim. of Margaret.
GRETCHEN: Dim. of Margaret.
GRISELDA: (Ger.) stone heroine; gray battle-maid. Dim. Grissel.
GUINIVERE: (Welsh) white-cheeked.
GUSSIE: Dim. of Augusta.
GWEN: Dim. of Guinivere, Gwendolyn.
GWENDOLYN: (Welsh) white-browed. Also, Gwendolen.
GWYNETH: (Welsh) blessed.
HADASSAH: (Heb.) myrtle.
HAGAR: (Heb.) forsaken.
HALLIE: Dim. of Harriet, Henrietta.
HANNAH: (Heb.) grace. Also, Hanna.
HARRIET: Fem. dim. of Henry. Also, Harriette, Harriot. Dim. Hattie.
HAZEL: From the name of the tree.
HEATHER: From the name of the plant. Also, Heath.
HEBE: (Gk.) youth.
HEDDA: Form of Hedwig.
HEDVA: (Heb.) joy.
HEDWIG: (Ger.) strife. Dim. Hedy.
HELEN: (Gk.) light; bright one. Also, Helaine, Helayne, Helena, Helene, Ellen, Eleanor. Dims. Nell, Nellie, Lena.
HELGA: (Norse) holy.
HELOISE: Form of Eloise.
HENRIETTA: Fem. dim. of Henry. Also, Henriette. Dims. Etta, Hetty.
HEPZIBAH: (Heb.) my delight is in her. Also, Hephzibah. Dim. Hepsy.
HERMIA: Fem. of Hermes.
HERMINE: Fem. of Herman.
HERMIONE: Fem. of Hermes. Also, Hermia.
HERTA: (Gk.) earth; strength. Also, Hertha.
HESTER: Form of Esther. Also, Hesther.
HETTY: Dim. Henrietta, Hester.
HILARY: Fem. of Hilary. Also, Hilaria, Hillary.
HILDA: (Ger.) form of Hildegard. Also, Hilde.
HILDEGARDE: (Ger.) battle-maid.
HOLLY: From the name of the plant.
HONEY: (Ger.) sweet.
HONORIA: (Lat.) honorable. Also, Honora.
HOPE: (A. S.) hope.
HORATIA: Fem. of Horace.
HORTENSE: (Lat.) lady in the garden. Also, Hortensia.
HULDA: (Heb.) weasel. Also, Huldah.
HYACINTH: From name of flower.
IANTHE: (Gk.) purple flower.
IDA: (Ger.) godlike; otherwise, youthful.
IDABELLE: (Ger.) godlike; fair. Also, Idabell.
ILENE: Form of Eileen; otherwise, form of Helen.
ILKA: Form of Ilona.
ILSE: German form of Elsie. Also, Ilsa.
IMOGEN: (Uncertain); otherwise, a literary name, from the heroine of Shakespeare's Cymbeline. Also, Imogene.

INA: Dim. of Katrina.
INEZ: Form of Agnes. Also, Ines, Ynes.
INGLIS: (A. S.) English.
INGRID: (Norse) ride of Ingvi (Norse hero).
IOLANTHE: (Gk.) flower of Iole, wife of the son of Hercules.
LONE: (Gk.) violet.
IRENE: (Gk.) beace. Also, Irna, Eirene. Dims. Rene, Renie.
IRIS: (Gk.) rainbow. Iris (Greek myth.) was the goddess of the rainbow.
IRITA: Form of Rita, with Ida or Irene added.
IRMA: (Ger.) power. Also, Erma.
ISA: (Ger.) iron.
ISABEL: Form of Elizabeth. Also, Isabella. Dims. Bella, Belle.
ISADORA: Fem. of Isidore.
ISHBEL: Scots form of Isabel. Also, Isabel.
ISOLDE: (Uncertain); otherwise, a literary name, after Isolde, the lover of Tristram. Also, Isolda.
JACKIE: Dim. Jacqueline.
JACQUELINE: Fem. of French form of James.
JANE: Fem. form of John.
JANET: Dim. of Jane. Also, Janot.
JANEY: Dim. Jane.
JANICE: Form of Jane. Also, Janis, Janith.
JASMINE: After the name of the flower. Also, Jessamyn, Yasmin.
JEAN: French form of Jane. Also, Jeanette, Jeanne, Jeanie.
JEANNINE: Dim. Jean.
JEMIMA: (Heb.) dove.
JENNIFER: Form of Guinivere.
JENNY: Form of Janey. Also, Jinny.
JERUSHA: (Heb.) possessed; married.
JESSAMYN: Form of Jasmine.
JESSE: (Heb.) wealth.
JESSICA: (Heb.) (uncertain); otherwise, a literary name, after the daughter of Shylock in Shakespeare's Merchant of Venice.
JESSIE: Scots form of Janet.
JEWEL: From jewel.
JILL: Dim. of Juliana.
JO: Dim. Joan, Josephine.
JOAN: Fem. of John. Also, Joann, Jo-ann, Jo Ann, Joanna. .
JOCELYN: Form of Joyce.
JODY: Form of Judy; otherwise, dim. of Joan.
JOSEPHA: Fem. of Joseph.
JOSEPHINE: Fem. of Joseph. Dims. Fifi, Jo, Josie, Phenie.
JOY: (Lat.) joy.
JOYCE: (Lat.) joyful; sportive.
JUANITA: Spanish form and dim. of Joan.
JUDITH: (Heb.) praised; otherwise, of Judah, as a place name. Dim. Judy.
JUDY: Dim. of Judith.
JULIA: Fem. of Julius.
JULIANA: Form of Julia. Dim. Liana.
JULIET: Dim. Julia. Also, Juliette.
JUNE: From the name of the month, in Latin the month of Juno (wife of Jupiter).
JUSTINE: Fem. of Justin. Also, Justina.
KAREN: Form of Katherine. Also, Karan, Karin.
KATE: Dim. Katherine.
KATHERINE: Form of Catherine. Also, Katharine. Dims. Karen, Kass, Kate, Kathie, Kay, Kathleen, Kitty.
KATHLEEN: Irish form of Katherine.
KATHY: Dim. of Katherine. Also, Kathe.
KETURAH: (Heb.) incense.
KEZIAH: (Heb.) cassia.
KITTY: Dim. Katherine.
LANA: (Uncertain).
LARAINE: Form of Laura, or Lorraine.
LAURA: (Lat.) laurel; otherwise, (uncertain).
LAURETTE: Dim. Laura.

LAVERNE: Fem. of Vernon. Also, La Verne.
LAVINIA: (Lat.) of Latium.
LEAH: (Heb.) strong.
LEATRICE: (Uncertain).
LEDA: In Greek myth., mother of Helen of Troy.
LEILA: (Arabic) dark as night.
LELIA: (Lat.) from a surname.
LENA: Dim. of Helen. Also, Lina.
LEONA: Fem. of Leon, a form of Leo.
LEONORA: Form of Eleanor. Also, Lenore.
LEOPOLDINE: Fem. of Leopold.
LEORA: Form of Leonora.
LESLEY: Fem. of Leslie. Also, Leslie, like the masculine.
LETITIA: (Lat.) happiness; joy. Also, Leticia. Lettice, Letizia, Letisha. Dims. Leta, Lettie, Letty.
LIANA: Dim. of Juliana.
LIBBY: Dim. of Elizabeth.
LILA: Form of Leila.
LILIAN: (Lat.) lily. Also, Lillian, Liliane.
LILLI: Form of Lily.
LILY: (Lat.) lily. Also, Lilli, Lillah. Dim. Lil.
LINDA: Dim. of Belinda, Melinda.
LISA: Dim. of Elizabeth.
LITA: Dim. of Carmelita.
LIVIA: Dim. of Olivia. Dim. Livvie.
LIZ: Dim. of Elizabeth. Also, Lizzie.
LIZA: Dim. of Elizabeth.
LOIS: (Gk.) good; desirable; otherwise, dim. of Louise.
LOLA: Dim. of Dolores.
LOLLY: Dim. of Laura.
LORA: Form of Laura.
LORELEI: (Ger.) alluring.
LORETTA: Dim. of Laura.
LORNA: Literary name, from heroine of R. D. Blackmore's novel Lorna Doone.
LORRAINE: (F.) of Lorraine (a place name).
LOTTIE: Dim. of Carlotta.
LOUELLA: Compound of Louise and Ella, or some similar invention. Dims. Lou, Lulu.
LOUISE: Fem. of Louis. Also, Louisa. Dims. Lou, Louie. Lulu.
LUCASTA: literary name, from Richard Lovelace's poem "To Lucasta, on Going to the Wars."
LUCIA: Italian form of Lucy.
LUCILLE: Form of Lucy. Also, Lucile.
LUCINDA: Form of Lucy.
LUCRETIA: (Lat.) gain; otherwise, light.
LUCY: Fem. of Lucius.
LULU: Dim. of Louise, Lucy.
LYDIA: (Gk.) of Lydia, country in Asia Minor.
LYNN: Fem. form same as masculine.
MABEL: Dim. of Amabel.
MADELEINE: Form of Magdalene. Also, Madelaine, Madeleina, Madeline, Madelon, Madelyn. Madlyn.
MAGDALENE: (Heb.) of Magdala, city in Galilee. Also, Magdalene, Magdaline. Dims. Magda, Matty.
MADGE: Dim. of Margaret.
MAE: Form af May.
MAGDA: Dim. of Magdalene.
MAGGIE: Dim. of Margaret.
MAGNA: Fem. of Magnus.
MAGNOLIA: From the name of the flower.
MAMIE: Dim. of Amry, May, Margaret. Also, Mame.
MANUELA: Spanish fem. form of Manuel.
MARA: Form of Mary.
MARCELLA: Fem. of Marcellus. Dim. Marcy.
MARCIA: Fem. of Marcius.
MARCY: Dim. of Marcella.
MARGARET: (Gk.) pearl. Also, Marguerita, Marguerite. Dims. Greta, Gretchen, Madge, Mag, Maggie, Maisie, Maisy, Margie, Margo,

Margot, Marjorie, Marjory, Meg, Meta, Peg, Peggie, Peggy, Rita.

MARGERY: Dim. of Margaret. Also, Marjorie.

MARGO: Dim. of Margaret. Also, Margot.

MARGUERITE: Form of Margaret.

MARIA: Form of Margaret.

MARIAN: French form of Mary. Also, Marion.

MARIANA: (Lat.) of the sea.

MARIANNE: Compound of Mary and Anne.

MARIE: French form of Mary.

MARILYN: Form of Mary.

MARIS: (Lat.) of the sea.

MARLENE: Form of Mary.

MARTHA: (Heb.) ruler of the house; otherwise, (Aramaic) lady. Dims. Marta, Marty, Matty.

MARTITIA: Form of Martha.

MARVA: Form of Marvela.

MARVELA: (Lat.) wonderful; marvel.

MARY: (Heb.) their rebellion; otherwise, bitter; otherwise, star of the sea. Also, Maria, Marie, Marion, Miriam. Dims. May, Moll, Mollie, Polly.

MATILDA: (Ger.) mighty battle-maiden; heroine. Also, Mathilda. Dims. Mat, Mattie, Maud, Maude.

MAUD: Dim. of Matilda. Also, Maude.

MAUREEN: Irish form of 'Mary.

MAVIS: (F.) thrush Also, Maeve.

MAXINE: Fem. of Max.

MAY: Dim. of Mary; otherwise, after the month.

MEG: Dim. of Margaret.

MEHITABEL: (Heb.) benefited of God. Also, Mehetabel. Dim. Hetty.

MELANIE: (Gk.) dark.

MELBA: From Melbourne, Australia, a place name.

MELICENT: (Lat.) sweet singer. Dim. Millie, Milly.

MELINDA: Form of Belinda.

MELISSA: (Gk.) bee.

MERCEDES: From Spanish title of the Blessed Virgin as Maria de Mercedes, Mother of Mercies.

MERCIA: From the place name, Mercia, one of the ancient divisions of England.

MERCY: (Lat.) pity; mercy.

MERLE: (Lat.) blackbird.

MERRIE: (A. S.) merry; pleasant; Also, Merry.

MERYL: Form of Muriel.

MIA: (It.) mine; my own.

MICHAELA: Fem. of Michael.

MICHELLE: French fem. form of Michel, or Michael. Also, Michele, Micheline.

MIGNON: (F.) dainty; delicate; petite.

MILDRED: (Ger.) mild speaker; otherwise, mild power. Dim. Millie.

MILLICENT: (Ger.) work-strength. Also, Melicent, Milicent.

MILLIE: Dim. of Mildred, Millicent, etc.

MIMI: Dim. of Miriam.

MINA: Dim. of Wilhelmina.

MINDY: Dim. of Aminta.

MINERVA: (Gk.) in myth., the Greek goddess of wisdom.

MINNA: (Ger.) memory; otherwise, (uncertain).

MINNIE: Dim. of Wilhelmina, Minerva.

MIRABEL: (Lat.) wonderful.

MIRANDA: (Lat.) admirable. Dim. Mira.

MIRIAM: Older form of Mary.

MITZI: Dim. Mary. Also, Mitzie.

MOIRA: Irish form of Mary.

MOLLIE: Dim. of Mary. Also, Molly.

MONA: (Lat.) one; single; unique; otherwise, (Irish) noble.

MONICA: (Lat.) adviser. Also, Monique.

MURIEL: (Irish) sea-bright.

MYRA: (Gk.) weeper; lamenter.

MYRTLE: From the name of the tree.

NADIA: (Slavic) hope. Also, Nadya.

NADINE: French form of Nadia.

NAN: Dim. of Anne, Nancy, etc.

NANCY: Dim. of Anna, Ann.

NANETTE: Dim. of Nan.

NAOMI: (Heb.) pleasant.

NATALIE: Fem. of Noel. Also, Nathalia.

NEDDA: Fem. of Edward.

NELIA: Dim. of Cornelia.

NELLY: Dim. of Eleanor, Ellen, Helen. Also, Nellie.

NEVA: (Lat.) snow.

NICOLE: French fem. form of Nicholas. Also, Nicolette.

NILA: (Lat.) of the Nile River.

NINA: Dim. of Anne.

NITA: Dim. of Juanita.

NOEL: Same as masculine name.

NONA: (Lat.) ninth born.

NORA: Irish dim. of Leonora, Honora. Also, Norah.

NOREEN: Irish dim. of Leonora, Honora.

NORMA: Fem. of Norman.

OCTAVIA: Fem. of Octavius.

ODETTE: French form of Ottilie.

OLGA: (Norse) holy.

OLIVE: (Lat.) olive. Also, Olivia. Dim. Livie.

OLIVIA: Form of Olive.

OLYMPIA: (Gk.) of Olympus (the mountain home of the Greek gods).

OONA: Form of Una.

OPAL: From the name of the jewel.

OPHELIA: (Gk.) help; useful.

ORA: (Lat.) golden.

OTTILLIE: (Ger.) fatherland.

PAMELA: Literary name, probably from the heroine of Samuel Richardson's novel Pamela.

PANSY: From name of the flower.

PAT: Dim. of Patricia. Also, Patty, Patsy.

PATIENCE: (Lat.) patience.

PATRICIA: Fem. of Patrick. Dims. Pat, Patsy, Patty.

PAULA: Fem. of Paul.

PAULINE: Fem. of Paul. Also, Paulina.

PEARL: From the name of the jewel.

PEGGY: Dim. of Margaret.

PENELOPE: (Gk.) weaver. Dims. Pen, Penny.

PEONY: From the name of the flower.

PERRY: Dim. of Pearl.

PERSIS: (Gk.) Persian woman.

PHEBE: Form of Phoebe.

PHILIPPA: Fem. of Philip.

PHILOMENA: (Gk.) strength of a friend. Also, Filomina.

PHOEBE: (Gk.) pure; radiant. Dim. Phebe.

PHYLLIS: (Gk.) green bough.

PIA: (Lat.) pious.

POLLY: Dim. of Mary.

PORTIA: (Lat.) from a surname.

PRISCILLA: (Lat.) somewhat old; ancient. Dim. Prissie.

PRUDENCE: (Lat.) prudent; wise.

PSYCHE: (Gk.) soul.

QUEENIE: Dim. of Queen.

QUINTA: Fem. of Quentin. Also, Quintilla.

RACHEL: (Heb.) ewe; lamb.

RAMONA: Spanish fem. of Ramon (Raymond).

REBECCA: (Heb.) of enchanting beauty; otherwise, yoke. Also, Rebekah. Dims. Beckie, Becky, Reba, Riva.

REGINA: (Lat.) Queen.

RENA: (Heb.) song.

RENATA: (Lat.) reborn; resurrected.

RENE: Dim. of Irene. Also, Renie.

RENÉE: (F.) reborn.

RHEA: (Gk.) in myth., the goddess mother of Zeus.

RHODA: (Gk.) rose; otherwise, from a place name, Rhodes (island).

RHONDA: From a place name.

RITA: Dim. of Margherita.

RIVA: Dim. of Rebecca. Also, Reeva.
ROBERTA: Fem. of Robert.
ROBIN: Same as the masculine.
ROCHELLE: (F.) little rock.
ROMA: (Lat.) of Rome; Roman.
ROSA: (Lat.) rose. Dim. Rosie.
ROSABEL: (Lat.) fair rose. Also, Rosabelle.
ROSALIE: (Lat.) Little blooming rose. Also, Rosalia, Rosaleen.
ROSALIND: (from Sp.) pretty rose; otherwise, (Lat.) beautiful as a rose. Also, Rosalinda. Dims. Rose, Linda.
ROSAMOND: (Lat.) pure rose; otherwise, (Ger.) horse-protection, or famous protection.
ROSE: (Lat.) rose.
ROSEMARY: Contraction of Rose and Mary. Also Rosemarie.
ROSINA: Dim. of Rose. Also, Rosine, Rosita.
ROWENA: (A. S.) fame-friend; otherwise, (Welsh) long white hair.
ROXANA: (Persian) dawn of the day. Also, Roxanna. Dims. Roxie, Roxy.
RUBY: From the jewel.
RUTH: (Heb.) beauty.
SABINA: (Lat.) Sabine woman.
SADIE: Dim. of Sara.
SALLY: Dim. of Sara. Also, Sallie.
SALOME: (Heb.) peaceful.
SAPPHIRA: (Heb.) gem; beautiful.
SAPPHO: (Gk.) after Sappho, Greek poetess.
SARA: (Heb.) princess. Also, Sarah, Dims. Sadie. Sal, Sallie, Sally.
SELINA: (Gk.) moon. Also, Selena.
SELMA: Fem. and dim. of Anselm.
SERAFINA: (Heb.) angel. Also, Seraphina.
SERENA: (Lat.) calm; peaceful.
SHARON: (Heb.) of Sharon.
SHEBA: (Heb.) oath.
SHEILA: Irish form of Celia. Also, Sheilah, Sheelah.
SHELLY: Dim. of Sheila, Shirley, Rochelle, etc. Also, Shelley.
SHERRY: (F.) dear one; otherwise, Dim. of Shirley, Sara, etc.
SHIRLEY: From a place name.
SIBYL: (Gk.) prophetess. Also, Sibylla, Sybil.
SILVIA: Form of Sylvia.
SIMONE: French fem. form of Simon.
SONDRA: Dim. of Alexandra. Also, Sandy, Sandra.
SONIA: Russian dim. of Sophia. Also, Sonja, Sonya.
SOPHIA: (Gk.) wisdom. Dims. Sophie, Sophy.
SOPHRONIA: (Gk.) of a sound mind.
STACY: Dim. of Anastasia.
STAR: (Eng.) star. Also, Starr.
STELLA: (Lat.) star.
STEPHANIE: Fem. of Stephen. Also, Stephana.
SUSAN: (Heb.) lily. Also, Susanna, Susannah. Dims. Sue, Susie, Suzy, Suky.
SYDNEY: Same as the masculine. Also, Sidney.
SYLVIA: (Lat.) wood; of the woods. Fem. of Sylvius (Sylvanus).
TABITHA: (Syrian) gazelle. Dim. Tabby.
TALLULAH: From a place name. Also, Tallula.
TAMARA: (Heb.) palm tree; otherwise, in myth., Queen of Caucasian Georgia.
TANAQUIL: (Lat.) after the wife of Tarquin.
TANYA: Dim. of Titania. Also, Tania.
TECLA: (Gk.) divine fame.
TERRY: Dim. of Theresa.
THALIA: (Gk.) in Greek literature, the muse of comedy.
THEA: Dim. of Dorothea.
THEDA: Dim. of Theodora.
THELMA: (Gk.) nursling.
THEODORA: Fem. of Theodore.
THEODOSIA: (Gk.) gift of the gods.

THERESA: (Gk.) bearing ears of corn; otherwise, to reap. Also, Teresa, Therese. Dims. Terry, Tess, Tessie.
THERESE: French form of Theresa.
THIRZA: (Heb.) linden tree. Also, Thurza, Tirza.
THISBE: (Gk.) from a place name.
THOMASINE: Fem. of Thomas.
TILLY: Dim. of Matilda.
TINA: Dim. of Christina, Evalina, etc. Also, Teena.
TONI: Dim. of Antoinette.
TRIXIE: Dim. of Beatrice.
ULRICA: Fem. of Ulric.
UNA: (Lat.) one. In Ireland, same as Agnes, Winifred.
UNDINE: (Lat.) wave. Also, Ondine.
URANIA: (Gk.) heavenly.
URSULA: (Lat.) bear.
VALENTINA: Fem. of Valentine.
VALERIE: (Lat.) strong. Also, Valeria.
VANESSA: A name created by Jonathan Swift in his Epistles.
VERA: (Lat.) true.
VERONICA: (Lat.) (uncertain); otherwise, (Gk. and Lat.) true image.
VICTORIA: (Lat.) victory. Dims. Vickie, Vicky.
VIDA: Fem. of David.
VIOLA: (Lat.) Violet. Dim. Vi.
VIOLET: From the name of the flower.
VIRGINIA: (Lat.) virgin; pure. Dims. Ginger, Ginny, Jennie, Jinnie, Virgie.
VIVIAN: (Lat.) lively. Also, Vivien, Vyvyan.
WALLIS: Fem. of Wallace. Dim. Wally.
WANDA: (Ger.) (uncertain).
WENDY: Dim. of Gwendolyn.
WILFREDA: Fem. of Wilfred.
WILHELMINA: Fem. of Wilhelm. Dims. Billie, Mina, Minella, Wilmett, Wilmot.
WILLA: Fem. of Will.
WILMA: Dim. of Wilhelmina.
WINIFRED: (A. S.) lover of peace; otherwise, (Welsh) white wave. Dims. Winnie, Freddie.
WINNIE: Dim. of Winifred.
XANTHE: (Gk.) golden yellow.
XANTIPPE: (Gk.) after Xantippe, the wife of Socrates.
XENIA: (Gk.) guest.
YASMIN: Form of Jasmine.
YETTA: Dim. of Henrietta.
YNEZ: Form of Inez.
YOLANDA: Form of Viola. Also, Yolande.
YVETTE: Form of Yvonne.
YVONNE: French fem. form of Yvor. See Ivor.
ZELDA: Dim. of Griselda.
ZENOBIA: (Gk.) having life from Zeus (Jupiter).
ZIPPORAH: (Heb.) bird.
ZITA: Dim. of Rosita, Teresita, etc.
ZOE: (Gk.) life.
ZONA: (Lat.) girdle.
ZULEIKA: (Arabic) fair.

National Battlefield Parks

KENNESAW MOUNTAIN: Ga.; established 1947; 3094 acres; important Civil War battle in Sherman's Atlanta Campaign.
RICHMOND: Va.; established 1944; 684 acres; scene of several battles in defense of Richmond during Civil War.

National Battlefield Sites

ANTIETAM: Md.; established 1890; 183 acres; site of battle that ended Lee's first invasion of the North in 1862.

BRICES CROSS ROADS: Miss.; established 1929; 1 acre; battle in which Forrest's cavalry took part, June 10, 1864.
COWPENS: S. C.; established 1929; 1 acre; site of Daniel Morgan's victory over the British on June 17, 1781.
FORT NECESSITY: Pa.; established 1931; 2 acres; scene of the opening battle of the French and Indian War.
TUPELO: Miss.; established 1929; 1 acre; commemorates Battle of Tupelo, July 13, 1864.
WHITE PLAINS: N. Y.; established 1926; marks positions of Washington's army at Battle of White Plains.

FORT DONELSON: Tenn.; established 1867; 15.34 acres.
FREDERICKSBURG: Va.; established 1865; 12.00 acres.
GETTYSBURG: Pa.; established 1863; 15.55 acres.
POPLAR GROVE: Va.; established 1866; 8.72 acres.
SHILOH: Tenn.; established 1866; 10.25 acres.
STONES RIVER: Tenn.; established 1865; 20.09 acres.
VICKSBURG: Miss.; established 1865; 119.76 acres.
YORKTOWN: Va.; established 1866; 2.91 acres.

National Book Awards

Note: The National Book Award, established in 1950, is an annual presentation by the American Booksellers' Association, and the Book Manufacturers' Institute of New York, for distinguished work in the categories of fiction, non-fiction, and poetry.

Fiction

1950: Nelson Algren, *The Man With the Golden Arm*.
1951: William Faulkner, *Collected Stories*. There was a special citation this year for *The Trouble of One House*, a novel by Brendan Gill.
1952: James Jones, *From Here to Eternity*.
1953: Ralph Ellison, *Invisible Man*.
1954: Saul Bellow, *The Adventures of Augie March*.
1955: John O'Hara, *Ten North Frederick*.
1956: Wright Morris, *A Field of Vision*.

Non-fiction

1950: Ralph L. Rusk, *The Life of Ralph Waldo Emerson*.
1951: Newton Arvin, *Herman Melville*.
1952: Rachel L. Carson, *The Sea Around Us*.
1953: Bernard DeVoto, *The Course of Empire*.
1954: Bruce Catton, *A Stillness at Appomattox*.
1955: Herbert Kubly, *American in Italy*.
1956: George F. Kennan, *Russia Leaves the War*.

Poetry

1950: William Carlos Williams, *Paterson (Book III)*, and also *Selected Poems*.
1951: Wallace Stevens, *The Auroras of Autumn*.
1952: Marianne Moore, *Collected Poems*.
1953: Archibald MacLeish, *Collected Poems, 1917-1952*.
1954: Conrad Aiken, *Collected Poems*.
1955: W. H. Auden, *The Shield of Achilles*.
1956: Richard Wilbur, *Things of This World*.

National Capital Parks

NATIONAL CAPITAL PARKS: D. C.-Va.-Md. established 1790; 29,023 acres; park system of the nation's capital.

National Cemeteries

ANTIETAM: Md.; established 1862; 11.36 acres.
BATTLEGROUND: D. C.; established 1864; 1.03 acres.

National Colors
See Colors

National Federal Historic Sites

ADAMS MANSION: Mass.; established 1946; 4 acres; home of Presidents John Adams and John Quincy Adams.
ATLANTA CAMPAIGN: Ga.; established 1944; 21 acres; marks significant point on Sherman's march from Chattanooga to Atlanta.
FEDERAL HALL MEMORIAL: N. Y.; established 1939; 0.49 acre; site of first seat of United States Goverment.
FORT RALEIGH: N. C.; established 1941; 16 acres; site of Sir Walter Raleigh's "Lost Colony."
HAMPTON: Md.; established 1948; 43 acres; one of the finest Georgian mansions in America. Completed about 1790.
HOME OF FRANKLIN D. ROOSEVELT: N. Y.; established 1944; 33 acres; Roosevelt's birthplace and home.
HOPEWELL VILLAGE: Pa.; established 1938; 848 acres; an early iron making village.
JEFFERSON NATIONAL EXPANSION MEMORIAL: Mo.; established 1935; 83 acres; commemorates territorial expansion.
MANNASSAS BATTLEFIELD: Va.; established 1940; 1605 acres; two significant Civil War battles were fought here.
OLD PHILADELPHIA CUSTOM HOUSE: Pa.; established 1939; 1 acre; fine example of Greek revival architecture.
SALEM MARITIME: Mass.; established 1938; 9 acres; early New England waterfront scene.
VANDERBILT MANSION: N.Y.; established 1940; 212 acres; example American palatial residence period 1880-1900.

National Historical Parks
See also Trails, American

ABRAHAM LINCOLN: Ky.; established 1939; 117 acres; log cabin believed to be that in which Lincoln was born, in memorial building on site of his birthplace.
CHALMETTE: La.; established 1939; 33 acres; part of ground on which was fought the Battle of New Orleans.
COLONIAL: Va.; established 1936; 7233 acres; Jamestown Island, site first permanent English settlement in America; Yorktown, scene American victory over Cornwallis.
MORRISTOWN: N. J.; established 1933; 958 acres; site of military encampment during Revolution, 1779-80.
SARATOGA: N. Y.; established 1948; 1865 acres; scene American victory over British General Burgoyne, 1777.

National Historic Sites Not Owned by Federal Government

GLORIA DEI: Pa.; established 1942. Second oldest Swedish church in United States. Erected about 1700. Administered by Corporation of Gloria Dei Church.

INDEPENDENCE HALL: Pa.; established 1943. Scene of the adoption of the Declaration of Independence. Administered by the city of Philadelphia.

JAMESTOWN: Va.; established 1940. Part of the site of the first permanent English settlement. Administered by Association for Preservation of Virginia Antiquities.

McLOUGHLIN HOUSE: Oreg.; established 1941. Home of John McLoughlin, "Father of Oregon." Administered by McLoughlin Memorial Association and municipality of Oregon City.

ST. PAUL'S CHURCH: N.Y.; established 1943. Eighteenth-cent. church connected with events leading to establishment of the Bill of Rights. Administered by Corporation of St. Paul's Church.

SAN JOSE MISSION: Tex.; established 1941. Fine example of a Spanish mission. Administered by the Catholic Church and State of Texas.

TOURO SYNAGOGUE: R. I.; established 1946. Illustrates Colonial religious architecture. Owned by Congregation Sherith Israel, New York City.

National Memorial Park

THEODORE ROOSEVELT: N. Dak.; established 1947; 58,341 acres; interesting Badlands and part of Roosevelt ranch.

National Memorials

HOUSE WHERE LINCOLN DIED: D.C.; established 1896; Lincoln died here on April 15, 1865.

KILL DEVIL HILL MONUMENT: N. C.; established 1927; 314 acres; site of Wright brothers' first airplane flight.

LEE MANSION: Va.; established 1925; 3 acres; antebellum home of Robert E. Lee.

LINCOLN MEMORIAL: D. C.; established 1922; classical structure with seated figure of Lincoln.

LINCOLN MUSEUM: D. C.; established 1932; formerly Ford's Theater, in which Lincoln was shot.

MOUNT RUSHMORE: S. Dak.; established 1929; 1686 acres; heads of four presidents carved on face of mountain.

NEW ECHOTA MARKER: Ga.; established 1930; 1 acre; site of last capital of Cherokee Indians in Georgia.

THOMAS JEFFERSON: D. C.; established 1943; 1 acre; colonnaded structure with heroic bronze statue of Jefferson.

WASHINGTON MONUMENT: D. C.; established 1885; obelisk, 555 feet high, in commemoration of George Washington.

National Military Parks

CHICKAMAUGA AND CHATTANOOGA: Ga.-Tenn.; established 1890; 8149 acres; Civil War battlefields around Chattanooga.

FORT DONELSON: Tenn.; established 1928; 103 acres; in capturing this fort in 1862, Grant earned sobriquet "Unconditional Surrender Grant."

FREDERICKSBURG AND SPOTSYLVANIA: Va.; established 1927; 2421 acres; important Civil War battlefields.

GETTYSBURG: Pa.; established 1895; 2463 acres; on this battlefield the tide turned against Confederate arms.

GUILFORD COURTHOUSE: N.C.; established 1917; 149 acres; commemorates Revolutionary battle, Mar. 15,1781.

KINGS MOUNTAIN: S. C.; established 1931; 4012 acres; site of 1780 victory of American frontiersmen over British.

MOORES CREEK: N. C.; established 1926; 30 acres; scene of battle between Whigs and Tories in 1776.

PETERSBURG: Va.; established 1926; 1325 acres; scene of the siege of Petersburg, 1864-65.

SHILOH: Tenn.; established 1894; 3729 acres; scene of Union victory in one of costliest battles of Civil War.

STONES RIVER: Tenn.; established 1927; 324 acres; scene of bloody Civil War engagement, 1862.

VICKSBURG: Miss.; established 1899; 1324 acres; scene of 47-day siege, which ended in a Union victory.

National Monuments
See also **Trails, American**

ACKIA BATTLEGROUND: Miss.; established 1938; 49 acres; site of Chickasaw Indian village and a Colonial battle.

ANDREW JOHNSON: Tenn.; established 1942; 17 acres; President Andrew Johnson's home, tailor shop, and grave.

APPOMATTOX COURT HOUSE: Va.; established 1940; 968 acres; scene of Lee's surrender to Grant, April 9, 1865.

ARCHES: Ut.; established 1929; 33,770 acres; extraordinary examples of erosion in form of giant arches.

AZTEC RUINS: N. Mex.; established 1923; 27 acres; ruins of prehistoric Indian town built in twelfth century.

BADLANDS: S. Dak.; established 1939; 122,972 acres; weirdly eroded area containing prehistoric animal fossils.

BANDELIER: N. Mex.; established 1916; 27,049 acres; ruins of prehistoric Indian homes.

BIG HOLE BATTLEFIELD: Mont.; established 1910; 200 acres; site of battle fought during retreat of . Chief Joseph.

BLACK CANYON OF THE GUNNISON: Colo.; established 1933; 13,176 acres; deep canyon of great geologic interest.

CABRILLO: Calif.; established 1913; 1 acre; memorial to Juan Rodriguez Cabrillo, discoverer of San Diego Bay.

CANYON DE CHELLY: Ariz.; established 1931; 83,840 acres; Indian ruins in caves in sheer canyon walls.

CAPITOL REEF: Ut.; established 1937; 33,069 acres; twenty-mile-long sandstone cliff of Gothic appearance.

CAPULIN MOUNTAIN: N. Mex.; established 1916; 680 acres; cone of a recently extinct volcano.

CASA GRANDE: Ariz.; established 1918; 473 acres; ruined adobe tower built by Indian farmers 600 years ago.

CASTILLO DE SAN MARCOS: Fla.; established 1924; 19 acres; oldest masonry fort in United States; built by Spanish.

CASTLE PINCKNEY: S. C.; established 1924;

4 acres; part of early defenses of Charleston Harbor.

CEDAR BREAKS: Ut.; established 1933; 6172 acres; spectacular natural amphitheater with pink rock walls.

CHACO CANYON: N. Mex.; established 1907; 18,039 acres; Indian ruins representing a high degree of culture.

CHANNEL ISLANDS: Calif.; established 1938; 1120 acres; sea-lion rookery; fossil beds. Undeveloped.

CHIRICAHUA: Ariz.; established 1924; 10,530 acres; wilderness of strange shaped rocks.

COLORADO: Colo.; established 1911; 18,121 acres; sheer-walled canyons, towering monoliths, and weird formations.

CRATERS OF THE MOON: Ida.; established 1924; 47,211 acres; cones, craters, and other volcanic phenomena.

CUSTER BATTLEFIELD: Mont.; established 1946; 765 acres; site of Custer's last stand.

DEATH VALLEY: Calif.-Nev.; established 1933; 1,850,565 acres; vast desert; lowest point in United States.

DEVIL POSTPILE: Calif.; established 1911; 798 acres; columnar remnant of a basaltic lava flow.

DEVILS TOWER: Wyo.; established 1906; 1194 acres; volcanic rock tower, 865 feet high. First national monument.

DINOSAUR: Ut.-Colo.; established 1915; 190,798 acres; rich fossil beds; rugged canyons.

EL MORRO: N. Mex.; established 1906; 240 acres; rock inscribed by Spanish and other early explorers.

FATHER MILLET CROSS: N. Y.; established 1925; memorial cross in memory of Father Pierre Millet.

FORT FREDERICA: Ga.; established 1945; 75 acres; built 1736 during struggle between Spain and England.

FORT JEFFERSON: Fla.; established 1935; 87 acres; built 1846 to control Florida Straits; bird and marine life.

FORT LARAMIE: Wyo.; established 1938; 214 acres; military post on route of '49ers and the Oregon Trail.

FORT MATANZAS: Fla.; established 1924; 228 acres; Spanish fort built in 1737 for protection of St. Augustine.

FORT McHENRY: Md.; established 1939; 48 acres; defense, 1814, inspired writing of "The Star-Spangled Banner."

FORT PULASKI: Ga.; established 1924; 5427 acres; used in defense of Savannah during War between the States.

FORT SUMTER: S. C.; established 1948; 2 acres; capture of this fort in Charleston Harbor by Confederates early in 1861 marked the beginning of the War between the States.

FOSSIL CYCAD: S. Dak.; established 1922; 320 acres; fossil beds. Undeveloped.

GEORGE WASHINGTON BIRTHPLACE: Va.; etablished 1930; 394 acres; memorial mansion on site of birthplace.

GILA CLIFF DWELLINGS: N. Mex.; established 1907; 160 acres; cliff dwellings in face of overhanging cliff.

GLACIER BAY: Alaska; established 1925; 2,297,456 acres; great tidewater glaciers and postglacial forests.

GRAND CANYON: Ariz.; established 1932; 196,051 acres; part of Grand Canyon of the Colorado River.

GRAN QUIVIRA: N. Mex.; established 1909; 451 acres; site of 17th-cent. Spanish mission.

GREAT SAND DUNES: Colo.; established 1932; 35,908 acres; among highest and largest dunes in United States.

HOLY CROSS: Colo.; established 1929; 1392 acres; snow-filled crevices in form of cross.

HOMESTEAD: Nebr.; established 1939; 163 acres; site of first claim under Homestead Act of 1862.

HOVENWEEP: Ut.-Colo.; established 1923; 299 acres; prehistoric towers, pueblos, and cliff dwellings.

JACKSON HOLE: Wyo.; established 1943; 173,065 acres; favorite haunt of trappers and traders. Teton foreground.

JEWEL CAVE: S. Dak.; established 1908; 1275 acres; cave decorated with fine calcite crystals.

JOSHUA TREE: Calif.; established 1936; 655,961 acres; fine stand of the rare Joshua tree.

KATMAI: Alaska; established 1918; 2,697,590 acres; dying volcanic region; Valley of Ten Thousand Smokes.

LAVA BEDS: Calif.; established 1925; 46,028 agres; scene of Modoc Indian War of 1873.

LEHMAN CAVES: Nev.; established 1922; 640 acres; caves of light gray and white limestone.

MERIWETHER LEWIS: Tenn.; established 1925; 300 acres; burial place of leader of Lewis and Clarke Expedition.

MONTEZUMA CASTLE: Ariz.; established 1906 783 acres; 5-story, 20-room Indian cliff dwelling.

MOUND CITY GROUP: O.; established 1923; 57 acres; famous group of prehistoric Indian mounds.

MUIR WOODS: Calif.; established 1908; 425 acres; virgin stand of coast redwoods, tallest of living things.

NATURAL BRIDGES: Ut.; established 1908; 2650 acres; three giant natural bridges eroded out of sandstone.

NAVAJO: Ariz.; established 1909; 360 acres; three of the largest and most elaborate of known cliff dwellings.

OCMULGEE: Ga.; established 1936; 683 acres; council chamber; ceremonial mounds, and other Indian remains.

OLD KASAAN: Alaska; established 1916; 38 acres; site of an abandoned Haida Indian village.

OREGON CAVES: Oreg.; established 1909; 480 acres; caves in limestone formation of great variety and beauty.

ORGAN PIPE CACTUS: Ariz.; established 1937; organ pipe cactus and other unusual desert plants.

PERRY'S VICTORY PEACE MEMORAL: O.; established 1936; 14 acres; commemorates naval victory in War of 1812.

PETRIFIED Forest: Ariz.; established 1906; 85,304 acres; spectacular petrified wood display: Painted Desert.

PINNACLES: Calif.; established 1908; 12,818 acres; spirelike rock formations 500 to 1200 feet high.

PIPE SPRING: Ariz.; established 1923; 40 acres; historic Mormon fort.

PIPESTONE: Minn.; established 1937; 116 acres; quarry from which Indians obtained materials for making peace pipes.

RAINBOW BRIDGE: Ut.; established 1910; 160 acres; largest known natural bridge in the world.

SAGUARO: Ariz.; established 1933; 53,669 acres; giant cacti.

SCOTTS BLUFF: Nebr.; established 1919; 2196 acres; landmark on Oregon Trail.

SHOSHONE CAVERN: Wyo.; established 1909; 212 acres; cave decorated with crystals. Not open to public.

SITKA: Alaska; established 1910; 57 acres; commemorates last stand of Kik-Siti Indians against Russian settlers.

STATUE OF LIBERTY: N. Y.; established 1924; 10 acres; colossal statue on Bedloe's Island; gift of French people.

SUNSET CRATER: Ariz.; established 1930; 3040 acres; truncated volcanic cone with brightly colored rim.

TIMPANAGOS CAVE: Ut.; established 1922; 250 acres; limestone cavern.

TONTO: Ariz.; established 1907; 1120 acres; two large well-preserved Pueblo cliff dwellings.

TUMACACORI: Ariz.; established 1908; 10 acres; historic Spanish mission building.

TUZIGOOT: Ariz.; established 1939; 43 acres; excavated ruins of a prehistoric pueblo occupied about 1000-1400 a.d.

VERENDRYE: N. Dak.; established 1917; 253 acres; commemorates the Verendrye explorations in North Dakota.

WALNUT CANYON: Ariz.; established 1915; 1642 acres; cliff dwellings in shallow caves built 1000 years ago.

WHEELER: Colo.; established 1908; 300 acres; an extinct volcanic region with pinnacles and deep gorges.

WHITE SANDS: N. Mex.; established 1933; 140,247 acres; glistening white gypsum sands drifting into high dunes.

WHITMAN: Wash.; established 1940; 46 acres; site of Indian mission and massacre of Whitman family.

WUPATKI: Ariz.; established 1924; 34,853 acres; red sandstone pueblo built by Indians nearly 1000 years ago.

YUCCA HOUSE: Colo.; established 1919; 10 acres; remnants of a once thriving prehistoric Indian village.

ZION: Ut.; established 1937; 33,921 acres; colorful Kolob Canyon and famous Hurricane Fault.

National Parks
See also **Trails, American**

ACADIA: Me.; established 1919; 28,308 acres; rugged coastal area on Mount Desert Island and nearby mainland.

BIG BEND: Tex.; established 1944; 691,339 acres; mountains and desert in the great bend of the Rio Grande.

BRYCE CANYON: Ut.; established 1928; 36,010 acres; grotesque fairyland of rock formations in many colors.

CARLSBAD CAVERNS: N. Mex.; established 1930; 45,527 acres; vast caverns with magnificent and curious formations.

CRATER LAKE: Oreg.; established 1902; 160,290 acres; deep blue lake in heart of extinct volcano.

EVERGLADES: Fla.; established 1947; 271,008 acres; subtropical swamps and prairies. Rich bird and animal life.

GLACIER: Mont.; established 1910; 997,248 acres; rocky mountain scenery with glaciers and lakes. Part of Waterton-Glacier International Peace Park, established 1932.

GRAND CANYON: Ariz.; established 1919; 645,296 acres; mile-deep gorge. World's most titanic example of erosion.

GRAND TETON: Wyo.; established 1929; 94,893 acres; majestic peaks, picturesque lakes, an unspoiled wilderness.

GREAT SMOKY MOUNTAINS: N. C.-Tenn.; established 1930; 451,004 acres; loftiest mountains east of the Black Hills, virgin forests.

HAWAII: T. H.; established 1916; 173,405 acres; active volcanoes, tropical vegetation fern forests.

HOT SPRINGS: Ark.; established 1921; 1019 acres; forty-seven mineral hot springs said to have therapeutic value.

ISLE ROYALE: Mich.; established 1940; 133,839 acres; great wilderness island in Lake Superior; moose herd.

KINGS CANYON: Calif.; established 1940; 452,905 acres; mountains, canyons, groves of giant sequoias.

LASSEN VOLCANIC: Calif.; established 1916; 103,269 acres; only recently active volcano in United States proper.

MAMMOTH CAVE: Ky.; established 1936; 50,585 acres; historic series of caverns; underground river.

MESA VERDE: Colo.; established 1906; 51,018 acres; large number of Indian cliff dwellings and other ruins.

MOUNT McKINLEY: Alas.; established 1917; highest mountain in North America. Unusual wildlife.

MOUNT RAINIER: Wash.; established 1899; 241,525 acres; greatest single-peak glacial system in United States.

OLYMPIC: Wash.; established 1938; 846,719 acres; mountain wilderness, rain forests, Roosevelt elk.

PLATT: Okla.; established 1906; 912 acres; cold mineral springs with distinctive properties.

ROCKY MOUNTAIN: Colo.; established 1915; 252,788 acres; magnificent section of Rocky Mountains.

SEQUOIA: Calif.; established 1890; 385,100 acres; groves of giant sequoias. Mount Whitney, highest in United States.

SHENANDOAH: Va.; established 1935; 193,473 acres; scenic portion of Blue Ridge Mountains with Skyline Drive.

WIND CAVE: S. Dak.; established 1903; 26,583 acres; limestone caverns in Black Hills; buffalo herd.

YELLOWSTONE: Wyo.-Mont.-Ida.; established 1872; 2,213,207 acres; world's greatest geyser area; spectacular falls and canyon; lakes; abundant wildlife.

YOSEMITE: Calif.; established 1890; 756,441 acres; inspiring gorge with sheer granite cliffs; waterfalls, three groves of giant sequoias; high Sierras.

Federal Recreational Areas
Not Part of National Park System

COULEE DAM: Wash.; established 1946; 98,500 acres. Part of Columbia River Basin project; recreational facilities being developed and administered by National Park Service under cooperative agreement with Bureau of Reclamation and Office of Indian Affairs.

LAKE MEAD: Ariz.-Nev.; established 1936; 1,772,533 acres. Third largest artificial lake in United States; recreational facilities administered by National Park Service under cooperative agreement with Bureau of Reclamation.

LAKE TEXOMA: Tex.-Okla.; established 1946; 161,137 acres. Recreational facilities are being developed and administered by National Park Service under cooperative agreement with Department of the Army.

MILLERTON LAKE: Calif.; established 1945; 11,605 acres. Development and administration of recreational facilities by National Park Service covered by cooperative agreement with Bureau of Reclamation.

ZION: Ut.; established 1919; 94,241 acres;

multicolored gorge in southern Utah's desert and canyon country.

National Parkways

BLUE RIDGE PARKWAY: Va.-N. C.; established 1933; 42,850 acres; scenic parkway averaging 3000 feet above sea level. Now completed or under construction, 333 miles.
GEORGE WASHINGTON MEMORIAL PARKWAY: Va.-Md.; established 1930; 2898 acres; parkway planned for Maryland and Virginia shores of Potomac River. Section completed between Washington and Mount Vernon.
NATCHEZ TRACE PARKWAY: Miss.-Tenn.-Ala.; established 1934; 13,649 acres; follows Indian trail, Nashville to Natchez. Completed or under construction, 147 miles.

Near Eastern Rulers, Ancient
See **Rulers**

New York Drama Critics Circle Awards
See also **Awards**

1935-36: *Winterset*, by Maxwell Anderson.
1936-37: *High Tor*, by Maxwell Anderson.
1937-38: *Of Mice and Men*, by John Steinbeck.
1938-39: None.
1939-40: *The Time of Your Life*, by William Saroyan.
1940-41: *Watch on the Rhine*, by Lillian Hellman.
1941-42: None.
1942-43: *The Patriots*, by Sidney Kingsley.
1943-44: None.
1944-45: *The Glass Menagerie*, by Tennessee Williams.
1945-46: None.
1946-47: *All My Sons*, by Arthur Miller.
1947-48: *A Streetcar Named Desire*, by Tennessee Williams.
1948-49: *Death of a Salesman*, by Arthur Miller.
1949-50: *The Member of the Wedding*, by Carson McCullers.
1950-51: *Darkness at Noon*, by Sidney Kingsley.
1951-52: *I Am a Camera*, by John Van Druten.
1952-53: *Picnic*, by William Inge.
1953-54: *The Teahouse of the August Moon*, by John Patrick.
1954-55: *Cat on a Hot Tin Roof*, by Tennessee Williams.
1955-56: *The Diary of Anne Frank*, by Frances Goodrich and Albert Hackett.
1956-57: *Long Day's Journey Into Night*, by Eugene O'Neill.

Nobel Prizes: Chemistry, Literature, Medicine and Physiology, Peace, Physics
See also **Awards**

Chemistry

1901: Jacobus Hendricus van't Hoff (Dutch). For the discovery of laws of chemical dynamics and of osmotic pressure.
1902: Emil Fischer (German). For his syntheses in the groups of sugars and purines.
1903: Svante August Arrhenius (Swedish). For his theory of electrolytic dissociation.
1904: Sir William Ramsay (English). For the discovery of gaseous, indifferent elements in the air and the determination of their place in the periodic system.
1905: Johann Friedrich Wilhelm Adolf von Baeyer (German). For his researches on organic dyestuffs and hydroaromatic compounds.
1906: Henri Moissan (French). For his research on the isolation of the element fluorine and for placing at the service of science the electric furnace which bears his name.
1907: Eduard Buchner (German). For his biochemical researches and his discovery of cellless fermentation.
1908: Ernest Rutherford (English). For his investigation into the disintegration of the elements and the chemistry of radioactive substances.
1909: Wilhelm Ostwald (German). For his work on catalysis and on the conditions of chemical equilibrium and velocities of chemical reactions.
1910: Otto Wallach (German). For his initiative work in the field of alicyclic substances.
1911: Marie Curie (French). For her services to the advancement of chemistry by the discovery of the elements radium and polonium, by the isolation of radium and the study of the nature and compounds of this remarkable element.
1912: Victor Grignard (French). For the discovery of the so-called Grignard reagent which has greatly helped in the development of organic chemistry during these last years.
1912: Paul Sabatier (French). For his method of hydrogenating organic compounds in the presence of finely divided metals.
1913: Alfred Werner (Swiss). In recognation of his work on the linkage of atoms in molecules, by which he has thrown fresh light on old problems and opened up new fields of research, particularly in inorganic chemistry.
1914: Theodore William Richards (American). For his exact determinations of the atomic weights of a great number of chemical elements.
1915: Richard Willstätter (German). For research on coloring matter in the vegetable kingdom, principally on chlorophyll.
1916: None.
1917: None.
1918: Fritz Haber (German). For the synthesis of ammonia from its elements, nitrogen and hydrogen.
1919: None.
1920: Walther Hermann Nernst (German). For his thermochemical work.
1921: Frederick Soddy (English). For his contributions to the chemistry of radioactive substances and his investigations into the origin and nature of isotopes.
1922: Francis William Aston (English). For his discovery, by means of his mass spectrograph, of the isotopes of a large number of nonradioactive elements, as well as for his discovery of the whole-number rule.
1923: Fritz Pregl (Austrian). For his invention of the method of microanalysis of organic substances.
1924: None.
1925: Richard Zsigmondy (German). For his elucidation of the heterogeneous nature of colloid solutions and for the methods he has devised in this connection, which have since become of fundamental importance in modern colloid chemistry.
1926: Theodor (The) Svedberg (Swedish). For his work on disperse systems.
1927: Heinrich Wieland (German). For his research on bile acids and analogous substances.

1928: Adolf Windaus (German). For his studies on the constitution of the sterols and their connection with the vitamins.

1929: Arthur Harden (English), Hans August Simon von Euler-Chelpin (German). For their investigations on the fermentation of sugar and of fermentative enzymes.

1930: Hans Fischer (German). For his researches into the constitution of hemin and chlorophyll, especially for his synthesis of hemin.

1931: Carl Bosch, Friedrich Bergius (German). In recognition of their contributions to the invention and development of chemical high-pressure methods.

1932: Irving Langmuir (American). For his discoveries and investigations in surface chemistry.

1933: None.

1934: Harold Clayton Urey (American). For his discovery of heavy hydrogen.

1935: Frédéric and Irène Joliot-Curie (French). For their synthesis of new radioactive elements.

1936: Peter Joseph Wilhelm Debye (b. Holland). For his contributions to the study of molecular structure through his investigations on dipole moments and on the diffraction of X-rays and electrons in gases.

1937: Sir Walter Norman Haworth (English). For his researches into the constitution of carbohydrates and vitamin C.

1937: Paul Karrer (Swiss). For his researches into the constitution of carotinoids, flavins, and vitamins A and B.

1938: Richard Kuhn (German). For his work on carotinoids and vitamins.

1939: Adolph Butenandt (German). For his work on sex hormones.

1939: Léopold Ružička (Swiss). For his work on polymethylenes and higher terpenes.

1940, 1941, 1942: None.

1943: Georg Hevesy (Hungarian). For his work on the use of isotopes as tracer elements in researches on chemical processes.

1944: Otto Hahn (German). For his discovery of the fission of heavy nuclei.

1945: Artturi Ilmari Virtanen (Finnish). For his researches and inventions in agricultural and nutritive chemistry, especially for his method of fodder preservation.

1946: James B. Summer (American). For his discovery that enzymes can be crystallized.

1946: John Northrop, Wendell M. Stanley (American). For their preparation of enzymes and virus proteins in a pure form.

1947: Sir Robert Robinson (English). For research on certain vegetable products of great biological importance, particularly alkaloids.

1948: Arne Tiselius (Swedish). For his researches on electrophoresis and adsorption analysis, especially for his discoveries concerning the complex nature of the serum proteins.

1949: William F. Giauque (American). For his work in the field of chemical thermodynamics, particularly concerning the behavior of substances at extremely low temperatures.

1950: Otto Diels, Kurt Adler (German). For the development of the diene synthesis.

1951: Edwin M. McMillan, Glenn I. Seaborg (American). For their discovery of plutonium. McMillan's work made possible the creation of cosmic rays in the laboratory (this in addition to his citation for work with Seaborg).

1952: Archer Martin (Canadian). For the development of paper partition chromatography, a method of separating compounds which is a modernization of a chemical technique said to have been known to the ancient Egyptians.

1953: Herman Staudinger (German). For the discovery, in 1927, of a way to synthesize fiber, thus laying the foundations of the modern plastics industry.

1954: Linus Pauling (American). For his work on the nature of chemical bonds, especially as applied to the structure of complicated substances.

1955: Vincent du Vigneaud (American). For his work in identifying oxytocin and vasopressin in a hormone produced by the pituitary gland and making a synthesis of the hormone.

1956: Sir Cyril N. Hinshelwood (English); Nikolai N. Semenov (Russian). For work on chemical reaction kinetics to improve the internal combustion engine and modern plastics.

Literature

Note: There were no awards in 1914, 1918, 1935, 1940-1943.

1901: René Sully Prudhomme (French). Poet.

1902: Theodor Mommsen (German). Historian.

1903: Björnstjerne Björnson (Norwegian). Novelist, dramatist.

1904: Frédéric Mistral (French). Poet. José Echegaray (Spanish). Dramatist.

1905: Henryk Sienkiewicz (Polish). Novelist.

1906: Giosué Carducci (Italian). Poet.

1907: Rudyard Kipling (English). Poet, novelist, short-story writer.

1908: Rudolf Eucken (German). Philosopher.

1909: Selma Lagerlöf (Swedish). Novelist.

1910: Paul von Heyse (German). Poet, novelist, dramatist.

1911: Maurice Maeterlinck (Belgian). Dramatist.

1912: Gerhart Hauptmann (German). Dramatist.

1913: Rabindranath Tagore (Indian). Poet.

1915: Romain Rolland (French). Novelist.

1916: Verner von Heidenstam (Swedish). Poet.

1917: Karl Gjellerup (Danish). Novelist, short-story writer, dramatist. Henrik Pontoppidan (Danish). Novelist, short-story writer.

1919: Carl Spitteler (Swiss). Poet.

1920: Knut Hamsun (Norwegian). Novelist.

1921: Anatole France (French). Novelist, critic.

1922: Jacinto Benavente (Spanish). Dramatist.

1923: William Butler Yeats (Irish). Poet, dramatist.

1924: Ladislaw Reymont (Polish). Novelist.

1925: George Bernard Shaw (English). Dramatist, critic.

1926: Grazia Deledda (Italian). Novelist.

1927: Henri Bergson (French). Philosopher.

1928: Sigrid Undset (Norwegian). Novelist.

1929: Thomas Mann (German). Novelist.

1930: Sinclair Lewis (American). Novelist.

1931: Erik Karlfeldt (Swedish). Poet.

1932: John Galsworthy (English). Novelist, dramatist.

1933: Ivan Bunin (Russian). Novelist, short-story writer.

1934: Luigi Pirandello (Italian). Dramatist.

1936: Eugene O'Neill (American). Dramatist.

1937: Roger Martin du Gard (French). Novelist.

1938: Pearl Buck (American). Novelist.

1939: Frans Eemil Sillanpää (Finnish). Novelist.

1944: Johannes V. Jensen (Danish). Novelist.

1945: Gabriela Mistral (Chilean). Poet.

1946: Hermann Hesse (Swiss). Poet, novelist.

1947: André Gide (French). Novelist, poet, critic, essayist.

1948: T. S. Eliot (English). Poet, dramatist, critic, essayist.

1949: William Faulkner (American). Novelist, short-story writer.

1950: Bertrand Russell (English). Philosopher, critic, short-story writer.

1951: Pär Lagerkvist (Swedish). Novelist, poet, playwright.
1952: François Mauriac (French). Novelist, playwright, poet, essayist.
1953: Winston Churchill (English). Historian.
1954: Ernest Hemingway (American). Novelist, short-story writer.
1955: Halldór Laxness (Icelandic). Novelist.
1956: Juan Ramon Jiminez (b. Spain). Poet.

Medicine and Physiology

1901: Emil von Behring (German). For his work on serum therapy, especially its application against diphtheria, by which he has opened a new road in the domain of medical science and thereby placed in the hands of the physicians a victorious weapon against illness and death.
1902: Sir Ronald Ross (English). For his work on malaria, by which he has shown how it enters the organism and thereby has laid the foundations for successful research on this disease and how to combat it.
1903: Niels Ryberg Finsen (Danish). In recognition of his contribution to the treatment of diseases, especially lupus vulgaris, with concentrated light-rays, whereby he has opened a new avenue to medical science.
1904: Ivan Petrovich Pavlov (Russian). In recognition of his work on the physiology of digestion, by which, in essential respects, he has transformed and enlarged our knowledge of this subject.
1905: Robert Koch (German). For his investigations and discoveries in regard to tuberculosis.
1906: Camillo Golgi (Italian). In recognition of his work on the structure of the nervous system.
1906: Santiago Ramon y Cajal (Spanish). In recognition of his work on the structure of the nervous system.
1907: Charles Louis Alphonse Laveran (French). In recognition of his work regarding the role played by protozoa in causing diseases.
1908: Paul Ehrlich (German). In recognition of his works on immunity.
1908: Élie Metchnikoff (b. Russia). In recognition of his works on immunity.
1909: Theodor Kocher (Swiss). For his works on the pysiology, pathology and surgery of the thyroid gland.
1910: Albrecht Kossel (German). In recognition of the contributions to the chemistry of the cell which he has made through his works on proteins, including the nucleic substances.
1911: Allvar Gullstrand (Swedish). For his work on the dioptrics of the eye.
1912: Alexis Carrel (French). In recognition of his works on vascular suture and the transplantation of blood-vessels and organs.
1913: Charles Robert Richet (French). In recognition of his work on anaphylaxis.
1914: Robert Bárány (Austrian). For his work on the physiology and pathology of the vestibular apparatus.
1915, 1916, 1917, 1918: None.
1919: Jules Bordet (Belgian). For his discoveries in regard to immunity.
1920: August Krogh (Danish). For his discovery of the capillary motor regulating system.
1921: None.
1922: Archibald Vivian Hill (English). For his discovery relating to the production of heat in the muscles.
1922: Otto Meyerhoff (German). For his discovery of the fixed relationship between the consumption of oxygen and the metabolism of lactic acid in muscle.

1923: Sir Frederick Grant Banting, John James Rickard MacLeod (Canadian). For their discovery of insulin.
1924: Willem Einthoven (Dutch). For his discovery of the mechanism of the electrocardiogram.
1925: None.
1926: Johan Fibiger (Danish). For his discovery of the Spiroptera carcinoma.
1927: Julius Wagner von Jauregg (Wagner-Jauregg) (Austrian). For his discovery of the therapeutic value of malaria inoculation in the treatment of dementia paralytica.
1928: Charles Jean Henri Nicolle (French). For his work on typhus.
1929: Sir Frederick Gowland Hopkins (English). For his discovery of the growth-stimulating vitamins.
1929: Christiaan Eijkman (Dutch). For his discovery of the anti-neuritic vitamin.
1930: Karl Landsteiner (American, b. Austria). For his discovery of the human blood groups.
1931: Otto Heinrich Warburg (German). For his discovery of the nature and mode of action of the respiratory enzyme.
1932: Sir Charles S. Sherrington, Edgar Douglas Adrian (English). For their discoveries regarding the function of the neurons.
1933: Thomas H. Morgan (American). For his discoveries concerning the function of the chromosome in the transmission of heredity.
1934: George Richards Minot, William P. Murphy, George H. Whipple (American). For their discoveries concerning liver therapy against anaemias.
1935: Hans Spemann (German). For his discovery of the organizer effect in embryonic development.
1936: Sir Henry H. Dale (English), Otto Loewi (Austrian). For their discoveries relating to the chemical transmission of nerve impulses.
1937: Albert Szent-Györgyi von Nagyrapolt (Hungarian). For his discoveries in connection with the biological combustion processes, with special reference to Vitamin C and the catalysis of fumaric acid.
1938: Corneille Heymans (Belgian). For his discovery of the role played by the sinus and aortic mechanisms in the regulation of respiration.
1939: Gerhard Domagk (German). For his discovery of the antibacterial effects of prontosil.
1940, 1941, 1942: None.
1943: Edward Adelbert Doisy (American). For his discovery of Vitamin K.
1943: Henrik Dam (Danish). For his discovery of the chemical nature of Vitamin K.
1944: Joseph Erlanger (American), Herbert Spencer Gasser (American). For their discoveries regarding the highly differentiated functions of single nerve fibers.
1945: Sir Alexander Fleming (English), Ernest Boris Chain (German), Sir Howard Florey English). For the discovery of penicillin and its curative value in a number of infectious diseases.
1946: Herman J. Muller (American). For his discovery of the production of mutations by means of X-ray irradiation.
1947: Carl Ferdinand Cori, Gerty Theresa Cori (American). For their discovery of how glycogen is catalytically converted.
1947: Bernardo Houssay (Argentinian). For his discovery of the part played by the hormone of the anterior pituitary lobe in the metabolism of sugar.
1948: Paul Mueller (Swiss). For his discovery of the high efficacy of DDT as a contact poison against several arthropods.

1949: Walter R. Hess (Swiss). For his discovery of the functional organization of the interbrain as a co-ordinator of the activities of the internal organs.

1949: Antonio Moniz (Portuguese). For his discovery of the therapeutic value of leucotomy in certain psychoses.

1950: Philip Showwalter Hench, Edward Calvin Kendal (American), Tadeus Reichstein (Swiss). For their discoveries about the hormones of the adrenal cortex.

1951: Max Theiler (American, b. South Africa). For his researches into the yellow fever virus and the development of the first effective vaccines against the disease.

1952: Selman A. Waxsman (American). For his work in the discovery of streptomycin (he was a co-discoverer of the drug made known in 1943) and its effects against tuberculosis.

1953: Fritz A. Lipmann (American), Hans Adolf Krebs (English) (both b. Germany). For their discoveries concerning the basic life processes carried on within human cells.

1954: Thomas H. Weller, Frederick C. Robbins, John F. Enders (American). For their discovery that poliomyelitis virus is capable of growing in cultures of different tissues.

1955: Hugo Theorell (Swedish). For his discoveries on the nature and action of oxidation enzymes.

1956: Dickinson W. Richards (American), André F. Cournand (American, b. France), Werner Forssmann (German). For their discoveries concerning heart catherization and pathological changes in the circulating system.

Peace

1901: Jean Henri Dunant (Swiss), Frédéric Passy (French).
1902: Elie Ducommun, Charles Albert Gobat (Swiss).
1903: Sir William Randal Cremer (English).
1904: Institute of International Law.
1905: Bertha von Suttner (Countess Kinsky) (Austrian).
1906: Theodore Roosevelt (American).
1907: Ernesto Teodore Moneta (Italian), Louis Renault (French).
1908: Klas Pontus Arnoldson (Swedish), Fredrik Bajer (Danish).
1909: August Marie Francois Beernaert (Belgian), Baron d'Estournelles de Constant (French).
1910: International Peace Bureau (Switzerland).
1911: Tobias Michael Carel Asser (Dutch), Alfred Hermann Fried (Austrian).
1912: Elihu Root (American).
1913: Henri LaFontaine (Belgian).
1914, 1915, 1916: None.
1917: International Red Cross of Geneva.
1918: None.
1919: Woodrow Wilson (American).
1920: Leon Victor Auguste Bourgeois (French).
1921: Karl Hjalmar Branting (Swedish), Christian Lange (Norwegian).
1922: Fridtjof Nansen (Norwegian).
1923, 1924: None.
1925: Charles Gates Dawes (American), Sir Austen Chamberlain (English).
1926: Aristide Briand (French).
1927: Ferdinand Buisson (French), Ludwig Quidde (German).
1928: None.
1929: Frank Billings Kellogg (American).
1930: Nathan Söderblom (Swedish).
1931: Nicholas Murray Butler, Jane Addams (American).
1932: None.
1933: Sir Norman Angell (English).

1934: Arthur Henderson (English).
1935: Carl von Ossietzky (German).
1936: Carlos Saavedra Lamas (Argentinian).
1937: Vixcount Cecil of Chelwood (Edgar Algernon Robert Cecil) (English).
1938: Nansen International Office for Refugees, Geneva.
1939, 1940, 1941, 1942, 1943: None.
1944: International Red Cross of Geneva.
1945: Cordell Hull (American).
1946: John R. Mott, Emily Balch (American).
1947: American Friends Service Committee (Quakers) and Friends Service Council, London
1948: None.
1949: Lord Boyd Orr (English).
1950: Ralph J. Bunche (American).
1951: Leon Jouhaux (French).
1952: Albert Schweitzer (French).
1953: Gen. Georg C. Marshall (American).
1954: The office of the United Nations Commissioner for Refuguess.
1955, 1956: None.

Physics

1901: Wilhelm Konrad Roentgen (German). For his discovery of X-rays.
1902: Hendrick Antoon Lorentz, Pieter Zeeman (Dutch). For their investigations concerning the influence of magnetism upon the phenomena of radiation.
1903: Antoine Henri Becquerel and Pierre and Marie Curie (French). For the discovery of spontaneous radioactivity.
1904: John William Strutt, Lord Rayleigh (English). For his work on the density of gases and his discovery, in this connection, of argon.
1905: Philipp Lenard (German). For his work on cathode rays.
1906: Joseph John Thomson (English). For his theoretical and experimental investigation into the transmission of electricity through gases.
1907: Albert Abraham Michelson (American). for his optical precision instruments and for the spectroscopic and metrological investigations made with them.
1908: Gabriel Lippmann (French). For his method of reproducing colors photographically, based on the phenomenon of interference.
1909: Guglielmo Marconi (Italian), Karl Ferdinand Braun (German). For their development of wireless telegraphy.
1910: Johannes Diderik van der Waals (Dutch). For his work concerning the equation of state of gases and liquids.
1911: Wilhelm Wien (German). For his discovries concerning the laws of heat radiation.
1912: Nils Gustaf Dalén (Swedish). For his invention of automatic regulators to be used in conjunction with gas accumulators for lighting beacons and light buoys.
1913: Heike Kamerlingh Onnes (Dutch). For his investigations into the properties of bodies at low temperatures, which led, among other things, to the preparation of liquid helium.
1914: Max von Laue (German). For his discovery of the diffraction of Roentgen rays in crystals.
1915: Sir William Henry Bragg, Sir William Lawrence Bragg (English). For their contributions to the study of crystal structure by means of X-rays.
1916: None.
1917: Charles Glover Barkla (English). For his discovery of the characteristic X-radiation of the elements.
1918: Max Planck (German). For his contribution

to the development of physics by his discovery of the quantum theory.

1919: Johannes Stark (German). For his discovery of the Doppler effect in Canal rays and of the splitting of spectral lines in an electric field.

1920: Charles Edouard Guillaume (Swiss). For the services he rendered to precision physics by his discovery of the anomalies in nickel-steel alloys.

1921: Albert Einstein (German). For his contribution to mathematical physics, and especially for his discovery of the law of photoelectric effect.

1922: Niels Bohr (Danish). For his studies on the structure af atoms and the radiation emanating from them.

1923: Robert Andrews Millikan (American). For his work on the elementary electric charge and on the photoelectric effect.

1924: Karl Manne Georg Siegbahn (Swedish). For his discoveries and investigations in X-ray spectroscopy.

1925: James Franck, Gustav Hertz (German). For their discovery of the laws governing the impact between an electron and an atom.

1926: Jean Baptiste Perrin (French). For his work on the discontinuous structure of matter, and especially for his discovery of the euqilibrium of sedimentation.

1927: Arthur Compton (American). For his discovery of the effect named after him.

1927: Charles Thomson Rees Wilson (English). For his discovery of the vapor condensation method of rendering visible the paths of electrically charged particles.

1928: Owen Willans Richardson (English). For his work on the thermionic phenomenon and more especially for the discovery of the law named after him.

1929: Louis Victor de Broglie (French). For his discovery of the wave nature of the electron.

1930: Chandrasekhara Venkata Raman (Indian). For his work on the scattering of light and for the discovery of the effect named after him.

1931: None.

1932: Werner Heisenberg (German). For the creation of quantum mechanics, the application of which has led, among other things, to the discovery of the allotropic forms of hydrogen.

1933: Paul Adrien Maurice Dirac (English), Erwin Schrödinger (Austrian). For the discovery of new and fruitful forms of atomic theory.

1934: None.

1935: Sir James Chadwick (English). For the discovery of the neutron.

1936: Carl David Anderson (American). For the discovery of the positron.

1936: Victor F. Hess (Austrian). For the discovery of cosmic radiation.

1937: Clinton Joseph Davisson (American), George Paget Thomson (English). For the experimental discovery of the interference phenomenon in crystals irradiated by electrons.

1938: Enrico Fermi (Italian). For the discovery of new radioactive elements produced by neutron irradiation and for the discovery of nuclear reactions brought about by slow electrons.

1939: Ernest Orlando Lawrence (American). For the discovery and development of the cyclotron, and for the results obtained by its aid, especially with regard to artificially radioactive elements.

1940: None.

1941: None.

1942: None.

1943: Otto Stern (American). For his contributions to the development of the molecular ray method and for his discovery of the magnetic moment of the proton.

1944: Isidor Isaac Rabi (American). For his application of the resonance method to the measurement of the magnetic properties of atomic nuclei.

1945: Wolfgang Pauli (Austrian). For the discovery of the exclusion principle, also called the Pauli Principle.

1946: Percy Williams Bridgeman (American). For the invention of apparatus for obtaining very high pressures, and for the discoveries which he made by means of this apparatus in the field of high pressure physics.

1947: Sir Edward Appleton (English). For his work on the physical properties of the high atmosphere, and especially for his discovery of the so-called Appleton Layer.

1948: Patrick Maynard Stuart Blackett (English). For his improvement of the Wilson Cloud-Chamber method and for the resulting discoveries in the field of nuclear physics and cosmic rays.

1949: Hideki Yukawa (Japanese). For having predicted, as a result of his theoretical work on nuclear physics, the existence of mesons.

1950: Cecil Frank Powell (English). For his development of the photographic method in the study of nuclear processes and for his discoveries concerning mesons.

1951: Sir John Cockcroft (English), E. T. S. Walton (Irish). For their atomic experiments in 1932, which paved the way for later atomic developments.

1952: Felix Bloch, Edward Mills Purcell (American). For their development of a new method to measure magnetic fields in atomic nuclei.

1953: Fritz Zernike (Dutch). For developing a special microscope which enables scientists to study living cells colored by light waves and which is widely used in cancer research.

1954: Max Born (English, b. Germany). For fundamental works in quantum mechanics, especially the statistical interpretation of wave function.

1954: Walter Bothe (German). For studies in cosmic radiation which led to a precision instrument enabling scientists to measure minute time spaces within the atom.

1955: Willis E. Lamb (American). For his discoveries regarding the hyperfine structure of the hydrogen spectrum.

1955: Polykarp Kusch (American). For the precision determination of the magnetic moment of the electron.

1956: John Bardeen, Walter H. Brattain, William B. Schockley (American). For their investigations on semiconductors and the discovery of the transistor effect.

Norse Gods
See **Gods** and **Goddesses**

Novelists and Prose Writers
See also **Detectives in Fiction; Nobel Prizes; Pulitzer Prizes; Satirists and Humorists**

ADAMIC, LOUIS: (1899-1951); b Yugoslavia; l. America; earthy novels of Yugoslavia and America; *The Native's Return.*

ADAMS, HENRY BROOKS: (1838-1918); America; man of letters, historian, scholar; member of Adams family of American statesmen;

Mont-Saint-Michel and Chartres, The Education of Henry Adams.

ADDISON, JOSEPH: (1672-1719); England; essayist; famous for essays contributed to *Tatler* and *Spectator.*

AESOP: (6th cent. B.C.); Greece; fabulist; Fables: "Androcles and the Lion," "Fox and the Grapes."

AIKEN, CONRAD POTTER: (1889-); America; poet, novelist; *Blue Voyage.*

ALARCÓN, PEDRO ANTONIO DE: (1833-1891); Spain; short-story writer, statesman, journalist; *El Sombrero de Tres Picos, El Niño de la Bola.*

ALCOTT, LOUISA MAY: (1832-1888); America; novelist and reformer; *Little Women, Little Men, Eight Cousins.*

ALDANOV M. A. (MARK A. LANDAU): (1889-); Russia; controversial novelist; *The Fifth Seal.*

ALDINGTON, RICHARD: (1892-); England; novelist, member of the Imagist group; *Death of a Hero.*

ALDRICH, THOMAS BAILEY: (1836-1907); America; man of letters, member of the Genteel Tradition group; *Marjorie Daw, Story of a Bad Boy.*

ALGER, HORATIO: (1834-1899); America; penny books for boys; *Struggling Upwards.*

ALGREN, NELSON: (1909-); America; novelist of the "lost men"; *The Man With the Golden Arm.*

ALLEN, JAMES LANE: (1849-1925); America; novelist of Kentucky; *A Kentucky Cardinal, The Blue Grass Region of Kentucky.*

ALLEN, WILLIAM HERVEY: (1899-1949); America; poet and novelist; *Anthony Adverse;* biography of Poe, *Israfel.*

AMMERS-KÜLLER, JOHANNA VAN: (1884-); Holland; best-selling novelist, widely translated; *The Rebel Generation.*

ANDERSEN, HANS CHRISTIAN: (1805-1875); Denmark; poet, novelist, dramatist; *Fairy Tales.*

ANDERSON, SHERWOOD: (1876-1941); America; realistic Chicago group; *Winesburg, Ohio, Poor White, Dark Laughter.*

ANDREYEV, LEONID (or ANDREIEV): (1871-1919); Russia; dramatist and novelist; *The Red Laugh.*

ANET, CLAUDE (JEAN SCHOPFER): (1868-1931); b. Switzerland; l. France; novelist of the exotic; *Petite ville.*

ANKER-LARSEN, JOHANNES: (1874-); Denmark; novelist; *The Philosopher's Stone.*

APULEIUS: (2nd cent. A.D.); Rome; philosopher and rhetorician; *Metamorphoses* or *The Golden Ass.*

ARAGON, LOUIS: (1897-); France; early associate of the Dadaist and Surrealist groups; *The Bells of Basle.*

ARLEN, MICHAEL (DIKRAN KUYUMJIAN): (1895-); b. Armenia; l. England; best seller of 1920's *The Green Hat.*

ARTSYBASHEV, MIKHAIL (or, ARTZYBASHEFF): (1878-1927); b. Russia; l. Russia, Poland; radical and naturalist writer; *Sanine.*

ASCH, SHOLEM: (1880-1957); b. Poland; l. America; Yiddish novelist; *Three Cities, The Nazarene.*

ATHERTON, GERTRUDE FRANKLIN: (1857-1948); America; novelist; *Black Oxen, The Conqueror.*

AUGUSTINE: (354-430); b. Algeria; saint, Bishop of Hippo, one of Fathers of Christian church; *Confessions, City of God.*

AUSTEN, JANE: (1775-1817); England; satirical novelist of English country gentry; *Pride and Prejudice.*

AYMÉ, MARCEL: (1902-); France; *Le Boeuf Clandestin.*

AZORÍN (JOSÉ MARTÍNEZ RUIZ): (1873-); Spain; *The Syrens and Other Stories.*

BACHELLER, IRVING ADDISON: (1859-1950); America; novelist; *A Man for the Ages.*

BALZAC, HONORÉ DE: (1799-1850); France; transitional figure between romantic and realist prose; *La Comédie Humaine,* a series of novels among which are *Eugénie Grandet* and *Le Pére Goriot.*

BARBUSSE, HENRI: (1873-1935); France; novelist with Socialist sympathies; *Under Fire.*

BARING, MAURICE: (1874-1945); England; novelist, journalist, playwright; *Roger Peckham.*

BAROJA Y NESSI, PÍO: (1872-); Spain; Basque physician, essayist, novelist; *Memorias de un Hombre de Acción.*

BARRÈS, MAURICE: (1862-1923); France; novelist who preached the restoration of natural energy; *L'Appel au Soldat.*

BARRIE, SIR JAMES MATTHEW: (1860-1937); Scotland; novelist and dramatist; *The Little Minister, Peter Pan* (play).

BAUM, VICKI: (1888-); b. Austria; l. America; *Grand Hotel.*

BAZIN, RENÉ: (1853-1932); France; protested against Zola and the Naturalist School; *La Terre qui Meurt; Les Oberlé.*

BEACH, REX ELLINGWOOD: (1877-1949) America; adventure stories; *The Spoilers.*

BEAUVOIR, SIMONE DE: (1909-); France; Existentialist novelist; *The Mandarins.*

BEERBOHM, SIR MAX: (1872-1956); England; novelist of satire; *Zuleika Dobson.*

BELLAMY, EDWARD: (1850-1898); America; Utopian novelist; *Looking Backward.*

BELLOC, HILAIRE: (1870-1953); b. France; l. England; Catholic man of letters; *The Bad Child's Book of Beasts.*

BELLOW, SAUL: (1915-); America; novelist; *The Adventures of Augie March.*

BEMELMANS, LUDWIG: (1898-); b. Austria; l. America; American writer and illustrator of humorous books; *Madeleine.*

BENÉT, STEPHEN VINCENT: (1898-1943); America; poet, novelist, short-story writer; *The Devil and Daniel Webster.*

BENNETT, ENOCH ARNOLD: (1867-1931); England; journalist and novelist; *Old Wives' Tale.*

BERNANOS, GEORGES: (1888-1948); France; novelist; *Diary of a Country Priest.*

BIERCE, AMBROSE GWINETT: (1842-1914?); America; journalist, satirist, short-story writer; *Can Such Things Be?*

BIGGERS, EARL DERR: (1884-1933); America; creator of detective Charlie Chan; *Seven Keys to Baldpate.*

BLACKMORE, RICHARD DODDRIDGE: (1825-1900); Scotland; *Lorna Doone.*

BLASCO-IBÁÑEZ, VINCENTE: (1867-1928); b. Spain; l. France; Spanish patriot, novelist of adventure stories; *The Four Horsemen of the Apocalypse.*

BOCCACCIO, GIOVANNI: (1313-1375); b. Paris; l. Naples, Florence; teller of tales, the father of classic Italian prose; *Decameron.*

BOETHIUS, ANICIUS MANLIUS SEVERINUS: (470?-525); Rome; philosopher and writer; *Consolaiton of Philosophy.*

BOJER, JOHAN: (1872-); Norway; novelist; *The Great Hunger.*

BORROW, GEORGE: (1803-1881); England; books based on his travels and the gypsies; *Romany Rye.*

BOSWELL, JAMES: (1740-1795); England;

among greatest of all biographers; *Life of Samuel Johnson.*

BOURGET, CHARLES JOSEPH PAUL: (1852-1935); France; social and psychological novelist; *L'Etape.*

BOWEN, ELIZABETH DOROTHEA COLE: (1899-); b. Ireland; l. England; sensitive contemporary novelist; *Death of the Heart, The Hotel.*

BOWLES, PAUL: (1911-); America; *The Sheltering Sky.*

BOYD, JAMES: (1888-1944); America; historical novelist; *Drums.*

BOYLE, KAY: (1903-); b. America; l. France; experimental writer; *Plagued by the Nightingale.*

BRADFORD, ROARK: (1896-1948): America; Negro stories; *Old Man Adam and his Chillun.*

BREMER, FREDRIKA: (1801-1865); b. Finland; l. Sweden; advocates women's rights in her novels; *Father and Daughter.*

BROMFIELD, LOUIS: (1896-1956); b. America; l. France, America; novelist of the American scene; *Early Autumn, The Rains Came.*

BRONTË, ANNE: (1820-1849); England; youngest of the Brontë sisters; *The Tenant of Wildfell Hall.*

BRONTË, CHARLOTTE: (1816-1855); England; most prolific of the Brontës; *Jane Eyre.*

BRONTË, EMILY: (1818-1848); England; wrote only one novel: *Wuthering Heights.*

BROWN, CHARLES BROCKDEN: (1771-1810); America; first American novelist to gain international attention; *Ormond, Jane Talbot.*

BRUSH, KATHARINE: (1902-1952); America; chronicler of the 1920's in New York City; *Young Man of Manhattan.*

BUCHAN, JOHN (LORD TWEEDSMUIR): (1876-1940); b. Scotland; l. England; correspondent of World War 1, romantic novelist; *Greenmantle, The Thirty-Nine Steps.*

BUCK, PEARL: (1892-); b. America; l. China, America; Pulitzer Prize winner, 1932, for *The Good Earth.*

BULWER-LYTTON, EDWARD GEORGE EARLE: (1803-1873); England; novelist and dramatist; *The Last Days of Pompeii.*

BUNIN, IVAN: (1870-1953); b. Russia; l. France; Russian man of letters; *The Village.*

BUNYAN, JOHN: (1628-1688); England; religious morality writer; *The Pilgrim's Progress.*

BURKE, THOMAS: (1887-1945); England; tales of old London; *Limehouse Nights.*

BURNETT, FRANCES HODGSON: (1849-1924); b. England; l. America; natural and romantic storyteller; *Little Lord Fauntleroy.*

BURNETT, WILLIAM RILEY: (1899-) America; *Little Caesar.*

BURT, MAXWELL STRUTHERS: (1882-1953); America; novelist of the Far West; *Hidden Creek.*

BUTLER, SAMUEL: (1612-1680); England; satirical poet; *Hudibras.*

BUTLER, SAMUEL- (1835-1902); b. England; l. New Zealand, England; novelist and freethinker; *Erewhon, The Way of All Flesh.*

BYRNE, DONN (BRIAN OSWALD DONN-BYRNE): (1889-1928); b. America; l. Ireland, America; last of the Irish storytellers; *Messer Marco Polo.*

CABELL, JAMES BRANCH: (1879-); America; allegorist; *Jurgen.*

CABLE, GEORGE WASHINGTON: (1844-1925); America; novels of Louisiana; *Old Creole Days.*

CAIN, JAMES MALLAHAN: (1892-); America; novelist and journalist, realistic school; *The Postman Always Rings Twice.*

CAINE, SIR HALL: (1853-1931); England; Pre-Raphaelite romantic; *The Eternal City.*

CALDWELL, ERSKINE: (1903-); America; social writer of the South; *God's Little Acre, Tobacco Road.*

CAMUS, ALBERT: (1914-); France; intellectual writer and novelist, Nobel Prize 1957; *The Plague, The Stranger.*

CANFIELD, DOROTHY: (Fisher, Dorothy C.) (1879-); America; novels about Vermont; *The Bent Twig.*

CAPOTE, TRUMAN: (1924-); America; novelist of the decadent South; *Other Voices, Other Rooms.*

CARCO, FRANCES: (1886-); France; one of the Paris Art Nouveau group; *The Last Bohemia.*

CARLYLE, THOMAS: (1795-1881); England; b. Scotland; prose writer; *Sartor Resartus.*

CARROLL, LEWIS (CHARLES LUDWIDGE DODGSON): (1832-1898); England; mathematician and writer of satiric fantasy; *Alice in Wonderland.*

CASTIGLIONE, BALDASSARE DE: (1478-1529); Italy; humanist and writer; *The Courtier.*

CATHER, WILLA SIBERT: (1876-1947); America; novelist of plains and prairies; *My Antonia, Death Comes for the Archbishop.*

CÉLINE, LOUIS-FERDINAND (LOUIS FUCHS DESTOUCHES): (1894-); France; physician and novelist; *Journey to the End of the Night.*

CENDRARS, BLAISE: (1887-); b. France; l. America, France; much traveled novelist of adventures; *Sutter's Gold.*

CERVANTES SAAVEDRA, MIGUEL DE: (1547-1616); Spain; satirist of Chivalry; *Don Quixote.*

CHAMBERS, ROBERT WILLIAM: (1865-1933); America; popular novelist; *The Rogue's Moon.*

CHAMSON, ANDRÉ: (1900-); France; realist novelist in reaction to "Art Nouveau"; *The Road.*

CHATEAUBRIAND, FRANÇOIS RENÉ DE: (1768-1848); France; novelist who started the French romantic movement; *Atala.*

CHEKHOV, ANTON PAVLOVICH: (1860-1904); Russia; nihilist writer of fiction and plays; *A Dreary Story, The Cherry Orchard* (play).

CHRÉTIEN DE TROYES: (fl. 2nd half 12th century); France; wrote medieval romances; *Lancelot, or the Knight of the Cart; Perceval; Yvain, or the Knight of the Lion.*

CHRISTIE, AGATHA: (-); England; mystery writer; *The Murder of Roger Ackroyd.*

CHURCHILL, WINSTON: (1871-1947); America; historical novelist; *Richard Carvel.*

CHURCHILL, SIR WINSTON LEONARD SPENCER: (1874-); England; author and noted statesman, Prime Minister during Second World War; *Blood, Sweat, and Tears; The Gathering Storm.*

CICERO, MARCUS TULLIUS: (106-43 B.C); Roman; orator, statesman, essayist; *Friendship, Old Age* (essays), *Catiline* (orations).

CLEMENS, SAMUEL LANGHORNE: See Twain, Mark.

COCTEAU, JEAN: (1891-); France; Surrealist poet and novelist; *Les Mariés de la Tour Eiffel.*

COLETTE (SIDONIE GABRIELLE CLAUDINE): (1871-1955); France; semi-autobiographical novelist; *Cheri.*

COLLIER, JOHN: (1901-); England; satirist, short-story writer; *Full Circle.*

COLLINS, WILKIE: (1824-1889); England; novelist; collaborator with Dickens; *The Moonstone.*

CONRAD, JOSEPH (TEODOR JÓSEF KONRAD KORZENIOWSKI): (1857-1924); b. Ukraine; l. England; novelist of sea tales. *An Outcast of The Islands, Lord Jim, The Rescue.*

COOPER, JAMES FENIMORE: (1789-1851); America; author of New York State's early history; *The Last of the Mohicans.*

COPPARD, ALFRED EDGAR: (1878-); England; short-story writer; *Adam and Eve and Pinch Me.*

CORELLI, MARIE (MARY MACKAY): (1855-1924); England; popular novelist; *The Sorrows of Satan.*

COUPERUS, LOUIS MARIE ANNE: (1863-1923); b. Holland; l. Batavia; Holland; early realist novelist; *Old People and the Things that Pass.*

COZZENS, JAMES GOULD: (1903- America; novelist of the American scene; *The Last Adam.*

CRANE, STEPHEN: (1871-1900); America; early realist; *The Red Badge of Courage.*

CRAWFORD, FRANCIS MARION: (1854-1909); b. Italy; l. America; novelist; *Dr. Claudius.*

CURWOOD, JAMES OLIVER: (1878-1927); America; stories of adventure in American Northwest: *Nomads of the North.*

DANA, RICHARD HENRY: (1815-1882); America; classic of sea adventure, *Two Years Before the Mast.*

DAUDET, ALPHONSE: (1840-1897); France; novelist; *Lettres de mon Moulin, Sapho.*

DAVIS, RICHARD HARDING: (1864-1916); America; journalist and novelist, romantic and adventure tales; *The Lion and the Unicorn.*

DAY, CLARENCE: (1874-1935); America; best known for humorous autobiographical sketches; *Life with Father, Life with Mother.*

DEEPING, WARWICK: (1877-1950); England; popular novelist; *Sorrell and Son.*

DEFOE, DANIEL: (1659?-1731); England; political journalist and novelist; *Robinson Crusoe, Moll Flanders.*

DELAND, MARGARET WADE: (1857-1945); America; novelist; *Old Chester Tales.*

DE LA ROCHE, MAZO: (1885-); Canada; many novels written about Whiteoak family; *Jalna.*

DELEDDA, GRAZIA: (1875-1936); Italy; novels of Sardinia, Nobel Prize winner; *Nell Azzuro.*

DELL, FLOYD: (1887-); America; voice of the younger generation of the 1920's; *Moon Calf.*

DE MORGAN, WILLIAM: (1837-1917); England; started writing for fun, became an immediate success; *Joseph Vance.*

DE QUINCEY, THOMAS: (1785-1859); England; critic and essayist; *Confessions of an English Opium Eater.*

DICKENS, CHARLES JOHN HUFFAM: (1812-1870); England; crusader against the Industrial Revolution and the condition of the poor; *Pickwick Papers, Oliver Twist, David Copperfield.*

DINESEN, ISAK (BARONESS KAREN BLIXEN): (1883-); b. Denmark; l. Africa, Denmark; novelist; *Seven Gothic Tales.*

DISRAELI, BENJAMIN: (1804-1881); England; statesman and novelist; *Vivian Grey.*

DIXON, THOMAS: (1864-1946); America; clergyman and writer; *The Clansman.*

DÖBLIN, ALFRED: (1878-); Germany; physician and novelist of the early psychological type; *Alexanderplatz.*

DODGSON, CHARLES: see Carroll, Lewis.

DOS PASSOS, JOHN RODERIGO: (1896-);

America; experimental writer of social and labor themes; *U.S.A.* (Trilogy).

DOSTOÉVSKI, FEDOR MIKHAILOVICH: (1821-1881); Russia; political and social novelist; *Crime and Punishment, The Brothers Karamazov.*

DOUGLAS, NORMAN: (1868-1952); b. England; l. Italy; satirist and novelist; *South Wind.*

DOYLE, SIR ARTHUR CONAN: (1859-1930); England; physician, occultist, novelist; *Sherlock Holmes.*

DREISER, THEODORE: (1871-1945); America; editor and writer, the realistic school; *Sister Carrie, An American Tragedy.*

DUBOIS, WILLIAM EDWARD BURGHARDT: (1868-); America; Negro educator and novelist; *The Souls of Black Folk.*

DUMAS, ALEXANDRE (FILS): (1824-1895); France; novelist and playwright of fashionable Paris; *La Dame aux Camélias.*

DUMAS, ALEXANDRE (PÈRE): (1803-1870); France; historical novelist; *The Three Musketeers, The Count of Monte Cristo.*

DU MAURIER, DAPHNE: (1907-); England; romantic novelist; *Rebecca.*

DU MAURIER, GEORGE: (1834-1896); b. France; l. England; illustrator and novelist of the romantic period; *Trilby.*

DUNSANY, LORD (EDWARD JOHN MORETON DRAX PLUNKETT: (1878-) England; writer of fantasy and dreams; *A Dreamer's Tales.*

DUUN, OLAV: (1876-1939); Norway; writer of the peasantry and the land; *Juvikfolke.*

EDMONDS, WALTER DUMAUX: (1903-); America; novelist of the New York State canal country; *Drums Along the Mohawk.*

EGGLESTON, EDWARD: (1837-1902); America; novelist of the State of Indiana; *The Hoosier Schoolmaster.*

EHRENBURG, ILYA: (1891-); b. Russia; l. Paris, Russia; novelist, newsman, political propagandist of the Soviet: *Out of Chaos.*

ELIOT, GEORGE (MARIAN EVANS): (1819-1888); England; classic novelist of history and local mores: *Silas Marner.*

ELIZABETH (COUNTESS ELIZABETH MARY RUSSELL): (1866-1941); b. Australia; l. England; popular novelist; *The Enchanted April.*

ELLISON, RALPH: (1914-); America; Negro satirical novelist; *Invisible Man.*

EMERSON, RALPH WALDO: (1803-1882); America; essayist and poet; among most influential writers of 19th century America; one of founders of Transcendentalism; *Essays.*

ERASMUS, DESIDERIUS: (1466?-1536); Holland; scholar and humanist of the Renaissance; *Praise of Folly.*

ERCKMANN-CHATRIAN: Emile Erckmann (1822-1899) and Alexandre Chatrian (1826-1890); France; joint authors of many successful novels; *L'Illustre Docteur Mathéus.*

ERSKINE, JOHN: (1879-1951); America; novelist and professor of English literature; *The Private Life of Helen of Troy.*

FALLADA, HANS: (Rudolf Ditzen) (1893-1947); Germany; social novelist of postwar Germany (World War I); *Little Man, What Now?*

FARNOL, JOHN JEFFERY: (1878-1952); England; novels of adventure; *The Amateur Gentleman.*

FARRELL, JAMES THOMAS: (1904-); America; sociological novelist of Chicago; *Studs Lonigan* (trilogy).

FAULKNER, WILLIAM: (1897-); America; novels and stories of Mississippi; Nobel Prize 1949; *The Sound and the Fury, As I Lay Dying, A Fable.*

FERBER, EDNA: (1887-); America; novelist of life in the Middle West; *Saratoga Trunk.*

FEUCHTWANGER, LION: (1884-); b. Germany; l. America; novelist of social statements; *Power.*

FIELDING, HENRY: (1707-1754); England; early realistic novelist; *Joseph Andrews, Tom Jones.*

FIRBANK, RONALD: (1886-1926); b. England; l. Italy; novelist of sensitivity and eccentricity; *The Flower Beneath the Foot.*

FISHER, VARDIS: (1895-); America; writer of the West; *Toilers of the Hills.*

FITZGERALD, F. SCOTT: (1896-1940); America; key novelist of Europe and America in the 1920's writing of the "International Set"; *The Great Gatsby, Tender is the Night.*

FLAUBERT, GUSTAVE: (1821-1880); France; stylist in the realistic manner; *Madame Bovary, Salammbô.*

FORBES, ESTHER: (1894?-); America; Pulitzer Prize winner, 1942; *Paul Revere and the World He Lived In.*

FORD, FORD MADOX: (1873-1939); England; collaborator with Joseph Conrad; *The Inheritors, Parade's End* (Tetralogy).

FORD, PAUL LEICESTER: (1865-1902); America; historian and novelist; *Janice Meredith.*

FORESTER, CECIL SCOTT: (1879-); b. Cairo; l. England; novelist of sea adventure and history; *Stores about Captain Horatio Hornblower.*

FORSTER, EDWARD MORGAN: (1879-); England; intellectual and novelist of style; *A passage to India, Howards End, Abinger Harvest* (essays).

FOUQUÉ: See La Motte-Fouqué, Friedrich Heinrich Karl.

FOURNIER, HENRI ALAIN: (1886-1941); France; visionary, idealistic novelist; *The Wanderer.*

FOWLER, GENE: (1890-); America; journalist and novelist of the "tough" school; *The Great McGoo.*

FOX, JOHN WILLIAM, Jr.: (1863-1919); America; short stories of the Southern mountain people; *The Little Shepherd of Kingdom Come.*

FRANCE, ANATOLE (JACQUES ANATOLE FRANÇOIS THIBAULT): (1844-1924); b. France; l. Italy, France; social reformer, stylist, satirist; Nobel Prize winner, 1921; *The Crime of Sylvestre Bonnard, Penguin Island.*

FRANK, WALDO: (1889-); America; rebel writer of the 1920's; *City Block.*

FREEMAN, MARY E. WILKINS: (1852-1930); America; novelist and short-story writer of rural New England; *A New England Nun.*

FREYTAG, GUSTAVE: (1816-1895); Germany; novelist and journalist, champion of liberalism; *Die Verlorene Handschrift.*

GABORIAU, EMILE: (1835-1874);France; writer of detective fiction; *Monsieur Lecoq.*

GALE, ZONA: (1874-1938); America; novelist; *Miss Lulu Bett.*

GALSWORTHY, JOHN: (1867-1933); England; chronicler of the British upper middle class; *The Forsythe Saga.*

GARDNER, ERLE STANLEY: (1889-) America; detective story writer; creator of Perry Mason character.

GARLAND, HAMLIN: (1860-1940); America; Typically American writer of the Middle West; Pulitzer Prize winner (1921); *Main-Traveled Roads, A Daughter of the Middle Border.*

GARNETT, DAVID: (1892-); England; fantasy writer; *Lady into Fox.*

GASKELL, ELIZABETH: (1810-1865); England; novels of 19th-cent. industrial England; *Mary Barton.*

GAUTIER, THÉOPHILE: (1811-1872); France; art and drama critic, Short stories, novels of the romantic period; *Mademoiselle de Maupin.*

GIBBS, ARTHUR HAMILTON: (1888-); b. England; l. America; novelist; *Soundings.*

GIDE, ANDRÉ: (1869-1951); France; leading figure in French letters; novelist, essayist, translator; *The Immoralist, The Counterfeiters.*

GIRAUDOUX, JEAN: (1882-1944); France; playwright, novelist, diplomat; *Simon, le Pathétique.*

GISSING, GEORGE ROBERT: (1857-1903); England; novelist of English middle-class life; *New Grub Street.*

GJELLERUP, KARL: (1857-1919); b. Denmark; l. Germany; Nobel Prize winner, 1917, *The Pilgrim Kamenita.*

GLASGOW, SUSAN: (1874-1945); America; social satirist of the "Old South"; *They Stooped to Folly.*

GLASS, MONTAGUE MARSDEN: (1877-1934); b. England; l. America; humorous fiction writer; *Potash and Perlmutter.*

GODWIN, WILLIAM: (1756-1836); England; satirist and philospher; *Adventures of Caleb Williams.*

GOETHE, JOHANN WOLFGANG VON: (1749-1832); Germany; poet, dramatist, novelist; leading figure in Romantic movement; *Wilhelm Meister.*

GOGOL, NIKOLAI VASILIEVICH: (1809-1852); b. Russia; l. Rome; father of realism in Russian literature; *Dead Souls.*

GOLDSMITH, OLIVER: (1728-1774); b. Ireland; l. England; poet, playwright, novelist, member of Samuel Johnson's group; *The Vicar of Wakefield.*

GOMEZ DE LA SERNA, RAMON: (1891-); Spain; play-boy novelist, leading exponent of Espressionism in Spain; *The Black and White Widow.*

GONCOURT, JULES & EDMOND: (19th cent.); France; collaborators as writers of realistic novels; bequeathed money for the French Goncourt Prize; *Germaine, Journal.*

GORDON, CAROLINE: (1895-); America; novelist, *The Malefactors.*

GORKY, MAXIM: (1868-1936): Russia; revolutionary novelist, short-story writer, playwright; *The Outcasts, And Other Stories.*

GOURMONT, RÉMY DE: (1858-1915); France; recluse scholar, early symbolist, Nietzschean novelist; *A Night at the Luxembourg.*

GRAHAME, KENNETH: (1859-1932); b. Scotland;.l. England; banker and writer of fantasy tales, *The Wind in the Willows.*

GRAND, SARAH: (1862-1943); b. Ireland; l. England; novelist and feminist; *The Winged Victory.*

GRAVES, ROBERT: (1895-); b. England; l. Majorca, Spain; poet, novelist, and classicist; *I, Claudius.*

GREEN, JULIAN: (1900-); b. France; l. America, France; expatriate novelist and essayist; *The Dark Journey.*

GREENE, GRAHAM: (1906-); England; Catholic novelist; *Brighton Rock.*

HAGGARD, SIR HENRY RIDER: (1856-1925); England; romantic novelist, gentleman farmer; *King Solomon's Mines, She.*

HALE, EDWARD EVERETT: (1822-1909); America; clergyman and author; *The Man Without a Country.*

HALÉVY, LUDOVIC: (1834-1908); France; playwright and novelist; *Un Mariage d'Amour.*

HALL, JAMES NORMAN: (1887-1951); America; traveler, adventurer, collaborator with

Charles Nordoff; *Mutiny on the Bounty.*

HALL, RADCLYFFE: (1886-1943); England; poet and realistic novelist; *The Well of Loneliness.*

HAMMETT, DASHIELL: (1894-); America; detective story writer; *The Maltese Falcon.*

HAMSUN, KNUT (KNUT PEDERSEN): (1860-1952); b. Norway; l. America; Norway; Nobel Prize winner, 1920; *Hunger.*

HARDY, ARTHUR SHERBURNE: (1847-1930); America; mathematician and writer; *The Wind of Destiny.*

HARDY, THOMAS: (1840-1928); England; poet and novelist, one of England's greats; *Far From the Madding Crowd, The Return of the Native, Tess of the d'Urbervilles.*

HARRIS, FRANK: (1854-1931); b. Ireland; l. America, Europe; autobiographer of great frankness, short-story writer, novelist; *Great Days.*

HARRIS, JOEL CHANDLER: (1848-1908); America; journalist and author; *Uncle Remus and Brer Rabbit.*

HARTE, FRANCIS BRETT: (1836-1902); America; writer of the early West; *The Luck of Roaring Camp, The Outcasts of Poker Flat* (stories).

HAWTHORNE, NATHANIEL: (1804-1864); America; member of Emerson—Thoreau group in New England; writer of American classic novels; *The Scarlet Letter, The House of the Seven Gables, The Marble Faun.*

HECHT, BEN: (1893-); America; newsman and realistic novelist; *Count Bruga.*

HEIDENSTAM, VERNER VON: (1859-1940); b. Sweden; l. Orient, Sweden; started a literary renaissance in Sweden by bringing an Oriental flavor to Swedish naturalism; Nobel Prize winner, 1916; *The Charles Men.*

HEMINGWAY, ERNEST: (1898-); b. America; l. Cuba; America's best-known novelist in Europe; hard-boiled, realistic style, member of the Paris *avant-garde* in the 1920's; *The Sun Also Rises, A Farewell To Arms, For Whom the Bell Tolls.*

HÉMON, LOUIS: (1880-1913); b. France; l. London, Canada; novelist of great promise, died young; *Maria Chapdelaine.*

HENRY, O. (WILLIAM SIDNEY PORTER): (1862-1910); America; adventurer, journalist, classic short-story writer, called the "American de Maupassant"; *The Four Million* (collection of stories).

HERGESHEIMER, JOSEPH: (1880-1953); America; romantic and popular novelist; *The Three Black Pennys.*

HERRICK, ROBERT: (1868-1938); America; novelist of American life; *Waste.*

HERSEY, JOHN: (1914-); America; novelist; *A Bell for Adano.*

HESSE, HERMAN: (1877-); b. Swabia; l. Switzerland; romantic, stylistic novelist of faith, Nobel Prize Winner, 1946; *Peter Camenzind.*

HEWLETT, MAURICE HENRY: (1861-1923); England; writer of medieval romances; *The Forest Lovers.*

HEYSE, PAUL VON: (1830-1914); Germany; novelist and playwright; Nobel Prize winner, 1910; *Meraner Novellen.*

HEYWARD, DUBOSE: (1885-1940); America; a Southerner, first to write realistically about the Southern Negro; *Porgy, Mamba's Daughters.*

HICHENS, ROBERT SMYTHE: (1864-1950); England; traveler, romantic novelist; *The Garden of Allah.*

HILTON, JAMES: (1900-1954); England; novelist; *Lost Horizon; Goodbye, Mr. Chips.*

HOLMES, OLIVER WENDELL: (1809-1894); America; man of letters and professor of anatomy and physiology at Harvard; *The Autocrat of the Breakfast Table* (essays).

HOPE, ANTHONY (HAWKINS, ANTHONY HOPE): (1863-1933); England; romantic novelist and playwright; *The Prisoner of Zenda.*

HOUSMAN, LAWRENCE: (1865-); England; political satirist and novelist; *Trimblerigg.*

HOWE, EDGAR WATSON: (1853-1937); America; author and journalist; *The Story of a Country Town.*

HOWELLS, WILLIAM DEAN: (1837-1920); America; man of letters; *The Rise of Silas Lapham.*

HUDSON, WILLIAM HENRY: (1841-1922); b. Argentina; l. England; nature writer; *Green Mansions.*

HUGHES, RICHARD: (1900-); England; playwright, novelist, short-story writer; *A High wind in Jamaica.*

HUGO, VICTOR MARIE: (1802-1885); France; man of letters; poet, playwright, novelist; *The Hunchback of Notre Dame, Les Misérables.*

HURST, FANNIE: (1889-); America; popular novelist; *Back Street.*

HUTCHINSON, ARTHUR STUART-MENTETH: (1879-); b. India; l. England; romantic journalist and novelist; *If Winter Comes.*

HUXLEY, ALDOUS: (1894-); b. England; l. America; experimental, intellectual novelist; *Point Counter Point, Brave New World.*

HUYSMANS, JORIS KARL: (1848-1907); France; realist novelist, antimaterialist; *Against the Grain.*

IRVING, WASHINGTON: (1783-1859); America; humorist, satirist, historian, novelist; "The Legend of Sleepy Hollow," a tale in the *Sketch Book.*

JACKSON, HELEN HUNT: (1830-1885): America; writer and reformer; *Ramona.*

JACOBS, WILLIAM WYMARK: (1863-1943); England; humorist and writer of sea stories; *Many Cargoes.*

JAMES, HENRY: (1843-1916); b. America; l. England; novelist of manners; *The American, Portrait of a Lady, The Ambassadors.*

JAMESON, MARGARET STORM: (1897-); England; social novelist; *The Captain's Wife.*

JENSEN, JOHANNES VILHELM: (1873-1950); Denmark; novelist and poet, Nobel Prize winner, 1944; *The Long Journey.*

JEWETT, SARAH ORNE: (1849-1909); America; novelist and short story writer; wrote local color stories of Maine; *Country By-Ways, The Country of the Pointed Firs.*

JOHNSON, DR. SAMUEL: (1709-1784); England; critic, lexicographer, conversationalist, satiric prose writer; *Rambler* (articles); *Rasselas, Prince of Abyssinia; Lives of the Poets* (biographies).

JOKAI, MAURUS: (1825-1904); Hungary; political and social novels and dramas; *A Hungarian Nabob.*

JORDAN, ELIZABETH: (1867-1947); America; writer and magazine editor; *Tales of the City Room.*

JOYCE, JAMES: (1882-1941); b. Dublin; l. Europe; poet, short story writer, novelist; influential innovator; *Portrait of the Artist as a Young Man, Ulysses, Finnegan's Wake.*

KAFKA, FRANZ: (1883-1924); b. Prague; l. Austria, Germany; mystic allegorist; *The Trial, The Castle, The Metamorphosis.*

KAGAWA, TOYOHIKO: (1888-); Japan; pacifist and Socialist writer; *Across the Death Line.*

KANTOR, MACKINLAY: (1904-); America; novelist and short-story writer; *Andersonville.*

KATAEV, VALENTIN PETROVICH: (1897-);
Russia; humorist and satirist; *The Embezzlers.*
KAYE-SMITH, SHEILA: (1888-); England;
writer of Sussex County, England; *Three
Against the World.*
KENNEDY, MARGARET: (1896-); England;
light novelist; *The Constant Nymph.*
KINGSLEY, CHARLES: (1819-1875); England;
novelist, clergyman, identified with 19th
cent. Christian Socialism; *Westward Ho!*
KIPLING, RUDYARD: (1865-1936); b. India;
l. England; Verses and tales of India; Nobel
Prize winner, 1907; *Plain Tales from the
Hills* (stories), *Jungle Books, Kim.*
KNIGHT, ERIC MOWBRAY: (1897-1943); b.
England; l. America; wrote in English York-
shire idiom; *The Flying Yorkshireman, Lassie
Come Home.*
KOESTLER, ARTHUR: (1905-); b. Hungary;
l. England; intellectual, political novelist and
essayist; *Darkness at Noon.*
KUPRIN, ALEXANDER IVANOVICH: (1870-
1938); Russia; realistic satirical novelist;
Yama (The Pit).
LAGERKVIST, PÄR: (1891-); Norway;
Nobel Prize winner, 1951; *Barabbas.*
LAGERLÖF, SELMA: (1858-1940); Sweden;
first woman Nobel Prize winner, 1909, novelist
of calm and naïve simplicity; *Gösta Berling.*
LAMB, CHARLES: (1775-1834). England;
essayist of Romantic period; *A Dissertation
on Roast Pig, Mrs. Battle's Opinions on
Whist* (essays).
LA MOTTE-FOUQUÉ, FRIEDRICH HEIN-
RICH KARL: (1777-1843); Germany; ro-
manticist; *Undine.*
LANDAU, MARK A.: see Aldanov, M. A.
LARDNER, RING (RINGGOLD WILMER):
(1885-1933); America; satirist, short-story
writer of American society in the 1920's; *You
Know Me Al.*
LAWRENCE, DAVID HERBERT: (1885-1930);
b. England; l. Italy, America, France; con-
troversial writer of the 1920's, naturalist novel-
ist; *Sons and Lovers, Lady Chatterly's
Lover.*
LAXNESS, HALLDÓR KILJAN: (1902-);
Iceland; novelist; *The Great Weaver of Cash-
mere.*
LEBLANC, MAURICE (1864-1941); France; de-
tective story writer; *Arsène Lupin.*
LEHMANN, ROSAMOND: (1903-); England;
novelist of lyrical delicacy; *Dusty Answer.*
LEONOV, LEONID: (1899-); Russia; pro-
Soviet novelist; *The Thief.*
LEROUX, GASTON: (1868-1927); France; de-
tective and mystery writer; *The Phantom
of the Opera.*
LESAGE, ALAIN RENÉ: (1668-1747); France;
early novel masterpiece; *L'Histoire de Gil
Blas de Santillane.*
LEVER, CHARLES JAMES: (1806-1872); b.
Dublin; l. Florence; rollicking, lighthearted
stories and novels; *Charles O'Malley.*
LEWIS, SINCLAIR: (1885-1951); b. America;
l. Europe, America; satiric novelist of Amer-
icans, home and abroad, Nobel Prize winner,
1930; *Main Street, Babbitt, Arrowsmith.*
LEWISOHN, LUDWIG: (1882-1955); b. Berlin;
l. America; novelist of Jews in America;
The Island Within.
LLEWELLYN, RICHARD: (1907-); adven-
turer and novelist of Wales; *How Green
Was My Valley.*
LOCKE, WILLIAM JOHN: (1863-1930); b.
Barbados, B. W. I.; l. England; architect and
romantic novelist; *The Beloved Vagabond.*
LONDON, JACK: (1876-1916); America; writer
of adventure in the West; *The Call of the
Wild, South Sea Tales.*

LOOS, ANITA (1893-); America; humorist
of the 1920's; *Gentlemen Prefer Blondes.*
LOTI, PIERRE (JULIEN VIAUD): (1850-1923);
France; sailor, romantic novelist; *The Mar-
riage of Loti.*
LOUŸS, PIERRE: (1870-1925); France; classi-
cal romanticist of amorous novels; *Psyche.*
LUCIAN (c. 120-200 A.D.); Greece; satirist and
humorist; *Veracious History, Dialogues of
the Dead.*
LYLY, JOHN: (1554-1606); England; leading
writer of artificial, highly balanced prose
style known as euphuistic, after his novel;
Euphues and His England.
LYTTON, EDWARD GEORGE: See Bulwer-
Lytton.
McCARTHY, MARY: (1912-); America; in-
tellectual satirist of the American scene; *The
Company She Keeps* (stories).
McCULLERS, CARSON: (1917-); America;
avant-garde writer of the South; *The Heart
is a Lonely Hunter.*
McCUTCHEON, GEORGE BARR: (1866-1925);
America; Hoosier school of writers; *Grau-
stark.*
McFEE, WILLIAM: (1881-); b. England; l.
America; novels of the sea; *Casuals of the
Sea.*
McKAY, CLAUDE: (1890-1948); b. Jamaica,
B. W. I.; l. America; realistic novelist of
workers, black and white; *Home to Harlem.*
MALORY, SIR THOMAS: (15th cent.); Eng-
land; compositor of prose epic; *Le Morte
d'Arthur.*
MALRAUX, ANDRÉ (1901-); France; intel-
lectual, art critic, and socialist novelist;
Man's Fate, Man's Hope.
MANN, THOMAS: (1875-1955); b. Germany;
l. America; contemporary stylist, social and
intellectual writer; Nobel Prize winner, 1929;
*Buddenbrooks, The Magic Mountain, Mario
and the Magician.*
MANSFIELD, KATHERINE: (1889-1923); b.
New Zealand; l. Europe; Sensitive writer of
short stories; *The Garden Party.*
MANZONI, ALESSANDRO: (1785-1873); Italy;
leader of the Italian romantic School; *I
Promessi Sposi, (The Betrothed Lovers).*
MARCH, WILLIAM (WILLIAM EDWARD
MARCH CAMPBELL): (1894-1954); Amer-
ica; novelist and short-story writer; *Com-
pany K.*
MARKS, PERCY,) (1891-); America; novelist
of college life in the 1920's; *The Plastic Age.*
MARQUAND, JOHN PHILLIPS: (1893-);
America; novelist of New England; Pulitzer
Prize, 1937; *The Late George Apley.*
MARQUIS, DON: (1878-1937); America; caus-
tic and humorous novelist; *The Old Soak's
History of the World, Archy and Mechitabel.*
MARRYAT, FREDRICK: (1792-1848); England;
novelist of sea life; *The Phantom Ship.*
MARTIN DU GARD, ROGER: (1881-):
France; novelist, Nobel Prize winner, 1937;
The Thibaults.
MARTÍNEZ ZUVIRIA, GUSTAVO ADOLPHO
(pseud., HUGO WAST): (1883-); Ar-
gentine; historical novelist of the Argentine;
Stone Desert.
MASON, VAN WYCK: (1897-); America;
historical novelist and detective writer; *Three
Harbours.*
MAUGHAM, WILLIAM SOMERSET: (1874-);
b. Paris; l. England, France; dramatist, nov-
elist, short-story writer; *Of Human Bondage,
The Moon and Sixpence.*
MAUPASSANT, GUY DE: (1850-1893); France;
realistic short-story writer; "The Diamond
Necklace," "The Rendezvous" (stories).
MAURIAC, FRANÇOIS) (1885-); France;

Nobel Prize 1952; Roman-Catholic novelist and critic; *Thérèse*.

MAUROIS, ANDRÉ: (1885-); France; biographer and stylistic and witty novelist; *The Family Circle*.

MELVILLE, HERMAN: (1819-1891); America; classic American novelist; *Moby Dick, Pierre, Billy Budd*.

MENCKEN, HENRY LOUIS: (1880-1956); American; journalist, essayist, literary critic; *The American Language*.

MEREDITH, GEORGE: (1828-1901); England; member of the Pre-Raphaelite Group; *The Egoist, Diana of the Crossways*.

MEREJKOWSKI, DIMITRI: (1866-1941). b. Russia; l. Paris; philosophical, historical novelist; *The Romance of Leonardo da Vinci*.

MÉRIMÉE, PROSPER: (1803-1870); France; novelist; *Colomba, Carmen*.

MICHENER, JAMES: (1907-); America; novelist; *Tales of the South Pacific*.

MILLER, HENRY: (1891-); b. America; l. France, California; *avant-garde* novelist; *The Tropic of Capricorn*.

MILNE, ALAN ALEXANDER: (1882-1956); England; dramatist and author of children's classic, *Winnie-the-Pooh*.

MILTON, JOHN: (1608-1674); England; poet and prose writer; *Areopagitica*.

MITCHELL, MARGARET: (1900-1949); America; one-novel phenomenon, Pulitzer Prize winner, 1937; *Gone with the Wind*.

MONTAIGNE, MICHEL EYQUEM DE: (1533-1595); France; one of earliest writers of personal essay; *Essays*.

MONTESQUIEU, BARON DE LA BREDE: (1689-1755); France; lawyer, philosopher, man of letters; *Lettres Persanes, L'Esprit des Lois*.

MONTGOMERY, LUCY MAUD: (1874-1942); Canada: popular writer for young people; *Anne of Green Gables*.

MOORE, GEORGE: (1852-1933); b. Ireland; l. England, France; naturalistic novelist, man of letters; *Esther Waters*.

MORAND, PAUL: (1888-); France; novelist and diplomat; *Open All Night*.

MORAVIA, ALBERTO: (1907-); Italy; novelist of the contemporary scene in Italy; *Woman of Rome*.

MORIER, JAMES JUSTINIAN: (1780-1849); b. England; l. Middle East; satirist of Western civilization; *The Adventures of Hajji Baba of Ispahan in England*.

MORLEY, CHRISTOPHER DARLINGTON: (1890-1957); America; journalist and novelist; *Kitty Foyle*.

MONTHERLANT, COMTE HENRI DE (1893-); France; aristocratic novelist of French tradition and classicism; *Les Célibataires*.

MORE, SIR THOMAS: (1478-1535); England; humanist and writer in both Latin and English; *Utopia*.

NASH or NASHE, THOMAS: (1567-1601); England; prose writer and dramatist; vigorously participated in controversies of the period; *Anatomy of Absurdities, Pierce Penniless, His Supplication to the Devil*.

NATHAN, ROBERT: (1894-); America; writer of fantasy; *Portrait of Jennie*.

NEUMANN, ALFRED: (1895-1952); Germany; historical novelist; *The Devil*.

NEXÖ, MARTIN ANDERSEN: (1869-1954); Denmark; social, proletarian novelist; *Ditte*.

NICHOLSON, MEREDITH: (1866-1947); America; romantic writer in American settings; *The House of a Thousand Candles*.

NORDHOFF, CHARLES BERNARD: (1887-

1947); America; travel and adventure writer, collaborator of James Norman Hall; *Mutiny on the Bounty*.

NORRIS, FRANK: (1870-1902); America; realistic novelist; *McTeague, The Octopus, The Pit*.

NORRIS, KATHLEEN: (1880-); America; popular novelist and short-story writer; *Saturday's Child*.

O'CONNOR, FRANK: (1903-); b. Ireland; l. America; short-story writer of contemporary Ireland; *Bones of Contention*.

O'FAOLÁIN, SEÁN: (1900-); Ireland; Irish patriot and novelist; *A Nest of Simple Folk*.

O'FLAHERTY, LIAM: (1897-); Ireland; writer of the Irish revolution, half-realistic, half-mystical; *The Informer*.

O'HARA, JOHN: (1905-); America; novelist of social patterns of urban and smalltown America; *Appointment in Samarra*.

OPPENHEIM, EDWARD PHILLIPS: (1866-1946); England; novels and short stories of international intrigue; *Ask Miss Mott*.

ORCZY, BARONESS EMMUSKA: (1865-1947); b. Hungary, l. France, England; romantic novelist; *The Scarlet Pimpernel*.

ORWELL, GEORGE: (1903-1950); b. India; l. England; anti-Communist novelist; *1984, Animal Farm*.

OUIDA (MARY LOUISE DE LA RAMÉE): (1839-1908); b. England; l. Florence; romances of 19th. cent. fashionable international set; *Under Two Flags*.

PAGE, THOMAS NELSON: (1853-1922); America; Southern novelist and diplomat; *The Old South*.

PARKER, DOROTHY: (1893-); America; satirist, short-story writer, witty conversationalist; *Here Lies*.

PARKER, SIR HORATIO GILBERT: (1862-1932); b. Canada; l. England; historical novelist; *The Seats of the Mighty*.

PASCAL, BLAISE: (1623-1662); France; mathematician, religious thinker, author; *Lettres Provinciales, Pensées*.

PATON, ALAN: (1903-); South Africa; social novelist of contemporary South Africa; *Cry the Beloved Country*.

PAUL, ELLIOT HAROLD: (1891-); b. America; l. France, Spain, America; versatile writer, member of the Paris group of experimentalists in 1920's, *The Last Time I Saw Paris*.

PEACOCK, THOMAS LOVE: (1785-1866); England; satiric novelist, friend of Shelley; *Nightmare Abbey*.

PEPYS, SAMUEL: (1633-1703); England, author and statesman; *Diary*.

PERELMAN, SIDNEY JOSEPH: (1904-); America; humorist; *Strictly From Hunger*.

PÉREZ DE AYALA, RAMON: (1880-) Spain; novelist, satirist of provincial life, critic; *Tiger Juan*.

PETROV, EUGENE: (1903-1942); Russia; short-story satirist; *Little Golden America*.

PHILLIPS, DAVID GRAHAM: (1867-1911); America; novelist, journalist, reformer; *Susan Lennox*.

PHILLPOTTS, EDEN: (1862-); b. India; l. England; prolific writer of the English scene; *The Human Boy*.

PIRANDELLO, LUIGI: (1867-1936); Italy; introspective novelist and playwright; *The Outcast*.

PLATO: (427?-347 B. C.) Greek philosopher, writer of famous dialogues; *Republic, Symposium, Phaedrus*.

PLINY THE YOUNGER (CAIUS PLINIUS CAECILIUS SECUNDUS): (c. 61 - c. 113);

Roman; administrator, wrote letters which have been preserved; *Letters.*

POE, EDGAR ALLAN: (1809-1848); America; poet and short-story writer; "The Gold Bug," "The Fall of the House of Usher," "The Masque of the Red Death" (stories).

PONTOPPIDAN, HENRICK: (1857-1943); Denmark; novelist, Nobel Prize winner, 1917; *Lucky Peter.*

PORTER, GENE STRATTON: (1868-1924); America; novelist and nature writer; *A Girl of the Limberlost.*

PORTER, KATHERINE ANNE: (1894-); America; short-story writer of style and sensitivity; *The Flowering Judas.*

PORTER, WILLIAM SYDNEY: See Henry, O.

POWYS, JOHN COWPER: (1872-); England; philosophical and mystical novels, *Wolf Solent.*

PRATOLINI, VASCO: (1913-); Italy; realistic writer; *A Hero of Our Time.*

PRÉVOST, ABBÉ (ANTOINE FRANÇOIS PRÉVOST D'EXILES) (1697-1763); France; Benedictine monk and novelist; *Histoire du Chevalier Des Grieux et de Manon Lescaut.*

PRÉVOST, MARCEL: (1862-1941); France; romantic shockers; *The Demi-Virgins.*

PRIESTLEY, JOHN BOYNTON: (1894-); England; popular novelist and playwright; *The Good Companions, Angel Pavement.*

PROUST, MARCEL: (1871-1922); France; recluse and writer of great style, chronicler of French society; *Remembrance of Things Past.*

PUSHKIN, ALEXANDER SERGEIVICH: (1799-1837); Russia; early revolutionary poet and novelist; *Boris Godunov.*

RABELAIS, FRANÇOIS: (1494-1553); France; earthy humorist and satirist, writer of two robust satires; *Pantagruel, Gargantua.*

RADCLIFFE, ANN: (1764-1823); England, romantic novelist; *The Mysteries of Udolpho, A Sicilian Romance.*

RADIGUET, RAYMOND: (1903-1923); France; poet and novelist, genius protegée of Cocteau; *The Devil in the Flesh.*

RAWLINGS, MARJORIE KINNAN: (1896-1953); America; writer of the Florida backwoods; Pulitzer Prize, 1938; *The Yearling.*

READE, CHARLES: (1814-1884); England; social and historical novelist and playwright; *The Cloister and the Hearth.*

REMARQUE, ERICH MARIA: (1897-); b. Germany; l. America; pacifist and anti-Nazi writer; *All Quiet on the Western Front.*

REYMONT, WLADYSLAW STANISLAW: (1868-1925); Poland; realistic novelist, Nobel Prize winner, 1924, *The Peasants.*

RICE, ALICE HEGAN: (1870-1942); America; charity worker and novelist; *Mrs. Wiggs of the Cabbage Patch.*

RICHARDSON, HENRY HANDEL (HENRIETTA RICHARDSON): (1880-1946); b. Australia; l. England; *Maurice Guest, The Fortunes of Richard Mahony* (trilogy).

RICHARDSON, SAMUEL: (1689-1761); England; novelist of manners; *Pamela, or Virtue Rewarded, Clarissa Harlowe.*

RICHTER, CONRAD: (1890-); America; writer of early Americana; *The Sea of Grass.*

RINEHART, MARY ROBERTS: (1876-); America; novelist and mystery-story writer; *The Circular Staircase.*

ROBERTS, ELIZABETH MADOX: (1886-1941); America; poetic prose-writer of the Kentucky hills; *The Great Meadow.*

ROBERTS, KENNETH LEWIS: (1885-1957); America; historical novelist; *Northwest Passage.*

ROLLAND, ROMAIN: (1866-1944); France;

writer of France's great political tradition; Nobel Prize winner, 1917; *Jean Christophe.*

RÖLVAAG, OLE EDVART: (1876-1931); b. Norway; l. America; writer of pioneer life in America; *Giants in the Earth.*

ROMAINS, JULES: (1885-); b. France; l. America; intellectual and poetic novelist of the masses; *Men of Good Will.*

ROMANOV, PANTELEIMON: (1884-); Russia; naturalist writer of Russia's transition; *Three Pairs of Silk Stockings.*

ROUSSEAU, JEAN JACQUES: (1712-1778); France; b. Switzerland; author and thinker; forerunner of Romantic movement; *Confessions; Julie, or the New Heloise; The Social Contract.*

RUNYON, DAMON: (1880-1946); America; journalist and humorous short-story writer of Broadway; *Guys and Dolls.*

RUSKIN, JOHN: (1819-1900); England; painter, critic, essayist; *The Stones of Venice, Unto This Last.*

RUSSELL, BERTRAND ARTHUR WILLIAM (EARL RUSSELL): (1872-); England; Nobel Prize 1950; philosopher and essayist; *Principia Mathematica, Marriage and Morals.*

RUSSELL, WILLIAM CLARK: (1844-1911); b. America; l. England; nautical tales of adventure, *The Wreck of the Grosvenor.*

SABATINI, RAFAEL: (1875-1950); b. Italy; l. England; romantic novelist; *Scaramouche, Captain Blood.*

SACKVILLE-WEST, VICTORIA MARY: (1892-); England; member of Bloomsbury group, romantic but unsentimental novelist; *All Passion Spent.*

SAGAN, FRANÇOISE: (1935-); France; novelist of contemporary France; *A Certain Smile.*

SAINT-EXUPÉRY, ANTOINE DE: (1900-1944); Poetic novels of flying; *Wind, Sand and Stars, The Little Prince.*

SAKI (HECTOR HUGO MONRO): (1870-1916); b. India; l. England; Humorous and ironic short stories and novels; *The Unbearable Bassington.*

SALTEN, FELIX: (1869-1945); b. Hungary; l. Austria, Switzerland; sentimental but sensitive stories of animals; *Bambi.*

SAND, GEORGE (AMANDINE AURORE LUCIE DUPIN): (1803-1876); France; feminist writer, member of the Paris artistic group; *Lélia, La Mare au Diable.*

SANTAYANA, GEORGE: (1863-1952); b. Spain; l. Italy, America; philosopher and naturalist novelist; *The Sense of Beauty* (philosophy) *The Last Puritan* (novel).

SAROYAN, WILLIAM: (1908-); America; novelist, short-story writer, playwright; *The Daring Young Man on the Flying Trapeze, The Trouble with Tigers.*

SARTRE, JEAN-PAUL: (1905-); France; Existentialist philosopher, novelist, playwright; *Nausée.*

SAYERS, DOROTHY LEIGH: (1893-); England; detective-story writer, created Lord Peter Wimsey; *Murder Must Advertise.*

SCHNITZLER, ARTHUR: (1862-1931); Austria; physician, playwright and novelist of Viennese decadence; *Fraülein Else, Daybreak.*

SCHOPFER, JEAN: see Anet, Claude.

SCHREINER, OLIVE: (1855-1926); South Africa; author and feminist; *The Story of an African Farm.*

SCOTT, SIR WALTER: (1771-1832); Scotland; classic historical novelist; *Waverly, Ivanhoe, Kenilworth.*

SEGHERS, ANNA: (1900-); b. Germany; l. Mexico; refugee novelist, antifascist, social writer; *The Seventh Cross.*

SENDER, RAMON J.: (1902-); b. Spain; l.

Mexico; Spanish Republican refugee, novelist, both realist and mystic; *Pro Patria.*

SHARP, MARGERY: (1905-); England; popular, humorous novelist and short-story writer; *The Nutmeg Tree.*

SHAW, IRWIN: (1913-); b. America; l. Paris; contemporary novelist; *The Young Lions.*

SHEEAN, VINCENT: (1899-); America; novelist and essayist; *Personal History.*

SHELLEY, MARY WOLLSTONECRAFT GODWIN: (1797-1851); England; Wife of poet Shelley and early science-fiction writer; *Frankenstein.*

SHOLOKHOV, MIKHAIL ALEKSANDROVICH: (1905-); Russia; Soviet writer; *And Quiet Flows the Don.*

SIENKIEWICZ, HENRYK: (1846-1916); Poland; novelist, Nobel Prize winner, 1905; *Quo Vadis?*

SILLANPÄÄ, FRANS EEMIL: (1888-1952); Finland; social novelist, Nobel Prize winner, 1939; *Meek Heritage.*

SILONE, IGNAZIO: (1900-); Italy; Socialist and antifascist novelist and essayist; *Fontamara, Bread and Wine.*

SIMENON, GEORGES (GEORGE SIM): (1903-); b. Belgium; l. France; prolific detective-story writer; *The Crime of Inspector Maigret.*

SINCLAIR, MAY: (1865?-1946); England; novelist, well known in the U.S., wrote in "stream of consciousness" style; *Anne Severn and the Fieldings.*

SINCLAIR, UPTON: (1878-); America; Socialist writer, very popular abroad; *The Jungle, World's End.*

SMITH, FRANCES HOPKINSON: (1838-1915); America; author and illustrator; *Caleb West, Master Diver.*

SMITH, THORNE: (1893-1934); America; farcical novelist; *Turnabout, Topper Takes a Trip.*

SMOLLETT, TOBIAS GEORGE: (1721-1771); England; prototype writer of mystery and horror stories; *Roderick Random, Ferdinand, Count Fathom.*

SPRING, HOWARD: (1889-); b. Wales; l. England; popular novelist; *My Son, My Son.*

STEEL, MRS. FLORA ANNIE: (1847-1929); b. India; l. India, England; champion of India and women's rights; novels which were careful studies of Indian myths; *On the Face of the Waters.*

STEELE, RICHARD: (1672-1729). England; b. Ireland; playwright and essayist; known for writings in the periodicals the *Tatler* and the *Spectator.*

STEIN, GERTRUDE: (1874-1946); b. America; l. France; leader of Paris experimental group; *Three Lives.*

STEINBECK, JOHN: (1902-); America; social and economic novelist, Pulitzer Prize winner; *The Grapes of Wrath, Of Mice and Men, The Moon is Down.*

STENDHAL (MARIE HENRI BEYLE): (1783-1842); romantic novelist of the French bourgeois class; *De l'Amour, The Red and the Black, La Chartreuse de Parme.*

STEPHENS, JAMES: (1882-1950); Ireland; poet and novelist; *The Crock of Gold.*

STERNE, LAURENCE: (1713-1768); b. Ireland; l. England; novelist of eccentricity, humor, and unconventionality; *Tristram Shandy.*

STEVENS, JAMES FLOYD: (1892-); America; writer of folk stories; *Paul Bunyan.*

STEVENSON, ROBERT LOUIS: (1850-1894); b. Scotland; l. America, Samoa; author of classic adventure stories; *Treasure Island, Dr. Jekyll and Mr. Hyde, Kidnapped.*

STILL, JAMES: (1906-); America; Southern poet and novelist; *River of Earth.*

STOUT, REX: (1886-); America; detective-story writer, creator of Nero Wolfe; *Black Orchids.*

STOWE, HARRIET BEECHER: (1811-1896); America; abolitionist, writer of importance in fight against slavery; *Uncle Tom's Cabin.*

STRINDBERG, AUGUST: (1849-1912); Sweden; Sweden's greatest playwright and novelist, both socialist and reactionary; *There Are Crimes and Crimes, The Road to Damascus.*

SUDERMANN, HERMANN: (1857-1928); Germany; liberal dramatist and novelist; *The Song of Songs.*

SUE, EUGÈNE: (1804-1857); France; popular French classicist; *The Wandering Jew.*

SVEVO, ITALO (ETTORE SCHMITZ): (1861-1928); Italy; experimental writer, sponsored by James Joyce; *The Confessions of Zeno.*

SWIFT, JONATHAN: (1667-1745); b. Ireland; l. England; rebellious satirist and misanthrope, novelist and essayist; *The Tale of a Tub, Gulliver's Travels, A Modest Proposal.*

SWINNERTON, FRANK: (1884-); England; popular novelist; *Nocturne.*

TAGORE, RABINDRANATH, SIR: (1861-1941); India; poet, philosopher, novelist, Nobel Prize winner, 1913; *The Home and the World.*

TARKINGTON, NEWTON BOOTH: (1869-1946); America; romantic novelist and stories of youth in America; *Monsieur Beaucaire, Penrod. The Magnificent Ambersons.*

THACKERAY, WILLIAM MAKEPEACE: (1811-1863); England; satirical novelist of fashionable society; *Vanity Fair, Henry Esmond, The Virginians.*

THOMAS, DYLAN: (1914-1953); b. Wales; d. America; *avant-garde* poet and short-story writer; *Portrait of the Artist as a Young Dog.*

THOREAU, HENRY DAVID: (1817-1862); America; poet, prose writer, naturalist; known for individualism and love of nature; *Walden.*

THURBER, JAMES: (1894-); America; satirist and illustrator, short-stories and plays; *My Life and Hard Times, My World — And Welcome to It.*

TOLSTOY, COUNT LEO NIKOLAEVICH: (1828-1910); Russia; moral and social philosopher, novelist and mystic; *War and Peace, Anna Karenina.*

TRILLING, LIONEL: (1905-); America; intellectual critic and novelist of contemporary America; *The Middle of the Journey.*

TROLLOPE, ANTHONY: (1815-1882); England; political and social novelist; *Phineas Finn.*

TULLY, JIM: (1888-1947); America; social novelist; *Jarnegan.*

TURGENEV, IVAN SERGEIVICH: (1818-1883); Russia; novelist of nihilist doctrines; *Fathers and Sons, Smoke.*

TWAIN, MARK (SAMUEL LANGHORNE CLEMENS): (1835-1910); America; satirist, novelist; disillusioned observer of humanity; *Tom Sawyer, Huckelberry Finn, Life on the Mississippi.*

UNDSET, SIGRID: (1882-1949); b. Norway; l. America; Norway's greatest novelist, Nobel Prize winner, 1928; *Kristin Lavransdatter.*

VAN VECHTEN, CARL: (1880-); America; eccentric writer of "clever" novels; *Nigger Heaven.*

VERNE, JULES: (1828-1905); France; semi-scientific romances of adventure; *Around the World in Eigthy Days, Twenty Thousand Leagues Under the Sea.*

VIGNY, ALFRED DE: (1797-1863); France; poet, playwright, novelist; *Cinq Mars.*

VOLTAIRE (FRANÇOIS MARIE AROUET) (1694-1778); greatest intellectual influence of the 18th cent. in Europe; philosopher and novelist; *Candide.*

WALPOLE, HORACE: (1717-1797); England; man of letters, author of supernatural romances; *The Castle of Otranto.*

WALPOLE, SIR HUGH: (1884-1941); b. New Zealand; l. England; prolific popular novelist; *Rogue Herries.*

WALTON, IZAAK: (1593-1683); England; prose writer; *The Compleat Angler.*

WARD, MARY AUGUSTA (MRS. HUMPHRY WARD): (1851-1920); b. Australia; l. England; novelist, philanthropist, antisuffragette; *Robert Elsmere.*

WASSERMAN, JAKOB: (1873-1934); Germany; novelist; *The World's Illusion.*

WAST, HUGO: See Martínez Zuviría, Gustavo Adolpho.

WAUGH, EVELYN: (1903-); England; satirist and novelist of the contemporary scene; *Vile Bodies, Brideshead Revisited, The Loved One.*

WEBB, MARY: (1881-1927); England; poetic novelist of nature; *Precious Bane.*

WELLS, HERBERT GEORGE: (1866-1946); England; satiric novelist and science-fiction writer; *The New Machiavelli, The Shape of Things to Come, You Can't Be Too Careful.*

WERFEL, FRANZ: (1890-1945); b. Czechoslovakia, l. Austria; antimilitarist journalist and novelist; *The Forty Days of Musa Dagh, The Song of Bernadette.*

WEST, REBECCA (CICILY ISABEL FAIRFIELD): (1892-); England; novelist, critic, journalist; *Harriet Hume, The Meaning of Treason.*

WESTCOTT, EDWARD NOYES: (1846-1898); America; banker and novelist; *David Harum.*

WHARTON, EDITH: (1862-1937); b. America; l. France; novelist of American society; *The Valley of Decision, Ethan Frome, The Age of Innocence.*

WILDE, OSCAR FINGAL O'FLAHERTIE WILLS, (1856-1900); b. Ireland; l. England, France; poet, wit, fiction writer, dramatist; *The Picture of Dorian Gray.*

WILDER, THORNTON NIVEN: (1897-); America; novelist and dramatist; Pulitzer Prize winner, 1927; *The Bridge of San Luis Rey.*

WIGGIN, KATE DOUGLAS: (1856-1923); America; novelist for young people; *Rebecca of Sunnybrook Farm.*

WILLIAMS, TENNESSEE: (1912-); America; novelist, short-story writer, and playwright of the decadent South; *One Arm.*

WILSON, EDMUND: (1895-); America, critic, journalist, fiction writer; *I Thought of Daisy, Axel's Castle* (essays), *Memoirs of Hecate County.*

WISTER, OWEN: (1860-1938); America; naturalistic novels of the West; *The Virginian.*

WODEHOUSE, Pelham Granville: (1881-); England; humorist in stories and novels; *Leave It to Psmith, The Crime Wave at Blandings.*

WOLFE, THOMAS CLAYTON: (1900-1938); America; novelist of America; *Look Homeward Angel, Of Time and the River, You Can't Go Home Again.*

WOOLF, VIRGINIA: (1882-1941); England; sensitive novelist and essayist in the "stream of consciousness" style; *Jacob's Room, Mrs. Dalloway, The Waves.*

WRIGHT, HAROLD BELL: (1872-1944); America; novels of the simple people of America; *The Shepherd of the Hills.*

WRIGHT, RICHARD: (1908-); America; Negro novelist and story writer; *Native Son.*

WYLIE, ELINOR: (1885-1928); America; poet and complex novelist; *The Orphan Angel.*

WYLIE, PHILLIP: (1902-); America; novels in criticism of contemporary America; *A Generation of Vipers, Finnley Wrenn.*

WYSS, JOHANN RUDOLPH: (1781-1830); Switzerland; collector folklore and Swiss Tales; *The Swiss Family Robinson.*

YOUNG, FRANCIS BRETT: (1884-1954); England; prolific popular novelist; *The Man About the House.*

ZOLA, EMILE: (1840-1902); France, leader of Naturalism in French literature; *Nana.*

ZWEIG, ARNOLD: (1887-); b. Germany; l. Palestine; writer on Jewish problems and politics; *The Case of Sergeant Grischa.*

ZWEIG, STEFAN: (1881-1942); Austria; playwright, author, biographer; *Passion and Pain, Conflicts.*

Oceans
See Salt Water Bodies

Operas, Grand
See also Characters from the Great Operas; Musical Compositions; Popular Names of Musical Compositions; Singing Voices, Types of

ADAM, ADOLPHE (1803-1856): *The Coachman of Longjumeau (Le Postillon de Longjumeau)*, 1836 (libretto: A. de Leuven, L. L. Brunswick).

AUBER, DANIEL FRANÇOIS (1782-1871): *The Dumb Girl of Portici (La Muette de Portici)*, 1828 (libretto: Scribe, Delavigne); *Fra Diavolo*, 1830 (libretto: Scribe).

BALFE, MICHAEL WILLIAM (1803-1870): *The Bohemian Girl*, 1843 (libretto: Alfred Bunn, based on *The Gipsy*, ballet-pantomime by Vernoy Saint-Georges).

BARTÓK, BÉLA (1881-1945): *Duke Bluebeard's Castle (A kékszakállú Herceg Vára)*, 1918 (libretto: B. Balázs).

BEETHOVEN, LUDVIG VAN (1770-1827): *Fidelio*, 1805 (libretto: Joseph Sonnleithner and Georg Friedrich Sonnleithner after the drama by Jean Nicolas Builly).

BELLINI, VINCENZO (1802-1835): *The Sleepwalker (La Sonnambula)*, 1831 (libretto: Felice Romani); *Norma*, 1831 (libretto: Felice Romani); *The Puritans (I Puritani)*, 1835 (libretto: Count Pepoli).

BERG, ALBAN (1885-1935): *Wozzeck*, 1925 (libretto: adapted by the composer from Georg Büchner's drama of the same name); *Lulu*, 1937 (libretto: adapted by the composer from Frank Wedekind's *Erdgeist* and *Die Buchse der Pandora*).

BERLIOZ, HECTOR (1803-1869): *Benvenuto Cellini*, 1838 (Libretto: De Wailly, Barbier); *The Damnation of Faust*, 1846 (libretto: Berlioz, Gerard, Gondonnière, after Gerald de Nerval's version of Goethe's play); *The Trojans (Les Trojans)*, Part I *(La Prise de Troie)*, 1869; the entire work, and the première of Part II, *Les Troyens à Carthage*, first given in 1890); *Béatrice et Bénédict*, 1862 (libretto: the composer, after Shakespeare's *Much Ado about Nothing*).

BIZET, GEORGES (1838-1875): *The Pearl Fishers (Les Pêcheurs de Perles)*, 1863 (libretto: Carré, Cormon); *Djamileh*, 1872, (libretto: Louis Gallet); *Carmen*, 1875 (libretto: Henri Meilhac, Ludovic Halévy, based on Merimée's novel).

BLITZSTEIN, MARC (1905-): *Regina*, 1953 (libretto by composer, based on the play *The Little Foxes*, by Lillian Hellman).

BOIELDIEU, FRANÇOIS ADRIEN (1775-1834): *The White Lady (La Dame Blanche)*, 1825 (libretto: Scribe, based on Scott's *Guy Mannering* and *The Monastery*).

BOÏTO, ARRIGO (1842-1918): *Mefistofele*, 1868 (libretto: the composer after Goethe); *Nero (Nerone)*, 1924 (libretto: the composer).

BORODIN, ALEXANDER (1834-1887): *Prince Igor*, 1890 (libretto: the composer, after a play by V. V. Stassov); the opera completed by Rimsky-Korsakov and Glazounov).

BOUGHTON, RUTLAND (1878-): *The Immortal Hour*, 1914 (libretto: adapted from the play and poems of Fiona Macleod).

BRITTEN, BENJAMIN (1913-): *Peter Grimes*, 1945 (libretto: Montagu Slater, after the poem by George Crabbe); *The Rape of Lucretia*, 1946 (libretto: Ronald Duncan, from André Obey's play, *Le Viol de Lucrèce*); *Albert Herring*, 1947 (libretto: Eric Crozier, from Maupassant's story "Le Rosier de Madame Husson"); *Let's Make an Opera!*, 1949 (libretto: Eric Crozier); *Billy Budd*, 1951 (libretto: E. M. Forster, Eric Crozier, based on Melville's story); *Gloriana*, 1953 (libretto: William Plomer).

BUSONI, FERRUCCIO (1866-1924): *Turandot*, 1917 (libretto: the composer); *Arlecchino*, 1917 (libretto: the composer); *Doctor Faust*, 1925 (libretto: the composer).

CADMAN, CHARLES WAKEFIELD (1881-1946): *Shanewis*, 1918 (libretto: Nelle Richmond Eberhart; *A Witch of Salem*, 1926 (libretto: Nelle Richmond Eberhardt).

CATALANI, ALFREDO (1854-1893): *La Wally*, 1892 (libretto: Luigi Illica); *Loreley*, 1919 (libretto: A. Zanardi and Carlo D'Ormville).

CHARPENTIER, GUSTAVE (1860-1956): *Louise*, 1900 (libretto: the composer).

CILÈA, FRANCESCO (1866-1950): *The Maid of Arles (L'Arlesiana)*, 1897 (libretto: Leopoldo Marenco, based on Daudet's story); *Adriana Lecouvreur*, 1902 (libretto: A. Colautti, from the play by Scribe and Legouvé).

CIMAROSA, DOMENICO (1749-1801): *Il Matrimonio Segreto*, 1792 (libretto: Giovanni Bertati after Colman's *The Clandestine Marriage*).

CONVERSE, FREDERICK SHEPHERD (1871-1940): *The Pipe of Desire*, 1906 (libretto: George Edward Burton); *The Sacrifice*, 1911 (libretto: the composer and John Macy).

CORNELIUS, PETER (1824-1874): *The Barber of Bagdad*, 1858 (libretto: the composer).

D'ALBERT, EUGEN (1864-1932): *The Lowlands (Tiefland)*, 1903 (libretto: Rudolph Lothar, after a Catalonian play, *Tierra Baixa*, by Angel Guimera).

DAMROSCH, WALTER (1862-1950): *The Scarlet Letter*, 1896 (libretto: George Parsons Lathrop, after Hawthorne); *Cyrano de Bergerac*, 1913 (libretto: W. J. Henderson, after Rostand); *The Man without a Country*, 1937 (libretto: Arthur Guiterman, after Edward Everett Hale).

DEBUSSY, CLAUDE (1862-1918): *Pelléas et Mélisande*, 1902 (libretto: from Maeterlinck's play of the same name.

DE KOVEN, REGINALD (1861-1920): *The Canterbury Pilgrims*, 1917 (libretto: Percy Mac Kaye, after Chaucer); *Rip Van Winkle*, 1920 (libretto: Percy Mac Kaye).

DELIBES, LÉO (1836-1891): *Lakmé*, 1883 (libretto: Edmond Gondinet, Philippe Gille, after Pierre Loti's *Le Mariage de Loti*).

DELIUS, FREDERICK (1862-1934): *A Village Romeo and Juliet*, 1907 (libretto: the composer, based on a story by Gottfried Keller).

DONIZETTI, GAETANO (1797-1848): *The Elexir of Love (l'Elisir d'Amore)*, 1832 (libretto: Felice Romani); *Lucrezia Borgia*, 1833 (libretto: Felice Romani after Victor Hugo); *Lucia di Lammermoor*, 1835 (libretto: Salvatore Cammarano after Sir Walter Scott's novel); *The Daughter of the Regiment*, 1840 (libretto: J. H. Vernoy Saint-Georges, F. Bayard); *La Favorita*, 1840 (libretto: Alphonse Royer, Gustav Waez); *Linda de Chamounix*, 1842 (libretto: Gaetano Rossi).

DUKAS, PAUL (1865-1935): *Ariadne and Blue Beard (Ariane et Barbe Bleu)*, 1907 (libretto: after Maeterlinck's play of the same name).

ERLANGER, CAMILLE (1863-1919): *Kermaria*, 1897; *Le Juif Polonaise*, 1900 (libretto; Henri Cain, P. B. Gheusi); *Aphrodité*, 1906 (libretto: Louis de Gramont, after Pierre Louÿs; Noël, 1906; *L'Aube Rouge*, 1912.

FALLA, MANUEL DE (1876-1946): *The Brief Life (La Vida Breve)*, 1913 (libretto: C. Fernandez Shaw: French version by P. Milliet).

FÉVRIER, HENRI (1876-): *Le Roi Aveugle*, 1906; *Monna Vanna*, 1909, American première, 1914 (libretto: Maurice Maeterlinck); *Gismonda*, 1915; *La Damnation de Blanche-Fleur*, 1920; *Aphrodité*, 1920; *La Femme Nue*, 1932.

FLOTOW, FRIEDRICH VON (1812-1883): *Medusa's Shipwreck*, 1839; *Camoen's Slave*, 1843; *Stradella*, 1844 (libretto: W. Friedrich); *The Soul in Pain*, 1846; *Martha*, 1847 (libretto: Vernoy Saint-Georges and W. Friedrich).

FRANCHETTI, ALBERTO (1860-1942): *Christopher Columbus*, 1892 (libretto: Luigi Illica); *Germania*, 1902 (libretto: Luigi Illica).

GAY, JOHN (1685-1732): *The Beggar's Opera*, 1728 (music arranged by John Christopher Pepusch; new version by Frederic Austin, 1920; new version by Benjamin Britten, 1948).

GERSHWIN, GEORGE (1898-1937): *Porgy and Bess*, 1935 (libretto; Du Bose Heyward, Ira Gershwin).

GIORDANO, UMBERTO (1867-1948): *Mala Vita*, 1892; *Andrea Chénier*, 1896 (libretto: Luigi Illica); *Fedora*, 1898 (libretto: A. Colautti, after Sardou); *Siberia*, 1908; *Madame Sans-Gêne*, 1915 (libretto: Renato Simoni, after Victorien Sardou and E. Moreau).

GLINKA, MICHAEL IVANOVITCH (1804-1857): *A Life for the Czar (Ivan Susanin)*, 1836 (libretto: G. F. Rozen); *Russlan and Ludmilla*, 1842 (libretto: V. F. Shirkov and K. B. Bakhturin after Pushkin).

GLUCK, CHRISTOPH WILLIBALD (1714-1787): *Orfeo ed Euridice*, 1762 (libretto: Raniero da Calzabigi); *Alceste*, 1767 (libretto: Raniero da Calzabigi); *Iphigénie en Aulide*, 1774 (libretto: Raniero da Calzabigi); *Iphigénie en Tauride*, 1779 (libretto: François Guillard).

GOLDMARK, KARL (1830-1915): *The Queen of Sheba (Die Königin von Saba)*, 1875 (libretto: Hermann von Mosenthal); *The Cricket on the Hearth (Das Heimchen am Herd)*, 1896 (libretto: M. Willner).

GOUNOD, CHARLES FRANÇOIS (1818-1893): *Faust*, 1869 (libretto: Barbier and Carré, after Goethe); *Mireille*, 1864 (libretto: Carré, after Frédéric Mistral's poem *Mireio*); *Romeo and Juliet*, 1867 (libretto: Barbier and Carré, after Shakespeare).

GRANADOS, ENRIQUE (1867-1916): *Goyescas*, 1916 (libretto: Fernando Periquet).

GRUENBERG, LOUIS (1883-): *The Emperor Jones*, 1933 (libretto: Kathleen de Jaffa).

HADLEY, HENRY K. (1871-1937): *Azora, the*

Daughter of Montezuma, 1917 (libretto: David Stevens); *Cleopatra's Night*, 1920 (libretto: Alice Leal Pollock, after Théophile Gautier).

HAGEMAN, RICHARD (1882-): *Caponsacchi*, 1932 (libretto: in German W. Wolff and J. Kapp; in English A. F. Goodrich, after *The Ring and the Book*, by Robert Browning).

HALÉVY, JACQUES FRANÇOIS (1799-1862): *La Juive*, 1835 (libretto: Augustin Eugène Scribe).

HANSON, HOWARD (1896-): *Merry Mount*, 1934 (libretto: Richard L. Stokes, after Hawthorne).

HERBERT, VICTOR (1859-1924): *Natoma*, 1911 (libretto: Joseph D. Redding); *Madeleine*, 1914 (libretto: Grant Stewart, after A. Decourcelles and L. Thiboust.

HINDEMITH, PAUL (1895-1957): *Mathias the Painter* (*Mathis der Maler*), 1938 (libretto: the composer).

HOLST, GUSTAV (1874-1934): *Savitri*, 1916 (libretto: the composer, from an episode in the *Mahabharata*).

HUMPERDINCK, ENGELBERT (1854-1921): *Hansel and Gretel*, 1893 (libretto: Adelheid Wette); *Die Königskinder*, 1910 (libretto: Ernest Rosmer, after the fairy tale by Elsa Bernstein).

JANÁČEK, LEOŠ (1865-1928): *Her Foster Daughter* (*Její Pastorkyňa Jenufa*), 1904 (libretto: the composer, based on a story by Gabriella Preissova); *Katya Kabanova*, 1921 (libretto: Cervinka, based on Ostrovsky's *The Storm*); *From a House of the Dead* (*Aus einem Totenhaus*), 1930 (libretto: the composer; based on Dostoevski's *Memoirs from a House of the Dead*).

KIENZL, WILHELM (1857-1941); *The Evangelist*, 1895.

KODALY, ZOLTAN (1882-): *Hary Janos*, 1926 (libretto: Bela Paulini, Zsolt Harsanyi).

KORNGOLD, ERICH WOLFGANG (1897-1957): *Die Tote Stadt* (The Dead City), 1920 (libretto: Schott, after the story *Bruges la Morte*, by Rodenbach).

KRENEK, ERNST (1900-) *Johnny Plays On*, 1927 (Jazz opera with libretto by the composer.

LALO, EDOUARD (1823-1892): *The King of Ys* (*Le Roi d'Ys*), 1888 (libretto: Edouard Blau).

LEONCAVALLO, RUGGIERO (1858-1919): *I Pagliacci*, 1892 (libretto: the composer); *Zaza*, 1900 (libretto: the composer).

LEONI, FRANCO (1864-1938): *L'Oracolo*, 1905 (libretto: Camillo Zanoni, after the play *The Cat and the Cherub*, by Chester Fernald).

LORTZING, ALBERT (1803-1851): *Czar and Carpenter* (Zar und Zimmerman), 1837 (text by the composer, founded on a French play by J. T. Merle); *The Poacher*, 1842 (text by the composer based on a play by A. von Kotzebue).

MASCAGNI, PIETRO (1863-1945): *Cavalleria Rusticana*, 1890 (libretto: G. Menasci, G. Targioni-Tozzetti); *L'Amico Fritz*, 1891 (libretto: P. Suardon); *Iris*, 1898 (libretto: Luigi Illica); *Lodoletta*, 1917 (libretto: Giacchino Forzano after the novel *Two Little Wooden Shoes* by Ouida).

MASSENET, JULES (1842-1912): *Manon*, 1884 (libretto: Meilhac and Gille, after Abbé Prévost); *Werther*, 1892 (libretto: Edouard Blau, Paul Milliet, Georges Hartmann, after Goethe's novel); *Thaïs*, 1894 (libretto: L. Gallet, after Anatole France); *Our Lady's Juggler* (*Le Jongleur de Notre Dame*), 1902 (libretto: M. Lena); *Don Quichotte*, 1910 (libretto:

Henry Cain, after Le Lorrain's play based on Cervantes' novel).

MENOTTI, GIAN-CARLO (1911-): *Amelia Goes to the Ball*, 1937 (libretto: by the composer); *The Island God*, 1942 (libretto: by the composer; English translation by Fleming McLeish); *The Old Maid and the Thief*, 1941 (libretto: the composer); *The Medium*, 1946 (libretto: the composer); *The Telephone*, 1947 (libretto: the composer); *The Consul*, 1950 (libretto: the composer); *Amahl and the Night Visitors*, 1951 (libretto: the composer); *The Saint of Bleecker Street*, 1955 (libretto: the composer).

MESSAGER, ANDRÉ (1853-1929): *Madame Chrysanthème*, 1893 (libretto: Hartmann and Alexandre, after the story by Pierre Loti).

MESSLER, VICTOR (1841-1890): *Fleurette*, 1864; *The Piper of Hamelin*, 1879 (libretto: Fr. Hofmann, after the version by Julius Wolff); *The Trumpeter of Säkkingen*, 1884 (libretto: Rudolf Bunge, after the poem by Victor von Scheffel).

MEYERBEER, JAKOB (1791-1864): *Robert le Diable*, 1831 (libretto: Scribe, Delavigne); *Les Huguenots*, 1836 (libretto: Scribe, after Deschamps); *Le Prophète*, 1849 (libretto: Scribe); *Dinorah, ou Le Pardon de Ploërmel*, 1859 (libretto: Barbier, Carré; *L'Africaine*, 1865 (libretto: Scribe).

MILHAUD, DARIUS (1892-): *Le Pauvre Matelot* (The Poor Sailor), 1927 (libretto: Jean Cocteau); Opera-Minutes: *L'Enlèvement d'Europe*, *L'Abandon d'Ariane*, *La Délivrance de Thésée*), 1928 (librettos: Henri Hoppenot); *Christophe Colomb*, 1930 (libretto: Paul Claudel).

MILLÖCKER, KARL (1842-1899): *The Beggar Student* (Der Bettelstudent), 1882 (libretto: Zell and Genee).

MONTEMEZZI, ITALO (1875-1952): *The Love of Three Kings* (*L'Amore dei Tre Re*), 1913 (libretto: Sem Benelli, from his play of the same name).

MONTEVERDI, CLAUDIO (1567-1643): *La Favola D'Orfeo*, 1607 (libretto: Alessandro Striggio); *Il Combattimento de Tancredi e Clorinda*, 1624 (libretto: Tasso); *Arianna*, 1608 (libretto: Rinuccini); *Il Ritorno D'Ulisse in Patria*, 1641 (libretto: G. Badoaro).

MOZART, WOLFGANG AMADEUS (1756-1791): *Idomeneo*, 1781 (libretto: Abbé Varesco, after a French opera by Campra and Danchet); *Die Entführung aus dem Serail*, 1782 (libretto: Gottlob Stephanie, from a play by C. F. Bretzner); *The Marriage of Figaro* (*Le Nozze de Figaro*), 1786 (libretto: Lorenzo da Ponte, after Beaumarchais); *The Impresario* (*Der Schauspieldirektor*, 1786; *Don Giovanni*, 1787 (libretto: Lorenzo da Ponte); *Cosí fan Tutte*, 1790 (libretto: Lorenzo da ponte); *The Clemency of Titus* (La Clemenza di Tito), 1791 (libretto: Mazzola, adapted from Metastasio); *The Magic Flute* (*Die Zauberflote*); 1791 (libretto: Emanuel Schikaneder)

MUSSORGSKY, MODEST (1839-1881): *The Khovanskys* (*Khovantchina*), 1886 (libretto: the composer and V. V Stassov); *The Fair at Sorochinsk*, 1911 (libretto: the composer, based on Gogol's *Evenings on a Farm near Dekanka*); *Boris Godounov*, 1874 (libretto: the composer, based on Pushkin's drama of same name).

NICOLAI, OTTO (1810-1849): *The Merry Wives of Windsor* (*Die Lustigen Weiber von Windsor*, 1849 (libretto: Hermann von Mosenthal, after Shakespeare's play).

OFFENBACH, JACQUES (1819-1880): *Orpheus in the Underworld* (*Orphée aux Enfers*), 1858 (libretto: Hector Crémieux, Ludovic Halévy);

The Tales of Hoffman (Les Contes d'Hoffmann), 1881 (libretto: Barbier).

PARKER, HORATIO (1863-1919): *Mona*, 1912 (libretto: Brian Hooker); *Fairyland*, 1915 (libretto: Brian Hooker).

PERGOLESI, GIOVANNI (1710-1736): *La Serva Padrona*, 1733 (libretto: G. A. Federico).

PFITZNER, HANS (1869-1949): *Palestrina*, 1917, (libretto: the composer).

PIZZETTI, ILDEBRANDO (1880-) *Debora e Jaele*, 1922 (libretto: the composer).

PONCHIELLI, AMILCARE (1834-1886): *La Gioconda*, 1876 (libretto: Arrigo Boïto).

PROKOFIEV, SERGE (1891-1953): *The Love for Three Oranges*, 1921 (libretto: the composer, after Carlo Gozzi's comedy).

PUCCINI, GIACOMO (1858-1924): *Manon Lescaut*, 1893 (libretto: Praga, Oliva, and Illica, after Abbé Prévost); *La Bohème*, 1896 (libretto: Giacosa, Illica); *Tosca*, 1900 (libretto: Giacosa, Illica); *Madam Butterfly*, 1904 (libretto: Giacosa, Illica); *The Girl of the Golden West (La Fanciulla del West)*, 1910 (libretto: G. Civinini, C. Zangarini, from David Belasco's play; *The Swallow (La Rondine)*, 1917 (libretto: G. Adami); *The Cloak (Il Tabarro)*, 1918 (libretto: G. Adami after the play *La Houppelande*, by Didier Gold); *Sister Angelica*, 1918 (libretto: G. Forzano); *Gianni Schicchi*, 1918 (libretto: G. Forzano); *Turandot*, 1926 (libretto: Adami, Simoni, based on Gozzi's fable).

PURCELL, HENRY (1658-1695): *Dido and Aeneas*, 1689 (libretto: Nahum Tate).

RABAUD, HENRI (1875-1949): *Mârouf*, 1914 (libretto: Lucien Nepoty).

RAVEL, MAURICE (1875-1937): *L'Heure Espagnole* (The Spanish Hour), 1911 (libretto: Franc Nohain); *L'Enfant et les Sortilèges*, 1925 (libretto: Colette).

RESPIGHI, OTTORINO (1879-1936): *The Sunken Bell (La Campana Sommersa)*; 1927 (libretto: Claudio Guastalla, after the play by Gerhart Hauptmann).

RIMSKY-KORSAKOV, NICOLAI ANDREIEVICH (1844-1908): *Pskovityanka (The Maid of Pskov, or Ivan the Terrible)*, 1873 (libretto: the composer, based on a play by L. A. Mei); *The Snow Maiden (Snegourochka)*, 1882 (libretto: the composer, from a play by N. Ostrovsky); *Sadko*, 1898 (libretto: the composer and V. I. Bielsky); *Le Coq d'Or*, 1909 (libretto: V. I. Bielsky, after Pushkin).

ROGERS, BERNARD (1893-)*The Warrior*, 1947 (libretto: Norman Corwin).

ROSSINI, GIOACCHINO ANTONIO (1792-1868): *L'Italiana in Algeri*, 1813 (libretto: A. Anelli); *The Barber of Seville (Il Barbiere de Siviglia)*, 1816 (libretto: Sterbini, founded on Beaumarchais); *Cinderella (La Cenerentola)*, 1817 (libretto: Jacopo Ferretti) *Semiramide*, 1823 (libretto: Gaetana Rossi); *William Tell*, 1829 (libretto: V. J. Etienne de Jouy, H. L. F. Bis, after Schiller).

SAINT-SAËNS, CAMILLE (1835-1921): *Samson et Dalila*, 1877 (libretto: Ferdinand Lemaire).

SEYMOUR, JOHN LAURENCE (1893-): *In the Pasha's Garden*, 1935 (libretto: Henry Tracy after the tale by H. G. Dwight).

SMETANA, BEDŘICH (1824-1884): *The Bartered Bride (Prodaná Nevěsta)*, 1866 (libretto: Karel Sabina); *Dalibor*, 1868 (libretto: J. Wenzig); *The Kiss (Hubicka)*, 1876 (libretto: E. Krasnohorska).

SMYTH, ETHEL (1858-1944): *The Wreckers (Standrecht)*, 1906 (libretto: Henry Brewster, (in French), from his Cornish drama, *Les Naufrageurs*); *The Boatswain's Mate*, 1916 (libretto: after W. W. Jacob's story of that name); *Fête Galante*, 1923 (book: after Maurice Baring's story of that name; poetic version by Edward Shanks).

SPONTINI, GASPARO LUIGI P. (1774-1851): *La Vestale*, 1807 (libretto: Etienne Jouy; *Ferdinand Cortez*, 1809; *Olympia*, 1819; *Agnes von Hohenstaufen*, 1829.

STRAUSS, JOHANN (1825-1899): *The Bat (Die Fledermaus)*, 1874 (libretto: Haffner and Genee); *The Gipsy Baron (Der Zigeunerbaron)*, 1885 (libretto: J. Schnitzer).

STRAUSS, RICHARD (1864-1949): *Fire Famine*, 1901 (libretto: Ernest von Wolzogen); *Salome*, 1905 (libretto: after Oscar Wilde's poem, translated into German by Hedwig Lachmann); *Elektra*, 1909 (libretto: Hugo von Hofmannsthal, after Sophocles); *Der Rosenkavalier (The Cavalier of the Rose)*, 1911 (libretto: Hugo von Hofmannsthal); *Ariadne auf Naxos*, 1912 (revised version 1916) (libretto: Hugo von Hofmannsthal); *Die Frau ohne Schatten (The Woman without a Shadow)*, 1919 (libretto: Hugo von Hofmannsthal); *Intermezzo*, 1924 (libretto: the composer); *Die Aegyptische Helena (The Egyptian Helen)*, 1928 (libretto: Hugo von Hofmannsthal); *Arabella*, 1933 (libretto: Hugo von Hofmannsthal); *Die Schweigsame Frau (The Silent Woman)*, 1935 (libretto: Stefan Zweig, freely adapted from Ben Jonson's *Epicoene*); *Friedenstag (Peace Day)*, 1938 (libretto: Josef Gregor); *Daphne*, 1938 (libretto: Josef Gregor); *Die Liebe der Danae (The Love of Danae)*, 1952 (official première; previously heard at a well-attended dress rehearsal in 1944, but a public performance then was prevented by a Nazi edict closing the theaters after the attempt on Hitler's life) (libretto: Josef Gregor); *Capriccio*, 1942 (libretto: Clemens Krauss).

STRAVINSKY, IGOR (1882-): *The Nightingale (Le Rossignol)*, 1914 (libretto: the composer, and S. Mitousoff, after Andersen's fairy tale); *Oedipus Rex*, 1927 (libretto: Jean Cocteau after Sophocles) translated into Latin by J. Danielou); *The Rake's Progress*, 1951 (libretto: W. H. Auden, Chester Kallman).

TAYLOR, DEEMS (1885-): *The King's Henchman*, 1927 (libretto: Edna St. Vincent Millay; *Peter Ibbetson*, 1931 (libretto: Constance Collier and Deems Taylor, after the novel by George Du Maurier); *Ramuntcho*, 1942 (libretto: the composer, after a novel by Pierre Loti).

TCHAIKOVSKY, PETER ILYICH (1840-1893): *Eugen Onegin*, 1879 (libretto: the composer and K. S. Shilovsky, after Pushkin); *The Queen of Spades (Pique Dame)*, 1890 (libretto: Modest Tchaikovsky, based on Pushkin).

THOMAS, CHARLES AMBROISE (1811-1896): *The Double Ladder*, 1837; *Mina*, 1843; *Betty*, 1846; *A Midsummer Night's Dream*, 1850; *The Carnival of Venice*, 1857; *Mignon*, 1866 (libretto: Barbier and Carré, after Goethe's *Wilhelm Meister)*; *Hamlet*, 1868 (libretto: Michel Carré and Jules Barbier, after Shakespeare); *Francesca da Rimini*, 1882.

THOMSON, VIRGIL (1896-): *Four Saints in Three Acts*, 1933 (libretto: Gertrude Stein); *The Mother of Us All*, 1947 (libretto: Gertrude Stein).

THUILLE, LUDWIG (1861-1907): *Lobaetnz*, 1898 (libretto: Otto Julius Bierbaum).

VERDI, GIUSEPPE (1813-1901): *Nabucco*, 1842 (libretto: Temistocle Solera); *Ernani*, 1844 (libretto: Francesco Maria Piave, after the drama by Victor Hugo; *Macbeth*, 1847 (libretto: Francesco Maria Piave); *Luisa Miller*, 1849 (libretto: S. Cammarano from Schiller's play *Kabale und Liebe*), *Rigoletto*, 1851 (li-

bretto: Francesco Maria Piave after Hugo's *Le Roi s'amuse); Il Trovatore,* 1853 (libretto: S. Cammarano); *La Traviata,* 1853 (libretto: Francesco Maria Piave after Dumas' *La Dame aux Camélias); The Sicilian Vespers (I Vespri Siciliani),* 1855 (libretto: Scribe and Charles Duveyier); *Simon Boccanegra,* 1857 (libretto: Francesco Maria Piave); *The Masked Ball (Un Ballo in Maschera),* 1859 (libretto: Somma, based on Scribe's text for Auber's opera *Gustave III, ou Le Bal Masqué); La Forza del Destino,* 1862 (libretto: Francesco Maria Piave); *Don Carlos,* 1867 (libretto: G. Mery and C. du Locle, in French, after Schiller); *Aïda,* 1871 (libretto: Antonio Ghislanzoni); *Otello,* 1887 (libretto: Arrigo Boïto, after Shakespeare's play); *Falstaff,* 1893 (libretto: Arrigo Boïto, after Shakespeare's The Merry Wives of Windsor and Henry IV).*
WAGNER, RICHARD (1813-1883): *Rienzi, 1842* (libretto: by the composer after Bulwer-Lytton); *The Flying Dutchman (Der Fliegende Holländer),* 1843 (libretto: by the composer, from an episode in Heine's *Memoirs of Herr von Schnabelewopski);* *Tannhäuser,* 1845 (libretto: the composer); *Lohengrin,* 1850 (libretto: the composer); *Tristan und Isolde,* 1865 (libretto: the composer); *Die Meistersinger von Nürnberg,* 1868 (libretto: the composer); *The Ring of the Nibelung (Der Ring des Nibelungen)* (complete cycle of four operas first performed at Bayreuth, 1876; libretto by the composer): *Das Rheingold,* 1869; *The Valkyrie (Die Walküre),* 1870; *Siegfried,* 1876; *The Twilight of the Gods (Die Götterdämmerung),* 1876; *Parsifal,* 1882 (libretto: the composer).
WALLACE, VINCENT (1814-1865): *Maritana,* 1845 (libretto: Edward Fitzball, based on the play *Don Cesar de Bazan).*
WEBER, CARL MARIA VON (1786-1826): *Der Freischütz,* 1821 (libretto; Johann Friedrich Kind); *Euryanthe,* 1823 (libretto: Helmine von Chezy); *Oberon,* 1826 (libretto: originally in English, James Robertson Planche).
WEINBERGER, JAROMIR (1896-): *Schwanda the Bagpiper (Švanda Dudák),* 1927 (libretto: M. Kareš).
VAUGHAN WILLIAMS, RALPH (1872-): *Hugh the Drover,* 1924 (libretto: Harold Child); *The Poisoned Kiss,* 1936 (libretto: Evelyn Sharpe, from a tale of Richard Garnett and Hawthorne's story of Rapaccini's daughter); *The Pilgrim's Progress,* 1951 (libretto: based on Bunyan's allegory).
WOLF, HUGO (1860-1903): *The Magistrate (Der Corregidor),* 1896 (libretto: Rosa Mayreder-Obermeyer).
WOLF-FERRARI, ERMANNO (1876-1948): *The School for Fathers (I Quattro Rusteghi),* 1906 (libretto: G. Pizzola from Goldoni; German text by H. Treibler); *Susanna's Secret (Il Segreto di Susanna),* 1909 (libretto: Enrico Golisciani; German version by Kalbeck); *The Jewels of the Madonna (I Giojelli della Madonna),* 1911 (libretto: Golisciani and Zangarini; German version by H. Liebstockl).
ZANDONAI, RICCARDO (1883-1944): *Francesca da Rimini,* 1914 (libretto: Tito Ricordi, after Gabriele d'Annunzio's play of the same name).

Oracles
See **Religious Allusions, References, and Symbols**

Orders
See **Religious Orders**

Oriental Gods
See **Gods and Goddesses; Gods of the World, A Checklist of Their Works and Patronage**

Oriental Orchestra

As Typified in the Azuma Kabuki Musicians' Orchestra

STRINGS: Samisen: three waxed silk strings, guitarlike, about 3' in length, both faces covered with skin, unfretted slender neck, plucked with a fan-shaped ivory pick.
PERCUSSION (METAL): Hontsurigane: small hanging bell. Dora; gong (always played with other instruments). Surigane: gong (indicates happiness, festivity).
DRUMS: Kozutsumi: small hand drum. Ozutsumi: large hand drum. Lkaidao, big drum.
FLUTES: Nokan (maintains rhythm). Shinobue (carries major melody).

Paintings, Famous

NOTE: The designation of nationality or locality is meant only to indicate what school or tradition has especially influenced a painter. It does not necessarily refer to a painter's native country.

AARON: Thomas Hart Benton (1889-); 1943. Pennsylvania Academy of Fine Arts, Philadelphia. American.
ABBEY OF SAINT-DENIS: Maurice Utrillo (1883-1955); 1910. Phillips Memorial Gallery, Washington, D.C. French.
ABDUCTION OF REBECCA, THE: Eugène Delacroix (1799-1863), 1846. Metropolitan Museum of Art, New York. French.
ABSTRACTION: C. S. Price (1874-), 1942. Valentine Gallery, New York. American.
ABSTRACT STILL LIFE WITH DOILY: Alfred Maurer (1868-1932). Phillips Memorial Gallery, Washington, D.C. American.
ACCORDIONIST: Pablo Picasso (1881-), 1911. Museum of Non-Objective Paintings, New York. French.
ACROBAT: Pablo Picasso (1881-), 1930. Owned by artist. French.
ACROBAT, THE: Alton Pickens (1917-), 1947. Curt Valentin, New York. American.
ACTOR, THE: Pablo Picasso (1881-), 1904-05. Mrs. Byron Foy. French.
ACTOR'S MASK: Paul Klee (1879-1940), 1925. Sidney Janis, New York. Swiss.
ADAM AND EVE: Paul Gauguin (1848-1903), 1902. Privately owned. French.
ADAM AND EVE: Fernand Léger (1881-1955), 1935-39. Privately owned, Milan. French.
ADAM WINNE: Artist unknown; early 18th cent. Henry Francis du Pont Winterthur Museum, Winterthur, Delaware. American.
ADDIE: Thomas Eakins (1844-1916), c. 1900. Philadelphia Museum of Art. American.
ADMIRAL SIR ISAAC COFFIN: Gilbert Stuart (1775-1828), c. 1810. Mr. William Amory, Boston. American.
ADMIRATION OF THE ORCHESTRELLE FOR THE CINEMATOGRAPH: Man Ray (1890-), 1919. Museum of Modern Art, New York. American.
ADORATION OF THE KINGS, THE: Leonardo da Vinci (1452-1519), 1481-82. Uffizi Gallery, Florence. Italian.
ADORATION OF THE MAGI, THE: Hieronymus Bosch (c. 1460-1516), Prado, Madrid. Flemish.

ADORATION OF THE MAGI, THE: Hieronymus Bosch (c. 1460-1516): Metropolitan Museum of Art, New York. Flemish.

ADORATION OF THE MAGI, THE: Albrecht Dürer (1471-1528), Uffizi Gallery, Florence. German.

ADORATION OF THE MAGI: Hans Memling (1430?-1494), 1479. Hospital of St. John, Bruges. Flemish.

ADORATION OF THE MAGI, THE: Ottaviano Nelli (c. 1375-1444), Worcester Art Museum, Worcester, Mass. Italian.

ADORATION OF THE MAGI, THE: Titian (Tiziano Vecellio) (1480?-1576), c. 1560. Arthur Sachs Collection. Venetian.

ADORATION OF THE MAGI, THE: Leonardo da Vinci (1452-1519), c. 1481. Uffizi Gallery, Florence. Florentine.

ADORATION OF THE SHEPHERDS, THE; ST. JOHN THE BAPTIST; ST. FRANCIS REVIVING THE STIGMATA (FRAMED AS A TRIPYCH): Gerard David (c. 1460-1523). Metropolitan Museum of Art, New York. Flemish.

ADORATION OF THE TRINITY, THE: Albrecht Dürer (1471-1528), 1511. Gemaldegalerie, Vienna. German.

AERIAL PHOTOGRAPHY—CHINA: Gyorgy Kepes (1906-), 1942. Herbert Ziebolz. Hungarian (lives in U.S.).

AFTERNOON WIND: Louis M. Eilshemius (1864-1941), 1899. Museum of Modern Art, New York. American.

AFTER THE BATH: Edgar Degas (1834-1917). Louvre, Paris. French.

AFTER THE HUNT: Gustave Courbet (1819-1877). Metropolitan Museum of Art, New York. French.

AFTER THE HUNT: William Michael Harnett (1848-1892), 1885. Mildred Anna Williams Collection, California Palace of the Legion of Honor, San Francisco. American.

AFTER THE TORNADO, BAHAMAS: Winslow Homer (1836-1910). Art Institute, Chicago. American.

AGNEW CLINIC, THE: Thomas Eakins (1844-1916), 1889. University of Pennsylvania. American.

AGONY IN THE GARDEN, THE: Giovanni Bellini (c. 1430-1517), 1455-70. National Gallery, London. Venetian.

AGONY IN THE GARDEN, THE: Andrea Mantegna (1431-1506). National Gallery, London. Paduan.

AITA PARAEI: ANNAH, THE JAVANESE WOMAN: Paul Gauguin (1848-1903), c. 1893. Privately owned. Zürich. French.

A LA MIE: Henry de Toulouse-Lautrec (1864-1901), 1891. Boston Museum of Fine Arts. French.

A LA TOURELLE ET RUE DU MONT CENIS: Maurice Utrillo (1883-1955), c. 1910. Privately owned, New York. French.

ALBA MADONNA, THE: Raphael (Raffaello Santi) (1483-1520). Mellon Collection of the National Gallery of Art, Washington, D. C. Umbrian.

ALDOBRANDINI MADONNA: Raphael (Raffaello Santi) (1483-1520), 1508. National Gallery, London. Umbrian.

ALLEGORY: Titian (Tiziano Vecellio) (1480?-1576), c. 1565. F. Howard Collection, London. Venetian.

ALL'S WELL: Winslow Homer (1836-1910), 1896. Boston Museum of Fine Arts. American.

ALPHONSE PROMAYET: Gustave Courbet (1819-1877). Metropolitan Museum of Art, New York. French.

ALTAR OF THE CRUCIFIXION, THE: Ro-

gier van der Weyden (1399?-1464), 1440-50. Gemaldegalerie, Vienna.

A MA FEMME: Marc Chagall (1887-), 1933-44. Owned by artist. French.

AMBASSADORS, THE: Hans Holbein the Younger (1497-1543), 1533. National Gallery, London. German.

AMERICAN GOTHIC: Grant Wood (1892-1942), 1930. Chicago Art Institute. American.

AMERICAN LANDSCAPE: Charles Sheeler (1883-), 1930. Museum of Modern Art, New York. American.

AMERICAN LANDSCAPE: L. Whitney(?). Newark Museum. American.

AMERICAN RADIATOR BUILDING: Georgia O'Keeffe (1887-). Stieglitz Collection, Fisk University, Nashville, Tennessee. American.

AMERICAN SCHOOL, THE: Matthew Pratt (1734-1805), 1765. Metropolitan Museum of Art, New York. American.

AMERICAN SEA CAPTAINS CAROUSING IN SURINAM: John Greenwood (1727-1792), 1757-58. City Art Museum, St. Louis. American.

AMORE VINCITORE: Caravaggio (Michelangelo Merisi) (1573-1610), c. 1598. Kaiser Friedrich Museum, Berlin. Italian.

AMOROUS PROCESSION: Francis Picabia (1878-1953), 1917. Mme. Simone Kahn, Paris. French.

AND THE GOLD OF THEIR BODIES: Paul Gauguin (1848-1903); 1901. Madame O. Sainsere. French.

ANGEL LEAVING TOBIAS AND HIS FAMILY, THE: Rembrandt van Rijn (1606-1669), 1637. Louvre, Paris. Dutch.

ANGELUS, THE: Jean-François Millet (1814-1875), 1859. Louvre, Paris. French.

ANNA HARDAWAY BUNKER: Chester Harding (1792-1866), c. 1857. John Herron Art Institute, Indianapolis. American.

ANNUNCIATION, THE: Jan van Eyck (1370?-1440?). Mellon Collection of the National Gallery of Art, Wash.. D.C. Flemish.

ANNUNCIATION, THE: Fra Angelico (1387-1455), c. 1438-45. Chapter House, San Marco, Florence. Italian.

ANNUNCIATION, THE: Simone Martini (1285?-1344), 1333. Uffizi Gallery, Florence. Sienese.

ANNUNCIATION, THE: Titian (Tiziano Vecellio) (1480?-1576), c. 1540. Scuola de San Rocco, Vneice. Venetian.

ANNUNCATION, THE: Titan (Tiziano Vecellio) (1480?-1576), c. 1565. S. Salvatore, Venice. Venetian.

ANSIDEI MADONNA: Raphael (Raffaello Santi) (1483-1520), 1507. National Gallery London. Umbrian.

ANTIQUE ERA, THE: Giorgio de Chirico (1888-), 1948. Privately owned, New York. French.

APOLLO AT THE FORGE OF VULCAN: Diego Velasquez (1599-1660), 1630. Prado, Madrid. Spanish.

APPARITION, THE: Paul Gauguin (1848-1903), 1902. Privately owned. French.

APPLE BLOSSOMS: Charles François Daubigny (1817-1878), 1873. Metropolitan Museum of Art, New York. French.

APRIL SHOWERS: Abraham Rattner (1893-), 1939. Mr. and Mrs. Roy R. Neuberger, New York. American.

APRIL SNOW: Maurice Prendergast (1859-1924), 1907. Phillips Memorial Gallery, Washington, D. C. American.

ARCADIAN SHEPHERDS, THE: See Et in Arcadio Ego.

ARCHANGEL GABRIEL, THE: Gerard David

(c. 1460-1523), Metropolitan Museum of Art, New York. Flemish.

ARCHITECT'S DREAM, THE: Thomas Cole (1801-1848), 1840. Toledo Museum of Art. American.

ARCTIC THAW: Paul Klee (1879-1940), 1920. Nierendorf Gallery, New York. Swiss.

AREAREA: JOYFULNESS: Paul Gauguin (1848-1903), 1892. Privately owned. French.

ARIADNE: John Vanderlyn (1775-1852), 1814. Pennsylvania Academy of Fine Arts. American.

ARIZONA # 1 : Amédée Ozenfant (1886-), 1938-44. Owned by artist. French (lives in U.S.A.).

ARLESIENNE, L': Pablo Picasso (1881-1912. Walter P. Chrysler, Jr. French.

ARLESIENNE, THE (AFTER A DRAWING BY GAUGUIN): Vincent van Gogh (1853-1890), 1890. Kröller-Müller State Museum, Otterlo, Holland. French.

THE ARNOLFINI MARRIAGE: Jan van Eyck (1370?-1440?). National Gallery of Art, London. Flemish.

AROUND THE FISH: Paul Klee (1879-1940), 1926. Museum of Modern Art, New York. Swiss.

ARRANGEMENT IN GRAY AND BLACK: James McNeill Whistler (1834-1903), c. 1871. Louvre, Paris. American.

ARRIVAL OF THE CIRCUS: Paul Klee (1879-1940), 1926. Phillips Memorial Gallery, Washington, D.C. Swiss.

ARRIVAL OF MARIA DE' MEDICI AT MARSEILLES, THE: Peter Paul Rubens (1577-1640), 1622-25. Louvre, Paris.

ARSENAL AT VENICE, THE: Francesco de' Guardi (1712-1793), 1780's. Gemaldegalerie, Vienna. Italian.

ARTIST IN HIS STUDIO, THE: Jan Vermeer (1632-1675). Kunsthistorisches Museum, Vienna. Dutch.

ARTIST SHOWING HIS PICTURE OF A SCENE FROM HAMLET TO HIS PARENTS, THE: William Dunlap (1766-1839), 1788. New York Historical Society, New York. American.

ARTIST'S SISTER THE: Pablo Picasso (1881-), 1899. Owned by artist. French.

ASCENSION, THE: John La Farge (1835-1910), 1888. Church of the Ascension, New York. American.

ASSUMPTION OF THE VIRGIN, THE: Giovanni de Paolo (1402?-1482?). Hyde Collection), Glens Falls, New York. Italian.

ASSUMPTION OF THE VIRGIN, THE: Titian (Tiziano Vecellio) (1480?-1576), 1516-18. Santa Maria Dei Frari, Venice. Venetian.

ATHENS: John La Farge (1835-1910), 1898. Bowdoin College Museum of Fine Arts. American.

AT THE MOULIN DE LA GALETTE: Henri de Toulouse-Lautrec (1864-1901), 1890. The Art Institute of Chicago. French.

AT THE MOULIN ROUGE: Henri de Toulouse-Lautrec (1864-1901), 1892. The Art Institute of Chicago. French.

AT THE MOULIN ROUGE: THE START OF THE QUADRILLE: Henri de Toulouse-Lautrec (1864-1901), National Gallery of Art, Washington, D.C. (Chester Dale Collection, loan). French.

AUNT FANNY: George Bellows (1882-1925), 1920. Des Moines Art Center. American.

AURORA: Guercino (Giovanni Francesco Barbieri) (1591-1666). Villa Ludovisi, Rome. Bolognese.

AUTUMNAL FANTASY: Charles Burchfield (1893-), 1916-45. K. M. Rehn Gallery, New York. American.

AUTUMN OAKS: George Inness (1825-1894), c. 1875. Metropolitan Museum of Art, New York. American.

BABY ROULIN: Vincent van Gogh (1853-1890), 1888. V. W. van Gogh Collection, Municipal Museum, Amsterdam. Dutch.

BACCHANALE: Titian (Tiziano Vecellio) (1480?-1576), c. 1518. Prado, Madrid. Venetian.

BACCHANALIAN REVEL BEFORE A TERM OF PAN: Nicolas Poussin (1594-1665), c. 1636-38. National Gallery, London. French.

BACCHANTE BY THE SEA: Jean Baptiste Camille Corot (1796-1875), 1865. Metropolitan Museum of Art, New York. French.

BACCHANTE IN A LANDSCAPE: Jean Baptiste Camille Corot (1796-1875). Metropolitan Museum of Art, New York. French.

BACCHUS: Caravaggio (Michelangelo Merisi) (1573-1610), c. 1596. Uffizi Gallery, Florence. Italian.

BACCHUS: Leonardo da Vinci (1452-1519) Louvre, Paris. Florentine.

BACCHUS AND ARIADNE: Gustavus Hesselius (1682-1755), c. 1720-30. Detroit Institute of Art. American.

BACCHUS AND ARIADNE: Tintoretto (Jacopo Robusti (1518-1594), 1578. Ducal Palace. Venice. Venetian.

BACCHUS AND ARIADNE: Titian (Tiziano Vecellio) (1480?-1576), 1523. National Gallery, London. Venetian.

BACK OF A WOMAN: André Derain (1880-1954), 1928. Dr. and Mrs. Harry Bakwin, New York. French.

BAIE DE FOURMIS, BEAULIEU: Eugène Boudin (1825-1898), 1892. Metropolitan Museum of Art, New York. French.

BALCONY, THE: William Baziotes (1911-) 1944. Owned by artist. American.

BALLERINA AND LADY WITH A FAN: Edgar Degas (1834-1917), 1885. (Pastel). Philadelphia Museum of Art. French.

BALLET OF ROBERT LE DIABLE, THE: Edgar Degas (1834-1917), 1872. Metropolitan Museum of Art, New York. French.

BANDINI SISTERS, THE: Silvestro Lega (1876-1895), 1890. Collection Tarragoni, Genoa Italian.

BANKS OF THE OISE: Charles François Daubigny (1817-1878), 1863. Metropolitan Museum of Art, New York. French.

BANKS OF THE OISE: Alfred Sisley (1839-1899); 1879. Chester Dale Collection, National Gallery of Art, Washington, D.C. French.

BANKS OF THE OISE: EARLY MORNING: Charles François Daubigny (1817-1878), 1875. Metropolitan Museum of Art, New York. French.

BANKS OF THE SEINE: Alfred Sisley (1839-1899). Louvre, Paris. French.

BANQUET OF THE OFFICERS OF THE CIVIL GUARD OF ST. GEORGE, A: Frans Hals (1580?-1666), 1616. Museum, Haarlem Dutch.

BAPTISM IN KANSAS: John Steuart Curry (1897-1946), 1928. Whitney Museum of American Art, New York, American.

BAPTISM OF CHRIST: Titian (Tiziano Vecellio) (1480?-1576), c. 1516. Pinacoteca Capitolina, Rome. Venetian.

BAR AT THE FOLIES-BERGÈRE, A: Édouard Manet (1832-1883), 1881. Courtauld Institute of Art, London. French.

BARBARIC TALES: Paul Gauguin (1848-1903). Folkwang Museum, Essen. French.

BAREBACK RIDER: Marc Chagall (1887-) 1928. Mrs. Edith Gregor Halpert, New York French.

BASIN AT ARGENTUIL: Claude Monet

(1840-1926), 1872. Rhode Island School of Design, Providence. French.

BATHERS: Jean Honoré Fragonard (1732-1806). Louvre, Paris. French.

BATHERS IN BRITTANY: Paul Gauguin (1848-1903), 1888. Privately owned. French.

BATHSHEBA: Rembrandt van Rijn (1606-1669), 1564. Louvre, Paris. Dutch.

BATTLE BETWEEN CARNIVAL AND LENT, THE: Pieter Bruegel the Elder (1520?-1569), 1559. Kunsthistorisches Museum, Vienna. Flemish.

BATTLE OF BUNKER'S HILL, THE: John Trumbull (1756-1843), 1786. Yale University Art Gallery. American.

BATTLE OF CARNIVAL AND FASTING, THE: Pieter Bruegel the Elder (1520?-1569), 1559. Gemaldegalerie, Vienna. Flemish.

BATTLE OF CONSTANTINE, THE: Piero della Francesca (1416?-1492), 1452-66. Church of San Francesco, Arezzo. Umbrian School.

BATTLE OF LIGHTS, CONEY ISLAND: Joseph Stella (1880-1946), 1913. Yale University Art Gallery. American.

BATTLE OF SANT' EGIDIO: Paolo Uccelo (c. 1397-1475), 1432. National Gallery, London. Florentine.

BATTLE OF THE CENTAURS AND THE LAPITHS: Piero de Cosimo (1462-1521?), c. 1485. National Gallery, London. Florentine.

BAY OF SAINTE-ADRESSE, THE: Raoul Dufy (1877-1953), 1924. Evelyn Sharp, New York, French.

BAY OF SAINT-TROPEZ, THE: André Dunoyer de Segonzac (1884-), 1926. Privately owned. French.

BEACH SCENE: Pablo Picasso (1881-), 1918. Owned by artist. French.

BEATRICE D'ESTE: Leonardo da Vinci (1452-1519). Pinacoteca Ambrosiana, Milan. Florentine.

BEFORE ENTERING THE RING: Camille Bombois (1883-), 1930-35. Museum of Modern Art, New York. French.

BELLE ANGELE, LA: Paul Gauguin (1848-1903). Louvre, Paris. French.

BELLE FERRONNIÈRE, LA: Leonardo da Vinci (1452-1519). Louvre, Paris. Florentine.

BELLE JARDINIÈRE, LA: Raphael (Raffaello Santi) (1483-1520), 1507. Louvre, Paris. Umbrian.

BELSHAZZAR'S FEAST: Washington Allston (1779-1843). Boston Museum of Fine Arts. American.

BENJAMIN FRANKLIN: Joseph Siffred Duplessis (1725-1802), 1778. Metropolitan Museum of Art, New York. French.

BENOIS MADONNA, THE: Leonardo da Vinci (1452-1519), 1478-80. Hermitage, Leningrad. Florentine.

BERCEUSE, THE (Mme. ROULIN): Vincent van Gogh (1853-1890), c. 1888. Kröller-Müller State Museum, Otterlo, Holland. French.

BERLIOZ HOUSE AND THE HUNTING LODGE OF HENRY IV, THE: Maurice Utrillo (1883-1955), c. 1917. The Art Gallery of Toronto, Canada. French.

BETRAYAL OF CHRIST, THE: Giotto (di Bondone) 1266-1336), 1305-06. Arena Chapel, Padua. Florentine.

BETRAYAL OF CUERNAVACA: Diego Rivera (1886-), 1929-30. Palacio de Cortes, Mexico. Mexican.

BIG CLOUD, THE: Jean Lurçat (1892-), 1929. Chester Dale Collection, National Gallery of Art, Washington, D.C. French.

BIRDCAGE AND PLAYING CARDS: Pablo Picasso (1881-), 1937. Mme. Elsa Schiaparelli. French.

BIRD SINGING IN THE MOONLIGHT: Morris Graves (1910-), 1938-39. Museum of Modern Art. American.

BIRDS OF AMERICA: John James Audubon (1785-1851), Folio Edition, 1827-38. American.

BIRDS NESTING: Pieter Bruegel the Elder (1530?-1569), 1568. Gemaldegalerie, Vienna. Flemish.

BIRTHDAY: Marc Chagall (1887-), 1915-23. Guggenheim Museum, New York. French.

BIRTH OF THE VIRGIN, THE: Sassetta (Stefano di Giovanni) (1392-1450). Collegiate Church of Asciano. Sienese.

BIRTH OF VENUS: Sandro Botticelli (Alessandro Filipepi) (1444?-1510), 1486-87. Uffizi Gallery, Florence. Florentine.

BIRTH OF VENUS, THE: Adolphe William Bouguereau (1825-1905), 1879. Luxembourg, Paris. French.

BISHOP GEORGE BERKELEY AND HIS FAMILY: John Smibert (1688-1751), 1729. Yale University Art Gallery. American.

BISTROS IN A SUBURB: Maurice Utrillo (1883-1955), c. 1910. Mr. and Mrs. Peter A. Rubel, New York. French.

BLACKFRIARS BRIDGE, LONDON: André Derain (1880-1954), 1906. Museum of Modern Art, New York. French.

BLACK LAKE, THE: Jan Preisler (1872-1918), 1904. Narodni Galerie, Prague. Czech.

BLESSING, THE: Jean Baptiste Chardin (1699-1779). Louvre, Paris. French.

BLIND LEADING THE BLIND, THE: Pieter Bruegel the Elder (1520?-1569), 1563. Museum, Naples. Flemish.

BLOND HALF-NUDE: Édouard Manet (1832-1883), 1878. Louvre, Paris. French.

BLOOD OF THE REDEEMER: Vittore Carpaccio (1472?-1527), 1496. Pinacoteca, Udine. Venetian.

BLOWING BUBBLES: Jean Baptiste Chardin (1699-1779). Metropolitan Museum of Art. New York. French.

BLUE BOAT, THE: Christopher Wood (1901-1930), 1930. Noel Coward, London. English.

BLUE BOY, THE: Erastus Salisbury Field (1805-1900?), 1830. owned by Colonial Williamsburg. American.

BLUE BOY, THE: Thomas Gainsborough (1727-1788), 1779. Huntington Gallery, San Marino, Calif. English.

BLUE BOY: Pablo Picasso (1881-), 1905. Edward M. M. Warburg. French.

BLUE CLOWN, THE: Walt Kuhn (1880-1949), 1931. Whitney Museum of American Art. American.

BLUE FOX, THE: Franz Marc (1880-1916). Stadt Museum, Wuppertal. German.

BLUE HORIZON: Luiz Martinez Pedro (1910 -), 1952. Privately owned. Cuban.

BLUE HORSE, THE: Franz Marc (1880-1916), c. 1911. Bernhard Koehler, Berlin. German.

BLUE HORSES: Franz Marc (1880-1916), 1911. Walker Art Center, Minneapolis. German.

BLUE LOBSTER, THE: Francis Tailleux (1913-), 1947. Galerie de France, Paris. French.

BLUE MOZART: Raoul Dufy (1877-1953), 1951. Privately owned, New York. French.

BLUE ROOM, THE: Pablo Picasso (1881-), 1901. Phillips Memorial Gallery, Washington, D.C. French.

BLUE SPACE: Balcomb Greene (1904-), 1941. Owned by artist. American.

BLUE TRAIN, THE: Raoul Dufy (1877-1953), 1935. Mrs. Albert D. Lasker, New York. French.

BLUE WINDOW, THE: Henri Matisse (1869-1954), c. 1912. Museum of Modern Art, New York. French.

BOARD OF THE CLOTHMAKERS' GUILD, THE (THE SYNDICS): Rembrandt van Rijn (1606-1669), 1662. Rijksmuseum, Amsterdam. Dutch.

BOAT, THE: Peter Blume (1906-), 1929. Museum of Modern Art, New York. American.

BOAT, THE: Leopold Survage (1879-), 1915. Robert Allerton, Chicago. French (born in Russia).

BOATMAN AMONG THE REEDS: Jean Baptiste Camille Corot (1796-1875); Metropolitan Museum of Art, New York. French.

BOAT ON THE BEACH: Georges Braque (1881-), 1928. M. Knoedler and Co., New York. French.

BOATS IN THE CANAL: Max Pechstein (1881-), 1923. National Gallery, Berlin. German.

BOATS ON SHORE: Charles François Daubigny (1817-1878), 1871. Metropolitan Museum of Art, New York. French.

BOATS ON THE BEACH: Vincent van Gogh (1853-1890), 1888. V. W. van Gogh Collection, Municipal Museum, Amsterdam. French.

BOTH MEMBERS OF THIS CLUB: George Bellows (1882-1925), 1909. National Gallery of Art, Washington, D.C. American.

BOULEVARDE DE CLICHY: Vincent van Gogh (1853-1890), 1886-88. V. W. van Gogh Collection, Municipal Museum, Amsterdam. French.

BOULEVARD MONTMARTRE: NIGHT EFFECT: Camille Pissarro (1831-1903), 1897. National Gallery, London. French.

BOUQUET, THE: Václav Spála (1885-1946), 1929. Narodni Galerie, Prague. Czech.

BOUQUET AND STOVE: Yasou Kuniyoshi (1893-), 1929. American.

THE BOWL: Reginald March (1898-1954), 1933. Brooklyn Museum. American.

BOY: Bernard Karfiol (1886-), c. 1925. Phillips Memorial Gallery, Washington, D.C. American.

BOY BITTEN BY A LIZARD: Caravaggio (Michelangelo Merisi) (1573-1610), 1592-93. Longhi Collection, Florence. Italian.

BOYHOOD OF RALEIGH, THE: John Everett Millais (1829-1896), Tate Museum, London. English.

BOY IN RED SWEATER, THE (LE CHANDAIL ROSE): Amadeo Modigliani (1884-1920), 1917. Jacques Gelman, Mexico. French.

BOY LEADING A HORSE: Pablo Picasso (1881-), 1905. William S. Paley, New York. French.

BOY WITH FRUIT (BACCHINO MALATO): Caravaggio (Michelangelo Merisi) (1573-1610), 1592. Borghese, Rome. Italian.

BOY WITH RABBIT: Sir Henry Raeburn (1756-1823). Burlington House, London. English.

BOY WITH THE SQUIRREL, THE: John Singleton Copley (1738-1815), c. 1765. Boston Museum of Fine Arts. American.

BRADFORD HUBBARD: Reuben Moulthrop (1763-1814), c. 1785. New Haven Colony Historical Society, New Haven, Conn. American.

BRANCHES ON BLOSSOMING ALMOND: Vincent van Gogh (1853-1890), 1889-90. V. W. van Gogh Collection, Municipal Museum, Amsterdam. French.

BRAWL, THE: Adriaen Brouwer (1605-1638). Metropolitan Museum of Art, New York. Flemish.

BREAD: Vincent van Gogh (1853-1890). 1886-88. V. W. van Gogh Collection, Municipal Museum, Amsterdam. French.

BREAKFAST ROOM, THE: Pierre Bonnard (1867-1947), 1930-31. Museum of Modern Art, New York. French.

BREEZING UP: Winslow Homer (1836-1910). Mellon Collection of National Gallery of Art, Washington, D.C. American.

BRETON GIRL IN PRAYER: See Girl from Britany in Prayer, A.

BRETON SHEPHERDESS, THE: Paul Gauguin (1848-1903), 1888. Privately owned. French.

BRIDE, THE: Marcel Duchamp (1887-), 1912. Arensberg Collection, Philadelphia Museum of Art. French.

BRIDE STRIPPED BARE BY HER OWN BACHELORS, THE: Marcel Duchamp (1887-), 1915-23. Miss Katherine Dreier. French.

BRIDGE, THE: Edvard Munch (1863-1944), 1905, Wallraf-Richartz-Museum, Cologne. Norwegian.

BRIDGE AT BRUGES: Camille Pissaro (1831-1903), 1903. City Art Gallery, Manchester. French.

BRIDGEWATER MADONNA, THE: Raphael (Raffaelo Santi) (1483-1520). Lord Ellesmere's Collection, London. Umbrian.

BRIDLE PATH, COOKHAM, THE: Stanley Spencer (1892-), 1938. Mrs. Thelma Cazalet-Keir, London. English.

BROOK BY MOONLIGHT: Ralph Albert Blakelock (1847-1919), c. 1890. Museum of Art, Toledo, Ohio. American.

BROOK OF THE BLACK WELL, THE: Gustave Courbet (1819-1877), Metropolitan Museum of Art, New York. French.

BROOKLYN BRIDGE: Joseph Stella (1880-1946), 1917-18. Yale University Art Gallery. American.

BROUWERSCANAL NEAR THE PRINSENCANAL, AMSTERDAM: George Hendrick Beritner (1857-1923), 1923. Stedelijk Museum, Amsterdam. Dutch.

BUILDERS, THE: Fernand Léger (1881-1955), 1950. Fernand Léger Collection, Paris. French.

BURIAL OF COUNT ORGAZ: El Greco (Domenicos Theotocopoulos) (1541-1614), 1586. Santo Tomé, Toledo. Spanish (born Crete).

BURIAL OF ST. LUCY, THE: Caravaggio (Michelangelo Merisi) (1573-1610), 1608. Santa Lucia, Syracuse. Italian.

BURIAL OF ST. PETRONILLA, THE: See Death of St. Petronilla, The.

BURIED TREASURE: Hyman Bloom (1913-), 1948. Durlacher Bros., New York. American.

BURST OF SUNLIGHT, THE: Jacob Ruisdael (c. 1628-1682), o. 1670. Louvre, Paris. Dutch.

BUTTE PINSON, LA: Maurice Utrillo (1883-1955), 1909. Privately owned, Paris. French.

CALAIS PIER: Joseph M. W. Turner (1775-1851), 1802-03. National Gallery, London. English.

CALLING OF SAINT MATTHEW, THE: Caravaggio (Michelangelo Merisi) (1573-1610), c. 1597. Contarelli Chapel, San Luigi dei Francesi, Rome. Italian.

CALM SEA: Gustave Courbet (1819-1877), 1869. Metropolitan Museum of Art, New York. French.

CANAL IN BRUSSELS, THE: Eugene-Louis Boudin (1825-1898), 1871. Mrs. Thelma Cazalet-Keir, London. French.

CANOEIST, THE: André Dunoyer de Segonzac (1885-), Privately owned, New York. French.

CARDINAL McCLOSKEY: George Peter Alexander Healy (1812-1894), 1862. Newberry Library, Chicago. American.

CARD PLAYER: Pablo Picasso (1881-), 1913-14. Museum of Modern Art, New York. French.

CARD PLAYERS, THE: Paul Cézanne (1839-1906), 1890. Stephen C. Clark Collection, New York. French.

CARD PLAYERS, THE: Fernand Léger (1881-1955), 1917. Rijksmuseum Kröller-Müller, Otterlo, Holland. French.

CARD SHAPERS, THE: Caravaggio (Michelangelo Merisi) (1573-1610); 1594-95. Palazzo Sciarra, Rome. Italian.

CARNIVAL: James Ensor (1860-1949). Stedelijk Museum, Amsterdam. Belgian.

CARNIVAL: Alton Pickens (1917-), 1949. Owned by artist. American.

CASINO AT NICE: Raoul Dufy (1877-1953), 1929. Mr. and Mrs. Peter A. Rubel, New York. French.

CASTLE OF AUVERS, THE: Vincent van Gogh (1853-1890), 1890. V. W. van Gogh Collection, Municipal Museum, Amsterdam. French.

CATALAN, LANDSCAPE (THE HUNTER): Joan Miro (1893-), 1923-24. Museum of Modern Art, New York. Spanish.

CAT AND BIRD: Paul Klee (1879-1940), 1928. Dr. F. H. Hirchland. Swiss.

CATTLE DEALER, THE: Marc Chagall (1887-), 1912. Mme. Walden Collection, Schinznach. French.

CATTLE LOADING, WEST TEXAS: Thomas Hart Benton (1899-), 1930. Addison Gallery of American Art, Andover, Mass. American.

CELLIST, THE: I. J. H. Bradley (active 1830-1855), 1832. Phillips Memorial Gallery, Washington, D.C. American.

CEMETERY, THE: Jacob van Ruisdael (1628-1682), c. 1652. Detroit Institute of Arts. Dutch.

CHAIR OF GAUGUIN, THE: Vincent van Gogh (1853-1890), 1888. V. W. van Gogh Collection, Municipal Museum, Amsterdam. French.

CHANT D'AMOUR, LE: Edward Burne-Jones (1833-1898). Metropolitan Museum of Art, New York. English.

CHARLES CALVERT: John Hesselius (1728-1778), 1761. Baltimore Museum of Art. American.

CHARLOTTE DE VAL D'OGNES: Jacques Louis David (1748-1825), c. 1795. Metropolitan Museum of Art, New York. French.

CHARTRES CATHEDRAL: Maurice Utrillo (1883-1955), c. 1913. Mrs. L. B. Wescott, Clinton, N. J. French.

CHATEAU DE LA SALLE: Maurice Utrillo (1883-1955), c. 1919. Jacob Goldschmidt, New York. French.

CHATEAU TOWER, THE: Maurice Utrillo (1883-1955), 1912. Perls Galleries, New York. French.

CHAUFFEUR, THE: Joan Miró (1893-), 1918. Walter P. Chrysler, Jr., Warrenton, Virginia. Spanish.

CHEMISE ENLEVÉE, LA: Jean Honoré Fragonard (1732-1806), 1665-72. Louvre, Paris. French.

CHEZ MOUQUIN: William Glackens (1870-1938), 1905. Art Institute of Chicago. American.

CHILD AT THE TABLE: Jan Sluijters (1881-), 1950. Owned by artist. Dutch.

CHILD CONSECRATED TO SUFFERING: Paul Klee (1879-1940), 1935. Albright Art Gallery, Buffalo. Swiss.

CHILDREN'S GAMES: Pieter Bruegel the Elder (c. 1520-1569), 1560. Kunsthistorisches Museum, Vienna. Flemish.

CHILDREN'S THEATER, THE: Jerome Myers (1867-1940). Detroit Institute of Arts. American.

CHILMARK: Thomas H. Benton (1889-), 1916. Privately owned. American.

CHILPERIC: Henri de Toulouse-Lautrec (1864-1901), 1896. Mr. and Mrs. John Hay Whitney, New York. French.

CHINESE RESTAURANT: Max Weber (1881-), 1915. Whitney Museum of American Art. American.

CHRIST AND MARY MAGDALENE: Titian (Tiziano Vecelli) (c. 1480-1576), c. 1514. National Gallery, London. Venetian.

CHRIST AND THE APOSTLES: Georges Rouault (1871-), c. 1925. Mr. and Mrs. Jacques Gelman, Mexico. French.

CHRIST AND THE PILGRIMS AT EMMAUS: Diego Velasquez (1599-1660), c. 1625-26. Metropolitan Museum of Art, New York. Spanish.

CHRIST APPEARING TO THE VIRGIN MARY: Titian (Tiziano Vecellio) (c. 1480-1576), c. 1554. Parish Church, Medole. Venetian.

CHRIST AT EMMAUS: Rembrandt van Rijn (1606-1669), 1648. Louvre, Paris. Dutch.

CHRIST AT EMMAUS: Titian (Tiziano Vecellio) (c. 1480-1576), 1525-45. Louvre, Paris. Venetian.

CHRIST BEARING THE CROSS: Hieronymus Bosch (c. 1460-1516), Musée des Beaux Arts, Ghent. Flemish.

CHRIST BEARING THE CROSS: Pieter Bruegel the Elder (c. 1520-1569), 1563. Gemaldegalerie, Vienna. Flemish.

CHRIST BEARING THE CROSS: Titian (Tiziano Vecellio (1480?-1576), c. 1560. Prado, Madrid. Venetian.

CHRIST CROWNED WITH THORNS: Titian (Tiziano Vecellio) (1480?-1576), c. 1542. Louvre, Paris. Venetian.

CHRISTINA: Bernard Karfiol (1886-), 1936. Carnegie Institute. American.

CHRISTINA'S WORLD: Andrew Wyeth (1917-), 1948. Museum of Modern Art, New York. American.

CHRIST IN LIMBO: Max Beckmann (1884-1950). Curt Valentin Gallery, New York. German.

CHRIST IN THE HOUSE OF MARTHA AND MARY: Jan Vermeer (1632-1675). National Gallery of Scotland, Edinburgh. Dutch.

CHRIST IN THE HOUSE OF MARY AND MARTHA: Diego Velasques (1599-1660), c. 1619. National Gallery, London. Spanish.

CHRIST IN THE TOMB: Hans Holbein the Younger (1497-1543), 1521. Museum, Basel. German.

CHRIST MOCKED BY SOLDIERS: Goerges Rouault (1871-), 1932. Museum of Modern Art, New York. French.

CHRIST ON LAKE GENNESARET: Eugène Delacroix (1796-1863). Metropolitan Museum of Art, New York. French.

CHRIST ON THE CROSS: Lucas Cranach (1472-1553), 1503. Alte Pinakothek, Munich. German.

CHRIST ON THE CROSS: Titian (Tiziano Vecellio) (1480?-1576), c. 1565. Monastery of St. Lawrence, El Escorial, Spain. Venetian.

CHRIST ON THE MOUNT OF OLIVES: Paul Gauguin (1848-1903), 1889. Privately owned. French.

CHRIST TAKING LEAVE OF HIS MOTHER: Gerard David (c. 1460-1523). Metropolitan Museum of Art, New York. Flemish.

CHURCH OF LA FERTE-MILON, THE: Maurice Utrillo (1883-1955), c. 1910. Dalzell Harfield, Los Angeles. French.

CHURCH OF LORETA, THE: Jan Bauch (1898-), 1942. Dr. Ing. F. Fabinger, Prague. Czech.

CHURCH OF SANTA MARIA DELLA SALUTE AT VENICE, THE: Francesco Guardi (1712-1793). Louvre, Paris. Venetian.

CHURCH STREET EL: Charles Sheeler (1883-), 1922. Mrs. Earle Horter. American.

CIRCUS, THE: Marc Chagall (1887-), 1926. Dr. F. Potvin Collection, Brussels. French.

CIRCUS, THE: Joan Miró (1893-), 1937. Pierre Matisse Gallery, New York. Spanish.

CIRCUS: Georges Rouault (1871-), 1906. Mrs. Dudley Thayer, West Grove, Penn. French.

CIRCUS (ACROBATS): Pablo Picasso (1881-), 1933. Owned by artist. French.

CIRCUS FERNANDO: THE RINGMASTER: Henri de Toulouse-Lautrec (1864-1901), 1888. Art Institute of Chicago. French.

CIRCUS RIDERS, THE: Marc Chagall (1887-), 1931. Laren, M. P. A. Regnault Collection. French.

CIRCUS WOMAN: Georges Rouault (1871-), 1906. Privately owned, New York. French.

CITY, THE: Fernand Léger (1881-1955), 1919. Philadelphia Museum of Art. French.

CITY INTERIOR: Charles Sheeler (1883-), 1936. Worcester Art Museum, Worcester, Mass. American.

CLARITY: Pablo Palazuelo (1916-), 1952. Galerie Maeght, Paris. Spanish.

CLASSICAL LANDSCAPE: Washington Allston (1779-1843), 1805-08. Addison Gallery of American Art, Andover, Mass. American.

CLATTER OF CROWS IN A SPRING WOOD: Charles Burchfield (1853-), 1949. Frank K. M. Rehn Gallery, New York. American.

CLIFF DWELLERS: George Bellows (1882-1925), 1913. Los Angeles County Museum. American.

CLOCK MAKER, THE: Paul Cézanne (1839-1906), c. 1896. Guggenheim Museum, New York. French.

CLOCK WHEELS: Man Ray (1890-), 1925. Yale University Art Gallery. American.

CLOWN, THE: Jesus Reyes Ferreira (1884-), 1947. Owned by artist. Mexican.

CLOWN: Georges Rouault (1871-), 1928. Privately owned. French.

COAST SCENE: Gustave Courbet (1819-1877). Metropolitan Museum of Art, New York. French.

COAST SCENE ON THE MEDITERRANEAN: Washington Allston (1779-1843), 1808-11. Privately owned. American.

COCK, THE: Marc Chagall (1887-), 1947. Private Collection, Paris. French.

COCK, THE: Charles Walch (1898-1948), French.

COFFEE BEARERS, THE: Candido Portinari (1903-). Helena Rubenstein, New York. Brazilian.

COLLAGE WITH SQUARES ARRANGED ACCORDING TO THE LAWS OF CHANCE: Hans Arp (1887-), 1916. Owned by artist. German.

COLLECTOR OF PRINTS, THE: Edgar Degas (1834-1917), 1866. Metropolitan Museum of Art, New York. French.

COLLINE DES PAUVRES, LA: See Poorhouse on the Hill, The.

COLONEL WILLIAM MONTRESOR: John Singleton Copley (1738-1815), c. 1772. Detroit Institute of Arts. American.

COLONEL WILLIAM TAYLOR: Ralph Earl (1751-1801), 1790. Albright Art Gallery, Buffalo. American.

COLONNA MADONNA, THE: Raphael (Raffaello Santi) (1483-1520), 1507. Berlin. Italian.

COMET, THE: Francesco Cristofanetti (1901-), 1942. Privately owned. Italian (lives in U.S.A.).

COMPIÈGNE BARRACKS: Maurice Utrillo (1883-1955), 1915. Perls Galleries, New York. French.

COMPOSITION: Arthur B. Carles (1882-), 1940. Owned by artist. American.

COMPOSITION: Jean Hélion (1904-), 1934. Valentine Gallery, New York. French (lives in U.S.A.).

COMPOSITION: Leonore Krassner (1911-), 1943. Owned by artist. American.

COMPOSITION: Fernand Léger (1881-1955), 1930. Dr. G. F. Reber, Lausanne-Chailly, Switzerland. French.

COMPOSITION: Joan Miró (1893-), 1933. Wadsworth Atheneum, Hartford, Conn. Spanish.

COMPOSITION: Joan Miró (1893-), 1933. Museum of Modern Art, New York. Spanish.

COMPOSITION: Joan Miró (1893-), 1948. Thomas Bouchard, New York. Spanish.

COMPOSITION: Piet Mondrian (1872-1944), 1915. Kröller-Müller State Museum, Otterlo, Holland. Dutch.

COMPOSITION I: Geer van Velde (1897-). Galerie Maeght, Paris. Dutch.

COMMUNICATIONS IN SPACE: Herbert Bayer (1900-), 1941. Owned by artist. Austrian (lives in U.S.A.).

CONCERT, THE: Cuno Amiet (1868-), 1915. Privately owned, Zurich, Switzerland. Swiss.

CONCERT CHAMPÊTRE: See Pastoral Symphony.

CONDOTTIERE, IL: Antonello da Messina (c. 1422-1479), 1475. Louvre, Paris. Venetian.

CONFERENCE OF THE AMERICAN COMMISSIONERS OF THE TREATY OF PEACE WITH ENGLAND: Benjamin West (1738-1820), 1783. Henry Francis du Pont Winterthur Museum, Winterthur, Delaware. American.

CONFIDENCE, THE: Joseph Hirsch (1910-), 1941. Samuel Spewack. American.

CONGRESS HALL: See Old House of Representatives, The.

CONGRESS VOTING INDEPENDENCE: Robert Edge Pine (1730-1788). 1788. Historical Society of Pennsylvania, Philadelphia. American.

CONTENTMENT: Louis Eilshemius (1864-1941), 1930. C. H. Kleeman, New York. American.

CONTES BARBARES: Paul Gauguin (1848-1903), 1902. Folkwang Museum, Essen. French.

CONTRASTE DE FORMES: Fernand Léger (1881-1955), 1914. Arensberg Collection, Philadelphia Museum of Art. French.

CONVERSATION: Kenneth Callahan (1906-), 1944-45. Brooklyn Museum. American.

CONVERSION OF ST. PAUL, THE: Caravaggio (Michelangelo Merisi) (1573-1610), 1601. Santa Maria del Popolo, Rome. Italian.

CONVERSION OF ST. PAUL, THE: Pieter Bruegel the Elder (c. 1520-1569), 1567. Kunsthistorisches Museum, Vienna. Flemish.

COPLEY FAMILY, THE: John Singleton Copley (1738-1815), 1785. National Gallery of Art, Washington, D.C. American.

CORNER IN THE MOULIN DE LA GALETTE, A: Henri de Toulouse-Lautrec (1864—1901), 1892. Chester Dale Collection, New York. French.

CORNFIELD WITH A BLACK TREE: Vincent van Gogh (1853-1890), c. 1889. Kröller-Müller State Museum, Otterlo, Holland. French.

CORNFIELD WITH CROWS: Vincent van Gogh (1853-1890), 1890. V. W. van Gogh Collection, Municipal Museum, Amsterdam. French.

CORONATION OF THE VIRGIN, THE: Sandro Botticelli (Alessandro Filipepi) (1444?-1510). Metropolitan Museum of Art, New York. Florentine.

CORONATION OF THE VIRGIN, THE:

Lorenzo Monaco (c. 1370-1425). National Gallery, London. Italian.

CORONATION OF THE VIRGIN, THE: Diego Velasquez (1599-1660), c. 1641. Prado, Madrid. Spanish.

CORSAGE JAUNE, LE: See Woman in Yellow.

CORSICAN LANDSCAPE: Maurice Utrillo (1883-1955), 1913. Privately owned, Paris. French.

COSMIC COMPOSITION: Paul Klee (1879-1940), 1919. Miss Helen R. Resor. Swiss.

COTE DE NORD: Maurice Utrillo (1883-1955), 1917. Niveau Gallery, New York. French.

COUNTRY CHURCH, A: Maurice Utrillo (1883-1955), c. 1920. Museum of Modern Art, New York. French.

COUNTRY FAIR: John A. Woodside (1781-1852), 1824. Mr. Harry T. Peters, Jr. American.

COUNTRY SCHOOL: Winslow Homer (1836-1910), 1871. City Art Museum of St. Louis, Mo. American.

COURSE OF EMPIRE, THE: Emanuel Leutze (1816-1868), 1861-63. United States Capitol. American.

COURT OF DEATH, THE: Rembrandt Peale (1778-1860), 1820. Detroit Institute of Art. American.

COURT SCENE: INTERIOR: Jean-Louis Forain (1852-1931). Corcoran Gallery of Art, Washington, D.C. French.

COURTYARD IN VENICE: Francesco Guardi (1712-1793). Wallace Collection, London. Italian.

COWPER MADONNA, LARGE: Raphael (Raffaello Santi) (1483-1520), 1508. Mellon Collection, National Gallery of Art. Washington, D.C. Umbrian.

COWPER MADONNA, SMALL: Raphael (Raffaello Santi) (1483-1520). Widener Collection, Philadelphia. Umbrian.

COW WITH A PARASOL, THE: Marc Chagall (1887-), 1946. M. Pierre Matisse Collection, New York. French.

CREATION: Abraham Walkowitz (1880-), 1918. Owned by artist. Russian (lives in U.S.A.).

CREATION OF ADAM, THE: Michelangelo (Michelangelo Buonarroti) (1475-1564). Sistine Chapel, Vatican, Rome. Florentine.

CRESCENDO: Arthur B. Davies (1862-1928), 1910. Whitney Museum of Modern Art, New York. American.

CROQUET MATCH, THE: Winslow Homer (1836-1910), 1872. Edwin S. Webster. American.

CRUCIFIED, THE: Walter Quirt (1902-), 1943. Durlacher Brothers, New York. American.

CRUCIFIXION, THE: Fra Angelico (1387-1455). Metropolitan Museum of Art, New York. Florentine.

CRUCIFIXION, THE: Gerard David (c. 1460-1523), Metropolitan Museum of Art, New York. Flemish.

CRUCIFIXION, THE: Mathias Grünewald (1487?-1530?), 1510-11. Museum, Colmar, Alsace. German.

CRUCIFIXION, THE: Antonello da Messina (c. 1430-1479), 1475. Musée des Beaux-Arts, Antwerp. Venetian.

CRUCIFIXION: Perugino (Pietro Vannucci) (1446-1523), c. 1495. Sta. Maria Maddalena dei Pazzi, Florence. Umbrian.

CRUCIFIXION: Georges Rouault (1871-), c. 1927. Mrs. John Alden Carpenter, Chicago. French.

CRUCIFIXION, THE: Tintoretto (Jacopo Robusti) (1518-1594). Church of San Cassiano, Venice. Venetian.

CRUCIFIXION: Anthony Van Dyck (1599-1641). Church at Malines, Belgium. Flemish.

CRUCIFIXION OF CHRIST, THE: Lucas Cranach the Elder (1472-1553), before 1502. German.

CRUCIFIXION OF ST. ANDREW, THE: Caravaggio (Michelangelo Merisi) (1573-1610), 1610. Museo, Toledo. Italian.

CRUCIFIXION OF ST. PETER, THE: Caravaggio (Michelangelo Merisi) (1573-1610), 1601. Santa Maria del Popolo, Rome. Italian.

CUPID AND PSYCHE: William Page (1811-1885), 1845. Mrs. Leslie Stockton Howell, West Palm Beach. American.

CUPID ASLEEP: Caravaggio (Michelangelo Merisi) (1573-1610), 1608. Pittino, Florence. Italian.

CYPRESSES: Vincent van Gogh (1853-1890). Metropolitan Museum of Art, New York. French.

CYPRESSES, THE: Vincent van Gogh (1853-1890), 1889. Kröller-Müller State Museum, Otterlo, Holland. French.

CYPRESSES AT CAGNES: Henri-Edmond Cross (1856-1910), c. 1900. National Museum of Modern Art, Paris. French.

CYPRESS WITH A STAR: Vincent van Gogh (1853-1890), Kröller-Müller State Museum, Otterlo, Holland. French.

DAMNED, THE: Luca Signorelli (1441-1523). San Brixio Chapel, Orvieto Cathedral, Italy. Umbrian.

DANA AND ACTAEON: Titian (Tiziano Vecellio) (1480?-1576), 1559. Bridgewater House, London. Venetian.

DANAE AND THE SHOWER OF GOLD: Titian (Tiziano Vecellio) (1480?-1576), 1554. Prado, Madrid. Venetian.

DANCE AT BOUGIVAL: Pierre Auguste Renoir (1841-1919), 1883. Boston Museum of Fine Arts. French.

DANCE AT THE SPRING: Francis Picabia (1879-1953), 1912. Walter Arensberg Collection, Philadelphia Museum. French.

DANCER: Pablo Picasso (1881-), 1907. Walter P. Chrysler, Jr. French.

DANCER, A: Constantin Guys (Ernest Adolphe) (1805-1892). Collection Albertina, Vienna. French.

DANCER LISTENING TO ORGAN MUSIC IN A GOTHIC CATHEDRAL: Joan Miró (1893-), 1945. Pierre Matisse Gallery, New York. Spanish.

DANCERS PRACTICING AT THE BAR: Edgar Degas (1834-1917), 1877. Metropolitan Museum of Art, New York. French.

DANCE YOU MONSTER TO MY SWEET SONG: Paul Klee (1879-1940), 1922. Guggenheim Museum, New York. Swiss.

DANTE AND VIRGIL IN HELL: Eugène Delacroix (1798-1863), 1821. Louvre, Paris. French.

DARK CORN: Georgia O'Keeffe (1887-), 1924. Metropolitan Museum of Art, New York. American.

DARK FIGURE, THE: Frederico Castellon (1914-), 1938. Whitney Museum of American Art, New York. American.

DAUGHTERS OF REVOLUTION: Grant Wood (1892-1942), 1932. Edward G. Robinsen. American.

DAVID AND GOLIATH: Caravaggio (Michelangelo Merisi) (1573-1610), 1599-1600. Prado, Madrid. Italian.

DAVID WITH HEAD OF GOLIATH: Caravaggio (Michelangelo Merisi) (1573-1610), c. 1595. Gemaldegalerie, Vienna. Italian.

DAVID WITH HEAD OF GOLIATH: Caravaggio (Michelangelo Merisi) (1573-1610), 1605. Borghese, Rome. Italian.

DAWN: Pablo Palazuelo (1916-), 1952. Galerie Maeght, Paris. Spanish.
DAWN IN PENNSYLVANIA: Edward Hopper (1882-), 1942. Mr. and Mrs. Otto L. Spaeth. American.
DAYDREAMS: Thomas Couture (1815-1879). Metropolitan Museum of Art, New York. French.
DEAD BIRD, THE: Albert Pinkham Ryder (1847-1917). Phillips Memorial Gallery, Washington, D.C. American.
DEAD CHRIST: Andrea Mantegna (1431-1506), after 1500. Brera, Milan. Paduan.
DEAD CHRIST WITH ANGELS: Giovanni Bellini (1435?-1516), c. 1468. Pinacoteca, Rimini. Venetian.
DEAD MAN REVIVED IN THE TOMB BY TOUCHING THE BONES OF THE PROPHET ELISHA, THE: Washington Allston (1779-1843), 1811-13. Pennsylvania Academy of Fine Arts, Philadelphia. American.
DEATH AND ASSUMPTION OF THE VIRGIN, THE: Fra Angelico (1387-1455), undated (early). Isabella Stewart Gardner Museum, Boston. Florentine.
DEATH IN THE ORCHARD: Franklin C. Watkins (1894-), 1938. John F. Steinman, Esq. American.
DEATH OF GENERAL MONTGOMERY AT THE SIEGE OF QUEBEC: John Trumbull (1756-1843), 1786. Yale University Art Gallery. American
DEATH OF JANE McCREA, THE: John Vanderlyn (1776-1852), 1803. Wadsworth Atheneum, Hartford, Conn. American.
DEATH OF MARAT, THE: Jacques Louis David (1748-1825). Royal Museum of Fine Arts, Brussels. French.
DEATH OF NELSON, THE: Daniel Maclise (1806-1870). Westminster Palace, London. English.
DEATH OF ST. FRANCIS, THE: Giotto (Giotto di Bondone) (1276?-1337?). Santa Croce, Florence. Florentine.
DEATH OF ST. PETRONILLA: Guercino (Giovanni Francesco Barbieri) (1591-1666), 1621. Capitoline Gallery, Rome. Bolognese.
DEATH OF SARDANAPALUS, THE: Eugène Delacroix (1799-1863), 1827. Louvre, Paris. French.
DEATH OF SOCRATES, THE: Jacuqes Louis David (1748-1825). Metropolitan Museum of Art, New York. French.
DEATH OF THE VIRGIN, THE: Caravaggio (Michelangelo Merisi) (1573-1610), 1606. Louvre, Paris. Italian.
DEATH ON THE PALE HORSE: Benjamin West (1738-1820), 1817. Philadelphia Academy of Fine Arts. American.
DEBORAH HALL: William Williams (1710?-1790), 1766. Brooklyn Museum. American.
DECOLLATION OF ST. JOHN THE BAPTIST, THE: Caravaggio (Michelangelo Merisi) (1573-1610), 1608. Cathedral of St. John, La Valletta, Malta. Italian.
DECORATION WITH CLOUD: Max Weber (1881-), 1913. Owned by artist. American.
DEER, THE: Gustave Courbet (1819-1877). Metropolitan Museum of Art, New York. French.
DEER, MOUNT STORM PARK: Worthington Whittredge (1820-1910), c. 1850. Worcester Art Museum, Worcester, Mass. American.
DEER IN THE FOREST: Franz Marc (1880-1916), 1913. Staatliche Galerie Moritzburg, Halle. German.
DEER ISLE, BOATS, AND PERTAINING THERETO: John Marin (1870-1953), 1927. Keith Warner, Ft. Lauderdale, Fla. American.
DELAWARE WATER GAP: George Innes (1825-

1894), 1861. Metropolitan Museum of Art, New York. American.
DELIGHTS OF THE POET: Giorgio di Chirico (1888-), c. 1913. Privately owned. French (born in Greece).
DELPHIC SIBYL: Michelangelo Buonarotti (1475-1564), 1508-09. Sistine Chapel, Rome. Florentine.
DEMOISELLES d'AVIGNON, LES: Pablo Picasso (1881-), 1907. Museum of Modern Art, New York. French.
DEMOISELLES DE VILLAGE, LES: Gustave Courbet (1819-1877). Metropolitan Museum of Art, New York. French.
DEMON ABOVE THE SHIPS: Paul Klee (1879-1940), 1916. Museum of Modern Art, New York. Swiss.
DEPARTURE (A TRIPTYCH): Max Beckmann (1884-1950), 1937. Museum of Modern Art, New York. German.
DEPOSITION, THE: Caravaggio (Michelangelo Merisi) (1573-1610), 1602. Pinacoteca Vaticana, Rome. Italian.
DEPOSITION, THE: Giotto (di Bondoni) (1266-1336), 1305-06. Arena Chapel, Padua. Florentine.
DEPOSITION, THE: Raphael (Raffaello Santi) (1483-1520), 1507. Originally for a chapel in the Perugia Cathedral, now in Borghese, Rome. Umbrian.
DEPOSITION, THE: Ugolino da Siena (act. 1290-1339), c. 1295. National Gallery, London. Italian.
DEPOSITION: Rogier van der Weyden (1400-1464), c. 1435. Prado, Madrid. Flemish.
DERBY VIEW: Dean Fausett (1913-), 1939. Museum of Modern Art, New York. American.
DESCENT FROM THE CROSS, THE: Peter Paul Rubens (1577-1640), 1611-14. Antwerp Cathedral. Flemish.
DESCENT FROM THE CROSS, THE: Rogier van der Weyden (1400-1464). Escorial, Madrid. Flemish.
DESCENT OF THE HOLY SPIRIT: Titian (Tiziano Vecellio) (1480?-1576), c. 1560. Santa Maria Della Salute, Venice. Venetian.
DESSERT, THE: Henri Matisse (1869-1954). New Museum of Modern Western Art, Moscow. French.
DESTRUCTION OF SODOM, THE: Jean Baptiste Camille Corot (1796-1875). Metropolitan Museum of Art, New York. French.
DEVELOPMENT IN MULTIPLICITY: John Ferren (1905-), 1937. Art of This Century Collection. American.
DEVIL AND TOM WALKER, THE: John Quidor (1801-1881), 1856. Mr. and Mrs. Lawrence A. Fleischman, Detroit. American.
DEWITT CLINTON: Samuel F. B. Morse (1791-1872), c. 1826. Metropolitan Museum of Art, New York. American.
DIANA: Paul Klee (1879-1940), 1931. Mr. and Mrs. Henry Clifford. Swiss.
DIANA AND CALLISTO: Titian (Tiziano Vecellio) (1480?-1576), 1559. Bridgewater House, London. Venetian.
DIFFRACTION # 1: I. Rice Pereira (1905-), 1942. Owned by artist. American.
DINNER PARTY, THE: Henry Sargent (1770-1845), c. 1815-20. Boston Museum of Fine Arts. American.
DISASTERS OF MYSTICISM, THE: Roberto (Matta) Echaurren (1912-), 1942. Mr. and Mrs. James Thrall Soby. Chilean (lives in U.S.A.).
DISPUTA DEL SACRAMENTO: Raphael (Raffaello Santi) (1483-1520), c. 1509. Stanza Della Segnatura, Vatican, Rome. Umbrian.
DISSOLUTE LIFE: Jan Steen (1626-1679), 1663. Gemaldegalerie, Vienna. Dutch.

DIVE BOMBER AND TANK: José Clemente Orozco (1883-1949), 1940. Museum of Modern Art, New York. Mexican.

DIVERS ON YELLOW BACKGROUND: Fernand Léger (1881-1955), 1941. Art Institute of Chicago. French.

DR. JOHNSON: Joshua Reynolds (1723-1792), 1772. National Gallery, London. English.

DR. MAX HERMANN-NEISSE: George Grosz (1893-), c. 1927. Eric Cohn Collection, New York. German.

DOGANA, VENICE, THE: Canaletto (Antonio Canal) (1697-1768). Gemaldegalerie, Vienna. Italian.

DOG AND COCK: Pablo Picasso (1881-), 1921. Museum of Modern Art, New York. French.

DOG BARKING AT THE MOON: Joan Miró (1900-), 1926. Gallery of Living Art, New York University. Spanish.

DOGE EMBARKING ON THE BUCENTAUR, THE: Francesco Guardi (1712-1793). Louvre, Paris. Venetian.

DOGE LEONARDO LOREDANO: Giovanni Bellini (1430?-1516), c. 1503. National Gallery, London. Venetian.

DONI MADONNA: See Holy Family (Michelangelo).

DON QUIXOTE: Honoré Daumier (1808-1876). Metropolitan Museum of Art, New York. French.

DON QUIXOTE AND SANCHO PANZA ENTERTAINED BY BASIL AND QUITERA: Gustave Doré (1832-1883). Metropolitan Museum of Art, New York. French.

DONNA ANTONIA DE IPENARRIETTA Y GALDOS AND HER SON: Diego Velasquez (1599-1660), c. 1631. Prado, Madrid. Spanish.

DRAWBRIDGE (PONT DE l'ANGLOIS): Vincent van Gogh (1853-1890), 1888. Kröller-Müller State Museum, Otterlo, Holland. French.

DRAWING: Alexander Calder (1898-), 1940. Willard Gallery, New York. American.

DREAM, THE: Henri Rousseau (1844-1910), 1910. Museum of Modern Art, New York. French.

DREAM OF THE GOOD LIFE: Mitchell Siporin (1910-), 1941. Downtown Gallery, New York. American.

DREAM OF ST. URSULA, THE: Vittore Carpaccio (1450?-1522), c. 1495. Academy, Venice. Venetian.

DRIFTWOOD: Zoltan Sepeshy (1898-), 1943. Midtown Galleries, New York. American.

DRIVING HOME THE CATTLE: Pieter Bruegel the Elder (c. 1520-1569), 1565. Gemaldegalerie, Vienna. Flemish.

DUCHESS OF DEVONSHIRE: Thomas Gainsborough (1727-1788), 1783. Metropolitan Museum of Art, New York. English.

DUKE OF NORFOLK, THE: See Portrait of Ippolito Riminaldi.

DUST BOWL: Alexandre Hogue (1898-), 1940. Fine Arts Department, I.B.M. Corporation. American.

DUTCH CARGO-BOAT, THE: André Lhote (1885-), 1948. French.

DUTCH COAST, THE: Paul Signac (1863-1935), 1906. Privately owned. French.

DUTCH COURTYARD, A: Pieter de Hooch (1629-1683?), c. 1656. National Gallery of Art, Washington, D.C. Dutch.

DUTCH INTERIOR: Joan Miró (1893-), 1928. Museum of Modern Art, New York. Spanish.

DWARF "EL PRIMO," THE: Diego Velasquez (1599-1660), 1644. Prado, Madrid. Spanish.

EARLY MORNING AFTER A STORM AT

SEA: Winslow Homer (1836-1910), 1902. Cleveland Museum of Art. American.

EARS OF CORN: Vincent van Gogh (1853-1890), 1890. V. W. van Gogh Collection, Municipal Museum, Amsterdam. French.

EASTER ON LAKE WALCHEN: Lovis Corinth (1858-1925), 1922. Privately owned. German.

EAST RIVER: Maurice Prendergast (1861-1924), 1901. Museum of Modern Art, New York. American.

ECCE HOMO: Titian (Tiziano Vecellio) (1480?-1576). Gemaldegalerie, Vienna. Venetian.

ECCE HOMO: Titian (Tiziano Vecellio) (1480?-1576), 1547. Prado, Madrid. Venetian.

ECHO-PLASM: Jimmy Ernst (1900-), 1944. Norlyst Gallery, New York. German (lives in U.S.A.).

EDUCATION OF CUPID, THE: Titian (Tiziano Vecellio) (1480?-1576), c. 1565. Arthur Sachs Collection. Venetian.

EDWARD VI AS PRINCE OF WALES: Hans Holbein the Younger (1497-1543), c. 1543. Metropolitan Museum of Art, New York. German.

EDWARD VI AS A CHILD: Hans Holbein the Younger (1497-1543). Mellon Collection of the National Gallery of Art, Washington, D.C. German.

EEL SPEARING AT SETAUKET: William Sidney Mount (1808-1868), 1845. New York State Historical Association, Cooperstown. American.

ELEVATION OF THE CROSS: Anthony Van Dyck (1599-1641). Courtrai. Flemish.

ELEVATION OF THE CROSS: Peter Paul Rubens (1577-1640), 1610-11. Antwerp Cathedral. Dutch.

ELIJAH FED BY THE RAVENS: Washington Allston (1779-1843), 1818. Boston Museum of Fine Arts. American.

EMBARKATION FOR THE ISLE OF CYTHERA, THE: Jean Antoine Watteau (1684-1721), 1717. Louvre, Paris. French.

EMPEROR, THE: Abraham Rattner (1895-), 1944. Whitney Museum of American Art, New York. American.

EMPLOYMENT AGENCY: Isaac Soyer (1907-), 1937. Whitney Museum of American Art, New York. American.

ENCHANTED ISLAND, THE: Jean Lurçat (1892-), 1928. Bernard David, Philadelphia. French.

ENCLOSED FIELD, THE: Vincent van Gogh (1853-1890), c. 1889. Kröller-Müller State Museum, Otterlo, Holland. French.

END OF THE WORLD, THE: Luca Signorelli (1441?-1523), 1500-04. Chapel of San Brizio, Orvieto. Umbrian.

ENTRANCE TO A VILLAGE: Meindert Hobbema (1638-1709), c. 1665. Metropolitan Museum of Art, New York. Dutch.

ENTRANCE TO THE VILLAGE: Camille Pissarro (1830-1903). Louvre, Paris. French.

ENVIRONS OF PARIS: Jean Baptiste Camille Corot (1796-1875). Metropolitan Museum of Art, New York. French.

EQUESTRIAN FIGURES: Marie Laurencin (1885-), 1924. Mrs. Solomon R. Guggenheim, New York. French.

ERASMUS OF ROTTERDAM: Hans Holbein the Younger (1497-1543), 1523. Louvre, Paris. German.

L'ESPAGNOLE: Henri Matisse (1869-1954). Robert Treat Paine, Boston. French.

ESTERHAZY MADONNA: Raphael (Raffaello Santi) (1483-1520), 1507-08. Budapest. Umbrian.

ET IN ARCADIA EGO: Nicolas Poussin (1594-1665), 1638-39. Louvre, Paris. French.

ETERNAL CITY, THE: Peter Blume (1906-),

1934-37. Museum of Modern Art, New York. American.

ÉTIENNE CHEVALIER, PRESENTED BY ST. STEPHEN: Jean Fouquet (1415-1481). Kaiser Friedrich Museum, Berlin. French.

EVANGELICAL STILL LIFE: Giorgio di Chirico (1888-   ), 1916. Privately owned. French.

EVENING: Charles François Daubigny (1817-1878). Metropolitan Museum of Art, New York. French.

EVENING IN MACHOV: Antonin Hudecek (1872-1942), 1910. National Gallery, Prague. Czech.

EXECUTION OF THE CITIZENS OF MADRID: Francisco Goya (y Lucientes) (1746-1828). Prado, Madrid. Spanish.

EXHIBITION GALLERY OF THE LOUVRE: Samuel F. B. Morse (1791-1872), 1833. College of Fine Arts, Syracuse University, Syracuse, New York. American.

EXHUMING OF THE MASTODON, THE: Charles Willson Peale (1741-1827), 1806. Mrs. Harry White. American.

EXOTIC: Paul Klee (1879-1940), 1939. Privately owned. Swiss.

EXOTIC GARDEN: Paul Klee (1879-1940), 1926. Privately owned. Swiss.

EXPULSION FROM PARADISE, THE: Masaccio (Tommaso Guidi). (1401-1428?), c. 1426. Church of the Carmine, Florence. Florentine.

EXPULSION FROM THE GARDEN OF EDEN, THE: Thomas Cole (1801-1842), 1828. Boston Museum of Fine Arts. American.

EYES CLOSED: Jean Dubuffet (1901-   ), 1954. Pierre Matisse Gallery, New York. French.

EYES TESTED: Reginald March (1898-1954), 1944. Frank K. M. Rehn Gallery, New York. American.

EZEKIEL GOLDTHWAIT: John Singleton Copley (1738-1815), c. 1770. Boston Museum of Fine Arts. American.

FABLE OF ARACHNE, THE: Diego Velasquez (1599-1660), c. 1657. Prado, Madrid. Spanish.

FACTORIES (LES FABRIQUES): Maurice Utrillo (1883-1955), c. 1911. Lewyt Collection, New York. French.

FACTORY, THE: Preston Dickinson (1891-1930), c. 1918. Boston Museum of Fine Arts. American.

FACTORY STREET: Maurice Utrillo (1883-1955), 1916-17. Jon Nicholas Streep, New York. French.

FALLING ANGEL, THE: Marc Chagall (1887-   ), 1947. Property of Artist. French.

FALL OF MAN, THE: Titian (Tiziano Vecellio) (1480?-1576), c. 1570. Prado, Madrid. Venetian.

FALLING LEAVES (LES ALYSCAMPS),: Vincent van Gogh (1853-1890), 1888. Kröller-Müller State Museum, Otterlo, Holland. French.

FALLS OF THE OHIO AND LOUISVILLE: Alexander Helwig Wyant (1836-1892), 1863. J. B. Speed Art Museum, Louisville, Kentucky. American.

FAMILY, THE: Mary Cassatt (1848-1926), c. 1887. Durand-Ruel, New York. American.

FAMILY, THE: Isaac Soyer (1907-   ), 1938. Midtown Gallery, New York. American.

FAMILY GROUP: Henry Moore (1898-   ), 1944-46. Philip James, London. English.

FAMILY OF JONATHAN TRUMBULL, THE: John Trumbull (1756-1843), 1777. Yale University Art Gallery. American.

FAMILY OF SALTIMBANQUES: Pablo Picasso (1881-   ), 1905. Art Institute of Chicago. French.

FAMILY PICTURE: Max Beckmann (1884-1950). Curt Valentin Gallery, New York. German.

FAMILY PORTRAIT: Rembrandt van Rijn (1606-1669), c. 1667-69. Herzog Anton Ulrich Museum, Brunswick. Dutch.

FANNY KEMBLE AS BIANCA: Thomas Sully (1783-1872), 1833. Pennsylvania Academy of the Fine Arts. American.

FAREWELL TO UNION SQUARE: Morris Kantor, (1896-   ), 1931. Newark Museum, New Jersey. American.

FARM, THE: Joan Miró (1893-   ), 1921-22. Ernest Hemingway, Havana. Spanish.

FARM, THE: Edvard Munch (1863-1944), 1905. Museum Folkwang, Essen. Norwegian.

FARMER'S DINNER, THE: Joan Miró (1893-   ), 1935. Thomas Adler, Lockland, Ohio. Spanish.

FARMER'S WIFE, THE: Joan Miró (1893-   ), 1922-23. Mrs. Pierre Matisse, New York. Spanish.

FATHER AND CHILD: Ben Shahn (1898-   ), 1946. James Thrall Soby. American.

FEAST IN THE HOUSE OF LEVI: Veronese (Paolo Cagliari) (1528-1588), 1573. Academy, Venice. Venetian.

FEDE, LA (VOTIVE PICTURE OF DOGE GRIMANI): Titian (Tiziano Vecellio) (1480?-1576), 1550-70. Palace of the Doges, Venice. Venetian.

FERNANDE: Pablo Picasso (1881-   ), 1909. Henry Church. French.

FERRY MAN, THE: Jean Baptiste Camille Corot (1796-1875). Metropolitan Museum of Art, New York. French.

FIELD AT AUVERS: Vincent van Gogh (1853-1890), 1890. V. W. van Gogh Collection Municipal Museum, Amsterdam. Dutch.

FIFER, THE: Édouard Manet (1832-1883). Louvre, Paris. French.

FIGHTING TEMERAIRE, THE: Joseph M. W. Turner (1775-1851), 1838-39. National Gallery, London. English.

FIGURE COMPOSITION: Émile Othon Friesz (1879-1949). Detroit Institute of Arts. French.

FIGURE IN A RED CHAIR: Pablo Picasso (1881-   ), 1932. Owned by artist. French.

FIGURES: André Dunoyer de Segonzac (1885-   ); 1917-18. Maurice Speiser, Philadelphia. French.

FIGURES AND MOUNTAINS: Joan Miró (1893-   ), 1936. Mr. and Mrs. Lee A. Ault, New Canaan, Conn. Spanish.

FIGURES IN THE PRESENCE OF A METAMORPHOSIS: Joan Miró (1893-   ), 1936. Mrs. Saidie A. May, Baltimore, Maryland. Spanish.

FIGURES UNDER THE MOON: Joan Miró (1893-   ), 1938. Valentine Gallery, New York. Spanish.

FIGURES WAITING: Abraham Rattner (1898-   ), 1946. Milton Lowenthal, New York. American.

FIGURE THROWING A STONE: Pablo Picasso (1881-   ), 1931. Owned by artist. French.

FIRE-EATER: Franklin C. Watkins (1894-   ), 1933-34. Philadelphia Museum of Art. American.

FIRE IN THE BORGO, THE: Raphael (Raffaello Santi) (1483-1520), c. 1514-17. Vatican, Rome. Umbrian.

FIRST WAR-WINTER: Charles Howard (1899-   ), 1940. San Francisco Museum of Art. American.

FISH BOWL: Pavel Tchelitchew (1898-   ), 1938. Durlacher Bros., New York. American.

FISHERMAN'S FAMILY: Julian Levi (1900-   ), 1939. Metropolitan Museum of Art, New York. American.

ISHERMAN'S LAST SUPPER: Marsden Hartley (1877-1943), 1940-41. Mr. and Mrs. Roy Neuberger. American.

IVE IN THE AFTERNOON: Robert Motherwell (1915-), 1950. Kootz Gallery, New York. American.

LAGELLATION OF CHRIST, THE: Caravaggio (Michelangelo Merisi) (1573-1610), 1607. San Domenico Maggiore, Naples. Italian.

LAYED OX, THE: Rembrandt van Rijn (1606-1669), 1655. Louvre, Paris. Dutch.

LAYING OF MARSYAS, THE: Titian (Tiziano Vecellio) (1480?-1576), e. 1570. Archiepiscopal Castle, Kremsier, Czechoslovakiet. Venetian.

LEET AT VILLEFRANCHE, THE: Raoul Dufy (1877-1953), 1926. Museum of Modern Art, New York. French.

LEMISH KERMIS, THE: Peter Paul Rubens (1577-1640), c. 1636. Louvre, Paris. Dutch.

LEMISH VILLAGE: Jan Bruegel the Younger (1601-1678). Metropolitan Museum of Art, New York. Flemish.

LIGHT INTO EGYPT, THE: Georges Rouault (1871-), 1948. Privately owned, Paris. French.

LIGHT OF A BIRD OVER THE PLAIN, III: Joan Miró (1893-), 1939. Pierre Matisse Gallery, New York. Spanish.

LIGHT OF A BIRD OVER THE PLAIN, IV: Joan Miró (1893-), 1939. Valentine Dudensing, New York. Spanish.

LIGHT OF FLORIMELL, THE: Washington Allston (1779-1843), 1819. Detroit Institute of Arts. American.

LIGHT OF NIGHT, THE: William Morris Hunt (1824-1879), 1878. Pennsylvania Academy of Fine Arts, Philadelphia. American.

LOWER GARDEN: Fannie Hillsmith (1911-), 1943. Norlyst Gallery, New York. American.

LOWERS: Henri Matisse (1869-1954), 1923. William Averell Harriman, New York. French.

LOWER SELLER: Diego Rivera (1886-), 1950. A. Schutz, Scarsdale, New York. Mexican.

LOWERS IN A BLUE VASE: Vincent van Gogh (1853-1890), . 1886-88. Kröller-Müller State Museum, Otterlo, Holland. French.

LOWERS OF DISASTER: Fautrier (c. 1900-), 1927. Phillips Memorial Gallery, Washington, D.C. French.

LOWER STILL LIFE: Maurice Utrillo (1883-1955), 1946. Miss Lily Pons, New York. French.

LOWER VENDOR, THE: Diego Rivera 1886-1957), 1935. San Francisco Museum of Art. Mexican.

LYING DUTCHMAN, THE: Albert Pinkham Ryder (1847-1917), c. 1887. National Collection of Fine Arts, Smithsonian Institute, Washington, D.C. American.

OR C IN LIMITED PALETTE: Ray Eames 1943. Charles Eames, Santa Monica, Calif. American.

ORD, THE: Claude Lorrain (1600-1682), c. 1650. Metropolitan Museum of Art, New York. French.

OREST, THE: Fernand Léger (1881-1955), 1942. Dr. F. Heer, Zurich, Switzerland. French.

OREST CITY: Arnold Friedman (1873-), 1945. Maurice Gallery, New York. American.

OREST OF ARDEN: Albert Pinkham Ryder (1847-1917), 1897. Stephen C. Clark. American.

ORGE, THE: Louis Le Nain (1593?-1648). Louvre, Paris. French.

ORTUNE-TELLER, THE (LA ZINGARA): Caravaggio (Michelangelo Merisi) (1573-1610), c. 1595. Louvre, Paris. Italian.

FOUR SAINTS: PETER, MARTHA, MARY MAGDALEN, AND LEONARD: Correggio (Antonio Allegri) (1489-1534). Metropolitan Museum of Art, New York. Lombard.

FOURTH OF JULY ORATOR: Ben Shahn (1898-), 1943. James Thrall Soby, Farmington, Conn. American.

FOX ISLAND, MAINE: Marsden Hartley (1877-1943), 1937-38. Addison Gallery of American Art, Andover, Mass. American.

FOYER, LE: Edgar Degas (1834-1917). Metropolitan Museum of Art, New York. French.

FRANCISCO LEZCANO: Diego Velasquez (1599-1660), c. 1638-42. Prado, Madrid. Spanish.

FRANKLIN DRAWING ELECTRICITY FROM THE SKY: Benjamin West (1738-1820), c. 1805. Privately owned. American.

FRESH GRASS IN THE PARK: Vincent van Gogh (1853-1890). Kröller-Müller State Museum, Otterlo, Holland. French.

FRIENDSHIP: Pablo Picasso (1881-), 1908. Museum of Modern Western Art, Moscow. French.

FRUITS OF AUTUMN: James Peale (1749-1831), 1827. Whitney Museum of American Art, New York. American.

FUNERAL, THE: Georges Rouault (1871-), 1930. Museum of Modern Art, New York. French.

FUNERAL OF PHOCION, THE: Nicolas Poussin (1594-1665), 1648. Louvre, Paris. French.

GALLANT, THE: Gerard Terborch (1617-1681), c. 1665. Louvre, Paris. Dutch.

GAME OF SKITTLES: Pieter de Hooch (1629-1677), c. 1665. Cincinnati Art Museum. Dutch.

GARDEN OF DAUBIGNY, THE: Vincent van Gogh (1853-1890), 1890. V. W. van Gogh Collection, Municipal Museum, Amsterdam. French.

GARDEN OF DELIGHTS (A TRIPTYCH: LEFT SHUTTER, THE CREATION OF EVE; CENTER PANEL, THE GARDEN OF DELIGHTS; RIGHT SHUTTER, HELL): Hieronymus Bosch (c. 1450-1516). Prado, Madrid. Dutch.

GARDEN OF EDEN, THE: Erastus Salisbury Field (1805-1900), 1860-70. Boston Museum of Fine Arts. American.

GARE ST. LAZARE: Claude Monet (1840-1926), 1877. Art Institute of Chicago. French.

GATE, THE: Raoul Dufy (1877-1953), 1930. Evelyn Sharp, New York. French.

GAY REPAST, A: Paul Klee (1879-1940), 1928. Privately owned. Swiss.

GAZELLE, THE: Franz Marc (1880-1916), 1912. Museum of Art, Rhode Island School of Design, Providence, Rhode Island. German.

GENERAL SAMUEL WALDO: Robert Feke (1705?-1750), c. 1748. Bowdoin College Museum of Fine Arts. American.

GENESIS, FIRST VERSION: Lorser Feitelson (1898-), 1934. San Francisco Museum of Art. American.

GENTLEMAN MOUNTING A HORSE: Anthony Van Dyck (1599-1641) Metropolitan Museum of Art, New York. Flemish.

GEORGE SAND'S GARDEN AT NOHANT: Eugène Delacroix (1799-1863). Metropolitan Museum of Art, New York. French.

GEORGE WASHINGTON (ATHENAEUM PORTRAIT): Gilbert Stuart (1755-1828), 1796. Boston Athenaeum. American.

GERTRUDE STEIN: Pablo Picasso (1881-), 1906. Metropolitan Museum of Art, New York. French.

GESTURE: Max Weber (1881-), 1921. Mr. and Mrs. F. H. Hirschland. American.

GILLES: Antoine Watteau (1684-1721). Louvre, Paris. French.

GINEVRA DE' BENCI: Leonardo da Vinci (1452-1519), 1474. Liechtenstein Gallery, Vienna. Florentine.

GIOCONDA, LA: See Mona Lisa.

GIPSY MADONNA, THE: Titian (Tiziano Vecellio) (1480?-1576), c. 1510. Gemaldegalerie, Vienna. Venetian.

GIPSY WOMAN WITH BABY: Amadeo Modigliani (1884-1920), 1919. Chester Dale Collection, Washington, D.C. French.

GIRL FROM BRITTANY IN PRAYER, A: Paul Gauguin (1848-1903), 1894. Privately owned. French.

GIRL IN PINK: Amadeo Modigliani (1884-1920). Samuel A. Lewisohn, New York. French.

GIRLS PLAYING CARDS: Karl Hofer (1878-), 1939. Bayerische Staatsgemalde-Sammlungen, Munich. German.

GIRLS WITH A TOY BOAT: Pablo Picasso (1881-), 1937. Art of This Century, New York. French.

GIRL WEAVING A GARLAND: Jean Baptiste Camille Corot (1796-1875). Metropolitan Museum of Art, New York. French.

GIRL WITH A COCK: Pablo Picasso (1881-), 1938. Mrs. Meric Callery. French.

GIRL WITH A FLUTE, A: Jan Vermeer (1632-1675), National Gallery of Art, Washington, D.C. Dutch.

GIRL WITH A MANDOLIN: Pablo Picasso (1881-), 1910. Roland Penrose. French.

GIRL WITH A RED HAT, A: Jan Vermeer (1632-1675). Kunsthistorisches Museum, Vienna. Dutch.

GIRL WITH CATS: Marie Laurencin (1885-), 1918. Privately owned, New York. French.

GIRL WITH DARK HAIR (PORTRAIT OF D. M.): Pablo Picasso (1881-), 1939. Privately owned. French.

GIRL WITH DISH OF FRUIT: Titian (Tiziano Vecellio) (1480?-1576), c. 1555. Kaiser Friedrich Museum, Berlin. Venetian.

GIRL WITH LOOSE HAIR: Vincent van Gogh (1853-1890), 1885-86. V. W. van Gogh Collection, Municipal Museum, Amsterdam. French.

GIRL WITH PIGEONS: Morris Hirschfield (1872-), 1942. Privately owned. American.

GIRL WRITING: Pablo Picasso (1881-), 1934. Peter Watson. French.

GIVE US THIS DAY: Marsden Hartley (1877-1943), 1938-39. Privately owned. American.

GLADIATORS: Giorgio di Chirico (1888-), c. 1928. Maurice Speiser, Philadelphia. French (born in Greece).

GLEANERS, THE: Jean François Millet (1814-1875), Louvre, Paris. French.

GLORIA, LA: Titian (Tiziano Vecellio) (1480?-1576), 1554. Prado, Madrid. Venetian.

GLORIOUS VICTORY OF THE SLOOP "MARIA": Lyonel Feininger (1871-1956), 1926. City Art Museum, St. Louis, Mo. American.

GNOME, THE: Odilon Redon (1840-1916), 1880. Art Institute of Chicago. French.

GOLDEN FISH, THE: Paul Klee (1879-1940), 1925-26. Privately owned, Holland. Swiss.

GOLDSMITH, THE: Joan Miró (1893-), 1918. Pierre Matisse Gallery, New York. Spanish.

GOSSIP: Giovanni Boldini (1845-1931), 1873. Metropolitan Museum of Art, New York. Italian.

GOULUE ENTERING THE MOULIN ROUGE, LA: Henri de Toulouse-Lautrec (1864-1901), 1892. Dr. and Mrs. David M. Levy, New York. French.

GOVERNOR PIETER STUYVESANT: Artist unknown, c. 1660-70. New York Historical Society, New York. American.

GRAHAM CHILDREN, THE: William Hogarth (1697-1764), 1742. National Gallery, London. English.

GRAIN ELEVATOR FROM BRIDGE: Ralston Crawford (1906-), 1942-43. Downtown Gallery, New York. American.

GRAND CANAL, VENICE: Joseph M. W. Turner (1775-1851), c. 1835. Metropolitan Museum of Art, New York. English.

GRAND DÉJEUNER, LE: See Three Women.

GRANDE JATTE, LA: See A Sunday Afternoon on The Island of La Grande Jatte.

GREAT JULIE, THE: Fernand Léger (1881-1955), 1945. Museum of Modern Art, New York. French.

GRAND LOGE, THE: Henri de Toulouse-Lautrec (1864-1901), 1897. Collection Mettler, St. Gallen, Switzerland. French.

GRAVELINES: André Derain (1880-1954), National Museum of Modern Art, Paris. French.

GRAY AND GOLD: John Rogers Cox (1915-), 1942. Cleveland Museum of Art. American.

GREEN DEPTH: I. Rice Pereira (1907-), 1944. Metropolitan Museum of Art, New York. American.

GREEN MAGAZINE: Joseph Solman (1909-), 1940. Phillips Memorial Gallery, Washington, D.C. Russian (lives in U.S.A.).

GREEN SEAS: Henry Mattson (1887-), 1938. Brooklyn Museum. American.

GREEN SHUTTER, THE: Raoul Dufy (1879-1953), 1913. Privately owned, New York. French.

GREYHOUNDS OF THE COMTE DE CHOISEUL, THE: Gustave Courbet (1819-1877), 1866. City Art Museum, St. Louis. French.

GREY ROCK, BLUE GREY SEA, AND BOAT: John Marin (1870-), 1938. Downtown Gallery, New York. American.

GROUP OF BATHERS: Paul Cézanne (1839-1906), 1892-94. Walter Arensberg Collection, Philadelphia Museum. French.

GUERNICA: Pablo Picasso (1881-), 1937. Museum of Modern Art, New York. French.

GUEYMARD IN THE ROLE OF ROBERT LE DIABLE: Gustave Courbet (1819-1877). Metropolitan Museum of Art, New York. French.

GUILLAUME BUDE: Jean Clouet (act. 1516-1540). Metropolitan Museum of Art, New York. French.

GUITAR PLAYER: André Derain (1880-1954), 1928. Privately owned. French.

GULF OF MARSEILLES SEEN FROM L'ESTAQUE, THE: Paul Cézanne (1839-1906). Metropolitan Museum of Art, New York. French.

GULF STREAM: Winslow Homer (1836-1910). Metropolitan Museum of Art, New York. American.

GUN FOUNDRY, THE: John F. Weir (1841-1926), 1867. Putnam County Historical Society, New York. American.

GYPSIES, THE: Jean Baptiste Camille Corot (1796-1875), 1872. Metropolitan Museum of Art, New York. French.

GYPSY WOMAN AND BABY: Amadeo Modigliani (1884-1920), 1916. Chester Dale Collection, Chicago. French (born in Italy).

HAERE TEMAI: LANDSCAPE WITH BLACK Hogs: Paul Gauguin (1848-1903), 1891. J. Thannhauser. French.

HAGAR IN THE WILDERNESS: Jean Baptiste Camille Corot (1796-1875), 1835. Metropolitan Museum of Art, New York. French.

HAIRDRESSER'S WINDOW: John Sloan (1871-1951), 1907. Wadsworth Atheneum. American.

HALF-PAST THREE: Marc Chagall (1887-),

1911. Walter Arensberg Collection, Philadelphia Museum. Russian.

HALL C. ENTRANCE R2: Paul Klee (1879-1940), 1920. Henry Church. Swiss.

HAMILTON FISH: Thomas Hicks (1823-1890), 1852. New York City Art Commission. American.

HANDBALL: Ben Shahn (1898-), 1939. Museum of Modern Art, New York. American.

HARBOR, THE: Joan Miró (1893-), 1945. Pierre Matisse Gallery, New York. Spanish.

HARLEM RIVER SIESTA: Julian Levi (1900-), 1938. Otto Soglow. American.

HARLEQUIN: Raoul Dufy (1877-1953), 1939. Privately owned, Paris. French.

HARLEQUIN: Pablo Picasso (1881-), 1901. Mr. and Mrs. Henry Clifford. French.

HARLEQUIN: Pablo Picasso (1881-), 1915. Privately owned. French.

HARLEQUIN'S CARNIVAL, THE: Joan Miró (1893-), 1924-25. Albright Art Gallery, Buffalo. Spanish.

HARLEQUIN'S FAMILY, THE: Pablo Picasso (1881-), 1905. Lewisohn Collection. French.

HARP OF THE WINDS, THE: Homer Martin (1836-1897), 1895. Metropolitan Museum of Art, New York. American.

HARVEST, THE: Vincent van Gogh (1853-1890), 1888. V. W. van Gogh Collection, Municipal Museum, Amsterdam. French.

HARVESTERS, THE: Pieter Bruegel the Elder (c. 1570-1569), 1565. Metropolitan Museum of Art, New York. Flemish.

HARVEST WAGON, THE: Thomas Gainsborough (1727-1788), 1784. Art Gallery of Toronto. English.

HAY FACTORY, GONESSE: Maurice Utrillo (1883-1955), 1914. Perls Galleries, New York. French.

HAYMAKING: Cuno Amiet (1868-), 1940. Owned by artist. Swiss.

HAYMARKET, THE: John Sloan (1871-1951), 1907. Brooklyn Museum. American.

HAYSTACKS: Claude Monet (1840-1926), 1891. Boston Museum of Fine Arts. French.

HAY WAIN, THE: John Constable (1776-1837). National Gallery of Art, London. English.

HAYWAIN, THE (A TRIPTYCH: LEFT SHUTTER, THE GARDEN OF EDEN; CENTER PANEL, THE HAYWAIN; RIGHT SHUTTER, THE TOWER OF HELL): Hieronymus Bosch (c. 1460-1516). Prado, Madrid. Dutch.

HEAD (FEMME AU NEZ EN QUART DE BRIE): Pablo Picasso (1881-), 1907. E.L.T. Messens. French.

HEADLESS HORSE WHO WANTS TO JUMP: Yasuo Kuniyoshi (1893-1953), 1945. Museum of Cranbrook Academy of Art. American.

HEAD OF A GIRL: Jan Vermeer (1632-1675). Maurithuis, The Hague. Dutch.

HEAD OF A WOMAN: Joan Miró (1893-), 1938. Pierre Matisse Gallery, New York. Spanish.

HEAD OF BORIS BLAI: Franklin C. Watkins (1894-), 1937. Phillips Memorial Gallery, Washington, D.C. American.

HEAD OF THE MOTHER OF THE ARTIST: Alberto Giacometti (1901-), 1947. Owned by artist. Italian.

HEAD OF THE SAVIOR: Leonardo da Vinci (1452-1519). Brera, Milan. Italian.

HEART OF THE ANDES: Frederick Edwin Church (1826-1900), 1859. Metropolitan Museum of Art, New York. American.

HEATAGE: David Hare (1917-), 1944. owned by artist. American.

HENRY VIII: Hans Holbein the Younger (1497-1543). Althorp Park. German.

HERCULES AND NESSUS: (Antonio) Pollaiuolo (1429?-1498), 1473. Gallery of Fine Arts, New Haven. Florentine.

HESTER STREET: George Luks (1867-1933), 1905. Brooklyn Museum. American.

HIDALGO Y COSTILLA: José Clemente Orozco (1883-1949). Government Palace, Guadalajara. Mexican.

HIDE AND SEEK: Pavel Tchelitchew (1898-). Museum of Modern Art, New York. American.

HIERONYMUS HOLZSCHUHER: Albrecht Dürer (1471-1528). Kaiser Friedrich Museum, Berlin. German.

HIGH PEAK: Matthew Barnes (1880-), 1936. Museum of Modern Art, New York. American.

HIGH YALLER: Reginald Marsh (1898-1954), 1934. Mrs. John S. Sheppard, New York. American.

HINA MARURU: FEAST OF HINA (GODDESS OF THE MOON): Paul Gauguin (1848-1903), 1893. Privately owned. French.

HINA TE FATOU: THE MOON AND THE EARTH: Paul Gauguin (1848-1903), 1893. Privately owned. French.

HISPANO-AMERICA: José Clemente Orozco (1883-), 1932-34. Baker Memorial Library, Dartmouth College. Mexican.

HOGARTH'S SERVANTS: William Hogarth (1697-1764). National Gallery, London. English.

HOGS KILLING RATTLESNAKE: John Steuart Curry (1897-1946), 1930. Art Institute of Chicago. American.

HOLY FAMILY: Michelangelo Buonarotti (1475-1564). Uffizi Gallery, Florence. Florentine.

HOLY FAMILY: Raphael (Raffaello Santi) (1483-1520). Hermitage, Leningrad. Umbrian.

HOLY FAMILY, THE: Rembrandt van Rijn (1606-1669), 1640. Louvre, Paris. Dutch.

HOLY FAMILY: Leonardo da Vinci (1452-1519), c. 1506. Hermitage, Leningrad. Florentine.

HOLY FAMILY OF FRANCIS I: Raphael (Raffaello Santi) (1483-1520), 1518. (executed by Giulio Romano). Louvre, Paris. Umbrian.

HOLY MOUNTAIN II: Horace Pippin (1888-1946), 1944. Edward A. Bragaline, New York. American.

HOLY ONE, THE: Paul Klee (1879-1940), 1921. Madame Galka E. Scheyer. Swiss.

HOMAGE TO DELACROIX: Ignace Fantin-Latour (1836-1904), 1864. Louvre, Paris. French.

HOMAGE TO RICHARD I, DUKE OF NORMANDY: Georges Mathieu (1921-), 1954. Richard B. Baker, New York. French.

HONORABLE MRS. GRAHAM, THE: Thomas Gainsborough (1727-1788), 1775. National Gallery of Scotland, Edinburgh. English.

HOPSCOTCH: Loren MacIver (1909-), 1940. Museum of Modern Art, New York. American.

HORSE AND RIDER: Anthony Van Dyck (1599-1641). Metropolitan Museum of Art, New York. Flemish.

HORSE FAIR, THE: Rosa Bonheur (1822-1899), 1853-55. Metropolitan Museum of Art, New York. French.

HORSES: Giorgio di Chirico (1888-), 1927. Miss Mary Hoyt Wiborg, New York. French (born in Greece).

HORSE'S HEAD: Pablo Picasso (1881-), 1937. Owned by artist. French.

HORSEWOMAN DE HAUTE ÉCOLE: Jacques Villon (1875-), 1950. Privately owned, Paris. French.

HÔTEL DE VILLE QUAY: Maurice Utrillo (1883-1955), 1912. Privately owned, Paris. French.

HOUSE BY THE RAILROAD: Edward Hopper (1882-   ), 1925. Museum of Modern Art, New York. American.
HOUSE OF CARDS, THE: Jean Baptiste Chardin (1699-1779). Mellon Collection of the National Gallery of Art, Washington, D.C. French.
HOUSE OF MYSTERY: Charles Burchfield (1893-   ), 1924. Art Institute of Chicago. American.
HOUSE OF VINCENT, THE: Vincent van Gogh (1853-1890); 1888. V. W. van Gogh Collection, Municipal Museum, Amsterdam. French.
HUMANE LANDSCAPE, THE: Georges Rouault (1871-), 1928. Mr. and Mrs. Nate B. Spingold, New York. French.
HUNTER, THE (CATALAN LANDSCAPE): See Catalan Landscape.
HUNTING DOGS: Gustave Courbet (1819-1877). Metropolitan Museum of Art, New York. French.
HUNTSMEN'S RETURN, THE: Pieter Bruegel the Elder (c .1520-1569), 1565. Gemaldegalerie, Vienna. Flemish.
I AND MY VILLAGE: Marc Chagall (1887-   ). Museum of Modern Art, New York. Russian.
IA ORANA MARIA: HAIL MARY: Paul Gauguin (1848-1903), 1891. A. Lewisohn Collection. French.
ICARUS: Johannes Molzahn (1892-), 1943. Owned by· artist. German (lives in U.S.A.).
IDEAL HEAD: Elihu Vedder (1836-1923), 1872. Privately owned, Detroit. American.
IDOL, THE: Paul Gauguin (1848-1903). Privately owned. French.
ILLUMINED PLEASURES: Salvador Dali (1904-   ), 1929. Privately owned. Spanish (lives in U.S.A.).
IMPROVISATION: Carl Robert Holty (1900-   ), 1942. Owned by artist. German (lives in U.S.A.).
IMPROVISATION: Wassily Kandinsky (1866-1944), 1915. Museum of Modern Art, New York. German.
IMPROVISATION NO. 30: Wassily Kandinsky (1866-1944). Art Institute, Chicago. German.
INCANTATION: Charles Sheeler (1883-), 1946. Brooklyn Museum. American.
INDIAN CHIEF SATURIBA AND THE FRENCH LEADER LAUDONNIÈRE AT RIBAUT'S COLUMN, THE: Jacques Le Moyne de Morgues (d. 1588), after 1562. James Hazen Hyde, New York. French.
INFANTA MARGARETA THERESA: Diego Velasquez (1599-1660), 1659. Gemaldegalerie, Vienna. Spanish.
INFANTA MARGARETA TERESA: Diego Velasquez (1599-1660), c. 1654. Prado, Madrid. Spanish.
INFANTA MARIA TERESA: Diego Velasquez (1599-1660), 1659. Gemaldegalerie, Vienna. rie, Vienna. Spanish.
INFANTA MARIA TERESA: Diego Velasuqez (1599-1660), c. 1651. Kunsthistorisches Museum, Vienna. Spanish.
INFANTE PHILIP PROSPER: Diego Velas-Z (1599-1660), 1659. Gemaldegalerie, Vienna. Spanish.
INN, THE: Jean Baptiste Camille Corot (1796-1875), 1831. Wellesley College Museum. French.
IN NATURE'S WONDERLAND: Thomas Doughty (1793-1856), 1835. Detroit Institute of Arts. American.
IN SPITE OF EVERYTHING, SPRING: Jacqueline Lamba (1910-   ), 1942. Norlyst Gallery, New York. French (lives in U.S.A.).
INSTITUTION OF THE ROSARY: Giovanni Battista Tiepolo (1696-1770). Santa Maria del Rosario, Venice. Italian.

INSTITUTION OF THE ROSARY: Giovanni Battista Tiepolo (1696-1770). Gesuati, Venice. Italian.
INTERIOR: Raoul Dufy (1877-1953), 1928. Privately owned, New York. French.
INTERIOR: Henri Matisse (1869-1954), Baltimore Museum. French.
INTERIOR OF A RESTAURANT: Vincent van Gogh (1853-1890), 1886-88. Kröller-Müller State Museum, Otterlo, Holland. French.
INTERIOR WITH A BOY: Pierre Bonnard (1867-1947), 1925. Phillips Memorial Gallery, Washington, D.C. French.
INTERIOR WITH A GIRL DRAWING: Pablo Picasso (1881-), 1935. Mrs. Meric Callery. French.
INTERNAL MOTION OF A FLUID: Gerome Kamrowski (1914-), 1943. Owned by artist. American.
INTERRUPTED SLEEP, THE: François Boucher (1703-1770), 1750. Metropolitan Museum of Art, New York. French.
IN THE COUNTRY: Leon Kroll (1884-), 1916. Detroit Institute of Art. American.
IN THE GRASS: Paul Klee (1879-1940), 1930. Sidney Janis Fallery, New York. Swiss.
INTRODUCING JOHN L. SULLIVAN: George Bellows (1882-1925). Mr. and Mrs. John Hay Whitney, New York. American.
IO: Corregio (Allegri da) (1494-1534), c. 1530. Gemaldegalerie, Vienna. Lombard.
IRISES, THE: Vincent van Gogh (1853-1890), 1890. V. W. van Gogh Collection, Municipal Museum, Amsterdam. French.
ISABELLA OF PORTUGAL: Titian (Tiziano Vecellio) (1480?-1576), Prado, Madrid. Venetian.
I SAW THE FIGURE FIVE IN GOLD: Charles Demuth (1883-1939), 1921. Metropolitan Museum of Art, New York. American.
ISLAND OF LA GRANDE-JATTE, THE: Alfred Sisley (1839-1899), 1873. Louvre, Paris. French.
ISOLATIONIST: William Gropper (1897-   ). Mr. and Mrs. Robert K. Rosenberg, White Plains, New York. American.
ITALIAN COMMEDIANS: Jean Antoine Watteau (1684-1721). Samuel H. Kress Collection of the National Gallery of Art, Washington, D.C. French.
ITALIAN LANDSCAPE: Jean Baptiste Camille Corot (1796-1875). Metropolitan Museum of Art, New York. French.
IVY, THE: Vincent van Gogh (1853-1890), 1890. V. W. van Gogh Collection, Municipal Museum, Amsterdam. French.
JACOB FOWLE: John Singleton Copley (1738-1815), c. 1763. Corcoran Gallery of Art, Washington, D.C. American.
JACOB HOUSEMAN: John Wesley Jarvis (1780-1840), 1809. Detroit Institute of Arts. American.
JACOB'S STRUGGLE WITH THE ANGEL: Paul Gauguin (1848-1903), 1889. Privately owned. French.
JAMES PEALE (THE LAMPLIGHT PORTRAIT): Charles Willson Peale (1741-1827), 1822. Detroit Institute of Arts. American.
JAMES STUART, DUKE OF RICHMOND AND LENNOX: Anthony Van Dyck (1599-1641). Metropolitan Museum of Art, New York Flemish.
JAMES TISSOT (1836-1902): Edgar Degas (1834-1917), c. 1868. Metropolitan Museum of Art, New York. French.
JANE SEYMOUR: Hans Holbein, the Younger (1497-1543), 1536-37. Gemaldegalerie, Vienna. German.
JEREMIAH: Michelangelo Buonarroti (1475-

1564), 1508-12. Detail, Sistine Chapel, Rome. Florentine.

JESTER, THE: Paul Klee (1879-1940), 1928. Privately owned. Swiss.

JEWISH WEDDING: Marc Chagall (1887-). Privately owned, New York. French.

JOHAN: Albert Pinkham Ryder (1847-1917). National Collection of Fine Arts, Smithsonian Institute, Washington, D.C. American.

JOHN ARNOLFINI AND HIS WIFE: Jan van Eyck (1385?-1441), 1434. National Gallery, London. Flemish.

JOHN, DUKE OF SAXONY: Lucas Cranach the Elder (1472-1553). Metropolitan Museum of Art, New York. German.

JOHN FREAKE: The Freake Limner, unknown artist (c. 1670-75), c. 1674. privately owned. American.

JOHN HANCOCK: John Singleton Copley (1738-1815). Boston Museum of Fine Arts. American.

JOHN WHEELWRIGHT(?): John Foster (1648-1681), 1677. Boston State House. American.

JOSEPH HENRI ALTES (1826-1895): Edgar Degas (1834-1917), 1868. Metropolitan Museum of Art, New York. French.

JOURNEY: Morris Graves (1910-), 1944. Benjamin Baldwin, New York. American.

JOURNEY OF THE MAGI: Sassetta (Stefano di Giovanni) (1392-1450). Metropolitan Museum of Art, New York. Sienese.

JOY OF LIFE: Henri Matisse (1869-1954), 1906. Barnes Foundation, Merion, Penn. French.

JUDGMENT OF JUPITER, THE: Samuel F. B. Morse (1791-1872), 1814. Privately owned. American.

JUDGMENT OF PARIS, THE: Lucas Cranach the Elder (1472-1553). Metropolitan Museum of Art, New York. German.

JUDGMENT OF PARIS, THE: Peter Paul Rubens (1577-1640). National Gallery of Art, London. Flemish.

JUDITH: Titian (Tiziano Vecellio) (1480?-1576), 1560-1570. Detroit Institute of Art. Venetian.

JUDITH BEHEADING HOLOFERNES: Caravaggio (Michelangelo Merisi) (1573-1610), c. 1599. Vincenzo Coppi Collection, Rome. Italian.

JUDITH WITH THE HEAD OF HOLOFERNES: Lucas Cranach the Elder (1472-1553). Metropolitan Museum of Art, New York. German.

JULY HAY: Thomas Benton (1889-), 1943. Metropolitan Museum of Art, New York. American.

JUPITER AND ANTIOPE: Correggio (1494-1534), 1521-22. Louvre, Paris. Lombard.

JUPITER AND ANTIOPE: Jean Antoine Watteau (1684-1721). Louvre, Paris. French.

KEY WEST BEACH: Peter Blume (1906-), 1940. James Thrall Soby. American.

KINDRED SPIRITS (WILLIAM CULLEN BRYANT AND THOMAS COLE): Asher B. Durand (1796-1886), 1849. New York Public Library. American.

KINETIC LIGHT: Robert J. Wolff (1905-), 1941. Owned by artist. American.

KINGDOM OF FLORA: Nicholas Poussin (1594-1665), c. 1635. Dresden Museum. French.

KING HENRY VIII: Hans Holbein the Younger (1497-1543), 1539. Corsini Gallery, Rome. German.

LACE MAKER, THE: Jan Vermeer (1632-1675), c. 1665. Louvre, Paris. Dutch.

LADY AND HER SON, A: John Vanderlyn (1775-1852), 1800. Senate House Museum, Kingston, New York. American.

LADY IN A RIDING HABIT — L'AMAZONE:

Gustave Courbet (1819-1877). Metropolitan Museum of Art, New York. French.

LADY WEIGHING GOLD: Jan Vermeer (1632-1675). National Gallery of Art, Washington, D.C. Dutch.

LADY WITH A FAN, A: Diego Velasquez (1599-1660), c. 1640. Wallace Collection, London. Spanish.

LADY WRITING A LETTER WITH HER MAID, A: Jan Vermeer (1632-1675). Sir Alfred Beit, London. Dutch.

LAFAYETTE: See Marquis de Lafayette.

LAIR OF THE SEA SERPENT, THE: Elihu Vedder (1836-1923), 1864. Boston Museum of Fine Arts. American.

LAKE ALBANO AND CASTEL GANDOLFO: Jean Baptiste Camille Corot (1796-1875). Metropolitan Museum of Art, New York. French.

LAKE GENEVA: Oskar Kokoschka (1886-). Paul Geier Collection, Cincinnati. German.

LANCES, THE: See Surrender of Breda, The.

LAND NEAR A SMALL TOWN, A: Alfred Sisley (1839-1899). Kunsthalle, Bremen. French.

LAND OF COCKAIGNE, THE: Pieter Bruegel the Elder (c. 1520-1569), 1567. Alte Pinakothek, Munich. Flemish.

LANDSCAPE: Gustave Courbet (1819-1877). Metropolitan Museum of Art, New York, French.

LANDSCAPE: Charles François Daubigny (1817-1878). Metropolitan Museum of Art, New York. French.

LANDSCAPE: Emile Othon Friesz (1879-1949). Samuel S. White, Philadelphia. French.

LANDSCAPE: André Dunoyer de Segonzac (1885-), 1927. Privately owned, New York. French.

LANDSCAPE: Chaim Soutine (1884-1943). Privately owned, New York. French (born in Lithuania).

LANDSCAPE AT ARLES NEAR THE ALYSCAMPS: Paul Gauguin (1848-1903), 1888. Louvre, Paris. French.

LANDSCAPE AT IDEN: Paul Nash (1889-1946), 1928. Tate Gallery, London. English.

LANDSCAPE: LE POULDU: Paul Gauguin (1848-1903), 1891. Durand-Ruel Collection. French.

LANDSCAPE NEAR CHICAGO: Aaron Bohrod (1907-), 1934. Whitney Museum of American Art, New York. American.

LANDSCAPE WITH A LEAF: Leopold Survage (1879-), 1928. Chester H. Johnson Gallery, Chicago. French (born in Russia).

LANDSCAPE WITH ROCKS: John Piper (1903-), 1946. Sir Kenneth Clark, London. English.

LANDSCAPE WITH STORKS: Charles François Daubigny (1817-1878), 1864. Metropolitan Museum of Art, New York. French.

LANDSCAPE WITH TREE TRUNK: Thomas Cole (1801-1842), c. 1827. Museum of Art, Rhode Island School of Design, Providence. American.

LANDSCAPE WITH VIADUCT: Paul Cézanne (1839-1906). Metropolitan Museum of Art, New York. French.

LAUNDRESS, THE: Henri de Toulouse-Lautrec (1864-1901), 1889. Collection Dortue, Le Vesinet, France. French.

LANE THROUGH THE TREES, A: Jean Baptiste Camille Corot (1796-1875). Metropolitan Museum of Art, New York. French.

LAPIN AGILE: Maurice Utrillo (1883-1955), c. 1930. Fine Arts Associates, New York. French.

LAPIN AGILE, LE: Maurice Utrillo (1883-1955). Calvet Museum, Avignon. French.

LARGE SELF-PORTRAIT, THE: Rembrandt

van Rijn (1606-1669), 1652. Gemaldegalerie, Vienna. Dutch.

LARGE VINE PERGOLA: Graham Sutherland (1903-), 1948. National Gallery of Canada, Ottowa. English.

LAST COMMUNION OF SAINT JEROME, THE: Sandro Botticelli (Alessandro Filipepi) (1444?-1510). Metropolitan Museum of Art, New York. Florentine.

LAST JUDGMENT: Michelangelo Buonarroti (1475-1564), 1535-41. Sistine Chapel, Vatican. Florentine.

LAST OF NEW ENGLAND, THE BEGINNING OF NEW MEXICO: Marsden Hartley (1877-1943), 1918. Art Institute of Chicago. American.

LAST OF OLD WESTMINSTER, THE: James McNeill Whistler (1834-1903), 1862. Boston Museum of Fine Arts. American.

LAST OF THE BUFFALO, THE: Albert Bierstadt (1830-1902). Corcoran Gallery of Art, Washington, D.C. American.

LAST SUPPER, THE: Titian (Tiziano Vecellio) (1480?-1576), 1564. Monastery of St. Lawrence, El Escorial, Spain. Venetian.

LAST SUPPER, THE: Leonardo da Vinci (1452-1519), 1497. Sta. Maria delle Grazie, Milan. Florentine.

LAUNDRESS, THE: Honoré Daumier (1808-1879). Metropolitan Museum of Art, New York. French.

LAURA DE DIANTI (ALLEGORY): Titian (Tiziano Vecellio) (1480?-1576). Louvre, Paris. Venetian.

LAVINIA, TITIAN'S DAUGHTER: Titian (Tiziano Vecellio) (1480?-1576), c. 1565. Dresden Gallery. Venetian.

LEAPING HORSE, THE: John Constable (1776-1837), 1825. Royal Academy, London. English.

LEISURE: Fernand Léger (1881-1955), 1944-49. Musée National d'Art Moderne, Paris. French.

LEMONS IN A BASKET: Vincent van Gogh (1853-1890), 1888. Kröller-Müller State Museum, Otterlo, Holland. French.

LETTER, THE: Jean Baptiste Camille Corot (1796-1875). Metropolitan Museum of Art, New York. French.

LIBERTY LEADING THE PEOPLE: Eugène Delacroix (1799-1863). Louvre, Paris. French.

LIGHTHOUSE, THE: Marsden Hartley (1877-1943), 1940-41. William A. M. Burden. American.

LIGHT SNOW AND HIGH WATER: Lee Gatch (1902-), 1942. Willard Gallery, New York. American.

LILY AND THE SPARROWS: Philip Evergood (1901-), 1939. Whitney Museum of American Art, New York. American.

LILY LILETH: Dante Gabriel Rossetti (1828-1882), 1867. Metropolitan Museum of Art, New York. English.

LION AND GLADIATORS: Giorgio di Chirico (1888-), 1927. Detroit Institute of Arts. French (born in Greece).

LISTEN TO LIVING: Matta (Matta Echaurren) (1912-), 1941. Museum of Modern Art, New York. Chilean.

LITTLE CIRCLES, NO. 555: Wassily Kandinsky (1866-1944), 1935. Guggenheim Museum, New York. German.

LITTLE GARDENS ON MONTMARTRE: Vincent van Gogh (1853-1890), 1886-88. V. W. van Gogh Collection, Municipal Museum, Amsterdam. French.

LITTLE GIRL WITH A DOLL: Pablo Picasso (1881-), 1938. Owned by artist. French.

LITTLE-KNOWN BIRD OF THE INNER EYE: Morris Graves (1910-), 1941. Museum of Modern Art, New York. American.

LITTLE MADONNA, THE: George Luks

(1867-1933), 1907. Addison Gallery of American Art. American.

LITTLE WHITE GIRL, THE: James McNeill Whistler (1834-1903), 1864. National Gallery, London. American.

LIVER IS THE COXCOMB, THE: Arshile Gorky (1904-1948), 1944. American.

LOGE, THE: Pierre Auguste Renoir (1841-1919). Courtauld Institute, London. French.

LONG BILL, THE: James Henry Beard (1812-1893). Cincinnati Art Museum. American.

LONG BRANCH, NEW JERSEY: Winslow Homer (1836-1910), 1869. Boston Museum of Fine Arts. American.

LONG ISLAND FARMHOUSES: William Sidney Mount (1807-1868), c. 1855. Metropolitan Museum, New York. American.

LOOKING EAST FROM DENNY HILL: Ralph Earl (1751-1801), 1801. Worcester Art Museum, Worcester, Mass. American.

LOOKING NORTH TO KINGSTON: Thomas Chambers (act. 1835-1855). Smith College Museum of Art. American.

LOOM, THE: Vincent van Gogh (1853-1890) 1884. V. W. van Gogh Collection, Municipal Museum, Amsterdam. French.

LOUISIANA RICE FIELDS: Thomas H. Benton (1889-), 1928. Brooklyn Museum. American.

LOVE LETTERS, THE: Jean Honoré Fragonard (1732-1806). Metropolitan Museum of Art, New York. French.

LOVESICK MAIDEN, THE: Jan Steen (c. 1626-1679), c. 1655. Metropolitan Museum of Art, New York. Dutch.

LOWER MANHATTAN: John Marin (1870-1953), 1920. Philip L. Goodwin. American.

LUCAS VAN UFFEL (d. 1637): Anthony Van Dyck (1599-1641). Metropolitan Museum of Art, New York. Flemish.

LUCRETIA AND TARQUIN: Titian (Tiziano Vecellio) (1480?-1576), c. 1560-70. Akademie der Bildenden Kunste, Vienna. Venetian.

LUCRETIA AND TARQUIN: Titian (Tiziano Vecellio) (1480 -1576), c. 1570. Fitzwilliam Museum, Cambridge. Italian.

LUNCHEON ON THE GRASS, THE: Édouard Manet (1832-1883), 1863. Louvre, Paris. French.

LUTE-PLAYER: Caravaggio (Michelangelo Merisi) (1573-1610), 1595-96. Uffizi Gallery, Florence. Italian.

MA: Paul Klee (1879-1940), 1922. Bernard Koehler, Berlin. Swiss.

McSORLEY'S BACK ROOM: John Sloan (1871-1951), 1912. Detroit Institute of Art. American.

MADAME BERTHE BADY: Henri de Toulouse-Lautrec (1864-1901), 1897. Museum of Albi, France. French.

MADAME CHARDIN WITH LILACS AND EGGS: Jean Baptiste Chardin (1699-1779). Metropolitan Museum of Art, New York. French.

MADAME GOBILLARD-MORISOT: Edgar Degas (1834-1917), 1869. Metropolitan Museum of Art, New York. French.

MADAME MARIE CROCQ: Gustave Courbet (1819-1877). Metropolitan Museum of Art, New York. French.

MADAME MOITESSIER, SEATED: Jean Auguste Dominique Ingres (1780-1867), 1844-56. National Gallery, London. French.

MADAME X: John Singer Sargent (1856-1925), 1884. Metropolitan Museum of Art, New York. American.

MLLE. MARIE DIHAU: Edgar Degas (1834-1917), 1872. Metropolitan Museum of Art, New York. French.

MADONNA ADORING THE SLEEPING CHILD: Giovanni Bellini (c. 1430-1516). Metropolitan Museum of Art, New York. Venetian.

MADONNA AND CHILD: Giovanni Bellini (c. 1430-1516). Metropolitan Museum of Art, New York. Venetian.

MADONNA AND CHILD: Bramantino (Bartolommeo Suardi) (act. 1490-1536). Metropolitan Museum of Art, New York. Milanese.

MADONNA AND CHILD: Filippo Lippi (1457?-1505?). New York Historical Society. Florentine.

MADONNA AND CHILD: Hans Memling (1430?-1494), 1487. Hospital of St. John, Bruges. Flemish.

MADONNA AND CHILD: Giovanni da Paolo (1402?-1482?), 1454. Metropolitan Museum of Art, New York. Sienese.

MADONNA AND CHILD ENTHRONED: Fra Angelico (1387-1455), c. 1433. M. Knoedler and Co., New York. Florentine.

MADONNA AND CHILD ENTHRONED WITH ANGELS: Jacobello del Fiore (act. 1385-1439). Fogg Art Museum, Harvard University, Cambridge, Mass. Venetian.

MADONNA AND CHILD ENTHRONED WITH ANGELS: Niccolo da Foligno (c. 1430-1502), c. 1468. Fogg Art Museum, Harvard University, Cambridge, Mass. Umbrian.

MADONNA AND CHILD IN THE ROSE GARDEN: Stefano da Verona (c. 1375-1438?). Worcester Art Museum, Worcester, Mass. Veronese.

MADONNA AND CHILD WITH A MUSICIAN ANGEL: Niccolo Rondinelli (act. 1480-c. 1520), c. 1510-20. High Museum of Art, Atlanta, Georgia. Venetian.

MADONNA AND CHILD WITH ANGELS: Taddeo di Bartolo (c. 1362-1422), 1418. Fogg Art Museum, Harvard University, Cambridge, Mass. Sienese.

MADONNA AND CHILD WITH ANGELS: Guidoccio Cozzarelli (1450?-1499). Samuel H. Kress Collection, New York. Sienese.

MADONNA AND CHILD WITH ANGELS: Vittorio Crivelli (act. 1481-1501), 1489. Philadelphia Museum of Art. Venetian.

MADONNA AND CHILD WITH ANGELS: Giovanni da Ponte (1385-1437). M. H. de Young Memorial Museum, San Francisco. Florentine. (Also known as Giovanni da Santo Stefano, or Giovanni di Marco).

MADONNA AND CHILD WITH ANGELS AND CHERUBIM: Matteo de Giovanni (c. 1430-1495), c. 1475-80. National Gallery of Art, Washington, D.C. Sienese.

MADONNA AND CHILD WITH SAINTS: Neroccio de' Landi (1447-1500), c. 1490. National Gallery of Art, Washington, D.C. Sienese.

MADONNA AND CHILD WITH SAINTS AND ANGELS: Matteo de Giovanni (c. 1430-1495), c. 1470-75. National Gallery of Art, Washington, D.C. Sienese.

MADONNA AND CHILD WITH SAINTS PETER, MARGARET, LUCY, AND JOHN THE BAPTIST: Giovanni Bellini (c. 1430-1516). Metropolitan Museum of Art, New York. Venetian.

MADONNA DEI PALAFRENIERI, THE: Caravaggio (Michelangelo Merisi) (1573-1610), 1605-06. Borghese, Rome. Italian.

MADONNA DEL FOLIGNO: Raphael (Raffaello Santi) (1483-1520), 1512. Vatican Gallery, Rome. Umbrian.

MADONNA DEL GRANDUCA: Raphael (Raffaello Santi) (1483-1520), c. 1505. Pitti Gallery, Florence. Umbrian.

MADONNA DE LORETTO, THE: Caravaggio (Michelangelo Merisi) (1573-1610), c. 1604. Sant' Agostino, Rome. Italian.

MADONNA DEL ROSARIO, THE: Caravaggio (Michelangelo Merisi) (1573-1610), c. 1605. Kunsthistorisches Museum, Vienna. Italian.

MADONNA IN ADORATION, THE: Cosimo Rosselli (1439-1507). Philbrook Art Center, Tulsa, Okla. Florentine.

MADONNA OF CHANCELLOR ROLIN: Jan van Eyck (1370?-1440?). Louvre, Paris. Flemish.

MADONNA OF MAYOR MEYER: Hans Holbein the Younger (1497-1543). Darmstadt Museum. German.

MADONNA OF ST. JEROME: Correggio (Allegri da) (1494-1534), c. 1523. Parma Gallery. Lombard.

MADONNA OF THE FISH: Raphael (Raffaello Santi) (1483-1520), 1513. Prado, Madrid. Umbrian.

MADONNA OF THE GOLDFINCH: Raphael (Raffaello Santi) (1483-1520), c. 1506. Uffizi Gallery, Florence. Umbrian.

MADONNA OF THE LAKE, THE: Giovanni Bellini (1435?-1516), c. 1487-88. Uffizi Gallery, Florence. Venetian.

MADONNA OF THE MAGNIFICAT: Sandro Botticelli (Alessandro Filipepi) (1444?-1510). Uffizi Gallery, Florence. Florentine.

MADONNA OF THE MEADOW: Raphael (Raffaello Santi) (1483-1520), 1505. Vienna. Umbrian.

MADONNA OF THE ROCKS: Leonardo da Vinci (1452-1519). Louvre, Paris. Florentine.

MADONNA WITH THE CHERRIES, THE: Titian (Tiziano Vecellio) (1480?-1576), c. 1515. Gemaldegalerie, Vienna. Venetian.

MADONNA WITH THE RABBIT: Titian (Tiziano Vecellio) (1480?-1576), c. 1530. Louvre, Paris. Venetian.

MADONNA WITH THE RED APPLE: See Madonna and Child (Memling).

MAGDALENA GANSEVOORT: Artist unknown, early 18th cent. Henry Francis du Pont Winterthur Museum, Winterthur, Delaware. American.

MAGNOLIAS: Stanley Spencer (1892-), 1938. Malcolm MacDonald, London. English.

MAIDS OF HONOR, THE: Diego Velasquez (1599-1660), c. 1656. Prado, Madrid. Spanish.

MAJESTY, THE: Duccio di Buoninsegna (1260?-1319?), 1308-11. Opera del Duomo, Siena. Sienese.

MA JOLIE (WOMAN WITH A GUITAR): Pablo Picasso (1881-), 1911-12. Museum of Modern Art, New York. French.

MAN: Marcel Gromaire (1892-), 1928. Privately owned, New York. French.

MANCHESTER VALLEY: Joseph Pickett (1848-1918), 1914?-18. Museum of Modern Art, New York. American.

MAN AND MACHINERY: Diego Rivera (1886-1957), c. 1933. Detroit Institute of Art. Mexican.

MAN IN A BLUE CAP: Paul Cézanne (1839-1906). Metropolitan Museum of Art, New York. French.

MAN IN THE CAFÉ: Juan Gris (1887-1927), 1912. Walter Arensberg Collection, Philadelphia Museum, of Art. Spanish.

MAN OF OPINION, A: George Grosz (1893-), 1928. Walker Galleries, New York. German.

MANOT, THE DANCER: André Derain (1880-1954), 1928. Phillips Memorial Gallery, Washington, D.C. French.

MANTLE, THE: Georges Braque (1881-), 1929. Paul Rosenberg and Co., New York. French.

MAN WITH A BEER KEG, A: Frans Hals (1580?-1666), c. 1635. Henry Reichhold Collection, Detroit. Dutch.

MAN WITH A GUITAR: Georges Braque (1882-), 1911. Museum of Modern Art, New York. French.

MAN WITH A ROSARY: Lucas Cranach the Elder (1472-1553). Metropolitan Museum of Art, New York. German.

MAN WITH A STRAW HAT — PORTRAIT OF BOYER: Paul Cézanne (1839-1906). Metropolitan Museum of Art, New York. French.

MAN WITH THE GLOVE, THE: Titian (Tiziano Vecellio) (1480?-1576), c. 1520. Louvre, Paris. Venetian.

MAN WITH THE HOE, THE: Jean-François Millet (1814-1875), 1863. San Francisco Museum. French.

MAN WITH GUITAR: Pablo Picasso (1881-), 1912. Walter Arensberg Collection, Philadelphia Museum of Fine Arts. French.

MAN WITH GUITAR: Pablo Picasso (1881-), 1913. Museum of Modern Art, New York. French.

MAN WITH ONE EYE: Vincent van Gogh (1853-1890), 1888. V. W. van Gogh Collection, Municipal Museum, Amsterdam. French.

MAN WITH THE LEATHER BELT: Gustave Courbet (1819-1877). Louvre, Paris. French.

MAN WITH THE WALKING STICK, THE: Paul Gauguin (1848-1903), c. 1893. Musée des Beaux-Arts, Paris. French.

MAN WITH VIOLIN: Pablo Picasso (1881-), 1910. Walter Arensberg Collection, Philadelphia Museum of Art. French.

MARCHESA DURAZZO, THE: Anthony Van Dyck (1599-1641). Metropolitan Museum of Art, New York. Flemish.

MARGARET BONI PLAYS THE RECORDER: Julian Levi (1900-), 1940.

MARIA TAYLOR BYRD: Charles Bridges (act. 1735-40). Metropolitan Museum of Art, New York. American.

MARINE — THE WATERSPOUT: Gustave Courbet (1819-1877), 1876. Metropolitan Museum of Art, New York. French.

MARITIME: Karl Knaths (1891-), 1931. Phillips Memorial Gallery, Washington, D.C. American.

MARKET AT SANARY, THE: Jean Puy (1876-), c. 1925. French.

MARKET CROSS, TREBOUL: Christopher Wood (1901-1930), 1930. Art Gallery, Buffalo. English.

MARKET PLACE (TLALTELOCO FRESCO): Diego Rivera (1886-1957), 1946-47. National Palace, Mexico City. Mexican.

MARQUESA DE PONTEJOS, THE: Francisco Goya (y Lucientes) (1746-1828). Mellon Collection of National Gallery of Art, Washington, D.C. Spanish.

MARQUIS DE LAFAYETTE: Samuel F. B. Morse (1791-1872), 1825-26. New York Art Commission, New York. American.

MARRIAGE À LA MODE, I: William Hogarth (1697-1764), 1744. Tate Gallery, London. English.

MARRIAGE AT CANA, THE: Veronese (Paolo Cagliari) (1528-1588), c. 1560. Dresden Museum, Venetian.

MARRIAGE AT CANA, THE: Veronese (Paolo Cagliari) (1528-1588), 1562-63. Louvre, Paris. Venetian.

MARRIAGE OF ISAAC AND REBECCA, THE: Claude Lorrain (1600-1682), 1647. National Gallery, London. French.

MARRIAGE OF ST. CATHERINE, THE: Giovanni Boccati (1445?-1480?), City Art Museum, St. Louis, Mo. Italian.

MARS: Diego Velasquez (1599-1660), c. 1640. Prado, Madrid. Spanish.

MARS AND VENUS: Veronese (Paolo Cagliari)

(1528-1588). Metropolitan Museum of Art, New York. Venetian.

MARTYRDOM OF ST. LAWRENCE, THE: Titian Tiziano Vecellio) (1480?-1576), c. 1550-55. Gesuiti, Venice. Venetian.

MARTYRDOM OF ST. LAWRENCE, THE: Titian (Tiziano Vecellio) (1480?-1576), c. 1550-Monastery of St. Lawrence, El Escorial, Spain. Venetian.

MARTYRDOM OF ST. MATTHEW, THE: Caravaggio (Michelangelo Merisi) (1573-1610), c. 1599-1603. San Luigi de' Francesi, Rome. Italian.

MARY AND ELIZABETH ROYALL: Iohn Singleton Copley (1738-1815), c. 1758. Boston Museum of Fine Arts. American.

MARY WARNER: Joseph Blackburn (in America 1753-1774), c. 1760. Warner House, Portsmouth, New Hampshire. American.

MASK OF FEAR: Paul Klee (1879-1940), 1932. Dr. Allan Roos. Swiss.

MASSACRE AT SCIO, THE: Eugène Delacroix (1799-1863). Louvre, Paris. French.

MASSACRE OF THE INNOCENTS: Pieter Bruegel the Elder (c. 1520-1569), 1563-66. Gemaldegalerie, Vienna. Flemish.

MASSACRE OF THE INNOCENTS, THE: Pieter Bruegel the Elder (c. 1520-1569), Kunsthistorisches Museum, Vienna. Flemish.

MATA MUA: ONCE UPON A TIME: Paul Gauguin (1848-1903), 1892. Privately owned. French.

MATER DOLOROSA: Titian (Tiziano Vecellio) (1480?-1576), 1554. Prado, Madrid. Venetian.

MATRIX OF AN UNFATHOMABLE WORLD: Boris Margo (1902-), 1942. Norlyst Gallery, New York. Russian (lives in U.S.A.).

MECHANIC, THE: Fernand Léger (1881-1955), 1920. Galerie Louis Carré, Paris. French.

MECHANICAL ELEMENTS: Fernand Léger (1881-1955), 1918-23. Privately owned, Paris. French.

MEDITATION: Benjamin Kopman (1887-), 1914. Mrs. Frederic Fairchild Sherman. American.

MEDITERRANEAN, THE: Raoul Dufy (1877-1953), 1923. Mrs. Louis S. Gimbel, Jr., New York. French.

MEDUSA: Caravaggio (Michelangelo Merisi) (1573-1610), 1596-97. Uffizi Gallery, Florence. Italian.

MEETING OF JOACHIM AND ANNA, THE: Giotto (di Bondoni) (1266-1336), c. 1305-06. Arena Chapel, Padua. Florentine.

MERCHANT'S EXCHANGE: John A. Woodside (1781-1852), 1836. Privately owned. American.

MERCURY AND ARGOS: Diego Velasquez (1599-1660), c. 1659. Prado, Madrid. Spanish.

MEXICAN VILLAGE: José Clemente Orozco (1883-1949). Detroit Institute of Art. Mexican.

MIDNIGHT RIDE OF PAUL REVERE: Grant Wood (1892-1942), 1931. Metropolitan Museum of Art, New York. American.

MIDTOWN MANHATTAN: Kurt Roesch (1905-), 1939. Metropolitan Museum of Art, New York. American.

MILITIA MUSTER, THE: David Claypoole Johnston (1799-1865), c. 1829. American Antiquarian Society, Worcester, Mass. American.

MILKMAID, THE: Jan Vermeer (1632-1675), c. 1658. Rijksmuseum, Amsterdam. Dutch.

MILKMAID OF BORDEAUX, THE: Francisco de Goya (y Lucientes) (1746-1828), 1827. Prado, Madrid. Spanish.

MILL, THE: Jakob van Ruysdael (1628-1682). Rijksmuseum, Amsterdam. Dutch.

MINERS' WIVES: Ben Shahn (1898-), 1948. Privately owned. American.

MIRACLE OF ST. MARK: Tintoretto (Jacopo Robusti) (1518-1594), 1548. Academy, Venice. Venetian.

MIRACLE OF ST. SYLVESTER, A: Il Pesellino (Francesco di Stefano). Doria-Pamphili Collection, Rome. Florentine.

MIRACLE OF THE TRUE CROSS: Giovanni Bellini (1430?-1516), 1500. Accademia, Venice. Venetian.

MIRROR, THE: Joan Miró (1893-), 1919. Pierre Matisse Gallery, New York. Spanish.

MIRROR, THE: Pablo Picasso (1881-), 1932. Owned by artist. French.

MIRROR, THE: Georges Rouault (1871-), 1906. Museum of Modern Art, Paris. French.

MR. AND MRS. THOMAS MIFFLIN: John Singleton Copley (1738-1815), 1773. Historical Society of Pennsylvania, Philadelphia. American.

MRS. ANNE POLLARD: Painter unknown, 1721. Massachusetts Historical Society, Boston. American.

MRS. CONSTANT STORRS: William Jennys (act. c. 1800-10). Pennsylvania Academy of Fine Arts, Philadelphia. American.

MRS. FREAKE AND BABY MARY: The Freak Limner (c. 1670-75), c. 1674. Privately owned. American.

MRS. JOHN EDWARDS: Joseph Badger (1708-1765), c. 1750. Boston Museum of Fine Arts. American.

MRS. RICHARD BRINSLEY SHERIDAN: Thomas Gainsborough (1727-1788). Mellon Collection of National Gallery of Art, Washington, D.C. English.

MRS. RICHARD YATES: Gilbert Stuart (1775-1828), c. 1793. Mellon Collection, National Gallery of Art, Washington, D.C. American.

MRS. SAMUEL CHANDLER: Winthrop Chandler (1747-1790). Colonel and Mrs. Edgar W. Garbisch. American.

MRS. SIDDONS: Thomas Gainsborough (1727-1788), 1784. National Gallery, London. English.

MRS. SYLVANUS BOURNE: John Singleton Copley (1738-1815), 1766. Metropolitan Museum of Art, New York. American.

MRS. THOMAS BOYLSTON: John Singleton Copley (1738-1815), 1766. Harvard University, Cambridge. American.

MIXED WEATHER: Paul Klee (1879-1940), 1929. Nierendorf Gallery, New York. Swiss.

MOCKER MOCKED, THE: Paul Klee (1879-1940), 1930. Museum of Modern Art, New York. Swiss.

MODERN CLASSIC: Charles Sheeler (1883-), 1931. Mrs. Edsel B. Ford, Detroit. American.

MODISTE, THE: Henri de Toulouse-Lautrec (1864-1901), 1900. The Museum of Albi, France. French.

MOHAWK VALLEY, THE: Alexander H. Wyant (1836-1892), 1866. Metropolitan Museum of Art, New York. American.

MONA LISA: Leonardo da Vinci (1452-1519), 1503. Louvre, Paris. Florentine.

MONASTERY: André Derain (1880-1954), 1928. Valentine Gallery, New York. French.

MONDAY MORNING: George Russell Drysdale (1912-), 1938. Metropolitan Museum of Art, New York. Australian.

MONKEY BARS: Henry Koerner (1915-), 1947. Mr. and Mrs. Robert Sherry. American.

MONOPRINT: Harry Bertoia (1915-), 1944. Owned by artist. American.

MONSIEUR SUISSE: Gustave Courbet (1819-1877). Metropolitan Museum of Art, New York. French.

MONSIEUR BOILEAU AT THE CAFÉ: Henri de Toulouse-Lautrec (1864-1901), 1893. Cleve-

land Museum of Art, Hinman B. Hurlbut Collection. French.

MONTAGNE SAINTE VICTOIRE, LA: Paul Cézanne (1839-1906), c. 1885-87. Courtauld Institute of Art, London. French.

MONTGOMERY AT SIEGE OF QUEBEC: See Death of General Montgomery at the Siege of Quebec.

MONTH OF NOVEMBER, THE: See Driving Home the Cattle.

MONTIGNY CHURCH: Maurice Utrillo (1883-1955). Privately owned, Paris. French.

MONTMARTRE: Vincent van Gogh (1853-1890), 1886-88. V. W. van Gogh Collection, Municipal Museum, Amsterdam. French.

MONTMARTRE: Maurice Utrillo (1883-1955), 1938. Schoneman Galleries, New York. French.

MOONLIGHT: Loren MacIver (1909-), 1940. American.

MOONLIGHT, HARBOURTOWN: Karl Knaths (1891-), 1940. Phillips Memorial Gallery, Washington, D.C. American.

MOONLIGHT LANDSCAPE: Washington Allston (1779-1843), 1819. Boston Museum of Fine Arts. American.

MOONLIGHT MARINE: Albert Pinkham Ryder (1847-1917). Metropolitan Museum of Art, New York. American.

MOON SONG: Darrel Austin (1907-), 1942. Edward A. Bragaline. American.

MOREAU DE SAINT-MÉRY: James Sharples (1751-1811), 1797. Metropolitan Museum of Art, New York. American.

MOTHER AND CHILD: Jean Baptiste Camille Corot (1796-1875). Metropolitan Museum of Art, New York. French.

MOTHER AND CHILD: Pablo Picasso (1881-), 1901. Maurice Werhein. French.

MOTHER AND CHILD: Pablo Picasso (1881-), 1921. French.

MOTHER AND SON: Morris Kantor (1896-), 1939. Frank K. M. Rehn Galleries. American.

MOTHER MEXICO: Diego Rivera (1886-1957), 1935. Art Institute of Chicago. Mexican.

MOULIN DE LA GALETTE: Raoul Dufy (1877-1953), 1951. Louis Bergman, New York. French.

MOULIN DE LA GALETTE, LE: Pablo Picasso (1881-), 1900. J. Thannhauser. French.

MOULIN DE LA GALETTE, LE: Pierre Auguste Renoir (1841-1919), 1876. John Hay Whitney. French.

MOUNT CALVARY, BRITTANY: Paul Gauguin (1848-1903), 1889. Musée Royal, Brussels. French.

MT. KATAHDIN, AUTUMN, NO. 1: Marsden Hartley (1877-1943), 1939-40. University of Nebraska Art Galleries, Lincoln. American.

MT. STE. VICTOIRE: Paul Cézanne (1839-1906). Phillips Collection, Washington, D.C. French.

MOUSME, LA: Vincent van Gogh (1853-1890). National Gallery of Art, Washington, D.C. French.

MOUTH OF THE SCHELDT: Jan van de Cappelle (1624?-1679), c. 1671. Metropolitan Museum of Art, New York. Dutch.

M2 430: Kurt Schwitters (1887-1948), 1922. Sidney Janis Gallery, New York. French.

MURAL FOR THE TERRACE PLAZA HOTEL IN CINCINNATI: Joan Miró (1893-), 1948. Spanish.

MUSE, THE—COMEDY: Jean Baptiste Camille Corot (1796-1875). Metropolitan Museum of Art, New York. French.

MUSIC: Janet Sobel (1894-), 1944. Owned by artist. Russian (lives in U.S.A.).

MUSICAL FORMS: Georges Braque (1882-), 1913. Walter Arensberg Collection, Philadelphia Museum of Art. French.

MUSICIAN, THE: Marc Chagall (1887-), 1912-13. French.

MUSIC IN THE RUE DE FLANDRE: James Ensor (1860-1949), 1891. Musée Royal des Beaux-Arts, Anvers, Belgium. Belgian.

MUSIC LESSON, THE: Gabriel Metsu (1629-1667), 1659. Metropolitan Museum of Art, New York. Dutch.

MUSIC MAKER: Milton Avery (1893-), 1946. American.

MUSIC MASTER, THE: Frank Duveneck (1848-1919), 1879. Mr. and Mrs. Charles F. Williams. American.

MUSIC PARTY, THE: Antoine Watteau (1684-1721), c. 1720. Wallace Collection, London. French.

MY EGYPT: Charles Demuth (1883-1935), 1925. Whitney Museum of American Art, New York. American.

MYSELF, PORTRAIT-LANDSCAPE, PRAGUE: Henri Rousseau (1844-1910), 1890. Museum of Modern Art, New York. French.

MYSTIC LAMB, THE: Anthony Van Dyck (1599-1641). St. Bavon Cathedral, Ghent. Flemish.

NARCISSUS: Caravaggio (Michelangelo Merisi) (1573-1610), 1599-1600. Galleria Nazionale D'Arte Antica, Rome. Italian.

NATHANIEL HURD: John Singleton Copley (1738-1815), c. 1765. Cleveland Museum of Art. American.

NATIVITY, THE: Albrecht Altdorfer (1480?-1538), c. 1520. German.

NATIVITY, THE: Botticelli (Alessandro Filipepi) (1444-1510), c. 1500. National Gallery, London. Florentine.

NATIVITY, THE: Piero della Francesca (1416-1492). National Gallery of Art, London. Umbrian.

NATIVITY, THE: Fra Angelico (1387-1455). Metropolitan Museum of Art, New York. Florentine.

NATIVITY, WITH DONORS AND PATRON SAINTS, THE: Gerard David (c. 1460-1523). Metropolitan Museum of Art, New York. Flemish.

NEAPOLITAN FISHERMAN: Raoul Dufy (1877-1953), 1914. Mr. and Mrs. Peter A. Rubel, New York. French.

NEW RICH, THE: Antonio Ruiz (1897-), 1941. Museum of Modern Art, New York. Mexican.

NEW YORK UNDER GASLIGHT: Stuart Davis (1894-), 1941. Herman Shulman estate. American.

NIAGARA: Frederick Edwin Church (1826-1900 1857. Corcoran Gallery, Washington, D.C. American.

NIGHT AND DAY: Max Ernst (1891-), 1942. Wright Ludington. German (lives in U.S.A.).

NIGHT CAFÉ, THE: Vincent van Gogh (1853-1890). Stephen C. Clark Collection, New York. French.

NIGHT FISHING AT ANTIBES: Pablo Picasso (1881-), 1939. Museum of Modern Art, New York. French.

NIGHTHAWKS: Edward Hopper (1882-), 1941-42. Chicago Art Institute. American.

NIGHT WATCH, THE: Rembrandt van Rijn (1606-1649), 1642. Rijksmuseum, Amsterdam. Dutch.

NIGHT WIND: Charles Burchfield (1893-), 1918. A. Conger Goodyear. American.

9:45 ACCOMMODATION, THE: Edward Lamson Henry (1841-1919), 1867. Metropolitan Museum of Art, New York. American.

NOCTURNE IN BLACK AND GOLD: THE FALLING ROCKET: James McNeill Whistler (1834-1903). Detroit Institute of Arts. American.

NO LET UP: George Grosz (1893-), 1940.

Mr. and Mrs. Frederick B. Adams, Jr., New York. American.

NOSTALGIA OF THE INFINITE: Giorgio de Chirico (1888-), 1911. Museum of Modern Art, New York. French (born Greece).

NOTRE DAME: Maurice Utrillo (1883-1955), 1913. Privately owned, Paris. French.

NOTRE-DAME DE CLIGNANCOURT: Maurice Utrillo (1883-1955), c. 1912. Mrs. Camille Dreyfus, New York. French.

NOTRE-DAME OF PARIS: Maurice Utrillo (1883-1955), 1914-15. Knoedler Galleries, New York. French.

NOVEMBER EVENING: Charles Burchfield (1898-), 1934. Metropolitan Museum of Art, New York. American.

NUDE: Moïse Kisling (1891-). Maurice Speiser, Philadelphia. French (born in Poland).

NUDE AT THE WINDOW: Morris Hirschfield (1872-1946), 1941. M. Martin Janis, Buffalo. American.

NUDE DESCENDING A STAIRCASE: Marcel Duchamp (1887-), c. 1913. Arensberg Collection, Philadelphia Museum of Art. French.

NUDE IN DOORWAY: Audrey Buller (1902-), 1933. Owned by artist. American.

NUDE MAJA, THE: Francisco de Goya (y Lucientes) (1746-1828), c. 1795-97. Prado, Madrid. Spanish.

NUDE ON A BLACK COUCH: Pablo Picasso (1881-), 1932. Mrs. Meric Callery. French.

NUDE ON A CHAIR: Vincent van Gogh (1853-1890), 1885-86. V. W. van Gogh Collection, Municipal Museum, Amsterdam. French.

NUDES: Pierre Auguste Renoir (1841-1919). Soho Gallery, London. French.

NUDES: Georges Rouault (1871-), c. 1907. Mr. and Mrs. Harry N. Abrams, New York. French.

NUDES IN THE FOREST: Fernand Léger (1881-1955), 1909-10. Rijksmuseum Kröller-Müller, Otterlo, Holland. French.

NUDE WITH A MUSICIAN: Pablo Picasso (1881-), 1942. Owned by artist. French.

NYMPH OF THE SPRING: Lucas Cranach (1472-1553), after 1537. Clarence Y. Palitz Collection, New York. German.

OAKS, THE: Théodore Rousseau (1812-1867). Louvre, Paris. French.

OARSMEN AT CHATOU: Pierre Auguste Renoir (1841-1919). National Gallery of Art, Washington, D.C. French.

OATH OF THE HORA III, THE: Jacques Louis David (1748-1825), 1785. Louvre, Paris. French.

OCEANSIDE: Evsa Model (1901-), 1943. M. Martin Janis. Russian (lives in U.S.A.).

ODALISQUE: Jean Dominique Ingres (1780-1867), 1858. Metropolitan Museum of Art, New York. French.

ODALISQUE: Henri Matisse (1869-1954). Chester Dale Collection, New York. French.

ODALISQUE WITH RAISED ARMS: Henri Matisse (1869-1954), 1923. National Gallery of Art, Washington, D.C. French.

OFFICE GIRLS: Raphael Soyer (1899-), 1936. Whitney Museum of American Art, New York. American.

OFFICER AND LAUGHING GIRL: Jan Vermeer (1632-1675). Frick Collection, New York. Dutch.

OLD BRIDGE, THE: André Derain (1880-1954), c. 1910. Chester Dale Collection, New York. French.

OLD CLOWN, THE: Georges Rouault (1871-), 1917. Edward G. Robinson. French.

OLD GUITARIST, THE: Pablo Picasso (1881-), 1903. Art Institute of Chicago. French.

OLD HOUSE OF REPRESENTATIVES, THE: Samuel F. B. Morse (1791-1872), 1821-22. Corcoran Gallery of Art, Washington, D.C. American.

OLD KING, THE: Georges Rouault (1871-   ), 1916-36. Carnegie Institute, Pittsburgh. French.

OLD MAN MOURNING: Vincent van Gogh (1853-1890), 1890. Kröller-Müller State Museum, Otterlo, Holland. French.

OLD MILL, THE: George Inness (1825-1894), 1849. Chicago Art Institute. American.

OLD MUSICIAN, THE: Édouard Manet (1832-1883), 1862. National Gallery of Art, Washington, D.C. French.

OLD NEW YORK: Louis C. Tiffany (1848-1933), c. 1878. Brooklyn Museum. American.

OLD OFFENDER, THE: Jean Louis Forain (1852-1931). Mr. and Mrs. Joseph J. Kerrigan, New York. French.

OLD QUARTER, QUEBEC: Preston Dickinson (1891-1930), 1927. Phillips Memorial Gallery, Washington, D.C. American.

OLD TOWER, THE: Vincent van Gogh (1853-1890), 1885. V. W. van Gogh Collection, Municipal Museum, Amsterdam. French.

OLD VIOLIN, THE: William Michael Harnett (1848-1892), 1886. Mr. and Mrs. Charles Finn Williams. American.

OLD WOMAN WITH A DOG: Adriaen Brouwer (1605-1638). Metropolitan Museum of Art, New York. Flemish.

OLD WOMAN WITH MASKS: James Ensor (1860-1949), 1899. R. Leten, Gand, Belgium.

OLIVE TREES: Vincent van Gogh (1853-1890), 1889. Kröller-Müller State Museum, Otterlo, Holland. French.

OLYMPIA: Édouard Manet (1832-1883), 1863. Louvre, Paris. French.

OMEN OF THE EAGLE, THE: Mark Rothko (1903-   ), 1942. Owned by artist. Russian (lives in U.S.A.).

ONE WHO UNDERSTANDS: Paul Klee (1879-1940), 1934. Leland Hayward. Swiss.

ON THE BEACH AT TROUVILLE: Eugène Boudin (1825-1898), 1863. Metropolitan Museum of Art, New York. French.

ON THE SEINE: MORNING: Charles François Daubigny (1817-1878), 1874. Metropolitan Museum of Art, New York. French.

ON THE UPPER DECK: Pablo Picasso (1881-   ), 1901. Art Institute of Chicago. French.

OPHELIA: Stanley William Hayter (1901-   ), 1936. Owned by artist. English (lives in U.S.A.).

ORCHESTRA, THE: Raoul Dufy (1877-1953), 1944. Stephen D. Heineman, Greenwich, Conn. French.

ORCHID AND HUMMING BIRD: Martin J. Heade (1819-1904). Detroit Institute of Arts. American.

ORIENTAL LION HUNT: Eugène Delacroix (1798-1863), 1834. Art Institute of Chicago. French.

ORPHEUS AND EURYDICE: Nicolas Poussin (1594-1665). Louvre, Paris. French.

OUT AT HOME: Fletcher Martin (1904-   ), 1940. Associated American Artists, New York. American.

OUTDOOR CAFÉ, STARRY NIGHT: Vincent van Gogh (1853-1890), 1888. Kröller-Müller State Museum, Otterlo, Holland. French.

OVER VITEBSK: Marc Chagall (1887-   ). Privately owned (Germany). French.

PAINTER IN HIS STUDIO, THE: Jan Vermeer (1632-1675), 1665-70. Gemaldegalerie, Vienna. Dutch.

PAINTER'S MOTHER, THE: Rembrandt van Rijn (1606-1669), 1639. Gemaldegalerie, Vienna. Dutch.

PAINTER'S TRIUMPH, THE: William S.

Mount (1807-1868), 1836. Pennsylvania Academy of the Fine Arts, Philadelphia. American.

PAINTING: Hans Hofmann (1880-   ), 1944. Owned by artist. German (lives in U.S.A.).

PALACE OF UBU ROI, THE: Georges Rouault (1871-   ). Mr. and Mrs. Ralph Coe, Cleveland. French.

PALUDES: Eugene Berman (1899-   ), 1937. M. Knoedler and Co., New York. American.

PARADE: Georges Rouault (1871-   ), 1907. Privately owned. French.

PARDO VENUS, THE: Titian (Tiziano Vecellio) (1480?-1576), c. 1535-40. Louvre, Paris. Venetian.

PARIS IN AUTUMN: Albert Marquet (1875-1947). French.

PARIS IN GRAY WEATHER: Albert Marquet (1875-1947), c. 1906. J. E. Wolfensberger, Zurich. French.

PARK AT ASNIÈRES: Vincent van Gogh (1853-1890), 1886-88. V. W. van Gogh Collection, Municipal Museum, Amsterdam. French.

PARK ON THE RIVER: William J. Glackens (1870-1938), 1905. Brooklyn Museum. American.

PARNASSUS: Raphael (Raffaello Santi) (1483-1520), 1511. Stanza Della Segnatura, Vatican, Rome. Umbrian.

PARSONAGE OF VINCENT'S PARENTS, THE: Vincent van Gogh (1853-1890), 1883-85. V. W. van Gogh Collection, Municipal Museum, Amsterdam. French.

PASSION OF SACCO AND VANZETTI, THE: Ben Shahn (1898-   ), 1931-32. Whitney Museum of American Art, New York. American.

PASTORALE: Paul Klee (1879-1940), 1927. Museum of Modern Art, New York. Swiss.

PASTORAL LANDSCAPE WITH SHEPHERDS: François Boucher (1703-1770), 1768. Metropolitan Museum of Art, New York. French.

PASTORAL STUDY: Albert Pinkham Ryder (1847-1917). National Collection of Fine Arts, Smithsonian Institute, Washington, D.C. American.

PASTORAL SYMPHONY: Giorgione (1478?-1510), c. 1505-10. Louvre, Paris. Venetian.

PAUL IN HARLEQUIN'S COSTUME: Pablo Picasso (1881-   ), 1923. William Goetz Collection, Los Angeles. French.

PEACEABLE KINGDOM, THE: Edward Hicks (1780-1849). Mr. and Mrs. Holger Cahill. American.

PEACOCK-MOTH, THE: Vincent van Gogh (1853-1890), 1889. V. W. van Gogh Collection, Municipal Museum, Amsterdam. French.

PEALE FAMILY GROUP: Charles Willson Peale (1741-1827), 1773. New York Historical Society, New York. American.

PEASANT DANCE: Pieter Bruegel the Elder (c. 1527-1569), c. 1568. Kunsthistorisches Museum, Vienna. Flemish.

PEASANTS' MEAL: Louis Le Nain (1593?-1648). Louvre, Paris. French.

PEASANT WEDDING: Pieter Bruegel the Elder (c. 1527-1569), c. 1568. Kunsthistorisches Museum, Vienna. Flemish.

PEASANT WITH A BIRD: Adriaen Brouwer (1605-1638). Metropolitan Museum of Art. New York. Flemish.

PENNINGTON MILLS, VIEW DOWNSTREAM Francis Guy (1760-1820), 1804. Peabody Institute, Baltimore. American.

PENN'S TREATY WITH THE INDIANS: Benjamin West (1738-1820), 1771. Pennsylvania Academy of Fine Arts. American.

PERSEUS AND ANDROMEDA: Titian (Tiziano Vecellio) (1480?-1576), c. 1555. Wallace Collection, London. Venetian.

PERSISTENCE OF MEMORY, THE: Salvador Dali (1904-   ), 1931. Museum of Modern

Art, New York. Spanish (worked in Paris, now in U.S.A.).

PERSON IN THE PRESENCE OF NATURE: Joan Miró (1893-), 1935. Walter Arensberg Collection, Philadelphia Museum of Art. Spanish.

PERSON THROWING A STONE AT A BIRD: Joan Miró (1893-), 1926. Museum of Modern Art, New York. Spanish.

PETER PAUL RUBENS (1577-1640): Anthony Van Dyck (1599-1641). Metropolitan Museum of Art, New York. Flemish.

PHILIP IV OF SPAIN: Diego Velasquez (1599-1660). Metropolitan Museum of Art, New York. Spanish.

PHILIP IV OF SPAIN: Diego Velasquez (1599-1660), 1636-38. National Gallery, London, Spanish.

PHILOSOPHER, THE: Jusepe de Ribera (La Spagnoletto) (1588?-1652). Prado, Madrid. Spanish.

PIASSETTA, VENICE, THE: Francesco Guardi (1712-1793). Wadsworth Atheneum, Hartford, Conn. Venetian.

PIAZZA ST. MARCO, VENICE: Michele Cammarano (1851-1920), c. 1895. Galleria d'Arte Moderna, Rome. Italian.

PIAZZA ST. MARCO IN VENICE, THE: Francesco Guardi (1712-1793), 1780's Gemaldegalerie, Vienna. Venetian.

PICNIC, THE: See Luncheon on the Grass, The.

PICTOGRAPH: Adolph Gottlieb (1903-) 1942. Jacques Seligmann and Co., New York. American.

PICTOGRAPH # 4: Adolph Gottlieb (1903-) 1943. Artist's Gallery, New York. American.

PICTURE ALBUM: Paul Klee (1879-1940), 1937. Mrs. Julius Wadsworth. Swiss.

PIERROT: Pablo Picasso (1881-), 1918. Adolph Lewisohn, New York. French.

PIERROT: Georges Rouault (1871-), 1911. Norbert Schimmel, Great Neck, New York. French.

PIERROT SEATED: Pablo Picasso (1881-), 1918. Lewisohn Collection. French.

PIETA: Titian (Tiziano Vecellio) (1480?-1567), 1573-76. Accademia, Venice. Venetian.

PIETER SCHUYLER: The Schuyler Painter, c. 1700-10. Mayor's Office, Albany, New York. American.

PILATE WASHING HIS HANDS: Rembrandt Van Rijn (1606-1669). Metropolitan Museum of Art, New York. Dutch.

PILOT, THE: Marcel Gromaire (1892-), 1927 Valentine Gallery, New York. French.

PINES AND ROCKS: Paul Cézanne (1838-1906), 1895-90. Museum of Modern Art, New York. French.

PINE TREE: Karl Knaths (1891-). Phillips Memorial Gallery, Washington, D.C. American.

PINK AND GREEN: Edgar Degas (1834-1917). Metropolitan Museum of Art, New York. French.

PINK PEACH TREE (SOUVENIR DE MAUVRE): Vincent van Gogh (1853-1890), 1888. Kröller-Müller State Museum, Otterlo, Holland. French.

PINK TABLE CLOTH, THE: Henry Varnum Poor (1888-), 1933. Cleveland Museum of Art. American.

PIPES OF PAN, THE: Pablo Picasso (1881-), 1923. Owned by artist. French.

PIT, THE: George Grosz (1893-), 1946. Murdock Collection, Wichita Art Museum. American.

PLACE DU TERTRE: Maurice Utrillo (1883-1955), c. 1913. Mr. and Mrs. John Hay Whitney, New York. French.

PLACE DU TERTRE: Maurice Utrillo (1883-

1955), c. 1911-12. Tate Gallery, London. French.

PLACE DU TERTRE, THE FOURTEENTH OF JULY: Maurice Utrillo (1883-1955), 1914. Alfred Schwabacher, New York. French.

PLAYGROUND: Paul Cadmus (1904-), 1948. Midtown Galleries, New York. American.

PLONGEURS CIRCULAIRES, LES: Fernand Léger (1881-1955), 1942. Valentine Gallery New York. French.

POÈMES BARBARES: Paul Gauguin (1848-1903), 1896. Privately owned. French.

POETESS, THE: Joan Miró (1893-), 1940. Mr. and Mrs. Ralph Colin, New York. Spanish.

POET LUUIS DE GONGORA, THE: Diego Velasquez (1599-1660), 1622. Boston Museum of Fine Arts. Spanish.

POLISH EXILE—MADAME DE BRAYER, THE: Gustave Courbet (1819-1877), 1858. Metropolitan Museum of Art, New York. French.

POLISH RIDER, THE: Rembrandt van Rijn (1606-1669), c. 1655. Frick Collection, New York. Dutch.

POND IN THE VALLEY: Gustave Courbet (1819-1877). Metropolitan Museum of Art, New York. French.

PONT NEUF, THE: Albert Marquet (1875-1947), 1906. Chester Dale Collection, Washington, D.C. French.

POORHOUSE ON THE HILL, THE: Paul Cézanne (1839-1906). Metropolitan Museum of Art, New York. French.

PORT FROM NEW YORK INTERPRETED, THE: Joseph Stella (1880-1946), 1920-21. Newark Museum. American.

PORT OF DIEPPE, THE: Eugène-Louis Boudin (1825-1898), 1896. Glasgow Art Gallery. French.

PORT OF MARSEILLES: Raoul Dufy (1877-1953), 1925. Perls Galleries, New York. French.

PORTRAIT OF A CHILD (ROSA BONHEUR?): Jean Baptiste Camille Corot (1796-1875). Metropolitan Museum of Art, New York. French.

PORTRAIT OF A GIRL: Amadeo Modigliani (1884-1920), 1917. French.

PORTRAIT OF A LADY: Anthony Van Dyck (1599-1641). Metropolitan Museum of Art, New York. Flemish.

PORTRAIT OF A LADY: Pablo Picasso (1881-), 1937. Owned by artist. French.

PORTRAIT OF A LADY: Rogier van der Weyden (1400-1464). Mellon Collection of the National Gallery of Art, Washington, D.C. Flemish.

PORTRAIT OF A LADY: John Wollaston (in America 1749-1767). Wendell Phillips Colton, New York. American.

PORTRAIT OF A LADY IN BLACK: Edvard Munch (1863-1944), 1892. Statens Museum for Kunst, Copenhagen. Norwegian.

PORTRAIT OF A MAN: Gustave Courbet (1819 -1877). Metropolitan Museum of Art, New York. French.

PORTRAIT OF A MAN: Anthony Van Dyck (1599-1641). Metropolitan Museum of Art, New York. Flemish.

PORTRAIT OF A MAN: Georges Rouault (1871-), 1911. Dikran G. Kelekian, New York. French.

PORTRAIT OF A MAN: Chaim Soutine (1884-1943). Chester Dale Collection, New York. French (born in Lithuania).

PORTRAIT OF A MAN AND HIS WIFE: Ulrich Apt, the Elder (c. 1481-1532), 1512. Metropolitan Museum of Art, New York. German.

PORTRAIT OF A MAN HOLDING A MANUSCRIPT: Rembrandt van Rijn (1606-1669),

1658. Metropolitan Museum of Art, New York. Dutch.

PORTRAIT OF A MEMBER OF THE SPINOLA FAMILY: Anthony Van Dyck (1599-1641). Metropolitan Museum of Art, New York. Flemish.

PORTRAIT OF AN ACTOR: Vincent van Gogh (1853-1890), 1888-89. Kröller-Müller State Museum, Otterlo, Holland. French.

PORTRAIT OF AN ENGLISH WOMAN: André Derain (1880-1954). Privately owned, New York. French.

PORTRAIT OF AN OLD MAN: Joseph Hirsch (1910-   ), 1939. Whitney Museum of American Art, New York. American.

PORTRAIT OF A RABBI: Rembrandt van Rijn (1606-1669), 1657. National Gallery, London. Dutch.

PORTRAIT OF A YOUNG MAN: Giovanni Bellini (c. 1430-1516). Metropolitan Museum of Art, New York. Venetian.

PORTRAIT OF A YOUNG MAN: Bronzino (Agnolo di Cosimo di Mariano) (1503-1572). Metropolitan Museum of Art, New York. Florentine.

PORTRAIT OF A YOUNG WOMAN: Edgar Degas (1834-1917). Metropolitan Museum of Art, New York. French.

PORTRAIT OF A YOUNG WOMAN AS VENUS BINDING THE EYES OF CUPID: Titian (Tiziano Vecellio) (1480?-1576). National Gallery of Art, Washington, D.C. Venetian.

PORTRAIT OF A YOUTH: Sandro Botticelli (Alessandro Filipepi) (1444?-1510). Mellon Collection, National Gallery of Art, Washington, D.C. Florentine.

PORTRAIT OF CECILIA GALLERANI: Leonardo da Vinci (1452-1519), c. 1483. Czartoryski Gallery, Cracow. Florentine.

PORTRAIT OF HIMSELF: Peter Paul Rubens (1577-1640), 1638-40. Gemaldegalerie, Vienna. Flemish.

PORTRAIT OF IPPOLITO RIMALDI ("YOUNG ENGLISHMAN"): Titian (Tiziano Vecellio) (1480?-1576). Pitti, Florence. Venet'an

PORTRAIT OF JACOPO STRADA: Titian (Tiziano Vecellio) (1480?-1576), 1568. Gemaldegalerie, Vienna. Venetian.

PORTRAIT OF KAHNWEILER: Pablo Picasso (1881-   ), 1910. Mrs. Charles B. Goodspeed. French.

PORTRAIT OF LUGNÉ POË: Jean Édouard Vuillard (1868-1940), 1891. Miss Mabel Choate, New York. French.

PORTRAIT OF MADAME HESSLING (Mme. JEAN RENOIR): André Derain (1880-1954), 1925. Joseph Stransky, New York. French.

PORTRAIT OF MADAME VAN LEER: Moïse Kisling (1891-   ), c. 1928. Privately owned, New York. French.

PORTRAIT OF MADAME X: Jean Lurçat (1892-   ), 1928. Chester Dale Collection, New York. French.

PORTRAIT OF MAFFEO BARBERINI: Caravaggio (Michelangelo Merisi) (1573-1610), c. 1596. Palazzo Corsini, Florence. Italian.

PORTRAIT OF MARIA LUISA, QUEEN OF SPAIN: Francisco Goya (y Lucientes) (1746-1828). Palacio Real, Madrid. Spanish.

PORTRAIT OF MRS. LOUIS BERGMAN: Raoul Dufy (1877-1953), 1951. Louis Bergman, New York. French.

PORTRAIT OF NATHANIEL HURD: John Singleton Copley (1737-1815). Museum of Art, Cleveland. American.

PORTRAIT OF THE ARTIST: Anthony Van Dyck (1599-1641). Metropolitan Museum of Art, New York. Flemish.

PORTRAIT OF THE ARTIST'S MOTHER READING: Henri de Toulouse-Lautrec (1864-1901), 1887. The Museum of Albi, France. French.

PORTRAIT OF THE ARTIST WITH A YELLOW CRUCIFIX: Paul Gauguin (1848-1903), c. 1890. Maurice Denis Collection. French.

PORTRAIT OF THEODORE DURET: Jean Édouard Vuillard (1868-1940), 1912. Chester Dale Collection, New York. French.

PORTRAIT OF THE PAINTER: Jean Baptiste Chardin (1699-1779). Louvre, Paris. French.

PORTRAIT OF THOMAS MIFFLIN AND HIS WIFE: John Singleton Copley (1737-1815). Historical Society of Pennsylvania, American.

POSE OF BUDDHA: Henri Matisse (1869-1954), 1924. Privately owned, New York. French.

POSTMAN ROULIN, THE: Vincent van Gogh (1853-1890), 1888-89. Kröller-Müller State Museum, Otterlo, Holland. French.

POST OFFICE: David Gilmor Blythe (1815-1865), c. 1863. Department of Fine Arts, Carnegie Institute, Pittsburgh. American.

POTATO, THE: Joan Miró (1893-   ), 1928. Privately owned, New York. Spanish.

POTATO-EATERS: Vincent van Gogh (1853-1890), 1885. V. W. van Gogh Collection, Municipal Museum, Amsterdam. French.

POUTING: Edgar Degas (1834-1917), 1875-76. Metropolitan Museum of Art, New York. French.

PRAYING JEW, THE: Marc Chagall (1887-   ), 1914. Chicago Art Institute. Russian.

PRESENTATION OF THE VIRGIN: Titian (Tiziano Vecellio) (1480?-1576), c. 1534-38. Accademia, Venice. Venetian.

PRIMAVERA: Sandro Botticelli (Alessandro Filipepi) (1444-1510), c. 1478. Uffizi Gallery, Florence. Florentine.

PRINCE BALTASAR CARLOS ON HIS PONY: Diego Velasquez (1599-1660), c. 1634. Prado, Madrid. Spanish.

PRINCE BALTASAR CARLOS WITH A DWARF: Diego Velasquez (1599-1660), 1631. Boston Museum of Fine Arts. Spanish.

PRINCE FELIPE PROSPER: Diego Velasquez (1599-1660), c. 1659. Kunsthistorisches Museum, Vienna. Spanish.

PRISONERS FROM THE FRONT: Winslow Homer (1836-1910), 1866. Metropolitan Museum of Art, New York. American.

PRIVATE ROOM AT "LE RAT MORT": Henri de Toulouse-Lautrec (1864-1901), 1899. Courtauld Institute of Art, London. French.

PROMENADE, THE: Jean Louis Forain (1852-1931). Mr. and Mrs. Joseph J. Kerrigan, New York. French.

PROMETHEUS (FRESCO): José Clemente Orozco (1883-1949), 1930. Frary Hall, Pomona College, Claremont, California. Mexican.

PROMETHEUS (TITYUS): Titian (Tiziano Vecellio) (1480?-1576), c. 1550. Prado, Madrid. Venet'an.

PROPHET JEREMIAH, THE: Michelangelo (Michelangelo Buonarroti) (1475-1564). Sistine Chapel, Vatican, Rome. Florentine.

PROSPERITY'S INCREASE: John Kane (1860-1934), 1933. William S. Paley, New York. American.

PUBLIC GARDEN AT ARLES: Vincent van Gogh (1853-1890), 1888. Jakob Goldschmidt Collection, New York. French.

PURIFICATION OF THE TEMPLE, THE: El Greco (Domenicos Theotocopoulos) (1541-1614), c. 1600-1610. National Gallery, London. Spanish (born Crete).

QUADROON, THE: George Fuller (1822-1884). Metropolitan Museum of Art, New York. American.

QUEEN OF SHEBA, THE: Piero della Francesca (1416?-1492), 1452-66. Church of San Francesco, Arezzo. Umbrian.

QUILTING PARTY, THE: Artist unknown, c. 1840-50. Museum of Modern Art, New York. American.

RABBI OF VITEBSK, THE. See praying jew, The.

RACE, THE: Pablo Picasso (1881-   ), 1922. Owned by artist. French.

RACE FOR THE DERBY AT EPSOM: Théodore Géricault (1791-1824). French.

RACE TRACK: Raoul Dufy (1877-1953), c. 1940. Alfred Schwagacher, New York. French.

RAFT, THE: Thomas Doughty (1793-1856), 1830. Museum of Art, Rhode Island School of Design, Providence. American.

RAFT OF THE MEDUSA, THE: Théodore Géricault (1791-1824), c. 1817. Louvre, Paris. French.

RAFTSMEN PLAYING CARDS: George Caleb Bingham (1811-1877), 1847-50. City Art Museum, St. Louis. American.

RAIN: Wassily Kandinsky (1866-1944), 1913. Karl Nierendorf. Russian.

RAIN, STEAM, AND SPEED: Joseph Mallord Turner (1775-1851). National Gallery of Art, London. English.

RAINBOW, THE: Max Beckmann (1884-   ), 1942. Buchholz Gallery, New York. German.

RAINY DAY IN CAMP: Winslow Homer (1836-1910). Metropolitan Museum of Art, New York. American.

RAISING OF LAZARUS, THE: Caravaggio (Michelangelo Merisi) (1573-1610), 1609. Museo Nazionale, Messina. Italian.

RAKE'S PROGRESS, THE: William Hogarth (1697-1764), 1735. Sir John Soane's Museum, London. English.

RAPALJE CHILDREN, THE: John Durand (fl. 1767-1782), c. 1768. New York Historical Society, New York. American.

RAPE OF EUROPA, THE: Titian (Tiziano Vecellio) (1480?-1576), 1559. Isabella Stewart Gardner Collection, Boston. Venetian.

RAPE OF HELEN, THE: Attributed to Benozzo Gozozli (1420-1498). National Gallery, London. Florentine.

REAPER, THE, (AFTER MILLET'S WORK IN THE FIELDS): Vincent van Gogh (1853-1890), 1889. V. W. van Gogh Collection, Municipal Museum, Amsterdam. French.

RECLINING NUDE: Amadeo Modigliani (1884-1920), 1920. Museum of Modern Art, New York. French (born Italy).

RECLINING VENUS: Giorgione (da Castelfranco) (c. 1478-1510). Dresden. Venetian.

RED AND BLUE: A. D. F. Reinhardt (1913-   ), 1941. Owned by artist. American.

RED BOAT, THE: Odilon Redon (1840-1916), 1912. Collection Hahnloser, Winterthur (Zurich). French.

RED CART: Stuart Davis (1894-   ). 1932. Addison Gallery of American Art, Andover, Mass. American.

RED CHIMNEYS: Charles Demuth (1883-1935), 1918. Phillips Memorial Gallery, Washington, D.C. American.

RED CONCERT: Raoul Dufy (1877-1953), 1946. Mr. and Mrs. Peter A. Rubel, New York. French.

RED FUNNEL, THE: Christopher Wood (1901-1930), 1930. Mrs. Lucy Carrington Wertheim, London. English.

RED HORSES: Franz Marc (1880-1916), c. 1911. Museum Folkwang, Essen. German.

RED STUDIO, THE: Henri Matisse (1869-1954), 1911. Museum of Modern Art, New York. French.

RED TABLECLOTH, THE: Pablo Picasso

(1881-   ), 1924. Miss Micheline Rosenberg. French.

REFUGE: Paul Klee (1879-1940), 1930. Mme. Galka E. Scheyer. Swiss.

REGRET, THE: Giorgio di Chirico (1888-   ), 1916. Munson-Williams-Proctor Institute, Utica New York. French (born Greece).

REHEARSAL OF THE BALLET ON THE STAGE: Edgar Degas (1834-1917). Metropolitan Museum of Art, New York. French.

REHEARSAL ROOM, THE: Edgar Degas (1834-1917). Metropolitan Museum of Art, New York. French.

RENOIR'S GARDEN: Maurice Utrillo (1883-1955), 1909-10. Gregoire Tarnapol, New York. French.

REPENTANT MAGDALENE, THE: Caravaggio (Michelangelo Merisi) (1573-1610), c. 1595. Galleria Doria-Pamphili, Rome. Italian.

REPENTANT MAGDALENE, THE: Georges de la Tour (1593-1652), c. 1635-40. Louvre, Paris. French.

RESIDENCE OF DAVID TWINING, THE: Edward Hicks (1780-1849). Museum of Modern Art, New York. American.

REST ON THE FLIGHT TO EGYPT, THE: Caravaggio (Michelangelo Merisi) (1573-1610), 1595-96. Galleria Doria-Pamphili, Rome. Italian.

REST ON THE FLIGHT INTO EGYPT, THE: Gerard David (c. 1460-1523). Metropolitan Museum of Art, New York. Flemish.

RESURRECTION: Piero della Francesca (c.1420-1492). Palazzo Communale, San Sepulchro. Umbrian.

RESURRECTION OF LAZARUS, THE: Geertgen Tot Sint Jans (c. 1460-1495), c. 1480. Louvre, Paris. Dutch.

RETURN OF THE HERD, THE: Pieter Bruegel the Elder (c. 1520-1569), 1565. Kunsthistorisches Museum, Vienna. Flemish.

RETURN OF THE PRODIGAL SON, THE: Jean Baptiste Greuze (1725-1805). Louvre, Paris. French.

RÊVERIE: Jean Baptiste Camille Corot (1796-1875). Metropolitan Museum of Art, New York. French.

RÊVIERE: Paul Gauguin (1848-1903), 1891. G. Wildenstein Collection. French.

RINGMASTER, THE: See Circus Fernando.

RISING OF A THUNDERSTORM AT SEA, THE: Washington Allston (1779-1843), 1804. Boston Museum of Fine Arts. American.

RIVER, THE: Maurice de Vlaminck (1876-   ). Chester Dale Collection, New York. French.

RIVER FRONT, THE: Charles François Daubigny (1817-1878), 1853. Metropolitan Museum of Art, New York. French.

RIVER MARNE: André Dunoyer de Segonzac (1885-   ), 1926. Privately owned, New York. French.

RIVERSIDE: Charles François Daubigny (1817-1878), 1872. Metropolitan Museum of Art, New York. French.

RIVER WITH A DISTANT TOWER: Jean Baptiste Camille Corot (1796-1875). Metropolitan Museum of Art, New York. French.

ROAD, THE: Camille Pissarro (1831-1903), 1870. Louvre, Paris. French.

ROASTING EARS: Thomas Hart Benton (1889-   ), 1938-39. Metropolitan Museum of Art, New York. American.

ROBERT FULTON: Benjamin West (1738-1820), 1806. New York State Historical Association, Cooperstown. American.

ROBERT LOUIS STEVENSON: John Singer Sargent (1856-1925), 1885. Mr. and Mrs. John Hay Whitney, New York. American.

ROBERT RICH, EARL OF WARWICK (1587-1658): Anthony Van Dyck (1599-1641). Metro-

politan Museum of Art, New York. Flemish.
ROCHELLE, LA: Edward Wadsworth (1889-1949), 1923. Mrs. von Bethmann-Hollweg, London. English.
ROCK, THE: Peter Blume (1906-   ), 1944-48. Edgar J. Kaufmann, Jr. American.
ROCKS—FOREST OF FONTAINEBLEAU: Paul Cézanne (1839-1906). Metropolitan Museum of Art, New York. French.
ROCKY MOUNTAINS, THE: Albert Bierstadt (1830-1902), 1863. Metropolitan Museum of Art, New York. American.
ROGER SHERMAN: Ralph Earl (1751-1801), c. 1777. Yale University Art Gallery. American.
ROMAN CAMPAGNA, THE: Thomas Cole (1801-1848), 1843. Wadsworth Atheneum, Hartford, Conn. American.
ROMANTIC PARK: Paul Klee (1879-1940), 1930. Mr. and Mrs. Edward M. M. Warburg. Swiss.
ROOM 203: Ivan Le Lorraine Albright 1897-   ), 1930-31. Owned by artist. American.
ROOT OF SAN ROMANO, THE: Paolo Uccello (1397?-1475), 1451-57. National Gallery, London. Florentine.
ROSES AND BEETLE: Vincent van Gogh (1853-1890), 1890. V. W. van Gogh Collection, Municipal Museum, Amsterdam. French.
ROWERS, THE: Hans von Marees (1837-1887), 1871. National Gallery, Berlin. German.
ROWING HOME: Winslow Homer (1836-1910), 1890. Phillips Memorial Gallery, Washington, D.C. American.
ROYAL YACHT CLUB, COWES, THE: Raoul Dufy (1877-1953), 1936. Mr. and Mrs. Harry N. Abrams, New York. French.
RUE CHAPPE: Maurice Utrillo (1883-1955), c. 1912. Privately owned, New York. French.
RUE DE CRIMÉE: Maurice Utrillo (1883-1955), 1910. Mrs. Henry Church, New York. French.
RUE DE LA JONQUIERE: Maurice Utrillo (1883-1955), c. 1909. Alex L. Hillman, New York. French.
RUE RAVIGNAN: Maurice Utrillo (1883-1955), c. 1911. Gregoire Tarnapol, New York. French.
RUSTIC LANDSCAPE WITH FIGURES BY A STREAM: François Boucher (1703-1770). 1768. Metropolitan Museum of Art, New York. French.
RYDAL FALLS, ENGLAND: John Frederick Kensett (1818-1872), 1858. George Walter Vincent Smith Art Museum, Springfield, Mass. American.
SACRE COEUR: Maurice Utrillo (1883-1955), 1916. Mr. and Mrs. Walter Hochschild, New York. French.
SACRE-COEUR DE MONTMARTRE AND PASSAGE COTTIN: Maurice Utrillo (1883-1955), 1934. William P. Seligman, New York. French.
SACRED AND PROFANE LOVE: Titian (Tiziano Vecellio) (1480?-1576), c. 1515-16. Galleria Borghese, Rome. Venetian.
SACRIFICE OF ISAAC, THE: Caravaggio (Michelangelo Merisi) (1573-1610), c. 1599. Uffizi Gallery, Florence. Italian.
SAILORS AT A BAR: Marcel Gromaire (1892-   ), 1927. Privately owned, New York. French.
ST. ANDREW AND ST. FRANCIS: El Greco (Domenicos Theotocopoulos) (1541-1614). Prado, Madrid. Spanish (born Crete).
ST. AUGUSTINE IN ECSTASY: Anthony Van Dyck (1599-1641). Antwerp. Flemish.
ST. CHRISTOPHER (FRESCO): Titian (Tiziano Vecellio) (1480?-1576), c. 1523. Ducal Palace, Venice. Venetian.
ST. CHRYSOGONUS: Michele Giambono (act.

1420-1462), after 1444. Church of SS. Gervasio e Protasio, Venetian.
ST. FRANCIS IN ECSTASY: Caravaggio (Michelangelo Merisi) (1573-1610), c. 1593. Wadsworth Atheneum, Hartford, Conn. Italian.
ST. FRANCIS IN PRAYER: Caravaggio (Michelangelo Merisi) (1573-1610), c. 1603. Santa Maria della Concezione, Rome. Italian.
ST. FRANCIS MEDITATING: Caravaggio (Michelangelo Merisi) (1573-1610), 1607. Museo Civico, Cremona. Italian.
ST. GEORGE: Andrea Mantegna (1431-1506), c. 1462. Academy, Venice. Paduan.
ST. GEORGE AND THE DRAGON: Raphael (Raffaello Santi) (1483-1520). Mellon Collection of the National Gallery of Art, Washington, D.C. Umbrian.
ST. JAMES LED TO EXECUTION: Andrea Mantegna (1431-1506), c. 1448-52. Eremitani, Padua. Paduan.
ST. JEROME: Caravaggio (Michelangelo Merisi) (1573-1610), c. 1604. Monastery, Montserrat. Italian.
ST. JEROME: Leonardo da Vinci (1452-1519), c. 1483. Vatican Gallery. Florentine.
ST. JEROME IN HIS STUDY: Antonello da Messina (1430?-1479?). National Gallery, London. Venetian.
ST. JOHN THE BAPTIST: Caravaggio (Michelangelo Merisi) (1573-1610), c. 1600-01. Galleria Doria-Pamphili, Rome. Italian.
ST. JOHN THE BAPTIST: Caravaggio (Michelangelo Merisi) (1573-1610), c. 1603. William Rockhill Nelson Gallery of Art, Kansas City. Italian.
ST. JOHN THE BAPTIST: Titian (Tiziano Vecellio) (1480?-1576), c. 1545. Accademia, Venice. Venetian.
ST. JOHN THE BAPTIST: Leonardo da Vinci (1452-1519), c. 1509-12. Louvre, Paris. Florentine.
ST. LOUIS DRAWING ROOM: Karl Zerbe (1903-   ), 1946. Owned by artist. American.
ST. MARTIN AND THE BEGGAR: El Greco (Domenicos Theotocopoulos) (1548-1614). Mellon Collection of the National Gallery of Art, Washington, D.C. Spanish (born Crete).
ST. MATTHEW AND THE ANGEL: Caravaggio (Michelangelo Merisi) (1573-1610), 1600. San Luigi de' Francesi, Rome. Italian.
ST. NICHOLAS DAY: Jan Steen (c. 1626-1679), c. 1665. Rijksmuseum, Amsterdam. Dutch.
ST. ROSALIE INTERCEDING FOR THE PLAGUE-STRICKEN OF PALERMO: Anthony Van Dyck (1599-1641). Metropolitan Museum of Art, New York. Flemish.
SAINT SEBASTIAN: Andrea Mantegna (1431-1506), before 1481. Louvre, Paris. Paduan.
ST. SEBASTIAN MOURNED BY SAINT IRENE: Georges de la Tour (1593-1652), c. 1633. Kaiser Friedrich Museum, Berlin. French.
ST. SEVERIN: Robert Delaunay (1882-   ), 1900. J. B. Neumann, New York. French.
SALISBURY CATHEDRAL: John Constable (1776-1837). National Gallery of Art, London. English.
SALISBURY CATHEDRAL FROM THE BISHOP'S GARDEN: John Constable (1776-1837). Metropolitan Museum of Art, New York. English.
SALOME WITH THE HEAD OF ST. JOHN: Caravaggio (Michelangelo Merisi) (1573-1610), c. 1607, Casita del Principe, El Escorial, Spain. Italian.
SALON IN THE RUE DES MOULINS: Henri de Toulouse-Lautrec (1864-1901), 1894. The Museum of Albi, France. French.
SALVATOR MUNDI: Albrecht Dürer (1471-

1528). Metropolitan Museum of Art, New York. German.

SAMUEL COATES: Thomas Sully (1783-1872), 1812. Pennsylvania Hospital. American.

SAND BARGE: Arthur G. Dove (1880-1946), 1930. Phillips Memorial Gallery, Washington D.C. American.

SAND, SEA, AND SKY: Lamar Dodd (1909-), 1938. Metropolitan Museum of Art, New York. American.

SAUL AND THE WITCH OF ENDOR: Benjamin West (1738-1820), 1777. Wadsworth Atheneum, Hartford, Conn. American.

SCENE IN MOROCCO: Charles Dufresne (1880-). Worcester Art Museum, Worcester, Mass. French.

SCENE IN THE CATSKILL MOUNTAINS: Frederick Edwin Church (1826-1900), 1852. Walker Art Center, Minneapolis. American.

SCENE IN VENICE: THE PIAZZETTA: Canaletto (1697-1768). Metropolitan Museum of Art, New York. Venetian.

SCHOOL OF ATHENS: Raphael (Raffaello Santi) (1483-1520), c. 1508-11. Vatican. Umbrian.

SCULPTOR AND HIS STATUE: Pablo Picasso (1881-), 1933. Privately owned. French.

SEA, THE: Gustave Courbet (1819-1877). Metropolitan Museum of Art, New York. French.

SEA, THE: Vincent van Gogh (1853-1890), 1888. V. W. van Gogh Collection, Municipal Museum, Amsterdam. French.

SEATED BATHER: Pablo Picasso (1881-), 1929. Mrs. Meric Callery. French.

SEATED BATHER: Auguste Renoir (1841-1919), 1913. Durand-Ruel. French.

SEATED CHOIR BOY: Chaim Soutine (1894-1943), 1930. Privately owned, Paris. French (born Lithuania).

SEATED NUDE: Henri Matisse (1869-1955), 1917. Samuel S. White, Philadelphia. French.

SEATED WOMAN, THE: Joan Miró (1893-), 1938-39. Miss Peggy Guggenheim, New York. Spanish.

SEATED WOMAN: Pablo Picasso (1881-), 1926-27. Museum of Modern Art, New York. French.

SEATED WOMAN: Pablo Picasso (1881-), 1927. James Thrall Soby. French.

SEATED WOMAN: Jean Édouard Vuillard (1868-1940), c. 1898. De Hauke and Co., New York. French.

SELF-PORTRAIT: Jacob Eichholtz (1776-1852), c. 1805-10. Mrs. James H. Beal, Pittsburgh. American.

SELF-PORTRAIT: Vincent van Gogh (1853-1890), 1885-86. V. W. van Gogh Collection, Municipal Museum, Amsterdam. French.

SELF-PORTRAIT: John Kane (1860-1932), 1929. Museum of Modern Art, New York. American.

SELF-PORTRAIT: Joan Miró (1893-), 1938. Pierre Matisse Gallery, New York. Spanish.

SELF-PORTRAIT: Amadeo Modigliani (1884-1920), 1919. Matarazzo Sobrinho Collection, São Paulo, Brazil. French (born Italy).

SELF-PORTRAIT: Pablo Picasso (1881-), 1901. Owned by artist. French.

SELF-PORTRAIT: Raphael (Raffaello Santi) (1483-1520). Uffizi Gallery, Florence. Umbrian.

SELF-PORTRAIT: Rembrandt van Rijn (1606-1669), 1659. National Gallery of Art, Washington, D.C. Dutch.

SELF-PORTRAIT: Titian (Tiziano Vecellio) (1480?-1576), c. 1550. Kaiser Friedrich Museum, Berlin. Venetian.

SELF-PORTRAIT: Titian (Tiziano Vecellio)

(1480?-1576), c. 1565. Prado, Madrid. Venetian.

SELF-PORTRAIT, WITH HAT: Alfred H. Maurer (1868-1932), 1928. Walker Art Center, Minneapolis. American.

SELF-PORTRAIT OF THE ARTIST WITH HIS FAMILY: Joseph Wright (1756-1793), c. 1793. Pennsylvania Academy of Fine Arts, Philadelphia. American.

SELF-PORTRAIT WITH GRAY HAT: Vincent van Gogh (1853-1890), 1886-88. V. W. van Gogh Collection, Municipal Museum, Amsterdam. French.

SELF-PORTRAIT WITH HIS DOG TRUMP: William Hogarth (1697-1764), 1745. National Gallery, London. English.

SELF-PORTRAIT WITH PIPE: Vincent van Gogh (1853-1890), 1887. V. W. van Gogh Collection, Municipal Museum, Amsterdam. French.

SELF-PORTRAIT WITH STRAW HAT: Vincent van Gogh (1853-1890), 1886-88. V. W. van Gogh Collection, Municipal Museum, Amsterdam. French.

SENATE, THE: William Gropper (1897-), 1935. Museum of Modern Art, New York. American.

SEVEN GIRLS: Paul Klee (1879-1940), 1910. Miss Anna Sweeney. Swiss.

SEVEN WORKS OF MERCY, THE: Caravaggio (Michelangelo Merisi) (1573-1610), 1607. Pio Monde della Misericordia, Naples. Italian.

SHE MOOS, WE PLAY: Paul Klee (1879-1940), 1928. Mrs. Paul Klee, Berne. Swiss.

SHEPHERD, THE: Paul Klee (1879-1940), 1929. Mr. and Mrs. Bernard J. Reis. Swiss.

SHE-WOLF: Jackson Pollock (1912-1956), 1943. Museum of Modern Art, New York. American.

SHIP GRAVEYARD: Julian Levi (1900-), 1941. Philip Loeb. American.

SHIP OF FOOLS, THE: Hieronymus Bosch (c. 1460-1516), c. 1500. Louvre, Paris. Dutch.

SHOOTING FOR THE BEEF: George Caleb Bingham (1811-1879), 1850. Brooklyn Museum, New York. American.

SHOPPER, THE: Kenneth Hayes Miller (1876-), 1928. Whitney Museum of American Art, American.

SHORE, THE: Max Beckmann (1884-), 1936. Frau M. Beckmann-Tube, Gauting. German.

SHRIMP GIRL, THE: William Hogarth (1697-1764), late. National Gallery, London. English.

SHRIMPS: Henri Matisse (1869-1954), 1919. Privately owned, New York. French.

SIBYL, THE: Jean Baptiste Camille Corot (1796-1875). .Metropolitan Museum of Art, New York. French.

SIDEBOARD, THE: Franklin C. Watkins (1894-), 1940. Whitney Museum of American Art, New York. American.

SIDE SHOW: Georges Seurat (1859-1891), 1889. Stephen C. Clark Collection. French.

SIDEWALK, THE: Loren MacIver (1909-), 1940. Addison Gallery of American Art, Andover, Mass. American.

SIEGFRIED AND THE RHINE MAIDENS: Albert Pinkham Ryder (1847-1917). Mellon Collection, National Gallery of Art. Washington, D.C. American.

SIGNORA D'ARZA: Thomas Eakins (1844-1916) 1902. Metropolitan Museum of Art, New York. American.

SILVAPLANERSEE: Ferdinand Hodler (1853-1918), 1907. Kunsthaus, Zurich. Swiss.

SIMULTANEOUS LINES: Enrico Prampolini (1894-), 1952. Collection Cassuto, Milan. Italian.

SIR THOMAS MORE: Hans Holbein the

Younger (1497-1543). Frick Collection, New York. German.

SISTINE MADONNA: Raphael (Raffaello Santi) (1483-1520), 1515-19. Dresden Gallery, Germany. Umbrian.

SIXTH AVENUE AND THIRD STREET, NEW YORK: John Sloane (1871-1951), 1928. Whitney Museum of American Art. American.

SKULL WITH CIGARETTE: Vincent van Gogh (1853-1890), 1885-86. V. W. van Gogh Collection, Municipal Museum, Amsterdam. French.

SLEEPING DRAGON, THE: Carlos Merida (1893-   ), 1948. Mr. and Mrs. Ricardo Martinez de Hoyos. Mexican.

SLEEPING GYPSY, THE: Henri Rousseau (1844-1910), 1897. Museum of Modern Art, New York. French.

SLEEPING VENUS: Giorgione (1478?-1510), c. 1508-10. Art Gallery, Dresden. Venetian.

SLEEP OF DIANA: Jean Baptiste Camille Corot (1796-1875), 1868. Metropolitan Museum of Art, New York. French.

SMALL SELF-PORTRAIT, THE: Rembrandt van Rijn (1606-1669), 1656-58. Gemaldegalerie, Vienna. Dutch.

SMOKERS, THE: Adriaen Brouwer (1605-1638). Metropolitan Museum of Art, New York. Flemish.

SNAKE AND MOON: Morris Graves (1910-   ), 1938-39. Museum of Modern Art, New York. American.

SNOW BOUND: Gina Knee (1898-   ), 1941. Willard Gallery, New York. American.

SNOW SCENE: Gustave Courbet (1819-1877). Metropolitan Museum of Art, New York. French.

SODA: Georges Braque (1882-   ), 1911. Museum of Modern Art, New York. French.

SOLITUDE: Charles François Daubigny (1817-1878), 1876 Metropolitan Museum of Art, New York. French.

SORTIE OF THE BRITISH GARRISON FROM GIBRALTAR: John Trumbull (1756-1843), 1789. Boston Athenaeum. American.

SOURCE, THE: Gustave Courbet (1819-1877). Metropolitan Museum of Art, New York. French.

SOURCE, LA: Jean Dominique Ingres (1780-1867), 1856. Louvre, Paris. French.

SOURCE OF THE LOUE, THE: Gustave Courbet (1819-1877). Metropolitan Museum of Art, New York. French.

SOUTHERN FRANCE: André Derain (1880-1954), 1927. Philips Memorial Gallery, Washington, D.C. French.

SOUTH OF SCRANTON: Peter Blume (1906-   ), 1931. Metropolitan Museum of Art, New York. American.

SOUVENIR OF NORMANDY: Jean Baptiste Camille Corot (1796-1875). Metropolitan Museum of Art, New York. French.

SOWER, THE: Jean François Millet (1814-1875), 1850. Boston Museum of Fine Arts. French.

SPACE MODULATOR IN PLEXIGLAS CH 4: L. Moholy-Nagy (1895-1946), 1941. Hungarian.

SPAIN: Salvador Dali (1904-   ), 1938. Edward James. Spanish (lives in U.S.A.).

SPANISH DANCER: Joan Miró (1893-   ), 1945. Mr. and Mrs. Lee A. Ault, New Canaan, Conn. Spanish.

SPANISH PRISON, THE: Robert Motherwell (1915-   ), 1943-44. Owned by artist. American.

SPIELERS, THE: George Luks (1867-1933), 1905. Addison Gallery of American Art, Andover, Mass. American.

SPINNERS, THE: See Fable of Arachne, The.

SPRING FLOWERS: Gustave Courbet (1819-

1877). Metropolitan Museum of Art, New York. French.

SPRING SHOWERS: Martin J. Heade (1819-1904), 1868. Boston Museum of Fine Arts. American.

SPRINGTIME: Édouard Manet (1832-1883), 1881. Fogg Museum, Harvard University, Cambridge, Mass. French.

SPRINGTIME: Franklin C. Watkins (1894-   ), 1935. Wright Ludington. American.

SPRINGTIME IN VIRGINIA: Winslow Homer (1836-1910). Privately owned, Detroit. American.

SQUARE AT MONTIGNY: Maurice Utrillo (1883-1955). Privately owned. French.

STAG AT SHARKEY'S: George Bellows (1882-1925), 1907. Cleveland Museum of Art. American.

STAIRCASE GROUP, THE: Charles Willson Peale (1741-1827), 1795. Philadelphia Museum of Art. American.

STAIRCASE OF QUEEN BERTHE, THE: Maurice Utrillo (1883-1955). Privately owned. French.

STAIRWAY, THE: Fernand Léger (1881-1955), 1913. Kunsthaus, Zurich, Switzerland. French.

STANDING NUDE: Pierre Bonnard (1867-1947) 1927. Privately owned, New York. French.

STANDING NUDE: Pablo Picasso (1881-   ), 1922. Wadsworth Atheneum, Hartford, Conn. French.

STARRY NIGHT, THE: Vincent van Gogh (1853-1890), 1889. Museum of Modern Art, New York. French.

STEAMER ODIN II, THE: Lyonel Feininger (1871-1956), 1927. Museum of Modern Art, New York. American.

STILL LIFE: Georges Braque (1881-   ), 1928. Phillips Memorial Gallery, Washington, D.C. French.

STILL LIFE: Paul Cézanne (1839-1906). Metropolitan Museum of Art, New York. French.

STILL LIFE: Henri Matisse (1869-1955), 1925. Mr. and Mrs. Samuel A. Lewisohn, New York. French.

STILL LIFE: Giorgio Morandi (1890-   ), 1916. Collection Mattioli, Milan. Italian.

STILL LIFE: André Dunoyer de Segonzac (1885-   ). James W. Barney, New York. French.

STILL LIFE: Maurice de Vlaminck (1876-   ), c. 1908. Mrs. Charles J. Liebman, New York. French.

STILL LIFE: Maurice de Vlaminck (1876-   ), 1928. Mrs. Thomas R. Coward. French.

STILL LIFE: Gabriel Zendel (1906-   ), 1951. Privately owned, Paris. French.

STILL LIFE: APPLES AND PRIMROSES: Paul Cézanne (1839-1906). Metropolitan Museum of Art, New York. French.

STILL LIFE IN RED AND GREEN: Mercedes Carles (1913-   ), 1935. Owned by artist. American.

STILL LIFE: JAR, CUP, AND FRUIT: Paul Cézanne (1839-1906), 1877. Metropolitan Museum of Art, New York. French.

STILL LIFE, JUG AND APPLES: Sir Matthew Smith (1879-   ), 1938. H. M. Queen Elizabeth, the Queen Mother. English.

STILL LIFE ON TABLE: Ben Nicholson (1894-   ), 1947. City Art Gallery, Aberdeen. English.

STILL LIFE—WHITE ROSES: Franklin C. Watkins (1894-   ), 1940. Wichita Museum, Kansas. American.

STILL LIFE WITH BASKET: Robert Macbryde (1913-   ). British Council, London. English.

STILL LIFE WITH COMPOTE: Charles Dufresne (1880-), 1928. Art Institute of Chicago. French.

STILL LIFE WITH A GUITAR: Pablo Picasso (1881-), 1942. Louise Leiris Gallery, Paris. French.

STILL LIFE WITH A PLASTER STATUETTE: Vincent van Gogh (1853-1890), 1886-88. Kröller-Müller State Museum, Otterlo, Holland. French.

STILL LIFE WITH A PLUCKED FOWL: Chaim Soutine (1894-1943). Maurice Speiser, Philadelphia. French (born Lithuania).

STILL LIFE WITH LANTERNS: John F. Peto (1854-1907), 1889. Brooklyn Museum. American.

STONE BREAKERS, THE: Gustave Courbet (1819-1877), 1850. Kunstmuseum, Dresden. French.

STORMING THE CITADEL: Jean Honoré Fragonard (1732-1806), 1772. Frick Collection, New York. French.

STORM IN THE JUNGLE: Henri Rousseau (1844-1910), 1891. Mr. and Mrs. Henry Clifford, Radnor, Pa. French.

STRANGE THING LITTLE KIOSAI SAW IN THE RIVER, THE: John La Farge (1835-1910), 1897. Metropolitan Museum of Art, New York. American.

STREET, THE: Alberto Giacometti (1901-), 1953. Galerie Maeght, Paris. French.

STREET AT MARLY, A: Alfred Sisley (1839-1899). Stadtische Kunsthalle, Mannheim. French.

STREET IN DELFT, A: Jan Vermeer (1632-1675). Rijksmuseum, Amsterdam. Dutch.

STREET IN ORTHEZ: Maurice Utrillo (1883-1955), 1923. Perls Galleries, New York. French.

STREET IN PARIS: Maurice Utrillo (1883-1955), 1914. Art Institute of Chicago. French.

STREET IN ROUEN: Camille Pissarro (1830-1903). Privately owned, Paris. French.

STREET SCENE: Maurice Utrillo (1883-1955), 1923. Knoedler Galleries, New York. French.

STRING QUARTETTE: Jack Levine (1915-), 1934-37. Metropolitan Museum of Art, New York. American.

STUDIO, THE: Raoul Dufy (1877-1953), 1942. Fine Arts Associates, New York. French.

STUDIO: John D. Graham (1890-), 1941. Dikran Kelekian. Russian (lives in U.S.A.).

STUDY OF AN OLD WORKER: Moses Soyer (1899-), 1939. Phillips Memorial Gallery, Washington, D.C. American.

STUDY OF VINES: Vincent van Gogh (1853-1890), 1888. Kröller-Müller State Museum, Otterlo, Holland. French.

STUYVESANT, PIETER: See Governor Pieter Stuyvesant.

SUBURBAN LANDSCAPE: Maurice Utrillo (1883-1955). Privately owned, Paris. French.

SUBURBAN LANDSCAPE: Maurice Utrillo (1883-1955), 1910. Perls Galleries, New York. French.

SUMMER: Max Weber (1881-), 1911. Whitney Museum of American Art, New York. American.

SUMMER LANDSCAPE: Stuart Davis (1894-), 1930. Museum of Modern Art, New York. American.

SUMMER'S DAY: Berthe Morisot (1841-1895), 1879. Tate Gallery, London. French.

SUMMER WIND: Alexander Brook (1898-), c. 1933. Mr. and Mrs. Otto L. Spaeth. American.

SUNDAY AFTERNOON ON THE ISLAND OF LA GRANDE JATTE, A: Georges Seurat (1859-1891), 1884-86. Art Institute of Chicago. French.

SUNFLOWERS: Vincent van Gogh (1853-1890),

1888. V. W. van Gogh Collection, Municipal Museum, Amsterdam. French.

SUNNY STREET, THE: August Macke (1887-1914), 1914. Privately owned. German.

SUNRISE: Claude Lorrain (1600-1682). Metropolitan Museum of Art, New York. French.

SUNSET: Peter Paul Rubens (1577-1640), c. 1638. National Gallery, London. Dutch.

SUNSET, CASCO BAY: John Marin (1870-1953), 1919. Miss Georgia O'Keeffe. American.

SUN SETTING BETWEEN THE HILLS: Graham Sutherland (1903-), 1937. Sir Kenneth Clark, London. English.

SUPREMIST COMPOSITION: Kasimir Malevich (1878-1935), c. 1915. Art of This Century Collection. Russian.

SURRENDER OF BREDA, THE: Diego Velasquez (1599-1660), c. 1635. Prado, Madrid. Spanish.

SURRENDER OF CORNWALLIS AT YORKTOWN, THE: John Trumbull (1756-1843), 1817-20. United States Capitol. American.

SUSANNA AND THE ELDERS: Tintoretto (Jacopo Robusti) (1518-1594), c. 1560. Gemaldegalerie, Vienna. Venetian.

SUSSEX LANDSCAPE, A: Paul Nash (1889-1946), 1928. Winifred Felce, London. English.

SWAN, THE: Andre Racz (1916-), 1941. Owned by artist. Born Transylvania (lives in U.S.A.).

SWEET TOOTH, THE: Pablo Picasso (1881-), 1902. Josef Stransky, New York. French.

SWIMMER, THE: Jean Bazaine (1904-), 1951. Willy Grubben, Brussels. French.

SWING, THE: Jean Honoré Fragonard (1732-1806), c. 1766-69. Wallace Collection, London. French.

SYNCHROMY IN BLUE AND ORANGE: S. MacDonald-Wright (1890-), 1916. Alfred Stieglitz, Fisk U. American.

SYNDICS, THE: See Board of the Clothmaker's Guild, The.

TABLE, THE: Georges Braque (1881-), 1928. Museum of Modern Art, New York. French.

TAORMINA: Raoul Dufy (1877-1953), 1923. Stephen D. Heineman, Greenwich, Conn. French.

TATA JESUCRISTO: Francisco Goitia (1884-), 1926-27. National Gallery of Painting, Mexico City. Mexican.

TE AA NO AREOIS: THE SEED OF THE AREOIS: Paul Gauguin (1848-1903), 1892. Privately owned. French.

TEA PARTY, THE: Henry Sargent (1770-1845), c. 1815-20. Boston Museum of Fine Arts. American.

TE ARII VAHINE: THE WOMAN WITH MANGOES: Paul Gauguin (1848-1903), 1896. Privately owned. French.

TEMOIN, LE: Yves Tanguy (1900-), 1940. Mr. and Mrs. Le Ray Berdeau. French.

TEMPEST: Oskar Kokoschka (1886-). Kunstmuseum, Basle. German.

TEMPEST, THE: Albert Pinkham Ryder (1847-1917). Detroit Institute of Art. American.

TEMPEST, THE: Giorgione (Barbarelli) (c. 1478-1510). Palazzo Giovanelli, Venice. Venetian.

TEMPI MADONNA: Raphael (Raffaello Santi) (1483-1520). 1505. Munich. Umbrian.

TEMPTATION OF CHRIST: Titian (Tiziano Vecellio) (1480?-1576), c. 1542. Minneapolis Art Museum. Venetian.

TEMPTATION OF ST. ANTHONY (TRIPTYCH): Hieronymos Bosch (c. 1460-1516). Lisbon Museum. Dutch.

TERRACE AT THE SEASIDE NEAR LE HAVRE: Claude Monet (1840-1926), 1866. Rev. T. Pitcairn, Bryn Athyn, Penn. French.

TERROR IN BROOKLYN: O. Louis Guglielmi

(1906-   ), 1941. Whitney Museum of American Art, New York. American.

THAT WHICH I SHOULD HAVE DONE I DID NOT DO: Ivan le Loraine Albright (1897-   ), 1941. Art Institute of Chicago. American.

THEATER BOX, THE: Pablo Picasso (1881-   ), 1921. Rosenberg and Helft, London. French.

THEY GUARD THE NIGHT: Raymond Breinin (1910-   ), 1945. Paul Baron. American.

THINKER, THE: Thomas Eakins (1844-1916), 1900. Metropolitan Museum of Art, New York. American.

THIRD - CLASS CARRIAGE, THE: Honoré Daumier (1808-1879). Metropolitan Museum of Art, New York. French.

THOMAS CARLYLE: James McNeill Whistler (1834-1903), 1872. Glasgow Corporation Art Gallery, Scotland. American.

THOMAS JEFFERSON: Gilbert Stuart (1755-1828), 1799. Bowdoin College, Brunswick, Maine. American.

THREADING LIGHT: Mark Tobey (1890-   ), 1942. Museum of Modern Art, New York. American.

THREE AGES OF MAN, THE: Dosso Dossi (Giovanni de Lutero) (1479-1542). Metropolitan Museum of Art, New York. Farrarese.

THREE CLOWNS: Georges Rouault (1871-   ), 1917. Mr. and Mrs. Joseph Pulitzer, Jr., St. Louis. French.

THREE DANCERS: Pablo Picasso (1881-   ), 1925. Owned by artist. French.

THREE FIGURES: Fernand Léger (1881-1955), 1910-11. Milwaukee Art Institute, Wisconsin. French.

THREE FRIENDS: Marsden Hartley (1877-1943), 1942. Mr. and Mrs. Henry R. Hope. American.

THREE GRACES: Pablo Picasso (1881-   ), 1924. Owned by artist. French.

THREE JUDGES: Georges Rouault (1871-   ), c. 1907. Mr. and Mrs. Samuel A. Marx, Chicago. French.

THREE LITERARY GENTLEMEN: Max Weber (1881-   ), 1945. A. P. Rosenberg and Co. American.

THREE MESSENGERS, THE: Carlos Merida (1893-   ), 1944. Clarita Kefkovitz. Mexican.

THREE MIRACLES OF SAINT ZENOBIUS: Sandro Botticelli (Alessandro Filipepi) (1444?-1510). Metropolitan Museum of Art, New York. Florentine.

THREE MUSICIANS: Pablo Picasso (1881-   ) 1921. Museum of Modern Art, New York. French.

THREE MUSICIANS: Pablo Picasso (1881-   ), 1921. Philadelphia Museum of Art. French.

THREE TREES, THE: See Woodland Scene.

THREE WOMEN (LE GRAND DÉJEUNER): Fernand Léger (1881-1955), 1921. Museum of Modern Art, New York. French.

THUNDERSTORM IN THE ROCKY MOUNTAINS: Albert Bierstadt (1830-1902), 1859. Boston Museum of Fine Arts. American.

TICKET OFFICE: Lamar Dodd (1909-   ), 1940. Telfair Academy, Savannah, Georgia. American.

TIGER, THE: Franz Marc (1880-1916). Bernhard Koehler, Berlin. German.

TIGHT ROPE: Raoul Dufy (1879-1953), 1925. Privately owned, New York. French.

TOILERS OF THE SEA: Rockwell Kent (1882-   ), 1907. Art Museum of the New Britain Institute, Conn. American.

TOILERS OF THE SEA: Albert P. Ryder (1847-1917), c. 1900. Addison Gallery, Phillips Academy, Andover, Mass. American.

TOILET OF VENUS, THE: François Boucher (1703-1770), 1751. Metropolitan Museum of Art, New York. French.

TOILETTE, LA: Mary Cassatt (1845-1926), 1894 R. A. Waller Memorial Collection, Chicago Art Institute. American.

TOILETTE, LA: Pablo Picasso (1881-   ), 1906 Albright Art Gallery, Buffalo. French.

TOILETTE, THE: Henri de Toulouse-Lautrec (1864-1901), 1896. Louvre. French.

TOPERS, THE: See Triumph of Bacchus, The.

TORNADO, BAHAMAS: Winslow Homer (1836-1910). Metropolitan Museum of Art, New York. American.

TORSO OF A WOMAN: Gustave Courbet (1819-1877). Metropolitan Museum of Art, New York. French.

TOTTENHAM CHURCH: John Constable (1776--1837). Metropolitan Museum of Art, New York. English.

TOWER OF BABEL, THE: Pieter Bruegel the Elder (c. 1520-1569), 1563. Kunsthistorisches Museum, Vienna. Flemish.

TRANSFIGURATION: Raphael (Raffaello Santi) (1483-1520), 1519. Vatican, Rome. Umbrian.

TRANSFIGURATION, THE: Titian (Tiziano Vecellio) (1480?-1576), c. 1560. San Salvatore, Venice. Venetian.

TRAPPERS' RETURN, THE: George Caleb Bingham (1811-1879), 1851. Detroit Institute of Arts. American.

TREE, SEA, MAINE: John Marin (1870-1953), 1919. Alfred Stieglitz, Fisk U. American.

TRIBUTE MONEY, THE: Masaccio (Tommaso Guidi) (c. 1401-1428). Brancacci Chapel, Sta. Maria del Carmine, Florence. Florentine.

TRIBUTE MONEY, THE: Titian (Tiziano Vecellio) (1480?-1576), c. 1518. Staatliche Gemaldegalerie, Dresden. Venetian.

TRIUMPHANT BOUQUET, THE: Charles Walch (1898-1948). Mme. Charles Walch, Paris. French.

TRIUMPH OF BACCHUS, THE: Diego Velasquez (1599-1660), 1628-29. Prado, Madrid. Spanish.

TRIUMPH OF CHASTITY: Lorenzo Lotto (1480-1556), c. 1528. Palazzo Rospigliosi, Florence. Italian.

TRIUMPH OF FLORA, THE: Nicolas Poussin (1594-1665), c. 1635. Louvre, Paris. French.

TRIUMPH OF NEPTUNE AND AMPHITRITE, THE: Nicolas Poussin (1594-1669), 1638-40. Museum of Art, Philadelphia. French.

TROUGH, THE: Marc Chagall (1887-   ), 1925. Viscomtesse de Noialles Collection, Paris. French.

TROUT POOL, THE: Worthington Whittredge (1820-1910). Metropolitan Museum of Art, New York. American.

TURKISH WOMEN AT THE BATH: Jean Auguste Dominique Ingres (1780-1867), 1862. Louvre, Paris. French.

TWITTERING MACHINE: Paul Klee (1879-1940), 1922. Museum of Modern Art, New York. Swiss.

TWO ACROBATS WITH A DOG: Pablo Picasso (1881-   ), 1905. Wright Ludington. French.

TWO CHILDREN ARE MENACED BY A NIGHTINGALE: Max Ernst (1891-   ), 1924. Museum of Modern Art, New York. German.

TWO COURTESANS ON A BALCONY: Vittore Carpaccio (1450?1522), c. 1510. Museo Correr, Venice. Venetian.

TWO HOUSES: Walter Stuempfig, Jr. (1914-   ), 1946. Corcoran Gallery of Art, Washington, D.C. American.

TWO LADIES IN A CARRIAGE: Constantin Guys (1802-1892), c. 1860. Metropolitan Museum of Art, New York. French.

TWO MEN: Eastman Johnson (1824-1906), 1881. Metropolitan Museum of Art, New York. American.

TWO MEN IN A SKIFF: Jean Baptiste Camille Corot (1796-1875). Metropolitan Museum of Art, New York. French.

TWO NUDES: Pablo Picasso (1881-   ), 1906. Rosenberg and Helft, London. French.

TWO PLUNGERS: Fernand Léger (1881-1955), 1942. Privately owned, New York. French.

TWO SEATED WOMEN: Pablo Picasso (1881-   ), 1920. Walter P. Chrysler, Jr. French.

TWO WOMEN: Eunice Pinney (1770-1849), c. 1815. Jean and Howard Lipman. American.

TWO WOMEN SEATED: Henry Moore (1898-   ), 1949. Andrew Revai, London. English.

TWO YOUNG BROTHERS IN BRITTANY: Paul Gauguin (1848-1903), 1888. Privately owned. French.

TWO ZEBRAS: Charles Dufresne (1880-   ), Maurice Speiser, Philadelphia. French.

UNA MUSICA: Caravaggio (Michelangelo Merisi) (1573-1610), 1593-94. Metropolitan Museum of Art, New York. Italian.

UNCLE DOMINIC: See Man in a Blue Cap.

UNFAITHFUL SHEPHERD, THE: Pieter Bruegel the Elder (c. 1520-1569). Johnson Collection, Philadelphia. Flemish.

UNION SQUARE: Morris Kantor (1896-   ), 1928. A. Conger Goodyear. American.

"UNITED STATES" AND THE "MACEDONIAN", THE: Thomas Birch (1779-1857), 1813. Historical Society of Pennsylvania, Philadelphia. American.

UPPER DECK: Charles Sheeler (1883-   ), 1929. Fogg Museum of Art, Harvard University, Cambridge, Mass. American.

URSINE PARK: Stuart Davis (1894-   ), 1942. Downtown Gallery, New York. American.

VANITY OF AN ARTIST'S DREAM: Charles Bird Kine (1785-1862), c. 1830. Fogg Museum of Art, Harvard University, Cambridge. American.

VASE, THE: Fernand Léger (1881-1955), 1927. Mr. and Mrs. Morton G. Neumann, Chicago. French.

VASE WITH FLOWERS: Vincent van Gogh (1853-1890), 1886-88. V. W. van Gogh Collection, Municipal Museum, Amsterdam. French.

VENETIAN SENATOR, A: Tintoretto (Jacopo Robusti) (1518-1594). Frick Collection, New York. Italian.

VENICE: DOGANA AND SAN GIORGIO MAGGIORE: Joseph Mallord Turner (1775-1851). Widener Collection in National Gallery of Art, Washington, D.C. English.

VENUS: Lucas Cranach (1472-1553), 1532. Frankfort Museum. German.

VENUS AND ADONIS: Titian (Tiziano Vecellio) (1480?-1576), 1554. National Gallery of Art, Washington, D.C. Venetian.

VENUS AND CUPID: Titian (Tiziano Vecellio) (1480?-1576), c. 1545. Uffizi Gallery, Florence. Venetian.

VENUS AND THE LUTE PLAYER: Titian (Tiziano Vecellio) (1480?-1576). Metropolitan Museum of Art, New York. Venetian.

VENUS AND THE ORGAN PLAYER: Raoul Dufy (1877-1953), 1949. Louis Bergman, New York. French.

VENUS AND THE ORGAN PLAYER: Titian (Tiziano Vecellio) (1480?-1576), c. 1545. Prado, Madrid. Venetian.

VENUS, CUPID, FOLLY, AND TIME: Angelo Bronzino (c. 1502-1572), c. 1546. National Gallery, London. Florentine.

VENUS OF URBINO: Titian (Tiziano Vecellio) (1480?-1576). Uffizi Gallery, Florence. Venetian.

VENUS WITH THE MIRROR: Titian (Tiziano Vecellio) (1480?-1576), c. 1555. Mellon Collection, National Gallery of Art, Washington, D.C. Venetian.

VENUS WITH THE MIRROR (THE ROKEBY VENUS): Diego Velasquez (1599-1660), c. 1642. National Gallery, London. Spanish.

VERDICT OF THE PEOPLE, THE: George Caleb Bingham (1811-1877), 1855. Boatmen's National Bank, St. Louis. American.

VERTICAL COMPOSITION: Rico Lebrun (1900-   ), 1945. Mr. and Mrs. George Dangerfield, New York. American.

VICTIMS, THE: José Clemente Orozco (1883-1949). University of Guadalajara. Mexican.

VICTORY BOOGIE WOOGIE: Piet Mondrian (1872-1944), 1943-44. Valentine Dudensing. Dutch.

VIE, LA: Pablo Picasso (1881-   ), 1903. Cleveland Museum of Art, Ohio. French.

VIENNA FROM THE BELVEDERE: Canaletto (Bernardo Belotto) (1720-1780). Gemaldegalerie, Vienna. Italian.

VIEW AT STOKE-BY-NAYLAND: John Constable (1776-1837). Metropolitan Museum of Art, New York. English.

VIEW FROM APPLE HILL: Samuel F. B. Morse (1791-1872), 1828-29. Stephen C. Clark. American.

VIEW FROM VINCENT'S ROOM (ANTWERP): Vincent van Gogh (1853-1890), 1885. V. W. van Gogh Collection, Municipal Museum, Amsterdam. French.

VIEW FROM VINCENT'S ROOM (RUE LEPIC, PARIS): Vincent van Gogh (1853-1890), 1886-88. V. W. van Gogh Collection, Municipal Museum, Amsterdam. French.

VIEW OF MARSEILLES: Raoul Dufy (1877-1953), 1908. Mr. and Mrs. Peter A. Rubel, New York. French.

VIEW OF THE CITY OF TOLEDO: El Greco (Domenicos Theotocopoulos) (1548-1614). Metropolitan Museum of Art, New York. Spanish.

VIEW OF THE KAATERSKILL HOUSE: Jasper Francis Cropsey (1828-1900), 1855. Minneapolis Institute of Arts. American.

VIEW OF WINDSOR CASTLE: Jean Piper (1903-   ), 1941. H. M. the Queen, London. English.

VIEW OVER PARIS: Vincent van Gogh (1853-1890), 1886-88. V. W. van Gogh Collection, Municipal Museum, Amsterdam. French.

VILLAGE: Ralph Rosenborg (1910-   ), 1940. Marion Willard. American.

VILLAGE POST OFFICE, THE: Thomas Waterman Wood (1823-1903), 1873. New York State Historical Association, Cooperstown. American.

VILLAGE STREET—DARDAGNY: Jean Baptiste Camille Corot (1796-1875). Metropolitan Museum of Art, New York. French.

VILLE D'AVRAY: Jean Baptiste Camille Corot (1796-1875). Metropolitan Museum of Art, New York. French.

VINCENT'S BEDROOM: Vincent van Gogh (1853-1890), 1889. V. W. van Gogh Collection, Municipal Museum, Amsterdam. French.

VIOLONIST, THE, (SI TU VEUX): Pablo Picasso (1881-   ), 1918. Privately owned. French.

VIRGIN AND CHILD, THE: Albrecht Dürer (1471-1528), 1516. Metropolitan Museum of Art, New York. German.

VIRGIN AND CHILD: Carlo Crivelli (1430?-1493?), c. 1470. Metropolitan Museum of Art, New York. Venetian.

VIRGIN AND THE CHILD, THE: Anthony Van Dyck (1599-1641). Metropolitan Museum of Art, New York. Flemish.

VIRGIN AND CHILD: Jean Fouquet (1415-1481), c. 1443. Museum of Fine Arts, Antwerp. French.

VIRGIN AND CHILD, THE: Masaccio (Tommaso Guidi) (1401-1428), 1426. National Gallery, London. Florentine.

VIRGIN AND CHILD WITH FOUR ANGELS: Taddeo di Bartolo (c. 1362-1422), c. 1400. John G. Johnson Collection, Philadelphia. Sienese.

VIRGIN AND CHILD WITH ST. ANNE, THE: Albrecht Dürer (1471-1528). Metropolitan Museum of Art, New York. German.

VIRGIN AND CHILD WITH ST. ANNE, THE: Leonardo da Vinci (1452-1519), 1508-10. Louvre Paris. Florentine.

VIRGIN AND CHILD WITH ST. ANNE AND ST. JOHN BAPTIST, THE: Leonardo da Vinci (1452-1519), c. 1498. Burlington House, London. Florentine.

VIRGIN AND CHILD WITH SS. JOHN THE BAPTIST AND MARY MAGDALENE, THE: Andrea Mantegna (1431-1506). National Gallery, London. Paduan.

VIRGIN OF THE ANNUNCIATION, THE: Gerard David (c. 1460-1523). Metropolitan Museum of Art, New York. Flemish.

VIRGIN OF THE BALANCES: Leonardo da Vinci (1452-1519), c. 1506. Hermitage Museum, Leningrad. Florentine.

VIRGIN OF THE DIVINE LOVE: Raphael (Raffaello Santi) (1483-1520). Naples. Umbrian.

VIRGIN OF THE ROCKS: Leonardo da Vinci (1452-1519), c. 1483-90. Louvre, Paris. Florentine.

VIRGIN OF THE ROCKS: Leonardo da Vinci (1452-1519), 1506-08. National Gallery, London. Florentine.

VIRGIN WITH A LAMB, THE: Raphael (Raffaello Santi) (1483-1520), 1507. Prado, Madrid. Umbrian.

VIRGIN WITH HER SON AND ST. ANNE: Leonardo da Vinci (1452-1519), c. 1503. Louvre, Paris. Florentine.

VIRGIN WITH THE DIADEM: Raphael (Raffaello Santi) (1483-1520), 1510. Louvre, Paris. Umbrian.

VISION OF SAINT PAUL: Caravaggio (Michelangelo Merisi) (1573-1610), 1600-01. Santa Maria del Popolo, Rome. Italian.

VISIT, THE: Max Weber (1881-   ), 1919. Mr. and Mrs. Milton Lowenthal. American.

VISITE, LA: RUE DES MOULINS: Henri de Toulouse-Lautrec (1864-1901), 1894. Chester Dale Collection, New York. French.

VIVIPAROUS QUADRUPEDS OF NORTH AMERICA (TWO-VOLUME EDITION OF COLORED PLATES): John James Audubon (1785-1851), 1842-45. American.

VOYAGE OF LIFE: MANHOOD, THE: Thomas Cole (1801-1848). Munson-Williams-Proctor Institute, Utica, New York. American.

VROUW BODOLPHE: Frans Hals (c. 1580-1666), 1643. Stephen C. Clark Collection, New York. Dutch.

VULCAN PRESENTING TO VENUS THE ARMS OF AENEAS: François Boucher (1703-1770), 1757. Louvre, Paris. French.

WAITING: Isabel Bishop (1902-   ), 1938. Newark Museum. American.

WAKE OF THE FERRY, THE: John Sloan (1871-1951), 1907. Phillips Collection, Washington, D. C. American.

WASHINGTON AT DORCHESTER HEIGHTS: Gilbert Stuart (1775-1828), 1806. City of Boston. American.

WASHINGTON AT THE PASSAGE OF THE DELAWARE: Thomas Sully (1783-1872), 1819. Boston Museum of Fine Arts. American.

WASHINGTON CROSSING THE DELAWARE: Emanuel Leutze (1816-1868), 1852. Metropolitan Museum of Art, New York. American.

WASHWOMAN: Honoré Daumier (1808-1879), c. 1863. Louvre, Paris. French.

WATCH, THE: Vincent van Gogh (1853-1890), 1889. V. W. van Gogh Collection, Municipal Museum, Amsterdam. French.

WATERING PLACE, THE: Alfred Sisley (1839-1899), 1874. Tate Gallery, London. French.

WATERMILL, THE: Meindert Hobbema (1638-1709), 1664. Louvre, Paris. Dutch.

WATER MILL WITH THE GREAT RED ROOF, THE: Meindert Hobbema (1638-1709), before 1670. Art Institute of Chicago. Dutch.

WATSON AND THE SHARK: John Singleton Copley (1738-1815), 1775. Boston Museum of Fine Arts. American.

WAVE, THE: William de Kooning (1904-   ), 1942-43. Owned by artist. Dutch (lives in U.S.A.).

WEARY: Eugene Higgins (1874-   ), 1905. Kleemann Gallery, New York. American.

WEDDING, THE: Fernand Léger (1881-1955), 1910-11. Musée National d'Art Moderne, Paris. French.

WEDDING DANCE, THE: Pieter Breugel the Elder (c. 1520-1569). Detroit Institute of Art. Flemish.

WESTERN LANDSCAPE: Thomas Moran (1837-1926), 1864. Art Museum, New Britain Institute, New Britain, Connecticut. American.

WESTWARD THE COURSE OF EMPIRE: See Course of Empire.

WHEELWRIGHT'S YARD ON THE SEINE: Jean Baptiste Camille Corot (1796-1875). Metropolitan Museum of Art, New York. French.

WHENCE DO WE COME? WHAT ARE WE? WHITHER ARE WE GOING?: Paul Gauguin (1848-1903), 1898. Privately owned. French.

WHISTLER'S MOTHER: See Arrangement in Gray and Black.

WHITE BARN, CANADA: Georgia O'Keeffe (1887-   ), 1932. Owned by artist. American.

WHITE CHATEAU, THE: Maurice Utrillo (1883-1955), 1911. Rhode Island School of Design. French.

WHITE HORSE, THE: Paul Gauguin (1848-1903). Louvre, Paris. French.

WHITE ORCHARD: Vincent van Gogh (1853-1890), 1888. V. W. van Gogh Collection, Municipal Museum, Amsterdam. French.

WHITE PLUMES: Henri Matisse (1869-1955), 1919. Privately owned, New York. French.

WHITHER NOW?: Max Weber (1881-   ), 1939. A. P. Rosenberg and Co., New York. American.

WHITSUN BRIDE, THE: Pieter Bruegel the Younger (1564-1637). Metropolitan Museum of Art, New York. Flemish.

WHY NOT USE THE "L": Reginald Marsh (1898-1954), 1930. Whitney Museum of American Art, New York. American.

WILLIAM WRAGG: Jeremiah Theüs (d. 1774), c. 1740-45. Detroit Institute of Arts. American.

WINDMILLS OF MONTMARTRE: Maurice Utrillo (1883-1955), 1949. Dr. and Mrs. Harry Bakwin, New York. French.

WINDOW IN THE UNION CLUB, A: Guy Pène du Bois (1884-   ), 1919. American.

WINDOW ON THE PARK, THE: André Derain (1880-1954), 1912. Privately owned, New York. French.

WINDY CORNER, A: Jerome Myers (1867-1940), 1907. Mrs. Mary Egner Malone. American.

WINGS OF THE MORNING: Henry E. Mattson (1887-   ), 1937. Metropolitan Museum of Art, New York. American.

WINGS OVER THE WATER: Frances Hodgkins (1869-1947), 1935. Temple Newsam Museum, Leeds. New Zealand.

WINSLOW FAMILY, THE: Joseph Blackburn (?-1763), 1755. Boston Museum of Fine Arts. American.

WINTER SCENE: Jan van de Cappelle (1624?-1679). Metropolitan Museum of Art, New York. Dutch.

WITHDRAWAL FROM DUNKIRK: Richard Eurich (1903-   ), 1940. Owned by British Government. British.

WIVENHOE PARK, ESSEX: John Constable (1776-1837). Widener Collection of National Gallery of Art, Washington, D.C. English.

WOLFERT'S WILL: John Quidor (1801-1881), 1856. Brooklyn Museum, New York. American.

WOMAN AND DOG: Pierre Bonnard (1867-1947), 1923. Phillips Memorial Gallery, Washington, D.C. French.

WOMAN AND STARS: Joan Miró (1893-   ), 1944. Pierre Matisse Gallery, New York. Spanish.

WOMAN AT A CRADLE: Vincent van Gogh (1853-1890), 1886-88. V. W. van Gogh Collection, Municipal Museum, Amsterdam. French.

WOMAN BATHING: Edgar Degas (1834-1917), 1885. Metropolitan Museum of Art, New York. French.

WOMAN BATHING, A: Rembrandt van Rijn (1606-1669), 1654. National Gallery, London. Dutch.

WOMAN GATHERING FAGGOTS—VILLE D'AVRAY: Jean Baptiste Camille Corot (1796-1875). Metropolitan Museum of Art, New York. French.

WOMAN IN A GARDEN: Pablo Picasso (1881-   ), 1938. Mrs. Meric Gallery. French.

WOMAN IN AN ARMCHAIR: Pablo Picasso (1881-   ), 1927. Owned by artist. French.

WOMAN IN AN ARMCHAIR: Pablo Picasso 1881-   ), 1929. Owned by artist. French.

WOMAN IN BLUE, THE: Fernand Léger (1881-1955), 1912. Kunstmuseum, Basel, Switzerland. French.

WOMAN IN THE CAFÉ DU TAMBOURIN: Vincent van Gogh (1853-1890), 1886-88. V. W. van Gogh Collection, Municipal Museum, Amsterdam. French.

WOMAN IN THE WAVES, THE: Gustave Courbet (1819-1877), 1868. Metropolitan Museum of Art, New York. French.

WOMAN IN YELLOW: Pablo Picasso (1881-   ), 1907. Mr. and Mrs. Joseph Pulitzer, Jr. French.

WOMAN IRONING: Edgar Degas (1834-1917), c. 1880. Metropolitan Museum of Art, New York. French.

WOMAN IRONING: Pablo Picasso (1881-   ), 1904. J. Thannhauser. French.

WOMAN LOOKING AT AQUARIUM: Henri Matisse (1869-1954). Art Institute of Chicago. French.

WOMAN READING: Jean Baptiste Camille Corot (1796-1875). Metropolitan Museum of Art, New York. French.

WOMAN READING IN A GARDEN: Mary Cassatt (1848-1926), 1880. Art Institute of Chicago. American.

WOMAN WITH A BOOK: Pablo Picasso

(1881-   ), 1909. Walter P. Chrysler, Jr. French.

WOMAN WITH A DOG: Mary Cassatt (1848-1926), c. 1889. Corcoran Gallery of Art, Washington, D.C. American.

WOMAN WITH A FAN: Pablo Picasso (1881-   ), 1905. Mr. and Mrs. William Averell Harriman. New York. French.

WOMAN WITH A FAN: Pablo Picasso (1881-   ), 1908. Leningrad Museum. French.

WOMAN WITH A NECKLACE: Amadeo Modigliani (1884-1920), 1917. Art Institute of Chicago. French (born Italy).

WOMAN WITH A PARROT: Gustave Courbet (1819-1877), 1866. Metropolitan Museum of Art, New York. French.

WOMAN WITH BUTTERFLIES: Fernand Léger (1881-1955), 1943. Saidenberg Gallery, New York. French.

WOMAN WITH CHRYSANTHEMUMS (MADAME HERTEL): Edgar Degas (1834-1917), 1865. Metropolitan Museum of Art, New York. French.

WOMAN WITH FOLDED ARMS: Pablo Picasso (1881-   ), 1901. Mr. and Mrs. Chauncey McCormick. French.

WOMAN WITH LOAVES: Pablo Picasso (1881-   ), 1906. Philadelphia Museum of Art. French.

WOMAN WITH PLANTS: Grant Wood (1892-1942), 1929. Cedar Rapids Fine Art Association. American.

WOMAN WITH THE HAT: Henri Matisse (1869-1954), 1905. Mr. and Mrs. Walter A. Haas, San Francisco. French.

WOMAN WITH THE MIRROR, THE—LA BELLE IRLANDAISE: Gustave Courbet (1819-1877), 1866. Metropolitan Museum of Art, New York. French.

WOMAN BATHERS: Paul Cézanne (1839-1906), 1898-1906. Philadelphia Museum of Art. French.

WOMEN REGENTS OF THE OLD MEN'S HOME: Frans Hals (1580?-1666), 1664. Museum, Haarlem. Dutch.

WOODEN HORSES: Reginald Marsh (1898-1954), 1936. Mr. and Mrs. Carl W. Kelly Collection, Winnetka, Ill. American.

WOODLAND SCENE: André Derain (1880-1954), c. 1922. Adolph Lewisohn, New York. French.

WOOD ON THE DOWNS: Paul Nash (1889-1946), 1928. Anna Wernher, London. English.

WOOLWORTH BUILDING: John Marin (1870-1953), 1915. Downtown Gallery, New York. American.

WORLD UPSIDE DOWN, THE: Jan Steen (1626-1679), c. 1663. Art Gallery, Vienna. Dutch.

WORSHIP OF VENUS, THE: Peter Paul Rubens (1577-1640), 1630-37. Gemaldegalerie, Vienna.

WORSHIP OF VENUS, THE: Titian (Tiziano Vecellio) (1480?-1576), c. 1518, Prado, Madrid. Venetian.

YELLOW CHRIST, THE: Paul Gauguin (1848-1903), 1889. Albright Art Gallery, Buffalo. French.

YELLOW CHRIST, BRITTANY, THE: Paul Gauguin (1848-1903), 1889. Paul Rosenberg Collection. French.

YONKER RAMP AND HIS SWEETHEART: Frans Hals (c. 1580-1666), 1623. Metropolitan Museum of Art, New York. Dutch.

YOUNG BATHER: Gustave Courbet (1819-1877) 1866. Metropolitan Museum of Art, New York. French.

YOUNG ENGLISHMAN: See Portrait of Ippolito Riminaldi.

YOUNG MAN IN THE SUN: Pierre Auguste Renoir (1841-1919). Louvre, Paris. French.
YOUNG MOTHER SEWING: Mary Cassatt (1848-1926). Metropolitan Museum of Art, New York. American.
YOUNG ROUTY: Henri de Toulouse-Lautrec (1864-1901), 1882. Kunstmuseum, Basel, Switzerland. French.
YOUNG SAILOR, THE: Henri Matisse (1869-1954). Mr. and Mrs. Leigh B. Block, Chicago. French.
YOUNG WOMAN WITH A WATER JUG: Jan Vermeer (1632-1675). Metropolitan Museum of Art, New York. Dutch.
ZACHARIAS AND THE ANGEL: William Blake (1757-1827). Metropolitan Museum of Art, New York. English.
ZAPATISTAS: José Clemente Orozco (1883-1949). Museum of Modern Art, New York. Mexican.
ZIRCHOW-7: Lyonel Feininger (1871-1956), 1917. American.
ZOO: Paul Klee (1879-1940), 1928. M. Martin Janis. Swiss.
ZOUAVE—BUGLER MILLIET, THE: Vincent van Gogh (1853-1890), 1888. Kröller-Müller State Museum, Otterlo, Holland. French.

Parables of Christ

The principal parables of Christ, exclusive of expressions that are merely parabolic

BARREN FIG TREE, THE: Luke XIII, 6-9.
BUILDER OF THE TOWER AND THE KING GOING TO BATTLE, THE: Luke XIV, 28-36.
FAITHFUL SERVANT, THE: Matt. XXIV, 45-51; Luke XII, 41-48.
GOOD SAMARITAN, THE: Luke X, 25-37.
GOOD SEED AND THE TARES (WEEDS), THE: Matt. XIII, 24-30, 36-43.
GREAT SUPPER, A: Luke XIV, 15-24.
HIDDEN TREASURE, THE: Matt. XIII, 44.
IMPORTUNATE FRIEND, THE: Luke XI, 5-8.
LABORERS IN THE VINEYARD, THE: Matt. XX, 1-16.
LOST COIN, THE: Luke XV, 8-10.
LOST SHEEP, THE: Matt. XVIII, 12-14; Luke XV, 4-7.
LOWEST (LAST) PLACE, THE: Luke XIV, 7-11.
MARRIAGE FEAST, THE: Matt. XXII, 1-14.
MUSTARD SEED AND THE LEAVEN, THE: Matt. XIII, 31-33; Mark IV, 30-32; Luke XIII, 18-21.
NET, THE: Matt. XIII, 47-50.
PEARL OF GREAT PRICE, THE: Matt. XIII, 45-46.
PHARISEE AND THE PUBLICAN, THE: Luke XVIII 9-14.
PRODIGAL SON, THE: Luke XV, 11-32.
RICH FOOL, THE: Luke XII, 16-21.
RICH MAN AND LAZARUS, THE: Luke XVI, 19-31.
SEED GROWING SECRETLY, THE: Mark IV, 26-29.
SOWER, THE: Matt. XIII, 3-9; Mark IV, 3-20; Luke VIII, 5-15.
STRAIT, THE (NARROW) GATE: Luke XIII, 23-30.
TALENTS, THE: Matt. XXV, 14-30.
TEN POUNDS, THE (OR, THE GOLD PIECES) Luke XIX, 11-27.
THIEF IN THE NIGHT, THE: Matt. XXIV, 42-44; Luke XII, 39.
TWO DEBTORS, THE: Luke VII, 40-43.

TWO SONS, THE: Matt. XXI, 28-32.
UNJUST JUDGE, THE: Luke XVIII, 1-8.
UNJUST STEWARD, THE: Luke XVI, 1-13.
UNMERCIFUL SERVANT, THE: Matt. XVIII, 23-35.
VINE-DRESSERS, THE: Matt. XXI, 33-46; Mark XII, 1-12; Luke XX, 9-19.
WATCHFUL SERVANTS, THE: Mark XIII, 33-37; Luke XIII, 35-38.
WAYWARD CHILDREN, THE (THE CHILDREN SITTING IN THE MARKET-PLACE): Matt. XI, 16-19; Luke VII, 31-35.
WISE AND FOOLISH VIRGINS, THE (THE TEN VIRGINS): Matt. XXV, 1-13.

Parks
See **State Parks** and listings under **Nationals**

Parkways
See **National Parkways**

Planets and Their Symbolic Gems
See also **Birthstones; Gem Stones; Gems and Days of the Week**

JUPITER: Cornelian.
MARS: Diamond.
MERCURY: Lodestone.
MOON: Crystal.
SATURN: Onyx.
SUN: Sapphire.
VENUS: Emerald.

Plays: Long Runs on Broadway

Dramas

LIFE WITH FATHER: 3224.
TOBACCO ROAD: 3182.
ABIE'S IRISH ROSE: 2327.
HARVEY: 1775.
BORN YESTERDAY: 1642.
THE VOICE OF THE TURTLE: 1557.
ARSENIC AND OLD LACE: 1444.
ANGEL STREET: 1295.
LIGHTNING: 1291.
MR. ROBERTS: 1157.
THE SEVEN YEAR ITCH: 1141.
THE TEAHOUSE OF THE AUGUST MOON: 1027.
ANNA LUCASTA: 957.
KISS AND TELL: 957.
THE MOON IS BLUE: 924.
THE BAT: 867.
MY SISTER EILEEN: 865.
WHITE CARGO: 864.
A STREETCAR NAMED DESIRE: 855.
YOU CAN'T TAKE IT WITH YOU: 837.
THREE MEN ON A HORSE: 835.
INHERIT THE WIND: 805.
THE LADDER: 789.
STATE OF THE UNION: 765.
THE FIRST YEAR: 760.
DEATH OF A SALESMAN: 742.
THE MAN WHO CAME TO DINNER: 739.
CLAUDIA: 722.
THE GOLD DIGGERS: 720.
NO TIME FOR SERGEANTS: 796.
DIARY OF ANNE FRANK: 717.
I REMEMBER MAMA: 714.
TEA AND SYMPATHY: 712.
JUNIOR MISS: 710.
SEVENTH HEAVEN: 704.
CAT ON A HOT TIN ROOF: 694.
PEG O' MY HEART: 692.
THE CHILDREN'S HOUR: 691.
DEAD END: 687.
THE LION AND THE MOUSE: 686.

DEAR RUTH: 683.
EAST IS WEST: 680.
THE DOUGHGIRLS: 671.
BOY MEETS GIRL: 669.
BLITHE SPIRIT: 657.
A TRIP TO CHINATOWN: 657.
THE WOMEN: 657.
THE FIFTH SEASON: 653.
RAIN: 648.
WITNESS FOR THE PROSECUTION: 646.
JANIE: 642.
THE GREEN PASTURES: 640.
THE FOUR POSTER: 632.
IS ZAT SO?: 618.
THE HAPPY TIME: 614.
SEPARATE ROOMS: 613.
AFFAIRS OF STATE: 610.
BROADWAY: 603.
ADONIS: 603.
STREET SCENE: 601.
THE MATCHMAKER: 589.
THE TWO MRS. CARROLLS: 585.
DETECTIVE STORY: 581.
BROTHER RAT: 577.
THE SHOW-OFF: 571.
HAPPY BIRTHDAY: 564.
THE GLASS MENAGERIE: 561.
STRICTLY DISHONORABLE: 557.
DIAL "M" FOR MURDER: 552.
WITHIN THE LAW: 541.
THE MUSIC MASTER: 540.
WHAT A LIFE: 538.
THE SOLID GOLD CADILLAC: 528.
THE BOOMERANG: 522.
VICTORIA REGINA: 517.
THE MEMBER OF THE WEDDING: 501.
PERSONAL APPEARANCE: 501.
BIRD IN HAND: 500.
ROOM SERVICE: 500.
SAILOR, BEWARE!: 500.
TOMORROW THE WORLD: 500.

Musicals

OKLAHOMA!: 2248.
SOUTH PACIFIC: 1925.
HELLZAPOPPIN: 1404.
THE KING AND I: 1246.
GUYS AND DOLLS: 1200.
ANNIE GET YOUR GUN: 1147.
PINS AND NEEDLES: 1108.
KISS ME KATE: 1070.
THE PAJAMA GAME: 1063.
DAMN YANKEES: 1030.
CAN-CAN: 892.
CAROUSEL: 890.
HATS OFF TO ICE: 889.
FANNY: 888.
FOLLOW THE GIRLS: 882.
SONG OF NORWAY: 860.
COMEDY IN MUSIC: 849.
WHERE'S CHARLEY?: 792.
SONS O' FUN: 742.
CALL ME MISTER: 734.
HIGH BUTTON SHOES: 727.
FINIAN'S RAINBOW: 725.
IRENE: 670.
BLOOMER GIRL: 654.
CALL ME MADAME: 644.
ANNIVERSARY WALTZ: 615.
STAR AND GARTER: 609.
THE STUDENT PRINCE: 608.
KIKI: 600.
WISH YOU WERE HERE: 598.
A SOCIETY CIRCUS: 596.
BLOSSOM TIME: 592.
BRIGADOON: 581.
KISMET: 580.
SHOW BOAT: 572.

SALLY: 570.
ONE TOUCH OF VENUS: 567.
ROSE MARIE: 557.
WONDERFUL TOWN: 556.
ZIEGFELD FOLLIES OF 1943: 553.
FLORADORA: 553.
GOOD NEWS: 551.
LET'S FACE IT: 547.
MY FAIR LADY: 752 (as of December 31, 1957).
PAL JOEY: 540.
THE RED MILL: 531.
ROSALINDA: 521.
CHAUVE SOURIS: 520.
BLACKBIRDS OF 1928: 518.
SUNNY: 517.
THE VAGABOND KING: 511.
THE NEW MOON: 509.
SHUFFLE ALONG (1921): 504.
UP IN CENTRAL PARK: 504.
CARMEN JONES: 503.
PANAMA HATTIE: 501.
THE MOST HAPPY FELLA: 678.

Popes

ST. PETER: Martyr, (42-67); Jew; considered to be author of two epistles.
ST. LINUS: Martyr; (67-79); of Tuscany.
ST. CLETUS: Martyr; (79-89); Roman.
ST. CLEMENT I: Martyr; (89-97); Roman; his first epistle is considered among the most important of early Christian documents.
ST. EVARISTUS: Martyr; (97-105); Greek.
ST. ALEXANDER I: Martyr; (105-115); Roman.
ST. SIXTUS I: Martyr; (115-125); Roman.
ST. TELESPHORUS: Martyr; (125-136); Greek.
ST. HYGINUS: Martyr; (136-140); Greek.
ST. PIUS I: Martyr; (140-155); of Aquileia.
ST. ANICETUS: Martyr; (155-166); Syrian.
ST. SOTER: Martyr; (166-174); of Campania.
ST. ELEUTHERUS: Martyr; (174-189); of Nicopolis in Epirus.
ST. VICTOR I: Martyr; (189-199); African.
ST. ZEPHYRINUS: Martyr; (199-217); Roman.
ST. CALLISTUS I: Martyr; (217-222); Roman.
ST. HYPPOLYTUS: Roman; antipope (217-235).
ST. URBAN I: Martyr; (222-230); Roman.
ST. PONTIAN: Martyr; (230-235); Roman.
ST. ANTHERUS: Martyr; (235-236); Greek.
ST. FABIAN: Martyr; (236-250); Roman.
ST. CORNELIUS: Martyr; (251-253); Roman; three important letters have been preserved; "the first indubitable utterances of a Roman bishop since the letter of Clement"—Shotwell and Loomis, *The See of Peter*, p. 352.
NOVATIAN: Roman; antipope in 251.
ST. LUCIUS I: Martyr; (253-254); Roman.
ST. STEPHEN I: Martyr; (254-257); Roman.
ST. SIXTUS II: Martyr; (257-258); Greek.
ST. DIONYSIUS: (259-268); Greek.
ST. FELIX I: Martyr; (269-274); Roman; wrote a letter attacking heretical doctrines regarding the Divinity of Christ.
ST. EUTYCHIAN: Martyr; (275-283); of Luni.
ST. CAIUS: Martyr; (283-296); Dalmatian.
ST. MARCELLINUS: Martyr; (296-304); Roman.
ST. MARCELLUS I: Martyr; (308-309); Roman.
ST. EUSEBIUS: Martyr; (309-310); Greek.
ST. MELCHIADES (MILTIADES): Martyr; (311-314); African.
ST. SYLVESTER I: (314-335); Roman.
ST. MARCUS: (Jan.-Oct., 336); Roman.
ST. JULIUS I: (337-352); Roman; wrote letters against the Arians.
LIBERIUS: (352-366); Roman.
FELIX II: Roman; antipope (355-365).

ST. DAMASUS I: (366-384); Spaniard; wrote defending the Nicene Creed during the Arian controversy.

URSINUS: Antipope (366-367).

ST. SIRICIUS: (384-398); Roman; wrote the first papal decretal that has come down to us.

ST. ANASTASIUS I: (398-401); Roman.

ST. INNOCENT I: (401-417); of Albano; wrote on the authority of the Roman see.

ST. ZOSIMUS: (417-418); Greek.

ST. BONIFACE I: (419-422); Roman; wrote strongly on papal authority.

EULALIUS: Antipope (418-419).

ST. CELESTIN I: (422-432); of Campania; wrote threatening Nestorius with excommunication.

ST. SIXTUS III: (432-440); Roman.

ST. LEO I (THE GREAT): (440-461); of Tuscany; the first of the great papal letter writers. Condemned heresies of Nestorius and Eutyches.

ST. HILARY: (461-468); Sardinian.

ST. SIMPLICIUS: (468-483); of Tivoli.

ST. FELIX III: (483-492); Roman.

ST. GELASIUS I: (492-496); African; wrote on relation of Church and state, stating the famous "Gelasian theory" of Church and state coexisting as distinct and legitimate powers, each supreme in its own sphere.

ANASTASIUS II: (496-498); Roman.

ST. SYMMACHUS: (498-514); Sardinian.

LAWRENCE: Antipope (498-505).

ST. HORMISDAS: (514-523); of Frosinone.

ST. JOHN I: Martyr; (523-526); of Tuscany.

ST. FELIX IV (III): (526-530); of Beneventum.

BONIFACE II: (530-532); Roman.

DIOSCORUS: Alexandrian; antipope (Sept.-Oct. 530).

JOHN II: (533-535); Roman.

ST. AGAPETUS I: (535-536); Roman.

ST. SILVERIUS: Martyr; (536-537); of Frosinone.

VIGILIUS: (537-555); Roman.

PELAGIUS I: (555-560); Roman.

JOHN III: (561-574); Roman.

BENEDICT I: (575-578); Roman.

PELAGIUS II: (579-590); Roman.

ST. GREGORY I, THE GREAT: (590-604); Roman; wrote extensively in connection with his works of reforming ecclesiastical discipline, Church prayer, and of encouraging missionary activities.

SABINIANUS: (604-606); of Tuscany.

BONIFACE III: (Feb.-Nov., 607); Roman.

ST. BONIFACE IV: (608-615); of Marsi.

ST. DEUSDEDIT (OR ADEODATUS) I: (615-618)· Roman.

BONIFACE V: (619-625); Neapolitan.

HONORIUS I: (625-638); of Campania.

SEVERINUS: (May-Aug., 640); Roman.

JOHN IV: (640-642); of Zara in Dalmatia.

THEODORE I: (642-649); Greek.

ST. MARTIN I: Martyr; (649-654); of Todi.

ST. EUGENIUS I: (654-657); Roman.

ST. VITALIAN: (657-672); of Segni.

DEUSDEDIT (ADEODATUS) II: (672-676); Roman.

DONUS: (676-678); Roman.

ST. AGATHO: (678-681); Sicilian.

ST. LEO II: (682-683); Sicilian.

ST. BENEDICT II: (684-685); Roman.

JOHN V: (685-686); of Antioch.

CONON: (686-687); of Thrace.

THEODORE: Antipope (Sept.-Oct. or Dec. 687).

PASCHAL: Antipope (687-692).

ST. SERGIUS I: (687-701); Syrian.

JOHN VI: (701-705); Greek.

JOHN VII: (705-707); Greek.

SISINNIUS: (Jan.-Feb., 708); Syrian.

CONSTANTINE I: (708-715); Syrian.

ST. GREGORY II: (715-731); Roman.

ST. GREGORY III: (731-741); Syrian.

ST. ZACHARY: (742-752); Greek.

STEPHEN II: 752; Roman. Not included in some lists. He was elected Pope, but died before his consecration. At the time, "the papal dignity was held to be conferred at the consecration."

STEPHEN III: (752-757); Sicilian.

ST. PAUL I: (757-767); Roman.

CONSTANTINE: B. Nepi; antipope (767-769).

PHILIP: Antipope (for a day in 768).

STEPHEN IV: (768-772).

ADRIAN I: (772-795); Roman.

ST. LEO III: (795-816); Roman.

STEPHEN V: (816-817); Roman.

ST. PASCHAL: (824-827); Roman.

EUGENIUS II: (824-827); Roman.

VALENTINE: (Sept., 827); Roman.

GREGORY IV: (828-844); Roman.

JOHN: Antipope (844).

SERGIUS II: (844-847); Roman.

ST. LEO IV: (847-858); Roman.

ANASTASIUS: Antipope (855).

BENEDICT III: (855-858); Roman.

ST. NICHOLAS I (THE GREAT): (858-867); Roman; wrote to the Council of the Bulgars concerning questions regarding baptism.

ADRIAN II: (867-872); Roman.

JOHN VIII: (872-882); Roman.

MARINUS I: (882-884); of Gallese.

ST. ADRIAN (HADRIANUS) III: (884-885); Roman.

STEPHEN VI: (885-891); Roman.

FORMOSUS: (891-896); Corsian(?); b. Portus.

BONIFACE VI: (Apr., 896); of Gallese.

STEPHEN VII: (896-897); Roman.

ROMANUS: (Aug.-Nov., 897); of Gallese.

THEODORE II: (897-898); Roman.

JOHN IX: (898-900); of Tivoli.

BENEDICT IV: (900-903); Roman.

LEO V: (July-Sept., 903); of Ardea in Latium. Leo V is sometimes listed as having been deposed. Roman Catholic teaching on this point, however, does not recognize deposition, holding that a pope validly in the office can leave the office only through death or genuine resignation.

CHRISTOPHER: Roman; antipope (903-904).

SERGIUS III: (904-911); Roman.

ANASTASIUS III: (911-913); Roman.

LANDO (LANDUS): (913-914); Sabine.

JOHN X: (914-928); of Ravenna; deposed; died in 928. (Cf. note on Leo V, 903).

LEO VI: (May-Dec. 929); Roman.

STEPHEN VIII: (929-931).

JOHN XI: (Feb.-Mar. 931); Roman; deposed; or 931-935. (Cf. note on Leo V, 903.)

LEO VII: (936-939); Roman.

STEPHEN IX: (939-942); German(?) or Roman(?).

MARINUS II: (942-946); Roman.

AGAPITUS II: (946-955); Roman.

JOHN XII: (955-963; deposed; or 964); Tusculum; Octavian. (Cf. note on Leo V, 903.)

LEO VIII: (963-965); Roman. The lawfulness and validity of his pontificate is disputed.

BENEDICT V: (May-June, 964 or 964-966); Roman; Grammaticus. His forced resignation may have been genuine, according to the theological reckoning. Thus the correct dates would depend upon the interior disposition of Benedict when he was forced to resign.

JOHN XIII: (965-972); Roman.

BENEDICT VI: (973-974); Roman.

BONIFACE VII: Roman; antipope (974).

BENEDICT VII: (974-983); Roman.

JOHN XIV: (983-984); of Pavia; Pietro of Pavia.

BONIFACE VII: (984-985); Roman. There is doubt whether Boniface in 984 was true pope or antipope for the second time.

JOHN XV: (985-996); Roman.

GREGORY V: (996-999); Saxony; Bruno of the House of Carinthin.

JOHN XVI: (997-998); Greek; John Philagatus; antipope, expelled, died 998.

SYLVESTER II: (999-1003); French; Gerbert d'Aurillac.

JOHN XVII: (June-Nov., 1003); Roman; Sicco.

JOHN XVII: (1003-1009); Roman.

SERGIUS IV: (1009-1012); Roman.

BENEDICT VIII: (1012-1024); Roman; John of the House of Tusculum.

JOHN XIX: (1024-1032); of Tusculum.

BENEDICT IX: (1032-1044); Tusculum; Theophylactus. Expelled in favor of Sylvester III and then shortly returned to office as his followers expelled Sylvester. Then Benedict sold the office to Gregory VI, but (in 1047) claimed to revoke his resignation. Sylvester would then seem to be antipope; and the validity of Gregory VI and of Clement II, who followed him, dependent upon the genuineness of Benedict's resignation.

SYLVESTER III: (Jan.-Mar., 1045); Roman; John, Bishop of Sabina. May be antipope; cf. note on Benedict IX (1032) and Benedict IX (1045).

BENEDICT IX: (1045); Tusculum; Theophylactus. Claimed papacy second time after deposition by Sylvester III; if original accession was valid, he would seem to be true pope until at least his resignation in favor of Gregory VI. And thus Sylvester III would be antipope. Cf. note on Benedict IX (1032).

GREGORY VI: (1045-1056); Roman; John Gratian. May be antipope; cf. notes on Benedict IX (1032), and on Benedict IX (1045). Also, if Gregory be considered a valid pope, his confession of invalidity regarding the means of accession is taken as termination of his pontificate through resignation.

CLEMENT II: (1046-1047); Saxony; Suidger of the House of Moresleve and Hornebuch. May be antipope; cf. notes on Boniface IX (1032).

BENEDICT IX: (1047-1048); Tusculum; Theophylactus. Benedict expelled Clement II by force and held possession of the Lateran for nine months until disloged by the Emperor. In this his third attempt upon the papacy it would seem certain to class him as antipope. Cf. also notes on Benedict IX (1032) and Benedict IX (1045).

DAMASUS II: (July-Aug., 1048); Bavarian, Poppo.

ST. LEO IX: (1049-1054); Alsatian; Bruno of the House of Egisheim-Dagsburg.

VICTOR II: (1055-1057); of the House of Tollestein-Hirschberg, Swabia; Gerhard.

STEPHEN X: (1057-1058); of Lorraine; Frederick.

BENEDICT X: (1058-1059); may be pope; "It cannot be affirmed that his title was certainly invalid...." Cath. Encyc.

NICHOLAS II: (1059-1061); Burgundian; Gerard.

ALEXANDER II: (1061-1073); Milanese; Anselm of the House of Baggio.

HONORIUS II: of Parma; Cadalo Pallavicino; antipope (1061-1073).

ST. GREGORY VII: (1073-1085); of Tuscia; Hildebrand Aldobrandesch. Wrote on the relation of the papacy with the emperor, occasioned by his conflict with Henry IV. Wrote also in connection with his great work of reforming the clergy and the government of the church.

CLEMENS III: B. Parma; Guibert; antipope (1080-1100).

BL. VICTOR III: (1086-1087); of Benvento; Desiderius Epifani.

BL. URBAN II: (1088-1099); French; Otto of the House of Chatillon.

PASCHAL II: (1099-1118); of Ravenna; Ranieri of Bieda.

THEODORIC: Antipope (Sept.-Dec., 1100).

ALBERT: Antipope (Feb.-Mar., 1102).

SYLVESTER IV: Roman; Maginulf; antipope (1105-1111).

GELASIUS II: (1118-1119); of Gaeta; Giovanni Crescentius Gaetani.

GREGORY VIII: French; Maurice Bourdin; antipope (1118-1121 or 1119).

CALISTUS II: (1119-1124); Burgundian; Guido of the House of Burgundy.

CELESTIN II: Theobald Boccadipecora; antipope on Dec. 15., 1124; abdicated at once.

HONORIUS II: (1124-1130); of Fiagnano; Lamberto Scannabecchi.

INNOCENT II: (1130-1143); Roman; Gregory Papareschi.

ANACLETUS II: Roman (Jewish); Pierleoni; antipope (1130-1138).

VICTOR IV: of Tusculum; Gregoria of the House of Tusculum; antipope (1138).

CELESTIN II: (1143-1144); of Castello; Guido of Città di Castello.

LUCIUS II: (1144-1145); of Bologna; Gerardo Caccianemici.

BL. EUGENE III: (1145-1153); of Pisa; Bernardo Paganelli.

ANASTASIUS IV: (1153-1154); Roman; Corrodo.

ADRIAN (HADRIANUS) IV: (1154-1159); Nicholas Breakspear, the only English pope.

ALEXANDER III: (1159-1181) of Siena; Orlando Bandinelli.

VICTOR IV: Of Mentecello; Octavian; antipope (1159-1164). Did not recognize his antipope predecessor of the same name (Victor IV, 1138).

PASCHAL III: Of Crema; Guido; antipope (1164-1168).

CALIXTUS III: Hungarian; John, Abbot of Struma; antipope (1168-1178).

INNOCENT III: (1179-1180); of Sezze; Lando Frangipane.

LUCIUS III: (1181-1185); of Lucca; Albaldo Allucingoli.

URBAN III: (1185-1187); Milanese; Alberto Crivelli.

GREGORY VIII: (Oct.-Dec., 1187); of Benuento; Alberto di Morra.

CLEMENT III: (1187-1191); Roman; Paolo Scolari.

CELESTIN III: (1191-1198); Roman; Giacinto Boboni-Orsini.

INNOCENT III: (1198-1216); of Anagni; of the House of Segni. At the height of the "political papacy," Innocent wrote defending the papacy's claim to temporal power.

HONORIUS III: (1216-1227); Roman; Cericio Sanelli.

GREGORIUS IX: (1227-1241); of Anagni; Ugolino of the House of Segni.

CELESTIN IV: (Oct.-Nov., 1241); Milanese; Godefrido Castiglioni.

INNOCENT IV: (1243-1254); Genoa; Sinibaldo di Fieschi.

ALEXANDER IV: (1254-1261); of Anagni; Rinaldo of the House of Segni.

URBAN IV: (1261-1264); of Troyes (French); Jacques Pantaléon.

CLEMENT IV: (1265-1268); French; Guy le Gros.

BL. GREGORY X: (1271-1276); of Piacenza; Teobaldo Visconti.

BL. INNOCENT V: (Jan.-June, 1276); of Savoy; Pierre de Tarentaise.

ADRIAN V: (July-Aug., 1276); of Genoa; Ottobuono de' Fieschi.

JOHN XXI: (1276-1277); Portuguese; Pedro Giuliano or Petrus Hispanus.

NICHOLAS III. (1277-1280); Roman; Giovanni Gaetano Orsini.

MARTIN IV: (1281-1285); French; Simon de Brie.

HONORIUS IV: (1285-1287); Roman; Giacomo Sanelli.

NICHOLAS IV: (1288-1292); of Ascoli; Girolamo Masci d'Ascoli-Piceno.

ST. CELESTIN V: (July-Dec., 1294); of Isernia; Pietro Angeleri Morroni; abdicated the papacy.

BONIFACE VIII: (1294-1303); of Anagni; Benedetto Gaetoni. Boniface issued the bull Clericus Laicos, which attacked the right of the state to impose taxes upon the Church. He also issued the famous bull Unam Sanctum, asserting the temporal authority of the Church as supreme, and making the classic statement of intransigent papal authority: "Indeed we declare, announce and define, that it is altogether necessary to salvation for every human ceature to be subject to the Roman pontiff." Boniface also attacked, in Excrabilis, the practice of appealing a papal decision to a council.

BL. BENEDICT XI: (1303-1304); of Treviso; Niccolo Bocasini.

CLEMENT V: (1305-1314); French; Bertrand de Goth.

JOHN XXII: (1316-1334); French; Jacques Arnaud d'Ossa.

NICHOLAS V: Of Rietti; Pietro Rainalducci; antipope (1328-1330, resigned).

BENEDICT XII: (1334-1342); French; Jacques Fournier.

CLEMENT VI: (1342-1352); French; Roger de Beaufort.

INNOCENT VI: (1352-1362); French; Étienne d'Aubert.

BL. URBAN V: (1362-1370); French; Guillaume Grimoard.

GREGORY XI: (1370-1378); French: Pierre Roger de Beaufort.

URBAN VI: (1378-1379); Neapolitan; Bartolomeo Prignani.

CLEMENT VII: Robert of the House of Geneva; antipope (1378-1394); sometimes listed as Avignon pope; not recognized by the Roman Catholic Church.

BONIFACE IX: (1389-1404); Neapolitan; Pietro Tomacelli.

BENEDICT XIII: Of Aragon; Pedro de Luna; antipope (1394-1423); sometimes listed as Avignon pope; not recognized by Roman Catholic Church.

INNOCENT VII: (1404-1406); of Sulmona; Cosimo di' Migliorati.

GREGORY XII: (1406-1415); Venetian; Angelo Corrario.

ALEXANDER V: Of Crete; Pietro Philargo; antipope (1410-1415); elected pope by the self-summoned Council of Pisa.

JOHN XXIII: Neapolitan; Baldassare Cossa; antipope (1410-1415); elected pope by the self-summoned Council of Pisa.

MARTIN V: (1417-1431); Roman; Otto Colonna.

CLEMENT VIII: Of Barcelona; Aegidius Sanchez Murroz; antipope (1423-1429); an Avignon pope.

BENEDICT XIX: Of Rodez; Bernard Carnier; antipope (1424-1425); an Avignon pope.

EUGENE IV: (1431-1447); Venetian; Gabriele Condulmieri.

FELIX V: (Duke of Savoy); Amadeus; antipope (1439-1449).

NICHOLAS V: (1446-1455); of Sarzana; Tomaso Parentucelli. Wrote bull Romanus Pontifex in 1455, and succeeding bulls that determined the extent of respective Spanish and Portuguese dominions in newly discovered territories, including those in the Americas.

CALLISTUS III: (1455-1458); of Valencia; Alphonso Borgia.

PIUS II: (1458-1464); Sienese; Aeneas Sylvius Piccolomini.

PAUL II: (1464-1471); Venetian; Pietro Barbo.

SIXTUS IV: (1471-1484); Ligurian; Francesco dello Rovere.

INNOCENT VIII: (1484-1492); Genoese; Giovanni Battista Cibo.

ALEXANDER VI: (1492-1503); of Valencia; Rodrigo Borgia.

PIUS III: (Sept.-Oct., 1503); Sienese; Francesco Todeschini-Piccolomini.

JULIUS II: (1503-1513); Ligurian; Giuliano della Rovere. His tomb designed by Michelangelo.

LEO X: (1513-1521); Florentine; Giovanni de' Medici.

ADRIAN VI: (1522-1523); of Utrecht; Adrian Dedel.

CLEMENT VII: (1523-1534); Florentine; Giulio de' Medici.

PAUL III: (1534-1549); Roman; Alessandro Farnese. In the bull, Pastorale Officium in 1537, Pope Paul condemned the enslavement of Indians.

JULIUS III: (1550-1555); Roman; Giovanni Maria Ciocchi del Monte.

MARCELLUS II: (Apr.9-30, 1555); of Montepulciano; Marcello Cervini.

PAUL IV: (1555-1559); Neopolitan; Giovanni Pietro Caraffa.

PIUS IV: (1559-1565); Milanese; Giovanni Angelo de' Medici.

ST. PIUS V: (1566-1572); B. Bosco; Michele Ghislieri. Wrote bull Regnans in excelsis, in which he formally excommunicated and deposed Elizabeth I of England, dated Feb.25, 1570.

GREGORY XIII: (1572-1585); Bolognese; Ugo Boncompagno.

SIXTUS V: (1585-1590); of Montalo; Felice Peretti.

URBAN VII: (Sept. 15-27, 1590); Genoese; Giovanni Battista Castagna.

GREGORY XIV: (1590-1591); of Cremona; Nicolo Sfondrato.

INNOCENT IX: (Oct.29-Dec.30, 1591); Bolognese; Giovanni Antonio Fachinetti.

CLEMENT VIII: (1592-1605); Florentine; Ippolito Aldobrandini.

LEO XI: (Apr.1-27, 1605); Florentine; Alessandro de' Medici.

PAUL V: (1605-1621); Roman; Camillo Borghese.

GREGORY XV: (1621-1623); Bolognese; Alessandro Ludovisi.

URBAN VIII: (1623-1644); Florentine; Maffeo Barberini.

INNOCENT X: (1644-1655); Roman; Giovanni Battista Pamfili.

ALEXANDER VII: (1655-1667); Sienese; Fabio Chigi.

CLEMENT IX: (1667-1669); Tuscan; Giulio Rospigliosi.

CLEMENT X: (1670-1676); Roman; Giovanni Battista Emilio Altieri.

INNOCENT XI: (1676-1689); of Como; Benedetto Odescalchi.

ALEXANDER VIII: (1689-1691); Venetian; Pietro Ottoboni.

INNOCENT XII: (1691-1700); Neopolitan; Antonio Pignatelli.

CLEMENT XI: (1700-1721); of Urbino; Giovanni Francesco Albani. Wrote the famous constitution *Unigenitus* (Sept. 8, 1713) attacking Jansenism and Gallicanism.

INNOCENT XIII: (1721-1724); Roman; Michele Angelo Conti.

BENEDICT XIII: (1724-1730); Roman; Vincenzo-Maria Orsini.

CLEMENT XII: (1730-1740); Florentine; Lorenzo Corsini.

BENEDICT XIV: (1740-1758); Bolognese; Prospero Lambertini. Wrote on marriage, usury, and other matters of economic morality, and on relations with Moslems. The first pope to use the term "encyclical." Wrote*Matrimonii, Annus Qui Hunc* (on sacred music), *Vix Peruenit* (on usury).

CLEMENT XIII: (1758-1769); Venetian; Carlo Rezzanico. Wrote a bull defending the Jesuits; and inaugurated the worship of the Sacred Heart.

CLEMENT XIV: (1769-1774); of Forli; Lorenzo Ganganelli. On July 21, 1773, wrote the encyclical *Dominus Ac Redemptor Noster*, dissolving the Jesuit Order.

PIUS VI: (1775-1799); of Cesena; Giovanni Angelo Braschi. Wrote against the Avignon defection in *Haec Nota*, and an encyclical concerning the Church in the French revolution *(Caritas Quae).*

PIUS VII: (1800-1823) of Cesena; Giorgio Barnabo Chiaramonti. In a bull of Aug. 7, 1814, restored the Society of Jesus. Wrote also on "mixed marriage."

LEO XII: (1823-1829); of Genga; Annibale Della Genga. Wrote encyclical *Caritate Christi Urgente Nos* on the sanctification of Sunday, and *Quo Graviora* on secret societies.

PIUS VIII: (1829-1830); of Cingoli, near Macerata; Francesco Saviero Castigliani. Wrote a bull *Litteris Alto* against mixed marriages, and encyclical *Traditi Humilitati* against religious indifferentism and heretical translations of Scripture.

GREGORY XVI: (1831-1846); of Belluno; Bartolomeo Alberto Cappellari. Wrote encyclical *Singulari Nos,* condemning Lamennais, and encyclical *Mirari Vos* against liberalism.

PIUS IX: (1846-1878); of Sinigaglia; Giovanni Maria Mastai-Ferretti. In the bull *Ineffabilis Deus,* Dec. 8, 1854, he proclaimed the dogma of the Immaculate Conception of the Virgin Mary. Wrote against liberalism, condemned "errors of our time" listed in the famous *Syllabus of Pius IX.*

LEO XIII: (1878-1903); of Carpineto; Gioacchino Pecci; wrote widely and influentially on dogmatic and social affairs: 86 encyclicals in all. Most important: *Rerum Novarum* on the condition of the working classes, *Aeterni Patris* on the philosophy of St. Thomas, and the 12 social encyclicals (including *Rerum Novarum)* called the *Leonine Corpus.*

ST. PIUS X: (1903-1914); of Riese; Guiseppe Sarto. Wrote encyclical *Pascendi* against the modernist heresy; wrote encouraging frequent reception of the Eucharist.

BENEDICT XV: (1914-1922); Genoese; Giacomo Della Chiesa. Wrote on problems of World War I; give his proposals for peace in *Ad Beatissimi,* Nov. 1, 1914.

PIUS XI: (1922-1939); of Desio, near Milan; Achille Ratti. Wrote important encyclical on labor questions, *Quaoragesimo Ano; Divini Redemptoris,* which states Church's opposition to communism; *Rappresentanti in Terra* on Christian education; *Casti Connubi* on Christian marriage.

PIUS XII: (1939-   ); Roman; Eugenio Pacelli. Wrote *Mystici Corpus* on the doctrine of the Mystical Body of Christ; *Mediator Dei* on the liturgy of the Church; *Summi Pontifi-* *catus* on the "Function of the State in th Modern World"; the theologically importan *Humani Gereris* dealing with the Church an modern philosophical and theological trends proclaimed the dogma of the Assumption o the Virgin Mary, in the Apostolic Constitutio *Munificentissimus Deus* on Nov. 2, 1950.

Popular, Programmatic, Literary and Alternative Names of Famou Musical Compositions
See also Ballets; Musical Composi tions; Operas, Grand

ABSENT-MINDED MAN SYMPHONY (IL DI STRATTO): Haydn's Symphony No. 60 i C Major.

ACTUS TRAGICUS: Bach's Cantata No. 106

ADIEUX, LES: Beethoven's Piano Sonata No 26 in E Flat Major, Op. 81a.

A LA GIGUE: Organ Fugue in G Major, Bach

ALEXANDERFEST: Handel's Concerto in (Major for Orchestra.

ALLA RUSTICA: Concerto in G Major fo Strings and Cembalo, Vivaldi.

ALLELUJA SYMPHONY: Haydn's Symphon No. 30 in C Major.

AMERICAN QUARTET: Dvořák's Quartet i F Major, Op. 96. Also called the Nigge Quartet.

ANTAR: Rimsky-Korsakov's Symphony No. 2

ANTARCTICA SYMPHONY: Vaughan Williams' Symphony No. 7.

APPASSIONATA SONATA: Beethoven's Pianc Sonata in F Minor, Op. 57.

ARCHDUKE TRIO: Beethoven's Piano Trio i B Flat, Op. 97.

ARPEGGIONE SONATA: Schubert's Cello Sonata in A Minor, Op. Posth.

BATTLE OF THE HUNS: Liszt's Symphonic Poem No. II.

BEAR SYMPHONY (L'OURS): Haydn's Symphony No. 82 in C Major.

BRANDENBURG CONCERTOS: Six orchestra concertos by Bach: No. 1 in F Major; No. 2 in F Major; No. 3 in G Major; No. 4 in G Major; No. 5 in D Major; No. 6 in B Flat Major.

BUFFOON BALLET: Prokofieff's *Chout* Ballet Op. 21.

BULLFINCH CONCERTO: Vivaldi's Concert in D Major for Flute, Op. 10, No. 3.

CETRA, LA: Vivaldi's Concertos for Violin, Strings, and Continuo, Op. 9, Nos. 1-12.

CHASSE, LA: See Hunt Symphony.

CHORAL SYMPHONY: Beethoven's Symphony No. 9 in D Minor, Op. 125.

"CHRIST LAG": Bach's Cantata No. 4.

CHRISTMAS CANTATA: Bach's Cantata No. 63.

CHRISTMAS CONCERTO: Corelli's Concerto Grosso No. 8 in G Minor.

CHRISTMAS ORATORIO: Bach's set of 6 church cantatas, based on Gospel story, to be sung successively at services on Christmas Day, the 2 days following, the feast of the Circumcision and the Sunday after, and on feast of Epiphany.

CHRISTMAS SYMPHONY: Haydn's Symphony No. 26 in D Minor. See Lamentations Symphony.

CIMENTO, IL: Vivaldi's Concertos for Violin, Op. 8, Nos. 1-12.

CLOCK SYMPHONY: Haydn's Symphony No. 101 in D Major. See London Symphonies.

COFFEE CANTATA: Bach's Cantata No. 211.

CORDOBA NOCTURNE: Albeniz' Nocturne No. 4, Op. 232.

CORONATION CONCERTO: Mozart's Piano Concerto No. 26 in D Major, K. 537.
CORONATION MASS: Mozart's Mass in C Major, K. 317.
CREATION, THE: Oratorio by Haydn.
CZECH SUITE: Dvořák's Suite in D Major, Op. 39.
DANCE MACABRE: Saint-Saëns' Symphonic Poem, Op. 40.
DANTE SONATA: Liszt's Piano Sonata "Après une lecture de Dante."
DANTE SYMPHONY: Liszt's Symphony to Dante's *Divina Commedia*.
DEATH AND THE MAIDEN: Schubert's String Quartet No. 14 in D Minor.
DISSONANT QUARTET: Mozart's Quartet No. 19 in C Major, K. 465.
DISTRATTO, IL: See Absent-Minded Man Symphony.
DORIAN TOCCATA AND FUGUE: Organ Toccata and Fugue in D Minor, Bach.
DOUBLE CONCERTO: Brahms' Concerto in A Minor, for Violin and Violoncello, Op. 102.
DREAM QUARTET: Haydn's Quartet in F Major, Op. 50, No. 5.
DRESDEN ORCHESTRA CONCERTO: See For the Dresden Orchestra.
DRUM ROLL SYMPHONY (PAUKENWIRBEL) Haydn's Symphony No. 103 in E Flat Major. See London Symphonies.
DUMKY TRIO: Dvořák's Piano Trio, Op. 90.
DUO SONATA: Schubert's Violin Sonata No. 5 in A Major, Op. 162.
EASTER CANTATA: Bach's Cantata No. 31; also Cantata No. 158.
EGMONT OVERTURE: Beethoven's Overture in C Minor, Op. 84, from his incidental music for Goethe's *Egmont.*
EINE KLEINE NACHTMUSIK: Mozart's Serenade for Strings in G Major, K. 525.
ELEGIAC TRIO: Rachmaninoff's Trio in D Minor.
ELIJAH: Mendelssohn's Oratorio, Op. 70.
EMPEROR CONCERTO: Beethoven's Piano Concerto No. 5 in E Flat Major, Op. 73.
EMPEROR QUARTET: Haydn's Quartet in C Major, Op. 76, No. 3.
EROICA SYMPHONY: Beethoven's Symphony No. 3 in E Flat Major, Op. 55.
EVENING SYMPHONY (LE SOIR): Haydn's Symphony No. 8 in G Major.
EYEGLASS DUET: Beethoven's Duet in E Flat Major for Viola and Cello.
FANTASIE: Chopin's Polonaise No. 7 in A Flat Major, Op. 61.
FANTASTIC SYMPHONY: Berlioz' *Symphonie Fantastique (Episode de la vie d'un artiste),* Op. 14.
FANTASY SONATA: Schubert's Piano Sonata in G Major, Op. 78.
FANTASY SUITE: Rachmaninoff's Suite No. 1 for Two Pianos, Op. 5.
FAREWELL SYMPHONY (ABSCHIED): Haydn's Symphony No. 45 in F Sharp Minor.
FIDELIO OVERTURE: Beethoven's Overture to his opera *Fidelio.* He wrote 3 other overtures for the opera. See Leonore Overtures.
FINGAL'S CAVE: Mendelssohn's Overture in B Minor, Op. 26, alternative title of Hebrides Overture.
FIRE SYMPHONY (FEUER): Haydn's Symphony No. 59.
FLOWER PIECE: Schumann's *Blumenstück,* Op. 19.
FLYING DUTCHMAN, THE: Wagner's Opera *Der Fliegende Holländer.*
FOR THE DRESDEN ORCHESTRA: Concerto in G Minor for orchestra, Vivaldi.
FORTY-EIGHT, THE: Bach's set of 48 Preludes and Fugues, in 2 books of 24 each.

His title for the first book was *Das wohltemperierte Clavier (The Well-Tempered Clavier).*
FROG QUARTET: Haydn's Quartet in D Major, Op. 50, No. 6.
"FROM MY LIFE": Smetana's String Quartet in E Minor.
FUNEBRE CONCERTO: Violin Concerto in B Flat Major, Vivaldi.
GEISTER TRIO: See Ghost Trio.
GENZINGER PIANO SONATA: Haydn's Piano Sonata No. 49 in E Flat Major.
GHOST (GEISTER) TRIO: Beethoven's Trio in D Major, Op. 70, No. 1, for Violin, Cello, and Piano.
GIANT, THE: Organ Fugue in D Minor, Bach.
GREAT CHACONNE: Purcell's Chaconne for Strings in G Minor.
GREAT C MAJOR SYMPHONY: Schubert's Symphony No. 7.
GREAT G MINOR FUGUE: Bach's Organ Fantasy and Fugue in G Minor.
GREAT MASS: Bruckner's Mass No. 3 in F Minor. Mozart's Mass in C Minor, K. 427.
GREAT ORGAN MASS: Haydn's Mass in E Flat Major.
GREAT PRELUDE AND FUGUE: Bach's Organ Prelude and Fugue in B Minor; also Organ Prelude and Fugue in E Minor; also Organ Prelude and Fugue in G Major.
HAFFNER MARCH: Mozart's March in D Major, K. 249.
HAFFNER SERENADE: Mozart's Serenade No. 7 in D Major, K. 250.
HAFFNER SYMPHONY: Mozart's Symphony No. 35 in D Major, K. 385.
HALLELUJAH CHORUS: Handel's *Messiah,* end of second part.
HAMMERCLAVIER, SONATA: Beethoven's Piano Sonata No. 29 in B Flat Major, Op. 106.
HARMONIEMESSE: Haydn's Missa Solemnis in B Flat Major.
HARMONIOUS BLACKSMITH: Air and variations from Handel's Fifth Harpsichord Suite, in E Major.
HAROLD IN ITALY: Berlioz' Symphony with Viola Obligato, based on Byron's *Childe Harold's Pilgrimage,* commissioned and rejected by Paganini.
HARP QUARTET: Beethoven's String Quartet in E Flat, Op. 74.
HAYDN QUARTETS: Mozart's String Quartets Nos. 14-19, K. 387, 421, 458, 464, 465.
HEBRIDES OVERTURE: See Fingal's Cave.
HELIGMESSE: Haydn's Missa Sancti Bernardi de Offida.
HEN SYMPHONY (LA POULE): Haydn's Symphony No. 83 in G Minor.
HOFBALL-MINUETS: Dances by Haydn.
HORNSIGNAL SYMPHONY: Haydn's Symphony No. 31 in D Major.
HORSEMEN QUARTET: Haydn's Quartet in G Minor, Op. 74, No. 3.
HUNT, THE: Mozart's String Quartet No. 17 in B Flat Major, K. 458.
HUNT SYMPHONY, THE (LA CHASSE): Haydn's Symphony No. 73 in D Major.
HYMN OF PRAISE SYMPHONY (LOBGESANG): Mendelssohn's Symphony No. 2, Op. 52.
ILYA MOUROMETZ: Gliere's Symphony No. 3, Op. 42.
IMPERIAL QUARTET: Haydn's String Quartet in F Major, Op. 74, No. 2.
IMPERIAL SYMPHONY: Haydn's Symphony No. 53 in D Major.
INEXTINGUISHABLE SYMPHONY: Nielsen's Symphony No. 4, Op. 29.
ITALIAN SYMPHONY: Mendelssohn's Symphony No. 4 in A Major, Op. 90.
"JAUCHZET GOTT": Bach's Cantata No. 51.

JAZZ CONCERTO: Copland's Concerto for Piano and Orchestra.

JENA SYMPHONY: Beethoven's Symphony in C Major.

JUPITER SYMPHONY: Mozart's Symphony No. 41 in C Major, K. 551.

KING OF PRUSSIA QUARTETS: Mozart's String Quartets Nos. 21-23, K. 575, 589, 590.

KREUTZER SONATA: Beethoven's Sonata No. 9 for Violin and Piano in A Major, Op. 47.

LAMENTATIONS SYMPHONY: Haydn's Symphony No. 26 in D Minor. Also called Christmas Symphony.

LARK QUARTET: Haydn's Quartet in D Major, Op. 64, No. 5.

LAUDON SYMPHONY: Haydn's Symphony No. 69.

LEBEWOHL SONATA: See Adieux, Les.

LEGGEREZZA, LA: Liszt's Etude de Concert No. 2 in F Minor.

LENINGRAD SYMPHONY: Shostakovitch's Symphony No. 7, Op. 60.

LEONORE OVERTURES: Beethoven wrote 4 overtures to his single opera *Fidelio*; 3 of them were entitled *Leonore* (the original title of the opera) and numbered 1, 2, 3.

LES ADIEUX: See Adieux, Les.

L'IMPERIALE: See Imperial Symphony.

LINZ SYMPHONY: Mozart's Symphony No. 36 in C Major, K. 425.

LITTLE G MINOR FUGUE: Organ Fugue in G Minor. Bach.

LITTLE PRELUDE AND FUGUE: Organ Prelude and Fugue in E Minor. Bach.

LITTLE RUSSIAN SYMPHONY: Tchaikovsky's Symphony No. 2 in C Minor, Op. 17.

LITURGICAL SYMPHONY: Honegger's Symphony No. 3.

LOBGESANG: See Hymn of Praise Symphony.

LONDON CHACONNE: Purcell's Chaconne for Strings in G Minor.

LONDON SYMPHONIES: Haydn's Symphonies No. 93-104 inclusive, including the Clock, Drum Roll, Military, Miracle, Surprise, & London.

LONDON SYMPHONY: Haydn's Symphony No. 104 is sometimes singled out as The London Symphony. (See London Symphonies.) Vaughan Williams' Symphony.

LONDON TRIO: Haydn's Trio No. 4 in C Major.

LORD NELSON MASS: Haydn's Missa Solemnis in D Minor.

MADRIGALESCO: Concerto in D Minor for Strings and Harpsichord, Vivaldi.

MANIATICO, IL: Brunetti's Symphony No. 33 in C Minor.

MANZONI REQUIEM: Verdi's Requiem Mass.

MARIA THERESA SYMPHONY: Haydn's Symphony No. 48 in C Major.

MARIAZELLERMESSE: Haydn's Missa Cellensis in C Major.

MATIN, LE: See Morning Symphony.

MELK CONCERTO: Haydn's Concerto in A Major for Violin.

MERCURY SYMPHONY (MERKUR): Haydn's Symphony No. 43 in E Flat Major.

MIDDAY SYMPHONY (LE MIDI): Haydn's Symphony No. 7 in C Major.

MIDI, LE: See Midday Symphony.

MILITARY SYMPHONY: Haydn's Symphony No. 100 in G Major, one of the London Symphonies.

MIRACLE SYMPHONY: Haydn's Symphony No. 96 in D Major, one of the London Symphonies.

MOONLIGHT SONATA: Beethoven's Piano Sonata No. 14 in C Sharp Minor, Op. 27, No. 2.

MOONLOVE SYMPHONY: Tchaikovsky's Symphony No. 5 in E Minor, Op. 64.

MORNING SYMPHONY (LE MATIN): Haydn's Symphony No. 6 in D Major.

MOURNING SYMPHONY (TRAUER): Haydn's Symphony No. 44 in E Minor.

MOZARTIANA: Tchaikovsky's Suite No. 4 in G Major, Op. 61.

MUNICH KYRIE: Mozart's Kyrie in D Minor for 4 Voices, K. 341.

NEW WORLD SYMPHONY: Dvořák's Symphony No. 5 in E Minor, Op. 95.

NIGGER QUARTET: See American Quartet.

NORDIC SYMPHONY: Hanson's Symphony No. 1.

NOTTE, LA: Vivaldi's Concerto in B Flat Major for Bassoon and Strings. Also, his Concerto for Flute in G Minor, Op. 10, No. 2.

OF A THOUSAND: Symphony No. 8 in E by Gustav Mahler.

OURS, L': See Bear Symphony.

OXFORD SYMPHONY: Haydn's Symphony No 92 in G Major.

PARIS OVERTURE: Mozart's Overture in B Flat Major, K. 311a.

PARIS SYMPHONIES: Haydn's Symphonies Nos. 82-87, including the Bear, the Hen, and the Queen.

PARIS SYMPHONY: Mozart's Symphony No. 31 in D Major, K. 297.

PASSIONE, LA: Haydn's Symphony No. 49 in F Minor.

PASTORAL SONATA: Beethoven's Piano Sonata No. 15 in D Major, Op. 28.

PASTORAL SYMPHONY: Beethoven's Symphony No. 6 in F, Op. 68. Vaughan Williams' Symphony No. 3. Bach's Symphony from the *Christmas Oratorio*. Handel's Symphony from the *Messiah*.

PASTORELLA, LA: Concerto in D Major, for Flute, Oboe, Violin, Bassoon, and Basso Continuo; Vivaldi.

PATHÉTIQUE: Tchaikovsky's Symphony No. 6 in B Minor, Op. 74.

PATHÉTIQUE, SONATA: Beethoven's Piano Sonata No. 8 in C Minor, Op. 13, the *Grand Sonate Pathétique*, is called simply the Pathétique.

PAUKENMESSE: Haydn's Mass in Time of War in C Major.

PAUKENSCHLAG: See Surprise Symphony.

PAUKENWIRBEL: See Drum Roll Symphony.

PEASANT CANTATA: Bach's Cantata No. 212.

PHILOSOPHER, THE: Haydn's Symphony No. 22 in E Flat Major.

PIACERE, IL: Vivaldi's Concerto in C Major for Violin, Op. 8, No. 6.

POST HORN SERENADE: Mozart's Serenade No. 9 in D Major, K. 320.

POULE, LA: See Hen Symphony.

PRAGUE SYMPHONY: Mozart's Symphony No 38 in D Major, K. 504.

QUEEN SYMPHONY, THE (LA REINE): Haydn's Symphony No. 85 in B Flat Major.

QUINTEN QUARTET: Haydn's Quartet in D Minor, Op. 76, No. 2.

RAINDROP PRELUDE: Chopin's Prelude in D Flat, No. 15 of the 24 Preludes, Op. 28.

RAIN SONATA: Brahm's Sonata No. 1 in G Major for Violin, Op. 78.

RÁKOCZY MARCH: Liszt's Hungarian Rhapsody No. 15.

RASOUMOVSKY QUARTETS: Beethoven's set of 3 string quartets in F, E Minor, and C, Op. 59.

REFORMATION SYMPHONY: Mendelssohn's Symphony No. 5 in D Major, Op. 107.

REINE, LA: See Queen Symphony.

RESURRECTION SYMPHONY: Mahler's Symphony No. 2 in C Minor.

REVOLUTIONARY ETUDE: Chopin's Etude No. 10 in C Minor, Op. 10.

RHENISH SYMPHONY: Schumann's Symphony No. 3 in E Flat Major.

RING, THE: Wagner's cycle of 4 operas, comprising prelude and trilogy: *Das Rheingold (The Rhine Gold)* 1869; *Die Walküre (The Valkyries)* 1870; *Siegfried* 1876; *Die Götterdämmerung (The Twilight of the Gods)* 1876.

RIPOSO, IL: Concerto in E Major for Violin, Vivaldi.

ROMANTIC SYMPHONY: Bruckner's Symphony No. 4 in E Flat Major. Hanson's Symphony No. 2.

RUSSIAN QUARTETS: Haydn's String Quartets, Op. 33. No. 1, B Minor; No. 2, E Flat Major; No. 3, C Major; No. 4, B Flat Major; No. 5, G Major; No. 6, D Major.

RUY BLAS OVERTURE: Mendelssohn's overture, written for Hugo's play *Ruy Blas*, 1839.

ST. ANNE'S: Organ Prelude and Fugue in E Flat Major, Bach.

SALOMON SYMPHONIES: Another name for Haydn's London Symphonies, Nos. 93-104.

SAMSON: Handel's Oratorio, based on Milton's *Samson Agonistes*.

SAN LORENZO: Vivaldi's Concerto in C Major for Orchestra.

SCHOOLMASTER, THE: Haydn's Symphony No. 55 in E Flat Major.

SCOTCH SYMPHONY: Mendelssohn's Symphony No. 3 in A Minor, Op. 56.

SEASONS, THE: Four concertos for violin, strings, and cembalo, Vivaldi. No. 1, *Spring*, E Major; No. 2, *Summer*, G Minor; No. 3, *Autumn*, F. Major; No. 4, *Winter*, F Minor.

SEA SYMPHONY: Vaughan Williams' Symphony No. 1.

SERIOUS QUARTET: Beethoven's String Quartet No. 11 in F Minor, Op. 95.

SINFONIA ESPANSIVA: Nielsen's Symphony No. 3, Op. 27.

SINFONIA SEMPLICE: Nielsen's Symphony No. 6.

SLATTER DANCES: Grieg's Norwegian Peasant Dances for Piano, Op. 72.

SOIR, LE: See Evening Symphony.

SONG OF THE NIGHT SYMPHONY: Mahler's Symphony No. 7 in B Minor.

SONGS WITHOUT WORDS: Several groups of piano pieces by Mendelssohn have this name.

SOSPETTO, IL: Vivaldi's Concerto in C Minor for Violin.

SOSPIRO, UN: Liszt's Etude de Concert No. 3 in D Flat Major.

SPRING SONATA: Beethoven's Sonata No. 5 in F Major for Violin and Piano, Op. 24.

SPRING SYMPHONY: Schumann's Symphony No. 1 in B Flat Major, Op. 38.

STRAVAGANZA, LA: Vivaldi's Concertos for Violin, Strings, and Continuo, Op. 4, Nos. 1-12.

SUITE CHARACTERISTIQUE: Tchaikovsky's Suite No. 2 in C Major, Op. 53.

SUNRISE QUARTET: Haydn's String Quartet in B Flat Major, Op. 76, No. 4.

SURPRISE SYMPHONY (PAUKENSCHLAG): Haydn's Symphony No. 94 in G Major.

TEMPESTA DI MARE, LA: Vivaldi's Concerto in E Flat Major for Violin, Op. 8, No. 5.

TEMPEST SONATA: Beethoven's Piano Sonata No. 17 in D Minor, Op. 31, No. 2.

THERESIENMESSE: Haydn's Mass in B Flat Major.

TITAN SYMPHONY: Mahler's Symphony No. 1 in D Major.

TOY SYMPHONY: Haydn's symphony for toy instruments (1788), has been attributed by some authorities to Leopold Mozart.

TRAGIC SYMPHONY: Schubert's Symphony No. 4 in C Minor.

TRAUER SYMPHONY: See Mourning Symphony.

TRIPLE CONCERTO: Beethoven's Concerto in C Major, Op. 56, for Piano, Violin, and Cello.

TROUT QUINTET: Schubert's Piano Quintet in A Major, Op. 114.

TRUMPET SONATA: Mozart's Piano Sonata No. 17 in D Major, K. 576.

TURKISH CONCERTO: Mozart's Violin Concerto No. 5 in A Major, K. 219.

TURKISH RONDO: Finale of Mozart's Piano Sonata in A Major, K. 331.

UNFINISHED SONATA: Mozart's Violin Sonata in C Major, K. 404.

UNFINISHED SYMPHONY: Schubert's Symphony No. 8 in B Minor.

VOCES INTIMAE: Sibelius' String Quartet in D Minor, Op. 56.

"WACHET AUF": Bach's Cantata No. 140.

WALDSTEIN SONATA: Beethoven's Piano Sonata No. 21 in C Major, Op. 53.

WANDERER FANTASIA: Schubert's Fantasia in C for Piano Solo, Op. 15, with variations on his song "Der Wanderer."

WEDDING, THE: Bach's Cantata No. 202.

WELLINGTON'S VICTORY SYMPHONY: Beethoven's Symphony, Op. 91.

WELL-TEMPERED CLAVIER, THE: See Forty-eight.

WITCHES' DANCE: Paganini's *Le Streghe*, Op. 8.

YOUTH SYMPHONY: Bruckner's Symphony in D Minor, Op. Posth.

Popular Songs
See Songs, Popular

Populations of the Countries of the World

Africa

AGALEGA: See British Dependencies.

AIN-SEFRA: See Algeria.

ALGERIA: (France: includes Algiers, Constantine, Oran, and Southern Territories of Ain-Sefra, Ghardaïa, Touggourt, and Oasis). 9,620,000.

ALGIERS: See Algeria.

ALHUCEMAS: See Spanish North Africa.

ANGOLA: (Portugal). 4,280,000.

ANNOBON: See Spanish Guinea.

BASUTOLAND: (Great Britain). 627,000.

BECHUANALAND: (Great Britain). 296.000.

BELGIAN CONGO: (Belgium). 12,600,000.

BRITISH DEPENDENCIES: (Diego Garcia, Peros Banhos, Agalega, Solomon, and Saint-Brandon). 2000. These Dependenciers are not separately listed elsewhere.

BRITISH SOMALILAND: (Great Britain). 640,000.

CAMEROONS: (British Trust). 1,500,000.

CAMEROONS: (French Trust). 3,146,000.

CAPE VERDE ISLANDS: (Portugal). 172,000.

CEUTA: See Spanish North Africa.

CHAD: See French Equatorial Africa.

CHAFARINAS: See Spanish North Africa.

COMORO ISLANDS: (France). 170,000.

CONSTANTINE: See Algeria.

CORISCO: See Spanish Guinea.

DAHOMEY: See French West Africa.

DAKAR: See French West Africa.

DIEGO GARCIA: See British Dependencies.

EGYPT: 22,934,000.

ELOBEYS: See Spanish Guinea.

ERITREA: See Ethiopia and Eritrea.

ETHIOPIA AND ERITREA: 20,000,000.

FERNANDO PO: See Spanish Guinea.

FRENCH EQUATORIAL AFRICA: (France: includes Chad, 2,452,000, Gabon, 392,000, Middle Congo, 733,000, and Oubangui-Chari, 1,103,000) 4,680,000.

FRENCH GUINEA: See French West Africa.

FRENCH SOMALILAND: (France) 63,000.

FRENCH SUDAN: See French West Africa.

FRENCH WEST AFRICA: (France: includes Dahomey, 1,614,000; French Guinea, 2,505,000; French Sudan, 3,642,000; Ivory Coast, 2,481,00 Mauritania, 615,000; Niger, 2,334,000; Senegal and Dakar, 2,214,000; and Upper Volta, 3,324,000). 18,729,000.

GABON: See French Euqatorial Africa.

GAMBIA: (Great Britain). 285,000.

GHANA (FORMERLY GOLD COAST): 4,191,000.

GHARDAIA: See Algeria.

GOLD COAST: See Ghana.

GREAT ELOBEY: See Spanish Guinea.

IFNI: See Spanish West Africa.

ILE DU PRINCE: See St. Thomas and Ile du Prince.

IVORY COAST: See French West Africa.

KENYA: (Great Britain). 6,048,000.

LIBERIA: 1,250,000.

LIBYA: 1,105,000.

LITTLE ELOBEY: See Spanish Guinea.

MADAGASCAR: (France: population figure does not include estimates for Iles Nossi-Bé, Iles Sainte-Marie, Iles Glorieuses, Iles Saint-Paul, Amsterdam, Marion, Crozet Archipelago, Kerguelan or Desolation Archipelago, or Terre Adélie) 4,776,000.

MAURITANIA: See French West Africa.

MAURITIUS: (Great Britain). 549,000.

MELILLA: See Spanish North Africa.

MIDDLE CONGO: See French Equatorial Africa.

MOROCCO, FORMER FRENCH ZONE: 8,495,000.

MOROCCO, FORMER SPANISH ZONE: 1,045,000.

MOROCCO, TANGIER: 183,000.

MOZAMBIQUE: (Portugal). 6,030,000.

NIGER: See French West Africa.

NIGERIA: (Great Britain). 31,254,000.

NORTHERN RHODESIA: See Rhodesia and Nyasaland.

NYASALAND: See Rhodesia and Nyasaland.

OASIS: See Algeria.

ORAN: See Algeria.

OUBANGUI-CHARI: See French Equatorial Africa.

PEMBA: See Zanzibar and Pemba.

PEÑON DE VÉLEZ-DE-LA-GOMERA: See Spanish North Africa.

PEROS BANHOS: See British Dependencies.

PORTUGUESE GUINEA: (Portugal). 541,000.

RÉUNION: (France). 278,000.

RHODESIA AND NYASALAND: (Great Britain: includes Northern Rhodesia, 2,130,000; Nyasaland, 2,540,000, and Southern Rhodesia, 2,399,000) 7,069,000.

RIO DE ORO: See Spanish West Africa.

RIO MUNI: See Spanish Guinea.

RODRIGUES: (Great Britain). 15,000.

RUANDA-URUNDI: (Belgian Trust). 4,280,000.

SAGUIA EL HAMRA: See Spanish West Africa.

SAINT-BRANDON: See British Dependencies.

ST. HELENA: (Great Britain). 5,000.

ST. THOMAS AND ILE DU PRINCE: (Portugal). 58,000.

SENEGAL: See French West Africa.

SEYCHELLES: (Great Britain). 39,000.

SIERRA LEONE: (Great Britain). 2,050,000.

SOLOMON: See British Dependencies.

SOMALILAND: (Italian Trust). 1,280,000.

SOUTHERN RHODESIA: See Rhodesia and Nyasaland.

SOUTH-WEST AFRICA: (Mandate of the Union of South Africa: includes Walvis Bay) 458,000.

SPANISH GUINEA: Spain: includes Annobon, Fernando Po, Río Muni, Corisco, and Great and Little Elobey) 208,000.

SPANISH NORTH AFRICA: (Spain: includes Ceuta, 60,000, Melilla, 83,000, and Alhucemas, Chafarinas, and Peñon de Vélez-de-la-Gomera with a combined population of 184) 143,184.

SPANISH WEST AFRICA: (Includes Ifni, Northern Zone, Río de Oro, and Saguia el Hamra) 83,000.

SWAZILAND: (Great Britain) 217,000.

TANGANYIKA: (British Trust) 8,324,000.

TANGIER: See Morocco, Tangier.

TOGOLAND: (British Trust) 429,000.

TOGOLAND: (French Trust) 1,080,000.

TOUGGOURT: See Algeria.

TUNISIA: 3,745,000.

UGANDA: (Great Britain) 5,508,000.

UNION OF SOUTH AFRICA: (Excluding Walvis Bay) 13,669,000.

UPPER VOLTA: See French West Africa.

WALVIS BAY: See South-West Africa.

ZANZIBAR AND PEMBA: (Great Britain). 278.000.

Asia

ADEN: (Great Britain: includes Colony, 140,000, and Protectorate, 650,000). 790,000.

AFGHANISTAN: 12,000,000.

AMAMI ISLANDS: See Japan.

ANDAMAN: See India.

BAHRAIN: 120,000.

BEECHEY ISLAND: See Bonin Islands.

BHUTAN: 623,000.

BONIN ISLANDS: (United States Military Government: includes Parry, Beechey, Volcano, and Marcus Islands, with 1950 population estimate of 170).

BRUNEI: (Great Britain). 56,000.

BURMA: 19,434,000.

CAMBODIA: 4,358,000.

CASHMERE: See Kashmir-Jammu under India

CEYLON: 8,589,000.

CHANDERNAGOR: See India.

CHINA: 582,603,000.

CYPRUS: (Great Britain). 520,000.

GAZA STRIP: See Palestine.

HOKKAIDO: See Japan.

HONG KONG: (Great Britain). 2,340,000.

HONSHU: See Japan.

INDIA: (Includes Chandernagor, Sikkim, Andaman, Nicobar, and Laccadive Islands, Kashmir-Jammu, Karikal, Mahé, Pondichéry, and Yanaon). 381,690,000.

INDONESIA: 81,900,000.

IRAN: 21,146,000.

IRAQ: 5,200,000.

ISRAEL:1,748,000.

JAPAN: (Includes Hokkaido, Honshu, Shikoku Kyushu, and small outlying islands, Tokar Archipelago and the Amami Islands transferred to Japan from Ryukyu Islands on December 1951 and 25 December 1953 respectively). 89,100,000.

JORDAN: (Including West Jordan, i.e., the par of Arab Palestine annexed 25 April 1950) 1,427,000.

KARIKAL: See India.

KASHMIR-JAMMU: See India.

KOREA: (Includes Republic of Korea, 21,526,000) 28,000,000.

KUWAIT: 203,000.

KYUSHU: See Japan.

LACCADIVE ISLANDS: See India.

AOS: 1,425,000.
EBANON: 1,425,000.
ACAU, OR MACAO: (Portugal). 200,000.
AHÉ: See India.
ALACCA: See Malaya, Federation of.
ALAYA, FEDERATION OF: (Great Britain: includes Federated Malay States, Unfederated Malay States, and the settlements of Penang and Malacca). 6,058,000.
ALDIVE ISLANDS: 89,000.
ARCUS ISLAND: See Bonin Islands.
ONGOLIAN PEOPLES' REPUBLIC: 1,000,000.
USCAT AND OMAN: 550,000.
EPAL: 8,431,537.
ICOBAR ISLANDS: See India.
ORTH BORNEO: (Great Britain). 370,000.
MAN: See Muscat and Oman.
AKISTAN: 82,439,000.
ALESTINE: (Former British Mandated Territory, now the Gaza Strip, or that part of Palestine under Egyptian administration since the Armistice of 1949). 325,000.
ARRY ISLAND: See Bonin Islands.
ENANG: See Malaya, Federation of.
HILIPPINES: 21,849,000.
ONDICHÉRY: See India.
ORTUGUESE INDIA: (Portugal). 644,000.
ORTUGUESE TIMOR: (Portugal). 469,000.
ATAR: 35,000.
YUKYU ISLANDS: (United States Military Government: includes those islands of the Ryukyu group south of the 29th degree of North latitude except the Tokara Archipelago and Amami Islands which reverted to Japan on 5th December and 25th December, 1953, respectively). 798,000.
ARAWAK: (Great Britain). 614,000.
AUDI ARABIA: 7,000,000.
HIKOKU: See Japan.
INGAPORE: (Great Britain: includes Christmas Island, 2,000, and Singapore Island, 1,211,000). 1,411,000.
IKKIM: See India.
OUTH KOREA: See Republic of Korea under Korea.
YRIA: (Includes nomads and semi-nomads, estimated at 288,400 in 1945). 4,145,000.
AIWAN: 8,907,000.
HAILAND: 20,302,000.
OKARA ARCHIPELAGO: See Japan.
RUCIAL OMAN: 80,000.
URKEY: 24,122,000.
NION OF SOVIET SOCIALIST REPUBLICS: See Europe.
IET-NAM: 26,300,000.
VEST JORDAN: See Jordan.
EST NEW GUINEA: (Netherlands). 700,000.
ANAON: See India.
EMEN: 4,500,000.

Europe

LBANIA: 1,394,000.
NDORRA: 6,000.
USTRIA: 6,974,000.
ZORES: See Portugal.
ALEARIC ISLANDS: See Spain.
ELGIUM: 8,868,000.
ERLIN, EAST AND WEST: See Germany.
UJE: See Yugoslavia.
ULGARIA: 7,548,000.
YELORUSSIAN SOVIET SOCIALIST REPUBLIC: See Union of Soviet Socialist Republics.
ANARY ISLANDS: See Spain.
HANNEL ISLANDS: (Great Britain: includes Guernsey, 45,000; and Jersey, 47,000), 102,000.

COMINO ISLAND: See Malta and Gozo.
CZECHOSLOVAKIA: 13,089,000.
DENMARK: 4,439,000.
EAST GERMANY: See Germany.
ENGLAND: See United Kingdom.
ESTONIA: See Union of Soviet Socialist Republics.
FAEROE ISLANDS: 34,000.
FEDERAL REPUBLIC OF GERMANY: See Germany.
FINLAND: 4,241,000.
FRANCE: 43,274,000.
GERMAN DEMOCRATIC REPUBLIC: See Germany.
GERMANY: (Includes German Democratic Republic, or East Germany, 16,700,000; Federal Republic, or West Germany, 49,995,000; East Berlin, 1,300,000; and West Berlin, 2,195,000). 70,190,000.
GIBRALTER: (Great Britain). 25,000.
GOZO: See Malta and Gozo.
GREECE: 7,973,000.
HUNGARY: 9,805,000.
ICELAND: 158,000.
IRELAND: 2,909,000.
IRELAND, NORTHERN: See United Kingdom.
ISLE OF MAN: (Great Britain). 56,000.
ITALY: 48,016,000.
JAN MAYEN ISLANDS: See Svalbard and Jan Mayen Islands.
KOPER: See Yugoslavia.
LATVIA: See Union of Soviet Socialist Republics.
LIECHTENSTEIN: 15,000.
LITHUANIA: See Union of Soviet Socialist Republics.
LUXEMBOURG: 309,000.
MADEIRA ISLANDS: See Portugal.
MALTA AND GOZO: (Great Britain: includes Comino Island). 314,000.
MONACO: 22,000.
NETHERLANDS: 10,751,000.
NORTHERN IRELAND: See United Kingdom.
NORWAY: 3,425,000.
POLAND: 27,278,000.
PORTUGAL: (Includes Azores and Madeira Islands). 8,756,000.
ROMANIA: 17,000,000.
RUSSIA: See Union of Soviet Socialist Republics.
SAAR: 992,000.
SAN MARINO: 14,000.
SCOTLAND: See United Kingdom.
SPAIN: (Includes Balearic and Canary Islands). 28,976,000.
SVALBARD AND JAN MAYEN ISLANDS: (Norway). 1,547.
SWEDEN: 7,262,000.
SWITZERLAND: 4,977,000.
UKRAINIAN SOVIET SOCIALIST REPUBLIC: See Union of Soviet Socialist Republics.
UNION OF SOVIET SOCIALIST REPUBLICS: (Population estimate for 1 April, 1956; the population of territories annexed during 1939-40, including Estonia, Latvia, and parts of Lithuania, Czechoslovakia, Finland, Poland, and Romania, was estimated at 23,000,000 in 1940; present territory also includes Tannu-Tuva, Southern Sakhalin, and the Kurile Islands, the rest of Lithuania, former parts of Germany; estimates for the Byelorussian Soviet Socialist Republic, 8,000,000, and for the Ukrainian Soviet Socialist Republic, 40,600,000, are included in the general population estimate). 200,200,000.
UNITED KINGDOM OF GREAT BRITAIN AND NORTHERN IRELAND: (Includes England and Wales, 44,623,000; Northern Ireland, 1,394,000; and Scotland, 5,198,000). 51,215,000.

VATICAN: 1,000.
WALES: See United Kingdom.
WEST GERMANY: See Germany.
YUGOSLAVIA: 17,628,000. This estimate does not include Koper and Buje, that part of the former Free Territory of Trieste, incorporated in 1954, with population estimated at 62,725 in 1953.

North America

ALASKA: (United States). 209,000.
ANGUILLA: See Leeward Islands.
ANTIGUA: See Leeward Islands.
ANTILLES, NETHERLANDS: See Netherlands Antilles.
ARUBO: See Netherlands Antilles.
BAHAMAS: (Great Britain; part of British West Indies). 94,000.
BARBADOS: (Great Britain; part of British West Indies). 229,000.
BERMUDA: (Great Britain; includes Carriacou and other dependencies in the Grenadines). 41,000.
BONAIRE: See Netherlands Antilles.
BRITISH HONDURAS: (Great Britain). 79,000.
BRITISH WEST INDIES: (Great Britain). See Bahamas, Barbados, Jamaica, Leeward Islands, Trinidad and Tobago, and Windward Islands.
CAICOS ISLANDS: See Turks and Caicos Islands.
CANADA: 15,601,000.
CANAL ZONE: (United States). 53,000.
CARRIACOU: See Bermuda.
CAYMAN ISLANDS: (Great Britain; part of British West Indies, dependency of Jamaica). 8,000.
COSTA RICA: 951,000.
CUBA: 5,829,000.
CURAÇAO: See Netherlands Antilles.
DOMINICA: See Windward Islands.
DOMINICAN REPUBLIC: 2,404,000.
EL SALVADOR: 2,193,000.
GREENLAND: (Denmark). 26,000.
GRENADA: See Windward Islands.
GRENADINES: See Bermuda.
GUADELOUPE: (France; includes Marie-Galante, la Désirade, les Saintes, Petite-Terre, St. Bartélemy, and part of St. Martin). 230,000.
GUATEMALA: 3,258,000.
HAITI: 3,305,000.
HONDURAS: 1,660,000.
JAMAICA: (Great Britain; part of British West Indies). 1,550,000. See Cayman Islands, Turks and Caicos Islands, for separate population estimates of Jamaican dependencies.
LA DÉSIRADE: See Guadeloupe.
LEEWARD ISLANDS: (Great Britain; part of British West Indies: includes Antigua, 52,000; Montserrat, 14,000; St.-Christophe-Nevis and Anguilla, 54,000; and Virgin Islands, 8,000). 128,000.
LES SAINTES: See Guadeloupe.
MARIE-GALANTE: See Guadeloupe.
MARTINIQUE: (France). 240,000.
MEXICO: 29,679,000.
MIQUELON: See St. Pierre and Miquelon.
MONTSERRAT: See Leeward Islands.
NETHERLANDS ANTILLES: (Netherlands: includes Arubo, Bonaire, Curaçao, Saba, St. Eustatius, and part of St. Martin). 230,000.
NICARAGUA: 1,245,000.
PANAMA: 910,000.
PETITE-TERRE: See Guadeloupe.
PUERTO RICO: (United States). 2,263,000.
SABA: See Netherlands Antilles.
ST. BARTHÉLEMY: See Guadeloupe.
ST.-CHRISTOPHE-NEVIS: See Leeward Islands.

ST. EUSTATIUS: See Netherlands Antilles.
ST. LUCIA: See Windward Islands.
ST. MARTIN: See Guadeloupe and Netherlands Antilles.
ST. PIERRE AND MIQUELON: (France). 5,000.
ST. VINCENT: See Windward Islands.
SWAN ISLANDS: (United States). 36.
TOBAGO: See Trinidad and Tobago.
TRINIDAD AND TOBAGO: (Great Britain; part of British West Indies). 721,000.
TURKS AND CAICOS ISLANDS: (Great Britain; part of British West Indies, dependency of Jamaica). 7,000.
UNITED STATES: 165,271,000 (estimate does not include 435,000 members of the armed forces stationed abroad.
VIRGIN ISLANDS: (United States: includes St. Croix, St. John, and St. Thomas). 24,000.
VIRGIN ISLANDS: (Great Britain). See Leeward Islands.
WINDWARD ISLANDS: (Great Britain; part of British West Indies: includes Dominica, 60,000; Grenada, 86,000; St. Lucia, 88,000; and St. Vincent, 74,000). 308,000.

Oceania

AMERICAN SAMOA: (United States). 22,000.
AUSTRALIA: 9,201,000. This estimate does not include full-blooded aborigines, estimated at 47,000 in 1944.
AUSTRAL ISLANDS: See French Oceania.
BISMARCK ARCHIPELAGO: See New Guinea.
BOUGAINVILLE ISLAND: See New Guinea.
BRITISH SOLOMON ISLANDS: (Great Britain). 103,000.
BUKA ISLAND: See New Guinea.
CAMPBELL ISLAND: See New Zealand.
CANTON ISLAND: See Gilbert and Ellice Islands.
CAROLINE ISLANDS: See Pacific Islands.
CHESTERFIELD ISLANDS: See New Caledonia.
CHRISTMAS ISLAND: See Gilbert and Ellice Islands.
COCOS, OR KEELING, ISLANDS: (Australia). 1,000.
COOK ISLANDS: (New Zealand). 16,000.
ELLICE ISLANDS: See Gilbert and Ellice Islands.
ENDERBURY ISLAND: See Gilbert and Ellice Island.
FANNING ISLAND: See Gilbert and Ellice Islands.
FATUNA ISLANDS: See New Caledonia.
FIJI ISLANDS: (Great Britain). 339,000.
FRENCH OCEANIA: (France: includes Austral, Gambier, Marquesas, Rapa, Society, and Tuamotu Islands). 69,000.
GAMBIER ISLANDS: See French Oceania.
GILBERT AND ELLICE ISLANDS: (Great Britain: includes Christmas, Fanning, Ocean, and Washington Islands; also the Phoenix Islands group, of which Canton and Enderbury Islands have been an Anglo-American condominium since 6 April, 1939. The population of Canton was 272 by a United States census taken in April, 1950, and Enderbury Island was uninhabited). 40,000.
GUAM: (United States). 36,000.
HAWAII: (United States). 560,000.
HUON ISLANDS: See New Caledonia.
JOHNSTON ISLAND: (United States). 46.
KEELING ISLANDS: See Cocos Islands.
KERMADEC ISLANDS: See New Zealand.
MARIANAS, OR MARIANA ISLANDS: See Pacific Islands.
MARQUESAS ISLANDS: See French Oceania.
MARSHALL ISLANDS: See Pacific Islands.

MIDWAY ISLANDS: (United States). 416.
NAURA: (Australian, British, and New Zealand Trust). 4,000.
NEW CALEDONIA: (France: includes dependencies of Wallis, Fatuna, Huon, and Chesterfield Islands). 63,000.
NEW GUINEA: (Australian Trust: includes Northeast New Guinea, the Bismarck Archipelago, Bougainville and Buka of the Solomon Islands group, and about 600 smaller islands). 1,254,000.
NEW HEBRIDES: (Anglo-French condominium). 54,000.
NEW ZEALAND: (Includes Campbell and Kermadec Islands, with population of 19 at 1951 census, but does not include the other minor uninhabited islands). 2,136,000.
NIUE: (New Zealand). 5,000.
NORFOLK ISLAND: (Australia). 1,000.
OCEAN ISLAND: See Gilbert and Ellice Islands.
PACIFIC ISLANDS: (United States Trust: includes the Caroline, Palau, Marshall, and Mariana, excluding Guam, Islands). 64,000.
PALAU ISLANDS: See Pacific Islands.
PAPUA: (Australia). 446,000.
PHOENIX ISLANDS: See Gilbert and Ellice Islands.
PITCAIRN ISLAND: (Great Britain). 125.
RAPA ISLAND: See French Oceania.
SAMOA: See American Samoa and also Western Samoa.
SOCIETY ISLANDS: See French Oceania.
SOLOMON ISLANDS: See British Solomon Islands.
TOKELAU ISLANDS: (New Zealand). 2,000.
TONGA ISLANDS: (Great Britain). 54,000.
TUAMOTU ISLANDS, OR ARCHIPELAGO: See French Oceania.
WAKE ISLAND: (United States). 349.
WALLIS ISLANDS: See New Caledonia.
WASHINGTON ISLAND: See Gilbert and Ellice Islands.
WESTERN SAMOA: (New Zealand Trust). 97,000.

South America

ARGENTINA: 19,111,000.
BOLIVIA: 3,198,000.
BRAZIL: 58,456,000 (estimate does not include Indian jungle population numbering 45,429 at 1950 census).
BRITISH GUIANA: (Great Britain). 485,000.
CAYENNE: See French Guiana.
CHILE: 6,761,000.
COLOMBIA: 12,657,000.
ECUADOR: 3,675,000.
FALKLAND ISLANDS: (Great Britain). 2,000.
FRENCH GUIANA: (France: includes Cayenne and Inini). 28,000.
ININI: See French Guiana.
PARAGUAY: 1,565,000.
PERU: 9,396,000.
SURINAM: (Netherlands). 225,000.
URUGUAY: 2,615,000.
VENEZUELA: 5,774,000 (estimate does not include Indian jungle population numbering 56,705 at 1950 special census of indigenous population).

Area Totals

AFRICA: (Includes Northern Africa, 78,000,000, and Tropical and Southern Africa, 145,000,000). 223,000,000, with possible error of 5%.
AMERICA: (Includes North America, 183,000,000, with possible error of 0.5%; Central America, 58,000,000, with possible error of 2 %; South America, 125,000,000, with possible error of 2 %). 366,000,000, with possible error of 1%.
ASIA: (Includes South-West Asia, 73,000,000, with possible error of 5%; South Central Asia, 499,000,000, with possible error of 1 %; South-East Asia, 185,000,000, with possible error of 5 %; and East Asia, 724,000,000, with possible error of 10%; Turkey is included in these estimates, but the Union of Soviet Socialist Republics is considered separately below). 1,481,000,000, with possible error of 5 %.
EUROPE: (Includes Northern and Western Europe, 137,00,000, with possible error of 0.5%; Central Europe, 134,000,000, with possible error of 0.5 %; and Southern Europe, 138,000,000, with possible error of 1 %; European Turkey is included in the estimates given for Asia, and the Union of Soviet Socialist Republics is listed separately below). 409,000,000, with possible error of 0.5%.
OCEANIA: 14,600,000, with possible error of 1 %.
UNION OF SOVIET SOCIALIST REPUBLICS: 200.200.000.
WORLD TOTAL: (Includes allowance for population of the Union of Soviet Socialist Republics). 2,691,000,000, with possible error of 5%.

Presidency
See also Rulers; Secretaries of State

Presidents of the United States

1. GEORGE WASHINGTON: 1789-1797.
2. JOHN ADAMS: 1797-1801.
3. THOMAS JEFFERSON: 1801-1809.
4. JAMES MADISON: 1809-1817.
5. JAMES MONROE: 1817-1825.
6. JOHN QUINCY ADAMS: 1825-1829.
7. ANDREW JACKSON: 1829-1837.
8. MARTIN VAN BUREN: 1837-1841.
9. WILLIAM HENRY HARRISON: 1841.
10. JOHN TYLER: 1841-1845.
11. JAMES KNOX POLK: 1845-1849.
12. ZACHARY TAYLOR: 1849-1850.
13. MILLARD FILLMORE: 1850-1853.
14. FRANKLIN PIERCE: 1853-1857.
15. JAMES BUCHANAN: 1857-1861.
16. ABRAHAM LINCOLN: 1861-1865.
17. ANDREW JOHNSON: 1865-1869.
18. ULYSSES S. GRANT: 1869-1877.
19. RUTHERFORD B. HAYES: 1877-1881.
20. JAMES A. GARFIELD: 1881.
21. CHESTER A. ARTHUR: 1881-1885.
22. GROVER CLEVELAND: 1885-1889.
23. BENJAMIN HARRISON: 1889-1893.
24. GROVER CLEVELAND: 1893-1897.
25. WILLIAM MCKINLEY: 1897-1901.
26. THEODORE ROOSEVELT: 1901-1909.
27. WILLIAM HOWARD TAFT: 1909-1913.
28. WOODROW WILSON: 1913-1921.
29. WARREN GAMALIEL HARDING: 1921-1923.
30. CALVIN COOLIDGE: 1923-1929.
31. HERBERT C. HOOVER: 1929-1933.
32. FRANKLIN DELANO ROOSEVELT: 1933-1945.
33. HARRY S. TRUMAN: 1945-1953.
34. DWIGHT D. EISENHOWER: 1953-

First Ladies with the Dates of Their Marriages to the Presidents

(Note: the sequence corresponds to the order in which the presidents succeeded to the White House)

1. MARTHA DANDRIDGE CUSTIS WASH-
   INGTON: 1759.
2. ABIGAIL QUINCY SMITH ADAMS: 1764.
3. MARTHA WAYLES SKELTON JEFFERSON:
   1772 (died in 1782, 19 years before Thomas
   Jefferson became president).
4. DOLLEY PAYNE TODD MADISON: 1794.
5. ELIZABETH KORTRIGHT MONROE: 1786.
6. LOUISA CATHERINE JOHNSON ADAMS:
   1797.
7. RACHEL DONELSON ROBARDS JACK-
   SON: 1791 (the validity of Mrs. Robards'
   divorce was challenged by her first husband,
   and the Jacksons were remarried in a second
   ceremony in 1794).
8. HANNAH HOES VAN BUREN: 1807 (Mrs.
   Van Buren died in 1819, 18 years before Martin
   Van Buren was elected president).
9. ANNA SYMMES HARRISON: 1795.
10. LETITIA CHRISTIAN TYLER: 1813 (the
    first Mrs. Tyler died in 1842 during John
    Tyler's term of office, and the president was
    married again in 1844 to Julia Gardiner
    Tyler).
11. SARAH CHILDRESS POLK: 1824.
12. MARGARET MACKALL SMITH TAYLOR:
    1810.
13. ABIGAIL POWERS FILLMORE: 1826 (the
    first Mrs. Fillmore died in 1853, and Millard
    Fillmore married Caroline Carmichael McIn-
    tosh in 1858, 5 years after he had left office).
14. JANE MEANS APPLETON PIERCE: 1834.
15. James Buchanan remained a bachelor.
16. MARY TODD LINCOLN: 1842.
17. ELIZA MCCARDLE JOHNSON: 1827.
18. JULIA DENT GRANT: 1848.
19. LUCY WARE WEBB HAYES: 1852.
20. LUCRETIA RUDOLPH GARFIELD: 1858.
21. ELLEN LEWIS HERNDON ARTHUR:
    1859.
22. FRANCES FOLSOM CLEVELAND: 1886.
23. CAROLINE LAVINIA SCOTT HARRISON:
    1853 (the first Mrs. Harrison died in 1892,
    and Benjamin Harrison married Mary Scott
    Dimmik Harrison in 1896, 3 years after he
    had left office).
24. FRANCES FOLSOM CLEVELAND: 1886.
25. IDA SAXTON MCKINLEY: 1871.
26. EDITH KERMIT CAROW ROOSEVELT:
    1886 (Theodore Roosevelt had been married
    previously to Alice Hathaway Lee, who died
    in 1884).
27. HELEN HERRON TAFT: 1886.
28. ELLEN LOUISA AXSON WILSON: 1885
    (the first Mrs. Wilson died in 1914 during
    Woodrow Wilson's first term of office, and
    the president was married in 1915 to Edith
    Bolling Galt).
29. FLORENCE KLING DEWOLFE HARDING
    1891
30. GRACE ANNA GOODHUE COOLIDGE:
    1905
31. LOU HENRY HOOVER: 1899.
32. ANNA ELEANOR ROOSEVELT: 1905.
33. ELIZABETH (BESS) VIRGINIA WALLACE
    TRUMAN: 1919.
34. MAMIE GENEVA DOUD EISENHOWER:
    1916.

President's Cabinet, as of 1958

ATTORNEY GENERAL.
POSTMASTER GENERAL.
SECRETARY OF AGRICULTURE.
SECRETARY OF COMMERCE.
SECRETARY OF DEFENSE.
SECRETARY OF HEALTH, EDUCATION &
   WELFARE.
SECRETARY OF THE INTERIOR.
SECRETARY OF LABOR.
SECRETARY OF STATE.
SECRETARY OF THE TREASURY.

Presidents and Their Professions

EDITOR: Warren G. Harding (owned and edited
   the Marion, Ohio, Star).
EDUCATOR: Woodrow Wilson (though Wilson
   was a qualified lawyer, and had been in
   practice in Atlanta, Georgia, in 1882, the major
   part of his career was spent in education: as
   an instructor in history at Bryn Mawr and
   Wesleyan, professor of jurisprudence at Prince-
   ton, and finally president of Princeton).
ENGINEER: Herbert C. Hoover.
FARMER: George Washington.
LAWYER: John Adams; Thomas Jefferson; James
   Madison; John Quincy Adams; Andrew Jack-
   son; Martin Van Buren; John Tyler; James
   Knox Polk; Millard Fillmore; Franklin Pierce;
   James Buchanan; Abraham Lincoln; Ruther-
   ford B. Hayes; James A. Garfield; Chester
   A. Arthur; Grover Cleveland; Benjamin Harri-
   son; William McKinley; William Howard Taft;
   Calvin Coolidge; Franklin Delano Roosevelt;
   Harry S. Truman.
SOLDIER: William Henry Harrison; Zachary
   Taylor; Ulysses S. Grant; Dwight D. Eisen-
   hower.
STATESMAN: James Monroe; Andrew Johnson;
   Theodore Roosevelt.

Presidents and the States Where They Were Born

IOWA: Herbert C. Hoover.
KENTUCKY: Abraham Lincoln.
MASSACHUSETTS: John Adams; John Quincy
   Adams.
MISSOURI: Harry S. Truman.
NEW JERSEY: Grover Cleveland.
NEW HAMPSHIRE: Franklin Pierce.
NEW YORK: Martin Van Buren; Millard Fill-
   more; Theodore Roosevelt; Franklin Delano
   Roosevelt.
NORTH CAROLINA: James Knox Polk; An-
   drew Johnson.
OHIO: Ulysses S. Grant; Rutherford B. Hayes;
   James A. Garfield; Benjamin Harrison; Wil-
   liam McKinley; William Howard Taft; War-
   ren G. Harding.
PENNSYLVANIA: James Buchanan.
SOUTH CAROLINA: Andrew Jackson.
TEXAS: Dwight D. Eisenhower.
VERMONT: Chester A. Arthur; Calvin Coo-
   lidge.
VIRGINIA: George Washington; Thomas Jeffer-
   son; James Madison; James Monroe; William
   Henry Harrison; John Tyler; Zachary Taylor;
   Woodrow Wilson.

Presidents and the States Where They Lived When They Were Elected

CALIFORNIA: Herbert C. Hoover.
ILLINOIS: Abraham Lincoln.
INDIANA: Benjamin Harrison.
LOUISIANA: Zachary Taylor.
MASSACHUSETTS: John Adams; John Quincy
   Adams; Calvin Coolidge.
MISSOURI: Harry S. Truman.
NEW HAMPSHIRE: Franklin Pierce.
NEW JERSEY: Woodrow Wilson.
NEW YORK: Martin Van Buren; Millard Fill-
   more; Chester A. Arthur; Grover Cleveland;

Theodore Roosevelt; Franklin D. Roosevelt; Dwight D. Eisenhower.

OHIO: William Henry Harrison; Rutherford B. Hayes; James A. Garfield; William McKinley; William Howard Taft; Warren G. Harding.

PENNSYLVANIA: James Buchanan.

TENNESSEE: Andrew Jackson; James Knox Polk; Andrew Johnson.

VIRGINIA: George Washington; Thomas Jefferson; James Madison; James Monroe; John Tyler.

WASHINGTON, D.C.: Ulysses S. Grant.

Presidents Who Were Related

JOHN QUINCY ADAMS: 6th President, was a son of John Adams, the 2nd President.

BENJAMIN HARRISON: 23rd President, was a grandson of William Henry Harrison, the 9th President.

FRANKLIN D. ROOSEVELT: 32nd President, was a 5th cousin, and his wife a niece of Theodore Roosevelt, the 26th President.

ZACHARY TAYLOR: 12th President, was a 2nd cousin of James Madison, the 4th President. (Madison and Taylor were great grandsons of James Taylor and Martha Thompson.)

Presidents Who Succeeded to Office

CHESTER ALAN ARTHUR: Served about 3½ years of James A. Garfield's term.

CALVIN COOLIDGE: Served about 1½ years of Warren G. Harding's term.

MILLARD FILLMORE: Served over half of Zachary Taylor's term.

ANDREW JOHNSON: Served three years and ten months of Lincoln's second term.

THEODORE ROOSEVELT: Served about 3½ years of William McKinley's second term.

HARRY S. TRUMAN: Succeeded to the Presidency less than 3 months after the commencement of Franklin D. Roosevelt's fourth term.

JOHN TYLER: Served all but a month of President William Henry Harrison's term.

Presidents Who Died in Office

JAMES A. GARFIELD.
WARREN GAMALIEL HARDING.
WILLIAM HENRY HARRISON.
ABRAHAM LINCOLN.
WILLIAM MCKINLEY.
FRANKLIN DELANO ROOSEVELT.
ZACHARY TAYOR

Prizes

See Academy Awards; Hall of Fame for Great Americans; New York Drama Critics' Circle Awards; Nobel Prizes; National Book Awards; Pulitzer Prizes

Products of the World: Their Origins and Uses

Major Products of the Countries of the World

ABACA: Central America (Canal Zone; Costa Rica; Guatemala; Honduras; Panama; North Borneo; Philippines.

AGAR: Japan.

AIRCRAFT: Australia; France; Germany; Italy; Japan; United Kingdom; U.S.A.; U.S.S.R.

ALUMINUM (ALUMINIUM): Albania; Austria; Canada; France; Germany; U.S.A.; U.S.S.R.

ANTIMONY: Alaska; Argentina; Bolivia; Burma; Chile; China; Mexico; Morocco (French); Morocco (Spanish); Pakistan; Peru; Sarawak; Union of South Africa; U.S.A. (Yellow Pine Mine at Stibnite, Idaho); Yugoslavia.

APPLES: Argentina; Australia; Austria; Belgium; Canada; Chile; Denmark; France; Germany (West); Greece; Italy; Japan; Korea; Luxembourg; Mexico; Netherlands; New Zealand; Norway; Spain; Sweden; Switzerland; Turkey; Union of South Africa; United Kingdom; U.S.A.

ARROWROOT: Cook Islands; Marshall Islands; Samoa (Eastern); Tubuai; Vietnam; Windward Islands.

ARSENIC (WHITE): Australia; Belgium; Brazil; Canada; France; Germany; Italy; Japan; Mexico; Peru; Southern Rhodesia; Sweden; U.S.A.

ASBESTOS: Bechuanaland; Canada; Cyprus; Egypt; Goa; Mozambique; Philippines; Southern Rhodesia; South West Africa; Swaziland; Union of South Africa; U.S.S.R.

ASPHALT: Barbados; Cuba; Goa; Philippines; Trinidad; Venezuela.

ASSES: See Horses, mules, asses.

ATTAR OF ROSES: Bulgaria.

AUTOMOBILES: Australia; Canada; France; Germany; Italy; United Kingdom; U.S.A.; U.S.S.R.

BABASSU NUT: Brazil.

BADDEYEYITE: Brazil.

BALSA (CORKWOOD): Ecuador.

BALSAM: Colombia; Peru; El Salvador.

BALATA (GUM FROM BULLY TREE): Brazil; Guiana (British); Guiana (Dutch); Peru; Venezuela.

BAMBOO: Goa; Japan; Marquesas Islands; Papua Territory; Vietnam.

BANANAS: Australia; Bahamas; Belgian Congo; Bermuda; Brazil; British Honduras; Brunei; Cameroons; Cameroun; Canary Islands; Colombia; Costa Rica; Cuba; Dominican Republic; Ecuador; Egypt; Eritrea; Fiji; Formosa; French West Africa; Guadaloupe; Guam; Guatemala; Guiana (French); Guiana (Dutch); Guinea (French); Hawaii; Honduras; Ivory Coast; Jamaica; Marquesas Islands; Marshall Islands; Martinique; Mexico; Mozambique; New Caledonia; Nicaragua; Nigeria; Niue; Norfolk Island; Panama; Papua Territory; Philippines; Principe; Puerto Rico; Samoa (Eastern); Samoa (Western); Solomon Islands (Northern); Somalia; Somaliland; Spain; Tanganyika; Tonga; Venezuela; Windward Islands; Zanzibar.

BARITE: England; Germany; Italy; U.S.A.

BARLEY: Aden Protectorate; Afghanistan; Albania; Algeria; Andorra; Argentina; Australia; Austria; Basutoland; Belgian Congo; Belgium; Bolivia; Canada; Chile; China; Cyprus; Czechoslovakia; Denmark; Ecuador; Egypt; Eritrea; Ethiopia; Finland; France; Germany; Greece; Hungary; Ifni; India; Iran; Iraq; Ireland; Israel; Italy; Japan; Jordan; Korea; Lebanon; Libya; Malta; Mexico; Morocco (French); Morocco (Spanish); Netherlands; New Zealand; Norway; Pakistan; Peru; Poland; Portugal; Rumania; Spain; Spanish Sahara; Swaziland; Sweden; Switzerland; Syria; Tangier; Tibet; Tunisia; Turkey; Union of South Africa; United Kingdom; U.S.A.; U.S.S.R.; Uruguay; Yemen; Yugoslavia.

BAUXITE: Brazil; British Guiana; Bulgaria; Dahomey; France; French West Africa; Ghana; Greece; Guiana (British); Guiana (Dutch);

Guinea (French); Hungary; India; Indonesia; Italy; Jamaica; Malayan Federation; Mozambique; Rumania; U.S.A.; U.S.S.R.; Vietnam; Yugoslavia.

BAY OIL: Virgin Islands; Windward Islands.

BAY RUM: Virgin Islands; Windward Islands.

BEANS, BROAD (FÈVES): Egypt; Ethiopia; France; Italy; Portugal; Spain; United Kingdom.

BEANS, DRY (HARICOTS SECS): Angola; Brazil; Burma; China; Chile; Colombia; Ethiopia; France; India; Italy; Japan; Mexico; Portugal; Ruanda-Urundi; Spain; Turkey; U.S.A.; Yugoslavia.

BÊCHE-DE-MER (TREPANG: SEA CUCUMBER): Australia (northern); Fiji; Solomon Islands.

BENZOIN (BENJAMIN; RESIN FROM A STORAX TREE): Java; Laos; Sumatra.

BERYL: Australia; Argentina; Brazil; India.

BIRD OF PARADISE PLUMES: New Guinea (Netherlands).

BISMUTH: Argentina (metal, ore); Bolivia; Canada (metal); China (ore); France (ore); Japan (metal); Korea, South; Mexico (impure bars); Peru (metal, alloy); Spain (metal); Yugoslavia (metal).

BITTERS: Venezuela; Virgin Islands; Windward Islands.

BREADFRUIT: Caroline Islands; Cook Islands; Gambier Islands; Guam; Mariana Islands; Marquesas Islands; Marshall Islands; Samoa (Eastern); Yap.

BRISTLES: China; U.S.S.R.

BUFFALOES: Brunei; Bulgaria; Burma; Cambodia; Ceylon; China; Egypt; India; Indonesia; Iraq; Lebanon; Pakistan; Malaya; Philippines; Taiwan Thailand; Tunisia; Turkey; Vietnam.

BURLAP: India; Pakistan.

BUTTER: Argentina; Australia; Austria; Belgium; Brazil; Canada; Denmark; Eire; Finland; France; Germany (West); Italy; Netherlands; New Zealand; Sweden; Switzerland; Union of South Africa; United Kingdom; U.S.A.

CACAO BEANS: Brazil; Cameroons; Ceylon; Colombia; Comoro Island; Dominican Republic; Ecuador; Fernando Po and Rio Muni; Guatemala; Guianas; French Equatorial Africa; French West Africa; Ghana; Jamaica; Liberia; Mariana Islands; Nicaragua; Nigeria; Panama; Peru; Principe; São Thomé; Tobago; Togoland; Trinidad; Venezuela.

CADMIUM: Australia; Belgian Congo; Belgium; Canada; France; Germany; Italy; Japan; Mexico; Norway; Peru; Poland; South West Africa; United Kingdom; U.S.A.

CALIPEE (TURTLE JELLY): Seychelles.

CAMELS: Aden Protectorate; Afghanistan; Algeria; Anglo-Egyptian Sudan; Eritrea; French Sudan; India; Iraq; Israel; Jordan; Libya; Mauritania; Mongolian Republic; Morocco (French); Niger; Pakistan; Qatar; Saudi Arabia; Somaliland; Somaliland (British); Spanish; Sahara; Syria; Tunisia.

CAMPHOR: Japan; Taiwan; Tanganyika; Zanzibar.

CARDAMON (GINGER SEEDS): India; Laos; Madagascar; Malabar; Sumatra; Vietnam.

CARNAUBA WAX (BRAZILIAN WAX PALM): Brazil.

CASSAVA (MANIOC, A STARCH): Argentina; Belgian Congo; Brazil; Caroline Islands; Colombia; Fiji; French Sudan; French Togoland; French West Africa; Ghana (and British Togoland); Guadaloupe; Guam; Guiana (French); Indonesia; Ivory Coast; Liberia; Madagascar; Mauritius; Mozambique; New Caledonia; New Hebrides; Niger; Nigeria; North Borneo;

Northern Rhodesia; Nyasaland; Palau Islands; Paraguay; Peru; Ruanda-Urundi; Senegal; Taiwan; Tanganyika; Togo; Togoland; Windward Islands; Venezuela; Yap.

CASTOR OIL: Brazil; India; U.S.S.R.

CATTLE: Anglo-Egyptian Sudan; Angola; Argentina; Australia; Austria; Basutoland; Bechuanaland; Belgian Congo; Belgium; Bolivia; Brazil; Bulgaria; Burma; Cambodia; Canada; Ceylon; Chile; China; Colombia; Costa Rica; Cuba; Czechoslovakia; Denmark; Dominican Republic; Ecuador; Egypt; Eire; El Salvador; Eritrea; Ethiopia; Falkland Islands; Finland; France; French Euqatorial Africa; French Morocco; French West Africa; Ghana (and British Togoland); Germany; Greece; Guatemala; Haiti; Hawaii; Honduras; Hungary; India; Indonesia; Iran; Iraq; Israel; Italy; Japan; Kenya; Korea; Laos; Madagascar; Malaya; Manchuria; Mexico; Mozambique; Netherlands; Nigeria and British Cameroons; New Caledonia; New Zealand; Nicaragua; Northern Rhodesia; Norway; Nyasaland; Pakistan; Panama; Paraguay; Peru; Philippines; Poland; Portugal; Portuguese Guinea; Puerto Rico; Ruanda-Urundi; Rumania; Somalia; Southern Rhodesia; South West Africa; Spain; Spanish Morocco; Swaziland; Sweden; Switzerland; Tanganyika; Thailand; Tunisia; Turkey; Uganda; Union of South Africa; United Kingdom; U.S.A.; U.S.S.R.; Uruguay; Venezuela; Yugoslavia.

CELESTITE: Mexico; England; Spain.

CEMENT: Albania; Argentina; Belgian Congo; Belgium; Bolivia; Canada; Chile; China; Colombia; Ecuador; Egypt; France; Germany; Hong Kong; Italy; Japan; Korea; Lebanon; Macao; Netherlands; Pakistan; Peru; Poland; Portugal; Spain; United Kingdom; U.S.A.; U.S.S.R.; Venezuela; Vietnam; Yugoslavia.

CHALK: England.

CHEESE: Australia; Canada; Czechoslovakia; Denmark; France; Netherlands; New Zealand; Norway; Portugal; Sweden; Switzerland; United Kingdom; U.S.A.

CHICK-PEAS (POIS CHICHES): Ethiopia; French Morocco; India; Italy; Mexico; Pakistan; Spain; Turkey.

CHROMITE: Albania; Cuba; Cyprus; Greece; Egypt; India; Japan; New Caledonia; Pakistan; Philippines; Sierra Leone; Southern Rhodesia; Turkey; Union of South Africa; U.S.A.; U.S.S.R.; Yugoslavia.

CITRUS FRUITS: (1) Oranges, tangerines, clementines; *(oranges, mandarines, clémentines)*: Algeria; Argentina; Australia; Brazil; Cuba; Egypt; French Morocco; French West Africa; Greece; Israel; Italy; Jamaica; Japan; Mexico; Spain; Turkey; Union of South Africa; U.S.A. (2) Grapefruit *(pamplemousse)*: Israel; U.S.A. (3) Lemons, limes, others *(citrons, limes, autres agrumes)*: Argentina; Chile; Egypt; Greece; Italy; Mexico; Spain; U.S.A.

CINNAMON: Ceylon; Malabar; Seychelles; Vietnam.

CITRONELLA: Ceylon; Singapore.

CLEMENTINES: See Citrus fruits.

COAL: Afghanistan; Alaska; Australia; Austria; Belgian Congo; Belgium; Bulgaria; Canada; Chile; China; Czechoslovakia; France; Germany; Goa; Hungary; India; Indonesia; Iran; Ireland; Japan; Korea; Malayan Federation; Mongolian Republic; Nepal; Netherlands; New Zealand; Nigeria; Philippines; Poland; Portugal; Rumania; Scotland; Southern Rhodesia; Spain; Turkey; Union of South Africa; United Kingdom; U.S.A.; U.S.S.R.; Venezuela; Vietnam; Yugoslavia.

CLOVES: Brazil; Ceylon; Guianas; Java; Madagascar; Mauritius; Spice Islands (Moluccas); Sumatra; Zanzibar.

COBALT: Australia; Belgian Congo; Bolivia; Burma; Canada; Chile; Finland; French Morocco; Iran; Italy; Japan; Northern Rhodesia; U.S.A.

COCA (SOURCE OF COCAINE): Bolivia; Bonin Islands; Peru.

COCOA: Bismarck Archipelago; Brazil; Cameroons; Cameroun; Ceylon; Costa Rica; Dominican Republic; Ecuador; French Equatorial Africa; French West Africa; Goa; Gold Coast; Guadaloupe; Guam; Guinea (Spanish); Haiti; Indonesia; Ivory Coast; Martinique; New Hebrides; Northeast New Guinea; Peru; Philippines; São Thomé; Sierra Leone; Timor; Togo; Togoland; Trinidad;, Venezuela; Windward Islands.

COCONUTS: Bismarck Archipelago; British Honduras; Ceylon; Cook Islands; Fiji; French Equatorial Africa; Gambier Islands; Gilbert Islands; Goa; Guiana (British); Guiana (Dutch); Honduras; Indonesia; Ivory Coast; Jamaica; Malayan Federation; Maldive Islands; Marquesas Islands; Marshall Islands; Mauritius; New Caledonia; New Guinea (Netherlands); New Hebrides; North Borneo; Northeast New Guinea; Palau Islands; Panama; Papua Territory; Principe; Puerto Rico; Sarawak; Seychelles; Singapore; Solomon Islands (northern); Thailand; Virgin Islands; Windward Islands; Yap.

COCONUT OIL: Ceylon; Fiji; Goa; Guam; Indonesia; Malaya; Philippines.

COFFEE: Angola; Belgian Congo; Bismarck Archipelago; Brazil; Cameroons; Cameroun; Cape Verde Islands; Colombia; Costa Rica; Cuba; Dominican Republic; Ecuador; Eritrea; Ethiopia; French Equatorial Africa; French West Africa; Guadaloupe; Guatemala; Guiana (British); Guiana (Dutch); Guinea (French); Guinea (Spanish); Haiti; Hawaii; Honduras; India; Indonesia; Ivory Coast; Jamaica; Kenya; Laos; Liberia; Madagascar; Martinique; Mexico; Mozambique; New Caledonia; New Hebrides; Nicaragua; Nigeria; Panama; Papua Territory; Peru; Principe; Puerto Rico; El Salvador; Sarawak; Saudi Arabia; Singapore; Tanganyika; Timor; Togo; Togoland; Trinidad; Uganda; Venezuela; Vietnam; Yemen; Zanzibar. 80 % of the world's supply of coffee comes from the Western Hemisphere; Africa supplies about 17 %, the rest comes from Asia and Oceania; in 1954-55. Brazil produced 42 %, and Colombia 19 %, of all the coffee in the world.

COKE (SPECIFIED): Belgium; Canada; Czechoslovakia; France; Germany; Great Britain; India; Italy; Japan; Netherlands; Poland; U.S.A.; U.S.S.R.

COLUMBITE: Nigeria.

COPPER: Afghanistan; Alaska; Albania; Australia; Austria; Belgian Congo; Belgium; Bolivia; Bulgaria; Burma; Canada; Chile; China; Cuba; Czechoslovakia; England; Finland; French Equatorial Africa; Germany; India; Iran; Italy; Japan; Korea; Mexico; Morocco (French); Nepal; New Caledonia; New Zealand; Northern Rhodesia; Norway; Pakistan; Papua Territory; Paraguay; Peru; Philippines; Portugal; Spain; Sweden; Turkey; Union of South Africa; U.S.A.; U.S.S.R.; Venezuela; Vietnam; Yugoslavia.

COPPER (SMELTER): Australia; Belgian Congo; Canada; Germany; Japan; Mexico; Northern Rhodesia; Peru; Sweden; Union of South Africa; U.S.A.; U.S.S.R.

COPRA (DRIED COCONUT MEAT, SOURCE OF OIL): Caroline Islands; Ceylon; Comoro Islands; Cook Islands; Dahomey; Fiji; Gam-

bier Islands; Gilbert Islands; Guam; Indonesia; Malayan Federation; Maldive Islands; Marshall Islands; Mauritius; Mexico; Mozambique; New Caledonia; New Guinea (Netherlands); New Hebrides; Niue; North Borneo; Northeast Guinea; Papua Territory; Philippines; Principe; Samoa (Eastern); Samoa (Western); Seychelles; Society Islands; Solomon Islands (Northern); Timor; Togo; Tokelau Islands; Tonga; Tuamotu; Tubuai; Vietnam; Windward Islands.

CORK: Algeria; Morocco (French); Morocco (Spanish); Portugal; Spain; Tunisia.

CORUNDUM: Union of South Africa.

COTTON: Afghanistan; Anglo-Egyptian Sudan; Angola; Argentina; Barbados; Belgian Congo; Brazil; Bulgaria; Burma; Cambodia; China; Colombia; Cyprus; Ecuador; Egypt; Ethiopia; Fiji; France; French Equatorial Africa; French Sudan; French West Africa; Gold Coast; Haiti; Hawaii; India; Indonesia; Iran; Iraq; Ivory Coast; Kenya; Korea; Leeward Islands; Malta; Mexico; Mozambique; Nepal; New Caledonia; Nicaragua; Niger; Nigeria; Northern Rhodesia; Nyasaland; Pakistan; Paraguay; Peru; Puerto Rico; El Salvador; Somaliland; Syria; Tanganyika; Thailand; Togo; Turkey; Uganda U.S.A.; U.S.S.R.; Venezuela; Vietnam; Zanzibar.

COTTON (LINT): Anglo-Egyptian Sudan; Argentina; Belgian Congo; Brazil; China; Egypt; Greece; India; Iran; Mexico; Mozambique; Nigeria; Pakistan; Peru; Syria; Turkey; Uganda; U.S.A.

COTTONSEED: Argentina; Brazil; China; Egypt; India; Mexico; Pakistan; Peru; Sudan; Turkey; Uganda; U.S.A.; U.S.S.R.

CRYOLITE: Greenland.

CUTCH (CATECHU; CASHOO): Brunei; North Borneo; Sarawak.

DATES: Aden Protectorate; Algeria; Anglo-Egyptian Sudan; Bahrain; Egypt; Eritrea; French Morocco; Iran; Iraq; Libya; Mauritania; Morocco (French); Niger; Oman; Qatar; Saudi Arabia; Trucial Oman; Tunisia.

DERRIS ROOT: North Borneo.

DIAMONDS: Angola; Australia; Belgian Congo; Brazil; British Togoland; Dahomey; French Equatorial Africa; French West Africa; Ghana; Guiana (British); India; Ivory Coast; Sierra Leone; Tanganyika; Union of South Africa; Venezuela; Zanzibar.

DIVIDIVI (TANNIN): Curaçao; Venezuela.

EGGS: Argentina; Australia; Belgium; Brazil; Canada; Denmark; France; Germany (West); Italy; Japan; Netherlands; Philippines; Sweden; United Kingdom; U.S.A.

ELECTRIC POWER: Australia; Belgium; Canada; Czechoslovakia; France; Italy; Japan; Norway; Sweden; Switzerland; Union of South Africa; United Kingdom; U.S.A.

EMENTINE: Brazil; Costa Rica; Nicaragua.

EMERY: Greece; Turkey; U.S.A.

FIBER, HARD CORDAGE: See Abaca, henequen, sisal.

FIGS: Algeria; Greece; Italy; Libya; Turkey; U.S.A.

FISH: Aden; Bahrain; Belgium; Bermuda; Bismarck Archipelago; Bonin Islands; British Honduras; Bulgaria; Cambodia; Canada; Canary Islands; Caroline Islands; Ceylon; Chile; China; Cuba; Curaçao; Cyprus; Damao; Denmark; Diu; Easter Island; Egypt; England; Finland; France; Gambier Islands; Germany; Gibralter; Gilbert Islands; Goa; Greece; Greenland; Guadaloupe; Hawaii; Hong Kong; Hungary; Iceland; Ifni; India; Iran; Ireland; Israel; Italy; Japan; Korea; Leeward Islands; Macao; Malayan Federation; Maldive Islands; Malta; Mariana Islands; Marshall Islands; Mexico; Morocco (French); Morocco (Spanish); Nauru; Netherlands; New Zealand; Norfolk Island; North Borneo; Norway; Pakistan; Paulu Islands; Peru; Philippines; Poland; Portugal; Ryukyu Islands; St. Pierre; Samoa (Western); Sarawak; Saudi Arabia; Senegal; Singapore; Spain; Spanish Sahara; Sweden; Thailand; Tokelau Islands; Tristan da Cunha; Trucial Oman; Tunisia; Turkey; U.S.A.; U.S.S.R.; Venezuela; Virgin Islands; Volcano Islands; Windward Islands; Yap; Yemen.

FLAX: Albania; Algeria; Austria; Belgium; Canada; Cyprus; Finland; Hungary; Ireland; Italy; Japan; Mexico; Netherlands; Northern Ireland; Peru; Poland; Rumania; Spain; United Kingdom; U.S.A.; U.S.S.R.; Yugoslavia.

FLAXSEED: Argentina; Austria; Belgium; Brazil; Canada; Czechoslovakia; France; French Morocco; India; Mexico; Netherlands; Poland; Turkey; Uruguay; U.S.A.; U.S.S.R.

FLUOR SPAR: France; Germany; U.S.A.; U.S.S.R.

GAMBIER (GAMBIR: FROM THE UNCARIA GAMBIR, A TYPICAL MALAYAN WOODY VINE OF THE MADDER FAMILY; A CUTCH, OR CATECHU): Malayan Federation.

GAS (MANUFACTURED): Australia; Austria; Belgium; Canada; France; Japan; Netherlands; United Kingdom; U.S.A.

GAS (NATURAL): Canada; U.S.A.; Venezuela.

GOATS: Albania; Algeria; Anglo-Egyptian Sudan; Angola; Argentina; Austria; Basutoland; Bechuanaland; Belgian Congo; Bolivia; Brazil; British Somaliland; Bulgaria; Chile; China; Colombia; Czechoslovakia; Dominican Republic; Ecuador; Egypt; Eritrea; France; French Cameroun; French Equatorial Africa; French West Africa; Germany; Ghana (and British Togoland); Greece; Haiti; India; Indonesia; Iran; Iraq; Israel; Jordan; Kenya; Lebanon; Libya; Liechtenstein; Malaya; Manchuria; Mexico; Nigeria (and British Cameroons); Pakistan; Peru; Philippines; Poland; Portugal; Ruanda-Urundi; Rumania; Somalia; Southern Rhodesia; South West Africa; Spain; Spanish Morocco; Syria; Tanganyika; Tunisia; Turkey; Uganda; Union of South Africa; U.S.A.; U.S.S.R.; Venezuela; Yugoslavia.

GOLD: Afghanistan; Alaska; Anglo-Egyptian Sudan; Argentina; Australia; Bechuanaland; Belgian Congo; Brazil; Burma; Canada; Chile; China; Colombia; Costa Rica; Dahomey; Dominican Republic; Ecuador; Eritrea; Ethiopia; Fiji; French Equatorial Africa; French West Africa; Ghana; Guatemala; Guiana (British); Guiana (French); Guiana (Dutch); Guinea (French); Honduras; India; Ivory Coast; Japan; Kenya; Korea; Madagascar; Malayan Federation; Mexico; Mongolian Republic; Mozambique; New Zealand; Nicaragua; Nigeria; North-East New Guinea; Nyasaland; Panama; Papua Territory; Peru; Philippines; Rumania; El Salvador; Sarawak; Saudi Arabia; Southern Rhodesia; Swaziland; Sweden; Tanganyika; Tibet; Union of South Africa; U.S.A.; U.S.S.R.; Uruguay; Venezuela; Vietnam; Zanzibar.

GRAIN, MIXED (MIXTURES OF BREAD GRAIN, FEED GRAIN, BREAD OR FEED GRAIN, OR GRAIN AND PULSES): Canada; Denmark; France; Germany; Greece; Sweden; Turkey; United Kingdom; Yugoslavia.

GRAPEFRUIT: See Citrus fruits.

GRAPES, TOTAL (VIGNE, ENSEMBLE DU VIGNOBLE): Algeria; Argentina; Australia; Austria; Brazil; Bulgaria; Cyprus; Czechoslovakia; Egypt; France; French Morocco; Germany (West); Greece; Hungary; Italy; Japan;

Portugal; Rumania; Spain; Switzerland; Syria; Tunisia; Turkey; U.S.A.; Yugoslavia.

GRAPES, WINE: Algeria; Argentina; Australia; France; French Morocco; Germany (West); Greece; Italy; Portugal; Spain; Switzerland; Tunisia; Union of South Africa; U.S.A.; Yugoslavia.

GRAPHITE: Canada; Ceylon (crystalline); India (crystalline); Japan; Madagascar (crystalline, flake); Mexico (lump).

GROUNDNUTS: Anglo-Egyptian Sudan; Argentina; Belgian Congo; Brazil; Burma; China; Dahomey; Fiji; French Cameroun; French Equatorial Africa; French Sudan; French West Africa; Gambia; Ghana; Guinea (French); Guinea (Portuguese); India; Indonesia; Ivory Coast; Japan; Kenya; Liberia; Madagascar; Mauritius; Mexico; Niger; Nigeria; North Borneo; Northern Rhodesia; Nyasaland; Senegal; Sierra Leone; Southern Rhodesia; Swaziland; Taiwan; Thailand; Togo; Togoland; Union of South Africa; U.S.A.; Vietnam.

GUM ARABIC (SENEGAL GUM): Anglo-Egyptian Sudan; Eritrea; Niger; Senegal; Tanganyika; Zanzibar.

HEMP: Italy; Tanganyika; U.S.S.R.

HENEQUEN (HARD CORDAGE FIBER): Cuba; Honduras; Mexico; El Salvador.

HIDES AND SKINS (FRESH OR RAW, UNLESS SPECIFIED): Argentina (dry cattle, dried sheep); Australia (cattle, calf, dry sheep); Austria (cattle, calf); Brazil (fresh, salted, dry cattle; salted pig; fresh sheep); Cambodia (cattle); Canada (cattle, calf, sheep); Colombia (dry cattle); Dominican Republic (cattle); Eritrea (cattle); Finland (cattle, calf); France (cattle); French Morocco (sheep, goat); French West Africa (dry sheep, goat); Germany, West (cattle, calf, horse); Greece (cattle, sheep, goat); Iceland (sheep); India (cattle); Italy (calf, sheep); Jamaica (cattle); Japan (wet-salted cattle); Netherlands (cattle, calf, goat); New Zealand (calf, pickled sheep); Pakistan (cattle, sheep); Paraguay (salted cattle); Portugal (cattle, calf, dry sheep); Southern Rhodesia (dry cattle); Spain (cattle, calf); Switzerland (dry cattle, calf); Syria (sheep); Tanganyika (raw, dry cattle; goat); Turkey (sheep, goat); Uganda (dry cattle); United Kingdom (cattle, calf, sheep); Union of South Africa (cattle, sheep).

HOGS: Argentina; Brazil; Canada; China; Czechoslovakia; France; Germany; Hungary; Italy; United Kingdom; U.S.A.; U.S.S.R.

HOPS: Austria; Belgium; Czechoslovakia; Germany (West); United Kingdom; U.S.A.

HORSES, MULES, ASSES: Algeria (H,M,A); Anglo-Egyptian Sudan (A); Argentina (H,M,A); Austria (H); Belgium (H); Brazil (H,M,A); Bulgaria (H,A); Canada (H); Chile (H); China (H,M,A); Colombia (H,M,A); Costa Rica (H); Cuba (H,M); Czechoslovakia (H); Denmark (H); Dominican Republic (H,M,A); Ecuador (H); Egypt (A); Finland (H); France (H,A); French Morocco (H,M,A); French West Africa (H,A); Germany (H); Greece (H,M,A); Guatemala (H,M); Haiti (H,A); Honduras (H); Hungary (H); India (H,A); Indonesia (H); Iran (H,A); Iraq (H,A); Eire, Republic of (H,A); Israel (A); Italy (H,M,A); Japan (H); Kenya (A); Manchuria (H,M,A); Mexico (H,M,A); Netherlands (H); New Zealand (H); Nicaragua (H); Nigeria (and British Cameroons) (H,A); Norway (H); Pakistan (H,A); Paraguay (H); Peru (H,M,A); Philippines (H); Poland (H); Portugal (H,M,A); Portuguese Timor (H); Puerto Rico (H); Rumania (H); El Salvador (H,M); Southern Rhodesia (A); South West Africa (A); Spain (H,M,A); Sweden (H); Switzerland (H); Syria (A); Tanganyika (A); Thailand (H); Tunis (H,M,A); Turkey (H,M,A); United Kingdom (H); Union of South Africa (H,M,A); Uruguay (H); U.S.A. (H,M); U.S.S.R. (H,A); Venezuela (H,A); Yugoslavia (H,A).

HYDROELECTRIC ENERGY (WATER POWER): Canada; France; Italy; Japan; Sweden; Switzerland; U.S.A.

HYOSCENE: Belgium; Egypt; France; Germany; Hungary; U.S.S.R.

INDIGO: Guinea (French); Senegal.

IODINE: Chile.

IRON ORE: Australia; Austria; Chile; France; Germany; India; Luxembourg; Spain; Sweden; United Kingdom; U.S.A.; U.S.S.R.

JUTE (RAW): Belgian Congo; Brazil; India (produces over 90 % of world's supply); Indo-China; Iran; Japan; Nepal; Pakistan; Taiwan.

KAPOK (CEIBA; SILK COTTON): Bismarck Archipelago; Cambodia; Dahomey; Ecuador; French Equatorial Africa; French Sudan; Indonesia; Mozambique; Niger; North Borneo; Papua Territory; Somaliland.

KOLA (KOLA NUT): Guinea (French); Ivory Coast; Sierra Leone; Togo.

KYANITE: India.

LAC (BASE OF SHELLAC): Bhutan.

LACE: Belgium; Cyprus; England; France; Malta; Portugal; St. Helena; Scotland.

LACQUER WARE: Burma; Japan.

LEAD: Afghanistan; Alaska; Argentina; Australia; Austria; Belgium; Bolivia; Bulgaria; Burma; Canada; China; Czechoslovakia; England; French Equatorial Africa; Germany; Greece; Hong Kong; Iran; Italy; Japan; Mexico; Mongolian Republic; Morocco (French); Morocco (Spanish); Nepal; New Caledonia; Nigeria; Peru; Poland; Rumania; Scotland; Spain; Sweden; Tunisia; U.S.A.; U.S.S.R.; Vietnam; Yugoslavia.

LEAD (SMELTER): Australia; Belgium; Burma; Canada; France; Germany; Italy; Mexico; Peru; Spain; U.S.A.; U.S.S.R.

LEATHER: Afghanistan; Albania; Argentina; Australia; Austria; Ceylon; Chile; Czechoslovakia; Dominican Republic; Finland; France; French Sudan; Germany; Greece; Hungary; Iceland; India; Iran; Israel; Lebanon; Liechtenstein; Luxembourg; Morocco (French); Netherlands; Niger; Norway; Pakistan; Peru; Poland; Syria; Tunisia; Uruguay; U.S.A.; U.S.S.R.; Venezuela.

LEMONS: See Citrus fruits.

LENTILS: Argentina; Egypt; Ethiopia; India; Pakistan; Syria; Turkey.

LIGNITE: Albania; Austria; Czechoslovakia; France; Germany; Greece; Hungary; Italy; Lebanon; Poland; Rumania; Spain; Tunisia; Turkey; U.S.S.R.; Yugoslavia.

LIMES: See Citrus fruits.

LOOFA SPONGES: Japan.

MAGNESIUM (METAL): Canada; France; Germany; Italy; Japan; Korea; Norway; Switzerland; United Kingdom; U.S.A.; U.S.S.R.

MAHOGANY: Brazil; French Equatorial Africa; Yucatan.

MANGANESE (ORE): Belgian Congo; Brazil; Chile; Cuba; Egypt; French Morocco; Ghana; India; Japan; Turkey; Union of South Africa; U.S.A.; U.S.S.R.

MAIZE: Albania; Argentina; Australia; Belgian Congo; Brazil; Canada; Cape Verde Islands; Chile; Costa Rica; Dominican Republic; Ecuador; Egypt; France; French Morocco; French Togoland; French West Africa; Guatemala; Honduras; India; Italy; Japan; Java (and Madura); Kenya; Mexico; Nicaragua; Northern Rhodesia; Pakistan; Panama; Philippines; Portugal; Ruanda-Urundi; El Salvador; Southern Rhodesia; Spain; Thailand; Turkey;

Uganda; Union of South Africa; Uruguay; U.S.A.; Venezuela; Yugoslavia.

MANILA: Philippines.

MEATS: Argentina; Australia; Belgium; Canada; Czechoslovakia; Denmark; Ireland; Netherlands; New Zealand; Poland; Sweden; Union of South Africa; United Kingdom; U.S.A.

MERCURY: Algeria; Canada; Chile; China; Czechoslovakia; Germany; Italy; Japan; Mexico; Spain; Union of South Africa; U.S.A.; U.S.S.R.; Yugoslavia.

MICA: Brazil; Canada; Madagascar; India; Union of South Africa.

MILK: Australia; Austria; Canada; Czechoslovakia; Denmark; Finland; Germany (West); Israel; Japan; Netherlands; Norway; Sweden; Switzerland; United Kingdom; U.S.A.

MILK, CONDENSED AND EVAPORATED: Argentina (whole); Australia (whole); Belgium (whole, skim); Canada (whole, skim, condensed, buttermilk); Chile (whole); Denmark (whole, skim); Eire; France; Germany, West (whole, skim); Japan (whole); Netherlands (whole, skim); New Zealand; Norway (whole); Peru (whole); Spain (whole); Sweden (whole, skim); Switzerland; Union of South Africa (whole); United Kingdom (whole, skim); U.S.A. (whole, skim, buttermilk).

MILK, DRIED: Argentina (skim); Australia (whole, skim, buttermilk, whey); Belgium (whole, skim); Brazil (whole); Canada (whole, skim, buttermilk, whey); Chile (whole); Denmark (whole, skim); Eire; France (whole, skim); Germany (whole, skim); Japan; Netherlands (whole, skim, whey); New Zealand (skim, buttermilk); Norway; Spain (whole); Sweden (whole, skim); Union of South Africa (whole, skim); United Kingdom (whole, skim, buttermilk; whey); Venezuela.

MILLET AND SORGHUM: Aden Protectorate (S); Argentina (M); Australia (S); Bechuanaland (M); Ceylon (M); Egypt (S); El Salvador (M); Eritrea (M); French Morocco (S); French Togoland (M); French West Africa (M,S); Guatemala (M); India (M,S); Japan (M); Jordan (S); Korea, South (M); Pakistan (M,S); Ruanda-Urundi (M,S); Somalia (M,S); Spanish Morocco (M,S); Syria (M); Tanganyika (M,S); Turkey (M); U.S.A. (S).

MOLASSES: Barbados; Cuba; Dominican Republic; Fiji; Guiana (British); Guiana (Dutch); Haiti; Hawaii; Leeward Islands; Mauritius; Puerto Rico; Virgin Islands; Windward Islands.

MOLYBDENUM: Canada; Chile; China; Finland; Japan; Korea; Manchuria; Mexico; Norway; Peru; U.S.A.; Yugoslavia.

MONAZITE: Brazil; India.

MOTHER-OF-PEARL: Anglo-Egyptian Sudan; Cook Islands; Eritrea; Society Islands; Somaliland.

MULES: See Horses, mules, asses.

NICKEL: Burma; Canada; Cuba; Finland; Germany; Greece; Indonesia; Iran; Japan; New Caledonia; Norway; Sweden; Union of South Africa; U.S.A.; U.S.S.R.

OATS: Albania; Algeria; Argentina; Australia; Austria; Basutoland; Belgian Congo; Belgium; Bulgaria; Canada; Chile; Cyprus; Czechoslovakia; Denmark; Finland; France; French Morocco; Germany; Greece; Hungary; Ireland; Italy; Japan; Luxembourg; Netherlands; New Zealand; Northern Ireland; Norway; Poland; Portugal; Rumania; Spain; Swaziland; Sweden; Switzerland; Tunisia; Turkey; U.S.A.; U.S.S.R.; Union of South Africa; United Kingdom; Uruguay; Yugoslavia.

OLIVE OIL: Albania; Algeria; Greece; Italy;

Jordan; Lebanon; Monaco; Portugal; Spain; Tunisia; Turkey.

OLIVES: Albania; Algeria; Cyprus; France; Greece; Italy; Jordan; Lebanon; Libya; Morocco (French); Portugal; Spain; Syria; Tunisia; Turkey.

ONIONS: Argentina; Australia; Bermuda; Brazil; Canada; Canary Islands; Egypt; France; Germany (West); Greece; Italy; Japan; Lebanon; Malta; Mexico; Netherlands; Spain; Turkey; United Kingdom; U.S.A.; Yugoslavia.

OPIUM: China; India; Japan; Saudi Arabia; Turkey; Yugoslavia.

ORANGES: See Citrus fruits.

PALM KERNELS: Angola; Belgian Congo; Brazil; Cameroons; Cameroun; French Equatorial Africa; French West Africa; Ghana; Guinea (Portuguese); Indonesia; Liberia; Nigeria; Sierra Leone; Togo.

PALM OIL: Belgian Congo; Dahomey; Guinea (French); Indonesia; Ivory Coast; Malayan Federation; Nigeria; Principe.

PAPRIKA: Hungary.

PEANUTS: Argentina; Belgian Congo; Brazil; Burma; Cameroons; China; French West Africa; Hong Kong; India; Indonesia; Japan; Mexico; Nigeria; Taiwan; Union of South Africa; U.S.A.; Uruguay.

PEARLS: Ceylon; Eritrea; Gambier Islands; Japan; Kuwait; Saudi Arabia; Society Islands; Tuamotu; Venezuela.

PEARS: Australia; Austria; Argentina; Belgium; Bulgaria; France; Germany (West); Greece; Italy; Japan; Netherlands; Spain; Switzerland; Turkey; United Kingdom; U.S.A.; Yugoslavia.

PEAS, DRY (POIS SECS): Belgian Congo; Ethiopia; French Morocco; Japan; Netherlands; Ruanda-Urundi; United Kingdom; U.S.A.

`PEPPER: Belgian Congo; Cambodia; Ceylon; India; Indo-China; Indonesia; Madagascar; Malaya; Nigeria; North Borneo; Sarawak; Singapore; Thailand.

PETROLEUM (CRUDE): Alaska; Albania; Algeria; Argentina; Austria; Bahrain; Bolivia; Brunei; Burma; Canada; China; Colombia; Ecuador; Egypt; Goa; Hungary; India; Indonesia; Iran; Iraq; Japan; Korea; Kuwait; Mexico; Netherlands; New Guinea (Netherlands); Pakistan; Peru; Philippines; Poland; Qatar; Rumania; Sarawak; Saudi Arabia; Trinidad; U.S.A.; U.S.S.R.; Venezuela; Yugoslavia.

PHOSPHATES: Cambodia; Caroline Islands; Curaçao; Egypt; Madagascar; Mariana Islands; Nauru; Poland; Society Islands; Tunisia; U.S.A.; U.S.S.R.; Venezuela.

PIG IRON (INCLUDING FERRO-ALLOYS): Australia; Belgium; Canada; Czechoslovakia; France; Germany; India; Japan; Luxembourg; Saarland; United Kingdom; U.S.A.; U.S.S.R.

PIGS: Angola; Argentina; Australia; Austria; Belgium; Bolivia; Brazil; Bulgaria; Burma; Cambodia; Canada; Chile; China; Colombia; Cuba; Czechoslovakia; Denmark; Dominican Republic; Ecuador; Finland; France; Germany; Greece; Guatemala; Haiti; Honduras; Hungary; India; Indonesia; Eire, Republic of; Italy; Japan; Korea; Laos; Madagascar; Malaya; Malta; Manchuria; Mexico; Netherlands; New Zealand; Nicaragua; Panama; Paraguay; Peru; Philippines; Poland; Portugal; Rumania; El Salvador; Southern Rhodesia; Spain; Sweden; Switzerland; Taiwan; Thailand; Trieste; Union of South Africa; U.S.A.; U.S.S.R.; Uruguay; Venezuela; Yugoslavia.

PINEAPPLES: Bahamas; Brunei; Cook Islands; Cuba; Fiji; Guam; Hawaii; Malayan Federation; Martinique; Mauritius; New Caledonia;

Paulu Islands; Panama; Philippines; Puerto Rico; Samoa (Eastern); Sarawak; Singapore; Taiwan; Union of South Africa.

PLATINUM: Alaska; Australia; Belgian Congo; Canada; Colombia; Ethiopia; Italy; New Caledonia; Northeast New Guinea; Norway; Union of South Africa; United Kingdom; U.S.A.; U.S.S.R.

PORCELAIN: Czechoslovakia; Denmark; France; Japan; Portugal; Sweden.

POTASH: Germany; Jordan; Spain; U.S.S.R.

POTATOES: Algeria; Andora; Australia; Austria; Belgian Congo; Belgium; Bolivia; Bulgaria; Canada; Canary Islands; Chile; Cyprus; Czechoslovakia; Denmark; England; Finland; France; Germany; Hungary; Iceland; Ireland; Israel; Italy; Japan; Lebanon; Luxembourg; Madagascar; Malta; Nepal; Netherland; Northern Ireland; Northern Rhodesia; Norway; Peru; Poland; Portugal; Rumania; St. Helena; Scotland; Southern Rhodesia; Spain; Sweden; Switzerland; Tristan da Cunha; Union of South Africa; United Kingdom; U.S.A.; U.S.S.R.

POULTRY (CHICKENS, DUCKS, GEESE, TURKEYS): Albania (C); Algeria (C;) Argentina (C,D,T); Australia (C,D,T); Austria (C); Belgium (C); Bolivia (C); Bulgaria (C); Brazil (C,D,T); Cambodia (C); Canada (C,T); China (C); Costa Rica (C); Cuba (C); Czechoslovakia (C); Denmark (C); Dominican Republic (C); Egypt (C,D,G); Eire (C,D,T); Finland (C); France (C,D,G,T); French Morocco (C); French West Africa (C); Germany (C,D,G); Greece (C); Haiti (C); Hungary (C,D,G); India (C,D); Iraq (C); Israel (C); Italy (C); Japan (C); Korea (C); Laos (C); Lebanon (C); Madagascar (C); Manchuria (C); Mexico (C); Netherlands (C,D); New Zealand (C); Nicaragua (C); Norway (C); Peru (C); Philippines (C); Poland (C,D,G,T); Portugal (C); Rumania (C,D,G); El Salvador (C); Somalia (C); Spain (C); Sweden (C); Switzerland (C); Syria (C); Taiwan (C,D); Tunisia (C); Turkey (C,T); Union of South Africa (C); United Kingdom (C,D,T); U.S.A. (C,D,G,T); U.S.S.R. (C,D,G,T); Uruguay (C); Vietnam (C,D); Yugoslavia (C).

PYRETHRUM: Japan; Kenya; Tanganyika.

QUARTZ: Brazil.

QUEBRACHO: Argentina; Paraguay.

QUININE (EXTRACT OF CINCHONA BARK): Australia; Ceylon; Colombia; Ecuador; India; Indonesia; Jamaica; Java; Laos; Netherlands East Indies (90 % of world's supply); Peru; Principe.

RADIUM: Belgian Congo; Canada.

RAISINS: Australia; Greece; Iran; U.S.A.

RAPESEED: China; France; Germany (West); India; Japan; Pakistan; Sweden.

RAPESEED OIL: China; India; Pakistan.

RAYON (FILAMENT): Belgium; Brazil; Canada; France; Germany; Italy; Japan; Netherlands; Spain; Switzerland; United Kingdom; U.S.A.; U.S.S.R.

RAYON (STAPLE): Austria; Belgium; Czechoslovakia; France; Germany; Italy; Japan; Poland; Spain; Sweden; Switzerland; United Kingdom; U.S.A.

RICE: Albania; Argentina; Australia; Belgian Congo; Bhutan; Brazil; British Honduras; Brunei; Burma; Cambodia; Ceylon; Chile; China; Colombia; Comoro Islands; Costa Rica; Damao; Dominican Republic; Equador; Egypt; Fiji; Formosa; French Sudan; French West Africa; Goa; Guiana (British); Guiana (French); Guiana (Dutch); Guinea (French); Guinea (Portuguese); Haiti; Hawaii; Honduras; Hong Kong; India; Indonesia; Iran; Iraq; Italy; Ivory Coast; Japan; Korea; Laos; Liberia;

Madagascar; Malayan Federation; Mauritius; Mexico; Morocco (Spanish); Nepal; New Caledonia; Nicaragua; Niger; Nigeria; North Borneo; Northern Rhodesia; Nyasaland; Pakistan; Panama; Papua Territory; Paraguay; Peru; Philippines; Portugal; Ryukyu Islands; Salvador; Sarawak; Saudi Arabia; Senegal; Sierra Leone; Sikkim; Singapore; Spain; Taiwan; Thailand; Tibet; Togoland; Turkey; U.S.A.; Uruguay; Venezuela; Vietnam.

ROSEWOOD ESSENCE: Guiana (French).

RUBBER: Belgian Congo; Bismarck Archipelago; Bolivia; Brazil; Brunei; Burma; Cambodia; Cameroons; Cameroun; Ceylon; Colombia; Ecuador; Fiji; French Equatorial Africa; Guatemala; Guiana (British); India; Indo-China; Indonesia; Liberia; Malayan Federation; Mexico; Netherlands East Indies; Nicaragua; Nigeria; North Borneo; Nyasaland; Papua Territory; Peru; Philippines; Sarawak; Singapore; Solomon Islands (Northern); Thailand; Togo; Uganda; Union of South Africa; Venezuela; Vietnam.

RUBBER, NATURAL (EXPORTS): British North Borneo; Burma; Ceylon; Indo-China; Indonesia; Malaya; Sarawak; Thailand.

RUBBER, SYNTHETIC: Canada; Germany; Sweden; U.S.A.; U.S.S.R.

RUBY: See Sapphire and ruby.

RUM: Barbados; British Honduras; Guadaloupe; Guiana (British); Guiana (French); Guiana (Dutch); Jamaica; Leeward Islands; Liberia; Martinique; Mauritius; Puerto Rico; Réunion; Society Islands; Trinidad; Virgin Islands; Windward Islands.

RUTILE: Australia; Brazil; U.S.A.

RYE: Albania; Argentina; Australia; Austria; Belgium; Brazil; Bulgaria; Canada; Czechoslovakia; Denmark; Finland; France; Germany; Greece; Hungary; Ireland; Italy; Korea; Luxembourg; Morocco (Spanish); Netherlands; Norway; Poland; Portugal; Rumania; Spain; Swaziland; Sweden; Switzerland; Turkey; Union of South Africa; United Kingdom; U.S.A.; U.S.S.R.; Yugoslavia.

SAGO: Brunei; New Guinea (Netherlands); North Borneo; Papua Territory; Sarawak.

SALT: Aden; Albania; Anglo-Egyptian Sudan; Austria; Bahamas; Bulgaria; Burma; Canada; Cape Verde Islands; Ceylon; China; Colombia; Czechoslovakia; Damao; Diu; Ecuador; Eritrea France; Germany; Goa; India; Iran; Iraq; Japan; Jordan; Kenya; Korea; Mauritania; Netherlands; Niger; Pakistan; Poland; Rumania; Saudi Arabia; Somaliland (British); Somaliland (French); Switzerland; Tanganyika; Tibet; U.S.A.; U.S.S.R.; Venezuela; Yugoslavia; Zanzibar.

SAPPHIRE AND RUBY: Burma; Ceylon; India; Siam; Union of South Africa.

SELENIUM: Canada; U.S.A.

SENNA: Egypt; India.

SESAME OIL: China.

SESAME SEED: Burma; China; Ethiopia; India; Mexico; Pakistan; Turkey; Uganda.

SHEA NUTS: Anglo-Egyptian Sudan; Dahomey; French Sudan; Nigeria.

SHEEP: Albania; Algeria; Anglo-Egyptian Sudan; Argentina; Australia; Austria; Basutoland; Belgian Congo; Bolivia; Brazil; British Somaliland; Bulgaria; Canada; Chile; China; Colombia; Cyprus; Czechoslovakia; Ecuador; Egypt; Eire; Eritrea; Falkland Islands; Finland; France; French Cameroun; French Equatorial Africa; French Morocco; French West Africa; Germany; Ghana (and British Togoland); Greece; Guatemala; Hungary; India; Indonesia; Iran; Iraq; Italy; Kenya; Libya; Liechtenstein; Manchuria; Mexico; Netherlands; New Zealand; Nigeria (and British

Cameroons); Norway; Pakistan; Peru; Poland; Portugal; Ruanda-Urundi; Rumania; Somalia; South West Africa; Spain; Spanish Morocco; Sweden; Syria; Tanganyika; Tunisia; Turkey; Uganda; Union of South Africa; United Kingdom; U.S.A.; U.S.S.R.; Yugoslavia.

SHELLAC: India; Indo-China; Siam.

SILVER: Afghanistan; Alaska; Argentina, Australia; Belgian Congo; Belgium; Bolivia; Brazil; Bulgaria; Burma; Canada; Chile; China; Colombia; Costa Rica; Czechoslovakia; Fiji; Germany; Honduras; Hong Kong; India; Japan; Kenya; Korea; Mexico; Mozambique; New Zealand; Nicaragua; Nigeria; Northeast New Guinea; Norway; Peru; Philippines; Rumania; El Salvador; Sweden; Union of South Africa; U.S.A.; U.S.S.R.

SISAL: Angola; Bahamas; Brazil; British East Africa; Comoro Islands; Eritrea; French Sudan; Haiti; Indonesia; Kenya; Madagascar; Mauritius; Mexico; Mozambique; Nyasaland; Papua Territory; Portuguese Africa; Senegal; Tanganyika; Zanzibar.

SORGHUM: See Millet and sorghum.

SOYBEANS: China; Indonesia; Japan; Korea; Manchuria; U.S.A.; Vietnam.

SOY SAUCE (SHOYU): China; Japan.

SPERM OIL: England; Germany; Japan; Norway.

SPONGES: Cyprus; Papua Territory; Tunisia.

STEEL: Austria; Belgium; Canada; Ceylon; Czechoslovakia; France; Germany; Italy; Japan; Luxembourg; Saarland; Sweden; United Kingdom; U.S.A; U.S.S.R.

SUGAR (CENTRIFUGAL): Brazil (cane); Cuba (cane); Hawaii (cane); India (cane); Indonesia (cane); Philippines (cane); Puerto Rico (cane); U.S.A. (beet, cane); U.S.S.R. (beet).

SUGAR BEETS: Austria; Belgium; Bulgaria; Canada; Czechoslovakia; Denmark; Finland; France; Germany; Hungary; Iran; Ireland; Israel; Italy; Netherlands; Poland; Portugal (and Azores); Rumania; Spain; Sweden; Switzerland; United Kingdom; U.S.A.; U.S.S.R.; Yugoslavia.

SUGAR CANE: Barbados; Brazil; British Honduras; Brunei; Canary Islands; China; Colombia; Comoro Islands; Costa Rica; Cuba; Dominican Republic; Egypt; Ethiopia; Fiji; Guadeloupe; Guam; Guatemala; Güiana (British); Guiana (French); Guiana (Dutch); Hong Kong; India; Indonesia; Jamaica; Kenya; Leeward Islands; Liberia; Madagascar; Marquesas Islands; Martinique; Nepal; Nicaragua; Niger; Oman; Pakistan; Panama; Paraguay; Philippines; Puerto Rico; Ryukyu Islands; El Salvador; Trinidad; Uganda; Union of South Africa; U.S.A.; Venezuela; Virgin Islands; Volcano Islands; Windward Islands.

SULPHUR: Argentina; Bolivia; Canada; Chile; France; Germany; Greece; Indonesia; Iran; Israel; Italy; Japan; Mexico; Norway; Pakistan; Peru; Portugal; Spain; Sweden; Turkey; U.S.A.; U.S.S.R.; Volcano Islands.

SUNFLOWER SEED: Argentina; Chile; Ethiopia; Turkey; Union of South Africa; Uruguay; Yugoslavia.

SWEET POTATOES AND YAMS: Argentina; Barbados; Belgian Congo; Brazil; Caroline Islands; China; Comoro Islands; Cook Islands; Cuba; Easter Island; Fiji; French Sudan; French Togoland; French West Africa; Ghana; Guadaloupe; Guam; Hong Kong; India; Indonesia (Java, Madura, and other islands); Ivory Coast; Japan; Korea, South; Mariana Islands; Marquesas Islands; Martinique; Mauritius; Mexico; New Guinea (Netherlands); New Hebrides; Nigeria; Niue; Papua Territory; Paulu Islands; Peru; Puerto Rico; Ruanda-Urundi; Ryukyu Islands; Samoa (Eastern);

Senegal; Singapore; Solomon Islands (Northern); Spain; Thailand; Togo; U.S.A.; Venezuela; Vietnam; Yap.

TAGUA NUT: Ecuador.

TALC: Egypt; India; Sardinia.

TANGERINES: See Citrus fruits.

TANTALITE: Australia; Belgian Congo; Brazil.

TARO: Caroline Islands; Cook Islands; Fiji; Guam; Marshall Islands; New Hebrides; Paulu Islands; Papua Territory; Samoa (Eastern); Samoa (Western); Solomon Islands (Northern); Tokelau Islands; Yap.

TEA: Brazil; Ceylon; China; India; Indonesia; Iran; Japan; Kenya; Laos; Malayan Federation; Mauritius; Mozambique; Nepal; Nyasaland; Pakistan; Taiwan; Union of South Africa; Vietnam.

TEAK: Goa; Laos; Malaya; Thailand.

TIN: Alaska; Australia; Belgian Congo (cassiterite); Belgium; Bolivia; Burma; China; Indonesia; Japan; Laos; Malayan Federation; Netherlands; Netherlands East Indies; Nigeria; Portugal; Singapore; Swaziland; Tanganyika; Thailand; Uganda; Union of South Africa; United Kingdom; Vietnam; Zanzibar.

TIN (SMELTER): Australia; Belgian Congo; Belgium; China; Germany; Indonesia; Japan; Malaya; Netherlands; Portugal; Union of South Africa; United Kingdom; U.S.A.

TITANIUM (COMMERCIALLY PURE METAL PRODUCTION): Australia (South); England; Japan; U.S.A.

TOBACCO: Aden Protectorate; Afghanistan; Albania; Algeria; Andorra; Angola; Argentina; Austria; Belgium; Brazil; Bulgaria; Burma; Cambodia; Cameroun; Canada; Cape Verde Islands; Ceylon; China; Colombia; Costa Rica; Cuba; Cyprus; Dominican Republic; Eritrea; Fiji; France; French Sudan; Greece; Guiana (Dutch); Hawaii; Honduras; Hungary; India; Indonesia; Iran; Iraq; Ireland; Israel; Italy; Ivory Coast; Jamaica; Japan; Korea; Libya; Luxembourg; Macao; Madagascar; Malayan Federation; Mauritius; Monaco; Mozambique; Nepal; New Caledonia; North Borneo; Northern Ireland; Northern Rhodesia; Nyasaland; Pakistan; Paraguay; Peru; Philippines; Puerto Rico; Rumania; El Salvador; Sarawak; Singapore; Somaliland; Southern Rhodesia; Swaziland; Switzerland; Syria; Tanganyika; Thailand; Togoland; Turkey; Uganda; Union of South Africa; U.S.A.; U.S.S.R.; Uruguay; Venezuela; Vietnam; Yugoslavia; Zanzibar.

TOBACCO (LATIKIA): Lebanon; Syria.

TROCHUS SHELL (TOP SHELL; SOURCE OF PEARL BUTTONS): Anglo-Egyptian Sudan; Fiji; New Caledonia; New Hebrides; Solomon Islands; Solomon Islands (Northern).

TUNG OIL: China.

TUNGSTEN (ORES): Argentina; Australia; Bolivia; Brazil; Burma; China; Korea; Malayan Federation; New Zealand; Portugal; Spain; Tanganyika; Thailand; Union of South Africa; Vietnam; Zanzibar.

URANIUM: Belgian Congo; Canada.

VANADIUM (ORES AND CONCENTRATES): Argentina; Mexico; Northern Rhodesia; Peru; South West Africa; U.S.A.

VANILLA: Bolivia; Comoro Islands; Guadaloupe; Réunion; Seychelles; Society Islands.

VEGETABLE IVORY: Anglo-Egyptian Sudan; Ecuador; Eritrea.

WHEAT: Aden Protectorate; Afghanistan; Albania; Algeria; Anglo-Egyptian Sudan; Argentina; Australia; Austria; Basutoland; Bechuanaland; Belgium; Brazil; Bulgaria; Canada; Chile; China; Colombia; Cyprus; Czechoslovakia; Damao; Denmark; Egypt; Eritrea; Ethiopia; Finland; France; Germany; Greece; Hungary; Ifni; India; Iran; Iraq; Ireland; Israel; Italy;

Japan; Jordan; Kenya; Korea; Lebanon; Libya; Luxembourg; Malta; Mauritania; Mexico; Morocco (French); Morocco (Spanish); Netherlands; New Caledonia; New Zealand; Niger; Northern Rhodesia; Norway; Nyasaland; Pakistan; Peru; Poland; Portugal; Rumania; Saudi Arabia; Southern Rhodesia; Spain; Swaziland; Sweden; Switzerland; Syria; Tanganyika; Tangier; Tibet; Tunisia; Turkey; Union of South Africa; United Kingdom; U.S.A.; U.S.S.R.; Uruguay; Yemen; Yugoslavia.

WHEAT FLOUR: Argentina; Australia; Canada; Chile; India; Ireland; Israel; Japan; Mexico; New Zealand; Union of South Africa; United Kingdom; U.S.A.; Yugoslavia.

WOOL: Afghanistan; Albania; Algeria; Argentina; Australia; Belgium; Chile; China; Easter Island; Falkland Islands; France; French North Africa; India; Iraq; Jordan; Kuwait; Mongolian Republic; New Zealand; Pakistan; Peru; Saudi Arabia; Spain; Syria; Tibet; Union of South Africa; United Kingdom; U.S.A.; U.S.S.R.; Uruguay.

YAMS: See Sweet potatoes.

ZINC: Alaska; Algeria; Argentina; Australia; Belgian Congo; Belgium; Bolivia; Burma; Canada; Chile; China; Czechoslovakia; French Equatorial Africa; Germany; Greece; Italy; Japan; Mexico; Morocco (French); Nepal; Nigeria; Norway; Peru; Poland; Rumania; Spain; Sweden; Tunisia; United Kingdom; U.S.A.; U.S.S.R.; Vietnam; Yugoslavia.

ZINC (SMELTER): Australia; Belgium; Canada; France; Germany; Japan; Mexico; Norway; Poland; United Kingdom; U.S.A.; U.S.S.R.

ZIRCON: Australia; Brazil; India.

The Nature and Uses of the Major Products of the World

ACONITE ROOT: Obtained from the plant aconite or monkshood; root is more or less conical, from 4 to 10 cm. in length and from 1 to 3.5 cm. in diameter at the crown; it is weak brown to moderate brown in color; powdered aconite root is pale brown to weak yellowish-brown in color. Uses: in medicine to slow the heart rate, and to lower the blood pressure; in dentistry, as a mild local anesthetic and counterirritant.

AGAR: Dried mucilaginous substance extracted from certain classes of algae; transparent, odorless, tasteless strips or powder, soluble in hot water, forming a viscid solution. Uses: bacteriological media, dental impressions, laxatives, photography, textiles, food.

ALCOHOL (ETHYL): Colorless, volatile, inflammable, organic liquid produced by fermentation of a sugar (molasses, grain, or wood cellulose) and distillation, or synthetically from various hydrocarbon gases, acetylene, or ethylene; in the U.S.A. nearly all synthetic alcohol is made from ethylene obtained from natural gas or petroleum refinery gases; ethylene is converted to ethyl sulphate by treatment with sulphuric acid and the ethyl sulphate is hydrolized with water to ethyl alcohol and sulphuric acid. Uses: chemical raw material, solvent, dehydrating agent, manufacture of protective coatings, plastics, pharmaceuticals, tetraethyl lead, antifreeze; production of chemical warfare gases and smokeless powders; alternative raw material to petroleum in the production of synthetic rubber.

ALUMINUM: Bluish-white metal valued for its lightness combined with strength, its non-corrosive quality, high heat of reaction, and excellent electrical conductivity; most abundant of all metallic elements, it is usually found as the oxide, of which bauxite, although not the most plentiful ore, is the richest and most easily processed; aluminium is produced by electrolytic reduction of alumina (produced from bauxite) with cryolite as a flux. See Bauxite. Uses: aircraft, train, truck, and bus bodies; transmission lines; machinery; structural uses; ship construction; electrical appliances; automotive equipment; cooking utensils; paint; foil; incendiaries; pontoons; smoke pots.

ANTIMONY: Hard, brittle metallic element of crystalline structure, tin-white in color; expands upon solidification; prepared chiefly from the ore stibnite (antimony sulphide) by roasting and reduction; imparts hardness and a smooth surface to soft-metal alloys. Uses: bearings and bearing metals; battery parts; paints and pigments; solders; lead hardening; many minor uses such as type metal, glass making, and cable coverings; flame-proofing textiles; camouflage paints; primers; pyrotechnics; hard lead bullet cores.

ARSENIC: Soft, brittle, poisonous element with steel-gray color and metallic luster; the principal source is as a by-product output from copper and lead ore smelting; white arsenic (arsenious oxide) is the principal arsenical. Uses: primarily an agricultural insecticide and weed killer; other uses include: wood preservation, glass decolorizer, and in certain medicines; chemical warfare gases such as Lewisite, Adamsite, and smokes.

ASBESTOS: Generic name for two principal fibrous minerals, amphibole and serpentine, which can be spun or felted; valued for their fine fibers, infusibility, toughness, flexibility and insulating properties. *Rhodesian chrysotile* is a variety of serpentine very low in iron, preferred where electrical insulation is important. Uses: high-grade asbestos cloth, gaskets; friction material (such as brake linings and clutch facings); principally flameproof Navy cable construction. *South African amosite* is an amphibole of well-developed fibrous structure with a high percentage of long fibers (4-7 inches long). Uses: high-temperature insulation, packings; flame-proof clothing; gas masks. *Canadian chrysotile* is a serpentine fiber, much of it too short for spinning, but constituting the bulk of commercial asbestos. Uses: paper and shingle stock, fireproofing material; heat and sound insulation; asbestos cement.

BALSA: Wood of a large tree native to tropical America and the West Indies; valued as one of the lightest woods, weighing only 8 lbs. per cubic foot; used where lightness is at a premium and great strength is not required. Uses: aircraft construction; life preservers and life rafts; sounding boards.

BARITE: White, opaque to translucent, crystalline salt whose texture is granular or fibrous; it is found associated with clays, occurring mostly in medium-sized deposits, although some underground veins have been worked; usually mined by open-pit methods; removal of impurities includes hand cobbing, grading, washing, and crushing; ground barite requires bleaching with sulphuric acid (to remove iron), drying and grinding. Uses: well drilling, lithopone pigments, chemicals, glass, filler for paints and rubber, tanning.

BAUXITE: Noncrystalline, earthy mineral, massive or in grains, varying in color from white to yellow or red; contains alumina in varying amounts, but best commercial grades should have at least 52 %; it is mined and the alumina in the ore converted into a usable form of alumina principally by the Boyer process; the alumina is then reduced by electrolysis to metallic aluminium; the lime-soda sinter process may be used to concentrate ores of less than 52%. Uses: primarily in the production of aluminum; other uses include artificial abrasives, aluminum chemicals and refractory brick, catalyst for oil cracking, synthetic rubber production.

BELLADONNA: Crude drug, belladonna or "deadly nightshade," consists of the dried leaves and roots of the plant *Atropa belladonna;* the active principles, atropine, hyoscyamine, and scopolamine are obtained by extraction. Uses: sedatives, dilation of eye.

BERYL (BERYLLIUM): Ore found in pegmatites from which the hard, brittle, light, crystalline metal beryllium is obtained; beryllium imparts to its alloys high tensile strength, hardness, fatigue-resistance, nonsparking and noncorrosive qualities, with good electrical and heat conductivity. Uses: beryllium copper alloys, high-speed bearings and bushings, springs, diaphragms, nonsparking tools, welding electrodes, X-ray and cyclotron tubes, steel deoxidizer, electronic tubes, ceramics, reverse brake and gear assemblies for landing craft, fire control instruments.

BISMUTH: Silvery-white metal with reddish tinge, brittle and easily powdered; its alloys characteristically have low melting points and a tendency to expand upon solidification; it is obtained as a by-product in the smelting and refining of copper, lead, and other nonferrous ores. Uses: pharmaceuticals, cosmetics, low melting alloys, solders, bearing metals, fuse parts in automatic safety valves; industrial applications such as jigs, spotting fixtures, die setting, anchoring machine tool bushings, tube bending, electro-forming, coating patterns and dies.

BRISTLES (PIG AND HOG): In the short, stiff, coarse hair found on these animals, the outer end is split or "flagged"; this flag increases the paint holding capacity and aids in uniform distribution of the paint; the bristles are tapered, giving stiffness at the base and resiliency at the tip. Uses: paint and varnish brushes, industrial and household brushes, tooth and shaving brushes, maintenance of military and maritime equipment, military construction.

BURLAP (JUTE): Fabric woven of jute yarns, "burlap" is used in an inclusive sense to refer to jute fabrics of various constructions, weights, and widths (see Cordage fibers). Uses: jute bags and sacks, backing for linoleum and oilcloth, asphalt roofing, felts, coverings for baled merchandise, sand bags, camouflage cloth, airfield surfacing material, packing and wrapping material.

BUTANOL (NORMAL BUTYL ALCOHOL): Colorless liquid with a vinous odor, soluble in water and miscible in all proportions with most of the common organic solvents; it is produced by the fermentation of starch and sugars, and also synthetically from petroleum or natural gas. Uses: solvent for drugs; shellac, varnish gums; manufacture of rayon, artificial leather, synthetic rubber, plastics; dehydrating nitrocellulose.

CADMIUM: Silvery-white metal occurring in the mineral greenockite, but obtained chiefly as a by-product of zinc smelting. Uses: protective finish in electroplating, solders, an alloy for hardening copper, cerium, gold, and silver; wearing surface for bearings; substitute for tin; chemical warfare agent.

CASTOR OIL: Oil obtained by crushing castor beans, the seed of the castor-oil plant *(Ricinus communis)*, grown in most tropical and semitropical countries; further recovery is obtained by pressing and extraction by solvents;

sulphonated castor oil used in the dye industry is known as Turkey red oil. Uses: medicine, paints and varnishes, dyeing, brake fluids, leather dressing, artificial leather, bombbay door mechanism, shock absorbers in recoil mechanism of guns.

CELESTITE: Gangue mineral usually associated with gypsum and sulphur; domestic grades contain 75 % to 90 % strontium sulphate and require crushing, jigging, and tabling; for chemical purposes further chemical extraction is necessary. Uses: refining beet sugar; fireworks; chemicals; well-drilling weight material; filler for paints, rubber, and plastics; tracer bullets; flares.

CHALK, ENGLISH: White or grayish, loosely cohesive kind of limestone; the powdered form is known as "whiting"; the crude lump chalk is crushed, washed, and dried. Uses: Manufacture of paints, rubber, putty, paper, also many lesser uses: putty and calking compounds, camouflage paints, filler for rubber insulation for wire.

CHROMITE: Essential mineral of chrome ore, from which commercial chronium and chromates are obtained; there are three grades used: metallurgical, refractory, and chemical; all require different treatments to obtain the finished products, namely, chromium and ferrochrome, refractories, and chemicals. *Metallurgical grade* is ore containing about 50% chromic oxide; it is classified as to chrome content, chrome-iron ratio, and physical form (lumpy, friable and fines, and concentrates); chromium, when added to steel, makes it stronger, harder, and corrosion-resistant. Uses: Alloying element in steel; particularly stainless; and wear- and heat-resistant steels; high-speed tool steel; automotive springs and axles; catalyst in gasoline and synthetic rubber production, projectiles; armor plate; rifle linings. *Refractory grade* is ore that contains combined chromic oxide and alumina; its use depends upon its chemical stability and neutral character; chromite refractories are very resistant to corrosion by metals, slags, and vapors; have a high melting point, and high thermal conductivity; are crushed, molded, and baked; or used as a cement. Uses: refractory brick and cement for lining marine boilers, open-hearth, and heat treating furnaces. *Chemical grade* of chromite: the concentrates and friable ores are crushed and roasted with soda ash and lime to yield sodium chromate from which other chromium salts are prepared. Uses: electroplating, dyes, pigments, tanning, oxidizing agent; many minor uses.

COAL: Black or brownish-black solid combustible mineral formed by the partial decomposition of vegetable matter under certain conditions; a series of coals can be traced from peat, lignite (brown coal), bituminous (soft coal); anthracite (hard coal), to graphite; the above order is based on increasing carbon content and decreasing volatility; the coal is mined, crushed, and sorted. Uses: primary requirement for industrial development; production of steel and mechanical power; fuel; destructive distillation.

COBALT: Highly magnetic white metal with a bluish tinge; resembling nickel in physical characteristics; hard, tough, malleable, and refractory, usually found associated with nickel and copper; obtained by smelting cobaltite or smaltite; used mainly in the metallic or oxide form. Uses: high-speed tool steel; hardsurfaced heat-resistant alloys; binder for tungsten carbide cutting tools; magnetic alloys; glaze in ceramics; pigment in glass; paint drier; plating chemicals; catalyst; chiefly in

stellite (cobalt-chromium-tungsten alloy) for high-speed tools, valve steel, welding rods; important in turbine buckets of jet-propelled aircraft.

COCONUT OIL: Obtained from the pressings of copra, the dried kernel of the coconut; desirable in soap manufacture for its quick lathering properties not possessed by most other fats and oils, the very high percentage of recoverable glycerine, and the hardness of soap manufactured from this oil. Uses: soap; minor uses such as paints, brake fluids, synthetic resins, and pharmaceuticals; margarine, mayonnaise, salad dressings, shortenings; the pressed copra is used as a cattle feed and fertilizer; in wartime the uses of coconut oil are generally restricted to soap because of its high recovery of glycerine which is used for explosives, synthetic rubber, and as a plasticizer.

COLUMBITE: Columbium-bearing ores are termed columbite; the ore is concentrated and reduced by electrolysis; available commercially in metallic form and as ferrocolumbium; alloyed with stainless steel, columbium increases the weldability, creep strength, impact strength, heat-resistance, and corrosion-resistance of the steel (see Tantalite). Uses: stainless steel additive; airplane engine parts and auxiliaries (such as exhaust stacks, manifolds, and collector rings); rocket propelled equipment; projectile cores.

COPPER: Reddish metal; ductile; malleable; very tenacious; and one of the best conductors of heat and electricity; its ores are mined, concentrated, smelted, and refined; considered one of the most essential metals because of the multitude of uses of copper and the principal alloys, brass and bronze. Uses: in the manufacture of electrical equipment, automobiles, building hardware, special alloys, chemicals, cartridge and shell cases, rotating bands, bullet jackets, propellers, machinery.

CORDAGE FIBERS; MANILA FIBER (ABACA): Hard fiber known commercially as Manila; obtained from the leaf of the abaca plant (*Musa textilis*) by stripping the sheathing leaves from the stalk; the process consists of milking the juice and pulp from the layers peeled from the stalk; an abaca plant consists of a group of stalks in various stages of development. Uses: rope, cordage, twine, manufacture of paper products; Manila drilling cables in oil wells, gas wells, mines; marine cordage, Manila torpedo lines, shot lines and breeches. *Sisal* is the hard fibers stripped from the leaves of the plant *Agave sisalana*; they are dried, then sorted and graded. Uses: binder twines and ropes, padding, wire rope cores, reinforcement for paper and plastics, best available substitute for Manila in heavy-duty cordage. True *hemp* is a soft fiber obtained from the inner bark of the plant *Cannabis sativa*, cultivated in most countries of the temperate zones; fiber is separated from stalk by retting; the long fibers ("line") are separated from the short, tangled fibers ("tow") by combing or "hacking." Uses: "line" for twines, houselines, marline, ropes up to one inch (usually tarred), webbing, coarse textiles, soles for sandals, fire hose yarn; "tow" is used for oakum in packing and calking, twine, toweling, and miscellaneous textiles; substitute for jute. *Henequen* is the hard fiber obtained from the plant *Agave fourcroydes*, which grows in Mexico and Cuba; often confused with sisal but is coarser, less flexible, darker, and weaker; sometimes called Mexican sisal. Uses: binder twines, padding, partial substitute for sisal and Manila fibers. *Jute* is the soft,

pliable, weak fiber obtained from the plant
Corchorus capsularis olitorious; easily spun and
cheap; imported mainly from India as fiber
and burlap (see Burlap). Uses: twine; carpet
and rug backing; upholstery; electrical insulation; jute paper; low-grade cordage; inner-
lining for clothing; cores for steel cable;
packing and wrapping materials; oakum and
calking materials; substitute for Manila and
sisal. *Flax* is the soft, fine, strong fiber from
the inner bark of the flax plant; *Linum
usitatissimum;* the long silky bast fibers are
freed from the stem by retting and various
mechanical processes. Uses: manufacture of
thread, yarns, fishlines, fish-nets, water hose,
towels, linen fabric; longer fibers, known as
dressed "line," are used in higher-quality
thread and fabrics, while shorter fibers ("tow")
are used in yarn, cordage, packing and canvas,
webbing and cords for parachute construction;
flax is preferred to cotton beause of its
length and strength. *Sunn fiber (sunn hemp)*
is a soft fiber with a wide range of color
(gray to brown) and quality due to differences
in preparation; it is obtained from the inner
bark of the sunn plant (*Crotalaria juncea*)
cultivated in India; some types such as Jubble-
pore are stronger and more durable than jute,
but are not as strong as true hemp; however,
Benares sunn "hemp," the principal type imported by the United States, is much inferior
to jute in strength and durability. Uses: manufacture of marine oakum, canvas, and paper
stock (cigarette paper), and to some extent
for tarred rigging and marline; the wartime
uses of sunn fiber are restricted to the manufacture of marine oakum and as a substitute
for other fibers.

CORK: Outer bark of the cork oak, grown in
commercial stands only in the Mediterranean
area; the bark is stripped from the tree,
steamed, flattened, scraped, and sorted; the
bark is filled with air cells so that air makes
up about 50 % of the volume; this entrapped
air accounts for its insulating properties,
buoyancy, lightness, resiliency, and imper-
viousness. Uses: low-temperature and acousti-
cal insulation; liners for bottle crowns; linoleum; stoppers; gaskets; washers; grease re-
tainers; plus many other minor uses; insulation
for tanks, aircraft, and submarines; cartridge
plugs and shell-case wads; life preservers;
buoys; shoe fillers; bomb parts.

CORUNDUM: Natural crystalline sesquioxide of
aluminum, containing a small amount of impurities such as silica, iron, lime, and water;
ruby and sapphire are a variety of pure corundum; second hardest mineral known; when
crushed it has the property of parting into
fragments with a cutting edge; artificial corundum (aluminum oxide) is manufactured by
fusing bauxite in an electric furnace. Uses:
primarily as an abrasive and polishing material
(the coarse grains in grinding wheels and fine
grains in the optical industry), and to a lesser
extent as a refractory.

COTTON: Raw cotton, which is almost pure
cellulose, is a soft white fiber obtained from
the cotton plant; after the "bolls" are picked
the fiber is separated from the seed by
ginning; the fiber is then processed by spinning,
weaving, and finishing to give an immense
variety of final fabric products. Uses: clothing;
household goods; industrial uses; surgical uses;
military clothing; individual and organizational
army equipment; airplane fabrics; cordage.

COTTON BY-PRODUCTS: *Linters.* The seed, after ginning, is sent to the cottonseed oil mills;
there the fuzz on the seed is removed by a
mechanical process similar to ginning; the fuzz

is called cotton linters. Uses: mattress and
upholstery stuffing; chemical cotton pulp for
rayon, plastics, and photographic film; pulp
for smokeless powders and explosives. *Cottonseed oil.* The seeds are crushed and the oil
refined; or the seeds are hulled and then
crushed; the oil is colorless and almost odorless; the solid residue after pressing is caked
and used as a cattle feed. Uses: primarily
as an edible oil; also in soap making and industrial uses such as lubricating, cutting, or
drying oils.

CRYOLITE (NATURAL): White or colorless
cleavable masses of sodium-aluminum fluoride
with a vitreous luster; it is mined in only
one place; Ivigtut, Greenland; valued because it is easily fused, carries electricity,
and dissolves alumina. Uses: primarily as flux
in the reduction of aluminum; minor uses include the manufacture of glass, enamels, abrasives, and insecticides.

DIAMOND DIES: Industrial diamonds through
which a hole of accurate size and contour
has been drilled (there are two classes, with
openings greater than and less than .002 inch;
openings as small as .0004 inch are produced).
Uses: drawing wires of very small and uniform diameter such as filaments for incandescent lamps and electronic tubes and wire
for measuring instruments.

DIAMONDS (INDUSTRIAL): Essentially pure
carbon, diamond is one of the hardest substances known; as it is unequaled in resistance
to abrasion and wear; it is one of the most important tools of modern industry. Uses: cutting
tools; abrasive wheels; an agent to true other
abrasives; drills and boring heads; dies; glass
cutters; saws; pivots and bearings.

EMERY: Common dark granular variety of corundum containing more or less magnetite or
hematite and possessing great hardness; it is
crushed, sorted, and made into blocks, wheels,
or ground and glued to paper. Uses: grinding
and polishing; non-slip, wear-resistant ingredient in concrete floors.

EMETINE: Derived by extraction from the dried
root or underground stem of the shrub ipecac,
which is native to Central America; generally
processed into emetine hydrochloride, a white
crystalline powder. Use: a medicine for treatment of amoebic dysentery.

ERGOT: Fungus growing on many grains, particularly rye; ergotized grains constitute a
dangerous impurity in grain used as food, but
when removed are valuable for preparing the
drug ergot; the active principles, ergotamine,
ergotoxine, etc., are extracted by various organic solvents. Uses: major use in obstetrics;
minor use as a circulatory stimulant, and in
treatment of migraine, delirium tremens, and
shock.

FLUOR SPAR: Calcium fluoride or fluorite;
a transparent or translucent mineral of many
colors occurring in crystalline or massive
forms; the ore is mined, beneficiated, and
purified into three commercial grades; metallurgical (minimum 85 % CaF_2), ceramic (minimum 95 % CaF_2), and acid (minimum 98 %
CaF_2); Uses: metallurgical: flux and purifying agent in steel manufacture; ceramic: preparation of enamels and glass; acid: preparation
of hydrofluoric acid, with particular emphasis
upon wartime uses of hydrofluoric acid in the
manufacture of atomic bombs; also aviation
gasoline, artificial cryolite, and freon (a re-
frigerant) for aerosol bombs.

GLYCERINE (GLYCEROL): Clear, odorless,
colorless or pale yellow, hygroscopic, sirupy,
sweet-tasting liquid, obtained from the spent
lye liquor of the soap industry. Uses: medi-

cines; leather finishing; foodstuffs; solvent; moistener; antifreeze; explosives; synthetic rubber production; plasticizer.

GRAPHITE: Native carbon often associated with various mineral impurities, varying from 50 % graphite (low grade) to 95 % or better (high grade); it is soft, black, greasy-feeling, with a metallic luster; it is infusible and a good conductor of electricity; it occurs as flakes or granular compact masses; there are two forms, crystalline and amorphous; after mining, it is cleaned, dressed, refined, and graded, the amorphous form is also produced artificially in the electric furnace. *Amorphous lump.* Uses: foundry facings; dry-cell batteries; carbon brushes; electrodes; lead pencils; lubricants; glazing of smokeless powders. *Flake.* Uses: crucibles, retorts, and stoppers, lubricants; foundry facings. *Crystalline fines.* Uses: lubricants, polishes, and paints.

HORSEHAIR: Raw horsehair is hair that has been cut or combed from horse tails and manes; it is generally classified as to color and length; dressed horsehair, in addition, has generally been washed, the root ends placed together (sorted to length), and the hair bundled. Uses: raw horsehair (unsorted): upholstery and mattress stuffing; dressed horsehair (sorted): brushes; hair cloth; upholstery cloth; violin bows; wigs; novelties; mattresses; parachute pads; saddle packs.

HYDRAZINE HYDRATE: Colorless, fuming liquid, prepared from sodium hypochlorite and ammonia. Uses: used in organic synthesis; rocket fuel.

HYDROGEN PEROXIDE: Colorless heavy liquid usually used in from 3 to 30% aqueous solutions as a rocket and submarine fuel; made either from barium peroxide or from persulphuric acid; the ordinary 30 % solution is concentrated by vacuum distillation to the desired strength. Uses: bleaching agent; antiseptic; preservative; disinfectant; oxidizing agent; submarine fuel; rocket fuel; synthetic rubber production.

HYOSCINE: Natural alkaloid extracted by organic solvents principally from the roots of the Australian dubusia *(Scopolia)* plant, and from henbane and various other plants; it is known technically as scopolamine hydrobromide. Uses: as a medicine to control motion sickness and as an analgesic in obstetrics.

INDIUM: Rare, soft, silvery-white, malleable, and easily fusible metal; it is obtained as a by-product of lead and zinc operations; the metallic form is obtained by electrolysis of the chloride; as an alloy additive to bearing metals, it lowers the coefficient of expansion, enhances fatigue resistance, and contributes marked resistance to corrosion by lubricating oil acids. Uses: coating to increase resistance of aircraft bearings to corrosion; coating hollow-steel propeller blades; decorative plating; solders; precious metal alloy; to give amber color or to glass.

IODINE: Gray or purple-black crystalline solid with a metallic appearance; a nonmetallic element, member of the halogen group, sparingly soluble in water but readily so in alcohol; a small amount is absolutely essential in the diet of human beings and animals; prepared as a by-product from Chilean nitrate or by extraction from oil-well brines by the activated carbon process or silver nitrate process. Uses: sensitizing solutions for photographic films; additive to stock feeds; antiseptic and germicide; chemical catalyst; minor uses in foods, dyes, plastics, and textiles.

IRON ORE: Iron-bearing minerals from which iron can be extracted commercially are, in decreasing order of world importance: hematite, magnetite, limonite, and siderite. Most ore mined in the U.S.A. is hematite and our iron and steel production facilities are geared almost exclusively to it as being relatively free from phosphorous and sulphur and therefore easily used in the Bessemer process; a large proportion (about 70 %) of our ore is mined by open-pit methods and is of such high grade as to be used directly in the blast furnace without treatment; ratio of iron ore input to pig iron output now averages about 1.80 to 1; adequate supplies of coking coal are a prerequisite to the transformation of ore to pig iron. Use: basis of iron and steel industry.

JEWEL BEARINGS: Most are made from natural and synthetic rubies and sapphires and a few from molded glass; it is a processed product of a multitude of types and sizes involving as many as sixty separate operations and requiring specialized labor and equipment; the major types are ring jewels (essentially bearing jewels with a hole in the center); end-stones (backing for other jewels); Vee jewels (having a precise conical depression on one face); and various timekeeping-device jewels. Uses: instrument jewels, pressure type instruments, dial indicators; Vee jewels: electrical indicating instruments; timekeeping-device jewels: chronographs, chronometers, watches, etc.

KAPOK: Soft lustrous floss obtained from the seed pods of the tropical kapok *(Ceiba pentandra)* tree; the material is distinguished by lightness, resiliency, water and moisture resistance, capacity for thermal and sound insulation, and resistance to rodents, vermin, and bacteria. Uses: stuffing and padding for upholstery, cushions, bedding, sleeping bags, sports equipment, life preservers; lining for arctic clothing; sound and heat insultation; pontoon bridges; cushioning and sound insulating in tanks and aircraft.

KYANITE, INDIAN: Gangue mineral generally occurring as clusters of crystals in schists; the crystals are extracted from the clay and processed; processing consists of grinding and sizing or calcining and sizing. Uses: firebrick or other refractory uses in furnaces of nonferrous metals; glass manufacturing.

LEAD: Soft heavy grayish metal obtained from the mineral galena by concentration, reduction, and refining. Uses: pigments; cable coverings; tetraethyl lead; storage batteries; solders; bearing metals; foil; construction material; ammunition; protective shield against radioactive materials.

LEATHER: Animal hide or skin or any part thereof that has been tanned, tawed, or otherwise dressed (except for use as furs) desirable because of its flexibility, resiliency, porosity; ventilating properties, high tensile and tear strength, and ease of working; various tanning and finishing methods impart the distinctive properties necessary for specific uses; there are two main tanning processes: vegetable and mineral. Distinction between hides and skins is simply a matter of size and is arbitrary; a small cattle hide, weighing less than 15 lbs., is called a "calfskin"; one from 15 to 30 lbs. a "kip"; and one above 30 lbs. a light or heavy "cattle hide." Uses: boots, shoes, and gloves; belting; harness equipment; upholstery; handbags; book bindings; rollers for textile and other machinery; sporting goods; aviator's clothing; military helmets; gas masks; gun slings; scabbards.

OOFA SPONGES: Fibrous body of a tropical gourd; the tough fiber is formed like loose felt in a round bar shape and is cream-yellow in color; cultivation is simple in rich, moist ground; the skin and centers are removed by soaking and washing in water and when nearly dry the seeds are shaken out; when dry the fiber is pressed flat; the process is done locally; the gourd is ready for processing about nine months after planting the seed; the fiber is effective in filtering free grease and oil from water. Uses: filters in marine engines; filtering and cleaning purposes in power plants, maintenance, and repair shops; household uses; inner soles of shoes.

MAGNESITE: Mineral carbonate of magnesium; occurs either as the crystalline or amorphous variety, in deposits or veins; used for manufacturing magnesia; it is quarried, hand sorted, crushed, and then calcined in kilns; for caustic magnesite, the kiln temperature is about 1200° C and for dead-burned magnesite, to which iron ore is added the temperature is about 1560° C. Uses: refractory brick; source of magnesium insulating material; paper industry; manufacture of carbon dioxide; preparation of oxychloride cement; medicines; flooring and wallboard material; ceramics; abrasives; accelerator for rubber processing.

MAGNESIUM: Silvery-white metallic element, malleable and ductile, extremely light (22 % of the weight of iron, 64 % that of aluminium), with great affinity for oxygen; very similar to aluminium; reduced from sea-water and brines by magnesium chloride process, and from dolomite or magnesite by the magnesium oxide process; to produce metallic magnesium the principal methods are the electrolysis of magnesium chloride and the thermal reduction of magnesium oxide. Uses: light alloys for airplane and automobile parts; appliances, etc.; deoxidizer in metallurgical operations; aircraft parts; bomb casings; pyrotechnics; incendiary bombs.

MANGANESE ORE: The oxide and carbonate ores (principally pyrolusite and manganite) are used commercially in four grades according to character and manganese content: battery; ferro; ferruginous; and manganiferous. *Battery grade* is used as a depolarizer in dry cells and for chemicals; the dioxide is necessary; the ore should contain about 72-87 % manganese and have a high content of available oxygen with a minimum of iron; it should also be relatively free of arsenic, copper, nickel, and cobalt, which are electronegative to zinc. Uses: chemicals, dry-cell batteries. Of the *metallurgical grades* the most important is the ferro grade ore, which contains over 35 % manganese and is used to produce ferromanganese; this is produced in either the blast or electric furnace. Ferromanganese is preferred to spiegel (see below) in spite of higher costs because of its greater efficiency in steel making. Ferruginous ores, 10-35 % manganese, are used to make spiegel (*spiegeleisen*), which is produced in the blast furnace in the same manner as pig iron, except at higher temperatures; the tapped metal is simply iron unusually high in manganese. The manganiferous ores, 5-10% manganese, are used mainly in producing a desirable high-manganese pig iron. The metallurgical grades are used in the manufacture of all types of steel and manganese steel alloys.

MAHOGANY: Heavy durable tropical wood used in the form of lumber, veneer, and plywood; valued for its strength, stability, size, and ability to take a finish. Uses: furniture, small boats, naval vessels, aircraft, gliders, pattern making.

MERCURY (QUICKSILVER): Silvery-white metallic element distinguished by the fact that it is the only metal that is liquid at normal temperatures; prepared by heating its ore, cinnabar, until it vaporizes, and then condensing the vapor; indispensable in the production of munitions and armaments. Uses: electrical apparatus; primers for explosives and blasting caps; chemicals; pharmaceuticals; industrial and control instruments; lamps; dental amalgams; vapor boilers; felt manufacture; antifouling paints; tracer composition; RM dry cells.

METHANOL (METHYL ALCOHOL): Two methods of production are used, natural and synthetic; the latter produced about 95 % of our requirements during World War II; natural (wood) alcohol is obtained from the destructive distillation of wood; synthetic is obtained by either catalytic synthesis of water gas and the use of high-pressure equipment or oxidation of some of the saturated lower hydrocarbons such as propane or butane; the first method produced about 95 % of the total synthetic supply. Uses: manufacture of formaldehyde, antifreeze, solvents, chemicals, denaturant, plastics, explosives such as RDX, PETN, and tetryl.

MICA: Complex silicate mineral of two major types: muscovite (or "white"), a potash silicate with superior dielectric properties, and phlogopite (or "amber") a magnesium silicate, which is softer but has better heat resistance. Mica is a flexible, tough, impervious nonconductor of heat and electricity that can be split into thin transparent sheets. Strategic grades are used in three forms: block or sheet (trimmed, well-formed crude crystals); film (division of the blocks into irregularly shaped pieces); and splittings (extremely thin pieces from lower-quality block). Mica is graded for size (1 sq. in. to over 100 sq. in.) and classed in six divisions, depending upon mineral imperfections and air bubbles, from clear, through degrees of staining, to black. For larger sheets, plates, and tape, built-up mica is made from splittings held together by insulating binder. *Muscovite block and film,* good stained and better, includes mica of the upper three divisions of quality; i.e., clear, fair stained, and good stained. Uses: insulation in radio and radar equipment; magnetos; gauge glasses. *Muscovite splittings.* Uses: built-up mica plates and tape for commutator segments, armature windings, slot insulation, and other electrical uses. *Phlogopite splittings.* Uses: same as muscovite splittings except used where high heat insulation is necessary; viewplates for ovens and furnaces. *Muscovite block, stained and lower,* includes the lower three divisions of staining: stained, heavy stained, and black. Uses: radio and electronic tube spacers, spark plugs, heating elements. *Phlogopite block.* Uses: electrical appliances, soldering irons, searchlights, spark plugs, heating elements.

MOLASSES: Thick brown or dark-colored sirupy mother liquor left after the removal of sucrose from sugar-cane or sugar-beet juice. Uses: major industrial use is as a source of alcohol; other uses include livestock feed, yeast production, and foodstuff.

MOLYBDENUM: Silvery-white malleable and ductile metal obtained principally from the ore molybdenite; the ore is concentrated and converted principally into molybdic oxide and reduced; molybdenum imparts toughness, creep resistance, and high impact resistance to its alloys. Uses: alloy of iron and steel; pigments; welding rod coatings; electrical equipment; radio tubes; applications where high temperature characteristics and ductility are required;

alloy steel; substitute for tungsten; armor; armor piercing projectiles; gun barrels.

MONAZITE: Yellow, red, or brown mineral containing the phosphates of the cerium metals occurring in certain sand or gravel deposits; it is the only commercial source of cerium, thorium, lanthanum, and other rare-earth elements; the metals are produced through fusion with alkalis; elution, and fractional crystallization. Uses: incandescent lighting; heat-resisting materials; pyrophoric alloys; special optical glasses; photographic industry; cores of position arc electrodes; sources of thorium for atomic energy.

NICKEL: Silvery-white metal valued for its alloying characteristics of strength, durability, toughness, and resistance to abrasion, heat, corrosion, and electrical action; the principal ores are the sulphide and a magnesium-nickel silicate; the ores are roasted and reduced; further purification, if desired, is done by electrolysis. Uses: alloying element in steel and nonferrous metals, widely used in various machinery and equipment parts; monel metal and plating for a corrosion-resistant; electrical equipment; utensils; coinage; catalytic agent; amor plate; gun forgings; recoil springs; marine shafting; condenser tubes and valves for naval equipment; naval cable sheathing.

NITROGEN: Colorless, odorless gas that forms 79 % of the atmosphere; alone, it shows little chemical activity; to be readily usable, it is obtained by purifying liquid air and combining with hydrogen to form ammonia, from which a vast variety of compounds can be formed; the principal method of conversion to ammonia is the Haber process, which is essentially mixing three volumes of hydrogen and one of nitrogen, under pressure and high temperature, and passing over a porous iron catalyst. Other sources of nitrogen include nitrates, organic nitrogeneous products such as fish scrap, cottonseed meal, etc., and as a by-product of coking coal. Uses: fertilizer, chemical manufacturing (using ammonia or nitric acid), metal treating, plastics; explosives.

NYLON: Group name for polyamides developed and manufactured solely by E. I. Du Pont de Nemours and Co.; it is a synthetic product made from benzene or phenol and ammonia (basically coal, water, and air) by means of elaborate equipment; it can be processed into yarn, strands, solutions, or molding powders. Yarn, the principal item, is made by forcing molten nylon through spinnerets and then, by a technique not used with other fibers, stretching or "drawing" the filaments, to convert inherent chemical properties into physical advantages of strength, elasticity, toughness, and translucency. Other properties of nylon are resistance to abrasion and mildew, low specific gravity, high dielectric value, and considerable resistance to heat, alkali, and many organic solvents. Uses: hosiery, clothing, parachutes, tires, tow ropes, various miscellaneous military equipment, substitute for silk and other fibers, bristles, screen cloths, wire insulation.

OPIUM: Dried milky juice from the unripe capsule of the opium poppy, which can be grown in many sections of the world (however, many countries do not choose to cultivate it); all supplies are imported and reach the United States in the form of gum opium, from which the opium alkaloids (principally morphine) are extracted. Uses: in medicine to reduce pain, produce sleep, or as a sedative.

OPTICAL GLASS: Specially manufactured, highly refined, stable, homogeneous, very transparent glass; free from color, striae, strains, bubbles, and seeds; refracts light through specific predetermined deviations. Uses: any high grade or precision instrument using lenses or prisms—cameras, transits, microscopes, fire control and navigation instruments, field glasses, periscopes, telescopes.

PALM OIL: Semisolid fat obtained from the outer fleshy part of the fruit of the oil palm (Elaesis quineensis), native to West Africa; its color ranges from pale yellow to deep orange or dark brown; properties that make it desirable for rolling sheet steel are its cheapness, lubricating action, and ability to act as a protective coating and to produce a glaze; for tin and terne plating it has the additional quality of facilitating the distribution of the metal coating. Uses: manufacture of tin and terne plate; rolling of steel sheet; edible oil in margarine and shortenings; soap making.

PEPPER: Black pepper is obtained by grinding the immature berry of the East Indian plant Piper nigrum; white pepper consists of ground dried ripe seed divested of the coatings. Use: as a condiment.

PETROLEUM: Heavy, inflammable, hydrocarbon mineral oil that is processed into a multitude of products with a great diversification of uses; the major classes of products include: avigation engine fuel; automotive gasoline; kerosene and light gas oils; Diesel fuels; fuel oils; guided missile and rocket propellants; chemicals; lubricants. It is a vitally needed raw material, requiring tremendous quantities for proper functioning in both a peacetime and a wartime economy (1.3 billion barrels of crude oil in 1939; 1.7 in 1944); supply in war is conditioned by reserves, refining capacities, transport facilities, demand, by locale and type of warfare, and effect of technological developments. Uses: basis of modern transport.

PLASTICS: Broad term "plastics" is considered by the industry to include only those materials capable of being molded, extruded, cast, or used in the form of an adhesive in laminated materials; there are three principal types: coal tar, non-coal tar, and cellulose. They are manufactured by two general chemical processes: condensation and polymerization; condensation is brought about by the union of two different chemical compounds; polymerization is a structural integration of a number of identical chemical molecules; both result in compounds of larger molecular structures than the starting materials; the resulting plastic is classified as thermosetting (when once set, retains form permanently), or thermoplastic (when reheated, returns to original plastic state). Plastics are relatively light, have a favorable ratio of tensile and compressive strength to weight, dielectric properties, resistance to moisture, acids, and alkalis; they vary in transparency from clear to opaque. Their one weakness is limited stability at moderately high temperatures; even the most recent "silicones" will not withstand temperatures above 500° F. Plastic are available in a variety of shapes and with a multitude of properties. Uses: multitudinous uses in airplane, automobile, radio, electrical, and household parts and equipment; coating material; weapon parts; military equipment.

PLATINUM METALS: Platinum and the metals similar in character—palladium, iridium, osmium, rhodium, and ruthenium—are usually found together; the metals are characterized by their high electric and thermal conductivity, low coefficient of expansion, and resistance to acids, reagents, high temperatures, and oxidation; they are obtained by placer mining or as by-products of copper, nickel, or gold mining; they are used as pure metals, and combined, clad, or alloyed with other metals. *Platinum*, a whitish-gray, relatively soft, ductile metal, is used in jewelry, electrical contacts, spark plugs, as a catalyst; spinnerets for rayon and fiber glass; laboratory and chemical equipment; thermocouples; dental alloys. *Iridium*, a very heavy, silvery-white, hard, brittle metal. Uses: jewelry; electric contacts; laboratory ware; resistors; fuses, spark plugs; surgical equipment. *Osmium*, a blue-white metal, is the hardest and heaviest metal known; it is not readily workable. Uses: hard tipping for pens and needles; special electric contacts; jewelry; pivot and bearing points; oxide for fingerprint detection. *Palladium*, a white, relatively soft metal, resembles platinum but is lighter and more easily fused; it is very ductile and easily worked, either hot or cold; has a great affinity for hydrogen. Uses: jewelry; platinum hardener; plating; spinnerets; dental alloys; catalyst for hydrogenation and dehydrogenation of organic compounds; detecting carbon monoxide. *Rhodium*, a very hard, brittle, white metal, ductile and malleable at red heat, is difficult to fuse. Uses: alloying additive to platinum for moderate hardness; thermocouples; catalysts; resistance windings for high temperature furnaces; chemical apparatus. *Ruthenium* is a hard, brittle, white metal, infusible and difficult to work. Uses: hardener for platinum and palladium; jewelry; plating; hydrogenation of organic compounds; hard tipping of pens.

PLYWOOD: Laminated product of two classifications, softwood and hardwood; made of an odd number of alternate layers of veneer (thin slices of wood) laid cross-grain to each other and bound by an adhesive; the logs may be sliced, sawn, or peeled by a rotary lathe to produce the veneer. Because of its construction, plywood is stronger than lumber of the same weight, does not easily split or warp, is available in large sizes, can be matched easily, and can be shaped or molded into many forms. Uses: aircraft parts, ship construction, vehicles, housing, furniture, shipping cases, landing craft.

PULPWOOD AND WOOD PULP: Pulpwood, obtained by logging from a comparitively few trees, such as spruce, balsam, fir, jack pine, hemlock, southern pine, cottonwood, and poplar, is the raw material for wood pulp; wood pulp is the fibrous material obtained by disintegrating wood by mechanical or chemical processes; the wood pulp may be used alone or with rags, waste paper, or fibrous parts of certain plants to produce the desired paper product. Uses: paperboards, coarse papers such as bag and wrapping, book papers, fine papers, newsprint, absorbent papers, substitute for cotton linters in the production of smokeless powders and rayon.

PYRETHRUM: Dried flower head of several species of chrysanthemums; prepared by grinding and extraction by kerosene or similar petroleum solvent; principal active ingredient is pyrethrin, which is present in the heads to the extent of $1/2$ to $1^1/2$ % and concentrated to about 20 % after extraction. Uses: agricultural and household insecticides; military uses such as malaria control, delousing, etc.

QUARTZ CRYSTALS: Form of silicon dioxide occurring in very limited deposits in both clear and colored forms that exhibit piezoelectric characteristics; the crystals are ground or etched to form small plates which are utilized to obtain a stable controlled frequency in radio apparatus of moderate frequencies. Uses: frequency control in radio transmitters and receivers, long distance telephone equipment, precision electrical measuring instruments, radar euqipment, submarine detection devices.

QUEBRACHO: Tree found in Argentina and Paraguay whose wood is the hardest, heaviest, and most durable known; it has many uses, but tannin is the main product; the trees mature in 100 years but may be cut in 50 years. Use: leather tanning.

QUINIDINE: Alkaloid similar to quinine, extracted solely from cinchona bark originating in the Netherlands East Indies; South American cinchona contains only a trace of this alkaloid. Use: cardiac therapy.

QUININE: Principal alkaloid derived from dried cinchona bark by extraction; it occurs as fine needle-like white crystals that darken on exposure to light; the crystals are colorless and have a very bitter taste; there is a wide variation in extractable alkaloids in various cinchona barks throughout the world. Uses: prophylaxis and treatment of malaria; treatment of various other diseases; scalp lotions; manufacture of polaroid glasses.

RADIUM: Rare white metallic element discovered by Pierre and Marie Curie; found in pitchblende and carnotite ores; a highly radioactive decomposition product of uranium, the atoms of which undergo spontaneous decomposition and give rise to a series of radioactive disintegration products and the element helium; the radium is extracted by a complicated wet process. Uses: curative medicine; detecting flaws in steels and other metals; salts used in luminous paints; used especially for aircraft and ship instrument dials; direction markers; gunsights; compasses.

RAPESEED OIL: Oil obtained from the seeds of rape, mustard, turnip, and other closely related species; known also as colza oil; although refined for edible purposes in some countries, it is used only as an inedible material in the U.S.A.; varying from yellow to dark brown in color, its characteristics include high viscosity, low saponification value, nonthickening property when heated and exposed to air, and keeping properties. Uses: marine engine oils; heavy machine lubricating oils; pneumatic tube oils; compounding of rubber substitutes; minor uses include paints, leather, textiles.

ROTENONE (DERRIS ROOT): Poisonous crystalline ketone; one of several insecticidal constituents of derris, cubé, and lonchocarpus roots; either the roots are ground into dust, or the rotenone is extracted with organic solvents to form a solution for spraying. Use: insecticides.

RUBBER (CRUDE): Obtained by tapping rubber trees (chiefly the *Hevae* species) and coagulating the sap or latex; it is shipped as sheets or crepe; crude rubber as such has few valuable properties; to increase its usefulness in specific applications it is compounded with pigments, softeners, accelerators, activators, age-resistors, and then vulcanized; vulcanization is essentially mixing with sulphur and heating; after this it is flexible, extensible; waterproof, impermeable to gases, and is a good insulator of electricity; it has marked resistance to abrasion, and to most chemicals. Uses: tires; tubes; hoses; mechanical rubber goods; footwear; wire and cable and other electrical insulation; tracks for tracklaying vehicles; pontoons; life rafts and small boats.

RUBBER (NATURAL LATEX): Sap of the *Hevae* tree, which has been prevented from coagulating by chemicals; it is concentrated by creaming or centrifuging and then shipped in the liquid state. Uses: spread or dipped rubber sundries; impregnated fabric and cord; sponges; air-tight containers; self-sealing fuel cells.

RUBBER (SYNTHETIC): Term usually applied to any vulcanizable elastomer; it includes a wide variety of rubberlike materials, none of which is like natural rubber in chemical composition but all of which more or less resemble it in psysical properties; some have particular qualities that make them superior for special uses; the main general purpose type is Buna-S; other important rubbers, in order of quantitative importance, include butyl, neoprene, and Buna-N. The type produced in government-owned plants are symbolized by "GR" followed by base abbreviation; for example: GR-S indicates "Government rubber; styrene base." Uses: same as natural rubber, plus special-purpose uses. *Buna-S (GR-S)* is made from butadiene and styrene; butadiene is obtained from alcohol, natural gas, or petroleum; styrene from coal and alcohol or natural gas; methods of processing and vulcanizing are similar to those used for natural rubber except that a longer processing period and more carbon black are required. Uses: tires and tubes; general replacement for natural rubber. *Butyl (GR-I)* is made from isobutene and isoprene, both of which may be obtained from petroleum or from natural gas; processing and vulcanizing methods are similar to those used for natural rubber except that it requires a very rapid accelerator. Uses: inner tubes, gas masks, coating of fabrics for impermeability. *Neoprene (GR-M)* is made from chloroprene that is synthesized from salt, sulphur, lime and coke; processing is similar to that of natural rubber, but vulcanizing can be done by heat alone. Uses: tank linings, conveyor belts, mechanical goods; hose for oils, solvents, and gases; life-saving equipment. *Buna-N (GR-A)* is made from butadiene (see Buna-S), acrylonitrile (which is obtained from petroleum or from alcohol), and sodium cyanide; processing and vulcanizing methods are similar to those used for natural rubber. Uses: self-sealing fuel tanks, cable coverings, packing, gaskets.

RUTILE: See Titanium.

SANTONIN: Colorless, odorless, bitter, lustrous white crystalline powder; derived from the dried flower heads of santonica and other species of artemisia. Uses: medicinal; intestinal worm destroyer.

SAPPHIRE AND RUBY: Pure variety of corundum or crystallized alumina found in blue (sapphire) or red (ruby) transparent or translucent crystals; the ruby generally occurs in bands of crystalline limestone associated with granitic or gneissic rock; sapphires generally occur as pebbles or rolled crystals in certain sand and gravel deposits. Uses: jewel bearings; minor uses include gauges, spinnerets, thread and wire guides, oil spray nozzles.

SCRAP, IRON AND STEEL: Necessary raw material in the production of steel; iron and steel scrap falls into two classifications—home and purchased; home scrap is the waste or by-product of iron and steel generated within steel mills and foundries in making new steel and castings and, with negligible exceptions, never enters the open market; purchased scrap represents the waste, by-products, accumulations and obsolescence from all other sources: metal working factories, railroads, shipyards, public utilities, farms, homes, detinning plants; in fact, it originates any place where iron and

steel are used. Uses: in manufacture of steel.

SELENIUM: Metal closely allied in physical and chemical properties with sulphur; exists in several allotropic forms; commercial form is a blackish powder, 99.5% pure; it occurs as selenides of copper, silver, gold, and nickel; selenium is obtained chiefly from the slimes deposited in the electrolytic refining of copper. Uses: glass industry (as a decolorizer and to produce ruby glass); in stainless steels to improve machinability; in rubber manufacture to improve resistance to heat and to increase resiliency; photo-electric cells; copper alloys.

SENNA: Dried leaflets *of Cassia senna*, grown in Egypt and southern India; senna contains a number of substances such as crysophanic and cathartic acids. Use: medicinal: laxative and cathartic.

SESAME OIL: Obtained by pressing the seed of the herbaceous plant *Sesamum indicum*. Uses: soap; insecticide; to some extent as an edible oil; aerosol bombs and ampules.

SHELLAC: Resinous material made from lac, the excretion of an East Indian insect; the insects feed on the sap of certain trees and exude a resinous liquid called "stick lac" when it hardens in air; it is purified, then twisted and stretched into sheets which are broken into flakes; it is very soluble in alcohol. Uses: phonograph records; binder in abrasive wheels; coating for electrical equipment; cements for electric light bulbs; aluminum and bronzing lacquers; varnishes; protective coating for cartridges; shell-cases; instruments and airplane parts; adhesive for fuses, shells, gaskets, and pyrotechnics; marine paints.

SILLIMANITE: Mineral occurring as slender prisms in aluminous crystalline rocks; crystals are extracted by grinding and concentrating. Uses: spark plugs, chemical wares, special refractories such as glass blowers and furnace linings.

SODIUM, POTASSIUM OR CALCIUM PERMANGANATE: Purple solid prepared from caustic soda, potash, or lime (sodium, potassium, or calcium hydroxide) by heating with manganese dioxide and a chlorate dissolved in water, followed by oxidation with chlorine or ozone; also prepared electrolytically from caustic soda, potash, or lime and fused manganese dioxide. Uses: bleaching agent; antiseptic; disinfectant; oxidizing agent; rocket fuel; gas masks.

SPERM OIL: Is processed from the spermaceti extracted from the sperm whale; the oil is non-gumming, oxidizes little, and is not influenced by temperature. Uses: lubricants, cutting oils, greases, softening agent for leather, finishing agent for textiles, navy torpedoes.

SQUILL: Dried inner bulb of *Urginea scilla*, found in the Mediterranean area; the white variety, by extraction with organic solvents, yields a number of glucosides, particularly scillain, scillaren, etc., used in medicine; the red variety is used as a rat poisoning agent since the rodents cannot expel the material after swallowing, whereas human beings can. Uses: in medicine as an expectorant, diuretic, and heart stimulant; rodent poison.

STRAMONIUM: Dried leaves and flowering tops of the species *Datura stramonium* (Jamestown weed, Jimson weed, or stinkweed); organic solvents extract a number of alkaloids, especially atropine, hyoscyamine, and scopolamine. Uses: medicinal, as a narcotic, sedative, and antispasmodic.

SUGAR: Sucrose; a sweet crystalline substance refined from sugar cane and sugar beets (see Molasses). Uses: food, condiment, food preservative.

TALC: Variety of soft hydrated magnesium silicate occurring naturally in many parts of the world in massive, foliated, or fibrous forms. *Steatite block* is a block or lava grade of steatite talc occurring in massive form; it is structurally capable of being machined to special shapes; more rare in occurrence than other forms and has more specialized uses. Uses: spacers for electronic tubes. *Steatite ground* is the foliated form, ground and pressed into usable shapes; it is a nonconductor of electricity and has a high dielectric strength; where purity is a factor, steatite is used in preference to other grades. Uses: heat and electrical insulators, especially high-frequency and radar equipment; spark plugs; light bulbs; filtering agent; talcum powders.

TANTALITE (TANTALUM): Tantalite is the generic term given to tantalum-bearing ores of economic worth; tantalite and its sister mineral columbite are usually found together as mixtures, and are designated tantalite or columbite depending on which predominates; tantalite is available as a concentrate containing 35-70% tantalum pentoxide; the oxide may be reduced to the metallic form electrolytically, (see Columbite). Uses: as a metal in radar and other electronic tubes; surgical and chemical equipment; as a fluoride catalyst in synthetic rubber manufacture; as oxides and carbides in manufacture of high-speed cutting tools and aerial camera lenses.

TIN: Soft bluish-white metal obtained from cassiterite by direct smelting; valued for its resistance to corrosion, miscibility with other metals, low melting point, and low surface tension in the molten state; solder is a mixture of lead, tin, and antimony; babbitt is a copper-tin-antimony alloy; bronze is a copper-tin alloy. Uses: plating; alloys; solders; foil and tubes; chemicals; babbitts and bronzes in guns, naval machinery, motors, and generators; anticorrosion coating for aircraft cables, radio and electrical wiring; innumerable indirect military uses.

TITANIUM: Metallic element ordinarily found and most used in the form of its oxides. *Ilmenite* is ores containing 44-60% titanium oxide; iron-black mineral of submetallic luster usually found in massive form but sometimes in crystalline; after processing, it is valuable as a white pigment because of its hiding power, color, tintability, and chalk resistance. Uses: chiefly in pigments; minor use in alloys; camouflage and protective coatings on ships, tanks, and planes. *Rutile* ores contain 90-94% titanium oxide; reddish-brown mineral with brilliant metallic luster occurring in crystalline or massive forms. Uses: coatings for welding rods; alloys (ferrotitanium); smoke screen material; arc light electrodes; steel deoxidizer; steel alloys subject to high temperatures.

TUNG OIL: Obtained from the nuts of the tung tree, which is native to China; the tree has been introduced to many countries but only in the U.S.A. has the experiment been successful; the oil, also known as China wood oil, has a high viscosity, dries rapidly through polymerization or molecular transformation; when heat treated, it produces a hard, quick-drying, waterproof coating, highly resistant to acids, alkalis, and weathering; when combined with phenolic resins, the oil has marked dielectric qualities preferred in electrical insulation. Uses: one of the most valuable dryers in paints, varnishes, etc.; insulation; linoleum and oilcloths; printing inks; protective and waterproof coatings; corrosion-resisting coatings for planes, ships, and guns; food container linings; synthetic resins; waterproofing shells, tents, tarpaulins, raincoats, etc.

TUNGSTEN: Heavy hard white metal that is resistant to acids, has a high tensile strength, and the highest melting point to all metals; the ore scheelite (calcium tungstate), the principal domestic ore, is concentrated and reduced; in alloys, tungsten imparts qualities of toughness, strength, hardness, and resistance to abrasion, even at high temperatures; tungsten carbide is second only to diamonds in hardness. Uses: high-speed tools; ferroalloys; cutting tools of stellite and tungsten carbide; electronic tube and incandescent lamp filaments; electrical contacts; chemicals; armor piercing projectiles; erosion-resisting gun liners; catalyst in production of high octane gasoline and TNT.

URANIUM: Ductile nickel-white radioactive metallic element that is one of the heaviest elements known; produces in the course of its atomic disintegration a series of substances including radium, helium, lead, and actinium, while emitting different forms of radiation known as alpha, beta, and gamma rays. Uranium has three known isotopes: U-234, U-235, and U-238; the element is extracted by complicated wet processes and the isotopes separated by four principal methods: gaseous, electromagnetic, centrifugal, and thermal diffusion. It is the essential raw material for the production of U-239, plutonium. Uses: salts used for coloring ceramics and glass; catalyst for chemical industry; mordant in dyeing; ferrouranium to alloy steel; atomic bomb.

VANADIUM: Metallic element having a grayish-white color with a silvery luster; it has a crystalline structure, is brittle, nonmagnetic, and has a high electrical resistivity; it readily alloys with iron and steel imparting hardness, strength, elasticity, and resistance to fatigue: it is also a powerful deoxidizer; obtained principally from carnotite and vanadinite, which are processed to the pentoxide or to ferrovanadium. Uses: alloying element in tool steels; alloy steels for springs, axles, gears, and machine parts that must withstand vibration and varying stress; salts are used to color pottery and glass; tools; parts for guns, ships, and engines; projectiles; torpedoes; catalyzer in production of high octane gasoline.

WOOL: Fine soft curly fleece shorn from sheep; after clipping it is scoured, then carded or combed, and spun, or otherwise processed. Uses: apparel wool for clothing and blankets; carpet wool for rugs and carpets; felts; uniform cloth; overcoats; underwear; shirting; gloves; socks; blankets; etc.

ZINC: Hard brittle bluish-white metal, very resistant to corrosion; the ore, zinc blende, is the chief source; the ore is concentrated and smelted producing "spelter" or zinc metal; brass, the principal zinc alloy, is a copper-zinc product. Uses: galvanizing of iron and steel; brass products; die castings; paints; dry-cell batteries. Brass for cartridge cases is the largest direct military use.

ZIRCONIUM ORES: The two principal ores of zirconium are baddeleyite and zircon; each with distinct properties and uses. *Baddeleyite* contains 68 to 98% zirconia (zirconium oxide); a white amorphous powder, baddeleyite is the chief source of metallic zirconium since the cost of reducing zircon is excessive; zirconia is a good conductor of heat but a poor conductor of electricity. Uses: alloying element in steel to increase impact strength; special refractories; electronic tubes; blasting caps; flares. *Zircon* is a zirconium silicate occurring in lustrous prisms or pyramids, brown or grayish in color. Uses: opacifier in porcelain enamels and other ceramics; refractories; water-repellent impregnation of cloth.

Prophets
See **Religious Allusions, References, and Symbols**

Prose Writers
See **Novelists and Prose Writers**

Prussian Rulers
See **Rulers**

Pseudonyms, Nicknames, Sobriquets, and Special Associations for Historical People
See also **Cities, Epithets of; Saints; Novelists and Prose Writers**

A: John Stuart Mill.
A.B.: Alexander Hamilton.
ABBÉ: Lord Byron.
ABBÉ CONSTANTIN: Léon Halévy.
ABDUL THE DAMNED: Abdul II of Turkey.
ACHITOPHEL: Anthony Ashley Cooper, Earl of Shaftesbury.
ADAGIA: Erasmus.
ADMIRABLE CRICHTON, THE: James Crichton.
ADONAIS: Percy Bysshe Shelley.
ADVANCE AGENT OF PROSPERITY, THE: William McKinley.
A.E. OR AE: George William Russell.
AFTERWIT, ANTHONY: Benjamin Franklin.
AGAPIDA, FRIAR ANTONIO: Washington Irving.
ALCIBIADES: Alfred, Lord Tennyson (in Punch), 1846.
ALCON, R.: Emily Bronte.
ALEXANDER THE COPPERSMITH: Alexander Hamilton.
ALEXANDRIA ZENOBIA: Anne Bronte.
ALIUNDE JOE: Justice Joseph Bradley.
A.M.B.A.: Stendhal.
AMERICAN, AN: John Adams; James Fenimore Cooper; Cotton Mather.
AMERICAN CITIZEN, AN: John Adams.
AMERICAN FLORENCE NIGHTINGALE: Anna Caroline Maxwell.
AMERICA'S SWEETHEART: Mary Pickford.
ANARCHISM: Mikhail Bakunin.
ANGEL OF THE SCHOOLS, THE: Thomas Aquinas.
ANGELIC DOCTOR, THE: Thomas Aquinas.
ANGLING, FATHER OF: Izaak Walton.
ANGLIPOLOSKI OF LITHUANIA: Daniel Defoe.
ANN, MOTHER: Ann Lee.
ANTHONY, C.L.: Dodie Smith.
ANTICANT, DR. PESSIMIST: Thomas Carlyle.
ANTI-MACHIAVEL: Jeremy Bentham.
A.O.B. (AN OLD BACHELOR): William Lloyd Garrison.
APOSTATA: Maximilian Harden.
APOSTATE, THE: Emperor Julian.
APOSTLE OF ANDALUSIA: Juan de Avila (1500-1569).
APOSTLE OF BRAZIL: José de Anchieta (1533-1597), a Jesuit.
APOSTLE OF CAMBRIA: St. Kentigern.
APOSTLE OF FREE TRADE: Richard Cobden (1804-1865).
APOSTLE OF HUNGARY: St. Anastatius.

APOSTLE OF INFIDELITY: Voltaire.
APOSTLE OF IRELAND: St. Patrick.
APOSTLE OF LIBERTY: Henry Clay.
APOSTLE OF NORTHUMBRIA: St. Cuthbert.
APOSTLE OF PERU: Alonzo de Barcena (1528-1598).
APOSTLE OF TEMPERENCE: Father Mathew.
APOSTLE OF THE ABYSSINIANS: St. Frumentius.
APOSTLE OF THE ALPS: Felix Neff (1798-1829).
APOSTLE OF THE ARDENNES: St. Hubert.
APOSTLE OF THE ARMENIANS: Gregory of Armenia.
APOSTLE OF THE ENGLISH: St. Augustine; St. George.
APOSTLE OF THE FRENCH: St. Denis.
APOSTLE OF THE FRISIANS: St. Willibrod.
APOSTLE OF THE GAULS: St. Irenaeus; St. Martin of Tours.
APOSTLE OF THE GENTILES: St. Paul.
APOSTLE OF THE GERMANS: St. Boniface.
APOSTLE OF THE HIGHLANDERS: St. Columba.
APOSTLE OF THE INDIANS: Bartolomé de Las Casas and John Eliot.
APOSTLE OF THE INDIES: St. Francis Xavier.
APOSTLE OF THE IROQUOIS: François Piquet (1708-1781).
APOSTLE OF THE NORTH: St. Ansgar (or Anscarius); Bernard Gilpin.
APOSTLE OF THE PEAK: William Bagshaw (1628-1702).
APOSTLE OF THE PICTS: St. Ninian.
APOSTLE OF THE SCOTTISH REFORMERS: John Knox.
APOSTLE OF THE SLAVS: St. Cyril.
APOSTLE OF THE SWORD: Mahomet.
APOSTLE OF TOLERATION: Roger Williams.
ARCHIMAGO: Edmund Spenser.
AREOPAGITICA: John Milton.
ARLEN, MICHAEL: Dikran Kouyoumdjian.
ARMENIAN, THE: Leo V, Emperor of Eastern Roman Empire.
ARTEMUS WARD: Charles Farrar Browne.
ASTRAEA, THE DIVINE: Mrs. Afra Behn.
ASTROPHEL: Edmund Spenser.
ATHEIST, THE: Aetius of Antioch.
ATTICUS: Joseph Addison.
AUNT MARGARET NICHOLSON, MY: Percy Bysshe Shelley.
AURORA LEIGH: Elizabeth Barrett Browning.
AUSTRALIAN PATRIOT, THE: William Charles Wentworth.
AUSTRIAN, THE (L'Autrichienne): Marie Antoinette.
AUTHOR, THE: Edward Gibbon.
AUTOCRAT: Oliver Wendell Holmes.
AUTUN, BISHOP OF: Talleyrand.
AVON, SWAN (BARD) OF: William Shakespeare.
AYRSHIRE PLOWMAN: Robert Burns.
BACHELOR, A TRAVELLING: James Fenimore Cooper.
ACKSIGHT-FORETHOUGHT: Sir Ernest Dunlop Swinton.
BAD, THE (Le Méchant): Charles II of Navarre.
BADINGUE: Napoleon III.
BAGMAN, THE: William II of Germany.
BAKER, THE (Le Boulanger): Louis XVI of France.
BAKER'S WIFE, THE (La Boulangère): Marie Antoinette.
BALACLAVA, CHARGE AT: Lord Cardigan.
BALANCHINE, GEORGE: Balanchivadze, Georgi.
BALD, THE (Le Chauve): Charles I of France.
BAL-WHIDDER, REV. MICAH: John Galt.
BAMBINO, THE: George Herman (Babe) Ruth.

BAMBOCCIO, IL: Pieter van Laar.
BAPTISTET: Alphonse Daudet.
BARBAROSSA: Frederick I (1123?-1190), Holy Roman Emperor.
BARD OF AYRSHIRE: Robert Burns.
BARLOW, MRS.: Lucy Walter.
BARNIVELT, ESDRAS, APOTH.: Alexander Pope.
BARTIMEUS: L.A. da Costa Ricci (Lewis Ritchie).
BASSETTO, CORNO DI: George Bernard Shaw.
BASTARD OF ORLEANS, THE: Jean Dunois.
BASTARDELLA, LA: Lucrezia Agujari.
BEAU BRUMMELL: George Brummell.
BEAUCLERC: Henry I of England.
BEAU JAMES: James John Walker.
BEAUDRIER, SIEUR DE: Jonathan Swift.
BECKERSTAFF, ISAAC: Jonathan Swift and Richard Steele.
BEEDING, FRANCIS: Hilary Aiden St. George Saunders and John Leslie Palmer.
BELL, ACTON: Anne Bronte.
BELL, CURRER: Charlotte Bronte.
BELL, ELLIS: Emily Bronte.
BELL, NEIL: Stephen Southwold.
BELL-THE-CAT: Archibald Douglas, Earl of Angus.
BELOVED DISCIPLE, THE: St. John.
BELOVED PHYSICIAN: Saint Luke; Sir Andrew Clark.
BENICIA BOY: John C. Heenan.
BENJAMINS, MR.: Disraeli.
BEREANUS, THEOSEBIS: William Hazlitt.
BERNADETTE, ST.: Bernadette Soubirous.
BERNHARD, KARL: Andreas Nicolai de Saint-Aubain.
BERNHARD, ROSINE: Sarah Bernhardt.
BERWICK, MARY: Adelaide Anne Procter.
BIEN AIMÉ: Louis XV.
BIGLOW, HOSEA: James Russell Lowell.
BILLINGS, JOSH: Henry Wheeler Shaw.
BILLY THE KID: William H. Bonney.
BLACK DAN: Daniel Webster.
BLACK JACK: John Alexander Logan.
BLAKE, NICHOLAS: Cecil Day Lewis.
BLAMELESS KING: King Arthur of England.
BLIND, THE (TEMNY): Basil II of Russia.
BLISS, JAMES T.: William Sydney Porter.
BLOOD AND IRON: Bismarck.
BLOODY MARY: Mary I of England.
BLUEBEARD: Gilles de Retz, Claude Perrault.
BLUETOOTH: Harold, King of Denmark.
BLUFF KING HAL: Henry VIII of England.
BOB: Sir William S. Gilbert.
BOBBIN BOY, THE: Gen. Nathaniel Prentiss Banks.
BOLD, THE (Le Téméraire): Charles, Duke of Burgundy.
BOLSHEVISM: Lenin, Trotsky.
BOLT CORT, SAGE OF: Samuel Johnson.
BOMBET, ALEXANDRE CESAR: Stendhal.
BONHOMME RICHARD, LE: Benjamin Franklin.
BONIN, BLAISE: George Sand.
BONNIE PRINCE CHARLIE: Charles Edward Stuart.
BOREL: Hugh II, Duke of Burgundy.
BOULGAROKTONOS (SLAYER OF THE BULGARIANS): Basil II of the Eastern Roman Empire.
BOUNTY, MUTINY OF THE: Fletcher Christian; Capt. William Bligh.
BOWDLERIZE: Thomas Bowdler.
BOWEN, MARJORIE: Gabrielle Margaret Vere Campbell Long.
BOY: Tadeusz Zelinski.
BOYD, NANCY: Edna St. Vincent Millay.
BOYES: John Dryden.
BOY ORATOR OF THE PLATTE, THE: William Jennings Bryan.

BOZ: Charles Dickens.
BOZZY: James Boswell.
BRANDY NAN: Queen Anne.
BRANDY NOSE: Queen Anne.
BRASS, SIR ROBERT: Robert Walpole.
BRAVEST OF THE BRAVE, THE: Marshal Michel Ney.
BREAD-POULTICE PRESIDENT, THE: Rutherford B. Hayes.
BRIDGET ELIA: Mary Lamb.
BRIDIE, JAMES: Dr. O. H. Mavor.
BRIGHT EYES: Susette La Flesche.
BRITANNICUS: Claudius Tiberius Germanicus.
BROAD-BOTTOM ADMINISTRATION: Henry Pelham.
BRONCO-BUSTER, THE: Theodore Roosevelt.
BROOK FARM: George Ripley, Nathaniel Hawthorne.
BROTHER JONATHAN: Gov. Jonathan Trumbull of Conn.; any American.
BROTHERS, TWO: Frederick, Charles, and Alfred Tennyson.
BROWN, THOMAS, THE YOUNGER: Thomas Moore.
BROWN BOMBER, THE: Joe Louis.
BRUCE, THE: Robert I, of Scotland.
BUFFALO BILL: Col. William Frederick Cody.
BULGARIANS, SLAYER OF THE (Boulgaroktonos): Basil II of the Eastern Roman Empire.
BULL, JOHN: John Arbuthnot; any Englishman.
BURTON, JUNIOR: Charles Lamb.
BUSINESS MAN IN POLITICS, THE: Mark Hanna.
BUSYBODY, THE: Benjamin Franklin.
BUTCHER, THE: William Augustus, Duke of Cumberland; Ulysses S. Grant.
BUTCHER, THE (Makeles): Leo I, Emperor of Eastern Roman Empire.
B.V. (BYSSHE VANOLIS): James Thomson.
B.W.: William Blake.
BYSTANDER: Goldwin Smith.
CABAL: Clifford, Shaftesbury (Ashley), Buckingham, Arlington, Lauderdale.
CADENUS: Jonathan Swift.
CAESAR: Alexander Hamilton.
CALAMITY JANE: Martha Jane Burke.
CALCULATING MACHINE: Charles Babbage.
CALIGULA (LITTLE BOOTS): Gaius Caesar.
CAMBUSCAN: Genghis Khan.
CANAL BOY, THE: James A. Garfield.
CANDIDUS: Samuel Adams.
CAPITANO, GRAN: Gonsalvo di Cordova.
CARBONARO: Napoleon III.
CARMEN SYLVA: Elizabeth of Rumania.
CARROLL, LEWIS: Charles L. Dodgson.
CARTHUSIANS: St. Bruno.
CASTLEMON, HARRY: Charles Austin Fosdick.
CATHASAIGH, P. O.: Sean O'Casey.
CATHOLIC, THE (CATOLICA, LA): Isabella I, Queen of Castile (and Aragon).
CATHOLICUS: John Henry, Cardinal Newman.
CATO: Joseph Addison; Robert Livingston.
CATO, THE AMERICAN: Samuel Adams.
CAUDILLO, EL: Francisco Franco.
CAUDLE, MRS.: Douglas Jerrold.
CAVALIER POET: John Cleveland.
CAVENDISH: Henry Jones.
CAXTON, PISISTRATUS: Bulwer-Lytton.
"CECILIA": Fanny Burney (Madame d'Arblay).
CENTURIATORS: Matthias Flacius Illyricus.
CESARION: Ptolemy XIV (or XVI).
CHAM: Armédée de Noé.
CHAM OF LITERATURE, GREAT: Samuel Johnson.
CHARTISM: Feargus E. O'Connor.
CHAUCER, DANIEL: Ford Madox Ford.
CHELSEA, SAGE OF: Thomas Carlyle.
CHET: Chester A. Arthur.

CHEVALIER DE ST. GEORGE: James Francis Edward Stuart.
CHEVALIER SANS PEUR ET SANS RE-PROCHE: Sieur de Bayard (Pierre Terrail).
CHIEF'S DAUGHTER, THE: Pocahantas.
CHILD OF MIRACLE: Comte de Chambord.
CHILLON, PRISONER OF: François de Bonivard (Bonnivard).
CHINESE GORDON: Charles George Gordon.
CID, THE: Don Roderigo Diaz, Count of Bivar.
CITIZEN-KING: Louis-Philippe.
CITIZEN OF GENEVA, A: Jean Jacques Rousseau.
CITIZEN OF NEW YORK, A: Authors of the Federalist Papers.
CLAIMANT, THE TICHBORNE: Arthur Orton.
CLEISBOTHAM, JEDEDIAH: Sir Walter Scott.
CLEOPHIL: William Congreve.
C.L.I.O.: Joseph Addison.
CLOSE, UPTON: Josef Washington Hall.
CLOUT, COLIN: John Skelton; Edmund Spenser.
CLUTTERBUCK, CAPT.: Sir Walter Scott.
COCKNEY POETS: John Keats; Leigh Hunt.
COEUR DE LION: Richard I of England; Louis VIII of France.
COFFIN, JOSIAH: Henry Wadsworth Longfellow.
COLETTE: Sidonie Gabrielle Claudine Colette.
COLKITTO: Marquis of Montrosa.
COLLODI, CARLO: Carlo Lorenzini.
COMMONER, THE GREAT: William Pitt, Earl of Chatham (the Elder); Thaddeus Stevens.
COMMUNISM: François Babeuf; François Fourier.
COMPTON, FRANCIS SNOW: Henry Adams.
CONNELL, NORREYS: Conal Holmes O'Riordan.
CONRAD, JOSEPH: Teodor Josef Konrad Korzeniowski.
CONSUELO: George Sand.
CONTENTED FREEMAN: Noah Webster.
gCOPALEEN, MYLES na: Brian O'Nolan.
CO-PARCENER TILDEN: Samuel J. Tilden.
COPPET: Mme. de Staël.
CORDELIERS: Danton; Desmoulins; Marat.
CORDIÈRE, LA BELLE: Louise Labé.
CORNISH WONDER: John Opie.
CORN-LAW RHYMER, THE: Ebenezer Elliott.
CORNWALL, BARRY: Bryan Waller Procter.
CORPORAL, LITTLE: Napoleon I.
CORSICAN, THE: Napoleon I.
CORVO, BARON: Frederick Rolfe.
COURTLY, SIR ROBERT: Robert Walpole.
COWLEY FATHERS: Richard Meux Benson.
CRADDOCK, CHARLES EGBERT: Mary Noailles Murfree.
CRAYON, GENT., GEOFFREY: Washington Irving.
CREATIVE EVOLUTION: Henri Bergson.
CRIB, TOM: Thomas Moore.
CRIMINOLOGY: Cesare Lombroso.
CRITO: Charles Lamb.
CROAKER, CROAKER & CO.: Joseph Rodman Drake and Fitz-Greene Halleck.
CROFTANGRY, CHRYSTAL: Sir Walter Scott.
CROMARTY, DEAS: Mrs. Elizabeth S. Watson.
CROWFIELD, CHRISTOPHER: Harriet Beecher Stowe.
CUBISM: Pablo Picasso, Georges Braque.
CUNCTATOR (THE DELAYER): Quintus Fabius Maximus.
CURTHOSE (Courte-Heuse): Robert II, Duke of Normandy.
CYNICS: Aristhenes; Diogenes.
CYNICUS: Martin Anderson.
CZAR REED: Thomas B. Reed.
C.3.3.: Oscar Wilde.

DADDY: Samuel Crisp; William Wordsworth.
DAGONET: George Robert Sims.
DANBERRY, MR.: Disraeli.
DANE, CLEMENCE: Winifred Ashton.
DANIEL, THE PROPHET: Daniel Defoe.
DANTE: Dante (Durante) Alighieri.
DEAR PRUE: Mary Scurlock (wife of Sir Richard Steele).
DEBONNAIRE, LE: Louis I of France.
DECADENTS: Paul Verlaine, Stephane Mallarmé.
DEFENDER OF THE FAITH: Henry VIII of England.
DELAFIELD, E.M.: Elizabeth Monica de la Pasture Dashwood.
DELAYER, THE: Quintus Fabius Maximus.
DELORME, JOSEPH: Charles Augustin Sainte-Beuve.
DEMOCRITUS JUNIOR: Robert Burton.
DENNIS, PATRICK: Edward Everett Tanner.
DÉSIRÉ, LE: Louis XVIII.
DESPAIR, POET OF: James Thompson.
DESSAUER, OLD: Duke Leopold.
DETERMINATUS: Samuel Adams.
DEVIL, THE (Le Diable): Robert I, Duke of Normandy.
DIAMOND JIM: James Buchanan Brady.
DIAMOND PITT: Thomas Pitt (1653-1726).
DIANA: Abigail Adams.
DICKENS, THE ITALIAN: Salvatore Farina.
DION: Bishop George Berkeley.
DISCIPLE WHOM JESUS LOVED, THE: St. John.
DISSENTER, A: Jonathan Swift.
DISTICH, DICK: Alexander Pope.
DIVINE LADY: Lady Hamilton.
DIVINE SARAH: Sarah Bernhardt.
DIZZY: Earl of Beaconsfield (Disraeli).
DOCTOR ANGELICUS: Thomas Aquinas.
DOCTOR CHRISTIANISSIMUS: Jean de Gerson.
DOCTOR ILLUMINATUS: Raymond Lully.
DOCTOR INVINCIBILIS: William of Ockham.
DOCTOR IRREFRAGIBILIS: Alexander of Hales.
DOCTOR JIM: Sir Leander S. Jameson.
DOCTOR MELLIFLUUS: St. Bernard.
DOCTOR MIRABILIS: Roger Bacon.
DOCTOR PROFUNDUS: Thomas Bradwardine.
DOCTOR SERAPHICUS: St. Bonaventura.
DOCTOR SINGULARIS: William of Ockham.
DOCTOR SOLEMNIS: Henry of Ghent.
DOCTOR SUBTILIS: Duns Scotus.
DOCTOR SYNTAX: William Combe.
DOGOOD, MRS. SILENCE: Benjamin Franklin.
DOLLAR DIPLOMACY: Philander Chase Knox.
DOOLEY, MR.: Finley Peter Dunne.
DOOLITTLE, DR.: Hugh Lofting.
DOMENICO: Kyriakos Theotokopoulos.
DOWD, T.B.: William Sydney Porter.
DOWNING, MAJOR JACK: Seba Smith.
DRAPER, A: Jonathan Swift.
DROLL, THE: Pieter Brueghel the Elder.
DRUID: Henry Hall Dixon.
DUCA MINIMO: Gabriele D'Annunzio.
DUCE, IL: Benito Mussolini.
DUKE, VERNON: Vladimir Dukelsky.
DUKE OF BRAINTREE, THE: John Adams.
DUNDREARY, LORD: Edward Sothern.
DUTCH GEORGE: George II of England.
DUTCHMAN, THE: William III of England.
EARTHAM, HERMIT OF: William Hayley.
EASTAWAY, EDWARD: Edward Thomas.
ECHO PROTEUS, ESQ.: Benjamin Franklin.
ECSTATIC DOCTOR, THE: Jan van Ruysbroeck.
EDAX: Charles Lamb.
EDITH SWAN-NECK: Harold II.
E.F.G.: Edward Fitzgerald.

EGALITÉ: Louis Philippe Joseph d'Orleans.
ELBERTUS, FRA: Elbert Green Hubbard.
EL CONQUISTADOR: James I of Aragon.
ELDER PITT, THE: William Pitt, Earl of Chatham (1708-1778).
ELEATIC SCHOOL: Xenophones, Parmenides, Zeno.
ELIA: Charles Lamb.
ELIA, BRIDGET: Mary Lamb.
ELIOT, GEORGE: Mary Ann (Marian) Evans.
ELIZABETH: Elizabeth Russell, Countess von Arnim.
EMINENCE GRISE: Father Joseph (François Le Clerc du Tremblay).
EMINENCE ROUGE: Cardinal Richelieu.
EMINENT HAND, AN: Alexander Pope.
ENCYCLOPEDISTES: Diderot, D'Alembert, Voltaire, Montesquieu, Buffon, Turgot, Quesnay, et al.
ENGLISHMAN, AN: Thomas Paine.
ENGLISHMAN, FREE-BORN: Daniel Defoe.
EPIGRAMMATIST: John Heywood.
ERASTUS, THOMAS: Thomas Lieber (Liebler).
ERROMANGO, MARTYR OF: John Williams.
ESEK, UNCLE: Henry Wheeler Shaw.
ESPARTERO, BALDOMERO: William Makepeace Thackeray.
ESPRIELLA, DON MANUEL ALVAREZ: Robert Southey.
ETTRICK SHEPHERD: James Hogg.
EUPHEMIUS: Robert Walpole.
EUPHUIST: John Lyly.
EVERGOOD: Eric I, King of Denmark.
E.V.L.: E.V. Lucas.
EXISTENTIALISM: Martin Heidegger, Jean Paul Sartre.
EXPOUNDER OF THE CONSTITUTION, THE Daniel Webster.
EYE WITNESS: Daniel Defoe.
FABIUS, THE AMERICAN: George Washington.
FAIR, THE (THE HANDSOME): Frederick III, King of Germany.
FAIRHAIRED, THE: Harold I of Norway.
FARMER GEORGE: George III.
FAT, THE (Le Gros): Charles II of France.
FAT CONTRIBUTOR, THE: William Makepeace Thackeray.
FATHER ABRAHAM: Abraham Lincoln.
FATHER ADAM: Adam, the first man, the father of humanity.
FATHER CHRISTMAS: St. Nicholas, or Santa Claus.
FATHER OF AMERICA: Samuel Adams (1722-1803), American statesman.
FATHER OF AMERICAN INDEPENDENCE: John Adams.
FATHER OF ANGLING: Izaak Walton.
FATHER OF BASEBALL: Alexander Cartwright.
FATHER OF BELIEVERS: Mahomet.
FATHER OF BOTANY: Joseph Pittou de Tournefort (1656-1708), Fr. botanist.
FATHER OF BRITISH INLAND NAVIGATION: Francis Egerton, Duke of Bridgewater (1736-1803), who planned and financed the Bridgewater Canal system.
FATHER OF BUSINESS EFICIENCY: Frederick Winslow Taylor (1865-1915).
FATHER OF CHEMISTRY: Arnauld de Villeneuve (1238-1314).
FATHER OF COMEDY: Aristophanes (b.c. 448-385).
FATHER OF COMSTOCKERY: Anthony Comstock (1844-1915).
FATHER OF DUTCH POETRY: Jakob Maerlant (1235-1300).
FATHER OF ECCLESIASTICAL (CHURCH) HISTORY: Eusebius of Caesarea (264-349).
FATHER OF ENGLISH BOTANY: William Turner (1520-1568).

FATHER OF ENGLISH CATHEDRAL MUSIC: Thomas Tallis (1510-1585).
FATHER OF ENGLISH POETRY: Caedmon; Chaucer.
FATHER OF ENGLISH PRINTING: William Caxton (1412-1491).
FATHER OF ENGLISH PROSE: Wycliffe (1324-1384); Roger Ascham (1515-1568).
FATHER OF ENGLISH SONG: Caedmon.
FATHER OF EPIC POETRY: Homer.
FATHER OF EQUITY: Heneage Finch, Earl of Nottingham (1621-1682), Lord Chancellor.
FATHER OF FREE SILVER: Richard Parks Bland.
FATHER OF FRENCH DRAMA: Etienne Jodelle (1532-1573).
FATHER OF FRENCH HISTORY: André Duchesne (1584-1640).
FATHER OF FRENCH PROSE: Geoffroi de Villehardouin (1167-1212).
FATHER OF FRENCH SATIRE: Mathurin Regnier (1573-1613).
FATHER OF FRENCH SURGERY: Ambrose Paré (1517-1590).
FATHER OF FRENCH TRAGEDY: Robert Garnier; Pierre Corneille.
FATHER OF GEOLOGY: Avicenna; Nicolas Steno; William Smith.
FATHER OF GERMAN LITERATURE: Gotthold Ephraim Lessing (1729-1781).
FATHER OF GOOD WORKS: Mahomet II.
FATHER OF GREEK DRAMA: Aeschylus; Thespis.
FATHER OF GREEK MUSIC: Terpander.
FATHER OF GREEK PROSE: Herodotus.
FATHER OF GREEK TRAGEDY: Aeschylus.
FATHER OF GREENBACKS: Elbridge Gerry Spaulding.
FATHER OF HIS COUNTRY: Cicero; Julius Caesar; Caesar Augustus; Cosimo de' Medici; Andronicus Palaeologus II; Andrea Doria; George Washington.
FATHER OF HIS PEOPLE: Louis XIV of France; Christian III of Denmark.
FATHER OF HISTORIC PAINTING: Polygnotos of Thaos.
FATHER OF HISTORY: Herodotus.
FATHER OF IAMBIC VERSE: Archilochus of Paros (fl. b.c. 700).
FATHER OF INDUCTIVE PHILOSOPHY: Francis Bacon, Lord Verulam (1561-1626).
FATHER OF INTERNATIONAL LAW: Hugo Grotius (1583-1645), Dutch jurist.
FATHER OF ITALIAN PROSE: Giovanni Boccaccio.
FATHER OF JESTS: Joseph Miller (1684-1738), English wit.
FATHER OF JURISPRUDENCE: Ranulph de Glanville, adviser of Henry II of England.
FATHER OF LANDSCAPE GARDENING: André Lenôtre.
FATHER OF LETTERS: Francis I of France.
FATHER OF MEDICINE: Aretaeos of Cappadocia; Hippocrates of Cos.
FATHER OF MODERN OIL PAINTING: Jan van Eyck.
FATHER OF MODERN PROSE FICTION: Daniel Defoe.
FATHER OF MODERN SKEPTICISM: Pierre Bayle.
FATHER OF MONKS: Ethelwold of Winchester (d. 984).
FATHER OF MORAL PHILOSOPHY: Thomas Aquinas.
FATHER OF MUSIC: Giovanni Pierluigi da Palestrina.
FATHER OF MUSICIANS: Jubal. (Gen. IV, 21).
FATHER OF NAVIGATION: Don Henrique, Duke of Viseo (1394-1460).

FATHER OF ORNITHOLOGY: George Edwards (1693-1773).
FATHER OF NAVIGATION: Athanasius, Bishop of Alexandria.
FATHER OF PARODY: Hipponax, Greek iambic poet, 6th century b.c.
FATHER OF PEACE: Andrea Doria.
FATHER OF PHILOSOPHY: Roger Bacon; Albrecht von Haller.
FATHER OF POETRY: Orpheus; Homer.
FATHER OF PROTECTIVE POLICY: Henry Clay.
FATHER OF RECLAMATION: Francis Emroy Warren.
FATHER OF REFORM: John Cartwright.
FATHER OF RIDICULE: François Rabelais.
FATHER OF ROMAN PHILOSOPHY: Cicero.
FATHER OF ROMAN SATIRE: Caius Lucilius.
FATHER OF SATIRE: Archilochus of Paros.
FATHER OF SCOTCH LANDSCAPE PAINTING: John Thomson of Duddington.
FATHER OF STATES RIGHTS: John Caldwell Calhoun.
FATHER OF THE AMERICAN NAVY: John Adams.
FATHERS OF THE CHURCH: Apostolic Fathers, contemporaries of the Apostles: Clement of Rome, Barnabas, Hermas, Ignatius, Polycarp; Primitive Fathers, of the first three centuries of the Christian era: Justin, Theophilus of Antioch, Irenaeus, Clement of Alexandria, Cyprian of Carthage, Origen, Gregory Thaumaturgus, Dionysius of Alexandria, Tertullian. See also Fathers of the Greek Church, Fathers of the Latin Church.
FATHER OF THE CONTINENTAL CONGRESS: Benjamin Franklin.
FATHER OF THE DECLARATION OF INDEPENDENCE: Thomas Jefferson.
FATHER OF THE FAITHFUL: Patriarch Abraham (Rom. IV).
FATHER OF THE FEDERAL RESERVE SYSTEM: George Carter Glass (1858-1946), statesman.
FATHERS OF THE GREEK CHURCH: Eusebius, Athanasius, Basil the Great, Gregory of Nyssa, Cyril of Jerusalem, Chrysostom, Epiphanius, Cyril of Alexandria, Ephraim of Edessa. See also Fathers of the Church, Fathers of the Latin Church.
FATHER OF THE HOMESTEAD: Andrew Johnson.
FATHER OF THE HUMAN RACE: Adam.
FATHER OF THE INDIAN ARMY: Stringer Lawrence.
FATHERS OF THE LATIN CHURCH: Origen, Tertullian, Clement of Rome, Ignatius, Justin, Irenaeus, Cyprian, Hilary of Poitiers, Ambrose, Optatus, Jerome, Augustine, Leo the Great, Prosper, Vincent of Lerins, Peter Chrysologus, Caesarius of Arles, Gregory the Great, Isidore of Seville, Venerable Bede, Peter Damian, Anselm, Bernard of Clairvaux.
FATHER OF THE NATIONAL ROAD: Henry Clay.
FATHER OF THE PEOPLE: Title of the absolute monarchs of Denmark (1660-1848): Frederick III, Christian V, Frederick IV, Christian VI, Frederick V, Christian VII, Frederick VI, Christian VIII; Louis XII of France; Gabriel du Pineau (1573-1644), French lawyer.
FATHER OF THE PHONOGRAPH: Thomas Edison.
FATHER OF THE POOR: Bernard Gilpin.
FATHER OF THE POTTERIES: Josiah Wedgwood.
FATHER OF THE SPANISH DRAMA: Lope de Vega.
FATHER OF THE STEAMBOAT: Robert Fulton.

FATHER OF THE SYMPHONY: Franz Joseph Haydn.
FATHER OF THE TARIFF: Alexander Hamilton.
FATHER OF TRAGEDY: Aeschylus; Thespis.
FATHER OF VAUDEVILLE: Olivier Basselin (c. 1400-1450), songwriter of Van-de-Vire, Normandy.
FATHER VIOLET: Napoleon I.
FAULTLESS, THE: Andrea del Sarto.
LES FAUVES (THE WILD BEASTS): Braque, Derain, Dufy, Matisse, Rouault, Vlaminck.
F.D.R.: Franklin Delano Roosevelt.
FEARLESS, THE: Richard of Normandy.
FEDERALIST PAPERS, THE: Alexander Hamilton, James Madison, John Jay.
FEMME, UNE: Anne Louise Germaine, Mme. de Staël.
FENIANS: James Stephens.
FERNEY: Voltaire.
FIGHTING BOB: Robley Dunglison Evans.
FIGHTING JOE: Gen. Joseph E. Hooker.
FIRST CONSUL: Napoleon I.
FIRST GENTLEMAN IN EUROPE: George IV.
FITCH, ENSIGN CLARK, U.S.N.: Upton Sinclair.
FITZBOODLE, GEORGE SAVAGE: William Makepeace Thackeray.
FITZVICTOR, JOHN: Percy Bysshe Shelley.
FIVE MEMBERS: Pym, Hampden, Holles, Haselrig, Strode.
FLOWER: Jan Brueghel the Elder.
FLYNT, JOSIAH: Josiah Flynt Willard.
FORD, FORD MADOX: Ford Madox Hueffer.
FOREIGNOR, THE (Le d'Outremer): Louis IV of France.
FORKBEARD: Svend, King of Denmark.
FOUCHER, PAUL: Victor Hugo.
FOWLER, THE: Henry I of Saxony.
FOX, THE (Le Renard): Louis XI of France.
FOX OF KINDERHOOK, THE: Martin Van Buren.
FRANCE, ANATOLE: Jacques Anatole François Thibault.
FRANKENSTEIN: Mary Wollstonecraft Shelley.
FREEMAN, MRS.: Duchess of Marlborough.
FROISSART, IEAN: Alphonse Daudet.
FÜHRER, DER: Adolf Hitler.
FUTURISM: Umberto Boccioni, Gino Severini, Emilio Marinetti.
GABERLUNZIE MAN: James V.
GADSHILL: Charles Dickens.
GASTON, MARIE: Alphonse Daudet.
GAY, MR. JOSEPH: Alexander Pope.
GAZUL, CLARA: Prosper Mérimeé.
G.B.S.: George Bernard Shaw.
GENDARME OF EUROPE, THE: Nicholas I of Russia.
GENTLE GEORGE: George Etherege.
GENTLEMAN GEORGE: George IV of England.
GENTLEMAN JIM: James J. Corbett.
GENTLEMAN OF CONNECTICUT, A: Lemuel Hopkins.
GENTLEMAN OF OXFORD, A: Percy Bysshe Shelley.
GENTLE SHEPHERD, THE: George Grenville.
GEORGE, OLD: George Monk.
GEORGE ELIOT: Mary Ann (Marian) Evans.
GEORGE SAND: Amandine Aurore Lucie Dupin.
GERALDA, LADY: Charlotte Brontë.
GERMANICUS: Nero Claudius Drusus; Claudius I; Nero; Britannicus.
GERONDISTS: Roland de La Platière; Pierre Vergniaud.
G.K.C.: Gilbert Keith Chesterton.
G.L.B.O.C.: Bishop George Berkeley.
GNATHO: Alexander Pope.
GODDEN, RUMER: Mrs. Laurence Foster.

GOLDSMITH, PETER: John Boynton Priestley.
G.O.M.: William E. Gladstone.
GOOD GREY POET: Walt Whitman.
GOOD QUEEN BESS: Elizabeth I of England
GOOSE, MOTHER: Mrs. Elizabeth Foster Goose.
GORDON PASHA: Charles George Gordon.
GORKI, MAXIM: Aleksei Maksimovich Peshkov.
GRACCHUS: François Babeuf.
GRADUATE OF OXFORD, A: John Ruskin.
GRAHAM, TOM: Sinclair Lewis.
GRAND DAUPHIN, LE: Louis de France.
GRAND MONARQUE, LE: Louis XIV.
GRAND OLD LADY OF LITERATURE: Henry James.
GRAND OLD MAN: William E. Gladstone.
GRAND OLD WOMAN, THE: William E. Gladstone.
GRAND, SARAH: Frances Elizabeth McFall.
GRAYFELL: Harold II of Norway.
GRAYSON, DAVID: Ray Stannard Baker.
GREAT, THE: Alexander of Macedon; Akbar of India; Catherine II of Russia; Charlemagne; Constantine; Frederick II of Prussia; Hugh of Cluny; Hugh, Count of Paris; Ivan III of Russia; Leo I of the Eastern Roman Empire; Otto I of Saxony; Peter I of Russia; Pope Leo I; Pope Gregory I.
GREAT COMMONER, THE: William Pitt, Earl of Chatham (1708-1778); Thaddeus Stevens.
GREAT COMPROMISER, THE: Henry Clay.
GREAT DUKE, THE: Duke of Wellington.
GREAT ELECTOR, THE: Frederick William (1620-1688), Elector of Brandenburg.
GREAT EMANCIPATOR, THE: Abraham Lincoln.
GREATEST HAPPINESS OF THE GREATEST NUMBER, THE: Joseph Priestley, Jeremy Bentham.
GREATEST SHOWMAN ON EARTH, THE: P. T. Barnum.
GREAT JOHN L., THE: John Lawrence Sullivan.
GREAT MAGICIAN, THE: Sir Walter Scott.
GREAT MARQUIS: James Graham, Earl Montrose.
GREAT PAINTER OF LITTLE PICTURES, THE: Jean Louis Meissonier.
GREAT PROFILE, THE: John Barrymore.
GREAT UNKNOWN, THE: Sir Walter Scott.
GRECO, EL: Kyriakos Theotokopoulos. Domenicos Theotocopoulos.
GREY EMINENCE: Père Joseph (François Le Clerc du Tremblay).
GRILE, DOD: Ambrose Bierce.
GUARD, THEODORE DE LA: Nathaniel Ward.
HALIBURTON, HUGH: James Logie Robertson
HAMMERGAFFERSTEIN, HANS: Henry Wadsworth Longfellow.
HAMMER OF: See also Malleus.
HAMMER OF HERETICS: Pierre d'Ailly.
HAMSUN, KNUT: Knut Pedersen.
HANDSOME, THE (Le Bel): Charles IV of France.
HANOVERIAN RAT, THE: George I of England.
HAPPY WARRIOR, THE: Al Smith.
HARDEN, MAXIMILIAN: Maximilian Witkowski.
HARD-RULER: Harold III of Norway.
HAREFOOT: Harold I of England.
HARLAND, MARION, OF RICHMOND, VA.: Mary Virginia Terhune.
HARRY OF THE WEST: Henry Clay.
HATTERAS, OWEN: George Jean Nathan and H. L. Mencken.
H.D.: Hilda Doolittle (Mrs. Aldington).
HEIR OF THE REPUBLIC, THE: Napoleon I.

HELL: Pieter Brueghel the Younger.
HELVIDIUS: John Jay.
HENRY, O.: William Sydney Porter.
HENRY, OLIVER: William Sydney Porter.
HEPTAMERON: Margaret of Navarre.
HERBERT, FRANCIS: William Cullen Bryant.
HERO OF TRAFALGAR, THE: Admiral Horatio Nelson.
HEXT, HARRINGTON: Eden Phillpotts.
H.H.: Helen Hunt Jackson.
HIGHLAND MARY: Robert Burns.
HILDEBRAND: Pope Gregory VII; Nikolaas Beets.
HIPPO, BISHOP OF: St. Augustine.
HIPPOCRATES, THE ENGLISH: Thomas Sydenham.
HIS FRAUDULENCY: Rutherford B. Hayes.
HISTORICUS: Sir William Harcourt.
HITLER: Adolf Schicklgruber.
HOBBES, JOHN OLIVER: Pearl Mary Teresa Craigie.
HOBSON'S CHOICE: Tobias Hobson.
HONEST ABE: Abraham Lincoln.
HONEST JOHN: John Kelly.
HOOSIER POET: James Whitcomb Riley.
HORN, ALOYSIUS: Alfred Aloysius Smith.
HORNEIN, HORACE: Lord Byron.
HOTSPUR: Henry Percy.
HUMANUS: Thomas Paine.
HUNGER: Olaf I, King of Denmark.
I. & Q.: Jonathan Edwards.
IBBETSON, PETER: George du Maurier.
ICARUS: Daniel Webster.
ICEBANKS: Vice-President Charles Warren Evans.
IDEALISM: Berkeley, Fichte, Schelling, Hegel.
ILLUMINATOR, THE: Gregory of Armenia.
IMAGISTS: T. E. Hulme, F. S. Flint, Richard Aldington, T. S. Eliot, Ezra Pound, Amy Lowell, John Gould Fletcher.
IMPARTIAL HAND: Samuel Johnson.
IMPARTIALIST, AN: Samuel Adams.
IMPRESSIONISM: Manet, Degas, Monet, Renoir, Pissaro, Sisley, Bazille, Berthe Morisot.
INCORRUPTIBLE, THE: Robespierre.
INFALLIBILITY: Pope Pius IX.
INGOLDSBY, THOMAS: Richard Harris Barham.
INTERNATIONAL, THE: Karl Marx, Friedrich Engels.
IRISH AGITATOR, THE: Daniel O'Connell.
IRISHMAN, AN: Thomas Moore.
IRISHMAN, BENIGHTED: William Makepeace Thackeray.
IRON, THE: Frederick II, Elector of Brandenburg.
IRON CHANCELLOR, THE: Bismarck.
IRON DUKE, THE: Arthur Wellesley, 1st Duke of Wellington.
IRON MAJOR, THE: Frank Cavanaugh.
IRON MAN, THE: Henry Louis (Lou) Gehrig.
IRON MASK, THE MAN IN THE: Nicholas Fouquet.
IRONQUILL: Eugene Fitch Ware.
ISAURIAN, THE: Leo III, Emperor of the Eastern Roman Empire (Constantine V, Leo IV, Constantine VI, and Irene were also "Isaurians," i.e. from Isauria).
JACKSON, STONEWALL: Gen. Thomas J. Jackson.
JACOBINS: Jacques René Hebert, Robespierre.
"JAMES III": James Francis Edward Stuart.
J***. B***.: James Boswell.
JEAMES: William Makepeace Thackeray.
JERSEY LILY: Lily Langtry.
JESUITS: Ignatius of Loyola.
JIM THE PENMAN: James G. Blaine.
JOHNSON, BENJAMIN F., OF BOONE: James Whitcomb Riley.

JOINER, THE *(Le Charpentier):* Louis XVI of France.
JORROCKS, MR. JOHN: Robert Smith Surtees.
JUST, THE: James II of Aragon.
KENT, HOLY NUN OF: Elizabeth Barton.
KERR, ORPHEUS C.: Robert Henry Newell.
KHAZAR, THE: Leo IV, Emperor of Eastern Roman Empire.
KING BOMBA: Ferdinand, King of Naples.
KING-MAKER: Richard Neville, Earl of Warwick.
KING OF THE COMMONS: James V.
KISKADDEN, MAUDE: Maude Adams.
KNICKERBOCKER, DIEDRICH: Washington Irving.
K. OF K.: Kichener of Khartoum.
LABRONIO, G.: Giovanni Marradi.
LACKLAND: John, King of England.
LADY, A: Jane Austen; Julia Ward Howe.
LADY WITH THE LAMP, THE: Florence Nightingale.
L'AIGLON: Napoleon II (François Charles Joseph Napoleon).
LAIRD OF LITTLEGRANGE: Edward FitzGerald.
LAIRD OF SKIBO, THE: Andrew Carnegie.
LAKE SCHOOL: Wordsworth, Coleridge, Southey.
LAMB, THE: Eric III, King of Denmark.
L'ANGLAIS MANGEUR D'OPIUM: Thomas De Quincey.
LANGWAY, A. HUGO: Andrew Lang.
LARKING, G.B.: George Bernard Shaw.
LAST OF THE BARONS: Richard Neville, Earl of Warwick.
LAST OF THE ENGLISH: Herewald (the Wake).
LAST OF THE GOTHS: Roderick.
LAST OF THE ROMANS: Cato Minor; Aetius; Cola di Rienzi.
LAST OF THE TRIBUNES: Cola di Rienzi.
LAUGHING PHILOSOPHER: Democritus.
LAYMAN, A: Sir Walter Scott.
LEARNED BLACKSMITH, THE: Elihu Burritt.
LELIA: George Sand.
LENIN, NIKOLAI: Vladimir Ilich Ulyanov.
LEOPOLD, ISAIAH EDWIN: Ed Wynn.
L'ESTRANGE, JOSEPH: Prosper Mérimée.
LIBERATOR: Simon Bolivar; Daniel O'Connell; Alexander II of Russia.
LIBERATOR OF CHILE: Bernardo O'Higgins.
LICENCIADO TOME DE BURGUILLOS, LE: Lope de Vega.
LICHFIELD, SWAN OF: Anna Seward.
LIGHT-HORSE HARRY: Henry Lee.
LION OF THE NORTH: Gustavus Adolphus.
LITTLE THOMAS: Thomas Moore.
LITTLE BEN: Benjamin Harrison.
LITTLE BOOTS (CALIGULA): Gaius Caesar.
LITTLE FLOWER, THE: Fiorello La Guardia.
LITTLE GIANT, THE: Stephen A. Douglas.
LITTLE MAC: Gen. George B. McClellan.
LITTLE MATTY: Martin Van Buren.
LITTLEPAGE, CORNELIUS: James Fenimore Cooper.
LITTLE PHIL: Gen. Philip Sheridan.
LITTLETON, MARK: John Pendleton Kennedy.
LONE FISHERMAN OF BATH, THE: Arthur Sewall.
LONG KNIFE: Daniel Boone.
LONGSHANKS: Edward I of England.
LONGSWORD: William I, Duke of Normandy.
LORRAIN, CLAUDE: Claude Gellée (Gelée).
LORRAIN, JEAN: Paul Duval.
LOT, PARSON: Charles Kingsley.
LOTHROP, AMY: Anna Bartlett Warner.
LOTI, PIERRE: Julien Viaud.
LOUIS, JOE: Joseph Louis Barrow.
LOUIS XVII: Eleazer Williams.

LOYAL SERVITEUR: Seigneur de Bayard.
LULU (LOU-LOU): Eugène Louis Napoleon, Prince Imperial.
LUTTERWOORTH, RECTOR OF: John Wycliffe.
LYNCH LAW: Charles Lynch (1733-96) of Virginia.
MACFLECKNOE: Thomas Shadwell.
MACLAREN, IAN: John Watson.
MAD ANTHONY: Gen. Anthony Wayne.
MAD CAVALIER: Prince Rupert, Count Palatine of Rhine.
MAD JACK: John Percival.
MADMAN OF MACEDONIA. THE: Alexander the Great.
MADMAN OF THE NORTH: Charles XII of Sweden.
MAD MONKS OF MEDMENHAM ABBEY: John Wilkes, Sir Francis Dashwood, Lord Sandwich, George Bubb Dodington.
MAD POET, THE: Nathaniel Lee.
MAEONIDES: Homer.
MAGISTER SENTENTIARUM: Peter Lombard.
MAGLANOWICH, HYACINTHE: Prosper Mérimeé.
MAID OF NORWAY: Margaret, Queen of Scotland.
MAID OF SARAGOSSA: Augustina.
MAINTENANT, MADAME DE: Marquise de Maintenon (Françoise d'Aubigné).
MAITLAND, THOMAS: Robert Buchanan.
MALAGROWTHER, MALACHI: Sir Walter Scott.
MALET, LUCAS: Mary St. Leger Kingsley Harrison.
MALLEUS ASIATICORUM: Joseph von Hammer-Purgstall.
MALLEUS CHRISTIANORUM: Almansor (al-Mansur).
MALLEUS MALEFICARUM: James Sprenger.
MALLEUS MONARCHORUM: Thomas Cromwell.
MAN, A: Horace Walpole.
MANASSA MAULER: Jack Dempsey.
MAN FROM NOWHERE, THE: Rudyard Kipling.
MAN OF BLOOD, THE: Charles I of England
MAN OF DESTINY: Napoleon I.
MAN OF FEELING: Henry Mackenzie.
MAN OF IRON, THE: Bismarck.
MAN OF THE REVOLUTION, THE: Samuel Adams.
MAN OF THE SECOND NOVEMBER: Napoleon III.
MANSFIELD, KATHERINE: Kathleen Beauchamp Murry.
MANTUAN, THE: Virgil.
MAN WHO WOULD BE KING, THE: Theodore Roosevelt.
MARCH, WILLIAM: William Edward Marcl Campbell.
MARCLIFF, THEOPHILUS: William Godwin
MARO: Virgil.
MARQUIS OF DOURO: Charlotte Brontë.
MARSHALL, WILLIAM, TRANSLATOR: Horace Walpole.
MARTYRED PRESIDENT, THE: Abraham Lincoln.
MARTYR KING, THE: Charles I of England
MARVEL, IK: Donald Grant Mitchell.
MARVELLOUS BOY, THE: Thomas Chatterton.
MASSA BOB: Robert E. Lee.
MATCH KING: Ivar Kreuger.
MATT: Matthew Prior.
MAUROIS, ANDRÉ: Emile Herzog.
MEAUX, BISHOP OF: Bossuet.
MELBA (MME. NELLIE): Helen Porter Mitchell.
MELMOTH, SEBASTIAN: Oscar Wilde.
MEMORABLE, THE: Eric II, King of Denmark

MEREDITH, OWEN: Robert Edward Bulwer-Lytton, 1st Earl of Lytton.
MERLIN: Alfred Lord Tennyson.
MERRY ANDREW: Andrew Borde.
MERRY MONARCH: Charles II.
MESMERISM: Franz (Friedrich) Anton Mesmer.
MEUDON, CURÉ OF: Rabelais.
MIDNIGHT, MRS. MARY: Christopher Smart.
MILL-BOY OF THE SLASHES, THE: Henry Clay.
MILLER, JOAQUIN: Cincinnatus Hiner Miller.
MISTRAL, GABRIELA: Lucila Godoy de Alcayaga.
MONADISM: Gottfried von Liebniz.
MONEYBAG (Kalita): Ivan I.
MONSEIGNEUR: Louis de France.
MORLEY, MRS.: Queen Anne.
MORNING STAR OF THE REFORMATION, THE: John Wycliff.
MOTHER JONES: Mary Harris Jones.
MOTHER OF THE CONFEDERACY, THE: Sallie Chapman Law.
MOUNTAIN, THE: Danton; Robespierre.
MULLIGAN GUARD DEMOSTHENES, THE: Bourke Cockran.
MULLIGAN OF KILBALLYMULLIGAN: William Makepeace Thackeray.
MURALTO, ONUPHRIO: Horace Walpole.
MYLES NA GCOPALEEN: Brian O'Nolan.
MYSTICISM: Philo, Paul, Clement of Alexandria, Origen, Plotinus, Porphyry, Augustine, Dionysus the Areopagite, Proclus, St. Macarius of Egypt, John Cassian, St. Gregory the Great, John Scotus Erigena, St. Peter Damian, St. Bruno, St. Anselm, St. Bernard of Clairvaux, St. Hildegard of Bingen, St. Elizabeth of Schonau, Nun Gertrude, St. Mechthild of Hackborn, Mechthild of Magdeburg, St. Gertrude the Great, St. Francis of Assisi, John of Parma, John of La Verna, Jacopone da Todi, Blessed Angela of Foligno, Bonaventura, Aquinas, Rabica, Al Ghazzali, Sadi, Jalalu'd Din, Hafiz, Dante, Meister Eckhart, John Tauler, Blessed Henry Suso, Blessed John Ruysbroeck, Gerald Groot, Thomas a Kempis, Nicolas of Cusa, Denis the Carthusian, Margery Kempe, Richard Rolle, Walter Hilton, Julian of Norwich, St. Bridget of Sweden, St. Catharine of Siena, Gerson, Joan of Arc, St. Catherine of Genoa, St. Peter of Alcantara, Ignatius Loyola, St. Teresa, St. John of the Cross, St. Rose of Lima, Jacob Boehme, George Fox, John Woolman, Thomas Vaughan, Henry Vaughan. Thomas Traherne, St. Jeanne Françoise de Chantal, St. Francis de Sales, Pascal, Miguel de Molinos, Madame Guyon, William Law, William Blake, the anonymous author of The Cloud of Unknowing.
NAMBY-PAMBY: Ambrose Philips.
NAPOLEON LE PETIT: Napoleon III.
NASBY, PETROLEUM V.: David Ross Locke.
NASIER, ALCOFRYBAS: Rabelais.
NASO: Ovid.
NATICK COBBLER, THE: Vice-President Henry Wilson.
NAUTICUS: Sir William Laird Clowes.
NEOPLATONISM: Plotinus, Porphyry, Ammonius Saccas, Proclus.
NESTOR OF THE PRESS, THE: Charles A. Dana.
NEW JERUSALEM CHURCH: Emanuel Swedenborg.
NEW TIMON: Baron Lytton of Knebworth.
NIGHTINGALE, THE AMERICAN FLORENCE: Anna Caroline Maxwell.
NIGHTMARE OF EUROPE, THE: Napoleon I.
NIHILISM: Herzen; Bakunin; Stepniak.
NINE WORTHIES, THE: Joshua, David, Judas Maccabeus, Hector, Alexander, Julius Caesar, Arthur, Godfrey de Bouillon.

NOLAN, THE: Giordano Bruno.
NOMINALISM: Roscellinus, Ockham.
NORTH, CHRISTOPHER: John Wilson.
NOVALIS: Baron Friedrich von Hardenberg.
NOVANGLUS: John Adams.
OBERON: Nathaniel Hawthorne.
O'BRIEN, FLANN: Brian O'Nolan.
OCCASIONALISM: Geulincx.
O'CONNOR, FRANK: Michael O'Donovan.
OGILVY, GAVIN: Sir James M. Barrie.
OLD BOY, AN: Thomas Hughes.
OLD BUCK: James Buchanan.
OLD BULLION: Thomas H. Benton.
OLD CATHOLICS: Johann von Dollinger, Joseph Reinkens.
OLD DREADNOUGHT: Edward Boscawen.
OLD FORWARD: Gebhard von Blucher.
OLD FRITZ (Alter Fritz): Friderick the Great of Prussia.
OLD FUSS AND FEATHERS: Gen. Winfield Scott.
OLD GEORGE: George Monk.
OLD HICKORY: Andrew Jackson.
OLD MAN ELOQUENT: Isocrates.
OLD MAN OF THE MOUNTAINS: Hassan-ibn-Sabbah.
OLD NOLL: Oliver Cromwell.
OLD PARIS MAN, AN: William Makepeace Thackeray.
OLD PRETENDER: James Francis Edward Stuart.
OLD PUBLIC FUNCTIONARY: James Buchanan.
OLD SPOONS: Gen. Benjamin Franklin Butler.
OLDSTYLE, JONATHAN: Washington Irving.
OLD TECUMP: Gen. William Tecumseh Sherman.
OLD WHIG, THE: Joseph Addison.
OLE LUK-OIE: Sir Ernest Dunlop Swinton.
OLYMPIO: Victor Hugo.
ONSLOW: John Calhoun.
OOM PAUL: Paul Kruger, President of Transvaal.
OOR RAB: Robert Burns.
OPIUM EATER, AN ENGLISH: Thomas De Quincey.
OPTIC, OLIVER: William T. Adams.
ORANGE PEEL: Sir Robert Peel.
ORATORY: St. Philip Neri.
ORWELL, GEORGE: Eric Arthur Blair.
OSSAWATOMIE BROWN: John Brown.
O'SULLIVAN, SEUMAS: James Starkey.
OUIDA: Marie Louise de la Ramée.
OUR ANDY: Andrew Johnson.
OUR FRITZ (Unser Fritz): Frederick II, Emperor of Germany.
OUR RANDY: Lord Randolph Churchill.
OUR TEDDY: Theodore Roosevelt.
PACIFICO, DON: Henry John Temple, Viscount Palmerston.
PADECOPEO, GABRIEL: Lope de Vega.
PAM: Henry John Temple, Viscount Palmerston.
PANSY: Mrs. Isabella M. Alden.
PANTOPHILE: Denis Diderot.
PAPA: Ernest Hemingway.
PAPAVERIUS: Thomas de Quincey.
P.A.P.O.I.L.A.: John Locke.
PARRICIDE, THE: John, Prince of Germany (1290-1313).
PARRICIDE, THE BEAUTIFUL: Beatrice Cenci.
PARTINGTON, MRS.: Sydney Smith.
PASQUIN, ANTHONY: John Williams.
PASSFIELD: Sidney Webb.
PASTON, GEORGE: E. M. Symonds.
PATER PATRIAE: Cicero; Cosimo de Medici.
PAUL, JOHN: John Paul Jones.
PEACEMAKER, THE: Isabel (or Elizabeth) of Aragon, Queen of Portugal.
PEASANT, THE: Pieter Brueghel the Elder.

PEASANT POET: John Clare.
PENN, ARTHUR: (James) Brander Matthews.
PENTWEAZLE, EBENEZER: Christopher Smart.
PEOPLE'S WILLIAM: William E. Gladstone.
PÈRE DUCHESNE: Jacques René Hébert.
PERFECTIONISTS: John Humphrey Noyes.
PERPETUAL CANDIDATE, THE: Grover Cleveland.
PERSON OF QUALITY, A: Jonathan Swift.
PERTINAX: Charles Gérault; André Géraud.
PESSIMISSM: Arthur Schopenhauer, Eduard von Hartmann.
PETER RABBIT: Rev. William Joseph Long.
PETROV, EVGENI: Evgeni Petrovich Kataev.
PHILADELPHUS: Increase Mather.
PHILIPPE-EGALITÉ: Louis Philippe Joseph d'Orleans.
PHILOMATH: Benjamin Franklin.
PHILOSOPHER, THE: Leo VI, Emperor of Eastern Roman Empire.
PHILOSOPHICAL PLEIAD: See Seven Wise Men of Greece.
PHIZ: Hablot Knight Browne.
PHYSICIAN, THE BELOVED: St. Luke; Sir Arthur Clarke.
PIEGAN PHIL: Gen. Philip Sheridan.
PIETISM: Philipp Jacob Spener.
PIG-IRON KELLY: William Kelly.
PILGRIM, DAVID: Hilary Aiden St. George Saunders and John Leslie Palmer.
PINDAR, PETER: John Wolcot.
PLATO: Aristocles.
PLATONISTS, CAMBRIDGE: Henry More, John Smith, Benjamin Whichcote, Peter Sterry, John Norris.
PLAYFAIR, I.: Oscar Wilde.
PLÉIADE: Du Bellay, Ronsard, Remi-Belleau, Baïf, Dorat, Jamin, Jodelle, Pontus de Thiard, Muret.
PLON-PLON: Prince Napoleon Bonaparte.
PLUMED KNIGHT, THE: James G. Blaine.
PLYMLEY, PETER: Sydney Smith.
POET-KING: James I.
POET OF THE SIERRAS, THE: Joaquin Miller.
POET'S POET, THE: Edmund Spenser.
POLPERRO: Sir Arthur Quiller-Couch.
POOR RICHARD: Benjamin Franklin.
POPLICOLA: Samuel Adams.
PORCUPINE, PETER: William Cobbett.
PORPHYROGENITUS: Constantine VII.
PORTIA: Abigail Adams.
PORT-ROYALISTS: Arnauld; Pascal; Nicole.
POSITIVISM: Auguste Comte.
POST-IMPRESSIONISTS: Cézanne, Matisse, Derain.
PRECEPTOR OF GERMANY, THE: Philip Melanchton.
PREEDY, GEORGE RUNNELL: Gabrielle Margaret Vere Campbell Long.
PRE-ESTABLISHED HARMONY: Gottfried von Leibniz.
PRE-RAPHAELITES: Dante Gabriel Rossetti, Christina Rossetti, William Rossetti, Holman Hunt, John Everett Millais, William Morris, Burne-Jones.
PRETTY FANNY: Fanny Kemble.
PREVIOUS, THE: William II of Germany.
PRINCE HAL: Henry V of England.
PRINCE OF PEACE: Christ.
PRINCE OF PLAYERS, THE: Edwin Booth.
PRINCE OF THE PEACE: Alcudia.
PRINCE OF THE RAILS, THE: Robert T. Lincoln.
PRINCE OF WALES, THE: Chester A. Arthur.
PRIOR, CAPT. SAMUEL: John Galt.
PROTECTOR, THE: Oliver Cromwell.
PROTESTANT DUKE, THE: James Scott, Duke of Monmouth (James Fitzroy or James Crofts).
PROTO-MARTYR, THE: St. Stephen.

PROUT, FATHER: Francis Sylvester Mahony.
P-SHAW: George Bernard Shaw.
PUBLICOLA: John Quincey Adams.
PUBLIUS: Alexander Hamilton, James Madison, John Jay.
PUCELLE, LA: Joan of Arc.
PUZZLE, PETER: Joseph Addison.
Q: Douglas Jerrold; Sir Arthur Quiller-Couch.
Q, OLD: William Douglas, Duke of Queensberry (1724-1810).
QUAD, M.: Charles Bertrand Lewis.
QUAKER POET: Bernard Barton; John Greenleaf Whittier.
QUAKERS: George Fox.
QUANTUM THEORY: Max Planck.
QUARRELER, THE (Le Hutin): Louis X of France.
QUEEN, ELLERY: Frederic Dannay and Manfred Lee.
QUEEN OF HEARTS: Elizabeth (Stuart), Queen of Frederick V of Bohemia.
QUIETISM: Miguel de Molinos; Mme. Guyon.
QUIRINUS: Lord Acton.
RAB: Abba Arika.
RABBIT'S FOOT STATESMAN, THE: William Jennings Bryan.
RAILSPLITTER, THE: Abraham Lincoln.
RAMAL, WALTER: Walter de la Mare.
RAMBAM: Maimonides.
RAPAGNETTA, GABRIELE: Gabriele D'Annunzio.
REALISM: William of Champeaux; Emile Zola.
RED, THE (Krasny): Ivan II.
RED ROSA: Rosa Luxemburg.
RED SHIRT HERO, THE: Giuseppe Garibaldi.
RED SPINNER: William Senior.
RE GALANTUOMO: Victor Emmanuel II.
REINHARDT, MAX: Max Goldman.
RELATIVITY: Einstein.
RELATIVITY OF KNOWLEDGE: Sir William Hamilton, Henry Mansel.
RENEGADE, THE: John Tyler.
RHODE, JOHN: Cecil John Charles Street.
RIBBONSON, HORATIO: George Bernard Shaw.
RICE, ELMER: Elmer Reizenstein.
RICHARDSON, HENRY HANDEL: Henrietta Richardson.
R.L.S.: Robert Louis Stevenson.
ROARING JACK: John Percival.
ROBERTSON, E. ARNOT: Eileen Robertson Turner.
ROBINSON CRUSOE: Daniel Defoe.
ROCK, CAPT.: Thomas Moore.
ROHMER, SAX: Arthur Sarsfield Ward.
ROI SOLEIL, LE: Louis XIV.
ROMANTICISM: Schiller, Goethe, Tieck, Macpherson, Collins, Grey, Percy, Keats, Byron, Shelley, Coleridge, Scott, Chenier, Hugo, de Musset, Dumas.
ROSCIUS, THE BRITISH: David Garrick.
ROSCIUS OF THE BOWERY, THE: Edwin Forrest.
ROSETTA STONE: Jean François Champollion.
ROSS, BARNABY: Frederic Dannay and Manfred Lee.
ROUGH AND READY: Zachary Taylor.
ROUSSEAU OF CHINA, THE: K'ang Yu-wei.
ROWANS, VIRGINIA: Edward Everett Tanner.
ROWLEY, THOMAS: Thomas Chatterton.
ROWLEY, OLD: Charles II.
ROYAL SAINT: Henry VI.
ROYCE, ASHLEY A.: Nathaniel Hawthorne.
RUFUS (THE RED): William II of England.
RUNNYMEDE: Disraeli.
RUPERT OF DEBATE: Edward George Stanley.
RUSSELL, LILLIAN: Helen Louise Leonard.
RUSSELL, R. H.: Peter Finley Dunne.
SACHARISA: Lady Dorothy Sidney.

SACKBEARER, THE: Ammonius Saccas.
SACRED HEART: Margaret Mary Alacoque.
SAGE OF CHELSEA, THE: Thomas Carlyle.
SAGE OF CONCORD, THE: Ralph Waldo Emerson.
SAILOR KING, THE: William IV of England.
ST. DENIS, RUTH: Ruth Denis.
SAKI: Hector Hugh Munro.
SALVATION ARMY: William Booth.
SAND, GEORGE: Amandine Aurore Lucie Dupin.
SAN JUAN HILL, THE HERO OF: Theodore Roosevelt.
SASSOON, SIEGFRIED: Saul Kain.
SATANIC SCHOOL: Shelley, Byron, Hugo, George Sand, Rossetti, Swinburne.
SATIRIST, A BLUDGEON: Lemuel Hopkins.
SAUNDERS, RICHARD: Benjamin Franklin.
SAXON, THE: Lothair II (or III).
SCOURGE OF GOD: Attila.
SCRIBLERUS, MARTINUS: Swift, Pope, Arbuthnot.
SCRIBLERUS SECUNDUS: Henry Fielding.
SEARCHLIGHT: Waldo Frank.
SE-BAPTIST: John Smith (Smyth).
SECOND-THOUGHTS, SOLOMON: John Pendleton Kennedy.
SEDGES, JOHN: Pearl Buck.
SEMIRAMIS OF THE NORTH: Margaret of Denmark; Catherine the Great; Queen Christina.
SENSATIONALISM: Etienne de Condillac.
SENTENCES, MASTER OF: Peter Lombard.
SERPENT OF THE NILE: Cleopatra.
SEVEN SAGES: See Seven Wise Men of Greece.
SEVEN WISE MEN OF GREECE: Bias, Chilon, Cleobulus, Periander, Pittacus, Solon, Thales. Some lists substitute Epimenides for Periander. Also called the Seven Sages and the Philosophical Pleiad.
SHAKERS, THE: Ann Lee.
SHAKESPEARE OF INDIA, THE: Kalidasa.
SHEARING, JOSEPH: Gabrielle Margaret Vere Campbell Long.
SHEPHERD OF THE OCEAN: Sir Walter Raleigh.
SHERRY: Richard Brinsley Sheridan.
SHIFTY DICK: Richard Croker.
SHUFFLEBOTTOM, ABEL: Robert Southey.
SIBYLLE DU FAUBOURG SAINT-GERMAIN, LA: Marie Anne Adelaide Lenormand.
SIDNEY, ALGERNON: John Quincy Adams.
SILENT, THE: William I of the Netherlands.
SILHOUETTE: Etienne de Silhouette.
SILLY BILLY: William IV of England.
SILURIST: Henry Vaughan.
SILVER DICK: Richard P. Bland.
SIMPLE, THE: Frederick III, King of Sicily.
SIMPLE, THE (Le Sot): Charles III of France.
SINGLE-SPEECH HAMILTON: William Gerard Hamilton (1729-96).
SINJOHN, JOHN: John Galsworthy.
THE SIX: Auric; Durey; Honneger; Milhaud; Poulenc; Taillefere.
SLEEPY PHIL: Philander Chase Knox.
SLICK, SAM: Thomas Chandler Haliburton.
SLUGGARD, THE (Le Fainéant): Louis V of France.
SMELFUNGUS: Tobias Smollett.
SMITH, JOHNSTON: Stephen Crane.
SMITH, MARY: Mary Pickford.
SMITH, S.S.: Thames Ross Williamson.
SNOW-KING, THE: Frederick V.
SOAPY SAM: Bishop Samuel Wilberforce.
SOCIALISM: Fourier, Proudhon, Lassalle, Marx.
SOCIOLOGY: Herbert Spencer.
SOLOMON, SCOTTISH: James VI and I.
SPALATIN, GEORG: Burckhardt, Georg.
SPANIARD, THE: Empress Eugénie.
SPARKS, GODFREY: Charles Dickens.

SPARKS, TIMOTHY: Charles Dickens.
SPIDER KING, THE: Louis XI of France.
SQUIRE GAWKEY: Richard Grenville, Earl Temple.
STAGIRITE: Aristotle.
STALIN, JOSEPH: Iosif Vissarionovich Dzhugashvili.
STAMMERER, THE (Le Bègue): Louis II of France.
STANLEY, SIR HENRY MORTON: John Rowlands.
S.T.C.: Samuel Taylor Coleridge.
STELLA: Lady Penelope Devereux; Esther Johnson.
STENDHAL: Marie Henri Beyle.
STIRLING, ARTHUR: Upton Sinclair.
STOICISM: Zeno; Cleanthes; Chrysippus.
STONEWALL JACKSON: Gen. Thomas J. Jackson.
STRAWBERRY HILL: Horace Walpole.
STRUTHER, JAN: Joyce Anstruther Maxtone Graham.
STUFFED PROPHET, THE: Grover Cleveland.
SULTAN OF SWAT: George Herman (Babe) Ruth.
SUN-KING, THE: Louis XIV.
SUPERB, THE: Winfield S. Hancock.
SUPERMEN: Nietzsche; George Bernard Shaw.
SURREALISM: Salvador Dali.
SUSPENSURUS: Charles Lamb.
SWEDISH NIGHTINGALE: Jenny Lind.
SYLVA, CARMEN: Elizabeth, Queen of Rumania.
SYMBOLISM: Rimbaud, Verlaine, Mallarmé, Maeterlinck, Verhaeren.
SYLVANDER: Robert Burns.
TALIESIN: Frank Lloyd Wright.
TEDDY THE FIRST: Theodore Roosevelt.
TÉMNY (THE BLIND): Basil II of Russia.
TEMPLETON, LAWRENCE: Sir Walter Scott.
TERMAGANT OF SPAIN: Elizabeth Farnese, Queen of Philip V.
TERRIBLE, THE: Ivan IV Vasilievich.
TERRIBLE TEDDY: Theodore Roosevelt.
TEUFELSDROECK, HERR: Thomas Carlyle.
THANET, OCTAVE: Alice French.
THAT MAN IN THE WHITE HOUSE: Franklin D. Roosevelt.
THAUMATURGUS OF THE WEST: Bernard Clairvaux.
THOUGHTFUL FATHER, THE: Nicholas Catinat.
THRYSIS: Arthur Hugh Clough.
THUNDERTENTRONCLE, ARMINIUS VON: Matthew Arnold.
TIBBS: Charles Dickens.
TIGER, THE: Georges Clemenceau.
TINKER OF ELSTOW: John Bunyan.
TINY TIM: Timothy L. Woodruff.
TITCOMB, TIMOTHY: Josiah Gilbert Holland.
TITMARSH, MICHAEL ANGELO: William Makepeace Thackeray.
TITO: Josip Broz (Brozovich).
TOM THUMB: Charles Sherwood Stratton.
TOOTHFUL TEDDY: Theodore Roosevelt.
TOPSY: William Morris.
TRACTARIANISM: Pusey, Newman, Keble, Froude.
TRAFALGAR, THE HERO OF: Admiral Horatio Nelson.
TRANSCENDENTALISM: Kant, Schelling, Fichte.
TRANSCENDENTALISTS: Emerson, Bronson Alcott, Theodore Parker, Margaret Fuller, Thoreau, Hawthorne, William Ellery Channing.
TRAVELLER, A: William Cullen Bryant.
TRENT AFFAIR, THE: James M. Mason, John Slidell, Capt. Charles Wilkes.
TRIPE, SIR ANDREW: Jonathan Swift.

TROTSKY, LEON: Leib (Lev) Davydovich Bronstein.
TRUST SLAYER, THE: Theodore Roosevelt.
TUMMY: Edward VII of England.
TWAIN, MARK: Samuel L. Clemens.
TYRANT OF SYRACUSE: Dionysius.
TYRANT OF THE CHERSONESE: Miltiades.
UNCLE BILLY: Gen. William Tecumseh Sherman.
UNCLE MARK: Mark Hanna.
UNCLE REMUS: Joel Chandler Harris.
UNCLE ROBERT: Robert E. Lee.
UNCOMMERCIAL TRAVELLER, THE: Charles Dickens.
UNCONDITIONAL SURRENDER: Ulysses S. Grant.
UN DES QUARANTES: Prosper Merimeé.
UNGODLY, THE: Aëtius of Antioch.
UNITED STATES: Ulysses S. Grant.
UNKNOWABLE, THE: Herbert Spenser.
UNREADY, THE: Ethelred, Saxon King of England.
URBAN, SYLVANUS: Edward Cave.
UTILITARIANISM: Jeremy Bentham; John Stuart Mill.
VALENTINO, RUDOLPH: Rodolpho d'Antonguola.
VANCE, ETHEL: Grace Zaring Stone.
VAN DINE, S.S.: Willard Huntington Wright.
VANOLIS, BYSSHE: James Thompson.
VATICAN, PRISONER OF THE: Pope Pius IX.
VEAL, MRS.: Daniel Defoe.
VELVET: Jan Brueghel the Elder.
VERNON, OLIVIA: Anne Brontë.
VERULAN: Francis Bacon.
VETO, MADAME: Marie Antoinette.
VINDEX: Samuel Adams.
VINEGAR JOE: Gen. Joseph W. Stilwell.
VIOLET, CORPORAL OR DADDY: Napoleon I.
VIRGIN QUEEN: Elizabeth I of England.
VOLTAIRE: François Marie Arouet.
VOYAGEUR, UN: George Sand.
WAGS, TWO: Frank Dempster Sherman, John Kendrick Bangs.
WAGSTAFF, THEOPHILE: William Makepeace Thackeray.
WAGSTAFFE, LAUNCELOT: Washington Irving.
WAITFORD, HANNAH: David Hume.
WALDEN, THE HERMIT OF: Henry David Thoreau.
WALTER: Tito.
WALTER, BRUNO: Bruno Schlesinger.
WARD, ARTEMUS: Charles Farrar Browne.
WARLIKE, THE: Frederick I, Elector of Saxony.
WARLOCK, PETER: Philip Arnold Heseltine.
WASH, REDBARN: George Bernard Shaw.
WASP OF TWICKENHAM, THE: Alexander Pope.
WATER DRINKER, A: Charles Lamb.
WATER POET, THE: John Taylor.
WEEPING PHILOSOPHER: Heraclitus.
WELLESLEY, LORD CHARLES: Charlotte Brontë.
WEST, REBECCA: Cicily Isabel Fairfield.
WETHERELL, ELIZABETH: Susan Bogert Warner.
W.H.: William Shakespeare.
WHITE, THE: Hugh, Count of Paris.
WIDOW, THE: Victoria of England.
WIDOW CAPET: Marie Antoinette.
WILBUR, HOMER: James Russell Lowell.
WILD BILL: William Joseph Donovan.
WILLIAMS, T. ZACHARIAH: Samuel Johnson.
WINNIE: Winston Churchill.
WINTER KING: Frederick V of Bohemia.

WISE, THE: Leo VI, Emperor of Eastern Roman Empire.
WISE, THE (Le Sage): Charles V of France.
WISEST FOOL IN CHRISTENDOM, THE: James VI and I.
WIZARD OF MENLO PARK, THE: Thomas A. Edison.
WIZARD OF THE NORTH: Sir Walter Scot
WOLFE, REGINALD: Thomas Frognall Dibdin
X.Y.Z.: Thomas De Quincey.
YANKEE: Jonathan Hastings.
YELLOWPLUSH, CHARLES JAMES: William Makepeace Thackeray.
YORICK: Laurence Sterne.
YOUNG, THE (Le Jeune): Louis VII of France
YOUNG AMERICA: Stephen A. Douglas, Edwin de Leon, George N. Sanders.
YOUNG CHEVALIER: Prince Charles Stewar
YOUNG ENGLAND: John Manners, Duke of Rutland; Disraeli.
YOUNGER PITT, THE: William Pitt (1759 1806).
YOUNGER SON: Edward Trelawney.
YOUNG GERMANY: Karl Gutzkow; Heinric Heine.
YOUNG IRELAND: Thomas Davis.
YOUNG ITALY: Guiseppe Mazzini.
YOUNG MAN: Charles II; Emperor William II.
YOUNG NAPOLEON, THE: Gen. George F McClellan.
YOUNG PRETENDER, THE: Prince Charle Edward Stuart.
YOUNG TURKEY: Mustafa Kemal; Enve Pasha.
YOUTH OF THIRTEEN, A: William Culle Bryant.
ZARATHUSTRA: Zoroaster; Nietzsche.
ZETA: James Anthony Froude.
ZZ: Louis Zangwill.

Pulitzer Prizes
See also **Awards**

Novels

(No awards in 1920, 1941, 1946, 1954, 1957
1918: *His Family*, by Ernest Poole.
1919: *The Magnificent Ambersons*, by Booth Tarkington.
1921: *The Age of Innocence*, by Edith Wharton
1922: *Alice Adams*, by Booth Tarkington.
1923: *One of Ours*, by Willa Cather.
1924: *The Able McLaughlins*, by Margaret Wilson.
1925: *So Big*, by Edna Ferber.
1926: *Arrowsmith*, by Sinclair Lewis (author declined award).
1927: *Early Autumn*, by Louis Bromfield.
1928: *The Bridge of San Luis Rey*, by Thornton Wilder.
1929: *Scarlet Sister Mary*, by Julia Peterkin
1930: *Laughing Boy*, by Oliver La Farge.
1931: *Years of Grace*, by Margaret Ayer Barnes
1932: *The Good Earth*, by Pearl Buck.
1933: *The Store*, by T. S. Stribling.
1934: *Lamb in His Bosom*, by Caroline Miller.
1935: *Now in November*, by Josephine Johnson
1936: *Honey in the Horn*, by H. L. Davis.
1937: *Gone with the Wind*, by Margaret Mitchell.
1938: *The Late George Apley*, by J. P. Marquand.
1939: *The Yearling*, by Marjorie Kinnan Rawlings.
1940: *The Grapes of Wrath*, by John Steinbeck
1942: *In This Our Life*, by Ellen Glasgow.
1943: *Dragon's Teeth*, by Upton Sinclair.
1944: *Journey in the Dark*, by Martin Flavin

1945: *A Bell for Adano*, by John Hersey.
1947: *All the King's Men*, by Robert Penn Warren.
1948: *Tales of the South Pacific*, by James Albert Michener.
1949: *Guard of Honor*, by James Gould Cozzens.
1950: *The Way West*, by Albert Bertram Guthrie, Jr.
1951: *The Town*, by Conrad Richter.
1952: *The Caine Mutiny*, by Herman Wouk.
1953: *The Old Man and the Sea*, by Ernest Hemingway.
1955: *A Fable*, by William Faulkner.
1956: *Andersonville*, by MacKinlay Kantor.

Drama

(No awards in 1919, 1942, 1944, 1947, 1951).
1918: *Why Marry?* by Jesse L. Williams.
1920: *Beyond the Horizon*, by Eugene O'Neill.
1921: *Miss Lulu Bett*, by Zona Gale.
1922: *Anna Christie*, by Eugene O'Neill.
1923: *Icebound*, by Owen Davis.
1924: *Hell-Bent for Heaven*, by Hatcher Hughes.
1925: *They Knew What They Wanted*, by Sidney Howard.
1926: *Craig's Wife*, by George Kelly.
1927: *In Abraham's Bosom*, by Paul Green.
1928: *Strange Interlude*, by Eugene O'Neill.
1929: *Street Scene*, by Elmer Rice.
1930: *The Green Pastures*, by Marc Connelly.
1931 *Alison's House*, by Susan Glaspell.
1932: *Of Thee I Sing*, by George S. Kaufman and Morrie Ryskind.
1933: *Both Your Houses*, by Maxwell Anderson.
1934: *Men in White*, by Sidney Kingsley.
1935: *The Old Maid*, by Zoë Akins.
1936: *Idiot's Delight*, by Robert E. Sherwood.
1937: *You Can't Take It With You*, by George S. Kaufman and Moss Hart.
1938: *Our Town*, by Thornton Wilder.
1939: *Abe Lincoln in Illinois*, by Robert E. Sherwood.
1940: *The Time of Your Life*, by William Saroyan (author declined award).
1941: *There Shall Be No Night*, by Robert E. Sherwood.
1943: *The Skin of Our Teeth*, by Thornton Wilder.
1945: *Harvey*, by Mary Chase.
1946: *State of the Union*, by Russel Crouse and Howard Lindsay.
1948: *A Streetcar Named Desire*, by Tennessee Williams.
1949: *Death of a Salesman*, by Arthur Miller.
1950: *South Pacific*, by Oscar Hammerstein II, Richard Rodgers, and Joshua Logan.
1952: *The Shrike*, by Joseph Kramm.
1953: *Picnic*, by William Inge.
1954: *The Teahouse of the August Moon*, by John Patrick.
1955: *Cat on a Hot Tin Roof*, by Tennessee Williams.
1956: *The Diary of Anne Frank*, by Frances Goodrich and Albert Hackett.
1957: *Long Day's Journey Into Night*, by Eugene O'Neill.

Poetry

(No award in 1946).
1922: *Collected Poems*, by Edwin Arlington Robinson.
1923: *The Harp-Weaver, and Other Poems*, by Edna St. Vincent Millay.
1924: *New Hampshire*, by Robert Frost.
1925: *The Man Who Died Twice*, by Edwin Arlington Robinson.
1926: *What's O'Clock?* by Amy Lowell.

1927: *Fiddler's Farewell*, by Leonore Speyer.
1928: *Tristram*, by Edwin Arlington Robinson.
1929: *John Brown's Body*, by Stephen Vincent Benét.
1930: *Selected Poems*, by Conrad Aiken.
1931: *Collected Poems*, by Robert Frost.
1932: *The Flowering Stone*, by George Dillon.
1933: *Conquistador*, by Archibald MacLeish.
1934: *Collected Verse*, by Robert Hillyer.
1935: *Bright Ambush*, by Audrey Wurdemann.
1936: *Strange Holiness*, by Robert Coffin.
1937: *A Further Range*, by Robert Frost.
1938: *Cold Morning Sky*, by Marya Zaturenska.
1939: *Selected Poems*, by John Gould Fletcher.
1940: *Collected Poems*, by Mark Van Doren.
1941: *Sunderland Capture*, by Leonard Bacon.
1942: *The Dust Which is God*, by William Rose Benét.
1943: *A Witness Tree*, by Robert Frost.
1944: *Western Star*, by Stephen Vincent Benét.
1945: *V-Letter and Other Poems*, by Karl Shapiro.
1947: *Lord Weary's Castle*, by Robert Lowell.
1948: *The Age of Anxiety*, by W. H. Auden.
1949: *Terror and Decorum*, by Peter Viereck.
1950: *Annie Allen*, by Gwendolyn Brooks.
1951: *Complete Poems*, by Carl Sandburg.
1952: *Collected Poems*, by Marianne Moore.
1953: *Collected Poems*, by Archibald MacLeish.
1954: *Collected Poems*, by Theodore Roethke.
1955: *Collected Poems*, by Wallace Stevens.
1956: *Poems, North and South*, by Elizabeth Bishop.
1957: *Things of This World*, by Richard Wilbur.

Biography

1917: Laura E. Richards, Maude Howe Elliott, in collaboration with Florence Howe Hall, *Julia Ward Howe*.
1918: William Cabell Bruce, *Benjamin Franklin, Self-Revealed*.
1919: Henry Adams (posthumous), *The Education of Henry Adams*.
1920: Albert J. Beveridge, *The Life of John Marshall*.
1921: Edward Bok, *The Americanization of Edward Bok*.
1922: Hamlin Garland, *A Daughter of the Middle Border* ("Family Chronicles," part 3).
1923: Burton J. Hendrick, *The Life and Letters of Walter H. Page*.
1924: Michael Pupin, *From Immigrant to Inventor*.
1925: Mark Antony DeWolfe Howe, *Barrett Wendel and His Letters*.
1926: Harvey Cushing, *The Life of Sir William Osler*.
1927: Emory Holloway, *Whitman — An Interpretation in Narrative*.
1928: Charles Edward Russell, *The American Orchestra and Theodore Thomas*.
1929: Burton J. Hendrick, *The Training of an American: The Earlier Life and Letters of Walter H. Page*.
1930: Marquis James, *The Raven, a Biography of Sam Houston*.
1931: Henry James, *Charles W. Eliot*.
1932: Henry F. Pringle, *Theodore Roosevelt*.
1933: Allan Nevins, *Grover Cleveland*.
1934: Tyler Dennett, *John Hay*.
1935: Douglas Southall Freeman, *R. E. Lee*.
1936: Ralph Barton Perry, *The Thought and Character of William James*.
1937: Allan Nevins, *Hamilton Fish — The Inner History of the Great Administration*.
1938: Odell Shepard, *Pedlar's Progress;* Marquis James, *Andrew Jackson*.
1939: Carl Van Doren, *Benjamin Franklin*.

1940: Ray Stannard Baker, *Woodrow Wilson —
Life and Letters.*
1941: Ola Elizabeth Winslow, *Jonathan Edwards.*
1942: Forrest Wilson, *Crusader in Crinoline* (Harriet Beecher Stowe).
1943: Samuel Eliot Morison, *Admiral of the
Ocean Sea* (Columbus).
1944: Carleton Mabie, *The American Leonardo:
The Life of Samuel F. B. Morse.*
1945: Russell Baline Nye, *George Bancroft:
Brahmin Rebel.*
1946: Linnie Marsh Wolfe, *Son of the Wilderness* (John Muir).
1947: William Allen White, *The Autobiography
of William Allen White* (posthumous).
1948: Margaret Clapp, *Forgotten First Citizen:
John Bigelow.*
1949: Robert E. Sherwood, *Roosevelt and Hopkins.*
1950: Samuel Flagg Bemis, *John Quincy Adams
and the Foundations of American Foreign
Policy.*
1951: Margaret Louise Coit, *John C. Calhoun:
American Portrait.*
1952: Merlo J. Pusey, *Charles Evans Hughes.*
1953: David J. Mays, *Edmund Pendleton, 1721-
1803.*
1954: Charles A. Lindbergh, *The Spirit of St.
Louis.*
1955: William S. White, *The Taft Story* (Robert
A. Taft).
1956: Talbot F. Hamlin, *Benjamin Henry
Latrobe.*
1957: Joseph Kennedy, *Profiles in Courage.*

History

1917: Jean Jules Jusserand, *With Americans of
Past and Present Days.*
1918: James Ford Rhodes, *A History of the
Civil War.*
1919: None.
1920: Justin Harvey Smith, *The War with
Mexico.*
1921: Rear Admiral William Snowden Sims, *The
Victory at Sea.*
1922: James Truslow Adams, *The Founding of
New England.*
1923: Charles Warren, *The Supreme Court in
United States History.*
1924: Charles Howard McIlwain, *The American
Revolution: A Constitutional Interpretation.*
1925: Frederic Logan Paxson, *A History of the
American Frontier.*
1926: Edward Channing, *History of the United
States,* Volume VI.
1927: Samuel Flagg Bemis, *Pinckney's Treaty.*
1928: Vernon Louis Parrington, *Main Currents
in American Thought,* first two of three
volumes.
1929: Fred Albert Shannon, *The Organization
and Administration of the Union Army, 1861-
1865.*
1930: Claude Halstead Van Tyne, *The War of
Independence, American Phase.*
1931: Bernadotte Everly Schmitt, *The Coming
of the War, 1914.*
1932: Gen. John Joseph Pershing, *My Experiences in the World War.*
1933: Frederick Jackson Turner, *The Significance
of Sections in American History.*
1934: Herbert Sebastian Agar, *The People's
Choice.*
1935: Charles McLean Andrews, *The Colonial
Period of American History.*
1936: Andrew Cunningham McLaughlin, *A Constitutional History of the United States.*
1937: Van Wyck Brooks, *The Flowering of New
England.*

1938: Paul Herman Buck, *The Road to Reunion.*
1939: Frank Luther Mott, *A History of American
Magazines.*
1940: Carl Sandburg, *Abraham Lincoln: The War
Years.*
1941: Marcus Lee Hansen, *The American Migration* (posthumous).
1942: Margaret Leech, *Reveille in Washington.*
1943: Esther Forbes, *Paul Revere and the World
He Lived In.*
1944: Merle Curti, *The Growth of American
Thought.*
1945: Stephen Bonsal, *Unfinished Business.*
1946: Arthur Meier Schlesinger, *The Age of
Jackson.*
1947: James Phinney Baxter, *Scientists Against
Time.*
1948: Bernard De Voto, *Across the Wide Missouri.*
1949: Roy F. Nichols, *The Disruption of
American Democracy.*
1950: O. W. Larkin, *Art and Life in America.*
1951: R. Carlyle Buley, *The Old Northwest,
Pioneer Period 1815-1840.*
1952: Oscar Handlin, *The Uprooted.*
1953: George Dangerfield, *The Era of Good
Feeling.*
1954: Bruce Catton, *A Stillness at Appomattox.*
1955: Paul Horgan, *The Rio Grande in North
American History.*
1956: Richard Hofstadter, *The Age of Reform.*
1957: George Kennan, *Russia Leaves the War.*

Music

1943: William Schuman, *Secular Cantata No. 2,
A Free Song.*
1944: Howard Hanson, *Symphony No. 4, Op.
34.* Special award to *Oklahoma!* by Richard
Rodgers and Oscar Hammerstein II.
1945: Aaron Copland, *Appalachian Spring.*
1946: Leo Sowerby, *The Canticle of the Sun.*
1947: Charles E. Ives, *Symphony No. 3.*
1948: Walter Piston, *Symphony No. 3.*
1949: Virgil Thomson, *Louisiana Story.*
1950: Gian-Carlo Menotti, *The Consul.*
1951: Douglas MacDowell Moore, *Giants in the
Earth.*
1952: Gail Kubik, *Symphony Concertante.*
1953: None.
1954: Quincy Porter, *Concerto for Two Pianos
and Orchestra.*
1955: Gian-Carlo Menotti, *The Saint of Bleecker
Street.*
1956: Ernest Toch, *Symphony No. 3.*
1957: Norman Dello Joio, *Meditation on Ecclesiastes.*

Religious Allusions, References,
and Symbols

ADVAITA: Doctrine of non-dualism in Vedic
philosophy, holding that spirit and matter,
self and non-self are manifestations of the
One Reality.
AGNUS DEI (LAMB OF GOD): Refers to St
John I. 29: "Behold the Lamb of God. Behold
him who taketh away the sins of the world,"
which John exclaims when he sees Christ
coming towards him.
ALPHA: See The Letters Alpha and Omega.
AHIMSA: Hindu doctrine prohibiting injury to
any form of sentient life.
AMENTA: The Egyptian hell.
THE ANCHOR: Among the earliest of Christian
symbols, used on catacombs and on ancient
gems, the anchor was an emblem of steadfast
hope and untiring patience. Heb. VI, 19.

THE APPLE: In Christian art, the apple symbolizes the fall of Adam.

ARALU: The Babylonian hell.

THE ARK: See the Ship.

THE ARK OF THE COVENANT: In the sanctuary of the Jewish Temple, the oblong chest in which were kept the two sacred stone tablets given to Moses on Mount Sinai. See the Ten Commandments.

ATMAN (ATMA): Hindu term which corresponds to the Christian soul, the Greek Psyche, and the Moslem Ruh; the death-surviving element.

AUREOLE: See Vesica Pisces.

AVATAR (AVATARA): Hindu term describing the incarnation, or taking on of bodily form, of a Master of life, i. e., one who has overcome Sangsara or Samsara (the Hindu cycle of births and deaths in which man is driven on by the force of Karma until, by gaining enlightenment, he frees himself from the revolving wheel); the most celebrated are the avatars of Vishnu, ten in number, four of which are subjects of Puranas, or sacred poems: in the Matsya avatar, Vishnu appeared in the form of a fish, to preserve the good king Satyavrata and his family while a flood destroyed the wicked people of the earth; in the Kurma or Kachyapa avatar, the god appeared in the form of a tortoise and supported Mount Mandara on his back while the gods churned the sea for the divine ambrosia; in the Varaha avatar, Vishnu appeared as a boar. again to save the earth from a flood; in Nara-sinah, he came as a man-lion to destroy the king who had been endowed by the gods with universal dominion as a reward for his austerities; he appeared in the Vamana avatar as a dwarf, and in the Parasurama as the son of Jamadagni; the seventh avatar took place after the Satya Yuga, or Golden Age, when Vishnu came as Rama, Lakshmana, Bharata, and Satrughna, the four sons of King Dasaratha, and destroyed the demons which infested the earth (the adventures of Rama in this avatar are recorded in the *Ramayana*); his appearance as Krishna in the eight avatar is told in the *Mahabharata*; in his ninth avatar, Vishnu appeared as Buddha; the tenth, or Kalki Avatara, has not yet occurred; in it Vishnu will appear on a white steed, armed with a sword, and bring the present Iron Age, or Kali Yuga, to a close, after which he will sleep on the waters, produce Brahma, and begin the cycle of a new order.

AVIDYA: The path of ignorance in Brahminism, leading to the recurrent lives and deaths of Sangsara, the opposite of Vidya, or the path of knowledge, which leads to Nirvana.

THE AX: In Christian art, a symbol of martyrdom.

BA: Egyptian bird-like figure which represents the soul.

THE BANNER, OR STANDARD: Symbol of victory in Christian art, belonging to military saints and to those who carried the gospel abroad. It is also carried by Christ after the Resurrection. St. Reparata and St. Ursula are the only female saints who are pictured with banners.

THE BEATITUDES: The eight (or nine) sayings of Matthew V, 3-12 spoken by Christ in the Sermon on the Mount: 1.) Blessed are the poor in spirit, for theirs is the kingdom of heaven; 2.) Blessed are the meek, for they shall possess the land; 3.) Blessed are they that mourn, for they shall be comforted; 4.) Blessed are they that hunger and thirst after justice, for they shall have their fill; 5.) Blessed are the merciful, for they shall obtain mercy; 6.) Blessed are the clean of heart, for they shall see God; 7.) Blessed are the peacemakers, for they shall be called the children of God; 8.) Blessed are they that suffer persecution for justice's sake, for theirs is the kingdom af heaven. A ninth is sometimes constructed from the following verses: 9.) Blessed are ye when they shall revile and persecute you and speak all that is evil against you, untruly, for my sake; Be glad and rejoice, for your reward in heaven is very great.

BEHESTH: The Persian heaven or Elysium.

THE BELL: In Christian art, a demonifuge, believed to have power to exorcise spirits.

BODHI: In the Buddhist system, wisdom; the Bodhi Path is the Path of Wisdom.

BODHISATTVA: In Buddhism, one who has progressed far enough along the path to Buddhahood to be considered as a potential Buddha, or Enlightened One.

BODIES, LITTLE NAKED: Symbols, in Christian art, of the souls of men. They are seen in pictures of St. Michael in his role as Lord of Souls. They are also placed in the hand which symbolizes God the Father.

THE BOOK: In Christian art, a book in the hands of St. Stephen represents the Old Testament; the evangelists are pictured carrying their own writings; in other cases it is the Scriptures or a symbol of the learning and writings of a particular saint.

BO-TREE: Buddha attained Enlightenment while meditating beneath the Bo-Tree, and the *ficus religiosa* is sacred to the Buddhists of India.

BUBBULU: In Babylonian mythology, the dark of the moon, when evil spirits were especially powerful.

BUDDHA AND BUDDHISM: Buddhism was founded by Siddhattha Gautama, known as Buddha, or the Enlightened, who was born c. 560 B. C. at Kapila, near the sacred city of Benares, son of a chief of the Sakiya clan; at the age of 29 he left his home and became a religious mendicant, and lived for the following six years with Brahmins, practicing asceticism and meditation; suddenly, while he was meditating under the Bo-Tree, illumination came to him; for the remainder of his life he lived as a recluse, and did not seek out a following; but students did come to him, and, in the course of his visits with them, he developed the system of philosophy which is summed up in his statement of the Middle Path: avoid the two extremes of self-gratification and self-mortification, and live by these Four Noble Truths: 1). All individual existence is misery; 2). The cause of this misery is attachment to sense-perceptions; 3). There is need to become unattached and passionless; and 4). To follow the Eight-Fold Path, which consists in: Right Views, Right Aspirations, Right Speech, Right Conduct, Right Means of Livelihood, Right Effort, Right Mindfulness, Right Contemplation; Buddha denied the existence of a permanent soul in the five aggregates of man (the Skandhas), and held that any permanent principle must be outside these, free of the changes which result from cause and effect (Karma); therefore, there exists a permanent something, a "non-born, non-becoming, non-created, non-caused" which cannot be reached by speculation but may be attained by the saint through his way of life; Buddha refused to answer questions of merely intellectual inquirers, though he was an adept at dialectic and suited his discourses to the capacities of his audiences; he held that the only important problem was that of deliverance from ignorance, sorrow, and suffering, and that this liberation would come to anyone who followed the Path; the teaching of Buddha was wholly practical and did not, like Brahminism and Christianity, lead towards theological definition and metaphysical speculation; in India, Buddhism was the predominant religion until about the 10th Century A. D.

THE CANDELABRUM: In Christian art, the candelabrum is the emblem of Christ and His Church, as the light of the world. With seven branches it refers to the seven gifts of the Holy Ghost, q.v., or to the seven churches (Rev. I, 20).

THE CANDLE: See the Lamp, Lantern, or Taper.

CASTE: In India, the division of society into classes; the chief castes are: Brahmins (priestly), Ksatriyas (warrior), Vaisyas (serf), and Sudras (menial); there are some 20 or more distinct castes, and expulsion from caste results in social ostracism.

CHAKRAVATIN: A Yogi who has mastered completely all of his inner forces.

THE CHALICE: In Christian art, symbolizes faith.

THE CHURCH: Generally, in Christian art, a church is usually a replica of a particular church, of which the bearer was the founder or first bishop; but in the hands of St. Jerome, it signifies his love and care for the whole Christian Church.

THE CIRCLE: Emblem of Eternity and of the Eternal God. Hermes Trisbegistus says: "God is a circle, whose center is every where, but whose circumference is nowhere to be found." The Circle was anciently represented by a serpent with its tail in its mouth.

THE CLUB: In Christian art, a symbol of martyrdom.

THE COMMANDMENTS: See the Ten Commandments.

CONFUCIUS: Confucius, or K'ung-Tsze (551-487 B.C.) was an official in Lu, his native state, who led a lifetime of no particular moment and was unrecognized, until two centuries after his death, as China's greatest teacher, and one of the outstanding sages of all times; he taught that virtue is natural and that man is by nature good; the principle which developed the best in man was self-control, for if each man does his duty, peace and equilibrium must result; the supreme Confucian virtue is "Jin," which is to "love all men and not do to others what you would not wish done to you," and appears to include also courage, reverence, justice, loyalty, and all of the idealistic positive virtues; the system of Confucius was agnostic.

CORN: See Ears of Corn and Bunches of Grapes.

THE CORPORAL AND SPIRITUAL WORKS OF MERCY: These are the traditional acts motivated by the virtue of mercy when it is considered as a radiation or emanation of divine love acting as a supplement to human weakness. For the specific works of mercy see The Corporal Works of Mercy and The Spiritual Works of Mercy.

THE CORPORAL WORKS OF MERCY: 1) To feed the hungry; 2) To give drink to the thirsty; 3) To clothe the naked; 4) To visit the prisoner; 5) To shelter the homeless; 6) To visit the sick; 7) To bury the dead.

CROSS: There are two principal forms of the Cross, the Latin and the Greek. The Latin Cross, or crux immissa, consisting of a longer upright than a crossbar, with the cross-bar mounted about one-quarter of the way down from the top of the upright, is the representation of the tree on which Christ suffered His crucifixion, and is the most prevalent cross in the works of art of the Latin (Western) Church. It was formerly called the Cross of the Passion, and is the Episcopal Cross. The Greek Cross, consisting of an upright and cross-bar of equal length which intersect at the center of the upright, is more spiritual in idea than the Latin Cross. It is said to represent the ministry of Christ, with the four equal arms representing the glad tidings of the Gospel spread throughout the entire world, as taught by the four evangelists and symbolized by the four arms pointing in the direction of the four winds of heaven. It is distinguished by its ornamental character and nearly all of the representations of the Cross, either heraldic or architectural, are modifications of this form. On the other hand, when the Cross is introduced as an accessory into pictures, it almost invariably takes the Latin form. The Cross of Calvary belongs to the Latin type, and is distinguished by being elevated on three steps, which are, symbolically, the three Christian graces of Faith, Hope, and Charity. The Cross, Patriarchal, is drawn with two horizontal bars; though usually said to be of the Latin type of cross, it is really a union of both Latin and Greek types, and is also called the Archbishop's Cross, or Cross of Lorraine. The Cross Crosslet in formed by four Latin crosses which are joined together at their bases. The Tau Cross, or St. Anthony's Cross, is called after the form and name of the Greek letter T. Traditionally it is the Tau Cross, rather than the Latin Cross, which is said to have been the cross on which Christ died. It is of very ancient origin, and is found among Egyptian hieroglyphics. The Mark spoken of by the prophet Ezechiel (Chap. IX, v, 4) is also supposed to be the Tau Cross. The Cross of Jerusalem, or Cross Potent, is the unity of four Tau crosses and, with four Greek crosses between the right angles of the four arms, forms the heraldic coat of Jerusalem (described technically, it is, on a field Argent, a cross potent, between four crosslets, or little crosses, Or—this exceptional display of metal upon metal being justified by reference to Psalm lxviii, 13). The eight-pointed Maltese Cross is a unity of four triangles, each of which has an even wedge-shape cut in the base. The eight points are said to symbolize the eight beatitudes. The Cross Patée resembles the Maltese Cross in form, and is often drawn and mistaken for it; but the triangles of the Cross Patée have regular bases and the intersection of the four apexes, where the triangles are joined together, is replaced by a small circle. St. Andrew's Cross, in shape like a printed capital letter X, is the national Cross of Scotland; combined with the Cross of St. George (see below), it forms the British Union Jack. The Cross of St. George is of the Greek form, and was anciently the badge of the kings of England. The Cross of Iona, Irish Cross (Celtic Cross) a heavy-bodied Latin or Greek Cross mounted upon a smaller circle, is often said to be more Greek than Latin in origin, and is used as an argument for an Eastern rather than Western introduction of Christianity into the British Islands. The Cross of Constantine is formed of the first two letters (X and P) with which the name of Christ is spelled in Greek. It is more like a monogram than a cross, and was used by the Emperor Constantine as a device upon his shield and upon his coins. As a symbol, it was often used by the early Christians, and is found on sepulchres in the Roman catacombs. The Monogram Cross, a heavy-bodied Greek

Cross with letters running through the arms, is an emblem of Christ as King of Heaven, Leader of Men, Prince of Peace, and Light of the World. In spite of these associations with Christianity, the cross did not, as a symbol, originate with the crucifixion of Christ. It has been discovered as an ornamental device in Carthage, in Scandinavia, in ancient Egypt and Rome, and among the Aztecs. In Cozumel it was an object of worship; in Tabasco it symbolized the rain-god; and in Palinque it is sculptured with a child held up adoring it.

THE CROWN: Symbol of supremacy and victory. In Christian art, it is used in representations of the Virgin as Queen of Heaven and of the Angels; when used with a martyr, it signifies victory over sin and death, and is usually accompanied by a palm branch; or it may indicate that a saint was of royal blood, in which case it is usually placed at the feet. In Jewish art, it is the symbol of a bride.

THE CRUCIFIXION: See the Passion and Crucifixion of Christ.

DAIBUTSU: Any large idol of Buddha, but especially the mammoth bronze image at Kamakura in Japan, dating from 1252.

DAI NICHI: In Japanese Buddhism, the Absolute, or the Ultimate Reality.

THE DECALOGUE: See the Ten Commandments.

DEMIURGE: In Platonic philosophy, a term used to denote the creator of the world; in Gnostic teaching, a creative spirit which is subordinate to God, and used to distinguish the creator of the universe from the Supreme God, hence, the world-soul.

THE DOUBLE TRIANGLE, OR SIX-POINTED STAR: Symbolizes Him who is the Creator of the elements, because the intersecting triangles were anciently held to represent the elements of fire and water.

THE DOVE: Emblem of the Holy Spirit and ancient symbol of innocence. Cant. VI. 9.

THE DRAGON: In Christian art, a symbol for sin and paganism.

EARS OF CORN AND BUNCHES OF GRAPES: In Christian art, symbols of the Eucharist.

ELYSIUM: See Heaven.

FIRE AND FLAMES: In Christian art, symbols of zeal and fervent souls; also, of the sufferings of martyrdom.

THE FISH: Refers to Christ, Who was called by many ancient writers "The Fish," because the first letters of the Greek sentence for *Jesus Christ, the Son of God, the Savior* form the letters of the *ichthus*, the Greek word for fish. The fish also symbolizes the regenerating waters of baptism, because the believer caught by those sent to be the "fishers of men" is figuratively a "little fish."

FIVE-POINTED STAR: Figured on the banner of Antiochus Soter and used throughout Asia in ancient times as a charm against witchcraft, by Pythagoras as an emblem of health, and by the Jews as a symbol of safety. A later popular Christian supposition held that this figure, when placed against the body, would so align itself that the angles pointed to the places where Christ was wounded; in time the star was considered a *Fuga Demonum*, because devils were thought to be afraid of it. Also called the Pentalpha, because it contains five repetitions of the letter A, and the endless triangle. The Magical Pentalpha figures in the west window on the south aisle of Westminster Abbey.

THE FIVE WOUNDS OF CHRIST: The wounds of Christ are symbolized by the hands and feet with a heart in the center, each pierced with one wound, or by a heart alone with five wounds.

THE FLAMING HEART: Symbol, in Christian art, of fervent piety and spiritual love.

THE FOUR HORSEMEN OF THE APOCALYPSE: The four riders of the four horses, symbols of the evils of war, mentioned in Chap. 6 of *Revelation* (or the *Apocalypse*). The horsemen are: Conquest, on a white horse; Death, on a pale horse; Famine, on a black horse; Slaughter, on a red horse.

FRUIT: In the hands of St. Catherine, fruit symbolizes "the fruit of the spirit."

FRUITS OF THE HOLY GHOST (OR OF THE SPIRIT): The fruits of the Holy Ghost are defined theologically as virtuous acts performed under the influence of grace and accompanied by a certain spiritual joy. As products of grace, which is given by the Holy Ghost, they are called fruits of the Third Person of the Christian Trinity. St. Paul (Gal. V, 22) enumerates twelve fruits of the Holy Ghost: charity, joy, peace, patience, kindness (or benignity), goodness, faith, modesty, and continency. This list has been expanded by tradition to include: long-suffering, mildness, and chastity. See also Gifts of the Holy Ghost.

GANGES (GANGA): The sacred river of India.

GAYATRI: See Savitra.

GEHENNA: A valley near Jerusalem where sacrifices were made to Moloch in early times; the name was afterwards given to the place of punishment of the dead.

GIFTS OF THE HOLY GHOST (OR OF THE SPIRIT): The gifts of the Holy Ghost are defined theologically as permanent dispositions of the soul that encourage response to the inspirations of the Holy Ghost. They are called gifts because they are given to the soul with grace at Baptism and Confirmation. Isaiah (Is. XI, 2) lists seven gifts: wisdom, understanding, counsel, fortitude, knowledge, piety, and fear of the Lord. See also Fruits of the Holy Ghost.

GRAPES: See Ears of Corn and Bunches of Grapes.

GURU: Hindu name for a moral and spiritual adviser.

HALO: See Vesica Pisces.

HEAVEN: In the Judeo-Christian cosmology, Heaven denotes the home of God and of His Angels ("Heaven is My throne," in both Isa. LXVI, 1 and Matt. V, 34). It is also used in the Bible and elsewhere to designate the upper air, which is the reference in such expressions as "the fowls of heaven," "the dew of heaven," "the clouds of heaven," "the cities are walled up to heaven" (Deut. I, 28), "Come, let us make a city and a tower, the top whereof may reach to heaven" (Gen. XI, 4), and, in Gen. I, 14, where the starry firmament is specified, "Let there be lights in the firmament of heaven." In the Ptolemaic system, the heavens were successive spheres or rings of space that encircled the central earth, each revolving at a different speed. The first seven were those of the so-called planets: the Moon, Mercury, Venus, the Sun, Mars, Jupiter, and Saturn; the eighth was the firmament of heaven containing all the fixed stars; the ninth was the crystalline sphere, invented by Hipparchus (2nd cent. b.c.) to account for the precession of the equinoxes. These were known as the Nine Heavens. The tenth — added much later — was the *primum mobile*.

Sometimes she deemed that Mars had from above

Left his fifth heaven, the powers of men
to prove.
          Hoole: *Orlando Furioso*, Bk. XIII.
The Mohammedans divided the realm of the
blessed into a system of seven heavens:
The first heaven is of pure silver, and
here the stars, each with its angel warder, are
hung out like lamps on golden chains. It
is the abode of Adam and Eve. *The second
heaven* is of pure gold and is the domain
of John the Baptist and Jesus. *The third
heaven* is of pearl, and is allotted to
Joseph. Here Azrael, the angel of death, is
stationed, and is forever writing in a large
book or blotting words out. The former are
the names of persons born, the latter those
of the newly dead. *The fourth heaven* is of
white gold, and is Enoch's. Here dwells the
Angel of Tears, whose height is "500 days'
Journey," and he sheds ceaseless tears for the
sins of man. *The fifth heaven* is of silver
and is Aaron's. Here dwells the Avenging
Angel, who presides over elemental fire.
The sixth heaven is composed of ruby
and garnet, and is presided over by Moses.
Here dwells the Guardian Angel of heaven
and earth, half snow and half fire. *The seventh
heaven* is formed of divine light beyond
the power of tongue to describe, and is ruled
by Abraham. Each inhabitant is bigger than
the whole earth, and has 70,000 heads, each
head 70,000 mouths, each mouth 70,000 tongues,
and each tongue speaks 70,000 languages, all
for ever employed in chanting the praises
of the Most High. TO BE IN THE SEVENTH
HEAVEN: To be supremely happy. The Cabalists maintained that there are seven heavens,
each rising in happiness above the other, the
seventh being the abode of God and the
highest class of angels. In Greek and Latin
poetry, heaven was Elysium, or the Elysian
fields. Homer describes Elysium as an ideally
happy land, and places it near Ocean on the
western part of the earth, where it formed
no part of the world of the dead. The Latin
poets identified Elysium with the lower world,
the abode of the blessed souls of the dead
departed. For the names of the heavens of
the different religions of the world see also
Gods and Goddesses: A Checklist of Their
Works and Attributes.
HERESY: Any doctrine opposed to the authorized teaching of the Church or society of
which one is a member is considered a heresy;
the Catholic is a heretic to the Protestant,
and vice versa; the Communist is a heretic
to the Capitalist, and vice versa; the word
derives from a Greek word, *hairesis*, meaning
choice, and refers to a man who makes his
own choice; the chief Christian heresies of
the early Christian centuries were: 1st Century
the Simonians (from Simon Magus), the Cerinthians, the Ebionites; 2nd Century: the Basilidians, the Cainites, the Marcionites; 3rd
Century: the Patripassians, the Novatians, the
Sabellians, the Manicheans; 4th Century: the
Arians, the Apollinarians, the Collyridians, the
Seleucians, the Jovinianists, the Bonosians; 5th
Century: the Pelagians, the Nestorians, the
Eutychians; 6th Century: the Predestinarians,
the Agnoetae, the Monothelites.
HOLY DAYS OF OBLIGATION: In the Catholic Church, days on which attendance at Mass
is obligatory. The following days are prescribed for the Universal Church: All Sundays
of the year; Circumcision, Jan. 1; Epiphany,
Jan. 6; St. Joseph, Mar. 19; Ascension, 40
days after Easter; Corpus Christi, Thursday
after Trinity Sunday; Sts. Peter and Paul,
June 29; Assumption, Aug. 15; All Saints,

Nov. 1; Immaculate Conception, Dec. 8;
Christmas, Dec. 25. In the United States,
Epiphany, St. Joseph, Corpus Christi, and
Sts. Peter and Paul, are not observed as
Holydays of Obligation. In Canada, St. Joseph,
Corpus Christi, Sts. Peter and Paul, and the
Assumption are not Holydays of Obligation.
I.H.S.: The abbreviated form of the Holy Name,
the mark over the middle letter being the
form of contraction. The monogram is of
Greek origin, the letters I.H.S. or I.H.C.
being the English representation of the Greek
letters J E S. Sometimes, when drawn with
capital letters, a cross, representing the sign of
contraction, is made through the letter H.
This has occasioned the supposition that the
letters could stand for *Jesus Hominum Salvator*
or *Jesus Hominum Consolator* (Jesus the Savior
— or Consoler — of Men), or even for
I Have Suffered. But the origin of the cipher
is Greek, not Latin or English. It was once
customary to use the monogram at the beginning of the alphabet in old horn-books, and
at the head of documents and parish records.
ISVARA: The supreme soul of Yoga. See Yoga.
JANNAB: The Garden of Paradise in Mohammedan myth.
JIN: In Confucianism, the highest virtue, which
is "to love all men and not to do to others
what you would not wish done to you." See
Confucius.
JUGGERNAUT (JAGGANATH): The huge
image of Vishnu which is kept in the temple
of Puri in Orissa, and once a year drawn
through the streets during a festival parade;
in earlier times, many devotees are said to
have flung themselves beneath the wheels in
a passionate climax of their religious ecstasy,
though contemporary investigators generally
hold that such demonstrations are an invention
of popular mythology.
KA: In the religion of ancient Egypt, a recurrent term of ambiguous meaning; it may
refer to the alter ego or double of a man,
the essence or spirit from which he derives
life; it may connote the spirit or ghost of
a man which is released by his death and
symbolized in the images of the dead buried
in Egyptian tombs; or it may signify the
guardian angel or genius which rejoins a man
when he dies.
KAABA (KA'BA): The goal of Moslem pilgrims, the building in the courtyard of El
Haram, the Great Mosque of Mecca, in which
is kept a small black sacred stone, thought to
be of meteoric origin.
KARMA: In Buddhism and Hinduism, the consequences of the interplay of cause and effect,
especially as the future existence of a man
is determined by his present acts. Roughly,
the equivalent of the Mohammedan Kismet.
KISMET (KISMAT): The Mohammedan fate or
destiny. See Karma.
LABORERS IN THE VINEYARD: In Christian
art, the laborers in the vineyard represent
those Christians who work in the vineyard
of the Lord.
THE LAMB OF GOD: See Agnus Dei.
THE LAMP, LANTERN, OR TAPER: All are
symbols of piety, but, when carried by St.
Lucia, the significance is that of heavenly
wisdom, or of spiritual light.
THE LANCE: In Christian art, a symbol of
martyrdom.
THE LETTERS ALPHA AND OMEGA: The
Greek capital letters A and O are used to
represent Him Who is "beginning and ending,
the first and the last."
THE LILY: Symbol of chastity and purity.
THE LION: In popular Eastern myth, the lion

cub is supposedly always still-born, and is
licked for three days by its sire until it comes
to life; the lion, therefore, became a symbol
of resurrection. As the "lion of Judah," it is
a symbol for Christ.

MAYA: In Hindu speculation, the term for
illusion, applied specifically to the world of
sense-perception and opposed to the Reality
or the One which is Brahma.

MOKSHA (MUKTI): In Hindu theology, the
word for salvation.

MUSHRUSSU: The dragon in Babylonian icono-
graphy, depicted with Ishtar on the Ishtar
gate of Babylon.

NAMES OF GOD: The Old Testament customarily lists seven "holy names of God." They
can be classified in three different groups:
(1) three referring to the relations of God to
His creation; (2) three referring to the chief
aspects of His intrinsic perfections; and (3)
the one name that is most characteristic of
God as the expression of His divine essence.
The three names that refer to the relations
of God to His creation are: (1) EL: The
oldest and most common name, used by the
Semites. It is believed to be the derivation
of an ancient word-root meaning "strong," and
is ordinarily used in combination with the
definite article, as "The El," or with a word
expressing some particular attribute of God,
such as "El Hai" ("Living God"), "El Hasha-
main" ("God of Heaven"), or, "El Elohim"
("God of Gods"). This name, however, is also
used in ways thought to have no specific
reference to God, and may designate other
gods than Jehovah. (2) ELOHIM: This occurs
as one of the two most common appellations
of God in the Old Testament. It is a plural
form (the singular, Eloah, is used in poetry),
and was also used to designate other gods and
superior beings, sometimes appearing in such
combination as "Elohim Sabaoth" ("God of
Hosts"). (3) ADONAI: It is derived from
the word meaning "to judge," and meaning
literally "My Lord." In the Old Testament,
Adonai refers to God alone. The three names
that refer to attributes of the Divine Perfection are: (1) SHADDAI: It is derived from
a root-word meaning "to employ force," and
usually is understood as "almighty" or "omni-
potent." It was customarily used with the
article, or in combination with El. (2) ELYON:
It is derived from the verb meaning "to mount,"
and is understood as "the Most High." It
appears frequently in combination with El.
(3) QADOSH: This name, meaning "the Holy
One," was used principally by the Prophets,
particularly Isaiah, to emphasize the peerless
sanctity of God. JHVH: This is the one
name most characteristic of the essence of
God, and more important than the other
names. The four consonants of this sacred word
were called the Tetragrammaton and they are
used over 6000 times in the Hebrew version
of the Bible as a purely literary title, never
spoken aloud. Like the Greeks and Romans,
who evolved special names to get around
specific references to certain deities, such as
Eumenides for the Erinys (or Furies), and
Mulciber for Vulcan, the Jews became accustomed to use Adonai in place of JHVH
in conversation. They also wrote JHVH with
the vowels of the word Adonai, which led
to the later supposition that the Name of
Names should be pronounced Jehovah. It is
now believed that the correct pronunciation
should be Yă·vä, and that the name was
derived from the verb-root "to be." If this
is true, JHVH means "He Who Is."

NARAKA: The hell of the Hindus, where sinners are punished, according to the sins, in
one of eight different "circles" or divisions.

NIMBUS: See Vesica Pisces.

THE NINE-POINTED STAR: Alludes to the
fruits of the Holy Spirit, q.v.

NIRVANA: In Buddhism, Nirvana is the peace
that surpasses all understanding, enlightenment, and the goal of all striving. The Hindu
Nirvana is the fulfillment of the individual
in his reunion with Brahma.

THE NOBLE ENLIGHTENED PATH: See
Path, The Noble Enlightened.

OLIVE BRANCHES: See Palm and Olive
Branches.

OMEGA: See The Letters Alpha and Omega.

ORACLE: (Lat. oraculum, from orare, "to speak,
to pray.") The answer of a god or inspired
priest to an inquiry respecting the future;
the deity giving responses; the place where the
deity could be consulted. Hence, a person
whose sayings are regarded as profound; or,
ironically, an infallible, dogmatic person. In
ancient Greece and Rome oracles were very
numerous and collected high fees for their
services. The most famous were: The Oracles
of Apollo at Delphi (where the priestess was
called the Pythoness), at Delos, and at Colchis;
The Oracle of Diana at Colchis; The Oracles
of Aesculapius at Epidaurus and at Rome;
The Oracles of Hercules at Athens and at
Gades; The Oracles of Jupiter at Dodona,
at Ammon in Libya, and at Crete; The Oracle
of Mars in Thrace; The Oracle of Minerva
at Mycenae; The Oracle of Pan in Arcadia;
The Oracle of Triphonius in Boeotia (where
only men made reponses); and The Oracles
of Venus at Paphos, at Aphaca, and in many
other places. In most of the temples, women,
sitting on a tripod, made the responses, many
of which were either ambiguous or so obscure
as to be misleading; to this day, our word
oracular is still used of obscure as well as
of authoritative pronouncements.

THE PALM: Symbolizes martyrdom.

THE PALM AND OLIVE BRANCHES: Emblems respectively of victory and peace.

PARSEES: See Zoroaster.

THE PASSION AND CRUCIFIXION OF
CHRIST: The symbols in Christian art of
the passion and crucifixion of Christ are: the
two swords of the Apostles, the ear of
Malchius, the sword of St. Peter, the pillar
and cord, the scourge, the crown of thorns,
the three dice, the spear, the sponge, the
nails, the cross, the thirty pieces of silver,
the hammer and pincers, the ladder, the lantern, the boxes of embalming spices, the seam-
less garment, the purse and the cock. See also
the Five Wounds of Christ.

PATH, THE NOBLE ENLIGHTENED: The
Noble Enlightened Path of the Buddhists is
the sacred way which leads to Nirvana or
Enlightenment; it is the Middle Way, or
Way of Perfection, and has eight stages: 1.
Right Understanding: Truth must be sought
before all else; 2. Right Resolution: Determination to achieve the highest degree of
wisdom; 3. Right Speech: All words which
are not kind, pure, and true, are forbidden,
no matter in what situation a man may be;
4. Right Conduct: Deeds and words must not
spring from likes and dislikes, but only from
desire to promote the law of unfailing love
and goodwill towards all; 5. Right Living:
Choosing, to the best of one's ability, a right
means of making a living, and avoiding all
of those which involve cruelty to man or
beast; 6. Right Effort: Continual need for
advancing in the path, and neither resting nor
falling back, an effort which is sustained by

remaining in harmony with the great law of life; 7. Right Meditation: the mind must be at peace, free of illusion and distortion, a state attained by meditation; 8. Right Rapture: The only true bliss is that of Nirvana, the peace which surpasses all understanding, and the goal of all striving.

THE PEACOCK: A frequent ancient funerary decoration, the peacock symbolized the transition from life to immortality. It was used in pagan art to represent the apotheosis of an empress, and was the special symbol of the goddess Juno.

THE PELICAN: Symbol of the Body and Blood of Christ, and of His atoning sacrifice, because the pelican was popularly believed to feed her young with her blood. The blood of the pelican was also held to have powers of regeneration, for when it was spilled by the mother bird over the bodies of her dead young, it was thought capable of reviving them — at the cost of the mother's own life.

PENTALPHA: See Five-pointed star.

THE PHOENIX: Symbol of the Resurrection from the Dead, usually inscribed with the motto *Resurgam,* I shall arise.

PIR: In Islam, a mystical religious guide, similar to the Hindu guru.

PITAKA: Literally "basket," the name for a collection of Buddhist Scriptures.

THE POMEGRANATE: A bursting pomegranate symbolizes a hopeful future.

PRAKRITI: In Hindu Sankhya philosophy, the essence of all material phenomena, thus the manifestation of the soul (Purusha).

PRAPATTI-MARGA: In Hindu religion, the method of total passive surrender to divine grace, an intensification of the way of devotion, Bhakti-marga.

PRETA: A ghost or spirit which is earth-bound. (Hindu).

PROPHET: In Judeo-Christian theology, a prophet is a man or a woman who has been chosen by God to reveal to the people of the earth the secrets of heaven or of the future. The major Biblical *prophets,* and their prophecies, are: *Ahijah* (c. 939 B.C.), who foretold the success of the rebellion of Jeroboam, the death of the child of Jeroboam, the fall of Jeroboam's house, and the beginning of the Divided Kingdom; *Amos in Tekoa in Judah* (805 B.C. - 747 B.C.), who prophesied a total solar eclipse, an earthquake which destroyed Hazall and Ben Haddad, and the descent of the Messiah from the house of David; *The Chronicler* (c. 350 B.C.); *Daniel* (c. 167 B.C.), who prophesied the triumph of Israel and the death of Belshazzar; *Deborah* (c.1150 B.C.), who was instrumental in the Israelite conquest of Canaan; the *Deuteronomists* (c. 690 B.C. - 500 B.C.); *Elisha, the son of Shaphat* (880 B.C. - 799 B.C.), among whose predictions was that of the birth of a child to the lady of Shunem (Elisha also had the power to restore life, as instanced by his resurrection of the same child whose birth he had foretold, the power to cure diseases, as instanced by his healing of Naaman the Syrian leper; it was also Elisha who anointed Jehu as king of Israel); *Elijah, the Tishbite* (880 B.C. - 849 B.C.), who predicted the drought because of the sins of Ahab and Jezebel; *Elizabeth, the mother of John the Baptist* (c. 60 B.C. - 7 B.C.), who anticipated the news of Mary's pregnancy; *Ezekiel, the son of Buzi* (622 B.C. - 565 B.C.), who prophesied the fall of Jerusalem and the blinding of King Zedekiah; *Ezra the Scribe* (c.397 B.C.); *Gad* (1005 B.C. - 990 B.C.), who foretold of David's journey from Adullam

to Judah; *Gideon* (c. 1160 B.C.); *Habakkuk, the Levite* (c.604 B.C.), who predicted the fall of Babylon; *Haggai* (after 549 B.C.), who forecast the restoration of the Temple; *Hosea, the son of Beeri* (780 B.C. - 735 B.C.), who predicted the destruction of Beth-Arbel and the fall of Samaria in 722 B.C.; *Isaiah, the son of Amoz* (790 B.C. - 696 B.C.), who prophesied the fall of Damascus and the birth of the Messiah to a Virgin; the *Second (or Deutero-) Isaiah* (c. 550 B.C.), who prophesied the end of the Babylonian captivity and foretold of the passion of Christ; the *Third Isaiah* (c.450 B.C.), who predicted the restitution of Jerusalem and the redemption of mankind; *Jehu, the con of Hannai* (c.889 B.C.), who forewarned of the fall of the house and dynasty of Baasha; *Jeremiah, the son of Hilkiah* (c.650 B.C. - 584 B.C.), who predicted the invasion of the Scythians; *Joel, the son of Pethuel* (c.300 B.C.), who prophesied the invasion of the Greeks and the profanation of the temples, the coming of the Kingdom of God and the triumph of the Church of Christ; *John the Baptist* (born c.7 B.C.), who announced the coming of Christ; *Jonah* (c.408 B.C.), who promised the salvation of a repentent Nineveh; *Jonah, the son of Amittai* (c.765 B.C.), who predicted the victory of Jeroboam II; *Joshua, the son of Nun* (late 13th century B.C.); *Malachi* (c.460 B.C.), who predicted the fall of Edom and the redemption of mankind; the *Man of God from Judah* (c.788 B.C.), who foretold of the birth of Josiah and the destruction of the altar of Jeroboam (3 Kings XIII); *Mary, the sister of Moses* (13th century B.C.); *Micah, the Morashtite* (c.780 B.C. - 696 B.C.), who predicted the conquest of Samaria by Sargon II, King of Assyria; *Micaiah, the son of Imlah* (c.853 B.C.), who prophesied the defeat of Jehosophat's army at Ramoth-Gilead; *Moses* (13th century B.C.); *Nahum, the Elkoshite* (c.612 B.C.), who predicted the fall of Nineveh; *Nathan* (c.985 B.C.), who inveighed against David's plan for a Temple and exposed his crime against Uriah; *Obadiah* (c.586 B.C.), who foretold the destruction of Edom and the triumph of Jerusalem; the *Priestly Writers* (c.550 B.C. - c.450 B.C.); the *Prophetess, wife of Isaiah* (c.790 B.C. -696 B.C.); *Samuel, the son of Elkanah of Ramah* (c.1075 B.C. - 1002 B.C.), who foretold of the destruction of Shiloh and of Amalek; *Saul* (c.1100 B.C. - 1011 B.C.); *Shemaiah of Judah* (c.935 B.C.), who warned against civil war; the *Wise Men of the Book of Proverbs* (c.590 B.C.); the *Yahwist* (c.850 B C.); *Zechariah, the son of Berechiah* (c.540 B.C.), who prophesied the erection of the second Temple and the redemption of mankind; the *Second Zechariah* (c.135 B.C.), who predicted the victory of the Maccabees; *Zedekiah, the False Prophet* (c.875 B.C.); *Zephaniah, the son of Cushi* (c.650 B.C.), who predicted the fall of Nineveh and Assyria. The alternate forms of these names in the Douay Bible are: Ezekiel, Ezechiel; Habakkuk, Habacuc; Haggai, Aggeus; Hosea, Osee; Isaiah, Isaias; Jeremiah, Jeremias; Jonah, Jonas; Joshua, Josue; Micah, Micheas; Obadiah, Abdias; Zechariah, Zacharias; Zephaniah, Sophonias.

PSYCHE: Greek word corresponding to the Christian concept of the soul, or death-surviving element. See also Atman, Ruh.

PUJA: Religious devotion in Hindu.

PURUSHA: In Hindu, the general term for the soul, whether of the universe or of the individual; the particular human soul is further distinguished as the Atman or Jivatman.

QUTB: In Moslem religion, a saint of extraordinary holiness.

RISHIS: Hindu wise men and seers.

RUH: The Moslem word for the soul, or death-surviving element. See also Psyche, Atman.

SACAEA: The festival of the ancient Babylonians, during which a condemned prisoner was dressed as a king, enthroned, permitted to act and live regally for five days, then stripped, whipped, and hanged.

SADHANA: The end of the Yogi's practice of meditation, the realization of unity.

SADHU (FEMININE, SADHUNI): A Hindu hermit who has renounced the world.

SAMADHI: The state of non-thought-formation towards which the Yogi strives in meditation, when the mind becomes one with the object of contemplation and all sense of separateness or individuality vanishes.

SAMHAIN: In Celtic religion, the November festival of the dead, when bonfires were burned and divination practiced; Hallowe'en is largely a continuation of the pagan Samhain, and some of the ancient ceremony survives in the Christian observance of All Souls Day (November 2).

SANNYASI (SANNYASIN): A Hindu ascetic, usually one who has passed the four stages (ashramas) of student, householder, hermit, and ascetic.

SAOSHYANT: In Zoroastrian religion, the prophet or Messiah who will come and found the Kingdom of God on earth.

SAVITRA: The most sacred of the Vedic stanzas, called the "golden text" of the Rig-Veda. Also called the Gayatri. See, in a separate listing, Scriptures of the Great World Religions.

THE SCOURGE: In Christian art, a symbol of penance.

THE SERMON ON THE MOUNT: See the Beatitudes.

THE SERPENT: Symbol of sin in Christian art.

THE SEVEN-POINTED STAR: Refers to Revelation V.6 (or Apocalypse V.6): ". . . and behold in the midst of the throne and of the four living creatures, and in the midst of the ancients, a Lamb standing, as it were slain, having seven horns and seven eyes: which are the seven Spirits of God, sent forth into all the earth." Like the Five-pointed star, this star is also called the Star of Bethlehem.

SHAIKH: A trained and recognized mystic in Islam.

SHAKINAH: The light, symbol of the Divine Presence, which rested above the "mercy-seat" in the Temple of Solomon in Jerusalem. Also Sheckinah.

SHAMANISM: The religious beliefs and practices of the Turanians of Siberia, directed by the Shaman or medicine-man who functions as both doctor and magician.

SHELL, THE: In Christian art, a symbol of pilgrimage.

SHEOL: In Hebrew religion, the place or abode of departed spirits.

SHIP, THE: In early Christian art, the ark stood for the Christian Church, but later on any ship came to be an acceptable substitute. The storm-tossed boat of St. Peter, which Christ is guiding in the usual representation, is a symbol of his watchfulness over the entire Church.

SHRUTI: The inspired scriptures of Hinduism (Vedas, Brahmanas, and Upanishads).

SIBYL: A prophetess of classical legend, who was supposed to prophesy under the inspiration of a deity. The name is now applied to any prophetess or woman fortuneteller. There were a number of sibyls, and they had their seats in widely separate parts of the world — Greece, Italy, Babylonia, and Egypt. Plato mentions only one, the Erythraean — identified with Amalthea, the Cumaean Sibyl, who was consulted by Aeneas before his descent into Hades and who sold the Sibylline Books to Tarquin; Martianus Capella speaks of two, the Erythraean and the Phrygian; Aelian of four, the Erythraean, Samian, Egyptian, and Sardian; Varro tells us there were ten: the Cumaean, the Delphic, the Egyptian, Erythraean, Hellespontine, Libyan, Persian, Phrygian, Samian, and Tiburtine. The medieval monks "adopted" the sibyls, as they did so much of papan myth; they made them twelve, and gave to each a separate prophecy and distinct emblem: (1) THE LIBYAN: "The day shall come when men shall see the King of all living things." Emblem: a lighted taper. (2) THE SAMIAN: "The Rich One shall be born of a pure virgin." Emblem: a rose. (3) THE CUMAN: "Jesus Christ shall come from heaven, and live and reign in poverty on earth." Emblem: a crown. (4) THE CUMAEAN: "God shall be born of a pure virgin, and hold converse with sinners." Emblem: a cradle. (5) THE ERYTHRAEAN: "Jesus Christ, Son of God, the Savior." Emblem: a horn. (6) THE PERSIAN: "Satan shall be overcome by a true prophet." Emblem: a dragon under the sibyl's feet, and a lantern. (7) THE TIBURTINE: "The Highest shall descend from heaven, and a virgin be shown in the valleys of the deserts." Emblem: a dove. (8) THE DELPHIC: "The Prophet born of the virgin shall be crowned with thorns." Emblem: a crown of thorns. (9) THE PHRYGIAN: "Our Lord shall rise again." Emblem: a banner and a cross. (10) THE EUROPEAN: "A virgin and her Son shall flee into Egypt." Emblem: a sword. (11) THE AGRIPPINE: "Jesus Christ shall be outraged and scourged." Emblem: a whip. (12) THE HELLESPONTIC: "Jesus Christ shall suffer shame upon the cross." Emblem: a cross. See the Sibylline Books.

THE SIBYLLINE BOOKS: (1) A collection of oracles of mysterious origin, preserved in ancient Rome, and consulted by the Senate in times of emergency or disaster. According to Livy there were originally nine; these were offered in sale by Amalthaea, the Sibyl of Cumae, in Aeolia, to Tarquin. The offer was rejected, and she burned three of them. After twelve months, she offered the remaining six at the same price. Again being refused, she burned three more, and after a similar interval asked the same price for the three left. The sum demanded was then given, and Amalthaea never appeared again. The three books were preserved in a stone chest underground in the temple of Jupiter Capitolinus, and committed to the charge of custodians chosen in the same manner as the high priests. The number of custodians was at first two, then ten, and ultimately fifteen. Augustus had some 2000 of the verses destroyed as spurious, and placed the rest in two gilt cases, under the base of the statue of Apollo, in the temple on the Palatine Hill, but the whole perished when the city was burned in the reign of Nero. (2) A Greek collection of eight books of poetical utterances relating to Jesus Christ, compiled in the 2nd century, is entitled *Oracula Sibylina*, or the *Sibylline Books*.

SIDDHIS: Meaning accomplishment, or fruition: the occult powers and supernatural knowledge gained by advanced Yogis.

SIX-POINTED STAR: See The Double Triangle.

SKANDHAS: In Buddhist doctrine, the aggregate of physical and psychical activities constituting human personality (the ego), the result of the Karmic forces; in Tibetan Yoga, they consist of five aggregates: body-aggregate, sensation-aggregate, emotion-aggregate, volition-aggregate, and consciousness-aggregate.

THE SKULL: In Christian art, a symbol of penance.

SPHINX OF GIZA: The Great Sphinx of Egypt probably considered in early times as a symbol of the sun-god.

THE SPIRITUAL WORKS OF MERCY: 1) To admonish the sinner; 2) To instruct the ignorant; 3) To counsel the doubtful; 4) To comfort the sorrowful; 5) To bear wrongs patiently; 6) To forgive all injuries; 7) To pray for the living and the dead. See The Corporal and Spiritual Works of Mercy.

THE STANDARD: See the Banner.

SURAS: The chapters into which the Koran is divided are called Suras.

SWORD, THE: In Christian art, a symbol of martyrdom. It is also the emblem of warrior saints, and sometimes represents a violent death, though it may not actually have been the instrument of death.

TABU (TABOO, TAPU): Among the Polynesians, a system which holds certain things sacred and prohibits their use.

TAPER, THE: See the Lamp, Lantern, or Taper.

TEN COMMANDMENTS, THE: In Exodus XX, 1-17, Moses is represented as receiving from God on Mount Sinai two sacred stone tablets on which were inscribed a series of commands to the children of Israel. The tablets were thereafter preserved in the Ark of the Covenant. The commandments, as constructed from the verses of the Old Testament, are: 1.) I am the Lord thy God, that brought thee out of the land of Egypt, out of the house of bondage. Thou shalt not make unto thyself a graven image in the likeness of anything that is in the heaven above, or in the earth beneath, or the waters under the earth. Thou shalt not adore them nor serve them; 2.) Thou shalt not take the name of the Lord thy God in vain; 3.) Remember that thou keep holy the Sabbath day; 4.) Honor thy father and thy mother; 5.) Thou shalt not kill; 6.) Thou shalt not commit adultery; 7.) Thou shalt not steal; 8.) Thou shalt not bear false witness against thy neighbor; 9.) Thou shalt not covet thy neighbor's wife; 10.) Thou shalt not covet thy neighbor's goods. Sometimes the injunctions of the first commandment are constructed as two separate commands, and the total of commandments is counted as eleven. From the Greek words for *ten* and *speech* or *word*, the Ten Commandments are also called the Decalogue.

TOHU BOHU: Chaos (without form and void), from the Hebrew Genesis 1.2.

TOPHET: Synonym for Gehenna, the Jewish name for hell.

TORAH: The Jewish term for the Mosaic Law.

TRIANGLE, THE: Emblematic of the Tribune God (three persons in one God), and of Christ.

TRIANGLE WITHIN A CIRCLE, THE: Emblem of the everlasting Trinity.

TRIRATNA: The Buddhist "three jewels," consisting of Buddha, the Dharma (Word of Truth), and Sangha (the Order of Monks).

UNICORN, THE: The fabulous one-horned unicorn was supposedly fleeter than all pursuers except a virgin pure of heart and mind; as the symbol of the Virgin Mary and of St. Justina, it is, therefore, the emblem of female chastity.

VEDANTA: The chief system of Hindu philosophy, representing a reaction of religious orthodoxy against the systems of philosophers; it teaches that Nature is a multiform manifestation of the universal soul, and all phenomena and apparent separateness of souls illusory; however, religious forms, ceremonies and sacrifices are necessary since the world, as a lower form of Reality, is apprehended by the senses; not until the soul becomes one with Brahma does it realize that all phenomena are illusion.

VESICA PISCES: A term used of the aureole, or halo, from its supposed resemblance to a fish. The nimbus, or glory around the head, is usually circular, but the nimbus of God the Father is often triangular, and the nimbus of the Trinity is an emanation of light whose rays form the three arms of a cross. The nimbus of the Virgin is ordinarily a simple ring, but sometimes a crown or diadem, but the aureole following the shape of the body is usually an elongated oval with sharp points which, from its fish-like form is called *Vesica Pisces* (Fish bladder). Also called "the divine oval" and "the mystical almond."

VINE AND VINE LEAF, THE: In Christian art, the vine and vine leaf represent Christ as the true vine of life.

YANG AND YIN: In Chinese philosophy, the great extremes of the First Cause, the Yang being the active male principle and the Yin the passive female principle; all phenomena are made up of the interacting principles of Yang and Yin.

YOGA: A development of the Sankhya Philosophy into which a supreme soul (Isvara) is introduced; Yoga is a practical system of physical, moral, and mental training among Eastern people and aims at the control and perfecting of body and mind, resulting in skill in action; Yogis are said to possess supernormal powers of various kinds.

ZEN: A Japanese Buddhist sect or school with two main divisions, Rinzai and Sodo, which maintains the ancient Hindu system of obtaining enlightenment by meditation (dhyana) and asserts that the truth is in man's heart if he will conscientiously work to find it.

ZION: Jerusalem, and, by metaphorical extension, the Christian heaven.

ZOROASTER: Founder of Zoroastrianism, a Persian religion (c. 1,000 B.C.); his teaching was dualistic; on the one side was Ahura Mazda (Ormuzd), the wise Creator of Good, and on the other Ahriman, Angra Mainyu (Hostile Spirit), Creator of Evil; attendant on Ahura Mazda are the six Amesha Spentas or archangels, personifying Good Thought, Righteousness, Sovereignty, Devotion, Health, and Immortality; allied to Ahriman are the Daevas or Demons (who are, in Hinduism, the devas or angels); fire is held sacred by the Zoroastrians and considered to be the source of all things; in early times Zoroastrianism was severely practical: man was to overcome evil by good in thought, word, and deed; it was only in later times that an elaborate ritual grew up as the society of priests (Magi) developed; Zoroastrianism was crushed out during the Mohammedan invasions (beginning in the 7th Century A.D.), and many Zoroastrians fled to India, where they have continued as the Parsees.

Religious Orders: Standard Abbreviations

A.A.: Assumptionist Fathers.

C.F.A.: Alexian Brothers.

C.F.C.: Brothers of Charity.
C.F.X.: Brothers of St. Francis Xavier
C.J.M.: Congregation of Jesus and Mary (Eudists)
C.M.: Congregation of the Mission (Vincentians).
C.M.F.: Claretian Missionary Fathers.
C.M.M.: Marianhill Fathers.
CONG. ORAT.: Oratorians.
C.P.: Passionist Fathers.
C.PP.S.: Society of the Precious Blood.
C.P.S.: Stigmatine Fathers.
C.R.: Congregation of the Resurrection.
C.R.: Theatini Fathers.
C.S.B.: Basilian Fathers.
C.S.C. Congregation of the Holy Cross.
C.S.P.: Paulist Fathers.
C.S.SP.: Holy Ghost Fathers.
C.SS.R.: Redemptorist Fathers.
C.S.V.: Clerks of St. Viator.
F.D.P.: Sons of Divine Providence.
F.I.C.: Brothers of Christian Instruction.
F.M.S.: Marist Brothers.
F.S.C.: Brothers of the Christian Schools.
F.S.C.H.: Brothers of the Christian Schools.
I.H.M.: Immaculate Heart of Mary Missioners.
M.I.C.: Marian Fathers.
M.M.: Maryknoll Missioners.
M.S.: Missionaries of the Sacred Heart.
M.S.: Missionaries of Our Lady of LaSolette.
M.S.C.: Missionaries of the Sacred Heart.
M.S.F.: Missionaries of the Holy Family.
M.S.SS.T.: Missionary Servants of the Most Holy Trinity.
O. CARM.: Carmelite Fathers.
O. CART.: Carthusian Order.
O.C.D.: Discalced Carmelites.
O. CIST.: Cistercian Order.
O.C.S.O.: Cistercians of the Strict Observance (Trappists).
O.D.M.: Order of Our Lady of Mercy.
O.F.M.: Franciscan Fathers.
O.F.M. CAP.: Capuchin Fathers.
O.F.M. CONV.: Friars Minor Conventual, or Black Franciscans.
O.M.: Order of Minims.
O.M.I.: Oblates of Mary Immaculate.
O.P.: Order of Preachers (Dominicans).
O. PRAEM.: Premonstratensians.
O.R.S.A.: Recollects of St. Augustine.
O.S.A.: Augustinian Fathers.
O.S.B.: Order of St. Benedict (Benedictines)
O.S.B.M.: Order of St. Basil the Great
O.S.C.: Holy Cross Canons.
OS.CAM.: Order of St. Camillus.
O.S.F.: Order of St. Francis.
O.S.F.S.: Oblates of St. Francis de Sales.
O.S.J.: Oblates of St. Joseph.
O.S.J.D.: Brothers of St. John of God.
O.S.M.: Servants of Mary (Servites).
O.SS.T.: Order of the Most Holy Trinity.
P.S.M.: Pious Society of Missions.
P.S.S.C.: Pious Society of the Missionaries of St. Charles.
S.A.: Franciscan Fathers of the Atonement.
S.C.: Brothers of the Sacred Heart.
S.C.: Salesian Congregation.
S.C.A.: Society of the Catholic Apostolate (Pallottine Fathers).
S.C.J.: Society of the Priests of the Sacred Heart.
S.D.B.: Salesians of Don Bosco.
S.D.S.: Salvatorians.
S.F.: Sons of the Holy Family.
S.J.: Jesuit Fathers.
S.M.: Marist Fathers.
S.M.M.: Company of Mary.
S.O.CIST.: Cistercians of the Common Observance.
S.O.S.B.: Sylvestrine Benedictines.
S.P.M.: Society of the Fathers of Mercy.

S.S.: Society of Priests of St. Sulpice.
S.S.C.: Saint Columban's Foreign Mission Society.
SS.CC.: Fathers of the Sacred Hearts of Jesus and Mary (Picpus Fathers).
S.S.E.: Society of St. Edmund.
S.S.J.: Saint Joseph's Society of the Sacred Heart.
S.S.P.: Pious Society of Saint Paul.
S.S.S.: Congregation of the Blessed Sacrament.
S.V.D.: Society of the Divine Word.
S.V.P.: Society of St. Vincent de Paul.
S.X.: Xaverian Missionary Fathers.
T.O.R.: Third Order Regular of Saint Francis.
T.O.S.F.: Franciscan Tertiaries.
W.F.: White Fathers.

Revolutionary War, American, Battles of
See also **Battles** and listings under **National**

1775

APRIL 19: Hostilities in America began at Lexington, Mass. A British detachment of 800 men, under Col. Smith and Maj. Pitcairn, set out to destroy some military stores that were known to be at Concord; the mission was supposedly secret, but news of the raid flew ahead of the marching men, as the countryside was alerted by the ringing of church bells and the firing of signal guns. At Lexington, on April 19, 70 Minute Men were assembled under arms near the meetinghouse; Maj. Pitcairn reached their rendezvous with his men, and challenged them: "Disperse, you rebels; throw down your arms and disperse." When he was not obeyed, he fired his pistol, and ordered his men to fire; on the first round, several Americans fell; the rest of the Minute Men fled, and the British continued to fire, killing eight of the fugitives. The British went on to Concord, where they destroyed considerable military stores; as they returned to Boston, they were harried all the way by snipers and guerilla bands. Fifty Americans died that day, and several more were wounded; 65 British soldiers were killed, and 186 wounded. The spirit of the Colonists was aroused, and Boston was soon ringed by an army of 20,000 men, mostly untrained militia, who were nevertheless determined to preserve their liberty at the expense of their lives, if need be.
MAY 10: Ticonderoga, New York: Ethan Allen forced British garrison to surrender.
MAY 12: Crown Point, New York, taken by Seth Warner.
MAY 27: Boston, Mass.; Putnam defeated British raiders on Hog Island.
JUNE 17: Bunker Hill (Breed's Hill), Boston: the British suffered heavy losses, but drove the Americans from their redoubt on Breed's Hill.
AUGUST 30: Stonington, Conn., attacked by British.
SEPT. 6: Americans under Schuyler began siege of St. John's, New Brunswick.
SEPTEMBER 25: Col. Ethan Allen with 83 men attempted to take Montreal; all were made prisoners.
OCTOBER 7: British ships fired upon Bristol, R. I.
OCTOBER 18: British burned Falmouth (Portland), Me.
NOVEMBER 2: Garrison at St. John, New

Brunswick, surrendered to Americans under Gen. Richard Montgomery.

NOVEMBER 13: Montreal taken by Montgomery; British commander, Sir Guy Carleton, narrowly escaped with his forces to Quebec.

DECEMBER 9-11: Norfolk, Va. (at Greatbridge): Gov. Dunmore of Virginia was defeated in an engagement with some 900 American troops and forced to withdraw from Norfolk.

DECEMBER 31: Quebec: American forces of Gen. Richard Montgomery and Benedict Arnold were decisively beaten; Montgomery killed; unable to rally enough men to renew the attack, Arnold eventually withdrew and Canada remained under British control.

1776

JAN. 1: British under Gov. Dunmore returned and burned Norfolk, Va.; the Americans adopted the same "scorched city" tactic and laid the standing portion of the city waste.

FEBRUARY 27: Moore's Creek Bridge, near Wilmington: Carolina patriots routed a detachment of Scottish loyalists.

MAR. 4: Americans bombarded British in Boston and occupied Dorchester Heights; within the next two weeks, Howe evacuated all of his forces to their ships.

MAY 19: Canada: Benedict Arnold and 900 Americans captured British post at the "Cedars."

JUNE 7: Three Rivers, Canada: Americans under command of Gen. Sullivan were defeated.

JUNE 15: British retook Montreal.

JUNE 21: Cherokee attack on fort at Watauga, Tenn., was repulsed.

JUNE 28: Fort Sullivan, Charleston, S. C.: British land-and-sea attack under Adm. Sir Peter Parker and Gens. Clinton and Cornwallis was checked, with heavy British losses.

JULY 5: New Haven, Conn., pillaged by British.

AUGUST 27: Battle of Long Island: on August 22, Gen. Howe landed his forces near New Utrecht, on the south side of Long Island; on August 27, the Americans were severely beaten in the Battle of Flatbush, and Gen. Sullivan and Lord Stirling were made prisoners; American losses in killed and wounded were about 2,000; the British losses were not over 400. After the disaster of Flatbush, Washington decided to retreat from Long Island, and unobserved by an enemy not more than 600 yards away, escaped with his army to Manhattan in a single night, August 29.

SEPTEMBER 16: Harlem Heights: Washington, retreating before the British advance up Manhattan Island, repulsed the troops that Howe brought up against him.

OCTOBER 11: Valcour Bay: British achieved naval victory over Arnold's jerry-built Lake Champlain "fleet."

OCTOBER 13: Split Rock: British annihilated the remainder of Arnold's fleet on Lake Champlain.

OCTOBER 28: White Plains, N. Y.: Howe, attempting to encircle the American army, engaged Washington's troops at White Plains, and, despite heavy losses, commanded the key positions; Washington continued his retreat.

NOVEMBER 16: Fort Washington, Manhattan Island, with the garrison left by Washington to cover the retreat of his army, fell to the British.

DECEMBER 26: Trenton, New Jersey: Washington surprised the British garrison, took nearly 1000 Hessian prisoners, and occupied the city.

1777

JANUARY 3: Princeton, N. J.: Washington outflanked the British troops that had been sent to relieve Trenton; in a series of sharp encounters, the British were driven back to New Brunswick, effectively leaving N. J. in American hands as a winter quarter.

APRIL 15: Indians attacked Boonesboro, Ky.

JULY 4: Boonesboro again attacked by Indians.

JULY 6: Gen. St. Clair abandoned Fort Ticonderoga, N. Y., to Gen. Burgoyne.

JULY 7: Hubbardton, Vt.: the American troops from Ticonderoga were beaten in an encounter with the British.

JULY 19: Indians besieged Logan's Fort, Ky.

AUGUST 2-23: British attacked Fort Stanwix, N. Y., until the siege was raised by the arrival of American reinforcements under Benedict Arnold.

AUGUST 6: Oriskany or Fort Schuyler, N. Y.: Americans effectively blocked the British advance down the Mohawk Valley.

AUGUST 16: Bennington, Vermont: British were defeated by American troops under Capt. John Stark.

SEPTEMBER 1: Indians attacked Fort Henry, W. Va. (Wheeling).

SEPTEMBER 11: Brandywine, Penn.: the Americans under Washington lost 300 killed and 600 wounded; the British (Cornwallis) lost 100 killed and 400 wounded; Lafayette was among the wounded; several hundred American prisoners were taken.

SEPTEMBER 18: Americans seized British posts at Lake George and at Fort Ticonderoga, N. Y.

SEPTEMBER 19: Stillwater, N Y.: Burgoyne, with heavy losses, drove back the Americans in the first Battle of Saratoga, on Bemis Heights.

SEPTEMBER 20: British defeated and massacred Americans under Gen. Anthony Wayne at Paoli, Penn.

SEPTEMBER 26: British troops under Gen. Howe took Philadelphia.

OCTOBER 4: Germantown, Penn.: the Americans (Washington) were defeated with losses of 200 killed, 600 wounded, and 400 prisoners; the British had 100 killed and 500 wounded.

OCTOBER 6: Forts Clinton and Montgomery, on the Hudson River, were taken by British.

OCTOBER 7: Saratoga, N. Y.: at Stillwater (Bemis Heights), near Saratoga, American forces under Gen. Horatio Gates met and defeated Gen. Burgoyne's forces.

OCTOBER 13: British burned Kingston, N. Y.

OCTOBER 17: Saratoga: Burgoyne's 5752 British troops surrendered to the Americans, along with arms, ammunition, and other supplies; the victory laid the foundation for an American alliance with France.

OCTOBER 22: Fort Mercer, N. J.; British forces besieged this strategic fort on the Delaware River.

NOVEMBER 16: Fort Mifflin, Penn.: the British took the second fort on the Delaware, which, with Fort Mercer, gave them control of the river.

1778

MAY 20: British surprised Lafayette at Barren Hill, Penn.

JUNE 28: Monmouth, N. J.: the British under Sir Henry Clinton were defeated in a hard-fought battle with Washington's forces and compelled to retreat with heavy losses.

JULY 2: Schoharie, N. Y.: Col. Butler, with his command of Tories and Indians, captured and massacred the 1000 inhabitants of the town.

JULY 4: Wyoming Valley, Penn., was raided by Tories and Indians, and the inhabitants massacred.

JULY 5: George Rogers Clark captured Kaskaskia, the British outpost in the Illinois Territory, and then drove the British from Cahokia and Vincennes.

AUGUST 29: Quaker Hill, R. I.: the British siege of Rhode Island (August 9-30) ended with the evacuation of Newport by the Americans (Gen. John Sullivan); the French fleet (Count D'Estaing) that had arrived at Newport on July 29 to lend aid to the American army retired to Boston.

NOVEMBER 11: Cherry Valley, N. Y.: Tories and Iroquois allies raided the settlements and massacred the inhabitants.

DECEMBER 17: British troops (Col. Hamilton) drove George Clark out of Vincennes.

DECEMBER 29: Savannah, Ga.: British captured the port and forced the Americans to retreat beyond the Savannah River.

DECEMBER 29: Indian Chief Brant raided Mohawk Valley, New York.

1779

JANUARY 9: Sunbury, Ga., was captured by the British.

JANUARY 29: Augusta, Ga., was taken by 2000 British (Gen. John Campbell).

FEBRUARY 3: Port Royal, S. C.: British defeated by Americans (Gen. William Moultrie).

FEBRUARY 14: Kettle Creek, Ga.: British defeated in skirmish with Americans.

FEBRUARY 25: George Rogers Clark reoccupied Vincennes, Ind.

MARCH 3: Brier's Creek, Ga.: British defeated Americans.

APRIL 18-24: Gen. Van Shaick destroyed Onandaga, N. Y.

MAY 14: Portsmouth and Norfolk, Va., were taken by British; the Navy Yard at Gosport, Va. burned.

MAY 31: Stony Point, N. Y., fell to the British.

JULY 5: Gov. Tryon of N. Y. took New Haven, Conn., in raid by his Loyalist party.

JULY 7: British and Tory (Governor Tryon of New York) party, after capturing and destroying military stores at Danbury, Conn., burned Fairfield.

JULY 11: British, under Tryon, burned Norwalk.

JULY 15: Stony Point, N. Y.: Americans (Gen. Anthony Wayne) raided by night and subdued the British garrison in hand-to-hand combat, taking 543 prisoners and large military stores; 63 British soldiers were killed.

AUGUST: Americans (Gen. John Sullivan) raided and destroyed Iroquois villages in Genesee Valley, N. Y.

AUGUST 19: Paulus Hook, N. J., fell to the Americans (Maj. Henry Lee).

AUGUST 29: Chemung, N. Y.: Americans (Gen. John Sullivan) defeated Tories and Indians in a battle near Elmira.

SEPTEMBER 23: John Paul Jones, in the *Bonhomme Richard*, captured the British frigate *Serapis* off the English coast.

OCTOBER 20: Savannah, Ga.; month-long American (Gen. Benjamin Lincoln) and French (Count D'Estaing) siege was abandoned.

1780

FEBRUARY 11: British attacked Charleston, S. C.

MARCH 14: Bernardo de Gálvez, Spanish governor of La., captured Mobile, Ala.

MAY 12: Charleston, S. C., capitulated to British (Sir Henry Clinton) after month-long siege; 2500 Americans (Gen. Benjamin Lincoln) taken prisoner.

JUNE 23: Springfield, N. J.: Americans (Gen. Nathaniel Greene) defeated British.

JULY 10: Newport, R. I.: 6000 French troops (Count de Rochambeau) arrived to aid Americans, but were cut off by the British (Sir Henry Clinton) and held inactive.

AUGUST 16: British (Lord Cornwallis) defeated Americans (Gen. Horatio Gates) at Camden, N. J.

SEPTEMBER 23: Maj. John André, British spy, captured by Americans, disclosed plot of Benedict Arnold to deliver West Point to the British; Arnold escaped to safety on the British ship *Vulture*.

OCTOBER 2: Maj. André, who had acted as British agent in Arnold's plot to surrender West Point, was hanged after the British declined General Washington's offer to exchange him for Arnold.

OCTOBER 7: King's Mountain, North Carolina: Americans defeated British and Tory forces (Maj. Ferguson).

OCTOBER 16: Royalton, Vt., attacked by Indians.

NOVEMBER 20: Indian battle at Boyd's Creek, Tenn.

1781

JANUARY 17: Cowpens, N. C.: Americans (Gen. Daniel Morgan) defeated the British (Col. Tarleton); British loss was 300 killed and wounded; 500 prisoners were taken, and large supplies of arms and military stores.

MARCH 15: Guilford Court House, North Carolina: Americans (Gen. Nathaniel Green) defeated by the British (Lord Cornwallis).

APRIL 2: Indian Battle of the Bluffs, Tenn.

APRIL 23: Col. Lee took Fort Watson, S. C., from British.

APRIL 25: Hobkirk's Hill, S. C.: Americans (Gen. Nathaniel Green) defeated by British.

APRIL 25: British took Petersburg, Va.

JUNE 18-19: Fort 96, S. C.: Americans (Gen. Greene) besieged British garrison, but were driven off.

JULY 6: Lafayette ordered Americans (Gen. Anthony Wayne) to attack the British (Lord Cornwallis) at Jamestown Ford, Va.; when the assault failed, the Americans retreated from Jamestown.

AUGUST 30 — September 5: Adm. de Grasse moved French fleet from the West Indies and defeated the British fleet (Adm. Graves) in a major naval battle in Chesapeake Bay.

SEPTEMBER 6: Benedict Arnold, sent on a raid by Sir Henry Clinton, burned and pillaged New London, Conn., captured Fort Griswold in Groton, and massacred the garrison after the fort had surrendered.

SEPTEMBER 8: Eutaw Springs, S. C.: the British lost 1100 men, and the Americans (Gen. Nathaniel Greene) 555, before the Americans retreated.

SEPTEMBER 28: Siege of Yorktown, Va. began; Gen. Washington, leading an American-French army of 12,000 men, crossed the Hudson River, moved through Philadelphia to

Virginia, where he attacked the British under Lord Cornwallis.

OCTOBER 19: Cornwallis surrendered to Washington, ending the American siege of Yorktown; 7037 British prisoners, not including seamen, were taken.

OCTOBER 20: Indians invaded Mohawk Valley, N. Y.

OCTOBER 20: Spaniards captured Fort St. Joseph, Ind.

1782

MAY 21: Wayne routed British near Savannah, Ga.

JUNE 5-6: Americans defeated by Indians at Sandusky, Ohio.

AUGUST 27: Last battle of the Revolution fought near Charleston, S. C.

Rivers, Principal World
See also Salt Water Bodies; Waterfalls

MISSISSIPPI-MISSOURI: 4200 miles; northwest and central U.S.A.
NILE: 4100 miles; northeast Africa.
AMAZON: 3700 miles; Peru, Brazil.
OB-IRTISH: 3200 miles; Siberia.
YANGTZE-KIANG: 3100 miles; China.
CONGO: 2900 miles; Central Africa.
AMUR-ARGUN-KERULEN: 2800 miles; northeast Asia.
LENA: 2800 miles; Siberia.
YENISEI: 2800 miles; Siberia.
HWANG-HO: 2700 miles; China.
PARANÁ-RIO GRANDE: 2700 miles; Brazil-Argentina.
NIGER: 2600 miles; West Africa.
MACKENZIE: 2514 miles (with tributaries); Northwest Territories, Canada.
MEKONG: 2500 miles; southeast Asia.
MURRAY-DARLING: 2310 miles; Australia.
VOLGA: 2300 miles; U.S.S.R.
YUKON: 2300 miles; Alaska.
MADEIRA-MAMORÉ: 2000 miles; western Brazil.
PURUS: 2000 miles; Peru, Brazil.
ST. LAWRENCE-GREAT LAKES WATERWAY: 2000 miles; Quebec, Ontario, Canada.
RIO GRANDE: 1800 miles; Colo., N. M., Texas, U.S.A.
SÃO FRANCISCO: 1800 miles; eastern Brazil.
SALWEEN: 1750 miles; Burma.
DANUBE: 1725 miles; central Europe.
COLORADO: 1700 miles; southwest U.S.A.
EUPHRATES: 1700 miles; Iraq.
INDUS: 1700 miles; India.
SYR DARYA: 1700 miles; U.S.S.R.
TOCANTINS: 1700 miles; Brazil.
YAPURA (JAPURÁ): 1700 miles; northwest South America.
BRAHMAPUTRA: 1680 miles; India.
NELSON-SASKATCHEWAN-BOW: 1660 miles; central Canada.
SI-KIANG: 1650 miles; China.
ORINOCO: 1600 miles; Venezuela.
ZAMBESI (ZAMBEZI): 1600 miles; southcentral and southeast Africa.
GANGES (GANGA): 1550 miles; India.
AMU DARYA: 1500 miles; U.S.S.R.
PARAGUAY: 1500 miles; southcentral South America.
ARKANSAS: 1450 miles; Colo., Kans., Okla., Ark., U.S.A.
DNIEPER: 1400 miles; U.S.S.R.
RIO NEGRO: 1400 miles; northwest South America.

URAL: 1400 miles; U.S.S.R.
IRRAWADDY: 1300 miles; Burma.
ORANGE: 1300 miles; South Africa.
RED: 1250 miles; Okla., Ark., La., U.S.A.
COLUMBIA: 1214 miles; Southwest Canada, northwest U.S.A.
TIGRIS: 1150 miles; Turkey, Iraq.
DON: 1100 miles; U.S.S.R.
PEACE: 1054 miles; western Canada.
SNAKE: 1038 miles; Wyo., Ida., Wash., U.S.A.
MAGDALENA: 1050 miles; Colombia.
CHURCHILL: 1000 miles; Sakatchewan, Manitoba, Canada.
PILCOMAYO: 1000 miles; southcentral South America.
SENEGAL: 1000 miles; West Africa.
URUGUAY: 1000 miles; southeast South America.
OHIO: 980 miles; Penn., O., Ind., Ill., U.S.A.
CANADIAN: 906 miles; N M., Tex., Okla., U.S.A.
BRAZOS: 870 miles; Texas, U.S.A.
TENNESSEE-FRENCH BROAD: 862 miles; N. C., Tenn., U.S.A.
COLORADO: 840 miles; Tex., U.S.A.
DNIESTER: 800 miles; southeast Europe.
RHINE: 800 miles; western Europe.
SUNGARI: 800 miles; Manchuria.
THEISS (TISZA): 800 miles; Ukraine, Hungary, Yugoslavia, Europe.
ATHABASKA: 765 miles; Alberta, Canada.
NORTH CANADIAN: 760 miles; Okla., N. M., U.S.A.
FRASER: 750 miles; British Columbia, Canada.
PECOS: 735 miles; N. M., Tex., U.S.A.
GREEN: 730 miles; Wyo., Colo., Ut., U.S.A.
JAMES (DAKOTA): 710 miles; N. D., S. D., U.S.A.
ELBE: 700 miles; Czechoslovakia, Germany.
RED RIVER OF THE NORTH: 700 miles; (with tributary); U.S.-Canada.
OTTAWA: 695 miles; Ontario, Quebec, Canada.
WHITE: 690 miles; Ark., U.S.A.
CUMBERLAND: 687 miles; Ky., Tenn., U.S.A.
YELLOWSTONE: 671 miles; Wyo., Mont., U.S.A.
TENNESSEE: 652 miles; Tenn., Ala., Ky., U.S.A.
LOIRE: 650 miles; France.
MOBILE-ALABAMA-COOSA: 639 miles; Ala., U.S.A.
VISTULA: 630 miles; Poland.
GILA: 625 miles; N. M., Ariz., U.S.A.
MILK: 625 miles; Canada-U.S.A.
NORTH PLATTE: 618 miles; Colo., Wyo., Nebr., U.S.A.
ALBANY: 610 miles; Ontario, Canada.
BACK (GREAT FISH RIVER): 605 miles; Northwest Territories, Canada.
CIMARRON: 600 miles; N. M., Kans., Okla., U.S.A.
MEUSE: 575 miles; France, Belgium, Holland.
TAGUS: 565 miles; Spain, Portugal.
ODER: 550 miles; Central Europe.
BUG (SOUTHERN BUG): 500 miles; Ukraine.
OSAGE: 500 miles; Kans., Mo., U.S.A.
RHONE: 500 miles; Switzerland, France.
EBRO: 475 miles; Spain.
GAMBIA: 475 miles; West Africa.
SEINE: 475 miles; France.
WABASH: 475 miles; Ind., Ill., U.S.A.
SUSQUEHANNA: 444 miles; N. Y., Pa., Md., U.S.A.
PO (ERIDANUS): 420 miles; Italy.
CONNECTICUT: 407 miles; Vt., N. H., Conn., U.S.A.
SACRAMENTO: 382 miles; Calif., U.S.A.
GARONNE: 370 miles; France.
JAMES: 340 miles; Va., U.S.A.
BIG HORN: 336 miles; Wyo., Mont., U.S.A.

MARNE: 320 miles; France.
HUDSON: 306 miles; N. Y., U.S.A.
DELAWARE: 296 miles; N. Y., Pa., N. J., Del., U.S.A.
POTOMAC: 287 miles (400 miles with North Branch and South Branch tributaries); W. V., Va.; U.S.A.
SHANNON: 240 miles; Ireland.
THAMES: 207 miles; southern England.
JORDAN: 200 miles; Israel.
CLYDE: 106 miles; southern Scotland.
RUBICON: Minor stream in northern Italy, crossed by Caesar and army 49 b.c.

Roman Empire
See **Barbaric Invaders of Rome**

Roman Gods
See **Gods and Goddesses**

Roman Rulers
See **Rulers**

Round Table
See **Knights of the Round Table**

Rulers
See also **Abdications and Depositions in European Royalty Since 1910; Popes; Presidency; Pseudonyms, Nicknames, and Special Associations for Historical Persons**

RULERS OF ANCIENT NEAR EASTERN COUNTRIES

Kings of the Hittites

PITKHANAS: About the 20th century B.C.
ANITTAS: c. 1900 B.C.
TUDHALIYAS I: 1740-10 B.C.
PU-SARRUMAS: 1710-1680 B.C.
LABARMAS I: 1680-50 B.C.
HATTUSILIS I: 1650-20 B.C.
MURSILIS I: 1620-1590 B.C.
HANTILIS: 1590-60 B.C.
ZIDANTAS I: 1560-50 B.C.
AMMUNAS: 1550-30 B.C.
HUZZIYAS I: 1530-25 B.C.
TELIPINUS: 1525-1500 B.C.
ALLUWANNAS: 1500-1490 B.C.
HANTILIS II: 1490-80 B.C.
ZIDANTAS II: 1480-70 B.C.
HUZZIYAS II: 1470-60 B.C.
TUDHALIYAS II: 1460-40 B.C.
ARNUWANDAS I: 1440-20 B.C.
HATTUSILIS II: 1420-1400 B.C.
TUDHALIYAS III: 1400-1385 B.C.
ARNUWANDAS II: 1385-75 B.C.
SUPPILULIUMAS: 1375-35 B.C.
ARNUWANDAS III: 1335-34 B.C.
MURSILUS II: 1334-06 B.C.
MUWATALLIS: 1306-1282 B.C.
URHI-TESHUB: 1282-75 B.C.
HATTUSILIS III: 1275-50 B.C.
TUDHALIYAS IV: 1250-20 B.C.
ARNUWANDAS IV: 1220-1190 B.C.
SUPPILULIUMAS II: c. 1190 B.C.

Kings of Macedonia

PERDICCAS I: End of 8th century B.C.
ARGAEUS: ?

PHILIP I: Beginning of 7th century.
AEROPUS: ?
ALCETAS: ?
AMYNTAS I: d. 498 B.C.
ALEXANDER I: 498-454 B.C.
PERDICCAS II: d. about 413 B.C.
ARCHELAUS: 413-399 B.C.
ARESTES: 399-394 B.C.
PAUSANIAS: 394-393 B.C.
AMYNTAS II: 393-369 B.C.
ALEXANDER II: 369-368 B.C.
PTOLEMY ALORITES: 367-364 B.C.
PERDICCAS III: 364-359 B.C.
PHILIP II: 359-336 B.C.
ALEXANDER III (THE GREAT): 336-323 B.C.
PHILIP III (ARRHIDAEUS): 323-317 B.C.
OLYMPIAS: 316-315 B.C.
CASSANDER: 316-297 B.C.
PHILIP IV: 296-295 B.C.
DEMETRIUS I (POLIORCETES): 294-283 B.C.
PYRRHUS: 287-286; 283-239 B.C.
LYSIMACHUS: 286-280 B.C.
PTOLEMY KERAUNOS: 280-277 B.C.
MELEAGER: 280-277 B.C.
ANTIPATER: 280-277 B.C.
SOSTHENES: 280-277 B.C.
ALEXANDER: 280-277 B.C.
ANTIGONUS II (GONATUS): 283-239 B.C. (Son of Demetrius Poliorcetes).
DEMETRIUS II: 239-229 B.C.
ANTIGONAS III (DOSON): 229-220 B.C.
PHILIP V: 220-179 B.C.
PERSEUS: 179-167 B.C.

Kings of Ancient Persia

CAMBYSES I: first half of 6th century B.C.
CYRUS (THE GREAT): c. 559-529 B.C.
CAMBYSES II: 529-522 B.C.
SMERDIS (THE FALSE): 522 B.C.
DARIUS I (HYSTASPIS): 521-486 B.C. (Also called Darius the Great.)
XERXES I (THE GREAT): 486-465 B.C.
ARTABANUS: 465 B.C.
ARTAXERXES I (LONGIMANUS): 465-425 B.C.
XERXES II: 424 B.C.
SOGDIANUS: 424 B.C.
DARIUS II (NOTHUS): 423-404 B.C.
ARTAXERXES II (MNEMON): 404-359 B.C.
ARTAXERXES II (OCHUS): 359-338 B.C.
XERXES III (ARSES): 338-336 B.C.
DARIUS III (CODOMANUS): 336-331 B.C.

Kings of Lydia

GYGES: 716-678 B. C.
ARDYS: 678-629 B. C.
SADYATTES: 629-617 B. C.
ALYATTES: 617-560 B. C.
CROESUS: 560-546 B. C.

Kings of Media

DEIOCES: c. 699-647 B. C.
PHRAORTES: c. 646-625 B. C.
CYAXARES: 625-585 B. C.
ASTYAGES: c. 584-550 B. C.

Kings of Pontus

(Note: There is confusion about the number of Kings named Mithridates before Mithridates Eupator. Some authorities only recognize three.)

ARIOBARZANES I: 5th century B. C.
MITHRIDATES I

ARIOBARZANES II: 363-337 B. C.
MITHRIDATES II: 337-302 B. C.
MITHRIDATES III: 302-266 B. C.
ARIOBARZANES III: 266-240 B. C.
MITHRIDATES IV: 240-190 B. C.
PHARNACES I: 190-156 B. C.
MITHRIDATES V (EUERGETES): 156-120 B. C.
MITHRIDATES VI EUPATOR (THE GREAT):
120-63 B. C.
PHARNACES II: 63-47 B. C.

Kings of Syria
(the Seleucidae)

SELEUCUS I (NICATOR): 358?-280 B. C.
ANTIOCHUS I (ANTIOCHUS SOTER): 280-261 B. C.
ANTIOCHUS II (ANTIOCHUS THEOS): 261-247 B. C.
SELEUCUS II (CALLINICUS): 247-226 B. C.
SELEUCUS III (SOTER): 226-223 B. C.
ANTIOCHUS III (THE GREAT): 223-187 B. C.
SELEUCUS IV (PHILOPATOR): 187-175 B. C.
ANTIOCHUS IV (ANTIOCHUS EPIPHANES): 175-163 B. C.
ANTIOCHUS V (ANTIOCHUS EUPATOR): 163-162 B. C.
DEMETRIUS I (SOTER): 162-150 B. C.
ALEXANDER BALA: 150-145 B. C.
DEMETRIUS II (NICATOR): 145-139 B.C.; 129-125 B. C.
ANTIOCHUS VI (ANTIOCHUS THEOS AND ANTIOCHUS DIONYSUS): 145-142 B. C.
ANTIOCHUS VII (ANTIOCHUS ENERGETES AND ANTIOCHUS SIDETES): 138-129 B. C.
ANTIOCHUS VIII (ANTIOCHUS PHILOMETOR AND ANTIOCHUS GRYPUS): 125-96 B. C.
ANTIOCHUS IX (ANTIOCHUS PHILOPATOR AND ANTIOCHUS CYZICENUS): 115-95 B. C.
SELEUCUS VI (EPIPHANES NICATOR): 96-93 B. C.
ANTIOCHUS X (ANTIOCHUS EUSEBES): 95-93 B. C.
DEMETRIUS III (EUCAERUS AND PHILOMETOR): 95-83 B. C.
ANTIOCHUS XI (ANTIOCHUS EPIPHANES): 95-92 B. C.
ANTIOCHUS XII (ANTIOCHUS DIONYSUS): 95-85 B. C.
TIGRANES: 83-69 B. C.
ANTIOCHUS XIII (ANTIOCHUS ASIATICUS): 69-64 B. C.

Kings of Pergamum

PHILETAERUS: 280-263 B. C.
EUMENES I: 263-241 B. C.
ATTALUS I (SOTER): 241-197 B. C.
EUMENES II: 197-160 B. C.
ATTALUS II (PHILADELPHUS): 160-138 B. C.
ATTALUS III (PHILOMETOR): 138-133 B. C.

RULERS OF AUSTRIA

FRANCIS I: 1804-1835 (ruled as Francis II of the Holy Roman Empire 1792-1806).
FERDINAND I: 1835-1848.
FRANCIS JOSEPH: 1848-1916 (Emperor of Austria and King of Hungary from 1867).
CHARLES I: 1916-1918.
REPUBLIC: 1918-1938.
ANSCHLUSS WITH GERMANY: 1938-1945.
ALLIED OCCUPATION: 1945-1955.
REPUBLIC: From 1955.

RULERS OF CHINA

HSIA DYNASTY: (2206?-?1766 B. C.)).
SHANG-YIN DYNASTY: (1766?-?1122 B. C.)).
CHOU DYNASTY: (1122?-?221 B. C.)).
CH'IN DYNASTY: (221?-206 B. C.)).
WESTERN HAN DYNASTY: (206 B. C.-9 A. D.).
INTERREGNUM: WANG MANG: (9-25).
EASTERN HAN DYNASTY: (25-220).
WEI DYNASTY: THE PERIOD OF THE THREE KINGDOMS: (220-264).
WESTERN CHIN DYNASTY: (265-317).
EASTERN CHIN DYNASTY: (317-419).
LIU SUNG DYNASTY: (420-479).
CHI'I DYNASTY (SOUTH): (479-502).
LIANG: (502-557).
CHOU DYNASTY (NORTH): (557-581).
SUI DYNASTY: (581-618).
T'ANG DYNASTY: (618-907).
THE FIVE DYNASTIES: (907-960).
SUNG DYNASTY, NORTHERN: (960-1127).
SUNG DYNASTY, SOUTHERN: (1127-1279).
TARTAR DYNASTIES, NORTH: (1127-1279).
YUAN DYNASTY: (1280-1368).
MING DYNASTY: (1368-1644).
CH'ING DYNASTY: (1644-1912).
REPUBLIC: From 1912.

RULERS OF ENGLAND

Saxons and Danes

EGBERT: 827-839.
ETHELWULF: 839-858.
ETHELBALD: 858-860.
ETHELRED: 866-871.
ALFRED: 871-901.
EDWARD: 901-925.
ATHELSTAN: 925-940.
EDMUND: 940-946.
EDRED: 946-955.
EDWY: 955-958.
EDGAR: 958-975.
EDWARD: 975-979.
ETHELRED II: 979-1016.
EDMUND: 1016.
CANUTE: 1017-1035.
HAROLD I: 1035-1040.
HARDICANUTE: 1040-1042.
EDWARD: 1042-1066.
HAROLD II: 1066.

House of Normandy

WILLIAM I: 1066-1087.
WILLIAM II: 1087-1100.
HENRY I: 1100-1135.

House of Blois

STEPHEN: 1135-1154.

House of Plantagenet

HENRY II: 1154-1189.
RICHARD I: 1189-1199.
JOHN: 1199-1216.
HENRY III: 1216-1272.
EDWARD I: 1272-1307.
EDWARD II: 1307-1327.
EDWARD III: 1327-1377.
RICHARD II: 1377-1399.

House of Lancaster

HENRY IV: 1399-1413.
HENRY V: 1413-1422.
HENRY VI: 1422-1461, 1470-1471.

House of York

EDWARD IV: 1461-1470, 1471-1483.
EDWARD V: 1483-1483.
RICHARD III: 1483-1485.

House of Tudor

HENRY VII: 1485-1509.
HENRY VIII: 1509-1547.
EDWARD VI: 1547-1553.
MARY I: 1553-1558.
ELIZABETH: 1558-1603.

House of Stuart

JAMES I: 1603-1625.
CHARLES I: 1625-1649.

The Commonwealth

OLIVER CROMWELL, LORD PROTECTOR:
1653-1658.
RICHARD CROMWELL: 1658-1659.

House of Stuart

CHARLES II: 1660-1685.
JAMES II: 1685-1688.
WILLIAM III AND MARY II: 1689-1702. Mary
died in 1694.
ANNE: 1702-1714.

House of Hanover

GEORGE I: 1714-1727.
GEORGE II: 1727-1760.
GEORGE III: 1760-1820.
GEORGE IV: 1820-1830.
WILLIAM IV: 1830-1837.
VICTORIA: 1837-1901.

House of Saxe-Coburg

EDWARD VII: 1901-1910.

House of Windsor

GEORGE V: 1910-1936.
EDWARD VIII: 1936 (abdicated).
GEORGE VI: 1936-1952.
ELIZABETH II: 1952-

RULERS OF FRANCE

The Carolingians

PEPIN THE SHORT: 751-768.
CHARLEMAGNE (CHARLES THE GREAT):
768-814.
LOUIS I (THE PIOUS OR LE DÉBON-
NAIRE): 814-840.
CHARLES I: 840-877.
LOUIS II: 877-879.
LOUIS III: 879-882.
CHARLES II: 884-888.
EUDES (ODO): 888-898.
CHARLES II: 898-922.

ROBERT: 922-936.
LOTHAIR: 954-986.
LOUIS V: 986-987.

The Capets

HUGH CAPET: 987-996.
ROBERT: 996-1031.
HENRY I: 1031-1060.
PHILIP I: 1060-1108.
LOUIS VI: 1108-1137 .
LOUIS VII: 1137-1180.
PHILIP II: 1180-1223.
LOUIS VIII: 1223-1226.
LOUIS IX: 1226-1270.
PHILIP III: 1270-1285.
PHILIP IV: 1285-1314.
LOUIS X: 1314-1316.
PHILIP V: 1316-1322.
CHARLES IV: 1322-1328.

House of Valois

PHILIP VI: 1328-1350.
JOHN II: 1350-1364.
CHARLES V: 1364-1380.
CHARLES VI: 1380-1422.
CHARLES VII: 1422-1461.
LOUIS XI: 1461-1483.
CHARLES VIII: 1483-1498.
LOUIS XII: 1498-1515.
FRANCIS I: 1515-1547.
HENRY II: 1547-1559.
FRANCIS II: 1559-1560.
CHARLES IX: 1560-1574.
HENRY III: 1574-1589.

House of Bourbon

HENRY IV: 1589-1610.
LOUIS XIII: 1610-1643.
LOUIS XIV: 1643-1715.
LOUIS XV: 1715-1774.
LOUIS XVI: 1774-1792 (beheaded 1793).

First Republic

NATIONAL CONVENTION: 1792-1795.
DIRECTORY: 1795-1799.
CONSULATE, NAPOLEON BONAPARTE,
FIRST CONSUL: 1799-1802.
NAPOLEON BONAPARTE ELECTED CON-
SUL FOR LIFE: 1802-1804.

First Empire

NAPOLEON, EMPEROR: 1804-1814.

Bourbons Restored

LOUIS XVIII: 1814-1824.
CHARLES X: 1824-1830.

House of Orléans

LOUIS PHILIPPE: 1830-1848.

Second Republic

LOUIS NAPOLEON: 1848-1852.

Second Empire

LOUIS NAPOLEON, emperor: 1852-1870.

Third Republic - Presidents

THIERS, LOUIS ADOLPHE: 1871-1873.
MACMAHON, MARSHAL PATRICE M.:
1873-1879.
GREVY, PAUL J.: 1879-1887.
SADI-CARNOT, M: 1887-1894.
CASIMIR-PERIER, JEAN P. P.: 1894-1895.
FAURE, FRANÇOIS FELIX: 1895-1899.
LOUBET, EMILE: 1899-1906.
FALLIERES, ARMAND: 1906-1913.
POINCARÉ, RAYMOND: 1913-1920.
DESCHANEL, PAUL: 1920-1920.
MILLERAND, ALEXANDRE: 1920-1924.
DOUMERGUE, GASTON: 1924-1931.
DOUMER, PAUL: 1931-1932.
LEBRUN, ALBERT: 1932-1940 (resigned).

Vichy Government

MARSHAL PHILIPPE PÉTAIN, CHIEF OF
STATE: 1940-1944.
PIERRE LAVAL, CHIEF OF GOVERNMENT:
1942-1944.

Presidents of the Provisional Government

CHARLES DE GAULLE: 1944-1946.
FÉLIX GOUIN: January 23, 1946.
GEORGES BIDAULT: June 19, 1946.
LÉON BLUM: December 12, 1946.

Fourth Republic - Presidents

AURIOL, VINCENT: 1947-1954.
COTY, RENÉ: 1954-

RULERS OF THE HOLY ROMAN EMPIRE

Note: The coronation of Charlemagne in 800 is usually dated the beginning of the Holy Roman Empire. Here the succession is traced from the Post-Carolingian Kings of East Frankland, though Conrad of Franconia and Henry I of Saxony were never crowned Emperor.

Post-Carolingian Kings of East Frankland and Emperors of the Holy Roman Empire

CONRAD OF FRANCONIA: 911-918.
HENRY I OF SAXONY (THE FOWLER):
919-936.
OTTO I OF SAXONY: 936-962 (crowned Emperor in 962).

Saxon Emperors

OTTO I: 962-973.
OTTO II: 973-983.
OTTO III: 983-1002.
HENRY II: 1002-1024.

Franconian Emperors

CONRAD II: 1024-1039.
HENRY III: 1039-1056.
HENRY IV: 1056-1106.
HENRY V: 1106-1125.
LOTHAIR III OF SAXONY: 1125-1137.

Hohenstaufen Emperors

CONRAD III: 1137-1152.
FREDERICK I, BARBAROSSA: 1152-1190.
HENRY IV: 1190-1197.
OTTO IV OF BRUNSWICK-WELF: 1198-1215
(rival Emperor with Philip of Swabia).
PHILIP OF SWABIA: 1198-1208 (rival Emperor
with Otto IV).
FREDERICK II: 1211-1250 (also King of Sicily).
CONRAD IV: 1250-1254.
INTERREGNUM: 1254-1273.
RUDOLPH I OF HAPSBURG: 1273-1291.
ADOLPH OF NASSAU: 1292-1298.
ALBERT I OF HAPSBURG: 1298-1308.
HENRY VII OF LUXEMBURG: 1308-1313.
LOUIS IV OF BAVARIA: 1314-1347.
CHARLES IV OF LUXEMBURG-BOHEMIA:
1347-1378.
WENCESLAUS OF LUXEMBURG: 1378-1400.
RUPERT OF BAVARIA: 1400-1410.
SIGISMUND OF LUXEMBURG: 1410-1437.
ALBERT II OF HAPSBURG: 1438-1439.
FREDERICK III OF HAPSBURG: 1440-1493.
MAXIMILIAN I OF HAPSBURG: 1493-1519.
CHARLES V OF HAPSBURG: 1519-1556.
FERDINAND I OF HAPSBURG: 1558-1564.
MAXIMILIAN II OF HAPSBURG: 1564-1576.
RUDOLPH II OF HAPSBURG: 1576-1612.
MATTHIAS OF HAPSBURG: 1612-1619.
FERDINAND II OF HAPSBURG: 1619-1637.
FERDINAND III OF HAPSBURG: 1637-1657.
LEOPOLD I OF HAPSBURG: 1658-1705.
JOSEPH I OF HAPSBURG: 1705-1711.
CHARLES VI OF HAPSBURG: 1711-1740.
CHARLES VII OF BAVARIA: 1742-1745.
FRANCIS I OF HAPSBURG-LORRAINE:
1745-1765.
JOSEPH II OF HAPSBURG-LORRAINE:
1765-1790.
LEOPOLD II OF HAPSBURG-LORRAINE:
1790-1792.
FRANCIS II OF HAPSBURG-LORRAINE:
1792-1806 (Napoleon declared the end of the
Holy Roman Empire in 1806).

RULERS OF ITALY

VICTOR EMMANUEL II: King of Sardinia,
1849-1861; King of Italy, 1861-1878.
HUMBERT: 1878-1900.
VICTOR EMMANUEL III: 1900-1946.
BENITO MUSSOLINI, DICTATOR: 1922-1945.
HUMBERT II: 1946; Republic declared, 1946.
PRESIDENT ENRICO DE NICOLA: 1946-1948
(provisional).
PRESIDENT LUIGI EINAUDI: 1948-1955.
PRESIDENT GIOVANNI GRONCHI: 1955-

RULERS OF PRUSSIA AND GERMANY

Prussia

FREDERICK WILLIAM THE GREAT, ELEC-
TOR OF BRANDENBURG: 1640-1688.
FREDERICK III: 1688-1713 (Frederick I, King
of Prussia 1701-1713).
FREDERICK WILLIAM I: 1713-1740.
FREDERICK II (THE GREAT): 1740-1786.
FREDERICK WILLIAM II: 1786-1797.
FREDERICK WILLIAM III: 1797-1840.
FREDERICK WILLAM IV: 1840-1861.

Germany

Part of the Holy Roman Empire until 1806; part of German Confederation 1815-1866.

WILLIAM I: 1861-1888 King of Prussia; 1871-1888 Emperor of Germany.
FREDERICK III: 1888.
WILLIAM II: 1888-1918.

Republic 1918-1933

PRESIDENT FRIEDRICH EBERT: 1919-1925.
PRESIDENT PAUL VON HINDENBURG: 1925-1933.

Third German Reich 1933-1945

REICHSFÜHRER ADOLF HITLER: 1933-1945 (appointed Chancellor by Hindenburg in 1933).
REICHSFÜHRER KARL DOENITZ: 1945.

Federal Republic of Western Germany

PRESIDENT THEODOR HEUSS: 1949-

Democratic Republic Government of Eastern Germany

PRESIDENT WILHELM PIECK: 1949-

RULERS OF ROME AND OF THE WESTERN AND EASTERN EMPIRES

Kings of Rome

ROMULUS: 753-715 B. C.
NUMA POMPILIUS: 715-673. B. C.
TULLUS HOSTILIUS: 673-641 B. C.
ANCUS MARCIUS: 641-616 B. C.
L. TARQUINIUS PRISCUS: 616-578 B. C.
SERVIUS TULLIUS: 578-534 B. C.
L. TARQUINIUS SUBERBUS: 534-510 B. C.

Emperors of Rome

AUGUSTUS (GAIUS JULIUS CAESAR OCTAVIANUS): 27 B. C.-14 A. D.
TIBERIUS (TIBERIUS CLAUDIUS NERO CAESAR): 14-37.
CALIGULA GAIUS CLAUDIUS NERO CAESAR GERMANICUS): 37-41.
CLAUDIUS (TIBERIUS CLAUDIUS NERO CAESAR DRUSUS): 41-54.
NERO (LUCIUS DOMITIUS AHENOBARBUS CLAUDIUS DRUSUS: 54-68.
GALBA (SERVIUS SULPICUS GALBA): 68-69.
OTHO (MARCUS SALVIUS OTHO): 69.
VITELLIUS (AULUS VITELLIUS GERMANICUS): 69.
VESPASIAN (TITUS FLAVIUS VESPASIANUS): 69-79.
TITUS (TITUS FLAVIUS VESPASIANUS): 79-81.
DOMITIAN (TITUS FLAVIUS DOMITIANUS): 81-96.
NERVA (MARCUS COCCEIUS NERVA): 96-98.
TRAJAN (MARCUS ULPIUS NERVA TRAIANUS): 98-117.
HADRIAN (PUBLIUS AELIUS TRAIANUS HADRIANUS): 117-138.
ANTONINUS PIUS (TITUS AURELIUS FULVIS BOIONIUS ARRIUS ANTONINUS PIUS): 138-161.

MARCUS AURELIUS (MARCUS ANNIUS AURELIUS VERUS): 161-180.
LUCIUS AURELIUS VERUS (LUCIUS CEIONIUS COMMODUS VERUS): 161-169.
COMMODUS (LUCIUS AELIUS MARCUS AURELIUS ANTONINUS COMMODUS): 180-192.
PERTINAX (PUBLIUS HELVIUS PERTINAX): 193.
DIDIUS JULIAN (MARCUS DIDIUS SALVIUS JULIANUS SEVERUS): 193.
SEPTIMUS SEVERUS (LUCIUS SEPTIMIUS SEVERUS): 193-211.
GETA (PUBLIUS SEPTIMIUS GETA): 211-212.
CARACALLA (MARCUS AURELIUS ANTONIUS BASSIANUS CARCALLUS): 211-217.
MACRINUS (MARCUS OPELLIUS SEVERUS MACRINUS): 217-218.
ELAGABULUS (MARCUS VARIUS AVITUS BASSIANUS AURELIUS ANTONIUS HELIOGABALUS): 218-222.
ALEXANDER SEVERUS (MARCUS ALEXIANUS BASSIANUS AURELIUS SEVERUS ALEXANDER): 222-235.
MAXIMIN (GAIUS JULIUS VERUS MAXIMINUS "THRAX"): 235-238.
GORDIAN I (MARCUS ANTONIUS GORDIANUS): 238.
PUPIENUS (MARCUS CLODIUS PUPIENUS MAXIMUS): 238.
BALBINUS (DECIMUS CAELIUS BALBINUS): 238.
GORDIAN III (MARCUS ANTONIUS GORDIANUS): 238-244.
PHILIPP "ARABS" (MARCUS JULIUS PHILIPPUS "ARABS"): 244-249.
DECIUS (GAIUS MESSIUS QUINTUS TRAIANUS DECIUS): 249-251.
GALLUS (GAIUS VIBIUS TREBONIANUS GALLUS): 251-253.
AEMILIAN (MARCUS JULIUS AEMILIUS AEMILIANUS): 253.
VALERIAN (GAIUS PUBLIUS LICINIUS VALERIANUS): 253-259.
GALLIEN (PUBLIUS LICINIUS EGNATIUS GALLIENUS): 259-268.
CLAUDIUS II (MARCUS AURELIUS CLAUDIUS GOTHICUS): 268-270.
AURELIAN (LUCIUS DOMITIUS AURELIANUS): 270-275.
TATICUS (MARCUS CLAUDIUS TACITUS): 275-276.
PROBUS MARCUS AURELIUS PROBUS): 276-282.
CARUS (MARCUS AURELIUS CARUS): 282-283.
DIOCLETIAN (GAIUS AURELIUS VALERIUS DIOCLES JOVIUS): 284-305.
MAXIMIAN (MARCUS AURELIUS VALERIUS MAXIMIANUS HERCULIUS): 286-305.
CONSTANTIUS I (FLAVIUS VALERIUS CONSTANTIUS CHLORUS): 305-306.
GALERIUS (GAIUS GALERIUS VALERIUS MAXIMIANUS): 305-311.
SEVERUS (FLAVIUS VALERIUS CONSTANTIUS CHLORUS): 306-307.
MAXIMIAN (MARCUS AURELIUS VALERIUS MAXIMIANUS): 306-308.
MAXENTIUS (MARCUS AURELIUS VALERIUS MAXENTIUS): 306-312.
LICINIUS (GAIUS FLAVIUS VALERIUS LICINIANUS LICINIUS): 311-324.
CONSTANTINE I, THE GREAT (FLAVIUS VALERIUS CONSTANTINUS): 311-337.
CONSTANTINE II (FLAVIUS VALERIUS CLAUDIUS CONSTANTINUS): 337-340.
CONSTANTIUS II (FLAVIUS VALERIUS JULIUS CONSTANTIUS): 337-361.

CONSTANS (FLAVIUS VALERIUS JULIUS CONSTANTIUS): 337-350.
JULIAN, THE APOSTATE (FLAVIUS CLAUDIUS JULIANUS): 361-363.
JOVIAN (FLAVIUS JOVIANUS): 363-364.
VALENTIAN I (FLAVIUS VALENTIANUS, IN THE WEST): 364-375.
VALENS (IN THE EAST): 364-378.
GRATIAN (FLAVIUS GRATIANUS AUGUSTUS IN TEH WEST): 375-383.
VALENTINIAN II (FLAVIUS VALENTIANUS, IN THE WEST): 375-392.
THEODOSIUS, THE GREAT (FLAVIUS THEODOSIUS, IN THE EAST, AND AFTER 392, IN THE WEST): 379-395.
MAXIMUS (MAGNUS CLEMENS MAXIMUS): 383-388.
EUGENIUS: 392-394.
ARCADIUS (IN THE EAST): 395-408.
HONORIUS (FLAVIUS HONORIUS, IN THE WEST): 395-423.
THEODOSIUS II (IN THE EAST): 408-450.
VALENTINIAN III (FLAVIUS PLACIDUS VALENTIANUS, IN THE WEST): 425-454.
MARCIAN (MARCIANUS, IN THE EAST): 450-457.
PETRONIUS (FLAVIUS ANCIUS PETRONIUS MAXIMUS, IN THE WEST): 455.
AVITUS (FLAVIUS MAECILIUS EPARCHUS AVITUS, IN THE WEST): 455-457.
MAJORIAN (JULIUS VALERIUS MAIORANUS, IN THE WEST): 457-461.
LEO I (LEO THRAX, MAGNUS, IN THE EAST): 457-474.
SEVERUS (LIBIUS SEVERIANUS SEVERUS, IN THE WEST): 461-465.
ANTHEMIUS (PROCOPIUS ANTHEMIUS, IN THE WEST): 467-472.
OLYBRIUS (ANCIUS OLYBRIUS, IN THE WEST): 472.
GLYCERIUS (IN THE WEST): 473-474.
JULIUS NEPOS (IN THE WEST): 473-475.
LEO II (IN THE EAST): 473-474.
ZENO (IN THE EAST): 474-491.
ROMULUS AUGUSTULUS (FLAVIUS MOMYLLUS ROMULUS AUGUSTUS, IN THE WEST): 475-476.

Emperors of Byzantine

ZENO: 474-491 A. D.
ANASTASIUS I: 491-518.
JUSTIN I (FLAVIUS JUSTINUS): 518-527.
JUSTINIAN THE GREAT (FLAVIANUS JUSTIANUS): 527-565.
JUSTIN II (FLAVIUS JUSTINUS): 565-578.
TIBERIUS (FLAVIUS CONSTANTINUS TIBERIUS): 578-582.
MAURICE (MAURITIUS): 582-602.
PHOCAS I: 602-610.
HERACLIUS I: 610-641.
CONSTANTINE III (CONSTANTINUS): 641.
HERACLEON (HERACLEONAS): 641.
CONSTANS II: 641-668.
CONSTANTINE IV (POGONATUS): 668-685.
JUSTINIAN II (RHINOTMETUS): 685-695 and 705-711.
LEONTIUS II: 695-698.
TIBERIUS III (APSIMAR): 698-705.
JUSTINIAN II: Restored.
PHILIPPICUS: 711-713.
ANASTASIUS II: 713-716.
THEODOSIUS III: 716-717.
LEO III (THE ISAURIAN): 717-741.
CONSTANTINE V (KOPRONYMUS): 741-775.
LEO IV: 775-780.
CONSTANTINE VI: 780-797.
IRENE (EMPRESS): 797-802.
NICEPHORUS I: 802-811.

STAURACIUS (STAURAKIUS): 811.
MICHAEL I (RHANGABÉ): 811-813.
LEO V (THE ARMENIAN): 813-820.
MICHAEL II (BALBUS): 820-829.
THEOPHILUS I: 829-842.
MICHAEL III: 842-867.
BARDAS: 842-866.
THEOPHILUS II: 867.
BASIL I (THE MACEDONIAN): 867-886.
LEO VI (THE WISE): 886-912.
ALEXANDER III: 912-913.
CONSTANTINE VII (PORPHYROGENITUS): 913-959.
ROMANUS I (LECAPENUS): 919-944.
ROMANUS II: 959-963.
BASIL II (BULGAROCTONUS): 963-1025.
NICEPHORUS II (PHOCAS): 963-969.
JOHN I (TZIMISCES): 969-976.
CONSTANTINE VIII: 1025-1028.
ZOË (EMPRESS): 1028-1050.
ROMANUS III (ARGYROPOLUS): 1028-1034.
MICHAEL IV (THE PAPHLAGONIAN): 1034-1041.
MICHAEL V (KALAPHATES): 1041-1042.
CONSTANTINE IX (MONOMACHUS): 1042-1054.
THEODORA (EMPRESS): 1054-1056.
MICHAEL VI (STRATIOTICUS): 1056-1057.
ISAAC I (COMNENUS): 1057-1059.
CONSTANTINE X (DUKAS): 1059-1067.
ANDRONICUS: 1067.
CONSTANTINE XI: 1067.
ROMANUS IV (DIOGENES): 1067-1071.
MICHAEL VII (PARAPINAKES): 1071-1078.
NICEPHORUS III (BOTANIATES): 1078-1081.
ALEXIUS I (COMNENUS): 1081-1118.
JOHN II (COMNENUS): 1118-1143.
MANUEL I: 1143-1180.
ALEXIUS II: 1180-1183.
ANDRONICUS I: 1183-1185.
ISAAC II (ANGELUS-COMNENUS): 1185-1195.
ALEXIUS III (ANGELUS): 1195-1203.
ISAAC II (RESTORED): 1203.
ALEXIUS IV: 1203-1204.
ALEXIUS V (DUKAS): 1204.

Latin Emperors

BALDWIN I: 1204-1205 A. D.
HENRY: 1205-1216.
PETER DE COURTENAY: 1216-1217.
ROBERT DE COURTENAY: 1218-1228.
BALDWIN II: 1228-1261.

Nicaen Emperors

THEODORE I (LASCARIS): 1206-1222 A. D.
JOHN DUKAS VATATZES: 1222-1254.
THEODORE II (LASCARIS): 1254-1259.
JOHN IV (LASCARIS): 1258-1261.
MICHAEL VIII (PALEOLOGUS): 1259-1261.

The Paleologi

MICHAEL VIII: 1261-1282.
ANDRONICUS II (THE ELDER): 1282-1328.
MICHAEL IX (CO-EMPEROR): 1295-1320.
ANDRONICUS III (THE YOUNGER): 1328-1341.
JOHN V (PALEOLOGUS): 1341-1347.
ANDRONICUS IV: 1376-1379.
JOHN V (RESTORED): 1379-1391.
JOHN VII: 1390.
MANUEL II: 1391-1425.
JOHN VII: 1425-1448.
CONSTANTINE XI: 1448-1453.

RULERS OF RUSSIA

IVAN III (THE GREAT): 1462-1505.
BASIL III: 1505-1533.
IVAN IV (THE TERRIBLE): 1533-1584.
THEODORE (FEODOR) I: 1584-1598.
BORIS GODUNOV: 1598-1605.
THEODORE (FEODOR) II: 1605.
DMITRI (DEMETRIUS): 1605-1606.
BASIL IV SHUISKI: 1606-1610.
INTERREGNUM: 1610-1613.
MICHAEL: 1613-1645.
ALEXIS: 1645-1676.
THEODORE (FEODOR) III: 1676-1682.
IVAN V AND PETER I: 1682-1689.
PETER I (THE GREAT): 1689-1725.
CATHERINE I: 1725-1727.
PETER II: 1727-1730.
ANNA: 1730-1740.
IVAN VI: 1740-1741.
ELIZABETH: 1741-1762.
PETER III: 1762.
CATHERINE II (THE GREAT): 1762-1796.
PAUL I: 1796-1801.
ALEXANDER I: 1801-1825.
NICHOLAS I: 1825-1855.
ALEXANDER II: 1855-1881.
ALEXANDER III: 1881-1894.
NICHOLAS II: 1894-1917.
REPUBLIC: 1917 (Provisional Government under Alexander Kerensky).

Union of Soviet Socialist Republics

PREMIER NIKOLAI LENIN: 1917-1924.
PREMIER ALEKSEI RYKOV: 1924-1930.
PREMIER VYACHESLAV MOLOTOV: 1930-1941.
PREMIER JOSEPH STALIN: 1941-1953 (General Secretary of the Communist Party and actual ruler of Russia 1924-1953).
PREMIER GEORGI MALENKOV: 1953-1955.
PREMIER NIKOLAI BULGANIN: 1955-.

RULERS OF SPAIN

FERDINAND OF ARAGON AND ISABELLA OF CASTILLE: 1479-1504.
FERDINAND AND PHILIP I: 1504-1506.
FERDINAND AND CHARLES I: 1506-1516.
CHARLES I (EMPEROR CHARLES V): 1516-1556.
PHILIP II: 1556-1598.
PHILIP III: 1598-1621.
PHILIP IV: 1621-1665.
CHARLES II: 1665-1700.
PHILIP V: 1700-1746.
FERDINAND VI: 1746-1759.
CHARLES III: 1759-1788.
CHARLES IV: 1788-1808.
JOSEPH BONAPARTE: 1808-1813.
FERDINAND VII: 1813-1833.
ISABELLA II: 1833-1868.
REPUBLIC: 1868-1870.
AMADEO: 1870-1873.
REPUBLIC: 1873-1875.
ALPHONSO XII: 1875-1885.
ALPHONSO XIII: 1886-1931.
REPUBLIC: 1931-1939.
FRANCISCO FRANCO, DICTATOR: 1939-.

Rulers, Titles of

AMEER (AMIR): Ruler of Afghanistan, Sind, and other Mohammedan states; also spelled Emir.
ARCHON: Chief of the nine magistrates of ancient Athens. The next in rank was called Basileus, and the third Polemarch (field marshal).
BEGLERBEG: See Bey.
BEGUM: A queen, princess, or lady of high rank in India.
BEY: In Turkey, a bey is usually a superior military officer, though the title is often assumed by those who hold no official position. The governor of a province is known as a beglar-bey or beglerbeg (lord of lords). It is also the title of a native chief in Tunis.
BRENN (BRENHIN) (WAR CHIEF): A dictator of the ancient Gauls, appointed by the Druids in times of danger.
BRETWALDA (WIELDER OF BRITAIN): A title of some of the Anglo-Saxon kings who held supremacy over the rest; a king of the Heptarchy.
CACIQUE: See Cazique.
CALIPH (CALIF) (SUCCESSOR): Successors of Mahomet in temporal and spiritual matters; the office formerly claimed by the Sultan of Turkey. The Turkish Assembly abolished the Caliphate in 1923.
CAZIQUE (CACIQUE): A native prince of the ancient Peruvians, Cubans, Mexicans, etc.
CHAGAN: The chief of the Avars.
CHAM: See Khan.
CRAL: The despot of ancient Servia.
CZAR: (From Lat. Caesar; see Kaiser). The popular title of the former emperors of Russia (assumed in 1547 by Ivan the Terrible), but officially his title only as King of Poland and a few other parts of his empire. His wife was the Czarina or Czaritza, his son the Czarevich, and his daughter the Czarevna. The sovereign of Bulgaria was officially styled Czar.
DEY: In Algiers, before it was annexed to France in 1830; also the 16th-cent. rulers of Tunis and Tripoli (Turk. Dai, Uncle).
DIWAN: The native chief of Palanpur, India.
DOGE: The ruler of the old Venetian Republic (697-1797); also of that of Genova (1339-1797).
DUKE: The ruler of a duchy; formerly in many European countries of sovereign rank. (Lat. Dux, a leader.)
ELECTOR: A Prince of the Holy Roman Empire (of sovereign rank) entitled to take part in the election of the Emperor.
EMIR: The independent chieftain of certain Arabian provinces, as Bokhara, Neljd, etc. The same as Amir.
EMPEROR: The paramount ruler of an empire (as India or Japan); especially, in medieval times, the Holy Roman Empire; from Lat. Imperator, one who commands.
EXARCH: The title of a viceroy of the Byzantine Emperors, especially the Exarch of Ravenna, who was de facto governor of Italy.
GAEKWAR: Formerly the title of the Monarch of the Mahrattas; now that of the native ruler of Baroda (his son being the Gaekwad). The word is Marathi for cowherd.
HOSPODAR: The title borne by the princes of Moldavia and Wallachia before the union of those countries with Rumania (Slavic, lord, master).
IMAM: A title of the Sultan as spiritual successor of Mahomet; also of the ruler of Yemen, Arabia. It is also used for certain religious leaders and the Shiites employ it for the expected Mahdi. The word means teacher or guide.
IMPERATOR: See Emperor.
INCA: The title of the sovereigns of Peru up to the conquest by Pizarro (1531).

KAISER: The German form of Lat. Caesar (see Czar); the old title of the Emperor of the Holy Roman Empire, and the Emperors of Germany and of Austria.

KHAN: The chief rulers of Tartar, Mongol, and Turkish tribes, as successors of Genghis Khan (d. 1227). The word means lord or prince.

KHEDIVE: The title conferred in 1867 by the Sultan of Turkey on the viceroy or governor of Egypt. In November, 1914, the Khedive, who had declared himself an adherant of the Central Powers, was deposed and a British Protectorate declared.

KING: The Anglo-Saxon cyning, literally "a man of good birth" (cyn, tribe, kin, or race, with the patronymic -ing.).

LAMA: The priest-ruler of Tibet, known as the Grand Lama or Dalai Lama. Also the ecclesiastical potentate of that country, known as the Tashai Lama.

MAHARAJAH: (Hind. the great king). The title of many of the native rulers of Indian states.

MIKADO: The popular title of the hereditary ruler of Japan, officially styled "Emperor." The name (like the Turkish Sublime Porte) means "The August Door." See Shogun.

MOGUL (OR GREAT MOGUL): The emperors of Delhi, and rulers of the greater part of India from 1526 to 1857, of the Mongol line founded by Baber.

MPRET: The old title of the Albanian rulers (from Lat. imperator), revived in 1913 in favor of Prince William of Wied, whose Mpretship, as a result of the outbreak of the Great War, lasted only a few months.

NAWAB: The native rulers of Bhopal, Tonk, Jaora, and some other Indian states.

PADISHAH: (Pers. protecting lord). A title of the Sultan of Turkey, the Shah of Persia, and of the former Great Moguls; also of the King of Great Britain as Emperor of India.

PENDRAGON: The title assumed by the ancient British overlord.

POLEMARCH: See Archon.

PRINCE: Formerly in common use as the title of a reigning sovereign, as it still is in a few cases, such as the Prince of Monaco and Prince of Liechtenstein.

RAJAH: Hindustani for king (see Maharajah): specifically the title of the native rulers of Cochin, Ratlam, Tippera, Chamba, Faridkot, Mandi, Pudukota, Rajgrh, Rajpipla, Sailana, and Tehri (Garhwal). See Rex.

RANEE (RANI): A Hindu queen, the feminine of Rajah.

REX (REG-EM): The Latin equivalent of our "king," connected with regere, to rule, and with Sanskrit rajan (whence Rajah), a king.

SACHEM (SAGAMORE): Chieftains of certain tribes of North American Indians.

SATRAP: The governor of a province in ancient Persia.

SHAH (PERS. KING): The supreme ruler of Persia and of some other Eastern countries. See Padishah.

SHEIKH: An Arab chief, or head man of a tribe.

SHOGUN: The title of the virtual rulers of Japan (representing usurping families who kept the true Emperor in perpetual confinement with some prestige of sovereignty but little power) from about the close of the 12th cent. to the revolution of 1867-1868. It means "leader of an army," and was originally the title of military governors. Also called Tycoon.

SIRDAR: The commander in chief of the Egyptian army and military governor of Egypt.

STADTHOLDER: Originally a viceroy in a province of the Netherlands, but later the chief executive officer of the United Provinces.

SULTAN (FORMERLY ALSO SOLDAN): The title of the rulers of many Mohammedan states, especially Turkey, before the formation of the new Turkish state.

TETRARCH: The governor of the fourth part of a province in the ancient Roman Empire.

TYCOON: An alternative title of the Japanese Shogun (which see). The word is from Chinese and means "great sovereign."

VALI: The title of the governors of Egypt prior to 1867, when the style Khedive (which see) was granted by the Sultan. Also a Turkish official.

VOIVODE (VAIVODE): Properly (Russ.) "the leader of an army." The word was for a time assumed as a title by the Princes of Moldavia and Wallachia, later called Hospodars (which see).

The following names have been adopted in varying degrees as royal titles among the peoples mentioned:

ABGARUS (THE GRAND): The kings of Edessa were so styled.

ABIMELECH (MY FATHER THE KING): The chief ruler of the ancient Philistines.

ATTABEG (FATHER PRINCE): Persia, 1118.

AUGUSTUS: The title of the reigning Emperor of Rome, when the heir presumptive was styled "Caesar."

CAESAR: Proper name adopted by the Roman emperors. See Kaiser; Czar.

CANDACE: Proper name adopted by the queens of Ethiopia.

CYRUS (MIGHTY): Ancient Persia.

DARIUS: Latin form of Darawesh (King). Ancient Persia.

MELECH (KING): Ancient Semitic tribes.

PHARAOH (LIGHT OF THE WORLD): Ancient Egypt.

PTOLEMY: Proper name adopted by Egypt after the death of Alexander.

SOPHY (SOPHI): A former title of the kings of Persia, from Cafi-ud-din, the founder of the ancient dynasty of the Cafi (or Cafavi).

Russian Rulers
See Rulers

Sacred Books
See Apocrypha; Bible; Scriptures

Saints
See also Angels; Apostles and Evangelists with Their Appropriate Symbols; Religious Allusions, References, and Symbols; Cathedrals and Churches; International Calendar of Saints and Special Days

Principal Saints and Their Symbols

GOD THE FATHER: The early Christian representation of God the Father pictured a hand in a gesture of bestowal, with rays issuing from each finger, extended from clouds. It was generally shown in the act of benediction, and the position of the hand revealed whether the picture belonged to the Greek (Eastern) or Latin (Western) Church. The Greek benediction was given with the forefinger extended, the middle finger slightly bent, the tumb crossed over the third finger, and the little finger bent, the entire gesture and placement of the fingers forming the monogram of the Son of God. The Latin benediction was given with the third and little fingers closed, while the thumb and two other fingers remained open and straight, the open fingers symbolizing the Trinity, and the closed the two natures of Christ (Christ as God and as man). Frequently the hand was surrounded by a cruciform nimbus, which in early art was used with God alone. Later symbols of God the Father were a face in the clouds, a bust, and, by the 14th century, a figure which was at first like the figure of Christ, but gradually was given the characteristics of aging. Since the 16th century, the symbol of God the Father has been a triangle surrounded by rays of light, an emblem of eternity.

CHRIST: The usual symbols for Christ are the glory, aureole or nimbus, fish, cross, lamb, and lion.

HOLY GHOST (HOLY SPIRIT): Dove.

THE TRINITY: Symbols of the Christian Trinity are three triangles, three circles, or three fishes.

ST. ADRIAN: An anvil and a sword, the instruments of his martyrdom.

ST. AGATHA: Is usually represented with a pair of pincers, which, in symbol of her martyrdom, hold a nipple between their teeth.

ST. AGNES: Always represented with a lamb, either beside her or in her hand, because of the similarity of *Agnus*, the Latin word for lamb, to Agnes, and because the lamb symbolizes her spotless purity.

ST. ALBAN: A sword and a cross.

ST. ALEXIS: A pilgrim's cloak and staff.

ST. ALPHEGE: Is represented with his chasuble full of stones. Sometimes he is holding a battle-ax, which symbolizes the instrument of his martyrdom.

ST. AMBROSE: A hive of bees.

ANGELS: The first great division of angels, the Councilors of the Most High, with their characteristic emblems are: Seraphim, represented as covered all over with eyes; Cherubim, standing on wheels, and each one having six wings; Thrones, with a throne or tower. The second division, or Governors, and their appropriate symbols are: Dominations, represented with a sword, triple crown, and scepter; Virtues, represented in full armor, carrying a battle-ax with an attached flying pennon, or with a crown and censer; Powers, represented as binding or beating devils, or as holding a baton. The third division, or Messengers, with their symbols are: Principalities (or Princedoms), represented in full armor and carrying each a lily; Archangels, who are Sts. Michael, Raphael, and Uriel—Uriel, described by Milton as "regent of the sun," is not identified with a specific symbol; Michael and Raphael are listed individually below; Angels, represented with wands.

ST. ANNE: Her symbol is a dove with a ring in his beak. She is usually holding a book in her hand.

ST. ANTHONY: A Tau cross and a pig with a bell around its neck.

ST. AUGUSTINE: Has no specific emblem.

ST. AUGUSTINE OF HIPPO: Is represented with a heart in his hand.

ST. BARBARA: The chalice.

ST. BARNABAS: A pilgrim's staff, symbolizing him as the companion of the apostle Paul, and a stone.

ST. BENEDICT: Is represented with a cup with a snake, emblematic of poison, issuing from it.

ST. BERNARD OF CLAIRVAUX: A beehive.

ST. BLASIUS: His symbol is a wool comb.

ST. BONIFACE: His emblem is a scourge or whip. He is also represented with a book pierced through with a sword.

ST. BRIDGET OF SWEDEN: A crozier and book.

ST. BRITIUS: Represented as carrying burning coals in his hands.

ST. CATHERINE: A wheel with spikes, because she was tortured and put to death on a wheel. She is sometimes represented with an inverted sword.

ST. CECILIA: Usually by organ-pipes. Sometimes she is pictured with a harp.

ST. CHAD: Has no specific emblem.

ST. CHRISTOPHER: A giant carrying the Christ-child over a river.

ST. CLEMENT: His symbols are a pot, which may have reference to an old St. Clement's Night custom of going about to beg party drinks, and anchor, which refers to the way he died, for he was thrown into the sea with an anchor around his neck. A papal crown is also his emblem.

ST. CRISPIN: A pair of shoes.

ST. CYPRIAN: A book and a sword.

ST. DAVID: The harp is his emblem. He is also represented by a leek.

ST. DENIS (DENYS): Is represented as a beheaded bishop, carrying his head in his hand.

ST. DOMINIC: Represented with a sparrow beside him, because the devil appeared to him as a sparrow, and a dog carrying a burning torch in its mouth, because his mother, while pregnant, dreamt she was delivered of such a dog, whose torch lighted the whole world.

ST. DOROTHEA: Is usually represented holding a branch of roses, wearing a wreath of roses, with a basket of roses and fruit beside her. Sometimes she is depicted with an angel who is carrying a basket with three apples and three roses.

ST. DUNSTAN: His emblem is a pair of tongs. Since he is said to have been a skilled harpist, the harp is also used as his emblem.

ST. EDMUND: Arrows.

ST. EDWARD: A cup and a dagger are his characteristic emblems.

ST. ELIZABETH, MOTHER OF JOHN THE BAPTIST: St. John and the lamb at her feet.

ST. ENURCHUS: Is represented with a dove lighting on his head.

ST. ETHELDREDA: Her emblems are a corsier, a crown, and a scepter.

ST. FABIAN: A book and a palm branch, and wearing the triple crown.

ST. FAITH: Represented with a bundle of rods, or carrying a brass bed in her hand.

ST. FRANCIS OF ASSISI: A seraph inflicting the five wounds of Christ.

ST. GENEVIEVE: Usually represented with the keys of Paris, because she is the patron of the city. Sometimes she appears with an angel and a devil who are struggling, respectively lighting and blowing out the candle she is carrying. She is also shown restoring her blind mother's sight and guarding her father's flocks.

ST. GEORGE: Is represented with a dragon. The shield with the St. George Cross is perhaps his most characteristic emblem.

ST. GERTRUDE: As patroness against rats and mice, she is represented as surrounded by them, or they are sporting on her spindle as she spins.

ST. GILES: Is usually represented with a crosier, and a hind with its front paws in his lap. Sometimes the neck of the hind is pierced with an arrow.

ST. GREGORY: Is represented with a dove.

ST. GUDULE (GUDILA): A lantern.

ST. HELENA: As Empress of Rome, she is represented as crowned and in royal robes. Sometimes she is carrying a model of the Holy Sepulcher, which was built by her command. Again, she is shown bearing a cross, or with the three spikes that nailed Christ to the cross.

ST. HILARY: Usually represented with three books, emblematic of his opposition to Arianism, and with his feet on serpents, symbolizing the false doctrine he vanquished. Sometime he has a Patriarchal Cross.

ST. HUBERT: Represented as a bishop holding a book with a stag on top of it, or as a hunter kneeling before a stag bearing a crucifix.

ST. HUGH: A swan.

ST. IGNATIUS: His emblem is a lion, or pride of ravening lions, because he was thrown to the lions, and so martyred.

ST. IGNATIUS LOYOLA: With the letters I.H.S. (Jesus) on his breast, or contemplating the same monogram displayed before him in the sky.

ST. JEROME: A Cardinal's hat, and a lion.

ST. JOACHIM: Usually represented as an old man carrying two doves in a basket.

ST. JOHN THE BAPTIST: Usually represented garbed in sheepskins, with a crude wooden cross and a pennon with the words *Ecce Agnus Dei* (Behold the Lamb of God), or with a book which is supporting a lamb. Sometimes he is holding a haloed lamb with a cross in its right foot.

ST. JOSEPH: Represented as an old man bearing a staff of budding lilies.

ST. JULIAN: Usually his emblem is a stag. Sometimes he is with a crowd of crippled and needy. Or he may be a ferryman, taking travelers across a river.

ST. KENTIGERN: With an episcopal cross in one hand, and a salmon and a ring in the other.

ST. LAMBERT: A palm branch, and a dart or spear.

ST. LAWRENCE: A gridiron, and a book.

ST. LEONARD: His symbols are chains and fetters.

ST. LUCIA: Her emblem is a sword-point sticking through her neck, a symbol of her martyrdom.

ST. LUCY: Her symbols are a lamp and a dish holding a pair of eyes.

ST. MACHUTUS: Has no specific emblem.

ST. MARGARET: Is usually represented in regal garments, and standing on a dragon which she is piercing with a long cross.

ST. MARTHA: Represented as a housewife, with a bunch of keys at her waist, and holding a pot of water.

ST. MARTIN: A cloak and a sword.

MARY: A Lily.

ST. MARY MAGDALEN: Her emblem is the "alabaster box of ointment."

ST. MICHAEL THE ARCHANGEL: Is represented by a spear and a pair of scales. See also Angels.

ST. NICHOLAS: Represented by three purses, a book, an anchor, or a ship.

ST. NICHOLAS OF BARI: A tub with naked infants in it.

ST. NICOMEDE: A spiked club.

ST. OLAF: Represented as a king bearing a sword which symbolizes his martyrdom. Sometimes he is carrying a loaf of bread.

ST. PANCRAS: Represented as a boy with a sword and palm branch.

ST. PATRICK: Usually represented in the act of banishing serpents. The shamrock is also his emblem.

ST. PERPETUA: Is usually represented with a cow standing beside her.

ST. PRISCA: Represented as a young girl, with a palm branch, and, at her feet, a lion. Sometimes she has a sword in her hand, and an eagle hovering over her.

ST. RAPHAEL THE ARCHANGEL: A pilgrim's staff. See also Angels.

ST. REMIGIUS: Represented with a dove carrying an oil-cruse in its beak.

ST. RICHARD: A plough or plough-share.

ST. ROCH: Represented in pilgrim's dress, with plague sores on his leg, and a ministering angel hovering near. Sometimes he is with a dog carrying a loaf of bread in its mouth.

ST. ROSALIE: A cave and cross and skull. Sometimes in the act of receiving a rosary from the Virgin.

ST. SEBASTIAN: Bound to a tree, and pierced with arrows.

ST. SILVESTER: Represented by a miter, which he is said to have invented.

ST. SIMEON: Represented with the Infant Jesus in his arms.

ST. STEPHEN THE PROTO-MARTYR: A book, and a stone in his hand.

ST. SWITHIN: In an old wooden stick calendar, or clog 'almanac, he is represented by a series of wavy lines, symbolizing a shower of rain.

ST. URSULA: A book and arrows.

ST. VALENTINE: A true lover's knot is his emblem.

ST. VINCENT: Represented as a deacon, with a gridiron full of spikes in his hand, and a raven hovering nearby.

ST. WINIFRED: Usually represented carrying her head in her hands, in symbol of her decapitation.

Local Saints and Patrons

ABERDEEN: St. Nicholas.

ALEXANDRIA: St. Mark (who founded the Church there).

ANTIOCH: St. Margaret.

ARDENNES REGION: St. Hubert, the "Apostle of the Ardennes."

BATH: St. David (?—c. 600; blessed the waters at Bath and imparted to them their warmth and invigorating nature).

BEAUVAIS: St. Lucian, the "Apostle of Beauvais."

BRUSSELS: The Virgin Mary, St. Godule.

CARTHAGE: St. Perpetua.

COLOGNE: St. Ursula.

CORFU: St. Spiridon.

CREMONA: St. Margaret.

DUMFRIES: St. Michael.

EDINBURGH: St. Giles.

EPHESUS: St. Elfisio.

FLORENCE: St. John the Baptist.
FRANCONIA: St. Kilian.
FRIESLAND: St. Wilbrod, the "Apostle of the Frisians."
GAUL: SS. Denys (the "Apostle of the Gauls"), Irenaeus, Martin.
GENOA: St. George of Cappadocia.
GLASGOW: St. Mungo (also called Kentigern).
LAPLAND: St. Nicholas.
LICHFIELD: St. Chad (who lived there).
LIÈGE: St. Albert.
LISBON: St. Vincent.
MILAN: St. Ambrose (Bishop of Milan, 374-397).
MOSCOW: St. Nicholas.
NAPLES: SS. Januarius, Thomas Aquinas.
OXFORD: St. Frideswide.
PADUA: SS. Anthony, Justina.
PARIS: St. Genevieve.
PISA: SS. Efeso, Ranieri.
POITIERS: St. Hilary.
ROCHESTER (ENGLAND): St. Paulinus.
ROME: SS. Peter and Paul.
SARAGOSSA: St. Vincent (his birthplace).
VENICE: SS. Lawrence Justiniani, Mark (who was buried there), Pantaleon.
VIENNA: St. Stephen.
YORKSHIRE: St. Paulinus.

Saints as Patrons

ACTORS: SS Genesius (Aug. 25), Vitus.
ACTRESSES: St. Pelagia of Antioch.
ALTAR BOYS: St. John Berchmans (Aug. 13).
ANIMALS: St. Francis of Assisi.
ARCHERS: St. Sebastian (Jan. 20).
ARCHITECTS: SS. Barbara, Bernward, Thomas the Apostle (Dec. 21).
ARMORERS: SS. Dunstan (May 19), George of Cappadocia, Lawrence, Maurice, Martin of Tours, Sebastian.
ART: SS. Agatha, Catherine of Bologna (Mar. 9), Luke (of painters, because he was one).
ARTISTS: SS. Agatha, Luke (Oct. 18).
ASTRONOMERS: St. Dominic (Aug. 4).
ATHLETES: St. Sebastian (Jan. 20).
AVIATORS: Our Lady of Loretto (Dec. 10); SS. Joseph of Cupertino (Sept. 18), Thérèse of Lisieux (Oct. 3).
BACKWARD CHILDREN: St. Hilary of Poitiers.
BAKERS: SS. Ambrose (bread made with honey), Aubertus, Albert of Ogna, Elizabeth of Hungary, Nicholas (Dec. 6), Peter, Vincent, Winifred (who was a baker).
BANKERS: St. Matthew (Sept. 21), Nicholas of Myra.
BARBERS: SS. Cosmas and Damien (Sept. 27), Louis (Aug. 25).
BASKETMAKERS: St. Anthony the Abbot (Jan. 17).
BEE KEEPERS: SS. Ambrose, Bernard of Clairvaux, Valentine.
BEGGARS: SS. Alexis (July 17), Elizabeth of Hungary, Giles (the slums of cities are sometimes called St. Giles), Lazarus the Beggar, Martin of Tours.
BELL-FOUNDERS: SS. Agatha, Forkernus.
BELTMAKERS: St. Alexius (July 17).
BISHOPS: SS. Timothy, Titus (Tim. 1,3; Tit. 1,7).
BLACKSMITHS: SS. Dunstan (May 19), Elegius, Giles, Hombonus (or Goodman), Peter (because he keeps the keys of heaven).
BLIND: Agathocles, Dunstan, Lucy (because she was blinded by Paschasius), Odilia (Dec. 13), Thomas à Becket.
BOATMEN: St. Julian Hospitaller.
BOMBARDIERS: St. Quentin.

BOOKBINDERS: SS. Bartholomew, John the Divine, Luke, Peter Celestine (May 19), Sebastian.
BOXMAKERS: St. Fiacre.
BOY SCOUTS: St. George (Apr. 23).
BREWERS: SS. Adrian, Armand, Arnulf of Metz, Arnulph of Soissons, Augustine of Hippo (Aug. 28), Boniface, Dorothy, Florian, Lawrence, Luke (Oct. 18), Meadard of Noyon, Nicholas of Myra (Dec. 16).
BRIDES: St. Nicholas (because he threw 3 dowries, in 3 stockings, in at the windows of 3 virgins, that they might marry their sweethearts and escape prostitution).
BRIDGE-BUILDERS: SS. John Nepomucene, Peter.
BRIDGES: St. Dorothy.
BROKERS: Charlemagne.
BRUSHMAKERS: St. Anthony the Abbot (Jan. 17).
BUILDERS: SS. Barbara, Hombonus (or Goodman), Thomas, Vincent Ferrer (April 5).
BURGLARS: St. Dismas, the penitent thief.
BURIAL SOCIETIES: St. Sebastian.
BUTCHERS: SS. Anthony the Abbot (Jan. 17), Bartholomew, Hadrian (Sept. 18), Luke (Oct. 18), Peter.
CABDRIVERS: St. Fiacre (Aug. 30).
CABINETMAKERS: SS. Anne (July 26), Gomer (Gummarus).
CAKEMAKERS: SS. Honoratus of Amiens, Macarius the Younger, Philip.
CANDLEMAKERS: SS. Honoratus of Amiens, Lucy, Lucian.
CANNONEERS: St. Barbara (who is usually represented in a fort or tower).
CAPTIVES: SS. Barbara, Felix of Valois, John of Marta, Leonard, Mark, Nicholas of Myra.
CARPENTERS: SS. Eulogius of Cordova, Joseph (who was a carpenter), Peter, Thomas.
CARPET-WEAVERS: St. Paul.
CARTERS: St. Willgis.
CATECHISTS: SS. Charles Borromeo (Nov. 14), Robert Bellarmine (May 13), Viator (Oct. 21).
CATTLE DEALERS: St. Theodard.
CAVALRY: SS. George, Martin of Tours.
CHAPLAINS: St. Quentin.
CHARCOAL-MAKERS: St. Alexander Carbonarius.
CHARITABLE SOCIETIES: SS. Elisabeth of Hungary, Vincent de Paul (July 19).
CHILDREN: SS. Abdon and Sennen, Felicitas, Germayne, Nicholas of Myra (Santa Claus), Raymond Nonnato, Solangia, Trophimus.
CHILDREN IN DANGER: St. Cunegund.
CHILDREN LEARNING TO WALK AND TALK: St. Zeno.
CHILDREN'S NURSES: SS. Agatha (Feb. 5), Margaret, Raymond Nonnatus.
CHILDREN WHO HAVE DIFFICULTY IN WALKING: St. Sabina.
CHIMNEY-SWEEPS: St. Florian.
CHOIR BOYS: The Holy Innocents (Dec. 28).
CHORISTERS: SS. Germanus of Paris, Gregory the Great, Leo the Great.
CLERGY: St. Charles Borromeo.
CLERICS: St. Gabriel of the Sorrowful Mother (Febr. 27).
CLOCKMAKERS: St. Peter.
CLOTH-WEAVERS: SS. Benno, John.
COAL-DEALERS: St. Alexander Carbonarius.
COBBLERS: SS. Crispin (who was a cobbler), Euseus.
COMEDIANS: St. Vitus (June 15).
COMPOSITORS: St. John the Apostle.
CONDEMNED CRIMINALS: St. Dismas, the penitent thief.
CONFECTIONERS: SS. Lawrence, Joseph.

CONFESSORS: SS. Charles Borromeo, Francis de Sales, John Nepomucene (May 16).

COOKS: SS. Lawrence (Aug. 10), Martha (July 29).

COOPERS: SS. Barnabas, Florian, Nicholas of Myra (Dec. 16).

COPPERSMITHS: SS. Benedict, Eulogius of Cordova, Fiacre.

COWBOYS: St. Theodard.

CRIMINALS: St. Dismas, the penitent thief.

CRIPPLES: St. Giles (who mortified his flesh by refusing cure of his accidental lameness).

CUTLERS: SS. Lawrence, Lucy.

DAIRY-WORKERS: SS. Bridget of Kildare (Feb. 1), Gunhildis.

DANCERS: St. Vitus (Jan. 20).

DEAF: St. Francis de Sales (Jan. 29).

DENTISTS: SS. Apollonia (Feb. 9), Lambert of Maestricht.

DIVINES: St. Thomas Aquinas.

DOCTORS: SS. Blaise, Cosmas and Damian, Lambert of Maestricht, Luke, Raphael.

DRAPERS: St. Wisula.

DRUGGISTS: SS. Cosmas and Damian (Sept. 27), James the Less (May 1), Emilian of Trevi, Raphael.

DRUNKARDS: SS. Martin (because Nov. 11, his Feast day, falls on the Venalia, or Feast of Bacchus), Urban.

DYERS: SS. Bartholomew, Helen, Maurice and Lydia (Aug. 3).

DYING, THE: St. Joseph.

ENGAGED COUPLES: SS. Agnes, Ambrose Sandedoni.

ENGINEERS: St. Ferdinand III (May 30).

ENGRAVERS: St. John the Divine.

EUCHARISTIC ACTION: St. Paschal Baylon (May 17).

FAMILY: St. Joseph.

FARMERS: SS. Abdon and Sennen, George (Apr. 23), Gratus of Aosta, Isidore (Mar. 22), Ulrich, Walpurga.

FARRIERS: St. John the Baptist (Aug. 29).

FERRYMEN: SS. Christopher (who was a ferryman), Julian Hospitaller.

FILE-MAKERS: St. Theodosius.

FIREMEN: St. Florian (May 4).

FIREWORKS-MAKERS: St. Barbara.

FIRST COMMUNICANTS: St. Tarcisius (Aug. 15).

FISHERMEN: SS. Andrew (Nov. 30), Benno, Peter (who was the Great Fisherman).

FISH-DEALERS: SS. Magnus, Peter.

FLORISTS: SS. Dorothy (Feb. 6), Fiacre, Honoratus of Amiens.

FLOUR MERCHANTS: St. Honoratus of Amiens.

FOOLS: St. Maturin (because the Greek word matin or maté means fool).

FREEMEN: St. John.

FUGITIVES: St. Bridget of Kildare (Feb. 1).

FULLERS: St. Sever (because St. Sever, on the Adour River, was famous for tanneries and fulleries).

FUNERAL DIRECTORS: St. Joseph of Arimathea (Mar. 17).

FURRIERS: St. Bartholomew.

GARDENERS: SS. Adelaide (Jan. 12), Agnes, Dorothy (Feb. 6), Fiacre (Aug. 30), Gertrude of Nivelles, Sebastian, Tryphon (Nov. 10).

GENTLEMEN: St. Eleazer De Sabran.

GLASSBLOWERS: St. Luke (Oct. 18).

GLAZIERS: SS. Lawrence, Lucy, Mark, Peter.

GLOVERS: St. Bartholomew.

GOLDSMITHS: SS. Anastasius, or Eloi (who was a goldsmith and sometimes called Eligius), Bernwald, Dunstan, Luke.

GOVERNORS: St. Chrysanthus.

GRAVEDIGGERS AND GRAVEYARDS: SS. Anthony the Abbot (Jan. 17), Joseph of Arimathea (Mar. 17), Lazarus.

GROCERS: St. Michael (Sept. 29).

GROOMS: SS. Anne, Hormisdas.

HANGED MEN: SS. Colman, Dismas (the penitent thief).

HATTERS: SS. James the Less (May 1), Jude, Maurice, Philip, Severus of Ravenna (Feb. 1).

HOG AND SWINEHERDS: St. Anthony.

HOLY WAFERS: St. Honoratus of Amiens.

HORSES AND HORSEMEN: SS. Colman, Ley (Thomas More, Work, 194: "St. Ley we make a horse leche, and must let our horse rather renne vnshod and marre his hoofe than to shode him on his day"), Martin of Tours, Stephen (Thomas More: "We must let al our horses bloud with a knife, because St. Stephen was killed with stones").

HOSIERS: St. Fiacre.

HOSPITALS: SS. Camillus de Lellis (July 18), John of God (Mar. 18), Jude Thaddeus (Oct. 28), Vincent de Paul.

HOUSE-HUNTERS: St. Joseph.

HOUSEMAIDS: SS. Blandina, Martha (July 29), Nothburga, Radegund, Zita (April 27).

HOUSEWIVES: SS. Anne (July 26), Francesca the Roman, Lazarus of Bethany, Martha (the sister of Lazarus), Osyth, Sabina.

HUNTERS: SS. Eustace, Hubert (Nov. 3, who lived in the famous Ardennes Hunting Forest).

HUSBANDS: St. Joseph.

INFANTRY: St. Maurice.

INFANTS: St. Felicitas, Nicholas.

INNKEEPERS: SS. Amand (Feb. 6), Goar, Julian Hospitaller, Martha, Theodotus.

INQUISITORS: St. Peter Martyr.

INSANE: St. Dymphna.

IRONMONGERS: St. Sebastian.

JEWELERS: SS. Agatha, Eligius (Dec. 1).

JOURNALISTS: St. Francis de Sales (Jan. 29).

JUDGES: St. Yves Helory.

JURISTS: St. Catherine of Alexandria (Nov. 25).

KNIFE-GRINDERS: SS. Lawrence, Maurice.

LABORERS: SS. Albert of Ogna, Isidore (May 10), James (July 25).

LACEMAKERS: SS. Elizabeth of Hungary, Teresa of Avila.

LAMP-MAKERS: SS. Lucy, Lucian.

LAUNDRESSES: SS. Hunna, Lawrence, Veronica.

LAWYERS: SS. Genesius (Aug. 25), Ivo (May 19).

LEAD-FOUNDERS: SS. Fabian, Fiacre, Sebastian.

LEARNING: SS. Acca (Nov. 27), Catherine of Alexandria.

LEPER COLONIES: St. Lazarus.

LIBRARIANS: SS. Aldhelm, Jerome (Sept. 30).

LINEN DRAPERS: St. Veronica.

LINSEED GROWERS: St. Claude of Besançon.

LITHOGRAPHERS: St. John the Divine.

LOCKSMITHS: SS. Baldomer, Dunstan (May 19), Quentin, Peter (who holds the keys of the Kingdom of Heaven).

LOVERS: SS. Valentine, Raphael (Oct. 24).

MADMEN: SS. Dymphna, Fillan.

MAIDENS: SS. Agnes, Margaret, Ursula, the Virgin Mary.

MARBLE-WORKERS: St. Clement I (Nov. 23).

MARINERS: SS. Christopher (who was a ferryman), Michael (Sept. 29), Nicholas of Tolentino (Sept. 10, who was once in danger of shipwreck and who calmed a tempest for pilgrims on route to the Holy Land).

MASONS: SS. Gregory the Great, Peter, Sebastian.

MATHEMATICIANS: St. Hubert.

MERCERS: St. Florian (son of a mercer).

MERCHANTS: SS. Francis of Assisi (Oct. 4), Hombonus (or Goodman), Nicholas of Myra (Dec. 6).
MESSENGERS: St. Gabriel (Mar. 24).
METAL WORKERS: SS. Eligius (Dec. 1), Hubert.
MIDWIVES: SS. Bridget of Kildare, Dorothy.
MILLERS: SS. Arnulph (Aug. 15), Victor of Marseilles (July 21).
MINERS: St. Barbara (Dec. 4).
MINSTRELS: St. Julian Hospitaller.
MISSIONS: SS. Francis Xavier (Dec. 3), Peter, Thérèse of Lisieux (Oct. 3).
MOTHERS: The Virgin Mary.
MOTORCYCLISTS: Our Lady of Grace (May 31).
MOTORISTS: St. Christopher (July 25).
MOUNTAIN-CLIMBERS: St. Bernard.
MUSICIANS: SS. Benedict, Cecilia (Nov. 22), Dunstan (May 19), Gregory the Great, Leo the Great, Odo of Cluny.
NAILSMITHS: St. Helen.
NAVIGATORS: SS. Brendan the Voyager, Christopher.
NEEDLEMAKERS: SS. Fiacre, Helen, Sebastian.
NEGRO MISSIONS: St. Peter Claver (Sept. 9).
NET-MAKERS: SS. James and John (Matt. IV,21), Peter.
NEWBORN INFANTS: St. Bridget of Kildare.
NEWLY-WEDS: SS. Dorothy, Valentine.
NIGHT WATCHMEN: St. Peter of Alcántara.
NOTARIES: SS. Luke (Oct. 18), Mark (Apr. 25).
NURSES: SS. Alexius (July 17), Camillus de Lellis (July 18), John of God (Mar. 8), Raphael (Oct. 24).
NURSING MOTHERS: St. Tryphena.
OIL REFINERS: St. John the Divine.
OLIVE-GROWERS: St. Bernard.
OPTICIANS: St. Fridolin (Mar. 6).
ORATORS: St. John Chrysostom (Jan. 27).
ORGAN BLOWERS: St. Genesius.
ORPHANS: St. Jerome Emiliani (July 20).
PAINTERS: SS. John the Divine, Lazarus, Luke, (Oct. 18, who was a painter), Michael the Archangel.
PARISH CLERKS: St. Nicholas.
PAPERMAKERS: St. John the Apostle.
PARISH PRIESTS: Cure D'Ars (Curate of Ars).
PARSONS: St. Thomas Aquinas.
PAWNBROKERS: SS. Catherine of Alexandria (Nov. 25), Justin (Apr. 14), Nicholas of Myra.
PEACE IN THE FAMILY: St. Baldus.
PEACEMAKERS: SS. Barnabas the Apostle, Francis Patrizzi.
PEASANTS: SS. Lucy, Margaret.
PEDLARS: St. Lucy.
PENCIL-MAKERS: St. Thomas Aquinas.
PHILOSOPHERS: SS. Acca (Nov. 27), Catherine of Alexandria (Nov. 25), Thomas Aquinas.
PHOTOGRAPHERS: St. Veronica.
PHYSICIANS: SS. Cosmas and Damian (Sept. 27), Luke (Oct. 18, Col. IV,14), Pantaleon (July 27), Raphael (Oct. 24).
PILGRIMS: SS. Alexius (July 17), James the Greater (July 25), James of Compostella, Julian Hospitaller, Raphael.
PIN-MAKERS: St. Sebastian (because his body was pierced with as many arrows as a pin-cushion is full of pins).
PLASTERERS: St. Bartholomew (Aug. 24).
POETS: SS. Cecilia (Nov. 22), David (Dec. 29).
POOR: SS. Anthony of Padua (June 13), Giles (because he gave up his possessions voluntarily to seek perfection), Lawrence (Aug. 10).
PORTERS: SS. Christopher (July 25), Quentin.

PORTRAIT-PAINTERS: St. Veronica (because the handkerchief with which she wiped Christ's face became impressed with His image).
POSTMEN: St. Gabriel (Mar. 24).
POTTERS: SS. Fiacre, Gore (who was a potter), Peter, Sebastian.
PREGNANT WOMEN: SS. Gerard Majella (Oct. 16), Margaret (July 20), Raymond Nonnatus (Aug. 31).
PRIESTS: St. Jean-Baptiste Vianney (Aug. 9).
PRINTERS: SS. Augustine of Hippo (Aug. 28), Genesius (Aug. 25), John of God (Mar. 8).
PRISONERS: SS. Barbara, Leonard, Sebastian.
PRISONS: St. Joseph Cafasso (June 23).
PUBLISHERS: St. John the Apostle.
RADIOLOGISTS: St. Michael (Sept. 29).
REPENTANT WOMEN: SS. Margaret of Cortona, Mary Magdalene, Thais.
RETREATS: St. Ignatius Loyola (July 31).
ROOFERS: St. Vincent.
ROPE-MAKERS: SS. Catherine of Alexandria (Nov. 25), Paul.
SADDLERS: Catherine of Alexandria (Nov. 25), Lucy, Crispin and Crispinian (Oct. 25).
SAILORS: SS. Andrew, Brendan the Voyager (May 16), Cuthbert (Mar. 20), Erasmus, (June 2), Eulalia (Feb. 12), Christopher, Nicholas of Tolentino (Sept. 10), Peter Gonzales (St. Elmo) (Apr. 15).
SCHOLARS: SS. Catherine of Alexandria (Nov. 25), Brigid (Feb. 1), Gregory the Great, Thomas Aquinas.
SCHOOL CHILDREN:
  Boys: SS. Benedict, Gregory the Great, Lawrence, Nicholas.
  Girls: SS. Osana of Mantua, Vincent.
SCHOOLS: SS. Joseph Calasanctius (Aug. 27), Thomas Aquinas.
SCIENTISTS: SS. Albert the Great, Thomas Aquinas.
SCULPTORS: SS. Bernwald, Claude (Nov. 8), Four Crowned Martyrs, John the Divine, Luke.
SEMINARIANS: St. Charles Borromeo.
SHEPHERDESSES: SS. Agatha, Genevieve.
SHEPHERDS: SS. Cuthbert, Paschal Baylon, Solangia, Windeline (who kept sheep, like David), Wolfgang.
SHIPWRIGHTS: St. Peter.
SHOEMAKERS: SS. Crispin and Crispinian (Oct. 25, who made shoes), Hombonus (or Goodman), Hugh.
SICK: SS. Camillus de Lellis (July 18), John of God (Mar. 8), Michael (Sept. 29).
SICK CHILDREN: St. Aldegondes.
SILVERSMITHS: SS. Andronicus (Oct. 11), Eloi (who worked in gold and silver).
SINGERS: SS. Cecilia (Nov. 22), Gregory (Mar. 12).
SKATERS: St. Lidwina (Apr. 14).
SOAP-MAKERS: St. Florian.
SOLDIERS: SS. Demetrius, George (Apr. 23), Hadrian (Sept. 8), Ignatius (July 23), Martin of Tours, Maurice, Michael the Archangel, Sebastian (Jan. 20), Theodore.
SOOTHSAYERS: St. Agabus (Acts XXI,10).
SPINSTERS: SS. Andrew (Nov. 30), Catherine of Alexandria (Nov. 25).
SPIRITUAL DIRECTORS: SS. Charles Borromeo, Frances de Sales, John Nepomucene.
SPORTSMEN: St. Hubert.
STAMMERERS: St. Notker Balbulus.
STATUARIES: St. Veronica.
STENOGRAPHERS: SS. Catherine of Alexandria (Nov. 25), Genesius (Aug. 25), Lucy.
STONECUTTERS: SS. Clement I (Nov. 23), Four Crowned Martyrs.
STONE MASONS: SS. Barbara (Dec. 4), Peter John I,42), Stephen (Dec. 26).

STUDENTS: SS. Aloysius Gonzaga, Catherine of Alexandria, Gregory the Great, Leo the Great, Jerome, Lawrence, Thomas Aquinas.
SURGEONS: SS. Cosmas and Damian (Sept. 27).
SWEETHEARTS: St. Valentine.
SWIMMERS: St. Adjutor.
SWINEHERDS AND SWINE: St. Anthony.
TAILORS: SS. Boniface, Hombonus (or Goodman, Nov. 13: who was a tailor), John the Baptist, Lucy, Quentin.
TANNERS: SS. Bartholomew, Clement (son of a tailor).
TAPESTRY MAKERS: St. Francis of Assisi.
TAX-COLLECTORS: St. Matthew (Sept. 21; Matt. IX,9).
TEACHERS: SS. Catherine of Alexandria (Nov. 25), Gregory the Great (Mar. 12).
TENTMAKERS: SS. Aquila, Paul (who were tentmakers, see Acts XVIII,3).
TERTIARIES: SS. Elizabeth of Hungary (Nov. 19), Louis of France (Aug. 24).
THEOLOGIANS: SS. Augustine of Hippo (Aug. 28), Thomas Aquinas, Thomas the Apostle.
THIEVES: SS. Dismas (the penitent thief), Ethlebert, Elian, Vincent, Vinden (all of whom caused stolen goods to be returned).
TILE-MAKERS: St. Fiacre.
TINNERS: Charlemagne, St. Pieran (who crossed the sea to Ireland on a millstone).
TOY-MAKERS: St. Claude of Besançon.
TOYS: SS. Claude of Besançon, Nicholas of Myra.
TRAVELERS: SS. Anthony of Padua (June 13), Brendan the Voyager, Christopher (July 25), Nicholas of Myra (Dec. 6), Raphael (Oct. 24), Valentine (Feb. 14).
UNDERTAKERS: St. Joseph of Arimathea.
UNHAPPILY MARRIED HUSBANDS: St. Gummarus.
UPHOLSTERERS: St. Paul.
VALETS: St. Adelmus.
VINTNERS AND VINEYARDS: SS. Amand (Feb. 6), Goar, Gratus of Aosta, Urban, Vincent, Walter of Pontoise.
VIRGINS: SS. Nicholas, Winifred.
WATCHMEN: St. Peter of Alcántara (Oct. 19).
WEAVERS: SS. Agatha, Barnabas, Crispin and Crispian, Severus, Stephen.
WHEELWRIGHTS: St. Boniface (son of a wheelwright).
WHISTLEMAKERS: St. Claude of Besançon.
WHITEWASHERS: St. Kilian.
WIDOWS: SS. Galla, Gertrude of Nivelles.
WIGMAKERS: St. Louis.
WOMEN: St. Margaret.
WOOLCOMBERS: St. Blaise (who was torn to pieces by "combes of yren").
WOULD-BE-MOTHERS: St. Margaret.
WRITERS: SS. Francis De Sales (Jan. 29), John the Apostle, Lucy (Dec. 13).
YACHTSMEN: St. Adjutor (Sept. 1).
YOUNG GIRLS: St. Agnes (Jan. 21).
YOUTH: SS. Aloysius Gonzaga (June 21), John Berchmans (Aug. 13), Gabriel Possinti (Feb. 27), Stanislaus Koska, Valentine, Vitus.

Saints of the Principal Countries

ABYSSINIA: St. Frumentius.
ARGENTINA: Our Lady of Luján.
ARMENIA: St. Gregory of Armenia.
AUSTRALIA: St. Francis Xavier.
BELGIUM: SS. Joseph, Boniface.
BOHEMIA (NOW IN CZECHOSLOVAKIA): SS. Wenceslaus, John of Nepomuk.
BRAZIL: The Immaculate Conception.
CANADA: St. Anne.
CAPPADOCIA (NOW IN TURKEY): St. Matthias.

CHINA: St. Joseph.
CZECHOSLOVAKIA: St. John of Nepomuk.
DENMARK: St. Anschar (See Norway); St. Canute.
ENGLAND: St. George.
ETHIOPIA (ABYSSINIA): St. Frumentius.
FINLAND: St. Henry.
FLANDERS (NOW IN BELGIUM AND FRANCE): St. Peter.
FRANCE: St. Denis (Denys); Joan of Arc; Remi (Remy), who is called the Great Apostle of the French (439-535).
GEORGIA (NOW IN U.S.S.R.): St. Nino.
GERMANY: SS. Boniface (the "Apostle of the Germans"), and Martin.
GREECE: St. Nicholas of Myra.
HOLLAND (NOW IN NETHERLANDS): The Virgin Mary.
HUNGARY: SS. Stephen; Louis; Mary of Aquisgrana (Aix-la-Chapelle); Anastasius.
IRELAND: SS. Patrick, Ingrid, and Columba.
ITALY: SS. Francis of Assisi, Catherine of Siena, and Anthony.
JAPAN: St. Peter Baptist.
MEXICO: Our Lady of Guadalupe.
NETHERLANDS: SS. Willibrod, Amand.
NORWAY: SS. Olaf and Anschar (also called Anscharius, Ansgar, Anskar, Ansgarius, and "Apostle of the North").
POLAND: SS. Casimir, Hedviga, Stanislaus.
PORTUGAL: SS. Vincent of Saragossa, Anthony of Padua, and Sebastian.
PRUSSIA: SS. Andrew and Albert.
RUSSIA: SS. Nicholas, Andrew, George, and the Virgin Mary.
SARDINIA: The Virgin Mary; St. Cagliari.
SCOTLAND: St. Andrew.
SICILY: St. Agatha (a Sicilian by birth).
SILESIA: St. Hedviga (Avoye).
SPAIN: St. James the Greater.
SWEDEN: St. Bridget.
SWITZERLAND: St. Gall.
UNITED STATES OF AMERICA: The Immaculate Conception.
WALES: St. David.

Saints Who Give Protection in Special Cases

AGUE: SS. Pernel, Petronella.
ALL BODILY AFFLICTIONS: Our Lady of Lourdes; SS. Roque, Sebastian.
BAD DREAMS: St. Christopher.
BARRENNESS IN WOMEN: SS. Anthony of Padua, Margaret.
BLEAR EYES: SS. Otilic, Clare.
BLINDNESS: St. Thomas à Becket.
BOILS AND BLAINS: SS. Roque, Cosmo.
CANCER OF THE BREAST: St. Agatha.
CATS: St. Gertrude of Nivelles.
CATTLE: St. Baldus, Bridget of Kildare, Cornelius, Leonard, Martin of Tours, Wendelin.
CATTLE DISEASES: St. Blaise.
CHASTITY: St. Susan.
CHILDBIRTH: St. Anne.
CHILDREN'S DISEASES: St. Blaise.
COLIC: St. Erasmus.
DEFILEMENT: St. Susan.
DESPERATE CASES: St. Jude Thaddeus.
DOGS: St. Vitus.
DOMESTIC ANIMALS: SS. Ambrose, Anthony the Abbot, Cornelius, Felix of Nola, Martin of Tours, Vitus.
DOUBTS: SS. Catherine, Thomas the Apostle.
DROUGHT AND RAIN: St. Scholastica.
DYING: SS. Barbara, Joseph.
EPILEPSY: SS. Cornelius, Valentine, Vitus.
FALSE ACCUSATIONS: SS. Mennas, Pancratius, Raymond Nonnatus.

FIRE: SS. Agatha, Catherine of Siena, Florian (if the fire has already broken out).
FLOOD, FIRE, AND EARTHQUAKE: St. Christopher.
FORTS: St. Barbara.
GEESE AND POULTRY: SS. Bridget of Kildare, Gall, Martin of Tours.
GENTILES: St. Paul the "Apostle of the Gentiles."
GOUT: SS. Maurice, Wolfgang.
HIGHLANDERS: St. Columb.
HILLS: St. Barbara.
HYDROPHOBIA: St. Hubert.
IDIOCY: St. Gildas (watches over idiots).
INFAMY: St. Susan.
INFECTION: St. Roque.
LEPROSY: St. Lazarus the Beggar.
LIGHTNING: St. Apollonia.
MADNESS: SS. Dymphna, Fillan.
MICE AND RATS: SS. Gertrude, Huldrick.
MOUNTAINS: St. Barbara.
NIGHT ALARMS: St. Christopher.
NORTH: SS. Ansgar, Bernard Gilpin.
PALSY: St. Cornelius.
PICTS: SS. Columb, Ninian.
PLAGUE: St. Roque.
POISON: St. Benedict.
RECOVERY OF LOST OBJECTS: St. Anthony of Padua.
RESPIRATORY DISEASES: St. Blaise.
QUINSY: St. Blaise.
RICHES: SS. Anne, Vincent.
ST. VITUS'S DANCE: St. Vitus.
SKIN DISEASES: St. Roque.
SMALLPOX: St. Martin of Tours.
SORE THROATS: St. Blaise.
STORMS AND TEMPESTS: St. Barbara.
SUDDEN DEATH: St. Martin.
TOOTHACHE: SS. Apollonia, Blaise.
VALLEYS: St. Agatha.
VEGETABLES: St. Werenfried.
VERMIN DESTROYERS: SS. Gertrude, Huldrick.
VINEYARDS: St. Urban.

Flowers and Plants Dedicated to the Saints or Associated with Specific Feasts and Holydays

(for the most part, the flowers dedicated to certain saints are in bloom at the time of the saint's feast day).

ALL SAINT'S DAY: Sweet Bay (Laurus nobilis); also Dark Red Sunflower (Helianthus atro rubens); November 1.
ANNUNCIATION OF THE BLESSED VIRGIN: Marigold (Calendula officinalis); March 25.
ASCENSION THURSDAY: Lily of Valley (Convallaria majalis); movable feast.
ASSUMPTION OF THE BLESSED VIRGIN MARY: Virgin's Bower (Clematis Vitalba); August 15.
CHILDERMAS DAY: See Holy Innocent's Day.
CHRISTMAS, OR THE NATIVITY OF OUR LORD: Holly (Ilex bacciflora); December 25.
CONVERSION OF ST. PAUL: Winter Hellebore (Helleborus hyemalis); January 25.
EASTER EVE: Same as Holy Saturday.
EASTER SUNDAY: White Lily (Lilium candidum); movable feast.
FEAST OF THE CIRCUMCISION: Laurustinus (Viburnum tinus); January 1.
FEAST OF THE EPIPHANY: Common Star of Bethlehem (Ornithogalum); January 6.
FINDING OF THE CROSS: See Invention of the Cross.

GOOD FRIDAY: Pasque-flower, or Long-sheathed Anemone (Anemone pulsatilla); movable feast.
HOLY ANGELS: See St. Michael and All the Angels.
HOLY CROSS DAY: Blue Passion-flower (Passiflora caerulea); September 14.
HOLY INNOCENTS' DAY (CHILDERMAS DAY): Bloody Heath (Erica cruenta); December 28.
HOLY NAME OF JESUS: Common Amaranth (Amaranthus hypochondriacus); August 7.
HOLY SATURDAY: Spear-leaved Violet (Viola lactea); movable feast.
HOLY THURSDAY: Laurel-leaved Passion-flower (Passiflora rubra); movable feast.
IMMACULATE CONCEPTION: Arbor Vitae Thuia occidentalis); December 8.
INVENTION OF THE CROSS: Poetic Narcisse (Narcissus poeticus); May 3.
LAMMAS DAY: See St. Peter's in Chains.
MARTYRDOM OF ST. JOHN THE BAPTIST: St. John's Wort (Hypericum elodes); August 29.
NATIVITY OF OUR LORD: See Christmas.
NATIVITY OF ST. JOHN THE BAPTIST: St. John's Wort (Hypericum pulchrum); also Tutsam (Hypericum Androsaemum); Chrysanthemums and Gooseberries are also appropriate to the feast day.
NATIVITY OF THE BLESSED VIRGIN MARY: Bryony, Our Lady's Seal; Red-berried Bryony (Bryonia dioica); September 8.
PALM SUMDAY: Common Palma Christi (Ricinus communis); movable feast.
PASSION SUNDAY: Christ's Thorn (Paliurus aculeatus); movable feast.
PENTECOST (WHITSUNDAY): Columbine (Aquilegia vulgaris); also White Thorn (Prunus spinosa); movable feast.
PURIFICATION OF THE BLESSED VIRGIN MARY: Snowdrop (Galanthus nivalis); February 2.
ST. AGATHA: Common Primrose (Primula vulgaris); February 5.
ST. AGATHA: Common Primrose (Primula vulgaris); February 5.
ST. AGNES: Black Hellebore or Christmas Rose (Helleborus niger, flore albo); January 21.
ST. ALBAN: Feather Grass (Stipa pennata), June 17.
ST. ALPHEGE: Ursine Garlic (Allium ursinum); April 19.
ST. AMBROSE: Meadow Orchis (Orchis mascula); April 4.
ST. ANDREW: St. Andrew's Cross, or Common Ascyrum (Ascyrus vulgaris); November 30.
ST. ANNE: Common Chamomile (Matricaria Chamomilla); July 26.
ST. AUGUSTINE: Rhododendron (Rhododendron ponticum); May 26.
ST. AUGUSTINE OF HIPPO: Goldenrod (Solidago virgaurea); August 28.
ST. BARNABAS: Midsummer Daisy (Chrysanthemum leucanthemum); June 11.
ST. BARTHOLOMEW: Sunflower (Helianthus annuus); August 24.
ST. BENEDICT: Herb Bennet (Genon urbanum); also Way Bennet or Wild Rye (Hordeum murinum), and Bulbous Fumitory (Fumaria bulbosa); March 21.
ST. BLASIUS: Great Water Moss (Fontinalis antepyretica); February 3.
ST. BONIFACE: Three-leaved Rose (Rosa sinica); June 5.
ST. BRITIUS (BRICE): Bay (Laurus poeticus); November 13.
ST. CATHERINE: Sweet Butter Bur (Petasites vulgaris); November 25.

ST. CECILIA: Trumpet-flowered Wood Sorrel *(Orchis tubiflora)*; November 22.

ST. CHAD (CEDDE): Dwarf Cerastium *(Cerastium pennilum)*; March 2.

ST. CLEMENT: Convex Wood Sorrel *(Oxalis convexula)*; November 23.

ST. CRISPIN: Flea-bane Star Wort *(Aster conizoides)*; October 25.

ST. CYPRIAN: Star Wort *(Aster tripolium)*; September 26.

ST. DAVID: Leek *(Allium porrum)*; March 1.

ST. DENIS (DENYS): Milky Agaric *(Agaricus lactiflorus)*; October 9.

ST. DUNSTAN: Monk's-hood *(Aconitum mapellus)*; May 19.

ST. EDMUND: Red Stapelia *(Stapelia rufa)*; November 20.

ST. EDWARD: Great Leopard Bane *(Doronicum pardalionetes)*; March 18.

ST. ETHELDREDA: Ten-leaved Sunflower *(Helianthus decapetalus)*; October 17.

ST. EUNURCHUS: Star Wort *(Callitriche autumnalis)*; September 7.

ST. FABIAN: Large Dead Nettle *(Lamium garganicum)*; January 20.

ST. FAITH: Late-flowering Feverfew *(Pyrethrum scrotinum)*; October 6.

ST. GEORGE: Harebell *(Hyacinthus non-scriptus)*; April 23.

ST. GILES: St. Giles' Orpine *(Sedum telephium)*; September 1.

ST. GREGORY: Channelled Ixia *(Ixia bulbocodium)*; March 12.

ST. HILARY: Barren Strawberry *(Fragaria sterilis)*; January 13.

ST. HUGH: Tree Stramony *(Datura arborea)*; November 17.

ST. JAMES THE APOSTLE: St. James' Wort *(Senecio Jacobaea)*; also St. James' Cross *(Amaryllis formosissima)*; July 25.

ST. JEROME: Golden Amaryllis *(Amaryllis aurea)*; September 30.

ST. JOHN THE EVANGELIST: Flame Heath *(Erica flamma)*; December 27.

ST. JUDE: See Sts. Simon and Jude.

ST. LAMBERT: Narrow-leaved Mallow *(Malva angustifolia)*; September 17.

ST. LAWRENCE: Common Balsam *(Impatiens balsama)*; August 10.

ST. LEONARD: Yew *(Taxus baccata)*; November 6.

ST. LUCIAN: Common Laurel *(Laurus)*; January 8.

ST. LUCY: Cypress Arbor Vitae *(Thuja cupressoides)*; December 13.

ST. LUKE: Floccose Agaric *(Agaricus floccosus)*; October 18.

ST. MACHUTUS: Sweet Coltsfoot *(Tussilago fragrans)*; November 15.

ST. MARGARET: Virginian Dragon's Head *(Dracocephalus Virginianum)*; July 20.

ST. MARK: Clarimond Tulip *(Tulipa praecox)*; April 25.

ST. MARTIN: Weymouth Pine *(Pinus strobus)*; November 11.

ST. MARY MAGDALEN: African Lily *(Agaphantus umbellatus)*; July 22.

ST. MATTHEW: Cilcated Passion-flower *(Passiflora cilcata)*; September 21.

ST. MATTHIAS: Mezereon *(Daphne mezereum)*; February 24.

ST. MICHEL AND ALL THE ANGELS: Michaelmas Daisy *(Aster tradescanti)*; September 29.

ST. NICHOLAS: Nest-flowered Heath *(Erica nidiflora)*; December 6.

ST. NICOMEDE: Single Yellow Rose *(Rosa lutea)*; June 1.

ST. PERPETUA: Early Daffodil *(Narcissus pseudo-narcissus simplex)*; March 7.

ST. PETER: Yellow Rattle *(Rhinanthus Galli)*; June 29.

ST. PETER'S IN CHAINS: Stramony *(Datura stramonium)*; Feast of Lammas Day.

ST. PHILIP: Red Tulip *(Tulipa gesneri)*; May 1.

ST. PRISCA: Four-toothed Moss *(Bryum pellucidum)*; January 18.

ST. REMIGIUS: Lowly Amaryllis or St. Remy's Lily *(Amaryllis humilis)*; October 1.

ST. RICHARD: Evergreen Alkanet *(Anchusa sempervirens)*; April 3.

STS. SIMON AND JUDE: St. Simon: Late Crysanthemum *(Chrysanthemum scrotinum)*; St. Jude: Scattered Star Wort *(Aster passiflorus)*; October 28.

ST. STEPHEN: Purple Heath *(Erica purpurea)*; December 26.

ST. SWITHIN: Small Cape Marigold *(Calendula pluvialis)*; July 15.

ST. SYLVESTER: Genista Heath *(Erica genistopha)*; December 31.

ST. THOMAS: Sparrow Wort *(Erica passerina)*; December 21.

ST. VALENTINE: Yellow Crocus *(Crocus maesiacus)*; February 14.

ST. VINCENT: Early Witlow Grass *(Draba verna)*; January 22.

TRANSFIGURATION OF OUR LORD: Common Meadow Saffron *(Colchicum autumnale)*; August 6.

TRINITY SUNDAY: Herb Trinity (also called Pansy, Violet, and Heartsease) *(Viola tricolor)*; also Commom White Trefoil *(Trifolium repens)*.

VENERABLE BEDE: Yellow Bachelor's Button *(Ranunculus acris plenus)*; May 27.

VISITATION OF THE BLESSED VIRGIN MARY: White Lily *(Lilium candidum)*; July 2.

WHITSUNDAY: See Pentecost.

Saints as Patrons: The Seven Champions of Christendom

(This is a medieval classification of the patron saints of seven of the leading countries of Christendom).

ST. ANDREW: Patron saint of Scotland.
ST. ANTHONY: Patron saint of Italy.
ST. DAVID: Patron saint of Wales.
ST. DENIS: Patron saint of France.
ST. GEORGE: Patron saint of England.
ST. JAMES: Patron saint of Spain.
ST. PATRICK: Patron saint of Ireland.

Salt Water Bodies: Bays, Gulfs, Oceans, Seas, Sounds, Straits
See also Lakes; Rivers; Waterfalls

ADRIATIC SEA: Arm of Mediterranean between Italy and Istria, Yugoslavia and Albania; 500 mi. long; 60-140 mi. wide; 4035' max. depth; area: 60,000 sq. mi.

AEGEAN SEA: Arm of Mediterranean between Aisa Minor and Greece; 400 mi. long, 200 mi. wide; area: 70,000 sq. mi.

ALBEMARLE SOUND: Inlet of Atlantic about 60 mi. long in NE N. Carolina; 5 to 15 mi. wide; area: 495 sq. mi.

ANDAMAN SEA: Part of Bay of Bengal; bounded by Andaman Island, Burma, Malaya, & Sumatra; 750 mi. north to south;

2850' average depth; 400 mi. wide; area: 308,000 sq. mi.

ARABIAN SEA: Arm of Indian Ocean; between Arabia and India; 1800 mi. wide.

ARCTIC OCEAN: North of Arctic Circle; covered with 7-10' of packed ice; greatest depth 17,850' in N. Bering Strait; shallowest depth 600'; average depth 4200'; area: 5,500,000 sq. mi.

ATLANTIC OCEAN: Separating North and South America from Europe and Africa; greatest depth 30,246' off Dominican Republic; area: about 31,500,000 sq. mi.

BAFFIN BAY: Inlet of Atlantic between Greenland and Baffin Island; 700 mi. long; 70-400 mi. wide; 1200-9000' deep.

BALTIC SEA: Enclosed by Denmark, Sweden, Finland, U.S.S.R., Poland, and Germany; 1056 mi. long; 157,000 sq. mi. in area; 1200' max. depth.

BASS STRAIT: Strait separating Australia and Tasmania; 80-150 mi. wide; 185 mi. long; area: 32,000 sq. mi.

BAY OF BISCAY: West coast of France and North coast of Spain; area: 160,000 sq. mi.

BAY OF FUNDY: Between New Brunswick and Nova Scotia, SW Canada; 145 mi. long; 48 mi. wide; area: 6300 sq. mi.; tides to 70'.

BERING SEA: Bounded by Alaska, Aleutian Islands, Kamchatka Peninsula, Siberia; 13,422' max. depth; area: 875,000 sq. mi.

BERING STRAIT: Connects Arctic Ocean and Bering Sea; separates U.S.S.R. & Alaska; 56 mi. wide.

BLACK SEA: Between Europe and Asia (Turkey and U.S.S.R.); 7200' max. depth; area: 878,000 sq. mi.

BOSPORUS: Strait between European and Asian Turkey; 20 mi. long; $1/2$ m. wide.

BUZZARDS BAY: Southeast Massachusetts; 30 mi. long; 5-10 mi. wide; area: 258 sq. mi.

CARIBBEAN SEA: Between West Indies and Central America; 1800 mi. long; 900 mi. wide; 22,788' max. depth; area: about 1,000,000 sq. mi.; average temperature 75 degrees F.; low salinity; blue water.

CHESAPEAKE BAY: Between Virginia and Maryland; 200 mi long; 4-10 mi. wide; area: 6000 sq.mi.

DARDANELLES: Strait between European and Asian Turkey; 40 mi. long; $3/4$ to 4 mi. wide.

DELAWARE BAY: Arm of Atlantic between New Jersey and Delaware; 52 mi. long; area: 1000 sq. mi.

EAST CHINA SEA: Off E. coast of China; 300-500 mi. wide; 600 mi. long; 8920' max. depth; 615' average depth; area: 482,300 sq. mi.

ENGLISH CHANNEL: Strait between England and France; 20-100 mi. wide; 350 mi. long; 564' max. depth; 175' average depth; area: 30,000 sq.mi.

GULF OF ADEN: Arm of Indian Ocean (Arabian Sea), between Arabia and Somaliland; 550 mi. long; 300 mi. wide; area: 85,000 sq.mi.

GULF OF BOTHNIA: Northern arm of Baltic Sea between Sweden and Finland; 400 mi. long; 50-150 mi. wide; area: 43,000 sq. mi.; low salinity; frozen in winter.

GULF OF CALIFORNIA: Arm of Pacific off coast of Mexico; 700 mi. long; 100-150 mi. wide; 8651' max. depth; 2660' mean depth; area: 64,000 sq. mi.

GULF OF CARPENTARIA: Inlet of Arafura Sea, off NE Australia; about 480 mi. long; about 420 mi. wide; area: 120,000 sq.mi.

GULF OF FINLAND: Between Finland and U.S.S.R.; 260 mi. long; 45-85 mi. wide; area: 15,000 sq. mi.; frozen in winter; low salinity.

GULF OF THE LION (GULF OF LIONS): Wide bay of Mediterranean off southern coast of France, from Spain to Toulon; Marseilles is chief port.

GULF OF MEXICO: Bounded by U.S.A., Cuba, and Mexico; 1000 mi. long; 800 mi. wide; max. depth 12,425' at Sigsbee Deep; area: 700,000 sq. mi.

GULF OF RIGA: Inlet of Baltic Sea in Latvia; 100 mi. long; 60 m. wide; area: 7,000 sq. mi.

GULF OF ST. LAWRENCE: Between Newfoundland and Canada; 500 mi. long; 250 mi. wide; area: 75,000 sq. mi.

GULF OF SIAM: Inlet of South China Sea bounded by Siam, Cambodia, and Annam; 385 mi. wide (at widest); 385 mi. long; area: 100,000 sq. mi.

GULF OF TONKIN: Arm of South China Sea; between Annam (Tonkin) and Hainan Island; 300 mi. long; 150 mi. wide; area: 45,000 sq. mi.

HUDSON BAY: Bounded by Northwest Territories; Manitoba, Ontario, and Quebec; 850 mi. long; 600 mi. wide; max. depth, 1500'; av. depth 420; area: 475,000 sq. mi.

INDIAN OCEAN: Bounded by Africa, Asia, Australia, and Antarctica; 24,440' max. depth (near Java); area: 28,356,300 sq.mi.

IRISH SEA: Bounded by Ireland and Great Britain; 130 mi. long; 130 mi. wide; 200' av. depth; area: 75,000 sq.mi.

JAPAN SEA: Branch of Pacific bounded by Japan, U.S.S.R., and Korea; about 12,276' max. depth; 4429' av. depth; 400,000 sq. mi.

KATTEGAT: Arm of North Sea between Sweden and Denmark; 137 mi. long; 37-80 mi. wide.

LONG ISLAND SOUND: Bounded by Connecticut and Long Island, N.Y.; 110 mi long; 10-25 mi. wide; area: 1500 sq. mi.

MEDITERRANEAN SEA: Bounded by Spain, France, Italy, Yugoslavia, Albania, Greece, Turkey, Syria, Lebanon, Israel, Egypt, Libia, Tunisia, Algeria, and Morocco; 2330 mi. long; 1,145,000 sq. mi.; max. depth 14,436' (off Cape Matapan).

MOZAMBIQUE CHANNEL: Strait between Madagascar and Mozambique; 950 mi. long; 250-625 mi. wide; area: 430,000 sq. mi.

NARRANGANSETT BAY: Inlet of Atlantic in Rhode Island, U.S.A.; 30 mi. long; 3-12 mi. wide; area: 140 sq. mi.

NORTH SEA: Bounded by Great Britain, Netherlands, Germany, Denmark, Norway; 350 mi. wide; 600 mi. long; 2165' max. depth; 180' av. depth; area: 222,100 sq. mi.

OKHOTSK SEA: Inlet of Pacific; W. of Kamchatka Peninsula, E. U.S.S.R.; 11,060' max. depth; 2750' av. depth; area: 589,800 sq. mi.

PACIFIC OCEAN: The largest ocean, bounded by the Arctic and Antarctic, North and South America, Asia and Australia; 11,000 mi. wide at max width; 34,440' max. depth; 14,000' av. depth; area: about 70,000,000 sq. mi.

PERSIAN GULF: Bounded by Arabia, Iran, Iraq, and Kuwait; 575 mi. long; 225 mi. wide; area: 89,000 sq. mi. 300' max. depth.

PUGET SOUND: Arm of Pacific in State of Washington; 90 mi. long; area 2000 sq. mi.

RED SEA: Between Arabia and NE Africa; 1450 mi. long; 7254' max. depth (off Sudan); area: 175,000 sq. mi.

ST. GEORGE'S CHANNEL: Between islands of New Ireland and New Britain; 100 mi. long; 20 mi. wide; area: 8000 sq. mi.

SAN FRANCISCO BAY: Arm of Pacific in California; 45 mi. long; 3-12 mi. wide; area: 350 sq. mi.; 100' max. depth.

SEA OF AZOV: NE Crimea, connected with Black Sea by Kerch Strait; 200 mi. long; 80 mi. wide; 49' max. depth; area: 14,520 sq. mi.

SEA OF JAPAN: See Japan Sea.

SEA OF MARMORA: Between European and Asian Turkey; 172 mi. long; 50 mi. wide; area: 4300 sq. mi.

SKAGERRAK STRAIT: Between Norway and Denmark; 150 mi. long; 80 mi. wide; over 2000' max. depth; area: 12,000 sq. mi.

SOUTH CHINA SEA: Bounded by China, Vietnam, Cambodia, Thailand, Malaya, Borneo, and Philippines; 1800 mi. long; 600 mi. wide; 600-15,000' deep; area: 895,400 sq. mi.

STRAITS OF GIBRALTAR: Between Spain and Morocco; connecting Atlantic and Mediterranean; 26 mi. long; 8-25 mi. wide; 1200' av. depth.

STRAIT OF MAGELLAN: Bounded by Chile and Tierra del Fuego; connecting Atlantic and Pacific; 360 mi. long; 2-20 mi. wide; area: 2000 sq.mi.

WHITE SEA: Inlet of Barents Sea in N. Russia; 365 mi. long; 1115' max. depth; area: 40,000 sq. mi.

YELLOW SEA: Between China and Korea; 400 mi. wide; 400 mi. long; area: 240,000 sq. mi.

Satirists and Humorists

Note: This is a list of writers who have achieved fame for their comic or satirical genius. In many cases, the authors have also been distinguished for other types of writing.

ADAMS, FRANKLIN PIERCE (F.P.A.): (1881-   ); American; journalist and satirical humorist.

ADDISON, JOSEPH: (1672-1719); b. England; l. Italy, England; essayist, spokesman and wit for rising middle class; essays in The Tatler, The Spectator.

AESOP: (6th cent. B. C.); Greece; fabulist, Egyptian and Indian sources; "Androcles and the Lion," "Fox and the Grapes," etc.

ARISTOPHANES: (c. 448-380 B. C.); Greece; comic playwright; Lysistrata, The Birds, The Wasps.

AUSTEN, JANE: (1775-1817); b. England; l. England; novelist, sharp observer of human nature; Pride and Prejudice.

BAGE, ROBERT: (1728-1801); England; novelist, influenced by French Revolutionary humanitarianism; Hermsprong.

BEAUMARCHAIS, PIERRE AUGUSTIN CARON DE: (1732-1799); France; playwright, attacked judicial injustice; Marriage of Figaro.

BEERBOHM, MAX: (1872-1956); b. England; l. Italy; critic, essayist, caricaturist; Zuleika Dobson.

BOILEAU-DESPREAUX, NICOLAS: (1636-1711); b. Paris; l. Paris; influenced by Horace, favorite at court of Louis XIV, satirist of society; Satires.

BUCHANAN, GEORGE: (1506-1581); b. Scotland; l. France, Scotland; scholar, teacher of Montaigne and James VI of Scotland; satires against the Franciscans, Franciscanus.

BURNS, ROBERT: (1759-1796); b. Scotland; l. Scotland; Scottish national poet, wrote satirical verses, squibs, epigrams of great warmth and sympathy; "Holy Willie's Prayer."

BUTLER, SAMUEL: (1612-1680); England; political and social satirist; Hudibras.

BUTLER, SAMUEL: (1835-1902); b. England; l. New Zealand, England; novelist and freethinker; Erewhon.

BYRON, LORD (GEORGE GORDON): (1788-1824); b. England; l. Italy; romantic poet, satirist, adventurer; Don Juan.

CARLYLE, THOMAS: (1795-1881); b. England; l. Germany, England; essayist and historian, attacked shams and corruption in society, Sartor Resartus.

CARROLL, LEWIS (CHARLES LUTWIDGE DODGSON): (1832-1898); England; mathematician, satiric fantasist of education; Alice in Wonderland.

CERVANTES SAAVEDRA, MIGUEL DE: (1547-1616); b. Spain; l. Italy, Spain; self-satirist, ultimate idealist; Don Quixote.

CHATTERTON, THOMAS: (1752-1770); England; poet, created fictitious character, Thomas Rowley, 15th-cent. monk; political diatribes in mannner of Junius.

CHAUCER, GEOFFRY: (1340?-1400); b. England; l. England; father of English poetry, transition between medieval and modern; Canterbury Tales.

CHESTERTON, GILBERT KEITH: (1874-1936); England; journalist, writer, master of verbal paradox; The Man who Was Thursday.

CHURCHILL, CHARLES: (1731-1764); England; poet, satirist; The Rosciad.

CLIEVELAND, JOHN: (1613-1659); England, Royalist satirical poet; Poems.

CONGREVE, WILLIAM: (1670-1729); b. England; l. England; playwright, graceful blending of reality and refinement; Way of the World.

COWLEY, ABRAHAM: (1618-1667); England; Royalist satirist.

DICKENS, CHARLES: (1812-1870); b. England; l. England; novelist, social satirist of 19th-cent. industrialism; Oliver Twist.

DISRAELI, ISAAC: (1766-1848); b. London; l. England; English man of letters, father of Benjamin Disraeli; Calamities of Authors.

DODINGTON, GEORGE BUBB: (1691-1764); England; satiric commentator; Diary.

DONNE, JOHN: (1573-1631); b. England; l. England; poet of disillusioned and romantic cynicism; Poems.

DOUGLAS, NORMAN: (1868-1952); b. England; l. Italy; sophisticated satirist of the 1920's; South Wind.

DRYDEN, JOHN: (1631-1700); b. England; l. England; early writer of elegant prose and polished satire; MacFlecknoe.

ERASMUS, DESIDERIUS: (1466-1536); b. Rotterdam; l. Italy; England, Switzerland; scholar and satirist of the Reformation; Encomium, Colloquies.

FIELDING, HENRY: (1707-1754); England; novelist of ironic satire; Jonathan Wild.

FRANCE, ANATOLE (JACQUES FRANÇOIS THIBAULT: (1844-1924); b. France; l. France; novelist, critic, poet, playwright, master of Satire; Penguin Island.

GAY, JOHN: (1688-1732); b. England; l. England; pastoral satirist; playwright; The Beggar's Opera.

GIFFORD, WILLIAM: (1756-1826); England; literary critic and poet, classical satirist; Baviad and Maeviad.

GILBERT, SIR WILLIAM SCHWENCK: (1836-1911); England; poet, librettist for Gilbert and Sullivan operettas; cynic of social and artistic sham; Patience, etc.

HALL, BISHOP JOSEPH: (1574-1656); England; father of English classic and formal satire, heroic meter; Satires.

HERBERT, ALAN PATRICK: (1890-   );

England; novelist, versifier in light, satiric vein; *Holy Deadlock.*

HERRICK, ROBERT: (1591-1674); England; Royalist satirist; *Hesperides.*

HONE, WILLIAM: (1780-1842); England; political satirist and bookdealer; *Political House that Jack Built.*

HOOD, THOMAS: (1799-1845); England; poet and humorist; *Song of the Shirt.*

HOOK, THEODORE: (1788-1841); England; humorist and novelist; *Tentamen.*

HORACE (QUINTUS HORATIUS FLACCUS): (65-8 B. C.): b. Venusia, Italy; l. Rome; ridiculed Stoics, influenced English and French satirists; *Odes.*

HUXLEY, ALDOUS LEONARD: (1894-   ); b. England; l. America; novelist, critic; detached hatred of modern civilization; *Point Counter Point.*

JERROLD, DOUGLAS WILLIAM: (1803-1857); England; playwright and humorist; *Black-eyed Susan.*

JOHNSON, SAMUEL: (1709-1784); b. England; l. England; conversationalist, satirist, poems in imitation of Juvenal; *London, Vanity of Human Wishes.*

JONSON, BENJAMIN: (1573-1637); b. England; l. England; playwright; bitter, realistic satire; *Volpone.*

JUNIUS (PSEUDONYM): Political satirist, father of English journalism; series of letters written 1768-1772, attacking British Ministry. Possibly written by Sir Philip Francis (1740-1818).

JUVENAL (DECIMUS JUNIUS JUVENALIS): (60?-140?); b. Rome; l. Rome; Roman satirist expressing moral indignation; *16 Satires.*

LA FONTAINE, JEAN DE: (1621-1695); b. France; l. France; sophisticated, satiric fabulist; *The Fables.*

LARDNER, RING (RINGGOLD WILMER): (1885-1933); American; humorist, short-story-writer, satirist of American society of 1920's; "Reunion."

LEWIS, SINCLAIR: (1885-1950); b. America; l. America; satirist of the American scene; *Main Street.*

LINDSAY, SIR DAVID: (1490-1555); b. Scotland; l. Scotland; most famous of old Scottish poets, "good sense" satirist; *Satire of the Three Estates.*

LUCIAN: (125-200); b. Syria; l. Egypt; traveled widely in ancient world; wittiest of ancients; *Dialogues.*

MAPES, WALTER: (12th cent.); b. Wales; l. England; clerical satirist; *Courtier's Triflings.*

MARVELL, ANDREW: (1621-1678); England; poet; wrote a number of verse-satires attacking the Restoration government.

MENCKEN, HENRY LOUIS: (1880-1956); America; editor and satirist; editor *American Mercury.*

MOLIÈRE (JEAN BAPTISTE POQUELIN): (1622-1673); b. France; l. France; playwright, moralist, realist; *Le Bourgeois Gentilhomme.*

MOORE, THOMAS: (1799-1852); b. Dublin; l. Italy, France; poet and prose writer of lampooning satire; *Lalla Rookh.*

NASH, OGDEN: (1902-   ); American; humorous and satiric verse; *Hard Lines.*

OLDHAM, JOHN: (1653-1683); England; called "English Juvenal"; *Satires upon the Jesuits.*

PARKER, DOROTHY: (1893-   ); America; contemporary satiric poetess; *Death and Taxes.*

PEACOCK, THOMAS LOVE: (1785-1866);

England; antiromantic novelist; *Nightmare Abbey.*

POPE, ALEXANDER: (1688-1744); b. England; l. England; poet and classicist, lived in world of fashion and lampooned it; *The Rape of the Lock.*

PULTENEY, WILLIAM: (1684-1764); England; political journalistic satire; editor, *The Craftsman.*

RABELAIS, FRANCOIS: (1494?-1553); b. Touraine; l. Paris; Renaissance man of good will; hearty realistic satire; *Gargantua.*

SAKI (HECTOR HUGH MUNRO): (1870-1916); b. Burma; l. England; political satire, humorous short stories and novels, cruel and elegant; "The Schartz-Metterklume Method."

SHAKESPEARE, WILLIAM: (1564-1616); not traditionally or consistently a satirist; characters of Falstaff, Hamlet, Lear; *Sonnets.*

SHAW, GEORGE BERNARD: (1856-1950); b. Dublin; l. England; playwright, critic, novelist, social satirist; *Men and Superman.*

SHERIDAN, RICHARD BRINSLEY: (1751-1816); b. Dublin; l. England; comic playwright of society; *The School for Scandal, The Rivals.*

SKELTON, JOHN: (Close of 15th cent.-1529); England; early Poet Laureate, wrote satiric doggerel attacking Cardinal Wolsey.

SOUTHEY, ROBERT: (1774-1843); England; poet and man of letters; "Devil's Walk" (with Coleridge).

STEELE, SIR RICHARD: (1672-1729); b. Ireland; l. England; political satirist; essays in *The Tatler, The Spectator.*

STERNE, LAWRENCE: (1713-1768); b. Ireland; l. England; satirist of novel construction; *Tristram Shandy.*

SWIFT, JONATHAN: (1667-1745); b. Ireland; l. England, Ireland; allegorist, philosophical satirist; *Gulliver's Travels.*

THACKERAY, WILLIAM MAKEPEACE: (1811-1863); b. England; l. England; novelist and journalist, satirist of fashionable society; *Vanity Fair.*

THURBER, JAMES GROVER: (1894-   ); America; satiric writer and cartoonist; *Is Sex Necessary?*

TWAIN, MARK (SAMUEL LANGHORNE CLEMENS): (1835-1910); America; humorist, observer of humanity; *Huckleberry Finn.*

VOLTAIRE (FRANÇOIS MARIE AROUET): (1694-1778); b. France; l. England, France, Germany, Switzerland; poet, playwright, satirist, essayist; *Candide.*

WOLCOT, JOHN: (1738-1819); England; poet, assumed name of Peter Pindar; satirical buffoonery; *Epistle to Peter Pindar.*

YOUNG, EDWARD: (1683-1765); England; satirist and poet; *The Love of Fame, the Universal Passion.*

School Colors
See **Academic Colors**

Schools of the United States:
Institutions of Higher Learning *
For famous people associated with specific philosophical, artistic, and literary schools, see **Pseudonyms, Nicknames, and Special Associations for Historical Persons**

*Indicates Ivy League college.

Alabama

ALABAMA, UNIVERSITY OF: University.
ALABAMA AGRICULTURAL AND ME-
CHANICAL COLLEGE Normal.
ALABAMA COLLEGE: Montevallo.
ALABAMA POLYTECHNIC INSTITUTE:
Auburn.
ALABAMA STATE COLLEGE: Montgomery.
ALABAMA STATE TEACHERS COLLEGE:
Florence.
ALABAMA STATE TEACHERS COLLEGE:
Jacksonville.
ALABAMA STATE TEACHERS COLLEGE:
Livingston.
ALABAMA STATE TEACHERS COLLEGE:
Troy.
ATHENS COLLEGE: Athens.
BIRMINGHAM-SOUTHERN COLLEGE:
Birmingham.
HOWARD COLLEGE: Birmingham.
HUNTINGDON COLLEGE: Montgomery.
JUDSON COLLEGE: Marion.
MARION INSTITUTE: Marion.
MILES COLLEGE: Birmingham.
OAKWOOD COLLEGE: Huntsville.
SACRED HEART JUNIOR COLLEGE:
Cullman.
ST. BERNARD COLLEGE: St. Bernard.
SNEAD JUNIOR COLLEGE: Boaz.
SOUTHEASTERN BIBLE COLLEGE:
Birmingham.
SOUTHERN UNION COLLEGE, THE:
Wadley.
SPRING HILL COLLEGE: Spring Hill.
STILLMAN COLLEGE: Tuscaloosa.
TALLADEGA COLLEGE: Talladega.
TUSKEGEE INSTITUTE: Tuskegee Institute.

Arizona

ARIZONA, UNIVERSITY OF: Tucson.
ARIZONA STATE COLEGE: Flagstaff.
ARIZONA STATE COLLEGE: Tempe.
EASTERN ARIZONA JUNIOR COLLEGE:
Thatcher.
GRAND CANYON COLLEGE: Phoenix.
PHOENIX COLLEGE: Phoenix.

Arkansas

ARKANSAS, UNIVERSITY OF: Fayetteville.
ARKANSAS AGRICULTURAL, MECHANI-
CAL & NORMAL COLLEGE: Pine Bluff.
ARKANSAS AGRICULTURAL AND ME-
CHANICAL COLLEGE: College Heights.
ARKANSAS COLLEGE: Batesville.
ARKANSAS POLYTECHNIC COLLEGE:
Russelville.
ARKANSAS STATE COLLEGE: State College.
ARKANSAS STATE TEACHERS COLLEGE:
Conway.
COLLEGE OF THE OZARKS: Clarksville.
FORT SMITH JUNIOR COLLEGE: Fort
Smith.
HARDING COLLEGE: Searcy.
HENDERSON STATE TEACHERS COLLEGE:
Arkadelphia.
HENDRIX COLLEGE: Conway.
JOHN BROWN UNIVERSITY: Siloam Springs.
LITTLE ROCK JUNIOR COLLEGE: Little
Rock.
OUACHITA BAPTIST COLLEGE: Arkadel-
phia.
PHILANDER SMITH COLLEGE: Little Rock.

SHORTER COLLEGE: North Little Rock.
SOUTHERN BAPTIST COLLEGE: Walnut
Ridge.
SOUTHERN STATE COLLEGE: Magnolia.

California

ALLAN HANCOCK COLLEGE: Santa Maria.
AMERICAN RIVER JUNIOR COLLEGE: Del
Paso Heights.
ANTELOPE VALLEY JUNIOR COLLEGE:
Lancaster.
ARMSTRONG COLLEGE: Berkeley.
ART CENTER SCHOOL, THE: Los Angeles.
BAKERSFIELD COLLEGE: Bakersfield.
BERKELEY BAPTIST DIVINITY SCHOOL:
Berkeley.
THE BIBLE INSTITUTE OF LOS ANGELES:
Los Angeles.
CALIFORNIA, UNIVERSITY OF: Campuses
at Berkeley, Los Angeles, San Francisco
(Medical Center), Santa Barbara (Santa Bar-
bara College), Davis, Riverside, La Jolla
(Scripps Institute of Oceanography), Mt.
Hamilton (Lick Observatory).
CALIFORNIA BAPTIST THEOLOGICAL
SEMINARY: Covina.
CLIFORNIA COLLEGE OF ARTS AND
CRAFTS: Oakland.
CALIFORNIA COLLEGE OF CHIROPODY:
San Francisco.
CALIFORNIA CONCORDIA COLLEGE: Oak-
land.
CALIFORNIA INSTITUTE OF TECHNOL-
OGY: Pasadena.
CALIFORNIA MARITIME ACADEMY:
Vallejo.
CALIFORNIA SCHOOL OF FINE ARTS:
San Francisco.
CALIFORNIA STATE POLYTECHNIC COL-
LEGE: San Luis Obispo.
CALIFORNIA WESTERN UNIVERSITY: San
Diego.
CHAFFEY JUNIOR COLLEGE: Ontario.
CHAPMAN COLLEGE: Orange.
CHICO STATE COLLEGE: Chico.
CHOUINARD ART INSTITUTE: Los Angeles.
CHURCH DIVINITY SCHOOL OF THE PA-
CIFIC: Berkeley.
CITRUS JUNIOR COLLEGE: Azusa.
CITY COLLEGE OF SAN FRANCISCO: San
Francisco.
CLAREMONT GRADUATE COLLEGE: Clare-
mont.
CLAREMONT MEN'S COLLEGE: Claremont.
COALINGA COLLEGE: Coalinga.
COGSWELL POLYTECHNICAL COLLEGE:
San Francisco.
COLLEGE OF NOTRE DAME: Belmont.
COLLEGE OF OSTEOPATHIC PHYSICIANS
AND SURGEONS: Los Angeles.
COLLEGE OF PHYSICIANS AND SUR-
GEONS: San Francisco.
COMPTON DISTRICT JUNIOR COLLEGE:
Compton.
DEEP SPRINGS COLLEGE: Deep Springs.
DOMINICAN COLLEGE OF SAN RAFAEL:
San Rafael.
EAST CONTRA COSTA COLLEGE: Concord.
EAST LOS ANGELES JUNIOR COLLEGE:
Los Angeles.
EL CAMINO COLLEGE: El Camino.
FRESNO JUNIOR COLLEGE: Fresno.
FRESNO STATE COLLEGE: Fresno.
FULLER THEOLOGICAL SEMINARY:
Pasadena.
FULLERTON JUNIOR COLLEGE: Fullerton.
GEORGE PEPPERDINE COLLEGE: Los An-
geles.

GLENDALE COLLEGE: Glendale.
GOLDEN GATE BAPTIST THEOLOGICAL SEMINARY: Berkeley.
GOLDEN GATE COLLEGE: San Francisco.
HARTNELL COLLEGE: Salinas.
HOLY NAMES, COLLEGE OF THE: Oakland.
HUMBOLDT STATE COLLEGE: Arcata.
IMMACULATE HEART COLLEGE: Los Angeles.
IMPERIAL VALLEY COLLEGE: El Centro.
JOHN MUIR COLLEGE: Pasadena.
LA SIERRA COLLEGE: Arlington.
LASSEN JUNIOR COLLEGE: Susanville.
LA VERNE COLLEGE: La Verne.
LONG BEACH CITY COLLEGE: Long Beach.
LONG BEACH STATE COLLEGE: Long Beach.
LOS ANGELES CITY COLLEGE: Los Angeles.
LOS ANGELES COLLEGE OF OPTOMETRY: Los Angeles.
LOS ANGELES CONSERVATORY OF MUSIC: Los Angeles.
LOS ANGELES COUNTY ART INSTITUTE: Los Angeles.
LOS ANGELES HARBOR JUNIOR COLLEGE: Los Angeles.
LOS ANGELES JUNIOR COLLEGE OF BUSINESS: Los Angeles.
LOS ANGELES PACIFIC COLLEGE: Los Angeles.
LOS ANGELES PIERCE JUNIOR COLLEGE: Woodland Hills.
LOS ANGELES STATE COLLEGE OF APPLIED ARTS AND SCIENCES: Los Angeles.
LOS ANGELES TRADE-TECHNICAL JUNIOR COLLEGE: Los Angeles.
LOS ANGELES VALLEY JUNIOR COLLEGE: Van Nuys.
LOYOLA UNIVERSITY OF LOS ANGELES: Los Angeles.
MARIN, COLLEGE OF: Kentfield.
MARYMOUNT COLLEGE: Los Angeles.
MEDICAL EVANGELISTS, COLLEGE OF: Loma Linda.
MENLO COLLEGE: Menlo Park.
MILLS COLLEGE: Oakland.
MODESTO JUNIOR COLLEGE: Modesto.
MONTEREY PENINSULA COLLEGE: Monterey.
MOUNT SAINT MARY'S COLLEGE: Los Angeles.
MOUNT SAN ANTONIO COLLEGE: Pomona.
NAPA COLLEGE: Napa.
NORTHROP AERONAUTICAL INSTITUTE: Inglewood.
OAKLAND JUNIOR COLLEGE: Oakland.
OCCIDENTAL COLLEGE: Los Angeles.
OCEANSIDE-CARLSBAD COLLEGE: Oceanside.
ORANGE COAST COLLEGE: Costa Mesa.
PACIFIC, COLLEGE OF THE: Stockton.
PACIFIC BIBLE COLLEGE OF AZUSA: Azusa.
PACIFIC LUTHERAN THEOLOGICAL SEMINARY: Berkeley.
PACIFIC SCHOOL OF RELIGION: Berkeley.
PACIFIC UNION COLLEGE: Angwin.
PALOMAR COLLEGE: San Marcos.
PALO VERDE JUNIOR COLLEGE: Blythe.
PASADENA CITY COLLEGE: Pasadena.
PASADENA COLLEGE: Pasadena.
POMONA COLLEGE: Claremont.
PORTERVILLE COLLEGE: Porterville.
REDLANDS, UNIVERSITY OF: Redlands.
REEDLEY COLLEGE: Reedley.
RIVERSIDE COLLEGE: Riverside.
SACRAMENTO JUNIOR COLLEGE: Sacramento.

SACRAMENTO STATE COLLEGE: Sacramento.
ST. JOHN'S COLLEGE: Camarillo.
ST. MARY'S COLLEGE OF CALIFORNIA: St. Mary's College.
ST. PATRICK'S SEMINARY: Menlo Park.
SAN BENITO COUNTY JUNIOR COLLEGE: Hollister.
SAN BERNARDINO VALLEY COLLEGE: San Bernardino.
SAN DIEGO COLLEGE FOR WOMEN: San Diego.
SAN DIEGO JUNIOR COLLEGE: San Diego.
SAN DIEGO STATE COLLEGE: San Diego.
SAN FRANCISCO, CITY COLLEGE OF: San Francisco.
SAN FRANCISCO, UNIVERSITY OF: San Francisco.
SAN FRANCISCO COLLEGE FOR WOMEN: San Francisco.
SAN FRANCISCO STATE COLLEGE: San Francisco.
SAN FRANCISCO THEOLOGICAL SEMINARY: San Anselmo.
SAN JOSE JUNIOR COLLEGE: San Jose.
SAN JOSE STATE COLLEGE: San Jose.
SAN LUIS OBISPO JUNIOR COLLEGE: San Luis Obispo.
SAN MATEO, COLLEGE OF: San Mateo.
SANTA ANA COLLEGE: Santa Ana.
SANTA BARBARA JUNIOR COLLEGE: Santa Barbara.
SANTA CLARA, UNIVERSITY OF: Santa Clara.
SANTA MONICA CITY COLLEGE: Santa Monica.
SANTA ROSA JUNIOR COLLEGE: Santa Rosa.
SCRIPPS COLLEGE: Claremont.
SEQUOIAS, COLLEGE OF THE: Visalia.
SHASTA COLLEGE: Redding.
SIERRA COLLEGE: Auburn.
SIMPSON BIBLE COLLEGE: San Francisco.
SOUTHERN CALIFORNIA, UNIVERSITY OF: Los Angeles.
SOUTHERN CALIFORNIA BIBLE COLLEGE: Costa Mesa.
STANFORD UNIVERSITY: Stanford.
STOCKTON COLLEGE: Stockton.
TAFT JUNIOR COLLEGE: Taft.
UNITED STATES NAVAL POSTGRADUATE SCHOOL: Monterey.
UNIVERSITY OF JUDAISM: Los Angeles.
UPLAND COLLEGE: Upland.
VALLEJO JUNIOR COLLEGE: Vallejo.
VENTURA COLLEGE: Ventura.
WEST CONTRA COSTA JUNIOR COLLEGE: Richmond.
WESTMONT COLLEGE: Santa Barbara.
WHITTIER COLLEGE: Whittier.
YUBA COLLEGE: Marysville.

Colorado

ADAMS STATE COLLEGE: Alamosa.
COLORADO, UNIVERSITY OF: Boulder.
COLORADO AGRICULTURAL AND MECHANICAL COLLEGE: Fort Collins.
COLORADO COLLEGE: Colorado Springs.
COLORADO SCHOOL OF MINES: Golden.
COLORADO STATE COLLEGE OF EDUCATION: Greeley.
COLORADO WOMEN'S COLLEGE: Denver.
CONSERVATIVE BAPTIST THEOLOGICAL SEMINARY: Denver.
DENVER, UNIVERSITY OF: Denver.
FORT LEWIS AGRICULTURAL AND MECHANICAL COLLEGE: Durango.
ILIFF SCHOOL OF THEOLOGY: Denver.

LAMAR JUNIOR COLLEGE: Lamar.
LORETTO HEIGHTS COLLEGE: Loretto.
MESA COUNTY JUNIOR COLLEGE: Grand
Junction.
NORTHEASTERN JUNIOR COLLEGE: Ster-
ling.
OTERO JUNIOR COLLEGE: La Junta.
PUEBLO JUNIOR COLLEGE: Pueblo.
REGIS COLLEGE: Denver.
TRINIDAD STATE JUNIOR COLLEGE:
Trinidad.
UNITED STATES AIR FORCE ACADEMY:
Denver.
WESTERN STATE COLLEGE OF COLO-
RADO: Gunnison.

Connecticut

ALBERTUS MAGNUS COLLEGE: New Haven.
BERKELEY DIVINITY SCHOOL: New Haven.
BRIDGEPORT, UNIVERSITY OF: Bridgeport.
CONNECTICUT, UNIVERSITY OF: Storrs.
CONNECTICUT COLLEGE: New London.
DANBURY STATE TEACHERS COLLEGE:
Danbury.
FAIRFIELD UNIVERSITY: Fairfield.
HARTFORD ART SCHOOL, INC.: Hartford.
HARTFORD COLLEGE: West Hartford.
HARTFORD SEMINARY FOUNDATION:
Hartford.
HARTT COLLEGE OF MUSIC: Hartford.
HILLYER COLLEGE: Hartford.
MITCHELL COLLEGE: New London.
NEW HAVEN STATE TEACHERS COL-
LEGE: New Haven.
NEW HAVEN YMCA JUNIOR COLLEGE:
New Haven.
QUINNIPIAC COLLEGE: Hamden.
RENSSELAER POLYTECHNIC INSTITUTE:
South Windsor.
ST. BASIL'S COLLEGE: Stamford.
ST. JOSEPH'S COLLEGE: West Hartford.
ST. MARY'S SEMINARY: Norwalk.
ST. THOMAS' SEMINARY: Bloomfield.
STATE TECHNICAL INSTITUTE: Hartford.
TEACHERS COLLEGE OF CONNECTICUT:
New Britain.
TRINITY COLLEGE: Hartford.
UNITED STATES COAST GUARD ACADE-
MY: New London.
WESLEYAN UNIVERSITY: Middletown.
WILLIMANTIC STATE TEACHERS COL-
LEGE: Willimantic.
*YALE UNIVERSITY: New Haven.

Delaware

DELAWARE STATE COLLEGE: Dover.
GOLDEY BEACOM SCHOOL OF BUSINESS:
Wilmington.
DELAWARE, UNIVERSITY OF: Newark.
WESLEY JUNIOR COLLEGE: Dover.

District of Columbia

AMERICAN UNIVERSITY, THE: Washing-
ton, D.C.
BENJAMIN FRANKLIN UNIVERSITY: Wash-
ington, D.C.
CAPITOL RADIO ENGINEERING INSTI-
TUTE: Washington, D.C.
CATHOLIC UNIVERSITY OF AMERICA:
Washington, D.C.
DISTRICT OF COLUMBIA TEACHERS COL-
LEGE: Washington, D.C.
DUNBARTON COLLEGE OF HOLY CROSS:
Washington, D.C.
GALLAUDET COLLEGE: Washington, D.C.

GEORGE WASHINGTON UNIVERSITY:
Washington.
GEORGETOWN UNIVERSITY: Washington.
GEORGETOWN VISITATION JUNIOR COL-
LEGE: Washington, D.C.
HOLTON-ARMS SCHOOL AND JUNIOR
COLLEGE: Washington, D.C.
HOWARD UNIVERSITY: Washington.
IMMACULATA JUNIOR COLLEGE: Washing-
ton.
MARJORIE WEBSTER JUNIOR COLLEGE:
Washington.
MODERN SCHOOL OF MUSIC, THE:
Washington, D.C.
MOUNT VERNON JUNIOR COLLEGE:
Washington, D.C.
ST. PAUL'S COLLEGE: Washington, D.C.
SCHOOL OF ADVANCED INTERNATION-
AL STUDIES OF THE JOHNS HOPKINS
UNIVERSITY: Washington, D.C.
SEVENTH-DAY ADVENTIST THEOLOGI-
CAL SEMINARY: Washington, D.C.
SOUTHEASTERN UNIVERSITY: Washington.
STRAYER COLLEGE OF ACCOUNTANCY:
Washington, D.C.
TRINITY COLLEGE: Washington.
UNITED STATES DEPARTMENT OF AGRI-
CULTURE GRADUATE SCHOOL: Washing-
ton, D.C.
WASHINGTON MISSIONARY COLLEGE,
THE: Washington.
WASHINGTON MUSICAL INSTITUTE:
Washington.
WASHINGTON SCHOOL OF PSYCHIATRY:
Washington, D.C.

Florida

BARRY COLLEGE: Miami.
BETHUNE-COOKMAN COLLEGE: Daytona
Beach.
CHIPOLA JUNIOR COLLEGE: Marianna.
EDWARD WATERS COLLEGE: Jacksonville.
FLORIDA, UNIVERSITY OF: Gainesville.
FLORIDA AGRICULTURAL AND MECHAN-
ICAL UNIVERSITY: Tallahassee.
FLORIDA CHRISTIAN COLLEGE, THE:
Tampa.
FLORIDA NORMAL AND INDUSTRIAL
MEMORIAL COLLEGE: St. Augustine.
FLORIDA SOUTHERN COLLEGE: Lakeland.
FLORIDA STATE UNIVERSITY: Tallahassee.
JACKSONVILLE COLLEGE OF MUSIC:
Jacksonville.
JACKSONVILLE UNIVERSITY: Jacksonville.
MIAMI, UNIVERSITY OF: Coral Gables.
ORLANDO JUNIOR COLLEGE: Orlando.
PALM BEACH JUNIOR COLLEGE: Lake
Worth.
PENSACOLA JUNIOR COLLEGE: Pensacola.
ROLLINS COLLEGE: Winter Park.
ST. PETERSBURG BIBLE INSTITUTE: St.
Petersburg.
ST. PETERSBURG JUNIOR COLLEGE: St.
Petersburg.
SOUTH-EASTERN BIBLE COLLEGE, INC.:
Lakeland.
STETSON UNIVERSITY: De Land.
TAMPA, UNIVERSITY OF: Tampa.
WASHINGTON JUNIOR COLLEGE: Pensa-
cola.
WEBBER COLLEGE: Babson Park.

Georgia

ABRAHAM BALDWIN AGRICULTURAL
COLLEGE: Tifton.
AGNES SCOTT COLLEGE: Decatur.
ALBANY STATE GOLLEGE: Albany.

ANDREW COLLEGE: Cuthbert.
ARMSTRONG COLLEGE OF SAVANNAH: Savannah.
ATLANTA ART INSTITUTE: Atlanta.
ATLANTA UNIVERSITY: Atlanta.
AUGUSTA, JUNIOR COLLEGE OF: Augusta.
BERRY COLLEGE: Mt. Berry.
BESSIE TIFT COLLEGE: Forsyth.
BRENAU COLLEGE: Gainesville.
BREWTON-PARKER JUNIOR COLLEGE: Mt. Vernon.
CLARK COLLEGE: Atlanta.
COLUMBIA THEOLOGICAL SEMINARY: Decatur.
EMMANUEL COLLEGE: Franklin Springs.
EMORY UNIVERSITY: Emory University.
FORT VALLEY STATE COLLEGE: Fort Valley.
GAMMON THEOLOGICAL SEMINARY: Atlanta.
GEORGIA, UNIVERSITY OF: Athens.
GEORGIA INSTITUTE OF TECHNOLOGY: Atlanta.
GEORGIA MILITARY COLLEGE: Milledgeville.
GEORGIA SOUTHWESTERN COLLEGE: Americus.
GEORGIA STATE COLLEGE FOR WOMEN: Milledgeville.
GEORGIA STATE COLLEGE OF BUSINESS ADMINISTRATION: Atlanta.
GEORGIA TEACHERS COLLEGE: Collegeboro, Statesboro.
GORDON MILITARY COLLEGE: Barnesville.
JUNIOR COLLEGE OF AUGUSTA: Augusta.
LA GRANGE COLLEGE: La Grange.
MEDICAL COLLEGE OF GEORGIA: Augusta.
MERCER UNIVERSITY: Macon.
MIDDLE GEORGIA COLLEGE: Cochran.
MOREHOUSE COLLEGE: Atlanta.
MORRIS BROWN COLLEGE: Atlanta.
NORMAN COLLEGE: Norman Park.
NORTH GEORGIA COLLEGE: Dahlonega.
OGLETHORPE UNIVERSITY: Oglethorpe University.
PAINE COLLEGE: Augusta.
PIEDMONT COLLEGE: Demorest.
REINHARDT COLLEGE: Waleska.
SAVANNAH STATE COLLEGE: Savannah.
SHORTER COLLEGE: Rome.
SOUTH GEORGIA COLLEGE: Douglas.
SOUTHERN COLLEGE OF PHARMACY: Atlanta.
SPELMAN COLLEGE: Atlanta.
TRUETT-MCCONNELL JUNIOR COLLEGE: Cleveland.
VALDOSTA STATE COLLEGE: Valdosta.
WESLEYAN COLLEGE: Macon.
WEST GEORGIA COLLEGE: Carrolton.
YOUNG L. G. HARRIS COLLEGE: Young Harris.

Idaho

BOISE JUNIOR COLLEGE: Boise.
IDAHO, COLLEGE OF: Caldwell.
IDAHO, UNIVERSITY OF: Moscow.
IDAHO STATE COLLEGE: Pocatello.
NORTHWEST NAZARENE COLLEGE: Nampa.
RICKS COLLEGE: Rexburg.

Illinois

AERONAUTICAL UNIVERSITY, INC.: Chicago.
AMERICAN CONSERVATORY OF MUSIC: Chicago.
AUGUSTANA COLLEGE: Rock Island.

AUGUSTANA THEOLOGICAL SEMINARY: Rock Island.
AURORA COLLEGE: Aurora.
BARAT COLLEGE OF THE SACRED HEART: Lake Forest.
BELLEVILLE TOWNSHIP JUNIOR COLLEGE: Belleville.
BETHANY BIBLICAL SEMINARY: Chicago.
BLACKBURN COLLEGE: Carlinville.
BRADLEY UNIVERSITY: Peoria.
CARTHAGE COLLEGE: Carthage.
CENTRALIA TOWNSHIP JUNIOR COLLEGE: Centralia.
CHICAGO, UNIVERSITY OF: Chicago.
CHICAGO ACADEMY OF FINE ARTS: Chicago.
CHICAGO CITY JUNIOR COLLEGE: Chicago.
CHICAGO COLLEGE OF CHIROPODY AND PEDIC SURGERY: Chicago.
CHICAGO COLLEGE OF OSTEOPATHY: Chicago.
CHICAGO CONSERVATORY: Chicago.
CHICAGO LUTHERAN THEOLOGICAL SEMINARY: Maywood.
CHICAGO MEDICAL SCHOOL: Chicago.
CHICAGO TEACHERS COLLEGE: Chicago.
CHICAGO TECHNICAL COLLEGE: Chicago.
CHICAGO THEOLOGICAL SEMINARY, THE: Chicago.
CHICAGO-KENT COLLEGE OF LAW: Chicago.
COLLEGE OF ST. FRANCIS: Joliet.
COLUMBIA COLLEGE: Chicago.
CONCORDIA TEACHERS COLLEGE: River Forest.
CONCORDIA THEOLOGICAL SEMINARY: Springfield.
COSMOPOLITAN SCHOOL OF MUSIC: Chicago.
DANVILLE JUNIOR COLLEGE: Danville.
DE PAUL UNIVERSITY: Chicago.
DE VRY TECHNICAL INSTITUTE: Chicago.
EASTERN ILLINOIS STATE COLLEGE: Charleston.
ELGIN COMMUNITY COLLEGE: Elgin.
ELMHURST COLLEGE: Elmhurst.
EUREKA COLLEGE: Eureka.
EVANGELICAL THEOLOGICAL SEMINARY: Naperville.
FELICIAN COLLEGE, THE: Chicago.
GARRETT BIBLICAL INSTITUTE: Evanston.
GEORGE WILLIAMS COLLEGE: Chicago.
GREENVILLE COLLEGE: Greenville.
ILLINOIS, UNIVERSITY OF: Urbana.
ILLINOIS COLLEGE: Jacksonville.
ILLINOIS COLLEGE OF CHIROPODY AND FOOT SURGERY: Chicago.
ILLINOIS COLLEGE OF OPTOMETRY: Chicago.
ILLINOIS INSTITUTE OF TECHNOLOGY: Chicago.
ILLINOIS STATE NORMAL UNIVERSITY: Normal.
ILLINOIS WESLEYAN UNIVERSITY: Bloomington.
JOHN MARSHALL LAW SCHOOL: Chicago.
JOLIET JUNIOR COLLEGE: Joliet.
KENDALL COLLEGE: Evanston.
KNOX COLLEGE: Galesburg.
LAKE FOREST COLLEGE: Lake Forest.
LA SALLE-PERU-OGLESBY JUNIOR COLLEGE: La Salle.
LEWIS COLLEGE OF SCIENCE AND TECHNOLOGY: Lockport.
LINCOLN BIBLE INSTITUTE: Lincoln.
LINCOLN COLLEGE: Lincoln.
LOYOLA UNIVERSITY: Chicago.
LYONS TOWNSHIP JUNIOR COLLEGE: La Grange.

MAC MURRAY COLLEGE: Jacksonville.
MALLINCKRODT COLLEGE: Wilmette.
MARYKNOLL SEMINARY: Glen Ellyn.
MC CORMICK THEOLOGICAL SEMINARY: Chicago.
MC KENDREE COLLEGE: Lebanon.
MEADVILLE THEOLOGICAL SCHOOL: Chicago.
MILLIKIN UNIVERSITY: Decatur.
MOLINE COMMUNITY COLLEGE: Moline.
MONMOUTH COLLEGE: Monmouth.
MONTICELLO COLLEGE: Alton.
MOODY BIBLE INSTITUTE: Chicago.
MORTON JUNIOR COLLEGE: Cicero.
MUNDELEIN COLLEGE: Chicago.
NATIONAL COLLEGE OF EDUCATION: Evanston.
NORTH CENTRAL COLLEGE: Naperville.
NORTH PARK COLLEGE AND THEOLOG-ICAL SEMINARY: Chicago.
NORTHERN BAPTIST THEOLOGICAL SEM-INARY: Chicago.
NORTHERN ILLINOIS STATE TEACHERS COLLEGE: De Kalb.
NORTHWESTERN UNIVERSITY: Evanston.
OLIVET NAZARENE COLLEGE: Kanakakee.
PESTALOZZI FROEBEL TEACHERS COL-LEGE: Chicago.
PRINCIPIA COLLEGE: Elsah.
QUINCY COLLEGE: Quincy.
ROCKFORD COLLEGE AND ROCKFORD MEN'S COLLEGE: Rockford.
ROOSEVELT UNIVERSITY: Chicago.
ROSARY COLLEGE: River Forest.
ST. BEDE COLLEGE: Peru.
ST. FRANCIS, COLLEGE OF: Joliet.
ST. MARY OF THE LAKE SEMINARY: Mundelein.
ST. PROCOPIUS COLLEGE: Lisle.
ST. XAVIER COLLEGE: Chicago.
SCHOOL OF THE ART INSTITUTE OF CHICAGO: Chicago.
SEABURY-WESTERN THEOLOGICAL SEM-INARY: Evanston.
SHERWOOD MUSIC SCHOOL: Chicago.
SHIMER COLLEGE: Mount Carroll.
SHURTLEFF COLLEGE: Alton.
SOUTHERN ILLINOIS UNIVERSITY: Car-bondale.
SPRINGFIELD JUNIOR COLLEGE: Spring-field.
THORNTON JUNIOR COLLEGE: Harvey.
TRINITY SEMINARY AND BIBLE COL-LEGE: Chicago.
VANDERCOOK COLLEGE OF MUSIC: Chicago.
WESTERN ILLINOIS STATE COLLEGE: Macomb.
WHEATON COLLEGE: Wheaton.

Indiana

ANCILLA DOMINI COLLEGE: Donaldson.
ANDERSON COLLEGE AND THEOLOGI-CAL SEMINARY: Anderson.
BALL STATE TEACHERS COLLEGE: Muncie.
BUTLER UNIVERSITY: Indianapolis.
CONCORDIA COLLEGE: Fort Wayne.
DE PAUW UNIVERSITY: Greencastle.
EARLHAM COLLEGE: Richmond.
EVANSVILLE COLLEGE: Evansville.
FORT WAYNE ART SCHOOL: Fort Wayne.
FORT WAYNE BIBLE COLLEGE: Fort Wayne.
FRANKLIN COLLEGE OF INDIANA: Franklin.
GOSHEN COLLEGE: Goshen.
GRACE THEOLOGICAL SEMINARY AND GRACE COLLEGE: Winona Lake.
HANOVER COLLEGE: Hanover.

INDIANA CENTRAL COLLEGE: Indianapolis.
INDIANA STATE TEACHERS COLLEGE: Terre Haute.
INDIANA TECHNICAL COLLEGE: Fort Wayne.
INDIANA UNIVERSITY: Bloomington.
JOHN HERRON ART SCHOOL: Indianapolis.
LAIN DRAFTING COLLEGE: Indianapolis.
MANCHESTER COLLEGE: North Manchester.
MARIAN COLLEGE: Indianapolis.
MARION COLLEGE: Marion.
NOTRE DAME, UNIVERSITY OF: Notre Dame.
PURDUE UNIVERSITY: Lafayette.
ROSE POLYTECHNIC INSTITUTE: Terre Haute.
ST. BENEDICT'S NORMAL COLLEGE: Ferdinand.
ST. FRANCIS COLLEGE: Fort Wayne.
ST. JOSEPH'S COLLEGE: Collegeville.
ST. MARY-OF-THE-WOODS COLLEGE: St. Mary-of-the-Woods.
ST. MARY'S COLLEGE: Notre Dame.
ST. MEINRAD SEMINARY: St. Meinrad.
TAYLOR UNIVERSITY: Upland.
TRI-STATE COLLEGE: Angola.
VALPARAISO TECHNICAL INSTITUTE: Valparasio.
VALPARAISO UNIVERSITY: Valparaiso.
VINCENNES UNIVERSITY: Vincennes.
WABASH COLLEGE: Crawfordsville.

Iowa

BOONE JUNIOR COLLEGE: Boone.
BRIAR CLIFF COLLEGE: Sioux City.
BUENA VISTA COLLEGE: Storm Lake.
BURLINGTON COLLEGE: Burlington.
CENTERVILLE COMMUNITY COLLEGE: Centerville.
CENTRAL COLLEGE: Pella.
CHICAGO EVANGELISTIC INSTITUTE: University Park.
CLARINDA JUNIOR COLLEGE: Clarinda.
CLARKE COLLEGE: Dubuque.
CLINTON JUNIOR COLLEGE: Clinton.
COE COLLEGE: Cedar Rapids.
CORNELL COLLEGE: Mt. Vernon.
CRESTON JUNIOR COLLEGE: Creston.
DES MOINES STILL COLLEGE OF OSTEOP-ATHY AND SURGERY: Des Moines.
DRAKE UNIVERSITY: Des Moines.
DUBUQUE, UNIVERSITY OF: Dubuque.
EAGLE GROVE JUNIOR COLLEGE: Eagle Grove.
ELLSWORTH JUNIOR COLLEGE: Iowa Falls.
EMMETSBURG JUNIOR COLLEGE: Emmets-burg.
ESTHERVILLE JUNIOR COLLEGE: Esther-ville.
FORT DODGE JUNIOR COLLEGE: Fort Dodge.
GRACELAND COLLEGE: Lamoni.
GRAND VIEW COLLEGE: Des Moines.
GRINNELL COLLEGE: Grinnell.
IOWA STATE COLLEGE OF AGRICUL-TURE AND MECHANIC ARTS: Ames.
IOWA STATE TEACHERS COLLEGE: Cedar Falls.
IOWA, STATE UNIVERSITY OF: Iowa City.
IOWA WESLEYAN COLLEGE: Mt. Pleasant.
KEOKUK COMMUNITY COLLEGE: Keokuk.
LORAS COLLEGE: Dubuque.
LUTHER COLLEGE: Decorah.
MARSHALLTOWN JUNIOR COLLEGE: Marshalltown.
MARYCREST COLLEGE: Davenport.
MASON CITY JUNIOR COLLEGE: Mason City.

MORNINGSIDE COLLEGE: Sioux City.
MOUNT MERCY JUNIOR COLLEGE: Cedar Rapids.
MOUNT ST. CLARE JUNIOR COLLEGE: Clinton.
MUSCATINE JUNIOR COLLEGE: Muscatine.
NORTHWESTERN JUNIOR COLLEGE: Orange City.
OTTUMWA HEIGHTS COLLEGE: Ottumwa.
PARSONS COLLEGE: Fairfield.
ST. AMBROSE COLLEGE: Davenport.
SIMPSON COLLEGE: Indianola.
UPPER IOWA UNIVERSITY: Fayette.
WALDORF COLLEGE: Forest City.
WARTBURG COLLEGE: Waverly.
WARTBURG THEOLOGICAL SEMINARY: Dubuque.
WEBSTER CITY JUNIOR COLLEGE: Webster City.
WESTMAR COLLEGE: Le Mars.
WILLIAM PENN COLLEGE: Oskaloosa.

Kansas

ARKANSAS CITY JUNIOR COLLEGE: Arkansas City.
BAKER UNIVERSITY: Baldwin City.
BETHANY COLLEGE: Lindsborg.
BETHEL COLLEGE: North Newton.
CENTRAL BAPTIST THEOLOGICAL SEMINARY: Kansas City.
CENTRAL COLLEGE: McPherson.
CHANUTE JUNIOR COLLEGE: Chanute.
COFFEYVILLE COLLEGE OF ARTS, SCIENCE, AND VOCATIONS: Coffeyville.
DONNELLY COLLEGE: Kansas City.
EMPORIA, COLLEGE OF: Emporia.
EL DORADO JUNIOR COLLEGE: El Dorado.
FORT HAYS KANSAS STATE COLLEGE: Hays.
FORT SCOTT JUNIOR COLLEGE: Fort Scott.
FRIENDS UNIVERSITY: Wichita.
GARDEN CITY JUNIOR COLLEGE: Garden City.
HESSTON COLLEGE: Hesston.
HIGHLAND JUNIOR COLLEGE: Highland.
HUTCHINSON JUNIOR COLLEGE: Hutchinson.
INDEPENDENCE COMMUNITY COLLEGE: Independence.
IOLA JUNIOR COLLEGE: Iola.
KANSAS, UNIVERSITY OF: Lawrence.
KANSAS CITY KANSAS JUNIOR COLLEGE: Kansas City.
KANSAS STATE COLLEGE OF AGRICULTURE AND APPLIED SCIENCE: Manhattan.
KANSAS STATE TEACHERS COLLEGE: Emporia.
KANSAS STATE TEACHERS COLLEGE: Pittsburg.
KANSAS WESLEYAN UNIVERSITY: Salina.
MANHATTAN BIBLE COLLEGE: Manhattan.
MARYMOUNT COLLEGE: Salina.
MC PHERSON COLLEGE: McPherson.
MILTONVALE WESLEYAN COLLEGE: Miltonvale.
MT. ST. SCHOLASTICA COLLEGE: Atchison.
OTTAWA UNIVERSITY: Ottawa.
PARSONS JUNIOR COLLEGE: Parsons.
PRATT JUNIOR COLLEGE: Pratt.
SACRED HEART COLLEGE: Wichita.
ST. BENEDICT'S COLLEGE: Atchison.
ST. JOHN'S LUTHERAN COLLEGE: Winfield.
ST. MARY COLLEGE: Xavier.

ST. MARY OF THE PLAINS COLLEGE: Dodge City.
SOUTHWESTERN COLLEGE: Winfield.
STERLING COLLEGE: Sterling.
TABOR COLLEGE: Hillsboro.
URSULINE COLLEGE OF PAOLA: Paola.
WASHBURN UNIVERSITY OF TOPEKA: Topeka.
WICHITA, UNIVERSITY OF: Wichita.

Kentucky

ASBURY COLLEGE: Wilmore.
ASBURY THEOLOGICAL SEMINARY: Wilmore.
ASHLAND JUNIOR COLLEGE: Ashland.
BELLARMINE COLLEGE: Louisville.
BEREA COLLEGE: Berea.
BETHEL COLLEGE: Hopkinsville.
BOWLING GREEN COLLEGE OF COMMERCE: Bowling Green.
BRESCIA COLLEGE: Owensboro.
CAMPBELLSVILLE COLLEGE: Campbellsville.
CANEY JUNIOR COLLEGE: Pippa Passes.
CARVER SCHOOL OF MISSIONS AND SOCIAL WORK: Louiseville.
CENTRE COLLEGE OF KENTUCKY: Danville.
COLLEGE OF THE BIBLE, THE: Lexington.
CUMBERLAND COLLEGE: Williamsburg.
EASTERN KENTUCKY STATE COLLEGE: Richmond.
GEORGETOWN COLLEGE: Georgetown.
KENTUCKY, UNIVERSITY OF: Lexington.
KENTUCKY STATE COLLEGE: Frankfort.
KENTUCKY WESLEYAN COLLEGE: Owensboro.
LEES JUNIOR COLLEGE: Jackson.
LINDSEY WILSON COLLEGE: Columbia.
LORETTO JUNIOR COLLEGE: Nerinx.
LOUISVILLE, UNIVERSITY OF: Louisville.
LOUISVILLE PRESBYTERIAN THEOLOGICAL SEMINARY: Louisville.
MIDWAY JUNIOR COLLEGE: Midway.
MOREHEAD STATE COLLEGE: Morehead.
MURRAY STATE COLLEGE: Murray.
NAZARETH COLLEGE: Louisville.
NAZARETH COLLEGE AND ACADEMY: Nazareth.
PADUCAH JUNIOR COLLEGE: Paducah.
PIKEVILLE COLLEGE: Pikeville.
ST. CATHARINE JUNIOR COLLEGE: Springfield.
ST. MARY'S COLLEGE: St. Mary.
SOUTHERN BAPTIST THEOLOGICAL SEMINARY: Louisville.
SUE BENNETT COLLEGE: London.
TRANSYLVANIA COLLEGE: Lexington.
UNION COLLEGE: Barbourville.
URSULINE COLLEGE: Louisville.
VILLA MADONNA COLLEGE: Covington.
WESTERN KENTUCKY STATE TEACHERS COLLEGE: Bowling Green.

Louisiana

ACADEMY OF THE HOLY ANGELS: New Orleans.
CENTENARY COLLEGE: Shreveport.
DILLARD UNIVERSITY: New Orleans.
GRAMBLING COLLEGE: Grambling.
LELAND COLLEGE: Baker.
LOUISIANA COLLEGE: Pineville.
LOUISIANA POLYTECHNIC INSTITUTE: Ruston.
LOUISIANA STATE UNIVERSITY AND AGRICULTURAL AND MECHANICAL COLLEGE: Baton Rouge.
LOYOLA UNIVERSITY: New Orleans.

MCNEESE STATE COLLEGE: Lake Charles.
NEW ORLEANS BAPTIST THEOLOGICAL SEMINARY: New Orleans.
NORTHEAST LOUISIANA STATE COLLEGE: Monroe.
NORTHWESTERN STATE COLLEGE OF LOUISIANA: Natchitoches.
NOTRE DAME SEMINARY: New Orleans.
ST. MARY'S DOMINICAN COLLEGE: New Orleans.
SOUTHEASTERN LOUISIANA COLLEGE: Hammond.
SOUTHERN UNIVERSITY AND AGRICULTURAL AND MECHANICAL COLLEGE: Baton Rouge.
SOUTHWESTERN LOUISIANA INSTITUTE: Lafayette.
TULANE UNIVERSITY: New Orleans.
XAVIER UNIVERSITY: New Orleans.

Maine

AROOSTOOK STATE TEACHERS COLLEGE: Presque Isle.
BATES COLLEGE: Lewiston.
BOWDOIN COLLEGE: Brunswick.
COLBY COLLEGE: Watersville.
GORHAM STATE TEACHERS COLLEGE: Gorham.
LA MENNAIS COLLEGE: Alfred.
MAINE, UNIVERSITY OF: Orono.
MAINE MARITIME ACADEMY: Castine.
NASSON COLLEGE: Springvale.
NORTHERN CONSERVATORY OF MUSIC: Bangor.
OBLATE COLLEGE AND SEMINARY: Bar Harbor.
RICKER COLLEGE: Houlton.
ST. JOSEPH'S COLLEGE: North Windham.
WASHINGTON STATE TEACHERS COLLEGE: Machias.
WESTBROOK JUNIOR COLLEGE: Portland.

Maryland

BALTIMORE, UNIVERSITY OF: Baltimore.
BALTIMORE COLLEGE OF COMMERCE: Baltimore.
BALTIMORE JUNIOR COLLEGE: Baltimore.
COPPIN STATE TEACHERS COLLEGE: Baltimore.
GOUCHER COLLEGE: Baltimore.
HAGERSTOWN JUNIOR COLLEGE: Hagerstown.
HOOD COLLEGE: Frederick.
JOHNS HOPKINS UNIVERSITY: Baltimore.
LOYOLA COLLEGE: Baltimore.
MARYLAND, UNIVERSITY OF: College Park.
MARYLAND SCHOOL OF ART AND DESIGN: Baltimore.
MARYLAND STATE COLLEGE: Princess Anne.
MARYLAND STATE TEACHERS COLLEGE: Bowie.
MARYLAND STATE TEACHERS COLLEGE: Frostburg.
MARYLAND STATE TEACHERS COLLEGE: Salisbury.
MARYLAND STATE TEACHERS COLLEGE: Towson.
MONTGOMERY JUNIOR COLLEGE: Tacoma Park.
MORGAN STATE COLLEGE: Baltimore.
MOUNT ST. AGNES COLLEGE: Mount Washington.
MOUNT SAINT MARY'S COLLEGE: Emmitsburg.
NER ISRAEL RABBINICAL COLLEGE: Baltimore.

NOTRE DAME OF MARYLAND, COLLEGE OF: Baltimore.
PEABODY INSTITUTE OF THE CITY OF BALTIMORE: Baltimore.
ST. CHARLES COLLEGE: Cantonsville.
ST. JOHN'S COLLEGE: Annapolis.
ST. JOSEPH COLLEGE: Emmitsburg.
ST. MARY'S SEMINARY AND UNIVERSITY: Baltimore.
ST. MARY'S SEMINARY JUNIOR COLLEGE: St. Mary's City.
UNITED STATES NAVAL ACADEMY: Annapolis.
WASHINGTON COLLEGE: Chestertown.
WESTERN MARYLAND COLLEGE: Westminster.

Massachusetts

AMERICAN INTERNATIONAL COLLEGE: Springfield.
AMHERST COLLEGE: Amherst.
ANDOVER NEWTON THEOLOGICAL SCHOOL: Newton Center.
ANNA MARIA COLLEGE FOR WOMEN: Paxton.
ASSUMPTION COLLEGE: Worcester.
ATLANTIC UNION COLLEGE: South Lancaster.
BABSON INSTITUTE OF BUSINESS ADMINISTRATION: Babson Park.
BOSTON COLLEGE: Chestnut Hill.
BOSTON CONSERVATORY OF MUSIC: Boston.
BOSTON SCHOOL OF OCCUPATIONAL THERAPY: Boston.
BOSTON UNIVERSITY: Boston.
BOUVÉ-BOSTON SCHOOL: Medford.
BRADFORD DURFEE TECHNICAL INSTITUTE: Fall River.
BRADFORD JUNIOR COLLEGE: Bradford.
BRANDEIS UNIVERSITY: Waltham.
CAMBRIDGE JUNIOR COLLEGE: Cambridge.
CLARK UNIVERSITY: Worcester.
CURRY COLLEGE: Milton.
EASTERN NAZARENE COLLEGE: Wollaston.
EMERSON COLLEGE: Boston.
EMMANUEL COLLEGE: Boston.
ENDICOTT JUNIOR COLLEGE: Beverly.
EPISCOPAL THEOLOGICAL SCHOOL: Cambridge.
FORSYTHE SCHOOL FOR DENTAL HYGIENISTS: Boston.
FRANKLIN TECHNICAL INSTITUTE: Boston.
GARLAND SCHOOL, THE, A JUNIOR COLLEGE: Boston.
GORDON COLLEGE: Beverly Farms.
*HARVARD UNIVERSITY: Cambridge.
HEBREW TEACHERS COLLEGE: Brookline.
HOLY CROSS, COLLEGE OF THE: Worcester.
HOLYOKE JUNIOR COLLEGE: Holyoke.
LASELL JUNIOR COLLEGE: Auburndale.
LESLEY COLLEGE: Cambridge.
LOWELL TECHNOLOGICAL INSTITUTE: Lowell.
MASSACHUSETTS, UNIVERSITY OF: Amherst.
MASSACHUSETTS COLLEGE OF OPTOMETRY: Boston.
MASSACHUSETTS COLLEGE OF PHARMACY: Boston.
MASSACHUSETTS INSTITUTE OF TECHNOLOGY: Cambridge.
MASSACHUSETTS MARITIME ACADEMY: Buzzards Bay.
MASSACHUSETTS SCHOOL OF ART: Boston.

MASSACHUSETTS STATE TEACHERS COLLEGE: Bridgewater.
MASSACHUSETTS STATE TEACHERS COLLEGE: Fitchburg.
MASSACHUSETTS STATE TEACHERS COLLEGE: Framingham.
MASSACHUSETTS STATE TEACHERS COLLEGE: Lowell.
MASSACHUSETTS STATE TEACHERS COLLEGE: Salem.
MASSACHUSETTS STATE TEACHERS COLLEGE: Westfield.
MASACHUSETTS STATE TEACHERS COLLEGE: Worcester.
MERRIMACK COLLEGE: Andover.
MT. HOLYOKE COLLEGE: South Hadley.
NEW BEDFORD INSTITUTE OF TEXTILES AND TECHNOLOGY: New Bedford.
NEW ENGLAND COLLEGE OF PHARMACY: Boston.
NEW ENGLAND CONSERVATORY OF MUSIC: Boston.
NEWTON COLLEGE OF THE SACRED HEART: Newton.
NEWTON JUNIOR COLLEGE: Newtonville.
NICHOLS JUNIOR COLLEGE: Dudley.
NORTHEASTERN UNIVERSITY: Boston.
OUR LADY OF THE ELMS, COLLEGE OF: Chicopee.
PINE MANOR JUNIOR COLLEGE: Wellesley.
RADCLIFFE COLLEGE: Cambridge.
REGIS COLLEGE: Weston.
ST. JOHN'S SEMINARY: Brighton.
SIMMONS COLLEGE: Boston.
SMITH COLLEGE: Northampton.
SPRINGFIELD COLLEGE: Springfield.
STALEY COLLEGE OF THE SPOKEN WORD, THE: Brookline.
STONEHILL COLLEGE: North Easton.
SUFFOLK UNIVERSITY: Boston.
TUFTS UNIVERSITY: Medford.
WELLESLEY COLLEGE: Wellesley.
WENTWORTH INSTITUTE: Boston.
WHEATON COLLEGE: Norton.
WHEELOCK COLLEGE: Boston.
WILLIAMS COLLEGE: Williamstown.
WOODS HOLE OCEANOGRAPHIC INSTITUTION: Woods Hole.
WORCESTER JUNIOR COLLEGE: Worcester.
WORCESTER POLYTECHNIC INSTITUTE: Worcester.

Michigan

ALBION COLLEGE: Albion.
ALMA COLLEGE: Alma.
AQUINAS COLLEGE: Grand Rapids.
BAY CITY JUNIOR COLLEGE: Bay City.
CALVIN COLLEGE: Grand Rapids.
CALVIN THEOLOGICAL SEMINARY: Grand Rapids.
CENTRAL MICHIGAN COLLEGE: Mt. Pleasant.
CLEARY COLLEGE: Ypsilanti.
COMMUNITY COLLEGE AND TECHNICAL INSTITUTE: Benton Harbor.
DETROIT, UNIVERSITY OF: Detroit.
DETROIT BIBLE INSTITUTE: Detroit.
DETROIT COLLEGE OF LAW: Detroit.
DETROIT INSTITUTE OF MUSICAL ART: Detroit.
DETROIT INSTITUTE OF TECHNOLOGY: Detroit.
DUNS SCOTUS COLLEGE: Detroit.
EASTERN MICHIGAN COLLEGE: Ypsilanti.
EMMANUEL MISSIONARY COLLEGE: Berrien Springs.
FERRIS INSTITUTE: Big Rapids.

FLINT JUNIOR COLLEGE: Flint.
GENERAL MOTORS INSTITUTE: Flint.
GOGEBIC COMMUNITY COLLEGE: Ironwood.
GRAND RAPIDS BAPTIST THEOLOGICAL SEMINARY AND BIBLE INSTITUTE: Grand Rapids.
GRAND RAPIDS JUNIOR COLLEGE: Grand Rapids.
HENRY FORD COMMUNITY COLLEGE: Dearborn.
HIGHLAND PARK JUNIOR COLLEGE: Highland Park.
HILLSDALE COLLEGE: Hillsdale.
HOPE COLLEGE: Holland.
JACKSON JUNIOR COLLEGE: Jackson.
KALAMAZOO COLLEGE: Kalamazoo.
LAWRENCE INSTITUTE OF TECHNOLOGY: Highland Park.
MADONNA COLLEGE: Livonia.
MARYGROVE COLLEGE: Detroit.
MERCY COLLEGE: Detroit.
MERRILL-PALMER SCHOOL: Detroit.
MICHIGAN, UNIVERSITY OF: Ann Arbor.
MICHIGAN COLLEGE OF MINING AND TECHNOLOGY: Houghton.
MICHIGAN STATE UNIVERSITY OF AGRICULTURE AND APPLIED SCIENCE: East Lansing.
MUSKEGON COMMUNITY COLLEGE: Muskegon.
NAZARETH COLLEGE: Nazareth.
NORTHERN MICHIGAN COLLEGE: Marquette.
NORTHWESTERN MICHIGAN COLLEGE: Traverse City.
OLIVET COLLEGE: Olivet.
OWOSSO BIBLE COLLEGE: Owosso.
PORT HURON JUNIOR COLLEGE: Port Huron.
SACRED HEART SEMINARY: Detroit.
SIENA HEIGHTS COLLEGE: Adrian.
ST. JOSEPH'S SEMINARY: Grand Rapids.
SOUTH MACOMB COMMUNITY COLLEGE: Van Dyke.
SPRING ARBOR JUNIOR COLLEGE: Spring Arbor.
SUOMI COLLEGE AND THEOLOGICAL SEMINARY: Hancock.
WAYNE STATE UNIVERSITY: Detroit.
WESTERN MICHIGAN COLLEGE OF EDUCATION: Kalamazoo.
WESTERN THEOLOGICAL SEMINARY: Holland.

Minnesota

AUGSBURG COLLEGE AND THEOLOGICAL SEMINARY: Minneapolis.
AUSTIN JUNIOR COLLEGE: Austin.
BETHANY LUTHERAN COLLEGE AND THEOLOGICAL SEMINARY: Mankato.
BETHEL COLLEGE AND SEMINARY: St. Paul.
BRAINERD JUNIOR COLLEGE: Brainerd.
CARLETON COLLEGE: Northfield.
CONCORDIA COLLEGE: Moorhead.
CONCORDIA COLLEGE: St. Paul.
ELY JUNIOR COLLEGE: Ely.
EVELETH JUNIOR COLLEGE: Eveleth.
GUSTAVUS ADOLPHUS COLLEGE: St. Peter.
HAMLINE UNIVERSITY: St. Paul.
HIBBING JUNIOR COLLEGE: Hibbing.
ITASCA JUNIOR COLLEGE: Coleraine.
LUTHER THEOLOGICAL SEMINARY: St. Paul.
MACALESTER COLLEGE: St. Paul.
MAC PHAIL COLLEGE OF MUSIC: Minneapolis.

MINNEAPOLIS COLLEGE OF MUSIC: Minneapolis.
MINNEAPOLIS SCHOOL OF ART: Minneapolis.
MINNESOTA, UNIVERSITY OF: Minneapolis.
MINNESOTA BIBLE COLLEGE: Minneapolis.
MINNESOTA STATE TEACHERS COLLEGE: Bemidji.
MINNESOTA STATE TEACHERS COLLEGE: Mankato.
MINNESOTA STATE TEACHERS COLLEGE: Moorhead.
MINNESOTA STATE TEACHERS COLLEGE: St. Cloud.
MINNESOTA STATE TEACHERS COLLEGE: Winona.
NORTHWESTERN COLLEGE: Minneapolis.
NORTHWESTERN LUTHERAN THEOLOGICAL SEMINARY: Minneapolis.
ROCHESTER JUNIOR COLLEGE: Rochester.
ST. BENEDICT, COLLEGE OF: St. Joseph.
ST. CATHERINE, COLLEGE OF: St. Paul.
ST. JOHN'S UNIVERSITY: Collegeville.
ST. MARY'S COLLEGE: Winona.
ST. OLAF COLLEGE: Northfield.
ST. PAUL BIBLE INSTITUTE: St. Paul.
ST. PAUL SEMINARY: St. Paul.
ST. SCHOLASTICA, COLLEGE OF: Duluth.
ST. TERESA, COLLEGE OF: Winona.
ST. THOMAS, COLLEGE OF: St. Paul.
VIRGINIA JUNIOR COLLEGE: Virginia.
WILLIAM MITCHELL COLLEGE OF LAW: St. Paul.
WORTHINGTON JUNIOR COLLEGE: Worthington.

Mississippi

ALCORN AGRICULTURAL AND MECHANICAL COLLEGE: Lorman.
ALL SAINTS' JUNIOR COLLEGE: Vicksburg.
BELHAVEN COLLEGE: Jackson.
BLUE MOUNTAIN COLLEGE: Blue Mountain.
CLARKE MEMORIAL COLLEGE: Newton.
COAHOMA JUNIOR COLLEGE: Clarksdale.
COPIAH-LINCOLN JUNIOR COLLEGE: Wesson.
DELTA STATE COLLEGE: Cleveland.
EAST CENTRAL JUNIOR COLLEGE: Decatur.
EAST MISSISSIPPI JUNIOR COLLEGE: Scooba.
GULF PARK COLLEGE: Gulfport.
HINDS JUNIOR COLLEGE: Raymond.
HOLMES JUNIOR COLLEGE: Goodman.
ITAWAMBA JUNIOR COLLEGE: Fulton.
JACKSON STATE COLLEGE: Jackson.
JONES COUNTY JUNIOR COLLEGE: Ellisville.
MARY HOLMES JUNIOR COLLEGE: West Point.
MERIDIAN MUNICIPAL JUNIOR COLLEGE: Meridian.
MILLSAPS COLLEGE: Jackson.
MISSISSIPPI, UNIVERSITY OF: University.
MISSISSIPPI COLLEGE: Clinton.
MISSISSIPPI INDUSTRIAL COLLEGE: Holly Springs.
MISSISSIPPI SOUTHERN COLLEGE: Hattiesburg.
MISSISSIPPI STATE COLLEGE: State College.
MISSISSIPPI STATE COLLEGE FOR WOMEN: Columbus.
MISSISSIPPI VOCATIONAL COLLEGE: Itta Bena.
NORTHEAST MISSISSIPPI JUNIOR COLLEGE: Booneville.

NORTHWEST MISSISSIPPI JUNIOR COLLEGE: Senatobia.
OKOLONA COLLEGE: Okolona.
PEARL RIVER JUNIOR COLLEGE: Poplarville.
PERKINSTON JUNIOR COLLEGE: Perkinston.
PINEY WOODS COUNTRY LIFE SCHOOL: Piney Woods.
PRENTISS NORMAL AND INDUSTRIAL INSTITUTE: Prentiss.
RUST COLLEGE: Holly Springs.
SOUTHWEST MISSISSIPPI JUNIOR COLLEGE: Summit.
SUNFLOWER JUNIOR COLLEGE: Moorhead.
TOUGALOO SOUTHERN CHRISTIAN COLLEGE: Tougaloo.
WILLIAM CAREY COLLEGE: Hattiesburg.
WOOD JUNIOR COLLEGE: Mathiston.

Missouri

CENTRAL BIBLE INSTITUTE: Springfield.
CENTRAL COLLEGE: Fayette.
CENTRAL MISSOURI STATE COLLEGE: Warrensburg.
CENTRAL TECHNICAL INSTITUTE, INC.: Kansas City.
CHRISTIAN COLLEGE: Columbia.
CONCEPTION SEMINARY: Conception.
CONCORDIA SEMINARY: St. Louis.
CONSERVATORY OF MUSIC OF KANSAS CITY: Kansas City.
COTTEY COLLEGE: Nevada.
CULVER-STOCKTON COLLEGE: Canton.
DRURY COLLEGE: Springfield.
EDEN THEOLOGICAL SEMINARY: Webster Groves.
HANNIBAL-LA GRANGE COLLEGE: Hannibal.
HARRIS TEACHERS COLLEGE: St. Louis.
JEFFERSON CITY JUNIOR COLLEGE: Jefferson City.
JOPLIN JUNIOR COLLEGE: Joplin.
JUNIOR COLLEGE OF FLAT RIVER: Flat River.
KANSAS CITY, UNIVERSITY OF: Kansas City.
KANSAS CITY, JUNIOR COLLEGE OF: Kansas City.
KANSAS CITY ART INSTITUTE AND SCHOOL OF DESIGN: Kansas City.
KANSAS CITY BIBLE COLLEGE: Kansas City.
KEMPER MILITARY SCHOOL: Booneville.
KENRICK SEMINARY: St. Louis.
KIRKSVILLE COLLEGE OF OSTEOPATHY AND SURGERY: Kirksville.
LINCOLN UNIVERSITY: Jefferson City.
LINDENWOOD COLLEGE FOR WOMEN: St. Charles.
MISSOURI, UNIVERSITY OF: Columbia.
MISSOURI VALLEY COLLEGE: Marshall.
MOBERLY JUNIOR COLLEGE: Moberly.
NORTHEAST MISSOURI STATE TEACHERS COLLEGE: Kirksville.
NORTHWEST MISSOURI STATE COLLEGE: Maryville.
PARK COLLEGE: Parkville.
ROCKHURST COLLEGE: Kansas City.
ST. JOSEPH JUNIOR COLLEGE: St. Joseph.
ST. LOUIS COLLEGE OF PHARMACY AND ALLIED SCIENCES: St. Louis.
ST. LOUIS INSTITUTE OF MUSIC: St. Louis.
ST. LOUIS PREPARATORY SEMINARY: St. Louis.
ST. LOUIS UNIVERSITY: St. Louis.
ST. PAUL'S COLLEGE: Concordia.
ST. TERESA, COLLEGE OF: Kansas City.

SOUTHEAST MISSOURI STATE COLLEGE: Cape Girardeau.
SOUTHWEST BAPTIST COLLEGE: Bolivar.
SOUTHWEST MISSOURI STATE COLLEGE: Springfield.
STEPHENS COLLEGE: Columbia.
TARKIO COLLEGE: Tarkio.
TRENTON JUNIOR COLLEGE: Trenton.
WASHINGTON UNIVERSITY: St. Louis.
WESTMINSTER COLLEGE: Fulton.
WILLIAM JEWELL COLLEGE: Liberty.
WILLIAM WOODS COLLEGE: Fulton.

Montana

CARROL COLLEGE: Helena.
CUSTER COUNTY JUNIOR COLLEGE: Miles City.
DAWSON COUNTY JUNIOR COLLEGE: Glendive.
EASTERN MONTANA COLLEGE OF EDUCATION: Billings.
GREAT FALLS, COLLEGE OF: Great Falls.
MONTANA SCHOOL OF MINES: Butte.
MONTANA STATE COLLEGE: Bozeman.
MONTANA STATE UNIVERSITY: Missoula.
NORTHERN MONTANA COLLEGE: Havre.
ROCKY MOUNTAIN COLLEGE: Billings.
WESTERN MONTANA COLLEGE OF EDUCATION: Dillon.

Nebraska

COLLEGE OF ST. MARY: Omaha.
CONCORDIA TEACHERS COLLEGE: Seward.
CREIGHTON UNIVERSITY: Omaha.
DANA COLLEGE: Blair.
DOANE COLLEGE: Crete.
DUCHESNE COLLEGE: Omaha.
FAIRBURY JUNIOR COLLEGE: Fairbury.
GRACE BIBLE INSTITUTE: Omaha.
HASTINGS COLLEGE: Hastings.
MCCOOK JUNIOR COLLEGE: McCook.
MIDLAND COLLEGE: Fremont.
NEBRASKA, UNIVERSITY OF: Lincoln.
NEBRASKA STATE TEACHERS COLLEGE: Chadron.
NEBRASKA STATE TEACHERS COLLEGE: Kearny.
NEBRASKA STATE TEACHERS COLLEGE: Peru.
NEBRASKA STATE TEACHERS COLLEGE: Wayne.
NEBRASKA WESLEYAN UNIVERSITY: Lincoln.
NORFOLK JUNIOR COLLEGE: Norfolk.
OMAHA, MUNICIPAL UNIVERSITY OF: Omaha.
SCOTTSBLUFF COLLEGE: Scottsbluff.
UNION COLLEGE: Lincoln.

Nevada

NEVADA, UNIVERSITY OF: Reno.

New Hampshire

COLBY JUNIOR COLLEGE FOR WOMEN: New London.
*DARTMOUTH COLLEGE: Hanover.
KEENE TEACHERS COLLEGE: Keene.
MOUNT SAINT MARY COLLEGE: Hooksett.
NEW HAMPSHIRE, UNIVERSITY OF: Durham.
NEW HAMPSHIRE TECHNICAL INSTITUTE: Manchester.
NEW HAMPSHIRE TECHNICAL INSTITUTE: Portsmouth.

PLYMOUTH TEACHERS COLLEGE: Plymouth.
RIVIER COLLEGE: Nashua.
ST. ANSELM'S COLLEGE: Manchester.

New Jersey

ALMA WHITE COLLEGE: Zarephath.
ASSUMPTION JUNIOR COLLEGE: Mallinckrodt Convent, Mendham.
BLOOMFIELD COLLEGE AND THEOLOGICAL SEMINARY: Bloomfield.
CALDWELL COLLEGE FOR WOMEN: Caldwell.
CENTENARY COLLEGE FOR WOMEN: Hackettstown.
DELAWARE, UNIVERSITY OF: Newark.
DON BOSCO COLLEGE: Newton.
DREW UNIVERSITY: Madison.
FAIRLEIGH DICKINSON COLLEGE: Rutherford.
GEORGIAN COURT COLLEGE: Lakewood.
IMMACULATE CONCEPTION JUNIOR COLLEGE: Lodi.
IMMACULATE CONCEPTION SEMINARY: Darlington.
INSTITUTE FOR ADVANCED STUDY, THE: Princeton.
JERSEY CITY JUNIOR COLLEGE: Jersey City.
MONMOUTH JUNIOR COLLEGE: West Long Branch.
MOTHER OF THE SAVIOR SEMINARY: Blackwood.
NEW BRUNSWICK THEOLOGICAL SEMINARY: New Brunswick.
NEW JERSEY STATE TEACHERS COLLEGE: Glassboro.
NEW JERSEY STATE TEACHERS COLLEGE: Jersey City.
NEW JERSEY STATE TEACHERS COLLEGE: Newark.
NEW JERSEY STATE TEACHERS COLLEGE: Paterson.
NEW JERSEY STATE TEACHERS COLLEGE: Trenton.
NEW JERSEY STATE TEACHERS COLLEGE: Upper Montclair.
NEWARK COLLEGE OF ENGINEERING: Newark.
PANZER COLLEGE OF PHYSICAL EDUCATION AND HYGIENE: East Orange.
PRINCETON THEOLOGICAL SEMINARY: Princeton.
*PRINCETON UNIVERSITY: Princeton.
RIDER COLLEGE: Trenton.
RUTGERS UNIVERSITY: New Brunswick.
ST. ELIZABETH, COLLEGE OF: Convent Station.
ST. JOSEPH'S COLLEGE: Princeton.
ST. PETER'S COLLEGE: Jersey City.
SETON HALL UNIVERSITY: South Orange.
SHELTON COLLEGE: Ringwood.
STEVENS INSTITUTE OF TECHNOLOGY: Hoboken.
TRENTON JUNIOR COLLEGE: Trenton.
UNION JUNIOR COLLEGE: Cranford.
UPSALA COLLEGE: East Orange.
VILLA WALSH JUNIOR COLLEGE: Morristown.
WESTMINSTER CHOIR COLLEGE: Princeton.

New Mexico

EASTERN NEW MEXICO UNIVERSITY: Portales.
NEW MEXICO, UNIVERSITY OF: Albuquerque.
NEW MEXICO COLLEGE OF AGRICUL-

TURE AND MECHANIC ARTS: State College.
NEW MEXICO HIGHLANDS UNIVERSITY: Las Vegas.
NEW MEXICO INSTITUTE OF MINING AND TECHNOLOGY: Socorro.
NEW MEXICO MILITARY INSTITUTE: Roswell.
NEW MEXICO WESTERN COLLEGE: Silver City.
ST. JOSEPH ON THE RIO GRANDE, COLLEGE OF: Albuquerque.
ST. MICHAEL'S COLLEGE: Santa Fe.

New York

ACADEMY OF AERONATICS: LaGuardia Airport, Flushing.
ADELPHI COLLEGE: Garden City.
ALFRED UNIVERSITY: Alfred.
AUBURN COMMUNITY COLLEGE: Auburn.
BANK STREET COLLEGE OF EDUCATION: New York.
BAPTIST BIBLE SEMINARY, INC.: Johnson City.
BARD COLLEGE: Annandale-on-Hudson.
BELLARMINE COLLEGE: Plattsburgh.
BENNETT JUNIOR COLLEGE: Millbrook.
BIBLICAL SEMINARY IN NEW YORK: New York.
BRIARCLIFF JUNIOR COLLEGE: Briarcliff Manor.
BROOKLYN COLLEGE: Brooklyn.
BROOKLYN LAW SCHOOL: Brooklyn.
BROOME TECHNICAL COMMUNITY COLLEGE: Binghamton.
BUFFALO, UNIVERSITY OF: Buffalo.
CANISIUS COLLEGE: Buffalo.
CATHEDRAL COLLEGE OF THE IMMACULATE CONCEPTION: Brooklyn.
CATHERINE MCAULEY JUNIOR COLLEGE: Rochester.
CAZENOVIA JUNIOR COLLEGE: Cazenovia.
CITY COLLEGE OF THE CITY OF NEW YORK: New York.
CLARKSON COLLEGE OF TECHNOLOGY: Potsdam.
COLGATE-ROCHESTER DIVINITY SCHOOL: Rochester.
COLGATE UNIVERSITY: Hamilton.
*COLUMBIA UNIVERSITY: New York.
CONCORDIA COLLEGIATE INSTITUTE: Bronxville.
COOPER UNION: New York.
*CORNELL UNIVERSITY: Ithaca.
DIVINE WORD SEMINARY: Conesus.
DOMINICAN JUNIOR COLLEGE OF BLAUVELT: Blauvelt, Rockland County.
D'YOUVILLE COLLEGE: Buffalo.
EASTMAN DENTAL DISPENSARY AND SCHOOL FOR DENTAL HYGIENISTS: Rochester.
ELMIRA COLLEGE: Elmira.
EPIPHANY APOSTOLIC COLLEGE: Newburgh.
ERIE COUNTY TECHNICAL INSTITUTE: Buffalo.
EYMARD PREPATORY SEMINARY: Hyde Park.
FASHION INSTITUTE OF TECHNOLOGY: New York.
FINCH COLLEGE: New York.
FORDHAM UNIVERSITY: New York.
GENERAL THEOLOGICAL SEMINARY: New York.
GOOD COUNSEL COLLEGE: White Plains.
HAMILTON COLLEGE: Clinton.
HARTWICK COLLEGE: Oneonta.
HERVEY JUNIOR COLLEGE: New York.

HOBART AND WILLIAM SMITH COLLEGES: Geneva.
HOFSTRA COLLEGE: Hempstead.
HOLY CROSS PREPARATORY SEMINARY: Dunkirk.
HOLY TRINITY ORTHODOX SEMINARY: Jordanville.
HOUGHTON COLLEGE: Houghton.
HUDSON VALLEY TECHNICAL INSTITUTE: Troy.
HUNTER COLLEGE: New York.
IONA COLLEGE: New Rochelle.
ITHACA COLLEGE: Ithaca.
JAMESTOWN COMMUNITY COLLEGE: Jamestown.
JEWISH INSTITUTE OF RELIGION: New York.
JEWISH THEOLOGICAL SEMINARY OF AMERICA: New York.
JULLIARD SCHOOL OF MUSIC: New York.
JUNIOR COLLEGE OF THE PACKER COLLEGIATE INSTITUTE: Brooklyn.
KEUKA COLLEGE: Keuka Park.
THE KING'S COLLEGE: Briarcliff Manor.
LADYCLIFF COLLEGE: Highland Falls.
LA SALETTE SEMINARY: Altamont.
LE MOYNE COLLEGE: Syracuse.
LONG ISLAND UNIVERSITY: Brooklyn.
MANHATTAN COLLEGE: New York.
MANHATTAN SCHOOL OF MUSIC: New York.
MANHATTANVILLE COLLEGE OF THE SACRED HEART: Purchase.
MANNES COLLEGE OF MUSIC: New York.
MARIAN COLLEGE: Poughkeepsie.
MARYKNOLL SEMINARY: Maryknoll.
MARYKNOLL TEACHERS COLLEGE: Maryknoll.
MARYMOUNT COLLEGE: Tarrytown.
MATER CHRISTI SEMINARY: Albany.
MERCY JUNIOR COLLEGE: Tarrytown.
MILLS COLLEGE OF EDUCATION: New York.
MOHAWK VALLEY TECHNICAL INSTITUTE: New Hartford.
MOLLOY CATHOLIC COLLEGE FOR WOMEN: Rockville Centre.
MOUNT ST. JOSEPH TEACHERS COLLEGE: Buffalo.
MOUNT SAINT MARY COLLEGE: Newburgh.
MT. ST. VINCENT, COLLEGE OF: New York.
NAZARETH COLLEGE: Rochester.
NEW ROCHELLE, COLLEGE OF: New Rochelle.
NEW SCHOOL FOR SOCIAL RESEARCH: New York.
NEW YORK CITY COMMUNITY COLLEGE OF APPLIED ARTS AND SCIENCES: Brooklyn.
NEW YORK COLLEGE OF PODIATRY: New York.
NEW YORK LAW SCHOOL: New York.
NEW YORK MEDICAL COLLEGE: New York.
NEW YORK, STATE UNIVERSITY OF, LIBERAL ARTS COLLEGE: Champlain.
NEW YORK, STATE UNIVERSITY OF, LIBERAL ARTS COLLEGE: Harpur.
NEW YORK, STATE UNIVERSITY OF, MEDICAL COLLEGE: New York.
NEW YORK, STATE UNIVERSITY OF, MEDICAL COLLEGE: Syracuse.
NEW YORK UNIVERSITY: New York.
NIAGARA UNIVERSITY: Niagara Falls.
NOTRE DAME COLLEGE OF STATEN ISLAND: New York.
NYACK MISSIONARY COLLEGE: Nyack.
ORANGE COUNTY COMMUNITY COLLEGE: Middletown.

OUR LADY OF HOPE MISSION SEMINARY: Newburgh.
PACE COLLEGE: New York.
PARSONS SCHOOL OF DESIGN: New York.
PAUL SMITH'S COLLEGE OF ARTS AND SCIENCES: Paul Smiths.
POLYTECHNIC INSTITUTE OF BROOKLYN: Brooklyn.
PRATT INSTITUTE: Brooklyn.
QUEENS COLLEGE OF THE CITY OF NEW YORK: Flushing.
RCA INSTITUTES, INC.: New York.
RENSSELAER POLYTECHNIC INSTITUTE: Troy.
ROBERTS WESLEYAN COLLEGE: North Chili.
ROCHESTER INSTITUTE OF TECHNOLOGY: Rochester.
ROCHESTER, UNIVERSITY OF: Rochester.
ROCKEFELLER INSTITUTE FOR MEDICAL RESEARCH: New York.
ROSARY HILL COLLEGE: Buffalo.
RUSSEL SAGE COLLEGE: Troy.
ST. BERNARDINE OF SIENA COLLEGE: Loudonville.
ST. BERNARD'S SEMINARY AND COLLEGE: Rochester.
ST. BONAVENTURE UNIVERSITY: St. Bonaventure.
ST. FRANCIS COLLEGE: Brooklyn.
ST. JOHN FISHER COLLEGE, INC.: Rochester.
ST. JOHN'S UNIVERSITY: Brooklyn.
ST. JOSEPH'S COLLEGE FOR WOMEN: Brooklyn.
ST. JOSEPH'S SEMINARY AND COLLEGE: Yonkers.
ST. JOSEPH'S SERAPHIC SEMINARY: Callicoon.
ST. LAWRENCE UNIVERSITY: Canton.
ST. ROSE, COLLEGE OF: Albany.
ST. THOMAS AQUINAS COLLEGE: Sparkill.
ST. VLADIMIR'S ORTHODOX THEOLOGICAL SEMINARY: New York.
SARAH LAWRENCE COLLEGE: Bronxville.
SKIDMORE COLLEGE: Saratoga Springs.
STATE UNIVERSITY OF NEW YORK: Albany.
SYRACUSE UNIVERSITY: Syracuse.
UNION COLLEGE AND UNIVERSITY: Schenectady.
UNION THEOLOGICAL SEMINARY: New York.
UNITED STATES MERCHANT MARINE ACADEMY: Kings Point.
UNITED STATES MILITARY ACADEMY: West Point.
VASSAR COLLEGE: Poughkeepsie.
WAGNER LUTHERAN COLLEGE: Staten Island.
WEBB INSTITUTE OF NAVAL ARCHITECTURE: Glen Cove, Long Island.
WELLS COLLEGE: Aurora.
WESTCHESTER COMMUNITY COLLEGE: White Plains.
YESHIVA UNIVERSITY: New York.

North Carolina

AGRICULTURAL AND TECHNICAL COLLEGE OF NORTH CAROLINA: Greensboro.
APPALACHIAN STATE TEACHERS COLLEGE: Boone.
ASHEVILLE-BILTMORE COLLEGE: Asheville.
ATLANTIC CHRISTIAN COLLEGE: Wilson.
BARBARA-SCOTIA COLLEGE: Concord.
BELMONT ABBEY COLLEGE: Belmont.
BENNETT COLLEGE: Greensboro.
BREVARD COLLEGE: Brevard.

CAMPBELL COLLEGE: Buies Creek.
CARVER COLLEGE: Charlotte.
CATAWBA COLLEGE: Salisbury.
CHARLOTTE COLLEGE: Charlotte.
CHOWAN COLLEGE: Murfreesboro.
DAVIDSON COLLEGE: Davidson.
DUKE UNIVERSITY: Durham.
EAST CAROLINA COLLEGE: Greenville.
ELIZABETH CITY STATE TEACHERS COLLEGE: Elizabeth City.
ELON COLLEGE: Elon College.
FAYETTEVILLE STATE TEACHERS COLLEGE: Fayetteville.
FLORA MACDONALD COLLEGE: Red Springs.
GARDNER-WEBB JUNIOR COLLEGE, INC.: Boiling Springs.
GREENSBORO COLLEGE: Greensboro.
GUILFORD COLLEGE: Guilford College.
HIGH POINT COLLEGE: High Point.
JOHNSON C. SMITH UNIVERSITY: Charlotte.
LEES-MCRAE COLLEGE: Banner Elk.
LENOIR-RHYNE COLLEGE: Hickory.
LIVINGSTONE COLLEGE: Salisbury.
LOUISBURG COLLEGE: Louisburg.
MARS HILL COLLEGE: Mars Hill.
MEREDITH COLLEGE: Raleigh.
MITCHELL COLLEGE: Statesville.
NORTH CAROLINA, UNIVERSITY OF: Chapel Hill.
NORTH CAROLINA COLLEGE AT DURHAM: Durham.
OAK RIDGE MILITARY INSTITUTE: Oak Ridge.
PEACE COLLEGE: Raleigh.
PEMBROKE STATE COLLEGE: Pembroke.
PFEIFFER COLLEGE: Misenheimer.
PINELAND JUNIOR COLLEGE AND EDWARDS MILITARY INSTITUTE: Salemburg .
PRESBYTERIAN JUNIOR COLLEGE FOR MEN: Maxton.
QUEENS COLLEGE: Charlotte.
SACRED HEART JUNIOR COLLEGE AND ACADEMY: Belmont.
ST. AUGUSTINE'S COLLEGE: Raleigh.
ST. MARY'S JUNIOR COLLEGE: Raleigh.
SALEM COLLEGE: Winston-Salem.
SHAW UNIVERSITY: Raleigh.
SOUTHEASTERN BAPTIST THEOLOGICAL SEMINARY: Wake Forest.
STATE COLLEGE OF AGRICULTURE AND ENGINEERING: Raleigh.
WAKE FOREST COLLEGE: Wake Forest.
WARREN WILSON COLLEGE: Swannanoa.
WESTERN CAROLINA COLLEGE: Cullowhee.
WILMINGTON COLLEGE: Wilmington.
WINGATE COLLEGE: Wingate.
WINSTON-SALEM TEACHERS COLLEGE: Winston-Salem.
WOMANS COLLEGE OF UNIVERSITY OF NORTH CAROLINA: Greensboro.

North Dakota

BISMARCK JUNIOR COLLEGE: Bismarck.
DEVILS LAKE JUNIOR COLLEGE. Devils Lake.
JAMESTOWN COLLEGE: Jamestown.
NORTH DAKOTA, UNIVERSITY OF: Grand Forks.
NORTH DAKOTA AGRICULTURAL COLLEGE: State College.
NORTH DAKOTA SCHOOL OF FORESTRY: Bottineau.
NORTH DAKOTA STATE SCHOOL OF SCIENCE: Wahpeton.
NORTH DAKOTA STATE TEACHERS COLLEGE: Dickinson.

NORTH DAKOTA STATE TEACHERS COL-
LEGE: Minot.
NORTH DAKOTA STATE TEACHERS COL-
LEGE: Valley City.
STATE NORMAL AND INDUSTRIAL COL-
LEGE: Ellendale.
STATE TEACHERS COLLEGE: Mayville.

Ohio

AKRON, UNIVERSITY OF: Akron.
ANTIOCH COLLEGE: Yellow Springs.
ASHLAND COLLEGE: Ashland.
BALDWIN-WALLACE COLLEGE: Berea.
BLUFFTON COLLEGE: Bluffton.
BOWLING GREEN STATE UNIVERSITY:
Bowling Green.
CAPITAL UNIVERSITY: Columbus.
CASE INSTITUTE OF TECHNOLOGY:
Cleveland.
CENTRAL STATE COLLEGE: Wilberforce.
CINCINNATI, UNIVERSITY OF: Cincinnati.
CLEVELAND INSTITUTE OF MUSIC: Cleve-
land.
COLLEGE OF STEUBENVILLE, THE: Steu-
benville.
COLLEGE-CONSERVATORY OF MUSIC OF
CINCINNATI: Cincinnati.
DAYTON, UNIVERSITY OF: Dayton.
DEFIANCE COLLEGE: Defiance.
DENISON UNIVERSITY: Granville.
FENN COLLEGE: Cleveland.
FINDLAY COLLEGE: Findlay.
FRANKLIN UNIVERSITY: Columbus.
HEBREW UNION COLLEGE—JEWISH IN-
STITUTE OF RELIGION: Cincinnati.
HEIDELBERG COLLEGE: Tiffin.
HIRAM COLLEGE: Hiram.
JOHN CARROLL UNIVERSITY: Cleveland.
KENT STATE UNIVERSITY: Kent.
KENYON COLLEGE: Gambier.
LAKE ERIE COLLEGE: Painesville.
MALONE COLLEGE: Cleveland.
MARIETTA COLLEGE: Marietta.
MARY MANSE COLLEGE: Toledo.
MIAMI UNIVERSITY: Oxford.
MOUNT ST. JOSEPH-ON-THE-OHIO, COL-
LEGE OF: Mount St. Joseph.
MT. UNION COLLEGE: Alliance.
MUSKINGUM COLLEGE: New Concord.
NOTRE DAME COLLEGE: Cleveland.
OBERLIN COLLEGE: Oberlin.
OHIO COLLEGE OF CHIROPODY: Cleveland.
OHIO MECHANICS INSTITUTE: Cincinnati.
OHIO NORTHERN UNIVERSITY: Ada.
OHIO STATE UNIVERSITY: Columbus.
OHIO UNIVERSITY: Athens.
OHIO WESLEYAN UNIVERSITY: Delaware.
OTTERBEIN COLLEGE: Westerville.
OUR LADY OF CINCINNATI COLLEGE:
Cincinnati.
RABBINICAL COLLEGE OF TELSHE:
Cleveland.
RIO GRANDE COLLEGE: Rio Grande.
ST. JOHN COLLEGE: Cleveland.
ST. MARY OF THE SPRINGS, COLLEGE
OF: Columbus.
SALMON P. CHASE COLLEGE: Cincinnati.
SINCLAIR COLLEGE: Dayton.
TOLEDO, UNIVERSITY OF: Toledo.
UNITED STATES AIR FORCE INSTITUTE
OF TECHNOLOGY: Wright-Patterson Air
Force Base.
UNITED THEOLOGICAL SEMINARY:
Dayton.
URBANA JUNIOR COLLEGE: Urbana.
URSULINE COLLEGE: Cleveland.
WESTERN COLLEGE FOR WOMEN: Oxford.

WESTERN RESERVE UNIVERSITY: Cleve-
land.
WILBERFORCE UNIVERSITY: Wilberforce.
WILMINGTON COLLEGE: Wilmington.
WITTENBERG COLLEGE: Springfield.
WOOSTER, COLLEGE OF: Wooster.
XAVIER UNIVERSITY: Cincinnati.
THE YOUNGSTOWN UNIVERSITY: Youngs-
town.

Oklahoma

BACONE COLLEGE: Bacone.
BENEDICTINE HEIGHTS COLLEGE, THE:
Tulsa.
BETHANY-NAZARENE COLLEGE: Bethany.
CAMERON STATE AGRICULTURAL COL-
LEGE: Lawton.
CENTRAL CHRISTIAN COLLEGE: Bartles-
ville.
CENTRAL STATE COLLEGE: Edmond.
CONNORS STATE AGRICULTURAL COL-
LEGE: Warner.
EAST CENTRAL STATE COLLEGE: Ada.
EASTERN OKLAHOMA AGRICULTURAL &
MECHANICAL COLLEGE: Willburton.
EL RENO JUNIOR COLLEGE: El Reno.
LANGSTON UNIVERSITY: Langston.
MURRAY STATE AGRICULTURAL COL-
LEGE: Tishomingo.
MUSKOGEE JUNIOR COLLEGE: Muskogee.
NORTHEASTERN OKLAHOMA AGRICUL-
TURAL AND MECHANICAL COLLEGE:
Miami.
NORTHEASTERN STATE COLLEGE: Tahle-
quah.
NORTHERN OKLAHOMA JUNIOR COL-
LEGE: Tonkawa.
NORTHWESTERN STATE COLLEGE: Alva.
OKLAHOMA, UNIVERSITY OF: Norman.
OKLAHOMA AGRICULTURAL AND ME-
CHANICAL COLLEGE: Stillwater.
OKLAHOMA BAPTIST UNIVERSITY:
Shawnee.
OKLAHOMA CITY UNIVERSITY: Oklahoma
City.
OKLAHOMA COLLEGE FOR WOMEN:
Chickasha.
OKLAHOMA MILITARY ACADEMY: Clare-
more.
PANHANDLE AGRICULTURAL AND ME-
CHANICAL COLLEGE: Goodwell.
PHILLIPS UNIVERSITY: Enid.
ST. GREGORY'S COLLEGE: Shawnee.
SAYRE JUNIOR COLLEGE: Sayre.
SOUTHEASTERN STATE COLLEGE: Durant.
SOUTHWESTERN STATE COLLEGE:
Weatherford.
TULSA, UNIVERSITY OF: Tulsa.

Oregon

CASCADE COLLEGE: Portland.
CONCORDIA COLLEGE: Portland.
DENTAL SCHOOL OF THE UNIVERSITY
OF OREGON: Portland.
EASTERN OREGON COLLEGE OF EDU-
CATON: La Grande.
GEORGE FOX COLLEGE: Newberg.
LEWIS AND CLARK COLLEGE: Portland.
LINFIELD COLLEGE: McMinnville.
MARYLHURST COLLEGE: Marylhurst.
MOUNT ANGEL SEMINARY: St. Benedict.
MOUNT ANGEL WOMEN'S COLLEGE:
Mount Angel.
MULTNOMAH COLLEGE: Portland.
MULTNOMAH SCHOOL OF THE BIBLE:
Portland.

NORTHWESTERN CHRISTIAN COLLEGE: Eugene.
OREGON, UNIVERSITY OF: Eugene.
OREGON COLLEGE OF EDUCATION: Monmouth.
OREGON STATE COLLEGE: Corvallis.
OREGON TECHNICAL INSTITUTE: Oretech.
PACIFIC BIBLE COLLEGE: Portland.
PACIFIC UNIVERSITY: Forest Grove.
PORTLAND, UNIVERSITY OF: Portland.
PORTLAND SCHOOL OF MUSIC: Portland.
PORTLAND STATE COLLEGE: Portland.
REED COLLEGE: Portland.
SOUTHERN OREGON COLLEGE OF EDUCATION: Ashland.
WESTERN EVANGELICAL SEMINARY: Portland.
WILLAMETTE UNIVERSITY: Salem.

Pennsylvania

ACADEMY OF THE NEW CHURCH: Bryn Athyn.
ALBRIGHT COLLEGE: Reading.
ALLEGHENY COLLEGE: Meadville.
ALLIANCE COLLEGE: Cambridge Springs.
BEAVER COLLEGE: Jenkintown.
BRYN MAWR COLLEGE: Bryn Mawr.
BUCKNELL UNIVERSITY: Lewisburg.
CARNEGIE INSTITUTE OF TECHNOLOGY: Pittsburgh.
CEDAR CREST COLLEGE: Allentown.
CHATHAM COLLEGE: Pittsburgh.
CHESTNUT HILL COLLEGE: Philadelphia.
CROZER THEOLOGICAL SEMINARY: Chester.
CURTIS INSTITUTE OF MUSIC, THE: Philadelphia.
DICKINSON COLLEGE: Carlisle.
DICKINSON SCHOOL OF LAW: Carlisle.
DIVINITY SCHOOL OF THE PROTESTANT EPISCOPAL CHURCH: Philadelphia.
DREXEL INSTITUTE OF TECHNOLOGY: Philadelphia.
DROPSIE COLLEGE: Philadelphia.
D. T. WATSON SCHOOL OF PSYCHIATRICS: Leetsdale.
DUQUESNE UNIVERSITY: Pittsburgh.
EASTERN BAPTIST COLLEGE: St. Davids.
EASTERN BAPTIST THEOLOGICAL SEMINARY, THE: Philadelphia.
EASTERN PILGRIM COLLEGE: Allentown.
ELIZABETHTOWN COLLEGE: Elizabethtown.
FAITH THEOLOGICAL SEMINARY: Philadelphia.
FRANKLIN AND MARSHALL COLLEGE: Lancaster.
GANNON COLLEGE: Erie.
GENEVA COLLEGE: Beaver Falls.
GETTYSBURG COLLEGE: Gettysburg.
GROVE CITY COLLEGE: Grove City.
GWYNEDD-MERCY JUNIOR COLLEGE: Gwynedd Valley.
HAHNEMANN MEDICAL COLLEGE AND HOSPITAL: Philadelphia.
HARCUM JUNIOR COLLEGE: Bryn Mawr.
HAVERFORD COLLEGE: Haverford.
HERSHEY JUNIOR COLLEGE: Hershey.
HOLY FAMILY COLLEGE: Philadelphia.
IMMACULATA COLLEGE: Immaculata.
JEFFERSON MEDICAL COLLEGE OF PHILADELPHIA: Philadelphia.
JUNIATA COLLEGE: Huntington.
KEYSTONE JUNIOR COLLEGE: La Plume.
KINGS COLLEGE: Wilkes-Barre.
LAFAYETTE COLLEGE: Easton.
LA SALLE COLLEGE: Philadelphia.
LEBANON VALLEY COLLEGE: Annville.
LEHIGH UNIVERSITY: Bethlehem.

LINCOLN UNIVERSITY: Lincoln University.
LINDEN HALL JUNIOR COLLEGE: Lititz.
LUTHERAN THEOLOGICAL SEMINARY: Gettysburg.
LUTHERAN THEOLOGICAL SEMINARY: Philadelphia.
LYCOMING COLLEGE: Williamsport.
MARY IMMACULATE SEMINARY: Northampton.
MARYWOOD COLLEGE: Scranton.
MERCYHURST COLLEGE: Erie.
MESSIAH COLLEGE: Grantham.
MISERICORDIA COLLEGE: Dallas.
MOORE INSTITUTE OF ART, SCIENCE, AND INDUSTRY: Philadelphia.
MORAVIAN COLLEGE: Bethlehem.
MOUNT ALOYSIUS JUNIOR COLLEGE: Cresson.
MOUNT MERCY COLLEGE: Pittsburgh.
MUHLENBERG COLLEGE: Allentown.
NATIONAL AGRICULTURAL COLLEGE: Doylestown.
PENN HALL JUNIOR COLLEGE AND PREPARATORY SCHOOL: Chambersburg.
*PENNSYLVANIA, UNIVERSITY OF: Philadelphia.
PENNSYLVANIA COLLEGE FOR WOMEN: Pittsburgh.
PENNSYLVANIA MILITARY COLLEGE: Chester.
PENNSYLVANIA STATE COLLEGE: State College.
PENNSYLVANIA STATE COLLEGE OF OPTOMETRY: Philadelphia.
PENNSYLVANIA STATE TEACHERS COLLEGE: Bloomsburg.
PENNSYLVANIA STATE TEACHERS COLLEGE: California.
PENNSYLVANIA STATE TEACHERS COLLEGE: Cheyney.
PENNSYLVANIA STATE TEACHERS COLLEGE: Clarion.
PENNSYLVANIA STATE TEACHERS COLLEGE: East Stroudsburg.
PENNSYLVANIA STATE TEACHERS COLLEGE: Edinboro.
PENNSYLVANIA STATE TEACHERS COLLEGE: Indiana.
PENNSYLVANIA STATE TEACHERS COLLEGE: Kutztown.
PENNSYLVANIA STATE TEACHERS COLLEGE: Lock Haven.
PENNSYLVANIA STATE TEACHERS COLLEGE: Mansfield.
PENNSYLVANIA STATE TEACHERS COLLEGE: Millersville.
PENNSYLVANIA STATE TEACHERS COLLEGE: Shippensburg.
PENNSYLVANIA STATE TEACHERS COLLEGE: Slippery Rock.
PENNSYLVANIA STATE TEACHERS COLLEGE: West Chester.
PENNSYLVANIA STATE UNIVERSITY, THE: University Park.
PHILADELPHIA BIBLE INSTITUTE: Philadelphia.
PHILADELPHIA COLLEGE OF OSTEOPATHY: Philadelphia.
PHILADELPHIA COLLEGE OF PHARMACY AND SCIENCE: Philadelphia.
PHILADELPHIA MUSEUM SCHOOL OF ART: Philadelphia.
PHILADELPHIA MUSICAL ACADEMY: Philadelphia.
PHILADELPHIA TEXTILE INSTITUTE: Philadelphia.
PITTSBURGH, UNIVERSITY OF: Pittsburgh.
PITTSBURGH-XENIA THEOLOGICAL SEMINARY: Pittsburgh.

REFORMED PRESBYTERIAN THEOLOGICAL SEMINARY: Pittsburgh.
ROSEMONT COLLEGE: Rosemont.
ST. CHARLES BORROMEO SEMINARY: Philadelphia.
ST. FIDELIS COLLEGE AND SEMINARY: Herman.
ST. FRANCIS COLLEGE: Loretto.
ST. JOSEPH'S COLLEGE: Philadelphia.
ST. VINCENT COLLEGE: Latrobe.
SCRANTON, UNIVERSITY OF: Scranton.
SETON HILL COLLEGE: Greensburg.
SPRING GARDEN INSTITUTE: Philadelphia.
SUSQUEHANNA UNIVERSITY: Selinsgrove.
SWARTHMORE COLLEGE: Swarthmore.
TEMPLE UNIVERSITY: Philadelphia.
THEOLOGICAL SEMINARY OF THE EVANGELICAL AND REFORMED CHURCH: Lancaster.
THIEL COLLEGE: Greenville.
URSINUS COLLEGE: Collegeville.
VILLA MARIA COLLEGE: Erie.
VILLANOVA COLLEGE: Villanova.
WASHINGTON AND JEFFERSON COLLEGE: Washington.
WAYNESBURG COLLEGE: Waynesburg.
WESTERN THEOLOGICAL SEMINARY: Pittsburgh.
WESTMINSTER COLLEGE: New Wilmington.
WESTMINSTER THEOLOGICAL SEMINARY: Philadelphia.
WILKES COLLEGE: Wilkes-Barre.
WILSON COLLEGE: Chambersburg.
WOMAN'S MEDICAL COLLEGE OF PENNSYLVANIA: Philadelphia.
WYOMISSING POLYTECHNIC INSTITUTE: Wyomissing.
YORK JUNIOR COLLEGE OF THE YORK COLLEGIATE INSTITUTE: York.

Rhode Island

*BROWN UNIVERSITY: Providence.
BRYANT COLLEGE: Providence.
CATHOLIC TEACHERS COLLEGE: Providence.
PROVIDENCE COLLEGE: Providence.
PROVIDENCE-BARRINGTON BIBLE COLLEGE: Providence.
RHODE ISLAND, UNIVERSITY OF: Kingston.
RHODE ISLAND COLLEGE OF EDUCATION: Providence.
RHODE ISLAND COLLEGE OF PHARMACY AND ALLIED SCIENCES: Providence.
RHODE ISLAND SCHOOL OF DESIGN: Providence.
ROGER WILLIAMS JUNIOR COLLEGE: Providence.
SALVE REGINA COLLEGE: Newport.

South Carolina

ALLEN UNIVERSITY: Columbia.
ANDERSON COLLEGE: Anderson.
BENEDICT COLLEGE: Columbia.
BOB JONES UNIVERSITY: Greenville.
CHARLESTON, COLLEGE OF: Charleston.
CITADEL, THE—THE MILITARY COLLEGE OF SOUTH CAROLINA: Charleston.
CLAFLIN COLLEGE: Orangeburg.
CLEMSON AGRICULTURAL COLLEGE: Clemson.
COKER COLLEGE: Hartsville.
COLUMBIA BIBLE COLLEGE: Columbia.
COLUMBIA COLLEGE: Columbia.
CONVERSE COLLEGE: Spartanburg.
ERSKINE COLLEGE: Due West.
FRIENDSHIP JUNIOR COLLEGE: Rock Hill.

FURMAN UNIVERSITY: Greenville.
LEANDER COLLEGE: Greenwood.
LIMESTONE COLLEGE: Gaffney.
LUTHERAN THEOLOGICAL SOUTHERN SEMINARY: Columbia.
MEDICAL COLLEGE OF SOUTH CAROLINA: Charleston.
MORRIS COLLEGE: Sumter.
NEWBERRY COLLEGE: Newberry.
NORTH GREENVILLE JUNIOR COLLEGE: Taylors.
PRESBYTERIAN COLLEGE: Clinton.
SOUTH CAROLINA, UNIVERSITY OF: Columbia.
SOUTH CAROLINA STATE COLLEGE: Orangeburg.
SPARTANBURG JUNIOR COLLEGE: Spartanburg.
VOORHEES SCHOOL AND JUNIOR COLLEGE: Denmark.
WESLEYAN METHODIST COLLEGE: Central.
WINTHROP COLLEGE: Rock Hill.
WOFFORD COLLEGE: Spartanburg.

South Dakota

AUGUSTANA COLLEGE: Sioux Falls.
BLACK HILLS TEACHER COLLEGE: Spearfish.
DAKOTA WESLEYAN UNIVERSITY: Mitchell.
FREEMAN JUNIOR COLLEGE: Freeman.
GENERAL BEADLE STATE TEACHERS COLLEGE: Madison.
HURON COLLEGE: Huron.
MOUNT MARTY COLLEGE: Yankton.
NORTHERN STATE TEACHERS COLLEGE: Aberdeen.
PRESENTATION JUNIOR COLLEGE: Aberdeen.
SIOUX FALLS COLLEGE: Sioux Falls.
SOUTH DAKOTA, UNIVERSITY OF: Vermillion.
SOUTH DAKOTA SCHOOL OF MINES AND TECHNOLOGY: Rapid City.
SOUTH DAKOTA STATE COLLEGE OF AGRICULTURE AND MECHANIC ARTS: Brookings.
SOUTHERN STATE TEACHERS COLLEGE: Springfield.
WESSINGTON SPRINGS COLLEGE: Wessington.
YANKTON COLLEGE: Yankton.

Tennessee

AUSTIN PEAY STATE COLLEGE: Clarksville.
BELMONT COLLEGE: Nashville.
BETHEL COLLEGE: McKenzie.
CARSON-NEWMAN COLLEGE: Jefferson.
CHATTANOOGA, UNIVERSITY OF: Chattanooga.
CHRISTIAN BROTHERS COLLEGE: Memphis.
CUMBERLAND UNIVERSITY: Lebanon.
DAVID LIPSCOMB COLLEGE: Nashville.
EAST TENNESSEE STATE COLLEGE: Johnson City.
FISK UNIVERSITY: Nashville.
FREED-HARDEMAN COLLEGE: Henderson.
GEORGE PEABODY COLLEGE FOR TEACHRS: Nashville.
HIWASSEE COLLEGE: Madisonville.
JOHNSON BIBLE COLLEGE: Kimberlin Heights.
KING COLLEGE: Bristol.
KNOXVILLE COLLEGE: Knoxville.
LAMBUTH COLLEGE: Jackson.

LANE COLLEGE: Jackson.
LEE COLLEGE: Cleveland.
LE MOYNE COLLEGE: Memphis.
LINCOLN MEMORIAL UNIVERSITY: Harrogate.
MADISON COLLEGE: Madison College.
MARTIN COLLEGE: Pulaski.
MARYVILLE COLLEGE: Maryville.
MEHARRY MEDICAL COLLEGE: Nashville.
MEMPHIS STATE COLLEGE: Memphis.
MIDDLE TENNESSEE STATE COLLEGE: Murfreesboro.
MILLIGAN COLLEGE: Milligan College.
MORRISTOWN NORMAL AND INDUSTRIAL COLLEGE: Morristown.
SCARRITT COLLEGE FOR CHRISTIAN WORKERS: Nashville.
SIENA COLLEGE: Memphis.
SOUTH, UNIVERSITY OF THE: Sewanee.
SOUTHERN COLLEGE OF OPTOMETRY: Memphis.
SOUTHERN MISSIONARY COLLEGE: Collegedale.
SOUTHWESTERN AT MEMPHIS: Memphis.
TENNESEE, UNIVERSITY OF: Knoxville.
TENNESSEE AGRICULTURAL AND INDUSTRIAL STATE UNIVERSITY: Nashville.
TENNESSE POLYTECHNIC INSTITUTE: Cookeville.
TENNESSEE WESLEYAN COLLEGE: Athens.
TREVECCA NAZARENE COLLEGE: Nashville.
TUSCULUM COLLEGE: Greeneville.
UNION UNIVERSITY: Jackson.
VANDERBILT UNIVERSITY: Nashville.
WILLIAM JENNINGS BRYAN UNIVERSITY: Dayton.

Texas

ABILENE CHRISTIAN COLLEGE: Abilene.
AGRICULTURAL AND MECHANICAL COLLEGE OF TEXAS: College Station.
ALVIN JUNIOR COLLEGE: Alvin.
AMARILLO COLLEGE: Amarillo.
ARLINGTON STATE COLLEGE: Arlington.
AUSTIN COLLEGE: Sherman.
AUSTIN PRESBYTERIAN THEOLOGICAL SEMINARY: Austin.
BAYLOR UNIVERSITY: Waco.
BIBLE BAPTIST SEMINARY: Fort Worth.
BISHOP COLLEGE: Marshall.
BLINN COLLEGE: Brenham.
BUTLER COLLEGE: Tyler.
CISCO JUNIOR COLLEGE: Cisco.
CLARENDON JUNIOR COLLEGE: Clarendon.
CORPUS CHRISTI, UNIVERSITY OF: Corpus Christi.
DALLAS THEOLOGICAL SEMINARY AND GRADUATE SCHOOL OF THEOLOGY: Dallas.
DECATUR BAPTIST COLLEGE: Decatur.
DEL MAR COLLEGE: Corpus Christi.
DE MAZENOD SCHOLASTICATE: San Antonio.
EAST TEXAS BAPTIST COLLEGE: Marshall.
EAST TEXAS STATE TEACHERS COLLEGE: Commerce.
FRANK PHILLIPS COLLEGE: Borger.
GAINESVILLE JUNIOR COLLEGE: Gainesville.
HARDIN-SIMMONS UNIVERSITY: Abilene.
HENDERSON COUNTY JUNIOR COLLEGE: Athens.
HOUSTON, UNIVERSITY OF: Houston.
HOWARD COUNTY JUNIOR COLLEGE: Big Spring.
HOWARD PAYNE COLLEGE: Brownwood.

HUSTON-TILLOTSON COLLEGE: Austin.
INCARNATE WORD COLLEGE: San Antonio.
JACKSONVILLE COLLEGE: Jacksonville.
JARVIS CHRISTIAN COLLEGE: Hawkins.
KILGORE COLLEGE: Kilgore.
LAMAR STATE COLLEGE OF TECHNOLOGY: Beaumont.
LAREDO JUNIOR COLLEGE: Laredo.
LEE COLLEGE: Baytown.
LE TOURNEAU TECHNICAL INSTITUTE OF TEXAS: Longville.
MARY ALLEN COLLEGE: Crockett.
MARY HARDIN-BAYLOR COLLEGE: Belton.
MCMURRY COLLEGE: Abilene.
MIDWESTERN UNIVERSITY: Wichita Falls.
NAVARRO JUNIOR COLLEGE: Corsicana.
NORTH TEXAS STATE COLLEGE: Denton.
ODESSA COLLEGE: Odessa.
OUR LADY OF THE LAKE COLLEGE: San Antonio.
OUR LADY OF VICTORY COLLEGE: Fort Worth.
PAN AMERICAN COLLEGE: Edinburg.
PANOLA COUNTY JUNIOR COLLEGE: Carthage.
PARIS JUNIOR COLLEGE: Paris.
PAUL QUINN COLLEGE: Waco.
PRAIRIE VIEW AGRICULTURAL AND MECHANICAL COLLEGE: Prairie View.
RANGER JUNIOR COLLEGE: Ranger.
RICE INSTITUTE: Houston.
SACRED HEART DOMINICAN COLLEGE: Houston.
ST. EDWARD'S UNIVERSITY: Austin.
ST. MARY'S UNIVERSITY OF SAN ANTONIO: San Antonio.
ST. PHILIP'S COLLEGE: San Antonio.
ST. THOMAS, UNIVERSITY OF: Houston.
SAM HOUSTON STATE TEACHERS COLLEGE: Huntsville.
SAN ANGELO COLLEGE: San Angelo.
SAN ANTONIO COLLEGE: San Antonio.
SCHREINER INSTITUTE: Kerrville.
SOUTH TEXAS COLLEGE: Houston.
SOUTHERN COLLEGE OF FINE ARTS: Houston.
SOUTHERN METHODIST UNIVERSITY: Dallas.
SOUTHWEST TEXAS JUNIOR COLLEGE: Uvalde.
SOUTHWEST TEXAS STATE TEACHERS COLLEGE: San Marcos.
SOUTHWESTERN BAPTIST THEOLOGICAL SEMINARY: Forth Worth.
SOUTHWESTERN BIBLE INSTITUTE: Waxahachie.
SOUTHWESTERN JUNIOR COLLEGE: Keene.
SOUTHWESTERN UNIVERSITY: Georgetown.
STEPHEN F. AUSTIN STATE COLLEGE: Nacogdoches.
SUL ROSS STATE COLLEGE: Alpine.
TARLETON STATE COLLEGE: Stephensville.
TEMPLE JUNIOR COLLEGE: Temple.
TEXARKANA COLLEGE: Texarkana.
TEXAS, UNIVERSITY OF: Austin.
TEXAS CHRISTIAN UNIVERSITY: Fort Worth.
TEXAS COLLEGE: Tyler.
TEXAS COLLEGE OF ARTS AND INDUSTRIES: Kingsville.
TEXAS LUTHERAN COLLEGE: Seguin.
TEXAS SOUTHERN UNIVERSITY: Houston.
TEXAS SOUTHMOST COLLEGE: Brownsville.
TEXAS STATE COLLEGE FOR WOMEN: Denton.
TEXAS TECHNOLOGICAL COLLEGE: Lubbock.
TEXAS WESLEYAN COLLEGE: Fort Worth.
TEXAS WESTERN COLLEGE: El Paso.

TRINITY UNIVERSITY: San Antonio.
TYLER JUNIOR COLLEGE: Tyler.
VICTORIA JUNIOR COLLEGE: Victoria.
WAYLAND BAPTIST COLLEGE: Plainview.
WEATHERFORD COLLEGE OF PARKER
COUNTY: Weatherford.
WEST TEXAS STATE COLLEGE: Canyon.
WHARTON COUNTY JUNIOR COLLEGE:
Wharton.
WILEY COLLEGE: Marshall.

Utah

BRIGHAM YOUNG UNIVERSITY: Provo.
CARBON COLLEGE: Price.
DIXIE JUNIOR COLLEGE: St. George.
ST. MARY-OF-THE-WASATCH, COLLEGE
OF: Salt Lake City.
SNOW COLLEGE: Ephraim.
SOUTHERN UTAH, COLLEGE OF: Cedar
City.
UTAH, UNIVERSITY OF: Salt Lake City.
UTAH STATE AGRICULTURAL COLLEGE:
Logan.
WEBER COLLEGE: Ogden.
WESTMINSTER COLLEGE: Salt Lake City.

Vermont

BENNINGTON COLLEGE: Bennington.
GODDARD COLLEGE: Plainfield.
GREEN MOUNTAIN JUNIOR COLLEGE:
Poultney.
MARLBORO COLLEGE: Marlboro.
MIDDLEBURY COLLEGE: Middlebury.
NORWICH UNIVERSITY: Northfield.
PUTNEY GRADUATE SCHOOL OF TEACH-
ER EDUCATION: Putney.
ST. MICHAEL'S COLLEGE: Winooski.
STATE TEACHERS COLLEGE: Castleton.
STATE TEACHERS COLLEGE: Johnson.
STATE TEACHERS COLLEGE: Lyndon Center.
TRINITY COLLEGE: Burlington.
VERMONT AND STATE AGRICULTURAL
COLLEGE, UNIVERSITY OF: Burlington.
VERMONT JUNIOR COLLEGE: Montpelier.

Virginia

APPRENTICE SCHOOL: Newport News.
AVERETT COLLEGE: Danville.
BLUEFIELD COLLEGE: Bluefield.
BRIDGEWATER COLLEGE: Bridgewater.
EASTERN MENNONITE COLLEGE: Harri-
sonburg.
EMORY AND HENRY COLLEGE: Emory.
FERRUM JUNIOR COLLEGE: Ferrum.
GENERAL ASSEMBLY'S TRAINING
SCHOOL FOR LAY WORKERS: Richmond.
HAMPDEN-SYDNEY COLLEGE: Hampden-
Sydney.
HAMPTON INSTITUTE: Hampton.
HOLLINS COLLEGE: Hollins College.
INSTITUTE OF TEXTILE TECHNOLOGY:
Charlottesville.
JUDGE ADVOCATE GENERAL'S SCHOOL,
THE: University of Virginia, Charlottes-
ville.
LONGWOOD COLLEGE: Farmville.
LYNCHBURG COLLEGE: Lynchburg.
MADISON COLLEGE: Harrisonburg.
MARION COLLEGE: Marion.
MARY BALDWIN COLLEGE: Staunton.
MARY WASHINGTON COLLEGE OF THE
UNIVERSITY OF VIRGINIA: Fredericks-
burg.
MARYMOUNT JUNIOR COLLEGE: Arlington.

MEDICAL COLLEGE OF VIRGINIA: Rich-
mond.
PROTESTANT EPISCOPAL THEOLOGICAL
SEMINARY IN VIRGINIA: Alexandria.
RADFORD COLLEGE, WOMAN'S DIVISION
OF VIRGINIA POLYTECHNIC INSTI-
TUTE: Radford.
RANDOLPH-MACON COLLEGE: Ashland.
RANDOLPH-MACON WOMEN'S COLLEGE:
Lynchburg.
RICHMOND, UNIVERSITY OF: Richmond.
ROANOKE COLLEGE: Salem.
ST. PAUL'S POLYTECHNIC INSTITUTE:
Lawrence.
SHENANDOAH COLLEGE: Dayton.
SHENANDOAH CONSERVATORY OF MU-
SIC: Dayton.
SOUTHERN SEMINARY AND JUNIOR
COLLEGE: Buena Vista.
STRATFORD COLLEGE: Danville.
SULLINS COLLEGE: Bristol.
SWEET BRIAR COLLEGE: Sweet Briar.
UNION THEOLOGICAL SEMINARY: Rich-
mond.
VIRGINIA, UNIVERSITY OF: Charlottes-
ville.
VIRGINIA INTERMONT COLLEGE: Bristol.
VIRGINIA MILITARY INSTITUTE:
Lexington.
VIRGINIA POLYTECHNIC INSTITUTE:
Blacksburg.
VIRGINIA STATE COLLEGE: Petersburg.
VIRGINIA THEOLOGICAL SEMINARY AND
COLLEGE: Lynchburg.
VIRGINIA UNION UNIVERSITY: Richmond.
WASHINGTON AND LEE UNIVERSITY:
Lexington.
WILLIAM AND MARY, COLLEGE OF:
Williamsburg.

Washington

CENTRAL WASHINGTON COLLEGE OF
EDUCATION: Ellensburg.
CENTRALIA JUNIOR COLLEGE: Centralia.
CLARK COLLEGE: Vancouver.
COLUMBIA BASIN COLLEGE: Pasco.
EASTERN WASHINGTON COLLEGE OF
EDUCATION: Cheney.
EVERETT JUNIOR COLLEGE: Everett.
GONZAGA UNIVERSITY: Spokane.
GRAYS HARBOR COLLEGE: Aberdeen.
HOLY NAMES COLLEGE: Spokane.
LOWER COLUMBIA JUNIOR COLLEGE:
Longville.
NORTHWEST BIBLE COLLEGE, INC.:
Seattle.
OLYMPIC COLLEGE: Bremerton.
PACIFIC LUTHERAN COLLEGE: Parkland.
PUGET SOUND, COLLEGE OF: Tacoma.
ST. EDWARD'S SEMINARY: Kenmore.
ST. MARTIN'S COLLEGE: Olympia.
SEATTLE PACIFIC COLLEGE: Seattle.
SEATTLE UNIVERSITY: Seattle.
SKAGIT VALLEY JUNIOR COLLEGE:
Mount Vernon.
WALLA WALLA COLLEGE: College Place.
WASHINGTON, STATE COLLEGE OF: Pull-
man.
WASHINGTON, UNIVERSITY OF: Seattle.
WENATCHEE JUNIOR COLLEGE: Wenatchee.
WESTERN WASHINGTON COLLEGE OF
EDUCATION: Bellingham.
WHITMAN COLLEGE: Walla Walla.
WHITWORTH COLLEGE: Spokane.
YAKIMA VALLEY JUNIOR COLLEGE:
Yakima.

West Virginia

ALDERSON-BROADDUS COLLEGE: Philippi.
BECKLEY COLLEGE: Beckley.
BETHANY COLLEGE: Bethany.
BLUEFIELD STATE COLLEGE: Bluefield.
CONCORD COLLEGE: Athens.
DAVIS AND ELKINS COLLEGE: Elkins.
FAIRMONT STATE COLLEGE: Fairmont.
GLENVILLE STATE COLLEGE: Glenville.
GREENBRIER JUNIOR COLLEGE: Lewisburg.
GREENBRIER MILITARY SCHOOL: Lewisburg.
MARSHALL COLLEGE: Huntington.
MORRIS HARVEY COLLEGE: Charlestown.
POTOMAC STATE COLLEGE OF WEST VIRGINIA UNIVERSITY: Keyser.
SALEM COLLEGE: Salem.
SHEPHERDS STATE COLLEGE: Shepherdstown.
WEST LIBERTY STATE COLLEGE: West Liberty.
WEST VIRGINIA INSTITUTE OF TECHNOLOGY: Montgomery.
WEST VIRGINIA STATE COLLEGE: Institute.
WEST VIRGINIA UNIVERSITY: Morgantown.
WEST VIRGINIA WESLEYAN COLLEGE: Buckhannon.

Wisconsin

ALVERNO COLLEGE: Milwaukee.
ASHLAND COUNTY TEACHERS COLLEGE: Ashland.
BARRON COUNTY TEACHERS COLLEGE: Rice Lake.
BELOIT COLLEGE: Beloit.
BUFFALO COUNTY TEACHERS COLLEGE: Alma.
CARDINAL STRITCH COLLEGE, THE: Milwaukee.
CARROLL COLLEGE: Waukesha.
COLUMBIA COUNTY TEACHERS COLLEGE: Columbus.
CONCORDIA COLLEGE: Milwaukee.
DODGE COUNTY TEACHERS COLLEGE: Mayville.
DOMINICAN COLLEGE: Racine.
DOOR-KEWAUNEE COUNTY TEACHERS COLLEGE: Algoma.
DUNN COUNTY TEACHERS COLLEGE: Menomonie.
EDGEWOOD COLLEGE OF THE SACRED HEART: Madison.
GREEN COUNTY TEACHERS COLLEGE: Monroe.
HOLY FAMILY COLLEGE: Manitowoc.
JUNEAU COUNTY TEACHERS COLLEGE: New Lisbon.
LAKELAND COLLEGE: Sheboygan.
LANGLADE COUNTY TEACHERS COLLEGE: Antigo.
LAWRENCE COLLEGE: Appleton.
LAYTON SCHOOL OF ART: Milwaukee.
LINCOLN COUNTY TEACHERS COLLEGE: Merrill.
MANITOWOC COUNTY TEACHERS COLLEGE: Manitowoc.
MARIAN COLLEGE: Fond du Lac.
MARINETTE COUNTY TEACHERS COLLEGE: Marinette.
MARQUETTE UNIVERSITY: Milwaukee.
MILTON COLLEGE: Milton.
MILWAUKEE INSTITUTE OF TECHNOLOGY: Milwaukee.
MILWAUKEE SCHOOL OF ENGINEERING: Milwaukee.

MILWAUKEE-DOWNER COLLEGE: Milwaukee.
MOUNT MARY COLLEGE: Milwaukee.
NASHOTAH HOUSE: Nashotah.
NORTHLAND COLLEGE: Ashland.
NORTHWESTERN COLLEGE: Watertown.
OUTAGAMIE COUNTY TEACHERS COLLEGE: Kaukauna.
POLK COUNTY TEACHERS COLLEGE: St. Croix Falls.
RACINE-KENOSHA COUNTY TEACHERS COLLEGE: Union Grove.
RICHLAND COUNTY TEACHERS COLLEGE: Richland Center.
RIPON COLLEGE: Ripon.
ST. FRANCIS COLLEGE: Burlington.
ST. FRANCIS SEMINARY: Milwaukee.
ST. LAWRENCE SEMINARY: Mt. Calvary.
ST. NORBERT COLLEGE: West De Pere.
SALVATORIAN SEMINARY: St. Nazianz.
SAUK COUNTY TEACHERS COLLEGE: Reedsburg.
SHEBOYGAN COUNTY TEACHERS COLLEGE: Sheboygan Falls.
STOUT STATE COLLEGE: Menomonie.
TAYLOR COUNTY TEACHERS COLLEGE: Medford.
VERNON COUNTY TEACHERS COLLEGE: Viroqua.
VITERBO COLLEGE: La Crosse.
WAUSHARA COUNTY TEACHERS COLLEGE: Wautoma.
WISCONSIN, UNIVERSITY OF: Madison.
WISCONSIN CONSERVATORY, INC.: Milwaukee.
WISCONSIN INSTITUTE OF TECHNOLOGY: Platteville.
WISCONSIN STATE COLLEGE: Eau Claire.
WISCONSIN STATE COLLEGE: La Crosse.
WISCONSIN STATE COLLEGE: Oshkosh.
WISCONSIN STATE COLLEGE: Platteville.
WISCONSIN STATE COLLEGE: River Falls.
WISCONSIN STATE COLLEGE: Stevens Point.
WISCONSIN STATE COLLEGE: Superior.
WISCONSIN STATE COLLEGE: Whitewater.
WOODS COUNTY TEACHERS COLLEGE: Wisconsin Rapids.

Wyoming

CASPER JUNIOR COLLEGE: Casper.
NORTHWEST CENTER OF THE UNIVERSITY OF WYOMING: Powell.
NORTHEAST AGRICULTURAL JUNIOR COLLEGE: Sheridan.
SOUTHEAST CENTER OF THE UNIVERSITY OF WYOMING: Torrington.
WYOMING, UNIVERSITY OF: Laramie.

School Songs
See **College Songs**

Scriptures: Sacred Books of the Great Religions of the World
See also **Bible**

1. BUDDHISM: a). The Hinayana (Little Vehicle) Buddhism of Ceylon, Burma and Siam, and the Mahayana (Great Vehicle) Buddhism of Nepal, Tibet, China, and Japan, both accept as their sacred canon Tipitaka (Three Baskets), the Sutta, and the Abidhamma, all of which are written in Pali; b). The chief Scriptures of the North Indian Mahayana Buddhism are the Mahavastu, the Saddharma-pundarika (Lotus of the True Law), and the philosophic Prajna-paramitas.

2. CHRISTIANITY: The Bible, consisting of the Old and New Testament Canon.

3. CONFUCIANISM: There are five Chinese classics, called the Five King: the Yi-king (Yih-king), or Book of Changes; the Shu-king, or Book of History; the Shi-king, or Book of Poetry (Odes); the Hi-ki (Li-king), or Book of Ceremonial Usage (Rites); the Chun-tsiu (Chun-chin), or Book of (Spring and Summer) Annals. They are supplemented by another group of sacred books called the Four Shu: the Lun-Yu, or Sayings of Confucius; the Chung Yung, or Book of Moral Conduct (the Doctrine of the Mean); the Ta-Hsuah (Ta-Hseuh), or Great Learning, Confucius' method for inculcating ideal character; the Ethical Writings of Mencius (Ming-tzu).

4. TAOISM: There are a number of expositions of Taoist (Chinese) doctrine, the chief being the Tâo-Teh-King, attributed to Lao-Tsze, and the philosophy of Chuang-Tsze.

5. HINDUISM: The sacred literature is complex and vast, but the principal books are: a). Early Literature: The Rig-Veda, a collection of 1,017 hymns produced by priestly families during many centuries; The Atharva-Veda, a collection of mantras, or texts of religion and magic; The Yagur-Veda, a group of liturgies; The Brahmanas, commentaries on the Vedas; The Aranyakas, or Forest Books, and The Upanishads, both of which are considered as inspired; b). Later Literature: The Sutras, or priestly commentaries of the Vedas; The Eighteen Puranas, which deal with cosmology, history, and religious philosophy; c). The popular Vaisnava, or Vishnu-worshiping literature of India has gathered around the two great epic poems, the Mahabharata and the Ramayana, which have been given religious (Vaisnavite) interest by the priests, and are a storehouse of philosophical and theological teaching; the celebrated Bhagavadgita is a poem within the Mahabharata; d). The Sankhya-Karita is the classic poem (4th cent. A. D.) of the Sankhya system, a Hindu philosophy among the oldest in the world and said to have originated with the sage Kapila; its theistic element is supplied by the Yoga-Sutra of Patanjali; e). The Vaisheshida-Sutra and the Nyaya-Sutra of Gautama are the chief books, respectively, of the Vaisheshika system (the Hindu philosophy which traces all things to indestructible atoms), and of the Nyaya system (the Hindu systems of logic); f). The Angas, forty-five in number, constitute the canonical scriptures of the Jains.

6. JUDAISM: The Bible, Old Testament; the Talmud (the code of Jewish civil and canonical law, composed of the Mishna, or text, and the Gemara, or commentary), of which there are two versions, the Jerusalem Talmud, closed at the end of the 4th cent. A. D., and the Babylonian Talmud, completed towards the end of the 5th cent. A. D. and derived from the former.

7. EGYPTIAN RELIGION: The chief surviving Scriptures are: a). The Book of the Dead, a collection of ritual and magic; b). The Pyramid Texts, a collection of prayers, myths, and hymns.

8. MOHAMMEDANISM: The Koran, a collection of prayers and inspirational utterances of Mohammed which was made fifteen years after his death (between 644-656 A. D.), regarded by the Mohammedans as inspired in every detail.

9. ZOROASTRIANISM: The Avesta, consisting of hymns, legal enactments, and liturgies, constitutes the chief Zoroastrian Scripture, and is supplemented by the Pahlavi books which are written in Pahlavi or Middle Persian. The Avesta (or Zend-Avesta) is divided into the Vendidad, Vispered, Yasna-Gathos, and Khordan Avesta. Among the later sacred writings of the Parsees are: Ard Viraf, Bundahishn, Dadistan-i-denig, Dinkard, Monogi Khrad, Shayist-ne-shayist, and Zadsparam.

10. OTHER WRITINGS: Held in esteem high enough to be considered as sacred, if not canonical, literature are: the Babylonian Great Epic; the Bhakti Hymns of India; the Book of Common Prayer (the book of services of the Anglican Catholic Church); the Book of Mormon; the Cabala (Judeo-Christian); the Chassidic Literature (Jewish); the Code of Khammurabi (Babylonian); the Fihrist (Manichean, being Mani's account of the creation of the world); Gilgamash (Sumerian epic, containing the story of the Babylonian flood); the Granth Sahib (Sikh, includes the Japji, Asa Ki War, and the Rahiras); the Hadith (Moslem traditional literature); *heaven and Hell*, by Emanuel Swedenborg; the Homeric Hymns (ancient Greek); the Hymn of the Arval Brethren, or Fratres Arvales (ancient Roman); the Hymn to Nyakopon (West African); the Jewish Prayer Book; the Midrash (Jewish); the Mo-ti Book (Chinese); the New Scriptures of the Japanese Konko Kyo Sect; the Orphic Hymns (Graeco-Roman); the Popul Vuh (sacred book of the ancient Quiche Maya Indians of Central America; *Science and Health with Key to the Scriptures*, by Mrs. Mary Baker Eddy (the metaphysics of Christian Science); the Shepherd of Hermas, by Hermas (fl. 140 A. D.) (an exposition of life among the early Christians); the Shinto Literature of Japan, including the Kojiki and Nihongi; and the Unique Necklace (Sufi).

Seas
See **Salt Water Bodies**

Secession of States
See **Admission, Secession, and Readmission of States**

Secretaries of State (U. S.)

JAY, JOHN[1]: Washington.
JEFFERSON, THOMAS: 1790, Washington.
RANDOLPH, EDMUND: 1794, Washington.
PICKERING, TIMOTHY: 1795, Washington.
PICKERING, TIMOTHY: 1797, J. Adams.
MARSHALL, JOHN: 1800, J. Adams.
MADISON, JAMES: 1801, Jefferson.
SMITH, ROBERT: 1809, Madison.
MONROE, JAMES: 1811, Madison.
RUSH, RICHARD: 1817, Monroe.
ADAMS, JOHN QUINCY: 1817, Monroe.
CLAY, HENRY: 1825, J. Q. Adams.
VAN BUREN, MARTIN: 1829, Jackson.
LIVINGSTON, EDWARD: 1831, Jackson.
MC LANE, LOUIS: 1833, Jackson.
FORSYTH, JOHN: 1834, Jackson.
FORSYTH, JOHN: 1837, Van Buren.
WEBSTER, DANIEL: 1841, W. H. Harrison.
WEBSTER, DANIEL: 1841, Tyler.

[1] John Jay acted as Secretary for Foreign Affairs from December, 1784, under the Continental Congress, and he continued unofficially to conduct the Department of State until Jefferson took office as Secretary.

UPSHUR, ABEL P.: 1843, Tyler.
CALHOUN, JOHN C.: 1844, Tyler.
BUCHANAN, JAMES: 1845, Polk.
CLAYTON, JOHN M.: 1849, Taylor.
WEBSTER, DANIEL: 1850, Fillmore.
EVERETT, EDWARD: 1852, Fillmore.
MERCY, WILLIAM L.: 1853, Pierce.
CASS, LEWIS: 1857, Buchanan.
BLACK, JEREMIAH S.: 1860, Buchanan.
SEWARD, WILLIAM H.: 1861, Lincoln.
SEWARD, WILLIAM H.: 1865, Johnson.
WASHBURNE, ELIHU B.: 1869, Grant.
FISH, HAMILTON: 1869, Grant.
EVARTS, WILLIAM M.: 1877, Hayes.
BLAINE, JAMES G.: 1881, Garfield.
FRELINGHUYSEN, FREDRICK: 1881, Arthur.
BAYARD, THOMAS F.: 1885, Cleveland.
BLAINE, JAMES G.: 1889, B. Harrison.
FOSTER, JOHN W.: 1892, B. Harrison.
GRESHAM, WALTER Q.: 1893, Cleveland.
OLNEY, RICHARD: 1895, Cleveland.
SHERMAN, JOHN: 1897, McKinley.
DAY, WILLIAM R.: 1898, McKinley.
HAY JOHN M.: 1898, McKinley.
HAY, JOHN M.: 1901, T. Roosevelt.
ROOT, ELIHU: 1905, T. Roosevelt.
BACON, ROBERT: 1909, T. Roosevelt.
KNOX, PHILANDER C.: 1909, Taft.
BRYAN, WILLIAM JENNINGS: 1913, Wilson.
LANSING, ROBERT: 1915, Wilson.
COLBY, BAINBRIDGE: 1920, Wilson.
HUGHES, CHARLES EVANS: 1921, Harding.
HUGHES, CHARLES EVANS: 1923, Coolidge.
KELLOGG, FRANK B.: 1925, Coolidge.
STIMSON, HENRY LEWIS: 1929, Hoover.
HULL, CORDELL: 1933, F. D. Roosevelt.
STETTINUIS, EDWARD, JR.: 1944,
　　F. D. Roosevelt
BYRNES, JAMES F: 1945, Truman:
MARSHALL, GEORGE C.: 1947, Truman.
ACHESON, DEAN G.: 1949. Truman.
DULLES, JOHN FOSTER: 1953, Eisenhower.

Senate Standing Committees
See Congress of the United States

Sermons
See Speeches and Sermons

Seven Champions of Christendom
See Saints

Seven Wonders of the Ancient World

(1) THE PYRAMIDS OF EGYPT: The pyramids, about 75 in number, and of varying size, were built as tombs in which the mummified bodies of kings and their families were preserved; the pyramids that have excited the greatest curiosity are: the Stepped Pyramid of Sakkara, which has been attributed to King Ouenephes of the First Dynasty, and the three great pyramids near Gizeh on the west bank of the Nile, the first and largest of which is said to have been erected as a tomb for King Choofoo (3733-3666 b. c.) of the Fourth Dynasty (called Cheops by the Greek historian Herodotus), and is measured to a height of 481 feet, with a base 774 feet square; the second of which is attributed to Chafra, or Chepren (3666-3633 b. c.); the third of which is said to have been built by Menkaura or Mycerinus, c. 3633 b. c.

(2) THE MAUSOLEUM BUILT BY QUEEN ARTEMISIA FOR HER HUSBAND, KING MAUSOLUS OF CARIA: Artemisia was the sister as well as the wife of Mausolus; they reigned as King and Queen of Caria 377-353 b. c. When he died she is said to have drunk down the ashes of his cremated body in a glass of liquor, and sponsored a lavish contest among the leading poets of the day for the best elegiac panegyric in his memory (won by Theopompus); ruled alone (352-c. 350 b. c.) and began construction at Halicarnassus of the mausoleum that was completed at about the time of her own death (c. 350 b. c.); a statue of Mausolus was brought (1857) to England by Sir C. T. Newton and placed in the British Museum; the word *mausoleum* is derived from the name of King Mausolus.

(3) THE TEMPLE OF DIANA AT EPHESUS: All of the Asiatic states contributed to the cost of the construction of a temple to Diana at Ephesus, and commissioned Ctesiphon as the chief architect (c. 552-544 b. c.); according to Pliny, work on the structure continued for 220 years; the temple, when completed, was 425 feet long, 225 feet wide, with 127 supporting columns of Parian marble, each of which was 60 feet high, weighed 150 tons, and was furnished by a different king; on the night of the birth of Alexander the Great, Herostratus (Eratostratus) set the temple afire (356 b. c.), claiming that his sole motive was to transmit his name to posterity; after the temple was rebuilt, it was burned again by the Goths during their naval invasion (c. 256-62 a. d.); in April, 1869, J. T. Wood discovered the site of the second temple and some sculptured columns were later brought to the British Museum.

(4) THE WALLS AND HANGING GARDENS OF BABYLON: The Walls and Hanging Gardens made Babylon the most magnificent city in the world; from the descriptions of Strabo and Diodorus, the Hanging Gardens are pictured as square in form, with terraces rising one above another as high as the walls of the city and mounted by flights of steps; the whole structure was supported by a series of arches, built one above another; on top were laid flat stones cemented together with bitumen plaster and covered with sheets of lead; garden mold was deposited on the lead sheets to nourish large trees, shrubs, flowers, and vegetables; there were five of these gardens in all, each with an area of about four acres, and forming a section of an amphitheater of gardens; by his time (23-79 a. d.) Pliny says that the gardens were a desolate wilderness.

(5) THE COLOSSUS OF RHODES: In honor of the sun, Chares of Lindus, a disciple of Lysippus, erected a brass statue of Apollo, 70 cubits (105 feet) high, in the harbor of Rhodes (c. 290-288 b. c.); it was thrown down by an earthquake (c. 224 b. c.); for nine centuries the statue lay in ruins until the Saracens took Rhodes and sold the metal (653 a. d.), weighing 720,900 pounds, to a Jewish merchant who is said to have loaded down 900 camels for the haul to Alexandria; the legend of the Colossus is that it stood upon two moles, a leg on either side of the harbor, so that a vessel in full sail could pass between.

(6) THE STATUE OF JUPITER OLYMPUS BY PHIDIAS: Phidias was commissioned to furnish a statue for the temple of Jupiter that the Eleans had authorized (c. 450 b. c.) Libon of Elis to build at Olympieum (near Pelopennesus) after the Elean conquest of that country; the Jupiter (or Zeus) that the

sculptor supplied (437-433 b. c.) was a colossus in gold and ivory, larger than his 39-feet ivory and gold statue of Minerva for the Parthenon; the intrinsic value of these statues made them enviable prizes of war and they have utterly disappeared from the historical record.

(7) THE PHAROS, OR LIGHTHOUSE, BUILT BY PTOLEMY PHILADELPHUS, KING OF EGYPT: At Pharos, an island on the Egyptian coast, Sostratus of Cnidus began work (298 b. c.) on a huge tower, which was completed by Ptolemy Philadelphus (c. 283 b.c.); the tower was 550 feet high, and is said to have been visible for 42 miles; fires were burned constantly at top to direct ships along the coast.

Shakespeare
See **Characters from Shakespeare's Plays; Songs from Shakespeare's Plays**

Sibyls
See **Religious Allusions, References, and Symbols**

Singing Voices, Types of, and Some Famous Singers
See also **Characters from the Great Operas**

ALTO: In choral and choir singing, and in four-part writing, the alto is the second highest voice, without reference to the sex of the singer; it is sometimes used to designate a very high male voice (countertenor), or a female voice lower than a soprano (contralto).

BARITONE: In the trio of normal male voices, the baritone falls between the high (tenor) and the low (bass); the baritone compass is about 2 octaves downward from G above middle C; in choral writing, the baritone is sometimes called "first bass."

Pasquale Amato, Manuel Ausensi, Frederic Austin, Mattia Battistini, Crane Calder, Giuseppe de Luca, Nelson Eddy, Geraint Evans, Dietrich Fischer-Dieskau, Ferdinand Frantz, Tito Gobbi, John Hargreaves, Mack Harrell, Ralph Herbert, Hans Hotter, Jacques Jansen, Herbert Janssen, Roderick Jones, Otakar Kraus, Erich Kunz, George London, Arnold Matters, Victor Maurel, Morley Meredith, Robert Merrill, José Mojica, Charles Panzera, Hernan Pelayo, Ivan Petroff, Heinz Rehfuss, Heinrich Rehkemper, Paul Robeson, Marko Rothmüller, Titta Ruffo, Charles Santley, Aksel Schiøtz, Heinrich Schlusnus, Paul Schoeffler, Joseph Schwarz, Antonio Scotti, Frederick Sharp, Paolo Silveri, Martial Singher, Rand Smith, Gerard Souzay, Mariano Stabile, Richard Standen, Riccardo Stracciari, John Charles Thomas, Thomas L. Thomas, Lawrence Tibbett, Giuseppe Valdengo, Jess Walters, William Warfield, Leonard Warren, Robert Weede, Tom Williams.

BASS: In the trio of normal male voices, the bass is the lowest, with a usual range of E above middle C down to C 2 octaves below middle C.

Hervey Alan, Norman Allin, Raphael Arie, Feodor Chaliapin, Boris Christoff, Stanley Clarkson, Norman Cordon, Fernando Corena, Frederick Dalberg, Adamo Didur, Otto Edelmann, Howell Glynne, Donald Gramm,

Alexander Kipnis, Emmanuel List, José Mardones, Richard Mayr, Ezio Pinza (also sang baritone), Alfred Poell, Mark Reizen, Edouard de Reszke, Nicola Rossi-Lemeni, Cesare Siepi, Wilhelm Strienz, Italo Tajo.

BASS-BARITONE: Michael Bohnen, Pol Plançon (sometimes listed as bass), Herman Schey, Randolph Symonetta.

COLORATURA SOPRANO: Coloratura refers to the elaboration of the vocal line with notes to a single syllable, and the runs, trills, and tricks of vocal ornamentation; it is her deftness and lightness of touch that distinguish the coloratura soprano from the dramatic or lyric soprano.

CONTRALTO: In the trio of normal female voices, the contralto is the lowest in pitch, with a customary range from F below middle C to about 2 octaves above.

Marion Anderson, Ruth Fernandez, Kathleen Ferrier, Herta Glaz, Sigrid Onegin, Nell Rankin, Ebe Stignani (can also sing mezzo-soprano).

FALSETTO: The falsetto is outside the range of the normal male voice, and refers to the high notes produced forcibly by a tightening of the glottis.

MEZZO-SOPRANO: Meaning *half,* mezzo, applied to soprano, indicates a female voice possessing qualities of both soprano and contralto.

Marie Brema, Edith Coates, Margarete Klose, Gloria Lane, Kirkby Lunn, Zelie de Lussan, Nan Merriman, Anna Pollak, Constance Shacklock (can sing contralto), Risë Stevens, Conchita Supervia (mezzo-contralto with soprano range), Blanche Thebom.

SOPRANO: In the trio of normal female voices, the soprano is the highest in pitch, above the mezzo-soprano and the contralto; the term also indicates the voices of boys before they have changed; the soprano range is usually from about middle C to 2 octaves above; sopranos are classified as dramatic, lyric, and coloratura; in vocal writing the soprano part is often called *treble.*

Pierette Alarie, Licia Albanese, Marie Louise Albani, Anna Maria Alberghetti, Victoria de los Angeles, Martha Angelici, Rose Bampton, Maria Barrientos, Erna Berger, Celestina Boninsegna, Lucrezia Bori, Geori Boue, Gre Brouwenstijn, Maria Meneghini Callas, Emma Calvé, Maria Caniglia, Margherita Carosio, Sara Carter, Lina Cavalieri, Maria Cebotari, Vivian Della Chiesa, Joan Cross, Maud Cunitz, Phyllis Curtin, Suzanne Danco, Ellabelle Davis, Emmy Destinn, Mattiwilda Dobbs, Marie Louise Lucinne Edvina, Victoria Elliott, Geraldine Farrar, Eileen Farrell, Ellen Farill, Sylvia Fisher, Kirsten Flagstad, Amelita Galli-Curci, Mary Garden, Christel Goltz, Margherita Grandi, Jacqueline Greissle, Giulia Grisi, Hilde Gueden, Margot Guilleaume, Joan Hammond, Janice Harsanyi, Ilse Hollweg, Gertraud Hopf, Elsie Houston, Alice Howland, Lydia Ibarrondo, Maria Ivogun, Florence Foster Jenkins, Maria Jeritza, Sena Jurinac, Dorothy Kirsten, Irma Kolassi, Miliza Korjus, Maria Kurenko, Selma Kurz, Magda Laszlo, Marjorie Laurence, Lilli Lehmann, Lotte Lehmann, Adele Leigh, Freida Leiker, Tiana Lemnitz, Jenny Lind, Colette Lorand, Mary Maddox, Liselotte Malkowsky, Amparo Guerra Margain, Virginie Mauret, Elfie Mayerhofer, Nellie Melba, Janine Micheau, Zinka Milanov, Martha Modl, Grace Moore, Claudia Muzio, Patricia Neway, Tii Niemela, Christine Nilsson, Alda Noni, Lillian Nordica, Lina Pagliughi, Jeanne Palmer, Adelina Patti, Roberta Peters, Lily Pons, Rosa Ponselle, Marie Powers, Rosa Raisa, Rosina

Raisbeck, Maria Reining, Josephine de Reszke, Elisabeth Rethberg, Esther Rethy, Traute Richter, Delia Rigal, Mado Robin, Elisabeth Roon, Anne Roselle, Marie Roze, Consuelo Rubio, Erna Sack, Sybil Sanderson, Bidu Sayao, Marjorie Schloss, Elisabeth Schumann, Elisabeth Schwarzkopf, Helena Scott, Irmgard Seefried, Marcella Sembrich, Amy Shuard, Victoria Sladen, Margaret Speaks, Eleanor Steber, Marion Studholme, Pia Tassinari, Renata Tebaldi, Luisa Tetrazzini, Maggie Teyte, Jennie Tourel, Helen Traubel, Margaret Truman, Eva Turner, Ninon Vallin, Astrid Varnay, Jennifer Vyvyan, Dorothy Warenskiold, Ljuba Welitsch, Camilla Williams, Hilde Zadek.

TENOR: In the trio of normal male voices, the tenor is the highest in pitch, with a customary range of about an octave below middle C to the octave above; tenors are classified as dramatic and lyric; in choral and choir music, the tenor is the 3rd part, the alto and soprano lying above it.

Giuseppe Anselmi, Kurt Baum, Jussi Björling, Allesandro Bonci, Enrico Caruso, John Coates (began as bass), Eugene Conley, Richard Crooks, Hugues Cuenod, Davis Cunningham, Gerald Davies, Alfred Deller (countertenor), Mario del Monaco, Fernando de Lucia, Anton Dermota, Murray Dickie, Edgar Evans, Miguel Fleta, Karl Friedrich, Miklos Gafni, Paul Gavert, Nicolai Gedda, Dunsan Georgevic, Beniamino Gigli, Herbert Ernst Groh, Carl Hague, Roland Hayes, Joseph Hislop, Luigi Ifantino, Allen Jones, Parry Jones, Rowland Jones, Trefor Jones, Oreste Kirkop, Mario Lanza, Hipolito Lazaro, Richard Lewis, Max Lichtegg, Walther Ludwig, Christopher Lynch, Norman MacKaye, Giovanni Matteo Mario, Giovanni Martinelli, Galliano Masini, John McCormack, Lauritz Melchior (began as baritone), James Melton, Walter Midgley, Frank Mullings, Lucien Maratore, Kenneth Neate (has full baritone range), Julius Patzak, Peter Pears, Aureliano Pertile, Gianni Poggi, Giacinto Prandelli, Sims Reeves, Jean de Reszke, Vladimir Rosing, Helge Roswaenge, Tito Schipa, Joseph Schmidt, Leopold Simoneau, Leo Slezak, Ante Soljanich, Set Svanholm, Ferruccio Tagliavini, Francesco Tamagno, Richard Tauber, Richard Tucker, Cesare Valletti, Marcel Wittrisch, Giovani Zenatello.

Songs, Popular
See also **Academy Award Songs, College Songs; Songs from Broadway Plays; Songs from Shakespeare's Plays**

Note: In some instances, the date of the song is the date of copyright, which is not necessarily the year when the song was most popular.

ABBA DABBA HONEYMOON: 1914; words and music: Fields, Arthur (1888-   ); Donovan, Walter (1888-   ).

ABOUT A QUARTER TO NINE: 1935 (movie: *Go Into Your Dance);* words: Dubin, Al (1891-1945); music: Warren, Harry (1893-   ).

ACCENTUATE THE POSITIVE: 1944 (movie: *Here Come the Waves);* words: Mercer, John H. (Johnny) (1909-   ); music: Arlen, Harold (1905-   ).

ACROSS THE WIDE MISSOURI: 1951; words and music: Drake, Ervin (1919-   ); Shirl, Jimmy (1909-   ).

AFTER GRADUATION DAY: 1947; words: Dee, Sylvia (1914-   ); music: Lippmann, Sidney (1914-   ).

AFTER I SAY I'M SORRY: 1926; words and music: Donaldson, Walter (1893-1947); Lyman, Abe (1897-   ).

AFTER THE BALL: 1892; words and music: Harris, Charles K. (1867-1930).

AFTER YOU'VE GONE: 1918; words and music: Creamer, Henry (1879-1930), Layton, Turner (-   ).

AH, BUT IS IT LOVE?: 1933; (movie: *Moonlight and Pretzels);* words: Harburg, E. Y. "Yip" (1898-   ); music: Gorney, Jay (1896-   ).

A-HUNTING WE WILL GO: 1935; words and music: Stride, Harry (1903-   ); Tobias, Charles (1898-   ); Tobias, Henry (1905-   ).

AINTCHA EVER COMIN' BACK: 1947; words: Taylor, Irving (1914-   ); music: Stordahl, Axel (1913-   ), Weston, Paul (1912-   ).

AIN'T SHE SWEET: 1927; words: Yellen, Jack (1892-   ); music: Ager, Milton (1893-   ).

AINT' WE GOT FUN: 1921; words: Kahn, Gus (1866-1941); music: Whiting, Richard A. (1891-1938).

ALABAMY BOUND: 1925; words: De Sylva, Buddy (George Gard de) (1895-1950); Green, Bud (1897-   ); music: Henderson, Ray (1896-   ).

ALEXANDER'S RAGTIME BAND: 1911; words and music: Berlin, Irving (1888-   ).

ALLEGHENY MOON: 1956; words and music: Hoffman, Al (1902-   ), Manning, Dick.

ALL I DO IS DREAM OF YOU: 1934 (movie: *Sadie McKee);* words: Freed, Arthur (1894-   ); music: Brown, Nacio Herb (1896-).

ALL I WANT FOR CHRISTMAS IS MY TWO FRONT TEETH: 1948; words and music: Gardner, Don (Donald Yetter Gardner) (1912-   ).

ALL MY LOVE: 1947; words and music: Akst, Harry (1894-   ); Chaplin, Saul (1912-   ); Jolson, Al (1886-1950).

ALL MY LOVE: 1950; (French original: "Bolero," by Contet and Durand; English words: Parish, Mitchell (1900-   ).

ALL OF A SUDDEN MY HEART SINGS: 1945 (movie: *Anchors Aweigh);* words and music: Rome, Harold J. (1908-   ).

ALL OF ME: 1931; words and music: Marks, Gerald (1900-   ); Simons, Seymour (1896-1949).

ALL OR NOTHING AT ALL: 1940; words and music: Altman, Arthur (   ), Lawrence, Jack (1912-   ).

ALL THIS AND HEAVEN TOO: 1939; words and music: De Lange, Eddie (Edgar) (1904-1939); Van Heusen, Jimmy (1913-   ).

ALL THROUGH THE DAY: 1946 (movie: *Centennial Summer);* words: Hammerstein II, Oscar (1895-   ); music: Kern, Jerome (1885-1945).

ALONE: 1935 (movie: *A Night at the Opera);* words: Freed, Arthur (1894-   ); music: Brown, Nacio Herb (1896-   ).

ALONE AT A TABLE FOR TWO: 1935; words and music: Fiorito, Ted (1900-   ), Hill, William J. "Billy" (1899-1940), Richman, Daniel.

ALWAYS: 1925; words and music: Berlin, Irving (1888-   ).

ALWAYS IN MY HEART: 1941 (movie: *Always in My Heart);* words: Gannon, Kim (James Kimball Gannon) (1900-   ); music: Lecuona, Ernesto.

ALWAYS YOU: 1954; Italian title: *Sempre Tu;* words: Mario, Johnny; Gray, Walter; Kreigsmann, James; music: Toto.

AMAPOLA: 1924; Spanish and English words and music: Joseph M. Lacalle.

AM I BLUE?: 1929 (movie: *On With the Show);* words: Clarke, Grant (1891-1931); music: Akst, Harry (1894-   ).

AMONG MY SOUVENIRS: 1927; words: Leslie, Edgar (1885-); music: Nicholls, Horatio.
AMOR: 1943; based on Spanish original by Ricardo Mendez and Gabriel Ruiz; English words: Skylar, Sunny (1913-   ).
ANCHORS AWEIGH: 1906; words: Miles, Alfred H. (1883-), Lovell, R. (-   ); music: Zimmermann, Charles A. (-   ).
ANDALUCIA: 1920; music: Lecuona, Ernesto. See The Breeze and I (1940), based on *Andalucia*.
AND HER TEARS FLOWED LIKE WINE: 1944; words and music: Green, Joe (Joseph Perkins) (1915-   ); Kenton, Stanley (Stan) (1912-   ); Lawrence, Charles; Moore, Phil (1918-   ).
AND MIMI: 1947; words and music: Simon, Nat (1900-   ); Kennedy, James.
AND THE GREEN GRASS GREW ALL AROUND: 1912; words: Jerome, William (1865-1932); music: Von Tilzer, Harry (1872-1946).
AND THEN SOME: 1935; words: Seymour, Tot; music: Lawnhurst, Vee (1905-   ).
ANGELA MIA: 1928; (movie: *Street Angel*); words: Pollack, Lew (1895-1946); music: Pollack and Rapee, Erno (1891-1945).
ANNIE DOESN'T LIVE HERE ANY MORE: 1933; words: Young, Joseph (1889-1939); music: Burke, Johnny (1908-   ); Spina, Harold (1906-   ).
ANNIVERSARY SONG: 1946 (movie: *Jolson Story*); words and music: Jolson, Al (1886-1950); Chaplin, Saul (1912-   ).
ANNIVERSARY WALTZ: 1941; words and music: Dubin, Al (1891-1945); Franklin, Dave (1895-   ).
AREN'T YOU GLAD YOU'RE YOU?: 1945; (movie: *The Bells of St. Mary's*); words: Burke, Johnny (1908-   ); music: Van Heusen, Jimmy (1913-   ).
ARE YOU LONESOME TONIGHT?: 1927; words: Turk, Roy (1892-1934); music: Handman, Lou (1894-   ).
ASK ANYONE WHO KNOWS: 1947; words: Seiler, Edward (1911-1952); music: Marcus, Sol (1912-   ).
ASLEEP IN THE DEEP: 1897; words: Lamb, Arthur J. (1870-1928); music: Petrie, Henry W. (1857-1925).
AS LONG AS I'M DREAMING: 1947; words: Burke, Johnny (1908-   ); music: Van Heusen, Jimmy (1913-   ).
AS YEARS GO BY: 1947; (movie: *Song of Love*); words and music: De Rose, Peter (1900-   ); Tobias, Charles (1898-   )—based on Brahms' Hungarian Dance No. 4.
AS YOU DESIRE ME: 1944; Wrubel, Allie (1905-   ).
AT A GEORGIA CAMP MEETING: 1897; words and music: Mills, Frederick Allen (Kerry Mills) (1869-1948).
A-TISKET, A-TASKET: 1938; words and music: Feldman, Al; Fitzgerald, Ella (1918-).
AT LAST: 1942; (movie: *Orchestra Wives*); words: Gordon, Mack (1904-   ); music: Warren, Harry (1893-   ).
AT SUNDOWN: 1927; words and music: Donaldson, Walter (1893-1947).
AT THE BALALAIKA: 1939; (movie: *Balalaika*); words and music: Forest, George (Chet) (1915-   ); Maschwitz, Eric; Wright, Robert (Bob) (1914-   ).
AT YOUR COMMAND: 1931; words and music: Barris, Harry (1905-   ); Crosby, Bing (1904-   ); Tobias, Harry (1905-   ).
AUF WIEDERSEHN, MY DEAR: 1932; words and music: Ager, Milton (1893-   ); Goodhart, Al (1905-   ); Hoffman, Al (1902-   ); Nelson, Ed G. (1896-   ).

AURA LEE: 1861; words: Fosdick, W. W.; music: Poulton, G. R.
AUTUMN LEAVES: 1955; English words: Mercer, Johnny (1909-   ); French words: Prevert, Jacques; music: Kosma, Joseph.
AUTUMN SERENADE: 1945; words and music: Gallop, Sammy (1915-   ); De Rose, Peter (1900-   ).
AVALON: 1920; words and music: De Sylva, Buddy (George Gard de) (1895-1950); Jolson, Al (1886-1950); Rose, Vincent (1880-1944).
A—YOU'RE ADORABLE (THE ALPHABET SONG): 1948; words and music: Lippman, Sidney (1914-   ); Kaye, Buddy (1918-   ); Wise, Fred (1915-   ).
BABY FACE: 1926; words and music: Davis, Benny (1895-   ); Akst, Harry (1894-   ).
BABY ME: 1939; words and music: Gottler, Archie (1896-   ); Handman, Lou (1894-   ); Harris, Harry (1901-   ).
BABY MINE: 1941 (movie: *Dumbo*); words: Washington, Ned (1901-   ); music: Churchill, Frank (1901-1942).
BABY TAKE A BOW: 1934; (movie: *Stand Up and Cheer*); words and music: Brown, Lew (1893-   ); Gorney, Jay (1896-   ).
BABY WON'T YOU PLEASE COME HOME?: 1919; words and music: Warfield, Charles; Williams, Clarence (1893-   ).
BACK HOME AGAIN IN INDIANA: 1917; Hanley, James Frederick (1892-1942).
BACK IN YOUR OWN BACKYARD: 1928; words and music: Dreyer, Dave (1894-   ); Jolson, Al (1886-1950); Rose, Billy (1899-   ).
BACK TO DONEGAL: 1942; words and music: Graham, Steve.
BAIA: 1944; words and music: De Lange, Edgar (Eddie) (1904-1949); Stept, Sammy H. (1897-   ).
BALLERINA: 1947; words: Russell, Bob (Sidney Keith) (1914-   ); music: Sigman, Carl (1909-   ).
BALLING THE JACK: 1913; words: Henry, James (Jim); music: Smith, Chris (1879-1949).
THE BAND PLAYED ON: 1895; words: Palmer, John E.; music: Ward, Charles B. (1865-1917).
BARNACLE BILL THE SAILOR: 1931; words and music: Luther, Frank (1905-   ); Robinson, Carson J. (1890-   ).
BEANS, BEANS, BEANS: 1912; words and music: Bowman, Elmer; Smith, Chris (1879-1949).
THE BEAT O'MY HEART: 1934; words and music: Burke, Johnny (1908-   ); Spina, Harold (1906-   ).
BEAUTIFUL LADY IN BLUE: 1935; words: Lewis, Samuel M. (1895-   ); music: Coots, J. Fred (1897-   ).
BEAUTIFUL OHIO: 1918; words: MacDonald, Ballard (1882-1935); music: Earl, Mary (King, Robert A.) (1862-1932).
BE CAREFUL, IT'S MY HEART: 1942 (movie: *Holiday Inn*); Berlin, Irving (1888-   ).
BE HONEST WITH ME, DEAR: 1941 (movie: *Riding on a Rainbow*); words: Rose, Fred; music: Autry, Gene (1907-   ).
BEI MIR BIST DU SCHOEN: 1937; words (English): Cahn, Sammy (1913-   ), Chaplin, Saul (1912-   ); words (original): Jacobs, Jacob; music: Secunda, Sholom.
BELOVED: 1928; words: Kahn, Gus (1886-1941); music: Sanders, Joe L. (1896-   ).
BE MY LITTLE BABY BUMBLE BEE: 1912; words: Murphy, Stanley (1875-1919); music: Marshall Henry I. (1883-   ).
BESAME MUCHO: 1943; words (English): Skylar, Sunny (1913-   ); words (Spanish) and music: Velasquez, Consuelo.

BE STILL, MY HEART: 1934; words and music: Egan, Jack (John C.) (1892-1940); Flynn, Allan (1894-   ).

BETWEEN THE DEVIL AND THE DEEP BLUE SEA: 1931; (movie: *Rhythmania*); words: Koehler, Ted (1894-   ); music: Arlen, Harold (1905-   ).

BEYOND THE BLUE HORIZON: 1930; (movie: *Monte Carlo*); words: Robin, Leo (1900-   ); Whiting, Richard A. (1891-1938); music: Harling, W. Franke (1887-   ).

BIBBIDI BOBBIDI BOO: 1950; (movie: *Cinderella*); David, Mack (1912-   ); Hoffman, Al (1902-   ); Livingston, Jerry (1909-   ).

B—I, BI: 1941; words: Russell, Sidney Keith (Bob) (1914-   ); music: Freedland, Beverley and Judy.

THE BIBLE TELLS ME SO: 1955; Dale Evans (1918-   ).

BILL BAILEY WON'T YOU PLEASE COME HOME?: 1902; words and music: Cannon, Hughie.

A BIRD IN A GILDED CAGE: 1900; words: Lamb, Arthur J. (1870-1928); music: Von Tilzer, Harry (1872-1946).

BLESS YOUR HEART: 1933; words and music: Drake, Milton (1912-   ); Enston, Duke; Stride, Harry (1903-   ).

BLOOP, BLEEP: 1947; Loesser, Frank (1910-   ).

BLUE BIRD OF HAPPINESS: 1934; words: Heyman, Edward (1907-   ); music: Harmati, Sandor.

BLUE CHAMPAGNE: 1941; Watts, Grady; and Ryerson, Frank.

BLUE HAWAII: 1937; (movie: *Waikiki Wedding*); words and music: Robin, Leo (1900-   ); Rainger, Ralph (1901-1942).

BLUE IS THE NIGHT: 1930; (movie: *Their Own Desire*); words and music: Fisher, Fred (1875-1942).

BLUE MOON: 1934; words: Hart, Lorenz (1895-1943); music: Rodgers, Richard (1902-   ).

BLUE PRELUDE: 1933; Bishop, Joe (1907-   ); Jenkins, Gordon (1910-   ).

BLUE RAIN: 1939; words: Mercer, Johnny (1909-   ); music: Van Heusen, Jimmy (1913-   ).

BLUES IN THE NIGHT: 1941 (movie: *Blues in the Night*); words: Mercer, Johnny (1909-   ); music: Arlen, Harold (1905-   ).

BLUE SKIES: 1927; Berlin, Irving (1888-   ).

BOB WHITE: 1937; words: Mercer, John H. (Johnny) (1909-   ); music: Hanighen, Bernard D. (1908-   ).

BOO HOO: 1937; words: Heyman, Edward (1907-   ); music: Loeb, John Jacob (1910-   ); Lombardo, Carmen (1903-   ).

BORN TO LOSE: 1943; Brown, Frankie.

THE BOULEVARD OF BROKEN DREAMS: 1933; (movie: *Moulin Rouge*); words: Dubin, Al (1891-1945); music: Warren, Harry (1893-   ).

BRAZIL: 1939; words (English): Russell, Sidney Keith (Bob) (1914-   ); music: Barroso, Ary.

THE BREEZE AND I: 1940; words: Stillman, Al (1906-   ); music: Lecuona, Ernesto (adapted from *Andalucia*).

BROADWAY MELODY: 1929; (movie: *Broadway Melody*); words: Freed, Arthur (1894-   ); music: Brown, Nacio Herb (1896-   ).

BROADWAY RHYTHM: 1935; (movie: *Broadway Melody of 1936*); words: Freed, Arthur (1894-   ); music: Brown, Nacio Herb (1896-   ).

BROKEN HEARTED: 1927; words: De Sylva, Buddy (George) (1895-1950); Brown, Lew (1893-   ); music: Henderson, Ray (1896-   ).

THE BROKEN RECORD: 1935; words and music: Bunch, Boyd (1906-   ); Friend, Cliff (1893-   ); Tobias, Charles (1898-   ).

BUT BEAUTIFUL: 1948; words and music: Burke, Johnny (1908-   ); Craig, Francis (1900-   ); Smith, Beasley (1901-   ).

BY A WATERFALL: 1933 (movie: *Footlight Parade*); words: Kahal, Irving (1903-1942); music: Fain, Sammy (1902-   ).

BY THE LIGHT OF THE SILVERY MOON: 1909; words: Madden, Edward (1878-1952); music: Edwards, Gus (1879-1945).

BY THE RIVER OF THE ROSES: 1943; words: Symes, Marty (1904-   ); music: Burke, Joseph A. (1884-1950).

BY THE RIVER SAINT MARIE: 1931; words: Leslie, Edgar (1885-   ); music: Warren, Harry (1893-   ).

CABIN IN THE COTTON: 1932; words: Parish, Mitchell (1900-   ); music: Perkins, Frank S. (1908-   ).

CALEDONIA, WHAT MAKES YOUR BIG HEAD SO HARD?: 1945; Moore, Fleecie.

CALIFORNIA HERE I COME: 1924; words: and music: De Sylva, Buddy (George) (1895-1950); Jolson, Al (1886-1950); Meyer, Joseph (1892-   ).

CALIFORN-I-AY: 1944; words: Harburg, E. Y. (1898-   ); music: Kern, Jerome (1895-1945).

THE CALL OF THE CANYON: 1940; Hill, William J. (Billy Hill) (1899-1940).

CALL ME DARLING, CALL ME SWEETHEART: 1931; words (German) and music: Fryberg, Mart (1890-   ); Reisfeld, Bert (1906-   ); Marbet, Rolf; words (English): Dick, Dorothy (1900-   ).

CANDY: 1944; words and music: David, Mack (1912-   ); Kramer, Alex Charles (1903-   ); Whitney, Joan (1914-   ).

CAN'T GET INDIANA OFF MY MIND: 1940; words: De Leon, Robert (1904-   ); music: Carmichael, Hoagy (1899-   ).

CAN'T YOU HEAR ME CALLIN', CAROLINE?: 1914; words: Gardner, William Henry (1865-1932); music: Rome, Caro (Carrie Northey) (1866-1937).

CARELESS: 1939; words and music: Howard, Eddy (1914-   ); Jurgens, Dick (1911-   ); Quadling, Lew (1906-   ).

CARELESSLY: 1936; words: Kenny, Nick (1895-   ); music: Kenny, Charles F. (1898-   ); Ellis, Norman.

CARIOCA: 1933 (movie: *Flying Down to Rio*); words: Kahn, Gus (1886-1941); Eliscu, Edward (1902-   ); music: Youmans, Vincent (1898-1946).

CAROLINA MOON: 1928; words and music: Burke, Joseph A. (1884-1950); Davis, Benny (1895-   ); Ringle, Dave (1894-   ).

CARRY ME BACK TO THE LONE PRAIRIE: 1934; Robinson, Carson J. (1890-   ).

CASEY JONES: 1909; words: Seibert, T. Lawrence; music: Newton, Eddie.

CASTLE OF DREAMS: 1919; words: McCarthy, Joseph (1885-1943); music: Tierney, Harry (1895-   ).

CECILIA: 1925; words and music: Dreyer, Dave (1894-   ); Ruby, Herman (1891-   ).

C'EST SI BON: 1950; words (English) and music: Seelen, Jerry (1912-   ); words (French) and music: Bette, Henri; Horney, André.

CHAMPAGNE WALTZ: 1934; words and music: Conrad, Con (1891-1938); Drake, Milton (1912-   ); Oakland, Ben (1907-   ).

CHANGE PARTNERS: 1938 (movie: *Carefree*); Berlin, Irving (1888-   ).

CHANGING PARTNERS: 1953; words: Darion, Joe; music: Coleman, Larry.

CHARLESTON: 1923; words and music: Mc-

Pherson, Richard C. (Cecil Mack) (1883-1944); Johnson, James P. (1894-   ).

CHARLEY, MY BOY: 1924; words: Kahn, Gus (1886-1941); music: Fiorito, Ted (1900-   ).

CHARMAINE: 1926; words and music: Pollack, Lew (1895-1946); Rapee, Erno (1891-1945).

THE CHARM OF YOU: 1945 (movie: *Anchors Aweigh*); words: Cahn, Sammy (1913-   ); music: Styne, Jule (1905-   ).

CHATTANOOGA CHOO-CHOO: 1941 (movie: *Sun Valley Serenade*); words: Gordon, Mack (1904-   ); music: Revel, Harry (1905-   ).

CHEEK TO CHEEK: 1935; (movie: *Top Hat*); Berlin, Irving (1888-   ).

CHI-BABA CHI-BABA: 1947; words and music: David, Mack (1912-   ); Hoffman, Al (1902-   ); Livingston, Jerry (1909-   ).

CHICAGO: 1922; Fisher, Fred (1875-1942).

CHICKERY CHICK: 1945; words: Dee, Sylvia (Josephine Moore Proffitt) (1914-   ); music: Lippman, Sidney (1914-   ).

CHINATOWN, MY CHINATOWN: 1906; words: Jerome, William (1865-1932); music: Schwartz, Jean (1878-   ).

CHIQUITA BANANA: 1938; words and music: Mackenzie, Leonard (1915-   ); Montgomery, Garth; Wirges, William F.

CHLOE: 1927; words: Kahn, Gus (1886-1941); music: Daniels, Charles N. (Neil Moret) (1878-1943).

CLOSE TO ME: 1936; words: Lewis, Samuel M. (1885-   ); music: De Rose, Peter (1900-   ).

COCKTAILS FOR TWO: 1934; (movie: *Murder At the Vanities*); words and music: Coslow, Sam (1902-   ); Johnston, Arthur James (1898-   ).

COME, JOSEPHINE, IN MY FLYING MACHINE: 1910; words: Bryan, Alfred (1871-   ); music: Fisher, Fred (1875-1942).

COME OUT, COME OUT, WHEREVER YOU ARE: 1933; words: Cahn, Sammy (1913-   ); music: Styne, Jule (1905-   ).

COMIN' IN ON A WING AND A PRAYER: 1943; words: Adamson, Harold (1906-   ); music: McHugh, Jimmy (1894-   ).

CONCHITA, MARQUITA, LOLITA, PEPITA, ROSETTA, JUANITA, LOPEZ: 1942 (movie: *Priorities on Parade*); words: Cahn, Sammy (1913-   ); music: Styne, Jule (1905-   ).

CONFUCIUS SAY: 1939; words and music: Friend, Cliff (1893-   ); Lombardo, Guy (1903-   ).

CONSTANTINOPLE: 1928; words: Brown, Lew (1893-   ); Carlton, Harry; De Sylva, Buddy (1895-1950); music: Henderson, Ray (1896-   ).

CONSTANTLY: 1942 (movie: *The Road to Morocco*); words: Burke, Johnny (1908-   ): music: Van Heusen, Jimmy (1913-   ).

COPENHAGEN: 1924; Davis, Charlie.

COQUETTE: 1928; words: Kahn, Gus (1886-1941); music: Green, Johnny (1908-   ); Lombardo, Carmen (1903-   ).

COSI—COSA: 1935; (movie: *A Night at the Opera*); words: Washington, Ned (1901-   ); music: Kaper, Bronislaw (1902-   ); Jurmann, Walter (1903-   ).

COUNT EVERY STAR: 1950; words: Gallop, Sammy (1915-   ); music: Coquatrix, Bruno.

COUNTING THE DAYS: 1945; words: Zaret, Hy (Hyman H. Zaret) (1907-   ); music: Kramer, Alex (1903-   ).

COW COW BOOGIE: 1941; words and music: Carter, Benny (1907-   ); De Paul, Gene (1919-   ); Raye, Don (Donald Mac Rae Wilhoite, Jr.) (1909-   ).

CRUISING DOWN THE RIVER: 1945; words and music: Beadell, Eily; Tollerton, Nell.

CRYING FOR THE CAROLINES: 1930; (movie: *Spring Is Here*); words: Lewis, Sam M. (1885-   ); music: Young, Joseph (1889-1939).

CUANTO LE GUSTA: 1948; (movie: *A Date With Judy*); words: Gilbert, Ray (1912-   ); music: Ruiz, Gabriel.

CUBAN PETE: 1936; Norman, José.

THE CURSE OF AN ACHING HEART (YOU MADE ME WHAT I AM TODAY): 1913; Fink, Henry (1893-   ); Piantadosi, Al (1884-   ).

DADDY'S LITTLE GIRL: 1905; words: Madden, Edward (1878-1952); music: Morse, Theodore F. (1873-1924).

DADDY, YOU'VE BEEN A MOTHER TO ME: 1920; words and music: Bryan, Alfred 1871-   ); Fischer, Fred (1875-1942).

DANCE OF THE PAPER DOLLS: 1928; words and music: Schuster, Joseph (1896-   ); Siras, John; Tucker, John A. (1896-   ).

DANCE WITH A DOLLY: 1940; words: Eaton, Jimmy (1906-   ); music: Kapp, David (1904-   ); Shand, Terry (1904-   ).

DANCING IN THE DARK: 1931; words: Dietz, Howard (1896-   ); music: Schwartz, Arthur (1900-   ).

DANCING WITH TEARS IN MY EYES: 1930; words: Dubin, Al (1891-1945); music: Burke, Joseph A. (1884-1950).

DANNY BOY: 1933; words: Weatherly, Frederick Edward; music: traditional Irish air.

DARDANELLA: 1919; words: Fisher, Fred (1875-1942); music: Bernard, Felix (1897-1944); Black, Johnny.

DARK EYES: 1926; music: arranged by Horlick, Harry and Stone, Gregory (1900-   ).

THE DARKTOWN STRUTTERS' BALL: 1917; Brooks, Shelton (1886-   ).

DAY BY DAY: 1945; words: Cahn, Sammy (1913-   ); music: Stordahl, Axel (1813-   ); Weston, Paul (1912-   ).

DAY DREAMING: 1941; words: Kahn, Gus (1886-1941); music: Kern, Jerome (1885-1945).

DAY IN, DAY OUT: 1939; words and music: Bloom, Rube (1902-   ); Mercer, Johnny (1909-   ).

DEAR HEARTS AND GENTLE PEOPLE: 1949; words: Hilliard, Bob (1918-   ); music: Fain, Sammy (1902-   ).

DEARIE: 1950; words: Hilliard, Bob (1918-   ); music: Mann, David (1916-   ).

DEAR LITTLE BOY OF MINE: 1918; words: Brennan, J. Keirn (1873-1948); music: Ball, Ernest R. (1878-1927).

DEARLY BELOVED: 1942; (movie: *You Were Never Lovelier*); Mercer, Johnny (1909-   ); Kern, Jerome (1885-1945).

DEAR OLD GIRL: 1903; words: Buck, Richard Henry (1870-   ); music: Morse, Theodore (1873-1924).

DEED I DO: 1936; words: Hirsch, Walter (1891-   ); music: Rose, Fred (1897-   ).

DEEP IN A DREAM: 1938; words: De Lange, Eddie (Edgar) (1904-1949); music: Van Heusen, Jimmy (1913-   ).

DEEP NIGHT: 1929; words: Vallee, Rudy, (Hubert P.) (1901-   ); music: Henderson, Charles E. (1907-   ).

DEEP PURPLE: 1934; words: Parish, Mitchell (1900-   ); music: De Rose, Peter (1900-   ).

DEEP RIVER: 1917; words and music: Burleigh, Harry T. (Henry Thacker Burleigh) (1866-1949); Fisher, Williams Arms (1861-1948).

DER FEUHRER'S FACE: 1942; words and music: Wallace, Oliver G. (1887-   ).

DIANE: 1927; (movie: *Seventh Heaven*);

words and music: Poallack, Lew (1895-1946); Rapee, Erno (1891-1945).

DID I REMEMBER?: 1936; (movie: *Suzy*); words: Adamson, Harold (1906-   ); music: Donaldson, Walter (1893-1947).

DID YOU EVER GET THAT FEELING IN THE MOONLIGHT?: 1944; words: Cavanaugh, James; music: Schuster, Ira (1889-1946), Stock, Larry (1896-   ).

DID YOU EVER SEE A DREAM WALKING?: 1933 (movie: *Sitting Pretty*); words: Gordon, Mack (1904-   ); music: Revel, Harry (1905-   ).

DIG YOU LATER (HUBBA, HUBBA, HUBBA): 1945; (movie: *Doll Face*); words: Adamson, Harold (1906-   ); music: McHugh, Jimmy (1894-   ).

DINAH: 1925; words: Lewis, Samuel M. (1885-   ); Young, Joseph (1889-1939); music: Akst, Harry (1894-   ).

DINNER FOR ONE, PLEASE, JAMES: 1935; Carr, Michael.

THE DIPSY DOODLE: 1937; Clinton, Larry (1909-   ).

DOCTOR, LAWYER, INDIAN CHIEF: 1945; (movie: *Stork Club*); words: Webster, Paul Francis (1907-   ); music: Carmichael, Hoagy (Hoagland) (1899-   ).

DOING THE UPTOWN LOWDOWN: 1933 (movie: *Broadway Thru' a Keyhole*); words: Gordon, Mack (1904-   ); music: Revel, Harry (1905-   ).

DO I WORRY: 1940; words and music: Cowan, Stanley (1918-   ); Worth, Bobby.

DOLORES: 1941 (movie: *Las Vegas Nights*); words: Loesser, Frank (1910-   ); music: Alter, Lou (1902-   ).

DONKEY SERENADE: 1937; (movie: *The Firefly*); words: Forrest, George (Chet) (1915-   ); Wright, Robert (1914-   ); music: Friml, Rudolf (1879-   ); Stothart, Herbert (d. 1949).

DO NOTHIN' TILL YOU HEAR FROM ME: 1943; words: Russell, Bob (Sidney Keith) (1914-   ); music: Ellington, Duke (1899-   ).

DON'T BLAME ME: 1933; words: Fields, Dorothy (1905-   ); music: McHugh, Jimmy (1894-   ).

DON'T BRING LULU: 1925; words: Brown, Lew (1893-   ); Rose, Billy (1899-   ); music: Henderson, Ray (1896-   ).

DON'T CRY: 1941; Skylar, Sunny (1913-   ).

DON'T CRY JOE: 1949; Marsala, Joe (1907-   ).

DON'T FENCE ME IN: 1944 (movie: *Hollywood Canteen*); Porter, Cole (1893-   ).

DON'T GET AROUND MUCH ANYMORE: 1942; words: Russell, Bob (Sidney Keith) (1914-   ); music: Ellington, Duke (1899-   ).

DON'T LET IT BOTHER YOU: 1934; (movie: *Gay Divorcee*); words: Gordon, Mack (1904-   ); music: Revel, Harry (1905-   ).

DON'T SIT UNDER THE APPLE TREE: 1942; words and music: Brown, Lew (1893-   ); Stept, Sam H. (1897-   ); Tobias, Charles (1898-   ).

DON'T SWEETHEART ME: 1943; words and music: Friend, Cliff (1893-   ); Tobias, Charles (1898-   ).

DON'T TAKE YOUR LOVE FROM ME: 1941; Nemo, Henry (1914-   ).

DOWN AMONG THE SHELTERING PALMS: 1915; words: Brockman, James (1886-   ); music: Olman, Abe (1888-   ).

DREAM: 1944; Mercer, John H. (Johnny) (1909-   ).

DREAMY MELODY: 1922; words and music: Magine, Frank (1888-   ); Koehler, Ted (1894-   ); Naset, C.

EASY COME, EASY GO: 1934; words: Heyman, Edward (1907-   ); music: Green, Johnny (1908-   ).

EASY TO LOVE: 1937; words and music: Cole Porter (1893-   ).

EBBTIDE: 1937; words: Robin, Leo (1900-   ); music: Rainger, Ralph (1901-1942).

EEENY MEENY MINEY MO: 1935; (movie: *To Beat the Band*); words and music: Malneck, Matty (1904-   ); Mercer, Johnny (1909-   ).

ELMER'S TUNE: 1941; words and music: Albrecht, Elmer (1901-   ); Gallop, Sammy (1915-   ); Jurgens, Dick (1911-   ).

EL RANCHO GRANDE: 1934; words: Costello, Bartley C. (1871-1941); music: Wranga, Emilio D.

EMPTY SADDLES: 1936; words: Brennan, J. Keirn (1873-1948); music: Hill, William J. (Billy Hill) (1899-1940).

ENJOY YOURSELF (IT'S LATER THAN YOU THINK): 1948; words: Magidson, Herbert (Herb) (1906-   ); music: Sigman, Carl (1909-   ).

EVERYBODY LOVES MY BABY (BUT MY BABY DON'T LOVE NOBODY BUT ME): 1924; words and music: Palmer, Jack (1900-   ); Williams, Spencer (1889-   ).

EVERYTHING DEPENDS ON YOU: 1935; words: Carpenter, Charles (1912-   ); Dunlap, Louis (-   ); music: Hines, Earl Kenneth (1905-   ).

EVERYTHING HAPPENS TO ME: 1941; words: Adair, Thomas M. (1913-   ); music: Dennis Matt (-   ).

EVERYTHING I HAVE IS YOURS: 1933; (movie: *Dancing Lady*); words: Adamson, Harold (1906-   ); music: Lane, Burton (1912-   ).

EVERYTIME: 1941; words: Martin, Hugh (1914-   ); music: Jenkins, Gordon (1910-   ).

FAIR AND WARMER: 1934; (movie: *Twenty Million Sweethearts*); words: Dubin, Al (1891-1945); music: Warren, Harry (1893-   ).

FAR AWAY PLACES: 1948; Kramer, Alex (1903-   ); Whitney, Joan (1914-   ).

FARE THEE WELL, ANNABELLE: 1934; (movie: *Sweet Music*); words: Dixon, Mort (1892-   ); music: Wrubel, Allie (1905-   ).

FAREWELL TO ARMS: 1933; Silver, Abner (-   ); Wrubel, Allie (1905-   ).

FERDINAND THE BULL: 1938; (Walt Disney's *Ferdinand the Bull*); words: Morey, Larry (1905-   ); music: Malotte, Albert Hay (1895-   ).

THE FERRYBOAT SERENADE: 1940; words and music: Adamson, Harold (1906-   ); El Di Lazarro.

FIVE FOOT TWO, EYES OF BLUE: 1925; words: Lewis, Samuel M. (1885-   ); Young, Joseph (1889-1939); music: Henderson, Ray (1896-   ).

FIVE MINUTES MORE: 1946 (movie: *Sweethearts of Sigma Chi*); words: Cahn, Sammy (1913-   ); music: Styne, Jule (1905-   ).

FLAT FOOT FLOOGIE: 1938; words and music: Gaillard, Bulee (Slim) (1916-   ); Green, Bud (1897-   ); Stewart, Slam.

FLIRTATION WALK: 1934; words: Dixon, Mort (1892-   ); music: Wrubel, Allie (1905-   ).

FLOWERS FOR MADAME: 1935; words: Newman, Charles; music: Menscher, Murray (Ted Murray) (1898-   ); Tobias, Charles (1898-   ).

FLYING DOWN TO RIO: 1933; (movie: *Flying Down to Rio*); words: Eliscu, Edward (1902-   ); Kahn, Gus (1886-1941); music: Youmans, Vincent (1898-1946).

A FOGGY DAY: 1937; (movie: *A Damsel in*

Distress); words: Gershwin, Ira (1896-);
music: Gershwin, George (1898-1937).
FOOLS RUSH IN: 1940; words: Mercer,
Johnny (1909-); music: Bloom, Rube
(1902-).
FOR ALL WE KNOW: 1934; words: Lewis,
Samuel M. (1885-); music: Coots, J. Fred
(1897-).
FOR ME AND MY GAL: 1917; words: Les-
lie, Edgar (1885-); Goetz, E. Ray (1886-
); music: Meyer, George W. (1885-).
FOR SENTIMENTAL REASONS: 1936; words:
Heyman, Edward (1907-); music: Sher-
man, Al (1897-); Silver, Abner (1899-).
FORTY-SECOND STREET: 1932; (movie:
Forty-second Street); words: Dubin, Al (1891-
1945); music: Warren, Harry (1893-).
FRENESI: 1939; words (English): Charles,
Ray; Russell, Bob (Sidney Keith) (1914-);
Whitcup, Leonard (1903-); words (Span-
ish) and music: Dominguez, Albert.
A FRIEND OF YOURS: 1944; (movie: *The
Great John L.);* words and music: Burke,
Johnny (1908-); Van Heusen, Jimmy
(1913-).
FROM THE TOP OF YOUR HEAD TO THE
TIP OF YOUR TOES: 1935; words: Gor-
don, Mack (1904-); music: Revel, Harry
(1905-).
FULL MOON AND EMPTY ARMS: 1946;
words and music: Kaye, Buddy (1918-);
Mossman, Ted (1912-).
FUNNY OLD HILLS: 1938; words: Robin,
Leo (1900-); music: Rainger, Ralph (1901-
1942).
FUZZY WUZZY: 1944; words and music:
Drake, Milton, (1912-); Hoffman, Al
(1902-); Livingston, Jerry (1909-).
A GAL IN CALICO: 1947; words: Robin,
Leo (1900-); music: Schwartz, Arthur
(1900-).
THE GAUCHO SERENADE: 1939; words:
Cavanaugh, James (Jimmy); music: Red-
mond, John (1906-); Simon, Nat (1900-
).
THE GENTLEMAN OBVIOUSLY DOESN'T
BELIEVE: 1935; words and music: Carr,
Michael; Pola, Edward (1907-).
GEORGIA ON MY MIND: 1930; words: Gor-
rell, Stuart; music: Carmichael, Hoagy (Hoag-
land) (1899-).
GET HAPPY: 1930; words: Koehler, Ted
(1894-); music: Arlen, Harold (1905-).
GET OUT AND GET UNDER THE MOON:
1928; words: Jerome, William (1865-1932);
Tobias, Charles (1898-); music: Shay,
Larry (1897-).
GHOST OF A CHANCE: words: Crosby,
Bing (1904-); Washington, Ned (1901-);
music: Young, Victor (1900-).
GIMME A LITTLE KISS, WILL YA HUH?:
1926; words and music: Pinkard, Maceo
(1897-); Smith, Jack; Turk, Roy (1892-
1934).
GIVE A LITTLE WHISTLE: 1940; words:
Washington, Ned (1901-); music: Harline,
Leigh (1907-).
GIVE ME THE SIMPLE LIFE: 1945; (movie:
Give Me the Simple Life); words: Ruby,
Harry (1895-); music: Bloom, Rube (1902-
).
GOD BLESS AMERICA: 1939; Berlin, Irving
(1888-).
GOING MY WAY: 1944; (movie: *Going My
Way);* words: Burke, Johnny (1908-);
music: Van Heusen, Jimmy (1913-).
GOLDEN EARRINGS: 1946; (movie: *Golden
Earrings);* words: Evans, Raymond B.
(1915-); Livingston, Jay Harold (1915-
); music: Young, Victor (1900-).

GOLDMINE IN THE SKY: 1938; words:
Kenny, Nick (1895-); music: Kenny,
Charles F. (1898-).
GONE FISHIN': 1950; words and music:
Kenny, Charles F. (1898-); Kenny, Nick
(1895-).
GOOD BYE BROADWAY, HELLO FRANCE:
1917; words and music: Baskette, Billy
(1884-1949); Davis, Benny (1895-); Reisner,
C. Francis.
GOOD, GOOD, GOOD: 1944; words and
music: Fisher, Doris (1915-); Roberts,
Allan (1905-).
GOODNIGHT, MY LOVE: 1936 (movie: *Stow-
away);* words: Gordon, Mack (1904-);
music: Revel, Harry (1905-).
GOODNIGHT, WHEREVER YOU ARE: 1944;
Hoffman, Al (1902-); Robertson, Dick
(1903-); Weldon, Frank.
GOODY GOODY: 1936; words and music:
Mercer, John H. (Johnny) (1909-); Mal-
neck, Matty (1904-).
GOT A DATE WITH AN ANGEL: 1931;
words and music: Grey, Clifford (1887-
1941); Miller, Sonnie; Tunbridge, Joseph;
Waller, Jack.
GOTTA BE THIS OR THAT: 1945; words
and music: Skylar, Sunny (1913-).
GOTTA GET ME SOMEBODY TO LOVE:
1946 (movie: *Duel in the Sun);* Wrubel, Allie
(1905-).
HAPPY DAYS ARE HERE AGAIN: 1929;
words: Yellen, Jack (1892-); music:
Ager, Milton (1893-).
HAVE YOU EVER BEEN LONELY?: 1933;
words and music: De Rose, Peter (1900-);
Hill, William J. (Billy) (1899-1940).
HAVE YOU GOT ANY CASTLES?: 1937;
words and music: Mercer, Johnny (1909-);
Whiting, Richard A. (1891-1938).
HAWAIIAN WAR CHANT: 1931; words:
Freed, Ralph (1907-); music: Noble, John-
ny (1892-1944); Lelelohoku.
HEARTACHES: 1931; words and music: Hoff-
man, Al (1902-); Klenner, John (1899-).
HEAVEN CAN WAIT: 1939; words and mu-
sic: De Lange, Eddie (Edgar) (1904-1949); Van
Heusen, Jimmy (1913-).
HEIGH HO: 1938; words: Morey, Larry
(1905-); music: Churchill, Frank E.
(1901-1942); Singer, Dolph (1900-1942).
HELLO FRISCO: 1915; words: Buck, Gene (Ed-
ward Eugene Buck) (1885-); music: Hirsch,
Louis Achille (1887-1924).
HERE COMES COOKIE: 1935 (movie: *Love
in Bloom);* words: Gordon, Mack (1904-);
music: Revel, Harry (1905-).
HERE COMES THE SHOW BOAT: 1927;
words: Rose, Billy (1899-); music: Pink-
ard, Maceo (1897-).
HERE LIES LOVE: 1932; words: Robin, Leo
(1900-); music: Rainger, Ralph (1901-1942).
HERE'S TO ROMANCE: 1935; (movie: *Here's
to Romance);* words and music: Conrad,
Con (1891-1938); Magidson, Herbert (Herb)
(1906-).
HE'S MY GUY: 1943; words and music:
Raye, Don (Donald MacRae Wilhoite, Jr.)
(1909-); De Paul; Gene (1919-).
HE'S 1-A IN THE ARMY (AND A-1 IN MY
HEART): 1941; words and music: Evans,
Reed (1912-).
HIGH ON A WINDY HILL: 1941; Kramer,
Alex (1903-); Whitney, Joan (1914-).
HITCHY KOO: 1912; words: Gilbert, L. Wolfe
(1886-); Muir, Lewis F.; music: Abrahams,
Maurice (Maurie) (1883-1931).
HOLD ME: 1920; words and music: Black,
Ben (1889-1950); Hickman, Art (1886-1930).

HOLIDAY FOR STRINGS: 1943; Gallop, Sammy (1915-   ); Rose, David (1910-   ).

HONEYSUCKLE ROSE: 1929; words: Razaf, Andy (Andreamenentania Paul Razafinkeriefo) (1895-   ); music: Waller, Thomas (Fats) (1904-1943).

HONG KONG BLUES: 1939; words and music: Carmichael, Hoagy (Hoagland) (1899-   ).

HOW ABOUT YOU?: 1941; words: Freed, Ralph (1907-   ); music: Lane, Burton (1912-   ).

HOW BLUE THE NIGHT: 1944; words: Adamson, Harold (1906-   ); music: McHugh, Jimmy (1894-   ).

HOW COME YOU DO ME LIKE YOU DO?: 1924; words and music: Austin, Gene (1904-   ); Bergere, Roy (1899-   ).

HOW MANY HEARTS HAVE YOU BROKEN?: 1943; words: Symes, Marty (1904-   ); music: Kaufman, Alvin S. (1910-   ).

HOW SWEET YOU ARE: 1943; words and music: Loesser, Frank (1910-   ); Schwartz, Arthur 1900-   ).

HOW YOU GONNA KEEP 'EM DOWN ON THE FARM, AFTER THEY'VE SEEN PAREE?: 1919; words: Lewis, Samuel M. (1885-   ); Young, Joseph (1889-1939); music: Donaldson, Walter (1893-1947).

THE HUCKLE BUCK: 1949; words: Alfred, Roy (1916-   ); music: Gibson, Albert Andrew (1913-   ).

HUGGIN' AND CHALKIN': 1947; words: Goell, Kermit (1915-   ); music: Hayes, Clancy.

HUMPTY DUMPTY HEART: 1941; (movie: Playmates); words: Burke, Johnny (1908-   ); music: Van Heusen, Jimmy (1913-   ).

HUT SUT SONG: 1939; words and music: Owens, John Milton (Jack) (1912-   ); Killian, Leo V.; McMichael, Ted.

I AIN'T GOT NOBODY: 1916; words: Lewis, Samuel M. (1885-   ); music: Baer, Abel (1893-   ); Williams, Spencer (1889-   ).

I CAME HERE TO TALK FOR JOE: 1943; words: Brown, Lew (1893-   ); music: Stept, Sam H. (1897-   ); Tobias, Charles (1898-   ).

I CAN DREAM, CAN'T I?: 1937; words: Kahal, Irving (1903-1942); music: Fain, Sammy (1902-   ).

I CAN'T GET STARTED: 1936; words: Gershwin, Ira (1896-   ); music: Duke, Vernon (Vladimir Dukelsky) (1903-   ).

I CAN'T GIVE YOU ANYTHING BUT LOVE, BABY: 1928; words: Fields, Dorothy (1905-   ); music: McHugh, Jimmy (1894-   ).

I CAN'T TELL WHY I LOVE YOU BUT I DO: 1900; words: Cobb, Will D. (1876-1930); music: Edwards, Gus (1879-1945).

I COULDN'T SLEEP A WINK LAST NIGHT: 1943 (movie: Higher and Higher); words: Adamson, Harold (1906-   ); music: McHugh, Jimmy (1894-   ).

I COVER THE WATERFRONT: 1932; words: Heyman, Edward (1907-   ); music: Green, Johnny (John W.) (1908-   ).

I CRIED FOR YOU: 1922; words: Freed, Arthur (1894-   ); music: Arnheim, Gus (1897-   ); Lyman, Abe (1897-   ).

IDA, SWEET AS APPLE CIDER: 1903; Leonard, Eddie (1875-1941); Munson, Eddie.

I'D CLIMB THE HIGHEST MOUNTAIN: 1926; words: Brown, Lew (1893-   ); music: Clare, Sidney (1892-   ).

I DIDN'T KNOW ABOUT YOU: 1944; words: Russell, Bob (Sidney Keith) (1914-   ); music: Ellington, Duke (Edward Kennedy Ellington) (1899-   ).

I DO, DO, DO LIKE YOU: 1947; Wrubel, Allie (1905-   ).

I DON'T KNOW WHY: 1931; words: Turk, Roy (1892-1934); music: Ahlert, Fred E. (1892-   ).

I DON'T SEE ME IN YOUR EYES ANYMORE: 1949; Benjamin, Bennie (1907-   ); Weiss, George David (1921-   ).

I DON'T STAND A GHOST OF A CHANCE WITH YOU: 1932; words: Crosby, Bing (Harry Lillis) (1904-   ); Washington, Ned (1901-   ); music: Young, Victor (1900-   ).

I DON'T WANT TO GET WELL: 1917; words: Johnson, Howard E. (1887-1941); music: Jentes, Harry (-   ); Pease, Harry (1886-1945).

I DON'T WANT TO SET THE WORLD ON FIRE: 1941; words: Seiler, Edward (1911-1952); music: Benjamin, Bennie (1907-   ); Marcus, Sol (1912-   ).

I DON'T WANT TO WALK WITHOUT YOU: 1942 (movie: Sweater Girl); words: Cahn, Sammy (1913-   ); music: Styne, Jule (1905-   ).

I DOUBLE DARE YOU: 1937; words: Eaton, Jimmy (1906-   ); music: Shand, Terry (1904-   ).

I DREAM OF YOU MORE THAN YOU DREAM I DO: 1944; words and music: Goetschius, Marjorie (1915-   ); Osser, Edna (1919-   ).

I FALL IN LOVE TOO EASILY: 1945; words: Cahn, Sammy (1913-   ); music: Styne, Jule (1905-   ).

I FALL IN LOVE WITH YOU EVERY DAY: 1946; words: Altman, Arthur; music: Stept, Sam H. (1897-   ).

I FEEL A SONG COMIN' ON: 1935; words: Fields, Dorothy (1905-   ); music: McHugh, Jimmy (1894-   ).

I FEEL LIKE A FEATHER IN THE BREEZE: 1936 (movie: Collegiate); words: Gordon, Mack (1904-   ); music: Revel, Harry (1905-   ).

IF I COULD BE WITH YOU ONE HOUR TONIGHT: 1926; words: Creamer, Henry (1879-1930); music: Johnson, Jimmy (James P.) (1894-   ).

IF I DIDN'T CARE: 1939; words amd music: Ager, Milton (1893-   ); Lawrence, Jack (1912-   ).

IF I HAD A TALKING PICTURE OF YOU: 1929; words: Brown, Lew (1893-   ); De Sylva, Buddy (1895-1950); music: Henderson, Ray (1896-   ).

IF I HAD MY WAY: 1913; words: Klein, James (1883-1946).

IF I KNEW YOU WERE COMING I'D HAVE BAKED A CAKE: 1950; words and music: Hoffman, Al (1902-   ); Merrill, Bob (1922-   ).Trace, Al (Albert, J. Trace Clem Watts) (1900-   ).

IF I LOVE AGAIN: 1932; words: Murray, John (1906-   ); music: Oakland, Ben (1907-   ).

IF YOU KNEW SUSIE: 1925; words: De Sylva, Buddy (1895-1950); music: Meyer, Joseph (1892-   ).

IF YOU WERE THE ONLY GIRL IN THE WORLD: 1929; words: Grey, Clifford (1887-1941); music: Ayer, Nat D.

I GET ALONG WITHOUT YOU VERY WELL: 1939; Carmichael, Hoagy (Hoagland) (1899-   ).

I GOT IT BAD AND THAT AIN'T GOOD: 1941; words: Webster, Paul Francis (1907-   ); music: Ellington, Duke (1899-   ).

I GUESS I'LL HAVE TO CHANGE MY PLAN: 1932; words: Dietz, Howard (1896-   ); music: Schwartz, Arthur (1900-   ).

I GUESS I'LL HAVE TO DREAM THE

REST: Stoner, Michael S. (Mickey Stoner) (1911-   ).

I HAD THE CRAZIEST DREAM: 1942; words: Gordon, Mack (1904-   ); music: Warren, Harry (1893-   ).

I HEARD YOU CRIED LAST NIGHT: 1943; Grouya, Theodor J. (Ted. Grouya) (1910-); Kruger, Jerrie.

I JUST CAN'T MAKE MY EYES BEHAVE: 1906; words: Cobb, Will D. (1876-1930); music: Edwards, Gus (1879-1945).

I KISS YOUR HAND MADAME: 1928; words: Rotter, Fritz (1900-   ); Young, Joseph (1889-1939); music: Erwin, Ralph.

I KNOW THAT YOU KNOW: 1926; words: O'Dea, Anne Caldwell (1867-1936); music: Youmans, Vincent (1898-1946).

I LIKE MOUNTAIN MUSIC: 1933; words: Cavanaugh, James (Jimmy); music: Weldon, Frank.

I LIKE NEW YORK IN JUNE (HOW ABOUT YOU): 1941; words: Freed, Ralph (1907-); music: Lane, Burton (1912-   ).

I'LL ALWAYS BE IN LOVE WITH YOU: 1929; Ruby, Harry (1895-   ); Stept, Sam H. (1897-   ).

I'LL BE HOME FOR CHRISTMAS: 1943; Gannon, Kim (James Kimball Gannon) (1900-   ); Kent, Walter (1911-   ); Ram, Buck (1908-   ).

I'LL BE SEEING YOU: 1944; words: Kahal, Irving (1903-1942); music: Fain, Sammy (1902-   ).

I'LL BE WITH YOU IN APPLE BLOSSOM TIME: 1920; words: Fleeson, Neville (1887-1945); music: Von Tilzer, Albert (1878-   ).

I'LL BUY THAT DREAM: 1945; (movie: *Sing Your Way Home*); words: Magidson, Herbert (Herb) (1906-); music: Wrubel, Allie (1905-   ).

I'LL CLOSE MY EYES: 1945; words; Kaye, Buddy (1918-   ); music: Alexander, Van (1915-   ); Tinturin, Peter (1910-   ).

I'LL DANCE AT YOUR WEDDING: 1947; words: Magidson, Herbert (Herb) (1906-   ); music: Oakland, Ben (1907-   ).

I'LL GET BY: 1928; words: Turk, Roy (1892-1934); music: Ahlert, Fred E. (1892-).

I'LL NEVER SMILE AGAIN: 1939; Lowe, Ruth (1914-   ).

I'LL REMEMBER APRIL: 1941; words: Johnston, Patricia (1922-   ); music: De Paul, Gene (1919-   ); Raye, Don (Donald MacRae Wilhoite, Jr.) (1909-   ).

I'LL SEE YOU IN MY DREAMS: 1924; words: Kahn, Gus (1886-1941); music: Jones, Isham (1894-   ).

I'LL SING YOU A THOUSAND LOVE SONGS: 1936; words: Dubin, Al (1891-1945); music: Warren, Harry (1893-   ).

I'LL TAKE YOU HOME AGAIN, KATHLEEN: 1875; words and music: Westendorf, Thomas P.

I'LL WALK ALONE: 1944 (movie: *Follow the Boys)*; words: Cahn, Sammy (1913-   ); music: Styne, Jule (1905-   ).

I LOVE AN OLD-FASHIONED SONG: 1946; (movie: *The Kid From Brooklyn)*; words: Cahn, Sammy (1913-   ); music: Styne, Jule (1905-   ).

I LOVE A PARADE: 1932; words: Koehler, Ted (1894-   ); music: Arlen, Harold (1905-   ).

I LOVE LOUISA: 1931; words: Dietz, Howard (1896-   ); Schwartz, Arthur (1900-   ).

I'M A BIG GIRL NOW: 1946; Drake, Milton (1912-   ); Hoffman, Al (1902-   ); Livingston, Jerry (1909-   ).

I'M A DREAMER (AREN'T WE ALL?):

1929; words: Brown, Lew (1893-   ); De Sylva, Buddy (1895-1950); music: Henderson, Ray (1896-   ).

I'M AFRAID THE MASQUERADE IS OVER: 1939; words: Magidson, Herb (1906-   ); music: Wrubel, Allie (1905-   ).

IMAGINATION: 1940; Burke, Johnny (1908-); Van Heusen, Jimmy (1913-).

I'M ALWAYS CHASING RAINBOWS: 1918; words: McCarthy, Joseph (1885-1943); music: Carroll, Harry (1892-   ).

I'M AN OLD COW HAND: 1936; Mercer, John H. (Johnny) (1909-   ).

I'M BEGINNING TO SEE THE LIGHT: 1944; Ellington, Duke (1899-   ); George, Don (1909-   ); Hodges, Johnny (1907-   ); James, Harry (1916-   ).

I'M BUBBLING OVER: 1937 (movie: *Wake Up and Live)*; words: Gordon, Mack (1904-); music: Revel, Harry (1905-   ).

I'M BUILDING UP TO AN AWFUL LETDOWN: 1935; Mercer, John H. (Johnny) (1909-   ).

I'M DANCING WITH TEARS IN MY EYES: 1930; words: Dubin, Al (1891-1945); music: Burke, Joseph A. (1884-1950).

I MET HER ON MONDAY: 1942; words: Newman, Charles; music: Wrubel, Allie (1905-   ).

I'M GETTING SENTIMENTAL OVER YOU: 1933; words: Washington, Ned (1901-   ); music: Bassman, George (1914-   ).

I'M GETTING TIRED SO I CAN SLEEP: 1942; Berlin, Irving (1888-   ).

I'M GLAD I WAITED FOR YOU: 1946 (movie: *Tars and Spars);* words: Cahn, Sammy (1913-   ); music: Styne, Jule (1905-   ).

I'M GONNA SIT RIGHT DOWN AND WRITE MYSELF A LETTER: 1935; words: Young, Joseph (1889-1939); music: Ahlert, Fred E. (1892-   ).

I'M IN THE MOOD FOR LOVE: 1935; words: Fields, Dorothy (1905-   ); music: McHugh, Jimmy (1894-   ).

I'M LOOKING OVER A FOUR LEAFED CLOVER: 1927; words: Dixon, Mort (1892-   ); music: Woods, Harry M. (1896-   ).

I'M MY OWN GRANDPAW: 1948; Jaffe, Moe (1901-   ); Latham, Dwight B. (1903-   ).

I'M NOBODY'S BABY: 1921; words: Davis, Benny (1895-   ); music: Ager, Milton (1893-   ); Santly, Lester (1894-   ).

I'M PUTTING ALL MY EGGS IN ONE BASKET: 1936; Berlin, Irving (1888-   ).

I'M SITTING ON TOP OF THE WORLD: 1925; words: Lewis, Samuel M. (1885-); Young, Joseph (1889-1939); music: Henderson, Ray (1896-   ).

I'M YOURS: 1930; words: Harburg, E. Y. ("Yip") (1898-   ); music: Green, Johnny (John W.) (1908-   ).

IN A LITTLE GYPSY TEAROOM: 1935; words: Leslie, Edgar (1885-   ); music: Burke, Joseph A. (1884-1950).

IN A LITTLE SPANISH TOWN: 1926; words: Lewis, Samuel M. (1885-   ); Young, Joseph (1889-1939); music: Wayne, Mabel (1904-   ).

IN A SHANTY IN OLD SHANTY TOWN: 1932; words: Young, Joseph (1889-1939); music: Little, Jack (Little Jack Little) (1900-   ); Schuster, Ira (1889-1946); Siras, John.

I NEVER MENTION YOUR NAME: 1943; words: Davis, Mack; music: George, Don R. (1909-   ); Kent, Walter (1911-   ).

IN LOVE IN VAIN: 1946; (movie: *Centennial Summer);* words: Robin, Leo (1900-   ); music: Kern, Jerome (1885-1945).

IN MY ARMS: 1943; words and music:

Grouya, Theodor J. (Ted Grouya) (1910-   );
Loesser, Frank (1910-   ).

IN MY MERRY OLDSMOBILE: 1905; words:
Bryan, Vincent; music: Edwards, Gus (1879-
1945).

IN THE BLUE OF EVENING: 1942; words:
Adair, Thomas M. (1913-   ); music: D'Arte-
ga, Alfonso (1907-   ).

IN THE EVENING BY THE MOONLIGHT:
1880; words and music: Bland, James A.

IN THE LAND OF BEGINNING AGAIN:
1918; words: Clarke, Grant (1891-1931); music: Meyer, George W. (1885-   ).

IN THE MOOD: 1939; words: Razaf, Andy
(Andreamenentania Paul Razafinkeriefo)
(1895-   ); music: Garland, Joseph C. (1903-
).

IN THE SHADE OF THE OLD APPLE
TREE: 1905; words: Williams, Harry (1895-
1922); music: Van Alstyne, Egbert Anson
(1882-1951).

IN THE STILL OF THE NIGHT: 1937;
Porter, Cole (1893-   ).

IN THE VALLEY OF THE MOON: 1933;
Burke, Joseph A. (1884-1950); Tobias, Charles
(1905-   ).

I PROMISE YOU: 1938; words: Lerner,
Sammy (Samuel M.) (1903-   ); music: Oakland, Ben (1907-   ).

I SAID NO: 1942 (movie: Sweater Girl);
words: Cahn, Sammy (1913-   ); music: Styne,
Jule (1905-   ).

I SCREAM, YOU SCREAM, WE ALL
SCREAM (FOR ICE CREAM): 1927; words:
Johnson, Howard E. (1887-1941); music: Moll,
Billy (1905-   ).

I SHOULD CARE: 1944; words: Cahn,
Sammy (1913-   ); music: Stordahl, Axel
(1913-   ); Weston, Paul (1912-   ).

IS IT TRUE WHAT THEY SAY ABOUT
DIXIE?: 1936; words: Caesar, Irving
(1895-   ); Lerner, Sammy (Samuel H.)
(1903-   ); music: Marks, Gerald (1900-   ).

I SURRENDER DEAR: 1932; words: Clifford, Gordon (1902-   ); music: Barris, Harry (1905-   ).

IT AIN'T GONNA RAIN NO MO': 1923;
Hall, Wendell Woods (1896-   ).

IT ALL DEPENDS ON YOU: 1926; words
and music: Brown, Lew (1893-   ); De Sylva,
Buddy (George) (1895-1950); Henderson, Ray
(1896-   ).

IT COULD HAPPEN TO YOU: 1944; words:
Burke, Johnny (1908-   ); music: Van Heusen, Jimmy (1913-   ).

IT DON'T MEAN A THING IF IT AIN'T
GOT THAT SWING: 1932; Ellington, Duke
(1899-   ); Mills, Irving (1894-   ).

IT HAD TO BE YOU: 1924; words: Kahn,
Gus (1886-1941); music: Jones, Isham (1894-
).

IT LOOKS LIKE RAIN IN CHERRY BLOS-
SOM LANE: 1937; words: Leslie, Edgar
(1885-   ); music: Burke, Joseph A. (1884-
1950).

I TOLD EVERY LITTLE STAR: 1932;
words: Hammerstein II, Oscar (1895-   );
music: Kern, Jerome (1885-1945).

IT'S A HAP-HAP-HAPPY DAY: 1939;
words: Neiburg, Al J. (Allen) (1902-   );
music: Sharpless, Winston S. (1909-   ); Tim-
berg, Sammy (1903-   ).

IT'S ALWAYS YOU: 1941 (movie: Road to
Zanzibar); words: Burke, Johnny (1908-   );
music: Van Heusen, Jimmy (1913-   ).

IT'S A MOST UNUSUAL DAY: 1948; words:
Adamson, Harold (1906-   ); music: McHugh,
Jimmy (1894-   ).

IT'S BEEN A LONG, LONG TIME: 1945;

words: Cahn, Sammy (1913-   ); music:
Styne, Jule (1905-   ).

IT'S BEEN SO LONG: 1935; words: Adamson, Harold (1906-   ); music: Donaldson,
Walter (1893-1947).

IT'S DELOVELY: 1936; Porter, Cole (1893-   ).

IT SEEMS I'VE HEARD THAT SONG BE-
FORE: 1942 (movie: Youth on Parade);
words: Cahn, Sammy (1913-   ); music:
Styne, Jule (1905-   ).

IT'S MAGIC: 1948 (movie: Romance on the
High Seas); words: Cahn, Sammy (1913-   );
music: Styne, Jule (1905-   ).

IT'S ONLY A PAPER MOON: 1933; words:
Harburg, E. Y. ("Yip") (1898-   ); Rose, Billy
(1899-   ); music: Arlen, Harold (1905-   ).

IT'S SO NICE TO HAVE A MAN AROUND
THE HOUSE: 1950; words and music: El-
liott, John M. (Jack) (1914-   ); Spina,
Harold (1906-   ).

IT'S SO PEACEFUL IN THE COUNTRY:
1941; Wilder, Alec (1907-   ).

IT'S THE TALK OF THE TOWN: 1933;
words: Neiburg, Al J. (Allen) (1902-   );
Symes, Marty (1904-   ); music: Levinson, J.

IT'S YOU OR NO ONE: 1948 (movie: Romance on the High Seas); words: Cahn,
Sammy (1913-   ); music: Styne, Jule (1905-
).

I USED TO LOVE YOU BUT IT'S ALL
OVER: 1920; words: Brown, Lew (1893-   );
music: Von Tilzer, Albert (1878-   ).

I'VE GOT A DATE WITH A DREAM: 1938;
(movie: My Lucky Star); words: Gordon,
Mack (1904-   ); music: Revel, Harry (1905-
).

I'VE GOT A FEELING I'M FALLING: 1929;
words: Rose, Billy (1899-   ); music: Link,
Harry (1896-   ); Waller, Thomas (Fats)
(1904-1943).

I'VE GOT A FEELING YOU'RE FOOLIN':
1936; words: Freed, Arthur (1894-   ); music:
Brown, Nacio Herb (1896-   ).

I'VE GOT A GAL IN KALAMAZOO: 1942;
words: Gordon, Mack (1904-   ); music: Warren, Harry (1893-   ).

I'VE GOT FIVE DOLLARS: 1931; words:
Hart, Lorenz (1895-1943); music: Rodgers,
Richard (1902-   ).

I'VE GOT MY HEART SET ON YOU: 1937;
(movie: Ali Baba Goes to Town); words:
Gordon, Mack (1904-   ); music: Revel, Harry (1905-   ).

I'VE GOT MY LOVE TO KEEP ME WARM:
1937; Berlin, Irving (1888-   ).

I'VE GOT YOU UNDER MY SKIN: 1936;
Porter, Cole (1893-   ).

I'VE HEARD THAT SONG BEFORE: 1942;
words: Cahn, Sammy (1913-   ); music:
Styne, Jule (1905-   ).

I WANT A GIRL (JUST LIKE THE GIRL
THAT MARRIED DEAR OLD DAD):
words: Dillon, William A. (1877-   ); music:
Von Tilzer, Harry (1872-1946).

I WANT TO BE HAPPY: 1924; words: Caesar, Irving (1895-   ); music: Youmans, Vincent (1898-1946).

I WISH I DIDN'T LOVE YOU SO: 1947
(movie: The Perils of Pauline); Loesser,
Frank (1910-   ).

I WISH I KNEW: 1945; words: Gordon, Mack
(1904-   ); music: Warren, Harry (1893-   ).

I WONDER WHAT'S BECOME OF SALLY:
1924; words: Yellen, Jack (1892-   ); music:
Ager, Milton (1893-   ).

I WONDER WHO'S KISSING HER NOW:
1909; words: Adams, Frank R. (1883-   );
Hough, Will M. (1882-   ); music: Howard,
Joseph E. (1878-   ); Orlob, Harold (1885-   ).

I WON'T DANCE: 1933; words: Fields, Dorothy (1905-   ); music: Kern, Jerome (1885-1945); McHugh, Jimmie (1894-   ).

JA DA: 1918; Carleton, Bob (Robert Louis) (1896-   ).

JAPANESE SANDMAN: 1920; words: Egan, Raymond B. (1890-   ); music: Whiting, Richard A. (1891-1938).

JEALOUSY: 1926; words: Bloom, Vera; music: Gade, Jacob.

JEANNINE, I DREAM OF LILAC TIME: 1928; words: Gilbert, L. Wolfe (1886-   ); music: Shilkret, Jack (1896-   ).

JEEPERS CREEPERS: 1938; Mercer, John H. (Johnny) (1909-   ); Warren, Harry (1893-   ).

JIM: 1941; Petrillo, Caesar (1898-   ); Samuels, Milton (1904-   ); Shawn, Nelson A. (1898-1945).

JINGLE JANGLE JINGLE: 1942; Lilly, Joseph J. (1913-   ); Loesser, Frank (1910-   ).

JUNE IN JANUARY: 1934; words: Robin, Leo (1900-   ); music: Rainger, Ralph (1901-1942).

JUST A COTTAGE SMALL BY A WATER-FALL: 1925; words: De Sylva, Buddy (1895-1950); music: Hanley, James Frederick (1892-1942).

JUST A GIGOLO: 1929; Caesar, Irving (1895-   ); Cassuci, Leonello; Bramer, Julius.

JUST A MEMORY: 1927; words: Brown, Lew (1893-   ); De Sylva, Buddy (George) (1895-1950); music: Henderson, Ray (1896-   ).

JUST A PRAYER AWAY: 1944; Kapp, David (1904-   ); Tobias, Charles (1898-   ).

JUST ONE MORE CHANCE: 1931; Coslow, Sam (1902-   ); Johnston, Arthur James (1898-   ).

KITTEN ON THE KEYS: 1921; Confrey, Edward E. (Zez) (1895-   ); Coslow, Sam (1902-   ).

K-K-K-KATY: 1915; O'Hara, Geoffrey (1882-   ).

THE LADY FROM TWENTYNINE PALMS: 1947; Wrubel, Allie (1905-   ).

THE LADY IN RED: 1935 (movie In Caliente); words: Dixon, Mort (1892-   ); music: Wrubel, Allie (1905-   ).

L'AMOUR, TOUJOURS L'AMOUR: 1922; words: Cushing, Catherine C. (   ); music: Friml, Rudolf (1897-   ).

LAMPLIGHTER'S SERENADE: 1942; words: Webster, Paul Francis (1907-   ); music: Carmichael, Hoagy (1899-   ).

LAROO LAROO LILLI BOLERO: 1948; words: Dee, Sylvia (Josephine Moore Proffitt) (1914-   ); Moore, Elizabeth Evelyn (1891-   ); music: Lippman, Sidney (1914-   ).

THE LAST ROUND-UP: 1933; Hill, William J. (Billy Hill) (1899-1940).

LAURA: 1945; Mercer, John H. (Johnny) (1909-   ); Raksin, David (1912-   ).

LAZY BONES: 1933; Carmichael, Hoagy (Hoagland) (1899-   ); Mercer, John H. (Johnny) (1909-   ).

LAZY RIVER: 1931; words: Arodin, Sidney; music: Carmichael, Hoagy (Hoagland) (1899-   ).

LEANIN' ON THE OLD TOP RAIL: 1939; words: Kenny, Nick (1895-   ); Kenny, Charles F. (1898-   ).

LET A SMILE BE YOUR UMBRELLA: 1927; words: Kahal, Irving (1903-1942); music: Fain, Sammy (1902-   ); Wheeler, Francis.

LET IT SNOW, LET IT SNOW, LET IT SNOW: 1945; words: Cahn, Sammy (1913-   ); music: Styne, Jule (1905-   ).

LET ME CALL YOU SWEETHEART: 1910; words: Whitson, Beth Slater (1879-1930); music: Friedman, Leo (1869-1927).

LET ME LOVE YOU TONIGHT: 1940; Parish, Mitchell (1900-   ); Touzet, René.

LET'S CALL THE WHOLE THING OFF: 1936; words: Gershwin, Ira (1896-   ); music: Gershwin, George (1898-1937).

LET'S FACE THE MUSIC AND DANCE: 1936; Berlin, Irving (1888-   ).

LET'S FALL IN LOVE: 1933; words: Koehler, Ted (1894-   ); music: Arlen, Harold (1905-   ).

LET'S GET AWAY FROM IT ALL: 1941; words: Adair, Thomas M. (1913-   ); music: Dennis, Matt.

LET'S GET LOST: 1943; Loesser, Frank (1910-   ); McHugh, Jimmy (1894-   ).

LET'S HAVE ANOTHER CUP OF COFFEE: 1927; Berlin, Irving (1888-   ).

LET'S K-NOCK K-NEES: 1934; (movie: Gay Divorcee); words: Gordon, Mack (1904-   ); music: Revel, Harry (1905-   ).

LET'S PUT OUT THE LIGHTS AND GO TO SLEEP: 1932; Hupfeld, Herman (1894-1951).

LET'S TAKE THE LONG WAY HOME: 1944; Arlen, Harold (1905-   ); Mercer, Johnny (1909-   ).

LET THE REST OF THE WORLD GO BY: 1919; words: Brennan, J. Keirn (1873-1948); music: Ball, Ernest R. (1878-1927).

LIGHTS OUT: 1936; Hill, William J. (Billy Hill) (1899-1940).

L'IL JOE: 1939; (movie: Destry Rides Again); Loesser, Frank (1910-   ).

LITTLE MAN YOU'VE HAD A BUSY DAY: 1934; words: Sigler, Maurice (1901-   ); music: Hoffman, Al (1902-   ); Wayne, Mabel (1904-   ).

THE LITTLE WHITE HOUSE (AT THE END OF HONEYMOON LANE): 1926; Dowling, Eddie (1895-   ); Henley, James Frederick (1892-1942).

LONG AGO AND FAR AWAY: 1943 (movie: Cover Girl); words: Gershwin, Ira (1896-   ); music: Kern, Jerome (1885-1945).

LOOK FOR THE SILVER LINING: 1920; words: Caldwell, Anne; music: Kern, Jerome (1885-1945).

LOUISE: 1929; words: Robin, Leo (1900-   ); music: Whiting, Richard A. (1891-1938.

LOVE: 1945; words: Martin, Hugh (1914-   ); music: Blane, Ralph (1914-   ).

LOVE BUG: 1937; Tomlin, Pinky (Truman) (1907-   ).

LOVE IN BLOOM: 1934; words: Robin, Leo (1900-   ); music: Rainger, Ralph (1901-1942).

LOVE IS A SONG: 1942 (movie: Bambi); words: Morey, Larry (1905-   ); music: Churchill, Frank (1901-1942).

LOVE IS JUST AROUND THE CORNER: 1934; words: Robin, Leo (1900-   ); music: Gensler, Lewis E. (1896-   ); Rainger, Ralph (1901-1942).

LOVE LETTERS IN THE SAND: 1931; words: Kenny, Nick (1895-   ); music: Coots, J. Fred (1897-   ); Kenny, Charles F. (1898-   ).

LOVELY TO LOOK AT: 1935; words: Fields, Dorothy (1905-   ); music: Kern, Jerome (1885-1945); McHugh, Jimmie (1894-   ).

LOVE ME OR LEAVE ME: 1928; Kahn, Gus (1886-1941).

LOVE ME AND THE WORLD IS MINE: 1906; words: Reed, David (Dave Reed) (1872-1946); music: Ball, Ernest R. (1878-1927).

LOVER: 1933; words: Hart, Lorenz (1895-1943); music: Rodgers, Richard (1902-   ).

LOVE THY NEIGHBOR: 1934 (movie: We're Not Dressing); words: Gordon, Mack (1904-   ); music: Revel, Harry (1905-   ).

THE LOVELINESS OF YOU: 1937 (movie:

You Can't Have Everything); words: Gordon, Mack (1904-); music: Revel, Harry (1905-).

LOVE, YOUR MAGIC SPELL IS EVERYWHERE: 1929; words: Janis, Elsie (1889-); music: Goulding, Edmund (1891-).

LOVE WALKED IN: 1938 (movie: *Gershwin Follies)*; words: Gershwin, Ira (1896-); music: Gershwin, George (1898-1937).

MAD ABOUT HIM, SAD WITHOUT HIM, HOW CAN I BE GLAD WITHOUT HIM BLUES: 1942; Charles, Dick (Richard Charles Krieg) (1919-); Markes, Lawrence W. (Larry) (1921-).

MADEMOISELLE FROM ARMENTIERES (HINKI DINKY PARLEZ VOUS): 1915; Rice, Gitz Ingraham (1891-1947).

MAGIC IS THE MOONLIGHT: 1930; Grever, Maria (1894-1951); Pasqualo, Charles.

MA, HE'S MAKING EYES AT ME: 1921; words: Clare, Sidney (1892-); music: Conrad, Con (Conrad K. Dober) (1891-1938).

MA, I MISS YOUR APPLE PIE: 1941; Loeb, John Jacob (1910-); Lombardo, Carmen (1903-).

MAIRZY DOATS: 1943; Drake, Milton (1912-); Hoffman, Al (1902-); Livingston, Jerry (1909-).

MAKIN' WHOOPEE: 1928; words: Kahn, Gus (1886-1941); music: Donaldson, Walter (1893-1947).

MAMA INEZ: 1931; words: Gilbert, L. Wolfe (1896-); music: Grenet, Eliseo (1893-1950).

MAMMY'S LITTLE COAL BLACK ROSE: 1916; words: Egan, Raymond B. (1890-); music: Whiting, Richard A. (1891-1938).

MAM'SELLE: 1947; words: Gordon, Mack (1904-); music: Goulding, Edmund (1891-).

MANAGUA NICARAGUA: 1946; Fields, Irving (1915-); Gamse, Albert.

MANHATTAN: 1925; words: Hart, Lorenz (1895-1943); music: Rodgers, Richard (1902-).

MANHATTAN SERENADE: 1928; words: Adamson, Harold (1906-); music: Alter, Louis (1902-).

THE MAN THAT BROKE THE BANK AT MONTE CARLO: 1892; words: and music: Gilbert, Fred; (introduced in *A Parlor Match*, by Charles H. Hoyt).

MARCHETA: 1913; Schertzinger, Victor (1890-1941).

MARGIE: 1920; words: Davis, Benny (1895-); music: Conrad, Con (Conrad K. Dober) (1891-1938); Robinson, J. Russel (1892-).

MARTA: 1931; words (English): Gilbert, L. Wolfe (1886-); music: Gilbert, Moises.

MARY IS A GRAND OLD NAME: 1905; Cohan, George M. (1878-1942).

MAYBE YOU'LL BE THERE: 1947; Bloom, Rube (1902-); Gallop, Sammy (1915-).

MAY I?: 1934; (movie: *We're Not Dressing)*; words: Gordon, Mack (1904-); music: Revel, Harry (1905-).

ME AND MY SHADOW: 1927; words: Rose, Billy (1899-); music: Dreyer, Dave (1894-1950); Jolson, Al (1886-1950).

MEET ME IN ST. LOUIS, LOUIS: 1904; words: Sterling, Andrew B. (1874-); music: Mills, Frederick Allen (Kerry Mills) (1869-1948).

MEET ME TONIGHT IN DREAMLAND: 1909; words: Whitson, Beth Slater, (1879-1930); music: Friedman, Leo (1869-1927).

MELANCHOLY BABY: 1912; words: Norton, George A. (1880-1923); music: Burnett, Ernie (1884-).

A MELODY FROM THE SKY: 1936 (movie: *The Trail of the Lonesome Pine)*; words:

Mitchell, Sidney D. (1888-1942); music: Alter, Louis (1902-).

THE MERRY GO ROUND BROKE DOWN: 1937; Franklin, Dave (1895-); Friend, Cliff (1893-).

MEXICALI ROSE: 1923; Tenney, Jack Breckinridge (1898-).

MILKMAN KEEP THOSE BOTTLES QUIET: 1944; De Paul, Gene (1919-); Raye, Don (Donald MacRae Wilhoite, Jr. (1909-).

MIMI: 1932; words: Hart, Lorenz (1895-1943); music: Rodgers, Richard (1902-).

MIRACLE OF FATIMA: 1952; Grace, Michael; Kresa, Helmy (1902-).

MISSOURI WALTZ: 1914; Logan, Frederick Knight (1871-1929); Shannon, James Royce (1881-1946).

MISS YOU: 1929; words: Tobias, Harry (1895-); music: Tobias, Charles (1898-); Tobias, Henry M. (1905-).

MOANIN' LOW: 1929; words: Dietz, Howard (1896-); music: Rainger, Ralph (1901-1942).

MOCKIN' BIRD HILL: 1949; Horton, Naughton.

MOOD INDIGO: 1931; Ellington, Duke (1899-); Mills, Irving (1894-).

MOONGLOW: 1934; De Lange, Eddie (Edgar) (1904-1949); Hudson, Will (1908-); Mills, Irving (1894-).

MOONLIGHT AND ROSES: 1925; Black, Ben (1889-1950); Daniels, Charles N. (Neil Moret) (1878-1943).

MOONLIGHT AND SHADOWS: 1937; words: Robin, Leo (1900-); music: Hollander, Frederick (1896-).

MOONLIGHT BAY: 1912; Madden, Edward (1878-1952); Wenrich, Percy (-1952).

MOONLIGHT BECOMES YOU: 1942; Burke, Johnny (1908-); Van Heusen, Jimmy (1913-).

MOONLIGHT COCKTAILS: 1941; Gannon, Kim (James Kimball Gannon) (1900-); Roberts, C. Luckey (Luckeyth) (1893-).

THE MOON OF MANAKOORA: 1937 (movie: *Hurricane)*; Loesser, Frank (1910-).

MOON OVER MIAMI: 1935; words: Leslie, Edgar (1885-); music: Burke, Joseph A. (1884-1950).

M-O-T-H-E-R: 1915; words: Johnson, Howard E. (1887-1941); music: Morse, Theodore (1873-1924).

MOTHER MACHREE: 1905; words: Young, Rida Johnson (1869-1926); music: Olcott, Chauncey (Chancellor John Olcott) (1858-1932); Ball, Ernest R. (1878-1927).

MR. FIVE BY FIVE: 1942; words: Rushing, James Andrew (1902-); music: De Paul, Gene (1919-); Raye, Don (Donald MacRae Whilhoite, Jr.) (1909-).

MULE TRAIN: 1949; (movie: *Singing Guns)*; Glickman, Fred; Heath; Hy; Lange, Johnny.

MULLIGAN GUARDS: 1873; words: Harrigan, Edward; music: Brahams, David.

MURDER HE SAYS: 1942; Loesser, Frank (1910-); McHugh, Jimmy (1894-).

MUSIC GOES ROUND AND ROUND: 1935; Farley, Edward J. (1904-); Hodgson, Rod; Riley, Mike (1904-).

MUSIC, MAESTRO, PLEASE: 1938; words: Magidson, Herbert (Herb) (1906-); music: Wrubel, Allie (1905-).

MY BLUE HEAVEN: 1927; words: Donaldson, Walter (1893-1947); music: Whiting, George (1884-1943).

MY BUDDY: 1922; words: Donaldson, Walter (1893-1947); music: Kahn, Gus (1886-1941).

MY CONCERTO: 1951; Tepper, Saul; Alstone, Alex.

MY DEVOTION: 1942; Hillman, Roc; Napton, Johnny.

MY DREAMS ARE GETTING BETTER ALL THE TIME: 1944; words: Kurtz, Manny (Emmanuel Kurtz) (1911-   ); music: Mizzy, Vic (1916-   ); Moore, Phil (1918-   ).

MY FICKLE EYE: 1946; words: Miller, Sidney (1916-   ); music: Gilbert, Ray (1912-   ).

MY FIRST AND LAST LOVE: 1951; Harris, Remus; Fisher, Marvin.

MY GAL SAL: 1905; Dresser, Paul (1857-1911).

MY HAPPINES: 1948 (Cash Box Award); words: Peterson, Betty (1918-   ); music: Bergantine, Borney (1909-   ).

MY IDEAL: 1930; words: Robin, Leo (1900-   ); music: Chase, Newell (1904-   ); Whiting, Richard A. (1891-1938)).

MY KINDA LOVE: 1929; Alter, Louis (1902-   ); Trent, Jo (1892-   ).

MY LITTLE BUCKAROO: 1937; words: Scholl, Jack (1903-   ); music: Jerome, M. K. (1893-   ).

MY LOVE LOVES ME: 1949 (movie: *The Heiress*); Livingston, Jay; Evans, Ray.

MY MOONLIGHT MADONNA: 1932; words: Webster, Paul Francis (1907-   ); music: Scotti, William.

MY OWN: 1925; Thompson, Harlan; Archer, Harry.

MY SHINING HOUR: 1943; Arlen, Harold (1905-   ); Mercer, Johnny (1909-   ).

MY SILENT LOVE: 1931; words: Heyman, Edward (1907-   ); music: Suesse, Dana (1911-   ).

MY SIN: 1921; words: Brown, Lew (1893-   ); De Sylva, Buddy (1895-1950); music: Henderson, Ray (1896-   ).

MY SISTER AND I: 1941; words: Zaret, Hy (Hyman H.) (1907-   ); music: Kramer, Alex Charles (1903-   ); Whitney, Joan (1914-   ).

MY SUGAR IS SO REFINED: 1946; words: Dee, Sylvia (Josephine Moore Proffitt) (1914-   ); music: Lippman, Sidney (1914-   ).

MY SWEETHEART'S THE MAN IN THE MOON: 1896; words and music: Thornton, James.

MY THRILL: 1952; Kaye, Buddy; Bruce, Gary.

MY TRULY, TRULY FAIR: 1951; Merrill, Bob.

MY WILD IRISH ROSE: 1889; Olcott, Chauncey (Chancellor John Olcott) (1858-1932).

NANCY (WITH THE SMILING FACE): 1944; words: Silvers, Phil (1912-   ); music: Van Heusen, Jimmy (1913-   ).

THE NEARNESS OF YOU: 1940; Carmichael, Hoagy (Hoagland) (1899-   ); Savitt, Jan (1913-1948).

NEAR YOU: 1947; words: Bryan, Alfred (1871-   ); Goell, Kermit (1915-   ); music: Craig, Francis (1900-   ).

NEVER IN A MILLION YEARS: 1937 (movie: *Wake Up and Live*); words: Gordon, Mack (1904-   ); music: Revel, Harry (1905-   ).

THE NIGHT IS YOUNG AND YOU'RE SO BEAUTIFUL: 1936; words: Kahal, Irving (1903-1942); Rose, Billy (1899-   ); music: Suesse, Dana (1911-   ).

THE NIGHT WAS MADE FOR LOVE: 1931; words: Harbach, Otto (1873-   ); music: Kern, Jerome (1885-1945).

NOT MINE: 1942; Mercer, Johnny (1909-   ); Schertzinger, Victor (1890-1941).

NOW I KNOW: 1943 (movie: *Up in Arms*); words: Koehler, Ted (1894-   ); music: Arlen, Harold (1905-   ).

NOW IS THE HOUR: 1948; Mauva Kaihan; Scott, Clement; Stewart, Dorothy M. (1897-   ).

OBJECT OF MY AFFECTION: 1934; Grier, James W. (Jimmie) (1902-   ); Price, Coy; Tomlin, Pinky (Truman) (1907-   ).

O, BY JINGO: 1919; words: Brown, Lew (1893-   ); music: Von Tilzer, Albert (1878-   ).

OH! BUT I DO: 1947; words: Robin, Leo (1900-   ); music: Schwartz, Arthur (1900-   ).

OH, HOW I MISS YOU TONIGHT: 1924; words: Davis, Benny (1895-   ); music: Burke, Joseph A. (1884-1950); Fisher, Mark (1895-1948).

OH LOOK AT ME NOW: 1941; words: De Vries, John (1915-   ); music: Bushkin, Joseph (Joe) (1916-   ).

OH JOHNNY, OH JOHNNY OH: 1917; words: Rose, Ed (1875-1935); music: Olman, Abe (1888-   ).

OH, MA MA! (THE BUTCHER BOY): 1938; Citovello, Paolo; Vallee, Rudy (Hubert P.) (1901-   ).

OH, WHAT IT SEEMED TO BE: 1945; Benjamin, Bennie (1907-   ); Weiss, George David (1921-   ); Carle, Frankie (1903-   ).

OH, YOU BEAUTIFUL DOLL: 1909; words: Brown, A. Seymour (1885-1947); music: Ayer, Nat.

OH, YOU CRAZY MOON: 1939; words: Burke, Johnny (1908-   ); music: Van Heusen, Jimmy (1913-   ).

OLD BUTTERMILK SKY: 1945; (movie: *Canyon Passage*); Brooks, Jack (1912-   ); Carmichael, Hoagy (Hoagland) (1899-   ).

THE OLD LAMPLIGHTER: 1946; Simon, Nat (1900-   ); Tobias, Charles (1898-   ).

THE OLD SPINNING WHEEL: 1933; Hill, William J. (Billy) (1899-1940).

ON A SLOW BOAT TO CHINA: 1948; Loesser, Frank (1910-   ).

ONCE IN A BLUE MOON: 1934 (movie: *We're Not Dressing*); words: Gordon, Mack (1904-   ); music: Revel, Harry (1905-   ).

ONCE IN A WHILE: 1937; Green, Bud (1897-   ); Edwards, Michael (1893-   ).

ONE DOZEN ROSES: 1942; Donovan, Walter (1888-   ); Jurgens, Dick (1911-   ); Lewis, Roger (1885-1948); Washburn, Country.

ONE HOUR WITH YOU: 1932; words: Robin, Leo (1900-   ); music: Whiting, Richard A. (1891-1938).

ONE NEVER KNOWS: 1936 (movie: *Stowaway*); words: Gordon, Mack (1904-   ); music: Revel, Harry (1905-   ).

ONE TWO BUTTON YOUR SHOE: 1936; Burke, Johnny (1908-   ); Johnston, Arthur James (1898-   ).

ONLY FOREVER: 1940; Burke, Johnny (1908-   ); Monaco, James V. (1885-1945).

ON MOBILE BAY: 1910; Daniels, Charles N. (Neil Moret) (1878-1943); Jones, Earle C.

ON THE BANKS OF THE WABASH FAR AWAY: 1896; words and music: Dresser, Paul (1857-1911).

ON THE BUMPY ROAD TO LOVE: 1938; Hoffman, Al (1902-   ); Mencher, Murray (Ted Murray) (1898-   ).

ON THE GOOD SHIP LOLLIPOP: 1934; words: Clare, Sidney (1892-   ); music: Whiting, Richard A. (1891-1938).

ON THE ISLE OF MAY: 1940; words: David, Mack (1912-   ); music: Kostelanetz, Andre (1901-   ).

ON THE SUNNY SIDE OF THE STREET: 1930; words: Fields, Dorothy (1905-   ); music: McHugh, Jimmy (1894-   ).

OPEN THE DOOR RICHARD: 1947; Clark, Frank; Howell, Dan; McVea, Jack; Kapp, David (1904-   ).

ORCHIDS IN THE MOONLIGHT: 1933; (movie: *Flying Down to Rio*); words: Kahn, Gus

(1886-1941); music: Eliscu, Edward (1902-   );
Youmans, Vincent (1898-1946).

ORGAN GRINDER'S SWING: 1937; Mills, Irving (1894-   ); Parish, Mitchell (1900-   );
Hudson, Will (1908-   ).

OVER THERE: 1917; Cohan, George M. (1878-
1942).

PAGAN LOVE SONG: 1929; (movie: *Pagan);*
words: Brown, Nacio Herb (1896-   ); music:
Freed, Arthur (1894-   ).

PARIS IN THE SPRING: 1935 (movie: *Paris
in the Spring);* words: Gordon, Mack (1904-
   ); music: Revel, Harry (1905-   ).

PEGGY O'NEIL: 1921; Dodge, Gilbert; Nelson, Ed G. (1886-   ); Pease, Harry (1886-
1945).

PEG O' MY HEART: 1913; words: Bryan,
Alfred (1871-   ); music: Fisher, Fred (1875-
1942).

PENNIES FROM HEAVEN: 1936; (movie:
Pennies from Heaven); Burke, Johnny (1908-
   ); Johnston, Arthur James (1898-   ).

PENNSYLVANIA POLKA: 1942; Lee, Lester
(1905-   ); Manners, Zeke (Leo Mannes) (1911-
).

PERFIDIA: 1940; words: Leeds, Milton (1909-
   ); music: Dominguez, Albert.

PERSONALITY: 1945; Burke, Johnny (1908-
   ); Van Heusen, Jimmy (1913-   ).

THE PICCOLINO: 1935; Berlin, Irving (1888-
).

PLAYMATES: 1917; words: Yellen, Jack (1892-
   ); music: Dowell, Saxie (Horace Kirby
Dowell) (1904-   ); Gumble, Albert (1883-
1946).

PLEASE: 1932; words: Robin, Leo (1900-   );
music: Rainger, Ralph (1901-1942).

POINCIANA: 1936; words: Bernier, Buddy
(1920-   ); music: Simon, Nat (1900-   ).

POOR BUTTERFLY: 1916; words: Golden,
John (1874-   ); music: Hubbell, Raymond
(1879-   ).

PRAISE THE LORD AND PASS THE AM-
MUNITION: 1942; Loesser, Frank (1910-   ).

PRETTY BABY: 1916; Kahn, Gus (1886-1941);
Van Alstyne, Egbert Anson (1882-1951).

PRETTY KITTY KELLY: 1920; Nelson, Ed
G. (1886-   ); Pease, Harry (1886-1945).

PRISONER OF LOVE: 1931; words: Colom-
bo, Russ; Robin, Leo (1900-   ); music:
Gaskill, Clarence (1892-1947).

PUDDIN HEAD JONES: 1934; words: Bryan,
Alfred (1871-   ); music: Handman, Lou
(1894-   ).

THE PUSSYCAT SONG (NYOT NYOW):
1948; Manning, Dick (1912-   ).

PUT ON YOUR OLD GREY BONNET: 1909;
words: Murphy, Stanley (1875-1919); music:
Wenrich, Percy (-1952).

PUT YOUR ARMS AROUND ME HONEY:
1910; words: McCree, Junie (1865-1918); music:
Von Tilzer, Albert (1878-   ).

RACING WITH THE MOON: 1941; (Vaughn
Monroe's Theme Song); Monroe, Vaughn
(1911-   ); Pope, Pauline; Watson, Johnny.

RAGTIME COWBOY JOE: 1902; words: Clarke,
Grant (1891-1931); music: Abrahams, Maurice
(Maurie) (1883-1931); Muir, Lewis M.

RAMONA: 1927; words: Gilbert, L. Wolfe
(1886-   ); music: Wayne, Mabel (1904-   ).;

REACHING FOR THE MOON: 1930; Berlin,
Irving (1888-   ).

RED SILK STOCKINGS AND GREEN PER-
FUME: 1947; words: Hilliard, Bob (1918-   );
Sanford, Dick (1896-   ); music: Mysels, Sam-
my (1906-   ).

RED WING: 1907; Chattaway, Thurland (1872-
1947); Mills, Frederick Allen (Kerry Mills)
(1869-1948).

REMEMBER: 1925; Berlin, Irving (1888-   ).

REMEMBER ME?: 1937; words: Dubin, Al
(1891-1945); music: Warren, Harry (1893-   ).

RHUMBOOGIE: 1940; words: Prince, Hugh Dun-
ham (Hughie Prince) (1906-   ); music: Raye,
Don (Donald MacRae Wilhoite, Jr.) (1909-
).

RIVER STAY WAY FROM MY DOOR: 1931;
words: Dixon, Mort (1892-   ); music: Woods,
Harry M. (1896-   ).

ROCKABY YOUR BABY WITH A DIXIE
MELODY: 1918; words: Lewis, Samuel H.
(1885-   ); Young, Joseph (1889-1939); music:
Schwartz, Jean (1878-   ).

ROCKIN' CHAIR: 1930; Carmichael Hoagy
(Hoagland) (1899-   ).

RODGER YOUNG, THE BALLAD OF: 1945;
Loesser, Frank (1910-   ).

ROSALIE: 1937 (movie: *Rosalie);* Porter, Cole
(1893-   ).

ROSE O'DAY: 1941; Lewis, Al (1901-   ); Tobias, Charles, (1898-   ).

ROSE OF NO MAN'S LAND: 1918; Brennan,
James A. (1885-   ); Caddigan, Jack J. (1879-
1952).

ROSES OF YESTERDAY: 1928; Berlin, Irving
(1888-   ).

ROSIE THE RIVETER: 1942; Evans, Reed
(1912-   ); Loeb, John Jacob (1910-   ).

ROW, ROW, ROW: 1912; words: Jerome, William (1865-1932); music: Monaco, James V.
(1885-1945).

RUM AND COCA COLA: 1944; words: Amsterdam, Morey (1912-   ); Sullivan, Jeri;
music: Baron, Paul (1910-   ).

RUMORS ARE FLYING: 1946; Benjamin,
Bennie (1907-   ); Weiss, George David (1921-
)

RUNNIN' WILD: 1922; words: Grey, Joseph
W. (1879-   ); music: Gibbs, Arthur H. (1895-
   ); Wood, Leo (1882-1929).

RUSSIAN LULLABY: 1927; Berlin, Irving
(1888-   ).

SAN FERNANDO VALLEY: 1943; Jenkins,
Gordon (1910-   ).

SANTA CLAUS IS COMING TO TOWN:
1934; words: Gillespie, Haven (1888-   ); music: Coots, J. Fred (1897-   ).

SATURDAY NIGHT IS THE LONELIEST
NIGHT OF THE WEEK: 1944; words: Cahn,
Sammy (1913-   ); music: Styne, Jule (1905-
).

SAY IT WISH MUSIC: 1921; Berlin, Irving
(1888-   ).

SAYS MY HEART: 1938; Lane, Burton (1912-
   ); Loesser, Frank (1910-   ).

SCATTERBRAIN: 1939; Burke, Johnny (1908-
   ); Keene, Kahn (1909-   ); Masters, Frankie (1904-   ).

SCHOOL DAYS: 1907; words: Cobb, Will D.
(1876-1930); music: Edwards, Gus (1879-1945).

SEEMS LIKE OLD TIMES: 1945; Loeb, John
Jacob (1910-   ); Lombardo, Carmen (1903-   ).

SEE WHAT THE BOYS IN THE BACK
ROOM WILL HAVE: 1939 (movie: *Destry
Rides Again);* Loesser, Frank (1910-   ).

SEPTEMBER IN THE RAIN: 1937; words:
Dubin, Al (1891-1945); music: Warren, Harry
(1893-   ).

THE SHEIK OF ARABY: 1921; words: Smith,
Harry Bache (1860-1936); music: Snyder, Ted
(1881-   ).

SHE'LL ALWAYS REMEMBER: 1942; Marks,
John D. (Johnnie) (1909-   ); Pola, Edward
(1907-   ).

SHE'S A LATIN FROM MANHATTAN: 1935;
words: Dubin, Al (1891-1945); music: Warren,
Harry (1893-   ).

SHINE ON HARVEST MOON: 1908; Norworth, Jack (1879-   ); Von Tilzer, Albert
(1878-   ).

SHOO FLY PIE AND APPLE PAN DOWDY: 1945; Gallop, Sammy (1915-   ); Wood, Guy B. (1912-   ).

SHOO SHOO BABY: 1943; Moore, Phil (1918-   ).

SHOULD I?: 1929; words: Freed, Arthur (1894-   ); music: Brown, Nacio Herb (1896-   ).

SHUFFLE OFF TO BUFFALO: 1932; words: Dubin, Al (1891-1945); music: Warren, Harry (1893-   ).

SIBONEY: 1929; words: Morse, Theodora (1890-   ); music: Lecuona, Ernesto (-   ).

SILVER ON THE SAGE: 1938; words: Robin, Leo (1900-   ); music: Rainger, Ralph (1901-1942).

SILVER THREADS AMONG THE GOLD: 1872; words: Rexford, Eben E.; music: Danks, Hart Pease.

THE SINGING HILLS: 1940; words: David, Mack (1912-   ); Sanford, Dick (1896-   ); music: Mysels, Sammy (1906-   ).

SINGING IN THE RAIN: 1929; words: Freed, Arthur (1894-   ); Raskin, William (1896-1942); music: Brown, Nacio Herb (1896-19).

SING YOU SINNERS: 1930; Coslow, Sam (1902-   ); Harling, W. Franke (1887-   ).

SIOUX CITY SUE: 1945; words: Greene, Mort (1912-   ); Freedman, Max C. (1895-   ); music: Siegel, Al (1898-   ); Signorelli, Frank (1901-   ).

SITTING ON TOP OF THE WORLD: 1925; words: Lewis, Samuel M. (1885-   ); Young, Joseph (1889-1939); music: Henderson, Ray (1896-   ).

SIX LESSONS FROM MADAME LA ZONGA: 1940; words: Newman, Charles; music: Monaco, James V. (1885-1945).

SKIP TO MY LOU: 1944; (movie: *Meet Me in St. Louis)*; words: Martin, Hugh (1914-19); music: Blane, Ralph (1914-   ).

SKYLARK: 1941; Carmichael, Hoagy (Hoagland) (1899-   ); Mercer, John H. (Johnny) (1909-   ).

SLEEPY LAGOON: 1930; Coates, Eric: Lawrence, Jack (1912-   ).

SLEEPY TIME GAL: 1926; words: Egan, Raymond B. (1890-   ); music: Alden, Joseph Reed; Lorenzo, Ange (1894-   ); Whiting, Richard A. (1891-1938).

SMILES: 1917; words: Callahan, J. Will (-   ); music: Roberts, Lee S. (1884-1949).

SOLITUDE: 1934; Dè Lange, Eddie (1904-1949); Ellington, Duke (1899-   ); Mills, Irving (1894-   ).

SO LONG MARY: 1905; Cohan, George M. (1878-1942).

SOMEBODY ELSE IS TAKING MY PLACE: 1937; Ellsworth, Bob (Robert H.) (1895-   ); Howard, Richard (1890-   ); Morgan, Russ (1904-   ).

SOMEBODY LOVES ME: 1924; words: MacDonald, Ballard (1882-1935); De Sylva, Buddy (George) (1895-1950); music: Gershwin, George (1898-1937).

SOMEBODY STOLE MY GAL: 1918; Wood, Leo (1882-1929).

SOME DAY MY PRINCE WILL COME: 1938 (movie: *Snow White and the Seven Dwarfs)*; words: Morey, Larry (1905-   ); music: Churchill, Frank E. (1901-1942).

SOME OF THESE DAYS: 1910; Brooks, Shelton (1886-   ).

SOMEONE'S ROCKING MY DREAMBOAT: 1941; words: Scott, Emmerson; music: Rene, Leon T. (1902-   ); Rene, Otis J., Jr. (1898-   ).

SOMEONE TO WATCH OVER ME: 1926; words: Gershwin, Ira (1896-   ); music: Gershwin, George (1898-1937).

SOME SUNDAY MORNING: 1917; words:

Egan, Raymond B. (1890-   ); Kahn, Gus (1886-1941); music: Whiting, Richard A. (1891-1938).

SOME SUNDAY MORNING: 1944; words: Koehler, Ted (1894-   ); music: Heindorf, Ray John (1908-   ); Jerome, M. K. (1893-   ).

SOME SUNNY DAY: 1922; Berlin, Irving (1888-   ).

SOMETHING TO REMEMBER YOU BY: 1930; words: Dietz, Howard (1896-   ); music: Schwartz, Arthur (1900-   ).

THE SONG IS ENDED BUT THE MELODY LINGERS ON: 1927; Berlin, Irvin (1888-   ).

THE SONG IS YOU: 1932; words: Hammerstein II, Oscar (1895-   ); music: Kern, Jerome (1885-1945).

SONNY BOY: 1928; words: Brown, Lew (1893-   ); De Sylva, Buddy (1895-1950); music: Henderson, Ray (1896-   ); Jolson, Al (1886-1950).

SO-O-O IN LOVE: 1945; words: Robin, Leo (1900-   ); music: Rose, David (1910-   ).

SOPHISTICATED LADY: 1933; words: Parish, Mitchell (1900-   ); music: Ellington, Duke (1899-   ); Mills, Irving (1894-   ).

SO YOU'RE THE ONE: 1940; words: Zaret, Hy (Hyman H.) (1907-   ); music: Kramer, Alex (1903-   ); Whitney, Joan (1914-   ).

SPOSIN': 1932; words: Razaf, Andy (Andreamenentania Paul Razafinkeriefo) (1895-   ); music: Denniker, Paul (1897-   ).

SPRING WILL BE A LITTLE LATE THIS YEAR: 1944; Loesser, Frank (1910-   ).

STAIRWAY TO THE STARS: 1939; words: Parish, Mitchell (1900-   ); music: Malneck, Matty (1904-   ); Signorelli, Frank (1901-   ).

STARDUST: 1929; words: Parish, Mitchell (1900-   ); music: Carmichael, Hoagy (1899-   ).

STAY AS SWEET AS YOU ARE: 1934 (movie: *College Rhythm)*; words: Gordon, Mack (1904-   ); music: Revel, Harry (1905-   ).

STEPPIN' OUT WITH MY BABY: 1947; Berlin, Irving (1888-   ).

STOMPIN' AT THE SAVOY: 1936; words: Razaf, Andy (Andreamenentania Paul Razafinkeriefo) (1895-   ); music: Goodman, Benny (1909-   ); Sampson, Edgar M. (1907-   ).

STOP, STOP, YOU'RE BREAKING MY HEART 1910; Berlin, Irving (1888-   ).

STORMY WEATHER: 1933; words: Koehler, Ted (1894-   ); music: Arlen, Harold (1905-   ).

STRAIGHT FROM THE SHOULDER: 1934 (movie: *She Loves Me Not)*; words: Gordon, Mack (1904-   ); music: Revel, Harry (1905-   ).

SUDDENLY IT'S SPRING: 1943; Burke, Johnny (1908-   ); Van Heusen, Jimmy (1913-   ).

SUNBONNET SUE: 1908; words: Cobb, Will D. (1876-1930); music: Edwards, Gus (1879-1945).

SUNDAY, MONDAY OR ALWAYS: 1943; Burke, Johnny (1908-   ); Van Heusen, Jimmy (1913-   ).

SUNNY SIDE UP: words: Brown, Lew (1893-   ); De Sylva, Buddy (1895-1950); music: Henderson, Ray (1896-   ).

SWANEE: 1919; words: Caesar, Irving (1895-   ); music: Gershwin, George (1898-1937).

SWEET ADELINE: 1903; Armstrong, Harry (1879-1951); Gerard, Richard H. (1876-1948).

SWEET AND LOVELY: 1931; words: Tobias, Harry (1895-   ); music: Arnheim, Gus (1897-   ); Daniels, Charles N. (Neil Moret) (1878-1943); Le Mare, Jules.

SWEET ELOISE: 1942; words: David, Mack (1912-   ); music: Morgan, Russ (1904-   ).

SWEET GEORGIA BROWN: 1925; Bernie, Ben

(1891-1943); Casey, Kenneth (1899-   ); Pinkard, Maceo (1897-   ).
SWEETHART DARLING: 1933; words: Kahn, Gus (1886-1941); music: Stothart, Herbert (-1949).
SWEETHEART OF SIGMA CHI: 1912; Stokes, Byron D.; Vernor, F. Dudleigh (1892-   ).
SWEET SUE: 1928; words: Harris, Will J. (1900-   ); music: Young, Victor (1900-   ).
SWINGIN' DOWN THE LANE: 1923; words: Kahn, Gus (1886-1941); music: Jones, Isham (1894-   ).
TAKE A NUMBER FROM ONE TO TEN: 1934 (movie: *College Rhythm*); words: Gordon, Mack (1904-   ); music: Revel, Harry (1905-   ).
TAKE ME OUT TO THE BALL GAME: 1903; Norworth, Jack (1879-   ); Von Tilzer, Albert (1878-   ).
TAMPICO: 1945; Fisher, Doris (1915-   ); Roberts, Allan (1905-   ).
TANGERINE: 1942; Mercer, Johnny (1909-   ); Sanders, Alma M. (1882-   ); Schertzinger, Victor (1890-1941).
TA-RA-RA-BOOM-DER-E: 1891; Metz, Theodore A. (1848-1936); Sayers, Henry J.
TEMPTATION: 1933; (movie: *Going Hollywood*); words: Freed, Arthur (1894-   ); music: Brown, Nacio Herb (1896-   ).
TEN LITTLE FINGERS AND TEN LITTLE TOES: 1921; Nelson, Ed G. (1886-   ); Pease, Harry (1886-1945); Schuster, Ira (1889-1946).
THANKS A MILLION: 1935; words: Kahn, Gus (1886-1941); music: Johnston, Arthur James (1898-   ).
THAT CERTAIN FEELING: 1925; words: Gershwin, Ira (1896-   ); music: Gershwin, George (1898-1937).
THAT OLD BLACK MAGIC: 1943; (movie: *Star-Spangled Rhythm*); Arlen, Harold (1905-   ); Mercer, Johnny (1909-   ).
THAT OLD FEELING: 1937; (movie: *Vogues of 1938*); words: Brown, Lew (1893-   ); music: Fain, Sammy (1902-   ).
THAT OLD GANG OF MINE: 1922; words: Dixon, Mort (1892-   ); Rose, Billy (1899-   ); music: Henderson, Ray (1896-   ).
THAT'S FOR ME: 1945; words: Hammerstein II, Oscar (1895-   ); music: Monaco, James V. (1885-1945); Rodgers, Richard (1902-   ).
THAT'S MY DESIRE: 1931; Loveday, Carroll (1896-   ); Kresa, Helmy (1904-   ).
THAT'S MY WEAKNESS NOW: 1928; Green, Bud (1897-   ); Stept, Sam H. (1897-   ).
THAT'S WHY DARKIES WERE BORN: 1931; words: Brown, Lew (1893-   ); music: Henderson, Ray (1896-   ).
THAT TUMBLE-DOWN SHACK IN ATHLONE: 1918; words: Carlo, Monte (1883-   ); Pascoe, Richard W. (1888-   ); music: Sanders, Alma M. (1882-   ).
THEM THERE EYES: 1930; words: Tracey, William G. (1893-   ); music: Pinkard, Maceo (1897-   ); Tauber, Doris (1908-   ).
THEN I'LL BE HAPPY: 1925; words: Brown, Lew (1893-   ); Clare, Sidney (1892-   ); music: Friend, Cliff (1893-   ).
THERE GOES THAT SONG AGAIN: 1944 (movie: *Carolina Blues*); words: Cahn, Sammy (1913-   ); music: Styne, Jule (1905-   ).
THERE, I'VE SAID IT AGAIN: 1941; Evans, Reed (1912-   ); Mann, David (1916-   ).
THERE MUST BE A WAY: 1945; Cook, Robert; Galop, Sammy (1915-   ); Saxon, David (1919-   ).
THERE'S DANGER IN YOUR EYES, CHERIE: 1929; words: Bryan, Alfred (1871-   ); Meskill, Jack (1897-   ); music: Richman, Harry (1895-   ).
THERE'S A HOME IN WYOMIN': 1933; De

Rose, Peter (1900-   ); Hill, William J. (Billy) (1899-1940).
THERE'S A LONG, LONG TRAIL: 1914; words: King, Stoddard (1889-1933); music: Elliott, Zo (Alonzo) (1891-   ).
THERE'S A LULL IN MY LIFE: 1937; (movie: *Wake Up and Live*); words: Gordon, Mack (1904-   ); music: Revel, Harry (1905-   ).
THERE'S A RAINBOW 'ROUND MY SHOULDER: 1928; words: Rose, Billy (1899-   ); music: Jolson, Al (1886-1950); Dreyer, Dave (1894-   ).
THESE FOOLISH THINGS REMIND ME OF YOU: 1935; Link, Harry (1896-   ); Marvell, Holt; Strachey, Jack.
THEY CAN'T TAKE THAT AWAY FROM ME: 1937; words: Gershwin, Ira (1896-   ); music: Gershwin, George (1898-1937).
THEY'RE EITHER YOO YOUNG OR TOO OLD: 1943; Loesser, Frank (1910-   ); Schwartz, Arthur (1900-   ).
THIS HEART OF MINE: 1943; words: Freed, Arthur (1894-   ); music: Warren, Harry (1893-   ).
THIS LOVE OF MINE: 1941; Parker, Sol; Savicola, Henry; Sinatra, Frank (1917-   ).
THE THREE CABALLEROS: 1941; (movie: *The Three Caballeros*); Cortazar, Ernesto M.; Esperon, Manuel; Gilbert, Ray (1912-   ).
THREE LITTLE FISHES: 1939; Dowel, Saxie (Horace Kirby Dowell) (1904-   ).
THREE LITTLE SISTERS: 1942; words: Taylor, Irving (1914-   ); music: Mizzy, Vic (1916-   ).
THREE LITTLE WORDS: 1930; words: Kalmar, Bert (1884-1947); music: Ruby, Harry (1895-   ).
TILL THE CLOUDS ROLL BY: 1917; words: Bolton, Guy; Wodehouse, Pelham Grenville (1881-   ); music: Kern, Jerome (1885-1945).
TILL THE END OF TIME: 1945; (Radio Annual Award); words: Kaye, Buddy (1918-   ); music: Mossman, Ted (1912-   ); Smith, Earl K. (1885-   ).
TILL THE REAL THING COMES ALONG: 1931; words: Holiner, Mann (1897-   ); music: Nichols, Alberta.
TILL WE MEET AGAIN: 1918; words: Egan, Raymond B. (1890-   ); music: Whiting, Richard A. (1891-1938).
TIME AFTER TIME: 1947; words: Cahn, Sammy (1913-   ); music: Styne, June (1905-   ).
TOO-RA-LOO-RA-LOO-RAL (IRISH LULLABY): Written for Chauncey Olcott and sung in his play *Shameen Dhu (My Little Dudeen)*, 1913; sung by Bing Crosby in *Going My Way*, 1945. Shannon, James Royce (1881-1946).
TOUCH OF YOUR HAND: 1933; words: Harbach, Otto (1873-   ); music: Kern, Jerome (1885-1945).
TRADE WINDS: 1940; words: Quenzer, Arthur (1905-   ); music: Friend, Cliff (1893-   ); Tobias, Charles (1898-   ).
TRAIL OF THE LONESOME PINE: 1913; words: MacDonald, Ballard; music: Carrol, Harry (1892-   ).
TREASURE OF SIERRA MADRE: 1948; words: Kaye, Buddy (1918-   ); music: Manning, Dick (1912-   ).
TREES: 1922; words: Kilmer, Joyce (1886-1918); music: Rasbach, Oscar (1888-   ).
THE TROLLEY SONG: 1943 (movie: *Meet Me in St. Louis*); words: Martin, Hugh (1914-   ); music: Blane, Ralph (1914-   ).
TRUCKIN': 1935; words: Koehler, Ted (1894-   ); music: Bloom, Rube (1902-   ).
TUXEDO JUNCTION: 1940; words: Feyne, Buddy (1912-   ); music: Dash, Julian; Haw-

kins, Erskine (1914-   ); Johnson, William
(1912-   ).
TWO CIGARETTES IN THE DARK: 1934;
words: Webster, Paul Francis (1907-   );
music: Pollack, Lew (1895-1946).
WAGON WHEELS: 1934; De Rose, Peter (1900-
); Hill, William J. (Billy) (1899-1940).
WAH! HOO!: 1936; Friend, Cliff (1893-   ).
WAITING FOR THE ROBERT E. LEE: 1912;
words: Gilbert L. Wolfe (1886-   ); music:
Muir, Lewis F.
WAIT TILL THE SUN SHINES NELLIE:
1905; words: Sterling, Andrew B. (1874-   );
music: Von Tilzer, Harry (1872-1946).
WALKING MY BABY BACK HOME: 1930;
words: Turk, Roy (1892-1934); music: Ahlert,
Fred E. (1892-   ); Richman, Harry (1895-   ).
WALTZ ME AROUND AGAIN WILLIE: 1906;
words: Cobb, Will. D. (1876-1930); music:
Shields, Ren (1868-1913).
WEDDING BELLS ARE BREAKING UP
THAT OLD GANG OF MINE: 1929; words:
Kahal, Irving (1903-1942), Raskin, William
(1896-1942); music: Fain, Sammy (1902-   ).
THE WEDDING OF THE PAINTED DOLL:
1929; words: Freed, Arthur (1894-   ); music:
Brown, Nacio Herb (1896-   ).
WE DID IT BEFORE AND WE CAN DO IT
AGAIN: 1941; Friend, Cliff (1893-   ); To-
bias, Charles (1898-   ).
WELL, ALL RIGHT: 1939; Faye, Francis;
Howell, Dan; Raye, Don (Donald MacRae
Wilhoite, Jr.) (1909-   ).
WE'RE IN THE MONEY: 1933; (movie: *Gold
Diggers of 1933);* words: Dubin, Al (1891-
1945); music: Warren, Harry (1893-   ).
WE SAW THE SEA: 1936; Berlin, Irving 1888-
WE THREE (MY ECHO, MY SHADOW, AND
ME): 1940; words: Cogane, Nelson (1902-   );
music: Robertson, Dick (1903-   ); Mysels,
Sammy (1906-   ).
WHAT A DIFFERENCE A DAY MADE: 1934;
words: Adams, Stanley (1907-   ); music:
Grever, Maria (1894-1951).
WHAT DID I DO?: 1948; words: Moira, Joe;
music: Myrow, Josef (1910-   ).
WHAT DO YOU WANNA MAKE THOSE
EYES AT ME FOR?: 1916; words: McCarthy,
Joseph (1885-1943); Johnson, Howard E. (1887-
1941); music: Monaco, James V. (1885-1945).
WHAT'LL I DO?: 1924; Berlin, Irving (1888-
).
WHAT MAKES THE SUN SET?: 1945; (movie:
Anchors Aweigh); words: Cahn, Sammy (1913-
); music: Styne, Jule (1905-   ).
WHAT'S THE GOOD WORD, MR. BLUE-
BIRD?: 1943; Hoffman, Al (1902-   ); Living-
ston, Jerry (1909-   ); Roberts, Allan (1905-
).
WHAT'S THE NAME OF THAT SONG?:
1936; words: Seymour, Tot; music: Lawn-
hurst, Vee (1905-   ).
WHAT WILL I TELL MY HEART?: 1937;
Lawrence, Jack (1912-   ); Tinturin, Peter
(1910-   ).
WHEN DAY IS DONE: 1924; words: De Sylva, Buddy (George) (1895-1950); music: Katscher, Robert (1894-1942). (Original publica-
tion, Vienna, under title "Madonna.")
WHEN DID YOU LEAVE HEAVEN?: 1936;
words: Bullock, Walter (1907-   ); music:
Whiting, Richard A. (1891-1938).
WHEN I GROW TOO OLD TO DREAM:
1935; words: Hammerstein II, Oscar (1895-
); music: Romberg, Sigmund (1887-1951).
WHEN IRISH EYES ARE SMILING: 1912;
words: Graff, George (1886-   ); music: Ball,
Ernest R. (1878-1927); Olcott, Chauncey (Chancellor John Olcott) (1858-1932).

WHEN I TAKE MY SUGAR TO TEA: 1931;
words: Kahal, Irving (1903-1942); music: Fain,
Sammy (1902-   ); Norman, Fred (1910-   ).
WHEN IT'S SLEEPYTIME DOWN SOUTH:
1931; Rene, Leon T. (1902-   ); Rene, Otis J.,
Jr. (1898-   ); Muse, Clarence (1889-   ).
WHEN IT'S SPRINGTIME IN THE ROCK-
IES: 1929; words: Woolsey, Mrs. Maryhale
(Maryhale Eugenie Hall) (1899-   ); music:
Sauer, Robert; Taggart; Milt.
WHEN MY BABY SMILES AT ME: 1920;
Lewis, Ted; Munroe, Bill; Sterling, Andrew
B. (1874-   ); music: Von Tilzer, Harry (1872-
1946).
WHEN MY DREAMBOAT COMES HOME:
1936; Friend, Cliff (1893-   ); Franklin, Dave
(1895-   ).
WHEN MY SUGAR WALKS DOWN THE
STREET: 1924; words: Austin, Gene (1900-
19); music: McHugh, Jimmy (1894-   ); Mills,
Irving (1894-   ).
WHEN THAT MIDNIGHT CHOO CHOO
LEAVES FOR ALABAM': 1912; Berlin, Ir-
ving (1888-   ).
WHEN THE BLUE OF THE NIGHT MEETS
THE GOLD OF THE DAY: 1931; (Bing
Crosby's Theme Song); words: Crosby, Bing
(Harry Lillis) (1904-   ); Turk, Roy (1892-
1934); music: Ahlert, Fred (1892-   ).
WHEN THE LIGHTS GO ON AGAIN ALL
OVER THE WORLD: 1942; Seiler, Edward
(1911-1952); Benjamin, Bennie (1907-   ); Mar-
cus, Sol (1912-   ).
WHEN THE MOON COMES OVER THE
MOUNTAIN: 1931; (Kate Smith's Theme
Song); words: Johnson, Howard E. (1887-1941);
Smith, Kate (1909-   ); music: Woods, Harry
M. (1896-   ).
WHEN THE RED RED ROBIN COMES BOB
BOB BOBBIN' ALONG: 1926; Woods, Har-
ry M. (1896-   ).
WHEN THERE'S A BREEZE ON LAKE
LOUISE: 1942 (movie: *Mayor of Forty-
Second Street);* words: Green, Mort (   );
music: Revel, Harry (1905-   ).
WHEN THE ROBINS NEST AGAIN: 1883;
words and music: Howard, Frank.
WHEN THE SWALLOWS COME BACK TO
CAPISTRANO: 1940; Rene, Leon T. (1902-
).
WHEN YOU'RE AWAY: 1914; words: Blos-
som, Henry (1866-1919); music: Herbert, Vic-
tor (1859-1924).
WHEN YOUR HAIR HAS TURNED TO SIL-
VER: 1930; words: Fletcher, Archie (1890-
); music: De Rose, Peter (1900-   ); To-
bias, Charles (1898-   ).
WHEN YOU WORE A TULIP AND I WORE
A RED, RED ROSE: 1914; Magidson, Her-
bert (Herb) (1906-   ); Mahoney, Jack (1882-
1945); music: Wenrich, Percy (-1952).
WHERE DO WE GO FROM HERE, BOYS?:
1917; words: Johnson, Howard E. (1887-1941);
music: Wenrich, Percy (-1952).
WHERE DO YOU WORKA JOHN?: 1926;
Marks, Charles B. (1890-   ); Warren, Harry
(1893-   ); Weinberg, Mortimer.
WHISPERING: 1920; words: Coburn, Richard
(1886-   ); music: Rose, Vincent (1880-1944);
Schonberger, John (1892-   ).
WHISTLE WHILE YOU WORK: 1938 (movie:
Snow White and the Seven Dwarfs); words:
Morey, Larry (1905-   ); music: Churchill,
Frank E. (1901-1942).
WHITE CLIFFS OF DOWER: 1941; words:
Burton, Nat (1901-1945); music: Kent, Walter
(1911-   ).
WHO'S AFRAID OF THE BIG BAD WOLF?:
1933; (movie: *Three Little Pigs);* Ronell, Ann;
Churchill, Frank E. (1901-1942).

WHO'S SORRY NOW?: 1923; words: Kalmar, Bert (1884-1947); music: Ruby, Harry (1895-); Snyder, Ted (1881-).

WHO'S YOUR LITTLE WHOOSIS?: 1931; words: Hirsch, Walter (1891-); music: Bernie, Ben (1891-1943); Goering, Al (1898)

WHO WOULDN'T LOVE YOU?: 1942; words: Carey, Bill (1916-); music: Gischer, Carl Theodore (1912-).

WHY DON'T WE DO THIS MORE OFTEN?: 1941; words: Newman, Charles; music: Wrubel, Allie (1905-).

WHY FIGHT THE FEELING?: 1950 (movie: Let's Dance); Loesser, Frank (1910-).

WHY WAS I BORN?: 1929; words: Hammerstein II, Oscar (1895-); music: Kern, Jerome (1885-1945).

WILL YOU LOVE ME IN DECEMBER AS YOU DO IN MAY?: 1905; words: Walker, James J. (1881-1946); music: Ball, Ernest R. (1878-1927).

WINTER WONDERLAND: 1934; Smith, Dick; Bernard, Felix (1897-1944).

WITH A SONG IN MY HEART: 1929; words: Hart, Lorenz (1895-1943); music: Rodgers, Richard (1902-).

WITH EVERY BREATH I TAKE: 1934; words: Robin Leo (1900-); music: Rainger, Ralph (1901-1942).

WITH MY EYES WIDE OPEN I'M DREAMING: 1934; words: Gordon, Mack (1904-); music: Revel, Harry (1905-).

WITH PLENTY OF MONEY AND YOU: 1936 (movie: Gold Diggers of 1936); words: Dubin, Al (1891-1945); Harburg, E. Y. ("Yip") (1898-); music: Arlen, Harold (1905-); Warren, Harry (1893-).

WITH THE WIND AND THE RAIN IN YOUR HAIR: 1940; Edwards, Clara (1925-); Lawrence, Jack (1912-).

THE WOODPECKER SONG: 1939; Adamson, Harold (1906-); Bruno, C., Di Lazarro, Eldo.

THE WOODY WOODPECKER SONG: 1948; (movie: Wet Blanket Policy); Idress, Ramez (1911-); Tibbles, George F. (1913-).

THE WORLD IS WAITING FOR THE SUNRISE: 1919; Lockhart, Gene (Eugene) (1891-); Seitz; Ernest J.

WOULD YOU?: 1936 (movie: San Francisco); words: Freed, Arthur (1894-); music: Brown, Nacio Herb (1896-).

WOULD YOU LIKE TO TAKE A WALK?: 1930; words: Dixon, Mort (1892-); music: Warren, Harry (1893-).

YAH-TA-TA, YAH-TA-TA: 1945; words: Burke, Johnny (1908-); music: Van Heusen, Jimmy (1913-).

YES, SIR THAT'S MY BABY: 1925; words: Kahn, Gus (1886-1941); music: Donaldson, Walter (1893-1947).

YES, WE HAVE NO BANANAS: 1922; Conn, Irving (1898-); Silver, Frank (1896-).

YOU ARE MY LUCKY STAR: 1935; words: Freed, Arthur (1894-); music: Brown, Nacio Herb (1896-).

YOU BELONG TO MY HEART: 1941; (movie: The Three Caballeros); Gilbert, Ray (1912-); Lara, Augustin.

YOU CAME ALONG: 1931; words: Heyman, Edward (1907-); music: Green, Johnny (1908-).

YOU CAN'T PULL THE WOOL OVER MY EYES: 1936; words: Newman, Charles; music: Ager, Milton (1893-); Mencher, Murray, (Ted Murray) (1898-).

YOU'D BE SO NICE TO COME HOME TO: 1943 (movie: Something to Shout About): Porter, Cole (1893-).

YOU GO TO MY HEAD: 1938; words: Gillespie, Haven; music: Coots, Fred J. (1897-).

YOU GOTTA BE A FOOTBALL HERO: 1933; Fields, Buddy (Arthur B.) (1899-); Lewis, Al (1901-); Sherman, Al (1897-).

YOU HIT THE SPOT: 1936 (movie: Collegiate); words: Gordon, Mack (1904-); music: Revel, Harry (1905-).

YOU KEEP COMING BACK LIKE A SONG: 1945; (movie: Blue Skies); Berlin, Irving (1888-).

YOU LUCKY PEOPLE YOU: 1941 (movie: Road to Zanzibar); words: Burke, Johnny (1908-); music: Van Heusen, Jimmy (1913-).

YOU MADE ME LOVE YOU: 1912; words: McCarthy, Joseph (1885-1943); music: De Rose, Peter (1900-); Monaco, James V. (1885-1945).

YOU MUST HAVE BEEN A BEAUTIFUL BABY: 1938; Mercer, Johnny (1909-); Warren, Harry (1893-).

YOU'RE AN OLD SMOOTHIE: 1932; words: De Sylva, Buddy (1895-1950); music: Brown, Nacio Herb (1896-); Whiting, Richard A. (1891-1938).

YOU'RE DANGEROUS: 1941 (movie: Road to Zanzibar); words: Burke, Johnny (1908-); music: Van Heusen, Jimmy (1913-).

YOU'RE MY EVERYTHING: 1931; words: Dixon, Mort (1892-); Young, Joseph (1989-1939); music: Warren, Harry (1893-).

YOU'RE THE CREAM IN MY COFFEE: 1928; words: Brown, Lew (1893-); De Sylva, Buddy (1895-1950); music: Henderson, Ray (1896-).

YOUR EYES HAVE TOLD ME SO: 1919; words: Kahn, Gus (1886-1941); music: Blaufuss, Walter (d. 1945); Van Alstyne, Egbert Anson (1882-1951).

YOU STARTED SOMETHING: 1941; words: Robin, Leo (1900-); music: Rainger, Ralph (1901-1942).

YOU TOOK ADVANTAGE OF ME: 1928; words: Fields, Herbert; Hart, Lorenz (1895-1943); music: Rodgers, Richard (1902-).

YOU TURNED THE TABLES ON ME: 1936; words: Mitchell, Sidney D. (1888-1942); music: Alter, Louis (1902-).

YOU'VE GOT ME CRYING AGAIN: 1933; words: Newman, Charles; music: Jones, Isham (1894-).

YOU WERE MEANT FOR ME: 1929; words: Freed, Arthur (1894-); Sissle, Noble (1889-); music: Brown, Nacio Herb (1896-).

YOU, YOU DARLIN': 1940; words: Scholl, Jack (1903-); Jerome, M. K. (1893-).

Songs from Broadway Plays:
The All-Time Hit-Tunes from the Great Broadway Musicals

ADELAIDE'S LAMENT: Guys and Dolls (Abe Burrows, Jo Swerling, Frank Loesser), 1950.

AFTER ALL, IT'S SPRING: Seventeen (Kim Gannon, Walter Kent), 1951.

AH, SWEET MYSTERY OF LIFE: Naughty Marietta (Rida Johnson Young, Victor Herbert), 1910.

AIN'T MISBEHAVIN': Hot Chocolates (Andy Razaf, Harry Brooks, "Fats" Waller), 1929.

ALICE BLUE GOWN: Irene (Joseph McCarthy, Harry Tierney), 1919.

ALL ALONE MONDAY: The Ramblers (Bert Kalmar, Harry Ruby), 1926.

ALL ER NOTHIN': Oklahoma! (Oscar Hammerstein II, Richard Rodgers), 1943.

ALLEZ-VOUS EN: Can-Can (Cole Porter, 1953.

ALL FOR HIM: *Paint Your Wagon* (Alan Jay Lerner, Frederick Loewe), 1951.

ALL OF YOU: *Silk Stockings* (Cole Porter), 1955.

ALL THE KING'S HORSES: *Three's a Crowd* (additional song by Howard Dietz, Alex Wilder, Edward Brandt), 1930.

ALL THE THINGS YOU ARE: *Very Warm for May* (Oscar Hammerstein II, Jerome Kern), 1939.

ALL THROUGH THE NIGHT: *Anything Goes* (Cole Porter), 1934.

ALMOST LIKE BEING IN LOVE: *Brigadoon* (Alan Jay Lerner, Frederick Loewe), 1947.

ALONE TOGETHER: *Flying Colors* (Howard Dietz, Arthur Schwartz), 1932.

ALONG WITH ME: *Call Me Mister* (Harold Rome), 1946.

ALWAYS TRUE TO YOU (IN MY FASHION): *Kiss Me Kate* (Cole Porter), 1948.

ALWAYS YOU: *Always You* (Oscar Hammerstein II, Herbert Stothart), 1920.

THE ANGELUS: *The Serenade* (Harry Bache Smith, Victor Herbert), 1897.

THE ANGELUS: *Sweethearts* (Robert Smith, Victor Herbert), 1913.

ANNA LILLA: *New Girl in Town* (Bob Merrill), 1957.

ANOTHER AUTUMN: *Paint Your Wagon* (Alan Jay Lerner, Frederick Loewe), 1951.

ANOTHER OP'NIN', ANOTHER SHOW: *Kiss Me Kate* (Cole Porter), 1948.

ANOTHER PRINCELY SCHEME: *Peter Pan* (Carolyn Leigh, Mark Charlap), 1954.

ANYTHING GOES: *Anything Goes* (Cole Porter), 1934.

ANYTHING YOU CAN DO: *Annie Get Your Gun* (Irving Berlin), 1942.

APRIL IN PARIS: *Walk a Little Faster* (E. Y. "Yip" Harburg, Vernon Duke), 1932.

ARE YOU HAVIN' ANY FUN?: *George White's Scandals of 1939* (Jack Yellen, Sammy Fain).

ARE YOU HAVIN' ANY FUN?: *Ziegfeld Follies of 1936-37* (Jack Yellen, Sammy Fain).

THE ARMY'S MADE A MAN OUT OF ME: *This Is The Army* (Irving Berlin), 1942.

AS ON THROUGH THE SEASONS WE SAIL: *Silk Stockings* (Cole Porter), 1955.

AT LAST: *Earl Carroll's Sketch Book of 1935* (Sam Lewis, Henry Tobias).

AT LONG LAST LOVE: *You Never Know* (Cole Porter), 1938.

AT THE CHECK APRON BALL: *New Girl in Town* (Bob Merrill), 1957.

AT THE RED ROSE COTILLION: *Where's Charley?* (Frank Loesser), 1948.

AUF WIEDERSEHEN: *The Blue Paradise* (Edgar Smith, Sigmund Romberg), 1915.

AUF WIEDERSEHEN: *The Boys and Betty* (George Hobart, Silvio Hein), 1908.

AUF WIEDERSEHEN: *The Catch of the Season* (Charles Taylor, William T. Francis), 1905.

AUF WIEDERSEHEN: *The Goddess of Truth* (Stanislaus Strange, Julian Edwards), 1896.

AUF WIEDERSEHEN: *The Gipsy* (Avery Hopwood, Gustav Luders), 1912.

AUTOGRAPH CHANT: *Hazel Flagg* (Bob Hilliard, Jule Styne), 1953.

AUTUMN IN NEW YORK: *Thumbs Up* (Vernon Duke), 1934.

THE BABBITT AND THE BROMIDE: *Funny Face* (Ira Gershwin, George Gershwin), 1927.

BABES IN THE WOODS: *Very Good Eddie* (Schuyler Green, Jerome Kern), 1915.

BABY: *Castles in the Air* (Raymond Peck, Percy Wenrich), 1926.

BABY MINE: *Blackbirds of 1930* (Flourney Miller, Andy Razaf, Eubie Blake).

THE BABY YOU LOVE: *Me and Juliet* (Oscar Hammerstein II, Richard Rodgers), 1953.

BALI HA'I: *South Pacific* (Oscar Hammerstein II, Richard Rodgers), 1949.

BALLAD OF MACK THE KNIFE: *The Threepenny Opera* (Marc Blitzstein, Kurt Weill), 1954.

BAMBALINA: *Wildflower* (Oscar Hammerstein II, Otto Harbach, Herbert Stothart, Vincent Youmans), 1923.

BAMBOO CAGE: *House of Flowers* (Truman Capote, Harold Arlen), 1954.

BANDANA DAYS: *Shuffle Along* (Noble Sissle, Eubie Blake), 1921.

THE BATTLE: *Peter Pan* (Carolyn Leigh, Mark Charlap), 1954.

BEAT OUT DAT RHYTHM ON THE DRUM: *Carmen Jones* (Oscar Hammerstein II; based on Bizet's *Carmen*), 1943.

BEAUTIFUL AND DAMNED: *The Passing Show of 1923* (Harold Atteridge, Sigmund Romberg, Jean Schwartz).

BECAUSE YOU'RE YOU: *The Red Mill* (Henry Blossom, Victor Herbert), 1906.

BEDELIA: *The Jersey Lily* (additional song by William Jerome, Jean Schwartz), 1903.

BEER BARREL POLKA: *Yokel Boy* (Lew Brown, Wladimir Timm, Jaromir Vejvoda), 1939.

BEGIN THE BEGUINE: *Jubilee* (Cole Porter), 1935.

BE KIND TO YOUR PARENTS: *Fanny* (Harold Rome), 1954.

BE LIKE THE BLUEBIRD: *Anything Goes* (Cole Porter), 1944.

THE BELLE OF AVENUE A: *Fad and Folly* (Paul West, Henry Waller), 1902.

BE MY LITTLE BABY BUMBLEBEE: *Ziegfeld Follies of 1911* (George V. Hobart, Raymond Hubbell).

BE STILL MY HEART: *Sunny* (Oscar Hammerstein II, Otto Harbach, Jerome Kern), 1925.

BESS, YOU IS MY WOMAN: *Porgy and Bess* (Ira Gershwin, George Gershwin), 1935.

THE BEST OF ALL POSSIBLE WORLDS: *Candide* (Richard Wilbur, Dorothy Parker, John La Touche, Leonard Bernstein), 1956.

THE BEST THINGS IN LIFE ARE FREE: *Good News* (Lew Brown, Buddy De Sylva, Ray Henderson), 1927.

BEWITCHED: *Pal Joey* (Lorenz Hart, Richard Rodgers), 1940.

BIDIN' MY TIME: *Girl Crazy* (Ira Gershwin, George Gershwin), 1930.

THE BIG, BLACK GIANT: *Me and Juliet* (Oscar Hammerstein II, Richard Rodgers), 1953.

BIG D: *The Most Happy Fella* (Frank Loesser), 1956.

BIG MOVIE SHOW IN THE SKY: *Texas Li'l Darlin'* (Johnny Mercer, Robert Emmett Dolan), 1949.

BILL: *Show Boat* (Oscar Hammerstein II, Jerome Kern), 1927.

BILLY BIGELOW'S SOLILOQUY: See Soliloquy.

BIRTHDAY SONG: *Fanny* (Harold Rome), 1954.

BIRTH OF THE BLUES: *George White's Scandals of 1926* (Lew Brown, Buddy De Sylva, Ray Henderson).

BLACK BOTTOM: *George White's Scandals of 1926* (Lew Brown, Buddy De Sylva, Ray Henderson).

BLOW, BLOW, GABRIEL: *Anything Goes* (Cole Porter), 1934.

THE BLUE ROOM: *The Girl Friend* (Lorenz Hart, Richard Rodgers), 1926.

BLUE SKIES: *Betsy* (additional song by Irving Berlin), 1926.

BODY AND SOUL: *Three's a Crowd* (additional song by Frank Eyton, Edward Heyman, Robert Sour, Johnny Green), 1930.

BONGA, BONGA, BONGA: See Civilization.

BONITA: *The Love Call* (Harry Smith, Sigmund Romberg), 1927.

BON VOYAGE: *Candide* (Richard Wilbur, Dorothy Parker, John La Touche, Leonard Bernstein), 1956.

THE BOWERY: *Smiles* (Harold Adamson, Clifford Gram, Ring Lardner, Vincent Youmans), 1930.

THE BOY FRIEND: *The Boy Friend* (Sandy Wilson), 1954.

BRIGADOON: *Brigadoon* (Alan Jay Lerner, Frederick Loewe), 1947.

BROTHER CAN YOU SPARE A DIME?: *Americana* (E. Y. "Yip" Harburg, Vernon Duke), 1932.

BROWN OCTOBER ALE: *Robin Hood* (Harry Smith, Reginald De Koven), 1890.

BRUSH UP YOUR SHAKESPEARE: *Kiss Me Kate* (Cole Porter), 1948.

BUCKLE DOWN, WINSOCKI: *Best Foot Forward* (Ralph Blane, Hugh Martin), 1941.

BUNNY, BUNNY, BUNNY: *Star and Garter* (Harold Rome), 1942.

A BUSHEL AND A PECK: *Guys and Dolls* Abe Burrows, Jo Swerling, Frank Loesser), 1950.

BUT NOT FOR ME: *Girl Crazy* (Ira Gershwin, George Gershwin), 1930.

BUTTON UP YOUR OVERCOAT: *Follow Through* (Lew Brown, Buddy Sylva, Ray Henderson), 1929.

BYE, BYE BABY: *Gentlemen Prefer Blondes* (Leo Robin, Jule Styne), 1949.

BY LANTERN LIGHT: *Plain and Fancy* (Arnold B. Horwitt, Albert Hague), 1955.

BY THE MISSISSINIWAH: *Something for the Boys* (Cole Porter), 1943.

CABIN IN THE SKY: *Cabin in the Sky* (John La Touche, Vernon Duke), 1941.

CALIFORNIA, HERE I COME: *Big Boy* (Buddy De Sylva, Al Jolson, Joseph Meyer), 1925.

CAMILLE, COLLETTE, FIFI: *Seventh Heaven* (Stella Unger, Victor Young), 1955.

CAN-CAN: *Can-Can* (Cole Porter), 1953.

CAN'T HELP LOVIN' DAT MAN: *Show Boat* (Oscar Hammerstein II, Jerome Kern), 1927.

CAPTAIN SPAULDING: See Hooray for Captain Spaulding.

CARELESS RHAPSODY: *By Jupiter* (Lorenz Hart, Richard Rodgers), 1942.

CARINO MIO: *Paint Your Wagon* (Alan Jay Lerner, Frederick Loewe), 1951.

CARNIVAL BALLET: *Plain and Fancy* (Arnold B. Horwitt, Albert Hague), 1955.

CARNIVAL TANGO: *The Boy Friend* (Sandy Wilson), 1954.

CAROLINA IN THE MORNING: *The Passing Show of 1922* (additional song by Gus Kahn, Walter Donaldson), 1922.

CECILIA: *Mamma's Baby Boy* (Junie McCree, Hans Linne), 1912.

C'EST LA VIE: *Seventh Heaven* (Stella Unger, Victor Young), 1955.

C'EST MAGNIFIQUE: *Can-Can* (Cole Porter), 1953.

CHARLESTON: *Running Wild* (Cecil Mack, James P. Johnson), 1923.

CHEERFUL LITTLE EARFUL: *Sweet and Low* (Ira Gershwin, Billy Rose, Harry Warren), 1930.

CHESS AND CHECKERS: *New Girl in Town* (Bob Merrill), 1957.

CHICAGO: *Pal Joey* (Lorenz Hart, Richard Rodgers), 1940.

CHICO'S REVERIE: *Seventh Heaven* (Stella Unger, Victor Young), 1955.

CHINATOWN, MY CHINATOWN: *Up and Down Broadway* (William Jerome, Jean Schwartz), 1910.

CHIQUITA: *Round the Town* (Walter Donaldson), 1924.

CHLOE: *Sinbad* (additional song by Buddy De Sylva, Al Jolson), 1918.

THE CHOCOLATE SOLDIER: *The Chocolate Soldier* (Rudolph Bernauer, Leopold Jacobson, Oscar Straus; based on *Arms and the Man*, by George Bernard Shaw), 1909.

CHOP STICKS: *Just Because* (Anne O'Ryan, Helen Woodruff, Madelyn Sheppard), 1922.

CHRISTOPHER STREET: *Wonderful Town* (Betty Comden, Adolph Green, Leonard Bernstein), 1953.

CINDERELLA BROWN: *International Revue* (Dorothy Fields, Jimmy McHugh), 1930.

CINDY: *Cinderella on Broadway* (Harold Atteridge, Alfred Goodman, Bert Grant), 1920.

CITY MOUSE, COUNTRY MOUSE: *Plain and Fancy* (Arnold B. Horwitt, Albert Hague), 1955.

CIVILIZATION (BONGA, BONGA, BONGA): *Angel in the Wings* (Robert Hilliard, Carl Sigman), 1947.

CLAP YOUR HANDS: *Oh, Kay* (Ira Gershwin, George Gershwin), 1926.

CLEOPATTERER: *Leave It to Jane* (Guy Bolton, P. G. Wodehouse, Jerome Kern; based on *The College Widow*, by George Ade), 1917.

CLIMB UP THE MOUNTAIN: *Out of This World* (Cole Porter), 1950.

CLOSE AS PAGES IN A BOOK: *Up in Central Park* (Dorothy Fields, Herbert Fields, Sigmund Romberg), 1942.

COCKEYED OPTIMIST: *South Pacific* (Oscar Hammerstein II, Richard Rodgers), 1949.

COLD CREAM JAR SONG: *Fanny* (Harold Rome), 1954.

COME ALONG WITH ME: *Can-Can* (Cole Porter), 1953.

COME, HERO MINE: *The Chocolate Soldier* Rudolph Bernauer, Leopold Jacobson, Oscar Straus; based on *Arms and the Man* by George Bernard Shaw), 1909.

COME RAIN OR COME SHINE: *St. Louis Woman* (Johnny Mercer, Harold Arlen), 1946.

COMES LOVE: *Yokel Boy* (Lew Brown, Sammy Stept, Charles Tobias), 1939.

COME TO ME, BEND TO ME: *Brigadoon* (Alan Jay Lerner, Frederick Loewe), 1947.

CONGA!: *Wonderful Town* (Betty Comden, Adolph Green, Leonard Bernstein), 1953.

CONQUERING NEW YORK: *Wonderful Town* (Betty Comden, Adolph Green, Leonard Bernstein), 1953.

COULD BE: *Wish You Were Here* (Harold Rome), 1952.

CRAZY RHYTHM: *Here's Howe* (Irving Caesar, Joseph Myer), 1928.

CUDDLE UP A LITTLE CLOSER, LOVEY MINE: *Three Twins* (Otto Harbach, Karl Hoschna), 1908.

A CUP OF COFFEE, A SANDWICH AND YOU: *Andre Charlot's Revue of 1925* (Billy Rose, Al Dubin, Joseph Meyer).

DANCE, DANCE, DANCE: *Artists and Models of 1930* (Ernie Golden, Harold Stern).

DANCE, DANCE, DANCE: *The Whirl of New York* (Edgar Smith, Alfred Goodman), 1921.

DANCE, LITTLE LADY: *This Year of Grace* (Noel Coward), 1928.

DANCE WITH ME: *Princess Flavia* (Harry Smith, Sigmund Romberg), 1925.

DANCING IN THE DARK: *The Band Wagon* (Howard Dietz, Arthur Schwartz), 1931.

DANCING ON THE CEILING: *Simple Simon* (Lorenz Hart, Richard Rodgers), 1930.

DARN THAT DREAM: *Swingin' the Dream* (Eddie De Lange, Jimmy van Heusen), 1939.

DAT'S LOVE: *Carmen Jones* (Oscar Hammerstein II; based on Bizet's *Carmen*), 1943.

DAY AFTER DAY: *Flying Colors* (Howard Dietz, Arthur Schwartz), 1932.

DAYS GONE BY: *Sitting Pretty* (Guy Bolton, P. G. Wodehouse, Jerome Kern), 1924.

DEEP IN MY HEART: *The Student Prince* (Dorothy Donnelly, Sigmund Romberg), 1924.

DEEP RIVER: *Deep River* (Lawrence Stallings, Franke Harling), 1926.

DESERT SONG: *The Desert Song* (Oscar Hammerstein II, Otto Harbach, Frank Mandel, Sigmund Romberg), 1926.

DIAMONDS ARE A GIRL'S BEST FRIEND: *Gentlemen Prefer Blondes* (Leo Robin, Jule Styne), 1949.

DID YOU CLOSE YOUR EYES?: *New Girl in Town* (Bob Merrill), 1957.

DIGA-DIGA-DOO: *Blackbirds of 1928* (Dorothy Fields, Jimmy McHugh).

DINAH: *How Come* (Harry Creamer, Will Vodery, Ben Harris), 1923.

DINAH: *When Claudia Smiles* (additional song by Stanley Murphy, Henry I. Marshall), 1914.

DISTANT MELODY: *Peter Pan* (additional song by Betty Comden, Adolph Green, Jule Styne), 1954.

DITES-MOI: *South Pacific* (Oscar Hammerstein II, Richard Rodgers), 1949.

DO-DO-DO: *Oh, Kay* (Ira Gershwin, George Gershwin), 1926.

DO I LOVE YOU, DO I?: *Du Barry Was a Lady* (Cole Porter), 1939.

DOIN' THE OLD YAHOO STEP: *Lend an Ear* (Charles Gaynor), 1948.

DOIN' WHAT COMES NATUR'LLY: *Annie Get Your Gun* (Irving Berlin), 1942.

DO IT AGAIN: *The French Doll* (Buddy De Sylva, George Gershwin), 1922.

DO IT THE HARD WAY: *Pal Joey* (Lorenz Hart, Richard Rodgers), 1940.

DOLORES: *Papa's Darling* (Harry Smith, Ivan Caryll), 1914.

DON JOSE: *Wish You Were Here* (Harold Rome), 1952.

DON'T BE AFRAID: *A Tree Grows in Brooklyn* (Dorothy Fields, Arthur Schwartz), 1951.

DON'T EVER LEAVE ME: *Sweet Adeline* (Oscar Hammerstein II, Jerome Kern), 1929.

DON'T GO IN THE LION'S CAGE TONIGHT: *The Blue Moon* (additional song by Jim Gilroy, E. Ray Goetz), 1906.

DON'T LIKE GOODBYES: *House of Flowers* (Truman Capote, Harold Arlen), 1954.

DRINKING SONG: *The Student Prince* (Dorothy Donnelly, Sigmund Romberg), 1924.

DRUMS IN MY HEART: *Through the Years* (Brian Hooker, Vincent Youmans), 1932.

EADIE WAS A LADY: *Take a Chance* (Buddy De Sylva, Lawrence Schwab, Nacio Herb Brown, Richard Whiting), 1932.

THE EAGLE AND ME: *Bloomer Girl* (E. Y. "Yip" Harburg, Harold Arlen), 1944.

EASTER PARADE: *As Thousands Cheer* (Irving Berlin), 1933.

EDELWEISS: *Louis the Fourteenth* (Arthur Wimperis, Sigmund Romberg), 1925.

EL DORADO: *Candide* (Richard Wilbur, Dorothy Parker, John La Touche, Leonard Bernstein), 1956.

ELIZABETH: *Wonder Bar* (Rowland Leigh, Robert Katscher), 1931.

EMBRACEABLE YOU: *Girl Crazy* (Ira Gershwin, George Gershwin), 1930.

ESTELLITA: *Princess Pat* (Henry Blossom, Victor Herbert), 1915.

EVELINA: *Bloomer Girl* (E. Y. "Yip" Harburg, Harold Arlen), 1944.

EVEN AS YOU AND I: *George White's Scandals of 1925* (Lew Brown, Buddy De Sylva, Ray Henderson).

EVERYBODY KNOWS I LOVE SOMEBODY: *Rosalie* (Ira Gershwin, P. G. Wodehouse, George Gershwin, Sigmund Romberg), 1928.

EVERYBODY LOVES EVERYBODY: *Wish You Were Here* (Harold Rome), 1952.

EVERYBODY LOVES TO MAKE A BOW: *Hazel Flagg* (Bob Hilliard, Jule Styne), 1953.

EVERYBODY STEP: *The Music Box Review of 1921* (Irving Berlin).

EVERY DAY IS LADIES DAY TO ME: *The Red Mill* (Henry Blossom, Victor Herbert), 1906.

EVERY MAN IS A STUPID MAN: *Can-Can* (Cole Porter), 1953.

EVERY STREET'S A BOULEVARD IN OLD NEW YORK: *Hazel Flagg* (Bob Hilliard, Jule Styne), 1953.

EVERYTHING HAPPENS TO ME: *Walk with Music* (Johnny Mercer, Hoagy Carmichael), 1940.

EVERYTHING I LOVE: *Let's Face It* (Cole Porter), 1941.

EVERYTHING I'VE GOT BELONGS TO YOU: *By Jupiter* (Lorenz Hart, Richard Rodgers), 1942.

EVERYTIME: *Best Foot Forward* (Ralph Blane, Hugh Martin), 1941.

EVERY TIME WE SAY GOODBYE: *Seven Lively Arts* (Cole Porter), 1944.

EXACTLY LIKE YOU: *International Revue* (Dorothy Fields, Jimmy McHugh), 1930.

EYES THAT LOVE: *The Love Call* (Harry Smith, Sigmund Romberg), 1927.

FALLING IN LOVE: *The Chocolate Soldier* (Rudolph Bernauer, Leopold Jacobson, Oscar Straus; based on *Arms and the Man* by George Bernard Shaw), 1909.

FALLING IN LOVE WITH LOVE: *The Boys from Syracuse* (Lorenz Hart, Richard Rodgers), 1938.

FANNY: *Fanny* (Harold Rome), 1954.

FASCINATING RHYTHM: *Lady Be Good* (Ira Gershwin, George Gershwin), 1924.

FEATHER IN THE BREEZE: *Everybody's Welcome* (Irving Kahal, Sammy Fain), 1931.

A FELLOW NEEDS A GIRL: *Allegro* (Oscar Hammerstein II, Richard Rodgers), 1947.

FEUDIN' AND FIGHTIN': *Laffing Room Only* (Burton Lane), 1944.

FINE AND DANDY: *Fine and Dandy* (Paul Jones, Kay Swift), 1930.

FIVE FOOT TWO: *Hello Lola* (Dorothy Donnelly, William B. Kernell; based on *Seventeen*, by Booth Tarkington), 1926.

FLATTERY: *Wish You Were Here* (Harold Rome), 1952.

FLINGS: *New Girl in Town* (Bob Merrill), 1957.

THE FLOWER GARDEN OF MY HEART: *Pal Joey* (Lorenz Hart, Richard Rodgers), 1940.

FOLLOW THE FOLD: *Guys and Dolls* (Abe Burrows, Jo Swerling, Frank Loesser), 1950.

FOLLOW YOUR HEART: *Plain and Fancy* (Arnold B. Horwitt, Albert Hague), 1955.

FOOLS FALL IN LOVE: *Louisiana Purchase* (Irving Berlin), 1940.

FRANKLIN D. ROOSEVELT JONES: *Sing Out the News* (Harold I. Rome), 1938.

FREDDY AND HIS FIDDLE: *Song of Norway* (George Forrest, Robert Wright; based on the music of Edvard Grieg), 1944.

FRENCH MARCHING SONG: *The Desert Song* (Oscar Hammerstein II, Otto Harbach, Frank Mandel, Sigmund Romberg), 1926.

FRIENDSHIP: *Du Barry Was a Lady* (Cole Porter). 1939.

FRIENDSHIP: *The Yankee Princess* (Buddy De Sylva, Emmerich Kalman), 1922.

FROM NOW ON: *La-La Lucille* (Buddy De Sylva, Arthur Jackson, George Gershwin), 1919.

FROM NOW ON: *Leave It to Me* (Cole Porter), 1938.

FROM THIS DAY ON: *Brigadoon* (Alan Jay Lerner, Frederick Loewe), 1947.

FUGUE FOR TIN HORNS: *Guys and Dolls* (Abe Burrows, Jo Swerling, Frank Loesser), 1950.

FUNNY FACE: *Funny Face* (Ira Gershwin, George Gershwin), 1927.

FUNNY LITTLE SAILOR MAN: *The New Moon* (Oscar Hammerstein II, Frank Mandel, Lawrence Schwab, Sigmund Romberg), 1928.

THE GAME: *Damn Yankees* (Richard Adler, Jerry Ross), 1955.

THE GENTLEMAN IS A DOPE: *Allegro* (Oscar Hammerstein II, Richard Rodgers), 1947.

GENTLEMEN PREFER BLONDES: *No Foolin'* (Gene Buck, Irving Caesar, J. P. McEvoy, Rudolf Friml), 1926.

GET HAPPY: *Nine-fifteen Revue* (Edward Eliscu, Harold Arlen), 1930.

GET ME TO THE CHURCH ON TIME: *My Fair Lady* (Alan Jay Lerner, Frederick Loewe), 1955.

GET OUT OF TOWN: *Leave It to Me* (Cole Porter), 1938.

GETTING TO KNOW YOU: *The King and I* (Oscar Hammerstein II, Richard Rodgers), 1951.

GIANNINA MIA: *The Firefly* (Otto Harbach, Rudolf Friml), 1912.

THE GIRL FRIEND: *The Girl Friend* (Lorenz Hart, Richard Rodgers), 1926.

GIRL OF MY DREAMS: *The Girl of My Dreams* (Otto Harbach, Karl Hoschna), 1911.

GIRL OF MY DREAMS: *Ziegfeld Follies of 1920* (Irving Berlin).

GIRLS, GIRLS, GIRLS: *The Merry Widow* (Adrian Ross, Franz Lehar), 1907.

THE GIRL THAT I MARRY: *Annie Get Your Gun* (Irving Berlin), 1946.

GIVE MY REGARDS TO BROADWAY: *Little Johnny Jones* (George M. Cohan), 1904.

GLITTER AND BE GAY: *Candide* (Richard Wilbur, Dorothy Parker, John La Touche, Leonard Bernstein), 1956.

GLOVE DANCE: *Seventh Heaven* (Stella Unger, Victor Young), 1955.

GOIN' HOME TRAIN: *Call Me Mister* (Harold Rome), 1946.

GO INTO YOUR DANCE: *The New Yorkers* (Cole Porter), 1930.

GO INTO YOUR DANCE: *The Passing Show of 1923* (Harold Atteridge, Sigmund Romberg, Jean Schwartz).

GOLDEN DAYS: *The Student Prince* (Dorothy Donelly, Sigmund Romberg), 1924.

GOODBYE LOVE: *Wish You Were Here* (Harold Rome), 1952.

GOODBYE OLD GIRL: *Damn Yankees* (Richard Adler, Jerry Ross), 1955.

GOOD NEWS: *Good News* (Lew Brown, Buddy De Sylva, Ray Henderson), 1927.

GOODNIGHT, SWEETHART: *Three Twins* (Otto Harbach, Karl Hoschna), 1908.

GOOD NIGHT, SWEETHEART: *Earl Carroll's Vanities of 1930* (James Campbell, Reg Connelly, Ray Noble).

GOOD NIGHT, SWEETHEART: *Earl Carroll's Vanities of 1931* (Jimmy Campbell, Reg Connelly, Ray Noble).

GOOD PALS: *The Love Call* (Harry Smith, Sigmund Romberg), 1927.

THE GOSSIPS: *Where's Charley?* (Frank Loesser), 1948.

GREAT DAY: *Great Day* (Billy Rose, Vincent Youmans), 1929.

THE GREATEST SHOW ON EARTH: *Lady in the Dark* (Ira Gershwin, Kurt Weill), 1941.

GUYS AND DOLLS: *Guys and Dolls* (Abe Burrows, Jo Swerling, Frank Loesser), 1950.

THE GYPSY IN ME: *Anything Goes* (Cole Porter), 1934.

HAIL, BIBINSKI: *Silk Stockings* (Cole Porter), 1955.

HALLELUJAH: *Hit the Deck* (Clifford Grey, Leo Robin, Vincent Youmans), 1927.

HAND ME DOWN THAT CAN OF BEANS: *Paint Your Wagon* (Alan Jay Lerner, Frederick Loewe), 1951.

HANDS ACROSS THE TABLE: *Continental Vanities* (Mitchell Parish, Maurice Aubert, Jean Delettre), 1934.

HAPPY HUNTING HORN: *Pal Joey* (Lorenz Hart, Richard Rodgers), 1940.

HAPPY IN LOVE: *Sons o, Fun* (Irving Kahal, Jack Yellen, Sammy Fain), 1940.

HAPPY LITTLE CROOK: *Seventh Heaven* (Stella Unger, Victor Young), 1955.

HAPPY TALK: *South Pacific* (Oscar Hammerstein II, Richard Rodgers), 1949.

HAPPY TO MAKE YOUR ACQUAINTANCE: *The Most Happy Fella* (Frank Loesser), 1956.

HARK TO THE SONG OF THE NIGHT: *Out of This World* (Cole Porter), 1950.

HARRIGAN: *Fifty Miles From Boston* (George M. Cohan), 1908.

HAS ANYBODY HERE SEEN KELLY?: *The Jolly Bachelors* (Glen MacDonough, Raymond Hubbell), 1910.

HAS I LET YOU DOWN?: *House of Flowers* (Truman Capote, Harold Arlen), 1954.

HAUNTED HEART: *Inside U.S.A.* (Howard Dietz, Arthur Schwartz), 1948.

HAVE YOU MET MISS JONES?: *I'd Rather Be Right* (Lorenz Hart, Richard Rodgers), 1937.

HEAD OVER HEELS IN LOVE: *Honeymoon Lane* (Eddie Dowling, James T. Hanley), 1926.

HEART: *Damn Yankees* (Richard Adler, Jerry Ross), 1955.

HEART OF A ROSE: *The Peasant Girl* (Harold Atteridge, Herbert Reynolds, Rudolf Friml), 1915.

HEART OF MY HEART: *Don Quixote* (Harry Smith, Reginald De Koven), 1889.

HEART OF MY HEART: *The Road to Mandalay* (William McKenna, Oreste Vessela), 1916.

HEART OF MY HEART: *Furs and Frills* (Edward Clark, Silvio Hein), 1917.

THE HEATHER ON THE HILL: *Brigadoon* (Alan Jay Lerner, Frederick Loewe), 1947.

HEAT WAVE: *As Thousands Cheer* (Irving Berlin), 1933.

HEAVEN WILL PROTECT THE WORKING GIRL: *Tillie's Nightmare* (Edgar Smith, A. Baldwin Sloane), 1910.

HE HAD REFINEMENT: *A Tree Grows In Brooklyn* (Dorothy Fields, Arthur Schwartz), 1951.

HEIDELBERG STEIN SONG: *The Prince of Pilsen* (Frank Pixley, Gustav Luders), 1900.

HELLO CENTRAL, GIVE ME NO MAN'S LAND: *Sinbad* (additional song by Joe Young, Sam Lewis, Jean Schwartz), 1918.

HELLO, FRISCO, HELLO: *The Ziegfeld Follies of 1915* (Gene Buck, Channing Pollock, Rennold Wolf, Louis Hirsch).

HELLO, HAZEL: *Hazel Flagg* (Bob Hilliard, Jule Styne), 1953.

HELLO YOUNG LOVERS: *The King and I* (Oscar Hammerstein II, Richard Rodgers), 1951.

HERE IN MY ARMS: *Dearest Enemy* (Lorenz Hart, Richard Rodgers), 1925.

HEY, GOOD LOOKIN': *Something for the Boys* (Cole Porter), 1943.

HOLD ME: *Century Revue* (Alfred Bryan, Jean Schwartz), 1920.

HOMEWORK: *Miss Liberty* (Irving Berlin), 1949.

HONEY BUN: *South Pacific* (Oscar Hammerstein II, Richard Rodgers), 1949.

HONEYMOON LANE: See A Little White House.

HOOK'S WALTZ: *Peter Pan* (additional song by Betty Comden, Adolph Green, Jule Styne), 1954.

HOORAY FOR CAPTAIN SPAULDING: *Animal Crackers* (Bert Kalmar, Harry Ruby), 1928.

THE HOSTESS WITH THE MOSTEST: *Call Me Madame* (Irving Berlin), 1950.

THE HOUSE I LIVE IN: *Let Freedom Ring* (Harold Rome), 1942.

HOUSE OF FLOWERS: *House of Flowers* (Truman Capote, Harold Arlen), 1954.

HOW ARE THINGS IN GLOCCA MORRA?: *Finian's Rainbow* (E. Y. "Yip" Harburg, Fred Saidy, Burton Lane), 1947.

HOW CAN I WAIT?: *Paint Your Wagon* (Alan Jay Lerner, Frederick Loewe), 1951.

HOW CAN I TELL YOU ARE AN AMERICAN?: *Knickerbrocker Holiday* (Maxwell Anderson, Kurt Weill), 1938.

HOW DID IT GET SO LATE SO EARLY?: *All in Fun* (June Sillman, William C. K. "Will" Irwin), 1940.

HOW DO YOU RAISE A BARN?: *Plain and Fancy* (Arnold Horwitt, Albert Hague), 1955.

HOW DO YOU SPEAK TO AN ANGEL?: *Hazel Flagg* (Bob Hilliard, Jule Styne), 1953.

HOW'D YOU LIKE TO SPOON WITH ME: *The Earl and the Girl* (additional song by Edward Laska, Jerome Kern), 1905.

HOW HIGH THE MOON: *Two for the Show* (Nancy Hamilton, Morgan Lewis), 1941.

HOW LONG HAS THIS BEEN GOING ON?: *Rosalie* (Ira Gershwin, P. G. Wodehouse, George Gershwin, Sigmund Romberg), 1928.

HOW WAS I TO KNOW?: *Love O'Mike* (Harry Smith, Jerome Kern), 1917.

HUSBAND CAGE: *House of Flowers* (Truman Capote, Harold Arlen), 1954.

A HYMN TO HIM: *My Fair Lady* (Alan Jay Lerner, Frederick Loewe), 1955.

I AM ASHAMED THAT WOMEN ARE SO SIMPLE: *Kiss Me Kate* (Cole Porter), 1948.

I AM LOVED: *Out of This World* (Cole Porter), 1950.

I CAIN'T SAY NO: *Oklahoma!* (Oscar Hammerstein II, Richard Rodgers), 1943.

I CAN DREAM, CAN'T I?: *Right This Way* (Irving Kahal, Sammy Fain), 1938.

I CAN'T DO THE SUN: *Babes in Toyland* (Glen MacDonough, Victor Herbert), 1903.

I CAN'T GET STARTED WITH YOU: *Ziegfeld Follies of 1936-37* (Ira Gershwin, Vernon Duke).

I CAN'T GIVE YOU ANYTHING BUT LOVE: *Blackbirds of 1928* (Dorothy Fields, Jimmy McHugh).

I COULD BE HAPPY WITH YOU: *The Boy Friend* (Sandy Wilson), 1954.

I COULD WRITE A BOOK: *Pal Joey* (Lorenz Hart, Richard Rodgers), 1940.

I DARE NOT LOVE YOU: *Princess Flavia* (Harry Smith, Sigmund Romberg), 1925.

IDA, SWEET AS APPLE CIDER: *Roly Boly Eyes* (additional song by Eddie Leonard), 1919.

I DIDN'T KNOW WHAT TIME IT WAS: *Too Many Girls* (Lorenz Hart, Richard Rodgers), 1939.

I DREAMT I DWELT IN MARBLE HALLS: *The Bohemian Girl* (Alfred Bunn, William Balfe), 1844.

I FEEL LIKE I'M GONNA LIVE FOREVER: *Hazel Flagg* (Bob Hilliard, Jule Styne), 1953.

IF I HAD MY DRUTHERS: *L'il Abner* (Johnny Mercer, Gene de Paul), 1956.

IF I LOVE AGAIN: *Americana of 1928* (additional song by John Murray, Ben Oakland).

IF I LOVED YOU: *Carousel* (Oscar Hammerstein II, Richard Rodgers), 1945.

IF IT'S A DREAM: *Seventh Heaven* (Stella Unger, Victor Young), 1955.

IF I WERE A BELL: *Guys and Dolls* (Abe Burrows, Jo Swerling, Frank Loesser), 1950.

I FOUGHT EVERY STEP OF THE WAY: *Top Banana* (Johnny Mercer), 1951.

I FOUND A MILLION DOLLAR BABY IN A FIVE-AND-TEN CENT STORE: *Billy Rose's Crazy Quilt* (Mort Dixon, Billy Rose, Harry Warren), 1931.

IF THAT WAS LOVE: *New Girl in Town* (Bob Merrill), 1957.

IF THERE IS SOMEONE LOVELIER THAN YOU: *Revenge with Music* (Howard Dietz, Arthur Schwartz), 1934.

IF THIS ISN'T LOVE: *Finian's Rainbow* (E. Y. "Yip" Harburg, Fred Saidy, Burton Lane), 1947.

IF YOU LOVED ME TRULY: *Can-Can* (Cole Porter), 1953.

I GET A KICK OUT OF YOU: *Anything Goes* (Cole Porter), 1934.

I GOT BEAUTY: *Out of This World* (Cole Porter), 1950.

I GOT LOST IN HIS ARMS: *Annie Get Your Gun* (Irving Berlin), 1942.

I GOT PLENTY OF NUTHIN': *Porgy and Bess* (Ira Gershwin, George Gershwin), 1935.

I GOT RHYTHM: *Girl Crazy* (Ira Gershwin, George Gershwin), 1930.

I GOT THE SUN IN THE MORNIN': *Annie Get Your Gun* (Irving Berlin), 1942.

I GUESS I'LL HAVE TO CHANGE MY PLAN: *First Little Show* (Howard Dietz, Arthur Schwartz), 1929.

I JUPITER, I REX: *Out of This World* (Cole Porter), 1950.

I JUST CAN'T MAKE MY EYES BEHAVE: *The Parisian Model* (additional song by Will Cobb, Gus Edwards), 1906.

I HATE MEN: *Kiss Me Kate* (Cole Porter), 1948.

I KNOW AND YOU KNOW: *Look Who's Here* (Edward Paulton, Silvio Hein), 1920.

I KNOW THAT YOU KNOW: *Oh, Please* (Anne Caldwell, Otto Harbach, Vincent Youmans), 1925.

I LEFT MY HEART AT THE STAGE DOOR CANTEEN: *This Is the Army* (Irving Berlin), 1942.

I LIKE YOU: *Fanny* (Harold Rome), 1954.

I LIVE, I DIE, FOR YOU: *The Love Call* (Harry Smith, Sigmund Romberg), 1927.

I'LL BE SEEING YOU: *Right This Way* (Irving Kahal, Sammy Fain), 1938.

I'LL BUILD A BUNGALOW: *Daffy Dill* (Guy Bolton, Oscar Hammerstein II, Herbert Stothart), 1922.

I'LL BUILD A STAIRWAY TO PARADISE: *George White's Scandals of 1922* (Buddy De Sylva, E. Ray Goetz, George Gershwin).

I'LL BUY YOU A STAR: *A Tree Grows in Brooklyn* (Dorothy Fields, Arthur Schwartz), 1951.

I'LL FOLLOW MY SECRET HEART: *Conversation Piece* (Noel Coward), 1934.

I'LL GO HOME WITH BONNIE JEAN: *Brigadoon* (Alan Jay Lerner, Frederick Loewe), 1947.

I'LL KNOW: *Guys and Dolls* (Abe Burrows, Jo Swerling, Frank Loesser), 1950.

I'LL SEE YOU AGAIN: *Bitter Sweet* (Noel Coward), 1929.

I'LL SEE YOU IN C-U-B-A: *Ziegfeld Midnight Frolic* (additional song by Irving Berlin), 1920.

I'LL SHOW HIM: *Plain and Fancy* (Arnold B. Horwitt, Albert Hague), 1955.

I LOVE LOUISA: *The Band Wagon* (Howard Dietz, Arthur Schwartz), 1931.

I LOVE PARIS: *Can-Can* (Cole Porter), 1953.

I LOVE THEM ALL: *Princess Flavia* (Harry Smith, Sigmund Romberg), 1925.

IMAGINATION: *Here's Howe* (Irving Caesar; additional music by Joseph Myer), 1928.

I'M ALWAYS CHASING RAINBOWS: *Oh, Look* (Joseph McCarthy, Harry Carrol; based on Frédéric Chopin's Fantasie Impromptu in C-sharp Minor), 1918.

I'M AN INDIAN, TOO: *Annie Get Your Gun* (Irving Berlin), 1942.

I'M AN ORDINARY MAN: *My Fair Lady* (Alan Jay Lerner, Frederick Loewe), 1955.

I MARRIED AN ANGEL: *I Married an Angel* (Lorenz Hart, Richard Rodgers), 1938.

I MAY BE WRONG BUT I THINK YOU'RE WONDERFUL: *Murray Anderson's Almanac* (additional song by Harry Ruskin, Henry Sullivan), 1929.

I'M EASILY ASSIMILATED: *Candide* (Richard Wilbur, Dorothy Parker, John La Touche, Leonard Bernstein), 1956.

I'M FALLING IN LOVE WITH SOMEONE: *Naughty Marietta* (Rida Johnson Young, Victor Herbert), 1910.

I'M FLYING: *Peter Pan* (Carolyn Leigh, Mark Charlap), 1954.

I'M GETTING TIRED SO I CAN SLEEP: *This Is the Army* (Irving Berlin), 1942.

I'M GLAD I'M LEAVING: *Hazel Flagg* (Bob Hilliard, Jule Styne), 1953.

I'M GONNA WASH THAT MAN RIGHT OUT OF MY HAIR: *South Pacific* (Oscar Hammerstein II, Richard Rodgers), 1949.

I'M HEAD OVER HEELS IN LOVE: *The City Chap* (Anne Caldwell, Jerome Kern), 1925.

I'M IN LOVE AGAIN: *Greenwich Village Follies of 1924* (Cole Porter).

I'M IN LOVE WITH A WONDERFUL GUY: *South Pacific* (Oscar Hammerstein II, Richard Rodgers), 1949.

I'M JUST WILD ABOUT HARRY: *Shuffle Along* (Noble Sissle, Eubie Blake), 1921.

I'M NOT IN LOVE: *Lend an Ear* (Charles Gaynor), 1948.

I'M ON MY WAY: *Paint Your Wagon* (Alan Jay Lerner, Frederick Loewe), 1951.

I'M YOUR GIRL: *Me and Juliet* (Oscar Hammerstein II, Richard Rodgers), 1953.

IN CALIFORN-I-A: *America's Sweetheart* (Lorenz Hart, Richard Rodgers), 1930.

INDIAN LOVE CALL: *Rose Marie* (Oscar Hammerstein II, Otto Harbach, Rudolf Friml), 1924.

INDIANS!: *Peter Pan* (Carolyn Leigh, Mark Charlap), 1954.

I NEVER HAS SEEN SNOW: *House of Flowers* (Truman Capote, Harold Arlen), 1954.

IN OLD NEW YORK: *Fritz in Tammany Hall* (William Jerome, Jean Schwartz), 1904.

IN OUR LITTLE DEN OF INIQUITY: *Pal Joey* (Lorenz Hart, Richard Rodgers), 1940.

IN RURITANIA: *Princess Flavia* (Harry Smith, Sigmund Romberg), 1925.

IN SAPPHIRE SEAS: *The Firefly* (Otto Harbach, Rudolf Friml), 1912.

INTERMISSION TALK: *Me and Juliet* (Oscar Hammerstein II, Richard Rodgers), 1953.

I OUGHT TO KNOW MORE ABOUT YOU: *Michael Todd's Peep Show* (Edward Heyman, Victor Young), 1950.

IS A PUZZLEMENT: *The King and I* (Oscar Hammerstein II, Richard Rodgers), 1951.

I SEE YOUR FACE BEFORE ME: *Between the Devil* (Howard Dietz, Arthur Schwartz), 1938.

I SLEEP EASIER NOW: *Out of This World* (Cole Porter), 1950.

THE ISLE OF OUR DREAMS: *The Red Mill* (Henry Blossom, Victor Herbert), 1906.

I STILL GET JEALOUS: *High Button Shoes* (Sammy Cahn, Jule Styne), 1947.

I STILL SEE ELISA: *Paint Your Wagon* (Alan Jay Lerner, Frederick Loewe), 1951.

IT: *The Desert Song* (Oscar Hammerstein II, Otto Harbach, Frank Mandel, Sigmund Romberg), 1926.

IT AIN'T NECESSARILY SO: *Porgy and Bess* (Ira Gershwin, George Gershwin), 1935.

ITALIAN STREET SONG: *Naughty Marietta* (Rida Johnson Young, Victor Herbert), 1910.

I TALK TO THE TREES: *Paint Your Wagon* (Alan Jay Lerner, Frederick Loewe), 1951.

IT ALL DEPENDS ON YOU: *Big Boy* (additional song by Lew Brown, Buddy De Sylva, Ray Henderson), 1925.

IT MUST BE SO: *Candide* (Richard Wilbur, Dorothy Parker, John La Touche, Leonard Bernstein), 1956.

IT NEVER ENTERED MY MIND: *Higher and Higher* (Lorenz Hart, Richard Rodgers), 1940.

IT'S A BEAUTIFUL DAY TODAY: *Whoopee* (Gus Kahn, Walter Donaldson), 1928.

IT'S A BIG WIDE, WONDERFUL WORLD: *All in Fun* (John Rox), 1940.

IT'S A CHEMICAL REACTION, THAT'S ALL: *Silk Stockings* (Cole Porter), 1955.

IT'S A HELLUVA WAY TO RUN A LOVE AFFAIR: *Plain and Fancy* (Arnold B. Horwitt, Albert Hague), 1955.

IT'S ALL RIGHT WITH ME: *Can-Can* (Cole Porter), 1953.

IT'S A LONG WAY TO TIPPERARY: *Chin Chin* (additional song by Harry Williams, Joe Judge), 1914.

IT'S A LONG WAY TO TIPPERARY: *Dancing Around* (additional song by Harry Williams, Joe Judge), 1914.

IT'S A LOVELY DAY TODAY: *Call Me Madam* (Irving Berlin), 1950.

IT'S A LOVELY DAY TOMORROW: *Louisiana Purchase* (Irving Berlin), 1940.

IT'S DELIGHTFUL DOWN IN CHILE: *Gentlemen Prefer Blondes* (Leo Robin, Jule Styne), 1949.

IT'S DE-LOVELY: *Red, Hot and Blue* (Cole Porter), 1936.

IT'S GOOD TO BE ALIVE: *New Girl in Town* (Bob Merrill), 1957.

IT SHOULD HAPPEN TO ME: *Crazy with*

the Heat (Richard Kollmar, Elsie Thompson), 1941.

IT'S LOVE: *Wonderful Town* (Betty Comden, Adolph Green, Leonard Bernstein), 1953.

IT'S ME: *Me and Juliet* (Oscar Hammerstein II, Richard Rodgers), 1953.

IT'S ME AGAIN: *Yokel Boy* (Lew Brown, Sammy Stept, Charles Tobias), 1939.

IT'S NEVER TOO LATE TO FALL IN LOVE: *The Boy Friend* (Sandy Wilson), 1954.

IT WONDERS ME: *Plain and Fancy* (Arnold B. Horwitt, Albert Hague), 1955.

I UPS TO HIM: *Show Girl* (additional song by Jimmy Durante), 1929.

I'VE COME TO WIVE IT WEALTHILY IN PADUA: *Kiss Me Kate* (Cole Porter), 1948.

IVE GOT A CRUSH ON YOU: *Treasure Girl* (Ira Gershwin, George Gershwin), 1928.

I'VE GOT A CRUSH ON YOU: *Strike Up the Band* (Ira Gershwin, George Gershwin), 1930.

I'VE GOT A FEELIN' I'M FALLIN': *Treasure Girl* (Ira Gershwin, George Gershwin), 1928.

I'VE GOT A RIGHT TO SING THE BLUES: *Earl Carroll's Vanities of 1932* (Ted Koehler, Harold Arlen), 1932.

I'VE GOT RINGS ON MY FINGERS AND BELLS ON MY TOES: *The Yankee Girl* (George Hobart, Silvio Hein), 1910.

I'VE GOT TO CROW: *Peter Pan* (Carolyn Leigh, Mark Charlap), 1954.

I'VE GROWN ACCUSTOMED TO HER FACE: *My Fair Lady* (Alan Jay Lerner, Frederick Loewe), 1955.

I'VE NEVER BEEN IN LOVE BEFORE: *Guys and Dolls* (Abe Burrows, Jo Swerling, Frank Loesser), 1950.

I'VE NEVER HEARD ABOUT LOVE: *The Student Prince* (Dorothy Donelly, Sigmund Romberg), 1924.

I'VE TOLD EVERY LITTLE STAR: *Music in the Air* (Oscar Hammerstein II, Jerome Kern), 1931.

I'VE WAITED FOR YOU: *Cherry Blossoms* (Harry Smith, Sigmund Romberg), 1927.

I WANNA BE LOVED BY YOU: *Goood Boy* (Bert Kalmar, Harry Ruby), 1928.

I WANNA GET MARRIED: *Follow the Girls* (Dan Shapiro, Milton Pascal; Phil Charig), 1944.

I WANT A KISS: *The Desert Song* (Oscar Hammerstein II, Otto Harbach, Frank Mandel, Sigmund Romberg), 1926.

I WANT MY MAMMA: *Earl Carroll's Vanities* (Albert Stillman, Jaraca and Vincente Paiva), 1940.

I WANT TO BE HAPPY: *No, No, Nanette* (Irving Caesar, Otto Harbach, Vincent Youmans), 1925.

I WANT TO BE THERE: *Cherry Blossoms* (Harry Smith, Sigmund Romberg), 1927.

I WANT TO DANCE ALL NIGHT: *My Fair Lady* (Alan Jay Lerner, Frederick Loewe), 1925.

I WANT WHAT I WANT WHEN I WANT IT: *Mlle. Modiste* (Henry Blossom, Victor Herbert), 1905.

I WENT TO A MARVELOUS PARTY: *Set to Music* (Noel Coward), 1939.

I WHISTLE A HAPPY TUNE: *The King and I* (Oscar Hammerstein II, Richard Rodgers), 1951.

I WISH I WERE IN LOVE AGAIN: *Babes in Arms* (Lorenz Hart, Richard Rodgers), 1937.

I WONDER AS I WANDER: *Polonaise* (John La Touche, Bronislaw Kaper; based on the music of Frédéric Chopin), 1945.

I WONDER WHO'S KISSING HER NOW: *The Prince of Tonight* (Joe Howard, Harold Orlob), 1909.

I WONDER WHY: *Iole* (Robert Chambers, William Peters), 1913.

I WONDER WHY: *Love O'Mike* (Harry Smith, Jerome Kern), 1917.

I WONDER WHY: *Sally, Irene and Mary* (Raymond Klages, J. Fred Coots), 1922.

I WONDER WHY: *My Princess* (Dorothy Donnelly, Sigmund Romberg), 1927.

I WON'T GROW UP: *Peter Pan* (Carolyn Leigh, Mark Charlap), 1954.

JENNY MADE HER MIND UP: See Saga of Jenny.

JINGLE BELLS: *Zig-Zag* (Jack Yellen, Milton Agar), 1922.

JOHNNY ONE NOTE: *Babes in Arms* (Lorenz Hart, Richard Rodgers), 1937.

JOSEPHINE: *Silk Stockings* (Cole Porter), 1955.

JOSHUA FIT DE BATTLE: *Shuffle Along of 1933* (Noble Sissle, Eubie Blake).

JUNE IS BUSTIN' OUT ALL OVER: *Carousel* (Oscar Hammerstein II, Richard Rodgers), 1945.

JUNE MOON: *June Moon* (George S. Kaufman, Ring Lardner), 1920.

JUST A KISS APART: *Gentlemen Prefer Blondes* (Leo Robin, Jule Styne), 1949.

JUST A REGULAR GIRL: *The Blushing Bride* (Cyrus Wood, Sigmund Romberg), 1922.

JUST ONE OF THOSE THINGS: *Jubilee* (Cole Porter), 1935.

JUST ONE WAY TO SAY I LOVE YOU: *Miss Liberty* (Irving Berlin), 1949.

JUST WE TWO: *The Student Prince* (Dorothy Donnelly, Sigmund Romberg), 1924.

JUST YOU AND I IN DREAMLAND: *The Lady of the Slipper* (James O'Dea, Victor Herbert), 1912.

JUST YOU WAIT: *My Fair Lady* (Alan Jay Lerner, Frederick Loewe), 1955.

KANSAS CITY: *Oklahoma!* (Oscar Hammerstein II, Richard Rodgers), 1943.

KATIE WENT TO HAITI: *Du Barry Was a Lady* (Cole Porter), 1939.

KATINKA: *Katinka* (Otto Harbach, Rudolf Friml), 1915.

KATINKA: *George White's Scandals of 1923* (Buddy De Sylva, E. Ray Goetz, Ballard MacDonald, George Gershwin).

KATINKA: *Vogues of 1924* (Clifford Grey, Jay Gorney, Herbert Stothart).

KEEPING COOL WITH COOLIDGE: *Gentlemen Prefer Blondes* (Leo Robin, Jule Styne), 1949.

KEEP IT GAY: *Me and Juliet* (Oscar Hammerstein II, Richard Rodgers), 1953.

A KISS IN THE DARK: *Orange Blossoms* (Buddy De Sylva, Victor Herbert), 1922.

KISS ME AGAIN: *Mlle. Modiste* (Henry Blossom, Victor Herbert), 1905.

THE LADY IS A TRAMP: *Babes in Arms* (Lorenz Hart, Richard Rodgers), 1937.

LADY OF THE EVENING: *The Music Box Review of 1922* (Irving Berlin).

LANTERN OF LOVE: *Castles in the Air* (Raymond Beck, Percy Wenrich), 1926.

THE LARK: *The Love Call* (Harry Smith, Sigmund Romberg), 1927.

THE LAST ROUND-UP: *Ziegfeld Follies of 1934* (William J. "Billy" Hill).

LAURA DE MAUPASSANT: *Hazel Flagg* (Bob Hilliard, Jule Styne), 1953.

LEAVE IT TO JANE: *Leave It to Jane* (Guy Bolton, P. G. Wodehouse, Jerome Kern; based on *The College Widow*, by George Ade), 1917.

LEGALIZE MY NAME: *St. Louis Woman*
(Johnny Mercer, Harold Arlen), 1946.
LET ME BE A FRIEND TO YOU: *Rosalie*
(Ira Gershwin, P. G. Wodehouse, George
Gershwin, Sigmund Romberg), 1928.
LET'S BE BUDDIES: *Panama Hattie* (Cole
Porter), 1940.
LET'S DO IT, LET'S FALL IN LOVE:
Paris (E. Ray Goetz, Cole Porter), 1928.
LET'S HAVE ANOTHER CUP OF COFFE:
Face the Music (Irving Berlin), 1932.
LET'S TAKE AN OLD-FASHIONED WALK:
The Honeymooners (George M. Cohan), 1907.
LET'S TAKE AN OLD-FASHIONED WALK:
Miss Liberty (Irving Berlin), 1949.
LET'S TAKE A WALK AROUND THE
BLOCK: *Life Begins at 8:40* (Sid Silvers,
Jack Yellen, Harold Arlen), 1934.
LIFE IS JUST A BOWL OF CHERRIES:
George White's Scandals of 1931 (Lew Brown,
Ray Henderson).
LIFE ON THE WICKED STAGE: *Show Boat*
(Oscar Hammerstein II, Jerome Kern), 1927.
LI'L AUGIE IS A NATCHAL MAN: *St. Louis
Woman* (Johnny Mercer, Harold Arlen), 1946.
LIMEHOUSE BLUES: *Andre Charlot's Revue
of 1924* (Douglas Furber, Philip Braham).
A LITTLE BIT OF HEAVEN: *The Heart of
Paddy Whack* (Rachel Crothers, Ernest Ball),
1914.
A LITTLE BRAINS, A LITTLE TALENT:
Damn Yankees (Richard Adler, Jerry Ross),
1955.
A LITTLE DREAM THAT LOST IT'S WAY:
Love Birds (Edgar Wolf, Ballard MacDonald,
Sigmund Romberg), 1920.
A LITTLE FISH IN A BIG POND: *Miss
Liberty* (Irving Berlin), 1949.
LITTLE GIRL: *Merry, Merry* (Harlan Thomp-
son, Harry Archer), 1925.
LITTLE GIRL BLUE: *Jumbo* (Lorenz Hart,
Richard Rodgers), 1935.
A LITTLE GIRL FROM LITTLE ROCK:
Gentlemen Prefer Blondes (Leo Robin, Jule
Styne), 1949.
LITTLE GYPSY SWEETHART (GYPSY LOVE
SONG: *The Fortune Teller* (Harry Smith,
Victor Herbert), 1898.
A LITTLE MORE HEART: *Hazel Flagg*
(Bob Hilliard, Jule Styne), 1953.
LITTLE OLD LADY: *The Show Is On* (Stan-
ley Adams, Hoagy Carmichael), 1936.
A LITTLE WHITE HOUSE AT THE END
OF HONEYMOON LANE: *Honeymoon Lane*
(Eddie Dowling, James T. Hanley), 1926.
LIVE AND LET LIVE: *Can-Can* (Cole Por-
ter), 1953.
LIZA: *Show Girl* (Gus Kahn, Ira Gershwin,
George Gershwin), 1929.
LOLITA: *Show Girl* (Gus Kahn, Ira Gersh-
win, George Gershwin), 1929.
LONELY HEARTS: *Blossom Time* (Dorothy
Donnelly, Sigmund Romberg), 1921.
LOOK AT 'ER: *New Girl in Town* (Bob Mer-
rill), 1957.
LOOK FOR THE SILVER LINING: *Sally*
(Buddy De Sylva, Clifford Gey, Jerome
Kern), 1920.
LOOK TO THE RAINBOW: *Finian's Rain-
bow* (E. Y. "Yip" Harburg, Fred Saidy, Bur-
ton Lane), 1947.
LOOK WHO'S DANCING: *A Tree Grows in
Brooklyn* (Dorothy Fields, Arthur Schwartz),
1951.
LOUISIANA HAYRIDE: *Flying Colors* (How-
ard Dietz, Arthur Schwartz), 1932.
LOVE IS A VERY LIGHT THING: *Fanny*
(Harold Rome), 1954.
LOVE IS QUITE A SIMPLE THING: *The
New Moon* (Oscar Hammerstein II, Frank

Mandel, Lawrence Schwab, Sigmund Rom-
berg), 1928.
LOVE IS SWEEPING THE COUNTRY: *Of
Thee I Sing* (Ira Gershwin, George Gersh-
win), 1931.
LOVELIER THAN EVER: *Where's Charley?*
(Frank Loesser), 1948.
LOVE, LOVE, LOVE: *Seventh Heaven* (Stella
Unger, Victor Young), 1955.
LOVELY LADY: *George White's Scandals of
1925* (Lew Brown, Buddy De Sylva, Ray
Henderson).
LOVELY LADY: *Lovely Lady* (Gladys Unger,
Cyrus Wood, Harold A. Levy, Dave Stam-
per), 1927.
LOVELY LADY: *Ain't Love Grand* (Gladys
Unger, Cyrus Wood, Harold A. Levy, Dave
Stamper), 1927.
LOVE MAKES THE WORLD GO ROUND:
The Magic Melody (Frederic Kummer, Sig-
mund Romberg), 1920.
LOVE ME, LOVE MY DOG: *Mlle. Modiste*
(Henry Blossom, Victor Herbert), 1905.
LOVE ME OR LEAVE ME: *Whoopee* (Gus
Kahn, Walter Donaldson), 1928.
LOVE ME OR LEAVE ME: *Simple Simon*
(additional song by Gus Kahn, Walter Donald-
son), 1930.
LOVER COME BACK TO ME: *The New
Moon* (Oscar Hammerstein II, Frank Man-
del, Lawrence Schwab, Sigmund Romberg),
1928.
LOVE'S HIGHWAY: *The Blushing Bride* (Cy-
rus Wood, Sigmund Romberg), 1922.
LOVE SNEAKS UP ON YOU: *Seventh Heaven*
(Stella Unger, Victor Young), 1955.
LOVE'S OWN SWEET SONG: *Sari* (C. C. S.
Cushing, E. P. Heath, Emmerich Kalman),
1914.
LOVE WHILE YOU MAY: *Springtime of
Youth* (Cyrus Wood, Matthew Woodward,
Walter Kollo, Sigmund Romberg), 1922.
LOVE WILL ALWAYS FIND A WAY: *Love
Birds* (Edgar Woolf, Ballard MacDonald, Sig-
mund Romberg), 1920.
LOVE WILL FIND A WAY: *Shuffle Along*
(Noble Sissle, Eubie Blake), 1921.
LUCK BE A LADY: *Guys and Dolls* (Abe
Burrows, Jo Swerling, Frank Loesser), 1950.
LUCKY IN LOVE: *The Dancing Girl* (Harold
Atteridge, Irving Caesar, George Gershwin,
Sigmund Romberg), 1923.
LUCKY IN LOVE: *Good News* (Lew Brown,
Buddy De Sylva, Ray Henderson), 1927.
MAD ABOUT THE BOY: *Set to Music* (Noel
Coward), 1939.
MADAME TANGO'S TANGO: *House of Flow-
ers* (Truman Capote, Harold Arlen), 1954.
MAD DOGS AND ENGLISHMEN: *Third Little
Show* (Noel Coward), 1931.
MAIDENS TYPICAL OF FRANCE: *Can-Can*
(Cole Porter), 1953.
MAKE A MIRACLE: *Where's Charley?* (Frank
Loesser), 1948.
MAKE BELIEVE: *Show Boat* (Oscar Ham-
merstein II, Jerome Kern), 1927.
MAKE OUR GARDENS GROW: *Candide* (Rich-
ard Wilbur, Dorothy Parker, John La
Touche, Leonard Bernstein), 1956.
MAKE THE MAN LOVE ME: *A Tree
Grows in Brooklyn* (Dorothy Fields, Arthur
Schwartz), 1951.
MAKING WHOOPEE: *Whoopee* (Gus Kahn,
Walter Donaldson), 1928.
MAMMY: *Sinbad* (additional song by Irving
Caesar, Walter Donaldson), 1918.
A MAN DOESN'T KNOW: *Damn Yankees*
(Richard Adler, Jerry Ross), 1955.
MANDY: *Yip, Yip, Yaphank* (Irving Berlin),
1918.

MANDY: *Ziegfeld Follies of 1919* (Irving Berlin).

MANDY: *This is the Army* (Irving Berlin), 1942.

THE MAN I LOVE: *Lady Be Good* (Ira Gershwin, George Gershwin), 1924.

THE MAN I LOVE: *Strike Up the Band* (Ira Gershwin, George Gershwin), 1930.

THE MAN OF THE YEAR THIS WEEK: *Top Banana* (Johnny Mercer), 1951.

MAN WITH A DREAM: *Seventh Heaven* (Stella Unger, Victor Young), 1955.

MANY A NEW DAY: *Oklahoma!* (Oscar Hammerstein II, Richard Rodgers), 1943.

MARCH OF THE SIAMESE CHILDREN: *The King and I* (Oscar Hammerstein II, Richard Rodgers), 1951.

MARCH OF THE TOYS: *Babes in Toyland* (Glen MacDonough, Victor Herbert), 1903.

MARDI GRAS: *House of Flowers* (Truman Capote, Harold Arlen), 1954.

MARIANNE: *The New Moon* (Oscar Hammerstein II, Frank Mandel, Lawrence Schwab, Sigmund Romberg), 1928.

MARRIAGE TYPE LOVE: *Me and Juliet* (Oscar Hammerstein II, Richard Rodgers), 1953.

MARY'S A GRAND OLD NAME: *Forty-Five Minutes From Broadway* (George M. Cohan), 1906.

MAXIM'S (I'M HAPPY AT MAXIM'S): *The Merry Widow* (Adrian Ross, Franz Lehar), 1907.

MAYBE: *Oh, Kay* (Ira Gershwin, George Gershwin), 1926.

THE MELODY OF LOVE: *Gypsy Love* (Harry Smith, Robert Smith, Franz Lehar), 1911.

MERRY WIDOW WALTZ (I LOVE YOU SO): *The Merry Widow* (Adrian Ross, Franz Lehar), 1907.

MINE TILL MONDAY: *A Tree Grows in Brooklyn* (Dorothy Fields, Arthur Schwartz), 1951.

A MISS YOU KISS: *Seventh Heaven* (Stella Unger, Victor Young), 1955.

MIX AND MINGLE: *Wish You Were Here* (Harold Rome), 1952.

MOANIN' LOW: *First Little Show* (Howard Dietz, Ralph Rainger), 1929.

MOON FLOWER: *Louie the Fourteenth* (Arthur Wimperis, Sigmund Romberg), 1925.

MONTMART': *Can-Can* (Cole Porter), 1953.

MORE I CANNOT WISH YOU: *Guys and Dolls* (Abe Burrows, Jo Swerling, Frank Loesser), 1950.

MORE THAN YOU KNOW: *Great Day* (Billy Rose, Vincent Youmans), 1929.

MORITAT: See Ballad of Mack the Knife.

THE MOST BEAUTIFUL GIRL IN THE WORLD: *Jumbo* (Lorenz Hart, Richard Rodgers), 1935.

THE MOST HAPPY FELLA: *The Most Happy Fella* (Frank Loesser), 1956.

MOTHER MACHREE: *Barry of Ballymore* (Rida Johnson Young, Ernest Ball), 1910.

MOTHER PIN A ROSE ON ME: *Coming Thru the Rye* (additional song by Bob Adams), 1906.

MOUNTAIN GREENERY: *Garrick Gaieties* (Lorenz Hart, Richard Rodgers), 1926.

MOVIN': *Paint Your Wagon* (Alan Jay Lerner, Frederick Loewe), 1951.

MR. AND MRS.: *The Blushing Bride* (Cyrus Wood, Sigmund Romberg), 1922.

MR. GALLAGHER AND MR. SHEAN: *Ziegfeld Follies of 1922* (additional song by Gallagher and Shean, Ernest Ball).

MR. WONDERFUL: *Mr. Wonderful* (Jerry Will Glickman, Larry Holofcener, Joseph Stein, George Weiss), 1956.

MY BABY JUST CARES FOR ME: *Whoopee* (Gus Kahn, Walter Donaldson), 1928.

MY DARLIN' EILEEN: *Wonderful Town* (Betty Comden, Adolph Green, Leonard Bernstein), 1953.

MY DARLING, MY DARLING: *Where's Charley?* (George Abbott, Frank Loesser), 1948.

MY DEFENSES ARE DOWN: *Annie Get Your Gun* (Irving Berlin), 1942.

MY FUNNY VALENTINE: *Babes in Arms* (Lorenz Hart, Richard Rodgers), 1937.

MY HEART BELONGS TO DADDY: *Leave It to Me* (Cole Porter), 1938.

MY HEART IS CALLING: *The Rose of Stamboul* (Harold Atteridge, Leo Fall, Sigmund Romberg), 1922.

MY HEART STOOD STILL: *A Connecticut Yankee* (Lorenz Hart, Richard Rodgers), 1927.

MY HERO: See Come, Hero Mine.

MY HOME IS IN MY SHOES: *Top Banana* (Johnny Mercer), 1951.

MY KINDA LOVE: *Americana of 1928* (additional song by Jo Trent, Louis Alter).

MY LUCKY STAR: *She's My Baby* (Lorenz Hart, Richard Rodgers), 1928.

MY LUCKY STAR: *Follow Through* (Lew Brown, Buddy De Sylva, Ray Henderson), 1929.

MY MAN: *Ziegfeld Follies of 1921* (English lyric by Channing Pollock; music by Maurice Yvain).

MY OWN: *Merry, Merry* (Harlan Thompson, Harry Archer), 1923.

MY ROMANCE: *Jumbo* (Lorenz Hart, Richard Rodgers), 1935.

MY SHIP: *Lady in the Dark* (Ira Gershwin, Kurt Weill), 1941.

MY SPRINGTIME THOU ART: *Blossom Time* (Dorothy Donnelly, Sigmund Romberg), 1921.

MYSTERIOUS Lady: *Peter Pan* (additional song by Betty Comden, Adolph Green, Jule Styne), 1954.

MY TIME OF DAY: *Guys and Dolls* (Abe Burrows, Jo Swerling, Frank Loesser), 1950.

NAMELY YOU: *L'il Abner* (Johnny Mercer, Gene de Paul), 1956.

NEAR TO YOU: *Damn Yankees* (Richard Adler, Jerry Ross), 1955.

'NEATH THE CHERRY BLOSSOM MOON: *Cherry Blossoms* (Harry Smith, Sigmund Romberg), 1927.

'NEATH THE SOUTHERN MOON: *Naughty Marietta* (Rida Johnson Young, Victor Herbert), 1910.

NEUROTIC YOU AND PSYCHOPATHIC ME: *Lend an Ear* (Charles Gaynor), 1948.

NEVER FELT THIS WAY BEFORE: *Wonderful Town* (Betty Comden, Adolph Green, Leonard Bernstein), 1953.

NEVER GIVE ANYTHING AWAY: *Can-Can* (Cole Porter), 1953.

NEVERLAND: *Peter Pan* (additional song by Betty Comden, Adolph Green, Jule Styne), 1954.

NEVERLAND WALTZ: *Peter Pan* (additional song by Betty Comden, Adolph Green, Jule Styne), 1954.

NEVER, NEVER, BE AN ARTIST: *Can-Can* (Cole Porter), 1953.

NEVER TOO LATE FOR LOVE: *Fanny* (Harold Rome), 1954.

THE NEW ASHMOLEAN MARCHING SOCIETY AND STUDENTS' CONSERVATORY BAND: *Where's Charley?* (Frank Loesser), 1948.

NEW YORK, NEW YORK: *On the Town* (Betty Comden, Adolph Green, Leonard Bernstein), 1944.

NIGHT AND DAY: *The Gay Divorcee* (Cole Porter), 1932.

THE NIGHT WAS MADE FOR LOVE: *The*

Cat and the Fiddle (Otto Harbach, Jerome Kern), 1931.

NIGHTY NIGHT: *Tip-Toes* (Ira Gershwin, George Gershwin), 1925.

NOBODY'S CHASING ME: *Out of This World* (Cole Porter), 1950.

NO LOVER FOR ME: *Out of This World* (Cole Porter), 1950.

NO OTHER LOVE: *Me and Juliet* (Oscar Hammerstein II, Richard Rodgers), 1953.

THE OCARINA: *Call Me Madam* (Irving Berlin), 1950.

OCTOPUS SONG: *Fanny* (Harold Rome), 1954.

ODE TO LOLA: *Seventeen* (Kim Gannon, Walter Kent), 1951.

OH BY JINGO, OH BY GEE: *Linger Longer Letty* (additional song by Lew Brown, Albert von Tilzer), 1919.

OH GEE, OH GOSH, OH GOLLY, I'M IN LOVE: *Ziegfeld Follies of 1922* (additional song by Ole Olson, Chic Johnson, Ernest Breuer).

OH HAPPY DAY: *L'il Abner* (Johnny Mercer, Gene de Paul), 1956.

OH, HAPPY WE: *Candide* (Richard Wilbur, Dorothy Parker, John La Touche, Leonard Bernstein), 1956.

OH, HOW I HATE TO GET UP IN THE MORNING: *Yip, Yip, Yaphank* (Irving Berlin), 1918.

OH, HOW I HATE TO GET UP IN THE MORNING: *This Is the Army* (Irving Berlin), 1942.

OHIO: *Wonderful Town* (Betty Comden, Adolph Green, Leonard Bernstein), 1953.

OH, JOHNNY, OH: *Follow Me* (additional song by Ed Rose, Abe Olman), 1916.

OH, LADY BE GOOD: *Lady Be Good* (Ira Gershwin, George Gershwin), 1924.

OH, PROMISE ME: *Robin Hood* (Clement Scott, Reginald De Koven), 1890.

OH, WHAT A BEAUTIFUL MORNIN': *Oklahoma!* (Oscar Hammerstein II, Richard Rodgers), 1943.

OKLAHOMA!: *Oklahoma!* (Oscar Hammerstein II, Richard Rodgers), 1943.

OLD DEVIL MOON: *Finian's Rainbow* E. Y. "Yip" Harburg, Fred Saidy, Burton Lane), 1947.

OLD-FASHIONED LOVE: *Running Wild* (Cecil Mack, James P. Johnson), 1923.

THE OLD SOFT SHOE: *Three To Make Ready* (Nancy Hamilton, Morgan Lewis), 1946.

OL' MAN RIVER: *Show Boat* (Oscar Hammerstein II, Jerome Kern), 1927.

ON A SUNDAY BY THE SEA: *High Button Shoes* (Sammy Cahn, Jule Styne), 1947.

ONCE IN A WHILE: *Revenge with Music* (Howard Dietz, Arthur Schwartz), 1934.

ONCE IN LOVE WITH AMY: *Where's Charley?* (Frank Loesser), 1948.

ONCE TO EVERY HEART: *Blossom Time* (Dorothy Donnelly, Sigmund Romberg), 1921.

ONE ALONE: *The Desert Song* (Oscar Hammerstein II, Otto Harbach, Frank Mandel, Sigmund Romberg), 1926.

ONE FLOWER ALONE GROWS IN YOUR GARDEN: *The Desert Song* (Oscar Hammerstein II, Otto Harbach, Frank Mandel, Sigmund Romberg), 1926.

THE ONE GIRL: *A Night in Venice* (J. Keirn Brennan, Moe Jaffe, music by Vincent Youmans), 1929.

ONE HUNDRED EASY WAYS: *Wonderful Town* (Betty Comden, Adolph Green, Leonard Bernstein), 1953.

ONE IN A MILLION: *Everybody's Welcome* (Irvin Kahal, Sammy Fain), 1931.

ONE KISS: *The New Moon* (Oscar Hammerstein II, Frank Mandel, Lawrence Schwab, Sigmund Romberg), 1928.

ONE MAN AIN'T QUITE ENOUGH: *House of Flowers* (Truman Capote, Harold Arlen), 1954.

ONE NIGHT OF LOVE: *A Night in Venice* (J. Keirn Brennan, Moe Jaffe, score by Lee Davis, Maurice Rubens), 1929.

ONLY A PAPER ROSE: *The Girl From Child's* (Phil Cook, Tom Johnstone), 1927.

ONLY A ROSE: *The Vagabond King* (Brian Hooker, W. H. Post, Rudolf Friml), 1925.

ONLY IF YOU'RE IN LOVE: *Top Banana* (Johnny Mercer), 1951.

ONLY ONE: *Princess Flavia* (Harry Smith, Sigmund Romberg), 1925.

ON THE FARM: *New Girl in Town* (Bob Merrill), 1957.

ON THE MIDWAY: *Plain and Fancy* (Arnold B. Horwitt, Albert Hague), 1955.

ON THE SIDEWALKS OF NEW YORK: *Sidewalks of New York* (additional song by James W. Blake, Charles B. Lawlor), 1927.

ON THE STREET WHERE YOU LIVE: *My Fair Lady* (Alan Jay Lerner, Frederick Loewe), 1955.

ON THE SUNNY SIDE OF THE STREET: *International Revue* (Dorothy Fields, Jimmy McHugh), 1930.

ON WITH THE DANCE: *Sally* (Buddy De Sylva, Clifford Grey, Jerome Kern), 1920.

ON WITH THE DANCE: *Garrick Gaities* (Lorenz Hart, Richard Rodgers), 1925.

OOH, WHAT YOU SAID: *Walk with Music* (Johnny Mercer, Hoagy Carmichael), 1940.

OO-OOO-OO, WHAT YOU DO TO ME: *Seventeen* (Kim Gannon, Walter Kent), 1951.

OTHER HANDS, OTHER HEARTS: *Fanny* (Harold Rome), 1954.

OUT OF MY DREAMS: *Oklahoma!* (Oscar Hammerstein II, Richard Rodgers), 1943.

OUT OF THE BLUE: *Sweet Adeline* (Oscar Hammerstein II, Jerome Kern), 1929.

OUTSIDE OF THAT I LOVE YOU: *Louisiana Purchase* (Irving Berlin), 1940.

OYSTERS, COCKLES AND MUSSELS: *Fanny* (Harold Rome), 1954.

PANESSE AND SON: *Fanny* (Harold Rome), 1954.

PARDON OUR FRENCH: *Michael Todd's Peep Show* (Edward Heyman, Victor Young), 1950.

PARIS GOWN: *Hazel Flagg* (Bob Hilliard, Jule Styne), 1953.

PARIS LOVES LOVERS: *Silk Stockings* (Cole Porter), 1955.

PARIS WAKES UP AND SMILES: *Miss Liberty* (Irving Berlin), 1949.

PASS THE FOOTBALL: *Wonderful Town* (Betty Comden, Adolph Green, Leonard Bernstein), 1953.

PEOPLE WILL SAY WE'RE IN LOVE: *Oklahoma!* (Oscar Hammerstein II, Richard Rodgers), 1943.

PERFECT YOUNG LADIES: *The Boy Friend* (Sandy Wilson), 1954.

PIRATE JENNY: *The Threepenny Opera* (Marc Blitzstein, Kurt Weill), 1954.

PIRATE SONG: *Peter Pan* (Carolyn Leigh, Mark Charlap), 1954.

PLAIN WE LIVE: *Plain and Fancy* (Arnold B. Horwitt, Albert Hague), 1955.

PLANT YOU NOW, DIG YOU LATER: *Pal Joey* (Lorenz Hart, Richard Rodgers), 1940.

PLAY A SIMPLE MELODY: *Watch Your Step* (Irving Berlin), 1914.

PLAY, GYPSIES, DANCE GYPSIES: *Countess Maritza* (Harry Smith, Emmerich Kalman), 1926.

PLENTY OF PENNSYLVANIA: *Plain and*

Fancy (Arnold B. Horwitt, Albert Hague), 1955.

POCKETFUL OF DREAMS: *Michael Todd's Peep Show* (Harold Rome), 1950.

PONY BOY: *Miss Innocence* (additional song by Charles O'Donell, Bobby Heath), 1908.

POOR BUTTERFLY: *The Big Show* (John Golden, Raymond Hubbell), 1916.

POOR LITTLE PIERRETTE: *The Boy Friend* (Sandy Wilson), 1954.

POOR LITTLE RHODE ISLAND: See Rhode Island Is Famous For You.

POPPA, WON'T YOU DANCE WITH ME?: *High Button Shoes* (Sammy Cahn, Jule Styne), 1947.

PORE JUD IS DAID: *Oklahoma!* (Oscar Hammerstein II, Richard Rodgers), 1943.

THE POW-WOW POLKA: *Peter Pan* (additional song by Betty Comden, Adolph Green, Jule Styne), 1954.

A PRETTY GIRL IS LIKE A MELODY: *Ziegfeld Follies of 1919* (Irving Berlin).

A PRINCELY SCHEME: *Peter Pan* (Carolyn Leigh, Mark Charlap), 1954.

A PRISONER OF LOVE: *The Red Petticoat* (Rida Johnson Young, Jerome Kern), 1912.

PUT 'EM BACK: *L'il Abner* (Johnny Mercer, Gene de Paul), 1956.

PUTTING ON THE RITZ: *Three Cheers* (Anne Caldwell, R. H. Burnside; Raymond Hubbell), 1928.

PUTTIN' ON THE RITZ: *Plain Jane* (Phil Cook, Tom Johnstone), 1924.

PUT YOUR ARMS AROUND ME, HONEY: *Madame Sherry* (Otto Harbach, Karl Hoschna), 1910.

PUT YOUR ARMS AROUND ME, HONEY: *The Fascinating Widow* (Otto Harbach, Karl Hoschna), 1911.

A QUIET GIRL: *Wonderful Town* (Betty Comden, Adolph Green, Leonard Bernstein), 1953.

THE RAIN IN SPAIN: *My Fair Lady* (Alan Jay Lerner, Frederick Loewe), 1955.

RANGER'S SONG (SONG OF THE RANGER: *Rio Rita* (Guy Bolton, Fred Thompson; Harry Tierney), 1927.

RECIPROCITY: *Seventeen* (Kim Gannon, Walter Kent), 1951.

THE RED BALL EXPRESS: *Call Me Mister* (Harold Rome), 1946.

THE RED BLUES: *Silk Stockings* (Cole Porter), 1955.

RED SAILS IN THE SUNSET: *Provincetown Follies* (Jimmy Kennedy, Hugh Williams), 1935.

REMARKABLE FELLOW: *Seventh Heaven* (Stella Unger, Victor Young), 1955.

RESTLESS HEART: *Fanny* (Harold Rome), 1954.

RHAPSODY IN BLUE: *Blackbirds of 1934* (additional music by Ira Gershwin, George Gershwin).

RHODE ISLAND IS FAMOUS FOR YOU: *Inside U.S.A.* (Howard Dietz, Arthur Schwartz), 1948.

RIDIN' HIGH: *Red, Hot and Blue* (Cole Porter), 1936.

RIO RITA: *Rio Rita* (Guy Bolton, Fred Thompson, Harry Tierney), 1927.

RISE AND SHINE: *Take a Chance* (Buddy De Sylva, Lawrence Schwab, Vincent Youmans), 1932.

RIVIERA: *The Boy Friend* (Sandy Wilson), 1954.

THE ROAD TO MANDALAY: *The Road to Mandalay* (Jack Appleton, Oreste Vessela), 1916.

ROCK-A-BYE YOUR BABY TO A DIXIE MELODY: *Sinbad* (Additional song by Joe Young, Sam Lewis, Jean Schwartz), 1918.

ROLL YER SOCKS UP: *New Girl in Town* (Bob Merrill), 1957.

ROMANCE: *The Desert Song* (Oscar Hammerstein II, Otto Harbach, Frank Mandel, Sigmund Romberg), 1926.

ROMANY LIFE: *The Fortune Teller* (Harry Smith, Victor Herbert), 1898.

A ROOM IN BLOOMSBURY: *The Boy Friend* (Sandy Wilson), 1954.

ROSE MARIE: *Rose Marie* (Oscar Hammerstein II, Otto Harbach, Rudolf Friml), 1924.

ROSE OF WASHINGTON SQUARE: *Ziegfeld's Midnight Frolics* (Ballard MacDonald), James F. Hanley), 1919.

ROSY POSY (GOODBYE): *The Blushing Bride* (Cyrus Wood, Sigmund Romberg), 1922.

ROW, ROW, ROW: *Ziegfeld Follies of 1912* (Harry Smith, Raymond Hubbell).

THE ROYAL SIAMESE CHILDREN: *The King and I* (Oscar Hammerstein II, Richard Rodgers), 1951.

THE RUTLAND BOUNCE: *Hazel Flagg* (Bob Hilliard, Jule Styne), 1953.

SAFETY IN NUMBERS: *The Boy Friend* (Sandy Wilson), 1954.

SAGA OF JENNY: *Lady in the Dark* (Ira Gershwin, Kurt Weill), 1941.

ST. JAMES INFIRMARY BLUES: *Blackbirds of 1934* (additional number by Joe Primrose).

ST. LOUIS BLUES: *Change Your Luck* (additional song by W. C. Handy), 1930.

SALLY: *Fad and Folly* (Paul West, Henry Waller), 1902.

SALLY: *Tommy Rot* (Safford Waters), 1902.

SALLY: *The Duchess* (Joseph Herbert, Harry Smith, Victor Herbert), 1911.

SALOME: *Hazel Flagg* (Bob Hilliard, Jule Styne), 1953.

THE SAME SILVER MOON: *My Maryland* (Dorothy Donnelly, Sigmund Romberg), 1927.

SANS SOUCI: *Top Banana* (Johnny Mercer), 1951.

SATIN AND SILK: *Silk Stockings* (Cole Porter), 1955.

SAY IT WITH MUSIC: *The Music Box Review of 1921* (Irving Berlin).

SAY SO: *Rosalie* (Ira Gershwin, P. G. Wodehouse, George Gershwin, Sigmund Romberg), 1928.

SEPTEMBER SONG: *Knickerbocker Holiday* (Maxwell Anderson, Kurt Weill), 1938.

SERENADE: *The Student Prince* (Dorothy Donnelly, Sigmund Romberg), 1924.

SERENADE WITH ASIDES: *Where's Charley?* (Frank Loesser), 1948.

SHADY LADY BIRD: *Best Foot Forward* (Ralph Blane, Hugh Martin). 1941.

SHAKE YOUR FEET: *Ziegfeld Follies of 1923* (Gene Buck, Dave Stamper).

SHALL WE DANCE?: *The King and I* (Oscar Hammerstein II, Richard Rodgers), 1951.

SHE DIDN'T SAY YES: *The Cat and the Fiddle* (Otto Harbach, Jerome Kern), 1931.

SHIKA, SHIKA: *Fanny* (Harold Rome), 1954.

SHINE ON HARVEST MOON: *Miss Innocence* (additional song by Jack Norworth, Nora Bayes), 1908.

SHOELESS JOE FROM HANNIBAL, MO: *Damn Yankees* (Richard Adler, Jerry Ross), 1955.

SHOPPING AROUND: *Wish You Were Here* (Harold Rome), 1952.

SHOW ME: *My Fair Lady* (Alan Jay Lerner, Frederick Loewe), 1955.

SHOW ME THE TOWN: *Rosalie* (Ira Gershwin, P. G. Wodehouse, George Gershwin, Sigmund Romberg), 1928.

THE SHUNNING: *Plain and Fancy* (Arnold B. Horwitt, Albert Hague), 1955.

SIBERIA: *Silk Stockings* (Cole Porter), 1955.

SILK STOCKINGS: *Silk Stockings* (Cole Porter), 1955.
THE SIMPLE LIFE: *A Dangerous Maid* (Arthur Jackson, George Gershwin), 1921.
THE SIMPLE LIFE: *The Girl Friend* (Lorenz Hart, Richard Rodgers), 1926.
SING A SONG OF SIXPENCE: *The Gypsy* (Frank Pixley, Gustav Luders), 1912.
SING FOR YOUR SUPPER: *The Boys From Syracuse* (Lorenz Hart, Richard Rodgers), 1938.
SING SOMETHING SIMPLE: *Second Little Show* (additional song by Herman Hupfeld) 1930.
SIT DOWN YOU'RE ROCKING THE BOAT: *Guys and Dolls* (Abe Burrows, Jo Swerling, Frank Loesser), 1950.
SIX MONTHS OUT OF EVERY YEAR: *Damn Yankees* (Richard Adler, Jerry Ross), 1955.
SLAUGHTER ON TENTH AVENUE: *On Your Toes* (Lorenz Hart, Richard Rodgers), 1936.
A SLEEPIN' BEE: *House of Flowers* (Truman Capote, Harold Arlen), 1954.
SLIDE, BOY, SLIDE: *House of Flowers* (Truman Capote, Harold Arlen), 1954.
THE SMALL HOUSE OF UNCLE THOMAS: *The King and I* (Oscar Hammerstein II, Richard Rodgers), 1951.
SMILES (THERE ARE SMILES THAT MAKE US HAPPY): *Passing Show of 1918* (additional song by J. Will Callahan, Lee S. Roberts).
SMOKE GETS IN YOUR EYES: *Roberta* (Otto Harbach, Jerome Kern), 1931.
SO FAR: *Allegro* (Oscar Hammerstein II, Richard Rodgers), 1947.
SOFTLY AS IN A MORNING SUNRISE: *The New Moon* (Oscar Hammerstein II, Frank Mandel, Lawrence Schwab, Sigmund Romberg), 1928.
SO IN LOVE: *Kiss Me Kate* (Cole Porter), 1948.
SOLILOQUY: *Carousel* (Oscar Hammerstein II, Richard Rodgers), 1945.
SO LONG MARY: *Forty-five Minutes From Broadway* (George M. Cohan), 1906.
SOME DAY: *Cherry Blossoms* (Harry Smith, Sigmund Romberg), 1927.
SOME DAY I'LL FIND YOU: *Kiki* (Schuyler Green, Zoel Parenteau), 1921.
SOME ENCHANTED EVENING: *South Pacific* (Oscar Hammerstein II, Richard Rodgers), 1949.
SOMEONE TO WATCH OVER ME: *Oh, Kay* (Ira Gershwin, George Gershwin), 1926.
SOMETHING OLD, SOMETHING NEW: *My Maryland* (Dorothy Donnelly, Sigmund Romberg), 1927.
SOMTHING SORT OF GRANDISH: *Finian's Rainbow* (E. Y. "Yip" Harburg, Fred Saidy, Burton Lane), 1947.
SOMETHING TO REMEMBER YOU BY: *Three's a Crowd* (Howard Dietz, Arthur Schwartz), 1930.
SOMETHING WONDERFUL: *The King and I* (Oscar Hammerstein II, Richard Rodgers), 1951.
SOMETIMES I'M HAPPY: *Hit the Deck* (Irving Caesar, Vincent Youmans), 1927.
THE SONG IS YOU: *Music in the Air* (Oscar Hammerstein II, Jerome Kern), 1931.
SONG OF LOVE: *Blossom Time* (Dorothy Donnelly, Sigmund Romberg; based on the Unfinished Symphony by Franz Schubert), 1921.
SONG OF VICTORY: *My Maryland* (Dorothy Donnelly, Sigmund Romberg), 1927.
SONG OF THE MOUNTIES: *Rose Marie* (Oscar Hammerstein II, Otto Harbach, Rudolf Friml), 1924.

SONG OF THE RANGER: See Ranger's Song.
SONG OF THE RIFFS: *The Desert Song* (Oscar Hammerstein II, Otto Harbach, Frank Mandel, Sigmund Romberg), 1926.
SONG OF THE VAGABONDS: *The Vagabond King* (Brian Hooker, W. H. Post, Rudolf Friml), 1925.
SOON: *Strike Up the Band* (Ira Gershwin, George Gershwin), 1930.
SOUTH AMERICAN WAY: *Streets of Paris* (Al Dubin, Jimmy McHugh), 1939.
SOUTH AMERICA, TAKE IT AWAY: *Call Me Mister* (Harold Rome), 1946.
SPAIN: *Show Girl* (gus Kahn, Ira Gershwin, George Gershwin), 1929.
SPEAK LOW: *One Touch of Venus* (Ogden Nash, Kurt Weill), 1944.
SPRING IS HERE: *Sweet Adeline* (Oscar Hammerstein II, Jerome Kern), 1929.
SPRING IS HERE: *Spring Is Here* (Lorenz Hart, Richard Rodgers), 1929.
SPRING IS HERE: *I Married an Angel* (Lorenz Hart, Richard Rodgers), 1938.
STANDIN' ON THE CORNER: *The Most Happy Fella* (Frank Loesser), 1956.
STAN' UP AND FIGHT: *Carmen Jones* (Oscar Hammerstein II; based on Bizet's *Carmen*), 1943.
STARLIT HOUR: *Earl Carroll's Vanities* (Mitchell Parish, Peter de Rose), 1940.
THE STARS REMAIN: *Meet the People* (Edward Eliscu, Henry Myers, Jay Gorney), 1940.
STAY WITH THE HAPPY PEOPLE: *Michael Todd's Peep Show* (Robert Hilliard, Jule Styne), 1950.
STEREOPHONIC SOUND: *Silk Stockings* (Cole Porter), 1955.
STOUT-HEARTED MEN: *The New Moon* (Oscar Hammerstein II, Frank Mandel, Lawrence Schwab, Sigmund Romberg), 1928.
STRANGE MUSIC: *Song of Norway* (George Forrest, Robert Wright; based on the music of Edvard Grieg), 1944.
THE STREETS OF NEW YORK: *The Red Mill* (Henry Blossom, Victor Herbert), 1906.
STRIKE ME PINK: *Strike Me Pink* (Lew Brown, Mack Gordon, Ray Henderson), 1933.
STRIKE UP THE BAND: *Strike Up the Band* (Ira Gershwin, George Gershwin), 1930.
SUE ME: *Guys and Dolls* (Abe Burrows, Jo Swerling, Frank Loesser), 1950.
SUMMERTIME: *Porgy and Bess* (Ira Gershwin, George Gershwin), 1935.
SUMMERTIME IS SUMMERTIME: *Seventeen* (Kim Gannon, Walter Kent), 1951.
SUN AT MY WINDOW, LOVE AT MY DOOR: *Seventh Heaven* (Stella Unger, Victor Young), 1955.
SUNBONNET SUE: *Sunbonnet Sue* (Robert Smith, Gus Edwards), 1923.
SUNNY: *Sunny* (Oscar Hammerstein II, Otto Harbach, Jerome Kern), 1925.
SUNSHINE GIRL: *New Girl in Town* (Bob Merrill), 1957.
SUPPOSING: *Sweet Little Devil* (Buddy De Sylva, George Gershwin), 1924.
SUR LA PLAGE: *The Boy Friend* (Sandy Wilson), 1954.
THE SURREY WITH THE FRINGE ON TOP: *Oklahoma!* (Oscar Hammerstein II, Richard Rodgers), 1943.
SWANEE: *Sinbad* (additional song by Irving Caesar, George Gershwin), 1918.
SWEET BYE-AND-BYE: *Naughty Marietta* (Rida Johnson Young, Victor Herbert), 1910.
SWEETHEART OF MINE: *Louis the Fourteenth* (Arthur Wimperis, Sigmund Romberg), 1925.

SWEETHEARTS: *Sweethearst* (Robert Smith, Victor Herbert), 1913.

SWING!: *Wonderful Town* (Betty Comden, Adolph Green, Leonard Bernstein), 1953.

'SWONDERFUL: *Funny Face* (Ira Gershwin, George Gershwin), 1927.

SYMPATHY: *The Chocolate Soldier* (Rudolph Bernauer, Leopold Jacobson, Oscar Straus; based on *Arms and the Man* by George Bernard Shaw), 1909.

SYMPATHY: *The Firefly* (Otto Harbach, Rudolf Friml), 1912.

TAKE BACK YOUR MINK: *Guys and Dolls* (Abe Burrows, Jo Swerling, Frank Loesser), 1950.

TAKE HIM: *Pal Joey* (Lorenz Hart, Richard Rodgers), 1940.

TAKE YOUR TIME AND TAKE YOUR PICK: *Plain and Fancy* (Arnold B. Horwitt, Albert Hague), 1955.

TAKING A CHANCE ON LOVE: *Cabin in the Sky* (John La Touche, Vernon Duke), 1941.

TEA FOR TWO: *No, No, Nanette* (Irving Caesar, Otto Harbach, Vincent Youmans), 1925.

TELL ME DUSKY MAIDEN: *The Sleeping Beauty and the Beast*, (additional song by Bob Cole, J. Rosamond Johnson), 1901.

TELL ME PRETTY MAIDEN: *Florodora* (Owen Hall, Leslie Stuart), 1900.

TENDER SHEPHERD: *Peter Pan* (Carolyn Leigh, Mark Charlap), 1954.

TEXAS, LI'L DARLIN': *Texas, Li'l Darlin'* (Johnny Mercer, Robert Emmett Dolan) 1949.

THAT RUSSIAN WINTER: *This Is the Army* (Irving Berlin), 1942.

THAT'S FOR SURE: *Top Banana* (Johnny Mercer), 1951.

THAT'S THE WAY IT HAPPENS: *Me and Juliet* (Oscar Hammerstein II, Richard Rodgers), 1953.

THAT'S WHY DARKIES WERE BORN: *George White's Scandals of 1931* (Lew Brown, Ray Henderson).

THAT TERRIFIC RAINBOW: *Pal Joey* (Lorenz Hart, Richard Rodgers), 1940.

THEN YOU·WILL KNOW: *The Desert Song* (Oscar Hammerstein II, Otto Harbach, Frank Mandel, Sigmund Romberg), 1926.

THERE AIN'T NO FLIES ON ME: *New Girl in Town* (Bob Merrill), 1957.

THERE BUT FOR YOU GO I: *Brigadoon* (Alan Jay Lerner, Frederick Loewe), 1947.

THERE IS NO PLACE LIKE HOME: *The Girl Question* (Will Hough, Frank Adams, Joe Howard), 1907.

THERE IS NOTHING LIKE A DAME: *South Pacific* (Oscar Hammerstein II, Richard Rodgers), 1949.

THERE'S A COACH COMIN' IN: *Paint Your Wagon* (Alan Jay Lerner, Frederick Loewe), 1951.

THERE'S A GREAT DAY COMING MANANA: *Hold On to Your Hats* (E. Y. "Yip" Harburg, Burton Lane), 1940.

THERE'S A HILL BEYOND A HILL: *Music in the Air* (Oscar Hammerstein II, Jerome Kern), 1931.

THERE'S A SMALL HOTEL: *On Your Toes* (Lorenz Hart, Richard Rodgers), 1936.

THERE'S NO BUSINESS LIKE SHOW BUSINESS: *Annie Get Your Gun* (Irving Berlin), 1942.

THEY CALL THE WIND MARIA: *Paint Your Wagon* (Alan Jay Lerner, Frederick Loewe), 1951.

THEY DIDN'T BELIEVE ME: *The Girl from Utah* (James T. Tanner, Jerome Kern), 1914.

THEY SAY IT'S WONDERFUL: *Annie Get Your Gun* (Irving Berlin), 1942.

THEY WONT KNOW ME: *Wish You Were Here* (Harold Rome), 1952.

THINE ALONE: *Eileen* (Henry Blossom, Victor Herbert), 1917.

THINGS: *Life Begins at 8:40* (Sid Silvers, Jack Yellen, Harold Arlen), 1934.

THIS CAN'T BE LOVE: *The Boys from Syracuse* (Lorenz Hart, Richard Rodgers), 1938.

THIS IS ALL VERY NEW TO ME: *Plain and Fancy* (Arnold B. Horwitt, Albert Hague), 1955.

THIS IS A REAL NICE CLAMBAKE: *Carousel* (Oscar Hammerstein II, Richard Rodgers), 1945.

THIS IS MY SONG OF LOVE: See Song of Love.

THIS IS THE ARMY, MR. JONES: *This Is the Army* (Irving Berlin), 1942.

THIS LITTLE PIG WENT TO MARKET: *Castles in the Air* (Charles Byrne, Gustave Kerker), 1890.

THIS NEARLY WAS MINE: *South Pacific* (Oscar Hammerstein II, Richard Rodgers), 1949.

THOSE WERE THE GOOD OLD DAYS: *Damn Yankees* (Richard Adler, Jerry Ross), 1955.

THE THOUGHT OF YOU: *Fanny* (Harold Rome), 1954.

THOU SWELL: *A Connecticut Yankee* (Lorenz Hart, Richard Rodgers), 1927.

THREE LITTLE MAIDS FROM SCHOOL: *Hello Daddy* (Dorothy Fields, Jimmy Mc Hugh), 1928.

THE THRILL IS GONE: *George White's Scandals of 1931* (Lew Brown, Ray Henderson).

THROUGH THE YEARS: *Through the Years* (Brian Hooker, Vincent Youmans), 1932.

TILL THE CLOUDS ROLL BY: *Oh, Boy* (Guy Bolton, P. G. Wodehouse, Jerome Kern), 1917.

TILL THE REAL THINGS COMES ALONG: *Rhapsody in Black* (Sammy Cahn, Mann Holiner, Alberta Nichols), 1931.

TIME ON MY HANDS: *Smiles* (Harold Adamson, Clifford Gray, Ring Lardner, Vincent Youmans), 1930.

THE TIME, THE PLACE, AND THE GIRL: *Mlle. Modiste* (Henry Blossom, Victor Herbert), 1905.

TOKAY: *Bitter Sweet* (Noel Coward), 1929.

TOM, DICK, OR HARRY: *Kiss Me Kate* (Cole Porter), 1948.

TOMMY ATKINS (ON DRESS PARADE): *The Firefly* (Otto Harbach, Rudolf Friml), 1912.

TO MY WIFE: *Fanny* (Harold Rome), 1954.

TONIGHT AT THE MARDI GRAS: *Louisiana Purchase* (Irving Berlin), 1940.

TOO CLOSE FOR COMFORT: *Mr. Wonderful* (Jerry Bock, Will Glickman, Larry Holofcener, Joseph Stein, George Weiss), 1956.

TOO DARN HOT: *Kiss Me Kate* (Cole Porter), 1948.

TOTEM TOM-TOM: *Rose Marie* (Oscar Hammerstein II, Otto Harbach, Rudolf Friml), 1925.

TO THE SHIP: *Peter Pan* (Carolyn Leigh, Mark Charlap), 1954.

THE TOUCH OF YOUR HAND: *Roberta* (Otto Harbach, Jerome Kern), 1931.

TOYLAND: *Babes in Toyland* (Glen MacDonough, Victor Herbert), 1903.

TRAMP, TRAMP, TRAMP ALONG THE HIGHWAY: *Naughty Marietta* (Rida Johnson Young, Victor Herbert), 1910.

TRUE HEARTS: *Louis the Fourteenth* (Arthur Wimperis, Sigmund Romberg), 1925.

TRY HER OUT AT DANCING: *The New Moon* (Oscar Hammerstein II, Frank Mandel, Lawrence Schwab, Sigmund Romberg), 1928.

TULIP TIME: *All Aboard* (E. Ray Goetz), 1913.

TULIP TIME: *Ziegfeld Follies of 1919* (Gene Buck, Dave Stamper).

TURKEY TROT: *A Certain Party* (Edgar Smith, Robin Hood Bowers), 1911.

TURTLE SONG: *House of Flowers* (Truman Capote, Harold Arlen), 1954.

TWINKLE, TWINKLE LITTLE STAR: *Somewhere Else* (Avery Hopwood, Gustav Luders), 1912.

TWINKLE, TWINKLE LITTLE STAR: *Ted Lewis Frolic* (Jack Yellen, Milton Agar), 1923.

TWO LADIES IN DE SHADE OF DE BANANA TREE: *House of Flowers* (Truman Capote, Harold Arlen), 1954.

TWO LITTLE GIRLS IN BLUE: *Two Little Girls in Blue* (Arthur Francis, Paul Lannin, Vincent Youmans), 1921.

TWO LOST SOULS: *Damn Yankees* (Richard Adler, Jerry Ross), 1955.

A TYPICAL DAY: *L'il Abner* (Johnny Mercer, Gene de Paul), 1956.

UGG-A-WUGG: *Peter Pan* (additional song by Betty Comden, Adolph Green, Jule Styne), 1954.

UNDER THE BAMBOO TREE: *Sally in Our Alley* (additional song by Bob Cole, J. Rosamond Johnson), 1902.

UNDER THE BAMBOO TREE: *Nancy Brown* (additional song by Bob Cole, J. Rosamond Johnson), 1903.

UNNECESSARY TOWN: *L'il Abner* (Johnny Mercer, Gene de Paul), 1956.

USE YOUR IMAGINATION: *Out of this World* (Cole Porter), 1950.

VALENCIA: *Great Temptations* (Clifford Grey, Jose Padilla), 1926.

VAMP YOUR MAN: *Louis the Fourteenth* (Arthur Wimperis, Sigmund Romberg), 1925.

VARSITY DRAG: *Good News* (Lew Brown, Buddy De Sylva, Ray Henderson), 1927.

VEN I VALSE: *New Girl in Town* (Bob Merrill), 1957.

A VERY SPECIAL DAY: *Me and Juliet* (Oscar Hammerstein II, Richard Rodgers), 1953.

VILIA: *The Merry Widow* (Adrian Ross, Franz Lehar), 1907.

VOODOO: *House of Flowers* (Truman Capote, Harold Arlen), 1954.

WAGON WHEELS: *Ziegfeld Follies of 1934* (William J. "Billy" Hill, Peter de Rose).

WAIT AND SEE: *Cherry Blossoms* (Harry Smith, Sigmund Romberg), 1927.

WAITIN': *House of Flowers* (Truman Capote, Harold Arlen), 1954.

WAITIN' FOR MY DEARIE: *Brigadoon* (Alan Jay Lerner, Frederick Loewe), 1947.

WALTZ ME AROUND AGAIN WILLIE: *His Honor the Mayor* (Kirke La Schelle, Julian Edwards), 1900.

WAND'RIN STAR: *Paint Your Wagon* (Alan Jay Lerner, Frederick Loewe), 1951.

WANTING YOU: *Blue Eyes* (additional song by Irving Caesar, George Gershwin), 1921.

WANTING YOU: *The New Moon* (Oscar Hammerstein II, Frank Mandel, Lawrence Schwab, Sigmund Romberg), 1928.

WAY DOWN YONDER IN NEW ORLEANS: *Spice of 1922* (additional song by Henry Creamer, Turner Layton).

WE DESERVE EACH OTHER: *Me and Juliet* (Oscar Hammerstein II, Richard Rodgers), 1953.

WE DID IT BEFORE: *Banjo Eyes* (Harold Adamson, John La Touche, Vernon Duke), 1941.

WE KISS IN A SHADOW: *The King and I* (Oscar Hammerstein II, Richard Rodgers), 1951.

WELCOME HOME: *Fanny* (Harold Rome), 1954.

WENDY: *Peter Pan* (additional song by Betty Comden, Adolph Green, Jule Styne), 1954.

WE OPEN IN VENICE: *Kiss Me Kate* (Cole Porter), 1948.

WE'RE HAVING A BABY, MY BABY AND ME: *Banjo Eyes* (Harold Adamson, John La Touche, Vernon Duke), 1941.

WE'RE HERE BECAUSE: *Lady Be Good* (Ira Gershwin, George Gershwin), 1924.

WERE THINE THAT SPECIAL FACE: *Kiss Me Kate* (Cole Porter), 1948.

WHAT A WASTE: *Wonderful Town* (Betty Comden, Adolph Green, Leonard Bernstein), 1953.

WHAT CARE I?: *Princess Flavia* (Harry Smith, Sigmund Romberg), 1925.

WHAT DO YOU THINK ABOUT MEN?: *Out of This World* (Cole Porter), 1950.

WHATEVER LOLA WANTS: *Damn Yankees* (Richard Adler, Jerry Ross), 1955.

WHAT IS A FRIEND FOR?: *House of Flowers* (Truman Capote, Harold Arlen), 1954.

WHAT IS THERE TO SAY?: *Ziegfeld Follies of 1934* (E. Y. "Yip" Harburg, Vernon Duke).

WHAT IS THIS THING CALLED LOVE?: *Wake Up and Dream* (Cole Porter), 1929.

WHAT'S THE USE?: *Candide* (Richard Wilbur, Dorothy Parker, John La Touche, Leonard Bernstein), 1956.

WHAT'S THE USE OF WONDERING?: *Carousel* (Oscar Hammerstein II, Richard Rodgers), 1945.

WHAT THE WELL-DRESSED MAN IN HARLEM WILL WEAR: *This Is the Army* (Irving Berlin), 1942.

WHEN A MAID COMES KNOCKING AT YOUR HEART: *The Firefly* (Otto Harbach, Rudolf Friml), 1912.

WHEN HEARTS ARE YOUNG: *The Lady in Ermine* (Harry Graham, Cyrus Wood, Sigmund Romberg), 1922.

WHEN I MARRY MR. SNOW: *Carousel* (Oscar Hammerstein II, Richard Rodgers), 1945.

WHEN I'M BLUE: *How Come* (Harry Creamer, Will Vodery, Ben Harris), 1923.

WHEN I'M NOT NEAR THE GIRL I LOVE: *Finian's Rainbow* (E. Y. "Yip" Harburg, Fred Saidy, Burton Lane), 1947.

WHEN IRISH EYES ARE SMILING: *Isle of Dreams* (George Graff, Chauncey Olcott, Ernest Ball), 1912.

WHEN SHE WALKS IN THE ROOM: *Up in Central Park* (Dorothy Fields, Herbert Fields, Sigmund Romberg), 1945.

WHEN THE EDELWEISS IS BLOOMING: *Hanky-Panky* (E. Ray Goetz, A. Baldwin Sloane), 1912.

WHEN THE IDLE POOR BECOME THE IDLE RICH: *Finian's Rainbow* (E. Y. "Yip" Harburg, Fred Saidy, Burton Lane), 1947.

WHEN YOU'RE AWAY: *The Only Girl* (Henry Blossom, Victor Herbert), 1914.

WHERE ARE YOU?: *Artists and Models of 1930* (Ernie Golden, Harold Stern).

WHERE DID THE NIGHT GO?: *Wish You Were Here* (Harold Rome), 1952.

WHERE IS THAT SOOMEONE FOR ME?: *Seventh Heaven* (Stella Unger, Victor Young), 1955.

WHERE IS THE LIFE THAT LATE I LED: *Kiss Me Kate* (Cole Porter), 1948.

WHERE OR WHEN: *Babes in Arms* (Lorenz Hart, Richard Rodgers), 1937.

WHERE YOU ARE: *Follow the Girls* (Dan Shapiro, Milton Pascal, Phil Charig), 1944.

WHO?: *Sunny* (Oscar Hammerstein II, Otto Harbach, Jerome Kern), 1925.

WHO COULD ASK FOR ANYTHING MORE?: *Of Thee I Sing* (Ira Gershwin, George Gershwin), 1931.

WHO DO YOU LOVE, I HOPE: *Annie Get Your Gun* (Irving Berlin), 1942.

WHO IS THE BRAVEST: *Hazel Flagg* (Bob Hilliard, Jule Styne), 1953.

WHOOP-TI-AY!: *Paint Your Wagon* (Alan Jay Lerner, Frederick Loewe), 1951.

WHOSE BABY ARE YOU?: *The Night Boat* (Anne Caldwell, Jerome Kern), 1920.

WHO'S GOT THE PAIN: *Damn Yankees* (Richard Adler, Jerry Ross), 1955.

WHY BE AFRAID TO DANCE?: *Fanny* (Harold Rome), 1954.

WHY CAN'T THE ENGLISH? (TEACH THEIR CHILDREN HOW TO SPEAK): *My Fair Lady* (Alan Jay Lerner, Frederick Loewe), 1955.

WHY CAN'T YOU BEHAVE?: *Kiss Me Kate* (Cole Porter), 1948.

WHY DO I LOVE YOU?: *Show Boat* (Oscar Hammerstein II, Jerome Kern), 1927.

WHY NOT KATIE?: *Plain and Fancy* (Arnold B. Horwitt, Albert Hague), 1955.

WHY SHOULDN'T I?: *Jubilee* (Cole Porter), 1935.

WHY WAS I BORN?: *Sweet Adeline* (Oscar Hammerstein II, Jerome Kern), 1929.

WILL YOU REMEMBER (SWEETHEART?): *Maytime* (Rida Johnson Young, Sigmund Romberg), 1917.

WINGS: *Take the Air* (Gene Buck, Dave Stamper), 1927.

WINTERGREEN FOR PRESIDENT: *Of Thee I Sing* (Ira Gershwin, George Gershwin), 1931.

WITH A LITTLE BIT OF LUCK: *My Fair Lady* (Alan Jay Lerner, Frederick Loewe), 1955.

WITH A SONG IN MY HEART: *Spring Is Here* (Lorenz Hart, Richard Rodgers), 1929.

WITH A TWIST OF THE WRIST: *Crazy with the Heat* (Irvin Graham), 1941.

WITHOUT A SONG: *Great Day* (Billy Rose, Vincent Youmans), 1929.

WITHOUT LOVE: *Silk Stockings* (Cole Porter), 1955.

WITHOUT YOU: *My Fair Lady* (Alan Jay Lerner, Frederick Loewe), 1955.

THE WOMAN IN HIS ROOM: *Where's Charley?* (Frank Loesser), 1948.

A WOMAN IS A SOMETIME THING: *Porgy and Bess* (Ira Gershwin, George Gershwin), 1935.

WOMAN'S PREROGATIVE: *St. Louis Woman* (Johnny Mercer, Harold Arlen), 1946.

WON'T YOU CHARLESTON WITH ME?: *The Boy Friend* (Sandy Wilson), 1954.

WON'T YOU MARRY ME?: *My Maryland* (Dorothy Donnelly, Sigmund Romberg), 1927.

A WORD A DAY: *Top Banana* (Johnny Mercer), 1951.

THE WORLD IS BEAUTIFUL TODAY: *Hazel Flagg* (Bob Hilliard, Jule Styne), 1953.

THE WORLD IS MINE: *Funny Face* (Ira Gershwin, George Gershwin), 1927.

WORLD WEARY: *This Year of Grace* (Noel Coward), 1928.

WOULDN'T IT BE LOVERLY?: *My Fair Lady* (Alan Jay Lerner, Frederick Loewe), 1955.

WOULD YOU LIKE TO TAKE A WALK?: *Sweet and Low* (Mort Dixon, Harry Warren), 1930.

WOULD YOU LIKE TO TAKE A WALK?: *Billy Rose's Crazy Quilt* (Mort Dixon, Harry Warren), 1931.

WRONG NOTE RAG: *Wonderful Town* (Betty Comden, Adolph Green, Leonard Bernstein), 1953.

WUNDERBAR: *Kiss Me Kate* (Cole Porter), 1948.

THE YEARS BEFORE US: *Where's Charley?* (Frank Loesser), 1948.

YER MY FRIEND AIN'TCHA?: *New Girl in Town* (Bob Merrill), 1957.

YESTERDAYS: *Roberta* (Otto Harbach, Jerome Kern), 1931.

YOU AND THE NIGHT AND THE MUSIC: *Revenge with Music* (Howard Dietz, Arthur Schwartz), 1934.

YOU APPEAL TO ME: *The Love Call* (Harry Smith, Sigmund Romberg), 1927.

YOU ARE LOVE: *Show Boat* (Oscar Hammerstein II, Jerome Kern), 1927.

YOU ARE NEVER AWAY: *Allegro* (Oscar Hammerstein II, Richard Rodgers), 1947.

YOU ARE SO FAIR: *Babes in Arms* (Lorenz Hart, Richard Rodgers), 1937.

YOU BETTER GO NOW: *New Faces of 1936* (Bix Reichner, Irvin Graham).

YOU CAN'T GET A MAN WITH A GUN: *Annie Get Your Gun* (Irving Berlin), 1942.

YOU CAN'T MISS IT: *Plain and Fancy* (Arnold B. Horwitt, Albert Hague), 1955.

YOU'D BE SURPRISED: *Ziegfeld Follies of 1919* (Irving Berlin).

YOU DID IT: *My Fair Lady* (Alan Jay Lerner, Frederick Loewe), 1955.

YOU DON'T WANT TO PLAY WITH THE BLUES: *The Boy Friend* (Sandy Wilson), 1954.

YOU DO SOMETHING TO ME: *Fifty Million Frenchmen* (Cole Porter), 1929.

YOU KNOW THAT I KNOW: *Nobody Home* (Guy Bolton, Paul Rubens, Jerome Kern), 1915.

YOU'LL NEVER WALK ALONE: *Carousel* (Oscar Hammerstein II, Richard Rodgers), 1945.

YOU MUSN'T KICK IT AROUND: *Pal Joey* (Lorenz Hart, Richard Rodgers), 1940.

YOUNG AND FOOLISH: *Plain and Fancy* (Arnold B. Horwitt, Albert Hague), 1955.

YOUNGER THAN SPRINGTIME: *South Pacific* (Oscar Hammerstein II, Richard Rodgers), 1949.

YOU'RE A BUILDER UPPER: *Life Begins at 8:40* (Sid Silvers, Jack Yellen, Harold Arlen), 1934.

YOU'RE A GRAND OLD FLAG: *George Washington Jr.* (George M. Cohan), 1906.

YOU'RE AN OLD SMOOTHIE: *Take a Chance* (Buddy De Sylva, Lawrence Schwab, Nacio Herb Brown, Richard Whiting), 1932.

YOU'RE A QUEER ONE, JULIE JORDAN: *Carousel* (Oscar Hammerstein II, Richard Rodgers), 1945.

YOU'RE DEVASTATING: *Roberta* (Otto Harbach, Jerome Kern), 1931.

YOU'RE GONNA DANCE WITH ME, WILLIE?: *Hazel Flagg* (Bob Hilliard, Jule Styne), 1953.

YOU'RE LONELY AND I'M LONELY: *Louisiana Purchase* (Irving Berlin), 1940.

YOU'RE MY EVERYTHING: *The Laugh Parade* (Mort Dixon, Joseph Young, Harry Warren). 1931.

YOU'RE SO BEAUTIFUL THAT — —: *Top Banana* (Johnny Mercer), 1951.

YOU ARE THE CREAM IN MY COFFEE: *Hold Everything* (Lew Brown, Buddy De Sylva, Ray Henderson), 1928.

YOU'RE THE TOP: *Anything Goes* (Cole Porter), 1934.

YOUR LAND AND MY LAND: *My Maryland* (Dorothy Donnelly, Sigmund Romberg), 1927.

YOURS IS MY HEART ALONE: *Yours Is My Heart Alone* (Ira Cobb, Karl Farkas, Harry Graham, Franz Lehar), 1946.
YOU TOOK ADVANTAGE OF ME: *Present Arms* (Lorenz Hart, Richard Rodgers), 1927.
YOU'VE NEVER BEEN LOVED: *Michael Todd's Peep Show* (Dan Shapiro, Sammy Stept), 1950.
YOU WERE DEAD YOU KNOW: *Candide* (Richard Wilbur, Dorothy Parker, John La Touche, Leonard Bernstein), 1956.
YULETIDE PARK AVENUE: *Call Me Mister* (Harold Rome), 1946.
ZING WENT THE STRINGS OF MY HEART: *Thumbs Up* (James Frederick Hanley), 1934.
ZIP: *Pal Joey* (Lorenz Hart, Richard Rodgers), 1940.

Songs from Shakespeare's Plays

"AND LET ME THE CANAKIN CLINK, CLINK": Sung by Iago; *Othello* (II, 3).
"AND OLD HARE HOAR": Sung by Mercutio; *Romeo and Juliet* (II, 4).
"BLOW, BLOW, THOU WINTER WIND": Sung by Amiens; *As You Like It* (II, 7).
"COME AWAY, COME AWAY, DEATH": Sung by Clown (Feste); *Twelfth Night* (II, 4).
"COME, THOU MONARCH OF THE VINE": Sung by Roman leaders led by Enobarbus; *Antony and Cleopatra* (II, 7).
"COME UNTO THESE YELLOW SANDS": Ariel's Song; *The Tempest* (I, 1).
"EARTH'S INCREASE, FOISON PLENTY": Sung by Ceres; *The Tempest* (IV, 1).
"FAREWELL, MASTER; FAREWELL, FAREWELL": Sung by Caliban; *The Tempest* (III, 1).
"FEAR NO MORE THE HEAT O' TH' SUN": Sung by Guiderius and Arviragus; *Cymbeline* (IV, 2).
"FIE ON SINFUL FANTASY!": Sung by Quick; *The Merry Wives of Windsor* (V, 5).
"FOR I THE BALLAD WILL REPEAT": Sung (?) by Clown; *All's Well That Ends Well* (I, 3).
"FULL FATHOM FIVE THY FATHER LIES": Ariel's Song; *The Tempest* (I, 1).
"GET YOU HENCE, FOR I MUST GO": Sung by Autolycus and Dorcas; *The Winter's Tale* (IV, 4).
"HARK, HARK! THE LARK AT HEAVEN'S GATE SINGS": Sung by Musicians; *Cymbeline* (II, 3).
"HEY ROBIN, JOLLY ROBIN": Sung by Clown (Feste); *Twelfth Night* (IV, 2).
"HONOUR, RICHES, MARRIAGE-BLESSING": Sung by Juno; *The Tempest* (IV, 1).
"HOW SHOULD I YOUR TRUE LOVE KNOW": Sung by Ophelia; *Hamlet* (IV, 5).
"IN YOUTH, WHEN I DID LOVE, DID LOVE": Sung by Clown (Gravedigger); *Hamlet* (V, 1).
"I SHALL NO MORE TO SEA, TO SEA": Sung by Stephano; *The Tempest* (II, 2).
"JOG ON, JOG ON, THE FOOT-PATH WAY": Sung by Autolycus; *The Winter's Tale* (IV, 4).
"KING STEPHEN WAS AND — A WORTHY PEER": Sung by Iago; *Othello* (II, 3).
"LAWN AS WHITE AS DRIVEN SNOW": Sung by Autolycus; *The Winter's Tale* (IV, 4).
"LOVE, LOVE, NOTHING BUT LOVE, STILL MORE": Sung by Pandarus; *Troilus and Cressida* (III, 1).
"ORPHEUS WITH HIS LUTE MADE TREES": Sung by Queen Katherine's woman; *Henry the Eight* (III, 1).
"OVER HILL, OVER DALE": Sung by Fairy; *A Midsummer Night's Dream* (II, 1).

"PARDON, GODDESS OF THE NIGHT": Sung by Claudio; *Much Ado About Nothing* (V, 3).
"SIGH NO MORE, LADIES, SIGH NO MORE": Sung by Balthasar; *Much Ado About Nothing* (II, 3).
"TAKE, O, TAKE THOSE LIPS AWAY: Sung by Boy with Mariana; *Measure for Measure* (IV, 1).
"TELL ME WHERE IS FANCY BRED": Sung by Portia; *The Merchant of Venice* (III, 2).
"THE MASTER, THE SWABBER, THE BOATSWAIN, AND I": Sung by Stephano; *The Tempest* (II, 2).
"THE POOR SOUL SAT SIGHING BY A SYCAMORE TREE": Sung by Desdemona; *Othello* (IV, 3).
"TOMORROW IS SAINT VALENTINE'S DAY": Sung by Ophelia; *Hamlet* (IV, 5).
"TO SHALLOW RIVERS, TO WHOSE FALL": Sung by Sir Hugh Evans; *The Merry Wives of Windsor* (III, 1).
"UNDER THE GREENWOOD TREE": Sung by Amiens; *As You Like It* (II, 5).
"WAS THIS FAIR FACE THE CAUSE, QUOTH SHE": Sung by Clown; *All's Well That Ends Well* (I, 3).
"WEDDING IS GREAT JUNO'S CROWN": Sung by Hymen; *As You Like It* (V, 4).
"WHEN DAFFODILS BEGIN TO PEER": Sung by Autolycus; *The Winter's Tale* (IV, 4).
"WHEN DAISIES PIED AND VIOLETS BLUE": Sung by Spring; *Love's Labour's Lost* (V, 2).
"WHEN ICICLES HANG BY THE WALL": Sung by Winter; *Love's Labour's Lost* (V, 2).
"WHEN THAT I WAS AND A LITTLE TINY BOY": Sung by Clown (Feste); *Twelfth Night* (V, 1).
"WHERE THE BEE SUCKS, THERE SUCK I": Sung by Ariel; *The Tempest* (V, 1).
"WHILE YOU HERE DO SNORING LIE": Sung by Ariel; *The Tempest* (II, 2).
"WHO DOTH AMBITION SHUN": Sung by all; *As You Like It* (II, 5).
"WHO IS SILVIA? WHAT IS SHE": Sung by Musicians, with Thurio; *Two Gentlemen of Verona* (IV, 2).
WILLOW SONG: See "The poor soul sat sighing by a sycamore tree."
"WILL YOU BUY ANY TAPE": Sung by Autolycus; *The Winter's Tale* (IV, 4).
"YOU SPOTTED SNAKES WITH DOUBLE TONGUE": Sung by Fairies; *A Midsummer Night's Dream* (II, 2).

Spanish-American War Battles
See also **Battles**

1898

FEBRUARY 15: U.S. battleship *Maine* destroyed by explosion in Havana, Cuba, harbor.
APRIL 11: Pres. McKinley asked Congress for right to intervene forcibly in Cuba to protect American sugar interests.
APRIL 20: Pres. McKinley signed the war resolution submitted to him by Congress.
APRIL 24: Spain declared war on the U.S.
APRIL 25: Congress, in a formal declaration, proclaimed that a state of war had existed between the U.S. and Spain since April 21.
APRIL 27: Matanzas, Cuba, batteries bombarded by U.S. ships.
MAY 1: Battle of Manila Bay: American Asian squadron, commanded by Com. George Dewey, destroyed Spanish fleet of ten vessels in Manila Bay.
MAY 12: San Juan, Puerto Rico, bombarded by U.S. fleet (Adm. William T. Sampson).

MAY 19: Admiral Pascual Cervera y Topete based Spanish fleet in Santiago harbor, Cuba.

MAY 31: Forts at entrance to Santiago harbor bombarded by U.S. ships (Com. Winfield Scott Schley), as blockade of Spanish fleet entered third day.

JUNE 10: Marines landed at Guantanamo Bay, Cuba.

JUNE 14-15: Spanish engaged in skirmish with U.S. Marines at Guantanamo; fort at Caimanera bombarded by U.S. ships.

JUNE 24: Spanish defeated at Las Guásimas, Cuba, in first infantry battle of the war, by advance party of American expeditionary force (Gen. Joseph Wheeler, Col. Theodore Roosevelt, Col. Leonard Wood).

JULY 1-2: Spanish earthworks at El Caney and San Juan, near Santiago, Cuba, taken in assault by American expeditionary force (Gen. William Shafter); American casualities: 1572.

JULY 3: Spanish fleet (Adm. Pascual Cervera y Topete), destroyed in attempt to run the American blockade (Adm. William T. Sampson) of Santiago, Cuba.

JULY 4: American Philippine expedition occupied Wake Island.

JULY 7: U.S. annexed Hawaii.

JULY 10: Santiago, Cuba, bombarded by U.S. ships.

JULY 11: Nipe, Cuba, bombarded by U.S. ships.

JULY 17: Santiago, Cuba, capitulated to American expeditionary force (Gen. William Shafter).

JULY 25: Puerto Rico occupied by American expeditionary force (Gen. Nelson A. Miles).

JULY 31: Spaniards repulsed by Americans at Malate, Philippines.

AUGUST 12: Spanish peace bid, providing for cessation of hostilities, signed in Washington.

AUGUST 13: Manila surrendered to combined U.S. land (Gen. Wesley Merritt) and sea (Adm. George Dewey) forces.

DECEMBER 10: Treaty of Paris: in the treaty, which ended the Spanish-American War, Spain recognized Cuban independence, ceded Puerto Rico and Guam to the U.S. as indemnity for the war, and sold the Phillipine Islands to the U.S. for 20 million dollars.

Spanish Rulers
See **Rulers**

Speeches and Sermons:
The Most Famous Addresses and Orations of History

ADAMS, CHARLES FRANCIS (1807-1886): Speech: On the States and the Union.

ADAMS, JOHN (1735-1826): Speech: On the Boston Massacre.

ADAMS, JOHN QUINCY (1767-1848): Speech: Oration at Plymouth.

ADAMS, SAMUEL (1722-1803): Speech: American Independence.

AESCHINES (389-314 b. c.): Speech: Against Crowning Demosthenes.

ANDOCIDES (467-391 b. c.): Speech: On the Mysteries.

ANTIPHON (480-411 b. c.): Speech: On the Murder of Herodes.

ANTONIUS, MARCUS (83?-30 b. c.) Speech: On the assassination of Caesar.

ARNOLD, MATTHEW (1822-1888): Address: On Emerson.

ARNOLD, THOMAS (1795-1842): Sermon: Alive in God.

AUGUSTINE, SAINT (354-430): Sermon: On the Lord's Prayer.

BEACONSFIELD, LORD (BENJAMIN DISRAELI) (1804-1881): Speeches: Conservatism; On the Berlin Congress.

BEDE, THE VENERABLE (673-735): Sermon: On the Nativity of St. Peter and St. Paul.

BEECHER, HENRY WARD (1813-1887): Speeches: Effect of the Death of Lincoln; At the Raising of "The Old Flag" at Fort Sumter.

BENJAMIN, JUDAH PHILIP (1811-1884): Speech: On the Property Doctrine, or the Right of Property in Slaves.

BEVERIDGE, ALBERT J. (1862-1927): Speeches: Denunciation of John Peter Altgeld, Governor of Illinois; Speech in favor of war with Spain.

BISMARCK, PRINCE (1815-1898): Speeches: A Plea for Imperial Armament; Against Liberalism: A Prussian Royalist Confession of Faith.

BJÖRNSON, BJÖRNSTJERNE (1832-1910): Speech: Address at the Grave of Ole Bull.

BLAINE, JAMES GILLESPIE (1830-1893): Speeches: Oration on Garfield; On the Remonetization of Silver.

BONAPARTE, NAPOLEON (1769-1821): Speeches: Address to Army at Beginning of Italian Campaign; Proclamation to the Army, May, 1796; Proclamation to the Soldiers on entering Milan; Address to Soldiers during the Siege of Mantua; Address at Conclusion of First Italian Campaign; Address to Troops after the War of the Third Coalition; Address to Troops on Beginning of the Russian Campaign; Farewell to the Old Guard.

BOSSUET, JACQUES BÉNIGNE (1627-1704): Sermon: Funeral Oration on Condé.

BOURDALOUE, LOUIS (1632-1704): Sermon: The Passion of Christ.

BRADLAUGH, CHARLES (1833-1891): Speech: At the Bar of the House of Commons.

BRIGHT, JOHN (1811-1889): Speeches: The *Trent* Affair; On Slavery in America.

BROOKS, PHILLIPS (1835-1893): Speeches: The Beauty of a Life of Service; Abraham Lincoln.

BROUGHAM, LORD (HENRY PETER BROUGHAM) (1778-1868): Speech: On Negro Emancipation.

BROWN, BENJAMIN GRATZ (1826-1885): Speech: On Slavery.

BROWN, JOHN (1800-1859): Speeches: Words to Governor Wise at Harper's Ferry; Last Speech to the Court.

BRYAN, WILLIAM JENNINGS (1860-1925): Speech: The "Cross of Gold."

BRYANT WILLIAM CULLEN (1794-1878): Speeches: Welcome to Louis Kossuth; Address at the Founding of the Metropolitan Art Museum.

BURKE, EDMUND (1729-1797): Speech: On Conciliation with America.

CAESAR, CAIUS JULIUS (102-44 b. c.): Speech: On the Treatment of the Catilinarian Conspirators.

CALHOUN, JOHN CALDWELL (1782-1850): Speech: On the Slavery Question.

CALVIN, JOHN (1509-1564): Sermon, On Enduring Persecution.

CAMBON, PIERRE JOSEPH (1754-1820): Speech: The Crisis of 1793.

CANNING, GEORGE (1770-1827): Speech: On Affording Aid to Portugal.

CARLYLE, THOMAS (1795-1881): Speech: Inaugural Address at Edinburgh University.

CARNOT, LAZARE NICOLAS MARGUERITE (1753-1823): Speech: Against Imperialism in France.

CATALINE, LUCIUS (c. 108-62 b. c.): Speech-

FISKE, JOHN (1842-1901): Speech: Oration on Columbus.

FLOOD, HENRY (1732-1791): Speech: Renunciation Speech.

FOX, CHARLES JAMES (1749-1806): Speech: On the Rejection of Bonaparte's Overtures.

FRANKLIN, BENJAMIN (1706-1790): Speeches: The Federal Constitution; Dangers of a Salaried Bureaucracy.

FREDERICK WILLIAM IV (1795-1861): Speech: Opening of the Prussian Diet.

GALLATIN, ALBERT (1761-1849): Speech: On the British Peace Treaty.

GAMBETTA, LÉON (1838-1882): Speech: On the Constitutional Laws.

GANDHI, MOHANDAS (1869-1948): Speech: Address to the Court on being sentenced for sedition.

GARFIELD, JAMES ABRAM (1831-1881): Speech: Inaugural Address.

GARIBALDI, GUISEPPE MARIA (1807-1882): Speeches: Last Speech as a Member of the Chamber; Address to His Soldiers.

GARRISON, WILLIAM LLOYD (1805-1879): Speech: Words of Encouragement to the Oppressed.

GAULLE, CHARLES DE (1890-   ): Speech: London radio address to the people of France, asking them to resist the German invaders.

GIDDINGS, JOSHUA R. (1795-1864): Speech: Denunciation of Slavery.

GLADSTONE, WILLIAM EWART (1809-1898): Speeches: On Domestic and Foreign Affairs; On the Beaconsfield Ministry.

GORDON, JOHN BROWN (1832-1904): Speech: On the Silver Coinage.

GORGIAS (c. 480-375 b.c.): Speech: Encomium on Helen.

GRACCHUS, CAIUS (158-121 b.c.): Speech: On the Revenue.

GRADY, HENRY WOODFEN (1850-1889): Speech: The New South.

GRANT, ULYSSES SIMPSON (1822-1885): Speeches: Inaugural Address; At Warren, Ohio.

GRATTAN, HENRY (1746-1820): Speech: Against English Imperialism.

GREELEY, HORACE (1811-1872): Speech: On the Union of Workers.

GUIZOT, FRANÇOIS PIERRE GUILLAUME (1787-1874): Speeches: Civilization and the Individual Man; At the University of Paris; At the Unveiling of the Statue of William the Conquerer.

HALE, EDWARD EVERETT (1822-1909): Speeches: New England Culture; The Sons of Massachusetts.

HALE, JOHN PARKER (1806-1873): Speech: On Secession.

HAMILTON, ALEXANDER (1757-1804): Speech: On the Federal Constitution.

HANCOCK, JOHN (1737-1793): Speech: The Boston Massacre.

HANNA, MARCUS ALONZO (MARK) (1837-1904): Speech: The Promotion of Commerce and Increase of Trade.

HARRISON, BENJAMIN (1833-1901): Speech: Inaugural Address.

HAYES, RUTHERFORD BIRCHARD (1822-1893): Speech: Campaign Speech.

HAYNE, ROBERT YOUNG (1791-1839): Speech: On Foote's Resolution.

HENRY, PATRICK (1736-1799): Speeches: "Give Me Liberty, or Give Me Death"; "We, the People, or We, the States?"; "A Nation—Not a Federation"; The Bill of Rights; Liberty or Empire?

HIGGINSON, THOMAS WENTWORTH (1823-1911),) Speeches: Decoration Day Address; Oration upon Grant; For Self-Respect and Self-Protection.

HITLER, ADOLF (1889-1945): Speech: Address to the Reichstag in defense of the purge of his enemies, July 13, 1934.

HOLMES, OLIVER WENDELL (1809-1894): Speeches: Lecture on Religious Poetry; Leave No Verbal Message; Tribute to Paul Morphy; At an Alumni Dinner.

HOUSTON, SAMUEL (1793-1863): Speech: On the Nebraska and Kansas Bill.

HUGHES, THOMAS (1823-1926): Speech: The Course of Freedom.

HUGO, VICTOR (1802-1885): Speeches: On the Centennial of Voltaire's Death; On Honoré de Balzac; On Capital Punishment.

INGERSOLL, ROBERT GREEN (1833-1899): Speeches: Blaine, the Plumed Knight; Oration at His Brother's Grave; Oration on Humboldt.

IRELAND, JOHN (ARCHBISHOP) (1838-1918): Speech: On Patriotism.

ISOCRATES (436-338 b.c.): Speech: Enconium on Evagoras.

JACKSON, ANDREW (1767-1845): Speech: State Rights and Federal Sovereignty.

JAY, JOHN (1745-1829): Speech: Address to the People of Great Britain.

JAY, JOHN (1817-1894): Speech: America Free —or America Slave.

JEFFERSON, THOMAS (1743-1826): Speech: Inaugural Address.

JOHNSON, ANDREW (1808-1875): Speech: At St. Louis.

KINGSLEY, CHARLES (1819-1875): Sermon: The Transfiguration.

KNOX, JOHN (1505-1572): Sermon: The First Temptation of Christ.

KOSSUTH, LOUIS (1802-1894): Speeches: At Faneuil Hall; At Plymouth; First Speech in New York.

LABORI, FERNAND GUSTAVE (1860-1917): Speech: The Conspiracy against Dreyfus.

LACORDAIRE, JEAN BAPTISTE HENRI (1802-1861): Speech: Panegyric on Daniel O'Connell.

LAMARTINE, ALPHONSE MARIE LOUIS 1790-1869): Speeches: Reply to Polish Deputations; Congratulatory Speech; Reply to Club Delegates.

LATIMER, HUGH (1480-1555): Sermon: On Christian Love.

LEE, HENRY (1756-1818): Speech: Eulogy on Washington.

LEE, RICHARD HENRY (1732-1794): Speech: Address to the Inhabitants of Great Britain.

LINCOLN, ABRAHAM (1809-1865): Speeches: Farewell Adress at Springfield; Cooper Institute Speech; Gettysburg Address; First Inaugural Address; Second Inaugural Address.

LIVINGSTON, ROBERT R. (1746-1813): Speech: Oration before the Cincinnati.

LLOYD GEORGE, DAVID (1863-1945): Speech: Plea for English volunteers to fight against the German Junkers, September 19, 1914.

LODGE, HENRY CABOT (1850-1924): Speeches: On Daniel Webster; At a Republican Convention.

LOWELL, JAMES RUSSELL (1819-1891): Speeches: Oration at the 250th Anniversary of the Founding of Harvard College; A Plea for the Modern Language.

LUTHER, MARTIN (1483-1546): Speech: Address to the Diet of Worms.

LYCURGUS (396-323 b.c.): Speech: Against Leocrates.

LYSIAS (c. 436-380 b.c.): Speech: Against Eratosthenes.

LYTTON, EDWARD GEORGE EARLE LYT-

TON BULWER, LORD (1803-1873): Speech: On the Crimean War.

MACARTHUR, DOUGLAS (1880-   ): Speech: Address to Congress in defense of his campaign in Korea ("Old soldiers never die").

MCCARTHY, JUSTIN (1830-1912): Speech: In Defense of His Colleagues.

MACAULAY, THOMAS BABINGTON (1800-1859): Speeches: On Parliamentary Reform; On Jewish Disabilities.

MCKINLEY, WILLIAM (1843-1901): Speeches: American Patriotism; Last Speech.

MACKINTOSH, SIR JAMES (1765-1832): Speech: On the Trial of Jean Peltier.

MADISON, JAMES (1751-1836): Speech: On the Federal Constitution.

MANN, HORACE (1796-1859): Speeches: On the Threatened Dissolution of the Union; The Institution of Slavery.

MANNING, HENRY EDWARD (1808-1892): Speech: The Triumph of the Church.

MANSFIELD, LORD (1705-1793): Speech: On the Right of England to Tax America.

MARAT, JEAN PAUL (1744-1793): Speech: Before the National Convention.

MARSHALL, JOHN (1755-1835): Speech: On the Federal Constitution.

MASSILON, JEAN BAPTISTE (1663-1742): Sermon: The Curse of a Malignant Tongue.

MATHER, COTTON (1663-1728): Sermon: The Bostonian Ebenezer.

MAZZINI, GIUSEPPE (1805-1872): Speech: To the Young Men of Italy.

MEAGHER, THOMAS FRANCIS (1823-1867): Speech: "Sword Speech."

MELANCHTHON, PHILIP (1497-1560): Speech: Funeral Oration over Martin Luther.

MIRABEAU, COUNT DE (HONORÉ GABRIEL VICTOR REQUETTI) (1749-1791): Speeches: On Necker's Financial Project; On the Accusation of Implication in the Insurrection of Oct. 5, 1789.

MONROE, JAMES (1758-1831): Speech: Federal Experiments in History.

MOODY, DWIGHT LYMAN (1837-1899): Sermon: What Think Ye of Christ?

MOREAU, JEAN VICTOR (1763-1813): Speech: In His Own Defense.

MORLEY, JOHN (VISCOUNT MORLEY OF BLACKBURN (1838-1923): Speech: On Home Rule.

MORRIS, GOUVERNEUR (1752-1816): Speech: On the Judiciary.

MORTON, OLIVER PERRY (1823-1877): Speech: On Reconstruction.

NAPOLEON III (1808-1873): Speeches: Speech in the National Assembly; First Inaugural Address as President; Address to the French Legislature.

NEWMAN, JOHN HENRY (1801-1890): Sermons: Communion with God; Second Spring.

NOTT, ELIPHALET (1773-1866): Sermon: How are the Mighty Fallen.

O'CONELL, DANIEL (1775-1847): Speech: Ireland Worth Dying for.

OTIS, HARRISON GRAY (1765-1848): Speech: Eulogy on Alexander Hamilton.

OTIS, JAMES (1725-1783): Speech: Against "Writs of Assistance."

PAINE, THOMAS (1737-1809): Speech: In the French National Convention.

PALMERSTON, LORD (HENRY JOHN TEMPLE) (1784-1865): Speech: The Affairs of Greece.

PARKER, THEODORE (1810-1860): Sermon: The State of the Nation.

PARKHURST, CHARLES HENRY (1842-1933): Sermon: On Garfield.

PARNELL, CHARLES STEWART (1846-1891):

Speeches: Against Non-Resident Landlords; On the Coercion Bill.

PEEL, SIR ROBERT (1788-1850): Speech: On the Repeal of the Corn Laws.

PERICLES (c. 495-429 b. c.): Speech: Funeral Oration.

PHELPS, EDWARD JOHN (1822-1900): Speech: Farewell Address.

PHELPS, WILLIAM WALTER (1839-1894): Speech: On Sound Currency.

PHILLIPS, CHARLES (1789-1859): Speech: At a Meeting of Roman Catholics at Cork.

PHILLIPS, WENDELL (1811-1884): Speeches: The Murder of Lovejoy; Eulogy on William Lloyd Garrison.

PINKNEY, WILLIAM (1764-1822): Speech: For the Relief of the Oppressed Slaves.

PITT, WILLIAM (1759-1806): Speech: On the Refusal to Negotiate.

PLINY THE YOUNGER (62-113): Speech: Panegyric in Praise of Trajan.

PLUNKET, WILLIAM CONYNGHAM (1764-1854): Speeches: On the Irish Parliament and the Union; Denunciation of the Union with England.

PULTENEY, WILLIAM (1684-1764): Speech: On a Motion for Reducing the Army.

PYM, JOHN (1584-1643): Speech: Against Strafford.

QUINCY, JOSIAH, JR. (1744-1775): Speech: In Defense of the Soldier.

RANDOLPH, JOHN (1773-1833): Speech: On Foreign Importations.

RED JACKET (1752-1830): Speeches: Speech at Fort Stanwix; Defense of Stiff-Armed George; Reply to Mr. Cram.

RHODES, CECIL (1853-1902): Speech: On the Crisis in South Africa.

ROBERTSON, FREDERICK WILLIAM (1816-1853): Sermon: The Loneliness of Christ.

ROBESPIERRE, MAXIMILIEN MARIE ISIDORE (1758-1794): Speech: Against Granting the King a Trial.

ROOSEVELT, FRANKLIN DELANO (1882-1945): Speeches: Before the Democratic Convention in Nomination of Alfred E. Smith for President (Happy Warrior speech); First Inaugural Address; Request to Congress for a declaration of war against Japan.

ROOSEVELT, THEODORE (1858-1919): Speeches: On National Questions; Seconding McKinley's Nomination; A Nation of Pioneers.

ROYER-COLLARD, PIERRE PAUL (1763-1845): Speeches: "Sacrilege" in Law; Against Press Censorship.

RUMBOLD, RICHARD (1622-1685): Speech: Speech from the Scaffold.

RUSKIN, JOHN (1819-1890): Lecture: On the Greek Myths.

RUTLEDGE, JOHN (1739-1800): Speech: Address to the General Assembly.

SACCO, NICOLA (1891-1927): Speech: Address to the Court on being found guilty of murder.

SAGASTA, PRAXETES MATEO (1827-1903): Speech: In Defense of the Unity of Italy.

SAINT-JUST, ANTOINE LOUIS LÉON DE (1767-1794): Speech: Arraignment of Danton.

SALISBURY, LORD (ROBERT ARTHUR GASCOYNE-CECIL) (1830-1903): Speeches: Tampering with the Constitution; The Egyptian Question; A Burning Question; On the Abandonment of General Gordon.

SAVONAROLA, GIROLAMO (1452-1498): Sermons: On the Apocalypse, 1486; Lenten Sermons on the Prophet Amos, 1496; On the Feast of the Ascension, May 12, 1496 ("In everything am I oppressed; even the spiritual power is against me with Peter's mighty key").

SCARLETT, SIR JAMES (1769-1844): Speech: Charge to the Jury.

SCHURZ, CARL (1829-1906): Speeches: Arraignment of Stephen A. Douglas; The Policy of Imperialism.

SCIPIO AFRICANUS (234-183 b. c.): Speech: In His Own Defense.

SEWARD, WILLIAM HENRY (1801-1872): Speech: On the Irrepressible Conflict.

SHEIL, RICHARD LALOR (1791-1851): Speeches: In Defense of Irish Catholics; On the Jewish Disabilities Bill.

SHERIDAN, RICHARD BRINSLEY B. (1751-1816): Speech: Impeachment of Warren Hastings.

SHERMAN, WILLIAM TECUMSEH (1820-1891): Speech: The Army and Navy.

SIMPSON, MATTHEW (1811-1884): Sermon: On the Resurrection of Our Lord.

SOCRATES (c. 470-399 b.c.): Speech: The Apology.

SPURGEON, CHARLES HADDON (1834-1892): Sermon: Condescension of Christ.

STALIN, JOSEPH (1879-1953): Speech: Address to the Russian people, asking them to resist the German invaders.

STANLEY, ARTHUR PENRHYN (1815-1881): Sermon: Jesus of Nazareth.

STEPHENS, ALEXANDER HAMILTON (1812-1883): Speeches: On the Evils of Secession; The "Corner-Stone" Speech.

STEVENS, THADDEUS (1792-1868): Speech: Against Webster and Northern Compromisers.

STEVENSON, ADLAI E. (1900-   ): Speeches: Acceptance speech before the Democratic National Convention, July 26, 1952; The Nature of Patriotism, August 27, 1952; Equal Rights, August 28, 1952; Faith in Liberalism, August 28, 1952; On Political Morality, September 11, 1952; The Proper Role of Government, October 9, 1952; On Liberty of Conscience, October 14, 1952.

STORRS, RICHARD SALTER (1821-1900): Speech: The Rise of Constitutional Liberty.

STRAFFORD, LORD (THOMAS WENTWORTH) (1593-1641): Speech: Before the House of Lords.

SUMNER, CHARLES (1811-1874): Speeches: The Crime against Kansas; The True Grandeur of Nations.

SUN YAT SEN (1866-1925): Lectures: The Three Principles of the People.

TALMAGE, THOMAS DE WITT (1832-1902): Sermon: Chant at the Corner-Stone.

TAYLOR JEREMY (1613-1667): Sermon: Christ's Advent to Judgment.

TECUMSEH (1768-1813): Speeches: At Vincennes; To General Proctor.

THIERS, ADOLPHE LOUIS (1797-1877): Speech: At Arcachon.

TILDEN, SAMUEL JONES (1814-1886): Speech: On Administrative Reform.

VALLANDIGHAM, CLEMENT LAIRD (1820-1871): Speech: On the War and its Conduct.

VANCE, ZEBULON BAIRD (1830-1894): Speech: The Slavery Question.

VANE, SIR HENRY (1612-1662): Speech: In His Own Defense.

VANZETTI, BARTOLOMEO (1888-1927): Speech: Address to the Court on being found guilty of Murder.

VERGNIAUD, PIERRE VICTURNIEN (1753-1793): Speech: On the Situation of France.

VOORHEES, DANIEL WOLSEY (1827-1897): Speeches: In Defense of John E. Cook; The Welfare of the Nation.

WADE, BENJAMIN FRANKLIN (1800-1878): Speech: On Secession.

WALPOLE, SIR ROBERT (1676-1745): Speech: On a Motion for Addressing the King for His Removal.

WARREN, JOSEPH (1741-1775): Speech: On the Boston Massacre.

WASHINGTON, BOOKER TALIAFERRO (1856-1915): Speeches: The Race Problem; At Harvard University; At the Shaw Monument; The Negro's Loyalty to the Stars and Stripes.

WASHINGTON, GEORGE (1732-1799): Speeches: Inaugural Address: Farewell Address.

WEBSTER, DANIEL (1782-1852): Speeches: The Reply to Hayne; Bunker-Hill Monument Oration; At Plymouth in 1820; Adams and Jefferson; On the Murder of Joseph White.

WELLINGTON, THE DUKE OF (1769-1852): Speech: On Catholic Emancipation.

WESLEY, JOHN (1703-1791): Sermon: God's Love to Fallen Man.

WHITE, ANDREW DICKSON (1832-1918): Speech: The Apostle of Peace among the Nations.

WHITEFIELD, GEORGE (1714-1770): Sermon: The Method of Grace.

WILBERFORCE, WILLIAM (1759-1833): Speech: Horrors of the British Slave Trade.

WILSON, WOODROW (1854-1924): Speeches: Address to the New Jersey Democratic Convention, 1910; Request to Congress for a declaration of war against Germany; In behalf of the League of Nations.

WINTHROP, JOHN (1588-1649): Speech: "Little Speech" on Liberty.

WIRT, WILLIAM (1772-1834): Speech: In the Trial of Aaron Burr.

XENOPHON (430-355 b. c.): Speech: In council of War.

ZOLA, EMILE (1840-1902): Speech: Appeal for Dreyfus.

ZWINGLI, ULRICH (1484-1531): Speech: The Evils of Foreign Military Service.

Stars, Brightest
See also **Constellations**

(Numbers refer to the apparent visual magnitude of stars, i.e., the order of their brightness as it is observed from the earth; the brightest stars are represented by the lowest numbers.)

SIRIUS (ALPHA CANIS MAJO): — 1.6
CANOPUS (ALPHA CARINAE): —0.9
ALPHA CENTAURI: +0.1
VEGA (ALPHA LYRAE): +0.1.
CAPELLA (ALPHA AURIGAE): +0.2
ARCTURUS (ALPHA BOÖTES): +0.2
RIGEL (BETA ORIONIS): +0.3
PROCYON (ALPHA CANIS MINORIS): +0.5
ACHERNAR (ALPHA ERIDANI): +0.6
BETA CENTAURI: +0.9
ALTAIR (ALPHA AQUILAE): +0.9
BETELGEUSE (ALPHA ORIONIS): +0.9
ALPHA CRUCIS: +1.0
ALDEBARAN (ALPHA TAURI): +1.1
POLLUX (BETA GEMINORUM): +1.2
SPICA (ALPHA VIRGINIS): +1.2
ANTARES (ALPHA SCORPII): +1.2
FORMALHAUT (ALPHA PISCIS AUSTRINI): +1.3
DENEB (ALPHA CYGNI): +1.3
REGULUS (ALPHA LEONIS): +1.3

States of the United States

For Congressional Representation by States see **Congress of the United States;** see also **Indians, American; Secretaries of State;**

Admission, Secession, and Readmission of States; Festivals, American; Presidency

State Birds

ALABAMA: Yellowhammer.
ARIZONA: Cactus wren.
ARKANSAS: Mockingbird.
CALIFORNIA: California valley quail.
COLORADO: Lark bunting.
CONNECTICUT: Robin; ruby-crowned kinglet.
DELAWARE: Cardinal.
FLORIDA: Mockingbird.
GEORGIA. Brown thrasher.
IDAHO: Mountain bluebird.
ILLINOIS: Cardinal.
INDIANA: Cardinal.
IOWA: Eastern goldfinch.
KANSAS: Western meadowlark.
KENTUCKY: Kentucky cardinal.
LOUISIANA: American brown pelican.
MAINE: Black-capped chickadee.
MARYLAND: Baltimore oriole.
MASSACHUSETTS: Black-capped chickadee; veery.
MICHIGAN: Robin red breast.
MINNESOTA: Scarlet tanager; American goldfinch.
MISSISSIPPI: Mockingbird.
MISSOURI: Bluebird.
MONTANA: Western meadowlark.
NEBRASKA: Western meadowlark.
NEVADA: Mountain bluebird.
NEW HAMPSHIRE: Purple finch.
NEW JERSEY: Eastern goldfinch.
NEW MEXICO: Road runner.
NEW YORK: Bluebird.
NORTH CAROLINA: Cardinal; Carolina chickadee.
NORTH DAKOTA: Western meadowlark.
OHIO: Cardinal.
OKLAHOMA: Bobwhite.
OREGON: Western meadowlark.
PENNSYLVANIA: Ruffed grouse.
RHODE ISLAND: Bobwhite.
SOUTH CAROLINA: Carolina wren.
SOUTH DAKOTA: Ring-necked pheasant; Carolina wren.
TENNESSEE: Mockingbird.
TEXAS: Western mockingbird.
UTAH: California sea gull.
VERMONT: Hermit thrush.
VIRGINIA: Cardinal; Robin.
WASHINGTON: Willow goldfinch.
WEST VIRGINIA: Cardinal; tufted titmouse.
WISCONSIN: Robin.
WYOMING: Western meadowlark.

State Flowers

ALABAMA: Goldenrod (Solidago patula).
ARIZONA: Giant Cactus (Cereus giganteus); water hyacinth (Eichhornia crassipes).
ARKANSAS: Apple blossom (Pyrus malus).
CALIFORNIA. Golden poppy (Eschecholtzia Californica).
COLORADO: Columbine, white and lavender (Aquilegia caerulea).
CONNECTICUT: Mountain laurel (Kalmia latifolia); narcissus (Narcissus pseudo-narcissus).
DELAWARE: Peach blossom (Prunus persica).
DISTRICT OF COLUMBIA: Goldenrod (genus Solidago); American beauty rose (genus Rosa).
FLORIDA: Florida blossom (Citrus trifoliata).
GEORGIA: Cherokee rose (Rosa sinica).
IDAHO: Syringa (Philadelphus lewisii).

ILLINOIS: Violet (genus Viola).
INDIANA: Zinnia (Zinnia elegans); formerly the tulip tree (Liriodendron tulipifera).
IOWA: Wild rose (Rosa virginiana); Indian corn (Zea mays).
KANSAS: Wild sunflower (Helianthus annuus).
KENTUCKY: Goldenrod (Solidago patula).
LOUISIANA: Magnolia (Magnolia grandiflora).
MAINE: Pine cone, tassel (Pinus strobus).
MARYLAND: Black-eyed Susan (Rudbeckia hirta).
MASSACHUSETTS: Mayflower (Epigaea repens).
MICHIGAN: Apple blossom (Pyrus coronaria).
MINNESOTA: Moccasin flower (Cypripedium calceolus).
MISSISSIPPI: Magnolia (Magnolia grandiflora).
MISSOURI: Hawthorne, downy (genus Crataegus).
MONTANA: Bitterroot (Lewisia rediviva).
NEBRASKA: Goldenrod (Solidago serotina).
NEVADA: Sagebrush (Artemisia tridentata); giant cactus (Cireus giganteus).
NEW HAMPSHIRE: Lilac, purple (Syringa vulgaris).
NEW JERSEY: Violet (genus Viola).
NEW MEXICO: Yucca (genus Yucca).
NEW YORK: Rose (genus Rosa); scarlet carnation (genus Dianthus).
NORTH CAROLINA: Goldenrod (genus Solidago).
NORTH DAKOTA: Wild rose (Rosa blanda).
OHIO: Scarlet carnation (genus Dianthus).
OKLAHOMA: Mistletoe (Phoradendron flavescens).
OREGON: Oregon grape (Berberis aquifolium).
PENNSYLVANIA: Mountain laurel (Kalmia latifolia).
RHODE ISLAND: Violet (genus: Viola); mountain laurel (Kalmia latifolia).
SOUTH CAROLINA: Yellow jessamine (Gelsemium sempervirens).
SOUTH DAKOTA: Pasque flower (Pulsatilla hirsutissima).
TENNESSEE: Iris (genus Iridaceae).
TEXAS: Blue bonnet (Lupinus subcarnosus).
UTAH: Sago lily (Calochortus muttallii).
VERMONT: Red clover (Trifolium pratense).
VIRGINIA: Dogwood (Cornus florida).
WASHINGTON: Rhododendron (Rhododendron macrophyllum); redwoods (Sequoia sempervirens).
WEST VIRGINIA: Rhododendron (Rhododendron maximum).
WISCONSIN: Violet (genus Viola).
WYOMING: Indian paint-brush (Castillija linariaefolia).

State Mottoes

ALABAMA: Andemus jura nostra defendere (We Dare to Defend Our Rights).
ARIZONA: Ditat Deus (God Enriches).
ARKANSAS: Regnat Populus (Let the People Rule!); Mercy and Justice.
CALIFORNIA: Eureka (I've Found It!).
COLORADO: Nil Sine Numine (Nothing without the Deity): Union and Constitution.
CONNECTICUT: Qui Transtulit, Sustinet (He Who Brought Us Across, Keeps Us Going).
DELAWARE: Liberty and Independence.
DISTRICT OF COLUMBIA: Justitia Omnibus (Justice to All).
FLORIDA: In God We Trust.
GEORGIA: Wisdom, Justice, and Moderation.
IDAHO: Esto Perpetua (Endure Forever!).
ILLINOIS: State Sovereignty—National Union.
INDIANA: The Crossroads of America.
IOWA: Our Liberties We Prize and Our Rights We Will Maintain.

KANSAS: Ad Astra per Aspera (To the Stars Through Difficulties).
KENTUCKY: United We Stand, Divided We Fall.
LOUISIANA: Union, Justice and Confidence.
MAINE: Dirigo (I Guide).
MARYLAND: Scuto Bonae Voluntatis Tuae Coronasti Nos (You Have Cloaked Us with the Shield of Your Good Will).
MASSACHUSETTS: Ense Petit Placidam sub Libertate Quietam (With the Sword She Seeks Peace Under Liberty).
MICHIGAN: Si Quaeris Peninsulam Amoenam, Circumspice (If You are Looking for a Pleasant Peninsula, Look Around You).
MINNESOTA: L'Etoile du Nord (The Northern Star).
MISSISSIPPI: Virtue et Armis (By Valor and Arms).
MISSOURI: Salus Populi Suprema Lex Esto (Let the Good of the People Be the Highest Law).
MONTANA: Oro y Plata (Gold and Silver).
NEBRASKA: Equality Before the Law.
NEVADA: All for Our Country.
NEW HAMPSHIRE: Live Free or Die.
NEW JERSEY: Liberty and Prosperity (unofficial).
NEW MEXICO: Crescit Eundo (It Grows as it Goes).
NEW YORK: Excelsior (Higher!).
NORTH CAROLINA: Esse Quam Videri (To Be, Rather than to Seem).
NORTH DAKOTA: Liberty and Union, Now and Forever, One and Inseparable.
OHIO: Imperium in Imperio (An Empire within an Empire) (unofficial).
OKLAHOMA: Labor Omnia Vincit (Work Accomplishes Everything).
OREGON: Alis Volat Propriis (She Flies with Her Own Wings).
PENNSYLVANIA: Virtue, Liberty, and Independence.
RHODE ISLAND: Hope.
SOUTH CAROLINA: Animis Opibusque Parati (Ready in Soul and Resource); Dum Spiro, Spero (Where There's Life, There's Hope).
SOUTH DAKOTA: Under God the People Rule.
TENNESSEE: Agriculture and Commerce.
TEXAS: Friendship.
UTAH: Industry.
VERMONT: Freedom and Unity.
VIRGINIA: Sic Semper Tyrannis (Thus Ever to Tyrants).
WASHINGTON: Alki (Chinook Indian for By and By).
WEST VIRGINIA: Montani Semper Liberi (Mountaineers Are Always Free Men).
WISCONSIN: Forward!
WYOMING: Cedant Arma Togae (Let Arms Yield to the Gown).

State Trees

ALABAMA: Officially, none.
ARIZONA: Palo Verde.
ARKANSAS: Oak.
CALIFORNIA: Redwood.
COLORADO: Blue spruce.
CONNECTICUT: White Oak.
DELAWARE: Holly Tree.
FLORIDA: Palm.
GEORGIA: Pine.
IDAHO: Western White Pine.
ILLINOIS: Oak.
INDIANA: Tulip.
IOWA: Officially, none.
KANSAS: Cottonwood.
KENTUCKY: Tulip.

LOUISIANA: Magnolia.
MAINE: Pine.
MARYLAND: White Oak.
MASSACHUSETTS: Elm.
MICHIGAN: Apple.
MINNESOTA: Norwegian Pine.
MISSISSIPPI: Magnolia.
MISSOURI: Hawthorne.
MONTANA: Yellow Pine.
NEBRASKA: American Elm.
NEVADA: Officially, none (some favor the Aspen).
NEW HAMPSHIRE: White Birch.
NEW JERSEY: White Cedar, Southern.
NEW MEXICO: Officially, none.
NEW YORK: Maple.
NORTH CAROLINA: Yellow Poplar.
NORTH DAKOTA: Green Ash.
OHIO: Buckeye.
OKLAHOMA: Red Bud.
OREGON: Douglas Fir.
PENNSYLVANIA: Hemlock.
RHODE ISLAND: Maple.
SOUTH CAROLINA: Palmetto.
SOUTH DAKOTA: Spruce (Black Hills).
TENNESSEE: Tulip Poplar.
TEXAS: Pecan.
UTAH: Blue Spruce.
VERMONT: Maple.
VIRGINIA: Dogwood.
WASHINGTON: Western Hemlock.
WEST VIRGINIA: Maple, Sugar.
WISCONSIN: Maple, Sugar.
WYOMING: Cottonwood.

State Parks and Recreation Systems

Note: The lists are selective.

Alabama

Parks, 11; monuments, 2; historic sites, 5; forests, 8. Total area, 81,326 acres.

BLADEN SPRINGS STATE PARK: 357 acres; undeveloped.
CEDAR CREEK HISTORIC SITE: 660 acres; camping, swimming, boating.
CHATTAHOOCHEE STATE PARK: 596 acres; cabins, swimming, fishing, boating.
CHEAHA STATE PARK: 2679 acres; historic sites, cabins, swimming, fishing, boating.
CHEWACLA STATE PARK: 852 acres; cabins, camping, swimming, fishing.
CHICKASAW STATE PARK: 560 acres; swimming.
CHOCCOLOCCO STATE FOREST: 4308 acres.
DE SOTO STATE PARK: 4650 acres; golf, cabins, camping, swimming, fishing, boating.
FORT GAINES HISTORIC SITE: 8 acres; 19th-cent. fort.
FORT MORGAN HISTORIC SITE: 435 acres; brick fort.
FORT TOULOUSE HISTORIC SITE: 7 acres; undeveloped.
GENEVA STATE FOREST: 7120 acres; cabins, swimming, fishing, boating.
GULF STATE PARK: 4681 acres; hotel or lodge, cabins, camping, swimming, fishing, boating.
LITTLE MOUNTAIN STATE PARK: 3740 acres; new.
LITTLE RIVER STATE FOREST: 2120 acres; cabins, camping, swimming, fishing, boating.
MONTE SANO STATE PARK: 2140 acres; hotel or lodge, cabins, swimming, riding.

MOND STATE MONUMENT: 298 acres; museum.
OAK MOUNTAIN STATE PARK: 9000 acres; cabins, camping, swimming, fishing.
PEA RIVER STATE FOREST: 35,000 acres.
VALLEY CREEK STATE PARK: 1080 acres; cabins, camping, swimming.
WEOGUFKA STATE FOREST: 803 acres; cabins, camping, swimming.

Arizona

State parks, 0; recreational areas, 2. Total area, 10,100 acres.

PAPAGO RECREATIONAL AREA: 1140 acres; fish hatchery.
SAGUARO FOREST RECREATIONAL AREA: 8960 acres; desert.

Arkansas

Parks, 8; wildlife preserves, 1. Total area, 20,199 acres.

ARKANSAS POST STATE PARK: 61 acres; early settlement.
BUFFALO RIVER STATE PARK: 1948 acres; hotel or lodge, cabins, camping, swimming, fishing.
CROWLEY'S RIDGE STATE PARK: 270 acres; cabins, camping, swimming, fishing, boating.
DEVIL'S DEN STATE PARK: 4885 acres; cabins, camping, swimming, fishing, boating, riding.
DONAGHEY STATE PARK: 20 acres; undeveloped.
LAKE CATHERINE STATE PARK: 2179 acres; cabins, camping, swimming, fishing, boating.
MOUNT NEBO STATE PARK: 3385 acres; cabins, camping.
PETIT JEAN STATE PARK: 4031 acres; hotel or lodge, cabins, camping, swimming, fishing, boating, riding.

California

Parks and beaches, 61; wildlife areas, 1; historic monuments, 18. Total area, 522,019 acres.

ALAMITOS BEACH STATE PARK: 11 acres; swimming, fishing, boating.
ANZA DESERT STATE PARK: 408,879 acres; camping, swimming.
ARMSTRONG REDWOODS STATE PARK: 400 acres; camping.
BIG BASIN REDWOODS STATE PARK: 9997 acres; cabins, camping, swimming, fishing, boating.
CALAVERAS BIG TREES STATE PARK: 1951 acres; hotel, camping, swimming, fishing.
CARLSBAD BEACH STATE PARK: 10 acres; swimming, fishing.
CARPINTERIA BEACH STATE PARK: 17 acres; camping, swimming, fishing.
CASTLE CRAGS STATE PARK: 3477 acres; camping, swimming, fishing.
CAYUCOS BEACH STATE PARK: 25 acres; swimming, fishing, boating.
COLUMBIA HISTORIC SITE: 5 acres; early mining town.
CUYAMACA RANCHO STATE PARK: 20,819 acres; camping, swimming, fishing, boating, riding.
DEL NORTE COAST REDWOODS STATE PARK: 5897 acres; fishing.

D. L. BLISS MEMORIAL: 957 acres; camping, swimming, fishing, boating.
DOHENY BEACH STATE PARK: 17 acres; camping, swimming, fishing.
DONNER HISTORIC SITE: 16 acres; memorial.
DRY LAGOON BEACH STATE PARK: 927 acres; swimming, fishing.
FORT ROSS HISTORIC SITE: 3 acres; site of Russian fort.
FREMONT PEAK STATE PARK: 287 acres; view.
GOLD DISCOVERY HISTORIC SITE: 9 acres; Sutter's Mill.
HUMBOLDT REDWOODS STATE PARK: 21,232 acres; hotel or lodge, cabins, camping, swimming.
HUNTINGDON BEACH STATE PARK: 29 acres; swimming.
JAMES D. PHELAN BEACH STATE PARK: 6 acres; swimming.
KRUSE RHODODENDRON RESERVE: 317 acres; May–June.
LA PURISIMA HISTORIC SITE: 526 acres; restored mission.
LITTLE RIVER BEACH STATE PARK: 111 acres; swimming, fishing.
MANHATTAN BEACH (LOS ANGELES): Swimming, fishing.
MARSHALL HISTORIC SITE: 23 acres; memorial.
MCARTHUR-BURNEY FALLS STATE PARK: 335 acres; camping, swimming, fishing, boating.
MENDOCINO WOODLANDS STATE FOREST: 5426 acres; camping.
MILL CREEK REDWOODS STATE PARK: 8768 acres; camping.
MISSION BAY STATE PARK: 60 acres; swimming, boating.
MONTGOMERY REDWOODS STATE PARK: 246 acres.
MORRO BAY STATE PARK: 1530 acres; golf, camping, swimming, fishing, boating.
MORRO STRAND STATE PARK: 15 acres; swimming, fishing.
MOUNT DIABLO STATE PARK: 2084 acres; view, camping, riding.
MOUNT SAN JACINTO STATE PARK: 12,708 acres; camping; fishing, riding.
MOUNT TAMALPAIS STATE PARK: 961 acres; view, camping, riding.
NATURAL BRIDGES BEACH STATE PARK: 27 acres; swimming, fishing.
NEW BRIGHTON BEACH STATE PARK: 48 acres; swimming, fishing.
PALOMAR MOUNTAIN STATE PARK: 1684 acres; camping, swimming.
PATRICK'S POINT STATE PARK: 420 acres; camping, swimming, fishing.
PFEIFFER BIG SUR STATE PARK: 707 acres; cabins, camping, swimming, fishing, boating, riding.
PISMO BEACH STATE PARK: 139 acres; swimming.
POINT LOBOS RESERVE: 336 acres; fishing.
PORTOLA STATE PARK: 1661 acres; mountains and forest.
PRAIRIE CREEK REDWOODS STATE PARK: 6468 acres; cabins, camping, swimming, fishing.
RUSSIAN GULCH STATE PARK: 1102 acres; camping, swimming, fishing.
SAMUEL F. TAYLOR STATE PARK: 2329 acres.
SAN CLEMENTE BEACH STATE PARK: 100 acres; camping, swimming, fishing.
SAN JUAN BAUTISTA HISTORIC SITE: 3 acres; restored mission.

SAN SIMEON CREEK BEACH STATE PARK:
42 acres; swimming, fishing.
SEA CLIFF BEACH STATE PARK: 23
acres; cabins, camping, swimming, fishing.
SILVER STRAND STATE PARK: 215 acres;
camping, swimming, fishing.
SONOMA COAST STATE PARK: 699 acres;
swimming, fishing.
SONOMA MISSION HISTORIC SITE: 1 acre.
TAHOE CAMPGROUND: 13 acres; camping,
swimming, fishing, boating.
TRINIDAD BEACH STATE PARK: 20 acres.
VALLEJO HOME HISTORIC SITE: 20 acres;
memorial.
VAN DAMME BEACH STATE PARK: 1729
acres; camping, swimming, fishing, boating.
WATSONVILLE - SUNSET BEACH STATE
PARK: 168 acres; swimming, fishing.
WILL ROGERS BEACH STATE PARK:
20 acres; swimming, fishing.
WILL ROGERS STATE PARK: 186 acres;
museum, riding.

Connecticut

Parks, 55; monuments and memorials, 9; waysides, 143. Total area, 15,743 acres.

ABOVE ALL STATE PARK: 31 acres; scenic.
BLACK POND STATE PARK: 100 acres;
camping, swimming.
BLACK ROCK STATE PARK: 713 acres;
camping, swimming, riding.
BOLTON NOTCH STATE PARK: 70 acres.
BUTTONBALL STATE PARK: 135 acres.
CAMPBELL FALLS STATE PARK: 102 acres;
scenic.
DENNIS HILL STATE PARK: 240 acres;
scenic.
DEVILS HOPYARD STATE PARK: 860
acres; swimming.
FORT GRISWOLD HISTORIC SITE: 40 acres.
FORT SHANTOCK STATE PARK: 177 acres;
swimming.
GAY CITY STATE PARK: 680 acres.
GILETTE CASTLE STATE PARK: 122
acres; museum.
HADDAM MEADOWS STATE PARK: 158
acres.
HAMMONASSET BEACH STATE PARK: 966
acres; camping, swimming.
HAYSTACK MOUNTAIN STATE PARK:
287 acres.
HOPEVILLE POND STATE PARK: 316 acres.
HOUSATONIC MEADOWS STATE PARK:
1060 acres; camping, swimming, fishing.
HUMASTON BROOK STATE PARK: 106
acres.
HURD PARK: 548 acres; scenery; boating.
INDIAN WELL STATE PARK: 189 acres;
swimming, boating.
ISRAEL PUTNAM MEMORIAL: 220 acres;
museum.
KENT FALLS STATE PARK: 275 acres;
scenic.
LAKE WARAMAUG STATE PARK: 95 acres;
camping, swimming, fishing, boating.
MACEDONIA BROOK STATE PARK: 1830
acres; camping.
MSHAMOQUET BROOK STATE PARK:
53 acres; swimming.
MOHAWK MOUNTAIN STATE PARK: 156
acres; camping.
MOUNT BUSHNELL STATE PARK: 84 acres;
scenic.
MOUNT TOM STATE PARK: 223 acres;
swimming, boating.
NATHANIEL LYON MEMORIAL STATE
PARK: 216 acres.

OLD FURNACE SITE STATE PARK: 15
acres; swimming.
PENWOOD STATE PARK: 800 acres; scenic.
ROCKY NECK STATE PARK: 560 acres;
camping, swimming.
SELDEN NECK STATE PARK: 527 acres;
camping, swimming, boating.
SHERWOOD ISLAND STATE PARK: 215
acres; swimming.
SLEEPING GIANT STATE PARK: 1071
acres; scenery; camping.
SOUTH FORD FALLS STATE PARK: 55
acres.
SQUANTZ POND STATE PARK: 173 acres;
camping, swimming, boating.
TRIMOUNTAIN STATE PARK: 127 acres;
scenic.
WADSWORTH FALLS STATE PARK: 285
acres.
WEST PEAK STATE PARK: 181 acres; scenic.
WHARTON BROOK STATE PARK: 72 acres;
camping.
WHITTEMORE GLEN STATE PARK: 120
acres.
WOLF DEN STATE PARK: 551 acres.
WOOSTER MOUNTAIN STATE PARK: 327
acres.

Florida

Parks, 17; recreational areas, 1; monuments, 7.
Total area, 48,685 acres.

COLLIER-SEMINOLE STATE PARK: 6423
acres; undeveloped.
DE SOTO BEACH STATE PARK: 216 acres.
New.
FLORIDA CAVERNS STATE PARK: 1187
acres. Cave. Camping, fishing.
FORT CLINCH STATE PARK: 1105 acres;
camping, swimming, fishing.
GOLD HEAD BRANCH STATE PARK:
1614 acres; cabins, camping, swimming, fish-
ing, boating.
HIGHLANDS HAMMOCK STATE PARK:
3800 acres; scenery, camping.
HILLSBOROUGH RIVER STATE PARK:
2637 acres; cabins, camping, swimming, fish-
ing, boating.
H. T. BIRCH STATE PARK: 180 acres;
swimming, fishing.
JUPITER STATE PARK: 11,124 acres. Unde-
veloped.
LAKE GRIFFIN STATE PARK: 725 acres;
New.
MYAKKA RIVER STATE PARK: 12,486
acres; cabins, camping, fishing, boating, rid-
ing.
O'LENO RECREATIONAL AREA: 1380 acres;
camping, swimming, fishing, boating.
PAN AMERICAN STATE PARK: 270 acres;
fishing, boating.
ST. ANDREWS STATE PARK: 570 acres.
New.
SANTA ROSA STATE PARK: 1339 acres;
New.
SUWANEE RIVER STATE PARK: 1703 acres.
Scenic. Fishing, boating.
TOMOKO STATE PARK: 729 acres; swim-
ming, fishing, boating.
TORREYA STATE PARK: 1098 acres; camp-
ing, fishing, boating.

Georgia

State parks, 21. Total area, 34,325 acres.

A. H. STEPHENS STATE PARK: 1175 acres;
camping, swimming.

CHEHAW STATE PARK: 600 acres; boating.
CLOUDLAND CANYON STATE PARK: 2770 acres. Scenic.
CROOKED RIVER STATE PARK: 592 acres; cabins, swimming, fishing, boating.
FORT MOUNTAIN STATE PARK: 1954 acres; swimming, fishing, boating.
FRANKLIN D. ROOSEVELT STATE PARK: 5064 acres; hotel, cabins, swimming, fishing, boating.
HARD LABOR CREEK STATE PARK: 5816 acres; cabins, camping, swimming, fishing, boating.
INDIAN SPRINGS STATE PARK: 152 acres; mineral spring.
JEFFERSON DAVIS MEMORIAL STATE PARK: 12 acres. Museum.
JEKYLL ISLAND STATE PARK: 11,000 acres; hotel, cabins, swimming, fishing, boating.
KOLOMOKI MOUNDS STATE PARK: 1284 acres. Indian site.
LAURA S. WALKER STATE PARK: 160 acres; cabins, swimming, fishing, boating.
LITTLE OCMULGEE STATE PARK: 1395 acres; cabins, swimming, fishing, boating, riding.
MAGNOLIA SPRINGS STATE PARK: 1107 acres; swimming, fishing, boating.
VETERANS LAKE STATE PARK: 1000 acres; swimming, fishing, boating.
VOGEL STATE PARK: 229 acres; hotel, cabins, swimming, fishing, boating, riding.

Idaho

Parks, 1; forests, 2; recreational areas, 1. Total area, 58,193 acres.

HEYBURN STATE PARK: 7905 acres; hotel, cabins, camping, swimming, fishing, boating, riding.
LAVA HOT SPRINGS RECREATIONAL AREA: 288 acres; camping, swimming.
PAYETTE LAKE STATE FOREST: 27,000 acres; camping, swimming, fishing, boating.
PRIEST LAKE STATE FOREST: 23,000 acres; camping, swimming, fishing, boating.

Illinois

Parks, 31; parkways, 1; nature areas, 1; vacation areas, 1; forests, 3; monuments, 45; waysides, 274. Total area, 39,275 acres.

APPLE RIVER CANYON STATE PARK: 157 acres; camping, fishing.
BLACK HAWK STATE PARK: 207 acres; hotel, camping, fishing, boating.
BUFFALO ROCK STATE PARK: 43 acres; camping fishing boating.
CAHOKIA MOUNDS STATE PARK: 145 acres; camping.
CAMPBELLS ISLAND HISTORIC SITE: 5 acres
CAVE-IN-ROCK STATE PARK: 64 acres; camping, fishing, boating.
CHAIN-O-LAKES STATE PARK: 4312 acres; camping, swimming, fishing, boating.
DICKSON MOUNDS STATE PARK: 25 acres.
DIXON SPRINGS STATE PARK: 391 acres.
FORT CHARTRES STATE PARK: 19 acres. Scenic.
FORT CLEVE COEUR HISTORICAL SITE: 15 acres. Historical.
FORT KASKASKIA STATE PARK: 201 acres; camping, swimming, fishing.
FORT MASSAC STATE PARK: 456 acres; camping.

FOX RIDGE STATE PARK: 690 acres; camping, fishing, boating.
FOX RIVER STATE PARK: 86 acres; scenic.
GEBHARD WOODS STATE PARK: 30 acres; camping, fishing.
GIANT CITY STATE PARK: 1523 acres; hotel, cabins, camping, fishing, riding.
GRAND MARAIS STATE PARK: 1125 acres.
ILLINI STATE PARK: 406 acres; camping, fishing, boating.
ILLINOIS BEACH STATE PARK: 1115 acres; swimming.
JUBILEE COLLEGE STATE PARK: 96 acres. Historical.
KANKAKEE RIVER STATE PARK: 266 acres; camping, fishing, boating.
KICKAPOO STATE PARK: Camping, fishing, boating.
LINCOLN HOME HISTORIC SITE.
LINCOLN LOG CABIN STATE PARK: 86 acres. Historical.
LINCOLN TOMB HISTORIC SITE.
LOWDEN MEMORIAL STATE PARK: 274 acres; camping, fishing.
MATHIESON STATE PARK: 174 acres. scenic.
METAMORA COURT HOUSE HISTORIC SITE.
MISSISSIPPI PALISADES STATE PARK: 898 acres; camping.
MOUNT PULASKI COURT HOUSE HISTORIC SITE.
NEW SALEM STATE PARK: 280 acres; camping, fishing.
PERE MARQUETTE STATE PARK: 2606 acres; hotel, cabins, camping, swimming, fishing, boating, riding.
PERE MARQUETTE VACATION AREA: 2574 acres; camping.
RED HILLS STATE PARK: 798 acres; scenic.
SILOAM SPRINGS STATE PARK: 2047 acres. Scenic.
SPITLER WOODS STATE PARK: 202 acres. Scenic.
STARVED ROCK STATE PARK: 1439 acres; hotel, cabins, camping, fishing, boating, riding.
U.S. GRANT HOME HISTORIC SITE: 4 acres.
VANDALIA STATE HOUSE HISTORIC SITES.
WHITE PINES FOREST STATE PARK: Hotel, cabins, camping, fishing, riding.

Indiana

Parks, 14; monuments, 10; forests, 13; waysides, 96. Total area, 169,279 acres.

ANGEL MOUNDS MEMORIAL: 421 acres. Indian site.
BASS LAKE STATE PARK: 8 acres; camping, swimming, fishing, boating.
BROWN COUNTY STATE PARK: 17,679 acres; hotel, cabins, camping, swimming, riding.
CLIFTY FALLS STATE PARK: 383 acres; hotel, camping, riding.
INDIANA DUNES STATE PARK: 2182 acres; hotel, cabins, camping, swimming.
J. F. D. LANIER HOME HISTORIC SITE.
LINCOLN STATE PARK: 1523 acres. Historic. Camping.
MC CORMICKS CREEK STATE PARK: 1,135 acres; hotel, camping, swimming, riding.
MOUNDS STATE PARK: 252 acres; camping, fishing, riding.
MUSCATUK STATE PARK: 201 acres; hotel, cabins, camping, fishing.
PIGEON ROOST MEMORIAL HISTORIC SITES: 5 acres.

POKAGON STATE PARK: 937 acres; hotel, cabins, camping, swimming, fishing, boating, riding.
SHAKAMAK STATE PARK: 1016 acres; cabins, camping, swimming, fishing, boating.
SPRING MILL STATE PARK: 1165 acres; hotel, cabins, camping, fishing, boating.
TIPPECANOE BATTLEGROUND HISTORIC SITE: 17 acres.
TIPPECANOE RIVER STATE PARK: 6336 acres; camping.
TURKEY RUN STATE PARK: 1520 acres; hotel, cabins, camping, swimming, fishing, riding.
VERSAILLES STATE PARK: 5204 acres; camping.

Iowa

Parks, 16; recreational reserves, 42; monuments, 12; parkways, 1; forests, 11; waysides, 81. Total area, 35,588 acres.

AMBROSE A. CALL RECREATIONAL AREA: 130 acres; camping.
BACKBONE STATE PARK: 1411 acres; cabins, camping, swimming, fishing.
BEEDS LAKE RECREATIONAL AREA: 290 acres; swimming, fishing.
BELLEVUE RECREATIONAL AREA: 148 acres. Golf; camping.
BLACK HAWK LAKE RECREATIONAL AREA: 173 acres; fishing.
CLEAR LAKE RECREATIONAL AREA: 27 acres; hotel, camping, swimming, fishing, boating.
COLD SPRING RECREATIONAL AREA: 60 acres; swimming.
DOLLIVER STATE PARK: 598 acres; hotel, camping, swimming, fishing, boating.
EAGLE LAKE RECREATIONAL AREA: 21 acres. Bird life.
ECHO VALLEY RECREATIONAL AREA: 101 acres; swimming.
FARMINGTON RECREATIONAL AREA: 127 acres; camping, fishing.
FORT DEFIANCE RECREATIONAL AREA: 181 acres; camping.
GEODE STATE PARK: 844 acres. Rock formations.
GITCHIE MANITOU HISTORIC SITE: 144 acres. Indian site.
GULL POINT RECREATIONAL AREA: 59 acres; camping.
HEERY WOODS RECREATIONAL AREA: 380 acres; camping, fishing, boating.
LACEY-KEOSAUQUA STATE PARK: 1613 acres; hotel, camping, swimming, fishing.
LAKE AHQUABI STATE PARK: 770 acres; hotel, camping, swimming, fishing.
LAKE KEOMAH RECREATIONAL AREA: 365 acres; hotel, camping, swimming, fishing, boating.
LAKE MACBRIDE STATE PARK: 773 acres; camping, swimming, fishing.
LAKE MANAWA RECREATIONAL AREA: 945 acres; swimming, fishing, boating.
LAKE OF THREE FIRES RECREATIONAL AREA: 386 acres; camping, swimming, fishing.
LAKE WAPELLO STATE PARK: 1130 acres; hotel, cabins, camping, swimming, fishing.
LEDGES STATE PARK: 793 acres; hotel, cabins, camping, swimming, fishing.
LEWIS AND CLARK RECREATIONAL AREA: 142 acres; swimming, fishing.
LOST ISLAND RECREATIONAL AREA: 28 acres; fishing.
MC GREGOR AREAS STATE PARK: 538 acres. Indian site; camping.

MAQUOKETA CAVES: 111 acres. Caverns; camping.
MILL CREEK RECREATIONAL AREA: 158 acres. Polo, swimming, fishing.
MINI-WAKAN RECREATIONAL AREA: 20 acres; fishing.
NINE EAGLES STATE PARK: 1139 acres. Undeveloped.
OAK GROVE RECREATIONAL AREA: 102 acres; camping.
OAKLAND MILLS RECREATIONAL AREA: 111 acres; camping, fishing.
OKAMANPEDAN RECREATIONAL AREA: 19 acres. Golf, hotel, fishing, boating.
PALISADES-KEPLER STATE PARK: 648 acres; hotel, cabins, camping, fishing.
PAMMEL RECREATIONAL AREA: 289 acres; hotel, camping.
PIKES POINT RECREATIONAL AREA: 5 acres; swimming, fishing, boating.
PILLSBURY POINT RECREATIONAL AREA: 6 acres; fishing.
PILOT KNOB STATE PARK: 368 acres; camping.
PINE LAKE RECREATIONAL AREA: 548 acres; hotel, cabins, camping, swimming, fishing.
PIONEER RECREATIONAL AREA: 14 acres. Old grist mill.
RED HAW HILL RECREATIONAL AREA: 419 acres; fishing.
RICE LAKE RECREATIONAL AREA: 46 acres.
RUSH LAKE RECREATIONAL AREA: 62 acres; fishing.
SHARON BLUFFS RECREATIONAL AREA: 144 acres. Scenic.
SPRINGBROOK STATE PARK: 720 acres; camping, swimming, fishing.
STONE STATE PARK: 881 acres; hotel, camping.
STORM LAKE RECREATIONAL AREA: 18 acres; fishing.
SWAN LAKE RECREATIONAL AREA: 230 acres; fishing.
TRAPPERS BAY RECREATIONAL AREA: 57 acres; fishing.
TWIN LAKES RECREATIONAL AREA: 19 acres; swimming, fishing.
UNION GROVE RECREATIONAL AREA: 270 acres; fishing, boating.
WALNUT WOODS RECREATIONAL AREA: 260 acres: hotel, camping.
WAPSIPINICON RECREATIONAL AREA: 249 acres; Golf, cabins, camping, fishing.
WAUBONSIE STATE PARK: 620 acres; camping.
WILDCAT DEN STATE PARK: 322 acres; camping.

Kansas

Parks, 22; forests, 1; game preserves, 2; waysides, 23. Total area, 39,734 acres.

BARTON COUNTY STATE PARK: 18,000 acres.
BUTLER COUNTY STATE PARK: 568 acres; camping, swimming, fishing, boating.
CLARK COUNTY STATE PARK: 1289 acres. Scenic.
CRAWFORD COUNTY NO. 1 STATE PARK: 418 acres; camping, swimming, fishing, boating.
CRAWFORD COUNTY NO. 2 STATE PARK: 446 acres; camping, swimming, fishing, boating.
DECATUR COUNTY STATE PARK: 98 acres. Lake.

FINNEY COUNTY STATE PARK: 854 acres; camping, swimming, fishing, boating.
KINGMAN COUNTY STATE PARK: 1562 acres; camping, swimming, fishing, boating.
KINGMAN STATE FOREST: 1600 acres; fishing.
LEAVENWORTH COUNTY STATE PARK: 506 acres; camping, swimming, fishing, boating.
LYON COUNTY STATE PARK: 582 acres; camping, swimming, fishing, boating.
MEADE COUNTY STATE PARK: 1240 acres; camping, swimming, fishing, boating.
MIAMI COUNTY STATE PARK: 277 acres.
NEHAMA COUNTY STATE PARK: 705 acres; camping, swimming, fishing, boating.
NEOSHO COUNTY STATE PARK: 216 acres; camping, swimming, fishing, boating.
OBERLIN-SAPPA COUNTY STATE PARK: 481 acres; camping, swimming, fishing, boating.
OTTAWA COUNTY STATE PARK: 711 acres; camping, swimming, fishing, boating.
POTTAWATOMIE COUNTY STATE PARK: 100 acres; camping, boating.
REPUBLIC COUNTY STATE PARK: 1064 acres; lake.
ROOKS COUNTY STATE PARK: 333 acres; fishing, boating.
SCOTT COUNTY STATE PARK: 1280 acres; camping, swimming, fishing, boating.
SHERIDAN COUNTY STATE PARK: 458 acres; camping, swimming, fishing, boating.
WOODSON COUNTY STATE PARK: 445 acres; camping, swimming, fishing, boating.

Kentucky

Parks, 15; historic sites, 6; recreational areas, 1. Total area, 35,581 acres.

AUDUBON STATE PARK: 320 acres. Museum; cabins, camping, fishing, boating.
BLUE LICKS BATTLEFIELD STATE PARK: 37 acres.
BUTLER STATE PARK: 421 acres; cabins, camping, swimming, fishing, boating, riding.
CARTER CAVES STATE PARK: 899 acres. Caverns.
COLUMBUS-BELMONT STATE PARK: 361 acres; cabins, camping.
CUMBERLAND FALLS STATE PARK: 593 acres; hotel, cabins, camping, swimming, fishing.
DAWSON SPRINGS STATE PARK: 460 acres; swimming, fishing, boating.
JEFFERSON DAVIS HISTORIC SITE: 22 acres. Birthplace.
KENTUCKY LAKE STATE PARK: 1200 acres; swimming, fishing, boating.
KENTUCKY RIDGE RECREATIONAL AREA: 12,000 acres; cabins.
LEVI JACKSON STATE PARK: 1315 acres; cabins, camping, fishing, boating, riding.
LINCOLN HOMESTEAD STATE PARK: 24 acres; golf.
MY OLD KENTUCKY HOME HISTORIC SITE: 235 acres; golf.
NATURAL BRIDGE STATE PARK: 1127 acres; hotel, camping.
OLD MULKEY MEETING HOUSE HISTORIC SITE: 30 acres.
PENNYRILE FOREST STATE PARK: 14.000 acres; hotel, cabins, camping, swimming, fishing, boating.
PINE MOUNTAIN STATE PARK: 2500 acres; hotel, camping.
PIONEER MEMORIAL STATE PARK: 28 acres, Fort Harrod.

Louisiana

Parks, 6; monuments, 2; waysides, 1; cemeteries, 1. Total area, 11,399 acres.

CHEMIN-A-HAUT-STATE PARK: 500 acres; hotel, cabins, fishing.
CHICOT STATE PARK: 6072 acres; cabins, camping, fishing, boating.
FONTAINEBLEAU STATE PARK: 2708 acres. swimming.
FORT MACOMB HISTORIC SITE: 16 acres; Ruins.
FORT PIKE HISTORIC SITE: 125 acres; ruins; fishing, boating.
LAKE BISTINEAU STATE PARK: 750 acres.
LONGFELLOW-EVANGELINE STATE PARK: 157 acres. Museum.
SAM HOUSTON STATE PARK: 1057 acres; Under development.

Maine

Parks, 10; historic sites, 11; forests, 1. Total area, 146,846 acres.

AROOSTOOK COUNTY STATE PARK: 430 acres; camping, swimming, fishing, boating.
BAXTER STATE PARK: 127,426 acres; hotel, cabins, camping, fishing.
BRADBURY MOUNTAIN STATE PARK: 172 acres; golf, camping, riding.
CAMDEN HILLS STATE PARK: 4964 acres; camping.
FORT KNOX STATE PARK: 125 acres. Historical. Camping.
LAKE ST. GEORGE STATE PARK: 5311 acres; camping, swimming, fishing, boating.
MOUNT BLUE STATE PARK: 4921 acres; camping, swimming, fishing, boating, riding.
REID STATE PARK: 250 acres. Undeveloped.
SALMON FALLS STATE PARK: 84 acres; camping.
SEBAGO LAKE STATE PARK: 1296 acres; camping, swimming, fishing, boating, riding.
SUGARLOAF ISLANDS STATE PARK: 3 acres.

Maryland

Parks, 7; forests, 8; memorials, 1; university owned forests, 1. Total area, 123,635 acres.

CEDARVILLE STATE FOREST: 3509 acres; camping, riding.
DONCASTER STATE FOREST: 1464 acres; camping.
ELK NECK STATE FOREST: 3762 acres; riding.
ELK NECK STATE PARK: 995 acres; cabins, camping, swimming, fishing, boating.
FORT FREDERICK STATE PARK: 279 acres; camping, fishing.
GAMBRILL STATE PARK: 1088 acres; camping, riding.
GREEN RIDGE STATE FOREST: 25,401 acres; camping, fishing, riding.
PATAPSCO STATE PARK: 1564 acres; camping, swimming, fishing, riding.
PLEASANT VALLEY STATE FOREST: 1800 acres; camping, swimming, boating.
POCOMOKE STATE FOREST: 12,337 acres; camping, fishing, boating, riding.
POTOMAC STATE FOREST: 12,628 acres; cabins, camping, fishing, riding.
SAVAGE RIVER STATE FOREST: 51,516 acres; cabins, camping, swimming, fishing, riding.
SWALLOW FALLS STATE FOREST: 7133

acres; camping, swimming, fishing, boating, riding.
WASHINGTON MONUMENT STATE PARK: 96 acres.

Massachusetts

Parks, 8; forests, 24; reservations, 8. Total area 108,505 acres.

BASH BISH STATE FOREST: 390 acres.
BEARTOWN STATE FOREST: 8004 acres; swimming, fishing, riding.
BRADLEY PALMER STATE PARK: 721 acres.
BRIMFIELD STATE FOREST: 3058 acres; swimming, fishing.
CAMPBELL'S FALLS STATE FOREST: 3 acres. Ski run.
CHESTER-BLANFORD STATE FOREST: 2328 acres; swimming, fishing.
D.A.R. STATE FOREST: 1237 acres; camping, swimming, fishing, boating.
DEER HILL RESERVATION: 259 acres; camping, fishing.
DOUGLAS STATE FOREST: 3468 acres; swimming, fishing, boating.
EAST MOUNTAIN STATE FOREST: 1553 acres. Ski run.
ERVING STATE FOREST: 5419 acres; swimming, fishing, boating.
FEDERATION OF WOMEN'S CLUBS STATE FOREST: 990 acres.
GRANVILLE STATE FOREST: 2233 acres; camping, swimming, fishing.
HAROLD PARKER STATE FOREST: 2906 acres; camping, swimming, fishing, boating, riding.
J. A. SKINNER STATE PARK: 375 acres.
J. C. ROBINSON STATE PARK: 1097 acres; swimming, riding.
LINDON BATES MEMORIAL STATE PARK: 224 acres.
MOHAWK TRAIL STATE FOREST: 5746 acres; cabins, camping, swimming, fishing.
MOUNT EVERETT RESERVATION: 1089.
MOUNT GREYLOCK RESERVATION: 8660 acres; camping, riding.
MOUNT GRACE STATE FOREST: 1224 acres; camping, fishing.
MOUNT SUGARLOAF RESERVATION: 89 acres; camping.
MOUNT TOM RESERVATION: 1800 acres; camping, swimming, fishing, riding.
MYLES STANDISH STATE FOREST: 10,910 acres; cabins, camping, swimming, fishing, boating, riding.
OCTOBER MOUNTAIN STATE FOREST: 14,189 acres; camping, swimming, fishing, riding.
OTTER RIVER STATE FOREST: 830 acres; camping, swimming, fishing.
PITTSFIELD STATE FOREST: 3854 acres; swimming, fishing, riding.
PURGATORY CHASM RESERVATION: 110 acres; camping.
R. C. NICKERSON STATE PARK: 1707 acres; camping, swimming, fishing, boating, riding.
SALISBURY BEACH STATE PARK: 500 acres; camping, swimming, fishing, boating.
SANDISFIELD STATE FOREST: 3923 acres; camping, swimming, fishing, boating.
SAVOY MOUNTAIN STATE FOREST: 10,641 acres; cabins, swimming, fishing, boating, riding.
SPENCER STATE FOREST: 1016 acres; swimming, fishing.
STANDISH MONUMENT STATE PARK: 25 acres. Historical.

TOLLAND STATE FOREST: 2940 acres; camping, swimming, fishing, boating.
WACHUSETT MOUNTAIN RESERVATION: 1560 acres; hotel, riding.
WAHCONAH STATE PARK: 47 acres. Scenic.
WALDEN POND RESERVATION: 147 acres; swimming, fishing, boating.
WILLARD BROOK STATE FOREST: 1617 acres; cabins, camping, swimming, fishing.
WINDSOR STATE FOREST: 1616 acres; camping, swimming, fishing.

Michigan

Parks, 78; recreational areas, 17; forest camps, 51; waysides, 70. Total area, 135,073 acres.

A. E. SLEEPER STATE PARK: 689 acres; camping, swimming, fishing.
ALGONAC STATE PARK: 895 acres; camping.
ALOHA STATE PARK: 37 acres; camping, swimming, fishing, boating.
BARAGA STATE PARK: Camping, swimming, fishing, boating.
BAY CITY STATE PARK: 179 acres; camping, swimming, fishing, boating.
BENZIE STATE PARK: 180 acres; camping, swimming.
BLOOMER NO. 1 STATE PARK: 36 acres; camping, fishing.
BLOOMER NO. 2 STATE PARK: 47 acres; camping.
BLOOMER NO. 3 STATE PARK: 100 acres; camping.
BLOOMER NO. 4 STATE PARK: 28 acres; camping.
BRIMLEY STATE PARK: 98 acres; camping, swimming, fishing, boating.
BURT LAKE STATE PARK: 430 acres; camping, swimming, fishing, boating.
DAY STATE PARK: 32 acres; camping, swimming.
26 acres; camping, fishing.
DODGE BROTHERS NO. 3 STATE PARK: 13 acres; camping.
DODGE BROTHERS NO. 4 STATE PARK: 78 acres; swimming, fishing, boating.
DODGE BROTHERS NO. 5 STATE PARK: 193 acres; camping.
DODGE BROTHERS NO. 6 STATE PARK: 36 acres; camping.
DODGE BROTHERS NO. 7 STATE PARK: 237 acres; camping.
DODGE BROTHERS NO. 8 STATE PARK: 41 acres; camping.
DODGE BROTHERS NO. 9 STATE PARK: 39 acres; camping.
DODGE BROTHERS NO. 10 STATE PARK: 114 acres; camping, swimming.
EAST TEWAS STATE PARK: 16 acres; camping, swimming, fishing, boating.
FLETCHER STATE PARK: 160 acres; camping.
FORT WILKINS STATE PARK: 106 acres; camping, swimming, fishing.
GLADWIN STATE PARK: 17 acres; camping, fishing.
GOGEBIC LAKE STATE PARK: 361 acres; camping, swimming, fishing, boating.
GRAND HAVEN STATE PARK: 44 acres; camping, swimming, fishing.
GRAND MARAIS STATE PARK: 1728 acres; camping.
GRAYLING WINTER RECREATIONAL AREA: 100 acres.
HARRISVILLE STATE PARK: 76 acres; camping, swimming, fishing.

HARTWICK PINES STATE PARK: 8596 acres; camping, swimming, fishing, boating.
HIGGENS LAKE STATE PARK: 271 acres; camping, swimming, fishing, boating.
HOEFT STATE PARK: 300 acres; camping; swimming.
HOLLAND STATE PARK: 43 acres; swimming, fishing.
INDIAN LAKE STATE PARK: 460 acres; camping, swimming, fishing, boating.
INTERLOCKEN STATE PARK: 278 acres; camping, swimming, fishing, boating.
ISLAND LAKE STATE PARK: 51 acres; camping, swimming, fishing, boating.
LAKEPORT STATE PARK: 374 acres; swimming.
LUDINGTON STATE PARK: 3436 acres; camping, swimming, fishing, boating.
MACKINAC ISLAND STATE PARK: 2800 acres; swimming, fishing, boating.
MCLAIN STATE PARK: 388 acres; camping, swimming.
MAGNUS STATE PARK: 16 acres; camping, swimming, fishing.
MEARS STATE PARK: 15 acres; camping, swimming.
MITCHELL STATE PARK: 121 acres; camping, swimming, fishing, boating.
MUSKEGON STATE PARK: 1357 acres; camping, swimming, fishing, boating.
NORTHPORT STATE PARK: 31 acres; camping.
OCEANA COUNTY STATE PARK: 1119 acres; camping.
OLD MISSION STATE PARK: 137 acres; camping.
ONAWAY STATE PARK: 158 acres; camping, swimming, fishing, boating.
ORCHARD BEACH STATE PARK: 211 acres; camping, swimming.
OSSINEKE STATE PARK: 220 acres; camping.
OTSEGO LAKE STATE PARK: 66 acres; camping, swimming, fishing, boating.
PALMS BROOK STATE PARK: 327 acres; large spring. Fishing.
PERE MARQUETTE STATE PARK: 15 acres; camping.
PICTURED ROCKS STATE PARK: 185 acres; camping.
POE REEF STATE PARK: 41 acres; camping.
PORCUPINE MOUNTAIN STATE PARK: 26,106 acres; camping, swimming, fishing, boating.
PORTAGE RIVER STATE PARK: 59 acres; camping.
ST. CLAIR STATE PARK: 16 acres; camping, swimming, boating.
SILVER LAKE STATE PARK: 25 acres; camping, swimming, fishing, boating.
STRAITS STATE PARK: 53 acres; camping, swimming, fishing.
STERLING STATE PARK: 554 acres; swimming.
TRAVERSE CITY STATE PARK: 38 acres; camping, swimming, fishing.
VAN BUREN STATE PARK: 68 acres; camping, swimming.
VAN ETTEN LAKE STATE PARK: 40 acres; camping.
WARREN DUNES STATE PARK: 985 acres; swimming.
WATERLOO RECREATIONAL AREA: 13,400 acres; camping, swimming, fishing, boating.
WELLS STATE PARK: 981 acres; camping, swimming.
WHITE CLOUD STATE PARK: 100 acres; camping.

WILDERNESS STATE PARK: 7656 acres; cabins, camping, swimming, fishing.
WILSON STATE PARK: 32 acres; camping, swimming, fishing.
W. J. HAYES STATE PARK: 671 acres; camping, swimming, fishing, boating.
YANKEE SPRINGS RECREATIONAL AREA: 4255 acres; camping, swimming, fishing, boating.
YOUNG STATE PARK: 559 acres; camping, swimming, fishing, boating.

Minnesota

Parks, 27; memorial parks, 5; historic sites, 9; forests, 12; waysides, 50. Total area, 1,516,788 acres.

ALEXANDER RAMSEY STATE PARK: 185 acres; scenic. Camping.
BAPTISM RIVER STATE PARK: 506 acres.
BEAVER CREEK STATE PARK: 325 acres; fishing.
BIRCH COULEE STATE PARK: 82 acres. Memorial.
BUFFALO RIVER STATE PARK: 242 acres; swimming.
CAMDEN STATE PARK: 470 acres; camping, swimming.
FLANDROU STATE PARK: 836 acres; camping, swimming, fishing, boating.
FORT RIDGELY STATE PARK: 225 acres; historic
GOOSEBERRY FALLS STATE PARK: 638 acres; camping, fishing.
INTERSTATE STATE PARK: 154 acres; cabins, camping, swimming, fishing, boating.
ITASCA STATE PARK: 31,976 acres; hotel, cabins, camping, swimming, fishing, boating, riding.
J. A. LATSCH STATE PARK: 350 acres; camping.
JAY COOKE STATE PARK: 8367 acres; camping, fishing.
KAPLAN WOODS STATE PARK: 180 acres.
KILLEN WOODS STATE PARK: 104 acres.
KODONES RIVER STATE PARK: 128 acres.
LAC QUI PARLE STATE PARK: 457 acres; camping, boating.
LAKE BEMIDJI STATE PARK: 205 acres; camping, swimming, fishing.
LAKE BRONSON STATE PARK: 746 acres; camping, swimming, fishing, boating.
LAKE CARLOS STATE PARK: 404 acres; camping, swimming.
LAKE SHETEK STATE PARK: 185 acres; camping, swimming, fishing, boating.
LINDBERGH STATE PARK: 110 acres; Memorial, museum.
MCCARTHY BEACH STATE PARK: 135 acres; Memorial.
MIDDLE RIVER STATE PARK: 285 acres; camping, swimming.
MINNEOPA STATE PARK: 110 acres.
MONSON LAKE STATE PARK: 199 acres. Memorial.
MOUND SPRING RECREATIONAL AREA: 195 acres. Scenic
NERSTRAND WOODS STATE PARK: 468 acres.
POMME DE TERRE RECREATIONAL AREA: Camping, swimming, boating.
ST. CROIX ISLANDS RECREATIONAL AREA: 39 acres.
ST. CROIX STATE PARK: 30,557 acres; cabins, camping, fishing.
SCENIC STATE PARK: 2121 acres; cabins, camping, swimming, fishing, boating.
SIBLEY, STATE PARK: 379 acres; camping, swimming, fishing, boating.

SPLIT ROCK CREEK RECREATIONAL AREA: 228 acres.
WHITEWATER STATE PARK: 688 acres. Golf, cabins, camping, swimming.
WILLIAM O'BRIEN STATE PARK: 180 acres.

Mississippi

Parks, 12. Total area, 11,009 acres.

CLARKCO STATE PARK: 793 acres; cabins, camping, swimming, fishing, boating.
GOLDEN SCHOOL STATE PARK: 120 acres. Memorial
HOLMES COUNTY STATE PARK: 463 acres; cabins, camping, swimming, fishing, boating.
LAKE SHELBY STATE PARK: 803 acres.
LEGION STATE PARK: 439 acres; cabins, camping, swimming, fishing, boating.
LEROY PERCY STATE PARK: 2442 acres; cabins, camping, swimming, fishing, boating.
MAGNOLIA STATE PARK: 250 acres; cabins, camping, swimming, fishing, boating.
PERCY QUIN STATE PARK: 2221 acres; hotel, cabins, swimming, fishing, boating.
ROOSEVELT STATE PARK: 550 acres; cabins, swimming, fishing, boating.
SPRING LAKE STATE PARK: 856 acres; cabins, swimming, fishing, boating.
TISHOMINGO STATE PARK: 1550 acres; cabins, swimming, fishing.
TOMBIGBEE STATE PARK: 522 acres; cabins, camping, swimming, fishing, boating.

Missouri

Parks, 23; forests and refuges 8; wayside, 35. Total area, 170,685 acres.

ALLEY SPRING STATE PARK: 407 acres; cabins, camping, swimming, fishing, riding.
ARROW ROCK STATE PARK: 34 acres; hotel, camping.
BABLER STATE PARK: 1837 acres; hotel, camping, riding.
BENNETT SPRING STATE PARK: 730 acres; hotel, cabins, camping, swimming, fishing, boating, riding.
BIG LAKE STATE PARK: 111 acres; hotel, cabins, camping, swimming, fishing, boating.
BIG OAK TREE STATE. PARK: 1007 acres. Botanical.
BIG SPRING STATE PARK: 4582 acres; hotel, cabins, camping, swimming, fishing, boating, riding.
CROWDER STATE PARK: 639 acres; camping.
CUIVRE RIVER STATE PARK: 5802 acres; cabins, swimming, fishing.
FORT ZUMWALT STATE PARK: 48 acres. Historical.
LAKE OF THE OZARKS STATE PARK: 16,148 acres; cabins, camping, swimming, fishing, boating.
LEWIS AND CLARK STATE PARK: 61 acres; camping, swimming, fishing, boating.
MARK TWAIN STATE PARK: 1185 acres. Museum. Camping, swimming, fishing.
MERAMEC STATE PARK: 7153 acres; hotel, cabins, camping, swimming, fishing, boating, riding.
MONTSERRAT STATE PARK: 3441 acres; cabins, camping.
MONTAUK STATE PARK: 758 acres; hotel, cabins, camping, swimming, fishing, boating, riding.
PERSHING STATE PARK: 1836 acres; camping.

ROARING RIVER STATE PARK: 2906 acres; hotel, cabins, camping, swimming, fishing, boating, riding.
ROUND SPRING STATE PARK: 76 acres; camping, swimming, fishing, boating.
SAM A. BAKER STATE PARK: 4761 acres; hotel, cabins, camping, swimming, fishing, boating, riding.
VAN METER STATE PARK: 546 acres; camping.
WALLACE STATE PARK: 161 acres; cabins, camping, fishing.
WASHINGTON STATE PARK: 1101 acres; cabins, camping, swimming, fishing, riding.

Montana

Parks, 2; waysides, 4. Total area, 2879 acres.

LEWIS AND CLARK CAVERN STATE PARK: 2777 acres.

Nebraska

Parks, 7; recreational areas, 31; waysides, 9. Total area, 9002 acres.

ARBOR LODGE STATE PARK: 65 acres. Museum.
ARNOLD RECREATIONAL AREA: 40 acres; camping, fishing.
BALLARD MARSH RECREATIONAL AREA: 1500 acres.
BLUE RIVER RECREATIONAL AREA: 14 acres; camping, fishing, boating.
CHADRON STATE PARK: 800 acres; hotel, cabins, camping, swimming, boating, riding.
CHAMPION RECREATIONAL AREA: 11 acres; camping, swimming, fishing.
COTTONMILL RECREATIONAL AREA: 100 acres; hotel, camping, swimming, fishing.
COTTONWOOD RECREATIONAL AREA: 160 acres; camping, swimming, fishing, boating.
CRYSTAL LAKE RECREATIONAL AREA: 55 acres; camping, fishing, boating.
DEAD TIMBER RECREATIONAL AREA: 200 acres; camping, swimming, fishing.
DUKE ALEXIS RECREATIONAL AREA: 100 acres; cabins, camping, swimming, fishing, boating.
FORT KEARNEY STATE PARK: 40 acres; camping.
FREMONT RECREATIONAL AREA: 307 acres; camping, swimming, fishing.
GOOSE LAKE RECREATIONAL AREA: 350 acres; camping
JEFFERSON COUNTY RECREATIONAL AREA: 40 acres; camping, swimming, fishing.
LITCHFIELD RECREATIONAL AREA: 20 acres; camping, fishing.
LONG LAKE RECREATIONAL AREA: 80 acres; camping.
LOUP CITY RECREATIONAL AREA: 50 acres; camping, swimming, fishing.
MEMPHIS RECREATIONAL AREA: 147 acres; camping, swimming, fishing, boating.
NIOBRARA STATE PARK: 408 acres; cabins, camping, swimming, fishing, boating.
OXFORD RECREATIONAL AREA: 30 acres.
PAWNEE LAKE RECREATIONAL AREA: 40 acres; camping, swimming, fishing, boating.
PIBEL LAKE RECREATIONAL AREA: 65 acres; camping, swimming, fishing, boating.
PLATTEVIEW RECREATIONAL AREA: 190 acres; camping, swimming, fishing.

PONCA STATE PARK: 80 acres; cabins, camping, swimming.
PRESSAY RECREATIONAL AREA: 1680 acres; camping, swimming, fishing.
RAT AND BEAVER RECREATIONAL AREA: 245 acres; fishing.
RAVENNA RECREATIONAL AREA: 80 acres; camping, fishing.
RICHARDSON COUNTY RECREATIONAL AREA: 55 acres; camping, fishing.
ROCK CREEK RECREATIONAL AREA: 100 acres; camping, swimming, fishing.
ROWELL RECREATIONAL AREA: 160 acres; camping.
SHELL LAKE RECREATIONAL AREA: 640 acres.
SMITH LAKE RECREATIONAL AREA: 640 acres.
STOLLEY STATE PARK: 43 acres; camping.
VICTORIA SPRINGS STATE PARK: 60 acres; camping, fishing, boating.
WALGREN RECREATIONAL AREA: 130 acres; camping, fishing, boating.
WELFLEET RECREATIONAL AREA: 200 acres; swimming.
WILDCAT HILLS RECREATIONAL AREA: 53 acres; camping.

Nevada

Parks, 5; waysides, 5. Total area, 11,520 acres.

BEAVER DAM STATE PARK: 719 acres; hot springs, camping.
CATHEDRAL GORGE STATE PARK: 1578 acres; scenic. Camping.
FORT CHURCHILL STATE PARK: 200 acres. Historical. Camping.
KERSHAW-CANYON-RYAN STATE PARK: 240 acres; camping.
VALLEY OF FORE STATE PARK: 8752 acres; cabins, camping.

New Hampshire

Parks, 18; resevations, 24; forests, 6. Total area, 38,656 acres.

BEAR BROOK STATE PARK: 6492 acres; camping, swimming, fishing.
BELKNAP RESERVATION: 545 acres. Scenic. Camping.
BELLAMY STATE PARK: 23 acres; swimming.
BLACK MOUNTAIN RESERVATION: 655 acres. Scenic.
CARDIGAN RESERVATION: 3090 acres. View. Camping.
CATHEDRAL AND WHITEHORSE RESERVATION: 205 acres; swimming.
CLOUGH STATE PARK: 309 acres; camping, fishing.
PETERBOROUGH STATE PARK: 12 acres; swimming.
CONNECTICUT LAKES STATE PARK: 1500 acres; scenic.
CRAWFORD NOTCH RESERVATION: 5950 acres; cabins, camping.
DIXVILLE NOTCH RESERVATION: 164 acres. Scenic.
ECHO LAKE STATE PARK: 83 acres; Undeveloped.
ENDICOTT ROCK STATE PARK: 3 acres; swimming.
FOREST LAKE STATE PARK: 420 acres; swimming.
FRANCONIA NOTCH RESERVATION: 6232 acres. Scenic. Camping.

GOVERNOR WENTWORTH FARM RESERVATION: 96 acres.
HAMPTON BEACH STATE PARK: 50 acres; swimming.
HEMMENWAY RESERVATION: 1958 acres. View. Camping.
INTERVALE SKI SLOPE RESERVATION: 13 acres
KEARSARGE RESERVATION: 2366 acres. View. Camping.
KINGSTON STATE PARK: 55 acres; camping, swimming.
MILAN HILL STATE PARK: 127 acres. View. Camping.
MILLER STATE PARK: 84 acres. View.
MONADNOCK RESERVATION: 699 acres; camping.
MOOSE BROOK STATE PARK: 755 acres; camping, swimming.
MOUNT PROSPECT STATE PARK: 430 acres. View.
PAWTUCKAWAY RESERVATION: 1071 acres; camping.
PILLSBURY RESERVATION: 3034 acres; camping.
WADLEIGH STATE PARK: 52 acres; swimming.
WELLINGTON STATE PARK: 104 acres; swimming.
WENTWORTH STATE PARK: 16 acres; swimming.
WHITE LAKE STATE PARK: 258 acres; camping, swimming.

New Jersey

Parks, 21; memorials, 1; forests, 9. Total area, 76,003 acres.

AIRPORT STATE PARK: 817 acres.
ALLAIRE STATE PARK: 1278 acres. New.
BASS RIVER STATE FOREST: 9270 acres; swimming, fishing.
BELLEPLAIN STATE FOREST: 6492 acres; hotel, swimming, fishing, boating.
CHEESEQUAKE STATE PARK: 962 acres; fishing.
CRANBERRY STATE PARK: 199 acres; swimming, fishing, boating.
FARNY STATE PARK: 803 acres. Undeveloped.
GREEN BANK STATE FOREST: 1833 acres; swimming.
HACKLEBARNEY STATE PARK: 193 acres; fishing.
HIGH POINT STATE PARK: 10,935 acres; hotel, cabins, camping, swimming, fishing, boating.
HOPATCONG STATE PARK: 107 acres; swimming, fishing, boating.
JENNY JUMP STATE FOREST: 967 acres; cabins, camping, fishing.
LEBANON STATE FOREST: 22,185 acres; cabins, camping, swimming, fishing, riding.
MOUNT LAUREL STATE PARK: 20 acres. Undeveloped.
MUSCONETCONG STATE PARK: 343 acres; cabins, camping, swimming, fishing, boating.
PALISADES INTERSTATE PARK: 1777 acres; cabins, camping, swimming, fishing, boating.
PARVIN STATE PARK: 967 acres; cabins, camping, swimming, fishing, boating.
PENN STATE FOREST: 2958 acres; cabins, swimming, fishing.
RINGWOOD MANOR STATE PARK: 470 acres. Historical.
STEPHENS STATE PARK: 237 acres; fishing.

SWARTSWOOD STATE PARK: 704 acres; swimming, fishing, boating.
VOORHEES STATE PARK: 429 acres; View.
WASHINGTON CROSSING STATE PARK: 373 acres; swimming.

New Mexico

Parks, 3; archeological sites, 8; waysides, 16. Total area, 3054 acres.

BOTTOMLESS LAKES STATE PARK: 1558 acres; swimming.
CONCHAS DAM STATE PARK: Hotel, camping, swimming, fishing, boating.
SANTA FE HYDE STATE PARK: 1135 acres; winter sports.

New York

Parks, 72; reservations, 6; parkways, 18; forest preserves, 2; historic sites, 30. Total area, 2,556,514 acres.

ADIRONDACK STATE FOREST: 2,171,690 acres; camping, swimming, boating.
ALLEGANY STATE PARK: 56,947 acres; hotel, cabins, camping, swimming, fishing, riding.
BATTLE ISLAND STATE PARK: 235 acres. Golf.
BEAR MOUNTAIN STATE PARK: 3621 acres; camping, swimming, boating, hotel.
BEAVER ISLAND STATE PARK: 722 acres. Scenic. Swimming.
BELMONT LAKE STATE PARK: 372 acres; boating, riding.
BENNINGTON BATTLEFIELD HISTORIC SITE: 171 acres.
BETHPAGE STATE PARK: 1405 acres; golf, riding.
BLAUVELT STATE PARK: 536 acres; riding.
BROOKS LAKE STATE PARK: 338 acres.
BUCKHORN ISLAND STATE PARK: 923 acres. Scenic.
BURNHAM POINT STATE PARK: 7 acres; camping, swimming, boating.
BUTTERMILK FALLS STATE PARK: 595 acres; cabins, camping, swimming.
CANOE PICNIC POINT STATE PARK: 70 acres; camping, swimming, boating.
CAPTREE STATE PARK: 298 acres.
CATSKILL FOREST PRESERVE: 232,423 acres; camping.
CAYUGA LAKE STATE PARK: 188 acres; cabins, camping, swimming, fishing, boating.
CEDAR ISLAND STATE PARK: 10 acres; camping, swimming, boating.
CEDAR POINT STATE PARK: 48 acres; camping, swimming, boating.
CHENANGO VALLEY STATE PARK: 928 acres; cabins, camping, swimming, fishing, boating, riding.
CHITTENANGO FALLS STATE PARK: 122 acres; camping, fishing.
CLARK RESERVATION: 225 acres; scenic.
CROWN POINT RESERVATION: 113 acres; camping, swimming, fishing.
CUBA LAKE RESERVATION: 650 acres; swimming, fishing, boating.
DEVIL'S HOLE STATE PARK: 42 acres. Niagara gorge.
DE WOLF POINT STATE PARK: 10 acres; cabins, swimming, boating.
ECHO LAKE STATE PARK: 64 acres.
FAHNSTOCK MEMORIAL: 3400 acres; camping, swimming, boating.
FAIR HAVEN BEACH STATE PARK:

816 acres; cabins, camping, swimming, fishing, boating.
FILIMORE GLEN STATE PARK: 856 acres; cabins, camping, swimming.
FIRE ISLAND STATE PARK: 800 acres; swimming, fishing, boating.
GILBERT LAKE STATE PARK: 1569 acres; cabins, camping, swimming, fishing, boating.
GILGO STATE PARK: 1223 acres.
GRASS POINT STATE PARK: 15 acres; camping, swimming, fishing, boating.
GREEN LAKES STATE PARK: 774 acres. Golf. Cabins, camping, swimming, boating.
HAMLIN BEACH STATE PARK: 751 acres; cabins, swimming.
HARRIMAN STATE PARK: 37,482 acres; camping, swimming, fishing, boating.
HAVERSTRAW STATE PARK: 73 acres; camping.
HECKSCHER STATE PARK: 1518 acres; swimming, riding.
HEMPSTEAD STATE PARK: 903 acres; riding.
HERKIMER HOME HISTORIC SITES: 143 acres.
HIGH TOR STATE PARK: 491 acres.
HITHER HILLS STATE PARK: 1755 acres; camping, swimming, fishing.
HOOK MOUNTAIN STATE PARK: 661 acres; swimming.
JAMES BAIRD STATE PARK: 580 acres. Golf, swimming.
JOHN BOYD THATCHER STATE PARK: 990 acres; camping.
JONES BEACH STATE PARK: 2413 acres. Boardwalk. Swimming, fishing.
KRING POINT STATE PARK: 39 acres; camping, swimming, fishing, boating.
LAKE ERIE STATE PARK: 240 acres; camping, swimming.
LAKE GEORGE BATTLEGROUND: 35 acres; camping, fishing.
LAKE TAGHKANIC STATE PARK: 750 acres; cabins, camping, swimming, fishing, boating.
LETCHWORTH STATE PARK: 6704 acres; hotel, cabins, camping.
LONG POINT STATE PARK: 12 acres; camping, swimming, fishing, boating.
MARY ISLAND STATE PARK: 13 acres; camping, swimming, boating.
MASSAPEQUA STATE PARK: 595 acres.
M. L. NORRIE STATE PARK: 323 acres; cabins, camping, fishing, boating.
MONTAUK POINT STATE PARK: 158 acres; fishing.
NELSON AND WHITNEY STATE PARK: 177 acres.
NEWTON BATTLEFIELD RESERVATION: 318 acres; camping.
NIAGARA RESERVATION: 425 acres. Niagara Falls.
NYACK BEACH STATE PARK: 60 acres; swimming.
OGDEN AND RUTH MILLS STATE PARK: 190 acres. Museum.
ORIENT BEACH STATE PARK: 342 acres; swimming.
ORISKANY BATTLEFIELD HISTORIC SITES: 5 acres.
PALISADES STATE PARK: 16 acres.
ROBERT H. TREMAN STATE PARK: 833 acres; cabins, camping, swimming, fishing.
SACKETS HARBOR BATTLEFIELD: 6 acres. Historical.
SELKIRK SHORES STATE PARK: 631 acres; cabins, camping, swimming, fishing.
STONY BROOK STATE PARK: 481 acres; Scenic. Camping, swimming, fishing.

STONY POINT RESERVATION: 45 acres. Museum. Swimming.
STORM KING STATE PARK: 1057 acres. Scenic.
SUNKEN MEADOW STATE PARK: 522 acres; swimming.
TACONIC STATE PARK: 6200 acres; cabins, camping, swimming, fishing, boating.
TALLMAN MOUNTAIN STATE PARK: 756 acres; camping. swimming.
TAUGHANNOCK FALLS STATE PARK: 535 acres; cabins, camping, swimming, fishing, boating.
VALLEY STREAM STATE PARK: 129 acres; boating.
VERONA BEACH STATE PARK: 520 acres; boating.
WATKINS GLEN STATE PARK: 540 acres. Scenic. Camping, swimming.
WATTERSON POINT STATE park: 6 acres; swimming.
WESTCOTT BEACH STATE PARK: 290 acres; swimming.
WHIRLPOOL STATE PARK: 109 acres; Niagara River.
WILDWOOD STATE PARK: 395 acres; swimming, camping.

North Carolina

Parks, 9; recreational areas, 2; archeological sites, 1. Total area, 35,309 acres.

CAPE HATTERAS STATE PARK: 1200 acres; cabins, swimming, fishing, boating.
CLIFFS OF THE NEUSE STATE PARK: 321 acres. Undeveloped.
CRABTREE CREEK STATE PARK: 5120 acres; camping.
FORT MACON STATE PARK: 500 acres; cabins, swimming.
HANGING ROCK STATE PARK: 3865 acres; camping, swimming, fishing.
JONES LAKE RECREATIONAL AREA: 1000 acres; swimming, fishing, boating.
MORROW MOUNTAIN STATE PARK: 4135 acres. Scenic. Camping, swimming.
MOUNT MITCHELL STATE PARK: 1224 acres; el. 6684 ft.
PETTIGREW STATE PARK: 16,800 acres; hotel, fishing.
RENDEZVOUS MOUNTAIN STATE PARK: 142 acres. Historical.
SINGLETARY LAKE RECREATIONAL AREA: 1000 acres; cabins, camping.

North Dakota

Parks, 4; recreational areas, 6; historic sites, 35. Total area, 3514 acres.

BEAVER LAKE RECREATIONAL AREA: 45 acres; swimming.
DE MORES HISTORIC SITES: 130 acres.
DOYLE MEMORIAL RECREATIONAL AREA: 21 acres. Historical.
FORT BUFORD HISTORIC SITE: 20 acres.
FORT CLARK HISTORIC SITE: 130 acres.
FORT LINCOLN STATE PARK: 750 acres. Museum.
FORT MANDAN HISTORIC SITE: 31 acres.
FORT UNION HISTORIC SITE: 8 acres.
INTERNATIONAL PEACE GARDEN: 888 acres; hotel, cabins.
LAKE METIGOSHE STATE PARK: 640 acres; cabins, camping, swimming, fishing, boating.
STREETER MEMORIAL RECREATIONAL AREA: 63 acres; swimming.

TURTLE RIVER STATE PARK: 475 acres; hotel, cabins, camping, swimming.

Ohio

Parks, 30; recreational areas, 3; forests, 19; memorials, 52. Total area, 180,608 acres.

BEAVER CREEK STATE PARK: 512 acres.
BLUE ROCK STATE FOREST: 4842 acres; camping.
BRUSH CREEK STATE FOREST: 8553 acres.
BUCKEYE FURNACE HISTORIC SITE: 267 acres.
BUCKEYE LAKE STATE PARK: 3962 acres. Golf. Hotel, camping, swimming, fishing, boating.
CASCADE STATE PARK: 69 acres; camping, fishing.
CATAWBA ISLAND STATE PARK: 7 acres; camping, fishing.
CLARK MEMORIAL: 243 acres.
COWAN CREEK STATE PARK: 1700 acres.
DEAN STATE FOREST: 1797 acres; camping.
EAST HARBOR BEACH STATE PARK: 1153 acres; swimming.
FALLEN TIMBERS HISTORIC SITES: 4 acres. Battle site.
FINDLEY STATE FOREST: 890 acres; camping.
FORT ANCIENT HISTORIC SITE: 680 acres. Museum. Camping.
FORT HILL HISTORIC SITE: 1116 acres. Indian site.
GUILFORD LAKE STATE PARK: 496 acres; camping, swimming, fishing, boating.
HARRISON LAKE STATE PARK: 196 acres; camping.
HOCKING STATE FOREST: 6651 acres; camping.
HUESTON WOODS STATE PARK: 1984 acres.
INDEPENDENCE DAM STATE PARK: 94 acres; camping, fishing boating.
INDIAN LAKE STATE PARK: 6300 acres; camping, fishing.
JACKSON LAKE STATE PARK: 359 acres; camping, swimming, fishing, boating.
JEFFERSON STATE PARK: 892 acres; camping, swimming, fishing, boating.
JOHN BRYAN STATE PARK: 751 acres; hotel, camping, swimming.
KISER LAKE STATE PARK: 647 acres; camping, swimming, fishing, boating.
LAKE LORAMIE STATE PARK: 1950 acres; camping, swimming, fishing, boating.
LAKE ST. MARY'S STATE PARK: 15,748 acres; camping, swimming, fishing, boating.
MIAMISBURG MOUND HISTORIC SITE: 36 acres. Indian mound.
MOHICAN STATE FOREST: 2287 acres; camping.
MOUND BUILDERS HISTORIC SITES: 73 acres. Eagle mound.
MOUNT GILEAD STATE PARK: 172 acres; camping, swimming, fishing, boating.
NELSON LEDGES STATE PARK: 65 acres. Scenic.
PIKE STATE FOREST: 6323 acres; cabins, camping, swimming, fishing, boating.
PORTAGE LAKES STATE PARK: 2250 acres; swimming, fishing, boating.
PYMATUNING LAKE STATE PARK: 5400 acres; camping, fishing.
RACCOON STATE FOREST: 5732 acres.
ROCKY FORK STATE PARK: 3600 acres.
SCHOENBRUNN VILLAGE HISTORIC SITE: 190 acres. Restoration.
SCIOTO TRAIL STATE FOREST: 9328 acres; camping, fishing.

SERPENT MOUND HISTORIC SITE: 61 acres. Effigy mound.
SHAWNEE STATE FOREST: 39,152 acres; camping.
SOUTH BASS ISLAND STATE PARK: 32 acres; camping, swimming, fishing, boating.
STARK CANAL STATE PARK: 82 acres; fishing.
STONE LICK STATE PARK: 1200 acres.
TAR HOLLOW STATE FOREST: 15,500 acres; camping.
THEODORE ROOSEVELT STATE PARK: 275 acres; camping, swimming, fishing.
VAN BUREN STATE PARK: 136 acres; camping, swimming, fishing, boating.
VIRGINIA KENDALL STATE PARK: 1575 acres; camping, swimming.
WELLSTON - LAKE ALMA STATE PARK: 231 acres; camping, fishing, boating.
ZALESKI STATE FOREST: 17,515 acres; hotel, cabins, camping, swimming, boating.

Oklahoma

Parks, 7; historic sites, 4; waysides, 46. Total area, 44,018 acres.

BEAVERS BEND STATE PARK: 1300 acres; cabins, camping, swimming, fishing, boating.
BOILING SPRINGS STATE PARK: 820 acres; cabins, camping, swimming, fishing.
LAKE MURRAY STATE PARK: 21,000 acres; cabins, camping, swimming, fishing, boating.
OLD FORT GIBSON STOCKADE HISTORIC SITE: 55 acres.
OSAGE HILLS STATE PARK: 740 acres; cabins, camping, fishing, boating.
QUARTZ MOUNTAIN STATE PARK: 11,000 acres; cabins, fishing.
ROBBERS CAVE STATE PARK: 8400 acres; cabins, camping, swimming, fishing, boating.
ROMAN NOSE STATE PARK: 520 acres; cabins, camping, swimming.
WILL ROGERS MEMORIAL: 27 acres. Museum.

Oregon

Parks and miscellaneous areas, 130; forests, 36; historic sites, 11. Total area, 433,555 acres.

BATTLE MOUNTAIN STATE PARK: 420 acres. Historical.
BENSON STATE PARK: 76 acres. Scenic.
BLACHLY MOUNTAIN STATE PARK: 319 acres; fishing.
BOOTH STATE PARK: 311 acres. Ponderosa pines.
CAMAS MOUNTAIN STATE PARK: 160 acres.
CAPE ARAGO STATE PARK: 134 acres; swimming, fishing.
CAPE LOOKOUT STATE PARK: 1172 acres; Scenic.
CAPE SEBASTIAN STATE PARK: 780 acres; Ocean view.
CASCADIA STATE PARK: 321 acres; camping, swimming.
CHAMPOEG STATE PARK: 107 acres. Historical.
CHANDLER STATE PARK: 57 acres. Scenic.
COVE PALISADES STATE PARK: 7156 acres; camping, fishing.
CROWN POINT STATE PARK: 29 acres; Columbia River.
DEVILS ELBOW STATE PARK: 97 acres; swimming.
ECOLA STATE PARK: 899 acres.

EMIGRANT SPRINGS STATE PARK: 1683 acres. Historical.
GEARHART STATE PARK: 286 acres.
GOLDEN FALLS STATE PARK: 129 acres. Scenic.
GUY W. TALBOT STATE PARK: 125 acres. Scenic.
HARRIS BEACH STATE PARK: 141 acres; swimming.
HUMBUG MOUNTAIN STATE PARK: 1675 acres; swimming, fishing.
J. B. YEON STATE PARK: 115 acres. Columbia River.
J. M. HONEYMAN STATE PARK: 522 acres; swimming, fishing, boating.
JOHN DAY FOSSIL BEDS STATE PARK: 1895 acres.
MAYER CREST STATE PARK: 260 acres. Scenic.
NEHALEM BEACH STATE PARK: 820 acres; swimming.
NEPTUNE STATE PARK: 331 acres; fishing.
NEWBURGH STATE PARK: 1937 acres.
OCHOCO STATE PARK: 141 acres.
PETER SKENE STATE PARK: 103 acres. Deep gorge.
PILOT BUTTE STATE PARK: 101 acres. View.
SADDLE MOUNTAIN STATE PARK: 2682 acres. Scenic.
SENECA FOUTS STATE PARK: 151 acres. Memorial.
SHELTON STATE PARK: 180 acres. Pine forest.
SHORE ACRES STATE PARK: 637 acres.
SHORT SAND BEACH STATE PARK: 2289 acres; swimming, fishing.
SILVER CREEK FALLS STATE PARK: 5997 acres; camping, fishing.
STARVATION CREEK STATE PARK: 145 acres. Scenic.
UMPQUA LIGHTHOUSE STATE PARK: 2636 acres. Scenic.
WYGANT STATE PARK: 585 acres. Scenic.

Pennsylvania

Parks and memorials, 65; picnic areas, 46. Total area, 97,881 acres.

ALAN SEEGAR STATE PARK: 155 acres. Memorial.
BEAR MEADOWS STATE PARK: 350 acres; fishing.
BLACK MOSHANNON STATE PARK: 2150 acres; cabins, swimming, fishing, boating.
BLUE KNOB STATE PARK: 5079 acres; camping, swimming.
BRUCE LAKE STATE PARK: 500 acres.
BUSHY RUN BATTLEFIELD STATE PARK: 132 acres. Museum.
CALEDONIA STATE PARK: 1795 acres. Golf. Hotel, camping, swimming.
CHERRY SPRING STATE PARK: 175 acres; trap shooting.
CLEAR CREEK STATE PARK: 150 acres; cabins, swimming, fishing.
COLERAIN STATE PARK: 239 acres; camping, swimming, fishing.
COLTON POINT STATE PARK: 150 acres; camping, swimming.
CONRAD WEISER STATE PARK: 26 acres. Undeveloped.
COOK FOREST STATE PARK: 6070 acres; hotel, cabins, camping, swimming, fishing.
COWANS GAP STATE PARK: 1346 acres; cabins, camping, swimming, fishing.
FORT NECESSITY STATE PARK: 318 acres.

FORT WASHINGTON STATE PARK: 354 acres.
FRENCH CREEK STATE PARK: 5349 acres; camping, swimming, fishing, boating.
GEORGE WILCOX STATE PARK: 124 acres.
GREENWOOD FURNACE STATE PARK: 382 acres; swimming.
HALFWAY STATE PARK: 972 acres; swimming, fishing.
HICKORY RUN STATE PARK: 13,386 acres; camping, swimming, fishing.
JOYCE KILMER STATE PARK: 21 acres; memorial. Camping, swimming.
KEYSTONE STATE PARK: 774 acres.
KOOSER STATE PARK: 510 acres; cabins, camping, swimming.
LAUREL HILL STATE PARK: 4226 acres; camping, swimming.
LEONARD HARRISON STATE PARK: 226 acres. Scenic.
LINN RUN STATE PARK: 2379 acres; cabins, swimming.
MC CONNELL NARROWS STATE PARK: 295 acres; swimming, fishing, boating.
MARTINS HILL STATE PARK: 500 acres; camping, fishing.
OLE BULL STATE PARK: 150 acres; camping, swimming.
PARKER DAM STATE PARK: 960 acres; cabins, swimming, boating.
PENNSYLVANIA STATE PARK: 3200 acres; swimming, fishing, boating.
PINE GROVE FURNACE STATE PARK: 3128 acres; hotel, cabins, camping, swimming.
POE VALLEY STATE PARK: 500 acres; camping, swimming, fishing.
PROMISED LAND STATE PARK: 2328 acres; cabins, camping, swimming, fishing, boating.
PYMATUNING STATE PARK: 18,000 acres; cabins, camping, fishing, boating.
RACCOON CREEK STATE PARK: 5530 acres; camping, swimming, fishing.
RALPH STOVER STATE PARK: 37 acres; hotel, camping, swimming.
RAVENSBURG STATE PARK: 150 acres; swimming.
RICKETTS GLEN STATE PARK: 5850 acres.
ROOSEVELT STATE PARK: 400 acres; swimming, fishing, boating, riding.
S. B. ELLIOTT STATE PARK: 721 acres; hotel, cabins, camping.
SIZERVILLE STATE PARK: 1390 acres; camping, swimming.
SMITH BROTHERS STATE PARK: 360 acres.
SNYDER-MIDDLESWORTH STATE PARK: 425 acres; camping, fishing.
TROUGH CREEK STATE PARK: 550 acres. Scenic.
VALLEY FORGE STATE PARK: 2030 acres. Historical.
VONEIDA STATE PARK: 100 acres.
WASHINGTON CROSSING STATE PARK: 480 acres; hotel, camping, swimming.
WHIPPLE DAM STATE PARK: 262 acres; swimming, fishing, boating.
WORLD'S END STATE PARK: 1891 acres; camping, swimming.

Rhode Island

Parks, 22; reservations, 6; parkways, 4; waysides, 10. Total area, 26,653 acres.

ARCADIA STATE FOREST: 8388 acres; swimming.
BEACH POND STATE PARK: 1186 acres; camping, swimming, fishing.
BURLINGAME STATE PARK: 3100 acres; camping, swimming, fishing.
DAWLEY STATE PARK: 200 acres; camping.

DIAMOND HILL STATE PARK: 372 acres; camping.
GEORGE WASHINGTON STATE FOREST: 244 acres; camping.
GODDARD STATE PARK: 472 acres. Golf. Camping, swimming.
HAINES STATE PARK: 102 acres; camping, swimming.
LINCOLN WOODS STATE PARK: 628 acres; camping, swimming, fishing.
PAWTUXET RIVER STATE PARK: 81 acres; camping, boating.
SAND HILL COVE STATE PARK: 27 acres; swimming, fishing.
SCARBOROUGH BEACH STATE PARK: 23 acres; swimming.
TEN MILE RIVER STATE PARK: 104 acres.
WICKABOXET STATE FOREST: 244 acres; camping.

South Carolina

Parks, 18; waysides, 6. Total area, 37,746 acres.

AIKEN STATE PARK: 867 acres; cabins, camping, fishing, boating.
BARNWELL STATE PARK: 252 acres; swimming.
CHERAW STATE PARK: 7361 acres; cabins, camping, swimming, fishing, boating.
CHESTER STATE PARK: 523 acres; fishing, boating.
EDISTO BEACH STATE PARK: 1255 acres; cabins, swimming, fishing, boating.
GIVHANS FERRY STATE PARK: 1235 acres; cabins, swimming, fishing, boating.
GREENWOOD STATE PARK: 1114 acres; fishing, boating.
HUNTING ISLAND STATE PARK: 5000 acres; swimming, fishing.
KINGS MOUNTAIN STATE PARK: 6141 acres; camping, swimming, fishing, boating.
LEE STATE PARK: 2839 acres; cabins, swimming, fishing, boating.
MYRTLE BEACH STATE PARK: 323 acres; cabins, camping, swimming.
OCONEE STATE PARK: 1165 acres; cabins, swimming, boating.
PARIS MOUNTAIN STATE PARK: 1301 acres; camping, swimming, boating.
POINSETT STATE PARK: 1000 acres; cabins, swimming, fishing, boating.
RIVERS BRIDGE STATE PARK: 390 acres; fishing, boating.
SANTEE STATE PARK: 2364 acres; fishing, boating.
SESQUICENTENNIAL STATE PARK: 1500 acres; swimming, fishing, boating.
TABLE ROCK STATE PARK: 2991 acres; cabins, swimming, boating.

South Dakota

Park and recreational areas, 31. Total area, 67,184 acres.

CUSTER STATE PARK: 61,000 acres; hotel, cabins, camping, swimming, fishing, boating, riding.
DURKEE LAKE STATE PARK: 200 acres.
FARM ISLAND STATE PARK: 1800 acres.
HARTFORD BEACH STATE PARK: 120 acres.
LAKE HERMAN STATE PARK: 170 acres.
LAKE HIDDENWOOD STATE PARK: 160 acres.
LAKE LOUISE STATE PARK: 320 acres.
LAKE RICHMOND STATE PARK: 300 acres.
NEWTON HILLS STATE PARK: 600 acres.
OAKWOOD LAKES STATE PARK: 900 acres.

ROY LAKE STATE PARK: 160 acres.

Tennessee

Parks, 16; memorials, 1. Total area, 117,974 acres.

BOOKER T. WASHINGTON STATE PARK: 350 acres; swimming.
CEDARS OF LEBANON STATE PARK: 8300 acres; cabins, swimming.
CHICKASAW STATE PARK: 11,215 acres; cabins, camping, swimming, fishing, boating.
COVE LAKE STATE PARK: 642 acres; cabins, swimming, fishing, boating.
CUMBERLAND MOUNTAIN STATE PARK: 1427 acres; cabins, swimming, fishing, boating.
FALL CREEK FALLS STATE PARK: 15,777 acres; camping, fishing.
HARRISON BAY STATE PARK: 1432 acres; fishing, boating.
MONTGOMERY BELL STATE PARK: 3744 acres; camping, swimming, fishing, boating.
NATCHEZ TRACE STATE PARK: 40,345 acres; cabins, camping, swimming, fishing, boating.
N. B. FORREST MEMORIAL STATE PARK: 77 acres; cabins, camping.
PARIS LANDING STATE PARK: 216 acres; boating.
PICKETT STATE PARK: 11,752 acres; cabins, camping, swimming, fishing, boating.
SHELBY ARCHEOLOGICAL STATE PARK: 510 acres.
SHELBY FOREST STATE PARK: 12,258 acres; boating.
SHELBY NEGRO STATE PARK: 469 acres.
STANDING STONE STATE PARK: 8764 acres; hotel, cabins, camping, swimming, fishing, boating.
WATAUGA STATE PARK: 773 acres; camping, swimming, fishing, boating.

Texas

Parks, 37; forests, 5; historic sites, 9; waysides, 519. Total area, 66,691 acres.

ABILENE STATE PARK: 507 acres.
BALMORHEA STATE PARK: 950 acres; cabins, swimming, fishing, boating.
BASTROP STATE PARK: 2100 acres. Golf. Hotel, cabins, swimming.
BENTSEN-RIO GRANDE VALLEY STATE PARK: 587 acres.
BIG SPRING STATE PARK: 363 acres. Scenic.
BLANCO STATE PARK: 110 acres; cabins, camping, fishing, boating.
BONHAM STATE PARK: 555 acres; swimming, fishing, boating.
BUESCHER STATE PARK: 1730 acres; camping.
CADDO LAKE STATE PARK: 485 acres; cabins, fishing, boating.
CLEBURNE STATE PARK: 483 acres; cabins, camping, swimming, fishing, boating.
DAINGERFIELD STATE PARK: Hotel, cabins, camping, fishing, boating.
DAVIS MOUNTAIN STATE PARK: 1540 acres; hotel, riding.
FANNIN BATTLEFIELD HISTORIC SITES: 13 acres.
FORT GRIFFIN STATE PARK: 503 acres; camping.
FORT PARKER STATE PARK: 1496 acres; hotel, camping, swimming, fishing, boating.

FRIO STATE PARK: 51 acres; camping, fishing.
GARNER STATE PARK: 640 acres; hotel, cabins, camping, swimming, fishing, riding.
GOLIAD HISTORIC SITE: 207 acres.
GONZALES HISTORIC SITE: 100 acres.
GOOSE ISLAND STATE PARK: 157 acres; camping, swimming, fishing, boating.
HUNTSVILLE STATE PARK: 2044 acres; swimming, fishing, boating.
INKS LAKE STATE PARK: 1194 acres; camping, fishing, boating.
JIM HOGG STATE PARK: 177 acres. Undeveloped.
KERRVILLE STATE PARK: 500 acres; camping, fishing, riding
LAKE CORPUS CHRISTI STATE PARK: 14,111 acres; camping, swimming, fishing, boating.
LOCKHART STATE PARK: 352 acres. Golf. Swimming.
LONGHORN CAVERN STATE PARK: 703 acres; camping.
MACKENZIE STATE PARK: 548 acres. Swimming.
MERIDIAN STATE PARK: 468 acres; cabins, camping, swimming, fishing, boating.
MINERAL WELLS STATE PARK: 55 acres; camping.
MOTHER NEFF STATE PARK: 256 acres; hotel, camping, fishing.
NORMANGEE STATE PARK: 500 acres; cabins.
PALMETTO STATE PARK: 320 acres; camping, swimming, fishing.
PALO DURO STATE PARK: 15,103 acres; hotel, cabins, camping, riding.
POSSUM KINGDOM STATE PARK: 6969 acres; hotel, cabins, camping, fishing, boating.
SAM HOUSTON HISTORIC SITE: 15 acres. Memorial.
SAN JACINTO HISTORIC SITE: 445 acres.
STATE FOREST NO. 1: 1700 acres; cabins, camping.
STATE FOREST NO. 3: 2360 acres; cabins, camping.
STEPHEN F. AUSTIN STATE PARK: 671 acres; fishing.
THE ALAMO HISTORIC SITE: 3 acres.
THIRTY-SIXTH DIVISION STATE PARK: 538 acres; hotel, cabins, camping, swimming, fishing, boating.
TYLER STATE PARK: 985 acres; hotel, swimming, fishing, boating.

Utah

Parks, 4. Total area, 85 acres.

JACOB HAMLIN STATE PARK: Undeveloped.
OLD STATE HOUSE STATE PARK: Historical.
"THIS IS THE PLACE" STATE PARK: 85 acres. Monument.
VERNAL STATE PARK: Museum.

Vermont

Parks, 21; forests, 9. Total area, 63,076 acres.

AINSWORTH STATE PARK: 432 acres.
ALLIS STATE PARK: 335 acres; camping.
ASCUTNEY STATE PARK: 1530 acres; camping.
BELLEVUE HILL STATE PARK: 69 acres. Skiing.
CALVIN COOLIDGE STATE FOREST: 9545 acres; camping.

CAMEL'S HUMP STATE FOREST: 7278 acres; Skiing.
CRYSTAL LAKE STATE PARK: 15 acres; swimming.
DARLING STATE PARK: 1747 acres. Skiing. Camping.
ELMORE STATE PARK: 785 acres; swimming, boating.
GIFFORD WOODS STATE PARK: 39 acres; camping.
GRAFTON STATE FOREST: 240 acres; camping.
GRANVILLE GULF STATE PARK: 1060 acres. Scenic. Camping.
GROTON STATE FOREST: 15,300 acres; camping, swimming, fishing.
HAZEN'S NOTCH STATE PARK: 60 acres. Scenic.
JAMAICA STATE PARK: 12 acres; swimming.
MAIDSTONE STATE FOREST: 405 acres; swimming.
MOLLY STARK STATE PARK: 148 acres. Scenic.
MONROE STATE PARK: 200 acres.
MOUNT MANSFIELD STATE FOREST: 20,994 acres; camping.
MOUNT PHILO STATE PARK: 160 acres. Scenic. Camping.
PROCTOR-PIPER STATE FOREST: 1487 acres.
ST. ALBANS BAY STATE PARK: 45 acres; swimming, boating.
SAND BAR STATE PARK: 10 acres; camping, swimming, fishing, boating.
THETFORD HILL STATE FOREST: 260 acres. Scenic.
TOWNSHEND STATE FOREST: 700 acres; camping.
WILGUS STATE PARK: 1530 acres; camping.

Virginia

Parks, 9; recreational areas, 5; waysides, 29. Total area, 26,576 acres.

BEAR CREEK RECREATIONAL AREA: 70 acres; swimming, fishing, boating.
DOUTHAT STATE PARK: 4493 acres; hotel, cabins, camping, swimming, fishing, boating, riding.
FAIRY STONE STATE PARK: 5027 acres; hotel, cabins, camping, swimming, fishing, boating.
GOODWYN LAKE RECREATIONAL AREA: 50 acres; swimming, fishing.
HOLLIDAY LAKE RECREATIONAL AREA: 190 acres; camping, swimming, boating.
HUNGRY MOTHER STATE PARK: 2134 acres; hotel, cabins, camping, swimming.
POCAHONTAS STATE PARK: 7605 acres; camping, swimming, fishing, boating, riding.
PRINCE EDWARD RECREATIONAL AREA: 30 acres; swimming, fishing.
SEASHORE STATE PARK: 2696 acres; cabins, swimming, fishing.
STAUNTON RIVER STATE PARK: 1254 acres; cabins, swimming.
WESTMORELAND STATE PARK: 1282 acres; cabins, swimming, fishing, boating.

Washington

Parks, 59; recreational areas, 6; historic sites, 3; scientific sites, 3; waysides, 9. Total area, 47,831 acres.

BEACON ROCK STATE PARK: 3206 acres; extinct volcano.
BOGACHIEL STATE PARK: 123 acres; camping, fishing.
BRIDLE TRAILS STATE PARK: 368 acres; riding.
BUSH PIONEER PACIFIC STATE PARK: 42 acres; camping.
DECEPTION PASS STATE PARK: 1724 acres; camping, swimming, fishing, boating.
DRY FALLS STATE PARK: 2200 acres. Scenic.
FIELDS SPRING STATE PARK: 93 acres; camping.
GINKGO PETRIFIED FOREST STATE PARK: 5980 acres.
ILWACO STATE PARK: 97 acres.
LAKE CHELAN STATE PARK: 140 acres; camping, swimming, fishing, boating.
LAKE SYLVIA STATE PARK: 234 acres; camping, swimming, fishing.
LARRABEE STATE PARK: 1350 acres; camping, swimming, fishing.
LEWIS AND CLARK STATE PARK: 530 acres; camping.
MILLERSYLVANIA STATE PARK: 765 acres; camping, swimming.
MORAN STATE PARK: 4804 acres; camping, swimming, fishing, boating.
MOUNT SPOKANE STATE PARK: 15,858 acres; camping.
PALOUSE FALLS STATE PARK: 95 acres. Undeveloped.
PEND O'REILLE STATE PARK: 393 acres; camping.
RAINBOW FALLS STATE PARK: 116 acres; camping.
RIVERSIDE STATE PARK: 5380 acres; camping, riding.
SALTWATER STATE PARK: 86 acres; camping, swimming.
SEQUIM BAY STATE PARK: 73 acres; camping, swimming, fishing.
TWANOH STATE PARK: 210 acres; camping, swimming.
TWIN HARBOR BEACH STATE PARK: 47 acres; camping, swimming.
WENATCHEE STATE PARK: 297 acres; camping.
ZILLAH STATE PARK: 87 acres.

West Virginia

Parks, 15; forests, 7; waysides, 8. Total area, 94,486 acres.

AUDRA STATE PARK: 316 acres.
BABCOCK STATE PARK: 3231 acres; hotel, cabins, swimming, fishing.
BLACKWATER FALLS STATE PARK: 446 acres; fishing.
CABWAYLINGS STATE FOREST: 6167 acres; cabins, fishing.
CACAPON STATE PARK: 5812 acres; hotel, cabins, swimming, fishing.
CARNIFAX FERRY STATE PARK: 275 acres. Historical.
CATHEDRAL STATE PARK: 118 acres.
COOPERS ROCK STATE FOREST: 12,973 acres; camping.
DROOP MOUNTAIN BATTLEFIELD STATE PARK: 265 acres; cabins.
GRANDVIEW STATE PARK: 52 acres. Scenic.
GREENBRIAR STATE FOREST: 5400 acres; cabins, riding.
HAWKES NEST STATE PARK: 142 acres. Scenic. Museum.
HOLLY RIVER STATE PARK: 7320 acres; cabins, swimming, fishing.
KANAWHA STATE FOREST: 6705 acres; camping.

KUMBRABOW STATE FOREST: 9425 acres; camping, swimming.
LOST RIVER STATE PARK: 3841 acres; hotel, cabins, swimming, fishing.
PANTHER CREEK STATE FOREST: 7724 acres; camping, swimming.
PINNACLE ROCK STATE PARK: 32 acres. Scenic.
SENECA STATE FOREST: 11,050 acres; cabins, swimming, fishing, boating.
TOMLISON RIVER STATE PARK: 1351 acres; camping, fishing, boating.
TYGART LAKE STATE PARK: 1775 acres.
WATOGA STATE PARK: 10,052 acres; cabins, swimming, riding.

Wisconsin

Parks, 21; forests, 8; waysides 124. Total area, 272,372 acres.

BRUNET ISLAND STATE PARK: 179 acres; camping, swimming, fishing, boating.
CASTLE MOUND ROADSIDE PARK: 222 acres; camping.
COPPER FALLS STATE PARK: 1200 acres; camping.
CUSHING STATE PARK: 9 acres. Memorial. Camping.
DEVILS LAKE STATE PARK: 2369 acres; Golf. Cabins, camping, swimming, fishing.
FIRST CAPITOL STATE PARK: 2 acres.
INTERSTATE STATE PARK: 581 acres; camping, swimming.
MERRICK STATE PARK: 124 acres; Golf. Camping, swimming.
NELSON DEWEY STATE PARK: 720 acres; camping.
NEW GLARUS WOODS STATE PARK: 43 acres; camping.
OJIBWA ROADSIDE PARK: 353 acres; camping, fishing.
PATTISON STATE PARK: 1160 acres; camping, swimming.
PENINSULA STATE PARK: 3649 acres; camping, swimming, boating.
PERROT STATE PARK: 937 acres; camping, fishing.
POTAWATOMI STATE PARK: 1046 acres; camping, fishing.
RIB MOUNTAIN STATE PARK: 494 acres; camping.
ROCKY ARBOR ROADSIDE PARK: 228 acres; camping.
TERRY ANDRAE STATE PARK: 167 acres; camping, swimming.
TOWER HILL STATE PARK: 108 acres; camping.
WYALUSING STATE PARK: 1671 acres; camping.

Wyoming

Parks, 3; battlefields, 1. Total area, 1356 acres.

FORT BRIDGER STATE PARK: 31 acres. Frontier fort.
HOT SPRINGS STATE PARK: 900 acres; hotel, cabins, swimming.
SARATOGA HOT SPRINGS STATE PARK: 420 acres; hotel, cabins.

Supreme Court
See Justices of the United States Supreme Court

Swords, Some Famous

ANGURVARDEL: (Icel. a stream of anguish) Sword of Frithiof, hero of the Icelandic saga transcribed by the Swedish poet, Bishop Tegner, as *Frithjof's Saga.*
ARONDIGHT: Sword of Launcelot of the Lake.
AZOTH: Sword of Paracelsus (Browning's *Paracelsus*, Bk. V).
BALISARDO: In Ariosto's *Orlando Furioso*, the sword made by the witch, Falerina, with which she intended to bring about Orlando's death; Balisardo was so potent that it could cut even enchanted objects; it became the weapon of Ruggiero.
BALMUNG: One of the swords of Siegfried in the *Nibelungenlied*, sometimes identified with Mimung; as a boy, Siegfried is said to have forged Balmung at a smithy deep within the forest, but the same sword is also said to have been one used by Wieland in his contest with Amilias when the latter was cut apart clear down from his helmet to his waist and did not know he was even wounded until he tried to stand up. See also Mimung.
CALIBURN: Another name of Excalibur (which see).
CHRYSAOR (SWORD AS GOOD AS GOLD): Artegal's sword (Spenser's *The Faërie Queene*).
COLADA: One of the dazzling golden-hilted swords of the Cid. See also Tizona.
CORROUGE: In the romances of chivalry, the sword of Sir Otuel, the haughty Saracen nephew of Ferragus (Ferracute), who was miraculously converted to Christianity and married the daughter of Charlemagne.
COURTAIN: (Fr. the short sword). One of the swords of Ogier the Dane (Ogier le Danois), hero of an old French romance who also appears in Ariosto's *Orlando Furioso*; he is identified with Holger Danske, the national hero of Denmark. See also Sauvagine.
CURTANA: The blunted sword of Edward the Confessor, a symbol of mercy, which is carried in the coronation processions before the kings of England between the swords of justice temporal and justice spiritual.
DURANDAL: (Probably from Fr. *dur*, hard, *durer*, to resist). The magic sword of Orlando (Roland), hero of French romances and of Orlando Furioso, with which he struck the crest of the Pyrenees and opened, with a single blow, the famous Breche de Roland, a deep defile 200-300 feet wide and 300-600 feet deep. Also written Durandart, Durandal, Durandana, Durindane, Durindale, Durindiana, Durenda, Durendal, Durlindana.
EXCALIBUR: The sword of King Arthur. (Ex cal [ce] liber [are], to liberate from the stone.)
FLAMBERGE OR FLOBERGE: (the flamecutter). One of the swords of Charlemagne; Rinaldo and the enchanter, Maligigi (or Maugis), cousins and heroes of the cycle of chivalric literature, and paladins of Charlemagne, each also possessed a sword with the same name.
FOOT-BREADTH: Sword of Thoralf Skolinson the Strong, companion of Hako I of Norway, distinguished for his bravery and strength. See also Quern-biter.
GLORIOUS: In the romances of chivalry, the sword with which Oliver (Olivier), one of the twelve peers of Charlemagne, hacked to shreds the nine swords made by Ansias, Galas, and Munifican.

GRAM: (grief). In the *Nibelungenlied*, one of the swords of Siegfried. See also Balmung, Mimung.

GREYSTEEL: The sword of Koll the Thrall.

HAUTE-CLAIRE: (very bright). Name given to the swords of Oliver and Closamont. See also Glorious.

JOYEUSE, LA: (Lat. *gaudiosa*). One of the swords of Charlemagne, which Galas spent three years in making; it was inscribed: *Decem praeceptorum custos Carolus.*

MERVEILLEUSE: (Fr. wonderful). In an old French romance of chivalry, the whistle-sharp sword of the hero, Doolin of Mayence; when stood on end, mere weight was enough to drive the keen blade through the tripod beneath the sword.

MIMUNG: A wonderful sword lent to Siegfried by Wittich, sometimes identified with Balmung.

MORGLAY: (Celt. mor, mawr, large, great, and glaif, a crooked sword. Claymore, or glaymore, derives from the word). The sword of Sir Bevis of Southhampton (Bevis of Hampton, a famous knight whose deeds are recorded in the second book of Michael Drayton's *Polylobion* (1612, 1622); he is the Beuves de Hantone of the French, and the Buovo d'Antona of the Italians; Morglay was so famous that it became a general name for a sword.

NAGELRING: (nail-ring). Sword of Dietrich of Bern (Theodoric the Great), who appears in many Middle High German romances, and especially in the *Niebelungenlied*.

PHILIPPAN: Sword of Marc Antony.

QUERN-BITER: Sword of Hako I, the Good, of Norway, with which he hewed a millstone in half. See also Foot-breadth.

SANGLAMORE: (the great and bloody) Sword of Braggadochio, the braggart, who typifies the Intemperate Tongue in *The Faërie Queene*, by Edmund Spenser.

SAUVAGINE: (the relentless). The sword of Ogier the Dane, on which, as on Courtain, Munifican the smith worked for three years. See also Courtain.

SCHRIT (OR SCHRITT) (? THE LOPPER): Biterolf's sword.

TIZONA: (the poker). One of the swords of the Cid, taken by the hero from King Bucar; like its companion-sword, Colada, it also had a hilt of gold. See Colada.

TRANCHERA: (It., from Fr. trancher, to cut). In Bojardo's *Orlando Innamorato*, the sword of Agricane, the fabulous king of Tartary, who besieges Angelica in the castle of Albracca, and is slain by Orlando in single combat.

WASKE: Sword of Iring.

WELSUNG: Sword of Sintram, hero of Baron La Motte Fouqué's German romance *Sintram and His Companions*, a tale of medieval Europe suggested by Albert Durer's engraving of the Knight, Death, and Satan; another German knight, Dietlieb, also had a sword named Welsung.

ZUFLAGER: Sword of Ali, cousin and son-in-law of Mohammed, whose beautiful eyes inspired the Persian accolade, *Ayn Hali, the eyes of Ali,* an expression reserved for things of surpassing beauty.

Symbolism
See Animals in Symbolism; Apostles and Their Appropriate Symbols; Colors; Religious A lusions, References, and Symbols; Flowers,

Plants, Leaves and Their Symbolic Meanings; Horses; Planets and Their Symbolic Gems; Saints; Swords.

Symphony Orchestra: Typical Composition
See also Oriental Orchestra: Typical Composition

STRINGS: 12-14 first violins, 10-12 second violins, 8-10 violas, 6-8 cellos, 4-6 double basses.

WOODWINDS: 2 flutes, 2 oboes, 2 clarinets, 2 bassoons.

BRASS: 2 trumpets, 2 or 4 horns, 2 or 3 trombones, 1 tuba.

PERCUSSION: 2 or 3 kettledrums and various instruments of definite pitch (glockenspiel, bells, xylophone) and indefinite pitch (snare drum, bass drum, cymbals, triangle).

HARPS: 2 or 1 (2 are called for more often than 1).

A larger orchestra would have this typical composition:

STRINGS: 16 first violins, 14 second violins, 12 violas, 10 cellos, 8 double basses.

WOODWINDS: 2 flutes and piccolo, 2 oboes and English horn, 2 clarinets and bass clarinet, 2 bassoons and contrabassoon.

BRASS: 3 trumpets, 4 horns, 3 trombones, 1 tuba.

PERCUSSION AND HARPS: As before.

Titles
See Rulers, Titles of

Trade, World
See Products of the World: Their Origins and Uses

Trails, Famous American
See also National Parkways

APPALACHIAN TRAIL: Completed in 1937, extends 2050 miles along the crest of the Appalachian Range from Mount Katahdin in Maine to Mount Oglethorpe in Georgia; the route, completely marked, traverses eight national forests and two national parks.

BOSTON POST ROAD: The mail and communication route in the New England Colonies, it is said to have started operations in January, 1673, when a mounted postman left New York and rode for three weeks until he reached Boston, on a mission described as an early version of a good-will tour; regular service began somewhat later, and was scheduled as a twice-weekly relay, with a rider from Boston and a rider from New York meeting midway and exchanging mail pouches.

CALIFORNIA TRAIL: Route of the '49ers followed the Oregon and Mormon trails to the Snake River in Idaho, then veered southward into the "California Trail" into the foothills of California.

CHISHOLM TRAIL: Route of the cattle-drivers between San Antonio, Texas, and Abilene, Kansas; it was blazed in 1865, after the close of the Civil War, when Texas began to build a cattle industry to supply Eastern markets with beef, and continued in use for 20 years, or until the general fencing-in of the grazing lands.

CUMBERLAND ROAD: Approved by Congress in 1807 as the first U.S. highway to be built with federal funds; begun at Cumberland, Maryland, in 1811, it cut the southwest corner of Pennsylvania, and eventually crossed Ohio, Indiana, and Illinois to the Mississippi River, carrying the main traffic in trade between the west and east.

ERIE CANAL: Officially opened by Governor De Witt Clinton of New York in 1825, immediately became the chief freight route between Buffalo and Albany, New York; it made New York City the major American port, greatly cut the freight rate on goods from the west, and paid off an original investment of $7 million within ten years.

LANCASTER PIKE: Two years in building, opened in 1794 as the first American road constructed according to plan; it ran for 62 miles between Philadelphia and Lancaster, Pennsylvania, and was a major stage in the transfer of passengers and goods between the Ohio Valley and the coast.

LITTLE RIVER TURNPIKE: After 1785, a major toll road in northern Virginia and the principal route for western produce on the way to Alexandria; extended from Aldie, on the Little River, to Snickers Gap, near Winchester, early in the nineteenth century; it continued in use, as a dual toll road, until 1896.

MORMON TRAIL: Nauvoo, Indiana, to Salt Lake City, Utah, 1300 miles, the route taken by Brigham Young when he led the Latter-day Saints to the west.

NATCHEZ-TRACE: Ran for 500 miles between Natchez, on the Mississippi River, and Nashville, Tennesee, and was the overland return route of traders who poled and floated cargoes down the Mississippi to New Orleans; since the flatboats could not return upstream against the current, they were sold for their lumber, and the crews took to the land on the way home; the Natchez Trace flourished barely a quarter-century, and was obsolete by 1830, when the steamboat made the double effort of the traders unnecessary, but legend and literature have increased its fame and it appears with undiminished vitality as a backdrop in many of the recent stories of Eudora Welty.

OREGON TRAIL: Blazed by 800 pioneers who set out from Independence, Missouri, in May, 1843, to try their luck in the new west lands described so glowingly in the accounts of Lewis and Clark; it is estimated that they were followed by a half-million settlers before the Oregon Trail receded into the continental chain of highways as part of U.S. 30.

PACIFIC CREST TRAIL: The Pacific Crest Trail system, which will eventually stretch 2265 miles from Canada to Mexico through Washington, Oregon, and California, traverses 19 national forests and half a dozen national parks. Although there is not yet a connected trail along the entire route, several sections have been completed.

SANTA FE TRAIL: Cut by William Bicknell, of Independence, Missouri, who established a trading route to the Mexican settlements of the Southwest; he began his trek after 1821, when Mexico had won independence from Spain, and the Spanish embargo on foreign trade ended; the route was used

for fifty years, until it could no longer compete with the railroads.

WILDERNESS ROAD: Cut through the forests between Cumberland Gap and Boonesboro, and later extended to the falls of the Ohio River, it followed a natural route, used in turn by the buffalo, the Indians, and the pioneers, Daniel Boone is credited with an original trail which the route later followed. The opening of the Wilderness Road in 1775 established a path through Kentucky and the West and stepped up the pace of westward migration.

OLD SPANISH TRAIL: Established by Spanish conquistadores and missionaries who pushed west out of St. Augustine, Florida, skirted the Gulf, and followed the Rio Grande to El Paso, where they were joined by soldiers and settlers from Mexico, who helped them to continue the route to Santa Fe.

Trees, American

ACACIA *ACACIA* (FAMILY LEGUMINOSAE): Emory acacia; sweet acacia; catclaw acacia; Wright acacia. Range: sweet acacia is widely cultivated and naturalized from Florida to Louisiana, in central and western Texas, and in southern California; the other species are found in the southwestern states, particularly in Texas.

ACHRAS *ACHRAS* (FAMILY SAPOTACEAE): Wild-dilly; sapodilla. In the U.S., the achras tree grows only in Florida.

AILANTHUS *AILANTHUS* (FAMILY SIMAROUBACEAE): Ailanthus; tree-of-heaven. Range: a native of China, the ailanthus is cultivated and widely naturalized as a "weed" tree throughout the U.S.

ALDER *ALNUS* (FAMILY BETULACEAE): European alder; seaside alder; Arizona alder; white alder; red alder; speckled alder; hazel alder; Sitka alder; thinleaf alder. Range: European, seaside, speckled, and hazel alder are Eastern species. The others range in the West from New Mexico to Alaska.

ANISE-TREE *ILLICIUM* (FAMILY MAGNOLIACEAE): Florida anise-tree; yellow anise-tree. Range: the Florida anise-tree grows in the Gulf States from Florida to Louisiana. The yellow anise-tree is local in eastern Florida.

APPLE *MALUS* (FAMILY ROSACEAE): Southern crap apple; sweet crab aple; Oregon crab apple; Baltimore crab apple; prairie crab apple; bigfruit crab apple; apple; Soulard crab apple. Range: species of apple tree occur generally throughout the U.S.

ARALIA *ARALIA* (FAMILY ARALIACEAE): Devil's walking-stick. Range: devil's walking-stick is widely distributed throughout the East and Midwest, as far south as Oklahoma and Texas. Other species are local and rare.

ASH *FRAXINUS* (FAMILY OLEACEA): White ash; singleleaf ash (typical); Lowell ash; Berlandier ash; Carolina ash; fragrant ash; fragrant ash (typical); Goodding ash; Gregg ash; Oregon ash; black ash; Chihuahua ash; green ash; pumpkin ash; blue ash; Texas ash; velvet ash. Range: species of ash are found everywhere in the U.S.

ASPEN: See Cottonwood.

BACCHARIS (SEA-MYRTLE) *BACCHARIS* (FAMILY COMPOSITAE): Baccharis; eastern baccharis. Range: the eastern baccharis ranges along the Coastal Plain.

BALDCYPRESS *TAXODIUM* (FAMILY PI-

NACEAE): Baldcypress; baldcypress (typical); pondcypress; Montezuma baldcypress. Range: baldcypress (typical) ranges through the states of the Coastal Plain and Mississippi Valley, and is rare in New York and New Jersey. The other species belong to the Coastal Plain and the Southwest.

BASSWOOD (LINDEN) *TILIA* (FAMILY TILIACEAE): American basswood; Carolina basswood; Florida basswood; white basswood. Range: species of basswood occur generally throughout the U.S.

BAYBERRY *MYRICA* (FAMILY MYRICACEAE): Pacific bayberry; southern bayberry; evergreen bayberry; odorless bayberry; northern bayberry. Range: species of bayberry grow along the Atlantic and Pacific coasts of the U.S.

BEECH *FAGUS* (FAMILY FAGACEAE): American beech. Range: Maine to Texas.

BIRCH *BETULA* (FAMILY BETULACEAE): Yellow birch; blueleaf birch; Yukon birch; Horne birch; sweet birch; river birch; water birch; paper birch; paper birch (typical); western paper birch; mountain paper birch; Alaska paper birch; Kenai birch; northwestern paper birch; gray birch; Purpus birch; Sandberg birch. Range: Yukon birch, Alaska paper birch, and Kenai birch grow in Alaska and Canada. Other species of birch are widely distributed throughout the U.S., especially in mountainous states of the Northeast and Northwest.

BLADDERNUT *STAPHYLEA* (FAMILY STAPHYLEACEAE): Sierra bladdernut; American bladdernut. Range: Sierra bladdernut is a California species; American bladdernut occurs in the eastern half of the U.S. from Michigan and Minnesota, to Georgia and Alabama.

BLUEBERRY *VACCINIUM* (FAMILY ERICACEAE): Tree sparkleberry. Range: southeast Virginia west to Kansas and Missouri, south to Texas and Florida.

BUCKEYE *AESCULUS* (FAMILY HIPPOCASTANACEAE): Texas buckeye; California buckeye; Ohio buckeye; yellow buckeye; red buckeye; painted buckeye. Range: Texas and California buckeye are generally restricted to those states. Ohio buckeye ranges the midwest from western Pennsylvania to Oklahoma. Yellow, red, and painted buckeye grow generally throughout the south Atlantic states.

BUCKTHORN *RHAMNUS* (FAMILY RHAMNACEAE): Birchleaf buckthorn; California buckthorn; Carolina buckthorn; hollyleaf buckthorn; great redberry buckthorn; glossy buckthorn; cascara buckthorn. Range: species of buckthorn occur generally throughout the U.S.

BUCKWHEAT-TREE *CLIFTONIA* (FAMILY CYRILLACEAE): Buckwheat-tree. Range: the Coastal Plain: South Carolina, northwest Florida, Georgia, and west to Louisiana.

BUFFALOBERRY *SHEPHERDIA* (FAMILY ELAEAGNACEAE): Silver buffaloberry. Range: Silver buffaloberry belongs to the western half of the U.S. from North Dakota to Arizona and New Mexico, and west to the coast.

BUMELIA *BUMELIA LANUGINOSA* (FAMILY SAPOTACEAE): Gum bumelia (typical); buckthorne bumelia; saffron-plum; tough bumelia. Range: these species of bumelia belong, generally, to the South, but buckthorn bumelia grows in southern Illinois and southern Indiana.

BURSERA *BURSERA* (FAMILY BURSERACEAE): Fragrant bursera; elephanttree; gumbo-limbo. Range: Gumbo-limbo grows in south Florida; fragrant bursera is exclusive and rare in southern Arizona (Pima County); the elephanttree grows throughout the desert mountains of Arizona and California.

BUTTONBUSH *CEPHALANTHUS* (FAMILY RUBIACEAE): Common buttonbush. Range: generally throughout the U.S.

CALIFORNIA-LAUREL *UMBRELLULARIA* (FAMILY LAURACEAE): California-laurel. Range: West Coast Ranges and Sierra Nevada from Oregon to California.

CAMPHOR-TREE: See Cinnamon.

CATALPA *CATALPA* (FAMILY BIGNONIACEAE): Southern catalpa; northern catalpa. Range Southern catalpa is, despite its name, found from southern New England to Texas. Northern catalpa ranges throughout the Midwest.

CEDAR: See Juniper.

CERCOCARPUS (MOUNTAIN MAHOGANY) *CERCOCARPUS* (FAMILY ROSACEAE): Birchleaf cercocarpus; birchleaf cercocarpus (typical); alderleaf cercocarpus; Catalina cercocarpus; hairy cercocarpus; curlleaf cercocarpus. Range: the West, generally.

CEREUS (SAGUARO) *CEREUS* (FAMILY CACTACEAE): Saguaro. Range: the saguaro is the giant, branched cactus of the Arizona and California deserts.

CHERRY: See Prunus.

CHESTNUT (CHINKAPIN) *CASTANEA* (FAMILY FAGACEAE): Alabama chinkapin; Florida chinkapin; American chestnut; chinknut; Ozark chinkapin; Allegheny chinkapin; Ashe chinkapin; golden chinkapin. Range: golden chinkapin is the only one of these species of chestnut that is found in the Far West. Other species range from Maine to Texas.

CHINABERRY *MELIA* (FAMILY MELIACEAE): Chinaberry. Range: a native of Himalaya, the chinaberry has been naturalized in southeastern U.S. and west through Texas, Oklahoma, and California.

CHINKAPIN: See Chestnut.

CINNAMON (CAMPHOR-TREE) *CINNAMOMUM* (FAMILY LAURACEAE): Camphortree. Range: a native of tropical Asia, widely cultivated in tropics around the world, the camphor-tree is naturalized in Florida, and has escaped from cultivation from Florida to Louisiana.

CITRUS *CITRUS* (FAMILY RUTACEAE): Lime; sour orange; lemon; citron; sweet orange. Range: all of these species are widely cultivated in tropical and subtropical regions.

CLETHRA *CLETHRA* (FAMILY CLETHRACEAE): Cinnamon clethra. Range: the mountains of the South.

CLIFFROSE *COWANIA* (FAMILY ROSACEAE): Cliffrose. Range: a western tree.

COFFEETREE *GYMNOCLADUS* (FAMILY LEGUMINOSAE): Kentucky coffeetree. Range: covers a broad area bounded by New York, Minnesota, Oklahoma, and Virginia.

CONDALIA *CONDALIA* (FAMILY RHAMNACEAE): Bitter condalia; bluewood. Range: bitter condalia grows in desert mountains of Arizona and California; bluewood in Texas.

CORALBEAN *ERYTHRENA* (FAMILY LEGUMINOSAE): Southwestern coralbean; eastern coralbean. Range: species of coralbean are found in southern and southwestern states.

COTTONWOOD; POPLAR *POPULUS* (FAMILY SALICACEAE): Lanceleaf cottonwood; narrowleaf cottonwood; balsam poplar; balsam poplar (typical); heartleaf balsam poplar; eastern cottonwood; Fremont cotton-

wood; Fremont cottonwood (typical); Rio Grande cottonwood; bigtooth aspen; swamp cottonwood; Palmer cottonwood; Parry cottonwood; quaking aspen; black cottonwood. Range: species of cottonwood occur generally throughout the U.S.
CYPRESS *CUPRESSUS* (FAMILY PINACEAE): Arizona cypress; Modoc cypress; Gowen cypress; Tecate cypress; McNab cypress; Monterey cypress; Range: each of these species grows in California; Arizona cypress is found in Texas, New Mexico, and Arizona; Modoc cypress grows in southwest Oregon.
DESERTWILLOW *CHILOPSIS* (FAMILY BIGNONIACEAE): Desertwillow. Range: throughout the Southwest.
DOGWOOD *CORNUS* (FAMILY CORNACEAE): Alternate-leaf dogwood; roughleaf dogwood; flowering dogwood; Pacific dogwood; western dogwood; blackfruit dogwood; red-osier dogwood; stiffcornel dogwood. Range: species of dogwood are found throughout the U.S.
DOUGLAS-FIR PSEUDOTSUGA (FAMILY PINACEAE): Bigcone Douglas-fir; Douglas-fir; Douglas-fir (typical). Range: Douglas-fir occurs in western U.S.
ELDER *SAMBUCUS* (FAMILY CAPRIFOLIACEAE): Pacific red elder; American elder; blueberry elder; blackbeard elder; Mexican elder; Florida elder; velvet elder; Range: species of elder occur generally throughout the U.S.
ELM *ULMUS* (FAMILY ULMACEAE): Winged elm; American elm; American elm (typical); Florida elm; cedar elm; Siberian elm; slippery elm; September elm; rock elm. Range: species of elm occur generally throughout the U.S., except in the Far West.
EUONYMUS *EUONYMOUS* (FAMILY CELASTRACEAE): Eastern wahoo; western wahoo; Range: these 2 species of euonymus are widely distributed, the first in the eastern states, the second in California, Oregon, Washington, and Sierra Nevada.
FIG *FICUS* (FAMILY MORACEAE): Florida strangler fig; common fig; shortleaf fig. Range: the common fig, escaped from cultivation, grows naturally in the Coastal Plain from Virginia to Florida and Texas, north to Arkansas and Tennessee. The other species are restricted to Florida.
FIR *ABIES* (FAMILY PINACEAE): Pacific silver fir; balsam fir; bracted balsam fir; Fraser fir; grand fir; subalpine fir (typical); corkbark fir; california red fir; Shasta red fir; noble fir. Range: species of fir, a mountain tree, are found from coast to coast in the U.S. and in Alaska.
FORESTIERA *FORESTIERA* (FAMILY OLEACEAE): Swamp-priver; desert-olive forestiera; Florida-privet; Texas forestiera. Range: swamp-privet is the most widely distributed of these species, ranging from Florida to southern Indiana, and west to Texas.
FRINGETREE *CHIONANTHUS* (FAMILY OLEACEAE): Fringetree. Range: from New Jersey to Texas, and, in the South, eastward to Florida.
GORDONIA (LOBLOLLY-BAY) *GORDONIA* (FAMILY THEACEAE): Loblolly-bay, Range: along the Coastal Plain from North Carolina to Mississippi.
HACKBERRY *CELTIS* (FAMILY ULMACEAE): Sugarberry; Lindheimer hackberry; hackberry; netleaf hackberry; Georgia hackberry. Range: species of hackberry are widely distributed throughout the U.S.
HACKMATACK: See Larch.

HAWTHORN *CRATAEGUS* (FAMILY ROSACEAE): St. Louis hawthorn; May hawthorn; Arnold hawthorn; Ashe hawthorn; barberryleaf hawthorn; Biltmore hawthorn; Boynton hawthorn; blueberry hawthorn; Brazoria hawthorn; pear hawthorn; Canada hawtnorn; Canby hawthorn; fireberry hawthorn; Kansas hawthorn; Cocks hawthorn; sandhill hawthorn; Columbia hawthorn; Dallas hawthorn; Dodge hawthorn; black hawthorn; Englemann hawthorn; Cerro hawthorn; St. Clair hawthorn; fanleaf hawthorn; yellow hawthorn; Jacksonville hawthorn; Gattinger hawthorn; Georgia hawthorn; Gregg hawthorn; Hannibal hawthorn; Harbison hawthorn; Holmes hawthorn; turkey hawthorn; Pensacola hawthorn; Mackenzie hawthorn; largeseed hawthorn; Margaret hawthorn; parsley hawthorn; Mohrs hawthorn; downy hawthorn; one-seed hawthorn; glossy hawthorn; Noel hawthorn; riverflat hawthorn; Palmer hawthorn; scarlet hawthorn; Pennsylvania hawthorn; prairie hawthorn; Washington hawthorn; Porter hawthorn; Pringle hawthorn; frosted hawthorn; dotted hawthorn; Putnam hawthorn; Ravenal hawthorn; Piedmont hawthorn; Reverchorn hawthorn; river hawthorn; Sabine hawthorn; willow hawthorn; Sargent hawthorn; pineland hawthorn; littlehip hawthorn; San Augustine hawthorn; fleshy hawthorn; Sutherland hawthorn; Opelousas hawthorn; Texas hawthorn; Tracy hawthorn; threeflower hawthorn; one-flower hawthorn; viburnum hawthorn; green hawthorn; Warner hawthorn; Williams hawthorn; Youngs hawthorn. Range: hawthorn has more species than any other U.S. tree, and much work remains before a list of species will be more than arbitrary. Here, only species that are definitely classified as trees, and not shrubs, are included. Many of them grow in restricted localities, but species of hawthorn are found throughout the U.S.
HAZEL (CALIFORNIA HAZEL) *CORYLUS* (FAMILY BETULACEAE): California hazel. Range: along the coasts of Washington and Oregon, and in the Coast Ranges and the Sierra Nevada to central California.
HEMLOCK *TSUGA* (FAMILY PINACEAE): Carolina hemlock; western hemlock; mountain hemlock. Range: western hemlock and mountain hemlock grow in the West, Carolina hemlock in the East.
HIBISCUS *HIBISCUS* (FAMILY MALVACEAE: Shrub-althea (rose-of-Sharon); sea hibiscus. Range: shrub-althea, a native of China and India, has escaped from cultivation in northeastern U.S., and now ranges south to Texas and Florida. Sea hibiscus grows in southern Florida.
HICKORY CARYA (FAMILY JUGLANDACEAE): Water hickory; Browns hickory; bitternut hickory; Demaree hickory; Dunbar hickory; scrub hickory; pignut hickory; pignut hickory; (typical); coast pignut hickory; pecan; shellback hickory; Laney hickory; bitter pecan; swamp hickory; Louisiana hickory; nutmeg hickory; Nussbaumer hickory; sand hickory; Schneck hickory; black hickory; mockernut hickory. Range: species of hickory are widely distributed throughout the U.S., but many grow in sharply restricted localities.
HOLLY *ILEX* (FAMILY AQUIFOLIACEAE): Carolina holly; Topel holly; dahoon; large gallberry; possumhaw; tawnyberry holly; smooth winterberry; Georgia holly; mountain winterberry; myrtle dahoon; American holly; American holly (typical); dune holly-common winterberry; yapon. Range: most

american species of holly grow in the South, along the Coastal Plain and to Texas. Smooth winterberry, mountain winterberry, and American holly range north to New England.

HONEYLOCUST (LOCUST) *GLEDETSIA* (FAMILY LEGUMINOSAE): Waterlocust, Texas honeylocust, honeylocust. Range: New England to Florida, and west to Texas and the Dakotas.

HOPHORNBEAM *OSTRYA* (FAMILY BETU-LACEAE): Knowlton hophornbeam; eastern hophornbeam. Range: eastern hophornbeam ranges from Maine to Texas; Knowlton hophornbeam is rare and local in the Southwest.

HOPTREE *PTELEA* (FAMILY RUTACEAE): Narrowleaf hoptree, common hoptree. Range: common hoptree occurs from New England to Texas; narrowleaf hoptree grows in the Southwest.

HORNBEAM (AMERICAN HORNBEAM) *CARPINUS* (FAMILY BETULACEAE): Range: widely distributed from Maine to Florida, and west to Texas.

INCENSE-CEDAR *LIBOCEDRUS* (FAMILY PINACEAE): Incense-cedar. Range: Pacific states and western Nevada.

JERUSALEM-THORN *PARKINSONIA* (FAMILY LEGUMINOSAE): Jerusalem-thorn. Range: the southern states from Florida to California.

JUJUBE *ZIZIPHUS* (FAMILY RHAMNACEAE): Common jujube. Range: escaped from cultivation, the common jujube, a native of southeast Europe and Asia, is naturalized from Alabama to Louisiana.

JUNIPER *JUNIPERUS* (FAMILY PINACEAE): Ashe juniper; California juniper; common juniper; alligator juniper; drooping juniper; one-seed-juniper; western juniper; Utah juniper; Pinchot juniper; Rocky Mountain juniper; southern redcedar; eastern redcedar. Range: southern redcedar grows in the Coastal Plain; eastern redcedar extends from Maine to Texas; the other species are found generally in the West.

KALMIA (MOUNTAIN LAUREL) *KALMIA* (FAMILY ERIACEAE): Mountain-laurel. Range: New England, the Midwest, and the South.

LARCH *LARIX* (FAMILY PINACEAE): Tamarack (hackmatack); subalpine larch; western larch. Range: the tamarack grows in the states bordering Canada and the Great Lakes, and locally in northern West Virginia and western Maryland. The other species belong to the Northwest.

LAUREL: See California-laurel; Kalmia.

LINDEN: See Basswood.

LOBLOLLY-BAY: See Gordonia.

LOCUST *ROBINIA* (FAMILY LEGUMINOSAE): Kelsey locust; New Mexican locust; black locust; clammy locust; clammy locust (typical); Hartwig locust. Range: New Mexican locust grows in the Southwest; the other species occur generally throughout the eastern half of the U.S.

LYONIA *LYONIA* (FAMILY ERICECEAE): Tree lyonia. Range: southeastern states.

MADRONE *ARBUTUS* (FAMILY ERIACEAE): Arizona madrone; Pacific madrone; Texas madrone. Range: species are found in the southwest and California.

MAGNOLIA *MAGNOLIA* (FAMILY MAGNOLIACEAE): Cucumbertree; yellow cucumbertree; Ashe magnolia; Fraser magnolia; southern magnolia; bigleaf magnolia; pyramid magnolia; umbrella magnolia; sweetbay. Range: umbrella magnolia grows in the Midwest and South; sweetbay follows the Coastal Plain from eastern Massachusetts to Texas.

Other species of magnolia are found in South.

MAPLE *ACER* (FAMILY ACERACEAE): Florida maple; vine maple; Rocky mountain maple; Douglas maple; bigtooth maple; Uvalde bigtooth maple; chalk maple; bigleaf maple; boxelder; black maple; striped maple; red maple (typical); Drummond red maple; silver maple; sugar maple; mountain maple. Range: The boxelder (also called ashleaf maple and Manitoba maple) occurs generally throughout the U.S. The Florida maple (or southern sugar maple) ranges from Virginia to eastern Texas, and north to Missouri. Vine maple, Rocky mountain maple, Douglas maple, bigtooth maple, chalk maple, and bigleaf maple are, generally, Western species follow the mountains of the East.

MESQUITE *PROSOPIS* (FAMILY LEGUMINOSAE): Mesquite; honey mesquite; western honey mesquite; velvet mesquite; screwbean mesquite. Range: the Southwest.

MOUNTAIN-ASH *SORBUS* (FAMILY ROSACEAE): American mountain-ash; European mountain-ash; showy mountain-ash; Sitka mountain-ash. Range: Sitka mountain-ash follows the mountains of the West, the other species follow the mountain of the East.

MOUNTAIN-LAUREL: See Kalmia.

MOUNTAIN-MAHOGANY: See Cercocarpus.

MULBERRY *MORUS* (FAMILY MORACEAE): White mulberry; Texas mulberry; black mulberry; red mulberry. Range: red mulberry ranges throughout the eastern half of the U.S. from Maine to Texas; the other species grow in the South.

OAK *QUERCUS* (FAMILY FAGACEAE): California live oak; white oak; Arizona white oak; Arkansas oak; Ashe oak; Albemarle oak; Beadle oak; Beaumont oak; Bebb oak; Bernard oak; swamp white oak; Bluffton oak; Bushes oak; Covington oak; caduca oak; Capesius oak; Chapman oak; canyon live oak; Palmer oak; scarlet oak; Compton oak; Carolina oak; Deam oak; Demaree oak; blue oak; California scrub oak; California scrub oak (typical); Alvord oak; McDonald oak; Durand oak; Durand oak (typical); Eggleston oak; northern pin oak; Emory oak; Englemann oak; Epling oak; shingleoin oak; southern red oak; southern red oak (typical); cherrybark oak; Faxon oak; Fernald oak; Fernow oak; Gambel oak; Gander oak; Garland oak; Oregon white oak; Georgia oak; Gifford oak; Chisos oak; Graves oak; gray oak; Guadalupe oak; Harbison oak; Hastings oak; Havard oak; Hawkins oak; Bartram oak; mounds oak; silverleaf oak; bear oak; shingle oak; bluejack oak; Livermore oak; Jacks oak; Jolon oak; Joor oak; California black oak; Lacey oak; turkey oak; laurel oak; Lea oak; California white oak; St. Landry oak; overcup oak; McNab oak; bur oak; blackjack oak; Mellichamp oak; swamp chestnut oak; Mohrs oak; oracle oak; Moulton oak; chinkapin oak; myrtle oak; Shumargra oak; Tharp live oak; water oak; Nuttall oak; Mexican blue oak; Oglethorpe oak; Organ Mountains oak; Fink oak; pin oak; willow oak; dwarf chinkapin oak; chestnut oak; sandpaper oak; sandpaper oak (typical); Vasey oak; Rehder oak; netleaf oak; Robbins oak; English oak; northern red oak; Rudkin oak; bottom oak; Saul oak; Schoch oak; Schuette oak; Shumard oak; Shumard oak (typical); Texas oak; Smalls oak; post oak; post oak (typical); sand post oak; Delta post oak; Stelloides oak; blackwater oak; Sterrett oak; substellata oak; Tharp oak; island live oak; Toumey oak; Towne oak; St.

Louis oak; shrub live oak; wavyleaf oak; black oak; live oak; live oak (typical); sand live oak; Walter oak; Willdenow oak; interior live oak. Range: species of oak occur generally throughout the U.S.

OLEANDER *NERIUM* (FAMILY APOCYNACEAE): Oleander. Range: the oleander has escaped from cultivation and is naturalized in the Gulf States from Florida to Texas.

OSAGE-ORANGE *MACLURA* (FAMILY MORACEAE): Osage-orange. Range: generally throughout the U.S.

OSMANTHUS *OSMANTHUS* (FAMILY OLEACEAE): Devilwood; bigfruit osmanthus. Range: Devilwood ranges through the states of the Coastal Plain; bigfruit osmanthus grows in central Florida.

PALMETTO *SABAL* (FAMILY PALMAE): Louisiana palmetto; cabbage palmetto; Texas palmetto. Range: palmettoes grow in the states of the Coastal Plain from North Carolina to Texas

PALOVERDE *CERCIDIUM* (FAMILY LEGUMINOSAE): Blue paloverde; border paloverde; yellow paloverde. Range: Texas, Arizona, and southeastern California.

PAPER-MULBERRY *BROUSSONETIA* (FAMILY MORACEAE): Paper-mulberry. Range: native of eastern Asia, the paper-mulberry, which supplies a bark used in paper-making, is naturalized in U.S. from New York to Missouri and southeastern Kansas, south to Texas and Florida.

PAULOWNIA *PAULOWNIA* (FAMILY BIGNONIACEAE): Royal Paulownia. Range: a native of China, Paulownia is cultivated and naturalized in the eastern, midwest, and southern states from Florida to Texas.

PAWPAW *ASIMINA* (FAMILY ANNONACEAE): Pawpaw. Range: eastern Texas to western New York, and south to Florida and Georgia.

PEACH: See Prunus.

PEAR *PYRUS* (FAMILY ROSACEAE): Pear. Range: pear is naturalized locally in the U.S. from Maine to Missouri, and from Texas to Florida.

PERSEA *PERSEA* (FAMILY LAURACEAE): Avocado (alligator-pear); redbay; silkbay; shorebay. Range: redbay ranges through the states of the Coastal Plain from Delaware to Texas; the other species grow in Florida.

PERSIMMON *DIOSPYROS* (FAMILY EBENACEAE): Texas persimmon; common persimmon. Range: Texas persimmon grows only in Texas in the U.S.; common persimmon ranges from New England through the Midwest to Texas, south to central Florida.

PINE *PINUS* (FAMILY PINACEAE): Whitebark pine; bristlecone pine; knobcone pine; foxtail pine; jack pine; Mexican pinyon; sand pine; lodgepole pine; Coulter pine; shortleaf pine; pinyon; slash pine; slash pine (typical); South Florida slash pine; Apache pine; limber pine; limber pine (typical); spruce pine; Jeffrey pine; sugar pine; Chihuahua pine; singleleaf pine; western white pine; bishop pine; longleaf pine; ponderosa pine; Arizona pine; Table-Mountain pine; Parry pinyon; Monterey pine; red pine; pitch pine; Digger pine; pond pine; Sonderegger pine; eastern white pine; Scotch pine; loblolly pine; Torrey pine; Virginia pine; Washoe pine; fishpoison-tree; Florida fishpoisin-tree. Range: species of pine occur generally throughout the U.S., though some are rare and local.

PLANERTREE (WATERELM) *PLANERA* (FAMILY ULMACEAE): Planertree. Range:

the states of the Coastal Plain, and in the Mississippi Valley.

PLUM: See Prunus.

POINCIANA *POINCIANA* (FAMILY LEGUMINOSAE): Paradise poinciana; Mexican poinciana; flowerfence. Range: flowerfence occurs in southern Florida; the other species grow in Texas and the Southwest.

POISON-SUMAC *TOXICODENDRON* (FAMILY ANACARDIACEAE): Poison-sumac. Range: widely throughout the eastern half of the U.S.

POPLAR: See Cottonwood.

PRICKLY-ASH *ZANTHOXYLUM* (FAMILY RUTACEAE): Common prickly-ash; Hercules-club; Hercules-club (typical); Biscayne prickley-ash; lime prickly-ash; yellowheart. Range: common prickly-ash grows generally in the northeast quarter of the U.S.; the other species grow in the Coastal Plain and Florida.

PRUNUS (CHERRY; PEACH; PLUM) *PRUNUS* (FAMILY ROSACEAE): Allegheny plum; American plum; inch plum; Chickasaw plum; mazzard; Carolina laurelcherry; sour cherry; garden plum; bitter cherry; desert apricot; hortulan plum; hollyleaf cherry; Bullace plum; Catalina cherry; Mahaleb cherry; Mexican plum; wildgoose plum; myrtle laurelcherry; Canada plum; pin cherry; peach; black cherry; black cherry (typical): **Alabama black cherry; Escarpment cherry; southwestern black cherry, sloe or blackthorn; Klamath plum; flatwoods plum; common chokecherry. Range: species occur generally throughout the U.S.

REDBUD *CERCIS* (FAMILY LEGUMINOSAE): Eastern redbud; Texas redbud; California redbud. Range: these 3 species have established the redbud throughout the U.S., and are named for the regions where they individually predominate.

RHODODENDRON *RHODODENDRON* (FAMILY ERICACEAE): Catawba rhododendron; Pacific rhododendron; rosebay rhododendron. Range: species of rhododendron are widely distributed throughout the U.S.

ROSE-OF-SHARON: See Hibiscus.

SAGEBRUSH ARTEMISIA (FAMILY COMPOSITAE): Big sagebrush. Range: generally throughout the West.

SAGUARO: See Cereus.

SAPIUM *SAPIUM* (FAMILY EUPHORBIACEAE): Jumping-bean sapium; Brazil sapium; tallowtree. Range: jumping-bean sapium, Maricopa and Pima counties, Arizona; Brazil sapium, northwestern Florida; tallowtree, Coastal Plain states, South Carolina to Louisiana.

SASSAFRAS *SASSAFRAS* (FAMILY LAURACEAE): Range: Sassafras covers the eastern half of the U.S. from Maine to Texas, east to Florida.

SAW-PALMETTO *SERENOA* (FAMILY PALMAE): Saw-palmetto. Range: through the states of the Coastal Plain from South Carolina to Louisiana.

SEA-MYRTLE: See Baccharis.

SEQUOIA *SEQUOIA* (FAMILY PINACEAE): Giant sequoia; redwood. Range: Giant sequoia grows in central California on the western slope of the Sierra Nevada; redwood, a coastal tree, grows from southwest Oregon to central California.

SERVICEBERRY *AMELANCHIER* (FAMILY ROSACEAE): Saskatoon serviceberry; downy serviceberry; Pacific serviceberry; inland serviceberry; Allegheny serviceberry; roundleaf serviceberry; Utah serviceberry. Range: the Utah serviceberry ranges through the West from Montana to Texas and New Mexico. The others belong to the northern tier of states, where species are found from coast to coast.

SILVERBELL *HALESIA* (FAMILY STYRACACEAE): Carolina silverbell; mountain silverbell; two-wing silverbell; little silverbell. Range: generally, the South.

SMOKETREE *COTINUS* (FAMILY ANACARDIACEAE): American smoketree. Range: rare and local in mountainous regions of Tennessee, Alabama, Missouri, Arkansas, and Oklahoma, the smoketree is common on Edwards Plateau in Texas, and is also found in Kentucky.

SNOWBELL (BIGLEAF SNOWBELL *STYRAX* (FAMILY STYRACECEAE): Bigleaf snowbell. Range: the Coastal Plain, southern Virginia to Louisiana, north to Arkansas.

SOAPBERRY *SAPINDUS* (FAMILY SAPINDACEAE): Western soapberry; Florida soapberry; wingleaf soapberry. Range: species of soapberry grow generally in the states of the South and the Southwest.

SOPHORA *SOPHORA* (FAMILY LEGUMINOSAE): Texas sophora; mescalbean. Range: Texas sophora grows from Louisiana to central Texas; the mescalbean ranges from eastern Texas to southeastern New Mexico.

SOURWOOD *OXYDENDRUM* (FAMILY ERICACEAE): Range: east as far as New Jersey, south to northern Florida, southeastern Louisiana.

SPRUCE *PICEA* (FAMILY PINACEAE): Brewer spruce; Engelmann spruce; white spruce; white spruce (typical); western white spruce; Porsild spruce; Lutz spruce; black spruce; blue spruce; red spruce; Sitka spruce. Range: species of spruce occur generally in the northern states of the U.S., particularly in rocky and mountanious regions.

STEWARTIA *STEWARTIA* (FAMILY THEACEAE): Virginia stewartia; mountain stewartia. Range: Virginia stewartia, states of the Coastal Plain, west to northern Mississippi; mountain stewartia, southern Appalachian Mountains.

SUMAC *RHUS* (FAMILY ANACARDIACEAE): Mearns sumac; shining sumac; smooth sumac; lemonade sumac; Kearney sumac; prairie sumac; laurel sumac; sugar sumac; staghorn sumac. Range: species of sumac occur generally throughout the U.S., especially smooth sumac, which apparently grows in every state.

SWEETGUM *LIQUIDAMBAR* (FAMILY HAMAMELIDACEAE): Sweetgum. Range: New England to eastern Texas and central Florida.

SWEETLEAF *SYMPLOCOS* (FAMILY SYMPLOCACEAE): Common sweetleaf. Range: states of the Coastal Plain from Delaware to Texas.

SYCAMORE *PLATANUS* (FAMILY PLATANACEAE): American sycamore; California sycamore; Arizona sycamore. Range: American sycamore ranges from Maine to Florida and central Texas; the other species are named for the regions where they occur.

TAMARACK: See Larch.

TAMARISK *TAMARIX* (FAMILY TAMARICACEAE): Smallflower tamarisk; five-stamen tamarisk. Range: smallflower tamarisk grows in southern California; five-stamen tamarisk is widely naturalized in southern and western U.S.

TANOAK *LITHOCARPUS* (FAMILY FAGACEAE): Tanoak. Range: the Pacific coast and in the Sierra Nevada.

THUJA *THUJA* (FAMILY PINACEAE):

Northern white-cedar; Oriental arborvitae; western redcedar. Range: northern white-cedar grows generally in the Northeast; Oriental arborvitae in Florida; western redcedar in Pacific Coast region.

TREE TOBACCO *NICOTIANA* (FAMILY SOLANACEAE): Tree tobacco. Range: a native of Argentina and Chile, occurs from Florida through Texas to California.

TUPELO *NYSSA* (FAMILY CORNACEAE): Water tupelo; Ogeechee tupelo; black tupelo or blackgum; black tupelo (typical); swamp tupelo or blackgum; bear tupelo. Range: water tupelo ranges through the southern states and northward in the Mississippi Valley to southern Illinois; black tupelo covers the entire East from Maine to Texas; the other species grow in the states of the Coastal Plain and in Florida.

VIBURNUM *VIBURNUM* (FAMILY CAPRIFOLIACEAE): Nannyberry; possumhaw viburnum; Walter viburnum; blackhaw; rusty blackhaw. Range: species of viburnum occur generally in the eastern half of the U.S., and nannyberry grows besides in the Black Hills of South Dakota, in Wyoming, and Colorado.

WAHOO: See Euonymus.

WALNUT *JUGLANS* (FAMILY JUGLANDACEAE): California walnut; butternut; Hinds walnut; Arizona walnut; little walnut; black walnut. Range: Butternut and black walnut grow in the Northeast, and range west and south to Wisconsin and Texas. The other species are found in California and in the Southwest.

WATERELM: See Planertree.

WASHINGTONIA *WASHINGTONIA* (FAMILY PALMAE): California washingtonia. Range: the canyons of the desert mountains of Arizona and California.

WHITE-CEDAR *CHAMAECYPARIS* (FAMILY PINACEAE): Port-Orford-cedar; Alaska cedar; Atlantic white-cedar. Range: Atlantic white-cedar grows throughout the Coastal Plain, and west to Mississippi. The other species belong to the Far West, western Canada, and Alaska.

WILLOW *SALIX* (FAMILY SALICACEAE): Feltleaf willow; white willow; Yakutat willow; peachleaf willow; littletree willow; weeping willow: Bebb willow; Bonpland willow; Coastal Plain willow; whiplash willow; Coulter willow; pussy willow; Missouri River willow; coyote willow; Florida willow; river willow; crack willow; Geyer willow; Glatfelter willow; Goodding willow; Hinds willow; Hooker willow; sandbar willow; red willow; Pacific willow; arroyo willow; strapleaf willow; shining willow; yellow willow; Mackenzie willow; dusky willow; black willow; serviceberry willow; meadow willow; balsam willow; Scouler willow; silky willow; northwest willow; Sitka willow; yewleaf willow; Tracy willow; basket willow. Range: Yakutat willow is an Alaskan species; the others occur generally throughout the U.S., though some have restricted ranges. The Florida willow is a rare species on the verge of extinction.

WITCH-HAZEL *HAMAMELIS* (FAMILY HAMAMELIDACEAE): Witch-hazel. Range: Maine to Texas and east to Florida.

YELLOW-POPLAR *LIRIODENDRON* (FAMILY MAGNOLIACEAE): Yellow-poplar. Range: New England to Missouri, Arkansas, Louisiana, and Florida.

YELLOWWOOD *CLADRASTIS* (FAMILY LEGUMINOSAE): Yellowwood. Range: rare and local in North Carolina, Tennessee, Kentucky, southern Indiana, southern Illinois, and south to Alabama and Georgia.

YEW *TAXUS* (FAMILY TAXACEAE): Pacific yew; Florida yew. Range: Florida yew grows in northwest Florida, rare and local; Pacific yew ranges through the mountains of the West.

YUCCA *YUCCA* (FAMILY LILIACEAE): Aloe yucca; Joshua-tree; Carneros yucca; soaptree yucca; Faxon yucca; moundlily yucca; Mohave yucca; beaked yucca; Schotts yucca; Torrey yucca; Trecul yucca. Range: Aloe yucca and moundlily yucca grow in the states of the Coastal Plain; the other species grow in the Southwest.

United States Congress
See **Congress of the United States**

United States Supreme Court
See **Justices of the United States Supreme Court**

Universities
See **Schools;** see also **Academic Colors;** for university degrees, see **Degree Abbreviations**

War,
Congressional Declarations of
See **Congress of the United States**

War of 1812, Battles of
See also **Battles**

1812

JUNE 18: War of 1812 period began.
JULY 12: Gen. Hull crossed Detroit River to capture Fort Malden, but failed.
JULY 17: American post at Mackinaw, Michigan, surrendered to British.
AUGUST 5: Americans defeated by British at Brownstown, Michigan.
AUGUST 13: British sloop-of-war *Alert* taken by the *Essex* (Capt. David Porter).
AUGUST 16: Gen. Hull surrendered Detroit to British; Hull and his American troops taken prisoner by Gen. Brock. See March 28, 1814.
AUGUST 19: In a twenty-five minute action, U.S. frigate *Constitution* (Capt. Isaac Hull) took British frigate *Guerriere* (Capt. Dacres).
SEPTEMBER 4-5: Indians attacked Fort Harrison, Indiana.
OCTOBER 4: British attack in boats repulsed at Ogdensburg, New York.
OCTOBER 5: Battle with Lotchaway and Alligator Indians, Georgia.
OCTOBER 13: Battle of Queenstown, Canada; Gen. Van Rensselaer of the New York militia attacked the British under Gen. Brock; Brock was killed in the engagement; after a stubborn battle, Van Rensselaer was taken prisoner; heavy American losses.
OCTOBER 18: British sloop-of-war *Frolic* captured by U.S. sloop-of-war *Wasp*.
OCTOBER 25: In an action lasting one and a half hours, British frigate *Macedon* (Capt. John S. Carden) taken by U.S. frigate *United States* (Capt. Stephen Decatur), off Madeira Islands.
DECEMBER 29: British frigate *Java* so cut

up in four-hour battle with U.S. *Constitution* (Com. William Bainbridge) that she was abandoned and burned at sea.

1813

JANUARY 11: Battle of Frenchtown, Michigan, on the River Raisin, in which Gen. Winchester, with 35 officers and 487 enlisted men surrendered prisoners to the British and Indians under Col. Proctor.
JANUARY 18: Frenchtown, Canada, was taken by Americans.
JANUARY 22: British retook Frenchtown.
FEBRUARY 5: Chesapeake Bay declared in a state of blockade.
FEBRUARY 7: Americans defeated British at Elizabeth, Canada.
FEBRUARY 22: Ogdensburg, New York, taken by British; public stores removed and destroyed.
FEBRUARY 24: British brig *Peacock* (Capt. Peake) captured by U.S. sloop-of-war *Hornet* (Capt. James Lawrence) after fifteen-minute action off British Guiana.
MARCH 26: American batteries at Black Rock, Canada, silenced lower British battery.
APRIL 6: British frigate *Belvidera* bombarded Lewiston, Delaware.
APRIL 13: Spanish garrison at Mobile, Alabama, surrendered to the U.S.
APRIL 27: Americans captured York, Canada, capital of Upper Canada, in raid by Gen. Dearborn; Gen. Pike killed in explosion of magazine.
APRIL 29: British burned storehouses and two ships at Frenchtown, plundered private houses.
MAY 1-5: Gen. W. H. Harrison besieged at Fort Meigs, Ohio, by British and Indians, but offered successful resistance.
MAY 3: Havre de Grace, Maryland, burned by British.
MAY 9: Fort Meigs, Ohio; British siege raised by Gen. Harrison.
MAY 27: Fort George, Canada, taken by Americans.
MAY 29: British repulsed in attack on Sackett's Harbor, New York.
JUNE 1: U.S. frigate *Chesapeake* (Capt. James Lawrence) captured by British frigate *Shannon* (Capt. Broke); Lawrence, mortally wounded, exclaimed in his delirium: "Don't give up the ship."
JUNE 6: Americans repulsed British at Burlington Heights, Canada.
JUNE 13: Defense of Hampton, Virginia.
JUNE 22: British naval attack on Craney Island, Virginia.
JUNE 23: Beaver Dam, Canada: Americans surrendered to the British.
JULY 17: British attack on Fort George, Canada, repulsed.
JULY 21: Gen. Proctor besieged Fort Meigs, Ohio.
JULY 27: Creek Indian battle on Burnt Corn Creek, Alabama.
AUGUST 2: British repulsed at Fort Stephenson on Lower Sandusky River by Maj. Croghan with 160 Americans opposing British and Indian force of 1300.
AUGUST 18: Spaniards ambushed Americans at San Antonio, Texas.
AUGUST 30: Creek Indians took Fort Mims, Ala., and massacred over 500 defenders.
SEPTEMBER 10: British squadron on Lake Erie (Capt. Barclay, commander), surrendered to American squadron (Com. Perry); Perry commanded nine small vessels and 54 guns; Barclay had six larger vessels and 63 guns,

and his sailors outnumbered the American sailors; American losses were 27 killed and 96 wounded; this was the occasion of Perry's famous report: "We have met the enemy and they are ours: two ships, two brigs, one schooner, and a sloop."

SEPTEMBER 30: Detroit reoccupied by American forces.

OCTOBER 5: Harrison defeated British on the River Thames, Canada, under command of Gen. Proctor; took 601 prisoners; the Indian chief Tecumseh was killed in the action, probably by Colonel Johnson.

NOVEMBER 3: Americans defeated Indians at Tallushatches, Ala.

NOVEMBER 9: Gen. Andrew Jackson, with 2000 Tennessee volunteers, attacked and defeated the Creek Indians at Talladega, Ala., killing 300, to American losses of 15 killed, 80 wounded.

NOVEMBER 12: "Canoe fight" with Indians, Alabama.

NOVEMBER 29: Auttose Indian towns destroyed by Gen. Floyd.

DECEMBER 10: Gen. McClure abandoned Fort George and burned the village of Newark, Upper Canada, giving the British an excuse for their subsequent burning of Washington, D.C., though they retaliated immediately and sufficiently by burning Buffalo and Black Rock (Dec. 30).

DECEMBER 19: Fort Niagara, New York, taken by British (Gen. Gordon Drummond).

DECEMBER 23: Indians defeated at "Holy Ground," Ala.

DECEMBER 30: Buffalo and Black Rock burned by British and Indian troops (Gen. Gordon Drummond). See December 10, 1813.

1814

JANUARY 22, 24: Indian battles at Emuckfau and Enotochopcs, Ala.

JANUARY 27: Indian battle at Calebee River.

FEBRUARY 21: British burned arsenal at Malone, New York, and pillaged the town.

MARCH 4: British defeated at Longwood, Canada.

MARCH 27: Jackson defeated Creeks at Great Horse-Shoe Bend, Ala.

MARCH 28: Gen. William Hull, who had surrendered Detroit to the British on August 16, 1812, was convicted of cowardice and neglect of duty and condemned by court-martial to be shot; the sentence was approved by the President (April 25) but remitted in the light of Hull's honorable Revolutionary War record.

MARCH 30: Americans were repulsed at La Colle, Canada.

APRIL 7: British attacked Saybrook, Connecticut.

APRIL 29: U.S. sloop-of-war Peacock (Capt. Warrington) captured the British sloop-of-war L'Epervier (Capt. Wales) in a forty-two minute action off the coast of Florida.

MAY 4-6: Fort Oswego captured by British; Lt. Col. Michell surrendered after 6 of his 300 men were killed, 38 wounded, and 26 missing; the British command of 1800 men lost 19 killed and 75 wounded.

JULY 3: Fort Erie, Canada, with a garrison of 137 men, surrendered to Maj. Gen. Brown without resistance.

JULY 5: Americans defeated British at Chippewa, Canada; Gen. Brown forced the British troops (Gen. Riall) to retreat to Fort George.

JULY 11: British fleet took Eastport, Maine.

JULY 25: Lundy's Lane, Canada; Gen. Brown

attacked the British (Gen. Drummond) and, after a bloody engagement lasting from 5 p.m. to midnight, drove them from their position, stormed and captured their artillery, then retreated at will to his own encampment; Gen. Drummond was wounded in the encounter.

AUGUST 4: British besieged Fort Erie, Canada.

AUGUST 9: British ships bombarded Stonington, Conn., with a squadron under command of Com. Hardy, and were driven off.

AUGUST 15: British assaulted Fort Erie, Canada, and were driven off by the American garrison.

AUGUST 24: Bladensburg, Md.: after blowing up his own flotilla in the Patuxent River, Com. Barney delayed the British at Bladensburg Heights and, though deserted by the militia, fought until surrounded and captured; Barney was wounded in the fighting.

AUGUST 24: Washington, D.C.; in the evening Gen. Proctor entered the city with 800 men, burned the Capitol, White House, the Library of Congress and Public Archives, and other public buildings, then retreated to his ships.

AUGUST 30: Creek Indians surprised Fort Mims, Ala.

SEPTEMBER 1: British sloop-of-war Avon (Capt. Arbuthnot) sunk by U.S. sloop-of-war Wasp, after an action lasting forty-six minutes.

SEPTEMBER 9: Americans attacked British near Plattsburg, N. Y.

SEPTEMBER 11: Americans under Macomb and Adm. McDonald defeated British under Gen. Prevost and Adm. Downie, at Plattsburg, N. Y.; while the British squadron engaged the American squadron (Com. Mc Donough) in the harbor, in an action lasting two hours and twenty minutes, Sir George Prevost, who had occupied Plattsburg with a British command of 14.000 men, led an unsuccessful attack against 1500 American regulars (Gen. Macomb) and 3000 Vermont and New York militia (Gens. Strong and Mooers).

SEPTEMBER 12-14: Five thousand British troops (Gen. Ross) joined the British fleet in a concerted land-and-sea attack upon Baltimore, Md., and were driven off.

SEPTEMBER 13: British ships bombarded Fort McHenry, which defended the harbor at Baltimore; during the night of the bombardment, Francis Scott Key wrote the words of "The Star-Spangled Banner", the British retired on the morning of September 14.

OCTOBER 5: Harrison defeated Proctor on Thames River, Canada.

NOVEMBER 3: Gen. Coffee surrendered to Indians at Tallushatches, Ala.

DECEMBER 23: Villeres Plantation, La.: Jackson attacked British camp 9 mi. below New Orleans.

DECEMBER 24: Treaty of peace, restoring territories occupied during the war to the status they had before hostilities began, signed by British and American commissions at Ghent, Belgium.

DECEMBER 28: Chalmette's Plantation: British attack on Jackson repulsed.

1815

JANUARY 1: British attacked Gen. Jackson's forces at Rodriguez' Canal.

JANUARY 8: Battle of New Orleans; the main body of the British, led by Gen.

Packenham, attempted to storm the American lines, but were driven off after losing 700 men, with 1400 more wounded, and 500 others taken prisoner; American losses totaled 6 killed and 7 wounded; Gen. Packenham was killed in the battle.

JANUARY 15: U.S. frigate *President* (Com. Decatur) taken by British squadron off Sandy Hook.

FEBRUARY 16: Congress ratified peace treaty signed at Ghent, Belgium on December 24, 1814.

FEBRUARY 20: U.S. frigate *Constitution* captured the British sloops-of-war *Cyane* and *Levant* off Madeira.

MARCH 23: U.S. sloop-of-war *Hornet* (Capt. Biddle) captured the British brig *Penguin* off the Cape of Good Hope.

Waterfalls of the World, Famous (in order of height)

ANGEL FALLS: E. of Caroni River, Venezuela; 3300 ft.

TUGELA FALLS: Tugela River, Natal, Union of South Africa; 2810 ft.

KUKENAAM FALLS: Kukenaam River, British Guiana; 2000 ft.

RORAIMA FALLS: At source of Amazon and Orinoco Rivers, Brazil - British Guiana - Venezuela; 2000 ft.

SUTHERLANDS FALLS: Arthur River, South Island, New Zealand; 1904 ft.

RIBBON FALLS: Tributary of the Yosemite River, Yosemite Park, Calif. U.S.; 1612 ft.

YOSEMITE FALLS, UPPER: Yosemite National Park, Calif., U.S.; 1430 ft.

GAVARNIE FALLS: Gave de Pau, France; 1385 ft.

KRIMMLER FALLS: Krimmler River, Austria; 1246 ft.

TAKKAKAW FALLS: Tributary of the Yoho River, British Columbia, Canada; 1200 ft.

WIDOW'S TEARS FALLS: Yosemite National Park, Calif., U.S.; 1170 ft.

STAUBBACH FALLS: Staubbach River, Switzerland; 980 ft.

TRUMMELBACH FALLS: Switzerland; 950 ft.

MIDDLE CASCADE: Tributary of the Merced River, Yosemite Park, Calif., U.S.; 910 ft.

MULTNOMAH FALLS: Multnomah Creek, Ore., U.S.; 850 ft.

VETTISFOSS: Mørkedola River, Norway; 850 ft.

KING EDWARD VIII FALLS: Tributary of the Mazaruni River, British Guiana; 840 ft.

GERSOPPA, FALLS OF: Sharavati River, India; 830 ft.

KAIETEUR FALLS: Potaro River, British Guiana; 741 ft.

FAIRY FALLS: Stevens Creek, Mt. Rainier Park, Wash., U.S.; 700 ft.

CASCATA DELLE MARMORE: Nera River, Italy; 650 ft.

MARADALSFOS: Tributary of the Ejkisdalsvand, Norway; 650 ft.

SKYKJEFOS: Inner Hardanger Fjord, Norway; 650 ft.

BRIDAL VEIL FALLS: Tributary of the Merced River; Yosemite Park, Calif., U.S.; 630 ft.

MALETSUNYANE FALLS: Maletsunyane River, Basutoland, Union of South Africa; 630 ft.

NEVADA FALLS: Merced River, Yosemite Park, Calif., U.S.; 594 ft.

VORINGFOSS: Bjoreia River, Norway; 535 ft.

SKJAEGGEDALSFOS: Inner Hardanger Fjord, Norway; 525 ft.

MARINA FALLS: Tributary of the Essequibo River, British Guiana; 500 ft.

TEQUENDAMA FALLS: Funza River, Colombia; 470 ft.

KING GEORGE'S FALLS (AUGHRABIES): Orange River, Cape Province, Union of South Africa; 450 ft.

VICTORIA FALLS: Zambesi River, Northern Rhodesia-Southern Rhodesia; 375 ft.

GUAIRA (GUAYRA) CATARACT: Parana River, Paraguay-Brazil; 374 ft.

ILLILOUETTE FALLS: Illilouette Creek, Yosemite Park, Calif., U.S.; 370 ft.

GRANITE FALLS: Granite Creek, Mt. Rainier Park, Wash., U.S.; 350 ft.

GREAT CATARACT: Cunene (Kunene) River, Angola - South West Africa; 330 ft.

COMET FALLS: Van Trump Creek; Mount Rainier Park, Wash., U.S.; 320 ft.

YOSEMITE FALLS, LOWER: Yosemite National Park, Calif., U.S.; 320 ft.

VERNAL FALLS: Yosemite National Park, Calif., U.S.; 317 ft.

VIRGINIA FALLS: South Nahanni River, Canada; 315 ft.

YELLOWSTONE FALLS, LOWER: Yellowstone River, Yellowstone National Park, Mont., U.S.; 308 ft.

GRAND FALLS: Hamilton River, Labrador, Canada; 302 ft.

REICHENBACH FALLS: Reichenbach River, Switzerland; 300 ft.

SLUISKIN FALLS: Paradise River, Mt. Rainier Park, Wash., U.S.; 300 ft.

GASTEIN, LOWER FALLS: Gasteiner Ache, Austria; 280 ft.

SNOQUALMIE FALLS: Snoqualmie River, Wash., U.S.; 270 ft.

MONTMORENCY FALLS: Montmorency River, Quebec, Canada; 265 ft.

PAULO AFONSO FALLS: São Francisco River, Brazil; 265 ft.

TALLULAH FALLS: Tallulah River, Ga., U.S.; 251 ft.

HARSPRANG: Lule River, Sweden; 246 ft.

HANDECKFALL: Aare River, Switzerland; 240 ft.

PISSEVACHE FALLS: Wildbach Salanfe River, Switzerland; 215 ft.

IGUASSU FALLS: Iguassu (Iguazu) River, Brazil-Argentina; 210 ft.

GASTEIN, UPPER FALLS: Gasteiner Ache, Austria; 207 ft.

SHOSHONE FALLS: Snake River, Ida., U.S.; 195 ft.

NARADA FALLS: Paradise River, Mt. Rainier Park, Wash., U.S.; 168 ft.

NIAGARA FALLS: Niagara River, New York-Ontario, U.S.-Canada; 167 ft.

HANDOL FALLS: Tributary of Lake Ann, Sweden; 148 ft.

TOWER FALLS: Yellowstone National Park, Wy., U.S.; 132 ft.

STORA SJORFALLET: Lule River, Sweden; 131 ft.

MURCHISON FALLS: Victoria Nile, Uganda; 120 ft.

YELLOWSTONE FALLS, UPPER: Yellowstone River, Yellowstone National Park, Montana, U.S.; 109 ft.

SCHAFFHAUSEN FALLS: Rhine River, Switzerland; 100 ft.

Wines: Great Clarets (Red Wines) of Bordeaux (Le Médoc)

Official Classification of 1855, by Château and Parish

FIRST GROWTHS: Château Lafite (Pauillac); Château Margaux (Margaux); Château Latour (Pauillac); Château Haut-Brion (Pessac, Graves).

SECOND GROWTHS: Château Mouton-Rothschild (Pauillac); Château Rausan-Ségla (Margaux); Château Rauzan-Gassies (Margaux); Château Léoville-Lascases (Saint-Julien); Château Léoville-Poyferré (Saint-Julien); Château Léoville-Barton (Saint-Julien); Château Durfort-Vivens (Margaux); Château Lascombes (Margaux); Château Gruaud-Larose-Sarget (Saint-Julien); Château Gruaud-Larose-Faure (Saint-Julien); Château Brane-Cantenac (Cantenac): Château Pichon-Longueville (Pauillac); Château Pichon-Longueville-Lalande (Pauillac); Château Ducru-Beaucaillou (Saint-Julien); Château Cos-d'Estournel (Saint-Estèphe); Château Montrose (Saint-Estèphe).

THIRD GROWTHS: Château Kirwan (Cantenac); Château Issan (Cantenac); Château Lagrange (Saint-Julien); Château Langoa (Saint-Julien); Château Giscours (Labarde); Château Malescot-Saint-Exupéry (Margaux); Château Cantenac-Brown (Cantenac); Château Palmer (Cantenac); Château La Lagune (Ludon); Château Desmirail (Margaux); Château Calon-Ségur (Saint-Estèphe); Château Ferrière (Margaux); Château Marquis d'Alesme-Becker (Margaux).

FOURTH GROWTHS: Château Saint-Pierre-Sevaistre (Saint-Julien); Château Saint-Pierre-Bontemps (Saint-Julien); Château Branaire-Ducru (Saint-Julien); Château Talbot (Saint-Julien); Château Duhart-Milon (Pauillac); Château Poujet (Cantenac); Château La Tour-Carnet (Saint-Laurent); Château Rochet (Saint-Estèphe); Château Beychevelle (Saint-Julien); Châteaux Le Prieuré (Cantenac); Châteaux Marquis-de-Terme (Margaux).

FIFTH GROWTHS: Château Pontet-Canet (Pauillac); Château Batailley (Pauillac); Château Grand-Puy-Lacoste (Pauillac); Château Grand-Puy-Ducasse (Pauillac); Château Lynch-Bages (Pauillac); Château Lynch-Moussas (Pauillac); Château Dauzac (Labarde); Château Mouton-d'Armailhacq (Pauillac); Château Le Tertre (Arsac); Château Haut-Bages-Libéral (Pauillac); Château Pédesclaux (Pauillac); Château Belgrave (Saint-Laurent); Château Camensac (Saint-Laurent); Château Cos-Labory (Saint-Estèphe); Château Clerc-Milon (Pauillac); Château Croizet-Bages (Pauillac); Château Cantemerle (Macau).

Wines: Great Sauternes of Bordeaux

Official Classification of 1855, by Château and Parish

GRAND FIRST GROWTH: Château Yquem (Sauternes).

FIRST GROWTHS: Château la Tour-Banche (Bommes); Château la Faurie-Peyraguey (Bommes); Château Clos Haut-Peyraguey (Bommes); Château Rayne-Vigneau (Bommes); Château Suduiraut (Preignac); Château Coutet (Barsac); Château Climens (Barsac); Château Guiraud (Sauternes); Château Rieussec (Fargues); Château Rabaud-Promis (Bommes); Château Sigalas-Rabaud (Bommes).

SECOND GROWTHS: Château de Myrat (Barsac); Château Doisy-Daëne (Barsac); Château Doisy-Dubroca (Barsac); Château Doisy-Védrines (Barsac); Château d'Arche (Sauternes); Château Filhot (Sauternes); Château Broustet (Barsac); Château Nairac (Barsac); Château Caillou (Barsac); Château Suau (Barsac); Château de Malle (Preignac); Château Romer (Preignac); Château Lamothe (Sauternes).

Wines of the World

Note: In each instance the locality in which the grape is grown is given, as is the type of wine, and some suggestions for serving. R.T. stands for Room Temperature.

Red Wines

ALOXE: Aloxe, France; table wine; R.T.; dry; all foods.

ALOXE-CORTON: Aloxe-Corton, France; table wine; R.T.; dry; all foods.

AMOUREUSES, LES: Chambolle-Musigny, France; table wine; R.T.; dry; all foods.

ARVELETS, LES: Pommard, France; table wine; R.T.; dry; all foods.

ASSMANNSHAUSEN: Rhineland, Germany; table wine; R.T.; dry; all foods.

BARBARESCO: Piedmont, Italy; table wine; R.T. dry; all foods.

BARBERA: Piedmont, Italy; table wine; R.T.; dry; all foods.

BARBERA: Alameda, Napa, Sonoma, Calif.; table wine, Burgundy-type; R.T.; dry; all foods.

BAROLO: Piedmont, Italy; table wine; R.T.; dry; all foods

BASSES-VERGELESSES, LES: Pernand, France; table wine; R.T.; dry; all foods.

BEAUJOLAIS: Burgundy, France; table wine; R.T.; dry; all foods.

BEAUNE: Beaune, France; table wine; R.T.; dry; all foods.

BEAUX MONTS: Vosne, France; table wine; R.T.; dry; all foods.

BONNES, MARES, LES: Morey, France; table wine; R.T.; dry; all foods.

BORDEAUX ROUGE: Palus, Côtes, Entre-Deux-Mers, France; table wine; R.T.; dry; all food.

BOUDOTS: Nuits-Saint-Georges, France; table wine; R.T.; dry; all foods.

BOURGOGNE ROUGE: Burgundy, France; table wine; R.T.; dry; all foods.

BRESSANDES, LES: Beaune, France; table wine; R.T.; dry; all foods.

BROUILLY: Odenas, France; table wine; R.T.; dry; all foods.

BURGUNDY: Napa, Santa Clara, Calif.; table wine, Burgundy-type; R.T.; dry; all foods.

CABERNET: Napa, Santa Clara, Calif.; table wine; R.T.; dry; all foods.

CADET BON, LE: Saint-Emilion, France; table wine; R.T.; dry; all foods.

CAILLERETS, LES: Volnay, France; table wine; R.T.; all foods.

CAILLES, LES: Nuits-Saint-Georges, France; table wine; R.T.; dry; all foods.

CANON LA GAFFELIÈRE: Saint-Emilion, France; table wine; R.T.; dry; all foods.

CAPITANS, LES: Julienas, France; table wine; R.T.; dry; all foods.

CARQUELINS, LES: Romanèche-Thorins, France; table wine; R.T.; dry; all foods.

CAVES, LES: Chenas, France; table wine; R.T.; dry; all foods.

CHALET BERGAT: Saint-Emilion, France;

CHAMBERTIN, LE: Gevrey-Chambertin, France; table wine; R.T.; dry; all foods.
CHAMBOLLE: Chambolle, France; table wine; R.T.; dry; all foods.
CHAMBOLLE-MUSIGNY: Burgundy, France; table wine; R.T.; dry; all foods.
CHAMPANS: Volnay, France; table wine; R.T.; dry; all foods.
CHAMP DECOURT GROSLIERS: Romanèche-Thorins, France; table wine; R.T.; dry; all foods.
CHAPELLE, LA: Fleurie, France; table wine; R.T.; dry; all foods.
CHAPELLE DE LA TRINITÉ: Saint-Emilion, France; table wine; R.T.; dry; all foods.
CHAPELLE DES BOIS: Fleurie; France; table wine; R.T.; dry; all foods.
CHAPÎTRE, LE: Fixin, France; table wine; R.T.; dry; all foods.
CHARBONO: Napa, Calif.; table wine, Burgundy-type; R.T.; dry; all foods.
CHARMES-CHAMBERTIN: Gevrey-Chambertin, France; table wine; R.T.; dry; all foods.
CHÂTEAU ALPHEN: South Africa; table wine; R.T.; dry; all foods.
CHÂTEAU AUSONE: Saint-Emilion, France; table wine; R.T.: dry; all foods.
CHÂTEAU BALEAU: Saint-Emilion, France; table wine; R.T.; dry; all foods.
CHÂTEAU BALESTARD LA TONNELLE: Saint-Emilion, France; table wine; R.T.; dry; all foods.
CHÂTEAU BARET: Graves, France; table wine; R.T.; dry; all foods.
CHÂTEAU BATAILLEY: Médoc, France; table wine; R.T.: dry; all foods.
CHÂTEAU BEAUREGARD: Pomerol, France; table wine; R.T.; dry; all foods.
CHÂTEAU BEAUSÉJOUR: Saint-Emilion, France; table wine; R.T.; dry; all foods.
CHÂTEAU BELAIR: Saint-Emilion, France; table wine; R.T.; dry; all foods.
CHÂTEAU BELAIR MARIGNAN: Saint Emilion, France; table wine; R.T.; dry; all foods.
CHÂTEAU BELGRAVE: Saint-Laurent, France; table wine; R.T.; dry; all foods.
CHÂTEAU BELLEGRAVE: Graves, France; table wine; R.T.; dry; all foods.
CHÂTEAU BELLEVUE: Saint-Emilion, France; table wine; R.T.; dry; all foods.
CHÂTEAU BERLIQUET: Saint-Emilion, France; table wine; R.T.; dry; all foods.
CHÂTEAU BEYCHEVELLE: Médoc, France; table wine; R.T.; dry; all foods.
CHÂTEAU BON-AIR: Graves, France; table wine; R.T.; dry; all foods.
CHÂTEAU BOYD-CANTENAC: Médoc, France; table wine; R.T.; dry; all foods.
CHÂTEAU BRANAIRE-DUCRU: Médoc, France; table wine; R.T.; dry; all foods.
CHÂTEAU BRANE-CANTENAC: Médoc, France; table wine; R.T.; dry; all foods.
CHÂTEAU BROWN-LEOGNAN: Graves, France; table wine; R.T.; dry; all foods.
CHÂTEAU CADET PIOLA: Saint-Emilion, France; table wine; R.T.; dry; all foods.
CHÂTEAU CALON-SÉGUR: Médoc, France; table wine; R.T.; dry; all foods.
CHÂTEAU CAMENSAC: Médoc, France; table wine; R.T.; dry; all foods.
CHÂTEAU CAMPONAC: Graves, France; table wine; R.T.; dry; all foods.
CHÂTEAU CANON: Saint-Emilion, France; table wine; R.T.; dry; all foods.
CHÂTEAU CANTEMERLE: Médoc, France; table wine; R.T.; dry; all foods.
CHÂTEAU CANTENAC-BROWN: Médoc, France; table wine; R.T.; dry; all foods.

CHÂTEAU DE CANTENAC-PRIEURÉ: Médoc, France; table wine; R.T.; dry; all foods.
CHÂTEAU CARBONNIEUX: Graves, France; table wine; R.T.; dry; all foods.
CHÂTEAU CARDINAL VILLEMAURINE: Saint-Emilion, France; table wine; R.T.; dry; all foods.
CHÂTEAU CHEVAL BLANC: Graves-Saint-Emilion, France; table wine; R.T.; dry; all foods.
CHÂTEAU CLERC-MILON: Pauillac, France; table wine; R.T.; dry; all foods.
CHÂTEAU CLERC-MILON-MONDON: Médoc, France; table wine; R.T.; dry; all foods.
CHÂTEAU CLINET: Pomerol, France; table wine; R.T.; dry; all foods.
CHÂTEAU LA CONSEILLANTE: Pomerol, France; table wine; R.T.; dry; all foods.
CHÂTEAU CORBIN MICHOTTE: Graves-Saint-Emilion, France; table wine; R.T.; dry; all foods.
France; table wine; R.T.; dry; all foods.
CHÂTEAU COS D'ESTOURNEL: Médoc, France; table wine; R.T.; dry; all foods.
CHÂTEAU COS-LABORY: Médoc, France; table wine; R.T.; dry; all foods.
CHÂTEAU COUTET: Saint-Emilion, France; table wine; R.T.; dry; all foods.
CHÂTEAU CROQUE-MICHOTTE: Graves-Saint-Emilion, France; table wine; R.T.; dry; all foods.
CHÂTEAU CROIZET-BAGES: Pauillac: France; table wine; R.T.; dry; all foods.
CHÂTEAU DAUZAC: Médoc, France; table wine; R.T.; dry; all foods.
CHÂTEAU DE RAYNE-VIGNEAU: Bommes, France; table wine; R.T.; dry; all foods.
CHÂTEAU DESMIRALL: Médoc, France; table wine; R.T.; dry; all foods.
CHÂTEAU DES REMPARTS LA CARTE: Saint-Emilion, France; table wine; R.T.; dry; all foods.
CHÂTEAU DUCRU-BEAUCAILLOU: Médoc, France; table wine; R.T.; dry; all foods.
CHÂTEAU DUHART-MILON: Médoc, France; table wine; R.T.; dry; all foods.
CHÂTEAU DU JARDIN VILLEMAURINE: Saint-Emilion, France; table wine; R.T.; dry; all foods.
CHÂTEAU DURFORT-VIVENS: Médoc, France: table wine: R.T.: dry: all foods.
CHÂTEAU DU TERTRE: Médoc, France; table wine; R.T.; dry; all foods.
CHÂTEAU FERRIÈRE: Médoc, France; table wine; R.T.; dry; all foods.
CHÂTEAU FIEUZAL: Graves, France; table wine; R.T.; dry; all foods.
CHÂTEAU FIGÉAC: Graves-Saint-Emilion, France; table wine; R.T.; dry; all foods.
CHÂTEAU FONPLEGADE: Saint-Emilion, France; table wine; R.T.; dry; all foods.
CHÂTEAU FONROQUE: Saint-Emilion, France; table wine; R.T.; dry; all foods.
CHÂTEAU GAZIN: Pomerol, France; table wine; R.T.; dry; all foods.
CHÂTEAU GISCOURS: Médoc, France; table wine; R.T.; dry; all foods.
CHÂTEAU GRAND PONTET: Saint-Emilion, France; table wine; R.T.; dry; all foods.
CHÂTEAU GRAND-PUY-DUCASSE: Médoc, France; table wine; R.T.; dry; all foods.
CHÂTEAU GRAND-PUY-LACOSTE: Médoc, France; table wine; R.T.; dry; all foods.
CHÂTEAU GRUAUD-LAROSE-FAURE: Médoc, France; table wine; R.T.; dry; all foods.
CHÂTEAU GRUAUD-LAROSE-FAURE: Saint-Julien, France; table wine; R.T.; dry; all foods.
CHÂTEAU GRUAUD-LAROSE-SARGET:

Saint-Julien, France; table wine; R.T.; dry; all foods.

CHÂTEAU GUILLOT: Pomerol, France; table wine; R.T.; dry; all foods.

CHÂTEAU HAUT-BAGES-LIBERAL: Médoc; France; table wine; R.T.; dry; all foods.

CHÂTEAU HAUT-BAILLY: Graves, France; table wine; R.T.; dry; all foods.

CHÂTEAU HAUT-BRION: Graves, France; table wine; R.T.; dry; all foods.

CHÂTEAU HAUT-GARDÈRE: Graves France; table wine; R.T.; dry; all foods.

CHÂTEAU ISSAN: Médoc, France; table wine; R.T.; dry; all foods.

CHÂTEAU JEAN CORBIN ET JEAN FAURE: Graves-Saint-Emilion, France; table wine; R.T.; all foods.

CHÂTEAU KIRWAN: Médoc, France; table wine; R.T.; dry; all foods.

CHÂTEAU LA CABANNE: Pomerol, France; table wine; R.T.; dry: all foods.

CHÂTEAU LA CLUSIÈRE: Saint-Emilion, France; table wine; R.T.; dry; all foods.

CHÂTEAU LA COUSPADE: Saint-Emilion, France; table wine; R.T.; dry; all foods.

CHÂTEAU LAFITE-ROTHSCHILD: Médoc, France; table wine; R.T.; dry; all foods.

CHÂTEAU LA FLEUR: Pomerol, France; table wine; R.T.; dry; all foods.

CHÂTEAU LA FLEUR PETRUS: Pomerol, France; table wine; R.T.; dry; all foods.

CHÂTEAU LA GAFFELIÈRE NAUDES: Saint-Emilion, France; table wine; R.T.; dry; all foods.

CHÂTEAU LAGRANGE: Médoc, France; table wine; R.T.; dry; all foods.

CHÂTEAU LA LAGUNE: Médoc. France; table wine; R.T.; dry; all foods.

CHÂTEAU LA LOUVIÈRE: Graves, France; table wine; R.T.; dry; all foods.

CHÂTEAU LA MARZELLE: Graves-Saint-Emilion, France; table wine; R.T.; dry; all foods.

CHÂTEAU LAMARZELLE FIGÉAC: Graves-Saint-Emilion, France; table wine; R.T.; dry; all foods.

CHÂTEAU LA MISSION-HAUT-BRION: Graves, France; table wine; R.T.; dry; all foods.

CHÂTEAU LANGOA: Médoc, France; table wine; R.T.; dry; all foods.

CHÂTEAU LASCOMBES: Margaux, France; table wine; R.T.; dry; all foods.

CHÂTEAU LA SERRE: Saint-Emilion, France; table wine; R.T.; dry; all foods.

CHÂTEAU LATOUR: Médoc, France; table wine; R.T.; dry; all foods.

CHÂTEAU LA TOUR-CARNET: Saint-Laurent, France; table wine; R.T.; dry; all foods.

CHÂTEAU LA TOUR DU PIN FIGÉAC MOURE: Graves - Saint-Emilion, France; table wine; R.T.; dry; all foods.

CHÂTEAU LA TOUR FIGÉAC: Graves-Saint-Emilion, France; table wine; R.T.; dry; all foods.

CHÂTEAU LE GAY: Pomerol, France; table wine; R.T.; dry; all foods.

CHÂTEAU LÉOVILLE-BARTON: Médoc, France; table wine; R.T.; dry; all foods.

CHÂTEAU LÉOVILLE-LASCASES: Médoc, France; table wine; R.T.; dry; all foods.

CHÂTEAU LÉOVILLE-POYFERRE: Médoc, France; table wine; R.T.; dry; all foods.

CHÂTEAU L'EVANGILE: Pomerol, France; table wine; R.T.; dry; all foods.

CHÂTEAU LIBERTAS: South Africa; table wine; R.T.; dry; all foods.

CHÂTEAU LYNCH-BAGES: Médoc, France; table wine; R.T.; dry; all foods.

CHÂTEAU LYNCH-MOUSSAS: Médoc, France; table wine; R.T.; dry; all foods.

CHÂTEAU MAGDELAINE: Saint-Emilion, France; table wine; R.T.; dry; all foods.

CHÂTEAU MALARTIC-LAGRAVIÈRE: Graves, France; table wine; R.T.; dry; all foods.

CHÂTEAU MALESCOT-SAINT-EXUPERY: Médoc, France; table wine; R.T.; dry; all foods.

CHÂTEAU MALINEAU: Saint-Emilion, France; table wine; R.T.; dry; all foods.

CHÂTEAU MARGAUX: Médoc, France; table wine; R.T.; all foods.

CHÂTEAU MARQUIS D'ALESME-BECKER: Médoc, France; table wine; R.T.; dry; all foods.

CHÂTEAU MARQUIS-DE-TERME: Médoc, France; table wine; R.T.; dry; all foods.

CHÂTEAU MONTROSE: Saint-Estèphe, France; table wine; R.T.; dry; all foods.

CHÂTEAU MOUTON-D'ARMAILHACQ: Médoc, France: table wine: R.T.: drv: all foods.

CHÂTEAU MOUTON-ROTHSCHILD: Médoc, France; table wine; R.T.; dry; all foods.

CHÂTEAU NENIN: Pomerol, France; table wine; R.T.; dry; all foods.

CHÂTEAUNEUF-DU-PAPA: Rhône, France; table wine; R.T.; dry; all foods.

CHÂTEAU OLIVIER (RED): Graves, France; table wine; R.T.; dry; all foods.

CHÂTEAU PALAT: Saint-Emilion, France; table wine; R.T.; dry; all foods.

CHÂTEAU PALMER-MARGAUX: Médoc, France; table wine; R.T.; dry; all foods.

CHÂTEAU PAPE-CLÉMENT: Graves, France; table wine; R.T.; dry; all foods.

CHÂTEAU PAVIE: Saint-Emilion, France; table wine; R.T.; dry; all foods.

CHÂTEAU PEDESCLAUX: Pauillac, France; table wine; R.T.; dry; all foods.

CHÂTEAU PETIT FAURIE DE SOUTARD: Saint-Emilion, France; table wine; R.T.; dry; all foods.

CHÂTEAU PETIT VILLAGE: Pomerol, France; table wine; R.T.; dry; all foods.

CHÂTEAU PETRUS: Pomerol. France; table wine; R.T.: drv: all foods.

CHÂTEAU PICHON-LONGUEVILLE: Médoc, France; table wine; R.Γ.; dry; all foods.

CHÂTEAU PICHON-LONGUEVILLE-LALANDE: Médoc, France; table wine; R.T.; dry; all foods.

CHÂTEAU PIQUE-CAILLOU: Graves, France; table wine; R.T.; dry; all foods.

CHÂTEAU PONTAC-MONTPLAISIR: Graves, France; table wine; R.T.; dry; all foods.

CHÂTEAU PONTET-CANET: Médoc, France; table wine; R.T.; dry; all foods.

CHÂTEAU PONTET-CARNET: Pauillac, France; table wine; R.T.; dry; all foods.

CHÂTEAU POUGET: Médoc, France; table wine; R.T.; dry; all foods.

CHÂTEAU RAUSAN-SÉGLA: Médoc, France; table wine; R.T.; dry; all foods.

CHÂTEAU RAUZAN-GASSIES: Médoc, France; table wine; R.T.; dry; all foods.

CHÂTEAU RIGAILHOU: Graves, France; table wine; R.T.; dry; all foods.

CHÂTEAU RIPEAU: Graves-Saint-Emilion. France; table wine; R.T.; dry; all foods.

CHÂTEAU ROCHET: Médoc, France; table wine; R.T.; dry; all foods.

CHÂTEAU ROCHET: Saint-Estèphe, France; table wine; R.T.; dry; all foods.

CHÂTEAU ROUGET: Pomerol, France; table wine; R.T.; dry; all foods.

CHÂTEAU SAINT-EMILION: Saint-Emilion, France; table wine; R.Γ.; dry; all foods.

CHÂTEAU SAINT-GEORGES (CÔTE PAVIE):

Saint-Emilion, France; table wine; R.T.; dry; all foods.
CHÂTEAU SAINT-JULIEN: Saint-Emilion, France; table wine; R.T.; dry; all foods.
CHÂTEAU SAINT-PIERRE-BONTEMPS: Médoc, France; table wine; R.T.; dry; all foods.
CHÂTEAU SAINT-PIERRE SEVAISTRE: Médoc, France; table wine; R.T.; dry; all foods.
CHÂTEAU SANSONNET: Saint-Emilion, France; table wine; R.T.; dry; all foods.
CHÂTEAU SMITH-HAUT-LAFITTE: Graves, France; table wine; R.T.; dry; all foods.
CHÂTEAU SOUTARD: Saint-Emilion, France; table wine; R.T.; dry; all foods.
CHÂTEAU TALBOT: Médoc, France; table wine; R.T.; dry; all foods.
CHÂTEAU TERTRE DAUGAY: Saint-Emilion, France; table wine; R.T.; dry; all foods.
CHÂTEAU TERTRE DE DAUGAY: Saint-Emilion, France; table wine; R.T.; dry; all foods.
CHÂTEAU TROIS MOULINS: Saint-Emilion, France; table wine; R.T.; dry; all foods.
CHÂTEAU TROPLONG MONDOT: Saint-Emilion, France; table wine; R.T.; dry; all foods.
CHÂTEAU TROTANOY: Pomerol, France; table wine; R.T.; dry; all foods.
CHÂTEAU TROTTEVILLE: Saint-Emilion, France; table wine; R.T.; dry; all foods.
CHÂTEAU VILLEMAURINE: Saint-Emilion, France; table wine; R.T.; dry; all foods.
CHIANTI: Tuscany, Italy; table wine; R.T.; dry; all foods.
CHIANTI (RED): Napa, San Joaquin, Santa Clara, Calif.; table wine; R.T.; dry; all foods.
CLARET: Napa, Santa Clara, Calif.; table wine, Claret-type; R.T.; dry; all foods.
CLAVOILLON: Puligny, France; table wine; R.T.; dry; all foods.
CLOS BERGAT BOSSON PIGASSE: Saint-Emilion, France; table wine; R.T.; dry; all foods.
CLOS COTE DAUGAY EX-MADELEINE: Saint-Emilion, France; table wine; R.T.; dry; all foods.
CLOS DE BÈZE: Gevrey-Chambertin, France; table wine; R.T.; dry; all foods.
CLOS DE FÈVES: Beaune, France; table wine; R.T.; dry; all foods.
CLOS FOURTET: Saint-Emilion, France; table wine; R.T.; dry; all foods.
CLOS DE LA COMMARAINE: Pommard, France; table wine; R.T.; dry; all foods.
CLOS DE LA MOUSSE: Beaune, France; table wine; R.T.; dry; all foods.
CLOS DE L'ANGELUS: Saint-Emilion, France; table wine; R.T.; dry; all foods.
CLOS DE LA PERRIÈRE: Fixin, France; table wine; R.T.; dry; all foods.
CLOS DE LA ROCHE: Morey, France; table wine; R.T.; dry; all foods.
CLOS DES GRANDES VIGNES: Pomerol, France; table wine; R.T.; dry; all foods.
CLOS DES LAMBRAYS: Morey France; table wine; R.T.; dry; all foods.
CLOS DES MOUCHES: Beaune, France; table wine; R.T.; dry; all foods.
CLOS DE TART: Morey, France; table wine; R.T.; dry; all foods.
CLOS DE VOUGEOT: Gilly-les-Vougeot, France; table wine; R.T.; dry; all foods.
CLOS DU COUVENT: Saint-Emilion, France; table wine; R.T.; dry; all foods.
CLOS DU ROI: Aloxe-Corton, France; table wine; R.T.; dry; all foods.
CLOS FOURTET: Saint-Emilion, France; table wine; R.T.; dry; all foods.

CLOS LA MAGDELEINE: Saint-Emilion, France; table wine; R.T.; dry; all foods.
CLOS L'EGLISE-CLINET: Pomerol, France; table wine; R.T.; dry; all foods.
CLOS MAUVEZIN: Saint-Emilion, France; table wine; R.T.; dry; all foods.
CLOS MORGEOT: Chassagne, France; table wine; R.T.; dry; all foods.
CLOS RAMONET: Saint-Emilion, France table wine; R.T.; dry; all foods.
CLOS SAINT-DENIS: Morey, France; table wine; R.T.; dry; all foods.
CLOS SAINT-JACQUES: Gevrey, France; table wine; R.T.; dry; all foods.
CLOS SAINT-MARTIN: Saint-Emilion. France; table wine; R.T.; dry; all foods.
CLOS TAVANNES: Santenay, France; table wine; R.T.; dry; all foods.
LA CLOTTE GRANDE CÔTE: Saint-Emilion, France; table wine; R.T.; dry; all foods.
COLLARES: Portugal; table wine; R.T; dry; all foods.
COMBOTTES, AUX: Gevrey-Chambertin, France; table wine; R.T.; dry; all foods.
CORTAILLOD: Switzerland; table wine; R.T.; dry; all foods.
CORTON: Aloxe, France; table wine; R.T.; dry; all foods.
CORVÉES: Prémeaux, France; table wine; R.T.; dry; all foods.
COTE ROTIE: Rhône, France; table wine; R.T.; dry; all foods.
CRAS, AUX: Nuits-Saint-Georges, France; table wine; R.T.; dry; all foods.
CRU DE L'ETOILE POURRET: Saint-Emilion, France; table wine; R.T.; dry; all foods.
CRU DE PAVIE DECESSE: Saint-Emilion, France; table wine; R.T.; dry; all foods.
CRU FRANK MAYNE: Saint-Emilion, France; table wine; R.T.; dry; all foods.
CRU GUADET SAINT-JULIEN: Saint-Emilion. France; table wine; R.T.; dry; all foods.
CRU HAUT-BRION-LARRIVET: Graves, France; table wine; R.T.; dry; all foods.
CRU LAGRANGE: Pomerol, France; table wine; R.T.; dry; all foods.
CRU L'ARROSSÉE: Saint-Emilion, France; table wine; R.T.; dry; all foods.
CRU SOUTARD CADET: Saint-Emilion, France; table wine; R.T.; dry; all foods.
CURÉ BON LA MADELEINE: Saint-Emilion, France; table wine; R.T.; dry; all foods.
DIDIERS: Prémeaux, France; table wine; R.T.; dry; all foods.
DOMAINE DE CHEVALIER: Graves, France; table wine; R.T.; dry; all foods.
DOMAINE DE COTE BIGUEY: Saint-Emilion, France; table wine; R.T.; dry; all foods.
DOMAINE DE GRAND FAURIE: Saint-Emilion, France; table wine; R.T.; dry; all foods.
DOMAINE DE LA GRAVE-TRIGANT-DE-BOISSET: Pomerol, France; table wine; R.T.; dry; all foods.
DOMAINE DE LA SALLE: Saint-Emilion, France; table wine; R.T.; dry; all foods.
DOMAINE DE PAVIE MACQUIN: Saint-Emilion, France; table wine; R.T.; dry; all foods.
DOMAINE DU CHATELET: Saint-Emilion, France; table wine; R.T.; dry; all foods.
DOMAINE DU HAUT CADET ET CHATEAU BRAGARD: Saint-Emilion, France; table wine; R.T.; dry; all foods.
DOMAINE DU JARDIN SAINT-JULIEN: Saint-Emilion, France; table wine; R.T.; dry; all foods.
LA DOMINIQUE: Graves - Saint-Emilion, France; table wine; R.T.; dry; all foods
DOUBY: Villie-Morgon, France; table wine; R.T.; dry; all foods.

DUBONNET: France; aromatized wine; iced; sweet; appetizer, cocktail, straight.

ECHÉZEAUX-DU-DESSUS, LES: Flagey-Echézeaux, France; table wine; R.T.; dry; all foods.

EGRI BIKAVER: Hungary; table wine; R.T.; dry; all foods.

EPENOTS, LES: Pommard, France; table wine; R.T.; dry; all foods.

FALERNO: Campania, Italy; table wine; R.T.; dry; all foods.

FÈVES: Beaune, France; table wine; R.T.; dry; all foods.

FLAGEY: Flagey, France; table wine; R.T.; dry; all foods.

FLEURIE: Fleurie, France; table wine; R.T.; dry; all foods.

FONTAINE LA MADELEINE: Saint-Emilion, France; table wine; R.T.; dry; all foods.

FORÊTS: Prémeaux, France; table wine; R.T.; dry; all foods.

GAMAY: Contra Costa, Napa, Calif., table wine. Burgundy-type; R.T.; dry; all foods.

GARRAUD, LE: Fleurie, France; table wine; R.1.; dry; all foods.

GAUDICHOTS, LES: Vosne, France; table wine; R.T.; dry; all foods.

GEVREY: Gevrey, France; table wine; R.T.; dry; all foods.

GEVREY-CHAMBERTIN: Gevrey-Chambertin, France; table wine; R.T.; dry; all foods.

GIRO DI SARDEGNA: Sardinia, Italy; dessert wine; R.T.; sweet; all purpose.

GRAGNANO: Campania, Italy; table wine; R.T.; dry; all foods.

LA GRANDE COTE: Saint-Emilion, France; table wine; R.T.; dry; all foods.

GRANDE COUR: Fleurie, France; table wine; R.T.; dry; all foods.

GRANDES MURAILLES: Saint-Emilion, France; table wine; R.T.; dry; all foods.

GRANDS ECHÉZEAUX, LES: Flagey-Echézeaux, France; table wine; R.T.; dry; all foods.

GRÈVES, LES: Beaune, France; table wine; R.T.; dry; all foods.

GUGNOLINO: San Bernardino, Cucamonga, Fresno, Solano, Calif.; table wine, Claret-type; R.T.; dry; all foods.

HERMITAGE (RED): Rhone, France; table wine; R.T.; or cold; dry; all foods.

HERVELETS, LES: Fixin, France; table wine; R.T.; dry; all foods.

HOSPICES DE BEAUNE: Beaune, France; table wine; R.T.; dry; all foods.

ILE DES VERGELESSES: Pernand, France; table wine; R.T.; dry; all foods.

INFERNO: Lombardy, Italy; table wine; R.T.; dry; all foods.

ITALIAN VERMOUTH: Italy; aromatized wine (brown); iced; bitter-sweet; straight, cocktail.

IVES: Silverton, Ohio; table wine; dry; all foods.

JARRONS, LES: Savigny-les Beaune, France; table wine; R.T.; all foods.

JULIÉNAS: Beaujolais, France; table wine; R.T.; dry; all foods.

LAMBRAYS, LES: Morey, France; table wine; R.T.; dry; all foods.

LARANCHE: Romanèche-Thorins, France; table wine; R.T.; dry; all foods.

LATRICIÈRES: Gevrey-Chambertin, France; table wine; R.T.; dry; all foods.

LAVIÈRES, LES: Savigny-les Beaune, France; table wine; R.T.; dry; all foods.

LISBON: Portugal; dessert wine; R.T.; sweet; appetizer, after dinner.

MÂCON: Mâcon, France; table wine; R.T.; dry; all foods.

MALAGA: Malaga, Spain; dessert wine (dark); R.T.; sweet; all foods.

MALCONSORTS, LES: Vosne-Romanée, France; table wine; dry; all foods.

MALMSEY: Madeira; dessert wine (dark); R.T.; sweet; all foods.

MARCO: Greece; table wine; R.T.; dry; all foods.

MARCONNETS, LES: Beaune, France; table wine; R.T.; dry; all foods.

MARSALA: Sicily, Italy; dessert wine (brown); R.T.; sweet; all purpose.

MAVRODAPHNE: Greece; dessert wine; R.T.; sweet; all purpose.

MAZIS-HAUTS, LES: Gevrey-Chambertin, France; table wine; R.T.; dry; all foods.

MAZY: Gevrey, France; table wine; R.T.; dry; all foods.

MÉDOC: Médoc, France; table wine; R.T.; dry; all foods.

LES MENUTS JACOBINS: Saint-Emilion, France; table wine; R.T.; dry; all foods.

MERCUREY: Côte Chalonnaise, France; table wine; R.T.; dry; all foods.

MONILLES, LES: Juliénas, France; table wine; R.T.; dry; all foods.

MOREY: Morey, France; table wine; R.T.; dry; all foods.

MORGON: Villie-Morgon, France; table wine; R.T.; dry; all foods.

MORIERS, LES: Fleurie, France; table wine; R.T.; dry; all foods.

MOULIN-A-VENT: Romanèche-Thorins, France table wine; R.T.; dry; all foods.

MOULIN DU CADET: Saint-Emilion, France; table wine; R.T.; dry; all foods.

MOULIN SAINT-GEORGES: Saint-Emilion, France; table wine; R.T.; dry; all foods.

MURGERS, AUX: Nuits-Saint-Georges, France; table wine; R.T.; dry; all foods.

MUSIGNY, LE: Chambolle-Musigny, France; table wine; R.T.; dry; all foods.

NEBBIOLO: Piedmont, Italy; table wine; R.T.; semi-sweet; all foods.

NIEDERBURG CABERNET: South Africa; table wine; R.T.; dry; all foods.

NOYER BART: Santenay, France; table wine; R.T.; dry; all foods.

NUITS: Nuits, France; table wine; R.T.; dry; all foods.

NUITS-SAINT-GEORGES: Nuits-Sant-Georges, France; table wine; R.T.; dry; all foods.

OEIL DE PERDRIX: Burgundy, France; sparkling wine (pink); iced; semisweet; all foods.

PAVILLON CADET: Saint-Emilion, France; table wine; R.T.; dry; all foods.

PERELLES: Romanèche-Thorins, France; table wine; R.T.; dry; all foods.

PERNAND-VERGELESSES: Pernand, France; table wine; R.T.; dry; all foods.

PERRIÈRE: Fixin, France; table wine; R.T.; dry; all foods.

PETITS MUSIGNY, LES: Chambolle-Musigny, France; table wine; R.T.; dry; all foods.

PETITS VOUGEOTS, LES: Vougeot, France; table wine; R.T.; dry; all foods.

PINOT NOIR: Napa, Sonoma, Calif.; table wine, Burgundy-type; R.T.; dry; all foods.

PIS, LE: Villie-Morgon, France; table wine; R.T.; dry; all foods.

POINT DE JOUR: Fleurie, France; table wine; R.T.; dry; all foods.

POIRETS, LES: Nuits-Saint-Georges, France; table wine; R.T.; dry; all foods.

POMEROL: Pomerol, France; table wine; R.T.; dry; all foods.

POMMARD: Pommard, France; table wine; R.T.; dry; all foods.

PONCIER: Fleurie, France; table wine; R.T.; dry; all foods.

PONGETS, LES: Aloxe-Corton, France; table wine; R.T.; dry; all foods.

PORT: Portugal; U.S.A.; dessert wine; R.T.; sweet; all purpose.

PRÉMEAUX: Prémeaux, France; table wine; R.T.; dry; all foods.

LE PRIEURÉ SAINT-EMILION: Saint-Emilion, France; table wine; R.T.; dry; all foods.

PRULIERS: Nuits-Saint-Georges, France; table wine; R.T.; dry; all foods.

QUINQUINA: France; aromatized wine (red); iced; bitter-sweet; straight, cocktail.

RENARDS, LES: Aloxe-Corton, France; table wine; R.T.; dry; all foods.

RICHEBOURG, LES: Vosne-Romanée, France; table wine; R.T.; dry; all foods.

RIOJA: Spain; table wine; R.T.; dry; all foods.

ROCHE GRÉ: Chenas, France; table wine; R.T.; dry; all foods.

ROCHELLE, LA: Chenas, France; table wine; R.T.; dry; all foods.

ROILETTE, LA: Fleurie, France; table wine; R.T.: dry; all foods.

ROMANÉE, LA: Vosne-Romanée, France; table France; table wine; R.T.; dry; all foods.

ROMANÉE-CONTI, LA: Vosne-Romanée, France; table wine; R.T.; dry; all foods.

ROMANÉE-SAINT-VIVANT, LA: Vosne-Romanée. France; table wine; R.T.; dry; all foods.

ROSÉ, VIN: France; Napa, California; table wine (pink); cold; dry; all foods.

RUBY PORT: Burgundy, France; table wine; R.T.: dry; all purpose.

RUCHOTTES, LES: Gevrey-Chambertin, France; table wine; R.T.; dry; all foods.

RUGIENS, LES: Pommard, France; table wine; R.T.; dry; all foods.

SAINT-EMILION: Saint-Emilion, France; table wine; R.T.; dry; all foods.

SAINT-GEORGES, LES: France; table wine; R.T.; drv: all foods.

SAINT-JACQUES: Gevrey-Chambertin, France; table wine; R.T. dry; all foods.

SANGIOVESE: Emilia, Italy; table wine; R.T.; dry; all foods.

SANTENOT: Meursault, France; table wine; R.T.; dry; all foods.

SANTENOTS-DU-MILIEU: Meursault, France; table wine; R.T.; dry; all foods.

SASSELA: Lombardy, Italy; table wine; R.T.; dry; all foods.

SPARKLING BURGUNDY: Burgundy, France; sparkling wine; iced; semisweet; all foods.

SUCHOTS, LES: Vosne-Romanée, France; table wine; R.T.; dry; all foods.

TACHE, LA: Vosne-Romanée, France; table wine; R.T.; dry; all foods.

TAVEL: Rhone, France; table wine (pink); iced; dry; all foods.

TAWNY PORT: Portugal; dessert wine; R.T.; sweet; all purpose.

TEGEA: Greece; table wine (pink); cold; dry; all foods.

TERTRE, LE: Arsac, France; table wine; R.T.; dry; all foods.

THOREY: Nuits-Saint-Georges, France; table wine; R.T.; dry; all foods.

THORINS: Romanèche-Thorins, France; table wine; R.T.; dry; all foods.

VALPOLICELLA: Veneto, Italy; table wine; R.T.; dry; all foods.

VALTELLINA: Veneto, Italy; table wine; R.T.; dry; all foods.

VAROILLES: Gevrey, France; table wine; R.T.; dry; all foods.

VAUCRAINS, LES: Nuits-Saint-Georges, France; table wine; R.T.; dry; all foods.

VERGELESSES: Savigny, France; table wine; R.T.; dry; all foods.

VERILLATS, LES: Chenas, France; table wine; R.T.; dry; all foods.

VIEUX CHÂTEAU-CERTAN: Pommerol, France; table wine; R.T.; dry; all foods.

VIEUX MOULIN DU CADET: Saint-Emilion, France; table wine; R.T.; dry; all foods.

VILLANYI-PECS: Pecs, Hungary; table wine; R.T.; dry; all foods.

VIVIER, LE: Fleurie, France; table wine; R.T.; dry; all foods.

VOLNAY: Volnay, France; table wine; R.T.; dry; all foods.

VOSLAU: Austria; table wine; R.T.; dry; all foods.

VOSNE: Vosne. France; table wine; R.T.; dry; all foods.

VOSNE-ROMANÉE: Vosne-Romanée, France; table wine; R.T.; dry; all foods.

ZINFANDEL: Fresno, Napa, Santa Clara, Calif.; table wine, Claret-type; R.T.; dry; all foods.

White Wines

ALELLA: Spain; table wine; cold; dry; all foods.

AMONTILLADO: Jerez, Spain; sherry (pale); slightly chilled; dry; appetizer.

AMOROSO: Jerez, Spain; sherry (golden); slightly chilled; dry; all purpose.

ANGELICA: California; dessert wine (straw, golden, or amber); R.T. or slightly chilled; sweet; all foods.

ANJOU: Anjou, France; table wine; cold; sweet; all foods.

ANNIGER PERLE: Austria; table wine; iced; dry; all foods.

ASTI SPUMANTI: Piedmont, Italy; sparkling wine; iced; semisweet; all foods.

BADACSONYI AUVERGNAC-GRIS: Hungary; table wine; cold; medium dry; all foods.

BADACSONYI RIZLING: Hungary; table wine; iced; dry; all foods.

BADACSONYI.. SZURKE-BARAT: Hungary; table wine; cold; dry; all foods.

BARSAC: Barsac, France; table wine; cold; sweet; all foods.

BÂTARD-MONTRACHET, LE: Puligny-Chassagne, France; table wine; cold; dry; all foods.

BERNKASTLER DOKTOR: Moselle, Germany; table wine; iced; dry; all foods.

BINGER SCHARLACHBERG: Rhineland, Germany; table wine; iced; dry; all foods.

BOAL: Madeira; dessert wine (golden); R.T.; sweet; all foods.

BORDEAUX BLANC: Bordeaux, France; table wine; iced; semisweet; all foods.

BORDEAUX BLANC: Palus, Côtes, Entre-Deux-Mers, France; table wine; iced; semisweet; all foods.

BOURGOGNE BLANC: Burgundy, France; table wine; iced; drv: all foods.

BRAUNEBERGER JUFFER: Moselle, Germany; table wine; iced; dry; all foods.

BUCELLAS: Portugal; table wine; cold; semisweet; all foods.

BURGUNDY, WHITE: Napa, Santa Clara, Calif.; table wine; cold; dry; all foods.

CAPRI: Capri, Italy; table wine; cold; dry; all foods.

CATAWBA, SPARKLING: Naples, New York, and Silverton, Ohio; sparkling wine (pale or golden); iced; semisweet; all foods.

CHABLIS: Lower Burgundy, France; table wine; iced; dry; all foods.

CHABLIS: Napa, Santa Clara, Sonoma, Calif.; table wine, Chablis-type; cold; dry; all foods.

CHAMPAGNE: Champagne, France; sparkling wine; iced; dry to sweet; all purpose.

CHAMPAGNE, BOTTLED: Alameda, Santa Clara, Calif., and Hammondsport, N.Y.; sparkling wine; iced; dry to sweet; all purpose.

CHAMPAGNE, BULK: Alameda, Napa, Santa Clara, Calif.; sparkling wine; iced; dry to sweet; all purpose.

CHASSAGNE-MONTRACHET: Chassagne-Montrachet, France; table wine; iced; dry; all foods.

CHÂTEAU D'ARCHE: Sauternes, France; table wine; cold; sweet; all foods.

CHÂTEAU BROUSTET: Barsac, France; table wine; cold; sweet; all foods.

CHÂTEAU CAILLOU: Barsac, France; table wine; cold; all foods.

CHÂTEAU CARBONNIEUX: Graves, France; table wine; iced; dry; all foods.

CHÂTEAU CLIMENS: Barsac, France; table wine; cold; sweet; all foods.

CHÂTEAU CLOS HAUT-PEYRAGUEY: Bommes, France; table wine; cold; sweet; all foods.

CHÂTEAU COUTET: Barsac, France; table wine; cold; sweet; all foods.

CHÂTEAU DOISY-DAËNE: Barsac, France; table wine; cold; sweet; all foods.

CHÂTEAU DOISY-VÉDRINES: Barsac, France; table wine; cold; sweet; all foods.

CHÂTEAU FILHOT: Sauternes, France; table wine; cold; sweet; all foods.

CHÂTEAU GRILLET: Côtes du Rhône, France; table wine; cold; sweet; all foods.

CHÂTEAU GUIRAUD: Sauternes, France; table wine; cold; sweet; all foods.

CHÂTEAU HAUT-BRION-BLANC: Pessac, France; table wine; iced; dry; all foods.

CHÂTEAU LAFAURIE - PEYRAGUEY: Bommes, France; table wine; cold; sweet; all foods.

CHÂTEAU LA TOUR-BLANCHE: Bommes, France; table wine; cold; sweet; all foods.

CHÂTEAU DE MALLE: Preignac, France; table wine; cold; sweet; all foods.

CHÂTEAU MYRAT: Barsac, France; table wine; cold; sweet; all foods.

CHÂTEAU NAIRAC: Barsac, France; table wine; cold; sweet; all foods.

CHÂTEAU OLIVIER: Graves, France; table wine; iced; dry; all foods.

CHÂTEAU RABAUD-PROMIS: Bommes, France; table wine; cold; sweet; all foods.

CHÂTEAU RIEUSSEC: Fargues, France; table wine; cold; sweet; all foods.

CHÂTEAU ROMER: Preignac, France; table wine; cold; sweet; all foods.

CHÂTEAU SIGALAS-RABAUD: Bommes, France; table wine; cold; sweet; all foods.

CHÂTEAU SUDUIRAUT: Preignac, France; table wine; cold; sweet; all foods.

CHÂTEAU YQUEM: Sauternes, France; table wine; cold; sweet; all foods.

CHEVALIER-MONTRACHET: Puligny-Montrachet, France; table wine; cold; dry; all foods.

CHIANTI, WHITE: Napa, San Joaquin, Santa Clara, Calif.; table wine; cold; dry; all foods.

CLOS GAENSBROENNEL: Alsace, France; table wine; iced; semisweet; all foods.

CLOS SAINTE-ODILE: Alsace, France; table wine; cold; medium dry; all foods.

CORTESE: Piedmont, Italy; table wine; iced; dry; all foods.

CORVO DI CASTELDACCIA: Sicily, Italy; table wine; iced; dry; all foods.

CSOPAKI FURMINT: Hungary; table wine; iced; dry; all foods.

DEBROI HARSLEVELU: Hungary; table wine; cold; medium sweet; all foods.

DIEDESHIEMER LEINHOHLE: Rhine, Germany; table wine; cold; dry; all foods.

DELAWARE: Naples, N.Y., and Cincinnati, O.; table wine, Rhine-wine type; cold; dry; all foods.

DHRONER HOFBERG: Moselle, Germany; table wine; iced; dry; all foods.

DIAMOND: Naples, N.Y.; table wine; cold; dry; all foods.

DIANA: Naples, N.Y.; table wine; cold; dry; all foods.

DUTCHESS: Hammondsport, N.Y.; table wine; cold; dry; all foods.

EAST INDIA BROWN: Jerez, Spain; sherry (dark brown); R.T.; sweet; after dinner and all purpose.

ELVIRA: Hammondsport, Naples, N.Y.; table wine; cold; dry; all foods.

EN CHARLEMAGNE: Burgundy, France; table wine; cold; dry; all foods.

ENKIRCHER STEFFENSBERG: Moselle, Germany; table wine; iced; dry; all foods.

ERDNER TREPPCHEN: Moselle, Germany; table wine; iced; dry; all foods.

EST, EST, EST: Latium. Italy; table wine; cold; dry; all foods.

FALERNO: Campania, Italy; table wine; cold; dry; all foods.

FINO: Jerez, Spain; sherry (pale); cold; dry; all foods.

FOLLE-BLANCHE: Napa, Santa Clara, Sonoma, California; table wine; Chablis-type; cold; dry; all foods.

FORSTER JESUITENGARTEN: Rhineland, Germany; table wine; cold; medium dry; all foods.

FORSTER KIRCHENSTUCK: Rhineland, Germany; table wine; cold; dry; all foods.

FRASCATI: Latium, Italy; table wine; cold; medium sweet; all foods.

FRENCH VERMOUTH: Midi, France; aromatized wine; cold; dry; appetizer and cocktails.

GENEVRIÈRES, LES: Burgundy, France; table wine; cold; dry; all foods.

GENTIL: Alsace, France; table wine; iced; medium dry; all foods.

GEWUERZ-TRAMINER: Alsace, France; table wine; cold; medium dry; all foods.

GOUTTES D'OR, LES: Burgundy, France; table wine; cold; dry; all foods.

GRASCHER HIMMELREICH: Moselle, Germany; table wine; iced; dry; all foods.

GRAVES: Bordeaux, France; table wine; cold; medium dry; all foods.

GRECO DI GERACE: Calabria, Italy; table wine; cold; medium dry; all foods.

GRINZING: Austria; table wine; iced; dry; all foods.

GRÜNHAÜSER (MAXIMIN GRUNHAUSER HERRENBERG): Moselle, Germany; table wine; iced; dry; all foods.

GUMPOLDSKIRCHNER STEINWEIN: Austria; table wine; iced; dry; all foods.

HALLGARTNER SCHÖNHELL: Rhineland, Germany; table wine; iced; dry; all foods.

HATTENHEIMER NUSSBRUNNEN: Rhineland, Germany; table wine; iced; dry; all foods.

HAUT-BARSAC: Bordeaux, France; table wine; cold; sweet; all foods.

HAUT-SAUTERNES: Bordeaux, France; table wine; cold; sweet; all foods.

HERMITAGE (WHITE): Rhône, France; table wine; R.T. or cold; dry; all foods.

HOCHHEIMER: Rhineland, Germany; table wine; iced; dry; all foods.
HOCHHEIMER KIRCHENSTUCK: Rhineland, Germany; table wine; iced; dry; all foods.
HOHENWARTHER: Austria; table wine; iced; dry; all foods.
JOHANNISBERGER HOLLE: Rhineland, Germany; table wine; iced; dry; all foods.
JOSEFSHOFER: Moselle, Germany; table wine; iced; dry; all foods.
KEKNYELU: Hungary; table wine; iced; dry; all foods.
KLOSTERNEUBERGER: Austria; table wine, iced; dry; all foods.
KNIPPERLÉ: Alsace, France; table wine; iced; dry; all foods.
LACRYMA CHRISTI: Campania, Italy; table wine; cold; medium dry; all foods.
LAUBENHEIMER: Rhineland, Germany; table wine; iced; dry; all foods.
LEANYKA EDES: Hungary; table wine; cold; medium sweet; all foods.
LEANYKA SZARAZ: Hungary; table wine; iced; dry; all foods.
LIEBFRAUMILCH: Rhineland, Germany; table wine; iced; medium dry; all foods.
MADEIRA: Madeira; dessert wine; golden; R.T.; dry-sweet; all foods.
MALVASIA DI LIPARI: Sicily, Italy; dessert wine; golden; R.T.; sweet; all foods.
MANZANILLA: Jerez, Spain; sherry (straw); iced; dry; all purpose.
MARKOBRUNN: Rhineland, Germany; table wine; iced; dry; all foods.
MEURSAULT: Burgundy, France; table wine; cold; dry; all foods.
MEURSAULT-CHARMES: Burgundy, France; table wine; cold; dry; all foods.
MEURSALT-LES-PERRIÈRES: Burgundy, France; table wine; cold; dry; all foods.
MONTILLA: Cordova, Spain; aperitif wine (straw); cold; dry; all foods.
MONTRACHET, LE: Marquis de la Guiche, France; table wine; cold; dry; all foods.
MOSCATEL DE MALAGA: Malaga, Spain; dessert wine (golden); R.T.; sweet; all purpose.
MOSCATEL DE SITGES: Catalonia, Spain; dessert wine (golden); R.T.; sweet; all purpose.
MOSCATO-FIOR D'ARANCIO: Sicily, Italy; dessert wine (golden); R.T.; sweet; all purpose.
MOSCATO DI PANTELLERIA: Sicily, Italy; dessert wine (golden); R.T.; sweet; all purpose.
MOSCATO DI SALENTO: Apulia, Italy; dessert wine (golden); R.T.; sweet; all purpose.
MOSELBLUMCHEN: Moselle, Germany; table wine; iced; dry; all foods.
MUSKOTALY: Hungary; table wine; iced; dry; all foods.
NACKENHEIMER ROTHENBERG: Rhineland, Germany; table wine; iced; dry; all foods.
NEUCHÂTEL: Switzerland; table wine; iced; dry; all foods.
NIERSTEINER DOMTHAL: Rhineland, Germany; table wine; iced; dry; all foods.
NIERSTEINER REHBACH: Rhineland, Germany; table wine; iced; dry; all foods.
OLOROSO SHERRY: Jerez, Spain; dessert wine (golden); R.T.; sweet; all purpose.
OPPENHEIMER HERRENBERG: Rhineland, Germany; table wine; iced; dry; all foods
OPPENHEIMER SACKTRÄGER: Rhineland, Germany; table wine; iced; dry; all foods.
ORVIETO: Umbria, Italy; table wine; iced; dry and sweet; all foods.
PERRIÈRES, LES: Burgundy, France; table wine; cold; dry; all foods.

PERRY: England; sparkling pear wine (straw); iced; sweet; all foods.
PFAFFSTATTER: Austria; table wine; iced; dry; all foods.
PIESPORTER GOLDTRÖPFSCHEN: Moselle, Germany; table wine; iced; dry; all foods.
PIESPORTER LAY: Moselle, Germany; table wine; iced; dry; all foods.
PUCELLE, LA: Burgundy, France; table wine; cold; dry; all foods.
PULIGNY-MONTRACHET: Burgundy, France; table wine; cold; dry; all foods.
QUINQUINA (WHITE): France; aromatized wine; iced; sweet to bitter; cocktails, straight.
RHINE WINE: Napa, Santa Clara, Sonoma, California; table wine, Rhine-wine type; cold; dry; all foods.
RIESLING: Austria, Hungary, Germany, and Alsace, France; table wine; iced; dry; all foods.
RIESLING: Napa, Santa Clara, Sonoma, California; table wine; Rhine-wine type; cold; dry; all foods.
RIZLING SZEMELT: Hungary; table wine; iced; dry; all foods.
RÜDESHEIMER HAUSEWEG: Rhineland, Germany; table wine; iced; dry; all foods.
RÜDESHEIMER HINTERHAUS: Rhineland, Germany; table wine; iced; dry; all foods.
RÜDESHEIMER SCHLOSSBERG: Rhineland, Germany; table wine; iced; dry; all foods.
RUPPERTSBERGER HOHEBURG: Rhineland, Germany; table wine; iced; dry; all foods.
SANSEVERO: Apulia, Italy; table wine; iced; dry; all foods.
SAUMUR: Anjou, France; table wine; cold; medium sweet; all foods.
SAUTERNE: Alameda, Napa, California; table wine; Sauternes type; cold; dry; medium, sweet; all foods.
SAUTERNES: Bordeaux, France; table wine; cold; sweet; all foods.
SAUVIGNON BLANC: Napa, Los Gatos, California; table wine, Sauternes-type; cold; dry; all foods.
SAUVIGNON BLANC: Napa, Sonoma, California; table wine, Sauternes-type; cold; sweet; all foods.
SCHLOSS JOHANNISBERG: Rhineland, Germany; table wine; iced; dry; all foods.
SCHLOSS REINHARDSHAUSEN: Rhineland, Germany; table wine; iced; dry; all foods.
SCHLOSS VOLLRADS: Rhineland, Germany; table wine; iced; dry; all foods.
SCUPPERNONG: Southeastern U.S.A.; table wine; cold; sweet; all foods.
SÉMILLON: Alameda, Napa, Sonoma, California; table wine; cold; dry; all foods.
SÉMILLON: Napa, Santa Clara, California; table wine; cold; semisweet; all foods.
SÉMILLON: Alameda, Napa, Santa Clara, California; table wine; cold; sweet; all foods.
SERCIAL: Madeira; dessert wine (golden); chilled; medium dry; all purpose.
SHERRY: Alameda, Napa, San Joaquin, Sonoma, California; sherry-type; slightly chilled; dry; appetizer.
SHERRY: San Joaquin, Sonoma, Tulare, California; sherry-type; R.T.; semisweet; dessert.
SHERRY: Alameda, Fresno, Sonoma, California; sherry-type; R.T.; sweet; dessert.
SOAVE: Veneto, Italy; table wine; cold, dry; all foods.
SOMLOYI FURMINT: Somloy, Hungary; table wine; iced; dry; all foods.
SPARKLING BURGUNDY (WHITE): Burgundy, France; sparkling wine; iced; medium sweet; all foods.
SPARKLING MOSELLE: Moselle, Germany

sparkling wine (white); iced; sweet; all foods.
STEINBERGER: Rhineland, Germany; table wine; iced; dry; all foods.
STEINWEIN: Wurzburg, Germany; table wine; iced; dry; all foods.
SYLVANER: Alsace, France; table wine; cold; medium dry; all foods.
SYLVANER: Alameda, Napa, Santa Clara, California; table wine; Rhine-wine-type; cold; dry; all foods.
SWEET CATAWBA: Ohio and New York, U.S.A.; table wine; cold; sweet; all foods.
SZILVANYI ZOLD: Hungary; table wine; cold; medium-sweet; all foods.
TOKAY ASZU: Hungary; R.T.; sweet; all purpose.
TOKAY SZAMORODNI: Hungary; cold; dry; all purpose.
TORRE GIULIA: Apulia, Italy; table wine; iced; medium dry; all foods.
TRAMINER: Alsace, France; table wine; cold; medium dry; all foods.
TRITTENHEIMER LAURENTIUSBERG: Moselle, Germany; table wine; iced; dry; all foods.
VALMUR: Chablis, France; table wine; iced; dry; all foods.
VAUDESIR: Chablis, France; table wine; iced; dry; all foods.
VERDICCHIO DI JESI: Marches, Italy; table wine; iced; dry; all foods.
VERNACCIA: Italy; table wine; cold; sweet; all foods.

VIGNE-BLANCHE, LA: Burgundy, France; table wine; iced; dry; all foods.
VINO DE PASTO: Jerez, Spain; sherry (pale); cold; dry; all purpose.
VIN SANTO: Tuscany, Italy; table wine; cold; sweet; all foods.
VOUVRAY: Touraine, France; table wine; cold; sweet; all foods.
WASSERBILLIG: Luxemburg; table wine; iced; dry; all foods.
WEHLENER SONNENUHR: Moselle, Germany; table wine; iced; dry; all foods.
WHITE PORT: Portugal; dessert wine (golden); R.T.; all purpose.
WILTINGER SCHARZHOFBERG: Moselle, Germany; table wine; iced; dry; all foods.
WILTINGER SCHLANGENGRABEN: Moselle, Germany; table wine; iced; dry; all foods.
WORMELDINGER: Luxemburg; table wine; iced; dry; all foods.
WÜRZBURGER LEISTE: Würzburg, Germany; table wine; iced; dry; all foods.
WÜRZBURGER STEIN: Würzburg, Germany; table wine; iced; dry; all foods.
ZELTINGER SCHLOSSBERG: Moselle, Germany; table wine; iced; dry; all foods.

Wonders of the World
See **Seven Wonders of the Ancient World**